KU-098-543

OXFORD LIBRARY OF PSYCHOLOGY

*Editor-in-Chief PETER E. NATHAN*

# The Oxford Handbook of Health Psychology

*Edited by*

Howard S. Friedman

OXFORD

UNIVERSITY PRESS

Oxford University Press is a department of the University of Oxford.
It furthers the University's objective of excellence in research, scholarship,
and education by publishing worldwide.

Oxford   New York
Auckland   Cape Town   Dar es Salaam   Hong Kong   Karachi
Kuala Lumpur   Madrid   Melbourne   Mexico City   Nairobi
New Delhi   Shanghai   Taipei   Toronto

With offices in
Argentina   Austria   Brazil   Chile   Czech Republic   France   Greece
Guatemala   Hungary   Italy   Japan   Poland   Portugal   Singapore
South Korea   Switzerland   Thailand   Turkey   Ukraine   Vietnam

Oxford is a registered trade mark of Oxford University Press
in the UK and certain other countries.

Published in the United States of America by
Oxford University Press
198 Madison Avenue, New York, NY 10016

© Oxford University Press 2011

First issued as an Oxford University Press paperback, 2014.

All rights reserved. No part of this publication may be reproduced, stored in a retrieval system,
or transmitted, in any form or by any means, without the prior permission in writing of
Oxford University Press, or as expressly permitted by law, by license, or under terms agreed with
the appropriate reproduction rights organization. Inquiries concerning reproduction outside the scope
of the above should be sent to the Rights Department, Oxford University Press, at the address above.

You must not circulate this work in any other form
and you must impose this same condition on any acquirer.

Library of Congress Cataloging-in-Publication Data
The Oxford handbook of health psychology / edited by Howard S. Friedman.
    p. ; cm. – (Oxford library of psychology)
  Handbook of health psychology
  Includes bibliographical references.
  ISBN: 978-0-19-534281-9 (hardcover); 978-0-19-936507-4 (paperback)
  1. Clinical health psychology–Handbooks, manuals, etc. 2. Medicine and
psychology–Handbooks, manuals, etc. I. Friedman, Howard S. II. Title:
Handbook of health psychology. III. Series: Oxford library of psychology.
[DNLM: 1. Behavioral Medicine–methods. 2. Disease–psychology.
3. Health Behavior. 4. Psychology, Medical.
WB 103]
R726.7.O94 2011
616.001'9–dc22                                    2011001676

9 8 7 6 5 4 3 2 1

Printed in the United States of America
on acid-free paper

NMC I FF

The Oxford Handbook of Health Psychology

# OXFORD LIBRARY OF PSYCHOLOGY

EDITOR-IN-CHIEF

Peter E. Nathan

AREA EDITORS:

*Clinical Psychology*
David H. Barlow

*Cognitive Neuroscience*
Kevin N. Ochsner and Stephen M. Kosslyn

*Cognitive Psychology*
Daniel Reisberg

*Counseling Psychology*
Elizabeth M. Altmaier and Jo-Ida C. Hansen

*Developmental Psychology*
Philip David Zelazo

*Health Psychology*
Howard S. Friedman

*History of Psychology*
David B. Baker

*Industrial/Organizational Psychology*
Steve W. J. Kozlowski

*Methods and Measurement*
Todd D. Little

*Neuropsychology*
Kenneth M. Adams

*Personality and Social Psychology*
Kay Deaux and Mark Snyder

# SHORT CONTENTS

# OXFORD LIBRARY OF PSYCHOLOGY

The *Oxford Library of Psychology*, a landmark series of handbooks, is published by Oxford University Press, one of the world's oldest and most highly respected publishers, with a tradition of publishing significant books in psychology. The ambitious goal of the *Oxford Library of Psychology* is nothing less than to span a vibrant, wide-ranging field and, in so doing, to fill a clear market need.

Encompassing a comprehensive set of handbooks, organized hierarchically, the *Library* incorporates volumes at different levels, each designed to meet a distinct need. At one level are a set of handbooks designed broadly to survey the major subfields of psychology; at another are numerous handbooks that cover important current focal research and scholarly areas of psychology in depth and detail. Planned as a reflection of the dynamism of psychology, the *Library* will grow and expand as psychology itself develops, thereby highlighting significant new research that will impact on the field. Adding to its accessibility and ease of use, the *Library* will be published in print and, later on, electronically.

The *Library* surveys psychology's principal subfields with a set of handbooks that capture the current status and future prospects of those major subdisciplines. This initial set includes handbooks of social and personality psychology, clinical psychology, counseling psychology, school psychology, educational psychology, industrial and organizational psychology, cognitive psychology, cognitive neuroscience, methods and measurements, history, neuropsychology, personality assessment, developmental psychology, and more. Each handbook undertakes to review one of psychology's major subdisciplines with breadth, comprehensiveness, and exemplary scholarship. In addition to these broadly conceived volumes, the *Library* also includes a large number of handbooks designed to explore in depth more specialized areas of scholarship and research, such as stress, health and coping, anxiety and related disorders, cognitive development, or child and adolescent assessment. In contrast to the broad coverage of the subfield handbooks, each of these latter volumes focuses on an especially productive, more highly focused line of scholarship and research. Whether at the broadest or most specific level, however, all of the *Library* handbooks offer synthetic coverage that reviews and evaluates the relevant past and present research and anticipates research in the future. Each handbook in the *Library* includes introductory and concluding chapters written by its editor to provide a roadmap to the handbook's table of contents and to offer informed anticipations of significant future developments in that field.

An undertaking of this scope calls for handbook editors and chapter authors who are established scholars in the areas about which they write. Many of the nation's and world's most productive and best-respected psychologists have agreed to edit *Library* handbooks or write authoritative chapters in their areas of expertise.

For whom has the *Oxford Library of Psychology* been written? Because of its breadth, depth, and accessibility, the *Library* serves a diverse audience, including graduate students in psychology and their faculty mentors, scholars, researchers, and practitioners in psychology and related fields. Each will find in the *Library* the information he or she seeks on the subfield or focal area of psychology in which he or she works or is interested.

Befitting its commitment to accessibility, each handbook includes a comprehensive index, as well as extensive references to help guide research. And because the *Library* was designed from its inception as an online as well as a print resource, its structure and contents will be readily and rationally searchable online. Further, once the *Library* is released online, the handbooks will be regularly and thoroughly updated.

In summary, the *Oxford Library of Psychology* will grow organically to provide a thoroughly informed perspective on the field of psychology, one that reflects both psychology's dynamism and its increasing interdisciplinarity. Once published electronically, the *Library* is also destined to become a uniquely valuable interactive tool, with extended search and browsing capabilities. As you begin to consult this handbook, we sincerely hope you will share our enthusiasm for the more than 500-year tradition of Oxford University Press for excellence, innovation, and quality, as exemplified by the *Oxford Library of Psychology*.

Peter E. Nathan
Editor-in-Chief
*Oxford Library of Psychology*

# ABOUT THE EDITOR

**Howard S. Friedman**

Howard S. Friedman, Ph.D., is Distinguished Professor of Psychology at the University of California, Riverside (UCR). His research is focused on lifespan psychosocial predictors and mediators of health and longevity. Dr. Friedman is the recipient of the career award for Outstanding Contributions to Health Psychology from the American Psychological Association (Division 38), the James McKeen Cattell award from the Association for Psychological Science for career achievements in applied psychology, and UCR's Distinguished Teaching Award.

# CONTRIBUTORS

**Nancy E. Adler**
Departments of Psychiatry and Pediatrics
University of California, San Francisco
San Francisco, California

**Leona S. Aiken**
Department of Psychology
Arizona State University
Tempe, Arizona

**Yael Benyamini**
Bob Shapell School of Social Work
Tel Aviv University
Tel Aviv, Israel

**Gary G. Berntson**
Department of Psychology
Ohio State University
Columbus, Ohio

**Kathrin Boerner**
Senior Research Scientist
Research Institute on Aging
Jewish Home Lifecare, New York
Associate Professor
Brookdale Department of Geriatrics &
Palliative Medicine
Mount Sinai School of Medicine,
New York

**Mary H. Burleson**
Division of Social & Behavioral Sciences
Arizona State University
Phoenix, Arizona

**John T. Cacioppo**
Department of Psychology
University of Chicago
Chicago, Illinois

**Charles S. Carver**
Department of Psychology
University of Miami
Coral Gables, Florida

**John P. Capitanio**
Department of Psychology
University of California, Davis
Davis, California

**Susan T. Charles**
Department of Psychology and Social
Behavior
University of California, Irvine
Irvine, California

**Cindy K. Chung**
Department of Psychology
The University of Texas at Austin
Austin, Texas

**Silvia Degni**
University of Rome, La Sapienza
Rome, Italy

**Mary Amanda Dew**
Department of Psychiatry
University of Pittsburgh School of Medicine
Pittsburgh, Pennsylvania

**Andrea F. DiMartini**
Department of Psychiatry
University of Pittsburgh School of Medicine
Pittsburgh, Pennsylvania

**Howard S. Friedman**
Department of Psychology
University of California, Riverside
Riverside, California

**Virginia Gil-Rivas**
Department of Psychology
University of North Carolina, Charlotte
Charlotte, North Carolina

**Judith A. Hall**
Department of Psychology
Northeastern University
Boston, Massachusetts

**Jutta Heckhausen**
Department of Psychology and Social Behavior
University of California, Irvine
Irvine, California

**Robert M. Kaplan**
Department of Health Services
University of California, Los Angeles
Los Angeles, California

**Margaret E. Kemeny**
Department of Psychiatry
University of California, San Francisco
San Francisco, California

**Heather Kitzman-Ulrich**
Texas Prevention Institute
University of North Texas
Health Science Center
Fort Worth, Texas

**Marta Gil Lacruz**
Department of Psychology and Sociology
University of Zaragoza
Zaragoza, Spain

**Andrew K. Littlefield**
Department of Psychological Sciences and the Midwest Alcoholism Research Center
University of Missouri
Columbia, Missouri

**Vanessa L. Malcarne**
Department of Psychology
San Diego State University
San Diego, California

**Julia A. Martinez**
Department of Psychology Colgate University
Hamilton, NY

**James W. Pennebaker**
Department of Psychology
The University of Texas at Austin
Austin, Texas

**Wade E. Pickren**
Professor and Chair of Psychology
Pace University
New York City, NY

**Hollie A. Raynor**
Department of Nutrition
University of Tennessee
Knoxville, Tennessee

**Britta Renner**
Department of Psychology
University of Konstanz
Konstanz, Germany

**Tracey A. Revenson**
Department of Psychology
The Graduate Center, City University of New York
New York, New York

**Michael J. Rohrbaugh**
Departments of Psychology and Family Studies/Human Development
University of Arizona
Tucson, Arizona

**Karen S. Rook**
Department of Psychology and Social Behavior
University of California, Irvine
Irvine, California

**Debra L. Roter**
Bloomberg School of Public Health
Johns Hopkins University
Baltimore, Maryland

**John Ruiz**
Department of Psychology
University of North Texas
Denton, TX

**Yosuke Sakairi**
Graduate School of Comprehensive Human Sciences
University of Tsukuba
Tsukuba, Japan

**Harald Schupp**
Department of Psychology
University of Konstanz
Konstanz, Germany

**Ralf Schwarzer**
Department of Psychology
Freie Universität Berlin
Berlin, Germany

**Suzanne C. Segerstrom**
Department of Psychology
University of Kentucky
Lexington, Kentucky

**Kenneth J. Sher**
Department of Psychological Sciences and
the Midwest Alcoholism Research Center
University of Missouri
Columbia, Missouri

**Varda Shoham**
Department of Psychology
University of Arizona
Tucson, Arizona

**Roxane Cohen Silver**
Department of Psychology and Social
Behavior
University of California, Irvine
Irvine, California

**Timothy W. Smith**
Department of Psychology
University of Utah
Salt Lake City, Utah

**Annette L. Stanton**
Department of Psychology
University of California, Los Angeles
Los Angeles, California

**Betsy A. Steeves**
Department of Nutrition
University of Tennessee
Knoxville, Tennessee

**Patrick Steffen**
Department of Psychology
Brigham Young University
Provo, Utah

**Genji Sugamura**
Department of Psychology
Kansai University
Osaka, Japan

**Jerry Suls**
Department of Psychology
University of Iowa
Iowa City, Iowa

**Masao Suzuki**
School of Human Sciences,
Department of Psychology
Waseda University
Tokorozawa, Japan

**Amelia E. Talley**
Department of Psychological Sciences and
the Midwest Alcoholism Research Center
University of Missouri
Columbia, Missouri

**Shelley E. Taylor**
Department of Psychology
University of California, Los Angeles
Los Angeles, California

**Lydia Temoshok**
Department of Medicine
University of Maryland School of
Medicine
Baltimore, Maryland

**Beverly E. Thorn**
Department of Psychology
University of Alabama
Tuscaloosa, Alabama

**Barbara J. Tinsley**
Division of Social & Behavioral
Sciences
Arizona State University
Phoenix, Arizona

**Irina L.G. Todorova**
Health Psychology Research Center
Sofia, Bulgaria

**Emily L. Van Walleghen**
Department of Nutrition
University of Tennessee
Knoxville, Tennessee

**Sara Vargas**
Department of Psychology
University of Miami
Coral Gables, Florida

**Barbara B. Walker**
Department of Medicine
National Jewish Health
Denver, Colorado

**J. Lee Westmaas**
Behavioral Research Center
American Cancer Society
Atlanta, Georgia

**Dawn K. Wilson**
Department of Psychology
University of South Carolina
Columbia, South Carolina

**Camille B. Wortman**
Department of Psychology
Stony Brook University
Stony Brook, New York

**Nicole Zarrett**
Department of Psychology
University of South Carolina
Columbia, South Carolina

# CONTENTS

**Part Six · Conclusion**

# PART 1

# Background, History, and Methods

# The Intellectual Roots of Health Psychology

Howard S. Friedman *and* Nancy E. Adler

**Abstract**

Health psychology has deep and broad intellectual roots. Although the field of health psychology did not formally organize as a scientific discipline until the 1970s, its concepts grew out of a long philosophical tradition and from scientific developments in medical and clinical psychology, epidemiology and public health, medical sociology and anthropology, and psychosomatic medicine. Appreciation of these roots encourages more sophisticated concepts and models, and it helps modern researchers avoid common intellectual traps and sterile research paths.

**Keywords**: History, intellectual roots of health psychology, psychosomatic, biopsychosocial

For thousands of years, the understanding of physical ailments was closely tied to age-old notions of the body's spiritual nature. In early philosophies, the body's health and its spirit are inextricably bound. The biblical proverbs taught that "A merry heart does good like a medicine" (Proverbs 17:22). In ancient Greece, patients visited temples to be cured by Asclepias, the god of healing. These retreats, probably the first hospitals, often contained gardens and fountains, and included bathing, nutrition, and sometimes exercise in their healing rituals (Longrigg, 1998). In ancient Rome, holistic health promotion became quite sophisticated in the integration of individual well-being and public health, nourishing the spirit while building accessible baths, removing sewage, and constructing aqueducts for clean water. After the fall of the western Roman Empire and the ensuing decline in science and hygiene, some of the spiritual aspects of these ancient practices were adopted and maintained by early Christians in the Dark Ages (Guthrie, 1945), as healing shrines were set up throughout Europe.

## The Ancient World
By the 4th century BCE, the Greeks had conceived of a world composed of air, water, fire, and earth,

and this in turn had led to the notion of the four bodily humors: blood, phlegm, choler (yellow bile), and melancholy (black bile). This was the age of Hippocrates, who came to be known as the Father of Medicine as he and his colleagues used striking skills of observation to lay the basis for much of modern medicine. Perhaps their major accomplishment was to move the conceptions of health and illness away from supernatural causes and cures. For example, Hippocrates declared that epilepsy was a disease (caused by surplus phlegm in the brain), not a sacred spell or divine affliction. Importantly, the observations of these early Greek scholars demonstrated that the likelihood of certain diseases could be affected by one's food, work, location, and endowments.

It was in the Roman era, several hundred years later, that Greek ideas of health and medicine were developed into the foundation of what would become modern approaches to wellness. Galen, a Greek doctor in second-century Rome, both philosopher and anatomist (who dissected animals), revealed the body to be a beautifully balanced creation, in constant interaction with its environment. Galen emphasized the importance of the balance of humors to the causes of disease. The predominant humor in a person was thought to produce his or her dominant temperament, and an excess of a particular humor led to disease. For example, an excess of black bile was thought to produce a melancholic personality, gluttony, eventual depression, and associated physical illness. Psychology and health, and mental and physical health, were seen as closely related. Although these ancient notions of bodily humors have been discarded, the idea that the health-relevant emotional states of individuals can be categorized as sanguine, repressed, hostile, and depressed, as well as balanced or imbalanced, remains with us. It is interesting that this scheme of emotional aspects of personality and health was sufficiently perceptive (or ambiguous) to influence the practice of medicine for 2,000 years. Now, however, we speak of hormones (not humors) associated with optimism, anxiety, anger, and depression.

Analogous concern with balance and harmony emerged in Eastern medicine. Ayurvedic medicine, originating in India more than 2,000 years ago, paralleled Western medicine in the use of herbs, foods, emetics, and bleeding to restore harmony. Like early Western medicine, it had its share of demons, magic spells, and potions, but it also emphasized spiritual balance and personal hygiene. Traditional Chinese medicine was based upon balance between the yin and the yang—the active male force and the passive female force (Venzmer, 1972). Acupuncture, the insertion of needles into the skin at strategic points in order to restore the proper flow of energy, is an example of an ancient Chinese practice that continues to this day, although modern scientific attention in this area has expanded from bodily "forces" to the roles of neurotransmitters.

## Religion, Spiritual Healing, and the Cartesian Dualism

The philosophy of the Middle Ages was heavily concerned with religious and spiritual matters, and this speculation about the human soul and its ties to God directed attention away from biology. The pilgrims depicted in Chaucer's 14th century work, *The Canterbury Tales*, are on a pilgrimage to the shrine of St. Thomas à Becket, at Canterbury. For more than 1,000 years, pilgrims sought such shrines and saints to heal their illnesses through divine intervention.

On their journeys, European pilgrims often stopped at *hospices*, a place of rest for travelers, the elderly, and the sick. Hospices were one of the origins of the modern hospital. Ironically, as modern medicine developed in the 20th century, and hospitals became centers of aggressive medical intervention, the elderly and the dying were often moved out—and the emotional and spiritual aspects of care often departed as well. Hospices were eventually reconstituted as programs to care for the terminally ill, a development that dates from St. Christopher's, a London hospice founded by Cicely Saunders in the 1960s (Stoddard, 1978). These programs focus on the psychological and spiritual needs of the dying, along with traditional medical and palliative care. Many modern hospitals have much they could learn from hospices, both ancient and modern (Greer & Mor, 1986).

With the coming of the Renaissance (and the rebirth of classical ideas), the philosopher and mathematician René Descartes (1596–1650) struggled with the relations between the mind or soul and the physical body. By freeing the body from its religious or spiritual aspects, Descartes helped establish the science of medical biology, less encumbered by religious orthodoxy. But by separating the mind from the body (including separating the mind from the brain), Descartes created a major philosophical conundrum. Although what we think affects what we do, and what we experience affects what we think and feel, how can an intangible spirit interact with a material physicality?

Struggling with this dichotomy, some subsequent philosophers argued that the mental and the physical are different aspects of the same substance. For Spinoza (1632–1677), the superordinate aspect is God. Others argued that the physical world exists only to the extent that it is perceived by a mind. Still others claimed that the psyche does not exist, but is simply an epiphenomenon of the physical workings of the body. This history of dichotomy is important to modern health psychology because 17th- and 18th-century philosophy had a crucial impact on modern notions of human nature, the proper structure of society, and what it means to be healthy.

These issues came to a head in the latter part of the 19th century, as new developments in biology (evolution), medicine/physiology (neurology), and psychology (sensation) opened wide new fields of inquiry. Most psychologists thereafter followed the lead of William James (1890/1910) and pushed aside the philosophical puzzles to instead focus directly on thinking, feeling, and learning, and on the brain, the nerves, and the hormonal system (Benjamin, 1988; Boring, 1950). Yet, incomplete or overly narrow understanding of mind–body matters continues to challenge modern health psychology.

## The Interdisciplinary Scientific Roots

The modern discipline of health psychology is, at its best, an interdisciplinary endeavor, emerging from a confluence of important 20th-century intellectual trends in the understanding of health.

One key thread in the scientific origins of health psychology traces back to the work of Charles Darwin. In his seminal work, Darwin (1859) not only proposed his theory of evolution, but also expended considerable effort describing the biological and anatomical similarities between humans and other species. The revelation that human attributes had many elements in common with animals reinforced the Cartesian split between those focused on the life of the mind and those concerned with the physical functioning of the body. At the same time, Darwin's observations inspired research (that continues to this day) on those evolutionary processes affecting human emotion and its relation to well-being (Ekman et al., 2003; Ekman & Davidson, 1994; Sinnott-Armstrong, 2008).

Darwin's work also inspired the Russian physiologist Ivan Pavlov to begin examining the relations among environmental stimulation, learning, and physiological responses, a second important thread of modern health psychology. It contributed directly as well to Sigmund Freud's search for ways in which the hidden workings of the brain might influence health, as Freud examined the evolutionary significance of mental functioning.

## Roots in Medical-Clinical Psychology

In the latter half of the 19th century, the American Medical Association (AMA, founded 1847) began to establish minimal standards for medical education and medical practice. This was a time when practices such as bleeding and quack nostrums were widespread, and patients who sought treatment had a higher chance of being harmed than helped. By the early part of the 20th century, physicians had organized into guilds and obtained legal status to regulate medical practice. The placing of strict control over the practice of medicine into the hands of physicians had two far-reaching results. First, it assured a certain level of quality and standardization in medical care. Second, it concentrated authority into the hands of one group of professionals—physicians—who controlled the definition of health and deemed other (nonmedical) aspects of health care to be ancillary or peripheral.

This professionalization of medicine extended to medical education. The AMA established a Council on Medical Education, with Abraham Flexner charged with surveying the existing medical schools and evaluating their training. The 1910 Flexner report, *Medical Education in the United States and Canada,* became the basis of the reform of medical education, which included standardization of entry requirements and the development of a scientifically based curriculum (in which an initial 2 years of laboratory-based science training preceded 2 years of clinical training). At about the same time, efforts were made to integrate psychology into medical training (Vevier, 1987). In 1911, Shepherd Ivory Franz, a psychologist and director of the Government Hospital for the Insane in Washington D.C., attended a conference on the integration of psychology and medicine hosted by the American Psychological Association (APA) (Franz, 1912, 1913). Franz discussed such issues as "the success of placebos . . ." in which "the mental effect of knowledge appears to be much greater than the chemical action of the drug" (1912, p. 910). Today, the power of placebos is implicitly recognized in the design of clinical trials of new drugs and procedures, in which the "double-blind" randomized trial is the gold standard of evidence, although the mechanisms accounting for placebo responses are still not fully understood.

Franz chaired an APA committee that surveyed U.S. medical schools and recommended increased cooperation between psychology and medicine, inclusion of psychology in the medical curriculum, and an undergraduate course in psychology as a prerequisite for medical school. By 1928, a psychology professor, E. A. Bott, produced an essay entitled the "Teaching of Psychology in the Medical Course." Noting that two decades of debate about the role of psychology in medical education had already occurred, Bott concluded: ". . . there seems to be a wide and growing acceptance of the view that psychological factors have an important place in the life adjustments of persons (and patients) in general, and that our conception of health must be broadened to take these mental factors fully into account. Some orientation of students towards an understanding and appreciation of these factors should therefore be attempted through formal instruction" (Bott, 1928, p. 291).

Although a number of psychologists have served on the faculties of medical schools over the past century and introduced medical students to a psychological perspective, rarely has psychology been viewed by physicians as a core science for the practice of medicine. Suggestions for requiring preparation in psychology as a prerequisite for medical school admission were also not acted upon. Rather, psychologists in medical schools, for the most part, have been called upon to address the so-called "art of medicine," involving communication skills, the relationship between the physician and patient, and the motivation of patients to follow treatment prescriptions. Because this "art of medicine" clearly involved psychology, psychologists were expected to help in the "humanizing" of doctor–patient relations.

Prior to the establishment of the field of health psychology, matters of the psychological aspects of medical care were often termed *medical psychology*. For the most part, clinical psychologists with appointments in departments of psychiatry focused on mental illness and its treatment, as well as on doing liaison psychology consultations for distressed patients with serious chronic disease. In some places and some countries (especially Great Britain), medical psychology was closely tied to psychiatry and the treatment of mental illnesses, but in the United States, medical psychologists also worked in medical schools alongside pediatricians, gerontologists, and even internists. As other scientific and social forces later pushed toward the need for a discipline of health psychology, the presence of a cadre of psychologists in medical settings provided a tremendous depth of relevant knowledge about medical care. For example, in 1969, clinical psychologist William Schofield analyzed psychological research in health domains and projected evolving demand for psychological service in both prevention and treatment (Schofield, 1969).

Although calls for the integration of psychology "back" into the medical curriculum and medical practice continue (Novack, 2003), psychology has never been a core piece of modern medicine and health care. Psychologists were primarily employed to deal with deviant behavior, family crises, and stressful situations (such as cancer, burns, assaults, and other forms of trauma); and, of course, psychology was often a key part of the practice of psychiatry. Psychology was not, however, seen as central to health, either by most physicians or even by most psychologists. The psychological aspects of health were and are often viewed (incorrectly) as an "art," whereas the reality is that research and practice in health psychology involve a difficult and complicated science.

Substantial integration of psychological theory and findings into medical school curricula continues to be challenging. Psychological material is often viewed by physicians as marginal, as it lies outside the traditional biomedical focus on disease. Nonetheless, progress has been made, with national boards for medical students now assessing behavioral science knowledge. Moreover, a report from the Institute of Medicine (Cuff & Vanselow, 2004) explicitly addresses the need for such a curriculum, as well as the obstacles to integrating it. The report identified 20 topics that should be included in a medical school curriculum. Many of these topics are within the purview of health psychology, including psychosocial contributions to chronic disease; developmental influences on disease; psychosocial factors in pain; determinants and modification of health-relevant behaviors; patient and physician beliefs, attitudes, and values; communication skills; and social disparities in health. Implementation of these recommendations has been advanced by grants from the U.S. National Institutes of Health (NIH) to a number of medical schools. Concurrently, Clinical and Translational Science Awards from NIH have encouraged academic health centers to foster a stronger translation of lab-based findings to treatment and out to communities, and these awards also call for increased psychosocial expertise. Although these developments are positive, significant intellectual, conceptual, and structural barriers remain to the real integration of psychological principles and knowledge into medical training.

**Roots in Psychosomatic Medicine**

The development and use of sulfa drugs in the 1930s and penicillin in the 1940s had given physicians, for the first time, dramatically effective treatments for many acute problems, and "internal medicine" began its rise to prominence. Medical students began receiving extensive training in biochemistry and microbiology. Matters of the "mind" were increasingly left to psychiatry, newly emerging as an important specialty.

Sigmund Freud, influenced by Darwin, began conducting evolutionary research early in his training but was unwilling to reduce psychology to biology. Freud was fascinated by bio-psychological problems like hysterical paralysis, and other physicians interested in mind–body relations soon gravitated to Freudian and related psychoanalytic concepts. The psychoanalyst Franz Alexander (1950) argued that various diseases are caused by specific unconscious emotional conflicts. For example, he posited that ulcers were linked to oral conflicts (an unconscious desire to have basic infantile needs satisfied) and asthma to separation anxiety (that is, an unconscious desire to be protected by one's mother). The Menningers (1936), pioneering and influential psychiatrists, noted that very aggressive and ambitious men seemed prone to heart disease.

Flanders Dunbar, at Columbia University, postulated that mental disturbance often contributed to organic disease (Dunbar, 1943). In 1938–39, Dunbar started the journal *Psychosomatic Medicine*, which subsequently became the official journal of the American Psychosomatic Society (founded in 1942) (www.psychosomatic.org). It was believed that inner psychic conflicts disrupted normal bodily functioning and that the resolution of these psychological conflicts would contribute to a cure. Interestingly, given current knowledge of disease processes, other conditions of primary interest to the early psychosomatic physicians were colitis, hypertension, diabetes, arthritis, and dermatitis, although little was known about immunology, psychobiology, and metabolism, especially in relation to psychological processes. Psychosomatic practitioners and researchers of the mid-20th century thus amassed clinical observations and proposed links between external stress, internal psychological conflict, and organic disease, but developed few validated scientific principles or specific efficacious treatments.

By the 1970s, the growth of biological knowledge (neurobiology, neurochemistry, genetics, neurophysiology) overwhelmed traditional psychosomatic psychiatry, and biological psychiatry rose to prominence. For example, the discovery (in 1982) that the bacterium *Helicobacter pylori* was a contributing factor to the development of ulcers called the psychosomatic basis of ulcers into question. But the two explanations are not mutually exclusive: Even in the presence of the bacteria, individual variation occurs in the experience of symptoms and in the effects of stress on the stomach environment, and these are linked to psychosocial experience. However, a pure "psychosomatic" explanation is inadequate, and certainly obsessive mothers are not the root cause. Analogously, although it is today not uncommon for psychiatrists to treat depression and attention deficit disorder primarily through medication, such biological approaches are often viewed as incomplete (by both practitioners and by the general public), with demands for more attention to be directed toward psychological, social, and environmental factors that affect and interact with the biological.

Psychosomatic medicine eventually began using more rigorous research methods and incorporating sociobehavioral science and biological science. There was increasing concern with the cumbersome psychoanalytic jargon and the basic premises that did not easily lend themselves to empirical validation. There was also better appreciation of the scientific possibilities of sociobehavioral and epidemiologic research.

For example, cardiologists, noticing a psychological predisposition to heart disease, turned to both psychophysiological studies of stress and longitudinal studies of "type A behavior" and coronary heart disease (Rosenman et al., 1964). They called for a reliable assessment of "coronary disease-proneness" and a fully empirical scientific approach, but it remained mostly for psychologists to apply multitrait, multimethod assessments and construct validation to this inquiry (Houston & Snyder, 1988).

## Roots in Medical Sociology and Anthropology

Medical sociology and medical anthropology have made important contributions to understanding the social aspects of illness and the social roles of patients and healers, as studies across cultures, ethnicities, and social classes and social roles showed that illness is not simply a biological condition, but is inherently social and cultural as well. In the period of rapid societal change and medical progress following World War II, the influential medical sociologist Talcott Parsons (1902–1979) and his colleagues began documenting the social nature of illness. Parsons began his career as a biologist, but moved into social science and primarily worked toward combining structural and functional approaches to understanding basic phenomena of society, including sickness and health. The pioneering medical sociologists described how people in any given society share certain expectations (norms) about the rights and responsibilities of a person who is ill. These roles (such as "sick roles"— norms applied to a category of people, namely patients) guide and facilitate the functioning of both the individual and the society. For example, to become a "patient," one must enter the sick role and be treated by a "healer" (usually a physician in American society) (Parsons, 1951, 1958). A sick person is relieved from certain responsibilities (such as going to work) but must seek medical help and profess a desire to get well. The doctor can validate this new status (i.e., confirm that the person is ill and can be a patient). A sick person who does not try to get well, does not seem uncomfortable in the role of patient, and simply shirks all usual responsibilities may be removed from the role of patient, that is, called a fake or malingerer. Such sociological analyses delineated how illness is a social phenomenon (Hollingshead, 1973) that must be agreed to or validated by the opinions of others in the society; it is not just a function of some internal organic state.

These ideas complemented and illuminated the many conundrums of psychosomatic medicine, such as the surprisingly low correlation often found between documentable tissue (organic) damage and patient reports of illness. The analyses provided an intellectual opening to such puzzling issues as individual differences in reactions to pain, and individual differences in seeking medical care. Pain is not isomorphic with organic disintegration and indeed is often more heavily determined by upbringing, personality, mood, social roles, and current social circumstances (Pennebaker, 1982).

With regard to help-seeking, social influences lead to problems of both too little and too much. Many people delay seeking treatment, both for life-threatening emergencies like heart attacks and strokes, and for dangerous progressive conditions such as precancerous lesions, infections, and small tumors. On the other hand, many other people are quick to demand medical attention for every minor ache. The shared social definitions of health and illness have serious consequences for both the individual and the society.

Medical anthropologists further illuminated the ways in which symptoms are noticed, interpreted, and reported across cultures and subcultures (Adler & Stone, 1979). For example, Mark Zborowski (1952) and Irving Zola (1966) documented ethnic differences in the experience of pain and responses to it. Further, many conditions that are considered diseases in the United States—ranging from depression to neurasthenia to hearing voices—are ignored, or seen as normal, or imbued with different meanings in different countries and cultures (Foster & Anderson, 1978; Kleinman, 1986; Scheff, 1967). This work presaged current debates about which conditions represent "illness" and therefore deserve coverage by medical plans or health insurance. It is also relevant to the struggles of clinical health psychologists to receive reimbursements as health practitioners.

The importance of medical sociology and medical anthropology have grown with the increasing cultural diversity of many Western populations, as well as with issues emerging from a global health perspective. Health care workers increasingly are being evaluated in terms of their "cultural competence" and ability to relate to patients from very different backgrounds, taking into account their patients' belief systems as these affect disease prevention, diagnoses, and treatment.

It is now clear that sociocultural, developmental, and sociodemographic forces, including age, gender, class, wealth, ethnicity, family, work, and nationality, are integral parts of a comprehensive understanding of health and illness (Adler, 2009). Modern health psychology, as a discipline partly rooted in social science, includes such concepts in its theories and its research, and addresses ethnic disparities in health, special issues in women's health, and sociodemographic considerations in health promotion.

## Roots in Epidemiology and Public Health

The late 19th century and the first half of the 20th century saw great changes in public health. First, the Industrial Revolution vastly increased the wealth of working people in Western societies and created a substantial middle class. Second, the work of French chemist Louis Pasteur and his colleagues on microorganisms, and the demonstrations of infection prevention by English surgeon Joseph Lister in the 1860s (see Metchnikoff, 1939) and others, led to the construction of *germ theory*—the idea that many diseases are caused by microorganisms. Together, these developments led to enormous changes in the quality of drinking water, the treatment of sewage, and the handling and storage of food (e.g., refrigeration).

As modern cities and suburbs developed, people gained access to safe drinking water, decent shelter, flush toilets, trash removal, and inspected, monitored, and nutritious food. On the individual level, hand-washing and other sanitary practices also increased, as people understood the transmission of infectious disease. Together, all these factors produced a dramatic decrease in the death rate from infectious disease (Grob, 1983; McKeown, 1976, 1979). Life expectancy in North America and Western Europe rose dramatically. The vivid decline in deaths from many infectious diseases occurred in advance of the availability of antibiotics, and even for diseases for which no vaccinations were available. For example, death rates from measles for children in England fell over 99% from 1850 to 1950 (McKeown, 1976), even though the measles vaccine was not introduced until the 1960s. Nevertheless, the introduction of vaccinations, beginning with a smallpox vaccine in the 1880s, paralleled the timeframe of the introduction of improved sanitation, nutrition, and living conditions, and further lowered the death rate and decreased morbidity from infectious agents. Together, these sanitation- and vaccination-related public health measures produced a remarkable improvement in health in the 100 years preceding the 1950s.

Interestingly, life expectancy in developed countries began to level off just as antibiotics fully entered the scene. As advances in biochemistry research created more and more antimicrobial drugs, the field of internal medicine came into its own—with the unintended side effect of obscuring the broader trends in public health. In other words, the dramatic increase in longevity was overattributed to "miracle drugs" (biomedical cures), rather than properly credited to plunging childhood mortality rates and new control of epidemics. Psychologically speaking, people could better understand cures as a result of miracle drugs than to make the connections between increased life expectancy and a largely invisible set of public health measures; this phenomenon still hinders public health efforts today.

As mortality from infectious diseases declined, death rates from cardiovascular disease skyrocketed to become the leading cause of death. Slowly, very slowly, the idea began to emerge (or, more accurately, *re-emerge*) that lifestyle—including behaviors like diet, cigarette smoking, and physical activity—might have significant effects on serious illnesses like heart disease. Starting in 1948, about 5,000 residents of Framingham, Massachusetts, were followed to see what behaviors and other risk factors might affect (predict) heart disease and stroke. The Framingham Study revealed that lifestyle-related conditions like hypertension (high blood pressure) were significant risk factors. By the 1970s, it began to seem both sensible and feasible to try *prevent* (rather than merely *treat*) the development of cardiovascular disease and other slow-developing conditions as well. The stage was thus set for the new field of health psychology to incorporate a public health perspective as a significant core concept; it would address psychological factors in the prevention of disease, as well as in treatment and recovery. Yet, it was not until 1990 that the U.S. government emphatically urged the adoption of lifestyles maximally conducive to good health (Healthy People 2000, 1990). The importance of behavior was underlined in a landmark article that showed that the primary "actual causes of death" in the United States were smoking, poor diet, lack of exercise, other risk behaviors (McGinnis & Foege, 1993).

The focus on prevention has remained a core concept in public health as well as in health psychology. The World Health Organization (WHO), an agency of the United Nations, was established in 1948 with a focus on complete physical, mental, and social well-being. It followed a predecessor organization in the League of Nations, set up to help control worldwide epidemics such as typhus and cholera. The WHO, along with other organizations addressing global health, has documented that chronic diseases tied to behavioral factors are increasing in the developing world (Yach, Hawkes,

Gould, & Hofman, 2004). It is not simply that, as infectious diseases are being reduced, there is more opportunity for chronic diseases to account for mortality. Rather, it appears that health-damaging behaviors, such as tobacco use and ingestion of excessive amounts of high-calorie foods, increase as nations experience economic development. Health promotion thus should be a critical component of global health. A WHO report presents a compelling case for the social determinants of health and their impact on the health inequities that now exist (Marmot et al., 2008). The more distal determinants work in part through behavioral and psychosocial pathways (Adler & Stewart, 2010).

Although medicine has traditionally paid less attention to prevention, changes in health care organization and delivery have encouraged a greater concern. Under fee-for-service arrangements, physicians have little financial incentive to spend time and resources on prevention since such activity is rarely compensated. In contrast, health maintenance organizations (HMOs) and similar groups that receive capitated payments (i.e., receive a lump sum per person per year) have greater motivation to help their patients avoid the need for medical care. HMOs such as Kaiser Permanente (begun in the 1930s in California) and HIP (Health Insurance Plan, begun in 1947, in New York), which care for patients over the long term, tend to invest more in prevention and have often integrated psychologists into their practices. This shift to managing health for populations opens opportunities for health psychologists in concepts, research, and practice.

### The Biopsychosocial Models

In the 1930s, researcher-physician Adolf Meyer proposed that stressful life events may be important in the etiology of illness (Meyer, 1948). He suggested that these events need not be negative or catastrophic to be pathogenic; they must simply be interpreted by the individual as an important life change. This work wrapped a social psychological context around the pioneering efforts of the experimental physiologist and physician, Walter Cannon. Cannon, following up on the investigations of the 19th-century French physiologist Claude Bernard, focused attention on the stress on the body from emotional activation. Bernard (1880) had emphasized the *milieu interne*—the internal environment—the idea that all living things must maintain a constant or balanced internal environment, thus making scientific the study of homeostasis. Cannon followed up on these ideas, discovering and explaining the relations among stress, the nervous system, and the endocrine system. He proposed one of the most important concepts in health psychology, the so-called "wisdom of the body" (Cannon, 1932).

In 1896, while still a medical student, Cannon began using the newly discovered x-rays to study digestion. He noticed that stomach movements seemed to be affected by emotional state (Benison, Barger, & Wolfe, 1987). Rather than viewing this finding as noisy data interfering with his study of the biology of digestion, Cannon went on to explore what causes the subjective feelings of a "knot in the stomach" when facing a stressful or fear-arousing situation. By 1932, Cannon was able to write a detailed analysis of how bodily alterations occur in conjunction with emotional strife and the experiencing of emotions such as anger or fear (Cannon 1932, 1942). He documented that stress causes an increase in the blood sugar level; a large output of adrenaline (epinephrine); an increase in pulse rate, blood pressure, and respiration rate; and an increase in the amount of blood pumped to the skeletal muscles—termed the *fight-or-flight response*.

Importantly, according to Cannon and his homeostasis approach, the body has developed a margin of safety, with allowance for contingencies that we count on in times of stress. In other words, the body naturally prepares itself for challenge, including the rare "extra" challenge. This robust internal regulation—this wisdom of the body to self-correct—is built around the hypothalamic-pituitary-adrenal (HPA) system, but extends to systems throughout the body. Cannon also observed that the body exists in a social and environmental context, and presciently argued that the study of psychophysiology should not ignore the larger issues of coping with environmental stress.

The idea that sundry noxious stimuli, be they emotional or physical, result in a biological, neuroendocrine response was championed in the 1930s by Hans Selye (1956), who studied the physiological consequences of an ongoing response to threat. In his view, just about any type of threat would produce an arousal in the body's system of defenses against noxious stimuli. But in Selye's model, stress would not necessarily lead to disease unless the adaptive responses are required for a prolonged period of time, an idea consistent with modern views on stress and disruption of metabolic and immune systems.

Harold Wolff (1953), a physician with great influence in psychiatric circles, continued this evolutionary view, with a focus on seeing stress as a response to *perceived* challenge or danger, rather than to a necessarily threatening or noxious stimulus. For Wolff, as for Selye, it was continuing but futile efforts to achieve homeostasis through maladaptive coping (such as constant worrying and arousal) that would lead to illness. Note that these models are more general and nonspecific than the "specific conflict to disease" models typically proposed by Dunbar and other founders of psychosomatic medicine. Even today, within modern neurobiology and psychoneuroimmunology, the debate continues about whether stress phenomena mostly begin with a general weakening and vulnerability, or instead involve mostly disease-specific disruptions of a particular biological mechanism.

More recently, neuroscientist Bruce McEwen built on the concept of allostasis introduced by Sterling and Eyer (1988) to capture the physiological effects of chronic stress exposure. Although homeostasis explains the body's response to an acute event, the associated process of allostasis maintains stability through change over time. This led to the important observation that responses that are functional in the short-term can exact a cost if maintained over time, leading to an "allostatic load" (McEwen, 1998, 2007). The processes of allostasis use the autonomic nervous system, the HPA axis, and the cardiovascular, metabolic, and immune systems to respond to challenge. Repeated stresses over time (many challenges, lack of adaptation, or lingering stress) cause ongoing and increased exposure to stress hormones, harming many physiological functions. The idea of allostasis, although not radically different from previous notions of stress and homeostasis, emphasizes the processes involved in the constant reestablishment of homeostasis and explains how even small degrees of dysregulation, when cumulated across systems, can contribute to disease susceptibility. It is striking how much of the most modern notions involve the same basic adaptation systems uncovered by Cannon and Selye.

This physiological work on stress response was paralleled by psychological research on the nature of stress and how individuals respond to (i.e., cope with) such stressors. In social psychology, Irving Janis (1958), in turning attention toward managing challenges, examined psychological coping mechanisms in facing the stress of surgery. His research showed that, before surgery, some patients were worried about their operation and felt very vulnerable; other patients were somewhat concerned and asked for information about their surgery; whereas still other patients were extremely cheerful and relaxed before their operation and did not want to know anything about it. Reactions differed after surgery, and these differences were related in systematic ways to the presurgery behaviors. The highly fearful and the totally fearless patients experienced poorer postoperative reactions compared to patients with a moderate amount of anticipatory fear. These successful patients rehearsed ways of dealing with the stresses they faced, a phenomenon referred to by Janis as "the work of worrying."

Around the same time, Richard Lazarus (1966) began research that showed that an individual's appraisal of the meaning of an event was critical for determining if it was experienced as stressful. Individuals experience stress when they perceive that they do not have the resources needed to address a given threat. An environmental event is not stressful if the individual appraises (interprets) it as manageable. Along with his collaborator, Susan Folkman, Lazarus elaborated the ways of coping with these threats and the implications of these efforts for health (Lazarus & Folkman, 1984). Such research helped launch the modern era of work on stress and coping.

Studying both the new developments in psychosomatic psychiatry and the emerging ideas of coping with stress, the physician George Engel (1968, 1977) helped bring together the various threads of mind–body approaches to health. Engel and his colleagues argued that a "giving up" response in the face of situations of loss may precede the development of various illnesses in individuals who have *predispositions* to the particular illnesses. Engel combined the environment (e.g., loss), the ability or inability to cope, and a set of common biological pathways to various health problems.

On the psychobiological side, health psychology was given a big push forward by Neal Miller (1976) and his colleagues. Miller was an eminent psychological researcher of learning and motivation during several decades at Yale University. In the 1960s, he moved to Rockefeller University (a center of brain research) and focused on integrating learning principles with the new discipline of behavioral neuroscience. As research techniques improved, Miller looked further into how the brain affected motivation and learning, and vice versa. By showing that organisms could sometimes learn to control bodily functions such as heartbeat, blood pressure, and intestinal contractions (that are regulated by the autonomic nervous system), Miller helped open the door to rigorous research on such topics as biofeedback, placebo effects, and relaxation training.

Also in the 1960s and 1970s, researchers overturned the assumption that the body's immune system acted autonomously, without input from the nervous system. For example, psychologist Robert Ader, who was studying the classical conditioning of learned taste aversion in rats, was puzzled when rats that had been injected with an immune-suppressing drug became ill during subsequent experiments, long after the drug was gone from their systems. Ader teamed with immunologist Nicholas Cohen and (using principles of conditioning) found that when the immune-suppressing drug (unconditioned stimulus) was paired with sweetened water (conditioned stimulus), the rats subsequently became ill when they received only the sweetened water (Ader & Cohen, 1975, 1985; Kemeny, 2011, Chapter 7, this volume). This work provided a clear demonstration that the immune system could be classically conditioned. The immune system had learned to respond to the environment and was communicating with the nervous system. Such research helped launch the modern field of psychoneuroimmunology, which postulates that environmental psychosocial challenges may cause or encourage disease through stress effects on suppressing or disrupting the immune system.

Together, these researchers (and others) thus demonstrated the importance of integrating the biological, the psychological, and the social, both conceptually and empirically. The general approach that emerged from the theorizing of Cannon, Selye, Engel, and others (Rodin & Stone, 1987) has come to be called the *biopsychosocial approach to health* (Fig. 1.1).

Consistent with the broad intellectual roots of health psychology, the founding health psychologists recognized that they themselves had not received training in the broad new field of health psychology. Rather, each brought to the field his or her own disciplinary background, but with an appreciation that this provided only part of the picture. They believed that psychologists would be better equipped if they were trained not only in their psychological disciplines but also in the issues of health and health care. It was not obvious, however, what the core training should be for this field. In May of 1983, a foundational conference was held at the Arden House, an old mansion on the Hudson River. The meeting was called the National Working Conference on Education and Training in Health Psychology (see Stone et al., 1987). We attended that gathering and remember it as an exhilarating blend of differing approaches to the same fundamental questions of psychology and health, with a fitting mountaintop location that allowed a glimpse of the "promised land."

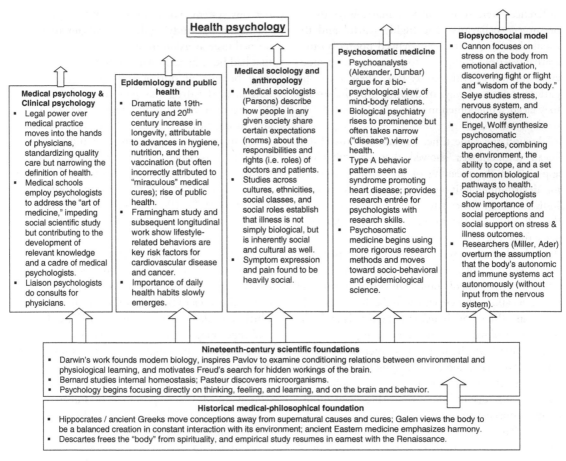

**Health psychology**

**Medical psychology & Clinical psychology**
- Legal power over medical practice moves into the hands of physicians, standardizing quality care but narrowing the definition of health.
- Medical schools employ psychologists to address the "art of medicine," impeding social scientific study but contributing to the development of relevant knowledge and a cadre of medical psychologists.
- Liaison psychologists do consults for physicians.

**Epidemiology and public health**
- Dramatic late 19th-century and 20th century increase in longevity, attributable to advances in hygiene, nutrition, and then vaccination (but often incorrectly attributed to "miraculous" medical cures); rise of public health.
- Framingham study and subsequent longitudinal work show lifestyle-related behaviors are key risk factors for cardiovascular disease and cancer.
- Importance of daily health habits slowly emerges.

**Medical sociology and anthropology**
- Medical sociologists (Parsons) describe how people in any given society share certain expectations (norms) about the responsibilities and rights (i.e. roles) of doctors and patients.
- Studies across cultures, ethnicities, social classes, and social roles establish that illness is not simply biological, but is inherently social and cultural as well.
- Symptom expression and pain found to be heavily social.

**Psychosomatic medicine**
- Psychoanalysts (Alexander, Dunbar) argue for a bio-psychological view of mind-body relations.
- Biological psychiatry rises to prominence but often takes narrow ("disease") view of health.
- Type A behavior pattern seen as syndrome promoting heart disease; provides research entrée for psychologists with research skills.
- Psychosomatic medicine begins using more rigorous research methods and moves toward socio-behavioral and epidemiological science.

**Biopsychosocial model**
- Cannon focuses on stress on the body from emotional activation, discovering fight or flight and "wisdom of the body." Selye studies stress, nervous system, and endocrine system.
- Engel, Wolff synthesize psychosomatic approaches, combining the environment, the ability to cope, and a set of common biological pathways to health.
- Social psychologists show importance of social perceptions and social support on stress & illness outcomes.
- Researchers (Miller, Ader) overturn the assumption that the body's autonomic and immune systems act autonomously (without input from the nervous system).

**Nineteenth-century scientific foundations**
- Darwin's work founds modern biology, inspires Pavlov to examine conditioning relations between environmental and physiological learning, and motivates Freud's search for hidden workings of the brain.
- Bernard studies internal homeostasis; Pasteur discovers microorganisms.
- Psychology begins focusing directly on thinking, feeling, and learning, and on the brain and behavior.

**Historical medical-philosophical foundation**
- Hippocrates / ancient Greeks move conceptions away from supernatural causes and cures; Galen views the body to be a balanced creation in constant interaction with its environment; ancient Eastern medicine emphasizes harmony.
- Descartes frees the "body" from spirituality, and empirical study resumes in earnest with the Renaissance.

**Fig. 1.1** The intellectual roots of health psychology.

This National Working Conference emphasized the coming rapprochement between psychology and health care. It recommended a focus on quality; a broad, interdisciplinary orientation; and significant attention to ethical, legal, and cultural issues. Anticipating the strain between science and practice, the recommendations also had a strong professional (clinical and public health) component embedded in science and emphasizing an integrated mix of theory and practice, training experience in health care settings, and the licensure of health psychologists (Stone, 1983). This interplay between science and practice should be synergistic, with clinical insights suggesting new hypotheses and research findings informing practice. However, a tension also exists between scientists and practitioners as health psychologists immersed in patient care seek specific advice and techniques for interventions, while health psychologists focused on the scientific underpinnings of health and health policy tend toward more complex and nuanced concepts and models. Nevertheless, the field of health psychology remains an excellent example of

the mutual benefits of reciprocal progress between theory and practice, research and application, and policy and implementation.

## Defining Health Psychology

As an academic discipline, health psychology might best be defined as *the scientific study of psychological processes related to health and health care*. As a professional and policy field, health psychology might best be defined as *the use of findings from basic psychological theory and peer-reviewed research to understand and encourage thoughts, feelings, and behaviors that promote health*.

These definitions are narrower than the foundational definitions from the 1980s, which talk about the educational, scientific, and professional contributions of psychology to the promotion of health, the maintenance of health, the prevention of illness, the treatment of illness, and the analysis and improvement of the health care system and health policy (Matarazzo, 1980, 1983; Stone, 1987; Wallston, 1997). Such broad definitions include almost everything having to do with psychology and health. Because almost every aspect of psychology has some implications for well-being, and because almost every aspect of health and health care involves some aspect of psychology (such as decision-making, communication, psychophysiology, or behavior), a broad definition of health psychology means that almost everything in psychology and almost everything in health care involves health psychology. In actuality, however, health psychologists largely focus on core psychological processes related to health. These include social support; coping with stress; communication and patient adherence; adaptation to chronic illness; health developmental issues in childhood, adolescence, and aging; health risk behavior and behavioral health promotion; resource allocation and decision-making in health care; psychopharmacology; personality and disease; pain management; social context and other social influences on health; and the central nervous system, hormones, and immunity. Increasing knowledge in genetics, epigenetics, and cellular biology is providing new frontiers of research, as health psychologists link psychological processes and biological mechanisms at fundamental levels. For example, new research ties stress to cellular aging and, in turn, to cardiovascular disease risk. (Epel et al., 2004, 2006). Interdisciplinary work, based in knowledge of its deep and broad roots, promises to continue to extend the purview and impact of the field of health psychology.

## References

Ader R., & Cohen N. (1975). Behaviorally conditioned immuno-suppression. *Psychosomatic Medicine, 37,* 333–340.

Ader, R., & Cohen, N. (1985). CNS-immune system interaction: Conditioning phenomena. *The Behavioral and Brain Sciences, 8,* 379–394.

Adler, N.E. (2009). Health disparities through a psychological lens. *American Psychologist, 64,* 663–673.

Adler, N.E., & Stewart, J (Eds.). (2010). *Biology of disadvantage: Socioeconomic status and health.* New York: Wiley Blackwell.

Adler, N.E., & Stone, G.C. (1979). Social science perspectives on the health system. In G.C. Stone, F. Cohen, & N.E. Adler (Eds.), *Health psychology—A handbook* (pp. 19–46). San Francisco: Jossey-Bass.

Alexander, F. (1950). *Psychosomatic medicine: Its principles and applications.* New York; Norton.

Bernard, C. (1880). *Leçons de pathologie expérimentale: Et leçons sur les propriétés de la moelle épinière.* Paris: Librarie J.-B. Baillière et fils.

Benjamin, L.T. Jr. (Ed.). (1988). *A history of psychology: Original sources and contemporary research.* New York: McGraw-Hill.

Benison, S., Barger, A.C., & Wolfe, E. (1987). *Walter B. Cannon: The life and times of a young scientist.* Cambridge: Harvard University Press.

Boring, E. (1950). *A history of experimental psychology.* New York: Appleton-Century-Crofts.

Bott, E.A. (1928). Teaching of psychology in the medical course. *Bulletin of the Association of American Medical Colleges, 3,* 289–304.

Cannon, W.B. (1932). *Wisdom of the body.* New York: W.W. Norton.

Cannon, W.B. (1942). Voodoo death. *American Anthropologist, 44,* 169–181.

Cuff, P.A., & Vanselow, N. (2004). *Improving medical education: Enhancing the behavioral and social science content of medical school education.* Washington DC: National Academies Press.

Darwin, C. (1859). *On the origin of species by means of natural selection.* London: J. Murray.

Dunbar, F.H. (1943). *Psychosomatic diagnosis.* New York: Hoeber.

Ekman, P., Campos, J.J., Davidson, R.J., & de Waal, F.B.M. (Eds.). (2003). Emotions inside out: 130 years after Darwin's: The expression of the emotions in man and animal. *Annals of the New York Academy of Sciences, 1000,* 152–179. New York, NY: New York University Press.

Ekman, P., & Davidson, R.J. (Eds.). (1994). *The nature of emotion: Fundamental questions.* New York: Oxford University Press.

Engel, G.L. (1968). A life setting conducive to illness: The giving up-given up complex. *Bulletin of the Menninger Clinic, 32,* 355–365.

Engel, G.L. (1977). The need for a new medical model: A challenge for biomedicine. *Science, 196,* 129–136.

Epel, E.S., Blackburn, E.H., Lin, J., Dhabhar, F.S., Adler, N.E., Morrow, J.D., & Cawthon, R.M. (2004). Accelerated telomere shortening in response to life stress. *Proceedings of the National Academy of Sciences, 101*(49), 17312–17315.

Epel, E.S., Lin, J., Wilhelm, F.H., Wolkowitz, O.M., Cawthon, R., Adler, N.E., et al. (2006). Cell aging in relation to stress arousal and cardiovascular disease risk factors. *Psychoneuroendocrinology, 31,* 277–287.

Foster, G.M., & Anderson, B.G. (1978). *Medical anthropology.* New York: Wiley.

Franz, S.I. (1912). The present status of psychology in medical education and practice. *Journal of the American Medical association, 58,* 909–911.

Franz, S.I. (1913). On psychology and medical education. *Science, 38,* 555–566.

Greer, D.S., & Mor, V. (1986). An overview of national hospice study findings. *Journal of Chronic Diseases, 39,* 5–7.

Grob, G.N. (1983). *Mental illness and American society, 1875–1940.* Princeton, NJ: Princeton University Press.

Guthrie, D. (1945). *A history of medicine.* London: T. Nelson and Sons.

Healthy People 2000. (1990). National Health Promotion and Disease Prevention. Washington DC: U.S. Department of Health and Human Services.

Hollingshead, A. (1973). Medical sociology: A brief review. *Milbank Memorial Fund Quarterly, 51,* 531–542.

Houston, B.K., & Snyder, C.R. (Eds.). (1988). *Type A behavior pattern: Research, theory, and intervention.* New York: Wiley.

James, W. (1890/1910). *The principles of psychology.* New York: Holt.

Janis, I.L. (1958). *Psychological stress: Psychoanalytic and behavioral studies of surgical patients.* New York: John Wiley.

Kemeny, M.E. (2011). Psychoneuroimmunology. In H.S. Friedman (Ed.), *The Oxford handbook of health psychology.* New York: Oxford University Press.

Kleinman, A. (1986). *Social origins of distress and disease: Depression, neurasthenia, and pain in modern China.* New Haven, CT: Yale University Press.

Lazarus, R.S. (1966). *Psychological stress and the coping process.* New York: McGraw-Hill.

Lazarus, R.S., & Folkman, S. (1984). *Stress, appraisal, and coping.* New York: Springer.

Longrigg, J. (1998). *Greek medicine: From the heroic to the Hellenistic age: A source book.* New York: Routledge.

Marmot, M., Friel, S., Bell, R., Houweling, T.A.J., & Taylor, S. (2008). *Commission on Social Determinants of Health. Final report.* Geneva: World Health Organization.

Matarazzo, J.D. (1980). Behavioral health and behavioral medicine. Frontiers for a new health psychology. *American Psychologist, 35*, 807–817.

Matarazzo, J.D. (1983). Education and training in health psychology: Boulder or Bolder. *Health Psychology, 2*, 73–113.

McEwen, B.S. (1998). Stress, adaptation and disease: Allostasis and allostatic load. *Annals of the New York Academy of Sciences, 840*, 33–44.

McEwen, B.S. (2007). Physiology and neurobiology of stress and adaptation: Central role of the brain. *Physiological Review, 87*, 873–904.

McGinnis, M., & Foege, W. (1993). Actual causes of death in the United States. *Journal of the American Medical Association, 270*(16), 2207–2211.

McKeown, T. (1976). *The modern rise of population.* London: Edward Arnold.

McKeown, T. (1979). *The role of medicine.* Princeton: Princeton University Press.

Menninger, K.A., & Menninger, W.C. (1936). Psychoanalytic observations in cardiac disorders. *American Heart Journal, 11*, 1–21.

Metchnikoff, E. (1939). *The founders of modern medicine: Pasteur, Koch, Lister; Including Etiology of wound infections, by Robert Koch, The antiseptic system, by Sir Joseph Lister, and Prevention of rabies, by Louis Pasteur.* Translated by D. Berger. New York: Walden Publications.

Meyer, A. (1948). Selected papers. In A. Lief (Ed.), *The commonsense psychiatry of Dr. Adolf Meyer.* New York: McGraw-Hill.

Miller, N.E. (1976). *Fact and fancy about biofeedback and its clinical implications.* Washington, DC: American Psychological Association.

Novack, D.H. (2003). Realizing Engel's vision: Psychosomatic medicine and the education of physician-healers. *Psychosomatic Medicine, 65*, 925–930.

Parsons, T. (1951). *The social system.* New York: Free Press.

Parsons, T. (1958). Definitions of health and illness in the light of American values and social structure. In E.G. Jaco (Ed.), *Physicians, patients, and illness: Sourcebook in behavioral science and medicine* (pp. 165–187). Glencoe, IL: Free Press.

Pennebaker, J.W. (1982). *The psychology of physical symptoms.* New York: Springer-Verlag.

Rodin, J., & Stone, G. (1987). Historical highlights in the emergence of the field. In G. Stone et al. (Eds.), *Health Psychology:* *A discipline and a profession* (pp. 15–26). Chicago: University of Chicago Press.

Rosenman, R.H., Friedman, M., Straus, R., Wurm, M., Kositcheck, R., Hahn, W., & Werthesson, N. (1964). A predictive study of coronary disease. The western collaborative group study. *Journal of the American Medical Association, 189*, 103–110.

Scheff, T.J. (Ed.). (1967). *Mental illness and social processes.* New York: Harper & Row.

Schofield, W. (1969). The role of psychology in the delivery of health services. *American Psychologist, 24*, 565–584.

Selye, H. (1956). *The stress of life.* New York: McGraw-Hill.

Sinnott-Armstrong, W. (Ed.). (2008). *Moral psychology: The evolution of morality: Adaptations and innateness.* Cambridge, MA: MIT Press.

Sterling P., & Eyer J. (1988). Allostasis: A new paradigm to explain arousal pathology. In S. Fisher & J. Reason (Eds.), *Handbook of life stress, cognition and health* (pp. 629–649). New York: Wiley & Sons.

Stoddard, S. (1978). *The hospice movement: A better way of caring for the dying.* New York: Vintage Books.

Stone, G.C. (1983). Summary of recommendations. *Health Psychology, 2*(5), 15–18.

Stone, G.C. (1987). The scope of health psychology. In Stone, G.C., Weiss, S.M., Matarazzo, J.D., Miller, N.E., Rodin, J. Belar, C.D., et al. (Eds.), *Health psychology: A discipline and a profession* (pp. 27–40). Chicago: University of Chicago Press.

Stone, G.C., Weiss, S.M., Matarazzo, J.D., Miller, N.E., Rodin, J., Belar, C.D., et al. (Eds.). (1987). *Health psychology: A discipline and a profession.* Chicago: University of Chicago Press.

Venzmer, G. (1972). Five thousand years of medicine. Translated from the German by M. Koenig. London: Macdonald and Co.

Vevier, C. (Ed.). (1987). *Flexner 75 years later: A current commentary on medical education.* Lanham, MD: University Press of America.

Wallston, K.A (1997). A history of Division 38 (Health Psychology). In D.A. Dewsbury (Ed.), *Unification through division: Histories of the divisions of the American Psychological Association* (Vol. 2, pp. 239–267). Washington, DC: American Psychological Association.

Wolff, H.G. (1953). *Stress and disease.* Springfield, IL: Thomas.

Yach, D., Hawkes, C., Gould, C.L., & Hofman, K. (2004). The global burden of chronic diseases. *Journal of the American Medical Association 291*(21), 2616–2622.

Zborowski, M. (1952). Cultural components in responses to pain. *Journal of Social Issues, 8*, 16–30.

Zola, I.K. (1966). Culture and symptoms: An analysis of patients presenting complaints. *American Sociological Review, 31*, 615–630.

CHAPTER

2

# A History of the Development of Health Psychology

Wade E. Pickren *and* Silvia Degni

**Abstract**

A long tradition of thought and practice has asserted important connections between psychological states and physical health. The possible mechanisms or paths of influence may have changed over time and varied across locations, but humans have long believed that how they think and what they feel may be intimately linked to whether they are healthy or sick. This chapter focuses on those ideas and practices that led to this tradition's eventual expression, in the late 20th century, in what came to be labeled health psychology. Beginning with developments in the mid to late 19th century, it tracks the convergence of thought and application that came together in the 20th century in a manner that made it possible to carve out a new area of disciplinary and professional expertise, that addressed health and disease from the perspective of the discipline of psychology.

**Keywords**: Psychological states, physical health, health psychology, Europe, North America, psychology

A long tradition of thought and practice has asserted important connections between psychological states and physical health. The possible mechanisms or paths of influence may have changed over time and varied across locations, but humans have long believed that how they think and what they feel may be intimately linked to whether they are healthy or sick. For a review of these developments over the course of human history, the reader is referred to Friedman and Adler (2007). In this chapter, we restrict our description of this tradition to ideas and practices that led to its eventual expression in the formation of what came to be labeled, in the late 20th century, as health psychology. We begin with developments in the mid to late 19th century and track the convergence of thought and application that came together in the 20th century in a manner that made it possible to carve out a new area of disciplinary and professional expertise that addressed health and disease from the perspective of the discipline of psychology. We cover events and material from Europe and the United States. In doing so, we

recognize the many important contributions made from outside these locales and only omit them due to space constrictions.

## "How to Live": Americans and the Search for Health in the 19th Century

The 19th century was a period of great change in the United States, with consequences for the eventual development of health psychology. As the century began, the United States was largely a rural society whose population, although not entirely homogeneous, was principally of Anglo-Saxon and Northern European descent. This changed, so that by the end of the century, the population was increasingly urban, and industrialization had replaced agriculture and trades as the predominant source of employment. Immigration in the second half of the century made the country more ethnically diverse, with large influxes of immigrants from southern and eastern Europe and China. By the end of the century, American life had been reshaped by these and other forces.

Americans also became better educated over the course of the century. By mid-century, the United States had the highest literacy rate in the world. One result of this was the increased demand for printed materials of all kinds, which proliferated, so that Americans were flooded with pamphlets, flyers, broadsides, magazines, and books. Each of these media fostered the dissemination of new ideas, along with the increasingly popular public lecture and demonstration. Through these avenues, Americans became aware of new developments that focused on mental life and its powers—like mesmerism, phrenology, New Thought, Spiritualism, and, by the end of the century, the New Psychology.

A vitally important part of this mix of new knowledge and practice was an emphasis on personal health, especially the purported importance of mental healing, diet, and wellness. For much of the century, the weight of this emphasis was on what one could do to obtain and maintain health. Thus, Americans from all walks of life came to be concerned about how to live the best life. Increasingly, the mind and psychological factors were thought to be keys to a healthy life.

These new approaches developed alongside formal medicine. As historians of medicine have pointed out, the 19th century was the era of great debate, contention, controversy, and competition among several models of disease, health, and medical practice: naturopathy, allopathy, and homeopathy, among others (Warner, 1997). Until the late 19th century, one could still become a physician through an apprenticeship, without any formal medical education (Cassedy, 1991; Starr, 1984). This reflected a different understanding about science, which most Americans—indeed most educated people in the Western world—understood as any form of systematic knowledge. This began to change under the influence of the German research universities, so that by the last third of the century, American colleges began to transform themselves into universities, with America's first such graduate research university, Johns Hopkins University, established at Baltimore in 1876.

The background of our history of health and psychology also must include another critical aspect. In post-Revolutionary War America, there arose a strong belief that every person could think and decide for himself, whether the matter concerned religion, medicine, personal health, or any other issue (Hatch, 1989). Historians often call this *Jacksonian populism* because of the character of the presidency of Andrew Jackson in the 1820s. Jackson was a rough-and-tumble "common man" who inspired an ethos of the self-made man and a disregard for the privileges typically accorded the elites. In this anti-authoritarian environment, the canons of traditional societies with their social hierarchies were challenged, along with the received authorities of medicine, religion, science, and other professions. Many individuals asserted their own interpretations of medicine and health, as well as science and religion. Thus, this was an age of exploration of new ideas about human nature, including new ideas about health (Delbourgo, 2006).

In this rich mix of people, ideas, population growth, and an expanding frontier, Americans took on the challenge of creating their own identity and asserted their right to decide for themselves the best way to live. The variegated nature of American society contained many movements and practices that held great import for the later development of psychology (Pickren & Rutherford, 2010; Schmit, 2005, 2010). These practices had great appeal to people in all strata of American society. Phrenology, mesmerism, spiritualism, New Thought, mental healing, diet, and exercise, often in combination, attracted followers from among the best-educated and from among the least-educated members of society. Each movement developed its own literature—books, magazines, journals, pamphlets—and had its own lecture circuit. These movements were far from marginal, no matter how strange or unscientific they seem today. For each movement, Americans wanted to know more and desired to benefit from whatever the movement promised. Americans used these new sciences to understand and improve their lives. In fact, these sciences and practices were crucially important in creating the psychological sensibility that we now take for granted in American life.

## "The Religion of Healthy-mindedness"[1]

One of the best-documented self-help movements of the late 19th and early 20th centuries is New Thought and its related practices, which are often referred to under the rubric of mental healing or mind cure. The background and sources of this diverse movement ranged from ancient esoteric philosophy to Native American practices to health practices brought from Africa by the slave trade to widely accepted Protestant beliefs (Albanese, 2007; Harrington, 2008) An early exposition of what came to be called New Thought was in the writings of Phineas P. Quimby (1802–1866). He drew upon older practices, such as mesmerism, to develop links between mind, behavior, and health. Quimby's work led to what became known as New Thought and influenced Mary Baker Eddy (1821–1910), the founder of Christian Science. Early in his career, Quimby had been a clock maker, but he became a mesmerist and healer after hearing a series of lectures on mesmerism in the late 1830s. By the 1850s, he had developed his system of thought about the influence of one mind on another to move beyond mesmerism to a practice of psychological healing. His method was one of intense empathy with the other person so that, as he said, he could then see the false belief (about disease) that was the true cause of the illness. He could then, he claimed, correct the false belief and the person experienced healing.

Quimby's influence was remarkable. In the charged atmosphere of the time, many embraced his psychology of health and disease. In addition to Mary Baker Eddy and Christian Science, there were, by the 1890s, a growing number of authors and practitioners who created a corpus of mental science that came to be called *New Thought*. Many of these writers, such as Warren Felt Evans (1817–1889), drew upon evidence from mesmerism to validate their claims of spiritual senses acting independently of the body. For those who embraced New Thought, mental science and healing were solidly grounded in an everyday psychology of human experience. This work held enormous appeal for many Americans well into the 20th century (Taves, 1999; Taylor, 1999). Indeed, several of the books by New Thought teachers sold more than a million copies each, and accompanying weekly magazines often had subscriptions in excess of 100,000 (Loss, 2002).

In addition to a wide following among many strata of society, the network of practitioners and followers included numerous religious leaders in both traditional denominations and in a variety of independent and nontraditional religious groups. This is not surprising, given that religion has played an important role in structuring human experiences of health and illness. The impact of this "religion of healthy-mindedness," to use William James's phrase, was to further strengthen American's belief in the importance of mind and body connections in health and disease and to help lay the groundwork for later receptivity to the ideas that these connections could be studied scientifically, as historian Anne Harrington (2008) has shown.

The 19th century was also a period when diet and exercise, along with other treatments designed to prevent or cure disease, flourished in the United States (Whorton, 1982). As one historian of the era pointed out, "No topic more occupied the Victorian mind than health—not religion or politics, or Improvement, or Darwinism" (Haley, 1978, p. 3). Exercise, sport, fitness, each had salutary effects on the nervous system (Owens, 1985; Park, 1994). Various health practices, including dietary regimens, included vegetarianism, herbalism, an emphasis on specific foods (e.g., the Graham cracker, fruitism, and so forth), all claimed to benefit mental functioning. The healthy person was one who was so in body, mind, and spirit.

These systems were not mutually exclusive. The benefits of exercise and diet were often joined, along with an emphasis on morally upright behavior. In addition, many of those who embraced dietary and fitness regimes also embraced one or more of the mind-cure approaches. Nor were individuals necessarily wedded to one approach for life; it was quite common for people to move from one system to another over the course of their lives.

The popularity of ideas and practices intended to bring spiritual and physical health was immense, so that, by the beginning of the 20th century, millions of Americans had embraced the importance of the mind or the psychological in the prevention of disease and the maintenance of health, even if they could not or did not articulate it in the language of the new scientific psychology (Whorton, 2002). It was this willingness to believe in the importance of the mental that later created the interest and attendant public resources in what came to be labeled behavioral medicine, health psychology, and mind–body medicine. In this sense, these 19th century developments helped make the direct involvement of psychologists possible (Harrington, 2008). As William James, America's preeminent psychologist, stated in 1902,

> The greatest discovery of my generation is that man can alter his life simply by altering his attitude of mind. The blind have been made to see, the halt to walk; lifelong invalids have had their health restored. The moral fruits have been no less remarkable. The deliberate adoption of a healthy-minded attitude has proved possible to many who never supposed they had it in them. (James, 1902, p. 95)

## Emotions, Disease, and Health in the First Half of the 20th Century

We turn now to a larger canvas and introduce developments from several arenas that proved important to the emergence of health psychology in the last quarter of the 20th century. Our focus will be on "railway spine," new theories about emotions and health, and psychosomatic medicine. We begin with the emergence of theories of health and disease in psychology and medicine in Europe and then turn to North America.

## Mind, Body, and Health: The Affirmation of the Psychosomatic in Europe

A puzzling new malady appeared in the middle of the 19th century. Men and women began to report a range of physical complaints, from minor to serious, after travel on the new railways. Physicians typically could not find an organic cause for most of these complaints, soon lumped together under the moniker, "railway spine" (Harrington, 2006). For some physicians, these complaints opened up the possibility of mental factors influencing physical health, in what were labeled *functional disorders* (Caplan, 1995). Although this diagnosis was controversial at the time, it heralded a new era of medicine focused on such "functional" maladies.

Later in the century, the brilliant Parisian neurologist, Jean-Martin Charcot, made a career out of the explication of such functional disorders, which he called *hysteria* (Micale, 1994). Charcot attracted many followers, and his work opened up new interpretations of mind–body relations in disease and health. The young Viennese neurologist Sigmund Freud spent a 6-month fellowship in Paris at the Salpêtrière Hospital, where he was able to observe Charcot's methods and hear his theories first-hand. Freud then embarked on a remarkable career in Vienna, where he used reason to show the limits of reason in human behavior. His work on the powerful role of the irrational in human affairs drew many disciples and not a few critics. By the 1920s, especially in German-speaking countries, his ideas of the power of unconscious influences were extended to the realm of physical diseases, first by Freud, then more fully by a number of his followers, perhaps most notably, Georg Groddeck (Avila, 2003; Groddeck, 1929). The extension of psychoanalytic thought to human illness came to be termed *psychosomatic medicine*.

The psychosomatic problem represented the original nucleus at the inception of the psychoanalytic movement that concerned itself precisely with those physical disorders devoid of an anatomo-pathological substratum. With the development of the libido theory and the resulting hypotheses regarding the development of neurosis, Freud proposed a model that integrated the somatic, psychic, and social components. His model convincingly represented how it was possible that physical diseases could occur as a result of psychological events

(Cremerius, 1978). The interest in these issues was already present in Freud's earlier writings, but took on greater importance when he devoted himself to the study of hysterical pathology. This problem had been highlighted since 1878, by Parisian neurologist Jean-Martin Charcot (1825–1893), in the course of his famous experiments with hypnosis on patients affected with hysteria, at the Salpêtrière hospital in Paris. According to Charcot's doctrine, hysteria was a hereditary functional disturbance of the nervous system, and thus a hereditary neurological infirmity and not a psychiatric disease. Nevertheless, on the basis of the results of applying hypnosis to hysteria, Charcot had hypothesized the possibility that paralysis could be produced by an idea, seeing that an opposite idea could make it disappear (Chertok, 1984; Aguayo, 1986). Theories such as this impressed Freud, who had spent a period of study with Charcot during the winter of 1885–1886. Freud had already been alerted to the phenomena of hysteria and the hypnosis treatment by Austrian physician Joseph Breuer, who told Freud about a patient, Anna O., whose hysterical symptoms he treated with hypnosis.

The reflection of the "founder of psychoanalysis" on such phenomena with Breuer is at the origin of the notion of "conversion," a founding idea for the incipient discipline of psychosomatics (Freud & Breuer, 1895). According to Freud, the inclination toward conversion would be a characteristic trait of hysterical patients: when a psychic content—an image, an impulse, a desire—is incompatible with the Ego, the affection associated with it is dismissed from consciousness by means of repression and converted into a sensory-motor disturbance that symbolizes and expresses on a bodily level the unacceptable content, thus partially solving the original psychological conflict. He hypothesized that hysterical symptoms derive from undischarged memories connected to past physical traumas. In the phenomenon of conversion there was thus inherent the problem of the "jump from the psychic to the somatic," which Freud defined as *mysterious* (Freud, 1909). The term introduced by Freud, although having a prevalently economic meaning—that is, it is a surplus of libidinous energy transformed and converted into the somatic—appears closely tied to a symbolic meaning: Transformation does not happen by chance but has a precise meaning of a forgotten language, or rather more precisely, the language that, in common usage, often escapes our attention. And the hidden significance of the symptom is tied to an organ, to a bodily function, which for various reasons has been invested with particular meanings. The problem to solve is why a conflict chose this path rather than choosing a neurotic symptom. Freud speaks of a predisposition, "the ability to convert" (Freud, 1894) and further clarified and defined "somatic complacence" (Freud, 1905), by which is meant the situation of a bodily function that has been invested with special significance in some special moment of life. In this sense, the body part or function held a particular symbolic meaning.

Simultaneously with the conversion model, Freud proposed another explanation of psychically conditioned somatic symptoms: the "equivalent of the anxiety attack" in anxiety neuroses (Freud, 1895). In this category of disorders associated with anxiety, somatic symptoms appear—palpitations, perspiration, nausea, diarrhea, trembling, respiratory alterations, headache—that are inconceivable as the product of a repressed representation or an intrapsychic conflict, but understandable instead as the result of the activation of the autonomous nervous system. In anxiety neurosis, unlike in hysteria and obsessional neurosis, anxiety could not be addressed through psychotherapy. Thus, it could not have originated from a removed representation. Therefore, the mechanism was that the organic symptom, understood as a deviation of the somatic excitation whose access to the psychic is blocked, should, according to Freud, be left to biomedical investigation. In this regard, therefore, Freud theoretically preceded the split of the psychosomatic movement into two distinct and noncommunicating approaches, the one focused on the physiological sense, the other on the psychoanalytic sense, which would take place about 50 years later with the rational application of the concept of stress to physiopathology (Ammon, 1974).

## From Pathology as Psychic Conflict to the Specificity of the Symptom

In Germany, the physician Georg Walther Groddeck (1866–1934) was a pioneer of psychosomatic medicine. He highlighted the need to carefully attend to unconscious forces and to the therapeutic value of the interpretation of symbolic language and psychic resistances. In 1897, he opened his own clinic in Baden-Baden, which in a short time drew patients from all of Europe. Even though he declared himself to be more of a "masseur" than a psychoanalyst,[2] the patients in his clinic were treated with psychoanalytic techniques, as well as with massage and an attentive alimentation. He refuted the distinction between psychic and organic disturbances by attempting to cure the whole person. Organic pathological processes and the symptoms of illness were the symbolic expression of a single unconscious entity (which, inspired by Nietzsche, he called Es, influencing Freud himself, who later used the term in his structural theory) that determines the behavior of each human being, both in the state of health and in that of illness (Grotjahn, 1945).

Analogously for Felix Deutsch (1858–1928), another pioneer of psychosomatic medicine, the "continuous current of conversion into the somatic," which was active also in healthy people, was considered a sort of "body language" that was used to unload, in a symbolic way, an unconscious overloaded with fragments of emotions and other psychic complexes (Deutsch, 1924; 1949; 1953).

The European idea of body language and of psychosomatic disturbance as a symbol of psychic conflict posed a series of problems as to how unconscious meanings could be transformed into symptoms of illness; whether there existed a rule of correlation between unconscious meanings, psychological contents and conflicts, and the material signs and symptoms of illness; how the choice was made of the organ to be struck by the psychosomatic disturbance; and how it was possible to verify the correctness of the analytic interpretation of the conversion phenomenon. For example, Harald Schultz-Hencke (1892–1953), who together with Werner Walther Kemper (1899–1975) made a decisive contribution to the establishment of psychosomatic medicine in Germany, developed the concept of "correlation of simultaneity." Schultz-Henke understood this organic symptomatology as a "somatic correlate" of psychic processes. The relation was not one of causality, but a relation of dependence characterized by simultaneity. In this way, the organic symptomatology was conceived as an "organic language" in which an unconscious meaning-motive-impulse-need, instead of expressing itself in words, expressed itself in the exalted functioning of an organ.[3]

Another important European contribution was that of the Heidelberg school, founded by the physician Viktor Freiherr von Weizsäcker (1886–1957). Interested in introducing within organic medicine the cognitions and foundations of psychoanalysis—he labeled his theoretical construction "medical anthropology," in that it paid particular attention to the physician–patient relation—he did not consider the psychic as simply an additional factor of the morbid event, but insisted that it represented another mechanism of the disturbed physiological machine. Weizsäcker tried to establish a relation between the psychophysiological dynamics of the morbid phenomenon with the external situation in which the individual happened to be and with the "individual's internal dynamics" (Weizsäcker, 1933; 1949). This position, so close to, although independent of, the developments of the contemporaneous psychoanalysis of the ego, remained in large part isolated in Europe, as is testified to by the orthodoxy professed even by his pupil Alexander Mitscherlich (1908–1982), who in any case dedicated himself to the theme of psychosomatics (Mitscherlich, 1954; 1973).

### Expression of the Emotions and Illness

The importance of the theory of conflict was such that it could be considered "the first important paradigm of psychosomatic medicine (Taylor, Bagby, & Parker, 1997). A large part of the efforts of the first generation of psychosomatic practitioners was therefore directed toward verifying this hypothesis, in the attempt to identify psychological conflicts characteristic of patients affected by those illnesses that were held to be of a psychosomatic nature. Toward the end of the 1950s, these great expectations were put into perspective, and the limits of the concept of neurosis applied to psychosomatics became evident (Lipowski, 1977).[4] The theory of unconscious psychic conflict was followed by one that attributed the greatest importance to the primary capacity of recognizing and expressing one's emotions.

The problem of the behavioral expression of emotions interested the scholars of the second generation of scientific psychosomatics, which developed in the 1950s both in Europe and in America, albeit with different itineraries. If Freud and psychoanalysis in general had tried to explain the "jump from the psychic to the somatic," another subject of research—whose most important precursors were the French physician Claude Bernard (1813–1878) and the American physiologist Walter Bradford Cannon (1871–1945)—began to explain how it occurred. This promising theme of investigation then became enriched by research conducted by Paul MacLean (1913–2007) and Giuseppe Moruzzi (1910–1986). In 1936, on the basis of similar pioneering investigations and parallel to the models of a psychoanalytic origin, the Austrian physician Hans Selye (1907–1982), discussed below, introduced to the United States the concept of stress

defined as a specific reaction of the organism to the various stimuli that act upon it.

In Europe, toward the end of the 1950s, several French psychoanalysts led by Pierre Marty (later known as the "Paris School") attempted to investigate the same question from the linguistic and symbolic point of view. Marty and his collaborators published a series of clinical observations concerning patients who had organic illnesses, and they hypothesized the existence of a personality structure—the psychosomatic personality—characterized by several deficits that make the individual unable to adequately elaborate emotions and psychic traumas, which are therefore expressed somatically. Although the neurotic patient possesses psychic defenses able to reduce the anxiogenic tension produced by unconscious conflicts, the psychosomatic patient is impaired in the use of symbolism and would use instead the body to unload internal tensions (Marty & M'Uzam, 1963). The psychosomatic personality was characterized by an attitude of hypernormality, with a conformist adaptation to the environment and to social demands, and by a particular cognitive style called "operative thought" (a concept originally introduced by Piaget), characterized by a series of deficits that would prevent a normal psychosomatic integration. The Paris School attributed operative thought to deficits in the organization of personality rather than to the action of pathological defenses, as in the neurotic patient. The authors attributed much importance to the energetic-propelled point of view, and they held that, in the psychosomatic personality, the drives cannot be sufficiently elaborated on a mental level, as a result of which they are expressed directly through the body. The theory of unconscious conflict is thus abandoned to the search for a new model that would better clarify the influence of the emotions on bodily functions. Attention thus shifted to precocious object relations, for which the psychosomatic personality was the consequence of a disorganized maternal attitude, incapable of sufficient empathetic care. The hypotheses formulated by the Paris School, in spite of some criticism, gave rise to a noteworthy consensus and interest within Europe. Later, their ideas were more broadly recognized, especially after Peter Sifneos and John Nemiah of the United States, independently from the French authors, reached basically the same conclusions and proposed the concept of *alexithymia*, which has today taken on a central importance also for the European psychosomatic discipline.

At the Laboratory of Clinical Research in Stockholm, Lennart Levi reconnected historically with the research of Cannon, Wolff, and Selye, and introduced the *psychosocial model*. According to this model, "psychosocial stimuli" become engraved on the "psychobiological program" of the individual and can provoke some "precursors of illness." Over time, these precursors may lead to somatic illness, with damage to organs and functions, as a result of the aspecific nature of the stress. Levi's psychosocial model offered a new vision of psychosomatics, no longer limited to the perspective of the individual reaction to emotions, but seen in individuals immersed in their social and environmental reality. This, among other things, gave rise to the psychosomatic branch of the medicine of work, throwing new light on professional illnesses, which were seen as an obvious consequence of the demonstrated alterations caused by the work of cardiovascular activity, metabolism, and the endocrine apparatus (Levi, 1972).

Since about 1970, within the European context, a new model of psychosomatics has been asserted. This model is characterized by *multicausality* (each physical or mental pathology derives from the interaction of biological, psychical, social, and cultural factors) and *interactive circularity* (the different causes act upon each other, reinforcing or restraining each other, thus making it difficult to establish a starting point).

Working upon the suggestions of the multiple models of explanation for psychosomatic pathology that were current in the United States, in Italy, Paolo Pancheri, in 1980 attempted a synthesis among the various models proposed to explain psychosomatic illness, and arrived at a *psychosomatic model*. According to this model, each stimulus, whether social and/or individual, produces psychological and biological modifications determined by the psychobiological program of the individual. The interest of this model lies in the fact that it covers various levels of analyses of psychosomatosis—psychosocial, psychological, biological, clinical—indicating the operative potentiality of psychosomatic medicine along the entire course of the illness, from prevention to therapy (Pancheri, 1980; 1984).

Some European contributions from this second generation of psychosomaticists are characterized by an existential curvature—according to which the psychical expresses the modality with which a body is in the world—to the psychosomatic question. An eminent representative of this approach is Medard Boss (1903–1990), a Swiss psychoanalytic psychiatrist, who holds that illness expresses either the only modality with which the body opens and relates to the world, or the modalities excluded, which, not expressing themselves in a global experience, are announced pathologically. From this viewpoint, those areas of the body affected by illness belong to the relation pathologically interrupted or exasperated with the world. That which determines bodily illness is thus neither a somatogenesis nor a psychogenesis nor an interaction between the two, but rather an alteration of the relation between the person and the world (Boss, 1963).

Finally, it is worth mentioning the contributions of several more recent psychoanalysts who place the accent on deficits of mental functioning that are closely connected with "precocious experiences of relation." Donald Winnicott (1896–1971), a well-known British psychoanalyst and pediatrician, wrote a fundamental article focused on psychosomatics (Winnicott, 1966). He proposed a focus on the "hyphen" that separates the two parts of the term, psyche-soma. The hyphen, Winnicott argued, was the most important part of the word because it defines the area that has to be studied, in that the hyphen at the same time "joins and separates the two aspects of medical practice" (Winnicott, 1966, p. 510). It is on this *trait d'union* that the specialist of psychosomatic illness works. According to Winnicott, the maturative process of a nonintegrated primary state depends upon the maternal attitude; if this is "good enough," the psychosomatic integration will take place; that is, the psyche will succeed in inhabiting the soma. An evolutive failure will instead provoke insecurity in this inner habitation and will lead to psychosomatic disorders (Winnicott, 1966).

Deserving of final mention is the contribution of the Hungarian psychoanalyst, Michael Balint (1896–1970), who emphasized the doctor–patient interaction and highlighted the use, on the part of the physician, of his or her personality in relations with the patient. This conception contains the expression of a new form of causality in pathology, a relational causality. The relational causality operates as a return to a unitary etiological theory, in which the meaning is to be sought in the relation that underlies the production of the symptoms. In this sense, Balint makes a distinction between the "autogenic illness" and the "iatrogenic illness" (Balint, 1956). According to Balint, inside the relationship, a symptom always has meaning, provided that there is someone able to decode it.

### Mind, Body, and Health: Psychosomatic Medicine in North America

In the United States, psychosomatic medicine emerged as a distinct field of interdisciplinary research and practice in the late 1930s. It was then concerned with the "interrelationships between emotional life and bodily processes both normal and pathological" (Dunbar, 1939, p. 3). These interrelationships were thought to be at the crux of such diverse illnesses as colitis, peptic ulcers, and asthma. Most histories of psychosomatic medicine have been written by physicians and, not surprisingly, have focused on the role of physicians, especially psychoanalytically oriented physicians, in its development (e.g., H. I. Kaplan & H. S. Kaplan, 1956; Kimball, 1970; Wittkower, 1960). In these standard accounts, the history of psychosomatic medicine is traced from Freud's concept of the symbolic conversion of psychic distress into somatic expression to the physiological representationalist views of Franz Alexander and Flanders Dunbar.

Such accounts have misrepresented the interdisciplinary character of the field and have neglected the important roles that psychologists and other scientists played. Although space will not permit a full account, in this section, we give a brief overview of the two ways in which psychologists contributed to the field's development and suggest that this was the beginning of events that led to the establishment of health psychology as a distinct subfield within the larger discipline of scientific psychology. First, psychologists provided the experimental research that served as the underpinning for the emergence of psychosomatic medicine as a recognized and coherent field of practice and theory. Second, psychologists provided leadership in the organization and institutionalization of the field.

Before we describe psychologists' role in the new field, we provide a general background for the development of psychosomatic medicine in the United States. Psychosomatic medicine's history is complex: it involved psychologists, psychiatrists, psychoanalysts, and medical practitioners of various specialties. It also reflected a philosophical reorientation in the life sciences toward organicism and away from reductionism; this was especially true in the explanation of the relations between mind and body (Cannon, 1932; Cross & Albury, 1987). Several of the largest American philanthropic foundations provided significant financial resources in an attempt to foster a more stable social order (Brown, 1987; Kohler, 1991). Thus, the putative role of mind–body relations in health and disease became more than a metaphor for a healthy body politic. It was hoped that understanding such relationships would literally make for a healthier society.

Helen Flanders Dunbar was the central figure in the promotion and establishment of psychosomatic medicine in America. Dunbar was broadly educated; she graduated from Bryn Mawr with majors in mathematics, pre-medicine, and psychology. She then earned a Ph.D. in philosophy, completed a degree in theology from Union Theological Seminary, and completed the requirements for her M.D. (Powell, 1977, 1978). Her psychology mentor was James Leuba, whose focus was the psychology of emotion in religious conversion experiences (Leuba, 1894, 1926). During her training tour in Europe in 1929, Dunbar learned about the new psychosomatic medicine from psychoanalyst and internist Felix Deutsch (Flagg, 1966; Lipsitt, 1989). While in Europe, Dunbar also served as an assistant to Carl Jung, at the Burgholzli Clinic in Zurich. When Dunbar returned to America, she was prepared to integrate the viewpoints gained from her diverse training. The result of the integration was a holistic, organismic approach to the understanding of human functioning that bore a strong relationship to the whole-organism psychobiology of Adolf Meyer and William Alanson White (Leys, 1991). Dunbar emphasized disease as disequilibrium within the person and within the environment. Emotions were perceived to play a vital role in maintaining or disrupting the person's equilibrium (Dunbar, 1934, 1935).

Upon receipt of her medical degree, Dunbar accepted a position at the Columbia-Presbyterian Medical Center in New York City, where many of the medical faculty and staff were sympathetic to or adherents of psychoanalysis and the role of psychological factors in disease (Schulman, 1969; Zubin & Zubin, 1977). The medical center proved to be an excellent base from which to influence the development of psychosomatic medicine. As historians of medicine and psychoanalysis have pointed out, an indigenous strain of psychoanalytic theory and practice, influenced by European psychoanalysis but with its own unique characteristics, had developed in American psychiatry (Hale, 1971, 1995; Powell, 1977; Scull & Schulkin, 2009; Taylor, 2000; White, 1926). Dunbar's work was congruent with this indigenous strain of a whole-organism approach to understanding health and disease.

To illustrate this psychological orientation at Columbia-Presbyterian at the time Dunbar became a member of the medical staff, we use the research of physician George Draper (Tracy, 1992). Draper established the Constitutional Clinic at Presbyterian Hospital in 1916 and was its director until his retirement in 1946. Constitutional medicine, Draper stated, studied "that aggregate of hereditarial characters, influenced more or less by environment, which determines the individual's reaction, successful or unsuccessful, to the stress of environment" (Draper, Dunn, & Seegal, 1924, p. 431). Draper developed his model of constitutional medicine over the years, eventually including four panels of personality: morphology, physiology, psychology, immunity. These four panels were collectively and individually influenced by both heredity and environment (Draper, 1934). Draper placed his views within the organismic/holistic movement in medicine and the life sciences, acknowledging his debt to Walter Cannon, Ivan Pavlov, Charles Sherrington, and George Coghill.

Research from the Constitutional Clinic reflected Draper's organismal views, including the reports of psychologists who worked with Draper. The first report by psychologists came in 1922, with a study of possible relations of endocrinological factors on intelligence (Naccarati & Lewy-Guinzburg, 1922). This was followed by a study of the relation of body type to motor intelligence (Naccarati & Garrett, 1923) and a report on morphology and intelligence (Heidbreder, 1926). Psychologist Cecil Murray analyzed case studies of patients suffering from disorders of the digestive tract. His analyses were informed by both constitutional theory and psychoanalysis, and he concluded that the bodily dysfunction was due to the inability to find an acceptable solution to psychological conflict. Murray suggested that these difficulties belonged to the psychological panel of the patients' constitution (Murray, 1930a, 1930b). The research of Draper and his colleagues at the Columbia-Presbyterian Constitutional Clinic is an illustration of the growing use of psychological concepts to understand and treat physical disorders. This was the research and clinical ethos that appealed to Dunbar.

In 1931, not long after taking the position at Columbia-Presbyterian, Dunbar received a grant from the Josiah Macy, Jr. Foundation to survey the extant literature on the relation of emotion to disease (Macy Foundation, 1955). The Macy Foundation had been established in 1930 to fund medical research and health, and its directors sought ways to promote holistic studies in medicine. The massive volume that resulted from Dunbar's survey, *Emotions and Bodily Changes* (1935), was a principal catalyst for the establishment of psychosomatic medicine as a new field within medicine in the United States. Dunbar reviewed and listed every relevant study published from 1910 to 1933. The scientific and disciplinary fields she drew from included, among others, endocrinology, anatomy, physiology, clinical medicine, psychoanalysis, experimental psychology, biochemistry, neurology, and psychiatry. She stated that her "aim was to bring together all the fragments of knowledge we possess, relevant to the problem of psychosomatic interrelationships," in order to facilitate further research in the emerging field and to serve as a guide for the young scientist (Dunbar, 1935, p. viii). The exhaustive review showed what had already been discovered about the relationship of mind and body in health and disease. As a result, the volume became a powerful impetus for further research by serving as a bibliographic guide to potential areas of fruitful research. Much of the research that bore directly on psychological or emotional aspects of health and disease was psychoanalytically or psychobiologically oriented. This volume was, in many ways, the single most important work in the institutionalization of psychosomatic medicine in the United States.

As noted, there was already a German-language literature, mostly psychoanalytic in orientation, which had evolved in the 1920s. Along with *Emotions and Bodily Changes*, the 1930s proved to be a richly productive era for North American research on psychological factors in health and disease. Early in the decade, American psychiatrists John Whitehorn and Gregory Zilboorg noted a growing trend among psychiatrists to consider multiple etiologic factors in mental disorders and an increasing concern about psychiatric factors in illness (1933). Perhaps the most important theorist to emerge at this time was the Hungarian émigré, Franz Alexander. Trained at the Berlin Psychoanalytic Institute under Karl Abraham, Alexander was invited to a professorship at the University of Chicago in 1931. Once there, he established the Chicago Institute for Psychoanalysis, and became one of America's leading public intellectuals for more than three decades. Beginning in the 1930s, Alexander, in a series of articles and books, argued for the necessity of considering both psychological and physiological factors in disease processes, and maintained that psychoanalysis provided the tools or techniques necessary for a full understanding of the psychological factors involved (e.g., Alexander, 1932, 1933, 1950). As an example, Alexander articulated the psychological contributions to peptic ulcer (Alexander, 1934). According to Alexander, the route to peptic ulcer lay in the identification of being fed with being loved, an identification that occurs in infancy. The emotional association that occurs at this time is the baseline for the connection in adulthood between unmet dependency needs and peptic ulcer. This was especially true for high-achieving men, those most likely to experience the stresses of corporate and political leadership. Alexander drew upon the work of Walter Cannon on the effects on the body of emotions to argue that the physiologic linkage occurred through the action of the sympathetic nervous system (Cannon, 1953).

Concurrent with Alexander's work on emotional factors in disease, Dunbar organized a symposium on psychological factors in specific disease states: hyperthyroidism (two papers), toxic goiter, diseases of the gastrointestinal tract, and coronary heart disease (Conrad, 1934; Daniels, 1934; Dunlap & Moersch, 1935; Katzenelbogen & Luton, 1935; Wolfe, 1934). In addition, Dunbar presented her synthesis of the relationships between physical and mental factors in illness (Dunbar, 1934). One of the most influential papers of the decade on psychosomatic disease was offered by Erich Wittkower (1935). His survey of research on emotional factors in bodily functions was exhaustive in its scope and served as a summation of current research on psychosomatic disease.

So far, we have focused on the theoretical and clinical formulations of physicians. What were the contributions of psychologists to the understanding of psychological and emotional factors in health and disease in this period? That is, how did psychologists contribute to the emerging field of psychosomatic medicine?

As we discussed earlier, William James wrote about what he called "healthy-mindedness" and referred his readers to much of the then current literature on mind-cure and New Thought. James, of course, was not an experimentalist, but he was a careful observer and brilliant synthesizer. By the 1920s, a small body of psychological research relevant to emotions and health had been developed as psychologists began to explore the role of emotions. Some of this early research was prompted by new equipment, such as that for measuring galvanic skin responses. Psychologists like William Marston used these new technologies to examine emotional responses relevant to legal questions, such as lie detection[5] (Bunn, 2007; Marston, 1917, 1938). Leipzig-trained psychologist George Stratton published several articles on emotions and their correlates, including incidence of disease (Stratton, 1926).

However, it was not until the 1930s that psychologists began to conduct more research relevant to health. When they began, psychoanalytic concepts were at the forefront of their work. In fact,

psychoanalysis provided an impetus for much of the research on experimental psychopathology conducted by psychologists in the 1930s. This body of work formed one of the pathways to the development of psychosomatic medicine at the end of the decade. It did so by providing a point of contact between psychologists and those physicians who were working on questions of psychosomatic relationships in health and disease. As has been well-documented, the relationship of psychoanalysis and American psychology has long been a mixture of both positive and negative features (Hornstein, 1992; Shakow & Rapaport, 1964).

David Shakow and David Rapaport provided a comprehensive review of the influence of Freudian ideas on American psychology (1964). Concerned primarily with showing the positive influence of Freud on academic psychology, they noted several obstacles that hindered psychologists' ability to understand psychoanalysis: lack of clearly articulated concepts, internal inconsistencies in psychoanalytic theory, and the commingling of theory with clinical application, among other problems. As a result, Shakow and Rapaport claimed, psychologists trained to privilege exact methods and to formulate testable hypotheses often misunderstood psychoanalytic concepts that resulted in either rejection or modification of psychoanalytic ideas into terms more amenable to mainstream American psychology.

Gail Hornstein characterized the relationship of psychoanalysis and American psychology as problematic (Hornstein, 1992). She argued that psychoanalysis represented a threat to academic psychology and that, during the interwar period, American academic psychologists retreated into positivism. This, Hornstein argues, was followed in the 1940s and 1950s by a strategy of cooptation or incorporation of psychoanalytic concepts through experimentation.

Beginning in the 1930s, a small number of experimental psychologists attempted a rapprochement between psychoanalysis and academic psychology. These psychologists believed that their adherence to the methodological demands of experimental psychology would profit psychoanalysis by lending precision and definition to its sometimes vague formulations. On the other hand, academic psychology, which was often charged with irrelevance in its research, would benefit from the experimental investigation of psychoanalytic concepts because real problems from everyday lives were confronted in the subject matter of psychoanalysis. Space constraints limit us to only a few examples; contemporaneous reviews may also be consulted for a more complete indication of the extent of psychologists' efforts to address psychoanalytic concepts (e.g., Hunt, 1944; Sears, 1943).

In 1929, Yale University entered into an agreement with the Rockefeller Foundation to establish a new interdisciplinary unit dedicated to the use of science to address deep-seated social problems. The Institute of Human Relations began with great promise and excitement as existing research programs were refurbished and revitalized, and new scientists were recruited to round out the ambitious program. One of those new scientists was Clark Hull, who had established himself as a promising researcher at the University of Wisconsin. Hull came to Yale in 1929, and by the mid-1930s had attracted a promising group of young male scientists as his graduate students. Among them were several of the future leaders of American psychology: Neal Miller, Leonard Doob, Robert Sears, and others. In the fall of 1935, Hull decided to initiate a program to correlate the tenets of psychoanalysis with conditioned reflex theory. Hull drew upon the prior and extensive discussions of possible links by the psychoanalysts Thomas French and Lawrence Kubie (French, 1933; Kubie, 1934) to formalize the program of research. As historian of psychology Jill Morawski has argued, Hull's efforts aimed to bring the irrational under the control of orderly, systematic science and formed one aspect of his larger project for a unified science (Morawski, 1986).

Numerous publications that engaged psychoanalytic constructs in the experimental psychology laboratory emerged from the Institute, as these young scientists threw themselves into the work. Perhaps the best known was the volume, *Frustration and Aggression* (Dollard et al., 1939). The authors acknowledged the formative influence of Freud by stating that he "more than any other scientist has influenced the formulation of our basic hypothesis" (p. ix). The book was an elaboration of the theme that aggression was the direct result of frustrated needs, which the authors explicated with results drawn from their experimental testing of psychoanalytic concepts. In difficult times like the Depression era, Dollard et al. suggested, frustration might lead to individual psychological problems, including illness, as well as to social problems such as crime, dysfunctional families, and labor unrest.

Young psychological scientists at some of the nation's leading centers of psychological research—Harvard, Yale, Brown, and elsewhere—became deeply involved in this effort to empirically test psychoanalytic constructs. Saul Rosenzweig, at both Harvard and Worcester State Hospital, tested the frustration hypothesis. A very young B. F. Skinner developed his auditory "inkblot" for use in psychodynamic research at the Harvard Psychological Clinic and elsewhere (Rutherford, 2003). At Brown University, a very talented group of young researchers, including Joe McVicker Hunt and Harold Schlosberg, were deeply engaged in testing psychoanalytic concepts. According to one participant, the attitude among the psychologists at Brown toward Freud was that "somehow science must seize on his [Freud's] ideas, straighten them out, and turn the magic of science and the laboratory on it and then we will truly have a theory and a practice to worship" (Bartlett, personal communication, February 9, 1995). All of these young scientists saw themselves as advancing psychological science in new directions that would have greater relevance to human problems, including health issues. Their most common term for this new approach was *experimental psychopathology*.

Organizationally, psychologists found themselves in a position to bring the disparate efforts together that led to the institutionalization of psychosomatic medicine as a new field. Walter Hunter, Chair of Psychology at Brown University, and Walter Miles, Yale University, were invited to participate in the planning of a new interdisciplinary initiative of the National Research Council (NRC). The NRC, with the support of philanthropies such as the Rockefeller and Macy Foundations, sought to stimulate research in areas that fell between established scientific disciplines (Bugos, 1989). A new initiative in 1937 was for research that had overlap among biology, psychology, anthropology, and the medical sciences, and resulted in a meeting of the NRC Division heads from each of these areas. From the perspective of the foundations and the NRC, the problem of "psychoneuroses," including psychosomatic disease, represented a society out of balance. Work in this borderland presented an opportunity to address human needs through cooperative science and, in doing so, to facilitate equilibrium in society.

Walter Hunter, as the head of the NRC Division of Psychology and Anthropology, suggested the experimental study of the functional nervous disorders. He proposed that the NRC bring together investigators doing similar research, which would increase probability of external funding. The general consensus of the group was that this was "the research of the hour," especially because the philanthropic foundations were interested in supporting it. Based on this meeting, the NRC formed the

Committee on Problems of Neurotic Behavior (CPNB). The Committee selected as its first topic of cooperative investigation, experimental neurosis and psychoanalysis. Over the next 2 years, Hunter and Miles chaired conferences, coordinated scientific papers, and sought funding to support a new journal to institutionalize the new approach. Ultimately, the Macy Foundation agreed to provide support if Hunter and Miles would consent to have Helen Flanders Dunbar lead the effort to establish a new journal. Reluctantly, they agreed, and in 1939, a new journal, *Psychosomatic Medicine*, was launched under the auspices of the NRC. One historian of psychosomatic medicine observed that the new journal was "an event of singular importance for the development of psychosomatic conceptions and medicine" (Lipowski, 1984, p. 156).

The journal served to give the nascent field a coherent, research-oriented identity instead of a loose, anecdotally based set of convictions about the importance of psychological factors in health or disease. An analysis of the first 5 years of publication indicates the crucial role psychologists played in the formation of this scientific identity. A content analysis of the first five volumes reveals that 167 articles were published. This count includes experimental investigations, case studies, and reviews of research. It does not include book reviews. Of the 167 articles, psychologists were authors or co-authors of 30 articles (17.9% of the total). More importantly, psychologists were the contributors most likely to publish reports that were experimental and laboratory based. For example, in the first volume, psychologists contributed six of the 14 experimental reports published. The same pattern continued over the next four volumes. The insights into psychoanalytic tenets and/or psychopathological states via experimental investigation gained psychologists a credible voice in the new field of psychosomatic medicine, which their work had helped create. In addition, the experimental work of psychologists gave credibility to the new field in the eyes of the medical and scientific communities. The role of experimental scientist was one that psychologists, of course, were well trained to fill, and it was this role that allowed them to gain a place in medical settings and to contribute relevant psychological research on medical topics. We will see this pattern again as we recount further developments after World War II.

The events described in this section were critical for the later emergence of psychologists' role in medicine and health care. By the time that the American Psychological Association (APA) Division 38, Health Psychology, was formed in 1978, psychologists had developed a sophisticated and impressive corpus of research and practice related to health and illness. The formation of the field of psychosomatic medicine in the United States was the first institutional step that made these later developments possible.

## New Models of Health and Disease in Post-War America

Psychosomatic medicine flourished during World War II, with many diseases being reconceptualized to encompass psychological factors in their etiology and/or treatment. A volume on wartime medicine, *Men Under Stress* (1945), by psychiatrists Roy Grinker and John Spiegel, greatly influenced American physicians back home to think about illness in psychoanalytic terms. Grinker and Spiegel (1945) illustrated their psychosomatic theories with brilliant case studies. For example, here is Case 11:

> A 27-year-old enlisted man developed enuresis after severe strafing and bombing. Since the bombing he has had much anxiety with tremor, dizzy spells, insomnia, and nightmares. The patient had always been closely attached to his mother with whom he had lived and he missed her greatly. He had never mixed socially with boys or girls and never had sexual relations. He had never been enuretic before. This passive dependent boy reacted to the combined deprivation of his mother and the dangerous situations of war by anxiety, depression, and regression to infantile enuresis. Brief psychotherapy making conscious the basis of his problem, which he had not recognized, resulted in cessation of the symptom. (p. 38)

In 1942, the American Society for Research in Psychosomatic Problems (changed to American Psychosomatic Society in 1948) was formed, with members drawn from many disciplines, including a significant number of psychologists. Over the years since its formation, numerous psychologists have, in fact, served as president of the Society. Through the influence of the Society, books such as Grinker's and Spiegel's and the classic founding text, *Psychosomatic Medicine*, by Weiss and English (1943), and the influence of Karl and William Menninger, psychoanalytic or psychosomatic ideas became widespread within American medicine.

After the war, psychosomatic and related psychodynamic models of disease etiology reached their greatest prominence in the first two decades post-World War II, reflecting the ascendancy of psychoanalytic theory in American medical and cultural life (Grob, 1991; Hale, 1995; Kimball, 1970).

Along with psychosomatics, new models of health and disease emerged. These models were not necessarily antithetic to psychosomatic approaches.

At Washington University in St. Louis, a dynamic team of clinicians and investigators formed the Department of Psychosomatic Medicine with a grant from the Commonwealth Fund. The team consisted of psychiatrist and physiologist George Saslow, internist Samuel Guze, and clinical psychologist Joseph Matarazzo. They termed their approach *comprehensive medicine*, by which they intended to convey the need for preventive medicine through a focus on the whole person. Comprehensive health care, they argued, must take into consideration the social and psychological aspects of human life, as well as specific disease agents. Such care considered each person; his or her hopes, dreams, past experiences, and present health practices; and insisted that health care, to be successful, must be relationally grounded (Matarazzo, 1955). Later, the team split up, with Matarazzo and Saslow moving to the Oregon Health Sciences Center, where Matarazzo established the nation's first department of medical psychology within a college of medicine (Matarazzo, 1994).

The endocrinologist Hans Selye prompted an extensive body of research in many medical and scientific fields with his model of stress, disease, and health, which he called general adaptation syndrome (GAS) (Mason, 1975; Selye, 1950, 1956). As noted already, the impact of emotions on health was one of the main contributions to psychosomatic medicine, and many publications appeared with this focus throughout the 1940s and early 1950s (e.g., Mittelman & Wolff, 1942; Wolff, 1953). Selye, however, used the results of years of laboratory research as the foundation of his model of how stress may lead to physical breakdown. The GAS proposed that various events could serve as stressors that may lead to a generalized response in the organism as it seeks to adapt to the event and return to normal functioning. The mobilization of the organism's defenses includes a first response from the hypothalamus, which leads to the activation of the adrenal glands, that then produce corticoid hormones. A variety of potentially negative health outcomes were possible if the organism was unable to return to its previous balance.

Selye's model was very influential among both the medical community and the general public, with one physician stating that Selye's theory of stress and adaptation has had greater influence than "any other theory of disease ever proposed" (Engel, cited in Mason, 1975, p. 10). Although this is perhaps an overstatement, we include it to indicate how influential Selye's theory was in this time period. It certainly influenced the research of psychologists and helped lay the groundwork for an expansion of psychological research, especially in the 1960s and into the 1970s.

Another homeostatic regulation model that emerged in the post-war era was that of George Engel and his colleagues at Rochester Medical Center. Engel proposed a theory of conservation-withdrawal by the organism that was intended to convey the complexity of intraindividual and interpersonal factors in health and disease. Engel and colleagues considered threats to the organism as likely to elicit withdrawal, which could then lead to depressed physiological functioning. If the individual gives up or withdraws due to the loss of a valued relationship, then this "giving up" sets the person up for illness. The illness, they proposed, would follow whatever predisposition the person had for particular diseases. Disrupted interpersonal relationships were at the heart of this model, with the impact of the disruption potentially powerful enough to cause serious illness (Engel & Schmale, 1972).

George Engel, of course, is best known among psychologists for his articulation of a biopsychosocial model of disease and health. Engel was influenced by the work on general systems theory that flowered during the 1950s and 1960s, inspired by the work of Ludwig von Bertalanffy (1968) and which had diverse interpretations, including that on living systems theory by psychiatrist-psychologist James Grier Miller (e.g., Miller, 1978). Engel only came to accept the critical role of personal and psychological factors in disease after a period of resistance (Smith & Strain, 2002). He was finally persuaded by a long association with the psychiatrist, John Romano, beginning in the early 1940s. After moving to Rochester Medical School and developing his conservation-withdrawal model in the 1950s, Engel continued to consider the importance of relational factors in health care. Over time, he expanded his notion of relationships to include the doctor–patient relationship, the patient's interpersonal relations, and the relationship of the doctor and patient to the larger world, including the hospital, neighborhood, city, and so forth. The health of a human being was shaped by all these relationships. Finally, in 1977, Engel published his model in the pages of *Science*, where it immediately created controversy, criticism, and, ultimately, acclaim and acceptance by many health care professionals, including those in the newly emergent fields of health psychology and behavioral medicine (Engel, 1977).

We give a brief history of the establishment of health psychology and behavioral medicine below. Here, we point out that the biopsychosocial construct was quickly incorporated into psychology. Psychologists readily embraced the biopsychosocial model, as it potentially gave them a critical role for research and intervention. An indicator of this acceptance can be found in the issue of the *Journal of Clinical and Consulting Psychology* (1982, volume 50, issue 6) devoted entirely to the theoretical and practical application of the model in the then-new fields of behavioral medicine and health psychology (Schwartz, 1982). The model continued to inform the field well into the 21st century, although it also was criticized for being vague (Marks, 1996) and was perceived by some as providing cover for the use of a stricter medical model in health intervention research and practice (Ghaemi, 2010; Lyons & Chamberlain, 2006).

## From Clinical Psychology to Health Psychology

American psychology was transformed after World War II. It moved from being a relatively small group of scientists to one of the fastest growing science-based professions in the country (Pickren & Schneider, 2005). This transformation was primarily due to the rapid growth of clinical psychology. The field of clinical psychology had held a small place in pre-war American psychology, but was reconstituted by several converging factors in the post-war period. First, the war brought sharpened awareness of mental health problems and led to a sense of urgency for an increased number of mental health professionals. Second, federal policy makers were concerned about the implications for public health of the alarming number of soldiers who suffered psychiatric casualties during the war, especially within the new era of atomic weaponry that Americans now had to live. Third, and positively, higher education was democratized by the new source of educational funding provided by the Serviceman's Readjustment Act of 1944 (better known as the G. I. Bill), thus making it possible for millions of discharged soldiers to attend college and graduate school.

World War II made it clear that mental disorders were likely more prevalent in the American population than previously thought. Almost 2 million men were rejected by the Selective Service for psychiatric problems or mental deficiencies, while another half-million-plus men were discharged due to mental disorders. This made the lack of mental health personnel much more visible to policy makers after the war. For example, there was a critical shortage of trained mental health workers in the Veterans Administration (VA), at a time when veterans with psychiatric disorders occupied 60% of VA hospital beds (Brand & Sapir, 1964). It was also clear that the nation as a whole did not have enough adequately trained personnel and that the nation's medical schools were not prepared to produce enough psychiatrists to meet the need. As a result, policy makers and legislators developed initiatives intended to increase the number of the nation's mental health service providers. These new programs targeted the professions of psychiatry, psychiatric nursing, social work, and clinical psychology for growth. As a result, for the first time, the federal government became involved in the large-scale support of training, research, and service in the mental health field (Farreras, 2005).

Two government agencies funded programs that proved critical in the transformation of American psychology. In 1946, the VA began working with the APA and several leading universities to develop a clinical psychology program (Baker & Pickren, 2007; Miller, 1946). In that same year, President Truman signed into law the National Mental Health Act (Public Law 487, 79th Congress) that created the National Institute of Mental Health (NIMH), which actually began providing funding in 1948 (Brand & Sapir, 1964). Together, the two agencies provided the financial resources for a massive expansion of psychological scientists and practitioners. The VA clinical psychology training program trained approximately 36,000 clinical psychologists from 1946 to 2005. The parallel funding program of the NIMH also generously supported clinical psychology training. In its first 20 years of funding (1948–1967), the NIMH provided funds for training almost 10,000 students ($58.89 million) in clinical psychology alone (Schneider, 2005).

### VA Clinical Psychology Research on Health and Illness

At the now-famous conference on clinical training held in Boulder, Colorado, in 1949, under the auspices of the NIMH, APA, and VA, delegates agreed to the *scientist-practitioner model* of training first proposed by David Shakow in 1942 (Baker & Benjamin, 2000; Shakow, 1942). The emphasis on the scientist identity was meant to indicate the priority of research over application, an emphasis that has been honored as much in the breach as in the implementation

(Pickren, 2007a). Nevertheless, many members of the rapidly growing cohort of post-war clinical psychologists found themselves in situations in which they were expected to conduct research relevant to clinical questions (Bronfenbrenner, 1947). The VA system employed many of these psychologists, and their research proved critically important in helping address questions relevant to health and disease (Baker & Pickren, 2007).

After the end of World War II, the VA was faced with the immense problem of health care for discharged soldiers. Along with other sectors of American health care, the VA sought to put its care on a solid scientific foundation. The VA expanded its hospital system and proactively sought arrangements with medical schools that made VA hospitals sites for training the full gamut of medical and allied professions, including clinical psychology. In most of these settings, it was hoped that the VA hospital would also serve as a site for medical research (Magnuson, 1960). Psychologists became intimately involved in many of these research endeavors, especially those relevant to mental health, as might be expected. In addition, VA psychologists also played critical roles in a range of other research, including the massive cooperative studies in psychopharmacology (Klett, 2003; Lasky, 1960). Perhaps surprisingly, VA psychologists were also involved in research directly relevant to health, for example, Joseph Brady's well-known studies on stress in "executive" monkeys (Brady, 1958).

The VA developed a rather ambitious plan for developing research programs within the system. The rationale for such a program was that clinical service would be improved, with the hope that medical research would lead to better patient care. It was also hoped that opportunities for research would make the VA system more attractive to highly qualified medical personnel. In addition, there was a need for research in order to have a more extensive knowledge base about the diseases relevant to the veteran population. Cardiovascular disease, cancer, psychiatric disorders, and tuberculosis (TB) were the leading foci of VA research programs. Tuberculosis was actually the first disease to be studied using the capacities of the VA multisite system for cooperative research. In 1946, the VA initiated a cooperative study of the effectiveness of drug treatments for TB, then a major problem in VA hospitals and among nonhospitalized military veterans. Tuberculosis remained a primary focus for more than a decade in the VA system, and psychologists became instrumental in its study. It should be noted that psychiatrist Thomas Holmes and sociologist Norman Hawkins developed the first assessment tool to indicate the relationship between major life events and disease states, the Schedule of Recent Experience (SRE), in the context of their research on TB. Later, Holmes and Richard Rahe revised the SRE into the Social Readjustment Rating Scale (Holmes & Rahe, 1967), which became a major instrument for psychological research and was an important part of the mix when the field of health psychology was institutionalized.

### Psychological Research on Health and Disease in the VA: Tuberculosis and Stress

Tuberculosis was a major problem among discharged soldiers, both among the VA clinical population and in the community. Tuberculosis represented a serious public health threat for the VA and was costly in terms of lives, professional hours, and custodial care. The number of TB patients in the VA system in 1954, for example, was in excess of 14,000 (Hildreth, 1954). Theories about the etiology and maintenance of the disease had emerged that suggested that psychological and behavioral factors may be important. These theories included psychosomatic approaches (e.g., Sparer, 1956; Wittkower, 1949) and stress models (e.g., Clark, Zahn, & Holmes, 1954). As noted, TB was the first disease targeted for a large scale cooperative study in the VA.

After the original cooperative study, psychologists initiated several smaller-scale cooperative studies that focused on TB. Research conducted by psychologists outside the VA system had already shown that psychological and behavioral factors were important for the understanding and treatment of the TB patient (Barker, Wright, & Gonick, 1943; Harrower, 1955). One immediate problem with TB patients that plagued clinicians was the issue of irregular discharge, which refers to patients leaving care before treatment is complete. This problem was thought to be due to the physical conditions of treatment. Sanitorium or hospital patients lived in a highly regulated environment, under conditions of confinement and isolation of indeterminate duration, which often led to dissatisfaction when the symptoms began to lessen; once strength returned, the patient would leave.

In 1949, the VA began to employ clinical psychologists in TB hospitals and sanitoria. It was hoped that psychologists could, in addition to their usual tasks of supervising graduate students and providing direct service in assessment, help reduce the number of patients leaving against medical advice. Not surprisingly, given their assessment skills, psychologists soon found that they could use psychological tests to determine which patients were likely to leave treatment early (irregular discharge). This became a critical function for psychologists, as it held potential to save money and improve care (Calden, Thurston, Stewart, & Vineberg, 1955).

From this beginning, psychologists moved into plans for a more extensive set of studies of TB patients (Vernier, Barrell, Cummings, Dickerson, & Hooper, 1961). A research protocol was developed, tests were chosen, and, in some cases, new tests were developed specifically for TB patients. The protocol also included measures of ward behavior and treatment responsivity. For the time period, the study was sizable in both number of participating hospitals (18) and number of patients (767). Psychological adjustment to treatment, hospitalization, and posttreatment community life were the foci of the study, with additional measures of intelligence and personality.

The results of the study were somewhat surprising. Those patients who were "good" hospital patients were also those who had a very difficult time adjusting to community life upon discharge. This, the psychologists argued, indicated that what counted as good behavior in the hospital—being passive and maintaining a low activity level—was not necessarily what helped a person adjust in the community. On the other hand, patients whose behavior was problematic during hospitalization—high activity level, independence—were much more likely to make a positive community adjustment. The authors argued that TB hospitals should be reorganized to encourage activity and independence. For those who were passive, programs should be put into place to teach social skills and foster independence. Most importantly, psychologists demonstrated that their research held positive implications for investigating the relationships among psychological variables and various disease states.

Stress–disease relationships were a focus of psychological research at the Perry Point, Maryland, VA Medical Center. Psychologist William Paré had begun his work on stress–disease relationships while still at Boston College (e.g., Paré, 1962) and continued after he was recruited to the VA in 1965. Early American research on possible stress and disease relationships dated back to the 1930s, much of it psychoanalytically oriented; especially well-known was the work of the Hungarian-born psychoanalyst, Franz Alexander (Alexander, 1934). As noted, other theoretical frameworks emerged in the 1950s, and the field of stress–disease research was truly multidisciplinary. Paré, like many others, was greatly influenced by Hans Selye's work on stress and disease.

Paré, however, used a different approach to induce stress on the organism. Whereas Selye typically induced stress through the use of restraint, Paré rejected this approach because of his distaste for the physical insult to the animals of Selye's methods. Paré developed an activity stress model in which one animal (rat) was placed in a running wheel cage and allowed to eat for 1 hour a day, while yoked to another nonactive rat. Both animals received the same amount of food. The nonactive rat survived nicely on the amount of food provided, but the activity-wheel rat ran excessively and developed significant ulcers within 12 days. A selection of a different rat strain allowed for Paré to induce ulcers more quickly. He concluded that this resembled the typical stress situation in the general population, in which some people develop stress reactions, while others are capable of handling much more stress without any ill effects (Paré, 1962). He pursued this for many years and found that the critical issue is to determine the relative impact of behavior, environment, physiology, and eventually, genetic heritage. Later, after publicity around the role of the *Helicobacter* bacterium in ulcers, Paré argued that the finding that stomach ulcers are caused by the *Helicobacter* bacterium did not invalidate his research, since about 80% of the population carries *Helicobacter* in their digestive system, yet only a small percentage has ulcers. For Paré, the role of behavior, physiology, and environment remained crucial factors in the onset of ulcers.

These two examples of psychological research on health and disease in the VA do not exhaust the range and variety of relevant research conducted in the immediate post-war era. However, they are typical examples and indicate how the scientific training of psychologists prepared them to conduct careful studies of mind–body, health–disease relationships. Work like that just described helped set the stage for much more extensive involvement in health research by psychologists in the 1970s.

Outside the VA health care system, another index of the growth of psychology in health-related fields can be found in the number of psychologists at work in medical schools and hospitals. Since the early 1900s, psychologists had been trying to get a foothold in medical settings (Pickren, 2007b). Until the post-war era, however, they had little success, with only a few psychologists functioning in such settings (e.g., Taylor, 1982, 2000). The post-war era brought many changes and reflected the growth of health care as an industry, as well as the emergence of clinical psychology as an allied health profession, initially in primary service to psychiatry (Starr, 1984). In 1953, there were 255 psychologists working full or part-time in medical schools (Mensh, 1953). Eleven years later, there were 993 psychologists in medical schools, and by 1976, that number had climbed to 2,336 (Matarazzo, Carmody, & Gentry, 1981). For most of this time, these psychologists were not practicing some early form of health psychology or behavioral medicine. By and large, they were teaching, conducting psychological assessments, or providing psychotherapy. There were exceptions, of course; in a handful of medical schools, psychologists had become involved in research or service related to medical care, for example, at the Oregon Health Sciences Center, where psychologist Joseph Matarazzo led the Department of Psychology (Matarazzo, 1994). This began to change by the mid-1970s, as a few psychologists began to conduct research and provide clinical services directly relevant to physical health.

## Lifestyle, Health, and Psychology

President-elect John F. Kennedy wrote an article on "The Soft American" for *Sports Illustrated* before his inauguration in 1961. In doing so, he heralded a change in American political and cultural life. President Eisenhower had established a Council on Youth Fitness in 1956, but had done little to promote it. Kennedy brought a new emphasis to physical health and activity as part of his argument for Cold War preparedness. He even changed the name to the Council on Physical Fitness, and his administration launched a campaign to encourage schoolchildren across the country to develop their fitness.

The 1960s marked a shift in American cultural life, as Kennedy's initiative illustrates. American life had changed since the end of World War II, and Americans were becoming much less physically fit than before. The nature of work from farms to factories had changed remarkably since the beginning of the century, with much of it becoming mechanized. Recreation had also changed, with much greater emphasis placed on spectator sports rather than participation. The lack of physical fitness in both young and old began to cause concern, especially in the Cold War era, when the need to be prepared became paramount.

Health research, much of it funded by the government, was beginning to show that many diseases had important behavioral and mental components. The paradigmatic issue was the link between smoking cigarettes and lung cancer. In 1957, the U. S. Surgeon General declared that a causal relationship existed between smoking and cancer. A panel of experts convened by President Kennedy in 1962 issued a report in 1964, *Smoking and Health: Report of the Advisory Committee to the Surgeon General.* The report stated that cigarette smoking was responsible for a 70% increase in the mortality rate of smokers over nonsmokers. The report indicated that risk for cancer rose with amount of usage, with heavy smokers having 20 times the risk for developing lung cancer than did nonsmokers. Cigarette smoking was implicated, as well, in other diseases, including bronchitis and coronary heart disease. The advisory committee noted that smoking during pregnancy reduced the average birth weight of infants. Legislation was passed that forbade advertising for cigarettes and required a warning label on each package of cigarettes. In retrospect, these events signaled a change of focus in American health policy. Behavior was clearly important in health and disease, and psychologists were the behavior experts.

By the 1960s, it was clear that patterns for death and disability had changed. No longer were the primary killers and disablers diseases such as polio, tuberculosis, influenza, or measles. Now, the primary causes of mortality and disability were coronary heart disease and its cognates, cancer, stroke, and accidents. In each of these leading causes, behavior was an important factor in both cause and treatment. Chronic diseases were costly in every sense, from personal distress to increased insurance expenditures, to lost wages and productivity.

President Kennedy's initiative pointed in this direction, and after his assassination, President Lyndon Johnson continued to place great emphasis on improving the nation's health. In February 1964, President Johnson delivered his "Health Message" to Congress, in which he stressed the need to develop the nation's medical resources and announced the establishment of a Commission on Heart Disease, Cancer, and Stroke. The Commission delivered its report in December 1964, with 35 recommendations for improving the nation's health, and in January, 1965, President Johnson articulated his plan in a special message to Congress on "Advancing the Nation's Health."

In this atmosphere, with its now recognizably unique emphasis on lifestyle factors in health and disease, psychologists found themselves "outside the loop," to use a Washington phrase, on one of the most important new government initiatives in years, one that held particular relevance to the field. As an example of how out of touch most psychologists and the APA were, when Medicare was established in this period and psychologists were offered the opportunity to be included as providers of mental health services, APA's leadership passed on the opportunity.[6] Tardily recognizing their need to be included in the wave of new government programs and funding, APA commissioned prominent clinical psychologist William Schofield to author a position paper on psychology in relation to health (Schofield, 1969). Schofield noted the increased federal interest in promoting health and preventing disease, and lamented that so few psychologists were involved in relevant health research or practice. His survey of articles on health-related topics in *Psychological Abstracts* for 1966–1967 found that the only areas in which psychologists had a significant presence were schizophrenia, psychotherapy, and mental retardation. In none of the areas outlined by President Johnson's Commission—coronary heart disease, stroke, and cancer—were psychologists substantively involved in either research or practice. Yet, as Schofield masterfully and subtly delineated, psychology was definitely a health profession, whether psychologists understood their field as such or not.

Schofield's report was one of the principal agents of change that helped move psychology toward a recognition of its many possible roles in health. In 1973, APA's Board of Scientific Affairs established the Task Force on Health Research and named Schofield as its chair. The Task Force carefully reviewed health research by psychologists and found that for the 8-year period, 1966–1973, an average of only 40 articles a year had been published out of the thousands of psychological research reports made each year. Nevertheless, the Task Force found that there was a great interest in the possibilities presented by health research. The group issued its report in 1976 (APA Task Force on Health Research, 1976). In the report, they noted the numerous possibilities for psychologists: illness behavior, adaptation to chronic disease, medical compliance, and health promotion, among others. By the time the report appeared, a small network of researchers had emerged, and it was this group that formed the APA Division 38, Health Psychology in 1978, thus institutionalizing the area within organized psychology (Wallston, 1997).

The new organization experienced great success. Within a few years, the division had established a first-rate journal, *Health Psychology*, and it quickly attracted a sizable membership of both researchers and clinicians. The organizational growth reflected, of course, the rapid growth of interest in psychological

aspects of health and disease. It also reflected the remarkable growth in funding resources provided by the National Institutes of Health and many private foundations.

At the same time that psychologists were organizing for what became the APA Division of Health Psychology, efforts were under way to establish a more explicitly interdisciplinary field. Led by senior psychologist Neal Miller, a group met at Yale University in 1977, in the Conference on Behavioral Medicine. Out of this conference and two subsequent conferences, the Society of Behavioral Medicine was formed, with membership drawn from a variety of scientific disciplines, although psychologists comprised the single largest discipline represented in the group.

## The Development of European Health Psychology

European health psychology, as an identifiable area, developed about a decade later than it did in the United States. Like the American field, the dominant approach has been the biopsychosocial model (Matarazzo, 1980) and, similarly to the United States, the clinical application of the model has been dominant.

During the last 30 years, European health psychology, in the wake of American health psychology, has developed an integrative paradigm that aims to overcome the traditional dualism of psyche and soma, indicating the basis of health deterioration in the dynamic interplay of biological, psychological, and social aspects (Engel, 1977). This new approach stresses the importance of specific levels of analysis, as well as the interdependence of the levels. Health psychology, on the basis of this model, proceeds from the study of the psychological level to the overall health of the person in the environment, with greater emphasis on promoting health than on the prevention of disease.

The development of European health psychology reflects significant interests and practices of the new contributions of scientific psychology to the promotion and maintenance of health. At the end of the World War II, scientific and professional contributions of psychology became part of the vast field of mental health, particularly in highly industrialized European societies. The number of psychologists multiplied rapidly, with the aim of providing mental health services to people seeking help for emotional and mental problems. The two main areas that developed in Europe in the post-war period are *clinical psychology*, which had its origin in hospitals and psychiatric clinics, and *counseling psychology*, which developed mainly in the fields of education. These fields were typically integrated with other professions involved in mental health, especially psychiatry. Another specialty that has made a substantial contribution to health psychology is the psychology applied to school contexts that arose from the need for specialized professional services related to problems of learning and development in children at school. Another traditional specialization within psychology involved in the health sector is that of industrial psychology. In this field, psychologists are interested in issues such as the development of capacities in relation to the demands of tasks, definition of tasks and environmental conditions to respond to the attitudes, assessment and increased satisfaction in work performance, the reduction of accidents, and stress reduction in the workplace.

In addition, in the 1970s, European health psychologists began to develop interventions on the community level, intended to reduce disease and mortality due to cardiovascular disease (Matarazzo et al., 1984). For example, the North Karelia Project was a pioneering work to improve national public health in Finland. It was launched in the Province of North Karelia, in Finland, in 1972, in response to a local petition for urgent and effective help to reduce the great burden of exceptionally high coronary heart disease mortality rates in the area, which at that time were the highest in the world. In cooperation with local and national authorities and experts, along with the World Health Organization, the North Karelia Project was formulated and implemented to carry out a comprehensive intervention through community organizations and the action of the people themselves. The Project has included a comprehensive evaluation, and has acted as a major demonstration program for national and international applications. Pekka Puska and his colleagues at the National Institute of Public Health in Helsinki designed and carried out a preventive intervention to reduce the risk factors in the population through dietary change and the reduction of smoking. The work was done through local community organizations and by the local people themselves. Comprehensive activities were used, involving health and other services, including schools, innovative media campaigns, local media, supermarkets, and the food industry. Over 5 years, the project successfully reduced levels of smoking and other known cardiovascular risk factors (such as high cholesterol, hypertension) among the population of North Karelia (Puska, 1984).[7]

During the 1970s, the discovery in Belgium that two chronic diseases, cardiovascular disorders and cancer, were responsible for more than 65% of mortality in the country, led researchers associated with the World Health Organization to pursue a plan of controlled, multifactorial intervention in some work environments in the country. Initial studies of the work environment showed the need for direct intervention on the community as a whole. Thus, researchers from four different cities (Brussels, Ghent, Leuven, and Liège), working together, planned a large-scale, targeted intervention for the inhabitants of some provinces, counties, and regions of Belgium (Kittel, 1984).

In recent years, many large-scale behavioral research projects in Britain, Germany, and France have utilized health psychology research. These programs are not limited to health education, but more broadly emphasize changing lifestyle through the application of the principles of social learning theory, community organization, and communication-persuasion. Along with the individually oriented model used to change the lifestyle, the environmental approach was developed from research on behavior in health and safety at work. As a result, knowledge gained from health psychology has been used to restructure work to improve psychosocial conditions and, consequently, the state of health. Particularly in Scandinavian countries, in the late 1970s, this research led to a broader concept of the work environment that has influenced legislation concerning work conditions (Gardell, 1981).

The European Health Psychology Society (EHPS) was established in 1986, with the aim of promoting empirical and theoretical research in and applications of health psychology within Europe. EHPS sought, as well, the interchange of information related to health psychology with other associations throughout the world. The inaugural meeting of the Society took place in Tilburg, the Netherlands, and was initiated by Stan Maes from Leiden University, the Netherlands. The EHPS has organized scientific meetings since 1986. The initial local groups of health psychologists, affiliated with EHPS, were from the United Kingdom, Ireland, the Netherlands, and Germany. Since that time, new members have also been drawn from Finland, France, Greece, Italy, Spain, Israel, Portugal, Norway, Sweden, Switzerland, and others and, in recent years, also from Central and Eastern Europe (Todorova & Renner, 2008). Also in 1986, the Special Group in Health Psychology—redesignated the Division of Health Psychology in 1997—of the British Psychological

Society was established, followed in 1992 by the Division of Health Psychology of the German Society of Psychology, in 1997 by the Italian Society of Health Psychology, and in 2001 by the Association Francophone de Psychologie de la Santé.

Since 1992, the European Federation of Professional Psychologists' Association (EFFPA) has had a Task Force on Health Psychology, with the objective of specifying training needs and objectives. Professionalization of health psychology in European countries is on average 10 to 20 years behind the United States (Nezu et al., 2003). The Education and Training Committee of the EHPS has published a reference guide of graduate programs in health psychology in Europe (McIntyre et al., 2000). In general, there are many master's and Ph.D. level programs, but few Psy.D. programs have been developed, with the result that training in practitioner skills is limited when compared with training in research skills (Nezu et al., 2003).

Since 1985, *Psychology and Health* has been the leading European journal. In 1996, the *Journal of Health and Medicine* was established with an international orientation in the field. Another journal, *Psychology, Health and Medicine*, has focused on psychological care for medical problems. Several national-level journals—*British Journal of Health Psychology*, *Revista de Psicologia de la Salud*, *Zeitschrift fur Gesundheitpsychologie*, *Psicologia della salute*— increased communication among health psychologists in Europe.

Therefore, in the 1990s, a considerable amount of research was initiated in Europe, reflecting some differences from country to country. The Anglo-Saxon approach to health psychology, closely associated with behavioral medicine, primarily focused on the development of new behavioral technologies for the promotion and preservation of physical health and on the study of behavioral factors that affect emergency treatment and foster the healing of physical illnesses. In France, health psychology has historically been characterized by the parallel development of two separate approaches: a cognitive behavioral orientation similar to the Anglo-Saxon approach and an approach derived from clinical and psychodynamic psychotherapy.

Italian health psychology has relied on two major precursors that have a solid tradition both in theory and application: medical psychology and psychosomatic medicine. Before the birth in the Italian universities of undergraduate courses in psychology, which occurred in the 1970s, and its subsequent transformation into faculties of psychology, which

took place in the 1980s, the focus of health psychology was expressed mainly in the psychological teaching in medical schools. This characteristic enabled psychology to cultivate and develop a comprehensive and detailed interest in psychological aspects of medical practice: the psychology of training of professionals working in health services, understanding the organizational aspects of health intervention, attention to the human patient, and understanding interpersonal processes that characterize the physician–patient relationship (cf. Canestrari, 1961; 1967; Bertini, 1972; Canestrari & Ricci Bitti, 1979; Cesa Bianchi, 1979; Giovannini et al., 1982). Another important trend that has influenced Italian health psychology is psychosomatic medicine, thanks to the presence of the Italian Society of Psychosomatic Medicine. Less interest was aroused in Italy by behavioral medicine, which received more attention in the same period in Anglo-Saxon and northern European countries and which has constituted in many of those countries the prerequisite for the development of health psychology, analogous to what happened in the United States.

Over time, there have emerged within European health psychology some areas that specifically address issues with different approaches: clinical health psychology, occupational health psychology, health psychology, community health psychology, and critical health psychology. The distinction among these different areas has not always been clear, however. Clinical health psychology represents the most important sector in the panorama of European health psychology and makes an important contribution to behavioral medicine in psychiatry. Clinical practice includes patient education, use of techniques of behavior change, and psychotherapy. Research abounds in this field in Europe, including research on behavior change models and behavior change interventions (Bridle et al., 2005; Hardeman et al., 2002; Michie & Abraham, 2004; Michie et al., 2007; Sniehotta et al., 2005; Ziegelman et al., 2006), illness perception and illness representations (Groarke et al., 2005; Hagger & Orbell, 2003, 2005; Moss-Morris et al., 2002), meanings in health and illness (Flowers et al., 2006; Goodwin & Ogden, 2007), and health-related cognitions (Panzer & Renner, 2008).

Although clinical health psychology is an important area of health psychology, not all European countries embrace this concept. For example, Italy has seen a particularly productive output of original contributions on the psychological and psychophysiological basis of health and welfare, the doctor–patient relationship, and health care quality, but not all psychologists who work in this area recognize themselves as serving in the field of health psychology. By contrast, in Britain, this tradition is very well defined with establishment, in 1998, within the Division of Clinical Psychology of a clinical health psychology interest group focused specifically on issues of physical health (Bennet, 2000).

Occupational health psychology is another field in European health psychology. The European Academy of Occupational Health Psychology was founded in 1999, in Britain, for the application of principles and practices of psychology to occupational health issues. Its main study object includes all the psychological, social, and organizational dynamics of the relationship between work and health. Although sharing the aims of American occupational health psychology, European policy also emphasizes the assessment of work organization and its impact not only on individual health but also on the welfare of the community. In this perspective, European health psychology is focused on issues concerning health maintenance organizations, quality of organizational climate, and the hospital as an organizational context, with attention to health of professionals, as well as more traditional patient satisfaction.

Public health psychology was introduced in the United States as a field to investigate the potential causal links between psychosocial factors and health at the population level (Ewart, 1991; Hepworth, 2006). In Europe, this trend of health psychology is quite active, especially with regards to the field of health communication, environmental initiatives, the negotiation of health behaviors, and participation and empowerment of the population in relation to decisions affecting their health (Kopp & Rethely, 2004; Kopp et al., 2000; Todorova & Todorov, 2006; Wardle & Steptoe, 2005).

Community health psychology, focused on those factors that contribute to the health and welfare of individuals as members of a community, aims to develop interventions to promote physical and mental health in the community. Although purposes, methods, and objectives are somewhat different, in recent years, health psychology and community psychology appear to be united by the study of issues such as social support, skills development, and self-determination. Thus, community health psychology has arisen at the intersection of these two disciplines. In European countries, many social psychologists and community psychologists have been engaged for several years in activities that fall into this area. Italian researchers have also contributed original work on

issues still not addressed on the international scene, for example, the study of the person–environment relationship in the urban context and health promotion and educational contexts (Petrillo, 2008; Zani, 2008).

Finally, the most recent sector to develop in European health psychology is critical health psychology. Established in Britain, critical health psychology deals with the distribution of power and its impact on health and behavior of individuals, health systems, and health policies (Crossley, 2008; Hepworth, 2006). The main theme of the approach is social justice and the universal right of all individuals to health and wellness, regardless of race and socioeconomic position. The goal is not limited to the study of inequality, but also addresses how to become an agent of change. The International Society of Critical Health Psychology, founded in Birmingham in 2001, is the organization that seeks to advance and represent studies in this area. Critical health psychology emphasizes a series of qualitative and participatory methods to understand health and disease, including the hermeneutic phenomenological approach, the narrative method, discourse analysis, grounded theory, action research, ethnography, and analysis of social representations. In Italy and other countries, such as France, many instances of methodological proposals in this field have been widely implemented since the discipline's emergence.

European health psychology, both Anglo-Saxon and northern and eastern European, shares with American health psychology a pragmatic approach to preventive interventions and the modification of health behaviors, while also paying greater attention to epistemological and operational models. The more philosophical approach of Europeans, especially in Mediterranean countries, which have a greater inclination to reflection, seems to have encouraged the discipline's migration away from medicine, thus reducing the biomedical emphasis that characterizes Anglo-Saxon tradition, while integrating qualitative approaches and constructivist processes that pay attention to not only psychological but also socioeconomic, cultural, political, and environmental factors (Ricci Bitti & Gremigni, 2008).

## Conclusion

Health psychology in both Europe and North America has been woven from many strands of thought and practice in medicine and other fields, including philosophy and diverse areas within the historically recent discipline and profession of psychology. As we have shown, European and North

American health psychology have many similarities, while simultaneously also having unique emphases. In a diverse world, this may prove to be one of the field's greatest strengths, as psychologists and the public learn how to adapt knowledge and practice gained in one setting to new settings. Ironically, health psychology in both Europe and North America has as its epistemological and practical foundation tenets laid down in the field of psychosomatic medicine during the 1930s. Now, however, psychologists have built on that foundation a multifaceted structure rich in complexity and the promise of improved health.

## Notes

1. William James, Lectures IV and V, *Varieties of Religious Experience*, 1902.
2. After Freud's recognition that had defined him as a "splendid analyst," he continued to define himself as a "wild psychoanalyst" and called jokingly his clinic "satanarium" instead of "sanatorium" (Ammon, 1974).
3. It is important to emphasize the absolute autonomy with which this proposal was developed in a period during which psychoanalysis in Germany was excluded from any contact with the contemporary developments of American psychoanalysis.
4. Above all, only few classical psychosomatic subjects were showing improvements under psychoanalytic treatment. Furthermore, the same data that at first had provoked a lot of enthusiasm turned out to be too weak and heterogeneous when submitted to the methodical analysis of modern research and statistics. Even though the relationship between susceptibility to illnesses and emotional factors has been several times confirmed, it has not been at all shown that this tie represents the psychic conflict consequence (Taylor, Bagby, & Parker, 1991).
5. Marston's real claim to fame is as the creator of Wonder Woman (Bunn, 1997).
6. This failure enraged and mobilized the emerging group of private-practice psychologists to get involved in APA's leadership in order to redirect at least some of APA's resources to the support of the practice of psychology. The resultant tensions and ill-will eventually led to the split of the organization and the establishment of what is now the Association for Psychological Science (Pickren & Rutherford, Chapter 12).
7. Over the years, the scope of the project has been enlarged to include broader objectives of integrated prevention of major noncommunicable diseases and health promotion, as well as prevention of risk-related lifestyles in childhood and youth. The 20-year results and experiences of the North Karelia Project show that a determined and well-conceived intervention can have a major impact on health-related lifestyles and on population risk factor levels, and that such a development, indeed, leads to reduced disease rates and improved health of the population. By 1995, the annual mortality rate of coronary heart disease in North Karelia in the working-age population had fallen approximately 75%, compared with the rate before the project (Puska et al., 1995).

## References

Aguayo, J. (1986). Charcot and Freud: Some implications of late 19th century French psychiatry and politics for the origins of psychoanalysis. *Psychoanalysis and Contemporary Thought, 9,* 223–260.

Albanese, C.L. (2007). *A republic of mind and spirit: A cultural history of American metaphysical religion.* New Haven, CT: Yale University Press.

Alexander, F. (1934). The influence of psychologic factors upon gastro-intestinal disturbances: A symposium. I. General principles, objectives, and preliminary results. *Psychoanalytical Quarterly, 3,* 501–539.

Alexander, F. (1932). Psychoanalysis and medicine. *Mental Hygiene, 16,* 63–84.

Alexander, F. (1933). Functional disturbances of psychogenic nature. *Journal of the American Medical Association 100,* 469–473.

Alexander, F. (1950). *Psychosomatic medicine.* New York: Norton.

Ammon, G. (1974). *Psychoanalyse und Psychosomatik* [Psychoanalysis and Psychosomatic]. München: Piper & Co. Verlag.

APA Task Force on Health Research. (1976). Contributions of psychology to health research: Patterns, problems, and potentials. *American Psychologist, 31,* 263–274.

Avila, L.A. (2003). Georg Groddeck: Originality and exclusion. *History of Psychiatry, 14,* 83–101.

Baker, D.B., & Benjamin, Jr., L.T. (2000). The affirmation of the scientist-practitioner: A look back at Boulder. *American Psychologist, 55,* 241–247.

Baker, R.R., & Pickren, W.E. (2007). *Psychology and the Department of Veterans Affairs: A Historical Analysis of Training, Research, Practice, and Advocacy.* Washington, DC: APA Books.

Balint, M. (1956). *The doctor, his patient and the illness.* London: Pitman Medical Publishing.

Barker, R.G., Wright, B.A., & Gonick, M.R. (1943). *Adjustment to physical handicap and illness.* New York: McGraw-Hill.

Bennett, P. (2000). *Introduction to clinical health psychology.* Buckingham: Open University Press.

Bertalanffy, L.V. (1968). *General systems theory: Foundations, development, applications.* New York: George Braziller.

Bertini, M. (1972). Problemi psicologici nei cosiddetti procedimenti "life extending" [Psychological problems in so-called process "life-extending"]. In AA.VV., *Rigetto psicologico di innesti, trapianti e plastiche* [Psychological rejection of grafts, transplants and plastic surgery] (pp. 101–112). Roma: Istituto Italiano di Medicina Sociale.

Boss, M. (1963). *Psychoanalysis and Daseinsanalysis.* New York: Basic Books.

Brady, J.V. (1958). Ulcers in "executive" monkeys. *Science, 199,* 95–100.

Brand, J., & Sapir, P. (1964). An historical perspective on the National Institute of Mental Health. In D.E. Woolridge (Ed.), *Biomedical science and its administration.* Unpublished report internal to NIH.

Bridle, C., Riesma, R.P., Pattenden, J., Sowden, A.J., Mather, L., Watt, I.S., & Walties, A. (2005). Systematic review of the effectiveness of health behavior interventions based on the transtheoretical model. *Psychology and Health, 20,* 283–301.

Bronfenbrenner, U. (1947). Research planning in neuropsychiatry and clinical psychology in the Veterans Administration. *Journal of Clinical Psychology, 3,* 33–38.

Brown, T.M. (1987). Alan Gregg and the Rockefeller Foundation's support of Franz Alexander's psychosomatic research. *Bulletin of the History of Medicine, 65,* 155–182.

Bugos, G.E. (1989). Managing cooperative research and border-land science in the National Research Council, 1922–1942. *Historical Studies in the Physical and Biological Sciences, 20,* 1–32.

Bunn G. (2007). Spectacular science: The lie detector's ambivalent powers. *History of Psychology, 10,* 156–178. doi: 10.1037/1093-4510.10.2.156.

Bunn, G. (1997). The lie detector, Wonder Woman and liberty: The life and work of William Moulton Marston. *History of the Human Sciences, 10,* 91–119. doi: 10.1177/095269519701000105.

Calden, G., Thurston, J.R., Stewart, B.M, & Vineberg, S.E. (1955). The use of the MMPI in predicting irregular discharge among tuberculosis patients. *Journal of Clinical Psychology, 11,* 374–377.

Canestrari, R., & Ricci Bitti, P.E. (1979). *Aspetti psicologici della pratica chirurgica* [Psychological aspects of surgical practice]. In R. Domini, P. Descovich & F. Maghetti (Eds.). *Trattato di tecnica chirurgica* [Treatise of surgical technique]. (vol. 1, pp. 15–29). Padova: Piccin.

Canestrari, R. (1961). L'insegnamento della psicologia nella formazione del medico [The teaching of psychology in the medical training]. *Giornale di Clinica Medica, 5,* 481–498.

Canestrari, R. (1967). Il rapporto medico-paziente in una società in trasformazione [The doctor-patient relationship in a changing society]. *Asclepieo, 2,* 29–32.

Cannon, W.B. (1932). *The wisdom of the body.* New York: Norton.

Cannon, W.B. (1953). *Bodily changes in pain, hunger, fear and rage.* Boston: Charles T. Branford Company.

Caplan, E.M. (1995). Trains, brains, and sprains: Railway spine and the origins of psychoneuroses. *Bulletin of the History of Medicine, 69,* 387–419.

Cassedy, J.H. (1991). *Medicine in America: A short history.* Baltimore: Johns Hopkins University Press.

Cesa-Bianchi, M. (Ed.). (1979). *Psicologia e ospedale generale* [Psychology and general hospital]. Milano: Franco Angeli.

Chertok, L. (1984). On the centenary of Charcot: Hysteria, suggestibility, and hypnosis. *British Journal of Medical Psychology, 57,* 111–120.

Clarke, E.R., Jr., Zahn, D.W., & Holmes, T.H. (1954). The relationship of stress, adrenocortical function, and tuberculosis. *American Review of Tuberculosis, 69,* 351–369.

Conrad, A. (1934). The anamnesis of the toxic goiter patient. *American Journal of Psychiatry, 91,* 517–527.

Cremerius, J. (1978). *Zur theorie und praxis der psychosomatischen medizin* [Theory and practice of psychosomatic medicine]. Frankfurt: Suhrkamp.

Cross, S.J., & Albury, W.R. (1987). Walter B. Cannon, L.J. Henderson, and the organic analogy. *Osiris, 2nd series, 3,* 165–192.

Crossley, M. (2008). Critical health psychology: Developing and refining the approach. *Social and Personality Psychology Compass, 2/1,* 21–33.

Daniels, G.E. (1934). Neuroses associated with the gastro-intestinal tract. *American Journal of Psychiatry, 91,* 527–540.

Delbourgo, J. (2006). *Electricity and enlightenment in early America.* Cambridge, MA: Harvard University Press.

Deutsch, F. (1924). Zur Bildung des Konversionssymptoms [Knowledge on conversion symptom]. *Internationale Zeitschrift für Psychoanalise, VIII,* 290–306.

Deutsch, F. (1949). *Applied psychoanalysis: Selected objectives of psychotherapy.* New York: Grune and Stratton.

Deutsch, F. (1953). *The psychosomatic concept in psychoanalysis.* New York: International Universities Press.

Dollard, J., Doob, L., Miller, N., Mowrer, O.H., & Sears, R.R. (1939). *Frustration and aggression.* New Haven, CT: Yale University Press.

Draper, G. (1934). Man as a complete organism-in health and disease. *New York State Journal of Medicine, 34,* 1052–1063.

Draper, G., Dunn, H., & Seegal, D. (1924). Studies in human constitution. I. Clinical anthropometry. *Journal of the American Medical Association, 82,* 431–434.

Dunbar, H.F. (1934). Physical-mental relationships in illness: Trends in modern medicine and research as related to psychiatry. *American Journal of Psychiatry, 91,* 541–562.

Dunbar, H.F. (1935). *Emotions and bodily changes: A survey of literature on psychosomatic relationships, 1910–1933.* New York: Columbia University Press.

Dunbar, H.F. (1939). Introductory statement. *Psychosomatic Medicine, 1,* 3–5.

Dunlap, H.F., & Moersch, F.P. (1935). Psychic manifestations associated with hyperthyroidism. *American Journal of Psychiatry, 91,* 1216–1236.

Engel, G.L., & Schmale, A.H. (1972). Conservation-withdrawal: A primary regulatory process for organismic homeostasis. In R. Porter & J. Knight (Eds.), *Physiology, emotion & psychosomatic illness,* Ciba Foundation Symposium 8, pp. 57–85. Amsterdam: Elsevier-Excerpta Medica.

Engel, G.L. (1977). The need for a new medical model: A challenge for biomedicine. *Science, 196,* 129–136.

Ewart, C.K. (1991). Social action theory for a public health psychology. *American Psychologist, 46,* 931–946.

Farreras, I.G. (2005). The historical context for National Institute of Mental Health support of American Psychological Association training and accreditation efforts. In W.E. Pickren & S.F. Schneider (Eds.), *Psychology and the National Institute of Mental Health: A historical analysis of science, practice, and policy* (pp. 153–179). Washington, DC: American Psychological Association.

Flagg, G.W. (1966). Felix Deutsch, 1884–1964. In F. Alexander, S. Eisenstein, & M. Grotjahn (Eds.), *Psychoanalytic pioneers* (pp. 299–307). New York: Basic Books.

Flowers, P., Davis, M., Hart, G., Rosengarten, M., Frankis, J., & Imrie, J. (2006). Diagnosis and stigma and identity amongst HIV positive Black Africans living in the UK. *Psychology and Health, 21,* 109–122.

French, T. (1933). Interrelations between psychoanalysis and the experimental work of Pavlov. *American Journal of Psychiatry, 89,* 1165–1203.

Freud, S., & Breuer, J. (1895). Studies on hysteria. In J. Strachey et al. (Eds.). *The standard edition of the complete works of Sigmund Freud* (vol. 2). London: The Hogarth Press and the Institute of Psychoanalysis, 1953–74.

Freud, S. (1894). The neuro-psychoses of defence. In J. Strachey et al. (Eds.). *The standard edition of the complete works of Sigmund Freud* (vol. 3, pp. 43–61). London: The Hogarth Press and the Institute of Psychoanalysis, 1953–74.

Freud, S. (1895). A project for a scientific psychology. In J. Strachey et al. (Eds.). *The standard edition of the complete works of Sigmund Freud* (vol. 1, pp. 283–397). London: The Hogarth Press and the Institute of Psychoanalysis, 1953–74.

Freud, S. (1905). Three essays on the theory of sexuality. In J. Strachey et al. (Eds.). *The standard edition of the complete works of Sigmund Freud* (vol. 7, pp. 125–245). London: The Hogarth Press and the Institute of Psychoanalysis, 1953–74.

Freud, S. (1909). Analysis of a phobia in a five-year-old boy. In J. Strachey et al. (Eds.). *The standard edition of the complete works of Sigmund Freud* (vol. 10, pp. 3–149). London: The Hogarth Press and the Institute of Psychoanalysis, 1953–74.

Friedman, H.S., & Adler, N.E. (2007). The history and background of health psychology. In H.S. Friedman & R.C. Silver (Eds.), *Foundations of health psychology* (pp. 3–18). New York: Oxford University Press.

Gardell, B. (1981). Strategies for reform programs on work organization and work environment. In B. Gardell & G. Johansson (Eds.). *Working life: A social science contribution to work reform* (pp. 3–13). Chichester: Wiley.

Ghaemi, S.N. (2010). *The rise and fall of the biopsychosocial model.* Baltimore: Johns Hopkins University Press.

Giovannini, D., Ricci Bitti, P.E., Sarchielli, G., & Speltini, G. (1982). *Psicologia e salute* [Psychology and Health]. Bologna: Zanichelli.

Goodwin, P., & Ogden, J. (2007). Women's reflections upon their past-abortions: An exploration of how and why emotional reactions change over time. *Psychology and Health, 22,* 231–248.

Grinker, R.R., & Spiegel, J.P. (1945). *Men under stress.* Philadelphia: The Blakiston Co.

Groarke, A., Curtis, R., Coughlan, R., & Gsel, A. (2005). The impact of illness representations and disease activity on adjustment in women with rheumatoid arthritis: A longitudinal study. *Psychology and Health, 20,* 597–613.

Grob, G.N. (1991). *From asylum to community: Mental health policy in modern America.* Princeton, NJ: Princeton University Press.

Groddeck, G. (1929). *The book of the it,* trans. by L.R. Clark. New York: Nervous and Mental Disease Publishing Company.

Grotjahn, M. (1945). Georg Groddeck and his teaching about man's innate need for symbolization. *Psychoanalytic Review, 32,* 9–24.

Hagger, M.S., & Orbell, S. (2003). A meta-analytic review of the common-sense model of illness representations. *Psychology and Health, 18,* 141–184.

Hagger, M.S., & Orbell, S. (2005). A confirmatory factor analysis of the revised illness perception questionnaire (IPQ-R) in a cervical screening context. *Psychology and Health, 20,* 161–173.

Hale, N.G. (1971). *Freud and the Americans: The beginnings of psychoanalysis in the United States, 1876–1917.* New York: Oxford University Press.

Hale, N.G. (1995). *The rise and crisis of psychoanalysis in the United States: Freud and the Americans, 1917–1985.* New York: Oxford University Press.

Haley, B. (1978). *The healthy body and Victorian culture.* Cambridge, MA: The Belknap Press.

Hardeman, W., Johnston, M., Johnston, D., Bonetti, D., Wareham, N., & Kimmonth, A.L. (2002). Application of the theory of planned behavior in behavior change interventions: A systematic review. *Psychology and Health, 17,* 123–258.

Harrington, A. (2008). *The cure within: A history of mind-body medicine.* New York: Norton.

Harrington, R. (2006). On the tracks of trauma: Railway spine reconsidered. *Social History of Medicine, 16,* 209–223.

Harrower, M.R. (1955). *Medical and psychological teamwork in the care of the chronically ill.* Springfield, IL: Charles C. Thomas.

Hatch, N.O. (1989). *The democratization of American Christianity.* New Haven, CT: Yale University Press.

Heidbreder, E. (1926). Intelligence and the height-weight ratio. *Journal of Applied Psychology, 10,* 52–62.

Hepworth, J. (2006). The emergence of critical health psychology: Can it contribute to promoting public health? *Journal of Health Psychology, 11,* 331–341.

Hildreth, H.M. (1954). Clinical psychology in the Veterans Administration. In E.A. Rubinstein and M. Lorr (Eds.), *Survey of clinical practice in psychology* (pp. 83–108). New York: International Universities Press.

Holmes, T.H., & Rahe, R.H. (1967). The social readjustments rating scales. *Journal of Psychosomatic Research, 11,* 213–218, 1967.

Hornstein, G.A. (1992). The return of the repressed: Psychology's problematic relations with psychoanalysis, 1909–1960. *American Psychologist 47,* 254–263.

Hunt, J.M. (Ed.). (1944). *Personality and the behavior disorders* (2 vols.). New York: Ronald Press.

Josiah Macy, Jr. Foundation. (1955). *The Josiah Macy, Jr. Foundation, 1930–1955: A review of activities.* New York: Josiah Macy, Jr. Foundation.

Kaplan, H.I., & Kaplan, H.S. (1956). An historical survey of psychosomatic medicine. *Journal of Nervous and Mental Disease, 124,* 546–568.

Katzenelbogen, S., & Luton, F.H. (1935). Hyperthyroidism and psychobiological reactions. *American Journal of Psychiatry, 91,* 975–981.

Kimball, C.P. (1970). Conceptual developments in psychosomatic medicine: 1939–1969. *Annals of Internal Medicine, 73,* 307–316.

Kittel, F. (1984). The interuniversity study on nutrition and health. In J.D. Matarazzo, S.M. Weiss, J.A. Herd, N.E. Miller, & S.M. Weiss (Eds.). *Behavioral health: A handbook of health enhancement and disease prevention* (pp. 1148–1153). New York: Wiley.

Klett, C.J. (2003, August). Oral history with Wade Pickren. Washington, DC: APA Archives.

Kohler, R.E. (1991). *Partners in science: Foundations and natural scientists, 1900–1945.* Chicago: University of Chicago Press.

Kopp, M., & Rethelyi, J. (2004). Where psychology meets physiology: Chronic stress and premature morality, the Central-Eastern European health paradox. *Brain Research Bulletin, 62,* 351–367.

Kopp, M., Skrabski, A., & Szedmak, S. (2000). Psychosocial risk factors, inequality and self-rated morbidity in a changing society. *Social Science and Medicine, 51,* 1351–1361.

Kubie, L. (1934). Relation of the conditioned reflex to psychoanalytic technique. *Archives of Neurology and Psychiatry, 32,* 1137–1142.

Lasky, J.J. (1960). Veterans Administration cooperative chemotherapy projects and related studies. In L. Uhr & J.G. Miller (Eds.), *Drugs and behavior* (pp. 540–554). New York: Wiley.

Leuba, J.H. (1894). A study in the psychology of religious phenomena. *American Journal of Psychology, 7,* 309–385.

Leuba, J.H. (1926). *The psychology of religious mysticism.* New York: Harcourt, Brace.

Levi, L. (1972). Stress and distress in response to psychosocial stimuli. *Acta Medica Scandinava, 191* (Suppl 528).

Leys, R. (1991). Types of one: Adolf Meyer's life chart and the representation of individuality. *Representations, 34,* 1–28.

Lipowski, Z.J. (1977). Psychosomatic medicine in the seventies: An overview. *American Journal of Psychiatry, 134,* 233–244.

Lipowski, Z.J. (1984). What does the word "psychosomatic" really mean? A historical and semantic inquiry. *Psychosomatic Medicine, 46,* 153–171.

Lipsitt, D.R. (1989). Anorexia nervosa, Felix Deutsch, and the associative anamnesis: A psychosomatic kaleidoscope. *Psychosomatic Medicine, 51*, 597–607.

Loss, C.P. (2002). Religion and the therapeutic ethos in twentieth century American history. *American Studies International, 40*, 61–76.

Lyons, A.C., & Chamberlain, K. (2006). *Health psychology: A critical introduction*. New York: Cambridge University Press.

Magnuson, P. (1960). *Ring the night bell: An American surgeon's story*. Boston: Little, Brown, and Company.

Marks, D.F. (1996). Health psychology in context. *Journal of Health Psychology, 1*, 7–21.

Marston, W.M. (1917). Systolic blood pressure symptoms of deception. *Journal of Experimental Psychology, 2*, 117–163.

Marston, W.M. (1938). *The lie detector test*. New York: Richard R. Smith.

Marty, P., M'Uzam, M. (1963). La pensée opératoire. *Revue Française de Psychoanalise, 27*, 345–356.

Mason, J.W. (1975). A historical view of the stress field. *Journal of Human Stress, 1*, 6–12.

Matarazzo, J.D. (1955). Comprehensive medicine: A new era in medical education. *Human Organization, 14*, 4–9.

Matarazzo, J.D. (1980). Behavioral health and behavioral medicine: Frontiers for a new health psychology. *American Psychologist, 35*(9), 807–817. doi: 10.1037/0003-066X.35.9.807.

Matarazzo, J.D. (1994). Psychology in a medical school: A personal account of a department's 35-year history. *Journal of Clinical Psychology, 50*, 7–36.

Matarazzo, J.D., Carmody, T.P., & Gentry, W.E. (1981). Psychologists on the faculties of United States schools of medicine: Past, present, and possible future. *Clinical Psychology Review, 1*, 293–317.

Matarazzo, J.D., Weiss, S.M., Herd, J.A., Miller, N.E., & Weiss, S.M. (Eds.). (1984). *Behavioral health: A handbook of health enhancement and disease prevention*. New York: Wiley.

McIntyre, T.M., Maes, S., Weinman, J., Wrzesniewski, K., & Marks, D.F. (2000). *Postgraduate programs in health psychology in Europe: A reference guide*. Leiden, The Netherlands: European Health Psychology Society Education and Training Committee.

Mensh, I.N. (1953). Psychology in medical education. *American Psychologist, 8*, 83–85.

Micale, M. (1994). *Approaching hysteria: Disease and its interpretations*. Princeton, NJ: Princeton University Press.

Michie, S., & Abraham, C. (2004). Interventions to change health behaviors: Evidence-based or evidence inspired? *Psychology and Health, 19*, 29–49.

Michie, S., Rothman, A., & Seeran, P. (2007). Current issues and new direction in psychology and health: Advancing the science of behavior change. *Psychology and Health, 22*, 249–253.

Miller, J.G. (1946). Clinical psychology in the Veterans Administration. *American Psychologist, 1*, 181–189.

Miller, J.G. (1978). *Living systems*. New York: McGraw-Hill.

Mitscherlich, A. (1954). Zur psychoanalytischen Auffassung psychosomatischer Krankheitsentstehung [The psychoanalytic point of view on the development of psychosomatic disease]. *Psyche, 8*, 561–578.

Mitscherlich, A., Boor, C. de (1973). Verstehende Psychosomatik: ein Stiefkind der Medizin [Psychosomatic: A stepchild of medicine]. *Psyche, 27*, 1–20.

Mittelman, B., & Wolff, H.G. (1942). Emotions and gastroduodenal function. *Psychosomatic Medicine, 4*, 5–61.

Morawski, J.G. (1986). Organizing knowledge and behavior at Yale's Institute of Human Relations. *Isis, 77*, 219–242.

Moss-Morris, R., Weinman, J., Petrie, K., Horne, R., Cameron, L., & Buick, D. (2002). The revised Illness Perception Questionnaire (IPQ-R). *Psychology and Health, 17*, 1–16.

Murray, C.D. (1930a). A brief psychological analysis of a patient with ulcerative colitis. *Journal of Nervous and Mental Disease, 72*, 617–627.

Murray, C.D. (1930b). Psychogenic factors in the etiology of ulcerative colitis and bloody diarrhea. *American Journal of Medical Sciences, 180*, 239–248.

Naccarati, S., & Garrett, H.E. (1923). The influence of constitutional factors on behavior. *Journal of Experimental Psychology, 6*, 455–465.

Naccarati, S., & Lewy-Guinzberg, R.L. (1922). Hormones and intelligence. *Journal of Applied Psychology 6*, 221–234.

Nezu, A.M., Maguth Nezu, C., Geller, P.A. (Eds.). (2003), Health psychology. In I.B. Weiner (Ed.). *Handbook of Psychology*, vol. 9. New York: Wiley.

Owens, L. (1985). Pure and sound government: Laboratories, playing fields, and gymnasia in the nineteenth-century search for order. *Isis, 76*, 182–194.

Pancheri, P. (1984). *Trattato di medicina psicosomatica* [Treatise of Psychosomatic Medicine]. Firenze: USES Edizioni Scientifiche.

Pancheri, P. (1980). *Stress, emozioni, malattia* [Stress, emotions and disease]. Milano: Mondadori.

Panzer, M., & Renner, B. (2008). To be or not to be at risk: Spontaneous reactions toward risk feedback. *Psychology and Health, 23*, 617–627.

Paré, W.P. (1962). The effect of conflict and shock stress on stomach ulceration in the rat. *Journal of Psychosomatic Research, 6*, 223–225.

Park, R.J. (1994). A decade of the body: Researching and writing about the history of health, fitness, exercise, and sport, 1983–1993. *Journal of Sport History, 21*, 51–82.

Petrillo, G. (2008). Promozione della salute e del benessere degli adolescenti nel contesto scolastico [Health Promotion and welfare of adolescents at school]. *Psicologia della salute, 3*, 59–82.

Pickren, W.E. (2007a). Tension and opportunity in post WWII American psychology. *History of Psychology, 10*, 279–299.

Pickren, W.E. (2007b). Psychology and medical education: A historical perspective from the United States. *Indian Journal of Psychiatry, 49*, 175–177.

Pickren, W.E., & Rutherford, A. (2010). *A history of modern psychology in context*. New York: Wiley.

Pickren, W.E., & Schneider, S.F. (Eds.). (2005). *Psychology and the National Institute of Mental Health: A historical analysis of science, practice, and policy*. Washington, DC: American Psychological Association Books.

Powell, R.C. (1977). Helen Flanders Dunbar (1902–1959) and a holistic approach to psychosomatic problems. I. The rise and fall of a medical philosophy. *Psychiatric Quarterly, 49*, 133–152.

Powell, R.C. (1978). Helen Flanders Dunbar (1902–1959) and a holistic approach to psychosomatic problems. II. The role of Dunbar's nonmedical background. *Psychiatric Quarterly, 50*, 144–157.

Puska, P. (1984). Community-based prevention of cardiovascular disease: The North Karelia Project. In J.D. Matarazzo,

S.M. Weiss, J.A. Herd, N.E. Miller & S.M. Weiss (Eds.). *Behavioral health: A handbook of health enhancement and disease prevention* (pp. 1140–1147). New York: Wiley.

Puska, P., Tuomilehto, J., Nissinen, A., & Vartiainen, E. (1995). *The North Karelia Project: 20-year results and experiences.* Helsinki: National Public Health.

Ricci Bitti, P.E., & Gremigni P. (2008). Quadri teorici e modelli operativi: Lo stato della psicologia della salute italiana nell'orizzonte internazionale [Theoretical frameworks and models: the situation of Italian health psychology on international horizon]. *Psicologia della salute, 3,* 21–31.

Rutherford, A. (2003). B.F. Skinner and the auditory inkblot: The rise and fall of the verbal summator as a projective technique. *History of Psychology, 4,* 362–378.

Schmit, D. (2005). Re-visioning American antebellum psychology: The dissemination of mesmerism, 1836–1854. *History of Psychology, 8,* 403–434.

Schmit, D. (2010). The Mesmerists inquire about "Oriental Mind Powers:" West meets East in the search for the universal trance. *Journal of the History of the Behavioral Sciences, 46,* 1–26.

Schneider, S.F. (2005). Reflections on psychology and the National Institute of Mental Health. In W.E. Pickren & S.F. Schneider (Eds.), *Psychology and the National Institute of Mental Health: A historical analysis of science, practice, and policy* (pp. 17–28). Washington, DC: American Psychological Association.

Schofield, W. (1969). The role of psychology in the delivery of health services. *American Psychologist, 24,* 565–584.

Schulman, J. (1969). *Remaking an organization.* Albany: State University of New York Press.

Schwartz, G. E. (1982). Testing the biopsychosocial model: The ultimate challenge facing behavioral medicine? *Journal of Consulting and Clinical Psychology, 50*(6), 1040–1053.

Scull, A., & Schulkin, J. (2009). Psychobiology, psychiatry, and psychoanalysis: The intersecting careers of Adolf Meyer, Phyllis Greenacre, and Curt Richter. *Medical History, 53,* 5–36.

Sears, R.R. (1943). *Survey of objective studies of psychoanalytic concepts.* New York: Social Science Research Council.

Selye, H. (1950). *The physiology and pathology of exposure to stress.* Montreal: Acta.

Selye, H. (1956). *The stress of life.* New York: McGraw-Hill.

Shakow, D., & Rapaport, D. (1964). *The influence of Freud on American psychology.* New York: International Universities Press.

Shakow, D. (1942). The training of the clinical psychologist. *Journal of Consulting Psychology, 6,* 277–288.

Smith, G.C., & Strain, J.J. (2002). George Engel's contribution to clinical psychiatry. *Australian and New Zealand Journal of Psychiatry, 36,* 458–466.

Sniehotta, F.F., Scholz, U., & Schwarzer, R. (2005). Bridging the intention-behavior gap: Planning, self-efficacy and action control in the adoption and maintenance of physical exercise. *Psychology and Health, 20,* 143–160.

Sparer, P.J. (1956). *Personality, stress, and tuberculosis.* New York: International Universities Press.

Starr, P. (1984). *The social transformation of American medicine.* New York: Basic Books.

Stratton, G.M. (1926). Emotions and the incidence of disease. *Journal of Abnormal and Social Psychology, 21,* 19–23.

Taves, A. (1999). *Fits, trances, and visions: Experiencing religion and explaining experience from Wesley to James.* Princeton, NJ: Princeton University Press.

Taylor, E. (1982). Louville Eugene Emerson: Psychotherapy, Harvard, and the early Boston scene. *Harvard Medical Alumni Bulletin, 56,* 42–48.

Taylor, E. (1999). *Shadow culture: Psychology and spirituality in America.* Washington, DC: Counterpoint.

Taylor, E. (2000). Psychotherapeutics and the problematic origins of clinical psychology in America. *American Psychologist, 55,* 1029–1033.

Taylor, G.J., Bagby, R.M., & Parker, J.D.A. (1997). *Disorders of affect regulation: Alexithymia in medical and psychiatric illness.* Cambridge: Cambridge University Press.

Todorova, I.L.G., & Renner, B. (2008). The European Health Psychology Society: History and prospects. *Psicologia della salute, 3,* 7–20.

Todorova, I., & Todorov, V. (2006). Gender and psychosocial aspects of health in Bulgaria. *Cognitie, Creier, Comportament, 10,* 31–51.

Tracy, S.W. (1992). George Draper and American constitutional medicine, 1916–1946: Reinventing the sick man. *Bulletin of the History of Medicine, 66,* 53–89.

Vernier, C.M., Barrell, R.P., Cummings, J.W., Dickerson, J.H., & Hooper, H.E. (1961). Psychosocial study of the patient with pulmonary tuberculosis. *Psychological Monographs: General and Applied, 75,* Whole No. 510, 1–32.

Wallston, K.A. (1997). A history of Division 38 (Health Psychology): Healthy, wealthy, and Weiss. In D.A. Dewsbury (Ed.), *Unification through division: Histories of the divisions of the American Psychological Association,* vol. 2 (pp. 239–267). Washington, DC: APA Books.

Wardle, J., & Steptoe, A. (2005). Public health psychology. *The Psychologist, 18,* 672–675.

Warner, J.H. (1997). *The therapeutic perspective: Medical practice, knowledge, and identity in America, 1820–1885.* Princeton, NJ: Princeton University Press.

Weiss, E., & English, O.S. (1943). *Psychosomatic medicine: The clinical application of psychopathology to general medical problems.* Philadelphia: W. B. Saunders Company.

Weizsäcker, V. von (1933). Körpergeschehen und Neurose. Analytische Studie über somatische Symptombildung [Body and neurosis. Analytical study of somatic symptom]. *Internationale Zeitschrift für Psychoanalyse, 19,* 16–116.

Weizsäcker, V. von (1949). Psychosomatische Medizin [Psychosomatic Medicine]. *Psyche, 3,* 331–341.

White, W.A. (1926). *The meaning of disease.* Baltimore: Williams & Wilkins.

Whitehorn, J.C., & Zilboorg, G. (1933). Present trends in American psychiatric research. *American Journal of Psychiatry, 90,* 303–312.

Whorton, J.C. (1982). *Crusaders for fitness: The history of American health reformers.* Princeton, NJ: Princeton University Press.

Whorton, J.C. (2002). *Nature cures: The history of alternative medicine in America.* New York: Oxford University Press.

Winnicott, D.W. (1966). Psychosomatic illness in its positive and negative aspects. *International Journal of Psychoanalysis, 47,* 510–516.

Wittkower, E. (1935). Studies on the influence of emotions on the functions of the organs. *Journal of Mental Science, 81,* 533–682.

Wittkower, E. (1960). Twenty years of North American psychosomatic medicine. *Psychosomatic Medicine, 22,* 308–316.

Wittkower, E.D. (1949). *A psychiatrist looks at tuberculosis.* London: National Association for the Prevention of Tuberculosis.

Wolfe, T. (1934). Dynamic aspects of cardiovascular symptomatology. *American Journal of Psychiatry, 91,* 563–574.

Wolff, H.G. (1953). *Stress and disease.* Springfield, IL: Charles C. Thomas.

Zani, B. (2008). L'intervento psico-sociale, psicologia di comunità e psicologia della salute [Psychosocial intervention, community psychology, and health psychology]. *Psicologia della salute, 3,* 83–93.

Ziegelman, J.P., Lippke, S., & Schwarzer, R. (2006). Adoption and maintenance of physical activity: Planning interventions in young, middle aged and older adults. *Psychology and Health, 21,* 145–163.

Zubin, D., & Zubin, J. (1977). From speculation to empiricism in the study of mental disorder: Research at the New York State Psychiatric Institute in the first half of the twentieth century. *Annals of the New York Academy of Sciences, 291,* 104–135.

# Measurement in Health Psychology Research

Timothy W. Smith

**Abstract**

This chapter provides an overview of basic principles and methods of measurement and illustrates their application in health psychology. Clearly articulated conceptual models and theoretical assumptions greatly facilitate sound measurement. In health psychology, several important considerations or contexts influence these conceptual models and other facets of the design, development, evaluation, and refinement of measurement procedures and techniques. Measures are useful to the extent that they permit valid inferences in the service of given research goals, and health psychology research encompasses a variety of goals and audiences.

**Keywords:** Health psychology, measurement methods, illness, medical care

Health psychology has always held the dual promise of a methodologically rigorous basic science and of applications for the improvement of health and well-being. With increasing methodological sophistication (Smith, 2003), remarkable progress has been made in fulfilling these goals. Early in the development of the field, book-length discussions illustrated convincingly that scientifically sound approaches to measurement were essential in the field's basic and applied agendas (Karoly, 1985; Keefe & Blumenthal, 1982).

From the outset, measurement has posed major challenges in health psychology, in part because the field is based on the biopsychosocial model (Engel, 1977). In contrast to the biomedical model, in which disease is seen as reflecting alterations in the function of cells, organs, and physiological systems, the biopsychosocial view describes health and disease in terms of the interplay of biological, psychological, and social/cultural processes. This framework involves reciprocally interacting and hierarchically arranged levels of analysis (von Bertalanffy, 1968) that shape research questions within and across levels of analysis. Each level of analysis has its own conceptual models, research methods, and related measurement procedures. The biopsychosocial model requires that these levels be integrated in research. For investigators, this imposes a requirement for considerable breadth in familiarity with measurement concepts and methods, and for care in the complex processes involved in bringing them together in meaningful ways.

Measurement remains a central concern for the field's progress, yet it rarely garners the attention that advances in basic research and application do. Reports of associations between psychosocial variables and disease or the usefulness of psychosocial interventions in the management of disease often receive considerable notice in the scientific literature, as well as in the science media. Even though such developments would not be possible without sound measurement procedures, this essential component of the research infrastructure generates little of the excitement associated with many instances of its use. Grand theories of behavior and health or mind and body, and related investigations, are nearly always more noteworthy than the smaller theories and seemingly lesser investigations regarding the associations between measures and the constructs they are intended to assess.

The gap between the centrality of measurement and the attention it receives is not unique to health psychology. Over the much longer history of psychological research, this same situation has been observed many times in many fields. Consider, for example, Judd and McClellend's (1998) observation of the state of measurement research and the usual level of attention to measurement concerns in social psychology:

> So why, one might ask, do we need a *Handbook* chapter on measurement, and why should one read it? The answer, we suggest, is that our discipline's lack of attention to measurement is a common dilemma. While the individual researcher can ignore measurement issues for the most part without consequence, the discipline as a whole suffers when the theories and methods of measurement are undeveloped and unscrutinized. Conceptual advances in science frequently follow measurement advances. The everyday practice of normal science can successfully operate without much attention to measurement issues. But for the discipline as a whole to advance and develop, measurement must be a focus of collective attention. (p. 180)

The authors' views could have just as appropriately been written about health psychology.

Definitions of measurement are plentiful and varied, but many share elements of Stevens's (1951, 1959, 1968) articulation of measurement as "the assignment of numbers to aspects of objects or events according to one or another rule or convention" (Stevens, 1968, p. 850). Judd and McClelland (1998) suggested that this view is not sufficient, because the assignment of numbers identified by Stevens as the core of this process actually constitutes measurement "only if the subsequent numbers ultimately represent something of meaning, some regularity of attributes or behaviors that permits prediction" (p. 181). Measuring a person's level of social support by counting the number of pieces of mail he or she receives in a week certainly involves an easily described rule, but at best it is indirectly related to social support as defined in most conceptual approaches and might actually be unrelated to the construct of interest.

Judd and McClelland endorse the refinement of Stevens's definition provided by Dawes and Smith (1985), who maintained that "the assignment of numbers not only must be orderly if it is to yield measurement but must also represent meaningful attributes and yield meaningful predictions" (p. 511). This emphasis on a systematic relationship between the numbers assigned in the process of observation and meaningful but indirectly observed attributes is a core assumption in most modern approaches to measurement. Judd and McClelland (1998) describe this correspondence as follows:

> The compact model or description that we construct of observations through measurement we will call a scale or a variable. The meaningful attribute or regularity that it is presumed to represent we will call a construct. Accordingly, measurement consists of rules that assign scale or variable values to entities to represent the constructs that are thought to be theoretically meaningful. (p. 181)

Following this definition, the construct of pain could be (and often is) measured with a 100 mm visual analogue scale anchored by the descriptors "no pain at all" and "worst pain imaginable." In the rule for assigning numbers to observations, pain is quantified as the distance in millimeters from the "no pain" end to the point a respondent marks as corresponding to his level of pain. As discussed later, such definitions underscore the fact that measurement is a complex process in which theory and conceptual models play an important role. The selection of constructs as meaningful—and the nonselection of others—is clearly a matter of theoretical models and related assumptions. Similarly, the selection of a method of observation and the rules involved in assigning numbers to observations are also theory-laden decisions. For example, in the visual analogue pain scale, it is assumed that individuals are able and willing to accurately describe their subjective experience. Hence, as discussed in detail later, the process of measurement is itself a theory-driven process (McFall, 2005).

For research on the grander theories and questions in health psychology to be maximally useful in the field's basic and applied agendas, these "smaller" embedded theories and questions regarding measurement must also be articulated and tested. Returning to the previous example, one could ask a variety of questions. What is the evidence that this visual analogue scale captures what the researcher intends when he or she sets out to measure "pain"? What constructs instead of or in addition to pain might be captured unintentionally using this method? For the visual analogue scale to be useful in understanding influences on the development of pain or in evaluating the benefits of a new treatment for pain, such questions must be addressed.

In behavioral science generally—and any field within psychology in particular—measurement is an ongoing and complex process. It involves theorizing, measurement development, evaluation, and refinement of both specific measurement techniques and the conceptual models underpinning those techniques. Measurement in health psychology is often particularly complex. A daunting variety of topics, methods, and levels of analysis seemingly requires encyclopedic knowledge within and beyond psychology, and researchers must be flexible and often creative in applying basic principles of measurement to novel questions and domains.

This chapter provides an overview of basic principles and methods of measurement, and illustrates their application in health psychology. Although the chapter cannot provide a thorough review of measurement in all areas of the field, it can illustrate the application of principles of measurement to the design and critical evaluation of measurement procedures in its main topics. Before turning to principles of measurement design and evaluation, it is important to discuss sources of complexity for measurement in health psychology. As discussed in virtually every section of this chapter, clearly articulated conceptual models and theoretical assumptions greatly facilitate sound measurement. In health psychology, several important considerations or contexts influence these conceptual models and other facets of the design, development, evaluation, and refinement of measurement procedures and techniques (Smith, 2003). Measures are useful to the extent that they permit valid inferences in the service of given research goals, and health psychology research encompasses a variety of goals and audiences.

## Sources of Complexity for Measurement in Health Psychology

In its emergence and subsequent development, health psychology has drawn heavily from concepts and methods in older fields in psychology, especially social, clinical, personality, experimental, and physiological psychology. Like the related fields of behavioral medicine and psychosomatic medicine, health psychology also draws on other behavioral and biomedical sciences, particularly medicine, epidemiology, public health, sociology, genetics, and nursing. Research and application in health psychology often—if not usually—involve collaborative efforts with investigators from these other sciences, and the resulting research methods, including measurement, are therefore both shaped by and intended to speak to multiple perspectives.

### *Three Domains of Health Psychology*

One source of complexity for measurement in health psychology is the wide variety of research topics in the field. These can be loosely organized into three overlapping domains (Smith, 2003). The first—*health behavior and prevention*—includes the association between daily habits and other behaviors (e.g., diet, physical activity level, smoking, alcohol use) and subsequent health outcomes. The initial goal of this research area is the identification of robust associations between potentially modifiable behaviors and subsequent health outcomes, as well as moderators of these associations (e.g., age, gender, ethnicity, family history of disease) that might indicate subgroups in which these behavioral risk factors are particularly important. Subsequent research examines determinants of these behavioral risk factors, in order to construct models that will facilitate the design of risk-reducing interventions. The array of influences on health behaviors that can inform intervention efforts is quite broad, including rapidly changing psychological variables (e.g., urges and other motivational variables, affect, appraisals), more stable psychological characteristics (e.g., beliefs, expectancies, attitudes), biological variables (e.g., homeostatic processes, chemical dependencies), and broader social and even cultural factors (e.g., socioeconomic status [SES], education).

Ideally, intervention research follows from the findings of studies of the nature, moderators, and determinants of behavioral risk factors. Intervention studies are intended to ask one or both of two questions. First, does the intervention produce meaningful changes in behavioral risk? In this context, meaningful refers not only to the magnitude of change but also to its duration, as many improvements in health behavior (e.g., smoking cessation, weight loss, increased physical activity) are short-lived. Second, do behavioral changes produced by these interventions reduce the incidence of disease or improve other health outcomes? In prevention research, a wide variety of intervention approaches can be used, ranging from individual or small-group–based approaches (e.g., behavior therapy, motivational interviewing, family or couple counseling), to larger group approaches (e.g., school, work site, or neighborhood programs), to population-based interventions (e.g., public policy, advertising, and public education).

This first health psychology domain illustrates one of the most important sources of complexity in health psychology measurement—the heterogeneity of constructs to be addressed. The health behaviors to be assessed range from seat belt, sunscreen, and health screening use to smoking, drinking, eating, and physical activity. The health outcomes these behavioral risks influence include longevity, morbidity or mortality from specific causes, and levels of functional activity (i.e., the inverse of disability). The determinants of these behaviors involve biological, psychological, social, cultural, and economic factors, and the types of interventions used to address them are similarly varied. Hence, in this one domain, the conceptual models of the relevant behaviors, moderators of their effects, their determinants, and intervention approaches can be highly varied and often complex. The methods of observation through which these constructs can be assessed and the rules for translating the related observations into numbers are similarly diverse.

The second domain—*stress and health,* or *psychosomatics*—poses similar challenges. Here, the focus is on more direct psychobiological influences on the development and course of disease. Psychological stress, negative emotions, and related personality traits and characteristics of the social environment are hypothesized to influence the onset and course of disease, through more direct physiological processes rather than behavioral mechanisms. Psychosocial epidemiology examines statistical associations of risk factors with the incidence and course of disease. These risk factors include characteristics or experiences of persons (e.g., personality traits, stressful life circumstances, emotional disorders), their social relationships (e.g., isolation, conflict), and their surroundings (e.g., neighborhood SES). The outcomes of interest include longevity and a variety of indications of the presence, severity, and course of disease that can be either general (e.g., hospitalization) or specific to a given condition (e.g., presence and severity of atherosclerosis, level of inflammation in arthritic joints).

Research in this second domain also tests models of mechanisms linking these risk factors with disease, including cardiovascular, neuroendocrine, immunologic, and other physiological processes that are plausibly influenced by the psychosocial constructs and plausibly linked to pathophysiology of disease. Beyond testing hypotheses about the influence of psychological experiences on health and disease, this research also informs the design of interventions intended to modify these risk factors or interrupt their psychobiological influences on pathophysiology. The outcomes targeted in such interventions (e.g., stress management) include change in the risk factor, alteration of the mediating mechanism, or in some instances, health outcomes such as morbidity or even mortality risk. Here again, the wide variety of constructs to be assessed and the complexity of the

conceptual models in which they are embedded pose major challenges in the design, evaluation, refinement, and use of measurement procedures.

The third major domain in health psychology involves *psychosocial aspects of medical illness and care.* Studies in this domain focus on the psychosocial impact of physical illness on patients and their families. The outcomes of interest include emotional, social, and physical functioning (i.e., activity vs. disability), the subjective impact of the condition or side effects of its usual medical/surgical care (e.g., pain, symptom severity), and sometimes the level and cost of health care utilization. The determinants of variations in these effects of illness are a major focus of such research, given that patients differ greatly in these outcomes. Potential influences on these impacts include aspects of the disease (e.g., severity, exacerbations) and its treatment (e.g., medication regimens, surgical procedures), characteristics of the person (e.g., personality, coping responses), and features of his or her social, cultural, and socioeconomic context (e.g., social support, SES, ethnicity). Once determinants of important outcomes have been identified, they can be useful in the design and implementation of adjunctive psychosocial interventions intended to improve well-being and even medical outcomes. Constructs to be measured in intervention research of this type include not only the wide array of psychosocial, biomedical, and even utilization outcomes described previously but also components of the delivery of these interventions (e.g., adherence to treatment protocols) and potential mediators and moderators of the intervention effects.

### Levels of Analysis in the Biopsychosocial Model

This brief description of the domains of health psychology indicates the remarkable breadth of research questions and settings in which basic principles of measurement must be applied. Much of this breadth stems from the fact noted previously that the biopsychosocial model (Engel, 1977) serves as the fundamental conceptualization in the field (Suls & Rothman, 2004). Typically, research questions in health psychology relate—at least in some manner—to the individual level of analysis, in that the behavior and/or health of individuals is assessed. However, these constructs at the individual level of analysis are often studied in relation to constructs within "higher" levels (e.g., social relations, socioeconomic factors), "lower" levels (e.g., physiological processes, biomedical outcomes), and, on occasion, to both higher and lower levels within a single study. For example, a study might examine the extent to which neighborhood SES as measured by median household income is related to the residents' ambulatory blood pressure levels, and whether that association is mediated by the individual residents' level of self-reported daily stress. Given that specific measures within these levels of analysis are often the purview of different disciplines, they are likely to reflect differing conceptual approaches, methods, and research traditions. As a result, the basic act of measurement in health psychology typically requires integration of a more diverse set of approaches than is usual within other areas of psychology.

Over the last 30 years, this aspect of health psychology has become the norm, rather than an unusual challenge. In fact, it is often seen as one of the novel and exciting characteristics of health psychology research, by both its producers and consumers. The increased demands on expertise can be managed, in part, through interdisciplinary collaboration; but, for such efforts to be maximally effective, investigators must often have at least some familiarity with methods outside of their basic discipline. Traditionally in the field, such efforts primarily occurred between the psychological and biological levels of analysis, but increasingly such translevel research is requiring health psychologists to become more familiar with issues in conceptualization and measurement at higher levels in the biopsychosocial model. For example, growing evidence that neighborhood characteristics are an important influence on leading causes of morbidity and mortality (Chaix, 2009) has raised important issues regarding the conceptualization and measurement of the health-relevant "active psychological ingredients" of neighborhoods (Nicotera, 2007) and how they might vary across urban and rural settings (DeMarco & DeMarco, 2010).

### Age, Sex, Ethnicity, and Culture

The nature of health problems varies as a function of demographic factors. Further, the importance of these factors in health psychology research is increasing, with changes in the age and ethnic composition of the population of the United States and other industrialized nations (Yali & Revenson, 2004). For example, the major sources of morbidity and mortality, psychosocial influences on these health outcomes, and the nature of related interventions change with age. The most prevalent threats to the health of children and adolescents are quite different from those that affect middle-aged adults, who in turn face different health threats than do the elderly. Psychosocial influences on these health outcomes

also vary with age, as do health-promoting interventions (Siegler, Bastain, Steffens, Bosworth, & Costa, 2002; Smith, Orleans, & Jenkins, 2004; Williams, Holmbeck, & Greeley, 2002). From the perspective of measurement, this poses challenges not only through the diversity of constructs to be assessed and the variety of conceptual models in which they are embedded. The appropriateness of methods of observation varies with age, as well. For example, pain, emotional distress, and functional activity (i.e., the inverse of disability) are often studied as consequences of chronic physical illness. Self-reports of these impacts of chronic disease are likely to be suspect in very young children. This method can yield much more useful measures of the same constructs in older children, adolescents, and adults, but the reliability and validity of measures must be carefully examined across these age groups (Huguet, Stinson, & McGrath, 2010; Solans, Pane, Estrada, Serra-Sutton, Berra, Herdman, et al., 2008).

This example of age as influencing the strengths and weaknesses of a given measurement procedure illustrates a broader issue. The properties of a measurement procedure are context specific. That is, investigators and consumers of research cannot assume that evidence regarding strengths and limitations of a measure generalizes to populations or settings beyond those in which the initial evidence was obtained. Such generalizations constitute hypotheses to be tested in measurement research.

Such generalizations are potentially problematic in health psychology research because the field has often disproportionately included middle- and upper-income white men in research samples (Park, Adams, & Lynch, 1998). Although women's health has received growing attention in recent years, these efforts have not yet eliminated the gender gap in understanding health and disease. Further, SES, ethnicity, and culture are increasingly but still insufficiently studied influences on the nature of health problems, their determinants, and effects of related interventions (Whitfield, Weidner, Clark, & Anderson, 2002; Yali & Revenson, 2004). From the perspective of measurement, these demographic dimensions and categories are themselves important topics for study in health psychology research. Also, the (non)equivalence of properties of any given measurement technique across these dimensions must be evaluated rather than assumed. For example, if a social support scale is found to capture the intended construct through measurement research with largely Caucasian samples, it must be demonstrated rather than assumed that the scale does so in Latino or other ethnic minority populations.

## Multiple Contexts and Audiences in Health Psychology Measurement

Its location at the intersection of several fields has implications for the design and evaluation of measurement procedures in health psychology, as does the fact that health psychology research has audiences beyond psychology. Perhaps the most obvious of these contexts and audiences is *medical science and care*. In the early years of health psychology research, tests of the association between psychosocial variables and subsequent health often used convenient, broad, and nonspecific measures of health outcomes. For example, the effect of stressful life changes on subsequent health was often studied using self-report symptom checklists as measures of health outcomes. Further, nonspecific "black box" models of the mechanisms linking psychosocial inputs and health outcomes were common. That is, it was presumed that effects of stressful life events on subsequent health were mediated by physiological effects of stress and emotion, but these pathophysiological mechanisms were typically not specified, let alone measured. Such work played an important role in the emergence of the field, but it had limited impact beyond psychology, perhaps because research traditions in medicine involve greater specificity in terms of health outcomes and underlying mechanisms.

One reflection of the maturing scientific status of health psychology research is that it is increasingly informed by current medical standards for assessing specific diseases, as well as an understanding of their pathophysiology. In this newer approach, health psychology research often addresses outcomes and criteria with established significance. Tests of hypotheses regarding psychosocial influences on disease are at least based on explicit and plausible mechanisms. These considerations obviously influence the selection of measures in research on stress and health or psychosomatics. Measures of health outcomes that are established in the context of a specific disease are important, as are established measures of mechanisms through which psychosocial factors might influence outcomes. For example, current research on the effects of depression on the development and course of cardiovascular disease uses widely accepted criteria of establishing the occurrence of disease (e.g., criteria for disease-specific morbidity and mortality) and describes—if not actually tests—autonomic or other physiological mechanisms linking such emotional stress to specific disease processes (Lett et al., 2004).

Similarly, studies of psychosocial adaptation to a given disease should include standard measures of the nature and severity of the condition used in the medical literature (e.g., specific cancer diagnoses, disease stages, related medical treatments). In this way, empirical ties to the medical literature on a given condition will be enhanced, making it more likely that, over time, health psychology research will have a growing impact on the broader field of health sciences. Similar considerations are important when selecting measures of outcomes for research on the effects of adjunctive psychosocial interventions. If psychosocial interventions have impacts on outcome measures typically used in traditional medical research on a given disease, then this health psychology research is more likely to capture the attention of a broader range of researchers and health care providers outside of psychology.

These suggestions should not be interpreted as an endorsement of uncritical acceptance of measures from medical research. In fact, a useful role health psychologists can play in interdisciplinary research is the application of principles of measurement design and evaluation to traditional medical measures and assessments. Evaluations of reliability, validity, and predictive utility are often relevant to these measures, and often the available research on a given approach suggests that such evaluations are lacking. This process can identify the strengths and weaknesses of widely used measures and diagnostic procedures, and the resulting refinements can enhance research in health psychology and related medical fields (Kaplan & Frosch, 2005; Shen et al., 2003).

Health care economics and health care financing form an important context for health research. Increasingly, measurement of health outcomes in ways that lend themselves to meaningful estimates of the clinical or practical significance of effects is useful. Ideally, such measurement procedures would lend themselves to comparisons across a wide range of conditions and interventions, in order to facilitate evaluations of the relative importance of observed effects. As discussed in more detail later, Kaplan (1994) has recommended the comprehensive and integrated measurement of several aspects of health status (e.g., symptoms, functional activity level) in standardized units called Quality-Adjusted Life Years. If these general health outcome assessments are used to express health benefits of interventions in standard units, then health psychology interventions can be compared with traditional medical or surgical interventions using the same outcome assessment. If the costs of such interventions are also quantified, then a wide variety of psychosocial and traditional medical interventions can be evaluated in terms of their cost-effectiveness or cost utility

(Kaplan & Groessel, 2002). This approach creates a "level playing field," in which the effects of traditional medical approaches are compared using a common and comprehensive metric with those obtained with psychosocial interventions. Measurement plays a key role in this important opportunity.

## Principles of Measurement Design and Evaluation

These sources of complexity in health psychology measurement make this fundamental aspect of the research endeavor challenging. Fortunately, basic principles developed over decades and more recently emerging quantitative methods combine to provide a trustworthy guide to measurement in these complex circumstances.

### *The Central Role of Theory*

In considering the role of theory and conceptual models in health psychology, one might understandably think first about fundamental questions about connections between psychosocial factors and health. In contrast to such important questions, questions about the nature of the relationship of measures to the constructs they are intended to reflect do not seem to involve "theories" or even conceptual models at all. Yet, they involve assumptions and hypotheses, and the field is better served when these are clearly articulated and tested (McFall, 2005).

Not all health psychology researchers would endorse the proposition that theory plays a central role in the development and evaluation of measures. The tradition of *operationism* or *operationalism* equates the concept to be measured with the specific research procedures used to accomplish the task. In the original form of this approach, the "concept is synonymous with the corresponding set of operations" (Bridgman, 1927, p. 5). For example, in a study evaluating the effects of an intervention to reduce chronic pain, pain might be defined (and measured) as the number of specific behaviors (e.g., grimacing, guarded movement) displayed during a structured set of movements. From this conceptual perspective on measurement, if the treatment reduces the frequency of these overt behaviors, it has *by definition* reduced pain. This philosophical view is integral in the behavioral tradition in psychology that was prominent during much of the last century and continues to be influential. Behavioral researchers of this orientation were highly involved in the emergence of health psychology and the overlapping field of behavioral medicine (Gentry, 1984). From this conceptual perspective, any inference or

generalization from specific research procedures to unobserved hypothetical constructs is fraught with peril, and "hard-line" versions of this perspective see such inferences as frankly unscientific. Interestingly, the author originally associated with this approach elsewhere in the physical sciences criticized what he saw as its simplistic application in psychology (Bridgman, 1945).

As with the waning prominence of behavioral analysis and other "operational" perspectives in psychology, behavioral medicine and health psychology have implicitly endorsed a broader philosophy of science, and as a result, a more theory-driven view of measurement (Strauss & Smith, 2009). Although the behavioral perspective remains influential, recognition that "operational" procedures of measurement have a complex rather than definitional relationship to the concepts of interest is now widespread. As a result, the need for careful delineation of the conceptual context of any measurement instrument or procedure as a critical aspect of the measurement process is more readily acknowledged. Further, although the strong version of operationalism has limited usefulness in current research, the skepticism associated with that tradition regarding inferences and generalizations about unobservable concepts on the basis of research procedures is useful when used constructively. That is, inferences about the meaning of measures are hypotheses. As in any research area, measurement research ideally involves the articulation of alternative hypotheses and the design of empirical tests pitting the rivals against each other.

The modern, "post-operationalism" approach arose in the middle of the last century (for a review, see Strauss & Smith, 2009) and emphasizes that any concept can be "operationalized" in multiple ways. Further, any specific operation contains both construct-relevant variance and construct-irrelevant variance. The process of developing and evaluating measures involves intensive critical analysis of the correspondence between research operations and unobserved constructs, rather than rejection of the issue.

The role of theory in measurement begins with clear and specific definitions of the construct to be assessed. Such definitions include a clear description of the domain or content of the construct, as well as specification of the boundaries or limits of that content. Beyond a sound definition, other characteristics of the conceptual model or theory of a construct must be articulated to guide the development and evaluation of a measure. In a broadly useful discussion of this essential component of the measurement

**Table 3.1 Questions to guide conceptualization in measurement**

| |
| --- |
| What is the expected degree of relationship among items or indicators? |
| What is the structure of the construct? |
| What is the stability of the construct? |
| What is the expected pattern of relationships of measures of the construct of interest with other measures of the same construct and with measures of other constructs? |

From West, S. G., & Finch, J. F. (1997). Personality measurement: Reliability and validity issues. In R. Hogan, J. Johnson, & S. Briggs (Eds.), *Handbook of personality psychology* (pp. 143–164). Dallas, TX: Academic Press.

process in personality research, West and Finch (1997, pp. 144–145) outline several questions to be answered in clarifying the nature of the construct (see Table 3.1).

The first question asks, "What is the expected degree of relationship among items that constitute the measure of the construct?" Although the wording of this question makes clear that it is most relevant to the case of multi-item scales, it is relevant to all cases in which multiple indicators are used in a scale or other summary variable. It is also a more complex question than it first appears.

In most instances in health psychology research, the association among items within a scale would be expected to be large, given that they are intended to reflect a single construct. Responses to the individual items are in essence *caused* by a latent trait or hypothetical construct (Bollen & Lennox, 1991). Hence, scale items intended to assess the personality trait of conscientiousness would be expected to correlate closely, as responses to scale items would be hypothesized to be caused by a single trait. However, not all sets of items making up scales would be expected to correlate in this way. For example, in measures of overall severity of recent physical symptoms, a variety of symptoms across multiple systems are assessed, and there may be little reason to expect that symptoms of upper respiratory infection (i.e., congestion, sneezing) would correlate highly with symptoms of intestinal or neurological conditions. Indeed, a high level of intercorrelation among such items could indicate that the scale assesses something (e.g., a general tendency for excessive somatic complaints) other than the construct of interest (i.e., a summary of generally unrelated aspects of recent health vs. actual illness).

In the case of the conscientiousness scale, responses to individual items are seen as effects of the person's standing on the hypothetical construct, and therefore the items should be highly correlated. In the case of the recent physical symptoms measure, severity of recent physical symptoms is not a general casual construct but instead is a higher-order emergent characteristic or construct that serves as a summary of the specific symptoms captured in individual items. Rather than the respondent's standing on a latent trait of overall sickness "causing" responses to the individual items, the individual items may be more accurately seen as "causes" of the higher-order variable reflected in the summary score for this emergent construct. Thus, a basic distinction among conceptual measurement models that influences the expected associations among indicators has to do with the nature of the causal direction between those indicators and the construct they assess. In "effect indicator" models, variations in item responses or other measured indicators are effects of unmeasured higher-order or latent casual variables or constructs. In "causal indicator" models, the opposite direction of causality is present; variation in the lower-order measured indicators or item responses cause variation in the unmeasured higher-order, emergent constructs (Bollen & Lennox, 1991).

Another example of this sort of emergent latent variable or causal indicator model commonly used in health psychology research is SES. As described by Bollen and Lennox (1991; see also Ozer, 1999), many different indicators of SES are available, such as years of education, grade of employment, and income. Yet variation in these indicators is not caused by variations in SES. Rather, education, grade of employment, and income can readily be seen as causes of SES. West and Finch (1997) describe how items within stressful life events scales (e.g., Holmes & Rahe, 1967) would also not be expected to be highly correlated because these are assumed to be generally unrelated occurrences. Hence, responses to individual items or indicators reflecting specific life events are not *effects* of the individual's standing on the latent variable or construct of major life events. Rather, responses to these items or indicators (or, more accurately, the events such responses are assumed to reflect) can be seen as causes of the person's standing on the construct of interest. As a result, one would not expect high levels of association among items; if low levels of intercorrelation are observed in the process of measurement evaluation, this would not challenge the measurement model. Interestingly, high levels of interitem correlation in a case such as a stressful life event checklist might raise questions regarding whether scale responses are influenced by different constructs or processes, such as general response styles (e.g., social desirability) or the effect of personality on the tendency to experience high versus low levels of stressful life change.

Thus, to answer to the first question posed by West and Finch (1997), one must determine if the measured items or indicators are effects or causes of the constructs they are intended to reflect. Effect indicator measurement models assume at least some intercorrelation among items or indicators, and the latent trait or construct explains these associations (i.e., they reflect a common cause). In causal indicator models, intercorrelations among indicators are not required. Health psychology contains many instances of both types of measurement models. Although interitem correlations (i.e., internal consistency) would be expected in effect indicator models, high levels of internal consistency could still reflect a measurement problem. If the conceptual domain to be assessed is broad, a high degree of internal consistency might indicate that too narrow a portion of the domain is sampled through the items within the measure. There are no firm guidelines for appropriate levels of interindicator correlation, but the observed level should be considered relative to the upper and lower limits implied by the conceptual definition of the construct to be measured.

The second question West and Finch (1997) pose is, "What is the structure of the construct?" Often, the assumption is that indicators or items reflect one unidimensional construct. In many instances, however, a construct may consist of multiple, lower-order intercorrelated components, each of which is assessed through several items or indicators. In the earlier example of the personality trait of conscientiousness, current versions of the five-factor model of personality maintain that this global trait contains distinct facets or components, such as achievement-striving, self-discipline, and deliberation (Costa & McCrae, 1992). As a result, all conscientiousness items or indicators should be correlated, but correlations among items within a subset reflecting the same facet should be larger than correlations among items tapping different facets.

Overall scale scores best represent unidimensional structures. When such structures are assumed rather than established, overall scores may inadvertently combine several specific, although perhaps intercorrelated components. Whether the use of overall summary scores for multidimensional measures is informed and intentional or inadvertent, a variety of interpretative and analytic challenges emerge (Carver, 1989; Hull, Lehn, & Tedlie, 1991). Associations of such complex scores with measures of other constructs may mask more specific associations involving components of the overall score. A lack of association between the overall score and other variables (i.e., null results) can similarly mask more specific associations. An early example of this issue was the personality trait of hardiness (Kobasa, 1979), a multifaceted trait that was hypothesized to confer emotional and physical resilience in the face of stressful life circumstances. Hardiness consisted of three specific components—belief in control over the events of one's life, commitment to a meaning or purpose, and viewing change as a challenge rather than threat. Hardiness scales contained subscales measuring these individual components. Therefore, analyses of total hardiness scale scores could mask the effects of the more specific dimensions (Carver, 1989; Hull et al., 1991). Regardless of how such multicomponent measures are managed in subsequent research, the design and evaluation of any measure must be informed by a clear answer to the question about the intended structure. This answer then becomes a hypothesis to be tested against other possible structures or measurement models.

The third question is, "What is the stability of the construct?" In health psychology research, some constructs are expected to be quite stable (e.g., personality traits), whereas others should be quite variable (e.g., acute pain, state affect). Still others would be expected to show intermediate levels of stability over time (e.g., health beliefs, disability). Despite the simplicity of this question, it is often overlooked in the selection of specific quantitative evaluations of measurements.

The final question posed by West and Finch (1997) contains a complex issue. "What is the pattern of relationships of measures of the construct of interest with other measures of the same construct and with measures of other constructs?" As these authors note, this refers to what Cronbach and Meehl (1955) called a *nomological net*. A nomological net consists of rules or hypotheses that specify the relationship of observable properties of hypothetical constructs to each other (e.g., associations among measures or other research operations), constructs to observables (i.e., latent variables to indicators or operations), or constructs to each other. Together, these interlocking specifications provide a set of hypotheses that can guide the development and evaluation of measurements. For example, a simple nomological net for the construct of hardiness described earlier might indicate that the three components would be expected to be associated more closely with each other than with conceptually distinct personality characteristics, such as trait anxiety or neuroticism. Hence, the three related component scales should be more closely correlated with each other than with scales assessing the conceptually distinct traits. Interestingly, poor support for this aspect of the nomological net for hardiness has been one of the most troubling challenges for the theory (Funk, 1992).

Nomological nets also contain assumptions about appropriate methods of observation (e.g., self-report, behavioral ratings, psychophysiological assessments) for a given construct, as well as likely levels of intercorrelations or convergence among such multiple indicators. For example, a nomological net for the construct *acute lower back pain* might specify that self-reports, facial expressions involving grimacing, and psychophysiological measures of increased muscle tension in the lower back would all correlate, and these associations would be larger than correlations of the pain measures with self-reports, facial expressions, and psychophysiological measures (e.g., electrodermal activity) of state anxiety.

In the process of measurement development and evaluation, the elements of nomological nets often emerge and change over time. This is because initial descriptions of the related conceptual models are often limited, and are elaborated and refined as research on the theory and related measurement models accumulates. In many instances, substantive research on a topic can provide relevant evidence regarding the related measurement models, as it typically involves elements of the surrounding nomological net. For example, evidence that scales assessing individual differences in trait anger or hostility are associated with increases in self-reported state anger, physiological arousal, and behavioral displays of aggressive or unfriendly behavior during potentially conflictual social interactions might indicate how these personality traits could influence physical health. Such evidence also supports the nomological net describing these traits and their measured manifestations (Smith, 1992). Similarly, evidence that anger is associated with the activation of approach motivation (e.g., mobilization of effort to remove obstacles to blocked goals) whereas other negative emotions (e.g., anxiety) are associated with avoidance motivation (Carver & Harmon-Jones, 2009) provides additional opportunities to evaluate measures relative to an expanded nomological net.

McFall (2005) has described a more extensive set of theoretical issues to be clarified in the development and evaluation of measures. Consideration of these issues serves the same function as West and Finch's (1997) questions, but does so in more detail. These issues are listed in Table 3.2. Like West and Finch (1997), McFall (2005) articulates and summarizes a general guiding principle in this approach to measurement—clear and critical thinking at each of these interrelated layers or levels is essential.

McFall's first level is *basic assumptions* or postulates. These theoretical propositions are often left unarticulated, but they exert critical influences on several decisions. For example, as we discuss elsewhere (Smith & Uchino, 2008), many studies of psychosocial influences on disease assume that physiological effects of psychological stress while the individual is awake link personality traits or aversive life circumstances with the development of disease. An alternative assumption suggests that the disruption of sleep and reduction in nighttime dipping of physiological stress responses links personality and negative life circumstances with disease (Cappucino, D'Elia, Strazzullo, & Miller, 2010). This assumption would obviously suggest very different decisions about stress measurement.

Based in these "givens" or basic postulates, *formal theoretical constructions* refer to conceptual definitions of hypothetical constructs and statements of

**Table 3.2 McFall's (2005) multiple levels of theory in measurement**

| Level | Issue or Activity |
| --- | --- |
| Postulates | Philosophical assumptions and untested "givens" |
| Formal theoretical constructions | Hypothetical constructs and nomological networks |
| Referents | Category labels for observable exemplars |
| Instrumental methods | Techniques and procedures for sampling exemplars |
| Measurement model | Conversion to units and assignment of numbers |
| Data reduction | Aggregation of numbers into statistical summaries |
| Data analysis | Processing of summary statistics by analytic method |
| Interpretation and inference | Evaluation of results relative to original question |

hypothesized relationships among them. The clarity and specificity of these theoretical constructions influences the quality of measurement. If such conceptualizations are vague or incomplete, irrelevant phenomena could be included in a measure or essential features overlooked. To facilitate theory-driven tests of convergent and discriminant aspects of construct validity, conceptual definitions and specifications must include descriptions of differences among conceptually related but distinct constructs and the expected relative levels of associations among them.

As discussed previously, these conceptual descriptions are essential elements of "nomological nets," which also include descriptions of the next level of conceptualization—*referents* or categories of observable exemplars that reflect unobserved constructs. Such categories of referents in health psychology commonly include subjective experience, overt behavior, and physiological functioning. Clear theory-based conceptualization regarding referents guides choices regarding specific research operations, such as the selection tasks or techniques labeled *instrumental methods* in McFall's taxonomy.

After selecting an instrumental method, a *measurement model* must be articulated. Referents assessed through specific instrumental methods are converted to appropriate units, and numerical values are assigned on a scale. Raw data derived from this guiding measurement model are then aggregated in the next step of *data reduction*, a process through which features are extracted from measured values and summarized to reflect the intended construct. For example, in measuring "cardiovascular reactivity"—a common study construct in research on stress and cardiovascular disease—measures of blood pressure recorded once every 90 seconds and scaled as mm Hg could be reduced and quantified to capture a mean increase over a previously recorded resting baseline. *Data analysis* refers to the use of a specific quantitative method to test the presence and magnitude of predicted covariation between values on the measure consideration and some other measured or manipulated variable. Each specific data analytic method has corollary assumptions about the variables involved and the question asked. These include, for example, assumptions regarding the level or scale of measurement (i.e., nominal, ordinal, interval, or ratio). If an analytic technique assumes a different level of measurement than the variable(s) being analyzed, invalid conclusions about the presence and magnitude of covariation can result. Therefore, choice of specific analytic techniques must be informed by prior levels of conceptualization.

The final level in McFall's model involves the evaluation of results of the analyses—*interpretation and inference*. At this point in the multilevel process, the knowledge gained is considered, and it is dependent upon the integrity of logic across prior conceptual levels or steps. McFall (2005) describes the issue addressed here as, "What, if anything, was learned from (7) the data analyses of (6) the summary statistics (5) generated by the measurement model (4) of the responses gathered by the instrumental methods (3) designed to sample the referents (2) for the formal theoretical constructs (1) supported by the basic assumptions?" (p. 318).

When expected results emerge from this process, the guiding theoretical models are supported, but only to the extent that, in each step, the decisions have been consistent with the guiding theoretical framework. Seemingly supportive results can be misleading if decisions at any level are inconsistent with this framework. Seemingly disconfirming results, in turn, could actually reflect difficulties at any of several levels, rather than challenging the basic conceptual hypothesis and theoretical formulation under evaluation.

Clear and precise conceptual definitions and answers to the questions posed by West and Finch (1997) and the issues outlined by McFall (2005) are an essential starting point in the design and evaluation of measurements in health psychology. In some instances, measures will have been developed and perhaps even widely adopted without sufficient thought and comment on these issues. In those cases, researchers can do a useful service by "doubling back" and "filling in" this missing work and evaluating the measurement procedure or technique in the new light of a more well-developed conceptual context.

## Key Concepts in Measurement
### LEVELS OF MEASUREMENT
Given the variety of topics, levels of analysis, and disciplines in health psychology research, measurement procedures often involve different levels of measurement. Importantly, levels of measurement are related to the usefulness of the measure in specific applications, as well as to the underlying quantitative models both for evaluating measurement procedures themselves and for testing substantive questions using them.

Measurements are typically classified in terms of *levels* or *scales*. In the most basic—*nominal* scales—numbers are assigned as labels to classes of objects. That is, numbers simply serve the function of names in identifying and distinguishing in a classification scheme. In *ordinal* scales, numbers are assigned in such a way as to reflect rank ordering on the characteristic of interest. For *interval* scales, numbers are assigned to attributes not only to reflect rank ordering but also so that differences between numbers correspond to meaningful differences on the measured construct. In ordinal scales, the difference between numbers refers only to rank order and implies nothing about the size of the difference on the measured characteristic. In contrast, interval scales consist of constant units of measurement, and therefore a given difference between scale values has a constant meaning relative to the measured construct. This consequence of constant units of measurement (i.e., constant meaning of differences between scale values) is true at all points along interval scales. For *ratio* scales, in addition to constant units of measurement, a true zero point can be designated.

In the behavioral sciences, the first three levels are common, and some debate has occurred about whether many continuous scale scores (e.g., scores on personality measures) represent ordinal or interval scales. For example, if it is an interval scale, then the difference between scores of 5 and 10 on the Beck Depression Inventory (BDI) should reflect the same magnitude of difference in the construct of severity of depressive symptoms as does the difference between scores of 25 and 30. Clearly, scores on the BDI convey much more information than an ordinal scale, but the difficulty in precisely determining the constancy of units makes it unclear if it is a true interval scale.

Given that scores of zero are possible on the BDI, one might wonder why it is not considered a ratio scale. For measures like the BDI and most measures in behavioral science, this does not represent a "true zero" because it does not imply the same sort of certainty about the total absence of depressive symptoms as does "0 pounds" in assessing weight or "0 beats per minute" in measuring heart rate.

The distinctions among levels of measurement are important in selecting appropriate statistical analyses and ensuring the accuracy of statistical conclusions. Although not without controversy, it is generally considered appropriate to treat scales or variables that clearly contain more information than ordinal scales, but that might not meet the precise requirements of constant units of measurement (e.g., state affect questionnaires; pain scales), as interval-level data for the purposes of analysis. In health psychology research, measurement often involves "true" interval and even ratio scales, and it is important to consider the level of measurement prior to selecting approaches to statistical analysis.

Schroeder, Carey, and Vanable (2003a) provide a valuable illustration of the issue of scales of measurement in the case of assessing sexual risk behavior. Most commonly, constructs such as the frequency of unprotected sexual intercourse are assessed through either count measures or relative frequency measures. Count measures ask respondents to indicate the exact number of times (during a specified interval) they engaged in a behavior (e.g., intercourse without a condom). Given the presence of a "true zero" and constant meaning of intervals, these measures, in theory, constitute true ratio scales. Relative frequency measures, in contrast, ask respondents about the occurrence of the target behavior (e.g., unprotected sexual activity) relative to a broader class of behavior (e.g., all occasions of sexual activity). These approaches to quantifying sexual risk behavior can take the form of several types of scales or levels of measurement, although perhaps most commonly ordinal- or interval-level measurements. These different levels of measurement typically result in different distributions, making different types of statistical analysis appropriate (e.g., parametric vs. nonparametric techniques). Further, count measures may provide a more direct indicator of true risk exposure and therefore may be more useful in some contexts, as when evaluating risk reduction interventions.

Except in the case of ratio scales used in health psychology (e.g., blood pressure, weight, etc.), most measurements in the field involve metrics that are arbitrary in two respects (Blanton & Jaccard, 2006); the individual's "true" standing on the construct of interest is unknown, as is the meaning of scale units. Only relative positions on the construct can be inferred. In these circumstances, care must be taken in interpreting scores as reflecting "low," "medium," or "high" standing on the construct of interest, or differences between individuals or groups as "small," "medium," or "large." Such inferences from arbitrary metrics require additional research relating observed scores to external criteria (Blanton & Jaccard, 2006). This is particularly important in efforts to describe the clinical significance of effects in intervention research (Kazdin, 2006).

## TRUE SCORES, ERROR, AND RELIABILITY
The ability to test any hypothesis in health psychology research depends on the extent to which scores on the measures used reflect the constructs of interest. The extent to which scores reflect the intended construct, in turn, depends on reliability and validity. In classical test theory, any given measurement or observed score ($X$) contains two components: "true score" ($T$)

and measurement error ($E$). Hence, $X = T + E$. In this view, $T$ theoretically represents the mean of a large number of measurements of a specific characteristic taken on one individual. $E$ combines a wide variety of random and changing factors that have influenced an observed score. In this model, the reliability of a measure is the ratio of true-score variance to observed-score variance, or the proportion of true-score variance in observed scores. Hence, a reliability coefficient of $rxt = .9$ means that 90% of the variance in observed scores reflects true-score variance; $1 - .9 = .1$ is the proportion of observed score variance that is due to random errors. If true scores reflect the construct of interest (see the following discussion of validity), then increasing levels of reliability in observed scores would translate into more accurate indicators of that construct.

In this view, there are many potential sources of unreliability (i.e., error), and as a result there are several types of reliability coefficients. Coefficients reflecting internal consistency quantify the degree of association or relationship among individual items within a given measure. The most common of these, Cronbach's (1951) coefficient $\alpha$, is the equivalent of the mean of the correlations between all possible split halves of a set of items. This is an important indication or estimate of the reliability of a measure consisting of multiple items intended to sample the same conceptual domain.

It is important to note that a high level of internal consistency does not necessarily indicate that a scale is unidimensional. Cronbach's $\alpha$, for example, is influenced positively by both the interrelatedness of the items and the number of items. Hence, especially in the case of longer scales, high levels of internal consistency can mask a multidimensional structure. Evidence of high levels of internal consistency is typically necessary but never sufficient as an indication of unidimensional structure. Other quantitative methods discussed later are required to evaluate structure. As noted previously, it is also possible that a high level of internal consistency could indicate that too narrow a range of indicators has been included in a measure of a construct that is conceptually defined as having greater breadth. This potential concern is related to the issue of content validity, discussed in a later section. Short scales often suffer from low internal consistency simply because of their length, and this can be problematic in health psychology research. For example, sometimes in the large surveys used in psychosocial epidemiology, space is at a premium, and researchers are forced to utilize shortened versions of scales intended to assess

important risk factors (e.g., personality traits or life experiences). The resulting low reliability can lead to an underestimate of the magnitude of associations between the risk factor and subsequent health outcomes.

Test–retest reliability refers to the stability of scores over time, or the correlation between scores on the same measure administered on two occasions. The level of agreement between independent judges or raters (i.e., interrater reliability) for categorical classification systems (e.g., psychiatric diagnoses) or rating scales (e.g., presence, type, and/or amount of pain behavior) is another common type of reliability assessed in health psychology research. As discussed previously, the relevance of any one type of reliability in the evaluation of a measure depends on the conceptual description of the construct it is intended to assess. Internal consistency of multiple items intended to reflect a single construct is commonly relevant, as is interrater agreement when behavioral observations or diagnostic classifications are used. Temporal stability is often highly relevant, especially if short intervals between testing occasions are employed. However, some constructs are described conceptually as changing rapidly enough (e.g., emotional states, acute pain) that test–retest reliabilities over longer periods are much less relevant. In such cases, high levels of temporal stability might actually raise concerns about the measure, as they suggest that it is not sufficiently sensitive to the expected change in the construct and instead reflects something more stable than implied by the conceptual definition of that construct. These and other potential sources of error can be combined in *generalizability theory*. Rather than treating all sources of error as equivalent, as is the case in the $X = T + E$ model of classical test theory, generalizability theory attempts to partition these sources of error into specific sources.

Reliability is a critical consideration in health psychology research for several reasons. The reliability of a measure sets an upper limit on the magnitude of observed associations that can be obtained with that measure. For example, if depressed mood and self-reported pain have a true correlation of $r = .50$ (i.e., depressed mood accounts for 25% of the variance in pain reports), the size of the observed association will depend on the reliabilities of the measures of depressed mood and pain. If the two measures both have reliability coefficients of .8, then the observed association will average $r = .4$ over multiple occasions of testing this effect. If the measures both have reliabilities of .6, the observed association will be $r = .3$. With perfectly reliable measures, of course, the observed association would be $r = .5$. Hence, low reliability of measures can produce underestimates of substantive associations.

This relationship between reliability of measurement and observed effect sizes has important implications for statistical hypothesis testing. For example, the reduction in observed effect size resulting from low reliability of measurement has a negative effect on statistical power (Cohen, 1992). In some health psychology research, the effects of psychosocial factors on health outcomes are small, given the complex, multifactorial etiology of many diseases. Therefore, reductions in observed effects sizes due to low reliability can produce artifactual null results, unless sample sizes are quite large. Further, these often-small effects of psychosocial variables (e.g., social support, depression) on health outcomes often compete in multivariate analyses (e.g., multiple linear or logistic regression) with characteristics that can be measured more reliably (e.g., body mass, cholesterol levels). It is possible that these psychosocial risk factors could appear less important in the prediction of health outcomes in part because of their relatively lower measurement reliability. In a similar vein, low reliability of measures of potential confounding or mediating variables results in the undercorrection of competing or confounding factors when the measured variable is controlled statistically. Because scores on the variable to be controlled contain relatively low levels of "true score," the statistical control procedure fails to adequately capture variance in this construct. Consider, for example, a mediational model in which chronic negative affect mediates the association between low SES and risk of disease (Matthews, Gallo, & Taylor, 2010). If the measure of chronic negative affect suffers from low reliability, then statistical analyses in which the effect of SES on health is tested with and without controlling the effects of negative affect might falsely contradict the mediational hypothesis.

## DEFINING AND TESTING VALIDITY

It should be noted that in the preceding discussion of reliability, classical test theory treats all of the measurement variance that is not due to error as "true-score" variance. In fact, true-score variance and error variance in the $X = T + E$ model are more accurately labeled *systematic* and *unsystematic* variance, respectively. Importantly, the systematic component of variance can reflect (a) a single intended construct, (b) a multidimensional construct, (c) a construct other than the intended one, or (d) a combination of these situations. That is, systematic variance is not necessarily a true score reflecting only the intended construct; it is not even necessarily a true score on only *one* construct. In behavioral science, measures rarely have the precision that the term "true score" seems to imply.

The issue of what the systematic variance captured by a more or less reliable measure actually reflects is called *validity*. Reliability is a necessary precondition for validity, because with increasing levels of error in measurement (i.e., increasing levels of unsystematic variance), there is by definition a decreasing amount of information about the construct of interest contained in any observed score. Hence, just as the (un)reliability of a measure limits the magnitude of its observed statistical association with other measures (un)reliability limits the magnitude of its association with the intended construct. The task of evaluating the validity of a measure goes beyond consideration of the relative amounts of systematic and unsystematic variance in scores to also involve partitioning the systematic measurement variance. Validity involves the question, "To what extent do observed scores reflect the intended construct, as opposed to something else?" Unreliability (i.e., error) of observed scores will limit this correspondence between measure and construct, but so will sources of systematic variance beyond the intended construct. It is essential to note that validity is not a property of measures. Rather, validity is a property of inferences or interpretations that are based on measures (Messick, 1995). That is, researchers do not validate tests or other measurement procedures per se. They validate interpretations, inferences, decisions, or judgments made on the basis of scores obtained with the measure.

Evidence of validity is easier to acquire and evaluate to the extent that the theory of the construct is well developed, including a description of its association with other constructs that could be sources of systematic variance in the observed scores (West & Finch, 1997). For example, a variety of conceptual models hypothesize an association of negative emotional conditions such as depression or anger with chronic pain, such that chronic pain often functions as a cause and/or consequence of negative affect. A statistical association between a measure of pain and a measure of negative affect could be seen as support for these models. However, an alternative interpretation of such an association could be that it reflects a correlation between two measures of a single construct (e.g., general distress). Hence, it would be important to determine the extent to which the measure of chronic pain can be distinguished from the measures of negative affect. That is, it would be useful to evaluate the extent to which the systematic variance in the measure of pain reflected that construct instead of a related but distinct construct, such as general distress. Research evaluating the validity of a given measure is never exhaustive and instead is typically ongoing. Hence, the validity of interpretations or inferences based on a measure is always at least somewhat tentative and subject to change (G.T. Smith, 2005; Strauss & Smith, 2009; West & Finch, 1997).

Because validity concerns hypotheses about what test scores mean, the degree of evidence in support of validity is a function of the amount of evidence consistent with the underlying measurement model and the nomological net in which it is embedded. Contradictory or disconfirming evidence, of course, challenges validity of a given interpretation of the measure. Further, the extent of the supportive evidence is in proportion to the cumulative severity of the tests of those hypotheses (Meehl, 1978), where the severity of a test of any given hypothesis refers to the likeliness of obtaining disconfirming results. For example, a simple t-test of the difference between two groups in their mean scores on a given measure evaluates the hypothesis that the groups do not have precisely the same mean level of this characteristic (i.e., $A >$ or $< B$). It is not terribly likely that any two groups would have exactly the same value, and therefore with a large enough sample size it is not particularly likely that the implicit prediction of "some difference, any difference" would be disconfirmed. Hence, findings of this sort provide weak—if any—evidence of validity. Specifying the direction of the difference between the two groups (i.e., $A > B$) increases the likelihood that the prediction could be disconfirmed, as would adding a third group and generating a more complex pattern prediction (i.e., $A > B > C$). More complex predictions entail a greater likelihood of disconfirmation, and as a result provide stronger evidence in support of the hypothesis.

Consistent with the principle of the importance of falsification in theory testing (Popper, 1959), the degree of support for a given hypothesis or theory is a function of the degree of risk of disconfirmation to which it has been subjected and survived (Meehl, 1978). In measurement research, predictions of patterns of associations involving simultaneous tests of multiple "strands" in the nomological net surrounding the construct and a specific measure provide greater risk of disconfirmation, and as a result, stronger evidence of validity than does a simple prediction involving a single association. For example, in contrast to a single predicted association (e.g., "Measure $A$ will correlate positively with measure $B$"), a prediction comprising a pattern of the relative magnitude of two,

three, or more associations (e.g., "Measure $A$ will correlate more closely with measure $B$ than it will with measure $C$") is easier to disconfirm. This is because there are more associations predicted, as well as specific predictions about their relative magnitude. Hence, failure to disconfirm the more complex prediction constitutes stronger evidence of validity than does failure to disconfirm the simpler prediction, providing both patterns are logically consistent with the conceptual description of the construct in the surrounding nomological net.

As described later, simultaneous evidence of larger associations between multiple measures of a single construct *and* smaller associations with measures of different constructs (i.e., convergent *and* discriminant validity) confers stronger evidence of validity than does the association between the measures of the same construct considered alone (i.e., only convergence). For example, evidence that two measures of social support correlate more closely with each other (association 1) than either of them do with a measure of the personality trait of extroversion (associations 2 and 3) confers stronger evidence of construct validity than does the significant correlation between the two measures of social support (association 1) alone. The former case represents a more complex pattern prediction (association 1 > than 2 and 3) and therefore would have been easier to disconfirm. Hence, support for the measurement model from the more complex and therefore "riskier" test provides stronger evidence of validity.

These "riskier" pattern predictions are particularly informative when they articulate and test plausible alternative interpretations of the simpler patterns. In the preceding example, the large and significant association between the two social support scales might reflect that both are valid measures of the intended construct. Alternatively, they could both be measuring an unintended third variable, such as individual differences in the personality trait extroversion. The more complex pattern prediction essentially articulates this alternative interpretation and pits it against the original interpretation in a context in which both patterns cannot occur; one interpretation must be discarded as unsupported. If the original rather than alternative interpretation is supported, the cumulative evidence of validity is increased.

Taxonomies of types of validity have changed over many years of measurement theory and research. The classic description by Cronbach and Meehl (1955) has been an important foundation for subsequent taxonomies. In their description, *content validity* referred to the extent to which items or other measured indicators of a construct are a representative sample of its conceptual domain. Specifically, a measure possesses content validity to the extent that all indicators fall within the conceptual definition of the construct, and the entire domain of the construct is adequately represented in the set of indicators. For example, as in the preceding description of the concept of hardiness, a measure should include items that pertain to the challenge, commitment, and change facets of the construct but not items that pertain to emotional distress. The closely related concept of *face validity* refers to the extent to which indicators or items appear to measure the intended construct. *Criterion validity* refers to the extent to which present (concurrent criterion validity) or future (predictive criterion validity) scores on a relevant criterion or outcome are related to scores on the measure. Finally, *construct validity* refers to the extent to which variance in scores on the measure reflects variation in the construct of interest, as opposed to other constructs.

Subsequent descriptions of types of validity have tended to view construct validity as the overarching concern, with the other types of validity simply aspects of this broader and more important consideration (Loevinger, 1957; Messick, 1989, 1995; G. T. Smith, 2005; Strauss & Smith, 2009). Obviously, this more modern view contrasts with the view that observed scores reflect a combination of "true score" and "error" that forms the core of classical test theory (John & Benet-Martinez, 2000). The construct approach holds that observed scores are more accurately seen as consisting of systematic variability (rather than true-score variability) and unsystematic variability, rather than "error." More important, however, the current view maintains that systematic variance is further partitioned into variance attributable to the construct of interest and variance attributable to other constructs. Hence, the validity of a measure (or, more accurately, interpretations based on a given measure) increases as the proportion of systematic, construct-relevant variance in scores increases relative to both of these other components—unsystematic or error variance and construct-irrelevant systematic variance.

An example of this view is presented in Figure 3.1. Self-reports of illness or physical symptoms have been used to measure the presence and severity of disease. Scores on such measures could reflect three sources, two of which are systematic. The unsystematic component could reflect careless responses to the scale items or other types of error (i.e., unreliability). The systematic component could reflect

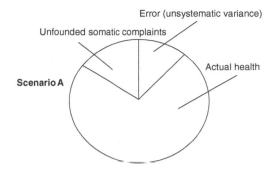

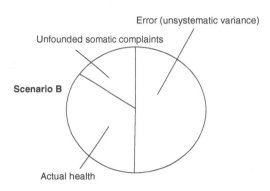

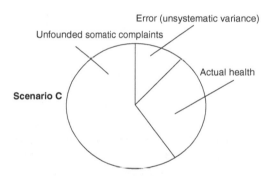

**Fig. 3.1** Portions of measurement variance in self-reported health.

(a) the presence and severity of actual illness (i.e., the intended construct), or (b) individual differences in the tendency to stoically minimize or deny physical illness versus excessive somatic complaints (i.e., an unintended construct). Three scenarios are presented in the figure. The first depicts a desirable level of validity; the construct-relevant component is large relative to the other two. In the second, the measure is invalid primarily because scores contain too much unsystematic variance—that is, the scale is unreliable. In this scenario, use of the scale is likely to produce misleading null results because little systematic variance is available to be involved in statistical covariation with measures of other constructs (e.g., social support). The third scenario indicates that the measure is reliable but invalid because it contains a large proportion of construct-irrelevant but systematic variance. Importantly, in this third scenario, results can produce misleading positive results, in that adequate systematic variance is available for covariation with other measures, but it does not reflect the intended construct.

There are several common sources of systematic construct-irrelevant variance. As a general class of such variance, method variance refers to variance that reflects the method or procedure used to measure the construct, rather than the construct itself. A widely discussed example of method variance involves response biases within self-report measures. Rather than simply reflecting the construct of interest, responses to self-report measures could reflect the tendency toward socially desirable responding. Situations vary in how strongly they encourage socially desirable responses (e.g., identifiable vs. anonymous responding). In addition, individuals may vary in the tendency to give socially desirable responses. Further, this tendency could reflect a motivation to avoid admitting socially undesirable characteristics to others or to oneself (Paulhus, 1991).

In a seminal contribution to the literature on construct validity, Campbell and Fiske (1959) proposed the multitrait, multimethod matrix (MTMM) as a technique for evaluating the extent to which scores on a given measure reflect the construct of interest, a different construct, and/or the method of measurement. The comparison construct(s) in MTMM studies can be either nuisance variables, such as socially desirable response styles, or substantive constructs that are potentially correlated with but distinct from the construct of interest. In this approach, two or more methods are used to measure two or more constructs, and the pattern of correlations among the measures is used to evaluate convergent and discriminant validity.

In addition to reliability coefficients (usually presented in the diagonal of MTMM tables), three types of correlations are included. Mono-trait, hetero-method correlations reflect the associations between different methods of assessing the same trait. These pairs of measures share variance due to the fact that they are intended to assess the same construct, but do not share common method variance. As noted previously, convergent validity refers to the extent to which different measures of a single construct correlate or converge. Discriminant validity refers to the extent to which a measure of a given construct does *not correlate* with (i.e., discriminates between or diverges from) a measure of a conceptually distinct construct. In the MTMM, the two other sets of associations are important in this regard. Hetero-trait, mono-method correlations represent the association between measures of separate constructs that share a common method. Hetero-trait, hetero-method correlations share neither a common construct nor method. As noted previously, evaluations of convergent and discriminant validity test predicted patterns of associations. Specifically, in the MTMM design, the pattern predicted is that convergent associations are larger than discriminant associations.

A recent topic in the study of psychosocial risk factors for cardiovascular disease provides an example of the MTMM approach. Suls and Bunde (2005) note that individual differences in anxiety, anger, and depressive symptoms have all been studied as risk factors for coronary heart disease (CHD). Usually, such studies implicitly conceptualize these emotional traits as distinct and typically measure only one of these three characteristics. However, anxiety, anger, and depressive symptoms are correlated components of the broader trait of neuroticism (Costa & McCrae, 1992). Studies of the health consequences of anxiety, depression, and anger rarely establish that measures of these three traits are in fact tapping distinct characteristics. To do so, a researcher could measure each of these three traits with two methods—self-reports and ratings by significant others. The Revised NEO Personality Inventory (NEO-PI-R; Costa & McCrae, 1992) is available in these two versions and includes scales to assess these dimensions. Given that prior theory and research suggest that anxiety, anger, and depression are components of a common underlying dimension (Costa & McCrae, 1992; Suls & Bunde, 2005), one would expect measures of these subtraits or facets to be correlated rather than truly independent. However, they should not be as closely correlated as two measures of the same subtrait.

Tables 3.3 and 3.4 present hypothetical results for two possible outcomes of an MTMM analysis of this issue. For both sets of results, two methods (i.e., self-reports and spouse reports) were used to assess the three traits of interest. In the first scenario, as depicted in Table 3.3, the convergent (i.e., mono-trait, hetero-method) correlations are larger than both of the sets of discriminant correlations (i.e., hetero-trait, mono-method; and hetero-trait, hetero-method). The three dimensions are clearly associated, as reflected in the nonzero, hetero-trait, mono-method and hetero-trait, hetero-method correlations. However, the convergent (i.e., mono-trait, hetero-method) associations are consistently larger. This pattern provides evidence of construct validity of the scales. In addition, the hetero-trait, mono-method correlations tend to

**Table 3.3** Hypothetical correlations in multitrait, multimethod analysis of self- and spouse reports of anxiety, anger, and depression: Example of good convergent and discriminant validity

|  | Self-Reports | | | Spouse Reports | | |
|---|---|---|---|---|---|---|
|  | Anxiety | Anger | Depression | Anxiety | Anger | Depression |
| *Self-reports* | | | | | | |
| Anxiety | (.86)* | | | | | |
| Anger | .48 | (.90) | | | | |
| Depression | .55 | .44 | (.87) | | | |
| *Spouse reports* | | | | | | |
| Anxiety | .60 | .32 | .36 | (.88) | | |
| Anger | .31 | .63 | .33 | .46 | (.85) | |
| Depression | .37 | .31 | .61 | .49 | .41 | (.89) |

*Reliabilities in parentheses.

be somewhat larger than the hetero-trait, hetero-method correlations, suggesting that some of the systematic variance in scale scores reflects method variance rather than the targeted construct.

In contrast, Table 3.4 depicts a pattern in which there is little evidence that the scales assess distinct dimensions. For example, the mono-trait, hetero-method correlations are generally smaller than the hetero-trait, mono-method associations. There is also clear evidence of method variance, in that the hetero-trait, mono-method associations are consistently larger than the hetero-trait, hetero-method associations. In this latter example, it would be concluded that the scales assess a single global dimension rather than the more specific (albeit, expected to be somewhat correlated) dimensions of anxiety, anger, and depression. Further, scale scores would include both variance reflecting this broad construct and a substantial degree of method variance.

These outcomes serve to illustrate the logic of the MTMM approach in depicting convergent and discriminant validity as essential aspects of construct validity. The actual quantitative evaluation of such studies has advanced in recent years with applications of structural equation modeling, but has remained a challenging undertaking (G. T. Smith, 2005). Full MTMM evaluations of construct validity are not common in most research areas in behavioral science,

**Table 3.4** Hypothetical correlations in multitrait, multimethod analysis of self- and spouse reports of anxiety, anger, and depression: Example of poor convergent and discriminant validity

|  | Self-reports | | | Spouse Reports | | |
|---|---|---|---|---|---|---|
|  | Anxiety | Anger | Depression | Anxiety | Anger | Depression |
| *Self-reports* | | | | | | |
| Anxiety | (.86)* | | | | | |
| Anger | .68 | (.90) | | | | |
| Depression | .71 | .67 | (.87) | | | |
| *Spouse reports* | | | | | | |
| Anxiety | .51 | .52 | .55 | (.88) | | |
| Anger | .49 | .48 | .47 | .66 | (.85) | |
| Depression | .53 | .50 | .50 | .70 | .68 | (.89) |

*Reliabilities in parentheses.

and certainly they are not common in health psychology. However, the basic logic of construct validation through the simultaneous consideration of convergent and discriminant associations (i.e., a pattern prediction) applies in far simpler measurement evaluation designs. The minimal requirement for testing a pattern of convergent and discriminant associations involves two measures of one construct (to examine convergence) and one measure of a different construct (to examine discriminant associations). Even such minimal approaches can often provide useful information.

## Methods in Measurement Evaluation

It is worthwhile to tie some of these basic issues in measurement to quantitative methods used to evaluate them. Many measurement evaluation issues are addressed with basic quantitative procedures that are well known to anyone with basic training in methodology. However, some techniques increasingly used in this context may be at least somewhat unfamiliar to health psychology researchers. This section describes three such techniques. It is well beyond the present scope to review these quantitative methods in detail, but it is useful to consider how these techniques are generally used.

### EXPLORATORY AND CONFIRMATORY FACTOR ANALYSIS

Factor analysis is commonly used to evaluate the structure of a measure. Exploratory factor analysis asks the question, "*What* is the structure of this set of indicators?" As the name implies, this family of analytic techniques holds few advanced assumptions about what the structure of a measure might be. In contrast, confirmatory factor analysis asks the question, "Is *this* the structure of this set of indicators?" In this manner, a specific, theory-driven prediction about the structure of a set of items or other indicators of a construct can be compared with the obtained pattern of covariation among indicators in a research sample. Therefore, confirmatory methods can provide "stronger" tests of structural hypotheses because the specific prediction can be disconfirmed by a poor fit with the obtained data. In an even stronger use of confirmatory factor analysis to test structural questions about measures, two or more competing structural hypotheses can be articulated a priori and pitted against each other in model comparison techniques.

For example, in the earlier situation in which anxiety, anger, and depressive symptoms are assessed, one might contrast two models of an 18-item measure containing three six-item subscales corresponding to each of the affective traits. A model in which these scales are hypothesized to reflect distinct but correlated dimensions (because they are three facets of a broader construct) would predict high levels of correlation among the three sets of six items and smaller but still significant correlations across sets. In a model in which these items were hypothesized to reflect indistinguishable aspects of a single broad dimension, correlations among the 18 items would be predicted to be high and generally uniform. These two a priori structural hypotheses can be compared directly. As with most measurement research, the yield from this sort of model testing is greater if the competing models are derived from related theory about the structure of the domain. It is important to note that if exploratory or confirmatory factor analyses indicate that a scale is actually multidimensional, a traditional index of internal consistency for the total scale score (e.g., Cronbach's $\alpha$) is potentially quite misleading. A large value would imply that the total scale is internally consistent (i.e., high reliability across items), when the more appropriate factor analytic methods for evaluating the scale structure suggest something quite different.

A special application of confirmatory factor analysis involves the evaluation of MTMM designs (Marsh & Grayson, 1995). In this case, the hypotheses to be articulated in advance and pitted against one another involve the degree of convergent and discriminant validity reflected in the obtained pattern of intercorrelations, as well as the presence and extent of method variance. Predictions, such as "The multiple measures of a single construct will correlate more closely with each other than with measures of a second construct" and "All measures in the matrix reflect a single construct," can be compared. Further, these predictions can be compared with the alternative hypothesis, "Scores of these measures reflect the method used to obtain them, rather than the intended construct." These various hypotheses can be translated into specific expected patterns involving the relative magnitude of the mono-method/hetero-method, hetero-trait/mono-method, and hetero-trait/hetero-method correlations (Eid, Lischetzke, Nussbeck, & Trierweiler, 2003; G. T. Smith, 2005).

### ITEM RESPONSE THEORY

Item response theory (IRT) is another relatively recent, complex quantitative method in measurement research (Schmidt & Embretson, 2003). Applied to multi-item or multi-indicator measures, IRT examines responses to items as a function of the individual's standing on the construct of interest. Specifically, items within a multi-item measure may provide more or less useful information depending on whether the individual displays a low, intermediate, or high level of the construct of interest. For example, in a true-false self-report scale measuring functional activity versus disability, the item "I have difficulty walking very long distances" might be useful in distinguishing mildly disabled persons from those with moderate levels of disability. This is because the former group is unlikely to endorse the item, whereas the latter is likely to endorse it. However, the item is less useful in distinguishing the moderately disabled from the severely disabled because both groups are likely to endorse it. In contrast, the item "I often have difficulty walking even very short distances" might not be useful in distinguishing the mildly and moderately disabled groups, since neither is likely to endorse the item. However, it could be quite useful in distinguishing the moderately and severely disabled groups.

Item response theory methods can be used to determine the extent to which a multi-item scale, for example, contains informative items across the full range of the construct as it is conceptually defined. In this way, it is a useful technique for addressing complex aspects of content validity. Item response theory can also be used in computerized interactive testing contexts to reduce the number of items used in an assessment, by decreasing the sampling of items well above and well below the emerging estimate of the individual's standing on the construct of interest and increasing the sampling with items that are maximally informative around the individual's estimated level. This latter use of IRT is clearly relevant to health psychology measurement, but it is not yet common.

### SIGNAL DETECTION THEORY

Another advanced technique in measurement evaluation uses concepts and quantitative methods from signal detection theory (SDT) in evaluations of criterion validity (McFall, 2005; McFall & Treat, 1999). In many measurement instances, a scale or similar procedure is used to predict an outcome criterion. For example, depressive disorders (i.e., major depression, minor depression, or dysthymia) are potentially serious conditions in need of treatment. They are more common among persons with chronic medical illness than in the general public (Steptoe, 2007). Further, in some medical populations, such as individuals with coronary heart disease, depression confers increased risk of recurrent coronary events

and cardiac mortality (Lett et al., 2004). Definitive clinical diagnoses of depressive disorders are usually made following diagnostic interviewing, a procedure that is typically considered too time-consuming and expensive to be feasible for all coronary patients. Therefore, various self-report or observer rating scales have been used as screening tools to identify patients who are sufficiently likely to be depressed to warrant referral for a more definitive diagnostic evaluation. Here, the basic measurement question involves the relationship of scores on the screening measure to the clinical criterion of diagnosed depressive disorder, clearly a question of the validity of such measures.

A variety of factors are considered in such evaluations. *Sensitivity,* or "hit rate," of tests in such applications refers to the proportion of true cases (i.e., actually depressed, according to diagnostic clinical interview) identified as cases on the basis of their score on the screening measure (e.g., scores on the BDI). *Specificity* refers to the proportion of true noncases identified as such on the basis of scores on the screening measure. Low specificity results in a high number of "false alarms." A critical influence on sensitivity and specificity is the cut point on the screening measure. For example, if a BDI score of equal to or greater than 2 is used to classify a coronary patient as depressed, virtually all truly depressed cases (as determined by subsequent diagnostic interviewing) would be identified. In this case, the screening measure would have high *sensitivity.* However, many truly nondepressed cases would be erroneously labeled as depressed, resulting in a high false-alarm rate or low *specificity.* In contrast, if a BDI score of 25 was used as the cut point, very few truly nondepressed patients would be identified as depressed on the basis of their screening score, producing few false alarms and high specificity. However, many truly depressed patients would be erroneously identified as nondepressed on the basis of having BDI scores below 25, indicating a low "hit rate" or low sensitivity.

In SDT, the function or curve depicting all possible combinations of values for hit rates and false alarm rates at all possible cut points is called a receiver operating curve (ROC). The area under this curve (AUC) can be calculated to quantify the information value for a given measure. Since this value reflects the relative degree of association between the measure and a criterion, it is clearly informative regarding criterion validity. AUC values of 0.50 reflect chance, in that the screening measure with this ROC (along or near the diagonal in a plot of false alarm rates vs. hit rates) does not improve criterion prediction at all. An AUC value of 1.0 is the upper limit, indicating that increasing hit rates does not increase false alarms, and decreasing false alarms does not decrease hits. Performance at this level is highly unlikely, of course, and the relative "information value" of measures is reflected in their AUC values.

In an application of this sort, Strik, Honig, Lousberg, and Denollet (2001) compared the criterion validity of several brief self-report scales and ratings in identifying depressed and nondepressed cardiac patients; it is likely that this approach will be increasingly common as health psychology researchers and practitioners alike have become more concerned with quantifying and comparing the utility of measurement and clinical assessment procedures. It is important to note that SDT analyses do not result in specification of optimal cutoffs for scale scores. That process involves judgments about the relative value or importance of specific outcomes. For example, in some applications, false positives are more worrisome than are false negatives (e.g., identifying candidates for an expensive and invasive medical procedure), whereas in other contexts, false negatives may be more worrisome (e.g., identifying suicidal risk). These considerations, along with the base rates of the outcome criterion in a given setting and other factors, are important in specifying cut points for decision making (McFall, 2005), but the SDT approach provides a broadly applicable approach for evaluating and comparing measures.

## Examples of Measurement Issues in the Three Domains of Health Psychology

To illustrate further the application of the basic principles and issues discussed previously to research in health psychology, the following section includes topics within each of the field's three major content domains. Across this wide range of specific topics, the importance of theory-driven decisions about the nature of constructs, the optimal methods of measuring them, and alternative interpretations of existing measures is clear.

### Health Behavior and Prevention

As in most behavioral and social science research, self-reports play a prominent role in research on health behavior and prevention. Self-reports of health behavior and its determinants are often used when other approaches are available, in large part because of their apparent simplicity and low cost. In other instances, such as survey studies with very large samples, self-reports are used because alternate measurement methods are simply not feasible. Most health behaviors are relatively specific and seemingly easily amenable to self-report (e.g., smoking, physical activity level, dietary intake, seat belt use). However, a large and growing body of research indicates that this measurement method is complex and often limited to the point of producing potentially misleading findings (Stone, Trukkan, et al., 2000).

All the previously described issues having to do with the reliability, structure, and validity of measures are relevant to self-reports of health behavior and self-reports of potential influences on health behavior. Importantly, the use of self-reports assumes that respondents are able and willing to provide accurate—that is, reliable and valid—information about their standing on the construct of interest. This is an implicit component of the nomological net surrounding any use of this method. As discussed previously, the tendency to give socially desirable responses is a pervasive threat to the validity of self-reports and can reflect the individual's interest in withholding information about socially undesirable characteristics from others or from him- or herself (Paulhus, 1991). Any time a self-report measure is used, this sort of method variance must be carefully considered as a potential source of systematic variance. Approaches to minimizing these threats to validity (e.g., anonymous responding) must be considered when designing and using such measures (Schaeffer, 2000).

In the case of health behavior, many if not most specific behaviors have obvious social desirability connotations. Smoking, physical inactivity, excessive calorie intake, alcohol or other substance abuse, unsafe sexual activity, and other unhealthy behaviors are generally seen as undesirable (e.g., Patrick et al., 1994; Schroeder, Carey, & Vanable, 2003b). If a measure of a predictor of health behavior (e.g., personality traits such as anger or hostility, social support, religious activity, self-efficacy) also contains systematic variance reflecting social desirability, the association between predictor and health behavior outcome may at least in part reflect this third variable (i.e., shared method variance) rather than the presumed association between the intended constructs.

Often, interventions intended to reduce unhealthy behavior and increase better habits communicate clear expectations for positive change. If self-reports of health behavior used as outcome measures in such intervention studies contain systematic variance reflecting the tendency to give socially desirable responses, then treatment effects can reflect—at least in part—an association between the social communication of expectancies for change (i.e., demand characteristics) and the tendency to provide socially desirable responses, rather than the substantive effect of the intervention on actual behavior change. In this instance, sources of invalidity in measurement can contribute to an overestimate of treatment effects. Non–self-report measures can be used as alternative or supplemental outcome measures, such as exhaled carbon monoxide or plasma cotinine as measures of smoking status (Glasgow et al., 1993) or mechanical monitors (e.g., actigraphs) to assess physical activity levels. In the case of some forms of physical activity measurement (e.g., walking), such monitors can even be integrated with global positioning technology (Maddison & Mhurchu, 2009). However, such measures are often not feasible in large-scale interventions or survey studies.

Even if individuals are willing to provide accurate self-reports, they may be unable to do so. A wide variety of cognitive and emotional processes can reduce the accuracy of self-reports (Kihlstrom, Eich, Sandbrand, & Tobias, 2000; Menon & Yorkston, 2000; Tourangeau, 2000). One consequence of these cognitive and affective threats to the accuracy of self-reports is reduced reliability. That is, they are sources of error in the form of unsystematic variance, and therefore would reduce observed effect sizes below "true" levels of association. However, when the accuracy of respondents' self-reports is low, they may rely on other processes in forming responses that are sources of construct-irrelevant systematic variance, thereby reducing the validity of the measure without necessarily reducing its reliability. For example, respondents' mood could influence their estimate of the frequency of a health behavior, such that they recall more positive behavior when in a positive mood and less when in a negative mood. Similar to the effects of socially desirable responding, if the predictor variables in related studies share this susceptibility to the influence of mood (or are themselves measures of current or characteristic mood), these influences on self-report measures of health behavior would lead to overestimates of the effects of interest. That is, the observed associations would reflect a combination of shared method variance and substantive effects.

In some measurement contexts, unreliable and invalid self-reports are more likely when individuals make global reports over long periods of time, as when they describe how much exercise they engage in during the usual week or how many hours of sleep they typically get. For this reason, "real-time" self-reports of daily or momentary experiences and activities obtained in the natural environment have become an important approach in health psychology and related fields (Affleck, Zautra, Tennen, & Armeli, 1999; Bolger, Davis, & Rafaeli, 2003; Kahneman, Krueger, Schkade, Schwartz, & Stone, 2005; Shiffman, 2000; Stone & Shiffman, 2002). One interesting type of measurement research involves testing the convergence of traditional global self-reports of a construct with measures of the same construct obtained through daily diary or experience sampling approaches. Results of such studies often indicate poor correspondence between global reports of behaviors such as smoking and reports obtained through the much more frequent experience sampling method (Shiffman, 2000). Such findings clearly suggest caution in interpreting traditional self-report measures but also suggest novel approaches to self-report assessment and a valuable paradigm for evaluating construct validity.

A final concern in studies of health behavior involves the measurement of influences on these actions. The potential influences on health behavior include a wide variety of characteristics, ranging from biochemical processes in addiction and appetite to sociocultural factors such as SES and acculturation. Basic issues of reliability and validity of measures of these constructs are obviously essential in the critical evaluation of related studies. Of particular importance is whether measures of factors influencing health behavior have sufficient evidence of convergent and discriminant validity to support the inference that it is the specific construct of interest and not another construct that is related to health behavior. As described previously, social desirability is one such alternative construct that has to do with measurement variance. Holding aside method artifacts and considering only substantive alternative constructs, these aspects of construct validity are often a source of concern.

A brief consideration of individual-level influences on health behavior will illustrate this concern. Conceptual descriptions of this domain of influences on health behavior include many individual difference characteristics. For example, simply within the cognitive-social perspective on the determinants of health behavior (Miller, Shoda, & Hurley, 1996), the list of important constructs includes the categories of health-relevant encodings (e.g., internal representations of health risks, attention to health information), health beliefs and expectations (e.g., outcome expectancies for health behavior, self-efficacy), health goals and values, and several others. Measures of these constructs are often developed for single studies, and even if used more frequently are often not subjected to extensive evaluations of their convergent and discriminant validity. As a result, evidence is often lacking as to the extent to which these scales actually measure the distinct and specific construct of interest *and do not* measure related constructs. Scale names often imply a great deal of specificity. For example, a measure of health-relevant goals implies it assesses goals but not outcome expectancies. However, this implied level of specificity is rarely evaluated through confirmatory structural analyses of the items of a specific scale and those of a scale intended to measure a related but conceptually distinct construct. The implicitly hypothesized structural model would predict the best fit from a two-factor model. However, if the item content is at all similar across the two item sets (and it often is), then a single-factor model is a viable alternative unless tested and discarded as fitting less well.

Further, evaluations of convergent and discriminant validity in the form of even partial MTMM studies are rare. The result is that this literature often seems to support conclusions about specific influences on health behavior that are much more definitive than is warranted given the limited support for the implicit hypothesis that these influences are measured with the level of specificity implied by scale labels. That is, it is possible that distinctly labeled but psychometrically overlapping scales are misinterpreted as supporting unique influences on health behavior. Greater attention to construct validity in this literature might identify broad or overlapping determinants of health behavior.

### Stress and Disease

As described previously, in the history of the field, the effects of stress, personality traits, and other psychosocial risk factors on physical health sometimes have been studied using self-report measures of health as the outcome variable. Self-rated health is reliably related to subsequent mortality (Idler & Benyamini, 1997; McGee, Liao, Cao, & Cooper, 1999), persuasively indicating that self-reports of health contain systematic variance related to the construct of interest. However, self-report measures of health also clearly contain systematic variance that is independent of actual health (Barsky, 2000; Pennebaker, 2000). Some individuals tend to report physical symptoms in excess of actual disease, whereas others tend to minimize symptoms. As a result, when a psychosocial predictor is found to be related to self-reported health, it is not clear if the association involves variance in the outcome measure that reflects actual health, the component that is unrelated to actual health, or a combination of these components.

This situation is further complicated by the fact that a broad individual difference variable—negative affectivity or neuroticism—predicts both actual health outcomes and complaints of health problems that are independent of actual illness (Suls & Bunde, 2005). This broad trait is also associated with measures of many other psychosocial risk factors (Smith & Gallo, 2001). Hence, whenever self-reported health is used as an outcome measure, it is possible that observed effects involve individual differences in the tendency to experience negative affect and report excessive physical health problems. Self-rated health is an important construct in and of itself, but these ambiguities undermine its usefulness when the research question involves the effects of psychosocial factors on actual disease. A similar issue arises when health outcome measures are heavily related to symptom reports rather than objective measures (e.g., reports of angina pectoris as an indicator of coronary disease, as opposed to medically verified myocardial infarction, ischemia, or coronary death). Finally, the tendency to make excessive somatic complaints can alter the process of selection into a medical study sample, potentially producing biases and misleading results. For example, a large literature indicates that the trait of negative affectivity or neuroticism is associated with actual coronary heart disease (Suls & Bunde, 2005). However, in studies of patients undergoing coronary angiography to assess the presence and severity of the underlying coronary artery disease, neuroticism is often found to be unrelated or even inversely related to the presence and severity of coronary disease. This finding could reflect the fact that individuals high in negative affectivity but otherwise healthy complain convincingly enough of possible cardiac symptoms that they are referred for this invasive diagnostic procedure. The resulting overinclusion of disease-free persons with high levels of neuroticism could produce misleading results.

Similar to the issue of individual difference predictors of health behaviors described previously, studies of psychosocial predictors of subsequent health often use individual difference measures that are insufficiently evaluated. On some occasions, the scales used in large epidemiological studies are by necessity quite brief, raising the concern that low reliability could attenuate the magnitude of associations with health outcomes. In other instances, the measures of psychosocial risk factors have not been subjected to even minimal construct validation, such as correlations with other measures of the same construct. It is common for measures to be used that have not been subjected to compelling tests of their convergent and discriminant validity. As a result, it is often possible that the measures used assess constructs are different from those which the scale label implies. Further, the proliferation of insufficiently validated scales used in such studies creates the possibility that previously identified risk factors are being "rediscovered" when unvalidated scales with novel labels unintentionally tap established risk constructs.

Several authors have argued that this psychometric cacophony could impede systematic progress in the field, and that the use of established construct validation methods and comparisons with well-validated individual differences in personality and social behavior could help to identify robust, broad risk factors studied under a variety of potentially misleading labels (Costa & McCrae, 1987; Friedman, Tucker, & Reise, 1995; Marshall, Wortman, Vickers, Kusulas, & Hervig, 1994; Smith & Gallo, 2001; Smith & Williams, 1992). Suls and Bunde (2005) provide a recent example of this issue in their review of the literature linking anxiety, depressive symptoms, and anger with the development and course of coronary disease. Without comprehensive measurement of these traits and thoughtful analysis of their overlapping and unique effects, it is difficult to discern if they represent distinct influences on cardiovascular health or aspects of a single broad risk factor involving the tendency to experience negative affect (cf. Friedman & Booth-Kewley, 1987).

The problems associated with the measurement of personality traits and similar psychosocial risk factors arise not only from the failure to employ thorough approaches to construct validation. They also often arise from an initial failure to thoroughly consider conceptual issues, such as the relationship of a proposed risk factor to previously established risk factors and well-validated taxonomies of related individual differences. In the latter regard, the five-factor model of personality and the interpersonal circumplex are useful nomological nets. Complete with clear conceptual definitions and many well-validated assessment procedures using multiple measurement methods, these models can facilitate comparing, contrasting, and integrating psychosocial risk factors (Gallo & Smith, 1998; Marshall et al., 1994; Smith & Williams, 1992).

As in the study of determinants of health behavior, self-reports of psychosocial risk factors for disease such as personality traits, social support, and stressful life experiences are commonly used, given their ease of administration and low cost. Given that some of these characteristics involve attitudes and subjective emotional experiences, this is not an unreasonable choice. The measurement model underlying such use implies that individuals can and will provide reliable and valid reports. However, there is some evidence to suggest that this assumption must be made with caution. For example, behavioral ratings of hostility from structured interviewers and spouse ratings of personality traits are more closely related to subsequent health outcomes than are self-reports of these characteristics (Miller et al., 1996; Smith et al., 2008). Similarly, in samples of heart patients, spouse reports of anger and other negative emotional characteristics are more closely related to disease severity and prognosis than are the patients' self-reports of the same characteristics (Ketterer et al., 2004). Low self-awareness of negative characteristics, social desirability artifacts, and patients' denial of emotional distress as they cope with serious illness are all possible sources of invalidity in self-reports of these risk factors. The net effect for research studies would be the tendency to find smaller—and potentially nonsignificant—effect sizes when self-report measures are employed. Hence, the optimal method of measurement is an important aspect of the conceptual model surrounding these risk factors.

The importance of conceptual models guiding measurement can also be seen in the study of mechanisms linking psychosocial risk factors and disease. The construct of cardiovascular reactivity (CVR) provides an important example in this regard. In its general meaning, CVR refers to increases in heart rate and blood pressure in response to stressful stimuli. Such responses are hypothesized to initiate and hasten the development of high blood pressure, atherosclerosis, and other manifestations of cardiovascular disease (Manuck, 1994). Although mounting evidence supports this view, measures of the post-stressor recovery of these physiological responses—a distinct but less frequently assessed construct—is at least as predictive of cardiovascular disease as are traditional measures of CVR (Chida & Steptoe, 2010).

However, in the guiding conceptual models in CVR research, this term is actually used to refer to two distinct characteristics. In the first, it is considered to be a stable individual difference variable that is consistent across time and situations. That is, some individuals display consistently large cardiovascular responses to potential stressors, whereas others display consistently smaller responses. The former group is hypothesized to be more prone to the development of cardiovascular disease. In an innovative and important application of the principles of measurement, Kamarck, Jennings, Pogue-Geile, and Manuck (1994) have demonstrated that the multiple measurements using multiple stressors increase the reliability of estimates of this trait, much like adding items to a self-report scale can increase estimates of internal consistency. Further, this more reliable estimate of CVR, not surprisingly, is more closely related to health outcomes (e.g., ambulatory blood pressure) than are single measurements of CVR, most likely due to the enhanced reliability of measurement. With this underlying conceptualization of CVR and the related measurement model, increasing the number of measurements and doing so across a wider range of stressors logically improves the measure—up to a point of diminishing returns.

However, CVR also refers to a mechanism hypothesized to link psychosocial risk factors to disease, as in the case of the personality trait of hostility (Williams, Barefoot, & Shekelle, 1985). In this specific model and many others like it, CVR is not necessarily a stable characteristic of the individual that is consistent across time and settings. Rather, it is a situation-specific response that is more pronounced among hostile persons than among their more agreeable counterparts. The personality trait is believed to be stable, as is the tendency for hostile persons to respond to some classes of stimuli (e.g., provocation, conflict, harassment) but not others (e.g., achievement challenge) with heightened CVR. Increasing the frequency of measurements of heart rate and blood pressure in relevant situations might improve the likelihood of detecting the hypothesized association between the personality trait and the unhealthy physiological response, through increased reliability of measurement of situation-specific CVR. However, simply increasing the number of measurements of CVR—if it includes nonrelevant situations—would not be expected to improve the reliability of measurement in this case.

The underlying conceptual model that should guide the measurement of this second conceptual view of CVR is quite different from that guiding assessments of broad cross-situational individual differences in CVR. Different views of the nature and location of the stability of the response, as well as different expectations regarding the stimuli used to evoke it, are implied in the nomological nets surrounding these two constructs, despite the use of the identical label. In the situation-specific view, more recent conceptual models from cognitive-social perspectives in personality (Mischel & Shoda, 1995) would provide a better guide for designing the assessment scheme for CVR than do the traditional views of the assessment of traits that underpin the model of measuring CVR proposed by Kamarck et al. (1994). In this newer perspective, individual differences are reflected in profiles or patterns of responses across specific situations, rather than levels of response across all situations. Measurement should be guided by theory, and care should be taken to make certain that the measurement model appropriately reflects other aspects of the nomological net surrounding the construct to be assessed.

In studies evaluating physiological mechanisms potentially linking psychosocial risk factors and health, care must also be taken in the measurement of the physiological response. For example, the sensitivity of assays to detect neuroendocrine or immune system responses and temporal aspects of these responses must guide the measurement protocol. Otherwise, insensitive or mistimed measures can contribute to erroneous results (Smith & Uchino, 2008). Similarly, the measurement of health outcomes must be guided by appropriate consideration of the likely occurrence and level of variability of medical endpoints during the study period. In studies of psychosocial determinants of the recurrence of myocardial infarction, for example, the likely frequency of recurrent events over follow-up periods of varying lengths must be considered before the protocol for measuring the health outcome of interest is finalized. Such decisions are often best informed through collaborations with other biomedical researchers.

### Psychosocial Aspects of Medical Illness and Care

Given the nature of many constructs in this third broad topic area (e.g., pain, emotion), self-reports are an essential approach to measurement. The nomological net surrounding most uses of global self-reports would predict convergence with measures of the same constructs obtained through daily diary or experience sampling methods. However, results often suggest little or no correspondence between these two methods of measuring constructs such as type of coping with stress or change in chronic pain (Porter, Stone, & Schwartz, 1999; Schwartz, Neale, Marco, Shiffman, & Stone, 1999; Stone, Broderick, Shiffman, & Schwartz, 2004; Stone et al., 1998). Hence, interpretations of findings obtained with global self-reports should be made cautiously. Further, the daily experience paradigm and recent variations (Kahneman et al., 2005) provide an important alternative for testing theories of adaptation in chronic disease, as well as a valuable context for evaluating other measures. Of course, self-report outcome measures of all types could contain systematic variance reflecting social desirability, again raising the previously described concerns about interpretations of their association with measures of predictor variables that also contain this component and their susceptibility to the inflation of estimates of intervention effects when those treatments contain demand characteristics.

In measuring predictors of adaptation in acute or chronic medical illness, the issues about construct validity described in the previous two content areas are again highly relevant. All too often, the labels applied to scales measuring predictor variables imply much more specificity than is supported by the available evidence of convergent and discriminant validity. Further, the outcomes these measures are used to predict typically involve emotional and physical distress. As a result, a measurement concern raised in the study of models of emotional adaptation in general is quite relevant here. Specifically, in their classic critique of research on cognitive models of depression, Coyne and Gotlib (1983) noted that some of the self-report measures of key cognitive constructs (e.g., dysfunctional attitudes, cognitive errors) often contain item wording that includes reference to emotional distress. This could result in what the authors described as "thinly veiled tautologies," in which associations between two measures with overlapping content are misinterpreted as evidence of the predicted substantive association between constructs. That is, common method variance in the form of similar item content contributes to—if not fully accounts for—the observed effect. In the literature on psychosocial predictors of adaptation to medical illness, few studies have demonstrated that predictor measures have sufficient discriminant validity relative to outcome measures to rule out this artifact as an alternative explanation for observed effects.

The study of adaptation to chronic disease also provides important examples of difficulties arising when measurement models previously studied in one context are applied in a novel context. As noted previously, depression is more common among persons with chronic medical illness than among medically healthy persons, presumably reflecting—at least in part—the stress of living with a serious health problem.

Hence, assessment of depression is an important component in studying adaptation to chronic disease (Steptoe, 2007). However, most of the measures of depression used in this body of research were initially developed and used to study depression in physically healthy populations. In the physically healthy population, physical symptoms included in depression inventories (e.g., sleep disturbance, fatigue, concerns about appearance) can be highly diagnostic. However, for persons with a serious physical (rather than mental) illness, these symptoms can reflect the medical condition rather than its emotional consequences (Blalock, DeVellis, Brown, & Wallston, 1989; Clark, Cook, & Snow, 1998; Mohr et al., 1997; O'Donnell & Chung, 1997; Peck, Smith, Ward, & Milano, 1989). This could lead to the overestimation of levels of depression in the medically ill. Further, correlates of these depression measures in such populations could in part reflect correlates of the severity of medical illness rather than only the construct of interest. Hence, use of a measure outside of the context where it was initially developed and validated could result in a circumstance in which it captures systematic variability beyond the construct of interest. Further, it is important to note that, although scores on self-report depression scales certainly are related to diagnosable clinical depressive disorders, such scales are best seen as measuring a broader dimension of negative affectivity that overlaps—but is not isomorphic with—depressive disorders (Coyne, 1994; Fechner-Bates, Coyne, & Schwenk, 1994). As a result, the scale names can be misleading.

The use of depression measures to assess the emotional impact of medical illness also raises a question about the appropriateness of the underlying conceptual model. Depression is certainly an important concern in this context. However, by conceptualizing emotional adaptation as the presence and severity of symptoms of depression, researchers are implicitly suggesting that varying the degrees of emotional maladjustment is a more appropriate approach than is variation in normal affective experience. Models of normal emotional experience (e.g., Watson & Tellegen, 1983) identify two dimensions—positive and negative affect. Chronic disease could have undesirable emotional consequences not only by increasing negative affect (NA) but also by reducing positive affect (PA). Importantly, measures of depression are associated with both higher NA and lower PA, and therefore depression measures combine NA and PA in a nonspecific affective index. Further, in chronic medical illness, NA and PA are influenced by different factors (Smith & Christensen, 1996; Zautra et al., 1995). As a result, use of depression measures to capture the emotional consequences of chronic illness can produce a loss of specificity in identifying influences on multifaceted aspects of adaptation. In this manner, the selection of a conceptual model and corresponding approach to measurement can result in an imprecise view of the phenomenon of interest.

Although increased specificity in measurement of outcomes is often highly desirable, valid global measures are also valuable. Kaplan (1994) has argued convincingly that a common metric for measuring health status would permit the comparative evaluation of the impact of various diseases and a wide range of health interventions. When combined with assessment of costs, such a broadly applicable, common metric also permits cost utility analyses in which health benefits of virtually any intervention for the prevention or management of virtually any condition can be compared relative to their related costs (Kaplan & Groessel, 2002). The Quality-Adjusted Life Year (QUALY; Kaplan, 1994) is one such index in which mortality and quality of life are combined. In this measurement model, quality of life is quantified as a combination of various aspects of morbidity and functional activity. The metric ranges from 0.0 (i.e., death or "zero quality of life") to 1.0 (i.e., asymptomatic, optimal functioning). By multiplying years alive by their quality, a common metric for health outcomes is derived. This is an example of a "cause indicator" measurement model rather than an "effect indicator" model, in that a given QUALY value is a result of the measured variables rather than a hypothetical construct that "causes" variability on the measured variables. It also is a clear example of how the health economic context of health psychology research and related issues of public policy are increasingly important in the development of new measurement procedures.

## Conclusion

As described in the preceding section, important issues involving the application of basic principles of measurement can be found in each of the major content domains of health psychology. This brief presentation provided illustrations rather than anything approaching an exhaustive review. There are many additional instances in which widely used measures are in need of further evaluation and refinement. Certainly, there are many research questions in the immediate future of the field where these basic measurement issues should be thoughtfully applied in the development of new measures and the use of existing measures in new contexts.

The interdisciplinary nature of the field creates the need for the application of principles of measurement development and evaluation to a wide-ranging set of biomedical, psychological, and social processes. Thorough attention to these issues is an essential aspect of the basic and applied research missions in health psychology. It is best seen as an ongoing process within an active and evolving field that is constantly addressing new research questions and extending the study of established topics to new contexts. As a result, the design, evaluation, and refinement of measurement procedures do not represent a research challenge to be addressed once and dispatched; instead, they must be continually considered when designing new research or evaluating prior work.

Fortunately, longstanding basic principles and a growing array of quantitative methods are available to address these complex challenges. It is essential to note that the application of these principles and techniques must be guided by theory. In this case, it is not the grand theories of health and behavior or mind and body central in the field's history that require consideration. Rather, it is the smaller—but no less important—theories of the construct to be assessed and methods of measurement that guide this work. These nomological nets have rarely been exhaustively studied in health psychology research. Hence, health psychology researchers and consumers of their efforts are well advised to exercise caution in making inferences about what measures actually reflect.

Perhaps more important, these unexplored measurement research questions present opportunities for useful contributions to the field. The evaluation of existing measures and development of new measures can be the primary focus of a research project, but useful contributions can also be made when measurement research is added as a secondary focus to research studies in which the primary focus is on some other substantive question. Whether measurement is a primary or secondary focus, and regardless of the quantitative complexity of the work, careful and clear thinking is the essential element of measurement research in health psychology (McFall, 2005). This includes consideration of the nature and structure of the construct of interest, delineation of the surrounding nomological net, critical evaluation of what can and cannot be concluded on the basis of available evidence, the articulation of alternative or competing interpretations of measures, and the design of "risky" tests of rival explanations. This type of sustained attention to measurement issues will strengthen the empirical foundations of the field and help to make its future as remarkable as its past.

## References

Affleck, G., Zautra, A., Tennen, H., Armeli, S. (1999). Multilevel daily process designs for consulting and clinical psychology: A primer for the perplexed. *Journal of Consulting and Clinical Psychology, 67,* 746–754.

Barsky, A.J. (2000). The validity of bodily symptoms in medical outpatients. In A.A. Stone, J.S. Turkkan, C.A. Bachrach, J.B. Jobe, H.S. Kurtzman, & V.S. Cain (Eds.), *The science of self-report: Implications for research and practice* (pp. 339–361). Mahwah, NJ: Erlbaum.

Blalock, S.J., DeVellis, R.F., Brown, G.K., & Wallston, K.A. (1989). Validity of the Center for Epidemiological Studies Depression scale in arthritic populations. *Arthritis and Rheumatism, 32,* 991–997.

Blanton, H., & Jaccard, J. (2006). Arbitrary metrics in psychology. *American Psychologist, 61,* 27–41.

Bolger, N, Davis, A., & Rafaeli, E. (2003). Diary methods: Capturing life as it is lived. *Annual Review of Psychology, 54,* 579–612.

Bollen, K.A., & Lennox, R. (1991). Conventional wisdom on measurement: A structural equation perspective. *Psychological Bulletin, 110,* 305–314.

Bridgman, P.W. (1927). *The logic of modern physics.* New York: Macmillan.

Bridgman, P.W. (1945). Some general principles of operational analysis. *Psychological Review, 52,* 246–249.

Campbell, D.T., & Fiske, D.W. (1959). Covergent and discriminant validation by the multitrait-multimethod matrix. *Psychological Bulletin, 56,* 81–105.

Cappuccio, F.P., D'Elia, F., Strazzullo, P., & Miller, M. (2010). Sleep duration and all-cause mortality: A systematic review and meta-analysis of prospective studies. *Sleep, 33,* 585–592.

Carver, C.S. (1989). How should multifaceted personality constructs be tested? Issues illustrated by self-monitoring, attributional style, and hardiness. *Journal of Personality and Social Psychology, 56,* 577–585.

Carver, C.S., & Harmon-Jones, E. (2009). Anger is an approach-related affect: Evidence and implications. *Psychological Bulletin, 135,* 183–204.

Chaix, B. (2009). Geographic life environments and coronary heart disease: A literature review, theoretical contributions, methodological updates, and a research agenda. *Annual Review of Public Health, 30,* 81–105.

Chida, Y., & Steptoe, A. (2010). Greater cardiovascular responses to laboratory mental stress are associated with poor subsequent cardiovascular risk status: A meta-analysis of prospective evidence. *Hypertension, 55,* 1026–1032.

Clark, D.A., Cook, A., & Snow, D. (1998). Depressive symptom differences in hospitalized medically ill, depressed psychiatric inpatients, and nonmedical controls. *Journal of Abnormal Psychology, 107,* 38–48.

Cohen, J. (1992). A power primer. *Psychological Bulletin, 112,* 155–159.

Costa, P.T., Jr., & McCrae, R.R. (1987). Neuroticism, somatic complaints, and disease: Is the bark worse than the bite? *Journal of Personality, 55,* 299–316.

Costa, P.T., Jr., & McCrae, R.R. (1992). *Professional manual: Revised NEO Personality Inventory (NEO-PI-R) and the NEO Five-Factor Inventory (NEO-FFI).* Odessa, FL: Psychological Assessment Resources.

Coyne, J.C. (1994). Self-reported distress: Analog or ersatz depression? *Psychological Bulletin, 116,* 29–45.

Coyne, J.C., & Gotlib, J. (1983). The role of cognition in depression: A critical review. *Psychological Bulletin, 94,* 472–505.

Cronbach, L.J. (1951). Coefficient alpha and the internal structure of tests. *Psychometrika, 16,* 297–334.

Cronbach, L.J., & Meehl, P.E. (1955). Construct validity in psychological tests. *Psychological Bulletin, 52,* 281–302.

Dawes, R.M., & Smith, T.L. (1985). Attitude and opinion measurement. In G. Lindzey & E. Aronson (Eds.), *The handbook of social psychology* (3rd ed., Vol. 1, pp. 509–566). New York: Random House.

DeMarco, A., & DeMarco, M. (2010). Conceptualization and measurement of the neighborhood in rural settings: A systematic review of the literature. *Journal of Community Psychology, 38,* 99–114.

Eid, M., Lischetzke, T., Nussbeck, F.W., & Trierweiler, L.I. (2003). Separating trait effects from trait-specific method effects in multitrait-multimethod models: A multiple-indicator CT-C(M-1) model. *Psychological Methods, 8,* 38–60.

Engel, G.L. (1977). The need for a new medical model: A challenge for biomedicine. *Science, 196,* 129–136.

Fechner-Bates, S., Coyne, J.C., & Schwenk, T.L. (1994). The relationship of self-reported distress to depressive disorders and other psychopathology. *Journal of Consulting and Clinical Psychology, 62,* 550–559.

Friedman, H.S., & Booth-Kewley, S. (1987). The "disease-prone personality": A meta-analytic view of the construct. *American Psychologist, 42,* 539–555.

Freidman, H.S., Tucker, J.S., & Reise, S.P. (1995). Personality dimensions and measures potentially related to health: A focus on hostility. *Annals of Behavioral Medicine, 17,* 245–251.

Funk, S. (1992). Hardiness: A review of theory and research. *Health Psychology, 11,* 333–345.

Gallo, L.C., & Smith, T.W. (1998). Construct validation of health-relevant personality units: Interpersonal circumplex and five-factor model analyses of the aggression questionnaire. *International Journal of Behavioral Medicine, 5,* 129–147.

Gentry, W.D. (Ed). (1984). *Handbook of behavioral medicine.* New York: Guilford.

Glasgow, R.E., Mullooly, J.P., Vogt, T.M., Stevens, V.J., Lichetenstein, E., Hollis, J.F., et al. (1993). Biochemical validation of smoking status in public health setting: Pros, cons and data from four low-intensity intervention trials. *Addictive Behaviors, 18,* 511–527.

Holmes, T.H., & Rahe, R.H. (1967). The social readjustment rating scale. *Journal of Psychosomatic Research, 14,* 213–218.

Huget, A., Stinson, J., & McGrath, P. (2010). Measurement of self-reported pain intensity in children and adolescents. *Journal of Psychosomatic Research, 64,* 329–336.

Hull, J.G., Lehn, D.A., & Tedlie, J.C. (1991). A general approach to testing multifaceted personality constructs. *Journal of Personality and Social Psychology, 61,* 932–945.

Idler, E.L., & Benyamini, Y. (1997). Self-rated health and mortality: A review of twenty-seven community studies. *Journal of Health and Social Behavior, 38,* 21–37.

John, O.P., & Benet-Martinez, V. (2000). Measurement: Reliability, construct validation, and scale construction. In H.T. Reis & C.M. Judd (Eds.), *Handbook of research methods in social and personality psychology* (pp. 339–369). Cambridge, England: Cambridge University Press.

Judd, C.M., & McClelland, G.H. (1998). Measurement. In D.T. Gilbert, S.T. Fiske, & G. Lindzey (Eds.), *Handbook of social psychology* (Vol. 2, pp. 180–232). Boston: McGraw-Hill.

Kahneman, D., Krueger, A.B., Schkade, D.A., Schwartz, N., & Stone, A.A. (2005). A survey method for characterizing daily life experiences: The day reconstruction method. *Science, 306,* 1776–1780.

Kamarck, T.W., Jennings, J.J., Pogue-Geile, M., & Manuck, S.B. (1994). A multidimensional measurement model for cardiovascular reactivity: Stability and cross-validation in two adult samples. *Health Psychology, 13,* 471–478.

Kaplan, R.M. (1994). The Ziggy theorem: Toward an outcomes-focused health psychology. *Health Psychology, 13,* 451–460.

Kaplan, R.M., & Frosch, D.L. (2005). Decision making in medicine and health care. *Annual Review of Clinical Psychology, 1,* 525–556.

Kaplan, R.M., & Groessel, E.J. (2002). Applications of cost-effectiveness methodologies in behavioral medicine. *Journal of Consulting and Clinical Psychology, 70,* 482–493.

Karoly, P. (Ed.). (1985) Measurement strategies in health psychology. New York: Wiley.

Kazdin, A.E. (2006). Arbitrary metrics: Implications for identifying evidence-based treatments. *American Psychologist, 61,* 42–49.

Keefe, F.J., & Blumenthal, J.A. (Eds.). (1982). *Assessment strategies in behavioral medicine.* New York: Grune and Stratton.

Ketterer, M.W., Denollet, J., Chapp, J., Thayer, B., Keteyian, S., Clark, V., et al. (2004). Men deny and women cry, but who dies? Do the wages of "denial" include early ischemic coronary disease? *Journal of Psychosomatic Research, 56,* 119–121.

Kihlstrom, J.F., Eich, E., Sandbrand, D., & Tobias, B.A. (2000). Emotion and memory: Implications for self-report. In A.A. Stone, J.S. Turkkan, C.A. Bachrach, J.B. Jobe, H.S. Kurtzman, & V.S. Cain (Eds.), *The science of self-report: Implications for research and practice* (pp. 81–99). Mahwah, NJ: Erlbaum.

Kobasa, S.C. (1979). Stressful life events, personality and health: An inquiry into hardiness. *Journal of Personality and Social Psychology, 37,* 1–11.

Lett, H.S., Blumenthal, J.A., Babyak, M.A., Sherwood, A., Strauman, T., Robins, C., et al. (2004). Depression as a risk factor for coronary artery disease: Evidence, mechanisms, and treatment. *Psychosomatic Medicine, 66,* 305–315.

Loevinger, J. (1957). Objective tests as instruments of psychological theory. *Psychological Reports, 3,* 635–694.

Manuck, S.B. (1994). Cardiovascular reactivity in cardiovascular disease: "Once more unto the breach." *International Journal of Behavioral Medicine, 1,* 4–31.

Marsh, H.W., & Grayson, D. (1995). Latent variable models of multitrait-multimethod data. In R.H. Hoyle (Ed.), *Structural equation modeling: Concepts, issues, and applications* (pp. 177–198). Thousand Oaks, CA: Sage.

Marshall, G.N., Wortman, C.B., Vickers, R.R., Kusulas, J.W., & Hervig, L.K. (1994). The five-factor model as a framework for personality-health research. *Journal of Personality and Social Psychology, 67,* 278–286.

Maddison, R., & Mhuchu, C. (2009). Global positioning system: A new opportunity in physical activity measurement. *International Journal of Behavioral Nutrition and Physical Activity, 6* (November 4), ArticleID73.

Matthews, K.A., Gallo, L.C., & Taylor, S.E. (2010). Are psychosocial factors mediators of socioeconomic status and health connections? A progress report and blueprint for the future. *Annals of the New York Academy of Sciences, 1186,* 146–173.

McFall, R.M. (2005). Theory and utility—key themes in evidence-based assessment: Comment on the special section. *Psychological Assessment, 17,* 312–323.

McFall, R.M., & Treat, T.A. (1999). Quantifying the information value of clinical assessments with signal detection theory. *Annual Review of Psychology, 50,* 215–241.

McGee, D.L., Liao, Y.L. Cao, G.C., & Cooper, R.S. (1999). Self-reported health status and mortality in a multi-ethnic U.S. cohort. *American Journal of Epidemiology, 149,* 41–46.

Meehl, P.E. (1978). Theoretical risks and tabular asterisks: Sir Karl, Sir Ronald, and the slow progress of soft psychology. *Journal of Consulting and Clinical Psychology, 46,* 806–834.

Menon, G., & Yorkston, E.A. (2000). The use of memory and contextual cues in the formation of behavioral frequency judgments. In A.A. Stone, J.S. Turkkan, C.A. Bachrach, J.B. Jobe, H.S. Kurtzman, & V.S. Cain (Eds.), *The science of self-report: Implications for research and practice* (pp. 63–79). Mahwah, NJ: Erlbaum.

Messick, S. (1989). Validity. In R.L. Linn (Ed.), *Educational measurement* (3rd ed., pp. 13–104). New York: Macmillan.

Messick, S. (1995). Validity of psychological assessment: Validation of inferences from persons' responses and performances as scientific inquiry into score meaning. *American Psychologist, 50,* 741–749.

Miller, S.M., Shoda, Y., & Hurley, K. (1996). Applying social-cognitive theory to health protective behavior: Breast self-examination in cancer screening. *Psychological Bulletin, 119,* 70–94.

Mischel, W., & Shoda, Y. (1995). A cognitive-affective system theory of personality: Reconceptualizing situations, dispositions, dynamics, and invariance in personality structure. *Psychological Review, 102,* 246–268.

Mohr, D.C., Goodkin, D.E., Likosky, W., Beutler, L., Gatto, N., & Langan, M.K. (1997). Identification of Beck Depression Inventory items related to multiple sclerosis. *Journal of Behavioral Medicine, 20,* 407–414.

Nicotera, N. (2007). Measuring neighborhood: A conundrum for human services researchers and practitioners. *American Journal of Community Psychology, 40,* 26–51.

O'Donnell, K., & Chung, J.Y. (1997). The diagnosis of major depression in end-stage renal disease. *Psychotherapy and Psychosomatics, 66,* 38–43.

Ozer, D.J. (1999). Four principles for personality assessment. In L.A. Pervin & O.P. John (Eds.), *Handbook of personality: Theory and research* (pp. 671–686). New York: Guilford.

Park, T.L., Adams, S.G., & Lynch, J. (1998). Sociodemographic factors in health psychology research: 12 years in review. *Health Psychology, 17,* 381–383.

Patrick, D.L., Cheadle, A., Thompson, D.C., Diebr, P., Koepsell, T., & Kinne, S. (1994). The validity of self-reported smoking: A review and meta-analysis. *American Journal of Public Health, 84,* 1086–1093.

Paulhus, D.L. (1991). Measurement and control of response bias. In J.P. Robinson, P.R. Shaver, & L.S. Wrightsman (Eds.), *Measures of personality and social psychological attitudes* (pp. 17–59). San Diego, CA: Academic Press.

Peck, J.R., Smith, T.W., Ward, J.R., & Milano, R. (1989). Disability and depression in rheumatoid arthritis: A multitrait, multi-method investigation. *Arthritis and Rheumatism 32*, 1100–1106.

Pennebaker, J.W. (2000). Psychological factors influencing the reporting of physical symptoms. In A.A. Stone, J.S. Turkkan, C.A. Bachrach, J.B. Jobe, H.S. Kurtzman, & V.S. Cain (Eds.), *The science of self-report: Implications for research and practice* (pp. 299–315). Mahwah, NJ: Erlbaum.

Popper, K. (1959). *The logic of scientific discovery.* New York: Basic Books.

Porter, L.S., Stone, A.A., & Schwartz, J.E. (1999). Anger expression and ambulatory blood pressure: A comparison of state and trait measures. *Psychosomatic Medicine, 61,* 454–463.

Schaeffer, N.C. (2000). Asking questions about threatening topics: A selective overview. In A.A. Stone, J.S. Turkkan, C.A. Bachrach, J.B. Jobe, H.S. Kurtzman, & V.S. Cain (Eds.), *The science of self-report: Implications for research and practice* (pp.105–121). Mahwah, NJ: Erlbaum.

Schmidt, K.M., & Embretson, S.E. (2003). Item response theory and measuring abilities. In I.B. Weiner (Series Ed.), J.A. Schinka & W. Velicer (Vol. Ed.), *Comprehensive handbook of psychology. Vol. 2: Research methods* (pp. 429–446). Hoboken, NJ: Wiley.

Schroeder, K.E., Carey, M.P., & Vanable, P.A. (2003a). Methodological challenges in research on sexual risk behavior: I. Item content, scaling, and data analytic options. *Annals of Behavioral Medicine, 26,* 76–103.

Schroeder, K.E., Carey, M.P., & Vanable, P.A. (2003b). Methodological challenges in research on sexual risk behavior: II. Accuracy of self-reports. *Annals of Behavioral Medicine, 26,* 104–123.

Schwartz, J.E., Neale, J., Marco, C., Shiffman, S.S., & Stone, A.A. (1999). Does trait coping exist? A momentary assessment approach to the evaluation of traits. *Journal of Personality and Social Psychology, 77,* 360–369.

Shen, B.-J., Todaro, J.F., Niaura, R., McCaffery, J.M., Zhang, J., Spiro, A, & Ward, K.D. (2003). Are metabolic risk factors one unified syndrome? Modeling the structure of the metabolic syndrome X. *American Journal of Epidemiology, 157,* 701–711.

Shiffman, S. (2000). Real-time self-report of momentary states in the natural environment: Computerized ecological momentary assessment. In A.A. Stone, J.S. Turkkan, C.A. Bachrach, J.B. Jobe, H.S. Kurtzman, & V.S. Cain (Eds.), *The science of self-report: Implications for research and practice* (pp. 277–298). Mahwah, NJ: Erlbaum.

Siegler, I.C., Bastain, L.A., Steffens, D.C., Bosworth, H.B., & Costa, P.T. (2002). Behavioral medicine and aging. *Journal of Consulting and Clinical Psychology, 70,* 843–851.

Smith, G.T. (2005). On construct validity: Issues of method and measurement. *Psychological Assessment, 17,* 396–408.

Smith, T.W. (1992). Hostility and health: Current status of a psychosomatic hypothesis. *Health Psychology, 11,* 139–150.

Smith, T.W. (2003). Health psychology. In I.B. Weiner (Series Ed.), J.A. Schinka & W. Velicer (Vol. Ed.), *Comprehensive handbook of psychology, Vol. 2: Research methods* (pp. 241–270). Hoboken, NJ: Wiley.

Smith, T.W., & Christensen, A.J. (1996). Positive and negative affect in rheumatoid arthritis: Increased specificity in the assessment of emotional adjustment. *Annals of Behavioral Medicine, 18,* 75–78.

Smith, T.W., & Gallo, L.C. (2001). Personality traits as risk factors for physical illness. In A. Baum, T. Revenson, & J. Singer (Eds.), *Handbook of health psychology.* Hillside, NJ: Erlbaum.

Smith, T.W., Orleans, T., & Jenkins, D. (2004). Prevention and health promotion: Decades of progress, new challenges, and an emerging agenda. *Health Psychology, 23,* 126–131.

Smith, T.W., & Uchino, B.N. (2008). Measuring physiological processes in biopsychosocial research: basic principles amid growing complexity. In L.J. Lueken & L.C. Gallo (Eds.), *Handbook of physiological research methods in health psychology* (pp. 11–33). Thousand Oaks, CA: Sage.

Smith, T.W., Uchino, B.N., Berg, C.A., Florsheim, P., Pearce, G., Hawkins, M., Henry, N., Beveridge, R., Skinner, M., Hopkins, P.N., & Yoon, H.C. (2008). Self-reports and spouse ratings of negative affectivity, dominance and affiliation in coronary artery disease: Where should we look and who should we ask when studying personality and health? *Health Psychology, 27,* 676–684.

Smith, T.W., & Williams, P.G. (1992). Personality and health: Advantages and limitations of the five-factor model. *Journal of Personality, 60,* 395–423.

Solans, M., Pane, S., Estrada, M., Serra-Sutton, V., Berra, S., Herdman, M., Alonso, J., & Rajil, L. (2008). Health-related quality of life measurement in children and adolescents: A systematic review of generic and disease-specific instruments. *Value in Health, 11,* 742–764.

Steptoe, A. (2007). *Depression and physical illness.* Cambridge, UK: Cambridge University Press.

Stevens, S.S. (1951). Mathematics, measurement, and psychophysics. In S.S. Stevens (Ed.), *Handbook of experimental psychology* (pp. 1–49). New York: Wiley.

Stevens, S.S. (1959). Measurement, psychophysics, and utility. In C.W. Christensen & P. Ratoosh (Eds.), *Measurement: Definitions and theories* (pp. 18–63). New York: Wiley.

Stevens, S.S. (1968). Measurement, statistics, and the schemapiric view. *Science, 161,* 849–856.

Stone, A.A., Broderick, J.E., Shiffman, S.S., & Schwartz, J.E. (2004). Understanding recall of weekly pain from a momentary assessment perspective: Absolute agreement, between- and within-person consistency, and judged change in weekly pain. *Pain, 107,* 61–69.

Stone A.A., Schwartz, J.E., Neale, J.M., Shiffman, S. Marco, C. Hickox, M., et. al. (1998). A comparison of coping assessed by ecological momentary assessment and retrospective recall. *Journal of Personality and Social Psychology, 74,* 1670–1680.

Stone, A.A., & Shiffman, S. (2002). Capturing momentary, self-report data: A proposal for reporting guidelines. *Annals of Behavioral Medicine, 24,* 236–243.

Stone, A.A., Turkkan, J.S., Bachrach, C.A., Jobe, J.B., Kurtzman, H.S., & Cain, V.S. (Eds.). (2000). *The science of self-report: Implications for research and practice.* Mahwah, NJ: Erlbaum.

Strauss, M.E., & Smith, G.T. (2009). Construct validity: Advances in theory and methodology. *Annual Review of Clinical Psychology, 5,* 1–25.

Strik, J., Honig, A., Lousberg, R., & Denollet, J. (2001). Sensitivity and specificity of observer and self-report questionnaires in major and minor depression following myocardial infarction. *Psychosomatics, 42,* 423–428.

Suls, J., & Bunde, J. (2005). Anger, anxiety, and depression as risk factors for cardiovascular disease: The problems and implications of overlapping affective disposition. *Psychological Bulletin, 131,* 260–300.

Suls, J., & Rothman, A. (2004). Evolution of the biopsychosocial model: Prospects and challenges for health psychology. *Health Psychology, 23,* 119–125.

Tourangeau, R. (2000). Remembering what happened: Memory errors and survey reports. In A.A. Stone, J.S. Turkkan, C.A. Bachrach, J.B. Jobe, H.S. Kurtzman, & V.S. Cain (Eds.), *The science of self-report: Implications for research and practice* (pp. 29–47). Mahwah, NJ: Erlbaum.

Von Bertalanffy, L. (1968). *General systems theory.* New York: Braziller.

Watson, D., & Tellegen, A. (1983). Toward a consensual structure of mood. *Psychological Bulletin, 98,* 219–225.

West, S.G., & Finch, J.F. (1997). Personality measurement: Reliability and validity issues. In R. Hogan, J. Johnson, & S. Briggs (Eds.), *Handbook of personality psychology* (pp. 143–164). Dallas, TX: Academic Press.

Whitfield, K.E., Weidner, G., Clark, R., & Anderson, N.B. (2002). Sociodemographic diversity and behavioral medicine. *Journal of Consulting and Clinical Psychology, 70,* 463–481.

Williams, P.G., Holmbeck, G.N., & Greenley, R.N. (2002). Adolescent health psychology. *Journal of Consulting and Clinical Psychology, 70,* 828–842.

Williams, R.B., Jr., Barefoot, J.C., & Shekelle, R.B. (1985). The health consequences of hostility. In M.A. Chesney & R.H. Rosenman (Eds.), *Anger and hostility in cardiovascular and behavioral disorders* (pp. 173–185). New York: Hemisphere.

Yali, A.M., & Revenson, T.A. (2004). How changes in population demographics will impact health psychology: Incorporating a broader notion of cultural competence into the field. *Health Psychology, 23,* 147–155.

Zautra, A., Burleson, M., Smith, C., Blalock, S., Wallston, K., BeVellis, R, et al. (1995). Arthritis and perceptions of quality of life: An examination of positive and negative affect in rheumatoid arthritis patients. *Health Psychology, 14,* 399–408.

# Designing and Conducting Interventions to Enhance Physical and Mental Health Outcomes

J. Lee Westmaas, Virginia Gil-Rivas, *and* Roxane Cohen Silver

**Abstract**

Health-focused interventions can prevent the devastating effects of many illnesses by encouraging changes in behavior. Interventions that recognize the multiple influences on behavior will have the greatest likelihood of success, but increased sensitivity to their costs, convenience, and reach has led to innovative new treatments, for example internet programs for post-traumatic stress disorder or smoking cessation. Nonetheless, although the landscape in which interventions can be delivered has changed, attention to principles of design and methodology remain the same. This chapter describes proven scientific methods in designing and evaluating interventions, and illustrates how understanding the causes of illnesses and health, and using theoretically driven and multilevel approaches to develop interventions, can save lives by promoting health and preventing illness.

**Keywords:** Interventions, mental health, physical health, methods, research design, theory

Coronary heart disease, cancers, and infectious diseases are among the top ten leading causes of death in both high-income and developing countries (WHO, 2008), but are largely preventable. Tobacco use, for example, was responsible for an estimated 5 million deaths worldwide in 2000 (Ezzati & Lopez, 2003), with 30% of these deaths due to cancers for which tobacco was a contributing factor (Ezzati, Henley, Lopez, & Thun, 2005). In addition, although human immunodeficiency virus (HIV) infection has been known for more than a decade to be mostly preventable by behaviors such as using a condom, in 2009, approximately 2.6 million people became infected with HIV, and 1.8 million deaths worldwide were due to acquired immune deficiency syndrome (AIDS)-related diseases (UNAIDS, 2010). These sobering statistics point out the need to develop—and the challenge of developing—effective interventions to promote health and prevent illness.

Although the task of persuading thousands or millions of people to change their behaviors may seem daunting, this is not an unrealistic goal. When the surgeon general announced that cigarette smoking was a leading cause of cancer in 1964, approximately 42% of the U.S. population smoked (Centers for Disease Control [CDC], 2004). Through a combination of laws restricting smoking in public places, advertising bans, tobacco taxes, the development of treatment programs for smoking cessation, and advances in pharmacotherapies, the rate of smoking in the United States in 2004 was reduced to approximately 21% (CDC, 2005), a 50% reduction in prevalence. In the early years of the AIDS epidemic in the United States, the increase in safer-sex activities among gay men that accompanied messages about the dangers of unprotected sex was also a remarkable example of the effectiveness of behavior change interventions (Revenson & Schiaffino, 2000; Shilts, 1987). However, the later increases in HIV risk behaviors among men who have sex with men (CDC, 2007; Williamson, Dodds, Mercey, Johnson, & Hart, 2006) and the increases in smoking rates observed among high school students in the 1990s (CDC, 1999), and among college students in the 2000s (Rigotti, Lee, & Wechsler, 2000; Wechsler, Kelley, Seibring, Juo, & Rigotti, 2001), demonstrate that effective prevention interventions need to be attuned to the dynamic, ongoing, and complex nature of human behavior. This chapter presents important conceptual and practical issues in designing and implementing behavioral and psychological interventions whose goal is to promote mental and physical health and prevent illness. Our aim is not to present a comprehensive review of each of these issues (readers will be provided with references to articles that provide more in-depth discussions) but to direct attention to their importance and their implications for conducting effective or informative prevention interventions. Examples that illustrate topics under discussion will be taken from the smoking cessation and HIV-prevention literatures, not only because of the substantial morbidity and mortality associated with smoking and HIV infection, but also because these topics have generated a substantial amount of research demonstrating the challenges of conducting effective prevention interventions.

## Primary, Secondary, and Tertiary Interventions

Interventions can be identified by the point along the health–illness continuum at which they occur. *Primary* prevention focuses on changing behaviors to prevent illness from occurring. For example, a primary prevention program for HIV-negative individuals would aim to prevent infection by promoting the use of condoms and other safe-sex strategies. *Secondary* prevention interventions occur after the individual has been diagnosed with a condition, disease, or illness and seek to stop or reverse its progression. In the case of HIV, a secondary prevention intervention would focus on behavior change to prevent other strains of the virus from infecting those already infected. Current health policy emphasizes secondary prevention, although it has been argued that devoting more resources to primary intervention might benefit population health more substantially (Kaplan, 2000). *Tertiary* prevention interventions seek to control the devastating complications of an illness or negative health condition. An intervention to get hospitalized cancer patients to give up smoking to promote recovery from their surgery is an example of a tertiary prevention intervention.

## Levels of Interventions
### *Population-level Interventions*

Interventions to promote health and prevent illness can also attempt to influence behavior at the individual,

organizational, community, or societal level. Action at the societal (population) level represents the broadest level of influence; interventions focused on this level of influence seek to motivate entire communities that differ on sociodemographic and other dimensions. These interventions may use the media and social organizations to educate and encourage people to adopt healthy behaviors and discourage unhealthy ones. For example, advertisements by the government of Canada encouraging physical activity in its populace (the ParticipAction campaign in the 1970s, 1980s, and 1990s) emphasized the positive health benefits of exercise and were expected to be viewed and acted upon regardless of age, gender, or socioeconomic status (Canadian Public Health Association, 2004). Population-based efforts usually involve simple messages that can be understood by the majority of a society's members. On their own, however, they can be less effective than other approaches in changing individual behavior. Population approaches can sometimes be cost-effective, however. If only a tiny fraction of the population is motivated to change its behavior as a result of the message, the cost savings resulting from the prevention of illness among these individuals can be significantly greater than the cost of the intervention (Thompson, Cornonado, Snipes, & Puschel, 2003).

Population-wide interventions also include laws that mandate health-promoting behaviors, for example, seat belt use, the wearing of protective headgear for motorcyclists in some jurisdictions, or laws restricting smoking in the workplace. These interventions can lead to behavior change not only by increasing levels of perceived threat but also by influencing individuals' attitudes, beliefs, and appraisals. At the interpersonal level, these campaigns may result in changes in social attitudes and norms that may further contribute to behavioral change. A population-level policy aimed at changing behavior can also be the final trigger for action among individuals contemplating behavioral change as a result of other prevention efforts. For example, in 2009, Virginia enacted a law to ban smoking in restaurants that, together with an increase in federal cigarette taxes, most likely led to the overwhelming increase in calls to Quitlines from Virginia smokers who decided it was time to quit (Brown, 2009).

### *Community- and Organizational-level Interventions*

Less broad in their reach are community and organizational activities that seek to promote healthy behavior in their members. Many community interventions have adopted a social ecological perspective, recognizing that behavior change is a result of social and environmental influences. The program components of community-level interventions are often supported by the results of individual-level or clinic-based research. Indeed, it has been argued that the costs of community-wide programs to promote healthy behaviors are justifiable only if prior research supports program components (Sorensen, Emmons, Hunt, & Johnston, 1998). An example of a community intervention to prevent the uptake of smoking in youth was the Healthy for Life Project conducted in the United States. Recognizing the various social influences on smoking, the intervention targeted peers, schools, and parents, as well as community agencies (Piper, 2000). A justification for the use of community prevention approaches is based on the concept of *population-attributable* risk, which refers to how much risk produces a given amount of disease in a population (Rose, 1985). According to the epidemiologist Geoffrey Rose (1992), changing the risk levels of a population to a small degree can impact public health more strongly than substantially changing the risk of a smaller number of people.

Some interventions are limited to specific institutions, such as work sites or schools. Considering that many individuals spend a substantial amount of time at places of employment or education, the proliferation of work site and school programs addressing a wide range of health issues, such as smoking, weight loss, and physical activity, is not surprising.

### Individual-level Interventions

In contrast to population-, community-, or organizational-level interventions, individual-level interventions are characterized by higher levels of personal interaction between the targets of the interventions and their providers, and they are more likely to be based on psychosocial or biomedical explanations for behavior. Many programs to reduce college student drinking, a significant cause of injuries, assaults, and deaths in this population, are individual-level interventions. The content of such interventions are typically dictated by specific theoretical orientations regarding behavior change. Further, the personal interaction afforded by individual-level interventions allows for the tailoring of their content to the unique characteristics of those targeted. A recent meta-analysis of individual-level interventions for alcohol abuse among undergraduates, some of which included tailored feedback, found them to be effective in reducing consumption and alcohol-related problems (Carey, Scott-Sheldon, Carey, & DeMartini, 2007). Family members or friends can also become involved in individual-level approaches. For example, an intervention to get tobacco chewers to quit enlisted the help of spouses to provide social support (i.e., be positive and noncritical) during abstinence (Danaher et al., 2009).

Advocates of ecological models of health promotion interventions recommend an integration of these various levels of influence in any effort to change health behaviors (Stokols, 2000). Nonetheless, the decision as to whether an intervention should be at the individual, community, or population level, and whether it should be primary, secondary, or tertiary, will be influenced by a number of factors. These include the amount of financial resources available, political considerations, findings from prior prevention/intervention research, the likelihood of community cooperation, and the believed causes of the behavior or illness in question. An important first step, however, is to understand the various influences on the illness- or health-promoting behavior and to use a theoretical model to guide the design and implementation of the intervention.

### Psychosocial and Other Pathways to Disease

Research in the last three decades has provided convincing evidence of the contribution of psychosocial, biological, and behavioral factors in illness and health, and several theories to explain these associations have been elaborated (Schneiderman, 2004). Understanding how these factors independently and interactively contribute to health is an important step in deciding when and how to intervene and who may be best helped by an intervention. Having a theoretical model as a template from which to understand the influence of these variables on health and behavior change is important in designing and implementing a successful and cost-effective intervention (Glanz & Bishop, 2010).

### Theoretical Models of Health Behavior Change

To date, prevention intervention efforts have been largely guided by individual-level theories that focus on social and cognitive variables (Kohler, Grimley, & Reynolds, 1999; Rutter & Quine, 2002) and that can also be characterized as decision-oriented theories.

These theories view individuals' health behaviors as the result of conscious decision-making processes based on considerations such as one's appraisals of one's susceptibility, or the severity of a threat. They include the health belief model (HBM; Rosentock, Strecher, & Becker, 1994); the theories of reasoned action (Ajzen & Fishbein, 1977, 1980) and planned behavior (Ajzen, 1991, 1988); social cognitive (learning) theory (Bandura, 1998, 2004); and the transtheoretical model of change (TTM; Prochaska & DiClemente, 1983). Although there is evidence that some of the constructs in health behavior theories individually predict behavior change, there are questions as to whether further testing of the theories will advance understanding of health behaviors. Noar and Zimmerman (2005) note that there is considerable overlap in their constructs, despite different terminology. They also argue that the theories are not falsifiable, that there is little consensus on whether one theory is more accurate than another in predicting a particular health behavior, and that the field would be better served if studies or interventions focused on *comparing* theories rather than testing a particular theory. Indeed, some recent work has been aimed at comparing the predictive ability of various theories (see Bish, Sutton, & Golombok, 2000; McClenahan, Shevlin, Adamson, Bennet, & O'Neill, 2007). Moreover, examining whether a particular theory may apply to specific health behaviors, among specific populations, or only in certain contexts would help advance their utility in designing interventions.

### Health Behavior Theories

One of the earliest and arguably the most researched health behavior theory is the HBM (Rosentock et al. 1994). According to the HBM, if people feel threatened by the prospect of an event occurring (e.g., skin cancer), and perceive both that the threat is severe enough and that the benefits of engaging in protective or preventative behavior (e.g., wearing sunscreen) outweigh the costs or barriers, they will engage in protective behavior(s). Prompting behavior change are cues to action (e.g., experiencing symptoms, or exposure to health messages). The HBM has been used to predict a variety of health behaviors, such as breast self-examination (Champion, 1994), safe-sex practices (Zimmerman & Olson, 1994), and exercise (Corwyn & Benda, 1999), among others. Although the HBM has been widely used, the relationship between key elements of the model and behavior change are rather modest (Abraham & Sheeran, 2005), suggesting the need to consider the

influence of factors in addition to those central to the model. More recently, this model has been extended to include principles of social-cognitive theory (i.e., self-efficacy, locus of control) in an effort to increase its predictive ability (Abraham & Sheeran, 2005; Gillibrand & Stevenson, 2006).

Social-cognitive (learning) theory (Bandura, 1998, 2004) posits five key contributors to health behavior, namely, knowledge of health risks and benefits, self-efficacy, outcome expectations, goals, and perceptions of barriers and aids to change. Prevention intervention programs based on social-cognitive theory typically include an informational component to increase perceptions of the risks and benefits associated with a particular behavior, as well as teaching social and cognitive skills that can be used to initiate behavior change, building self-efficacy to promote behavior maintenance, and building social support to sustain change (Kohler et al., 1999). Self-efficacy (one's perceived ability to take the action necessary to achieve the desired effects or outcomes) is viewed as the most important component as it has direct and indirect effects on all other key determinants of behavior (Bandura, 2004). Self-efficacy beliefs are the result of direct and vicarious experience and verbal persuasion. For example, an overweight person's self-efficacy beliefs about his ability to lose weight is likely to be higher if he observes a similar peer who has lost weight, if he has lost weight on a previous occasion, and if a health professional persuades him that it is possible to lose weight with appropriate exercise and diet regimes, compared to someone who has not had these experiences. Bandura (1998) suggests that self-efficacy beliefs play an influential role in health in two ways: (a) by influencing biological pathways (i.e., sympathetic nervous system activation, immune functioning) involved in the relationship between stress and illness, and (b) by its impact on individuals' decisions to make behavioral changes, their motivation to maintain these changes, and their ability to resume those efforts when they face a setback. For example, higher levels of diet-related self-efficacy should lead to dietary changes, as well as to reducing the stress levels and sympathetic activation that in turn decrease urges to consume foods high in fat and carbohydrates. These processes in turn would be posited to maintain the dietary changes.

Social learning theory also proposes that outcome expectations regarding the physical effects of a health behavior (e.g., discomfort), the social reactions it evokes (i.e., whether others reinforce or punish the change), and self-evaluative reactions to one's behavior are important influences on behavior (Bandura, 2004). Also important are barriers to the initiation and maintenance of behavioral change, which can be internal (such as whether the individual has the resources and skills needed), situational, or the result of larger social and structural factors. For example, having many friends who smoke would constitute a structural barrier for a smoker who wants to quit, whereas occasionally being offered cigarettes would be a situational barrier.

An extensive body of research has documented the influence of self-efficacy beliefs in implementing and maintaining health behavior changes. These include dietary changes (McCann et al., 1995), physical activity and exercise adherence (McAuley, Jerome, Marquez, Elavsky, & Blissmer, 2003; Plotnikoff, Lippke, Courneya, Birkett, & Sigal, 2008), preventive health behaviors (Myers & Horswill, 2006), smoking cessation (Shiffman et al., 2000), condom use (Baele, Dusseldorp, & Maes, 2001), alcohol use (Maisto, Connors, & Zywiak, 2000), and drug use (Reilly et al., 1995).

In contrast to the centrality of self-efficacy in the HBM, a strong *intention* to change is a primary motivating factor in the theories of reasoned action (TRA; Ajzen & Fishbein, 1977, 1980) and planned behavior [TPB]; Ajzen, 1988, 1991). Behavioral intentions, in turn, are predicted by (a) expectations that a behavior will produce a particular outcome and the evaluation of that outcome (behavioral beliefs), (b) beliefs about what others think is appropriate behavior (normative beliefs) and motivation to comply with others' opinions (subjective norms), and (c) beliefs about the existence of factors that may facilitate or impede behavior and the power of these factors (control beliefs) (Ajzen, 2002). The relative contribution of each component of the model to intentions and behavior is posited to vary across behaviors and populations (Fishbein, 2000). Furthermore, behavior is expected to be predicted not only by intentions, but also by the amount of actual control individuals' have over the behavior (Ajzen, 2002). For example, an individual may be more likely to have an annual mammogram if she thinks that mammograms permit early detection of breast cancer, if she believes that members of her social network have annual mammograms, and if she believes that few barriers exist to obtaining a mammogram.

The TPB has garnered a great deal of research attention, and the empirical evidence supports its utility for predicting intentions and behavior (Armitage & Conner, 2001). Health interventions guided by TPB have shown weak to moderate associations between key elements of the theory and condom use (Albarracin, Johnson, Fishbein, & Muellerleile, 2001; Fishbein et al., 2001), contraceptive use (Adler, Kegeles, Irwin, & Wibbelsman, 1990), initiation (Abraham & Sheeran, 2004) and maintenance of physical activity (Armitage, 2005), alcohol use (Johnston & White, 2003; Norman, Armitage, & Quigley, 2007), preventive health screening (Bish et al., 2000; Sheeran, Conner, & Norman, 2001), and smoking (Higgins & Conner, 2003), among others.

Another theory of health behavior change that has elicited a substantial amount of research in a variety of health domains is the TTM (Prochaska & DiClemente, 1983). Key constructs include stages of change, the process of change, decisional balance (pros and cons of change), and situational self-efficacy. The stages of change are precontemplation (not ready to change within the next 6 months), contemplation (thinking about change within the next 6 months), preparation (ready to change in the next 30 days), action, and maintenance (more than 6 months of sustained action). The TTM has been used to predict a wide range of health behaviors, including alcohol and drug use (Prochaska, DiClemente, & Norcross, 1992), physical activity (Marshall & Biddle, 2001), and sexual risk behaviors (Grimley, Prochaska, & Prochaska, 1993).

The TTM also posits that tailoring interventions to individuals' readiness to change based on their current stage will be more likely to produce behavioral changes compared to using interventions not matched to individuals' stage. For example, in a TTM stage-matched intervention, smokers in the precontemplation stage would receive information regarding the causes and consequences of smoking, whereas those in the preparation stage would receive more immediate advice on quitting, such as how to substitute healthy behaviors for smoking, or how to avoid cues that could trigger urges. Current empirical evidence, however, provides limited support for the idea that tailoring interventions to stage-of-change facilitates stage progression (Adams & White, 2005; Bridle et al., 2005). In addition to the lack of evidence for stage-matching (cf. Aveyard, Massey, Parsons, Manaseki, & Griffin, 2009), other investigators have stated that the TTM does not fulfill criteria for a stage theory (Herzog, 2008; Herzog & Blagg, 2007) or have proposed abandoning the TTM because of this and other methodological reasons (West, 2005).

Other theoretical models guiding health promotion research include cognitive/information processing

(Joos & Hickam, 1990), social support theories (Gonzalez, Goeppinger, & Lorig, 1990), the health action process approach (Schwarzer, 2008), the common-sense model of self-regulation of health and illness (Leventhal, Brissette, & Leventhal, 2003), and the precaution adoption process model (Weinstein & Sandman, 2002).

Based on research demonstrating the value of key concepts from the preceding models in predicting behavior change, Elder, Ayala, and Harris (1999) summarized the important ingredients for successful health promotion and prevention programs. Specifically, for a person to change, she or he must "(1) have a strong positive intention or predisposition to perform a behavior; (2) face a minimum of information processing and physical, logistical, and social environmental barriers to performing the behavior; (3) perceive her-/himself as having the requisite skills for the behavior; (4) believe that material, social, or other reinforcement will follow the behavior; (5) believe that there is normative pressure to perform and none sanctioning the behavior; (6) believe that the behavior is consistent with the person's self-image; (7) have a positive affect regarding the behavior; and (8) encounter cues or enablers to engage in the behavior at the appropriate time and place" (p. 276).

## Psychological Variables Influencing Health Behaviors

In addition to the constructs from health behavior theories described above, other psychosocial variables have been singled out for their relationships with health behavior change and as the focus of interventions. Sobel (1995) argued that psychosocial variables, such as a sense of control and optimism, in addition to self-efficacy, not only directly impact health behaviors but also have direct effects on physiological processes that in turn influence health. Interventions that attempt to increase levels of these "shared determinants of health," he believes, are important in changing any health-relevant behavior but have not been given the attention they deserve. For example, although feelings of self-efficacy have been found to be an important predictor of behavior change, few interventions have been developed in which creating feelings of self-efficacy regarding the targeted behaviors is an important goal. The studies of Lorig and colleagues at the Stanford Arthritis Center were offered by Sobel as an example in which the finding that improvement in symptoms (reduced pain) was predicted most strongly by an enhanced sense of control over symptoms led to

a change in intervention focus (Lorig & Fries, 1990; Lorig et al., 1989). The result was a restructuring of the intervention to focus on enhancing feelings of self-efficacy based on achievable goals (e.g., walking up two steps rather than a whole flight of stairs), and which produced significant reductions in pain and subsequent physician visits.

Psychosocial factors unique to a population have also been targeted for interventions after being linked to health outcomes. For example, the research of Kemeny and colleagues (Cole, Kemeny, & Taylor, 1997; Kemeny, 2003) with HIV-positive patients found that negative expectancies about their future health, negative appraisals of the self, and rejection sensitivity due to HIV status or sexual orientation were important predictors of CD4 counts or rate of progression to AIDS (controlling for a variety of confounding factors such as baseline health status or immune functioning). Interventions to alter cognitive appraisals of the disease process among these men, in addition to cognitive-behavioral stress management, were found to produce significant changes in physiological parameters relevant to HIV, such as CD4 T cell levels and viral load (Schneiderman, Antoni, & Ironson, 2003).

Studies have also discovered visceral and unconscious influences on health behaviors that may be relevant to interventions aimed at changing these behaviors. The research of Ditto and colleagues indicate that bodily motivations such as sexual arousal, for example, can affect decision-making about protective health behaviors such as using a condom (Ditto, Pizarro, Epstein, Jacobson, & Macdonald, 2006). Unconscious and conscious thoughts of death, or of one's mortality, play a central role in health behavior change from a terror management theory perspective (Pyszczynski, Greenberg, & Solomon, 1999). Goldenberg and Arndt (2008) recently laid out a terror management health model in which being presented with evidence of one's mortality and consciously acknowledging this evidence leads to health protective behaviors. In contrast, unconscious thoughts triggered by less direct evidence of mortality lead to efforts to increase self-esteem and a sense of meaning rather than to behavioral change. An application of this model would dictate how health messages should be presented to maximize behavioral change.

Personality factors have also been singled out for their relationships to health (Friedman, 2000). Type A personality, and its core features of hostility and anger (Smith, Glazer, Ruiz, & Gallo, 2004), in addition to dispositional optimism (Steptoe, Wright,

Kunz-Ebrecht, & Iliffe, 2006), repressive coping (Denollet, Martens, Nyklicek, Conraads, & de Gelder, 2008), and other personality dimensions have been directly, or in interaction with social/environmental factors, linked to health outcomes. The personality factors of impulsivity and sensation-seeking, in particular, are associated with alcohol and drug use, and interventions focused on these dispositional qualities have been developed and shown to be effective (e.g., Conrod, Castellanos, & Mackie, 2008).

Personality-based interventions can also take the form of tailoring health messages to maximize their effectiveness. In Higgins' (1998) self-regulation model, individuals differ in whether they are promotion-focused (i.e., achievement-oriented and focused on positive outcomes) or prevention-focused (i.e., motivated by security needs and avoidance of threat). Higgins and colleagues found that health messages to increase fruit and vegetable consumptions were more effective if they were congruent with participants' regulatory focus (i.e., whether they emphasized the benefits of the behavior versus avoiding the costs of not engaging in the behavior; Latimer et al., 2008). Promotion- and prevention-focused information processing styles may share conceptual overlap with reward and punishment sensitivities as captured by self-report measures of Behavioral Inhibition (or Activation) Systems (Brenner, Beauchaine, & Sylvers, 2005). These dispositional styles are believed to be mediated by serotonergic and dopaminergic functioning and their associated emotional systems (Gray, 1994a, 1994b). They have been examined for their ability to predict how individuals respond to messages about health risks (cf. Westmaas & Woicik, 2005).

Although the constructs described above have demonstrated associations with health and health behavior change, there have been some criticisms that health behavior change theories or interventions need to take a more ecological or multilevel approach to achieve the greatest change. Health behavior theories have perhaps received the most criticism possibly because they assume rational and conscious decision-making about health risks and ignore other important influences or motivations, such as personality, visceral or unconscious motivations, or situational or emotional factors (Weinstein, 2006). They also tend to explain health behaviors or behavior change at a single level of analysis, assume that the associations among their constructs do not differ for different populations, and do not specify the expected relationships among all constructs in

the model (Rothman, 2008). Although comparisons among health behavior theories will improve understanding of the most important constructs in these theories, a more social-ecological or multilevel approach to interventions (described later), along with attention to the above concerns, is likely to improve our ability to develop effective theory-based interventions.

### Social Influences and Interventions to Improve Mental and Physical Health

Regardless of the theoretical orientation or focus of interventions, they occur in a social context, whether at the individual-, group-, organizational-, or community-level. The influence of social relationships can take the form of direct or indirect social pressure to engage in healthful behaviors, social norms (beliefs about whether others are engaging in the same behavior), observational learning (as described in social learning theory), and the actual provision of emotional, informational, or instrumental support to help individuals achieve behavior change or improve mental health outcomes. The provision of social support to help individuals improve health behaviors or outcomes is arguably a key focus of many interventions. Examples of these include support groups for cancer patients that lead to improvements in a patient's emotional state (i.e., depression and anxiety symptoms), illness adaptation, and quality of life (e.g., Zabalegui, Sanchez, Sanchez, & Juando, 2005), or assigning smokers to buddies who provide emotional support during the stressful process of quitting (May & West, 2000; Park, Schultz, Tudiver, Campbell, & Becker, 2004).

In many cases, however, the promise of social support has not lived up to expectations. For example, some studies have found null or adverse effects of critical-incident stress debriefing (CISD), a form of immediate social support provided to survivors of acute trauma, on the incidence of posttraumatic stress disorder (McNally, Bryant, & Ehlers, 2003). In addition, a critical review of psychosocial interventions for cancer patients found no evidence that they prolonged life, a conclusion that was attributed partly to the confounding of medical care with the actual intervention, along with other methodological problems (Coyne, Stefanek, & Palmer, 2007).

The extent to which social influences predict health outcomes may be determined by other factors (e.g., personality), but few studies have examined how individual difference variables interact with social influences to predict mental and physical health or illness. Possible candidates are hostility

(Lepore, 1995) and defensiveness (Strickland & Crowne, 1963; Westmaas & Jamner, 2006), as experimental studies have found these dispositional qualities to moderate the extent to which social support reduces subjective and physiological reactions to stressors.

In the smoking cessation literature, some intervention studies that have sought to increase the amount of social support for smokers from peers or family members have proven to be ineffective (May & West, 2000; Westmaas, Bontemps-Jones, & Bauer, 2010) possibly because the support was in addition to that provided by professionals. Still, attention to potential moderators such as gender and the use of theoretical models to guide research may be valuable in understanding how social support can be used effectively in interventions (May & West, 2000). For example, one mechanism through which social support might facilitate smoking cessation is by buffering responses to daily hassles or the stress of quitting, thereby reducing the intensity of negative affect and cravings that can lead to lapses. However, gender of the support provider or recipient may be a moderating factor in the extent to which this effect is demonstrated, given differences in gender socialization experiences that emphasize nurturance and communality for females, and autonomy and instrumentalism for males. An example of the potential benefit of considering gender in developing an intervention involving social support is provided by Fals-Stewart and colleagues (2006). They first examined gender differences in the etiology and successful treatment of alcohol abuse and, using these data, developed an intervention involving teaching the spouse to provide appropriate support for abstinence. The intervention was successful in reducing the number of drinking days, negative consequences from drinking, and partner violence (Fals-Stewart et al., 2006).

Attention to how social support is defined (structural, emotional, social pressure, etc.) is also critical (Westmaas et al., 2010). For example, although a quitline counselor or family members may provide emotional support to a smoker during quitting, structural aspects of support, such as the size of a smoker's social network and the proportion of the network that smokes, may be important factors in the success of an intervention. For example, Christakis and Fowler (2008) found that stopping smoking tended to spread within socially connected networks, such that "people appeared to act under collective pressures within niches in the network" (p. 2256). Their data suggest that providing tools to nonsmoking members to assist their smoking peers, or encouraging smokers' peers to quit could facilitate declines in smoking rates. Social capital (connectedness among individuals in a social network) can also contribute to health though the diffusion of knowledge. Considering the most relevant aspect of social influence for changing behavior in a given population and the use of standardized measures and process evaluation are also important in evaluating the effects of social support components.

The provision and receipt of social support for health behavior change is currently being transformed with the popularity of the internet. Online interventions have been developed for a variety of mental and physical health problems (Portnoy, Scott-Sheldon, Johnson, & Carey, 2008), with the aim of replacing or supplementing the expertise of a health care professional. For example, a recent study found that adults who were randomly assigned to an internet-based structured cognitive-behavioral intervention for insomnia versus a waiting-list control group demonstrated superior sleep outcomes up to 6 months after the intervention had ended (Ritterband et al., 2009). Many online interventions also include a forum to allow patients to provide each other with reassurance and encouragement for behavior change. One initial evaluation of an internet smoking cessation system, albeit uncontrolled, found that greater use of an online module for peer social support was associated with significantly greater abstinence (point-prevalence and continuous) 3 months post-intervention (Cobb, Graham, Bock, Papandonatos, & Abrams, 2005). Apart from formal interventions, social networking sites such as Facebook and MySpace have online communities of individuals trying to change behaviors, and these can also provide mutual support. An inherent appeal of social networking sites for prevention and intervention research is their ability to reach a large population at relatively low cost. For example, an analysis of the social networking site usage of young lesbian, gay, and bisexual individuals concluded that an intervention to reduce suicide ideation and attempts in this population had the capability of reaching 18,409 individuals (Silenzio, Duberstein, Tang, Lu, Tu, & Homan, 2009). A fruitful area of research will be to evaluate the effectiveness of these sites in helping individuals change and the processes underlying these effects.

## A Social Ecological Approach to Health Behavior Change

Social ecological models of behavior change address multiple sources of influence on health-relevant behaviors. In a model described by Sorensen and colleagues (1998), these sources of influence cut across various disciplines by considering biomedical or biophysiological theories of disease causation, psychosocial factors (e.g., individual-level factors such as personality, a sense of control, and self-efficacy), epidemiological factors (such as disease patterns and risk factors within populations), and cultural, social, economic, and political processes. According to Sorenson, the social ecological model thus offers a "theoretical framework that integrates multiple perspectives and theories," and "recognizes that behavior is affected by multiple levels of influence, including intrapersonal factors, interpersonal processes, institutional factors, community factors, and public policy" (p. 390).

Social ecological models to promote healthful behaviors can also address the influence of physical environments. According to Stokols (1992), in a social ecological approach "the healthfulness of a situation and the well-being of its participants are assumed to be influenced by multiple facets of both the physical environment (e.g., geography, architecture, and technology) and the social environment (e.g., culture, economics, and politics)" (p. 7). Of five health-related functions of the socio-physical environment noted by Stokols, one is environment as "an enabler of health behavior exemplified by the installation of safety devices in buildings and vehicles, geographic proximity to health care facilities, and exposure to interpersonal modeling or cultural practices that foster health-promotive behavior" (pp. 13–14).

An example of the interplay between physical and social environments and how they impact health behaviors is provided by research conducted by Landrine and Corral (2009). Their research has demonstrated that residential segregation accounts for black–white health disparities in cancer morbidity and mortality because black neighborhoods are more likely to have inadequate health care facilities staffed by less competent physicians, higher environmental exposures, and inferior built environments than do white neighborhoods. Racial discriminatory practices by supermarkets, and the targeting of black neighborhoods by fast-food outlets, for example, contribute to these differences in built environments that have implications for health-promoting behaviors such as purchasing fresh fruit and vegetables.

Designing interventions to achieve health behavior changes in communities, and that use a social ecological model to guide the intervention, requires the collaboration and integration not only of various scientific disciplines but also that of community members and multiple organizations and institutions (Stokols, 2006). A transdisciplinary research approach, and the inclusion of community organizations, is itself becoming a topic of study (Stokols, 2006) that will likely lead to recommendations on how best to achieve the vital collaborations that lead to the most effective behavioral changes. Community-based research demonstrating health behavior changes is likely to have the greatest chances of impacting communities in the long term.

## Multiple Influences on Health Behavior Change: The Case of Smoking

A good example of the multiple levels of influence that comprise a social ecological approach to behavior change is the case of smoking. Smoking is implicated in many illnesses, and the ability to quit appears to be a function of societal, psychosocial, and biological variables. Cigarette smoking is believed to account for approximately 87% of all lung cancer cases (U.S. Department of Health and Human Services [USDHHS], 2004), but not all smokers will develop lung cancer. Polymorphisms in certain genes influence the degree to which carcinogens in cigarette smoke are metabolized, and by implication, the likelihood of developing lung cancer (Cote et al., 2009; Rossini, de Almeida Simao, Albano, & Pinto, 2008). These and other advancements in understanding biological differences that contribute to the negative health effects of smoking offer the possibility of future biologically based interventions to prevent the development of lung cancer among smokers (secondary prevention).

Individual-level psychosocial factors are also associated with smoking initiation, such as parental or sibling smoking, and perceived norms about the acceptability of smoking. School-based primary interventions have addressed these psychosocial factors. Recent meta-analyses of school-based interventions found that the most effective approaches were those that included a focus on social reinforcement for not smoking, whereas the least effective were those that sought only to increase awareness of the dangers of starting to smoke (Levinthal, 2005).

In addition to psychosocial factors as contributors to smoking behavior, societal-level factors are implicated, such as the price of cigarettes and the portrayal of smoking among actors in movies (Anderson & Hughes, 2000). The ease with which youth can purchase cigarettes is also a crucial factor

(Klonoff & Landrine, 2004). Sociodemographic and cultural variables, such as age, gender, ethnicity, and/or socioeconomic status, may moderate the impact of biological, psychosocial, and societal influences on smoking. For example, gender or ethnic differences in smoking initiation, in reasons for smoking, and in smoking prevalence or ability to quit have been demonstrated (Mermelstein, 1999; Perkins, 2001; Perkins, Donny, & Caggiula, 1999), thus suggesting their potential role as moderators of intervention effectiveness. Similarly, although depression or negative emotions have been linked in many studies to smoking initiation, maintenance, and difficulty quitting, this association may not exist for black smokers (Klonoff & Landrine, 2001).

Although a social-ecological perspective in designing health promotion interventions has been promulgated and extensively implemented (see reviews by Merzel & D'Afflitti, 2003; Sorensen et al., 1998), a single unifying framework that integrates multiple levels of influence on a particular health behavior, and that acknowledges possible interactions among them, has been absent (Merzel, & D'Afflitti, 2003). Goodman and colleagues have also argued that, without the specificity of an integrative social-ecological model with which to test hypotheses, it is difficult to properly evaluate the effects of community-level prevention interventions (Goodman, Liburd, & Green-Phillips, 2001). Other challenges for the social ecological approach include deciding which variables from each level should be the focus of interventions, and determining the most appropriate data analytic techniques to address hypotheses.

## Selecting the Population

An initial step in designing prevention interventions is deciding who should be the target of the intervention. This decision should be partly related to whether the focus of the intervention is primary, secondary, or tertiary prevention. Many illness-promoting behaviors begin during youth or adolescence, and so primary interventions will often need to target individuals in these age groups. Good examples are school-based prevention interventions targeting smoking, obesity, or pregnancies and sexually transmitted diseases. However, primary interventions can also target older individuals, such as HIV-negative men who have sex with men, or college students who are in danger of starting to smoke or binge drink. Age and gender differences are important considerations because they are related

to maturational or sociocultural factors that are likely to influence whether the health behavior is adopted. For example, the use of explicit sexual language in print messages urging gay men to use condoms to prevent HIV infection, although believed to have been effective for this population, could be offensive if applied to young women who are also in danger of becoming infected.

If the target population for an intervention consists of specialized groups such as ethnic and racial minorities, immigrant populations, children, the elderly, or the physically ill, other challenges exist. For example, cultural beliefs may play a significant role in the adoption of the behavior, and culture-appropriate materials may be needed to deliver the intervention. In an intervention to reduce the likelihood of HIV infection among male migrant farm workers in California who have sex with other men, but who would not self-identify as gay, Conner and colleagues distributed a novella (ongoing sagas presented in comic book format) to promote condom use (Mishra, Sanudo, & Conner, 2004). In this particular socioethnic group, such an approach was seen as a legitimate source of information compared with other possible options.

In addition to cultural factors, specialized groups may also differ on other sociodemographic characteristics, such as literacy or socioeconomic status, which will dictate the methods used to deliver the intervention. If English is not the native language of the intended recipients, the intervention will of course need to be presented in their language. If reading ability is limited, print media are not appropriate.

The sociodemographic and cultural characteristics of a targeted population can also influence whether an intervention should be undertaken at the individual, community, or societal level. If the targeted population is difficult to recruit for face-to-face interactions, then community- or society-level interventions, rather than individual-level prevention approaches, may be more appropriate. If individuals from some communities have to endure a long commute to attend a cognitive-behavioral smoking cessation clinic provided by a hospital, or do not have the financial resources to make the trip, public service messages on radio stations or campaigns delivered through church groups may have a better chance at reaching them. For example, Brandon and colleagues recruited recently quit smokers for a relapse-prevention intervention through newspaper, radio, and media advertisements that provided them with a toll-free number to call to register for the program (Brandon et al., 2004). The intervention consisted of brochures that were mailed directly to participants. This technique was effective in decreasing relapse rates.

Sometimes an intervention seeks to target those who are most at risk. If reducing risk in the most at-risk individuals is the overarching goal, it might be assumed that increasing the intensity of the intervention will be needed to change behavior. However, even moderately intense prevention efforts could increase the attrition rate in such a population. Equally important, the intervention may be less likely to show positive effects among those most at risk. For example, the aim of the Community Intervention Trial for Smoking Cessation (COMMIT) was to increase cessation rates among heavy smokers (i.e., those smoking more than 25 cigarettes a day). However, post-intervention analyses indicated that COMMIT succeeded in increasing quit rates among light and moderate smokers (i.e., those smoking less than 25 cigarettes a day), but not among heavy smokers (Fisher, 1995).

Another important consideration in selecting participants is how generalizable the results of the intervention are intended to be, which in turn will influence whether the intervention is likely to be adopted by others. The RE-AIM (Reach, Effectiveness, Adoption, Implementation, Maintenance) framework, developed by Glasgow and colleagues, is a system of evaluating health promotion interventions that includes an assessment of the representativeness of participants and the settings in which the intervention was conducted (Glasgow, Bull, Gillette, Klesges, & Dzewaltowski, 2002). Among the components of RE-AIM, Reach refers to "the percentage of potential participants who will take part in an intervention, and to how representative they are of the population from which they are drawn" (p. 63). For example, although telephone counseling for smokers (i.e., quitlines) is an effective cessation intervention (Lichtenstein, Zhu, & Tedeschi, 2010), estimates are that it reaches only 1%–2% of smokers (Cummins, Bailey, Campbell, Koon-Kirby, & Zhu, 2007). More research is thus needed to address why some smokers who want to quit do not use a quitline. Although sociodemographic variables such as age, gender, or ethnicity may play a role in preferences for different cessation treatment modalities (e.g., web-based interventions) other factors may also be operating. For example, many smokers may simply be unaware of the availability of free quitlines, assume that medications alone are sufficient to help them quit, or hold negative views of psychosocial interventions. Investigating the potential reach of a planned intervention can inform recruitment, indicate how generalizable the intervention will be, and suggest how likely the desired population will adopt it if it is shown to be efficacious.

## Selecting the Appropriate Design

To be able to conclude that an intervention is effective, plausible alternative explanations for behavior change must be ruled out. Randomization of individuals, schools, work sites, or communities to intervention and control groups represents the best strategy for ruling out alternative explanations, but participant responses to and reactions against the randomization process must be attended to and minimized, if possible (Wortman, Hendricks, & Hillis, 1976). In addition, other designs, including longitudinal research, can be used to support causal inferences. However, longitudinal designs are based on the assumption that certain parameters do not change over time, and there is still the possibility of spuriousness that needs to be accounted for in order to make causal inferences (Kenny, 1979).

One threat to the ability to make causal inferences is the problem of selection bias. Selection bias occurs if the units making up the intervention and control groups differ before the intervention is even implemented (Larzelere, Kuhn, & Johnson, 2004). These biases can lead to both overestimating and underestimating the effects of interventions. In some interventions, selection biases operate so that the sickest or riskiest groups are targeted for behavior change. Regression to the mean by these individuals, defined as the tendency over time to approach mean levels of a behavior (Cook & Campbell, 1979), can give the appearance that the intervention produced positive effects. Without randomization to intervention and control groups of the most at-risk individuals, regression to the mean as a plausible alternative interpretation of results cannot be eliminated.

Well-designed randomized clinical trials represent one of the most powerful means of assessing health behavior theories and the effectiveness of interventions. However, as Helgeson and Lepore (1997) note, designing a randomized clinical intervention will often require balancing "the needs of the individual patient with the requirements of the research protocol" and "the practical or logistical issues in conducting an intervention with the theoretical and experimental issues." Helgeson and Lepore further note that this balancing act will sometimes require unforeseen modifications to the research protocol in order to ensure patient recruitment and retention and/or the cooperation of clinic staff. As an example, they mention the occasional cancer patient who is dismayed by his or her assignment to the control group and asks to be put in the intervention group. The authors resolved this issue in their own research by favoring patients' well-being (e.g., providing them with referrals to other support groups in the community; see Hohmann & Shear, 2002, for another discussion of these problems).

When there is nonrandomization of units to intervention and control groups, assessing possible preexisting differences between intervention and control groups on variables that may influence the targeted behavior becomes paramount. These principles have not always been followed in community interventions to prevent the uptake of smoking in young people, however. According to a recent Cochrane database review, among the 17 community intervention studies designed to prevent youth smoking that included control groups and assessed baseline characteristics (their criteria for inclusion in the review), in eight studies the allocation of communities or schools to the intervention or control groups was nonrandom, and some studies did not account for baseline differences in smoking in their follow-up analyses (Sowden, Arblaster, & Stead, 2005).

In the absence of randomization to intervention and control groups, matching individuals or communities from intervention and comparison groups on variables associated with the targeted behavior is appropriate. In a review of 32 community interventions to reduce smoking in adults that included a control group, however, only five studies demonstrated that the intervention and control communities were comparable on demographic variables at baseline (Secker-Walker, Gnich, Platt, & Lancaster, 2005).

In randomized controlled interventions conducted at the community level, the need to maintain scientific rigor through standardization and control can sometimes conflict with community goals and priorities. A certain amount of flexibility in accommodating the needs of participating community organizations is important for ensuring intervention integrity and can ultimately influence the effectiveness of the intervention. Involving communities in the design and implementation process will help both researchers and communities understand each other's perspectives and can ensure that the goals and priorities of both parties are met.

The expense of randomized controlled trials at the community level, in which the unit of allocation to experimental and comparison groups is the community or organization, can be a motivating factor in considering alternative designs, especially if required levels of statistical power are to be achieved. Sorensen and colleagues (1998) have stated that in designing interventions at the community level, "an expanded range of research methodologies is required to address the diverse needs for scientific rigor, appropriateness to research questions, and feasibility in terms of cost and setting" (p. 401). They describe other designs that could supplement the randomized control trial in answering questions about the effectiveness of community interventions, including observational studies, qualitative research methods, and action research methods. For example, qualitative research methods would be appropriate for understanding community needs, priorities, and resources before an intervention is designed.

With the increased popularity of the internet, a number of Web-based interventions have also been developed. Web-based interventions offer the advantages of accessibility, low cost, data completeness, standardization, personalization or tailoring of information, and potentially greater accuracy for reporting symptoms or illegal or stigmatizing behaviors. Subjects can also participate in program elements in the privacy of their own homes and at their own convenience, and the degree of program participation can be easily assessed. Recent reviews or meta-analyses of internet-based interventions to promote positive physical or mental health, for example those that address smoking cessation, substance use, depression, and posttraumatic stress disorders, have demonstrated positive treatment effects compared with control groups (Barr Taylor, & Luce, 2003; Bock et al., 2004; Copeland & Martin, 2004; Kessler et al., 2009; Litz, Engle, Bryant, & Papa, 2007; Portnoy et al., 2008).

### Power Analyses

For any research endeavor, conducting power analyses is an important means of determining the number of units to be assigned to experimental and control groups in order to answer questions about the intervention's effectiveness. If a proposed study is not adequately powered, the absence of reliable (significant) differences between groups could be attributed to lack of power. Power analyses can also determine whether there are sufficient data points to adequately evaluate if intervention effects on outcome variables are moderated by other variables (e.g., motivation to quit smoking or gender). Such analyses represent the testing of "group by moderating variable" interactions and provide valuable information, especially if no main effects are obtained.

In individual-level interventions, the unit of allocation is the participant, with power analyses indicating the number of participants that should be recruited in each group in order to detect significant main or interaction effects at predetermined levels of power (usually 80%). In community interventions, the unit of allocation is the work site, school, hospital, city, or town. Power analysis to determine adequate sample sizes in community interventions needs to account for statistical dependencies of responses within each unit or cluster (Donner & Klar, 1996; Koepsell et al., 1992). When only one community receives the intervention, with another community serving as the control group, conducting power analysis is difficult if results are to be analyzed at the cluster level. Indeed, it has been argued that the modest or nonsignificant effects of several community interventions to promote health and prevent illness may have been due to insufficient power to detect positive effects, even small ones (Secker-Walker et al., 2005).

### Enlisting Cooperation for Interventions

In clinic-based interventions, the goal is often to evaluate the efficacy of a specific treatment on a specific outcome. An example is determining whether a cognitive-behavioral intervention for smoking cessation is effective in getting hospitalized patients to quit. Clinic-based interventions usually involve nurses, doctors, or other health care professionals (e.g., therapists, psychologists, and psychiatrists). Helgeson and Lepore (1997) provide several guidelines and comments that are useful in enlisting the cooperation of medical personnel. For example, they note that, to gain access to a medical population, the first step is to identify a physician who values research and can be convinced that the results of the intervention will translate to benefits for the patient and the medical community. Including physicians in designing the intervention itself may be challenging, given the time constraints that many have, but nurses, whose training emphasizes the psychosocial needs of the patient, can often provide valuable information about patients and the operation of the institution (Holman, 1997). This information can be especially valuable in the design phase of the intervention. Because of the multitude of demands faced by clinic staff, minimizing the amount of work required of them (e.g., by developing a list of eligible patients for the study) will be important in maintaining their interest and cooperation.

Maintaining contact with staff, particularly nurses, who are often vital to the successful implementation of the project, rewarding them for their cooperation, and providing updates and evidence of the intervention's value will also help to achieve this goal (Helgeson & Lepore, 1997; Grady & Wallston, 1988).

For interventions at the community level, the skills and priorities of the individuals, agencies, and institutions participating in the intervention are more varied. Altman (1995a) summarized four recommendations for improving community-level interventions, at least two of which refer to the importance of community cooperation. The four recommendations include "(i) integrate interventions into the community infrastructure, (ii) use comprehensive, multilevel intervention approaches, (iii) facilitate community participation and promote community capacity-building, and (iv) conduct thorough needs assessment/social reconnaissance in order to tailor interventions to the community context." Spending the time to understand the priorities of community organizations, whose assistance is required for the intervention to be implemented, and incorporating their needs into the intervention goals will help to sustain their cooperation during the research phase. At the same time, demonstrating how the intervention goals can benefit the community, and obtaining consensus for their importance, will help ensure that the needs of all parties are adequately met. Some flexibility is required on the part of the academically oriented research team so that the intervention is tailored to the community context. These recommendations undergird the effectiveness of community-based participatory research.

### Process Evaluation

Designing, planning, and executing an intervention, especially one that requires the cooperation of researchers, community agencies, workplaces, and media, involves a tremendous amount of effort. To be able to determine whether these considerable efforts are effective in producing the intended changes, and are cost-effective, a rigorous evaluation of intervention delivery is required. Without extensive process evaluation, interpreting a lack of differences between intervention and control groups is particularly problematic. For example, if teachers implementing a smoking resistance program among middle schoolers deviates significantly from activities geared to changing norms about smoking and resisting offers to smoke, then nonsignificant effects of the intervention could be attributed to the intervention group having received a weaker dose of the treatment than intended. Ongoing evaluation of program activities and delivery can also be used to appropriately modify program components once the intervention is under way.

A model example of rigorous process evaluation occurred in the COMMIT trial, a 5-year community intervention trial to decrease smoking prevalence among heavy smokers (Fisher, 1995). Monitoring of program delivery was extensive, with logs completed by staff and volunteers and computerized record keeping of intervention activities. Process evaluation in other community interventions has included surveys completed by the targeted population and deliverers of the intervention, either by phone or through the mail, focus groups and semi-structured interviews, and tracking and documenting program activities. In some trials, these functions were performed by computerized systems (Secker-Walker et al., 2005).

Process evaluation in community interventions can also include a determination of its *reach* and *penetration*. Reach refers to how aware members of the target population are of program activities, through radio or television advertisements, newspaper articles, health fairs, workplace programs, treatment clinics, self-help kits, and so on. Penetration refers to the extent to which the targeted population participated in these activities. Polling of representative samples of individuals from the targeted population can determine reach and penetration, which can be presented as the number or proportion of individuals who partook of intervention activities. This information should be an important part of the dissemination of trial results because low rates of awareness and/or penetration could account for nonsignificant differences between intervention and comparison groups on key outcomes. Penetration (intervention dose) can also be used to determine dose–response relationships, a measure of the effect of the intervention.

Because there may be diffusion or "spillover" of the treatment from the experimental group or community into the comparison group or community, assessing the reach and penetration in comparison groups or communities for activities that are similar to intervention components should also be performed. At the community level, this scenario is likely to occur if the media extensively cover intervention activities. Comparison communities may also independently conduct their own health fairs, enact legislation, or provide media messages that produce effects similar to those of the intervention.

For example, in the Alliance of Black Churches Project to reduce smoking through counseling by church members, the difference between the intervention group and the comparison group in whether they received information about smoking from a church member was 29% versus 20%, respectively (Schorling et al., 1997). In the COMMIT trial, differences in indices of penetration for the intervention and control communities were relatively small.

Secular trends in awareness of and engagement in behaviors that promote health and prevent illness may also lead to behavioral changes in the control group that are comparable to those in the intervention group. For example, the decreased social acceptability of smoking, facilitated first by the surgeon general's report and subsequently by tobacco taxes, public health campaigns, and the Master Tobacco Settlement Agreement, may be contributing to a decline in smoking rates in many geographic areas. The secular trend of reducing smoking levels has been cited for the observation of a greater decrease in smoking prevalence in the control compared with the intervention community in the Pawtucket Heart Health program (Carleton, Lasater, Assaf, Feldman, & McKinlay, 1995). Secular trends in smoking reduction may have also precluded finding stronger effects in the COMMIT trial (Bauman, Suchindran, & Murray, 1999). A greater intensity of intervention dosage may be needed to overcome secular trends observed in comparison communities. In addition, to better assess intervention effectiveness, investigators should determine the extent to which secular trends in behavior change are occurring prior to the implementation of the intervention (Secker-Walker et al., 2005).

## Outcome Evaluation

For any health promotion or disease prevention intervention, what the outcome variables should be, by what means they should be assessed (questionnaires, interviews, etc.), and how often and when they should be measured, need to be determined. In community-level interventions, outcome variables should be relevant or salient to the individuals from the communities or populations being studied (Hohmann & Shear, 2002). Hohmann and Shear (2002) suggest that, although symptoms and diagnostic categories may be important for comparative purposes, for participants the important or expected outcomes may be different (e.g., an increase in level of daily functioning). The use of standardized measures with demonstrated reliability and validity, or measures that have been used in prior research, should be encouraged because they allow for easier comparison with results of prior research.

Who the intervention is targeting, as discussed previously, may play a role in determining which methods should be used to assess outcome variables. Self-report measures are often the most convenient and may be the best option if highly personal information, such as sexual practices or illegal activity, is sought. Structured interviews conducted over the telephone or computer-assisted interviews also provide some degree of anonymity and are probably less subject to the problem of missing data than are questionnaires. Both questionnaire and interview formats allow some degree of control of the testing context and data quality by researchers, but the degree of control needed will depend on the question being asked. For example, in a study investigating why women stay in abusive relationships, Herbert and colleagues used a strategy that ensured that women who completed the sensitive questionnaires could do so without the knowledge of their abusive spouses (Herbert, Silver, & Ellard, 1991).

For interventions conducted at the individual level, demand characteristics are more likely to be a problem. For example, smokers who undergo a cognitive-behavioral intervention to quit smoking may be motivated to misrepresent their actual levels of smoking at the end of the intervention because of the expectation by clinic staff that they should have quit or reduced their smoking. This consideration has led many smoking cessation programs to include biochemical validation of smoking status. In general, however, the more limited the contact between participants and clinic staff, the less likely smokers are to misrepresent their actual levels of smoking (Velicer, Prochaska, Rossi, & Snow, 1992). In addition, findings from randomized experiments document that when research participants respond to questions without interacting directly with an interviewer, they are more likely to reveal sensitive and/or personal information (Lau, Thomas, & Liu, 2000; Turner et al., 1998). Moreover, socially desirable responding may differ for cultural reasons. For example, black smokers were 3.5 to 8.9 times more likely to deny smoking compared to age-/gender-matched whites in the National Health and Nutrition Education Survey (NHANES III) (Fisher, Taylor, Shelton, & Debanne, 2008). Socially desirable responding among blacks decreases when black interviewers are used, consistent with evidence that such discrepancies are due to blacks' distrust of white researchers and to avoid negative evaluations by whites (Corbie-Smith, Thomas, & St. George, 2002; Krysan & Couper, 2003).

The reliability of participants' responses can also be assessed through the use of "collateral" reports from subjects' romantic partners, family, and/or friends. Convergence of evidence from these sources provides a greater degree of confidence about the reliability of responses. In addition to self-report or interview format, observational or archival measures can be useful indicators of intervention effectiveness. An example would be documentation of the number of teenage pregnancies before, during, and after an intervention promoting condom use in adolescents. These methods of assessment differ in convenience and amount of resources required. As noted earlier, Web-based questionnaire assessments have been used with increasing success in health psychology research because of their convenience and low cost, and it is likely that they will be seriously considered for use in future health-promoting interventions. (See also Schlenger & Silver, 2006, for additional information on the pros and cons of the use of the Web for data collection.)

The assessment of outcomes, and of potential mediating or moderating variables, should be conducted before, during, and after the intervention. Assessing outcomes some time after the intervention has ended can answer important questions about its long-term efficacy. For example, follow-up of cognitive-behavioral smoking cessation programs has found impressive quit rates soon after the intervention ended, but a substantial number of smokers relapse within the subsequent year (Tonnesen, 2009). This has led to a focus on devising relapse prevention programs for smokers, some of which have been successful (e.g., Brandon et al., 2004). Many community-level prevention efforts have also led to short-lived behavioral changes. However, some of the health effects of interventions may take years to be realized. This has stimulated efforts to encourage the sustainability or maintenance of interventions after researchers have collected and published their data.

## Sustaining Interventions at the Community Level

If intervention activities are to be transferred to community organizations, their leaders should be involved in the planning and implementation of the intervention, which will need to be sensitive to the priorities and limitations of community resources (Altman, 1995b). According to Altman, questions of ownership and control of community programs should be addressed prior to implementation, and any conflicts resolved, so that there is "broad-based support from a cross-section of community constituencies" (p. 529), both during the intervention and after the research phase has ended. An exchange of skills, through education and training, between researchers and community staff, and fostering a sense of empowerment in communities to obtain resources for programs also contribute to sustainability. For example, educating community leaders on effective performance evaluation should foster a sense of empowerment and produce skills that leaders can use to design and implement unique interventions that address the same health behaviors.

## Disseminating Research Findings

Although expenditures on health promotive research have been substantial, knowledge of how to disseminate findings from research to primary care clinics and community agencies that deliver health services is only now emerging as a research endeavor in its own right (Kerner, Rimer, & Emmons, 2005). Much work remains, however, for dissemination research to advance as a science. As Kerner et al. note, the best research methods for evaluating dissemination strategies have not yet been established, which limits the amount of guidance available for researchers who want to conduct dissemination research. These authors also recommend more infrastructure support from private and public sectors, along with greater consensus among journal reviewers and editors on how to evaluate dissemination research projects. Nonetheless, it is critical to translate the empirical results of scientific investigations into practical recommendations for health care professionals, schools, work sites, and community organizations. Working effectively with the media and others to disseminate research findings to the public—to ensure that they are effectively applied to both policy and practice—should be an important goal of researchers. With increasing attention to these issues, the efforts devoted to designing effective health-promoting interventions will hopefully translate to evidence-based practices that improve the public health.

## Ethical Issues

Any research whose goal is to change behaviors, even health-promoting ones, must attend to ethical issues involving the use of human subjects. Because of concerns regarding the use of community samples in intervention research, nonprofit agencies, health care settings, schools, and work sites may serve as gatekeepers to block access to potential research subjects. Convincing these gatekeepers of the value of one's research often requires demonstrating sensitivity to the ethics of human subject experimentation (Sieber, 1998). Moreover, conducting interventions at any level of analysis must also involve the review of research plans by institutional review boards housed in academic institutions, as well as in individual research settings (e.g., hospitals). The provision of an inherently more appealing treatment may require eventually offering it as an option to the control group at a later date (e.g., designing a "waiting list" control group). Sometimes, implementing a waiting list means withholding treatment for a period and depriving individual participants of current best practices. In such cases, this design is not ethically feasible (see Devilly & McFarlane, 2009, for statistical suggestions to deal with this problem). Designing research on specialized populations, such as geriatric, pediatric, or medically ill samples, requires special attention to issues of informed consent, avoiding coercive procedures, and providing ample opportunity for refusal and termination of participation in the research effort over time. It is important that the individual researcher conduct a careful cost–benefit analysis, weighing the personal rights of individual participants against the potential benefits for society of the research. Although ethical issues surrounding the design and implementation of community-based intervention research may be challenging and will undoubtedly require creativity and persistence, conducting methodologically rigorous research on human participants is required for the science of health promotion and illness prevention to advance.

## Conclusion

The value of health promotion and intervention programs to improve health and reduce illness has been amply demonstrated in several domains of behavior. Indeed, it can be argued that intervention programs are victims of their own success when individuals in control groups show the same improvements in health behaviors as those in intervention groups. However, for progress to continue in our dynamic environment, where new threats to mental and physical health emerge (e.g., bioterrorism) and old ones adopt new faces (e.g., water pipes for smoking), lessons learned from prior intervention research must be considered. Attention to such principles as the use of theoretical models to guide research; consideration of individual, cultural, and sociodemographic differences and their moderating effects on intervention outcomes; the equivalence of intervention and control groups; and the appropriate use of statistical analyses and methods should provide the foundation for health promotion and intervention research. However, to improve the health of the greatest number of individuals, the expertise of others who are invested in advancing our ability to promote health and prevent illness is needed. Their involvement, as well as that of the targets of our research, will necessarily contribute to our understanding of the most effective ways to initiate and sustain health behavior change. As science progresses, however, new questions and methods will emerge that offer the potential to further improve the health and well-being of all members of societies. In the final section below, we discuss areas in which further research is needed or in which new perspectives may change the way we design or implement interventions.

## Future Directions

Although addressing negative mental and physical health outcomes are appropriate targets for intervention, the relatively new field of positive psychology (Snyder, Lopez, & Pedrotti, 2010) offers the possibility that more interventions will capitalize on human strengths, such as creativity, altruism, capacity for growth, and resilience. The aim of these interventions will be to promote positive emotional and physical states that buffer against illness. At the same time, advances in understanding genetic and other biological contributors to mental and physical health will point to their importance in developing interventions with the highest impact. With the sequencing of the human genome and increasingly advanced statistical techniques for identifying genes involved in physical and mental conditions, the possibility for tailored treatments that include both pharmacological and behavioral components will be enhanced. These advances will be efficiently disseminated through the internet and other technologies, such as mobile phones (Whittaker et al., 2009), text messaging (Prestwich, Perugini, & Hurling, 2010), and pod-casts (Turner-McGrievy et al., 2010), providing an additional avenue for social influences to effect behavior change and health outcomes. In this new world, identifying the most important constructs and levels of influence on behavior, and specifying the strengths of their interrelationships for different populations, will be crucial in developing and testing theories of mental and physical health behavior change that can be translated to effective interventions.

## References

Abraham, C., & Sheeran, P. (2005). The health belief model. In M. Conner, & P. Norman (Eds.), *Predicting health behavior* (2nd ed.), pp. 23–61. Buckingham: Open University Press.

Abraham, C., & Sheeran, P. (2004). Deciding to exercise: The role of anticipated regret. *British Journal of Health Psychology, 9,* 269–278.

Adams, J., & White, M. (2005). Why don't stage-based activity promotion interventions work? *Health Education Research, 20,* 237–243.

Adler, N.E., Kegeles, S.M., Irwin, C.E., & Wibbelsman, C. (1990). Adolescent contraceptive behavior: An assessment of decision processes. *Journal of Pediatrics, 116,* 463–471.

Ajzen, I. (1988). *Attitudes, personality and behavior.* Milton Keynes, UK: Open University.

Ajzen, I. (1991). The theory of planned behavior. *Organizational Behavior and Human Decision Processes, 50,* 179–211.

Ajzen, I. (2002). *Constructing a TPB questionnaire: Conceptual and methodological considerations.* Retrieved from http://www.people.umass.edu/aizen/pdf/tpb.measurement.pdf.

Ajzen, I., & Fishbein, M. (1977). Attitude-behavior relations: A theoretical analysis and review of empirical research. *Psychological Bulletin, 84,* 888–918.

Ajzen, I., & Fishbein, M. (1980). *Understanding attitudes and predicting social behavior.* Englewood Cliffs, NJ: Prentice Hall.

Albarracin, D., Johnson, B.T., Fishbein, M., & Muellerleile, P.A. (2001). Theories of reasoned action and planned behavior as models of condom use: A meta-analysis. *Psychological Bulletin, 127,* 142–161.

Altman, D. (1995a). Strategies for community health intervention: Promises, paradoxes, pitfalls. *Psychosomatic Medicine, 57,* 226–233.

Altman, D.G. (1995b). Sustaining interventions in community systems: On the relationship between researchers and communities. *Health Psychology, 14,* 526–536.

Anderson, P., & Hughes, J.R. (2000). Policy interventions to reduce the harm from smoking. *Addiction, 95*(Suppl), S9–S11.

Armitage, C.J. (2005). Can the theory of planned behavior predict the maintenance of physical activity? *Health Psychology, 24,* 235–245.

Armitage J.C., & Conner, M. (2001). Efficacy of the theory of planned behaviour: A meta-analytic review. *British Journal of Social Psychology, 40,* 471–499.

Aveyard, P., Massey, L., Parsons, A., Manaseki, S., & Griffin, C. (2009). The effect of transtheoretical model based interventions on smoking cessation. *Social Science & Medicine, 68*(3), 397–403.

Baele, J., Dusseldorp, E., & Maes, S. (2001). Condom use self-efficacy: Effect on intended and actual condom use in adolescents. *Journal of Adolescent Health, 28,* 421–431.

Bandura, A. (1998). Health promotion from the perspective of social cognitive theory. *Psychology and Health, 13,* 623–649.

Bandura, A. (2004). Health promotion by social cognitive means. *Health Education & Behavior, 31,* 143–164.

Barr Taylor, C., & Luce, K.H. (2003). Computer- and Internet-based psychotherapy interventions. *Current Directions in Psychological Science, 12,* 18–22.

Bauman, K.E., Suchindran, C.M., & Murray, D.M. (1999). The paucity of effects in community trials: Is secular trend the culprit? *Preventive Medicine, 28,* 426–429.

Bish, A., Sutton, S., & Golombok, S. (2000). Predicting uptake of a routine cervical smear test: A comparison of the health belief model and the theory of planned behavior. *Psychology and Health, 15*, 35–50.

Bock, B.D., Graham, A.L., Sciamanna, C.N., Krishnamoorthy, J., Whiteley, J., Carmona-Barros, R.N. et al. (2004). Smoking cessation treatment on the Internet: Content, quality, and usability. *Nicotine and Tobacco Research, 6*, 207–219.

Brandon, T.H., Meade, C.D., Herzog, T.A., Chirikos, T.N., Webb, M.S., & Cantor, A.B. (2004). Efficacy and cost-effectiveness of a minimal intervention to prevent smoking relapse: Dismantling the effects of amount of content versus contact. *Journal of Consulting and Clinical Psychology, 72*, 797–808.

Brenner, S.L., Beauchaine, T.P., & Sylvers, P.D. (2005). A comparison of psychophysiological and self-report measures of BAS and BIS activation. *Psychophysiology, 42*(1), 108–115.

Bridle, C., Riemsma, R.P., Pattenden, J., Sowden, A.J., Mather, L., Watt, I.S., & Walker, A. (2005). Systemic review of the effectiveness of health behavior interventions based on the transtheoretical model. *Psychology and Health, 20*, 283–301.

Brown, D. (2009, April 3). *Cigarette tax boost prods some to quit.* P. A6. Washington Post: Katherine Weymouth.

Canadian Public Health Association. (2004). Participaction—The mouse that roared: A marketing and health communications success story. *Canadian Journal of Public Health, 95*(Suppl), 1–46.

Carey, K.B., Scott-Sheldon, L.A.J., Carey, M.P., & DeMartini, K.S. (2007). Individual-level interventions to reduce college student drinking: A meta-analytic review. *Addictive Behaviors, 32*, 2469–2494.

Carleton, R.A., Lasater, T.M., Assaf, A.R., Feldman, H.A., & McKinlay, S.(1995). The Pawtucket heart health program: Community changes in cardiovascular risk factors and projected disease risk. *American Journal of Public Health, 85*, 777–785.

Centers for Disease Control and Prevention. (1999). Cigarette smoking among high school students: 11 States, 1991–1997. *Morbidity and Mortality Weekly Report, 48*, 686–692.

Centers for Disease Control and Prevention. (2004). *The health consequences of smoking: A report of the Surgeon General.* Rockville, MD: U.S. Department of Health and Human Services, Public Health Service.

Centers for Disease Control and Prevention. (2005). Cigarette smoking among adults—United States, 2004. *MMWR Highlights, 54*(44), 1121–1124.

Centers for Disease Control and Prevention. (2007). *HIV/AIDS among men who have sex with men.* Retrieved from http://www.cdc.gov/hiv/topics/msm/resources/factsheets/msm.htm.

Champion, V.L. (1994). Strategies to increase mammography utilization. *Medical Care, 32*, 118–129.

Christakis, N.A., & Fowler, J.H. (2008). The collective dynamics of smoking in a large social network. *The New England Journal of Medicine, 358*(21), 2249–2258.

Cobb, N.K., Graham, A.L., Bock, B.C., Papandonatos, G., & Abrams, D.B. (2005). Initial evaluation of a real-world Internet smoking cessation system. *Nicotine & Tobacco Research, 7*(2), 207–216.

Cole, S.W., Kemeny, M.E., & Taylor, S.E. (1997). Social identity and physical health: Accelerated HIV progression in rejection-sensitive gay men. *Journal of Personality and Social Psychology, 72*, 320–335.

Conrod, P.J., Castellanos, N., & Mackie, C. (2008). Personality-targeted interventions delay the growth of adolescent drinking and binge drinking. *Journal of Child Psychology and Psychiatry, 49*(2), 181–190.

Cook, T., & Campbell, D. (1979). *Quasi-experimental design.* Chicago: Rand McNally.

Copeland, J., & Martin, G. (2004). Web-based interventions for substance use disorders: A qualitative review. *Journal of Substance Abuse Treatment, 26*, 109–116.

Corbie-Smith, G., Thomas, S.B., & St. George, D.M. (2002). Distrust, race, and research. *Archives of Internal Medicine, 162*, 2458–2463.

Corwyn, R.F., & Benda, B.B. (1999). Examination of an integrated theoretical model of exercise behavior. *American Journal of Health Behavior, 23*, 381–392.

Cote, M.L., Chen, W., Smith, D.W., Benhamou, S., Bouchardy, C., & Butkiewicz, D. (2009). Meta- and pooled analysis of GSTP1 polymorphism and lung cancer: a HuGE-GSEC review. *American Journal of Epidemiology, 169* (7), 802–814.

Coyne, J.C., Stefanek, M., & Palmer, S.C. (2007). Psychotherapy and survival in cancer: The conflict between hope and evidence. *Psychological Bulletin, 133*(3), 367–394.

Cummins, S.E., Bailey, L,. Campbell, S., Koon-Kirby, C., & Zhu, S.-H. (2007). Tobacco cessation quitlines in North America: A descriptive study. *Tobacco Control,16*(Suppl I), i9- i15.

Danaher, B.G., Lichtenstein, E., Andrews, J.A., Severson, H.H., Akers, L., & Barckley, M. (2009). Women helping chewers: Effects of partner support on 12-month tobacco abstinence in a smokeless tobacco cessation trial. *Nicotine & Tobacco Research, 11*(3), 332–335.

Denollet, J., Martens, E.J., Nyklicek, I., Conraads, V.M., & de Gelder, B. (2008). Clinical events in coronary patients who report low distress: Adverse effect of repressive coping. *Health Psychology, 27*(3), 302–308.

Devilly, G.J., & McFarlane, A.C. (2009). When wait lists are not feasible, nothing is a thing that does not need to be done. *Journal of Consulting and Clinical Psychology, 77*, 1159–1168.

Ditto, P.H., Pizarro, D.A., Epstein, E.B., Jacobson, J.A., & Macdonald, T.K. (2006). Visceral influences on risk-taking behavior. *Journal of Behavioral Decision Making, 19*, 99–113.

Donner, A., & Klar, N. (1996). Statistical considerations in the design and analysis of community intervention trials. *Journal of Clinical Epidemiology, 49*, 435–439.

Elder, J.P., Ayala, G.X., & Harris, S. (1999). Theories and intervention approaches to health-behavior change in primary care. *American Journal of Preventive Medicine, 17*, 275–284.

Ezzati, M., & Lopez, A.D. (2003). Estimates of global mortality attributable to smoking in 2000. *Lancet, 362*, 847–852.

Ezzati, M., Henley, S.J., Lopez, A.D., & Thun, M.J. (2005). Role of smoking in global and regional cancer epidemiology: Current patterns and data needs. *International Journal of Cancer, 116*, 963–971.

Fals-Stewart, W., Birchler, G.R., & Kelley, M.L. (2006). Learning sobriety together: A randomized clinical trial examining behavioral couples therapy with alcoholic female patients. *Journal of Consulting and Clinical Psychology, 74*(3), 579–591.

Fishbein, M. (2000). The role of theory in HIV prevention. *AIDS Care, 12*, 273–278.

Fishbein, M., Hennessy, M., Kamb, M., Bolan, G.A., Hoxworth, T., Iatesta, M., et al. (2001). Using intervention theory to model factors influencing behavior change: Project Respect. *Evaluation and the Health Professions, 24*, 363–384.

Fisher, E.B. (1995). The results of the COMMIT trial. *American Journal of Public Health, 85*, 159–160.

Fisher, M.A., Taylor, G.W., Shelton, B.J., & Debanne, S. (2008). Age and race/ethnicity-gender predictors of denying smoking. United States. *Journal of Health Care for the Poor and Underserved, 19*, 7589.

Friedman, H.S. (2000). Long-term relations of personality and health: Dynamisms, mechanisms, tropisms. *Journal of Personality, 68*(6), 1089–1107.

Gillibrand, R., & Stevenson, J. (2006). The extended health belief model applied to the experience of diabetes in young people. *British Journal of Health Psychology, 11*, 155–169.

Glanz, K., & Bishop, D.B. (2010). The role of behavioral science theory in development and implementation of public health interventions. *Annual Review of Public Health, 31*, 399–418.

Glasgow, R.E., Bull, S.S., Gillette, C., Klesges, L.M., & Dzewaltowski, D.A. (2002). Behavior change intervention research in health care settings: A review of recent reports with emphases on external validity. *American Journal of Preventive Medicine, 23*, 62–69.

Goldenberg, J.L., & Arndt, J. (2008). The implications of death for health: A terror management health model for behavioral health promotion. *Psychological Review, 115*(4), 1032–1053.

Gonzalez, V., Goeppinger, J., & Lorig, K. (1990). Four psychosocial theories and their application to patient education and clinical practice. *Arthritis Care and Research, 3*, 132–143.

Goodman, R.M., Liburd, L.C., & Green-Phillips A. (2001). The formation of a complex community program for diabetes control: Lessons learned from a case study of Project DIRECT. *Journal of Public Health Management and Practice, 7*, 19–29.

Grady, K.E., & Wallston, B.S. (1988). *Research in health care settings*. Newbury Park, CA: Sage.

Gray, J.A. (1994a). Personality dimensions and emotion systems. In P. Ekman, & R.J. Davidson (Eds.), *The nature of emotion: Fundamental questions* (pp. 329–331). New York: Oxford University Press.

Gray, J.A. (1994b). Three fundamental emotion systems. In P. Ekman, & R.J. Davidson (Eds.), *The nature of emotion: Fundamental questions* (pp. 243–247). New York: Oxford University Press.

Grimley, D.M., Prochaska, G.E., & Prochaska, J.O. (1993). Condom use assertiveness and the stages of change with main and other partners. *Journal of Applied Biobehavioral Research, 12*, 152–173.

Helgeson, V.S., & Lepore, S.J. (1997). The hurdles involved in conducting a randomized clinical intervention. *Health Psychologist, 18*(4), 4–5, 14–16.

Herbert, T.B., Silver, R.C., & Ellard, J.H. (1991). Coping with an abusive relationship: 1. How and why do women stay? *Journal of Marriage and the Family, 53*, 311–325.

Herzog, T.A. (2008). Analyzing the transtheoretical model using the framework of Weinstein, Rothman, and Sutton (1998): The example of smoking cessation. *Health Psychology, 27*(5), 548–556.

Herzog, T.A., & Blagg, C.O. (2007). Are most precontemplators contemplating smoking cessation? Assessing the validity of the Stages of Change. *Health Psychology, 26*(2), 222–231.

Higgins, E.T. (1998). Promotion and prevention: Regulatory focus as a motivational principle. *Advances in Experimental Social Psychology, 30*, 1–46.

Higgins, A., & Conner, M. (2003). Understanding adolescent smoking: The role of the Theory of Planned Behavior and implementation intentions. *Psychology, Health, and Medicine, 8*(2), 173–186.

Hohmann, A.A., & Shear, M.K. (2002). Community-based intervention research: Coping with the "noise" of real life in study design. *American Journal of Psychiatry, 159*, 201–207.

Holman, E.A. (1997). The nursing profession's role in health psychology research: A reply to Helgeson and Lepore. *Health Psychologist, 19*(2), 8.

Johnston, K.L., & White, K.M. (2003). Binge-drinking: A test of the role of group norms in the theory of planned behavior. *Psychology and Health, 18*, 63–77.

Joos, S., & Hickam, D. (1990). How health professionals influence health behavior: Patient provider interaction and health care outcomes. In K. Glanz, F. Lewis, & B. Rimer (Eds.), *Health behavior and health education: Theory, research and practice* (pp. 216–241). San Francisco: Jossey Bass.

Kaplan, R.M. (2000). Two pathways to prevention. *American Psychologist, 55*, 382–396.

Kemeny, M.E. (2003). An interdisciplinary research model to investigate psychosocial cofactors in disease: Application to HIV-1 pathogenesis. *Brain, Behavior, and Immunity, 17*(Supplement), S62–S72.

Kenny, D.A. (1979). *Correlation and causality*. New York: Wiley.

Kerner, J., Rimer, B., & Emmons, K. (2005). Introduction to the special section on dissemination. Dissemination research and research dissemination: How can we close the gap? *Health Psychology, 24*, 443–446.

Kessler, D., Lewis, G., Kaur, S., Wiles, N., King, M., Weich, S., Sharp, D.J., Araya, R., Hollinghurst, S., & Peters, T.J. (2009). Therapist-delivered internet psychotherapy for depression in primary care: A randomised controlled trial. *Lancet, 374*, 628–634.

Klonoff, E.A., & Landrine, H. (2001). Depressive symptoms and smoking among US Black adults: Absence of a relationship. *Journal of Health Psychology, 6*(6), 645–649.

Klonoff, E.A., & Landrine, H. (2004). Predicting youth access to tobacco: The role of youth versus store-clerk behavior and issues of ecological validity. *Health Psychology, 23*(5), 517–524.

Koepsell, T.D., Wagner, E.H., Cheadle, A.C., Patrick, D.L., Martin, D.C., Diehr, P.H., et al. (1992). Selected methodological issues in evaluating community-based health promotion and disease prevention programs. *Annual Review of Public Health, 13*, 31–57.

Kohler, C.L., Grimley, D., & Reynolds, K. (1999). Theoretical approaches guiding the development and implementation of health promotion programs. In J.M. Raczynski, & R.J. DiClemente (Eds.), *Handbook of health promotion and disease prevention* (pp. 23–46). New York: Kluwer/Plenum.

Krysan, M., & Couper, M.P. (2003). Race in the live and the virtual interview: Racial differences, social desirability, and activation effects in attitude surveys. *Social Psychology Quarterly, 66*(4), 364–383.

Landrine, H., & Corral, I. (2009). Separate and unequal: Residential segregation and black health disparities. *Ethnic Disparities, 19*(2), 179–184.

Larzelere, R.E., Kuhn, B.R., & Johnson, B. (2004). The intervention selection bias: An underrecognized confound in intervention research. *Psychological Bulletin, 130*, 289–303.

Latimer, A.E., Williams-Pichota, P., Katulak, N.A., Cox, A., Mowad, L., & Higgins, E.T. (2008). Promoting fruit and vegetable intake through messages tailored to individual differences in regulatory focus. *Annals of Behavioral Medicine, 35*, 363–369.

Lau, J.T.F., Thomas, J., & Liu, J.L.Y. (2000). Mobile phone and interactive computer interviewing to measure HIV-related risk behaviours: The impacts of data collection methods on research results. *AIDS, 14*, 1277–1278.

Lepore, S.J. (1995). Cynicism, social support, and cardiovascular reactivity. *Health Psychology, 14*, 210–216.

Leventhal, H., Brissette, I., & Leventhal, E.A. (2003). The common-sense model of self-regulation of health and illness. In L.D. Cameron, & H. Leventhal (Eds.), *The self-regulation of health and illness behavior* (pp. 42–65). New York: Routledge.

Levinthal, C.F. (2005). *Drugs, behavior, and modern society.* Boston: Allyn and Bacon.

Lichtenstein, E., Zhu, S-H, Tedeschi, G. (2010). Smoking cessation quitlines: an underrecognized intervention success. *American Psychologist, 65*(4), 252–261.

Litz, B.T., Engel, C.C., Bryant, R.A., & Papa, A. (2007). A randomized, controlled proof-of-concept trial of an internet-based, therapist-assisted self-management treatment for post-traumatic stress disorder. *American Journal of Psychiatry, 164*, 1676–1683.

Lorig, K., & Fries, J.F. (1990). *The arthritis helpbook: A tested self-management program for coping with your arthritis.* Reading, MA: Addison-Wesley.

Lorig, K., Seleznick, M., Lubeck, D., Ung, E., Chastain, R.L., & Holman, H.R. (1989). The beneficial outcomes of the arthritis self-management course are not adequately explained by behavior change. *Arthritis and Rheumatism, 31*, 91–95.

Maisto, S.A., Connors, G.J., & Zywiak, W.H. (2000). Alcohol treatment, changes in coping skills, self-efficacy, and levels of alcohol use and related problems 1 year following treatment initiation. *Psychology of Addictive Behaviors, 14*, 257–266.

Marshall, S.J., & Biddle, S.J.H. (2001). The transtheoretical model of behavior change: A meta-analysis of applications to physical activity and exercise. *Annals of Behavioral Medicine, 23*, 229–246.

May, S., & West, R. (2000). Do social support interventions ("buddy systems") aid smoking cessation? A review. *Tobacco Control, 9*, 415–422.

McAuley, E., Jerome, G.J., Marquez, D.X., Elavsky, S., & Blissmer, B. (2003). Exercise self-efficacy in older adults: Social, affective, and behavioral influences. *Annals of Behavioral Medicine, 25*, 1–7.

McCann, J.M., Bovbjerg, V.E., Brief, D.J., Turner, C., Follette, W.C., Fitzpatrick, V., et al. (1995). Relationship of self-efficacy to cholesterol lowering and dietary change in hyperlipidemia. *Annals of Behavioral Medicine, 17*, 221–226.

McClenahan, C., Shevlin, M., Adamson, G., Bennet, C., & O'Neill, B. (2007). Testicular self-examination: a test of the health belief model and the theory of planned behavior. *Health Education Research, 22*, 272–284.

McNally, R.J., Bryant, R.A., & Ehlers, A. (2003). Does early psychological intervention promote recovery from post-traumatic stress? *Psychological Science in the Public Interest, 4*, 45–79.

Mermelstein, R. (1999). Ethnicity, gender and risk factors for smoking initiation: An overview. *Nicotine and Tobacco Research, 1*(Suppl 2), S69–S70.

Merzel, C., & D'Afflitti, J. (2003). Reconsidering community-based health promotion: Promise, performance, and potential. *American Journal of Public Health, 93*, 557–574.

Mishra, S.I., Sanudo, F., & Conner, R.F. (2004). Collaborative research toward HIV prevention among migrant farmworkers. In B.P. Bowser, S.I. Mishra, et al. (Eds.), *Preventing AIDS: Community-science collaborations* (pp. 69–95). New York: Haworth.

Myers, L.B., & Horswill, M.S. (2006). Social cognitive predictors of sun protection intention and behavior. *Behavioral Medicine, 32*, 57–63.

Norman, P., Armitage, C.J., & Quigley, C. (2007). The theory of planned behavior and binge drinking: Assessing the impact of binge drinker prototypes. *Addictive Behaviors, 32*, 1753–1768.

Noar, S.M., & Zimmerman, R.S. (2005). Health behavior theory and cumulative knowledge regarding health behaviors: Are we moving in the right direction? *Health Education Research: Theory & Practice, 20*(3), 275–290.

Park, E., Schultz, J.K., Tudiver, F., Campbell, T., & Becker, L. (2004). Enhancing partner support to improve smoking cessation. *Cochrane Database of Systematic Review, 1*, CD002928.

Perkins, K.A. (2001). Smoking cessation in women: Special considerations. *CNS Drugs, 15*, 391–411.

Perkins, K.A., Donny, E., & Caggiula, A.R. (1999). Sex differences in nicotine effects and self-administration: Review of human and animal evidence. *Nicotine and Tobacco Research, 1*, 301–315.

Piper, D.L. (2000). The Health for Life Project: Behavioral outcomes. *Journal of Primary Prevention, 21*, 47–73.

Plotnikoff, R.C., Lippke, S., Courneya, K.S., Birkett, N., & Sigal, R.J. (2008). Physical activity and social cognitive theory: A test in a population sample of adults with Type 1 or Type 2 diabetes. *Applied Psychology: An International Review, 57*, 628–643.

Portnoy, D.B., Scott-Sheldon, L.A.J., Johnson, B.T., & Carey, M.P. (2008). Computer-delivered interventions for health promotion and behavioral risk reduction: A meta-analysis of 75 randomized controlled trials, 1988–2007. *Preventive Medicine, 47*, 3–16.

Prestwich, A., Perugini, M., & Hurling, R. (2010). Can implementation intentions and text messages promote brisk walking? A randomized trial. *Health Psychology, 29*, 40–49.

Prochaska, J.O., & DiClemente, C.C. (1983). Stages and processes of self-change of smoking: Toward an integrative model of change. *Journal of Consulting and Clinical Psychology, 51*, 390–395.

Prochaska, J.O., DiClemente, C.C., & Norcross, J.C. (1992). In search of how people change: Applications to addictive behaviors. *American Psychologist, 47*, 1102–1114.

Pyszczynski, T., Greenberg, J., & Solomon, S. (1999). A dual-process model of defense against conscious and unconscious death-related thoughts: An extension of terror management theory. *Psychological Review, 106*, 835–845.

Reilly, P.M., Sees, K.L., Shopshire, M.S., Hall, S.M., Delucchi, K.L., Tusel, D.J., et al. (1995). Self-efficacy and illicit opioid use in a 180-day detoxification treatment. *Journal of Consulting and Clinical Psychology, 63*, 158–162.

Revenson, T.A., & Schiaffino, K.M. (2000). Community-based health interventions. In J. Rappaport, & E. Seidman (Eds.), *Handbook of community psychology* (pp. 471–493). New York: Kluwer Academic/Plenum.

Rigotti, N.A., Lee, J.E., & Wechsler, H. (2000). US college students' use of tobacco products: Results of a national survey. *Journal of the American Medical Association, 9*, 699–705.

Ritterband, L.M., Thorndike, F.P., Gonder-Frederick, L.A., Magee, J.C., Bailey, E.T., & Saylor, D.K., et al. (2009). Efficacy of an internet-based behavioral intervention for adults with insomnia. *Archives of General Psychiatry, 66*(7), 692–698.

Rose, G. (1985). Sick individuals and sick populations. *International Journal of Epidemiology, 14*, 32–38.

Rose, G. (1992). *The strategy of preventive medicine.* New York: Oxford University Press.

Rosentock, I.M., Strecher, V.J., & Becker, M.H. (1994). The health belief model and HIV risk behavior change. In R.J. DiClemente, & J.L. Peterson (Eds.), *Preventing AIDS: Theories and methods of behavioral interventions* (pp. 5–24). New York: Plenum.

Rossini, A., de Almeida Simão, T., Albano, R.M., & Pinto, L.F. (2008). CYP2A6 polymorphisms and risk for tobacco-related cancers. *Pharmacogenomics, 9*(11), 1737–1752.

Rothman, A. (2008, June). *Structures of health behavior theories.* Presentation at the 2008 Advanced Training Institute of Health Behavior Theory, Madison, Wisconsin.

Rutter, D., & Quine, L. (2002). *Changing health behavior: Intervention and research with social cognition models.* Buckingham, PA: Open University Press.

Schlenger, W.E., & Silver, R.C. (2006). Web-based methods in terrorism and disaster research. *Journal of Traumatic Stress, 19*, 185–193.

Schneiderman, N. (2004). Psychosocial, behavioral, and biological aspects of chronic disease. *Current Directions in Psychological Science, 13*, 247–251.

Schneiderman, N., Antoni, M.H., & Ironson, G. (2003). Behavioral medicine in HIV infection. *Psychotherapeutics, 48*, 342–347.

Schorling, J.B., Roach, J., Siegel, M., Baturka, N. Hunt, D.E., Guterbock, T.M., et al. (1997). A trial of church-based smoking cessation interventions for rural African Americans. *Preventive Medicine, 26*, 92–101.

Secker-Walker, R.H., Gnich, W., Platt, S., & Lancaster, T. (2005). Community interventions for reducing smoking among adults. *Cochrane Database of Systematic Review, 1*, CD001745.

Schwarzer, R. (2008). Modeling health behavior change: How to predict and modify the adoption and maintenance of health behaviors. *Applied Psychology: An International Review, 57*, 1–29.

Sheeran, P., Conner, M., & Norman, P. (2001). Can the theory of planned behavior explain patterns of health behavior change? *Health Psychology, 20*, 12–19.

Shiffman, S., Balabanis, M.H., Paty, J.A., Engberg, J., Gwaltney, C.J., Liu, K.S., et al. (2000). Dynamic effects of self-efficacy on smoking lapse and relapse. *Health Psychology, 19*, 315–323.

Shilts, R. (1987). *And the band played on: Politics, people, and the AIDS epidemic.* New York: St. Martin's.

Sieber, J.E. (1998). Planning ethically responsible research. In L. Bickman, & D.J. Rog (Eds.), *Handbook of applied social research methods* (pp. 127–156). Thousand Oaks, CA: Sage.

Silenzio, V.M.B., Duberstein, P.R., Tang, W., Lu, N., Tu, X., & Homan, C.M. (2009). Connecting the invisible dots: Reaching lesbian, gay, and bisexual adolescents and young adults at risk for suicide through online social networks. *Social Science & Medicine, 69*(3), 469–474.

Smith, T.W., Glazer, K., Ruiz, J.M., & Gallo, L.C. (2004). Hostility, anger, aggressiveness, and coronary heart disease: An interpersonal perspective on personality, emotion, and health. *Journal of Personality, 72*(6), 1217–1270.

Sobel, D.S. (1995). Rethinking medicine: Improving health outcomes with cost-effective psychosocial interventions. *Psychosomatic Medicine, 57*, 234–244.

Sorensen, G., Emmons, K., Hunt, M.K., & Johnston, D. (1998). Implications of the results of community intervention trials. *Annual Review of Public Health, 19*, 379–416.

Sowden, A., Arblaster, L., & Stead, L. (2005). Community interventions for preventing smoking in young people. *Cochrane Database of Systematic Review, 1*, CD001291.

Steptoe, A., Wright, C., Kunz-Ebrecht, S.R., & Iliffe, S. (2006). Dispositional optimism and health behaviour in community-dwelling older people: Associations with health ageing. *British Journal of Health Psychology, 11*(Pt 1), 71–84.

Stokols, D. (1992). Establishing and maintaining healthy environments: Toward a social ecology of health promotion. *American Psychologist, 47*, 6–22.

Stokols, D. (2000). Social ecology and behavioral medicine: Implications for training, practice, and policy. *Behavioral Medicine, 26*(3), 129–138.

Stokols, D. (2006). Toward a science of transdisciplinary action research. *American Journal of Community Psychology, 38*, 63–77.

Strickland, B.R., & Crowne, D.P. (1963). Need for approval and the premature termination of psychotherapy. *Journal of Consulting and Clinical Psychology, 27*, 95–101.

Snyder, C.R., Lopez, S.J., & Pedrotti, J.T. (2010). Positive psychology: The scientific and practical explorations of human strengths. Thousands Oaks, CA: Sage.

Thompson, B., Coronado, G., Snipes, S.A., & Puschel, K. (2003). Methodological advances and ongoing challenges in designing community-based health promotion programs. *Annual Review of Public Health, 24*, 315–340.

Tonnesen, P. (2009). Smoking cessation: How compelling is the evidence? A review. *Health Policy, 91*(Suppl 1), S15–25.

Turner, C.F., Ku, L., Rogers, S.M., Lindberg, L.D., Pleck, J.H., & Sonenstein, F.L. (1998). Adolescent sexual behavior, drug use, and violence: Increased reporting with computer survey technology. *Science, 280*, 867–873.

Turner-McGrievy, G.M., Campbell, M.K., Tate, D.F., Truesdale, K.P., Bowling, J.M, & Crosby, L. (2010). Pounds Off Digitally Study: A randomized podcasting weight-loss intervention. *American Journal of Preventive Medicine, 37*, 263–269.

Joint United Nations Programme on HIV/AIDS (UNAIDS). (2010). *Report on the global AIDS epidemic.* Geneva, Switzerland.

U.S. Department of Health and Human Services. (2004). *The health consequences of smoking: A report of the surgeon general.* Rockville, MD: U.S. Department of Health and Human Services, Centers for Disease Control and Prevention, National Center for Chronic Disease Prevention and Health Promotion, Office on Smoking and Health.

Velicer, W.F., Prochaska, J.O., Rossi, J.S., & Snow, M.G. (1992). Assessing outcome in smoking cessation studies. *Psychological Bulletin, 111*, 23–41.

Weinstein, N.D. (2006, June). *Decision-oriented theories of health behavior.* Presentation at the 2006 Advanced Training Institute of Health Behavior Theory, Madison, Wisconsin.

Weinstein, N.D., & Sandman, P.M. (2002). The Precaution Adoption Process Model and its application. In R.J. DiClemente, R.A. Crosby, & M.C. Kegler (Eds.), *Emerging theories in health promotion practice and research* (pp. 16–39). San Francisco: Jossey-Bass.

Wechsler, H., Kelley, K., Seibring, M., Juo, M., & Rigotti, N.A. (2001). College smoking policies and smoking cessation programs: Results of a survey of college health center directors. *Journal of American College of Health, 50*, 141–142.

West, R. (2005). Time for a change: Putting the transtheoretical (stages of change) model to rest. *Addiction, 100*, 1036–1039.

Westmaas, J.L., Bontemps-Jones, J., & Bauer, J.E. (2010). Social support in smoking cessation: Reconciling theory and evidence. *Nicotine and Tobacco Research, 12*(7), 695–707.

Westmaas, J.L., & Jamner, L.D. (2006). Paradoxical effects of social support on blood pressure reactivity among defensive individuals. *Annals of Behavioral Medicine, 31*, 238–247.

Westmaas, J.L., & Butler-Woicik, P. (2005). Dispositional motivations and genetic risk feedback. *Addictive Behaviors, 30*(8), 1524–1534.

Whittaker, R., Borland, R., Bullen, C., Lin, R.B., McRobbie, H., & Rodgers, A. (2009). Mobile phone-based interventions for smoking cessation. *Cochrane Database of Systematic Reviews, 7*, CD006611.

Williamson, L.M., Dodds, J.P., Mercey, D.E., Johnson, A.M., & Hart, G.J. (2006). Increases in HIV-related sexual risk behavior among community samples of gay men in London and Glasgow: How do they compare? *Journal of Acquired Immune Deficiency Syndromes, 42*(2), 238–241.

World Health Organization (2008). The top ten causes of death. Fact sheet No 310. Retrieved from http://www.who.int/mediacentre/factsheets/fs310/en/index.html.

Wortman, C.B., Hendricks, M., & Hillis, J.W. (1976). Factors affecting participant reactions to random assignment in ameliorative social programs. *Journal of Personality and Social Psychology, 33*, 256–266.

Zabalegui, A., Sanchez, S., Sanchez, P.D., & Juando, C. (2005). Nursing and cancer support groups. *Journal of Advanced Nursing, 51*, 369–381.

Zimmerman, R.S., & Olson, K. (1994). AIDS-related risk behavior and behavior change in a sexually active, heterosexual sample: A test of three models of prevention. *AIDS Education and Prevention, 6*, 189–205.

# Uncertainty, Variability, and Resource Allocation in the Health Care Decision Process

Robert M. Kaplan

**Abstract**

Medicine is not a mechanical science. Instead, it is a social science that requires complex decisions based on ambiguous evidence. Uncertainty often exists about the correctness of the diagnosis, regarding whether treatments will make patients better, and regarding variability in beliefs that treatments are safe. This chapter presents evidence showing that substantial variability arises in physician decisions. It reviews several lines of research to demonstrate remarkable variation in the decisions to use diagnostic tests and therapeutic interventions. It argues that physician decisions are influenced by incentives to increase the number of patients receiving a chronic disease diagnoses through aggressive testing and through changes in the definition of what we label as "disease." These incentives can have substantial impacts on health care costs, patient anxiety, and the organization and delivery of health care. Because of these problems, patients need to be much more active in sharing decisions about their own care. The final section of the chapter reviews the emerging literature on shared medical decision making.

**Keywords:** Medical decision making, health care decision making, medical diagnosis, patient participation

Health psychology has played a tentative role in the enterprise of health care. Health psychologists have concerned themselves with how patients adapt to illness or how psychological factors might contribute to a medical diagnosis (Miller, Sherman, & Christensen, 2010; Mollen, Ruiter, & Kok, 2010). They have also studied how diagnosis affects mood, cognitive functioning, and other psychological variables. It is typically assumed that diagnoses are correct and that all patients placed in diagnostic categories should receive treatment. Considerable effort has been devoted to training patients to adhere to physician orders or instructions. It is assumed that physician orders describe the most likely path to positive patient outcomes. Rarely has the patient's perspective been given equal consideration. For example, health psychology devotes insufficient attention to whether treatment results in improved health, damaged health through side effects, or reduced financial resources, or to how patients can gain equal partnership in decisions concerning their medical care.

One common assumption is that medical diagnoses are "correct." By correct, we assume that a diagnosis identifies true pathology, and that identification of this problem initiates a course of action that will result in patient improvement. The physician plays a mechanical role. He or she finds the problem and then proceeds to fix it. This chapter argues that medicine is not a mechanical science. Instead, it is a social science that requires complex decisions based on ambiguous evidence. Uncertainty often exists about the correctness of the diagnosis, regarding whether treatments will make patients better, and regarding variability in beliefs that treatments are safe. This chapter focuses on uncertainty, variability, and resource allocation. First, evidence will be presented to show that substantial variability arises in physician decisions. Several lines of research will be reviewed to demonstrate remarkable variation in the decisions to use diagnostic tests and therapeutic interventions. Second, it will be argued that physician decisions are influenced by incentives to increase the number of patients receiving a chronic disease diagnoses through aggressive testing and through changes in the definition of what we label as "disease." These incentives can have substantial impacts on health care costs, patient anxiety, and the organization and delivery of health care. Third, because of these problems, patients need to be much more active in sharing decisions about their own care. The final section of the chapter will review the emerging literature on shared medical decision making.

## Expenditures and Outcomes

Good health is, perhaps, the most valued state of being. In many ways, we orient our lives to achieve wellness for ourselves and for our families and friends. Health services are used to achieve better health, maintain good health, or prevent health-damaging conditions. Because these services come at a cost, we are willing to use financial resources to purchase health. But, are we using our resources wisely in the pursuit of better population health? To address this question, we must consider the financial implications of purchasing health care. A good starting point is the comparison of medical decisions and health care expenditures in the United States in relation to other countries.

Health care costs in the United States have grown exponentially since 1940. Although a temporary slowdown occurred in the early 1990s, the rate of increase began to accelerate again by the turn of the century. Health care in the United States now consumes about 17% of the gross domestic product (GDP), whereas no other country in the world spends more than 10%. Although the rate of growth has slowed, health care costs rose by 1.1% between 2008 and 2009 (about $2,400,000,000 (Sessions & Detsky, 2010). And health care costs continue to grow at a rate faster than the rest of the economy. Between 1980 and 2010, the rate at which health care costs grew more rapidly than other costs was about 2.8% per year (Fuchs, 2010). Figure 5.1, based on data reported to the Organization for Economic Development and Cooperation (OEDC), shows that the expense of health care in the United States exceeds that in virtually all developed countries.

One of the most unexplored assumptions is that greater expenditure will result in greater health benefit. We know from international studies that developed countries that spend considerably less than the United States on health care have about equal health outcomes. The United Kingdom, for example, spends less than half as much per capita on health care as the United States. However, life expectancy in the United Kingdom (81.6 years for women, 77.2 years for men) is slightly longer than it is in the United States (80.8 years for women, 75.6 years for men), and infant mortality is slightly lower (4.8/1,000 vs. 6.3/1,000; [2010 data found at

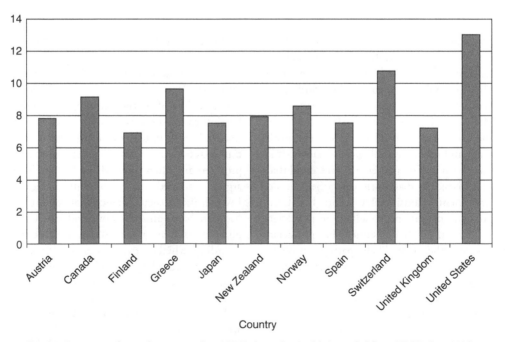

**Fig. 5.1** Percentage of gross domestic product (GDP) devoted to health (compiled from OECD data, 2003).

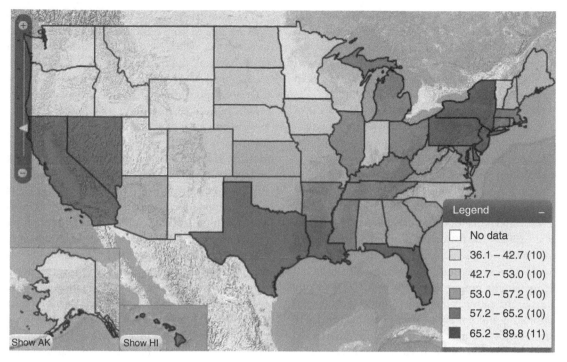

**Fig. 5.2** Physician visits during last 6 months by state. Compiled from data from Dartmouth Atlas of Healthcare.

Widopedia.com]). Among 13 countries in one comparison, the United States ranked 12th when compared on 16 health indicators (Starfield, 2000). Neither country is a world leader on these indicators. For infant mortality, the United Kingdom ranks 22nd and the United States ranks 33rd.

Within the United States, there is considerable variability in spending. Figure 5.2 shows average number of physician visits by the Medicare during the last 2 years of life, broken down by state. The data come from the 2010 Dartmouth Atlas of Healthcare. In California, decedents had an average of 72.8 visits, whereas in Oregon there were only about half as many visits (37.9). In California, the Medicare program spent an average of $33,706 per recipient during the last 6 months of life, whereas in Oregon, average per recipient spending was $18, 935. Quality is typically defined as adherence to defined

standards of patient care. For example, it is possible to estimate the extent to which physicians adhere to defined patient guidelines. Evaluations have suggested that essentially no relationship exists between per capita spending and quality across the U.S. states. Figure 5.3 uses 2010 data from the Dartmouth Atlas to summarize the relationship between per capita spending during the last 2 years of life and family ratings of satisfaction with the care. As the figure demonstrates, spending more does not buy more satisfaction. In fact, there appears to be a negative relationship—states with high spending tend to have lower patient satisfaction.

Another, related assumption is that patients will be better off if they have access to high-technology centers. For example, neonatal intensive care units (NICUs) offer dramatic benefits to premature and low-birth-weight infants. It is assumed that there

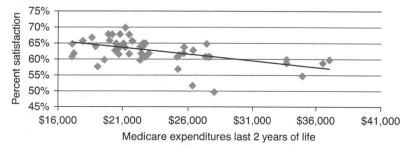

**Fig. 5.3** Satisfaction by Expenditures: Dartmouth Atlas 2010.

will be more NICUs in areas where there are concentrations of low-birth-weight infants. However, systematic evaluation of this issue suggests that the concentration of neonatologists and specialized units is unrelated to the areas where there is a need for these services (Goodman et al., 2002).

We would assume that babies born in areas of plentiful care have a higher chance of survival. However, evidence suggests that this is not the case. It does appear that survival is poor for low-birth-weight infants born in areas in the bottom 20% of NICU availability. Beyond this lower quintile, however, being born in a area with a high density of NICUs makes very little difference (Goodman et al., 2002). The reason for this finding may be that we may have more neonatologists and NICUs than necessary. For example, the number of births per neonatologist ranges from 390 to 8,197. In many areas of the country, there are simply too many neonatologists and not enough work for them to do. In other words, we may have significantly overtrained and overinvested in neonatal intensive care. With an overabundance of providers, some unnecessary procedures may be done. Further, building an overabundance of NICUs might use resources that could have been applied for other purposes. For example, many communities that have an oversupply of NICUs do not support appropriate prenatal care due to lack of resources. Spain has many fewer NICUs than the United States, but it devotes more resources to supportive care. Spain's infant mortality rate is lower than the that of the United States (3.9 vs. 6.9/1,000; OECD 2003 data).

## Opportunity Cost Problem

Managed care and other pressures have forced new competition among health care providers. Health care resources are limited, and there is constant pressure to spend more on attractive new treatments or diagnostic procedures. Without containment, health care could grow to the point at which it would use such a large portion of the GDP that there would not be enough money left for high-quality public services in other sectors, such as education, energy, or national defense (Blumenthal, 2001; Mechanic & Altman, 2010). Although most provider groups understand that health care costs must be contained, few acknowledge that their own expenditures should be subject to evaluation. Successful lobbying to obtain reimbursement for a specific service may necessarily mean that another service is excluded.

Suppose, for example, that the amount that can be spent on health care is fixed, and $3 of each $100

(3%) is devoted to behavioral services. If psychologists are able to get $10 of each $100 spent on their services, less will be available to spend on other nonbehavioral health services. This is called the *opportunity cost problem*. Opportunity costs are the forgone opportunities that are surrendered when resources are used to support a particular decision. If we spend a lot of money in one sector of health care, we necessarily spend less money elsewhere. How do we decide which services should get more and which should get fewer resources?

When confronted with the choice between two good programs, it is always tempting to support both. The difficulty is that it costs more to offer multiple programs. No public policy has ever been shown to effectively control costs in the American health care system (Blumenthal, 2001). The cost of programs is represented in the fees for health insurance or the cost of health care to taxpayers. A society can choose to offer as many health programs as it wants. However, more programs require more funding. Employees do not want the fees for their health insurance to rise, and taxpayers do not want tax increases. The goal of formal decision models is to get higher-quality health care without increasing costs.

## Uncontrollable Demand for Heath Care

There are many explanations for why it is difficult to control health care costs (Gilmer & Kronick, 2005; Quinn, 2010). Providing an exhaustive list of these explanations is beyond the scope of this chapter; however, two important issues will be probed. First, the demand for health care is elastic, expandable, and perhaps infinite. It might be argued that health concerns should receive first priority in the allocation of public resources. Once population health is achieved, policy makers can move on to other priorities, such as education, national defense, or homeland security. However, if all desired health services were provided, resources would be exhausted quickly, and insufficient resources may be left to address other societal concerns. The problem is compounded by a continual supply of new, expensive services and products. Further, we have no assurance that investments in health care will improve population health because many services produce limited benefits.

Many have argued that society has a moral obligation to provide all necessary services for those who are sick and in need of help. The challenge is in determining how many people are in need of help and whether services will really help them. The medical care system has been motivated to expand the number of people who are "sick" and, therefore, in need of medical service. This has been accomplished through screening programs that identify disease at very early phases. Once an individual is identified as "sick," it is incumbent upon the system to treat the problem. In many cases, however, attention to early stages of disease may offer little or no benefit. Mass screening programs may produce harm, but not for the obvious reasons. There is little evidence that they harm people physiologically; the concern is connected to opportunity costs. Some expensive programs may divert significant resources away from public health and behavioral programs that might offer greater potential to improve population health.

## How Much Health Care Do We Need? The Geographic Distribution of Health Services

The difference in disease rates in various communities is complicated by another variable. Society has often assumed that if a doctor diagnoses an illness, the illness exists. Further, we assume that any qualified doctor, presented with the same problem, will come to the same diagnosis. However, substantial evidence suggests that diagnosis rates vary widely. Professionals do not always come to the same conclusion when presented with very similar cases. Thus, if the distribution of disease is the same in different communities, we would expect the rates of reporting to be roughly equivalent. However, physicians vary markedly in the rates of illness they detect and the rates of service they recommend. Wennberg and his colleagues have devoted 35 years to the description of this problem (Mittler, Landon, Fisher, Cleary, & Zaslavsky, 2010; Weeks et al., 2010; Wennberg, 1996; Wennberg & Gittelsohn, 1982). They report that a major factor in the use of medical services is supplier-induced demand; in other words, providers create demand for their services by diagnosing illnesses. When new diagnostic technologies gain acceptance from physician groups, new epidemics of "disease" appear. One of the earliest documented cases of supplier-induced demand was described by Glover in the United Kingdom. Glover recorded the rates of tonsillectomy in the Hornse Burrough school district. In 1928, 186 children in the district had their tonsils surgically removed. The next year, the doctor who enthusiastically supported tonsillectomy was replaced by another physician who was less attracted to the procedure. In 1929, the number of tonsillectomies was reduced to only 12 (Wennberg, 1990).

Often, surgeons agree on the need to perform surgery. For example, there are high-consensus diagnoses, such as resection of the colon for colon cancer and surgery for appendicitis. Other areas of high agreement might include amputation of a toe with gangrene, removal of well-defined tumors, or intervention to repair a compound fracture. For most surgical procedures, however, there is substantial discretion, and rates for surgery vary (Birkmeyer, 2009; Birkmeyer & Dimick, 2009; Englesbe, Dimick, Fan, Baser, & Birkmeyer, 2009).

### Los Angles Versus San Diego: A Case Example

Between the completion of the first and second editions of this book, I moved from San Diego to Los Angeles. My physical move was only about 100 miles, and most aspects of the two communities are very similar. However, health care in Los Angeles is remarkably different from that in San Diego. In 2009, an estimated $2.4 trillion was spent for health care in the United States. In other words, we spent nearly $8,000 per person on health care (the data is from the US Center for Medicare and Medicaid Services (www.cms.gov) U.S. Center for Health Statistics). Of course, that amount was not spent on each individual. You may not have been hospitalized in 2–11, but some people were hospitalized for extended periods or for services that were very expensive. Averages do not tell us much about individual cases. Still, important lessons are to be learned by looking at the overall expenditures data for different locales. Within the United States, we would expect the average costs to be similar in regions serving an equal number of people. Yet, that is not the case. For most of my career, I worked at the medical school at the University of California, San Diego. A few years ago, I moved to the University of California, Los Angeles. My physical move took me only about 100 miles, and the communities are demographically very similar. However, the differences in how medicine is practiced are surprisingly different. In 2006, Medicare was spending an average of $11,639 per recipient in Los Angeles and $6,654 in San Diego for services offered during the last 2 years of life. In other words, Medicare is spending $1.75 in Los Angeles to purchase the same package of services that they spend $1.00 on, just 120 miles down the road. Differences between total Medicare (Parts A and B) 2005 expenditures in San Diego and Los Angeles health services areas are summarized in Figure 5.4. The lowest-cost Los Angeles health service area (Torrence) was more expensive than the highest-cost community (La Mesa) in San Diego County. Considering Los Angeles as a benchmark,

Glendale had 2005 expenditures that were 97% of those in Los Angeles. The most expensive San Diego community of La Mesa had mean per recipient expenditures that were 69% of what was spent per recipient in Los Angeles. The San Diego County community of La Jolla had expenditures that were only half those in Los Angeles. There was very little overlap between the San Diego and the Los Angeles markets for total Medical reimbursements, total Part A expenditures, total Part B expenditures, percent of Medicare deaths occurring within a hospital, inpatient hospital reimbursement, hospital admission during the last 6 months of life, Part B reimbursements to physicians, and reimbursements for professional and laboratory services. The analysis of Medicare claims has an important methodological advantage over virtually any other database because Medicare pays for health care for essentially all individuals 65 years or older. The analyses use essentially the entire claims database or a representative 5% sample. These include hundreds of millions of claims, so the usual sources of sampling error are essentially absent from these analyses. What is most striking about these studies is that the amount of health care delivered in different geographic regions is highly variable. Some regions get much more than others. However, we have very little evidence that those living in areas that receive more care have better health outcomes than do those living in areas that receive less care (Wennberg, Freeman, & Culp, 1987).

The Los Angeles–San Diego comparison is particularly interesting from a public policy perspective. U.S. Medicare is a federal program that aims to provide equal benefit to all its recipients. Yet, on average, Medicare spends at least 50% more per recipient in Los Angeles than it does in San Diego (Kaplan, 2009; Wennberg et al., 1987). Are San Diego residents getting a bad deal? Because the government spends less on San Diego residents, it might be argued that the health of San Diego residents will suffer because they receive insufficient medical attention. However, evidence does not show that residents of Los Angeles residents are any healthier than residents of San Diego. In fact, some evidence implies that Los Angeles residents may be worse off. For example, evidence from a publicly available database run by the Medicare program (hospitalcompare.gov) consistently shows that San Diego has the edge on measures of patient satisfaction (Fisher & Welch, 1999). Further, the chances of dying within 30 days of major heart surgery are lower in San Diego in comparison to Los Angeles. The basis for these geographic comparisons comes from a group of investigators at the Dartmouth Medical School who created an atlas of maps that show health care utilization broken down by geographic region. The atlas attempts to link the substantial variation in service to a variety of other factors. Figure 5.4 for example, shows Medicare spending mapped by hospital service area. It shows that Medicare spends about twice as much per recipient in southern Texas as it does in New Mexico. Yet, we have no evidence that people in southern Texas get better health care or have better health outcomes than do people in Albuquerque. One factor that does not explain the variation is the prevalence of disease in the different communities.

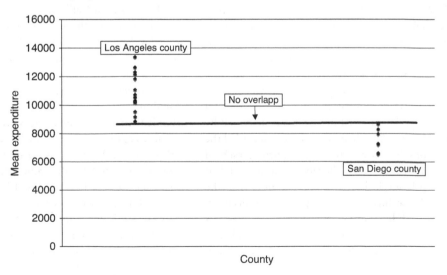

**Fig. 5.4** Differences in Medicare spending between Los Angeles and San Diego. Data compiled from Dartmouth Atlas of Healthcare.

On the other hand, some evidence suggests that the availability of doctors and hospitals informs how much medical service a community will receive. For example, *The Dartmouth Atlas of Health Care* also shows remarkable variability in the distribution of physicians and physician specialists. For example, there are 43.9 psychiatrists per 1,000 persons in White Plains, New York, and there are 38.4 in San Francisco. Manhattan is not far behind (35.5). On the other hand, there are only 2.8 psychiatrists per 1,000 persons in Oxford, Mississippi, and 3.0 per 1,000 in Fort Smith, Arkansas. The map shows that psychiatrists tend to live in major metropolitan areas and to be focused on the West or East Coast. They have a strong concentration in New England. There is also a substantial concentration near the ski areas of Colorado and in southeast Arizona (Wennberg, 1998).

Some medical conditions are associated with higher variation and health care use than are others. For example, the variation for problems such as fracture of the hip is not large; patients who fracture their hips are likely to be admitted to the hospital wherever they live. However, as the maps show, most health problems are associated with high variation. The Dartmouth group estimates that 80% of patients who are admitted to hospitals have been diagnosed with high-variation medical conditions such as pneumonia, chronic obstructive pulmonary disease, gastroenteritis, and congestive heart failure. They argue that hospital capacity has a major influence on the likelihood that a patient will be hospitalized. This relationship is illustrated in Figure 5.5, which shows the relationship between hospital beds per 1,000 residents and hospital discharges for ambulatory care–sensitive conditions. The figure suggests that the bed supply explains more that half of the variance in discharges for conditions such as pneumonia, heart failure, and chronic obstructive pulmonary disease. The correlation between hospital beds and admissions is a remarkable .75. In hospital referral regions where there are fewer than 2.5 beds per 1,000 residents, the hospital discharge rate for high-variation conditions was 145 per 1,000. Among regions that had more 4.5 beds per 1,000 residents, the rate was 219.8. More beds mean more hospital discharges. These data indicate that the decision to admit individuals to the hospital is influenced by factors other than their medical condition. When beds are available, they are more likely to be used. When more hospital beds are used, health care costs go up.

It seems plausible that communities with greater hospital resources are better able to care for their populations. More health care should lead to more health. However, several analyses have shown that people are slightly more likely to die in communities where more acute hospital care is used. An obvious explanation is that these communities have people who are older, sicker, or poorer. However, careful analyses controlled for age, sex, race, income, and a variety of variables related to illness and the need for care. None of these variables was able to explain the relationship (Fisher et al., 2003). In other words, the analysis suggests that more is not better. In fact, it implies that more may be worse.

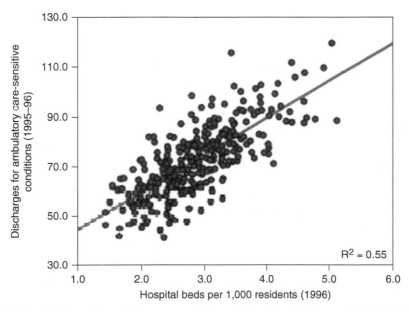

**Fig. 5.5** Hospital beds and discharges for ambulatory care–sensitive conditions (from *The Dartmouth Atlas of Health Care*, p. 129).

## Is Preventive Medicine Using the Wrong Model?

How could there be so much variation in the use of medical care services? Are some doctors missing important diagnoses, and others diagnosing diseases that do not exist? Following the dictum that all who are sick must receive treatment, it might be argued that everyone with a medical diagnosis must be given the very best treatment. Nowhere is this more apparent than in the field of clinical preventive medicine, which is moving toward more aggressive screening and treatment of mild-spectrum disease. We define mild-spectrum as values close to the population norm. One thrust of preventive medicine has been directed toward the use of high-cost pharmaceutical products for the management of large numbers of patients. There are many alternative uses of the same resources, including public health approaches that might prevent risk factors from developing in the first place. These approaches may not be part of the medical care system but might produce substantial health benefit. For example, programs to prevent youths from using cigarettes may produce substantial public health benefit even though they do not require medical diagnosis or the use of medical or surgical treatments (Kaplan, 2000).

Disease is often characterized as a binary variable. A "diagnosis" is either present or absent. However, many biological variables are normally distributed in the population. Clinical judgment and evidence-based reviews have been used to set cut points that divide these continuous distributions into disease–nondisease dichotomies. Little is known about the effect of setting different disease cut points upon costs and health outcomes.

## Finding Better Ways to Make Health Care Decisions

If the decisions made in heath care are not optimal in terms of resource use and patient outcomes, how might a better system be designed? The remainder of this chapter introduces decision models that might contribute to solving this problem. Before reviewing applications of the models, two conceptual issues will be introduced. The first is a conceptualization of health outcomes, and the second is a "disease reservoir model" that probes our understanding of the need for health services.

### Defining Health Outcomes

The traditional biomedical model of health and the outcomes model focus on different measures for the evaluation of health care. The traditional biomedical model is regarded as successful if disease is found and fixed. The outcomes model of health care suggests that resources should be used to make people live longer and feel better (Kaplan, 2000, 2009). Finding and fixing disease may or may not contribute to this objective.

To quantify the benefits of health care, it is necessary to build a comprehensive model of health benefit. Traditional measures of health outcome were very general. They included life expectancy, infant mortality, and disability days. The difficulty with these indicators is that they did not reflect most of the benefits of health care. For example, life expectancy and infant mortality are good measures because they allow for comparisons between programs with different specific objectives. The difficulty is that neither is sensitive to minor variations in health status. Treatment of most common illnesses may have relatively little effect on life expectancy. Infant mortality, although sensitive to socioeconomic variations, does not register the effect of health services delivered to people who are older than 1 year.

Survival analysis, which gives a unit of credit for each year of survival, is an attractive generic measure of health status. Suppose, for example, that a person has a life expectancy of 80 years and dies prematurely at age 50. In survival analysis, the person is scored as 1.0 for each of the first 50 years and 0 for each year thereafter. The problem is that years with disability are scored the same as those years in perfect health. For example, a person with severe arthritis who is alive is scored exactly the same as someone in perfect health. To address this problem, we have proposed using adjusted survival analysis, a method that allows us to summarize outcomes in terms of quality-adjusted life years (QALYs). In quality-adjusted survival analysis, years of wellness are scored on a continuum ranging from 0 for death to 1.0 for optimum function (Kaplan, 1994).

QALYs are measures of life expectancy with adjustments for quality of life (Fryback et al., 2007; Garster, Palta, Sweitzer, Kaplan, & Fryback, 2009; Gold, Franks, & Erickson, 1996; Gold, Stevenson, & Fryback, 2002; Kaplan, 1990; Kaplan & Anderson, 1996; Kaplan & Mehta, 1994; Weinstein, Siegel, Gold, Kamlet, & Russell, 1996). QALYs integrate mortality and morbidity to express health status in terms of equivalents of well years of life. If a woman dies of breast cancer at age 50 and one would have expected her to live to age 75, the disease was associated with 25 lost life years. If 100 women died at age 50 (and also had a life expectancies of 75 years), 2,500 (100 × 25 years) life years would be lost.

Death is not the only outcome of concern in cancer. Many adults suffer from the disease, leaving them somewhat disabled over long periods of time. Although they are still alive, the quality of their lives has diminished. QALYs take into consideration the quality-of-life consequences of these illnesses. For example, a disease that reduces quality of life by one-half will take away 0.5 QALYs over the course of one year. If it affects two people, it will take away 1 year (or $2 \times 0.5$) over a 1-year period. A pharmaceutical treatment that improves quality of life by 0.2 for each of five individuals will result in the equivalent of one QALY if the benefit is maintained over a 1-year period. The basic assumption is that 2 years scored as 0.5 add up to the equivalent of 1 year of complete wellness. Similarly, 4 years scored as 0.25 are equivalent to 1 completely well year of life. A treatment that boosts a patient's health from 0.5 to 0.75 produces the equivalent of 0.25 QALYs. If applied to four individuals, and the duration of the treatment effect is 1 year, the effect of the treatment would be equivalent to 1 completely well year of life. This system has the advantage of considering both benefits and side effects of programs in terms of the common QALY units. Although QALYs are typically assessed for patients, they can also be measured for others, including caregivers who are placed at risk because they experience stressful life events. The Institute of Medicine recommended that population health metrics be used to evaluate public programs and to assist the decision-making process (Field & Gold, 1998).

In addition to health benefits, programs also have costs. Resources are limited, and good policy requires allocation to maximize life expectancy and health-related quality of life. Thus, in addition to measuring health outcomes, costs must also be considered. Methodologies for estimating costs have now become standardized (Gold, 1996; Kaplan, 1994, 2009; Ramsey, Sullivan, & Kaplan, 2008; Weinstein, 1996). From an administrative perspective, cost estimates include all costs of treatment and costs associated with caring for any side effects of treatment. Typically, economic discounting is applied to adjust for using current assets to achieve a future benefit. From a social perspective, costs are broader and may include costs of family members staying home from work to provide care. Comparing programs for a given population with a given medical condition, cost-effectiveness is measured as the change in costs of care for the program compared with the existing therapy or program, relative to the change in health measured in a standardized unit

such as the QALY. The difference in costs over the difference in effectiveness is the *incremental cost-effectiveness* and is usually expressed as the cost/QALY. Since the objective of all programs is to produce QALYs, the cost/QALY ratio can be used to show the relative efficiency of different programs (Kaplan & Anderson, 1996).

### When Finding and Fixing Disease Does Not Matter: The Disease Reservoir Hypothesis

Using a traditional biomedical approach, much of contemporary preventive medicine is oriented toward finding disease early and applying aggressive treatments. However, there may be circumstances in which early detection of disease does not lead to improvement in patient outcomes. To understand this, it may be valuable to introduce an idea known as the *disease reservoir hypothesis* (Kaplan, 2009).

Undiagnosed disease is probably quite common, particularly among older people. Cancers of the breast and prostate have been identified in as many as 30% (breast) and 40% (prostate) of older adults who die from other causes (Black & Welch, 1997). Only about 3% of elderly men will die of prostate cancer, and only about 3% of elderly women will die of breast cancer. Autopsy studies consistently show that more than 90% of young adults who died early in life from noncardiovascular causes have fatty streaks in their coronary arteries indicating the initiation of coronary disease (Strong et al., 1999). The harder we look, the more likely it is that cases will be found. A very sensitive test for prostate cancer may detect disease in ten men for each man who will eventually die of this condition. Advanced magnetic resonance imaging (MRI) technology has revealed surprisingly high rates of undiagnosed stroke. One cross-sectional study of 3,502 men and women over age 65 found that 29% had evidence of mild stokes and that 75% had plaque in their carotid arteries (Manolio et al., 1999).

As diagnostic technology improves, the health care system will be challenged because these common problems will be identified in many individuals who may not benefit from treatment. The problem has been fiercely debated in relation to cancer screening tests such as mammography and prostate-specific antigen (PSA) (Welch & Black, 1997; Welch, Schwartz, & Woloshin, 2000).

According to the American Cancer Society, screening and early detection of cancers save lives (*Cancer Facts and Figures 2010*). It is believed that a reservoir of undetected disease exists that might be eliminated through more aggressive intervention.

Screening guidelines have been proposed, and those who fail to adhere to these guidelines are regarded as irresponsible. One national survey found that 87% of adults think that cancer screening is almost always a good idea, and 74% believe that early detection saves lives. Nearly 70% of the respondents considered a 55-year-old woman who did not get a mammogram to be irresponsible (Schwartz, Woloshin, Fowler, & Welch, 2004). Although early detection messages have been pushed for more than a century (Aronowitz, 2001), evidence that early detection results in better outcomes is very limited (Welch, 2001, 2004).

To better understand the problem, it is necessary to understand the natural history of disease. Public health campaigns assume that disease is binary; either a person has the "diagnosis," or they do not. However, most diseases are processes. It is likely that chronic disease begins long before it is diagnosed. For example, if smokers are screened for lung cancer, many cases can be identified. However, clinical trials have shown that the course of the disease is likely to be the same for those who are screened and those not subjected to screening, even though screening leads to more diagnosis and treatment (Marcus et al., 2000).

Black and Welch make the distinction between disease and *pseudodisease* (Black & Welch, 1997). Pseudodisease is disease that will not affect life duration or quality of life at any point in a patient's lifetime. When the disease is found, it is often "fixed" with surgical treatment. However, the fix may have consequences, often leaving the patient with new symptoms or problems. The outcomes model considers the benefits of screening and treatment from the patient's perspective (Kaplan, 2000, 2009). Often, using information provided by patients, we can estimate the quality-adjusted life expectancy for a population and determine if they are better off with or without screening and treatment (Kaplan et al., 1997).

### The Value of Screening

Screening tests are often used to detect disease early. Although screening is clearly worthwhile for detecting cases of disease, some of these cases will actually be pseudodisease. Cases of pseudodisease are unlikely to benefit from clinical intervention, thus raising questions about whether resources commonly devoted to early disease detection might be better used for other purposes. To illustrate the complexity of these decisions, three case examples will be offered: prostate cancer, breast cancer, and heart disease.

### PROSTATE CANCER SCREENING

The disease reservoir hypothesis helps explain controversies surrounding several cancer screening tests. One example of the differences between the traditional biomedical model and the outcomes models concerns screening and treatment for prostate cancer. Most cancer prevention efforts follow a traditional "find it–fix it" secondary prevention model. The identification of cancer dictates treatment, which in turn is evaluated by changes in biological process or disease activity. In the case of prostate cancer, a digital rectal exam may identify an asymmetric prostate, leading to a biopsy and the identification of prostate cancer. Diagnosis of cancer often leads to a radical prostatectomy (surgical removal of the prostate gland). The success of the surgery would be confirmed by eradication of the tumor, reduced PSA, and patient survival.

Studies have demonstrated that serum PSA is elevated in men with clinically diagnosed prostate cancer (Fowler, Bigler, & Farabaugh, 2002; Schroder & Wildhagen, 2002; Vis, 2002) and that high PSA levels have positive predictive value for prostate cancer. Despite the promise of PSA screening, there are also significant controversies. Prostate cancer is common for men aged 70 and older (Adami, 2010; Adolfsson, 2010). Averaging data across eight autopsy studies, it has been estimated that the prevalence of prostate cancer is as high as 39% in 70- to 79-year-old men (Adami, 2010: Adolfsson, 2010). The treatment of this disease varies dramatically from country to country and within regions of the United States. For example, radical prostatectomy was done nearly twice as often in the Pacific Northwest as it was in New England a few years ago (Lu-Yao et al., 1997), although the disparities have declined slightly in recent years (Bubolz, Wasson, Lu-Yao, & Barry, 2001).Yet, survival rates and deaths from prostate cancer are no different in the two regions. PSA screening finds many cases. In the great majority of cases, however, the men would have died of another cause long before developing their first symptom of prostate cancer. In other words, much of the prostate cancer that is detected is probably pseudodisease.

Several decision models have been developed to assess the value of screening and treatment of prostate cancer. One model considered three options for the treatment of prostate cancer: radical prostatectomy (surgical removal of the prostate gland), external beam radiation therapy, and "watchful waiting." Both radical prostatectomy and radiation therapy carry high risks of complications that may reduce life satisfaction. For example, there are significant increases in the chances of becoming impotent and/or incontinent (Fowler, Barry, Lu-Yao, Wasson, & Bin, 1996; Fowler et al., 1998). Watchful waiting, on the other hand, does not require therapy, but only evaluation and supervision by a physician. The watchful waiting option has been used least often because it does not treat the cancer (Fowler et al, 2006; McNaughton-Collins et al 2004).

Decision models have been used to estimate QALYs under these three treatment options. For example, one decision model was to estimate whether prostatectomy results in longer quality-adjusted survival in men with clinically localized prostate cancer. The analysis considered the QALYs with conservative treatment and prostatectomy for men aged 55, 60, and 65 with clinically localized well, moderately, and poorly differentiated prostate cancer. Well-differentiated cancer cells have a regular cell structure and are associated with a good prognosis. Poorly differentiated cancers have an irregular cell structure and are associated with a high chance of spread.

Figure 5.6 summarizes the results of the analysis. For men with well-differentiated tumors, conservative treatment (waiting) was about equivalent to prostatectomy. For men with moderately differentiated tumors, prostatectomy was preferred to conservative treatment. This was also so for men with poorly differentiated tumors. In terms of QALYs, conservative therapy may be the most appropriate approach for well-differentiated cancer. Men with moderately differentiated cancer had a marginal benefit from prostatectomy at age 55 and 60, but the benefit did not extend to men beyond the age of 65. With poorly differentiated cancer, all men appeared to benefit from surgery. However, the model also showed that, in many cases, the results are altered when different values are used to weight the quality-of-life outcomes. For example, if men have moderately differentiated cancer but assign a low quality-of-life value to impotence, the model is more likely to recommend conservative treatment. For men less concerned about the quality-of-life effects of impotence, the model suggests that surgery may be the best option (Bhatnagar, Kaplan, Stewart, & Bonney, 2001).

Similar decision models have been used to evaluate screening for prostate cancer. Using QALYs as an outcome measure, simulations suggest there are few benefits of screening. For example, Krahn and colleagues (1994) estimated the population benefit of programs to screen 70-year-old men for prostate cancer. They found that the benefits, on average, were improvements in the life expectancy from a

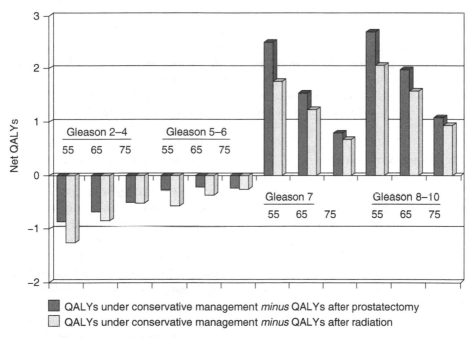

**Fig. 5.6** Net quality-adjusted life years (QALYs) at ages 55, 65, and 75. QALYs after prostatectomy or radiation therapy (RT) minus QALYs under conservative management for patients diagnosed at 55, 65, or 75 years old. Conservative management was preferred for well-differentiated cancers (Gleason scores 2–4 and 5–6) (negative net QALYs). Prostatectomy or RT was preferred over conservative management for moderately differentiated and poorly differentiated cancers (Gleason score 7 and 8–10). Treatment benefit decreased with increasing age. From Bhatnagar et al., 2004. Reprinted with permission of Elsevier.

few hours to 2 days. However, when they adjusted the life expectancy for quality of life, they discovered that screening programs actually reduced quality-adjusted life days. The reason for this negative impact is that screening identifies many men who would have died of other causes. These men, once identified with prostate cancer, are then likely to engage in a series of treatments that would significantly reduce their quality of life. For these men, the treatment causes harm without producing substantial benefits. Because the traditional model and the outcomes model focus on different outcome measures, they come to different conclusions about the value of screening.

One of the major problems is that it is very hard to evaluate the effect of screening with PSA testing and digital rectal examination on the number of deaths from prostate cancer that are prevented. To investigate this issue, the National Institutes of Health (NIH) included screening for prostate cancer as a component of the epic Prostate, Lung, Colorectal, and Ovarian (PLCO) Cancer Screening Trial. For 6 years, 38,343 men were offered annual PSA testing. Another 38,350 men received usual care, which sometimes included screening, but screening was not prompted. As expected, the screening group was screened more often (86% vs. less than 50% in the usual care group), and 22% more cancer was detected in the screening group. However, after 7 years of follow-up, the cancer death rate was 2.0 per 10,000 in the screened group and slightly lower 1.7 per 10,000 in the usual care group. In other words, there was no evidence that prostate cancer screening resulted in longer life, despite that fact that it identified more tumors (Andriole et al., 2009).

### SCREENING FOR BREAST CANCER

Controversy surrounding the use of screening mammography for women 40 to 50 years of age is another example. The *Dartmouth Atlas of Health Care* systematically reviews variation in the use of a wide variety of medical services. One example is the use of techniques for the diagnosis and treatment of breast cancer. Controversy exists about the age for initiating screening for breast cancer using mammography (Gotzsche & Nielsen, 2009; Javitt & Hendrick, 2010; Jorgensen, Brodersen, Hartling, Nielsen, & Gotzsche, 2009). However, the analyses consistently show that screening women older than 50 produces at least some health benefit. Among women between the ages of 50 and 74, periodic screening results in slightly lower rates of death from

breast cancer (Navarro & Kaplan, 1996). Thus, screening of women of Medicare age is commonly advocated. Nevertheless, there is substantial variation in the percentage of female Medicare recipients who had had one or more mammograms. As a result (Wennberg, 1998), for women diagnosed with breast cancer, substantial variation exists in the treatments delivered. In 1992–1993, more than 100,000 women in the Medicare program had surgery for breast cancer. For women who have breast cancer, the surgeon has at least two major options: lumpectomy, which involves removal of the tumor, or mastectomy, which requires either the removal of a larger portion of tissue (partial mastectomy) or complete removal of the breast (total mastectomy). Clinical trials have shown little or no difference in survival rates between women who receive lumpectomy followed by radiation or chemotherapy and women who receive total mastectomy. Because the outcomes are likely to be similar, the woman's own preference should play an important role in the decision process. However, The *Dartmouth Atlas of Health Care* shows that there are some regions in the country where mastectomy is typically done and other regions where lumpectomy is typically done. For example, considering the proportion of women who had breast-sparing surgery (lumpectomy), women were 33 times more likely to have lumpectomy if they lived in Toledo, Ohio, than if they lived in Rapid City, South Dakota (48% vs. 1.4%). Figure 5.7 shows the variation map for breast-sparing surgery. The proportion of women having breast-sparing surgery in Patterson, New Jersey, and Ridgewood, New Jersey, was 37.8% and 34.8%, respectively. At the other extreme, only 1.9% had breast-sparing surgery in Ogden, Utah, as did 3.8% in Yakima, Washington. In general, breast-sparing surgery is more widely used in the Northeast than anywhere else in the United States, and the rates tend to be low in the South, Midwest, and Northwest.

Surgery rates are affected by the number of new cases detected. Evidence also suggests that cancer screening rates vary from community to community. Mammography offers an excellent example. In February 2002, Health and Human Services secretary Tommy Thompson used endorsement of mammography for women 40 years of age and older as evidence supporting the Bush administration's commitment to preventive medicine. Thompson held a press conference to advise women, "If you are 40 or older, get screened for breast cancer with mammography every 1 to 2 years." When President Barach Obama delivered his first message to congress to

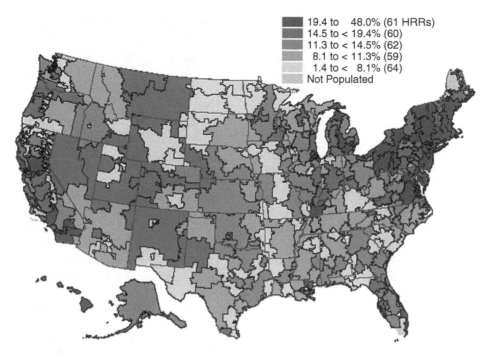

19.4 to 48.0% (61 HRRs)
14.5 to < 19.4% (60)
11.3 to < 14.5% (62)
8.1 to < 11.3% (59)
1.4 to < 8.1% (64)
Not Populated

**Fig. 5.7** Percentage of inpatient breast cancer surgery in Medicare women that was breast-sparing by hospital referral region (HRR), 1992–1993; compiled from *Dartmouth Atlas of Health Care*.

promote health care reform, he emphasized support for mammograms "because they work and save lives". However, the public health benefit of promoting screening mammography for 40- to 50-year-old women may be somewhat limited. Clinical trials and meta-analyses have failed to show a population benefit of screening women in this age group (Barton et al., 2001; Fletcher, 1997; Gelmon & Olivotto, 2002; McLellan, 2002; Miettinen et al., 2002; Nystrom et al., 2002).

In January 1997, the NIH convened a panel to make recommendations about the use of screening mammography for women 40 to 50 years of age. In contrast to diagnostic testing used when a woman is in a high-risk group or has felt a lump, screening mammography is used to evaluate asymptomatic women. The conclusion of the panel review shocked the American Cancer Society. The headline of *USA Today* (January 24, 1997) read, "Mammogram Panel Only Adds to Furor." Commentators on morning talk shows were outraged by the committee's decision. Richard Klausner, the director of the National Cancer Institute, decided to disregard the report of his own expert panel. Shortly thereafter, the American Cancer Society appointed a panel of experts chosen because each already believed that screening was valuable for 40- to 50-year-old women. To no one's surprise, this ACS panel recommended that 40- to 50-year-old women should be screened (Fletcher, 1997).

The controversy died down for a brief time but reemerged in 2002. Two Norwegian epidemiologists reanalyzed earlier trials and classified studies by methodological quality. In their analysis, they noted that the only studies supporting screening mammography for women of any age were of low quality, and that those studies not supporting screening mammography tended to have greater methodological rigor (Gotzsche, Hartling, Nielsen, Brodersen, & Jorgensen, 2009; Gotzsche & Nielsen, 2009). The findings are summarized in Figure 5.8. Remarkably, there appeared to be no benefit at all for screening— the relative risk ratio was nearly 1.0. Although the analysis was conducted as part of the highly respected Cochrane collaboration, the Cochrane group disowned the analysis in the wake of a public controversy, although the protocol for the study had been approved by the group before the results were known (Horton, 2001). Even though many scholars agree with the Norwegian investigators, the controversy continues. For example, data from a key Swedish study have been reanalyzed and shown to support screening mammography (Nystrom et al., 2002). However, all reviews of the data indicate that any benefit of screening mammography are very small and that screening offers little or no benefit in terms of increasing life expectancy when all causes of mortality are considered (Black, Haggstrom, & Welch, 2002). Decisions are very difficult to evaluate in

| Study | Screened<br>Number of deaths/<br>number of women | Not screened<br>Number of deaths/<br>number of women | Relative risk*<br>(95% CI) | Weight<br>(%) | Relative risk*<br>(95% CI) |
|---|---|---|---|---|---|
| Maimö 1976 | 2537/21088 | 2593/21195 | | 70.08 | 0.98 (0.93–1.04) |
| Canada 1980a | 418/25214 | 414/25216 | | 11.22 | 1.01 (0.88–1.16) |
| Canada 1980b | 734/19711 | 690/19694 | | 18.70 | 1.06 (0.96–1.18) |
| Subtotal | 3689/66013 | 3697/66105 | | 100.00 | 1.00 (0.96–1.05) |

Test for heterogeneity: $\chi^2 = 1.80$, df = 2 (p = 0.41)
Test for overall effect: z = 0.05 (p = 0.96)

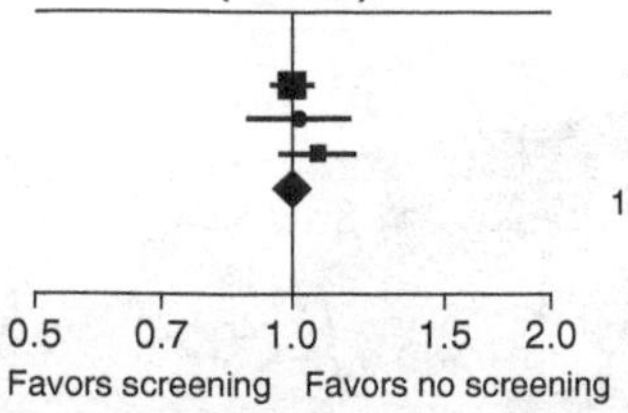

**Fig. 5.8** Relative risk and confidence intervals for mammography randomized controlled trials (from Olsen and Gotzsche, 2001). Cochrane review on screening for breast cancer with mammography (*Lancet* 358: 1340–1342). Reprinted with permission of Elsevier.

individual cases. For example, many women get screened, have surgical treatment, and go on to live long and healthy lives. In many cases, these women attribute their survival to early detection and treatment. However, it is difficult to determine whether the screening saved their lives, or if the outcomes would have been the same without screening. The clinical trials indicate that the contribution of screening is very small.

Once again, the controversy died down for a few years. But, in 2009, the United States Preventive Services Task Force (USPSF) released a report that was essentially the same as all previous reviews. They suggested that screening offered little benefit, particularly for women prior to age 50. Because the issues were so well known, they did not expect the same negative reactions that followed previous releases of the same information. They were wrong. Within days, there was a major social and political rebellion, and there were assurances from politicians and insurance companies that mammography would continue to be a covered service (Javitt & Hendrick, 2010).

Since many experts believe the benefit of screening is very small, we must call on decision analysis to evaluate the policies promoted by the American Cancer Society and by other groups. The cost-effectiveness of mammography has been estimated in several analyses. These analyses are difficult because most meta-analyses fail to show that screening mammography has any benefit for 40- to 49-year-old women (there is less debate about the value of screening for women 50–69 years of age). Under the assumption of no benefit, the cost/QALY goes toward infinity because the model would require division by zero. Using studies suggesting some benefit of mammography for women 40–49 years of age, Eddy (1989, 1997) estimated the cost to produce a QALY at $240,000. One analysis used newer data to evaluate the cost-effectiveness of guidelines requiring screening for women aged 40–49 (Salzmann, Kerlikowske, & Phillips, 1997).

They noted that screening women 50–64 years of age produces a QALY at about $21,400. By contrast, the expected benefit of screening women 40–49 years of age increases life expectancy by only 2.5 days at a cost of $676 per woman, resulting in an incremental cost utility of $105,000/QALY.

Analyses in all aspects of health care suggest that there is plenty of disease to be discovered and that newer technology will find even more cases. But are all these cases clinically important? The disease reservoir hypothesis leads to some controversial predictions concerning breast and prostate cancer screening. One hypothesis is that greater screening for disease will create the false appearance of epidemics. Figure 5.9 shows increases in breast cancer (left panel) and increases in prostate cancer (right panel) as a function of increased screening. With a reservoir of undetected disease, the more you look, the more you find. Figure 5.9 also shows the mortality from breast cancer and prostate cancer. If these were true epidemics, we would expect increases in deaths from these serious diseases. However, in each case, mortality is relatively stable (Kaplan, 2000).

Stable mortality rates appear to contradict the suggestion that survival from cancer is increasing and is attributable to better screening and treatment. Although there appeared to be a small increase in prostate cancer deaths in the 1980s, it has since declined and may have been an artifact (Fowler et al., 2002). The disease reservoir hypothesis would argue that screening changes the point at which disease is detected (lead time) without necessarily changing the course of the illness. If the date of death is unchanged, earlier detection will make the interval between diagnosis and death appear longer, even when screening has no effect on life expectancy. This is known as *lead-time bias*.

**CHOLESTEROL SCREENING**

The controversy over screening extends beyond cancer. In cancer screening, a judgment is made about whether or not a tumor is present. Clinicians

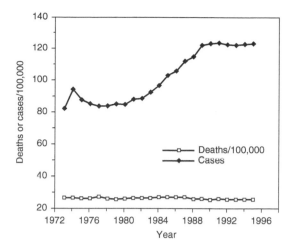

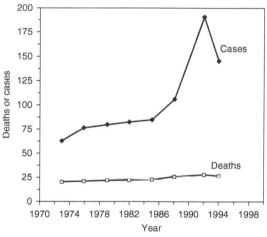

**Fig. 5.9** (A) Breast cancer cases and deaths: 1974–1995 (Surveillance Epidemiology and End Results [SEER] data); (B) Prostate cancer cases and deaths: 1972–1994 (SEER data).

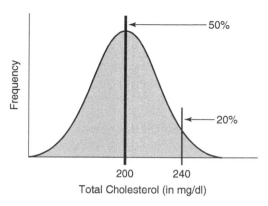

**Fig. 5.10** Percentage of U.S. population with total cholesterol over 240 mg/dL and 200 mg/dL (National Health and Nutrition Examination Survey [NHANES] data).

sometimes challenge whether the tumor had meaningful clinical consequences. In many areas of medicine, the definition of *disease* is somewhat arbitrary. Many biological processes are approximately normally distributed in the general population. Diagnostic thresholds are often set toward the tail of the distribution (see Figure 5.10). For example, total cholesterol values greater than 240 mg/dL were once used as the diagnostic threshold for hypercholesterolemia. Recently, diagnostic thresholds have been reduced, and some groups advocate treatment for individuals closer to the center of the distribution. In the total cholesterol example, the third National Health and Nutrition Examination Survey (NHANES III) showed that about 20% of the adult population have values above 240 mg/dL. However, more than half of the adult population has total cholesterol levels over 200 mg/dL. If some group advocated changing the diagnostic threshold

from 240 to 200, the policy change would identify an additional 30% of the adult population as in need of treatment.

There are several other examples of the problem with changing disease definitions (Kaplan, Ganiats, & Frosch, 2004, Kaplan & Ong, 2007, Kaplan, 2009)). The National Heart Lung and Blood Institute (NHLBI) has administered the National High Blood Pressure Education Program (NHBPEP) for more than three decades. In May 2003, the commission released its seventh national report, known as JNC-7 (Chobanian et al., 2003). Successive JNC reports have pushed for lower diagnostic thresholds for high blood pressure. JNC-6 defined high-normal blood pressure as systolic blood pressure of 130–139 mm Hg and diastolic blood pressure 85–89 mmHg. JNC-7 goes a step further by defining a new condition known as *prehypertension*. Individuals in this category have a systolic blood pressure of 120–139 mm Hg or a diastolic blood pressure of 80–89 mm Hg (Chobanian et al., 2003). Although many people will be labeled as prehypertensive, the report does not suggest the use of antihypertensive drugs in this category. Instead, behavioral intervention is indicated. On the surface, the rationale for creating the new category of prehypertension is compelling. Epidemiologic studies of adults between the ages of 40 and 70 years suggest that each increase in systolic blood pressure of 20 mmHg and each increase in diastolic blood pressure of 10 mmHg results in a doubling of risk for cardiovascular disease, except for those with blood pressures lower than 115/75 mm Hg (Lewington, 2002). The report argued that management of blood pressure using medication results in a 40% reduction in the incidence of stroke, a 25% reduction in the incidence of myocardial infarction, and a 50% reduction in the incidence of heart failure (Neal, 2000). However, large clinical trials have not shown benefits for lowering high-normal to optimal blood pressure, and there are no outcome studies assessing the effects of behavioral interventions upon mortality. Further, it is unclear what benefit to expect from lifestyle intervention among those in the prehypertension range. Analysis of data from NHANES III suggests that nearly 90% of older adults will qualify for a diagnosis of pre-hypertension or hypertension. Similar examples are available for type 2 diabetes (with a change in diagnostic threshold for fasting blood glucose from 140 mg/dL to 126 mg/dL), overweight (reduction of threshold to body mass index of 25 kg/m$^2$), and several other health problems. Some common health problems, such as subsyndromal depression, could include as much as 50% of the adult population. This is important because those with the mildest disease (values closest to the mean) usually have the lowest risk of complications from their "disease," yet they often face the same risks of treatment side effects as those more clearly in need of therapy.

At the same time, pharmaceutical costs have become the strongest driver of increases in health care costs. The most recent evidence suggests that pharmaceutical costs rose twice as fast as other components of heath care expenditures during the 1990s (Liberman & Rubinstein, 2002). Currently, the costs of prescription medications for Medicare patients are rising about 20% each year. To address the policy issues, we need to understand the impact of lowering diagnostic thresholds upon population health status and health care costs. For most of these conditions, an expensive pharmaceutical product is available, with treatment costs approaching $5 per day. For older adults with multiple diagnoses, the costs of medications may exceed the cost of food.

Given the lower potential benefit and the higher costs of treating the large number of patients with mild-spectrum conditions, the cost-effectiveness of treating mild-spectrum disease is less than that for directing resources toward the severe-spectrum group. It is even less than treating the average group evaluated in clinical trials. For this reason, we must explore the incremental cost-effectiveness associated with changing diagnostic thresholds. Spending significant resources on mild-spectrum conditions may foreclose opportunities to invest in other aspects of health care. For example, the cost/QALY for treating some mild-spectrum condition might be $800,000/QALY. Using resources to screen and treat this hypothetical condition might reduce the opportunity to support a program that produces a QALY for $50,000. In other words, each QALY gained by pursuing mild-spectrum conditions might take resources away from a program that could produce 16 QALYs at the same cost.

Screening and treatment for high cholesterol offers an interesting case study. The National Cholesterol Education Program developed detailed guidelines on screening for high cholesterol (Executive Summary of The Third Report of The National Cholesterol Education Program [NCEP] Expert Panel on Detection, Evaluation, and Treatment of High Blood Cholesterol in Adults [Adult Treatment Panel III]; American Medical Association, 2001). A national campaign was developed with the emphasis on screening all Americans for high cholesterol. The evidence supporting this campaign came from two sources. First, epidemiologic investigations have shown significant correlations between elevated serum cholesterol and deaths from coronary heart disease (Grundy et al., 1997). Second, clinical trials have demonstrated that reductions in total cholesterol and in the low-density lipoprotein subfraction of cholesterol resulted in reductions in deaths from coronary heart disease (Van Horn & Ernst, 2001). The national policy was based on the mechanistic thinking that high cholesterol is bad and lower cholesterol improves health status. Consumers were led to believe that those with elevated cholesterol were likely to die of heart disease, whereas those with normal levels would survive.

Many difficulties in these analyses have now become apparent. First, the NCEP recommended cholesterol screening tests for all Americans independent of age, gender, or ethnicity. However, the clinical trials supporting the policies were based exclusively on middle-aged men, and there was no specific evidence for children or for older adults. A second concern was that systematic clinical trials consistently failed to demonstrate improvements in life expectancy resulting from cholesterol lowering (Kaplan, 1984). In all clinical trials, reductions in deaths from heart disease were offset by increases in deaths from other causes (Golomb, 1998; Golomb, Stattin, & Mednick, 2000; Kaplan & Groessl, 2002). For example, the Coronary Primary Prevention Trial (CPPT) showed that a drug effectively lowered cholesterol in comparison to placebo. Further, those taking the cholesterol-lowering medication were significantly less likely to die of heart disease than those taking the placebo. However, over the period these participants were followed, there were more deaths from other causes among those taking the drug, and the chances of being alive were comparable in the two groups (The Lipid Research Clinics Coronary Primary Prevention Trial results. II. The relationship of reduction in incidence of coronary heart disease to cholesterol lowering, 1984). More recent evidence also demonstrates systematic increases in deaths from other causes for those taking cholesterol-lowering agents. Biological mechanisms for these increases have been proposed (Golomb, 1998).

In contemporary medicine, most patients with high cholesterol are treated with a class of expensive medications known as statins. Although the great majority of physicians encourage the use of statins, there is some controversy (Kaplan & Golomb, 2001). A meta-analysis based on studies published before the release of statins showed a mortality benefit with cholesterol-lowering treatment for high-risk populations; studies enrolling low-cardiac risk populations showed that cholesterol-lowering drugs may be associated with an increased risk of death (Smith, Song, & Sheldon, 1993). Although risk–benefit profiles may be more favorable for statins than for other cholesterol-lowering treatments, a truly low-risk primary prevention group has not been studied. Among statin trials, the study enrolling those at lowest risk for heart disease mortality showed no overall mortality benefit, but rather an insignificant trend toward harm (80 vs. 77 deaths; Downs et al., 1998).

The focus on overall mortality is important because reduced deaths from heart disease may be compensated for by increased risk of death from other causes (Annoura et al., 1999). Statins have been linked to modest but significant reductions in cognitive functioning (Muldoon et al., 2000), a finding of particular relevance to the older elderly— in whom cognitive function is potently related to survival (Frisoni, Fratiglioni, Fastbom, Viitanen, & Winblad, 1999). Other statin effects have been reported that may impact quality of life, including sleep disturbance, peripheral neuropathy, erectile dysfunction, pain (Bruckert, Giral, Heshmati, & Turpin, 1996), and depression (Golomb et al., 2008; Davidson et al., 1996).

There have been several cost-utility analyses of cholesterol screening and treatment. Goldman and colleagues (1991) modeled the value of screening for high cholesterol and treatment with statin medications. Their model considered recurrent heart attack rates using data from the Framingham Heart Study. One simulation considered men with total cholesterol values in excess of 300 mg/dL but no other risk factors for heart disease. For these men, the cost to produce a year of life was estimated to be between $71,000 and $135,000. For women,

estimates ranged from $84,000 to $390,000 per life year. If the threshold for initiating treatment is lowered to 250 mg/dL, the cost to produce a year of life increases to between $105,000 and $270,000 for men. Campaigns have attempted to increase the number of adults undergoing medical treatment. Until recently, the threshold for a diagnosis of hypercholesterolemia was 240 mg/dL. Under that definition, about one in five adults qualified. With the more recent push toward defining high cholesterol as greater than 200 mg/dL, about half of all adults will be deemed abnormal (Fisher & Welch, 1999). However, as shown by the simulations, the lower the diagnostic threshold, the less cost-effective screening and treatment will be.

## WHAT OPPORTUNITIES ARE BEING MISSED?

As noted previously, most resources in preventive medicine are devoted to screening programs. The public health benefits of many (but certainly not all) of these programs have been limited. The common feature of the screening programs is that they require a medical diagnosis. The intent is not to prevent disease but to diagnose established pathology at an early phase. Once diagnosed, the screened individual becomes a patient who requires significant medical attention. Changes in diagnostic thresholds assure that large proportions of the general population will become patients. Half of all adults qualify for a diagnosis of high serum cholesterol, and well over half qualify for a diagnosis of overweight or obesity. In many cases, changes in diagnostic thresholds allow large portions of the population the opportunity to enter a disease category from which they were previously excluded. Often, the decision to lower diagnostic thresholds follows the availability of a high-cost pharmaceutical product to treat the condition. In many cases, individuals with mild-spectrum conditions have very little potential to benefit from treatment.

While enormous resources are being devoted to screening approaches to preventive medicine, remarkably little effort has been devoted to true disease prevention. In primary prevention, diagnosis is irrelevant because there is no disease to diagnose. Intervention is typically behavioral and might include exercise, dietary change, or the avoidance or reduction of tobacco use. Interventions might also include public policy change such as water sanitation or highway improvements (Kaplan, 2009). For example, there is mounting evidence that people are more physically active if they live in communities that are designed for walking and cycling (Ayala et al, 2011, Kistler et al, 2011, Sallis 2011).

## SHARED DECISION MAKING

This chapter argues that health care in the United States is too expensive, and that resources are often used to treat pseudo-diseases. A central component of the problem is that the role of uncertainty in medical decision making is underappreciated. Although patients accept treatment with high expectations of benefit, experienced health care providers may recognize that the potential benefit of many treatments is probabilistic. One approach to this problem is greater patient involvement in decisions about care. This section reviews the emerging study of shared medical decision making, in which choices of treatment pathways are a collaborative effort between provider and patient (Frosch & Kaplan, 1999).

In an ideal world, a patient could approach a physician with a list of symptoms and problems. The physician would identify the problem and administer a remedy. The service should be inexpensive and painless. However, this scenario is not common. For most medical decisions, judgments about disease are not perfectly reliable, and even when an early diagnosis is available, it is not always clear that treatment is the best option (Eddy, 2005). Choices about what treatments should be offered have typically been left to the physician. For a variety of reasons, however, patients are becoming active in the decision process.

One example of the greater need for information is illustrated by reactions to information the British National Health Services was giving women about breast cancer screening. A brochure informed women that screening could extend their lives and that there were very few risks. After reviewing the evidence on screening, an international group of experts wrote to the *London Times* in protest. They argued that the government should tell the women the truth. According to the 2009 Cochrane review, there was little evidence that screening increased life expectancy, and there was evidence for harm. For each 2,000 women screened, it is possible that one will have her life extended. But, about 10 times as many women (about 1 in 200) will undergo unnecessary treatment as a result of screening, and one women in each 10 may suffer psychological harm as a result of a false-positive test (Brodersen, Jorgensen, & Gotzsche, 2010; Jorgensen & Gotzsche, 2010). As a result of this protest, the National Health Service revised its brochure and now distributes information that is more consistent with the evidence-based reviews.

Shared decision making is the process by which a patient and physician join in partnership to decide whether the patient should undergo diagnostic testing or receive therapy. Often, shared decision making involves formal decision aids that provide patients with detailed information about their options. The information is usually presented through interactive video disks, decision boards, descriptive consultations, or the internet (O'Connor, Graham, & Visser, 2005). Using these decision aids, patients complete exercises to inform them of the risks and benefits of treatment options. Sometimes they provide preferences for outcomes in the shared decision-making process (Frosch & Kaplan, 1999).

Decision aids are valuable for both patients and physicians. One of the challenges of contemporary primary care medicine is that patient visits are short. Typically, the entire visit is limited to 15 minutes. During this time, the physician must greet the patient, then do routine evaluations such as taking blood pressure, reviewing medical history, determining the presenting complaint, performing a physical examination, making a diagnosis, writing a prescription, discussing treatment plans, writing notes in the patient's chart, and move on to the next patient. If, at the end of this interaction, the patient asks the difficult questions such as, "Should I be on hormone replacement therapy?" or "Should I get a PSA test?" or "Do I need a mammogram?" the physician knows that not enough time is available to discuss the issue properly. For each of these issues, the literature is complex and conflicting. Instead of dealing with the complexity, it is much easier to simply say that the test or treatment is recommended. However, each of these decisions has important consequences for the patient.

Shared decision making is not patient decision making. In other words, there are technical aspects of medical decisions for which patients are not well equipped. For example, patients are not expected to know what approach to surgery is best or the advantages or disadvantages of particular medications. On the other hand, patients have a perspective that only they fully understand. For instance, surgical treatment of prostate cancer may make a man impotent. For some men, this is a major concern, even at older ages. Other men may not be sexually active, and for them impotence may not be a concern. The patient provides the perspective that is typically unknown to the physician. Use of decision aids allows these preferences to be expressed. The personal issues brought by the patient can be merged with the technical concerns of the physicians.

Because time in medical encounters is so limited, shared decision making often involves a referral to a decision laboratory. The doctor may advise the patient to use a decision aid, often under the supervision of another health care professional. Once the patient has interacted with the decision aid, he or she can return to the physician prepared to deal with the decision in a relatively short period of time.

Although shared decision making is a relatively new field, several decision aids have now been evaluated. In one example, Frosch, Kaplan, and Feletti (2001) considered a decision aid to help men decide whether they should be screened for prostate cancer using the PSA test. The men were all enrolled in a clinic that provides a wide variety of medical screening tests. In an experiment, the men were randomly assigned to one of four groups in a $2 \times 2$ factorial design. One factor was for use of a decision video. Men either watched or did not watch a video that systematically reviewed the risks and benefits of PSA screening. The video featured a debate between a urologist who favored PSA screening and an internist who opposed it. Further, the video systematically reviewed the probabilities of false positives, false negatives, and the risks of prostate cancer. It also systematically reviewed the evidence for the benefits of treatment for prostate cancer. The other factor in the experimental design was whether or not men had the opportunity to discuss the decision with others. The design resulted in four groups: usual care, discussion alone, video alone, and video plus discussion. All men were asked if they wanted the PSA test, and medical records were obtained to determine whether the test was completed.

The study showed that there was a systematic effect of the video and discussion groups. In the usual care control group, virtually all men (97%) got the PSA test. In other words, with no new information, men will typically take the test. In the other groups, having more information led to a conservative bias. In contrast to the usual care control, those in the other groups were more sensitive to the risks of the test in relation to its benefits. Among those participating in the discussion group, 82% got the PSA test. For those watching the video, 63% completed the test. Those watching the video and participating in discussions had only a 50% PSA completion rate (see Figure 5.11). The study demonstrates that, as patients become better informed, they are less likely to take the PSA test. The study also obtained information on patient knowledge. As knowledge increased, the likelihood of getting the PSA test deceased, again stressing that better-informed patients make more conservative decisions.

There are a variety of other approaches to shared decision making. Sometimes, patient preferences for outcomes are measured directly. One example concerns treatment for prostate cancer. In this case, decision models can be used to simulate the likely benefit of a particular choice. These models often yield a decision map, which shows the best choice for a particular patient, given his or her medical history and individual values. Figure 5.12 is an example of one of these maps. This particular map considers patient preferences for becoming impotent. In this

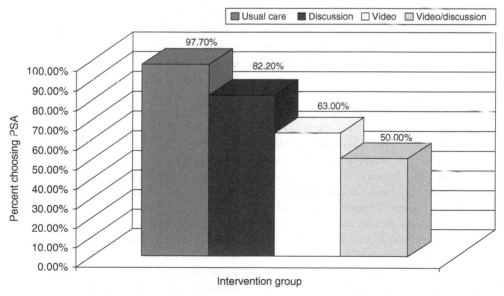

**Fig. 5.11** Men choosing prostate specific antigen (PSA) test by intervention group (from Frosch, Kaplan, & Felitti, 2001). Reprinted with permission of John Wiley and Sons.

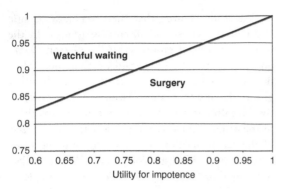

**Fig. 5.12** Decision map relating patient utility for impotence to treatment choice. Preferred alternatives for men age 55 with localized prostate cancer. Original figure by R. M. Kaplan.

case, if the patient has a high disutility for impotence, below .67, and the probability of impotence is greater than .8, watchful waiting is the appropriate choice. However, if the disutility for impotence is higher (.85), probability of impotence being as high as .90 might be tolerated (Bhatanagar et al., 2001).

The internet offers significant advantages for shared decision making. Because medical knowledge changes so quickly, the internet provides a great opportunity to continually update information. However, we do not know how effective the internet is at delivering information. New evidence suggests that large proportions of the American population have internet access. Yet, how good of a platform is the internet for delivering shared decision making? In one study, 226 men, 50 years of age or older, who were scheduled for a complete physical exam, were randomly assigned to access a web site or to view a 23-minute videotape about the risks and benefits of being screened for prostate cancer using the PSA test. Both methods of delivering the information were effective, but those watching the video were more likely to review the materials than were those using the internet. In addition, those watching the video were more likely to increase their knowledge about the PSA test and were more likely to decline the test than were those assigned to the internet group. Further, those who watched the video were more likely to express confidence that watchful waiting was the best treatment for prostate cancer. Thus, it appeared that the video may have been the best channel for delivering the information. However, using cookies from the internet, it was possible to determine how much time each participant spent using the program. The analysis indicated that many of the men spent very little time with the internet program. Among those men who participated in the entire internet program, the results were identical to the results for those who watched the video. In other words, the internet and the video worked about equally well if people exposed themselves to the entire program. When motivated to use the internet, patients can gain significant benefits (Frosch, Kaplan, & Felitti, 2003).

## Conclusion

Contemporary health care is in crisis. Despite relentless increases in cost, there is little evidence that high expenditures are related to patient or population benefit. To address these problems, new methods must be applied to find the best use of limited resources. Preventive medicine is a medical specialty that should help address this problem by applying technologies that will prevent expensive episodes of illness. However, the primary focus of preventive medicine has been toward the identification of established disease at an early phase. The tools of preventive medicine emphasize medical diagnosis and pharmacological treatment. Analyses of many large-scale screening and treatment programs indicate that the benefits have been limited (Kaplan, 2000). Nevertheless, we are currently witnessing greater emphasis on population screening and lowering of diagnostic thresholds for many disease categories. This will result in significant increases in health care costs with unknown population health benefits.

A major contributor to the expense of contemporary heath care is that considerable uncertainty exists about the potential benefit of many preventive treatments. Typically, the safest option is to assume all minor health problems will grow into major health concerns. The favored option is to medically treat these conditions. However, the benefit of these treatments is typically uncertain, and the treatments usually carry some risks. Further, aggressive treatment of mild-spectrum conditions is costly, with little evidence of benefit at the population level.

Although the uncertain benefit of many programs for screening and treatment of mild-spectrum disease is well documented in the medical literature, most patients are unaware of the controversies. When uncertainty exists among providers, approaches to treatment are often highly variable. This is reflected in the medical care use maps. Typically, the variation represents differences in physician preferences. Shared medical decision making is a new paradigm in health care that uses decision aids to help patients understand the risks and benefits of treatment. Early studies suggest that allowing patients a greater role in decision making usually results in more conservative decisions. The selection of less aggressive care results in reduced health care costs. Further shared medical decision making typically results in greater patient satisfaction. By offering a better basis for informed consent, shared medical decision making may also protect physicians from litigation.

Shared decision making is a new paradigm in medicine and health care. There will be ample opportunities to develop new methodologies and to evaluate the effect of these methods on patient outcomes, patient satisfaction, and medical care costs.

## References

American Medical Association. (2001). Executive summary of the third report of the national cholesterol education program (NCEP) expert panel on detection, evaluation, and treatment of high blood cholesterol in adults (Adult Treatment Panel III). *Journal of the American Medical Association, 285*(19), 2486–2497.

Adami, H.O. (2010). The prostate cancer pseudo-epidemic. *Acta Oncology, 49*(3), 298–304.

Adolfsson, J. (2010). Screening for prostate cancer: Will we ever know? *Acta Oncology, 49*(3), 275–277.

Andriole, G.L., Crawford, E.D., Grubb, R.L., 3rd, Buys, S.S., Chia, D., Church, T.R., et al. (2009). Mortality results from a randomized prostate-cancer screening trial. *New England Journal of Medicine, 360*(13), 1310–1319.

Annoura, M., Ogawa, M., Kumagai, K., Zhang, B., Saku, K., & Arakawa, K. (1999). Cholesterol paradox in patients with paroxysmal atrial fibrillation. *Cardiology, 92*(1), 21–27.

Aronowitz, R.A. (2001). Do not delay: Breast cancer and time, 1900–1970. *Milbank Quarterly, 79*(3), 355–386, III.

Ayala, G.X., Gammelgard, A., Sallis, J.F., & Elder, J.P. (2011). The association of physical activity and work-related characteristics among latino adults. *Journal of Physical Activity and Health, 8*(1), 79–84.

Barton, M.B., Moore, S., Polk, S., Shtatland, E., Elmore, J.G., & Fletcher, S.W. (2001). Increased patient concern after false-positive mammograms: Clinician documentation and subsequent ambulatory visits. *Journal of General Internal Medicine, 16*(3), 150–156.

Bhatnagar, V., Kaplan, R., Stewart, S., & Bonney, W. (2001). Prostatectomy compared to conservative treatment for localized prostate cancer: A decision analysis. *Medical Decision Making, 21*(6), 548.

Bhatnagar, V., Stewart, S.T., Bonney, W., & Kaplan, R. (2004). Treatment options for localized prostate cancer: Quality-adjusted life years and the effects of lead-time. *Urology, 63*(1), 103–9.

Birkmeyer, J.D. (2009). Improving outcomes with lung cancer surgery: Selective referral or quality improvement? *Annals of Surgical Oncology, 16*(1), 1–2.

Birkmeyer, J.D., & Dimick, J.B. (2009). Understanding and reducing variation in surgical mortality. *Annual Review of Medicine, 60*, 405–415.

Black, W.C., Haggstrom, D.A., & Welch, H.G. (2002). All-cause mortality in randomized trials of cancer screening. *Journal of the National Cancer Institute, 94*(3), 167–173.

Black, W.C., & Welch, H.G. (1997). Screening for disease. *American Journal of Roentgenology, 168*(1), 3–11.

Blumenthal, D. (2001). Controlling health care expenditures. *New England Journal of Medicine, 344*(10), 766–769.

Brodersen, J., Jorgensen, K.J., & Gotzsche, P.C. (2010). The benefits and harms of screening for cancer with a focus on breast screening. *Polskie Archiwum Medycyny Wewnętrznej, 120*(3), 89–94.

Bruckert, E., Giral, P., Heshmati, H.M., & Turpin, G. (1996). Men treated with hypolipidaemic drugs complain more frequently of erectile dysfunction. *Journal of Clinical Pharmacy and Therapeutics, 21*(2), 89–94.

Bubolz, T., Wasson, J.H., Lu-Yao, G., & Barry, M.J. (2001). Treatments for prostate cancer in older men: 1984–1997. *Urology, 58*(6), 977 982.

Chobanian, A.V., Bakris, G.L., Black, H.R., Cushman, W.C., Green, L.A., Izzo, J.L., Jr., et al. (2003). The seventh report of the joint national committee on prevention, detection, evaluation, and treatment of high blood pressure: The JNC 7 report. *Journal of the American Medical Association, 289*(19), 2560–2572.

Davidson, K.W., Reddy, S., McGrath, P., Zitner, D., & MacKeen, W. (1996). Increases in depression after cholesterol-lowering drug treatment. *Behavioral Medicine, 22*(2), 82–84.

Downs, J.R., Clearfield, M., Weis, S., Whitney, E., Shapiro, D.R., Beere, P.A., et al. (1998). Primary prevention of acute coronary events with lovastatin in men and women with average cholesterol levels: Results of AFCAPS/TexCAPS. Air Force/Texas Coronary Atherosclerosis Prevention Study [see comments]. *Journal of the American Medical Association, 279*(20), 1615–1622.

Eddy, D.M. (1989). Screening for breast cancer. *Ann Intern Med, 111*(5), 389–399.

Eddy, D.M. (1997). Breast cancer screening in women younger than 50 years of age: what's next? *Ann Intern Med, 127*(11), 1035–1036.

Eddy, D.M. (2005). Evidence-based medicine: A unified approach. *Health Affairs (Millwood), 24*(1), 9–17.

Englesbe, M.J., Dimick, J.B., Fan, Z., Baser, O., & Birkmeyer, J.D. (2009). Case mix, quality and high-cost kidney transplant patients. *Am Journal of Transplantation, 9*(5), 1108–1114.

Field, M.J., & Gold, M.R. (1998). *Summarizing population health.* Washington, DC: Institute of Medicine, National Academy Press.

Fisher, E.S., & Welch, H.G. (1999). Could more health care lead to worse health? *Hospital Practice (Off Ed), 34*(12), 15–16, 21–12, 25.

Fisher, E.S., Wennberg, D.E., Stukel, T.A., Gottlieb, D.J., Lucas, F.L., & Pinder, E.L. (2003). The implications of regional variations in Medicare spending. Part 2: Health outcomes and satisfaction with care. *Annals of Internal Medicine, 138*(4), 288–298.

Fletcher, S.W. (1997). Whither scientific deliberation in health policy recommendations? Alice in the Wonderland of breast-cancer screening. *New England Journal of Medicine, 336*(16), 1180–1183.

Fowler, F.J., Jr., Barry, M.J., Lu-Yao, G., Wasson, J.H., & Bin, L. (1996). Outcomes of external-beam radiation therapy for prostate cancer: A study of Medicare beneficiaries in three surveillance, epidemiology, and end results areas. *Journal of Clinical Oncology, 14*(8), 2258–2265.

Fowler, F.J., Jr., Barry, M.J., Walker-Corkery, B., Caubet, J.F., Bates, D.W., Lee, J.M., et al.(2006). The impact of a suspicious prostate biopsy on patients' psychological, socio-behavioral, and medical care outcomes. *Journal of General Internal Medicine,* 21(7), 715–721.

Fowler, F.J., Jr., Bin, L., Collins, M.M., Roberts, R.G., Oesterling, J.E., Wasson, J.H., et al. (1998). Prostate cancer screening and beliefs about treatment efficacy: A national survey of primary care physicians and urologists. *American Journal of Medicine,* 104(6), 526–532.

Fowler, J.E., Jr., Bigler, S.A., & Farabaugh, P.B. (2002). Prospective study of cancer detection in black and white men with normal digital rectal examination but prostate specific antigen equal or greater than 4.0 ng/mL. *Cancer,* 94(6), 1661–1667.

Frisoni, G.B., Fratiglioni, L., Fastbom, J., Viitanen, M., & Winblad, B. (1999). Mortality in nondemented subjects with cognitive impairment: The influence of health-related factors. *American Journal of Epidemiology,* 150(10), 1031–1044.

Frosch, D., & Kaplan, R.M. (1999). Shared medical decision making. *American Journal of Preventive Medicine, 17(4),* 285–94.

Frosch, D.L., Kaplan, R.M., & Felitti, V.J. (2001). The evaluation of two methods to facilitate shared decision making for men considering the prostate-specific antigen test. *Journal of General Internal Medicine,* 16(6), 391–398.

Frosch, D.L., Kaplan, R.M., & Felitti, V.J. (2003). A randomized controlled trial comparing internet and video to facilitate patient education for men considering the prostate specific antigen test. *Journal of General Internal Medicine,* 18(10), 781–787.

Fryback, D.G., Dunham, N.C., Palta, M., Hanmer, J., Buechner, J., Cherepanov, D., et al. (2007). US norms for six generic health-related quality-of-life indexes from the National Health Measurement study. *Medical Care,* 45(12), 1162–1170.

Fuchs, V.R. (2010). Health care is different—that's why expenditures matter. *Journal of the American Medical Association,* 303(18), 1859–1860.

Garster, N.C., Palta, M., Sweitzer, N.K., Kaplan, R.M., & Fryback, D.G. (2009). Measuring health-related quality of life in population-based studies of coronary heart disease: Comparing six generic indexes and a disease-specific proxy score. *Quality of Life Research,* 18(9), 1239–1247.

Gelmon, K.A., & Olivotto, I. (2002). The mammography screening debate: Time to move on. *Lancet,* 359(9310), 904–905.

Gilmer, T., & Kronick, R. (2005). It's the premiums, stupid: Projections of the uninsured through 2013. *Health Affairs (Millwood),* 24, W5-143–W5-151.

Gold, M., Franks, P., & Erickson, P. (1996). Assessing the health of the nation. The predictive validity of a preference-based measure and self-rated health. *Medical Care,* 34(2), 163–177.

Gold, M.R., Stevenson, D., & Fryback, D.G. (2002). HALYS and QALYS and DALYS, oh my: Similarities and differences in summary measures of population health. *Annual Review of Public Health,* 23, 115–134.

Goldman, L., Weinstein, M.C., Goldman, P.A., & Williams, L.W. (1991). Cost-effectiveness of HMG-CoA reductase inhibition for primary and secondary prevention of coronary heart disease. *Journal of the American Medical Association,* 265(9), 1145–1151.

Golomb, B.A. (1998). Cholesterol and violence: Is there a connection? *Annals of Internal Medicine,* 128(6), 478–487.

Golomb, B.A., Dimsdale, J.E., White, H.L., Ritchie, J.B., & Criqui, M.H. (2008). Reduction in blood pressure with statins: Results from the UCSD Statin Study, a randomized trial. *Archives of Internal Medicine,* 168(7), 721–727.

Golomb, B.A., Stattin, H., & Mednick, S. (2000). Low cholesterol and violent crime. *Journal of Psychiatric Research,* 34(4–5), 301–309.

Goodman, D.C., Fisher, E.S., Little, G.A., Stukel, T.A., Chang, C.H., & Schoendorf, K.S. (2002). The relation between the availability of neonatal intensive care and neonatal mortality. *New England Journal of Medicine,* 346(20), 1538–1544.

Gotzsche, P.C., Hartling, O.J., Nielsen, M., Brodersen, J., & Jorgensen, K.J. (2009). Breast screening: The facts—or maybe not. *British Medical Journal, 338,* b86.

Gotzsche, P.C., & Nielsen, M. (2009). Screening for breast cancer with mammography. *Cochrane Database of Systematic Reviews* (4), CD001877.

Grundy, S.M., Balady, G.J., Criqui, M.H., Fletcher, G., Greenland, P., Hiratzka, L.F., et al. (1997). Guide to primary prevention of cardiovascular diseases. A statement for healthcare professionals from the Task Force on Risk Reduction. *American Heart Association Science Advisory and Coordinating Committee. Circulation,* 95(9), 2329–2331.

Horton, R. (2001). Screening mammography—An overview revisited. *Lancet,* 358(9290), 1284–1285.

Javitt, M.C., & Hendrick, R.E. (2010). Revealing Oz behind the curtain: USPSTF screening mammography guidelines and the hot air balloon. *American Journal of Roentgenology,* 194(2), 289–290.

Jorgensen, K.J., Brodersen, J., Hartling, O.J., Nielsen, M., & Gotzsche, P.C. (2009). Informed choice requires information about both benefits and harms. *Journal of Medical Ethics,* 35(4), 268–269.

Jorgensen, K.J., & Gotzsche, P.C. (2010). Who evaluates public health programmes? A review of the NHS breast screening programme. *Journal of the Royal Society of Medicine,* 103(1), 14–20.

Kaplan, R., & Anderson, J. (1996). The general health policy model: An integrated approach. In B. Spilker (Ed.), *Quality of life and pharmacoeconomics in clinical trials* (pp. 309–322). New York: Raven.

Kaplan, R.M. (1984). The connection between clinical health promotion and health status. A critical overview. *American Psychologist,* 39(7), 755–765.

Kaplan, R.M. (1990). Behavior as the central outcome in health care. *American Psychologist,* 45(11), 1211–1220.

Kaplan, R.M. (1994). The Ziggy theorem - Toward an outcomes-focused health psychology. *Health Psychology,* 13(6), 451–460.

Kaplan, R.M. (2000). Two pathways to prevention. *American Psychologist,* 55(4), 382–396.

Kaplan, R. (2009). *Diseases, diagnoses, and dollars.* New York: Cupernicus Press.

Kaplan, R.M., Ganiats, T.G., & Frosch, D.L. (2004). Diagnostic and treatment decisions in US healthcare. *Journal of Health Psychology,* 9(1), 29–40.

Kaplan, R.M., & Golomb, B.A. (2001). Cost-effectiveness of statin medications. *American Psychologist,* 56(4), 366–367.

Kaplan, R.M., & Groessl, E.J. (2002). Cost-effectiveness analysis in behavioral medicine. *Journal of Consulting and Clinical Psychology,* 70(3), 482–493.

Kaplan, R.M., & Mehta, R. (1994). Outcome measurement in kidney disease. *Blood Purification,* 12(1), 20–29.

Kaplan, R.M., & Ong, M. (2007). Rationale and public health implications of changing CHD risk factor definitions. *Annual Review of Public Health,* 28, 321–344.

Kaplan, R.M., Patterson, T.L., Kerner, D.N., Atkinson, J.H., Heaton, R.K., & Grant, I. (1997). The quality of well-being scale in asymptomatic HIV-infected patients. HNRC group. HIV neural behavioral research center. *Quality of Life Research, 6*(6), 507–514.

Kistler, K.D., Brunt, E.M., Clark, J.M., Diehl, A.M., Sallis, J.F., & Schwimmer, J.B. (2011). Physical activity recommendations, exercise intensity, and histological severity of nonalcoholic fatty liver disease. *American Journal of Gastroenterology.* doi: ajg2010488 [pii]10.1038/ajg.2010.488.

Krahn, M.D., Mahoney, J.E., Eckman, M.H., Trachtenberg, J., Pauker, S.G., & Detsky, A.S. (1994). Screening for prostate cancer. A decision analytic view. *Journal of the American Medical Association, 272*(10), 773–780.

Lewington, S., Clarke, R., Qizilbash, N., Peto, R., & Collins, R. (2002). Age-specific relevance of usual blood pressure to vascular mortality: A meta-analysis of individual data for one million adults in 61 prospective studies. *Lancet, 360*(9349), 1903–1913.

Liberman, A., & Rubinstein, J. (2002). Health care reform and the pharmaceutical industry: Crucial decisions are expected. *Health Care Management (Frederick), 20*(3), 22–32.

Lipid Research Group. (1984). The lipid research clinics coronary primary prevention trial results. II. The relationship of reduction in incidence of coronary heart disease to cholesterol lowering. *Journal of the American Medical Association, 251*(3), 365–374.

Lu-Yao, G.L., Friedman, M., & Yao, S.L. (1997). Use of radical prostatectomy among Medicare beneficiaries before and after the introduction of prostate specific antigen testing. *Journal of Urology, 157*(6), 2219–2222.

Manolio, T.A., Burke, G.L., O'Leary, D.H., Evans, G., Beauchamp, N., Knepper, L., et al. (1999). Relationships of cerebral MRI findings to ultrasonographic carotid atherosclerosis in older adults: The cardiovascular health study. CHS collaborative research group. *Arteriosclerosis, Thrombosis, and Vascular Biology, 19*(2), 356–365.

Marcus, P.M., Bergstralh, E.J., Fagerstrom, R.M., Williams, D.E., Fontana, R., Taylor, W.F., et al. (2000). Lung cancer mortality in the Mayo lung project: Impact of extended follow-up. *Journal of the National Cancer Institute, 92*(16), 1308–1316.

McLellan, F. (2002). Independent US panel fans debate on mammography. *Lancet, 359* (9304), 409.

McNaughton-Collins, M., Fowler, F.J., Jr., Caubet, J.F., Bates, D.W., Lee, J.M., Hauser, A., & Barry, M.J. (2004). Psychological effects of a suspicious prostate cancer screening test followed by a benign biopsy result. *American Journal of Medicine, 117*(10), 719–725.

Mechanic, R., & Altman, S. (2010). Medicare's opportunity to encourage innovation in health care delivery. *New England Journal of Medicine, 362*(9), 772–774.

Miettinen, O.S., Henschke, C.I., Pasmantier, M.W., Smith, J.P., Libby, D.M., & Yankelevitz, D.F. (2002). Mammographic screening: No reliable supporting evidence? *Lancet, 359*(9304), 404–405.

Miller, S.M., Sherman, A.C., & Christensen, A.J. (2010). Introduction to special series: The great debate—evaluating the health implications of positive psychology. *Annals of Behavioral Medicine, 39*(1), 1–3.

Mittler, J.N., Landon, B.E., Fisher, E.S., Cleary, P.D., & Zaslavsky, A.M. (2010). Market variations in intensity of Medicare service use and beneficiary experiences with care. *Health Services Research, 45*(3), 647–669.

Mollen, S., Ruiter, R.A., & Kok, G. (2010). Current issues and new directions in Psychology and Health: What are the oughts? The adverse effects of using social norms in health communication. *Psychology and Health, 25*(3), 265–270.

Muldoon, M.F., Barger, S.D., Ryan, C.M., Flory, J.D., Lehoczky, J.P., Matthews, K.A., et al. (2000). Effects of lovastatin on cognitive function and psychological well-being. *American Journal of Medicine, 108*(7), 538–546.

Navarro, A.M., & Kaplan, R.M. (1996). Mammography screening: Prospects and opportunity costs. *Womens Health, 2*(4), 209–233.

Neal, B., MacMahon, S., & Chapman, N. (2000). Effects of ACE inhibitors, calcium antagonists, and other blood-pressure-lowering drugs: Results of prospectively designed overviews of randomised trials. Blood Pressure Lowering Treatment Trialists' Collaboration. *Lancet, 356*(9246), 1955–1964.

Nystrom, L., Andersson, I., Bjurstam, N., Frisell, J., Nordenskjold, B., & Rutqvist, L.E. (2002). Long-term effects of mammography screening: Updated overview of the Swedish randomised trials. *Lancet, 359*(9310), 909–919.

O'Connor, A.M., Graham, I.D., & Visser, A. (2005). Implementing shared decision making in diverse health care systems: the role of patient decision aids. *Patient Education and Counseling, 57*(3), 247–249.

Quinn, K. (2010). Achieving cost control, care coordination, and quality improvement in the Medicaid program. *Journal of Ambulatory Care Management, 33*(1), 38–49; discussion 69–70.

Ramsey, S.D., Sullivan, S.D., & Kaplan, R.M. (2008). Cost-effectiveness of lung volume reduction surgery. *Proceedings of the American Thoracic Society, 5*(4), 406–411.

Sallis, J.F. (2011). Leisure-time physical activity and depression in adolescence. *Clinical Journal of Sports Medicine, 21*(1), 72.

Salzmann, P., Kerlikowske, K., & Phillips, K. (1997). Cost-effectiveness of extending screening mammography guidelines to include women 40 to 49 years of age. *Annals of Internal Medicine, 127*(11), 955–965.

Schroder, F.H., & Wildhagen, M.F. (2002). Low levels of PSA predict long-term risk of prostate cancer: Results from the Baltimore longitudinal study of aging. *Urology, 59*(3), 462.

Schwartz, L.M., Woloshin, S., Fowler, F.J., Jr., & Welch, H.G. (2004). Enthusiasm for cancer screening in the United States. *Journal of the American Medical Association, 291*(1), 71–78.

Sessions, S.Y., & Detsky, A.S. (2010). Incorporating economic reality into medical education. *Journal of the American Medical Association, 304*(11), 1229–1230.

Smith, G.D., Song, F., & Sheldon, T.A. (1993). Cholesterol lowering and mortality: The importance of considering initial level of risk. *British Medical Journal, 306*(6889), 1367–1373.

Starfield, B. (2000). Is US health really the best in the world? *Journal of the American Medicinal Association, 284*(4), 483–485.

Strong, J.P., Malcom, G.T., McMahan, C.A., Tracy, R.E., Newman, W.P., 3rd, Herderick, E.E., et al. (1999). Prevalence and extent of atherosclerosis in adolescents and young adults: Implications for prevention from the Pathobiological Determinants of Atherosclerosis in Youth study. *Journal of the American Medical Association, 281*(8), 727–735.

Van Horn, L., & Ernst, N. (2001). A summary of the science supporting the new National Cholesterol Education Program dietary recommendations: What dietitians should know. *Journal of the American Dietetic Association, 101*(10), 1148–1154.

Vis, A.N. (2002). Does PSA screening reduce prostate cancer mortality? *Canadian Medical Association Journal, 166*(5), 600–601.

Weeks, W.B., Gottlieb, D.J., Nyweide, D.E., Sutherland, J.M., Bynum, J., Casalino, L.P., et al. (2010). Higher health care quality and bigger savings found at large multispecialty medical groups. *Health Affairs (Millwood)*, *29*(5), 991–997.

Weinstein, M.C., Siegel, J.E., Gold, M.R., Kamlet, M.S., & Russell, L.B. (1996). Recommendations of the panel on cost-effectiveness in health and medicine. *Journal of the American Medical Association*, *276*(15), 1253–1258.

Welch, H.G. (2001). Informed choice in cancer screening. *Journal of the American Medical Association*, *285*(21), 2776–2778.

Welch, H.G. (2004). *Should I be tested for cancer?* Berkeley, CA: University of California Press.

Welch, H.G., & Black, W.C. (1997). Using autopsy series to estimate the disease "reservoir" for ductal carcinoma in situ of the breast: How much more breast cancer can we find? *Annals of Internal Medicine*, *127*(11), 1023–1028.

Welch, H.G., Schwartz, L.M., & Woloshin, S. (2000). Do increased 5-year survival rates in prostate cancer indicate better outcomes? *Journal of the American Medical Association*, *284*(16), 2053–2055.

Wennberg, J. (1996). On the appropriateness of small-area analysis for cost containment. Researchers should abandon their microscopic inspection of medical practice and refocus their gaze on what patients want, what works, and how much is enough. *Health Affairs*, *15*(4), 164–167.

Wennberg, J., & Gittelsohn, A. (1982). Variations in medical care among small areas. *Scientific American*, *246*(4), 120–134.

Wennberg, J.E. (1990). *Small area analysis and the medical care outcome problem*. In Sechrest L, Perrin E, & Binker J, (Eds.), Research methodology: Strengthening causal interpretations of non-experimental data (pp. 177–206). Rockville, MD: U.S. Dept. of Health and Human Services.

Wennberg, J.E. (1998). *The Dartmouth atlas of health care in the United States*. Hanover, NH: Trustees of Dartmouth College.

Wennberg, J.E., Freeman, J.L., & Culp, W.J. (1987). Are hospital services rationed in New Haven or over-utilised in Boston? *Lancet*, *1*(8543), 1185–1189.

PART 2

# Core Concepts in
# Health Psychology

# The Brain, Homeostasis, and Health: Balancing Demands of the Internal and External Milieu

John T. Cacioppo *and* Gary G. Berntson

**Abstract**

Communications among the nervous system, neuroendocrine system, and immune system are bidirectional to better balance the demands of the internal and external milieu. By producing feelings of fever and fatigue, not only is the immune system better able to defend against an infection (e.g., invading microbes do not flourish at elevated body temperatures), but the individual who, due to fever and fatigue, withdraws from daily stresses to the comfort of his or her bedroom also diminishes the release of neural and hormonal signals that can compromise immune function. This chapter traces the historical development of integrative principles regarding the regulatory and restorative forces of the autonomic nervous system, neuroendocrine function, and immune actions, and their modulation by the brain in transaction with the environment. The intention is to examine from a global perspective how the brain integrates the regulatory and restorative processes of the body to foster health and adaptation to environmental challenges.

**Keywords:** Autonomic nervous system, neuroendocrine system, immune system, brain function, regulatory process, restorative process, homeostasis, allostasis

The biologist Richard Lewontin (2000) characterized living organisms as electromechanical devices made up of articulated physical parts that, for purely thermodynamic reasons, eventually wear out and fail to function. Lithgow and Kirkwood (1996), in their review of research on the biology of aging, observed that it is "disadvantageous to increase maintenance beyond a level sufficient to keep the organism in good shape through its natural life expectancy in the wild, because the extra cost will eat into resources that in terms of natural selection are better used to boost other functions that will enhance fitness" (p. 80). We are only now beginning to understand how the brain integrates the regulatory and restorative forces of the body to foster health and adaptation to environmental challenge. This chapter examines these forces as they relate to psychology and health.

In their normal state, regulatory processes (e.g., homeostasis) buffer organisms from the effects of internal and external changes, and restorative processes (e.g., wound healing, humoral immunity) operate to refresh, buttress, and repair various forms of cellular damage. Regulatory devices work only within certain limits of perturbation in buffering the organism from changes in the internal milieu, however, and the restorative components of these regulatory devices work only within certain limits to return the organism to an earlier condition. If the disturbance is too great or enduring, the very parameters around which these regulatory devices operate (e.g., basal levels of functioning or set points) can be affected. Psychological stress has also been shown to influence the operation of these regulatory (Berntson & Cacioppo, 2007; McEwen, 1998) and restorative (Cacioppo, Hawkley, & Berntson, 2003; Kiecolt-Glaser, Page, Marucha, MacCallum, & Glaser, 1998) devices, meaning that anticipated or imagined events, as well as specific physical assaults, can disrupt mind and biology. For example, the sympathetic activation of the heart and cardiovascular system promotes adaptive responding by adjusting the circulation of blood to sleeping, walking, and running (Sterling & Eyer, 1988). Surges of blood pressure in the face of job stress, however, provide the metabolic support needed for anticipated and actual physical activity; if repeated and persisting, these cardiovascular responses may promote hypertension and atherosclerosis (McEwen, 1998).

Among the peripheral regulatory and restorative devices orchestrated by the brain in mammalian species are the autonomic, endocrine, and immune systems. Not long ago, these systems were thought to function largely independently, outside the reach of social and cultural influences. Research on the molecular aspects of neuroimmunomodulation has now shown that the autonomic, endocrine, and immune systems communicate by shared ligands (compounds that bind to receptors and exert functional actions, such as cytokines, hormones, and neurotransmitters) coordinated at multiple levels of the neuraxis (i.e., brain and nervous system; e.g., McCann et al., 1998). The nervous system can communicate with the endocrine system through direct innervation, whereas the endocrine system signals the nervous system through hormones and neurotransmitters that cross the blood–brain barrier or act directly on viscera.

The nervous system and endocrine system communicate with the immune system through a variety of means, including autonomic innervation of lymphoid organs and through adrenergic (Madden, Thyagarajan, & Felton, 1998) and glucocorticoid (Bauer, 1983) receptors on immune cells. For example, previous studies have demonstrated the impact of psychological stress on the steady-state expression/reactivation of latent Epstein-Barr virus (EBV). Most adults have been exposed to EBV (mononucleosis), but they do not show symptoms of this virus because the immune system holds it in check. The virus is said to be "latent" in the body. When a person is under stress, cellular immune function can be impaired (through the effects of stress hormones on lymphocytes), resulting in less control over the expression of the latent virus, increases in antibody to the virus, and in some cases, the clinical manifestation of the virus. Cacioppo, Kiecolt-Glaser, et al. (2002) investigated whether the steady-state expression of latent EBV in vivo differed between high- and low-stress reactors, as defined by sympathetic cardiac reactivity (Cacioppo, 1994; Cacioppo, Uchino, & Berntson, 1994). Results revealed that women who were high-stress reactors were characterized by

higher antibody titers to the latent virus than low-stress reactors. Moreover, an in vitro study suggested that the frequency and amplitude of the release of pituitary and adrenal hormones, such as the powerful stress hormone cortisol, may be sufficient to account for this result.

That is, daily stressors can activate the autonomic nervous system and promote the release of pituitary and adrenal hormones, especially in high reactors. The release of these glucocorticoid hormones, in turn, may contribute to the weakened immunologic conditions required for the reactivation of the virus in latently infected cells throughout the body. If these individuals are not able to retreat from the stresses of their environment to recuperate, or, worse yet, if their weakened immunologic state only increases the stressors they are confronting, then a positive feedback system results, which fosters conditions for the development of frequent and chronic disease. This circumstance is more likely to characterize individuals from low than high socioeconomic status, because they are less likely to be able to afford to miss work due to illness, and individuals who are socially isolated rather than integrated, because they are less likely to have someone help them to at least temporarily deal with their daily stresses. One of the implications of this positive feedback system is that it creates physiological conditions that make illness more likely and more ravaging. What physiological forces have evolved to counteract the creation of this positive feedback loop in everyone?

The immune system, long thought to consist of isolated circulating sentinels against disease, is now recognized as communicating with the central nervous system, autonomic nervous system, and endocrine system. Catecholamines and peptides (e.g., neuropeptide Y) modulate lymphocytic actions, and peripheral immune cytokines (lymphocyte secretions) are transduced into a neuronal signal and conveyed to the brain via afferent fibers in the vagus nerve (Maier & Watkins, 2009) and influence behavior (Dantzer, et al., 1998; see Kemeny, 2011, Chapter 7, this volume). As Maier and Watkins (1998) noted:

> If the immune system is conceived of as a diffuse sense organ that communicates the status of infection- and injury-related events to the brain, it is then sensible to inquire how sense organs generally communicate to the brain. They do not generally do so by accumulating chemical signals in the blood that then cross into the brain. Rather, they do so by activating peripheral nerves that go to the brain. Indeed, there is a nerve that innervates regions of the

body in which immune responses occur (the gut, spleen, thymus, lymph nodes, etc.) and provides afferent input to the brain from these regions, which is called the *vagus nerve*. Although the vagus has traditionally been viewed as an efferent nerve providing parasympathetic input from the brain to visceral organs, modern anatomy has revealed that many of the vagal fibers (roughly 70%) are actually sensory, sending afferent messages from the innervated organs to the brain. (p. 88)

Maier and Watkins (1998, 2009) review further evidence that fever, increases in pain responsivity, brain norepinephrine changes, glucocorticoid increases, and conditioned taste aversions produced by cytokines may be attenuated in animals in which the vagus had been lesioned. These results suggest that, in addition to direct actions of immune signals in the brain, the afferent (sensory) aspect of the vagus is an important route through which information from the peripheral immune system (e.g., cytokines) can be conveyed to the brain, where such effects are controlled (Hansen, O'Connor, Goehler, Watkins, & Maier, 2001).

In short, communications among the nervous system, neuroendocrine system, and immune system are bidirectional to better balance the demands of the internal and external milieu. By producing feelings of fever and fatigue, not only is the immune system better able to defend against an infection (e.g., invading microbes do not flourish at elevated body temperatures), but the individual who, due to fever and fatigue, withdraws from daily stresses to the comfort of his or her bedroom also diminishes the release of neural and hormonal signals that can compromise immune function.

We organize the present chapter in terms of the historical development of integrative principles regarding the regulatory and restorative forces of the autonomic nervous system, neuroendocrine function, and immune actions and their modulation by the brain in transaction with the environment. Our intention is not to focus in detail on any one regulatory device but to examine from a global perspective how the brain integrates the regulatory and restorative processes of the body to foster health and adaptation to environmental challenges. We begin with an overview of why an integrative analysis may be profitable for understanding health and disease.

## The Organism in Transaction with the Environment

The social and behavioral sciences are influenced by societal problems, just as the medical sciences are driven by health problems. Changes in society and health over the past century have drawn the social, behavioral, and biological sciences together to address how the brain integrates the regulatory forces of the body to cultivate health while also promoting adaptation to the physical, psychological, and social challenges posed by extended life in contemporary society (Cacioppo, Berntson, Sheridan, & McClintock, 2000). A century ago, antibiotics were nonexistent, public health was underdeveloped, and germ-based diseases were among the major causes of adult morbidity and mortality. The mortality statistics point to the most important killers as being diphtheria, smallpox, tuberculosis, bronchitis, pneumonia, and measles. Medical scientists at the turn of the 20th century focused on the major health problems of the day about which they could do something. By the end of the 20th century, public health improvements, widespread vaccinations, and advances in medical and pharmacological treatments were paralleled by diminished mortality from infectious diseases.

The decreased mortality from infectious diseases during the 19th and 20th centuries may not be primarily attributable to these medical or public health innovations, however. Lewontin (2000) notes, for instance, that the death rates from infectious diseases were decreasing by the 1830s, and that more than 90% of the reduction in these death rates had occurred before antibiotics were introduced after World War I. Even improvements in sanitation may not be an adequate explanation for the decreases in deaths from infectious diseases because the principal killers were airborne, not waterborne. Measles, the principal killer of children in the 19th century, was still contracted by most children in the first half of the 20th century, but the mortality rate from the disease had greatly diminished (Lewontin, 2000). Thus, reductions in mortality from infectious diseases could not be explained adequately in terms of measures designed to prevent the spread of diseases.

The reduction may be attributable to a general trend of increases in real wage, an increase in the state of nutrition, and a decrease in the number of hours worked—that is, *a decrease in the wear and tear on the organism* and *improved opportunities for the organism to heal itself*. As Lewontin (2000) notes: "As people were better nourished and better clothed and had more rest time to recover from taxing labor, their bodies, being in a less stressed physiological state, were better able to recover from the further severe stress of infection" (p. 104). If this analysis is correct, the social and behavioral sciences have a great deal to contribute to understanding morbidity and mortality, in particular as they help illuminate the operations and dysfunction of regulatory and restorative processes. It also follows that health psychology should consider not only the effects of stress and catabolic processes but also the effects of restorative and anabolic processes.[1]

Demographic changes during the 20th century have direct implications for health care, problems, and costs. Only 4% of the U.S. population lived to be more than 65 years of age, compared with more than 17% today. The fastest-growing segment of the population is now older adults, with the number of persons under the age 65 in the United States increasing by a factor of three during the 20th century, while the number of persons 65 and over is increasing by a factor of 11 (Hobbs & Stoops, 2002). Although threats from infectious diseases demand continued vigilance (Garrett, 2000), and research and advances in molecular biology provide powerful new weapons with which to combat the devastation of diseases (Kandel & Squire, 2000), entry into the 21st century has brought into view a new set of health problems. Among the leading causes of death in industrialized nations are now heart disease, cancer, cerebrovascular disease, accidents, chronic lung disease, infectious diseases, diabetes, suicide and homicide, and chronic liver disease/cirrhosis (e.g., Blumenthal, Matthews, & Weiss, 1994). Chronic diseases are now the most frequent sources of complaints and the largest causes of morbidity and mortality in older adults, and the cost of these diseases is stunning. According to estimates by Luskin and Newell (1997), by the early 1990s, individuals 65 and older (who at that time accounted for 11% of the U.S. population) accounted for 36% of all hospital stays and 48% of total days of doctor care. These percentages and the corresponding health costs are increasing dramatically, not only because the costs of health care are rising but also because the number of elderly individuals is increasing rapidly (as is the percentage of the total population that is elderly). To better understand the etiology of these new sources of morbidity and mortality, we need to consider the effects of stress and restoration on the cumulative wear and tear of the organism.

## Regulated Variables, Perturbations, and Adaptive Responses

With impressive advances in molecular biology and genetics, it is easy to think about the organism as indifferent to the physical and social environment, and health problems as best addressed exclusively at the level of the gene or cell (cf. Temple, McLeod, Gallinger, & Wright, 2001). Claude Bernard's (1878/1974) seminal observations more than a century ago speak eloquently against such a notion. He observed that the extracellular fluid constitutes the immediate environment—the internalized sea—for plants and animals. He noted the relative constancy of this internal milieu and regarded this constancy, and the physiological mechanisms that served to maintain it, as providing protection against the powerful entropic forces that threaten to disrupt the biological order essential for life. Without mechanisms to stabilize the cellular environment, organisms would be confined to a limited ecological niche. In Bernard's terms, the existence of these mechanisms permitted animals to live a *free and independent* existence.

The notion of an integrative regulatory biology in animals that enables a free and independent existence, and the exquisite role of the brain and behavior in this process, is illustrated in the regulatory mechanisms that maintain body temperature. Metabolic activity is impaired at temperatures discrepant from 98.60° F, so this equilibrium point is usually defended by multiple mechanisms. One of the simplest is a self-produced atmosphere that surrounds the human body and helps insulate it from the outer air (Lewontin, 2000). Specifically, the body is surrounded by a layer of higher-density air that is warmed and moistened by the body's metabolic heat and water. (This phenomenon helps explain the windchill factor, which is the result of wind stripping away this insulating layer.) In Lewontin's (2000) terms, "Organisms not only determine what aspects of the outside world are relevant to them by peculiarities of their shape and metabolism, but they actively construct, in the literal sense of the word, a world around themselves" (p. 54) that helps buffer the internal milieu from environmental variations.

In addition, normal metabolic activity, such as the breaking down of food to composite packets and energy, creates heat in excess of 98.60° F. Consequently, the body activates the eccrine (sweat) glands (to foster perspiration and a consequent loss of body heat) and peripheral vasodilation (to foster a shunting of blood from the hot viscera and muscles to cutaneous tissue beds near the surface of the skin to allow heat to dissipate). These adaptive responses go unnoticed under normal circumstances, leaving the individual's limited cognitive resources and behavioral options untouched. When body temperature falls below 98.60° F, eccrine gland activity decreases to minimize perspiration and the consequent loss of body heat, and peripheral vasoconstriction occurs to retain the heated blood within the deep recesses of the brain and body. These automated and unnoticed peripheral adjustments are often sufficient to maintain body temperature within the narrow range needed for orderly metabolic activity, thereby permitting a "free and independent existence."

If the organism is exposed to a greater drain on its heat output, an involuntary rhythmical tensing of small muscles throughout the body (i.e., shivering) begins to occur. Each time a muscle fiber contracts, millions of adenosine triphosphate molecules are cleaved, liberating energy in the form of heat, and the biomechanics of muscle contraction produces yet additional heat. As the need for heat increases, more and larger muscles are recruited. Heat production can increase for several critical minutes, although some muscle coordination is forfeited in the process. Broader systems can be called into action, including additional autonomic (e.g., Collins & Surwit, 2001) and neuroendocrine (e.g., Arancibia, Rage, Astier, & Tapia-Arancibia, 1996) adjustments. Still higher-order regulatory mechanisms are called into play, including attention, behavioral adjustments, and decision making. Although especially well known in cold-blooded animals that have a body temperature that varies with the temperature of its surroundings, if given the opportunity all vertebrates will contribute to thermal regulation by moving to a region of warmer or cooler temperature. The individual notices (i.e., attends to) being cold, and cognitive resources and behavioral options that were available for other tasks are usurped to reestablish a constancy of the balance within. The individual might do so by donning a sweater, turning on a heater, moving to a warmer location, or huddling with others. In doing so, however, the individual surrenders, at least temporarily, some of the freedom and independence of existence that characterizes the integrative physiology of animals. If even these devices prove insufficient, extravagances of the organism such as coordinated movement, consciousness, and maintenance of appendages are sacrificed, at least temporarily, while the remaining heated blood is directed to the organs (e.g., heart and brain) that are vital to survival, thereby increasing the chances that the physical or social environment changes to restore the balance within and, consequently, the likelihood of survival.

Anticipatory responses, planning, and decision making are also empowered, as individuals can change their behaviors and environments to minimize perturbations to the balance within. Migration to warmer climates with the changing seasons and construction of dwellings to buffer changes in temperature are illustrative. As Claude Bernard (1878/1974) observed, mammals are far from being indifferent to their surroundings but must be in close and intimate relation to it, continually compensating for and counterbalancing external variations. This interplay between organismic and environmental conditions is orchestrated at multiple levels to maintain a balance within.

The same principle applies to the endocrine and immune systems. The latter must defend the organism against an unknowable variety of infectious agents by surveying, identifying, isolating, and eradicating rapidly reproducing microorganisms. Accordingly, the immune system cannot be too insensitive in initiating, developing, or expanding, else effector functions can be overwhelmed by pathogens (e.g., cancer, viral, and infectious diseases; Cohn & Langman, 1990), and it cannot be too sensitive because the cellular and chemical agents meant to combat pathogens are themselves capable of substantial destruction of host tissues (i.e., autoimmune diseases; Germain, 2000). For a review of the regulatory agents and mechanisms that characterize the immune system, see Kemeny (2011, Chapter 7, this volume).

In sum, the autonomic, neuroendocrine, and immune systems are orchestrated in part to preserve conditions compatible with life, in what Claude Bernard (1878/1974) called the *milieu intérieur*—a state Esther Sternberg (2000) has called "the balance within." Humans do not reside in an unchanging, nurturant ecological niche but rather explore, accommodate, and tame hostile and hospitable environments alike. In the process, disturbing forces (e.g., stressors) operate on the *milieu intérieur*. The resulting disequilibrium can trigger counteracting normalizing forces (Chrousos, 2000), followed by repair and maintenance.

## Homeostasis

It remained for subsequent investigators to delineate the general nature of these regulatory mechanisms. A dominant perspective for most of the 20th century was Walter Cannon's (1939) notion of *homeostasis*, in which adaptive reactions were equated with processes that maintained the constancy of the fluid matrix (see Berntson & Cacioppo, 2007).

Cannon argued that the variations from basal physiological levels ("set points") do not reach the dangerous extremes that impair the functions of the cells or threaten the existence of the organism because adaptive reactions are automatically triggered to return the affected physiological system to a basal state.

In Cannon's model (1929), the sympathetic branch of the autonomic nervous system (as the primary homeostatic regulator) and the parasympathetic branch provide a fine-tuning of visceral responses. Homeostasis was thought to be maintained by a self-regulating feedback mechanism (i.e., servocontrolled reflexes; Cannon, 1929, 1939). Slight variations in the magnitude of activation notwithstanding, the sympathetic and parasympathetic branches were thought to be reciprocally activated and synergistic in their actions (Berntson & Cacioppo, 2007). The baroreceptor–heart rate reflex, which serves to maintain blood pressure, illustrates this reciprocal relationship between the activation of the sympathetic and parasympathetic branches (Berntson, Cacioppo, & Quigley, 1991). Elevations in blood pressure activate the baroreceptors (pressure-sensitive receptors) mostly within the carotid sinus, which then increase firing in afferent (sensory) fibers to the nucleus of the tractus solitarius (NTS). The activation of the NTS, in turn, inhibits sympathetic motor neurons in the intermediolateral cell column of the spinal cord and excites the parasympathetic source nuclei in the nucleus ambiguous and dorsal motor nucleus of the vagus. That is, increased blood pressure reflexively leads to a decrease in sympathetic activation of the heart and a reciprocal increase in parasympathetic activation of the heart. This decrease in sympathetic activation slows the heart rate and reduces ventricular contractility, whereas the reciprocal increase in parasympathetic activation also slows the beat of the heart, all of which reduce cardiac output. Together with reductions in sympathetic adrenergic vasoconstrictor tone, the baroreceptor actions compensate for the disturbance and restore blood pressure to normal levels. The opposite pattern of autonomic control (i.e., sympathetic activation and reciprocal parasympathetic withdrawal) is triggered by a sudden lowering of blood pressure (e.g., during assumption of an upright posture) to elevate and stabilize blood pressure.

As this example illustrates, the baroreflex displays the essential characteristics of a feedback-regulated, homeostatic mechanism that responds to perturbations of blood pressure and acts to restore basal blood pressure. But blood pressure regulation is not limited to servomechanisms like the baroreflex. Indeed, blood pressure changes can be seen in anticipation of a perturbation, before any change in baroreceptor afference. Examples include the increased blood pressure just prior to physical exercise, the assumption of an upright posture, or the anticipated confrontation of a threatening or dangerous stimulus. To some extent, these anticipatory changes likely reflect simple Pavlovian conditioning, in which stimuli (environmental or cognitive) that predict an impending perturbation can serve as conditioned stimuli (CS) for an anticipatory, compensatory adjustment (Dworkin & Dworkin, 1995). In addition to this simple form of heterotopic conditioning (i.e., conditioning in which the CS and the unconditioned stimuli, or UCS, are in different modalities), there is a growing probability of homotopic conditioning of the baroreflex and other autonomic systems (Dworkin, 2000). In homotopic conditioning, the CS and UCS are in the same modality (e.g., baroreceptor afference), wherein a modest baroreceptor activation (CS) that evokes a small compensatory response (unconditioned response or UCR) may trigger a larger conditioned response (CR) that acts synergistically with the UCR to actually preclude a subsequent perturbation (Dworkin, 2000). This serves to make adjustments that not only precede physiological perturbation but also dampen or eliminate the perturbation. Thus, when fine-tuned by consistent homotopic conditioning, regulatory systems may act preemptively to prevent, rather than simply react to, perturbations.

These specific examples, although not exclusively servomechanisms, still represent homeostasis because they represent negative feedback systems that operate to maintain physiological functioning around a given set point. Conditioned anticipatory responses, however, are not limited to homeostatic effects, as they can also produce a change in set point or an inhibition of set point regulation (Dworkin, Elbert, & Rau, 2000). The reflex-based homeostatic model also has limitations, as the same excitatory stimulus (e.g., stressor) can have profoundly different effects on physiological activation across individuals or life circumstances, and higher-level behavioral circuits come into play. Accordingly, the reciprocal activation of the sympathetic and parasympathetic branches may be true for brainstem baroreceptor reflexes, but it does not provide a comprehensive account of the autonomic responses supporting more complex behaviors (Berntson et al., 1991; Berntson, Cacioppo, & Quigley, 1993).

In an illustrative study, Berntson et al. (1994) quantified the sympathetic and parasympathetic responses to postural (orthostatic) and active coping (e.g., mental arithmetic) stressors using autonomic blockades. At the nomothetic level, orthostatic and psychological stressors produced what appeared to be reciprocal activation—whether individuals moved from a sitting to a standing posture or whether they moved from a quiescent baseline to an active coping task (i.e., mental arithmetic, competitive reaction time, and public speaking tasks), mean sympathetic activation of the heart increased and vagal (parasympathetic) activation of the heart decreased. Based on the known physiology, the postural effect is largely attributable to reciprocal autonomic control by the baroreflex. Indeed, the correlation between the quantitative estimates of sympathetic and parasympathetic contributions to the cardiac response to orthostatic stressor was large and significant, confirming reciprocal cardiac activation at the idiographic level consistent with Cannon's conception of homeostasis. The autonomic determinants of the cardiac responses to the psychological stressors, in contrast, revealed large and reliable individual differences in sympathetic and parasympathetic activation. Unlike that found for posture, for instance, the correlation between the quantitative estimates of sympathetic and parasympathetic contributions to the cardiac response to psychological stressors were nonsignificant (Berntson et al., 1994). The autonomic control of the heart in response to each of the psychological stressors is modulated by more rostral (higher-order) brain systems. These higher regions of the brain are rich in input from environmental and associative (including personal historical) events (Berntson, Sarter, & Cacioppo, 1998). Accordingly, they produce cardiac responses to psychological stressors that exceed metabolic demands (Turner, 1989) and reveal more interindividual variation in the mode of cardiac control (Berntson et al., 1994).

To account for these and related findings, Berntson and colleagues (e.g., Berntson et al., 1991, 1993) proposed a model of autonomic space in which sympathetic and parasympathetic activation not only could be reciprocal but could also be uncoupled, coactivated, or coinhibited. Reciprocal activation fosters a rapid and dramatic change in effector status (e.g., heart rate), uncoupled activation affords more fine-tuning (e.g., vagal withdrawal in response to mild exercise), and coactivation or coinhibition can regulate or mute the functional consequences of underlying neural adjustments.

These latter adjustments, which fall outside the rubric of homeostasis (Berntson et al., 1991), nevertheless represent regulatory adjustments to support the demands, perceived or real, of the external world. Of what importance is this to health?

Although high blood pressure is generally asymptomatic, approximately 30% of individuals with high blood pressure will suffer some adverse health outcome, such as heart disease, and 5%–10% will die from a stroke (Temple et al., 2001). High heart rate (HR) reactivity to active coping tasks has received considerable attention because of its association with elevated blood pressure and cardiovascular disease in later life (e.g., Light, Dolan, Davis, & Sherwood, 1992). High HR reactivity has also been associated with poorer recovery following myocardial infarction (e.g., Krantz & Manuck, 1984), heightened sympathetic adrenomedullary activity, and impaired cellular immune function (Manuck, Cohen, Rabin, Muldoon, & Bachen, 1991; Sgoutas-Emch et al., 1994).

Although high HR reactivity has been regarded to be a risk factor for hypertension, an individual's classification as high in HR reactivity could originate from elevated sympathetic reactivity, vagal withdrawal, or reciprocal activation of the sympathetic and vagal outflows to the heart. Research on cardiac reactivity, however, has generally emphasized variations in HR reactivity rather than variations in the autonomic origins of HR reactivity. According to Berntson and colleagues' (1991) theory of autonomic organization and function, the classification of individuals in terms of HR reactivity relegates variations in the autonomic origins of HR reactivity to the error term. In other words, one cannot distinguish between a level of HR reactivity that reflects sympathetic activation or vagal withdrawal—and blurring this distinction can obscure relationships between autonomic responses to stressors and behavioral, humoral, or clinical outcomes (Cacioppo, 1994). Indeed, reliable differences exist not only in HR reactivity to psychological stressors but also in sympathetic cardiac activation and in vagal cardiac activation (Berntson et al., 1994; Cacioppo, Berntson, et al., 1994; Cacioppo, Uchino, & Berntson, 1994); it is the sympathetic component that best predicts the activation of the hypothalamic pituitary axis and cellular immunity (Benschop et al., 1998; Cacioppo et al., 1995; Uchino, Cacioppo, Malarkey, Glaser, & Kiecolt-Glaser, 1995). In different health domains, such as when predicting the recovery from myocardial infarction, both sympathetic and vagal components may be important for understanding separable, potentially pathophysiological mechanisms of action (Berntson et al., 1997).

Sympathetic activation is not the unidimensional construct that was ascribed to Cannon, either. Contrary to the notion that sympathetic nervous activation is global and diffuse, highly specific regional sympathetic activation has been observed in response to stressors (Johnson & Anderson, 1990), even in extreme conditions such as panic attacks (Wilkinson et al., 1998). Obrist, Light, and colleagues demonstrated that active coping tasks (those with which one copes by doing something; e.g., mental arithmetic) tend to elicit β-adrenergic (e.g., cardiac) activation and increased blood pressure, whereas passive coping tasks (those with which one copes by enduring; e.g., cold pressor) tend to elicit α-adrenergic (e.g., vasomotor) activation (Light, Girdler, & Hinderliter, 2003) and increased blood pressure. Again, individual differences have been found, with some individuals showing greater cardiac reactivity and others greater vasomotor reactivity (Kasprowicz, Manuck, Malkoff, & Krantz, 1990; Light, Turner, Hinderliter, Girdler, & Sherwood, 1994; Llabre, Klein, Saab, McCalla, & Schneiderman, 1998; Sherwood, Dolan, & Light, 1990). An integration of these apparently disparate effects is suggested by the research showing that individuals who approach active coping tasks with the belief that they can meet task demands ("challenge appraisals") also tend to show primarily cardiac activation to the task, whereas those who approach the tasks with the belief that they cannot meet task demands ("threat appraisals") tend to show primarily vascular activation (Tomaka, Blascovich, Kibler, & Ernst, 1997). Whether it is threat/challenge appraisals or active/passive coping strategies for dealing with the stressors that produce the different patterns of sympathetic activation remains to be determined, but it is becoming clear that sympathetic activation does not represent a simple arousal mechanism, and that not all responses to stressors are the same (Berntson, Cacioppo, & Sarter, 2003; Hawkley & Cacioppo, 2003).

## Allostasis

The research reviewed in the preceding section suggests that not all regulatory mechanisms are homeostatic and that the balance within is not maintained by a system of rigid servocontrollers operating around immutable set points. The regulated response of the brain and body serves a constancy of the internal milieu, not only in an immediate sense, like most homeostatic adjustments, but also in the long term under conditions of changing physiological capacities or resilience. The complexity of the regulatory devices required to achieve this constancy led Sterling and Eyer (1988) and McEwen and Stellar (1993) to propose the concept of *allostasis*. Thus, the concept of allostasis is an abstraction to guide our study and understanding of the many autonomic, endocrine, and immune dimensions that are regulated by multiple, interacting mechanisms that are subjected to broader modulatory influences, whether from external challenges or endogenous processes.

Allostatic regulation (in contrast to homeostatic regulation) reflects the operation of higher neural systems that serve to control and integrate a broad range of homeostatic reflexes (Berntson & Cacioppo, 2003). Allostatic regulation, therefore, may achieve greater flexibility in maintaining integrative regulation both within and across autonomic, neuroendocrine, and immune function than is possible through homeostasis alone. An illustration is the alteration in body temperature set point associated with a fever (Berntson & Cacioppo, 2007). The increase in body temperature during illness does not represent a failure of homeostasis. Rather, the increased temperature of a fever is actively regulated and defended, and reductions in body temperature are met with active compensatory thermogenic processes (e.g. shivering, behavioral thermoregulation). The elevation in temperature associated with a fever may be of benefit in slowing bacterial growth and proliferation (Maier & Watkins, 1998, 2009). Despite its potential adaptive significance, fever is not readily subsumed within homeostatic regulation because it reflects the adoption of a new regulatory set point.

In sum, the term *allostasis* was coined by Sterling and Eyer (1988) to refer to active deviations from homeostatic levels that often appear under conditions of adaptive challenge.[2] Interestingly, the seeds of this idea can be found in Selye's (1973) concept of heterostasis, in which altered chemical and hormonal conditions associated with exogenous stimuli were seen as contributing to resistance and adaptation by rendering tissues less sensitive to pathogenic stimuli and/or neutralizing or destroying pathogens. The anti-inflammatory effects of adrenocorticoids, such as cortisol, are an example of the former mechanism, as corticoids make tissue less sensitive to irritation. An example of the latter mechanism is the centrally regulated increase in body temperature (fever) associated with illness, which may promote an optimal host defense.

## Short-term Gains Versus Long-term Costs

Both homeostasis and allostasis exist to buffer organisms from the effects of internal and external changes—for instance, from the effects of environmental stressors. Stressors and stress responses are neither inherently good nor inherently bad, however. Homeostasis and allostasis evolved because there were reproductive benefits to being able to respond to environmental stressors. The counteracting forces triggered by disturbances of the internal milieu can have long-term costs but can also promote growth, adaptation, and resilience—especially if the resources that can be marshaled are sufficient to meet adaptive demands and the associated restorative (e.g., anabolic) processes promote adaptive responding to subsequent exposures to the same kind of demands. Learning, muscular development, and humoral immunity are illustrative of the empowering aspects of the restorative powers of the body. A defensive lineman who makes the transition from college to professional football may initially be in awe of the strength of the offensive linemen he must block and muscularly fatigued after practices. The same events, however, become less and less demanding as the lineman's muscles have time to repair and grow following each practice.[3] Thus, at least some long-term costs of stress may be minimized, or in some cases reversed, if appropriate repair and maintenance processes also unfold. Indeed, vaccinations work in this way. A weakened antigen is inserted to immunologically challenge the body to produce the antibodies needed to eradicate the pathogen and repair the body. An individual who is vaccinated may suffer a brief, mild bout of the illness but subsequently will have an acquired immunity to future exposures to this antigen.

In the remainder of this section, we focus on the short-term benefits and the long-term costs of stress responses. We return, in a later section on clinical implications, to the importance of dealing with these long-term costs not only by decreasing exposures to stressors but also by increasing the opportunity and salubrity of restorative physiological processes.

### Sympathetic Adrenomedullary System

Cannon (1929) studied not only the physiological basis of homeostasis but also the influence of emotional disturbances on various physiological processes. This latter work focused on what he termed the *emergency reaction*. In Cannon's (1929) formulation, autonomic and neuroendocrine activation associated with emotional disturbances serves to mobilize metabolic resources to support the requirements of fight or flight, thereby promoting the protection and survival of the organism. The sympathetic nervous system, via a sympathetic nerve called the *splanchnics,* directly stimulates the medullary cells of the adrenal gland, causing the release of the catecholamine hormones epinephrine and norepinephrine. Cannon (1929) believed that the sympathetic-adrenomedullary (SAM) system was activated primarily during fight-or-flight responses and played a role in maintaining homeostasis within the body and adapting to environmental stressors.

The actions of the SAM system—which include an increase in muscular efficiency, release of energy stores (glycogenolysis), and increased arterial blood pressure and muscle blood flow—are attributable in large part to epinephrine. Because of differences in the receptors of the arterial walls, catecholamines cause vasodilation within the internal organs (e.g., via β-adrenergic receptors in skeletal muscles) and vasoconstriction in the periphery (e.g., by α-adrenergic receptors in cutaneous tissue beds). This pattern of perfusion (blood flow) has adaptive utility. By shifting blood flow to muscles, the organism is better able to mobilize and cope with the situation. The constriction of peripheral areas not only facilitates the rapid redistribution of blood within the body but also minimizes the loss of blood should an injury occur. Additionally, with the presence of pressure-sensitive receptors in the arterial walls, circulatory changes initiated by the release of catecholamines can feed back and alter the activity of the brain. Blood pressure elevations, for instance, have been shown to diminish pain—a useful short-term adjustment in response to attack but a costly long-term adjustment if it occurs in response to chronic psychological stress and results in hypertension (Dworkin et al., 2000).

### Hypothalamic Pituitary Adrenocortical System

Although sympathetic activation from the release of norepinephrine from sympathetic terminals produces more specific effects than Cannon had envisioned (1928), the SAM response to stress, with the release of epinephrine and norepinephrine into and transport by the blood to visceral organs throughout the body, is capable of producing generalized effects from which the organism recovers more slowly than from sympathetic or parasympathetic (i.e., direct neural) activation. Cannon's historic characterization of the SAM response to stress as adaptive but fixed or rigid (i.e., stereotypic) was elaborated upon in Selye's (1956) general adaptation syndrome (GAS) theory, which emphasized the hypothalamic-pituitary-adrenocortical (HPA) response to stressors. The SAM system is directly innervated by the sympathetic nervous system and therefore can respond more quickly to stressors than the HPA system and more slowly than the autonomic nervous system. The HPA system, on the other hand, has more general and enduring effects than either the SAM or the autonomic nervous system.

Briefly, a release of adrenocorticotropic hormone (ACTH) from the pituitary can be initiated from the hypothalamus and cause the adrenal gland to secrete carbohydrate-active steroids (e.g., glucocorticoids) that have wide-ranging effects on the body's metabolism. These include muscular efficiency, energy resources and cellular metabolism, inflammatory and allergic responses, and brain function, including alertness, learning, and memory processes underlying behavioral adaptation. Selye's work on GAS theory provided early support for the notion that physiological activation in response to stressors is beneficial up to a point, but excessive or prolonged activation may indeed have long-term costs. The initial physiological reaction in the general adaptation syndrome is an emergency fight-or-flight response believed to be adaptive, at least in most instances in the short term. If ineffective behavioral coping results, additional compensatory actions occur, such as increased and sustained secretions of steroids and decreased secretions of catecholamines, and a consequent alteration in homeostatic levels for a number of physiological systems (e.g., water retention, circulatory pressure). If the stress continues for a protracted period without relief, the physiological coping mechanisms may not be able to prevent permanent physiological damage to organs or the demise of the organism.

Cortisol levels are generally held in check by a negative feedback mechanism, in which dual glucocorticoid and mineralocorticoid receptors in the hippocampal region of the brain inhibit further HPA activity (De Kloet, Vreugdenhil, Oitzl, & Joels, 1998). Relatedly, psychological stress in animals has been shown to increase the number of hippocampal mineralocorticoid receptors and produce greater inhibition of HPA activity (Geising et al., 2001). However, continued glucocorticoid and mineralocorticoid excess, which can result from sustained psychological stress, may contribute ultimately to the down-regulation of these hippocampal receptors and to hippocampal atrophy

(Sapolsky, 1996). Such anatomical changes, in turn, diminish the ability of circulating stress hormones to reduce or terminate HPA activation. In other words, chronically elevated circulating cortisol levels can lead to a down-regulation (decreased sensitivity) of the glucocorticoid receptors in the hippocampal region, which in turn decreases the efficacy of the negative feedback mechanism that, under normal conditions, applies brakes to the activation of the HPA axis. With weakened brakes on this stress system, the individual will come to be characterized by a higher set point for circulating cortisol (McEwen, 1998; Selye, 1973).[4]

Importantly, Selye studied physical stressors in animals, but subsequent work has shown that the same general mechanisms may operate in response to psychological stressors in humans (Mason, 1975). Thus, idiosyncratic construals (i.e., cognitive appraisals; Lazarus & Folkman, 1984) of an event can produce variations in autonomic, neuroendocrine, and immune adjustments to the event (Cacioppo, 1994), as well as variations in recovery (Davidson, 1998; McEwen & Seeman, 2003).

### Immune Modulation

The pituitary and adrenal hormones and other neuropeptides (short-chain proteins in the nervous system that are capable of acting as a neurotransmitters) play an important role in the modulation of the immune system (Munck, Guyre, & Holbrook, 1984), as well. Circulating hormones such as epinephrine, norepinephrine, and cortisol can act on visceral as well as cellular immune receptors; they constitute an important gateway through which psychological stressors affect the cellular immune response (Ader, 2007). As we discussed earlier, psychological stress is associated with increases in antibody titers to latent EBV (mononucleosis). In an early study, Kasl and colleagues (1979) followed cadets at West Point, over a 4-year period, who were seronegative for EBV at entry into the Academy. Consistent with the notion that stress can down-regulate the cellular immune response and adversely affect the body's ability to respond to infection with EBV, they found that poor academic performance, high levels of motivation for a military career, and an overachieving father were associated with a greater risk for seroconversion to EBV, longer hospitalization in the infirmary following infection (i.e., more severe illness episodes), and higher EBV antibody titers among those who seroconverted but had no clinical symptoms. Similarly, using an academic stress model with medical students,

Glaser and colleagues measured EBV antibody titers over time, both at baseline periods in which the students were less stressed and during examination periods, when the medical students reported more stress. Results showed reliable changes in antibody titers to EBV virus capsid antigen (VCA) concomitant with the down-regulation of several components of the cellular immune response (Glaser et al., 1987, 1991, 1993).

In sum, autonomic and neuroendocrinological activation in response to stressors serves to mobilize metabolic resources to support the requirements of fight or flight. Stress may be necessary for survival, but it can also alter susceptibility to disease. Stress, particularly if prolonged or repeated, can produce cardiovascular changes that can contribute to a narrowing of blood vessels and to heart attacks or strokes and reduce the strength of immunologic activities in the body (Baum, 1994; Cohen, 1996). Stress may obscure symptoms, increase appraisal and patient delays, and reduce medical compliance (Andersen, Cacioppo, & Roberts, 1995). Stress can activate maladaptive behaviors that reflect attempts to cope with negative emotional responses. Persons experiencing psychological stress, for example, may engage in unhealthy practices such as smoking, not eating or sleeping properly, and not exercising; these behaviors may foster accidents, cardiovascular disease, and suppressed immune function (e.g., Baum, 1994).

Many of the powerful elicitors of emotion in contemporary society—personal affronts, traffic congestion, pressing deadlines, public speaking engagements, unreasonable bosses, perceived injustices—do not require or even allow behavioral fight or flight, and the reactions in response to these events can substantially exceed metabolic requirements. Thus, although physiological activation in response to stressors is beneficial up to a point, excessive autonomic and neuroendocrine activation can diminish health across time. That is, a design for the brain and stress physiology that worked well in human evolution may have maladaptive aspects that manifest as life expectancy has increased well beyond the reproductive years. Indeed, according to Lithgow and Kirkwood's (1996) disposable soma theory of aging, it may be disadvantageous to increase maintenance beyond a level sufficient to keep the organism in good shape through its natural life expectancy in the wild. Given that the metabolic requirements posed by the psychological stressors in today's society are often minimal, physiological reactivity to quotidian stressors in the absence of restorative

breaks may increase the wear and tear on the organism and contribute to broad-based morbidity and mortality.

**Allostatic Load**
The concept of allostasis was introduced earlier in this chapter. In this section, we introduce the related concept of allostatic load. The damage to the balance within, although potentially occurring in response to acute environmental events during an especially sensitive period of development (Anisman, Zaharia, Meaney, & Merali, 1998; Meaney et al., 1996), more typically reflects the accrual of wear and tear on the regulatory and restorative systems of the body in response to stressors over an extended period of time—an accrual termed *allostatic load*. Among the allostatic responses that have been studied most extensively are the autonomic nervous system and the two neuroendocrine systems covered in the preceding section—the SAM and HPA systems. As outlined earlier, the activation of these systems results in the release of neurotransmitters at the viscera, catecholamines from the adrenal medulla, corticotropin from the pituitary, and cortisol from the adrenal cortex. Although inactivation of these systems normally occurs when the perceived danger is past, inefficient inactivation or delayed recovery may result in an overexposure to stress hormones. Thus, high and prolonged exposure to glucocorticoids may result in degenerative changes in the hippocampus, as discussed earlier, with a consequent loss in ability to diminish or terminate potent aspects of the stress response (Sapolsky, 1996).

The adaptive utility of stress reactions is inherent in the concept of allostasis, as is the notion that they come at a cost over the long term (e.g., Crimmins, Johnston, Hayward, & Seeman, 2006; Sabbath, Watt, Sheiham, & Tsakos, 2008; Seeman, Singer, Ryff, Love, & Levy-Storms, 2002). McEwen and Steller (1993) proposed that specific patterns of stress response vary considerably across individuals and contexts, but that they also show common allostatic features. Specifically, in contrast to simple homeostatic systems that are focused on a single dimension (e.g., blood gases) and regulated around a fixed set point, allostatic systems entail multiple dimensions, integrated and orchestrated by central, autonomic, and endocrine processes. Within allostatic systems, functional set points are subject to change, and disturbances in one dimension may lead to compensatory fluctuations in another. McEwen and Stellar (1993) propose that repeated or prolonged allostatic fluctuations extract a physiological cost, a sort of "wear and tear." This wear and tear is seen to be cumulative, largely irreversible, and disposed toward stress pathology. Prolonged stress-related elevations in cortisol and increases in insulin secretion, for instance, accelerate atherosclerosis and contribute to hypertension (McEwen & Stellar, 1993). These latter changes are largely irreversible by normal restorative devices and increase the risk for disease.

McEwen (1998) discussed four specific situations associated with allostatic load. First and most obvious, frequent exposure to stressors increases allostatic load. The frequency of stressors, for instance, has been shown to accelerate atherosclerosis and increase the risk of myocardial infarction (e.g., Kaplan & Manuck, 2003). The stressors need not be physically present either, as, for reasons outlined earlier, repeated feelings of threat or worry can also trigger stress reactions that over time contribute to the deterioration of cellular and organ function and regulatory mechanisms (i.e., allostatic load).

Second, allostatic load can result from a failure to adapt or habituate to repeated stressors of the same type. The metabolic requirements posed by the psychological stressors to which people are typically exposed in contemporary society are minimal (e.g., public speaking, daily commutes), yet these stressors continue to elicit strong autonomic and neuroendocrine activation. Individuals who fail to show adaptation to these stressors may also be at risk for pathophysiological developments (Cacioppo et al., 1998).

Third, allostatic load results when there is an inability or inefficiency in terminating the allostatic response after the stressor is removed. Some individuals, for instance, recover more slowly than others from psychological stressors such as mental arithmetic, and the latter are thought to be at greater risk for hypertension (Gehring & Pickering, 1995). Consistent with this reasoning, McEwen (1998) reviews evidence that the failure to efficiently terminate sympathetic and HPA responses to stressors is a feature of an age-related functional decline in nonhuman animals, a process that likely operates in humans as well.

Finally, inadequate responses by some allostatic systems trigger compensatory increases in others. If cortisol secretion does not increase in response to stress, secretion of inflammatory cytokines, which is usually down-regulated by cortisol, increases, with potentially pathophysiological effects (Munck et al., 1984).

In sum, we have emphasized that what is adaptive or maladaptive, healthy or unhealthy, depends on context, and what may be good for one tissue may be lifesaving, but may have a negative impact on another tissue, with mortal consequences in the long run. The regional positioning of immunocytes in response to acute stress may provide the host with a selective advantage should aggressive behavioral interactions lead to cutaneous wounding and the possibility of infection (Dhabhar & McEwen, 1997). The selective advantage that may accompany acute stress does not extend to chronic forms of stress, however, as the prolonged activation of the HPA axis and sympathetic nervous system seen in chronic stress tends to suppress cellular immunity (Lupien & McEwen, 1997; Sheridan, 1998), reduce response to vaccination (Kiecolt-Glaser, Glaser, Gravenstein, Malarkey, & Sheridan, 1996), and slow the healing of experimental cutaneous and mucosal wounds (Kiecolt-Glaser et al., 1995; Marucha, Kiecolt-Glaser, & Favagehi, 1998; Padgett, Marucha, & Sheridan, 1998). *These complexities underscore the interdependence between organisms and their physical and social environments.* Restorative mechanisms such as a balanced diet, moderate exercise, sleep, and rich social connections can have salutogenic (e.g., stress-buffering) effects, whereas a diet high in fat, the use of tobacco and alcohol, a sedentary lifestyle, and hostility and isolation exacerbate the deleterious effects of chronic stress. Our understanding of the complex regulative and restorative processes of the organism—and the balance within—is therefore fostered by a multilevel integrative analysis.

## Clinical Implications

In his book on genetics, evolution, and biology, Lewontin (2000) argued that we would not fully understand living organisms if we continue to think of genes, organisms, and environments as separate entities. "In a curious sense," he suggested, "the study of the organisms is really a study of the shape of the environmental space, the organisms themselves being nothing but the passive medium through which we see the shape of the external world" (p. 44). We have sounded a resonant theme here, suggesting that a multilevel integrative analysis is needed if we are to develop a comprehensive explanation of morbidity and mortality. Given the complexity of the regulatory mechanisms in the brain and body, clinical interventions that target a single peripheral process (e.g., β-adrenergic blockades) should not be expected to be broadly protective or to have only protective effects. Pharmacological interventions designed to affect peripheral cellular processes, therefore, might best be conceptualized as a component of a broad, multimodal (e.g., behavioral, psychosocial) therapeutic intervention.

The concept of stress has also received a great deal of attention in health psychology, with numerous studies showing that stress is associated with acute responses that mimic pathophysiological states (e.g., elevated blood pressure, diminished lymphocyte proliferation) and higher rates of morbidity and mortality. It would be easy to conclude from these studies that stress is bad and to develop clinical interventions based on this premise. Clinical interventions designed to either decrease a person's exposure to stressors (e.g., simplify living) or diminish the person's reactivity to stressors (e.g., cognitive behavior therapy; stress buffering by friends and family) certainly have a place, but not all stressors are or should be avoided, and many may offer opportunities for growth or an expansion of capacities.

In these cases, the value of temporary respites from the stresses of everyday life might be considered. As noted in the introductory section of this chapter, stress hormones can diminish important aspects of cellular immunity. If these individuals are not able to retreat from the stresses of their environment to recuperate or, worse yet, if their weakened immunologic state only increases the stressors they are confronting, then a positive feedback system results that fosters the conditions for the development of frequent and chronic disease. That is, a positive feedback loop may be created that makes illness more likely and more ravaging. Unfortunately, those individuals who are least likely to be able to take these respites are, perhaps not coincidentally, those who are also at risk for broad-based morbidity and mortality.

Relatedly, we have reviewed evidence emphasizing not only the potentially different short- and long-term effects of stress reactions but the additional importance of the repair and maintenance processes of the body. Individuals who feel socially connected, for instance, may live longer and healthier lives in part because they enjoy more efficient sleep (and restorative physiological processes) than people who feel socially isolated (Cacioppo, Hawkley, et al., 2002). More scientific and clinical research is needed on how the toxic effects of stressors may be reduced by the repair and maintenance processes of the brain and body.

## Conclusion

The topics we have discussed fall under five general principles: (1) the autonomic, neuroendocrine, and immune systems are orchestrated in part to buffer the organism against the effects of internal and external changes by regulatory and restorative devices; (2) disturbances of the constancy of internal conditions trigger counteracting forces that can have both beneficial, acute effects and detrimental, chronic effects for the organism (i.e., what may be good for one tissue may be lifesaving, but may have negative impact on another tissue, with mortal consequences in the long run); (3) the organization of these regulatory devices is not static across circumstances and the life span; (4) whether these adjustments are adaptive or maladaptive, healthy or unhealthy, depends in part on the physical and social environment (external milieu) and in part on the status of the organism and the nature of the response itself (internal milieu); and (5) a design for the brain and stress physiology that worked well in human evolution is now a contributing factor to broad-based morbidity and mortality. These principles operate at the level of the aggregate, covering a range of specific pathophysiological processes.

We have also emphasized that the etiology and course of chronic disease have biological substrates, but that these biological substrates are influenced profoundly by the physical and social world. We have discussed a variety of issues bearing on this assertion, including the mechanisms by which adaptive reactions are achieved (e.g., Berntson et al., 1991), including homeostasis and allostasis (McEwen & Stellar, 1993; Sterling & Eyer, 1988). Evidence has been reviewed that allostatic load—the accrued effects of a lifetime of stress—alters the efficiency of effectors, as well as the regulatory and restorative devices that control them. Accordingly, there is profit from conceptualizing organismic functioning within an environmental (physical, psychological, social) context and from confronting the new questions that such a conceptualization brings into focus.

It remains to be determined, for instance, to what extent individual differences in allostatic load are the consequence of differential exposure to stressors, differential reactivity to stressors, and differential recovery from stressors—and why. A good deal is now known about stress physiology (e.g., Chrousos, 2000), but the rostral neurobehavioral systems that orchestrate organismic–environmental transactions (Berntson et al., 1998; Berntson, Cacioppo, & Sarter, 2003) and the psychological transduction mechanisms (e.g., health behaviors, health utilization, stress buffering) remain only partially mapped. "Stress" has been assigned a special role in the development of allostatic load, but the concept of stress itself is often vaguely (or circularly) defined. Operationalizations and measures across studies, especially across animal and human studies, were regularly so different (e.g., restraint, hypoglycemic, orthostatic, mathematic stressors) that results are sometimes difficult to compare or reconcile (Lovallo, 1997). Stressors are not always negative, either, as positive as well as negative events are considered stressors in studies focused on predicting health (Holmes & Rahe, 1967). Further complicating matters, the measurements of stress within a given study are often so weakly correlated that they provide poor convergent validity for the construct of stress (e.g., Lacey, 1959; Johnson & Anderson, 1990). In short, neither stress nor health is a simple, unitary concept, and the search for a singular universal mechanism relating stress to health is doomed to failure. The concept of allostatic load, too, although useful at a molar level of analysis, is misleading if applied to specific underlying mechanisms as if there were a single cause of wear and tear. The concept is useful because it represents a broad, multifarious category of specific and largely unrelated transduction mechanisms that contribute to wear and tear on the organism.

Why not simply ignore the molar constructs of integrative physiology and focus on the details of the cellular machinery? As Claude Bernard (1878/1974) opined more than a century ago, and Lewontin (2000) and we (Cacioppo et al., 2000) have echoed more recently, the organization and function of the elemental parts of an organism can be understood comprehensively only within the context of its transactions with its physical and social environment. Lewontin's (2000) analysis suggesting that the reduction in mortality from infectious diseases during the late 1800s and early 1900s is attributable to a general trend of increases in real wage, an increase in the state of nutrition, and a decrease in the number of hours worked—that is, a decrease in the wear and tear on the organism and improved opportunities for the organism to heal itself—hints at causal factors and targets of interventions to which we would be blind if we focused on cellular mechanisms alone. Although we are beginning to understand how the brain integrates the regulatory and restorative forces of the body to foster health and adaptation to environmental challenges, it is clear that health psychology will have much to contribute to this understanding for a long time to come.

## Acknowledgments

Funding was provided by the National Institute of Aging Grant No. RO1AG034052–01.

## Notes

1. *Catabolic processes* refers to the phase of metabolism in which complex molecules are broken down into simpler ones, often resulting in a release of energy (e.g., stress reactivity), whereas *anabolic processes* refers to the phase of metabolism in which simple substances are synthesized into the complex materials of living tissue.
2. Allostasis further holds that the modulation of homeostatic or regulatory mechanisms can be achieved through local (peripheral) or central processes (Berntson & Cacioppo, 2007).
3. The current framework also points to a qualification in this statement. If the lineman is overtraining that is, if he is not getting sufficient nutrition and rest to allow his body to repair and grow as a result of the training, then the training will not provide the same physiological benefits.
4. This example also illustrates how the physiological systems activated by events in daily life not only can protect and restore some aspects or functions of the body but can simultaneously damage others, either through behavioral channels (e.g., a person persisting in the face of stressors and thereby putting himself in a position to suffer additional damage), alteration of the equilibrium or set point of a homeostatic system, increased reactivity to stressors, or slowed and less potent recovery and restoration following stressors.

## References

Ader, R. (Ed.). (2007). *Psychoneuroimmunology* (4th ed.). San Diego, CA: Academic Press.

Andersen, B.L., Cacioppo, J.T., & Roberts, D.C. (1995). Delay in seeking a cancer diagnosis: Delay stages and psychophysiological comparison processes. *British Journal of Social Psychology, 34,* 33–52.

Anisman, H., Zaharia, M.D., Meaney, M.J., & Merali, Z. (1998). Do early-life events permanently alter behavioral and hormonal responses to stressors? *International Journal of Developmental Neuroscience, 16,* 149–164.

Arancibia, S., Rage, F., Astier, H., & Tapia-Arancibia, L. (1996). Neuroendocrine and autonomous mechanisms underlying thermoregulation in cold environment. *Neuroendocrinology, 64,* 257–267.

Bauer, G. (1983). Induction of Epstein-Barr virus early antigens by corticosteroids: Inhibition by TPA and retinoic acid. *International Journal of Cancer, 31,* 291–295.

Baum, A. (1994). Behavioral, biological, and environmental interactions in disease processes. In S. Blumenthal, K. Matthews, & S. Weiss (Eds.). (1994). *New research frontiers in behavioral medicine: Proceedings of the national conference* (pp. 61–70). Washington, DC: NIH Publications.

Benschop, R.J., Geenen, R., Mills, P.J., Naliboff, B.D., Kiecolt-Glaser, J.K., Herbert, T.B., et al. (1998). Cardiovascular and immune responses to acute psychological stress in young and old women: A meta-investigation. *Psychosomatic Medicine, 60,* 290–296.

Bernard, C. (1878/1974). *Lecons sur les phenomenes de la vie communes aux animaux et aux vegetaux.* [Lectures on the phenomena of life common to animals and plants] (H.E. Hoff, R. Guillemin, & L. Guillemin, Trans.). Springfield, IL: Thomas. (Original work published 1878, Paris: B. Bailliere et Fils).

Berntson, G.G., Bigger, J.T., Jr., Eckberg, D.L., Grossman, P., Kaufmann, P.G., Malik, M., et al. (1997). Heart rate variability: Origins, methods, and interpretive caveats. *Psychophysiology, 34*, 623–648.

Berntson, G.G., & Cacioppo, J.T. (2007). Integrative physiology: Homeostasis, allostasis and the orchestration of systemic physiology. In J.T. Cacioppo, L.G. Tassinary, & G.G. Berntson (Eds.), *Handbook of psychophysiology* (3rd ed., pp. 433–452). New York: Cambridge University Press.

Berntson, G.G., & Cacioppo, J.T. (2003). A contemporary perspective on multilevel analyses and social neuroscience. In F. Kessel, P. Rosenfeld & N. Anderson (Eds.), *Expanding the boundaries of health and social science: Case studies in interdisciplinary innovation* (pp. 18–40). New York: Oxford University Press.

Berntson, G.G., Cacioppo, J.T., Binkley, P.F., Uchino, B.N., Quigley, K.S., & Fieldstone, A. (1994). Autonomic cardiac control. III. Psychological stress and cardiac response in autonomic space as revealed by pharmacological blockades. *Psychophysiology, 31*, 599–608.

Berntson, G.G., Cacioppo, J.T., & Quigley, K.S. (1991). Autonomic determinism: The modes of autonomic control, the doctrine of autonomic space, and the laws of autonomic constraint. *Psychological Review, 98*, 459–487.

Berntson, G.G., Cacioppo, J.T., & Quigley, K.S. (1993). Cardiac psychophysiology and autonomic space in humans: Empirical perspectives and conceptual implications. *Psychological Bulletin, 114*, 296–322.

Berntson, G.G., Cacioppo, J.T., & Sarter, M. (2003). Bottom-up: Implications for neurobehavioral models of anxiety and autonomic regulation. In R.J. Davidson, K.R. Sherer, & H.H. Goldsmith (Eds.), *Handbook of affective sciences* (pp. 1105–1116). New York: Oxford University Press.

Berntson, G.G., Sarter, M., & Cacioppo, J.T. (1998). Anxiety and cardiovascular reactivity: The basal forebrain cholinergic link. *Behavioural Brain Research, 94*, 225–248.

Blumenthal, S., Matthews, K.A., & Weiss, S. (1994). *New research frontiers in behavioral medicine: Proceedings of the national conference.* Washington, DC: NIH Publications.

Cacioppo, J.T. (1994). Social neuroscience: Autonomic, neuroendocrine, and immune responses to stress. *Psychophysiology, 31*, 113–128.

Cacioppo, J.T., Berntson, G.G., Malarkey, W.B., Kiecolt-Glaser, J.K., Sheridan, J.F., Poehlmann, K.M., et al. (1998). Autonomic, neuroendocrine, and immune responses to psychological stress: The reactivity hypothesis. *Annals of the New York Academy of Sciences, 840*, 664–673.

Cacioppo, J.T., Berntson, G.G., Sheridan, J.F., & McClintock, M.K. (2000). Multi-level integrative analyses of human behavior: Social neuroscience and the complementing nature of social and biological approaches. *Psychological Bulletin, 126*, 829–843.

Cacioppo, J.T., Burleson, M.H., Poehlmann, K.M., Malarkey, W.B., Kiecolt-Glaser, J.K., Berntson, G.G., et al. (2000). Autonomic and neuroendocrine responses to mild psychological stressors: Effects of chronic stress on older women. *Annals of Behavioral Medicine, 22*, 140–148.

Cacioppo, J.T., Hawkley, L.C., & Berntson, G.G. (2003). The anatomy of loneliness. *Current Directions in Psychological Science, 12*, 71–74.

Cacioppo, J.T., Hawkley, L.C., Berntson, G.G., Ernst, J.M., Gibbs, A.C., Stickgold, R., et al. (2002). Lonely days invade the nights: Social modulation of sleep efficiency. *Psychological Science, 13*, 384–387.

Cacioppo, J.T., Kiecolt-Glaser, J.K., Malarkey, W.B., Laskowski, B.F., Rozlog, L.A., Poehlmann, K.M., et al. (2002). Autonomic glucocorticoid associations with the steady state expression of latent Epstein-Barr virus. *Hormones and Behavior, 42*, 32–41.

Cacioppo, J.T., Malarkey, W.B., Kiecolt-Glaser, J.K., Uchino, B.N., Sgoutas-Emch, S.A., Sheridan, J.F., et al. (1995). Heterogeneity in neuroendocrine and immune responses to brief psychological stressors as a function of autonomic cardiac activation. *Psychosomatic Medicine, 57*, 154–164.

Cacioppo, J.T., Uchino, B.N., & Berntson, G.G. (1994). Individual differences in the autonomic origins of heart rate reactivity: The psychometrics of respiratory sinus arrhythmia and preejection period. *Psychophysiology, 31*, 412–419.

Cannon, W.B. (1928). The mechanism of emotional disturbance of bodily functions. *New England Journal of Medicine, 198*, 877–884.

Cannon, W.B. (1929). Organization for physiological homeostasis. *Physiological Reviews, 9*, 399–431.

Cannon, W.B. (1939). *The wisdom of the body* (2nd ed.) London: Kegan Paul, Trench, Trubner.

Chrousos, G.P. (2000). The stress response and immune function: Clinical implications. The 1999 Novera H. Spector Lecture. *Annals of the New York Academy of Sciences, 917*, 38–67.

Cohen, S. (1996). Psychological stress, immunity, and upper respiratory infections. *Current Directions in Psychological Science, 5*, 86–90.

Cohn, M., & Langman, R.E. (1990). The protection: The unit of humoral immunity selected by evolution. *Immunological Review, 115*, 11–147.

Collins, S., & Surwit, R.S. (2001). The beta-adrenergic receptors and the control of adipose tissue metabolism and thermogenesis. *Recent Progress in Hormone Research, 56*, 309–328.

Crimmins, E.M., Johnston, M.L., Hayward, M., & Seeman, T. (2006). Age differences in allostatic load: An index of frailty. In Y. Zeng, et al. (Eds.), *Longer life and healthy aging* (pp. 111–126). Netherlands: Springer.

Dantzer, R., Bluthe, R., Laye, S., Bret-Dibat, J., Parnet, P., & Kelley, K.W. (1998). Cytokines and sickness behavior. *Annals of the New York Academy of Sciences, 840*, 586–590.

Davidson, R.J. (1998). Affective style and affective disorders: Perspectives from affective neuroscience. *Cognition and Emotion, 12*, 307–330.

De Kloet, E.R., Vreugdenhil, E., Oitzl, M.S., & Joels, M. (1998). Brain cortico-steroid receptor balance in health and disease. *Endocrine Review, 19*, 269–301.

Dhabhar, F.S., & McEwen, B.S. (1997). Acute stress enhances while chronic stress suppresses cell-mediated immunity in vivo: A potential role for leukocyte trafficking. *Brain, Behavior, and Immunity, 11*, 286–306.

Dworkin, B.R. (2000). Introception. In J.T. Cacioppo, L.G. Tassinary, & G.G. Berntson (Eds.), *Handbook of psychophysiology* (pp. 459–481). Cambridge, UK: Cambridge University Press.

Dworkin, B.R., & Dworkin, S. (1995). Learning of physiological responses: II. Classical conditioning of the baroreflex. *Behavioral Neuroscience, 109*, 1119–1136.

Dworkin, B.R., Elbert, T., & Rau, H. (2000). Blood pressure elevation as a coping response. In P. McCabe, N. Schneiderman, T.M. Field, & A.R. Wellens (Eds.), *Stress, coping and the cardiovascular system* (pp. 51–69). Mahwah, NJ: Erlbaum.

Garrett, L. (2000). *Betrayal of trust: The collapse of global public health.* New York: Hyperion.

Gehring, W., & Pickering, T.G. (1995). Association between delayed recovery of blood pressure after acute mental stress and parental history of hypertension. *Journal of Hypertension, 13,* 603–610.

Geising, A., Bilang-Bleurel, A., Droste, S.K., Linthorst, A.C.E., Holsboer, F., & Reul, J.M.H.M. (2001). Psychological stress increases hippocampal mineralocorticoid receptor levels: Involvement of corticotropin-releasing hormone. *Journal of Neuroscience, 21,* 4822–4829.

Germain, R.N. (2000). The art of the probable: System control in the adaptive immune system. *Science, 293,* 240–245.

Glaser, R., Pearson, G.R., Bonneau, R.H., Esterling, B.A., Atkinson, C., & Kiecolt-Glaser, J.K. (1993). Stress and the memory T-cell response to the Epstein-Barr virus in healthy medical students. *Health Psychology, 12,* 435–442.

Glaser, R., Pearson, G.R., Jones, J.F., Hillhouse, J., Kennedy, S., Mao, H., & Kiecolt-Glaser, J.K. (1991). Stress related activation of Epstein-Barr virus. *Brain Behavior Immunology, 5,* 219–232.

Glaser, R., Rice, J., Sheridan, J., Fertel, R., Stout, J., Speicher, C.E., et al. (1987). Stress-related immune suppression: Health implications. *Brain Behavior Immunology, 1,* 7–20.

Hansen, M.K., O'Connor, K.A., Goehler, L.E., Watkins, L.R., & Maier, S.F. (2001). The contribution of the vagus nerve in interleukin-1β–induced fever is dependent on dose. *American Journal of Regulatory Integrative Comparative Physiology, 280,* R929–R934.

Hawkley, L.C., & Cacioppo, J.T. (2003). Loneliness and pathways to disease. *Brain, Behavior, and Immunity, 17*(Suppl. 1), S98–S105.

Hobbs, F., & Stoops, N. (2002). *Demographic trends in the 20th century.* U.S. Census Bureau, Census 2000 Special Reports, Series CENSR-4. Washington, DC: U.S. Government Printing Office.

Holmes, T.H., & Rahe, R.H. (1967). The social readjustment rating scale. *Journal of Psychosomatic Research, 11,* 213–218.

Johnson, A.K., & Anderson, E.A. (1990). Stress and arousal. In J.T. Cacioppo, & L.G. Tassinary (Eds.), *Principles of psychophysiology* (pp. 216–252). New York: Cambridge University Press.

Kandel, E.R., & Squire, L.R. (2000). Breaking down scientific barriers to the study of brain and mind. *Science, 290,* 1113–1120.

Kaplan, J.R., & Manuck, S.B. (2003). Monkeying around with coronary disease: Status, stress, and atherosclerosis. In F. Kessel, Rosenfield, & N. Anderson (Eds.), *Expanding the boundaries of health and social science: Case studies in interdisciplinary innovation* (pp. 68–94*).* New York: Oxford University Press.

Kasl, S.V., Evans, A.S., & Niederman, J.C. (1979). Psychosocial risk factors in the development of infectious mononucleosis. *Psychosomatic Medicine, 41,* 445–466.

Kasprowicz, A.L., Manuck, S.B., Malkoff, S.B., & Krantz, D.S. (1990). Individual differences in behaviorally evoked cardiovascular response: Temporal stability and hemodynamic patterning. *Psychophysiology, 27,* 605–619.

Kemeny, M.E. (2011). Psychoneuroimmunology. In H.S. Friedman (Ed.), *The Oxford handbook of health psychology.* New York: Oxford University Press.

Kiecolt-Glaser, J.K., Glaser, R., Gravenstein, S., Malarkey, W.B., & Sheridan, J. (1996). Chronic stress alters the immune response to influenza virus vaccine in older adults. *Proceedings of the National Academy of Sciences: United States of America, 93,* 3043–3047.

Kiecolt-Glaser, J.K., Marucha, P.T., Malarkey, W.B., Mercado, A.M., & Glaser, R. (1995). Slowing of wound healing by psychological stress. *Lancet, 346,* 1194–1196.

Kiecolt-Glaser, J.K., Page, G.G., Marucha, P.T., MacCallum, R.C., & Glaser, R. (1998). Psychological influences on surgical recovery. *American Psychologist, 53,* 1209–1218.

Krantz, D.S., & Manuck, S.B. (1984). Acute psychophysiologic reactivity and risk of cardiovascular disease: A review and methodologic critique. *Psychological Bulletin, 96,* 435–464.

Lacey, J.I. (1959). Psychophysiological approaches to the evaluation of psychotherapeutic process and outcome. In E.A. Rubinstein, & M.B. Parloff (Eds.), *Research in psychotherapy* (pp. 160–208). Washington, DC: American Psychological Association.

Lazarus, R.S., & Folkman, S. (1984). *Stress, appraisal, and coping.* New York: Springer.

Lewontin, R. (2000). *The triple helix.* Cambridge, MA: Harvard University Press.

Light, K.C., Dolan, C.A., Davis, M.R., & Sherwood, A. (1992). Cardiovascular responses to an active coping challenge as predictors of blood pressure patterns 10 to 15 years later. *Psychosomatic Medicine, 54,* 217–230.

Light, K.C., Girdler, S.S., & Hinderliter, A.L. (2003). Genetic and behavioral factors in combination influence risk of hypertensive heart disease. In N. Anderson, F. Kessel, & P. Rosenfield (Eds.), *Expanding the boundaries of health: Bio-behavioral-social perspectives* (pp. 41–67). New York: Oxford University Press.

Light, K.C., Turner, J.R., Hinderliter, A.L., Girdler, S.S., & Sherwood, A. (1994). Comparison of cardiac versus vascular reactors and ethnic groups in plasma epinephrine and nor-epinephrine responses to stress. *International Journal of Behavioral Medicine, 3,* 229–246.

Lithgow, G.J., & Kirkwood, T.B.L. (1996). Mechanisms and evolution of aging. *Science, 273,* 80–81.

Llabre, M.M., Klein, B.R., Saab, P.G., McCalla, J.B., & Schneiderman, N. (1998). Classification of individual differences in cardiovascular responsivity: The contribution of reactor type controlling for race and gender. *International Journal of Behavioral Medicine, 5,* 213–229.

Lovallo, W.R. (1997). *Stress and health.* Thousand Oaks, CA: Sage.

Lupien, S.J., & McEwen, B.S. (1997). The acute effects of corticosteroids on cognition: Integration of animal and human model studies. *Brain Research Reviews, 24,* 1–27.

Luskin, F., & Newell, K. (1997). Mind-body approaches to successful aging. In A. Watkins (Ed.), *Mind-body medicine: A clinician's guide to psychoneuroimmunology* (pp. 251–268). New York: Churchill Livingstone.

Madden, K.S., Thyagarajan, S., & Felten, D.L. (1998). Alterations in sympathetic noradrenergic innervation in lymphoid organs with age. *Annals of the New York Academy of Sciences, 840,* 262–268.

Maier, S.F., & Watkins, L.R. (1998). Cytokines for psychologists: Implications of bidirectional immune-to-brain communication for understanding behavior, mood, and cognition. *Psychological Review, 105*, 83–107.

Maier, S.F., & Watkins, L.R. (2009). Neuroimmunology. In G.G. Berntson, & J.T. Cacioppo (Eds.), *Handbook of neuroscience for the behavioral sciences* (pp. 119–135). New York: John Wiley & Sons.

Manuck, S.B., Cohen, S., Rabin, B.S., Muldoon, M.F., & Bachen, E.A. (1991). Individual differences in cellular immune response to stress. *Psychological Science, 2*, 111–115.

Marucha, P.T., Kiecolt-Glaser, J.K., & Favagehi, M. (1998). Mucosal wound healing is impaired by examination stress. *Psychosomatic Medicine, 60*, 362–365.

Mason, J.W. (1975). An historical view of the stress field: Part II. *Journal of Human Stress, 1*, 22–35.

McCann, S.M., Lipton, J.M., Sternberg, E.M., Chrousos, G.P., Gold, P.W., & Smith, C.C. (Eds.). (1998). Neuro-immunomodulation: Molecular aspects, integrative systems, and clinical advances. *Annals of the New York Academy of Sciences, 840*, 1–856.

McEwen, B.S. (1998). Protective and damaging effects of stress mediators. *New England Journal of Medicine, 338*, 171–179.

McEwen, B.S., & Seeman T. (2003). Stress and affect: Applicability of the concepts of allostasis and allostatic load. In R.J. Davidson, K.R. Sherer, & H.H. Goldsmith (Eds.), *Handbook of affective sciences* (pp. 1117–1138). New York: Oxford University Press.

McEwen, B.S., & Stellar, E. (1993). Stress and the individual: Mechanisms leading to disease. *Archives of Internal Medicine, 153*, 2093–2101.

Meaney, M.J., Bhatnagar, S., Larocque, S., McCormick, C.M., Shanks, N., Sharma, S., et al. (1996). Early environment and the development of individual differences in the hypothalamic-pituitary-adrenal stress response. In C.R. Pfeffer (Ed.), *Severe stress and mental disturbance in children* (pp. 85–127). Washington, DC: American Psychiatric Press.

Munck, A., Guyre, P.M., & Holbrook, N.J. (1984). Physiological functions of glucocorticoids in stress and their relation to pharmacological actions. *Endocrine Reviews, 5*, 25–44.

Padgett, D.A., Marucha, P.T., & Sheridan, J.F. (1998). Neuro-endocrine effects on wound healing in SKH-1 female mice. *Brain, Behavior, and Immunity, 12*, 64–73.

Sabbah, W., Watt, R.G., Sheiham, A., & Tsakos, G. (2008). Effects of allostatic load on the social gradient in ischaemic heart disease and periodontal disease: Evidence from the Third National Health and Nutrition Examination Survey. *Journal of Epidemiology and Community Health, 62*, 415–420.

Sapolsky, R.M. (1996). Why stress is bad for your brain. *Science, 273*, 749–750.

Seeman, T.E., Singer, B.H., Ryff, C.D., Love, G.D., & Levy-Storms, L. (2002). Social relationships, gender, and allostatic load across two age cohorts. *Psychosomatic Medicine, 64*, 395–406.

Selye, H. (1956). *The stress of life.* New York: McGraw-Hill.

Selye, H. (1973). Homeostasis and heterostasis. *Perspectives in Biology and Medicine, 16*, 441–445.

Sgoutas-Emch, S.A., Cacioppo, J.T., Uchino, B., Malarkey, W., Pearl, D., Kiecolt-Glaser, J.K., et al. (1994). The effects of an acute psychological stressor on cardiovascular, endocrine, and cellular immune response: A prospective study of individuals high and low in heart rate reactivity. *Psychophysiology, 31*, 264–271.

Sheridan, J.F. (1998). Stress-induced modulation of anti-viral immunity. *Brain, Behavior and Immunity, 12*, 1–6.

Sherwood, A., Dolan, C.A., & Light, K.C. (1990). Hemodynamics of blood pressure responses during active and passive coping. *Psychophysiology, 27*, 656–668.

Sterling, P., & Eyer, J. (1988). Allostasis: A new paradigm to explain arousal pathology. In S. Fisher, & J. Reason (Eds.), *Handbook of life stress, cognition and health* (pp. 629–649). New York: Wiley.

Sternberg, E. (2000). *The balance within.* New York: Freeman.

Temple, L.K.F., McLeod, R.S., Gallinger, S., & Wright, J.G. (2001). Defining disease in the genomics era. *Science, 293*, 807–808.

Tomaka, J., Blascovich, J., Kibler, J., & Ernst, J.M. (1997). Cognitive and physiological antecedents of threat and challenge appraisal. *Journal of Personality and Social Psychology, 73*, 63–72.

Turner, R.J. (1989). Individual differences in heart rate response during behavioral challenge. *Psychophysiology, 26*, 497–505.

Uchino, B.N., Cacioppo, J.T., Malarkey, W.B., Glaser, R., & Kiecolt-Glaser, J.K. (1995). Appraisal support predicts age-related differences in cardiovascular function in women. *Health Psychology, 14*, 556–562.

Wilkinson, D.J., Thompson, J.M., Lambert, G.W., Jennings, G.L., Schwarz, R.G., Jefferys, D., et al. (1998). Sympathetic activity in patients with panic disorder at rest, under laboratory mental stress, and during panic attacks. *Archives of General Psychiatry, 55*, 211–220.

# Psychoneuroimmunology

Margaret E. Kemeny

**Abstract**

Psychoneuroimmunology is an interdisciplinary field that involves the investigation of the bidirectional relationships among the mind, brain, immune system, and health. In this chapter, studies are reviewed demonstrating that exposure to stressful life experience can impact immune function, with relations depending on psychological and behavioral responses. In addition, our evolving understanding that the immune/inflammatory system can impact the brain and behavioral processes, including mood, motivation, and cognition, will be described. The implications of brain–immune communication for health and disease will be discussed.

**Keywords:** Psychoneuroimmunology, immune system, immune function, stress, brain, emotion, cognition, immunity

One of the fundamental goals of the scientific field of health psychology is to define the psychological and social factors that influence health and disease. A necessary condition for defining these relationships is the ability to specify the physiological pathways that underlie these linkages. Psychoneuroimmunology is an interdisciplinary field that is central to this goal, in that it involves the investigation of the bidirectional relationships among the mind, brain and immune system and the implications of these relationships for clinical disease. The immune system is a major pathophysiological system; dysfunctions in this system can play a critical role in the etiology and progression of a variety of diseases, including infections, autoimmune diseases (such as rheumatoid arthritis), some forms of cancer, and cardiovascular disease, as well as mortality. By understanding how psychological factors and their neurophysiological correlates affect the immune system, it is possible to flesh out important components of the physiological pathway that link social and psychological factors to disease etiology and progression. Specifying a mechanistic or mediational pathway is central to establishing a causal relationship between a specific

psychological factor and a health outcome (see Figure 7.1 for a schematic representation of central components of this pathway [Kemeny, 2003]). Psychoneuroimmunology studies can provide evidence for each of the links in this pathway and can point to critical social and psychological elicitors, mediating systems, and potentially sensitive points for intervention or prevention of disease.

In addition to "top-down" effects of the mind and brain on the immune system, the immune system can affect the brain, and alter learning, memory, mood, cognition, and motivation. Findings related to these effects can foster a greater understanding of the psychological sequelae of immune-related diseases, and can contribute to the development of effective interventions for reducing the adverse psychological effects of such conditions. For example, alterations in cognition and mood can occur with inflammatory diseases, such as systemic lupus erythematosus (SLE), and some of these neurophysiological effects may be a function of inflammatory processes acting on the brain. In fact, under certain circumstances, cognitive and affective disorders may be directly tied to inflammatory activity in the brain

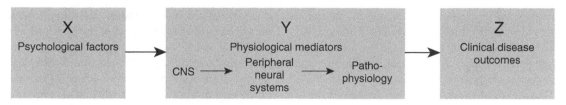

**Fig. 7.1** The X-Y-Z model for investigating linkages between psychological processes, physiological mediators, and disease progression. Reprinted from Kemeny, M. E. (2003). An interdisciplinary research model to investigate psychosocial cofactors in disease: Application to HIV-1 pathogenesis. *Brain, Behavior, and Immunity, 17*, S67–S72, with permission from the publisher, Elsevier.

and periphery. On a conceptual level, research in psychoneuroimmunology can shed light on the adaptive bidirectional linkages across the neurophysiological, behavioral, and immune systems. For example, research in this field has demonstrated that behavior can be shaped by products of the immune system as part of an integrated recuperative response following injury or infection.

## Historical Overview

The nervous system is known to regulate most organ systems (e.g., the endocrine system, cardiovascular system, respiratory system). However, until relatively recently, the immune system was assumed to be autonomous, without major input from the brain. Research in psychoneuroimmunology over the past 40 years has challenged this assumption by documenting bidirectional communication between the central nervous system (CNS; the brain and spinal cord) and the immune system (the cells and organs that play a role in response to pathogens; see Ader, Felten & Cohen, 2001). The earliest findings formed the groundwork for the conceptual leap that was necessary for investigators to begin to consider possible linkages between these two systems. For example, in the early 1960s, Rasmussen and colleagues (Solomon, 1969) demonstrated that stressor exposure in animals could affect the course of viral infections. A critical first chapter in our recognition that the CNS is capable of modulating immune processes began with the work of psychologist Robert Ader and immunologist Nicholas Cohen. In 1975, Ader and Cohen reported that the immune system could be classically conditioned. Using a rodent model, an immunosuppressive drug, cyclophosphamide (the unconditioned stimulus), was paired with saccharin (the conditioned stimulus), resulting in immune suppression (Ader & Cohen, 1975). Subsequent exposure to saccharin alone was able to induce immune suppression. Clearly, such learning occurs in the brain, so these studies were among the very first to demonstrate brain-to-immune system communication. At about the same time,

Russian investigators made another significant contribution at a neurophysiological level by demonstrating that lesions of the hypothalamus in rodents could alter immune responses in the periphery (Korneva, 1967).

The first "speculative theoretical integration" that laid out a framework for understanding possible linkages between the brain and the immune system was written in 1964 by George Solomon and Rudolph Moos (Solomon & Moos, 1964). They suggested that neuroendocrine processes could regulate immunity, and introduced the notion that "experience" could impact this system. Solomon and his immunologist colleague Alfred Amkraut went on to show effects of early experience, stressors, and spontaneous behavior on immunity in animals. Another critical milestone in this field was the demonstration by David Felten and Suzanne Felten (Felten & Felten, 1988) that sympathetic nervous system (SNS) fibers innervate immune organs and alter the activity of resident immune cells, thereby providing a "hardwired" link between the brain and the immune system. The field was catapulted forward in the early 1980s, when the team headed by Janice Kiecolt-Glaser and Ronald Glaser began their program of research documenting the effects of stressful life experience on a wide array of immune functions in humans (Kiecolt-Glaser et al., 1984). It was not until the 1990s, however, that researchers began to recognize that not only could behavior and the CNS affect the immune system but immune products could affect the brain and behavior, suggesting a fully bidirectional relationship across these systems (Maier & Watkins, 1998).

## An Adaptive Integrated System

The changes in immune processes coincident with exposure to stressors and particular psychological responses and behaviors are likely not mere side effects of the neurophysiological impact of such exposures. Activation of stress-responsive systems, such as the hypothalamic-pituitary-adrenal axis (HPA), in response to a threat involves a coordinated and adaptive set of physiological changes, such as the release of bodily fuels to ready the organism for action. However, until recently, the immunologic changes that often occur following such provocations were believed to be nonfunctional side effects of activation of these stress systems. There is growing evidence that some immune system changes play a critical *adaptive* role in responding not only to pathogen assault but to behavioral conditions as well. These immune changes can be viewed as part of an integrated psychobiological response to specific eliciting conditions (Weiner, 1992).

It is now clear that the brain and the immune system have the "hardwiring" to allow this kind of ongoing communication to occur. As described in more detail below, there are a variety of ways that the brain can "talk" to the immune system. For example, immune cells express receptors not only for proteins produced by other immune cells, but also for molecules produced by the brain and neuroendocrine system. Thus, the immune system is equipped to "hear" the messages communicated by these molecules and to be regulated by these systems. In addition, all types of immune organs are innervated by autonomic nervous system (ANS) fibers, and these fibers have functional connections with the immune cells resident in these organs. This neural hardwiring allows the ANS to directly influence the activities of these immune cells, regulating their response to pathogens, for example.

The immune system can play an adaptive role in at least three behavioral responses—the fight-or-flight response, recuperation from injury or infection, and a more general disengagement/withdrawal response (Kemeny, 2009). The well-articulated *fight-or-flight response* involves higher brain region recognition of a threat that may necessitate physical action and the mobilization of resources to promote bodily systems that can be utilized in such a situation, while down-regulating systems that are not a priority under threatening conditions, such as growth and reproduction (Sapolsky, 1993). This goal shift from resource building in a nonthreat context to resource utilization during a threat activates the SNS, the HPA, and other regulatory systems. Under these circumstances, patterned changes in the immune system are also occurring. Across animal species, white blood cells are shunted from the bloodstream to immune organs such as lymph nodes, bone marrow, the gastrointestinal tract, and the skin (Dhabhar, 2003), and "first line of defense" cells such as natural killer (NK) cells are increased in number. Dhabhar and McEwen (2001) argue that

this redistribution of immune cells to immune organs may be an integral part of the fight-or-flight response, which mobilizes physiological systems that can adaptively respond to physical threats, such as predation. One part of this adaptive response may be preparation for the challenge of wounding or infection that may occur during physical stressors that involve fighting or fleeing, for example (Dhabhar, 2003; Dhabhar & McEwen, 2001). Higher levels of white blood cells in these "battle station" organs would increase the likelihood of effective response to wounding and infection. A rapid increase in a particular subclass of white blood cells (the first line of defense cells) would also allow for rapid and nonspecific killing of pathogens that may enter the system through wounds or other injury (Kemeny & Gruenewald, 2000). Thus, just as activation of stress systems increases respiratory and heart rates to prepare the organism for a challenge, these fight-or-flight systems may also ready the organism for wounding and increase chances of survival following exposure to infectious agents. Mediation of these acute effects may be via the SNS, since SNS products increase heart rate and, at the same time, influence the trafficking of white blood cells as well as the expression of immune molecules that play a central role in that trafficking (Ottaway & Husband, 1992).

The immune system also plays a major role in supporting *behavioral recuperation* following infection or injury. As will be described in more detail below, proteins called *proinflammatory cytokines* are released during infection or injury, and these substances orchestrate a number of the immune activities that play a role in killing the pathogen and repairing damaged tissue. At the same time, these molecules act on the brain and cause the animal to withdraw from its normal activities (sexual behavior, exploration, grooming) and engage in recuperative activities, including sleeping. This reorganization of priorities, with resulting changes in behavior, is adaptive because it lowers energy utilization so that available energy can support processes necessary to fight the infection (e.g., fever) and also facilitates the restorative processes required to recuperate from illness and injury (Maier & Watkins, 1998).

In addition to the behavioral disengagement required for efficient recuperation from injury or infection, the immune system can play a role in a more generalized *behavioral disengagement* in response to specific psychological stressors. In humans and other animals, the proinflammatory cytokines that are induced with infection can also be activated with exposure to psychological stressors, outside the context of infection or injury (Maier & Watkins, 1998). The behavioral disengagement that is produced as a result of activation of these cytokines would be a particularly adaptive response to uncontrollable stressors, such as confrontation with a more aggressive or dominant animal (Kemeny, Gruenewald, & Dickerson, 2004). In such contexts, cytokine-induced behaviors such as withdrawal and inhibition of aggression, sexual behavior, and social exploration would be adaptive in that they would reduce the likelihood of attack and injury.

The notion of a link between proinflammatory cytokine activity and adaptive behavioral disengagement in response to uncontrollable threats is supported by studies of social reorganization using an intruder confrontation model. Proinflammatory cytokine responses to confrontation depend on the behavior of the animal. Social reorganization (introducing a dominant rodent into the home cage of other rodents) increases the inflammatory response to an infectious agent and increases systemic levels of corticosterone in home caged animals, suggesting a state of "glucocorticoid resistance" in immune cells. Normally, glucocorticoids, including cortisol, are immunosuppressive. Glucocorticoid resistance indicates that immune cells are resistant to the immunosuppressive effects of cortisol, for example, and continue to produce inflammatory mediators, even when glucocorticoids are present. Further work has confirmed that the subordinate animals in the context of social reorganization show glucocorticoid resistance resulting in elevated proinflammatory cytokine levels, and the level of glucocorticoid resistance is correlated with the frequency of submissive behaviors (Avitsur, Stark, & Sheridan, 2001).

These correlational findings are corroborated in an experimental model in which healthy animals are injected with a proinflammatory cytokine. Normally, in response to a confrontation with another animal, animals typically display offensive behavior and then switch to defensive behavior if it becomes clear that the contest is uncontrollable and they are likely to lose. However, animals injected with a proinflammatory cytokine display no offensive behavior but instead display only defensive elements such as upright defensive posture and submissive posture (Cirulli, De Acetis, & Alleva, 1998). Thus, an uncontrollable social threat may induce the release of these cytokines, or resistance to the anti-inflammatory effects of corticosteroids, resulting in increased levels of proinflammatory cytokines, which then promote or

maintain the behavioral disengagement that is observed in subordinate animals exhibiting submissive behavior and a defeated posture. Since subordinate animals are more likely to be wounded than dominants, this cytokine activation would also be adaptive in promoting wound healing.

Do these immunological patterns hold in humans? In some human studies of acute laboratory stressors, levels of proinflammatory cytokines are increased, but in other cases they are not. A perusal of the elicitors across these studies indicates that those studies that utilized an uncontrollable social threat (performing difficult tasks without the possibility of success in front of an evaluative audience) showed consistent increases in these cytokines, whereas those without this type of uncontrollable social threat did not (Ackerman, Martino, Heyman, Moyna, & Rabin, 1998; Dickerson, Gruenewald, & Kemeny, 2004). In fact, when comparing the immunological consequences of a relatively uncontrollable social and nonsocial threat, only the social threat induced glucocorticoid resistance (Dickerson, Gable, Irwin, Aziz, & Kemeny, 2009) which may explain the findings linking social threat to greater inflammatory activity. Uncontrollable social threats may represent a set of conditions that are capable of activating the production of proinflammatory cytokines and eliciting behavioral disengagement in animals and humans.

Although activation of stress systems and resulting alterations in the immune system may be adaptive under certain circumstances in the short run, persistent alteration in these systems could result in vulnerability to disease. *Allostatic load*, a concept coined by Bruce McEwen, refers to the consequences of prolonged exposure to stress hormones, or a cumulative toll on the body due to chronic overactivation of stress-responsive systems (McEwen, 1998). These response patterns are thought to increase the risk of a number of negative health outcomes, such as diabetes, hypertension, cancer, and cardiovascular disease (McEwen, 1998). In the case of the immune system, long-term down-regulation of certain immune parameters as a result of chronic exposure to stressors, could increase vulnerability to infection or, in certain cases, tumors. At the same time, chronic *overactivation* of certain immune processes, as in the systems described above that regulate inflammation, could increase vulnerability to autoimmune disorders (which involve overactivity of certain immune processes) or cardiovascular disease (which can be promoted by inflammatory mediators). As described above, glucocorticoid resistance, which results in the inability of immune cells to be down-regulated by cortisol, is one pathway to overactive inflammatory activity. Exposure to chronically stressful conditions is associated with glucocorticoid resistance (Miller, Chen et al., 2008; Miller, Chen et al., 2009), and this linkage may explain, at least in part, the relationship between chronic stress and inflammatory diseases.

## The Immune System

The immune system serves a variety of functions, including destruction and clearance of foreign pathogens (viruses, bacteria), and destruction of host cells that have become altered, as in the case of the formation of tumor cells. A number of "key players" form the central cellular components of the immune response. Immune cells are leukocytes or white blood cells that fall into three classes: polymorphonuclear granulocytes (e.g., neutrophils), lymphocytes (e.g., T cells, B cells), and monocytes. These cells can be found in the bloodstream, the lymphatic vessels and nodes, as well as in a variety of immune organs such as the bone marrow, thymus, spleen, and gastrointestinal tract. When a pathogen enters the body (e.g., is breathed in) and is not ejected or destroyed by the body's nonimmunological defenses (e.g., coughing), it can come into contact with immune cells in the local tissue or in the lymphatic vessels or nodes. Without adequate defense, the consequence of infection of local tissue can be tissue damage and organ impairment. For example, viruses can infect host cells, replicate within those cells, and destroy them.

A first line of defense against invading organisms is the process of inflammation. Inflammation is a complex set of events that bring immune cells into infected areas, so that pathogens can be destroyed or inactivated and damage to the infected area can be limited. As a result of the production of mediators of inflammation, blood vessels to the infected area are dilated and become more permeable, so that immune products can enter the area. Immune cells are chemically attracted to the area (chemotaxis), the tissue swells from increased release of immune fluids, the invader is attacked and often destroyed, and the area is walled off and tissue is repaired. Systemic fever can be induced as part of this adaptive response, because immune cells can proliferate more efficiently at higher than normal temperatures and many pathogens are less effective at these temperatures.

One cell plays a primary role in the initial first line of defense process: the macrophage. *Macrophages* (also monocytes) can engulf, digest, and process foreign organisms, alert other cells to the infection, and produce specific proteins called cytokines, which coordinate immune reactions. A number of proinflammatory cytokines play a key role in this process, including interleukins 1 and 6 (IL-1, IL-6) and tumor necrosis factor (TNF)$\alpha$. There are also anti-inflammatory cytokines, such as interleukin-10, that dampen the inflammatory response and inhibit specific immune cell functions relevant to inflammation.

Another cell that is capable of acting quickly in a nonspecific way at this early stage is the NK cell. Natural killer cells are lymphocytes that can kill virally infected cells and can produce substances (for example, interferon) that inhibit viral replication. These cells can also kill tumor cells in vitro and may play this role in the body as well.

The second line of defense involves two other types of cells, the T and B cells, and requires specificity (a match between receptors expressed on the immune cell and the specific pathogen or pathogen component, called the *antigen*). The CD8 suppressor/cytotoxic T cell is capable of killing virally infected cells. The CD4 helper T cell releases a variety of types of cytokines that promote the functioning of cytotoxic T cells and B cells, for example (see Table 7.1). B cells produce antibody molecules that can neutralize the activity of other cells, participate in a number of other immune responses (such as the complement cascade), and facilitate cytotoxicity by T cells and NK cells. A great deal of the orchestration and balance of help and suppression of various immune processes results from the activities of various types of the communication molecules called cytokines (Sherwood, 1993).

A number of methods are used to assess immune processes to determine if psychological factors are capable of altering this system. First, immune cells can be enumerated, or counted. Knowing the impact of a stressor, for example, on the number and proportion of various immune subsets is important since an immune response requires adequate numbers of the various subclasses of cells. For example, the human immunodeficiency virus (HIV) is capable of infecting and killing the CD4 helper T cell, resulting in significant loss of these cells. This loss plays a major role in the immune deficiency that can result from HIV infection, leaving the host vulnerable to a range of diseases. The number of CD4 helper T cells (per cubic millimeter of blood) is a critically important value that predicts acquired immune deficiency syndrome (AIDS) onset and mortality.

Second, immune assays can test the functions of immune cells. For example, assays can determine if

**Table 7.1  Immune cell functions (% of total leukocytes)**

| | | |
|---|---|---|
| Macrophage/Monocytes (2%–8%) | | |
| | Engulf/digest organism | |
| | Antigen presentation | |
| | Cytokine production (IL-1, IL-6, TNF-α) | |
| Lymphocytes (20%–40%) | | |
| | Natural Killer Cell | |
| | | Kills virally infected cells non-specifically |
| | | Produces interferon |
| | | Kills tumor cells |
| | T Helper (CD4) Cell | |
| | | Cytokine production (Il-2, γ IFN) |
| | | Activates T cytotoxic cells |
| | | Stimulates B-cell maturation and antibody production |
| | T Cytotoxic/Suppressor (CD8) Cell | |
| | | Kills virally infected cells specifically |
| | B Cell | |
| | | Antibody production |
| | | Neutralizes viruses |
| | | Destroys viruses via complement cascade or facilitation of T or NK cytotoxicity |
| Polymorphonuclear Granulocytes (50%–70%) | | |
| | Neutrophils | |
| | | Digest bacteria |
| | Eosinophils | |
| | | Kill parasites |
| | Basophils | |
| | | Increase vessel permeability in inflammatory response |

immune cells produce antibody in response to stimuli, are capable of killing virally infected cells or tumor cells, produce different classes of cytokines, and the like. No one immune assay can determine the capacity of the immune system to defend the body from pathogens, but functional testing can determine the capacity of cells to engage in a wide array of essential immune functions. A variety of immune assays are utilized in psychoneuroimmunology studies. For example, the *natural killer cell activity* assay (NKCA) determines whether NK cells are capable of killing tumor cells in a test tube. *Lymphocyte proliferative capacity* captures a central function of lymphocytes— the ability to proliferate in response to a foreign challenge. This proliferation (cell division) provides the "army" of cells required to mount a defense against a particular pathogen. *Cytokine production* can be measured, so that the ability of cells to produce these critical communication molecules can be determined. This assay involves incubating leukocytes with antigens or mitogens, collecting the resulting fluids produced by the cells in vitro, and then assessing these fluids for levels of various cytokines. There is a great deal of interest in cytokines since these proteins coordinate a variety of immune functions. Many other assays utilized in this field allow investigators to pinpoint the immune functions affected by stress and other inputs.

Although most immune cells utilized in these methods are derived from the bloodstream, it is important to determine the functioning of immune cells in immune organs and tissues that are directly involved in the immune response to pathogens. For example, investigators are now creating injuries or wounding of the skin and looking at tissue repair and wound healing mechanisms. Also, foreign substances (e.g., antigens) can be placed under the skin to elicit an immune response, and the tissue can be examined using immunohistochemistry to determine which cells are present and activated, for example. Cells from the lungs, gastrointestinal tract, and other organs can be obtained for assessments similar to those used to examine the functions of immune cells in the blood.

## Physiological Systems That Affect the Immune System

How does the brain come in contact with the immune system and play a role in its regulation? One pathway is via the ANS. The second pathway is via factors released in the brain that activate organs to produce hormones that affect immune cells and organs. The HPA axis that releases the glucocorticoids (e.g., cortisol) is a major endocrine relay from the CNS to the immune system.

### Hypothalamic-Pituitary-Adrenal Axis

The HPA is a system that can become activated in response to specific stressful stimuli. Neural pathways link perception and appraisal of a stimulus to an integrated response in the hypothalamus, which results in the release of corticotropin-releasing hormone (CRH). CRH travels to the anterior pituitary gland and stimulates adrenal cells to release adrenocorticotropic hormone (ACTH) into the blood stream. Adrenocorticotropic hormone travels to the adrenal glands and causes the adrenal cortex to release cortisol into the blood stream and other bodily fluids. These changes occur as a part of normal physiological functioning and can become accentuated during stressful encounters. The glucocorticoids are part of a complicated signaling system that integrates brain and body in response to the environment, regulating behaviors such as wake–sleep cycles with physiological responses such as metabolism (McEwen et al., 1997).

Cortisol can have profound effects on a variety of physiological systems, including the immune system (Webster, Tonelli, & Sternberg, 2002). Cortisol can act on lymphocytes and inhibit a wide variety of lymphocyte functions, including the ability to proliferate. It can also slow integrated immune responses such as wound healing. Cortisol is one of the body's important anti-inflammatory components because it can act on immune cells to inhibit the production of proinflammatory cytokines (such as IL-1, IL-6), just as its synthetic form, cortisone, reduces inflammation on the skin or in various organs. At the same time, proinflammatory cytokines can activate the HPA, causing the release of cortisol. Over the past 10 years, it has become clear that a bidirectional cytokine–HPA network exists that is responsive to exposure to stressful circumstances.

## Autonomic Nervous System

The ANS is divided into three parts: the SNS, the parasympathetic nervous system, and the enteric nervous system (which regulates the gastrointestinal tract). The SNS controls a variety of involuntary bodily functions that must be up-regulated in response to threats, for example, the cardiovascular system and the respiratory system. It is considered to be a system designed for mobilization. Thus, in response to acute stressors, individuals often experience symptoms that reflect activation of this system (e.g., acceleration of heart rate, breathing rate). The parasympathetic nervous system controls involuntary resting functions (such as digestion, reproduction), and activates organ systems to play a restorative role when the organism is not threatened. In addition, it actively inhibits sympathetic activity, for example by inhibiting heart rate, resulting in a

calming of the individual. The neurotransmitter released by sympathetic fibers is norepinephrine (noradrenalin), and the neurotransmitter released by parasympathetic fibers is acetylcholine. Walter Cannon, in the 1930s (Cannon, 1932), demonstrated that exposure to emergency situations resulted in the release of the hormone epinephrine (adrenalin) from the adrenal medulla. It is sympathetic innervation of the adrenal medulla and release of norepinephrine that causes the release of epinephrine from the adrenal medulla into the blood stream. The release of sympathetic neurotransmitters from nerve terminals can be inhibited by the glucocorticoids.

Autonomic nervous system fibers are directly connected to the immune system. Noradrenergic fibers innervate virtually all immune organs, including primary immune organs (thymus and bone marrow) and secondary organs (lymph nodes, Peyer's patches in the gut). These neural fibers release their neurotransmitters in close proximity to immune cells in these organs. Immune cells express receptors for these neurotransmitters (α– and β–adrenergic receptors) allowing them to be affected by the ANS. Studies that involve interfering with ANS connections to immune organs (e.g., by chemically denervating these organs) demonstrate alterations in the functioning of resident immune cells, thus indicating a functional link between the ANS and the activity of cells residing in these organs. Sympathetic modulation of the immune system can be both potentiating and inhibiting (Bellinger et al., 2008).

A variety of human studies demonstrate linkages between these two systems. For example, administration of epinephrine can greatly alter the number of circulating CD4 helper T cells within 15 minutes. Evidence also suggest that sympathetic activity mediates effects of acute stressful experience on certain immune functions since administration of β blockers, which block the activity of sympathetic hormones, can eliminate effects of acute stressors on certain immune functions (Benschop et al., 1996; Elenkov, Wilder, Chrousos, & Vizi, 2000).

## Other Physiological Systems

Other physiological systems also affect the immune system and may play a role in the relationship between psychological factors and immune processes. For example, other hormones, such as growth hormone and prolactin, can alter immune functions (Kelley, Weigent, & Kooijman, 2007). Other neuropeptides, such as the opioids (including β-endorphin and the enkephalins) have been shown to influence immune functions in vitro (Carr & Weber, 2001).

## Learning and the Immune System

One of the most important sets of studies demonstrating a link between the mind, brain, and immune system involves the ability of the immune system to be classically conditioned. As noted above, Ader and Cohen first demonstrated in 1975 that the taste of saccharin initially paired with an immunosuppressive drug acquired the ability to suppress antibody response in a classical conditioning paradigm (Ader & Cohen, 1975). These findings have been replicated and extended to studies of different conditioned and unconditioned stimuli, and different responses. For example, conditioned immunoenhancement has also been demonstrated (Solvason, Ghanta, & Hiramoto, 1988). The mechanisms that underlie these effects are unclear; however, Ader and colleagues have demonstrated that they are not due to a conditioned stress response since these effects can be elicited in animals whose adrenal glands have been removed. An interesting question is the nature of the constraints on these effects. Can any kind of immunologic alteration be "learned" and therefore affected by the CNS, or are there specific limits to the nature of the effects that can be conditioned?

One of the important implications of this area of research is the possibility that such paradigms could be used to alter immune processes in such a way as to benefit health. These conditioned immune changes, although small, have in fact been shown to be clinically significant in animals. Specifically, the conditioning paradigm was applied to mice genetically susceptible to an SLE-like autoimmune disease. In these mice, the immunosuppressive drug cyclophosphamide prolongs life because it controls the overactive immune response that is central to the pathogenesis of this autoimmune disease. Mice given a schedule of saccharin-flavored water that had been paired with cyclophosphamide showed prolonged survival (Ader & Cohen, 1975). These studies confirm that the CNS can control immunoregulatory processes and suggests that these relationships have clinical significance (an example of X-Y-Z mechanistic pathways). A few studies suggest that immune responses may be able to be conditioned in humans as well. For example, nausea following chemotherapy can become conditioned to the hospital environment, explaining the frequent observation that cancer patients begin to become nauseous once they enter the hospital for their chemotherapy treatments (Bovjberg et al., 1990; Goebel et al., 2002).

A number of possible applications of this area of research may follow from this body of work. For example, it may be possible to pair an innocuous substance with an effective drug that has toxic side effects and then, following conditioning, reduce the dosage of the toxic drug, substituting the conditioned substance for some dosages. The innocuous substance could not fully replace the pharmacologic agent, however, since the conditioned effects would eventually extinguish. Also, it may be possible to determine whether certain negative physiological or health effects are conditioned to particular environments or other stimuli. If so, detrimental health effects could be reduced via extinction processes. Given the findings above, nausea associated with chemotherapy that has become conditioned to the hospital environment could be reduced with trials of exposure to the hospital environment without subsequent chemotherapy.

Another potentially useful application of our understanding of classical conditioning of the immune system relates to placebo effects in immune-relevant diseases. In the placebo literature, there is evidence of improvement in a variety of diseases with administration of placebo pills or other non-specific treatments (Guess, Kleinman, Kusek, & Engel, 2002), as well as enhancement in physiological processes relevant to disease, such as bronchoconstriction following exposure to allergen in asthmatics (Kemeny et al., 2007). There is a great deal of controversy in this area regarding the symptoms and conditions amenable to placebo effects; renewed interest in this area should lead to findings that can determine when, under what conditions, and how placebo effects occur. One area of interest and investigation focuses on whether some placebo effects are due to prior experience with the pairing of an effective treatment (the unconditioned stimulus) with pill taking (the conditioned stimulus), such that pill taking alone (without the pharmacologic stimulus; i.e., the placebo) can elicit similar beneficial physical responses. For example, a placebo pill for the treatment of pain related to joint inflammation may reduce pain because patients have had experience taking effective treatments for reducing these symptoms in the past. In this case, pill taking has been paired with effective pharmacologic agents and can therefore alter symptom experience alone. In other words, one possibility is that "harnessing the power of the placebo" might depend on setting up a conditioning trial to maximize the efficacy of the conditioned stimulus (Ader, 2000). An alternative explanation for placebo effects centers on potential mediation by positive treatment-specific expectancies induced by receiving treatment (see expectancy section below). Recent research involving a placebo manipulation in the context of pain supports the notion that representations of expectations within certain brain regions may modulate neural activity relevant to placebo outcomes (Wager et al., 2004).

## Stress and the Immune System

A large literature indicates that stress can impact the immune system. The literature often uses the term *stress* in a vague and inconsistent way, sometimes referring to stress as a stimulus, sometimes as a psychological response, and sometimes as the physiological responses to difficult circumstances. A number of more specific terms are preferable. *Stressors* or stressful life experiences are circumstances that threaten a major goal. The prototype is a predator attack that threatens the goal of maintaining survival and physical integrity. Other major goals include the maintenance of a positive social self (status), social connectedness, and resources. *Distress* is a negative psychological response to goal threats that can involve a variety of affective and cognitive responses, including fear, hopelessness, a sense of being overwhelmed, sadness, anxiety, frustration, and the like. A few models are now utilized to determine the impact of stressor exposure on immune activity. For example, *acute stressors* can be modeled in the laboratory with exposure to 20–30 minutes of stressful procedures, such as performance of difficult tasks in front of an evaluative audience. *Acute or short-term naturalistic stressors* are time-limited circumstances that last days to weeks, such as taking school exams. *Major life change events* are usually defined as exposure to a discrete event that disrupts one's normal life experience in a significant away but is time-limited, for example, marital separation or bereavement. *Chronic stressors* are prolonged, lasting weeks, months or years, with a waxing and waning of impact (e.g., caring for a family member with a chronic or life-threatening disease, job loss; see Cohen, 1981 for stress definitions).

Exposure to a wide variety of naturalistic stressors can impact the immune system. In animals, stressors such as electric shock, restraint, cold water swim, maternal separation, and social defeat have been shown to cause both enumerative and functional alterations in the immune system (Ader, 2007).

In humans, short-term stressors such as medical school examinations, major life change events such as the death of a spouse or divorce, and chronic ongoing difficulties such as caregiving for a loved one with Alzheimer disease have been found to be associated with changes in the number and proportion of various lymphocyte subsets. Often, following a stressful circumstance, the number of helper T cells, cytotoxic T cells, and NK cells is reduced. In addition, these stressors are associated with deficits in the ability of immune cells in vitro to proliferate, kill tumor cells, produce antibody, respond to cytokine signals, and engage in other immune functions (Segerstrom & Miller, 2004). Stressors, such as taking exams, have also been associated with increased levels of antibody to latent viruses such as the Epstein-Barr virus (EBV) and the herpes simplex virus (HSV), suggesting a decreased capacity of the immune system to control viral latency (Kiecolt-Glaser & Glaser, 2001). Using medical school examinations as a model, Kiecolt-Glaser and Glaser have demonstrated reliable alterations in the immune system with short-term naturalistic stressor exposure (Kiecolt-Glaser et al., 1984, 1986). Also, whole, integrated local immune responses have been evaluated; for example, naturalistic stressors have been shown to slow wound healing (Kiecolt-Glaser, Marucha, Malarkey, Mercado, & Glaser, 1995). In addition to the direct health-relevant immune effects just described, stress has been shown to have a negative impact on influenza and other respiratory virus infections, influenza virus vaccine response, local and systemic evidence of inflammation, and cellular markers of cell aging in leukocytes. Together, these are the most significant stress studies in many ways because alterations in these parameters are most directly related to health and disease (Glaser & Kiecolt-Glaser, 2005). Stressed individuals can engage in deleterious health behaviors, such as drug or alcohol use, reduced exercise, or altered nutrition that can affect their immune systems directly. However, these stress-related immune changes are not due solely to the negative impact of these health behaviors. Exposure to stressful circumstances and their psychological and physiological effects contribute to immune system dysfunction, over and above the effects of stress-related behavior change. Stressor exposure can also *enhance* certain immune functions. For example, as described above, certain stressors can increase the inflammatory response by increasing levels of proinflammatory cytokines. Although inflammation is an adaptive response to orchestrate the elimination of pathogens and repair damaged tissue, chronic and inappropriate inflammation (along with other factors) plays an important role in the etiology and progression of inflammatory diseases, such as rheumatoid arthritis and inflammatory bowel disease. The ability of stressor exposure to increase mediators of inflammation may be a result of a stress-related reduction in the sensitivity of immune cells to the inhibitory effects of cortisol, or glucocorticoid resistance (GCR) as described above (Miller, Cohen, & Ritchey, 2002). Specifically, immune cells express glucocorticoid receptors that allow them to be affected by cortisol; for example, cortisol inhibits the production of a variety of cytokines. When these receptors are down-regulated, however, the cells do not respond to cortisol signals, so that they do not become inhibited when exposed to increased levels of cortisol. Exposure to chronically stressful experience can reduce the sensitivity of immune cells to the inhibitory effects of cortisol, thus leading to increases in inflammatory mediators normally constrained by cortisol (Miller, Cohen, & Ritchey, 2002). Even acute laboratory stressors that involved social threat can increase glucocorticoid resistance (Dickerson, Gable, Irwin, Aziz, & Kemeny, 2009). An important point here is that stress can affect the immune system not only by activating the release of chemical messengers from various arousal systems but also by acting on the receptors expressed on immune cells that "hear" these signals.

The size of the effects of stressors on the immune system varies widely, depending on the nature and chronicity of the stressor and the type of immune parameter evaluated. In most cases, it is not known whether the types of immune alterations generated as a result of stressor exposure can in fact increase vulnerability to disease (discussed in more detail below).

A large number of studies have demonstrated that acute exposure to *laboratory* stressful experiences can also alter immune processes. Typical laboratory paradigms expose individuals to brief (e.g., 20 min) stressors, such as mental arithmetic, loud noise, difficult puzzles, or giving a speech. Blood is drawn before and after the stressful task. As with naturalistic studies, these brief exposures can impair lymphocyte functions, such as the proliferative response, and decrease the number of B cells and CD4 helper T cells (Herbert & Cohen, 1993b). However, in contrast to effects of naturalistic studies, NK cell activity and the number of NK cells (as well as CD8 cells) *increases* after an acute laboratory stressor. The functional changes may be due to increases in the number of NK cells in the blood stream following a stressor, not to changes in the function of cells on a per-cell basis. The immune effects observed with acute laboratory stress occur quickly, within 5 minutes, and return back to baseline within 30 minutes to 1 hour. The presence of chronic life stressors may accentuate the effects of acute laboratory stressors on certain immune functions (Pike et al., 1997).

### Stressor Specificity

Different types of stressors and stressor characteristics may be capable of eliciting distinctive patterns of immunologic alteration. The duration, intensity, and timing of a stressor can impact the nature of the immune effects. For example, an increasing number of foot shocks per session progressively decreased the proliferative response in rats (Lysle, Lyte, Fowler, & Rabin, 1987). Continuous versus intermittent stress can have different immune consequences in rodents (Shavit et al., 1987). However, little is known about the relationship between stressor characteristics and immune effects in humans. Although acute laboratory stressors versus acute naturalistic stressors have different immune effects, as described above, it is unclear whether these differences are due to the length of the stressors, the context, or other parameters, for example, timing or the specific nature of the stressors. For example, laboratory stressors (such as giving a speech) are shorter than naturalistic stressors (such as final exams), do not have the lengthy anticipatory period, have different potential consequences and different social contexts, and may therefore induce different cognitive and affective responses. These distinctive psychological responses may then have different neurohormonal correlates and immunological consequences.

It is possible that the specific nature of the stressor, apart from timing and other issues, may elicit a distinctive pattern of neurobiological and peripheral changes to support an adaptive response to the specific nature of the context (Weiner, 1992). Studies in humans that systematically vary these stressor characteristics have not been conducted, so it is unclear which factors explain the different pattern of immune effects. However, evidence that different types of stressors elicit distinct patterns of physiological changes in systems that affect the immune system, such as the HPA and ANS, suggest that the specific nature of the stressor may also be relevant to the pattern of immune effects (Blascovich & Tomaka, 1996).

## Physiological Mediators of Stressor Effects

Sympathetic arousal appears to mediate some of the effects of acute stressors on NKCA and other immune outcomes. For example, in a study of parachute jumping as a stressor, significant elevations in measures of sympathetic arousal occurred during and after the jump, including increases in heart and respiratory rates and release of epinephrine and nor-epinephrine. In addition, the number of NK cells and NKCA against tumor targets increased during the stressor (the numbers doubled on average). Sympathetic mediation of NK effects was suggested by the fact that the greater the level of norepinephrine produced during the jump, the greater the NKCA increase (Schedlowski et al., 1993). The increases in NK number and activity following acute laboratory stressors also appear to be mediated by sympathetic arousal, because of the correlation between sympathetic activation and NK enhancement (Herbert et al., 1994). Strong support for the mediating role of ANS products comes from studies that show that similar immune effects can be induced with an injection of epinephrine (Van Tits et al., 1990) and that stress effects on this aspect of immunity can be abolished with a β-adrenergic antagonist (Benschop et al., 1994).

Since exposure to some stressors can increase levels of glucocorticoids, and glucocorticoids are potent immunosuppressive substances, it has long been assumed that the HPA axis plays a major mediating role in the immune suppressive effects of stressors on the immune system. Although there is data to support this contention, a number of studies fail to find this relationship. For example, stress-induced immunosuppression can occur in animals whose adrenal glands have been removed (Keller, Weiss, Schleifer, Miller, & Stein, 1983). And, in some cases, it appears that the glucocorticoids can permit the induction of stress-related immune changes, but these steroids may not be sufficient by themselves (Moynihan & Stevens, 2001). Other systems have been shown to affect the immune system and mediate stress effects, including the opioid peptides. It is likely that the physiological mediation of stress effects involve multiple, interacting systems and depend on a number of factors, including the nature of the stressor, the condition of the host, the presence of pathogens, and the specific immune parameters under study (e.g., see Webster Marketon & Glaser, 2008).

## Individual Difference Factors

Although stressors impact a variety of immune parameters, the effects are not uniform across individuals.

Even when the specific nature of the stressor and other contextual factors are held constant as much as possible, some individuals show immune alterations and some do not. There is a great deal of variability in the magnitude of the changes and their trajectory (speed of onset and recovery), and in the aspects of immune function that become altered. A variety of potential sources of this variance exist, including the genetic makeup of the individuals, their health status, the impact of behaviors on their immune status (including recreational drug and alcohol use, exercise, nutrition, smoking), the medication they are taking, and more. Despite the relative paucity of research on, for example, the moderating role of genetic factors on the relationship between stressor exposure and immune alteration in humans, it is likely to be a highly fruitful area of research that will produce much more useful findings than studies of environmental or psychological factors alone. For example, studies of strain differences using Lewis versus Fischer rats led to a wealth of information on the linkage between the HPA and inflammatory disease. Specifically, Sternberg and colleagues (1997) found that Lewis and Fisher rats, which differ in the reactivity of the HPA, also vary in their susceptibility to experimentally induced rheumatoid arthritis and encephalomyelitis. Lewis rats show reduced activity in an open field (a measure of anxiety), have lower HPA activity, and are much more susceptible to these autoimmune diseases.

Individual differences related to psychological states and traits are of great interest in the field of psychoneuroimmunology. There can be a great deal of difference in the psychological response to stressors across individuals and within individuals over time. These responses can be tied to individual differences in stable characteristics, such as personality and temperament. The specific nature of the psychological response to a stressor may play a critical role in shaping the neurophysiological and consequent immunologic responses observed (Kemeny & Laudenslager, 1999; Segerstrom, Kemeny, & Laudenslager, 2001). Key individual differences in response to circumstances would include cognitive appraisal and affective response.

## Affect and the Immune System

Growing evidence suggests that affective response may play an important role in determining the immunological changes associated with exposure to a stressor. A number of studies suggest a relationship between affective traits and basal immune status or response to stressors. One area that appears promising is the utilization of brain electrical activity recording in the left and right prefrontal cortex as a measure of affectivity. Davidson has shown that greater relative right prefrontal activation is associated with less positive and more negative trait affect (Davidson, 1998). Individuals with this activation pattern also respond more strongly to negative affective challenges and have higher basal cortisol levels (Kalin, Larson, Shelton, & Davidson, 1998). Davidson and his colleagues have also shown lower basal immune function (NKCA) and a greater reduction in function after an examination stressor in individuals with greater right prefrontal activation (Davidson, Coe, Dolski, & Donzella, 1999; Kang et al., 1991). Thus, this neurophysiological emotion-relevant pattern may predict both basal and stressor-induced immune changes. Other emotion regulation styles, such as trait worry and repressive style, have also been shown to predict immune response to laboratory and naturalistic stressors in some studies (Esterling, Antoni, Kumar, & Schneiderman, 1990; Segerstrom, Glover, Craske, & Fahey, 1999; Segerstrom, Solomon, Kemeny, & Fahey, 1998).

A great deal is known about the relationship between depression and the immune system. Major depression is associated with immune alterations, including functional changes that are similar to those observed with naturalistic stressors (Irwin, Daniels, Bloom, & Weiner, 1986; Schleifer et al., 1984). A meta-analytic review has shown that depression is associated with reliable increases in certain immune subsets (e.g., neutrophils) and decreases in others (B and T cells). Decrements in proliferative capacity are common as well as in NKCA and other measures of T-cell function (Herbert & Cohen, 1993a). Depressed individuals most vulnerable to immune suppression appear to be those with more severe depression, older age, and those who also have a sleep disorder or alcoholism (Irwin, 2001). There is also some evidence that increases in these immune functions can be observed in depressed patients following treatment (Irwin, Lacher, & Caldwell, 1992).

Recent evidence suggests immune *enhancement* can also occur with depression. In initial studies by Maes and his colleagues, patients with depressive symptoms or syndromal depression showed evidence of increased levels of proinflammatory cytokines, although these findings are not always consistent (Maes et al., 1994). Controlling for a host of potential alternative explanations, such as

presence of other medical conditions, medications, and health behaviors such as cigarette smoking, individuals meeting criteria for clinical depression have been shown to have higher levels of IL-6 when compared to demographically matched controls (Miller, Stetler, Carney, Freedland, & Banks, 2002). In some studies, pharmacologic treatment was associated with a reduction in these levels. It has been argued that the relationship between depression and increased levels of proinflammatory cytokines may be mediated by glucocorticoid resistance, as described earlier in relation to exposure to chronic stressors.

One of the most provocative aspects of the research on depression and proinflammatory cytokines is the hypothesis that these cytokines may play an etiologic role in depression (see Kent, Bluthe, Kelley, & Dantzer, 1992; Maier & Watkins, 1998; Yirmiya et al., 1999). Four sets of findings support this possibility. First, studies, as described above, demonstrate a link between a diagnosis of depression and increased levels of these cytokines. Second, injections of proinflammatory cytokines in humans can induce depression-like symptoms, including dysphoria, anhedonia, helplessness, fatigue, and apathy, which regress when treatment has ended. Third, patients with inflammatory diseases that are often accompanied by elevated levels of proinflammatory cytokines have an increased risk for depression. And finally, animals injected with these cytokines either peripherally or centrally show an increase in a number of behaviors that overlap with depression (Dantzer et al., 2001; Kent et al., 1992). Specifically, these cytokines can induce what is called *sickness behavior*, which includes locomotor retardation, immobility, sleep disorders, anorexia, hyperalgesia, decreased social exploration, inhibition of sexual behavior, and anhedonia. These are symptoms of many illnesses but most also overlap with the vegetative symptoms of depression. The behavioral changes observed following administration of a proinflammatory cytokine are not the result of physical weakness or debilitation, but the expression of a shift in motivational state that alters priorities to deal preferentially with combating infection (Dantzer et al., 2001). The changes are adaptive in that they reduce the utilization of unnecessary energy, which can then be redirected to energy-draining aspects of the inflammatory process, such as the development of a fever (Maier & Watkins, 1998). Interestingly, sickness behavior in rats due to injection with proinflammatory cytokines can be prevented if the animals are pretreated with certain antidepressant medications (Castanon, Bluthe, & Dantzer, 2001).

Maier and Watkins (1998) have argued that exposure to stressors can increase the production of proinflammatory cytokines, which then contributes to the onset of depression via cytokine effects on the CNS. In other words, the known association between exposure to stressful life experience and depression may be mediated, in some cases, by stress-induced increases in the proinflammatory cytokines and the sickness behaviors that are engendered. This notion is supported by the research reviewed above that a variety of acute stressors have been associated with elevations in these cytokines, both in animals and humans. However, it appears that *uncontrollable* stressors may preferentially activate this network, leading to depression since the motivational shifts demonstrated following an injection of IL-1β are consistent with behavioral responses to uncontrollable contexts. As described above, animals injected with IL-1 exhibit defensive and defeated postures during a confrontation, postures they would assume if the context was uncontrollable and they were destined to lose. And animals that are socially defeated show a greater production of these cytokines than those who are not (Avitsur et al., 2001; Stark et al., 2001). In humans, the results are inconclusive. However, among the small number of laboratory stress studies conducted, those that utilize an uncontrollable social evaluative threat demonstrate a consistent increase in these cytokines, whereas those without this social threat do not (Ackerman et al., 1998; Dickerson et al., 2009). It would be adaptive for uncontrollable stressors to be capable of eliciting cytokine-induced depression-like disengagement from a conservation-withdrawal perspective, for example. However, these behavioral indicators of depression would be maladaptive in response to a controllable circumstance. Other affective states associated with motivational disengagement may also be linked to increases in proinflammatory cytokines (see evidence for increases in these cytokines with shame; Dickerson, Kemeny, Aziz, Kim, & Fahey, 2004).

A growing but still limited literature suggests that positive affective states may also be associated with immune system changes (Marsland, Pressman, & Cohen, 2007). Older literature suggests that positive affect is associated with increases in secretory immunoglobulin A (SIga), an antibody found in the mucosal immune system (e.g., in saliva). Increases have been demonstrated in response to positive mood inductions, such as watching a funny movie, and in tandem with positive mood measured

on a day-to-day basis. However, the relevance of this type of change to disease is not clear. Positive affect may also be correlated with increases in the number of certain subsets of white blood cells, although the results are not entirely consistent, and the direction of effects is similar to that found with a stressor exposure. Fewer studies have examined the relationship between positive affect and functional measures of immune response or whole integrated immune responses (e.g., placing an antigen under the skin and examining the immune response on the skin (Marsland et al., 2007).

Different affective states may have distinctive effects on the immune system. One major support for this premise rests on the emerging evidence that distinctive affective states have different CNS and ANS correlates. For example, neuroimaging studies find that different regions of the brain become activated with different emotional states (Damasio et al., 2000; Lane, Reiman, Ahern, Schwartz, & Davidson, 1997). And studies that induce diverse affective states have shown different patterns of autonomic arousal with certain emotional states (Ekman, Levenson, & Friesen, 1983). For example, skin temperature increases more with anger than with fear. These distinct neural patterns may result in different effects on the immune system since autonomic fibers innervate immune organs and regulate the activity of the resident immune cells. A few studies suggest different immunological correlates of affective states. For example, Futterman and colleagues (Futterman, Kemeny, Shapiro, & Fahey, 1994) conducted an experimental study that manipulated positive and negative mood over a 25-minute period. Results indicated that both positive and negative mood increased NKCA; however, the proliferative response was increased with positive mood and decreased with negative mood. Differential antigen-specific IgA antibody responses have been found to be associated with positive and negative daily mood ratings (Stone, Cox, Valdlmarsdottir, Jandorf, & Neale, 1987). Less work has been conducted differentiating immune correlates of different negative emotions. In a disclosure study, participants wrote about a trivial topic or a situation in which they blamed themselves, in order to elicit the experience of shame (Dickerson et al., 2004). The self-blame condition induced significantly more shame and guilt thanother emotions and also increased the levels of TNF-α receptor, a marker of proinflammatory cytokine activity. The greatest increases in TNF were observed in those individuals who reported the greatest increases in shame during the mood induction, whereas changes in other emotions were not correlated with this immune parameter. These findings suggest that acute affective experience may have immunologic correlates and that the nature and extent of the immune change may depend on the specific nature of the emotion experienced. Insufficient evidence to date, however, exists from studies that directly test this specificity hypothesis to draw firm conclusions one way or the other.

## Cognitive Representations and the Immune System

Individuals differ in the way in which they think about themselves, their lives, and others. Representations of the self have been investigated in psychology as powerful contributors to mood and motivation. A number of studies suggest that self representations may also affect neurophysiological systems and the immune system. As described below, negative appraisals of self have been shown to predict activation of the HPA in healthy individuals, as well as important immune and health endpoints in those infected with HIV (Dickerson, Gruenewald, & Kemeny, 2004). In addition, following priming of self-representations, greater self-discrepancy (or the difference between one's perceived "actual" self and one's "ought" self or "ideal" self) was associated with lower NKCA (Strauman, Lemieux, & Coe, 1993).

Representations of the future have also been linked to the immune system. Although dispositional optimism, or the tendency to expect positive outcomes, has been shown to predict a variety of health outcomes, a number of studies have not found health correlates of this style, reflecting the possibility that this disposition may be adaptive in some contexts and for some individuals but not across the board. However, there is a body of literature demonstrating that optimistic individuals show enhanced indices of immune function (Segerstrom & Sephton, 2010). In addition, state representations of the future (e.g., expectations about future health) have been shown to predict health outcomes in HIV (see section on HIV research). Affective states are proposed to mediate the relationships between cognitive representations and physiological parameters; however, it is also possible that cognitive states and their neural substrates can activate physiological changes without the intermediary role of affect (Kemeny & Gruenewald, 2000).

There has been a great deal of interest in the role that social support may play in promoting and maintaining physical health. Across a large number of studies, individuals with confidants (someone they can talk to about problems) and those who have more satisfying social relationships have superior physical health compared to those with less social support. One possible mechanism underlying some of these effects is the immune benefits associated with social support. Individuals who have greater social support may have stronger immune systems (main effect hypothesis), or social support may buffer the effects of stressors on immune processes (buffering hypothesis) or both (Cohen & Wills, 1985).

Increasing evidence indicates that social support is capable of moderating the effects of stressful experience on the immune response. For example, in infant squirrel monkeys, the presence of peers moderated both the hormonal and immunological effects of maternal separation (Coe, Rosenberg, & Levine, 1988). In medical students confronting major exam periods, the extent of immune alteration (NKCA, antibody response to EBV) was associated with the degree of loneliness experienced (Kiecolt-Glaser et al., 1984). In another context, the extent of immune alteration following separation or divorce depended on level of attachment to the ex-spouse (Kiecolt-Glaser et al., 1984). These conclusions are bolstered by the literature demonstrating protective effects of social support with regard to physiological systems that impact the immune system (e.g., the autonomic nervous system and the HPA).

Social hierarchy is another important social process that appears to play a critical role in regulating social relationships and physiology in almost all animal species including humans. Dominant and subordinant animals do not manifest the same neurophysiological and immunological changes in response to social confrontations. Submissives show more negative physiological alterations (inhibited production of antibody) even 3 weeks after an encounter with dominant animals (Fleshner, Laudenslager, Simons, & Maier, 1989). The amount of time spent in the defeated posture and antibody levels were highly correlated in this study ($r = -.80$). Immune differences in dominant versus subordinant animals have been demonstrated in a variety of species including fish, rodents, and primates. For example, in one set of studies by Stefanski and colleagues (1998), rats were exposed to social confrontation, and the behavioral response of the intruder was characterized as either submissive (defeat posture) or subdominant (without defeat). Basal immune parameters did not differ across the groups; however, after 7 days of confrontation, shifts in lymphocyte subsets were observed, with the largest decreases in the subdominant. Sheridan and colleagues (Avitsur et al., 2001) showed that when rodents were confronted with a very aggressive intruder, they demonstrated nonverbal displays of social defeat and more glucocorticoid resistance than did animals who were not exposed to this confrontation. The degree of glucocorticoid resistance correlated with the extent of submissive displays. A larger literature indicates that submissive animals also show increased levels of corticosteroid, with the level correlated positively with the amount of displayed submissive behavior. Thus, altered patterns of HPA activation could mediate immune correlates of low status. Extrapolation of these findings to status differences in humans have been undertaken (Kemeny, Gruenewald, & Dickerson, 2004).

## Interventions

If stressors, negative mood, and negative cognitive appraisals can adversely affect the immune system, can psychological interventions that reduce negative states of mind induce immune improvements? At least 100 intervention studies have been conducted with immune endpoints in healthy individuals, or those with cancer, autoimmune disease, and other conditions. A number of studies have demonstrated short-term immune enhancement following interventions, although the extent of benefit appears to depend on the type of intervention and the aspect of immunity examined (Kemeny & Miller, 1999; Miller & Cohen, 2001).

One of the interesting findings in this area of research indicates that the interventions that have been found in the past to show the most robust effects on depression, for example, do not appear to show the strongest effects on the immune system. For example, cognitive behavioral interventions, which focus on altering maladaptive cognitive responses and have shown psychological benefits for individuals with depression, have shown inconsistent immunologic effects. This may be due to the fact that the majority of participants in these intervention studies do not have elevated levels of depression and are therefore less likely to derive the benefit that a depressed sample would derive (Miller & Cohen, 2001).

Disclosure paradigms involve writing essays about traumatic events. Writing takes place in short sessions (e.g., 20 minutes), over 4 or more days. Engaging in this form of expressive writing has been found to positively impact health care utilization,

autonomic nervous system reactivity, and other processes; however, effects on the immune system are mixed. For example, benefits were shown by Petrie, Booth, and colleagues (Petrie, Booth, Pennebaker, Davison, & Thomas, 1995), who studied disclosure in 40 medical students who were given a hepatitis B vaccine with boosters at 1 and 4 months post disclosure sessions. Antibody titers to hepatitis B were significantly higher at 1, 4, and 6 months post vaccination in the disclosure group compared to the control group. Effects on other immune parameters, including NKCA and lymphocyte subsets, were not observed. Consistent effects of disclosure on specific immune parameters have not yet been demonstrated.

Despite the large literature documenting reductions in distress and physiological arousal with relaxation, research does not suggest consistent immune benefits (Miller & Cohen, 2001). In these studies, a wide array of techniques were used to induce a relaxed state, including progressive muscle relaxation, biofeedback, imagery, and meditation, or combinations of these techniques. In some cases, significant benefits were obtained. For example, in an early study of older individuals in nursing homes, participants were randomly assigned to receive relaxation exercises once a week for 6 weeks, social contact with a college student over the same time frame, or no intervention (Kiecolt-Glaser et al., 1985). Significant increases in NKCA and decreases in antibody to HSV (suggesting more control over viral latency) were found immediately after the intervention. HSV effects were maintained at the 1-month follow-up. The social support condition showed no benefits. On the other hand, other relaxation intervention studies have shown no immune benefits. It may be that certain relaxation approaches are more beneficial than others. For example, an 8-week meditation program (mindfulness-based stress reduction) significantly increased antibody levels to a flu vaccine in participants compared to a control condition (Davidson et al., 2003). Interestingly, significantly greater left prefrontal cortex activation resulted from the intervention, using recordings of brain electrical activity from the scalp, and those who showed this pattern of neural activation showed the greatest increase in antibody levels following the intervention. Individuals with greater relative left prefrontal activation have been shown to report less negative and more positive dispositional mood and respond less negatively to emotional challenges (Davidson, 1998). Therefore, meditation may impact neural processes that underlie emotional responses tied to immune activity.

Such effects may be due to increased attention and awareness, or relaxation or both. On the other hand, there is some consistent evidence of immune benefit for hypnosis and conditioning. These interventions are interesting because, rather than focusing on decreasing negative mood and distress, they involve a directed manipulation of "expectation" about the specific immune processes being examined. Thus, these studies are based on the premise that it is possible to manipulate the direction of an immune response via neurophysiological pathways. These studies differ in a number of ways from the other intervention studies. For example, many studies of the impact of hypnosis and conditioning evaluated hypersensitivity reactions as outcomes. An antigen is placed under the skin, and the wheal that forms is measured as an index of the immune response to the antigen. These studies are unique in that an entire in vivo immune response is measured rather than the activity of immune cells isolated from their biological context. Also, only highly hypnotizable participants are included in the hypnosis studies. Any of these factors may explain the successes in this area.

More recently, multimodal interventions have been designed and tested for effects on the immune system and disease. As of yet, no clear understanding of the intervention type best able to affect immune system functioning has emerged. However, promising research suggests the potential for multimodal group stress management approaches in affecting health-relevant immune parameters in HIV-positive individuals (Antoni, 2007).

### Development

Early experience can have a profound effect on the developing immune system, as well as on adult immunity. For example, in very early work in rats, Solomon and colleagues (1968) showed that handling in the first 21 days of life was associated with more vigorous antibody responses in adulthood. Maternal separation has been studied in young nonhuman primates as it relates to immune outcomes. Maternal separation results in elevations in a variety of markers of distress, alterations in sleep patterns, and effects on the CNS, SNS, the HPA, and other hormone systems. The extent and nature of these changes depend on the species, presence of others, length of the separation, and other factors. Alterations in a wide variety of immune parameters are also observed, including reductions in the proliferative response and the primary antibody response as well as increases in markers of macrophage

activation (Worlein & Laudenslager, 2001). Effects depend on behavioral response, with evidence that more vocalized distress and more behavioral withdrawal may be associated with greater physiological alteration. Even brief separations at an early age can affect adult behavioral patterns and physiological responses, including immune responses.

### Do Stress-related Immune Changes Explain the Relationship Between Stress and Disease?

Although stressor exposure and psychological responses can influence the immune system, and these psychological processes have also been found to be risk factors for certain diseases, another important direction of current research focuses on the extent to which immune changes mediate the stress–disease relationship (see Glaser, 2005; Kemeny & Schedlowski, 2007). A major thrust of research in health psychology is aimed at examining these links, as described in the X-Y-Z model (Kemeny, 1991; see Figure 7.1). For example, in animal studies, alterations in NKCA may mediate the effects of stress on metastases to the lung in rats with a breast tumor (Ben-Eliyahu, Yirmiya, Liebeskind, Taylor, & Gale, 1991). And in infectious disease, HSV pathogenesis following exposure to a stressor may be related to suppression of HSV-specific cytotoxic T cells and NKCA in rodents (Bonneau, Sheridan, Feng, & Glaser, 1991a, 1991b).

Research is burgeoning in the area of immunological mediators of the relationship between stress and disease in humans. For some diseases, it has been difficult to specify clear mediational pathways. For example, excellent work has been done to show that chronic exposure to stressful experience is associated with vulnerability to a respiratory infection following inoculation with a rhinovirus (Cohen et al., 1998). However, the immune (or other physiological) mediators of this relationship have yet to be determined. Importantly, research in HIV infection, cardiovascular disease, and cancer have begun to define these important pathways.

### Predictors of HIV Disease

HIV-1 infection has been used as a model for studying psychoneuroimmunological relationships and disease endpoints for a variety of reasons, but particularly because immune and virologic processes that are highly predictive of disease course are known and easily quantifiable. This fact may not seem particularly noteworthy, but it is important to recognize that, even for diseases known to be affected by the immune system, such as infectious or auto-immune diseases, immune assays whose values can predict disease course in humans are often not readily available. This problem has limited the ability of researchers to conduct studies of psychological factors, immune mediators, and disease etiology or course. In addition, HIV is a good model because there is unexplained variability in disease course even in individuals on antiretroviral medication. Also, some of the immunologic processes that can contain the virus have been shown to be modifiable in other populations by stressful life experience and psychological factors. And, HIV infection occurs frequently in younger, otherwise healthy individuals, so that comorbidities do not complicate models. Finally, many HIV-positive individuals are exposed to profoundly stressful circumstances (e.g., death of close others to HIV, stigma), and so it is possible to compare physiological processes and disease course in samples differing on psychological responses to these stressors.

A number of studies have shown that psychological factors can predict HIV disease course, controlling for demographic, behavioral, and medical factors (see Kemeny, 2003; Sloan, Collado-Hidalgo, & Cole, 2007). For example, HIV-positive individuals with high levels of depression show accelerated rates of clinical disease progression, as well as evidence of more rapid immune decline in some studies, but relationships vary depending on the disease outcome measured (Cole & Kemeny, 2001). A simple count of the number of stressful life events encountered over intervals such as the past year does not consistently predict disease course. However, the presence of significant stressors, defined in terms of the nature of the individual's specific context, has predicted immune decline in HIV-positive individuals (Leserman et al., 2000). These findings are supported by studies in rhesus macaques inoculated with the simian immunodeficiency virus (SIV) showing that exposure to social stressors, such as housing changes and separation, predict accelerated disease progression and immune alteration (Capitanio & Lerche, 1998; Capitanio, Mendoza, Lerche, & Mason, 1998). Social support and active coping processes have both been shown to predict less rapid progression of HIV disease (e.g., Leserman et al., 2000).

As described above, cognitive appraisal processes can have profound effects on psychological and physiological responses to threats. A number of studies suggest that one set of appraisal processes—expectations of disease course—predict clinical and immunologic evidence of HIV disease progression. Even at the same stage of disease, individuals with HIV vary widely in their expectations about the future course of their disease. Some expect to remain healthy, whereas others are "preparing" for disease progression and death. Longitudinal studies show that those with more pessimistic expectations develop HIV-related symptoms more quickly and die of AIDS more rapidly (Reed, Kemeny, Taylor, & Visscher, 1999; Reed, Kemeny, Taylor, Wang, & Visscher, 1994). Expectations also predict an array of immune changes that are associated with disease progression, including CD4 T-cell decline, deficits in proliferative capacity, and high levels of immune activation (which have been shown to trigger replication of the virus and CD4 T-cell death). These associations, across studies, are strongest in HIV-positive individuals who have lost a close friend to AIDS in the past year. Pessimistic expectations in this context may lead to a "giving up" or goal disengagement, which is then associated with immune alteration. Treatment of HIV infection has improved since most of these studies were conducted, so it will be important to see if such psychological states continue to predict disease course in this context.

A second consistent cognitive predictor of immune changes relevant to HIV progression is negative appraisals of the self. A growing literature suggests that threats to one's "social self" or threats to social esteem, status, and acceptance are associated with specific negative cognitive and affective responses, including shame and humiliation. More recently, evidence suggests that such threats are also accompanied by specific physiological changes (Dickerson, Kemeny, Aziz, Kim, & Fahey, 2004). Social Self-preservation theory argues that these affective and physiological responses are integral components of a coordinated psychobiological response to threats to "social self-preservation," in the same way that fear and its physiological correlates are aspects of the response to threats to physical self-preservation (Kemeny et al., 2005). Although these affective and physiological changes may be adaptive in an acute threat context, persistence of these psychobiological responses may have negative consequences for health. Persistence could occur under two conditions: chronic exposure to conditions of social self threat (such as evaluative, rejecting conditions as experienced by those with a stigma) or the presence of individual difference factors that increase vulnerability to experience negative self-related emotions and cognitions (e.g., rejection sensitivity).

HIV is a good model for investigations in this area because HIV infection occurs among stigmatized groups (gay and bisexual men, minority individuals, drug abusers) and is a stigmatizing sexually transmitted disease itself (See Kemeny, 2009).

Consistent with theoretical predictions, HIV-positive gay and bisexual men who are particularly sensitive to rejection concerning their homosexuality show more rapid progression of HIV disease than do those who are less sensitive to these social self threats. Specifically, individuals with more rejection sensitivity concerning their homosexuality showed faster CD4 T-cell decline, and faster times to AIDS onset and death over a 9-year follow-up period (Cole, Kemeny, & Taylor, 1997). Rejection-sensitive individuals died, on average, 2 years faster than their less sensitive counterparts. Effects were not explained by health behaviors, medications, demographics, and other possible confounding factors. In addition, rejection sensitivity predicts response to antiviral medication. Among HIV-positive men initiating the highly active antiretroviral therapy (HAART) regimen to control viral replication, those with psychological characteristics that include increased sensitivity to rejection showed a weaker response to the medication over the next year than did the less sensitive individuals. Specifically, those less rejection-sensitive showed greater beneficial changes in HIV viral load (amount of HIV in the blood) and CD4 T-cell levels (Cole, Kemeny, Fahey, Zack, & Naliboff, 2003). This relationship was mediated by increased ANS arousal to a variety of stimuli in the more sensitive individuals.

Perceptions of rejection and negative self-related cognitions also predict indicators of HIV progression. In a multiethnic sample of women with HIV and a sample of HIV-positive men, the interpersonal rejection/self-reproach component of depression predicted accelerated CD4 T-cell decline over time, when the other depression components did not (Kemeny & Dean, 1995). HIV-positive gay men who characteristically blame themselves for negative events showed more rapid CD4 declines than did those who did not manifest this attributional style (Segerstrom, Taylor, Kemeny, Reed, & Visscher, 1996). Thus, cognitions associated with self-blame and social rejection are capable of predicting indicators of HIV progression, whether or not they occur in the context of depression. Social self-preservation theory predicts that the experience of shame and related self-conscious emotions may be an important affective component of the psychobiological response to social self threats.

Overall, these findings may help to reconcile the inconsistent pattern of results regarding the ability of depression to predict various indictors of HIV progression. In a highly stigmatized group, the perceived social rejection or negative self component of depression and the experience of the shame family of emotions may be more salient feelings that have more powerful and persistent physiological correlates. These physiological changes may then play a role in immunologic control of this latent virus. Intervention studies could provide confirmation of the causal direction of these relationships.

Two potential physiological pathways that may explain the relationships between psychological factors and HIV progression have been studied. The first pathway centers on the HPA. Glucocorticoids may play a role in HIV progression, since elevated levels of cortisol predict HIV progression indices in vivo (Capitanio et al., 1998; Leserman, 2000). Also, in vitro studies show that corticosteroids can enhance HIV-1 replication (Markham, Salahuddin, Veren, Orndorff, & Gallo, 1986) and may prolong viral gene expression (Ayyavoo et al., 1997).

Social self threats can activate the HPA axis, resulting in increased levels of cortisol. In a meta-analytic review of 208 laboratory stress studies, those laboratory conditions that involved uncontrollable social self threats (e.g., uncontrollable motivated performance tasks in front of an evaluative audience) showed higher cortisol responses and slower recovery times than those that did not contain this threat (Dickerson & Kemeny, 2004). A subsequent experiment confirmed this synthesis—exposure to a motivated performance task that included an evaluative audience provoked the HPA, resulting in elevations of cortisol, whereas exposure to tasks without this component did not (Gruenewald, Kemeny, Aziz, & Fahey, 2006). In animals, social threats, such as social defeat and subordination, are associated with activation of the HPA (Shively, Laber-Laird, & Anton, 1997). These data support the notion that social self threats and their affective sequelae in humans and other animals are associated with activation of the HPA. This activation may serve as one mediator of the effects of social self threat on HIV progression.

A second pathway linking psychological factors to HIV progression involves the autonomic nervous system. Cole and colleagues have shown that HIV-positive individuals who demonstrate higher SNS activity to a variety of challenging tasks show poorer benefit following initiation of HAART—they show less suppression of viral replication (Cole et al., 2001). Supporting these findings, the SNS neurotransmitter, norepinephrine (NE), has been shown to enhance HIV replication in vitro, and there is a dose–response relationship between level of NE and replication rate (Cole, Korin, Fahey, & Zack, 1998; Cole et al., 2001). This effect involves the cyclic AMP/protein kinase A signaling pathway (Cole et al., 1998, 2001). As described above, SNS fibers innervate immune organs and release NE in close proximity to lymphocytes that express β- adrenoreceptors capable of responding to this signal. Since stressful experience and psychological factors have been shown to activate the SNS, this system may mediate effects of psychological processes on HIV replication, CD4 T-cell decline, and clinical disease progression.

## Cardiovascular Disease

Cardiovascular disease is another excellent model for studies in psychoneuroimmunology and disease. In the past, risk factors for cardiovascular disease have centered on hypertension, lipids, diabetes, and similar physical factors. However, more recently, increasing attention has been focused on the role of inflammatory processes in atherosclerotic diseases. Inflammation plays a role in atherogenesis (Fahdi, Gaddam, Garza, Romeo, & Mehta, 2003) and contributes to plaque instability. Increases in markers of inflammation, such as C-reactive protein (CRP), have been shown to predict a higher risk of stroke and myocardial infarction in healthy individuals (Ridker, Cushman, Stampfer, Tracy, & Hennekens, 1997). These inflammatory processes may explain the consistent ability of depression to predict increased risk of first and recurrent cardiac events within relatively short time intervals (Kop, 1999), since depression is associated with elevated levels of a variety of mediators of inflammation, as described above. It is interesting to note that increased levels of inflammatory cytokines, particularly IL-6, have been shown to predict a variety of diseases. In fact, elevated IL-6 levels in healthy adults have been found to predict all-cause mortality (Ershler & Keller, 2000). Thus, the bidirectional interaction between psychological factors and the inflammatory network is a critically important area of psychoneuroimmunology.

It is important not to presume immune mediation in the relationship between psychological factors and disease progression, even when a particular psychological state can predict both endpoints. The problem with this assumption can be clearly seen in the results of an intervention study conducted with patients with malignant melanoma. The impact of a psychoeducational group intervention was evaluated in relation to mood, coping, the NK system, melanoma recurrence, and mortality over a 6-year period (Fawzy et al., 1990, 1990a, 1993). The intervention involved health education, training in problem-solving skills, stress management, and social support. Those randomly assigned to the 6-week intervention showed improved mood and active coping relative to the controls, as well as increases in the number of NK cells and in NKCA at 6 months. Most significantly, the intervention group had fewer melanoma recurrences and fewer deaths during the 5- to 6-year follow-up period when compared with the control condition. However, despite the fact that NK cells may play a role in tumor surveillance, results indicated that the NKCA changes induced by the intervention did not mediate the health benefits observed. Thus, health effects may have been due to other unmeasured immune or nonimmune physiological changes produced by the intervention, or to behavioral changes of some kind.

## Conclusion

Stressful life circumstances can suppress aspects of immune functioning. Although true, this oversimplification does not do justice to the complexity of the bidirectional relationships between the mind and the immune system. First, the "mind" is not included in the equation. Although the majority of research focuses on stressful life experience, it is becoming increasingly clear that it is one's perception of circumstances, and the neurophysiological activation patterns that accompany those perceptions, that play a central role in shaping the bodily response to context. In other words, a "stress response," involving activation of the HPA and SNS, along with consequent alterations in the immune system, may depend more heavily on the individual's pattern of responses to his or her life contexts than to the specific nature of the circumstance presented to them. Studies demonstrate that when appraisals are manipulated, distinctive physiological effects can result (Gross & John, 2002; Tomaka & Blascovich, 1994).

The potential health effects of these psychological response differences are highlighted in a study predicting mortality in HIV-positive individuals. In this study, HIV-positive gay and bisexual men who concealed their homosexuality (i.e., were "in the closet") showed accelerated rates of HIV progression, including a more rapid loss of CD4 T cells, and a more rapid onset of AIDS and death (Cole, Kemeny, Taylor, & Visscher, 1996), controlling for biobehavioral confounds. However, the relationship between concealment and HIV progression also depended on the extent to which these men were sensitive to rejection concerning their homosexuality. Concealing one's homosexuality was unrelated to disease progression among men who were highly rejection sensitive, presumably because failing to tell others about one's sexual identify reduced the likelihood of experiencing the outright rejection that these individuals fear (Cole et al., 1998). Overall, then, there may have been a health price of "passing" in individuals due potentially to the inhibition of a core aspect of one's identity or the chronic fear of the consequences of being discovered. However, among rejection-sensitive individuals, concealment appeared to be protective. Thus, the relationship between one's social context—whether or not the social world is aware of one's stigma—and health depended on one's level of sensitivity to rejection from members of that social world. These interactions between context and psychological response provide a clearer picture of the relationship between the mind and health. Adding to these models other critical moderators, such as genetic predispositions and behavioral factors that play a critical role in disease etiology and progression, will improve our ability to predict disease outcomes.

It is also important to note that a relationship between a psychological factor and a change in the immune system may be due to the impact of the mind on the immune system, the effects of the immune system on the mind, both, or neither. Simple cross-sectional correlations across these systems can no longer be interpreted in a unidirectional way. It is now becoming clearer that the immune system can impact the way we think and feel, even in individuals without illness or disease. This research area has provided a new and novel way to understand the predictors of disengagement-related affective states, in particular depression. These findings and new conceptualizations of depression may lead to the development of innovative therapeutic strategies to control these difficult states of mind.

At a conceptual level, we can include the immune system in the list of stress-relevant systems that may play a central role in shaping adaptive responses to both pathogen threats, as well as other environmental threats. Many years ago, fever was viewed as a nuisance side effect of exposure to infectious agents, one to be eliminated as soon as possible. Now, fever is widely recognized to be an important physiological response to pathogens that supports the body's ability to fight infection. Findings in the field of psychoneuroimmunology have demonstrated that the same molecules that control temperature regulation can also regulate our motivation and behavior in the service, again, of supporting immunologic defense mechanisms and recovery from illness. It can be argued that these immune products play a role in adaptation to stressful circumstances and are a fundamental component of the adaptive physiological response to certain environmental threats. Future research will more carefully spell out the elicitors of this response and the way in which it is integrated with the other important aspects of the body's adaptive reaction to stressful situations.

# References

Ackerman, K.D., Martino, M., Heyman, R., Moyna, N.M., & Rabin, B.S. (1998). Stressor-induced alteration of cytokine production in multiple sclerosis patients and controls. *Psychosomatic Medicine, 60*(4), 484–491.

Ader, R. (2000). The placebo effect: If it's all in your head, does that mean you only think you feel better? *Advances in Mind Body Medicine, 16*(1), 7–11.

Ader, R., & Cohen, N. (1975). Behaviorally conditioned immunosuppression. *Psychosomatic Medicine, 37*, 333–340.

Ader, R. (Ed.). (2007). *Psychoneuroimmunology* (4th ed.). Burlington, MA: Elsevier Academic Press.

Antoni, M.H., Schneiderman, N., Penedo, F. (2007). Behavioral interventions: immunologic mediators and disease outcomes. In R. Ader (Ed.), *Psychoneuroimmunology* Vol. 1 (4th ed., pp. 675–703). San Diego, CA: Academic Press.

Avitsur, R., Stark, J.L., & Sheridan, J.F. (2001). Social stress induces glucocorticoid resistance in subordinate animals. *Hormones and Behavior, 39*(4), 247–257.

Ayyavoo, V., Rafaeli, Y., Nagashunmugam, T., Mahalingham, S., Phung, M.T., Hamam, A., et al. (1997). HIV-1 viral protein R(Vpr) as a regulator of the target cell. *Psychoneuroendocrinology, 22*(Suppl. 1), S41–49.

Bellinger, D.L., Millar, B.A., Perez, S., Carter, J., Wood, C., ThyagaRahan, S., et al. (2008). Sympathetic modulation of immunity: Relevance to disease. *Cellular Immunology, 252*, 27–56.

Ben-Eliyahu, S., Yirmiya, R., Liebeskind, J.C., Taylor, A.N., & Gale, R.P. (1991). Stress increases metastatic spread of a mammary tumor in rats: Evidence for mediation by the immune system. *Brain, Behavior, and Immunity, 5*, 193–205.

Benschop, R.I., Nieuwenhuis, E., Tromp, E., Godaert, G., Ballieux, R.E., & van Doornen, L. (1994). Effects of B-adrenergic blockade on immunologic and cardiovascular changes induced by mental stress. *Circulation, 89*, 762–769.

Benschop, R.J., Jacobs, R., Sommer, B., Schurmeyer, T.H., Raab, J.R., Schmidt, R.E., & Schedlowski, M. (1996). Modulation of the immunologic response to acute stress in humans by beta-blockade or benzodiazepines. *Journal of the Federation of American Societies for Experimental Biology, 10*(4), 517–524.

Blascovich, J., & Tomaka, J. (1996). The biopsychosocial model of arousal regulation. *Advances in Experimental Social Psychology, 28*, 1–51.

Bonneau, R.H., Sheridan, J.F., Feng, N., & Glaser, R. (1991a). Stress- induced effects on cell mediated innate and adaptive memory components of the murine immune response to herpes simplex virus infection. *Brain, Behavior, and Immunity, 5*, 274–295.

Bonneau, R.H., Sheridan, J.F., Feng, N., & Glaser, R. (1991b). Stress-induced suppression of herpes simplex virus (HSV)-specific cytotoxic T lymphocyte and natural killer cell activity and enhancement of acute pathogenesis following local HSV infection. *Brain, Behavior, and Immunity, 5*, 170–192.

Bovjberg, D.H., Redd, W.H., Maier, L.A., Holland, J.C., Lesko, L.M., Niedzwiecki, D., et al. (1990). Anticipatory immune suppression in women receiving cyclic chemotherapy for ovarian cancer. *Journal of Consulting and Clinical Psychology, 58*, 153–157.

Cannon, W.B. (1932). *The wisdom of the body.* New York: Norton.

Capitanio, J.P., & Lerche, N.W. (1998). Social separation, housing relocation, and survival in simian AIDS: A retrospective analysis. *Psychosomatic Medicine, 60*(3), 235–244.

Capitanio, J.P., Mendoza, S.P., Lerche, N.W., & Mason, W.A. (1998). Social stress results in altered glucocorticoid regulation and shorter survival in simian acquired immune deficiency syndrome. *Proceedings of the National Academy of Sciences USA, 95*(8), 4714–4719.

Carr, D.J.J., & Weber, R.J. (2001). Opioidergic modulation of the immune system. In R. Ader, D. Felten, & N. Cohen (Eds.), *Psychoneuroimmunology* (3rd ed., pp. 405–414). New York: Elsevier Press.

Castanon, N., Bluthe, R.M., & Dantzer, R. (2001). Chronic treatment with the atypical antidepressant tianeptine attenuates sickness behavior induced by peripheral but not central lipopolysaccharide and interleukin-1beta in the rat. *Psychopharmacology (Berl), 154*(1), 50–60.

Cirulli, F., De Acetis, L., & Alleva, E. (1998). Behavioral effects of peripheral interleukin-1 administration in adult CD-1 mice: Specific inhibition of the offensive components of intermale agonistic behavior. *Brain Research, 791*(1–2), 308–312.

Coe, C.L., Rosenberg, L.T., & Levine, S. (1988). Effect of maternal separation on the complement system and antibody response in infant primates. *International Journal of Neuroscience, 40*, 289–302.

Cohen, F. (1981). Stress and bodily illness. *Psychiatric Clinics of North America, 4*(2), 269–286.

Cohen, S., Frank, E., Doyle, W.J., Skoner, D.P., Rabin, B.S., & Gwaltney, J.M., Jr. (1998). Types of stressors that increase susceptibility to the common cold in healthy adults. *Health Psychology, 17*(3), 214–223.

Cohen, S., & Wills, T.A. (1985). Stress, social support, and the buffering hypothesis. *Psychological Bulletin, 98*, 310–357.

Cole, S.W., & Kemeny, M.E. (2001). Psychosocial influences on the progression of HIV infection. In R. Ader, D.L. Felten, & N. Cohen (Eds.), *Psychoneuroimmunology* Vol. 2 (3rd ed., pp. 583–612). San Diego: Academic Press.

Cole, S.W., Kemeny, M.E., Fahey, J.L., Zack, J.A., & Naliboff, B.D. (2003). Psychological risk factors for HIV pathogenesis: Mediation by the autonomic nervous system. *Biological Psychiatry, 54*, 1444–1456.

Cole, S.W., Kemeny, M.E., & Taylor, S.E. (1997). Social identity and physical health: Accelerated HIV progression in rejection-sensitive gay men. *Journal of Personality and Social Psychology, 72*(2), 320–335.

Cole, S.W., Kemeny, M.E., Taylor, S.E., & Visscher, B.R. (1996). Elevated physical health risk among gay men who conceal their homosexual identity. *Health Psychology, 15*(4), 243–251.

Cole, S.W., Korin, Y.D., Fahey, J.L., & Zack, J.A. (1998). Norepinephrine accelerates HIV replication via protein kinase A-dependent effects on cytokine production. *Journal of Immunology, 161*(2), 610–616.

Cole, S.W., Naliboff, B.D., Kemeny, M.E., Griswold, M.P., Fahey, J.L., & Zack, J.A. (2001). Impaired response to HAART in HIV-infected individuals with high autonomic nervous system activity. *Proceedings of the National Academy of Sciences USA, 98*(22), 12695–12700.

Damasio, A.R., Grabowski, T.J., Bechara, A., Damasio, H., Ponto, L.L., Parvizi, J., & Hichwa, R.D. (2000). Subcortical and cortical brain activity during the feeling of self-generated emotions. *Nature Neuroscience, 3*(10), 1049–1056.

Dantzer, R., Bluthe, R., Castanon, N., Cauvet, N., Capuron, L., Goodall, G., et al. (2001). Cytokine effects on behavior. In R. Ader, D.L. Felten, & N. Cohen (Eds.), *Psychoneuroimmunology* Vol. 1 (3rd ed., pp. 703–727). New York: Academic Press.

Davidson, R.J. (1998). Affective style and affective disorders: Perspectives from affective neuroscience. *Cognition and Emotion, 12*, 307–330.

Davidson, R.J., Coe, C.C., Dolski, I., & Donzella, B. (1999). Individual differences in prefrontal activation asymmetry predict natural killer cell activity at rest and in response to challenge. *Brain, Behavior, and Immunity, 13*(2), 93–108.

Davidson, R.J., Kabat-Zinn, J., Schumacher, J., Rosenkranz, M., Muller, D., Santorelli, S.F., et al. (2003). Alterations in brain and immune function produced by mindfulness meditation. *Psychosomatic Medicine, 65*(4), 564–570.

Dhabhar, F.S. (2003). Stress, leukocyte trafficking, and the augmentation of skin immune function. *Annals of the New York Academy of Sciences, 992*, 205–217.

Dhabhar, F.S., & McEwen, B.S. (2001). Bidirectional effects of stress and glucocorticoid hormones on immune function: Possible explanations for paradoxical observations. In R. Ader, D.L. Felten, & N. Cohen (Eds.), *Psychoneuroimmunology* Vol. 1 (3rd ed., pp. 301–338). New York: Academic Press.

Dickerson, S.S., Gable, S.L., Irwin, M.R., Aziz, N., & Kemeny, M.E. (2009). Social-evaluation threat and proinflammatory cytokine regulation: An experimental laboratory investigation. *Psychological Science, 20*(10), 1237–1244.

Dickerson, S.S., Gruenewald, T.L., & Kemeny, M.E. (2004). When the social self is threatened: Shame, physiology, and health. *Journal of Personality, 72*(6), 1191–1216.

Dickerson, S.S., & Kemeny, M.E. (2004). Acute stressors and cortisol responses: A theoretical integration and synthesis of laboratory research. *Psychological Bulletin, 130*(3), 355–391.

Dickerson, S.S., Kemeny, M.E., Aziz, N., Kim, K.H., & Fahey, J.L. (2004). Immunological effects of induced shame and guilt. *Psychosomatic Medicine, 66*(1), 124–131.

Ekman, P., Levenson, R.W., & Friesen, W.V. (1983). Autonomic nervous system activity distinguishes among emotions. *Science, 221*(4616), 1208–1210.

Elenkov, I.J., Wilder, R.L., Chrousos, G.P., & Vizi, E.S. (2000). The sympathetic nerve—an integrative interface between two supersystems: The brain and the immune system. *Pharmacological Reviews, 52*(4), 595–638.

Ershler, W.B., & Keller, E.T. (2000). Age-associated increased interleukin-6 gene expression, late-life diseases, and frailty. *Annual Review of Medicine, 51*, 245–270.

Esterling, B.A., Antoni, M.H., Kumar, M., & Schneiderman, N. (1990). Emotional repression, stress disclosure responses, and Epstein-Barr viral capsid antigen titers. *Psychosomatic Medicine, 52*, 397–410.

Fahdi, I.E., Gaddam, V., Garza, L., Romeo, F., & Mehta, J.L. (2003). Inflammation, infection, and atherosclerosis. *Brain, Behavior, and Immunity, 17*(4), 238–244.

Fawzy, F.I., Cousins, N., Fawzy, N.W., Kemeny, M.E., Elashoff, R., & Morton, D. (1990a). A structured psychiatric intervention for cancer patients: I. Changes over time in methods of coping and affective disturbance. *Archives of General Psychiatry, 47*(8), 720–725.

Fawzy, F.I., Fawzy, N.W., Hyun, C.S., Elashoff, R., Guthrie, D., Fahey, J.L., & Morton, D.L. (1993). Malignant melanoma. Effects of an early structured psychiatric intervention, coping, and affective state on recurrence and survival 6 years later. *Archives of General Psychiatry, 50*(9), 681–689.

Fawzy, F.I., Kemeny, M.E., Fawzy, N.W., Elashoff, R., Morton, D., Cousins, N., & Fahey, J.L. (1990). A structured psychiatric intervention for cancer patients: II. Changes over time in immunological measures. *Archives of General Psychiatry, 47*(8), 729–735.

Felten, D.L., & Felten, S.Y. (1988). Sympathetic noradrenergic innervation of immune organs. *Brain, Behavior, and Immunity, 2*(4), 293–300.

Fleshner, M., Laudenslager, M.L., Simons, L., & Maier, S.F. (1989). Reduced serum antibodies associated with social defeat in rats. *Physiology and Behavior, 45*(6), 1183–1187.

Futterman, A.D., Kemeny, M.E., Shapiro, D., & Fahey, J.L. (1994). Immunological and physiological changes associated with induced positive and negative mood. *Psychosomatic Medicine, 56*(6), 499–511.

Glaser, R. (2005). Stress-associated immune dysregulation and its importance for human health: A personal history of psychoneuroimmunology. *Brain, Behavior, and Immunity, 19*(1), 3–11. doi: S0889–1591(04)00076–5 [pii].

Glaser, R., & Kiecolt-Glaser, J.K. (2005). Stress-induced immune dysfunction: Implications for health. *Nature Reviews Immunology, 5*(3), 243–251. doi: nri1571 [pii] 10.1038/nri1571 [doi].

Goebel, M.U., Trebst, A.E., Steiner, J., Xie, Y.F., Exton, M.S., Frede, S., et al. (2002). Behavioral conditioning of immunosuppression is possible in humans. *Journal of the Federation of American Societies for Experimental Biology, 16*(14), 1869–1873. doi: 10.1096/fj.02–0389com.

Gross, J.J., & John, O.P. (2002). Wise emotion regulation. In L.F. Barrett, & P. Salovey (Eds.), *The wisdom of feelings: Psychological processes in emotional intelligence*. New York: Guilford.

Gruenewald, T.L., Kemeny, M.E., Aziz, N., & Fahey, J.L. (2006). Acute threat to the social self: Subjective social status, self-conscious emotions and HPA activity. *Brain, Behavior & Immunity, 20*(4), 410–419.

Guess, H.A., Kleinman, A., Kusek, J.W., & Engel, L.W. (2002). *The science of the placebo: Toward an interdisciplinary research agenda*. London: BMJ Books.

Herbert, T.B., & Cohen, S. (1993a). Depression and immunity: A meta-analytic review. *Psychological Bulletin, 113*, 472–486.

Herbert, T.B., & Cohen, S. (1993b). Stress and immunity in humans: A meta-analytic review. *Psychosomatic Medicine, 55*, 364–379.

Herbert, T.B., Cohen, S., Marsland, A.L., Bachen, E.A., Rabin, B.S., Muldoon, M.F., & Manuck, S.B. (1994). Cardiovascular reactivity and the course of immune response to an acute psychological stressor. *Psychosomatic Medicine, 56*, 337–344.

Irwin, M. (2001). Depression and immunity. In R. Ader, D.L. Felten, & N. Cohen (Eds.), *Psychoneuroimmunology* Vol. 2 (3rd ed., pp. 383–398). New York: Academic Press.

Irwin, M., Daniels, M., Bloom, E.T., & Weiner, H. (1986). Life events, depression, and natural killer cell activity. *Psychopharmacology Bulletin, 22*(4), 1093–1096.

Irwin, M.R., Lacher, U., & Caldwell, C. (1992). Depression and reduced natural killer cytotoxicity: A longitudinal study of depressed patients and control subjects. *Psychological Medicine, 22*, 1045–1050.

Kalin, N.H., Larson, C., Shelton, S.E., & Davidson, R.I. (1998). Asymmetric frontal brain activity cortisol, and behavior associated with fearful temperament in Rhesus monkeys. *Behavioral Neuroscience, 112*, 286–292.

Kang, D.H., Davidson, R.I., Coe, C.L., Wheeler, R.W., Tomarken, A.J., & Ershler, W.B. (1991). Frontal brain asymmetry and immune function. *Behavioral Neuroscience, 105*, 860–869.

Keller, S.E., Weiss, J.M., Schleifer, S.J., Miller, N.E., & Stein, M. (1983). Stress-induced suppression of immunity in adrenalectomized rats. *Science, 221*, 1301–1304.

Kelley, K.W., Weigent, D.A., & Kooijman, R. (2007). Protein hormones and immunity. *Brain, Behavior, and Immunity, 21*(4), 384–392. doi: S0889–1591(06)00361–8 [pii] 10.1016/j.bbi.2006.11.010 [doi].

Kemeny, M.E. (1991). Psychological factors, immune processes and the course of herpes simplex and human immunodeficiency virus infection. In N. Plotnikoff, A. Murgo, R. Faith, & J. Wybran (Eds.), *Stress and immunity* (pp. 199–210). Boca Raton, FL: CRC Press, Inc.

Kemeny, M.E. (2003). An interdisciplinary research model to investigate psychosocial cofactors in disease: Application to HIV-1 pathogenesis. *Brain, Behavior, and Immunity, 17*, 62–72.

Kemeny, M.E (2009). Presidential Address: Psychobiological responses to social threat: evolution of a psychological model in psychoneuroimmunology. *Brain, Behavior & Immunity, 23*(1), 1–9.

Kemeny, M.E., & Dean, L. (1995). Effects of AIDS-related bereavement on HIV progression among New York City gay men. *AIDS Education and Prevention, 7*(Suppl.), 36–47.

Kemeny, M.E., & Gruenewald, T.L. (2000). Affect, cognition, the immune system and health. In E.A. Mayer, & C.B. Saper (Eds.), *The biological basis for mind body interactions* Vol. 122 (1st ed., pp. 291–308). New York: Elsevier Science.

Kemeny, M.E., Gruenewald, T.L. & Dickerson, S.S. (2004). Shame as the emotional response to threat to the social self: implications for behavior, physiology, and heath. *Psychological Inquiry, 15*(2), 153–160.

Kemeny, M.E., & Laudenslager, M. (1999). Beyond stress: The role of individual differences factors in psychoneuroimmunologic relationships. *Brain, Behavior, and Immunity, 13*, 73–75.

Kemeny, M.E., & Miller, G. (1999). Effects of psychosocial interventions on the immune system. In M. Schedlowski, & U. Tewes (Eds.), *Psychoneuroimmunology: An interdisciplinary introduction* (pp. 373–416). New York: Plenum Publishing.

Kemeny, M.E., Rosenwasser, L.J., Panettieri, R.A., Rose, R.M., Berg-Smith, S.M., & Kline, J.N. (2007). Placebo response in asthma: A robust and objective phenomenon. *Journal of Allergy and Clinical Immunology, 119*(6), 1375–1381. doi: S0091–6749(07)00577–5 [pii] 10.1016/j.jaci.2007.03.016 [doi].

Kemeny, M.E., & Schedlowski, M. (2007). Understanding the interaction between psychosocial stress and immune-related diseases: A stepwise progression. *Brain, Behavior, and Immunity, 21*(8), 1009–1018. doi: S0889–1591(07)00160–2 [pii] 10.1016/j.bbi.2007.07.010 [doi].

Kent, S., Bluthe, R.M., Kelley, K.W., & Dantzer, R. (1992). Sickness behavior as a new target for drug development. *Trends in Pharmacological Sciences, 13*, 24–28.

Kiecolt-Glaser, J.K., Garner, W., Speicher, C., Penn, G.M., Holliday, J., & Glaser, R. (1984). Psychosocial modifiers of immunocompetence in medical students. *Psychosomatic Medicine, 46*, 7–17.

Kiecolt-Glaser, J.K., Glaser, J., Williger, D., Stout, J., Messick, G., Sheppard, S., et al. (1985). Psychosocial enhancement of immunocompetence in a geriatric population. *Health Psychology, 4*, 25.

Kiecolt-Glaser, J.K., & Glaser, R. (2001). Psychological stress and wound healing: Kiecolt-Glaser et al. (1995). *Advances in Mind Body Medicine, 17*(1), 15–16.

Kiecolt-Glaser, J.K., Glaser, R., Strain, E.C., Stout, I.C., Tarr, K.L., Holliday, I.E., & Speicher, C.E. (1986). Modulation of cellular immunity in medical students. *Journal of Behavioral Medicine, 9*, 5–21.

Kiecolt-Glaser, J.K., Marucha, P.T., Malarkey, W.B., Mercado, A.M., & Glaser, R. (1995). Slowing of wound healing by psychological stress. *Lancet, 346*(8984), 1194–1196.

Kop, W.J. (1999). Chronic and acute psychological risk factors for clinical manifestations of coronary artery disease. *Psychosomatic Medicine, 61*(4), 476–487.

Korneva, E.A. (1967). The effect of stimulating different mesencephalic structures on protective immune response patterns. *Sechenov Physiological Journal of the USSR, 53*, 42–50.

Lane, R.D., Reiman, E.M., Ahern, G.L., Schwartz, G.E., & Davidson, R.J. (1997). Neuroanatomical correlates of happiness, sadness, and disgust. *American Journal of Psychiatry, 154*(7), 926–933.

Leserman, J. (2000). The effects of depression, stressful life events, social support, and coping on the progression of HIV infection. *Current Psychiatry Reports, 2*(6), 495–502.

Leserman, J., Petitto, J.M., Golden, R.N., Gaynes, B.N., Gu, H., Perkins, D.O., et al. (2000). Impact of stressful life events, depression, social support, coping, and cortisol on progression to AIDS. *American Journal of Psychiatry, 157*(8), 1221–1228.

Lysle, D.T., Lyte, M., Fowler, H., & Rabin, B.S. (1987). Shock-induced modulation of lymphocyte reactivity: Suppression, habituation, and recovery. *Life Sciences, 41*, 1805–1814.

Maes, M., Scharpe, S., Meltzer, H.Y., Okayli, G., Bosmans, E., D'Hondt, P., et al. (1994). Increased neopterin and interferon-gamma secretion and lower availability of L-tryptophan in major depression: Further evidence for an immune response. *Psychiatry Research, 54*, 143–160.

Maier, S.F., & Watkins, L.R. (1998). Cytokines for psychologists: Implications of bidirectional immune-to-brain communication for understanding behavior, mood, and cognition. *Psychological Review, 105*, 83–107.

Markham, P.D., Salahuddin, S.Z., Veren, K., Orndorff, S., & Gallo, R.C. (1986). Hydrocortisone and some other hormones enhance the expression of HTLV-III. *International Journal of Cancer, 37*(1), 67–72.

Marsland, A.L., Pressman, S., & Cohen, S. (2007). Positive Affect and Immune Function. In R. Ader (Ed.), *Psychoneuroimmunology* (4th ed.) (761–780). Burlington, MA: Elsevier Academic Press.

McEwen, B.S. (1998). Protective and damaging effects of stress mediators. *New England Journal of Medicine, 338*, 171–179.

McEwen, B.S., Biron, C.A., Brunson, K.W., Bulloch, K., Chambers, W.H., Dhabhar, F.S., et al. (1997). The role of adrenocorticoids as modulators of immune function in health and disease: Neural, endocrine and immune interactions. *Brain Research, 23*(1–2), 79–133.

Miller, G.E., Chen, E., Fok, A.K., Walker, H., Lim, A., Nicholls, E.F., et al. (2009). Low early-life social class leaves a biological residue manifested by decreased glucocorticoid and increased proinflammatory signaling. *Proceedings of the National Academy of Sciences USA, 106*(34), 14716–14721. doi: 10.1073/pnas.0902971106.

Miller, G.E., Chen, E., Sze, J., Marin, T., Arevalo, J.M., Doll, R., et al. (2008). A functional genomic fingerprint of chronic stress in humans: Blunted glucocorticoid and increased NF-kappaB signaling. *Biological Psychiatry, 64*(4), 266–272. doi: S0006–3223(08)00361–2 [pii] 10.1016/j.biopsych.2008.03.017 [doi].

Miller, G.E., & Cohen, S. (2001). Psychological interventions and the immune system: A meta-analytic review and critique. *Health Psychology, 20*(1), 47–63.

Miller, G.E., Cohen, S., & Ritchey, A.K. (2002). Chronic psychological stress and the regulation of pro-inflammatory cytokines: A glucocorticoid-resistance model. *Health Psychology, 21*(6), 531–541.

Miller, G.E., Stetler, C.A., Carney, R.M., Freedland, K.E., & Banks, W.A. (2002). Clinical depression and inflammatory risk markers for coronary heart disease. *American Journal of Cardiology, 90*(12), 1279–1283.

Moynihan, J.A., & Stevens, S.Y. (2001). Mechanisms of stress-induced modulation of immunity in animals. In R. Ader, D. Felten, & N. Cohen (Eds.), *Psychoneuroimmunology* (3rd ed., pp. 227–249). New York: Elsevier Press.

Ottaway, C.A., & Husband, A.J. (1992). Central nervous system influences on lymphocyte migration. *Brain, Behavior, and Immunity, 6*(2), 97–116.

Petrie, K.L., Booth, R.J., Pennebaker, J.W., Davison, K.P., & Thomas, M.G. (1995). Disclosure of trauma and immune response to a hepatitis B vaccination program. *Journal of Consulting and Clinical Psychology, 63*, 787–792.

Pike, J.L., Smith, T.L., Hauger, R.L., Nicassio, P.M., Patterson, T.L., McClintick, J., et al. (1997). Chronic life stress alters sympathetic, neuroendocrine, and immune responsivity to an acute psychological stressor in humans. *Psychosomatic Medicine, 59*(4), 447–457.

Reed, G.M., Kemeny, M.E., Taylor, S.E., & Visscher, B.R. (1999). Negative HIV-specific expectancies and AIDS-related bereavement as predictors of symptom onset in asymptomatic HIV-positive gay men. *Health Psychology, 18*(4), 354–363.

Reed, G.M., Kemeny, M.E., Taylor, S.E., Wang, H.Y., & Visscher, B.R. (1994). Realistic acceptance as a predictor of decreased survival time in gay men with AIDS. *Health Psychology, 13*(4), 299–307.

Ridker, P.M., Cushman, M., Stampfer, M.J., Tracy, R.P., & Hennekens, C.H. (1997). Inflammation, aspirin, and the risk of cardiovascular disease in apparently healthy men. *New England Journal of Medicine, 336*(14), 973–979.

Sapolsky, R.M. (1993). Endocrinology alfresco: Psychoendocrine studies of wild baboons. *Recent Progress in Hormone Research, 48,* 437–468.

Schedlowski, M., Jacobs, R., Alker, J., Prohl, F., Stratmann, G., Richter, S., et al. (1993). Psychophysiological, neuroendocrine and cellular immune reactions under psychological stress. *Neuropsychobiology, 28,* 87–90.

Schleifer, S.J., Keller, S.E., Meyerson, A.T., Raskin, M.J., Davis, K.L., & Stein, M. (1984). Lymphocyte function in major depressive disorder. *Archives of General Psychiatry, 41,* 484.

Segerstrom, S., Kemeny, M.E., & Laudenslager, M. (2001). Individual differences in immunologic reactivity. In R. Ader, D.L. Felten, & N. Cohen (Eds.), *Psychoneuroimmunology* (3rd ed., pp. 87–109). New York: Academic Press.

Segerstrom, S.C., Glover, D.A., Craske, M.G., & Fahey, J.L. (1999). Worry affects the immune response to phobic fear. *Brain, Behavior, and Immunity, 13*(2), 80–92.

Segerstrom, S.C., & Miller, G.E. (2004). Psychological stress and the human immune system: A meta-analytic study of 30 years of inquiry. *Psychological Bulletin 130*(4), 601–630.

Segerstrom, S.C., & Sephton, S.E. (2010). Optimistic expectancies and cell-mediated immunity: The role of positive affect. *Psychological Science, 21*(3), 448–455. doi: 10.1177/0956797 610362061.

Segerstrom, S.C., Solomon, G.F., Kemeny, M.E., & Fahey, J.L. (1998). Relationship of worry to immune sequelae of the Northridge earthquake. *Journal of Behavioral Medicine, 21*(5), 433–450.

Segerstrom, S.C., Taylor, S.E., Kemeny, M.E., Reed, G.M., & Visscher, B.R. (1996). Causal attributions predict rate of immune decline in HIV-seropositive gay men. *Health Psychology, 15*(6), 485–493.

Shavit, Y., Martin, F.C., Yirmiya, R., Ben-Eliyahu, S., Terman, G.W., Weiner, H., et al. (1987). Effects of a single administration of morphine or footshock stress on natural killer cell cytotoxicity. *Brain, Behavior, and Immunity, 1*(4), 318–328.

Sherwood, L. (1993). *Human physiology: From cells to systems* (2nd ed.). St. Paul, MN: West Publishing Company.

Shively, C.A., Laber-Laird, K., & Anton, R.F. (1997). Behavior and physiology of social stress and depression in female cynomolgus monkeys. *Biological Psychiatry, 41*(8), 871–882.

Sloan, E., Collado-Hidalgo, A., & Cole, S. (2007). Psychobiology of HIV infection. In R. Ader (Ed.), *Psychoneuroimmunology* Vol. 1 (pp. 1053–1076). New York: Academic Press.

Solomon, G. (1969). Stress and antibody response in rats. *Archives of Allergy, 35,* 97–104.

Solomon, G.F. (1968). Early experience and immunity. *Nature, 220*(169), 821–822.

Solomon, G.F., & Moos, R.H. (1964). Emotions, immunity, and disease: A speculative theoretical integration. *Archives of General Psychiatry, 11,* 657–674.

Solvason, H.B., Ghanta, V.K., & Hiramoto, R.N. (1988). Conditioned augmentation of natural killer cell activity: Independence from nociceptive effects and dependence on interferon-beta. *Journal of Immunology, 140,* 661–665.

Stark, J.L., Avitsur, R., Padgett, D.A., Campbell, K.A., Beck, F.M., & Sheridan, J.F. (2001). Social stress induces glucocorticoid resistance in macrophages. *American Journal of Physiology: Regulatory, Integrative, Comparative, Physiology, 280*(6), R1799–1805.

Stefanski, V. (1998). Social stress in loser rats: Opposite immunological effects in submissive and subdominant males. *Physiology and Behavior, 63,* 605–613.

Sternberg, E.M. (1997). Neural-immune interactions in health and disease. *Journal of Clinical Investigation, 100,* 2641–2647.

Stone, A.A., Cox, D.S., Valdlmarsdottir, H., Jandorf, L., & Neale, J.M. (1987). Evidence that secretory IgA antibody is associated with daily mood. *Journal of Personality and Social Psychology, 52,* 988–993.

Strauman, T.J., Lemieux, A.M., & Coe, C.L. (1993). Self-discrepancy and natural killer cell activity: Immunological consequences of negative self-evaluation. *Journal of Personality and Social Psychology, 64,* 1042–1052.

Tomaka, J., & Blascovich, J. (1994). Effects of justice beliefs on cognitive appraisal of and subjective, physiological, and behavioral responses to potential stress. *Journal of Personality and Social Psychology, 67*(4), 732–740.

Van Tits, L.J.H., Michel, M.C., Grosse-Wilde, H., Rappel, M., Eigler, F.W., Soliman, A., & Brodde, O.E. (1990). Catecholamines increase lymphocyte β2-adrenergic receptors via a β2-andrenergic, spleen-dependent process. *American Journal of Physiology, 258,* E191–E202.

Wager, T.D., Rilling, J.K., Smith, E.E., Sokolik, A., Casey, K.L., Davidson, R.J., et al. (2004). Placebo-induced changes in FMRI in the anticipation and experience of pain. *Science, 303*(5661), 1162–1167.

Webster, J.I., Tonelli, L., & Sternberg, E.M. (2002). Neuroendocrine regulation of immunity. *Annual Review of Immunology, 20,* 125–163. doi: 10.1146/annurev. immunol.20.082401.104914.

Webster Marketon, J.I., & Glaser, R. (2008). Stress hormones and immune function. *Cell Immunology, 252*(1–2), 16–26. doi: 10.1016/j.cellimm.2007.09.006.

Weiner, H. (1992). *Perturbing the organism: The biology of stressful experiences.* Chicago, IL: The University of Chicago Press.

Worlein, J.M., & Laudenslager, M.L. (2001). Effects of early rearing experiences and social interactions on immune function in nonhuman primates. In R. Ader, D.L. Felten, & N. Cohen (Eds.), *Psychoneuroimmunology* Vol. 2 (3rd ed., pp. 73–85). New York: Academic Press.

Yirmiya, R., Weidenfeld, J., Pollak, U., Morag, M., Morag, A., Avitsur, R., et al. (1999). Cytokines, "depression due to a general medical condition," and antidepressant drugs. In R. Dantzer, E. Wollman, & R. Yirmiya (Eds.), *Cytokines, stress and depression* (pp. 283–316). New York: Kluwer Academic.

# Stress, Coping, and Health

Charles S. Carver *and* Sara Vargas

**Abstract**

This chapter addresses the confluence of two sets of processes—stress and coping—as they come to bear on health. It first addresses the following questions: What defines the experience of stress? What defines coping? What sorts of distinctions among coping responses are useful, or even necessary? Finally, how do processes of stress and coping interweave to influence health? Addressing this last question entails confronting at least two further issues: What boundaries must be placed around the construct of "health," and by what pathways might health be affected by stress and coping? After considering these issues, the chapter describes selected evidence from several areas of research on how stress and coping influence health.

**Keywords:** Stress, coping, health impact, coping response

This chapter addresses the confluence of two sets of processes as they come to bear on a class of outcomes. The processes are stress and coping. The outcome is health. This topic is enormous in its scope (see, e.g., Compas, Connor-Smith, Saltzman, Thomsen, & Wadsworth, 2001; Folkman & Moskowitz, 2004: Folkman, 2009; Skinner, Edge, Altman, & Sherwood, 2003). It will be obvious, then, that this chapter does not fully survey all of the relevant research and theory. Rather, it addresses a set of basic issues, problems, and conceptual themes that have arisen in several distinct literatures bearing on these topics.

To begin, we must consider some questions. First, exactly what defines the experience of stress? Although models have been proposed over the years that differ somewhat in focus, it appears possible to extract from them a common core of shared themes. Next, what defines coping? Furthermore, what sorts of distinctions among coping responses are useful, or even necessary? Finally, how do processes of stress and coping interweave to influence health? Addressing this last question entails confronting at

least two further issues: What boundaries must be placed around the construct of "health," and by what pathways might health be affected by stress and coping? After considering these issues, we describe selected evidence from several areas of research on how stress and coping influence health.

## What Is Stress?

What is the nature of stress? We adopt here the view that stress should be viewed within the context of behavior more generally. For that reason, before turning to stress per se, we briefly sketch a view of some of the processes involved in behavior. Although there are many ways to think about how people go about their activities, the family of viewpoints that tends to dominate discussions of motivated action today derives from a long tradition of expectancy-value models of motivation.

### Self-regulation of Action

A common view in contemporary psychology is that human behavior is organized around the pursuit of goals or incentives (Austin & Vancouver, 1996;

Bandura, 1986; Carver & Scheier, 1998; Elliott, 2008; Higgins, 1996; Pervin, 1989). Such a view assumes that goals energize and direct activities, that goals give meaning to people's lives, that understanding a person means understanding that person's goals. Indeed, in this view, it is often implicit that the self consists partly of the person's goals (starting with the desired sense of self and ranging downward or outward to goals of less complexity) and the organization among them.

It is important to realize that, although some goals have a static endpoint quality (to have a task completed), others are dynamic. The goal of taking a vacation is not to be sitting in your driveway at the end of 2 weeks but to experience the events of the vacation. The goal of developing a relationship is not to create a static endpoint, because relationships continue to grow and evolve over time. Some goals are moving targets. An example is career development. Just about the time you reach the level of complexity you had in mind for your career, you realize there is something else you want to add in. Goals vary substantially in their breadth. Some concern what kind of person you want to be; some concern things you want to do.

Goals provide the "value" in the expectancy-value model of motivation. When a person has an aspiration, a desired goal, the incentive value is what pulls behavior into motion. In this view, if there were no goals (not even trivial ones), there would be no action. A goal, an incentive, provides something to strive toward. This is true even when the goal is mundane—for example, reaching out to pick up a coffee cup at breakfast.

Although it may be less obvious, there also exist what might be viewed as "anti-goals": values, endpoints, or events that people want to avoid and distance themselves from. Examples are traffic tickets, public ridicule, physical pain, and premature death. People's behavior sometimes is motivated by the attempt to escape or avoid these sorts of aversive values, rather than by the attempt to approach incentives.

It is now widely believed that avoidance is managed by one set of neural mechanisms and approach by a somewhat different set (e.g., Davidson, 1998; Depue & Collins, 1999; Gray, 1994; Rothbart & Hwang, 2005). Sometimes both sets of processes are engaged at once, because sometimes attaining a desired incentive will simultaneously forestall a threat that the person wants to avoid. Sometimes, however, behavior is dominated largely by either approach or avoidance.

If goals provide the "values" in expectancy-value models of motivation, the "expectancy" is provided by—well, goal-related expectancies. Expectancies are the degree of confidence or doubt that a given outcome can be attained successfully. Sometimes this is expressed as a probability of attaining the outcome; sometimes it is expressed instead as a dichotomy. Effects of confidence and doubt can be seen even before a behavior is begun. If the person is doubtful enough about a successful outcome, the behavior will not even be attempted. It requires some degree of confidence to try, and it requires a degree of confidence to keep trying when things get difficult. It is undeniable that goal-directed efforts often become entangled in impediments of various sorts. Diverse theories propose that even under conditions of extreme impediment, people's efforts will be determined partly by their expectancies of success (e.g., Bandura, 1986; Brehm & Self, 1989; Carver & Scheier, 1981, 1998; Klinger, 1975; Wortman & Brehm, 1975; Wright, 1996).

No view of action can be complete without emotions. Emotions often arise when people engage in (or even think about) behavior. Emotions are also an important aspect of stress (Lazarus, 1999). Carver and Scheier (1998) have argued that feelings arise from a system that monitors the effectiveness with which people move toward incentives and away from threats. In essence, feelings are an internal signal that progress toward a goal either is too slow (negative affect) or is faster than necessary (positive affect). Although the details of that view are more complex, the main point for now is simply that negative feelings arise when there are obstacles to goal attainment (or anti-goal avoidance). These negative feelings are related to the sense of confidence versus doubt, but they are also partly distinct from it.

Mentioning obstacles also serves as a reminder that not every behavior produces its intended outcome, not even with extreme exertion of effort. Sometimes the obstacles are just too great. Sometimes people stop trying, and sometimes they give up the goal they had been pursuing. Indeed, giving up on some of our goals is a developmental necessity of life (Wrosch, Scheier, Miller, Schulz, & Carver, 2003).

A basis exists for arguing that certain kinds of negative feelings (depression) are critical to the process by which people turn aside from one incentive and search for another one (Klinger, 1975; Nesse, 2000). As long as the person remains committed to a particular goal, inability to move in the appropriate direction remains distressing. If the person is able to disengage from commitment to that goal, however, there no longer is a basis for the distress. It may be that the level of the distress (and its duration) provides the impetus to give up. Interestingly, some evidence suggests that disengagement is more likely, and more successful, in the context of goal seeking than in the context of anti-goal avoidance (Lench & Levine, 2008).

Generally speaking, when a goal is abandoned, it is important that the person eventually take up another. The absence of a goal yields a sense of emptiness that can be quite problematic (Carver & Scheier, 2003). Disengagement seems to be a valuable and adaptive response in life when it leads to—or is tied to—the taking up of other goals (Aspinwall & Richter, 1999; Miller & Wrosch, 2007; Wrosch et al., 2003). By taking up an attainable alternative, the person remains engaged in activities that have meaning for the self, and life continues to have purpose.

An alternative to giving up on an unattainable goal is to scale it back to something more restricted (Carver & Scheier, 2003). This is a kind of disengagement, in the sense that the initial goal no longer remains in place once the scaling back has occurred. It avoids a complete disengagement from the behavioral domain in question, however, by substituting the more restricted goal. This shift thus keeps the person involved in that area of life, at a level that holds the potential for successful outcomes.

The principles just outlined are about behavior in general. They also have value when thinking more specifically about stress and coping. We now turn to models of stress and show how that may be so.

### Stress: Lazarus and Folkman

Most contemporary views of stress and coping trace in one way or another to the work of Richard Lazarus and Susan Folkman and their colleagues (e.g., Lazarus, 1966, 1999; Lazarus & Folkman, 1984). The model they developed assumes that stress exists when a person confronts circumstances that tax or exceed his or her ability to manage them. This places the experience of stress in the domain of behavior in which obstacles or difficulties are being confronted. When people find themselves hard-pressed to deal with some impediment or some looming threat, stress exists.

The Lazarus and Folkman model incorporates several themes that have had a large impact on others' thinking. One theme is that stress arises from the person's appraisal of circumstances, rather than the objective circumstances. The appraisal depends both on information contained in the situation and

on information inside the person. This initial appraisal is a perception of threat, harm, or challenge. Threat appraisal is the perception of the impending occurrence of a bad or harmful event. Harm appraisal is the perception that something bad has already happened. Challenge appraisal is the perception that one can gain or grow from what nonetheless will be a demanding encounter.

In all these cases, there are impediments to desired conditions either looming or already in place. Work in the Lazarus and Folkman tradition has typically focused on the experience of the stress per se, rather than on the broader matrix of behavior within which the stressor emerges. However, it seems clear that threats often represent imminent interference with pursuit of desired activities, goals, or conditions. For example, a serious illness threatens one's life goals, one's golf game, and one's perception of reality. In the same way, many kinds of harm are actually instances of loss (a term that is sometimes used in place of harm). Loss is the perception that a desired object or condition is no longer present or available. Loss thus precludes the continued existence of a desired state of affairs. For example, the death of a spouse prevents continuation of the relationship.

Sometimes threat and harm involve impediments to desired goals. But sometimes threat and harm appraisal involve impending anti-goals. An example is the experience of pain (e.g., Affleck, Tennen, Pfeiffer, & Fifield, 1987). Chronic pain does disrupt effort to engage in desired activities (i.e., to move toward goals), but that usually is a secondary effect of pain. Pain is, at its core, an aversive experience that the person would rather not have (an anti-goal). Some harm events represent the occurrence of such anti-goals (pain being only one example). Some threats similarly represent perceptions of the imminent arrival of an anti-goal. Thus, threat and harm can involve the avoidance motivational system as well as the approach system.

Here are some more examples. With respect to approach, a person can be threatened by doubt about receiving a sought-after promotion. With respect to avoidance, a person can be threatened by a sudden movement in a dark alley or the sound of a tornado. There are differences in the affects that arise from failing in approach and failing in avoidance (Carver, 2004; Carver & Harmon-Jones, 2009; Higgins, 1996). Although general distress is common to both cases, threat in a purely approach context should yield frustration and anger, whereas threat in a purely avoidance context should yield anxiety and fear.

Challenge in the Lazarus and Folkman model is a special case, one that is quite different conceptually from those of threat and harm. A challenge appraisal reveals a situation in which the person's efforts must be fully engaged, but in which the person perceives an opportunity for gain or growth—a chance to move forward. Challenge is a situation in which the person confronts what might be viewed as an "optimal" obstacle—one that appears surmountable (given appropriate effort) and the removal of which will lead to a better state of affairs than just a return to the status quo (see also Carver, 1998).

Challenge seems to involve engagement of the approach system but not the avoidance system. Further, challenge seems to imply confidence about being able to reach the goal (unless the challenge is accompanied by threat). Affects stemming from challenge are such positive feelings as hope, eagerness, and excitement (Lazarus & Folkman, 1984). Although Lazarus and Folkman posited challenge to be stressful, its characteristics (and its consequences) appear to be different enough from those of threat and loss as to cast doubt on that view (see Blascovich, 2008).

Another theme embedded in the Lazarus–Folkman model is that there is a dynamic, continuous evaluation of both the situation and one's readiness to respond to it. This is reflected in a second appraisal process. People don't always respond to stress reflexively. They often appraise their chances of being able to deal with the stressor effectively. They weigh various options and consider the consequences of those options before acting. Decisions about how to cope depend in part on implicit confidence or doubt about the usefulness of a particular response. Thus, issues of confidence and doubt, as well as the disruption of intended courses of behavior, are embedded in this theoretical model.

The two appraisal processes are presumed to be interwoven, so that they mutually influence each other. For example, if a threat is appraised as being strong enough, it begins to cast doubt on one's ability to handle it. Similarly, the recognition that one has a perfect response available for use can diminish the experience of threat. Although the Lazarus and Folkman model is usually presented as a sequence of processes, its authors were explicit in indicating that both processes are continuous and interdependent.

### Conservation of Resources: Hobfoll
Another view on the experience of stress, developed by Stevan Hobfoll (1989, 1998), begins with the idea that people have an accumulation of resources that they try to protect, defend, and conserve. A person's resources can be physical (e.g., a house, a car, clothing); they can be conditions of current life (e.g., having friends and relatives, stable employment, sound marriage); they can be personal qualities (e.g., a positive view of the world, work skills, social prowess); or they can be energy resources (e.g., money, credit, or knowledge). Resources are anything that the person values.

This theory holds that people try to conserve the resources they have, and acquire further resources. From this viewpoint, stress occurs when resources are threatened or lost, or when people invest resources somehow and fail to receive an adequate return on the investment. Hobfoll (1989) argued that loss of resources is the central experience in stress (see also Hobfoll, Freedy, Green, & Solomon, 1996). Threat is an impending loss. One might think of the failure to receive an adequate return on investment of resources as being the loss of an anticipated new resource.

Hobfoll (1989) has argued that this theory differs in important ways from other models of stress (and he has generated hypotheses that would not be as readily derived from other models). His stress theory uses an economic metaphor for human experience, which differs from the orientation of other models. In this metaphor, people acquire resources, defend them, and use them to acquire more resources. Stress occurs when the market has a downturn in the value of your resources or when an event of some sort wipes out part of your resource base.

Of particular importance may be social and psychological resources. Holahan, Moos, Holahan, and Cronkite (1999) followed a large sample of adults across a 10-year period, assessing negative and positive life events and changes in personal and social resources. They found that an increase in the balance of negative events to positive events was related to a decline in social and personal resources, whereas a decrease in negative events was related to increase in resources. The changes in resources, in turn, predicted changes in depression. Holahan et al. concluded that the resources people use to protect themselves against stresses are themselves vulnerable to being eroded by stress. They subsequently replicated this pattern in a sample of people who were followed after treatment for depression (Holahan et al., 2000). Other recent work has implicated loss of interpersonal resources in the emergence of symptoms of depression and cancer-related posttraumatic stress disorder (PTSD) among women with cancer (Banou, Hobfoll, & Trochelman, 2009).

Although the economic metaphor is a useful one, it may be desirable to step back from the resources and ask what about them makes them important. It does not seem too far a stretch to say that resources matter to people inasmuch as they facilitate people's movement toward desired goals or avoidance of anti-goals (and this view does not seem intrinsically to contradict Hobfoll's theoretical position). What use is a car? It can take you places you want to go, and it can make an impression on other people. What use are friends? They can help you feel better when you are upset, and you can do interesting things of mutual enjoyment with them. What use is a positive life view? It keeps you moving toward a variety of other goals. Work skills permit you to complete projects, achieve things, and hold a job that fosters continued movement toward goals. Money and influence are means to a variety of ends.

In short, for most people, resources appear to be closely bound up in the continuing pursuit of goals. Thus, the attempt to conserve resources typically occurs in the implicit service of continued goal attainment. A loss of resources represents a threat to that continued goal attainment. Once again, there appear to be strong implicit connections to general principles of self-regulation.

### Illness Representations: Leventhal

Another viewpoint on stress, which is focused specifically on health-related stress, is Leventhal's common-sense model of illness representation (e.g., Leventhal, Brisette, & Leventhal, 2003; Leventhal, Meyer, & Nerenz, 1980; Leventhal et al., 1997). This viewpoint focuses on how people form representations of their experience of illnesses, and how they then respond to those representations. This view shares with that of Lazarus and Folkman the assumption that people's experiences and understandings are driven partly by the objective situation and partly by what the people bring to those situations.

The perception of an illness generally begins with some current somatic experience. Whether it is identified as illness-related, and thus threatening, depends on the person's preexisting prototypes of illness. These prototypes are based partly on the person's illness history and partly on external information. Comparing the current symptom to the available prototypes results in an illness representation (or potentially a representation of something other than an illness). The representation may include a label as the identity of the illness, assumptions about its causes, timeline, consequences, and how

curable it is. These illness representations then guide the person's responses.

This model includes the assumption that illness perceptions are hierarchically organized. There are higher-level, abstract representations (and corresponding coping strategies) and lower-level, concrete representations (and corresponding specific coping tactics). For example, at the abstract level, an experience might be identified as cancer, with various kinds of high-level associations about treatment and prognosis. At the concrete level, a specific symptom might be identified only as an ache (for example), leading to different of associations about treatment pertaining to that symptom (Benyamini, McClain, Leventhal, & Leventhal, 2003).

This model focuses on the complexity of the processes by which people evaluate their subjective experiences as threats or not. It is oriented more than the other models toward the process of defining to oneself the very existence of a threat. In that sense, its logic represents an elaboration on the first step of the stress experience assumed by Lazarus and Folkman: that stress begins with the perception of a threat, in this case a threat that is defined by one's representation of subjective symptoms in terms of illness.

### Section Summary

The preceding sections outlined some of the principles that are widely used to think about stress (for discussions of how to measure stress, see Cohen, Kessler, & Gordon, 1997; Ice & James, 2007). These sections also suggested ways in which models of the experience of stress resemble the general principles of self-regulation that were described initially. Most basically, the experience of stress occurs when a person perceives a threat (either an impending anti-goal or the impending inability to attain a goal) or perceives loss or harm (the actual occurrence of an anti-goal or removal of access to a goal). From the self-regulatory view, these experiences constitute the broad realm of behavior under adversity. People respond to their perceptions of threat or loss in a variety of ways. Such responses are the subject of the next section.

## What Is Coping?

The words *stress* and *coping* are often used together as a phrase, as though the two concepts were intimately joined. After all, there can hardly be coping without the existence of a stressor, and where there is a stressor there usually are coping efforts. Indeed, Lazarus and Folkman's analysis included the effort to cope as a component of the stress experience. What, then, is coping?

Coping is often defined as efforts to deal in some manner with the threatening or harmful situation, to remove the threat or to diminish the various ways in which it can have an impact on the person. That sounds reasonably clear, but it leaves a good deal up in the air. For example, is coping necessarily planful, or can it be automatic? A considerable difference of opinion exists here. Some prefer to limit the concept of coping to voluntary responses (Compas et al., 2001; Connor-Smith, Compas, Wadsworth, Thomsen, & Saltzman, 2000). Others are content to include automatic and involuntary responses within the coping construct (Carver, Scheier, & Weintraub, 1989; Eisenberg, Fabes, & Guthrie, 1997; Skinner & Zimmer-Gembeck, 2007). Of course, distinguishing between voluntary and involuntary responses to stress is not always simple. Indeed, responses that at first are intentional and effortful may become more and more automatic with repetition, further blurring the distinction.

Even if one restricts oneself to responses that are volitional, the sort of definition given in the previous paragraph covers a lot of ground. Indeed, it covers so much ground that theorists have had to make several distinctions within the concept (see Compas et al., 2001; Folkman & Moskowitz, 2004; Skinner et al., 2003). Some of these distinctions are described in the next sections.

## Problem-focused versus Emotion-focused Coping

A distinction that was made early on by Lazarus and Folkman (1984) and their colleagues is between problem-focused coping and emotion-focused coping. Problem-focused coping is aimed at the stressor itself. It may involve taking steps to remove the obstacle that the threat represents or to evade the threatening stimulus. For example, if you are driving on a highway and a car jumps the median strip and heads in your general direction, steering out of its path would be problem-focused coping. If you are driving to an important appointment and unexpected work being done on the highway disrupts traffic and threatens to make you late, you can exit the highway and drive around the obstacle via side streets. This would also be problem-focused coping. These two kinds of coping would allow you to evade or escape from the threat.

Other kinds of problem-focused coping do not evade the threat completely but rather diminish its impact. For example, if a hurricane is forecast, people can put up shutters and bring potted plants and patio furniture into the garage. When the storm hits, the likelihood of damage to the home is thereby reduced. This is problem-focused coping because it deals with the physical impact of the stressor. As another example, if a person knows that the company he works for is on a shaky financial footing, he can try to put some savings aside. If the company fails and he loses his job, he will have something to fall back on. This is also problem-focused coping because it deals with the financial impact of the stressor.

Emotion-focused coping reflects the fact that stress experiences typically elicit distress emotions. Emotion-focused coping is aimed at reducing those emotions. There are many ways to try to reduce feelings of distress. Thus, many coping responses have been characterized as being emotion focused. If the point of a given response is to try to make oneself feel better, that response would seem to be emotion-focused coping. Relaxation exercises would represent emotion-focused coping; going to the movies to take one's mind off the problem might be seen as emotion-focused coping; for some people, shopping is emotion-focused coping.

The concept of emotion-focused coping has taken on something of a life of its own in recent years—under the label *emotion regulation*—as more psychologists have become interested in the effectiveness of the various ways in which people try to reduce unwanted emotions (e.g., Gross, 2007; Kamholz, Hayes, Carver, Gulliver, & Perlman, 2006; Larsen & Prizmic, 2004). A particular focus in this literature has been on the contrast between efforts to suppress emotion, which are not very effective, and efforts to construe stressful situations in ways that diminish their emotional impact, which is much more effective in reducing the emotions (Ochsner & Gross, 2004).

Problem-focused and emotion-focused coping are distinguishable from each other on the basis of their immediate, proximal goal: addressing the problem versus the emotions. However, some coping strategies can serve either function, depending on the focus of their use. An example is the use of social support (e.g., Carver et al., 1989). People can turn to others for emotional support and reassurance, which would represent emotion-focused coping. Alternatively, people often can turn to others for physical assistance (e.g., putting up those shutters before the storm hits). This mobilizing of instrumental assistance is problem-focused coping.

It should also be noted that these two kinds of responses can have interrelated effects on one another.

If a person engages in effective problem-focused coping, the threat may now seem to be diminished. If so, the distress emotions prompted by the threat should also diminish. Thus, problem-focused coping can result in the reduction or prevention of emotional upheaval. Similarly, if a person engages in effective emotion-focused coping, he or she can now consider the problem more calmly. This may permit the person to undertake problem-focused coping more effectively. It may even permit him or her to think of problem-focused responses that were not previously apparent. Thus, emotion-focused coping can result in better problem-focused coping.

These classes of response probably occur in different balances as a function of the nature of the stressor. Problem-focused coping presumably is most likely if the stressor is something the person views as controllable; emotion-focused coping presumably is more likely if the person sees the stressor as uncontrollable (e.g., Park, Armeli, & Tennen, 2004; Terry & Hynes, 1998; Vitaliano, DeWolfe, Maiuro, Russo, & Katon, 1990). Threats vary in controllability. However, usually there is nothing that can be done about loss, making losses less controllable than threats. In general, the more the situation can be characterized as one that simply has to be endured (as is the case in instances of harm and loss), the less common is the attempt to engage in problem-focused coping.

The distinction made between problem-focused and emotion-focused coping is a useful and valuable one. Initially, it led researchers to classify every coping response as being either one or the other. This may have been a mistake. Some reactions that people have when confronting threat or loss appear not to be motivated either by an attempt to remove the stressor or by an attempt to dampen distress emotions. For example, people under stress sometimes engage in self-blame. Although self-blame is often characterized as emotion-focused coping, it is hard to see how it represents an attempt to diminish negative feelings. The realization that the problem versus emotion distinction did not capture everything of importance in coping led to further distinctions.

### Engagement Versus Disengagement or Avoidance Coping

Another particularly important distinction is between engagement or approach coping, in which the effort is aimed at dealing with the stressor either directly or indirectly (via emotion regulation), and what is often called avoidance or disengagement coping (e.g., Moos & Schaefer, 1993; Roth & Cohen,

1986; Skinner et al., 2003). Engagement coping includes all forms of problem-focused coping and some forms of emotion-focused coping, such as seeking of emotional support, cognitive restructuring, and acceptance. Disengagement coping includes responses such as avoidance, denial, and wishful thinking.

Disengagement coping is often emotion focused because it involves an attempt to escape feelings of distress. Sometimes disengagement coping is almost literally an effort to continue on as though the stressor does not exist, so that it does not have to be reacted to, behaviorally or emotionally. Wishful thinking and fantasy distance the person from the stressor, at least temporarily, and denial creates a boundary between reality and the person's experience.

Sometimes the concept of avoidance coping is extended to include giving up on goals the stressor is threatening (Carver et al., 1989). This sort of avoidance coping differs conceptually from the others just described in that it deals with both the stressor's existence and its emotional impact by giving up an investment in something else. By disengaging from the goal that is being threatened, the person avoids the negative feelings associated with the threat.

As just indicated, avoidance coping often is seen as emotion focused, because it often is an attempt to evade or escape from feelings of distress. Avoidance coping is generally not effective in escaping distress, however, particularly in the long term. The problem with avoidance coping is that it does nothing about the stressor's existence and its eventual impact. If you are experiencing a real threat in your life and you respond by going to the movies, the threat will remain when the movie is over. Eventually it must be dealt with.

Indeed, many stressful experiences have a time course that is difficult to change. The longer you avoid dealing with a problem of this sort, the less time is available to deal with the problem when you finally turn to it. This can make the situation worse, in any number of ways. Yet another potential problem with avoidance coping is that some kinds of avoidance create additional problems of their own. Excessive use of alcohol or drugs can create social and health problems. Shopping as an escape sometimes leads to unwise spending binges.

There is some evidence that avoidance coping is not as dysfunctional in cases of loss as it is in cases of threat. Bonnano, Keltner, Holen, and Horowitz (1995) studied bereaved persons at 6 months after bereavement and again 8 months later. They separated them according to the degree to which they were displaying signs of emotional avoidance at the 6-month point. Persons who displayed this pattern at 6 months were also less likely to display grief symptoms 8 months later.

Even in this sort of case, however, evidence is mixed. In another study, Folkman and her colleagues found that bereaved men who tried to distance themselves from thoughts about the loss of their partner had more depression over time than those who did not try to distance themselves (Folkman, Chesney, Collette, Boccellari, & Cooke, 1996). In another study, a coping intervention for men and women diagnosed with human immunodeficiency virus (HIV) infection led to decreases in avoidant coping strategies, and through that to decreases in depression and grief (Smith, Tarakeshwar, Hansen, Kochman, & Sikkema, 2009).

One reason there is controversy over the role of avoidance coping as a way of dealing with loss is that there is a broader controversy about exactly what a recovery from loss entails (Wortman & Silver, 1989). For example, it is commonly held that loss must be mourned, "worked through," examined, questioned, and assimilated (e.g., Lannen, Wolfe, Prigerson, Onelov, & Kreicbergs, 2008). Meaning must be found in the loss, so that the person can come to terms with it. If this were so, avoidance coping would interfere with this process. However, there is evidence that not everyone goes through this process, and that engagement in this process is not good for everyone. For some people, failing to dwell on the loss seems to be the way to get past it (Stroebe, Schut, & Stroebe, 2005; Wortman & Silver, 1989).

### Other Aspects of Coping

Additional categories of coping responses have also been suggested. To some extent, they can be placed within the context of either problem versus emotion focus or engagement versus disengagement. One such category is called *accommodative* or *secondary control coping* (Morling & Evered, 2006; Skinner et al., 2003). This notion has its origins in part in views of successful aging (Brandtstädter & Renner, 1990). Accommodation refers to adjustments within the self that are made in response to (usually external) constraints. It represents a continuation of engagement, but with an acceptance that the constraints have to be adjusted to rather than overcome.

In the realm of coping, accommodation applies to responses such as acceptance, cognitive restructuring, and scaling back one's goals in the face of insurmountable interference (Carver, Scheier, &

Weintraub 1989; Morling & Evered, 2006; Skinner et al., 2003; Wade et al., 2001). Accommodative coping seems to permit the person both to feel better about the situation and to remain engaged in other kinds of coping efforts (Carver et al., 1993; Connor-Smith et al., 2000; Kennedy et al., 2000).

A somewhat related concept is what Folkman (1997) called meaning-focused coping (see also Folkman, 2008; Park & Folkman, 1997). In this response, people draw on their beliefs and values to find (or to remind themselves of) benefits in stressful experiences (Tennen & Affleck, 2002). Meaning-focused coping may include reordering of life priorities. It may entail infusing ordinary events with broader meaning. The construct of meaning-focused coping has roots in evidence that positive as well as negative emotions are common during stressful experiences (e.g., Andrykowsky, Brady, & Hunt, 1993), that positive feelings influence outcomes, and particularly that people try to find benefit and meaning in adversity (Helgeson, Reynolds, & Tomich, 2006; Park, Lechner, Antoni, & Stanton, 2009; Tedeschi & Calhoun, 2004). This idea is discussed in more detail later on. Although this construct emphasizes the positive changes a stressor can bring to a person's life, it is noteworthy that meaning-focused coping also typically is an accommodation to the constraints of one's situation. This kind of coping appears most likely when stressful experiences are uncontrollable or going badly (Folkman, 2008).

Yet another aspect of coping is called *emotional-approach coping* (Stanton et al., 2000). This term refers to actively processing and expressing one's emotions, in a fashion that represents an engagement with, rather than either a venting of the feelings or a direct soothing of them. Emotional-approach coping entails an effort to be clear about what feelings mean and to accept that these feelings are important. This approach can result in less distress later on, as long as it does not turn into rumination (Stanton et al., 2000). There is evidence that emotional-approach coping can be adaptive for medical populations, including those diagnosed with cancer or chronic pain, or experiencing infertility (Austenfeld & Stanton, 2004).

Although most analyses of coping emphasize its role during the experience of threat and loss, not all do so. Aspinwall and Taylor (1997) argued that a good deal of coping occurs well before the occurrence of any stressor. They call this *proactive coping*. Proactive coping is intended to prevent threatening or harmful situations from arising. Aspinwall and Taylor distinguished between proactive coping and anticipatory coping. The latter involves preparing for an upcoming event that is very likely to occur. As an example, putting up shutters for an approaching hurricane would be anticipatory coping. Proactive coping is aimed at keeping the stressful experience from ever arriving, or at least from arriving in a fully potent form. Proactive coping is partly a matter of scanning the experiential horizon for signs that a threat may be building. Should the beginnings of a threat be perceived, the person can put into motion strategies that will prevent it from appearing or that will remove the person from its path.

If the anticipation of an emerging threat helps the person to avoid the occurrence of the event, the person will have fewer really stressful experiences and will undergo stress of less intensity when the experiences are unavoidable. To the extent that stressful events can be averted or minimized, the person will therefore have a lower level of chronic stress. In keeping with this idea, proactive coping has been associated with positive mood and cognitions, as well as positive motivational states (Greenglass & Fiksenbaum, 2009). There are potential liabilities to this strategy, however. Most obviously, people who are ever-vigilant to the possibility of threat may already be creating stress experiences for themselves by placing themselves in the continuous posture of vigilance.

## Positive Emotions and Positive Coping Responses

An issue that has emerged as important in the coping literature concerns the possible role played by positive experiences during the period of the stressful event. People experience distress emotions during a period of stress, but they also experience positive emotions during the same period (e.g., Andrykowski et al., 1993; Folkman, 2008). There is some basis for believing that positive emotions can have positive effects on health (e.g., Folkman & Moskowitz, 2000, 2004; Fredrickson, Mancuso, Branigan, & Tugade, 2000). One review suggests that such effects on health per se are fairly mixed (Pressman & Cohen, 2005). On the other hand, there is evidence that interventions aimed at enhancing positive experiences enhance subjective well-being and reduce depression (Sin & Lyubomirsky, 2009).

Beyond positive emotions per se, another class of positive experience that is sometimes associated with stress is variously referred to as stress-related growth (Park, Cohen, & Murch, 1996), posttraumatic growth (Tedeschi & Calhoun, 2004), or benefit

finding (Tomich & Helgeson, 2004). Many persons who are under great stress report finding meaning in the stressor, growing as a person, or experiencing other positive life changes as a result of the stressor, including stresses associated with disease (Affleck & Tennen, 1996; Bower, Kemeny, Taylor, & Fahey, 1998; Carver & Antoni, 2004; Cordova, Cunningham, Carlson, & Andrykowski, 2001; Helgeson et al., 2006; Jim & Jacobsen, 2008; Low, Bower, Kawn, & Seldon, 2008; Norekvål et al., 2008; Park & Folkman, 1997; Sears, Stanton, & Danoff-Burg, 2003; Taylor, 1983; Tomich & Helgeson, 2004). There is evidence that this broad class of positive experiences incorporates several subgroups (Sears et al., 2003; Weaver, Llabre, Lechner, Penedo, & Antoni, 2008). There is also evidence that these reactions can be induced by therapeutic interventions, as well as occurring spontaneously (Antoni et al., 2001, 2006).

This broad topic has generated a great deal of interest in the past decade (Park, Lechner, Antoni, & Stanton, 2009). These types of positive experiences have been associated with better psychosocial and physiological outcomes. For example, Helgeson, Reynolds, and Tomich (2006) found that benefit finding was related to less depression, more positive well-being, and less intrusive and avoidant thoughts about a stressor. Bower and colleagues (2008) reviewed evidence which suggests that these types of coping responses may even influence health outcomes by lowering stress reactivity, increasing rate of habituation to stressors, and enhancing quicker recovery from stress-related arousal.

## Some Methodological Issues in Coping Research

Before concluding this discussion of coping, at least brief mention should be made of several methodological issues in the study of coping. These issues are raised here as cautionary points. Unfortunately there is no clear resolution to them. The existence of the issues should be kept in mind, however, in considering evidence later on pertaining to the relationships between stress and coping and health.

One very basic issue is that coping can be examined concurrently with the relevant outcome, or coping can instead be examined as a prospective predictor of the outcome. It is clear that any cross-sectional analysis of coping and health (or stress and health, for that matter) is subject to important limitations on inference. Given only concurrent relations, it is impossible to draw any conclusions about causal influence. After all, ill health can create stress and induce certain kinds of coping responses, just as easily as it can be influenced by stress and coping responses. With concurrent associations, there is no way to untangle the meaning of the association. Measuring coping (or stress) at one point and health outcomes at a subsequent point at least permits one to establish temporal precedence of the one compared with the other. Although this falls short of showing cause and effect, it at least establishes the plausibility of a causal relation.

Another set of issues concerns the attempt to measure coping over an extended period of time, rather than at a specific moment. What should be the time frame for assessment? Should people in the study be asked about their current coping (i.e., at this moment) with a particular stressor, and be asked repeatedly over multiple instances? Should people be asked instead to rate the extent to which they have used each of a set of coping reactions with the accumulated stressors of the day or the week? Attempting to measure coping with specific stressors repeatedly over time is labor-intensive. Yet, there are important reasons to consider such a strategy. Most important, there is evidence that people do not do a very good job of remembering what they did to cope with even fairly salient stressors, once some time has passed (Ptacek, Smith, Espe, & Raffety, 1994), though they do better when the time frame is more limited (Todd, Tennen, Carney, Armeli, & Affleck, 2004).

Another, related issue is how long a time lag to use in examining prospective effects of coping. Should you measure coping on one day and the outcome variable the next day? A week later? A month later? Three months later? With some outcome variables, it would seem to be necessary to permit a fairly substantial delay before assessment of the outcome. With others it is less clear. How much sense does it make, for example, to measure coping with a stressor at one time point, then measure emotional well-being a year later? Tennen, Affleck, Armeli, and Carney (2000) have argued for the usefulness of a strategy in which coping and outcomes are measured daily, at least for certain kinds of coping effects.

Another set of questions concerns how to deal with people's responses on self-reports of coping. Typically, people are asked to indicate the extent to which they used (or involuntarily experienced) each of several responses to the stressor, on a rating scale that ranges from zero to some high value. One question that has been raised occasionally is this: What if a particular coping response is very important, but different people need to do more of it in order to function adaptively? If the study combines these people, some who report moderate use of the strategy will be using it more than enough, and some might be using it less than they need to. Yet, they will be treated as using the strategy equivalently in the analyses. This can obscure a potentially important relationship between the coping strategy and the outcome.

Another question concerns how to deal with the fact that some people report many different coping reactions at a given time, whereas others report far fewer. Should the researcher assume that the extent of use of each strategy is the critical issue? Or should the researcher assume that a person who used this strategy and almost nothing else is relying on this one more than a person who used this strategy and six others as well? Tennen et al. (2000) have argued that, in general, people use emotion-focused coping only after they have tried problem-focused coping and found it to be ineffective. This suggests an approach to examining coping in which the question is whether the individual changes from one sort of coping to another across successive days as a function of lack of effectiveness of the first coping response used.

These various ways of viewing the information lead to very different analytic strategies. The first view presented would treat the raw information as predictors of the outcome. The second view might lead the researcher to create an index of the percentage of total coping that was devoted to this particular coping strategy (cf. Vitaliano, Russo, Young, Teri, & Maiuro, 1991). The third view entails use of multilevel analytic strategies (see Tennen et al., 2000). Yet another possibility is to use all available information about coping to create aggregations of people whose profiles of coping responses are similar, through such techniques as cluster analysis. If several common profiles can be identified, perhaps these more accurately reflect coping differences in large samples of people.

One last issue to be noted briefly is that people choose coping responses partly on the basis of the situational context and the nature of the threat, but also partly on the basis of who they are as people. Personality has a substantial impact on many important outcomes in life (see Ozer & Benet-Martínez, 2006), and coping is one of them (Carver & Connor-Smith, 2010; Connor-Smith & Flachsbart, 2007; Solberg Nes & Segerstrom, 2006). (Health is another: Rasmussen, Scheier, & Greenhouse, 2009.) When we talk about differences in coping responses in a study being related to some outcome, we cannot be sure that what we are really referring to are not differences in personality. If these responses derive from personality, they may have roots that are much deeper than we realize.

As indicated earlier, the issues raised in this section are unresolved. It is clear that some strategies have built-in problems (e.g., cross-sectional studies cannot be informative about causality). With respect to other issues (such as the use of raw scores or indices), there is no clear indication that one approach is right and the other wrong. Readers should be aware, however, that different positions on these issues were taken in various studies that bear on stress, coping, and health. These are not the only issues we have to worry about, though. Further issues are raised when we add in the concept of health.

## Stress Effects on Health: Issues

In considering how stress and coping may influence health, we must decide what we mean by "health." At first glance, health seems a simple concept with an obvious meaning. However, further reflection reveals that it has some fuzzy boundaries.

### *What Is Health?*

A good deal of research has been conducted on the impact of stress and coping on emotional well-being. Emotional well-being is important in its own right, and there are some indications that variations in emotional well-being influence health. However, for the purposes of this chapter, we must consider emotional responses as being at least a step away from health.

A literature is also beginning to develop regarding the impact of stress and coping on physiological parameters of various sorts, such as blood pressure, neurotransmitters, and immune activity. Should these variables be thought of as constituting health? This question is harder to answer (see also Cohen & Rodriguez, 1995). Shifts in the values of some physiological indices are considered to be disorders in and of themselves. An example is blood pressure. When resting blood pressure is consistently above a certain level, the person is diagnosed as having the illness called hypertension. In other cases, it is less clear that shifts in a physiological parameter—even fairly extreme shifts—would be viewed as reflecting illness. In general, changes in these parameters are viewed as perhaps having influences on health, but not as representing health effects per se.

Generally, when we talk about health in this context, we are talking about the presence or absence of a diagnosable, verifiable illness or disorder. Even within that framework, however, there is a great deal

of potential diversity (cf. Carver & Scheier, 1998, Chapter 18). In some cases research focuses on disease promotion, in which the issue is who gets the disease and who does not. An example is research on women who have the human papilloma virus, which is a predisposing factor for cervical cancer. Some of these women will develop cancer; others will not. In other cases, the research focus is on disease progression—how quickly an early form of a disease evolves into a more advanced form. In yet other cases, the focus is on recurrence of a disease that has been successfully treated. An example is studies of women who have been treated successfully for breast cancer and are continuing their posttreatment lives. Sometimes research even examines illness that occurs as a side effect of treatment for a different illness. An example is the rehospitalization for infection that often follows successful heart surgery. Finally, in some cases, the health outcome is literally life or death. In these studies, the focus is on mortality rates or survival times among people who have a severe disease. For example, do stress and coping processes influence the longevity of acquired immune deficiency syndrome (AIDS) patients?

All the possibilities described in the preceding paragraph are legitimately regarded as studies of "health." The diversity among them, however, raises further issues. For example, it might be the case that stress and coping variables play a role in some kinds of health outcomes but not in others—perhaps stress influences disease promotion but not survival time, or vice versa. The possibility of an influence on specific health outcomes rather than health outcomes more broadly means that unsupportive findings must be evaluated more tentatively. What becomes important is patterns of effects on particular classes of outcomes.

### *Behavioral Pathways of Influence*

Another set of issues to be considered is what constitutes the functional pathways by which stress and coping might influence health. There are, in fact, several possibilities, which have very different implications.

Some potential pathways are quite behavioral, pathways in which health consequences arise from the nature of the behaviors themselves. For example, people sometimes engage in risky behaviors, such as unprotected sex. If risky behaviors are more likely when people are under stress, the result would be that stress creates greater potential for exposure to sexually transmitted diseases (see Antoni, 2002).

As another example, certain kinds of behavior, such as smoking and drug use, are intrinsically antagonistic to health. If such behaviors are more likely when people are under stress (cf. Cohen, Schwartz, Bromet, & Parkinson, 1991; Holohan, Moos, Holohan, Cronkite, & Randall, 2003; Horwitz & White, 1991), the result would be that stress increases exposure to harmful agents (in these cases, chemical agents) and ultimately causes adverse health effects. Indeed, the use of drugs and alcohol can have further ripple effects by increasing the tendency to engage in other kinds of high-risk behaviors (e.g., Ostrow et al., 1990).

Yet another area of behavioral influence concerns adherence to medical regimens. Failure to adhere to a prescribed medical regimen can seriously compromise the benefit of the treatment. If nonadherence or erratic adherence is more likely when people are under stress, the result would be a reduced exposure to the curative agent and eventually poorer medical outcomes (Dunbar-Jacob & Schlenk, 1996; Sherbourne, Hays, Ordway, DiMatteo, & Kravitz, 1992). A parallel case can be made for maintaining exercise and a well-balanced diet. Exercise and proper eating are often the first things to be disregarded when stress arises, and doing so keeps the person from benefits he or she would otherwise experience (Chandola et al., 2008; Smith & Leon, 1992).

A final sort of behavioral effect is the failure to seek either diagnosis or treatment for a condition that turns out to be an illness (Andersen & Cacioppo, 1995). Failure to seek medical consultation can result in the progression of the disease well beyond its initial level. The result sometimes is that a medical condition that would have been fairly easily treated becomes sufficiently advanced as to be more difficult to treat effectively.

Each of these cases represents a purely "behavioral" pathway to illness. That is, each case involves either an increase in potential exposure to a pathogen or a decrease in exposure to a beneficial agent as a result of the person's action. However, none of these cases assumes a direct link between the person's behavior (or psychological state) and changes in aspects of the body's internal functioning.

We will say very little more about these behavioral pathways, but they obviously are important. Dysfunctional coping tactics such as smoking, drinking, binge eating, and high-risk sex represent clear ways in which adverse health effects can be created (for review of issues and findings, see Dunbar-Jacob, Schlenk, & Caruthers, 2002). To the extent that failure to seek diagnosis or treatment (or to follow instructions regarding treatment) can be thought of as avoidance coping, such pathways would reflect

yet further instances in which avoidance coping produces adverse effects. These effects are quite straightforward. For the remainder of this chapter, however, we focus on other pathways that involve links between psychological and physiological responses, links that typically are more covert and subtle (Miller, Chen, & Cole, 2009).

### Psychophysiological Pathways of Influence

Many kinds of psychological experiences produce involuntary physiological changes within the body. Some of these changes are disruptive of important health-protective functions. In these hypothesized pathways, stress and coping processes influence the body's reactions in some way that renders the person more vulnerable to the promotion or progression of disease.

Typically, this sort of pathway is assumed to begin with the experience of emotional distress (although that aspect of the sequence is not always addressed directly in the research). Intense emotional states are associated with a variety of cardiovascular responses and neuroendocrine changes. Given the broad array of responses that are associated with negative emotions, there again are diverse potential pathways of influence on health.

For example, one line of reasoning holds that extensive and repeated cardiovascular stress responses place an abnormally high burden on arteries, resulting (over the long term) in small tears and the depositing of protective plaques. Too much depositing of plaques, however, eventually turns into a case of atherosclerosis (e.g., Krantz & McCeney, 2002; Rozanski, Blumenthal, & Kaplan, 1999; Smith & Ruiz, 2002). Similarly, the processes by which blood pressure is regulated may be responsive over repeated cardiovascular demands, leading to eventual development of hypertension (cf. Fredrikson & Matthews, 1990). Nor are these the only mechanisms by which stress can contribute to cardiovascular disease.

Another focal point in analyses of stress-related physiological responding is the hypothalamic-pituitary-adrenocortical (HPA) axis. This set of structures has proved to have major involvement in the body's stress response (Michelson, Licinio, & Bold, 1995). We will not describe the functioning of the HPA axis in any detail here, except to say that it is involved in sympathetic nervous system activation under stress (for a broader treatment, see Chapter 6, this volume, by Cacioppo and Berntson, 2011). This pattern of physiological changes represents the body's pattern of preparation for intense physical activity, more colloquially known as the fight-or-flight response.

HPA activation is reflected in increased levels of several hormones, including the catecholamines (epinephrine and norepinephrine) and cortisol.

Cortisol is believed to be a particularly important stress hormone because of its links to other processes in the overall stress response. Perhaps most important, elevation of cortisol can suppress immune functions (Webster, Marketon, & Glaser, 2008). The effects include decreasing antibody production, decreasing numbers of T cells, decreasing lymphocyte proliferative responses, and inhibition of natural killer cell (NK) activation (Kronfol, Madhavan, Zhang, Hill, & Brown, 1997). Maier et al. (1994) argued that this suppression stems from a very simple principle: The body can devote its energies either to the fight-or-flight response or to elimination of internal pathogens, but it cannot easily do both at the same time. When strong demands are made on one (fight-or-flight), the other (immune surveillance) is suppressed (see also Miller, Cohen, & Ritchey, 2002).

Indeed, another target in analyses of stress-related physiological responding is the immune system itself (Segerstrom & Miller, 2004). The immune system is an aspect of the body that obviously has important implications for health. The immune system is the body's main line of defense against disease agents ranging from bacteria to cancer cells. If immune functioning is impaired, the person thereby becomes more vulnerable both to opportunistic infectious agents and to agents of disease that had already been at work in the body. The result may be either disease promotion or disease progression (Glaser & Kiecolt-Glaser, 1994). The immune system is far more complicated than was assumed three decades ago, and there are several ways in which stress can influence immune function (for reviews see Gouin, Hantsoo, & Kiecolt-Glaser, 2008; Kemeny, 2011, Chapter 7, this volume; Kiecolt-Glaser, McGuire, Robles, & Glaser, 2002; Marin, Chen, Munch, & Miller, 2009; Robles, Glaser, & Kiecolt-Glaser, 2005; Vidovíc et al., 2009).

One last point should perhaps be made here about the nature of psychophysiological response patterns. One of the earliest writers in the literature of stress, Hans Selye (1956), described the course of stress using the phrase *general adaptation syndrome*. It consists of three stages. First, an alarm reaction occurs, in which an array of physiological changes occur, in an immediate effort to counter the damaging agent. If the stress continues, a stage of resistance develops in which the body develops inflammation and bodily resources are expended to heal any damage that has occurred. If the stress is severe enough, or if

it continues for long enough, a third stage ensues: exhaustion. The depletion of resources that defines exhaustion produces a cessation of struggling.

Most of the focus on psychophysiological pathways in today's health psychology is on the phases of the stress response that Selye termed *alarm* and *resistance*. Generally, we are looking for signs of struggle from the mechanisms of the body. However, sometimes it is the exhaustion part of the response that is critical to the impact of stress on health (Segerstrom & Miller, 2004). Selye's depiction of exhaustion has some commonality with the psychological state of depression. Depression represents a condition in which the person has given up struggling to move forward. Giving up can also have adverse effects, although the experience differs in many ways from that of a repeated or prolonged struggle.

### Section Summary

Let us summarize parts of what has been said thus far and preview some things that are yet to be described by means of a visual illustration. Figure 8.1 depicts a set of hypothetical links among stress, coping, emotional distress, physiological responses, and health. One way to read the links in the figure is as paths of potential influence. Another way to read them is as relationships that might be examined in a given study. (We hasten to add, however, that we know of no study that has examined all the relationships that are shown in Figure 8.1).

Models of stress and illness that are not primarily behavioral in their focus often assume a logic involving the paths that are aligned in a vertical column in the center of Figure 8.1: That is, adverse events (actual or anticipated) induce the stress experience (path 1), which causes negative emotions (path 2). These emotions incorporate a variety of physiological changes. If the emotional reactions are intense, prolonged, or repeated, a potential exists for disruption in one or more physiological systems (path 3). In one way or another, this disruption then makes disease more likely (path 4).

Most studies, however, jump past one or more of these steps. Some examine the impact of stress on physiological changes (path 5); some examine the impact of stress on disease outcomes (path 6). Some start with emotional distress rather than stress, and examine its impact on disease outcomes (path 7). The ideal study would incorporate data on all the classes of variables shown in Figure 8.1: stress level, coping responses, emotional distress, physiological parameters, and disease outcomes. However, this ideal is not often encountered in the literature.

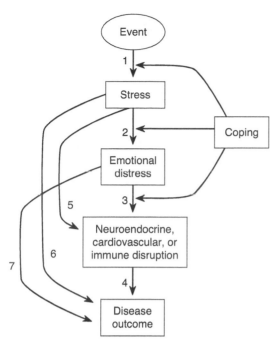

**Fig. 8.1** Hypothetical pathways by which stress and coping might influence disease outcomes. Each path can also be read as an association that might be examined in a given study. It should be noted that this diagram is an oversimplification in several respects. For one thing, at least some of the arrows actually go in both directions, rather than just one.

Coping is shown in this figure as a moderator, which potentially interacts at three places in the stream of influence. In each case, if the coping is effective, it would dampen the response that is next in line; if the coping is dysfunctional, it might increase the next response. Coping can be proactive, and if engaged sufficiently, it can prevent the stress from arising in the first place (path 1). Coping can influence how intense or prolonged are the distress emotions involved in the event (path 2). And coping can potentially change how emotions are translated into physiological disruptions (path 3). Of course, if a particular study were to disregard emotional distress, or physiological reactions, any interaction that involved coping might instead appear as impinging on paths 5, 6, or 7 (interactions that are omitted from Figure 8.1).

## Impact of Stress on Psychological and Physiological Responses

Let us now turn to some of the evidence bearing on some of the pathways shown in Figure 8.1. With respect to effects of preventive or proactive coping (Aspinwall & Taylor, 1997), little evidence exists. At present, that hypothesis must be viewed as a line of reasoning that appears worth testing explicitly.

### From Stress to Distress and the Role of Coping

With respect to the link between stress and distress, the path is unquestionable. There is no doubt that stressful events produce emotional distress. A variety of studies of chronic stress make this case readily, as do studies of acute stress. As an example, it has been shown that poorer marital quality relates to higher levels of depression (Kiecolt-Glaser, Fisher et al., 1987), as does being a caregiver for someone with Alzheimer disease (Kiecolt-Glaser, Glaser et al., 1997). These findings are straightforward, and there are many more that make conceptually similar points.

There is also not much doubt that coping can have an influence on the link between stress and distress—effects that range from helpful to harmful. One illustration of these effects of coping comes from a study done some time ago examining how women deal with treatment for early-stage breast cancer across the first year after treatment (Carver et al., 1993). In this study, coping with the diagnosis and treatment of the cancer and mood were assessed the day before surgery, 10 days after surgery, and at three follow-ups. Because all the women in this study had just been diagnosed with early-stage breast cancer, the stressor they were exposed to was roughly uniform (differences in stage, surgical treatment, and adjuvant therapy were also examined, however).

Several coping tactics related to distress. Coping that revolved around accepting the reality of the situation (acceptance), placing as good a light on it as possible (positive reframing), and trying to relieve the situation with humor all related to less concurrent distress, both before surgery and afterward. Coping that involved trying to push the reality of the situation away (denial) and giving up the attempt to reach threatened goals (behavioral disengagement) related to greater concurrent distress at all measurement points.

Prospective effects also occurred, both from coping to distress and from distress to coping. Indeed, these effects seemed to form a spiral of influence. Presurgical acceptance predicted less postsurgical distress (controlling for presurgical distress); postsurgical distress, in turn, predicted greater use of denial and disengagement at the 3-month point. Finally, denial and disengagement at 3 months predicted more distress at 6 months after surgery (controlling for 3-month distress), whereas use of humor at 3 months predicted less distress at 6 months (additional evidence of such a spiral in another sample was reported by Culver, Arena, Antoni, & Carver, 2002).

This pattern makes several points. First, it is clear that some coping responses were helpful with regard to future distress (acceptance, use of humor), and others were disruptive (denial and disengagement). Second, the coping responses that were most useful in this situation were emotion focused (acceptance and use of humor). There was little to be done in this situation except to adapt to it and follow the doctors' orders. As a result, the responses that were most useful were those that involved accommodation yet engagement. Finally, the overall pattern of findings appears to be consistent with elements of the self-regulation model of behavior described earlier.

This study is a single example of a large number of studies of how differences in coping reactions can result in different levels of emotional distress among persons dealing with stresses. The literature is a very broad one (see also Folkman & Moskowitz, 2004). A couple of caveats about this literature should be kept in mind, however. First, as indicated earlier in the chapter, many studies of stress, coping, and distress are cross-sectional rather than prospective. Although there sometimes are reasons for using cross-sectional designs, the design has very serious drawbacks.

A second caveat concerns the nature of the effect observed, even when the study is prospective. Specifically, the logic underlying studies of this topic is that coping interacts with stress to determine level of emotional distress. Adequately testing such a moderator, or "stress buffering," hypothesis (Cohen & Wills, 1985), requires that there be varying levels of both stress and coping. In the study just described, for example (Carver et al., 1993), this was not the case. All participants in that study were cancer patients, with roughly equivalent stressors. Thus, that study does not deal with the question of whether coping would have had a comparable set of relations to distress level even among women who were not experiencing the stresses associated with breast cancer. Such a finding might be interpretable, but it would not fit the interactive view depicted in Figure 8.1.

### Links from Emotional Distress to Physiological Responses

The next step in the logical chain shown in Figure 8.1 is from distress emotions to physiological responses. A great many potential physiological responses are possible, and evidence has accumulated pertaining to many of them. Consider first cardiovascular effects. There is no question that many negative emotions, such as anxiety and anger, produce increases in cardiovascular responses.

An illustration of such effects comes from research on marital interactions. In this research, married couples are asked to discuss a topic on which they have a conflict, and their physiological responses are monitored over time. One early study of this design found that when hostile behavior occurred during these interactions, it produced sizable changes in blood pressure (Ewart, Taylor, Kraemer, & Agras, 1991). In fact, a more recent study found that simply recalling an instance of marital conflict is enough to raise a person's blood pressure (Carels, Sherwood, & Blumenthal, 1998). These findings are particularly compelling because they focus on an experience that is very common in day-to-day life: conflict with significant others.

Emotional distress has also been related to elevations of cortisol and other neuroendocrines (Biondi & Picardi, 1999; Michelson et al., 1995), particularly in the context of social threat (Dickerson & Kemeny, 2004; Kemeny, 2009). Research on marital interaction also provides a good illustration of these effects. Hostile behavior during marital conflict has been found to lead to increases in epinephrine and norepinephrine, both among newlyweds (Malarkey, Kiecolt-Glaser, Pearl, & Glaser, 1994) and among couples in long-term marriages (Kiecolt-Glaser et al., 1997). Among wives, elevations in norepinephrine and cortisol were also found when their own negative behavior was met by withdrawal on the part of their husbands (Kiecolt-Glaser, Newton, et al., 1996), a pattern that has also been linked to marital distress (e.g., Heavey, Layne, & Christensen, 1993). Effects on negative affect and cortisol responses after conflict discussion are less pronounced among newlyweds who report higher spousal satisfaction, suggesting a buffering effect (Heffner, Kiecolt-Glaser, Loving, Glaser, & Malarkey, 2004). It is of some interest that elevations in neuroendocrine function predict likelihood of divorce 10 years later (Kiecolt-Glaser, Bane, Glaser, & Malarkey, 2003).

These marital interaction effects on neuroendocrines are typically stronger among women than men (Kiecolt-Glaser & Newton, 2001). Interestingly, however, cortisol reactivity to harassment by an experiment accomplice has been found to be twice as great among men as among women (Earle, Linden, & Weinberg, 1999). Perhaps this is because the harassment is experienced by men as a greater threat to their social dominance (cf. Smith, Allred, Morrison, & Carlson, 1989; Smith, Nealey, Kircher, & Limon, 1997; Smith, Ruiz, & Uchino, 2000).

Thus, distress associated with social challenge often leads to increases in cortisol (Dickerson & Kemeny, 2004). Interestingly, just as coping can influence distress, there is also evidence that coping responses influence cortisol levels. In general, problem-focused and approach coping styles are related to lower overall levels of cortisol, more favorable diurnal cortisol rhythms, and faster recovery to normal after a stressor (Mikolajczak, Roy, Luminet, Fillee, & de Timary, 2007; Nicolson, 1992; O'Donnell, Badrick, Kumari, & Steptoe, 2008; Sjogren, Leanderson, & Kristenson, 2006). A number of qualities that reflect social support have also been linked to favorable cortisol profiles. Use of social support relates to lower daily cortisol levels (O'Donnell, Badrick, Kumari, & Steptoe, 2008). In contrast, social isolation (living alone and little contact with friends and family) predicts a greater cortisol response at awakening and greater cortisol output over the day (Grant, Hamer, & Steptoe, 2009).

Evidence from other sources suggests that elevation of cortisol can suppress immune function (Antoni & Schneiderman, 1998; Kronfol et al., 1997; O'Leary, 1990). Thus, it would seem reasonable to suggest that distress can influence immune function. Indeed, that does seem to be true. For example, Kiecolt-Glaser et al. (2005) found that negative marital interactions were associated with increases in proinflammatory cytokines. Depression has been related to suppressed immune function in many studies (see Herbert & Cohen, 1993, for a meta-analytic review; see Robles et al., 2005, for a more recent analysis of depression and cytokines). A synergistic effect also seems to exist between depression and other adverse factors. One study found that depression status interacts with smoking, with the lowest NK cell activity appearing in depressed smokers (Jung & Irwin, 1999).

Other research has linked the stress of the long-term stress of caring for a sick relative to adverse immune effects. In one study (Glaser, Sheridan, Malarkey, MacCallum, & Kiecolt-Glaser, 2000), caregivers received a pneumococcal bacterial vaccination and had immune measures collected at several points afterward. Caregivers showed poorer antibody responses at 3 and 6 months after the vaccination than did controls. In another study (Gallagher, Phillips, Drayson, & Carroll, 2009), parental caregivers of children with disabilities received the same vaccine and showed poorer antibody responses at 1- and 6-month follow-ups.

There appear to be two different patterns of cortisol response and related immune response (Segerstrom & Miller, 2004). Loss, epitomized by bereavement, tends to relate to increases in cortisol production and decreased NK cytotoxicity. In contrast, trauma and posttraumatic disorders tend to relate to decreases in cortisol production. That decrease has consequences for immune function, but consequences that are different from those associated with chronic stress.

As with cortisol, there is also evidence that coping relates to variations in immune system functioning. For example, in a study of HIV patients, those who showed difficulty in recognizing and expressing their emotions had higher levels of an immune marker related to HIV disease progression (Temoshok et al., 2008). Also among HIV patients, those expressing disengagement tendencies had higher viral loads and lower immune cell counts (Wald, Dowling, & Temoshok, 2006). In a nonpatient sample, task-focused engagement coping was linked to better immune system functioning, along with lower HPA activation (Olff et al., 1995).

Recall that Figure 8.1 placed cardiovascular, neuroendocrine, and immune disruptions at the same step of the hypothetical sequence of processes. As suggested by the preceding paragraph, however, it is not clear whether such an equivalent placement actually is warranted (cf. Maier et al., 1994). Some studies appear to suggest that one set of these physiological parameters influences another set. On the other hand, there is also evidence that several systems are mutually entrained. For example, Cacioppo et al. (1998) found that brief psychological stressors increased cardiac sympathetic activation, elevated catecholamines, and affected cellular immune responses. Persons who showed the greatest stress-related changes in HPA activation also showed the greatest reduction in cellular immune response. Everything seemed tied to everything else in these data.

As if all this were not complicated enough, there is also evidence that influence can be exerted in the opposite direction. Reichenberg and colleagues (2001) injected volunteer research participants with two different substances at two different times. One was a mild dose of a toxin; the other was a placebo. Participants' bodies reacted to the toxin by producing an immune response—for example, increase in circulating levels of interleukin-6. An hour after the injection of the toxin (but not the placebo), participants reported an elevation in anxiety. Two hours after that (while the immune response was still elevated), they reported an elevation in depressed feelings. This pattern of findings suggests the possibility that emotional responses can be influenced by the body's immune response. Indeed, a set of symptoms commonly experienced among cancer patients, called "sickness behavior," includes lethargy, depression, and cognitive impairment, and is thought to be induced by proinflammatory cytokines (see Myers, 2008).

As indicated by this brief review of a handful of studies, a great deal of information links stress and distress to physiological reactions of diverse types. This sort of research is ongoing, and the picture of how different systems interweave or influence each other should become clearer in the next decades. As noted earlier, however, there is a considerable difference between showing that stress and distress predict changes in physiological responses and showing that stress and distress play a role in actual health outcomes. We now turn to the question of whether stress and coping have implications for physical well-being over the longer term.

## Stress and Health

The evidence on the links between stress and physical well-being is scattered across many literatures. There remain many questions about mechanisms of influence. There appears to be no question, however, that such a relationship does exist.

### From Stress to Cardiovascular Disruption and Disease

One literature bearing on this relationship focuses on cardiovascular diseases (see, e.g., Krantz & McCeney, 2002; Rozanski et al., 1999; Smith & Ruiz, 2002; Sparrenberger et al., 2009). The studies range from laboratory and field research on humans to studies of nonhuman animals. The stresses range from acute to chronic. The outcome measures range from the very focalized and specific (such as myocardial ischemia, and the occurrence of myocardial infarction), to broader and longer-term (such as development of atherosclerosis).

Part of this literature examines the impact of chronic stress on cardiovascular disease. Chronic work stress seems to exert a variety of pathophysiological effects, including raising blood pressure (Chandola et al., 2008; Schnall et al., 1990; Schnall, Schwartz, Landsbergis, Warren, & Pickering, 1998). A recent review of seven studies concluded that chronic stress predicts sustained elevations in blood pressure (Sparrenberger et al., 2009).

Although people tend to think of chronic stress solely in terms of work, social disruptions can also create chronic stress, which can lead to cardiovascular problems. As an example, many years ago Ratcliffe

and Cronin (1958) described the impact of social disruption among zoo animals. They argued that crowding and disruption of normal social patterns had led to an increase in atherosclerosis among the animals. More recently, it was found that social isolation, as well as crowding, can create similar problems (Shively, Clarkson, & Kaplan, 1989). In the latter study, monkeys housed alone had four times as much atherosclerosis as those housed in social groups.

Emotional distress has also been studied as a predictor of cardiovascular problems over the long term (e.g., Krantz & McCeney, 2002). Among initially healthy persons, symptoms of anxiety and depression have been found to predict incidence of coronary heart disease (CHD) later on (Barefoot & Schroll, 1996; Everson-Rose & Lewis, 2005; Ford et al., 1998; Kubzansky et al., 1997). Furthermore, among patients who already have clinical evidence of CHD, symptoms of anxiety and depression predict recurrent coronary events and earlier death (Ahern et al., 1990; Barefoot et al., 1996; Barefoot et al., 2000; Frasure-Smith, Lesperance, & Talajic, 1995; Moser & Dracup, 1996; for reviews, see Januzzi, Stern, Pasternak, & DeSanctis, 2000 and Steptoe & Brydon, 2009). Depression has also proved to be a risk factor for CHD among persons with diabetes (Kinder, Kamarck, Baum, & Orchard, 2002). Other constructs related to depression, such as symptoms of exhaustion (Appels, Golombeck, Gorgels, de Vreede, & van Breukelen, 2000), pessimism (Scheier et al., 1999), loneliness (Thurston & Kubzansky, 2009), and hopelessness (Everson et al., 1996; Everson, Kaplan, Goldberg, Salonen, & Salonen, 1997), also predict adverse effects and more negative prognoses relating to CHD.

It is not just chronic stress that influences cardiovascular disease. Acute stressors can also have major cardiovascular effects (e.g., Krantz & McCeney, 2002), although findings have been somewhat inconsistent (e.g., see Sparrenberger et al., 2009). An acute stressor that has long been associated with elevated rates of cardiac events is bereavement (Kaprio, Koskenvuo, & Rita, 1987; Parkes, 1964). In one very large study (95,647 persons followed for 4 to 5 years), the highest relative mortality by heart attack occurred immediately after bereavement (Kaprio et al., 1987). During the first month after bereavement, men's risk of sudden death doubled, and women's risk tripled. After the first month, mortality rates returned to population levels.

Bereavement is probably the best known of acute stressors with cardiovascular implications, but it is not the only one. For instance, during the Los Angeles earthquake of 1994, the number of sudden cardiac deaths rose from a daily average of 4.6 in the preceding week to 24 on the day of the earthquake (Leor, Poole, & Kloner, 1996). A similar sharp increase occurred in the number of deaths on the first day of missile strikes on Israeli cities during the Gulf War of 1991 (Meisel et al., 1991). The stress of a major sporting event can also influence cardiac episodes (Wilbert-Lampen et al., 2008). Even an event as simple as a bout of anger can trigger myocardial infarction (MI; Mittleman et al., 1995). In this study, a sample of post-MI patients were asked to reconstruct the events preceding their infarctions. Their reports revealed a relative risk of MI that was more than double after an anger episode.

Research on animals shows that acute stress can have a wide range of very specific adverse effects on the cardiovascular system. Among other things, there is evidence that acute stress can trigger myocardial ischemia, promote arrhythmias, stimulate platelet function, and increase blood viscosity (for more detail concerning mechanisms, see Rozanski et al., 1999). Consistent with this view, evidence from a number of studies links the experience of anxiety to elevated risk of fatal ischemic heart disease (Hemingway & Marmot, 1999). Indeed, one review has concluded that of anger, anxiety, and depression, the evidence was strongest for anxiety as a causal factor in ischemic heart disease (Kubzansky & Kawachi, 2000). A wide variety of research has linked anger proneness to other aspects of coronary heart disease (Krantz & McCeney, 2002; Miller, Smith, Turner, Guijarro, & Hallet, 1996; Smith, Glazer, Ruiz, & Gallo, 2004; Williams et al., 2000), but recent research also indicates a unique role for anxiety in MI above and beyond that played by anger (Shen et al., 2008).

### From Stress to Viral Infection

The effects of stress on the cardiovascular system represent one very important aspect of today's research on stress and health, but there are many other focuses as well. Another body of work that is particularly interesting examines vulnerability to infection. Vulnerability or resistance to infection can be shown in a great many ways, and research bearing on the issue has approached it from several directions. One line of research concerns an infection that most people encounter repeatedly over the course of a lifetime: the common cold.

Does stress influence who catches a cold and who does not? The procedure used in research on this question has been to collect a sample of healthy participants, assess them in several ways, expose them to various doses of cold virus in a carefully controlled environment, then see what happens. Cohen, Tyrrell, and Smith (1991) did this, assessing participants' preexisting stress level (using a measure that blended stress and subjective distress). Lower stress levels predicted greater resistance to infection.

Subsequent work has found several other things about this vulnerability (Cohen, 2005). For example, relatively brief stressful events (less than a month in length) did not predict relative infection risk, but chronic stress (events lasting a month or longer) did (Cohen et al., 1998). The long-term stresses in this study were primarily unemployment (or underemployment) and long-lasting interpersonal problems with family or friends. In other research, having chronically high positive emotionality was protective against infection (Cohen, Doyle, Turner, Alper, & Skoner, 2003). That result has since been replicated and extended to an influenza virus (Cohen, Alper, Doyle, Treanor, & Turner, 2006).

Evidence from a study of monkeys indicates that vulnerability to colds is greater among individuals of lower status than among those of higher status (Cohen et al., 1997). Evidence from adult humans similarly indicates that higher perceived socioeconomic status, though not objective socioeconomic status, was associated with decreased susceptibility to colds (Cohen et al., 2008).

The investigators carrying out this line of research have also collected a variety of other measures to determine the pathway by which stress (or emotional distress) exerts its effects. These measures included endocrine and immune measures that were collected before the exposure to the virus. Interestingly enough, the relation between stressors and susceptibility to colds could not be explained by changes occurring in these other variables. How, then, was the effect mediated?

The answer, which has begun to emerge in subsequent studies (Cohen, 2005), requires going deeper into the immune system, to examine proinflammatory cytokines. These substances trigger the symptoms associated with upper respiratory viral infections. The evidence suggests that stress impairs the body's ability to turn off the production of these cytokines when they are no longer needed (e.g., Miller et al., 2002). Cohen (2005) has pointed out that the conclusion was rather different from what had originally been expected: This effect of stress occurs not because stress suppresses an immune function, but because stress interferes with the ability of the overall immune system to regulate itself properly—it makes it harder to turn the immune function off when it should turn off.

The common cold provides a good example of research on stress, coping, and health partly because it is an experience to which we can all relate. However, it is perhaps important to point out that the viruses responsible for colds stand as representatives of a far broader class of pathogen. Although it is unclear how far the findings described here will generalize, there is good reason to think the principles are likely to be applicable to susceptibility to infection from other viral agents as well (see Cohen & Herbert, 1996).

### Stress and Wound Healing

Another focus for research dealing with infectious agents has been on the processes by which wounds, or breaks in the skin, heal over time. Wound healing is a complex process that involves a variety of immune functions. Research on this topic has included both examination of the immune response per se and study of the overall time required for the wound to heal (for reviews, see Christian et al., 2007; Vileikyte, 2007). Some of this research creates wounds in the form of blisters; more recently, a common procedure has been to create a punch wound of a controlled diameter and depth.

Glaser et al. (1999) reported data bearing on an immune effect that may represent the first step toward wound healing. This is the inflammatory response that occurs shortly after the event causes the wound. Glaser et al. created blisters on people's forearms, had them rate their stress levels, and also measured the presence of two cytokines that are responsible for the inflammation response. Those who reported higher levels of stress also produced lower levels of these cytokines, which are important for the first stages of wound healing.

And what of wound healing per se? A number of studies have now been reported on this topic. Kiecolt-Glaser and colleagues (Kiecolt-Glaser, Marucha, Malarkey, Mercado, & Glaser, 1995) investigated the effects of the stress resulting from caring for a relative with Alzheimer disease on wound healing. They compared women caring for demented relatives with control women matched for age and family income. All the women underwent a wound that was carefully controlled in size. Healing was assessed by photography of the wound and by response to hydrogen peroxide (healing defined as no foaming). Wound healing took significantly longer in caregivers than in controls. Secondary evidence from this

study suggested that the caregivers were also experiencing immune suppression.

Another demonstration of this stress effect on wound healing made use of dental students as research participants (Marucha, Kiecolt-Glaser, & Favagehi, 1998). These students underwent punch wounds on the oral hard palate at two different times: 3 days before the first major exam of the semester (a highly stressful time), and during a vacation period (a low-stress time). On average, the students took 40% longer (3 days longer) to heal during the high-stress period than during the control period. This study also found a decline in production of a substance relevant to the immune response during the exam period, again suggesting a possible immune pathway. However, the researchers did not test the path statistically, leaving open the question of whether the difference in immune response was behind the difference in healing time.

Another study of oral hard palate wounds investigated the effects of loneliness and depressive symptoms on wound healing in a sample of undergraduates (Bosch et al., 2007). High levels of depressive symptoms were associated with slower wound healing, even after controlling for a number of demographic variables and health behaviors. Loneliness and diurnal cortisol secretion, however, were not related to wound healing.

Another study examined wound healing as a function of perceived stress at the time of the wound (Ebrecht, Hextall, Kirtley, Taylor, Dyson, & Weinman, 2004). Those reporting lower stress levels experienced faster healing. They also were less likely to display a morning elevation in cortisol. Although the authors suggested that the cortisol elevations played a role in the difference in wound healing, again there was no statistical test for mediation.

Another interesting topic is the role of pain-related stress on wound healing (for review see Soon & Acton, 2006). As an example, a relatively small study of women who underwent gastric bypass surgery ($N = 17$) indicated that those who reported higher levels of pain immediately afterward and for the following 4 weeks had slower healing of the surgical wounds (McGuire et al., 2006). The relationship between pain and healing did not appear to be a function of health habits (e.g., smoking), depressive symptoms, presurgical (i.e., preexisting) pain, type of surgery, or medical complications.

The question of how stress influences wound healing is one that has important practical implications. As suggested by the previous paragraph, it seems likely that the same processes involved in healing of small, controlled wounds are also involved in the process of recovery from major surgery (Broadbent, Petrie, Alley, & Booth, 2003; Kiecolt-Glaser, Page, Marucha, MacCallum, & Glaser, 1998). If so, a more complete understanding of how to foster healing may have a large payoff in promoting faster recovery from surgery.

One limitation of the studies in this topic area is that they fairly uniformly focus on acute wounds. It has been suggested that research should also look at chronic wounds, such as diabetic foot ulcers, as chronic wounds are associated with a distinct set of immunologic factors (Vileikyte, 2007).

### Section Summary

The preceding sections have touched on research in several areas in which evidence suggests that stress (or distress) plays a role in some aspect of physical health. This description is clearly not anywhere close to being exhaustive. Even in the areas we did touch on, a great deal more information exists than was presented here. There are also many other areas in which research is actively examining questions about stress, coping, and physical health—areas that include (but are by no means limited to) such diseases as cancer, HIV and AIDS, and rheumatoid arthritis.

## Conclusion

This chapter has addressed a set of questions concerning the interrelations among stress, coping, and health. We began by considering some definitions of stress and coping, and trying to link those experiences to a general model of motivation and self-regulated action. In so doing, we tried to make the case that coping is not a special event but is normal behavior that takes place under circumstances of adversity. Stress is the adversity; coping is the attempt to make it go away or to diminish its impact.

These experiences are important to the behavioral scientist, but they are also important to the health scientist. Dealing with adversity creates emotional responses. It also changes the activities of the systems that handle the flow of blood to various parts of the body, the systems that manage immune responses, and the systems that manage communication among other subsystems. These various consequences of stress and coping change the person's internal environment in ways that ultimately influence health. The attempt to understand how this happens is an important part of health psychology.

The efforts to untangle these links have been ongoing for decades, but in a sense they are only just beginning. The human body is exceedingly complex; the reasons for many of its functions are not well understood. The paths of influence shown earlier, in Figure 8.1, represent a simplified view of how experience may create a long-lasting adverse impact on the body. The diagram is far too simple to be complete, and it may even be quite wrong. For example, it is possible that the effects of stress on health depend less on emotional reactions than is now generally believed. Similarly, today's understanding of the neuroendocrine system and the immune system remains limited. Perhaps the keys to disease processes lie in areas as yet unexplored.

We know now that stress has several kinds of adverse effects on health. Establishing that fact in effect took health psychologists through the first level of the puzzle. The key questions now are different. They are questions about the mechanisms by which disease is created and worsened. An increasing focus on mechanisms of causality will force health scientists to refine and extend their research strategies. One change that is certain to come in the near future will be an increased emphasis on studies (and on statistical analyses) that test pathways of influence from one variable to another to another, in order to obtain a closer grasp of the mechanisms of action. Only in this way will we really be able to claim that we understand how stress and coping influence health.

## References

Affleck, G., & Tennen, H. (1996). Construing benefits from adversity: Adaptational significance and dispositional underpinnings. *Journal of Personality, 64*, 899–922.

Affleck, G., Tennen, H., Pfeiffer, C., & Fifield, J. (1987). Appraisals of control and predictability in adapting to a chronic disease. *Journal of Personality and Social Psychology, 53*, 273–279.

Ahern, D.K., Gorkin, L., Anderson, J.L., Tierney, C., Hallstrom, A., Ewart, C., et al. (1990). Biobehavioral variables and mortality or cardiac arrest in the Cardiac Arrhythmia Pilot Study (CAPS). *American Journal of Cardiology, 66*, 59–62.

Andersen, B.L., & Cacioppo, J.T. (1995). Delay in seeking a cancer diagnosis: Delay stages and psychophysiological comparison processes. *British Journal of Social Psychology, 34*, 33–52.

Andrykowski, M.A., Brady, M.J., & Hunt, J.W. (1993). Positive psychosocial adjustment in potential bone marrow transplant recipients: Cancer as a psychosocial transition. *Psychooncology, 2*, 261–276.

Antoni, M.H. (2002). HIV and AIDS. In A.J. Christensen, & M.H. Antoni (Eds.), *Chronic physical disorders: Behavioral medicine's perspective* (pp. 191–219). Oxford, England: Blackwell.

Antoni, M.H., Lechner, S.C., Kazi, A., Sifre, T., Phillips, K., Carver, C.S., et al. (2006). How stress management improves quality of life after treatment for breast cancer. *Journal of Consulting and Clinical Psychology, 74*, 1143–1152.

Antoni, M.H., Lehman, J.M., Kilbourn, K.M., Boyers, A.E., Culver, J.L., Alferi, S.M., et al. (2001). Cognitive-behavioral stress management intervention decreases the prevalence of depression and enhances benefit finding among women under treatment for early-stage breast cancer. *Health Psychology, 20,* 20–32.

Antoni, M.H., & Schneiderman, N. (1998). HIV/AIDS. In A. Bellack, & M. Hersen (Eds.), *Comprehensive clinical psychology* (pp. 237–275). New York: Elsevier Science.

Appels, A., Golombeck, B., Gorgels, A., de Vreede, J., & van Breukelen, G. (2000). Behavioral risk factors of sudden cardiac arrest. *Journal of Psychosomatic Research, 48,* 463–469.

Aspinwall, L.G., & Richter, L. (1999). Optimism and self-mastery predict more rapid disengagement from unsolvable tasks in the presence of alternatives. *Motivation and Emotion, 23,* 221–245.

Aspinwall, L.G., & Taylor, S.E. (1997). A stitch in time: Self-regulation and proactive coping. *Psychological Bulletin, 121,* 417–436.

Austenfeld, J.L., & Stanton, A.L. (2004). Coping through emotional approach: A new look at emotion, coping, and health-related outcomes. *Journal of Personality, 72,* 1335–1364.

Austin, J.T., & Vancouver, J.B. (1996). Goal constructs in psychology: Structure, process, and content. *Psychological Bulletin, 120,* 338–375.

Bandura, A. (1986). *Social foundations of thought and action: A social cognitive theory.* Englewood Cliffs, NJ: Prentice-Hall.

Banou, E., Hobfoll, S.E., & Trochelman, R.D. (2009). Loss of resources as mediators between interpersonal trauma and traumatic and depressive symptoms among women with cancer. *Journal of Health Psychology, 14,* 200–214.

Barefoot, J.C., Brummett, B.H., Helms, M.J., Mark, D.B., Siegler, I.C., & Williams, R.B. (2000). Depressive symptoms and survival of patients with coronary artery disease. *Psychosomatic Medicine, 62,* 790–795.

Barefoot, J.C., Helms, M.S., Mark, D.B., Blumenthal, J.A., Califf, R.M., Haney, T.L., et al. (1996). Depression and long-term mortality risk in patients with coronary artery disease. *American Journal of Cardiology, 78,* 613–617.

Barefoot, J.C., & Schroll, M. (1996). Symptoms of depression, acute myocardial infarction, and total mortality in a community sample. *Circulation, 93,* 1976–1980.

Benyamini, Y., McClain, C.S., Leventhal, E.A., & Leventhal, H. (2003). Living with the worry of cancer: Health perceptions and behaviors of elderly people with self, vicarious, or no history of cancer. *Psycho-Oncology, 12,* 161–172.

Biondi, M., & Picardi, A. (1999). Psychological stress and neuroendocrine function in humans: The last two decades of research. *Psychotherapy and Psychosomatics, 68,* 114–150.

Blascovich, J. (2008). Challenge and threat. In A.J. Elliot (Ed.), *Handbook of approach and avoidance motivation* (pp. 431–445). New York: Psychology Press.

Bonnano, G.A., Keltner, D., Holen, A., & Horowitz, M.J. (1995). When avoiding unpleasant emotions might not be such a bad thing: Verbal-autonomic response dissociation and midlife conjugal bereavement. *Journal of Personality and Social Psychology, 69,* 975–989.

Bosch, J.A., Engeland, C.G., Cacioppo, J.T., & Marucha, P.T. (2007). Depressive symptoms predict mucosal wound healing. *Psychosomatic Medicine, 69,* 597–605.

Bower, J., Kemeny, M., Taylor, S., & Fahey, J. (1998) Cognitive processing, discovery of meaning, CD4 decline, and AIDS-related mortality among bereaved HIV-seropositive men. *Journal of Consulting and Clinical Psychology, 66,* 979–986.

Bower, J.E., Low, C.A., Moskowitz, J.T., Sepah, S., & Epel, E. (2008). Benefit finding and physical health: Positive psychological changes and enhanced allostasis. *Social and Personality Psychology Compass, 2/1,* 223–244.

Brandtstädter, J., & Renner, G. (1990). Tenacious goal pursuit and flexible goal adjustment: Explication and age-related analysis of assimilative and accommodative strategies of coping. *Psychology and Aging, 5,* 58–67.

Brehm, J.W., & Self, E.A. (1989). The intensity of motivation. *Annual Review of Psychology, 40,* 109–131.

Broadbent, E., Petrie, K.J., Alley, P.G., & Booth, R.J. (2003). Psychological stress impairs early wound repair following surgery. *Psychosomatic Medicine, 65,* 865–869.

Cacioppo, J.T., & Berntson, G.G. (2011). The brain, homeostasis, and health: balancing demands of the internal and external milieu. In H.S. Friedman (Ed.), *The Oxford handbook of health psychology.* New York: Oxford University Press.

Cacioppo, J.T., Berntson, G.G., Malarkey, W.B., Kiecolt-Glaser, J.K., Sheridan, J.F., Poehlmann, K.M., et al. (1998). Autonomic, neuroendocrine, and immune responses to psychological stress: The reactivity hypothesis. In S.M. McCann, J.M. Lipton, et al. (Eds.), *Annals of the New York Academy of Sciences* Vol. 840: *Neuroimmunomodulation: Molecular aspects, integrative systems, and clinical advances* (pp. 664–673). New York: New York Academy of Sciences.

Carels, R.A., Sherwood, A., & Blumenthal, J.A. (1998). Psychosocial influences on blood pressure during daily life. *International Journal of Psychophysiology, 28,* 117–129.

Carver, C.S. (1998). Resilience and thriving: Issues, models, and linkages. *Journal of Social Issues, 54,* 245–265.

Carver, C.S. (2004). Negative affects deriving from the behavioral approach system. *Emotion, 4,* 3–22.

Carver, C.S., & Antoni, M.H. (2004). Finding benefit in breast cancer during the year after diagnosis predicts better adjustment 5 to 8 years after diagnosis. *Health Psychology, 26,* 595–598.

Carver, C.S., & Connor-Smith, J. (2010). Personality and coping. *Annual Review of Psychology, 61,* 679–704.

Carver, C.S., & Harmon-Jones, E. (2009). Anger is an approach-related affect: Evidence and implications. *Psychological Bulletin, 135,* 183–204.

Carver, C.S., Pozo, C., Harris, S.D., Noriega, V., Scheier, M.F., Robinson, D.S., et al. (1993). How coping mediates the effect of optimism on distress: A study of women with early stage breast cancer. *Journal of Personality and Social Psychology, 65,* 375–390.

Carver, C.S., & Scheier, M.F. (1981). *Attention and self-regulation: A control-theory approach to human behavior.* New York: Springer Verlag.

Carver, C.S., & Scheier, M.F. (1998). *On the self-regulation of behavior.* New York: Cambridge University Press.

Carver, C.S., & Scheier, M.F. (2003). Three human strengths. In L.G. Aspinwall, & U.M. Staudinger (Eds.), *A psychology of human strengths: Perspectives on an emerging field* (pp. 87–102). Washington, DC: American Psychological Association.

Carver, C.S., Scheier, M.F., & Weintraub, J.K. (1989). Assessing coping strategies: A theoretically based approach. *Journal of Personality and Social Psychology, 56,* 267–283.

Chandola, T., Britton, A., Brunner, E., Hemingway, H., Malik, M., Kumari, M., et al. (2008). Work stress and coronary heart disease: What are the mechanisms? *European Heart Journal, 29*, 640–648.

Christian, L.M., Graham, J.E., Padgett, D.A., Glaser, R., & Kiecolt-Glaser, J.K. (2007). Stress and wound healing. *Neuroimmunoiodulation, 13*, 337–346.

Cohen, S. (2005). The Pittsburgh common cold studies: Psychosocial predictors of susceptibility to respiratory infectious illness. *International Journal of Behavioral Medicine, 12*, 123–131.

Cohen, S., Alper, C.M., Doyle, W.J., Adler, N., Treanor, J.J., & Turner, R.B. (2008). Objective and subjective socioeconomic status and susceptibility to the common cold. *Health Psychology, 27*, 268–274.

Cohen, S., Alper, C.M., Doyle, W.J., Treanor, J.J., & Turner, R.B. (2006). Positive emotional style predicts resistance to illness after experimental exposure to rhinovirus or influenza a virus. *Psychosomatic Medicine, 68*, 809–815.

Cohen, S., Doyle, W.J., Turner, R.B., Alper, C.M., & Skoner, D.P. (2003). Emotional style and susceptibility to the common cold. *Psychosomatic Medicine, 65*, 652–657.

Cohen, S., Frank, E., Doyle, W.J., Skoner, D.P., Rabin, B.S., & Gwaltney, J.M., Jr. (1998). Types of stressors that increase susceptibility to the common cold in healthy adults. *Health Psychology, 17*, 214–223.

Cohen, S., & Herbert, T.B. (1996). Health psychology: Psychological factors and physical disease from the perspective of human psychoneuroimmunology. *Annual Review of Psychology, 47*, 113–142.

Cohen, S., Kessler, R.C., & Gordon, L.U. (Eds.). (1997). *Measuring stress: A guide for health and social scientists.* New York: Oxford University Press.

Cohen, S., Line, S., Manuck, S.B., Rabin, B.S., Heise, E.R., & Kaplan, J.R. (1997). Chronic social stress, social status, and susceptibility to upper respiratory infections in nonhuman primates. *Psychosomatic Medicine, 59*, 213–221.

Cohen, S., & Rodriguez, M.S. (1995). Pathways linking affective disturbances and physical disorders. *Health Psychology, 14*, 374–380.

Cohen, S., Schwartz, J.E., Bromet, E.J., & Parkinson, D.K. (1991). Mental health, stress, and poor health behaviors in two community samples. *Preventive Medicine, 20*, 306–315.

Cohen, S., Tyrrell, D.A., & Smith, A.P. (1991). Psychological stress and susceptibility to the common cold. *New England Journal of Medicine, 325*, 606–612.

Cohen, S., & Wills, T.A. (1985). Stress, social support, and the buffering hypothesis. *Psychological Bulletin, 98*, 310–357.

Compas, B.E., Connor-Smith, J.K., Saltzman, H., Thomsen, A.H., & Wadsworth, M.E. (2001). Coping with stress during childhood and adolescence: Problems, progress, and potential in theory and research. *Psychological Bulletin, 127*, 87–127.

Connor-Smith, J.K., Compas, B.E., Wadsworth, M.E., Thomsen, A.H., & Saltzman, H. (2000). Responses to stress in adolescence: Measurement of coping and involuntary stress responses. *Journal of Consulting and Clinical Psychology, 68*, 976–992.

Connor-Smith, J.K., & Flachsbart, C. (2007). Relations between personality and coping: A meta-analysis. *Journal of Personality and Social Psychology, 93*, 1080–1107.

Cordova, M.J., Cunningham, L.L.C., Carlson, C.R., & Andrykowski, M.A. (2001). Posttraumatic growth following breast cancer: A controlled comparison study. *Health Psychology, 20*, 176–185.

Culver, J.L., Arena, P.L., Antoni, M.H., & Carver, C.S. (2002). Coping and distress among women under treatment for early stage breast cancer: Comparing African Americans, Hispanics, and non-Hispanic whites. *Psycho-Oncology, 11*, 495–504.

Davidson, R.J. (1998). Affective style and affective disorders: Perspectives from affective neuroscience. *Cognition and Emotion, 12*, 307–330.

Depue, R.A., & Collins, P.F. (1999). Neurobiology of the structure of personality: Dopamine, facilitation of incentive motivation, and extraversion. *Behavioral and Brain Sciences, 22*, 491–517.

Dickerson, S.S., & Kemeny, M.E. (2004). Acute stressors and cortisol responses: A theoretical integration and synthesis of laboratory research. *Psychological Bulletin, 130*, 355–391.

Dunbar-Jacob, J., & Schlenk, E.A. (1996). Treatment adherence and clinical outcome: Can we make a difference? In R.J. Resnick, & R.H. Rozensky (Eds.), *Health psychology through the life span: Practice and research opportunities* (pp. 323–343). Washington, DC: American Psychological Association.

Dunbar-Jacob, J., Schlenk, E.A., & Caruthers, D. (2002). Adherence in the management of chronic disorders. In A.J. Christensen, & M.H. Antoni (Eds.), *Chronic physical disorders: Behavioral medicine's perspective* (pp. 69–82). Oxford, UK: Blackwell.

Earle, T.L., Linden, W., & Weinberg, J. (1999). Differential effects of harassment on cardiovascular and salivary cortisol stress reactivity and recovery in women and men. *Journal of Psychosomatic Research, 46*, 125–141.

Ebrecht, M., Hextall, J., Kirtley, L. -G., Taylor, A., Dyson, M., & Weinman, J. (2004). Perceived stress and cortisol levels predict speed of wound healing in healthy male adults. *Psychoneuroendocrinology, 29*, 798–809.

Eisenberg, N., Fabes, R.A., & Guthrie, I. (1997). Coping with stress: The roles of regulation and development. In J.N. Sandler, & S.A. Wolchik (Eds.), *Handbook of children's coping with common stressors: Linking theory, research, and intervention* (pp. 41–70). New York: Plenum.

Elliot, A.J. (Ed.). (2008). *Handbook of approach and avoidance motivation.* New York: Psychology Press.

Everson, S.A., Goldberg, D.E., Kaplan, G.A., Cohen, R.D., Pukkala, E., Tuomilehto, J., et al. (1996). Hopelessness and risk of mortality and incidence of myocardial infarction and cancer. *Psychosomatic Medicine, 58*, 113–121.

Everson, S.A., Kaplan, G.A., Goldberg, D.E., Salonen, R., & Salonen, J.T. (1997). Hopelessness and 4-year progression of carotid atherosclerosis. *Arteriosclerosis, Thrombosis, and Vascular Biology, 17*, 1490–1495.

Everson-Rose, S.A., & Lewis, T.T. (2005). Psychosocial factors and cardiovascular disease. *Annual Review of Public Health, 26*, 469–500.

Ewart, C.K., Taylor, C.B., Kraemer, H.C., & Agras, W.S. (1991). High blood pressure and marital discord: Not being nasty matters more than being nice. *Health Psychology, 10*, 155–163.

Folkman, S. (1997). Positive psychological states and coping with severe stress. *Social Science and Medicine, 45*, 1207–1221.

Folkman, S. (2008). The case for positive emotions in the stress process. *Anxiety, Stress, and Coping, 21*, 3–14.

Folkman, S. (2009). Questions, answers, issues, and next steps in stress and coping research. *European Psychologist, 14*, 72–77.

Folkman, S., Chesney, M., Collette, L., Boccellari, A., & Cooke, M. (1996). Postbereavement depressive mood and its prebereavement predictors in HIV+ and HIV–gay men. *Journal of Personality and Social Psychology, 70*, 336–348.

Folkman, S., & Moskowitz, J.T. (2000). Positive affect and the other side of coping. *American Psychologist, 55*, 647–654.

Folkman, S., & Moskowitz, J.T. (2004). Coping: Pitfalls and promise. *Annual Review of Psychology, 55*, 745–774.

Ford, D.E., Mead, L.A., Chang, P.P., Cooper-Patrick, L., Wang, N., & Klag, M.J. (1998). Depression is a risk factor for coronary artery disease in men. *Archives of Internal Medicine, 158*, 1422–1426.

Frasure-Smith, N., Lesperance, F., & Talajic, M. (1995). The impact of negative emotions on prognosis following myocardial infarction: Is it more than depression? *Health Psychology, 14*, 388–398.

Fredrickson, B.L., Mancuso, R.A., Branigan, C., & Tugade, M.M. (2000). The undoing effect of positive emotions. *Motivation and Emotion, 24*, 237–258.

Fredrikson, M., & Matthews, K.A. (1990). Cardiovascular responses to behavioral stress and hypertension: A meta-analytic review. *Annals of Behavioral Medicine, 12*, 30–39.

Gallagher, S., Phillips, A.C., Drayson, M.T., & Carroll, D. (2009). Parental caregivers of children with developmental disabilities mount a poor antibody response to pneumococcal vaccination. *Brain, Behavior, & Immunity, 23*, 338–346.

Glaser, R., & Kiecolt-Glaser, J.K. (Eds.). (1994). *Handbook of human stress and immunity*. San Diego, CA: Academic Press.

Glaser, R., Kiecolt-Glaser, J.K., Marucha, P.T., MacCallum, R.C., Laskowski, B.F., & Malarkey, W.B. (1999). Stress-related changes in proinflammatory cytokine production in wounds. *Archives of General Psychiatry, 56*, 450–456.

Glaser, R., Sheridan, J., Malarkey, W.B., MacCallum, R.C., & Kiecolt-Glaser, J.K. (2000). Chronic stress modulates the immune response to a pneumococcal pneumonia vaccine. *Psychosomatic Medicine, 62*, 804–807.

Gouin, J.P., Hantsoo, L., & Kiecolt-Glaser, J.K. (2008). Immune dysregulation and chronic stress among older adults: A review. *Neuroimmunomodulation, 15*, 251–259.

Grant, N., Hamer, M., & Steptoe, A. (2009). Social isolation and stress-related cardiovascular, lipid, and cortisol responses. *Annals of Behavioral Medicine, 37*, 29–37.

Gray, J.A. (1994). Personality dimensions and emotion systems. In P. Ekman, & R.J. Davidson (Eds.), *The nature of emotion: Fundamental questions* (pp. 329–331). New York: Oxford University Press.

Greenglass, E.R., & Fiksenbaum, L. (2009). Proactive coping, positive affect, and well-being: Theoretical and empirical consideration. *European Psychologist, 14*, 29–39.

Gross, J.J. (Ed.). (2007). *Handbook of emotion regulation*. New York: Guilford.

Heavey, C.L., Layne, C., & Christensen, A.A. (1993). Gender and conflict structure in marital interaction: A replication and extension. *Journal of Consulting and Clinical Psychology, 61*, 16–27.

Heffner, K.L., Kiecolt-Glaser, J.K., Loving, T.J., Glaser, R., & Malarkey, W.B. (2004). Spousal support satisfaction as a modifier of physiological responses to marital conflict in younger and older couples. *Journal of Behavioral Medicine, 27*, 233–254.

Helgeson, V.S., Reynolds, K.A., & Tomich, P.L. (2006). A meta-analytic review of benefit finding and growth. *Journal of Consulting and Clinical Psychology, 74*, 797–816.

Hemingway H., & Marmot, M. (1999). Psychosocial factors in the aetiology and prognosis of coronary heart disease: Systematic review of prospective cohort studies. *British Medical Journal, 318*, 1460–1467.

Herbert, T., & Cohen, S. (1993). Stress and immunity in humans: A meta-analytic review. *Psychosomatic Medicine, 55*, 364–379.

Higgins, E.T. (1996). Ideals, oughts, and regulatory focus: Affect and motivation from distinct pains and pleasures. In P.M. Gollwitzer, & J.A. Bargh (Eds.), *The psychology of action: Linking cognition and motivation to behavior* (pp. 91–114). New York: Guilford.

Hobfoll, S.E. (1989). Conservation of resources: A new attempt at conceptualizing stress. *American Psychologist, 44*, 513–524.

Hobfoll, S.E. (1998). *Stress, culture, and community*. New York: Plenum.

Hobfoll, S.E., Freedy, J.R., Green, B.L., & Solomon, S.D. (1996). Coping in reaction to extreme stress: The roles of resource loss and resource availability. In M. Zeidner, & N.S. Endler (Eds.), *Handbook of coping: Theory, research, applications* (pp. 322–349). New York: Wiley.

Holahan, C.J., Moos, R.H., Holahan, C.K., & Cronkite, R.C. (1999). Resource loss, resource gain, and depressive symptoms: A 10-year model. *Journal of Personality and Social Psychology, 77*, 620–629.

Holahan, C.J., Moos, R.H., Holahan, C.K., & Cronkite, R.C. (2000). Long-term posttreatment functioning among patients with unipolar depression: An integrative model. *Journal of Consulting and Clinical Psychology, 68*, 226–232.

Holahan, C.J., Moos, R.H., Holahan, C.K., Cronkite, R.C., & Randall, P.K. (2003). Drinking to cope and alcohol use and abuse in unipolar depression: A 10-year model. *Journal of Abnormal Psychology, 112*, 159–165.

Horwitz, A.V., & White, H.R. (1991). Becoming married, depression, and alcohol problems among young adults. *Journal of Health and Social Behavior, 32*, 221–237.

Ice, G.H., & James, G.D (Eds.). (2007). *Measuring stress in humans: A practical guide for the field*. New York: Cambridge University Press.

Januzzi, J.L., Stern, T.A., Pasternak, R., & DeSanctis, R.W. (2000). The influence of anxiety and depression on outcomes of patients with coronary artery disease. *Archives of Internal Medicine, 160*, 1913–1921.

Jim, H.S., & Jacobsen, P.B. (2008). Posttraumatic stress and posttraumatic growth in cancer survivorship: A review. *Cancer* Journal, *14*, 414–419.

Jung, W., & Irwin, M. (1999). Reduction of natural killer cytotoxic activity in major depression: Interaction between depression and cigarette smoking. *Psychosomatic-Medicine, 61*, 263–270.

Kamholz, B.W., Hayes, A.M., Carver, C.S., Gulliver, S.B., & Perlman, C.A. (2006). Identification and evaluation of cognitive affect-regulation strategies: Development of a self-report measure. *Cognitive Therapy and Research, 30*, 227–262.

Kaprio J., Koskenvuo, M., & Rita, H. (1987). Mortality after bereavement: A prospective study of 95,647 persons. *American Journal of Public Health, 77*, 283–287.

Kemeny, M.E. (2009). Psychobiological responses to social threat: Evolution of a psychological model in psychoneuroimmunology. *Brain, Behavior, & Immunity, 23*, 1–9.

Kemeny, M.E. (2011). Psychoneuroimmunology. In H.S. Friedman (Ed.), *The Oxford handbook of health psychology*. New York: Oxford University Press.

Kennedy, P., Marsh, N., Lowe, R., Grey, N., Short, E., & Rogers, B. (2000). A longitudinal analysis of psychological impact and coping strategies following spinal cord injury. *British Journal of Health Psychology, 5*, 157–172.

Kiecolt-Glaser, J.K., Bane, C., Glaser, R., & Malarkey, W.B. (2003). Love, marriage, and divorce: Newlyweds' stress hormones foreshadow relationship changes. *Journal of Consulting and Clinical Psychology, 71*, 176–188.

Kiecolt-Glaser, J.K., Fisher, L.D., Ogrocki, P., Stout, J.C., Speicher, C.E., & Glaser, R. (1987). Marital quality, marital disruption, and immune function. *Psychosomatic Medicine, 49*, 13–34.

Kiecolt-Glaser, J.K., Glaser, R., Cacioppo, J.T., MacCallum, R.C., Snydersmith, M., Kim, C., et al. (1997). Marital conflict in older adults: Endocrinological and immunological correlates. *Psychosomatic Medicine, 59*, 339–349.

Kiecolt-Glaser, J.K., Loving, T.J., Stowell, J.R., Malarkey, W.B., Lemeshow, S., Dickinson, S.L., & Glaser, R. (2005). Hostile marital interactions, proinflammatory cytokine production, and wound healing. *Archives of General Psychiatry, 62*, 1377–1384.

Kiecolt-Glaser, J.K., Marucha, P.T., Malarkey, W.B., Mercado, A.M., & Glaser, R. (1995). Slowing of wound healing by psychological stress. *Lancet, 346*, 1194–1196.

Kiecolt-Glaser, J.K., McGuire, L., Robles, T.F., & Glaser, R. (2002). Emotions, morbidity, and mortality: New perspectives from psychoneuroimmunology. *Annual Review of Psychology, 53*, 83–107.

Kiecolt-Glaser, J.K., & Newton, T.L. (2001). Marriage and health: His and hers. *Psychological Bulletin, 127*, 451–471.

Kiecolt-Glaser, J.K., Newton, T., Cacioppo, J.T., MacCallum, R.C., Glaser, R., & Malarkey, W.B. (1996). Marital conflict and endocrine function: Are men really more physiologically affected than women? *Journal of Consulting and Clinical Psychology, 64*, 324–332.

Kiecolt-Glaser, J.K., Page, G.G., Marucha, P.T., MacCallum, R.C., & Glaser, R. (1998). Psychological influences on surgical recovery: Perspectives from psychoneuroimmunology. *American Psychologist, 53*, 1209–1218.

Kinder, L.S., Kamarck, T.W., Baum, A., & Orchard, T.J. (2002). Depressive symptomatology and coronary heart disease in type I diabetes mellitus: A study of possible mechanisms. *Health Psychology, 21*, 542–552.

Klinger, E. (1975). Consequences of commitment to and disengagement from incentives. *Psychological Review, 82*, 1–25.

Krantz, D.S., & McCeney, M.K. (2002). Effects of psychological and social factors on organic disease: A critical assessment of research on coronary heart disease. *Annual Review of Psychology, 53*, 341–369.

Kronfol, Z., Madhavan, N., Zhang, Q., Hill, E.E., & Brown, M.B. (1997). Circadian immune measures in healthy volunteers: Relationship to hypothalamic-pituitary-adrenal axis hormones and sympathetic neurotransmitters. *Psychosomatic Medicine, 59*, 42–50.

Kubzansky, L.D., & Kawachi, I. (2000). Going to the heart of the matter: Do negative emotions cause coronary heart disease? *Journal of Psychosomatic Research, 48*, 323–337.

Kubzansky, L.D., Kawachi, I., Spiro, A., III, Weiss, S.T., Vokonas, P.S., & Sparrow, D. (1997). Is worrying bad for your heart? A prospective study of worry and coronary heart disease in the Normative Aging Study. *Circulation, 95*, 818–824.

Lannen, P.K., Wolfe, J., Prigerson, H.G., Onelov, E., & Kreicbergs, U.C. (2008). Unresolved grief in a national sample of bereaved parents: Impaired mental and physical health 4 to 9 years later. *Journal of Clinical Oncology, 26*, 5870–5876.

Larsen, R.J., & Prizmic, Z. (2004). Affect regulation. In R.F. Baumeister, & K.D. Vohs (Eds.), *Handbook of self-regulation: Research, theory, and applications* (pp. 40–61). New York: Guilford Press.

Lazarus, R.S. (1966). *Psychological stress and the coping process.* New York: McGraw-Hill.

Lazarus, R.S. (1999). *Stress and emotion: A new synthesis.* New York: Springer.

Lazarus, R.S., & Folkman, S. (1984). *Stress, appraisal, and coping.* New York: Springer.

Lench, H.C., & Levine, L.J. (2008). Goals and responses to failure: Knowing when to hold them and when to fold them. *Motivation and Emotion, 32*, 127–140.

Leor, J., Poole, W.K., & Kloner, R.A. (1996). Sudden cardiac death triggered by an earthquake. *New England Journal of Medicine, 334*, 413–419.

Leventhal, H., Brissette, I., & Leventhal, E.A. (2003). The common-sense model of self-regulation of health and illness. In L.D. Cameron, & H. Leventhal (Eds.), *The self-regulation of health and illness behavior* (pp. 42–65). New York: Routledge.

Leventhal, H., Benyamini, Y., Brownlee, S., Diefenbach, M., Leventhal, E.A., Patrick-Miller, L. et al. (1997). Illness representations: Theoretical foundations. In K.J. Petrie, & J. Weinman (Eds.), *Perceptions of health and illness: Current research and applications* (pp. 19–45). Amsterdam: Harwood.

Leventhal, H., Meyer, D., & Nerenz, D.R. (1980). The common sense representation of illness danger. In S. Rachman (Ed.), *Contributions to medical psychology* Vol. 2 (pp. 17–30). New York: Pergamon.

Low, C.A., Bower, J.E., Kwan, L., & Seldon, J. (2008). Benefit finding in response to BRCA1/2 testing. *Annals of Behavioral Medicine, 35*, 61–69.

Maier, S.F., Watkins, L.R., & Fleshner, M. (1994). Psychoneuroimmunology: The interface between behavior, brain, and immunity. *American Psychologist, 49*, 1004–1017.

Malarkey, W., Kiecolt-Glaser, J.K., Pearl, D., & Glaser, R. (1994). Hostile behavior during marital conflict alters pituitary and adrenal hormones. *Psychosomatic Medicine, 56*, 41–51.

Marin, T.J., Chen, E., Munch, J.A., & Miller, G.E. (2009). Double-exposure to acute stress and chronic family stress is associated with immune changes in children with asthma. *Psychosomatic Medicine, 71*, 378–384.

Marucha, P.T., Kiecolt-Glaser, J.K., & Favagehi, M. (1998). Mucosal wound healing is impaired by examination stress. *Psychosomatic Medicine, 60*, 362–365.

McGuire, L., Heffner, K., Glaser, R., Needleman, B., Malarkey, W., Dickinson, S., et al. (2006). Pain and wound healing in surgical patients. *Annals of Behavioral Medicine, 31*, 165–172.

Meisel, S.R., Kutz, I., Dayan, K.I., Pauzner, H., Chetboun, I., Arbel, Y., et al. (1991). Effects of Iraqi missile war on incidence of acute myocardial infarction and sudden death in Israeli civilians. *Lancet, 338*, 660–661.

Michelson, D., Licinio, J., & Bold, P.W. (1995). Mediation of the stress response by the hypothalamic-pituitary-adrenal axis. In M.J. Friedman, D.S. Charney, & A.Y. Deutch (Eds.), *Neurobiological and clinical consequences of stress* (pp. 225–238). Philadelphia: Lippincott-Raven.

Mikolajczak, M., Roy, E., Luminet, O., Fillée, C., & de Timary, P. (2007). The moderating impact of emotional intelligence on free cortisol responses to stress. *Psychoneuroendocrinology, 32*, 1000–1012.

Miller, G., Chen, E., & Cole, S.W. (2009). Health psychology: Developing biologically plausible models linking the social world and physical health. *Annual Review of Psychology, 60,* 501–524.

Miller, G.E., Cohen, S., & Ritchey, A.K. (2002). Chronic psychological stress and the regulation of pro-inflammatory cytokines: A glucocorticoid-resistance model. *Health Psychology, 21,* 531–541.

Miller, T.Q., Smith, T.W., Turner, C.W., Guijarro, M.L., & Hallet, A.J. (1996). A meta-analytic review of research on hostility and physical health. *Psychological Bulletin, 119,* 322–348.

Miller, G.E., & Wrosch, C. (2007). You've gotta know when to fold'em: Goal disengagement and systemic inflammation in adolescence. *Psychological Science, 18,* 773–777.

Mittleman, M.A., Maclure, M., Sherwood, J.B., Mulry, R.P., Tofler, G.H., Jacobs, S.C., et al. (1995). Triggering of acute myocardial infarction onset by episodes of anger. *Circulation, 92,* 1720–1725.

Moos, R.H., & Schaefer, J.A. (1993). Coping resources and processes: Current concepts and measures. In L. Goldberger, & S. Breznitz (Eds.), *Handbook of stress: Theoretical and clinical aspects* (2nd ed., pp. 234–257). New York: Free Press.

Morling, B. & Evered, S. (2006). Secondary control reviewed and defined. *Psychological Bulletin, 132,* 269–296.

Moser, D.K., & Dracup, K. (1996). Is anxiety early after myocardial infarction associated with subsequent ischemic and arrhythmic events? *Psychosomatic Medicine, 58,* 395–401.

Myers, J.S. (2008). Proinflammatory cytokines and sickness behavior: Implications for depression and cancer-related symptoms. *Oncology Nursing Forum, 35,* 802–807.

Nesse, R.M. (2000). Is depression an adaptation? *Archives of General Psychiatry, 57,* 14–20.

Nicolson, N.A. (1992). Stress, coping and cortisol dynamics in daily life. In M.W. de Vries (Ed.), *The experience of psychopathology: Investigating mental disorders in their natural settings* (pp. 219–232). Cambridge: Cambridge University Press.

Norekvål, T.M., Moons, P., Hanestad, B.R., Nordrehaug, J.E., Wentzel-Larsen, T., & Fridlund, B. (2008). The other side of the coin: Perceived positive effects of illness in women following acute myocardial infarction. *European Journal of Cardiovascular Nursing, 7,* 80–87.

Ochsner, K.N., & Gross, J.J. (2004). Thinking makes it so: A social cognitive neuroscience approach to emotion regulation. In R.F. Baumeister, & K.D. Vohs (Eds.), *Handbook of self-regulation: Research, theory, and applications* (pp. 229–255). New York: Guilford Press.

O'Donnell, K., Badrick, E., Kumari, M., & Steptoe, A. (2008). Psychological coping styles and cortisol over the day in healthy older adults. *Psychoneuroendocrinology, 33,* 601–611.

O'Leary, A. (1990). Stress, emotion, and human immune function. *Psychological Bulletin, 108,* 363–382.

Olff, M., Brosschot, J.F., Godeart, G., Benschop, R.J., Ballieux, R.E., Heijnen, C.J., et al. (1995). Modulatory effects of defense and coping on stress-induced changes in endocrine and immune parameters. *International Journal of Behavioral Medicine, 2,* 85–103.

Ostrow, D.G., VanRaden, M., Fox, R., Kingsley, L.A., Dudley, J., & Kaslow, R.A. (1990). Recreational drug use and sexual behavior change in a cohort of homosexual men. *AIDS, 4,* 759–765.

Ozer, D.J., & Benet-Martínez, V. (2006). Personality and the prediction of consequential outcomes. *Annual Review of Psychology, 57,* 401–421.

Park, C.L., Armeli, S., & Tennen, H. (2004). Appraisal–coping goodness of fit: A daily internet study. *Personality and Social Psychology Bulletin, 30,* 558–569.

Park, C.L., Cohen, L.H., & Murch, R.L. (1996). Assessment and prediction of stress-related growth. *Journal of Personality, 64,* 71–105.

Park, C.L., & Folkman, S. (1997). Meaning in the context of stress and coping. *Review of General Psychology, 1,* 115–144.

Park, C.L., Lechner, S.C., Antoni, M.H., & Stanton, A.L. (Eds.). (2009). *Medical illness and positive life change.* Washington DC: American Psychological Association.

Parkes, C.M. (1964). Effects of bereavement on physical and mental health: A study of the medical records of widows. *British Medical Journal, 2,* 274–279.

Pervin, L.A. (Ed.). (1989). *Goal concepts in personality and social psychology.* Hillsdale, NJ: Erlbaum.

Pressman, S.D., & Cohen, S. (2005). Does positive affect influence health? *Psychological Bulletin, 131,* 925–971.

Ptacek, J.T., Smith, R.E., Espe, K., & Raffety, B. (1994). Limited correspondence between daily coping reports and retrospective coping recall. *Psychological Assessment, 6,* 41–49.

Rasmussen, H.N., Scheier, M.F., & Greenhouse, J.B. (2009). Optimism and physical health: A meta-analytic review. *Annals of Behavioral Medicine, 37,* 239–256.

Ratcliffe, H.L., & Cronin, N.T. (1958). Changing frequency of atherosclerosis in mammals and birds at the Philadelphia Zoological Garden. *Circulation, 18,* 41–52.

Reichenberg, A., Yirmiya, R., Schuld, A., Kraus, T., Haack, M., Morag, A., & Pollmacher, T. (2001). Cytokine-associated emotional and cognitive disturbances in humans. *Archives of General Psychiatry, 58,* 445–452.

Robles, T.F., Glaser, R., & Kiecolt-Glaser, J.K. (2005). Out of balance: A new look at chronic stress, depression, and immunity. *Current Directions in Psychological Science, 14,* 111–115.

Roth, S., & Cohen, L.J. (1986). Approach, avoidance, and coping with stress. *American Psychologist, 41,* 813–819.

Rothbart, M.K., & Hwang, J. (2005). Temperament and the development of competence and motivation. In A.J. Elliot, & C.S. Dweck (Eds.), *Handbook of competence and motivation* (pp. 167–184). New York: Guilford.

Rozanski, A., Blumenthal, J.A., & Kaplan, J. (1999). Impact of psychological factors on the pathogenesis of cardiovascular disease and implications for therapy. *Circulation, 99,* 2192–2217.

Scheier, M.F., Matthews, K.A., Owens, J.F., Schulz, R., Bridges, M.W., Magovern, G.J., Jr., et al. (1999). Optimism and rehospitalization after coronary artery bypass graft surgery. *Archives of Internal Medicine, 159,* 829–833.

Schnall, P.L., Pieper, C., Schwartz, J.E., Karasek, R.A., Schlussel, Y., Devereux, R.B., et al. (1990). The relationship between job strain, workplace diastolic blood pressure, and left ventricular mass index. *Journal of the American Medical Association, 263,* 1929–1935.

Schnall, P.L., Schwartz, J.E., Landsbergis, P.A., Warren, K., & Pickering, T.G. (1998). A longitudinal study of job strain and ambulatory blood pressure: Results from a three-year follow-up. *Psychosomatic Medicine, 60,* 697–706.

Sears, S.R., Stanton, A.L., & Danoff-Burg, S. (2003). The yellow brick road and the emerald city: Benefit finding, positive reappraisal coping, and post-traumatic growth in women with early-stage breast cancer. *Health Psychology, 22,* 487–497.

Segerstrom, S.C., & Miller, G.E. (2004). Psychological stress and the human immune system: A meta-analytic study of 30 years of inquiry. *Psychological Bulletin, 130*, 601–641.

Selye, H. (1956). *The stress of life*. New York: McGraw-Hill.

Shen, B.J., Avivi, Y.E., Todaro, J.F., Spiro III, A., Laurenceau, J.-P., Ward, K.D., & Niaura, R. (2008). Anxiety characteristics independently and prospectively predict myocardial infarction in men: The unique contribution of anxiety among psychological factors. *Journal of the American College of Cardiology, 51*, 113–119.

Sherbourne, C.D., Hays, R.D., Ordway, L., DiMatteo, M.R., & Kravitz, R.L. (1992). Antecedents of adherence to medical recommendations: Results from the Medical Outcomes Study. *Journal of Behavioral Medicine, 15*, 447–468.

Shively, C.A., Clarkson, T.B., & Kaplan, J.R. (1989). Social deprivation and coronary artery atherosclerosis in female cynomolgus monkeys. *Atherosclerosis, 77*, 69–76.

Sin, N.L., & Lyubomirsky, S. (2009). Enhancing well-being and alleviating depressive symptoms with positive psychology interventions: A practice-friendly meta-analysis. *Journal of Clinical Psychology, 65*, 467–487.

Sjogren, E., Leanderson, P., & Kristenson, M. (2006). Diurnal saliva cortisol levels and relations to psychosocial factors in a population sample of middle-aged Swedish men and women. *International Journal of Behavioral Medicine, 13*, 193–200.

Skinner, E.A., & Zimmer-Gembeck, M.J. (2007). The development of coping. *Annual Review of Psychology, 58*, 119–144.

Skinner, E.A., Edge, K., Altman, J., & Sherwood, H. (2003). Searching for the structure of coping: A review and critique of category systems for classifying ways of coping. *Psychological Bulletin, 129*, 216–269.

Smith, T.W., Allred, K.D., Morrison, C.A., & Carlson, S.D. (1989). Cardiovascular reactivity and interpersonal influence: Active coping in a social context. *Journal of Personality and Social Psychology, 56*, 209–218.

Smith, T.W., Glazer, K., Ruiz, J.M., & Gallo, L.C. (2004). Hostility, anger, aggressiveness, and coronary heart disease: An interpersonal perspective on personality, emotion, and health. *Journal of Personality, 72*, 1217–1270.

Smith, T.W., & Leon, A.S. (1992). *Coronary heart disease: A behavioral perspective*. Champaign-Urbana, IL: Research Press.

Smith, T.W., Nealey, J.B., Kircher, J.C., & Limon, J.P. (1997). Social determinants of cardiovascular reactivity: Effects of incentive to exert influence and evaluative threat. *Psychophysiology, 34*, 65–73.

Smith, T.W., & Ruiz, J.M. (2002). Coronary heart disease. In A.J. Christensen, & M.H. Antoni (Eds.), *Chronic physical disorders: Behavioral medicine's perspective* (pp. 83–111). Oxford, UK: Blackwell.

Smith, T.W., Ruiz, J.M., & Uchino, B.N. (2000). Vigilance, active coping, and cardiovascular reactivity during social interaction in young men. *Health Psychology, 19*, 382–392.

Smith, N.G., Tarakeshwar, N., Hansen, N.B., Kochman, A., & Sikkema, K.J. (2009). Coping mediates outcome following a randomized group intervention for HIV-positive bereaved individuals. *Journal of Clinical Psychology, 65*, 319–335.

Solberg Nes, L., & Segerstrom, S.C. (2006). Dispositional optimism and coping: A meta-analytic review. *Personality and Social Psychology Review, 10*, 235–251.

Soon, K., & Acton, C. (2006). Pain-induced stress: A barrier to wound healing. *Wounds, 2*, 92–101.

Sparrenberger, F., Cichelero, F.T., Ascoli, A.M., Fonseca, F.P., Wiess, G., Berwanger, O., et al. (2009). Does psychosocial stress cause hypertension? A systematic review of observational studies. *Journal of Human Hypertension, 23*, 12–19.

Stanton, A.L., Danoff-Burg, S., Cameron, C.L., Bishop, M., Collins, C.A., et al. (2000). Emotionally expressive coping predicts psychological and physical adjustment to breast cancer. *Journal of Consulting and Clinical Psychology, 68*, 875–882.

Steptoe, A., & Brydon, L. (2009). Emotional triggering of cardiac events. *Neuroscience & Biobehavioral Reviews, 33*, 63–70.

Stroebe, M.S., Schut, H., & Stroebe, W. (2005). Attachment in coping with bereavement: A theoretical integration. *Review of General Psychology, 9*, 48–66.

Taylor, S.E. (1983). Adjustment to threatening events: A theory of cognitive adaptation. *American Psychologist, 38*, 1161–1173.

Tedeschi, R.G., & Calhoun, L.G. (2004). Posttraumatic growth: Conceptual foundations and empirical evidence. *Psychological Inquiry, 15*, 1–18.

Temoshok, L.R., Waldstein, S.R., Wald, R.L., Garzino-Demo, A., Synowski, S.J., Sun, L., et al. (2008). Type C coping, alexithymia, and heart rate reactivity are associated independently and differentially with specific immune mechanisms linked to HIV progression. *Brain, Behavior, & Immunity, 22*, 781–792.

Tennen, H., & Affleck, G. (2002). Benefit-finding and benefit-reminding. In C.R. Snyder, & S.J. Lopez (Eds.), *Handbook of positive psychology* (pp. 584–597). New York: Oxford University Press.

Tennen, H., Affleck, G., Armeli, S., & Carney, M.A. (2000). A daily process approach to coping: Linking theory, research, and practice. *American Psychologist, 55*, 626–636.

Terry, D.J., & Hynes, G.J. (1998). Adjustment to a low-control situation: Reexamining the role of coping responses. *Journal of Personality and Social Psychology, 74*, 1078–1092.

Thurston, R.C., & Kubzansky, L.D. (2009). Women, loneliness, and incident coronary heart disease. *Psychosomatic Medicine, 71*, 836–842.

Todd, M., Tennen, H., Carney, M.A., Armeli, S., & Affleck, G. (2004). Do we know how we cope? Relating daily coping reports to global and time-limited retrospective assessments. *Journal of Personality and Social Psychology, 86*, 310–319.

Tomich, P.L., & Helgeson, V.S. (2004). Is finding something good in the bad always good? Benefit finding among women with breast cancer. *Health Psychology, 23*, 16–23.

Vidovíc, D., Vilibíc, M., Sabioncello, A., Gotovac, K., Rabatíc, S., Folnegovíc-Šmalc, V., et al. (2009). Changes in immune and endocrine systems in posttraumatic stress disorder–Prospective study. *Acta Neuropsychiatrica, 21*, 46–50.

Vileikyte, L. (2007). Stress and wound healing. *Clinics in Dermatology, 25*, 49–55.

Vitaliano, P.P., DeWolfe, D.J., Maiuro, R.D., Russo, J., & Katon, W. (1990). Appraised changeability of a stressor as a modifier of the relationship between coping and depression: A test of the hypothesis of fit. *Journal of Personality and Social Psychology, 59*, 582–592.

Vitaliano, P.P., Russo, J., Young, H., Teri, L., & Maiuro, R.D. (1991). Predictors of burden in spouse caregivers of individuals with Alzheimer's disease. *Psychology and Aging, 6*, 392–402.

Wade, S.L., Borawski, E.A., Taylor, H.G., Drotar, D., Yeates, L.O., & Stancin, T. (2001). The relationship of caregiver coping to family outcomes during the initial year following pediatric traumatic injury. *Journal of Consulting and Clinical Psychology, 69*, 406–415.

Wald, R.L., Dowling, G.C., & Temoshok, L.R. (2006). Coping styles predict immune system parameters and clinical outcomes in patients with HIV. *Retrovirology, 3*, P65.

Weaver, K.E., Llabre, M.M., Lechner, S.C., Penedo, F., & Antoni, M.H. (2008). Comparing unidimensional and multidimensional models of benefit finding in breast and prostate cancer. *Quality of Life Research, 17*, 771–781.

Webster Marketon, J.I., & Glaser, R. (2008). Stress hormones and immune function. *Cell Immunology, 252*, 16–26.

Wilbert-Lampen, U., Leistner, D., Greven, S., Pohl, T., Sper, S., Volker, C., et al. (2008). Cardiovascular events during World Cup Soccer. *New England Journal of Medicine, 358*, 475–483.

Williams, J.E., Paton, C.C., Siegler, I.C., Eigenbrodt, M.L., Nieto, F.J., & Tyroler, H.A. (2000). Anger proneness predicts coronary heart disease risk: Prospective analysis from the Atherosclerosis Risk in Communities (ARIC) study. *Circulation, 101*, 2034–2039.

Wortman, C.B., & Brehm, J.W. (1975). Responses to uncontrollable outcomes: An integration of reactance theory and the learned helplessness model. In L. Berkowitz (Ed.), *Advances in experimental social psychology* Vol. 8 (pp. 277–336). New York: Academic Press.

Wortman, C., & Silver, R. (1989). The myths of coping with loss. *Journal of Consulting and Clinical Psychology, 57*, 349–357.

Wright, R.A. (1996). Brehm's theory of motivation as a model of effort and cardiovascular response. In P.M. Gollwitzer, & J.A. Bargh (Eds.), *The psychology of action: Linking cognition and motivation to behavior* (pp. 424–453). New York: Guilford.

Wrosch, C., Scheier, M.F., Miller, G.E., Schulz, R., & Carver, C.S. (2003). Adaptive self-regulation of unattainable goals: Goal disengagement, goal re-engagement, and subjective well-being. *Personality and Social Psychology Bulletin, 29*, 1494–1508.

# Social Support: A Review

Shelley E. Taylor

**Abstract**

Social support, which is the perception or experience that one is cared for, esteemed, and part of a mutually supportive social network, has beneficial effects on mental and physical health. We review the psychobiological pathways whereby these effects may occur and detail the circumstances under which socially supportive efforts may misfire. Origins of social support include genetic factors and the early environment. We examine gender and cultural differences in how social support is experienced. Under some circumstances, providing social support confers the same benefits as receiving it. A myriad number of social support interventions, including those delivered via the internet, have been evaluated and have the potential to provide emotional and informational support to people who might otherwise lack social support.

**Keywords:** Social support, stress, emotional support, informational support, instrumental support, gender, culture, genes, early environment, interventions, support groups

Group living is perhaps the most significant adaptation of primate species, including human beings. Whereas other animals are armed with weapons, such as sharp teeth or claws, and defensive resources, such as thick skin and speed, primate species depend critically on group living for survival (Caporeal, 1997; Dunbar, 1996). This tendency to come together is especially great under threat. Even chimpanzees, known for their solitary behavior, may abandon this style in favor of group activity when an enhanced risk of predation exists (Boesch, 1991). In times of intense stress, humans are much the same. Following the September 11 terrorist attacks, some of the most common methods people reported using to cope with this threatening event involved turning to others, including family, friends, and even strangers (Galea et al., 2002). There are, of course, tangible benefits to social affiliation under threat. For example, following a disaster, such as a fire, a flood, or a bombing, the presence of many hands can locate survivors and get them to safety. But the presence of others has long been known to foster adjustment to threatening events in other ways, specifically by protecting against adverse changes in mental and physical health that may otherwise occur in response to stress. Social support is now so widely acknowledged as a critical resource for managing stressful occurrences that over 1,100 articles on the topic appear in the research and clinical literatures each year.

## *What Is Social Support?*

Social support is defined as the perception or experience that one is loved and cared for by others, esteemed and valued, and part of a social network of mutual assistance and obligations (Wills, 1991). Social support may come from a partner, relatives, friends, coworkers, social and community ties, and even a devoted pet (Allen, Blascovich, & Mendes, 2002). Taxonomies of social support have usually classified support into several specific forms. *Informational support* occurs when one individual helps another to understand a stressful event better and to ascertain what resources and coping strategies may be needed to deal with it. Through such information or advice, a person under stress may determine exactly what potential costs or strains the stressful event may impose and decide how best to manage it. *Instrumental support* involves the provision of tangible assistance such as services, financial assistance, and other specific aid or goods. Examples include driving an injured friend to the emergency room or providing food to a bereaved family. *Emotional support* involves providing warmth and nurturance to another individual and reassuring a person that he or she is a valuable person for whom others care. But as the definition makes clear, social support can also involve simply the *perception* that such resources are available, should they be needed. For example, knowing that one is cared for and/or that one could request support from others and receive it is comforting in its own right. Thus, social support may involve specific transactions whereby one person explicitly receives benefits from another, or it may be experienced through the perception that such help and support is potentially available.

Social support is typically measured either in terms of the structure of socially supportive networks or the functions that network members may provide (e.g., Wills, 1998). Structural social support, often referred to as social integration, involves the number of social relationships in which an individual is involved and the structure of interconnections among those relationships. Social integration measures assess the number of relationships or social roles a person has, the frequency of contact with various network members, and the density and interconnectedness of relationships among the network members. Functional support is typically assessed in terms of the specific functions (informational, instrumental, and emotional) that a specific member may serve for a target individual and is often assessed in the context of coping with a particular stressor. Thus, an individual might be asked how much of different kinds of support each member of a supportive network provided during a stressful event.

An early debate in the social support literature centered on the circumstances under which social support may be beneficial. One hypothesis, known as the direct effects hypothesis, maintains that social support is generally beneficial to mental and physical health during nonstressful times as well as during stressful times. The other hypothesis, known as the buffering hypothesis, maintains that the health and mental health benefits of social support are chiefly evident during periods of high stress; when there is little stress, social support may have few physical or mental health benefits. According to this hypothesis, social support acts as a reserve and resource that blunts the effects of stress or enables an individual to deal with stress more effectively, but otherwise is less consequential for mental and physical health (Cohen & Wills, 1985). After decades of research, evidence for both types of effects have emerged. Measures of social integration typically show direct associations with mental and physical health, but not buffering effects (Thoits, 1995). In contrast, the perception that emotional support is available is associated both with direct benefits to physical and mental health and also with buffering effects (e.g., Wethington & Kessler, 1986).

## Benefits of Social Support and Reasons for the Benefits

### MENTAL AND PHYSICAL HEALTH BENEFITS

Research consistently demonstrates that social support reduces psychological distress such as depression or anxiety during times of stress (e.g., Fleming, Baum, Gisriel, & Gatchel, 1982; Lin, Ye, & Ensel, 1999; Sarason, Sarason, & Gurung, 1997). It has been found to promote psychological adjustment to chronically stressful conditions, such as coronary artery disease (Holahan, Moos, Holahan, & Brennan, 1997), diabetes, HIV (Turner-Cobb et al., 2002), cancer (Penninx et al., 1998; Stone, Mezzacappa, Donatone, & Gonder, 1999), rheumatoid arthritis (Goodenow, Reisine, & Grady, 1990), kidney disease (Dimond, 1979), childhood leukemia (Magni, Silvestro, Tamiello, Zanesco, & Carl, 1988), and stroke (Robertson & Suinn, 1968), among other disorders. Social support also protects against cognitive decline in older adults (Seeman, Lusignolo, Albert, & Berkman, 2001), heart disease among the recently widowed (Sorkin, Rook, & Lu, 2002), and psychological distress in response to traumatic events, such as 9/11 (Simeon, Greenberg, Nelson, Schmeider, & Hollander, 2005).

Social support also contributes to physical health and survival (e.g., Rutledge et al., 2004). In a classic study that documented this point, epidemiologists Lisa Berkman and Leonard Syme (1979) followed nearly 7,000 California residents over a 9-year period to identify factors that contributed to their longevity or early death. They found that people who lacked social and community ties were more likely to die of all causes during the follow-up period than were those who cultivated or maintained their social relationships. Having social contacts predicted an average 2.8 years increased longevity among women and 2.3 years among men, and these differences persisted after controlling for socioeconomic status (SES), health status at the beginning of the study, and health habits (Berkman & Syme, 1979). Of particular significance is the fact that the positive impact of social ties on health is as powerful, and in some cases, more powerful a predictor of health and longevity than well-established risk factors for chronic disease and mortality, with effect sizes on par with smoking, blood pressure, lipids, obesity, and physical activity (House, Landis, & Umberson, 1988).

These benefits are realized in part by the fact that social support appears to help people to stave off illness altogether. For example, Cohen and associates (1997) intentionally infected healthy community volunteers with a cold or flu virus by swabbing the inside of their nasal passages with virus-soaked cotton swabs. They found that people experiencing a high level of stress were more likely to develop infections than were people under less stress, and the colds and flus they developed were more serious as well. However, those with more social ties were less likely to become ill following exposure to the virus, and if they did, they were able to recover more quickly than were those with fewer social ties (Cohen, Doyle, Skoner, Rabin, & Gwaltney, 1997).

On the whole, though, evidence for the impact of social support on the likelihood of becoming ill is not as consistently positive as evidence for its impact on course of illness or recovery (Seeman, 1996; Taylor & Seeman, 2000). It may be that social contacts both contribute to illness likelihood, as through contagion or the creation of stress (e.g., Hamrick, Cohen, & Rodriguez, 2002), but also promote health via social support, leading, on balance, to the only moderately positive net effect on illness likelihood.

Social support has been tied to a variety of specific health benefits among individuals sustaining health risks. These include fewer complications during pregnancy and childbirth (Collins, Dunkel-Schetter, Lobel, & Scrimshaw, 1993), less susceptibility to herpes attacks among infected individuals (VanderPlate, Aral, & Magder, 1988), lower rates of myocardial infarction among individuals with diagnosed disease, a reduced likelihood of mortality from myocardial infarction (Kulik & Mahler, 1993; Wiklund et al., 1988), faster recovery from coronary artery disease surgery (King, Reis, Porter, & Norsen, 1993; Kulik & Mahler, 1993), better diabetes control (Marteau, Bloch, & Baum, 1987), better compliance and longer survival in patients with end-stage renal disease (Cohen et al., 2007),

and less pain among arthritis patients (Brown, Sheffield, Leary, & Robinson, 2003).

The impact of social support on mortality is also clearly established, as the seminal study by Berkman and Syme (1979) suggests. In prospective studies controlling for baseline health status, people with a higher quantity and quality of social relationships have consistently been shown to be at lower risk of early death (Herbst-Damm & Kulik, 2005; Seeman, 1996), and in studies of both humans and animals, social isolation has been found to be a major risk factor for early mortality (House et al., 1988).

## PATHWAYS LINKING SOCIAL SUPPORT TO HEALTH

Considerable effort has gone into exploring the pathways whereby social support is beneficial to health. Early research examined the possibility that social support may be associated with good health habits which, in turn, beneficially affect health. For example, family living has been tied to a broad array of good health habits, including a lower likelihood of drug or alcohol abuse and smoking, and an enhanced likelihood of a balanced diet and good sleep habits (e.g., Umberson, 1987). Social isolation has been tied to unhealthy responses to stress, such as smoking and alcohol abuse, which can adversely affect health (Broman, 1993). However, although social support may be helpful to people initially in developing or changing health habits, such as stopping smoking, it may have less consistent effects on maintenance (Carlson, Goodey, Bennett, Taenzer, & Koopmans, 2002). If the social support network itself is engaged in a behavior change program, social support may beneficially affect ongoing maintenance. In one study (Fraser & Spink, 2002), for example, women for whom exercise had been prescribed for medical problems were less likely to drop out if they experienced social support in the group. Similarly, when families are engaged in behavior change programs (such as dietary change following diagnosis of cardiovascular disease), such involvement may promote better adherence to an otherwise taxing set of changes (Wilson & Ampey-Thornhill, 2001). Social support may also increase commitment to medical regimens because it enhances feelings of self-efficacy (DiMatteo, 2004; Resnick, Orwig, Magaziner, & Wynne, 2002) or because it affects responsiveness to social influence efforts by others (Cohen & Lemay, 2007). But some social networks may also promote unhealthy behaviors, such as smoking, drug abuse, and drinking (Wills & Vaughan, 1989). On the whole, the impact of social support on health appears to exist over and above any influence it exerts on health habits.

Accordingly, researchers have focused heavily on potential physiological, neuroendocrine, and immunologic pathways by which social support may achieve its health benefits. What are these pathways? During times of stress, the body releases the catecholamines epinephrine and norepinephrine with concomitant sympathetic nervous system (SNA) arousal and may also engage the hypothalamic-pituitary-adrenocortical (HPA) axis, involving the release of corticosteroids including cortisol. These responses have short-term protective effects under stressful circumstances, because they mobilize the body to meet the demands of pressing situations. However, with chronic or recurrent activation, they can be associated with deleterious long-term effects, with implications for health (e.g., Seeman & McEwen, 1996; Uchino, Cacioppo, & Kiecolt-Glaser, 1996). For example, excessive or repeated discharge of epinephrine or norepinephrine can lead to the suppression of cellular immune function, produce hemodynamic changes such as increases in blood pressure and heart rate, provoke abnormal heart rhythms such as ventricular arrhythmias, and produce neurochemical imbalances that may relate to psychiatric disorders (McEwen & Stellar, 1993). Intense, rapid, and/or long-lasting sympathetic responses to repeated stress or challenge have been implicated in the development of hypertension and coronary artery disease.

Recently, evidence for these pathways has been found at the neural level (Eisenberger, Taylor, Gable, Hilmert, & Lieberman, 2007). In a study in which participants kept daily social support diaries, participated in a functional magnetic resonance imaging (fMRI) task assessing neurocognitive reactivity to a social stressor, and participated in laboratory stress tasks during which neuroendocrine responses were assessed, those who interacted regularly with supportive individuals across a 10-day period showed diminished cortisol reactivity to a social stressor. Moreover, greater social support and diminished cortisol responses were associated with diminished activity in the dorsal anterior cingulate cortex (dACC) and Brodmann area 8, brain regions whose activity has previously been tied to social distress. Differences in this neurocognitive reactivity mediated the relationship between social support and low cortisol reactivity. Thus, this study helps to identify the pathways whereby social support affects neural regulation of neuroendocrine processes in response to stress, and this may contribute to health outcomes.

Social support may also protect against immune-related disorders and promote healthy responses to influenza vaccine (Pressman et al., 2005). Stress may increase the risk for adverse health outcomes by suppressing the immune system in ways that leave a person vulnerable to opportunistic diseases and infections. Corticosteroids have immunosuppressive effects, and stress-related increases in cortisol have been tied to decreased lymphocyte responsivity to mitogenic stimulation and to decreased lymphocyte cytotoxicity. Such immunosuppressive changes may be associated with increased susceptibility to infectious disorders and to destruction of neurons in the hippocampus as well (McEwen & Sapolsky, 1995).

An immunosuppression model does not explain how stress might influence diseases whose central feature is excessive inflammation, however; such diseases include allergic, autoimmune, rheumatologic, and cardiovascular disorders, among other disorders that are known to be exacerbated by stress. Miller, Cohen, and Ritchey (2002) hypothesized that chronic stress may diminish the immune system's sensitivity to glucocorticoid hormones that normally terminate the inflammatory cascade that occurs during stress. In support of their hypothesis, they found a clear buffering effect of social support on this process, such that among healthy individuals, glucocorticoid sensitivity bore no relation to social support; however, among parents of children with cancer (a population under extreme stress), those who reported receiving a high level of tangible support from others had higher glucocorticoid sensitivity. Relatedly, social integration has been tied to lower levels of C-reactive protein, a marker of inflammation (Loucks, Berkman, Gruenewald, & Seeman, 2006).

Extensive evidence suggests that all these systems—the HPA axis, the immune system, and the SNA—influence each other and thereby affect each other's functioning. For example, links between HPA axis activity and SNA activity suggest that chronic activation of the HPA axis could potentiate overactivation of sympathetic functioning (Chrousos & Gold, 1992). Proinflammatory cytokines, which are involved in the inflammatory processes just noted, can activate the HPA axis and may contribute not only to the deleterious effects that chronic activation of this system may cause, but also, potentially to depressive symptoms, which have previously been tied to HPA axis activation (Maier & Watkins, 1998; Capuron, Ravaud, & Dantzer, 2000). To the extent, then, that social support can keep SNA or HPA axis responses to stress low, it may have a beneficial impact on other systems as well (Seeman & McEwen, 1996; Uchino et al., 1996). In turn, these benefits may affect health in a positive direction.

A variety of empirical studies has yielded evidence consistent with these hypotheses. For example, a considerable experimental literature demonstrates that the presence of a supportive person when one is going through a stressful task can reduce cardiovascular and HPA axis responses to stress; these benefits can be experienced whether the supportive person is a partner, a friend, or a stranger (e.g., Christenfeld et al., 1997; Gerin, Milner, Chawla, & Pickering, 1995; Gerin, Pieper, Levy, & Pickering, 1992; Kamarck, Manuck, & Jennings, 1990; Kors, Linden, & Gerin, 1997; Lepore, Allen, & Evans, 1993; Sheffield & Carroll, 1994; see Lepore, 1998 for a review).

Not all research shows beneficial effects of social support in challenging circumstances, however. Sometimes the presence of a friend or stranger actually increases sympathetic reactivity among those undergoing stress (e.g., Allen, Blascovich, Tomaka, & Kelsey, 1991; Mullen, Bryant, & Driskell, 1997). For example, Allen et al. (1991) found that relative to a control condition in which they remained alone, women who completed a stressful task in the presence of a female friend had higher physiological reactivity and poorer performance (see also Kirschbaum, Klauer, Filipp, & Hellhammer, 1995; Smith, Gallo, Goble, Ngu, & Stark, 1998). Whereas the presence of a partner seems to reduce stress-related physiological and neuroendocrine reactivity among men, the presence of a male partner more reliably enhances reactivity among women (Kiecolt-Glaser & Newton, 2001). The presence of a friend or partner may increase evaluation apprehension over whether important others' perceptions of the self may decline, and so this apprehension may eliminate any effect of support (Lepore, 1998).

Other biological processes may underlie the benefits of social support as well. A growing literature suggests a potential role for oxytocin in the neuroendocrine and physiological benefits of social support. In response to stress, animals and humans experience a cascade of hormonal responses that begins, at least in some stressors, with the rapid release of oxytocin. Consistent evidence suggests that (1) oxytocin is associated with affiliative activities in response to stress, (2) oxytocin is released in response to stress, and (3) oxytocin is associated with reduced SNS and HPA axis responses to stress (see Taylor, Dickerson, & Klein, 2002).

Research from both animal (e.g., Grippo et al., 2007) and human (e.g., Taylor, Gonzaga et al., 2006) studies has found that, in response to the social stressor of social isolation, oxytocin levels rise; one possible explanation for this effect is that oxytocin acts as a biological signal to the organism to seek social company. Indeed, the relation of oxytocin to affiliative activity is very strong. Exogenous administration of oxytocin reliably leads to increases in a broad array of prosocial activities, including seeking proximity, grooming, and mothering, and has been tied to empathy and trust in humans. Both animal (e.g., Witt, Carter, & Walton, 1990; McCarthy, 1995) and human (e.g., Grewen, Girdler, Amico, & Light, 2005) studies have found that oxytocin is consistently associated with signs of relaxation, including an increase in social contact and in grooming in animals (e.g., Carter, DeVries, & Getz, 1995), and relaxation and calm in humans (e.g., Uvnäs-Moberg, 1996), and lower blood pressure and heart rate (Light, Grewen, & Amico, 2005). Oxytocin appears to inhibit the secretion of adrenocorticotropin (ACTH) hormone and cortisol in humans as well (Chiodera & Legros, 1981; Legros, Chiodera, & Demy-Ponsart, 1982).

The potential roles of oxytocin, both in the down-regulation of SNS and HPA axis responses to stress and in the tendency to turn to others, at present, are hypotheses with a great deal of animal evidence to support them, but less evidence from human studies. Consequently, this issue represents a direction for research, rather than an established biological pathway by which social support may exert protective effects on health. Moreover, there may be roles for other hormones both in promoting social support initially and in regulating its biological effects, which include vasopressin, norepinephrine, serotonin, prolactin, and endogenous opioid peptides (Nelson & Panksepp, 1998; Taylor et al., 2002).

## WHY IS SOCIAL SUPPORT BENEFICIAL?

Much early research on social support took for granted that its impact on mental and physical health came largely from the specific benefits furnished by social support transactions. That is, when one person helps another, that other is benefited tangibly or emotionally in ways that can contribute to the well-documented beneficial outcomes described. A variety of observations, however, have led researchers to rethink whether all the benefits, or indeed, the primary benefits of social support come from its actual utilization.

The fact that structural measures of social support are associated with mental and physical health benefits is implicit support for questioning this account. If merely knowing the number of social ties an individual has leads to insights about that individual's health, then it would appear that the activation of those ties may not be essential for benefits to be experienced. Research suggests that the mere perception of social support, whether or not it is actually utilized, can be stress-reducing with concomitant benefits for well-being. For example, Broadwell and Light (1999) brought married men and women into the laboratory and had them fill out a questionnaire about how much support they felt they had at home (or a questionnaire assessing matters unrelated to support). Each person was then put through several stressful tasks such as computing difficult arithmetic problems in his or her head. The men who reported a lot of support from their families had lower blood pressure responses to the stressful tasks than did those who had less social support, suggesting that their families were providing support to them even though they were not physically present; the effect was not significant for women. In fact, beliefs about the availability of emotional support actually appear to exert stronger effects on mental health than the actual receipt of social support does (e.g., Wethington & Kessler, 1986; Dunkel-Schetter & Bennet, 1990; see Thoits, 1995 for discussion).

This point suggests that the receipt of social support may have costs. Consistent with this idea, Bolger, Zuckerman, and Kessler (2000) documented that actually making use of one's social support network can be associated with enhanced rather than reduced stress. In their studies, couples completed daily diaries regarding the stressors they experienced, how distressed they were in response to them, and whether they had provided or received support from their partner. Supportive acts that were reported by the support recipient did not promote adjustment to stress, but rather, were associated with poorer adjustment, suggesting that when explicit support efforts are recognized, there can be emotional costs to the recipient. However, when supportive acts were reported by the support provider, but were unrecognized by the recipient, stress-protective effects were found (Bolger & Amarel, 2007). The results suggest that the most effective support is "invisible" to the recipient; that is, it occurs without his or her awareness. Thus, it may be that one set of benefits that social support confers is the availability of a supportive network that may act in a supportive manner without one's realization, thereby reducing distress in response to threatening events. Indeed, merely thinking about one's supportive ties can reduce stress (Smith, Ruiz, & Uchino, 2004).

An important implication of results such as these is that, at least under some circumstances, people can carry their social support networks around in their heads to buffer them against stress without ever having to recruit their networks in active ways that may produce the costs just noted. Findings like these suggest that it is important to distinguish exactly when supportive efforts from others may be beneficial for mental and physical health and when they may not show these benefits (Bolger & Amarel, 2007).

## WHEN IS SOCIAL SUPPORT BENEFICIAL?

Whether social contacts are experienced as supportive may depend on several factors. These include how large or dense one's social support networks are, whether the support provided is appropriate for meeting the stressor, and whether the right kind of support comes from the right person.

Considerable research has explored the characteristics of socially supportive networks. As noted, people who belong to more formal and informal organizations in their communities, such as church groups, the PTA, clubs, and the like, enjoy the health and mental health benefits of social support. This may be because such people are more socially skilled to begin with and thus seek out contacts from others, or it may be a direct consequence of participation in supportive networks. Social networks may also be important for accessing specific types of assistance during times of stress (such as social services) (Lin & Westcott, 1991). However, the beneficial effects of social support are not cumulative in a linear fashion. It is clear that having a confidant (such as a spouse or a partner) may be the most effective social support (Collins & Feeney, 2000; Cohen & Wills, 1985), especially for men (e.g., Broadwell & Light, 1999; Wickrama, Conger, & Lorenz, 1995). Accordingly, married people report higher perceived support than unmarried people do (Thoits, 1995). With respect to friends, research documents the benefits of at least one close friend, but having a dozen or more close friends may be little more beneficial for health and mental health than having a few close friends (Langner & Michael, 1960). Indeed, one of the risks of social support networks is that overly intrusive social support may actually exacerbate stress (Shumaker & Hill, 1991).

People who belong to dense social networks of friends or family who are highly interactive may find themselves overwhelmed by the advice and interference that is available to them in times of stress. As comedian George Burns noted, "happiness is having a large, loving, caring, close-knit family in another city."

Sometimes support providers give poor advice, fail at providing tangible assistance, or provide inappropriate or too little emotional support, thereby reducing or eliminating the effectiveness of the effort (Bolger, Foster, Vinokur, & Ng, 1996; Burg & Seeman, 1994). Social support efforts, too, may be well-intentioned, but perceived as controlling or directive by the recipient. For example, when a spouse is pulled into the management of a chronic disease, such as coronary artery disease, the "support" of encouraging exercise and changing a partner's diet may be perceived as interference by the patient (Franks et al., 2006). Although such well-intentioned support may achieve some benefits in modifying behaviors in a healthy direction, the potential to produce interpersonal conflict and psychological distress is clearly present as well (e.g., Fisher, La Greca, Greco, Arfken, & Schneiderman, 1997; Lewis & Rook, 1999; Wortman & Lehman, 1985). Socially supportive efforts may misfire for other reasons. When significant others' responses to a person's expression of symptoms or distress is contingent on that expression, such "support" may unwittingly reinforce symptom experiences and actually enhance emotional distress (Itkowitz, Kerns, & Otis, 2003).

Effective social support may depend on an appropriate balance between the needs of the recipient and what that recipient gets from those in the social network (Cohen & McKay, 1984; Cohen & Wills, 1985). This "matching hypothesis" suggests that, to be supportive, the actions of the provider must meet the specific needs of the recipient (Thoits, 1995). Thus, for example, if a person needs emotional support but receives advice instead, the misfired effort at support may actually increase psychological distress (Horowitz et al., 2001; Thoits, 1986). Research generally supports this hypothesis. Different kinds of support, for example, may be valued from different members of a social support network. Emotional support may be most helpful from intimate others and actually resented when casual friends attempt to provide it, whereas information and advice may be especially valuable from experts but regarded as inappropriate from well-intentioned friends or family with questionable expertise (e.g., Benson, Gross, Messer, Kellum, &

Passmore, 1991; Dakof & Taylor, 1990). Consistent with this perspective, Helgeson and Cohen (1996) reviewed research on the impact of social support on adjustment to cancer. They found that emotional support was most desired by patients and appeared to have the greatest beneficial influence on adjustment. However, peer support group interventions whose goal was providing emotional support did not, for the most part, have benefits; rather, educational groups that provided information were perceived more positively. Although there are several possible interpretations of these findings, it may be that emotional needs were best met by those close to cancer patients, rather than by the relative strangers in the peer group, and that educational interventions in peer groups better met the cancer patients' specific informational needs.

Other threats to obtaining social support may come from the support recipient. People who are under extreme stress often express their distress to others and over time, can drive their social support networks away (Matt & Dean, 1993; McLeod, Kessler, & Landis, 1992). For example, depressed, disabled, or ill people can inadvertently repel their families and friends by persistently expressing their negative emotions (Alferi, Carver, Antoni, Weiss, & Duran, 2001; Coyne et al., 1987; Fyrand, Moum, Finset, & Glennas, 2002). In a longitudinal investigation of 405 elderly individuals, Gurung, Taylor, and Seeman (2003), found that men and women who were depressed or who had cognitive dysfunction reported more problems with social relationships at follow-up several years later (see also Honn & Bornstein, 2002; Alferi et al., 2001). They concluded that those most in need for social support were potentially less likely to receive it and to instead experience gaps in their social support.

The positive impact of social support on adjustment to stressful events may be attenuated in especially high-stress environments. For example, Ceballo and McLoyd (2002) found that the usually positive impact of social support on parenting behavior was attenuated in high-stress neighborhoods. Gurung, Taylor, Kemeny, and Myers (2004) found that, although high levels of social support were associated with lower levels of depression in a sample of low-income HIV-seropositive women, social support resources were not sufficient to moderate the relation between chronic burden and high levels of depression. Thus, like most resources, the effectiveness of social support in reducing distress due to stressful circumstances may have its limits at especially high levels of stress. Related to these observations is the fact that the perception of social support as available is positively correlated with SES (Taylor & Seeman, 2000; Thoits, 1984).

A *New Yorker* cartoon shows one woman enthusiastically telling another woman that what she likes best about their friendship is that they never have to see each other or talk. Indeed, many relationships may be better for the having of them than for the using of them. Social relationships are fraught with the potential for discord as well as support, and so relationships are a potential double-edged sword. In a study of 120 widowed women, Rook (1984) found that negative social interactions were consistently and more strongly related (negatively) to well-being than were positive social interactions. Having one's privacy invaded by family and friends, having promises of help not come through, and being involved with people who provoked conflict or anger were among the events that worsened adjustment in this vulnerable sample. Similarly, Schuster, Kessler, and Aseltine (1990) found that negative interactions with a spouse or close friends augmented depression more than positive, supportive interactions reduced it. Research examining the neuroendocrine correlates of marital relationships likewise reveal that conflict can lead to elevated cortisol levels (Heffner et al., 2006), to delayed wound healing, and to a lower cytokine response at wound sites (Kiecolt-Glaser et al., 2005). Negative social interactions also contribute to negative self-rated health and to more adverse health conditions as well (Newsom, Mahan, Rook, & Krause, 2008). These findings not only underscore the double-edged nature of social relationships, but also imply that avoiding social relationships or situations that actually tax well-being may be helpful for managing stress.

## *Origins of Social Support*
### WHO GETS SOCIAL SUPPORT?
The fact that social relationships can be either supportive or unhelpful, and the fact that support recipients substantially affect which outcome occurs raises an intriguing issue. Is social support largely "outside" in the social environment or "inside" the person, in the form of abilities to extract support from the environment or construe support as available? Although social support no doubt involves aspects of both, attention to the qualities of the support recipient has yielded some important findings.

Research has suggested that there may be heritable aspects of social support. Specifically, research using twin-study methodology has uncovered a moderately high degree of heritability, either in the ability to construe social support as available or in the ability to experience one's network of friends and relatives as supportive (Kessler, Kendler, Heath, Neale, & Eaves, 1992). Similarly, heritability estimates suggest that genetic factors may account for about 50% of the variance in loneliness (Boomsma, Willemsen, Dolan, Hawkley, & Cacioppo, 2005). Although there are a number of potential interpretations of these findings, at the very least, they suggest that genes may play a role in some of the benefits of social support.

Some of these heritable factors may involve social competence. Some people are more effective than others in extracting the social support that they need, suggesting that social support involves a considerable degree of skill. People who have difficulty with social relationships, those who are chronically shy (Naliboff et al., 2004) or who anticipate rejection from others (Cole, Kemeny, Fahey, Zack, & Naliboff, 2003), are at risk for isolating themselves socially, with concomitant risks for health. Being a socially competent individual appears to be especially important for getting emotional support, but it may not predict as strongly the ability to get tangible assistance or information (Dunkel-Schetter, Folkman, & Lazarus, 1987).

Researchers are beginning to identify some of the specific genes that may be involved in the development (or not) of social skills. This work is in its infancy, and so some caution regarding these points is warranted. The μ-opioid receptor gene (*OPRM1*) appears to be implicated in the experience of social support. Specifically, people with the G allele of the polymorphism (A118G) appear to be more sensitive to potential rejection and also experience greater increases in salivary cortisol during laboratory stress tasks (Way, Taylor, & Eisenberger, 2009). Carriers of the G allele, relative to individuals with two copies of the A allele, also exhibit greater activity in the dACC during a social exclusion fMRI task. Thus, across multiple measures of social sensitivity, the G allele is associated with the potential for greater social distress. Recent research with monkeys shows similar findings (Barr et al., 2008; Miller et al., 2004).

Similarly, within the gene coding for monoamine oxidase (MAOA), the low expression variants of MAOA-uVNTR are tied to activation in the dACC in response to a social exclusion fMRI task; that activation is correlated with self-reported distress in response to social exclusion (Eisenberger, Way, Taylor, Welch, & Lieberman, 2007). Thus, it appears that the MAOA gene also influences distress experienced in response to social exclusion or rejection.

Other genes that contribute to social support (or its absence) are also likely to be uncovered. For example, genes that help to regulate the dopamine system may also be involved in the experiences of social support or social rejection (Way & Taylor, 2011). In addition, carriers of the A allele of the oxytocin receptor gene are less likely to show sensitive parenting (Bakermans-Kranenburg & van IJzendoorn, 2008), thereby pointing in a preliminary way to a gene that may be implicated in maternal nurturance. A polymorphism within the vasopressin 1A receptor (AVPR1A) has been tied to empathy and altruistic behavior, and may thereby contribute to social support processes (Bachner-Melman et al., 2005; Knafo et al., 2008). (For a review of genetic factors in social distress/social support, see Way & Taylor, 2011).

## A DEVELOPMENTAL APPROACH TO SOCIAL SUPPORT

The fact that social support may have heritable aspects and that it may depend, in part, on social skills, suggests that focusing on its early familial antecedents may also be enlightening regarding why this vital resource seems to come so easily to some people and more rarely to others. The thesis to be offered here is that (a) the beneficial effects of social support on physical and mental health begin with supportive familial contact; (b) these contacts, in turn, lay the groundwork for the development of social competencies and corresponding abilities to enlist and provide social support and/or construe social support as available; and (c) these skills are transferred intergenerationally, through both genomic and nongenomic pathways.

Evidence that socially supportive contacts in early life have beneficial effects on responses to stress, mental health, and health is manifold and may be readily seen in both human and animal studies. In some of the earliest work on this topic, Harlow and Harlow (1962) found that monkeys who were raised with an artificial terrycloth mother and who were isolated from other monkeys during the first 6 months of life showed disruptions in their adult social contacts. They were less likely to engage in normal social behavior, such as grooming, their sexual responses were inappropriate, mothering among the females was deficient, and they often showed either highly fearful or abnormally aggressive behavior toward their peers. Not surprisingly, these social behaviors led to peer rejection. In sum, a broad array of social skills were compromised by the absence of early nurturant contact with the mother.

Building on work like this, Meaney and colleagues (Francis, Diorio, Liu, & Meaney, 1999; Liu et al., 1997) explicitly linked early nurturant maternal contact to the development of stress responses in offspring and showed that these contacts affect emotional and neuroendocrine responses to stress across the lifespan. In their paradigm, infant rats are removed from the nest, handled by a human experimenter and then returned to the nest. The response of the mother to this separation and reunification is intense licking and grooming and arched-back nursing, which provides the pup with nurturant and soothing immediate stimulation. On the short term, this contact reduces SNS and HPA axis responses to stress in the pups (and in the mother as well). Over the long term, this maternal behavior results in a better regulated HPA axis response to stress and novelty, and better regulation of somatic growth and neural development, especially hippocampal synaptic development in the pup. These rat pups also showed more open field exploration, which suggests lower levels of fear. This compelling animal model suggests that nurturant stimulation by the mother early in life modulates the responses of offspring to stress in ways that have permanent effects on the offspring's HPA axis responses to stress, on behavior suggestive of anxiety/fearfulness, and on cognitive function (see also Suomi, 1999).

Warm, nurturant, and supportive contact with a caregiver affects physiological and neuroendocrine stress responses in human infants and children, just as in these animal studies. Early research on orphans reported high levels of emotional disturbance, especially depression, in infants who failed to receive nurturant stimulating contact from a caregiver (Spitz & Wolff, 1946). More recent findings from Eastern European abandoned infants confirm that, without the affectionate attentions of caregivers, infants may fail to thrive, and many die (Carlson & Earls, 1997).

Not surprisingly, attachment processes are implicated in these relations. Gunnar and her associates, studying 15-month-old children receiving well-baby examinations, found that securely attached infants were less likely to show elevated cortisol responses to normal stressors, such as inoculations, than were less securely attached infants (Gunnar, Brodersen, Krueger, & Rigatuso, 1996; see also Nachmias, Gunnar, Mangelsdorf, Parritz, & Buss, 1996). The protective effects of secure attachment were especially evident for socially fearful or inhibited children (see also Levine & Wiener, 1988; Hart, Gunnar, & Cicchetti, 1996; see Collins & Feeney,

2000, for a discussion of attachment in adult supportive relationships).

Research also consistently suggests that families characterized by unsupportive relationships have damaging outcomes for the mental, physical, and social health of their offspring, not only on the short term, but across the lifespan. Overt family conflict, manifested in recurrent episodes of anger and aggression, deficient nurturing, and family relationships that are cold, unsupportive, and/or neglectful have been associated with a broad array of adverse mental and physical health outcomes long into adulthood (Repetti, Taylor, & Saxbe, 2007; Repetti, Taylor, & Seeman, 2002). The chronic stress of unsupportive families produces repeated or chronic SNS activation in children, which, in turn, may lead to wear and tear on the cardiovascular system. Over time, such alterations may lead to pathogenic changes in sympathetic or parasympathetic functioning or both. Such changes may contribute to disorders such as essential hypertension (e.g., Ewart, 1991) and coronary heart disease (e.g., Woodall & Matthews, 1989).

As appears to be true in the animal studies previously described, early nurturant and supportive contacts appear to be important for human offspring's emotional responses to stress as well, especially those involving anxiety or fear. Infants begin life with emergent abilities to monitor the environment, especially for potential threats. The amygdala is activated any time there is something new or unexpected in the environment, especially if it involves suggestions of danger. Early in life, the amygdala sends off many messages of alarm. Any loud noise, for example, will alarm an infant, and a few months later, strangers typically provoke distress. Through the comforting attentions of parents, infants begin to learn about and adjust to the social world. Over time, they learn that strangers are not necessarily threatening and that loud noises are not inevitably associated with danger, among other moderations of automatic responses to threat. As the prefrontal cortex develops, children learn additional ways to moderate the signals that they get from the amygdala, storing information about both the threatening and the comforting aspects of the social world.

The development of this system is critically affected by early nurturant contact. Infants form comforting bonds with others and, in turn, give rise to the emotion regulation skills and social skills that ultimately enable children to manage potentially threatening events autonomously, skills that become vital to managing stress across the lifespan (Taylor, 2002). That is, a broad array of evidence demonstrates that children from supportive families are more likely than those from unsupportive families to develop effective emotion regulation skills and social competencies (Repetti et al., 2002), as judged, for example, by teachers and peers. Similarly, adults whose interpersonal styles are marked by hostility and cynicism, a style that has been tied to an unsupportive or conflict-ridden early family environment, are less likely to report having social support (e.g., Smith, 1992) and/or support may be a less effective buffer against stress (e.g. Lepore, 1995).

Epigenetic factors appear to be involved in these pathways. That is, maternal nurturance can induce long-lasting changes in the function of genes, which is an additional mechanism by which experiences of early social support can induce long-term behavioral alterations in emotional and social functioning.

Meaney and colleagues have shown that rat pups exposed to highly nurturant mothering show less emotionality to novel circumstances and more normative social behavior, including mothering in adulthood, compared to recipients of normal mothering (Francis et al., 1999; Weaver et al., 2004). Studies with monkeys have shown similar effects. For example, Suomi (1987) reports that highly reactive monkeys cross-fostered to nurturant mothers develop good socioemotional skills and achieve high status in the dominance hierarchy, whereas monkeys with reactive temperaments who are peer-raised develop poor socioemotional skills and end up at the bottom of the dominance hierarchy.

Such long-term effects of maternal care appear to be a result of epigenetic structural alterations (methylation) to the glucocorticoid receptor gene that occur in the first week after birth and affect its expression throughout the lifespan (Meaney & Szyf, 2005). This process is affected by each of the neurochemical systems discussed in this chapter, and thus polymorphisms in these systems that affect signaling are likely to have downstream effects upon this process. Mothers showing high levels of nurturant behavior exhibit greater increases in oxytocin receptors during pregnancy, which is thought to trigger maternal responsivity (Meaney, 2001), and they have higher levels of dopamine release when caring for their pups (Champagne et al., 2004). This more nurturant mothering triggers greater increases in serotonin turnover in the pup, which initiates the cascade leading to the altered glucocorticoid receptor expression that affects adulthood reactivity to stress (Meaney & Szyf, 2005).

Related evidence has been uncovered with humans. For example, the harshness or nurturance of the early environment is implicated in the expression of the serotonin transporter gene (*5-HTTLPR*). People with two copies of the *5-HTTLPR* short allele (short/short) who have experienced childhood maltreatment are more likely to be diagnosed with major depressive disorder than are individuals with one or two copies of the long allele who have experienced similar environments (Caspi et al., 2003; Kaufman et al., 2004). A study from our laboratory (Taylor et al., 2006) suggests that the short allele may not only function as a risk allele for depression in the face of an adverse environment, but as an allele reflecting general sensitivity to the environment, providing protection from symptoms of depression when the environment is nurturant. Using a non-clinical sample of 118 adult men and women, we assessed nurturance of the early family environment, depressive symptomatology, and *5-HTTLPR* genotype. As expected, a stressful early family environment by itself was significantly related to depressive symptomatology. However, a significant gene-by-environment interaction between *5-HTTLPR* and the nurturance of the early family environment qualified the risk for depression. Specifically, individuals with two copies of the short allele had greater depressive symptomatology if they had experienced early familial adversity compared with participants with the short/long or long/long genotypes, but significantly less depressive symptomatology if they reported a supportive early environment. Notably, the adverse early family environments studied were ones in which the degree of social pain was fairly mild, consisting of some conflict, moderate household chaos, and/or cold, unaffectionate, and distant behaviors, rather than explicit maltreatment in the form of physical or sexual abuse.

Of interest, this differential sensitivity to the environment does not appear to be limited to childhood, but is present in adulthood as well. Thus, people with the short/short genotype who reported being in a currently highly stressful environment had higher levels of depressive symptomatology, relative to those with short/long or long/long variants, whereas those who reported currently being in a low-stress environment had significantly lower levels of depressive symptomatology (Taylor, Way et al., 2006). Reports of the early and current environment were only modestly correlated with each other, and so these results are fairly independent of each other. Thus, with respect to depressive symptoms, the short/short genotype of the serotonin transporter

gene appears to be risky in harsh environments but protective in nurturant environments. Consistent with this latter point, short/short individuals have been found to be more responsive to the protective effects of social support as well (Kaufman et al., 2004; Kilpatrick et al., 2007).

In essence, then, the early family environment may provide the groundwork for social competence and the abilities to enlist social support across the lifespan. In families that are warm and nurturant, children learn to manage threat effectively with a lesser physiological/neuroendocrine toll, and through exposure to good models, they may develop social skills of their own. If they are raised in cold, non-nurturant, or conflict-ridden families, children instead experience threatening events more commonly and learn fewer social competencies, with the result that social support networks may be difficult to develop or use effectively. As such, early nurturance of offspring in response to stress might be thought of as a prototype for social support, which is mirrored throughout life in the many more modest supportive contacts a person encounters across the lifespan.

Are the benefits of being raised in a socially supportive environment conferred genetically or through the environment? In other words, do particularly nurturant parents have particularly socially skilled offspring by virtue of their shared genetic heritage, or does nurturance itself play a role in the acquisition of social skills? Both mechanisms appear to be involved. On the one hand, certain species show genetically based high levels of "licking and grooming" in response to stress (Liu et al., 1997), which are transmitted to offspring as styles that appear in the offspring's nurturant behavior. On the other hand, by cross-fostering offspring to high- or low-nurturant caretakers, the impact of the behavior itself on physiological and social functioning becomes clear. For example, Suomi (1987) assigned rhesus monkeys selectively bred for differences in temperamental reactivity to foster mothers who were either unusually nurturant or within the normal range of mothering behavior. Highly reactive infants cross-fostered to normal mothers exhibited deficits in social behavior, and in adulthood, they tended to drop and remain low in the dominance hierarchy (Suomi, 1991). Highly reactive infants cross-fostered to exceptionally nurturant females, in contrast, showed higher levels of social skills, and in adulthood were more likely to rise to the top of the dominance hierarchy. When highly reactive females became mothers, they adopted the maternal style of their foster mothers, independent of their own reactivity profile (Suomi, 1987). Studies such as these provide evidence of the behavioral intergenerational transfer of nurturance over and above genetic predispositions (see also Francis et al., 1999).

These studies are significant for several reasons. First, they suggest clear developmental origins for social competencies that may affect social support availability across the lifespan. Second, they provide clear evidence that maternal nurturance can moderate genetic risks typically associated with the potential for maladaptive social behavior. Third, they demonstrate the nongenomic intergenerational transfer of social skills via exposure to nurturant supportive behavior. In short, then, whereas genetic factors may contribute to whether or not an individual is able to develop social competence, early nurturant experience can also be a contributing factor that may extend not only across one's own lifespan, but to one's offspring as well. Although the evidence for such a model is primarily from animals, one would expect that genomic and nongenomic factors may be involved in the intergenerational transfer of social skills and deficits in humans as well.

## Gender, Culture, and Social Support
### GENDER AND SOCIAL SUPPORT

The previous discussion places a heavy role on mothering, at least in the animal studies implicating nurturance in offspring's social and physiological behavior. This raises the question of whether there are gender differences in the ability to provide social support to others, in its extraction from others, and in its benefits. The research evidence suggests that women provide more social support to others, draw on socially supportive networks more consistently in times of stress, and may be more benefited by social support (e.g., Taylor, Klein, Lewis, Gruenewald, Gurung, & Updegraff, 2000).

Although men typically report larger social networks than women do, in part because of men's historically greater involvement in employment and in community organizations, studies find that women are consistently more invested in their relationships and that their relationships with others are more intimate (Belle, 1987). Women are more involved in both the giving and receiving of social support than are men (Thoits, 1995). Across the lifecycle, women are more likely to mobilize social support, especially from other women, in times of stress. Adolescent girls report more informal sources of support than do boys, and they are more likely to turn to their same-sex peers than are boys (e.g., Copeland

& Hess, 1995; see Belle, 1987 for a review). College student women report more available helpers and report receiving more support than do college men (e.g., Ptacek, Smith, & Zanas, 1992; see Belle, 1987 for a review). Adult women maintain more same-sex close relationships than do men, they mobilize more social support in times of stress than do men, they turn to female friends more often than men turn to male friends, they report more benefits from contacts with their female friends and relatives (although they are also more vulnerable to psychological stress resulting from stressful network events), and they provide more frequent and more effective social support to others than do men (Belle, 1987; McDonald & Korabik, 1991; Ogus, Greenglass, & Burke, 1990).

Women are also more invested in their social networks than are men. They are better at reporting most types of social network events, and they are more likely to report getting involved if there is a crisis in the network (Wethington, McLeod, & Kessler, 1987). In an extensive study of social networks, Veroff, Kulka, and Douvan (1981) reported that women were 30% more likely than men to have provided some type of support in response to network stressors. These findings appear to generalize across a number of cultures as well (Edwards, 1993; Whiting & Whiting, 1975).

Studies of caregiving also bear out these observations. Over 80% of this care is provided by mothers, daughters, and wives. For example, in the United States, the typical caregiver is a 60-year-old, low-income woman with a disabled or ill spouse. However, daughters care for aging parents (sons are only one-fourth as likely to give parental care), mothers care for disabled children, and a growing number of caregivers are grandmothers caring for the offspring of their own children who may have drug or alcohol problems or HIV infection (Taylor, 2002). Several studies suggest that men, in contrast, are more likely to institutionalize their wives in response to common causes of the need for caregiving, such as stroke or Alzheimer disease (Freedman, 1993; Kelly-Hayes et al., 1998).

As the previous analysis suggests, women are not only disproportionately the providers of social support, they are also more likely to seek social support in response to stress. Two meta-analyses (Luckow, Reifman, & McIntosh, 1998; Tamres, Janicki, & Helgeson, 2002) examined gender differences in coping with stress and found that women were significantly more likely to seek and use social support to deal with a broad array of stressors. For example, in the Luckow et al. review, of the 26 studies that tested for gender differences in coping via social support, one showed no differences and 25 showed that women favored social support more. These gender differences are more apparent in the domain of seeking emotional support than for other types of social support.

One might expect that if women seek social support more, are more invested in their social support networks, and report that social support is more important to them than is the case for men, they might be benefited more by social support. A meta-analysis conducted by Schwarzer and Leppin (1989) found support for this hypothesis. Across many investigations, the correlation between social support and good health was approximately .20 for women, but for men, the correlation was only .08.

Women may be somewhat more effective providers of social support than men are as well. For example, Wheeler and colleagues (Wheeler, Reis, & Nezlek, 1983) studied students who remained at college during the December holidays to see who became depressed and lonely in response to this stressful circumstance. The students kept track of how they spent their days, with whom they spent them, and what emotions they experienced during that period. The strongest determinant of how lonely the students were was how much contact they had each day with women. The more time a student, whether man or woman, spent with women, the less lonely he or she was. The amount of time spent with other men, for the most part, did not affect mental health.

Research consistent with this point has also come from studies of the differences between men's and women's abilities to provide social support for each other in times of stress and the protective effects of such efforts. An array of evidence suggests that women may be better providers of social support to men than men are to women (Thoits, 1995). For example, when men are asked where their emotional support comes from, most men name their wife as their chief source of social support and many name her as the only person to whom they confide their personal problems or difficulties (see Glaser & Kiecolt-Glaser, 1994; New England Research Institutes, 1997; Phillipson, 1997); women report that they are likely to turn to a female friend or relative, as well as to their spouse.

These differences appear to translate directly into health benefits. Although marriage benefits both men and women, it benefits men more (Chesney & Darbes, 1998). Thus, for example, the health of married men is better than that of single men, but

the health of women is less strongly influenced by marital status. Mortality rates among widowed men are higher than among widowed women, and widowed men who remarry die later in life than those who do not remarry; among widowed women, remarrying has no effect on age of death (Helsing, Szklo, & Comstock, 1981; Stroebe & Stroebe, 1983). As noted earlier, in experimental studies, when women and men are asked to bring their partner with them when they undergo stressful laboratory tasks, men's SNS and HPA axis responses to stress tend to be buffered by the presence of a female partner, but females' responses to stress are often stronger in the presence of a partner than when alone (see Kiecolt-Glaser, & Newton, 2001). Moreover, the downside of social contacts discussed earlier, namely the potential for conflict and other negative interactions, appear to weigh more heavily on women than on men. Specifically, in a large-scale review, Kiecolt-Glaser and Newton (2001) report that wives show stronger heart rate, blood pressure, and HPA axis changes during marital conflict than do husbands.

In a theoretical model that provides a framework for these observations, Taylor and colleagues (2000) suggested that gender differences in the seeking and giving of social support may reflect, in part, a robust and biologically based difference in how men and women cope with stress. They suggested that, whereas the behaviors of fight-or-flight, namely aggression or withdrawal in response to stress, may be especially characteristic of men, a pattern termed *tend-and-befriend* may be more characteristic of women in response to stress. Tending involves nurturant activities designed to protect the self and offspring that may promote safety and reduce distress. Befriending is the creation and maintenance of social networks, especially those involving other women, that may aid in this process. Their argument is predicated on the evolutionary assumption that, during human prehistory, men and women faced somewhat different adaptive challenges, and as a result may have developed different stress responses to meet those different challenges. Specifically, females of most species, including humans, have primary responsibility for the early nurturing of offspring through pregnancy, nursing, and care in early life. Stress responses in females, then, are likely to have evolved in such a way as to simultaneously protect mothers and offspring. Whereas fight and flight constitute responses to stress that can protect an individual well, tending to offspring and befriending others in a social group may facilitate the joint protection of self and offspring.

Taylor and colleagues suggested that these stress responses may be influenced, in part, by neuroendocrine underpinnings, such as the release of oxytocin and endogenous opioid peptides. As noted earlier, oxytocin is thought to be an affiliative hormone that may underlie at least some forms of maternal and social contact. Because the impact of oxytocin is enhanced by the effects of estrogen, oxytocin's effects are thought to be stronger in females than in males and may be implicated in the maternal tending of offspring seen in response to stress (Taylor et al., 2000).

In summary, then, although both men and women benefit from social support, women tend to give and receive social support from different sources. Women are disproportionately the support providers to children, to men, and to other women. The support that they provide also appears to translate directly into health benefits. When men seek social support, on the other hand, they are most likely to do so from a partner, and they show clear health benefits from having a marital partner. Overall, women are somewhat more likely to give social support, seek it out in times of stress, and benefit from it, patterns that may have evolutionary significance and biological underpinnings (Taylor et al., 2000; Taylor, 2002).

## CULTURE AND SOCIAL SUPPORT

Culture is another variable that may moderate how social support is perceived or received. On the one hand, there is a large literature to suggest that the benefits of social support for mental and physical health extend across many cultures. On the other hand, the possibility that support is experienced differently in different cultures is an important issue that has not been widely addressed. Is there any reason to believe that particular cultural dimensions might be related to how and whether social support is experienced or used in response to stress?

Considerable research suggests that people from East Asian cultural contexts view the maintenance of harmony within the social group as an overarching goal. Any effort to bring personal problems to the attention of others to enlist their help may be seen as undermining that harmony or making inappropriate demands on the social group. Accordingly, the appreciation of these norms may lead people to avoid taxing the system by bringing their problems to the attention of others for the purpose of enlisting social support. By contrast, European Americans tend to see ongoing relationships as resources for helping to meet personal needs (Kim, Sherman, &

Taylor, 2008). To the extent that social support is seen as a resource, Western Europeans may seek the explicit help of family and friends to help themselves cope more successfully with stressful events. In a series of three studies, Taylor, Sherman, Kim, Jarcho, Takagi, and Dunagan (2004) found evidence consistent with these points. Across multiple studies, European Americans, relative to Asian Americans and Asians, reported drawing on their social relationships more to help them cope with stressful events. Concern over disrupting the harmony of the group, concern over social criticism or losing face, and the belief that one should be self-reliant in solving one's personal problems were found to mediate the nonuse of social support among those of Asian background.

Social support is thought to be a universally helpful resource, however, which suggests that there may be cultural differences in the ways that it is used or experienced. Forms of social support that do not risk disturbing relationships may be more sought out and be more beneficial for those from Asian cultural backgrounds. Thus, implicit social support, similar to perceived support, may be commonly experienced by East Asians; it refers to the comfort provided through the awareness of a support network rather than through the use of a support network. By contrast, explicit social support, which is used by European Americans, may correspond more closely to the conventional Western definition of a social support transaction; that is, as the use of social networks that involve solicitation of advice, instrumental aid, and emotional support.

The utility of this distinction was demonstrated in an experimental study (Taylor, Welch, Kim, & Sherman, 2007) in which Asian Americans and European Americans were primed with either an implicit or explicit support manipulation. Participants in an implicit support condition thought about a group they were close to and wrote about the aspects of the group that were important to them, whereas participants in the explicit support condition were told to think about people they were close to and to write a letter asking for advice and support during upcoming stressful tasks. Subsequently, participants went through several laboratory stressors. Asian Americans who had completed the implicit support task experienced less stress and had lower cortisol responses to stress compared with those who completed the explicit support task, whereas the reverse was found for European Americans.

Like the research on perceived support noted earlier, implicit social support may have many of the same mental health and health benefits as social support that is explicitly drawn on in times of stress. There is a potential broader lesson to be learned from these beginning studies of cultural differences in the experience of social support. As research has clarified the ways in which extracting support from others may be costly, the benefits of just knowing that others care for you have come into view.

## Providing Social Support

### COSTS AND BENEFITS OF PROVIDING SOCIAL SUPPORT

Conceptualizations of social support have been guided by the implicit assumption that support is beneficial for the recipient but costly for the provider. On the surface, this is a fairly sensible assumption. The provision of advice, emotional support, or tangible assistance can be costly to a support provider, at least in time, and potentially in resources as well. Virtually all acts of social support, ranging from listening to a friend's woes about her marriage to taking in family members who are out of work, involve an outlay of at least some resources.

This viewpoint may also have been shaped by evolutionary perspectives on altruism, which encompasses some of the actions usually construed as social support. Altruistic behavior has presented something of a problem for traditional evolutionary theory. Put in its simplest form, the paradox is, how do we pass on our altruistic genes to future generations if those very genes can put us at risk, thereby reducing the probability that we will pass on our genes at all? The warning cry of the sentinel, common to some rodent species, is often presented as an example. On the lookout for danger, the sentinel sees a predator such as a hawk and then lets out a loud and distinctive warning cry that not only sends his companions scampering for safety, but attracts the attention of the predator, increasing the likelihood that the sentinel itself will be the predator's meal. Although the kinds of social support that we commonly find in contemporary society do not typically put people at potentially fatal risk, in our early prehistory, giving aid to another person facing a severe threat (such as a predator) may well have done so, under at least some circumstances, and thus the question is a fair one.

Altruism has largely been rescued by the concept of reciprocal altruism (Hamilton, 1963; Trivers, 1971), which maintains that altruists do not dispense altruism at random but are more likely to aid genetically related others and behave altruistically toward others when there is some expectation of reciprocity. Providing social support is normative, and to the extent that people typically spend their time in the company of familiar social networks of mutual obligation, there is every reason to expect that a favor done by one person may be reciprocated by another at another time.[1]

The idea that support provision is inherently costly is also given credence by research on caregiving. Many people are involved in giving care to elderly parents, spouses, and disabled children. The costs of caregiving can be substantial, as it can be a difficult, grinding, chronic stressor. Over half of contemporary caregivers work outside the home, and many need to modify their job or reduce their hours to accommodate their caregiving. For older people, such caregiving can be a fatal undertaking, with caretakers at high risk for physical and mental health problems. Nearly 60% of elderly caregivers show signs of clinical depression. Evidence of immunocompromise is often present in caregivers, which can leave them vulnerable to flu and respiratory disorders, and they show a poorer response to the influenza vaccine as well (Kiecolt-Glaser, Glaser, Gravenstein, Malarkey, & Sheridan, 1996; Newsom & Schulz, 1998; see also Esterling, Kiecolt-Glaser, & Glaser, 1996). Other studies have found that the stress of caregiving can have adverse effects on wound repair (Kiecolt-Glaser, Marucha, Malarkey, Mercado, & Glaser, 1995), on the regulation of SNS responses to stress (Mills et al., 1997), and on declines in natural killer (NK) cell function (Esterling et al., 1996). Moreover, these immune alterations can persist well after caregiving activities have ceased (Esterling, Kiecolt-Glaser, Bodnar, & Glaser, 1994). Caregivers shake off infectious disease very slowly and are at heightened risk for death. Schulz and Beach (2000), for example, found that the chances of dying in a given 4-year period for an elderly person involved in stressful caregiving were 63% higher than for elderly people without these responsibilities (see also Cacioppo, et al., 2000; King, Oka, & Young, 1994; Spitze, Logan, Joseph, & Lee, 1994; Wu, Wang, Cacioppo, Glaser, Kiecolt-Glaser, & Malarkey, 1999).

Evidence like this would seem to bear out the viewpoint that giving social support is costly. However, the majority of these studies have focused on populations in which any adverse effects of providing care would be expected to be seen. A number of the situations studied involve particularly burdensome caregiving. A number of the samples involved the elderly, who are at particular risk for health problems. Many others have focused on samples with extreme demands on their time. It is reasonable to think that, although caregiving may provide a glimpse into the extremes of social support provision, it may not characterize support provision generally.

In recent years, the potential benefits of giving social support have become better understood. There are a number of reasons to believe that providing social support to another might be stress reducing for the provider, as well as for the recipient. As the reciprocal altruism perspective just described suggests, providing support to others, as in the form of specific aid, increases the likelihood that there will be people there for you when your needs arise, a perception that can be comforting in its own right, as the perceived social support literature shows. Giving support to others may cement a personal relationship, provide a sense of meaning or purpose, and signify that one matters to others, all of which have been found to promote well-being (e.g., Batson, 1998; Taylor & Turner, 2001). Empirical research suggests that helping others may reduce distress and contribute to good health (Brown, Brown, House, & Smith, 2008; Li & Ferraro, 2005; Schwartz, Meisenhelder, Ma, & Reed, 2003). A study by Brown, Nesse, Vinokur, and Smith (2003) assessed giving and receiving social support in an older married sample and related it to mortality over a 5-year period. Death was significantly less likely for those people who reported providing instrumental support to friends, relatives, and neighbors and to those who reported providing emotional support to their spouses. Receiving support did not affect mortality, once giving support was statistically controlled. The study also statistically controlled for a wide variety of potential contributors to these effects, and the relationships held. This study thus provides important evidence that the giving of support can promote health and/or retard illness progression.

Although the exact mechanisms underlying the benefits of support provision are not yet understood, the animal studies on the impact of nurturant behavior on offspring that were described earlier may be instructive. These studies found that, not only were offspring soothed by nurturant contact, but also the animal providing the nurturant contact was benefited as well. Specifically, benefits to offspring were mirrored in the nurturers in the form of reduced sympathetic arousal and higher observed calm (Wiesenfeld, Malatesta, Whitman, Grannose, & Vile, 1985; Uvnäs-Moberg, 1996; see also Adler, Cook, Davison, West, & Bancroft, 1986; Altemus,

Deuster, Galliven, Carter, & Gold, 1995). Thus, it is possible that the benefits of providing social support operate through some of the same physiological and neuroendocrine pathways whereby the receipt of support from others seems to achieve its benefits. In addition, if oxytocin and other hormones are implicated in the provision of social support, the anxiolytic properties of oxytocin, coupled with its established role in down-regulating SNS and HPA axis responses to stress, may provide a second potential point of departure for understanding the health benefits of providing social support, as well as receiving it.

### Social Support Interventions: Clinical Implications

The implications of social support research for clinical practice and interventions are substantial. As one of the best established resources contributing to psychological well-being and health, clinical efforts to enhance or improve social support are well-placed. Moreover, when people are experiencing intensely stressful events, social support is not inevitably forthcoming. Even when people in a social network make efforts to provide social support, those efforts may not always be effective, as noted earlier. Consequently, a broad array of clinical support interventions have arisen to augment social support, especially for those experiencing gaps in the support they receive from others.

Some of these are family support interventions. For example, when a person has been diagnosed with a chronic condition or illness, the family's participation in an intervention may be enlisted to improve the diagnosed patient's adjustment to the condition. In addition, as noted earlier, involving the family in health behavior change programs may be beneficial for effective management of the disorder (see Taylor, 2008).

Family support interventions may also be emotionally soothing to family members as well, in part by alleviating anxiety that may be generated by incomplete understanding or misinformation. Explaining exactly what the patient's condition is, what treatments will be needed, and how the family can help can mean that support provided by family members may be more forthcoming and effective. In addition, family members may receive guidance in well-intentioned actions that should nonetheless be avoided because they are experienced as aversive by patients (e.g., Dakof & Taylor, 1990; Martin, Davis, Baron, Suls, & Blanchard, 1994).

For the most part, people who need help managing stressful events turn to their family, to friends, and to experts, such as medical caregivers, for the support that they need in times of stress. In some cases, however, that support is not forthcoming. Family and friends may be ill-equipped to provide the kind of support that a person needs for any of several reasons. Some conditions for which a person may require social support are stigmatizing ones, such as HIV, cancer, or epilepsy, and stigmatizing conditions can drive friends and family away (Wortman & Dunkel-Schetter, 1979). In other cases, a person's particular problems, such as the discovery of a chronic disease, can lead to questions and concerns that can be answered only by people with similar problems. Consequently, social support groups have arisen, as potential low-cost and efficient vehicles for meeting unmet social support needs. As of 1979, over 15 million Americans were using social support groups as a primary vehicle for their mental health services (Evans, 1979), and those numbers have grown over the past 25 years. Recent studies estimate that about 25 million individuals participate in support groups at some point during their life (Kessler, Mickelson, & Zhao, 1997), with whites and women more likely to participate than non-whites and men (Davison, Pennebaker, & Dickerson, 2000).

Social support groups were originally conceived of as small, face-to-face voluntary groups of individuals who came together to solve a problem or help each other cope with handicaps or illnesses, especially through the provision of emotional support (Katz & Bender, 1976). Some of these groups originally were grass-roots organizations formed by patients themselves, but more commonly, these support groups included a professional clinician, either as an initiator and organizer, or as an ongoing counselor who facilitated group interaction. Self-help groups, a particular type of social support group, do not include the participation of a trained professional, once the group is established (Katz & Bender, 1976). Originally, social support groups developed to treat a broad array of problems, disorders, and disabilities, including alcoholism, drug abuse, chronic diseases, loss of a partner through divorce or death, and most commonly, obesity (see Taylor, Falke, Shoptaw, & Lichtman, 1986 for an early review).

Social support groups continue to be a vital resource for the chronically ill and to people managing problems, such as obesity and alcoholism. These groups provide a format for discussions of mutual concern that arise as a result of illness, provide specific information about how others have dealt with similar problems, and provide people with the opportunity to share their emotional responses with others sharing the same problem (Gottlieb, 1988). Such groups can potentially fill gaps in social support not filled by family and friends or may act as an additional source of support provided by those going through the same event.

How effective are these groups? A large number of studies have evaluated the efficacy of social support groups by comparing people who have actually participated in such groups with those who have been waitlisted for participation and/or with non-participants, and these studies have generally found beneficial effects (see Hogan & Najarian, 2002 for a review). For example, social support groups have been found to reduce psychological distress for rheumatoid arthritis patients (e.g., Bradley, et al., 1987), cancer patients (e.g, Telch & Telch, 1986), and patients who have had a myocardial infarction (e.g., Dracup, 1985), among many others. As noted, self-help groups may especially benefit those with disorders that are stigmatizing, such as AIDS, alcoholism, breast and prostate cancer, and epilepsy (Davison, Pennebaker, & Dickerson, 2000; Droge, Arntson, & Norton, 1986).

Other benefits include helping patients to develop the motivation and techniques to adhere to complicated treatment regimens (Storer, Frate, Johnson, & Greeenberg, 1987). Support groups may encourage adherence for several reasons. In the course of interacting with others, a participant may learn techniques that others have used successfully to maintain adherence or to cope effectively with a disorder, and adopt those techniques to combat his or her particular barriers to adherence. Because people may commit themselves to change their behavior in front of others in the support group, they may be especially motivated to maintain adherence (e.g., Cummings, Becker, Kirscht, & Levin, 1981). Emotional support and the encouragement that others with similar problems provide can also encourage adherence to treatment.

Although social support groups have the potential to provide both emotional and informational support to participants, they may be better at providing educational than emotional benefits. In a review of cancer support groups described earlier, Helgeson and Cohen (1996) found that educational groups were more effective in meeting patients' needs than were support groups specifically aimed at the provision of emotional support. As noted, because relationships among support group members may seem artificial or not as intimate as "natural" relationships, relations in the support group may be more appropriate for providing information about the target problem or for managing it, whereas family or close friends may be better sources of emotional support.

A controversial issue in the support group literature has been whether participation in support groups among the chronically or terminally ill may promote better health and long-term survival. An early study of advanced breast cancer patients in a weekly cancer support group provided evidence that participants survived longer than nonparticipants (Spiegel, Bloom, Kraemer, & Gottheil, 1989). However, a follow-up investigation was unable to replicate this finding (Spiegel et al., 2007), and so whether the benefits of support group participation include the slowing of disease progression remains at issue.

Social support groups were widely heralded early in their history because they presaged a low-cost, convenient treatment option for people who might otherwise not have a therapeutic venue for their problems. Some studies, however, suggested that self-help groups actually reach only a small proportion of potentially eligible members (Taylor, Falke, Shoptaw, & Lichtman, 1986), appealing disproportionately to well-educated, middle-class white women. Not only is this the segment of the population that is already served by traditional treatment services, but at least one study (Taylor et al., 1986) suggested that participants in self-help groups were actually the same individuals who were using support services of all kinds, including therapists, ministers, family, friends, and medical experts.

Other factors can limit the effectiveness of support groups as well. In an evaluation of sources of satisfaction and dissatisfaction among members of cancer support groups, reported difficulties included logistical problems of getting to the face-to-face support group on a regular basis, irritation or annoyance over a particular individual or individuals in the group, concerns that meetings were too large, and concern that topics were too narrow and did not cover the issues in which prospective participants were interested (Taylor, Falke, Mazel, & Hilsberg, 1988).

The limited appeal of face-to-face groups has been somewhat offset by the rise of formal and informal internet support groups (Davison, Pennebaker, & Dickerson, 2000). Social networks are clearly expanding. MySpace and other social networking sites have more than 90 million members (Hulbert, 2006), indicating shifting patterns in social ties. In addition to these networking ties, informal social support groups have increased substantially in number over the past decade. While not providing the benefit of face-to-face social contact, they are logistically much easier to access, they are inexpensive (once one has a computer and an internet connection), they provide opportunities to come and go at will and at times of personal need, and they may be a more acceptable mode of help-seeking for men than traditional support groups have been (e.g., Bunde, Suls, Martin, & Barnett, 2006; Fogel, Albert, Schnabel, Ditkoff, & Neugut, 2002). The wealth of information that is now available on the web also means that answers to many specific questions can be answered without long-term participation in a support group.

Because internet-based support groups are a rapidly growing means of providing social support, especially for individuals with chronic illnesses or other stressful conditions, efforts have now gone into evaluating their effectiveness. For example, in one study (Barrera, Glasgow, McKay, Boles, & Feil, 2002), 160 type II diabetes patients were randomized into one of four conditions: diabetes information only; a personal self-management coach; a social support intervention; or a personal self-management coach coupled with the social support intervention. All four conditions were implemented via the internet. After 3 months, individuals in the two social support conditions (both with and without the personal coach) reported significant increases in perceived support, both with respect to their disease specifically and in general.

Internet social support can be useful with children as well. For example, STARBRIGHT World is a computer network that serves hospitalized children, providing interactive health education and opportunities to meet online with children in other hospitals who have similar disorders (Hazzard, Celano, Collins, & Markov, 2002). In one study evaluating the effectiveness of this program, children who participated reported more support, were found to be more knowledgeable about their illness, and were rated as lower in negative coping.

To date, a large-scale evaluation of internet social support resources has not been undertaken, largely because it is difficult to identify all of the sources that are available and all of the ways in which people distinctively use them. What research literature there is, however, suggests that these internet resources are used for many of the same purposes as face-to-face groups are (Davison et al., 2000), and that, as such, they can be a valuable source of both informational and emotional support.

## Conclusion

Across the lifespan, nurturant, supportive contact with others, a sense of belonging or mattering to others, and participation in social groups have been tied to a broad array of mental health and health benefits. Indeed, the social environment appears to be instrumental in helping people develop the abilities to build emotionally supportive ties with others and to construe social support as available.

Socially supportive ties are clearly beneficial in times of stress and may achieve these benefits in large part by helping individuals to control their emotional responses to stressful situations, such as anxiety and depression, and by keeping physiological, neuroendocrine, and immunologic responses to stress at low levels or by promoting faster recovery of these systems following stress. As such, social support has translated into mental and physical health benefits across numerous studies.

Social relationships are inherently double-edged, and so ties with others are not inevitably supportive; gaps in support, misfired efforts at support, and blatantly unsupportive behavior from others in times of stress are well-documented. In part because of these observations, researchers and practitioners are increasingly recognizing that the perception of social support, even in the absence of its utilization, may account for many of its benefits.

Many important issues remain for investigation. Among the most important conceptual issues is the integration of social support into our understanding of the psychological and biological concomitants of relationships more generally. The growing literature on developmental antecedents of social support may be especially helpful in building such an integrative model. The biological mechanisms underlying the benefits of social support also merit continued investigation. In particular, animal studies have been very useful for identifying underlying mechanisms relating social contacts to health outcomes, and this rich source of insights should continue to be mined. Much emphasis has been placed on SNS and HPA axis responses to stress as primary pathways affected by social support. Continued exploration of the possible roles of oxytocin, endogenous opioid peptides, and other hormones is warranted.

Why the mere perception of support has such strong effects on well-being and health merits continued consideration. Does perceived support operate through similar mechanisms as actual social support, or are other factors, such as genetic predispositions, more significant influences? Some issues that will merit additional research are only just being recognized, and these include cultural differences in the experience of social support and the psychological/biological benefits of providing support to others.

On the clinical side, perhaps the most compelling and provocative issues center on the potential health benefits of social support interventions, social support groups, and the enormous role that internet support increasingly plays in people's lives. Targeting people who otherwise may lack sufficient or effective social support, such as patients with stigmatizing conditions and their families and the isolated and/or infirm elderly (Weber, Roberts, Yarandi, Mills, Chumbler, & Wajsman, 2007; Winningham & Pike, 2007), needs to assume high priority.

What is, perhaps, most striking about social support research is the astonishing expansion of contexts and vehicles that have arisen to provide support and to address potentially unmet support needs. Once the value of social support for health and mental health was identified, it became understood for the valuable resource it is. As such, social support is a cornerstone of the important insights that health psychology has yielded.

## Acknowledgments

Preparation of this manuscript was supported by grants from the NSF (SES-0525713 and BCS-0729532).

## Notes

1. Of interest in this context is the observation that, in communal relationships, there are norms explicitly *against* reciprocity (Clark & Mills, 1979), favoring instead the notion that a communal relation with another transcends what would otherwise be obligations for reciprocity.

## References

Adler, E.M., Cook, A., Davison, D., West, C., & Bancroft, J. (1986). Hormones, mood and sexuality in lactating women. *British Journal of Psychiatry, 148*, 74–79.

Alferi, S.M., Carver, C.S., Antoni, M.H., Weiss, S., & Duran, R.E. (2001). An exploratory study of social support, distress, and life disruption among low-income Hispanic women under treatment for early stage breast cancer. *Health Psychology, 20*, 41–46.

Allen, K., Blascovich, J., & Mendes, W.B. (2002). Cardiovascular reactivity and the presence of pets, friends, and spouses: The truth about cats and dogs. *Psychosomatic Medicine, 64*, 727–739.

Allen, K.M., Blascovich, J., Tomaka, J., & Kelsey, R.M. (1991). Presence of human friends and pet dogs as moderators of autonomic responses to stress in women. *Journal of Personality and Social Psychology, 61*, 582–589.

Altemus, M.P., Deuster, A., Galliven, E., Carter, C.S., & Gold, P.W. (1995). Suppression of hypothalamic-pituitary-adrenal axis response to stress in lactating women. *Journal of Clinical Endocrinology and Metabolism, 80*, 2954–2959.

Bachner-Melman, R., Dina, C., Zohar, A.H., Constantini, N., Lerer, E., Hoch, S., et al. (2005). AVPR1a and SLC6A4 gene polymorphisms are associated with creative dance performance. *PLoS Genetics, 1*, e42.

Bakermans-Kranenburg, M.J., & van IJzendoorn, M.H. (2008). Oxytocin receptor (*OXTR*) and serotonin transporter (*5-HTT*) genes associated with observed parenting. *Social Cognitive and Affective Neuroscience, 3*, 128–134.

Barr, C.S., Schwandt, M.L., Lindell, S.G., Higley, J.D., Maestripieri, D., Goldman, D., et al. (2008). Variation at the mu-opioid receptor gene (OPRM1) influences attachment behavior in infant primates. *Proceedings of the National Academy of Sciences U S A, 105*, 5277–5281

Barrera, M. Jr., Glasgow, R.E., McKay, H.G., Boles, S.M., & Feil, E.G. (2002). Do Internet-based support interventions change perceptions of social support?: An experimental trial of approaches for supporting diabetes self-management. *American Journal of Community Psychology, 30*, 637–654.

Batson, C.D. (1998). Altruism and prosocial behavior. In D.T. Gilbert, & S.T. Fiske (Eds.), *The handbook of social psychology* Vol. 2 (pp. 282–316). New York, New York: McGraw Hill.

Belle, D. (1987). Gender differences in the social moderators of stress. In R.C. Barnett, L. Biener, & G.K. Baruch (Eds.), *Gender and stress* (pp. 257–277). New York: The Free Press.

Benson, B.A., Gross, A.M., Messer, S.C., Kellum, G., & Passmore, L.A. (1991). Social support networks among families of children with craniofacial anomalies. *Health Psychology, 10*, 252–258.

Berkman, L.F., & Syme, S.L. (1979). Social networks, host resistance, and mortality: A nine-year follow-up study of Alameda County residents. *American Journal of Epidemiology, 109*, 186–204.

Boesch, C. (1991). The effects of leopard predation on grouping patterns in forest chimpanzees. *Behaviour, 117*, 220–242.

Bolger, N., & Amarel, D. (2007). Effects of social support visibility on adjustment to stress: Experimental evidence. *Journal of Personal and Social Psychology, 92*, 458–475.

Bolger, N., Foster, M., Vinokur, A.D., & Ng, R. (1996). Close relationships and adjustments to a life crisis: The case of breast cancer. *Journal of Personality and Social Psychology, 70*, 283–294.

Bolger, N., Zuckerman, A., & Kessler, R.C. (2000). Invisible support and adjustment to stress. *Journal of Personality and Social Psychology, 79*, 953–961.

Boomsma, D.I., Willemsen, G., Dolan, C.V., Hawkley, L.C., & Cacioppo, J.T. (2005). Genetic and environmental contributions to loneliness in adults: The Netherlands twin register study. *Behavioral Genetics, 35*, 745–752.

Bradley, L.A., Young, L.D., Anderson, K.O., Turner, R.A., Agudelo, C.A., McDaniel, L.K., et al. (1987). Effects of psychological therapy on pain behavior of rheumatoid arthritis patients: Treatment outcome and six-month followup. *Arthritis and Rheumatism, 30*, 1105–1114.

Broadwell, S.D., & Light, K.C. (1999). Family support and cardiovascular responses in married couples during conflict and other interactions. *International Journal of Behavioral Medicine, 6*, 40–63.

Broman, C.L. (1993). Social relationships and health-related behavior. *Journal of Behavioral Medicine, 16*, 335–350.

Brown, S.L., Brown, R.M., House, J.S., & Smith, D.M. (2008). Coping with spousal loss: Potential buffering effects of self-reported helping behavior. *Personality and Social Psychology Bulletin, 34*, 849–861.

Brown, S.L., Nesse, R.M., Vinokur, A.D., & Smith, D.M. (2003). Providing social support may be more beneficial than receiving it: Results from a prospective study of mortality. *Psychological Science, 14*, 320–327.

Brown, J.L., Sheffield, D., Leary, M.R., & Robinson, M.E. (2003). Social support and experimental pain. *Psychosomatic Medicine, 65*, 276–283.

Bunde, M., Suls, J., Martin, R., & Barnett, K. (2006). Hystersisters online: Social support and social comparison among hysterectomy patients on the internet. *Annals of Behavioral Medicine, 31*, 271–278.

Burg, M.M., & Seeman, T.E. (1994). Families and health: The negative side of social ties. *Annals of Behavioral Medicine, 16*, 109–115.

Cacioppo, J., Burleson, M., Poehlmann, K., Malarky, W., Kiecolt-Glaser, J., Bernston, G., Uchino, B., & Glaser, R. (2000). Autonomic and neuroendocrine responses to mild psychological stressors: Effects of chronic stress on older women. *Annals of Behavioral Medicine, 22*, 140–148.

Caporeal, L.R. (1997). The evolution of truly social cognition: The core configuration model. *Personality and Social Psychology Review, 1*, 276–298.

Capuron, L., Ravaud, A., & Dantzer, R. (2000). Early depressive symptoms in cancer patients receiving interleukin-2 and/or interferon alpha-2b therapy. *Journal of Clinical Oncology, 18*, 2143–2151.

Carlson, L.E., Goodey, E., Bennett, M.H., Taenzer, P., & Koopmans, J. (2002). The addition of social support to a community-based large-group behavioral smoking cessation intervention: Improved cessation rates and gender differences. *Addictive Behaviors, 27*, 547–559.

Carlson, M., & Earls, F. (1997). Psychological and neuroendocrinological sequelae of early social deprivation in institutionalized children in Romania. *Annals of the New York Academy of Sciences, 807*, 419–428.

Carter, C.S., DeVries, A.C., & Getz, L.L. (1995). Physiological substrates of mammalian monogamy: The prairie vole model. *Neuroscience and Biobehavioral Reviews, 19*, 303–314.

Caspi, A., Sugden, K., Moffitt, T.E., Taylor, A., Craig, I.W., Harrington, H., et al. (2003). Influence of life stress on depression: moderation by a polymorphism in the 5-HTT gene. *Science, 301*, 386–389.

Ceballo, R., & McLoyd, V.C. (2002). Social support and parenting in poor, dangerous neighborhoods. *Child Development, 73*, 1310–1321.

Champagne, F.A., Chretien, P., Stevenson, C.W., Zhang, T.Y., Gratton, A., & Meaney, M.J. (2004). Variations in nucleus accumbens dopamine associated with individual differences in maternal behavior in the rat. *Journal of Neuroscience, 24*, 4113–4123.

Chesney, M., & Darbes, L. (1998). Social support and heart disease in women: Implications for intervention. In K. Orth-Gomer, M. Chesney, & N.K. Wenger (Eds.), Women, stress, and heart disease (pp. 165–182). Mahwah, NJ: Erlbaum.

Chiodera, P., & Legros, J.J. (1981). L'injection intraveineuse d'osytocine entraine unediminution de la concentration plasmatique de cortisol chez l'homme normal. *C. R. Soc. Bio. (Paris), 175*, 546.

Christenfeld, N., Gerin, W., Linden, W., Sanders, M., Mathur, J., Deich, J.D., & Pickering, T.G. (1997). Social support effects on cardiovascular reactivity: Is a stranger as effective as a friend? *Psychosomatic Medicine, 59*, 388–398.

Chrousos, G.P., & Gold, P.W. (1992). The concepts of stress and stress system disorders: Overview of physical and behavioral homeostasis. *Journal of the American Medical Association, 267*, 1244–1252.

Clark, M.S., & Mills, J. (1979). Interpersonal attraction in exchange and communal relationships. *Journal of Personality and Social Psychology, 37*, 12–24.

Cohen, S., & Lemay, E.P. (2007). Why would social networks be linked to affect and health practices? *Health Psychology, 26*, 410–417.

Cohen, S., & McKay, G. (1984). Social support, stress, and the buffering hypothesis: A theoretical analysis. In A. Baum, S.E. Taylor, & J. Singer (Eds.), *Handbook of psychology and health* Vol. 4 (pp. 253–268). Hillsdale, NJ: Erlbaum.

Cohen, S., & Wills, T.A. (1985). Stress, social support, and the buffering hypothesis. *Psychological Bulletin, 98*, 310–357.

Cohen, S., Doyle, W.J., Skoner, D.P., Rabin, B.S., & Gwaltney, J.M., Jr. (1997). Social ties and susceptibility to the common cold. *Journal of the American Medical Association, 277*, 1940–1944.

Cohen, S.D., Sharma, T., Acquaviva, K., Peterson, R.A., Patel, S.S., & Kimmel, P.L. (2007). Social support and chronic kidney disease: An update. *Advances in Chronic Kidney Disease, 14*, 335–344.

Cole, S.W., Kemeny, M.E., Fahey, J.L., Zack, J.A., & Naliboff, B.D. (2003). Psychological risk factors for HIV pathogenesis: Mediation by the autonomic nervous system. *Biological Psychiatry, 54*, 1444–1456.

Collins, N.L., Dunkel-Schetter, C., Lobel, M., & Scrimshaw, S.C.M. (1993). Social support in pregnancy: Psychosocial correlates of birth outcomes and post-partum depression. *Journal of Personality and Social Psychology, 65*, 1243–1158.

Collins, N.L., & Feeney, B.C. (2000). A safe haven: An attachment theory perspective on support seeking and caregiving in intimate relationships. *Journal of Personality and Social Psychology, 78*, 1053–1073.

Copeland, E.P., & Hess, R.S. (1995). Differences in young adolescents' coping strategies based on gender and ethnicity. *Journal of Early Adolescence, 15*, 203–219.

Coyne, J.C., Kessler, R.C., Tal, M., Turnbull, J., Wortman, C.B., & Greden, J.F. (1987). Living with a depressed person. *Journal of Consulting and Clinical Psychology, 55*, 347–352.

Cummings, K.M., Becker, M.H., Kirscht, J.P., & Levin, N.W. (1981). Intervention strategies to improve compliance with medical regimens by ambulatory hemodialysis patients. *Journal of Behavioral Medicine, 4*, 111–128.

Dakof, G.A., & Taylor, S.E. (1990). Victims' perceptions of social support: What is helpful from whom? *Journal of Personality and Social Psychology, 58*, 80–89.

Davison, K.P., Pennebaker, J.W., & Dickerson, S.S. (2000). Who talks? The social psychology of illness support groups. *American Psychologist, 55*, 205–217.

DiMatteo, M.R. (2004). Social support and patient adherence to medical treatment: A meta-analysis. *Health Psychology, 23*, 207–218.

Dimond, M. (1979). Social support and adaptation to chronic illness: The case of maintenance hemodialysis. *Research in Nursing and Health, 2*, 101–108.

Dracup, K. (1985). A controlled trial of couples' group counseling in cardiac rehabilitation. *Journal of Cardiopulmonary Rehabilitation, 5*, 436–442.

Droge, D., Arntson, P., & Norton, R. (1986). The social support function in epilepsy self-help groups. *Small Group Behavior, 17*, 139–163.

Dunbar, R. (1996). *Grooming, gossip, and the evolution of language.* Cambridge, MA: Harvard University Press.

Dunkel-Schetter, C., & Bennet, T.L. (1990). Differentiating the cognitive and behavioral aspects of social support. In B.R. Sarason, & I.G. Sarason, et al. (Eds.), *Social support: An interactional view. Wiley series on personality processes* (pp. 267–296). Oxford, England: John Wiley & Sons.

Dunkel-Schetter, C., Folkman, S., & Lazarus, R.S. (1987). Correlates of social support receipt. *Journal of Personality and Social Psychology, 53*, 71–80.

Edwards, C.P. (1993). Behavioral sex differences in children of diverse cultures: The case of nurturance to infants. In M.E. Pereira, & L.A. Fairbanks (Eds.), *Juvenile primates: Life history, development, and behavior* (pp. 327–338). New York: Oxford University Press.

Eisenberger, N.I., Taylor, S.E., Gable, S.L., Hilmert, C.J., & Lieberman, M.D. (2007). Neural pathways link social support to attenuated neuroendocrine stress responses. *NeuroImage, 35*, 1601–1612.

Eisenberger, N.I., Way, B.M., Taylor, S.E., Welch, W.T., & Lieberman, M.D. (2007). Understanding genetic risk for aggression: Clues from the brain's response to social exclusion. *Biological Psychiatry, 61*, 1100–1108.

Esterling, B.A., Kiecolt-Glaser, J.K., & Glaser, R. (1996). Psychosocial modulation of cytokine-induced natural killer cell activity in older adults. *Psychosomatic Medicine, 58*, 264–272.

Esterling, B.A., Kiecolt-Glaser, J.K., Bodnar, J.C., & Glaser, R. (1994). Chronic stress, social support, and persistent alterations in the natural killer cell response to cytokines in older adults. *Health Psychology, 13*, 291–298.

Evans, G. (1979). *The family-wise guide to self-help.* New York: Ballentine, 1979.

Ewart, C.K. (1991). Familial transmission of essential hypertension: Genes, environments, and chronic anger. *Annals of Behavioral Medicine, 13*, 40–47.

Fisher, E.B., La Greca, A.M., Greco, P., Arfken, C., & Schneiderman, N. (1997). Directive and nondirective social support in diabetes management. *International Journal of Behavioral Medicine, 4*, 131–144.

Fleming, R., Baum, A., Gisriel, M.M., & Gatchel, R.J. (1982). Mediating influences of social support on stress at Three Mile Island. *Journal of Human Stress, 8*, 14–22.

Fogel, J., Albert, S.M., Schnabel, F., Ditkoff, B.A., & Neugut, A.I. (2002). Internet use and social support in women with breast cancer. *Health Psychology, 21*, 398–404.

Francis, D., Diorio, J., Liu, D., & Meaney, M.J. (1999). Non-genomic transmission across generations of maternal behavior and stress responses in the rat. *Science, 286*, 1155–1158.

Franks, M.M., Stephens, M.A., Rook, K.S., Franklin, B.A., Ketevian, S.J., & Artinian, N.T. (2006). Spouses' provision of health-related support and control to patients participating in cardiac rehabilitation. *Journal of Family Psychology, 20*, 311–318.

Fraser, S.N., & Spink, K.S. (2002). Examining the role of social support and group cohesion in exercise compliance. *Journal of Behavioral Medicine, 25*, 233–249.

Freedman, V.A. (1993). Kin and nursing home lengths of stay: A backward recurrence time approach. *Journal of Health and Social Behavior, 34,* 138–152.

Fyrand, L., Moum, T., Finset, A., & Glennas, A. (2002). The impact of disability and disease duration on social support of women with rheumatoid arthritis. *Journal of Behavioral Medicine, 25,* 251–268.

Galea, S., Ahern, J., Resnick, H., Kilpatrick, D., Bucuvalas, M., Gold, J., & Vlahov, D. (2002). Psychological sequelae of the September 11 terrorist attacks in New York City. *New England Journal of Medicine, 346,* 982–987.

Gerin, W., Milner, D., Chawla, S., & Pickering, T.G. (1995). Social support as a moderator of cardiovascular reactivity: A test of the direct effects and buffering hypothesis. *Psychosomatic Medicine, 57,* 16–22.

Gerin, W., Pieper, C., Levy, R., & Pickering, T.G. (1992). Social support in social interaction: a moderator of cardiovascular reactivity. *Psychosomatic Medicine, 54,* 324–336.

Glaser, R., & Kiecolt-Glaser, J.K. (Eds.). (1994). *Handbook of human stress and immunity.* San Diego, CA: Academic Press.

Goodenow, C., Reisine, S.T., & Grady, K.E. (1990). Quality of social support and associated social and psychological functioning in women with rheumatoid arthritis. *Health Psychology, 9,* 266–284.

Gottlieb, B.H. (1988). *Marshalling social support: Formats, processes, and effects.* Newbury Park, CA: Sage.

Grewen, K.M., Girdler, S.S., Amico, J., & Light, K.C. (2005). Effects of partner support on resting oxytocin, cortisol, norepinephrine, and blood pressure before and after warm partner contact. *Psychosomatic Medicine, 67,* 531–538.

Grippo, A.J., Gerena, D., Huang, J., Kumar, N., Shah, M., Ughreja, R., & Carter, C.S. (2007). Social isolation induces behavioral and neuroendocrine disturbances relevant to depression in female and male prairie voles. *Psychoneuroendocrinology, 32,* 966–980.

Gunnar, M.R., Brodersen, L., Krueger, K., & Rigatuso, J. (1996). Dampening of adrenocortical responses during infancy: Normative changes and individual differences. *Child Development, 67,* 877–889.

Gurung, R.A.R., Taylor, S. E, & Seeman, T.E. (2003). Accounting for changes in social support among married older adults: Insights from the MacArthur studies of successful aging. *Psychology and Aging, 18,* 487–496.

Gurung, R.A.R., Taylor, S.E., Kemeny, M., & Myers, H. (2004). "HIV is not my biggest problem": The impact of HIV and chronic burden on depression in women at risk for AIDS. *Journal of Social and Clinical Psychology, 23,* 490–511.

Hamilton (1963). The evolution of altruistic behavior. *The American Naturalist, 97,* 354–356.

Hamrick, N., Cohen, S., & Rodriguez, M.S. (2002). Being popular can be healthy or unhealthy: Stress, social network diversity, and incidence of upper respiratory infection. *Health Psychology, 21,* 294–298.

Harlow, H.F., & Harlow, M.K. (1962). Social deprivation in monkeys. *Scientific American, 207,* 136–146.

Hart, J., Gunnar, M., & Cicchetti, D. (1996). Altered neuroendocrine activity in maltreated children related to symptoms of depression. *Development and Psychopathology, 8,* 201–214.

Hazzard, A., Celano, M., Collins, M., & Markov, Y. (2002). Effects of STARBRIGHT World on knowledge, social support, and coping in hospitalized children with sickle cell disease and asthma. *Children's Health Care, 31,* 69–86.

Heffner, K.L., Loving, T.J., Kiecolt-Glaser, J.K., Himawan, L.K., Glaser, R., & Malarkey, W.B. (2006). Older spouses' cortisol responses to marital conflict: Associations with demand/withdraw communication patterns. *Journal of Behavioral Medicine, 29,* 317–325.

Helgeson, V.S., & Cohen, S. (1996). Social support and adjustment to cancer: Reconciling descriptive, correlational, and intervention research. *Health Psychology, 15,* 135–148.

Helsing, K.J., Szklo, M., & Comstock, G.W. (1981). Factors associated with mortality after widowhood. *American Journal of Public Health, 71,* 802–809.

Herbst-Damm, K.L., & Kulik, J.A. (2005). Volunteer support, marital status, and the survival times of terminally ill patients. *Health Psychology, 24,* 225–229.

Hogan, B.E., & Najarian, B. (2002). Social support interventions: Do they work? *Clinical Psychology Review, 22,* 381–440.

Holahan, C.J., Moos, R.H., Holahan, C.K., & Brennan, P.L. (1997). Social context, coping strategies, and depressive symptoms: An expanded model with cardiac patients. *Journal of Personality and Social Psychology, 72,* 918–928.

Honn, V.J., & Bornstein, R.A. (2002). Social support, neuropsychological performance and depression in HIV infection. *Journal of the International Neuropsychological Society, 8,* 436–447.

Horowitz, L.M., Krasnoperova, E.N., Tatar, D.G., Hansen, M.B., Person, E.A., Galvin, K.L., & Nelson, K.L. (2001). The way to console may depend on the goal: Experimental studies of social support. *Journal of Experimental Social Psychology, 37,* 49–61.

House, J.S., Landis, K.R., & Umberson, D. (1988). Social relationships and health. *Science, 241,* 540–545.

Hulbert, A. (2006 July 16). Confidant Crisis: Americans have fewer close friends than before. Is that a problem? *New York Times Magazine,* p. 15.

Itkowitz, N.I., Kerns, R.D., & Otis, J.D. (2003). Support and coronary heart disease: The importance of significant other responses. *Journal of Behavioral Medicine, 26,* 19–30.b

Kamarck, T.W., Manuck, S.B., & Jennings, J.R. (1990). Social support reduces cardiovascular reactivity to psychological challenge: A laboratory model. *Psychosomatic Medicine, 52,* 42–58.

Katz, A.H., & Bender, E.I. (1976). Self-help in society–the motif of mutual aid. In A. Katz, and E. Bender (Eds.), *The strength in us: Self-help groups in the modern world* (pp. 2–13). New York: New Viewpoints.

Kaufman, J., Yang, B.Z., Douglas-Palumberi, H., Houshyar, S., Lipschitz, D., Krystal, J.H., & Gelernter, J. (2004). Social supports and serotonin transporter gene moderate depression in maltreated children. *Proceedings of the National Academy of Sciences USA, 101,* 17316–17321.

Kelly-Hayes, M., Wolf, P.A., Kannel, W.B., Sytkowski, D., D'Agostino, R.B., & Gresham, G.E. (1988). Factors influencing survival and need for institutionalization following stroke: The Framingham Study. *Archives of Physical and Medical Rehabilitation, 69,* 415–418.

Kessler, R.C., Kendler, K.S., Heath, A.C., Neale, M.C., & Eaves, L.J. (1992). Social support, depressed mood, and adjustment to stress: A genetic epidemiological investigation. *Journal of Personality and Social Psychology, 62,* 257–272.

Kessler, R.C., Mickelson, K.D., & Zhao, S. (1997). Patterns and correlates of self-help group membership in the United States. *Social Policy, 27,* 27–46.

Kiecolt-Glaser, J.K., Glaser, R., Gravenstein, S., Malarkey, W.B., & Sheridan, J. (1996). Chronic stress alters the immune response to influenza virus vaccine in older adults. *Proceedings of the National Academy of Science USA, 93,* 3043–3047.

Kiecolt-Glaser, J.K., Loving, T.J., Stowell, J.R., Malarkey, W.B., Lemeshow, S., Dickenson, S.L., & Glaser, R. (2005). Hostile marital interactions, proinflammatory cytokine production, and wound healing. *Archives of General Psychiatry, 62,* 1377–1384.

Kiecolt-Glaser, J.K., Marucha, P.T., Malarkey, W.B., Mercado, A.M., & Glaser, R. (1995). Slowing of wound healing by psychological stress. *Lancet, 346,* 1194–1196.

Kiecolt-Glaser, J.K., & Newton, T.L. (2001). Marriage and health: His and hers. *Psychological Bulletin, 127,* 472–503.

Kilpatrick, D.G., Koenen, K.C., Ruggiero, K.J., Acierno, R., Galea, S., Resnick, H.S., et al. (2007). The serotonin transporter genotype and social support and moderation of post-traumatic stress disorder and depression in hurricane-exposed adults. *American Journal of Psychiatry, 164,* 1693–1699.

Kim, H.S., Sherman, D.K., & Taylor, S.E. (2008). Culture and social support. *American Psychologist, 63,* 518–526.

King, A., Oka, B., & Young, D. (1994). Ambulatory blood pressure and heart rate responses to stress of work and caregiving in older women. *Journal of Gerontology, 49,* 239–245.

King, K.B., Reis, H.T., Porter, L.A., & Norsen, L.H. (1993). Social support and long-term recovery from coronary artery surgery: Effects on patients and spouses. *Health Psychology, 12,* 56–63.

Kirschbaum, C., Klauer, T., Filipp, S., & Hellhammer, D.H. (1995). Sex-specific effects of social support on cortisol and subjective responses to acute psychological stress. *Psychosomatic Medicine, 57,* 23–31.

Knafo, A., Israel, S., Darvasi, A., Bachner-Melman, R., Uzefovsky, F., Cohen, L., et al. (2008). Individual differences in allocation of funds in the dictator game associated with length of the arginine vasopressin 1a receptor RS3 promoter region and correlation between RS3 length and hippocampal mRNA. *Genes, Brain, and Behavior, 7,* 266–275.

Kors, D., Linden, W., & Gerin, W. (1997). Evaluation interferes with social support: Effects on cardiovascular stress reactivity. *Journal of Social and Clinical Psychology, 16,* 1–23.

Kulik, J.A., & Mahler, H.I.M. (1993). Emotional support as a moderator of adjustment and compliance after coronary artery bypass surgery: A longitudinal study. *Journal of Behavioral Medicine, 16,* 45–64.

Langner, T., & Michael, S. (1960). *Life stress and mental health.* New York: Free Press.

Legros, J.J., Chiodera, P., & Demy-Ponsart, E. (1982). Inhibitory influence of exogenous oxytocin on adrenocorticotropin secretion in normal human subjects. *Journal of Clinical Endocrinology and Metabolism, 55,* 1035–1039.

Lepore, S.J. (1995). Cynicism, social support, and cardiovascular reactivity. *Health Psychology, 14,* 210–216.

Lepore, S.J. (1998). Problems and prospects for the social support-reactivity hypothesis. *Annals of Behavioral Medicine, 20,* 257–269.

Lepore, S.J., Allen, K.A.M., & Evans, G.W. (1993). Social support lowers cardiovascular reactivity to an acute stress. *Psychosomatic Medicine, 55,* 518–524.

Levine, S., & Wiener, S.G. (1988). Psychoendocrine aspects of mother-infant relationships in nonhuman primates. *Psychoneuroimmunology, 13,* 143–154.

Lewis, M.A., & Rook, K.S. (1999). Social control in personal relationships: Impact on health behaviors and psychological distress. *Health Psychology, 18,* 63–71.

Li, Y., & Ferraro, K.F. (2005). Volunteering and depression in later life: Social benefit or selection processes? *Journal of Health and Social Behavior, 46,* 68–84.

Light, K.C., Grewen, K.M., & Amico, J.A. (2005). More frequent partner hugs and higher oxytocin levels are linked to lower blood pressure and heart rate in premenopausal women. *Biological Psychology, 69,* 5–21.

Lin, N., & Westcott, J. (1991). Marital engagement/disengagement, social networks, and mental health. In J. Eckenrode (Ed.), *The social context of coping* (pp. 213–237). New York: Plenum.

Lin, N., Ye, X., & Ensel, W. (1999). Social support and depressed mood: A structural analysis. *Journal of Health and Social Behavior, 40,* 344–359.

Liu, D., Diorio, J., Tannenbaum, B., Caldji, C., Francis, D., Freedman, A., et al. (1997). Maternal care, hippocampal glucocorticoid receptors, and hypothalamic-pituitary-adrenal responses to stress. *Science, 277,* 1659–1662.

Loucks, E.B., Berkman, L.F., Gruenewald, T.L., & Seeman, T.E. (2006). Relation of social integration to inflammatory marker concentrations in men and women 70–79 years. *American Journal of Cardiology, 97,* 1010–1016.

Luckow, A., Reifman, A., & McIntosh, D.N. (1998, August). *Gender differences in coping: A meta-analysis.* Poster session presented at the 106th annual convention of the American Psychological Association, San Francisco, CA.

Magni, G., Silvestro, A., Tamiello, M., Zanesco, L., & Carl, M. (1988). An integrated approach to the assessment of family adjustment to acute lymphocytic leukemia in children. *Acta Psychiatrica Scandinavica, 78,* 639–642.

Maier, S.F., & Watkins, L.R. (1998). Cytokines for psychologists: Implications of bidirectional immune-to-brain communication for understanding behavior, mood, and cognition. *Psychological Review, 105,* 83–107

Marteau, T.M., Bloch, S., & Baum, J.D. (1987). Family life and diabetic control. *Journal of Child Psychology and Psychiatry, 28,* 823–833.

Martin, R., Davis, G.M., Baron, R.S., Suls, J., & Blanchard, E.B. (1994). Specificity in social support: Perceptions of helpful and unhelpful provider behaviors among irritable bowel syndrome, headache, and cancer patients. *Health Psychology, 13,* 432–439.

Matt, G.E., & Dean, A. (1993). Social support from friends and psychological distress among elderly persons: Moderator effects of age. *Journal of Health and Social Behavior, 34,* 187–200.

McCarthy, M.M. (1995). Estrogen modulation of oxytocin and its relation to behavior. In R. Ivell, & J. Russell (Eds.), *Oxytocin: Cellular and molecular approaches in medicine and research* (pp. 235–242). New York: Plenum Press.

McDonald, L.M., & Korabik, K. (1991). Sources of stress and ways of coping among male and female managers. *Journal of Social Behavior and Personality, 6,* 185–198.

McEwen, B.S., & Sapolsky, R.M. (1995). Stress and cognitive function. *Current Opinion in Neurobiology, 5,* 205–216.

McEwen, B.S., & Stellar, E. (1993). Stress and the individual: Mechanisms leading to disease. *Archives of Internal Medicine, 153,* 2093–2101.

McLeod, J.D., Kessler, R.C., & Landis, K.R. (1992). Speed of recovery from major depressive episodes in a community sample of married men and women. *Journal of Abnormal Psychology, 101,* 277–286.

Meaney, M.J. (2001). Maternal care, gene expression, and the transmission of individual differences in stress reactivity across generations. *Annual Review of Neuroscience, 24,* 1161–1192.

Meaney, M.J., & Szyf, M. (2005). Environmental programming of stress responses through DNA methylation: life at the interface between a dynamic environment and a fixed genome. *Dialogues in Clinical Neuroscience, 7,* 103–123.

Miller, G.E., Cohen, S., & Ritchey, A.K. (2002). Chronic psychological stress and the regulation of pro-inflammatory cytokines: A glucocorticoid-resistance model. *Health Psychology, 21,* 531–541.

Miller, G.M., Bendor, J., Tiefenbacher, S., Yang, H., Novak, M.A., & Madras, B.K. (2004). A mu-opioid receptor single nucleotide polymorphism in rhesus monkey: association with stress response and aggression. *Molecular Psychiatry, 9,* 99–108.

Mills, P.J., Ziegler, M.G., Patterson, T., Dimsdale, J.E., Haugher, R., Irwin, M., & Grant, I. (1997). Plasma catecholamine and lymphocyte beta2-adrenergic alterations in elderly Alzheimer caregivers under stress. *Psychosomatic Medicine, 59,* 251–256.

Mullen, B., Bryant, B., & Driskell, J.E. (1997). Presence of others and arousal: An integration. *Group dynamics: Theory, research, and practice, 1,* 52–64.

Nachmias, M., Gunnar, M.R., Mangelsdorf, S., Parritz, R.H., & Buss, K. (1996). Behavioral inhibition and stress reactivity: The moderating role of attachment security. *Child Development, 67,* 508–522.

Naliboff, B.D., Mayer, M., Fass, R., Fitzgerald, L.Z., Chang, L., Bolus, R., & Mayer, E.A. (2004). The effect of life stress on symptoms of heartburn. *Psychosomatic Medicine, 66,* 426–434.

Nelson, E., & Panksepp, J. (1998). Brain substrates of infant-mother attachment: contributions of opioids, oxytocin, and norepinephrine. *Neuroscience and Biobehavioral Reviews, 22,* 437–452.

New England Research Institutes. (1997, Spring/Summer). Gender differences in social supports: Data from the Massachusetts Male Aging Study and the Massachusetts Women's Health Study. *Network,* p. 12.

Newsom, J.T., Mahan, T.L., Rook, K.S., & Krause, N. (2008). Stable negative social exchanges and health. *Health Psychology, 27,* 78–86.

Newsom, J.T., & Schulz, R. (1998). Caregiving from the recipient's perspective: Negative reactions to being helped. *Health Psychology, 17,* 172–181.

Ogus, E.D., Greenglass, E.R., & Burke, R.J. (1990). Gender-role differences, work stress and depersonalization. *Journal of Social Behavior and Personality, 5,* 387–398.

Penninx, B.W.J.H., van Tilburg, T., Boeke, A.J.P., Deeg, D.J.H., Kriegsman, D.M.W., & van Eijk, J. Th.M. (1998). Effects of social support and personal coping resources on depressive symptoms: Different for various chronic diseases? *Health Psychology, 17,* 551–558.

Phillipson, C. (1997). Social relationships in later life: A review of the research literature. *International Journal of Geriatric Psychiatry, 12,* 505–512.

Pressman, S.D., Cohen, S., Miller, G.E., Barkin, A., Rabin, B.S., & Treanor, J.J. (2005). Loneliness, social network size, and immune response to influenza vaccination in college freshmen. *Health Psychology, 24,* 297–306.

Ptacek, J.T., Smith, R.E., & Zanas, J. (1992). Gender, appraisal, and coping: A longitudinal analysis. *Journal of Personality, 60,* 747–770.

Repetti, R.L., Taylor, S.E., & Saxbe, D. (2007). The influence of early socialization experiences on the development of biological systems. In J. Grusec, and P. Hastings (Eds.), *Handbook of socialization* (pp. 124–152). New York, NY: Guilford.

Repetti, R.L., Taylor, S.E., & Seeman, T.E. (2002). Risky families: Family social environments and the mental and physical health of offspring. *Psychological Bulletin, 128,* 330–366.

Resnick, B., Orwig, D., Magaziner, J., & Wynne, C. (2002). The effect of social support on exercise behavior in older adults. *Clinical Nursing Research, 11,* 52–70.

Robertson, E.K., & Suinn, R.M. (1968). The determination of rate of progress of stroke patients through empathy measures of patient and family. *Journal of Psychosomatic Research, 12,* 189–191.

Rook, K.S. (1984). The negative side of social interaction: Impact on psychological well-being. *Journal of Personality and Social Psychology, 46,* 1097–1108.

Rutledge, T., Reis, S.E., Olson, M., Owens, J., Kelsey, S.F., Pepine, C.J., et al. (2004). Social networks are associated with lower mortality rates among women with suspected coronary disease: The National Heart, Lung, and Blood Institute-sponsored women's ischemia syndrome evaluation study. *Psychosomatic Medicine, 66,* 882–888.

Sarason, B.R., Sarason, I.G., & Gurung, R.A.R. (1997). Close personal relationships and health outcomes: A key to the role of social support. In S. Duck (Ed.), *Handbook of personal relationships* (pp. 547–573). New York: Wiley.

Schulz, R., & Beach, S. (2000). Caregiving as a risk factor for mortality: The caregiver health effects study. *Journal of the American Medical Association, 282,* 2215–2219.

Schuster, T.L., Kessler, R.C., & Aseltine, R.H., Jr. (1990). Supportive interactions, negative interactions, and depressed mood. *American Journal of Community Psychology, 18,* 423–438.

Schwartz, C., Meisenhelder, J.B., Ma, Y., & Reed, G. (2003). Altruistic social interest behaviors are associated with better mental health. *Psychosomatic Medicine, 65,* 778–785.

Schwarzer, R., & Leppin, A. (1989). Social support and health: A meta-analysis. *Psychology and Health, 3,* 1–15.

Seeman, T.E. (1996). Social ties and health: The benefits of social integration. *Annals of Epidemiology, 6,* 442–451.

Seeman, T.E., & McEwen, B. (1996). Impact of social environment characteristics on neuroendocrine regulation. *Psychosomatic Medicine, 58,* 459–471.

Seeman, T.E., Lusignolo, T.M., Albert, M., & Berkman, L. (2001). Social relationships, social support, and patterns of cognitive aging in healthy, high-functioning older adults: MacArthur studies of successful aging. *Health Psychology, 20,* 243–255.

Sheffield, D., & Carroll, D. (1994). Social support and cardiovascular reactions to active laboratory stressors. *Psychology and Health, 9,* 305–316.

Shumaker, S.A., & Hill, D.R. (1991). Gender differences in social support and physical health. *Health Psychology, 10,* 102–111.

Simeon, D., Greenberg, J., Nelson, D., Schmeider, J., & Hollander, E. (2005). Dissociation and post-traumatic stress 1 year after the World Trade Center disaster: Follow-up of a longitudinal study. *Journal of Clinical Psychiatry, 66,* 231–237.

Smith, T.W. (1992). Hostility and health: Current status of a psychosomatic hypothesis. *Health Psychology, 11,* 139–150.

Smith, T.W., Gallo, L.C., Goble, L., Ngu, L.Q., & Stark, K.A. (1998). Agency, communion, and cardiovascular reactivity during marital interaction. *Health Psychology, 17*, 537–545.

Smith, T.W., Ruiz, J.M., & Uchino, B.N. (2004). Mental activation of supportive ties, hostility, and cardiovascular reactivity to laboratory stress in young men and women. *Health Psychology, 23*, 476–485.

Sorkin, D., Rook, K.S., & Lu, J.L. (2002). Loneliness, lack of emotional support, lack of companionship, and the likelihood of having a heart condition in an elderly sample. *Annals of Behavioral Medicine, 24*, 290–298.

Spiegel, D., Bloom, J.R., Kraemer, H.C., & Gottheil, E. (1989). Effect of psychosocial treatment on survival of patients with metastatic breast cancer. *The Lancet, 2*, 888–891.

Spiegel, D., Butler, L.D., Giese-Davis, J., Koopman, C., Miller, E., DiMiceli, S., et al. (2007). Effects of supportive-expressive group therapy on survival of patients with metastatic breast cancer: A randomized prospective trial. *Cancer, 110*, 1130–1138.

Spitz, R.A., & Wolff, K.M. (1946). Anaclitic depression: An inquiry into the genesis of psychiatric conditions in early childhood, II. In A. Freud, et al. (Eds.), *The psychoanalytic study of the child* Vol. 2 (pp. 313–342). New York: International Universities Press.

Spitze, G., Logan, J., Joseph, G., & Lee, E. (1994). Middle generation roles and the well-being of men and women. *Journal of Gerontology, 49*, 107–116.

Stone, A.A., Mezzacappa, E.S., Donatone, B.A., & Gonder, M. (1999). Psychosocial stress and social support are associated with prostate-specific antigen levels in men: Results from a community screening program. *Health Psychology, 18*, 482–486.

Storer, J.H., Frate, D.M., Johnson, S.A., & Greenberg, A.M. (1987). When the cure seems worse than the disease: Helping families adapt to hypertension treatment. *Family Relations, 36*, 311–315.

Stroebe, M.S., & Stroebe, W. (1983). Who suffers more? Sex differences in health risks of the widowed. *Psychological Bulletin, 93*, 279–301.

Suomi, S.J. (1987). Genetic and maternal contributions to individual differences in rhesus monkey biobehavioral development. In N.A. Krasnagor, E.M. Blass, M.A. Hofer, & W.P. Smotherman (Eds.), *Perinatal development: A psychobiological perspective* (pp. 397–420). New York: Academic Press.

Suomi, S.J. (1991). Up-tight and laid-back monkeys: Individual differences in the response to social challenges. In S. Brauth, W. Hall, & R. Dooling (Eds.), *Plasticity of development* (pp. 27–56). Cambridge, MA: MIT Press.

Suomi, S.J. (1999). Attachment in rhesus monkeys. In J. Cassidy, & P. Shaver (Eds.), *Handbook of attachment: Theory, research, and clinical applications* (pp.181–197). New York: Guilford Press.

Tamres, L., Janicki, D., & Helgeson, V.S. (2002). Sex differences in coping behavior: A meta-analytic review. *Personality and Social Psychology Review, 6*, 2–30.

Taylor, J., & Turner, R.J. (2001). A longitudinal study of the role of significance of mattering to others for depressive symptoms. *Journal of Health and Social Behavior, 42*, 310–325.

Taylor, S.E. (2002). *The tending instinct: How nurturing is essential to who we are and how we live*. New York: Holt.

Taylor, S.E. (2008). *Health Psychology* (7th ed.). New York: McGraw-Hill.

Taylor, S.E., Dickerson, S.S., and Klein, L.C. (2002). Toward a biology of social support. In C.R. Snyder, & S.J. Lopez (Eds.), *Handbook of positive psychology* (pp. 556–569). London: Oxford University Press.

Taylor, S.E., Gonzaga, G., Klein, L.C., Hu, P., Greendale, G.A., & Seeman S.E. (2006). Relation of oxytocin to psychological stress responses and hypothalamic-pituitary-adrenocortical axis activity in older women. *Psychosomatic Medicine, 68*, 238–245.

Taylor, S.E., Falke, R.L., Mazel, R.M., & Hilsberg, B.L. (1988). Sources of satisfaction and dissatisfaction among members of cancer support groups. In B. Gottlieb (Ed.), *Marshalling social support* (pp. 187–208). Beverly Hills, CA: Sage Publications.

Taylor, S.E., Falke, R.L., Shoptaw, S.J., & Lichtman, R.R. (1986). Social support, support groups, and the cancer patient. *Journal of Consulting and Clinical Psychology, 54*, 608–615.

Taylor, S.E., Klein, L.C., Lewis, B.P., Gruenewald, T.L., Gurung, R.A.R., & Updegraff, J.A. (2000). Biobehavioral responses to stress in females: Tend-and-befriend, not fight-or-flight. *Psychological Review, 107*, 411–429.

Taylor, S.E., & Seeman, T.E. (2000). Psychosocial resources and the SES-health relationship. In N. Adler, M. Marmot, & B. McEwen (Eds.), *Socioeconomic status and health in industrial nations: Social, psychological, and biological pathways* (pp. 210–225). New York: New York Academy of Sciences.

Taylor, S.E., Sherman, D.K., Kim, H.S., Jarcho, J., Takagi, K., & Dunagan, M.S. (2004). Culture and social support: Who seeks it and why? *Journal of Personality and Social Psychology, 87*, 354–362.

Taylor, S.E., Way, B.M., Welch, W.T., Hilmert, C.J., Lehman, B.J., & Eisenberger, N.I. (2006). Early family environment, current adversity, the serotonin transporter polymorphism, and depressive symptomatology. *Biological Psychiatry, 60*, 671–676.

Taylor, S.E., Welch, W.T., Kim, H.S., & Sherman, D.K. (2007). Cultural differences in the impact of social support on psychological and biological stress responses. *Psychological Science, 18*, 831–837.

Telch, C.F., & Telch, M.J. (1986). Group coping skills instruction and supportive group therapy for cancer patients: A comparison of strategies. *Journal of Consulting and Clinical Psychology, 54*, 802–808.

Thoits, P.A. (1984). Explaining distributions of psychological vulnerability: Lack of social support in the face of life stress. *Social Forces, 63*, 453–481.

Thoits, P.A. (1986). Social support as coping assistance. *Journal of Consulting and Clinical Psychology, 54*, 416–423.

Thoits, P.A. (1995). Stress, coping and social support processes: Where are we? What next? *Journal of Health and Social Behavior, 35*, 53–79.

Trivers, R.L. (1971). The evolution of reciprocal altruism. *Quarterly Review of Biology, 46*, 35–37.

Turner-Cobb, J.M., Gore-Felton, C., Marouf, F., Koopman, C., Kim, P., Israelski, D., & Spiegel, D. (2002). Coping, social support, and attachment style as psychosocial correlates of adjustment in men and women with HIV/AIDS. *Journal of Behavioral Medicine, 25*, 337–353.

Uchino, B., Cacioppo, J., & Kiecolt-Glaser, J. (1996). The relationship between social support and physiological processes: A review with emphasis on underlying mechanisms and implications for health. *Psychological Bulletin, 119*, 488–531.

Umberson, D. (1987). Family status and health behaviors: Social control as a dimension of social integration. *Journal of Health and Social Behavior, 28,* 306–319.

Uvnäs-Moberg, K. (1996). Neuroendocrinology of the mother-child interaction. *Trends in Endocrinology and Metabolism, 7,* 126–131.

Uvnäs-Moberg, K. (1997). Oxytocin linked antistress effects - the relaxation and growth response. *Acta Psychologica Scandinavica, 640* (Suppl.), 38–42.

VanderPlate, C., Aral, S.O., & Magder, L. (1988). The relationship among genital herpes simplex virus, stress, and social support. *Health Psychology, 7,* 159–168.

Veroff, J., Kulka, R., & Douvan, E. (1981). *Mental health in America: Patterns of help-seeking from 1957 to 1976.* New York: Basic Books.

Way, B.M., & Taylor, S.E. (2011). Genetic factors in social pain. In G. MacDonald, & L.A. Jensen-Campbell (Eds.), *Social pain: A neuroscientific, social, clinical, and developmental analysis* (pp. 95–119). Washington, DC: American Psychological Association.

Way, B.M., Taylor, S.E., & Eisenberger, N.I. (2009). Variation in the mu-opioid receptor gene (OPRM1) is associated with dispositional and neural sensitivity to social rejection. Proceedings of the National Academy of Sciences, 106, 15079–84.

Weaver, I.C., Cervoni, N., Champagne, F.A., D'Alessio, A.C., Sharma, S., Seckl, J.R., et al. (2004). Epigenetic programming by maternal behavior. *Nature Neuroscience, 7,* 847–854.

Weber, B.A., Roberts, B.L., Yarandi, H., Mills, T.L., Chumbler, N.R., & Wajsman, Z. (2007). The impact of dyadic social support on self-efficacy and depression after radical prostatectomy. *Journal of Aging and Health, 19,* 630–645.

Wethington, E., & Kessler, R.C. (1986). Perceived support, received support, and adjustment to stressful life events. *Journal of Health and Social Behavior, 27,* 78–89.

Wethington, E., McLeod, J.D., & Kessler, R.C. (1987). The importance of life events for explaining sex differences in psychological distress. In R.C. Barnett, L. Biener, & G.K. Baruch (Eds.), *Gender and stress* (pp. 144–156). New York: The Free Press.

Wheeler, L., Reis, S., & Nezlek, J. (1983). Loneliness, social interaction, and sex roles. *Journal of Personality and Social Psychology, 45,* 943–953.

Whiting, B., & Whiting, J. (1975). *Children of six cultures.* Cambridge, MA: Harvard University Press.

Wickrama, K., Conger, R.D., & Lorenz, F.O. (1995). Work, marriage, lifestyle, and changes in men's physical health. *Journal of Behavioral Medicine, 18,* 97–111.

Wiesenfeld, A.R., Malatesta, C.Z., Whitman, P.B., Grannose, C., & Vile, R. (1985). Psychophysiological response of breast- and bottle-feeding mothers to their infants' signals. *Psychophysiology, 22,* 79–86.

Wiklund, I., Oden, A., Sanne, H., Ulvenstam, G., Wilhemsson, C., & Wilhemsen, L. (1988). Prognostic importance of somatic and psychosocial variables after a first myocardial infarction. *American Journal of Epidemiology, 128,* 786–795.

Wills, T.A. (1991). Social support and interpersonal relationships. In M.S. Clark (Ed.), *Prosocial behavior* (pp. 265–289). Newbury Park, CA: Sage.

Wills, T.A. (1998). Social support. In E.A. Blechman, & K.D. Brownell (Eds.), *Behavioral medicine and women: A comprehensive handbook* (pp. 118–128). New York: Guilford Press.

Wills, T.A., & Vaughan, R. (1989). Social support and substance use in early adolescence. *Journal of Behavioral Medicine, 12,* 321–340.

Wilson, D.K., & Ampey-Thornhill, G. (2001). The role in gender and family support on dietary compliance in an African-American adolescent hypertension prevention study. *Annals of Behavioral Medicine, 23,* 59–67.

Winningham, R.G., & Pike, N.L. (2007). A cognitive intervention to enhance institutionalized older adults' social support networks and decrease loneliness. *Aging and Mental Health, 11,* 716–721.

Witt, D.M., Carter, C.S., & Walton, D. (1990). Central and peripheral effects of oxytocin administration in prairie voles (*Microtus ochrogaster*). *Pharmacology, Biochemistry, and Behavior, 37,* 63–69.

Woodall, K.L., & Matthews, K.A. (1989). Familial environment associated with type A behaviors and psychophysiological responses to stress in children. *Health Psychology, 8,* 403–426.

Wortman, C.B., & Dunkel-Schetter, C. (1979). Interpersonal relationships and cancer: A theoretical analysis. *Journal of Social Issues, 35,* 120–155.

Wortman, C.B., & Lehman, D.R. (1985). Reactions to victims of life crises: Support attempts that fail. In I.G. Sarason, and B.R. Sarason (Eds.), *Social support: Theory, research, and applications* (pp. 463–489). Dordrecht, The Netherlands: Martinus Nijhoff.

Wu, H., Wang, J., Cacioppo, J.T., Glaser, R., Kiecolt-Glaser, J.K., & Malarkey, W.B. (1999). Chronic stress associated with spousal caregiving of patients with Alzheimer's dementia is associated with downregulation of B-lymphocyte GH mRNA. *Journal of Gerontology, Series A, Biological Sciences and Medical Sciences, 54,* M212–215.

# Personality, Disease, and Self-healing

Howard S. Friedman

## Abstract

Individuals vary significantly in disease-proneness, recuperation, health, and longevity. Some of this variability can be predicted from personality, which captures biopsychosocial patterns that unfold across the lifespan. This is especially true when considering how personality interacts with psychosocial contexts. This chapter presents conceptual models of and reviews research linking core personality traits to health and longevity. Conscientiousness predicts better physical health and longevity, for a variety of reasons. The influences of extraversion, sociability, and agreeableness depend on a variety of situations and lifestyles tied to particular social groups. Neuroticism and negative affectivity are often conceptualized as negative traits that lead to illness, but the evidence is mixed; in light of certain social stresses, realistic pessimism and worrying may be health protective. Studying deeper and more sophisticated models of links between personality and health leads to an enhanced understanding of individual differences in life pathways toward health or illness.

**Keywords:** Personality, self-healing, conscientiousness, neuroticism, optimism, health

One of the oldest and most puzzling questions in the field of health is why some people become sick while other seemingly similar people remain well or quickly recover from disease. And, why do some live long while others die young? Do the answers lie primarily in chance exposure to pathogens and other threats, or are individual factors—especially psychological matters—of key importance? Is it true that worriers develop ulcers and suffer heart attacks, while shy people face cancer? Is relaxation an elixir, and will keeping a smile on your face make you live longer?

The relationships among individual differences, disease, and health have been investigated scientifically for more than 100 years. The general verdict (subject to numerous exceptions and qualifications) is that a person who is chronically irritated, depressed, hostile, impulsive, bored, frustrated, unstable, lonely, or powerless is indeed more likely to develop illnesses and to die prematurely than is someone who is generally emotionally balanced and effective,

is in a satisfying job and engaged with life, has stable and supportive social relationships, and is well integrated into the community (Booth-Kewley & Friedman, 1987; Cacioppo & Berntson, 2011, Chapter 6, this volume; Cohen & Williamson, 1991; Friedman & Booth-Kewley, 1987; Friedman & Martin, 2011; House, Landis, & Umberson, 1988; Kiecolt-Glaser, Glaser, Cacioppo, & Malarkey, 1998; Miller, Smith, Turner, Guijarro, & Hallett, 1996; Repetti, Taylor, & Seeman, 2002; Smith & MacKenzie, 2006). Yet the various efforts to measure and precisely characterize such people have often led to a muddle of weak and hard to replicate findings.

To help clarify this muddle with a more structured and scientific framework, I developed the constructs termed *disease-prone personalities* and *self-healing personalities* (Friedman 1991/2000; 1998; Friedman & Booth-Kewley, 1987; Friedman & VandenBos, 1992). These constructs direct theory and research away from associations of single predictors and single outcomes, focusing instead on multiple-predictor, multiple-outcome developments over long periods of time. For example, instead of a medical focus on type A behavior and myocardial infarction, attention moves to biopsychosocial homeostasis and overall well-being and mortality risk, in a sociocultural context. As we shall see, some clarity can emerge from a modern and theoretically sophisticated personality approach to these matters, but the conceptual and methodological issues are complex. Addressing the key goal of improving health, well-being, and longevity requires distilling an accurate understanding of the core causal relationships.

All too often, when dealing with illness, medical investigators, as well as laypersons, think they are asking the question, "*Why* do people become sick?" but they are really often studying "*Who* becomes sick?" There is astounding variability in susceptibility to various illnesses and in the speed and likelihood of recovery. This variability in vulnerability and recuperation is usually at least as important as the average levels of disease, but yet is underappreciated and understudied.

Most so-called "risk factors" do a poor job of predicting who will succumb, and when and why they will succumb. Most worriers who self-medicate with chocolate-chip cookies do not develop breast cancer, most couch potatoes do not suffer strokes, and it is even the case that most smokers do not develop lung cancer. Typically, a solitary risk factor, even if well-documented (as many are not), produces only a marginal increase in an individual's risk for a particular disease, again revealing the marked variability. Multiple risk factors, if coupled with detailed knowledge of sociobehavioral environments and of paths across time, can, however, do a fairly good job in predicting subpopulation risk.

Despite the limits on prognostic power, there is a striking motivation to look for simple causal models of personality, health, and longevity. When one hears of someone becoming ill or dying at a young age, an immediate thought is, "What can I (as an individual) do to avoid that fate?" (Or, "Why am I different?") Even scientists and physicians, hearing of an association between a stable characteristic or persistent activity and morbidity, often show a strong tendency to imagine fairly simple causal links. For example, a well-done study of milk consumption in midlife and the future risk of Parkinson disease found those in the highest intake group were at a substantially increased risk when compared to those who consumed no milk, even controlling for overall calcium intake and certain other factors (Park et al., 2005). A primary conclusion was: "Whether observed effects are mediated through nutrients other than calcium or through neurotoxic contaminants [in milk] warrants further study" (p. 1047). In other words, the search for explanation quickly turns to a straightforward biomedical model of direct biochemical mediation. Overall, even though scientists well appreciate (in theory) that correlation does not mean causation, the research corpus is full of studies that focus on a single variable and include potentially misleading assumptions of causality. Such matters point to the existence of a more fundamental conceptual problem regarding disease-proneness. That is, we need better ways of and new models for thinking about why an individual stays healthy.

Many people are exposed to harmful bacteria, viruses, and other microorganisms but do not become ill. This situation was documented a half century ago in a pioneering study by two pediatricians who followed a number of families for about a year, doing throat cultures for streptococcal bacteria every few weeks. In a surprising result, they found that most of the time, the strep infections did not produce any symptoms of illness. The strep bacteria by themselves did not cause illness. When the people and families were stressed, however, the strep illness was more likely to develop (Meyer & Haggerty, 1962). On the other hand, no one developed the strep illness without exposure to the bacteria. Today, we have the paradoxical situation that social stress is generally taken for granted as an influence on upper respiratory illness (Cohen, Doyle & Skoner, 1999), yet the focus of medical practice remains on the microorganism.

Traditional approaches to health are dominated by the biomedical model of disease, in which health care is seen primarily as a curing or repair system, needed when medical problems strike. It emphasizes physiology, pathology, procedures, and pharmaceuticals. Although it is well known that many biopsychosocial factors influence whether an individual will stay well, the dominant biomedical model of disease exerts constant pressure to focus either on internal genetics or on the external threats of infectious agents and toxins. In contrast, consideration of the individual and his or her personality forces a broader and deeper analysis, which is closer to the true complexity of illness and well-being. This topic is the subject of this chapter.

## Historical Context

The idea of links between personality and health dates back thousands of years and clearly appears in the writings of Hippocrates, Galen, and their followers. The ancient Greeks, keen observers of the human condition, saw four essentials—the so-called bodily humors—as key to both individuality and health. People with a healthy, balanced supply of blood would likely be sanguine—having the healthy temperament and ruddy complexion characteristic of a person dominated by this humor. It nowadays refers to someone who is cheerful, confident, passionate, and optimistic. Excessive black bile (or melancholy—sadness, gloom, splenic moroseness) might lead to depression and degenerative diseases or cancer. Yellow bile (or choler—characterizing peevish, bilious people) would produce (if present in excess) a bitter, angry personality and associated feverish diseases. Finally, phlegm was said to be characteristic of a phlegmatic (sluggish, unemotional), cold apathy, associated for example with rheumatism. Although notions of bodily humors have been discarded, the underlying conception that individuals can be categorized as sanguine, depressed, hostile, and repressed remains with us. It turns out that personality is indeed very relevant to understanding health.

The ancient Greek notion of humoral *balance* likewise appears in modern ideas of biopsychosocial homeostasis, which developed from the psychophysiological models of French physiologist Claude Bernard (1880) and "fight-or-flight" discoverer Walter Cannon (1932). Physicians no longer regularly, intentionally bleed and purge their patients, but they do search for anomalies as a sign of illness. In the late 1940s, a number of medical students at Johns Hopkins University were studied in terms of their biological and psychological characteristics, categorized as either slow and solid (wary, self-reliant), rapid and facile (cool, clever), or irregular and uneven (moody, demanding). They were then followed for 30 years, during which time about half of them developed some serious health problem. Most (77%) of the previously labeled "irregular and uneven" types developed a serious disorder during these 30 years, but only about a quarter of the rest suffered a major health setback. In a follow-up, the "irregular and uneven" temperament types were again much more likely to have disease or to have died (Betz & Thomas, 1979). A later study found those physicians who seemed to have social and emotional problems (were repressed loners) were more likely to develop cancer (Shaffer, Graves, Swank, & Pearson, 1987), raising interest in various possible causal links. Such early work on personality balance helped set the stage for the current-day

focus on allostasis—the ability to achieve stability through change (McEwen, 1998). The processes of allostasis use the autonomic nervous system, the hypothalamic-pituitary-adrenal axis, and the cardiovascular, metabolic, and immune systems to respond to challenge.

With the dominance of psychoanalytic and neo-analytic theory in the emergence of the field of psychiatry in the first half of the 20th century, many interesting ideas in psychosomatic medicine grew out of the psychodynamic framework. (Freud himself used hypnosis and related psychodynamic techniques in the 1890s to cure hysterical paralysis [Freud, 1955].) In classic work beginning in the 1930s, Flanders Dunbar (1955) described conflicted patients, such as one named Agnes, an unhappy and unattractive women of 50 plagued with a serious heart condition that her doctors labeled "cause unknown." Agnes went in and out of hospitals until, finally, she died in the hospital on her birthday because, Dunbar said, Agnes had always wanted to show her resentment at being born. The influential psychoanalyst Alexander (1950) suggested that various diseases are caused by specific unconscious emotional conflicts. For example, ulcers were linked to oral conflicts (an unconscious desire to have basic infantile needs satisfied) and asthma to separation anxiety (that is, an unconscious desire to be protected by one's mother). Thus, although internal medicine exploded in influence on the medical scene in the 1950s and 1960s with pharmaceuticals based on biochemistry, a substantial but underappreciated history in medicine considered the importance of the psychology of the individual. However, like much psychoanalytic work, most of the early psychosomatic work could not be directly studied in a scientific manner and so was often ignored by those working in scientific psychology.

### The Example of Coronary-proneness, Type A Behavior, and Heart Disease

Perhaps the most researched topic in personality and disease involves the long-observed association between certain patterns of emotional behavior and the development of heart disease. The topic is of special interest in part because cardiovascular disease (heart disease and stroke) is by far the greatest cause of premature mortality in Western countries. Of course, it has been known for thousands of years that excitement increases pulse rate and that emotions like fear and love can cause pain in one's chest. But in the late 19th century, the medical educator Sir William Osler proposed a direct link between high-pressure activity and coronary heart disease (CHD) (Leibowitz, 1970). In the 1930s, Karl and William Menninger (1936), well-known American psychiatrists, asserted that CHD is related to repressed aggression.

Despite extensive clinical observations, systematic study of the association between emotional behavior and heart disease did not begin until the 1950s, when type A people were defined as those involved in a constant struggle to do more and more things in less and less time, and who were often quite hostile or aggressive in their efforts to achieve them (M. Friedman & Rosenman, 1974). Type A people always seem to be under the pressure of time, and live a life characterized by competitiveness. They are hasty, impatient, impulsive, hyperalert, and tense. When under pressure, most people may exhibit some behaviors that are similar to this type A pattern, but type A individuals exhibit this behavior very often, for example, turning even the most potentially relaxing situation (recreational sports such as tennis) into a high-pressure event (Chesney & Rosenman, 1985).

The initial aim was to simplify and objectify the concept by choosing a neutral term ("type A"), viewing it as a medical syndrome of coronary-proneness, and avoiding related psychological (especially psychodynamic) concepts and theories. However, it soon became apparent that the disease-relevant psychological characteristics and behavior patterns of individuals cannot be adequately explained in such a sterile manner. That is, researchers soon turned to trying to understand the trait correlates of type A behavior, the components of type A behavior, the developmental bases of type A behavior, the various sociobehavioral consequences of being type A, and the health aspects of the type A pattern beyond coronary disease. Furthermore, in a formulation in which type A behavior is defined as synonymous with coronary-proneness, the approach begs the question of whether this type of personality does indeed *predict* coronary disease.

Interestingly, people who do not show type A characteristics are called type B. Consistent with the traditional biomedical approach to health and disease, type B was defined as a default state, with no independent consideration as to what a healthy personality style might be. This approach shunned the usual scientific practice of establishing construct validity by showing that (a) the assessment is related to what it should theoretically be related to (convergent validation) and (b) the assessment is not related to what it should not be related to (discriminant

validation) (Campbell & Fiske, 1959). This purposeful disregard of construct validity did not make the phenomenon simpler to study, but, on the contrary led to numerous meandering and unspecified studies. Further, only a theory can tell us what our construct should and should not relate to, and the early type A approach lacked such a theory. It was not proposed to be related or unrelated to any other psychological phenomena.

A half century and thousands of studies on the possible links between type A and heart disease produced mixed results (Booth-Kewley & Friedman, 1987; Dembroski et al., 1978; Houston & Snyder, 1988; Jenkins, 1979; Matthews, 1982; Miller, Turner, Tindale, Posavac, & Dugoni, 1991). The type A pattern is reliable and can be best assessed through the type A structured interview (rather than through questionnaires). Excessive competitiveness and constant hostility do seem, for some people in some circumstances, to increase the likelihood of CHD (see the section on Neuroticism below). But being hurried or working hard at one's job are generally not risk factors. Thus, the original formulation was only very partially confirmed.

By inspiring so much empirical research, the flawed type A idea helped the establishment of a broader and deeper approach. For example, the construct of a disease-prone personality (Friedman & Booth-Kewley, 1987) was developed to simultaneously consider multiple aspects of personality and multiple diseases. Conversely, the construct of a self-healing personality (Friedman, 1991/2000) examines a multidimensional healing emotional style involving a match between the individual and the environment across time, which maintains a physiological and psychosocial homeostasis. Such perspectives encourage and even necessitate a conceptually and methodologically more appropriate concern with rich theoretical traditions, multiple predictive measures, and multiple outcomes across time. For instance, rather than an uninformative "type B" default formulation, self-healing personalities emerge as similar to the mentally healthy orientations that have been extensively described by humanistic and positive psychologists. Such approaches in turn involve sophisticated concern with mediators, moderators, and constraints on the associations between personality and health.

**EXTENDED TYPOLOGIES**

Other researchers subsequently also have pursued the typology approach, looking for a pattern or a collection of psychobiological symptoms associated with a particular disease. The type C personality is proposed to be cancer-prone (Temoshok, 2000; Temoshok et al., 1985). This type C personality is repressed, apathetic, and hopeless. A type D personality describes distressed people who are at increased risk of cardiac events (Denollet, 2000; Mols & Denollet, 2010); type D people are high on both negative affectivity (tendency to experience negative emotions) and social inhibition (tendency to inhibit the expression of emotions). As we shall see, such conceptions remain popular because they do capture certain elements of the full relationship between personality and health.

On the other side of the coin, pioneering work by Salvador Maddi and Suzanne Ouellette Kobasa (1984) on *hardiness* helped provide a basic framework for thinking about staying healthy in the face of challenge. First, they suggest that a hardy personality maintains a sense of control. This is not necessarily a wild sense of optimism, but rather a sense that one can control one's own behaviors. Second, there is a commitment to something that is important and meaningful in their lives. This may also involve values and goals. Third, hardy people welcome challenge. For example, they may view change as an exciting challenge to their growth and development. Hardiness generally involves a productive orientation, in which one shows a zest for life. Although drawing much-needed attention to the positive side of personality and health (the idea derives from humanistic-existential personality theories), early approaches to hardiness had a number of flaws. Most basically, the problems revolved around unreliable or narrow measurement, and piecemeal research that could not capture the richness of a healthy personal style (Ouellette & DiPlacido, 2001). Such deficiencies again point to the need for a more comprehensive approach.

## What Is Personality, and Why Is Personality Important to Health and Disease?

Why worry about a difficult-to-define construct like personality when one could concentrate directly on infectious agents, antimicrobial drugs, immunology, and so on? The answer is that a focus on the individual personality captures not only the individual's characteristic health-relevant patterns—his or her psychobiological predispositions, usual behaviors, and emotional reactions—but it also apprehends the individual's perception of the social milieu and why some people are more likely to be exposed to infectious agents, develop unhealthy habits, and enter stress-inducing situations in the first place.

Personality can be defined as the biopsychosocial patterns that make people uniquely themselves, and it is a very useful "unit of analysis" for studying health because it corresponds to the whole biological organism rather than to components or collectives (Friedman & Schustack, 2012). In other words, it is the person who is born, the person who behaves, and the person who ultimately dies. There are many reasons to believe that there is some coherence to or something systemic about being an individual; individuals are not merely random collections of cells and organs. Similarly, although persons are born into families and communities, there is some independence of the individual from what happens to the broader social collectives. For example, although people of lower socioeconomic status (SES) are at higher risk for morbidity and premature mortality, substantial individual variation exists.

The study of personality and health is especially significant because it leads directly to the issue of causal linkages. In other words, personality is of interest here to the extent that it allows better intervention to improve health, or at the very least, good prediction of future health and disease. By studying personality and health, we are forced to gather research on genetics, development, psychoimmunology, stress, and unhealthy habits, and see how the pieces fit together in the whole person. Similarly, after examining social relations or SES or social integration, we are forced to return to study how these forces affect the individual. In the applied sphere, the study of personality encourages a focus on individual differences in reactions to interventions, and it cultivates attention to the individual's selection of health-relevant environments (Friedman, 2000). That is, personality—the individual's biopsychosocial patterns of behavior—is a construct that connects well with biopsychosocial approaches to health.

In sum, personality is important because it is the individual person who lives a unique life path, becomes ill or stays well, and lives long or dies prematurely. It matters to some extent whether one's cells or organs are uninfected and functioning well, but only because these affect the whole person. It matters whether a city has polluted air or uncooperative patients, but only because these may affect or characterize the individual. No isomorphism exists between risk factors and an individual's outcomes. Indeed, any health care provider comes to appreciate the complexity and resiliency of the human organism and the complex causal pathways to better health.

## Models of Linkages Between Personality and Health

At conception, a genetic endowment is inherited from the mother and the father, but the developing organism immediately encounters a unique environment. The in utero environment varies in its supplies of nutrition, toxins, and hormones, thus affecting genetically programmed development, including physiology, the sensory organs, and especially the developing brain. For example, sex hormones affect later sexual behaviors and masculinity–femininity; and stress hormones and mother's personality may affect later robustness (Copper et al., 1996; Lobel, DeVincent, Kaminer, & Meyer, 2000; Parsons, 1980). Nine months later, the newborn enters the world with certain predispositions and orientations.

The newborn's body and brain are still rapidly developing and changing, and so early experiences can have long-term significant effects, on both biological and psychological adaptability and resistance to challenge. Importantly, the newborn, who already has an incipient personality of sorts, immediately begins to affect his or her environment. For example, one infant may cry incessantly, thereby affecting the behaviors of the mother and perhaps the whole family (in a manner significantly different from that of a quiet baby who soon sleeps through most of the night). However, mothers differ in how they respond to a crying infant, thus further complicating the individual patterns.

By the time the child enters preschool or other significant social interactions with peers at around age 3, certain relatively consistent patterns of response are apparent. Some toddlers are more shy or fearful or irritable or impulsive or distractible or sociable than others (Kagan, 1994; Plomin, 1986; Thomas, Chess, & Korn, 1982). These consistencies in emotional and motivational responses are often termed *temperament*. Temperament captures the biopsychological patterns of responses that have begun to stabilize by about this age. But because these patterns will strongly interact with experiences of childhood, especially cognitive and social experiences, it is useful to distinguish them from personality, which begins to stabilize later in childhood.

By age 5 or 6, when formal schooling and more extensive cognitive and social influences begin, the relations among the health-relevant characteristics are already complex. The genetic endowment at conception already has been influenced in myriad ways, and so only the strongest genetic influences (such as trisomy 21/Down syndrome, or ganglioside accumulation in the brain/Tay-Sachs) would be expected to have straightforward, direct effects on personality and health. Most influences of genetics, in utero experiences, and sensory/emotional/cognitive inclinations will be much more subtle and complicated.

Throughout life, aspects of personality may change, although usually gradually (Roberts, Walton, & Viechtbauer, 2006; Twenge, 2000, 2001, 2002). Personality captures a combination of genetic, familial, experiential, and sociocultural elements, and so it provides a useful approach to the big picture. But because personality and health are affected by so many internal and external and interactional variables, the causal links are multidimensional.

A key problem for personality researchers is that we cannot randomly assign a person to personality (at least not until the human genome project develops further, as one wag put it). So, because we are stuck with correlational designs, we need rich data collected across many years. The studies with the best research designs are longitudinal and use time-lagged correlational statistics or survival analyses to uncover associations between personality and health. Such longitudinal studies can ascertain whether and when personality is a reliable predictor of health (Hampson & Friedman, 2008). Unfortunately, most investigations of personality and disease usually focus on adults and are cross-sectional or of limited time frame. Even with longitudinal studies, it is easy to slip into unjustified conclusions about causal relations. For example, if people with repressed emotions are found to be more prone to develop cancer, it is often implicitly or explicitly (and incorrectly) assumed that decreasing one's repression will necessarily decrease one's risk of cancer. Yet, there is reason to believe that broad socioeconomic policies that improve children's well-being along many dimensions can be fruitfully considered to be policies of health promotion (Friedman & Martin, 2011; Haas, 2008; Hayward & Gorman, 2004).

A number of key models of causal linkages exist between personality and health, each of which may have its own subsets and variations. In many instances, more than one linkage is *simultaneously* causing an observed association. Most study designs, however, are not set up to detect multiple causal linkages.

### Personality Caused Disease: The Behavioral Route

A commonly investigated causal model proposes that personality can lead directly to disease through patterns of unhealthy behaviors, such as poor diet and lack of physical activity. A frequent and sensible step in examining links between personality and disease is thus to isolate and control for known behavioral causes of disease, such as cigarette smoking. Mediational analyses of behavior help point to likely causal pathways. For example, if extroverted or anxious people are more likely to smoke (and to be ill), and controlling for smoking eliminates (statistically explains) a link between personality and a smoking-relevant disease, then these findings are evidence (but not proof) that cigarettes are a smoking gun linking personality and disease. It might also be the case, however, that other factors are correlated with smoking, extroversion, and the disease. Further, note that even if a causal link is tentatively established, alterations in extroversion or treatments for the anxiety will not necessarily prevent the disease unless the smoking is also affected. And, even if the mediator (e.g., smoking) is affected, the disease risk many not diminish if another unhealthy behavior (such as overeating) takes its place.

Sometimes researchers improperly use statistics to control social or behavioral variables to eliminate "known risk factors," rather than systematically testing mediator models. For example, if controlling for SES eliminates a personality-to-disease association, it would be improper to dismiss personality as an irrelevant abstraction. Socioeconomic status is a very broad variable, with no unitary explanatory power as to mechanism of disease causation. Simple approaches may overlook a more complex but important web of associations among individual differences, environments, behaviors, and disease. The full models need to be developed and tested.

Broadly speaking, evidence supports the idea that health-relevant behavior can be an important mediator of some of the associations between personality and health (Bogg & Roberts, 2004; Kassel, Stroud, & Paronis, 2003; Smith & Gallo, 2001; Vollrath & Torgersen, 2008). Personality docs predict a wide variety of health-relevant behaviors. The evidence is much weaker, however, that limiting certain unhealthy behaviors will eliminate disease risk. For example, public health warnings in the 1980s to reduce cholesterol and fat intake did little to improve the dietary and obesity profile of Americans 30 years later. Similarly, it is not known whether directly targeting the relevant unhealthy personality is generally effective.

We need to think about how a personality trait will play out in the situations one commonly encounters, *and* the situations to which it will lead us. This is the well-known interaction of personality and situation. Psychologists talk a lot about this, but too often ignore it in practice.

Special research attention should be directed at smoking, because smoking is by far the most powerful common behavioral influence on health. Smoking is often discussed in a broader health behavioral context—including dietary changes, such as eating more vegetables, and alcohol use, such as eliminating that double martini at lunch—but in fact, other such behavioral interventions usually will have a relatively minor effect compared to stopping smoking. The importance of smoking has implications for research design and analysis, because smoking is likely to emerge as such a potent mediator in many populations where it is present. Note also that, although Americans (especially men) smoked a lot in the 1950s through the 1970s, today, smoking has dropped by more than half in many states. So, a certain personality characteristic that might predispose one to smoke in some times or places might be much less relevant in other times and places.

Injury—violence and accidents—is a health outcome that is often strongly affected by personality-influenced health behaviors; this is especially true before middle age (Zuckerman & Kuhlman, 2000). Risky sports, unsafe driving, and exposure to violent situations (including those that increase the risk of homicide and suicide) are a major threat to health and longevity; but usually the causes of injury are multifactorial.

### Personality Caused Disease: The Psychophysiological Route
Personality can affect disease directly through physiological mechanisms. That is, individual reaction patterns can trigger unhealthy neurohormonal states. This pathway is the one that laypersons most often assume when they speak about individual differences and disease.

Models of personality causing disease through psychophysiological-mediating mechanisms often begin with a focus on poor coping with stress. Depending upon the challenge, individuals who are depressed, introverted, repressed, unconscientious, or otherwise unbalanced are often less successful in bringing to bear necessary psychological, social, and behavioral resources to face challenge (Aspinwall & Taylor, 1997). However, although there is no doubt that the resulting psychosocial stress involves harmful bodily reactions (Cacioppo & Berntson, 2011, Chapter 6, this volume; Kemeny, 2011, Chapter 7, this volume), there is not yet a body of longitudinal work showing relations among well-measured personality characteristics, subsequent psychophysiological meditating mechanisms, and consequent disease outcomes (Friedman, 2008). The key questions concern which links are important and common for which kinds of people.

Stress affects the cardiovascular system and metabolism both through the nervous system and the neuroendocrine system (hormones), and so mechanisms have been sought in such matters as changes in heart rate, blood pressure, and plasma lipids, with generally encouraging results (e.g., Sutin et al., 2010). There is also good evidence that chronic psychological states are related to immune functioning, and immune functioning is related to disease susceptibility (Kemeny, 2011, Chapter 7, this volume). But again here, there is only weak evidence that psychoneuroimmunological effects are a key factor in explaining links between personality and health (Kemeny, 2011, Chapter 7, this volume; Segerstrom, 2011, Chapter 30, this volume; Segerstrom & Miller, 2004). It may turn out to be the case that psychoneuroimmunological mechanisms will need to be understood in conjunction with stable biological predispositions, health-relevant behaviors, and selection and interpretation of situations for a robust explanatory picture to emerge. Interestingly, cardiovascular and metabolic investigations (usually focused on CHD) have almost always proceeded independently of psychoneuroimmunological investigations (usually focused on cancer or human immunodeficiency virus [HIV] infection), thus lessening the chances that common pathways and processes (such as inflammation) will be discovered.

More speculative and rarely investigated are mechanisms involving the so-called "will to live." Some individuals appear able to employ mental efforts to improve their physiological function, but reports of such successes tend to be isolated and speculative. That is, although there are many well-documented reports of extraordinary individuals and startling recoveries, generally, a well-replicated and scientifically reviewed body of rigorous follow-up research does not exist. Advances in brain imaging may lead to better understanding of emotion, motivation, and well-being (Davidson, 2010; Rosenkranz et al., 2003; Urry et al., 2004).

### Personality Caused Disease: Selection into Situations

One of the least understood but most interesting likely causal link between personality and disease involves gravitating toward or even choosing unhealthy situations (Friedman, 2000). The usual model of a person randomly encountering various stressful events is untenable; the fact is that the individual helps create and select events (Bolger & Zuckerman, 1995). For example, neuroticism tends to predict to negative life events. That is, neurotic people are more likely to experience objectively more stressful events (Magnus, Diener, Fujita, & Payot, 1993; Taylor, Repetti, & Seeman, 1997). Others, who are well-socialized, conscientious, and agreeable, are more likely to wind up well-educated and surrounded by mature adults.

A hostile, aggressive child may disrupt his family interactions (thereby creating an unsettled home environment) and may then run out to spend the evening with a like-minded gang. Or, in terms of a more a clearly biological example, so-called "super-tasters" have more receptors (taste buds) on their tongues and are three times as sensitive to bitterness than people of low taste sensitivity (Bartoshuk et al., 2001); such people might be likely to avoid eating various vegetables, thereby missing their health-protective effects. Many such biologically based individual differences have not yet been discovered nor applied to the implications for healthy or unhealthy pathways and choices.

In short, in such examples, it is not that personality leads directly to unhealthy behaviors or unhealthy psychophysiological reactions, but rather that personality facilitates entering the unhealthy situations.

### Biological Underlying (Third) Variables

Genetic endowments and early experiences can affect both later personality and later health. In the simplest or most extreme case, a severe genetic defect is present, shaping both personality and disease. For example, people with Down syndrome (trisomy 21) are at high risk for congenital heart disease, as well as for premature mortality, usually dying before age 50. Although personality varies, there are clearly differences from people without this condition, such as in average mental acuity. Another chromosomal disorder, Angelman syndrome (deleted area in chromosome 15), leads to children who are unusually happy and laugh excessively. They develop movement and seizure disorders, as well as mental retardation.

In such cases, an association exists between personality and health, but influencing the personality would not change the health. Only an intervention that affected the biological sequelae of the genetic abnormality would have consequences. Yet, such examples are a useful entry to thinking about more subtle and complex underlying biological variables. In many people, biological third variables are affecting both personality and health.

When challenged, some people react more than others do, with changes in their blood pressure and heart rate. That is, there are individual differences in psychophysiological reactivity (also called cardiovascular reactivity). Someone who is easily aroused emotionally, who tends to perceive threats-to-self in the environment, and whose coping resources are taxed is likely to respond to stressful events with high levels of unhealthy physiological arousal—symptoms of chronic catecholamine release. It is not yet clear the extent to which this variable is a reliable individual difference that is relevant to both personality and overall disease risk (Suls & Rittenhouse, 1990; Swain & Suls, 1996).

Hans Eysenck argued that such temperament-related psychobiological systems produce many associations between personality and disease, but also that some psychobiological characteristics are potentially modifiable, thus producing changes in both personality and disease risk. Eysenck's Big Three construct of psychoticism (Eysenck & Eysenck, 1976; Eysenck, 1991, 1992) describes a predisposition toward sociopathic or psychotic behavior (but high scorers are not necessarily "psychotic" in the clinical sense). Individuals high on this dimension are hostile, solitary, impulsive, novelty-seeking, manipulative, and without fear. This dimension may be linked to health in a number of ways—both behaviorally and psychophysiologically. More recently, researchers have focused on individual differences in neurotransmitters, looking at relations between dopamine and sensation seeking, serotonin and conscientiousness, and norepinephrine and extroversion or reward seeking (Bond, 2001; Carver & Miller, 2006; Cloninger, 1998). Overall, the study of the genetic and early biological influences on personality and associations to disease is still in its infancy.

Finally, it is also the case that people with chronic anxiety are more likely to feel pain and other symptoms. They also may be especially vigilant about bodily sensations (Pennebaker, 1982). This is discussed further in the later section on neuroticism. Again, in such relationships (of biological underlying third variables), interventions addressing personality will not necessarily do anything to affect health and longevity.

## Disease-caused Personality Changes
Many observed associations between personality and health are the result of patterns that follow from the onset of disease. That is, the disease "causes" (affects) the personality. However, this area is understudied, and the extent of this phenomenon is unknown.

### BRAIN-MEDIATED
Not surprisingly, diseases that affect the brain also have a dramatic impact on personality. Consider Parkinson disease and Parkinson-like syndromes, characterized by tremor, muscle rigidity, and movement problems. It has long been noticed that people with Parkinson disease tend to appear stoic. Since Parkinson disease involves a deficiency of dopamine (as neurons in the substantia nigra degenerate), it may be the case that this defect produces this aspect of personality. Even here, there can be multiple causal links, although the cause is usually unknown. For example, Parkinson disease may sometimes result from brain infection, which then affects personality; but there also can be an underlying third variable, as when people who mine manganese or live in regions with volcanic soil (high in manganese) sometimes become compulsive fighters and later develop Parkinson disease (due to this heavy metal poisoning). Ironically, professional boxers who receive multiple blows to the head can also develop Parkinson disease as a result (so-called pugilistic Parkinson syndrome).

Well-documented personality change is associated with excessive alcohol consumption. Alcoholism can lead to anxiety and depression, although it is sometimes anxiety and depression that contributed to the drinking. At the extreme, in Wernicke-Korsakoff syndrome, there are memory problems, confusion, and delusions, due to brain damage from severe deficiency of thiamine (Vitamin $B_1$) in malnourished chronic alcoholics. Analogously, drugs such as cocaine and lysergic acid diethylamide (LSD) can occasionally produce long-lasting, dramatic alterations in personality.

Other diseases that commonly affect personality through effects on the brain include strokes (which affect personality differentially as a function of the location of the stroke), metabolic disorders involving the thyroid, or conditions that involve glycemic control (such as diabetes). Sometimes, the personality changes result from medical treatment effects, as in the postperfusion syndrome of mental status changes after coronary bypass surgery (Newman et al., 2001) (occasionally nicknamed "pump head"). Further, many widely prescribed drugs, especially psychotropic drugs like tranquilizers, sleeping pills, and antidepressants may have significant effects on personality. The psychological side effects of many prescription drugs are underinvestigated.

With diseases that may develop slowly, such as Alzheimer disease, syphilis, and acquired immune deficiency syndrome (AIDS), the changes in personality may become apparent long before the changes in organic brain function are diagnosed, and so it may appear that the personality is predicting or even causing the disease, when the reality is that the disease is changing the personality (Woodward, 1998).

### PSYCHOLOGICALLY MEDIATED

Encounters with serious illness, such as suffering a myocardial infarction or receiving a diagnosis of cancer, can sometimes precipitate a dramatic change in personality. This is similar in some respects to a religious conversion (and indeed sometimes a religious conversion is the response).

### BEHAVIORALLY MEDIATED

Disease may cause changes in motivation (or cravings) and in social status, as occurs if a stroke or cancer victim loses a job, gets divorced, and becomes hostile and depressed. New pressures and social groups may then alter the likelihood of smoking, drinking, risky behavior, and so on, thereby further changing both the individual's personality and health.

### SOCIAL PSYCHOLOGICALLY MEDIATED

Illness often changes the reactions of others to the ill person. For example, the well-documented physical attractiveness stereotype (Dion, 1972) shows positive expectations and subsequent behavioral effects of "beautiful" people, and the opposite kinds of effects can sometimes be expected of people stigmatized due to disease (Crocker, Major & Steele, 1998; Goffman, 1963).

In all these cases, a link exists between personality and disease, but it is caused by the disease or the treatment.

### Person–Situation Interactions

Many times, it is important to know about both the personality and the situation to understand the links to health.

Widely prescribed legal drugs such as tranquilizers (Valium), sleeping pills (Halcion), and antidepressants (Prozac), as well as widely available illegal drugs such as cocaine, are known to have short-term and sometimes long-term effects on personality. Importantly, it is not random who takes these drugs; certain personalities are more likely to seek them, or have them prescribed, or to become addicted.

Furthermore, when encountering a significant life stress, a significantly negative effect on health is more likely if there is a predisposing genetic condition. That is, there can be a gene-by-environment interaction, in which an individual's response to environmental insults is moderated by his or her genetic makeup (Caspi et al., 2003).

Or, consider the case in which a person is tending toward unhealthy environments but these environments are inaccessible. For example, if an impulsive, unstable person is raised in a supportive family, with safe schools, in a tight-knit supportive community, with perhaps a supportive religion, then the opportunity for unhealthy behavior greatly diminishes.

The various ways in which personality tends to remain stable, even though it is possible to change, has been summarized into a model termed *cumulative continuity* (Roberts & Caspi, 2003). By interpreting situations as similar, by eliciting similar reactions from others, and by seeking out certain similar situations, as well as by responding to stable genetic influences and stable environments (social and economic), the average adult maintains a fairly consistent personality. Understanding these individual consistencies, without oversimplifying them, can likely take us a long way toward understanding personality and health. Note, however, that unusual circumstances (such as the major psychosocial disruptions of a war, economic depression, terrorism, or natural disaster) can produce dramatic personality change and unexpected effects on health.

In sum, when we examine development across long periods of time, we find a complex but understandable interplay between traits and situations. Especially with a focus on processes, the development of healthy or unhealthy states becomes predictable (Friedman, 2000; Roberts & Pomerantz, 2004).

### Self-healing

Although most research focuses on disease, it is equally important to examine those people in whom there is a self-healing personality, which maintains a physiological and psychosocial homeostasis (Friedman, 1991/2000). Such individuals tend to wind up in certain healthy environments, evoke positive reaction from others, and have a healing emotional style that matches the individual with the environment. In these people, good mental health tends to promote good physical health, and good physical health tends to promote good mental health. Various healthy patterns go together, which can be termed *cosalubrious effects*.

As one good pattern or reaction leads to another, positive results cumulate. There is evidence that a process of "broaden-and-build" develops, as coping skills improve, social networks expand, and recuperation processes improve (Fredrickson, 2001). Because medical care is typically focused on pathology, such links have been mostly ignored in health care.

## Specific Traits and Health

A variety of evidence suggests that good mental health is associated with good physical health. As noted, people who are well-adjusted are at lower risk for serious conditions like heart disease than are those who are seriously or chronically hostile, depressed, anxious, or unstable. Another way of viewing this association is to say that health is health, and that the distinction between mental and physical health is not of greater scientific utility than distinctions among various illnesses. However, one major difference involves age: Chronically hostile and depressed people in their 20s are not likely to die of cancer or heart disease until their 50s or 60s (no matter what the relation between personality and disease). It makes sense to examine specific personality traits and health, because certain recognizable patterns of responding, when considered over long time periods, put one at higher or lower risk for various chronic diseases and for premature mortality. This is especially true when personality is considered in conjunction with the social, economic, and physical environments. Then, one must consider the various causal models described above, to see which are applicable in each case.

Personality psychologists use sundry theories, perspectives, methods, and classifications (Friedman & Schustack, 2012). It is useful to employ an expanded version of the five-factor approach to traits. The five factors, which often emerge from factor analyses of trait labels, are conscientiousness, agreeableness, neuroticism, extroversion, and openness. I have added other characteristics (such as "optimism" to the agreeableness category) to simplify matters, but all the characteristics considered under each of the five trait factors should not be considered synonymous. Indeed, important distinctions often exist among related trait constructs.

### Conscientiousness

Conscientiousness is a consistent a tendency to be prudent, planful, persistent, and dependable. One of the major dimensions of the five-factor approach to personality, conscientiousness is not highly related to personality concepts and measures historically used in health research (Booth-Kewley & Vickers, 1994; Friedman, Tucker, & Reise, 1995; Marshall et al., 1994). I will use the example of conscientiousness, which increasing evidence reveals to be highly relevant to pathways to health, as a detailed illustration of fruitful conceptual models and revealing methods of analysis.

For more than 20 years, my colleagues and I have studied personality and longevity in the Terman cohort, derived from the Terman Gifted Children Study that began in 1921. The 1,528 Terman participants were, for the most part, first studied as elementary school children and have been followed ever since. It is the longest study of a single cohort ever conducted so intensively, with rich data collected regularly throughout the lifespan (from childhood to late adulthood and death). The sample was later characterized as a productive, intelligent segment of 20th-century middle-class American men and women (mostly white) (Sears, 1984; Subotnik, Karp, & Morgan, 1989). Importantly, we have collected death certificates and have professionally coded date and cause of death (Friedman, Tucker, Schwartz, Tomlinson-Keasey et al., 1995).

Starting with the childhood data, our project first tested whether variables representing major dimensions of personality could predict longevity across the lifespan (Friedman et al., 1993). We examined all items collected by Terman in 1922 that seemed relevant to personality. In 1922, one of each participant's parents (usually the mother, or both parents together) and each participant's teacher were asked to rate the participant on 25 trait dimensions chosen to measure intellectual, volitional, moral, emotional, aesthetic, physical, and social functioning. We constructed a measure of Conscientiousness–Social Dependability that included the four items of prudence, conscientiousness, freedom from vanity/egotism, and truthfulness. This corresponds roughly to the five-factor model (McCrae & John, 1992) dimension of Conscientiousness, and we have documented the correspondence between conscientiousness measured with this scale and the contemporary NEO-PI-R conscientiousness (although the measure is not identical to the NEO-PI measure) (Martin & Friedman, 2000). Childhood conscientiousness was clearly related to survival in middle to old age. For example, a person at the 75th percentile on conscientiousness had only 77% of the risk of a person at the 25th percentile of dying in any given year (Friedman et al., 1993).

We then derived (from the archival Terman data) personality measures for adulthood that we likewise validated by showing them to be consistent with the five-factor contemporary conceptions (Martin & Friedman, 2000; Martin & Friedman Schwartz, 2007). Adult conscientiousness was "measured" when the participants were in their 30s and 40s. As of 2000, 70% of the men and 51% of the women in this sample had verified deaths, with the median age of death for those who had died being 72.7 years for men and 74.0 years for women. We again found conscientiousness (now measured in adulthood) to be significantly related to mortality risk. Those low on adult conscientiousness died sooner.

The Friedman et al. findings on conscientiousness and longevity now have been confirmed in follow-up studies by others. One study examined the relation of personality to mortality in 883 older Catholic clergy members, about two-thirds of whom were female. The NEO Five-Factor Inventory was administered at baseline, and the clergy were followed for a little more than 5 years, during which time 182 died. Those scoring very high on conscientiousness were about half as likely to die as those with a very low score (Wilson, Mendes de Leon, Bienias, Evans, & Bennett, 2004). Another key study examined participants in a Medicare demonstration study with over 1,000 participants, aged 65–100 (Weiss, Costa, Karuza, Duberstein, & Friedman, 2004). The participants in this prospective study were older, sicker, and more representative of the elderly population, and over the 5 years of follow-up, persons high in conscientiousness were significantly less likely to die (see also M. Taylor et al., 2009). Meta-analysis confirms that across 20 samples (over 8,900 participants), conscientiousness is protective from mortality risk (Kern & Friedman, 2008).

A study of conscientiousness and renal deterioration in patients with diabetes found that time to renal failure was longer in those with high conscientiousness (Brickman, Yount, Blaney, Rothberg, & De-Nour, 1996), and another prospective study of chronic renal insufficiency found that patients with low conscientiousness had a substantially increased mortality rate over the 4-year term of the study (Christensen et al., 2002). (Both of these studies also found effects of neuroticism.) Evidence of the generality of the importance of conscientiousness comes from a study using the Midlife Development in the United States Survey, a nationally representative sample of 3,032 noninstitutionalized civilian adults (Goodwin & Friedman, 2006). This study examined the association between the five-factor traits of personality and common mental and physical disorders and found that Conscientiousness (protectively) was reliably associated with reduced risk of illness: Those with diabetes, hypertension, sciatica, urinary problems, stroke, hernia, TB, joint problems, and a variety of mental illnesses and substance abuse problems had significantly lower levels of conscientiousness, compared with those without each disorder.

Such pervasive associations between conscientiousness and health go well beyond adherence effects, as is well illustrated by a randomized study of medication after a myocardial infarction (Horwitz et al., 1990). Patients who did not adhere to their prescribed treatment regimen (that is, who took less than 75% of the prescribed medication) were 2.6 times more likely than good adherers to die within a year of follow-up; but most interestingly, the unconscientious adherers (poor adherers) had an increased risk of death whether they were on the β-blocker propranolol (odds ratio = 3.1) or *placebo* (odds ratio = 2.5). This effect was not accounted for by the severity of the myocardial infarction, marital status, education, smoking, or social isolation. In other words, being conscientious enough to fully cooperate with treatment (even if with a placebo) emerged as a more important predictor of mortality risk than the medication.

In short, research following the Friedman et al. (1993) study has shown substantial confirmation of the importance of conscientiousness to health and longevity. Although surprising because of the traditional research emphasis on frustration and hostile moods, it turns out that conscientiousness is a key personality predictor of health and longevity.

## MODELS

The question then arises as to *why* conscientiousness is related to health. The causal pathways are probably not simple ones.

First, as noted, there is good reason to suspect that conscientiousness is a good predictor of health because of its many associations with healthy behaviors. A meta-analysis of 194 studies examined conscientiousness-related traits and leading behavioral contributors to mortality—tobacco use, diet and activity patterns, excessive alcohol use, violence, risky sexual behavior, risky driving, suicide, and drug use (Bogg & Roberts, 2004). Conscientiousness-related traits were negatively related to all the risky health-related behaviors and positively related to all these beneficial health-related behaviors (see also Hampson, Goldberg, Vogt, & Dubanoski, 2007).

Among the Terman participants, possible behavioral mechanisms for the robust association between conscientiousness and longevity were examined by gathering cause of death information and by considering the possible mediating influences of drinking alcohol, smoking, and overeating (Friedman, Tucker, Schwartz, Martin et al., 1995). Survival analyses suggested that the protective effect of conscientiousness was somewhat but not primarily due to accident avoidance. About 9% of the low-conscientious quartile, and 5% of the high-conscientious quartile, died as a result of injury (accidents and violence); those who died from injury were more likely to be in the low-conscientiousness quartile. But, overall, relatively few people died as the result of injury, and so the overall effect of conscientiousness was not simply explained. Similarly, the protective effect of conscientiousness could not be mostly explained by abstinence from unhealthy substance intake (heavy drinking and smokers). Conscientiousness seems to have a more far-reaching and general involvement.

Second, there is emerging evidence for various psychophysiological mechanisms linking conscientiousness and health. For example, one study examined conscientiousness (NEO-PI) and subclinical cardiovascular disease (atherosclerosis) in a healthy community sample of 353 (51% female). This study used sonography to measure intima-media thickness and collected physiological measures including 24-hour urinary catecholamines. As expected, conscientiousness was associated with less thickening, with urinary norepinephrine emerging as a partial mediator (Witzig, Kamarck, Muldoon, & Sutton-Tyrrell, 2003).

It is not known the extent to which conscientious people develop more modulated physiological reaction patterns or whether an underlying biopsychological tendency leads both to conscientiousness and salutary reaction patterns. In terms of psychophysiological mechanisms involving underlying third variables, there is evidence that serotonin function may be relevant (Carver & Miller, 2006; Manuck et al., 1998; Williams et al., 2004) Researchers studying the effects of a μ-opioid receptor mutation found that not only did chemical blocking of opioids result in differential cortisol responses and increases in adrenocorticotropic hormone (ACTH) for those with the variant polymorphism, but that these individuals also scored significantly lower on NEO-PI-R Conscientiousness than did those without it. Those with the variant serotonin transporter might have abnormal hypothalamus-pituitary-adrenal (HPA) axis responses to

stress and corresponding personality traits that are regulated by μ-opioid receptor activation (Uhart & Wand, 2009; Wand et al., 2002).

Third, there is evidence that conscientious individuals seek out or find themselves in healthier environments. In many cultures, imprudent, impulsive people are more likely to find themselves in environments and subcultures that are dangerous, involving for example, smoking, fast driving, unprotected sexual activity, or gang or military violence. People lacking persistence and dependability are likewise more likely to wind up with poor career prospects and lower SES, with all the accompanying threats to health (Adler et al., 1994). Those who are more controlled, secure, and hard-working by age 18 are headed to better careers within a decade, which in turn can further enhance their health and their subsequent conscientiousness (Hogan & Ones, 1997; Judge & Ilies, 2002; Kern, Friedman, Martin, Reynolds, & Luong, 2009; Roberts, Caspi, & Moffitt, 2003).

Even social support is relevant here, as there is self-selection and partner selection into marriage. A heritable influence on propensity to marry exists (Johnson, McGue, Krueger, & Bouchard, 2004), with conscientious college women experiencing lower rates of divorce (Roberts & Bogg, 2004). Early individual traits affect later marital stability (Larson & Holman, 1994); divorce is not a random stressor but rather is somewhat predictable. For example, in the Terman study, the association between marital history at midlife (in 1950) and mortality (as of 1991) was investigated (Tucker, Friedman, Wingard, & Schwartz, 1996). Consistently married individuals lived longer than those who had experienced marital breakup, but this was not only due to the protective effects of marriage itself. Participants who were currently married, but had previously experienced a divorce, were at significantly higher mortality risk compared with consistently married individuals. Consistently married individuals had been more conscientious children than were inconsistently married individuals, and there was evidence for selection into marriage. That is, part of the relationship between marital history and mortality risk was explained by childhood conscientiousness, associated with both future marital history and mortality risk (cf. Sbarra & Nietert, 2009).

In short, the example of conscientiousness reveals the complexity of the relations among personality, physiology, behavior, environments, and health. Multiple pathways likely coexist, and it is unwise to focus only on one path. Further, although conscientiousness is a valuable predictor, interventions to improve health will profitably take advantage of knowledge of this complexity.

### Agreeableness, Optimism, and Cheerfulness

Research findings usually confirm the popular assumption that people who are happier, optimistic, and better adjusted are also healthier, but such findings are especially susceptible to an uncritical overinterpretation. Because studies almost never manipulate happiness and optimism and then show a direct and lasting effect on physical health compared with a control group, there is scant empirical justification for advising people to "cheer up" as a means of promoting their health. Rather, it appears that many of the causal pathways described earlier in this chapter play a role in these associations.

There is fairly good evidence that cheerful people, who are generally in good moods, are healthier, at least over the short term (Pressman & Cohen, 2005; Salovey, Rothman, Detweiler, & Steward, 2000). But this summary statement does not mean that good moods are causing good health. Further, good moods are not a simple and strong correlate of any basic aspect of personality. For example, agreeable people—who are straightforward, altruistic, trusting, and modest—may find themselves in long-term situations in which they are not particularly happy.

Much of the research on this topic focuses on psychophysiological mediation and derives from the idea that challenge is not stressful if it is not interpreted as stressful; that is, construal is key (Cohen & Lazarus, 1983; Segerstrom, Taylor, Kemeny, & Fahey, 1998). Various lines of research thus examine the positive cognitions (or rose-colored glasses) through which some individuals cope with life's challenges, thus avoiding stressful physiological arousal. Further, people with good coping skills can be resilient in the face of stress and strain (Garmezy, 1993; Ryff & Singer, 2001).

Considerable evidence suggests that positive illusions can lead to better health, especially when there is little one can do objectively to reduce the threat or vulnerability (Taylor & Brown, 1988; Taylor et al., 1992). Similarly, individuals with an optimistic explanatory style tend to be healthier, although this may primarily be due an avoidance of the health threats associated with depression (Peterson, Seligman, Yurko, Martin, & Friedman, 1998; Peterson et al., 2001). On the other hand, the case has often been made that people who think that they or their situation is better than it really is are less in touch with

the true demands of reality and with the actions that are needed to deal effectively with challenge, including threats to health (Aldwin, 1994; Colvin & Block, 1994; Colvin, Block, & Funder, 1995; Lazarus & Folkman, 1984). These contradictory conceptions about positive illusions often cannot be resolved until the particular implications of the cognitive states or illusions are addressed. For example, if adherence to a difficult treatment regimen is health-promoting, then those individuals who can use their good coping or good humor to stick with it are likely to be more successful. Similarly, if the situation is relatively uncontrollable, then accepting one's condition with good humor may prove adaptive. However, if one's cheerfulness leads one to ignore the difficult regimen with the idea that "everything will work out anyway," then the positive illusion is maladaptive.

Despite the general association between optimism and health, there has long been an underlying thread of theory and research questioning this generalization. As noted, various ways of coping can be either good or bad, depending on the context. (See also Chapter 19, by Wortman & Boerner, 2011, this volume.) Moreover, highly positive moods can be a sign of emotional imbalance. For example, a study of survival in patients with end-stage renal disease found those who had "an even mixture of unhappiness and happiness" lived longer than those who were very happy (Devins et al., 1990). Importantly, some people show irrational decision-making processes, such as believing that "I don't smoke too much and don't inhale deeply." Many individuals show a reliable tendency to believe that they are less likely than their peers to suffer harm, and this tendency is difficult to challenge (Dillard, Midboe & Klein, 2009; Weinstein & Klein, 1995).

Sometimes people are happy and optimistic because they have successfully overcome a health challenge; the better health is thus causing their sense of well-being. Such effects may even occur long-term, such as if one gets in great physical condition during the decade after suffering a mild heart attack. At other times, a cheerful persona may actually be an attempt to cover up some difficult emotional or health challenge. That is, humor can sometimes be an attempt to deal with stress or a difficult childhood (Dixon, 1980). Comics do not live any longer than their peers (Rotton, 1992), and many face addiction or substance abuse. Furthermore, if people are feeling bad about their challenges but cannot get themselves to put on a smile or learn optimism, they might instead spiral downward (Held, 2004).

In the Terman lifespan study, children who were rated by their parents and teachers as more cheerful/optimistic, and as having a sense of humor, died *earlier* in adulthood than those who were less cheerful (Friedman et al., 1993). A follow-up study attempted to see whether cheerful children were less willing to take precautions, more risk-taking, were less prepared for future stressful challenges, or were covering up some psychological problem (Martin et al., 2002). The cheerful children did grow up to drink more alcohol, smoke more cigarettes, and engage in more risky hobbies and activities, but these had only a minor effect in explaining the relation of cheerfulness and mortality risk. Further, the cheerful children did not grow up to show evidence of poor adjustment. Unrealistic optimism or insufficient caution (Weinstein, 1982) remains a possible explanation, although the data are weak in this regard.

One circumscribed situation in which optimism and cheerfulness might be expected to have a regular and significant effect on health involves those people facing a difficult and trying medical challenge. For example, an optimistic elderly person facing a painful and difficult medical regimen may be more likely to persevere and thus survive. This conception is consistent with the idea that optimism functions as a self-regulating mechanism, with optimistic people more likely to persevere in goal-directed behavior (Carver & Scheier, 1981). A feeling of self-efficacy often predicts a healthy response to challenge.

The medical sociologist Aaron Antonovsky proposed a theory of salutogenesis—a theory of how people stay healthy (Antonovsky, 1979, 1987). Central to successful coping with the challenges of the world is what Antonovsky calls a *sense of coherence*—the person's confidence that the world is understandable, manageable, and meaningful. The world must not necessarily be controllable but controlled—for example, such as occurs in someone with a strong sense of divine order (cf. Wallston et al., 1999). Hopelessness is generally found to be associated with poor health (Everson et al., 1996), but the reasons for this association are probably multifactorial. Antonovsky's approach grew in part from the insightful observation of those in Nazi concentration camps, who noticed that those inmates quickest to die were those who had their sense of identity and purpose taken away from them (Bettelheim, 1960; Frankl, 1962; see also Lutgendorf et al., 1999). One large-scale study that followed over 20,000 European adults for up to 6 years found that those with a strong sense of coherence were 30% less likely to die, even after adjusting for risk factors such as smoking, blood pressure, cholesterol, social class, hostility, and neuroticism (Surtees, Wainwright, Luben, Khaw, & Day, 2003). But it may often be the case that the same underlying psychosocial relations that promote psychological fulfillment also promote physical health—such things as success at work, with friends, and in marriage; in such cases, promoting happiness or optimism per se would not necessarily have any effect on health (unless the underlying psychosocial relations were also affected) (Friedman & Martin, 2011).

Disagreeableness and pessimism are often associated with hostility and depression. Much of this research as related to health is done under the rubric of Neuroticism, and this is considered next.

### Neuroticism: Worrying, Hostility, and Depression

Perhaps the most complex associations between personality and health involve neuroticism. Neuroticism, or Emotional Instability, refers to people who tend to be anxious, high-strung, tense, and worrying; they are also often hostile and prone to depression, as they cope poorly with stress. (Some prefer to call this "negative affectivity"—experiencing too many or chronic negative emotions.) There is longstanding, incontrovertible evidence that many diseases are associated with higher levels of hostility, anxiety, and depression (Barefoot & Schroll, 1996; Friedman & Booth-Kewley, 1987; Goodwin & Friedman, 2006; Kubzansky, Kawachi, Weiss, & Sparrow, 1998; Miller, Smith, Turner, Guijarro, & Hallet, 1996; Schulz, Martire, Beach, & Scheier, 2000), but the causal pathways have rarely been elucidated.

Neurotic people are more likely to feel and report symptoms, and disease can cause distress (Costa & McCrae, 1987; Watson & Pennebaker, 1989). Hence some links of neuroticism to disease are correlational, artifactual, or reverse causal. Such associations do not in any way mean that neuroticism is not also sometimes a causal factor in disease. If neuroticism is correlated with disease because of artifacts associated with the way that disease is assessed, then we should find such associations stronger when medical diagnosis depends on interviews and self-report measures (as does the assessment of personality). Fortunately, this artifact has become less worrisome as studies have focused less on the self-reported, little-varying "health" of college students and more on physician-diagnosed health and longevity.

In 1987, a meta-analysis revealed that not only anxiety and hostility, but also depression was reliably associated with cardiovascular disease (Booth-Kewley & Friedman, 1987). This finding ran counter to the prevailing wisdom about the importance of type A behavior and was viewed skeptically at the time (Mathews, 1988). However, the general association between depression and risk of heart disease has since been confirmed in a many studies. Depression and related states of chronic anxiety, pessimism, and vital exhaustion predict risk of heart disease in both initially healthy persons and those who already have heart disease (Appels, Golombeck, Gorgels, de Vreede, & van Breukelen, 2000; Barefoot & Schroll, 1996; Barefoot et al., 2000; Ford et al., 1998; Januzzi, Stern, Pasternak, & DeSanctis, 2000; Frasure-Smith, Lesperance, & Talajic, 1995; Rugulies, 2002; Scheier et al., 1999). Further, when the appropriate broader framework is used, depression also predicts other adverse health outcomes.

With a typical approach that views a risk factor as a direct causal agent, many clinicians began treating depression in a effort to prevent the exacerbation of heart disease. Surprising to some researchers, treating depression in recent heart attack patients does not reduce the risk of death or second heart attack (ENRICHD, 2003). Given the societal toll taken by heart disease, such a rush to intervention is understandable, but the confusion that then results from an unexpected research result is reminiscent of the confusion and disappointment that surrounded failed type A intervention studies decades earlier. How and why is depression predicting heart disease, and why only in some people? Viewing depression as a simple "medical risk factor" outside the interconnected web of associations is short-sighted.

There is increasing evidence for contributions by an underlying biological third variable. That is, there appears to be a common genetic vulnerability to depression and CHD (Bondy, 2007; McCaffery et al., 2006; Vaccarino et al., 2009). To the extent that such a relation holds, the ordinary risk factor intervention ("treat depression") will fail.

Furthermore, neurotic people, including depressives, are more likely to encounter negative events and to interpret them in a more negative manner (Bolger & Zuckerman, 1995; Magnus et al., 1993; Middeldorp, Cath, Beem, Willemsen, & Boomsma, 2008; Mroczek & Almeida, 2004; Taylor, Repetti, & Seeman, 1997). Neuroticism is also associated with a host of psychophysiological states, generally harmful, including impaired immunity and cardiovascular damage; but more attention needs to be paid to ongoing, long-term pathways (Fredericks et al., 2010; Herbert & Cohen, 1993; Kern & Friedman, 2011;

Schneiderman, Weiss, & Kaufmann, 1989; Smith, 2010; Terracciano, Lockenhoff, Zonderman, Ferrucci, & Costa, 2008; Williams, 1994).

The elements of neuroticism—anxiety, depression, and anger-hostility—are predictive of and play some causal role in illness but their interrelations are not much studied (Friedman & Booth-Kewley, 1987; Suls & Bunde, 2005). We do not really understand whether one of these elements often leads to another (e.g., chronic anger leading to depression), whether these elements have independent or additive effects, and whether they are being optimally conceptualized and assessed (Suls & Bunde, 2005). Also, little is known about how they relate to patterns of healthy social support (Gallo & Smith, 1999), although anger and hostility are clearly implicated in multiple links to disease, including psychosocial pathways (Smith, 2010; Smith, Glazer, Ruiz, & Gallo, 2004).

What about the other side of the coin? Can neuroticism sometimes be healthy, thus explaining inconsistent findings? Consider now a broader view, which adds the context of worrying about health and of feeling and reporting symptoms. Neurotic people sometimes have the motivation to be very vigilant about avoiding dangerous or polluted environments, noting symptoms needing attention, keeping up with medical developments, and cooperating with treatment. Such a worrying neurotic person—a health nut—might remain very healthy (Friedman, 2000). There is indeed scattered evidence for this view.

In a study of renal deterioration (Brickman et al., 1996), patients moderate in neuroticism did better than patients who were low in neuroticism (and also better than those too high in neuroticism). Aspects of neuroticism, such as self-reports of psychological distress and mental strain, sometimes predict lower mortality risk (Gardner & Oswald, 2004; Korten et al., 1999; Weiss & Costa, 2005). Analogously, a paradox was found in the well-known Western Collaborative Group study of type A and heart disease, in which type A clearly predicted heart disease; but *after* a heart attack, type A patients (male) were less likely to die during the subsequent dozen years (Ragland & Brand, 1988). It may be that these type A patients worked especially hard at their treatment regimen for recovery. In the Terman sample, neuroticism was protective for widowed men, suggesting that in certain cases, neuroticism may become especially protective (Taga, Friedman, & Martin, 2009). Further, even before disease develops, some people thrive on challenge and competition, and so there are "healthy type A's"; these are people who rush around with heavy workloads but do not want to live any other way (Friedman, Hall, & Harris, 1985). In short, it appears that two distinct sorts of health-related outcomes result from neuroticism, some positive and some negative. The strength of any causal role for neuroticism in disease (out of context) is difficult to ascertain without a broad conceptual and methodological approach.

There are many subject (patient) selection artifacts in personality and health studies, which are especially related to neuroticism. These can arise as a function of the control group used in a study, if certain people are more likely than others to enter the health care system. For example, people who are neurotic and complain about chest pain are much more likely to have angiograms than are people who are stoic. This artifact changes the association between depression and observed artery blockage from positive to negative (Friedman, 2000). That is, because random samples of the full population are rarely taken for invasive or risky studies, people who are less neurotic and complaining are unknowingly left out of the study.

By not taking a broader view of overall disease-proneness, studies in this area are also susceptible to faulty inferences that result from restriction of range. The range or variance of the predictor or the outcome (or both) may be unduly restricted. For example, type A behavior is associated with CHD in initially healthy samples, but not in high-risk samples selected from clinical populations (Miller, Turner, Tindale, Posavac, & Dugoni, 1991). It appears that restriction of range hides a phenomenon that may truly be present in a more representative (broader) sample. One should be alert for such artifacts whenever the sample is selected on the basis of clinical diagnosis (e.g., angry men) or on the basis of disease (e.g., myocardial infarction; death from heart disease).

To add yet another complication, sometimes the neuroticism is not apparent because it is repressed. A number of studies find poor health associated with repressed anxiety or "repressive coping" (e.g., Jensen, 1987; Matthews et al., 1998; Pettingale, Morris, Greer, & Haybittle, 1985; see also Chapter 18, by Pennebaker & Chung, 2011, this volume) or suppressed anger (Wilson et al., 2003). A similar pattern in which individuals are unable to express emotion and seem at higher risk for disease progression is sometimes studied under the rubric of *alexithymia* (a condition described by the ancient Greeks as an absence of words for emotions; a condition in which individuals are apathetic, stoic, unemotional,

or repressed; Marchesi, Brusamonti, & Maggini, 2000). There is speculation and scattered research that such conditions promote the development or the progression of some cancers (Butow, 2000), but, as usual, the relationship of this constellation of traits to other traits, other behaviors, and other illnesses has not been much studied.

With all of these clarifications and caveats surrounding neuroticism and disease, it is not surprising that simple and clear associations have failed to appear. For example, people with migraines and ulcers and related pain are very likely to be high on anxiety, but the relations have been shown to occur through a wide variety of pathways including recall bias, general distress, a variety of unhealthy behaviors, pituitary-adrenal activation, altered blood flow, and more. These combinations of causal pathways lead to varying results and failures to replicate specific links from study to study.

### Extroversion and Sociability

When it comes to matters of health, extroversion is a double-edged sword. Extroverted people are warm, assertive, sociable, active, talkative, and seeking of stimulation and excitement. This tendency has been shown to lead to both health-promoting and health-damaging behavioral patterns.

The seeking of stimulation and excitement can of course be health-damaging, especially for young men in today's societies. Even children with accident-related injuries tend to be more extroverted (Vollrath, Landolt, & Ribi, 2003). Extroverts are generally at greater risk for smoking and alcohol abuse, although most of the evidence comes from adolescents or young adults (Grau & Ortet, 1999; Martsh & Miller, 1997; Tucker et al., 1995). Studies confirm that such associations with extroversion are best understood in context (Ham & Hope, 2003; Watson, 2000). Note that although extroverts may perform risky behaviors, it is generally to increase positive rewards and experiences; in certain circumstances, the health effects may be different. For example, to the extent that extroverts sometimes tend to be more physically active, they gain the health benefits of activity (exercise), despite some risk of injury.

If sociability leads to good social relations and social integration, then the sociability aspect of extroversion is likely to be health-promoting. However, the most sociable people do not necessarily have the best social relations. An example of the context-dependent effects of sociability comes from Terman's Life Cycle study. Using ratings by parents and teachers in childhood, Sociability was defined in terms of fondness for large groups, popularity, leadership, preference for playing with several other people, and preference for social activities such as parties. Sociable individuals did not live longer than their unsociable peers (Friedman et al., 1993). There was simply no evidence that sociable children were healthier or lived longer across many decades. In fact, sociable children were somewhat more likely to grow up to smoke and drink (Tucker et al., 1995). To further analyze this finding, Terman's own grouping of the men in the sample into "scientists and engineers" versus "businessmen and lawyers" were examined. (Terman had found the former group much more unsociable and less interested in social relations at school and in young adulthood). It turned out that the scientist and engineer group were at slightly *less* risk of premature mortality, despite their unsociable nature (Friedman et al., 1994). For example, these studious men often wound up in those well-adjusted, socially stable, and well-integrated life situations well known to be healthy.

Some research suggests that sociability is associated with greater resistance to developing colds when persons were experimentally exposed to a cold virus (thus controlling for differential exposure) (Cohen, Doyle, Turner, Alper, & Skoner, 2003). However, extensive efforts failed to uncover any likely mediators for this effect. Here again, it may be that sociability is too broad a construct or too tied to the co-occurring contexts to be simply understood (Cohen & Janicki-Deverts, 2009).

Because extroversion seems closely tied to the sensitivity of the nervous system (Eysenck, 1990, 1991), it may also be the case that extraversion has a genetic basis that is linked to physiological processes that directly affect proneness to disease. The relation could be an underlying third variable that produces a spurious association. Or, the physiological processes may produce strong motivations toward certain sociobehavioral patterns. Such causal models of extroversion and health have not been much studied.

A somewhat different approach to understanding the possible deleterious effects of introversion or unsociability is to focus on the psychological construct of loneliness—feelings of social isolation. This has been a path taken by John Cacioppo and colleagues (Cacioppo et al., 2002; Cacioppo & Patrick, 2008; Hawkley, Burleson, Berntson, & Cacioppo, 2003; Hawkley & Cacioppo, 2004). Characteristics of lonely people include a poorer quality of sleep and subtle alterations in cardiovascular function

(total peripheral resistance) and immune health. But no striking behavioral or psychophysiological differences have emerged. Such findings are consistent with the idea that a narrow focus on unsociability will be less fruitful than a broader consideration of what it means to be embedded in a social network.

### Openness and Intelligence

People high on Openness tend to be creative and to value aesthetic and intellectual pursuits, and they tend to seek a wide range of experiences. In some personality schemes, openness is closely tied to intelligence, but in other schemes, it is more related to creativity and imagination (McCrae & Costa, 1987; Peabody & Goldberg, 1989).

Popular stereotypes that intelligent people are frail, weak, and "nerdy," as compared to their robust but not-so-clever counterparts, have long been discredited by research; bright people tend to be healthy (Friedman & Markey, 2003; Terman & Oden, 1947). The issue here again, however, is a complex one, as intelligence may serve as a marker for various other health factors and conditions. Further, although intelligence and openness potentially provide a number of health advantages, these advantages are sometimes outweighed by other factors.

Well-conducted lifespan longitudinal research indicates that more intelligent people are at lower risk of disease and premature mortality (Batty, Deary, & Gottfredson, 2007; Deary, 2009; Deary & Der, 2005; Deary, Whiteman, Starr, Whalley, & Fox, 2004; Osler et al., 2003). This relation sometimes holds even after correcting for education, occupational social class, and smoking. Similarly, people with lower intellectual abilities among the elderly in the Berlin Aging Study were at higher mortality risk (Maier & Smith, 1999). But all sorts of causal links may be simultaneously operating.

First, it is possible that intelligence and openness are frequently related to health and longevity due to a variety of biological factors. These include genetic, developmental, and behavioral influences. In fact, IQ has been posited as an indirect measure of both bodily insults and system integrity (Whalley & Deary, 2001.) In terms of underlying variables, healthy early developmental experiences combined with robust genes set the stage for both high-functioning brains and long-living bodies. It is also the case that individuals who resist disease suffer fewer brain insults; since the brain is a biological organ that communicates in various ways with the rest of the body, it is not surprising that the brain is impaired by many diseases. Further, it has been suggested that high levels of cognitive functioning may delay the clinical expression of disease and postpone the physical decline associated with aging (Snowdon, 1997; Snowdon et al., 1996).

Second, SES is often correlated with both intelligence and health-related behaviors and activities. It is well established that people of higher income and education are healthier and live longer (the so-called SES-health gradient; Adler et al., 1994), probably for a myriad of reasons. It is generally very difficult to fully disentangle the various interrelating causes, but at the very least, SES often both leads to and results from higher cognitive abilities and interests.

Third, bright individuals are certainly better able to receive and understand health information, and so may be able to avoid harmful substances (e.g., tobacco products, pesticides, saturated fats) and better utilize beneficial substances (e.g., medication). Further, high intelligence might lead to better decision making in regards to health and health care utilization. Nonetheless, creative and smart people die at high rates in their 60s and 70s, just as do less intelligent people. Creative, avant-garde individuals might, in some circumstances, also be more likely to use illegal recreational drugs, drink excessively, travel to exotic locations with exotic pathogens, and weaken their community ties. In some highly intellectual, aesthetic subgroups, dangerous sexual activity may be more common.

In the Terman cohort, when the Terman participants' mortality rates are compared to the mortality rates of the general U.S. population born in 1910, the Terman sample lived longer than their general population peers, even after taking into account the fact (artifact) that the Terman participants, by study design, lived at least until age 10. However, the patterns of mortality risk and overall risk later in life are not strikingly different. That is, the risk pattern is remarkably similar to that of the full 1910 birth cohort of the United States (although somewhat delayed) (Friedman & Markey, 2003). The Terman men were more likely to drink significant amounts of alcohol than was the general male population, and they also smoked more, in keeping with the fashionable expectations of the time. Overall, the highly intelligent Terman participants, just like their peers of average intelligence, were highly susceptible to behavioral and psychosocial threats to health and longevity.

## Conclusion

Remarkable variability exists in susceptibility to illness and in the likelihood of recovery. Traditional biological and behavioral risk factors like blood pressure and diet do a mediocre job of telling us when or why someone will be well or ill. The search for understanding of individual differences is thus scientifically necessary, but it also leads to a wider and deeper analysis, closer to the true nature of illness and well-being. Employing the methods of the science of personality to study health, we are pressed to see how the various pieces of the biopsychosocial organism fit together and develop across time.

Studies (and newspaper headlines) continually appear, claiming that a personality trait is (or is not) related to some disease. Such articles are not much more sophisticated than approaches that query, "Does the mind really affect the body?" It is not helpful to keep asking which traits constitute a cancer-prone personality, or whether a smiling face makes you live longer. Further, it is practically useless to give general advice to patients to "relax," "cheer up," and "avoid stress." Instead, we need research attention to focus on the complex links and pathways associated with better or worse health, and interventions that point and move individuals to their own best pathways.

First, we need to understand which causal mechanisms are common in certain subpopulations and which are present in any given instance. If the personality is being influenced by the disease, or if both the personality and the disease are being influenced by underlying genetic or physiological factors, then there is often no value in focusing on changing personality to improve health. Second, we need to understand the relevant context to see what influences (if any) will pull a person toward or away from available healthy environments. Finally, if personality is exerting a causal influence on health, we need to specify the interrelated sets of mediating mechanisms and interrelated outcomes.

Many individual differences in likelihood of illness and recovery go well beyond chance expectations. Personality psychology provides a window into these processes, and the research tools to investigate them. Risky behavior, harmful psychophysiological patterns, and unsupportive social environments are not independent but generally tend to cluster. Analogously, self-healing patterns are just that—they are patterns, rather than litanies of random health components. As the example of conscientiousness well illustrates, various sorts of links exist between personality and health and longevity, sometimes operating simultaneously and sometimes more important for different people at different times. For example, conscientiousness is closely tied to many health behaviors; it is linked to impulsive risk-taking;

it is associated with levels of hormones and neurotransmitters; and it often predicts whether individuals will seek out or find themselves in healthier environments.

Approaching health with the biomedical model of disease leads one to focus on genetics or on infectious agents and toxins. In most cases, such approaches are substantially incomplete; although a large number of diseases can be mostly understood in biomedical terms, they account for a small proportion of morbidity and mortality in developed countries. Rather, the major conditions—including cardiovascular disease, cancer, diabetes, injury, and addiction—are most often best prevented and addressed by considering long-term biopsychosocial patterns. Consideration of the individual and his or her personality forces a more profound analysis, which is closer to the true complexity of illness and well-being.

## Acknowledgments

Supported in part by NIA grants AG08825 and AG027001. The views expressed are those of the author.

## References

Adler, N.E., Boyce, T., Chesney, M., Cohen, S., Folkman, S., Kahn, R.L. & Syme, S.L. (1994). Socioeconomic status and health: The challenge of the gradient. *American Psychologist, 49*, 15–24.

Aldwin, C.M. (1994). *Stress, coping, and development: An integrative perspective.* New York: Guilford Press.

Alexander, F. (1950). *Psychosomatic medicine.* New York: W. W. Norton.

Antonovsky, A. (1979). *Health, stress, and coping.* San Francisco: Jossey-Bass.

Antonovsky, A. (1987). *Unraveling the mystery of health: How people manage stress and stay well.* San Francisco: Jossey-Bass.

Appels, A., Golombeck, B., Gorgels, A., de Vreede, J., & van Breukelen, G. (2000). Behavioral risk factors of sudden cardiac arrest. *Journal of Psychosomatic Research, 48*, 463–469.

Aspinwall, L.G., & Taylor, S.E. (1997). A stitch in time: Self-regulation and proactive coping. *Psychological Bulletin, 121*, 417–436.

Barefoot, J.C., & Schroll, M. (1996). Symptoms of depression, acute myocardial infarction, and total mortality in a community sample. *Circulation, 93*, 1976–1980.

Barefoot, J.C., Brummett, B.H., Helms, M.J., Mark, D.B., Siegler, I.C., & Williams, R.B. (2000). Depressive symptoms and survival of patients with coronary artery disease. *Psychosomatic Medicine, 62*, 790–795.

Bartoshuk, L.M., Duffy, V.B., Fast, K., Kveton, J.F., Lucchina, L.A., Phillips, M.N., et al. (2001). What makes a supertaster? *Chemical Senses, 26*, 1074.

Batty, G.D., Deary, I.J., & Gottfredson, L.S. (2007). Premorbid (early life) IQ and later mortality risk: Systematic review. *Annals of Epidemiology, 17*, 278–288.

Bernard, C. (1880). *Leçons de pathologie expérimentale: Et leçons sur les propriétés de la moelle épinière.* Paris: Librairie J. -B. Baillière et fils.

Bettelheim, B. (1960). *The informed heart: Autonomy in a mass age.* Glencoe, IL: Free Press.

Betz, B., & Thomas, C. (1979). Individual temperament as a predictor of health or premature disease. *Johns Hopkins Medical Journal, 144*, 81–89.

Bogg, T., & Roberts, B.W. (2004). Conscientiousness and health-related behaviors: A meta-analysis of the leading behavioral contributors to mortality. *Psychological Bulletin, 130*(6), 887–919.

Bolger, N., & Zuckerman, A. (1995). A framework for studying personality in the stress process. *Journal of Personality & Social Psychology, 69*(5), 890–902.

Bond, A.J. (2001). Neurotransmitters, temperament and social functioning. *European Neuropsychopharmacology, 11*, 261–274.

Bondy, B. (2007), Common genetic factors for depression and cardiovascular disease. *Dialogues in Clinical Neuroscience, 9*, 19–28.

Booth-Kewley, S., & Friedman, H.S. (1987). Psychological predictors of heart disease: A quantitative review. *Psychological Bulletin, 101*, 343–362.

Booth-Kewley, S., & Vickers, R.R., Jr. (1994). Associations between major domains of personality and health behavior. *Journal of Personality, 62*, 282–298.

Brickman, A.L., Yount, S.E., Blaney, N.T., Rothberg, S.T., & De-Nour, A.K. (1996). Personality traits and long-term health status: The influence of neuroticism and conscientiousness on renal deterioration in Type-1 diabetes. *Psychosomatics: Journal of Consultation Liaison Psychiatry, 37* (5), 459–468.

Butow, P.N., Hiller, J.E., Price, M.A., Thackway, S.V., Kricker, A., & Tennant, C.C. (2000). Epidemiological evidence for a relationship between life events, coping style, and personality factors in the development of breast cancer. *Journal of Psychosomatic Research, 49*, 169–181.

Cacioppo, J.T., & Berntson, G.G. (2011). The brain, homeostasis, and health: balancing demands of the internal and external milieu. In H.S. Friedman (Ed.), *The Oxford handbook of health psychology.* New York: Oxford University Press.

Cacioppo, J.T., Hawkley, L.C., Crawford, L.E., Ernst, J.M., Burleson, M.H., Kowalewski, R.B., et al. (2002). Loneliness and health: Potential mechanisms. *Psychosomatic Medicine, 64*(3), 407–417.

Cacioppo, J.T., & Patrick, W. (2008). Loneliness: Human nature and the need for social connection. New York: Norton.

Campbell, D.T., & Fiske, D.W. (1959). Convergent and discriminant validation by the multitrait-multimethod matrix. *Psychological Bulletin, 56*, 81–105.

Cannon, W.B. (1932). *Wisdom of the body.* New York: W. W. Norton.

Carver, C.S., & Miller, C.J. (2006). Relations of serotonin function to personality: Current views and a key methodological issue. *Psychiatry Research, 144*, 1–15.

Carver, C.S., & Scheier, M.F. (1981). *Attention and self-regulation: A control-theory approach to human behavior.* New York, NY: Springer-Verlag.

Caspi, A., Sugden, K., Moffitt, T.E., Taylor, A., Craig, I.W., Harrington, H., et al. (2003). Influence of life stress on depression: moderation by a polymorphism in the 5-HTT gene. *Science, 301*(5631), 291–293.

Chesney, M.A., & Rosenman, R.H. (Eds.) (1985). *Anger and hostility in cardiovascular and behavioral disorders.* New York: Hemisphere.

Christensen, A.J., Ehlers, S.L. Wiebe, Moran, J.S., Raichle, P.J., Ferneyhough, K., & Lawton, W.J. (2002). Patient personality and mortality: A 4-year prospective examination of chronic renal insufficiency. *Health Psychology, 21*, 315–320.

Cloninger, C.R. (1998). The genetics and psychobiology of the seven-factor model of personality. In K.R. Silk (Ed.), *Biology of personality disorders* (pp. 63–92). Washington, DC: American Psychiatric Press.

Cohen, F., & Lazarus, R.S. (1983). Coping and adaptation in health and illness. In D. Mechanic (Ed.), *Handbook of health, health care, and the health professions* (pp. 608–635). New York: Free Press.

Cohen, S., & Janicki-Deverts, D. (2009). Can we improve our physical health by altering our social networks? *Perspectives on Psychological Science, 4*, 375–378.

Cohen, S., & Williamson, G.M. (1991). Stress and infectious disease in humans. *Psychological Bulletin, 109*, 5–24.

Cohen, S., Doyle, W.J., & Skoner, D.P. (1999). Psychological stress, cytokine production, and severity of upper respiratory illness. *Psychosomatic Medicine, 61*, 175–180.

Cohen, S., Doyle, W.J., Turner, R.B., Alper, C.M., & Skoner, D.P. (2003). Sociability and susceptibility to the common cold. *Psychological Science, 14*, 389–395.

Colvin C.R., Block, J., & Funder, D.C. (1995). Overly positive self-evaluations and personality: negative implications for mental health. *Journal of Personality and Social Psychology, 68*, 1152–1162.

Colvin, C.R., & Block, J. (1994). Do positive illusions foster mental health? An examination of the Taylor and Brown formulation. *Psychological Bulletin, 116*, 3–20.

Copper, R.L., Goldenberg, R.L., Das, A., Elder, N., Swain, M., Norman, G., et al. (1996). The preterm prediction study: Maternal stress is associated with spontaneous preterm birth at less than thirty-five weeks' gestation. *American Journal of Obstetrics and Gynecology, 175*, 1286–1292.

Costa, P.T., & McCrae, R.R. (1987). Neuroticism, somatic complaints, and disease: Is the bark worse than the bite? *Journal of Personality, 55*, 299–316.

Crocker, J., Major, B., & Steele, C. (1998). Social stigma. In D.T. Gilbert, et al (Eds.), *The handbook of social psychology* Vol. 2 (4th ed., pp. 504–531). Boston, MA: McGraw-Hill.

Davidson, R.J. (2010). Empirical explorations of mindfulness: Conceptual and methodological conundrums. *Emotion, 10*, 8–11.

Deary, I.J. (2009). Introduction to the special issue on cognitive epidemiology. *Intelligence, 37*, 517–519.

Deary, I.J., & Der, G. (2005). Reaction time explains IQ's association with death. *Psychological Science, 16*(1), 64–69.

Deary, I.J., Whiteman, M.C., Starr, J.M., Whalley, L.J., & Fox, H.C. (2004). The impact of childhood intelligence on later life: Following up the Scottish Mental Surveys of 1932 and 1947. *Journal of Personality and Social Psychology, 86*, 130–147.

Dembroski, T.M., Weiss, S.M., Shields, J.L., Haynes, S.G., & Feinlieb, M. (Eds.). (1978). *Coronary-prone behavior.* New York: Springer-Verlag.

Denollet, J. (2000). Type D personality: A potential risk factor refined. *Journal of Psychosomatic Research, 49*(4), 255–266.

Devins, G.M., Mann, J., Mandin, H., Paul, L.C., Hons, R.B., Burgess, E.D., et al. (1990). Psychosocial predictors of survival in end-stage renal disease. *Journal of Nervous and Mental Disease, 178*(2), 127–133.

Dillard, A.J., Midboe, A.M., & Klein, W.M.P. (2009). The dark side of optimism: Unrealistic optimism about problems with alcohol predicts subsequent negative event experiences. *Personality and Social Psychology Bulletin, 35*, 1540–1550.

Dion, K. (1972). Physical attractiveness and evaluation of children's transgressions. *Journal and Personality and Social Psychology, 24*, 207–213.

Dixon, N.F. (1980). Humor: A cognitive alternative to stress? In I.G. Sarason, & C.D. Spielberger (Eds.), *Stress and anxiety* Vol. 7 (pp. 281–289). Washington, DC: Hemisphere.

Dunbar, F. (1955). *Mind and body: Psychosomatic medicine.* New York: Random House.

ENRICHD Investigators (2003). Effects of treating depression and low perceived social support on clinical events after myocardial infarction: The enhancing recovery in coronary heart disease patients (ENRICHD) randomized trial. *Journal of the American Medical Association, 289*, 3106–3116.

Everson, S.A., Goldberg, D.E., Kaplan, G.A., Cohen, R.D., Pukkala, E., Tuomilehto, J., & Salonen, J.T. (1996). Hopelessness and risk of mortality and incidence of myocardial infarction and cancer. *Psychosomatic Medicine, 58*, 113–121.

Eysenck, H.J. (1990). Biological dimensions of personality. In L.A. Pervin (Ed.), *Handbook of personality: Theory and research* (pp. 244–276). New York, NY: Guilford Press.

Eysenck, H.J. (1991). *Smoking, personality, and stress: Psychosocial factors in the prevention of cancer and coronary heart disease.* New York: Springer-Verlag.

Eysenck, H.J. (1992). Four ways five factors are not basic. *Personality and Individual Differences, 13*, 667–673.

Eysenck, H.J., & Eysenck, S.B.G. (1976). *Psychoticism as a dimension of personality.* London: Hodder & Stoughton.

Ford, D.E., Mead, L.A., Chang, P.P., Cooper-Patrick, L., Wang, N., & Klag, M.J. (1998). Depression is a risk factor for coronary artery disease in men. *Archives of Internal Medicine, 158*, 1422–1426.

Frankl, V.E. (1962). *Man's search for meaning: An introduction to logotherapy* (Rev. ed., I. Lasch, Trans.). Boston: Beacon Press.

Frasure-Smith, N., Lesperance, F., Talajic, M. (1995). Depression and 18-month prognosis after myocardial infarction. *Circulation, 91*(4), 999–1005.

Fredericks, C.A., Drabant, E.M., Edge, M.D., Tillie, J.M., Hallmayer, J., Ramel, W., et al. (2010). Healthy young women with serotonin transporter SS polymorphism show a pro-inflammatory bias under resting and stress conditions. *Brain, Behavior, and Immunity, 24*, 350–357.

Fredrickson, B.L. (2001). The role of positive emotions in positive psychology: The broaden-and-build theory of positive emotions. *American Psychologist, 56*, 218–226.

Freud, S. (1955). *Collected works: Vol. 2. Studies of Hysteria.* NY: Hogarth Press.

Friedman, H.S. (1998). Self-healing personalities. In H.S. Friedman (Editor-in-chief), *Encyclopedia of Mental Health* Vol. 3 (pp. 453–459). San Diego: Academic Press.

Friedman, H.S. (2000). Long-term relations of personality and health: Dynamisms, mechanisms, tropisms. *Journal of Personality, 68*, 1089–1108.

Friedman, H.S. (2008). The multiple linkages of personality and disease. *Brain, Behavior, and Immunity, 22*, 668–675.

Friedman, H.S., & Booth-Kewley, S. (1987). The "disease-prone personality": A meta-analytic view of the construct. *American Psychologist, 42*, 539–555.

Friedman, H.S., & Markey, C.N. (2003). Paths to longevity in the highly intelligent Terman cohort. In C.E. Finch, J.-M. Robine, & Y. Christen (Eds.), *Brain and longevity* (pp. 165–175). New York: Springer.

Friedman, H.S., & Martin, L.R. (2011). *The longevity project: Surprising discoveries for health and long life from the landmark eight-decade study*. New York: Hudson Street Press.

Friedman, H.S., & Schustack, M.W. (2012). *Personality: Classic theories and modern research, 5th edition*. Boston: Pearson/Allyn & Bacon.

Friedman, H.S., & VandenBos, G. (1992). Disease-prone and self-healing personalities. *Hospital and Community Psychiatry: A Journal of the American Psychiatric Association, 43*, 1177–1179.

Friedman, H.S., Hall, J.A., & Harris, M.J. (1985). Type A behavior, nonverbal expressive style, and health. *Journal of Personality and Social Psychology, 48*, 1299–1315.

Friedman, H.S., Tucker, J.S., & Reise, S. (1995). Personality dimensions and measures potentially relevant to health: A focus on hostility. *Annals of Behavioral Medicine, 17*, 245–253.

Friedman, H.S., Tucker, J.S., Martin, L.R., Tomlinson-Keasey, C., Schwartz, J.E., Wingard, D.L. & Criqui, M.H. (1994). Do non-scientists really live longer? *The Lancet, 343*, 296.

Friedman, H.S., Tucker, J., Schwartz, J.E., Martin, L.R., Tomlinson-Keasey, C., Wingard, D., & Criqui, M. (1995). Childhood conscientiousness and longevity: Health behaviors and cause of death. *Journal of Personality and Social Psychology, 68*, 696–703.

Friedman, H.S., Tucker, J.S., Schwartz, J.E., Tomlinson-Keasey, C., Martin, L.R., Wingard, D.L., & Criqui, M.H. (1995). Psychosocial and behavioral predictors of longevity: The aging and death of the "Termites." *American Psychologist, 50*, 69–78.

Friedman, H.S., Tucker, J., Tomlinson-Keasey, C., Schwartz, J., Wingard, D., & Criqui, M.H. (1993). Does childhood personality predict longevity? *Journal of Personality and Social Psychology, 65*, 176–185.

Friedman, H.S. (2000). *Self-healing personality: Why some people achieve health and others succumb to illness*. New York: iUniverse, Inc. (Original work published 1991).

Friedman, M., & Rosenman, R.H. (1974). *Type A behavior and your heart*. New York: Knopf.

Gallo, L.C., & Smith, T.W. (1999). Patterns of hostility and social support: Conceptualizing psychosocial risk factors as characteristics of the person and the environment. *Journal of Research in Personality, 33*, 281–310.

Gardner, J., & Oswald, A. (2004). How is mortality affected by money, marriage and stress? *Journal of Health Economics, 23*, 1181–1207.

Garmezy, N. (1993). Children in poverty: Resilience despite risk. *Psychiatry, 56*, 127–136.

Goffman, E. (1963). *Stigma: Notes on the management of spoiled identity*. Englewood Cliffs, NJ: Prentice-Hall.

Goodwin, R.G., & Friedman, H.S. (2006). Health status and the Five Factor personality traits in a nationally representative sample. *Journal of Health Psychology, 11*, 643–654.

Grau, E., & Ortet, G. (1999). Personality traits and alcohol consumption in a sample of non-alcoholic women. *Personality and Individual Differences, 27*, 1057–1066.

Haas, S. (2008). Trajectories of functional health: The "long arm" of childhood health and socioeconomic factors. *Social Science & Medicine, 66*, 849–861.

Ham, L.S., & Hope, D.A. (2003). College students and problematic drinking: A review of the literature. *Clinical Psychology Review, 23*(5), 719–759.

Hampson, S.E., & Friedman, H.S. (2008). Personality and health: A lifespan perspective. In O.P. John, R.W. Robins, & L.A. Pervin (Eds.), *The handbook of personality: Theory and research* (3rd ed., pp. 770–794). New York: Guildford Press.

Hampson, S.E., Goldberg, L.R., Vogt, T.M., & Dubanoski, J.P. (2007). Mechanisms by which childhood personality traits influence adult health status: Educational attainment and healthy behaviors. *Health Psychology, 26*, 121–125.

Hawkley, L.C., & Cacioppo, J.T. (2004). Stress and the aging immune system. *Brain, Behavior, and Immunity, 18*, 114–119.

Hawkley, L.C., Burleson, M.H., Berntson, G.G., & Cacioppo, J.T. (2003). Loneliness in everyday life: Cardiovascular activity, psychosocial context, and health behaviors. *Journal of Personality and Social Psychology, 85*, 105–120.

Hayward, M.D., & Gorman, B.K. (2004). The long arm of childhood: The influence of early-life social conditions on men's mortality. *Demography, 41*, 87–107.

Held, B.B. (2004). The negative side of positive psychology. *Journal of Humanistic Psychology, 44*, 9–46.

Herbert, T.B., & Cohen, S. (1993). Depression and immunity: A meta-analytic review. *Psychological Bulletin, 113*, 472–486.

Hogan, J., & Ones, D.S. (1997). Conscientiousness and integrity at work. In R. Hogan, J.A. Johnson, & S.R. Briggs (Eds.), *Handbook of personality psychology* (pp. 849–870). San Diego, CA: Academic Press.

Horwitz, R.I., Viscoli, C.M., Berkman, L., Donaldson, R.M., Horwitz, S.M., Murray, C.J., et al. (1990). Treatment adherence and risk of death after a myocardial infarction. *Lancet, 336*(8714), 542–545.

House, J.S., Landis, K.R., & Umberson, D. (1988). Social relationships and health. *Science, 241*, 540–545.

Houston, B.K., & Snyder, C.R. (1988). *Type A behavior pattern: Research, theory and intervention*. New York: Wiley.

Januzzi, J.L., Stern, T.A., Pasternak, R., & DeSanctis, R.W. (2000). The influence of anxiety and depression on outcomes of patients with coronary artery disease. *Archives of Internal Medicine, 160*, 1913–1921.

Jenkins, C.D. (1979). The coronary prone personality. In W.D. Gentry, & R.B. Williams (Eds.), *Psychological aspects of myocardial infarction and coronary care* (2nd ed., pp. 5–30). St. Louis: C.V. Mosby.

Jensen, M.R. (1987). Psychobiological factors predicting the course of breast cancer. *Journal of Personality, 55*, 317–342.

Johnson, W., McGue, M., Krueger, R.J., & Bouchard, T.J., Jr. (2004). Marriage and personality: A genetic analysis. *Journal of Personality and Social Psychology, 86*, 285–294.

Judge, T.A., & Ilies, R. (2002). Relationship of personality to performance motivation: A meta-analytic review. *Journal of Applied Psychology, 87*(4), 797–807.

Kagan, J. (1994). *Galen's prophecy: Temperament in human nature*. New York: Basic Books.

Kassel, J.D., Stroud, Laura R., & Paronis, C.A. (2003). Smoking, stress, and negative affect: Correlation, causation, and context across stages of smoking. *Psychological Bulletin, 129*, 270–304.

Kemeny, M.E. (2011). Psychoneuroimmunology. In H.S. Friedman (Ed.), *The Oxford handbook of health psychology*. New York: Oxford University Press.

Kern, M.L., & Friedman, H.S. (2008). Do conscientious individuals live longer? A quantitative review. *Health Psychology, 27*, 505–512.

Kern, M.L., & Friedman, H.S. (2011). Personality and pathways of influence on physical health. *Social and Personality Psychology Compass, 5*, 76–87.

Kern, M.L., Friedman, H.S., Martin, L.R., Reynolds, C.A., & Luong, G. (2009). Conscientiousness, career success, and longevity: A lifespan analysis. *Annals of Behavioral Medicine, 37,* 154–163.

Kiecolt-Glaser, J.K., Glaser, R., Cacioppo, J.T., & Malarkey, W.B. (1998). Marital stress: Immunologic, neuroendocrine, and autonomic correlates. In S.M. McCann, & J.M. Lipton (Eds.), *Annals of the New York Academy of Sciences,* Vol. 840: *Neuroimmunomodulation: Molecular aspects, integrative systems, and clinical advances* (pp. 565–663). New York: New York Academy of Sciences.

Korten, A.E., Jorm, A.F., Jiao, Z., Letenneur, L., Jacomb, P.A., Henderson, A.S., et al. (1999). Health, cognitive, and psychosocial factors as predictors of mortality in an elderly community sample. *Journal of Epidemiology and Community Health, 53,* 83–88.

Kubzansky, L.D., Kawachi, I., Weiss, S.T., & Sparrow, D. (1998). Anxiety and coronary heart disease: A synthesis of epidemiological, psychological, and experimental evidence. *Annals of Behavioral Medicine, 20,* 47–58.

Larson, J.H., & Holman, T.B. (1994). Premarital predictors of marital quality and stability. *Family Relations: Interdisciplinary Journal of Applied Family Studies, 43,* 228–237.

Lazarus, R.S., & Folkman, S. (1984). *Stress, appraisal, and coping.* New York: Springer.

Leibowitz, J.O. (1970). *The history of coronary heart disease.* Berkeley: University of California Press.

Lobel, M., DeVincent, C.J., Kaminer, A., & Meyer, B.A. (2000). The impact of prenatal maternal stress and optimistic disposition on birth outcomes in medically high-risk women. *Health Psychology, 19,* 544–553.

Lutgendorf, S.K., Vitaliano, P.P., Tripp-Reimer, T., Harvey, J.H., & Lubaroff, D.M. (1999). Sense of coherence moderates the relationship between life stress and natural killer cell activity in healthy older adults. *Psychology & Aging, 14*(4), 552–563.

Maddi, S.R., & Kobasa, S.C. (1984). *The hardy executive: Health under stress.* Homewood, IL: Dow Jones-Irwin.

Magnus, K., Diener, E., Fujita, F., & Payot, W. (1993). Extraversion and neuroticism as predictors of objective life events: A longitudinal analysis. *Journal of Personality & Social Psychology, 65,* 1046–1053.

Maier, H., & Smith, J. (1999). Psychological predictors of mortality in old age. *Journals of Gerontology: Series B: Psychological Sciences & Social Sciences, 54B,* 44–54.

Manuck, S.B., Flory, J.D., McCaffery, J.M., Matthews, K.A., Mann, J.J., & Muldoon, M.F. (1998). Aggression, impulsivity, and central nervous system serotonergic responsivity in a nonpatient sample. *Neuropsychopharmacology, 19,* 287–299.

Marchesi, C., Brusamonti, F., & Maggini, C. (2000). Are alexithymia, depression, and anxiety distinct constructs in affective disorders? *Journal of Psychosomatic Research, 49,* 43–49.

Marshall, G.N., Wortman, C.B., Vickers, R.R., Jr., Kusulas, J.W., & Hervig, L.K. (1994). The five-factor model of personality as a framework for personality-health research. *Journal of Personality and Social Psychology, 67,* 278–286.

Martin, L.R., & Friedman, H.S. (2000). Comparing personality scales across time: An illustrative study of validity and consistency in life-span archival data. *Journal of Personality, 68,* 85–110.

Martin, L.R., Friedman, H.S., & Schwartz, J.E. (2007). Personality and mortality risk across the lifespan. The importance of conscientiousness as a biopsychosocial attribute. *Health Psychology, 26,* 428–436.

Martin, L.R., Friedman, H.S., Tucker, J.S., Tomlinson-Keasey, C., Criqui, M.H. & Schwartz, J.E. (2002). A life course perspective on childhood cheerfulness and its relation to mortality risk. *Personality and Social Psychology Bulletin, 28,* 1155–1165.

Martsh, C.T., & Miller, W.R. (1997). Extraversion predicts heavy drinking in college students. *Personality and Individual Differences, 23,* 153–155.

Matthews, K.A. (1982). Psychological perspectives on the Type A behavior pattern. *Psychological Bulletin, 91,* 293–323.

Matthews, K.A. (1988). Coronary heart disease and type A behaviors: Update on and alternative to the Booth-Kewley and Friedman (1987) quantitative review. *Psychological Bulletin, 3,* 373–380.

Matthews, K.A., Owens, J.F., Kuller, L.H., Sutton-Tyrrell, K., & Jansen-McWilliams, L. (1998). Are hostility and anxiety associated with carotid atherosclerosis in healthy postmenopausal women? *Psychosomatic Medicine, 60,* 633–638.

McCaffrey, J.M., Frasure-Smith, N., Dubé, M.P., Théroux, P., Rouleau, G.A., Duan, Q., & Lespérance, F. (2006). Common genetic vulnerability to depressive symptoms and coronary artery disease: A review and development of candidate genes related to inflammation and serotonin. *Psychosomatic Medicine, 68,* 187–200.

McCrae, R.R., & Costa, P.T., Jr. (1987). Validation of the five-factor model of personality across instruments and observers. *Journal of Personality and Social Psychology, 52,* 81–90.

McCrae, R.R., & John, O. (1992). An introduction to the five-factor model and its applications. *Journal of Personality, 60,* 175–215.

McEwen, B.S. (1998). Stress, adaptation and disease: Allostasis and allostatic load. *Annals of the New York Academy of Sciences, 840,* 33–44.

Menninger, K.A., & Menninger, W.C. (1936). Psychoanalytic observations in cardiac disorders. *American Heart Journal, 11,* 1–12.

Meyer, R., & Haggerty, R. (1962). Streptococcal infections in families. *Pediatrics, 29,* 539–549.

Middeldorp, C.M., Cath, D.C., Beem, A.L., Willemsen, G., & Boomsma, D.I. (2008). Life events, anxious depression and personality: A prospective and genetic study. *Psychological Medicine: A Journal of Research in Psychiatry and the Allied Sciences, 38,* 1557–1565.

Miller, T.Q., Smith, T.W., Turner, C.W., Guijarro, M.L., & Hallet, A.J. (1996). A meta-analytic review of research on hostility and physical health. *Psychological Bulletin, 119,* 322–348.

Miller, T.Q., Turner, C.W., Tindale, R.S., Posavac, E.J., & Dugoni, B.L. (1991). Reasons for the trend toward null findings in research on Type A behavior. *Psychological Bulletin, 110,* 469–485.

Mols, F., & Denollet, J. (2010). Type D personality among non-cardiovascular patient populations: A systematic review. *General Hospital Psychiatry, 32,* 66–72.

Mroczek, D.K., & Almeida, D.M. (2004). The effect of daily stress, personality, and age on daily negative affect. *Journal of Personality, 72,* 355–378.

Newman, M.F., Kirchner, J.L., Phillips-Bute, B., Gaver, V., Grocott, H., Jones, R.H., et al. (2001). Longitudinal assessment of neurocognitive function after coronary-artery bypass surgery. *New England Journal of Medicine, 344,* 395–402.

Osler, M., Andersen, A.-M.N., Due, P., Lund, R., Damsgaard, M.T., & Holstein, B.E. (2003). Socioeconomic position in early life, birth weight, childhood cognitive function, and adult mortality. A longitudinal study of Danish men born in 1953. *Journal of Epidemiology and Community Health, 57*(9), 681–686.

Ouellette, S.C., & DiPlacido, J. (2001). Personality's role in the protection and enhancement of health: Where the research has been, where it is stuck, how it might move. In A. Baum, T.A. Revenson, & J. Singer (Eds.), *Handbook of health psychology* (pp. 175–194). Lawrence Erlbaum Associates.

Park, M., Ross, G.W., Petrovitch, H., White, L.R., Masaki, K.H., Nelson, J.S., et al. (2005). Consumption of milk and calcium in midlife and the future risk of Parkinson disease. *Neurology, 64*, 1047–1051.

Parsons, J.E. (1980). *The psychobiology of sex differences and sex roles*. Cambridge, UK: Hemisphere.

Peabody, D., & Goldberg, L.R. (1989). Some determinants of factor structures from personality-trait descriptors. *Journal of Personality and Social Psychology, 57*, 552–567.

Pennebaker, J.W., & Chung, C.K. (2011). Expressive writing: Connections to physical and mental health. In H.S. Friedman (Ed.), *The Oxford handbook of health psychology*. New York: Oxford University Press.

Pennebaker, J.W. (1982). *The psychology of physical symptoms*. New York: Springer-Verlag.

Peterson, C., Bishop, M.P., Fletcher, C.W., Kaplan, M.R., Yesko, E.S. Moon, C.H., et al. (2001). Explanatory style as a risk factor for traumatic mishaps. *Cognitive Therapy and Research, 25*, 633–649.

Peterson, C., Seligman, M.E.P., Yurko, K.H., Martin, L.R., & Friedman, H.S. (1998). Catastrophizing and untimely death. *Psychological Science, 9*, 49–52.

Pettingale, K.W., Morris, T., Greer, S., & Haybittle, J.L. (1985). Mental attitudes to cancer: An additional prognostic factor. *Lancet, 1*(8431), 750.

Plomin, R. (1986). *Development, genetics, and psychology*. Hillsdale, NJ: Erlbaum.

Pressman, S.D., & Cohen, S. (2005). The influence of positive affect on health: a review. *Psychological Bulletin, 131*, 925–971.

Ragland, D.R., & Brand, R.J. (1988). Type A behavior and mortality from coronary heart disease. *New England Journal of Medicine, 318*, 65–69.

Repetti, R.L., Taylor, S.E., & Seeman, T.E. (2002). Risky families: Family social environments and the mental and physical health of offspring. *Psychological Bulletin, 128*, 330–366.

Roberts, B.W., & Bogg, T. (2004). A longitudinal study of the relationships between conscientiousness and the social environmental factors and substance use behaviors that influence health. *Journal of Personality, 72*, 325–353.

Roberts, B.W., & Caspi, A. (2003). The cumulative continuity model of personality development: Striking a balance between continuity and change in personality traits across the life course. In R.M. Staudinger, & U. Lindenberger (Eds.), *Understanding human development: Lifespan psychology in exchange with other disciplines* (pp. 183–214). Dordrecht, NL: Kluwer Academic Publishers.

Roberts, B.W., & Pomerantz, E.M. (2004). On traits, situations, and their integration: A developmental perspective. *Personality and Social Psychology Review, 8*, 402–416.

Roberts, B.W., Caspi, A., & Moffitt, T. (2003). Work experiences and personality development in young adulthood. *Journal of Personality and Social Psychology, 84*, 582–593.

Roberts, B.W., Walton, K., & Viechtbauer, W. (2006). Patterns of mean-level change in personality traits across the life course: A meta-analysis of longitudinal studies. *Psychological Bulletin, 132*, 1–25.

Rosenkranz, M.A., Jackson, D.C., Dalton K.M., Dolski, I., Ryff, C.D., Singer, B.H., et al. (2003). Affective style and in vivo immune response: Neurobehavioral mechanisms. *Proceedings of the National Academy of Sciences, 100*, 11148–11152.

Rotton, J. (1992). Trait humor and longevity: Do comics have the last laugh? *Health Psychology, 11*, 262–266.

Rugulies, R. (2002). Depression as a predictor for coronary heart disease: A review and meta-analysis. *American Journal Of Preventive Medicine, 23*, 51–61.

Ryff, C.D., & Singer, B.H. (Eds.) (2001). *Emotion, social relationships, and health*. New York: Oxford University Press.

Salovey, P., Rothman, A.J., Detweiler, J.B., & Steward, W. (2000). Emotional states and physical health. *American Psychologist, 55*, 110–121.

Sbarra, D.A., & Nietert, P.J. (2009). Divorce and death: Forty years of the Charleston Heart Study, *Psychological Science, 20*, 107–113.

Scheier, M.F., Matthews, K.A., Owens, J.F., Schulz, R., Bridges, M.W., Magovern, G.J., Jr., & Carver, C.S. (1999). Optimism and rehospitalization after coronary artery bypass graft surgery. *Archives of Internal Medicine, 159*, 829–833.

Schneiderman, N., Weiss, S.M., & Kaufmann, P.G. (Eds.) (1989). *Handbook of research methods in cardiovascular behavioral medicine*. New York: Plenum Press.

Schulz, R., Martire, L.M., Beach, S.R., & Scheier, M.F. (2000). Depression and mortality in the elderly. *Current Directions in Psychological Science, 9*, 204–208.

Sears, R.R. (1984). The Terman gifted children study. In S.A. Mednick, M. Harway, & K.M. Finello (Eds.), *Handbook of longitudinal research* (Vol. 1, pp. 398–414). New York: Praeger.

Segerstrom, S.C. (2011). Dispositional optimism, psychophysiology, and health. In H.S. Friedman (Ed.), *The Oxford handbook of health psychology*. New York: Oxford University Press.

Segerstrom, S.C., & Miller, G.E. (2004). Psychological stress and the human immune system: A meta-analytic study of 30 years of inquiry. *Psychological Bulletin, 104*, 601–630.

Segerstrom, S.C., Taylor, S.E., Kemeny, M.E., & Fahey, J.L. (1998). Optimism is associated with mood, coping, and immune change in response to stress. *Journal of Personality and Social Psychology, 74*, 1646–1655.

Shaffer, J., Graves, P.L., Swank, R.T., & Pearson, T.A. (1987). Clustering of personality traits in youth and the subsequent development of cancer among physicians. *Journal of Behavioral Medicine, 10*(5), 441–444.

Smith, T.W. (2010). Depression and chronic medical illness: Implications for relapse prevention. In C.S. Richards, & M.G. Perri (Eds.), *Relapse prevention for depression* (199–225). Washington, DC: American Psychological Association.

Smith, T.W., & Gallo, L.C. (2001). Personality traits as risk factors for physical illness. In A. Baum, T. Revenson, & J. Singer (Eds.), *Handbook of health psychology* (pp. 139–172). Hillsdale, NJ: Lawrence Erlbaum.

Smith, T.W., Glazer, K., Ruiz, J.M., & Gallo, L.C. (2004). Hostility, anger, aggressiveness, and coronary heart disease:

An interpersonal perspective on personality, emotion, and health. *Journal of Personality, 72*, 1217–1270.

Smith, T.W., & MacKenzie, J. (2006). Personality and risk of physical illness. *Annual Review of Clinical Psychology, 2*, 435–467.

Snowdon, D.A. (1997). Aging and Alzheimer's disease: Lessons from the Nun Study. *Gerontology, 37*, 150–156.

Snowdon, D.A., Kemper, S.J., Mortimer, J.A., Greiner, L.H., Wekstein, D.R., & Markesbery, W.R. (1996). Linguistic ability early in life and cognitive function and Alzheimer's disease in late life: Findings from the Nun Study. *Journal of the American Medical Association, 275*, 528–532.

Subotnik, R.F., Karp, D.E., and Morgan, E.R. (1989). High IQ children at midlife: An investigation into the generalizability of Terman's genetic studies of genius. *Roeper Review, 11*(3), 139–145.

Suls, J., & Bunde, J. (2005). Anger, anxiety, and depression as risk factors for cardiovascular disease: The problems and implications of overlapping affective dispositions. *Psychological Bulletin, 131*, 260–300.

Suls, J., & Rittenhouse, J.D. (1990). Models of linkages between personality and disease. In: H.S. Friedman (Ed.), *Personality and disease* (pp. 38–64). New York: John Wiley & Sons, pp. 38–64.

Surtees, P., Wainwright, N., Luben, R., Khaw, K.T., & Day, N. (2003). Sense of coherence and mortality in men and women in the EPIC-Norfolk United Kingdom prospective cohort study. *American Journal of Epidemiology, 158*, 1202–1209.

Sutin, A.R., Terracciano, A., Deiana, B., Uda, M., Schlessinger, D., Lakatta, E.G., & Costa, P.T., Jr. (2010). Cholesterol, triglycerides, and the Five-Factor model of personality. *Biological Psychology, 84*, 186–191.

Swain, A., & Suls, J. (1996). Reproducibility of blood pressure and heart rate reactivity: A meta-analysis. *Psychophysiology, 33*, 162–174.

Taga, K.A., Friedman, H.S., & Martin, L.R. (2009). Early personality traits as predictors of mortality risk following conjugal bereavement. *Journal of Personality, 77*, 669–690.

Taylor, M.D., Whiteman, M.C., Fowkes, G.R., Lee, A.J., Allerhand, M., & Deary, I.J. (2009). Five Factor model personality traits and all cause mortality in the Edinburgh Artery Study cohort. *Psychosomatic Medicine, 71*, 631–641.

Taylor, S.E., & Brown, J.D. (1988). Illusion and well-being: A social psychological perspective on mental health. *Psychological Bulletin, 103*, 193–210.

Taylor, S.E., Kemeny, M.E., Aspinwall, L.G., Schneider, S.G., Rodriguez, R., & Herbert, M. (1992). Optimism, coping, psychological distress, and high-risk sexual behavior among men at risk for acquired immune deficiency syndrome. *Journal of Personality and Social Psychology, 63*, 460–473.

Taylor, S.E., Repetti, R.L., & Seeman, T. (1997). Health psychology: What is an unhealthy environment and how does it get under the skin? *Annual Review of Psychology, 48*, 411–447.

Temoshok, L.R. (2000). Complex coping patterns and their role in adaptation and neuroimmunomodulation: Theory, methodology, and research. In A. Conti, G.J.M. Maestroni, S.M. McCann, E.M. Sternberg, & J.M. Lipton (Eds.), *Annals of the New York Academy of Sciences* Vol. 917: *Neuroimmunomodulation: Perspectives at the new millennium* (pp. 446–455). New York: New York Academy of Sciences.

Temoshok, L., Heller, B.W., Sagebiel, R., Blois, M., Sweet, D.M., DiClemente, R.J., & Gold, M.L. (1985). The relationship of psychosocial factors to prognostic indicators in cutaneous malignant melanoma. *Journal of Psychosomatic Research, 29*, 139–154.

Terman, L.M., & Oden, M.H. (1947). *The gifted child grows up: Twenty-five years' follow-up of a superior group*. Stanford, CA: Stanford University Press.

Terracciano, A., Lockenhoff, C.E., Zonderman, A.B., Ferrucci, L., & Costa, P.T. (2008). Personality predictors of longevity: Activity, emotional stability, and conscientiousness. *Psychosomatic Medicine, 70*, 621–627.

Thomas, A., Chess, S., & Korn, S.J. (1982). The reality of difficult temperament. *Merrill-Palmer Quarterly, 28*, 1–20.

Tucker, J., Friedman, H.S., Tomlinson-Keasey, C., Schwartz, J.E., Wingard, D.L., & Criqui, M.H. (1995). Childhood psychosocial predictors of adulthood smoking, alcohol consumption, and physical activity. *Journal of Applied Social Psychology, 25*, 1884–1899.

Tucker, J.S., Friedman, H.S., Wingard, D.L. & Schwartz, J.E. (1996). Marital history at mid-life as a predictor of longevity: Alternative explanations to the protective effect of marriage. *Health Psychology, 15*, 94–101.

Twenge, J.M. (2000). The age of anxiety? Birth cohort change in anxiety and neuroticism, 1952–1993. *Journal of Personality and Social Psychology, 79*(6), 1007–1021.

Twenge, J.M. (2001). Birth cohort changes in extraversion: A cross-temporal meta-analysis, 1966–1993. *Personality and Individual Differences, 30*, 735–748.

Twenge, J.M. (2002). Birth cohort, social change, and personality: The interplay of dysphoria and individualism in the 20th century. In D. Cervone, & W. Mischel (Eds.), *Advances in Personality Science* (pp. 196–218). New York: Guilford.

Uhart M., & Wand G.S. (2009). Stress, alcohol and drug interaction: An update of human research. *Addiction Biology, 14*, 43–64.

Urry, H.L., Nitschke, J.B., Dolski, I., Jackson, D.C., Dalton, K.M., Mueller, C.J., et al. (2004). Making a life worth living: Neural correlates of well-being. *Psychological Science, 15*, 367–372.

Vaccarino, V., Votaw, J., Faber, T., Veledar, E., Murrah, N.V., Jones, L.R., et al. (2009). Major depression and coronary flow reserve detected by positron emission tomography. *Archives of Internal Medicine, 169*(18), 1668–1676.

Vollrath, M., Landolt, M.A., & Ribi, K. (2003). Personality of children with accident-related injuries. *European Journal of Personality, 17*, 299–307.

Vollrath, M.E., & Torgersen, S. (2008). Personality types and risky health behaviors in Norwegian students. *Scandinavian Journal of Psychology, 49*, 287–292.

Wallston, K.A., Malcarne, V.L., Flores, L., Hansdottir, I., Smith, C.A., Stein, M.J., et al. (1999). Does God determine your health? The God locus of health control scale. *Cognitive Therapy & Research, 23*, 131–142.

Wand, G.S., McCaul, M., Yang, X., Reynolds, J., Gotjen, D., Lee, S., & Ali, A. (2002). The mu-opioid receptor gene polymorphism (A188G) alters HPA axis activation induced by opioid receptor blockade. *Neuropsychopharmacology, 26*, 106–114.

Watson, D., & Pennebaker, J.W. (1989). Health complaints, stress, and distress: Exploring the central role of negative affectivity. *Psychological Review, 96*, 234–254.

Watson, D. (2000). *Mood and temperament*. New York: Guilford Press.

Weinstein, N.D., & Klein, W.M. (1995). Resistance of personal risk perceptions to debiasing interventions. *Health Psychology, 14*, 132–140.

Weinstein, N.D. (1982). Unrealistic optimism about susceptibility to health problems. *Journal of Behavioral Medicine, 5*, 441–460.

Weiss, A., & Costa, P.T. (2005). Domain and facet personality predictors of all-cause mortality among Medicare patients aged 65 to 100. *Psychosomatic Medicine, 67*, 724–733.

Weiss, A., Costa, P.T., Karuza, J., Duberstein, P.R., & Friedman, B. (2004, March). *Personality as predictors of cardiovascular disease and mortality in patients aged 65–100*. Presented at the 62nd annual meeting of the American Psychosomatic Society, Orlando, FL.

Whalley, L.J., & Deary, I.J. (2001). Longitudinal cohort study of childhood IQ and survival up to age 76. *British Medical Journal, 322*(7290), 819–829.

Williams, R. (1994). *Anger Kills*. New York: Harper Collins.

Williams, R.B., Kuhn, C.M., Helms, M.J., Siegler, I.C., Barefoot, J.C., Ashley-Kocy, A., et al. (2004, March). *Central nervous system (CNS) serotonin function and NEO-PI personality profiles*. Presented at the 62nd annual meeting of the American Psychosomatic Society, Orlando, FL.

Wilson, R.S., Bienias, J.L., de Leon, C.F.M., Evans, D.A., & Bennett, D.A. (2003). Negative affect and mortality in older persons. *American Journal of Epidemiology, 158*, 827–835.

Wilson, R.S., Mendes de Leon, C.F., Bienias, J.L., Evans, D.A., & Bennett, D.A. (2004). Personality and mortality in old age. *Journal of Gerontology B: Psychological Sciences and Social Science, 59*, 110–116.

Witzig, M.E., Kamarck, T.W., Muldoon, M.F., & Sutton-Tyrrell, K. (2003). Examining the relationship between conscientiousness and atherosclerosis: The Pittsburgh healthy heart project. Presented at the 61st annual meeting of the American Psychosomatic Society Phoenix, Arizona.

Woodward, J.L. (1998). Dementia. In H.S. Friedman (Editor-in-chief), *Encyclopedia of Mental Health*, Vol. 1 (pp. 693–713). San Diego: Academic Press.

Wortman, C.B., & Boerner, K. (2011). Beyond the myths of coping with loss: Prevailing assumptions versus scientific evidence. In H.S. Friedman (Ed.), *The Oxford handbook of health psychology*. New York: Oxford University Press.

Zuckerman, M., & Kuhlman, D.M. (2000). Personality and risk-taking: Common biosical factors. *Journal of Personality, 68*(6), 999–1029.

# Adjustment to Chronic Disease: Progress and Promise in Research

Annette L. Stanton *and* Tracey A. Revenson

**Abstract**

Chronic illnesses carry important psychological and social consequences that demand significant psychological adjustment. The literature is providing increasingly nuanced conceptualizations of adjustment, demonstrating that the experience of chronic disease necessitates adaptation in multiple life domains. Heterogeneity in adjustment is apparent between individuals and across the course of the disease trajectory. Focusing primarily on cancer and rheumatic diseases, we review longitudinal investigations of proximal (personality attributes, cognitive appraisals, coping processes, interpersonal relationships) and distal (socioeconomic variables, culture/ethnicity, gender-related processes) risk and protective factors for adjustment across the illness trajectory. We conclude that the past decade has seen a surge in research that is longitudinal in design, involves adequately characterized samples of sufficient size, and includes statistical control for initial values on dependent variables. A progressively convincing characterization of risk and protective factors for favorable adjustment to chronic illness has emerged. We identify important issues for future application and research.

**Keywords:** Coping, adjustment, adaptation, social support, personality, chronic disease, cancer, arthritis, clinical intervention, biopsychosocial model

In 1961, a seminal, observational study of adjustment to chronic disease appeared in the *Archives of General Psychiatry* (Visotsky, Hamburg, Goss, & Lebovits, 1961). Its authors posed questions regarding adjustment to polio that continue to stimulate research on chronic disease today: "How is it possible to deal with such powerful, pervasive, and enduring stresses as are involved in severe polio? What are the types of coping behavior that contribute to favorable outcomes?" (p. 28). Fifty years later, theoretical and empirical consideration of these questions has produced multifaceted conceptualizations of adjustment to chronic disease, theoretical frameworks for understanding determinants of adjustment, and empirical evidence regarding factors that contribute to untoward or favorable outcomes. In this chapter, we begin with a brief discussion of the prevalence and impact of chronic disease and then consider what is meant by adjustment to chronic disease. We go on to discuss themes in theories of contributors to adjustment. Finally, we address implications for intervention and future research.

The knowledge base on adjustment to major chronic diseases (e.g., cancer, cardiovascular disease, diabetes, arthritis) is large and growing. In this chapter, we attempt to offer cross-cutting observations that have emerged from our analysis of relevant theory and research. Although we draw broadly from the literature on adjustment to various chronic diseases, the reader will notice an emphasis on those diseases closer to our own areas of expertise (i.e., cancer and rheumatic disease). We focus on psychosocial processes as they influence adjustment to chronic disease, rather than as causal factors in chronic disease, although we provide references to this burgeoning literature where relevant. Further, we do not address the important areas of adjustment to chronic disease in childhood (e.g., Roberts & Steele, 2009) or caregiver adjustment

(Martire & Schulz, in press; Vitaliano, Zhang, & Scanlan, 2003).

## Definition and Impact of Chronic Disease

The Centers for Disease Control and Prevention (CDC) define *chronic diseases* as "noncommunicable illnesses that are prolonged in duration, do not resolve spontaneously, and are rarely cured completely" (Centers for Disease Prevention [CDC], 2009). According to this definition, approximately 133 million Americans live with chronic diseases, which account for 70% of all deaths and more than 75% of medical care costs in the United States (CDC, 2009). Chronic diseases do not affect all groups equally; in 2006, age-adjusted mortality for black Americans exceeded that of whites for major chronic diseases (heart disease, cancer, stroke) by a magnitude of 22%–46% (National Center for Health Statistics, 2009).

In addition to shortening survival, chronic diseases are the leading cause of disability, which leads to economic, social, and psychological declines. Approximately 25% of adults with chronic illness experience significant limitations of daily activities (CDC, 2009). Arthritis, the most common cause of disability in the United States, limits activity for 19 million adults (CDC, 2009).

The global burden of chronic disease also is striking, with noncommunicable chronic diseases accounting for 60% of deaths worldwide, a figure that is double the mortality that results from combined infectious conditions (human immunodeficiency virus/acquired immune deficiency syndrome [HIV/AIDS], tuberculosis, malaria), maternal and perinatal conditions, and nutritional deficiencies (Daar et al., 2007). The number of people living with one or more chronic conditions is projected to increase in the next decades, particularly in the developing world (Daar et al., 2007). Many infectious diseases have been eradicated. Increases in both life expectancy and the proportion of older people are accompanied by an increased prevalence of chronic disease. Thanks to medical advances, many diseases that were formerly considered to be acute and/or rapidly terminal—including AIDS and some types of cancer—are now being redefined as chronic.

Chronic diseases vary along several dimensions, and even individual chronic diseases reveal a good deal of heterogeneity. No standard exists for defining what is meant by *chronic*. From a psychological perspective, the definition of chronic disease is complex: When does one stop being a cancer patient? Is it when one is informed by the medical team that no detectable cancer is present? When treatment is complete or symptoms subside? When one celebrates the 5-year anniversary after diagnosis? The meaning of chronicity, as with so many other aspects of disease, lies in the eye of the beholder, although researchers probably would concur that the disease process must persist over at least several months to constitute *chronic* disease.

Rapidity of onset, degree of ambiguity in symptom presentation, level of life threat, prominence of pain, disease course (e.g., progressive vs. relapse-remitting), degree of daily life disruption from symptoms and treatment, and treatment effectiveness represent other dimensions that demonstrate variability across and within chronic diseases. Although some of the consequences of chronic disease are sudden and obvious, such as the surgical excision of a body part, others are gradual and insidious, such as the loss of muscle strength (Thompson & Kyle, 2000). Compromised performance of roles and daily activity, progressive fatigue, and changes in interpersonal relations can proceed subtly and follow an uneven course. It is with acknowledgment of this great variation in what constitutes *chronic disease* that we attempt to present some generalizations culled from our analysis of the literature on adjustment to chronic disease. In attempting to address questions regarding what constitutes "optimal" adjustment to chronic disease, however, it is clear to us from the outset that there is no such thing as "one size fits all."

## What Does It Mean to Adjust to Chronic Disease?

Prior to considering determinants of adjustment to chronic disease, we must define what it means to adjust. The words *adjustment* and *adaptation* often are used interchangeably in the literature, and will be in this chapter as well. Analysis of the literature leads us to the conclusions that (a) chronic disease necessitates adjustment in multiple life domains; (b) both positive and negative indicators of adjustment are relevant; (c) adjustment is not static, but rather represents a process that unfolds over time; (d) adjustment cannot be understood adequately without reference to contextual factors; and (e) heterogeneity in adjustment is the rule rather than the exception.

### Adjustment Is Multifaceted

Studies such as that of Visotsky and colleagues (1961) marked an early attempt to broaden conceptualization of adjustment to chronic disease from a sole focus on (the absence of) psychopathology and toward multifaceted conceptualizations. At least five related conceptualizations of adjustment to chronic disease appear consistently in the literature (Hoyt & Stanton, in press): mastery of the adaptive tasks of disease, maintenance of adequate functional status and social roles, absence of diagnosable psychological disorder, reports of relatively low negative affect, and perceived quality of life in various domains.

Reviewing observational studies of adjustment to major life transitions, including serious disease, Hamburg and Adams (1967) suggested several central adaptive tasks: keeping distress within manageable limits, maintaining a sense of personal worth, restoring relations with significant other people, enhancing prospects for recovery of bodily functions, and increasing the likelihood of attaining a personally valued and socially acceptable situation once maximum physical recovery has been accomplished. Taylor's (1983) theory of cognitive adaptation to threatening events, which used adjustment to breast cancer as its exemplar, also emphasized self-esteem enhancement and preservation of a sense of mastery, and added resolution of a search for meaning as a central adaptive task. Moos and Schaefer (1984) added the disease-related tasks of managing pain and symptoms, negotiating the medical treatment environment, and maintaining adequate relationships with health care professionals.

A related conceptualization of adjustment focuses on functional status as the central indicator (e.g., Spelten, Sprangers, & Verbeek, 2002). Operationalizations of functional status include resumption of paid employment or routine activities, mobility, and adherence to a prescribed physical rehabilitation protocol or other medical regimen. The presence or absence of psychological disorder, whether assessed via diagnostic interview or suggested by self-report questionnaire, often is used as a marker of adjustment (e.g., Fann et al., 2008; Müller-Tasch et al., 2008). Other researchers examine reports of negative or positive affect. In a review on coping with rheumatoid arthritis (RA; Zautra & Manne, 1992), most studies relied on the absence of negative affect to indicate adjustment. Reports of life quality in various domains also denote adjustment to chronic disease. In this regard, researchers often examine health-related quality of life in physical, functional, social, sexual, and emotional domains (e.g., Cella, 2001; Eton & Lepore, 2001; Fitzpatrick, 2004; Majerovitz & Revenson, 1994).

These conceptualizations of adjustment to chronic disease reveal that adjustment is multidimensional, including intrapersonal and interpersonal domains, with cognitive, emotional, physical, and behavioral components. Further, domains of adjustment are interrelated. For example, depressive symptoms contribute to functional status (e.g., poor glycemic control) in people with diabetes (Lustman & Clouse, 2005), and restriction of daily activities accounts for significant variance in depressive symptoms in breast cancer patients (Williamson, 2000) and arthritis patients (DeVellis, Revenson, & Blalock, 1997). Negative emotions can intensify morbidity in chronic conditions such as cardiovascular disease, osteoporosis, and cancer (for a review, see Kiecolt-Glaser, McGuire, Robles, & Glaser, 2002).

## Adjustment Involves Both Positive and Negative Outcome Dimensions

It is understandable that researchers primarily have studied psychological disorder and negative affect in individuals who confront chronic disease. The growth of American clinical psychology in the latter half of the 20th century emphasized pathological processes and an individually based approach (Sarason, 1989). Moreover, identifying the prevalence of and contributors to maladjustment is important for the development of effective interventions. A relative lack of attention to positive psychosocial and behavioral processes has persisted until recent years, despite early observations that "many patients are remarkably resourceful even in the face of a catastrophic situation" (Hamburg & Adams, 1967, p. 278).

A number of good reasons exist for evaluating positive indicators of adjustment. First, positive adjustment may more accurately represent the experience of most individuals with chronic disease than does psychopathology. Studies of long-term cancer survivors suggest that the greatest degree of distress and disruption occurs within the first year after diagnosis, which corresponds to the initial treatment phase, with adjustment indicators improving after that (Dorval, Maunsell, Deschenes, Brisson, & Masse, 1998; Tomich & Helgeson, 2002). In addition, many individuals extract benefit from the experience of chronic illness (see Park, Lechner, Antoni, & Stanton, 2009). For example, women report more positive change associated with their experience of breast cancer, particularly in life appreciation, relations with others, and spiritual change, than do age- and education-matched healthy comparison women reporting on changes experienced during the same time period (Cordova, Cunningham, Carlson, & Andrykowski, 2001). In a study of married couples in which one partner had rheumatic disease (Revenson, 2003), even the most psychologically distressed couples reported high levels of personal growth because of the disease. Similarly, large percentages of people with RA (Danoff-Burg & Revenson, 2005), lupus (Katz, Flasher, Cacciapaglia, & Nelson, 2001), HIV/AIDS (Siegel & Schrimshaw, 2000), and heart disease (Affleck, Tennen, Croog, & Levine, 1987) report illness-related benefits. Although questions remain regarding the conceptualization, operationalization, and correlates of reports of stressor-related positive change (see Tedeschi & Calhoun, 2004 for target article and commentaries; Tennen & Affleck, 2009), many people with chronic disease appear able to thrive. In addition, positive affect experienced during chronic illness may influence health outcomes (e.g., Moskowitz, 2003).

Second, positive adjustment is not simply the absence of psychopathology—a disease that provokes distress in some realms will not necessarily preclude the experience of life's joys. For example, HIV-positive and HIV-negative caregivers of men with AIDS evidenced the combined presence of high depressive symptoms and positive morale (Folkman, Moskowitz, Ozer, & Park, 1997). Zautra, Smith, Affleck, and Tennen (2001) found that the presence of positive affect reduced the magnitude of the relationship between pain and negative affect among fibromyalgia and arthritis patients. Although positive and negative affect may become less differentiated under stressful conditions (e.g., Zautra et al., 2001), focusing solely on psychopathology will result in a limited understanding of adjustment.

Third, positive and negative indicators of adjustment may have different determinants. Distinct coping strategies are related to positive and negative indicators of adjustment (e.g., Echteld, van Elderen, & van der Kamp, 2003; Felton & Revenson, 1984; Stanton, Tennen, Affleck, & Mendola, 1992). Understanding the environmental, interpersonal, and intrapsychic dynamics of individuals who remain resilient or adjust well to chronic disease may enhance our ability to specify protective factors, which in turn will promote intervention development.

Finally, the social construction of chronic disease as guaranteeing clinical depression or unremitting suffering may carry negative consequences. This stereotype may provoke inordinate fear or despair in those who face serious disease and may even discourage some individuals from seeking life-saving medical treatments. It also may result in stigmatization of the chronically ill by the layperson, the withholding of support by friends and family, or the overprescription of psychological intervention or psychoactive medications by health care professionals.

Of course, unbalanced attention to positive adjustment has a downside. Social construction of the unfailingly "strong" patient allows the chronically ill little room for having a bad day (or a bad year). Worse is the possibility that presenting a positive face becomes so prescriptive that one falls prey to the notion that any distress or negative thinking contributes to physical disease. Holland and Lewis (2000) referred to the "tyranny of positive thinking" (p. 14) in cautioning against such a prescription.

### Adjustment Is a Dynamic Process

Although psychologists tend to use language suggesting that adjustment is a static outcome ("Women who were well-adjusted . . ." or "These factors lead to poor adjustment . . ."), we are of the view that adjustment to chronic disease is a dynamic process. As treatment demands, life threat, disability, and prognosis change over time, so do the adaptive tasks of illness. Although stage theories of adaptation to disease or traumatic events have been proposed, there is little evidence supporting such stage models (Wortman & Boerner, 2011, Chapter 19, this volume). Owing to changing contextual factors, adaptation is neither linear nor lock-step. Medical advances, such as the development of potent antiretroviral therapies for AIDS; twists and turns in disease progression, such as an arthritis flare or cancer recurrence; and changes in the individual's life context, such as taking on new family or work roles, create more circuitous pathways.

A breast cancer diagnosis provides a vivid illustration of how adaptation must be seen as a dynamic process. Upon being informed that a breast lump is malignant, women are faced with making medical decisions, informing family members, setting aside, at least temporarily, other demands in one's life (e.g., work), and acknowledging the threat that the diagnosis places on survival. During the postoperative phase, patients are faced with new treatment decisions, and then may undergo noxious side effects of treatment. During treatment and in the reentry period following treatment, patients are working to maintain relationships, resume or reconfigure work and family roles, and grapple with the long-term meaning of the disease. Women also may be faced with an altered self-concept, late effects of medical treatments, repeated or novel treatments, fear of disease recurrence, and, in some cases, actual disease recurrence.

Disease progression also colors the adaptational process. Initial severity and prognosis of the disease, how fast or slow the disease worsens, and whether there are symptomatic and asymptomatic periods (and how long they last) all shape adjustment. For example, a slower disease process may allow gradual adaptation, as people cope with their disease in smaller bites and anticipatory coping efforts are enacted. A disease course marked with frequent transitions from relative health to illness or ability to disability—sometimes without warning—may prove a harder road to follow. For example, the nature of RA involves a long time horizon, with periods of relative severity of joint pain, swelling, and stiffness alternating with periods of relative comfort. Medications may be effective for some time and then stop working, necessitating adjustment to a new medical regimen. Interactions with health care providers also change, as patients move from crisis phases to more stable, long-term phases of medical care (Newman, Fitzpatrick, Revenson, Skevington, & Williams, 1996, Chapter 6). Moreover, interactions with intimate others can involve alternating periods of relative independence and dependence in functional and emotional realms.

### Adjustment Is Embedded in Context
Adjustment to chronic disease can best be understood in conjunction with the life context in which disease occurs and the coping tasks it poses (Revenson, 1990, 2003). Sociocultural characteristics such as gender, age, and social class shape culturally acceptable modes of coping and adjustment and, at the same time, place boundaries around coping resources. For example, in a multiethnic sample of women treated for early-stage breast cancer, women's strongest concerns included cancer recurrence, pain, death, harm from adjuvant treatment, and financial issues (Spencer et al., 1999). However, concerns varied as a function of patient characteristics, such that younger women had more prominent sexual and partner-related concerns than older women, and Hispanic women reported a greater degree of concern in almost all areas than African American or non-Hispanic white women.

Moreover, these contextual factors are often interdependent. Chronic disease and functional disability are more prevalent in old age, and women live longer than men; therefore, women are likely to be living with at least one chronic condition for some part of their life. It also is important to consider whether the disease is occurring "on-time" or "off-time" in the normative life cycle (Neugarten, 1979). "Off-time" onset, such as being diagnosed with Parkinson disease in one's 30s, is likely to be more stressful than when the disease occurs "on-time." One is not prepared for the life transitions or bodily changes that disease brings—there is no period of anticipatory coping. And, relatively few age peers are simultaneously experiencing the same life situation, so there are fewer individuals with whom to share concerns.

### Heterogeneity in Adjustment Is the Rule
Prospective research convincingly demonstrates that chronic disease confers risk for distress and life disruption. For example, Polsky and colleagues (2005) examined five biennial waves of the Health and Retirement Study in more than 8,000 adults aged 51–61 without significant depressive symptoms at study onset. Within 2 years after an initial diagnosis of cancer, diagnosed individuals had the highest risk of significant depressive symptoms (hazard ratio = 3.55 vs. no incident disease), which decreased over the next 6 years. Risk of onset of depressive symptoms also increased significantly within the first 2 years of a diagnosis of heart disease or chronic lung disease (but not hypertension, arthritis, diabetes, or stroke), and higher risk persisted over the next 6 years for those with heart disease. Those diagnosed with arthritis had increased risk for depressive symptoms 2–4 years after diagnosis.

Chronic disease does not invariably compromise psychological and functional status, however. Research on trajectories of adjustment over time in individuals with chronic disease demonstrates wide individual variability (Dew et al., 2005; Helgeson, Snyder, & Seltman, 2004). In a large cross-sectional study, Stewart and colleagues (1989) assessed 9,385 adults at medical office visits in three U.S. cities. Fifty-four percent had at least one of nine conditions (i.e., hypertension, myocardial infarction, congestive heart failure, arthritis, diabetes, angina, chronic lung problems, back problems, gastrointestinal complaints). Compared with those with no chronic disease, chronic disease patients (except hypertension) reported lower functioning in physical, social, mental health, health perceptions, pain, and role-related domains. Mental health was the domain least affected by chronic condition, however, and chronic condition presence explained only a minority of variance in functioning and well-being.

Research examining clinical levels of psychological dysfunction in groups with chronic disease suggests that a subgroup manifests such disorders, although rates vary widely across studies. Reviewing research with validated instruments that assessed psychological sequelae of cancer, van't Spijker,

Trijsburg, and Duivenvoorden (1997) reported that 0%–46% of patients qualified for depressive disorder and 0.9%–49% for anxiety disorder across studies. For patients with advanced cancer, the median point prevalence of depression ranged from 22% to 29% (Hotopf, Chidgey, Addington-Hall, & Ly, 2002) and was significantly higher than that of the general population. The prevalence of depression, however, varies as a function of many contextual factors, including how it is measured, cancer type, and gender (Massie, 2004).

In a review of the literature on end-stage renal disease (Christensen & Ehlers, 2002), 12%–40% of patients meet criteria for depressive disorder, rates that varied as a function of assessment methods and diagnostic criteria used. A meta-analysis demonstrated that 19% of individuals with heart failure experience depression as determined by diagnostic interview and 33.6% as assessed via self-report questionnaire (Rutledge, Reis, Linke, Greenberg, & Mills, 2006). In a meta-analysis of 12 studies comparing individuals with RA and healthy controls on measures of depression, Dickens, McGowan, Clark-Carter, and Creed (2002) reported a greater rate of depressive symptoms in the group with RA, although effect sizes were heterogeneous across studies ($r = .07–.43$). In a meta-analytic review of 42 studies of depression in adults with type 1 or type 2 diabetes (Anderson, Clouse, Freedland, & Lustman, 2001), prevalence estimates ranged from 0% to 60.7%. Rates varied as a function of a number of factors, such that depression was more prevalent in diabetic women than men, uncontrolled than controlled studies, clinical than community samples, and when assessed by self-report questionnaires versus standardized diagnostic interviews.

Rather than potentiating global psychological dysfunction, chronic disease is likely to carry more circumscribed impact for most people. Andersen and colleagues (e.g., Andersen, Anderson, & deProsse, 1989a, 1989b) observed that cancer is more likely to produce "islands" of life disruption in particular life realms and at specific points in the disease trajectory than to confer substantial risk for global maladjustment. For example, common sources of distress for breast cancer patients are fears of recurrence, including future treatment (Vickberg, 2003) and a more general sense of vulnerability (Bower, Meyerowitz, Bernaards, Rowland, & Ganz, 2005). Persons with diabetes often worry about long-term complications and report anxiety/guilt when problems in self-management occur (Polonsky et al., 1995). Any specific disease represents multiple potential stressors or adaptive tasks, which are differentially relevant to individuals in particular life contexts and at different times in the disease's life cycle. Thus, theoretical frameworks that specify risk and protective factors for (mal)adjustment should acknowledge the marked variability in adjustment to chronic disease across persons, time, and settings and should aid in accounting for this variation. Specification of such contributors will allow targeting for intervention individuals and groups with particular characteristics or experiencing particular contexts.

## Determinants of Adjustment to Chronic Disease

Over the past quarter century, general psychological theories of stress and coping, self-regulation, personality, and social processes have formed the foundation for understanding adjustment to chronic disease. Rather than describing discrete theories, we adopt the approach of specifying constructs that emerge *across* theories as important determinants of adjustment. We focus on personality orientations, cognitive appraisals, coping processes, and interpersonal support as more proximal determinants of adjustment and on socioeconomic variables, culture, ethnicity, and gender roles as more macro-level determinants of adjustment.

### *Dispositional Factors*

Dispositional variables are likely to have both a direct influence on adjustment to chronic disease and an indirect effect, mediated through appraisals and coping processes. Optimism (Scheier & Carver, 1985), a generalized expectancy for positive outcomes, serves as an example in this regard. In a study of ischemic heart disease patients, optimism assessed 1 month after hospital discharge predicted lower depressive symptoms 1 year later, controlling for depressive symptoms and other variables at study entry (Shnek, Irvine, Stewart, & Abbey, 2001). Assessed prior to coronary artery bypass graft surgery, optimism predicted faster in-hospital recovery and return to normal life activities 6 and 12 months later (Scheier et al., 1989, 2003). Controlling for prior distress, optimism predicted lower distress in women with breast cancer over the year after surgery (Carver et al., 1993; cf. Stanton & Snider, 1993). Optimism also was related to lower distress in HIV-positive and HIV-negative men (Lutgendorf, Antoni, Schneiderman, Ironson, & Fletcher, 1995). Thus, holding a generalized expectancy for favorable outcomes constitutes a protective factor for individuals adjusting to chronic disease and may be accompanied by physical health benefits (e.g., Rasmussen, Scheier, & Greenhouse, 2009; Tindle et al., 2009). Optimism appears to work through promoting the use of approach-oriented coping strategies and social support and reducing threat appraisals and avoidance-oriented coping (Brissette, Scheier, & Carver, 2002; Scheier et al., 2003; Schou, Ekeberg, & Ruland, 2005; Trunzo & Pinto, 2003).

Dispositional factors also can interact with other variables to influence adjustment. For example, interpersonal stress predicted increases in negative affect and disease activity only for those arthritis patients who had excessive dispositional sensitivity to others' feelings and behavior (Smith & Zautra, 2002). Coping through expressing emotions regarding breast cancer predicted a decline in distress and fewer medical appointments for cancer-related morbidities for women high in hope, a construct reflecting a sense of goal-directed determination and ability to generate plans to achieve goals (Stanton et al., 2000).

Dispositional factors can be assessed in the earliest phases of diagnosis to identify those who might be at risk for unfavorable adjustment. Understanding the mechanisms through which dispositional variables contribute to adjustment will enable researchers to target mediating mechanisms for intervention. Whether psychosocial interventions will promote changes of sufficient magnitude and endurance to affect health and well-being for individuals with longstanding dispositional risk (e.g., Antoni et al., 2001; Zautra et al., 2008) requires further study.

## Cognitive Appraisal Processes

Although they differ in the specific cognitive processes that receive emphasis, theories of adjustment to chronic disease converge to suggest that how individuals view their disease is a central determinant of subsequent actions, emotions, and adjustment. A man who believes that his diagnosis of heart disease is a death sentence is likely to make very different decisions regarding treatment than one who sees his disease as curable, and the two men are likely to manifest distinct adjustment trajectories. In his stress and coping paradigm that underlies much of the literature on adjustment to disease, Richard Lazarus (Lazarus, 1981; Lazarus & Folkman, 1984) assigned central importance to cognitive appraisals in determining coping processes and adjustment. Two sets of appraisal processes are crucial: primary appraisal, which involves assessment of the degree and nature of threat (i.e., potential for harm) and challenge (i.e., potential for benefit), and secondary appraisal, in which the individual evaluates the situation's changeability or controllability and available coping resources. Cognitive variables that have received considerable theoretical and empirical attention as determinants of disease-related adjustment include perceived threats to health and life goals, disease-related expectancies, and finding meaning in the disease experience. Because these have been the central constructs in the past 20 years of research, each will be reviewed briefly.

### PERCEIVED THREATS TO LIFE GOALS

Many theorists have emphasized cognitive appraisals of disease with regard to consequences for life goals. In 1991, Lazarus revised his conceptualization of primary appraisal to include goal relevance, goal congruence, and type of ego involvement. The self-regulation theory of Carver and Scheier (e.g., 1998), applied to chronic disease (Scheier & Bridges, 1995, pp. 261–262), posits that "illness represents one general and significant class of events that can interfere with the pursuit of life's activities and goals, both those that are health related and those that are not. . . . [Illness] can interfere, to a greater or lesser extent, with the general set of plans and activities that give a person's life its form and meaning." To the extent that one perceives chronic disease as blocking cherished life goals, psychological distress is likely. For example, primary appraisals of threat and harm/loss were important predictors of subsequent anxiety and depression in male cardiac patients (Waltz, Badura, Pfaff, & Schott, 1988). In a daily process study (Affleck et al., 2001), goal barriers perceived by fibromyalgia patients were associated with pain and fatigue across time; moreover, dispositional optimism affected the relations among goal processes, fatigue, and pain. In a study of Latinas with arthritis, Abraído-Lanza (1997; Abraído-Lanza & Revenson, 2006) found that inability to perform valued roles (including housewife/homemaker) as a result of the disease was associated with worse mental health (also see Neugebauer, Katz, & Pasch, 2003). Lepore and Eton (2000) found that men with prostate cancer who accommodated to their illness by changing significant life goals were less negatively affected by physical dysfunction than were men who did not make such accommodations.

The self-regulation theory of Leventhal and colleagues (e.g., Leventhal, Leventhal, & Cameron, 2001) also points to the centrality of appraisals and threats to the self-system with regard to disease cause, identity, timeline, controllability, and consequences. For example, individuals who view their cancer as chronic or cyclic report more distress than those who perceive it as an acute disease, controlling for disease stage (Rabin, Leventhal, & Goodin, 2004).

## DISEASE-RELATED EXPECTANCIES

Expectancies regarding the controllability of chronic disease and its consequences are an important cognitive contributor to adjustment (e.g., Lazarus & Folkman, 1984; Thompson & Kyle, 2000). Chronic disease can undermine perceptions of control in several realms, including control of bodily integrity and functioning, daily schedules, performance in valued roles, and life itself. A hallmark of chronic disease is that individuals' active participation in medical treatments and lifestyle modifications cannot ensure control over its course and outcome. Most individuals are likely to discover controllable aspects of their experience, perceiving greater control over disease consequences (e.g., symptoms, daily management) than over disease outcome (e.g., Affleck, Tennen, Pfeiffer, & Fifield, 1987, on RA; Thompson, Nanni, & Levine, 1994, on AIDS; Thompson, Sobolew-Shubin, Galbraith, Schwankovsky, & Cruzen, 1993, on cancer).

Reviewing research on control perceptions in people with chronic disease, Thompson and Kyle (2000) reported nearly uniform findings that greater general and disease-specific perceived control is associated with favorable psychosocial outcomes and suggestive evidence that physical parameters also are affected. A sense of control predicted less angina in patients following coronary artery bypass grafts (Fitzgerald, Tennen, Affleck, & Pransky, 1993) and better functional status for osteoarthritis surgery patients (Orbell, Jonston, Rowley, Espley, & Davey, 1998). Recent longitudinal research also documents the benefits of perceived control (e.g., Bárez, Blasco, Fernández-Castro, & Viladrich, 2009; Barry, Kasl, Lictman, Vaccarino, & Krumholz, 2006). Control appraisals also influence the choice of coping strategies, in that higher perceived control is associated with the use of more approach-oriented coping (e.g., Felton, Revenson, & Hinrichsen, 1984; Folkman, Chesney, Pollack, & Coates, 1993).

Thompson and Kyle (2000) suggested that having control over aspects of the disease is useful only to the extent that one desires such control. They also concluded that expectancies for control did not need to match realistic opportunities for control to be useful, although others have suggested that the adaptive potential of control appraisals may depend on whether the threat is responsive to control attempts (Christensen & Ehlers, 2002; Helgeson, 1992).

For example, Thompson and colleagues (1993) found that cancer patients' belief that they could control daily emotional and physical symptoms was a stronger predictor of adjustment than was perceived control over disease progression. Affleck and colleagues (1987) found that individuals with severe rheumatic disease who perceived more control over *symptoms* reported less mood disturbance, whereas those who perceived more control over *disease course* had greater mood disturbance. Similarly, Schiaffino and Revenson (1992) showed that perceived control over symptoms—an aspect of RA that is controllable—as opposed to perceived control over disease course was instrumental in generating better adjustment. Disease course can condition the influence of control appraisals; higher perceived control over breast cancer predicted a decline in mental and physical health for women who experienced disease recurrence, whereas women who remained disease free benefitted from high control appraisals (Tomich & Helgeson, 2006).

Individuals' expectancies regarding their disease-related responses, efficacy, and disease outcomes also contribute to adjustment. For example, self-efficacy expectancies predict symptom management and adjustment in individuals with arthritis and other chronic conditions (DeVellis & DeVellis, 2001; Keefe, Smith, et al., 2002; Schiaffino, Revenson, & Gibofsky, 1991). In a study of breast cancer patients, Montgomery and Bovbjerg (2001) found that response expectancies regarding nausea predicted anticipatory nausea prior to the third chemotherapy infusion, even after controlling for severity of prior post-treatment nausea and prior anticipatory nausea. Several types of disease-related expectancies (e.g., response, control, and outcome expectancies) can affect adaptive outcomes, and their relative predictive power in specific contexts requires continued scrutiny (Carver et al., 2000; Tennen & Affleck, 2000).

## FINDING MEANING

What does it mean to "find meaning" in chronic disease (Calhoun & Tedeschi, 2006; Park et al., 2009)? Janoff-Bulman and Frantz (1997) wrote of two different forms of meaning sought by individuals in the aftermath of trauma, which may apply to the context of chronic illness. First, meaning as comprehensibility represents an attempt to determine whether and how an event makes sense and often involves causal attribution processes. In her cognitive adaptation theory, Taylor (1983) focused on the search for meaning as an individual's attempts to address the question, "Why me?" Taylor found that more than 90% of a breast cancer sample advanced some causal attribution for the cancer. The specific content of the attribution was not important for psychological adjustment, but simply making some attribution for the cancer was related to adjustment. In a review addressing the experience of threatening events in general, including chronic disease, Tennen and Affleck (1990) reported a consistent relationship between the specific external attribution of blaming others for an event and poorer well-being.

According to Janoff-Bulman and Frantz (1997), a second form of finding meaning involves meaning as significance, which reflects the value of the experience to the individual. The two forms of finding meaning are linked in that the search for comprehensibility often prompts a newfound awareness of personal vulnerability and randomness, which in turn paves the way for an attempt to create meaning in life "by generating significance through appraisals of value and worth" (Janoff-Bulman & Berger, 2000, p. 33). If the diagnosis of chronic disease is sufficiently disruptive to core beliefs (i.e., meaningfulness of the world, self-worthiness), it should prompt such a search for meaning and concomitant greater awareness of and attention to living. Commenting on this enhanced awareness, a participant in the first author's research lamented that she was beginning to lose "the edge." She went on to explain that, 2 years after her breast cancer diagnosis, she found herself living more on "automatic pilot," losing the sense of immediacy and appreciation for the present moment that her cancer diagnosis had catalyzed.

Janoff-Bulman and Berger (2000) argued that if the reality of death is prompted by the trauma, then a greater appreciation for what it means to be alive can ensue: "That which we may lose suddenly is perceived as valuable" (p. 35). If benevolence and self-worth are questioned, then others' reactions can assume special significance and, depending on their content, can promote greater appreciation for intimate relationships. Self-appreciation also can increase as individuals discover their own competencies in overcoming adversity. Thus, the search for meaning as significance can lead one to find benefits in the chronic disease experience, perhaps particularly to the extent that the disease is perceived as life-threatening.

The contention that highly threatening experiences can prompt finding benefit has received empirical support. A review of 29 independent, quantitative studies of cancer patients, and seven additional substudies based on those samples, demonstrated that more life disruption and perceived threat were associated with more perceived growth from the experience of cancer (Stanton, Bower, & Low, 2006; also see Helgeson, Reynolds, & Tomich, 2006, for a meta-analysis of cross-sectional studies across a variety of stressors). Intentional engagement with the experience of cancer, as evidenced through dispositional approach tendencies and approach-oriented coping strategies such as problem-focused coping, active acceptance of the cancer diagnosis, and intentional positive reappraisal, also was related to more perceived benefit.

Does finding benefit in chronic illness affect psychological or physical health? Notable positive findings exist: finding positive meaning in the cancer experience at 1–5 years after diagnosis predicted an increase in positive affect 5 years later in a sample of 763 breast cancer patients (Bower et al., 2005), finding benefit in the year after surgery predicted lower distress and depressive symptoms 4–7 years later in another sample of women diagnosed with breast cancer (Carver & Antoni, 2004), and finding positive meaning in the loss of a close other to AIDS predicted a less rapid decline in CD4 T cells and lower mortality in HIV-positive men over a 2- to 3-year follow-up (Bower, Kemeny, Taylor, & Fahey, 1998). However, reviews of the literature (Algoe & Stanton, 2009; Helgeson et al., 2006; Stanton et al., 2006) reveal mixed findings for the relation between benefit finding and psychological adjustment (note that the relations of benefit finding with better physical health appear somewhat more consistent). The reviewers conclude that relations of finding benefit with adjustment are likely to be conditioned by individual differences in motivational functions of benefit finding, the timing of finding benefit relative to disease diagnosis and treatment, how benefit finding is assessed, and other factors. For example, reports of benefit might reflect motivations to approach the stressful experience actively or to deny the stressor's negative impact, with distinct consequences for adjustment (e.g., Stanton, Danoff-Burg, & Huggins, 2002).

### Coping Processes

It is difficult to imagine that the behaviors the individual initiates in response to the demands of chronic disease would not make a difference in that person's adjustment. Indeed, although limited by problems in conceptualization, measurement, and methodology (Coyne & Racioppo, 2000; Danoff-Burg,

Ayala, & Revenson, 2000; Somerfield & McCrae, 2000), findings from the large literature on coping processes as contributors to adjustment warrant a conclusion that coping matters (Taylor & Stanton, 2007).

Broadly, coping efforts may be directed toward relative approach toward or avoidance of the experience of chronic disease (e.g., Suls & Fletcher, 1985). This approach–avoidance continuum reflects a fundamental motivational construct in humans and other animals (Carver & Scheier, 1998; Davidson, Jackson, & Kalin, 2000; Fox, 1991) and thus maps easily onto broader theories of functioning. Examples of approach-oriented coping processes are information seeking, problem solving, seeking social support, actively attempting to identify benefits in one's experience, and creating outlets for emotional expression. Coping oriented toward avoidance involves both cognitive (e.g., denial, distraction, suppression) and behavioral strategies (e.g., behavioral disengagement). Other processes, such as spiritual coping, potentially can serve either approach-oriented or avoidance goals (e.g., Abraído-Lanza, Guier, & Revenson, 1996).

Because chronic disease is by definition a long-term stressor, both the types of coping strategies that are used and their utility are likely to vary over time and disease-related adaptive tasks. Although avoidant coping may be useful at specific, acute points of crisis, reviewers of the literature concur that avoidance typically is associated with maladjustment over time (e.g., Maes, Leventhal, & De Ridder, 1996). An example is a study of male cardiac patients (Levine et al., 1987), in which men who denied their disease spent fewer days in the coronary care unit and had fewer indications of cardiac dysfunction during hospitalization than nondeniers. However, deniers were less adherent to exercise training and had more days of rehospitalization in the year after discharge. As another example, breast cancer patients who were high on coping through cognitive avoidance prior to breast biopsy reported more distress at that point, after cancer diagnosis, and after surgery than did less avoidant women (Stanton & Snider, 1993; see also Carver et al., 1993). Similarly, a meta-analysis of 63 studies in HIV/AIDS (Moskowitz, Hult, Bussolari, & Acree, 2009; note that most studies were cross-sectional) revealed that avoidant coping strategies were associated with lower positive and higher negative affect, poorer health behaviors, and poorer physical health. Coping through avoidance may involve harmful behaviors (e.g., alcohol use), paradoxically prompt intrusion of disease-relevant thoughts and emotions (Wegner & Pennebaker, 1992), or impede other coping attempts.

Are active coping processes oriented toward approaching stressful aspects of chronic disease more useful than avoidant strategies? Although the findings are not as consistent as those for avoidant coping (Maes et al., 1996), evidence exists for the utility of approach-oriented strategies. For example, Young (1992) concluded from the literature on RA that "active, problem-focused coping attempts (e.g., information seeking, cognitive restructuring, pain control, and rational thinking) were consistently associated with positive affect, better psychological adjustment, and decreased depression" (p. 621; see also Keefe, Smith, et al., 2002). In the Moskowitz et al. meta-analysis (2009), approach-oriented coping attempts, and particularly coping through direct action and positive reappraisal, were associated with higher positive and lower negative affect, healthy behaviors, and better physical health in individuals living with HIV/AIDS (also see Duangdao & Roesch, 2008 on diabetes; Roesch et al., 2005, on prostate cancer). Momentary assessment research yields similar findings: among heart failure patients, a day that included efforts to improve symptoms was followed by a day of fewer illness symptoms, whereas a day that included trying to distract oneself from the illness was followed by a day with more symptoms, for example (Carels et al., 2004). The demonstrated efficacy of interventions that encourage the use of approach-oriented strategies, such as problem solving and cognitive or emotional processing, also suggests the utility of approach-oriented coping (e.g., Antoni et al., 2006; Smyth, Stone, Hurewitz, & Kaell, 1999). Of course, some approach-oriented strategies may not be particularly effective for immutable aspects of the disease. In addition, avoidance- and approach-oriented strategies may be differentially predictive of negative and positive outcomes (e.g., Blalock, DeVellis, & Giorgino, 1995; Echteld et al., 2003). Thus, the exclusion of positive adjustment indicators in many studies may obscure the potentially beneficial effects of approach-oriented coping processes.

It is unreasonable to expect that coping processes alone would determine adjustment to chronic disease. Rather, coping strategies are likely to mediate relations of personal and contextual attributes with adjustment and to interact with other factors in affecting adjustment. For example, the combination of high avoidance-oriented coping and low social support was identified as a risk factor for post-transplant psychological disturbance in adults awaiting bone marrow transplant for cancer (Jacobsen et al., 2002), and breast cancer patients who had high perceived personal control had low distress when they used active, problem-focused coping strategies (Osowiecki & Compas, 1999). Illustrating mediational effects, an unsupportive social context can prompt use of avoidance-oriented coping, which in turn predicts an increase in distress in women with breast cancer (Manne, Ostroff, Winkel, Grana, & Fox, 2005) and poorer adherence and higher viral load in HIV-positive individuals (Weaver et al., 2005). Holahan et al. (1997) found that a positive social context at study entry predicted greater relative use of approach-oriented coping by cardiac patients 4 years later, which in turn predicted a reduction in depressive symptoms. Rather than focusing solely on coping processes as contributors to adjustment, researchers testing more complex models (i.e., examining mediation and moderation) in longitudinal designs are producing stronger and more ecologically relevant findings.

### Social Resources and Interpersonal Support

Nearly four decades of research demonstrates that social support is a strong predictor of adjustment to chronic disease (Uchino, 2004; Wills & Ainette, in press). In particular, support from spouses or intimate partners is an important predictor of patients' adaptation (Revenson & DeLongis, 2011), including arthritis (e.g., Holtzman & DeLongis, 2007), cancer (e.g., Manne et al., 2004) and heart disease (Case, Moss, Case, McDermott, & Eberly, 1992).

Most of the adaptive tasks of chronic disease require help from others. Thus, patients need an available and satisfying network of interpersonal relations on which they can count for both emotional sustenance and practical help during periods of pain, disability, and uncertainty. Broadly defined, *social support* refers to the processes by which interpersonal relationships promote psychological well-being and protect people from health declines, particularly when they are facing stressful circumstances. Supportive behaviors involve demonstrations that one is loved, valued, and cared for, as well as provision of helpful information and tangible assistance.

An important distinction has been made between structural aspects of social ties and the functional resources that flow through existing ties (Berkman & Glass, 1999; Wills & Ainette, in press). Examples of structural measures are marital status, frequency of social activities, social network size, and network density (i.e., how many members know each other). In contrast, the functions of support include (1) expressing positive affect; (2) validating beliefs, emotions and actions; (3) encouraging communication of feelings; (4) providing information or advice; (5) providing material aid; and (6) reminding recipients that they are part of a meaningful social group. Although, in principle, functional measures of support should not be dependent on social network size, the networks and social activities of ill or disabled individuals often are restricted because of the disease. Both structural aspects of social ties and functional dimensions have been related to better health outcomes (e.g., Ertel, Glymour, & Berkman, 2008).

The psychological benefits of supportive relationships have been examined in many studies of persons with chronic disease. Compared with those reporting less support, patients receiving more support from friends and family exhibit greater emotional well-being, cope more effectively, perform fewer risky behaviors, and exhibit fewer depressive symptoms (see review by Wills & Ainette, in press). The positive relationship between social support and better psychosocial adjustment is robust across studies of populations with different disease durations, when different measures of support are used, and in both cross-sectional and longitudinal analyses. Moreover, social support contributes to psychosocial adjustment after controlling for prior levels of adjustment (i.e., social support helps explain *changes* in psychosocial adjustment).

Most studies of the effects of support on adjustment to disease are cross-sectional; thus, whether support benefits can be maintained over the course of a chronic disease is at question. Social support is often conceptualized and measured as fairly stable, whereas stressors, coping efforts, and patterns of psychological adjustment are assumed to fluctuate as disease status changes. Yet the composition of patients' social networks—even the closest family ties—may change over time in quantity or quality. For example, in a longitudinal study of breast cancer survivors, women who were treated with breast-conserving surgery reported less social support 3 months after surgery than women who were treated with mastectomy, although there had been no differences in perceived support immediately after surgery (Levy et al., 1992). Whether this is a result of the fact that women who had breast-conserving surgery were younger or that others saw them as healthier and as needing less support could not be discerned.

## MECHANISMS THROUGH WHICH SUPPORT CONFERS BENEFITS

Social support affects adjustment through a number of physiological, emotional, and cognitive pathways (see Wills & Ainette, in press, Figure 2, for an array of mediational models). Social support enables recipients to use effective coping strategies by helping them come to a better understanding of the problem faced, increasing motivation to take instrumental action, and reducing emotional stress, which may impede other coping efforts. Support may encourage the performance of positive health behaviors, thus preventing or minimizing disease and symptom burden. Or it may minimize physiological reactivity to stress or boost immune function, thus affecting health outcomes (Uchino, 2006).

A number of theoretical models have been used to identify the psychological mechanisms by which social support confers its beneficial effects. An early approach that maintains sticking power is the stress-buffering model (Cohen & Wills, 1985). This model holds that support acts as a protective factor at times of crisis, serving to cushion the individual against the deleterious effects of stress. In contrast, the direct effects model proposes that support is beneficial regardless of the degree of stress experienced (i.e., more support is correlated with a better outcome across the board). Overall, empirical evidence for the direct effects model is found when support is conceptualized in terms of social integration (structural measures), whereas the stress-buffering model seems to describe the data when the functions of support are measured.

The matching hypothesis (Cutrona & Russell, 1990) maintains that certain types of social support are beneficial when they fit the contextual features of the stressor, including desirability, controllability, duration, timing, and social roles. The matching hypothesis also suggests that the effectiveness of support may hinge on a fit between the recipient's support needs and the amount or type of support received. For example, a recently diagnosed patient may desire concrete information to make a medical decision; a more disabled patient may prefer help with daily activities combined with companionship (Lanza, Cameron, & Revenson, 1995). Alternately, misfit may involve discrepancies between amount and quality of support desired and received; if the support provided exceeds the support required, feelings of infantilization or dependency may ensue (Revenson, 1993). *Who* is providing support may be another critical aspect of the matching hypothesis. Different people serve distinct supportive functions, so that it is the support network *as a whole* that fulfills the individual's needs (Dakof & Taylor, 1990; Lanza et al., 1995).

Work by Bolger and colleagues (e.g., Bolger, Zuckerman, & Kessler, 2000; Bolger & Amarel, 2007) suggests that social support that is "invisible" leads to better outcomes. Invisible support involves transactions in which recipients are not aware that support has been provided. As a result, support recipients do not feel obligated to reciprocate; nor is self-worth lost because they cannot reciprocate (because of the illness) or because they label themselves as needy or inadequate. Research has not tested this model with medical populations, but it is likely that especially for persons with greater disability, the invisibility of support may promote its success.

## THE NEGATIVE EFFECTS OF SOCIAL SUPPORT

Most research on the effects of social relationships on health has focused on its benefits. Yet, receiving, using, or requesting social support has its costs as well. It is important to distinguish between negative social interactions and social support attempts that backfire. The former involves outright negative behaviors including criticism ("You never handle your pain well"), avoidance ("I don't want to hear about it any more"), or angry outbursts ("*Your* pain is ruining *my* life!") that never were meant to be supportive or helpful. In a study of cancer patients and spouses, Manne and colleagues (2006) described three communication styles: mutual constructive communication, mutual avoidance, and demand–withdraw communication. All three styles were related to distress 9 months later, with demand–withdraw communication associated with the highest distress and lowest relationship satisfaction for both patients and partners. At the same time, many well-intended attempts at helping go awry, for example, giving advice or providing feedback that patients do not perceive as helpful. Support may be perceived as problematic when it is neither desired, needed, nor requested, or when the type of support offered does not match the recipient's needs (e.g., Lanza et al., 1995; Hagedoorn et al., 2000).

People with chronic illness often need to disclose thoughts and feelings to others in order to process their emotions, maintain or reestablish a positive self-concept, and make sense of their illness (Lepore, 2001). Disclosure of stressful experiences may regulate emotion by changing the focus of attention, increasing habituation to negative emotions, and facilitating positive cognitive reappraisals of threats (Stanton & Danoff-Burg, 2002). The perception of others as unreceptive to these emotional disclosures has been referred to as *social constraints* (Lepore & Revenson, 2007). Social constraints may emerge because of objective social conditions or as a result of individuals' appraisals of those conditions that lead people to refrain from or modify their disclosure of stress- related thoughts, feelings, or concerns. Persons with chronic illness who perceive that others are unreceptive to hearing about their experiences evidence poorer adjustment (e.g., greater depressive symptoms) than those who view their social networks as more receptive (e.g., Badr & Carmack Taylor 2006; Cordova et al., 2001; Danoff-Burg, Revenson, Trudeau, & Paget, 2004; Manne & Badr, 2008).

For example, Badr and Carmack Taylor (2006) examined social constraints in communication between recently diagnosed lung cancer patients and their spouses. Slightly over a third of the sample reported avoiding or having difficulties talking about the cancer in general, and two-thirds of the spouses had difficulties or avoided discussing prognosis, death or funeral arrangements, for fear of upsetting the patient. Some patients reported that their partner's denial and avoidance were distressing, made them change how they interacted with the partner, and strained the relationship. The investigators also found that social constraints can change over time, perhaps as the "reality" of cancer sets in and denial abates. For example, one female patient reported: "[My husband] told me the other day he just didn't realize about what's going on with me, how hard that is, because initially, he just kind of really shut down and didn't do very much at all . . . he was sorry he wasn't there for me at the beginning. And I understood" (p. 677).

In a study of patients with gastrointestinal cancer (Porter, Keefe, Baucom, Hurwitz, Moser, Patterson, & Kim, 2009), there was great variation in how much patients and spouses discussed cancer-related concerns, with some disclosing many concerns and some holding back a great deal. Spouses disclosed fewer concerns, reflecting a dyadic coping style termed "protective buffering" (Coyne & Smith, 1991). For both patients and spouses, nondisclosure was related to more cancer-related intrusive thoughts.

## DIRECTIONS IN RESEARCH ON SOCIAL SUPPORT IN CHRONIC ILLNESS

In the past decade, research on interpersonal relationships and health has refocused itself to conceptualize supportive transactions as part of dyadic coping (Revenson & DeLongis, 2011; Revenson, Kayser, & Bodenmann, 2005; Manne & Badr, 2008).

Broadly cast, dyadic coping recognizes mutuality and interdependence in coping responses to a specific shared stressor, indicating that couples respond to stressors as interpersonal units rather than as individuals in isolation. Interpersonal support is a central component in most definitions (e.g., Berg & Upchurch, 2007; Manne & Badr, 2008).

A diagnosis of chronic illness unleashes multiple stressors or adaptive tasks for the couple, which is why illness needs to be understood as an interpersonal experience. When spouses report receiving helpful support, they tend to engage in more adaptive ways of coping with chronic stress. For example, Holtzman, Newth, and DeLongis (2004) examined the role of support in coping and pain severity among patients with RA and found that such support influences pain severity indirectly, both through encouraging the use of specific coping strategies, such as positive reappraisal, as well as by impacting the effectiveness with which these coping strategies were employed. Moreover, support from the spouse attenuated the impact of maladaptive responses to pain, disrupting the vicious cycle of catastrophizing and pain (Holtzman & DeLongis, 2007).

Whether assessed objectively or subjectively, as social networks or functional aspects of those relationships, and as emerging from formal or informal helping systems, social support has been related to more positive adjustment to illness. Factors such as timing, source of support, and balance of positive and problematic aspects of support moderate this relationship. In recent years, research has linked social support to intermediate processes such as positive or negative affect and coping, and linked support to broader models of emotional disclosure and emotion regulation. As studies accumulated over the past three decades, it became clear that social support is a complex, multifaceted construct and that different aspects of support (or different ways of measuring support) produce distinct effects on adjustment.

### Macro-Level Contextual Factors

Previously, we suggested that adaptational processes are best understood in conjunction with the life context in which disease occurs. Macro-level contextual factors such as socioeconomic status (SES), culture, ethnicity, and gender most likely affect adjustment through more proximal psychosocial mechanisms. Culture may influence adjustment, for example, by shaping beliefs and cognitions (Landrine & Klonoff, 1992), which are then strengthened by feedback from social ties and socialization practices (Berkman & Glass, 1999).

In the next sections, we briefly describe the major macro-contextual factors that need to be considered in understanding variation in psychosocial adaptation. But we preface these sections with a caveat: At this time, more research documents the effects of macro-level contextual factors on the development of disease than on psychosocial adjustment to illness once it occurs. We urge health psychology researchers to consider these macro-level contextual factors in their work. Why? Berkman and Glass (1999) distinguish between upstream and downstream contextual factors that affect health. Culture, SES, politics, and social change (e.g., urbanization) affect social network structure and social capital; these are the upstream or more distal influences. Social networks and social capital, in turn, provide opportunities for psychosocial mechanisms (e.g., social support, access to resources, community participation) to influence adjustment through behavioral and physiological pathways; these are the downstream or more proximal factors. Taylor, Repetti, and Seeman (1997) propose a similar conceptualization. In their model, SES and race most likely affect health indirectly through their influence on key environments, including the physical environment in which one lives and works, and the social environment of interpersonal relationships. Greater social support, access to more resources/people, and neighborhoods with greater social capital have been shown to lead to resilience, even among populations facing adversity (Saegert, Thompson, & Warren, 2001).

## CULTURE

A central component of context is culture: contexts, and the behaviors and interactions that take place within them, are infused with values, belief systems, and worldviews that emanate from cultural phenomena. The concept of culture is applicable across standard social categories, including gender, sexual orientation, race/ethnicity, nationality, religious preference, and disability status. Most conceptualizations of culture include external referents, such as customs, artifacts, and social institutions, and internal referents such as ideologies, belief systems, attitudes, expectations, and epistemologies.

Adaptation to disease occurs within one or more cultural contexts. It is useful to think of cultural contexts as supplying the blueprints for adaptation to disease—how meaning is given to events, which behaviors are appropriate in which situations, and what competencies are valued by group members. These blueprints or cultural schemata provide the various cultural lenses that inform people's worldviews,

for example, whether one should follow the advice of "traditional" medical providers or turn to culturally sanctioned healers (McClain, 1989). Cultural blueprints also shape cognitive appraisals of disease (Landrine & Klonoff, 1992), guide treatment decisions (Rubel & Garro, 1992), and determine how illness is defined and expressed. For example, in Latina cultures the condition of *nervios* blurs the distinction between physical and mental illness, and in some societies with high poverty rates or a totalitarian government, the expression of illness is a behavioral manifestation of powerlessness, particularly among women (Low, 1995). Culture also may define the acceptability of particular coping responses, such as emotional expression or anger, and thus their value as adaptive mechanisms. Moreover, most individuals are members of multiple cultural or social groups that condition the meaning of other social categories.

## SOCIOECONOMIC STATUS

Although the United States has prided itself on being a classless society in which anyone can better her or his life circumstances, disparities between the "haves" and "have-nots" are marked and growing. In social science research, SES has been conceptualized alternately as financial status (income), occupational status, educational status (or some combination of these), the position in society into which one is born (which creates hierarchies of majority and minority statuses), or subjective perceptions of social status or relative deprivation (Ghaed & Gallo, 2007). These different socioeconomic indices affect health at distinct times in the life course, operate at different levels (e.g., individual vs. neighborhood), and work through different causal pathways (Braverman et al., 2005). Changes in SES over time, including unemployment and loss of income, can affect later health and have cumulative health effects. For example, childhood SES can influence later health (Chen, Martin, & Matthews, 2006), independent of adult SES (Cohen, Doyle, Turner, Alper, & Skoner, 2004).

Quite simply, people of lower SES consistently appear to have worse health outcomes (Adler & Rehkopf, 2008; Adler, Marmot, McEwan, & Stewart, 1999). Reviewing a number of large-scale studies in the United States and Western Europe, Adler and colleagues (1994, 1999) documented an inverse graded association between SES and morbidity, mortality, and prevalence and disease course at all levels of SES; that is, morbidity and mortality are greater not only at the lowest levels of SES, but rather a graded relationship occurs at all levels of SES. However, it still holds that rates of chronic disease are higher among those in poverty, as are rates of activity restrictions and the extent of impairment and decrement in functional abilities that stem from chronic disease.

SES affects health both directly and indirectly, through its linkages with psychosocial factors, such as attitudes and emotion, health behaviors, including both risk and preventive behaviors, and access to and quality of medical care, particularly preventive care. That is, persons of lower SES may not only experience more psychosocial risks and deficits in the care they receive, but also may be more vulnerable to them (Williams, 1990). Access to medical care, however, is not a sufficient explanatory variable for the SES-health gradient (Adler, Boyce, Chesney, Folkman, & Syme, 1993; Meyerowitz, Richardson, Hudson, & Leedham, 1998; Williams, 1990). Recent work has given greater attention to psychosocial and behavioral variables as mediating mechanisms. For example, low SES is linked both to risky health behaviors, such as smoking and alcohol use, and to fewer health-protective factors, such as exercise, health attitudes, and social ties (Adler & Rehkopf, 2008; Ruiz, Steffen, & Prather, in press). Gallo and Matthews (2003) offered the *reserve capacity model* as a framework for understanding the psychosocial factors that mediate the relationship between SES and health. Individuals of lower SES experience more stressful life events and events of greater magnitude and have fewer social and psychosocial resources to cope with them, which leads to poorer mental and physical health, and worse adaptation to illness. Evidence for the reserve capacity model is accumulating (Gallo, Espinosade los Monteros, Ferent, Urbina, & Talavera, 2007; Matthews, Räikkönen, Gallo, & Kuller, 2008); research on the model's application to psychosocial adaptation to illness is needed.

Poverty and its correlates (e.g., low education) can provide a qualitatively different context in which individuals cope (Evans, 2003). In addition to signaling a lack of fundamental resources, poverty often creates a sense of helplessness and hopelessness. In a study of more than 1,400 individuals with RA followed over 5 years (Callahan, Cordray, Wells, & Pincus, 1996), a higher sense of helplessness entirely mediated the relation between lower education and early mortality. The constant struggle for resources to meet basic human needs can severely constrain coping resources.

## RACE/ETHNICITY

Social science researchers typically use demographic markers (e.g., Hispanic, black, nationality, immigrant status) to define ethnic minority or nonmainstream cultural groups. However, it is more likely that ethnic minority groups' experiences with racism, discrimination and social exclusion, on both interpersonal and structural levels, lie at the root of many race/ethnicity-based health disparities (Brondolo, Brady ver Halen, Pencille, Beatty, & Contrada, 2009; Brondolo, Gallo, & Myers, 2009; Mays, Cochran, & Barnes, 2007; Paradies, 2006). Meyerowitz and her colleagues (1998) reviewed the literature on ethnic differences in cancer outcomes and predictors of those outcomes, and found overall differences in screening behavior, delay in seeking treatment, and follow-up of abnormal findings, all of which can lead to being diagnosed with less treatable stages of cancer, and subsequent greater stress, fewer coping options, and lower quality of life. Interactions with health care providers also differed among ethnic groups, which were related to treatment decisions and anxiety around them. Meyerowitz and her coauthors also examined macro-level contextual influences that might affect or be confounded with these findings, such as SES, and concluded that broad ethnic group markers are insufficient to define any cultural group.

Between-group studies based on nominal categories as ethnic group membership do little to illuminate the mediating pathways that explain these group differences (Yali & Revenson, 2004). For example, Barger and Gallo (2008) found large differences in health behaviors among individuals who identified themselves as Mexican versus Mexican American in the National Health Interview study, although these two self-identified groups are often grouped together for analyses as "Hispanic." Statistically controlling for age, gender, and SES, individuals who identified as Mexican American were 43% more likely to smoke and have a body mass index (BMI) classifying them as obese than those self-identifying as Mexican. Thus, studies that fail to differentiate among subgroups within the broad Census classifications may be missing important within-group heterogeneity.

Ethnic categorization does not lead us to those answers when it is confounded with poverty or SES. Similarly, poverty does not fully account for race differences in health; as explained earlier, these differences occur at every level of the SES gradient (Mays et al., 2007). Instead, our understanding of variation in adjustment to illness might increase if we consider the psychological manifestations of race/ethnicity, such as discrimination, racism, and social exclusion. A number of studies have found that

African American women who attributed interpersonal mistreatment to racial discrimination exhibit greater blood pressure reactivity and recovery to laboratory stressors that bear similarities to an encounter with racial prejudice (e.g., Guyll, Matthews, & Bromberger, 2001; Lepore et al., 2006). These findings suggest that perceived racism may act as a chronic stressor. Place of birth and immigration status are often overlooked when race/ethnicity and SES differences are examined but they, too, are an important factor in health disparities (Adler & Rehkopf, 2008). Immigration status, including years in the United States and acculturation level may explain paradoxical effects in ethnic minority populations, for example, why Latinas have worse health relative to non-Latino whites, but have lower all-cause mortality rates (e.g., Abraído-Lanza, Chao, & Flóres, 2005).

No individual-level coping strategy has emerged as effective for offsetting the impact of racism on health (Brondolo et al., 2009). It is likely that changes will need to occur at structural, economic and political levels in order to have the broadest impact on reducing health disparities. Mays et al. (2007) describe several of the race-discrimination-health pathways including segregation, residential stratification, conditions of violence, lack of social capital and growing up in poor neighborhoods. Eloquently, they argue that the persistent racial stratification in the United States serves as a "structural lattice for maintaining discrimination" and subsequent poor mental and physical health (Mays et al., 2007, p. 24.6).

GENDER ROLES

Many psychological theories of "healthy adjustment" are influenced by beliefs about gender roles. For example, dominant assumptions of mental health are that one should fight an illness; use active, instrumental, problem-solving efforts; and be self-reliant, drawing on one's inner resources. These ways of coping not only are correlated with better adjustment in many studies but in some cases, constitute the definition of better adjustment. The finding that female chronic disease patients have lower psychological well-being than their male counterparts (e.g., Hagedoorn et al., 2008) mirrors the literature on gender differences in depression in the general population (Gore & Colten, 1991). Although depression is often related to pain, disability, and disease severity, these factors do not fully explain observed gender differences in adjustment to disease (Helgeson, in press).

Two examples may help illustrate how gender socialization translates into differentially effective modes of coping with illness that ultimately affect adjustment. In the area of personality, the gender-linked personality orientations of *agency* and *communion* (and their extreme forms, *unmitigated agency* and *unmitigated communion*) are related to adjustment to a number of chronic diseases (Helgeson, 2003a, Helgeson, in press). Individuals with an agentic orientation focus more on themselves and use more instrumental strategies to cope with stress. Individuals with a more communal orientation focus on others' needs and interpersonal relationships, and are more emotionally expressive. Unmitigated agency involves orientation toward oneself without regard for others and difficulty expressing emotions, whereas unmitigated communion refers to an extreme orientation toward others, in which individuals become overinvolved with others to the detriment of their own well-being.

Agency has been linked to better physical and mental health across a number of chronic diseases, including coronary heart disease (Helgeson, 1993), prostate cancer (Helgeson & Lepore, 2004), diabetes (Helgeson, 1994), and RA (Trudeau, Danoff-Burg, Revenson, & Paget, 2003). Unmitigated agency, however, has been related to greater difficulty in expressing emotions, which in turn was associated with negative general and cancer-related adjustment in a group of men with prostate cancer (Helgeson & Lepore, 2004) and to maladjustment in women with breast cancer (Prio, Zeldow, Knight, Mytko, & Gradishar, 2001). Unmitigated communion has been associated with poor health behavior, negative social interactions, and greater depression and cardiac symptoms following a first coronary event (Fritz, 2000), poorer metabolic control and greater psychological distress among adolescents with diabetes (Helgeson, Escobar, Siminerio, & Becker, 2007), and greater functional disability and depressive symptoms among women and men with RA (Danoff-Burg et al., 2004; Trudeau et al., 2003) and women with breast cancer (Helgeson, 2003b).

Interpersonal relationships are essential components of women's coping with major stressors, including chronic illness. Women draw on their support networks more often; these interpersonal contacts serve as a place to express emotions, acquire feedback on coping choices, and obtain assistance with life tasks, such as child care. Women are more likely to ask for support, use support, and not feel demeaned by it (Shumaker & Hill, 1991). Women's focus on interpersonal relationships may create both additional stresses (Wethington, McLeod, & Kessler, 1987) and benefits (Brown, Nesse, Vinokur, & Smith, 2003); women are often taking care of others while they, themselves, are coping with a chronic condition (Abraído-Lanza & Revenson, 2006; Revenson, Abraído-Lanza, Majerovitz, & Jordan, 2005). A meta-analysis of couples coping with cancer (Hagedoorn et al., 2008) revealed that women report more psychological distress than men whether they are the patient or the caregiver (see similar findings for arthritis, Revenson, 2003, and heart disease, Rohrbaugh et al., 2002). One prominent explanation is that caring for others is a more central aspect of women's identity (Gilligan, 1982), and the loss of that role is too great a threat to self-esteem and well-being to abandon (Abraído-Lanza & Revenson, 2006). Thus, whether they are the patient or the caregiver, women continue to focus on others and maintain their domestic roles, both of which can create added stress (see also Hagedoorn et al., 2008).

It is difficult to isolate the effect of gender on adaptation to disease. Because many diseases vary in their prevalence among men and women, most studies of adaptation to disease include respondents of only one sex or couples in which either men or women have the chronic disease (e.g., men with prostate cancer and their wives). Thus, if we detect differences in adjustment to disease, we cannot disentangle the influences of the disease context and of gender, or conclude whether the experience of coping with the "same" disease differs for men and women. For example, the majority of studies of adaptation to myocardial infarction involve male patients and female spouses. After a heart attack, men tend to reduce their work activities and responsibilities and are nurtured by their wives. In contrast, after returning home from the hospital, women resume household responsibilities more quickly, including taking care of other family members, and report receiving a greater amount of help from adult daughters and neighbors than from their healthy husbands (Rose, Suls, Green, Lounsbury, & Gordon, 1996). Michela (1987) found such substantial differences in husbands' and wives' experience that he wrote, "*His* experience is filtered through concerns about surviving and recovering from the MI with a minimum of danger or discomfort, while *her* experience is filtered through the meaning of the marital relationship to her—what the marriage has provided and, hence, what is threatened by the husband's potential death or what is lost by his disability" (p. 272). Are these completely different *his* and *her* experiences, or are they experiences created by the role of patient versus partner/caregiver? Hagedoorn et al.'s (2008) meta-analysis would suggest that gender role trumps patient/partner role, at least for couples with cancer.

Gender seldom has been examined in conjunction with other contextual factors for their synergistic influences. For example, the literature on gender differences in mortality or morbidity rarely examines whether these gender differences are influenced by SES. Yet the magnitude of socioeconomic gradients in health and mortality varies by gender; for example, cardiovascular mortality and morbidity exhibit a steeper gradient for women than for men (MacIntyre & Hunt, 1997). Moreover, gender often places constraints on financial, educational, and occupational aspirations (Coriell & Adler, 1996).

Taylor and colleagues (2000) proposed a tend-and-befriend model to characterize stress responses that are more uniquely female. Drawing evidence from hundreds of studies of humans and other animals, they argued that adaptive responses to stress in females is likely to involve efforts to tend, that is, to nurture the self and others, and to befriend, that is, to create and maintain social networks in order to provide protection from external threats. They suggested that these behaviors are likely to be prompted by the biobehavioral attachment/caregiving system, which depends in part on hormonal mechanisms in interaction with social, cultural, and environmental input. The intersection of biological and environmental influences on gender differences in adjustment to chronic disease is a promising area for study.

## Interventions to Enhance Adjustment to Chronic Disease: Implications of the Person-Context Fit

The fact that adaptation is a function of both persons and their environments (French, Rodgers, & Cobb, 1974; Lewin, 1951/1997) suggests multiple points for intervention, some directed at changing persons, some aimed at changing environments, and others targeted toward improving person-environment fit. The macro-level contextual factors described earlier—SES, culture, ethnicity, and gender roles—cannot be changed (or changed easily) without social intervention. System-level interventions are necessary to decrease barriers to health care and socioeconomic disparities, for example.

Practitioners also can work toward improving the interpersonal context through teaching patients how to develop and maintain social ties, recognize and accept others' help and emotional encouragement, and change their appraisals of the support they are receiving. Involving family members in psychological interventions for individuals with chronic illness can confer benefits. A meta-analysis comparing randomized, controlled trials of family-oriented versus patient-oriented interventions revealed a small advantage of family interventions (Martire & Schulz, 2007; see also Nezu, Nezu, Felgoise, McClure, & Houts, 2003). In addition to bringing the partner into the patient's treatment (Martire, Lustig, Schulz, Miller, & Helgeson, 2004), couple-focused interventions can enhance disclosure and communication between partners (e.g., Martire, Schulz, Keefe, Rudy, & Starz, 2007; Porter et al., 2009), teach coping skills (Keefe et al., 2004), or combine several strategies (Northouse et al., 2007; Scott, Halford, & Ward, 2004).

Most psychosocial interventions are directed primarily toward individual-level change (although they often are conducted in a group format) and are multimodal, involving cognitive-behavioral, educational, and interpersonal support components. Reviews of such interventions demonstrate their potential for success in improving adjustment and disease-related outcomes. For example, a meta-analysis of 37 studies of psychoeducational (health education and stress management) interventions for coronary heart disease patients suggested that the programs yielded positive effects on depression and anxiety, as well as cardiac risk factors (e.g., blood pressure, physical activity) and mortality (Dusseldorp, van Elderen, Maes, Meulman, & Kraaij, 1999; also see Linden, Phillips, & Leclerc, 2007). In a systematic review, Thombs et al. (2008) concluded that cognitive behavioral or medication treatment of depression in individuals with cardiovascular disease results in modest improvement in depressive symptoms. Multiple reviews provide examples of individual-level interventions for people with cancer (e.g., Andersen, 2002; Meyer & Mark, 1995; Newell, Sanson-Fisher, & Savolainen, 2002; Tatrow & Montgomery, 2006), diabetes (Gonder-Frederick, Cox, & Ritterband, 2002), AIDS (Carrico & Antoni, 2008; Crepaz et al., 2008; Scott-Sheldon, Kalichman, Carey, & Fielder, 2008), and arthritis (Keefe, Smith et al., 2002). Many of these reviews call for increased empirical attention to person-intervention fit and for targeting of interventions toward those most at risk for poor adjustment (e.g., Andersen, 2002; Gonder-Frederick et al., 2002; Scott-Sheldon et al., 2008).

Current theories of adjustment to chronic disease can guide the design of interventions. An example is Folkman and colleagues' (1991) coping effectiveness training. Successful in improving such outcomes as perceived stress and burnout, effects mediated by an increase in coping self-efficacy (Chesney, Folkman, & Chambers, 1996; Chesney, Chambers, Taylor, Johnson, & Folkman, 2003) in HIV-positive men, this intervention included appraisal training to disaggregate global stressors into specific coping tasks and to distinguish between changeable and immutable aspects of stressors; coping training to tailor application of particular coping strategies to specific stressors; and social support training to increase effectiveness in choosing and maintaining support resources. Successful interventions often have been developed only after years of basic research on the nature of the disease juxtaposed with the nature of coping with disease-related stressors. For example, Keefe (Keefe, Smith, et al., 2002) developed a pain coping intervention for arthritis patients based on his research showing the adverse effects of catastrophizing on adjustment to disease. As another example, a brief intervention directed toward illness perceptions (Leventhal et al., 2001) produced faster return to work in myocardial infarction patients compared with standard care, as well as positive effects on a number of other outcomes (Broadbent, Ellis, Thomas, Gamble, & Petrie, 2009).

In light of the evidence that most individuals who confront chronic disease adjust well, a fruitful intervention approach will involve targeting especially challenging points in the disease trajectory, specific islands of disruption, and individuals who are most at risk, for example, those with clinical levels of depression, low social support, or high social constraints. For example, Zautra and colleagues (2008) demonstrated that intervention approaches were differentially effective for RA patients with or without a history of recurrent depression. Identification of targets for intervention can be informed by research on contributors to adjustment to chronic disease. Research on predictors of adjustment also can aid in understanding *how* interventions work (e.g., through altering coping strategies or illness-related cognitions), which will allow the design of more effective treatments. A special issue of the *Journal of Consulting and Clinical Psychology* on behavioral medicine/clinical health psychology (2002) calls for greater investigation of moderators of and mechanisms for intervention effects, greater attention in interventions to environmental influences on adjustment, and increased attention to both biological and specific psychosocial endpoints (Andersen, 2002; Christensen & Ehlers, 2002; Gonder-Frederick et al., 2002; Keefe, Buffington,

Studts, & Rumble, 2002; Keefe, Smith, Buffington, Gibson, Studts, & Caldwell, 2002). Interventions which are responsive to the person-context fit hold promise for enhancing health and well-being in individuals and their loved ones contending with chronic disease.

## Future Research in Adjustment to Chronic Disease: The Promise of Both Broad Integration and Fine-Grained Focus

If you are a student researcher reading this chapter, you might feel daunted by the multiplicity of intersecting factors that deserve consideration in research on adjustment to chronic disease. Even though we have been researchers in the area for the past 25 years, *we* still feel daunted by this complexity. To the extent that a researcher attempts to examine both contextual and individual contributors to adjustment using methodologically sound research designs (i.e., longitudinal or experimental methods, clinical trials), she or he is likely to require large samples, relatively lengthy time frames, additional instrument development, and assurance that interventions are culturally anchored across diverse samples. This is a tough enough challenge to send even the most seasoned researchers running in the opposite direction. However, progress in the social sciences can be gauged by "small wins" (Weick, 1984), which involve recasting large problems into smaller, less knotty problems that present controllable opportunities to produce visible results. We believe that we need both broad and narrowly focused research in this area, and we encourage the readers of this chapter to take the next steps.

As a journal editor said to one of us, we do not need another cross-sectional study of the relations between individual coping strategies and distress in newly diagnosed breast cancer patients, to take but one example of the type of research most commonly found in the field. Rather, theoretically guided and methodologically definitive research examining individual and contextual biopsychosocial predictors, moderators of, and mechanisms for adaptive and biologic outcomes in chronic disease is what will advance the knowledge base.

To realize this goal, multiple sources of expertise will need to be integrated in order to produce the best conceptual frameworks and research designs. This need is especially urgent as researchers are making strides investigating how physiological processes interact with psychosocial factors in chronic disease. This linkage can go in both directions. Psychosocial processes, such as stress and inadequate coping responses, can lead to poorer health outcomes.

For example, chronic stress has been linked to premature physiological aging (Epel et al., 2004). At the same time, physiological processes can lead to poorer adjustment outcomes. For example, not only has fatigue, a major symptom of cancer treatment, been linked to depression and maladaptive coping, but also biological mechanisms such as anemia, blunted cortisol responses, and proinflammatory cytokine activity have been associated with persistent fatigue in cancer survivors (Bower et al., 2007). Similar findings link inflammatory markers with fatigue in patients with rheumatic disease (Davis et al., 2008).

There is an increased interest in understanding biobehavioral mediators of health outcomes. Exemplars include understanding the biopsychosocial mechanisms underlying the effects of personality attributes (e.g., Helgeson, 2003; Martin et al., 2002; Smith & Gallo, 2001) and interpersonal variables (e.g., Taylor, Dickerson, & Klein, 2002; Uchino, Cacioppo, & Kiecolt-Glaser, 1996) on outcomes of chronic disease; the link between spirituality and health (e.g., Seeman, Dubin, & Seeman, 2003); and the relation of depression to both chronic disease onset (e.g., Carney, Jones, Woolson, Noyes, & Doebbeling, 2003; Wulsin & Singal, 2003) and resulting morbidity and mortality (e.g., Brown, Levy, Rosberger, & Edgar, 2003; de Groot, Anderson, Freedland, Clouse, & Lustman, 2001; Kinder, Kamarck, Baum, & Orchard, 2002; Sullivan, LaCroix, Russo, & Walker, 2001; Van Tilberg et al., 2001). Studies such as these require sophisticated research planning and implementation.

Interdisciplinary collaboration is a critical mechanism for pursuing research that is truly biopsychosocial (or biopsychosociocultural). A multidisciplinary team representing expertise in psychosocial and biological processes involved in specific diseases, relevant theoretical frameworks, and quantitative methods provides the basic vehicle for conducting such research. If we are to address the complex questions that we have posed in this chapter, then scholars from other social sciences (e.g., sociology, anthropology) and from public health, as well as patients and community gatekeepers, also will contribute to the team, offering knowledge of macro-level contextual factors and community-level interventions.

At the same time as integrative research is needed, investigations with a sharp, hypothesis-driven focus on unanswered questions in chronic disease (e.g., mechanisms for gender-related effects on adjustment to chronic disease; behavioral and biologic mechanisms for the relation between avoidant coping and disease outcomes) also can move the field forward.

Such research may alternate between basic research with healthy samples responding to experimentally induced stressors, experimental and quasi-experimental investigations of populations experiencing chronic disease, and clinical intervention trials to document causal mechanisms more conclusively. Longitudinal studies focusing on in-depth analysis of single contributors to adjustment (e.g., upward and downward social comparison, benefit finding, emotional expression) can set the stage for research to understand how these processes work in context and with diverse populations. Particularly in new areas of inquiry, qualitative studies can frame research questions and provide a way to "get inside" patients' experiences of chronic disease. Participatory action research also can provide feedback on research directions, questions, and approaches, as research participants play a role in framing the research questions and interpreting the data. Intensive, daily process methodologies also may illuminate interacting individual and contextual contributors to adjustment. These methodologies are particularly appropriate for diseases for which coping and self-management demands occur daily. Certainly, there is room for large-scale research that examines multiple and interacting determinants of adjustment to chronic disease, as well as sharply honed, micro-analytic investigations of processes underlying both positive and negative adaptive outcomes.

## Directions for Research and Application: Summary

Directions for research and application in adjustment to chronic disease can be distilled into several broad recommendations: (1) map the trajectory of various domains of adjustment to chronic illness in order to identify crucial targets for intervention and optimal points at which to intervene; (2) move toward including macro-level contextual factors in models of adjustment to illness to produce socioeconomically and culturally-informed frameworks; (3) investigate the interactions of multiple contributors to characterize issues of person-environment fit in adjustment to chronic disease; (4) elaborate biological and psychosocial mechanisms underlying the effects of intrapersonal and interpersonal factors on adjustment to chronic disease; and (5) translate findings on contributors to adjustment into interventions and submit them to test in experimental designs.

## Conclusion

How far has our knowledge of adjustment to chronic disease advanced over the past 50 years, since that seminal, observational study of adjustment to chronic disease appeared in the *Archives of General Psychiatry* (Visotsky et al., 1961)? We still study how it is possible to deal with such powerful, pervasive, and enduring stresses as are involved in chronic disease, though the focus now is not on polio but on life-threatening diseases such as cancer and heart disease, as well as on non–life-threatening but severely disabling conditions such as arthritis. Considerable progress is evident in the development of multi-faceted conceptualizations and operationalizations of adjustment, theories to specify contributors to adaptation, and the knowledge base regarding specific factors that contribute to unfavorable outcomes (although we know less about determinants of favorable outcomes). We now know that understanding discrete coping behaviors is not enough; investigating the intersections of emotions, cognition, and culture with behavior in the context of interpersonal relationships and life roles may provide more adequate answers. We are beginning to use this knowledge to guide clinical interventions, though (in the spirit of twentieth-century American psychology) we still rely largely on individual treatment models. We have made small wins, and the biggest gains—adequately capturing the interconnections among biological, psychological, and sociocultural mechanisms for adjustment to chronic disease—are still to come.

## References

Abraído-Lanza, A.F. (1997). Latinas with arthritis: Effects of illness, role identity, and competence on psychological well-being. *American Journal of Community Psychology, 25*, 601–627.

Abraído-Lanza, A.F., Chao, M.T., & Flóres, K.R. (2005). Do healthy behaviors decline with acculturation?: Implications for the Latino mortality paradox. *Social Science & Medicine, 61*, 1243–1255.

Abraído-Lanza, A.F., Guier, C., & Revenson, T.A. (1996). Coping and social support resources among Latinas with arthritis. *Arthritis Care and Research, 9*, 501–508.

Abraído-Lanza, A.F., & Revenson, T.A. (2006). Illness intrusion and psychological adjustment to rheumatic diseases: A social identity framework. *Arthritis and Rheumatism: Arthritis Care & Research, 55*, 224–232.

Adler, N.E., Boyce, T., Chesney, M., Cohen, S., Folkman, S., Kahn, R.L., et al. (1994). Socioeconomic status and health: The challenge of the gradient. *American Psychologist, 49*, 15–24.

Adler, N.E., Boyce, T., Chesney, M., Folkman, S., & Syme, S.L. (1993). Socioeconomic inequalities in health: No easy solution. *Journal of the American Medical Association, 269*, 3140–3145.

Adler, N.E., Marmot, M., McEwan, B.S., & Stewart, J. (Eds.) (1999). *Annals of the New York Academy of Sciences* Vol. 896: *Socioeconomic status and health in industrialized nations.* New York: New York Academy of Sciences.

Adler, N.E., & Rehkopf, D.H. (2008). U.S. disparities in health: Descriptions, causes, mechanisms. *Annual Review of Public Health, 29,* 235–252.

Affleck, G., Tennen, H., Croog, S., & Levine, S. (1987). Causal attribution, perceived benefits, and morbidity after a heart attack: An 8-year study. *Journal of Consulting and Clinical Psychology, 55,* 29–35.

Affleck, G., Tennen, H., Pfeiffer, C., & Fifield, J. (1987). Appraisals of control and predictability in adapting to chronic disease. *Journal of Personality and Social Psychology, 53,* 273–279.

Affleck, G., Tennen, H., Zautra, A., Urrows, S., Abeles, M., & Karoly, P. (2001). Women's pursuit of personal goals in daily life with fibromyalgia: A value-expectancy analysis. *Journal of Consulting and Clinical Psychology, 69,* 587–596.

Algoe, S.B., & Stanton, A.L. (2009). Is benefit finding good for individuals with chronic disease? In C.L. Park, S.C. Lechner, M.H. Antoni, & A.L. Stanton (Eds.), *Medical illness and positive life change: Can crisis lead to personal transformation?* (pp. 173–193). Washington, DC: American Psychological Association.

Andersen, B.L. (2002). Biobehavioral outcomes following psychological interventions for cancer patients. *Journal of Consulting and Clinical Psychology, 70,* 590–610.

Andersen, B.L., Anderson, B., & deProsse, C. (1989a). Controlled prospective longitudinal study of women with cancer: I. Sexual functioning outcomes. *Journal of Consulting and Clinical Psychology, 57,* 683–691.

Andersen, B.L., Anderson, B., & deProsse, C. (1989b). Controlled prospective longitudinal study of women with cancer: II. Psychological outcomes. *Journal of Consulting and Clinical Psychology, 57,* 692–697.

Anderson, R.J., Clouse, R.E., Freedland, K.E., & Lustman, P.J. (2001). The prevalence of comorbid depression in adults with diabetes: A meta-analysis. *Diabetes Care, 24,* 1069–1078.

Antoni, M.H., Lechner, S.C., Kazi, A., Wimberly, S.R., Sifre, T., Urcuyo, K.R., et al. (2006). How stress management improves quality of life after treatment for breast cancer. *Journal of Consulting and Clinical Psychology, 74,* 1143–1152.

Antoni, M.H., Lehman, J.M., Kilbourn, K.M., Boyers, A.E., Culver, J.L., Alferi, S.M., et al. (2001). Cognitive-behavioral stress management intervention decreases the prevalence of depression and enhances benefit finding among women under treatment for early-stage breast cancer. *Health Psychology, 20,* 20–32.

Badr, H., & Carmack Taylor, C.L. (2006). Social constraints and spousal communication in lung cancer. *Psycho-Oncology, 15,* 673–683.

Bárez, M., Blasco, T., Fernández-Castro, J., & Viladrich C. (2009). Perceived control and psychological distress in women with breast cancer: A longitudinal study. *Journal of Behavioral Medicine, 32,* 187–196.

Barger, S.D., & Gallo, L.C. (2008). Ability of ethnic self-identification to partition modifiable health risk about US residents of Mexican ancestry. *American Journal of Public Health, 98,* 1971–1978.

Barry, L.C., Kasl, S.V., Lichtman, J., Vaccarino, V., & Krumholz, H.M. (2006). Perceived control and change in physical functioning after coronary artery bypass grafting: A prospective study. *International Journal of Behavioral Medicine, 13,* 229–236.

Berg, C.A., & Upchurch, R. (2007). A developmental-contextual model of couples coping with chronic illness across the adult life span. *Psychological Bulletin, 133,* 920–954.

Berkman, L.F., & Glass, T. (1999). Social integration, social networks, social support, and health. In L.F. Berkman, & T. Glass (Eds.), *Social epidemiology* (pp. 137–173). New York: Oxford University Press.

Blalock, S.J., DeVellis, B.M., & Giorgino, K.B. (1995). The relationship between coping and psychological well-being among people with osteoarthritis: A problem-specific approach. *Annals of Behavioral Medicine, 17,* 107–115.

Bolger, N., & Amarel, D. (2007). Effects of social support visibility on adjustment to stress: Experimental evidence. *Journal of Personality and Social Psychology, 92,* 458–475.

Bolger, N., Zuckerman, A., & Kessler, R.C. (2000). Invisible support and adjustment to stress. *Journal of Personality and Social Psychology, 79,* 953–961.

Bower, J.E., Ganz, P.A., Aziz, N., Olmstead, R., Irwin, M.R., & Cole, S.W. (2007). Inflammatory responses to psychological stress in fatigued breast cancer survivors: Relationship to glucocorticoids. *Brain, Behavior, & Immunity, 21,* 251–258.

Bower, J.E., Kemeny, M.E., Taylor, S.E., & Fahey, J.L. (1998). Cognitive processing, discovery of meaning, CD4 decline, and AIDS-related mortality among bereaved HIV-seropositive men. *Journal of Consulting and Clinical Psychology, 66,* 979–986.

Bower, J.E., Meyerowitz, B.E., Desmond, K.A., Bernaards, C.A., Rowland, J.H., & Ganz, P.A. (2005). Perceptions of positive meaning and vulnerability following breast cancer: Predictors and outcomes among long-term breast cancer survivors. *Annals of Behavioral Medicine, 29,* 236–245.

Braverman, P.A., Cubbin, C., Egerter, S., Chideya, S., Marchi, S.S., Metzler, M., & Posner, S. (2005). Socioeconomic status in health research: One size does not fit all. *Journal of the American Medical Association, 294,* 2879–2888.

Brissette, I., Scheier, M.F., & Carver, C.S. (2002). The role of optimism in social network development, coping, and psychological adjustment during a life transition. *Journal of Personality and Social Psychology, 82,* 102–111.

Broadbent, E., Ellis, C.J., Thomas, J., Gamble, G., & Petrie, K.J. (2009). Further development of an illness perception intervention for myocardial infarction patients: A randomized controlled trial. *Journal of Psychosomatic Research, 67,* 17–23.

Brondolo, E., Brady ver Halen, N., Pencille, M., Beatty, D., & Contrada, R.J. (2009). Coping with racism: A selective review of the literature and a theoretical and methodological critique. *Journal of Behavioral Medicine, 32,* 64–88.

Brondolo, E., Gallo, L.C., & Myers, H.F. (2009). Race, racism, and health: Disparities, mechanisms, and interventions. *Journal of Behavioral Medicine, 32,* 1–8.

Brown, K.W., Levy, A.R., Rosberger, Z., & Edgar, L. (2003). Psychological distress and cancer survival: A follow-up 10 years after diagnosis. *Psychosomatic Medicine, 65,* 636–643.

Brown, S.L., Nesse, R.M., Vinokur, A.D., & Smith, D.M. (2003). Providing social support may be more beneficial than receiving it: Results from a prospective study of mortality. *Psychological Science, 14,* 320–327.

Calhoun, L.G., & Tedeschi, R.G. (Eds.). (2006). *Handbook of posttraumatic growth: Research and practice.* Mahwah, NJ: Lawrence Erlbaum Associates.

Callahan, L.F., Cordray, D.S., Wells, G., & Pincus, T. (1996). Formal education and five-year mortality in rheumatoid arthritis: Mediation by helplessness scale scores. *Arthritis Care and Research, 9,* 463–472.

Carels, R.A., Musher-Eizenman, D., Cacciapaglia, H., Perez-Benitez, C.I., Christie, S., & O'Brien, W. (2004). Psychosocial functioning and physical symptoms in heart failure patients: A within-individual approach. *Journal of Psychosomatic Research, 56,* 95–101.

Carney, C.P., Jones, L., Woolson, R.F., Noyes, R., & Doebbeling, B.N. (2003). Relationship between depression and pancreatic cancer in the general population. *Psychosomatic Medicine, 65,* 884–888.

Carrico, A.W., & Antoni, M.H. (2008). Effects of psychological interventions on neuroendocrine hormone regulation and immune status in HIV-positive persons: A review of randomized controlled trials. *Psychosomatic Medicine, 70,* 575–584.

Carver, C.S., & Antoni, M.H. (2004). Finding benefit in breast cancer during the year after diagnosis predicts better adjustment 5 to 8 years after cancer. *Health Psychology, 23,* 595–598.

Carver, C.S., Harris, S.D., Lehman, J.M., Durel, L.A., Antoni, M.H., Spencer, S.M., et al. (2000). How important is the perception of personal control? Studies of early stage breast cancer patients. *Personality and Social Psychology Bulletin, 26,* 139–149.

Carver, C.S., Pozo, C., Harris, S.D., Noriega, V., Scheier, M.F., Robinson, D.S., et al. (1993). How coping mediates the effect of optimism on distress: A study of women with early stage breast cancer. *Journal of Personality and Social Psychology, 65,* 375–390.

Carver, C.S., & Scheier, M.F. (1998). *On the self-regulation of behavior.* New York: Cambridge University Press.

Case, R.B., Moss, A.J., Case, N., McDermott, M., & Eberly, S. (1992). Living alone after myocardial infarction: Impact on prognosis. *Journal of the American Medical Association, 267,* 515–519.

Cella, D. (2001). Quality-of-life measurement in oncology. In A. Baum, & B.L. Andersen (Eds.), *Psychosocial interventions for cancer* (pp. 57–76). Washington, DC: American Psychological Association.

Centers for Disease Control and Prevention, U.S. Department of Health and Human Services. (2009). *Chronic diseases: The power to prevent, the call to control.* Retrieved from http://www.cdc.gov/nccdphp/publications/AAG/chronic.htm.

Chen, E., Martin, A.D., & Matthews, K.A. (2006). Socioeconomic status and health: Do gradients differ within childhood and adolescence? *Social Science & Medicine, 62,* 2161–2170.

Chesney, M.A., Chambers, D.B., Taylor, J.M., Johnson, L.M., & Folkman, S. (2003). Coping effectiveness training for men living with HIV: Results from a randomized clinical trial testing a group-based intervention. *Psychosomatic Medicine, 65,* 1038–1046.

Chesney, M., Folkman, S., & Chambers, D. (1996). Coping effectiveness training for men living with HIV: Preliminary findings. *International Journal of STD and AIDS, 7*(Suppl 2), 75–82.

Christensen, A.J., & Ehlers, S.L. (2002). Psychological factors in end-stage renal disease: An emerging context for behavioral medicine research. *Journal of Consulting and Clinical Psychology, 70,* 712–724.

Cohen, S., Doyle, W.J., Turner, R.B., Alper, C.M., & Skoner, D.P. (2004). Childhood socioeconomic status and host resistance to infectious illness in adulthood. *Psychosomatic Medicine, 66,* 553–558.

Cohen, S., & Wills, T.A. (1985). Stress, support and the buffering hypothesis. *Psychological Bulletin, 98,* 310–357.

Cordova, M.J., Cunningham, L.L., Carlson, C.R., & Andrykowski, M.A. (2001). Posttraumatic growth following breast cancer: A controlled comparison study. *Health Psychology, 20,* 176–185.

Coriell, M., & Adler, M. (1996). Socioeconomic status and women's health: How do we measure SES among women? *Women's Health: Research on Gender, Behavior, and Policy, 2,* 141–156.

Coyne, J.C., & Racioppo, M.W. (2000). Never the twain shall meet? Closing the gap between coping research and clinical intervention research. *American Psychologist, 55,* 655–664.

Coyne, J.C., & Smith, D.A. (1991). Couples coping with a myocardial infarction: A contextual perspective on wives' distress. *Journal of Personality and Social Psychology, 61,* 404–412.

Crepaz, N., Passin, W.F., Herbst, J.H., Rama, S.M., Malow, R.M., Purcell, D.W., Wolitski, R.J. & HIV/AIDS Prevention Research Synthesis Team. (2008). Meta-analysis of cognitive-behavioral interventions on HIV-positive persons' mental health and immune functioning. *Health Psychology, 27,* 4–14.

Cutrona, C.E., & Russell, D.W. (1990). Type of social support and specific stress: Toward a theory of optimal matching. In B.R. Sarason, I.G. Sarason, & G.R. Pierce (Eds.), *Social support: An interactional view* (pp. 319–366). New York: Wiley.

Daar, A.S., Singer, P.A., Persad, D.L., Pramming, S.K., Matthews, D.R., Beaglehole, R., et al. (2007). Grand challenges in chronic non-communicable diseases. *Nature, 450,* 494–496.

Dakof, G., & Taylor, S.E. (1990). Victims' perceptions of social support: What is helpful from whom? *Journal of Personality and Social Psychology, 58,* 80–89.

Danoff-Burg, S., Ayala, J., & Revenson, T.A. (2000). Researcher knows best? Toward a closer match between the concept and measurement of coping. *Journal of Health Psychology, 5,* 183–194.

Danoff-Burg, S., & Revenson, T.A. (2005). Benefit-finding among patients with rheumatoid arthritis: Positive effects on interpersonal relationships. *Journal of Behavioral Medicine, 28,* 91–103.

Danoff-Burg, S., Revenson, T.A., Trudeau, K.J., & Paget, S.A. (2004). Unmitigated communion, social constraints, and psychological distress among women with rheumatoid arthritis. *Journal of Personality, 72,* 29–46.

Davidson, R.J., Jackson, D.C., & Kalin, N.H. (2000). Emotion, plasticity, context, and regulation: Perspectives from affective neuroscience. *Psychological Bulletin, 126,* 890–909.

Davis, M.C., Zautra, A.J., Younger, J., Motivala, S.J., Attrep, J., & Irwin, M.R. (2008). Chronic stress and regulation of cellular markers of inflammation in rheumatoid arthritis: Implications for fatigue. *Brain, Behavior, & Immunity, 22,* 22–23.

de Groot, M., Anderson, R., Freedland, K.E., Clouse, R.E., & Lustman, P.J. (2001). Association of depression and diabetes complications: A meta-analysis. *Psychosomatic Medicine, 63,* 619–630.

DeVellis, B.M., & DeVellis, R.F. (2001). Self-efficacy and health. In A. Baum, T.A. Revenson, & J.E. Singer (Eds.), *Handbook of health psychology* (pp. 235–247). Mahwah, NJ: Erlbaum.

DeVellis, B.M., Revenson, T.A., & Blalock, S. (1997). Arthritis and autoimmune diseases. In S. Gallant, G.P. Keita, & R. Royak-Schaler (Eds.), *Health care for women: Psychological, social and behavioral issues* (pp. 333–347). Washington, DC: American Psychological Association.

Dew, M.A., Myaskovsky, L., Switzer, G.E., DiMartini, A.F., Schulberg, H.C., & Kormos, R.L. (2005). Profiles and predictors of the course of psychological distress across four years after heart transplantation. *Psychological Medicine, 35,* 1215–1227.

Dickens, C., McGowan, L., Clark-Carter, D., & Creed, F. (2002). Depression in rheumatoid arthritis: A systematic review of the literature with meta-analysis. *Psychosomatic Medicine, 64,* 52–60.

Dorval, M., Maunsell, E., Deschenes, L., Brisson, J., & Masse, B. (1998). Long-term quality of life after breast cancer: Comparison of 8-year survivors with population controls. *Journal of Clinical Oncology, 16,* 487–494.

Duangdao, K.M., & Roesch, S.C. (2008). Coping with diabetes in adulthood: A mcta-analysis. *Journal of Behavioral Medicine, 31,* 291–300.

Dusseldorp, E., van Elderen, T., Maes, S., Meulman, J., & Kraaij, V. (1999). A meta-analysis of psychoeducational programs for coronary heart disease patients. *Health Psychology, 18,* 506–519.

Echteld, M.A., van Elderen, T., & van der Kamp, L.J.T. (2003). Modeling predictors of quality of life after coronary angioplasty. *Annals of Behavioral Medicine, 26,* 49–60.

Epel, E.S., Blackburn, E.H., Lin, J., Dhabhar, F.S., Adler, N.E., Morrow, J.D., & Cawthon, R. (2004). Accelerated telomere shortening in response to life stress. *Proceedings of the National Academy of Sciences USA, 101*(49), 17312–17315.

Ertel, K.A., Glymour, E.M., & Berkman, L.F. (2008). Social networks and health: A life course perspective integrating observational and experimental evidence. *Journal of Social and Personal Relationships, 26,* 73–92.

Eton, D.T., & Lepore, S.J. (2001). Prostate cancer and quality of life: A review of the literature. *Psycho-Oncology, 10,* 1–20.

Evans, G.W. (2003). A multimethodological analysis of cumulative risk and allostatic load among rural children. *Developmental Psychology, 39*(5), 924–933.

Fann, J.R., Thomas-Rich, A.M., Katon, W.J., Cowley, D., Pepping, M., McGregor, B.A., & Gralow, J. (2008). Major depression after breast cancer: A review of epidemiology and treatment. *General Hospital Psychiatry, 30,* 112–126.

Felton, B.J., & Revenson, T.A. (1984). Coping with chronic illness: A study of illness controllability and the influence of coping strategies on psychological adjustment. *Journal of Consulting and Clinical Psychology, 52,* 343–353.

Felton, B.J., Revenson, T.A., & Hinrichsen, G.A. (1984). Stress and coping in the explanation of psychological adjustment among chronically ill adults. *Social Science and Medicine, 18,* 889–898.

Fitzgerald, T.E., Tennen, H., Affleck, G., & Pransky, G.S. (1993). The relative importance of dispositional optimism and control appraisals in quality of life after coronary artery bypass surgery. *Journal of Behavioral Medicine, 16,* 25–43.

Fitzpatrick, R. (2004). Quality of life: Measurement. In N.B. Anderson (Ed.), *Encyclopedia of health and behavior* (pp. 685–690). Thousand Oaks, CA: Sage.

Folkman, S., Chesney, M., McKusick, L., Ironson, G., Johnson, D.S., & Coates, T.J. (1991). Translating coping theory into intervention. In J. Eckenrode (Ed.), *The social context of coping* (pp. 239–259). New York: Plenum.

Folkman, S., Chesney, M., Pollack, L., & Coates, T. (1993). Stress, control, coping, and depressive mood in human immunodeficiency virus-positive and -negative gay men in San Francisco. *Journal of Nervous and Mental Disease, 181,* 409–416.

Folkman, S., Moskowitz, J.T., Ozer, E.M., & Park, C.L. (1997). Positive meaningful events and coping in the context of

HIV/AIDS. In B.H. Gottlieb (Ed.), *Coping with chronic stress* (pp. 293–314). New York: Plenum.

Fox, N.A. (1991). If it's not left, it's right: Electroencephalograph asymmetry and the development of emotion. *American Psychologist, 46,* 863–872.

French, J.R.P., Jr., Rodgers, W., & Cobb, S. (1974). Adjustment as person-environment fit. In G.V. Coelho, D.A. Hamburg, & J.E. Adams (Eds.), *Coping and adjustment* (pp. 316–333). New York: Basic Books.

Fritz, H.L. (2000). Gender-linked personality traits predict mental health and functional status following a first coronary event. *Health Psychology, 19,* 420–428.

Gallo, L., Espinosa de los Monteros, K., Ferent, V., Urbina, J., & Talavera, G. (2007). Educational attainment, psychosocial resources, and metabolic syndrome variables in Latinas. *Annals of Behavioral Medicine, 34,* 14–25.

Gallo, L.C., & Matthews, K.A. (2003). Understanding the association between socioeconomic status and physical health: Do negative emotions play a role? *Psychological Bulletin, 129,* 10–51.

Ghaed, S.G., & Gallo, L.C. (2007). Subjective social status, objective socioeconomic status, and cardiovascular risk in women. *Health Psychology, 26,* 668–674.

Gilligan, C. (1982). *In a different voice: Psychological theory and women's development.* Cambridge, MA: Harvard University Press.

Gonder-Frederick, L.A., Cox, D.J., & Ritterband, L.M. (2002). Diabetes and behavioral medicine: The second decade. *Journal of Consulting and Clinical Psychology, 70,* 611–625.

Gore, S., & Colten, M.E. (1991). Gender, stress, and distress. In J. Eckenrode (Ed.), *The social context of coping* (pp. 139–163). New York: Plenum.

Guyll, M., Matthews, K.A., & Bromberger, J.T. (2001). Discrimination and unfair treatment: Relationship to cardiovascular reactivity among African American and European American women. *Health Psychology, 20,* 315–325.

Hagedoorn, M., Kuijer, R.G., Buunk, B.P., DeJong, G.M., Wobbes, T., & Sanderman, R. (2000). Marital satisfaction in patients with cancer: Does support from intimate partners benefit those who need it most? *Health Psychology, 19,* 274–282.

Hagedoorn, M., Sanderman, R., Bolks, H.N., & Coyne, J.C. (2008). Distress in couples coping with cancer: A meta-analysis and critical review of role and gender effects. *Psychological Bulletin, 134,* 1–30.

Hamburg, D.A., & Adams, J.E. (1967). A perspective on coping behavior: Seeking and utilizing information in major transitions. *Archives of General Psychiatry, 17,* 277–284.

Helgeson, V.S. (1992). Moderators of the relation between perceived control and adjustment to chronic illness. *Journal of Personality and Social Psychology, 63,* 656–666.

Helgeson V.S. (1993). Implications of agency and communion for patient and spouse adjustment to a first coronary event. *Journal of Personality and Social Psychology, 64,* 807–816.

Helgeson, V.S. (1994). Relation of agency and communion to well-being: Evidence and potential explanations. *Psychological Bulletin, 116,* 412–428.

Helgeson, V.S. (2003). Cognitive adaptation, psychological adjustment, and disease progression among angioplasty patients: 4 years later. *Health Psychology, 22,* 30–38.

Helgeson, V.S. (2003a). Gender-related traits and health. In J. Suls, & K.A. Wallston (Eds.), *Social psychological foundations of health and illness* (pp. 367–394). Oxford, England: Blackwell Publishing.

Helgeson, V.S. (2003b). Unmitigated communion and adjustment to breast cancer: Associations and explanations. *Journal of Applied Social Psychology, 33,* 1643–1661.

Helgeson, V.S. (in press). Gender and health. In A. Baum, T.A. Revenson, & J.E. Singer (Eds), *Handbook of health psychology,* 2nd ed. New York: Taylor & Francis.

Helgeson, V.S., Escobar, O., Siminerio, L., & Becker, D. (2007). Unmitigated communion and health among adolescents with and without diabetes: The mediating role of eating disturbances. *Personality and Social Psychology Bulletin, 33,* 519–536.

Helgeson, V.S., & Lepore, S.J. (2004). Quality of life following prostate cancer: The role of agency and unmitigated agency. *Journal of Applied Social Psychology, 34,* 2559–2585.

Helgeson, V.S., Reynolds, K.A., & Tomich, P.L. (2006). A meta-analytic review of benefit finding and growth. *Journal of Consulting and Clinical Psychology, 74,* 797–816.

Helgeson, V.S., Snyder, P., & Seltman, H. (2004). Psychological and physical adjustment to breast cancer over 4 years: Identifying distinct trajectories of change. *Health Psychology, 23,* 3–15.

Holahan, C.J., Moos, R.H., Holahan, C.K., & Brennan, P.L. (1997). Social context, coping strategies, and depressive symptoms: An expanded model with cardiac patients. *Journal of Personality and Social Psychology, 72,* 918–928.

Holland, J.C., & Lewis, S. (2000). *The human side of cancer: Living with hope, coping with uncertainty.* New York: HarperCollins.

Holtzman, S., & DeLongis, A. (2007). One day at a time: The impact of daily satisfaction with spouse responses on pain, negative affect and catastrophizing among individuals with rheumatoid arthritis. *Pain, 131,* 202–213.

Holtzman S, Newth S, & DeLongis A. (2004). The role of social support in coping with daily pain among patients with rheumatoid arthritis. *Journal of Health Psychology, 9,* 677–695.

Hotopf, M., Chidgey, J. Addington-Hall, J., and Ly, K.L. (2002). Depression in advanced disease: A systematic review. Part 1. Prevalence and case finding. *Palliative Medicine, 16,* 81–97.

Hoyt, M.A., & Stanton, A.L. (in press). Adjustment to chronic illness. In A.S. Baum, T.A. Revenson, & J.E. Singer (Eds.), *Handbook of health psychology* (2nd ed.). New York: Taylor & Francis.

Jacobsen, P.B., Sadler, I.J., Booth-Jones, M., Soety, E., Weitzner, M.A., & Fields, K.K. (2002). Predictors of posttraumatic stress disorder symptomatology following bone marrow transplantation for cancer. *Journal of Consulting and Clinical Psychology, 70,* 235–240.

Janoff-Bulman, R., & Berger, A.R. (2000). The other side of trauma: Towards a psychology of appreciation. In J.H. Harvey, & E.D. Miller (Eds.), *Loss and trauma: General and close relationship perspectives* (pp. 29–44). Philadelphia: Taylor and Francis.

Janoff-Bulman, R., & Frantz, C.M. (1997). The impact of trauma on meaning: From meaningless world to meaningful life. In M. Power, & C.R. Brewin (Eds.), *The transformation of meaning in psychological therapies* (pp. 91–106). New York: Wiley.

Katz, R.C., Flasher, L., Cacciapaglia, H., & Nelson, S. (2001). The psychosocial impact of cancer and lupus: A cross-validation study that extends the generality of "benefit-finding" in

patients with chronic disease. *Journal of Behavioral Medicine, 24,* 561–571.

Keefe, F.J., Blumenthal, J., Baucom, D., Affleck, G., Waugh, R., Caldwell, D.S., & Lefebvre, J. (2004). Effects of spouse-assisted coping skills training and exercise training in patients with osteoarthritic knee pain: A randomized controlled study. *Pain, 110,* 539–549.

Keefe, F.J., Buffington, A.L.H., Studts, J.L., & Rumble, M.E. (2002). Behavioral medicine: 2002 and beyond. *Journal of Consulting and Clinical Psychology, 70,* 852–856.

Keefe, F.J., Smith, S.J., Buffington, A.L.H., Gibson, J., Studts, J.L., & Caldwell, D.S. (2002). Recent advances and future directions in the biopsychosocial assessment and treatment of arthritis. *Journal of Consulting and Clinical Psychology, 70,* 640–655.

Kiecolt-Glaser, J.K., McGuire, L., Robles, T.F., & Glaser, R. (2002). Emotions, morbidity, and mortality: New perspectives from psychoneuroimmunology. *Annual Review of Psychology, 53,* 83–107.

Kinder, L.S., Kamarck, T.W., Baum, A., & Orchard, T.J. (2002). Depressive symptomatology and coronary heart disease in Type I diabetes mellitus: A study of possible mechanisms. *Health Psychology, 21,* 542–552.

Landrine, H., & Klonoff, E. (1992). Culture and health-related schemas: A review and proposal for interdisciplinary integration. *Health Psychology, 11,* 267–276.

Lanza, A.F., Cameron, A.E., & Revenson, T.A. (1995). Helpful and unhelpful support among individuals with rheumatic diseases. *Psychology and Health, 10,* 449–462.

Lazarus, R.S. (1981). The stress and coping paradigm. In C. Edisdorfer, D. Cohen, A. Kleinman, & P. Maxim (Eds.), *Models for clinical psychopathology* (pp. 177–214). New York: Spectrum Medical and Scientific Books.

Lazarus, R.S. (1991). *Emotion and adaptation.* New York: Oxford University Press.

Lazarus, R.S., & Folkman, S. (1984). *Stress, appraisal, and coping.* New York: Springer.

Lepore, S.J. (2001). A social-cognitive processing model of emotional adjustment to cancer. In A. Baum, & B.L. Andersen (Eds.), *Psychosocial interventions for cancer* (pp. 99–116). Washington, DC: American Psychological Association.

Lepore, S.J., & Eton, D.T. (2000). Response shifts in prostate cancer patients: An evaluation of suppressor and buffer models. In C. Schwartz, & M. Sprangers (Eds.), *Adaptations to changing health: Response shift in quality-of-life research* (pp. 37–51). Washington, DC: American Psychological Association.

Lepore, S.J., & Revenson, T.A. (2007). Social constraints on disclosure and adjustment to cancer. *Social and Personality Psychology Compass, 1*(1), 313–333. doi:10.1111/j.1751-9004.2007.00013.

Lepore, S.J., Revenson, T.A., Weinberger, S., Weston, P., Frisina, P.G., Robertson, R., et al. (2006). Effects of social stressors on cardiovascular reactivity in black and white women. *Annals of Behavioral Medicine, 31,* 120–127.

Leventhal, H., Leventhal, E.A., & Cameron, L. (2001). Representations, procedures, and affect in illness self-regulation: A perceptual-cognitive model. In A. Baum, T.A. Revenson, & J.E. Singer (Eds.), *Handbook of health psychology* (pp. 19–47). Mahwah, NJ: Erlbaum.

Levine, J., Warrenburg, S., Kerns, R., Schwartz, G., Delaney, R., Fontana, A., et al. (1987). The role of denial in recovery from coronary heart disease. *Psychosomatic Medicine, 49,* 109–117.

Levy, S.M., Haynes, L.T., Herberman, R.B., Lee, J., McFeeley, S., & Kirkwood, J. (1992). Mastectomy versus breast conservation surgery: Mental health effects at long-term follow-up. *Health Psychology, 11*, 349–354.

Lewin, K. (1997). *Resolving social conflicts and field theory in social science.* Washington, DC: American Psychological Association. (Original work published 1951).

Linden, W., Phillips, M.J., & Leclerc, J. (2007). Psychological treatment of cardiac patients: A meta-analysis. *European Heart Journal, 28*, 2972–2984.

Low, S. (1995). Embodied metaphors: Nerves as lived experience. In T. Csordas (Ed.), *Embodiment and experience: The existential ground of culture and self* (pp. 139–162). Cambridge, England: Cambridge University Press.

Lustman, P.J., & Clouse, R.E. (2005). Depression in diabetic patients: The relationship between mood and glycemic control. *Journal of Diabetes and Its Complications, 19*, 113–122.

Lutgendorf, S.K., Antoni, M.H., Schneiderman, N., Ironson, G., & Fletcher, M.A. (1995). Psychosocial interventions and quality of life changes across the HIV spectrum. In J.E. Dimsdale, & A. Baum (Eds.), *Quality of life in behavioral medicine research* (pp. 205–239). Hillsdale, NJ: Erlbaum.

MacIntyre, S., & Hunt, K. (1997). Socio-economic position, gender and health: How do they interact? *Journal of Health Psychology, 2*, 315–334.

Maes, S., Leventhal, H., & De Ridder, D.T.D. (1996). Coping with chronic diseases. In M. Zeidner, & N. Endler (Eds.), *Handbook of coping: Theory, research, applications* (pp. 221–251). New York: Wiley.

Majerovitz, S.D., & Revenson, T.A. (1994). Sexuality and rheumatic disease: The significance of gender. *Arthritis Care and Research, 7*, 29–34.

Manne, S.L., & Badr, H. (2008). Intimacy and relationship processes in couples' psychosocial adaptation to cancer. *Cancer, 112*, 2541–2555.

Manne, S., Ostroff, J., Norton, T., Fox, K., Goldstein, L., & Grana, G. (2006). Cancer-related relationship communication in couples coping with early stage breast cancer. *Psycho-Oncology, 15*, 234–247.

Manne, S.L., Ostroff, J., Winkel, G., Grana, G., & Fox, K. (2005). Partner unsupportive responses, avoidant coping, and distress among women with early stage breast cancer: Patient and partner perspectives. *Health Psychology, 24*, 635–641.

Manne, S.L., Sherman, M., Ross, S., Ostroff, J., Heyman, R.E., & Fox, K. (2004). Couples' support-related communication, psychological distress, and relationship satisfaction among women with early stage breast cancer. *Journal of Consulting and Clinical Psychology, 72*, 660–670.

Martin, L.R., Friedman, H.S., Tucker, J.S., Tomlinson-Keasey, C., Criqui, M.H., & Schwartz, J.E. (2002). A life course perspective on childhood cheerfulness and its relation to mortality risk. *Personality and Social Psychology Bulletin, 28*, 1155–1165.

Martire, L.M., Lustig, A.P., Schulz, R., Miller, G.E., & Helgeson, V.S. (2004). Is it beneficial to involve a family member? A meta-analysis of psychosocial interventions for chronic illness. *Health Psychology, 23*, 599–611.

Martire, L.M., & Schulz, R. (2007). Involving family in psychosocial interventions for chronic illness. *Current Directions in Psychological Science, 16*, 90–94.

Martire, L.M., & Schulz, R. (in press). Caregiving and carereceiving in later life: Recent evidence for health effects and promising intervention approaches. In A. Baum, T.A. Revenson,
& J.E. Singer (Eds.), *Handbook of health psychology* (2nd ed.). New York: Taylor & Francis.

Martire, L.M., Schulz, R., Keefe, F.J., Rudy, T.E., & Starz, T.W. (2007). Couple-oriented education and support intervention: Effects on individuals with osteoarthritis and their spouses. *Rehabilitation Psychology, 52*, 121–132.

Massie, M.J. (2004). Prevalence of depression in patients with cancer. *Journal of the National Cancer Institute Monographs, 32*, 57–71.

Matthews, K.A., Räikkönen, K., Gallo, L. & Kuller, L.H. (2008). Association between socioeconomic status and metabolic syndrome in women: Testing the reserve capacity model. *Health Psychology, 27*, 576–583.

Mays, V.M., Cochran, S.D., & Barnes, N.W. (2007). Race, race-based discrimination, and health outcomes among African Americans. *Annual Review of Psychology, 58*, 24.1–24.25

McClain, C.S. (Ed.). (1989). *Women as healers: Cross-cultural perspectives.* New Brunswick, NJ: Rutgers University Press.

Meyer, T.J., & Mark, M.M. (1995). Effects of psychosocial interventions with adult cancer patients: A meta-analysis of randomized experiments. *Health Psychology, 14*, 101–108.

Meyerowitz, B.E., Richardson, J., Hudson, S., & Leedham, B. (1998). Ethnicity and cancer outcomes: Behavioral and psychosocial considerations. *Psychological Bulletin, 123*, 47–70.

Michela, J.L. (1987). Interpersonal and individual impacts of a husband's heart attack. In A. Baum & J.E. Singer (Eds.), *Handbook of psychology and health* Vol. 5 (pp. 255–301). Hillsdale, NJ: Erlbaum.

Montgomery, G.H., & Bovbjerg, D.H. (2001). Specific response expectancies predict anticipatory nausea during chemotherapy for breast cancer. *Journal of Consulting and Clinical Psychology, 69*, 831–835.

Moos, R.H., & Schaefer, J.A. (1984). The crisis of physical illness. In R. Moos (Ed.), *Coping with physical illness* (pp. 3–26). New York: Plenum.

Moskowitz, J.T. (2003). Positive affect predicts lower risk of AIDS mortality. *Psychosomatic Medicine, 65*, 620–626.

Moskowitz, J.T., Hult, J.R., Bussolari, C., & Acree, M. (2009). What works in coping with HIV? A meta-analysis with implications for coping with serious illness. *Psychological Bulletin, 135*, 121–141.

Müller-Tasch, T., Frankenstein, L., Holzapfel, N., Schellberg, D., Löwe, B., Nelles, M., et al. (2008). Panic disorder in patients with chronic heart failure. *Journal of Psychosomatic Research, 64*, 299–303.

National Center for Health Statistics. (2009). *Health, United States, 2008 with chartbook.* Hyattsville, MD: National Center for Health Statistics.

Neugarten, B. (1979). Time, age and the life cycle. *American Journal of Psychiatry, 136*, 887–894.

Neugebauer, A., Katz, P.P., & Pasch, L.A. (2003). Effect of valued activity disability, social comparison, and satisfaction with ability on depressive symptoms in rheumatoid arthritis. *Health Psychology, 22*, 253–262.

Newell, S.A., Sanson-Fisher, R.W., Savolainen, N.J. (2002). Systematic review of psychological therapies for cancer patients: Overview and recommendations for future research. *Journal of the National Cancer Institute, 94*, 558–584.

Newman, S., Fitzpatrick, R., Revenson, T.A., Skevington, S., & Williams, G. (1996). *Understanding rheumatoid arthritis.* London: Routledge and Kegan Paul.

Nezu, A.M., Nezu, C.M., Felgoise, S.H., McClure, K.S., & Houts, P.S. (2003). Project Genesis: Assessing the efficacy of problem-solving therapy for adult distressed adult cancer patients. *Journal of Consulting and Clinical Psychology, 71*, 1036–1048.

Northouse, L.L., Mood, D.W., Schafenacker, A. Montie, J.E., Sandler, H.M., Forman, J.D., & Kershaw, T. (2007). Randomized clinical trial of a family intervention for prostate cancer patients and their spouses. *Cancer, 110*, 2809–2818.

Orbell, S., Jonston, M., Rowley, D., Espley, A., & Davey, P. (1998). Cognitive representations of illness and functional and affective adjustment following surgery for osteoarthritis. *Social Science and Medicine, 47*, 93–102.

Osowiecki, D.M., & Compas, B.E. (1999). A prospective study of coping, perceived control and psychological adjustment to breast cancer. *Cognitive Therapy and Research, 23*, 169–180.

Paradies, Y. (2006). A systematic review of empirical research on self-reported racism and health. *International Journal of Epidemiology, 35*, 888–901.

Park, C.L., Lechner, S.C., Antoni, M.H., & Stanton, A.L. (Eds.). (2009). *Medical illness and positive life change: Can crisis lead to personal transformation?* Washington, DC: American Psychological Association.

Piro, M., Zeldow, P.B., Knight, S.J., Mytko, J.J., & Gradishar, W.J. (2001). The relationship between agentic and communal personality traits and psychosocial adjustment to breast cancer. *Journal of Clinical Psychology in Medical Settings, 8*, 263–271.

Polonsky, W.H., Anderson, B.J., Lohrer, P.A., Welch, G., Jacobson, A.M., Aponte, J.E., et al. (1995). Assessment of diabetes-related distress. *Diabetes Care, 18*, 754–760.

Polsky, D., Doshi, J.A., Marcus, S, Oslin, D., Rothbard, A., Thomas, N., & Thompson, C.L. (2005). Long-term risk for depressive symptoms after a medical diagnosis. *Archives of Internal Medicine, 165*, 1260–1266.

Porter, L.S., Keefe, F.J., Baucom, D.H., Hurwitz, H., Moser, B., Patterson, E., & Kim, H.J. (2009). Partner-assisted emotional disclosure for patients with gastrointestinal cancer. *Cancer, 115* (18 suppl), 4326–4338.

Rabin, C., Leventhal, H., & Goodin, S. (2004). Conceptualizations of disease timeline predicts posttreatment distress in breast cancer patients. *Health Psychology, 23*, 407–412.

Rasmussen, H.N., Scheier, M.F., & Greenhouse, J.B. (2009). Optimism and physical health: A meta-analytic review. *Annals of Behavioral Medicine, 37*, 239–256.

Revenson, T.A. (1990). All other things are *not* equal: An ecological perspective on the relation between personality and disease. In H.S. Friedman (Ed.), *Personality and disease* (pp. 65–94). New York: Wiley.

Revenson, T.A. (1993). The role of social support with rheumatic disease. In S. Newman, & M. Shipley (Eds.), *Psychological aspects of rheumatic disease. Bailliere's Clinical Rheumatology* 7(2) (pp. 377–396). London: Bailliere Tindal.

Revenson, T.A. (2003). Scenes from a marriage: Examining support, coping, and gender within the context of chronic illness. In J. Suls, & K. Wallston (Eds.), *Social psychological foundations of health and illness* (pp. 530–559). Oxford, England: Blackwell.

Revenson, T.A., Abraído-Lanza, A.F., Majerovitz, S.D., & Jordan, C. (2005). Couples' coping with chronic illness: What's gender got to do with it? In T.A. Revenson, K. Kayser, & G. Bodenmann (Eds.), *Emerging perspectives on couples'*

coping with stress* (pp. 137–156). Washington, DC: American Psychological Association.

Revenson, T.A., & DeLongis, A. (2011). Couples coping with chronic illness. In S. Folkman (Ed.), *Oxford handbook of stress, health, and coping* (pp. 101-123). NY: Oxford University Press.

Revenson, T.A., Kayser, K., & Bodenmann, G. (Eds.). (2005). *Couples coping with stress: Emerging perspectives on dyadic coping.* Washington, DC: American Psychological Association.

Roberts, M.C., & Steele, R.G. (Eds.). (2009). *Handbook of pediatric psychology* (4th ed.). New York: Guilford.

Roesch, S.C., Adams, L., Hines, A., Palmores, A., Vyas, P., Tran, C., et al. (2005). Coping with prostate cancer: A meta-analytic review. *Journal of Behavioral Medicine, 28*, 281–293.

Rohrbaugh, M.J., Cranford, J.A., Shoham, V., Nicklas, J.M., Sonnega, J., & Coyne, J.C. (2002). Couples coping with congestive heart failure: Role and gender differences in psychological distress. *Journal of Family Psychology, 16*, 3–13.

Rose, G., Suls, J., Green, P.J., Lounsbury, P., & Gordon, E. (1996). Comparison of adjustment, activity, and tangible social support in men and women patients and their spouses during the six months post-myocardial infarction. *Annals of Behavioral Medicine, 18*, 264–272.

Rubel, A.J., & Garro, L.C. (1992). Social and cultural factors in the successful control of tuberculosis. *Public Health Reports, 107*, 626–636.

Ruiz, J.M., Steffen, P., & Prather, C.C. (in press). Socioeconomic status and health. In A. Baum, T.A. Revenson, & J.E. Singer (Eds.), *Handbook of health psychology* (2nd ed.). New York: Taylor & Francis.

Rutledge, T., Reis, V.A., Linke, S.E., Greenberg, B.H., & Mills, P.J. (2006). Depression in heart failure a meta-analytic review of prevalence, intervention effects, and associations with clinical outcomes. *Journal of the American College of Cardiology, 48*, 1527–1537.

Saegert, S., Thompson, J.P., & Warren, M.R. (2001). *Social capital and poor communities.* New York: Russell Sage Foundation Publications.

Sarason, S.B. (1989). *The making of an American psychologist.* San Francisco: Jossey-Bass.

Scheier, M.F., & Bridges, M.W. (1995). Person variables and health: Personality predispositions and acute psychological states as shared determinants for disease. *Psychosomatic Medicine, 57*, 255–268.

Scheier, M.F., & Carver, C.S. (1985). Optimism, coping and health: Assessment and implications of generalized outcome expectancies. *Health Psychology, 4*, 219–247.

Scheier, M.F., Matthews, K.A., Owens, J.F., Magovern, G.J., Lefebvre, R.C., Abbott, A.R., & Carver, C.S. (2003). Dispositional optimism and recovery from coronary artery bypass surgery: The beneficial effects on physical and psychological well-being. In P. Salovey, & A.J. Rothman (Eds.), *Social psychology of health: Key readings in social psychology* (pp. 342–361). New York, NY: Psychology Press.

Scheier, M.F., Matthews, K.A., Owens, J.F., Magovern, G.J., Lefebvre, R.C., Abbott, R.A., et al. (1989). Dispositional optimism and recovery from coronary artery bypass surgery: The beneficial effects on physical and psychological well-being. *Journal of Personality and Social Psychology, 57*, 1024–1040.

Schiaffino, K.M., & Revenson, T.A. (1992). The role of perceived self-efficacy, perceived control, and causal attributions in adaptation to rheumatoid arthritis: Distinguishing mediator vs. moderator effects. *Personality and Social Psychology Bulletin, 18*, 709–718.

Schiaffino, K.M., Revenson, T.A., & Gibofsky, A. (1991). Assessing the role of self-efficacy beliefs in adaptation to rheumatoid arthritis. *Arthritis Care and Research, 4*, 150–157.

Schou, I., Ekeberg, Ø., & Ruland, C.M. (2005). The mediating role of appraisal and coping in the relationship between optimism-pessimism and quality of life. *Psycho-Oncology, 14*, 718–727.

Scott, J.L., Halford, W.K., & Ward, B.G. (2004). United we stand? The effects of a couple-coping intervention on adjustment to early stage breast or gynecologic cancer. *Journal of Consulting and Clinical Psychology, 72*(6), 1122–1135.

Scott-Sheldon, L.A., Kalichman, S.C., Carey, M.P., & Fielder, R.L. (2008). Stress management interventions for HIV+ adults: A meta-analysis of randomized controlled trials, 1989 to 2006. *Health Psychology, 27*, 129–139.

Seeman, T.E., Dubin, L.F., & Seeman, M. (2003). Religiosity/spirituality and health: A critical review of the evidence for biological pathways. *American Psychologist, 58*, 53–63.

Shnek, Z.M., Irvine, J., Stewart, D., & Abbey, S. (2001). Psychological factors and depressive symptoms in ischemic heart disease. *Health Psychology, 20*, 141–145.

Shumaker, S., & Hill, D.R. (1991). Gender differences in social support and physical health. *Health Psychology, 10*, 102–111.

Siegel, K., & Schrimshaw, E.W. (2000). Perceiving benefits in adversity: Stress-related growth in women living with HIV/AIDS. *Social Science and Medicine, 51*, 1543–1554.

Smith, B.W., & Zautra, A.J. (2002). The role of personality in exposure and reactivity to interpersonal stress in relation to arthritis disease activity and negative affect in women. *Health Psychology, 21*, 81–88.

Smith, T.W., & Gallo, L.C. (2001). Personality traits as risk factors for physical illness. In A. Baum, T.A. Revenson, & J.E. Singer (Eds.), *Handbook of health psychology* (pp. 139–173). Mahwah, NJ: Erlbaum.

Smyth, J., Stone, A., Hurewitz, A., & Kaell, A. (1999). Effects of writing about stressful experiences on symptom reduction in patients with asthma or rheumatoid arthritis: A randomized trial. *Journal of the American Medical Association, 281*, 1304–1309.

Somerfield, M.R., & McCrae, R. (2000). Stress and coping research: Methodological challenges, theoretical advances, and clinical applications. *American Psychologist, 55*, 620–625.

Spelten, E.R., Sprangers, M.A.G., & Verbeek, J.H.A.M. (2002). Factors reported to influence the return to work of cancer survivors: A literature review. *Psycho-Oncology, 11*, 124–131.

Spencer, S.M., Lehman, J.M., Wynings, C., Arena, P., Carver, C.S., Antoni, M.H., et al. (1999). Concerns about breast cancer and relations to psychosocial well-being in a multiethnic sample of early-stage patients. *Health Psychology, 18*, 159–168.

Stanton, A.L., Bower, J.E., & Low, C.A. (2006). Posttraumatic growth after cancer. In L.G. Calhoun & R.G. Tedeschi (Eds.), *Handbook of posttraumatic growth: Research and practice* (pp. 138–175). Mahwah, NJ: Lawrence Erlbaum Associates.

Stanton, A.L., & Danoff-Burg, S. (2002). Emotional expression, expressive writing, and cancer. In S. Lepore, & J. Smyth (Eds.). *The writing cure: Theory and research on the expressive writing paradigm* (pp. 31–51). Washington, DC: American Psychological Association.

Stanton, A.L., Danoff-Burg, S., Cameron, C.L., Bishop, M.M., Collins, C.A., Kirk, S.B., et al. (2000). Emotionally expressive coping predicts psychological and physical adjustment to breast cancer. *Journal of Consulting and Clinical Psychology, 68*, 875–882.

Stanton, A.L., Danoff-Burg, S., & Huggins, M.E. (2002). The first year after breast cancer diagnosis: Hope and coping strategies as predictors of adjustment. *Psycho-Oncology, 11*, 93–102.

Stanton, A.L., & Snider, P.R. (1993). Coping with a breast cancer diagnosis: A prospective study. *Health Psychology, 12*, 16–23.

Stanton, A.L., Tennen, H., Affleck, G., & Mendola, R. (1992). Coping and adjustment to infertility. *Journal of Social and Clinical Psychology, 11*, 1–13.

Stewart, A.L., Greenfield, S., Hays, R.D., Wells, K., Rogers, W.H., Berry, S.D., et al. (1989). Functional status and well-being of patients with chronic conditions: Results from the Medical Outcomes Study. *Journal of the American Medical Association, 262*, 907–913.

Sullivan, M.D., LaCroix, A.Z., Russo, J.E., & Walker, E.A. (2001). Depression and self-reported physical health in patients with coronary disease: Mediating and moderating factors. *Psychosomatic Medicine, 63*, 248–256.

Suls, J., & Fletcher, B. (1985). The relative efficacy of avoidant and nonavoidant coping strategies: A meta-analysis. *Health Psychology, 4*, 249–288.

Tatrow, K., & Montgomery, G.H. (2006). Cognitive behavioral therapy techniques for distress and pain in breast cancer patients: A meta-analysis. *Journal of Behavioral Medicine, 29*, 17–27.

Taylor, S.E. (1983). Adjustment to threatening events: A theory of cognitive adaptation. *American Psychologist, 38*, 1161–1173.

Taylor, S.E., Dickerson, S.S., & Klein, L.C. (2002). Toward a biology of social support. In C.R. Snyder, & S.J. Lopez (Eds.), *Handbook of positive psychology* (pp. 556–569). New York: Oxford University Press.

Taylor, S.E., Klein, L.C., Lewis, B.P., Gruenewald, T.L., Gurung, R.A.R., & Updegraff, J.A. (2000). Biobehavioral responses to stress in females: Tend-and-befriend, not fight-or-flight. *Psychological Review, 107*, 411–429.

Taylor, S.E., Repetti, R., & Seeman, T.E. (1997). Health psychology: What is an unhealthy environment and how does it get under the skin? *Annual Review of Psychology, 48*, 411–447.

Taylor, S.E., & Stanton, A.L. (2007). Coping resources, coping processes, and mental health. *Annual Review of Clinical Psychology, 3*, 377–401.

Tedeschi, R.G., & Calhoun, L.G. (2004). Posttraumatic growth: Conceptual foundations and empirical evidence. *Psychological Inquiry, 15*, 1–18.

Tennen, H., & Affleck, G. (1990). Blaming others for threatening events. *Psychological Bulletin, 108*, 209–232.

Tennen, H., & Affleck, G. (2000). The perception of personal control: Sufficiently important to warrant careful scrutiny. *Personality and Social Psychology Bulletin, 26*, 152–156.

Tennen, H., & Affleck, G. (2009). Assessing positive life change: In search of meticulous methods. In Park, C.L., Lechner, S.C., Antoni, M.H., & Stanton, A.L. (Eds.) *Medical illness and positive life change: Can crisis lead to personal transformation?*

(pp. 31–49). Washington, DC: American Psychological Association.

Thombs, B.D., De Jonge, P., Coyne, J.C., Whooley, M.A., Frasure-Smith, N., Mitchell, A.J., et al. (2008). Depression screening and patient outcomes in cardiovascular care: A systematic review. *Journal of the American Medical Association, 300*, 2161–2171.

Thompson, S.C., & Kyle, D.J. (2000). The role of perceived control in coping with the losses associated with chronic illness. In J.H. Harvey, & E.D. Miller (Eds.), *Loss and trauma: General and close relationship perspectives* (pp. 131–145). Philadelphia: Brunner-Routledge.

Thompson, S.C., Nanni, C., & Levine, A. (1994). Primary versus secondary and central versus consequence-related control in HIV-positive men. *Journal of Personality and Social Psychology, 67*, 540–547.

Thompson, S.C., Sobolew-Shubin, A., Galbraith, M.E., Schwankovsky, L., & Cruzen, D. (1993). Maintaining perceptions of control: Finding perceived control in low-control circumstances. *Journal of Personality and Social Psychology, 64*, 293–304.

Tindle, H.A., Chang, Y.F., Kuller, L.H., Manson, J.E., Robinson, J.G., Rosal, M.C., et al. (2009). Optimism, cynical hostility, and incident coronary heart disease and mortality in the Women's Health Initiative. *Circulation, 120*, 656–662.

Tomich, P.L., & Helgeson, V.S. (2002). Five years later: A cross-sectional comparison of breast cancer survivors with healthy women. *Psycho-Oncology, 11*, 154–169.

Tomich, P.L., & Helgeson, V.S. (2006). Cognitive adaptation theory and breast cancer recurrence: Are there limits? *Journal of Consulting and Clinical Psychology, 74*, 980–987.

Trudeau, K.J., Danoff-Burg, S., Revenson, T.A., & Paget, S. (2003). Gender differences in agency and communion among patients with rheumatoid arthritis. *Sex Roles, 49*, 303–311.

Trunzo, J.J., & Pinto, B.M. (2003). Social support as a mediator of optimism and distress in breast cancer survivors. *Journal of Consulting and Clinical Psychology, 71*, 805–811.

Uchino, B.N. (2004). *Social support and physical health: Understanding the health consequences of relationships.* New Haven: Yale University Press.

Uchino, B.N. (2006). Social support and health: A review of physiological processes potentially underlying links to disease outcomes. *Journal of Behavioral Medicine, 29*, 377–387.

Uchino, B.N., Cacioppo, J.T., & Kiecolt-Glaser, J.K. (1996). The relationship between social support and physiological processes: A review with emphasis on underlying mechanisms and implications for health. *Psychological Bulletin, 119*, 488–531.

Van Tilberg, M.A.L., McCaskill, C.C., Lane, J.D., Edwards, C.L., Bethel, A., Feinglos, M.N., et al. (2001). Depressed mood is a factor in glycemic control in type I diabetes. *Psychosomatic Medicine, 63*, 551–555.

van't Spijker, A., Trijsburg, R.W., & Duivenvoorden, H.J. (1997). Psychological sequelae of cancer diagnosis: A meta-analytical review of 58 studies after 1980. *Psychosomatic Medicine, 59*, 280–293.

Vickberg, S.M.J. (2003). The Concerns about Recurrence Scale (CARS): A systematic measure of women's fears about the possibility of breast cancer recurrence. *Annals of Behavioral Medicine, 25*, 16–24.

Visotsky, H.M., Hamburg, D.A., Goss, M.E., & Lebovits, B.Z. (1961). Coping behavior under extreme stress: Observations of patients with severe poliomyelitis. *Archives of General Psychiatry, 5*, 27–52.

Vitaliano, P.P., Zhang, J., & Scanlan, J.M. (2003). Is caregiving hazardous to one's physical health? A meta-analysis. *Psychological Bulletin, 129*, 946–972.

Waltz, M., Badura, B., Pfaff, H., & Schott, T. (1988). Marriage and the psychological consequences of a heart attack: A longitudinal study of adaptation to chronic illness after 3 years. *Social Science and Medicine, 27*, 149–158.

Weaver, K.E., Llabre, M.M., Duran, R.E., Antoni, M.M., Penedo, F.J., Ironson, G., & Schneiderman, N. (2005). A stress and coping model of medication adherence and viral load in HIV+ men and women on highly active antiretroviral therapy (HAART). *Health Psychology, 24*, 385–392.

Wegner, D., & Pennebaker, J. (Eds.). (1992). *Handbook of mental control.* New York: Prentice-Hall.

Weick, K. (1984). Small wins: Redefining the scale of social problems. *American Psychologist, 39*, 40–49.

Wethington, E., McLeod, J.D., & Kessler, R. (1987). The importance of life events for explaining sex differences in mental health. In R.C. Barnett, L. Biener, & G.K. Baruch (Eds.), *Gender and stress* (pp. 144–155). New York: Free Press.

Williams, D.R. (1990). Socioeconomic differentials in health: A review and redirection. *Social Psychology Quarterly, 53*, 81–99.

Williamson, G.M. (2000). Extending the activity restriction model of depressed affect: Evidence from a sample of breast cancer patients. *Health Psychology, 19*, 339–347.

Wills, T.A., & Ainette, M.G. (in press). Social networks and social support. In A.S. Baum, T.A. Revenson, & J.E. Singer (Eds.), *Handbook of health psychology* (2nd ed.). New York: Taylor & Francis.

Wortman, C.B., & Boerner, K. (2011). Beyond the myths of coping with loss: Prevailing assumptions versus scientific evidence. In H.S. Friedman (Ed.), *The Oxford handbook of health psychology.* New York: Oxford University Press.

Wulsin, L.R., & Singal, B.M. (2003). Do depressive symptoms increase the risk for the onset of coronary disease? A systematic quantitative review. *Psychosomatic Medicine, 65*, 201–210.

Yali, A.M., & Revenson, T.A. (2004). How changes in population demographics will impact health psychology: Incorporating a broader notion of cultural competence into the field. *Health Psychology, 23*, 147–155.

Young, L.D. (1992). Psychological factors in rheumatoid arthritis. *Journal of Consulting and Clinical Psychology, 60*, 619–627.

Zautra, A.J., & Manne, S.L. (1992). Coping with rheumatoid arthritis: A review of a decade of research. *Annals of Behavioral Medicine, 14*, 31–39.

Zautra, A.J., Davis, M.C., Reich J.W., Nicassio P., Tennen H., Finan P., et al. (2008). Comparison of cognitive behavioral and mindfulness meditation interventions on adaptation to rheumatoid arthritis for patients with and without history of recurrent depression. *Journal of Consulting and Clinical Psychology, 76*, 408–421.

Zautra, A.J., Smith, B., Affleck, G., & Tennen, H. (2001). Examinations of chronic pain and affect relationships: Applications of a dynamic model of affect. *Journal of Consulting and Clinical Psychology, 69*, 785–796.

# Social Comparison Processes: Implications for Physical Health

Jerry Suls

**Abstract**

Social comparisons in the physical health domain can serve several motives, including self-evaluation, self-enhancement, and the finding of common bonds. Comparisons may be made with actual people, media role models, or with implicit "created-in-the-head" norms. Such norms, including the false consensus effect and unrealistic optimism, can undermine health-promotive practices. Comparisons also affect the interpretation of ambiguous somatic changes that might be indicative of physical illness. Symptom appraisal via comparison is discussed in the context of the lay referral network and mass psychogenic illness. Experiencing acute or chronic illness produces uncertainty and threat, which elicit both self-evaluation and self-enhancement motives. These instigate comparisons, leading to assimilation or contrast with better- or worse-off or more knowledgeable targets. Implications of social comparison research and theory for public health campaigns and medical practice are discussed.

**Keywords:** Social comparison, unrealistic optimism, false consensus effect, upward comparison, downward comparison, social support groups, self-enhancement, self-evaluation

By comparing with others, people may assess the correctness of their opinions and whether they have sufficient ability to accomplish their goals (Festinger, 1954; Suls & Wheeler, 2000). The objects of comparisons, however, extend far beyond abilities and opinions to emotional states, income satisfaction, self-concept, and subjective well-being. Social comparisons may be actively sought or arrive unbidden through everyday interactions. They are pervasive and affect every domain of human conduct and experience, including physical illness and well-being. The comic strip "Non Sequitur" recently depicted a couple reclining in lawn chairs next to a cemetery with the husband asserting, "I've never felt so alive" (April 20, 2010). The scenario is preposterous but makes its point. In this chapter, I describe three domains—health prevention, medical treatment-seeking, and adaptation to physical illness—in which social comparisons have been shown to play an important role. First, I provide a brief survey of basic theory and evidence about social comparisons.

## Conceptual Background

The following is a brief survey of the 60-year history of social comparison study. The interested reader is referred to the classic formulation (Festinger, 1954) and revisions and relevant compendia for more detail (Brickman & Bulman, 1977; Goethals & Darley, 1977; Mussweiler, 2003; Stapel & Koomen, 2000; Suls, Martin, & Wheeler, 2000; Wheeler, Martin, & Suls, 1997; Wills, 1981; Wood, 1989).

### Self-evaluation

Social comparison may serve several different motives, including self-evaluation, self-enhancement, and the finding of common bonds (Helgeson & Mickelson, 1995). Festinger's (1954) original formulation emphasized self-evaluation. When people lack objective standards to assess the adequacy of their abilities and accuracy of their opinions, uncertainty creates a drive to socially compare. Comparisons with persons similar to oneself are seen to have the greatest utility. Festinger assumed people wanted to find agreement with others on opinions because consensus implied validity (it may also create a common bond). When considering ability, similarity is important, but there also is a tendency, emphasized in Western culture and referred to as the *unidirectional drive upward*, for people to want to be more like those they see as better than themselves. These two countervailing forces motivate people to compare with and aspire toward slightly better others (Wheeler, 1966). The original theory had a serious ambiguity, however: although similarity figured prominently, the basis of the similarity was unspecified.

This problem was resolved by borrowing two insights from attribution theory (Kelley, 1967): that ability can only be inferred from performance, and that performance is affected not only by ability but also by other attributes, such as motivation, age, experience, etc.; these are referred to as *related attributes*. To draw inferences about ability by comparing level of performance with someone else, it is necessary to be matched with them on these attributes— otherwise one cannot discern whether performing the same or differently is due to ability or to the other attributes. Goethals and Darley (1977) concluded that comparisons with persons who are similar to oneself on related attributes resolve the conceptual ambiguity left by the original theory. More recent perspectives would add a refinement, which is that such comparisons best answer the question, "Am I as good I ought to be (given my background, circumstances, etc.)."

An equally important, but separate question, driven by uncertainty, is "Can I do X?" To arrive at the answer, I must find someone (a proxy) who has already attempted "X" and learn how he or she performed. His or her success or failure signals my future outcome only if both of us performed similarly on a prior task, and my proxy was known to have exerted maximal effort on that prior occasion (e.g., if my proxy was fatigued, his or her performance might have been a serious underestimate of what he or she could accomplish, and therefore a poor prognosticator of my own personal future success). If I do not know my proxy exerted maximum effort, then related attributes become relevant: knowing how we stand on related attributes can suffice to decide whether my proxy is an appropriate comparison (Wheeler, Martin, & Suls, 1997).

As for opinion comparison, the related attribute approach distinguishes between belief and value opinions. Beliefs refer to verifiable facts, whereas values are personal preferences. Comparisons with similar others on related attributes, such as background and general worldview, are of most utility for preference evaluation (Goethals & Darley, 1977). For beliefs, however, someone who is dissimilar on related attributes is hypothesized to be more useful because he or she provides a different perspective to "triangulate on" the truth. A modification proposed by Suls, Martin, and Wheeler (2000) agrees with the prediction about preferences; however, to assess facts, people prefer to compare with someone who is more advantaged on related attributes (and therefore has more expertise) but who still shares their general worldview. The utility of such a comparison person, referred to as a *similar expert*, is illustrated by the finding that gay men are more likely to adopt safe-sex practices if they are advocated by someone who is both more knowledgeable and who shares their sexual orientation (Kelly, Lawrence, Diaz, Stevenson et al. 1991).

### Self-enhancement

Social comparisons, driven by cognitive and affective factors (rather than uncertainty), also can enhance or protect subjective well-being. A popular theory of downward comparison (Wills, 1981) posits that people whose self-esteem is threatened or who have chronic low self-esteem prefer to compare with others who are worse off than themselves. Exposure to a less fortunate person (downward target) is thought to boost subjective well-being via a contrastive process. Downward comparison also was conceived as a coping strategy. Initial evidence for the theory was encouraging (e.g., Buunk & Gibbons, 1997), and it became a major source of ideas for research and intervention among health psychologists who were interested in how people use social comparisons to adapt to the challenges posed by acute and chronic illness (described in more detail later) (Tennen, McKee, & Affleck, 2000).

As more evidence was collected, doubts surfaced about the solidity of downward comparison theory. Taylor and Lobel (1989) proposed that comparing with someone worse off might make oneself feel better, but comparison or contact with someone more fortunate can provide inspiration and information for self-improvement. The picture was further complicated when researchers found evidence that both upward or downward comparisons can elicit positive or negative responses (Buunk, Collins, Taylor, Van Yperen, & Dakoff, 1990). Comparison direction seemed less critical than the implication of the comparison: "Will I get better, or will I get worse?" Since then, experimental evidence has shown that upward comparisons can be inspiring and elicit positive affect (Lockwood & Kunda, 1997), but only if an upward comparison induces the person to assimilate or identify with those who are better off. Prior to these results, self-enhancement was mainly seen as a contrastive outcome; recent research, however, suggests assimilation also is possible.

## Social Cognition Meets Social Comparison

Contemporary theories emphasize how cognitive processes elicit self-evaluations toward (assimilation) or away (contrast) from a target (Mussweiler, 2003). One relevant process, described by cognitive psychologists, is *selective accessibility*; that is, the kind of information about the self and the target that is made cognitively accessible. The other is the automatic process by which the mind searches selectively for information consistent with whichever hypothesis is salient (Klayman & Ha, 1987). If an initial exposure to a target signals a holistic impression of similarity, based on sex or age, then a selective cognitive search automatically is set in motion to find additional similarities—resulting in assimilation with the comparison target. However, if the holistic impression suggests dissimilarity, then the cognitive search is for dissimilarities—resulting in contrast (see Stapel, 2007, for an alternative perspective). The insight that social comparison can eventuate in assimilation or contrast, depending on situational factors, is perhaps the most significant recent advance in this field of study.

## Constructed Norms

Besides actual comparison, another kind of information might be considered a kind of "pseudo-comparison." Often, people assess their abilities and opinions based on their implicit ideas about the distribution of opinions, personal attributes, and behavioral practices in the population. These are "in-the-head" norms, based on some combination of memory, guesswork, and projection. Although not strictly based on real comparisons, these norms may be treated as real. When people have limited capacity or motivation to socially compare with actual people, they may rely on such implicit norms (see Alicke, 1985; Krueger & Clement, 1994; Suls, 1986; Weinstein, 1980). As described in the next section, constructed norms can have as real consequences for health behaviors as actual comparisons.

## Comparison, Social Norms, and Preventive Behavior

Peoples' health-relevant attitudes, perceptions of personal risk, and behaviors are based in part on normative expectations (e.g., Ajzen & Fishbein, 1980): Do others agree or disagree? Are their risks greater or less than mine? And, do they behave as I do? Normative expectations are partly based on comparisons with friends or family members, and sometimes with casual acquaintances or with general norms of the population. The latter might be the most useful—What do most people feel, think, or do?—but precise estimates are only available from scientific polling. Lacking such information, however, people rely on their impressions of social norms based on the unrepresentative, "thin slice" of the population to which they are exposed or can imagine. Lay people use cognitive heuristics, or rules of thumb, to "construct" this norm (Nisbett & Kunda, 1985). Of course, people are not disinterested observers of social norms because they have a vested interest in perceiving their views and practices as appropriate and their personal risks to be low. Not surprisingly, then, perceptions of norms are subject to cognitive and motivated biases, which can lead to distorted perceptions of social norms—three of which are directly relevant to physical health.

### False Consensus and Health Behaviors

One rule of thumb is the *availability heuristic*, whereby behavior or attitudes that are memorable or cognitively accessible tend to be perceived to be more common (Kahneman & Tversky, 1973). Because one's own opinions and practices are typically the most accessible, the tendency is to distort the social norm in the direction of one's own behavior: "What I believe or what I do is more prevalent among my peers." This is commonly referred to as the *false consensus effect* (FCE; Krueger & Clement, 1994; Ross, Greene, & House, 1977). Because the cognitive machinery responsible for norm estimates is unconscious, people are unaware that they are fooling themselves. Adolescents who frequently use alcohol, cigarettes, and marijuana (vs. those who do not) estimate that a higher proportion of their peers also drink, smoke and use marijuana (Suls, Wan, & Sanders, 1988). The FCE also applies to attitudes, experiences, and traits. Lay people and physicians tend to assume that illnesses they have personally experienced tend to be more prevalent in the population (Jemmott, Croyle, & Ditto, 1988). Nurses, who are instructed to adopt so-called "universal standards," such as wearing gloves when taking blood, think that other nurses adopt the same practices. For example, nurses who use gloves estimate that 78% of their peers also do; nurses who rarely wear gloves think only 37% of their peers do (Burns & Knussen, 2005).

The FCE provides a consensus for personal health practices and also projects a "common bond" (Gibbons, Gerrard, & Boney-McCoy, 1995). In this way, cigarette smokers can assume their behavior is normative; binge drinkers can assume their behavior is unexceptional. A fictional consensus also can instigate the adoption of unhealthy practices. Adolescents who initially think they have the same attributes as the prototypical "smoker," are more likely to start smoking (Andrews, Hampson, Backley, Gerrard, & Gibbons, 2008; Gibbons & Eggleston, 1996).

### Unrealistic Optimism

People also tend to believe that negative events are less likely to happen to them than to their peers; in other words, they are at less risk of disease and being injured in natural disasters. This is referred to as *unrealistic optimism* (UR), although "unrealistic *comparative* optimism," is probably a more appropriate term. (UR is analogous to the better-than-average effect, the tendency for a majority of people to rate themselves as higher on positive attributes and lower on negative attributes than their peers; Chambers & Windschitl, 2004). Unrealistic optimism is found for a wide range of health events, including heart attack (Avis, McKinlay, & Smith, 1989), developing skin cancer (Clarke, Williams, & Arthey, 1997), breast cancer (Skinner, Kreuter, Kobrin, & Strecher, 1998), lung cancer (Strecher, Kreuter, & Kobrin, 1995), or contracting human immunodeficiency virus (HIV) infection (Gold & Aucote, 2003). Unrealistic optimism is a group-level effect and considered biased because most people in a group cannot have lower than average risk unless the distribution of risk is greatly skewed (Klein & Cooper, 2008).

The roots of UR are both cognitive and motivational. People may believe they are less vulnerable because they are more familiar with the things they do to prevent harm or injury than with the things other people do (Moore & Small, 2007). They also may be motivated to perceive themselves as less vulnerable to protect their sense of self-esteem (Taylor & Brown, 1988), which may be conceived as another manifestation of the unidirectional drive upward described earlier.

This illusion of invulnerability can be reduced, but it requires special measures. Neither highlighting

a subject's risky behaviors ("I get drunk three or four times a week") versus their nonrisky behaviors, nor asking them to focus on factors that create the problem or risk, are effective (Weinstein & Klein, 1995). In fact, the latter procedure may lead to more optimism, by providing people with more opportunities to think of reasons why their own risk is low (Weinstein, 2003). But learning about the average risk status of peers on factors (which tend to be similar to the subject's) contributing to the disease can reduce UR. Weinstein (2003) concluded the UR is primarily a motivated bias: "people welcome the idea that their relative risk is low but resist the idea that their relative risk is high" (p. 37). The most direct and reliable method to reduce UR may be to provide explicit, personalized feedback about relative risk using information about a person's actual standing on different risk factors (i.e., absolute risk), but this is generally not feasible in large public educational campaigns.

Believing one is comparatively invulnerable has implications for health because UR is associated with less worry and motivation to reduce health-damaging behaviors or to seek medical screening (Blalock DeVellis, Afifi, & Sandler, 1990; Klein, 1997; Lipkus, Klein, Skinner. & Rimer, 2005; Zajac, Klein, & McCaul, 2006). Although absolute risk also plays a role, comparative risk is more important in some health contexts. In an experimental study, Klein (1997) manipulated absolute and comparative risk and showed that only comparative risk influenced levels of worry (cf. Mason, Prevost, & Suttton, 2008).

The FCE and UR seem contradictory: People perceive consensus for their personal practices, but simultaneously think they have superior attributes and better prospects. Both perceptions can coexist, however, if people believe that their peers tend to be similar but they, personally, are somewhat ahead of the "pack", thus satisfying both the need for consensus and self-enhancement.

### Pluralistic Ignorance

False consensus effect and UR reflect positively on the person, but the third bias, pluralistic ignorance (PI), is qualitatively different. It refers to the belief that one's private attitudes and judgments are different from those of others, even though everyone's public behavior appears to be identical (Miller & McFarland, 1987). The classic case is of a small community in the 1930s, in which everyone condemned alcohol and card playing in public, but behaved differently at home (Schanck, 1932). Because of the absence of these (scandalous!) practices in public and the fear of disapproval or embarrassment about expressing their personal views, the citizens mistakenly inferred others' public behavior reflected their private sentiments: "even if no one believes . . . everyone believes that everyone else believes," (Miller & McFarland, 1991, p. 287–288). As a consequence, people continued to publicly advocate and perpetuate a norm no one privately supported. Pluralistic ignorance, in short, creates a feeling of personal distinctiveness and even alienation. Ultimately, such feelings may prompt the individual to conform to the erroneous norm.

Unlike the other normative biases, PI emerges when a disjunction exists between peoples' public expressions and what they privately believe. Pluralistic ignorance is probably less pervasive than FCE or UR, but no less pernicious in its consequences. On college campuses, the apparent approval of alcohol consumption by other students, combined with fear of social disapproval for being different, may make the individual reluctant to publicly express any misgivings—based on his or her own experiences or exposure to hung-over roommates and inappropriate behavior. Consequently, college students infer that they are more uncomfortable with excessive drinking and its consequences than are their peers (Bourgeosie & Bowen, 2001; Prentice & Miller, 1993; Suls & Green, 2003). Pluralistic ignorance tends to be strongest among college men because masculinity is more closely associated with alcohol consumption on campus, and the stigma and pressure for not conforming is perceived to be greater (Suls & Green, 2003). Consistent with these ideas, male students are more apt to increase their drinking over the course of a school year in conformity to the erroneous norm (Prentice & Miller, 1993). Once one becomes a heavy drinker, the reservations may fade away; instead, the social norm is recalibrated—perceiving that others share their approving views about alcohol (Wild, 2002).

## Social Norms, Role Models, and Public Campaigns

The health-relevant norms that people cognitively construct are susceptible to FCE, UR, and PI biases and thereby create apparent support for damaging behaviors and undermine health-promoting activities. In addition, societal trends stemming from political, cultural, or business sources can promote comparison "role models" that serve to skew the perception of normative practices. A prime example would be the smoking campaigns launched by tobacco companies depicting people who smoke as "popular," "cool," and sophisticated.

Another example concerns physical appearance, which figures significantly in self-esteem and is implicated in eating disorders. Physical appearance comparisons with more attractive targets such as fashion models and TV and movie celebrities (O'Brien et al., 2009) are common and perhaps unavoidable. In contemporary society, particularly for women, body thinness tends to be held up as a standard and is promoted widely in the media (e.g., Levine & Murnen, 2009). In this way, thinness becomes the norm to which to aspire and use as a standard.

Archival evidence from television, magazine, movies, and other literature document the prevalence of the thinness standard (e.g., Grabe, Ward, & Hyde, 2008). Furthermore, meta-analyses (Grabe et al., 2008; Groesz, Levine, & Murnen, 2002) find small to moderate effect sizes for the impact of media images on body dissatisfaction and eating disorders. For example, level of media exposure predicts increases in negative body image and disordered eating in longitudinal studies of children and early adolescents (see Levine & Murnen, 2009). Even laboratory experiments manipulating experimental exposure to television commercials featuring the thin ideal showed higher levels of body dissatisfaction and drive for thinness 2 years later (Hargreaves & Tiggemann, 2003).

In everyday life, exposure to fit and unfit peers is even more common than media exposure to models. Wasilenko, Kulik, and Wanic (2007) conducted a field experiment manipulating exposure to a fit versus an unfit model (or no model) on the exercise behavior of female undergraduates who were working out at a recreation center. Each woman's time exercising on the apparatus was unobtrusively recorded before she was asked to complete a brief questionnaire about body satisfaction. If women had happened to exercise in the presence of a fit peer, they reported lower body satisfaction than did women exercising near an unfit peer or no-peer, with no difference between the two latter conditions. The women exposed to the fit exerciser also devoted less time to exercise, regardless of their body mass index. The media may provide idealized standards for attractiveness or fitness, but "an unfavorable comparison with a model from Victoria Secret would itself have no direct implications for one's dating prospects, whereas unfavorable comparisons with everyday peers well could" (Wasilenko et al., 2007, p. 743).

### Recalibrating Norms with Comparison Feedback

Biased perceptions of social norms, which are subject to cognitive heuristics and motivated reasoning, and extreme comparison standards broadcast in the media can undermine health-promotive behaviors. Health psychologists have devised interventions to recalibrate norms and standards. Some of these efforts are based on prior research demonstrating that people do worry about level of risk when they believe they are at higher risk than their peers (Dillard, McCaul, Kelso, & Klein, 2006; Lipkus & Klein, 2006). Therefore, inclusion of veridical social comparison information in tailored communication materials should affect perceived risk, worry, and, in turn, screening and protective behaviors.

As one example, researchers have found that providing realistic feedback about misperceived norms reduced excessive drinking among college students (Agostinelli, Brown, & Miller, 1995). Receipt of accurate normative comparison information reduced drinking at 1- and 2-month follow-ups (LaBrie, Hummer, Neighbors, & Pedersen, 2008).

In the cancer domain, Lipkus and Klein (2006) recruited community residents for a study of colorectal cancer screening. After collecting information about risk factors, subjects were stratified to high- and low-risk groups, based on presence of absence of actual risk factors. Participants were also informed that they had more or less than the average number of risk factors of a group of 100 other people also tested. Those given high comparison feedback (vs. low or no feedback) made higher comparative risk estimates. Also, individuals provided with social comparison information had the highest intentions and the highest screening rates. One problem was that some subjects, despite receiving information that they had more risk factors for cancer, contended that they still were at lower risk. This means that special measures are required to prompt patients to veridically process comparison feedback.

### Comparison and Medical Treatment-seeking

When a person experiences somatic changes, which may be symptomatic of illness, how do they decide whether they are physically ill and require medical attention? Apart from traumatic injuries, illness episodes often begin with ambiguous somatic changes (Pennebaker, 1982), such as an ache or pain, scratchy throat, or vague feelings of nausea. Uncertainty about the physical changes should initiate affiliation, appraisal, and comparison (Safer, Tharps, Jackson, & Leventhal, 1979; Schachter, 1959). Consultation with family members and friends—members of the lay referral network—is often sought for support and to obtain clarity about what the symptoms mean (Friedson, 1961; Mechanic, 1971). Such informal consultation may involve social comparison to reduce uncertainty (Suls, Martin, & Leventhal, 1997). If the symptoms are reminiscent of a contagious illness, then knowing whether people with whom one has had close contact currently or recently had a cold or the flu is relevant information. Similarly, a lower gastrointestinal (GI) symptom might engender a comparison with others with whom one recently shared a meal to assess whether they had or have a similar reaction.

In other instances, members of the lay referral network may be consulted to exchange opinions—opinion comparison—about what the particular constellation of symptoms might mean and what they should do (e.g., "Will the symptoms pass quickly?" "Should I take an over-the-counter medication or seek a physician's care?" based on the conversants' lay models of illness (Leventhal, Meyer, & Nerenz, 1980; Martin, Rothrock, Leventhal, & Leventhal, 2003).

With the advent of the internet, some comparison in lay referral occurs in chat rooms especially designed for particular kinds of patients. One example is the hystersisters.com website, which allows women anticipating or soon to have a hysterectomy the opportunity to share concerns and post questions to other women who are or have undergone the same medical experience. Surveys with "hystersisters" show that whom ones consults with depends on the type of concern. For factual issues, such as how much bed rest is necessary and what type of exercises to do during recovery from the surgery, someone similar but with more expertise was preferred—a similar expert, as mentioned above. For issues with a value component, such as spiritual concerns, similarity of values was a more critical basis of preference (Bunde, Suls, Martin, & Barnett, 2006), consistent with the belief/value distinction.

Implicit social comparisons also can play a role in symptom interpretation. Martin et al. (2003) described a familiar scenario in which "sitting next to a sniffling, sneezing stranger on a crowded airplane will prompt several days of monitoring for respiratory symptoms" (p. 215). The sneezing stranger may be immediately brought to mind if, a few days later, one has a raspy throat or stuffy noise, symptoms that are common and, in most cases, benign. Similarly, when chronic heartburn sufferers learned from press reports about a medical article that heartburn could be a symptom of esophageal cancer, thousands of people immediately made appointments with their physicians (Brody, 1999). Their symptoms, previously thought to merely reflect dyspepsia, were relabeled as a sign of possible cancer.

Comparison may make salient the perceived prevalence of a symptom or diagnosis and ironically render it less serious. Jemmott, Ditto, and Croyle (1986) demonstrated that subjects who were informed of an alleged enzyme deficiency were more distressed by the information if they were only one of five persons tested who had a positive diagnosis than if a majority also received a positive diagnosis. The belief seems to be: "If everyone has it, then it can't be serious." This phenomenon is replicated in medical anthropology where, among certain disadvantaged communities in the Southwest, chronic low-grade GI distress is so prevalent that the people ignore their symptoms and do not seek medical attention although they suffer from a serious pathogen.

Under certain circumstances, comparisons can mistakenly lead people to believe they are ill. *Mass psychogenic illness* refers to occasions of widespread symptoms among groups of individuals in places like schools, factories, and military bases, where stress and anxiety tend to be high (Colligan, Pennebaker, & Murphy, 1982), but where no objective evidence of illness is found. The classic example is the "June Bug" incident, occurring at a textile plant, and documented by Kerckhoff and Back (1968). Scores of employees reported nausea and feverishness, some of whom required hospitalization, despite no physical cause being found. This happened at a very busy time at the plant, when initially a few employees claimed to have been bitten by a bug prior to symptom onset. The "bug" spread rapidly, and the plant had to be closed. Apparently, symptoms of psychological stress were mislabeled as markers of physical illness.

When such episodes are documented, the victims tend to be acquainted, report ambiguous symptoms, and share a common environment and personal attributes (Stahl & Lebedun, 1974), and the group is under some form of stress, such as a challenging deadline—thus resulting in a kind of hysterical contagion. The reader will appreciate that certain key features that instigate social comparisons tend to be present: uncertainty, stress, and people who tend to share attributes. The frequency of these episodes is difficult to estimate, but, even if they are rare, the present-day threat of terrorism and biological warfare increases societal vulnerability to such epidemics (Balaratnasingama & Janca, 2006). No psychological or personality disorders appear to be strongly associated with vulnerability (Bartholomew & Wessely, 2002); given conditions of fear and uncertainty, anyone may be susceptible (Wessely, 2000).

## Adaptation to Illness

In the 1980s, interest in downward comparisons received a significant boost with the publication of a field study of how breast cancer survivors adjusted to their condition (Wood, Taylor, & Lichtman, 1985). Without prompting, a majority of survivors who were being interviewed reported that they were coping better than other cancer patients. A representative statement was: "I only had a lumpectomy, but those other women lost a breast"—a comparison with someone less fortunate. This empirical support for Wills' (1981) theory inspired many correlational descriptive studies of how medical patients cope with the threat and challenges of physical illness (see Buunk & Gibbons, 1997; Gibbons & Gerrard, 1991). The emphasis was on self-enhancement or self-protection because of the threatening nature of medical treatment and illness, but uncertainty also can be a common outcome, so self-evaluation is a second salient motive for patients.

### Acute Medical Threats

Some types of medical threats are acute, such as undergoing a stressful medical examination or a painful surgery. Besides coping with the impeding procedure, patients may wonder how they should be feeling ("How worried should I be?") and what can they expect to happen. Comparison theory originally focused on peoples' uncertainty about the appropriateness of their feelings—emotional comparison (Schachter, 1959). In accord with the theory, people who feel miserable want to affiliate with people experiencing the same feelings. Indeed, findings suggested "misery loves miserable company," a confirmation of the similarity hypothesis. Kulik and Mahler (1987) observed that patients also want concrete details about what will happen, or comparison for cognitive clarity, and recognized that someone who recently experienced the procedure might be a better source of information.

In several field studies, they observed patients both before and after cardiac surgery. Some patients were randomly assigned to roommates who previously had undergone the surgery (post-op), whereas others were assigned to other pre-op roommates. Not only did the patients prefer to talk with another patient who already had the procedure, but these patients recovered more quickly (Kulik, Mahler, & Moore, 1996). Such results suggest that cognitive clarity is an important consideration for patients, and it is served by comparing with a similar expert. Since patients are assigned to hospital rooms, these findings might be implemented to speed recovery in cardiology practice.

## Chronic Illness Threats

Since Wood et al. (1985), many studies with different medical populations report patients making downward comparisons (Tennen, McKee, & Affleck, 2000), but whether this is a uniformly helpful strategy is unclear. First, correlational methodologies, used in much of this research, cannot distinguish between the *effect* of using comparison versus a *belief*, which is a function of wishful thinking or actual status (Tennen et al., 2000). Second, contrary to the downward comparison theory prediction that people under threat look downward, people in a good mood tend to report more downward comparisons; those in a bad mood report more upward comparisons (Wheeler & Miyake, 1992). Finally, some individuals seem to benefit from comparing with the more fortunate (Taylor & Lobel, 1989), consistent with the idea patients can find positive meaning in either direction (Buunk et al., 1990) depending on whether assimilation or contrast is produced (Suls, Martin, & Wheeler, 2002). Experimental evidence, requiring replication with patient samples, yields the comforting conclusion, consistent with self-enhancement, that people tend to resist assimilation with less fortunate others (Wheeler & Suls, 2007).

A factor implicated in experimental research is whether the person believes higher status is attainable, which should facilitate a cognitive selective search for similarities with more fortunate targets and thereby produce upward assimilation (Lockwood & Kunda, 1997; Major, Testa, & Bylsma, 1991). A belief in attainability can be situational and therefore, is potentially amenable to psychological intervention. Attainability also is probably related to optimism, which has been associated with positive health outcomes (e.g., Scheier, Matthews, Owens, et al., 1989). On a less positive note, patients who are higher in neuroticism exhibit more interest in social comparison, but react less favorably to comparisons with both more fortunate and less fortunate others (Van der Zee, Oldersma, Buunk, & Bos, 1998). Neuroticism is associated with feelings of uncertainty—prompting frequent comparisons—but also with pessimism—leading to negative responses to better or worse off others.

Social comparison interventions to improve the well-being of chronically ill patients are still rare, but a pioneering effort was conducted by Stanton, Danoff-Burg, Cameron, Snider, and Kirk (1999). Breast cancer patients were assigned to listen to an audio taped interview of a (supposed) patient whose comments reflected good, poor, or unspecified psychological and physical status. Patients who listened to a poorly adjusted patient rated their own adjustment as better than did those exposed to the well-adjusted patient. But even those who listened to a high-functioning survivor rated their own adjustment and prognosis as better than that described by the patient in the interview. Benefits were derived from being exposed to either type of comparison, and assimilation with someone less fortunate was resisted. Such results have the potential to inform medical professionals about the most effective patient models that should be presented in psycho-educational materials used in patient rehabilitation (Mahler & Kulik, 1998).

## Comparison Processes in Support Groups

Patients frequently are referred or refer themselves to medical support groups for disclosure and discussion of their health problems, treatment, and recovery. In such groups, social comparisons among group members occur spontaneously, but costs or benefits of this aspect of the group experience have not been systematically assessed. The rule is that all patients with a particular disease, regardless of need for psychosocial treatment, are recruited. This means the groups are heterogeneous in terms of distress level. Although nondistressed patients may not have need for the group, they are not excluded because health professionals think they serve an important function as role models, sources of information, and inspiration for other group members (Carmack-Taylor et al., 2007). Such speculations are consistent with experimental social comparison evidence, reviewed above.

A concern remains that the initially nondistressed members may become dispirited by being around patients who are coping poorly. Only one study thus far has shown any evidence that such patients can be harmed by the group experience (Helgeson, Cohen, Schulz, & Yasko, 2000). The relevant experimental research in social comparison suggests that people resist downward assimilation, but this requires systematic studies before making conclusions for medical practice.

## Conclusion

Social comparison can satisfy three motives: self-evaluation, self-enhancement, and the finding of common bonds, all of which are relevant to preventive health beliefs, symptom interpretation, medical treatment, and patient recovery. This chapter presented a selective survey of conceptual and empirical developments in the psychology of social comparison over the last six decades and described how this knowledge has been applied to several health domains. Constructed or actual social comparisons influence the perceived level of support, level of worry and, in turn, increase or decrease motivation for health-promotive behaviors, such as cancer screening. Comparison models representing unhealthy practices, promoted by the mass media, can contribute to distorted self-perceptions and dysfunctional behavior. Of course, this also means that systematic exposure to positive comparison models can reverse these effects.

The interpretation of somatic changes as indicative of physical illness is a necessary condition for people to seek medical attention. Often, however, these signs are ambiguous; social comparison is commonly used to reduce uncertainty and appraise the significance of these signs. An important source of comparison information is the person's lay referral network, consisting of others with whom he or she is close and with whom he or she shares similar attributes and experiences. For matters of preference, similar others are valuable; for facts or beliefs, similar experts play a larger role. In stressful, contained areas, such as schools and factories, like-minded people who experience ambiguous symptoms may mistakenly think they are physically ill, exhibiting a kind of hysterical mass contagion based on comparison.

People suffering from acute or chronic medical conditions use comparisons to cope, to reduce the threat, and to find ways to meet challenges. Psychological benefits can be obtained from upward and downward comparisons, although this depends on cognitive and motivational factors that encourage assimilation or contrast. For acute threats, such as surgery, emotional comparison with similar others may reduce uncertainty about how one should be feeling, but comparing with others who have already experienced the threat may provide the cognitive details that patients desire to anticipate the experience. Finally, social support groups for medical patients afford many opportunities for social comparison. Whether the benefits exceed the costs for patients who are already coping well needs additional study because they do serve as important role models for those who are coping less well.

In the last 30 years, a rich and deepening collaboration has occurred between the psychology of social comparison and health psychology by both basic research scientists and clinicians/practitioners. These efforts resemble a busy street intersection, with questions, methods, results, and implications coming and going both ways. There are surely more advances to come. Contrary to the cartoon from "Non Sequitur," described in the introduction, it is too early to pull-up a lawn chair (next to a cemetery or not) and relax.

## References

Agostinelli, G., Brown, J.M., & Miller, W.R. (1995). Effects of normative feedback on consumption among heavy drinking college students. *Journal of Drug Education, 25*, 31–40.

Ajzen, I., & Fishbein, M. (1980). *Understanding attitudes and predicting behavior*. Englewood Cliffs, NJ: Prentice-Hall.

Alicke, M. (1985). Global self-evaluations as determined by the desirability and controllability of trait adjectives. *Journal of Personality and Social Psychology, 49*, 1621–1630.

Andrews, J., Hampson, S., Barckley, M., Gerrard, M., & Gibbons, F.X. (2008). The effect of early cognitions on cigarette and alcohol use during adolescence. *Psychology of Addictive Behaviors, 22*, 96–106.

Avis, N., McKinlay, J., & Smith, K. (1989). Is cardiovascular risk factor knowledge sufficient to influence behavior? *American Journal of Preventive Medicine, 6*, 137–144.

Balaratnasingama, S., & Janca, A. (2006) Mass hysteria revisited. *Current Opinion in Psychiatry, 19*, 171–174.

Bartholomew, R.E., & Wessely, S. (2002). Protean nature of mass sociogenic illness. *British Journal of Psychiatry, 180*, 300–306.

Blalock, S.J., DeVellis, B.M., Afifi, R.A., & Sandler, R.S. (1990). Risk perceptions and participation in colorectal cancer screening. *Health Psychology, 9*, 792–806.

Brickman, P., & Bulman, R.J. (1977). Pleasure and pain in social comparison. In J. Suls, & R.L. Miller (Eds.), *Social comparison processes: Theoretical and empirical perspectives* (pp. 149–186). Washington, DC: Hemisphere.

Bourgeois, M., & Bowen, A. (2001). Self-organization of alcohol-related attitudes and beliefs in a campus housing complex: An initial investigation. *Health Psychology, 20*, 434–437.

Brody, J.E. (1999, April 27). Chronic heartburn, an ominous warning. *The New York Times*, p. D6.

Bunde, M., Suls, J., Martin, R., & Barnett, K. (2006). Hystersisters on-line: Social support and social comparison of hysterectomy patients on the internet. *Annals of Behavioral Medicine, 31*, 271–278.

Burns, L., & Knussen, C. (2005). False consensus and accuracy of perceptions of nurses regarding universal precaution practices. *Psychology, Health & Medicine, 10*, 344–354.

Buunk, B.P., Collins, R.L., Taylor, S.E., Van Yperen, N.W., & Dakof, G.A. (1990). The affective consequences of social comparison: Either direction has its ups and downs. *Journal of Personality and Social Psychology, 59*(6), 1238–1249.

Buunk, B., & Gibbons, F.X. (Eds.). (1997). *Health, coping and well-being: Perspectives from social comparison theory*. Mahwah, NJ: Lawrence Erlbaum Associates.

Carmack Taylor, C.L., Kulik, J., Badr, H., Smith, M., Basen-Engquist, K., Penedo, F., & Gritz, E.R. (2007). A social comparison theory analysis of group composition and efficacy of cancer support group programs. *Social Science & Medicine, 65*, 262–273.

Chambers, J., & Windschitl, P. (2004). Biases in social comparative judgments: The role of nonmotivated factors in the above-average and comparative-optimism effects. *Psychological Bulletin, 130*, 813–838.

Clarke, V., Williams, T., & Arthey, S. (1997). Skin type and optimistic bias in relation to the sun protection and suntanning behaviors of young adults. *Journal of Behavioral Medicine, 20*, 207–222.

Colligan, M., Pennebaker, J., & Murphy, L. (Eds.). (1982). *Mass psychogenic illness: A social psychological analysis.* Hillsdale, NJ: Lawrence Erlbaum.

Dillard, A.J., McCaul, K.D., Kelso, P.D., & Klein, W.M.P. (2006). Resisting good news: Reactions to breast cancer risk communication. *Health Communication, 19*, 115–123.

Festinger, L. (1954). A theory of social comparison processes. *Human Relations, 7*, 117–140.

Friedson, E. (1961). *Patients' views of medical practice.* New York: Russell Sage.

Gibbons, F., & Eggleston, T. (1996). Smoker networks and the "typical smoker": A prospective analysis of smoking cessation. *Health Psychology, 15*, 469–477.

Gibbons, F.X., & Gerrard, M. (1991). Downward comparison and coping with threat. In J. Suls, & T.A. Wills (Eds.), *Social comparison: Contemporary theory and research* (pp. 317–346). Hillsdale, NJ: Lawrence Erlbaum.

Gibbons, F., Gerrard, M., & Boney-McCoy, S. (1995). Prototype perception predicts (lack of) pregnancy prevention. *Personality and Social Psychology Bulletin, 21*, 85–93.

Goethals, G., & Darley, J. (1977). Social comparison theory: An attributional approach. In J. Suls, & R. Miller (Eds.), *Social comparison processes: Theoretical and empirical perspectives* (pp. 259–278). Washington, DC: Hemisphere.

Gold, R.S., & Aucote, H.M. (2003). I'm less at risk than most guys: Gay men's unrealistic optimism about becoming infected with HIV. *International Journal of STD & AIDS, 14*, 18–23.

Grabe, S., Ward, L., & Hyde, J. (2008). The role of media in body image concerns among women: A meta-analysis of experimental and correlational studies. *Psychological Bulletin, 134*, 460–476.

Groesz, L., Levine, M., & Murnen, S. (2002). The effects of experimental presentations of thin media images on body satisfaction: A meta-analytic review. *International Journal of Eating Disorders, 31*, 1–16.

Hargreaves, D., & Tiggemann, M. (2003). The effect of "thin ideal" television commercials and body dissatisfaction and schema activation during early adolescence. *Journal of Youth and Adolescence, 32*, 367–373.

Helgeson, V.S., Cohen, S., Schulz, R., & Yasko, J. (2000). Group support interventions for women with breast cancer: Who benefits from what? *Health Psychology, 19*, 107–114.

Helgeson, V.S., & Mickelson, K.D. (1995). Motives for social comparison. *Personality and Social Psychology Bulletin, 21*, 1200–1209.

Jemmott, J.B., Ditto, P., & Croyle, R.T. (1986). Judging health status: Effects of perceived prevalence and personal relevance. *Journal of Personality and Social Psychology, 50*, 899–905.

Jemmott, J.B., Croyle, R.T., & Ditto, P. (1988). Commonsense epidemiology: Self-based judgments from laypersons and physicians. *Health Psychology, 7*, 55–73.

Kahneman, D., & Tversky, A. (1973). On the psychology of prediction. *Psychological Review, 80*, 237–251.

Kelley, H. (1967). Attribution theory in social psychology. In D. Levine (Ed.), *Nebraska symposium on motivation* (pp. 192–240). Lincoln, NE: University of Nebraska Press.

Kelly, J., Lawrence, J., Diaz, Y., Stevenson, L.Y et al. (1991). HIV risk behavior reduction following intervention with key opinion leaders of the population: An experimental analysis. *American Journal of Public Health, 81*, 168–171.

Kerckhoff, A., & Back, K. (1968). *The June bug: A study of hysterical contagion.* New York: Appleton-Century-Crofts.

Klayman, J., & Ha, Y.-W. (1987). Confirmation, disconfirmation and information in hypothesis-testing. *Psychological Review, 94*, 211–228.

Klein, W.M. (1997). Objective standards are not enough: Affective, self-evaluative, and behavioral responses to social comparison information. *Journal of Personality and Social Psychology, 72*, 763–774.

Klein, W.M.P., & Cooper, K.L. (2008). On the physical health costs of self-enhancement. In E. Chang (Ed.), *Self-criticism and self-enhancement: Theory, research, and clinical implications* (pp. 141–158). Washington, DC: American Psychological Association.

Krueger, J., & Clement, R. (1994). The truly false consensus effect: An ineradicable and egocentric bias in social perception. *Journal of Personality and Social Psychology, 67*, 596–610.

Kulik, J.A., & Mahler, H.I.M. (1987). Effects of preoperational roommate assignment on preoperative anxiety and postoperative recovery from coronary bypass surgery. *Health Psychology, 6*, 525–543.

Kulik, J., Mahler, H., & Moore, P. (1996). Social comparison and affiliation under threat: Effects of recovery from major surgery. *Journal of Personality and Social Psychology, 71*, 967–979.

LaBrie, J., Hummer, J., Neighbors, C., & Pedersen, E. (2008). Live interactive group-specific normative feedback reduces misperceptions and drinking in college students: A randomized cluster trial. *Psychology of Addictive Behaviors, 22*, 141–148.

Leventhal, H., Meyer, D., & Nerenz, D. (1980). The commonsense representation of illness danger. In S. Rachman (Ed.), *Medical psychology* Vol. 2 (pp. 7–30). New York: Pergamon Press.

Levine, M., & Murnen, S. (2009). "Everybody knows that mass media are/are not [*pick one*] a cause of eating disorders": A critical review of evidence for a causal link between media, negative body image, and disordered eating in females. *Journal of Social and Clinical Psychology, 28*, 9–42.

Lipkus, I., & Klein, W. (2006) Effects of communicating social comparison information on risk perceptions for colorectal cancer. *Journal of Health Communication, 11*, 391–407.

Lipkus I., Klein, W., Skinner, C., & Rimer, B. (2005). Breast cancer risk perceptions and breast cancer worry: What predicts what? *Journal of Risk Research, 8*, 439–452.

Mason, D., Prevost, A.B. & Suttton, S. (2008). Perceptions of absolute versus relative differences between personal and comparison health risk. *Health Psychology, 27*, 87–92.

Lockwood, P., & Kunda, Z. (1997). Superstars and me: Predicting the impact of role models on the self. *Journal of Personality and Social Psychology, 73*, 91–103.

Mahler, H., & Kulik, J. (1998). Effects of videotape preparations on self-efficacy beliefs and recovery of coronary bypass surgery patients. *Annals of Behavioral Medicine, 20*, 39–46.

Major, B., Testa, M., & Blysma, W. (1991). Responses to upward and downward social comparisons: The impact of esteem-relevance and perceived control. In J. Suls, & T.A. Wills (Eds.), *Social comparison: Contemporary theory and research* (pp. 237–260). Hillsdale, NJ: Lawrence Erlbaum Associates.

Martin, R., Rothrock, N., Leventhal, H., & Leventhal, E. (2003). Common sense models of illness: Implications for symptom perception and health-related behaviors. In J. Suls, & K. Wallston (Eds.), *Social psychological foundations of health and illness* (pp. 199–225). Malden, MA: Blackwell.

Mechanic, D. (1971). Social psychological factors affecting the presentation of bodily complaints. *New England Journal of Medicine, 286*, 1132–1139.

Miller, D., & McFarland, C. (1987). Pluralistic ignorance: When similarity is interpreted as dissimilarity. *Journal of Personality and Social Psychology, 53*, 298–305.

Miller, D., & McFarland, C. (1991). When social comparison goes awry: The case of pluralistic ignorance. In J. Suls, & T.A. Wills (Eds.), *Social comparison: Contemporary theory and research* (pp. 287–313). Hillsdale, NJ: Lawrence Erlbaum.

Moore, D., & Small, D. (2007). Error and bias in comparative judgment: On being better and worse than we think we are. *Journal of Personality and Social Psychology, 92*, 972–989.

Mussweiler, T. (2003). Comparison processes in social judgment: Mechanisms and consequences. *Psychological Review, 110*, 472–489.

Nisbett, R., & Kunda, Z. (1985). Perception of social distributions. *Journal of Personality and Social Psychology, 48*, 297–311.

O'Brien, K.S., Caputi, P., Minto, R., Peoples, G., Hooper, C., Kell, S., & Sawley, E. (2009). Upward and downward physical appearance comparisons: Development of scales and examination of predictive qualities. *Body Image, 6*, 201–206.

Pennebaker, J.W. (1982). *The psychology of physical symptoms.* New York: Springer-Verlag.

Prentice, D., & Miller, D. (1993). Pluralistic ignorance and alcohol use on campus: Some consequences of misperceiving the social norm. *Journal of Personality and Social Psychology, 64*, 243–256.

Ross, L., Greene, D., & House, P. (1977). The "false consensus effect": An egocentric bias in social perception and attribution processes. *Journal of Experimental Social Psychology, 13*, 279–301.

Safer, M., Tharps, D., Jackson, T., & Leventhal, H. (1979). Determinants of three stages of delay in seeking care at a medical clinic. *Medical Care, 17*, 11–209.

Schanck, R.L. (1932). A study of community and its group institutions conceived of as behavior of individuals. *Psychological Monographs, 43*, 1–133.

Schachter, S. (1959). *The psychology of affiliation.* Stanford, CA: Stanford University of Press.

Scheier, M., Matthews, K., Owens, J., Magovern, G., Lefebvre, R.C., Abbott, R.A., & Carver, C.S. (1989). Dispositional optimism and recovery from coronary artery bypass surgery: The beneficial effects on physical and psychological well-being. *Journal of Personality and Social Psychology, 57*, 1024–1040.

Skinner, C., Kreuter, M., Kobrin, S., & Strecher, V. (1998). Perceived and actual breast cancer risk: Optimistic and pessimistic biases. *Journal of Health Psychology, 3*, 181–193.

Stahl, S.M., & Lebedun, M. (1974). Mystery gas: An analysis of mass hysteria. *Journal of Health and Social Behavior, 15*, 44–50.

Stanton, A., Danoff-Burg, S., Cameron, C., Snider, P., & Kirk, S. (1999). Social comparison and adjustment to breast cancer: An experimental examination of upward affiliation and downward evaluation. *Health Psychology, 18*, 151–158.

Stapel, D.A. (2007). In the mind of the beholder: The interpretation comparison model of accessibility effects. In D.A. Stapel, & J. Suls (Eds.), *Assimilation and contrast in social psychology* (pp. 143–164). New York & Hove, UK: Psychology Press.

Stapel, D.A., & Koomen, W. (2000). Distinctiveness of others, mutability of selves: Their impact on self-evaluations. *Journal of Personality and Social Psychology, 79*(6), 1068–1087.

Strecher, V., Kreuter, M., & Kobrin, S. (1995). Do cigarette smokers have unrealistic perceptions of their heart attack, cancer and stroke risks? *Journal of Behavioral Medicine, 18*, 45–54.

Suls, J. (1986). Notes on the occasion of Social Comparison Theory's thirtieth birthday. *Personality and Social Psychology Bulletin, 12*, 289–296.

Suls, J., & Green, P.J. (2003). Pluralistic ignorance and college student perceptions of gender-specific alcohol norms. *Health Psychology, 22*, 479–486.

Suls, J., Martin, R., & Leventhal, H. (1997). Social comparison, lay referral, and the decision to seek medical care. In B. Buunk, & F. Gibbons (Eds.), *Health, coping and well-being: Perspectives from social comparison theory* (pp. 195–226). Mahwah NJ: Lawrence Erlbaum Associates.

Suls, J., Martin, R., & Wheeler, L. (2000). Three kinds of opinion comparison: The Triadic Model. *Personality and Social Psychology Review, 4*, 219–237.

Suls, J., Martin, R., & Wheeler, L. (2002). Social comparison: Why, with whom and with what effect? *Current directions in psychological science, 11*, 159–163.

Suls, J., Wan, C.K., & Sanders, G. (1988). False consensus and false uniqueness in estimating the prevalence of health-protective behaviors. *Journal of Applied Social Psychology, 18*, 66–79.

Suls, J., & Wheeler, L. (Eds.) (2000). *Handbook of social comparison.* New York: Kluwer/Plenum.

Taylor, S.E., & Brown, J.D. (1988). Illusion and well-being: A social psychological perspective on mental health. *Psychological Bulletin, 103*, 193–210.

Taylor, S., & Lobel, M. (1989). Social comparison under threat: Downward evaluation and upward contacts. *Psychological Review, 96*, 569–575.

Tennen, H., McKee, T.E., & Affleck, G. (2000). Social comparison processes in health and illness. J. Suls, & L. Wheeler (Eds.), *Handbook of social comparison: Theory and Research* (pp. 443–486). New York: Kluwer Academic/Plenum.

Van der Zee, K., Oldersma, F., Buunk, B., & Bos, D. (1998). Social comparison preferences among cancer patients as related to cancer patients as related to neuroticism and social comparison orientation. *Journal of Personality and Social Psychology, 75*, 801–810.

Wasilenko, K., Kulik, J., & Wanic, R. (2007.) Effects of social comparisons with peers on women's body satisfaction and exercise behavior. *International Journal of Eating Disorders, 40*, 740–745

Weinstein, N. (1980). Unrealistic optimism about future life events. *Journal of Personality and Social Psychology, 39*, 806–820.

Weinstein, N. (2003). Exploring the links between risk perceptions and preventive health behavior. In J. Suls, & K. Wallston (Eds.), *Social psychological foundations of health and illness* (pp. 22–53). Malden, MA: Blackwell.

Weinstein, N., & Klein, W. (1995). Resistance of personal risk perceptions to debiasing interventions. *Health Psychology, 14,* 132–140.

Wessely, S. (2000). Responding to mass psychogenic illness. *New England Journal of Medicine, 342,* 129–130.

Wheeler, L. (1966). Motivation as a determinant of upward comparison. *Journal of Experimental Social Psychology, 2,* Suppl. 1, 27–31.

Wheeler, L., Martin, R., & Suls, J. (1997). The proxy social comparison model for self-assessment of ability. *Personality and Social Psychology Review, 1,* 54–61.

Wheeler, L., & Miyake, K. (1992). Social comparison in everyday life. *Journal of Personality and Social Psychology, 62,* 760–733.

Wheeler, L., & Suls, J. (2007) Assimilation in social comparison: Can we agree on what it is? *International Review of Social Psychology, 20,* 31–51.

Wild, C.T. (2002). Personal drinking and sociocultural drinking norms: A representative population study. *Journal of Studies in Alcohol, 63,* 469–475.

Wills, T.A. (1981). Downward comparison principles in social psychology. *Psychological Bulletin, 90,* 245–271.

Wood, J.V. (1989). Theory and research concerning social comparison of personal attributes. *Psychological Bulletin, 106,* 231–248.

Wood, J.V., Taylor, S., & Lichtman, R. (1985). Social comparison in adjustment to breast cancer. *Journal of Personality and Social Psychology, 49,* 1169–1183.

Zajac, L., Klein, W., & McCaul, K. (2006). Absolute and comparative risk perceptions as predictors of cancer worry: Moderating effects of gender and psychological distress. *Journal of Health Communication, 11,* 37–49.

Yael Benyamini

**Abstract**

This chapter describes the contents and structure of subjective perceptions of health and illness, which are coherent theories in which individuals' health-related knowledge is integrated and that then serve to guide their coping with health issues as part of dynamic self-regulation processes that take place over time. These perceptions are not always medically accurate, yet they are rational and internally logical from the person's subjective point of view. They serve as the objective reality for the individual in their role as major influences on behaviors and outcomes. The chapter discusses how such perceptions are formed on the basis of a variety of sources and their sensitivity to experiential, rather than to purely medical knowledge. Different quantitative and qualitative ways to assess health perceptions are described. Next, the processes involving these perceptions are discussed: The reasons why people form these perceptions, their associations with various physical and psychological outcomes, the mechanisms explaining these associations, and the personal and sociocultural factors affecting these perceptions. Finally, directions for future research are outlined.

**Keywords:** Illness perceptions, illness representations, lay beliefs of health and illness, self-regulation, illness cognitions, subjective health perceptions, disease prototypes, personal models of illness, explanatory models

Archeologists have found skulls with holes cut through them, dated as early as the Neolithic period or the late Stone Age, almost 10,000 years ago (Rice, 1998). Similar skulls have been found in many regions of the world, showing that the practice of trephination had been conducted throughout history, up until the Renaissance, and in some places even into recent times. There must have been quite a few successful cases, otherwise this practice would likely have been abandoned over the years. Indeed, analyses of these skulls showed that many of the patients treated in this way survived. One of the explanations for this phenomenon is that these patients were believed to be possessed by an evil spirit and were therefore treated by cutting a hole in their skull, to allow the spirit to leave the body. This "surgery" may have relieved intracranial pressure and thus led to improvements in the patient's symptoms. The unsuccessful cases were also easy to explain within this theory: In those cases, one could argue that the evil spirit was too powerful to vanquish.

This theory is a wonderful example of illness perceptions and the way they operate. It provides a coherent story, explaining a person's weird behavior and showing how a solution could be logically derived from the story. Moreover, the treatment outcomes, regardless of whether they are favorable or not, offer further support for the theory, thus providing an example of how illness perceptions are substantiated by experience and therefore could be quite resistant to change. This is also one of many illustrations of how old the concept of illness perceptions is: Long before the term was coined or any formal medical knowledge had accumulated, people have tried to interpret symptoms and illnesses that they and those close to them encountered and thus give meaning to their experiences.

The story behind trephination, as well as additional examples of illness perceptions from other times and places, may seem esoteric. Yet, anthropologists and cultural psychiatrists have noted that although at first glance conceptualizations of illness and healing in industrialized societies seem to be very different from those in preindustrial societies, they share the same basic principles: "In industrial as well as in primitive societies, illness may create noxious emotions, raise moral issues, disturb the patient's image of himself, and estrange him from his compatriots" (Frank, 1964, p. viii). All these emotional, cognitive, moral, and social aspects combine together in the subjective understanding of one's illness, which must be taken into account if we wish to understand how people cope with illnesses and how professionals could help them.

Trephination is an example of a subjective perception of illness that seems to have been universally accepted. However, in many cases, people with the same condition differ greatly in their perception of their condition, for a variety of reasons ranging from differences in the manifestations of the disease to individual variations. These perceptions are an important key to understanding people's health and illness behavior, no less important than the objective indicators of the disease. They can be as narrow as perceptions of specific symptoms, which then feed into the perception of the illness and vice versa. Perceptions of illnesses affect our overall perception of our health; in this case too, the effect could go both ways: Our overall perception of health can influence the way we perceive specific illnesses. Our perception of health is part of our self—it affects our self-perception and is affected by our self-identity and personality. Finally, both health and illness are not merely states of the individual, experienced and interpreted at the physical and psychological levels, they are also evaluated within the culture and social structures to which the individual belongs (Parsons, 1958). These levels, from symptoms to their sociocultural context, can be viewed as increasingly widening circles with interrelations between them (see Figure 13.1). To understand perceptions of health and illness, we need to attend to each and all of them.

This chapter reviews modern theory and research on perceptions of health and illness. First, the definition, contents, and structure of illness perceptions will be described. Next, we will examine ways of

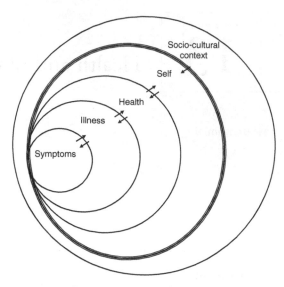

**Fig. 13.1** A schematic presentation of the associations between widening circles of illness and health perceptions and the way in which they are embedded in the self system and the sociocultural system.

assessing illness perceptions and related perceptions, such as those concerning treatment. Then, we will attend to basic questions that need to be answered in order to understand the importance and meaning of these perceptions: How are illness perceptions formed? How stable are illness perceptions? Why are illness perceptions formed? Are illness perceptions related to health outcomes? How are they related to outcomes? How can this knowledge guide effective interventions? Whose perceptions should we be interested in (in addition to the patient's)—family members, health professionals, nonpatients? Then, we will attend to the influence of individual differences such as personality, age, gender, and culture. Finally, directions for the future will be suggested.

## What Are Illness Perceptions?

Illness perceptions contain and organize the knowledge and beliefs that people hold regarding symptoms, illnesses, diseases, medical conditions and health threats. They are people's subjective understanding of these conditions. They are also known as patients' theories of illness or illness representations (Leventhal, Meyer, & Nerenz, 1980), mental representations in health and illness or illness schemata (Skelton & Croyle, 1991), illness cognitions (Leventhal & Diefenbach, 1991), implicit models of illness (Turk, Rudy, & Salovey, 1986), disease prototypes (Bishop, Briede, Cavazos, Grotzinger, & McMahon, 1987), lay beliefs of illness (Donovan, Blake, & Fleming, 1989), explanatory models of illness (Kleinman, 1988b), or personal models of illness (Lange & Piette, 2006). These approaches mainly emphasize their cognitive components although some also refer to emotional components.

Many of these descriptive terms have been developed within the Leventhal common-sense model of self-regulation (Leventhal et al., 1980; Leventhal, Nerenz, & Steele, 1984) or inspired by it. This theoretical model argues that, when an individual is faced with a health-related Stimulus, which could be internal (e.g., a bodily sensation) or external (e.g., hearing about a health problem on TV), s/he forms a representation of the danger, which is a cognitive representation of the health problem, and a representation of the fear it elicits, which is an emotional representation. Each type of representation guides the choice of procedures selected to cope with the danger and with the fear. Ultimately, the individual appraises the outcomes of these coping procedures. As a result of this appraisal process, s/he might adjust the representations and/or the procedures to fit the actual outcomes experienced so far. Thus, two related feedback loops flow from the illness perceptions to the coping procedures to the appraisal of outcomes, one through a "cold" cognitive path and the other through a "hot" emotional path.

The basic tenet underlying this model is that people are active problem solvers: We actively seek information about health-related issues and process it within the relevant personal and social contexts to formulate action plans and implement them. This model's name emphasizes commonsense because it attempts to delineate the commonsense processes by which people interpret their symptoms and illnesses and react to them. The model is not "commonsense"; it is a theoretical model of people's commonsense thinking.

To illustrate this conceptual framework, imagine that you have just realized that you are suffering from a headache. You would probably find yourself first trying to characterize it: Is it a sharp, piercing pain? Is it a dull, bothersome pain? Is it focused in a specific area, or spread throughout the head? Is it similar to other headaches I've had? You are dealing with several questions: *What* is it? i.e., the *identity* of the headache. Next, you may try to understand what could have caused this headache: Is it because I didn't sleep well last night? Because I didn't drink enough water today? Is it related to the virus I have just barely recovered from? You are now answering the question: *Why* is this happening? i.e., the *cause* of the headache. You may try to reconstruct how this headache had developed: Did it come

about suddenly? Has it been waxing and waning? This is the question of the *timeline* of this headache. You may also be deliberating its *consequences*: How bad is it? Can I carry on like this, or is my functioning so impaired that I should take the rest of the day off? The answers to these questions will also provide you with clues as to the possibility of curing this headache or at least improving your condition: If the headache is due to dehydration, I should drink a lot in the next hour or two; if it's the type of headache that usually subsides when I take pain medication, I could try this solution. If you cannot come up with a tentative solution, you might feel out of control over this headache. Now you are engaging in thoughts about the *curability* or *controllability* of this headache.

Note that, in this process, you have used your past and present experiences to characterize the nature, timeline, and consequences of this headache and have come up with *working cognitions* (Leventhal & Benyamini, 1997) about its causes and controllability. These working cognitions can now be put to a test: You can form action plans, which translate the perceptions into behavior (Leventhal et al., 1997). Let's say you believe the symptom may be a sign of dehydration, and you choose not to take medication but to drink quite a lot of water in the next few hours. After a while, you are likely to find yourself reappraising your situation: Has the headache subsided? If not, you may decide to drink even more, which means that you are still employing the same working cognition but have modified your action plan, or you may decide that the working cognition is invalid and an alternative one should be formulated.

The headache example has referred so far only to cognitive representations of this headache. Your emotional reaction to a seemingly benign symptom is not expected to be dramatic—at most, this headache may be somewhat annoying. However, if the same headache continues to bother you and disrupts your day for several days or weeks, you may consider the possibility that it is not a acute benign symptom. This change in your representation would lead to a change in your action plan (Should I consult my doctor about these recurring headaches?) and a more dramatic emotional reaction (for example, fear that it indicates a chronic disease or a brain tumor).

As this example shows, the contents of illness perceptions are organized into components, which can be identified and clearly defined. We will now turn to a more in-depth review of these components.

## The Contents of Illness Perceptions

Studies by Leventhal and colleagues (1980) have identified four main components of illness perceptions—identity, timeline, consequences, and cause—to which a fifth main component was soon added: curability or controllability (first suggested by Lau & Hartman, 1983). Over the years, additional distinctions within the timeline and controllability components have been identified, and a meta-cognition of coherence, or one's understanding of the health problem, has been added (Moss-Morris et al., 2002). Research on these "building blocks" of illness perceptions has provided better understanding of the contents and further support for the claim that people form them in a very active way, as will be presented below.

### Identity of the Illness

The identity of the illness is comprised of its label and symptoms. The early studies by Leventhal and colleagues (e.g., Nerenz & Leventhal, 1983) drew attention to the process by which we attempt to label our somatic experiences. Symptoms are typically the starting point. People seek information to label their symptoms (an idea further developed by the psychophysiological comparison theory; Cacioppo, Andersen, Turnquist, & Tassinary, 1989). Another related approach, the *prototype approach* (Bishop, 1991), suggested that information about symptoms is organized in a way that facilitates this process: People hold beliefs about the associations between particular sets of symptoms and specific diseases (Bishop & Converse, 1986). When encountering symptoms, they perform a "prototype check" by judging the similarity between the symptoms experienced and available prototypes of various diseases. The greater the fit, the more confident they would be regarding the appropriate label for their symptoms. The perceived associations among symptoms belonging to the same illness prototype were also supported by experiments inducing symptom suggestibility (Skelton, Loveland, & Yeagley, 1996).

What happens when the label is not easily found or does not fit the symptoms? People seek care for symptoms that are difficult to label, and feel frustrated when physicians cannot provide a clear disease label for their recurring symptoms (Moss-Morris & Wrapson, 2003). Patients are baffled by discordant experiences: Patients with chest pain who were told that their condition was *not* cardiac viewed it as less controllable and understandable than did patients with cardiac chest pain (Robertson, Javed,

Samani, & Khunti, 2008). They are also more likely to be at loss regarding the correct way of coping: Among women who were eventually diagnosed with breast cancer, those with nonlump symptoms were more likely to delay seeking care, presumably because their symptoms did not fit their prototype of breast cancer (Burgess, Ramirez, Richards, & Love, 1998); similarly, myocardial infarction (MI) patients whose symptoms did not match their expectations regarding an MI were more likely to delay seeking care (Horne, James, Petrie, Weinman, & Vincent, 2000).

Interestingly, symmetry exists between symptoms and label: People not only seek a label for symptoms they experience, they also seek symptoms that provide a concrete manifestation of a label. For example, although hypertension is *a*symptomatic, both normotensives and hypertensives have been found to believe that symptoms are associated with it and could be used to monitor blood pressure (Baumann & Leventhal, 1985; Meyer, Leventhal, & Gutmann, 1985). Under laboratory conditions, participants who were given a high blood pressure reading reported more symptoms commonly associated with blood pressure (Baumann, Cameron, Zimmerman, & Leventhal, 1989). In real life, perceived hypertension, but not actual blood pressure level, led to anxiety during blood pressure measurement and to greater "white coat effects" (Spruill et al., 2007). Both real hypertensives and falsely aware ones who perceived a high symptom level reported more sickness absence than did normotensives or unaware hypertensives (Melamed, Froom, & Green, 1997). Together, these experimental and real-life findings suggest that the perception of hypertension has a stronger impact on illness perceptions and behaviors than does actual blood pressure.

This tendency to attach symptoms to an existing label can have both beneficial and detrimental consequences. On the negative side, people may attribute to their disease symptoms that are unrelated to it, especially in highly symptomatic and not well-known conditions such as pseudo-tumor cerebri (Kesler, Kliper, Goner-Shilo, & Benyamini, 2009). This may lead them to refrain from seeking care for these symptoms, which may be diagnosable and treatable. On the positive side, people who have been diagnosed with a disease and are aware of the label, are likely to be more vigilant regarding symptoms related to it and thus assess their health status more accurately (Idler, Leventhal, McLaughlin, & Leventhal, 2004).

The original conceptualization of the common-sense model referred to the nature of an illness identity. For many chronic patients, there is no question about the nature of the identity: They have been diagnosed and have received clear information about the label, as well as the symptoms that characterize the disease. Yet, variability can be seen in the extent to which people accept this identity. The few studies that have assessed this component of the *acceptance of the identity* found it to be strongly related to the identity and perceived consequences of the disease (Benyamini, Medalion, & Garfinkel, 2007) and to make a unique contribution to mental health, controlling for other components of the illness perception (Kemp, Morley, & Anderson, 1999).

## Timeline of the Illness

One of the most intuitive ways in which we test the nature of a symptom is to follow its course over time (Leventhal & Diefenbach, 1991). Throughout human history, most diseases were acute. This may be the reason why health care systems, as well as personal belief systems, are constructed around an initial model of illness as acute. New patients with hypertension often hold an acute model of their disease, whereas continuing patients are more likely to hold a chronic model of the disease; those who do hold a chronic model are more likely to adhere to treatment than those with an episodic or acute model (Meyer et al., 1985). Among women treated for breast cancer, 29% viewed their disease as acute in the early stages of treatment but only 11% still held this view 6 months later (Leventhal, Easterling, Coons, Luchterhand, & Love, 1986). Most serious diseases nowadays are likely to be chronic; their perceptions could be mapped onto a dimension ranging from acute to chronic, or they can be characterized as episodic or cyclic (Moss-Morris et al., 2002).

## Consequences

This component includes people's overall evaluation of the seriousness of their conditions, as well as the extent to which these conditions affect specific domains of their lives—physical, social, financial, occupational, and so on. Since these consequences are highly salient, more so than aspects such as the illness timeline or causes, this component is often the major player in explaining or predicting outcomes such as quality of life (e.g., Stafford, Berk, & Jackson, 2009) or recovery from illness (e.g., Petrie, Weinman, Sharpe, & Buckley, 1996). The most interesting findings are from studies showing that one's perceptions of the severity and consequences of the disease have an independent and often stronger effect on these physical (e.g., Whittaker, Kemp, & House, 2007) and emotional outcomes (Laubmeier & Zakowski, 2004) than do more objective measures of disease severity.

## Causes

Most people form hypotheses about the causes of their illness, and the tendency to do so increases with the severity of the diagnosis (see review by Turnquist, Harvey, & Andersen, 1988). The relationship between causal attributions and health has been extensively studied under many theoretical frameworks. Such investigations emphasized the importance of attributions as a determinant of adjustment to illness, in themselves and not within a wider view of causes as part of the overall illness perception. Hall, French, and Marteau (2003), who reviewed 65 studies, many involving attributions for one's own illness, found little evidence of a relationship between attributions and outcomes, although Roesch and Weiner (2001), who reviewed 27 studies, found evidence of an indirect relationship of attribution with adjustment, mediated through ways of coping.

These inconsistencies suggest that causal attributions cannot be studied in isolation: The meaning of an attribution and its consequences could differ as a function of the disease model within which it is made (Benyamini, Leventhal, & Leventhal, 2007). Different models prescribe different functions for causal beliefs: In attributing cause, cancer patients may worry about recurrence and seek ways to prevent it; hypertension and diabetes patients seek ways to control their disease; and post-MI patients juggle between asserting control over recovery and avoiding blame for the event. When arthritis patients were asked for the causes of ambiguous symptoms, almost all provided an answer but only those with a cancer history were preoccupied with the cause (Benyamini, McClain, Leventhal, & Leventhal, 2003). Attributions to internal factors led to better metabolic control among diabetes patients (Brown, Kaslow, Sansbury, Meacham, & Culler, 1991) but worse control over diet among overweight women (Ogden & Wardle, 1990).

How do patients deduce the causes of their disease? They seem to follow simple but very logical (even if erroneous) causal rules, such as "causes should be temporally and spatially close to effects" (Taylor, 1982; e.g., a blow to one's breast could cause cancer), and "causes should resemble effects" (Salmon, Woloshynowych, & Valor, 1996; e.g., musculoskeletal symptoms are caused by "wearing out," whereas gastrointestinal symptoms are caused by lifestyle factors). Such ways of thinking lead to widespread misperceptions, such as the belief that arthritis pain is related to the weather (Redelmeier & Tversky, 1996) or the belief that only the maternal genetic line is relevant for judging risk of breast cancer (Shiloh, 2006). Additional heuristics that patients apply in order to identify the cause for their illness also follow a clear logic (Leventhal, Weinman, Leventhal, & Phillips, 2008). In the case of diseases suspected to result from environmental exposure, these could include social comparisons—comparisons to other people who have also been exposed to the same conditions (if I am experiencing digestion problems a few hours after eating at a restaurant, I would probably first ask the people who also ate there whether they felt anything). In other cases, the stress–illness rule is used—the tendency to attribute symptoms to stress in the presence of stressors (Cameron, Leventhal, & Leventhal, 1995), or the age–illness rule is used—the tendency to attribute slow-developing, not too severe symptoms, to age (Leventhal & Diefenbach, 1991). The latter two rules result in attributions to nondisease sources, a tendency that is particularly noticeable in the early stages of illness episodes when symptoms are ambiguous and slowly developing. Note that both interpretations could lead to delays in seeking professional care. Thus, causal attributions are important because they are related to behavioral as well as emotional responses (Prohaska, Keller, Leventhal, & Leventhal, 1987).

## Controllability/Curability

For chronic conditions, this component is all about the extent to which the illness could be controlled (i.e., the belief that something can be done to improve health status or at least prevent deterioration in health status). For acute conditions, this component involves the extent to which the condition is curable. It is easy to see how this component is related to one's actions: For example, students who held stronger beliefs in the curability of their illness were also more likely to visit a physician (Lau, Bernard, & Hartman, 1989). It is possible to distinguish between several types of controllability: Personal controllability and medical/treatment controllability (Moss-Morris et al., 2002). Each type could involve control over the outcomes and control over the symptoms. When complex treatment regimens are involved (e.g., for cancer or infertility), both personal and treatment control over the outcomes may be low; however, patients may also hold beliefs about the extent to which they can exert control over the course of the treatment and its interference with their lives (Benyamini, 2003).

Note that perceived control is among the basic concepts in many theoretical frameworks (Walker, 2001). Similar to the "causes" component, perceived control has been extensively studied in the health and illness area, so that a fuller discussion is beyond the scope of this chapter. Our interest here lies more with these components as part of an integrated illness perception, and therefore it is important to discuss the structure of illness perceptions.

## The Structure of Illness Perceptions

Illness perceptions are integrated schemas constructed from the relationships among their components and among hierarchical levels within each component. One could visualize a top-down structure within each component, from very abstract to very concrete perceptions within each component, with a network of associations among them.

### Relationships Among the Components of Illness Perceptions

The components of the illness perception are strongly interrelated, so that together they form a coherent, logical story of the illness. Many of these relationships are quite intuitive: For example, if one views a medical condition as chronic, its perceived consequences are likely to be more severe, its curability/controllability lower, and the emotional reaction stronger than if it is viewed as acute or short-lasting (Benyamini, Gozlan, & Kokia, 2004); if one views the cause as lifestyle-related, it is likely that perceptions of controllability would be stronger than if the cause was believed to be genetic or environmental (Shiloh, Rashuk-Rosenthal, & Benyamini, 2002). Many studies have reported a pattern of intercorrelations among the components that follows along these lines (see meta-analysis by Hagger & Orbell, 2003). These components also interact in their effects on various outcomes. For example, participants led to believe that they have high blood pressure reported more symptoms, especially if they attributed their high blood pressure to stress (Baumann et al., 1989).

### Relationships Between Hierarchical Levels of the Illness Perception

The Leventhal self-regulation model posits that illness perceptions and their related coping strategies and tactics are hierarchically organized in a formation constructed from abstract high-level representations to concrete, experiential low-level ones (Leventhal et al., 1984); similarly, illness causal attributions were also found to be organized in a hierarchical structure (Shiloh et al., 2002). This formation can be put to action in a bottom-up fashion: For instance, an individual's realization that she or he may be having a heart attack that is likely due to lifestyle factors might be represented at the concrete level with specific symptoms indicating a heart attack, as well as with specific risk behaviors that could have led to it and thus make this label plausible (which would also lead to quick care-seeking). It could also work top-down: Knowing a disease label, such as cancer, from personal or vicarious experience, can not only lead to general cancer worry but also to vigilance regarding specific symptoms (Benyamini, McClain et al., 2003).

## How Are Illness Perceptions Assessed?

As theories of illness perceptions developed, reliable and valid ways to assess them were needed. Turk et al. (1986) reviewed many early attempts to uncover the structure and contents of illness perceptions. Some of these attempts used predetermined dimensions believed to underlie the perception of all diseases. Others used exploratory techniques, with closed-ended or open-ended questions, to uncover the main dimensions. Both approaches contributed to further development of closed-ended questionnaires that can be used across diseases and populations.

The early studies conducted by Leventhal and colleagues explored patient's perception of their disease by asking them to describe it in their own words. Patients' responses then served to uncover the components of the illness perception. Structured interviews included general questions, such as "In your own words, what do you think [high blood pressure] means?," followed by specific probes (Meyer et al., 1985). The probes were designed to enable a clear distinction to be made between the patient's report of what she or he had been told and believed about their disease and its treatment, and what she or he believed to be true in general and thought was true about his or her disease. Interestingly, patients had no problem making these distinctions or acknowledging inconsistencies between medical knowledge and their own beliefs (and most of them asked that their beliefs not be communicated to the treating physician!).

Another example of such open-ended questioning appeared in a study by Lau et al. (1989). They asked respondents to think back to the last time they had a cold and to "tell us everything you remember about this illness" (p. 201). Additional questions inquired about why one became sick and why one had recovered. The open-ended responses were coded into distinct thoughts that were categorized into the predetermined categories of identity, timeline, consequences, cause, and cure.

When the self-regulation model became more established, some studies used it to construct a semistructured interview that inquired about each of the components of the illness perception. This approach yields data that are more difficult to analyze compared with closed-ended assessments of these components (see below) but that also provide a richer understanding of the illness in question and its manifestations and meanings for specific populations (e.g., O'Neill & Morrow, 2001).

An opposite approach used various quantitative clustering methods to uncover the dimensions underlying the perception of symptoms and diseases. In one study, participants were asked to rate 45 symptoms on eight semantic properties. Three main factors emerged from a factor analysis of the data: (1) the extent to which the symptom is threatening, disruptive, and painful; (2) the familiarity of the symptoms and the perceived personal responsibility for their occurrence; and, (3), how embarrassing these symptoms were (Jones, Wiese, Moore, & Haley, 1981). These factors resemble the consequences, causes, and controllability components mentioned above.

A similar approach at the disease level was employed by Rounds and Zevon (1993). Participants were asked to rate the similarity of cancer and 11 other medical conditions and to rate them on various attribute scales. When these data were submitted to multidimensional scaling, two dimensions were found to underlie the perceptions of these illnesses: the first dimension ranged from physical impairments on one end (e.g., cancer, arthritis) to psychological/functional impairments on the other end (e.g., schizophrenia, visual impairment). The second dimension ranged from more "normal" conditions (diabetes, alcoholism) to less normal ones (cerebral palsy, epilepsy).

In another study, participants sorted 35 illnesses into piles on the basis of their similarity. Seven clusters emerged from an analysis based on the similarity scores; five of them involved the nature of the typical sufferer from the diseases in that cluster. This led to additional explorations of illness prototypes, which included dimensions such as the consequences, causes, and controllability of the illness along with a characterization of the typical person who gets it. These findings enable investigation of the prototype check conducted by people who encounter a set of symptoms and engage in lay diagnosis of the illness (Lalljee, Lamb, & Carnibella, 1993).

These studies provided support for the existence of universal illness perceptions that are held even by nonpatients. These perceptions have important implications for the way in which lay people react to new symptoms they encounter and to symptoms and diseases in others. However, these methods were not used to study people's perceptions of their own illness. Turk et al. (1986) attempted to operationalize the constructs proposed by Leventhal et al. (1980) and Lau and Hartman (1983) in the Implicit Model of Illness Questionnaire (IMIQ) in a way that could be useful for studying lay people's perceptions of different illnesses as well as patients' perceptions of their own illnesses. Both exploratory and confirmatory factor analyses supported a four-factor solution, with the factors seriousness, personal responsibility, controllability, and changeability. These factors roughly correspond to the consequences, causes, controllability, and (episodic) timeline components mentioned above. Further explorations of illness perceptions using the IMIQ highlighted its utility in identifying differences between patient and nonpatient populations: Patients with a chronic disease—multiple sclerosis or rheumatoid arthritis—were much more aware of the variability in symptoms over time and assigned much less personal responsibility for the disease than did students (Schiaffino & Cea, 1995).

In 1996, the Illness Perception Questionnaire (IPQ) was published by Weinman, Petrie, Moss-Morris, and Horne. Since then, the bulk of research on illness perceptions has been carried out with this instrument, in its different versions. The IPQ includes a checklist of symptoms and four multi-item subscales assessing perceived causes, timeline, consequences, and control/cure. Its subscales were interrelated in expected ways (e.g., a longer timeline is related to more severe perceived consequences) and were related concurrently and prospectively among MI patients to measures of self-rated health and perceived likelihood of a future MI. Much of the research on illness perceptions carried out with this instrument was summarized in a meta-analysis by Hagger and Orbell (2003). Illness perceptions were found to be related to many of the coping strategies investigated, as well as to adaptive outcomes

such as psychological well-being, role and social functioning, and vitality.

A revised version of the IPQ (the IPQ-R) includes several modifications (Moss-Morris et al., 2002):

- In the symptom subscale, respondents were asked to rate each symptom twice: Once indicating whether or not they had experienced each symptom since their illness, and a second time indicating whether or not they believed this symptom was specifically related to their illness.
- In addition to the acute-to-chronic timeline subscale, a *cyclic* subscale was added to assess the extent to which the disease waxed and waned in episodes.
- The perceived control scale was split into *personal* control and *treatment* control.
- An emotional representations subscale was added, assessing the extent to which the illness led one to be upset, angry, worried, etc.
- A new component was added: Coherence, or the degree to which a person holds a coherent understanding of the illness. Coherence is purported to be a meta-cognition that taps whether the illness "makes sense" to the patient and reflects the way in which the patient evaluates the usefulness of his or her illness perception.

In addition, the checklist of causes was expanded (for a more extensive instrument, see the Illness Attribution Scale, Shiloh et al., 2002). This instrument also showed good psychometric properties, including predictive validity.

The length of the full IPQ-R (about 70 items) motivated the development of the Brief Illness Perception Questionnaire (BIPQ), designed to provide a quick assessment of the illness perception using nine items (Broadbent, Petrie, Main, & Weinman, 2006). The items, each assessing a component of the illness perception, are highly correlated with the corresponding IPQ-R subscales. The items were also found to be correlated with various measures of health, physical, and psychological functioning, and they discriminated between different illness populations. This recently published instrument has already been used in several studies, often with adaptations to the specific illness at question, and was found to be related to measures of health and adherence (e.g., Kesler et al., 2009; Mann, Ponieman, Leventhal, & Halm, 2009).

The ease of administration of the IPQ, along with its robust theoretical basis, has led to a rapid increase in the quantity of such research over the past decade and has enabled quantitative analyses of changes over time in illness perceptions, as well as comparisons across populations; however, it has also exposed the limitations of using a "generic" measure in diverse disease contexts (French & Weinman, 2008). The general underlying structure was confirmed in some contexts (e.g., cervical screening; Hagger & Orbell, 2005), whereas in others the structure differed among illnesses (e.g., Heijmans & de Ridder, 1998). Differences were found even among subpopulations with the same disease (heart disease) that differed only in type of treatment (Hirani, Pugsley, & Newman, 2006). The authors of the IPQ were aware of the limitations and encouraged researchers to add or modify items to ensure that they cover those areas relevant to the disease studied and perceived as such by the respondents (Moss-Morris et al., 2002; Weinman et al., 1996). However, this advice was not often implemented. As French and Weinman (2008) pointed out in their critique, many studies may have missed critical patient beliefs that are specific to their disease. Without identifying those beliefs, it may be impossible to understand their behavior or change it.

These limitations point to the need to integrate research on illness perceptions with qualitative health research. Many phenomenological studies have explored people's experience of their illness in depth and uncovered recurring themes. Illness narratives have been extensively studied (see Kleinman's 1988a seminal work). Due to the sheer number of such studies, a full discussion of this literature is beyond the scope of this chapter. However, it is important to note that the basic principles arising from these studies are similar to those identified by more structured approaches: People construct narratives of their illness that help them make sense of their experience and provide meaning to it (Kleinman, 1988a; Williams, 1984). The findings are typically specific to a health condition or even to a study, thus limiting the ability to compare across studies and diseases (although several reviews of this literature have succeeded in identifying recurring themes; see Hydén, 1997; Thorne et al., 2002).

Despite these limitations, qualitative studies provide an initial understanding of the context of the disease, which could help in developing semistructured interviews that could in turn guide the development of adapted versions of a closed-ended instrument such as the IPQ. As in any other field of study, when both qualitative and quantitative findings accumulate, the field becomes richer and

our knowledge advances. In the case of illness perceptions, using qualitative methods and drawing on their findings holds promise as a way to further inspire quantitative studies. In addition, researchers can use mixed-method questioning of the same patients to gain in-depth understanding of their unique circumstances. This was recently illustrated with the development of the Barts Explanatory Model Inventory (BEMI), which includes an interview and several checklists that can be used across diseases and cultures (Rüdell, Bhui, & Priebe, 2009).

One additional limitation of the IPQ and similar instruments must be noted: They are all verbal and thus tap structured knowledge and therefore may be culture-specific. Recently, several studies by Broadbent and colleagues have shown the utility of using patients' drawings to explore their illness perception: For example, MI patients' drawings of their hearts were found to be related to the severity of their condition and predicted recovery better than did the medical measures (Broadbent, Ellis, Gamble, & Petrie, 2006; Broadbent, Petrie, Ellis, Ying, & Gamble, 2004). Similarly, headache sufferers' drawings were related to their physical and psychological functioning as well as to their illness perceptions (Broadbent, Niederhofferb, Haguec, Cortera, & Reynolds, 2009). Nonverbal methods, including music, could also facilitate the understanding of illness perceptions across cultures (Bastien, 2009).

In sum, the assessment of illness perceptions is not a trivial, technical matter because methods of assessment can constrain or expand our ability to gain insights into the role of these perceptions. Substantial developments have been made in the area of assessment of illness perceptions, yet more work lies ahead. Developing easy-to-administer yet disease- and culture-relevant measures is important not only for research: Patients do not usually disclose their illness perceptions spontaneously to health care providers; questionnaires can provide a rapid, reliable, and legitimate way to elicit these perceptions (Petrie & Weinman, 2006).

## Treatment Perceptions and Their Assessment

Let us return to the headache example from the beginning of the chapter: What would determine if you take a pill to alleviate the pain? Is it only your perception of the headache, or also your perception of medications in general and this one in particular? To understand how people cope with a medical procedure, it is necessary to understand their perception of the disease, but also of the procedures aimed at treating it and the interactions between them (Benyamini, 2007). For example, if you believe you have diabetes only when your sugar is high, then you are unlikely to take your medicine regularly (Mann et al., 2009). Similarly, if you believe the severity of your disease can be judged by your symptoms (Baumann & Leventhal, 1985; McAndrew, Schneider, Burns, & Leventhal, 2007), then you are likely to take your medication as prescribed only when you experience symptoms (Chakraborty, Avasthi, Kumar, & Grover, 2009; Meyer et al., 1985). Note that these behaviors reflect people's concerns about taking medication regularly. Their decisions about taking their medication seem to balance the concerns against the perceived necessity of the medication. Indeed, *concerns* and *necessity* are the two components of the treatment representation identified by Horne, Weinman, and Hankins (1999). Both components are comprised of a cognitive and an emotional representation, similar to illness perceptions, and can be measured with the Beliefs about Medicines Questionnaire (BMQ) developed by Horne et al. (1999) to assess beliefs about medicines in general and about perceptions of the specific medication prescribed to the respondent.

## How Are Illness Perceptions Formed?

How do people form illness perceptions? What sources do they draw upon? This topic is one of the least studied in this area. It is likely that illness perceptions are drawn from a variety of sources and are consolidated as we develop and accumulate knowledge and experience from these sources. Within this developmental approach, the basic source would be one's family. Do you remember what your mother did when she had a headache? Did she lie down and rest? Did she take a pill? Did she run to the doctor? How did your parents react when you were ill? Which questions did they ask you about your feeling at that time? These questions could have disclosed their theory about your illness (and about illnesses in general), and their actions revealed their beliefs about how to handle it. One of the few studies that tested this found that arthritis patients who reported that their parents avoided routine activities in response to minor acute illness, such as the flu, tended to restrict their own behavior and report more helplessness and depression compared with patients with the same disease severity who reported that their parents did not avoid activities when ill (Elfant, Gall, & Perlmuter, 1999).

An additional important source is our personal experience with diseases—whether it is direct experience or exposure to ill people around us. Personal experiences provide a wealth of sensory, emotional, and cognitive information that is integrated into our view of the illness. Past experience helps set this within the overall trajectory of our health. Social comparison helps us set this within a context and "calibrate" our feelings in comparison to others' (Suls, 2003). Added to that is the knowledge obtained from cultural sources—the myths and perceptions that are common in our society (Leventhal et al., 2008), as well as information distributed by the media. Diseases such as cancer and human immunodeficiency virus (HIV) infection are likely to receive media attention that is disproportionate to the actual risk, in comparison to major causes of death such as heart disease (Frost, Frank, & Maibach, 1997). The media tends to emphasize certain aspects of the disease, such as fear in the case of cancer, and certain types of the diseases, with no relation to actual incidence rates (Clarke, 2004). Media accounts can also promote stereotypes regarding the type of person who is likely to contract a disease, as can be seen in gendered accounts of migraine in pharmaceutical marketing (Kempner, 2006). Note that, in these ways, the media contributes to biases in the perception of illnesses that can lead to over- or underutilization of health care services.

What role does information from health care providers play in our illness perceptions? On the one hand, such information is among the main sources that we rely upon to judge our health status (Benyamini, Leventhal, & Leventhal, 2003). On the other hand, studies show that it is only one of the many sources on which we base our perceptions of diseases (Goodman, Morrissey, Graham, & Bossingham, 2005; Hunt, Jordan, & Irwin, 1989). The greater the incongruence between our own feelings and the information we receive from health care providers, the less we trust that information and the more we keep seeking for explanations for our symptoms that make sense in our own eyes. This is especially prominent in functional symptom syndromes, which are not easily diagnosed and are often attributed by physicians to psychological factors (Moss-Morris & Wrapson, 2003). These issues will be further discussed below.

## How Stable Are Illness Perceptions?

Illness perceptions are quite stable over periods of several weeks, although their test–retest reliability tends to become lower as months pass (Moss-Morris et al., 2002; Weinman et al., 1996). In light of the variable nature of illnesses, this is not surprising. Indeed, lower consistency over time is seen in the perceptions of identity and timeline, whereas greater consistency is seen in attributions of disease cause (Cameron, Petrie, Ellis, Buick, & Weinman, 2005a; Moss-Morris et al., 2002). Changes in illness perceptions are not always toward more negative perceptions: Over time, people often adjust to the burden of disease and experience less burdensome consequences (Schenkman, Cutson, Zhu, & Whetten-Goldstein, 2002) and emotional reactions (Goodman et al., 2005); or, they feel more control over time and consequently worry less (Mora, Halm, Leventhal, & Ceric, 2007).

Illness representations are part of a dynamic process that evolves over time (Leventhal, Leventhal, & Contrada, 1998). Therefore, their relative stability (Lawson, Bundy, & Harvey, 2008; Rutter & Rutter, 2007) is more puzzling than the changes reported. The reason may be partly methodological: Open-ended interviews suggest that the changes occur as stages and at specific points (Goodman et al., 2005); quantitative studies, even longitudinal ones, may miss these crucial time points. The main changes may occur in the initial period following diagnosis, after which it may be more difficult to influence illness perceptions (Lawson et al., 2008; Rutter & Rutter, 2007).

What is puzzling in the stability of illness perceptions is their resistance to change in face of medical information that indicates otherwise (Baker & Wiginton, 1997; Cameron et al., 2005a; Wold, Bycrs, Crane, & Ahnen, 2005). This is most clearly illustrated by chronic patients' disbelief that their disease is chronic and that it is unlikely that they can be completely cured; this disbelief leads to other problematic misconceptions: The belief that symptoms are a good measure of both the severity of the disease and the need for medication (Lange & Piette, 2006; Meyer et al., 1985); and the belief that each attack or flare-up is an acute episode and not a worsening of a chronic condition (Baker & Wiginton, 1997). Illness perceptions are more closely linked to one's personal experience—symptoms and the consequences of coping efforts—and to information provided by similar patients than to medical facts (Godoy-Izquierdo, Lopez-Chicheri, Lopez-Torrecillas, Velez, & Godoy, 2007; Leventhal et al., 1980). Therefore, they tend to change over time as experience and information from other people accumulate, but are more resistant to

change in face of medical information. A definite diagnosis, even of a serious disease such as cancer, could lead to a belief in a shorter timeline, as compared with similarly symptomatic people who were not diagnosed with cancer (Orbell et al., 2008); it is only after patients take medication or undergo treatment for several months that they are more likely to comprehend that their disease is chronic (Leventhal et al., 1986).

The process of forming illness perceptions provides an explanation for these seemingly irrational tendencies. In most cases, this process is well under way before we reach the doctor and are exposed to a medical opinion. In fact, seeking care is one of the outcomes of this process. Thus, by the time we receive information from physicians and medical tests, it is not assessed in itself but rather in the context of the information that we have already gathered about the illness in question and the working cognitions that we have formed on the basis of this information. This temporal unfolding of the process explains why medical information, although it is considered reliable, often has less impact on one's perceptions and ways of coping with illness in comparison to other types of information that are likely to be more subjective. One way that people use to work out this seeming paradox is to accept the medical information in general, yet view their own case as unique, for which the given information is not necessarily relevant (e.g., Murphy & Kinmonth, 1995).

Moreover, medical information usually does not replace one's prior perceptions; it is integrated into them in a way that is most consistent with them and with one's general view of life and health. This sometimes results in refusal to accept the information, as can be seen with patients diagnosed with cancer or infertility, who first react with denial (Menning, 1980; Vos & de Haes, 2007). It could also have the opposite effect, leading to quick changes in illness perceptions: People referred to coronary angiography who received results indicating diseased arteries did not change their illness perception, presumably because they had already perceived themselves as patients with heart disease, whereas those who received a favorable result quickly changed their illness perception (Devcich, Ellis, Gamble, & Petrie, 2008).

Ample evidence shows that people do not easily change their risk perceptions even when provided with information about risk. Even when they remember the information, apparently it is not integrated into their view of their own risk, as that would lead to appropriate action. This does not necessarily happen, as can be seen by the number of people who are aware of the risk of smoking yet continue to do so. Even individualized feedback that is inconsistent with a personal theory about the symptoms is likely to be discarded: Patients who believed they were hypersensitive to electromagnetic fields did not change their symptom reports or symptom attributions when provided with evidence that they were unable to detect electromagnetic signals (Nieto-Hernandez, Rubin, Cleare, Weinman, & Wessely, 2008). *Fuzzy trace theory* provides additional support for these notions: It argues that, even when people are aware of the facts, in the process of making decisions, they rely on the gist of the information, its subjective meaning, and not necessarily on all the details (Reyna, 2008). This may be why people often use metaphors to describe the meaning of their subjective experiences (Kirmayer, 1992): These metaphors best capture their experience. To conclude, illness perceptions are generally stable but are likely to change when symptom experience changes (Foster et al., 2008). However, they are less responsive to medical information that is inconsistent with prior or current beliefs, behavior, or sensations.

## Why Are Illness Perceptions Formed?

Life is a continuous process of experience organization. We long for order and meaning, but we live in a world that may not have any (Dwidevi & Gardner, 1997). A health problem often brings into our lives more ambiguity, loss of control, and feelings of threat, so that life becomes chaotic and unpredictable. To create some order and regain control, we seek ways to interpret somatic experiences in meaningful ways and to organize them into a coherent narrative that provides a continuity with our experiences and our self system. We construct a personal theory of our condition, which stems out of our personal narrative of our lives, is deeply intertwined with our self-identity and basic relationships, and enables us to interpret the new experiences and find meaning and order in them (Frank, 1995; Williams, 1984). Thus, both cognitive and emotional factors drive the formation of illness perceptions.

On the cognitive side, if illness perceptions are used to organize information in an efficient way, they should assist in information storage and retrieval. Indeed, participants more readily identified a disease when it was indicated by a more prototypical cluster of symptoms and were more

confident of their judgment; they also recalled more symptoms from prototypical sets (Bishop & Converse, 1986). When primed for a specific illness, participants showed an attentional bias to words related to that illness (but not to another), and the bias was related to their perceptions of the illness, as measured by the IPQ-R; these findings were repeated for two illnesses with which people are generally familiar: an acute illness, the common cold, as well as a chronic one, cardiovascular disease (Henderson, Orbell, & Hagger, 2007). Moreover, priming an illness also increases attention to coping strategies that have been used in the past to deal with this illness (Henderson, Orbell, & Hagger, 2009). These results show that the information about physical symptoms is organized and processed according to people's preexisting beliefs about the association between symptoms and diseases.

These findings support the argument that illness perceptions organize illness-related information in coherent ways that include logical links between representations and coping. Additional evidence for this argument comes from a study showing that individuals hold internally consistent beliefs about causes and solutions: When presented with a vignette about an illness, they recommended a treatment that corresponded with their perception of the cause—psychological or biomedical (Ogden & Jubb, 2008). Another example comes from a study of patients who received an abnormal colorectal cancer screening result: Those who perceived more personal control over the disease also made more efforts to change behavior (Orbell et al., 2008).

On the emotional side, managing uncertainty is often one of the main challenges in coping with an illness (Nicholls, Glover, & Pistrang, 2004). Illness perceptions can play an important role in relieving uncertainty and reducing anxiety. That is why the self-regulation model emphasizes the coherence between different perceptions rather than their independent effects (Leventhal, Benyamini, & Shafer, 2007). The overall picture created by a coherent theory about the illness can tie together seemingly disparate experiences—such as fatigue, breathlessness, difficulty walking—that occurred at different times and therefore were considered to be acute and only mildly severe, to a single chronic and severe disease, congestive heart failure (Horowitz, Rein, & Leventhal, 2004). Only when the individual sees the connections between these experiences and unites them under one conceptual framework will she or he react appropriately (i.e., seek immediate care).

The emotional benefits of reducing uncertainty may be why a search for causal attributions is more likely the more serious the disease (Turnquist et al., 1988). The formulation of an illness perception, by definition, relieves uncertainty as it replaces a potentially disorganized, threatening, and incomprehensible assortment of information and thoughts with a coherent theory that organizes them. Individuals are clearly motivated to find explanations for uncertain physiological signs and symptoms, and the strength of this motivation is related to the salience and perceived personal consequences of these bodily changes (Cacioppo, Andersen, Turnquist, & Petty, 1986). However, when medical information does not provide any clue as to the nature of one's symptoms and how to organize the knowledge about them (as in medically unexplained symptoms), subjective perceptions cannot fill the gap alone, and they are often negative and related to worse mental health (Frostholm et al., 2007). When the subjective perception is not perceived as legitimate by health care providers and is not validated by objective tests, as often happens in conditions that are difficult to diagnose, such as back pain, illness perceptions are insufficient to reduce uncertainty and the accompanying distress (Rhodes, McPhillips-Tangum, Markham, & Klenk, 1999), although they can motivate patients to challenge medical uncertainty and consequently reach a clearer diagnosis (Lillrank, 2003).

Illness perceptions are part of the self-regulation process that takes place in face of a health threat. This approach assumes that people are motivated to avoid and treat health threats. To this end, it seem that an accurate perception of their situation would be most beneficial because it would be more likely to lead to ways of coping that best fit the situation and consequently result in the most favorable outcome. However, this assumption does not take into account the emotional ramifications that an accurate perception of a threatening situation could have. Patients strive to feel like survivors and not like victims (Baker & Wiginton, 1997) and to assert control but not blame. Therefore, like many self-related perceptions, perceptions of illness can also show self-serving biases aimed at reducing anxiety and distress.

Many chronic illnesses are affected by genetics and environmental factors, but also by behavioral factors such as smoking, diet, exercise, and exposure to the sun. Thus, there is great potential for self-blame, which could lead to emotional distress. Yet, if one recognized that these behavioral factors caused the illness, it could also increase feelings of controllability over it. The solution to this seeming paradox is to frame illness perceptions in a way that lowers self-blame for the disease yet increases responsibility—and therefore controllability—over recovery. A series of experiments about recovery attributions supported the role of self-serving motivational processes in these attributions and suggested that these processes may be most effective when they are not entirely conscious (Shiloh, Peretz, Iss, & Kiedan, 2007).

Not surprisingly, the best examples for these biases were reported regarding perceptions of one of the most threatening diseases, cancer. For example, recently diagnosed cancer patients were less likely to attribute their diagnosis to behavioral causes, compared with patients with similar symptoms but a benign diagnosis (Orbell et al., 2008). Cancer survivors often cite genetic and environmental factors, as well as stress, as causes of their type of cancer and underestimate the role of behavioral factors known to be associated with cancer risk; the bias is even greater when asked about the causes of one's own cancer (Wold et al., 2005). Although this may be partly due to greater familiarity with one's own behavior—if you know you don't smoke and do exercise, there is no contradiction between believing that smoking or lack of exercise cause your type of cancer and reporting that they didn't cause *your* cancer. However, the differences in the Wold et al. (2005) study were far greater than expected, in light of the frequency of smoking or of being sedentary; even current smokers more often reported that they thought smoking was a risk factor for others than for themselves.

The emotional advantage can be gained, as noted above, from an opposite bias in perceptions of the factors responsible for recovery: Among cancer survivors, personal and behavioral factors were low on the list of illness attributions, but high on the list of attributions for the prevention of recurrence (Stewart et al., 2001). Among these factors were a positive attitude, exercise, diet, and a healthy lifestyle.

Similar biases were reported for another serious disorder: heart disease. Patients seemed to frame the causes for their heart attack in a way that reduced blame yet asserted control (French, Maissi, & Marteau, 2005). When searching for a causal factor, they often focused on a single uncontrollable one, which may have been the trigger for the event (e.g., stress), and not on the underlying cause, such as long-term lifestyle habits. At the same time, they described these same causes as controllable in the future. Similar to the findings from the cancer studies, the authors argued that, although these perceptions may not be epidemiologically accurate, they are emotionally and behaviorally adaptive.

Despite humans' ability to create and use self-serving biases, these biases typically do not provide a leap too far from reality (Taylor & Brown, 1988). Thus, although illness perceptions can serve to control distress in the face of illness, through the reduction of uncertainty or the creation of self-serving beliefs, they are not rosy glasses through which people examine their situation. Grave changes in our health can result in negative perceptions of the disease in question, and these can and do lead to further distress (Dickens et al., 2008). On the positive side, self-serving attempts to minimize risk perception do not necessarily prevent people from implementing risk-reducing lifestyle changes (Farrimond, Saukko, Qureshi, & Evans, 2010) or monitoring their bodies for signs of disease (Benyamini, McClain et al., 2003).

## Are Illness Perceptions Related to Health Outcomes?

Why should we be interested in illness perceptions? Are they simply a way to improve our understanding of the patients and our communication with them by acknowledging the way they think about their illness? Improving doctor–patient communication is a worthy goal but it can also be promoted in other ways. Are illness perceptions a more accurate and sensitive measure of disease severity? Measurement of disease severity is quite accurate in many areas with today's advanced technology; yet, subjective reports may still be essential for illnesses in which there are no objective manifestations (e.g., many of the musculoskeletal conditions). Are illness perceptions causally related to the patient's physical, functional, and psychological state? This question of the causal relationship between illness perceptions and outcomes is the most intriguing one but also the most difficult to answer.

Let us first examine the evidence relevant to the possibility that illness perceptions are an accurate measure. People's illness perceptions are based on their knowledge of their own behavior and history, as can be seen by the correspondence between their risk perceptions and attributions and their actual risk profiles (Stafford, Jackson, & Berk, 2008). However, an examination of the main components of illness perceptions—consequences, timeline, identity and control/cure—showed that, cross-sectionally,

they are unrelated or only weakly related to disease state (see meta-analysis by Hagger & Orbell, 2003), which is puzzling. Are illness perceptions unrelated to actual disease state? Or, do they contain different types of information that may be more accurate than objective measures of disease state? There are additional reasons not to "trust" illness perceptions: They can be affected by self-serving biases, as discussed above, and they can be manipulated (e.g., by priming; see Crane & Martin, 2003).

However, a large body of research suggests that illness perceptions are important and may be valid as predictors of outcomes other than disease state. First, the same meta-analysis (Hagger & Orbell, 2003) also found that illness perceptions are related to a variety of outcomes: physical, role and social functioning; vitality; psychological distress and well-being. Second, several longitudinal studies point to a *unique* contribution of illness perceptions to outcomes, beyond that of more objective measures: Illness perceptions reported shortly after a heart attack were stronger predictors of return to work and functioning in the following months than illness severity measures (Petrie et al., 1996). Illness perceptions more strongly predicted physical function, pain, depression, and anxiety among women with rheumatoid arthritis, compared with disease status (Groarke, Curtis, Coughlan, & Gsel, 2005). Cross-sectional research provided evidence from additional disease populations: Among psoriasis patients, illness perceptions accounted for almost twice as much variance in disability as did demographic and clinical variables together, when all these variables were tested together in a single model (Fortune, Richards, Griffiths, & Main, 2002); in another study of chronic patients (with psoriasis, rheumatoid arthritis, or chronic obstructive pulmonary disease), similar associations emerged between illness perceptions and functioning measures, after controlling for clinical measures and disease duration (Scharloo et al., 1998). Together, these findings suggest that the most important contribution of subjective illness perceptions is their greater sensitivity as measures of physical and psychological functioning, compared with objective measures of disease status. Further support for this notion comes from longitudinal studies (Frostholm et al., 2007; Hampson, Glasgow, & Strycker, 2000).

Additional convincing evidence comes from a study of patients after a heart attack: More negative representations predicted a greater risk of complications, after controlling for demographic and clinical variables; depression and anxiety did not predict these complications (Cherrington, Moser, Lennie, & Kennedy, 2004). Note that the Hampson et al. (2000) study mentioned above also reported that personal models of illness predicted both mental and physical functioning, whereas depression predicted only mental health. These findings suggest that the effects of illness perceptions are not limited to associations between similar measures of positive (or negative) emotions or expectations or to the mental or physical effects of depression.

To get back to this section's opening questions: Are illness perceptions independently related to outcomes because they contain valid information that is not tapped by objective measures, or are they related to outcomes because they affect present and future outcomes? This question resembles a similar debate regarding global self-ratings of health (Idler & Benyamini, 1997). In both cases, the answer is the same: It is difficult to tease apart the two explanations, which emphasize accuracy versus causal effect.

To understand why it is difficult, imagine a chronic patient who complains of constant fatigue. On the one hand, this may be an accurate measure of the state of his or her disease, a "proxy" for more sophisticated measures, and thus it will be concurrently and prospectively related to various outcomes. This is not to be taken lightly: A measure that is closely related to one's quality of life and/or provides a more accurate assessment of disease status than that provided by medical tests is important. On the other hand, negative perceptions of fatigue and the condition responsible for it may lead the person to cope passively, to conserve energy, refrain from physical activity, and remain at home for longer stretches of time, so that social activities are also compromised (Heijmans, 1998). These behaviors may lead to further deterioration of the person's health status, as well as to depression, which can also lead to lower activity, poor diet, and other unhealthy behaviors and could possibly have direct effects on physiological systems. The negative illness perceptions can also lead directly to depression, thus exacerbating these processes (Dickens et al., 2008; Sharpe, Sensky, & Allard, 2001). In sum, it is difficult to know whether fatigue in this case was an accurate portrayal of this person's deteriorating health status or a causal factor contributing to further deterioration of health. If we wish to fully understand the importance of illness perceptions as a potential causal factor, we need to identify possible mechanisms that could account for such effects.

## How Are Illness Perceptions Related to Outcomes?

Illness perceptions guide coping procedures, according to the self-regulation model. Thus, they can ultimately affect outcomes through the choice of actions arising from these perceptions. Very few studies tested this (i.e., tested coping procedures as mediators between illness perceptions and outcomes), and most of them found null results (see Hagger & Orbell, 2003). This may be due to the level of specificity in which these predictors were measured: Whereas illness perceptions are typically measured with scales asking about very specific aspects of one's illness, which were sometimes adapted to the illness at question, coping strategies are usually measured with generic instruments aimed at assessing coping with a stressful situation. Indeed, several studies that did support the mediation hypothesis adapted the measure of illness perceptions to the health condition they studied *and* used a situation-specific coping questionnaire (such as the Coping with Infertility Questionnaire; Benyamini et al., 2008), or at least used an illness-specific coping questionnaire (Gray & Rutter, 2007) or asked about coping with a specific illness state (such as coping with the symptoms at their worst rather than with the illness in general; Rutter & Rutter, 2002).

Two main ways of coping are of interest here and have been often investigated: People's decisions to seek care and their adherence to medical recommendations. As for decisions to seek care, research has provided ample evidence for associations between illness perceptions and the use of primary care (Frostholm et al., 2005), emergency care (Walsh, Lynch, Murphy, & Daly, 2004), complementary and alternative care (Bishop, Yardley, & Lewith, 2008), and genetic counseling (Shiloh, 2006). Such effects are found along all stages of coping with a health threat, from initial realization that one needs to seek care to rehabilitation and prevention of future incidents. The most striking examples can be seen in the area of cardiovascular care. Beliefs about symptoms, causal beliefs, and illness perceptions determine time to care-seeking among patients with a heart attack (Perkins-Porras, Whitehead, Strike, & Steptoe, 2008; Schoenberg, Peters, & Drew, 2003). Illness perceptions predict attendance at cardiac rehabilitation (see review by Cooper, Jackson, Weinman, & Horne, 2002); not surprisingly, attenders are more likely to view their illness as severe but to believe it is controllable (see also Whitmarsh, Koutantji, & Sidell, 2003).

Regarding adherence to recommendations about medical treatment and lifestyle, despite its documented effectiveness, many studies showed high rates of *non*adherence, especially for chronic patients who are instructed to take medication on a regular basis for many years (Horne, 1998) or to make substantial lifestyle changes (Wiles, 1998). This cannot be simply explained by problems in doctor–patient communication without acknowledging the major role that patients' perceptions play (Conrad, 1994). Indeed, accurate illness perceptions can lead to greater lifestyle changes. Patients with hypercholesterolemia who held more accurate perceptions at baseline showed greater dietary modifications in the following year (Coutu, Dupuis, D'Antono, & Rochon-Goyer, 2003). Asthma patients who realized that their disease is chronic yet viewed it as controllable, were more likely to be adherent to their medication.

As time passes, patients drift further away from the official medical explanation for their disease and tend to form and follow their own account (Wiles, 1998). Thus, the subjective illness perceptions become the major determinant of people's decisions to act in ways intended to preserve their health.

Treatment perceptions add an important independent dimension to the prediction of adherence. Strong beliefs in necessity, a strong identity, and high consequences all lead to better adherence (Llewellyn, Miners, Lee, Harrington, & Weinman, 2003). Illness perceptions can also influence adherence indirectly through treatment beliefs: Among asthma patients, perceptions of greater consequences and a more chronic timeline led to doubts about treatment necessity, which in turn predicted lower adherence (Horne & Weinman, 2002; see also Ross, Walker, & MacLeod, 2004 for similar findings among patients with hypertension).

The investigation of treatment perceptions uncovered the inherent conflict between necessity and concerns that is experienced even by overall healthy people, who, on the one hand, wish to alleviate occasional bothersome symptoms (such as headaches) and on the other hand, wish to maintain a natural body ideal (Hansen, Holstein, & Hansen, 2009). The conflict can be much stronger among people who are instructed to take medications for a chronic disease on a regular basis (Horne, 2006). Investigations of treatment perceptions showed that they can be used to differentiate between intentional and nonintentional nonadherers. The latter do not differ much from adherers whereas the former use nonadherence as a strategy to cope with

the necessity–concerns conflict (Clifford, Barber, & Horne, 2008) and with side effects (Johnson & Neilands, 2007). Additional, less frequent, combinations of necessity and concerns were also found to be related to nonadherence, such as skeptical patients (low necessity, high concerns) and indifferent ones (low on both; Horne, Parham, Driscoll, & Robinson, 2009).

In sum, although from a medical view nonadherence seems to be irrational and deviant, when we take into account patients' experience and their active management of their disease, nonadherence seems to follow quite logically from their understanding of their condition, within the context of their own lives (Ingadottir & Halldorsdottir, 2008). When people realize that the risks they face are not just general threats but personal, familial risks, they are more likely to choose healthy behaviors (Pijl et al., 2009); when they believe in a medical model of a disease, they are more adherent to medication whereas a stress-related model leads to stress-reducing behaviors (Hekler et al., 2008); when they believe their disease is controllable, they are more likely to take their meds (Ross et al., 2004). The common theme in all these findings is that people's actions are normal and rational, even if medically "incorrect," and that understanding their perceptions is the key to understanding their behaviors.

## Interventions

If insights into people's subjective views of their illness can help us understand and predict their behaviors, can they also assist us in intervening to affect these behaviors? For example, if we know that patients who feel little control over their heart disease are less likely to attend a rehabilitation program (Petrie et al., 1996), we can tailor the promotion of this program to people with low feelings of control or, alternatively, attempt to increase their perceived control. Similarly, if patients who believe hypertension is caused by stress are less likely to use their medication (Hekler et al., 2008), we may want to challenge their causal beliefs and/or their beliefs about treatment necessity and concerns regarding the medication. If the patient wrongly believes that having undergone a serious heart attack means that she should refrain from activity, we can challenge this notion and help her construct an action plan that is appropriate for her medical condition and personal life circumstances. Thus, focusing on illness perceptions can guide us in planning patient-centered interventions that may be more effective than standardized ones that do not take into account the person's beliefs (Lauver et al., 2002). Even if we are unable to provide personally tailored interventions, illness perceptions can help us cluster patients, so that relevant treatments can be provided to each group (Hobro, Weinman, & Hankins, 2004).

This concept of patient-centered treatment proved effective in an intervention for patients after a first heart attack. In addition to standard care, they met with a psychologist for three sessions in which their illness perceptions were explored, negative perceptions were challenged, and an action plan for recovery was constructed (Petrie, Cameron, Ellis, Buick, & Weinman, 2002). The intervention significantly altered participants' beliefs about their disease: Compared to patients who received only standard care, intervention participants viewed the consequences of their illness as less severe, the timeline as shorter, and the disease as more controllable, and reported that they understood their condition better. These differences persisted for 3 months. More importantly, intervention participants returned to work faster (and the difference was significant even after adjustment for clinical measures). These findings were recently replicated in another sample (Broadbent, Ellis, Thomas, Gamble, & Petrie, 2009b). A parallel intervention was conducted with the patients' spouses, leading to changes in their understanding of the illness and the expected pattern of recovery, as well as in their causal attributions and level of concern (Broadbent, Ellis, Thomas, Gamble, & Petrie, 2009a).

Another prominent example is the DESMOND program for individuals newly diagnosed with type 2 diabetes (Davies et al., 2008; Skinner et al., 2006). Tests of this theoretically driven program showed that a 6-hour structured self-management education session can be successful in changing illness perceptions: Participants were more likely to understand their illness and to accept that it is a chronic and serious yet controllable disease. Changes in perceptions were also found to be related to outcomes: A change in perceived personal responsibility was related to weight loss.

These studies inspired other researchers to plan interventions based on exploring and changing illness perceptions in an attempt to change patients' actions (e.g., adherence to treatment; Karamanidou, Weinman, & Horne, 2008) and outcomes (e.g., decrease in symptom levels; Deary, 2008; McAndrew et al., 2008). These and other examples can be found in a special issue of the *British Journal of Health Psychology* that was devoted to therapeutic techniques for interventions based on Leventhal's commonsense model (Wearden & Peters, 2008).

These studies and similar ones are very promising. However, some were effective in changing perceptions but not behaviors (e.g., Karamanidou et al., 2008), and others are still in various stages of testing. The state of the art at the moment raises more questions than it answers (Benyamini, 2005). Two main issues need to be addressed. The first stems from the assumption underlying these interventions that we (providers of the intervention) know something that the patient does not; we attempt to feed the subjective mind with objective information. From research on the stability and resistance of illness perceptions to change, we know this is not a simple task yet the few successful studies published to date show that it can be achieved, if enough resources are devoted to it (such as personal sessions for each patient with a psychologist trained at administering the intervention). What we don't know is whether and when we may be wrong in doing so: Are negative illness perceptions always invalid? Are positive illness perceptions always the standard to strive for? Take, for example, a woman with diabetes who views her disease as uncontrollable. What happens if we convince her that it is controllable, that lifestyle changes can reduce her risk or complications—will she then feel more at ease to exercise control over her medication by altering the regimen according to her feelings? And what if she believes her disease is very serious, but her physician does not think so? Should we try to change *her* belief? Most probably, her physician is right. But what if he's not? What if he is missing another diagnosis or underestimating the effects of comorbidity of her diabetes and additional chronic diseases from which she is suffering? Or, what if we succeed in convincing her that her condition is not that serious, and she lowers the dosage of her medication without consulting her doctor? Such questions underscore the importance of being cautious in implementing such interventions and the need for long-term follow-up of their participants. Such follow-up would enable us to assess desirable and undesirable changes in beliefs and behaviors that the interventions triggered.

The second issue involves the need for in-depth understanding of what part of an intervention worked to achieve its goals. What were the critical components of such an intervention? Was it the information that patients received, which was provided in a more intimate setting than is typical in standard care? Was it the tailoring of this information to the patient's beliefs and life circumstances? (Or is it the belief that the information was tailored?

see Webb, Simmons, & Brandon, 2005). Was it simply the personal attention that the patient received? To improve the effectiveness of such interventions, we should also strive for better understanding of their mechanisms. This understanding can, in turn, improve our understanding of the theory underlying them.

## In Whose Perceptions Should We Be Interested?

Although the label "illness perceptions" implies that the focus is on the perceptions of people afflicted with a certain medical condition, this is only a piece of the larger picture. In some form, we all hold perceptions of each condition we have ever encountered. Whether we heard about it in the media or met a person with the condition, if we know about it, we have organized the information we have as a schema or prototype of the condition. If we have only little information (and little interest) in it, this prototype may not be detailed, well-organized, and highly coherent. However, it is the basis to which additional information is added and, more importantly, it determines the way we cope with anything related to this illness, from our own health behaviors to our reactions to people afflicted with it. Thus, illness perceptions are relevant not only in patients, and patients do not cope with illnesses in a social vacuum. The perceptions of people surrounding them are important in understanding the self-regulation processes of patients and others. Research that has expanded the study of illness perceptions to nonpatient populations has focused on three main types: family members, health care professionals, and nonpatients. The principles underlying the formation and use of these illness perceptions are similar and resemble those of patients.

### Family Members' Perceptions

Every component of the self-regulation process typically takes place within the family (Leventhal, Leventhal, & Van Nguyen, 1985). The vast social support literature provides ample evidence of the importance of close relationships in stressful situations (underscoring both beneficial and detrimental effects). These relationships can affect a person's illness perceptions directly, by serving as an additional source of information, and indirectly, by increasing or alleviating the illness-related stress (Knoll, Schwarzer, Pfuller, & Kienle, 2009). Perceptions of family members are of the same form as those of the patient and are similarly only partly related to objective measures of illness (Barrowclough, Lobban,

Hatton, & Quinn, 2001). They can affect the patient's perceptions, interact with them, be affected by them, and affect ways of coping chosen by family members (Weinman, Heijmans, & Figueiras, 2003), including the support they provide to the patient in his or her coping with the disease (Benyamini, Medalion et al., 2007). They may also underlie negative social experiences, such as undermining (Benyamini, Medalion et al., 2007) and delegitimizing (Dickson, Knussen, & Flowers, 2007; in that study family members' perceptions were not directly studied). Most studies involved patients and spouses (Weinman et al., 2003), although some also looked at parents and children (e.g., Olsen, Berg, & Wiebe, 2008).

Researchers have been particularly interested in the degree of congruence between patient and carer perceptions. Patient and family members' illness perceptions often concur (e.g., Heijmans, de Ridder, & Bensing, 1999; Weinman, Petrie, Sharpe, & Walker, 2000), but when they do not, the disagreement could affect both partners' adjustment to the disease and its impact on their lives. Incongruence was shown to be associated with outcomes related to the patient (Figueiras & Weinman, 2003; Heijmans et al., 1999), the spouse (Kuipers et al., 2007), and the dyad (Peterson, Newton, & Rosen, 2003). This research has raised debates about the methodology of determining incongruence and about the importance of studying interactions between patient and carer perceptions (Benyamini, Medalion et al., 2007). Findings differ by type of illness, component of illness perception, and gender, but in general, most studies show that discrepancies between patient and spouse are detrimental and that underestimation of the illness by the spouse/carer is most likely to be related to negative outcomes. See, for example, differences in perceptions of controllability over infertility (Benyamini, Gozlan, & Kokia, 2009), in perceptions of severity of pain in osteoarthritis (Cremeans-Smith et al., 2003), or in perceived consequences of rheumatoid arthritis (Sterba et al., 2008). In sum, there is sufficient evidence regarding the importance of expanding our view of illness perceptions to include family members.

### Health Care Providers

Do health care providers perceive illnesses in the same way that lay people do? Or, do they hold scientific, objective, explanations of illnesses, so that a gap exists between these representations and those of their patients? Historically, if we go as far back as Hippocrates, there was no gap. The physician treated the person as a whole, paid special notice to all patient symptoms and reports, interpreted these within the person's physical and social environment, and constructed his view of the illness and its causes on the basis of all these observations; the disease did not possess an existence independent and apart from the patient (Chadwick & Mann, 1950; Schober & Lacroix, 1991). It is only in the past century that doctors tended to treat patient reports with skepticism, thus gradually creating a chasm between what the physicians learn of the person's inner body and the way the person perceives his or her condition and speaks about it (Hydén, 1997).

Today, it is quite clear that health care providers construct their own illness perceptions and that these perceptions can differ from those of patients (Insel, Meek, & Leventhal, 2005). This most often means that providers' perceptions are likely to represent a narrow biomedical view, compared to the more varied views of their patients (Bar-On & Cristal, 1987). Paradoxically, with unexplained symptoms, the opposite phenomenon occurs: Patients seeking legitimacy search for biomechanical explanations in the face of providers' psychosomatic model (Hardwick, 2005) or doubt about the cause, which leads them to suggest psychological causes (May, Rose, & Johnstone, 2000). This is to be expected, if we remember why and how illness perceptions are created: They are created to cope with uncertainty; and, they are created in a process of integrating medical information into preexisting understandings of health and illness as well as contextual factors (Armstrong & Murphy, 2008). Health care professionals interpret their observations of a specific patient in the context of knowledge regarding the typical patient and evidence-based research findings (Whelan, 2009), whereas patients judge their symptoms in the context of their personal direct and vicarious experiences. Thus, even if the objective information held by patient and professional regarding the patient's disease is identical, its interpretation could vastly differ.

When health care providers see that their patients receive and understand medical information, they are often unaware of the way people use this information, getting the "gist" of the matter, as they interpret it (Reyna, 2008), and therefore not necessarily relying on the full information for making decisions regarding their behavior. People often use metaphors to describe and create meaning for their subjective experiences; these metaphors work best for them but often clash with the rational biomedical language used by their physicians

(Kirmayer, 1992). Training practitioners to elicit illness representations and action plans can change doctor–patient communication style and content and enable an open discussion of these matters (see intervention study by de Ridder, Theunissen, & van Dulmen, 2007).

In sum, research on providers' illness perceptions is important for two main reasons. The first is that gaps between professionals and patients could lead to misunderstandings and consequently to patient nonadherence. The second is that professionals' perceptions guide their own professional behavior and decisions about implementing various treatments (Eccles, Grimshaw, Walker, Johnston, & Pitts, 2005), including their perceptions of their patients' beliefs (Horne, Kovacs et al., 2009). Furthermore, professionals from different disciplines could hold very different models of the same illness, greatly affecting shared decision making in multidisciplinary teams (Colombo, Bendelow, Fulford, & Williams, 2003). In light of these reasons and the extensive literature on doctor–patient communication, as well as on medical decision-making, it is surprising that so little has been done to investigate the role of providers' illness perceptions.

### Nonpatients

How do nonpatients perceive illnesses? Are they less knowledgeable than providers, yet more objective than patients? Or, are they less knowledgeable than patients, as they do not possess firsthand experience of the disease, and just as subjective as patients are because they are also threatened by the risk of disease? Research in this area has focused on two different populations: Lay people—nonpatients whose perceptions represent the general social stereotype of the illness—and healthy people who are at risk for a disease. Just as patients would rather attribute their disease to uncontrollable factors to avoid blame, both of these healthy populations are similar in their motivation to perceive the disease in ways that would enable them to feel safer. However, these two subpopulations also differ in many respects.

#### HEALTHY INDIVIDUALS

For healthy individuals, the most important component of the illness perception is identity (Rees, Fry, Cull, & Sutton, 2004). Their knowledge about diseases is most often focused on the characteristic symptoms as well as the nature of typical sufferers and typical causes (Lalljee et al., 1993), which is the information that one needs to assess personal risk (or rather to convince yourself that you are not at risk). Research with a version of the IPQ-R adapted for lay people has shown that, at least when actively prompted, their perceptions span all components of the illness perceptions and are similar in structure and reliability to those of different patient groups (Figueiras & Alves, 2007). Another study showed that the associations between causal attributions and illness perceptions differed between patients and nonpatients (Shiloh et al., 2002). Nonpatients are more likely to attribute illness to controllable factors and less to stress or chance (French, Senior, Weinman, & Marteau, 2001) or conversely to heredity (Arcury, Skelly, Gesler, & Dougherty, 2004) and other factors that are considered to be dispositions of the patient. They are also likely to assign more personal responsibility to patients than patients do (Schiaffino & Cea, 1995). All these attributions are self-serving as they allow people to create a prototype of the typical patient that they can distance from themselves.

Research on other aspects of healthy people's perception of disease and of patients conducted with regards to breast cancer, also showed that non-patients have a biased view of the disease and its consequences and, at the same time, believe they know how patients feel, which can impact on the appropriateness of the support they provide to patients (Buick & Petrie, 2002). This can lead patients to feel misunderstood and increase their distress; conversely, social stigma can lead patients to delay seeking care (see an example regarding tuberculosis in Johansson, Diwan, Huong, & Ahlberg, 1996). Note that direct comparisons between patients and nonpatients may be biased by methodological artifacts and differences in the interpretation of the questions (French et al., 2001). Nevertheless, research on illness perceptions of the general public has important implications for prevention of disease and for stigmatization of patients.

INDIVIDUALS "AT RISK"

Increasing progress in epidemiological knowledge of risk factors as well as genetic diagnostics constantly increases the number of people who are medically or socially defined as being "at risk" for a serious health problem (Kenen, 1996). Such individuals form perceptions of the disease and its causes that can interact with cultural beliefs about the disease, as well as with their self-perceptions (Shiloh, 2006). People at risk use various strategies to defend themselves against excessive distress. Smokers and x-ray technicians were found to have biased risk perceptions; women at genetic risk for breast cancer used defensive discounting of cancer causal attributions along with self-enhanced self-assessments of health (Shiloh, Drori, Orr-Urtreger, & Friedman, 2009). The increasing number of "at risk" people calls for more research on their perceptions of the diseases for which they are at risk and the associations of these perceptions with behavioral and emotional coping strategies. The aim should be to learn which perceptions lead to the fine line between acknowledging risk and taking appropriate preventive measures on the one hand, while not suffering from excessive anxiety on the other.

## Individual Differences In Illness Perceptions

Illness perceptions are embedded within a personal and a cultural context. The personal context includes personality dispositions and personal characteristics, such as age and gender, that affect the way people experience health threats and interpret these experiences.

### Personality

Personality traits have been found to predict illness perceptions (Lawson et al., 2008). Among the studies of illness perceptions that have included measures of personality dispositions, some found smaller effects for personality as a predictor of future outcomes, in comparison with illness perceptions (see for example, Millar, Purushotham, McLatchie, George, & Murray, 2005, who studied neuroticism), whereas others found stronger effects for personality (see for example, Llewellyn, Weinman, McGurk, & Humphris, 2008; Treharne, Kitas, Lyons, & Booth, 2005; both studied optimism). Overall, despite those findings and reports of associations between illness perceptions and personality dispositions (Goetzmann et al., 2005), very little research in this area has focused on the role of personality.

This is surprising because personality dispositions (e.g., traits such as neuroticism or optimism) tint the lens through which we perceive the world. Illness perceptions involve our perceptions and expectations in the present and future, specific to our disease. Therefore, one would expect them to be related to our general overview of the world and our generalized expectancies for the future (see Armor & Taylor, 1998, for a discussion of the theoretical relationship between dispositional and situated optimism and the empirical evidence).

Furthermore, personality dispositions can affect people's interpretation of their symptoms (see the effects of type A personality on time to the decision to seek care for symptoms of a heart attack; Matthews, Seigel, Kuller, Thompson, & Varat, 1983) and their vigilance about their symptoms (see effect of trait affectivity on asthma worry and attention to symptoms; Mora et al., 2007); they can moderate the effects of other predictors of disease outcomes (see interaction between optimism and disease duration on pain; Treharne et al., 2005); and they can affect the effectiveness of interventions (see interaction between intervention for myocardial infarction patients and trait negative affectivity; Cameron, Petrie, Ellis, Buick, & Weinman, 2005b). Therefore, the illness perception area could benefit from more research on its associations with personality traits, especially as attempts to implement the existing knowledge in interventions become more frequent.

## *Age*

Most research on illness perceptions has been conducted with adults, and age merely served as a covariate in the analyses. The two extremes of the life cycle deserve more attention: Children and older adults. Children's illness perceptions and the factors influencing them provide insights regarding the development of illness perceptions. Older adults' illness perceptions provide insights into the interactions between aging and health and between self and health perceptions. In addition, understanding illness perceptions in specific subpopulations such as these is useful in planning interventions aimed at increasing knowledge about health and illness and engagement in health behaviors.

### CHILDREN'S ILLNESS PERCEPTIONS

Understanding health and illness is part of the content of our socialization into society and is therefore the product of an interaction between personal characteristics; the intentional actions of social agents, such as families; peers; the educational system; and the media (Tinsley, 1992), as well as the often unintentional exposure to various social and physical conditions (Irwin, Johnson, Henderson, Dahinten, & Hertzman, 2006). Children's understanding of health and illness develops in correspondence with the stages of cognitive development (Bibace & Walsh, 1980). Thus, younger children often describe more mechanistic biomedical models of disease (Piko & Bak, 2006) and focus on contagion as the main causal factor (Schmidt &

Fröhling, 2000). Similar to adults, there is great variability among children at any age in their perceptions of health and illness (Perrin & Gerrity, 1981; Schmidt & Fröhling, 2000). However, systematic differences also exist: Older children who are capable of more abstract thinking, those with greater verbal intelligence, and those from a higher socioeconomic status report more sophisticated conceptualizations of health and illness (Boles & Roberts, 2007; Eiser & Kopel, 1997; Paterson, Moss-Morris, & Butler, 1999).

Research on chronically ill children shows that both age and experience contribute to children's understanding of illness (Crisp, Ungerer, & Goodnow, 1996). Even though they almost always cope with disease within the family context, their knowledge and understanding do not necessarily correspond with those of their parents (Crisp et al., 1996; McQuaid, Howard, Kopel, Rosenblum, & Bibace, 2002; Olsen et al., 2008; Salewski, 2003), suggesting that age and personal experience may be stronger effects. However, differences in perceptions are all the more reason to attend to the family context: For example, parents' responses to their asthmatic children's symptom perceptions were found to account for part of the relationship between child perceptions and morbidity (McQuaid et al., 2007).

Children also vary in their understanding of health promotion and prevention of disease (Piko & Bak, 2006). In general, knowledge about illnesses and their etiology seems to develop earlier than the understanding of prevention (Paterson et al., 1999; Rubovits & Wolynn, 1999). Note that even when knowledge and understanding of illness in general and one's illness in particular become quite sophisticated, this does not ensure adherence to the medical regimen (McQuaid, Kopel, Klein, & Fritz, 2003). This may be related to parents' knowledge and attitudes, which often do not correspond with the prescribed regimen (McQuaid et al., 2002) and seem to influence those of their children (DePaola, Roberts, Blaiss, Frick, & McNeal, 1997). Alternatively, social or other factors may prevent their knowledge from translating into adherence.

The assessment of illness perceptions among children obviously needs to be adapted to their abilities. Most studies used structured interviews with simple questions. Some supplemented these with drawings that provide children with a nonverbal route to express their perceptions (Sartain, Clarke, & Heyman, 2000). Such drawings have been found to be valid aids in the diagnosis of headaches among children (Stafstrom, Rostasy, & Minster, 2002).

These findings suggest that further uses of children's drawings of their illness should be investigated, not only to circumvent limitations in verbal ability but also to elicit valid information. As for verbal questioning, a children's version of the IPQ was recently published (Walker, Papadopoulos, Lipton, & Hussein, 2006). The data support its reliability and make this new instrument a promising means of studying illness perceptions among children.

## OLDER ADULTS' ILLNESS PERCEPTIONS

As we age, we carry with us our perceptions of health and illness and the experience that we have had with health threats throughout our life. Therefore, there are no dramatic changes in our understanding of illnesses (such as those that children undergo as they develop). The processes by which older people derive their illness perceptions are similar to those employed by younger people. For example, comparisons to oneself in the past, social comparisons, and assessments of current causal factors all entail the use of such rules as the "age-illness" and the "stress-illness" forms mentioned earlier (Leventhal & Crouch, 1997). Yet, the amount of information available to old people when making these comparisons and assessments is vast in comparison to young adults. From middle age on, experience accumulates at an exponential rate because not only is the individual more likely to have first-hand experience with health problems, but his own age cohort and that of his parents and age peers provide ample opportunity to learn about illness from close experience. Although all this may lead to denial and avoidance in middle age, older adults tend to be risk averse; therefore, they attend closely to health information and are likely to be more adherent to prevention and treatment recommendations (Leventhal & Crouch, 1997).

This does not mean that older adults' illness perceptions are necessarily accurate. First, they are affected by myths about aging and illness (Berkman, Rohan, & Sampson, 1994; Coupland & Coupland, 1994). If one believes that, in old age, the treatment for cancer is worse than the disease itself (or that once you have it, it's too late), or that nothing can be done about joint pains because they come with age, then one is less likely to seek diagnosis or treatment. Second, age attributions combined with greater experience can lead to more confidence in self-diagnosis, followed by attempts at self-care. This is sometimes beneficial because greater knowledge of one's body and close attention to the trajectory of

health can lead to accurate perceptions of health (Ferraro & Kelley-Moore, 2001; Idler & Benyamini, 1997), but it may also lead older people to discount new symptoms. Third, older people often evaluate symptoms and illnesses with much more background "noise" created by comorbidity. This makes it more difficult to form accurate perceptions of one's illness.

Finally, in old age, more than at any other period of life, perceptions of health and illness have significant implications for one's self-identity and self-perception. Although most elderly people are independent and functioning well physically, mentally, and socially, most have been diagnosed with at least one chronic disease (Hooyman & Kiyak, 1999). Accepting the illness identity is related to more severe consequences (Benyamini, Medalion et al., 2007); accepting its identity and chronic nature (in contrast with perceiving it as acute or episodic) leads to a stronger effect of the disease on the person's view of him/herself (Nerenz & Leventhal, 1983). When diseases such as cancer are accompanied by serious illness burden and perceived as chronic, they increase the discrepancy between actual and ideal self (Heidrich, Forsthoff, & Ward, 1994). Visible diseases, such as Parkinson's disease, are especially likely to be perceived as serious and disruptive to one's sense of an integrated and autonomous self (Bramley & Eatough, 2005). Negative perceptions of a chronic disease, such as coronary heart disease, can affect one's global self-perception of health (Aalto et al., 2006), which can have a pervasive effect on self-perception and quality of life.

### Gender and Illness Perceptions

Biological and social differences between women and men, as well as the interaction between them, lead to gender differences in the perceptions of health and illness. On the biological side, some of the illnesses are unique to one or the other sex (gynecological problems; prostate problems), some differ in prevalence between the sexes (e.g., women are more likely to cope with invisible or unexplained diseases and symptoms), and some are common in both sexes but women often experience them differently (e.g., heart disease). On the social side, social norms and gender roles prescribe different expectations from women and men and thus provide a different context for judging symptoms, performing prototype checks, and formulating illness perceptions. These factors can also interact, so that different symptoms or diseases experienced within a different social context, which yields gender-based expectations, can lead to greater differences than are accounted for by the biological or social factors separately (Hader, Smith, Moore, & Holmberg, 2001).

The most striking examples come from the area of cardiovascular diseases, in which gendered views of the disease combine with gender stereotypes of the patients. A review by Martin and Suls (2003) showed that gender stereotypes of cardiac disease might be an important factor in explaining the greater delay in seeking care for cardiac symptoms among women, in comparison to men. Uncertainty in symptom interpretation underlies delay in care-seeking for both genders but is more likely to occur with women because the symptoms are judged in light of the available (male) prototype of the disease (Schoenberg et al., 2003). Moreover, since the prototypical heart disease patient is a middle-aged man with several risk factors (sedentary, smoking, obese) and who is experiencing acute chest pain, many women judge their condition to be quite different from this prototype and therefore are late in realizing that they may be having a heart attack.

The rules by which people determine the nature of a symptom (Leventhal et al., 2008) can help illuminate the findings regarding women's misperception of cardiac symptoms. First, the symmetry rule—people's tendency to connect symptoms with labels (and when provided with labels, to report more symptoms). Women do not ignore their symptoms; however, because women often experience heart disease and even a heart attack not as severe acute chest pain but with more vague pains and discomfort, their first tentative label is more likely to be indigestion or another noncardiac label. Second, the age–illness rule—the tendency, with age, to attribute milder symptoms to aging processes. Women are afflicted with heart disease on average at a higher age than are men; they are more likely to experience cardiac symptoms along with other bodily changes and to find it difficult to discern these symptoms from other changes and therefore to attribute them to age. Third, the stress–illness rule, or the tendency to attribute new symptoms to stress in the presence of a recent stressor. Since women with heart disease are likely to be older, they are less likely to be experiencing work stress but more likely to be coping with stressful family demands, such as taking care of an ill spouse. This makes it easy to attribute symptoms to the stressor and not seek care. Evidence that the tendency to attribute symptoms to stress is stronger for women comes from research showing that external judges are more likely to use the stress–illness rule

for women, even for diseases in which no gender differences in the somatic experience are expected, thus discounting the severity of their symptoms and the need of swift care-seeking (Martin & Lemos, 2002).

Note that the same happens with additional illnesses that have different manifestations among men (e.g., depression; Johansson, Bengs, Danielsson, Lehti, & Hammarstrom, 2009) or gender-biased stereotypes that could lead to different rates of care-seeking and diagnosis. For example, men with breast cancer tend to be diagnosed at an older age than women and with later-stage disease (Giordano, 2005). This is the mirror image of the findings on heart disease among women, which goes largely unnoticed because breast cancer in men is relatively rare, but reflects the same issues of misattribution of symptoms and related delays in care-seeking.

Providers are also affected by their prototypes of diseases and stereotypes of women and men. This is seen in their diagnoses of mental health conditions— the higher prevalence of mental health problems among women often leads to misdiagnosis. Most important are those physical disorders that have symptoms that could be mistaken to be psychiatric (e.g., endocrinological disorders, seizure disorders, multiple sclerosis, lupus). Not surprisingly, misattribution of the symptoms of these disorders to mental health problems are more often made by both female patients and their physicians (Klonoff & Landrine, 1997).

Another area in which providers' perceptions are likely to be affected by gender stereotypes is the diagnosis of "invisible" diseases, such as pain and unexplained symptoms, which are more prevalent among women. In these conditions, the subjective experience often does not correspond to objective medical examinations. To complicate matters further, gender differences in pain can be explained mostly in terms of gender disparities in life circumstances rather than in biological terms (Bingefors & Isacson, 2004). All this makes diagnosis difficult and uncertain, and often leaves women feeling misunderstood and disrespected because of providers who discount the seriousness of their symptoms or "blame the victim" (Ballweg, 1997; Huntington & Gilmour, 2005; Lillrank, 2003). Women strive to reach a coherent representation of their illness that portrays them as credible patients with legitimate pain complaints, thus rejecting psychological or alternative interpretations of their somatic experiences (Werner, Isaksen, & Malterud, 2004).

Providers' decisions about referral to treatment can also be affected by gender stereotypes of illnesses and patients. Again, this is most often seen with heart disease and may be one of the reasons why women are less likely to be referred to coronary bypass surgery and coronary angioplasty (Shaw et al., 2004). Research may also be biased in similar ways: Meyerowitz and Hart (1996) argued that women with breast cancer have been especially targeted for research, as compared with women with cancers in other sites, and that this bias cannot be fully explained by differences in survival and incidence rates among different types of cancer. They proposed that the bias results from an assumption that the breast is so central to womanhood that any assault to the breast will destroy a woman's psychological integrity. This is in contrast with evidence that breast cancer is no more devastating to women than other cancers (e.g., Mendelsohn, 1990).

In sum, the process of forming illness perceptions cannot be isolated from the gender stereotypes so prevalent in our society. These stereotypes bias our prototypes of illnesses and of the typical patient. It is of utmost importance that both lay people and providers recognize this because of the substantial effects on patients' care-seeking and providers' diagnoses and priorities in treatment and research. Furthermore, viewing illness perceptions within the entire self-regulation process highlights additional important effects of gender: Individuals may hold illness perceptions that could have led them to take appropriate action, yet their actions are often limited by social constraints. Examples can be seen with women in traditional societies, in which they are prohibited by their husbands from undergoing gynecological examinations (Givaudan, Pick, Poortinga, Fuertes, & Gold, 2005) or are limited in their ability to practice safe sex (O'Leary, 1999); among men, masculine socialization can hinder help-seeking (Addis & Mahalik, 2003). A more detailed discussion of the self-regulation process from a gender perspective can be found in Benyamini (2009).

## Culture

Western cultures tend to emphasize biomedical explanations for illness. This is in contrast with views expressed by non-Western cultures, which typically assign a greater role to social and moral aspects (Karasz, 2005), religious factors (Alqahtani & Salmon, 2008; Pérez-Stable, Sabogal, Otero-Sabogal, Hiatt, & McPhee, 1992), and experiential models (Chesla, Skaff, Bartz, Mullan, & Fisher, 2000), and often identify with a more fatalistic view

of health and illness (Landrine & Klonoff, 1994; Pérez-Stable et al., 1992). It seems impossible to understand illness perceptions without attending to the cultural context in which they are formulated. Communal cultures that view the self primarily as a relational concept, interpret health and illness differently than do individualistic cultures (Capstick, Norris, Sopoaga, & Tobata, 2009). Cultures in which spirituality is an integral part of life view illness through these lens too: Like every other element of life, illness has a purpose, illness is a price to be paid (Cox, 1998). Therefore, the contents of illness representations greatly differ across cultures. Medical anthropologists have been studying these issues for decades, and this area is beyond the scope of this chapter.

In contrast with the vast differences in content, the principles underlying illness perceptions and their effects are similar across cultures: The components of illness perceptions are similar across cultures and historical times (Schober & Lacroix, 1991); perceptions of health and illness are meaningfully interrelated (Mulatu, 1999) and are logically related to actions taken (Chesla et al., 2000); they can be medically erroneous, yet internally consistent and seemingly rational within the cultural context in which they were formulated (Pérez-Stable et al., 1992). Moreover, they affect individuals' perceptions of medications (Horne et al., 2004), their beliefs about the actions to be taken to preserve health and treat illness (Liddell, Barrett, & Bydawell, 2005), and the type of provider they turn to (Quah & Bishop, 1996).

Providers and researchers should be aware of the discrepancies in health perceptions between their culture and that of their patients (Shih, 1996). Even seemingly trivial semantic differences can be very meaningful: In English, the term "hypertension" is often taken by people to reflect an established association between nervousness, social stress, and elevated blood pressure. In the Philippines, tuberculosis is highly stigmatized, but references to "weak lungs" are acceptable (Nichter, 1994). Attending to these often subtle semantic differences is essential in communicating with patients to promote their health.

From a methodological point of view, it is important to remember that researchers often come from a Western worldview, and patients may be providing them with responses they perceive as corresponding with that view. Closed-ended items and checklists that include a variety of illness causes and characteristics make it more legitimate to acknowledge factors such as supernatural causes (Landrine & Klonoff, 1994).

## Conclusion

Perceptions of health and illness organize our health-related knowledge and experience into meaningful structures that we use to interpret new experiences and determine how to cope with them. They are the main and pivotal component of the dynamic process of self-regulation of health and illness. Our perceptions and interpretations are constructed in an internally coherent way, with logical connections among the levels of abstraction we use to store and process the components of the perception and the actions guided by them. They are based on a variety of sources of information and are created through the application of commonsense heuristics that help us judge new symptom experiences against existing perceptions. These perceptions may at times seem irrational but provide an integration of our knowledge that is usually very logical from our personal, commonsense point of view.

These perceptions encompass perceptions of symptoms, for which we seek illness labels and characteristics, and that then feed into our general sense of health (see Figure 13.1). Our general perception of our health status is part of our self-identity. This process of forming and using perceptions of health and illness is part of a dynamic and complex process of self-regulation that is affected by a multitude of contextual factors, ranging from individual characteristics through our cultural values and beliefs. Despite their subjective nature, these perceptions are important because they predict physical, functional, and psychological outcomes. Their effects on these outcomes are direct as well as indirect, because they determine ways of coping, including health and illness behaviors. They also influence our attitudes and behaviors toward people afflicted with a disease. In sum, regarding perceptions of health and illness, *the subjective is the objective*. These perceptions serve as the lens through which we view health information and experience, and therefore they are key to patient-centered and patient-tailored care that can improve health care and health outcomes.

### *Future Directions*

The ultimate challenge is to understand perceptions of health and illness in depth as they take part in the dynamic self-regulation process over time, effecting coping and outcomes and influenced by coping, outcomes, the self, and the sociocultural system. Since this is an ambitious aim, each section of this chapter outlined specific issues that should be addressed by future research in order to advance knowledge in this field:

- How are coherence and acceptance of illness identity (the most recently proposed components of the illness perception) formed, and what is their role in the self-regulation process?
- How can we enrich the assessment of illness perceptions? Drawing upon both quantitative and qualitative methods, including verbal and nonverbal information, may help us develop better means of uncovering the unique and crucial characteristics of the perception of each health threat.
- What are the sources for the formation of perceptions of health and illness, and how do people integrate information from diverse sources into a coherent representation of a health threat? What are the rules they use to form their perceptions and to modify them upon further appraisal? Most importantly, how do these processes evolve over time?
- How do perceptions of illness affect one's overall perception of health, and vice versa?
- Which additional factors mediate the associations of illness perceptions and outcomes, and how do they explain what are currently reported to be direct relationships?
- How can we study the dynamic nature of the associations between perceptions and outcomes? Most studies predicted outcomes from baseline perceptions; more sophisticated methods may help uncover the dynamics of the self-regulation process and the internal (self-system) and external (sociocultural system) contextual effects on this process.
- When prescribing interventions, how can we better utilize the knowledge about illness perceptions, the way they are formed, and their effects, to enable people to collect information and integrate it into their perceptions in ways that will eventually contribute to better health?
- When and how do social and cultural constructions affect illness perceptions and their translation into effective ways of coping? Adding ethnicity or culture as covariates in a model is insufficient to understanding how personal and cultural perceptions of health and illness interact.

- Similarly, adding personal characteristics as covariates—gender, age, personality dispositions—is insufficient to uncover their interactions with illness perceptions or the extent to which their effects on outcomes are mediated through specific illness perceptions.
- How are illness perceptions formed within a family? How do family members mutually affect each other's perceptions?
- How can we encourage health care professionals to treat *subjective* health perceptions as a crucial part of the *objective* reality of their patients and consequently use them to achieve better communication with their patients and provide better health care?

# References

Aalto, A.M., Aro, A.R., Weinman, J., Heijmans, M., Manderbacka, K., & Elovainio, M. (2006). Sociodemographic, disease status, and illness perceptions predictors of global self-ratings of health and quality of life among those with coronary heart disease One year follow-up study. *Quality of Life Research, 15*(8), 1307–1322.

Addis, M.E., & Mahalik, J.R. (2003). Men, masculinity, and the contexts of help seeking. *American Psychologist, 58*(1), 5–14.

Alqahtani, M., & Salmon, P. (2008). Cultural influences in the aetiological beliefs of Saudi Arabian primary care patients about their symptoms: The association of religious and psychological beliefs. *Journal of Religion and Health, 47*(3), 302–313.

Arcury, T.A., Skelly, A.H., Gesler, W.M., & Dougherty, M.C. (2004). Diabetes meanings among those without diabetes: Explanatory models of immigrant Latinos in rural North Carolina. *Social Science & Medicine, 59*(11), 2183–2193.

Armor, D.A., & Taylor, S.E. (1998). Situated optimism: specific outcome expectancies and self-regulation. In M.P. Zanna (Ed.), *Advances in experimental social psychology* Vol. 30 (pp. 310–379). San Diego, CA: Academic Press.

Armstrong, N., & Murphy, E. (2008). Weaving meaning? An exploration of the interplay between lay and professional understandings of cervical cancer risk. *Social Science & Medicine, 67*(7), 1074–1082.

Baker, J.A., & Wiginton, K. (1997). Perceptions and coping among women living with Lupus. *American Journal of Health Behavior, 21*(2), 129–136.

Ballweg, M.L. (1997). Blaming the victim: The psychologizing of endometriosis. *Obstetrics & Gynecology Clinics of North America, 24*(2), 441–453.

Bar-On, D., & Cristal, N. (1987). Causal attributions of patients, their spouses and physicians, and the rehabilitation of the patients after their first myocardial infarction. *Journal of Cardiopulmonary Rehabilitation, 7*, 285–298.

Barrowclough, C., Lobban, F., Hatton, C., & Quinn, J. (2001). An investigation of models of illness in carers of schizophrenia patients using the Illness Perception Questionnaire. *British Journal of Clinical Psychology, 40*(Pt. 4), 371–385.

Bastien, S. (2009). Reflecting and shaping the discourse: The role of music in AIDS communication in Tanzania. *Social Science & Medicine, 68*(7), 1357–1360.

Baumann, L.J., Cameron, L.D., Zimmerman, R.S., & Leventhal, H. (1989). Illness representations and matching labels with symptoms. *Health Psychology, 8*(4), 449–469.

Baumann, L.J., & Leventhal, H. (1985). "I can tell when my blood pressure is up, can't I?" *Health Psychology, 4*(3), 203–218.

Benyamini, Y. (2003). Hope and fantasy among women coping with infertility and its treatments. In R. Jacoby, & G. Keinan (Eds.), *Between stress and hope: From a disease-centered to a health-centered perspective* (pp. 141–166). Westport, CT: Praeger Publishers/Greenwood Publishing Group.

Benyamini, Y. (2005). *Discussion: Symposium on "changing patients' perceptions to improve health outcomes."* Paper presented at the 19th annual conference of the European Health Psychology Society, Galway, Ireland.

Benyamini, Y. (2007). Coping with stressful medical procedures. In S. Ayers, A. Baum, C. McManus, S. Newman, K. Wallston, J. Weinman, & R. West (Eds.), *Cambridge handbook of psychology, health and medicine* (2nd ed., pp. 59–63). Cambridge, UK: Cambridge University Press.

Benyamini, Y. (2009). A self-regulation approach to stress and coping with women's health issues. *European Psychologist, 14*(1), 63–71.

Benyamini, Y., Gefen-Bardarian, Y., Gozlan, M., Tabiv, G., Shiloh, S., & Kokia, E. (2008). Coping specificity: the case of women coping with infertility treatments. *Psychology & Health, 23*(2), 221–241.

Benyamini, Y., Gozlan, M., & Kokia, E. (2004). On the self-regulation of a health threat: Cognitions, coping, and emotions among women undergoing treatment for infertility. *Cognitive Therapy and Research, 28*(5), 577–592.

Benyamini, Y., Gozlan, M., & Kokia, E. (2009). Women's and men's perceptions of infertility and their associations with both partners' psychological adjustment. *British Journal of Health Psychology, 14*, 1–16.

Benyamini, Y., Leventhal, E.A., & Leventhal, H. (2003). Elderly people's ratings of the importance of health-related factors to their self-assessments of health. *Social Science & Medicine, 56*(8), 1661–1667.

Benyamini, Y., Leventhal, E.A., & Leventhal, H. (2007). Attributions and health. In S. Ayers, A. Baum, C. McManus, S. Newman, K. Wallston, J. Weinman, & R. West (Eds.), *Cambridge handbook of psychology, health and medicine* (2nd ed., pp. 26–32). Cambridge, UK: Cambridge University Press.

Benyamini, Y., McClain, C.S., Leventhal, E.A., & Leventhal, H. (2003). Living with the worry of cancer: Health perceptions and behaviors of elderly people with self, vicarious, or no history of cancer. *Psycho-Oncology, 12*(2), 161–172.

Benyamini, Y., Medalion, B., & Garfinkel, D. (2007). Patient and spouse perceptions of the patient's heart disease and their associations with received and provided social support and undermining. *Psychology & Health, 22*(7), 765–785.

Berkman, B., Rohan, B., & Sampson, S. (1994). Myths and biases related to cancer in the elderly. *Cancer, 74*(S7), 2004–2008.

Bibace, R., & Walsh, M.E. (1980). Development of children's concepts of illness *Pediatrics, 66*(6), 912–917.

Bingefors, K., & Isacson, D. (2004). Epidemiology, co-morbidity, and impact on health-related quality of life of self-reported headache and musculoskeletal pain—A gender perspective. *European Journal of Pain, 8*(5), 435–450.

Bishop, F.L., Yardley, L., & Lewith, G.T. (2008). Treatment appraisals and beliefs predict adherence to complementary therapies: A prospective study using a dynamic extended self-regulation model. *British Journal of Health Psychology, 13*(4), 701–718.

Bishop, G.D. (1991). Understanding the understanding of illness: Lay disease representations. In J.A. Skelton, & R.T. Croyle (Eds.), *Mental representation in health and illness* (pp. 32–59). New York: Springer-Verlag.

Bishop, G.D., Briede, C., Cavazos, L., Grotzinger, R., & McMahon, S. (1987). Processing illness information: The role of disease prototypes. *Basic and Applied Social Psychology, 8*(1 & 2), 21–43.

Bishop, G.D., & Converse, S.A. (1986). Illness representations: A prototype approach. *Health Psychology, 5*(2), 95–114.

Boles, R.E., & Roberts, M.C. (2007). Children's perceptions of illness and death. In A. Baum, C. McManus, S. Newman, J. Weinman, & R. West (Eds.), *Cambridge handbook of psychology, health and medicine* (pp. 38–41). Cambridge, UK: Cambridge University Press.

Bramley, N., & Eatough, V. (2005). The experience of living with Parkinson's disease: An interpretive phenomenological analysis case study. *Psychology & Health, 20*(2), 223–235.

Broadbent, E., Ellis, C.J., Gamble, G., & Petrie, K.J. (2006). Changes in patient drawings of the heart identify slow recovery after myocardial infarction. *Psychosomatic Medicine, 68*, 910–913.

Broadbent, E., Ellis, C.J., Thomas, J., Gamble, G., & Petrie, K.J. (2009a). Can an illness perception intervention reduce illness anxiety in spouses of myocardial infarction patients? A randomized controlled trial. *Journal of Psychosomatic Research, 67*(1), 11–15.

Broadbent, E., Ellis, C.J., Thomas, J., Gamble, G., & Petrie, K.J. (2009b). Further development of an illness perception intervention for myocardial infarction patients: A randomized controlled trial. *Journal of Psychosomatic Research, 67*(1), 17–23.

Broadbent, E., Niederhofferb, K., Haguec, T., Cortera, A., & Reynolds, L. (2009). Headache sufferers' drawings reflect distress, disability and illness perceptions. *Journal of Psychosomatic Research, 16*, 465–470.

Broadbent, E., Petrie, K.J., Ellis, C.J., Ying, J., & Gamble, G. (2004). A picture of health - myocardial infarction patients' drawings of their hearts and subsequent disability: A longitudinal study. *Journal of Psychosomatic Research, 57*(6), 583–587.

Broadbent, E., Petrie, K.J., Main, J., & Weinman, J. (2006). The brief illness perception questionnaire. *Journal of Psychosomatic Research, 60*(6), 631–637.

Brown, R.T., Kaslow, N.J., Sansbury, L., Meacham, L., & Culler, F.L. (1991). Internalizing and externalizing symptoms and attributional style in youth with diabetes. *Journal of the American Academy of Child and Adolescent Psychiatry, 30*(6), 921–925.

Buick, D.L., & Petrie, K.J. (2002). "I Know Just How You Feel": The validity of healthy women's perceptions of breast-cancer patients receiving treatment. *Journal of Applied Social Psychology, 32*(1), 110–123.

Burgess, C.C., Ramirez, A.J., Richards, M.A., & Love, S.B. (1998). Who and what influences delayed presentation in breast cancer? *British Journal of Cancer, 77*(8), 1343–1348.

Cacioppo, J.T., Andersen, B.L., Turnquist, D.C., & Petty, R.E. (1986). Psychophysiological comparison processes: Interpreting cancer symptoms. In B.L. Andersen (Ed.), *Women with cancer: Psychological perspectives* (pp. 141–171). New York: Springer-Verlag.

Cacioppo, J.T., Andersen, B.L., Turnquist, D.C., & Tassinary, L.G. (1989). Psychophysiological comparison theory: On the experience, description, and assessment of signs and symptoms. *Patient Education and Counseling, 13*, 257–270.

Cameron, L.D., Leventhal, E.A., & Leventhal, H. (1995). Seeking medical care in response to symptoms and life stress. *Psychosomatic Medicine, 57*(1), 37–47.

Cameron, L.D., Petrie, K.J., Ellis, C.J., Buick, D., & Weinman, J. (2005a). Symptom experiences, symptom attributions, and causal attributions in patients following first-time myocardial infarction. *International Journal of Behavioral Medicine, 12*(1), 30–38.

Cameron, L.D., Petrie, K.J., Ellis, C.J., Buick, D., & Weinman, J. (2005b). Trait negative affectivity and responses to a health education intervention for myocardial infarction patients. *Psychology & Health, 20*(1), 1–18.

Capstick, S., Norris, P., Sopoaga, F., & Tobata, W. (2009). Relationships between health and culture in Polynesia— A review. *Social Science & Medicine, 68*(7), 1341–1348.

Chadwick, J., & Mann, W.N. (1950). *The medical works of Hippocrates.* Oxford, UK: Blackwell Scientific.

Chakraborty, K., Avasthi, A., Kumar, S., & Grover, S. (2009). Attitudes and beliefs of patients of first episode depression towards antidepressants and their adherence to treatment. *Social Psychiatry and Psychiatric Epidemiology, 44*(6), 482–488.

Cherrington, C.C., Moser, D.K., Lennie, T.A., & Kennedy, C.W. (2004). Illness representation after acute myocardial infarction: Impact on in-hospital recovery. *American Journal of Critical Care, 13*(2), 136–145.

Chesla, C.A., Skaff, M.M., Bartz, R.J., Mullan, J.T., & Fisher, L. (2000). Differences in personal models among Latinos and European Americans: Implications for clinical care. *Diabetes Care, 23*(12), 1780–1785.

Clarke, J.N. (2004). A comparison of breast, testicular and prostate cancer in mass print media (1996–2001). *Social Science & Medicine, 59*(3), 541–551.

Clifford, S., Barber, N., & Horne, R. (2008). Understanding different beliefs held by adherers, unintentional nonadherers, and intentional nonadherers: Application of the necessity-concerns framework. *Journal of Psychosomatic Research, 64*(1), 41–46.

Colombo, A., Bendelow, G., Fulford, B., & Williams, S. (2003). Evaluating the influence of implicit models of mental disorder on processes of shared decision making within community-based multi-disciplinary teams. *Social Science & Medicine, 56*(7), 1557–1570.

Conrad, P. (1994). The meaning of medications: Another look at compliance. In P. Conrad, & R. Kern (Eds.), *The sociology of health and illness: Critical perspectives* (4th ed., pp. 149–161). New York: St. Martin's Press.

Cooper, A.F., Jackson, G., Weinman, J., & Horne, R. (2002). Factors associated with cardiac rehabilitation attendance: A systematic review of the literature. *Clinical Rehabilitation, 16*(5), 541–552.

Coupland, J., & Coupland, N. (1994). "Old age doesn't come alone": Discursive representations of health-in-aging in geriatric medicine. *International Journal of Aging and Human Development, 39*(1), 81–95.

Coutu, M.-F., Dupuis, G., D'Antono, B., & Rochon-Goyer, L. (2003). Illness representation and change in dietary habits in hypercholesterolemic patients. *Journal of Behavioral Medicine, 26*(2), 133–152.

Cox, G.R. (1998). Illness, medicine, and spirituality: Native American healing practices among Apache, Sioux, and Navajo. *Illness, Crisis & Loss, 6*(1), 67–82.

Crane, C., & Martin, M. (2003). Illness schema and level of reported gastrointestinal symptoms in irritable bowel syndrome. *Cognitive Therapy and Research, 27*(2), 185–203.

Cremeans-Smith, J.K., Stephens, M.A., Franks, M.M., Martire, L.M., Druley, J.A., & Wojno, W.C. (2003). Spouses' and physicians' perceptions of pain severity in older women with osteoarthritis: Dyadic agreement and patients' well-being. *Pain, 106*(1–2), 27–34.

Crisp, J., Ungerer, J.A., & Goodnow, J.J. (1996). The impact of experience on children's understanding of illness. *Journal of Pediatric Psychology, 21*(1), 57–72.

Davies, M.J., Heller, S., Skinner, T.C., Campbell, M.J., Carey, M.E., Cradock, S., et al. (2008). Effectiveness of the diabetes education and self management for ongoing and newly diagnosed (DESMOND) programme for people with newly diagnosed type 2 diabetes: Cluster randomised controlled trial. *British Medical Journal, 336*(7642), 491–495.

de Ridder, D.T.D., Theunissen, N.C.M., & van Dulmen, S.M. (2007). Does training general practitioners to elicit patients' illness representations and action plans influence their communication as a whole? *Patient Education and Counseling, 66*(3), 327–336.

Deary, V. (2008). A precarious balance: Using a self-regulation model to conceptualize and treat chronic fatigue syndrome. *British Journal of Health Psychology, 13*, 231–236.

DePaola, L.M., Roberts, M.C., Blaiss, M.S., Frick, P.J., & McNeal, R.E. (1997). Mothers' and children's perceptions of asthma medication. *Children's Health Care, 26*(4), 265–283.

Devcich, D.A., Ellis, C.J., Gamble, G., & Petrie, K.J. (2008). Psychological responses to cardiac diagnosis: Changes in illness representations immediately following coronary angiography. *Journal of Psychosomatic Research, 65*(6), 553–556.

Dickens, C., McGowan, L., Percival, C., Tomenson, B., Cotter, L., Heagerty, A., et al. (2008). Negative illness perceptions are associated with new-onset depression following myocardial infarction. *General Hospital Psychiatry, 30*(5), 414–420.

Dickson, A., Knussen, C., & Flowers, P. (2007). Stigma and the delegitimation experience: An interpretative phenomenological analysis of people living with chronic fatigue syndrome. *Psychology & Health, 22*(7), 851–867.

Donovan, J.L., Blake, D.R., & Fleming, W.G. (1989). The patient is not a blank sheet: Lay beliefs and their relevance to patient education. *British Journal of Rheumatology, 28*, 58–61.

Dwidevi, K.N., & Gardner, D. (1997). Theoretical perspectives and clinical approaches. In K.N. Dwidevi (Ed.), *The therapeutic use of stories* (pp. 19–41). London: Routledge.

Eccles, M., Grimshaw, J., Walker, A., Johnston, M., & Pitts, N. (2005). Changing the behavior of healthcare professionals: The use of theory in promoting the uptake of research findings. *Journal of Clinical Epidemiology, 58*(2), 107–112.

Eiser, C., & Kopel, S.J. (1997). Children's perceptions of health and illness. In K.J. Petrie, & J. Weinman (Eds.), *Perceptions of health and illness: Current research and applications* (pp. 47–76). Amsterdam: Harwood Academic Publishers.

Elfant, E., Gall, E., & Perlmuter, L.C. (1999). Learned illness behavior and adjustment to arthritis. *Arthritis Care and Research, 12*(6), 411–416.

Farrimond, H., Saukko, P.M., Qureshi, N., & Evans, P.H. (2010). Making sense of being at "high risk" of coronary heart disease within primary prevention. *Psychology & Health, 25*(3), 289–304.

Ferraro, K.F., & Kelley-Moore, J.A. (2001). Self-rated health and mortality among Black and White adults: Examining the dynamic evaluation thesis. *Journal of Gerontology: Social Sciences, 56*(4), S195–S205.

Figueiras, M.J., & Alves, N.C. (2007). Lay perceptions of serious illnesses: An adapted version of the revised illness perception questionnaire (IPQ-R) for healthy people. *Psychology & Health, 22*(2), 143–158.

Figueiras, M.J., & Weinman, J. (2003). Do similar patient and spouse perceptions of myocardial infarction predict recovery? *Psychology & Health, 18*(2), 201–216.

Fortune, D.G., Richards, H.L., Griffiths, C.E.M., & Main, C.J. (2002). Psychological stress, distress and disability in patients with psoriasis: Consensus and variation in the contribution of illness perceptions, coping and alexithymia. *British Journal of Clinical Psychology, 41*, 157–174.

Foster, N.E., Bishop, A., Thomas, E., Main, C., Horne, R., Weinman, J., et al. (2008). Illness perceptions of low back pain patients in primary care: What are they, do they change and are they associated with outcome? *Pain, 136*(1–2), 177–187.

Frank, A.W. (1995). *The wounded storyteller: Body, illness, and ethics.* Chicago: The University of Chicago Press.

Frank, J.D. (1964). Foreword. In A. Kiev (Ed.), *Magic, faith, and healing: Studies in primitive psychiatry today* (pp. xiii–xiv). London: The Free Press of Glencoe.

French, D.P., Maissi, E., & Marteau, T.M. (2005). The purpose of attributing cause: Beliefs about the causes of myocardial infarction. *Social Science & Medicine, 60*(7), 1411–1421.

French, D.P., Senior, V., Weinman, J., & Marteau, T.M. (2001). Causal attributions for heart disease: A systematic review. *Psychology & Health, 16*(1), 77–98.

French, D.P., & Weinman, J. (2008). Current issues and new directions in Psychology and Health: "Assessing illness perceptions: Beyond the IPQ." *Psychology & Health, 23*(1), 5–9.

Frost, K., Frank, E., & Maibach, E. (1997). Relative risk in the news media: A quantification of misrepresentation. *American Journal of Public Health, 87*(5), 842–845.

Frostholm, L., Fink, P., Christensen, K.S., Toft, T., Oernboel, E., Olesen, F., et al. (2005). The patients' illness perceptions and the use of primary health care. *Psychosomatic Medicine, 67*(6), 997–1005.

Frostholm, L., Oernboel, E., Christensen, K.S., Toft, T., Olesen, F., Weinman, J., et al. (2007). Do illness perceptions predict health outcomes in primary care patients? A 2-year follow-up study. *Journal of Psychosomatic Research, 62*(2), 129–138.

Giordano, S.H. (2005). A review of the diagnosis and management of male breast cancer. *The Oncologist, 10*(7), 471–479.

Givaudan, M., Pick, S., Poortinga, Y.H., Fuertes, C., & Gold, L. (2005). A cervical cancer prevention programme in rural Mexico: Addressing women and their context. *Journal of Community & Applied Social Psychology, 15*(5), 338–352.

Godoy-Izquierdo, D., Lopez-Chicheri, I., Lopez-Torrecillas, F., Velez, M., & Godoy, J.F. (2007). Contents of lay illness models dimensions for physical and mental diseases and implications for health professionals. *Patient Education and Counseling, 67*(1–2), 196–213.

Goetzmann, L., Scheuer, E., Naef, R., Klaghofer, R., Russi, E.W., Buddeberg, C., et al. (2005). Personality, illness perceptions, and lung function (FEV1) in 50 patients after lung transplantation. *GMS Psycho-Social-Medicine, 2.*

Goodman, D., Morrissey, S., Graham, D., & Bossingham, D. (2005). Illness representations of systemic lupus erythematosus. *Qualitative Health Research, 15*(5), 606–619.

Gray, S.E., & Rutter, D.R. (2007). Illness representations in young people with chronic fatigue syndrome. *Psychology & Health, 22*(2), 159–174.

Groarke, A., Curtis, R., Coughlan, R., & Gsel, A. (2005). The impact of illness representations and disease activity on adjustment in women with rheumatoid arthritis: A longitudinal study. *Psychology & Health, 20*(5), 597–613.

Hader, S.L., Smith, D.K., Moore, J.S., & Holmberg, S.D. (2001). HIV Infection in women in the United States: Status at the Millennium. *Journal of the American Medical Association, 285*(9), 1186–1192.

Hagger, M.S., & Orbell, S. (2003). A meta-analytic review of the common-sense model of illness representations. *Psychology & Health, 18*(2), 141–184.

Hagger, M.S., & Orbell, S. (2005). A confirmatory factor analysis of the revised illness perception questionnaire (IPQ-R) in a cervical screening context. *Psychology & Health, 20*(2), 161–173.

Hall, S., French, D.P., & Marteau, T.M. (2003). Causal attributions following serious unexpected negative events: a systematic review. *Journal of Social and Clinical Psychology, 22*(5), 515–536.

Hampson, S.E., Glasgow, R.E., & Strycker, L.A. (2000). Beliefs versus feelings: A comparison of personal models and depression for predicting multiple outcomes in diabetes. *British Journal of Health Psychology, 5*, 27–40.

Hansen, D.L., Holstein, B.E., & Hansen, E.H. (2009). "I'd rather not take it, but . . .": Young women's perceptions of medicines. *Qualitative Health Research, 19*(6), 829–839.

Hardwick, P.J. (2005). Engaging families who hold strong medical beliefs in a psychosomatic approach. *Clinical Child Psychology and Psychiatry, 10*(4), 601–616.

Heidrich, S.M., Forsthoff, C.A., & Ward, S.E. (1994). Psychological adjustment in adults with cancer: the self as mediator. *Health Psychology, 13*(4), 346–353.

Heijmans, M. (1998). Coping and adaptive outcome in chronic fatigue syndrome: Importance of illness cognitions. *Journal of Psychosomatic Research, 45*(1), 39–51.

Heijmans, M., & de Ridder, D. (1998). Assessing illness representations of chronic illness: Explorations of their disease-specific nature. *Journal of Behavioral Medicine, 21*(5), 485–503.

Heijmans, M., de Ridder, D., & Bensing, J. (1999). Dissimilarity in patients' and spouses' representations of chronic illness: Exploration of relations to patient adaptation. *Psychology & Health, 14*, 451–466.

Hekler, E., Lambert, J., Leventhal, E.A., Leventhal, H., Jahn, E., & Contrada, R. (2008). Commonsense illness beliefs, adherence behaviors, and hypertension control among African Americans. *Journal of Behavioral Medicine, 31*(5), 391–400.

Henderson, C.J., Orbell, S., & Hagger, M.S. (2007). Does priming a specific illness schema result in an attentional information-processing bias for specific illnesses? *Health Psychology, 26*(2), 165.

Henderson, C.J., Orbell, S., & Hagger, M.S. (2009). Illness schema activation and attentional bias to coping procedures. *Health Psychology, 28*(1), 101–107.

Hirani, S.P., Pugsley, W.B., & Newman, S.P. (2006). Illness representations of coronary artery disease: An empirical examination of the Illness Perceptions Questionnaire (IPQ) in patients undergoing surgery, angioplasty and medication. *British Journal of Health Psychology, 11*, 199–220.

Hobro, N., Weinman, J., & Hankins, M. (2004). Using the self-regulatory model to cluster chronic pain patients: The first step towards identifying relevant treatments? *Pain, 108*(3), 276–283.

Hooyman, N., & Kiyak, H.A. (1999). *Social gerontology: A multidisciplinary perspective* (5th ed.). Boston: Allyn & Bacon.

Horne, R. (1998). Adherence to medication: A review of the existing literature. In L. Myers, & K. Midence (Eds.), *Adherence to treatment in medical conditions* (pp. 285–310). Amsterdam: Harwood Academic Press.

Horne, R. (2006). Compliance, adherence, and concordance. *Chest, 130*(1 suppl.), 65S–72S.

Horne, R., Graupner, L., Frost, S., Weinman, J., Wright, S.M., & Hankins, M. (2004). Medicine in a multi-cultural society: The effect of cultural background on beliefs about medications. *Social Science & Medicine, 59*(6), 1307–1313.

Horne, R., James, D., Petrie, K.J., Weinman, J., & Vincent, R. (2000). Patients' interpretation of symptoms as a cause of delay in reaching hospital during acute myocardial infarction. *Heart, 83*(4), 388–393.

Horne, R., Kovacs, C., Katlama, C., Clotet, B., Fumaz, C.R., Youle, M., et al. (2009). Prescribing and using self-injectable antiretrovirals: How concordant are physician and patient perspectives? *AIDS Research and Therapy, 6*(2).

Horne, R., Parham, R., Driscoll, R., & Robinson, A. (2009). Patients' attitudes to medicines and adherence to maintenance treatment in inflammatory bowel disease. *Inflammatory Bowel Diseases, 15*(6), 837–844.

Horne, R., & Weinman, J. (2002). Self-regulation and self-management in asthma: Exploring the role of illness perceptions and treatment beliefs in explaining non-adherence to preventer medication. *Psychology & Health, 17*(1), 17–32.

Horne, R., Weinman, J., & Hankins, M. (1999). The beliefs about medicines questionnaire: the development and evaluation of a new method for assessing the cognitive representation of medication. *Psychology & Health, 14*(1), 1–24.

Horowitz, C.R., Rein, S.B., & Leventhal, H. (2004). A story of maladies, misconceptions and mishaps: Effective management of heart failure. *Social Science & Medicine, 58*(3), 631–643.

Hunt, L.M., Jordan, B., & Irwin, S. (1989). Views of what's wrong: Diagnosis and patients' concepts of illness. *Social Science & Medicine, 28*(9), 945–956.

Huntington, A., & Gilmour, J.A. (2005). A life shaped by pain: Women and endometriosis. *Journal of Clinical Nursing, 14*(9), 1124–1132.

Hydén, L.-C. (1997). Illness and narrative. *Sociology of Health & Illness, 19*(1), 48–69.

Idler, E.L., & Benyamini, Y. (1997). Self-rated health and mortality: A review of twenty-seven community studies. *Journal of Health & Social Behavior, 38*(1), 21–37.

Idler, E.L., Leventhal, H., McLaughlin, J., & Leventhal, E.A. (2004). In sickness but not in health: Self-ratings, identity, and mortality. *Journal of Health & Social Behavior, 45*(3), 336–356.

Ingadottir, B., & Halldorsdottir, S. (2008). To discipline a "dog": The essential structure of mastering diabetes. *Qualitative Health Research, 18*(5), 606–619.

Insel, K.C., Meek, P.M., & Leventhal, H. (2005). Differences in illness representation among pulmonary patients and their providers. *Journal of Health Psychology, 10*(1), 147–162.

Irwin, L.G., Johnson, J.L., Henderson, A., Dahinten, V.S., & Hertzman, C. (2006). Examining how contexts shape young children's perspectives of health. *Child: Care, Health, and Development, 33*(4), 353–359.

Johansson, E., Bengs, C., Danielsson, U., Lehti, A., & Hammarstrom, A. (2009). Gaps between patients, media, and academic medicine in discourses on gender and depression: A metasynthesis. *Qualitative Health Research, 19*(5), 633–644.

Johansson, E., Diwan, V.K., Huong, N.D., & Ahlberg, B.M. (1996). Staff and patient attitudes to tuberculosis and compliance with treatment: An exploratory study in a district in Vietnam. *Tubercle and Lung Disease, 77*(2), 178–183.

Johnson, M., & Neilands, T. (2007). Coping with HIV treatment side effects: Conceptualization, measurement, and linkages. *AIDS and Behavior, 11*(4), 575–585.

Jones, R.A., Wiese, H.J., Moore, R.W., & Haley, J.V. (1981). On the perceived meaning of symptoms. *Medical Care, 19*(7), 710–717.

Karamanidou, C., Weinman, J., & Horne, R. (2008). Improving haemodialysis patients' understanding of phosphate-binding medication: A pilot study of a psycho-educational intervention designed to change patients' perceptions of the problem and treatment. *British Journal of Health Psychology, 13*, 205–214.

Karasz, A. (2005). Cultural differences in conceptual models of depression. *Social Science & Medicine, 60*(7), 1625–1635.

Kemp, S., Morley, S., & Anderson, E. (1999). Coping with epilepsy: Do illness representations play a role? *British Journal of Clinical Psychology, 38*, 43–58.

Kempner, J. (2006). Gendering the migraine market: Do representations of illness matter? *Social Science & Medicine, 63*(8), 1986–1997.

Kenen, R.H. (1996). The at-risk health status and technology: A diagnostic invitation and the "gift" of knowing. *Social Science & Medicine, 42*(11), 1545–1553.

Kesler, A., Kliper, E., Goner-Shilo, D., & Benyamini, Y. (2009). Illness perceptions and quality of life among women with pseudo-tumor cerebri. *European Journal of Neurology, 16*, 931–936.

Kirmayer, L.J. (1992). The body's insistence on meaning: Metaphor as presentation and representation in illness experience. *Medical Anthropology Quarterly, 6*(4), 323–346.

Kleinman, A. (1988a). *The illness narratives: Suffering, healing, and the human condition.* New York: Basic Books.

Kleinman, A. (1988b). *Rethinking Psychiatry: from Cultural Category to Personal Experience.* New York: Free Press.

Klonoff, E.A., & Landrine, H. (1997). *Preventing misdiagnosis of women: A guide to physical disorders that have psychiatric symptoms* Thousand Oaks, California: Sage.

Knoll, N., Schwarzer, R., Pfuller, B., & Kienle, R. (2009). Transmission of depressive symptoms: A study with couples undergoing assisted reproduction treatment. *European Psychologist, 14*(1), 7–17.

Kuipers, E., Watson, P., Onwumere, J., Bebbington, P., Dunn, G., Weinman, J., et al. (2007). Discrepant illness perceptions, affect and expressed emotion in people with psychosis and their carers. *Social Psychiatry and Psychiatric Epidemiology, 42*(4), 277–283.

Lalljee, M., Lamb, R., & Carnibella, G. (1993). Lay prototypes of illness: Their content and use. *Psychology & Health, 8*(1), 33–49.

Landrine, H., & Klonoff, E.A. (1994). Cultural diversity in causal attributions for illness: The role of the supernatural. *Journal of Behavioral Medicine, 17*(2), 181–193.

Lange, L., & Piette, J. (2006). Personal models for diabetes in context and patients' health status. *Journal of Behavioral Medicine, 29*(3), 239–253.

Lau, R.R., Bernard, T.M., & Hartman, K.A. (1989). Further explorations of common-sense representations of common illnesses. *Health Psychology, 8*(2), 195–219.

Lau, R.R., & Hartman, K.A. (1983). Common sense representations of common illnesses. *Health Psychology, 2*(2), 167–185.

Laubmeier, K.K., & Zakowski, S.G. (2004). The role of objective versus perceived life threat in the psychological adjustment to cancer. *Psychology & Health, 19*(4), 425–437.

Lauver, D.R., Ward, S.E., Heidrich, S.M., Keller, M.L., Bowers, B.J., Brennan, P.F., et al. (2002). Patient-centered interventions. *Research in Nursing & Health, 25*(4), 246–255.

Lawson, V.L., Bundy, C., & Harvey, J.N. (2008). The development of personal models of diabetes in the first 2 years after diagnosis: a prospective longitudinal study. *Diabetic Medicine, 25*(4), 482–490.

Leventhal, E.A., & Crouch, M. (1997). Are there differences in perceptions of illness across the lifespan? In K.J. Petrie, & J. Weinman (Eds.), *Perceptions of health and illness: Current research and applications* (pp. 77–102). Amsterdam: Harwood Academic Publishers.

Leventhal, H., & Benyamini, Y. (1997). Lay beliefs about health and illness. In A. Baum, C. McManus, S. Newman, J. Weinman, & R. West (Eds.), *Cambridge handbook of psychology, health and medicine* (pp. 131–135). Cambridge, UK: Cambridge University Press.

Leventhal, H., Benyamini, Y., Brownlee, S., Diefenbach, M., Leventhal, E.A., Patrick-Miller, L., & Robitaille, C. (1997). Illness representations: Theoretical foundations. In K.J. Petrie, & J. Weinman (Eds.), *Perceptions of health and illness: Current research and applications* (pp. 19–45). Amsterdam: Harwood Academic Publishers.

Leventhal, H., Benyamini, Y., & Shafer, C. (2007). Lay beliefs about health and illness. In S. Ayers, A. Baum, C. McManus, S. Newman, K. Wallston, J. Weinman, & R. West (Eds.), *Cambridge handbook of psychology, health and medicine* (2nd ed., pp. 124–128). Cambridge, UK: Cambridge University Press.

Leventhal, H., & Diefenbach, M. (1991). The active side of illness cognition. In J.A. Skelton, & R.T. Croyle (Eds.), *Mental representation in health and illness* (pp. 247–272). New York: Springer-Verlag.

Leventhal, H., Easterling, D.V., Coons, H., Luchterhand, C., & Love, R.R. (1986). Adaptation to chemotherapy treatments. In B.L. Andersen (Ed.), *Women with cancer: Psychological perspectives* (pp. 177–203). New York: Springer-Verlag.

Leventhal, H., Leventhal, E.A., & Contrada, R.J. (1998). Self-regulation, health, and behavior: A perceptual-cognitive approach. *Psychology & Health, 13*(4), 717–733.

Leventhal, H., Leventhal, E.A., & Van Nguyen, T. (1985). Reactions of families to illness: Theoretical models and perspectives. In D. Turk, & R. Kerns (Eds.), *Health, illness, and families: A life-span perspective* (pp. 108–145). New York: John Wiley & Sons.

Leventhal, H., Meyer, D., & Nerenz, D.R. (1980). The common sense representation of illness danger. In S. Rachman (Ed.), *Contributions to medical psychology* Vol. 2 (pp. 17–30). New York: Pargamon.

Leventhal, H., Nerenz, D.R., & Steele, D.J. (1984). Illness representations and coping with health threats. In A. Baum, S.E. Taylor, & J.E. Singer (Eds.), *Handbook of psychology and health* Vol. 4 (pp. 219–252). Hillsdale, New Jersey: Erlbaum.

Leventhal, H., Weinman, J., Leventhal, E.A., & Phillips, L.A. (2008). Health psychology: The search for pathways between behavior and health. *Annual Review of Psychology, 59,* 477–505.

Liddell, C., Barrett, L., & Bydawell, M. (2005). Indigenous representations of illness and AIDS in Sub-Saharan Africa. *Social Science & Medicine, 60*(4), 691–700.

Lillrank, A. (2003). Back pain and the resolution of diagnostic uncertainty in illness narratives. *Social Science & Medicine, 57*(6), 1045–1054.

Llewellyn, C.D., Miners, A.H., Lee, C.A., Harrington, C., & Weinman, J. (2003). The illness perceptions and treatment beliefs of individuals with severe haemophilia and their role in adherence to home treatment. *Psychology & Health, 18*(2), 185–200.

Llewellyn, C.D., Weinman, J., McGurk, M., & Humphris, G. (2008). Can we predict which head and neck cancer survivors develop fears of recurrence? *Journal of Psychosomatic Research, 65*(6), 525–532.

Mann, D., Ponieman, D., Leventhal, H., & Halm, E. (2009). Predictors of adherence to diabetes medications: The role of disease and medication beliefs. *Journal of Behavioral Medicine, 32*(3), 278–284.

Martin, R., & Lemos, K. (2002). From heart attacks to melanoma: Do common sense models of somatization influence symptom interpretation for female victims? *Health Psychology, 21*(1), 25–32.

Martin, R., & Suls, J. (2003). How gender stereotypes influence self-regulation of cardiac health care-seeking and adaptation. In L.D. Cameron, & H. Leventhal (Eds.), *The self-regulation of health and illness behavior.* New York: Routledge.

Matthews, K.A., Seigel, J.M., Kuller, L.H., Thompson, M., & Varat, M. (1983). Determinants of decisions to seek medical treatment by patients with acute myocardial infarction symptoms. *Journal of Personality and Social Psychology, 44,* 1144–1156.

May, C.R., Rose, M.J., & Johnstone, F.C.W. (2000). Dealing with doubt: How patients account for non-specific chronic low back pain. *Journal of Psychosomatic Research, 49,* 223–225.

McAndrew, L., Musumeci, S., Tamara, J., Mora, P.A., Vileikyte, L., Burns, E., et al. (2008). Using the common sense model to design interventions for the prevention and management of chronic illness threats: From description to process. *British Journal of Health Psychology, 13,* 195–204.

McAndrew, L., Schneider, S.H., Burns, E., & Leventhal, H. (2007). Does patient blood glucose monitoring improve diabetes control? A systematic review of the literature. *The Diabetes Educator, 33*(6), 991–1010.

McQuaid, E.L., Howard, K., Kopel, S.J., Rosenblum, K., & Bibace, R. (2002). Developmental concepts of asthma: Reasoning about illness and strategies for prevention. *Journal of Applied Developmental Psychology, 23*(2), 179–194.

McQuaid, E.L., Koinis Mitchell, D., Walders, N., Nassau, J.H., Kopel, S.J., Klein, R.B., et al. (2007). Pediatric asthma morbidity: The importance of symptom perception and family response to symptoms. *Journal of Pediatric Psychology, 32*(2), 167–177.

McQuaid, E.L., Kopel, S.J., Klein, R.B., & Fritz, G.K. (2003). Medication adherence in pediatric asthma: Reasoning, responsibility, and behavior. *Journal of Pediatric Psychology, 28*(5), 323–333.

Melamed, S., Froom, P., & Green, M.S. (1997). Hypertension and sickness absence: The role of perceived symptoms. *Journal of Behavioral Medicine, 20*(5), 473–487.

Mendelsohn, G.A. (1990). Psychosocial adaptation to illness by women with breast cancer and women with cancer at other sites. *Journal of Psychosocial Oncology, 8*(4), 1–25.

Menning, B.E. (1980). The emotional needs of infertile couples. *Fertility & Sterility, 34*(4), 313–319.

Meyer, D., Leventhal, H., & Gutmann, M. (1985). Common-sense models of illness: The example of hypertension. *Health Psychology, 4*(2), 115–135.

Meyerowitz, B.E., & Hart, S. (1996). Women and cancer: Have assumptions about women limited our research agenda? In A.L. Stanton, & S.J. Gallant (Eds.), *The psychology of women's health: Progress and challenges in research and application* (pp. 51–84). Washington, DC: American Psychological Association.

Millar, K., Purushotham, A.D., McLatchie, E., George, W.D., & Murray, G.D. (2005). A 1-year prospective study of individual variation in distress, and illness perceptions, after treatment for breast cancer. *Journal of Psychosomatic Research, 58*(4), 335–342.

Mora, P., Halm, E., Leventhal, H., & Ceric, F. (2007). Elucidating the relationship between negative affectivity and symptoms: The role of illness-specific affective responses. *Annals of Behavioral Medicine, 34*(1), 77–86.

Moss-Morris, R., Weinman, J., Petrie, K.J., Horne, R., Cameron, L.D., & Buick, D. (2002). The revised illness perception questionnaire (IPQ-R). *Psychology & Health, 17,* 1–16.

Moss-Morris, R., & Wrapson, W. (2003). Representational beliefs about functional somatic syndromes. In L.D. Cameron, & H. Leventhal (Eds.), *The self-regulation of health and illness behavior* (pp. 119–137). London: Routledge.

Mulatu, M.S. (1999). Perceptions of mental and physical illnesses in North-western Ethiopia: Causes, treatments, and attitudes. *Journal of Health Psychology, 4*(4), 531–549.

Murphy, E., & Kinmonth, A.L. (1995). No symptoms, no problem? Patients' understandings of non-insulin dependent diabetes. *Family Practice, 12*(2), 184–192.

Nerenz, D.R., & Leventhal, H. (1983). Self-regulation theory in chronic illness. In T.G. Burish, & L.A. Bradley (Eds.), *Coping with chronic disease: Research and applications* (pp. 13–37). New York: Academic Press.

Nicholls, C., Glover, L., & Pistrang, N. (2004). The illness experiences of women with fibroids: An exploratory qualitative study. *Journal of Psychosomatic Obstetrics and Gynecology, 25,* 295–304.

Nichter, M. (1994). Illness semantics and international health: The weak lungs/TB complex in the Philippines. *Social Science & Medicine, 38*(5), 649–663.

Nieto-Hernandez, R., Rubin, G.J., Cleare, A.J., Weinman, J.A., & Wessely, S. (2008). Can evidence change belief? Reported mobile phone sensitivity following individual feedback of an inability to discriminate active from sham signals. *Journal of Psychosomatic Research, 65*(5), 453–460.

O'Leary, A. (1999). Preventing HIV infection in heterosexual women: What do we know? What must we learn? *Applied & Preventive Psychology, 8*(4), 257–263.

O'Neill, E.S., & Morrow, L.L. (2001). The symptom experience of women with chronic illness. *Journal of Advanced Nursing, 33*(2), 257–268.

Ogden, J., & Jubb, A. (2008). How consistent are beliefs about the causes and solutions to illness?: An experimental study. *Psychology, Health & Medicine, 13*(5), 505–515.

Ogden, J., & Wardle, J. (1990). Control of eating and attributional style. *British Journal of Clinical Psychology, 29*(Pt. 4), 445–446.

Olsen, B., Berg, C.A., & Wiebe, D.J. (2008). Dissimilarity in mother and adolescent illness representations of type 1 diabetes and negative emotional adjustment. *Psychology & Health, 23*(1), 113–129.

Orbell, S., O'Sullivan, I., Parker, R., Steele, B., Campbell, C., & Weller, D. (2008). Illness representations and coping following an abnormal colorectal cancer screening result. *Social Science & Medicine, 67*(9), 1465–1474.

Parsons, T. (1958). Definitions of health and illness in light of American values and social structure. In E.G. Jaco (Ed.), *Patients, physicians, and illness: Sourcebook in behavioral science and medicine* (pp. 165–187). New York: The Free Press.

Paterson, J., Moss-Morris, R., & Butler, S.J. (1999). The effect of illness experience and demographic factors on children's illness representations. *Psychology & Health, 14*(1), 117–129.

Pérez-Stable, E.J., Sabogal, F., Otero-Sabogal, R., Hiatt, R.A., & McPhee, S.J. (1992). Misconceptions about cancer among Latinos and Anglos. *Journal of the American Medical Association, 268*(22), 3219–3223.

Perkins-Porras, L., Whitehead, D., Strike, P., & Steptoe, A. (2008). Causal beliefs, cardiac denial and pre-hospital delays following the onset of acute coronary syndromes. *Journal of Behavioral Medicine, 31*(6), 498–505.

Perrin, E.C., & Gerrity, P.S. (1981). There's a demon in your belly: Children's understanding of illness. *Pediatrics, 67*(6), 841–849.

Peterson, B.D., Newton, C.R., & Rosen, K.H. (2003). Examining congruence between partners' perceived infertility-related stress and its relationship to marital adjustment and depression in infertile couples. *Family Process, 42*(1), 59–70.

Petrie, K.J., Cameron, L.D., Ellis, C.J., Buick, D., & Weinman, J. (2002). Changing illness perceptions after myocardial infarction: An early intervention randomized controlled trial. *Psychosomatic Medicine, 64*(4), 580–586.

Petrie, K.J., & Weinman, J. (2006). Why illness perceptions matter. *Clinical Medicine, 6*(6), 536–539.

Petrie, K.J., Weinman, J., Sharpe, N., & Buckley, J. (1996). Role of patients' view of their illness in predicting return to work and functioning after myocardial infarction: Longitudinal study. *British Medical Journal, 312*, 1191–1194.

Pijl, M., Timmermans, D.R.M., Claassen, L., Janssens, A.C.J.W., Nijpels, G., Dekker, J.M., et al. (2009). Impact of communicating familial risk of diabetes on illness perceptions and self-reported behavioral outcomes. *Diabetes Care, 32*(4), 597–599.

Piko, B.F., & Bak, J. (2006). Children's perceptions of health and illness: Images and lay concepts in preadolescence. *Health Education Research, 21*(5), 643–653.

Prohaska, T.R., Keller, M.L., Leventhal, E.A., & Leventhal, H. (1987). Impact of symptoms and aging attribution on emotions and coping. *Health Psychology, 6*(6), 495–514.

Quah, S.-H., & Bishop, G.D. (1996). Seeking help for illness: The roles of cultural orientation and illness cognition. *Journal of Health Psychology, 1*(2), 209–222.

Redelmeier, D.A., & Tversky, A. (1996). On the belief that arthritis pain is related to the weather. *Proceedings of the National Academy of Sciences of the United States of America, 93*(7), 2895–2896.

Rees, G., Fry, A., Cull, A., & Sutton, S. (2004). Illness perceptions and distress in women at increased risk of breast cancer. *Psychology & Health, 19*(6), 749–765.

Reyna, V.F. (2008). A theory of medical decision making and health: Fuzzy trace theory. *Medical Decision Making, 28*(6), 850–865.

Rhodes, L.A., McPhillips-Tangum, C.A., Markham, C., & Klenk, R. (1999). The power of the visible: The meaning of diagnostic tests in chronic back pain. *Social Science & Medicine, 48*(9), 1189–1203.

Rice, P.L. (1998). *Health Psychology.* Pacific Grove, CA: Brooks/Cole Publishing Company.

Robertson, N., Javed, N., Samani, N.J., & Khunti, K. (2008). Psychological morbidity and illness appraisals of patients with cardiac and non-cardiac chest pain attending a rapid access chest pain clinic: A longitudinal cohort study. *Heart, 94*(3), e12.

Roesch, S.C., & Weiner, B. (2001). A meta-analytic review of coping with illness: Do causal attributions matter? *Journal of Psychosomatic Research, 50*(4), 205–219.

Ross, S., Walker, A., & MacLeod, M.J. (2004). Patient compliance in hypertension: Role of illness perceptions and treatment beliefs. *Journal of Human Hypertension, 18*(9), 607–613.

Rounds, J.B., & Zevon, M. (1993). Cancer stereotypes: A multidimensional scaling analysis. *Journal of Behavioral Medicine, 16*(5), 485–495.

Rubovits, D.S., & Wolynn, T.H. (1999). Children's illness cognition: What mothers think. *Clinical Pediatrics, 38*(2), 99–105.

Rüdell, K., Bhui, K., & Priebe, S. (2009). Concept, development and application of a new mixed method assessment of cultural variations in illness perceptions: Barts Explanatory Model Inventory. *Journal of Health Psychology, 14*(2), 336–347.

Rutter, C.L., & Rutter, D.R. (2002). Illness representation, coping and outcome in irritable bowel syndrome (IBS). *British Journal of Health Psychology, 7*, 377–391.

Rutter, C.L., & Rutter, D.R. (2007). Longitudinal analysis of the illness representation model in patients with irritable bowel syndrome (IBS). *Journal of Health Psychology, 12*(1), 141–148.

Salewski, C. (2003). Illness representations in families with a chronically ill adolescent differences between family members and impact on patients outcome variables. *Journal of Health Psychology, 8*(5), 587–598.

Salmon, P., Woloshynowych, M., & Valor, R. (1996). The measurement of beliefs about physical symptoms in English general practice patients. *Social Science & Medicine, 42*(11), 1561–1567.

Sartain, S., A., Clarke, C., L., & Heyman, R. (2000). Hearing the voices of children with chronic illness. *Journal of Advanced Nursing, 32*(4), 913–921.

Scharloo, M., Kaptein, A.A., Weinman, J., Hazes, J.M., Willems, L.N., Bergman, W., & Rooijmans, H.G.M. (1998). Illness perceptions, coping and functioning in patients with rheumatoid arthritis, chronic obstructive pulmonary disease and psoriasis. *Journal of Psychosomatic Research., 44*(5), 573–585.

Schenkman, M., Cutson, T.M., Zhu, C.W., & Whetten-Goldstein, K. (2002). A longitudinal evaluation of patients' perceptions of Parkinson's disease. *Gerontologist, 42*(6), 790–798.

Schiaffino, K.M., & Cea, C.D. (1995). Assessing chronic illness representations: The implicit models of illness questionnaire. *Journal of Behavioral Medicine, 18*(6), 531–548.

Schmidt, L.R., & Fröhling, H. (2000). Lay concepts of health and illness from a developmental perspective. *Psychology & Health, 15*(2), 229–238.

Schober, R., & Lacroix, J.M. (1991). Lay illness models in the Enlightenment and the 20th century: Some historical lessons. In J.A. Skelton, & R.T. Croyle (Eds.), *Mental representation in health and illness* (pp. 10–31). New York: Springer-Verlag.

Schoenberg, N.E., Peters, J.C., & Drew, E.M. (2003). Unraveling the mysteries of timing: Women's perceptions about time to treatment for cardiac symptoms. *Social Science & Medicine, 56*(2), 271–284.

Sharpe, L., Sensky, T., & Allard, S. (2001). The course of depression in recent onset rheumatoid arthritis: The predictive role of disability, illness perceptions, pain and coping. *Journal of Psychosomatic Research, 51*, 713–719.

Shaw, M., Maxwell, R., Rees, K., Ho, D., Oliver, S., Ben-Shlomo, Y., et al. (2004). Gender and age inequity in the provision of coronary revascularisation in England in the 1990s: Is it getting better? *Social Science & Medicine, 59*(12), 2499–2507.

Shih, F.J. (1996). Concepts related to Chinese patients' perceptions of health, illness and person: Issues of conceptual clarity. *Accident and Emergency Nursing, 4*(4), 208–215.

Shiloh, S. (2006). Illness representations, self-regulation, and genetic counseling: A theoretical review. *Journal of Genetic Counseling, 15*(5), 325–337.

Shiloh, S., Drori, E., Orr-Urtreger, A., & Friedman, E. (2009). Being "at-risk" for developing cancer: Cognitive representations and psychological outcomes. *Journal of Behavioral Medicine, 32*(2), 197–208.

Shiloh, S., Peretz, G., Iss, R., & Kiedan, R. (2007). Recovery attributions: Explicit endorsement of biomedical factors and implicit dominance of psycho-social factors. *Journal of Behavioral Medicine, 30*(3), 243–251.

Shiloh, S., Rashuk-Rosenthal, D., & Benyamini, Y. (2002). Illness causal attributions: An exploratory study of their structure and associations with other illness cognitions and perceptions of control. *Journal of Behavioral Medicine, 25*(4), 373–394.

Skelton, J.A., & Croyle, R.T. (Eds.). (1991). *Mental representation in health and illness*. New York: Springer-Verlag.

Skelton, J.A., Loveland, J.E., & Yeagley, J.L. (1996). Recalling symptom episodes affects reports of immediately-experienced symptoms: Inducing symptom suggestibility. *Psychology & Health, 11*(2), 183–201.

Skinner, T.C., Carey, M.E., Cradock, S., Daly, H., Davies, M.J., Doherty, Y., et al. (2006). Diabetes education and self-management for ongoing and newly diagnosed (DESMOND): Process modelling of pilot study. *Patient Education and Counseling, 64*(1–3), 369–377.

Spruill, T., Pickering, T., Schwartz, J., Mostofsky, E., Ogedegbe, G., Clemow, L., et al. (2007). The impact of perceived hypertension status on anxiety and the white coat effect. *Annals of Behavioral Medicine, 34*(1), 1–9.

Stafford, L., Berk, M., & Jackson, H.J. (2009). Are illness perceptions about coronary artery disease predictive of depression and quality of life outcomes? *Journal of Psychosomatic Research, 66*(3), 211–220.

Stafford, L., Jackson, H.J., & Berk, M. (2008). Illness beliefs about heart disease and adherence to secondary prevention regimens. *Psychosomatic Medicine, 70*(8), 942–948.

Stafstrom, C.E., Rostasy, K., & Minster, A. (2002). The usefulness of children's drawings in the diagnosis of headache. *Pediatrics, 109*(3), 460–472.

Sterba, K.R., DeVellis, R.F., Lewis, M.A., Jordan, J.M., Baucom, D.H., & DeVellis, B.M. (2008). Effect of couple illness perception congruence on psychological adjustment in women with rheumatoid arthritis. *Health Psychology, 27*(2), 221–229.

Stewart, D.E., Cheung, A.M., Duff, S., Wong, F., McQuestion, M., Cheng, T., et al. (2001). Attributions of cause and recurrence in long-term breast cancer survivors. *Psycho-Oncology, 10*(2), 179–183.

Suls, J. (2003). Contributions of social comparison to physical illness and well-being. In J. Suls, & K.A. Wallston (Eds.), *Social psychological foundations of health and illness* (pp. 226–255). Malden, MA: Blackwell Publishing.

Taylor, S.E. (1982). Social cognition and health. *Personality and Social Psychology Bulletin, 8*(3), 549–562.

Taylor, S.E., & Brown, J.D. (1988). Illusions and well-being: A social psychological perspective on mental health. *Psychological Bulletin, 103*, 193–210.

Thorne, S., Paterson, B., Acorn, S., Canam, C., Joachim, G., & Jillings, C. (2002). Chronic illness experience: Insights from a metastudy. *Qualitative Health Research, 12*(4), 437–452.

Tinsley, B.J. (1992). Multiple influences on the acquisition and socialization of children's health attitudes and behavior: An integrative review *Child Development, 63*(5), 1043–1069.

Treharne, G.J., Kitas, G.D., Lyons, A.C., & Booth, D.A. (2005). Well-being in rheumatoid arthritis: The effects of disease duration and psychosocial factors. *Journal of Health Psychology, 10*(3), 457–474.

Turk, D.C., Rudy, T.E., & Salovey, P. (1986). Implicit models of illness. *Journal of Behavioral Medicine, 9*(5), 453–474.

Turnquist, D.C., Harvey, J.H., & Andersen, B.L. (1988). Attributions and adjustment to life threatening illness. *British Journal of Clinical Psychology, 27*(Pt. 1), 55–65.

Vos, M.S., & de Haes, J.C.J.M. (2007). Denial in cancer patients, an explorative review. *Psycho-Oncology, 16*(1), 12–25.

Walker, C., Papadopoulos, L., Lipton, M., & Hussein, M. (2006). The importance of children's illness beliefs: The children's illness perception questionnaire (CIPQ) as a reliable assessment tool for eczema and asthma. *Psychology, Health & Medicine, 11*(1), 100–107.

Walker, J. (2001). *Control and the psychology of health: Theory, measurement and applications*. Buckingham, UK: Open University Press.

Walsh, J.C., Lynch, M., Murphy, A.W., & Daly, K. (2004). Factors influencing the decision to seek treatment for symptoms of acute myocardial infarction: An evaluation of the self-regulatory model of illness behavior. *Journal of Psychosomatic Research, 56*, 67–73.

Wearden, A., & Peters, S. (2008). Therapeutic techniques for interventions based on Leventhal's common sense model. *British Journal of Health Psychology, 13*, 189–193.

Webb, M.S., Simmons, V.N., & Brandon, T.H. (2005). Tailored interventions for motivating smoking cessation: Using placebo tailoring to examine the influence of expectancies and personalization. *Health Psychology, 24*(2), 179–188.

Weinman, J., Heijmans, M., & Figueiras, M.J. (2003). Carer perceptions of chronic illness. In L.D. Cameron, & H. Leventhal (Eds.), *The self-regulation of health and illness behavior* (pp. 207–219). London: Routledge.

Weinman, J., Petrie, K.J., Moss-Morris, R., & Horne, R. (1996). The illness perception questionnaire: A new method for assessing the cognitive representation of illness. *Psychology & Health, 11*, 431–445.

Weinman, J., Petrie, K.J., Sharpe, N., & Walker, S. (2000). Causal attributions in patients and spouses following first-time myocardial infarction and subsequent lifestyle changes. *British Journal of Health Psychology, 5,* 263–273.

Werner, A., Isaksen, L.W., & Malterud, K. (2004). "I am not the kind of woman who complains of everything": Illness stories on self and shame in women with chronic pain. *Social Science & Medicine, 59*(5), 1035–1045.

Whelan, E. (2009). Negotiating science and experience in medical knowledge: Gynaecologists on endometriosis. *Social Science & Medicine, 68*(8), 1489–1497.

Whitmarsh, A., Koutantji, M., & Sidell, K. (2003). Illness perceptions, mood and coping in predicting attendance at cardiac rehabilitation. *British Journal of Health Psychology, 8*(2), 209–221.

Whittaker, R., Kemp, S., & House, A. (2007). Illness perceptions and outcome in mild head injury: A longitudinal study. *Journal of Neurology, Neurosurgery and Psychiatry, 78*(6), 644–646.

Wiles, R. (1998). Patients' perceptions of their heart attack and recovery: The Influence of epidemiological "evidence" and personal experience. *Social Science & Medicine, 46*(11), 1477–1486.

Williams, G. (1984). The genesis of chronic illness: Narrative re-construction. *Sociology of Health and Illness, 6*(2), 175–200.

Wold, K., Byers, T., Crane, L., & Ahnen, D. (2005). What do cancer survivors believe causes cancer? (United States). *Cancer Causes and Control, 16*(2), 115–123.

PART 3

# Core Issues in Clinical Health

# Physician–Patient Communication

Judith A. Hall *and* Debra L. Roter

**Abstract**

This chapter focuses on the various aspects of physician–patient communication. It begins with a discussion of relationship-centered medicine, which considers the relationship as part of the therapeutic picture, depending not just on the patient's attributes (values, background, etc.) but also on those of the physician in a dynamic relation with the patient. It then discusses the theoretical and philosophical basis of the therapeutic relationship, the assessment of physician–patient communication, quantitative approaches to interaction analysis, correlates of physician–patient communication, and the clinical outcomes of communication.

**Keywords:** Physician–patient relationship, patient care, patient-centered medicine, communication, relationship-centered care

Everyone who has been a medical patient—and of course, this is everyone—knows that interactions with physicians can be rewarding and productive, but more often than not such interactions are upsetting and frustrating. Encounters with doctors are highly charged, and patients often remember (and recount for family and friends) every word exchanged at important moments in the medical visit. Patients also remember, usually too late, things they wished they or the doctor had talked about. The fact that patients focus on how they communicate with their doctor should not, of course, be a surprise considering that most of what doctors and patients do is talk. Fortunately, current models of medical care fully acknowledge the centrality of talk—and communication more broadly—to the practice of medicine.

Although good medical care depends crucially on the cognitive skills of the clinician (e.g., diagnostic ability and knowledge base), in combination with the wise use of technology and physiologically based treatments, these are not all of what good medical care is about. An understanding of good medical care includes finding the sources of a range of positive (and often negative) outcomes, including dissatisfaction, doctor shopping, litigation, poor adherence to medical regimens, skipping appointments, poor understanding and recall of information, and ultimately, less than optimal resolution of health problems.

## Evolving Models of the Physician–Patient Relationship

The physician–patient relationship and its expression through the medical dialogue have been described or alluded to in the history of medicine since the time of the Greeks (Plato, 1961) and in the modern medical and social sciences literature for the past 50 years (Engel, 1977; Freidson, 1970; Parsons, 1951; Szasz & Hollender, 1956). Nevertheless, historians of modern medicine have tracked an undeniable decline in the centrality of communication to the care process. In his study of the history of doctors and patients, Shorter (1985) attributes the denigration of communication to the ascendancy of the molecular and chemistry-oriented sciences as the predominant 20th-century medical paradigm. This change was fundamental in directing medical inquiry away from the person of the patient to the biochemical makeup and pathophysiology of the patient. It was not coincidental that the practice of interviewing patients from a written outline designed around a series of yes–no hypothesis-testing questions replaced unstructured medical histories at this point in the history of medicine.[1]

The resulting loss of focus on the patient as person was well captured in Kerr White's (1988) lament that physicians failed to recognize that "apples are red and sweet as well as being composed of cells and molecules" (page 6). Lacking a pathway to collaboration and partnership, many see the need for fundamental reform in medicine's vision. Just as the molecular and chemistry-oriented sciences were adopted as the 20th-century medical paradigm, incorporation of the patient's perspective into medicine's definition of patient need has been suggested as the medical paradigm of the 21st century (White, 1988). George Engel's articulation of the biopsychosocial model of medical interviewing in the 1970s (Engel, 1977, 1988), later translated into a patient-centered clinical method by McWhinney (1988, 1989), has given substance to *patient-centeredness* as a key philosophy underlying medical communication curricula and research (Lipkin, Putnam, & Lazare, 1995; Mead & Bower, 2000).

Patient-centeredness has been defined both loosely and also somewhat inconsistently by different authors (Epstein et al., 2005). At the heart of all conceptions are two key notions. The first is that the patient is a whole person, not just a set of symptoms or an organ system. Emotional and psychosocial issues are therefore to be accorded the attention they deserve as causes, exacerbators, and consequences of the state of a person's health. It follows from such a perspective that the patient's expectancies, beliefs, attitudes, values, experiences, and cultural background (as well as other sociodemographic characteristics, such as gender) move to the forefront as influences on the process of care and as matters on which the patient is a crucial source of information and decision-making authority. The patient is thus a player in a much more active way than the earlier "doctor-centric" paradigm, in which the physician assesses the facts of a situation and decides what is to be done, would allow. The acknowledgment that patients are experts on their own experience, values, and history is reflected in the title of Tuckett, Boulton, Olson, and Williams's (1985) book on physician–patient communication, *Meetings Between Experts*.

The second key aspect of the patient-centered approach is that communication is the vehicle by which medical care takes place, and it is therefore a subject deserving of intense scrutiny by researchers, medical educators, and clinicians in practice and their patients. Indeed, the two key elements we have identified can be joined in a parsimonious definition of medical care as the combination of mutual expertise and interpersonal communication in the service of solving health issues.

Although widely used, the term *patient-centered medicine* has been criticized as representing a semantic disregard for the powerful nature of the patient–provider *relationship*. The Pew-Fetzer Task Force on Advancing Psychosocial Health Education (Tresolini, 1994) suggests the more encompassing term *relationship-centered medicine* as recognizing the role of relationships in the optimal integration and synthesis of both the biomedical and lifeworld perspectives. According to this perspective, the relationship itself is part of the therapeutic picture, and this in turn depends not just on the patient's attributes (values, background, etc.) but also on those of the physician, in a dynamic relation with the patient (Beach et al., 2006). Thus, just as the patient-centered perspective puts a face on the patient, so the relationship-centered perspective puts a face on the physician as well. Medical care is seen as a dynamic process between individuals, not just a formulaic or role-based interchange.

A further expansion of the concept of relationship-centered care includes such notions as medically functional, facilitative, responsive, informative, and participatory (Cohen-Cole, 1991; Kurz, Silverman, & Draper, 1998; Lipkin et al., 1995; Stewart et al., 1995; Stone, 1979). The relative importance of each of these characteristics may vary depending on the care setting, the health status of the patient, and the nature and extent of prior relationship, and other exigencies.

First, the *medically functional* aspect of relationship-centered care is the extent to which the relationship fulfills the medical management functions of the visit within the constraints of a given health delivery system. Provision of quality care demands accomplishment of basic medical tasks. If the relationship inhibits performance of these tasks, it fails both patients and physicians in a primary way. Included among these tasks are structuring the visit, efficient use of time and resources, smooth organization and sequencing of the visit, and team building among health professionals (Kurz et al., 1998; Stewart et al., 1995), as well as technical tasks related to physical exam, diagnosis, and treatment.

Second, the relationship must be *facilitative* in eliciting the patient's full spectrum of concerns and visit agenda. Within this context, the patient's ability to tell the story of his or her illness holds the key to the establishment and integration of the patient's perspective in all subsequent care. Telling the story is the method by which the meaning of the illness and the meaning of the disease are integrated and interpreted by both doctor and patient. Particularly critical is elicitation in the psychosocial realm of experience. A patient's experience of illness is often reflected in how illness affects quality of life and daily function, family, social and professional functioning and relations, and feelings and emotions. Awareness of how these coping challenges are faced is critical to the finding of common ground and establishment of authentic dialogue (Cohen-Cole, 1991; Kurz et al., 1998; Lazare, Putnam, & Lipkin, 1995; Stewart et al., 1995).

Third, the visit must be *responsive* to the patient's emotional state and concerns. Physicians are not simply expert consultants; they are also individuals to whom people go when they are particularly vulnerable. Expressions of verbal and nonverbal support, empathy, concern, and legitimation, as well as explicit probes regarding feelings and emotions, are important elements of rapport building and are key to a patient feeling known and understood (Cohen-Cole, 1991; Kurz et al., 1998; Lazare et al., 1995; Roter et al., 1995; Stewart et al., 1995). Responsiveness carries the potent assumption that the patient is a person and not just an object.

Fourth, the relationship must be *informative,* providing both technical information and expertise and behavioral recommendations in a manner that is understandable, useful, and motivating. A singularly consistent finding in studies of doctors and patients conducted over the past 25 years has been that patients want as much information as possible from their physicians. Receiving information appears to be as important in contributing to the patient's capacity to cope with the overwhelming uncertainty and anxieties of illness as it is in making a substantive contribution to directing patient actions (Roter & Hall, 2006).

Finally, the fifth element of the relationship is that it must be *participatory.* Physicians have a responsibility and obligation to help patients assume an authentic and responsible role in the medical dialogue and in decision making. The first definition of *doctor* in *Webster's* is "teacher." The word *teacher* implies helping, but this help is not limited to the usual clinical sense of providing correct diagnosis and treatment, or empathy and reassurance. A teacher helps by equipping learners (patients) with what

they need to help themselves; this includes not just information but also confidence in the value of their own contributions. The educator model is more egalitarian and collaborative than the traditional doctor–patient model, and as such is core to the building of a mutual partnership (Freire, 1970). Moreover, patient participation and autonomy can be traced back even farther to how the physicians were educated in medical school—whether on an autonomy-promotive or controlling (authoritarian) model (Williams & Deci, 1998).

### The Theoretical and Philosophical Basis of the Therapeutic Relationship

The relationship center of care can be viewed from another perspective. Bioethicists Emanuel and Emanuel (1992) suggest that power relations in medical visits are expressed through several key elements, including (a) who sets the agenda and goals of the visit (the physician, the physician and patient in negotiation, or the patient); (b) the role of patients' values (assumed by the physician to be consistent with their own, jointly explored by the patient and physician, or unexamined); and (c) the functional role assumed by the physician (guardian, adviser, or consultant). Application of these core elements can be useful in recognizing the variety of power relations expressed in models of the doctor–patient relationship.

The upper left quadrant of Table 14.1, demonstrating mutuality, reflects the strengths and resources of each participant on a relatively even footing. Inasmuch as power in the relationship is balanced, the goals, agenda, and decisions related to the visit are the result of negotiation between partners; both the patient and the physician become part of a joint venture. The medical dialogue is the vehicle through which patient values are explicitly articulated and explored. Throughout this process the physician acts as a counselor or adviser.

Most prevalent, but not necessarily most efficient or desirable, is the prototype of paternalism, shown in the lower left quadrant. In this model of relations, physicians dominate agenda setting, goals, and decision making in regard to both information and services; the medical condition is defined in biomedical terms, and the patient's voice is largely absent. The physician's obligation is to act in the patient's "best interest." The determination of best interest, however, is largely based on the assumption that the patient's values and preferences are the same as those of the physician. The guiding model is that of physician as guardian, acting in the patient's best interest regardless of patient preferences.

**Table 14.1    Prototypes of the physician–patient relationship**

| Patient power | Physician power | |
|---|---|---|
| | High physician power | Low physician power |
| **High patient power** | MUTUALITY | CONSUMERISM |
| Goals and agenda | Negotiated | Patient set |
| Patient values | Jointly examined | Unexamined |
| Physician's role | Adviser, technical | consultant |
| **Low patient power** | PATERNALISM | DEFAULT |
| Goals and agenda | Physician set | Unclear |
| Patient values | Assumed | Unclear |
| Physician's role | Guardian | Unclear |

The top right quadrant of the table represents consumerism. Here, the more typical power relationship between doctors and patients may be reversed. Patients set the goal and agenda of the visit and take sole responsibility for decision making. Patient demands for information and technical services are accommodated by a cooperating physician. Patient values are defined and fixed by the patient and unexamined by the physician. This type of relationship redefines the medical encounter as a marketplace transaction. *Caveat emptor,* "let the buyer beware," rules the transaction, with power resting in the buyer (patient) who can make the decision to buy (seek care) or not, as seen fit (Haug & Lavin, 1983). The physician role is limited to technical consultant, with the obligation to provide information and services contingent on patient preferences (and within professional norms).

When patient and physician expectations are at odds, or when the need for change in the relationship cannot be negotiated, the relationship may come to a dysfunctional standstill, a kind of relationship default, as represented in the lower right quadrant of the table. Default can be seen as characterized by unclear or contested common goals, obscured or unclear examination of patient values, and an uncertain physician role. It is here that medical management may be least effective, with neither the patient nor the physician sensing progress or direction. A frustrated and angry patient may make inappropriate time and service demands and ultimately drop out of care because of failed expectations. For physicians, these visits represent the most frustrating aspects of medicine, reflecting "the difficult and hateful patient." Unless recalibration of the relationship is undertaken with direct intervention,

the relationship is likely to continue to unravel and ultimately fail.

It can be argued that, because each form of relationship brings some benefit, it should be left to patients to decide which form they prefer (Haug & Lavin, 1983; Quill, 1983). A different perspective, however, can be taken. Even when patients and physicians have mutually agreed upon a paternalistic relationship, questions regarding the appropriateness of the relationship may still be raised. Patients and doctors are often on so unequal a footing that few patients can really play an equal role with physicians in shaping the relationship. The possibility exists, then, that patients may adopt a passive patient role without being fully aware of alternatives or able to negotiate a more active stance (President's Commission, 1982). Certainly they lack role modeling by their physicians much of the time. According to a study of community practicing physicians, a full three-quarters of physicians did not promote a participatory style of interaction with their patients (Gotler et al., 2000).

Just as the paternalistic model can be criticized for its narrow exclusion of the patient's perspective, fault can also be found with the consumerist model as too narrowly limiting the physician's role. Patients may limit physician participation in decision making without appreciating the full benefit in terms of both decision making and coping that could be added by the inclusion of the physician's perspective (Roter & Hall, 2006; Schneider, 1998).

Relatively little is known about what kinds of patients are likely to prefer more or less passive and dependent relationships with their physicians. Several sociodemographic variables do appear to be associated with a more dependent relationship preference; the strongest of these is older age (alternatively, earlier age-cohort). Male gender, lower income, and lower level of occupation are also associated with this preference (Arora & McHorney, 2000; Ende, Kazis, Ash, & Moskowitz, 1989; Haug & Lavin, 1983). Other investigators have suggested that the wide gap in educational background and socioeconomic status between most patients and physicians contributes to the deference of lower social class patients and their adoption of a passive and dependent role in the doctor–patient relationship (Waitzkin, 1985). Ende and colleagues (Ende et al., 1989; Ende, Kazis, & Moskowitz, 1990) also suggest that illness severity plays a crucial role in patient deference to physicians in medical decision making, even for physicians.

There are significant nurturing and supportive aspects to a dependent or paternalistic doctor–patient relationship. Patients may draw comfort and support from a doctor "father" figure. Indeed, the supportive nature of paternalism appears to be all the more important when patients are very sick and at their most vulnerable (Ende et al., 1989, 1990). Relief of the burden of worry is curative in itself, some argue, and the trust and confidence implied by this model allow the doctor to do "medical magic." There is also evidence that idealization of the physician can have an important therapeutic effect, as placebo studies have demonstrated. Respondents who reported having greater faith in doctors, and being more dependent on them, were much less likely than others to adopt a consumerist orientation (Hibbard & Weeks, 1985, 1987).

In many regards, the primary methodological challenge to the field is the transition from the conceptual underpinnings of relationship-centered care to operational indicators of communication that are observable and measurable. Indeed, a number of measurement systems address at least some component of relationship-centered care consistent with the characteristics listed earlier (Roter, 2000a). Although none of the systems is explicitly contradictory with other systems or suggests exclusivity in its measurement, little attempt has been made to find common measurement ground. This is problematic; no single magic measurement bullet is evident or likely to soon emerge.

## How Physician–Patient Communication is Studied

A debate of longstanding intensity concerning the assessment of medical dialogue centers on the distinction between qualitative and quantitative evaluative approaches (Roter & Frankel, 1992). In a qualitative approach, a narrative account of medical interaction or a verbatim transcript of a medical exchange is studied in terms of the substantive themes that emerge, with reliance on interpretation of the underlying meaning embodied in the discourse. In contrast, in a quantitative approach, one gives numerical values to events, behaviors, verbal statements, and personal/situational characteristics using instruments and methods that aim for objectivity and reliability, and that allow for statistical analysis. The heat of the debate is derived not merely from a disagreement over the relative advantages and disadvantages of qualitative and quantitative methods but from the broader perception that these approaches reflect incompatible paradigms. Advocates of each of these methods not only have argued their own relative merits but also have maintained unusually critical and intellectually isolated positions.

A well recognized list of attributes distinguishes the quantitative and qualitative paradigms and their adherents. The quantitative worldview is characterized as hypothetico-deductive, particularistic, atomistic, objective, and outcome oriented; its researchers are logical positivists. In contrast, the qualitative worldview is characterized as social anthropological, inductive, holistic, subjective, and process oriented; its researchers are phenomenologists (Reichardt & Cook, 1969). An allegiance to a particular paradigm implies not only a worldview but also a paradigm-specific method of inquiry and even of styles of presentation.

The extension of the qualitative and quantitative paradigm controversy to evaluation of medical dialogue has been made by several authors. Quantitative approaches have been characterized as reflective of and consistent with the biomedical model's emphasis on scientific method and a tendency to translate observations into numbers. For instance, quantitative researchers typically present statistical summaries and correlates of objectively measured and investigator-defined patient and provider behaviors. Qualitatively inclined researchers, on the other hand, rarely assign numerical values to their observations but prefer instead to record data in the language of their subjects, almost always presenting actual speech through verbatim transcripts of audio and video recordings. In this tradition, special respect is paid to trying to capture the patient's perspective and worldview (Mishler, 1984).

As argued elsewhere (Roter & Frankel, 1992), it is our view that the paradigmatic perspective that promotes mutual exclusivity is in error; we see no inherent logic to the limitations established by tradition, other than tradition itself. Much of the debate in medical interaction research has focused on comparing methods independent of particular contexts, questions, or outcomes. Methods of research should be judged on the extent to which they succeed in answering the questions posed by the investigator. Qualitative and quantitative methods may each be best suited to answer certain kinds of questions. Moreover, respect for alternative methods does not preclude combining or hybridizing methods to maximize discovery and insight. An example of combining is Beckman and Frankel's (1984) study of physician–patient exchanges at the beginning of the medical interview, which we summarize later. Examples of hybridization would be to ask the patient directly using quantitative assessment about his or her own perspectives and interpretations or to measure qualitative concepts such as amount of dominance or boredom using quantitative methods (e.g., raters' impressions). The question for researchers should be one of practical utility and theoretical relevance: Under what conditions does each method, or a combination of methods, make sense and advance the theory and practice of medical interviewing?

## Qualitative Approaches

A wide variety of approaches to qualitative assessment of patient–physician interaction is evident in the literature, with several of these reflecting particular theoretical and methodological roots and the use of formalized transcription and analytic guidelines (Mishler, 1984; Sacks, Schegloff, & Jefferson, 1974). The three primary formalized approaches are discourse analysis, conversational analysis, and narrative analysis. Although there is a good deal of overlap, discourse analysis approaches tend to focus on how talk within medical interactions changes, establishes, or maintains social/power relationships, while conversational analysis addresses structural features of talk that obligate participants to certain courses of action, for instance, turn-taking rules and question-and-answer sequences. Narrative analysis focuses on the stories of participants' experiences (Roter & McNeilis, 2003). Other approaches are more ad hoc in nature and idiosyncratic in their methods (Roter & Frankel, 1992). Nevertheless, the common ground shared across all qualitative approaches is the preservation of the verbatim record of spoken dialogue in the participants' own words.

Beckman and Frankel's (1984) study of the opening segments of medical visits is perhaps the most frequently cited qualitative study in medical communication and represents an integrated qualitative-quantitative assessment of patient–physician interaction. These segments were evaluated for total number of patient concerns expressed, number of concerns expressed before physician interruption, time from onset of the study segment to the point of interruption if present, and the total time for the study segment. The studied segment usually began with the physician's solicitation of the chief complaint and ended with the physician's recount of the history of the present illness, or a patient statement indicating completion of concerns.

Overall, patients completed their statements in only 23% of the visits analyzed. Only one of the interrupted patients completed his or her statement. For the other 69% of patients, the interruption appeared to halt the spontaneous flow of information from the patient and marked a transition to a series of closed-ended, physician-initiated questions, although there was no evidence that the patients had finished answering the opening question, "What problems are you having?" On average, patients were interrupted 18 seconds after they began to speak, most often after the expression of a single stated concern.

At the same time that they conducted these quantitative analyses, Beckman and Frankel (1984) also analyzed the dialogue itself, as shown in these examples of completed and interrupted statements. A completed statement went as follows:

D: How you been doing?
P: Oh, well, I been doing okay, except for Saturday, well Sunday night. You know I been kinda nervous off and on, but I had a little incident at my house Saturday and it kinda shook me up a little bit.
D: Okay.
P: And, my ulcer, its been burning me off and on, like when I eat something if it don't agree, then I'll find out about it.
D: Right, okay.
P: But lately, I've been getting this funny . . . like, I'll lay down on my back, and my heart'll go "brr" you know like that. Like it's skipping a beat or something, and then it'll just start on back off beating like when I get upset it'll just start beating boom-bom-bom, and it'll just go back to its normal beat.
D: Okay.
P: Is that normal?
D: That's, that's a lot of things. Anything else that's bothering you?
P: No.

In contrast to this segment, the following exchange was interrupted by the physician after the first stated problem:

D: What brings you here today?
P: My head is killing me.
D: Have you had headaches before?

The authors argued that premature interruption, as in the second example, could give the physician an incomplete picture of the patient's needs, resulting in an inappropriate treatment plan and use of time. For instance, in a similar study (Marvel, Epstein, Flowers, & Beckman, 1999), investigators found that patients who completed their statement of concern in the opening moments of the encounter were significantly less likely to raise concerns toward the end of the visit. It is interesting to note that, although most interruptions occurred within 5–50 seconds of the physician's initial question, most completed statements took less than 1 minute, and no patient took more than 3 minutes to complete his or her statement.

These studies highlight not only insightful use of qualitative analysis but also a combined methodology that allowed them to quantify key aspects of the communication process for purposes of description as well as prediction. These studies can thus be seen as a prototype of a combined qualitative–quantitative approach.

## Quantitative Approaches to Interaction Analysis

It is only since the mid-1960s that the actual dynamics of the therapeutic dialogue have been observed in any systematic manner and an attempt to recast this aspect of medicine as science has been made. The evolution of methodological and technological sophistication has made observation and analysis of the medical visit easier over the years; indeed, the number of empirical studies of doctor–patient communication doubled from 1982 to 1987 (Roter, Hall, & Katz, 1988). A review of studies directly assessing provider–patient communication and its correlates found 28 different analysis systems used in 61 studies (Roter et al., 1988). Half the studies used audiotape as their primary method of observation; the remaining studies were equally likely to use videotape or impartial observers. There was a great deal of diversity in the content and process analysis approaches applied to the medical interactions. More than half the investigators employed an analysis system uniquely designed for their current study; the other investigators used a coding approach, usually with some minor modifications, employed in a prior study by the same or other investigators.

Even the most commonly used coding systems at the time of the review were used in only a handful of studies (ranging from five to seven studies each) and included Bales' Interaction Process, which was originally designed to assess group dynamics, Stiles' Verbal Response Mode, and the Roter Interaction Analysis System (RIAS). A subsequent review of communication assessment instruments, covering the period 1986 to 1996, identified a total of 44 instruments (Boon & Stewart, 1998). Approximately one-third of these instruments were designed to evaluate medical student performance in communication skills training programs; of these, only three were used by an investigator other than the system's author. Also identified in the review were 28 systems used primarily for assessment of communication in research studies. In this category, four systems based on an analysis of an empirical record were used by multiple investigators, including the three identified in the earlier review and the patient-centered method (Henbest & Stewart, 1989).

We are not aware of a published catalogue of communication coding systems subsequent to 1996, although our current informal review of the literature similarly finds that many authors continue to develop and apply unique coding approaches to their studies with very few of these systems replicated by researchers other than the system's author. Two systems that were not highlighted in the earlier reviews but appear to be growing in popularity in the current literature with at least several replications are the Davis Observation Code (Callahan & Bertakis, 1991) and the Four Habits Coding System (Krupat, Frankel, Stein, & Irish, 2006). A brief overview of the four historically prominent systems is provided here with the caveat that we are not aware of studies using the Bales System of Interaction Process since the early 1980s or the Verbal Response Mode since 2001. The RIAS has gained prominence in the literature over the past 30 years and has been used in over 250 studies worldwide.

### Process Analysis System (Bales)

Concerned with group dynamics, Bales (1950) developed an analysis scheme for assessing patterns of interaction, communication, and the decision-making processes of small groups. Since its original conceptualization, Bales's scheme has been more widely modified than any other single approach to increase understanding of the dynamics of the medical encounter. Bales's approach focuses on ways in which the process and structure of communication among persons in a group reflect how they differentially participate in problem solving. The theoretical rationale of this method conceives of problem solving in two domains, the task area and the socioemotional area. Interaction is described in terms of 12 mutually exclusive categories; 6 are conceived as affectively neutral and ascribed to the task dimension (e.g., gives suggestion or asks for orientation), and 6 are viewed as representing the social-emotional dimension of communication, divided into positive and negative affective categories (e.g., agrees or disagrees; shows tension release or shows tension).

Analysis using Bales's method is based on literal transcripts of the verbal events of the encounter that are operationally defined as the smallest discriminable speech segment to which the rater can assign classification. A unit may be as short as a single word or as long as a lengthy sentence; compound sentences are usually divided at the conjunction, and sentence clauses are scored as separate units when they convey a single item of thought or behavior, such as an acknowledgment, evaluation, or greeting. Inasmuch as Bales's system was originally devised as a method for studying group interaction, many researchers who derived theoretical direction from the system substantially changed the substantive categories to more directly reflect dyadic medical interaction. Nevertheless, the first studies of medical dialogue in which Bales's Process Analysis System was applied in the late 1960s and 1970s are still cited as the seminal studies in doctor–patient communication (Davis, 1969, 1971; Freemon, Negrete, Davis, & Korsch, 1971; Korsch, Gozzi, & Francis, 1968). Additional work in the 1980s with adults (Stewart, 1984) was also closely modeled on Bales's system.

### The Verbal Response Mode

An alternative theoretical approach to Bales's Process Analysis, based on linguistic theory, was introduced by William Stiles as the Verbal Response Mode (VRM; Stiles, 1992). Like Bales's system, the VRM taxonomy is a general-purpose system for coding speech acts and consequently is not specific to medical encounters. The unit of analysis is a speech segment (similar to Bales's system), defined grammatically to be equivalent to one psychological unit of experience, or a single utterance.

The system forms a taxonomy that implies a particular interpersonal intent or micro-relationship between communicator and recipient. There are three principles of classification: the source of experience, operationalized as attentiveness (to the other speaker) or informativeness (speaker's own experience); presumption about experience, operationalized as directive (controlling dialogue) or acquiescent (deferring to the other's viewpoint); and, finally, the frame of reference, defined as presumptuous (presuming knowledge about the other person) or unassuming (not presuming particular knowledge). Each of these classification principles is dichotomous, taking the value of either "the speaker" or "the other." The taxonomy assigns language segments to the following categories: disclosure, edification, advisement, confirmation, question, acknowledgment, interpretation, and reflection. Using this taxonomy, each speech segment is coded twice, once with respect to its grammatical form, or literal meaning, and once with respect to its communicative intent, or pragmatic meaning. Thus, there are 64 possible form–intent combinations—eight pure modes in which form and intent coincide, and 56 mixed modes in which they differ.

Reliability of VRM coding appears to be good, with reports of 81% agreement for form and 66% for intent (based on Cohen's $\kappa$) in a study of parent–child interaction (Stiles & White, 1981), and an average of 78% agreement over categories was reported in a Dutch study of primary care visits (Meeuwesen, Schaap, & van der Staak, 1991).

The VRM has been used by its author and others in studies in the United States, the United Kingdom, and the Netherlands. As noted by Stiles in his review, these studies included patients in primary care as well as patients with particular types of problems, including hypertensive expectant mothers, breast cancer patients, those with a psychological component to their physical complaint, and the institutionalized aged (see Stiles, 1992).

### Roter Interaction Analysis System

The Roter Interaction Analysis System (RIAS) has been described in detail elsewhere (Roter & Larson, 2002). Briefly, it is derived loosely from social exchange theories related to interpersonal influence and problem solving (Bales, 1950). It provides a tool for viewing the dynamics and consequences of patients' and providers' exchange of resources through their medical dialogue. The social exchange orientation is consistent with health education and empowerment perspectives that view the medical encounter as a "meeting between experts," grounded in an egalitarian model of patient–provider partnership that rejects expert domination and passive patient roles (Freire, 1983; Roter, 1987, 2000a, 2000b; Roter & Hall, 1991; Tuckett et al., 1985; Wallerstein & Bernstein, 1988).

A useful framework for organizing and grounding RIAS-coded communication in the clinical encounter is the functional model of medical interviewing (Cohen-Cole, 1991). Task behaviors fall within two of the medical interview functions: gathering data to understand the patient's problems and educating and counseling patients about their illness and to motivate patients to adhere to treatment. Affective behaviors generally reflect the third medical interview function of building a relationship through the development of rapport and responsiveness to the patient's emotions. A fourth function of the visit can be added—activating and partnership building—to enhance patients' capacity to engage in an effective partnership with their physician. Although not explicitly defined by the authors of the functional model, the use of verbal strategies to help patients integrate, synthesize, and translate between the biomedical and psychosocial paradigms of the therapeutic dialogue deserves special note. The "activating" function facilitates the expression of patients' expectations, preferences, and perspectives, so that they may more meaningfully participate in treatment and management decision making (Roter, 2000a).

The RIAS is applied to the smallest unit of expression or statement to which a meaningful code can be assigned, generally a complete thought, expressed by each speaker throughout the medical dialogue. These units are assigned to mutually exclusive and exhaustive categories that reflect the content and form of the medical dialogue. Form distinguishes statements that are primarily informative (information giving), persuasive (counseling), interrogative (closed- and open-ended questions), affective (social, positive, negative, and emotional), and process oriented (partnership building, orientations, and transitions). In addition to form, content areas are specified for exchanges about medical condition and history, therapeutic regimen, lifestyle behaviors, and psychosocial topics relating to social relations and feelings and emotions.

In addition to the verbal categories of exchange, coders rate each speaker on 6-point scales reflecting a range of affective dimensions, including anger, anxiety, dominance, interest, and friendliness. These ratings have been found to reflect voice tone independent of literal verbal content (Hall, Roter, & Rand, 1981).

The system is flexible and responsive to study context by allowing for the addition of tailored categories. Coders may also mark the phases of the visit, so that the opening, history segment, physical exam, counseling and discussion segment, and closing are specified, and communication falling within these parts of the visit can be analyzed and summarized separately (e.g., Roter, Lipkin, & Korsgaard, 1991).

Since the unit of analysis is the smallest unit of expression or statement to which a meaningful code can be assigned, and these are mutually exclusive and exhaustive, the RIAS categories can be used individually or combined to summarize the dialogue in a variety of ways. For instance, medical questions and psychosocial questions can be separately tallied, subclassified as open or closed, combined to form superordinate categories, or made into ratios (e.g., open to closed questions, biomedical to psychosocial questions). Similar groupings can be derived from information-giving and counseling categories. Other variable combinations represent composites of partnership building, emotional talk, and positive talk. Patient-centeredness scores can be computed by calculating a ratio of patient versus physician communication control: the sum of physician information giving (including both biomedical and psychosocial) and patient psychosocial information giving and question asking divided by the sum of physician question asking and patient biomedical information giving (Roter et al., 1997; Wissow et al., 1998). The RIAS has demonstrated substantial reliability and predictive validity to a variety of patient outcomes. In its author's own studies, the reliability has ranged across categories from roughly .70 to .90 based on Pearson correlation coefficients, with lower reliabilities reflecting infrequent categories (Levinson, Roter, Mullooly, Dull, & Frankel, 1997; Roter, Hall, & Katz, 1987; Roter et al., 1997; Wissow et al., 1998). Other researchers have reported similar reliabilities (Bensing & Dronkers, 1992; Inui, Carter, Kukull, & Haigh, 1982; Mead & Bower, 2000; Van Dulmen, Verhaak, & Bilo, 1997).

The RIAS has been used widely in the United States and Europe, as well as in Asia, Africa, and Latin America, in primary care and in specialty practice, and in relation to many correlates; examples are physicians' malpractice experience (Levinson et al., 1997), physicians' satisfaction (Roter et al., 1997; Suchman, Roter, Green, & Lipkin, 1993), and patients' satisfaction (Bertakis, Roter, & Putnam, 1991; Hall, Irish, Roter, Ehrlich, & Miller, 1994b; Roter et al., 1987, 1991, 1997). It has also been used to evaluate several types of communication training programs, including residency and medical student training (Kalet, Earp, & Kowlowitz, 1992; Roter, Cole, Kern, Barker, & Grayson, 1990) and continuing medical education (Roter et al., 1995). (An annotated list of more than 250 RIAS-related studies is available on the RIAS Web site: https://rias-works.org).

### Patient-Centered Measure

Specifically to assess the behaviors of patients and doctors according to the patient-centered clinical method (McWhinney, 1989; Stewart et al., 1995), a method of scoring the "patient-centeredness" of audio taped or video taped medical encounters was developed (Brown, Weston, & Stewart, 1989; Levenstein, McCracken, McWhinney, Stewart, & Brown, 1986; Stewart et al., 1995). The scoring procedure is described in detail elsewhere (Brown, Stewart, & Tessier, 1995; Henbest & Stewart, 1989; Stewart et al., 1995); briefly, scores range from 0 (not at all patient-centered) to 100 (very patient-centered) based on assessment of three main components. The first component is "understanding of the patient's disease and experience" (statements related to symptoms, prompts, ideas, expectations, feelings, and impact on function). For each of the six elements, every pertinent statement (as many as are applicable) made by the patient is recorded verbatim on the coding sheet. The coder assigns a score to the statement as to whether the physician provided preliminary exploration (yes or no) or further exploration (yes or no), or cut off discussion (yes or no). The second component, "understanding the whole person," explores the context of a patient's life setting (e.g., family, work, social supports) and stage of personal development (e.g., life cycle). The third component is "finding common ground" (mutual understanding and agreement on the nature of the problems and priorities, the goals of treatment and management, and the roles of the doctor and patient).

Interrater reliability, reported by the system's authors, ranges between .69 and .83 (Brown, Stewart, McCracken, McWhinney, & Levenstein, 1986; Stewart et al., 1996). Mead and Bower (2000) report an intraclass correlation coefficient of .58 for the system in their study.

### Comparison Studies

Two studies have contrasted multiple coding systems in an attempt to compare these approaches and draw some conclusions regarding their relative practical and predictive value, or to validate one approach through its comparison with another. In the first of these studies, Bales's original Process Analysis System, the RIAS, and the VRM were compared by Inui et al. (1982). The three interaction analysis systems were applied to 101 new-patient visits at a general medical clinic for which patient knowledge, satisfaction, recall of prescribed medications, and compliance had been measured. The investigators found that the explanatory power of the three systems differed. For instance, Bales's system explained 19% of the variation between patients who took prescribed drugs correctly, compared with 28% for the RIAS and none for the VRM. Explanation of variation in knowledge was somewhat better for the RIAS than for Bales's system and the VRM, and satisfaction also favored the RIAS and Bales systems.

In the second study, three measures of patient-centeredness were applied to the same sample of 55 videotaped general practitioner (GP) consultations (Mead & Bower, 2000). The RIAS was used to construct a single summary measure of patient-centeredness as a ratio of patient-centered categories of talk (all physician and patient questions and information giving about psychosocial or lifestyle-related issues, physician information about biomedical topics, all patient biomedical questions, all physician emotionally focused talk, and physician partnership talk) divided by physician-centered categories of talk (summation of all physician question asking, physician directive statements, and patient biomedical information giving). The second measure of patient-centeredness was devised using the Henbest and Stewart coding approach (1989), and the third measure was a global rating scale designed by the authors for use in the Euro-Communication Study, a six-nation comparative study of physician–patient communication (Mead & Bower, 2000). Correlations were of similar magnitude between the Euro-Communication rating scale and the RIAS (Pearson correlation = .37; $p < .01$) and between the Euro-Communication rating scale and the Henbest and Stewart measure (Pearson correlation = .37; $p < .01$), and somewhat lower between the RIAS and Henbest and Stewart measure (Pearson correlation = .21; $p < .12$).

The Euro-Communication rating scale was significantly correlated with five variables: physician age, perceived acquaintance with the patient, consultation length, proportion of patient-directed eye gaze in the consultation, and physician ratings of the importance of psychological factors. The RIAS was also significantly correlated with all these variables, with the exception of GP age. In addition, the RIAS was correlated with the patient's score on the General Health Questionnaire, a validated measure of emotional distress (Goldberg & Williams, 1988), patient age, and patient health status. The Henbest and Stewart measure was significantly associated with only one of the measures—patient-directed eye gaze.

## Description of Communication Process

Despite the differences in approaches to assessment of the medical dialogue just described, a large degree of overlap occurs in the variables that are extracted from these studies. In our review of 61 published studies in the field prior to 1987 (Hall, Roter, & Katz, 1988; Roter et al., 1988), we found 247 unique communication variables based on observations of patient and physician interaction. Few of the variables, at least in the form in which they were reported, were common to more than one or two studies. However, virtually all the variables fit within five mutually exclusive categories: information giving, question asking, social conversation, positive talk, and negative talk. An additional category, partnership building, was necessary for physician interaction only. A more recent review of communication studies addressing physician gender differences produced a very similar array of variables and subsuming categories (Roter, Hall, & Aoki, 2002).

How do these categories translate into a portrait of the medical encounter? We addressed this question in an earlier summary across a variety of studies (Roter & Hall, 2006). First, reviewing physician talk, we found that what physicians do most is give information (38% of all utterances on average). This includes all forms of information giving, including the mere reciting of facts ("Your blood pressure is high today, 180/95"); counseling ("It is very important that you take all the medication I am prescribing. You have to get your blood pressure under control, and this medication will do it, but only if you take it as you are supposed to"); and directions and instructions ("Put your clothes back on and sit down. Now, take these pills twice a day for a week and drink plenty of water"). Each of these has a different intent—to inform, to persuade, or to control (respectively). From our own work, it appears that the giving of facts constitutes about half of this category, and both counseling and directing patient behavior contribute in equal parts to the remainder.

Question asking by physicians also accounts for a good proportion of the visit (23% of the physician's utterances); this is usually done during history taking and mostly consists of closed-ended questions. Closed-ended questions are those questions for which a one-word answer, usually yes or no, is expected (e.g., "Are your leg symptoms worse after standing for several minutes?"). In contrast, open-ended questions are those that allow patients some discretion in the direction they take in answering (e.g., "Tell me about your leg pain. What seems to be the problem?").

Closed questions limit responses to a narrow field set by the physician; the patient knows that an appropriate response is one or two words and does not normally elaborate any further. In contrast, open questions suggest to the patient that elaboration is appropriate and that the field of inquiry is wide enough to include the patient's thoughts about what might be relevant. These two types of questions have very different implications for control of the medical visit; closed questions imply high physician control of the interaction, whereas open questions are much less controlling. In routine practice, closed questions outnumber open questions by a factor of two or three, perhaps because they are thought to be less time-consuming and more efficient at providing the information needed to make a diagnosis.

Positive talk constitutes a smaller share of physician talk (15% of the utterances) and serves two functions. One is obvious. Approval (e.g., "Your blood pressure is great! You've been doing a good job on your diet and taking your pills"), shared laughter, encouragement, and empathy all increase a positive bond between speakers. The second purpose of statements in this category is to signal that the listener is attentive and eager for the speaker to continue. Often included are communications more aptly described as noises than as words; *hm, huh, aha,* and *ahh* serve this purpose. The Beckman and Frankel study described earlier found that the more a physician used these noises in the first 90 seconds of the visit, the more likely the physician was to uncover fully the patient's major concerns and reason for the visit (Beckman & Frankel, 1984). Patients readily defer to the physician and are easily diverted from giving their thoughts. Attentive noises, however, encourage elaboration, so that a patient's full agenda for the visit can be revealed.

Partnership building (about 11% of utterances) represents the physician's attempts to engage the patient more fully in the medical dialogue. These may be considered, in some respect, as attempts to activate the patient, perhaps directed at particularly passive or noncommunicative patients.

Social, nonmedical conversation constitutes some 6% of interaction. It includes greetings, casual remarks, and niceties ("Hello Mr. Waller, nice to see you. That was some baseball game last night"). This talk is important as a social amenity—it is usually positive, and we are accustomed to greetings and a certain amount of chit-chat in most encounters, at least initially, to put people at ease.

Finally, negative talk is quite rare from physicians (less than 2% of utterances). This includes disagreements, confrontations, and antagonisms ("You've gained weight since your last visit, and I am disappointed in you. You're not really trying at all"). However, although negative talk is not often made explicit by physicians, a negative message can be expressed in other ways. Professional etiquette and training discourage unpleasantness and the high emotions that may arise from direct criticisms and contradictions. Reprimands may be expressed as forceful counseling or imperatives on the need to follow recommendations better. For the unsuccessful dieter, for instance, this could mean exhortation for the patient to do better on his or her diet and to follow a prescribed regimen. The physician may also express displeasure in an angry, anxious, or dominant tone of voice or by cutting patients off in various ways.

It should not be surprising to find that about half of patient talk is information giving, much of this in response to the physician's questions. What is surprising, however, is how little interaction, only some 7%, is devoted to the patient's questions. This is particularly troubling because many studies have demonstrated that patients often have questions they would like to ask their physicians but simply do not. It has been suggested that this reticence may reflect a reluctance to appear foolish or inappropriate, or it may be that physicians, in myriad ways, signal that the time is not right to ask questions. The right time, however, is never quite there. Whatever the reason, patients ask questions relatively rarely.

Although the proportion of positive talk was roughly equivalent for physicians and patients, negative talk reported in the studies we reviewed was seven times as great for patients as for physicians. It is notable how much more frequent direct contradiction or criticism of the physician is by the patient than vice versa. Patients may be more direct in this regard than their physicians because they have fewer communication options; they cannot easily express their disagreements through lecture, counseling, or imperatives. However, patients engaged in more positive as well as negative talk. The expression of these emotionally laden statements generally marks greater interpersonal engagement. The patient is

likely to have a far greater emotional investment in the proceedings than the physician, and this is expressed in both positive and negative terms.

## Correlates of Physician-Patient Communication

Individuals coming together in medical dialogue bring with them all their personal characteristics—their personalities, social attitudes and values, personal histories, gender, sexual orientation, age, education, ethnicity, and physical and mental health, to name a few. This applies to the physician as well as to the patient. Furthermore, the end points we might wish to measure, such as satisfaction or clinical outcomes, have many determinants besides the nature of physician–patient interaction.

Always, when interpreting nonexperimental comparisons, which constitute most of the literature on physician–patient communication, it is important not to make assumptions about the causal relations among variables. Even when potentially confounding variables (such as sociodemographic variables or health status) are controlled for statistically, strong inferences of causality are often not justified. Causation may lie in unmeasured variables, and even when one has measured the right variables, complex paths of causation can exist. A given behavior could have many different origins—it may be caused by a stable or transient characteristic of the person engaging in it, by how that person responds to the other person's characteristics, or by how that person is treated by the other person, to name a few possibilities. To illustrate those just named, a patient may act negatively because he feels sick, because he does not like his physician's ethnicity, or because the physician is inconsiderate and he is responding in kind. The physician–patient interaction is a prime setting for the operation of interpersonal self-fulfilling prophecies (Rosenthal & Rubin, 1978). Such processes not only are illustrative of complex reciprocal causation but also are generally out of awareness, producing serious errors of attribution—for example, a physician attributes passivity in the patient to the patient's lack of interest, when the patient is simply responding to the physician's own uninviting and cursory behavior, which is brought on by the physician's belief that the patient is uninterested. Another example of likely reciprocal causation is the physician's liking for the patient. Physicians like some of their patients more than others, and this is related to how much the patient likes the physician, as well as to patient characteristics (e.g., gender and health status; Hall, Epstein, DeCiantis, & McNeil, 1993;

Hall, Horgan, Stein, & Roter, 2002; Levinson, Frankel, Roter, & Drum, 2006).

In the sections that follow, we present research relating physician–patient communication to antecedent and outcome variables that have been frequently studied.

## Predictors of Communication
### Patient Health

The state of a patient's physical and mental health is related to both patient and physician communication (Bertakis, Callahan, Helms, Rahman, & Robbins, 1993; Hall, Roter, Milburn, & Daltroy, 1996). When the patient is more distressed, either physically or mentally, both the patient and the physician engage in less social conversation and make more emotionally concerned statements, engage in more psychosocial discussion, and ask more biomedical questions. Sicker patients also provide more biomedical information. The research also suggests that physicians may respond ambivalently to sicker patients; physicians report less satisfaction after visits with sicker patients, and they report liking sicker patients less than they do healthier patients (Hall et al., 1993, 1996, 2002).

This apparent ambivalence, in conjunction with numerous findings showing that people with worse health status are less satisfied with their care (as reviewed by Hall, Feldstein, Fretwell, Rowe, & Epstein, 1990), raises the question of whether physicians produce dissatisfaction in their sicker patients by displaying negative behaviors toward them. Hall, Milburn, Roter, and Daltroy (1998) used structural equation modeling to test this hypothesis and an alternative hypothesis that the dissatisfaction stems directly from the sicker patient's negative outlook. In general, the direct path was supported over the physician-mediation path, with one exception: Physicians' curtailing of social conversation with sicker patients accounted for some of these patients' dissatisfaction. This is unfortunate, for in curtailing this "expendable" category of interaction (perhaps in the service of devoting time to more pressing medical issues, or perhaps because sicker patients are not so fun to interact with) physicians may unknowingly undermine their relationships with the very patients for whom the quality of the relationship may matter most.

### Physician Gender

A large amount of research conducted in nonclinical settings has found gender differences in communication style (e.g., Brody & Hall, 2008; Dindia & Allen, 1992; Eagly & Johnson, 1990; Hall,1984). Indeed, the magnitude of gender differences in nonverbal expression rivals or exceeds the gender differences found for a wide range of other psychological variables (Hall, 2006). Men have been shown to engage in less smiling and laughing, less interpersonal gazing, greater interpersonal distances and less direct body orientation, less nodding, less hand gesturing, and fewer back-channel responses (interjections such as "mm hmm," which serve to facilitate a partner's speech); they also have more restless lower bodies, more expansive arm and leg movements, and weaker nonverbal communication skills (in terms of accuracy in judging the meanings of cues and expressing emotions accurately through nonverbal cues) than do women. Men have also been found to use less verbal empathy, to be less democratic as leaders, and to engage in less personal self-disclosure than do women. Also relevant is research suggesting that women report experiencing many emotions both more frequently and more intensely than do men, and refer more to emotions in their language.

There are several reasons to investigate the communication behavior of male and female physicians. Of most practical significance is the relevance of the "female" behavioral repertoire to the goals of medical education in the era of the biopsychosocial model. As mentioned earlier, the concept of relationship-centered medicine, with its emphasis on viewing the patient as a whole person, is reminiscent of "female" interaction goals such as minimizing status differentials, sharing personal information, relating effectively to emotional concerns, and showing sensitivity to others' needs and states. Furthermore, it appears that patients experience better clinical outcomes when their physicians have a more patient-centered approach (Stewart, 1996).

In undertaking a review of communication differences between male and female physicians, we entertained two contrasting hypotheses (Roter et al., 2002). The first was that the gender differences commonly seen in nonclinical settings would not be present in physicians. Considering that medical school is still widely regarded as a highly "masculine" institution, we considered it possible that selection bias (resulting from either self-selection or school admissions policies) would produce female physicians whose behavioral style is similar to that of male physicians. Furthermore, even without this bias, the process of medical education (learning to suppress one's feelings, exert authority, and generally model oneself on the "male" physician prototype) might level out initial differences.

The second hypothesis was that male and female physicians would differ in the same ways that men and women differ in other walks of life. Finding such differences among physicians would attest to the strength of gender-role socialization across the lifespan, which creates gender differences in communication style that resist homogenization in the course of medical education.

Our review of this literature generally supported the second hypothesis. Male and female physicians did not differ in how much biomedical information they conveyed, but male physicians' talk included less psychosocial discussion. Male physicians also asked fewer questions of all sorts, engaged in fewer partnership-building behaviors (enlisting the patient's active participation and reducing physician dominance), produced less positively toned talk and less talk with emotional content, used less positive nonverbal behavior (e.g., smiling and nodding), and had overall shorter visits than did female physicians (Roter et al., 2002). Consistent with these direct observational effects, male physicians report liking their patients less than female physicians report (Hall et al., 1993, 2002) and hold less patient-centered values than female physicians (where a patient-centered response would be to believe that the patient's expectations, feelings, and life circumstances are critical elements in the treatment process and that the physician's role includes sharing information and caring for the whole patient; Krupat et al., 2000).

Although in a statistical sense these gender differences are often small, they are not trivial and likely have an important impact when generalized over many medical visits and many patients. To the extent that male physicians' behavior and attitudes are less patient-centered than those of female physicians, there may be implications for overall quality of care and health outcomes. And, considering that the gender differences among physicians closely mirror those found in the general population, it should come as no surprise that female physicians seem to have fewer barriers to overcome when learning to apply the biopsychosocial model in medical practice (Roter & Hall, 2004).

Meta-analytic review has also shown that, in primary care practice, patients communicate differently *toward* male versus female physicians as well, in a pattern that either matches or complements the physician gender effects described above (Hall & Roter, 2002). Patients talk more to female than male physicians, disclose more biomedical and psychosocial information, and make more positive statements.

Patients also behave more assertively toward female physicians, perhaps as a response to female physicians' more participatory and status-leveling style.

In spite of the communication style differences suggesting that female physicians are more patient centered, and evidence that patients prefer and are more satisfied with patient-centered behavior (Hall et al., 1988; Swenson, Buell, Zettler, White, Ruston, & Lo, 2004), patients are barely more satisfied with female than male physicians, according to a meta-analysis by Hall, Blanch-Hartigan, and Roter (in press). Variation in the gender difference across studies permitted examination of moderating variables. The difference favored female physicians most when physicians were less experienced, when physicians and patients were newly acquainted, when satisfaction pertained to a specific visit, when satisfaction was measured right after a visit, and when patients were younger.

Possibly, the fact that female physicians engage in higher levels of desirable, patient-centered behaviors is offset by masculine-biased values and expectations that put female physicians at a disadvantage in patients' eyes; alternatively, even though female physicians are more patient centered than male physicians, they still may violate the female stereotype in not being as "soft" and approachable as patients expect women to be (Hall, Irish, Roter, Ehrlich, & Miller, 1994b). Thus, female physicians may experience something of a double bind. A particularly intriguing possibility is that female physicians' communication style is seen by patients as good "female" behavior rather than good "doctor" behavior, meaning that patients do not give female physicians adequate credit for their professional skills (Blanch-Hartigan, Hall, Roter, & Frankel, 2010). Hopefully, social attitudes are changing as more women enter medicine and as patients develop less paternalistic expectations regarding their medical care. However, medicine will never be a gender-neutral domain, as expectations for how men and women behave will still shape both physicians' and patients' attitudes and behavior. As an example, satisfaction with male and female physicians is correlated with how much their behavior style conforms to normative expectations for their gender (Schmid Mast, Hall, Klöckner, & Choi, 2008).

### Patient Gender

Among patients with chronic disease, females are more likely than males to prefer an active role in medical decision making (Arora & McHorney, 2000). Indeed, this preference appears to be borne out in practice, as female patients report that they experience more opportunity for decision making in their relations with their physicians than male patients report (Kaplan, Gandek, Greenfield, Rogers, & Ware, 1995). In that study, patient participation in decision making was particularly low when male patients interacted with male physicians, a finding consistent with the finding that in male patient–male physician interactions, the contribution of the patient relative to the physician is the least of all gender combinations (Hall, Irish, Roter, Ehrlich, & Miller, 1994a).

Waitzkin (1985) found that female patients were given more information than male patients, and that the information was given in a more comprehensible manner. The same data set also revealed that the greater amount of information directed toward women was largely in response to women's tendency to ask more questions in general and to ask more questions following the doctor's explanation (Wallen, Waitzkin, & Stoeckle, 1979). Similar conclusions were reached by Pendleton and Bochner (1980), who found in an English study that female patients were given more information than males and that this information was in answer to their more frequent questions.

Investigators have also found that female patients receive more positive talk and more attempts to include them in discussion than males. In one study, physicians were more likely to express "tension release" (mainly laughter) with female patients and to ask them more for their feelings (Stewart, 1983).

Although stereotypes about females' agreeableness and politeness might lead to the expectation that they would be more satisfied with care than men, the literature does not support this hypothesis (Hall & Dornan, 1990). Indeed, the trend suggests, if anything, less satisfaction among women than among men (Hall & Dornan, 1990; Hargraves et al., 2001; Thi, Briançon, Empereur, & Guillemin, 2002).

### Patient Age

Visits with elderly patients are complex. Older patients are plagued by multiple and complicated medical problems, as well as hearing impairment and sometimes dementia. Stressful life events of old age often occur simultaneously in the elderly, resulting in depression, fear of losing independence and control, and threats to self-esteem and identity (Greene & Adelman, 1996). As their health declines, the elderly are confronted with the treatment and management of debilitating or life-threatening conditions and are asked to make difficult decisions regarding end-of-life planning. While faced with these challenges, the elderly may be at a special disadvantage in fully understanding the complex choices they are asked to make. The elderly typically demonstrate lower levels of literacy and have had less exposure to formal education than younger birth cohorts (Gazmararian et al., 1999).

Particularly relevant to these decision-making demands, older patients are more passive and less actively engaged in the treatment decision-making process than younger patients. The Medical Outcomes Study (MOS; Kaplan et al., 1995), based on surveys of more than 8,000 patients sampled from the practices of 344 physicians, found that patients aged 75 and over reported significantly less participatory visits with their doctors than all but the youngest age cohorts of patients (those younger than 30 years). Interestingly, the most participatory visits were among only slightly younger patient groups, including those aged 65 to 74, and the middle-aged group ranging from 45 to 64 years. In addition to age, both poor health status and lower educational achievement were associated with lower reports of participation. Thus, the oldest patients may be at triple risk for low levels of participatory engagement with their doctors; each of these factors—cohort expectations, health status, and educational attainment—may act alone and in concert to diminish the likelihood that full patient–physician partnerships will develop.

As measured by physician time during interviews, elderly patients do not receive greater physician attention (Keeler, Solomon, Beck, Mendenhall, & Kane, 1982; Mann et al., 2001; Radecki, Kane, Solomon, Mendenhall, & Beck, 1988). However, older patients go to the doctor three times more often than their younger counterparts, so cumulatively they may accrue more physician contact. There is some indication, however, that how the time is spent may differ. Several investigators have concluded that older patients appear to have an advantage over younger patients in communication with physicians. A meta-analysis of more than 40 studies published between 1965 and 1985 in which video or audio tapes of medical visits were analyzed found consistent relationships between patient age and physicians' interviewing skills (Hall et al., 1988; Roter et al., 1988). The review found that older patients received more information, more total communication, and more questions concerning drugs than did younger patients.

Studies comparing communication directed toward older and younger patients found differences in what topics were addressed and the emotional tone of the visit. Greene and colleagues found physicians were less responsive to the psychosocial issues the elderly raised during visits than to similar concerns of younger patients (Greene, Hoffman, Charon, & Adelman, 1987). Inadequate response in this domain may be associated with patient or physician reticence to introduce psychosocial problems into an already complicated biomedical visit, and a tendency to attribute sensory failings to the aging process. Other studies, however, have not reported similar results. Mann et al. (2001) found no decrease in counseling on medical or psychosocial topics, or physician satisfaction with patient visits, with increasing age of patients. Indeed, many studies have found that increasing age is associated with higher levels of patient satisfaction (see meta-analysis of Hall & Dornan, 1990).

Older patient visits are distinguished from those of younger adults by the frequent presence of a visit companion; estimates of the percentages of all visits that include a companion range between 20% and 57% (Prohaska & Glasser, 1996). There are only a few empirical studies of the effect of companions on the dynamics of exchanges in discussions, but their presence appears to change communication patterns (Roter, 2003; Tates & Meeuwesen, 2001). Greene et al. (1987) found that when a companion was present, older patients raised fewer topics, were less responsive to topics they did raise, and were less assertive and expressive. Moreover, patients were sometimes excluded completely from the conversation when a companion was present. Additional communication difficulties have been identified, including a tendency for a family member to take on the information-giving role in the visit, sometimes contradicting the patient or disclosing information the patient had not wanted revealed (Hasselkus, 1994). It appears that the content, tone, and nature of the medical discussion may be shaped by the roles adopted by the patient companion; these may range from advocate and supporter to antagonist (Adelman, Greene, & Charon, 1987; Greene, Adelman, Friedmann, & Charon, 1994).

More positive descriptions of the contribution of a patient companion have been reported in two more recent studies. Analysis of audio tape–recorded medical encounters found visit companions to commonly facilitate physician and patient understanding by clarifying or expanding on patient history, asking questions of the physician, and prompting patient involvement. Patients who were older and in worse health held greater expectations for companion involvement (Ishikawa, Roter, Yamazaki, & Takayama, 2005) and companions of older and

sicker patients were in turn more verbally active (Clayman, Roter, Wissow, & Bandeen-Roche, 2005; Ishikawa et al., 2005). Moreover, patients whose visit companions prompted their engagement in medical dialogue were more than four times as likely to be actively engaged in decision making (Clayman et al., 2005). Collectively, these studies suggest the presence and roles assumed by visit companions are salient to quality of patient–provider communication and delivery of patient-centered care.

Results of the Medicare Current Beneficiary Survey (MCBS) similarly indicate that visit companions tend to accompany patients who are older, less educated, and in worse health than their unaccompanied counterparts, and that companions have a significant impact on patients' experience of care (Wolff & Roter, 2008). Patient satisfaction with physicians' interpersonal skills and informativeness were found to be a positive function of the intensity of companions' involvement in visit communication. The strength of this relationship is most evident among individuals with the worst self-rated health. That the inverse relationship generally found between health status and satisfaction is attenuated with greater companion involvement in visit communication suggests that the presence and actions of visit companions may bridge communication barriers in the care of especially vulnerable patients, thus suggesting that companions are a potentially valuable but largely unrecognized quality of care resource.

An intriguing question is the effect on communication of having "baby boomers" as companions in the medical visits of their aging parents, compared with spouses or contemporaries acting as visit companions. We might speculate that these adult children bring a consumerism to their encounters that can dominate the visit and perhaps contribute to a verbal withdrawal by the patient from the medical dialogue (as described by Greene et al., 1987); alternatively, the presence of a consumerist companion may spur assertive behavior on the part of some patients.

### Patient Ethnicity and Social Class
Physicians deliver less information, less supportive talk, and less proficient clinical performance to black and Hispanic patients and patients of lower economic class than they do to more advantaged patients, even in the same care settings (Bartlett et al., 1984; Epstein, Taylor, & Seage, 1985; Hooper, Comstock, Goodwin, & Goodwin, 1982; Ross, Mirowsky, & Duff, 1982; Waitzkin, 1985; Wasserman, Inui, Barriatua, Carter, & Lippincott, 1984). Race discordance between physicians and patients (e.g., an

African American patient seen by a white physician) is associated with patient reports of lowered involvement, less partnership, lower levels of trust, and lower levels of satisfaction, as well as with shorter length and more negative affect (e.g., Cooper-Patrick et al., 1999; Cooper et al., 2003; Young & Klingle, 1996).

Interpreting sociodemographic effects is complex. Inadequacies of communication in visits involving minority or low-income patients may result because physicians devalue them and their needs; or, poor performance could stem from erroneous beliefs about the expectations, capacities, and desires of such patients; yet another possibility is that, as a result of cultural norms or lack of confidence, such patients do not request or demand a high level of performance from their physicians (which could, of course, confirm whatever stereotypes the physicians may already have; van Ryn, 2002).

### Physician and Patient Training

Educators and researchers have often commented on the ironic fact that physicians perform thousands of medical interviews during their career with virtually no formal training in communication skills (Epstein, Campbell, Cohen-Cole, McWhinney, & Smilkstein, 1993). The assumption was, for a long time, that physicians naturally have adequate skill or that skill inevitably develops through experience. Now, medical educators agree that training is necessary, that a solid foundation of behavioral science research exists to support training programs, and that training improves the communication skills of physicians (Rao, Anderson, Inui, & Frankel, 2007). Communication skills training during medical school has been shown to have effects lasting as long as five years (Maguire, Fairburn, & Fletcher, 1986).

Despite variations in the length and format of physician training programs, all or most of these programs focus on the principles of relationship-centered medicine as defined in this chapter (e.g., Bensing & Sluijs, 1985; Cohen-Cole, 1991; Novack, Dube, & Goldstein, 1992; Putnam, Stiles, Jacob, & James, 1988; Roter et al., 1995). For example, the study of Novack et al. (1992) found improvements in sensitivity to psychosocial aspects of the patient's illness, ability to relate to patients, ability to elicit information from patients, and ability to communicate empathy. Roter et al.'s (1995) training program emphasized physicians' ability to recognize and handle psychosocial problems; after only eight hours of training, physicians did better with their actual patients (who were audio-taped several weeks after training) in terms of emotion handling, recognizing

psychological problems, and taking a problem-solving approach, with no increase in the overall length of the medical visit.

Smith et al.'s (2000) training program for primary care residents improves residents' knowledge, attitudes, and self-confidence, as well as their skills in interviewing patients and dealing with relationships, in managing and communicating with somatizing patients, and in educating patients. Elements in Smith's training program include setting the stage (e.g., welcoming the patient, using the patient's name, introducing self, removing barriers to communication, putting the patient at ease); agenda setting (e.g., indicating time available, indicating own needs, obtaining list of all issues the patient wants to discuss, summarizing and finalizing the agenda); nonfocused interviewing (e.g., appropriate use of open- and closed-ended questions, observing the patient's cues); and focused interviewing (e.g., symptom discovery, learning personal context of symptoms, addressing emotions).

In contrast to the many programs aimed at physicians and many published evaluations of such programs, relatively little research has tried to intervene with patients to improve the communication process. Classic is Roter's (1977) waiting-room intervention to increase patients' question asking. As described later, the waiting-room interventions by Greenfield and colleagues also influenced patients' behaviors during the medical visit. Recently, an even simpler intervention, consisting of a mailed booklet designed to heighten patients' skills and awareness when communicating with their physicians, had significant effects on patients' information seeking and success in obtaining information, and on how much information they gave to their physicians (Cegala, McClure, Marinelli, & Post, 2000). In a systematic review of intervention studies, Harrington, Noble, and Newman (2004) concluded that patients' rate of participation is often increased by interventions, more so for face-to-face than written interventions (such as a booklet or workbook).

### Clinical Outcomes of Communication

From a functional perspective, the assessment of physician–patient communication serves the purpose of predicting important outcomes for patients. In the following sections, we describe three categories of outcomes—satisfaction, adherence, and health status/quality of life. These categories do not, of course, exhaust all the desirable short- and long-term effects of communication processes within medical care. Others include recall of medical advice, physician–patient concordance (e.g., about the purpose of the visit), relief of worry, physician satisfaction, self-confidence, and sense of control (Beckman, Kaplan, & Frankel, 1989).

It is important to be reminded again of the causal uncertainties intrinsic to correlational data. As indicated earlier, experimentally controlled studies are rare in this literature. Even quite strong and consistent predictive relations do not necessarily mean direct causal paths.

### Satisfaction

Satisfaction with medical care is mostly measured with reference to a medical visit that has just occurred. However, the referent can also be a particular physician, one's care in general, or doctors in general. Researchers sometimes favor asking about one's care in general, or doctors in general, because this does not emphasize the patient's own experience and therefore produces average levels of satisfaction that are not as extremely high as typically found with physician-specific or visit-specific measures (Hall & Dornan, 1988). This ceiling effect has often been noted as a problem for two reasons. The first is psychometric, in that a restriction of range may attenuate correlations with other variables of interest. The second relates to validity: The extremely high level of satisfaction found in many studies seems to contradict the everyday impression that many patients are disappointed and frustrated in their interactions with physicians. Despite the ceiling effect, which can be extreme, the validity of patient satisfaction measurement is supported by many correlations with antecedent, process, and outcome variables.

Although much satisfaction research has proceeded without a strong theoretical basis (Cleary & McNeil, 1988), it is reasonable to think of satisfaction as the end result of the patient's comparison of ideal hopes, realistic expectations, and actual care. Satisfaction has been operationally defined with many instruments that tap a dozen or so aspects of care, in addition to overall or global satisfaction. Some aspects are asked about frequently (e.g., physician's humaneness and physician's informativeness) and some very infrequently (e.g., outcome of care and physician's attention to psychosocial problems; Hall & Dornan, 1988). Although instruments often cover noninterpersonal aspects of care such as access, availability, facilities, and bureaucracy, satisfaction with physician behavior during the medical visit is most relevant to the present chapter.

Physicians' behaviors are often classified as task related or technical, versus socioemotional or affective. For example, not explaining findings or procedures fully or using too much jargon would be considered task-related failings, whereas treating the patient disrespectfully or acting in a hurry would be considered socioemotional failings. This distinction can be difficult to draw, however, when one considers, first, that task-related behaviors have affective significance (the patient attributes a respectful or caring attitude to the physician who provides clear explanations) and, second, that the biopsychosocial model specifically places attention to the patient's psychosocial concerns within the scope of physicians' task obligations (Roter & Hall, 2006; Roter et al., 1987).

Satisfaction instruments are typically designed with psychometric standards in mind (e.g., reliability) and typically consist of Likert-scaled items (agree–disagree) or direct evaluative scales (not satisfied to very satisfied). Although investigators often conceptualize satisfaction as multifactorial, nevertheless different aspects of satisfaction tend to be highly related, and often a one-dimensional structure is revealed, although sometimes the distinction between technical and interpersonal aspects is supported (Hagedoorn et al., 2003; Marshall, Hays, Sherbourne, & Wells, 1993; Roter et al., 1987).

The term *satisfaction* suggests a response that is both affective (how did this experience make me feel?) and evaluative (did this experience meet my standards of quality?), and indeed instruments often capture these elements. However, about half of all satisfaction studies operationally define "satisfaction" in terms of factual descriptions (e.g., my physician seemed to be in a hurry; my physician answered all of my questions) that embody "satisfaction" only to the extent that the investigator makes assumptions about what values and expectations are held by the patient (Hall & Dornan, 1988). Thus, the patient whose physician does not seem to be in a hurry is assumed to be the more satisfied. This could be a wrong assumption if the patient was not particularly troubled by that aspect of the physician's behavior. Measures designed on this format are positively related to those that ask the patient to evaluate his care or indicate satisfaction directly, supporting their use as satisfaction measures. Nevertheless, it is interesting to point out the conceptual ambiguity of items that in one context would be taken as description of the physician's behavior and in another context as an evaluative response to the physician's behavior.

Many studies have found relations between physician behaviors measured during the medical visit and patient satisfaction measured after the visit.

Speaking broadly, many findings can be subsumed under several broad categories of physician behavior (see reviews by Hall et al., 1988; Ong, de Haes, Hoos, & Lammes, 1995; Thompson, 1994; Williams, Weinman, & Dale, 1998). Greater satisfaction is associated with a physician style that includes more information giving, more social (i.e., nonmedical) talk, and more supportive behavior (partnership building, positive talk, psychosocial and emotional talk). Although less studied than verbal behavior, the physician's nonverbal behavior is also an important influence on patient satisfaction (e.g., gaze, forward lean, and voice tone; Hall, Harrigan, & Rosenthal, 1995; Haskard, Williams, DiMatteo, Heritage, & Rosenthal, 2008; Roter, Frankel, Hall, & Sluyter, 2006; Schmid Mast, 2007). Greater physician competence in both task and socioemotional domains predicts satisfaction, suggesting that patients are able to discriminate on objective quality dimensions. Longer visits predict satisfaction, which may be no surprise considering that the previously named categories together account for most physician–patient conversation. On the patient's side, higher levels of activation also contribute to improvements in satisfaction (Bertakis et al., 1998).

Consistent with these behavioral predictors, physician attitudes also predict satisfaction. Krupat et al. (2000) found that patients were more satisfied when their physicians responded favorably to items such as "Patients should be treated as if they were partners with the doctor, equal in power and status." Patients' responses are particularly favorable when physician and patient share corresponding attitudes about patient control and involvement (Kiesler & Auerbach, 2006). Several physician behaviors have emerged as negative predictors of satisfaction. Although psychosocial questioning is very well received by patients, there is evidence that more questioning on biomedical topics is associated with lower satisfaction (Bertakis et al., 1991; Roter et al., 1987). At least two interpretations of this finding are possible. One is that more biomedical questioning by the physician occurs when the patient's health is worse, and, as discussed earlier, poor health is associated with lower satisfaction. Another interpretation is that more biomedical questioning by the physician is indicative of greater physician dominance, with the questions (which are most often the closed, yes–no type) reflecting physician control over the dialogue. Indeed, a number of studies find that greater physician dominance predicts lower satisfaction, whether measured objectively (as in a higher ratio of physician-to-patient talk; Bertakis

et al., 1991) or in patients' ratings of physician dominance (Buller & Buller, 1987; Burgoon et al., 1987).

There are not many intervention studies in the satisfaction literature; Hall and Dornan (1988) found that only 14% of the 221 satisfaction studies in their meta-analysis had experimental designs. Many studies report simple correlations that do not attempt to control statistically for potentially confounding variables. One needs to be cautious, therefore, in assuming that causality goes from communication behavior to patients' subsequent satisfaction. When controlled studies are done, they do support a causal interpretation; for example, interventions aimed at improving physicians' communication skills have been shown to produce not only changes in physician behavior but also improvements in patient satisfaction (Evans, Kiellerup, Stanley, Burrows, & Sweet, 1987). But even so, there can be other causal paths, such as when low patient satisfaction is expressed in negative behaviors, which are then reciprocated by the physician.

At its extreme, low satisfaction can culminate in a malpractice suit. Research finds that disappointment in one's relationship with a physician often overshadows the objective severity of the physician's errors of medical judgment. Objectively measured quality of care does not appear to be the primary determinant in a patient's decision to initiate a malpractice claim. It is estimated that fewer than 2% of patients who have suffered a significant injury due to negligence initiate a malpractice claim (Localio, Lawthers, & Brennan, 1991). There is evidence that patients and families are more likely to sue a physician when faced with a bad outcome if they think the physician failed to communicate in a timely and open manner or perceive the physician as being uncaring or indifferent (Beckman, Markakis, Suchman, & Frankel, 1994).

Observational research has revealed how communication actually differed between physicians who were never sued and those who were (Ambady, LaPlante, Nguyen, Rosenthal, Chaumeton, & Levinson, 2002; Levinson et al., 1997). Never-sued doctors had longer visits, engaged in more laughter, were more likely to orient the patient to what to expect in regard to the flow of the visit, used more partnership-type exchanges (i.e., asking for the patient's opinion, understanding of what was said and expectations for the visit, showing interest in patient disclosures, and paraphrasing and interpreting what the patient said), and had nonverbal voice tone that was less dominant and more concerned/anxious than physicians who had been sued.

Although most research on patient satisfaction has been conducted in primary care, outpatient settings, research in other settings confirms the findings. For example, Ong, Visser, Lammes, and de Haes (2000) found that cancer patients' satisfaction was related to the affective quality of the consultation. Like most patients, those with cancer typically want more information than they get, are unsure of their diagnosis and prognosis, and are unsure of what diagnostic tests are needed and what they mean; indeed, oncologists themselves report being stressed by their poor training in communication (Fallowfield & Jenkins, 1999). A smaller amount of attention has been paid to studying communication issues for hospitalized patients, some of whom have cancer; in this setting, the preference for receiving information is high and receipt of information is predictive of satisfaction (Krupat, Fancey, & Cleary, 2000). Hospital patients complain about inadequate time talking with nurses and doctors, not being told about hospital routine, not being told whom to ask for help, and not getting enough information about postdischarge care (Delbanco et al., 1995).

Another tradition of research examines a different kind of physician skill, namely ability to communication emotions accurately and their ability to identify the affective meanings of nonverbal cues, as measured with tests designed for this purpose. Physicians' tested ability to express emotions through facial expressions and tones of voice, and their ability to judge the meanings of nonverbal expressions on a standard test, predicted their patients' satisfaction (DiMatteo, Taranta, Friedman, & Prince, 1980). The ability of medical students to identify emotions in nonverbal cues has been shown to predict positively the behavior of standardized patients during a simulated clinical examination, as well as impressions made on viewers of the videotaped interaction who watched while imagining they were the patient (Hall, Roter, Blanch, & Frankel, 2009). Research has not yet documented the path through which nonverbal sensitivity might translate into a favorable impact in the medical visit, although Robbins, Kirmayer, Cathébras, Yaffe, and Dworkind (1994) found that more nonverbally sensitive physicians had heightened vigilance for signs of emotional distress in their patients.

## Adherence

The extent to which patients follow their treatment or lifestyle recommendations and show up for scheduled visits has long been a subject of concern for health services researchers because failure in either of these areas is likely to jeopardize health and waste health resources (Becker, 1985). For many years, the term *compliance* was used by investigators, but more recently, in keeping with changes in how the field conceptualizes the physician–patient relationship, *adherence* has become the preferred term. As long as the implicit model of the relationship was a paternalistic one in which influence was assumed to flow one way, it followed that the patient's job was to do what the doctor said to do (i.e., comply). With the advent of other models of patienthood, a wider range of goals and commitments is now considered relevant to health outcomes. Accordingly, the term *adherence* suggests that the patient may engage in behaviors relevant to self-set and mutually negotiated goals, as well as to physician-set goals.

Research finds that adherence is often shockingly low, as reviewed by Haynes, Taylor, and Sackett (1979) and subsequently corroborated by many other reviewers. Estimates of nonadherence rates with prescribed therapeutic regimens typically range from 30% to 60%, with most researchers agreeing that at least 50% of patients for whom drugs are prescribed fail to receive full benefit through inadequate adherence (Rogers & Bullman, 1995). Moreover, it has been estimated that almost one-third of patients who received prescriptions were using them in a manner that posed a serious threat to their health (Boyd, Covington, Stanaszek, & Coussons, 1974). Nevertheless, doctors infrequently suspect that their patients are not taking their drugs exactly as prescribed, and are poor at estimating their patients' rate of adherence. Patients rarely volunteer adherence information to their doctor, and doctors do not often explicitly ask, instead blaming nonadherence on the patient's personality (Becker, 1985; Steele, Jackson, & Gutmann, 1990).

Measures of adherence are varied and include self-reports of medication adherence, diet, exercise, and prevention; physiological outcomes (such as blood pressure and blood glucose) that are deemed to be sensitive to medication and/or lifestyle adherence; indirect measures such as refill records and pill counts; and utilization measures, which include appointment making, appointment keeping, and use of preventive services such as mammography (Roter et al., 1998). These measures differ in their validity; self-reports of adherence, for example, may be exaggerated (although research suggests they are positively related to other methods of assessment;

Becker, 1985), and physiological indicators are subject to influences other than adherence to regimen.

Meta-analysis has revealed, perhaps not surprisingly, that how physicians communicate is related to adherence (Haskard Zolnierek & DiMatteo, 2009), based on studies of direct observation during patient visits. Those investigators also concluded that programs of communication skills training for physicians improved adherence in the patients of those physicians. DiMatteo, Hays, and Prince (1986) found that the patients of physicians who scored as higher in sensitivity to nonverbal cues, as measured with a standardized test, were more adherent to their scheduled appointments than patients of less sensitive physicians. We do not yet know how it is that such physicians induce better adherence, but it is known that patients are more adherent when their physicians deliver more information, ask more questions about adherence (but fewer questions overall), and engage in more positive talk (Hall et al., 1988). In this context, the patient intervention study of Roter (1977), mentioned earlier, is relevant: Patients who were encouraged by the investigator to ask more questions during their medical visits were subsequently more likely to keep their scheduled appointments than were untrained patients. Although it is possible that improvements in appointment keeping resulted from the added information patients received from their physicians, other findings of the study suggested that the higher rates of appointment keeping were related to an enhanced internal sense of control in health-related matters. The patients who participated in the activation intervention scored significantly higher than other patients on a measure of health locus of control.

The sources of patients' nonadherence are many, with some related to deficiencies in the physician–patient relationship. Patients need to understand the treatment recommendations, believe in them, and have the ability and resources to follow them. When they do not understand what they are to do or doubt a recommendation's usefulness, they ignore it; and when they lack appropriate circumstances or supports, they are less likely to follow through as recommended (DiMatteo, 1994; DiMatteo, Reiter, & Gambone, 1994).

Poor adherence can also be the end result of reciprocity processes between patient and physician. Roter and Hall (2006) suggested that resentment toward a disappointing or aggravating physician can lead patients to reciprocate the negativity by not doing what the physician wants. Unfortunately, in deciding how to behave, a patient may be more influenced by the anticipated satisfaction of "getting even" with the doctor than by the likely damage to his or her own health resulting from nonadherence. Although our emphasis has been on communication skill as a physician trait, it is possible of course that situational stresses and other contextual variables impair physician performance as well. Consistent with such an interpretation, when physicians were less satisfied with their jobs, their patients reported poorer treatment adherence as much as two years later (DiMatteo et al., 1993).

Many intervention studies have been designed to improve adherence. A meta-analysis of 153 studies classified the intervention strategies broadly as educational, behavioral, and affective (Roter et al., 1998). Educational interventions could emphasize pedagogical methods intended to increase patients' knowledge through one-to-one and group teaching, as well as the use of written and audio-visual materials. Behaviorally focused interventions were designed to change adherence by targeting, shaping, or reinforcing specific behavioral patterns and included skill-building and practice activities, behavioral modeling and contracting, packaging and dosage modifications, and mail and telephone reminders. Affectively focused strategies attempted to influence adherence through appeals to feelings and emotions or social relationships and social supports, including family support, counseling, and supportive home visits. Interventions were further subclassified according to how many distinct components and strategies were represented.

The meta-analysis of Roter et al. (1998) found that interventions had positive effects that ranged from small to large in magnitude. Overall effects were almost always significant, regardless of whether the outcome measures were physiological indicators such as disease severity, direct indicators such as blood or urine tests, indirect indicators such as refill records, subjective measures such as self-reports, or utilization measures such as appointment keeping. Larger studies produced smaller effects, possibly because they used less tailored or less intensive interventions. Interventions profited from combining more than one kind of strategy, for example, educational plus behavioral. Finally, interventions appeared to be effective across different diagnostic categories (cancer, hypertension, diabetes, and mental health problems), although some kinds of interventions worked better than others for different diagnoses.

All in all, it is encouraging that interventions can do some good, considering that adherence is also influenced by many extraneous factors, including personality, health beliefs, and sociodemographic factors. The question that is most germane to the present chapter is whether it is possible and practical for physicians to incorporate adherence-improving activities in routine practice. We strongly believe that it is, and that a large part of the battle consists in simply persuading physicians to increase their currently low level of discussing the topic with their patients. Once that barrier is overcome, it should be relatively easy to teach physicians to engage in a few targeted behaviors. Furthermore, studies showing that satisfaction and adherence are positively related and our earlier discussion of reciprocity suggest that the quality of the physician–patient relationship itself can motivate adherence, above and beyond any particular adherence-inducing behaviors enacted by the physician.

An example of the potential for incorporating simple interventions into routine practice is the study of Cegala, Marinelli, and Post (2000), in which a workbook was mailed to patients before their scheduled visit that was designed to instruct them in seeking, verifying, and providing information during the medical visit and to give patients the opportunity to write down their concerns and questions. Adherence, as determined in a telephone survey two weeks later, was significantly greater than in two control groups.

### Health and Quality of Life

Some of the same measures that are used as indicators of adherence are also used as health status end points, for example, glucose, blood pressure, and cholesterol control. A number of self- or physician-reported instruments exist, typically checklists of health conditions. Other measures of health status are more global, reflecting a patient's or an observer's (typically a physician's) assessment of health on various dimensions, including physiological, emotional, cognitive, and social (Hall et al., 1996; Jenkinson, 1994; Stewart & Ware, 1992). Instruments such as these serve also as predictor measures and covariates in many studies.

Research finds that behaviors that can collectively be considered relationship centered, including physician informativeness, partnership building, and emotional rapport and support, are related to a range of health outcomes, such as improvements in emotional health, symptom resolution, physical functioning and quality-of-life assessments, physiological indicators of disease management (blood pressure, blood sugar), and pain control (Arora, 2003; Stewart, 1996). For example, blood pressure control improved more if patients were allowed to tell their whole story to their doctor and the doctor provided more information to the patient (Orth et al., 1987); health status improved more over time when the physician's communication style included more psychosocial counseling (Bertakis et al., 1998).

Consistent with these results, a meta-analysis of randomized studies of the effects of psychosocial interventions on health and quality of life in cancer patients found positive and significant effects for a range of outcomes, including emotional adjustment, functional adjustment, and reduction in disease- and treatment-related symptoms (Meyer & Mark, 1995). These positive effects were evident across a range of psychosocial interventions, including cognitive-behavioral methods, informational-educational methods, and various kinds of counseling and verbal psychotherapy. The impact on disease outcomes was also positive but not significant (there were few studies in this category).

More striking still are experimental studies showing that communication interventions can have significant effects on health outcomes. In one type of study, a research assistant reviews the medical record with the patient, helps the patient identify decisions to be made, rehearses negotiation skills, encourages the patient to ask questions, reviews obstacles such as embarrassment and intimidation, and afterward gives the patient a copy of the medical record for that visit. In a sample of diabetic patients, such an intervention reduced blood sugar, reduced patients' reports of functional limitations (mobility, role functions, physical activities), and improved patients' perceptions of their overall health (Greenfield, Kaplan, Ware, Yano, & Frank, 1988). Mechanisms accounting for these effects are not entirely understood because the intervention contained a number of elements but are likely related both to information exchange and to feelings of empowerment; in that study, experimental patients elicited more information from physicians, talked more, and were more assertive. Encouraging results have occurred in similarly designed studies using different patient populations, for example, patients with ulcer disease (Kaplan, Greenfield, & Ware, 1989). G. C. Williams and Deci (2001) intervened experimentally with physicians' manner of communicating about smoking cessation and found that an autonomy-supportive style increased patient participation, which then reduced smoking rates for as long as 30 months after the visit.

A review of studies on the relation between physician behavior style and patients' health outcomes in chronic disease made a distinction between studies that measured how much the physician elicited and discussed patients' beliefs versus how much the physician tried to activate the patient to take control in the consultation and in the management of the illness (Michie, Miles, & Weinman, 2003). Studies involving patient activation showed more consistent effects.

Interventions to improve physicians' communication skills also hold promise to improve health status. As mentioned earlier, Roter et al. (1995) randomly assigned community-based physicians either to an eight-hour course on improving their recognition and management of psychosocial distress in primary care or to a control group. Patients of trained physicians showed improvements in their emotional distress for as long as six months after the intervention.

Although only a relatively small number of studies relate communication process to health outcomes, some studies allow an inference about ultimate health effects by showing that communication is related to important proximal variables or that patient reports of physician behavior predict health outcomes. A good example regarding a proximal variable is the pediatric study of Wissow, Roter, and Wilson (1994), in which parents were more likely to disclose information about their child's mental health when the pediatricians asked more questions about psychosocial issues, expressed support, and displayed interest and attention while listening. If we assume that disclosure of a psychosocial problem is the first step toward treating and relieving it, then such a study again points to physician communication as a potent influence in this process. An example based on patient reports of physician behavior is G. C. Williams, Freedman, and Deci's (1998) study in which diabetic patients' reports of autonomy-supportive behaviors by their physicians predicted improvements in their glucose levels.

Yet another pathway to improved health outcomes is through adherence to medical regimens; although one would like to assume that adherence promotes health, this should not be a foregone conclusion, because many factors contribute to health outcomes. Fortunately, the meta-analysis of DiMatteo, Giordani, Lepper, and Croghan (2002) demonstrated that better adherence is associated with better health outcomes, especially when adherence is to a nonmedication regimen. Tracing the path backward from adherence to communication, these results further support the idea that communication has an important impact on health status.

## Conclusion
### Limitations in Research to Date and Future Directions

There are a number of fundamental issues with which the field must contend for progress to continue. Among these important considerations are the need for guiding theoretical models, current methodological limitations, and the application of research methods and results to physician training and assessment.

First, we can point to a lack of theoretical models, and a general lack of theoretical depth, in physician–patient research (Hall & Schmid Mast, 2009; Roter, 2000a; Roter & Hall, 2006). This deficit has contributed to the largely exploratory nature of this work, with little conceptual framing of the studies' meaning. In this regard, the application of meta-analytic methods can be helpful in uncovering common underlying dimensions in this body of research. Many of the coding systems are complementary and could potentially be combined in creative and powerful ways. Furthermore, measurement approaches must be subject to both construct and predictive tests of validity. In particular, they must be designed to capture the theoretical constructs that guide a study's hypotheses. A recent review concluded, for example, that even though investigators are eager to study patient involvement in decision making, few instruments exist that are specifically designed to measure this aspect of clinical communication (Elwyn et al., 2001).

Second, methodological limitations are evident in all individual systems of interaction analysis. One such limitation is the field's still rudimentary success in accounting for interaction *sequence*. A basic assumption has been that summary profiles based on frequencies of verbal behaviors occurring during the encounter adequately reflect the communication process. However, as pointed out by Inui and Carter (1985), this is analogous to describing *Hamlet* as a play in which the principal characters include ghosts, witches, lords, ladies, officers, soldiers, sailors, messengers, and attendants—one of whom is already dead, one of whom dies by drowning, one by poisoned drink, two by poisoned sword, and one by sword and by drink! Although in the qualitative approach there is great respect paid to the sequence in which events occur, capturing temporal phenomena in a generalizable way is still an elusive goal. Another weakness is that most research has been cross-sectional, with little attention to longitudinality or continuity of care; two exceptions are studies by Stewart (1995) and van Dulmen et al. (1997). In a meta-analysis reported earlier, only 40% of the studies even specified whether the patient and physician were previously acquainted (Roter et al., 1988). Our current work is moving in this direction; we have analyzed the health maintenance visits of 192 new babies over a 1-year period (for a total of 700 visits) to 30 pediatricians. Surprisingly, we found that a longitudinal relationship was not associated with more frequent discussion of psychosocial topics or with improved physician awareness of maternal distress (Wissow et al., 2000). Although there is reason to believe that continuity of care provides great advantages to the therapeutic relationship (it is related to patient satisfaction, for example), we really know very little about continuity's black box. In fact, it may be that there are some negative aspects of continuity, such as the presumptuousness of familiarity, labeling, and simply the need for a fresh perspective. Better specification of the ongoing relationship can be accomplished through more conscientious reporting by investigators and through more creative research designs.

The gulf between basic research and clinical application could be better bridged. More intervention studies are needed in which teaching methods are evaluated in light of actual changes in physicians' communication style and, further, validated against changes in patient outcomes. Those physicians responsible for training in clinical interviewing courses could particularly benefit from this area of work by collaborating with researchers to develop analysis schemes pertinent to quality-of-care assessment. And, even without new research, the wealth of existing research on the communication process could be better utilized, so that practicing physicians have a better sense of what communication behaviors and skills are important and why.

We will mention a few more areas for future research. Most intervention studies have targeted physicians, but they are not the only targets for behavior change. There should be more research using patient interventions. Several studies that evaluated patient interventions found favorable effects. This is clearly an area that needs further elaboration and has tremendous potential for health education trials.

There should be more analysis of relationships under stress, for example, under circumstances of trauma or terminal illness. Most of what is known know about patient–physician communication has come from the context of routine primary care. As mentioned earlier, a growing and important body of studies with cancer patients will help us better understand nonroutine care and the management of life-threatening illness episodes. Insight into these areas is important because it could improve the care of large numbers of patients who will remain outside of the primary care system, as well as improve coordination and integration of care for the majority of patients straddling primary and specialty care.

The biopsychosocial model brings attention to mind–body connections in illness and health. Integration of psychotherapeutic techniques and theories into communication assessment and primary care training will help the field meet the challenges of psychosomatic and psychosocial distress among so many patients.

Communication researchers must also confront emerging ethical and philosophical issues. These include decision-making processes related to conditions of uncertainty such as end-of-life planning, enrollment in clinical trials, treatment of the cognitively impaired, and decisions regarding genetic testing and its consequences.

Insight is needed into the social context of the therapeutic relationship, with more attention to issues of gender, social class, and ethnicity. Of these social context variables, gender has received the most attention within communication studies, although as noted earlier the number of studies is still small. More recently, there has been an upsurge in studies of disadvantaged groups and the sources of health disparities. This work should continue.

Knowledge of the basic social psychology of the therapeutic relationship continues to mature but still shows vulnerable gaps. We cannot yet consistently increase patient understanding and recall, improve participatory decision making, or optimize adherence and commitment to therapeutic regimens. These are continuing and critical challenges for communication researchers. Better integration of theories from cognitive and social psychology could help.

Researchers must embrace the challenge of new interactive computer technologies at all levels of their work. Use of interactive CD-ROMs, Web-based programming, and interactive videos foreshadows this tremendously exciting new frontier.

Finally, one further issue is worthy of consideration: The basic characteristics of the provider–patient relationship may be undergoing substantial evolutionary change (Inui & Carter, 1985). There is considerable evidence that patients are becoming more consumerist in orientation, and particularly the new generation of patients is likely to directly challenge physician authority within the medical encounter (Haug & Lavin, 1983). There is, likewise, evidence that physicians may be accommodating their patients with a more egalitarian relationship and tolerance for patient participation in decision making. The implications of these changes are tremendous, and they must be given full and serious consideration in conceptualizing how the patient–physician relationship may be articulated in the medical encounter. Important strides have been made in the understanding of doctor–patient relations, but challenges remain. The most significant of these challenges is to push forward our conceptual and methodological imagination to approach the field in new and meaningful ways.

## Notes

1. We refer throughout this chapter to *physicians* and *doctors* (terms we use interchangeably), but a great deal of what we report is relevant to other health professionals, including nurses, dentists, physical and occupational therapists, and pharmacists. Furthermore, each of these professions has been the focus of its own communication research.

## References

Adelman, R.D., Greene, M.G., & Charon, R. (1987). The physician elderly patient companion triad in the medical encounter. *Gerontologist, 27*, 729–734.

Ambady, N., LaPlante, D., Nguyen, T., Rosenthal, R., Chaumeton, N., & Levinson, L. (2002). Surgeons' tone of voice: A clue to malpractice history. *Surgery, 132*, 5–9.

Arora, N.K. (2003). Interacting with cancer patients: The significance of physicians' communication behavior. *Social Science and Medicine, 57*, 791–806.

Arora, N.K., & McHorney, C.A. (2000). Patient preferences for medical decision-making: Who really wants to participate? *Medical Care, 38*, 335–341.

Bales, R.F. (1950). *Interaction process analysis*. Cambridge, MA: Addison-Wesley.

Bartlett, E.E., Grayson, M., Barker, R., Levine, D.M., Golden, A., & Libber, S. (1984). The effects of physician communication skills on patient satisfaction, recall, and adherence. *Journal of Chronic Diseases, 37*, 755–764.

Beach, M.C., Inui, T., & Relationship-Centered Care Research Network (2006). Relationship-centered care: A constructive reframing. *Journal of General Internal Medicine, 21*, S3–8.

Becker, M.H. (1985). Patient adherence to prescribed therapies. *Medical Care, 23*, 539–555.

Beckman, H.B., & Frankel, R.M. (1984). The effect of physician behavior on the collection of data. *Annals of Internal Medicine, 101*, 692–696.

Beckman, H., Kaplan, S.H., & Frankel, R. (1989). Outcome based research on doctor–patient communication: A review. In M. Stewart, & D. Roter (Eds.), *Communicating with medical patients* (pp. 223–227). Newbury Park, CA: Sage.

Beckman, H.B., Markakis, K.M., Suchman, A.L., & Frankel, R.M. (1994). The doctor-plaintiff relationship: Lessons from plaintiff depositions. *Archives of Internal Medicine, 154*, 1365–1370.

Bensing, J.M., & Dronkers, J. (1992). Instrumental and affective aspects of physician behavior. *Medical Care, 30*, 283–298.

Bensing, J.M., & Sluijs, E.M. (1985). Evaluation of an interview training course for general practitioners. *Social Science and Medicine, 20*, 737–744.

Bertakis, K.D., Callahan, E.J., Helms, L.J., Azari, R., Robbins, J.A., & Miller, J. (1998). Physician practice styles and patient outcomes: Differences between family practice and general internal medicine. *Medical Care, 36*, 879–891.

Bertakis, K.D., Callahan, E.J., Helms, L.J., Rahman, A., & Robbins, J.A. (1993). The effect of patient health on physician practice style. *Family Medicine, 25*, 530–535.

Bertakis, K.D., Roter, D.L., & Putnam, S.M. (1991). The relationship of physician medical interview style to patient satisfaction. *Journal of Family Practice, 32*, 175–181.

Blanch-Hartigan, D., Hall, J.A., Roter, D.L., Frankel, R.M. (2010). Gender bias in patients' perceptions of patient-centered behaviors. *Patient Education and Counseling, 80*, 315–320.

Boon, H., & Stewart, M. (1998). Patient–physician communication assessment instruments: 1986 to 1996 in review. *Patient Education and Counseling, 35*, 161–176.

Boyd, J.R., Covington, T.R., Stanaszek, W.F., & Coussons, R.T. (1974). Drug defaulting: Part I. Determinants of compliance. *American Journal of Hospital Pharmacy, 31*, 485–491.

Brody, L.R., & Hall, J.A. (2008). Gender and emotion in context. In M. Lewis, J.M. Haviland-Jones, & L. Feldman Barrett (Eds.), *Handbook of emotions* (3nd ed., pp. 395–408). New York: Guilford.

Brown, J.B., Stewart, M.A., McCracken, E.C., McWhinney, I.R., & Levenstein, J.H. (1986). The patient-centered clinical method: 2. Definition and application. *Family Practice: An International Journal, 3*, 75–79.

Brown, J.B., Stewart, M., & Tessier, S. (1995). *Assessing communication between patients and doctors: A manual for scoring patient-centered communication*. Working paper series (Paper No. 95). University of Western Ontario, Centre for Studies in Family Medicine, London, Ontario, Canada.

Brown, J.B., Weston, W.W., & Stewart, M.A. (1989). Patient-centered interviewing. Part II: Finding common ground. *Canadian Family Physician, 35*, 153–157.

Buller, M.K., & Buller, D.B. (1987). Physicians' communication style and patient satisfaction. *Journal of Health and Social Behavior, 28*, 375–388.

Burgoon, J.K., Pfau, M., Parrott, R., Birk, T., Coker, R., & Burgoon, M. (1987). Relational communication, satisfaction, compliance-gaining strategies, and compliance in communication between physicians and patients. *Communication Monographs, 54*, 307–324.

Callahan, E.J., & Bertakis, K.D. (1991). Development and validation of the Davis Observation Code. *Family Medicine, 23*, 19–26.

Cegala, D.J., Marinelli, T., & Post, D. (2000). The effects of patient communication skills training on compliance. *Archives of Family Medicine, 9*, 57–64.

Cegala, D.J., McClure, L., Marinelli, T.M., & Post, D.M. (2000). The effects of communication skills training on patients' participation during medical interviews. *Patient Education and Counseling, 41*, 209–222.

Clayman, M., Roter, D., Wissow, L., & Bandeen-Roche, K. (2005). Autonomy-related behaviors of patient companions and their effect on decision-making activity in geriatric primary care visits. *Social Science and Medicine, 60*, 1583–1591.

Cleary, P.D., & McNeil, B.J. (1988). Patient satisfaction as an indicator of quality care. *Inquiry, 25*, 25–36.

Cohen-Cole, S. (1991). *The medical interview: The three function approach.* St. Louis, MO: Mosby.

Cooper, L.A., Roter, D.L., Johnson, R.L., Ford, D.E., Steinwachs, D.M., & Powe, N.R. (2003). Patient-centered communication, ratings of care, and concordance of patient and physician race. *Annals of Internal Medicine, 139*, 907–915.

Cooper-Patrick, L., Gallo, J.J., Gonzales, J.J., Vu, H.T., Powe, N.R., Nelson, C., et al. (1999). Race, gender, and partnership in the patient–physician relationship. *Journal of the American Medical Association, 282*, 583–589.

Davis, M. (1969). Variations in patients' compliance with doctors' advice: An empirical analysis of patterns of communication. *American Journal of Public Health, 58*, 274–288.

Davis, M. (1971). Variation in patients' compliance with doctors' orders: Medical practice and doctor–patient interaction. *Psychiatry in Medicine, 2*, 31–54.

Delbanco, T.L., Stokes, D.M., Cleary, P.D., Edgman-Levitan, S., Walker, J.D., Gerteis, M., et al. (1995). Medical patients' assessments of their care during hospitalization: Insights for internists. *Journal of General Internal Medicine, 10*, 679–685.

DiMatteo, M.R. (1994). Enhancing patient adherence to medical recommendations. *Journal of the American Medical Association, 271*, 79–83.

DiMatteo, M.R., Giordani, P.J., Lepper, H.S., & Croghan, T.W. (2002). Patient adherence and medical treatment outcomes: A meta-analysis. *Medical Care, 40*, 794–811.

DiMatteo, M.R., Hays, R.D., & Prince, L.M. (1986). Relationship of physicians' nonverbal communication skills to patient satisfaction, appointment noncompliance, and physician workload. *Health Psychology, 5*, 581–594.

DiMatteo, M.R., Reiter, R.C., & Gambone, J.C. (1994). Enhancing medication adherence through communication and informed collaborative choice. *Health Communication, 6*, 253–265.

DiMatteo, M.R., Sherbourne, C.D., Hays, R.D., Ordway, L., Kravitz, R.L., McGlynn, E.A., et al. (1993). Physicians' characteristics influence patients' adherence to medical treatment: Results from the Medical Outcomes study. *Health Psychology, 12*, 93–102.

DiMatteo, M.R., Taranta, A., Friedman, H.S., & Prince, L.M. (1980). Predicting patient satisfaction from physicians' nonverbal communication skills. *Medical Care, 18*, 376–387.

Dindia, K., & Allen, M. (1992). Sex differences in self-disclosure: A meta-analysis. *Psychological Bulletin, 112*, 106–124.

Eagly, A.H., & Johnson, B.T. (1990). Gender and leadership style: A meta-analysis. *Psychological Bulletin, 108*, 233–256.

Elwyn, G., Edwards, A., Mowle, S., Wensing, M., Wilkinson, C., Kinnersley, P., et al. (2001). Measuring the involvement of patients in shared decision-making: A systematic review of instruments. *Patient Education and Counseling, 43*, 5–22.

Emanuel, E.J., & Emanuel, L.L. (1992). Four models of the physician–patient relationship. *Journal of the American Medical Association, 267*, 2221–2226.

Ende, J., Kazis, L., Ash, A., & Moskowitz, M.A. (1989). Measuring patients' desire for autonomy: Decision making and information-seeking preferences among medical patients. *Journal of General Internal Medicine, 4*, 23–30.

Ende, J., Kazis, L., & Moskowitz, M.A. (1990). Preferences for autonomy when patients are physicians. *Journal of General Internal Medicine, 5*, 506–509.

Engel, G.L. (1977). The need for a new medical model: A challenge for biomedicine. *Science, 196*, 129–136.

Engel, G.L. (1988). How much longer must medicine's science be bound by a seventeenth century world view? In K. White (Ed.), *The task of medicine: Dialogue at Wickenburg* (pp. 113–136). Menlo Park, CA: Henry J. Kaiser Family Foundation.

Epstein, A.M., Taylor, W.C., & Seage, G.R. (1985). Effects of patients' socioeconomic status and physicians' training and practice on patient-doctor communication. *American Journal of Medicine, 78*, 101–106.

Epstein, R.M., Campbell, T.L., Cohen-Cole, S.A., McWhinney, I.R., & Smilkstein, G. (1993). Perspectives on patient-doctor communication. *Journal of Family Practice, 37*, 377–388.

Epstein, R.M., Franks, P., Fiscella, K., Shields, C.G., Meldrum, S.C., Kravitz, R.L., & Duberstein, P.R. (2005). Measuring patient-centered communication in patient–physician consultations: Theoretical and practical issues. *Social Science and Medicine, 61*, 1516–1528.

Evans, B.J., Kiellerup, F.D., Stanley, R.O., Burrows, G.D., & Sweet, B. (1987). A communication skills programme for increasing patients' satisfaction with general practice consultations. *British Journal of Medical Psychology, 60*, 373–378.

Fallowfield, L., & Jenkins, V. (1999). Effective communication skills are the key to good cancer care. *European Journal of Cancer, 35*, 1592–1597.

Freemon, B., Negrete, V., Davis, M., & Korsch, B. (1971). Gaps in doctor patient communication. *Pediatric Research, 5*, 298–311.

Freidson, E. (1970). *Professional dominance.* Chicago: Aldine.

Freire, P. (1970). *Pedagogy of the oppressed.* New York: Seabury.

Freire, P. (1983). *Education for critical consciousness.* New York: Continuum.

Gazmararian, J.A., Baker, D.W., Williams, M.V., Parker, R.M., Scott, T.L., Green, D.C., et al. (1999). Health literacy among Medicare enrollees in a managed care organization. *Journal of the American Medical Association, 281*, 545–551.

Goldberg, D., & Williams, P. (1988). *A user's guide to the general health questionnaire.* Windsor, Berkshire, UK: NFER-Nelson.

Gotler, R.S., Flocke, S.A., Goodwin, M.A., Zyzanski, S.J., Murray, T.H., & Stange, K.C. (2000). Facilitating participatory decision-making: What happens in real-world community practice? *Medical Care, 38*, 1200–1209.

Greene, M.G., & Adelman, R.D. (1996). Psychosocial factors in older patients' medical encounters. *Research on Aging, 18*, 84–102.

Greene, M.G., Adelman, R.D., Friedmann, E., & Charon, R. (1994). Older patient satisfaction with communication during an initial medical encounter. *Social Science and Medicine, 38*, 1279–1283.

Greene, M.G., Hoffman, S., Charon, R., & Adelman, R.D. (1987). Psychosocial concerns in the medical encounter: A comparison of the interactions of doctors with their old and young patients. *Gerontologist, 27*, 164–168.

Greenfield, S., Kaplan, S.H., Ware, J.E., Jr., Yano, E.M., & Frank, H.J.L. (1988). Patients' participation in medical care: Effects on blood sugar control and quality of life in diabetes. *Journal of General Internal Medicine, 3*, 448–457.

Hagedoorn, M., Uijl, S.G., Van Sonderen, E., Ranchor, A.V., Grol, B.M.F., Otter, R., et al. (2003). Structure and reliability of Ware's patient satisfaction questionnaire. III: Patients' satisfaction with oncological care in the Netherlands. *Medical Care, 41*, 254–263.

Hall, J.A. (1984). *Nonverbal sex differences: Communication accuracy and expressive style*. Baltimore: Johns Hopkins University Press.

Hall, J.A. (2006). How big are nonverbal sex differences? The case of smiling and nonverbal sensitivity. In K. Dindia, & D.J. Canary (Eds.), *Sex differences and similarities in communication* (2nd ed., pp. 59–81). Mahwah, NJ: Erlbaum.

Hall, J.A., Blanch-Hartigan, D., & Roter, D.L. (in press). Patients' satisfaction with male versus female physicians: A meta-analysis. *Medical Care*.

Hall, J.A., & Dornan, M.C. (1988). Meta-analysis of satisfaction with medical care: Description of research domain and analysis of overall satisfaction levels. *Social Science and Medicine, 27*, 637–644.

Hall, J.A., & Dornan, M.C. (1990). Patient socio-demographic characteristics as predictors of satisfaction with medical care: A meta-analysis. *Social Science and Medicine, 30*, 811–818.

Hall, J.A., Epstein, A.M., DeCiantis, M.L., & McNeil, B.J. (1993). Physicians' liking for their patients: More evidence for the role of affect in medical care. *Health Psychology, 12*, 140–146.

Hall, J.A., Feldstein, M., Fretwell, M.D., Rowe, J.W., & Epstein, A.M. (1990). Older patients' health status and satisfaction with medical care in an HMO population. *Medical Care, 28*, 261–270.

Hall, J.A., Harrigan, J.A., & Rosenthal, R. (1995). Nonverbal behavior in clinician-patient interaction. *Applied and Preventive Psychology, 4*, 21–37.

Hall, J.A., Horgan, T.G., Stein, T.S., & Roter, D.L. (2002). Liking in the physician–patient relationship. *Patient Education and Counseling, 48*, 69–77.

Hall, J.A., Irish, J.T., Roter, D.L., Ehrlich, C.M., & Miller, L.H. (1994a). Gender in medical encounters: An analysis of physician and patient communication in a primary care setting. *Health Psychology, 13*, 384–392.

Hall, J.A., Irish, J.T., Roter, D.L., Ehrlich, C.M., & Miller, L.H. (1994b). Satisfaction, gender, and communication in medical visits. *Medical Care, 32*, 1216–1231.

Hall, J.A., Milburn, M.A., Roter, D.L., & Daltroy, L.H. (1998). Why are sicker patients less satisfied with their medical care? Tests of two explanatory models. *Health Psychology, 17*, 70–75.

Hall, J.A., & Roter, D.L. (2002). Do patients talk differently to male and female physicians? A meta-analytic review. *Patient Education and Counseling, 48*, 217–224.

Hall, J.A., Roter, D.L., Blanch, D.C., & Frankel, R.M. (2009). Nonverbal sensitivity in medical students: Implications for clinical interactions. *Journal of General Internal Medicine, 24*, 1217–1222.

Hall, J.A., Roter, D.L., & Katz, N.R. (1988). Meta-analysis of correlates of provider behavior in medical encounters. *Medical Care, 26*, 657–675.

Hall, J.A., Roter, D.L., Milburn, M.A., & Daltroy, L.H. (1996). Patients' health as a predictor of physician and patient behavior in medical visits: A synthesis of four studies. *Medical Care, 34*, 1205–1218.

Hall, J.A., Roter, D.L., & Rand, C.S. (1981). Communication of affect between patient and physician. *Journal Health and Social Behavior, 11*, 18–30.

Hall, J.A., & Schmid Mast, M. (2009). Five ways of being "theoretical": Applications to provider-patient communication research. *Patient Education and Counseling, 74*, 282–286.

Hargraves, J.L., Wilson, I.B., Zaslavsky, A., James, C., Walker, J.D., Rogers, G., et al. (2001). Adjusting for patient characteristics when analyzing reports from patients about hospital care. *Medical Care, 39*, 635–641.

Harrington, J., Noble, L.M., & Newman, S.P. (2004). Improving patients' communication with doctors: A systematic review of intervention studies. *Patient Education and Counseling, 52*, 7–16.

Haskard, K.B., Williams, S.L., DiMatteo, M.R., Heritage, J., & Rosenthal, R. (2008). The provider's voice: Patient satisfaction and the content-filtered speech of nurses and physicians in primary medical care. *Journal of Nonverbal Behavior, 32*, 1–20.

Haskard Zolnierek, K.M., & DiMatteo, M.R. (2009). Physician communication and patient adherence to treatment: A meta-analysis. *Medical Care, 47*, 826–834.

Hasselkus, B.R. (1994). Three-track care: Older patients, family member, and physician in the medical visit. *Journal of Aging Studies, 8*, 291–307.

Haug, M., & Lavin, B. (1983). *Consumerism in medicine: Challenging physician authority*. Beverly Hills, CA: Sage.

Haynes, R.B., Taylor, D.W., & Sackett, D.L. (1979). *Compliance in health care*. Baltimore: Johns Hopkins University Press.

Henbest, R.J., & Stewart, M.A. (1989). Patient-centeredness in the consultation I: A method for measurement. *Family Practice: An International Journal, 6*, 249–253.

Hibbard, J.H., & Weeks, E.C. (1985). Consumer use of physician fee information. *Journal of Health and Human Resources Administration, 7*, 321–335.

Hibbard, J.H., & Weeks, E.C. (1987). Consumerism in health care: Prevalence and predictors. *Medical Care, 25*, 1019–1032.

Hooper, E.M., Comstock, L.M., Goodwin, J.M., & Goodwin, J.S. (1982). Patient characteristics that influence physician behavior. *Medical Care, 20*, 630–638.

Inui, T.S., & Carter, W.B. (1985). Problems and prospects for health services research on provider patient communication. *Medical Care, 23*, 521–538.

Inui, T.S., Carter, W.B., Kukull, W.A., & Haigh, V.H. (1982). Outcome-based doctor–patient interaction analysis: I. Comparison of techniques. *Medical Care, 10*, 535–549.

Ishikawa, H., Roter, D., Yamazaki, Y., & Takayama, T. (2005). Physician-elderly patient-companion communication and roles of companions in Japanese geriatric encounters. *Social Science and Medicine, 60*, 2307–2320.

Jenkinson, C. (Ed.). (1994). *Measuring health and medical outcomes*. London: UCL Press.

Kalet, A., Earp, J., & Kowlowitz, V. (1992). How well do faculty evaluate the interviewing skills of medical students? *Journal of General Internal Medicine, 7*, 499–505.

Kaplan, S.H., Gandek, B., Greenfield, S., Rogers, W., & Ware, J.E. (1995). Patient and visit characteristics related to physicians' participatory decision-making style: Results from the Medical Outcomes Study. *Medical Care, 33*, 1176–1183.

Kaplan, S.H., Greenfield, S., & Ware, J.E., Jr. (1989). Assessing the effects of physician–patient interactions on the outcomes of chronic disease. *Medical Care, 27*, S110–S127.

Keeler, E.B., Solomon, D.H., Beck, J.C., Mendenhall, R.C., & Kane, R.L. (1982). Effect of patient age on duration of medical encounter with physicians. *Medical Care, 20*, 1101–1108.

Kiesler, D.J., & Auerbach, S.M. (2006). Optimal matches of patient preferences for information, decision-making and interpersonal behavior: Evidence, models and interventions. *Patient Education and Counseling, 61,* 319–341.

Korsch, B.M., Gozzi, E.K., & Francis, V. (1968). Gaps in doctor–patient communication: I. Doctor–patient interaction and patient satisfaction. *Pediatrics, 42,* 855–871.

Krupat, E., Fancey, M., & Cleary, P.D. (2000). Information and its impact on satisfaction among surgical patients. *Social Science and Medicine, 51,* 1817–1825.

Krupat, E., Frankel, R., Stein, T., & Irish, J. (2006). The Four Habits Coding Scheme: validation of an instrument to assess clinicians' communication behavior. *Patient Education and Counseling, 62,* 38–45.

Krupat, E., Rosenkranz, S.L., Yeager, C.M., Barnard, K., Putnam, S.M., & Inui, T.S. (2000). The practice orientations of physicians and patients: The effect of doctor–patient congruence on satisfaction. *Patient Education and Counseling, 39,* 49–59.

Kurz, S.M., Silverman, J.D., & Draper, J.D. (1998). *Teaching and learning communication skills in medicine.* Oxford, England: Radcliffe Medical Press.

Lazare, A., Putnam, S.M., & Lipkin, M. (1995). Three functions of the medical interview. In M. Lipkin, S. Putnam, & A. Lazare (Eds.), *The medical interview: Clinical care, education, and research* (pp. 3–19). New York: Springer-Verlag.

Levinson, W., Frankel, R.M., Roter, D., & Drum, M. (2006). How much do surgeons like their patients? *Patient Education and Counseling, 61,* 429–434.

Levenstein, J.H., McCracken, E.C., McWhinney, I.R., Stewart M.A., & Brown, J.B. (1986). The patient-centered clinical method. I. A model for the doctor–patient interaction in family medicine. *Family Practice, 3,* 24–30

Levinson, W., Roter, D.L., Mullooly, J., Dull, V., & Frankel, R. (1997). Doctor–patient communication: A critical link to malpractice in surgeons and primary care physicians. *Journal of the American Medical Association, 277,* 553–559.

Lipkin, M., Putnam, S., & Lazare, A. (Eds.). (1995). *The medical interview: Clinical care, education, and research.* New York: Springer-Verlag.

Localio, A.R., Lawthers, A.G., & Brennan, T.A. (1991). Relation between malpractice claims and adverse events due to negligence: Results of the Harvard medical practice study III. *New England Journal of Medicine, 325,* 245–251.

Maguire, P., Fairburn, S., & Fletcher, C. (1986). Consultation skills of young doctors: Benefits of feedback training in interviewing as students persist. *British Medical Journal, 292,* 1573–1576.

Mann, S., Sripathy, K., Siegler, E., Davidow, A., Lipkin, M., & Roter, D.L. (2001). The medical interview: Differences between adult and geriatric outpatients. *Journal of the American Geriatric Society, 49,* 65–71.

Marshall, G.N., Hays, R.D., Sherbourne, C.D., & Wells, K.B. (1993). The structure of patient satisfaction with outpatient medical care. *Psychological Assessment, 5,* 477–483.

Marvel, M.K., Epstein, R.M., Flowers, K., & Beckman, H.B. (1999). Soliciting the patient's agenda: Have we improved? *Journal of the American Medical Association, 281,* 283–287.

McWhinney, I. (1988). Through clinic method to a more humanistic medicine. In K. White (Ed.), *The task of medicine: Dialogue at Wickenburg* (pp. 218–231). Menlo Park, CA: Henry J. Kaiser Family Foundation.

McWhinney, I. (1989). The need for a transformed clinical method. In M. Stewart, & D. Roter (Eds.), *Communicating with medical patients* (pp. 25–40). Newbury Park, CA: Sage.

Mead, N., & Bower, P. (2000). Measuring patient-centeredness: A comparison of three observation-based instruments. *Patient Education and Counseling, 39,* 71–80.

Meeuwesen, L., Schaap, C., & van der Staak, C. (1991). Verbal analysis of doctor–patient communication. *Social Science and Medicine, 10,* 1143–1150.

Meyer, T.J., & Mark, M.M. (1995). Effects of psychosocial interventions with adult cancer patients: A meta-analysis of randomized experiments. *Health Psychology, 14,* 101–108.

Michie, S., Miles, J., & Weinman, J. (2003). Patient-centredness in chronic illness: What is it and does it matter? *Patient Education and Counseling, 51,* 197–206.

Mishler, E.G. (1984). *The discourse of medicine: Dialectics of medical interviews.* Norwood, NJ: Ablex.

Novack, D.H., Dube, C., & Goldstein, M.G. (1992). Teaching medical interviewing: A basic course on interviewing and the physician–patient relationship. *Archives of Internal Medicine, 152,* 1814–1820.

Ong, L.M.L., de Haes, J.C.J.M., Hoos, A.M., & Lammes, F.B. (1995). Doctor–patient communication: A review of the literature. *Social Science and Medicine, 40,* 903–918.

Ong, L.M.L., Visser, M.R.M., Lammes, F.B., & de Haes, J.C.J.M. (2000). Doctor–patient communication and cancer patients' quality of life and satisfaction. *Patient Education and Counseling, 41,* 145–156.

Orth, J.E., Stiles, W.B., Scherwitz, L., Hennrikus, D., & Vallbona, C. (1987). Patient exposition and provider explanation in routine interviews and hypertensive patients' blood pressure control. *Health Psychology, 6,* 29–42.

Parsons, T. (1951). *The social system.* Glencoe, IL: Free Press.

Pendleton, D.A., & Bochner, S. (1980). The communication of medical information in general practice consultations as a function of patients' social class. *Social Science and Medicine, 14A,* 669–673.

Plato. (1961). (E.J. Emanuel, Trans.). In E. Hamilton, & H. Cairns (Eds.), *The collected dialogues.* Princeton, NJ: Princeton University Press.

President's Commission for the Study of Ethical Problems in Medicine and Biomedical and Behavioral Research. (1982). *Making health care decisions and ethical and legal implications of informed consent in the patient-practitioner relationship* (Vol. 1). Washington, DC: U.S. Government Printing Office.

Prohaska, T.R., & Glasser, M. (1996). Patients' views of family involvement in medical care decisions and encounters. *Research on Aging, 18,* 52–69.

Putnam, S.M., Stiles, W.B., Jacob, M.C., & James, S.A. (1988). Teaching the medical interview: An intervention study. *Journal of General Internal Medicine, 3,* 38–47.

Quill, T.E. (1983). Partnerships in patient care: A contractual approach. *Annals of Internal Medicine, 98,* 228–234.

Radecki, S.E., Kane, R.L., Solomon, D.H., Mendenhall, R.C., & Beck, J.C. (1988). Do physicians spend less time with older patients? *Journal of the American Geriatrics Society, 36,* 713–718.

Rao, J.K., Anderson, L.A., Inui, T.S., & Frankel, R.M. (2007). Communication interventions make a difference in conversations between physicians and patients: A systematic review of the evidence. *Medical Care, 45,* 340–349.

Reichardt, C.S., & Cook, T.D. (1969). *Qualitative and quantitative methods in evaluation research.* Beverly Hills, CA: Sage.

Robbins, J.M., Kirmayer, L.J., Cathébras, P., Yaffe, M.J., & Dworkind, M. (1994). Physician characteristics and the recognition of depression and anxiety in primary care. *Medical Care, 32,* 795–812.

Rogers, P.G., & Bullman, W.R. (1995). Prescription medicine compliance: A review of the baseline of knowledge. A report of the National Council on Patient Information and Education. *Journal of Pharmacoepidemiology, 2,* 3–36.

Rosenthal, R., & Rubin, D.B. (1978). Interpersonal expectancy effects: The first 345 studies. *Behavioral and Brain Sciences, 3,* 377–386.

Ross, C.E., Mirowsky, J., & Duff, R.S. (1982). Physician status characteristics and client satisfaction in two types of medical practice. *Journal of Health and Social Behavior, 23,* 317–329.

Roter, D. (1977). Patient participation in the patient-provider interaction: The effects of patient question asking on the quality of interaction, satisfaction, and compliance. *Health Education Monographs, 5,* 281–315.

Roter, D. (1987). An exploration of health education's responsibility for a partnership model of client-provider relations. *Patient Education and Counseling, 9,* 25–31.

Roter, D.L. (2000a). The enduring and evolving nature of the patient–physician relationship. *Patient Education and Counseling, 39,* 5–15.

Roter, D.L. (2000b). The medical visit context of treatment decision-making and the therapeutic relationship. *Health Expectations, 3,* 17–25.

Roter, D.L. (2003). Observations on methodological and measurement challenges in the assessment of communication during medical exchanges. *Patient Education and Counseling, 50,* 17–21.

Roter, D.L., Cole, K.A., Kern, D.E., Barker, L.R., & Grayson, M. (1990). An evaluation of residency training in interviewing skills and the psychosocial domain of medical practice. *Journal of General Internal Medicine, 5,* 347–354.

Roter, D., & Frankel, R. (1992). Quantitative and qualitative approaches to the evaluation of the medical dialogue. *Social Science and Medicine, 34,* 1097–1103.

Roter, D.L., Frankel, R.M., Hall, J.A., & Sluyter, D. (2006). The expression of emotion through nonverbal behavior in medical visits: Mechanisms and outcomes. *Journal of General Internal Medicine, 21,* S28–34.

Roter, D.L., & Hall, J.A. (1991). Health education theory: An application to the process of patient-provider communication. *Health Education Research Theory and Practice, 6,* 185–193.

Roter, D.L., & Hall, J.A. (2004). Physician gender and patient-centered communication: A critical review of empirical research. *Annual Review of Public Health, 25,* 497–519.

Roter, D.L., & Hall, J.A. (2006). *Doctors talking with patients/patients talking with doctors: Improving communication in medical visits* (2nd ed.). Westport, CT: Praeger.

Roter, D.L., Hall, J.A., & Aoki, Y. (2002). Physician gender effects in medical communication: A meta-analytic review. *Journal of the American Medical Association, 288,* 756–764.

Roter, D.L., Hall, J.A., & Katz, N.R. (1987). Relations between physicians' behaviors and analogue patients' satisfaction, recall, and impressions. *Medical Care, 25,* 437–451.

Roter, D.L., Hall, J.A., & Katz, N.R. (1988). Patient–physician communication: A descriptive summary of the literature. *Patient Education and Counseling, 12,* 99–119.

Roter, D.L., Hall, J.A., Kern, D.E., Barker, L.R., Cole, K.A., & Roca, R.P. (1995). Improving physicians' interviewing skills and reducing patients' emotional distress. *Archives of Internal Medicine, 155,* 1877–1884.

Roter, D.L., Hall, J.A., Merisca, R., Nordstrom, B., Cretin, D., & Svarstad, B. (1998). Effectiveness of interventions to improve patient compliance: A meta-analysis. *Medical Care, 36,* 1138–1161.

Roter, D.L., & Larson, S. (2002). The Roter Interaction Analysis System (RIAS): Utility and Flexibility for Analysis of Medical Interactions. *Patient Education and Counseling, 46,* 243–251.

Roter, D., Lipkin, M., Jr., & Korsgaard, A. (1991). Gender differences in patients' and physicians' communication during primary care medical visits. *Medical Care, 29,* 1083–1093.

Roter, D.L., & McNeilis, K.S. (2003). The nature of the therapeutic relationship and the assessment and consequences of its discourse in routine medical visits. In T. Thompson, A. Dorsey, K. Miller, & R. Parrott (Eds.) *Handbook of health communication* (pp. 121–140). Mahway, NJ: Lawrence Erlbaum.

Roter, D.L., Stewart, M., Putnam, S., Lipkin, M., Stiles W., & Inui, T. (1997). Communication patterns of primary care physicians. *Journal of the American Medical Association, 270,* 350–355.

Sacks, H., Schegloff, E.A., & Jefferson, G. (1974). A simplest systematic for the organization of turn-taking for conversation. *Language, 50,* 696–735.

Schmid Mast, M. (2007). On the importance of nonverbal communication in the physician–patient interaction. *Patient Education and Counseling, 67,* 315–318.

Schmid Mast, M., Hall, J.A., Klöckner, C., & Choi, E. (2008). Physician gender affects how physician nonverbal behavior is related to patient satisfaction. *Medical Care, 46,* 1212–1218.

Schneider, C.E. (1998). *The practice of autonomy: Patients, doctors, and medical decisions.* New York: Oxford University Press.

Shorter, E. (1985). *Bedside manners.* New York: Simon and Schuster.

Smith, R.C., Marshall-Dorsey, A.A., Osborn, G.G., Shebroe, V., Lyles, J.S., Stoffelmayr, B.E., et al. (2000). Evidence-based guidelines for teaching patient-centered interviewing. *Patient Education and Counseling, 39,* 27–36.

Steele, D.J., Jackson, T.C., & Gutmann, M.C. (1990). Have you been taking your pills? The adherence monitoring sequence in the medical interview. *Journal of Family Practice, 30,* 294–299.

Stewart, A.L., & Ware, J.E., Jr. (Eds.). (1992). *Measuring functioning and well-being: The medical outcomes study approach.* Durham, NC: Duke University Press.

Stewart, M. (1983). Patient characteristics which are related to the doctor–patient interaction. *Family Practice, 1,* 30–35.

Stewart, M.A. (1984). What is a successful doctor–patient interview? A study of interactions and outcomes. *Social Science and Medicine, 19,* 167–175.

Stewart, M. (1995). Patient-doctor relationships over time. In M. Stewart, J.B. Brown, W.W. Weston, I. McWhinney, C.L. McWilliam, & T.R. Freeman (Eds.), *Patient-centered medicine: Transforming the clinical method* (p. 216–228). Thousand Oaks, CA: Sage.

Stewart, M.A. (1996). Effective physician–patient communication and health outcomes: A review. *Canadian Medical Association Journal, 152,* 1423–1433.

Stewart, M., Brown, J.B., Weston, W.W., McWhinney, I., McWilliam, C.L., & Freeman, T.R. (Eds.). (1995). *Patient-centered medicine: Transforming the clinical method.* Thousand Oaks, CA: Sage.

Stewart, M., Brown, J.B., Donner, A., McWhinney, I.R., Oates, J., & Weston, W. (1996). *The impact of patient-centered care on patient outcomes in family practice.* Final report, Health Services Research, Ministry of Health, Ontario, Canada.

Stiles, W.B. (1992). *Describing talk: A taxonomy of verbal response modes*. Newbury Park, CA: Sage.

Stiles, W.B., & White, M.L. (1981). Parent-child interaction in the laboratory: Effects of role, task, and child behavior pathology on verbal response mode use. *Journal of Abnormal Child Psychology, 9*, 229–241.

Stone, G.C. (1979). Patient compliance and the role of the expert. *Journal of Social Issues, 35*(1), 34–59.

Suchman, A.L., Roter, D.L., Green, M., & Lipkin, M., Jr. (1993). Physician satisfaction with primary care office visits. *Medical Care, 31*, 1083–1092.

Swenson, S.L., Buell, S., Zettler, P., White, M., Ruston, D.C., & Lo, B. (2004). Patient-centered communication: Do patients really prefer it? *Journal of General Internal Medicine, 19*, 1069–1079.

Szasz, P.S., & Hollender, M.H. (1956). A contribution to the philosophy of medicine: The basic model of the doctor–patient relationship. *Archives of Internal Medicine, 97*, 585–592.

Tates, K., & Meeuwesen, L. (2001). Doctor-parent-child communication: A (re)view of the literature. *Social Science and Medicine, 52*, 839–851.

Thi, P.L.N., Briançon, S., Empereur, F., & Guillemin, F. (2002). Factors determining inpatient satisfaction with care. *Social Science and Medicine, 54*, 493–504.

Thompson, T.L. (1994). Interpersonal communication and health care. In M.L. Knapp, & G.R. Miller (Eds.), *Handbook of interpersonal communication* (2nd ed., pp. 696–725). Thousand Oaks, CA: Sage.

Tresolini, C.P., and the Pew-Fetzer Task Force on Advancing Psychosocial Health Education. (1994). *Health professions education and relationship-centered care*. San Francisco: Pew Health Professions Commission.

Tuckett, D., Boulton, M., Olson, C., & Williams, A. (1985). *Meetings between experts*. New York: Tavistock.

Van Dulmen, A.M., Verhaak, P.F.M., & Bilo, H.J.G. (1997). Shifts in doctor–patient communication during a series of outpatient consultations in non-insulin-dependent diabetes mellitus. *Patient Education and Counseling, 30*, 227–237.

van Ryn, M. (2002). Research on the provider contribution to race/ethnicity disparities in medical care. *Medical Care, 40*, I140–I151.

Waitzkin, H. (1985). Information giving in medical care. *Journal of Health and Social Behavior, 26*, 81–101.

Wallen, J., Waitzkin, H., & Stoeckle, J.D. (1979). Physician stereotypes about female health and illness. *Women and Health, 4*, 135–146.

Wallerstein, N., & Bernstein, E. (1988). Empowerment education: Freire's ideas adapted to health education. *Health Education Quarterly, 15*, 379–394.

Wasserman, R.C., Inui, T.S., Barriatua, R.D., Carter, W.B., & Lippincott, P. (1984). Pediatric clinicians' support for parents makes a difference: An outcome-based analysis of clinician-parent interaction. *Pediatrics, 74*, 1047–1053.

White, K. (1988). Physician and professional perspectives. In K. White (Ed.), *The task of medicine: Dialogue at Wickenburg* (pp. 30–46). Menlo Park, CA: Henry J. Kaiser Family Foundation.

Williams, G.C., Freedman, Z.R., & Deci, E.L. (1998). Supporting autonomy to motivate patients with diabetes for glucose control. *Diabetes Care, 21*, 1644–1651.

Williams, G.C., & Deci, E.L. (1998). The importance of supporting autonomy in medical education. *Annals of Internal Medicine, 129*, 303–308.

Williams, G.C., & Deci, E.L. (2001). Activating patients for smoking cessation through physician autonomy support. *Medical Care, 39*, 813–823.

Williams, S., Weinman, J., & Dale, J. (1998). Doctor–patient communication and patient satisfaction: A review. *Family Practice, 15*, 480–492.

Wissow, L.S., Roter, D., Bauman, L.J., Crain, E., Kercsmar, C., Weiss, K., et al. (1998). Patient-provider communication during the emergency department care of children with asthma. *Medical Care, 36*, 1439–1450.

Wissow, L.S., Roter, D., Larson, S., Wang, M-C, Hwang, W.T., & Johnson, R. (2000, July). *Longitudinal pediatric care and discussion of maternal psychosocial issues*. Paper presented at the Mental Health Services research meetings, Washington, DC. (Abstract pages 52–53).

Wissow, L.S., Roter, D.L., & Wilson, M.E.H. (1994). Pediatrician interview style and mothers' disclosure of psychosocial issues. *Pediatrics, 93*, 289–295.

Wolff, J.L., & Roter, D.L. (2008). Hidden in plain sight: Medical visit companions as a resource for vulnerable older adults. *Archives of Internal Medicine, 168*, 1409–1415.

Young, M., & Klingle, R.S. (1996). Silent partners in medical care: A cross-cultural study of patient participation. *Health Communication, 8*, 29–53.

# Aging and Health

Karen S. Rook, Susan Turk Charles, *and* Jutta Heckhausen

**Abstract**

The biopsychosocial model of health views health and illness in old age as resulting not only from biological and physical factors but also from the cumulative effects of a lifetime of psychological, social, and behavioral processes. This model recognizes the biological trajectory of decline throughout the adult lifespan and the fact that physical changes increase older adults' susceptibility to acute and chronic conditions. In addition, this model acknowledges that psychological and social processes interact over time with biological changes to influence physical functioning, onset and progression of disease, and adaptation to illness. The chapter is organized in three main sections. The first section emphasizes the biological component of the model, discussing trajectories of physical functioning and health in old age, including physical decline, morbidity, and mortality. The second section focuses on the psychosocial component of the biopsychosocial model, emphasizing psychosocial factors that influence physical health and functioning in old age. The chapter concludes by discussing two very different scenarios that researchers have projected for the health of future cohorts of older adults.

**Keywords:** Older adults, elderly, biopsychosocial model, aging, health, life expectancy

In the past century, economically developed nations experienced unprecedented changes in the age structure of their populations, as a result of improved public health measures and medical advances that extended life expectancy. Throughout human history, there have always been individuals who lived to an advanced age, but such survival was unusual before the 20th century. During the 20th century, life expectancy increased markedly and birth rates declined, ushering in an era of dramatic societal aging among developed nations. Since 1900, for example, the total population of the United States tripled in size, but the population of people over age 65 grew 12-fold (American Administration on Aging [AAA], 2009). Average life expectancy at birth in the United States was 48 years in 1900, whereas it is now 74.8 years for men and 80.1 years for women (Hoyert, Kung, & Smith, 2005). Similarly, in 1900, only 4% of the population in the United States was older than 65 years of age, but

that figure has risen to 12.4% and is expected to climb to 20% by the year 2030 (AAA, 2009). With the overall growth of the population, these percentage increases represent a very substantial, and rapidly growing, increase in the absolute numbers of people living to age 65 and beyond.

Accompanying this demographic shift has been a change in the major threats to health, and corresponding changes in medical research and treatment. Infectious and parasitic acute illnesses have been replaced by chronic, degenerative illnesses as the dominant health concerns in modern societies, and it is older adults who are most likely to experience chronic conditions (Centers for Disease Control and Prevention & The Merck Institute of Aging & Health [CDC/MIAH], 2007). Many of these chronic conditions, moreover, have roots in longstanding behaviors or lifestyles that compromise health over time. The traditional medical model, in which disease is conceptualized as the result of specific pathogens or physical changes that can be treated by medical technology, is not well suited to address the chronic conditions that contribute to morbidity and mortality in later adulthood. Instead, health researchers have turned to the biopsychosocial model of health, in which health and illness in old age are viewed as resulting not only from biological and physical factors, but also from the cumulative effects of a lifetime of psychological, social, and behavioral processes (Engel, 1977; Ryff & Singer, 2009). This model recognizes the biological trajectory of decline throughout the adult lifespan and the fact that physical changes increase older adults' susceptibility to acute and chronic conditions. In addition, this model acknowledges that psychological and social processes interact over time with biological changes to influence physical functioning, onset and progression of disease, and adaptation to illness (Engel, 1977).

The biopsychosocial model can be applied to people of all ages, but this chapter focuses on older adults. The chapter is organized in three main sections. In the first section, we emphasize the biological component of the model, discussing trajectories of physical functioning and health in old age, including physical decline, morbidity, and mortality. We provide illustrations of normative changes that occur with age in the functioning of organ and sensory systems, noting the considerable variability in aging processes that exists within and across people. We then consider how these primary aging processes affect older adults' vulnerability to chronic illnesses and mortality. This leads to a discussion of how aging processes affect older adults' experiences of illness and medical intervention, as well as their perceptions of their physical health and their ability to carry out daily activities.

The second section of the chapter focuses on the psychosocial component of the biopsychosocial model, emphasizing psychosocial factors that influence physical health and functioning in old age. We approach this complex topic by illustrating several classes of psychosocial factors that influence health in later life, including ones that (a) operate very early in life to increase the risk of illness and disability in later adulthood, (b) emerge in later adulthood to influence concurrent health status, (c) influence adaptation to illness and disease in later adulthood, and (d) influence the issues involved in, and optimal strategies for, health promotion and rehabilitation in late adulthood. A review of research that bears on these different classes of psychosocial factors is beyond the scope of the chapter,

but we illustrate each one with a relevant research example.

We conclude by discussing two very different scenarios that researchers have projected for the health of future cohorts of older adults. One scenario forecasts that future increases in life expectancy are likely to be accompanied by corresponding gains in health and declines in disability. Another scenario projects that future increases in life expectancy are unlikely to be unaccompanied by such health gains and, instead, will only lengthen the period of illness and disability in later life. These starkly different scenarios should serve as a call to arms for researchers to contribute knowledge to efforts to forestall the darker forecast. We link our examination of these different scenarios to a discussion of alternative conceptions of what constitutes successful aging. As will be seen, health psychologists have an important role to play in identifying factors that slow or postpone chronic illness, decrease the severity and duration of disability, and help to preserve well-being even when functional limitations develop in later life.

Given the breadth and complexity of the topic of health and aging, this chapter necessarily considers some issues at the expense of others. We emphasize findings and conclusions derived from research conducted primarily in modern, economically developed nations, and these findings may not generalize to less developed nations. Similarly, we provide only a limited treatment of the substantial heterogeneity that exists in the elderly population, although we highlight well-documented sociodemographic variations in health and illness in later life. Finally, we emphasize the individual level of analysis, given our background as psychologists and the focus of this volume on health psychology. A more complete treatment of the topic of aging and health ultimately will require integration of research on individual and social structural factors that interact to influence health and functioning over the lifespan (Riley, 1998).

## Physical Functioning and Health in Old Age

It is an unavoidable fact that biological and physiological functioning decline throughout the adult lifespan. Considerable intra- and interindividual variability exists in the rate and extent of change, however, making these declines difficult to characterize. Organ systems and functional abilities decline at different rates, and people also vary in the rate and extent of physical changes they experience over time. Complicating matters further, the implications of such declines for susceptibility to illness and for daily activities also vary. Some declines are unalterable, whereas others are potentially reversible. In addition, some declines can be mitigated by compensatory gains in other areas of physiological functioning. The changes that accompany normal aging, referred to as primary aging, generally can be characterized as relatively benign (M. E. Williams, 1994); these changes should be distinguished from pathological processes that accompany disease, or changes referred to as secondary aging (Birren & Cunningham, 1985; see Blumenthal, 2003, for a more complete discussion of the aging–disease distinction).

## Primary Aging

Age-related declines in the functioning of sensory and organ systems have been documented extensively, with many declines beginning as early as the middle to late 20s (see review by Whitbourne, 1996). For example, hearing changes with age, making it more difficult to understand sounds at higher frequencies, and vision changes, resulting in greater difficulty focusing on close objects and seeing under conditions of glare or low illumination (Fozard & Gordon-Salant, 2001; Schieber, 2006). The size and efficiency of many organs decline gradually with age. Lung capacity, for example, diminishes by about 40% from age 20 to 70 (NIA, 1996). Such decreases in organ size or capacity can signal changes in biological functioning. For example, the thymus gland shrinks considerably with age, resulting in fewer or less efficient T cells in the bloodstream. This decrease in a gland important to the immune system may contribute to increased susceptibility to, and prolonged recovery from, infections in later life (Terpenning & Bradley, 1991).

Primary aging also includes declines in higher-order regulatory processes, which may influence older adults' susceptibility to environmental challenges and other stressors. *Homeostasis* refers to the automatic and constantly occurring adjustments that the human body makes to maintain equilibrium, such as adjusting body temperature to changes in room temperature. With advancing age, maintaining homeostasis becomes more difficult, and this may increase older adults' vulnerability to morbidity and mortality. Greater difficulty regulating body temperatures with age, for example, may lead to conditions that partly account for the elevated death rates among older adults during significant heat waves (Semenza et al., 1996).

## VARIABILITY AND MALLEABILITY OF PHYSICAL DECLINE

Declines in organ functioning and homeostatic processes tend to be gradual, however, and they also vary considerably within and across individuals (Ryff & Singer, 2009). For example, an older person may exhibit marked decline in one area, such as pulmonary functioning, but little decline in other areas. Chronological age per se is an imperfect predictor of the nature or extent of decline in physiological functioning, as some older individuals exhibit few of the typical changes associated with aging, whereas others exhibit many changes.

In addition, declines in functioning in some areas may be offset by gains or compensatory responses in other areas. For example, among adults who are free of heart disease, the ability of the heart to pump blood rapidly during periods of cardiovascular demand (such as exercise) declines with age, but overall blood flow declines relatively little because the volume of blood pumped with each stroke increases with age (NIA, 2005). Similarly, although age-related declines in brain volume, neurotransmitter production, and neuronal connective structures (axons, dendrites, synapses) are common, compensatory changes within the brain may help to mitigate negative effects on cognitive functioning (Raz, 2000; Reuter-Lorenz & Lustig, 2005). The growth of new dendrites, for example, improves neuronal connectivity, and bilateral frontal lobe activation improves performance on some cognitive tasks (Cabeza, Anderson, Locantore, & McIntosh, 2002; Greenwood, 2007). Moreover, lifestyle factors, such as physical exercise that reduce risks for a broad range of chronic illnesses in later life, may also slow or reverse some of the declines in physical functioning that often occur in later life. For example, in the absence of exercise, muscle mass declines by more than 20% for both men and women from age 30 to age 70, but regular exercise can slow the rate of age-related muscle loss (NIA, 2006).

## RESERVE CAPACITY AND EVERYDAY FUNCTIONING

The existence of a reserve capacity in most organ systems minimizes the impact of common age-related declines on everyday activities. This extra capacity allows organ systems to function at four to ten times their normal capacity, if needed, under stressful conditions (Fries & Crapo, 1981). Kidney functioning declines by 30% after age 30, for example, but the remaining capacity is more than adequate to allow wastes to be extracted from the bloodstream under ordinary circumstances (NIA, 1996). In the context of very stressful circumstances or unusually challenging environmental conditions, however, the demands on an organ system may overwhelm even this reserve capacity, leading to organ failure. Cardiovascular functioning that is sufficient to allow an older person to take daily walks, for example, may be insufficient to allow the person to shovel snow or lift heavy boxes without increasing the risk of a heart attack. Thus, despite common declines in physical functioning, older adults often do not experience substantial adverse effects on their ability to carry out daily activities (until advanced old age, as we discuss later). Such adverse effects become evident most often when older adults exert themselves beyond their customary levels of activity, such as walking up a steep flight of stairs or fighting an illness.

Reserve capacity is not a static resource, however, but tends to decline with age (Fries, 1980; Hayflick, 1998). This decline may be partly responsible for the fact that older adults are more adversely affected by, and even more likely to die from, conditions that tend not to be lethal at younger ages, such as influenza or pneumonia (Koivula, Sten, & Makela, 1999).

## PRIMARY AGING AND ACUTE ILLNESS

Primary aging refers to age-related declines in physical functioning, not disease processes. Declines in reserve capacity and homeostasis make older adults more vulnerable, however, to the effects of acute disease processes (Sahyoun, Lentzner, Hoyert, & Robinson, 2001). Acute illnesses tend to be more common in young adulthood, but they often affect older adults more severely. More than 5% of deaths among older adults are attributable to conditions such as pneumonia, influenza, and septicemia, and some researchers believe that the death rate from these conditions has increased in recent years (Sahyoun et al., 2001). Some epidemiologists have cautioned, moreover, that infectious diseases may be reemerging as significant causes of morbidity and mortality in economically developed nations due to increased international trade and migration, ecological disruption, and the spread of antibiotic-resistant pathogens (Barrett, Kuzawa, McDade, & Armelagos, 1998). If this should prove to be the case, existing views of the dominant threats to health in later life might need to be revised.

## Secondary Aging

The fact that progressive declines in physiological functioning are common in later adulthood makes it challenging to distinguish changes that reflect intrinsic processes of aging (primary aging) from those that reflect the accumulated effects of disease, disuse, or exposure to environmental hazards (secondary aging). For example, osteoarthritis was once considered a normative age change, or the result of primary aging (Bennett, Waine, & Bauer, 1942). Only in the past 20 years did researchers determine that this condition represents a disease process that is associated with but not caused by age (e.g., Dequeker, 1989; Oddis, 1996). Atherosclerosis, in contrast, is now regarded as an essentially universal change that occurs with advancing age, or an outcome of primary aging (NIA, 1996). Distinguishing between changes that result from primary aging and those that result from secondary aging requires longitudinal studies that span decades (T. F. Williams, 1992).

Early and influential examples of longitudinal studies undertaken for this purpose include the Duke Longitudinal Study of Aging (Busse et al., 1985) and the Baltimore Longitudinal Study of Aging (NIA, 1996, 2008; Shock et al., 1984). Both studies were initiated in the 1950s, and both administered extensive batteries of physiological and psychological tests to participants on a regular basis over a period of decades. The Baltimore Longitudinal Study, for example, which began in 1958 and is still ongoing, brings participants ranging in age from their 20s to their 90s to Baltimore every two years to undergo as many as 100 different assessments of physiological, psychological, and social functioning; the study has yielded more than 800 scientific papers to date (NIA, 1996). Longitudinal studies have proved to be crucial to efforts to identify the timing and predictors of significant health-related changes in later life, such as the transitions between physical decline, functional impairment, and disability, as well as possible transitions between disease and recovery (Verbrugge, Reoma, & Gruber-Baldini, 1994). For example, Fozard, Metter, and Brant (1990) observed that major transitions in the rate of decline in strength occur in young and middle adulthood, rather than in old age.

### ALLOSTATIC LOAD

The cumulative effects of stressors experienced over the course of a lifetime may contribute to secondary aging by causing permanent shifts in the organism's ability to regulate its physiological parameters (such as blood pressure or immune functioning) in response to external demands (Robinson-Whelen, Kiecolt-Glaser, & Glaser, 2000). Allostatic load is defined as the accumulated wear and tear on the body that results from having to adapt repeatedly to physical and psychological stressors (McEwen, 2006). It is commonly measured by relatively stable indicators of physiological reactivity to physiological dysregulation, such as cholesterol levels, body mass index, glucose levels, or blood-clotting ability (McEwen, 2006): The more risk factors that are present at elevated levels, the greater the allostatic load. The precursors of high allostatic load may begin with conditions that develop relatively early in life, such as childhood obesity or hypertension. Stressful life events experienced throughout the lifespan can lead to gradual alterations in the various components of allostatic load.

The physiological toll of severe or persistent stressors affects all age groups, but allostatic load generally increases with age, with significant implications for the health of older adults. Allostatic load predicts cognitive decline and increased functional impairment among older adults (Seeman, Singer, Rowe, Horwitz, & McEwen, 1997). The generally higher allostatic load among older adults, coupled with age-related declines in reserve capacity and the ability to maintain homeostasis, can contribute to higher morbidity and mortality among older adults even when their stress levels resemble those of younger age groups.

## SECONDARY AGING AND CHRONIC ILLNESS
Secondary aging is generally attributed to the cumulative effects of disease, disuse, or exposure to hazards; as such, it is closely linked to chronic illness in later life. Chronic illnesses last for long periods of time, cannot be cured, and have the potential to interfere with daily functioning and to detract from the quality of life. Unlike acute illnesses, chronic illnesses are more common in later adulthood, and approximately 80% of adults older than 65 have at least one chronic condition (He, Sengupta, Velkoff, & DeBarros, 2005). Like acute conditions, chronic conditions tend to be associated with greater medical complications and greater restrictions of activity among older adults (CDC/MIAH, 2007). For example, having one or more chronic conditions is associated with restrictions of daily activities among fewer than 10% of people under the age of 45 as compared with 25% of those aged 65–74 and 45% of those aged 75 and older (Schiller & Bernadel, 2004). The greater prevalence of chronic health problems in later life is partly attributable to the aging of young and middle-aged adults with disabilities, but it primarily reflects the increased incidence of chronic illness in later adulthood (Lollar & Crews, 2003).

The most common chronic conditions among older men and women in the United States include arthritis, hypertension, heart disease, cancer, diabetes, and sinusitis (AAA, 2009). Sensory impairments are common, as well. Some chronic conditions are age-related, such as heart disease; others are not, such as paraplegia resulting from a spinal cord injury, but they may have significantly greater physical complications at advanced ages (e.g., Gerhard, Bergstrom, Charlifue, Menter, & Whitencck, 1993). Chronic conditions experienced in old age tend to be more disabling, to require more care, and to be more difficult to treat than the conditions that affect younger age groups (NAAS, 1999a). In fact, chronic conditions are estimated to account for about half of all disability among older adults in the United States (Merck Institute of Aging/ Gerontological Society of America [MIAH/GSA], 2002) and contribute to older adults' greater health care utilization (including hospitalization) and expenditures (AAA, 2009). Although some chronic illnesses may not impact daily life significantly (e.g., successfully controlled hypertension), others can be debilitating and can impair daily functioning (e.g., chronic obstructive pulmonary disease [COPD]).

The chronic illnesses from which older adults suffer tend to be degenerative and to develop relatively slowly over many years or decades. Chronic illness may exist at a subclinical level for many years in middle adulthood and old age before symptoms become evident or severe in late life (Fries & Crapo, 1981). For example, the onset of coronary heart disease may begin in young adulthood, with the advent of elevated cholesterol and small arterial plaques. The underlying coronary disease processes may progress with the development of larger arterial plaques in middle age before symptoms appear or adversely affect functioning. Although the progression from symptom onset to disability may unfold relatively slowly over time, this transition can be hastened by risk factors that are relatively acute, such as sudden stress or vasospasm in the case of cardiovascular disease (Kaplan, Haan, & Wallace, 1999). The extent to which age at the time of onset may influence the severity and subsequent course of a disease (e.g., development of prostate cancer at age 75 vs. age 60) is not yet fully understood (Siegler, Bastian, & Bosworth, 2001).

## COMORBIDITY
Many older adults have multiple chronic conditions, which can magnify health risks and complicate treatment. One large study of later-life comorbidity

among five chronic conditions found that 29% of the elderly participants had two or more physician-diagnosed conditions, with substantial co-occurrence of hypertension, coronary artery disease, cerebro-vascular disease, and diabetes (Fillenbaum, Pieper, Cohen, Cornoni-Huntley, & Guralnik, 2000). Among people aged 75 and older, 37% have three or more chronic conditions, compared with just 7% of people in their mid-40s to mid-50s (National Center for Health Statistics, 2007). Comorbidity magnifies health risks. Diabetes, for example, significantly increases the risk of developing fatal coronary heart disease (Huxley, Barzi, & Woodward, 2006). Similarly, the pain and stiff-ness associated with arthritis may aggravate a coexisting condition, such as diabetes, by discour-aging physical exercise. Arthritis, the inactivity to which it contributes, and its exacerbation of comorbid conditions are major sources of disabil-ity in later life (Song, Chang, & Dunlop, 2006). Mental health problems, particularly depression, often co-occur with physical health problems, which may accelerate the rate of decline and complicate treatment plans (e.g., Sullivan, Newton, Hecht, Russo, & Spertus, 2004). More generally, comor-bidity may affect the manifestation, detection, and outcomes of various health conditions (Kaplan et al., 1999).

## FRAILTY

Advancing age, coupled with declining reserves and increasing impairment across multiple organ sys-tems, increases the likelihood that an older adult will be regarded as frail. *Frailty* is characterized by wasting of the body (unintentional weight loss of 10 or more pounds), general muscular weakness, slow walking speed, limited physical activity, and reduced resistance to acute illness and emotional or physical stress (Fried et al. 2001; Gillick, 2001). These signs of decline may be present in frail older adults even in the absence of a dominant chronic illness (Fries, 2004). By some estimates, as many as 40% of adults in their 80s and older may be frail (Fried, Ferrucci, Darer, Williamson, & Anderson, 2004). Gillick (2001) described a "cycle of frailty" characterized by a pattern of declining physiological reserves that decrease an older person's ability to "withstand acute illness or emotional upheaval or physical dislocation" (p. M135). Frailty tends to worsen over time and is linked to a cascade of prob-lems that include increased risks for falls, injuries, hospitalization, nursing-home placement, and mortality (Fried et al., 2004).

## MORTALITY

The leading causes of death among adults aged 65 and older in the United States are heart disease, cancer, stroke, COPD, pneumonia and influenza, and diabetes (Himes, 2001). Together, these condi-tions account for 75% of the deaths among older adults, with just two conditions—heart disease and cancer—accounting for more than half of the deaths among older adults. Additionally, progressive declines in organ reserves make frail older adults increasingly vulnerable to small perturbations that may cause death (Fries, 2004). Fries (2004, p. M604) has referred to frailty as "the ultimate competing risk for mortality, that of 'old age.'" It is not surprising, given the association between advanced age and both chronic illness and frailty, that death is a phenomenon that is concentrated in later life in most developed nations. In the United States, for example, approximately three-quarters of all deaths occur among people aged 65 and older (Sahyoun et al., 2001).

It is important to bear in mind, of course, that death is not concentrated in later adulthood in all regions of the world. Extreme poverty and high rates of disease in many areas of the developing world have contributed to a problem of "shortevity" rather than "longevity" (Butler, 2002). In less eco-nomically developed nations, infectious diseases still figure prominently as causes of mortality, and life expectancies are correspondingly short (Butler, 2002). In the poorest countries of Africa and the Middle East, average life expectancy is only about 45 years of age (United Nations [U.N.], 2009), and the disability-adjusted life expectancy (the number of years a person can expect to live in good health) is considerably shorter, averaging only 25 years in some cases (Mathers, Sadana, Salomon, Murray, & Lopez, 2001).

Even in economically developed societies, researchers worry about the extent to which gains in life expectancy can be sustained. On the one hand, reductions in such behavioral risk factors as ciga-rette smoking contributed to significant decreases in death rates due to heart disease and stroke over the past two decades in the United States (Himes, 2001). Mortality rates for cancer also declined in recent decades for men, due largely to decreases in lung cancer attributed to reduced rates of smoking. Yet, burgeoning rates of obesity in the population cast a troubling shadow over the longevity gains observed until recently in the United States, as obe-sity elevates the risk for a number of serious chronic conditions (Wadden, Brownell, & Foster, 2002).

In fact, a recent analysis of the implications of high rates of childhood obesity for life expectancy offered the chilling forecast that the current generation of children may be the first in modern history to lead sicker and shorter lives than those of their parents (Olshansky et al., 2005).

## Disease Manifestation and Perceptions

The manifestations and perceptions of symptoms of disease may differ for younger and older people. Myocardial infarctions, for example, are more often "clinically silent" in older adults, relative to younger adults, particularly among men (Kaplan et al., 1999). Other chronic diseases or disease events may go undetected for longer periods in later life because their symptom manifestations are more subtle or vague (Kaplan et al., 1999). Perceptions and reports of pain appear to change with age, with older adults exhibiting greater reticence to report pain (although not under conditions of strong pain stimulation; Yong, Gibson, Horne, & Helme, 2001), less confidence in their judgments of pain sensations, and greater reluctance to label sensations as painful (Yong et al., 2001). Older adults tend to "normalize" at least some of the physical symptoms they experience, attributing them to aging rather than to illness (George, 2001). Older adults also sometimes misconstrue symptoms of disease or acute disease events (such as a heart attack or ulcer) as normal aspects of aging (Leventhal & Prohaska, 1986; Stoller, 1993) or feel reluctant to burden or inconvenience others with their symptoms (Jurgens, Hoke, Byrnes, & Riegel, 2009). Both older adults' knowledge of disease symptoms and progression and the socioemotional context in which they experience symptoms influence the timeliness with which they seek medical care (Leventhal, Leventhal, & Contrada, 1998).

## Medical Intervention

The primary focus of medical intervention traditionally has been on curing illness rather than providing palliative care or assisting with the management of a chronic, degenerative disease process. Yet, the epidemiological and demographic revolutions that have occurred in developed nations, and that are under way in many developing nations (Murray & Lopez, 1996), are prompting a shift in public health priorities, from the prevention and treatment of communicable diseases to the prevention and management of chronic conditions, pain, and disability.

Efforts to treat chronic illnesses often frustrate both the physician and the patient. Besides being frustrating, treating older adults is often more challenging than treating younger adults. Understanding age-related changes in biological and physiological processes is vital for successful medical treatment, yet such information has been scarce until relatively recently. Norms, diagnostic criteria, and treatment plans for a variety of conditions have been based on predominantly middle-aged men (Meyerowitz & Hart, 1995). Determining appropriate medication dosages for older adults is often difficult, for example, because older adults generally have a greater percentage of fatty tissue and a slower metabolism than do middle-aged adults, and both of these factors magnify drug effects. Metabolism in the liver declines, as does kidney blood flow and functioning, resulting in reduced renal clearance and a potential increase in the accumulation of drugs in the bloodstream (Kaplan et al., 1999). Thus, medication may have longer-lasting effects in older adults as compared with younger age groups, and smaller doses may achieve the desired therapeutic effects (Steiner, 1996). Comorbidity often increases the complexity of medication regimens, with a corresponding increase in the number of medications taken and the risk of drug interactions and compliance problems (Roberts & Snyder, 2001).

Achieving adherence to medical regimens also presents unique challenges in later life. Older adults often need to recall and synchronize multiple medication schedules, and they may experience added difficulties reading medication labels or instructions, opening medication packaging (e.g., childproof bottles), and swallowing large medication capsules (Miller, 2003). Some older adults also attempt to self-regulate drug dosages based on their perceptions of their health status, believing, for example, that they can forgo blood pressure medication for hypertensive illness on days when they do not feel stressed. Such mistaken beliefs can have grave health consequences.

Medical researchers and practitioners have called for fundamental changes in prevailing approaches to the management of chronic disease. Some have urged consideration of models in which patients function less as passive recipients of health care than as active partners who collaborate with health care providers in the complex and continuous processes of managing chronic disease over time (Holman, 2002). Arguments for such a partnership model grow out of recognition that the course of chronic disease in individual patients is characterized by considerable uncertainty and that patients often have greater awareness than do physicians of potentially important trends and transitions in their disease progression. This greater awareness of internal states can be joined with the physicians' knowledge to make effective joint decisions about care and to allow for timely interventions when the patient's illness course departs from an expected trajectory (Kane, Priester, & Totten, 2005). In addition, the long-term management of chronic illnesses requires patients to understand and accept more responsibility and a wider range of practices than is typically the case with acute illness, and this, too, is likely to require an effective partnership between patients and physicians (Holman, 2002; Kane et al., 2005).

Advances in medical technology also have begun to allow forms of medical care to be administered at home that were once the province of hospitals and nursing homes, such as inhalation therapies and intravenous medication regimens (Kane, 1995). Such home-based "high-tech" health care has the potential to contain treatment costs, but it creates new challenges for individual patients and their family caregivers, including the need to understand and properly administer technologically complex care and the need to adapt to a medicalized home environment (Kane, 1995). Emerging technologies that allow for the remote monitoring of patients' health status have the potential to improve patient care by increasing the ease and efficiency of ongoing health-status monitoring and the regularity of patient–physician exchanges (Wasson et al., 1992). Such technologies have the potential to be particularly useful for elderly patients whose chronic conditions limit mobility and make visits to physicians' offices arduous ordeals. Yet here, too, a great deal remains to be learned about patients' understanding and acceptance of remote-monitoring technologies and the psychological impacts of such regular health-status monitoring and feedback. This discussion illustrates that medical care practices are beginning to undergo transformations in response to population aging and the ascendance of chronic disease as the dominant threat to health in developed countries (Kane, 1995).

## Implications of Age-related Declines for Functional Health and Self-rated Health

As noted earlier, the declines in physiological functioning and health status that often occur with advancing age do not inevitably impair older adults' day-to-day functioning and qualify of life. The impact of such changes is typically gauged by examining how they affect older adults' ability to carry out their daily activities (functional health) and how they influence older adults' evaluations of their health (self-rated health). Moreover, as indicated earlier, the heterogeneity that exists within the elderly population makes broad generalizations difficult. Bearing this caveat in mind, we describe some of the common patterns that have been documented in the literature and highlight departures from these patterns that have been associated with sociodemographic variations.

It warrants noting that statistics regarding the percentage of older adults who exhibit some degree of functional impairment are often interpreted in two different ways. For example, a statistic indicating that 25% of older adults experience difficulty performing at least some tasks that are essential to maintaining independence (AAA, 2009) is applauded by some as evidence that 75% of older adults do not experience such difficulties. For others, the 25% figure commands serious attention because it translates into huge numbers of people, in an absolute sense, who may be on a health trajectory that culminates in the loss of independence. This basic tension between emphasizing the "good" or "bad" news about aging recurs throughout the literature on aging and health and, indeed, throughout much of the history of gerontology (Carstensen & Charles, 2003). This is a theme to which we will turn in the concluding section of the chapter because it is tied centrally to differing conceptions of what constitutes optimal aging.

### Functional Health

Chronic conditions generally do not take a substantial toll on older adults' daily functioning until relatively advanced old age. Among people aged 65–74, only 29% report limiting their daily activities because of a chronic condition, but this figure rises to 51% among those aged 75 and older (AARP, 2001). A more complete view of the impact of chronic illness and declines in physiological function emerges when researchers examine older adults' ability to carry out everyday tasks of living. The terms *activities of daily living* (ADLs) and *instrumental activities of daily living* (IADLs) have come to refer to two classes of everyday activities that reflect the ability to carry out self-care tasks. ADLs refer to basic self-care activities, such as eating, bathing, dressing, and being able to get in and out of a chair or bed. IADLs refer to more complex activities that allow people to function independently in the community, such as shopping, preparing meals, and managing personal finances (Katz, 1983; Nagi, 1965).

Older adults who are able to perform ADLs, but who have difficulty with IADLs, may able to continue living in their own homes with the assistance of others (who can buy groceries, help with household tasks, etc.). Older adults who experience ADL impairment, in contrast, are more likely to need long-term care and to have an elevated risk for nursing home placement (Gaugler, Duval, Anderson, & Kane, 2007). Estimates of functional impairment among older adults vary, but one recent study found that 25% of older adults had difficulty performing at least some ADLs, and an additional 14.6% had difficulties performing IADLs (AAA, 2009).

Because the conditions that contribute to disability in later life often develop gradually over the life course, considerable research attention is focused on understanding stages in the transition from initial pathology to significant impairment, and factors that hasten or slow these transitions (Femia, Zarit, & Johansson, 2001; Taylor, 2010). A prominent theoretical model developed by Verbrugge and Jette (1994) posits that the disablement process involves a progression from a *pathological condition* (disease onset or injury) to *impairment* (dysfunction in specific bodily systems) to *functional limitations* (difficulties performing basic activities of daily living, such as handling objects or ambulating) to *disability* (difficulties performing instrumental activities of daily life, such as household management or meal preparation). Empirical evidence has confirmed some of the core assumptions of this model, such as the assumption that functional limitations represent a major cause of subsequent disability, and that some limitations (such as lower body limitations) are more consequential than others (such as upper body limitations; Lawrence & Jette, 1996; Penninx et al., 2000). Additional evidence, however, suggests that some older adults experience disability even in the absence of identifiable functional limitations (Fried, Ettinger, Lind, Newman, & Gardin, 1994). For these individuals, factors such as social isolation, depression, and poor self-rated health—rather than physical impairment per se—may play a role in the development of disability (Femia et al., 2001).

### Self-rated Health

Self-rated health in later life has been studied intensively both because it is a legitimate dimension of health in its own right and because it has been found to predict important health outcomes. For example, self-rated health has been found to predict the severity of disability in later life, after controlling for functional limitations (Femia et al., 2001) and,

further, has been found to predict mortality, after controlling for physical health, chronic illnesses, and functional limitations (Deeg & Bath, 2003; Strawbridge & Wallhagen, 1999). Significant associations have been found between older adults' ratings of their health and objective assessments of their health (e.g., Fillenbaum, 1979), although self-reported health often predicts mortality better than these assessments or even physician ratings (e.g., Benyamini & Idler, 1999; Borawski, Kinney, & Kahana, 1996).

Despite the age-related declines in physiological functioning and increases in chronic illness that we have discussed, older adults' perceptions of their health tend, on average, to be positive (although sociodemographic variations, discussed later, qualify this conclusion). In one recent large study, 42% of participants aged 65–74, and even 25% of those aged 85 and over, described their health as "excellent" or "very good" (NIA, 2007). Chronic illness does detract from self-rated health (NIA, 2007), but even older adults with chronic conditions often rate their health more favorably than might be expected given their physical impairments. Older adults may view their health favorably in part because they evaluate it with reference to age peers rather than with reference to their own health at a younger age (Robinson-Whelen & Kiecolt-Glaser, 1997). Most older adults do not identify themselves as "old," and they tend to regard their life circumstances, including their own health, as better than those of same-aged peers (National Council on Aging, 2002). Research also suggests that self-rated health is based on more than functional health and, rather, reflects mood states, engagement in social activities, and the extent to which daily pursuits feel meaningful; the full "illness–wellness continuum" may be important, therefore, in understanding how older adults appraise their health status (Benyamini, Idler, Leventhal, & Leventhal (2000). Important sociodemographic variations also exist in how older adults view their health and in the health conditions they experience.

### Sociodemographic Variations in Health, Illness, and Mortality

Later life unfolds over an expansive time frame, encompassing the experiences of people in their 60s to those of people over 100, and it includes a heterogeneous group of people who have accumulated diverse life experiences. Age itself is an important source of variation within the elderly population, and gerontological researchers often have found it useful to distinguish between the "young-old" (often defined as those aged 65–80) and the "old-old" (defined as those older than 80 or 85). Compared with the young-old, the old-old tend to have more chronic conditions and to experience more adverse effects of both acute and chronic illnesses. The higher rates of chronic illness and disability among the oldest members of the elderly population, coupled with the fact that more people are surviving to very advanced old age with conditions that formerly would have resulted in an earlier death (MIAH/ GSA, 2002), may account for their somewhat less positive health assessments. As noted earlier, whereas 42% of the young-old (aged 65-74) describe their health as "excellent" or "very good," only 25% of the old-old (aged 85 and older) describe their health in such favorable terms (NIA, 2007). Additionally, the proportion of the old-old who describe their health as "excellent" or "very good" has declined slightly over time, in contrast to the gains seen for the young-old (AARP, 2001). The health status of the very old is of special interest to gerontological researchers because individuals aged 85 and older constitute the fastest-growing segment of the elderly population.

The great heterogeneity among older adults in terms of other sociodemographic characteristics results in different trajectories of health, which often underscore how differences throughout the lifespan affect health. Unfortunately, groups that historically have faced discrimination also commonly experience poorer health outcomes in old age. These differences are apparent when people are asked to rate their health. Older African Americans less often describe their health as "excellent" or "very good" than do their European American counterparts, and few of the gains in self-reported health noted earlier in this discussion for European Americans generalized to African Americans. For example, only 26% of African Americans aged 65–74 endorsed these positive health descriptions in 1992, a figure that had increased by only 2% from 1982 (AARP, 2001).

Women live longer than men, but they experience more, if less lethal, chronic conditions (Austad, 2006; Verbrugge, 2001). Consistent with this, women generally rate their health less favorably and report more restrictions of activity and more days of bed rest when they feel ill (Verbrugge, 1989, 2001). This gender difference in self-rated health is evident across the lifespan, leading Verbrugge (1989) to conclude that women feel sicker for more of their lives than do men of the same age; women survive to live longer, but one price for this greater longevity is a higher prevalence and duration of disability (Stuck et al., 1999). Across a number of studies, older women have been found to exhibit more activity limitations because of underlying health conditions than have men (Verbrugge, 2001). From this perspective, the everyday burden of chronic illness in later life seems to be greater for women than for men (Verbrugge, 1985). Older men are more likely than older women to suffer from heart disease, in contrast, which poses a greater risk of death and partly accounts for the greater longevity of women (Gold, Malmberg, McClearn, Pedersen, & Berg, 2002).

Analyses of racial and ethnic differences in health and illness in later adulthood often are limited to comparisons between European Americans and African Americans, although Hispanic Americans are sometimes included, as well. In these studies, members of ethnic minority groups generally have higher rates of chronic illness. African American men are at higher risk for hypertension and experience more rapid progression of end-organ damage from hypertension than do European American men (see review by Wagner, 1998). They also exhibit greater cardiovascular reactivity to stressors (Guyll, Matthews, & Bromberger, 2001), another possible precursor to heart disease. Similarly, elderly Hispanic Americans and African Americans have higher rates of diabetes than do elderly European Americans (CDC/MIAH, 2007), as well as higher rates of strokes and heart attacks (Cooper et al., 2000).

The major causes of death among older adults exhibit relatively little variability across sociodemographic groups, but the rank ordering of specific causes varies. Diabetes emerges as a more prominent cause of death among older African Americans and American Indians, for example, than among other groups of older adults (Sahyoun et al., 2001). More notably, members of ethnic minority groups generally exhibit higher rates of mortality than do European Americans for almost every condition, as a result of lifelong experiences of economic hardship and discrimination that limit access to adequate health care and increase exposure to stress and environmental hazards (Williams & Collins, 1995). Consistent with this, life expectancies are shorter for members of ethnic minority groups. For example, life expectancies calculated at birth for African American men and women are roughly 7 and 5 years shorter, respectively, than for their European American counterparts (Himes, 2001).

Life expectancies calculated at age 65 or beyond, among those who have survived to old age, often narrow or reveal a reverse pattern, with African Americans of advanced age living longer than age-matched European Americans (e.g., Corti et al., 1999). This reversal, which has come to be known as the *racial cross-over* in mortality, may reflect robustness in the population of African Americans of advanced old age, although data-quality issues need to be ruled out (Lynch, Brown, & Harmsen, 2003). The possibility of a mortality cross-over does not, in any event, belie the significant disadvantages in health status and overall life expectancy experienced by many members of ethnic minority groups.

Such findings suggest that real gains in the overall health of the elderly population will not be achieved until these disparities in health and longevity are addressed (Sahyoun et al., 2001). This will require research directed toward identifying modifiable behavioral risk factors and developing intervention strategies that take into account ethnic and cultural diversity, as well as life stage. Such work is needed not only to address current health disparities but also to anticipate and plan for the changing makeup of future elderly cohorts, which will be characterized by considerably greater racial, ethnic, and socioeconomic diversity than is the case now (NAAS, 1999b).

## Psychosocial Factors and Physical Health

Psychosocial factors are intimately linked to physical functioning, as reviewed extensively in this volume. In this section, we illustrate some of the many ways that psychosocial factors affect health in later life. Our discussion emphasizes four pathways through which psychosocial factors influence physical health in old age, including (1) psychosocial factors that operate early in life to influence health status in later adulthood, (2) psychosocial factors in later adulthood that influence concurrent health status, (3) psychosocial factors that influence adaptation to illness and disease in later adulthood, and (4) psychosocial factors that influence health promotion and rehabilitation in late adulthood. For each of these four pathways, we provide an example to illustrate the kinds of interrelationships that have been reported in the literature.

### Psychosocial Factors Early in Life that Influence Health Status in Later Adulthood

The importance of psychosocial factors for health in old age begins early in life. For example, it is now widely accepted that unhealthy behaviors and lifestyles account for a substantial proportion of deaths in the United States, with estimates often converging on a figure of 50% (McGinnis & Foege, 1993; U.S. Department of Health and Human Services [USDHHS], 1979). Many important health behaviors that have consequences for health and illness in later adulthood represent established patterns that emerge in childhood and young adulthood, with adverse health effects often becoming evident by middle adulthood (Gatz, Harris, & Turk-Charles, 1995). Other psychosocial factors that predict morbidity may begin even earlier in the life course, with some researchers arguing that the precursors of risk factors for cardiovascular disease and other chronic illnesses common to old age are present at birth (e.g., Sandman, Wadhwa, Chicz-DeMet, Porto, & Garite, 1999).

### THE EXAMPLE OF PERSONALITY

Personality traits refer to relatively stable patterns of thoughts, emotional experiences, and behaviors. These habitual patterns are believed to influence physiological functioning and eventual health outcomes through both direct and indirect pathways (for a comprehensive review, see Friedman, 2011, Chapter 10, this volume). Researchers who endorse direct pathway paradigms examine personality traits related to high levels of emotional instability, or emotional reactivity, such as hostility and neuroticism. They endorse the classic stress process model of health (Pearlin, Menaghan, Lieberman, & Mullan, 1981), which states that constant physiological reactivity leads to wear and tear on the system. The effects of constant physiological reactivity accumulate, eventually resulting in greater morbidity and earlier mortality (e.g., Wilson, Mendes de Leon, Bienias, Evans, & Bennett, 2004). People who are high on the dimension of trait hostility, for example, exhibit greater physiological reactivity to negative events than do people who are low on this dimension (Suarez, Kuhn, Schanberg, Williams, & Zimmermann, 1998). In addition, hostility is related to a higher incidence of cardiovascular disease and earlier mortality (Friedman, 2011, Chapter 10, this volume).

When examining other personality traits, researchers find that higher levels of neuroticism and lower levels of conscientiousness are related to higher levels of interleukin-6 (IL-6; Sutin et al., 2010), a proinflammatory cytokine linked to greater inflammation and associated with slower wound healing. Years of emotional instability are posited to explain why higher levels of neuroticism predict the prevalence of chronic health conditions ranging from ulcerative colitis to cardiovascular disease 25 years later (Charles, Gatz, Kato, & Pedersen, 2008), and why higher levels of neuroticism are related to mortality (e.g., Mroczek & Spiro, 2007; Shipley, Weiss, Der, Taylor, & Dreary, 2007), even among a fairly homogeneous sample (elderly Catholic clergy members; Wilson et al., 2004).

Researchers studying indirect pathways from personality to health in later life often study health behaviors mediating these relationships. For example, conscientiousness may predispose people to avoid dangerous behaviors and adhere to the recommendations of health professionals, and agreeableness may lead people to engage in unhealthy but social behaviors, such as drinking alcohol, smoking, and eating to excess (Booth-Kewley & Vickers, 1994; Kern & Friedman, 2008). Although people scoring high on agreeableness are more likely to smoke and drink than are people scoring low on this measure, these health behaviors do not completely explain the relationship between agreeableness and longevity (Martin et al., 2002). In addition, the likelihood of fatal accidents based on impulsive behavior appears to be lower among those high in conscientiousness but, again, this association does not explain the relationship between conscientiousness and mortality (Friedman et al., 1995). Moreover, personality traits are independently related to health behaviors and to socioeconomic status, and all of these factors contribute to mortality (Chapman, Fiscella, Kawachi, & Duberstein, 2010). These effects influence people of all ages, but their aggregated effects become stronger as time passes and when people are most physically vulnerable, which is usually at the end of the lifespan. Regardless of the specific mechanisms involved, personality traits are linked to physical health outcome, and their effects are large (Friedman et al., 1995; Friedman, Tomlinson-Keasey, & Schwartz, 1993).

These relationships are likely to begin relatively early in life. For example, low levels of conscientiousness and high levels of agreeableness in childhood predict all-cause mortality after age 50 (Friedman, 2011, Chapter 1, this volume; Friedman et al., 1993; Friedman et al., 1995; Martin, Friedman, & Schwartz, 2007). In another study, men who were more pessimistic and less optimistic in their 20s had worse health beginning in middle age (Peterson, Seligman, & Vaillant, 1988). These associations are not immutable, however; although

neuroticism has been linked to higher morbidity and mortality in several studies (e.g., Charles et al., 2008; Wilson et al., 2004), people who decrease in neuroticism over time show reduced risk for mortality compared to peers whose high scores remain constant over time (Mroczek & Spiro, 2007).

### Psychosocial Factors in Later Adulthood that Influence Concurrent Health Status

Psychosocial factors also may operate to influence concurrent health status in later life. Some factors, such as the nature of day-to-day affective experience or the quality of one's interactions with social network members, influence health and well-being in other life stages and, therefore, do not necessarily have unique effects in old age. For example, affective experience is associated with sympathetic nervous system activation (e.g., Kunzmann & Grühn, 2005) and changes in immune functioning in both older and younger adults (e.g., Futterman, Kemeny, Shapiro, Polonsky, & Fahey, 1992; see review by Herbert & Cohen, 1993). Similarly, the quality of one's interactions with social network members has important implications for health and well-being across the lifespan (see reviews by Berkman, Glass, Brissette, & Seeman, 2000; House, Landis, & Umberson, 1988; Seeman, 1996; Uchino, Cacioppo, & Kiecolt-Glaser, 1996), including old age (e.g., Antonucci, 2001; Seeman, 2000).

Yet, the changing circumstances of later adulthood can create challenges that are relatively unique to this life stage or that alter previously stable psychosocial processes. For example, the loss or disruption of close relationships is a common experience in later life, with nearly 60% of women and 22% of men likely to be widowed by their mid-70s (U.S. Bureau of the Census, 2004). The loss of friends is common, as well. In one longitudinal study, 59% of men and 42% of women older than 85 reported that a close friend had died in the preceding year (Johnson & Troll, 1994). Such losses disrupt existing support networks and have the potential to detract from health and well-being (Goldman, Koreman, & Weinstein, 1995), creating adaptational demands in their own right (Rook, 2000; Zettel & Rook, 2004).

Similarly, although affective experiences influence health across the life course, the nature of affective experiences and the processes of emotion regulation exhibit developmental shifts. In the following section, we examine some of the commonalities and differences across age groups in the interplay between emotion and health.

## THE EXAMPLE OF EMOTION

The association between physical health and emotion is often similar among age groups, and studies have found evidence for bidirectional causation, in which both health symptoms and emotional experience influence each other (Charles & Almeida, 2006; Diefenbach, Leventhal, Leventhal, & Patrick-Miller, 1996). For example, negative mood states have been found to predict physical health symptoms six months later (Leventhal, Hansell, Diefenbach, Leventhal, & Glass, 1996). Conversely, self-rated physical health has been found to predict subsequent depressive symptoms (Aneshensel, Frerichs, & Huba, 1984). Additionally, as functional status and physical conditions improve for older adults, so does their affective well-being (Lieberman et al., 1999).

Given these associations between affect and health, perhaps one of the more counterintuitive findings in gerontology is what is *not* happening in the interplay of age-related losses, health status, and emotion. Older adults experience more losses than do younger adults in multiple areas of their lives, including social, economic, and health domains. Friends and family members die, retirement is often accompanied by reductions in social prestige and income, and chronic conditions increase. In addition, older adults experience reductions in physical reserve capacity, loss of homeostasis, and greater allostatic load, all risk factors that lead to greater physical vulnerability. In view of these changes, older adults might be expected to report reduced life satisfaction and lower affective well-being compared with younger adults. Surprisingly, this is not the case. Older adults do not differ from younger adults in life satisfaction or affective well-being, and they report less negative affect and relatively stable (and sometimes higher) levels of positive affect (see review by Charles & Carstensen, 2010). In fact, older adults with two chronic illnesses report the same level of affective well-being as younger adults reporting no physical health conditions (Piazza, Charles, & Almeida, 2007).

The theory of strength and vulnerability integration (SAVI) explains how older adults can experience reductions in physical health yet maintain relatively high levels of affective well-being (Charles & Carstensen, 2010; Charles & Piazza, 2009). Older adults do so because they are motivated to optimize emotionally meaningful experiences and emotional well-being in later life as a result of greater realization that time remaining in life is growing shorter (as posited by socioemotional selectivity theory; Carstensen, 2006), and they have the necessary self-awareness and knowledge to do so based on their accumulated life experiences. According to socioemotional selectivity theory, all people have a conscious or unconscious awareness of how much time they have left to live, and chronological age is associated with this recognition of limited time. When time is limited, as in advanced old age, people focus on emotional goals, seeking to minimize involvement in emotionally unrewarding activities and focusing, instead, on emotionally meaningful experiences.

By combining this increased motivation with increased self-knowledge, older age is related to an increased ability to avoid negative experiences and instead engage in positive experiences. This selective avoidance is evident in studies using attentional and memory paradigms, as well studies examining how people appraise potentially negative information (see review by Charles & Carstensen, 2010). When older adults cannot avoid negative situations, however, SAVI predicts that age-related reductions in reserve capacity, coupled with any physical health problems they may be experiencing, may make regulating physiological arousal that accompanies negative distress more difficult (Charles & Piazza, 2009).

Threats to health and longevity shift one's focus to emotionally meaningful events (Carstensen & Fredrickson, 1998) and may lead to increased efforts to attain emotional goals. In a related vein, Leventhal and his colleagues (Leventhal, Rabin, Leventhal, & Burns, 2001) argue that emotional reactions to potential health threats influence ensuing plans for dealing with the threats and may become action goals themselves. Older adults have been found to be more risk averse in this regard, as reflected in a shorter latency from the onset of physical symptoms to the seeking of medical care (Leventhal, Leventhal, Schaefer, & Easterling, 1993). Less tolerance for the emotional distress and uncertainty associated with an unknown risk appears to underlie older adults' vigilant, risk-averse approach to potential health threats and may partly explain, as well, older adults' greater adherence to treatment regimens and generally lower rates of health-compromising behavior (Leventhal et al., 2001).

Thus, emotional experiences and the processes of emotion regulation are related to health status and the management of potential health threats in later life. We have emphasized affective processes that exhibit distinct developmental trends over the lifespan, but it is also important to recognize that genes and temperament contribute a degree of stability to affective processes. Emotions are physiological phenomena that can be influenced by the same factors that determine physical health and reserve capacity (Leventhal et al., 1998). This genetic influence persists into old age, suggesting that genes continue to play an important role in the associations between psychosocial factors and both objective and subjective dimensions of health, despite older adults' greater lifetime exposure to environmental influences (Lichtenstein & Pedersen, 1995; Lichtenstein, Pedersen, Plomin, de Faire, & McClearn, 1989). The recognition that biologically based tendencies and psychosocial factors interact to influence the health–emotion relationship in old age underscores, yet again, the complexities of studying health in old age and the usefulness of the biopsychosocial approach in understanding these interrelationships.

### Psychosocial Factors that Influence Adaptation to Illness and Disease in Later Adulthood

A key challenge in later life, and an important area of inquiry for health psychologists, is the process of adapting to declining health. How older people seek to adapt to such declines has significant implications for their quality of life and sense of self-worth, as well as for subsequent health and functioning. Adaptation to chronic illness is a broad topic with many facets, and it is reviewed extensively elsewhere (see Stanton & Revenson, 2011, Chapter 11, this volume). We accordingly limit our attention to psychosocial factors—and specifically processes of primary and secondary control—that hold promise for understanding how older adults seek to preserve their psychological well-being in the face of declining health.

#### THE EXAMPLE OF CONTROL STRIVINGS AND PROCESSES

Theoretical models of developmental regulation provide a useful framework for thinking about how people respond to declining health and functional capabilities with advancing age. The lifespan theory of control, recently also referred to as the *motivational theory of lifespan development* (Heckhausen & Schulz, 1995; see review by Heckhausen, Wrosch, & Schulz, 2010), differentiates between primary control strategies directed toward maintaining and expanding control of outcomes in the environment and in one's physical state, and secondary control strategies directed toward influencing one's internal

psychological resources, such as one's motivation, emotional well-being, or hopefulness. When outcomes are controllable, adaptive behavior is aimed at achieving primary control through a variety of goal engagement strategies (Heckhausen, 1999; Heckhausen & Schulz, 1995; Heckhausen et al., 2010). In contrast, when outcomes are uncontrollable, the adaptive form of control striving is to disengage from the futile goal and to focus instead on ameliorating the adverse effects of the loss of control on one's internal resources. Such goal disengagement protects resources from being expended on unattainable goals and allows them to be directed toward other goals.

The control model of developmental regulation has been applied to study responses to health problems, disease, and disability in adulthood and old age. In one large study, for example, older and middle-aged adults reported both greater persistence in addressing health stressors (primary control strivings) and more positive reappraisal (self-protective disengagement from primary control strivings) than did young adults (Wrosch, Heckhausen, & Lachman, 2000). Similarly, in another study, a majority of adults in advanced old age (79–98 years) reported using either primary control strivings only (42%) or a combination of primary and secondary control strategies (16%) to deal with the consequences of illness and disability on everyday functioning (Haynes, Heckhausen, Chipperfield, Perry, & Newall, 2009). Such evidence of continued primary control striving regarding health among older and middle-aged adults is noteworthy because it suggests that, even though the actual potential to control health outcomes may decline with age, these individuals continue to engage in health maintenance behavior. At the same time, however, primary control strivings contributed less to the psychological well-being of middle-aged and older adults than did strategies of positive reappraisal. Thus, health-related primary control strivings were still used by aging individuals, albeit with less effectiveness.

This conclusion was reinforced and extended in a study of that found that primary control strategies had positive health consequences for the young-old but more negative consequence for the old-old (Chipperfield, Perry, & Menec, 1999). The oldest participants are likely to have suffered more chronic conditions, and such uncontrollable health problems would have rendered primary control attempts futile and wasteful of psychological resources. In contrast, among older adults experiencing acute, controllable illnesses, primary control behavior (engaging in health-promoting behavior) has been found to be associated with better psychological health (Wrosch, Schulz, & Heckhausen, 2002). Thus, primary control striving appears to be adaptive for controllable physical illnesses.

Recent studies have expanded and qualified what constitutes adaptive control striving in advanced old age. Wrosch and his colleagues (Wrosch, Schulz, Miller, Lupien, & Dunne, 2007) showed that older adults' health engagement control strategies helped to buffer the detrimental effects of health problems on depressive mood and diurnal cortisol secretion. Older adults not using such health engagement control strategies were more susceptive to the negative emotional and biological consequences of their health problems. Similarly, Wrosch and Schulz (2008) found that health engagement control strategies protected older adults with daily physical symptoms (e.g., shortness of breath, joint pain) from declines in functional health over a 2-year period. The adpativeness of primary control striving was underscored in the Aging in Manitoba study (Hall, Chipperfield, Heckhausen, & Perry, 2010), which showed that goal engagement strategies predicted lower mortality for individuals with acute, reversible conditions (e.g., heart attack, stroke), but poorer physical health for those with chronic, irreversible conditions (e.g., osteoarthritis, chronic heart disease). Conversely, goal disengagement was associated with poorer physical health for patients with acute conditions, but better health for those with chronic conditions and very old adults. As proposed by the theory, effective control striving is calibrated to whether or not desired outcomes are controllable. Goal engagement with primary control striving is adaptive when controllability is high. Under conditions of low controllability, goal disengagement and self-protective positive reappraisal strategies are most beneficial for subjective well-being and physical health (Hall et al., 2010).

Disengagement from primary control has its limits, however, and at more severe levels of disability, the control system may fail to compensate for the losses, thus increasing the individual's vulnerability to anxiety, despair, and eventually clinical depression (see model in Schulz, Heckhausen, & O'Brien, 2000). Research on the use and consequences of different control strategies in diverse populations of individuals with chronic and/or life-threatening conditions may allow us to identify the major steps and shifts in individuals' control strategies when facing chronic, progressive disease.

Research on older adults' coping with progressive visual impairment is providing significant insights into the timing and sequencing of losses of functioning and phases of primary control striving, goal adjustment, partial goal disengagement, and reengagement with attainable goals (Boerner, Brennan, Horowitz, & Reinhardt, 2010; Wahl, Becker, & Burmedi, 2004; Wahl, Schilling, & Becker, 2007). Several lines of defense may exist, each with its own cycle of initial primary control striving, superseded by compensatory secondary control strategies when primary control potential is compromised (Heckhausen, 2002).

### Psychosocial Factors that Affect Health Promotion and Rehabilitation in Later Adulthood

Psychosocial factors influence health in later adulthood not only by influencing psychological adaptation to declining health, as discussed earlier, but also by the influencing the degree of success that is experienced in efforts to initiate and sustain health-enhancing behavior, whether in the context of prevention or treatment and rehabilitation. In this section, we consider whether modifiable risk factors for disease onset or progression known to be important in earlier life stages retain their importance in later life, and whether efforts to modify them have comparable benefits in later life. We also consider unique issues that arise in considering health promotion with older adults, and we illustrate how psychosocial factors may affect health behavior change efforts in later life by considering the role of social network influences.

It is often assumed that potentially modifiable risk factors that predict disease onset or progression in young adulthood and middle age have less relevance in later life. A review by Kaplan et al. (1999) suggests that this belief is not substantiated by available evidence. The association between some risk factors and disease does decline with age (e.g., smoking and ischemic stroke), but the association between other risk factors and disease persists or even increases with age (e.g., elevated systolic blood pressure and coronary heart disease); other risk factors exhibit no consistent age-related associations with disease outcomes (Kaplan et al., 1999). Even in advanced old age, some known risk factors continue to predict an increased risk of morbidity and mortality. For example, elevated cholesterol has been found to be a risk factor for mortality even among even among men aged 75–97 (Sorkin, Andres, Muller, Baldwin, & Fleg, 1992), and pharmacological interventions to lower lipid levels have been found to reduce the probability of coronary events among high-risk individuals aged 65 and older (Dombrook-Lavender, Pieper, & Roth, 2004; but see Muldoon, Kaplan, & Manuck, 2000). Risk-factor modification in middle and later adulthood does appear to yield significant health benefits (Rowe & Kahn, 1998) in cases where the modifiable factor plays a concurrent role in the disease process.

In a related vein, some researchers question whether preventive health behaviors in old age are as effective in younger ages or whether they constitute an example of too little, too late (e.g., Keysor & Jette, 2001). Health promotion and disease prevention tend to be targeted toward younger age groups, reflecting the belief that health-promoting behavior yields few discernible benefits for older adults. The title of an editorial in the *Journal of Gerontology: Medical Sciences* suggests an alternative view: "It's Never Too Late: Health Promotion and Illness Prevention in Older Persons" (Morley & Flaherty, 2002). Health behavior change and risk factor modification have been shown to have benefits even in old age, contributing to improved health and slowing the progression of disease (Fries, 2003; Kaplan et al., 1999; Leventhal et al., 2001; Rakowski, 1992, 1997; Smith, Orleans, & Jenkins, 2004). Improvements in aerobic fitness and arterial stiffness have been obtained in later life with vigorous physical exercise (Vaitkevicius et al., 1993; see review by Singh, 2002). Similarly, moderate to intense resistance training, even among relatively frail or disabled older adults, has been shown to reduce disability and arthritis pain, increase gait stability, and reduce rates of injurious falls (Singh, 2002). Olshansky, Hayflick, and Carnes (2002) concluded in this regard that health and fitness can be enhanced in later life, as in other life stages, "primarily through the avoidance of behaviors . . . that accelerate the expression of age-related diseases, and by the adoption of lifestyles . . . that take advantage of a physiology that is inherently modifiable" (p. B295).

The effectiveness of specific strategies to promote health is likely to vary across age groups, however, and the identification and evaluation of age-appropriate strategies represent important priorities for future research (Smith et al., 2004). As noted earlier, comorbidity is common in later life, and a preexisting condition may limit the effectiveness of a behavioral intervention intended to address a different condition (Rakowski, 1992). For example,

engaging in daily walks or other physical exercise in the context of a cardiac rehabilitation program may be discomforting or hazardous for an older person with impaired vision. Shortness of breath associated with COPD can cause anxiety and a reluctance to engage in physical activity that might trigger episodes of breathlessness, leading to further cardiopulmonary deconditioning. To increase physical activity, it may be necessary for health care providers to anticipate and address older patients' concerns about breathing-related symptoms (Cousins, 2000; Leventhal et al., 2001). Moreover, health is itself a resource for initiating and maintaining lifestyle modifications, and even highly motivated older adults may lack the energy and physical reserves to engage in preventive behaviors (Rakowski, 1992). Low rates of physical exercise among older adults, relative to the other age groups, represent an exception to the general tendency for older adults to engage in fewer health-risk behaviors; this may be partly attributable to older adults' subjective experience of exercise programs as draining rather than augmenting energy reserves (Brownlee, Leventhal, & Leventhal, 1996), to their potential misinterpretation of some of the physical effects of exercise as cardiac symptoms (Leventhal et al., 2001), and to perceived or real environmental barriers to exercise (Leventhal et al., 2001; Rakowski, 1992). Rakowski (1992) also has cautioned against assuming that the formats for physical exercise favored by many young and middle-aged adults, such as sports club facilities or other group settings that afford little privacy, will necessarily be preferred by older adults.

More generally, the design and evaluation of strategies for promoting health in later life must take into account older adults' representations of and experiences with health threats and options for managing health risks, as well as the physical and social environments in which health promotion efforts occur. We explore the role of the social environment next, in a brief discussion of the role of social network members in health promotion and rehabilitation in later life (see Siegler, Bastian, Steffens, Bosworth, & Costa, 2002, for a discussion of the patient–physician relationship as another important element of the social environment for health promotion in later life).

### THE EXAMPLE OF SOCIAL NETWORK INFLUENCES

People's efforts to manage a health threat by making changes in their health behavior probably rarely occur in a vacuum; rather, their efforts are likely to be observed and, often, shaped by members of the social environment, such as family members and friends (Berg & Upchurch, 2007). For example, spouses often monitor, and seek to influence, each other's health behavior (Lewis & Rook, 1999; Tucker, Orlando, Elliott & Klein, 2006), and this is particularly likely to be true in the context of chronic illness (Stephens, Fekete, Franks, Rook, Druley, & Greene, 2009). Moreover, efforts to modify health behaviors and adhere to a treatment regimen in the context of a chronic disease, such as diabetes, often must be sustained over lengthy periods of time and, to be effective, must be capable of being renewed in the wake of setbacks. Spouses and other close social network members have the potential to facilitate or interfere with lifestyle modifications, treatment adherence, and the management of setbacks over the course of a chronic illness.

Most discussions of the role of social networks in health promotion and rehabilitation have emphasized the emotional and instrumental support provided by close relationships. A substantial literature has documented the health benefits of social support among various patient groups, including individuals diagnosed with cardiovascular disease (e.g., Sayers, Riegel, Pawlowski, Coyne, & Samaha, 2008), cancer (e.g., Broadhead & Kaplan, 2006), diabetes (e.g., Williams & Bond, 2002), and arthritis (e.g., Strating, Suurmeijer, & Van Schuur, 2006). A meta-analysis that focused specifically on the implications of social support for adherence to prescribed treatment regimens documented that social support, particularly practical support, was significantly related to greater adherence (DiMatteo, 2004). A similar benefit was observed in studies that assessed the participants' family environments, with greater family cohesiveness associated with greater adherence.

This meta-analysis also revealed that family conflict was associated with less adherence, serving as a reminder that social networks can be a source of stress and demands, as well as support (Rook, 1994, 1998). Ironically, distressing interactions that occur with social network members in the context of efforts to make and sustain health behavior changes sometimes result from support attempts that go awry over time (Coyne, Wortman, & Lehman, 1988). Research on the effects of health-related social control, or social regulation, in close relationships is gaining momentum and offers a way to conceptualize some of the well-intentioned efforts of social network members that have the effect of inadvertently undermining rather than enhancing health behavior change and treatment adherence.

Social control involves efforts by social network members to regulate the health behaviors of a focal person, either by discouraging an established health-compromising behavior or by encouraging the development of a health-enhancing behavior (Lewis & Rook, 1999; Umberson, 1987). Early work on health-related social control was guided by the view that social control should contribute to physical health by fostering better health behaviors yet, at the same time, might detract from psychological health by constraining target individuals' autonomy. Hughes and Gove (1981) stated this "dual-effects hypothesis" succinctly: "Constraint may be the source of considerable frustration; at the same time it tends to reduce the probability of problematic or maladaptive behaviors" (p. 71). Subsequent formulations of the dual-effects hypothesis have elaborated on the expectation of adverse psychological effects by noting that social network members' efforts to regulate a target person's health behavior convey, even if implicitly, a message that the target person's capacity for self-regulation is deficient (Franks et al., 2006; Rook, 1990, 1995).

Empirical research testing the effects of health-related social control in older adults (Rook, Thuras, & Lewis, 1990; Tucker, 2002) and other age groups (e.g., Lewis & Rook, 1999; Tucker & Anders, 2001;Westmaas, Wild, & Ferrence, 2002) has yielded mixed evidence for the dual-effects hypothesis. In the few studies that have focused specifically on illness management among chronically ill individuals, social control has been linked both to better (Fekete, Geaghan, & Druley, 2009; Stephens et al., 2009) and worse treatment adherence (Franks et al., 2006; Helgeson, Novak, Lepore, & Eton, 2004; Thorpe, Lewis, & Sterba, 2008). More consistent evidence of adverse effects on psychological health has emerged from this work, with studies reporting social control (particularly heavy-handed forms of control) to be related to greater psychological distress and lower self-efficacy (Franks et al., 2006; Helgeson et al., 2004; Thorpe et al., 2008; Tucker et al., 2006). It seems plausible that social network members' efforts to be supportive of a patient's efforts to adhere to a prescribed medical regimen give way over time to more controlling, and even coercive, efforts to induce behavior change if the patient's own efforts achieve little success (Franks et al., 2006; Rook, 1990; Thorpe et al., 2008).

This discussion has focused on the potential roles of social network members, particularly those involving close relationships, in older adults' efforts to initiate and sustain changes in important health behaviors. Enduring behavior change is often difficult to achieve, and it is not surprising that frustrations develop, not only among those attempting to effect such behavior change but also among the people who are close to them. The fact that social network interactions at such times have the potential to be problematic does not mean that they cannot be powerfully supportive and health enhancing at other times. Nonetheless, understanding how older adults' close social relationships may affect their health behavior is likely to benefit from considering negative, as well positive, influences (Newsom, Mahan, Rook, & Krause, 2008; Seeman, 2000) and control, as well as support (Gallant, 2003; Rook et al., 1990).

## Projections for the Health Status of Future Older Adults

A key question that surfaces in many discussions of the health of the elderly population is what the future holds. Will the future bring continued increases in life expectancy, and if so, will the added years of life represent a time of good health or only a time of extended disability? The answers to these questions have important implications for public health planning and priorities, as well as for the lives of older individuals, potentially affecting their personal longevity expectations, health behavior and health care utilization, financial and retirement decisions, residential changes, and planning and decision making in other important areas of their lives. Developing scientific models that allow such forecasts for the future to be offered with any degree of certainty is a difficult undertaking; it is not surprising that scientific opinion is mixed regarding the most probable future scenarios (e.g., see review by Robine & Michel, 2004, and commentaries published in the same issue).

### Life Expectancy of Future Elderly Cohorts

Scientists disagree regarding the prospects for further increases in human life expectancy. Some argue that further increases are unlikely, at least on a scale that resembles the dramatic increases that occurred in the 20th century (e.g., Fries, 1980; Olshansky et al., 2002). Arguments mustered in support of this position (see Fries & Crapo, 1981) have included evidence of apparently finite life spans in many species, a limit in the number of times that normal human cells can divide and replicate (the Hayflick limit), and the failure to find

scientific validation for the claims of extraordinary old age among purportedly long-lived peoples in various regions of the world. Other scientists challenge some of these data and argue, in contrast, that the preponderance of available evidence supports the conclusion that human life expectancy will continue to increase (Vaupel et al., 1998). The Hayflick limit already has been overturned in laboratory experiments in recent years through genetic engineering. Caloric restriction has been found to increase the lifespan of rodents and nonhuman primates, although extrapolation to humans is not yet warranted (Olshansky et al., 2002). The substantial growth in the number of centenarians now alive challenges the notion that further increases in average life expectancy cannot be achieved (Oeppen & Vaupel, 2002). Moreover, some scientists note that the actual empirical record of mortality improvements points to gains in life expectancy of approximately 2.5 years per decade for more than a century, and it is reasonable to expect continued gains in the future (Oeppen & Vaupel, 2002; but see Fries, 2003). Oeppen and Vaupel (2002) concluded that "modest annual increments in life expectancy will never lead to immortality . . . but centenarians may become commonplace within the lifetimes of people alive today" (p. 1031). They caution, as well, that underestimating possible increases in life expectancy is risky from a public policy standpoint because even modest increases can translate into large numbers of very old individuals, contributing to a burgeoning demand for health care services.

Extending the human lifespan will have limited value, of course, unless this is accompanied by corresponding improvements in the health status of older adults. Closely tied to questions about the life expectancy of future elderly cohorts, therefore, are questions about the probable health status of such future cohorts.

### Health Status of Future Elderly Cohorts

Many medical researchers and epidemiologists predict, with some caveats, that the health of future cohorts of older adults in developed nations such as the United States will be better than that of current and past cohorts. This optimistic projection is based on declines in recent decades in the rates of some chronic diseases and disability in the older population (AARP, 2001). As noted earlier, mortality due to heart disease declined in the United States in the 1980s and 1990s, reflecting a reduction in rates of smoking and improved control of hypertension. Lung cancer mortality has declined among older men as a result of declining rates of smoking (NAAS, 1999b), and the prevalence of some other chronic conditions is declining (Rowe, 1997). Levels of education have increased among older adults (U.S. Department of Health and Human Services [USDHHS], 2001). All of these factors, coupled with improvements in medical care and technology, may have contributed to a decline in the prevalence of disability in the elderly population in recent years (NAAS, 1999a; Waidmann & Liu, 2000), although they may not fully account for it (Fries, 2002a).

Such patterns are consistent with the *compression of morbidity* hypothesis first proposed in the early 1980s (Fries, 1980; Fries & Crapo, 1981). This hypothesis posited that the burden of illness in an aging society can be reduced most effectively not through efforts to find cures for the leading causes of disability and mortality but, instead, through efforts to postpone the onset of chronic illness to a time in life that approaches the average age of death. The duration of time spent living with chronic illness, accordingly, would be compressed into fewer years, with correspondingly less pain and disability. Notably, the total number of years lived does not increase in this scenario; rather, by delaying functional decline, the period of life that is relatively free of disability (i.e., active life expectancy) is extended. Postponing the onset of chronic illness would require an emphasis on the prevention or modification of well-established behavioral risk factors for disease. Fries (2002b, 2003) recently took stock of evidence bearing on the compression of morbidity hypothesis and concluded that little evidence of such compression was apparent in the 1980s, but more promising evidence began to emerge by the 1990s, including declining rates of some chronic illness and disability in older adults. More compelling evidence for the compression of morbidity hypothesis has emerged from studies indicating that the age of disability onset began to shift in the 1990s to later ages among individuals with fewer behavioral risk factors, such as smoking, lack of exercise, and obesity. This postponement was found to correspond to 7–8 years in several studies and was related not only to substantially reduced disability but also to reduced medical care costs among individuals exhibiting fewer behavioral risk factors (Fries, 2002b). Additional, and also compelling, support for the compression of morbidity perspective has emerged from analyses indicating that disability rates declined more sharply during this period than did mortality rates (Fries, 2003, 2004).

The optimism engendered by these signs of a compression of morbidity in later adulthood (Fries, 1980; Rowe, 1997) is tempered, however, by other developments that threaten to undo these trends toward improved health. Increased rates of smoking among women, for example, suggest that future cohorts of elderly women may experience higher rates of lung cancer mortality (NAAS, 1999b). Similarly, soaring rates of childhood and adult obesity have the potential to contribute to a significant increase in the prevalence of chronic illness and disability among future cohorts of older adults. In addition, the old-old constitute the fastest-growing segment of the elderly population (Kinsella & Velkoff, 2001), and this traditionally has been the age-group in which rates of functional impairment and disability are highest (MIAH/GSA, 2002; USDHHS, 2001). Thus, even though rates of disability have declined among older adults overall, the growing size of the 85 and older subgroup is anticipated to lead to an increase in the sheer number of people with disability and an increase in the family and societal burdens of care (NAAS, 1999b; Waidmann & Liu, 2000). The number of disabled older adults living in and out of institutions, for example, is estimated to increase by 300% from 1985 to 2050 (Manton, Corder, & Stallard, 1997).

Even the widely cited declines in rates of disability among older adults appear, on closer scrutiny, to provide a basis for more guarded optimism. These declines in disability do not appear to have followed a linear or accelerating trajectory; additionally, they apply only to routine care disability and not to severe personal care disability (Freedman, Martin, & Schoeni, 2002; Schoeni, Freedman, & Wallace, 2001). Equally important, the gains in health that have been observed in later life in recent decades have not been evenly distributed across the elderly population. Fewer gains have been observed among older adults with less education and lower socioeconomic status and among older members of ethnic minority groups (AARP, 2001; Schoeni et al., 2001).

### Prospects for an Antiaging Medicine
The declining physical vigor and increasing risk of disability that accompany old age, despite the gains in selected areas that some groups have begun to enjoy, lead many people to invest hope in the prospect that a viable antiaging medicine will emerge someday. This hope can be traced, in various permutations, through centuries of human history (Binstock, 2004; Haber, 2004). Recently, several

groups of biogerontologists have joined forces to condemn an antiaging industry that exploits fears of aging by marketing an astonishing variety of products and therapies purported to extend longevity and to prevent or reverse the physical signs of aging. (e.g., Binstock, 2004; Butler et al., 2002; Hayflick, 2004; Olshansky et al., 2002). These scientists soundly reject claims of the validity of any existing antiaging remedies, and most express strong doubts that effective interventions for halting or reversing fundamental aging processes will emerge in the foreseeable future. Still others suggest that public debate and discussion should begin now to consider the social and ethical implications of possible antiaging remedies that could be discovered to be effective at some point in the future (Binstock, 2004).

## Conclusion: Resilient Aging in the Absence of a Fountain of Youth

Hopes for the discovery of a fountain of youth that could undo the effects of aging and guarantee a disease-free old age have long fueled human imagination, but such hopes lack a foundation in modern biomedical science and, thus, remain elusive. In the absence of a fountain of youth, more realistic prospects and goals for successful, or resilient, aging should command our attention. These include the prevention of premature deaths associated with modifiable risk factors, the postponement of functional impairment and disability to later ages, and the preservation of independence and psychological well-being to the fullest extent possible even after the onset of functional limitations.

Successful aging, therefore, is unlikely to involve a process of growing old with minimal illness or impairment, and conceptions of successful aging have been evolving to reject both overly pessimistic and overly optimistic views. The concept of successful aging was propelled to a place of prominence in the gerontological literature by Rowe and Kahn (1987) in the late 1980s. They argued that many of the decrements often attributed to aging were, in fact, the result of disease. They juxtaposed this concept of "usual aging" with the concept of "successful aging," or growing old without disease-related decrements. This formulation of successful aging, and its explicit contrast with usual aging, excited many researchers and practitioners, who were pleased by the challenge it presented to prevailing notions of what is possible in later life. It also stimulated a considerable amount of empirical work directed toward identifying the biopsychosocial determinants of successful aging. Critics of the concept of successful

aging, however, felt that it inadvertently championed an elite few whose genetic or socioeconomic advantages made healthy aging possible (Masoro, 2001). Other critics objected that the concept of successful aging, as originally defined by Rowe and Kahn (1987), precluded the possibility that individuals with disabilities acquired early in life could age successfully (Strawbridge, Wallhagen, & Cohen, 2002).

Rowe and Kahn (1998) subsequently expanded their definition of successful aging to include three main components: a low probability of suffering from disease or a disease-related disability, a high level of cognitive and physical functioning, and active engagement with life. This expanded definition has blunted much of the criticism and has broadened the appeal of the construct, although some gerontologists favor models of successful aging (Baltes, 1997; Baltes & Baltes, 1990; Baltes & Carstensen, 1996; Heckhausen & Schulz, 1995) that emphasize the processes by which well-being is preserved in the face of age-related declines in health and functioning. These models of successful aging, thus, are compatible rather than contradictory, with complementary emphases on adaptive outcomes and processes, and Kahn (2002) has urged the theoretical integration of these different models.

A common element of many current perspectives on what it means to age well is an emphasis, explicit or implicit, on resilience. Resilience is defined as succeeding in the face of adversity (Ryff, Singer, Love, & Essex, 1998). Being resilient in later adulthood is contingent not on health status per se but, rather, on how people manage health-related challenges. Given the virtual inevitability of physical decline with advancing age, an individual's capacity to deal with its consequences for everyday activities and psychological health is a key determinant of successful, or resilient, aging. In this sense, successful aging is not merely a state but a process over time (Menec, 2003; von Farber et al., 2001). Successful aging may be evaluated, moreover, with reference to subjective and objective criteria, and these sets of criteria may differ and may follow distinctive trajectories over time (Baltes & Baltes, 1990; Staudinger, Marsiske, & Baltes, 1995).

Health psychologists have a great deal to contribute to the understanding and promotion of processes and conditions that are important in efforts to prevent premature death, postpone disability, and encourage resilience in the face of physical declines and functional limitations. Such work has both tremendous importance and considerable urgency in view of the burgeoning of the elderly population that lies ahead. Underscoring this urgency, Fries (2003) observed that "our greatest national health problem is the health of the elderly" (p. 458), and Kane (2004) warned, "Whatever the final shape of the morbidity and disability projections, they will be dwarfed in the United States by the demographic shifts of an aging baby boomer population" (p. 608). Given the centrality of behavioral and psychosocial factors to health and adaptation in later adulthood, and given their expertise in these areas, health psychologists can make significant contributions to efforts to meet the challenges of population aging. At the same time, health psychology as a discipline is likely to be enriched by adopting a lifespan perspective on health and by integrating concepts and methods from research on aging and adult development (Siegler et al., 2002; Smith, Kendall, & Keefe, 2002).

## References

American Administration on Aging. (2009). *A profile of older Americans: 2009*. U.S. Department of Health and Human Services. Retrieved February 17, 2010 from http://www.aoa.gov/AoARoot/Aging_Statistics/Profile/2009.

American Association of Retired Persons (AARP). (2001). *The health of people age 50 and older*. Washington, DC.: American Association of Retired Persons.

Aneshensel, C.S., Frerichs, R.R., & Huba, G.J. (1984). Depression and physical illness: A multiwave, nonrecursive causal model. *Journal of Health and Social Behavior, 25*, 350–371.

Antonucci, T.C. (2001). Social relations: An examination of social networks, social support, and sense of control. In J.E. Birren & K. Warner Schaie (Eds.), *Handbook of the psychology of aging* (5th ed., pp. 427–453). San Diego, CA: Academic Press.

Austad, S.N. (2006). Why women live longer than men: Sex differences in longevity. *Gender Medicine, 3*(2), 79–92.

Baltes, P.B. (1997). On the incomplete architecture of human ontogeny: Selection, optimization, and compensation as a foundation of developmental theory. *American Psychologist, 52*, 366–380.

Baltes, P.B., & Baltes, M. (1990). Psychological perspectives on successful aging: The model of selective optimization with compensation. In P.B. Baltes & M. Baltes (Eds.), *Successful aging: Perspectives from the behavioral sciences* (pp. 1–34). New York: Cambridge University Press.

Baltes, M.M., & Carstensen, L.L. (1996). The process of successful aging. *Ageing and Society, 16*, 397–422.

Barrett, R., Kuzawa, C.W., McDade, T., & Armelagos, G.J. (1998). Emerging and re-emerging infectious diseases: The third epidemiologic transition. *Annual Review of Anthropology, 27*, 247–271.

Bennett, G.A., Waine, H., & Bauer, W. (1942). *Changes in the knee joint at various ages*. New York: Commonwealth Fund.

Benyamini, Y., & Idler, E.L. (1999). Community studies reporting association between self-rated health and mortality. *Research on Aging, 21*, 392–401.

Benyamini, Y., Idler, E.L., Leventhal, H., & Leventhal, E.A. (2000). Positive affect and function as influences on self-assessments of health: Expanding our view beyond illness and disability. *Journal of Gerontology B: Psychological Sciences and Social Sciences, 55*, P107–P116.

Berg, C.A., & Upchurch, R. (2007). A developmental-contextual model of couples coping with chronic illness across the adult life span. *Psychological Bulletin, 133.*, 920–954.

Berkman, L.F., Glass, T., Brissette, I., & Seeman, T.E. (2000). From social integration to health: Durkheim in the new millennium. *Social Science and Medicine, 51*, 843–857.

Binstock, R.H. (2004). Anti-aging medicine and research: A realm of conflict and profound societal implications. *Journal of Gerontology A: Biological Sciences and Medical Sciences, 59*, B523–533.

Birren, J.E., & Cunningham, W. (1985). Research on the psychology of aging: Principles, concepts, and theory. In J.E. Birren & K.W. Schaie (Eds.), *Handbook of the psychology of aging* (2nd ed., pp. 3–34). New York: Van Nostrand Reinhold.

Blumenthal, H.T. (2003). The aging-disease dichotomy: True or false? *Journal of Gerontology A: Biological Sciences and Medical Sciences, 58*, 138–145.

Boerner, K., Brennan, M., Horowitz, A., & Reinhardt, J.P. (2010). Tackling vision-related disability in old age: An application of the life-span theory of control to narrative data. *Journal of Gerontology: Psychological Sciences and Social Sciences,65*, P22–P31.

Booth-Kewley, S., & Vickers, R.R. (1994). Associations between major domains of personality and health behavior. *Journal of Personality, 62*, 281–298.

Borawski, E.A., Kinney, J.M., & Kahana, E. (1996). The meaning of older adults' health appraisals. *Journal of Gerontology B: Psychological Sciences and Social Sciences, 51*, S157–S170.

Broadhead, W.E., & Kaplan, B.H. (2006). Social support and the cancer patient. Implications for future research and clinical care. *Cancer, 67*(S3), 794–799.

Brownlee, S., Leventhal, E.A., & Leventhal, H. (1996). Self-regulation, health, and behavior. In J.E. Birren (Ed.), *Encyclopedia of gerontology* (Vol. 2, pp. 467–477). San Diego, CA: Academic Press.

Busse, E.W., Maddox, G.L., Buckley, C.E., Burger, P.C., George, L.K., Marsh, G.R.L., et al. (1985). *The Duke longitudinal studies of normal aging: 1955–1980*. New York: Springer.

Butler, R.N. (2002). Report and commentary from Madrid: The United Nations World Assembly on Ageing. *Journal of Gerontology A: Biological Sciences and Medical Sciences, 57*, M770–M771.

Butler, R.N., Fossel, M., Harman, S.M., Heward, C.B., Olshansky, S.J., Perls, T.T., et al. (2002). Is there an antiaging medicine? *Journal of Gerontology A: Biological Sciences and Biological Sciences, 57*, B333–B338.

Cabeza, R., Anderson, N.D., Locantore, J.K., & McIntosh, A.R. (2002). Aging gracefully: compensatory brain activity in high-performing older adults. *Neuroimage, 17*(3), 1394–1402.

Carstensen, L.L. (2006). The influence of a sense of time on human development. *Science, 312*,1913–1915.

Carstensen, L.L., & Charles, S.T. (2003). Human aging: Why is even good news taken as bad? In L. Aspinwall & U. Staudinger (Eds.), *A psychology of human strengths: Perspectives on an emerging field* (pp. 75–86). Washington, DC: American Psychological Association.

Carstensen, L.L., & Fredrickson, B.F. (1998). Influence of HIV status and age on cognitive representations of others. *Health Psychology, 17,* 494–503.

Centers for Disease Control and Prevention and The Merck Institute of Aging & Health. (2007). The state of aging and health in America. Retrieved October 20, 2008 from http://www.cdc.gov/Aging/pdf/saha_2007.pdf.

Chapman, B.P., Fiscella, K., Kawachi, I., & Duberstein, P.R. (2010). Personality, socioeconomic status, and all-cause mortality in the United States. *American Journal of Epidemiology, 171,* 83–92.

Charles, S.T., & Almeida, D.M. (2006). Daily reports of symptoms and negative affect: Not all symptoms are the same. *Psychology & Health, 21,* 1–17.

Charles, S.T., & Carstensen, L.L. (2010). Social and emotional aging. *Annual Review of Psychology, 61,* 383–409.

Charles, S.T., Gatz, M., Kato, K., & Pedersen, N.L. (2008). Physical health 25 years later: The predictive ability of neuroticism. *Health Psychology, 27,* 369–378.

Charles, S.T., & Piazza, J.R. (2009). Age differences in affective well being: ontext matters. *Social and Personality Psychology Compass, 3,* 711–724.

Chipperfield, J.G., Perry, R., & Menec, V.H. (1999). Primary and secondary control enhancing strategies: Implications for health in later life. *Journal of Aging and Health, 11,* 517–539.

Cooper, R., Cutler, J., Desvigne-Nickens, P., Fortmann, S.P., Friedman, L., Havlik, R., et al. (2000). Trends and disparities in coronary heart disease, stroke, and other cardiovascular diseases in the United States: Findings of the National Conference on Cardiovascular Disease Prevention. *Circulation, 102,* 3137–3147.

Corti, M.C., Guralnik, J.M., Ferrucci, L., Izmirlian, G., Leville, S.G., Pahor, M., et al. (1999). Evidence for a black-white crossover in all-cause and coronary heart disease mortality in an older population: The North Carolina EPESE. *American Journal of Public Health, 89,* 308–314.

Cousins, S.O. (2000). My heart couldn't take it: Older women's beliefs about exercise benefits and risks. *Journal of Gerontology B: Psychological and Social Sciences, 55,* P283–P294.

Coyne, J.C., Wortman, C.B., & Lehman, D.R. (1988). The other side of support: Emotional overinvolvement and miscarried helping. In B.H. Gottlieb (Ed.), *Marshalling social support: Formats, processes, and effects* (pp. 305–330). Newbury Park, CA: Sage.

Deeg, D.J.H., & Bath, P.A. (2003). Self-rated health, gender, and mortality in older persons: Introduction to a special issue. *Gerontologist, 43,* 369–371.

Dequeker, J. (1989). Triggering factors for pathological joint changes. In G. Ehrlich & G. Gallacchi (Eds.), *The elderly rheumatic patient: Diagnostic, prognostic and therapeutic aspects. Report of a symposium held during the XIth European Congress of Rheumatology, Athens, 1987* (pp. 18–28). Lewiston, NY: Huber.

Diefenbach, M.A., Leventhal, E.A., Leventhal, H., & Patrick-Miller, L. (1996). Negative affect relates to cross-sectional but not longitudinal symptom reporting: Data from elderly adults. *Health Psychology, 15,* 282–288.

DiMatteo, R.M. (2004). Social support and patient adherence to medical treatment. *Health Psychology, 23,* 207–218.

Dombrook-Lavender, K.A., Pieper, J.A., & Roth, M.T. (2004). Primary prevention of coronary heart disease in the elderly. *Annals of Pharmacotherapy, 37,* 1653–1663.

Engel, G.L. (1977). The need for a new medical model: A challenge for biomedicine. *Science, 196,* 129–136.

Fekete, E.M., Geaghan, T.R., & Druley, J.A. (2009). Affective and behavioural reactions to positive and negative health-related social control in HIV+ men. *Psychology and Health, 24,* 501–515.

Femia, E.E., Zarit, S.H., & Johansson, B. (2001). The disablement process in very late life: A study of the oldest-old in Sweden. *Journal of Gerontology B: Psychological and Social Sciences, 56,* P12–P23.

Fillenbaum, G.G. (1979). Social context and self-assessments of health among the elderly. *Journal of Health and Social Behavior, 20,* 45–51.

Fillenbaum, G.G., Pieper, C.F., Cohen, H.J., Cornoni-Huntley, J.C., & Guralnik, J.M. (2000). Comorbidity of five chronic health conditions in elderly community residents: Determinants and impact on mortality. *Journals of Gerontology Series A: Biological and Medical Sciences, 55*(2), M84–M89.

Fozard, J., & Gordon-Salant, S. (2001). Changes in vision and hearing with aging. In J.E. Birren & K.W. Schaie (Eds.), *Handbook of the psychology of aging.* (5th ed., pp. 241–266). San Diego, CA: Academic Press.

Fozard, J.L., Metter, E.J., & Brant, L.J. (1990). Next steps in describing aging and disease in longitudinal studies. *Journal of Gerontology, 45,* P116–P127.

Franks, M.M., Stephens, M.A.P., Rook, K.S., Franklin, B.A., Keteyian, S.J., & Artinian, N.T. (2006). Spouses' provision of health-related support and control to patients participating in cardiac rehabilitation. *Journal of Family Psychology, 20,* 311–318.

Freedman, V.A., Martin, L.G., & Schoeni, R.F. (2002). Recent trends in disability and functioning among older adults in the United States: A systematic review. *Journal of the American Medical Association, 288,* 3137–3146.

Fried, L.P., Ettinger, W.H., Lind, B., Newman, A.B., & Gardin, J. (1994). Physical disability in older adults: A physiological approach. *Journal of Clinical Epidemiology, 47,* 747–760.

Fried, L.P., Ferrucci, L., Darer, J., Williamson, J.D., & Anderson, G. (2004). Untangling the concepts of disability, frailty, and comorbidity: Implications for improved targeting and care. *Journal of Gerontology A: Biological Sciences and Medical Sciences, 59,* M255–263.

Fried, L.P., Tangen, C.M., Walston, J., Newman, A.B., Hirsch, C., Gottdiener, J., et al. (2001). Frailty in older adults: Evidence for a phenotype. *Journal of Gerontology A: Biological Sciences and Medical Sciences, 56,* M146–M156.

Friedman, H.S. (2011). Personality, disease, and self-healing. In H.S. Friedman (Ed.), *The Oxford handbook of health psychology.* New York: Oxford University Press.

Friedman, H.S., Tomlinson-Keasey, C., & Schwartz, J.E. (1993). Does childhood personality predict longevity? *Journal of Personality and Social Psychology, 65,* 176–185.

Friedman, H.S., Tucker, J.S., Schwartz, J.E., Martin, L.R., Tomlinson-Keasey, C., Wingard, D.L., et al. (1995). Childhood conscientiousness and longevity: Health behaviors and cause of death. *Journal of Personality and Social Psychology, 68,* 696–703.

Fries, J.F. (1980). Aging, natural death, and the compression of morbidity. *New England Journal of Medicine, 303,* 130–135.

Fries, J.F. (2002a). Editorial: Reducing disability in old age. *Journal of the American Medical Association, 288,* 3164–3165.

Fries, J.F. (2002b). Successful aging: An emerging paradigm of gerontology. *Clinics in Geriatric Medicine, 18,* 371–382.

Fries, J.F. (2003). Measuring and monitoring success in compressing morbidity. *Archives of Internal Medicine, 139*, 455–459.

Fries, J.F. (2004). Robine and Michel's "Looking forward to a general theory on population aging": Commentary. *Journal of Gerontology A: Biological Sciences and Medical Sciences, 59*, M603–M605.

Fries, J.F., & Crapo, L.M. (1981). *Vitality and aging*. San Francisco: Freeman.

Futterman, A.D., Kemeny, M.E., Shapiro, D.P., Polonsky, W., & Fahey, J.L. (1992). Immunological variability associated with experimentally-induced positive and negative affective states. *Psychological Medicine, 22*, 231–238.

Gallant, M.P. (2003). The influence of social support on chronic illness self-management: a review and directions for research. *Health Education & Behavior, 30*, 170–195.

Gatz, M., Harris, J.R., & Turk-Charles, S. (1995). The meaning of health for older women. In A.L. Stanton & S.J. Gallant (Eds.), *The psychology of women's health: Progress and challenges in research and application* (pp. 491–529). Washington, DC: American Psychological Association.

Gaugler, J. E, Duval, S., Anderson, K. A, & Kane, R.L. (2007). Predicting nursing home admission in the US: A meta-analysis. *BMC Geriatrics, 19*, 7–13.

Gerhard, K.A., Bergstrom, E., Charlifue, S.W., Menter, R.R., & Whiteneck, G.G. (1993). Long-term spinal cord injury: Functional changes over time. *Archives of Physical Medicine and Rehabilitation, 74*, 1030–1034.

George, L.K. (2001). The social psychology of health. In R.H. Binstock & L.K. George (Eds.), *Handbook of aging and the social sciences* (pp. 217–237). San Diego, CA: Academic Press.

Gillick, M. (2001). Pinning down frailty. *Journal of Gerontology A: Biological Sciences and Medical Science, 56*, M134–M135.

Gold, C.H., Malmberg, B., McClearn, G.E., Pedersen, N.L., & Berg, S. (2002). Gender and health: A study of older unlike-sex twins. *Journal of Gerontology B: Psychological Sciences and Social Sciences, 57*, S168–S176.

Goldman, N., Koreman, S., & Weinstein, R. (1995). Marital status and health among the elderly. *Social Science and Medicine, 40*, 1717–1730.

Greenwood, P.M. (2007). Functional plasticity in cognitive aging: Review and hypothesis. *Neuropsychology, 21*(6), 657–673.

Guyll, M., Matthews, K.A., & Bromberger, J.T. (2001). Discrimination and unfair treatment: Relationship to cardiovascular reactivity among African American and European American women. *Health Psychology, 20*, 315–325.

Haber, C. (2004). Life extension and history: The continual search for the fountain of youth. *Journal of Gerontology B: Biological Sciences and Medical Sciences, 59*, B512–B522.

Hall, N.C., Chipperfield, J.G., Heckhausen, J., & Perry, R.P. (2010). Control striving in older adults with serious health problems: A 9-year longitudinal study of survival, health, and well-being. *Psychology and Aging, 25*, 432–445.

Hayflick, L. (1998). How and why we age. *Experimental Gerontology, 33*(7–8), 639–653.

Hayflick, L. (2004). "Anti-aging": is an oxymoron. *Journal of Gerontology A: Biological Sciences and Medical Sciences, 59*, M573–M578.

Haynes, T.L., Heckhausen, J., Chipperfield, J.G., Perry, R.P., & Newall, N.E. (2009). Primary and secondary control strategies: Implications for health and well-being among older adults. *Journal of Social and Clinical Psychology, 28*, 165–195.

He, W., Sengupta, M., Velkoff, V.A., & DeBarros, K.A. (2005). *65+in the United States: 2005*. U.S. Census Bureau, Current Population Reports, P23–P209. Washington, DC: U.S. Government Printing Office.

Heckhausen, J. (1999). *Developmental regulation in adulthood: Age-normative and sociostructural constraints as adaptive challenges*. New York: Cambridge University Press.

Heckhausen, J. (2002). Developmental regulation of life-course transitions: A control theory approach. In L. Pulkkinen & A. Caspi (Eds.), *Paths to successful development: Personality in the life course* (pp. 257–280). Cambridge, England: Cambridge University Press.

Heckhausen, J., & Schulz, R. (1995). A life-span theory of control. *Psychological Review, 102*, 284–304.

Heckhausen, J., Wrosch, C., & Schulz, R. (2010). A motivational theory of life-span development. *Psychological Review, 117*, 32–60.

Helgeson, V.S., Novak, S.A., Lepore, S.J., & Eton, D.T. (2004). Spouse social control efforts: Relations to health behavior and well-being among men with prostate cancer. *Journal of Social and Personal Relationships, 21*, 53–68.

Herbert, T.B., & Cohen, S. (1993). Stress and immunity in humans: A meta-analytic review. *Psychosomatic Medicine, 55*, 364–379.

Himes, C.L. (2001). Elderly Americans. *Population Bulletin, 56*, 3–42.

Holman, H. (2002). Patients as partners in managing chronic disease. *British Medical Journal, 320*, 526–527.

House, J.S., Landis, K.R., & Umberson, D. (1988). Social relationships and health. *Science, 241*, 540–545.

Hoyert, D.L., Kung, H.C., & Smith, B.L. (2005). *Deaths: Preliminary data for 2003*. National Vital Statistics Reports, 53 (15). Hyattsville, MD: National Center for Health Statistics.

Hughes, M., & Gove, W.R. (1981). Living alone, social integration, and mental health. *American Journal of Sociology, 87*, 48–74.

Huxley, R., Barzi, F., & Woodward, M. (2006). Excess risk of fatal coronary heart disease associated with diabetes in men and women: meta-analysis of 37 prospective cohort studies. *British Medical Journal, 332*(7533), 73–78.

Johnson, C.L., & Troll, L. (1994). Constraints and facilitators to friendships in late life. *Gerontologist, 34*, 79–87.

Jurgens, C.Y., Hoke, L., Byrnes, J., & Riegel, B. (2009). Why do elders delay responding to heart failure symptoms? *Nursing Research, 58*(4), 274–282.

Kahn, R.L. (2002). On "Successful Aging and Well-Being: Self-Rated Compared With Rowe and Kahn." *The Gerontologist, 42*, 725–726.

Kane, R.L. (1995). Comment: Health care reform and the care of older adults. *Journal of the American Geriatrics Society, 43*, 718–719.

Kane, R.L., Priester, R., & Totten, A.M. (2005). *Meeting the challenge of chronic illness*. Baltimore: Johns Hopkins.

Kane, R.L. (2004). Robine and Michel's "Looking forward to a general theory on population aging": Commentary. *Journal of Gerontology A: Biological Sciences and Medical Sciences, 59*, M608.

Kaplan, G.A., Haan, M.N., & Wallace, B.R. (1999). Understanding changing risk factor associations with increasing age in adults. *Annual Review of Public Health, 20*, 89–108.

Katz, S. (1983). Assessing self-maintenance: Activities of daily living, mobility and instrumental activities of daily living. *Journal of the American Geriatrics Society, 31*, 721–727.

Kern, M.L., & Friedman, H.S. (2008). Do conscientious individuals live longer? A quantitative review. *Health Psychology*, *27*, 505–512.

Keysor, J.J., & Jette, A.M. (2001). Have we oversold the benefit of late-life exercise? *Journal of Gerontology A: Biological Sciences and Medical Sciences, 56*, M412–M423.

Kinsella, K., & Velkoff, V.A. (2001). *An aging world.* U.S. Census Bureau, Series P95/01–1. Washington, DC: U.S. Government Printing Office.

Koivula, I., Sten, M., & Makela, P.H. (1999). Prognosis after community-acquired pneumonia in the elderly. *Archives of Internal Medicine, 159*, 1550–1555.

Kunzmann, U., & Grühn, D. (2005). Age differences in emotional reactivity: the sample case of sadness. *Psychology and Aging, 20*, 47–59.

Lawrence, R.H., & Jette, A.M. (1996). Disentangling the disablement process. *Journal of Gerontology B: Psychological Sciences and Social Sciences, 51*, S173–S182.

Leventhal, E.A., Hansell, S., Diefenbach, M., Leventhal, H., & Glass, D.C. (1996). Negative affect and self-reports of physical symptoms: Two longitudinal studies of older adults. *Health Psychology, 15*, 282–288.

Leventhal, E.A., Leventhal, H., Schaefer, P., & Easterling, D. (1993). Conservation of energy, uncertainty reduction, and swift utilization of medical care among the elderly. *Journal of Gerontology B: Psychological Sciences and Social Sciences, 48*, P78–P86.

Leventhal, E.A., & Prohaska, T.R. (1986). Age, symptom interpretation, and health behavior. *Journal of the American Geriatrics Society, 34*, 185–191.

Leventhal, H., Leventhal, E.A., & Contrada, R.J. (1998). Self-regulation, health, and behavior: A perceptual-cognitive approach. *Psychology and Health, 13*, 717–733.

Leventhal, H., Rabin, C., Leventhal, E.A., & Burns, E. (2001). Health risk behaviors and aging. In J.E. Birren & K. Warner Schaie (Eds.), *Handbook of the psychology of aging* (5th ed., pp. 186–214). San Diego, CA: Academic Press.

Lewis, M.A., & Rook, K.S. (1999). Social control in personal relationships: Impact on health behaviors and psychological distress. *Health Psychology, 18*, 63–71.

Lichtenstein, P., & Pedersen, N.P. (1995). Social relationship, stressful life events, and self-reported physical health: Genetic and environmental influences. *Psychology and Health, 10*, 295–319.

Lichtenstein, P., Pedersen, N.P., Plomin, R., de Faire, U., & McClearn, G.E. (1989). Type A behavior pattern, related personality traits and self-reported coronary heart disease. *Personality and Individual Differences, 10*, 419–426.

Lieberman, D., Galinsky, D., Fried, V., Grinshpun, Y., Mytlis, N., Tylis, R., et al. (1999). Geriatric Depression Screening Scale (GDS) in patients hospitalized for physical rehabilitation. *International Journal of Geriatric Psychiatry, 14*, 549–555.

Lollar, D.J., & Crews, J.E. (2003). Redefining the role of public health in disability. *Annual Review of Public Health, 24*, 195–208.

Lynch, S.M., Brown, J.S., & Harmsen, K.G. (2003). Black-white differences in mortality compression and deceleration and the mortality crossover reconsidered. *Research on Aging, 25*, 456–483.

Manton, K.G., Corder, L., & Stallard, E. (1997). Chronic disability trends in the elderly United States populations: 1982–1994. *Proceedings of the National Academy of Sciences, Medical Sciences, 94*, 2593–2598.

Martin, L.R., Friedman, H.S., & Schwartz, J.E. (2007). Personality and mortality risk across the life span: The importance of conscientiousness as a biopsychosocial attribute. *Health Psychology, 26*(4), 428–436.

Martin, L., Friedman, H.S., Tucker, J.S., Tomlinson-Keasey, C., Criqui, M.H., & Schwartz, J.E. (2002). A life course perspective on childhood cheerfulness and its relation to mortality risk. *Personality and Social Psychology Bulletin, 28*, 1155–1165.

Masoro, E.J. (2001). "Successful aging": Useful or misleading concept? *Gerontologist, 41*, 415–418.

Mathers, C.D., Sadana, R., Salomon, J.A., Murray, C.J.L., & Lopez, A.D. (2001). Healthy life expectancy in 191 countries, 1999. *Lancet, 357*, 1685–1690.

McEwen, B.S. (2006). Stress, adaptation, and disease: Allostasis and allostatic load. *Annals of the New York Academy of Sciences, 840*, 33–44.

McGinnis, J.M., & Foege, W.H. (1993). Actual causes of death in the United States. *Journal of the American Medical Association, 270*, 2207–2212.

Menec, V.H. (2003). The relation between everyday activities and successful aging: A 6-year longitudinal study. *Journal of Gerontology B: Psychological Sciences and Social Sciences, 58*, S74–S82.

Merck Institute of Aging, Health, & Gerontological Society of America. (2002). *The state of aging and health in America*. Washington, DC: Gerontological Society of America.

Meyerowitz, B.E., & Hart, S.L. (1995). Women and cancer: Have assumptions about women limited our research agenda? In A.L. Stanton & S.J. Gallant (Eds.), *The psychology of women's health: Progress and challenges in research and application* (pp. 51–84). Washington, DC: American Psychological Association.

Miller, C.A. (2003). Safe medication practices: Administering medications to elders who have difficulty swallowing. *Geriatric Nursing, 24*, 378–379.

Morley, J.E., & Flaherty, J.H. (2002). It's never too late: Health promotion and illness prevention in older persons. *Journal of Gerontology A: Biological Sciences and Medical Sciences, 57*, M338–M342.

Mroczek, D.K., & Spiro, A. (2007). Personality change influences mortality in older men. *Psychological Science, 18*, 371–376.

Muldoon, M.F., Kaplan, J.R., & Manuck, S.B. (2000). Uncertain health effects of cholesterol reduction in the elderly. In S.B. Manuck, R.J. Jennings, B.S. Rabin, & A. Baum (Eds.), *Behavior, health and aging* (pp. 225–244). Mahwah, NJ: Erlbaum.

Murray, C.J.L., & Lopez, A.D. (1996). Evidence-based health policy: Lessons from the Global Burden of Disease Study. *Science, 274*, 740–743.

Nagi, S. (1965). Some conceptual issues in disability and rehabilitation. In M. Sussman (Ed.), *Sociology and rehabilitation* (pp. 100–113). Washington, DC: American Sociological Association.

National Academy on an Aging Society. (1999a). Chronic and disabling conditions. *Challenges for the 21st Century*, 1, 1–6. Washington, DC.: National Academy on an Aging Society.

National Academy on an Aging Society. (1999b). *Demography is not destiny*. Washington, DC.: National Academy on an Aging Society.

National Center for Health Statistics. (2007). *Health, U.S., 2007 with chartbook on trends in the health of Americans*. Retrieved

October 20, 2008 from http://www.cdc.gov/nchs/data/hus/hus07.pdf.

National Council on the Aging. (2002). *American perceptions of aging in the 21st century: The NCOA's continuing study of the myths and realities of aging.* Washington, DC: The National Council on the Aging, Inc.

National Institute on Aging. (1996). *In search of the secrets of aging* (2nd ed.). Bethesda, MD: U.S. Government Printing Office.

National Institute on Aging. (2005). *Aging hearts and arteries.* Retrieved March 15, 2010 http://www.nia.nih.gov/NR/rdonlyres/0BBF820F-27D0–48EA-9820–736B7F9F08BB/0/HAFinal_0601.pdf.

National Institute on Aging. (2006). *Aging under the microscope: A biological quest.* Retrieved July 12, 2007 from http://www.nia.nih.gov/NR/rdonlyres/0161ED5A-4D01–4649-8B90-EAAA2A3624E6/0/Aging_Under_the_Microscope2006.pdf.

National Institute on Aging. (2007). *Growing older in America: The Health and Retirement Study.* Retrieved October 27, 2008 from http://www.nia.nih.gov/ResearchInformation/ExtramuralPrograms/BehavioralAndSocialResearch/HRS.htm.

National Institute on Aging. (2008). *Healthy aging: Lessons from the Baltimore Longitudinal Study of Aging.* Retrieved March 15, 2010 from http://www.nia.nih.gov/NR/rdonlyres/F1B25F15-BB89–4A73–842A-5E7A2A2F69C2/0/BLSA_FNL_110708FinalPDF.pdf.

Newsom, J.T., Mahan, T.L., Rook, K.S., & Krause, N. (2008). Stable negative social exchanges and health. *Health Psychology, 27,* 78–86.

Oddis, C.V. (1996). New perspectives on osteoarthritis. *American Journal of Medicine, 100,* 10S–15S.

Oeppen, J., & Vaupel, J.W. (2002). Broken limits to life expectancy. *Science, 296,* 1029–1031.

Olshansky, S.J., Hayflick, L., & Carnes, B.A. (2002). Position statement on human aging. *Journal of Gerontology A: Biological Sciences and Medical Sciences, 57,* B292–B297.

Olshansky, S.J., Passaro, D.J., Hershow, R.C., Layden, J., Carnes, B.A., Brody, J., et al. (2005). A potential decline in life expectancy in the United States in the 21st century. *New England Journal of Medicine, 352,* 1138–1145.

Pearlin, L.I., Menaghan, E.G., Lieberman, M.A., & Mullan, J.T. (1981). The stress process. *Journal of Health and Social Behavior, 22,* 337–356.

Penninx, B.W.J.H., Ferrucci, L., Leveille, S.G., Rantanen, T., Pahor, M., & Guralnik, J.M. (2000). Lower extremity performance in nondisabled older persons as a predictor of subsequent hospitalization. *Journal of Gerontology A: Biological Sciences and Medical Sciences, 55,* M691–M697.

Peterson, C., Seligman, M.E., & Vaillant, G. (1988). Pessimistic explanatory style is a risk factor for physical illness: A thirty-five-year longitudinal study. *Journal of Personality and Social Psychology, 55,* 23–27.

Piazza, J.R., Charles, S.T., & Almeida, D.M. (2007). Living with chronic health conditions: age differences in affective well-being. *The Journals of Gerontology: Psychological Sciences and Social Sciences, 62,* 313–321.

Rakowski, W. (1992). Disease prevention and health promotion with older adults. In M. Ory, R. Abeles, & P. Lipman (Eds.), *Aging, health, and behavior* (pp. 239–275). Newbury Park, CA: Sage.

Rakowski, W. (1997). Health behavior in the elderly. In D.S. Gochman (Ed.), *Handbook of health behavior research*

*III: Demography, development, and diversity* (pp. 97–117). New York: Plenum.

Raz, N. (2000). Aging of the brain and its impact on cognitive performance: Integration of structural and functional findings. In F.I.M. Craik & T.A. Salthouse (Eds.), *The Handbook of aging and cognition* (2nd ed., pp. 1–90). Mahwah, NJ: Lawrence Erlbaum.

Reuter-Lorenz, P.A., & Lustig, C. (2005). Brain aging: Reorganizing discoveries about the aging mind. *Current Opinion in Neurobiology, 15*(2), 245–251.

Riley, M.W. (1998). Letter to the editor. *Gerontologist, 38,* 151.

Roberts, J., & Snyder, D.L. (2001). Drug Interactions. In G.L. Maddox, R.C. Atchley, J.G. Evans, C.E. Finch, R.A. Kane, M.D. Mezey, et al. (Eds.), *Encyclopedia of aging: A comprehensive multidisciplinary resource in gerontology and geriatrics,* 3rd ed. (pp. 310–313). New York: Springer.

Robine, J.M., & Michel, J.P. (2004). Looking forward to a general theory on population aging. *Journal of Gerontology A: Biological Sciences and Medical Sciences, 59,* M590–M597.

Robinson-Whelen, S., & Kiecolt-Glaser, J. (1997). The importance of social versus temporal comparison appraisals among older adults. *Journal of Applied Social Psychology, 27,* 959–966.

Robinson-Whelen, S., Kiecolt-Glaser, J.K., & Glaser, R. (2000). Effects of chronic stress on immune function and health in the elderly. In S.B. Manuck & R. Jennings (Eds.), *Behavior, health, and aging* (pp. 69–82). Mahwah, NJ: Erlbaum.

Rook, K.S. (1990). Social networks as a source of social control in older adults' lives. In H. Giles, N. Coupland, & J. Wiemann (Eds.), *Communication, health, and the elderly* (pp. 45–63). Manchester, England: University of Manchester Press.

Rook, K.S. (1994). Assessing the health-related dimensions of older adults' social relationships. In M.P. Lawton & J. Teresi (Eds.), *Annual review of gerontology and geriatrics* (Vol. 14, pp. 142–181). New York: Springer.

Rook, K.S. (1995). Social support, companionship, and social control in older adults' social networks: Implications for well-being. In J. Nussbaum & J. Coupland (Eds.), *Handbook of communication and aging research* (pp. 437–463). Mahwah, NJ: Erlbaum.

Rook, K.S. (1998). Investigating the positive and negative sides of personal relationships: Through a glass darkly? In B.H. Spitzberg & W.R. Cupach (Eds.), *The dark side of close relationships* (pp. 369–393). Mahwah, NJ: Lawrence Erlbaum.

Rook, K.S. (2000). The evolution of social relationships in later adulthood. In S. Qualls & N. Abeles (Eds.), *Psychology and the aging revolution* (pp. 173–191). Washington, DC: American Psychological Association.

Rook, K.S., Thuras, P., & Lewis, M. (1990). Social control, health risk taking, and psychological distress among the elderly. *Psychology and Aging, 5,* 327–334.

Rowe, J.W. (1997). The new gerontology. *Science, 278,* 367.

Rowe, J.W., & Kahn, R.L. (1987). Human aging: Usual and successful. *Science, 237,* 143–149.

Rowe, J.W., & Kahn, R.L. (1998). *Successful aging.* New York: Pantheon.

Ryff, C., & Singer, B. (2009). Understanding healthy aging: Key components and their integration. In V.L. Bengtson, D. Gans, N.M. Putney, & M. Silverstein (Eds.), *Handbook of theories of aging,* 2nd ed. (pp. 117–144). New York: Springer.

Ryff, C., Singer, B., Love, G.D., & Essex, M.J. (1998) Resilience in adulthood and later life: Defining features and dynamic processes. In J. Lomranz (Ed.), *Handbook of aging and mental health: An integrative approach* (pp. 6996). New York: Plenum.

Sahyoun, N.R., Lentzner, H., Hoyert, D., & Robinson, K.N. (2001). Trends in causes of death among the elderly. *Aging Trends, 1,* 1–9. Hyattsville, MD: National Center for Health Statistics.

Sandman, C., Wadhwa, P.D., Chicz-DeMet, A., Porto, M., & Garite, T.J. (1999). Maternal corticotropin-releasing hormone and habituation in the human fetus. *Developmental Psychobiology, 34,* 163–173.

Sayers, S.L., Riegel, B., Pawlowski, S., Coyne, J.C., & Samaha, F.F. (2008). Social support and self-care of patients with heart failure. *Annals of Behavioral Medicine, 35,* 70–79.

Schieber, F. (2006). Vision and aging. In J.E. Birren & K.W. Schaie (Eds.), *Handbook of the psychology of aging* (pp. 129–161). San Diego, CA: Academic Press.

Schiller J.S., & Bernadel, L. (2004). *Summary health statistics for the U.S. population: National Health Interview Survey, 2002.* National Center for Health Statistics. Vital Health Statistics 10(220). Washington, DC: U.S. Government Printing Office.

Schoeni, R.F., Freedman, V.A., & Wallace, R.B. (2001). Persistent, consistent, widespread, and robust? Another look at recent trends in old-age disability. *Journal of Gerontology B: Psychological Sciences and Social Sciences, 55,* S206–S218.

Schulz, R., Heckhausen, J., & O'Brien, A. (2000). Negative affect and the disablement process in late life: A life-span control theory approach. In S.B. Manuck, R. Jennings, B.S. Rabin, & A. Baum (Eds.), *Behavior, health, and aging* (pp. 119–133). Mahwah, NJ: Erlbaum.

Seeman, T.E. (1996). Social ties and health. *Annals of Epidemiology, 6,* 442–451.

Seeman, T.E. (2000). Health promoting effects of friends and family: The impact of the social environment on health outcomes in older adults. *American Journal of Health Promotion, 14,* 362–370.

Seeman, T.E., Singer, B.H., Rowe, J.H., Horwitz, R.I., & McEwen, B.S. (1997). Price of adaptation-Allostatic load and its health consequences: MacArthur studies of successful aging. *Archives of Internal Medicine, 157,* 2259–2268.

Semenza, J.C., Rubin, C.H., Falter, K.H., Selanikio, J.D., Flanders, D.W., Howe, H.L., et al. (1996). Heat-related deaths during the July 1995 heat wave in Chicago. *New England Journal of Medicine, 335,* 84–90.

Shipley, B.A., Weiss, A., Der, G., Taylor, M.D., & Deary, I.J. (2007). Neuroticism, extraversion, and mortality in the UK Health and Lifestyle Survey: a 21-year prospective cohort study. *Psychosomatic Medicine, 69,* 923–931.

Shock, N.W., Greulich, R.C., Andres, R.A., Arenberg, D., Costa, P.T., Jr., Lakatta, E.W., et al. (1984). *Normal human aging: The Baltimore Longitudinal Study of Aging.* Washington, DC: U.S. Department of Health and Human Services.

Siegler, I.C., Bastian, L.A., & Bosworth, H.B. (2001). Health, behavior, and aging. In A. Baum, T.A. Revenson, & J.E. Singer (Eds.), *Handbook of health psychology* (pp. 469–476). Mahwah, NJ: Erlbaum.

Siegler, I.C., Bastian, L.A., Steffens, D.C., Bosworth, H.B., & Costa, P.T. (2002). Behavioral medicine and aging. *Journal of Consulting and Clinical Psychology, 70,* 843–851.

Singh, M.A.F. (2002). Exercise comes of age: Rationale and recommendations for a geriatric exercise prescription. *Journal of Gerontology A: Biological Sciences and Medical Sciences, 57,* M262–M282.

Smith, T.W., Kendall, P.C., & Keefe, F.J. (2002). Behavioral medicine and clinical health psychology: Introduction to the special issue, A view from the decade of behavior. *Journal of Consulting and Clinical Psychology, 70,* 459–462.

Smith, T.W., Orleans, C.T., & Jenkins, C.D. (2004). Prevention and health promotion: Decades of progress, new challenges, and emerging agenda. *Health Psychology, 23,* 126–133.

Song, J., Chang, R.W., & Dunlop, D.D. (2006). Population impact of arthritis on disability in older adults. *Arthritis and rheumatism, 55*(2), 248–255.

Sorkin, J.D., Andres, R., Muller, D.C., Baldwin, H.L., & Fleg, J.L. (1992). Cholesterol as a risk factor for coronary heart in disease in elderly men: The BLSA. *Annals of Epidemiology, 2,* 59–67.

Stanton, A.L., & Revenson, T.A. (2011). Adjustment to chronic disease: progress and promise in research. In H.S. Friedman (Ed.), *The Oxford handbook of health psychology.* New York: Oxford University Press.

Staudinger, U.M., Marsiske, M., & Baltes, P.B. (1995). Resilience and reserve capacity in later adulthood: Potentials and limits of development across the life span. In D. Ciccetti & D.J. Cohen (Eds.), *Developmental psychopathology:* Vol. 2: Risk, disorder, and adaptation, pp. 801–847). New York: Wiley.

Steiner, J.F. (1996). Pharmacotherapy problems in the elderly. *Journal of the American Pharmaceutical Association, 36,* 431–437.

Stephens, M.A.P., Fekete, E., Franks, M.M., Rook, K.S., Druley, J.A., & Greene, K. (2009). Spouses' use of persuasion and pressure to promote patients' medical adherence after orthopedic surgery. *Health Psychology, 28,* 48–55.

Strating, M.M.H., Suurmeijer, T.P.B.M., & Van Schuur, W.H. (2006). Disability, social support, and distress in rheumatoid arthritis: results from a thirteen-year prospective study. *Arthritis Care & Research, 55*(5), 736–744.

Stoller, E.P. (1993). Interpretations of symptoms by older people: A health diary study of illness behavior. *Journal of Aging and Health, 5,* 58–81.

Strawbridge, W.J., & Wallhagen, M.I. (1999). Self-rated health and mortality over three decades: Results from a time-dependent covariate analysis. *Research on Aging, 21,* 402–416.

Strawbridge, W.J., Wallhagen, M.I., & Cohen, R.D. (2002). Successful aging and well-being: Self-rated compared with Rowe and Kahn. *Gerontologist, 42,* 727–733

Stuck, A.E., Walthert, J.M., Nikolaus, T., Buela, C.J., Hohmann, C., & Beck, J.C. (1999). Risk factors for functional status decline in community-living elderly people: A systematic literature review. *Social Science and Medicine, 48,* 445–469.

Suarez, E.C., Kuhn, C.M., Schanberg, S.M., Williams, R.B., & Zimmermann, E.A. (1998). Neuroendocrine, cardiovascular, and emotional responses of hostile men: The role of interpersonal challenge. *Psychosomatic Medicine, 60,* 78–88.

Sullivan, M.D., Newton, K., Hecht, J., Russo, J.E., & Spertus, J.A. (2004). Depression and health status in elderly patients with heart failure: A 6-month prospective study in primary care. *The American Journal of Geriatric Cardiology, 13*(5), 252–260.

Sutin, A.R., Terracciano, A., Deiana, B., Naitza, S., Ferrucci, L., Uda, M., et al. (2010). High neuroticism and low conscientiousness are associated with interleukin-6. *Psychological Medicine, 40,* 1485–1493.

Taylor, M.G. (2010). Capturing transitions and trajectories: the role of socioeconomic status in later life disability. *Journal of Gerontology B: Psychological Sciences and Social Sciences.* 65B, 733–743.

Terpenning, M.S., & Bradley, S.F. (1991). Why aging leads to increased susceptibility to infection. *Geriatrics, 46,* 77–80.

Thorpe, C.T., Lewis, M.A., & Sterba, K.R. (2008). Reactions to health-related social control in young adults with type 1 diabetes. *Journal of behavioral medicine, 31,* 93–103.

Tucker, J.S. (2002). Health-related social control within older adults' relationships. *Journal of Gerontology B: Psychological Sciences and Social Sciences, 57,* P387–P395.

Tucker, J.S., & Anders, S.L. (2001). Social control of health behaviors in marriage. *Journal of Applied Social Psychology, 31,* 467–485.

Tucker, J.S., Orlando, M., Elliott, M.N., & Klein, D.J. (2006). Affective and behavioral responses to health-related social control. *Health Psychology, 25,* 715–722.

Uchino, B.N., Cacioppo, J.T., & Kiecolt-Glaser, J.K. (1996). The relationship between social support and physiological processes: A review with emphasis on underlying mechanisms and implications for health. *Psychological Bulletin, 119,* 488–531.

Umberson, D. (1987). Family status and health behaviors: Social control as a dimension of social integration. *Journal of Health and Social Behavior, 28,* 306–319.

United Nations (2009). *World population ageing.* Retrieved March 16, 2010 from http://www.un.org/esa/population/publications/WPA2009/WPA2009_WorkingPaper.pdf.

U.S. Bureau of the Census. (2004). *Statistical Abstract of the U.S. Section 1: Population* Washington, DC: U.S. Government Printing Office.

U.S. Department of Health and Human Services. (1979). *Healthy people: The surgeon general's report on health promotion and disease prevention.* Washington, DC: U.S. Government Printing Office.

U.S. Department of Health and Human Services. (2001). *A profile of older Americans: 2001.* Washington, DC: U.S. Government Printing Office.

Vaitkevicius, P.V., Fleg, J.L., Engel, J.H., O'Connor, F.C., Wright, J.G., Lakatta, L.E., et al. (1993). Effects of age and aerobic capacity on arterial stiffness in healthy adults. *Circulation, 88,* 1456–1462.

Vaupel, J.W., Carey, J.R., Christensen, K., Johnson, T.E., Yashin, A.I., Holm, N.V., et al. (1998). Biodemographic trajectories of longevity. *Science, 280,* 855–860.

Verbrugge, L.M. (1985). The twain meet: Empirical explanations of sex differences in health and mortality. *Journal of Health and Social Behavior, 30,* 282–304.

Verbrugge, L.M. (1989). The twain meet: Empirical explanations of sex differences in health and mortality. *Journal of Health and Social Behavior, 30,* 282–304.

Verbrugge, L.M. (2001). Sex differences in health. In G.L. Maddox, R.C. Atchley, J.G. Evans, C.E. Finch, R.A. Kane, M.D. Mezey, et al. (Eds.), *Encyclopedia of aging: A comprehensive multidisciplinary resource in gerontology and geriatrics* (3rd ed., pp. 850–854). New York: Springer.

Verbrugge, L.M., & Jette, A.M. (1994). The disablement process. *Social Science and Medicine, 38,* 1–14.

Verbrugge, L.M., Reoma, J.M., & Gruber-Baldini, A.L. (1994). Short-term dynamics of disability and well-being. *Journal of Health and Social Behavior, 35,* 97–117.

von Farber, M., Bootsma-van der Wiel, A., van Exel, E., Gussekloo, J., Lagaay, A.M., van Dongen, E., et al. (2001).

Successful aging in the oldest old: Who can be characterized as successfully aged? *Archives of Internal Medicine, 161,* 2694–2700.

Wadden, T.A., Brownell, K.D., & Foster, G.D. (2002). Obesity: Responding to the global epidemic. *Journal of Consulting and Clinical Psychology, 70,* 510–525.

Wagner, L. (1998). Hypertension in African-Americans. *Clinical Excellence for Nurse Practitioners: The International Journal of NPACE, 2*(4), 225–231.

Wahl, H.-W., Becker, S., & Burmedi, D. (2004). The role of primary and secondary control in adaptation to age-related vision loss: A study of older adults with macular degeneration. *Psychology and Aging, 19,* 235–239.

Wahl, H.-W., Schilling, O., & Becker, S. (2007). Age-related macular degeneration and change in psychological control: Role of time since diagnosis and functional ability. *Journal of Gerontology: Psychological Sciences and Social Sciences, 62,* P90–P97.

Waidmann, T.A., & Liu, K. (2000). Disability trends among elderly persons and implications for the future. *Journal of Gerontology B: Psychological Sciences and Social Sciences, 55,* S298–S307.

Wasson, J., Gaudette, C., Whaley, F., Sauvigne, A., Baribeau, P., & Welch, H.G. (1992). Telephone care as a substitute for routine clinic follow-up. *Journal of the American Medical Association, 267,* 1788–1829.

Westmaas, J.L., Wild, T.C., & Ferrence, R. (2002). Effects of gender in social control of smoking cessation. *Health Psychology, 21,* 368–376.

Whitbourne, S.K. (1996). Psychological perspectives on the normal aging process. In L.L. Carstensen, B.A. Edelstein, & L. Dornbrand (Eds.), *The practical handbook of clinical gerontology* (pp. 3–25). Thousand Oaks, CA: Sage.

Williams, D.R., & Collins, C. (1995). U.S. socioeconomic and racial differences in health: Patterns and explanations. *Annual Review of Sociology, 21,* 349–386.

Williams, K.E., & Bond, M.J. (2002). The roles of self-efficacy, outcome expectancies and social support in the self-care behaviors of diabetics. *Psychology, Health, and Medicine, 7,* 127–141.

Williams, M.E. (1994). Clinical management of the elderly patient. In W.R. Hazzard, E.L. Bierman, J.P. Blass, W.H. Ettinger Jr., & J.B. Halter (Eds.), *Principles of geriatric medicine and gerontology* (3rd ed., pp. 195–201). New York: McGraw-Hill.

Williams, T.F. (1992). Aging versus disease: Which changes seen with age are the result of "biological aging"? *Generations, 16,* 21–25.

Wilson, R.S., Mendes de Leon, C.F., Bienias, J.L., Evans, D.A., & Bennett, D.A. (2004). Personality and mortality in old age. *Journal of Gerontology B: Psychological Sciences and Social Sciences, 59,* P110–P116.

Wrosch, C., Heckhausen, J., & Lachman, M.E. (2000). Primary and secondary control strategies for managing health and financial stress across adulthood. *Psychology and Aging, 15,* 387–399.

Wrosch, C., & Schulz, R. (2008). Health-engagement control strategies and 2-year changes in older adults' physical health. *Psychological Science, 19,* 537–541.

Wrosch, C., Schulz, R., & Heckhausen, J. (2002). Health stresses and depressive symptomatology in the elderly: The importance of health engagement control strategies. *Health Psychology, 21,* 340–348.

Wrosch, C., Schulz, R., Miller, G.E., Lupien, S., & Dunne, E. (2007). Physical health problems, depressive mood and cortisol secretion in old age: Buffer effects of health engagement control strategies. *Health Psychology, 26,* 341–349.

Yong, H.H., Gibson, S.J., de L. Horne, D.J., & Helme, R.D. (2001). Development of a Pain Attitudes Questionnaire to assess stoicism and cautiousness for possible age differences. *Journal of Gerontology B: Psychological Sciences and Social Sciences, 56,* P279–P284.

Zettel, L.A., & Rook, K.S. (2004). Substitution and compensation in the social networks of older women. *Psychology and Aging, 19,* 433–443.

# Chronic Pain: Closing the Gap Between Evidence and Practice

Beverly E. Thorn *and* Barbara B. Walker

**Abstract**

Chronic pain devastates lives and leads to staggering health care costs. Because chronic pain is one of the most common complaints seen in health care settings and is commonly associated with other health problems, it is critical that health psychologists have a thorough understanding of pain disorders. In this chapter, we describe the problematic gap that exists between what we know about chronic pain and our ability to provide effective treatments in practice. After reviewing the evidence from several different perspectives, we argue that this gap exists in large part because of a collision between the biopsychosocial and biomedical models. Specifically, the evidence supports conceptualizing and treating chronic pain using a biopsychosocial model, but the prevailing model practiced within our current health care system is biomedical. With their extensive experience and training in both the biopsychosocial model and evidence-based practice, health psychologists are uniquely qualified to narrow this gap.

**Keywords:** Chronic pain, pain clinics, health psychology, back pain, treatment outcome, biopsychosocial

It is difficult for most people to imagine the effects of severe, unremitting pain. Not only does it devastate lives, pain can kill. In one of the largest surveys on pain to date, 18% of Americans with severe or unbearable pain did not consult a professional because they did not believe anyone could help (Sternbach, 1986); there is little doubt that this fatalistic view contributes to the high rate of suicide among chronic pain sufferers (Tang & Crane, 2006). Perhaps the most disturbing aspect of these findings is that there *are* effective ways to help people with chronic pain. Unfortunately, an undeniable gap also exists between our understanding of chronic pain and our ability to provide adequate treatment.

In this chapter, we examine this gap carefully and argue that it exists in large part because, although the evidence supports treating chronic pain from a biopsychosocial perspective, it is the biomedical model that prevails in practice. Given this, our view is that health psychologists, with their extensive experience and training in the biopsychosocial model and evidence-based practice, are uniquely qualified

to bring about change. The overarching goal of this chapter is to provide health psychologists with the information needed to begin working toward changes that will help close this gap. With this deeper understanding, our hope is that new approaches to both research and clinical care will come that will ultimately reduce suffering among patients with persistent debilitating pain.

To begin, we will set the stage for considering chronic pain as a critical, central health care issue: Chronic pain is defined and the magnitude of the problem in terms of its prevalence and its enormous impact on individuals, families, and the health care system is described. Next, we will present chronic pain from three different vantage points: past, present, and future. Looking back in time, we will trace the development of the biomedical and biopsychosocial models and describe how chronic pain has been conceptualized historically within these two models. These models do not operate in a vacuum, however, so we transition to the present by discussing them first within the context of our current health care system and then within the context of the growing and compelling literature regarding the psychobiology of chronic pain. Using the example of chronic low back pain, we will then review the current evidence base for treatments that have grown out of the biomedical and biopsychosocial models. Based upon a critical review of this evidence, we will outline key components of treatment that, given our current state of knowledge, are important for health psychologists to consider. Finally, we will discuss the strengths and limitations of our current state of knowledge, and, with an eye toward the future, discuss several ways that health psychologists can contribute to improving the care we can offer patients suffering from chronic pain.

## Background

To say that chronic pain is a central health care issue is an understatement. Here, we provide common definitions of chronic pain and information regarding the emotional and financial burdens of this problem.

### Definitions

The International Association for the Study of Pain (IASP), with over 6,500 members from 123 countries, is the world's largest multidisciplinary organization focused on pain research and treatment. Consistent with the biopsychosocial model, IASP defines "pain" as an unpleasant experience that encompasses both sensory and emotional modalities; may or may not be accompanied by identifiable tissue damage; and is influenced by multiple factors, including cognitive, affective, and environmental (http://www.iasp-pain.org/).

Chronic pain is usually regarded as pain that persists beyond the normal time of healing, but this conceptualization is insufficient for at least two reasons: First, the time required for healing is variable depending upon the injury, and the operational definition of "healing" is subjective. Second, many conditions are conceptualized and treated as chronic pain syndromes even though normal healing has not occurred, such as arthritic conditions, spinal stenosis, nerve entrapment, and in some cases, malignancies (Mersky & Bogduk, 1994). Generally, pain that persists for at least 3 months following an acute injury, or pain that occurs and persists due to unknown causes is considered "chronic." Chronic pain is often not explained by underlying disease processes, and although biomedical health care interventions are frequently sought, they are rarely curative (Turk, 2001). Since neither a specific timeline nor a normal period for healing are sufficient

criteria to delineate chronic pain, it is perhaps better described as "a persistent pain that is not amenable, as a rule, to treatments based upon specific remedies, or to the routine methods of pain control, such as non-narcotic analgesics" (Mersky & Bogduk, 1994, p. xii). *Recurrent pain* is similar to chronic pain in that it occurs across an extended period of time, but it involves periods with little or no pain (remission), followed by recurrence, as, for example, in migraine headaches. It is generally agreed that chronic pain is not just acute pain that lasts a long time. We shall come back to this point.

### Prevalence and Costs

Worldwide lifetime prevalence rate of chronic pain is estimated to be 35.5%, with individual studies reporting lifetime prevalence rates ranging from 11.5% to 55.2% (Ospina & Harstall, 2002) Over 205 million Americans have severe headache, back, neck, or face pain (Lethbridge-Cejku, Schiller, & Bernadel, 2004). In a survey of 800 patients with chronic pain 76% reported they experience pain at least daily, and almost half reported their pain as always present and "not under control." More than 75% of the sample reported that their pain interferes with daily activities and 25% reported that their pain has caused problems with their family and friends. Eighty-six percent of patients who reported taking prescription and over-the-counter medications said that they experienced unwanted side effects, with half of these patients reporting concerns about addiction to medications (American Chronic Pain Association, 2004). Lifetime prevalence rates of suicide attempts are reported to be between 5% and 14% in those with chronic pain, and the prevalence of suicidal ideation is approximately 20%. The risk of death by suicide is at least doubled in patients with chronic pain (Tang & Crane, 2006).

The economic costs of chronic pain are also striking. In the ACPA survey cited above, 55% of the patients interviewed were not employed. National survey data indicate that over a 2-week interval, 13% of workers lose an average of 4.6 hours per week of work time due to headache, back, arthritis, or another musculoskeletal pain, which represents $61.2 billion in lost productivity per year for American businesses (Stewart, Ricci, Chee, Morganstein, & Lipton, 2003). When other cost factors (including health care, disability, and legal services) are considered, chronic back pain alone costs approximately $100 billion per year in the United States (Frymoyer & Durett, 1997). These data underscore the staggering impact of chronic pain on every facet of a patient's life.

To summarize, chronic pain, which is among the most common presenting complaints seen in medical settings, is associated with depression, substance abuse, extremely poor quality of life, loss of wages, and staggering health care costs. Even more concerning is the fact that chronic pain sufferers attempt and commit suicide at a rate higher than do those with other medical and psychiatric disorders. Later in this chapter, we will demonstrate that many commonly prescribed treatments have been found to be ineffective. Taken together, all these factors converge to create an imperative that health psychologists educate themselves and others about the theoretical underpinnings of chronic pain and their implications for treatment. We begin this effort by first discussing the emergence of the biomedical and biopsychosocial models, and then we explore these two models within the context of the current health care system and recent neurobiological evidence.

## Emergence of the Biomedical and Biopsychosocial Models

As mentioned earlier, most health care professionals believe that biological, psychological, and social factors all play a role in health, but simply believing this is not enough. It is critical that health psychologists understand not only the different assumptions that underlie the biomedical and biopsychosocial models of health, but also the implications of these assumptions for both research and the delivery of care. As will become clear, choosing the biomedical or the biopsychosocial model will, in large part, determine the research and/or treatment one decides to pursue with regard to chronic pain.

The biomedical model became popular with the advent of modern medicine in the 19th century. This model stemmed in part from Descartes who, in the 17th century, declared that the mind and body are separate entities; the body could be studied scientifically, whereas the mind could not. The mind was relegated to study by philosophers and the clergy. This view became even more entrenched when Darwin published his theory of evolution; man was an animal like all others and should be studied accordingly. Strong opposition to this viewpoint later emerged within both medicine and psychology in the 20th century, and in 1977, George Engel formally challenged the biomedical model in a key paper describing the biopsychosocial model (Engel, 1977). Since then, the fields of psychosomatic medicine (which emerged from within psychiatry), behavioral medicine, and health psychology (which emerged from within psychology) all developed and

continue to be strong proponents of the biopsychosocial model.

To appreciate the profound differences between the two models, it is important to examine first what lies at the core of each one. The key core issue is this: What causes illness? Within the biomedical model, illness is thought to be caused by outside forces that affect the body. As a result, the patient plays a relatively passive role, whereas health care providers assume responsibility for fixing the problem, which is biologically based. Without necessarily realizing it, many health care providers and chronic pain patients enter treatment adhering to this view in part because this model worked well for them in the past when dealing with acute pain problems. If a person had a broken leg, for example, the physician likely put on a cast, the leg healed, and the pain disappeared. If a person suffered from strep throat, the physician prescribed an antibiotic, and the pain was relieved.

Most current health care problems are chronic and not acute, however, and the biomedical model has significant shortcomings when applied to chronic illness. In contrast to the biomedical model, the biopsychosocial model views illness as caused by a multitude of converging biological, psychological, and social factors emanating from both outside and inside the person. As a result, patients are asked to actively collaborate with their providers instead of playing a passive role. In the biopsychosocial model, mind and body are seen as highly interconnected, working together in a complex system. The ultimate goal in the biomedical model is for the provider to cure the patient, whereas the goal in the biopsychosocial model is for the patient and health care providers to collaborate to reinstate regulation within a complex, intricate system of biological, psychological, and social factors that have become disregulated.

### The Two Models in the Context of Our Current Health Care System

Traditionally, physicians in training have had very little exposure to chronic pain management, following instead a curriculum focused on acute pain. The classic (biomedical) model of pain asserts that pain is caused by tissue damage, which is thought to generate and maintain pain signals going to the brain. Not surprisingly, health care providers who are exposed to the classic model of pain (but with little in the way of a chronic pain curriculum) will come to assume that chronic pain is acute pain that lasts for a long time. In this biomedical conceptualization, the focus of assessment is on finding the anatomic cause of the pain (the antecedent pain generator), and treatment is focused on removal of the cause. When it is not possible to remove the cause of the pain (e.g., in the case of arthritic conditions), palliative approaches such as analgesic medications are used. Unfortunately, this focus reinforces a passive patient in pursuit of curative or palliative care, does little to promote functional restoration, and increases the probability of disability.

Society is also more accepting of a biomedical model of illness (and chronic pain) than of a biopsychosocial model. Certainly, the prevailing health care model, reimbursement system, and laws encourage the perception that the mind and body are separate entities. The health care system has been touted as one that is curative, and patients understandably wish to be rid of pain—quickly. As medical technology continues to advance, and interventional techniques as well as medicines become increasingly formulated and marketed by industry, our society expects (indeed, demands) cures for any variety of "*dis*-ease," including chronic pain. Another reason that consumers may be loathe to embrace a biopsychosocial model is that substantial social stigma is still associated with any illness that is perceived to have a "mental illness" component, a stigma that is perceived by patients themselves (Moses, 2009; Von Korff, Katon, Unutzer, Wells, & Wagner, 2001) and promulgated by health care professionals (Ross & Goldner, 2009). Unfortunately, as the patient continues to limit activity and seek diagnoses and cures, he or she may spiral downward into a difficult to escape disability syndrome. Subsequently, the patient develops the identity of a "disabled pain patient" and assumes the role of the passive recipient of diagnosis, treatment, and cure (Thorn, 2004).

### The Models in the Context of Current Research on Chronic Pain

The entrenched biomedical system just described presents a quandary, particularly when it comes to the evidence supporting (or not supporting) the classic (biomedical) model of pain perception. Several lines of evidence argue strongly against the separation of mind and body with regard to chronic pain; here, we present three that are particularly intriguing.

### Lack of Association Between Tissue Damage or Vital Signs and Severity of Pain

As just one of many examples, in a study of asymptomatic persons with no history of back pain, magnetic resonance imaging (MRI) of their lumbar spines revealed that only 36% had normal intervertebral disks at all levels. The other 64% had bulges or protrusions of at least one, but often more than one, lumbar disk (Jensen et al., 1994). Disk extrusions (the most extreme extension of the disk beyond the intervertebral space) were not typical in this asymptomatic sample, suggesting that the most severe pathophysiology may more likely be associated with pain reports. The crucial finding from this study, however, is that verifiable tissue abnormalities do not predict reports of present pain nor are they associated with a history of pain.

It is also the case that, despite clinical lore suggesting that bona fide pain is associated with abnormal vital signs (e.g., tachycardia, hypertension), there is no support for this assumption. In a large study of patients presenting to an emergency department with verifiable biomedical diagnoses associated with severe acute pain (e.g., bone fracture, kidney stones), there was no clinically significant association between self-reported pain scores and heart rate, blood pressure, or respiratory rate (Marco, Plewa, Buderer, Hymel, & Cooper, 2006). Thus, neither tissue pathology nor secondary physiological markers are good predictors of pain report. On the other hand, psychosocial variables, such as catastrophizing/fear of pain, depression, and satisfaction with one's job, have been found to be important predictors of a variety of pain-related outcomes, including loss of work time (Bigos et al., 1992; Bruns & Disorbio, 2009; Carragee, Alamin, Miller, & Carragee, 2005; Jarvik et al., 2005; Krause, Ragland, Fisher, & Syme, 1998; Sullivan et al., 2001).

### Chronic Pain Alters Structure and Function of the Nervous System

Sensations coming from skin, muscles, or viscera (including pain sensations) are part of the somatosensory system. Free nerve endings, which can be stimulated by mechanical, thermal, chemical, or electrical means, serve as pain receptors. Once free nerve endings are stimulated, axonal nerve fibers transmit the message to the spinal cord and then on to the brain via several different potential pathways. Interneurons along the way serve as relay stations in the transmission process. Some of the crucial pain pathways travel through areas of the brain that we already know to be important in emotion and cognition, such as the thalamus and the limbic system. Typically thought of as the final destination of pain signals, the somatosensory cortex of the brain is arranged into multiple somatotopic maps of the body surface.

In addition to various behavioral, emotional, and cognitive ramifications, persistent pain produces long-lasting (perhaps permanent) changes in the central nervous system (CNS). The capacity of neurons to change their structure, their chemical profile, or their function is termed *neural plasticity* (Woolf & Salter, 2000). In acute pain, brain-related pain processing is temporarily altered (*modulated*) in a way that increases the sensitivity of neurons to pain signals. Once the tissue is healed, the hypersensitivity typically returns to baseline. Long-lasting alterations in neurons (*modifications*) can also result from the experience of pain. Documented modifications of the nervous system include such structural changes as an increase in the number of pain receptors in the spinal cord following tissue damage and inflammation, and a reduction in brain inhibitory processes following nerve injury (Woolf & Salter, 2000). The phenomenon of neural plasticity may help explain certain conditions such as *allodynia*, a condition in which nonpainful stimulation (e.g., light touch) produces pain; *hyperalgesia*, a situation in which a mildly painful stimulus produces intense pain; and *referred pain*, the perception of pain spread to noninjured tissue (Covington, 2000; Iadarola & Caudle, 1997). Often, these processes persist after the damaged tissue has healed.

Very recent evidence suggests that in addition to altering CNS function in pain-specific ways, chronic pain also alters global (non–pain-related) nervous system function via disruption of vital homeostatic networks. An experiment with patients with chronic back pain revealed that, although their performance on a minimally demanding visual attention task was equal to that of healthy controls, there were pronounced differences in the way their brains processed this nonpain information. In these patients, functional activity was altered in several key areas of the brain's "default mode" network (related to the organized activity of the brain in a resting state). Furthermore, the disruption in functional connectivity showed a linear relation to pain duration, such that those with longer histories of back pain showed greater aberration (Baliki, Geha, Apkarian, & Chialvo, 2008). Findings such as this may help to explain why patients with chronic pain often report difficulties in simple cognitive activities requiring concentration. In addition to CNS disruptions highlighted above, patients with chronic pain also show evidence of disregulation of the autonomic nervous system (ANS), which may be a result of the long-term stress associated with chronic pain (Gockel, Lindholm, Niemisto, & Hurri, 2008; Tracey & Mantyh, 2007).

## The Gate Control Theory Emphasizes the Critical Nature of Cognitive and Affective Factors

Based on what we know about CNS and ANS dysregulation that occurs with the experience of chronic pain, why would a biopsychosocial approach make sense? In the 1960s, Melzack and Wall proposed a revolutionary theory of pain perception, the *gate control theory of pain* (Melzack & Wall, 1965). They suggested that the brain is a *dynamic* participant in pain perception rather than merely a passive recipient of pain signals. Their original hypothesis was that descending signals from the brain could either dampen or amplify pain signals being transmitted from the spinal cord by allowing relatively more, or fewer, pain signals to ultimately reach the brain. Melzack and Wall emphasized the possibility that psychological factors could influence the way in which the brain ultimately responds to painful stimulation through the inhibition or enhancement of the sensory flow of pain signals. The gate control theory thus opened the door for pain to be included within the biopsychosocial model of illness, and pointed to the tremendous potential of psychological interventions for chronic pain.

There is growing research support for the gate control theory (more recently renamed the *neuromatrix model of pain*; Melzack, 2001, 2005). For example, functional MRI (fMRI) research has identified the prefrontal and anterior cingulate cortices (ACC) as important structures involved in the descending pain inhibitory system (Kupers, Faymonville, & Laureys, 2005). These areas are crucial components of cognitive and affective neural networks. A related study using combined psychophysical and fMRI was able to isolate the brain regions associated with expected pain versus actual experienced pain. Although there were areas unique to each, some overlap in activation occurred in the anterior insula and ACC. When expected pain was manipulated to decrease, activation decreased in areas of the brain related to expectancy. More importantly, when expectation of pain decreased, the activation of areas related to actual experienced pain, including the somatosensory cortex, was also decreased (Koyama, McHaffie, Laurienti, & Coghill, 2005). This finding strongly supports the idea that cognitive factors can shape the brain processes that formulate the sensory experience of pain. Another study showed that other cognitive experiences, such as attention and reappraisal, result in activation of the ventrolateral prefrontal cortex and lead to a change in the emotional significance of pain (Wiech, Ploner, & Tracey, 2008).

Earlier, we described how chronic pain can be conceptualized from a biomedical or a biopsychosocial perspective, we explored how the biomedical model prevails within our current health care system, and then we reviewed some compelling new research evidence. Taken together, findings that the extent of tissue damage and vital signs are not necessarily associated with severity of pain, that psychological factors can predict chronic pain outcomes, that experiencing chronic pain can alter both pain and nonpain neuronal structure and function, and that psychological factors can significantly influence pain sensation all argue against the separation of mind and body when it comes to chronic pain (Gatchel, Peng, Peters, Fuchs, & Turk, 2007). Ironically, although current research on the psychoneurobiology of pain supports taking a biopsychosocial approach, our current health care system widely supports the biomedical model. Given this discrepancy, it seems critical that we examine the current research on the effectiveness of common treatments for chronic pain. In the next section, we ask: How effective are biomedical and/or biopsychosocial treatments for one of the most common chronic pain conditions: chronic low back pain?

## An Evidence-based Approach to Effective Treatments for Chronic Low Back Pain

Given the vast proliferation of scientific research in recent years, there is a growing need for psychologists to be able to quickly and efficiently answer questions concerning the effective treatment of chronic pain. In response to these and other concerns within the field of medicine, a new paradigm emerged in the 1990, one termed *evidence-based medicine* (EBM) by a group at McMaster University, who defined it as the "conscientious, explicit, and judicious use of current best evidence in making decisions about the care of individual patients" (Sackett, Rosenberg, Gray, Haynes, & Richardson, 1996, p. 71). Since then, every major health care field, including psychology, has adopted a policy of evidence-based health care. Within psychology, evidence-based practice in psychology (EBPP) was defined as "the integration of the best available research with clinical expertise in the context of patient characteristics, culture, and preferences" (APA Presidential Task Force, 2006, p. 273). This general method is now widely known as evidence-based practice (EBP) to reflect its applicability to multiple disciplines, and attempts have been made to form a common transdisciplinary language (Satterfield et al., 2009).

Evidence-based practice proposes specific methods for asking and answering questions (such as that posed

earlier); specialized tools and resources have been developed to support this effort, and these can be of great value to psychologists (Walker & London, 2007). For the question about chronic pain treatment, the first step is to determine what, where, and how to search for the best evidence available. To support this evidence-based endeavor, a new literature has evolved. This literature is comprised of papers that gather, appraise, and synthesize the results of primary studies. The centerpiece of this new literature is a body of evidence called *systematic reviews*.

Most psychologists are familiar with traditional reviews, in which authors search the literature and generate conclusions based on their findings; systematic reviews are quite different from these. Unlike traditional reviews, systematic reviews follow highly specific, predetermined methods for capturing the evidence, appraising it, and synthesizing it in a manner that is easily accessible to clinicians. They focus on a clear, clinically relevant question and end with a statement about the "clinical bottom-line." Systematic reviews apply the same scientific rigor to the review process that is applied in primary research, and they are designed to avoid the biases that can occur in traditional reviews. Traditional reviews, for example, often rely exclusively upon findings that have been published in English. This can bias the conclusions of the review since negative findings are more likely to appear in (a) non-English than English journals and (b) unpublished than published studies (Dickersin, 2005). In contrast, systematic reviews attempt to locate *all* relevant articles in order to minimize bias. Unlike traditional reviews, an explicit goal of systematic reviews is that their results be replicable. Systematic reviews are essentially research on research.

### Results from Cochrane Systematic Reviews

The Cochrane Collaboration (http://www.cochrane.org/) is the premier resource for up-to-date, evidence-based systematic reviews on the effects of health care interventions. Earlier, we asked the question: How effective are biomedical and/or biopsychosocial treatments for chronic low back pain? To answer this question, we searched the Cochrane Database of Systematic Reviews (CDSR), which contains high-quality, regularly updated systematic reviews that have been performed or commissioned by the Cochrane Collaboration. Specifically, we searched for systematic reviews with "back pain" in the title, and we retrieved 29 reviews. We excluded 16 of them,[1] leaving 13 systematic reviews that were highly relevant. In addition to searching the CDSR, we searched the titles of systematic reviews performed by the Cochrane Back Group and the Cochrane Behavioral Medicine Group[2] and found two more systematic reviews that were not included in our first search.

Table 16.1 illustrates these 15 systematic reviews on the effectiveness of various treatments for chronic low back pain. Treatments are ordered from the most biomedically oriented at the top (surgery, injections, medications, etc.) to the most biopsychosocially oriented at the bottom (behavioral treatment, exercise, back school). We extracted the following information from each review for Table 16.1: (a) the title and author of the review; (b) the percentage of total papers initially found that were later included in the review; (c) of those that were included, the percentage that were later rated as high quality; (d) the adverse effects of the treatment; (e) the main conclusions of the review, and finally, (e) the "bottom line" regarding effectiveness.

The most striking findings in Table 16.1 are those regarding the main conclusions. Scanning down the last ("bottom line") column from the most biomedical to the most biopsychosocial interventions, one notes a definite trend from less to more effectiveness. It is noteworthy that reviewers were unable to draw any conclusions due to poor study quality and/or insufficient or conflicting evidence in six of the 15 reviews (as indicated by "??" in the table). Of the remaining nine reviews, four of them (injections, traction, spinal manipulation, and antidepressants) concluded that the intervention studied was not effective for chronic low back pain, and it is of interest to note that each of these interventions fall clearly on the biomedical end of the spectrum. Toward the middle of the spectrum, it is interesting to note that opioids and three herbal medications were found to have effects on pain but not on functioning. Clearly, the most promising results in the table are associated with the last three reviews at the biopsychosocial end of the spectrum. These systematic reviews concluded that behavioral treatments such as relaxation training, biofeedback, cognitive therapy, back schools, and exercise are all effective for pain and some showed effects on functioning as well.

Several other features of the table are also worth noting. When beginning a systematic review of effectiveness, authors perform a comprehensive search of all the literature in the area and then exclude all papers that are not randomized controlled trials meeting their predetermined criteria for inclusion, are not relevant to the question, and/or that omit information critical for the review. The third column contains the percentage of papers that were included in reviews, compared with the number of papers originally identified. For the seven systematic reviews that contained these data, the average percentage was only 16%, illustrating that only a small subset of studies performed were ultimately included in these systematic reviews. After deciding which studies to include, Cochrane reviewers then assess their quality by systematically rating each one on 12 validity criteria recommended by the Cochrane Back Review Group (van der Velde et al., 2007; van Tulder, Furlan, Bombardier, Bouter, & Editorial Board Cochrane, 2003). A high-quality study (i.e., low risk of bias) is defined as fulfilling at least six (50%) of the 12 validity criteria. This score is important because conclusions drawn from high-quality studies are obviously more convincing than conclusions drawn from primarily low-quality studies. The third column illustrates the wide variability among reviews; the percentage of high-quality studies ranged from 0% to 100%, with an average of only 45%.

Taken together, the results in Table 16.1 illustrate how complex it becomes to find simple answers to very important clinical questions. Systematic reviews developed as a way of synthesizing primary studies, but when one finds numerous systematic reviews on the same topic, it becomes difficult to synthesize those results. In response to this, a level of synthesis has developed that extends beyond systematic reviews; these are often systematic reviews or meta-analyses of systematic reviews and are called *evidence-based guidelines*. Given the findings presented in Table 16.1, it becomes of interest to examine the evidence-based guidelines for chronic pain. Within the United States, many (but not all) evidence-based guidelines can be found in the National Guideline Clearinghouse (http://www.guideline.gov/), which offers free access to its database on its public website.

### Evidence-based Practice Guidelines for Chronic Pain

Within the area of chronic pain, an evidence-based practice guideline on nonpharmacologic treatments was recently commissioned by the American Pain Society and the American College of Physicians (Chou & Huffman, 2007). Development of the guideline was motivated in part by the finding that clinicians vary substantially in how they manage low back pain (Cherkin, Deyo, Wheeler, & Ciol, 1995), coupled with the fact that much of the evidence on

**Table 16.1   Fifteen systematic reviews on the effectiveness of various treatments for chronic low back pain**

| Cochrane Review | Objective | Numbers included/total numbers retrieved (%) | Numbers high quality/total numbers included (%) | Adverse Effects | Main Conclusions | The Bottom Line |
|---|---|---|---|---|---|---|
| Surgery for degenerative lumbar spondylosis (Gibson & Waddell, 2005) | To review evidence on the effectiveness of surgical interventions for degenerative lumbar spondylosis | 31/** [1] | ** | Not reported | Conflicting and insufficient evidence | ??[2] |
| Prolotherapy injections for chronic low-back pain (Dagenais, Yelland, Del Mar, & Schoene, 2007) | To determine the efficacy of prolotherapy in adults with chronic low-back pain | 5/7 (71%) | 5/5 (100%) | Increased back pain and stiffness following injections | When used alone, not an effective treatment for CLBP[3]; weak evidence when combined with manipulation and exercise | Not effective alone for pain or functioning |
| Injection therapy for subacute and chronic low-back pain (Staal, de Bie, de Vet, Hildebrandt, & Nelemans, 2008) | To determine if injection therapy is more effective than placebo or other treatments for patients with subacute or CLBP | 18/56 (32%) | 9/18 (50%) | Headache, dizziness, transient local pain, tingling, numbness, & nausea | Insufficient evidence to support the use of injection therapy in chronic low back pain | ?? |
| Antidepressants for nonspecific low back pain (Urquhart, Hoving, Assendelft, Roland, & van Tulder, 2008) | To determine whether antidepressants are more effective than placebo for LBP | 9/** | 6/9 (66%) | Dry mouth, constipation, tachycardia, sedation, orthostatic hypotension, & tremor | No clear evidence that antidepressants are any more effective than placebo in CLBP | Not effective for pain |
| Opioids for chronic low back pain (Deshpande, Furlan, Mailis-Gagnon, Atlas, & Turk, 2007) | To determine the efficacy of opioids in adults with CLBP | 5/5043 (0.1%) | 3/4 (75%) | Headaches and nausea | Weak evidence that Tramadol reduces pain more than placebo and that weak opioids reduce pain more than Naproxen, but neither significantly improved function | Effective for pain but not for functioning |
| Herbal Medications for nonspecific low back pain (Gagnier, van Tulder, Berman, & Bombardier, 2006) | To determine the effectiveness of herbal medicine for nonspecific low back pain | 10/295 (3%) | 8/10 (80%) | Mild transient GI complaints | Devil's claw and white willow bark both reduced pain more than placebo and about the same as a daily dose of Vioxx. Cayenne reduced pain more than placebo | Three herbal medications effective for pain |

| Study | Purpose | | | Adverse effects | Conclusions | Not effective for pain or functioning |
|---|---|---|---|---|---|---|
| Traction for low back pain with or without sciatica (Clarke et al., 2007) | To determine traction's effectiveness, compared to placebo, sham traction or no treatment | ** | 5/25 (20%) | Increased pain | No more effective than placebo, sham treatment or other treatments | Not effective for pain or functioning |
| Superficial heat or cold for low back pain (French, Cameron, Walker, Reggars, & Esterman, 2006) | To assess the effects of superficial heat and cold therapy for low back pain in adults | 3/1178 (0.2%) | 0/3 (0%) | None | No conclusions can be drawn from the three poor-quality studies | ?? |
| Spinal manipulative therapy for low back pain (Assendelft, Morton, Yu, Suttorp, & Shekelle, 2004) | To compare spinal manipulative therapy with numerous other therapies | 29/1153 (2.5%) ** | | None | No statistically or clinically significant advantage over general practitioner care, analgesics, physical therapy, exercises, or back school | Not effective for pain or functioning |
| Lumbar supports for prevention and treatment of low back pain (van Duijvenbode, Jellema, van Poppel, & van Tulder, 2008) | To assess the effects of lumbar supports for prevention and treatment of non-specific low-back pain | 3/820 (0.3%) | 1/3 (33.3%) | Restricted movement, general discomfort | Conflicting evidence; poor quality studies | ?? |
| Exercise therapy for treatment of non-specific low back pain (Hayden, van Tulder, Malmivaara, & Koes, 2005) | To evaluate the effectiveness of exercise therapy in adult non-specific acute, subacute and chronic low-back pain versus no treatment and other conservative treatments | 43/** | 6/43 (14%) | Increased low back pain and muscle soreness in a small number of patients | Slightly effective at decreasing pain and improving function but poor study quality limits conclusions | ?? |
| Individual patient education for low back pain (Engers et al., 2008) | To determine whether individual patient education is effective in the treatment of non specific low back pain and which type is most effective | 24/** | 14/24 (58%) | None | Effectiveness of individual education remains unclear for patients with CLBP | ?? |
| Behavioral treatment for chronic low back pain (Henschke et al., 2010) | To determine if behavioural therapy is more effective than reference treatments for CLBP, and which type of behavioral treatment is most effective | 21/** | 6/21 (29%) | Not reported | Relaxation training, biofeedback, and cognitive therapy are more effective than WLC for short-term pain relief. Long-term effects unknown. No significant differences between behavioral treatments and exercise therapy | More effective than no treatment for pain; conflicting evidence for functioning |

(continued)

**Table 16.1** *(Cont'd)*

| Cochrane Review | Objective | Numbers included/total numbers retrieved (%) | Numbers high quality/total numbers included (%) | Adverse Effects | Main Conclusions | The Bottom Line |
|---|---|---|---|---|---|---|
| Conservative treatment of acute and chronic nonspecific low back pain (vanTulder, Koes, & Bouter, 1997) | To assess the effectiveness of the most common conservative types of treatment for patients with acute and chronic nonspecific low back pain | 80/** | 20/80 (25%) | Not reported | Strong evidence for short-term effectiveness of manipulation, back schools (*in occupational settings*), and exercise therapy. Limited evidence for the effectiveness of behavior therapy | Manipulation, back schools (in an occupational setting) and exercise are effective for the outcome that was measured [4] |
| Back schools for nonspecific low back pain (Heymans, van Tulder, Esmail, Bombardier, & Koes, 2005) | To assess the effectiveness of back schools (education, skill-building and exercise) for patients with non-specific LBP | 19/** | 6/19 (32%) | Not reported | Moderate evidence that back schools (*in occupational settings*) reduce pain and improve function compared to exercise, manipulation, myofascial therapy, advice, placebo or WLC in CLBP | Effective for pain and functioning in occupational settings |

[1]** indicates that these data were not reported in the review.
[2]Unable to draw conclusions due to poor study quality, insufficient and/or conflicting evidence.
[3]Chronic low back pain
[4]The authors of this review compared studies measuring different outcomes making it impossible to separate results for pain and functioning.

treating low back pain is conflicting. To prepare this guideline, the authors examined the systematic reviews from the Cochrane Library along with systematic reviews and individual studies published elsewhere. Consistent with results presented in Table 16.1, they concluded that cognitive-behavioral therapy (CBT), relaxation training, exercise, functional restoration, spinal manipulation, and interdisciplinary rehabilitation show good evidence of moderate efficacy for chronic low back pain. One of the most interesting findings was that they found little evidence of consistent differences between interventions—with one fascinating exception: Intensive interdisciplinary rehabilitation was more effective than noninterdisciplinary efforts.

It is interesting to note that another recent evidence-based guideline came to a similar conclusion. In their recent practice guideline on chronic back pain, The National Institute for Clinical Evidence in England (NICE; http://guidance.nice.org.uk) recommended against a wide variety of unidisciplinary techniques (e.g., injections, lumbar supports, traction, etc.) and suggested referring patients to an intensive interdisciplinary program if a less intensive treatment was not significantly helpful and a patient has a high degree of disability and/or psychological distress. Their intensive review of the best recent evidence led them to recommend that an intensive treatment program include at least CBT and exercise.

Thus, the Cochrane reviews shown in Table 16.1, as well as very recent clinical practice guidelines, lead to an interesting hypothesis: that biopsychosocially oriented, interdisciplinary interventions are more effective than unidisciplinary biomedically oriented interventions. To explore this further, we next take a closer look at the evidence supporting interdisciplinary pain programs.

### Interdisciplinary Pain Rehabilitation Programs

In marked contrast to a purely biomedical intervention approach, inpatient and outpatient interdisciplinary pain rehabilitation programs (IPRPs) were developed and originated in the 1970s. The rationale for such programs was to provide intensive pain management approaches that utilize the expertise of a variety of specific disciplines, but in a coordinated fashion. These tertiary clinics/programs were developed specifically for patients with pain; these patients are often those with complex pain problems who have not responded to a variety of other interventions. Although IPRPs vary considerably, the theoretical framework is decidedly biopsychosocial and

the team works with patients to reduce pain; address social and environmental factors that may trigger, exacerbate, or maintain pain; and to increase physical functioning. It is important to note that the primary goal of treatment is not to *eliminate* pain. Instead, the focus is on helping patients increase activity levels and muscle strength, decrease pain behaviors, reduce or eliminate reliance on analgesic medications (particularly narcotic analgesics and/or muscle relaxants), and reduce depression, anxiety, and social isolation. Traditionally, IPRPs include physicians, psychologists, and physical therapists, among other team members, with ancillary services included as needed (e.g., dietetics, recreational therapy).

The existing evidence for the efficacy of IPRPs is strong. In an early meta-analysis including 3,089 chronic pain patients, 45%–65% of patients were reported to return to work after completing an IPRP treatment, compared to only 20% following surgery for pain and 25% following implantation of pain control devices (Flor, Fydrich, & Turk, 1992). Follow-up reviews comparing IPRPs to traditional medical interventions reported almost equal efficacy in terms of pain reduction, but IPRPs showed superior increases in functional activities, return to work, reduction in depression, lower health care costs, and termination of disability claims (Turk, 2001, 2002).

The most comprehensive systematic review to date recently confirmed these early findings and extended them even further (Scascighini, Toma, Dober-Spielmann, & Sprott, 2008). These authors reported strong evidence that multidisciplinary treatments are more effective than standard medical treatment and moderate evidence that multidisciplinary treatments are more effective than non-multidisciplinary treatments. Based on their findings, they were able to isolate some components of multidisciplinary treatment that seem critical to be maximally effective: CBT, exercise, relaxation training, patient education, and physical therapy. Their evidence was so convincing that they concluded that, "[a] standard of multidisciplinary programmes should be internationally established to guarantee generally good outcomes in the treatment of chronic pain" (Scascighini et al., 2008, p. 670), and strongly suggest that chronic pain patients be referred to specialized multidisciplinary treatment programs rather than to single disciplines sequentially.

### Challenges for the Present and Hope for the Future

To fully appreciate the enormous challenges associated with treating chronic pain, it is important to view the problem of chronic pain within the broader context of our health care system. We next discuss the striking effect of our health care system on treating chronic pain and highlight some of the most pressing challenges ahead. In this final section, we argue that, because of their expertise in EBP and the biopsychosocial model, health psychologists are uniquely qualified to play an integral role in transforming our health care system to better meet the needs of people suffering from chronic pain.

## The Current Health Care System

In this chapter, we have presented strong evidence that chronic pain is a biopsychosocial problem that demands biopsychosocially oriented treatment. Unfortunately, when providers attempt to transport biopsychosocial interventions into our current health care system, they find it increasingly difficult. Our current health care system is essentially biomedically oriented, with very little support for the interdisciplinary, biopsychosocially oriented programs that have been found to be most effective for chronic pain.

One reason for this relates to the way that providers are currently reimbursed for their services. Third-party payers sustain the biomedical model of pain management in several ways. First, there is continued insistence on the separation of mental health and physical health benefits. Indeed, by federal law, the Health Insurance Portability and Accountability Act (HIPAA, 1996) promotes the separation of mental and physical health by providing unique laws for each (http://www.hhs.gov/ocr/privacy/index.html). Mental health benefits have historically been afforded a much lower coverage rate, if they are covered at all. On the other hand, the number (and cost) of invasive biomedical treatments for chronic pain has risen dramatically, a direct reflection of an increase in reimbursement for such services. For example, from 1997 to 2006, there was a 197% increase in interventional treatments for chronic pain conditions in Medicare-covered patients (Manchikanti, Singh, Pampati, Smith, & Hirsch, 2009) and from 1996 to 2001, the rate of spinal fusions alone rose by 113% in the United States (Deyo, Gray, Kreuter, Mirza, & Martin, 2005). Ironically, the era of managed care and capitation may have increased incentives for providers to reduce utilization of health care services, but this may actually have had the unintended effect of forcing patients to express their symptoms more urgently in order to gain access to the (biomedical) health care system (Barsky & Borus, 1995).

The taxonomies through which patients receive pain-related diagnoses also encourage separation of mind and body and thus remain inadequate. Patients can receive pain-related diagnoses via the International Classification of Diseases (ICD; World Health Organization, 1992) or via the *Diagnostic and Statistical Manual of Mental Disorders* (DSM; American Psychiatric Association, 2000). The ICD system used by physicians specifically separates pain disorders into those thought to be of psychogenic etiology and those thought to be of nonpsychogenic etiology (the classic "functional" vs. "organic" distinction). The DSM system lists Pain Disorders under the broader category of Somatoform Disorders, and a hallmark of somatoform disorders is that the patient experiences physical symptoms with no known physiological basis. Indeed, in the case of Pain Disorder, it is specified that if the pain results from a medical condition and psychological factors are judged to play a minimal role, this subtype of pain disorder is not considered a mental illness (and is therefore coded under Axis III). The major problem is that patients receiving a DSM Pain Disorder diagnosis are by definition classified as mentally ill. The net result of receiving a mental illness diagnosis for a chronic pain disorder is that patients suffer not only the associated stigma, but also fewer health care benefits.

Turk (2001, 2002) argues that widespread use of IPRPs could substantially reduce the iatrogenic complications that about 50% of pain patients experience from medication or surgical side effects and could save the health care system well over $11 billion per year. Ironically, financial support for IPRPs through third-party insurers has shown a steady decrease, whereas the number and cost of biomedical interventional treatments continues to escalate (Deyo et al., 2005; Gatchel et al., 2007; Manchikanti et al., 2009) Part of the issue is the tendency for payers to unbundle the multidisciplinary pain package into biological and psychosocial components, renewing the dualistic separation of mind and body. Interdisciplinary pain programs have been forced to drop their psychologist members, not because psychologists are not valued but because of organizational systemic barriers. Other barriers to integrated biopsychosocial treatment are that many insurers refuse to pay more than one provider to treat a particular problem on the same day, and it is rare for any system to reimburse providers for time spent communicating with other providers—an essential component of interdisciplinary pain treatment.

For these reasons, at least in the U.S. private sector, IPRPs have been transformed into single-discipline clinics with treatment consisting of evaluation and intervention only from the discipline involved. In a national survey of physicians (Cherkin et al., 1995), it was found that clinicians vary widely in how they manage back pain. With chronic pain, for example, it is not unusual for patients to be referred for a course of physical therapy. If physical therapy is not helpful, they may be referred to an anesthesiologist for nerve blocks. When nerve blocks fail to provide significant relief, patients often receive more medication and/or another type of single-discipline treatment (e.g., acupuncture, massage, or yoga), leading to a vicious cycle that ultimately leads both patients and providers feeling helpless and hopeless.

In summary, the evidence is clear that integrated, interdisciplinary treatment of chronic pain is the treatment of choice for a significant proportion of chronic pain patients, but it is not available to the vast majority of chronic pain sufferers in the United States today. Ironically, in the area of chronic pain, our health care system currently supports and encourages treatment that is inconsistent with the best evidence at the same time that it encourages EBP.

## A Paradigm Shift in the Offing?

Thankfully, the news is not all bad. The possibility of health care reform that values behavioral health, new biopsychosocial treatment guidelines and laws, and the recent addition of health and behavior procedural codes all provide hope that the biopsychosocial model can be revitalized as the health care system undergoes transformation.

### Transforming Practice Guidelines into Biopsychosocial Laws

In a previous section, both the NICE guidelines and the guidelines commissioned by the American Pain Society and the American College of Physicians (Chou & Huffman, 2007) were cited as promulgating interdisciplinary rather than single-discipline treatment for chronic pain. Two other recent guidelines (one from the American College of Occupational and Environmental Medicine (ACOEM; American College of Occupational and Environmental Medicine, 2008) and the other from the Colorado Division of Worker Compensation (Colorado Division of Worker Compensation, 2009) are particularly noteworthy because they resulted in the passage of new laws regarding reimbursement for the management of chronic pain. In spite of the controversy generated by the ACOEM guideline related to its limited expert review panel, consensus opinion statements, and recommended elimination of a

variety of tests, therapies, and interventions (Manchikanti et al., 2008) both this guideline and the one from Colorado led to the advent of biopsychosocial laws pertaining to the assessment and treatment of chronic pain treatment. Such laws are now in place in Colorado (Colorado Division of Worker Compensation, 2009), California (California Medical Treatment Utilization Schedule, 2009), Texas (Texas Division of Worker's Compensation Adopted Rules, 2006) Kansas (Kansas Division of Workers Compensation, 2008), Delaware (Delaware Health care Advisory Panel, 2009), and Oklahoma (Oklahoma Physician Advisory Committee, 2007). These regulations are based upon a biopsychosocial conceptualization, are enforceable in a court of law, and recommend or, in certain cases, require that psychological services be provided prior to invasive biomedical interventions.

### Procedural Terminology: Health & Behavior Codes

Another example of the move toward integrating medical and psychological interventions is the relatively recent change in the way psychologists can be reimbursed for treating biopsychosocial problems such as chronic pain. Traditionally, psychologists could be reimbursed only for assessing and treating problems classified as mental disorders. As mentioned earlier, that required psychologists to give DSM diagnoses to patients with chronic pain, which, in many cases, was inappropriate. That changed in 2002, through the combined efforts of the APA Practice Directorate and the Interdivisional Health Care Committee, represented by Divisions 17, 22, 38, 40, and 54 of the APA (http://apa.org/apapractice/cpt_2002.html). Health and Behavior (H&B) procedural codes now allow psychologists to be reimbursed for assessing and treating patients with a primary medical diagnosis. Provided that a physician has previously diagnosed a patient with a medical condition using the ICD diagnostic system, psychologists can now use H&B codes to assess and treat the problem. Thus, for the first time, procedure codes are available that accurately reflect what health psychologists actually do to help patients manage chronic painful conditions. Furthermore, H&B codes are paid out of a patient's medical benefits rather than from a "behavioral health" carve-out plan.

Unfortunately, these codes are not yet universally accepted by health insurance carriers (although by law, Medicare must accept them), and many practitioners remain hesitant to use them for this reason.

However, with health care moving steadily toward increased integration, the growing emphasis on evidence-based medicine, and the advent of biopsychosocial practice guidelines and laws, there is cause for optimism that a paradigm shift toward the biopsychosocial treatment of chronic pain is coming.

## The Role of Health Psychologists in Advancing the Biopsychosocial Treatment Model

A generous portion of this chapter has been devoted to detailing the challenges associated with assessment and treatment of chronic pain in the current health care climate. Rather than view these challenges as obstacles, our stance is that they present a wealth of opportunities for health psychologists to advance the application of the biopsychosocial model in the care of patients with chronic pain. In this final section, we outline some of the pressing needs that health psychologists are uniquely qualified to meet. Although a comprehensive list of current needs is beyond the scope of this chapter, our aim is to whet the appetite with a few specific examples related to research, clinical practice, and advocacy.

### Research Needs

Virtually every systematic review on the topic of chronic pain has concluded that not enough high-quality randomized controlled trials are available on which to base conclusions regarding the efficacy of treatment for chronic pain. This is not a concern unique to psychosocial or biopsychosocial treatments for chronic pain, nor is this problem limited to the field of pain management; rather, this is a consistent and continuing problem in the extant research literature. When systematic reviews are conducted, it is frequently the case that a substantial number of trials cannot be included because they did not report necessary details or because they were poor quality studies. For example, statistics needed to calculate effect sizes are sometimes missing in the primary study, full details of treatment content are often omitted, and treatment implementation is often not measured (e.g., adherence to the manual, quality of therapy). Since a single clinical trial has less power to answer efficacy questions than combined clinical trials, it is critically important that future clinical trials be designed in such a way that they are eligible for inclusion into systematic reviews. Clinical trials are costly in many ways, and biopsychosocial treatments require intensive effort on the part of the interventionists as well the patients. The harsh reality is that trials excluded from systematic reviews represent wasted effort because they do not contribute to our existing knowledge (Eccleston, Williams, & Morley, 2009).

In an effort to enhance the internal validity of studies, the Consolidated Standards of Reporting Trials (CONSORT; http://www.consort-statement.org) group has published a checklist of items that should be reported in clinical trials (Moher, Schulz, & Altman, 2001). Furthermore, guidelines for reporting information in clinical trials that are relevant to external validity have been proposed (Green & Glasgow, 2006); many of these factors (e.g., the type of site where the treatment is intended to be adopted, acceptable alterations of the treatment, and applicability of the treatment in heterogeneous or high-risk populations) are not commonly addressed in clinical trials. Both sets of rating criteria share the common goal of encouraging clinical researchers to report more details regarding all aspects of a clinical trial, which would enhance both the internal and external validity of studies, increase the likelihood that a clinical trial would meet the criteria for inclusion in a systematic review, and ultimately, facilitate the translation of clinical research into clinical practice.

In addition to enhanced reporting standards, increased attention to the issue of outcome assessment is important. Outcome variables and the instruments used to assess these variables vary widely. This may explain some of the variability in outcomes among studies of treatments for chronic pain. The Initiative on Methods, Measurement, and Pain Assessment in Clinical Trials (IMMPACT) group has suggested six assessment domains that pain researchers should attend to when designing clinical trials (Dworkin et al., 2008): pain, physical functioning, emotional functioning, participant ratings of improvement and satisfaction with treatment, symptoms and adverse events, and participant disposition. Of these, adverse events are particularly worth noting; they are rarely reported in psychosocial treatment literature, even though there is evidence that some patients may deteriorate with treatment (Morley, Williams, & Hussain, 2008). Furthermore, measuring health care utilization (e.g., physician and hospital visits, analgesic medication use), would greatly increase the clinical utility of the findings (Dworkin et al., 2008).

### Clinical Needs

It is imperative that health psychologists not underestimate the complexity of behavior change or discount the social and psychological factors promoting and maintaining disability in patients with chronic pain (Blyth, Macfarlane, & Nicholas, 2007). Although manualized treatments have given us much in terms of promoting standardized treatment, a temptation exists to assume that, as long as one adheres to the manual, high-quality treatment has been delivered. It is fair to say that the manual is necessary, but not sufficient for delivering an evidence-based treatment. Nonspecific factors remain a key ingredient of active treatments, and we should not underemphasize the need for empathy, building rapport, and providing a sound, reasonable rationale for treatment that is geared to the particular needs of the patient. Close examination of the literature reveals that manualized treatments offered under the label of CBT often contain a mixture of different modules with varying content, and the relationships between the aims of treatment, the modules offered, and the outcomes measured are often unclear and/or disjointed. In clinical practice, there is likely even more variability due to pragmatics, practitioner preferences, and constraints imposed by the treatment setting. To complicate the situation even further, our current health care system encourages offering the shortest possible course of treatment delivered by the lowest-level provider possible, but "good clinical outcomes should perhaps not be expected from dilute and brief treatments delivered by inexperienced staff to severely distressed patients" (Eccleston et al., 2009, p. 22).

One way to enhance the success of treatments geared toward lifestyle changes (pain self-management) is to find ways to help patients actually apply what they have learned (e.g., through homework or practicing skills that were learned in treatment). This is a key variable that has been given inadequate attention in both clinical research and practice. For example Scharff and Marcus (1994) found that headache participants who practiced the skills taught in treatment were more likely to maintain their treatment gains when measured at follow-up. Likewise, completion of homework assignments was significantly related to treatment outcome in patients with irritable bowel syndrome participating in group CBT (Tkachuk, Graff, Martin, & Bernstein, 2003). This is a general finding in medical research (i.e., adherent patients have better outcomes), and it may be that these individuals are different in other ways, such as having more conscientious personality characteristics. Even if this is the case, if we can find ways to reinforce what is learned in the treatment, perhaps by enhancing skills practice, long-term outcomes may be improved. Although it is scant, the literature focusing on enhancing skills acquisition is

important, and clinicians and researchers alike would be well advised not to ignore this aspect of treatment (Johnson & Kazantzis, 2004).

Since pain self-management requires modifying a wide range of behaviors, it is likely that the relatively brief courses of psychosocial treatment typically offered (8–12 weeks) are less than ideal for maintaining treatment gains. Recent innovations using therapeutic interactive voice response therapy (TIVR) hold promise; TIVR uses a telephone interaction via a recorded voice to ask specific questions, with the caller inputting responses through a telephone keypad. Studies have found that TIVR not only maintained, but actually enhanced treatment gains following CBT interventions for chronic pain (Naylor, Helzer, Naud, & Keefe, 2002; Naylor, Keefe, Brigidi, Naud, & Helzer, 2008) Although these technological advances may seem out of the realm of possibility for a typical clinical practice today, telephone and internet-administered therapies hold enormous potential to provide efficient, cost-effective ways of enhancing pain self-management strategies learned in face-to-face therapy. As more high-quality research in this area emerges, hopefully more opportunities will emerge to use this and other types of technology in practice.

### Advocacy Needs
A final avenue that health psychologist can take in advancing the biopsychosocial model is to advocate strongly for it at local, community and national levels. At the most local level, health psychologists bear a responsibility to educate other professionals about our unique role within the health care system. Given that the strict dichotomy between biological and psychological problems continues to pervade health care, it is not surprising that many health care professionals continue to assume that psychologists assess and treat only mental health problems. The properly trained health psychologist is in a unique position to dispel this antiquated view. Specific to chronic pain, one can create opportunities to converse with patients as well as other professionals about the implications of the biopsychosocial model for chronic pain. This educational process can be slow; it often occurs in one patient, one community talk, one support group, and/or one colleague at a time. Because of this, it is important to keep the enormous rewards in mind. As we have emphasized throughout this chapter, greater adherence to the biopsychosocial model has the potential to reduce suffering among patients who may be suffering needlessly. This is a critically important goal.

In addition to advocating at a local level, health psychologists can also advocate with private health insurance companies to reimburse psychologists for health and behavior assessment and intervention services. The APA practice directorate provides a free tutorial on using H&B codes and sample letters that can be personalized and/or modified and sent to local private insurance companies (http://apa.org/apapractice/hbcodes).

The highest level of advocacy involves the political/legislative process. Since the health care system is poised to change dramatically in the coming years, it is critically important that health psychologists become active and involved in these changes to ensure that the health care system fosters, encourages, and incentivizes the growth of the biopsychosocial approach to chronic diseases. As a specific example, although the current H&B codes list six procedures, Medicare covers only five; it does not cover services provided to a family without the patient present. Private insurers are typically stricter in their coverage of H&B codes than Medicare, so it is likely that this particular code (96155) is rarely covered. A sorely needed additional H&B code would allow an interdisciplinary team to discuss the treatment of a patient without the patient present. Although this service is the glue that holds interdisciplinary treatment together, it is currently not covered under any insurance reimbursement plan. This lack of reimbursement for providers to talk with one another without the patient present has been a major reason why so many interdisciplinary, colocated chronic pain management teams have been dismantled.

## Conclusion
### Future Directions
Our ultimate goal, of course, is to improve the care of our patients who suffer from persistent debilitating pain. In this chapter, we have argued that although the biomedical model (and single-discipline treatment) still prevails in the treatment of chronic pain, the best available scientific evidence supports a biopsychosocial model (and interdisciplinary treatment). Thus, it is clear that a paradigm shift is desperately needed to advance patient care in the area of chronic pain, and, in our view, health psychologists are among the most qualified professionals to promote such a shift. We have highlighted several avenues that could be taken: among others, these include becoming engaged in writing systematic reviews and biopsychosocially oriented practice guidelines, advocating for health care reform that includes biopsychosocial laws and expanding reimbursement of Health and Behavior Codes, and aggressively educating others at the local, community, state, and national levels about the importance of integrating behavioral and mental health into treatment of chronic pain.

In this chapter, we have pointed out the gaps that exist between what we know about chronic pain and what we actually do in practice. Based upon this, it is apparent that certain changes must occur for our patients with chronic pain to receive the very best care. If that is true, health psychologists have a professional obligation to pursue those changes relentlessly. Our hope is that as we do so, the standard of care for chronic pain will move toward a more psychosocially oriented model, thereby diminishing the troubling gaps that currently exist between evidence and practice.

## Notes
1. Ten reviews were excluded because they did not focus on chronic pain, one was excluded because it focused on a procedure not performed in the United States, three were excluded because it was impossible to separate acute from chronic pain, one was replaced by a later review, and one review was withdrawn prior to completion.
2. The Cochrane Collaboration has assembled review groups that include people from around the world who share an interest in developing and maintaining systematic reviews in a particular area. A list of the review groups, their contact information, and reviews each group has completed can be viewed at http://www.cochrane.org/contact/entities.htm#CRGLIST.

## References
American Chronic Pain Association. (Endo Pharmaceuticals, Sponsor). (2004). *Americans living with pain survey.* Retrieved from http://www.theacpa.org/.

American College of Occupational and Environmental Medicine. (2008). *Occupational medicine practice guidelines* (2nd revised ed.). Beverly Farms, Mass: OEM Press.

American Psychiatric Association. (2000). *Diagnostic and statistical manual of mental disorders* (4th revised ed.). Washington, D.C.: American Psychiatric Association.

APA Presidential Task Force. (2006). Evidence-based practice in psychology. *American Psychologist, 61*(4), 271–285.

Assendelft, W.J.J., Morton, S.C., Yu, E.I., Suttorp, M.J. & Shekelle, P.G. (2004). Spinal manipulative therapy for low-back pain. *Cochrane Database of Systematic Reviews 2004*, (1). doi: CD000447. DOI: 10.1002/14651858.CD000447.pub2.

Baliki, M.N., Geha, P.Y., Apkarian, A.V., & Chialvo, D.R. (2008). Beyond feeling: Chronic pain hurts the brain, disrupting the default-mode network dynamics. *Journal of Neuroscience, 28*(6), 1398–1403.

Barsky, A.J., & Borus, J.F. (1995). Somatization and medicalization in the era of managed care. *Journal of the American Medical Association, 274*(24), 1931–1934.

Bigos, S.J., Battie, M.C., Spengler, D.M., Fisher, L.D., Fordyce, W.E., Hansson, T., et al. (1992). A longitudinal, prospective study of industrial back injury reporting. *Clinical Orthopaedics and Related Research, 279*, 21–34.

Blyth, F.M., Macfarlane, G.J., & Nicholas, M.K. (2007). The contribution of psychosocial factors to the development of chronic pain: The key to better outcomes for patients? *Pain, 129*(1–2), 8–11.

Bruns, D., & Disorbio, J.M. (2009). Assessment of biopsychosocial risk factors for medical treatment: A collaborative approach. *Journal of Clinical Psychology in Medical Settings, 16*(2), 127–147.

California Department of Industrial Relations. (2009). *California Medical Treatment Utilization Schedule.* Retrieved from http://www.dir.ca.gov/dwc/DWCPropRegs/MTUS_Regulations/MTUS_Regulations.htm.

Carragee, E.J., Alamin, T.F., Miller, J.L., & Carragee, J.M. (2005). Discographic, MRI and psychosocial determinants of low back pain disability and remission: A prospective study in subjects with benign persistent back pain. *Spine Journal, 5*(1), 24–35.

Cherkin, D.C., Deyo, R.A., Wheeler, K., & Ciol, M.A. (1995). Physician views about treating low back pain- The results of a national survey. *Spine, 20*(1), 1–9.

Chou, R., & Huffman, L.H. (2007). Nonpharmacologic therapies for acute and chronic low back pain: A review of the evidence for an American pain Society/American college of physicians clinical practice guideline. *Annals of Internal Medicine, 147*(7), 492–504.

Clarke, J.A., van Tulder, M.W., Blomberg, S.E.I., de Vet, H.C.W., van der Heijden, G.J., Brønfort, G. & Bouter, L.M. (2007). Traction for low-back pain with or without sciatica. *Cochrane Database of Systematic Reviews 2007*, (2). doi: CD003010. DOI: 10.1002/14651858.CD003010.pub4.

Colorado Division of Worker Compensation. (2009). *Rule 17: Medical Treatment Guidelines.* Retrieved from http://www.coworkforce.com/dwc/Medical_Treatment.asp.

Covington, E.C. (2000). The biological basis of pain. *International Review of Psychiatry, 12*(2), 128–147.

Dagenais, S., Yelland, M.J., Del Mar, C., & Schoene, M.L. (2007). Prolotherapy injections for chronic low-back pain. *Cochrane Database of Systematic Reviews 2007*, (2). doi: 10.1002/14651858. CD004059.pub3.

Delaware Health care Advisory Panel. (2009). *Practice guidelines: Title 19 Labor Delaware Administrative Code.* Retrieved from http://dowe.ingenix.com/info.asp?page=pracguid.

Deshpande, A., Furlan, A.D., Mailis-Gagnon, A., Atlas, S. & Turk, D. (2007). Opioids for chronic low-back pain. *Cochrane Database of Systematic Reviews 2007*, (3). doi: 10.1002/14651858.CD004959.pub3.

Deyo, R.A., Gray, D.T., Kreuter, W., Mirza, S., & Martin, B.I. (2005). United States trends in lumbar fusion surgery for degenerative conditions. *Spine, 30*(12), 1441–1445.

Dickersin, K. (2005). Publication bias: Recognizing the problem, understanding its origins and scope, and preventing harm. In H.R. Rothstein, A.J. Sutton, & M. Borenstein (Eds.), *Publication bias in meta-analysis: Prevention, assessment and adjustments* (pp. 11–33). Sussex, England: John Wiley & Sons.

Dworkin, R.H., Turk, D.C., Wyrwich, K.W., Beaton, D., Cleeland, C.S., Farrar, J.T., et al. (2008). Interpreting the clinical importance of treatment outcomes in chronic pain clinical trials: IMMPACT recommendations. *Journal of Pain, 9*(2), 105–121.

Eccleston, C., Williams, A.C.D., & Morley, S. (2009). Psychological therapies for the management of chronic pain (excluding headache) in adults. *Cochrane Database of Systematic Reviews* (2).

Engel, G.L. (1977). The need for a new medical model: A challenge for biomedicine. *Science, 196*(4286), 129–136.

Engers, A.J., Jellema, P., Wensing, M., van der Windt, D.A.W.M., Grol, R. & van Tulder, M.W. (2008). Individual patient education for low back pain. *Cochrane Database of Systematic Reviews 2008*, (1). doi: 10.1002/14651858.CD004057.pub3.

Flor, H., Fydrich, T., & Turk, D.C. (1992). Efficacy of multidisciplinary pain treatment centers: A meta-analytic review. *Pain, 49*(2), 221–230.

French, S.D., Cameron, M., Walker, B.F., Reggars, J.W. & Esterman, A.J. (2007). Superficial heat or cold for low back pain. *Cochrane Database of Systematic Reviews 2006*, (1). doi: 10.1002/14651858.CD004750.pub2.

Frymoyer, J.W., & Durett, C.L. (1997). The economics of spinal disorders. In T.I. Whitecloud (Ed.), *The adult spine: Principles and practice* (2nd ed.). 1, 143–150. Philadelphia, PA: Lippincott-Raven.

Gagnier, J.J., van Tulder, M.W., Berman, B.M. & Bombardier, C. (2006). Herbal medicine for low back pain. *Cochrane Database of Systematic Reviews 2006*, (2). doi: 10.1002/14651858.CD004504.pub3.

Gatchel, R.J., Peng, Y.B., Peters, M.L., Fuchs, P.N., & Turk, D.C. (2007). The biopsychosocial approach to chronic pain: Scientific advances and future directions. *Psychological Bulletin, 133*(4), 581–624.

Gibson, J.A. & Waddell, G. (2005). Surgery for degenerative lumbar spondylosis. *Cochrane Database of Systematic Reviews 2005*, (4). doi: CD001352. DOI: 10.1002/14651858.CD001352.pub3.

Gockel, M., Lindholm, H., Niemisto, L., & Hurri, H. (2008). Perceived disability but not pain is connected with autonomic nervous function among patients with chronic low back pain. *Journal of Rehabilitation Medicine, 40*(5), 355–358.

Green, L.W., & Glasgow, R.E. (2006). Evaluating the relevance, generalization, and applicability of research - Issues in external validation and translation methodology. *Evaluation & the Health Professions, 29*(1), 126–153.

Hayden, J., van Tulder, M.W., Malmivaara, A. & Koes, B.W. (2005). Exercise therapy for treatment of non-specific low back pain. *Cochrane Database of Systematic Reviews 2005*, (3). doi: CD000335. DOI: 10.1002/14651858.CD000335.pub2.

Health Insurance Portability and Accountability Act of 1996, 42 U.S.C. § 1320d-9 (2010).

Henschke, N., Ostelo, R.W.J.G., van Tulder, M.W., Vlaeyen, J.W.S., Morley, S., Assendelft, W.J.J. & Main, C.J. (2010). Behavioural treatment for chronic low-back pain. *Cochrane Database of Systematic Reviews 2010*, (7). doi: CD002014. DOI: 10.1002/14651858.CD002014.pub3.

Heymans, M.W., van Tulder, M.W., Esmail, R., Bombadier, C., & Koes, B.W. (2005). Back schools for nonspecific low back pain: A systematic review within the framework of the Cochrane Collaboration Back Review Group. *Spine, 30*(19), 2153–2163.

Iadarola, J.M., & Caudle, R.M. (1997). Good pain, bad pain. *Science, 278*(5336), 239–240.

Jarvik, J.G., Hollingworth, W., Heagerty, P.J., Haynor, D.R., Boyko, E.J., & Deyo, R.A. (2005). Three-year incidence of low back pain in an initially asymptomatic cohort - Clinical and imaging risk factors. *Spine, 30*(13), 1541–1548.

Jensen, M.C., Brantzawadzki, M.N., Obuchowski, N., Modic, M.T., Malkasian, D., & Ross, J.S. (1994). Magnetic-resonance-imaging of the lumbar spine in people without back pain. *New England Journal of Medicine, 331*(2), 69–73.

Johnson, M.H., & Kazantzis, N. (2004). Cognitive behavioral therapy for chronic pain: Strategies for the successful use of homework assignments. *Journal of Rational-emotive and Cognitive-behavior Therapy, 22*, 189–218.

Kansas Division of Workers Compensation. (2008). *Official Disability Guidelines*. Retrieved from http://www.dol.ks.gov/wc/html/wc_odg.asp.

Koyama, T., McHaffie, J.G., Laurienti, P.J., & Coghill, R.C. (2005). The subjective experience of pain: Where expectations become reality. *Proceedings of the National Academy of Sciences of the United States of America, 102*(36), 12950–12955.

Krause, N., Ragland, D.R., Fisher, J.M., & Syme, S.L. (1998). 1998 Volvo Award winner in clinical studies - Psychosocial job factors, physical workload, and incidence of work-related spinal injury: A 5-year prospective study of urban transit operators. *Spine, 23*(23), 2507–2516.

Kupers, R., Faymonville, M.E., & Laureys, S. (2005). The cognitive modulation of pain: Hypnosis- and placebo-induced analgesia. *Boundaries of Consciousness: Neurobiology and Neuropathology, 150*, 251–269, 599–600.

Lethbridge-Cejku, M., Schiller, J.S., & Bernadel, L. (2004). *Summary health statistics for U.S. adults: National health interview survey 2002*, Vol. 10 (222) (pp. 1–151). Washington, DC: US Department of Health and Human Services.

Manchikanti, L., Singh, V., Derby, R., Schultz, D.M., Benyamin, R.M., Prager, J.P., et al. (2008). Reassessment of evidence synthesis of occupational medicine practice guidelines for interventional pain management. *Pain Physician, 11*(4), 393–482.

Manchikanti, L., Singh, V., Pampati, V., Smith, H.S., & Hirsch, J. (2009). Analysis of growth of interventional techniques in managing chronic pain in the medicare population: A 10-year evaluation from 1997 to 2006. *Pain Physician, 12*(1), 9–33.

Marco, C.A., Plewa, M.C., Buderer, N., Hymel, G., & Cooper, J. (2006). Self-reported pain scores in the emergency department: Lack of association with vital signs. *Academic Emergency Medicine, 13*(9), 974–979.

Melzack, R. (2001). Pain and the neuromatrix in the brain. *Journal of Dental Education, 65*(12), 1378–1382.

Melzack, R. (2005). Evolution of the neuromatrix theory of pain. The Prithvi Raj lecture. Presented at the third world congress of World Institute of Pain, Barcelona, 2004. *Pain Pract, 5*(2), 85–94.

Melzack, R., & Wall, P.D. (1965). Pain mechanisms: A new theory. *Science, 150*(3699), 971–979.

Mersky, H., & Bogduk, N. (1994). *Classification of chronic pain: Descriptions of chronic pain syndromes and definitions of pain terms*. Seattle: IASP Press.

Moher, D., Schulz, K.F., & Altman, D. (2001). The CONSORT statement: Revised recommendations for improving the quality of reports of parallel-group randomized trials. *Journal of the American College of Surgeons, 193*(4), A71–A76. (Reprinted from *Journal of the American Medical Association, 285*:1987–1991).

Morley, S., Williams, A., & Hussain, S. (2008). Estimating the clinical effectiveness of cognitive behavioural therapy in the clinic: Evaluation of a CBT informed pain management programme. *Pain, 137*(3), 670–680.

Moses, T. (2009). Self-labeling and its effects among adolescents diagnosed with mental disorders. *Social Science & Medicine, 68*(3), 570–578.

Naylor, M.R., Helzer, J.E., Naud, S., & Keefe, F.J. (2002). Automated telephone as an adjunct for the treatment of chronic pain: A pilot study. *Journal of Pain, 3*(6), 429–438.

Naylor, M.R., Keefe, F.J., Brigidi, B., Naud, S., & Helzer, J.E. (2008). Therapeutic interactive voice response for chronic pain reduction and relapse prevention. *Pain, 134*(3), 335–345.

Oklahoma Physician Advisory Committee. (2007). *Oklahoma guidelines for treatment of chronic pain disorders, adopted by the administrator of the Oklahoma workers' compensation court*. Retrieved from http://www.owcc.state.ok.us/PDF/Guidelines%20for%20Treatment%20of%20Chronic%20Pain%20Disorders.pdf.

Ospina, M., & Harstall, C. (2002). *Prevalence of chronic pain: An overview*. Prepared for the Alberta Heritage Foundation for Medical Research, Health Technology Assessment. (*Edmonton, AB. Report No. 28*). Alberta Heritage Foundation, Alberta: Canada.

Ross, C.A., & Goldner, E.M. (2009). Stigma, negative attitudes and discrimination towards mental illness within the nursing profession: A review of the literature. *Journal of Psychiatric and Mental Health Nursing, 16*(6), 558–567.

Sackett, D.L., Rosenberg, W.M.C., Gray, J.A.M., Haynes, R.B., & Richardson, W.S. (1996). Evidence based medicine: What it is and what it isn't - It's about integrating individual clinical expertise and the best external evidence. *British Medical Journal, 312*(7023), 71–72.

Satterfield, J.M., Spring, B., Brownson, R.C., Mullen, E.J., Newhouse, R.P., Walker, B.B., et al. (2009). Toward a transdisciplinary model of evidence-based practice. *Milbank Quarterly, 87*(2), 368–390.

Scascighini, L., Toma, V., Dober-Spielmann, S., & Sprott, H. (2008). Multidisciplinary treatment for chronic pain: A systematic review of interventions and outcomes. *Rheumatology, 47*(5), 670–678.

Scharff, L., & Marcus, D.A. (1994). Interdisciplinary outpatient group treatment of intractable headache. *Headache, 34*(2), 73–78.

Staal, J.B., de Bie, R., de Vet, H.C.W., Hildebrandt, J., & Nelemans, P. (2008). Injection therapy for subacute and chronic low-back pain. *Cochrane Database of Systematic Reviews 2008*, (3). doi: 10.1002/14651858.CD001824.pub3.

Sternbach, R.A. (1986). Survey of pain in the United States: The Nuprin pain report. *Clinical Journal of Pain, 2*(1), 49–53.

Stewart, W.F., Ricci, J.A., Chee, E., Morganstein, D., & Lipton, R. (2003). Lost productive time and cost due to common pain conditions in the US workforce. *Journal of the American Medical Association, 290*(18), 2443–2454.

Sullivan, M.J.L., Thorn, B., Haythornthwaite, J.A., Keefe, F., Martin, M., Bradley, L.A., et al. (2001). Theoretical perspectives on the relation between catastrophizing and pain. *Clinical Journal of Pain, 17*(1), 52–64.

Tang, N.K.Y., & Crane, C. (2006). Suicidality in chronic pain: A review of the prevalence, risk factors and psychological links. *Psychological Medicine, 36*(5), 575–586.

Texas Department of Insurance. *Texas Division of Worker's Compensation adopted rules*. (2006). Retrieved from http://www.tdi.state.tx.us/wc/rules/adopted/dmaorder1206.html.

Thorn, B.E. (2004). *Cognitive therapy for chronic pain: A step-by-step guide*. New York: Guilford Publications.

Tkachuk, G.A., Graff, L.A., Martin, G.L., & Bernstein, C.N. (2003). Randomized controlled trial of cognitive-behavioral group therapy for irritable bowel syndrome in a medical setting. *Journal of Clinical Psychology in Medical Settings, 10*(1), 57–69.

Tracey, I., & Mantyh, P.W. (2007). The cerebral signature and its modulation for pain perception. *Neuron, 55*(3), 377–391.

Turk, D.C. (2001). Treatment of chronic pain: Clinical outcomes, cost-effectiveness, and cost benefits. *Drug Benefit Trends, 13*, 36–38.

Turk, D.C. (2002). Clinical effectiveness and cost-effectiveness of treatments for patients with chronic pain. *Clinical Journal of Pain, 18*(6), 355–365.

Urquhart, D.M., Hoving, J.L., Assendelft, W.J.J., Roland, M. & van Tulder, M.W. (2008). Antidepressants for non-specific low back pain. *Cochrane Database of Systematic Reviews 2008*, (1). doi: CD001703. DOI: 10.1002/14651858.CD001703.pub3.

van der Velde, G., van Tulder, M., Cote, P., Hogg-Johnson, S., Aker, P., Cassidy, J.D., et al. (2007). The sensitivity of review results to methods used to appraise and incorporate trial quality into data synthesis. *Spine, 32*(7), 796–806.

van Duijvenbode, I., Jellema, P., van Poppel, M. & van Tulder, M.W. (2008). Lumbar supports for prevention and treatment of low back pain. *Cochrane Database of Systematic Reviews 2008*, (2). doi:10.1002/14651858.CD001823. pub3.

van Tulder, M., Furlan, A., Bombardier, C., Bouter, L., & Editorial Board of the Cochrane Collaboration Back Review Group. (2003). Updated method guidelines for systematic reviews in the Cochrane Collaboration Back Review Group. *Spine, 28*(12), 1290–1299.

Van Tulder, M.W., Koes, B.W. & Bouter, L.M. (1997). Conservative treatment of acute and chronic nonspecific low back pain: A systematic review of randomized controlled trials of the most common interventions. *Spine, 22*(18), 2128–2156.

Von Korff, M., Katon, W., Unutzer, J., Wells, K., & Wagner, E.H. (2001). Improving depression care: Barriers, solutions, and research needs. *Journal of Family Practice, 50*(6), E1.

Walker, B.B., & London, S. (2007). Novel tools and resources for evidence-based practice in psychology. *Journal of Clinical Psychology, 63*(7), 633–642.

Wiech, K., Ploner, M., & Tracey, I. (2008). Neurocognitive aspects of pain perception. *Trends in Cognitive Sciences, 12*(8), 306–313.

Woolf, C.J., & Salter, M.W. (2000). Neuroscience—neuronal plasticity: Increasing the gain in pain. *Science, 288*(5472), 1765–1768.

World Health Organization. (1992). *ICD-10: International Statistical Classification of Diseases and Related Health Problems* (10th ed.). Geneva: World Health Organization.

# Coping with Cancer

Vanessa L. Malcarne

**Abstract**

This chapter addresses coping within the context of the adult cancer experience. It does not provide a comprehensive overview of the enormous literature on coping with cancer, but rather considers a range of relevant issues that have challenged coping researchers in the past, and are expected to do so in the future. The chapter first describes how coping has been conceptualized and measured in relation to both appraisals and outcomes, then discusses methodological concerns about research to date. Next, the efficacy of coping interventions and potential underlying mechanisms are considered. The challenge of translating research to practice, including whether interventions are cost-effective and relevant, is addressed, followed by a discussion of the provocative question of whether coping interventions can impact survival parameters. The chapter concludes by presenting specific coping strategies that will likely be the focus of future research, and key issues to be addressed by future cancer coping researchers.

**Keywords:** Cancer, coping, stress, appraisal, interventions, measurement, survival

Worldwide, more than 12 million people are diagnosed with cancer each year. Cancer is a leading cause of mortality, responsible for an estimated 7.6 million deaths annually, and an estimated 17.5 million deaths by 2050, based on growth and aging trends (American Cancer Society, 2009). In addition, an estimated 25 million cancer survivors diagnosed within the past 5 years are living with the diagnosis, some still in treatment, and others posttreatment but managing disease sequelae and the threat of recurrence (American Cancer Society, 2007). A very large literature has documented the negative impact of cancer on a broad range of psychosocial outcomes for survivors, in addition to its physical effects. For example, although the rate of psychiatric disorders attributed to the cancer experience is unknown, reviews have suggested that between one-fifth and one-quarter of cancer survivors may meet criteria for major depressive disorder, the psychiatric syndrome most often diagnosed in survivors (DeFlorio & Massie, 1995; Sellick & Crooks, 1999). A recent study of advanced cancer found that 12% met

criteria for a major psychiatric condition, mainly depression, and 28% had accessed a mental health intervention since their cancer diagnosis (Kadan-Lottick, Vanderwerker, Block, Zhang, & Prigerson, 2005). Estimates of rates of more general distress are even higher, and may characterize 30%–40% of survivors (Carlson et al., 2004; Zabora et al., 1997; Zabora, Brintzenhofeszoc, Curbow, Hooker, & Piantadosi, 2001).

However, in addition to describing the negative impact of cancer, research has documented wide variability in psychosocial adjustment and quality of life in people with similar medical profiles, prognoses, treatments, and medical outcomes. This raises the essential question of why some people do so well handling the myriad stressors encompassed by the word "cancer" and others do so poorly. Although many psychosocial variables have been identified and studied, none has received more attention than coping, with the assumption that the distress, impaired quality of life, and even physiological effects associated with cancer can be at least partially addressed by effective coping.

## Definitions and Typologies
### Definitions

What is coping? In a seminal paper three decades ago, coping was conceptualized by Folkman and Lazarus as "cognitive and behavioral efforts made to master, tolerate, or reduce external and internal demands and conflicts among them" (Folkman & Lazarus, 1980, p. 223). These authors have provided variations of their definition since, including "ongoing cognitive and behavioral efforts to manage specific external and/or internal demands that are appraised as taxing or exceeding the resources of the person" or, more simply, "cognitive and behavioral efforts to manage psychological stress" (Lazarus, 1993, p. 237). When Lazarus and Folkman first introduced their stress and coping model in the early 1980s (Folkman & Lazarus, 1980, 1985; Lazarus & Folkman, 1984), they strongly emphasized that coping was a process that unfolded moment by moment over time, reciprocally influenced by and influencing appraisals of the stressor (see "Context," below), as well as proximal and distal outcomes. Further, they attempted to distinguish coping processes from coping styles, arguing that the former were situation-specific, whereas the latter implied consistency of coping across varied situations and circumstances.

There is no question that the Lazarus and Folkman conceptualization is the most widely used, although it is also true that there is no single agreed-upon definition. Other variations include "action-oriented and intrapsychic efforts to manage the demands created by stressful events" (Taylor & Stanton, 2007, p. 377), and "cognitive and/or behavioral attempts to manage (reduce or tolerate) situations that are appraised as stressful to an individual" (Franks & Roesch, 2006, p. 1028). Luecken and Compas (2002) have conceptualized coping as a self-regulatory process involving "conscious, volitional efforts to regulate one's cognitive, behavioral, emotional, and physiological responses to stress" (p. 337). Although these definitions are all slightly different, they share certain key concepts: Coping is conscious and effortful, is a response to internal or environmental demands perceived as stressful, involves cognitions and behaviors, evolves over time, and is not defined by its effectiveness or lack thereof.

### Typologies

A number of coping typologies have been proposed, but none more influential than the original breakdown proposed by Lazarus and Folkman: that coping could be broadly conceptualized as problem-focused or emotion-focused (Folkman & Lazarus, 1980, 1985; Lazarus, 1993, 2000; Lazarus & Folkman, 1984). The distinction between these two types of coping is based on the immediate goal (Carver, 2007). Problem-focused coping aims to change either the stressful event or the person–environment relationship that is the source of stress. In contrast, emotion-focused coping aims to change the way to which the stressor is related or attended to, or to regulate emotions resulting from the stressor (Folkman & Lazarus, 1980; Lazarus, 1993; Lazarus & Folkman, 1984). So, for example, if one imagines a man with prostate cancer who wants to travel for vacation but is worried about accidents due to urinary incontinence, his problem-focused coping might involve attempting to identify medical interventions that would reduce incontinence, problem-solving ways to reduce the likelihood of accidents on the trip (e.g., by making frequent bathroom stops), or making use of aids such as incontinence pads. In contrast, his emotion-focused coping might focus on reducing his distress and frustration; distracting himself through other, more easily accessed pleasant activities; seeking emotional support from other men with similar experiences; refocusing on activities close to home; reframing his situation to find its positive aspects; or trying to process and understand his emotional responses to the cancer.

Another important typology distinguishes between approach and avoidance coping (Holahan & Moos, 1987; Moos & Schaefer, 1993). Approach coping engages with the stressor in some way, whether directly or indirectly; in contrast, avoidance coping represents efforts to disengage from the stressor. Avoidance has often been conceptualized as emotion-focused coping, because it doesn't involve efforts to reduce stress or associated distress through directly changing the stressor or related circumstances, but instead attempts to reduce distress by avoiding the stressor entirely. However, some specific types of emotion-focused coping (e.g., positive reappraisal, maintaining positive expectancies and optimism, exercising self-control, examining and expressing emotions, acceptance) are seen by experts as representing approach rather than avoidance coping (Austenfeld & Stanton, 2004; Franks & Roesch, 2006; Roesch et al., 2005), so avoidance and emotion-focused coping should not be seen as synonymous.

Although these categorizations have been widely employed throughout the literature on coping with cancer, the use of such broad typologies, which mix coping strategies such as seeking advice with seeking support, cognitive restructuring with avoidance, or emotional expression with mental disengagement, may obscure important consideration of individual coping strategies (Carver, Scheier, & Weintraub, 1989). Increasingly, attention is being paid to the adaptational implications of specific strategies for coping with various aspects of the cancer experience; this will be discussed in more depth below.

## Methodological Concerns

Coping has been the object of an extensive literature in the context of chronic illness in general, as well as specifically in cancer (Folkman & Moskowitz, 2004). In January 2010, a quick search of the PsycINFO database, restricting the search to publications between 1990 and 2009, and entering the key words "cancer" and "coping," yielded 1,127 studies; the same search in Medline yielded 3,591 publications. Although overlap obviously occurs between these two databases, it is clear that much effort has been devoted to understanding the role of coping in the cancer experience. However, in parallel to concerns raised about the broader literature examining how coping influences outcomes in response to all types of stressors (including cancer), there has been fairly extensive criticism about the quality of the research on coping with cancer (e.g., Carver, 2007; Coyne & Racioppo, 2000; de Ridder & Schreurs, 2001; Franks & Roesch, 2006; Roesch et al., 2005; Somerfield & McCrae, 2000; Stanton, Revenson, & Tennen, 2007; Taylor & Stanton, 2007). These criticisms can be broadly grouped into concerns about measurement strategies, consideration of the context in which coping occurs (including how that context is appraised), and how coping effectiveness is conceptualized and determined. Each of these areas will be considered in turn.

### Measurement Strategies

Lazarus and Folkman intended, and their model necessitates, that coping be studied in a moment-by-moment, process-oriented manner, within the context of a specific stressor. As Lazarus himself has written, the intention was to measure what a person is thinking and doing "repeatedly over time and across diverse stressful encounters in research designs that are intraindividual as well as interindividual" (Lazarus, 1993, p. 236). However, the introduction of the stress and coping model led instead to a proliferation of self-report surveys that were used in cross-sectional studies focused on inter- rather than intraindividual relationships. Inconsistent with Lazarus and Folkman's conceptualization, some

coping questionnaires continued to measure coping as a trait that was expected to be expressed consistently across stressors. Other questionnaires, including Folkman and Lazarus's own widely used Ways of Coping Checklist and its revisions (Folkman & Lazarus, 1980; Vitaliano, Russo, Carr, Maiuro, & Becker, 1985), and the COPE (Carver, 2010; Carver et al., 1989) and Brief COPE (Carver, 1997), were designed to be completed with regard to a specific stressor identified by the respondent (e.g., cancer or some stressor associated with cancer, such as chemotherapy). Still other coping questionnaires were developed to focus on very specific stressors associated with the cancer experience (e.g., cancer-related fatigue, fear of recurrence) or are specific to subtypes of cancer.

All of these checklists offer advantages in terms of ease of use, and can be applied efficiently in large samples, and on repeated occasions in longitudinal studies. However, they may unfortunately be a major contributor to why the literature on coping with cancer has had limited impact, despite its quantity. Coyne and Racioppo (2000) have decried a "crisis of research using coping checklists" (p. 656), and others, including both Folkman and Lazarus, have also argued that coping checklists have a number of inherent limitations (see, for example, Folkman & Moskowitz, 2004; Lazarus, 1993, 2000). Strategies may be inadequately sampled, leaving respondents unable to accurately describe how they coped. Variations in recall periods across instruments are common and may contribute to poor reliability, as respondents struggle to remember and accurately report what strategies they used to cope with some aspect of their cancer experience over the past week or month, and with what frequency. In some surveys, items are confounded with outcomes. For example, the Mental Adjustment to Cancer (MAC) Scale (Watson et al., 1988) has been used and interpreted as a measure of coping in some studies, despite being developed as a measure of adjustment, as indicated in its name. Also, significant overlap between MAC subscales and measures of anxiety and depression has been revealed through factor analysis, suggesting that the MAC is better used as a measure of outcome than of coping (Nordin, Berglund, Terje, & Glimelius, 1999).

How coping should be represented by scores on available measures has also caused confusion in the field. Some researchers have used total scores, which are difficult to interpret. More typically, researchers have attempted to create scores representing the major categories of coping (e.g., problem-focused or emotion-focused, approach or avoidance), typically by combining scores from specific coping subscales that are presumed to represent the broader category. For example, the Ways of Coping Checklist was originally developed to yield scores representing problem- and emotion-focused coping, and has often been used in this manner. However, structural analysis of this instrument has rarely yielded such a clean division, and the developers' own research has supported the existence of more than two factors (e.g., Folkman, Lazarus, Dunkel-Schetter, DeLonis, & Gruen, 1986). Carver et al. (1989) argue that scoring coping strategies separately is preferable to combining them into such broad groupings, and this is reflected in scoring instructions for their widely-used checklist, the COPE, and its shorter derivative, the Brief COPE. These instruments yield scores for more than a dozen different coping strategies, and research suggests that the subscale scores do not intercorrelate strongly, although they do form higher-order factors generally representing active/problem-focused coping, emotion-focused coping, disengagement/denial, and acceptance/positive reinterpretation, with turning to religion often loading separately. The authors do not currently recommend the use of aggregates and overall coping scores, and specifically urge users to investigate the measurement properties of these instruments in their own samples if higher-order composites are desired (Carver, 2010).

A related and unresolved issue regarding the use of coping checklists is how scores should be calculated. Although many use raw scores, representing the frequency of use or total amount of any type of coping, this approach has significant shortcomings. First, it is not clear what it means to use more coping strategies, versus fewer, or more different types of coping, versus a more restricted range, particularly when most of the research literature is cross-sectional. Often studies find heavy use of coping to be associated with more distress; in cross-sectional research, this may mean that people who are particularly distressed are engaging in high-frequency use of a single type of coping or trying many types of coping in order to find a solution, rather than that heavy or diverse use of coping strategies leads to distress. Twenty-five years ago, Vitaliano and colleagues argued that we need to adopt a profile-based approach to understanding coping (Vitaliano, Maiuro, Russo, & Becker, 1987), using "relative" scores that represent the percent of overall coping effort devoted to any particular coping strategy versus others. Carver (2007) has echoed the importance of considering

such indices of overall coping, and has raised the related question of whether heavy reliance on one type of coping, versus employment of diverse strategies, has implications for adjustment. In addition, the sequence of coping efforts may be important, as people may move from one coping strategy to try another when the first approach fails to work (Tennen, Affleck, Armeli, & Carney, 2000), and this may in and of itself reflect an adaptive approach in some circumstances.

Unfortunately, heavy reliance on the use of self-report checklists has generally limited measurement to a broad "snapshot" overview of people's coping behavior, as these surveys are inherently unable to measure the dynamic process of coping originally conceptualized by Lazarus and Folkman (1984). Lazarus, among others, has expressed his disappointment in the way coping has been conceptualized and measured to date, noting that, "few studies on coping pay more than lip service to the basic idea . . ." that "coping changes with the context and over time as the status of a problem changes" (Lazarus, 1993, p. 239). Coyne and Racioppo (2000) were extremely critical of the failure of studies to capture the true process of coping, due to their heavy reliance on retrospective recall of coping through self-report questionnaires, and have gone so far as to "call for a moratorium on such studies" (p. 659), combined with warning labels on the existing literature. Although there is clear disagreement about whether such a radical step is necessary, and whether there is truly no worthwhile research on coping to date (see, for example, Lazarus's [2000] response to Coyne & Racioppo, 2000), there is no question that much of the research to date on coping with cancer has indeed been dependent on cross-sectional designs using checklist methodologies, and that this has limited the contribution of the literature (Somerfield & McCrae, 2000).

In response to this, efforts have been made to measure coping in a more process-oriented way. Stone and Neale's (1984) Daily Coping Assessment (DCA) was one of the earliest daily process measures developed, and it has been used to measure coping in cancer survivors. The DCA asks about coping with the most stressful event of the day in terms of stressfulness of the event, controllability, and which of several types of coping strategies were employed; respondents are then asked to provide written descriptions of exactly how they coped within these types. A study comparing the DCA to the Mental Adjustment to Cancer (MAC) Scale in persons with gastrointestinal (GI) cancer found different results depending on which measure was considered; the MAC showed participants predominantly used "fighting spirit" as their coping response; the DCA showed acceptance, relaxation, distraction, and direct action were frequently used. Factor analysis of the DCA and MAC with measures of anxiety and depression showed that the DCA was generally independent of outcomes, whereas the MAC was not (Wasteson, Glimelius, Sjödén, & Nordin, 2006).

Since the introduction of the DCA, a variety of open-ended daily diaries have been used to study coping in cancer. These vary in format, with some asking respondents to write brief entries at given timepoints, and others asking for more in-depth narratives. These have the advantage of obtaining rich qualitative data on coping efforts, reported much closer in time to the corresponding stressor than can be typically achieved by checklists. For example, cancer survivors can create diary entries reporting on their coping strategies while they are in the hospital for chemotherapy treatments or directly after receiving disease-related communication from their healthcare team. Tennen and colleagues have noted that daily (or more frequently completed) diaries can help to clarify how different types of coping reciprocally influence one another; for example, whether problem-focused coping attempts alternate with emotion-focused coping efforts over the course of a stressor (Tennen et al., 2000).

Since the introduction of written daily diaries as an alternative to checklists, more sophisticated and process-oriented measurement technologies for sampling self-monitored behavior in real time and in natural environments have emerged, grouped under the rubric of ecological momentary assessment (EMA; Shiffman, Stone, & Hufford, 2008; Smyth & Stone, 2003; Stone & Shiffman, 1994, 2002). The development of sophisticated and ambulatory computer-based devices has opened the door to tremendous opportunities in this approach to assessment. People can be regularly or randomly signaled to report their coping efforts, as well as concomitant psychological and physiological experiences, on tiny devices in real time, yielding many datapoints. Ecological momentary assessment is widely believed to present significant advantages over the use of checklists, and in particular may be more sensitive to person–situation interactions (Fahrenberg, Myrtek, Pawlik, & Perrez, 2007), which would be particularly advantageous in the study of coping. However, it is not without limitations (Coyne & Racioppo, 2000; Folkman & Moskowitz, 2004). First and foremost, EMA is

likely to be reactive. Asking people how they are coping with aspects of their cancer on a moment by moment, or even an hourly or daily basis, necessarily changes their experience of their cancer, if only by heightening their awareness of how they are coping (and perhaps also how well their coping efforts appear to be working). Ecological momentary assessment asks people to report how they are coping at a particular moment at time, and thus may lead people to focus on more concrete and discrete coping efforts, and overlook coping efforts that are more abstract or long-term (Folkman & Moskowitz, 2004). Also, there is evidence of poor adherence to EMA, even when signaling is used (e.g., Broderick, Schwartz, Shiffman, Hufford, & Stone, 2003; Broderick & Stone, 2006; Stone & Shiffman, 2002). This could be a particular problem when attempting to get regular assessments from persons with cancer who are actively undergoing treatment and/or are physically compromised.

All of these approaches rely on self-report, and there has long existed widespread concern about the ability of people to retrospectively or concurrently report their psychological or physical states. Although often it is difficult to come up with alternatives for measuring internal processes, a probe detection paradigm was recently used to measure both conscious/ voluntary and non-conscious/automatic cognitive engagement (i.e., attentional bias) to cancer-related words (Glinder, Beckjord, Kaiser, & Compas, 2007). Self-report of engagement coping was associated with attention to consciously presented, but not subconsciously presented, cancer-related words on the probe detection task. Interestingly, voluntary engagement (measured via self-report or probe detection task) appeared to be adaptive, whereas involuntary engagement was associated with poorer outcomes.

Self-report, even EMA, has particular limitations when measuring physical outcomes. This has relevance for studies that attempt to link coping to physiological changes or improvements in cancer survivors. For example, in their meta-analysis of studies linking mindfulness interventions to cancer outcomes, Ledesma and Kumano (2009) reported that effect sizes for self-reported physical outcomes were moderate and significant, compared to effect sizes for objective measures of physical outcomes, which were small and nonsignificant.

### Context

Coping must always be considered within the context of the stressor to which it is a response.

When a stressor is relatively simple and discrete (e.g., an argument with a friend), its parameters can be more easily defined, and a direct connection can be made between the stressor and the coping responses it elicits. However, major life stressors are rarely so circumscribed; even what may seem to be a relatively unitary and straightforward stressor such as a car accident may involve dealing with insurance claims, injuries, financial costs, daily inconveniences due to lack of transportation, purchasing a new car, and so forth. Cancer represents a remarkably complex stressor, with many facets. First, there is no one type of cancer. Cancer is "a group of diseases characterized by uncontrolled growth and spread of abnormal cells" (American Cancer Society, 2009, p. 1), not a single disease. There are more than 100 different types of cancer, generally named for their point of origin, and each can present with different levels of severity; at different stages; at different sites; with differing degrees of pain, discomfort, and functional disability; and with different prognostic severity. My father and mother-in-law both died of cancer during the time I was writing this chapter, and their disparate experiences reinforced my conviction that there is no single common stressor known as "cancer," although there are clearly common experiences within that stressor. Coping with cancer means coping with a variety of disease-related challenges, over an extended period of evolving circumstances. As Lazarus (1993) noted,

> If one asks patients how they cope post-surgically with, say, breast cancer, the answer is apt to be misleading because the coping strategy depends on whether, at any given time, they are dealing with one or another of the diverse threats engendered by the disease . . . The threat focused on by the patient at any moment might be the likelihood of recurrence of the malignancy—depending, of course, on whether it is near the time at which a post-surgical diagnostic examination is scheduled. If it is, then the danger of recurrence will probably be at the center of attention . . . Alternatively, the focus of threat may be having to tell a spouse, friends, parents, or children about what is happening. The stage of the illness, that is, whether the cancer is early or well-advanced, strongly influences the patient's state of mind. An advanced cancer may create the need in a patient to think about whether to continue or discontinue debilitating treatment, to deal with the growing imminence of death . . . (p. 236)

The context of the stressor is defined in part by an individual's appraisals, or perceptions, of that stressor. Lazarus and Folkman's stress and coping model distinguished between primary and secondary appraisals. These were defined as cognitive processes "through which an event is evaluated with respect to what is at stake (primary appraisal) and what coping resources and options are available (secondary appraisal)" (Folkman & Lazarus, 1980; p. 223). Primary appraisals could involve harm/loss (the perception that damage has already occurred from the stressor), threat (anticipated possibility of harm/loss), or challenge (anticipated opportunity for mastery or gain). In cancer, primary appraisals could include, for example, the belief that health has been lost (harm/loss); the perception that one may experience physical discomfort or assaults to physical condition, for example as the result of chemotherapy (threat); and/or the sense that there is a possibility of experiencing a new depth of understanding about life from the experience (challenge).

Coping arises in response to appraisals, but a reciprocal influence is hypothesized between coping and appraisals throughout one's response to a stressor. In secondary appraisal, people identify what options they have, weigh costs and benefits of various coping approaches, and evaluate whether they have the resources to effectively address the stressor. This reciprocally influences primary appraisal; for example, people who don't perceive themselves to have many coping resources will likely begin to view cancer-related stressors as more threatening and likely to cause harm/loss than challenging.

## IS CANCER A UNIQUE STRESSOR?

An often overlooked issue concerning cancer as a context for coping is: Does cancer present a unique set of stressors that require a separate field of study? Or, would it be sufficient to study coping within the broader context of chronic illness, assuming that the same general principles and patterns of findings would apply? There are without question many commonalities across chronic diseases (i.e., most serious illnesses require coping with significant physical discomfort, making decisions about treatment and dealing with its side effects, and adapting to functional limitations). However, de Ridder and Schreurs (2001) point out that different diseases can present different challenges. They note, for example, that diabetes requires a great deal of daily self-management, whereas cancer can present the challenge of preparing for death. Similarly, Stanton et al. (2007) distinguish features more common across chronic illnesses (e.g., fears about the future, physical limitations, impact on financial status and daily activities) versus features that are more specific to a particular illness, and give the example of life threat as a stressor that is more characteristic of cancer than of some other chronic illnesses. Overall, clearly, many stressors are associated with cancer that are also associated with other chronic illnesses, and it benefits our understanding of the coping process when we consider the effectiveness of people's coping with these common stressors across different diseases. At the same time, it is essential that researchers elucidate what is unique to a particular illness. It would be advantageous to identify stressors more specifically, defining the problems and challenges faced by survivors with different types of cancer, at different stages, undergoing different treatments, and facing different associated life challenges. This way, survivors' choice of coping strategies, and the effectiveness of those strategies, can be understood as a "fit" between coping and a cancer-related stressor.

### APPRAISAL-COPING FIT

An important contextual issue is the fit, or match, between coping and the context in which it is applied. The choice of coping strategies is expected to vary depending on the parameters of the stressor encountered. Lazarus and Folkman's (1984) model predicted that people facing a stressor will appraise that stressor across a variety of dimensions and choose their coping strategies accordingly. For example, Lazarus (1993) predicted that, when a person appraises a stressor as controllable, they will be more likely to choose problem-focused strategies, but when a stressor is perceived as uncontrollable or unmodifiable, emotion-focused strategies would be chosen. In the context of cancer, this means that survivors would appraise cancer-related stressors as they arise and engage in coping that "matched" their appraisals. In a recent meta-analysis, Franks and Roesch (2006) examined the relationship between appraisals and coping in people living with cancer. Coping strategies were categorized within two typologies: as either approach or avoidance, and/or as either emotion-focused or problem-focused. The meta-analysis found evidence of coping being at least in part determined by appraisals of the stressor. Cancer survivors who made threat appraisals were significantly more likely to engage in problem-focused coping, those who made harm/loss appraisals engaged in significantly greater use of avoidance, and those who made challenge appraisals reported significantly greater use of approach strategies.

### *Effectiveness*

Coping is not, in and of itself, effective or ineffective. Coping refers to the *efforts* people make to manage a stressor, in this case a stressor related to their cancer, and not to their *success* in these efforts. As Lazarus (1993) himself has noted, "coping thoughts and actions under stress must be measured separately from their outcomes in order to examine, independently, their adaptiveness or maladaptiveness" (p. 235). Although it might be assumed that it is preferable to try to directly impact the stressor, resolving, reducing, or eliminating it, rather than simply trying to modulate or moderate one's reaction to the stressor, there is actually no assumption that one way is better than the other. Actually, the assumption is that they may influence one another in a reciprocal fashion (Lazarus, 2000).

### APPRAISAL-COPING FIT AND EFFECTIVENESS

The "fit" between coping and the demands of the stressor, and/or one's appraisals of those demands (as described above) is believed to have important implications for coping effectiveness (de Ridder & Schreurs, 2001; Folkman & Moscowitz, 2004; Taylor & Stanton, 2007). It has been argued that a "match" between appraisals and coping, or between objective disease or stressor parameters and coping, will result in better outcomes, based on the notion that coping efforts will be more likely to be effective if they closely match the demands of the stressful situation. More active, problem-focused strategies are hypothesized to better match appraisals that the stressor can be directly changed, whereas more passive, emotion-focused strategies are believed to better match appraisals that the stressor is not modifiable, and thus coping efforts should be focused on one's response to the stressor. Similarly, coping that matches appraisals of environmental characteristics and resources should be more adaptive. For example, in a prospective study of early-stage breast cancer survivors, Stanton et al. (2000) found that coping through emotional expression was associated with better outcomes 3 months later. Interestingly, for quality of life (although not for other measured outcomes), the effect of emotional expression was moderated by social context, such that high levels of emotional expression were related to improved quality of life over time only for women who perceived themselves to be in highly receptive social contexts. In addition, high levels of emotional expression were also beneficial over time for women high in hope, with regard to reductions in both psychological distress and medical appointments; there were no such effects for women low in hope. However, although intriguing, evidence in support of the importance of the appraisal-coping match is still limited in cancer research.

## SELECTING AND REPORTING OUTCOMES

The question of the effectiveness of any particular coping strategy depends on its relationship to relevant and important cancer and adjustment outcomes. However, selecting which outcomes are most relevant and important, and understanding the relationship of coping to those outcomes, has proven challenging (Folkman & Moskowitz, 2004; Sharpe & Curran, 2006; Somerfield & McCrae, 2000).

In most cancer coping research, measured outcomes can be conceptualized as representing positive and negative aspects of quality of life. Quality of life is a broad construct, incorporating not only the person's physical health status, but also his or her psychological state, level of functional independence, social relationships, personal values and beliefs, and relationship to important environmental features and contexts (World Health Organization, 1997). Correspondingly, research on coping with cancer has assessed an enormous variety of outcomes, including psychosocial (e.g., psychological symptoms or presence of diagnosable disorders, positive experiences, self-evaluation, interpersonal relationships), functional (e.g., disability, role fulfillment), and physiological/medical (e.g., biological markers, disease progression, and survival itself). Outcomes are sometimes very general (e.g., overall quality of life, general distress level) or very specific (e.g., level of depressive symptoms, degree of sleep difficulty, whether or not clinical criteria are met). Often, the reasons behind selection of outcomes are not explicit.

The goals of people with cancer are rarely considered in determining relevant outcomes. Although reducing distress or returning to premorbid levels of functioning might be seen as important goals, it is not clear that these are desirable or achievable for all cancer survivors, and the issue of what represents a successful outcome may need to be reconsidered, or defined by survivors themselves (Coyne & Racioppo, 2000; Nezu, Nezu, Friedman, Faddis, & Houts, 1998; Sharpe & Curran, 2006). Rarely assessed but highly relevant and desired outcomes might include more effective communication with loved ones or medical professionals, maintaining or returning to normal routines, enjoying previously enjoyed or newly discovered leisure activities, or helping others facing similar challenges.

Another problem in understanding the relationship of coping to outcomes is that sometimes researchers confound the two, defining coping as anything that results in successful outcomes (Lazarus, 1993; Sharpe & Curran, 2006). Folkman and Moskowitz (2004) also stress the importance of distinguishing coping from successful resolution of stressful challenges, noting that some stressors, such as chronic illness, rarely can be successfully resolved. Use of different methods for measuring coping and adaptation would help to address this problem; the shared variance resulting from reliance on retrospective or concurrent self-report for measuring both predictors and outcomes makes it difficult to disentangle cause from effect (Coyne & Racioppo, 2000; Sharpe & Curran, 2006). Folkman and Moskowitz (2004) have noted the importance of distinguishing between proximal and distal outcomes, recognizing that coping may have differential relationships to more or less immediate outcomes, and that these outcomes may not act in concert.

The plethora of cross-sectional research on coping with cancer has made it difficult to establish whether variations in coping influence proximal or distal outcomes. Carver (2007) stresses the need to measure coping at one time point, and relevant health outcomes at subsequent time points, in order to at least "establish temporal precedence of the one, compared with the other" (p. 126), even if cause and effect cannot definitively be established. In addition, he has suggested that, although the appropriate time period will vary by the outcome of interest, in many cases, the time period should be much shorter than it is. Carver raises this important question: "Should you measure coping on one day and the outcome variable the next day? A week later? A month later? Three months later? . . . How much sense does it make, for example, to measure coping with a stressor at one time point, then measure emotional well-being a year later?" (p. 127).

It may also make sense in many studies to limit the number of outcomes considered. In studies employing multiple measures of similar or related outcomes, it would be important to statistically examine overlap, using factor analytic techniques to identify common elements and thus reducing redundancies that contribute to inflated error rates. Carefully choosing outcomes with clinical relevance, measuring these using varied assessment techniques (i.e., not solely self-report) with well established reliability and validity for use in cancer, and committing a priori to a focused and circumscribed analytic strategy will build confidence in research findings (Coyne, Lepore, & Palmer, 2006).

One particularly exciting but controversial distal outcome that has received increased attention in recent years is medical status, including survival. This research examines the potential of coping to actually impact the course of the cancer and its outcomes;

that is, to decrease progression of cancer and reduce mortality. This literature will be reviewed below, in the section Can Coping Interventions Cure Cancer?

## DO SOME COPING STRATEGIES WORK BETTER THAN OTHERS?

Despite the premise that no coping strategy can be seen as effective or ineffective by itself, but must be considered in terms of its "fit" to the demands of the stressor and its relationship to independently assessed, conceptually orthogonal, and temporally subsequent outcomes, does research support the notion that there are no consistent differences among strategies for coping with cancer? Or, do we find that some coping strategies are consistently associated with better outcomes in cancer, and some are consistently associated with worse outcomes?

In general, studies in cancer have found stronger evidence supporting the relationship of problem-focused coping to positive outcomes, in contrast to emotion-focused coping, which seems to more often be associated with elevated distress. However, even this finding is not consistent. A recent meta-analysis of studies of coping with prostate cancer found that emotion-focused coping was positively associated with adjustment outcomes, as were problem-focused and approach coping (Roesch et al., 2005). Coping strategies measured in the different prostate cancer studies considered were categorized as problem-focused or emotion-focused, or alternately as representing approach versus avoidance. Most of the coping strategies that were classified as emotion-focused represented approach-oriented strategies; strategies such as avoidance, self-blame, distancing, and disengagement were not included as emotion-focused strategies. These latter coping strategies, grouped under the general rubric of avoidance, were associated with more negative outcomes. Similarly, some have urged caution before concluding that emotion-focused coping is maladaptive, noting that such findings may result from problems in how emotion-focused coping is conceptualized and measured. Emotion-focused coping, as commonly measured, may be confounded with distress (Austenfeld & Stanton, 2004; Coyne & Racioppo, 2000), and some strategies commonly classified as emotion-focused (e.g., becoming upset, self-blame, denial) may, at least in some circumstances, not represent effortful coping at all (Austenfeld & Stanton, 2004; Malcarne, Compas, Epping-Jordan, & Howell, 1995; Vos & deHaes, 2007).

Given the many methodological shortcomings of the current research, it is difficult to reach any firm conclusions about whether any coping approaches are consistently effective or ineffective. In future research, it would be helpful to investigate, using prospective designs, how specific coping strategies impact carefully selected outcomes, rather than combining potentially disparate strategies in motley groupings and expecting to show broad psychological and physiological improvements.

## Coping Interventions

Fairly extensive efforts have been made to develop and test coping interventions for cancer survivors. Whether these interventions have their intended impact, and by what mechanism(s), are crucial issues to address. Translation of research into practice continues to be a challenge, especially given the need, in today's health care climate, to demonstrate that coping interventions are cost-effective. Whether cancer survivors want interventions to improve coping, and in what format, are important and underexplored concerns. Finally, there is the provocative question of whether coping interventions can prevent, slow the progression of, or even cure cancer. Each of these intervention issues will be addressed in turn.

### Efficacy of Coping Interventions

Ultimately, the goal of determining how coping relates to outcomes in cancer is to help survivors deal successfully with their disease through development of efficient and useful coping-based interventions. However, despite a number of randomized controlled trials investigating the efficacy of various interventions designed, at least in part, to change coping in cancer survivors, answering the question of whether these interventions work is difficult for a number of reasons. First, very few studies have specifically examined whether coping is an/the essential mechanism of change in a cancer-related intervention. Rather, coping is typically addressed as one of several components in a cognitive-behavioral intervention, and its specific impact is not examined (de Ridder & Schreurs, 2001). Second, coping is rarely examined as a mediator. If an intervention is designed to change coping behavior, it is essential to measure whether changes in coping do, in fact, occur, and whether those changes are responsible or account for changes in the outcomes of interest. Also, moderators of the impact that coping interventions have on outcomes are often not considered, so it is difficult to know for whom these interventions work, or work best. Finally, many of the interventions studies in cancer that have included coping as a component have been criticized for methodological flaws, including use of multiple dependent measures without controlling for inflated error rates; reporting significant but failing to report null findings when multiple dependent measures are used (i.e., confirmatory bias); lack of randomization to treatment conditions; lack of assessment of widely used "usual care" control conditions; poor handling of missing data and failure to use intent-to-treat analytic strategies; failure to consider the clinical meaningfulness of effect sizes; lack of attention to CONSORT standards in designing or reporting research; and failure to consider whether interventions are acceptable to survivors or can be applied in community/clinic settings (Coyne et al., 2006; Coyne & Racioppo, 2000; Lepore & Coyne, 2006). And, unfortunately, most of the samples in cancer coping intervention studies have been composed of middle-aged, educated Caucasians; ethnic minority groups, the uninsured, the elderly, and rural inhabitants have been less likely to be included.

It is essential that intervention studies systematically examine whether changes in coping mediate changes in cancer-related outcomes, and a small number of studies have done so (e.g., Andersen, Shelby, & Golden-Kreutz, 2007; Antoni et al., 2001, 2006; Helgeson, Cohen, Schulz, & Yasko, 1999; Manne et al., 2008; Penedo et al., 2004, 2006). In a recent randomized controlled trial enrolling 353 women with gynecological cancers, Manne et al. (2008) compared two interventions designed to reduce depression (i.e., coping and communication-enhancing intervention [CCI] and supportive counseling [SC]) to a usual care control. They proposed that the effects of the CCI on depression would be mediated by the coping stategies specifically targeted by this intervention, which included positive reappraisal, acceptance, problem-solving, emotional processing and expression, and seeking of support. In contrast, the SC intervention was hypothesized to influence emotional processing and expression. Measures of coping and depression were taken repeatedly over time. Results supported specific intervention-targeted coping strategies as full or partial mediators of the effects of the CCI on depression; mediators of SC were less clear. This approach to research is essential, not only to understanding whether coping is a key mechanism of change in multicomponent interventions, but also to simplifying and increasing the efficiency of interventions by reducing them to their essential components.

In addition, the magnitude of outcome change effected by coping interventions needs to be more carefully considered and translated into clinically meaningful parameters. Statistically significant findings regarding small to moderate effect sizes on self-report questionnaires will be unlikely to convince others to adopt the coping interventions reported as efficacious in the literature, to justify the time and energy of participants, or to provide evidence supporting reimbursement by third-party payers (Coyne et al., 2006).

### Translation to Practice
Our record in translating coping research to practice has been "dismal," according to Lazarus (2000), who lamented both the failure of researchers to responsibly communicate the clinical applicability of their findings to practitioners, and of practitioners to stay abreast of and incorporate research findings in their work. Part of the problem lies in the inherent complexity of the relevant literature. Across studies, researchers are testing interventions that vary in their components, their duration, their intensity, whether they are delivered face-to-face or via media, whether they are individually or group-administered, where they are delivered, whether only the individual survivor is involved or other family members, the degree of training of the individual(s) delivering the intervention, and the characteristics of the survivors receiving the intervention (e.g., types of cancer, treatment parameters, prognoses, personal goals and needs, existing coping skills) (Lewis, 1997). This makes it difficult for clinicians to select and apply interventions, or to be confident they will prove effective.

### Cost-effectiveness
An essential consideration in the translation of research to practice is whether coping interventions are cost-effective. Successful translation from research to practice will require, in today's health care market, that the interventions we develop and test can be implemented in a manner that is economically feasible, and it has become incumbent upon researchers to demonstrate the cost effectiveness of their interventions. Unfortunately, comparative cost has rarely been considered in the literature on interventions designed to promote effective coping with cancer. Rather, researchers have shown a tendency to develop and test interventions that are delivered personally (either individually or in groups), often by highly trained professionals, to cancer survivors who are either able to travel to central locations to receive the intervention or who receive personal visits in their home. This means that interventions demonstrated to be efficacious are likely to be very expensive to deliver in real-life settings, and rarely have researchers

explicitly considered costs in evaluating the potential effectiveness of the interventions they study.

Carlson and Bultz (2004), in their discussion of whether psychosocial interventions can not only be effective, but also economical, review studies that have performed cost–benefit analyses of quality-of-life interventions for chronic illness. Only a few of these studies examined interventions for coping with cancer, but results were promising. For example, early-stage breast cancer survivors who were randomized to receive a 6-week intervention that included instruction in coping with cancer showed improved depression levels and quality of life (Simpson, Carlson, & Trew, 2001). Billing costs from post-intervention to 2-year follow-up showed average savings per survivor, based on billing for medical costs and after taking intervention costs into account, of approximately $45. The authors argue that, because the sample was subclinical (anyone with a Structured Clinical Interview for DSM Disorders [SCID] diagnosis was excluded), and the intervention could be delivered by lower-cost workers than were used in the study, these may be underestimates of potential cost savings.

Studies of expressive writing interventions suggest the possibility of this being a cost-effective intervention. In a small pilot study of men with prostate cancer, Rosenberg et al. (2002) compared an expressive writing intervention (20 minutes per day for 4 days) to treatment as usual. In the writing condition, men's health care contacts decreased significantly, while the control group stayed relatively stable over the 6-month follow-up. Although cost estimates were not calculated, the low cost of the intervention, which could be initiated by paraprofessionals and is largely self-delivered (there was one reinforcing phone call in the intervention), combined with the substantial decrease in health care contacts, suggest that it could be highly cost-effective. Similarly, in women with breast cancer, Stanton et al. (2002) demonstrated that expressive writing interventions resulted in fewer physical symptoms and decreased cancer-related medical visits.

In a very simple and inexpensive intervention, Bennett, Phelps, Brain, Hood and Gray (2007) evaluated a two-page self-help leaflet on distraction-based coping designed to reduce stress (versus standard written information) distributed to women awaiting results from genetic risk assessments. The leaflet simply instructed women to limit thinking about risk assessment to a short time period each day, and to actively distract from related thoughts at other times; examples of distraction strategies were provided.

There was no overall effect on distress in this generally nondistressed sample, but there was a significant reduction in distress among women who received the leaflet who were more distressed at baseline, with no corresponding reduction in the control group. Although the authors did not conduct a formal cost effectiveness analysis, the incredibly low cost of this intervention, combined with its ability to significantly decrease distress among women most at need, present a strong basis for it being considered cost-effective.

Computers can be highly economical, and computer-mediated communications probably represent the wave of the future for delivering behavioral medicine interventions (Budman, 2000). Currently in the United States, more than two-thirds of Americans have home-based internet access, and this is expected to continue to increase rapidly (Nielsen//NetRatings, 2010; U.S. Census Bureau, 2009). In addition, virtually all American schools and public libraries provide internet access, typically free or at very low cost. Cancer survivors are increasingly turning to the internet for information about their disease (e.g., Meric et al., 2002), and this has expanded interest in the internet as a medium for delivering cancer coping interventions, especially to rural and home-bound survivors. A recent review of the small literature examining the effects of internet- or interactive computer-based programs for women with breast cancer, many of which contained coping skills training, showed positive increases for a variety of outcomes, but strongest effects were found for increased cancer knowledge (Ryhänen, Siekkinen, Rankinen, Korvenranta, & Leino-Kilpi, 2010). Although these communication options present exciting new ways to address coping, there is evidence that turning to online technology to deliver health-related psychosocial and educational interventions may contribute, at least in the near future, to health disparities, as people with more education and of higher socioeconomic status are more likely to use and benefit from these interventions (Beacom & Newman, 2010; Bush, Vanderpool, Cofta-Woerpel, & Wallace, 2010). It has been recommended that training in computer skills be provided, and there is evidence that these interventions can be delivered in hospital and clinic settings at reasonably low cost, perhaps while survivors are visiting treatment settings for medical reasons (e.g., Edgar, Greenberg, & Remmer, 2002).

Research on coping interventions should routinely assess and report costs of delivering the intervention, as well as potential savings resulting from measurable outcomes such as reduced health care visits, decreased hospital stays, and decreased medication usage (Carlson & Bultz, 2004). If coping interventions can be found to reduce actual medical costs—the "medical cost-offset effect" (Chiles, Lambert, & Hatch, 1999)—it will make adoption of interventions more likely and ease the process of translation from research to practice.

### Do People Want Coping Interventions?

Coyne et al. (2006) have posed the important question: "Are these the kinds of interventions that would have high uptake and sustained use in the community?" (p. 108). Or, put more simply: Do people with cancer want our interventions? Many cancer survivors do not avail themselves of any of the coping interventions available to them. A number of barriers may inhibit participation. People may perceive their problems as normative within the context of cancer, and not see a need for what they perceive as "therapy" or "professional help." They may not want to discuss their personal situations with strangers, and many interventions are offered in a group format. This may be a bigger problem than we have recognized, especially in the current climate in which costs must be kept to a minimum. Relatedly, people may want to learn techniques on how to manage their specific cancer experience from their health care team, rather than spending time sharing concerns with other survivors or receiving instruction on coping from people less familiar with their circumstances. Also, most survivors experience significant physical discomfort and fatigue, and may be disinclined to spend their very limited time and energy developing coping skills. Relatedly, they may face logistic obstacles to participation, such as distance, transportation problems, complicated schedules, and lack of financial resources. Privacy concerns may be an issue, especially in smaller communities.

In one of the few studies specifically examining cancer survivors' interest in participating in a psychosocial intervention, women with breast cancer undergoing radiotherapy were assessed on anxiety, depression, and interest in psychosocial support (Söllner, Maislinger, König, Devries, & Lukas, 2004). Only half of the moderately or severely distressed women, and fewer of the mildly distressed women, expressed interest in psychosocial support services, and even fewer took part in the services when they were offered. Interestingly, a high percentage expressed a desire for psychosocial support from their oncologists and nurses, rather than from mental health staff.

Studies examining accrual rates to descriptive investigations or clinical trials testing coping interventions have found that recruitment is difficult,

even when only questionnaires are used, participation is highly convenient, the interventions are free, and/or there is compensation provided (e.g., Coyne & Racioppo, 2000; Sadler et al., 2007; Shipman et al., 2008). Shipman et al. interviewed people with advanced cancer to determine why they chose or declined to take part in longitudinal questionnaire-based research about their cancer experiences. They found that people wanted to: (a) participate from their homes rather than in treatment settings, due to privacy concerns and difficulty travelling; (b) have face-to-face interviews rather than phone interviews or self-administered questionnaires, due to administration challenges and the desire to express themselves fully; and (c) have afternoon and highly flexible scheduling, due to the need for rest and the problem of unpredictable symptom fluctuations. The desired characteristics of participation expressed by these individuals are a poor match for how research studies are typically conducted, or for how interventions are offered.

Buss et al. (2008) reported on recruitment to two randomized controlled trials testing a web-based information, coping, and support intervention for people with advanced cancer and their caregivers. There were significant incentives, including financial compensation for questionnaires completed and for internet usage and, in some conditions, people could keep the laptops they were provided. Despite this, only half of the hundreds of survivors approached chose to participate. Reasons included lack of familiarity with computers, not seeing any benefits to the program beyond what they could already find on the internet, wanting information from their physician rather than from a computer, wanting medical rather than psychosocial interventions, not wanting to burden their caregivers, and not wanting to take on anything new because they felt overwhelmed. Buss et al. also noted that their 50% participation rate was high compared to other published accrual rates, and they suggest that poor functional status, limited life expectancy, lack of interest, and the real or perceived burden of data collection procedures likely discourage participation in psychosocial interventions. In addition, oncologists and health care staff represent important gatekeepers in the process, and their support is essential (Buss et al., 2008; Sadler et al., 2007). In both research and practice, oncologists are often the primary source of referrals to interventions, and if they lack familiarity with the intervention, are unconvinced of its (potential) utility for their clientele, or oppose its application, it is highly unlikely that survivors will participate.

Despite widespread endorsement of the need to develop tailored coping interventions carefully matched to the needs and characteristics of the people who will benefit from them, reality has not matched our best intentions. Most of the coping interventions reported in the literature are fairly generic, perhaps aiming to meet diverse survivors' needs by offering instruction on a variety of different coping strategies. And, participants in our intervention studies are also not representative of the diverse individuals and communities we seek to reach, but instead tend to be white, highly educated, earlier in the cancer process, and less ill (e.g., Ledesma & Kumano, 2009). We need to develop and test coping interventions that are relevant and tailored to diverse populations, whether the diversity is cultural, developmental, socioeconomic, religious, or other. Recent highly encouraging efforts have been made toward this goal. Rose and colleagues developed and evaluated a relatively low-cost coping intervention for middle-aged and older cancer survivors, delivered by advanced practice nurses primarily via phone contacts (Rose, Radzierwicz, Bowman, & O'Toole, 2008). Many of the typical coping components were included in the intervention, but they were tailored to address the unique concerns of these age groups, versus younger survivors. Penedo and colleagues adapted a cognitive-behavioral stress management group intervention for use with Spanish-monolingual Hispanic men with prostate cancer (Penedo et al., 2007). All intervention and study materials were translated into Spanish, and the intervention was delivered by bilingual medical personnel with experience in providing services to this population. In addition, the intervention was modified to include issues considered culturally relevant to Hispanic men with prostate cancer, and to use cultural terms and phrases throughout; also, cultural values such as *allocentrism*, *simpatia*, and *familialism* were incorporated. Results from a randomized controlled trial showed improvement in quality-of-life outcomes compared with men who participated in a half-day psychoeducational seminar. These sorts of tailored coping interventions are promising. In the future, finding ways to actually involve communities in the development of coping interventions, building from the ground up and taking cultural and logistic considerations into account from the onset, should deliver great return on investment.

To date, coping interventions have primarily been delivered in group formats over multiple weeks, often in formats that approximate courses. Typically, these are offered at medical or academic settings to which participants must travel, and that may be perceived as remote, unfamiliar, or unwelcoming by many cancer survivors. Even when interventions are offered at cancer centers or clinics at which survivors are receiving services, they are often offered independently of medical treatment and require additional visits, time, and energy. To expand the appeal and adoption of interventions, we need to take greater steps to meet cancer survivors where they are, whether that is at home, in the community, or in medical treatment. Lewis (1997) has suggested that coping interventions might better reach nontraditional communities if they were a better fit to their lifestyles. This can mean, for example, delivering interventions in easily accessed and familiar community settings, using mass media popular with a particular community (e.g., telenovelas for Spanish-speaking populations in the United States; Wilkin et al., 2007), or engaging trusted community leaders or members in disseminating interventions.

### Can Coping Interventions Cure Cancer?

The issue of whether coping can actually influence the course of disease and potentially prevent or delay recurrence or mortality has ignited much controversy. Some have argued that attention to survival-related outcomes may distract us from the importance of psychosocial benefits that may result from modifications to coping, and may have negative implications for the perceived value of, and investment in, coping interventions shown to have impact on quality-of-life outcomes but not survival (Coyne, Stefanek, & Palmer, 2007; Goodwin, 2004). Although these points are well taken, the notion that changes in coping might influence disease parameters, including progression and survival, is provocative.

What does the literature show? None of the dozen or so studies claiming to show effects of psychosocial interventions on progression, recurrence, and/or survival has specifically evaluated coping interventions, although some of the interventions incorporate some variant of coping skills training as one of several components. Perhaps the most famous of these studies (Spiegel, Bloom, Kraemer, & Gottheil, 1989) reported an almost doubling of survival time in women with metastatic breast cancer who received 1 year of structured group therapy versus women in a control group. Group therapy content included discussions of coping with cancer, emotional expression, beliefs and priorities, building social support, and management of the physical impact of cancer. In another study of a group intervention, Fawzy and colleagues (Fawzy et al., 1993;

Fawzy, Canada, & Fawzy, 2003) reported decreased risk of recurrence and lower mortality in men and women with malignant melanoma at 5–6 and 10 years after a relatively short (6-week) intervention that included attention to coping skills. Several other studies have examined some variant of cognitive, behavioral, supportive, and/or expressive group or individual therapies with content that included at least some specific structured attention to coping. Some have reported therapeutic effects on improved survival (Andersen et al., 2008; Richardson, Shelton, Krailo, & Levine, 1990) although most have not, including some studies that sought to replicate Spiegel et al.'s intervention (Cunningham et al., 1998; Edelman, Lemon, Bell, & Kidman, 1999; Goodwin et al., 2001; Kissane et al., 2004).

In a series of reviews and communications, Coyne, Stefanek, Palmer, and Thombs have raised serious concerns about methodological and statistical shortcomings of studies claiming that psychotherapeutic interventions influenced progression and survival parameters (e.g., Coyne et al., 2007; Palmer & Coyne, 2004; Stefanek, Palmer, Thombs & Coyne, 2009). These criticisms include not a priori identifying survival as an endpoint, insufficient sample sizes, capitalizing on chance findings, and overanalysis of data. The same group has noted that some of the studies have incorporated medical treatment into the psychological intervention, through, for example, including the health care team as part of the intervention or discussing survivor progress in the psychological intervention with the health care team. The findings from these studies are difficult to evaluate due to the confounding of medical intervention with psychological intervention (Palmer & Coyne, 2004). It has been countered that this represents the real state of cancer treatment, and that one would not expect nor desire a lack of coordination and communication between psychological and medical care (Spiegel & Giese-Davis, 2004). Although this is certainly true, from a research perspective it makes it difficult to attribute changes in people's medical status to psychological components of interventions such as coping. The study by Richardson et al. (1990) provides an interesting intersection of these points of view. Richardson et al.'s intervention focused on self-management (including adherence), taking quick action to resolve side effects and complications, and improving communication with the health care team. Although the intervention clearly incorporated coping, the coping skills appeared to be very specifically targeted to addressing the medical aspects of the cancer stressor, including the health care

system. In this case, improved medical care may have mediated a relationship between coping and cancer outcomes.

Other studies have not examined interventions, but instead related coping to recurrence and survival in prospective studies. Petticrew, Bell, and Hunger (2002) reviewed 26 studies examining the association between coping and cancer survival, and 11 studies of the association between coping and recurrence. They concluded that there was little support for a role of coping in survival or recurrence, although they noted methodological limitations throughout the extant literature.

A related question is, does coping cause cancer or influence cancer risk? Butow et al. (2000) reviewed the small (five study) literature on the relationship between coping style and the development of breast cancer, and concluded that "the evidence for an association between breast cancer and short-term coping styles is scant, inconsistent, and thus, insufficient to conclude that coping strategies contribute to breast cancer" (p. 174).

If coping did influence disease parameters, ranging from disease onset to survival, what is the proposed mechanism? The basic premise for medical benefits of coping has relied on the idea that coping may influence (increase/decrease) stress and distress; these in turn impact neuroendocrine and immune function, which then affect cancer outcomes (for a review, see Luecken & Compas, 2002). Luecken and Compas (2002) proposed that decreased distress resulting from coping efforts by cancer survivors may prevent activation of the hypothalamic-pituitary-adrenal (HPA) axis and elevated cortisol levels. Elevated cortisol is immunosuppressive; immunosuppression may contribute to tumor growth and metastasis, although these processes are still not well understood, nor fully accepted. In survival analyses of their intervention study, Andersen et al. (2008) found that participation by women with breast cancer in a 26-week intervention that included attention to coping, versus an assessment-only control, predicted differences in survival 11 years later. Andersen et al. point to decreases in stress, and resultant alterations in endocrine and immune pathways, as the likely mechanisms, and present supportive physiological evidence. Their findings are exciting, but have been challenged on methodological and statistical grounds (Stefanek et al., 2009). Research that systematically and prospectively examines the intersection of coping with neuroendocrine and immune system functioning, and medical parameters, is needed before we can truly draw conclusions about whether coping has implications for disease progression and survival in cancer.

## Coping Strategies of Future Interest

Many different coping strategies have been studied in relation to cancer, often within the course of the same study, given the wide use of checklists yielding scores for multiple coping strategies. However, in recent years, both descriptive and intervention studies have emerged that focus more exclusively and extensively on single coping strategies and their implications for cancer-related quality of life. A few specific strategies may be of particular significance in the process of adapting to cancer and are the focus of expanding bodies of research. These are problem solving, benefit finding, emotional expression, religious/spiritual coping, and mindfulness. Given their likely prominence in coping research in the near future, they are reviewed briefly here.

### Problem Solving

Problem solving (PS; generally considered to be a type of problem-focused coping although also incorporating emotion-focused aspects) represents a strategic approach to coping that includes maintaining a positive and constructive orientation to solving problems associated with a given stressor, generating and selecting among coping alternatives, and implementing and evaluating solutions (D'Zurilla & Nezu, 1999). The focus is not on the particular coping strategies chosen, but on the process of choosing the strategies. Studies have supported the notion that more effective PS skills predict more positive quality-of-life outcomes in cancer (e.g., Nezu, Nezu, Friedman et al., 1999).

Just over a decade ago, Art and Christine Nezu and their colleagues expanded problem-solving therapy (PST), previously established as efficacious for treatment of depression, to application with cancer survivors (Nezu et al., 1998; Nezu, Nezu, Houts, Friedman, & Faddis, 1999). It was anticipated that PST should be effective at improving quality of life in cancer because it reduces depression, which is experienced by many persons with cancer, and also because PST focuses on developing and promoting PS skills, which represent a problem-focused approach to coping that has been shown to be generally adaptive in the context of cancer-related stressors. Improvements in PS were expected to buffer the relationship between the major and associated daily stressors represented by the cancer experience and poor quality-of-life outcomes (Nezu, Nezu, Felgoise, McClure, &

Houts, 2003). Problem-solving therapy interventions for cancer have been delivered in both individual and group formats, with a focus on providing cancer survivors with an active, optimistic appraisal set, followed by specific training in problem identification and formulation, generating and performing cost–benefit analyses of alternative solutions, implementing optimal coping choices, and monitoring and evaluating the resulting outcome (see Nezu et al., 1998, for a detailed description of the intervention). Although few randomized controlled trials have been completed, results to date provide general support for the efficacy of PST interventions for cancer survivors (e.g., Allen et al., 2002; Nezu et al., 2003) and suggest that changes in PS coping are the essential mechanism underlying the success of the intervention (Nezu et al., 2003). Recently, a computer-assisted personal digital assistant (PDA)-based PST intervention was tested for Spanish-speaking mothers of children with cancer, with results suggesting equivalent efficacy to standard PST (Askins et al., 2009). Although in this case both interventions included traditional PST delivered in person, these results raise the intriguing possibility that technology could be used to deliver PST interventions in a highly cost-effective and convenient manner.

### Benefit Finding

Although there is no question that the cancer experience impacts people negatively in many ways, in recent years attention has been paid to the possibility that people with cancer may also find their lives changed in positive ways. This has been referred to as *posttraumatic growth* or *benefit finding* (BF); these terms are generally used interchangeably in the literature. Several recent reviews (Algoe & Stanton, 2009; Helgeson, Reynolds, & Tomich, 2006; Stanton, Bower, & Low, 2006) have provided evidence that BF has positive, albeit generally small, relationships to some mental health outcomes but not others, and few relationships to physical health outcomes, although the literature is limited by reliance on cross-sectional studies, and it is still unclear exactly how BF would be expected to relate to outcomes such as psychological distress (Stanton et al., 2006). All of the reviews published to date have concluded that this is an exciting but still developing field, and there have been widespread calls for prospective studies with improved methodology, including nonretrospective measurement of BF over the process of a stressful encounter such as cancer (see Tennen & Affleck, 2008, for a detailed discussion of methodological concerns).

One crucial issue is whether benefit finding represents a coping strategy, or the result of coping. Helgeson et al. (2006) raised this important issue, noting that researchers in this area may be mixing definitions of benefit finding, with some attending to the process of finding benefits, and others treating benefit finding as an outcome. Most measures used in the literature define benefit finding as something that has already occurred, with items asking what sort of growth/change has occurred as the result of a stressor, or specifically of an illness. Studies have typically measured BF as an outcome of psychosocial interventions in cancer (e.g., stress management; see Antoni et al., 2001, in breast cancer; Penedo et al., 2006, in prostate cancer). In their review of prospective studies of BF in chronic illness, Algoe and Stanton (2009) specifically excluded studies in which BF was conceptualized as coping, although they noted that some coping questionnaires have subscales with items that appear to measure efforts to find benefits. Helgeson et al. note that BF very likely is related to coping, but that the field is still at an early stage in making fine distinctions among constructs. The few studies to date that have examined BF in relation to similarly operationalized coping strategies suggest a positive relationship between more active coping approaches (e.g., positive reappraisal, planning, problem-focused) and BF, and little to no relationship with more passive/avoidant approaches (Stanton et al., 2006).

Although little attention has been paid to cancer survivors' active efforts to identify benefits, likely due at least in part to the fact that this is a sensitive issue and that individuals might be resistant to or upset by suggestions that they should engage in attempts to see positive aspects to their illness (Stanton et al., 2006), intervention research suggests that engaging people in active efforts to find benefits in their cancer experience may have positive results. Stanton et al. (2002) evaluated written BF and expressive disclosure (ED) interventions, versus a fact-writing control, in women with breast cancer. Women in the BF intervention were asked to write on four occasions about their positive thoughts and feelings regarding their cancer; in other words, to engage in active efforts to find benefits. Women in the ED intervention wrote about their deepest thoughts and feelings about having cancer. Women who received either intervention, versus a fact-writing control, had fewer physical symptoms and cancer-related medical appointments post intervention.

## Emotional Expression

Emotional expression, also known as emotional disclosure or expressive coping, has garnered significant interest as a potential adaptive coping mechanism for cancer. Clinical interventions using emotional expression have primarily focused on writing, based on a now widely used paradigm introduced by Pennebaker and Beall (1986). Recent meta-analyses (Frattaroli, 2006; Frisina, Borod, & Lepore, 2004) have concluded that written emotional expression has positive effects on psychological and/or physical outcomes in chronic illness, including cancer (e.g., de Moor et al.'s 2002 study of metastatic renal cell carinoma; Rosenberg et al.'s 2002 study of prostate cancer survivors; Stanton et al.'s 2000 and 2002 studies of breast cancer survivors). However, little is known about the mechanisms by which written emotional expression influences outcomes.

Stanton and colleagues have attempted to investigate these mechanisms in the context of their above-described study of early-stage breast cancer survivors comparing BF and ED writing interventions to a fact-writing control. Stanton et al. (2002) found that, for psychological outcomes, interventions interacted with cancer-related avoidance, such that ED was more effective for women low in avoidance, and BF was more effective for women high in avoidance. This interaction suggests that the fit between coping strategies (type of emotional expression and degree of avoidance) may be important in determining outcomes. In follow-up analyses, Low, Stanton, and Danoff-Burg (2006) examined possible mechanisms by which either ED or BF may be influencing physical outcomes. They hypothesized that autonomic habituation to negative thoughts and feelings about cancer would be at least in part responsible for the health effects seen for the ED group. In contrast, they hypothesized that the degree of positive emotions would account for the outcomes realized by the BF group. Interestingly, within-in-session heart rate habituation was greater for the ED group than for either BF or control groups. This supports the notion that ED may be producing positive health outcomes via decreases in autonomic arousal, and subsequent lowering of the impact of stress on the body. The authors were unable to clearly identify mechanisms for the BF group. A subsequent content analysis of the writing exercises by the same group (Creswell et al., 2007) determined that self-affirmation, rather than cognitive processing or discovery of meaning, may have had a stress-buffering effect on physical symptoms for both intervention groups, although the effect was not through heart rate habituation, thus suggesting an independent pathway.

## Religious/Spiritual Coping

Many cancer survivors report that religion and spirituality are very important factors in their adjustment to their illness, and this may be particularly true for members of minority groups (e.g., Culver, Arena, Antoni, & Carver, 2002; Culver, Arena, Wimberly, Antoni, & Carver, 2004). Consequently, there has been an expansion of interest in religious and spiritual aspects of coping in recent years, and the number of publications addressing this issue has expanded rapidly. Religious coping strategies may bridge or lie outside of the traditional problem-focused/emotion-focused distinction applied to coping. Although religious coping has traditionally been viewed as emotion-focused, and has even been inappropriately presumed to necessarily represent avoidance of responsibility for addressing one's problems, many religious coping strategies (e.g., praying that one will get better, turning to one's religious community for support or services) may have a distinctly problem-focused aspect.

Thuné-Boyle, Stygall, Keshtgar, and Newman (2006) recently reviewed the literature linking religious/spiritual coping strategies to quality-of-life outcomes in cancer survivors. Many of the studies reviewed found that use of religious coping was not associated with adaptational outcomes, and some studies published since this review have reported similarly weak findings (e.g., Gall, Kristjansson, Charbonneau, & Florack, 2009), although others have reported stronger positive associations (e.g., Tarakeshwar et al., 2006). Overall, as Thuné-Boyle et al. noted, the literature on religious coping is not methodologically strong. Most of the studies have been cross-sectional, samples have been primarily Christian and generally small, and measurement of religious coping has often been limited to short questionnaires such as the Brief Measure of Religious Coping (Pargament, Smith, Koenig, & Perez, 1998), the two-factor short form of the much longer and more comprehensive RCOPE (Pargament, Koenig, & Perez, 2000), despite the much richer data that can be gained from the multiple subscales of the longer scale. A report by a blue-ribbon panel of experts in religiosity/spirituality and health/illness, published as a joint effort of National Institute on Aging and the Fetzer Institute, strongly recommended that religiosity and spirituality cannot be measured simply or represented by scores from one or a few scales; rather, these are complex variables that must be measured multidimensionally (Fetzer Institute, 1999). Because this presents logistic challenges for researchers studying a variety of aspects of the cancer experience, the NIA/Fetzer working group recommended that researchers choose specific mechanisms that would be most relevant to their research questions and study those in depth. In the case of coping, this would mean careful selection of assessment strategies to permit a multifaceted measurement of subtypes of religious/spiritual coping efforts (Hill & Pargament, 2008).

More prospective research on religious and spiritual coping with cancer is needed, of people from various religious backgrounds, that employs multifaceted assessment of religious/spiritual coping, and that links specific coping approaches to specific outcomes rather than to general distress. In a recent longitudinal study comparing women with breast cancer to women with a benign diagnosis, Gall, Guirguis-Younger, Charbonneau, and Florack (2009) showed changes in use of subtypes of religious coping from prediagnosis through presurgery, and several time points post surgery. Of particular interest was that the implications of religious coping for adjustment varied with the specific religious coping strategy used, as well as when it was used during the cancer experience. Another intriguing recent study by Phelps et al. (2009) identified a prospective relationship between religious coping and a very specific outcome: intensive life-prolonging care at the end of life for persons with terminal cancer. In a multisite sample of 345 predominantly Christian individuals with advanced cancer, positive religious coping (relying on faith to promote healthy adaptation, measured using the Brief RCOPE) at baseline entry into the study predicted reception of mechanical ventilation and resuscitation in the last week of life, even after controlling for demographics, some medical characteristics, and other coping mechanisms. Although the mechanism is not clear, the authors speculated that desire for intensive end-of-life care may be associated with individuals' belief in miracles, moral conviction that life must be extended no matter its condition or prognosis, perception that engaging in intensive end-of-care represents an opportunity for God to heal them, or sense that they are collaborating with God in the fight for recovery. These findings underscore the very important role that religious coping may play in understanding adjustment to various aspects of the cancer experience.

## Mindfulness

Mindfulness, as conceptualized in the current psychological literature, is derived from Buddhist constructs of moment-to-moment awareness and nonjudgmental perception of experiences, thoughts, and feelings. In the context of cancer, it can be considered a coping strategy. Two decades ago, Kabat-Zinn (1990) developed a structured mindfulness-based stress reduction (MBSR) intervention that has enjoyed increasing popularity as an intervention in chronic illness, and more recently has since been evaluated, sometimes in modified form (e.g., Foley, Baillie, Huxter, Price, & Sinclair, 2010; Lengacher et al., 2009), for cancer. Survivors are taught, typically in a several-week course, how to be mindful of the body, beginning with the breath and expanding to include one's bodily experiences and reactions to stress. Sitting and walking meditation, body scan exercises, and relaxation strategies are used to increase awareness and promote the application of mindfulness in stress reduction. A recent meta-analysis of MBSR interventions for cancer survivors showed moderate effect sizes for psychological outcomes, such as anxiety and depression, and small effects for physical outcomes (Ledesma & Kumano, 2009). Unfortunately, many of the studies to date have not specifically measured changes in mindfulness, or have not analyzed changes in mindfulness as a mediator of health outcomes. Also, significant concerns about the measurement of mindfulness have been raised (Grossman, 2008).

## Conclusion

We have made much progress in understanding the process of coping with cancer, but we still have a long way to go. The effort and expense expended in conducting thousands of studies of coping with cancer have not been in vain, as there have been important gains made in theory, research, and practice. Recent critiques of the current literature have at times been harsh, pointing to a host of problems ranging from methodological missteps to premature conclusions. However, it is essential that we carefully consider these criticisms in the interest of advancing the field, coming to a true understanding of the role of coping in adaptation, and ultimately promoting improved outcomes in cancer.

## Future Directions

Throughout this chapter, I have raised a number of questions and challenges for coping researchers to address, struggle with, and ultimately, resolve. In future work, the following issues are key:

1. We need to move beyond "snapshots" of self-reported coping. Calls for a moratorium on the use of coping checklists may be extreme but underscore the importance of moving beyond self-report questionnaires into more sophisticated process-oriented methods of assessing coping. Ultimately, we can't understand the process of coping from a single overview measurement, and we need to move to prospective longitudinal research on coping with specific aspects of cancer, measuring changes in the appraised stressor, coping processes, and relevant outcomes as they unfold and reciprocally influence one another over time. A corresponding focus on smaller time periods, examining coping within the time frame of minutes, hours, or days, instead of weeks and months, will complement existing research and provide a more fine-grained examination of the coping process.

2. We must develop and evaluate more focused interventions, with greater attention to mechanisms. Not surprisingly, evidence suggests that multicomponent cognitive-behavioral therapies are effective in reducing depression and anxiety for cancer patients, as well as for other clinical populations. In the future, we should focus our efforts on identifying coping interventions that target specific cancer-related problems via tailored approaches. A coping intervention for breast cancer surgery may appropriately be very different from a coping intervention for cancer-related fatigue.

3. It is essential that our interventions reach the survivors they were designed to help. Translation of interventions research to practice, including special attention to cost concerns, is our responsibility, and we need to take dissemination into account when designing our interventions. Rather than taking the traditional approach of offering multiple-session interventions at medical centers, we should strive to design interventions that can be brought to and evaluated in the community. This will likely force us to consider new ways of delivering interventions that will ultimately broaden their appeal and accessibility to currently underserved communities. This will mean finding ways to involve communities in the development of interventions, taking cultural and logistic considerations into account from the onset.

4. Attending to cultural considerations is another way to expand our understanding of

coping and broaden the appeal and utility of our interventions. Culture does not equate to race/ethnicity; rather, it is a complex construct that includes nationality, geographic location, gender identity, sexuality, religiosity, and socioeconomic status, among others. As Stanton and Revenson (2007) have pointed out, "Cultural contexts supply blueprints for adaptation to disease" and "also may define the acceptability of particular coping responses, such as emotional expression or anger, and thus their value as adaptive mechanisms" (p. 217).

5. We should continue to investigate the physiological effects of coping. Coping may not cure cancer, but at least some types of coping used in the context of some cancer-related circumstances are likely to affect physiological processes, perhaps with real consequences for cancer survivors.

## Dedication

This chapter is dedicated to my father, Don Malcarne, and my mother-in-law, Evelyn Kashima.

## Notes

1. The term "survivor" is used throughout this chapter instead of "patient," consistent with the National Cancer Institute definition that "an individual is considered a cancer survivor from the time of diagnosis until the end of life" (National Cancer Institute, 2010).

## References

Algoe, S.B., & Stanton, A.L. (2009). Is benefit finding good for individuals with chronic disease? In C.L. Park, S.C. Lechner, M.H. Antoni, & A.L. Stanton (Eds.), *Medical illness and positive life change: Can crisis lead to personal transformation?* (pp. 173–193). Washington, DC: American Psychological Association.

Allen, S.M., Shah, A.C., Nezu, A.M., Nezu, C.M., Ciambrone, D., Hogan, J., & Mor, V. (2002). A problem-solving approach to stress reduction among younger women with breast carcinoma: A randomized controlled trial. *Cancer, 94,* 3089–3100.

American Cancer Society (2007). *Global facts and figures 2007.* Atlanta: Author.

American Cancer Society (2009). *Cancer facts and figures 2009.* Atlanta: Author.

Andersen, B.L., Shelby, R.A., & Golden-Kreutz, D.M. (2007). RCT of a psychological intervention for patients with cancer: I. Mechanisms of change. *Journal of Consulting and Clinical Psychology, 75,* 927–938.

Andersen, B.L., Yang, H.-C., Farra, W.B., Golden-Kreutz, D.M., Emery, C.F., et al. (2008). Psychological intervention improves survival for breast cancer patients: A randomized clinical trial. *Cancer, 113,* 3450–3458.

Antoni, M.H., Lechner, S.C., Kazi, A., Wimberly, S.R., Sifre, T., Urcuyo, K.R., et al. (2006). How stress management improves quality of life after treatment for breast cancer. *Journal of Consulting and Clinical Psychology, 74,* 1143–1152.

Antoni, M.H., Lehman, J.M., Kilbourn, K.M., Boyers, A.E., Culver, J.L., Alferi, S.M., et al. (2001). Cognitive-behavioral stress management intervention decreases the prevalence of depression and enhances benefit finding among women under treatment for early-stage breast cancer. *Health Psychology, 20,* 20–32.

Askins, M.A., Sahler, O.J.Z., Sherman, S.A., Fairclough, D.L., Butler, R.W., Katz, E.R., et al. (2009). Report from a multi-institutional randomized clinical trial examining computer-assisted problem-solving skills training for English- and Spanish-speaking mothers of children with newly diagnosed cancer. *Journal of Pediatric Psychology, 34,* 551–563.

Austenfeld, J.L., & Stanton, A.L. (2004). Coping through emotional approach: A new look at emotion, coping, and health-related outcomes. *Journal of Personality, 72,* 1335–1363.

Beacom, A.M., & Newman, S.J. (2010). Communicating health information to disadvantaged populations. *Family & Community Health, 33,* 152–162.

Bennett, P., Phelps, C., Brain, K., Hood, K., & Gray, J. (2007). A randomized controlled trial of a brief self-help coping intervention designed to reduce distress when awaiting genetic risk information. *Journal of Psychosomatic Research, 63,* 59–64.

Broderick, J., Schwartz, J., Shiffman, S., Hufford, M., & Stone, A. (2003). Signaling does not adequately improve diary compliance. *Annals of Behavioral Medicine, 26,* 139–148.

Broderick, J.E., & Stone, A.A. (2006). Paper and electronic diaries: Too early for conclusions on compliance rates and their effects–Comment on Green, Rafaeli, Bolger, Shrout, and Reis (2006). *Psychological Methods, 11,* 106–111.

Budman, S.H. (2000). Behavioral health care dot-com and beyond: Computer-mediated communications in mental health and substance abuse treatment. *American Psychologist, 55,* 1290–1300.

Bush, N., Vanderpool, R., Cofta-Woerpel, L., & Wallace, P. (2010). Profiles of 800,000 users of the National Cancer Institute's cancer information service since the debut of online assistance, 2003–2008. *Preventing Chronic Disease, 7,* A31.

Buss, M.K., DuBenske, L.L., Dinauer, S., Gustafson, D.H., McTavish, F., & Cleary, J.F. (2008). Patient/caregiver influences for declining participation in supportive oncology trials. *The Journal of Supportive Oncology, 6,* 168–174.

Butow, P.N., Hiller, J.E., Price, M.A., Thackway, S.V., Kricker, A., & Tennant, C.C. (2000). Epidemiological evidence for a relationship between life events, coping style, and personality factors in the development of breast cancer. *Journal of Psychosomatic Research, 49,* 169–181.

Carlson, L.E., Angen, M., Cullum, J., Goodey, E., Koopmans, J., Lamont, L., et al. (2004). High levels of untreated distress and fatigue in cancer patients. *British Journal of Cancer, 90,* 2297–2304.

Carlson, L.E., & Bultz, B.D. (2004). Efficacy and medical cost offset of psychosocial interventions in cancer care: Making the case for economic analyses. *Psycho-Oncology, 13,* 837–849.

Carver, C.S. (1997). You want to measure coping but your protocol's too long: Consider the brief COPE. *International Journal of Behavioral Medicine, 4,* 92–100.

Carver, C.S. (2007). Stress, coping, and health. In H.S. Friedman, & R.C. Silver (Eds.), *Foundations of health psychology* (pp. 117–144). New York: Oxford University Press.

Carver, C.S. (2010). *COPE: Complete version.* Retrieved from http://www.psy.miami.edu/faculty/ccarver/sclCOPE.html.

Carver, C.S., Scheier, M.F., & Weintraub, J.K. (1989). Assessing coping strategies: A theoretically based approach. *Journal of Personality and Social Psychology, 56*, 267–283.

Chiles, J.A., Lambert, M.J., & Hatch, A.L. (1999). The impact of psychological interventions on medical cost offset: A meta-analytic review. *Clinical Psychology: Science and Practice, 6*, 204–220.

Coyne, J.C., Lepore, S.J., & Palmer, S.C. (2006). Efficacy of psychosocial interventions in cancer care: Evidence is weaker than it first looks. *Annals of Behavioral Medicine, 32*, 104–110.

Coyne, J.C., & Racioppo, M.W. (2000). Never the twain shall meet? Closing the gap between coping research and clinical intervention research. *American Psychologist, 55*, 655–664.

Coyne, J.C., Stefanek, M., & Palmer, S.C. (2007). Psychotherapy and survival in cancer: The conflict between hope and evidence. *Psychological Bulletin, 133*, 367–194.

Creswell, J.D., Lam, S., Stanton, A., Taylor, S.E., Bower, J.E., & Sherman, D.K. (2007). Does self-affirmation, cognitive processing, or discovery of meaning explain cancer-related health benefits of expressive writing? *Personality and Social Psychology Bulletin, 33*, 238–250.

Culver, J.L., Arena, P.L., Antoni, M.H., & Carver, C.S. (2002). Coping and distress among women under treatment for early stage breast cancer: Comparing African Americans, Hispanics, and non-Hispanic Whites. *Psycho-Oncology, 11*, 495–504.

Culver, J.L., Arena, P.L., Wimberly, S.R., Antoni, M.H., & Carver, C.S. (2004). Coping among African-American, Hispanic, and non-Hispanic white women recently treated for early stage breast cancer. *Psychology and Health, 19*, 157–166.

Cunningham, A.J., Edwards, C.V.I., Jenkins, G.P., Pollack, H., Lockwood, G.A., & Warr, D. (1998). A randomized controlled trial of the effects of group psychological therapy on survival in women with metastatic breast cancer. *Psycho-Oncology, 7*, 508–517.

DeFlorio, M., & Massie, M.J. (1995) Review of depression in cancer: Gender differences. *Depression, 3*, 66–80.

De Moor, C. Sterner, J., Warneke, C., Gilani, Z., Hall, M., Amato, R., & Cohen, L. (2002). A pilot study of the effects of expressive writing on psychological and behavioral adjustment in patients enrolled in a phase II trial of vaccine therapy for metastatic renal cell carcinoma. *Health Psychology, 21*, 615–619.

De Ridder, D., & Schreurs, K. (2001). Developing interventions for chronically ill patients: Is coping a helpful concept? *Clinical Psychology Review, 21*, 205–240.

D'Zurilla, T.J., & Nezu, A.M. (1999). *Problem-solving therapy: A social competence approach to clinical intervention* (2nd ed.). New York: Springer.

Edelman, S.U., Lemon, J., Bell, D.R., & Kidman, A.D. (1999). Effects of group CBT on the survival time of patients with metastatic breast cancer. *Psycho-Oncology, 8*, 474–481.

Edgar, L., Greenberg, A., & Remmer, J. (2002). Providing internet lessons to oncology patients and family members: A shared project. *Psycho-Oncology, 11*, 439–446.

Fahrenberg, J., Myrtek, M., Pawlik, K., & Perrez, M. (2007). Ambulatory assessment–monitoring behavior in daily life settings: A behavioral-scientific challenge for psychology. *European Journal of Psychological Assessment, 23*, 206–213.

Fawzy, F.I., Fawzy, N.W., Hyun, C.S., Elashoff, R., Guthrie, D., Fahey, J.L., & Morton, D.L. (1993). Malignant melanoma: Effects of an early structured psychiatric intervention, coping, and affective state on recurrence and survival 6 years later. *Archives of General Psychiatry, 50*, 681–689.

Fawzy, F.I., Canada, A.L., & Fawzy, N.W. (2003). Malignant melanoma: Effects of a brief, structured psychiatric intervention on survival and recurrence at 10-year follow-up. *Archives of General Psychiatry, 60*, 100–103.

Fetzer Institute (1999). *Multidimensional measurement of religiousness/spirituality for use in health research.* Retrieved from http://www.fetzer.org/research/248-dses.

Foley, E., Baillie, A., Huxter, M., Price, M., & Sinclair, E. (2010). Mindfulness-based cognitive therapy for individuals whose lives have been affected by cancer: A randomized controlled trial. *Journal of Consulting and Clinical Psychology, 78*, 72–79.

Folkman, S., & Lazarus, R.S. (1980). An analysis of coping in a middle-aged community sample. *Journal of Health and Social Behavior, 21*, 219–239.

Folkman, S., & Lazarus, R.S. (1985). If it changes it must be a process: Study of emotion and coping during three stages of a college examination. *Journal of Personality and Social Psychology, 48*, 150–170.

Folkman, S., Lazarus, R.S., Dunkel-Schetter, C., DeLongis, A., & Gruen, R.J. (1986). Dynamics of a stressful encounter: Cognitive appraisal, coping, and encounter outcomes. *Journal of Personality and Social Psychology, 50*, 992–1003.

Folkman, S., & Moskowitz, J.T. (2004). Coping: Pitfalls and promises. *Annual Review of Psychology, 55*, 745–774.

Franks, H., & Roesch, S.C. (2006). Appraisals and coping in people living with cancer: A meta-analysis. *Psycho-Oncology, 15*, 1027–1037.

Frattaroli, J. (2006). Experimental disclosure and its moderators: A meta-analysis. *Psychological Bulletin, 132*, 823–865.

Frisina, P.G., Borod, J.C., & Lepore, S. (2004). A meta-analysis of the effects of written emotional disclosure on the health outcomes of clinical populations. *The Journal of Nervous and Mental Disease, 192*, 629–634.

Gall, T.L., Guirguis-Younger, M., Charbonneau, C., & Florack, P. (2009). The trajectory of religious coping across time in response to the diagnosis of breast cancer. *Psycho-Oncology, 18*, 1165–1178.

Gall, T.L., Kristjansson, E., Charbonneau, C., & Florack, P. (2009). A longitudinal study on the role of spirituality in response to the diagnosis and treatment of breast cancer. *Journal of Behavioral Medicine, 32*, 174–186.

Glinder, J.G., Beckjord, E., Kaiser, C.R., & Compas, B.E. (2007). Psychological adjustment to breast cancer: Automatic and controlled responses to stress. *Psychology and Health, 22*, 337–359.

Goodwin, P.J., Leszcz, M., Ennis, M., Koopmans, J., Vincent, L., Guther, H. et al. (2001). The effect of group psychosocial support on survival in metastatic breast cancer. *New England Journal of Medicine, 345*, 1719–1726.

Goodwin, P.J. (2004). Support groups in breast cancer: When a negative result is positive. *Journal of Clinical Oncology, 22*, 4244–4246.

Grossman, P. (2008). On measuring mindfulness in psychosomatic and psychological research. *Journal of Psychosomatic Research, 64*, 405–408.

Helgeson, V.S., Cohen, S., Schulz, R., & Yasko, J. (1999). Education and peer discussion group interventions and adjustment to breast cancer. *Archives of General Psychiatry, 56*, 340–347.

Helgeson, V.S., Reynolds, K.A., & Tomich, P.L. (2006). A meta-analytic review of benefit finding and growth. *Journal of Consulting and Clinical Psychology, 74*, 797–816.

Hill, P.C., & Pargament, K.I. (2008). Advances in the conceptu-alization and measurement of religion and spirituality: Implications for physical and mental health research. *Psychology of Religion and Spirituality, 5*, 3–17.

Holahan, C.J., & Moos, R.H. (1987). Personal and contextual determinants of coping strategies. *Journal of Personality and Social Psychology, 52*, 946–955.

Kabat-Zinn, J. (1990). *Full catastrophe living: Using the wisdom of your body and mind to face stress, pain, and illness.* New York: Delacorte.

Kadan-Lottick, N.S., Vanderwerker, L.C., Block, S.D., Zhang, B., & Prigerson, H.G. (2005). Psychiatric disorders and mental health service use in patients with advanced cancer: A report from the coping with cancer study. *Cancer, 104*, 2872–2881.

Kissane, D.W., Love, A., Hatton, A., Bloch, S., Smith, G., Clarke, D.M., et al. (2004). Effect of cognitive-existential group therapy on survival in early-stage breast cancer. *Journal of Clinical Oncology, 22*, 4255–4260.

Lazarus, R.S. (1993). Coping theory and research: Past, present, and future. *Psychosomatic Medicine, 55*, 234–247.

Lazarus, R.S. (2000). Toward better research on stress and coping. *American Psychologist, 55*, 665–673.

Lazarus, R.S., & Folkman, S. (1984). *Stress, appraisal, and coping.* New York: Springer.

Ledesma, D., & Kumano, H. (2009). Mindfulness-based stress reduction and cancer: A meta-analysis. *Psycho-Oncology, 18*, 571–579.

Lengacher, C.A., Johnson-Mallard, V., Post-White, J., Moscoso, M.S., Jacobsen, P.B., Klein, T.W., et al. (2009). Randomized controlled trial of mindfulness-based stress reduction (MBSR) for survivors of breast cancer. *Psycho-Oncology, 18*, 1261–1272.

Lepore, S.J., & Coyne, J.C. (2006). Psychological interventions for distress in cancer patients: A review of reviews. *Annals of Behavioral Medicine, 32*, 85–92.

Lewis, F.M. (1997). Behavioral research to enhance adjustment and quality of life among adults with cancer. *Preventive Medicine, 26*, S19–S29.

Low, C.A., Stanton, A.L., & Danoff-Burg, S. (2006). Expressive disclosure and benefit finding among breast cancer patients: Mechanisms for positive health effects. *Health Psychology, 24*, 181–189.

Luecken, L.J., & Compas, B.E. (2002). Stress, coping, and immune function in breast cancer. *Annals of Behavioral Medicine, 24*, 336–344.

Malcarne, V.L., Compas, B.E., Epping-Jordan, J.E., & Howell, D.C. (1995). Cognitive factors in adjustment to cancer: Attributions of self-blame and perceptions of control. *Journal of Behavioral Medicine, 18*, 401–417.

Manne, S.L., Winkel, G., Rubin, S., Edelson, M., Rosenblum, N., Bergman, C., et al. (2008). Mediators of a coping and communication-enhancing intervention and a supportive counseling intervention among women diagnosed with gynecological cancers. *Journal of Consulting and Clinical Psychology, 76*, 1034–1045.

Meric, F., Bernstam, E.V., Mirza, N.Q., Hunt, K.K., Ames, F.C., Ross, M.I., et al. (2002). Breast cancer on the world wide web: Cross sectional survey of quality of information and popularity of websites. *British Medical Journal, 324*, 577–581.

Moos, R.H., & Schaefer, J.A. (1993). Coping resources and pro-cesses: Current concepts and measures. In L. Goldberger, & S. Breznitz (Eds.), *Handbook of stress: Theoretical and clinical aspects* (pp. 234–257). New York: Free Press.

National Cancer Institute (2010). *Cancer Terms.* Retrieved from http://www.cancer.gov/dictionary/?CdrID=450125.

Nielsen//Netratings (2010). *Three out of four Americans have access to the Internet, according to Nielsen//Netratings.* Retrieved from www.nielsen-online.com/pr/pr_040318.pdf.

Nezu, A.M., Nezu, C.M., Felgoise, S.H., McClure, K.S., & Houts, P.S. (2003). Project Genesis: Assessing the efficacy of problem-solving therapy for distressed adult cancer patients. *Journal of Consulting and Clinical Psychology, 71*, 1036–1048.

Nezu, A.M., Nezu, C.M., Friedman, S.H., Faddis, S., & Houts, P.S. (1998). *Helping cancer patients cope: A problem-solving approach.* Washington, DC: American Psychological Association.

Nezu, A.M., Nezu, C.M., Friedman, S.H., Houts, P.S., DelliCarpini, L.A., Nemeth, C.B., & Faddis, S. (1999). Cancer and psychological distress: Two investigations regarding the role of problem solving. *Journal of Psychosocial Oncology, 16*, 27–40.

Nezu, A.M., Nezu, C.M., Houts, P.S., Friedman, S.H., & Faddis, S. (1999). Relevance of problem-solving therapy to psycho-social oncology. *Journal of Psychosocial Oncology, 16*, 5–26.

Nordin, K., Berglund, G., Terje, I., & Glimelius, B. (1999). The mental adjustment to cancer scale–A psychometric analysis and the concept of coping. *Psycho-Oncology, 8*, 250–259.

Palmer, S.C., & Coyne, J.C. (2004). Examining the evidence that psychotherapy improves the survival of cancer patients. *Biological Psychiatry, 56*, 61–62.

Pargament, K.I., Smith, B., Koenig, H., & Perez, L. (1998). Patterns of positive and negative religious coping with major life stres-sors. *Journal of the Scientific Study of Religion, 37*, 710–724.

Pargament, K.I., Koenig, H.G., & Perez, L. (2000). The many methods of religious coping: Development and initial validation of the RCOPE. *Journal of Clinical Psychology, 56*, 519–543.

Penedo, F., Dahn, J., Molton, I., Gonzalez, J., Kinsinger, D., Roos, B., et al. (2004). Cognitive behavioral stress manage-ment improves stress management skills and quality of life in men recovering from treatment of prostate cancer. *Cancer, 100*, 192–200.

Penedo, F.J., Molton, I., Dahn, J.R., Shen, B-J, Kinsinger, D., Traeger, L., et al. (2006). A randomized clinical trial of group-based cognitive-behavioral stress management in localized prostate cancer: Development of stress manage-ment skills improves quality of life and benefit finding. *Annals of Behavioral Medicine, 31*, 261–270.

Penedo, F.J., Traeger, L., Dahn, J., Molton, I., Gonzalez, J.S., Schneiderman, N., & Antoni, M.H. (2007). Cognitive behav-ioral stress management intervention improves quality of life in Spanish monolingual Hispanic men treated for localized prostate cancer: Results of a randomized controlled trial. *International Journal of Behavioral Medicine, 14*, 164–172.

Pennebaker, J.W., & Beall, S.K. (1986). Confronting a traumatic event: Toward an understanding of inhibition and disease. *Journal of Abnormal Psychology, 95*, 274–281.

Petticrew, M., Bell, R., & Hunter, D. (2002). Influence of psycho-logical coping on survival and recurrence in people with cancer: Systematic review. *British Medical Journal, 325*, 1066–1069.

Phelps, A.C., Maciejewski, P.K., Nilsson, M., Balboni, T.A., Wright, A.A., Paulk, M.E., et al. (2009). Religious coping and use of intensive life-prolonging care near death in patients with advanced cancer. *Journal of the American Medical Association, 301*, 1140–1147.

Richardson, J.L., Shelton, D.R., Krailo, M., & Levine, A.M. (1990). The effect of compliance with treatment on survival among patients with hematologic malignancies. *Journal of Clinical Oncology, 8,* 356–364.

Roesch, S.C., Adams, L., Hines, A., Palmores, A., Vyas, P., Tran, C., et al. (2005). Coping with prostate cancer: A meta-analytic review. *Journal of Behavioral Medicine, 28,* 281–293.

Rose, J.H., Radzierwicz, R., Bowman, K.F., & O'Toole, E.E. (2008). A coping and communication support intervention tailored to older patients diagnosed with late-stage cancer. *Clinical Interventions in Aging, 3,* 77–95.

Rosenberg, H.J., Rosenberg, S.D., Ernstoff, M.S., Wolford, G.L., Amdur, R.J., Elshamy, M.R., et al. (2002). Expressive disclosure and health outcomes in a prostate cancer population. *International Journal of Psychiatry in Medicine, 32,* 37–53.

Ryhänen, A.M., Siekkinen, M., Rankinen, S., Korvenranta, H., & Leino-Kilpi, H. (2010). The effects of Internet or interactive computer-based patient education in the field of breast cancer: A systematic literature review. *Patient Education and Counseling, 79,* 5–13.

Sadler, G.R., Ko, C.M., Malcarne, V.L., Banthia, R., Gutierrez, I., & Varni, J.W. (2007). Costs of recruiting couples to a clinical trial. *Contemporary Clinical Trials, 28,* 423–432.

Sellick, S.M., & Crooks, D.L. (1999). Depression and cancer: An appraisal of the literature for prevalence, detection, and practice guideline development for psychological interventions. *Psycho-Oncology, 8,* 315–333.

Sharpe, L., & Curran, L. (2006). Understanding the process of adjustment to illness. *Social Science & Medicine, 62,* 1153–1166.

Shiffman, S., Stone, A.A., & Hufford, M.R. (2008). Ecological momentary assessment. *Annual Review of Clinical Psychology, 4,* 1–32.

Shipman, C., Hotopf, M., Richardson, A., Murray, S., Koffman, J., Harding, R., Speck, P., & Higginson, I.J. (2008). The views of patients with advanced cancer regarding participation in serial questionnaire studies. *Palliative Medicine, 22,* 913–920.

Simpson, J.S.A., Carlson, L.E., & Trew, M. (2001). Effect of group therapy for breast cancer on healthcare utilization. *Cancer Practice, 9,* 19–26.

Smyth, J.M., & Stone, A.A. (2003). Ecological momentary assessment research in behavioral medicine. *Journal of Happiness Studies, 4,* 35–52.

Söllner, W., Maislinger, S., König, A., Devries, A., & Lukas, P. (2004). Providing psychosocial support for breast cancer patients based on screening for distress within a consultation-liaison service. *Psycho-Oncology, 13,* 893–897.

Somerfield, M.R., & McCrae, R.R. (2000). Stress and coping research: Methodological challenges, theoretical advances, and clinical applications. *American Psychologist, 55,* 620–625.

Spiegel, D., Bloom, J.R., Kraemer, H.C., & Gottheil, E. (1989). Effect of psychosocial treatment on survival of patients with metastatic breast cancer. *Lancet, 2,* 888–891.

Spiegel, D., & Giese-Davis, J. (2004). Examining the evidence that psychotherapy improves the survival of cancer patients: Reply. *Biological Psychiatry, 56,* 62–64.

Stanton, A.L., Bower, J.E., & Low, C.A. (2006). Posttraumatic growth after cancer. In L.G. Calhoun, & R.G. Tedeschi (Eds.), *Handbook of posttraumatic growth: Research and practice* (pp. 138–175). Mahwah, NJ: Lawrence Erlbaum.

Stanton, A.L., Danoff-Burg, S., Cameron, C.L., Bishop, M.M., Collins, C.A., Kirk, S.B., et al. (2000). Emotionally expressive coping predicts psychological and physical adjustment to breast cancer. *Journal of Consulting and Clinical Psychology, 68,* 875–882.

Stanton, A.L., Danoff-Burg, S., Sworowski, L.A., Collins, C.A., Branstetter, A.D., Rodriguez-Hanley, A., et al. (2002). Randomized, controlled trial of written emotional expression and benefit finding in breast cancer patients. *Journal of Clinical Oncology, 20,* 4160–4168.

Stanton, A.L., & Revenson, T.A. (2007). Adjustment to chronic disease: Progress and promise in research. In H.S. Friedman, & R.C. Silver (Eds.), *Foundations of health psychology* (pp. 203–233). New York: Oxford University Press.

Stanton, A.L., Revenson, T.A., & Tennen, H. (2007). Health psychology: Psychological adjustment to chronic disease. *Annual Review of Psychology, 58,* 565–592.

Stefanek, M.E., Palmer, S.C., Thombs, B.D., & Coyne, J.C. (2009). Finding what is not there: Unwarranted claims of an effect of psychosocial intervention on recurrent and survival. *Cancer, 115,* 5612–5616.

Stone, A.A., & Shiffman, S. (1994). Ecological momentary assessment (EMA) in behavioral medicine. *Annals of Behavioral Medicine, 16,* 199–202.

Stone, A.A., & Shiffman, S. (2002). Capturing momentary, self-report data: A proposal for reporting guidelines. *Annals of Behavioral Medicine, 24,* 236–243.

Stone, A.A., & Neale, J.M. (1984). New measure of daily coping: Development and preliminary results. *Journal of Personality and Social Psychology, 46,* 892–906.

Tarakeshwar, N., Vanderwerker, L.C., Paulk, E., Pearce, M.J., Kasl, S.V., & Prigerson, H.G. (2006). Religious coping is associated with the quality of life of patients with advanced cancer. *Journal of Palliative Medicine, 9,* 646–656.

Taylor, S.E., & Stanton, A.L. (2007). Coping resources, coping processes, and mental health. *Annual Review of Clinical Psychology, 3,* 377–401.

Tennen, H., & Affleck, G. (2008). Assessing positive life change: In search of meticulous methods. In C.L. Park, S.C. Lechner, M.H. Antoni, & A.L. Stanton (Eds.), *Medical illness and positive life change: Can crisis lead to personal transformation?* (pp. 31–49). Washington, DC: American Psychological Association.

Tennen, H., Affleck, G., Armeli, S., & Carney, M.A. (2000). A daily process approach to coping: Linking theory, research, and practice. *American Psychologist, 55,* 626–636.

Thuné-Boyle, I.C., Stygall, J.A., Keshtgar, M.R., & Newman, S.P. (2006). Do religious/spiritual coping strategies affect illness adjustment in patients with cancer? A systematic review of the literature. *Social Science & Medicine, 63,* 151–164.

U.S. Census Bureau (2009). *Internet use in the United States: October 2009.* Retrieved from http://www.census.gov/population/www/socdemo/computer/2009.html.

Vitaliano, P.P., Maiuro, R.D., Russo, J., & Becker, J. (1987). Raw versus relative scores in the assessment of coping strategies. *Journal of Behavioral Medicine, 10,* 1–18.

Vitaliano, P.P., Russo, J., Carr, J.E., Maiuro, R.D., & Becker, J. (1985). The ways of coping checklist: Revision and psychometric properties. *Multivariate Behavioral Research, 20,* 3–26.

Vos, M.S., & de Haes, J.C.J.M. (2007). Denial in cancer patients, an explorative review. *Psycho-Oncology, 16,* 12–25.

Watson, M., Greer, S., Young, J., Inayat, Q., Burgess, C., & Robertson, B. (1988). Development of a questionnaire measure of adjustment to cancer: The MAC scale. *Psychological Medicine, 18,* 203–209.

Wasteson, E., Glimelius, B., Sjödén, P., & Nordin, K. (2006). Comparison of a questionnaire commonly used for measuring coping with a daily-basis prospective coping measure. *Journal of Psychosomatic Research, 61,* 813–820.

Wilkin, H.A., Valente, T.W., Murphy, S., Cody, M.J., Huang, G., & Beck, V. (2007). Does entertainment-education work with Latinos in the United States? Identification and the effects of a telenovela breast cancer storyline. *Journal of Health Communication, 12*, 455–469.

World Health Organization (1997). *WHOQOL: Measuring quality of life.* Retrieved from www.who.int/mental_health/media/68.pdf.

Zabora, J.R., Blanchard, C.G., Smith, E.D., Roberts, C.S., Glajchen, M., Sharp, J.W., et al. (1997). Prevalence of psychological distress among cancer patients across the disease continuum. *Journal of Psychosocial Oncology, 15*, 73–87.

Zabora, J., Brintzenhofeszoc, K., Curbow, B., Hooker, C., & Piantadosi, S. (2001). The prevalence of psychological distress by cancer site. *Psycho-Oncology, 10*, 19–28.

# Expressive Writing: Connections to Physical and Mental Health

James W. Pennebaker *and* Cindy K. Chung

## Abstract

This paper presents a broad overview of the expressive writing paradigm. Since its first use in the 1980s, dozens of studies have explored the parameters and boundary conditions of its effectiveness. In the laboratory, consistent and significant health improvements are found when individuals write or talk about personally upsetting experiences. The effects include both subjective and objective markers of health and well-being. The disclosure phenomenon appears to generalize across settings, many individual difference factors, and several Western cultures, and is independent of social feedback.

**Keywords:** Mental health, language, expressive writing, trauma, emotional upheaval, cognitive change

There is a long history in psychology and medicine linking the occurrence of traumatic experiences with subsequent physical and mental health problems. What is it about a trauma that influences health? Several candidates immediately come to mind. Psychologically, personal upheavals provoke intense and long-lasting emotional changes. The unexpected events are generally associated with cognitive disruption, including rumination and attempts to understand what happened and why. Socially, traumas are known to cause wholesale disruptions in people's social networks. Due in part to these social and psychological changes, traumas often influence lifestyle changes, such as unhealthy smoking, drinking, exercise, sleeping, and eating patterns. Each of these psychological, social, and behavioral effects results in a cascade of biological changes, including elevations in cortisol, immune disruption, cardiovascular changes, and a cascade of neurotransmitter changes.

Individuals who are highly reactive to novel stimuli (Vaidya & Garfield, 2003), highly anxious (Miller, 2003), avoidant, and self-blaming (Sutker, Davis, Uddo, & Ditta, 1995), or high in hypnotic ability (Bower & Sivers, 1998) may be particularly susceptible to traumatic experiences. Similarly, the more extreme the trauma and the longer time over which it lasts are predictors of posttraumatic stress disorder (PTSD) incidence (e.g., Breslau, Chilcoat, Kessler, & Davis, 1999). It is also generally agreed that people most prone to PTSD have had a history of depression, trauma, and other PTSD episodes in the past, even prior to their most recent traumatic experience (Cabrera, Hoge, Bliese, Castro, & Messer, 2007; Miller, 2003).

A cursory reading of the literature might lead many intelligent people to assume that mental and health problems are standard responses to all great traumas. Surprisingly, the opposite is true: Most people deal with traumatic experiences quite well, with no major changes in their mental or physical health. In a classic article, Wortman and Silver (1989) summarized a large number of studies indicating that at least half of people who have faced the death of a spouse or child did not experience intense anxiety, depression, or grief. Numerous studies report that at least 65% of male and female soldiers who have lived through horrific battles or war zone stress never show any evidence of PTSD (Keane, 1998; Murray, 1992). Multiple studies with individuals who have survived major motor vehicle accidents (Brom, Kleber, & Hofman, 1993) or witnessed tragic airplane accidents (Carlier & Gersons, 1997) find that the majority did not experience depression or PTSD in the weeks or months after their experiences. Across studies, 40%–80% of rape survivors did not evidence symptoms of PTSD (Kilpatrick, Resnick, Saunders, & Best, 1998; Resnick, Kilpatrick, & Lipovsky, 1991).

Why is it that some people seem to deal with major upheavals better than others? What is the profile of healthy coping? This, of course, is a central question among trauma researchers. We know, for example, that people with an intact social support group weather upheavals better than do others (e.g., Murray, 1992). Beyond basic genetic predispositions, do some people adopt certain coping strategies that allow them to move past an upheaval more efficiently? If such coping strategies exist, can they be trained? If such techniques are available, how do they work?

Given that as many as 30% of people who face massive traumatic experiences will experience PTSD, what can we, as researchers and clinicians, do to reduce this rate? It is likely that many (perhaps most) PTSD-prone individuals will not benefit from any simple interventions. The nature of their trauma, their genetic, biological, and/or personality predispositions, or pre-trauma life experiences will override social or psychological therapies. Nevertheless, some PTSD-prone individuals, as well as the majority of distressed but subclinical cases, may benefit by focusing on their psychological and social worlds in the wake of their traumatic experiences.

A central premise of this chapter is that when people transform their feelings and thoughts about personally upsetting experiences into language, their physical and mental health often improve. The links to PTSD are still tenuous. However, an increasing number of studies indicate that having people write about emotional upheavals can result in healthy improvements in social, psychological, behavioral, and biological functioning. As with the trauma–illness link, however, there is probably not a single mediator that can explain the power of writing. One promising candidate that is proposed concerns the effects of translating emotions into language format, or as we suggest, the metaphorical translation of an analog experience into a digital one.

## Emotional Upheavals, Disclosure, and Health

Not all traumatic events are equally toxic. By the 1960s, Holmes and Rahe (1967) suggested that the health impact of a trauma varied with the degree that the trauma disrupted a person's life. Interestingly, the original scales tapping the health risks of traumas generally measured socially acceptable traumas—the death of a spouse, the loss of a job. No items asked if the participant had been raped, had a sexual affair, or had caused the death of another. By the mid-1980s, investigators started to notice that upheavals that were kept secret were more likely to result in health problems than were those that could be spoken about more openly. For example, individuals who were victims of violence and who had kept this experience silent were significantly more likely to have adverse health effects than were those who openly talked with others (Pennebaker & Susman, 1988). In short, having any type of traumatic experience is associated with elevated illness rates; having any trauma and not talking about it further elevates the risk. These effects actually are stronger when controlling for age, sex, and social support. Apparently, keeping a trauma secret from an intact social network is more unhealthy than not having a social network to begin with (cf. Cole, Kemeny, Taylor, & Visscher, 1996).

If keeping a powerful secret about an upsetting experience is unhealthy, can talking about it, or putting it into words in some way be beneficial? This is a question we asked over two decades ago. Going on the untested assumption that most people would have had at least one emotional upheaval that they had not disclosed in great detail, we began a series of studies that involved people writing and, in some cases, talking about these events.

In the first study, people were randomly assigned to write about a trauma or about superficial topics for four days, 15 minutes per day. We found that confronting the emotions and thoughts surrounding deeply personal issues promoted physical health, as measured by reductions in physician visits in the months following the study, fewer reports of aspirin usage, and overall more positive long-term evaluations of the effect of the experiment (Pennebaker & Beall, 1986). The results of that initial study have led to a number of similar disclosure studies, in our laboratory and by others, with a wide array of intriguing results.

## The Basic Writing Paradigm

The standard laboratory writing technique has involved randomly assigning participants to one of two or more groups. Most writing groups are asked to write about assigned topics for 1–5 consecutive days, for 15–30 minutes each day. Writing is generally done in the laboratory, with no feedback given. Those assigned to the control conditions are typically asked to write about superficial topics, such as how they use their time. The standard instructions for those assigned to the experimental group are a variation on the following:

> For the next 3 days, I would like for you to write about your very deepest thoughts and feeling about the most traumatic experience of your entire life. In your writing, I'd like you to really let go and explore your very deepest emotions and thoughts. You might tie this trauma to your childhood, your relationships with others, including parents, lovers, friends, or relatives. You may also link this event to your past, your present, or your future, or to who you have been, who you would like to be, or who you are now. You may write about the same general issues or experiences on all days of writing or on different topics each day. Not everyone has had a single trauma but all of us have had major conflicts or stressors—and you can write about these as well. All of your writing will be completely confidential. Don't worry about spelling, sentence structure, or grammar. The only rule is that once you begin writing, continue to do so until your time is up.

Whereas the original writing studies asked people to write about traumatic experiences, later studies expanded the scope of writing topics to general emotional events or to specific experiences shared by other participants (e.g., diagnosis of cancer, losing a job, coming to college). The amount of time people have been asked to write has also varied tremendously from 10 to 30 minutes for 3, 4, or 5 days—sometimes within the same day, to once per week for up to 4 weeks.

The writing paradigm is quite powerful. Participants—from children to the elderly, from honor students to maximum security prisoners—disclose a remarkable range and depth of human experiences. Lost loves, deaths, sexual and physical abuse incidents, and tragic failures are common themes in all of our studies. If nothing else, the paradigm demonstrates that when individuals are given the opportunity to disclose deeply personal aspects of their lives, they readily do so. Even though a large number of participants report crying or being deeply upset by the experience, the overwhelming majority report that the writing experience was valuable and meaningful in their lives.

The interest in the expressive writing method has grown over the years. The first study was published in 1986. By 1996, approximately 20 studies had been published. By 2009, over 200 had been published in English language journals. Although many studies have examined physical health and biological outcomes, an increasing number have explored writing's effects on attitude change, stereotyping, creativity, working memory, motivation, life satisfaction, school performance, and a variety of health-related behaviors. It is beyond the scope of this chapter to provide a detailed review of the findings of the writing paradigm. Rather, we briefly summarize some of the more promising findings before focusing on the underlying mechanisms that may be at work.

### Effects of Disclosure on Health-related Outcomes

Researchers have relied on a variety of physical and mental health measures to evaluate the effect of writing. Writing or talking about emotional experiences relative to writing about superficial control topics has been found to be associated with significant drops in physician visits from before to after writing among relatively healthy samples. Over the last decade, as the number of expressive writing studies has increased, several meta-analyses either have been conducted or are being conducted as of this writing.

The original expressive writing meta-analysis, published by Joshua Smyth (1998), was based on 14 studies using *healthy participants*. His primary conclusions were that the writing paradigm is significantly associated with positive outcomes with a weighted mean effect size of $d = .47$ ($r = .23$), noting that this effect size is similar to or larger than those produced by other psychological interventions. The highest significant effect sizes were for psychological ($d = .66$) and physiological outcomes ($d = .68$), which were greater than those for health ($d = .42$) and general functioning outcomes ($d = .33$). A nonsignificant effect size was found for health behaviors. He also found that longer intervals between writing sessions produced larger overall effect sizes, and that males benefited more from writing than did females.

Frisina, Borod, and Lepore (2004) performed a similar meta-analysis on nine writings studies using *clinical populations*. They found that expressive writing significantly improved health outcomes ($d = .19$, $p < .05$). However, the effect was stronger for physical ($d = .21$, $p = .01$) than for psychological ($d = .07$, $p = .17$) health outcomes. The authors suggested that a possible reason for these small effect sizes was the heterogeneity of the samples. Writing was less effective for psychiatric than physical illness populations. Almost 7 years after the first meta-analysis (Smyth,

1998) was published, another meta-analysis by Meads (2003) was released by the Cochran Commission. In an analysis of dozens of studies, the author concluded that there was not sufficient evidence to warrant adopting the writing method as part of clinical practice. One problem that the report underscored was the lack of any large randomized clinical trials (RCTs) that were based on large, clearly identified samples. Coming from a medical background, the Meads article was befuddled by the fact that most of the experimental studies of expressive writing were more theory-oriented and not aimed at clinical application. Since the release of the Meads paper, a new wave of RCTs has started with a diverse group of patient populations.

Harris (2006) recently reported on a meta-analysis of RCTs using expressive writing. Harris compared the use of health care services in 30 independent samples who had participated in expressive writing about stressful experiences. Using a random effects approach, he found effect sizes (Hedges's $g$) of .16 (.02, .31) for healthy samples, .21 (-.02, .43) for samples with preexisting medical conditions, and .06 (-.12, .24) for samples who had been prescreened for psychological criteria. He concluded that expressive writing only had an effect for healthy samples. These results were similar to those found in Mead's (2003) meta-analysis, but with the Harris (2006) study having more power to detect such effects. Harris defended the findings as potentially significant to the health care of healthy samples, and to the health care system itself. In addition, he stated that the findings pointed toward the need to identify people with medical and psychological conditions for whom expressive writing might be contraindicated, as well as an assessment of preexisting over- or underuse of health care services, in order to better interpret the results.

Finally, Frattaroli (2006) published the largest meta-analysis on the effects of expressive writing. Her meta-analysis included *all randomized expressive writing experiments* that had used some variation of the original Pennebaker and Beall (1986) writing instructions, along with the presentation of outcome data. Using a random effects approach, she found an overall effect size of $d = .15$ (equivalent to an $r = .075$), which she noted was meaningful given that her meta-analysis had included unpublished studies (which tend to contribute to much lower average effect sizes) and a methodologically heterogeneous set of studies. She also noted that the effect size was important, given that expressive writing is time- and cost-effective, perceived by participants to be helpful, and easy to administer.

Researchers have relied on a variety of physical and mental health measures to evaluate the effect of writing. Across multiple studies in laboratories around the world, writing or talking about emotional experiences relative to writing about superficial control topics has been found to be associated with significant drops in physician visits from before to after writing among relatively healthy samples. Writing and/or talking about emotional topics has also been found to influence immune function in beneficial ways, including T-helper cell growth (using a blastogenesis procedure with the mitogen PHA), antibody response to Epstein-Barr virus, and antibody response to hepatitis B vaccinations (for reviews, see Lepore & Smyth, 2002; Pennebaker & Graybeal, 2001; Sloan & Marx, 2004a).

Activity of the autonomic nervous system is also influenced by the disclosure paradigm. Among those participants who disclose their thoughts and emotions to a particularly high degree, skin conductance levels are significantly lower during the trauma disclosures than when describing superficial topics. Systolic blood pressure and heart rate drop to levels below baseline following the disclosure of traumatic topics but not superficial ones (Pennebaker, Hughes, & O'Heeron, 1987). In short, when individuals talk or write about deeply personal topics, their immediate biological responses are congruent with those seen among people attempting to relax. McGuire, Greenberg, and Gevirtz (2005) have shown that these effects can carry over to the long term in participants with elevated blood pressure. One month after writing, those who participated in the emotional disclosure condition exhibited lower systolic and diastolic blood pressure (DBP) than before writing. Four months after writing, DBP remained lower than baseline levels.

Similarly, Sloan and Marx (2004b) found that participants in a disclosure condition exhibited greater physiological activation, as indexed by elevated cortisol levels, during their first writing session, relative to controls. Physiological activation then decreased and was similar to that of controls in subsequent writing sessions. The initial elevation in cortisol from the first writing session predicted improved psychological but not physical health at 1 month follow-up. It is possible that confronting a traumatic or distressing experience led to reactions aimed for in exposure-based treatments (e.g., Foa & Kozak, 1986). Biological support for exposure effects of expressive writing was found in another study that looked at individuals diagnosed with PTSD. Although expressive writing did not lead to decreases in PTSD-related symptom severity, Smyth, Hockemeyer, and Tulloch (2008) found decreases in cortisol levels during trauma-related imaginal exposure 3 months following expressive writing, along with decreases in negative mood states and increases in posttraumatic growth (i.e., hope for the future, personal strength, and appreciation for life).

Behavioral changes have also been found. Students who write about emotional topics evidence improvements in grades in the months following the study (e.g., Lumley & Provenzano, 2003; Pennebaker, Colder, & Sharp, 1990). Senior professionals who have been laid off from their jobs get new jobs more quickly after writing (Spera, Buhrfeind, & Pennebaker, 1994). Consistent with the direct health measures, university staff members who write about emotional topics are subsequently absent from their work at lower rates than are controls (Francis & Pennebaker, 1992). Interestingly, relatively few reliable changes emerge using self-reports of health-related behaviors. That is, in the weeks after writing, experimental participants do not exercise more or smoke less. The one exception is that the study with laid-off professionals found that writing reduced self-reported alcohol intake.

Self-reports also suggest that writing about upsetting experiences, although painful in the days of writing, produces long-term improvements in mood and indicators of well-being compared to controls. Although some studies have failed to find clear mood or self-reported distress effects, Smyth's (1998) meta-analysis on written disclosure studies indicates that, in general, writing about emotional topics is associated with significant reductions in distress.

## *Procedural Differences That Affect Expressive Writing*

Writing about emotional experiences clearly influences measures of physical and mental health. In recent years, several investigators have attempted to define the boundary conditions of the disclosure effect. Some of the most important findings are as follows:

### TOPIC OF DISCLOSURE
Although two studies have found that health effects only occur among individuals who write about particularly traumatic experiences (Greenberg & Stone, 1992; Lutgendorf, Antoni, Kumar, & Schneiderman, 1994), most studies have found that disclosure is more broadly beneficial. Choice of topic, however, may selectively influence outcomes. Although most studies find that writing about emotional topics has positive effects on physical health, only certain

assigned topics appear to be related to changes in grades. For beginning college students, for example, when asked to write specifically about emotional issues related to coming to college, both health and college grades improve. However, when other students are asked to write about emotional issues related to traumatic experiences in general, only health improvements—and not academic performance—are found (see Pennebaker, 1995; Pennebaker & Keough, 1999).

Over the last decade, an increasing number of studies have experimented with more focused writing topics. Individuals diagnosed with breast cancer, lung cancer, or human immunodeficiency virus (HIV) infection, have been asked to write specifically about their living with the particular disease (e.g., de Moor et al., 2002; Mann, 2001; Petrie, Fontanilla, Thomas, Booth, & Pennebaker, 2004; Stanton & Danoff-Burg, 2002). Similarly, people who have lost their jobs have been asked to write about that experience (Spera et al., 1994). In each case, however, participants are asked to write about this topic in a very broad way and are encouraged to write about other topics that may be only remotely related. For example, in the job lay-off project, participants in the experimental conditions were asked to explore their thoughts and feeling about losing their jobs. Fewer than half of the essays dealt directly with the lay-off. Others dealt with marital problems, issues with children, money, and health.

It has been our experience that traumatic experiences often bring to the fore other important issues in people's lives. As researchers, we assume that, say, the diagnosis of a life-threatening disease is the most important issue for a person to write about in a cancer-related study. However, for many, this can be secondary to a cheating husband, an abusive parent, or some other trauma that may have occurred years earlier. We recommend that writing researchers and practitioners provide sufficiently open instructions to allow people to deal with whatever important topics they want to write about. As described in greater detail below, the more that the topic or writing assignment is constrained, the less successful it usually is.

### TOPIC ORIENTATION: FOCUSING ON THE GOOD, THE BAD, OR THE BENEFITS
There are a number of theoretical and practical reasons to assume that some strategies for approaching emotional upheavals might be better than others. With the growth of the field of positive psychology, several researchers have reported on the benefits of having a positive or optimistic approach to life

(Carver & Scheier, 2000; Diener, Lucas, & Oishi, 2002; Seligman, 2000). Particularly persuasive have been a series of correlational studies on benefit finding—that is, people who are able to find benefits to negative experiences generally report less negative affect, milder distress, fewer disruptive thoughts, and greater meaningfulness in life. People who engage in benefit-finding fare better on objective physical and mental health outcomes (e.g., children's developmental test scores, recurrence of heart attacks) even after controlling for a host of possible confounding factors (for a review, see Affleck & Tennen, 1996). Being able to see things in a positive light, then, might be a critical component to successful adjustment.

In one study examining adjustment to college, Cameron and Nicholls (1998) had participants previously classified as dispositional optimists or pessimists write in one of three conditions: a self-regulation condition (writing about thoughts and feelings toward coming to college and then formulating coping strategies), a disclosure condition (writing about thoughts and feelings only), or a control task (writing about trivial topics). Overall, participants in the disclosure task had higher grade point average (GPA) scores at follow-up, but only those in the self-regulation task experienced less negative affect and better adjustment to college over the control participants. Optimists visited their doctors less in the following month if they had participated in either of the experimental writing conditions. On the other hand, only pessimists in the self-regulation condition had significantly fewer visits to the doctor after the study. With the added encouragement of formulating coping strategies, pessimists may be able to reap the same health benefits from writing about their thoughts and feelings as optimists naturally might do.

When confronting traumatic experiences, is it best to ask people to simply write about them, or to write about the positive sides of the experiences? Several studies have addressed this question. Particularly interesting has been a series of studies by Laura King and her colleagues. When asked to write about intensely positive experiences (IPE) or control topics, participants who wrote about IPEs reported significantly better mood and fewer illness-related health center visits than did those who wrote about trivial topics (Burton & King, 2004). In another study, students were asked to write about traumas in the standard way (King & Miner, 2000). In the benefit-finding condition, participants were encouraged to focus on the benefits that have come from the trauma. Finally, in the mixed condition,

participants were first asked to write about the trauma, and then to switch to the perceived benefits arising from the trauma experience. Counter to predictions, the trauma-only and benefits-only participants evidenced health improvements, whereas the mixed group did not. It could be that writing about the perceived benefits is enough to organize thoughts and feelings about a trauma and to cope effectively. However, as evidenced from the mixed condition, if people aren't able to integrate their perceived benefits into their trauma story in their own way, writing may be ineffective.

Other studies suggest that focusing on positive emotions in writing may have mixed effects. With a sample of breast cancer patients, Stanton and colleagues (2002) found that a traditional writing group exhibited slightly more health improvements than their positive-feelings-only writing group. More recently, Lyubomirsky, Sousa, and Dickerhoof (2006) conducted an ingenious series of studies wherein students wrote about either their best or worst life experiences. Further, some students were asked to either replay the events in their mind, whereas others were asked to analyze them in detail. The analysis of negative events resulted in better health and life satisfaction, whereas the analysis of positive experiences resulted in slightly worse health and satisfaction. Similarly, Ullrich and Lutgendorf (2002) found that participants who were instructed to write about the cognitive and emotional aspects of a trauma fared better than those who were instructed to focus only on emotional aspects.

Several unpublished studies from our own lab paint a similar picture about the problems of constraining participants' orientations. For her dissertation, Cheryl Hughes (1994) asked students to write either about the positive or the negative aspects of their coming to college for 3 days. Neither group evidenced any benefits of writing compared to a nonemotional control condition. Indeed, both groups complained that there were some real negative (in the positive condition) and positive (in the negative condition) aspects of coming to college that they also wanted to write about. Similarly, in an unpublished project by Lori Stone (2003), students were asked to write about their thoughts and feelings about the September 11 attacks. In one condition, they received the standard unconstrained instructions. In a second condition, participants were asked to focus on their own feelings on one day and on other perspectives on alternating days. The perspective-switching instructions proved to be less beneficial than the unconstrained methods.

Although several variations on the expressive writing method have been tested, none has been found to be consistently superior to the original trauma writing or other methods that encourage the participants' freely choosing their writing topic. Forcing individuals to write about a particular topic or in a particular way may cause them to focus on the writing itself rather than the topic and the role of their emotions in the overall story.

## WRITING VERSUS TALKING ALONE VERSUS TALKING TO OTHERS

Most studies comparing writing alone to talking either into a tape recorder (Esterling et al., 1994) or to a therapist in a one-way interaction (Donnelly & Murray, 1991; Murray, Lamnin, & Carver, 1989) find comparable biological, mood, and cognitive effects. Talking and writing about emotional experiences are both superior to writing about superficial topics.

A striking exception to this was a study by Gidron, Peri, Connolly, and Shalev (1996), in which a group of 14 Israeli PTSD patients were randomly assigned to either write about traumas ($N$ = 8) or about superficial topics ($N$ = 6) on three occasions. After writing, experimental participants were asked to discuss their most traumatic events with a group, whereas controls were asked to describe a daily routine. Unlike all other published writing studies, this one found that experimental participants were significantly more distressed with poorer health at 5-week follow-up. Because other studies have been conducted with participants coping with PTSD, the findings are not solely due to the nature of the participants or disorder. Rather, reading or discussing one's traumas in a group format after writing may pose unexpected problems. Clearly, additional research is needed to help understand this process.

## ACTUAL OR IMPLIED SOCIAL FACTORS

Indeed, unlike psychotherapy and everyday discussions about traumas, the writing paradigm does not employ feedback to the participant. Rather, after individuals write about their own experiences, they are asked to place their essays into an anonymous-looking box with the promise that their writing will not be linked to their name. In one study comparing the effects of having students either write on paper that would be handed in to the experimenter or on a magic pad (wherein the writing disappears when the person lifts the plastic writing cover), no autonomic or self-report differences were found (Czajka, 1987). The benefits of writing, then, occur without explicit social feedback. Nevertheless, the degree to which people write holding the belief that some symbolic other person may "magically" read their essays can never be easily determined.

Several studies have shown that self-disclosure through blogging can increase perceived social support (Baker & Moore, 2008), subjective well-being (Ko & Kuo, 2009), and success in weight loss (Chung & Pennebaker, 2011), primarily through receiving and sending comments on a blog or within a blog community. However, blogging is a very different enterprise than solitary expressive writing. Not only do people share their entries with others but they clearly seek feedback from others. Blogging, then, is a social process—perhaps more so than a self-reflective and insight-seeking or insight-provoking self-change strategy. On the other hand, expressive writing provides benefits to the writers themselves, with later improvements in social relationships as one of many potential indirect effects.

## TIMING: HOW LONG AFTER A TRAUMA?

In the last 30 years, advances in emergency medicine have been astounding. Although we know how to treat people medically in the first hours and days after a trauma, our knowledge about psychological interventions during the same time period has grown very little. Without the guidance of any research, several groups have created immediate crisis intervention businesses. Perhaps the most commercially successful, now called Critical Incident Stress Management (CISM, e.g., Mitchell & Everly, 1996), argues that people victimized by trauma should be attended to within the first 72 hours after a trauma. Although the CISM system has many components, the most interesting and controversial encourages individuals to openly acknowledge their emotions and thoughts within a group concerning the trauma. The CISM system has now been adopted by thousands of businesses, governmental organizations, and other groups around the world. Despite the intuitive appeal of CISM, there is very little evidence that it works. Indeed, most studies suggest that it is more likely to cause harm than benefits (McNally, Byrant, & Ehlers, 2003).

The CISM findings, as well as other projects interested in self-disclosure immediately after an upheaval, have relevance for the timing for an expressive writing intervention. For example, one study asked women who had recently given birth to talk about their deepest thoughts, feelings, and fears to their midwives. These women were actually more likely to subsequently experience depression than women not asked to talk about these topics (Small, Lumley, Donohue, Potter, & Waldenstrom, 2000). Women who were asked to write about the treatment they were undergoing for breast cancer during the last week of radiation treatment evidenced no benefits for any measures compared to controls (Walker, Nail, & Croyle, 1999).

Is there an optimal time after a trauma during which expressive writing would most likely work? Unfortunately, no parametric studies have been conducted on this. Over the years, we have been involved in several projects that have attempted to tap people's natural disclosure patterns in the days and weeks after upheavals. For example, using a random digit dialing in the weeks and months after the 1989 Loma Prieta Earthquake in the San Francisco Bay area, we asked different groups of people the number of times that they had thought about and talked about the earthquake in the previous 24 hours. We used a similar method a year later to tap people's responses to the declaration of war with Iraq during the first Persian Gulf War. In both cases, we found that people talked with one another at very high rates in the first 2–3 weeks. By the fourth week, however, talking rates were extremely low. Rates of thinking about the earthquake and war showed differing patterns: It took considerably longer (about 8 weeks) before people reported thinking about them at low rates (from Pennebaker & Harber, 1993).

More recently, we have analyzed the blogs of almost 1,100 frequent users of an internet site in the 2 months before and 2 months after the September 11 attacks. Rates of writing increased dramatically for about 2 weeks after the attacks. More striking was the analysis of word usage. Use of first-person singular (I, me, and my), dropped almost 15% within 24 hours of the attacks and remained low for about a week. Over the next 2 months, I-word usage remained below baseline (Cohn, Mehl, & Pennebaker, 2004). Usage of first-person singular is significant because it correlates with depression (Rude, Gortner, & Pennebaker, 2004). What was striking was that these bloggers—who expressed an elevated rate of negative moods in the days after 9/11—were generally quite healthy. They were psychologically distancing themselves from the emotional turmoil of the event.

Considering the current evidence, it is likely that defenses such as denial, detachment, distraction, and distancing may, in fact, be quite healthy in the hours and days after an upheaval. A technique such as expressive writing may be inappropriate until several weeks or months later. Indeed, we now encourage clinicians to delay their use of expressive writing until at least 1–2 months after an upheaval or until they think their patient is thinking "too much" about the event. Obsessing and ruminating about a trauma a few weeks after it has occurred is probably not too much. Thinking about it at the same high rate 6 months later might, in fact, signal that expressive writing might be beneficial.

## TIMING OF WRITING SESSIONS

Although Smyth's (1998) meta-analysis found no effect for the length of writing sessions, Frattaroli's (2006) meta-analysis suggested that writing sessions of greater than 15 minutes were more potent than writing sessions of less than 15 minutes. Recently, in an admirably brazen test of the lower boundary of expressive writing's effectiveness, Burton and King (2008) had 49 healthy participants write about a negative event, a positive event, or a control topic for just 2 minutes a day for 2 consecutive days (for a grand total of 4 minutes). Both of the expressive (negative event and positive event) writing groups reported experiencing fewer physical symptoms at 4–6 weeks follow-up than did controls. The authors suggested that perhaps the 2 minutes is all that was needed in order to kick-start the processing of emotional events. Indeed, it was likely that the 2-minute writing session left participants with "unfinished business," suggesting that the time between writing sessions was spent processing the writing topic.

## TIMING BETWEEN WRITING SESSIONS

Different experiments have variously asked participants to write for 1 to 5 days, ranging from consecutive days to sessions separated by a week, ranging from 10 to 45 minutes for each writing session, for anywhere from one to seven sessions. In Smyth's (1998) meta-analysis, he found a trend suggesting that the more days over which the experiment takes place, the stronger the impact on outcomes. Two subsequent studies that actually manipulated the times between writing failed to support Smyth's findings.

The first, by Sheese, Brown, and Grazziano (2004), asked students to write either once per week for 3 weeks or for 3 continuous days about traumatic experiences or superficial topics. Although the experimental–control difference was significant for health center differences, no trend emerged concerning the relative benefits of once a week versus daily writing. More recently, the authors randomly assigned 100 students to write either about major life transitions or about superficial topics. Participants wrote three times, 15 minutes each time, either once a day for 3 days, once an hour for 3 hours, or three times in a little more than an hour (Chung & Pennebaker, 2008). Immediately after the last writing session and again at 1 month follow-up, no differences were found between the daily versus three times per hour condition. Indeed, at follow-up, the three experimental groups evidenced lower symptom reports ($p - .05$, one-tailed test) than the controls after controlling for prewriting symptom levels. Several later studies also support that benefits can accrue from short 10–15 minute breaks between expressive writing sessions (e.g., Baddeley & Pennebaker, in press; Smyth et al., 2008).

## TIME UNTIL FOLLOW-UP

Another suspect for inconsistent or null results across writing studies is the varied duration between the final writing session and the follow-up assessment. Expressive writing outcomes have been measured up to about 6 months after the writing sessions are completed. While some psychological and physical health changes may be immediately apparent, they may be fleeting. On the other hand, some effects may take days, weeks, months, or even years to emerge as significant changes on various health measures, if at all. The timing of improvements may also vary as a function of sampling characteristics. In an expressive writing study examining those suffering from asthma or rheumatoid arthritis (RA), health benefits were seen in asthmatic patients in the experimental writing condition as early as 2 weeks after writing. However, the health profile of RA patients in the experimental writing condition did not differ from those in the control condition until the 4-month assessment period (Smyth, Stone, Hurewitz, & Kaell, 1999).

Considering all the other variants on the writing method already mentioned, it would be difficult to come up with some standard time for follow-up. Instead, knowing the general time course of proposed underlying mechanisms and providing multiple convergent measures to validate specific outcomes may be a more practical approach in thinking about follow-up assessments.

## INDIVIDUAL DIFFERENCES

No consistent personality measures have distinguished who does versus who does not benefit from writing. A number of variables have been unrelated to outcomes, including age, anxiety (or negative affectivity), and inhibition or constraint. A small number of studies that have either preselected participants or performed a median split on a particular variable have reported some effects. However, given the small number of studies, these effects should probably be viewed as promising rather than definitive.

Christensen et al. (1996) preselected students on hostility and found that those high in hostility benefited more from writing than those low in hostility. A couple of studies have found that individuals high on alexithymia (a trait that taps the inability of people to label or distinguish particular negative emotions) tended to benefit from writing more than those low on alexithymia (Paez, Velasco, & Gonzalez, 1999; Solano, Donati, Pecci, Persicheeti, & Colaci, 2003). Indeed, a recent study by Baikie (2008) showed that alexithymics and splitters (those who tend to see the world as all good or all bad) experienced fewer health visits after expressive writing, than did repressive copers (those who tend to avoid and deny emotional responses). Baikie suggested that the structure and time limit of expressive writing allowed alexithymics and splitters to feel more comfortable processing emotional events than did talking therapies, for which they tend to experience poorer outcomes. However, research by Lumley (2004) suggests that, unlike the participants in the aforementioned studies, alexithymics suffering from chronic illnesses or elevated stress may not reap the same benefits after writing. Similarly, Wong and Rochlen (2009) had men who tend to be emotionally restricted write expressively about their best possible emotional connectedness with an imagined romantic partner (current, imaginary, or future) or about a control topic. The authors found decreased distress for the expressive writing group, but they found no other effects on relationship quality or likelihood of being in a relationship between the experimental and control writing groups.

Finally, there has been a great deal of interest in knowing if sex differences exist in the potential benefits of expressive writing. Smyth's (1998) meta-analysis revealed that males tend to benefit more from the writing paradigm than do females. Several studies have explored this with reasonably large samples—usually with college students—and have not replicated the meta-analytic results. However, expressive writing studies with heterosexual romantic couples have found improved relationship outcomes when the male is assigned to the expressive writing condition. Slatcher and Pennebaker (2006) found a nonsignificant trend for a couple to be more likely to experience relationship stability if the male was assigned to the expressive writing condition. A more recent study confirmed this finding in heterosexual military couples. Baddeley and Pennebaker (in press) found decreases in aggressive behaviors within the dyad when the male was assigned to the expressive writing condition. Interestingly, when the female had been assigned to the expressive writing condition, there was a strong decrease in marital satisfaction within the couple. Taken together, the results corroborate what women have known for centuries: When it comes to relationships, men need to talk (or rather, write) about their feelings more.

## EDUCATIONAL, LINGUISTIC, OR CULTURAL EFFECTS

Within the United States, the disclosure paradigm has benefited senior professionals with advanced degrees at rates comparable to rates of benefit in maximum security prisoners with sixth-grade educations (Richards, Beal, Segal, & Pennebaker, 2000; Spera et al., 1994). Among college students, we have not found differences as a function of the students' ethnicity or native language. The disclosure paradigm has produced positive results among French-speaking Belgians (Rimé, 1995), Spanish-speaking residents of Mexico City (Dominguez et al., 1995) and northern Spain (Paez et al., 1999), multiple samples of adults and students in the Netherlands (Schoutrop, Lange, Brosschot, & Everaerd, 1997) and Italy (e.g., Solano et al., 2003), English-speaking New Zealand medical students (Petrie et al., 1995), Japanese undergraduates (Yogo & Fujihara, 2008), and Korean/English and Spanish/English bilinguals in the United States (Kim, 2008).

## Summary

When individuals write or talk about personally upsetting experiences in the laboratory, consistent and significant health improvements are found. The effects include both subjective and objective markers of health and well-being. The disclosure phenomenon appears to generalize across settings, many individual difference factors, and several Western cultures, and is independent of social feedback.

## Why Does Expressive Writing Work?

Psychology, like most sciences, is dedicated to understanding how things work. We are also driven by the law of parsimony and assume that, ideally, a single explanatory mechanism for a phenomenon should exist. If you are expecting a clean and simple explanation for the effectiveness of writing, we have some very bad news: There is no single reason that explains it. Over the last two decades, a daunting number of explanations have been put forward, and many have been found to be partially correct. Ultimately, there is no such thing as a single cause for a complex phenomenon. The reason is two-fold. First, any causal explanation can be dissected at multiple levels of analysis, ranging from social explanations to changes in neurotransmitter levels. Second, an event that takes weeks or even months to unfold will necessarily have multiple determinants that can inhibit or facilitate the process over time.

In this section, we briefly summarize some of the more compelling explanations for the expressive writing–health relationship. Keep in mind that many of these processes occur simultaneously or may influence one another.

### Individual and Social Inhibition

The first expressive writing projects were guided by a general theory of inhibition (cf. Pennebaker & Beall, 1986; Pennebaker, 1989). Earlier studies had discovered that people who had experienced one or more traumas in their lives were more likely to report health problems if they did not confide in others about their traumas than if they had done so (e.g., Pennebaker & Susman, 1988). The inhibition idea was that the act of inhibiting or in some way holding back thoughts, emotions, or behaviors is associated with low-level physiological work—much the way that Sapolsky (2004) or Selye (1978) thought about stress. Further, people were especially likely to inhibit their thoughts and feelings about traumatic experiences that were socially threatening. Hence, individuals who had experienced a sexual trauma would be far less likely to talk about it with others than if they had experienced the death of a grandparent.

Following the logic of inhibition, it was assumed that if people were encouraged to talk or write about a previously inhibited event, health improvements would be seen. Perhaps, we reasoned, once people put their experience into words, they would no longer have the need to inhibit. Despite the helpfulness of the theory in generating interesting and testable hypotheses, the supporting evidence has been decidedly mixed. Several early studies attempted to evaluate the degree to which people wrote about secret versus more public traumas and previously disclosed versus not previously disclosed events. In no case did these factors differentially predict improvements in health (e.g., Greenberg & Stone, 1992; Pennebaker, Kiecolt-Glaser, & Glaser, 1988).

Some evidence for the inhibition theory comes from a recent study of gay men in a community sample with social constraints on self-expression

(Swanbon, Boyce, & Greenberg, 2008). Sixty-two gay men were asked to write either about gay-related thoughts and feelings, or about control topics. The authors found that the expressive writing group experienced less avoidance about being gay and reported experiencing fewer somatic symptoms relative to the control group, suggesting that disclosure could help to decrease the cognitive load of inhibiting thoughts about the self. However, the sample included older, more educated, and openly gay men. Future studies would have to test closeted gay men in order to provide a better test of the inhibition theory of expressive writing.

Promising research in this vein has been conducted by Steve Lepore and his colleagues (e.g., Lepore, Fernandez-Berrocal, Ragan, & Ramos, 2004; Lepore, Ragan, & Jones, 2000). Across several studies, they find that people who are encouraged to talk about an emotional experience, such as a movie, are less reactive to the movie if what they say is validated. That is, if their comments about seeing the movie on the first occasion are supported by another person, they find the movie less aversive on a second screening on another day. However, if another person disagrees with their thoughts and feelings about the movie, the participants are more biologically aroused on a second screening—even though they are watching the movie alone.

Ultimately, real-world inhibitory processes are almost impossible to measure. For example, people have great difficulty in evaluating the degree to which they have been actively holding back in telling others about an emotional experience. Some people who don't tell others about an upsetting experience may never think about the event, whereas others do. Of those who think about it, some may want to tell others; others may not. Of these various cases, it is not clear which people are inhibiting or even who might benefit most from writing. Although experimental studies may be effective in demonstrating the potential dangers of inhibition, the task of isolating these psychological processes in the real world will be a far more difficult enterprise. As described in a later section on the social dynamics of expressive writing, one potential strategy is to simply track changes in people's social behaviors after expressive writing in order to infer the possibility of inhibition.

### Emotions and Emotional Expression
Emotional reactions are part of all important psychological experiences. From the time of Breuer and Freud (1957/1895), most therapists have explicitly or tacitly believed that the activation of emotion is necessary for therapeutic change. The very first expressive writing study found that if people just wrote about the facts of a trauma, they did not evidence any improvement (Pennebaker & Beall, 1986). Consistent with an experiential approach to psychotherapeutic change, emotional acknowledgment ultimately fosters important cognitive changes (Ullrich & Lutgendorf, 2002).

Although experiencing emotions while writing is clearly a necessary component of the expressive writing effects, cognitive work is required as well. As an example, students were randomly assigned to either express a traumatic experience using bodily movement, or to express an experience using movement and then write about it, or to exercise in a prescribed manner for 3 days, 10 minutes per day (Krantz & Pennebaker, 2007). Whereas the two movement expression groups reported that they felt happier and mentally healthier in the months after the study, only the movement plus write group evidenced significant improvements in physical health and GPA. The mere emotional expression of a trauma is not sufficient. Health gains appear to require translating experiences into language.

### Habituation to Emotional Stimuli
A variation on the emotional expression idea is that the benefits of writing accrue because individuals habituate to the aversive emotions associated with the trauma they are confronting. The role of habituation to emotional stimuli has a long and rich history in classical conditioning and a variety of behavioral therapies (e.g., Wolpe, 1968). More nuanced approaches have been proposed by Edna Foa and her colleagues (e.g., Foa & Kozak, 1986; Meadows & Foa, 1999). Repeated exposure to emotional stimuli can help to extinguish the classically conditioned link between an event and people's reactions to it. At the same time, these authors note, people change in their understanding and/or representation of it.

Sloan, Marx, and Epstein (2005) tested the idea that repeated exposure to a writing topic might be a more potent strategy than topic switching. Undergraduate students with mild PTSD symptoms in their "same disclosure" condition wrote about a single event over three writing sessions; the "different disclosure" condition wrote about a different traumatic event during each writing session; controls wrote about trivial, nontraumatic topics. Participants in the "same disclosure" group reported the greatest improvements in physical health and PTSD symptom severity at 4- and 8-week follow-ups relative to the other two groups, supporting their theory of expressive writing as exposure therapy. In addition, they found that the degree of salivary cortisol increases in response to the first writing session were strongly associated with decreases in PTSD symptom severity.

Another test of a habituation model would be to see if people who wrote about the same topic in the same general way from essay to essay would benefit more than people who changed topics. In earlier studies (e.g., Pennebaker & Francis, 1996), judges evaluated the number of different topics people wrote about across a 3-day writing study. Number of topics was unrelated to health improvements. A more elegant strategy involved the use of latent semantic analysis (LSA, Landauer, Foltz, & Laham, 1998). Latent semantic analysis, a technique developed by experts in artificial intelligence, is able to mathematically evaluate the similarity of content of any sets of text, such as essays. Using LSA, we attempted to learn if the content similarity of essays written by people in the experimental conditions in three previous writing studies was related to health improvements. The answer is no. If anything, the more similar the writing content was from day to day, the less likely was health to improve (Campbell & Pennebaker, 2003).

A pure habituation argument is probably insufficient in explaining the expressive writing effects. The findings from the emotion-only condition in the Pennebaker and Beall (1986) study together with the expressive movement-only condition in the Krantz and Pennebaker (2007) experiment both suggest that the mere activation of emotions associated with a trauma can provide only limited benefits. Beyond any habituation processes, some form of cognitive change is also important.

### Language and Emotions: Toward an A-to-D Theory of Emotional Processing

What happens when emotions or emotional experiences are put into words? Research has shown that verbally labeling an emotion may itself influence the emotional experience. Keltner, Locke, and Audrain (1993) found that, after reading a depressing story, participants who were given the opportunity to label their emotions subsequently reported higher life satisfaction than those who did not label them. Berkowitz and Troccoli (1990) found that after labeling their own emotions, participants were more magnanimous in evaluating others than if not given the emotion labeling opportunity. These approaches are consistent with the findings of Schwarz (1990), who has demonstrated that defining and making

attributions for internal feelings can affect the feelings themselves. Similarly, Wilson (2002) summarized several studies indicating that when individuals focus on their feelings, the correspondence between attitudes and behaviors increases, whereas attending to the reasons for one's attitudes reduces attitude–behavior consistency.

Indeed, changing any sensory experience into language affects the experience. In an important study on language's effects on sensory experience, Schooler and Engstler-Schooler (1990) suggested that, once an individual attempts to translate a picture into words, it changes the memory of the picture. Most experiences are like pictures. Sights, sounds, smells, and feelings are often vague, complicated, and dynamic. To provide a detailed image of any experience would require more than the presumed 1,000-word limit. However, because language is flexible, anywhere from relatively few words to several thousand words can be used to describe a single experience.

The problem of capturing an experience with language is comparable to the engineering difficulty of defining an analog signal using digital technology. In the world of measuring skin conductance, for example, a person's fingers will change in their sweatiness almost continuously. Skin conductance level (SCL), as measured by an old-fashioned polygraph, initially increases after the person hears a loud tone and then gradually returns to normal. For this signal to be computer analyzed, the analog line must be converted into numbers using an analog-to-digital (A-to-D) converter. To convert the line to numbers, however, one needs to decide how frequently the numbers should be sampled. Should one sample SCL hundreds of times per second, once per second, once every 5 seconds? Obviously, the more times one samples, the truer the representation of the line will be. However, sampling at such a high frequency can be a tremendous waste of time and computer space since most of the adjacent readings will be redundant. Similarly, if the sampling rate is once every 5 seconds, most of the information of the change in SCL will be lost.

Verbally labeling an emotion is much like applying a digital technology (language) to an analog signal (emotion and the emotional experience). Assume that novel or emotion-provoking experiences tend to remain in awareness until they are either cognitively understood or they extinguish with time. It is hypothesized that if an emotion or experience remains in analog form, it cannot be understood or conceptually tied to the meaning of an event. The only way by which an emotion or experience in nonlinguistic form can leave awareness is through habituation, extinction, or the introduction of a new or competing emotion. Once an experience is translated into language, however, it can be processed in a conceptual manner. In language format, the individual can assign meaning, coherence, and structure. This would allow for the event to be assimilated and, ultimately, resolved and/or forgotten, thereby alleviating the maladaptive effects of incomplete emotional processing on health.

Following from the above reasoning, if an experience and its emotions are described too briefly, the experience will not adequately capture or represent the event (hereafter referred to as *verbal underrepresentation*). In this case, it would be predicted that the many parts of the experience that were not represented in the brief linguistic description would continue to be processed until they gradually extinguished over time. If a moderate number of words are used to describe the experience (*moderate representation*), its representation should adequately mirror the event. This should reduce the degree to which the event takes up cognitive capacity, and, at the same time, enhance self-regulation, coping, and health. On the other hand, if the emotional event is described in exhaustive detail (*overrepresentation*), the experience is essentially reconfigured in its entirety, but in a new format.

The argument, based on the A-to-D emotion theory, is that once an event is adequately represented in language format, the verbal/conceptual processing takes over. In theory, one could argue that the ideal way to talk about an emotional event is to employ language in the form of moderate representation. The moderate representation view is that the most efficient way to process an event is to use as few words as possible that adequately capture the entire emotional experience. The event, then, would be summarized in a relatively tight way that would allow for later leveling and sharpening. Alternatively, the overrepresentation view would argue that representing the event in detailed linguistic form would lessen the possibility for reappraisal or assimilation into broader knowledge structures and identity.

Lisa Feldman Barrett (Feldman, 1995; Feldman Barrett, 1998) has distinguished between individuals who describe their emotional experience using highly differentiated emotion terms, and those who more or less categorize their emotional experience using like-valenced terms interchangeably. In her studies, participants are asked to keep a daily diary for 2 weeks to rate their most intense emotional experience each day on several affect terms using a Likert scale. Emotional differentiation is reflected by a small correlation between positive emotion words (e.g., happiness, joy, enthusiasm, and amusement), and a small correlation between negative emotion words (e.g., nervous, angry, sad, ashamed, guilty). Feldman Barrett, Gross, Conner, Christensen, and Benvenuto (2001) showed that the more individuals differentiated their negative emotions, the more they endorsed engaging in various emotion regulation strategies (situation selection, situation modification, attentional deployment, cognitive change, and response modulation) over the course of the study, especially for more intense negative emotional experiences. These findings provide support for the A-to-D theory. That is, individuals who more precisely identify a verbal label representing their actual emotion experience are more likely to make attributions and effectively plan for future actions.

### Use of Emotion Words in Writing

The A-to-D approach is a valuable working model by which to understand the connection between emotional experience and its translation into words. A complementary approach to the understanding of emotional processes in the expressive writing paradigm is to look at the words people use while describing traumatic experiences. If we merely counted the ways people use emotion words in natural text, could we begin to capture the underlying emotional processes that occur during writing?

Although a number of computerized text analysis programs have been developed (for a review, see Pennebaker, Mehl, & Niederhoffer, 2003), we are most familiar with Linguistic Inquiry and Word Count (LIWC), which was initially created to analyze essays from emotional writing studies. LIWC was developed by having groups of judges evaluate the degree to which about 2,000 words or word stems were related to each of several dozen categories (for a full description, see Pennebaker, Francis, & Booth, 2001). The categories include negative emotion words (sad, angry), positive emotion words (happy, laugh), causal words (because, reason), and insight words (understand, realize). For each essay, LIWC computes the percentage of total words that these and other linguistic categories represent.

The LIWC program enabled language explorations into previous writing studies, linking word usage among individuals in the experimental conditions with various health and behavioral outcomes (Pennebaker, Mayne, & Francis, 1997). One reanalysis of data was based on six writing studies: two studies involving college students writing about traumas in which blood immune measures were collected (Pennebaker, Kiecolt-Glaser, & Glaser, 1988; Petrie et al., 1995), two studies included first-year college students who wrote about their deepest thoughts and feelings about coming to college (Pennebaker, Colder, & Sharp, 1990; Pennebaker & Francis, 1996), one study of maximum security prisoners in a state penitentiary (Richards et al., 2000), and one study using professional men who had unexpectedly been laid-off from their jobs after over 20 years of employment (Spera et al., 1994).

Analyzing the use of negative and positive emotion word use yielded two important findings. First, the more that people used positive emotion words, the more their health improved. Negative emotion word use, however, was curvilinearly and not linearly related to health change after writing. Individuals who used a moderate number of negative emotions in their writing about upsetting topics evidenced the greatest drops in physician visits in the months after writing. The curvilinear emotion indices were computed using the absolute value of the difference between each person's emotion word use and the means of the sample. The simple correlations between change in physician visits with the curvilinear negative emotion index was $r(152) = .27$, $p < .05$ whereas the positive words were unrelated, $r = -.14$, $ns$.

Individuals who use very few negative emotion words or who use a very high rate of them are the ones most likely to remain sick after writing, compared with those who use a moderate number of negative emotion words. The findings support the A-to-D theory, and, in many ways, also square with other literatures. Individuals who maintain verbal underrepresentation and tend to use very few negative emotion words are most likely to be characterized as repressive copers (cf. Schwartz & Kline, 1995) or alexithymics (Lumley, Tojek, & Macklem, 2002). Those who overuse negative emotion words may well be the classic high negative affect individuals described by Watson and Clark (1984). That is, those individuals who describe their negative conditions in such detail may simply be in a recursive loop of complaining without attaining closure (overrepresentation). Indeed, as discussed below, this may be exacerbated by the inability of these individuals to develop a story or narrative (Nolen-Hoeksema, 2000).

### Beyond Emotions: The Construction of a Story

One of the basic functions of language and conversation is to communicate coherently and understandably. By extension, writing about an emotional experience in an organized way is healthier than writing in a chaotic way. Indeed, growing evidence from several labs suggest that people are most likely to benefit if they can write a coherent story (e.g., Smyth, True, & Sotto, 2001). Any technique that disrupts the telling of the story or the organization of the story is undoubtedly detrimental. For example, those who have a brooding ruminative style (where a coherent story is perhaps not formed and does not change or gets more negative over time) are more likely to benefit from expressive writing than are those who have a reflective pondering ruminative style (i.e., those who tend to organize their thoughts about their situation in order to engage in adaptive problem solving; Sloan, Marx, Epstein, & Dobbs, 2008).

Unfortunately, we are not yet at the point of being able to precisely define what is meant by coherent, understandable, or meaningful when it comes to writing about emotional upheavals (cf. Graybeal, Seagal, & Pennebaker, 2002). One person's meaning may be another's rumination. Many times in our own research we have been struck by how a person appears to be writing in a way that avoids dealing with what we see as a central issue. Nevertheless, the person's health improves and he or she exclaims how beneficial the study was. Meaning, then, may ultimately be in the eyes of the writer.

Although talking about the upsetting experience will help to organize and give it structure, talking about such a monumental experience may not always be possible. Others may not want to or even be able to hear about it. Within the discourse literature, particular attention has been paid to the role of written language in demanding more integration and structure than spoken language (Redeker, 1984; see also Brewin & Lennard, 1999). It would follow that writing—and to a lesser degree talking—about traumatic experiences would require a structure that would become apparent in the ways people wrote or talked about the events.

### The Components of a Story: The Analysis of Cognitive Words

It is beyond the bounds of this chapter to explore the philosophical definitions of knowledge, narrative, or meaning. For current purposes, knowledge of an event can encompass a causal explanation of it or the ability to understand the event within a broader context. The degree to which individuals are able to cognitively organize the event into a coherent narrative is a marker that the event has achieved knowledge status. In many ways, it is possible to determine the degree to which people have come to know their emotions and experiences by the language they use. Words or phrases such as, "I now realize that . . . ," or "I understand why . . ." suggest that people are able to identify when they have achieved a knowing state about an event.

The LIWC analyses find promising effects for changes in insight and causal words over the course of emotional writing (see also Klein & Boals, 2001; Petrie, Booth, & Pennebaker, 1998). Specifically, people whose health improves, who get higher grades, and who find jobs after writing go from using relatively few causal and insight words to using a high rate of them by the last day of writing. In reading the essays of people who show this pattern of language use, judges often perceive the construction of a story over time (Graybeal et al., 2002). Building a narrative, then, may be critical in reaching understanding or knowledge. Interestingly, those people who start the study with a coherent story that explained some past experience generally do not benefit from writing.

Those who use more insight and causal words in their emotional writing tend to gain the most improvements in working memory, and, at the same time, report drops in intrusive thinking about negative events (Boals & Klein, 2005; Klein & Boals, 2001). Consistent with the A-to-D emotion theory, for those in the experimental condition, the writing experience packages the event in a way that frees their minds for other cognitive tasks. Another way to interpret the salutary effects of using insight and causal words is that, together with the use of positive emotion words, this type of language reflects a positive reappraisal of events, which fuels cognitive broadening (Fredrickson, 1998; 2001). Narrating an emotional event into the bigger picture might help to integrate the experience into one's greater knowledge structures and personal identity.

Either way, the findings are consistent with current views on narrative and psychotherapy (e.g., Mahoney, 1995) in suggesting that it is critical for the client to create and come to terms with a story to explain and understand behavioral or mental problems and their history. Merely having a story may not be sufficient since the quality of stories, as well as the people themselves, change over time. A story, then, is a type of knowledge. Further, a narrative that provides knowledge must label and organize the emotional effects of an experience, as well as the experience itself.

### Writing As a Way to Change Perspective

A central tenet of all insight-oriented therapies is that, through psychotherapy, people are able to develop a better understanding of their problems and reactions to them (e.g., Rogers, 1980). Inherent in this understanding is the ability to stand back and look at oneself from different perspectives. Although most therapists would agree with the importance of shifting perspectives, the difficulty for a researcher is in devising a way to track this shift. Some recent linguistic analyses offer some promising new strategies.

As described earlier, LSA is a powerful mathematical tool that allows investigators to determine the similarity of any sets of essays. Latent semantic analysis was originally designed to look at the linguistic content of text samples. Consequently, most LSA applications routinely delete all noncontent words. These noncontent or "junk" words include pronouns, prepositions, conjunctions, articles, and auxiliary verbs. A more formal designation of junk words would be closed-class words, function words, or particles. Function words can be thought of as the glue that holds content words together. Rather than reflecting what people are saying, these function words connote how they are speaking. In short, function words reflect linguistic style (cf. Pennebaker & King, 1999; Pennebaker et al., 2003).

Is it possible that peoples' linguistic styles can predict who benefits from writing? Using LSA, we discovered that the answer is yes. Analyzing three previous expressive writing studies, we discovered that the more that people change in their use of function words from day to day in their writing, the more their health improved (Campbell & Pennebaker, 2003). Closer analyses revealed that these effects were entirely due to changes in pronoun use. Specifically, the more that people oscillated in their use of first-person singular pronouns (I, me, my) and all other personal pronouns (e.g., we, you, she, they), the more people's health improved. If individuals wrote about emotional upheavals across the 3–4 days of writing, but they approached the topic in a consistent way—as measured by pronoun use—they were least likely to show health improvements. The findings suggest that the switching of pronouns reflects a change in perspective from one writing day to the next. Interestingly, it doesn't matter if people oscillate between an I-focus to a we- or them-focus or vice versa. Rather, health improvements merely reflect a change in the orientation and personal attention of the writer.

A note on causality is in order. The various studies that have examined the relationship between word use and health outcomes in the emotional writing conditions imply a causal arrow: People who change perspectives, use positive emotion words, and who construct a story ultimately evidence better health. Be cautious in interpreting these findings. The use of these word patterns may simply be reflecting some underlying cognitive and emotional changes occurring in the person. As noted earlier, some studies have attempted to get people to write with more positive emotion words, changing perspectives, and even constructing a story. These manipulations have not been particularly successful. The issues of mediation, moderation, and emergent properties of word use, cognitive and emotional activity, and long-term health will provide fertile grounds for research in the years to come.

In recent years, there has been a call for finding the boundaries of expressive writing (Smyth & Pennebaker, 2008). In one study that was published in a special issue examining the boundary effects of expressing writing, Seih and his colleagues (2008) adapted Psychological Displacement in Diary Writing (PDDP; Jin 2005) for expressive writing. PDDP is a paradigm in which people write diary entries from a first-person perspective. Next, they write about the same event using a second-person perspective. Finally, they write about the same event from a third-person perspective. Seih and his colleagues found that experimental manipulations of changing perspectives were successful in reducing levels of anxiety and anger. Ongoing studies in our lab suggest that requiring people to switch perspectives does not confer benefits above standard writing instructions (Seih, Chung, & Pennebaker, in press). These intriguing findings indicate that changes in writing perspectives are more an emergent property of successful writing. That is, it reflects psychological improvement rather than necessarily causing it.

## Expressive Writing and Social Dynamics

One of the popular appeals of the expressive writing paradigm is that it sounds almost magical. Write for 15 minutes a day for 3 days (a total of 45 minutes), and your health will improve for months. You may also get a job, fall in love, and make better grades. This is a bit of an overstatement. When people write about emotional upheavals for 3 or 4 days, they report thinking about the topics quite frequently. Many spontaneously tell us that they have been dreaming about the topics. Expressive writing's effects exist beyond the walls of the experiment.

Even more striking have been some of the social changes that occur as a result of expressive writing. Across multiple studies, individuals report that they talk to others about their writing topics. Many years ago, we conducted a study with Holocaust survivors

and asked them to tell their stories orally. Prior to the study, approximately 70% reported that they had not talked about their experiences during World War II in any detail to anyone. After the interview, all participants were given a copy of their video taped testimony. A month later, the average person reported watching the videotape 2.3 times and showing it to 2.5 other people (Pennebaker, Barger, & Tiebout, 1989). Disclosure begets disclosure.

Recently, we have developed a digital recording device called the *electronically activated recorder*, or the EAR (Mehl & Pennebaker, 2003). The EAR has been engineered to record for 30 seconds every 12–13 minutes. The recordings are then transcribed and rated by judges concerning where the participant is and what he or she is doing. Recently, Youngsuk Kim (2008) had 95 bilingual students either write about traumatic experiences or participate in control tasks for 4 days, 15 minutes each day. Prior to writing and assignment to condition, individuals wore the EAR for 2 days. Approximately 1 month after writing, they wore the EAR again for 2 days. Overall, those who wrote about emotional upheavals talked more with others after writing than before writing. An earlier pilot study of approximately 50 students had found a similar effect (Pennebaker & Graybeal, 2001).

Across the various studies, we are now becoming convinced that one of the powers of expressive writing is that it brings about changes in people's social lives. Consider that writing has been shown to increase working memory and that these effects apparently last several weeks (Klein & Boals, 2001). After people write about troubling events, they devote less cognitive effort on them. This allows them to be better listeners, better friends. The writing may also encourage people to talk more openly with others about the secrets that they have been keeping.

## The Big Picture: Life Course Correction

Part of the human experience is that we all deal with a variety of major and minor life issues. Often, we are taken off guard by an upheaval and don't have sufficient time to think about it or to explore the broader implications the event might have on us and those around us. One reason that we believe that expressive writing has been effective is that it serves as a life course correction. Occasionally, most of us benefit from standing back and examining our lives. This requires a perspective shift and the ability to detach ourselves from our surroundings. If we are still in the midst of a massive upheaval, it is virtually impossible to make these corrections.

The idea of expressive writing as a life course correction has not been tested empirically. The idea is certainly consistent with McAdam's (2001) life story approach. It is also relevant to work in autobiographical memory (e.g., Neisser & Fivush, 1994; Conway, 1990). There are times when we are forced to stop and look back at our lives and evaluate what issues and events have shaped who we are, what we are doing, and why.

## Conclusion

The purpose of this chapter has been to provide a broad overview of the expressive writing paradigm. Since its first use in the 1980s, dozens of studies have explored the parameters and boundary conditions of its effectiveness. Perhaps most interesting has been the growing awareness that its value cannot be explained by a single cause or theory. Expressive writing ultimately sets off a cascade of effects.

There is a certain irony that the original explanation for the writing phenomenon was inhibition. In the 1980s, our belief was that when people didn't talk about emotional upheavals, the work of inhibition ultimately led to stress and illness. That explanation was partially correct. Now, however, we are all beginning to appreciate the nuances of the problem. Not talking about a traumatic experience is also associated with a breakdown of one's social network, a decrease in working memory, sleep disruptions, alcohol and drug abuse, and an increased risk for additional traumatic experiences. Expressive writing or the unfettered talking about a trauma can often short circuit this process.

Writing forces people to stop and reevaluate their life circumstance. The mere act of writing also demands a certain degree of structure, as well as the basic labeling or acknowledging of their emotions. A particularly rich feature of the process is that these inchoate emotions and emotional experiences are translated into words. This analog-to-digital process demands a different representation of the events in the brain, in memory, and in the ways people think on a daily basis.

All of these cognitive changes have the potential for people to come to a different understanding of their circumstances. The cognitive changes themselves now allow the individuals to begin to think about and use their social worlds differently. They talk more; they connect with others differently. They are now better able to take advantage of social support. And with these cognitive and social changes, many of their unhealthy behaviors abate. As recent data suggest, expressive writing promotes sleep, enhanced immune function, reduced alcohol consumption, and more.

Despite the large number of promising studies, expressive writing is not a panacea. The overall effect size of writing is modest at best. We still don't know for whom it works best, when it should be used, or when other techniques should be used in its place. One of the difficulties of studying expressive writing is that the best studies have found that writing influences slow moving but important outcome measures such as physician visits, illness episodes, and other real-world behaviors that may take months to see. Self-report outcomes, although common and easy to use, generally do not bring about extremely strong findings. Future researchers would be wise to try to agree on one or more outcome measures that are sufficiently robust and also easy to measure.

After two decades of research on expressive writing, two strategies must continue to grow. The first is applying the method to large samples of people with differing diagnoses using rigorous RCT designs. This "big science, big medicine" approach is essential. At the same time, we should continue to nurture innovative smaller science. It will be the individual labs around the world that will ultimately tell us the boundary conditions of the phenomenon and the underlying mechanisms that explain its effectiveness.

## Acknowledgments

Preparation of this paper was aided by funding from the National Institutes of Health (MH52391), Army Research Institute (W91WAW-07-C-0029), NSF (NSF-NSCC-090482), and START (DHS Z934002). An earlier version of this paper was published as Pennebaker and Chung (2007).

## References

Affleck, G., & Tennen, H. (1996). Construing benefits from adversity: Adaptational significance and dispositional underpinnings. *Journal of Personality, 64*, 899–922.

Baddeley, J.L., & Pennebaker, J.W. (in press). An expressive writing intervention for military couples. *Journal of Traumatic Stress Studies.*

Baikie, K.A. (2008). Who does expressive writing work for? Examination of alexithymia, splitting, and repressive coping style as moderators of the expressive writing paradigm. *British Journal of Health Psychology, 13*, 61–66.

Baker, J.R., & Moore, S.M. (2008). Blogging as a social tool: A psychological examination of the effects of blogging. *CyberPsychology & Behavior, 11*, 747–774

Berkowitz, L. & Troccoli, B.T. (1990). Feelings, direction of attention, and expressed evaluations of others. *Cognition and Emotion, 4*, 305–325.

Boals, A., & Klein, K. (2005). Word use in emotional narratives about failed romantic relationships and subsequent mental health. *Journal of Language and Social Psychology, 24*, 252–268.

Bower, G.H., & Sivers, H. (1998). Cognitive impact of traumatic events. *Developmental & Psychopathology, 10*, 625–653.

Breuer, J., & Freud, S. (1957). *Studies on hysteria* (J. Strachey, Trans.). New York: Basic Books. (Original work published 1895).

Breslau, N., Chilcoat, H.D., Kessler, R.C., & Davis, G.C. (1999). Previous exposure to trauma and PTSD effects of subsequent trauma: Results from the Detroit area survey of trauma. *American Journal of Psychiatry, 156*, 902–907.

Brewin, C.R., & Lennard, H. (1999). Effects of mode of writing on emotional narratives. *Journal of Traumatic Stress, 12*, 355–361.

Brom, D., Kleber, R.J., & Hofman, M.C. (1993). Victims of traffic accidents: Incidence and prevention of post-traumatic stress disorder. *Journal of Clinical Psychology, 49*, 131–140.

Burton, C.M., & King, L.A. (2004). The health benefits of writing about intensely positive experiences. *Journal of Research in Personality, 38*, 150–163.

Burton, C.M., & King, L.A. (2008). Effects of (very) brief writing on health; The two-minute miracle. *British Journal of Health Psychology, 13*, 9–14.

Cabrera, O.A., Hoge, C.W., Bliese, P.D. Castro, C.A., & Messer, S.C. (2007). Childhood adversity and combat as predictors of depression and post-traumatic stress in deployed troops. *American Journal of Preventive Medicine, 33*, 77–82.

Campbell, R.S., & Pennebaker, J.W. (2003). The secret life of pronouns: Flexibility in writing style and physical health. *Psychological Science, 14*, 60–65.

Cameron, L.D., & Nicholls, G. (1998). Expression of stressful experiences through writing: Effects of a self-regulation manipulation for pessimists and optimists. *Health Psychology, 17*, 84–92.

Carlier, I.V.E., & Gersons, B, P.R. (1997). Stress reactions in disaster victims following the Bijlmermeer plane crash. *Journal of Traumatic Stress, 10*, 329–335.

Carver, C.S., & Scheier, M.F. (2000). Optimism. In C.R. Snyder, & S.J. Lopez (Eds.), *Handbook of positive psychology* (pp. 231–243). London: Oxford University Press.

Christensen A.J., Edwards D.L., Wiebe J.S., Benotsch E.G., McKelvey L., Andrews M., & Lubaroff D.M. (1996). Effect of verbal self-disclosure on natural killer cell activity: Moderating influence of cynical hostility. *Psychosomatic Medicine, 58*, 150–155.

Chung, C.K., & Pennebaker, J.W. (2008). Variations in the spacing of expressive writing sessions. *British Journal of Health Psychology, 13*, 15–21.

Chung, C.K., & Pennebaker, J.W. (2011). *Predicting weight loss using computerized text analysis*. Manuscript in preparation.

Cohn, M.A., Mehl, M.R., & Pennebaker, J.W. (2004). Linguistic markers of psychological change surrounding September 11, 2001. *Psychological Science, 15*, 687–693.

Cole, S.W., Kemeny, M.E., Taylor, S.E., & Visscher, B.R. (1996). Elevated physical health risk among gay men who conceal their homosexual identity. *Health Psychology, 15*, 243–251.

Conway, M.A. (1990). *Autobiographical memory: An introduction*. Buckingham, England: Open University Press.

Czajka, J.A. (1987). *Behavioral inhibition and short term physiological responses*. Unpublished master's thesis, Southern Methodist University, Dallas, TX.

De Moor, C., Sterner, J., Hall, M., Warneke, C., Gilani, Z., Amato, R., et al. (2002). A pilot study of the effects of expressive writing on psychological and behavioral adjustment in patients enrolled in a phase II trial of vaccine therapy for metastatic renal cell carcinoma. *Health Psychology, 21*, 615–619.

Diener, E., Lucas, R., & Oishi, S.E. (2002). Subjective well-being: The science of happiness and well-being. In C.R. Snyder, and S.J. Lopez (Eds.), *Handbook of positive psychology*, pp. 463–473. London: Oxford University Press.

Dominguez, B., Valderrama, P., Meza, M., Perez, S., Silva, A., Martinez, G., et al. (1995). The roles of emotional reversal and disclosure in clinical practice. In J.W. Pennebaker (Ed.), *Emotion, disclosure, and health* (pp. 255–270). Washington, DC: American Psychological Association.

Donnelly, D.A., & Murray, E.J. (1991). Cognitive and emotional changes in written essays and therapy interviews. *Journal of Social & Clinical Psychology, 10*, 334–350.

Esterling, B.A., Antoni, M.H., Fletcher, M.A., Margulies, S. et al. (1994). Emotional disclosure through writing or speaking modualtes latent Epstein-Barr virus antibody titers. *Journal of Consulting & Clinical Psychology, 62*, 130–140.

Feldman, L. (1995). Valence focus and arousal focus: Individual differences in the structure of affective experience. *Journal of Personality and Social Psychology, 69*, 153–166.

Feldman Barrett, L. (1998). Discrete emotions or dimensions? The role of valence focus and arousal focus. *Cognition and Emotion, 12*(4), 579–599.

Feldman Barrett, L., Gross, J., Conner Christensen, T., & Benvenuto, M. (2001). Knowing what you're feeling and knowing what to do about it: Mapping the relation between emotion differentiation and emotion regulation. *Cognition & Emotion, 15*, 713–724.

Foa, E.B., & Kozak, M.J. (1986). Emotional processing of fear: Exposure to corrective information. *Psychological Bulletin, 99*, 20–35.

Francis, M.E. & Pennebaker, J.W. (1992). Putting stress into words: Writing about personal upheavals and health. *American Journal of Health Promotion, 6*, 280–287.

Frattaroli, J. (2006). Experimental disclosure and its moderators: A meta-analysis. *Psychological Bulletin, 132*, 823–865.

Fredrickson, B.L. (1998). What good are positive emotions? *Review of General Psychology: Special Issue: New Directions in Research on Emotion, 2*, 300–319.

Fredrickson, B.L. (2001). The role of positive emotions in positive psychology: The broaden-and-build theory of positive emotions. *American Psychologist, 56*, 218–226.

Frisina, P.G., Borod, J.C., & Lepore, S.J. (2004). A meta-analysis of the effects of written emotional disclosure on the health outcomes of clinical populations. *The Journal of Nervous and Mental Disease, 192*, 629–634.

Gidron, Y., Peri, T., Connolly, J.F., & Shalev, A.Y. (1996). Written disclosure in posttraumatic stress disorder: Is it beneficial for the patient? *Journal of Nervous & Mental Disease, 184*, 505–507.

Graybeal, A., Seagal, J.D., & Pennebaker, J.W. (2002). The role of story-making in disclosure writing: The psychometrics of narrative. *Psychology and Health, 17*, 571–581.

Greenberg, M.A., & Stone, A.A. (1992). Emotional disclosure about traumas and its relation to health: Effects of previous disclosure and trauma severity. *Journal of Personality and Social Psychology, 63*, 75–84.

Harris, A.H.S. (2006). Does expressive writing reduce health care utilization? A meta-analysis of randomized trials. *Journal of Consulting and Clinical Psychology, 74*, 243–252.

Hughes, C.F. (1994). Effects of expressing negative and positive emotions and insight on health and adjustment to college. *Dissertation Abstracts International: Section B: The Sciences & Engineering, 54*, 3899.

Holmes, T.H., & Rahe, R.H. (1967). The Social Readjustment Rating Scale. *Journal of Psychosomatic Research, 11*, 213–218.

Jin S.R. (2005). *The dialectical effect of psychological displacement: A narrative analysis.* Taipei: National Science Council.

Keane, T.M. (1998). Psychological effects of military combat. In B.P. Dohrenwend (Ed.), *Adversity, stress, and psychopathology* (pp. 52–65). London: Oxford University Press.

Keltner, D., Locke, K.D., & Audrain, P.C. (1993). The influence of attributions on the relevance of negative feelings to personal satisfaction. *Personality and Social Psychology Bulletin, 19*, 21–29.

Kilpatrick, D.G., Resnick, H.S., Saunders, B.E., & Best, C.L. (1998). Rape, other violence against women, and posttraumatic stress disorder. In B.P. Dohrenwend (Ed.), *Adversity, stress, and psychopathology* (pp. 161–176). London: Oxford University Press.

Kim, Y. (2008). Effects of expressive writing among bilinguals: Exploring psychological well-being and social behaviour. *British Journal of Health Psychology, 13*, 43–47.

King, L.A., & Miner, K.N. (2000). Writing about the perceived benefits of traumatic events: Implications for physical health. *Personality & Social Psychology Bulletin, 26*, 220–230.

Klein, K., & Boals, A. (2001). Expressive writing can increase working memory capacity. *Journal of Experimental Psychology: General, 130*, 520–533.

Ko, H.-C., & Kuo, F.-Y. (2009). Can blogging enhance subjective well-being through self-disclosure? *CyberPsychology & Behavior, 12*, 75–79.

Krantz, A.M. & Pennebaker, J.W. (2007). Expressive dance, writing, trauma, and health: When words have a body. In I.A. Serlin, J. Sonke-Henderson, R. Brandman, & J. Graham-Pole (Eds.), *Whole person healthcare Vol. 3: The arts and health* (pp. 201–229). Westport, CT: Praeger.

Landauer, T.K., Foltz, P.W., & Laham, D. (1998). An introduction to latent semantic analysis. *Discourse Processes, 25*, 259–284.

Lepore, S.J., Fernanadez-Berrocal, P., Ragan, J., & Ramos, N. (2004). It's not that bad: Social challenges to emotional disclosure enhance adjustment to stress. *Anxiety, Stress & Coping: An International Journal, 17*, 341–361.

Lepore, S.J., Ragan, J., & Jones, S. (2000). Talking facilitates cognitive-emotional processes of adaptation to an acute stressor. *Journal of Personality & Social Psychology, 78*, 499–508.

Lepore, S.J., & Smyth, J.M. (2002). *Writing cure: How expressive writing promotes health and emotional well-being.* Washington, DC, US: American Psychological Association.

Lumley, M.A. (2004). Alexithymia, emotional disclosure, and health: A program of research. *Journal of Personality, 72*, 1271–1300.

Lumley, M.A., & Provenzano, K.M. (2003). Stress management through written emotional disclosure improves academic performance among college students with physical symptoms. *Journal of Educational Psychology, 95*(3), 641–649.

Lumley, A., Tojek, T.M., & Macklem, D.J. (2002). Effects of written emotional disclosure among repressive and alexithymic people. In S.J. Lepore, & J.M. Smyth (Eds.), *The writing cure: How expressive writing promotes health and emotional well-being* (pp. 75–95). Washington, DC: American Psychological Association.

Lutgendorf, S.K., Antoni, M.H., Kumar, M., & Schneiderman, N. (1994). Changes in cognitive coping strategies predict EBV-antibody titre change following a stressor disclosure induction. *Journal of Psychosomatic Research, 38*, 63–78.

Lyubomirsky, S., Sousa, L., & Dickerhoof, R. (2006). The costs and benefits of writing, talking, and thinking about life's triumphs and defeats. *Journal of Personality and Social Psychology, 90*, 692–708.

Mahoney, M.J. (1995). *Cognitive and constructive psychotherapies: Theory, research, and practice.* New York: Springer.

Mann, T. (2001). Effects of future writing and optimism on health behaviors in HIV-infected women. *Annals of Behavioral Medicine, 23*, 26–33.

McAdams, D.P. (2001). The psychology of life stories. *Review of General Psychology, 5*, 100–122.

McGuire, K.M.B., Greenberg, M.A., & Gevirtz, R. (2005). Autonomic effects of expressive writing in individuals with elevated blood pressure. *Journal of Health Psychology, 10*, 197–207.

McNally, R.J., Bryant, R.A., & Ehlers, A. (2003). Does early psychological intervention promote recovery from posttraumatic stress? *Psychological Science in the Public Interest, 4*, 45–79.

Meadows, E.A., & Foa, E.B. (1999). Cognitive-behavioral treatment of traumatized adults. In P.A. Saigh, & J.D. Bremmer (Eds.), *Posttraumatic stress disorder: A comprehensive text* (pp. 376–390). Needham Heights, MA: Allyn & Bacon.

Meads, C. (2003, October). *How effective are emotional disclosure interventions? A systematic review with meta-analyses.* Paper presented at the 3rd international conference on the (Non) Expression of Emotions in Health and Disease. Tilburg, NL.

Mehl, M.R., & Pennebaker, J.W. (2003). The social dynamics of a cultural upheaval: Social interactions surrounding September 11, 2001. *Psychological Science, 14*, 579–585.

Miller, M.W. (2003). Personality and the etiology and expression of PTSD: A three-factor model perspective. *Clinical Psychology: Science & Practice, 10*, 373–393.

Mitchell, J.T., & Everly, G.S. (1996). *Critical Incident Stress Debriefing (CISD): An operations manual.* Ellicott City, MD: Chevron.

Murray, J.B. (1992). Posttraumatic stress disorder: A review. *Genetic, Social, & General Psychology Monographs, 118*, 313–338.

Murray, E.J., Lamnin, A.D., & Carver, C.S. (1989). Emotional expression in written essays and psychotherapy. *Journal of Social & Clinical Psychology, 8*, 414–429.

Neisser, U., & Fivush, R. (1994). *The remembering self: Construction and accuracy in the self-narrative.* New York, NY: Cambridge University Press.

Nolen-Hoeksema, S. (2000). The role of rumination in depressive disorders and mixed anxiety/depressive symptoms. *Journal of Abnormal Psychology, 109*, 504–511.

Paez, D., Velasco, C., & Gonzalez, J.L. (1999). Expressive writing and the role of alexithymia as a dispositional deficit in self-disclosure and psychological health. *Journal of Personality and Social Psychology, 77*, 630–641.

Pennebaker, J.W. (1989). Confession, inhibition, and disease. In L. Berkowitz (Ed.), *Advances in experimental social psychology* Vol. 22 (pp. 211–244). New York: Academic Press.

Pennebaker, J.W. (1995). *Emotion, disclosure, & health.* Washington, DC: American Psychological Association.

Pennebaker, J.W., Barger, S.D., & Tiebout, J. (1989). Disclosure of traumas and health among Holocaust survivors. *Psychosomatic Medicine, 51*, 577–589.

Pennebaker, J.W., & Beall, S. (1986). Confronting a traumatic event: Toward an understanding of inhibition and disease. *Journal of Abnormal Psychology, 95*, 274–281.

Pennebaker, J.W. & Chung, C.K. (2007). Expressive writing, emotional upheavals, and health. In H. Friedman, & R. Silver (Eds.), *Handbook of health psychology* (pp. 263–284). New York: Oxford University Press.

Pennebaker, J.W., Colder, M., & Sharp, L.K. (1990). Accelerating the coping process. *Journal of Personality & Social Psychology, 58*(3), 528–537.

Pennebaker, J.W., & Francis, M.E. (1996). Cognitive, emotional, and language processes in disclosure. *Cognition & Emotion, 10*(6), 601–626.

Pennebaker, J.W., Francis, M.E., & Booth, R.J. (2001). *Linguistic inquiry and word count (LIWC): LIWC2001.* Mahwah, NJ: Erlbaum Publishers.

Pennebaker, J.W., & Graybeal, A. (2001). Patterns of natural language use: Disclosure, personality, and social integration. *Current Directions, 10*, 90–93.

Pennebaker, J.W. & Harber, K.D. (1993). A social stage model of collective coping: The Persian Gulf war and other natural disasters. *Journal of Social Issues, 49*, 125–145.

Pennebaker, J.W., Hughes, C.F., & O'Heeron, R.C. (1987). The psychophysiology of confession: Linking inhibitory and psychosomatic processes. *Journal of Personality & Social Psychology, 52*, 781–793.

Pennebaker, J.W., & Keough, K.A. (1999). Revealing, organizing, and reorganizing the self in response to stress and emotion. In R. Ashmore, & L. Jussim (Eds.), *Self and social identity* Vol. II (pp. 101–121). New York: Oxford.

Pennebaker, J.W., Kiecolt-Glaser, J., & Glaser, R. (1988). Disclosure of traumas and immune function: Health implications for psychotherapy. *Journal of Consulting and Clinical Psychology, 56*, 239–245.

Pennebaker, J.W., & King, L.A. (1999). Linguistic styles: Language use as an individual difference. *Journal of Personality and Social Psychology, 77*, 1296–1312.

Pennebaker, J.W., Mayne, T.J., & Francis, M.E. (1997). Linguistic predictors of adaptive bereavement. *Journal of Personality and Social Psychology, 72*, 166–183.

Pennebaker, J.W., Mehl, M.R., & Niederhoffer, K.G. (2003). Psychological aspects of natural language use: Our words, our selves. *Annual Review of Psychology, 54*, 547–577.

Pennebaker, J.W., & Susman, J.R. (1988). Disclosure of traumas and psychosomatic processes. *Social Science & Medicine, 26*, 327–332.

Petrie, K.P., Booth, R.J., & Pennebaker, J.W. (1998). The immunological effects of thought suppression. *Journal of Personality and Social Psychology, 75*, 1264–1272.

Petrie, K.J., Booth, R., Pennebaker, J.W., Davison, K.P., & Thomas, M. (1995). Disclosure of trauma and immune response to Hepatitis B vaccination program. *Journal of Consulting and Clinical Psychology, 63*, 787–792.

Petrie, K.J., Fontanilla, I., Thomas, M.G., Booth, R.J., & Pennebaker, J.W. (2004). Effect of written emotional expression on immune function in patients with human immunodeficiency virus infection: A randomized trial. *Psychosomatic Medicine, 66*, 272–275.

Redeker, G. (1984). On differences between spoken and written language. *Discourse Processes, 7*, 43–55.

Resnick, H.S., Kilpatrick, D.G., & Lipovsky, J.A. (1991). Assessment of rape-related posttraumatic stress disorder: Stressor and symptom dimensions. *Psychological Assessment, 3*, 561–572.

Richards, J.M., Beal, W.E., Seagal, J.D., & Pennebaker, J.W. (2000). Effects of disclosure of traumatic events on illness behavior among psychiatric prison inmates. *Journal of Abnormal Psychology, 109*(1), 156–160.

Rime, B. (1995). Mental rumination, social sharing, and the recovery from emotional experience. In J.W. Pennebaker (Ed.), *Emotion, disclosure, & health* (pp. 271–291). Washington, DC: American Psychological Association.

Rogers, C.R. (1980). *A way of being.* Boston: Houghton Mifflin.

Rude, S.S., Gortner, E.M., & Pennebaker, J.W. (2004). Language use of depressed and depression-vulnerable college students. *Cognition and Emotion, 18*, 1121–1133.

Sapolsky, R.M. (2004). *Why zebras don't get ulcers.* New York, NY: Henry Holt and Company.

Schooler, J.W., & Engstler-Schooler, T.Y. (1990). Verbal overshadowing of visual memories: Some things are better left unsaid. *Cognitive Psychology, 22*, 36–71.

Schoutrop, M.J.A., Lange, A., Brosschot, J., & Everaerd, W. (1997). Overcoming traumatic events by means of writing assignments. In A. Vingerhoets, F. van Bussel, & J. Boelhouwer (Eds.), *The (Non)expression of emotions in health and disease* (pp. 279–289). Tilburg, The Netherlands: Tilburg University Press.

Schwartz, G.E., & Kline, J.P. (1995). Repression, emotional disclosure, and health: Theoretical, empirical, and clinical considerations. In J.W. Pennebaker (Ed.), *Emotion, disclosure, and health* (pp. 177–194). Washington, DC: American Psychological Association.

Schwarz, N. (1990). Feelings as information: Informational and motivational functions of affective states. In E.T. Higgins, & R.M. Sorrentino (Eds.), *Handbook of motivation and cognition: Foundations of social behavior* Vol. 2 (pp. 527–561). New York: Guilford.

Seih, Y.T., Lin, Y.C., Huang, C.L., Peng, C.W., & Huang, S.P. (2008). The benefits of psychological displacement in diary writing when using different pronouns. *British Journal of Health Psychology, 13*, 39–41.

Seih, Y.T., Chung, C.K., & Pennebaker, J.W. (in press). Experimental manipulations of perspective taking and perspective switching in expressive writing. *Cognition and Emotion.*

Seligman, M.E.P. (2000). Positive psychology. In J.E. Gillman (Ed.), *Science of optimism and hope: Research essays in honor of Martin E. P. Seligman* (pp. 415–429). Philadelphia, PA: Templeton Foundation Press.

Seyle, H. (1978). *The stress of life.* Oxford, England: McGraw Hill.

Sheese, B.E., Brown, E.L., & Graziano, W.G. (2004). Emotional expression in cyberspace: Searching for moderators of the Pennebaker disclosure effect via email. *Health Psychology, 23*, 457–464.

Slatcher, R.B., & Pennebaker, J.W. (2006). How do I love thee? Let me count the words: The social effects of expressive writing. *Psychological Science, 17*, 660–664.

Sloan, D.M. & Marx, B.P. (2004a). Taking pen to hand: Evaluating theories underlying the written disclosure paradigm. *Clinical Psychology: Science & Practice, 11*, 121–137.

Sloan, D.M., & Marx, B.P. (2004b). A closer examination of the structured written disclosure procedure. *Journal of Consulting & Clinical Psychology, 72*, 165–175.

Sloan, D.M., Marx, B.P., & Epstein, E.M. (2005). Further examination of the exposure model underlying the efficacy of written emotional disclosure. *Journal of Consulting and Clinical Psychology, 73*, 549–554.

Sloan, D.M., Marx, B.P., Epstein, E.M., & Dobbs, J.L. (2008). Expressive writing buffers against maladaptive rumination. *Emotion, 8*, 302–306.

Small, R., Lumley, J., Donohue, L., Potter, A., & Waldenstrom, U. (2000). Randomised controlled trial of midwife led debriefing to reduce maternal depression after childbirth. *British Medical Journal, 321*, 1043–1047.

Smyth, J.M. (1998). Written emotional expression: Effect sizes, outcome types, and moderating variables. *Journal of Consulting and Clinical Psychology, 66*, 174–184.

Smyth, J.M., Hockemeyer, J.R., & Tulloch, H. (2008). Expressive writing and post-traumatic stress disorder: Effects on trauma symptoms, mood states, and cortisol reactivity. *British Journal of Health Psychology, 13*, 85–93.

Smyth, J.M., & Pennebaker, J.W. (2008). Exploring the boundary conditions of expressive writing: In search of the right recipe. *British Journal of Health Psychology, 13*, 1–7.

Smyth, J.M., Stone, A.A., Hurewitz, A., & Kaell, A. (1999). Effects of writing about stressful experiences on symptom reduction in patients with asthma or rheumatoid arthritis: A randomized trial. *Journal of the American Medical Association, 281*, 1304–1309.

Smyth, J.M., True, N., & Souto, J. (2001). Effects of writing about traumatic experiences: The necessity for narrative structuring. *Journal of Social and Clinical Psychology, 20*, 161–172.

Solano, L., Donati, V., Pecci, F., Persicheeti, S., & Colaci, A. (2003). Post-operative course after papilloma resection: Effects of written disclosure of the experience in subjects with different alexithymia levels. *Psychosomatic Medicine, 65*, 477–484.

Spera, S.P., Buhrfeind, E.D., & Pennebaker, J.W. (1994). Expressive writing and coping with job loss. *Academy of Management Journal, 37*(3), 722–733.

Stanton, A.L., & Danoff-Burg, S. (2002). Emotional expression, expressive writing, and cancer. In S.J. Lepore, & J.M. Smyth (Eds.), *Writing cure: How expressive writing promotes health and emotional well-being* (pp. 31–51). Washington, DC: American Psychological Association.

Stanton, A.L., Danoff-Burg, S., Sworowski, L.A., Collins, C.A., Branstetter, A.D., Rodriguez-Hanley, A., et al. (2002). Randomized, controlled trial of written emotional expression and benefit finding in breast cancer patients. *Journal of Clinical Oncology, 20*, 4160–4168.

Stone, L. (2003*). Expressive writing and perspective change: Applications to September 11*. Poster presented at the 2003 conference for the Society for Personality and Social Psychology, Savannah, GA.

Sutker, P.B., Davis, J.M., Uddo, M., & Ditta, S.R. (1995). War zone stress, personal resources, and PTSD in Persian Gulf war returnees. *Journal of Abnormal Psychology, 104*, 444–452.

Swanbon, T., Boyce, L., & Greenberg, M.A. (2008). Expressive writing reduces avoidance and somatic complaints in a community sample with constraints on expression. *British Journal of Health Psychology, 13*, 53–56.

Ullrich, P.A., & Lutgendorf, S.L. (2002). Journaling about stressful events: Effects of cognitive processing and emotional expression. *Annals of Behavioral Medicine, 24*, 244–250.

Vaidya, N.A., & Garfield, D.A.S. (2003). A comparison of personality characteristics of patients with posttraumatic stress disorder and substance dependence: Preliminary findings. *Journal of Nervous & Mental Disease, 191*, 616–618.

Walker, B.L., Nail, L.M., & Croyle, R.T. (1999). Does emotional expression make a difference in reactions to breast cancer? *Oncology Nursing Forum, 26*, 1025–1032.

Watson, D., & Clark, L.A. (1984). Negative Affectivity: The disposition to experience aversive emotional states. *Psychological Bulletin, 96*, 465–490.

Wilson, T.D. (2002*). Strangers to ourselves: Discovering the adaptive unconscious*. Cambridge, MA: Belknap Press/ Harvard University Press.

Wolpe, J. (1968). Psychotherapy by reciprocal inhibition. *Conditional Reflex, 3*, 234–240.

Wong, Y.J., & Rochlen, A.B. (2009). Potential benefits of expressive writing for male college students with varying degrees of restrictive emotionality. *Psychology of Men & Masculinity, 10*, 149–159.

Wortman, C.B., & Silver, R.C. (1989). The myths of coping with loss. *Journal of Consulting & Clinical Psychology, 57*, 349–357.

Yogo, M., & Fujihara, S. (2008). Working memory capacity can be improved by expressive writing: A randomized experiment in a Japanese sample. *British Journal of Health Psychology, 13*, 77–80.

# Beyond the Myths of Coping with Loss: Prevailing Assumptions Versus Scientific Evidence

Camille B. Wortman *and* Kathrin Boerner

**Abstract**

This chapter reviews those developments in the field of bereavement that have led to changes in prevailing views about how people cope with the loss of a loved one. The first section provides a brief review of the most influential theories of grief and loss. Some of these theories have contributed to the myths of coping, whereas others have helped generate new questions about the grieving process. The second section discusses each myth of coping, summarizing available evidence and highlighting ways in which myths have changed over time as research evidence has accumulated. The final section discusses the implications of this work for researchers, clinicians, and the bereaved themselves. In so doing, it considers the efficacy of grief counseling or therapy. It also addresses the question of what physicians, funeral directors, employers, and friends can do to support the bereaved in their efforts to deal with loss.

**Keywords:** Bereavement, grieving, grief, death, loss, coping

The death of a loved one is a ubiquitous human experience and is often regarded as a serious threat to health and well-being. Coming to terms with personal loss is considered to be an important part of successful adult development (Baltes & Skrotzki, 1995). In this chapter, we draw from our own research and that of others to explore how people are affected by the death of a loved one. In our judgment, such losses provide an excellent arena in which to study basic processes of stress and adaptation to change. Unlike many stressful life experiences, bereavement cannot be altered by the coping efforts of survivors. Indeed, the major coping task faced by the bereaved is to reconcile themselves to a situation that cannot be changed and find a way to carry on with their own lives. By learning more about how people react to a loved one's death, and how they come to terms with what has happened, we can begin to clarify the theoretical mechanisms through which major losses can have deleterious effects on subsequent mental and physical health.

In our judgment, one of the most fascinating things about studying bereavement is the extraordinary variability that has been found regarding how people react to the death of a loved one. Some people are devastated and never again regain their psychological equilibrium; others emerge from the loss relatively unscathed and perhaps even strengthened (Bonanno et al., 2002; Elison & McGonigle, 2003; Parkes & Weiss, 1983). Yet, at this point, we know relatively little about the diverse ways that people respond to the loss of a loved one, and why some people react with intense and prolonged distress while others do not. Do people who have the most rewarding and satisfying relationships with their loved one suffer the most following the loved one's death? Or, do those with conflictual or ambivalent relationships experience the most distress following the loss of a loved one, as clinicians have frequently argued (see, e.g., Freud, 1917/1957; Rando, 1993; Parkes & Weiss, 1983)? Among those who fail to show distress following the loss, is this best understood as denial, lack of attachment, or resilience in the face of loss?

Over the years, we carried out several systematic evaluations of common assumptions about coping with loss that appear to be held by professionals in the field, as well as by laypersons (Bonanno & Kaltman, 2001; Wortman & Boerner, 2007; Wortman & Silver, 1987, 1989, 2001). We identified these assumptions by reviewing some of the most important theoretical models of the grieving process, such as Freud's (1917/1957) grief work perspective and Bowlby's (1980) early attachment model (see Bonanno & Kaltman, 1999; Wortman & Silver, 2001). In addition, we examined books and articles written by and for clinicians and other health care providers that describe the grieving process (see, e.g., Jacobs, 1993; Malkinson, Rubin, & Witztum, 2000; Rando, 1993; Worden, 2008). Finally, we reviewed books and articles written by and for bereaved individuals themselves (e.g., Elison & McGonigle, 2003; Gowell, 1992; Sanders, 1999; Umberson, 2003). The following assumptions were identified:

- Bereaved persons are expected to exhibit significant distress following a major loss, and the failure to experience such distress is regarded as indicative of a problem (e.g., that the bereaved person will experience a delayed grief reaction).
- Positive emotions are implicitly assumed to be absent during this period. If they are expressed, they tend to be viewed as an indication that people are denying or covering up their distress.
- Following the loss of a loved one, the bereaved must confront and "work through" his or her feelings about the loss. Efforts to avoid or deny feelings are regarded as maladaptive in the long run.
- It is important for the bereaved to relinquish his or her attachment to the deceased loved one.
- Within a year or two, the bereaved will be able to come to terms with what has happened, recover from the loss, and resume his or her earlier level of functioning.

Because these assumptions about the grieving process seemed to be firmly entrenched in Western culture, we anticipated that they would be supported by the available scientific data. However, our reviews of the literature provided little support for any of these assumptions. For this reason, we labeled them "myths of coping with loss."

Initially, studies in the field of grief and loss were plagued by major methodological shortcomings, including the use of convenience samples, low response rates, attrition, and the failure to include control groups. There was a dearth of scientific evidence on important concepts like "working through"

and recovery from loss. Hence, in our earliest papers discussing these assumptions (Wortman & Silver, 1987, 1989), it was difficult to evaluate the validity of some of them. Over the past few decades, however, research on bereavement has burgeoned. In fact, just in the last 10 years, over 5,000 articles have appeared on grief and/or bereavement. In addition to a large number of sound empirical studies, three editions of an influential handbook of bereavement have appeared in the literature (Stroebe, Hansson, Schut, & Stroebe, 2008; Stroebe, Hansson, Stroebe, & Schut, 2001; Stroebe, Stroebe, & Hansson, 1993). As a result of the accumulation of research evidence, as well as related theoretical developments in the field of bereavement, some shifts have occurred in prevailing views about how people cope with the loss of a loved one. In this chapter, we review these developments.

In the first section of the chapter, we provide a brief review of the most influential theories of grief and loss. Some of these theories have contributed to the myths of coping, whereas others have helped generate new questions about the grieving process. In the second section, we discuss each myth of coping, summarizing available evidence and highlighting ways in which the myths have changed over time as research evidence has accumulated. In these sections, we also identify what we believe to be the most important new areas of research. In the final section, we discuss the implications of this work for researchers, clinicians, and the bereaved themselves. In so doing, we consider the efficacy of grief counseling or therapy. We also address the question of what physicians, funeral directors, employers, and friends can do to support the bereaved in their efforts to deal with loss.

## Theories of Grief and Loss

Many different theoretical formulations have influenced the current understanding of the grief process (for a more detailed review, see Archer, 1999, 2008; Bonanno & Kaltman, 1999; Rando, 1993; Stroebe & Schut, 2001).

### Classic Psychoanalytic View

One of the most influential approaches to loss has been the classic psychoanalytic model of bereavement, which is based on Freud's (1917/1957) seminal paper, "Mourning and Melancholia." According to Freud, the primary task of mourning is the gradual surrender of one's psychological attachment to the deceased. Freud believed that relinquishment of the love object involves a painful internal struggle.

The individual experiences intense yearning for the lost loved one, yet is faced with the reality of that person's absence. As thoughts and memories are reviewed, ties to the loved one are gradually withdrawn. This process, which requires considerable time and energy, was referred to by Freud as "the work of mourning." At the conclusion of the mourning period, the bereaved individual is said to have "worked through" the loss and to have freed himself or herself from an intense attachment to an unavailable person. Freud maintained that when the process has been completed, the bereaved person regains sufficient emotional energy to invest in new relationships and pursuits. This view of the grieving process has dominated the bereavement literature over much of the past century, and only more recently has been called into question (Bonanno & Kaltman, 1999; Stroebe, 1992–1993; Wortman & Silver, 1989). For example, it has been noted that the concept of grief work is overly broad and lacks clarity because it fails to differentiate between such processes as rumination, confrontative coping, and expression of emotion (Stroebe & Schut, 2001).

## ATTACHMENT THEORY

Another theoretical framework that has been extremely influential is Bowlby's attachment theory (Bowlby, 1969, 1973, 1980; see also Fraley & Shaver, 1999; Shaver & Tancredy, 2001). In this work, Bowlby integrated ideas from psychodynamic thought, from the developmental literature on young children's reactions to separation, and from work on the mourning behavior of primates. Bowlby maintained that, during the course of normal development, individuals form instinctive affectional bonds or attachments, initially between child and parent and later between adults. He believed that the nature of the relationship between a child and his or her mother or caregiver has a major impact on subsequent relationships. He suggested that when affectional bonds are threatened, powerful attachment behaviors are activated, such as crying and angry protest. Unlike Freud, Bowlby believed that the biological function of these behaviors is not withdrawal from the loved one but rather reunion. However, in the case of a permanent loss, the biological function of assuring proximity with attachment figures becomes dysfunctional. Consequently, the bereaved person struggles between the opposing forces of activated attachment behavior and the reality of the loved one's absence.

Bowlby maintained that, to deal with these opposing forces, the mourner goes through four stages of grieving: (a) initial numbness, disbelief, or shock; (b) yearning or searching for the deceased, accompanied by anger and protest; (c) despair and disorganization as the bereaved gives up the search, accompanied by feelings of depression and hopelessness; and (d) reorganization or recovery as the loss is accepted, and there is a gradual return to former interests. By emphasizing the survival value of attachment behavior, Bowlby was the first to give a plausible explanation for responses such as searching or anger in grief. Bowlby was also the first to maintain that a relationship exists between a person's attachment history and how he or she will react to the loss of a loved one. For example, children who endured frequent separations from their parents may form anxious and highly dependent attachments as adults, and may react with intense and prolonged grief when a spouse or partner dies (see Shaver & Tancredy, 2001, or Stroebe, Schut, & Stroebe, 2005a, for a more detailed discussion). Because it provides a framework for understanding individual differences in response to loss, Bowlby's attachment model has continued to be influential in the study of grief and loss (see, e.g., Shear et al., 2007).

## STAGES OF GRIEF

Another aspect of Bowlby's work that has been influential in determining how we think about grief is his idea that grieving involves stages of reaction to loss. Drawing from this work, several theorists have proposed that people go through stages or phases in coming to terms with loss (see, e.g., Horowitz, 1976, 1985; Ramsay & Happee, 1977; Sanders, 1989). Perhaps the most well known of these models is the one proposed by Kübler-Ross (1969) in her highly influential book *On Death and Dying*. This model, which was developed to explain how dying persons react to their own impending death, posits that people go through denial, anger, bargaining, depression, and ultimately acceptance. It is Kübler-Ross's model that popularized stage theories of bereavement. For many years, stage models have been taught in medical, nursing, and social work schools, and in many cases, these models are firmly entrenched among health care professionals. Kübler-Ross's model has also appeared in articles in newspapers and magazines written for bereaved persons and their family members. As a result, stage models have strongly influenced the common understanding of grief in our society.

## BEYOND STAGE MODELS

As research has begun to accumulate, it has become clear that there is little support for the view that these systematic stages exist. Although some studies purport to support stage models (Maciejewski, Zhang, Block, & Prigerson, 2007), the weight of the evidence suggests that reactions to loss vary considerably from person to person, and that few people pass through the stages in the expected fashion (see Archer, 1999, or Attig, 1996, for a review). Several major weaknesses of stage models have been identified (Neimeyer, 1998). First, they cannot account for the variability in response that follows a major loss. Second, they place grievers in a passive role when, in fact, grieving requires the active involvement of the survivor. Third, such models fail to consider the social or cultural factors that influence the process. Fourth, stage models focus too much attention on emotional responses to the loss and not enough on cognitions and behaviors. Finally, stage models tend to pathologize people who do not pass through the stages As a result of these and other critiques and a lack of empirical support, most researchers have come to believe that the idea of a fixed sequence of stages is not particularly useful (Stroebe, Hansson et al., 2001).

More recent theoretical models, such as Neimeyer's model of meaning reconstruction (Neimeyer, 1997, 1999), have attempted to address these shortcomings by portraying grief as a more idiosyncratic process in which people strive to make sense of what has happened. For example, Neimeyer (2000, 2006) has maintained that major losses challenge a person's sense of identity and narrative coherence. Narrative disorganization can range from relatively limited and transient to more sweeping and chronic, depending on the nature of the relationship and the circumstances surrounding the death. According to Neimeyer, a major task of grief involves reorganizing one's life story to restore coherence and maintain continuity between the past and the future.

## STRESS AND COPING APPROACH

Over the past two decades, a theoretical orientation referred to as the *stress and coping approach*, or the *cognitive coping approach* (Lazarus & Folkman, 1984; see also Chapter 8, by Carver, & Vargas, 2011, this volume), has become highly influential in the field of bereavement. Stress and coping theorists maintain that life changes like the death of a loved one become distressing if a person appraises the situation as taxing or exceeding his or her resources. An important feature of this model is that it highlights the role of cognitive appraisal in understanding how people react to loss. A person's appraisal, or subjective assessment of what has been lost, is hypothesized to

influence his or her emotional reaction to the stressor and the coping strategies that are employed. As Folkman (2001) has indicated, however, there is surprisingly little research on specific coping strategies that people use to deal with loss and the impact of these various strategies.

To explain why a given loss has more impact on one person than another, stress and coping researchers have focused on the identification of potential risk factors, such as a history of mental health problems, as well as protective factors, such as optimism or social support (For a review, see Stroebe, Schut, & Stroebe, 2007; see also Chapter 9, by Taylor, 2011, this volume). The appraisal of the loss, as well as the magnitude of physical and mental health consequences that result from the loss, are thought to depend on these factors. Those with fewer risk factors and more protective factors are expected to recover more quickly and completely.

## TOWARD MORE COMPREHENSIVE MODELS OF BEREAVEMENT

Stage models and the stress and coping model can be applied to bereavement, but they were not developed specifically to account for people's reactions to the death of a loved one. Within the past few years, two new theoretical models have been developed: Bonanno's four-component model (Bonanno & Kaltman, 1999), and Stroebe and Schut's (1999, 2001) dual-process model. Not only do these models focus specifically on bereavement, but each attempts to integrate elements from diverse theoretical approaches into a comprehensive model. Bonanno's goal was to develop a conceptually sound and empirically testable framework for understanding individual differences in grieving. He identified four primary components of the grieving process— the context in which the loss occurs (e.g., was it sudden or expected, timely or untimely?); the subjective meanings associated with the loss (e.g., was the bereaved person resentful that he or she had to care for the loved one prior to the death?); changes in the representation of the lost loved one over time (e.g., does the bereaved person maintain a continuing connection with the deceased?); and the role of coping and emotion regulation processes that can mitigate or exacerbate the stress of loss. Bonanno's model makes the prediction that recovery is most likely when negative grief-related emotions are regulated or minimized and when positive emotions are instigated or enhanced (Bonanno, 2001). This hypothesis, which is diametrically opposed to what would be derived from the psychodynamic approach, has generated considerable interest and support in recent years.

The dual-process model of coping with bereavement (Stroebe & Schut, 1999, 2001) indicates that following a loved one's death, bereaved people alternate between two different kinds of coping: loss-oriented coping and restoration-oriented coping. While engaged in loss-oriented coping, the bereaved person focuses on and attempts to process or resolve some aspect of the loss itself. Dealing with intrusive thoughts is an example of loss-oriented coping. Restoration-oriented coping involves attempting to adapt to or master the challenges inherent in daily life, including life circumstances that may have changed as a result of the loss. Examples of restoration-oriented coping include distracting oneself from the grief, doing new things, or mastering new skills. Stroebe and Schut (2001) have proposed that bereaved individuals alternate between loss- and restoration-oriented coping, and that such oscillation is necessary for adaptive coping. Restorative activities not only provide respite from the painful work of facing the loss, but help the bereaved to replenish psychological resources, such as energy and hope.

Stroebe and Schut (2001) have maintained that, early in the process, most people focus primarily on loss-oriented coping but that, over time, a shift occurs to more restoration-oriented coping. They have also indicated that the model provides a way to understand individual differences in coping. For example, they pointed out that considerable evidence indicates that women tend to be more loss-oriented than men (Stroebe & Schut, 2001), thus suggesting a possible explanation for gender differences in response to loss. As Archer (1999) has noted, one of the most important features of this model is that it provides an alternative to the view that grief is resolved solely through confrontation with the loss.

More recently, Stroebe, Folkman, and colleagues proposed an integrative risk factor framework, which incorporates an analysis of stressors, risk, and protective factors, as well as appraisal and coping processes that are thought to affect adjustment to bereavement (see Stroebe, Folkman, Hansson, & Schut, 2006). The model is meant to encourage a more systematic analysis of individual differences in response to bereavement, and, in particular to guide research that examines interactions among the different model components (i.e., among risk factors, appraisal, and coping processes). For example, intrapersonal risk factors such as gender are best considered in combination with differences in type of stressors that bereaved men and women may face, or with differences in their stress appraisals or coping styles.

Throughout the years, the theoretical models discussed here have influenced and, at the same time, have been influenced by the empirical work on coping with loss. As noted above, accumulating evidence regarding variability in response to loss led researchers to move away from traditional grief models and to instead employ a stress and coping framework that can account for divergent responses to loss. In turn, the empirical evidence that has come out of this effort to account for variability in response to loss has led to further theoretical development. The most recent bereavement models have drawn from these studies to develop new insights about what questions are important to study. The following sections provide a review of the empirical work that in some ways has been the "engine" behind recent changes in our thinking about bereavement.

## Revisiting the "Myths Of Coping"

Over the past decade, bereavement research has continued to become more methodologically sophisticated, with many researchers employing powerful longitudinal designs to study the impact of loss. Some longitudinal studies have examined the reactions of the bereaved from a few months after the loss through the first 5 years (e.g., Bonanno, Keltner, Holen, & Horowitz, 1995; Murphy, Johnson, Chung, & Beaton, 2003; Murphy, Johnson, & Lohan, 2002). Others have focused on people whose loved one is ill, and have assessed relevant variables before and at various intervals after the death (e.g., Folkman, Chesney, Collette, Boccellari, & Cooke, 1996; Haley et al., 2008; Nolen-Hoeksema & Larson, 1999; Nolen-Hoeksema, McBride, & Larson, 1997; Schulz, Mendelson, & Haley, 2003). Still others have followed large community samples across time and studied those who became bereaved during the course of the study (e.g., Bonanno et al., 2002; Carnelley, Wortman, & Kessler, 1999; Lichtenstein, Gatz, Pederson, Berg, & McClearn, 1996; Mendes de Leon, Kasl, & Jacobs, 1994). Most studies have relied solely on respondents' assessments of key variables such as depression. However, some have used clinical assessments, and a few have included nonverbal data (e.g., Bonanno & Keltner, 1997) or assessments from others (e.g., Bonanno, Moskowitz, Papa, & Folkman, 2005).

The vast majority of bereavement studies have focused on the loss of a spouse. In the past decade, however, important new studies have appeared on reactions to the loss of a child (e.g., Dyregrov,

Nordanger, & Dyregrov, 2003; Murphy, 1996; Murphy et al., 1999; Murphy, Johnson, & Lohan, 2003; Wijngaards-de Mej et al., 2008); parent (e.g., Jacobs & Bovasso, 2009; Silverman, Nickman, & Worden, 1992); and sibling (e.g., Balk, 1983; Batten & Oltjenbruns, 1999; Cleiren, 1993; Hogan & DeSantis, 1994). In one study, reactions to various kinds of familial loss were compared (Cleiren, 1993; Cleiren, Diekstra, Kerkhof, & van der Wal, 1994). Most studies have focused on respondents who are heterogeneous with respect to cause of death. However, some have examined reactions to specific losses, such as parents whose children experienced a sudden, traumatic death (e.g., Dyregrov et al., 2003; Murphy, Johnson, & Lohan, 2003), or gay male caregivers whose partners died of acquired immune deficiency syndrome (AIDS; e.g., Folkman, 1997a; Folkman et al., 1996; Moskowitz, Folkman, & Acree, 2003; Moskowitz, Folkman, Collette, & Vittinghoff, 1996). A few studies have compared two or more groups of respondents who lost loved ones under different circumstances (e.g., natural causes, accident, or suicide; e.g., Cleiren, 1993; Dyregrov et al., 2003; Middleton, Raphael, Burnett, & Martinek, 1998; Murphy, Johnson, Wu, Fan, & Lohan, 2003). Consequently, it is now possible to determine whether the "myths of coping" hold true across different kinds of deaths that occur under varying conditions.

Of course, there are still some areas where relatively little is known. For example, the vast majority of studies on the loss of a spouse focus on middle-aged or elderly white women. This is ironic, since the available evidence (see, e.g., Miller & Wortman, 2002; Stroebe, Stroebe, & Schut, 2001) suggests that men are more vulnerable to the effects of conjugal loss than are women. In recent years, there has been increasing interest in how men grieve (see, e.g., Martin & Doka, 2000), and in gender differences in grieving (see, e.g., Wolff & Wortman, 2006; Wortman, Wolff, & Bonanno, 2004). There are very few studies on reactions to the death of a sibling, despite evidence that this is a profound loss, particularly for adult women (Cleiren, 1993). With few exceptions (e.g., Carr, 2004), there is also a paucity of studies that include blacks or Hispanics. Hence, it is difficult to determine whether the findings reported in the literature will generalize to these or other culturally diverse groups.

In the material that follows, each assumption about coping with loss is discussed in some detail. As we will show, beliefs about some of these assumptions have shifted over time as the evidence has continued to accumulate. For example, because several studies have identified a variety of emotional reactions among the bereaved, researchers have become more skeptical about the assumption that most people go through a period of intense distress following a loss. In the discussion that follows, each myth is updated, the available evidence is presented, and gaps in our knowledge base are identified.

### The Expectation of Intense Distress
DESCRIPTION

Several of the most influential theories in the area, such as classic psychoanalytic models (e.g., Freud, 1917/1957) and Bowlby's (1980) attachment model, are based on the assumption that at some point, people will confront the reality of their loss and go through a period of depression. Many books written by grief researchers, as well as those written by and for the bereaved, also convey the view that following the death of a loved one, most people react with intense distress or depression. For example, Sanders (1999) has maintained that once the bereaved person has accepted the reality of the loss, he or she will go through a phase of grief that can seem frightening "because it seems so like clinical depression" (p. 78). Similarly, Shuchter (1986) has indicated that "virtually everyone whose spouse dies exhibits some signs and symptoms of depression" (p. 170). It is anticipated that depression or distress will decrease over time as the bereaved comes to terms with the loss.

Historically, the failure to exhibit grief or distress following the loss of a spouse has been viewed as an indication that the grieving process has gone awry (e.g., Deutsch, 1937; Marris, 1958). Bowlby (1980) identified "prolonged absence of conscious grieving" (p. 138) as one of two possible types of disordered mourning, along with chronic mourning. Marris (1958) has indicated that "grieving is a process which 'must work itself out' . . . if the process is aborted from too hasty a readjustment . . . the bereaved may never recover" (p. 33). In recent years, some investigators have challenged the assumption that the failure to experience distress is indicative of pathology. For example, M. Stroebe, Hansson, and Stroebe (1993) have argued that there are many possible reasons why a bereaved person may fail to exhibit intense distress that would not be considered pathological (e.g., early adjustment following an expected loss; relief that the loved one is no longer suffering).

However, available evidence suggests that most practicing clinicians continue to maintain, either explicitly or implicitly, that there is something wrong with individuals who do not exhibit grief or depression following the loss of a loved one. In a survey of expert clinicians and researchers in the field of loss (Middleton, Moylan, Raphael, Burnett, & Martinek, 1993), a majority (65%) endorsed the belief that "absent" grief exists, that it typically stems from denial or inhibition, and that it is generally maladaptive in the long run. An important component of this view is that it assumes that if people fail to experience distress shortly after a loss, problems or symptoms of distress will erupt at a later point. For example, Bowlby (1980) has argued that individuals who have failed to mourn may suddenly, inexplicably become acutely depressed at a later time (see also Rando, 1984; Worden, 2008). These authors have also maintained that the failure to grieve will result in subsequent health problems (Bowlby, 1980; Worden, 2008).

Consistent with the notion that "absent" grief signals unhealthy denial and repression of feelings, there is a great deal of clinical literature to suggest that people who have lost a loved one, but who have not begun grieving, will benefit from clinical intervention designed to help them work through their unresolved feelings (see, e.g., Bowlby, 1980; Deutsch, 1937; Jacobs, 1993; Lazare, 1989; Rando, 1993; Worden, 2008). In a report published by the Institute of Medicine, for example, Osterweis, Solomon, and Green (1984) concluded that "professional help may be warranted for persons who show no evidence of having begun grieving" (p. 136). Similarly, Jacobs (1993) has suggested that the bereaved individuals who experience "inhibited grief . . . ought to be offered brief psychotherapy by a skilled therapist" (p. 246).

The failure to exhibit distress following the loss of a loved one has also been viewed as evidence for character weakness in the survivor. In a classic paper, Deutsch (1937) maintained that grief-related affect was sometimes absent among individuals who were not emotionally strong enough to begin grieving. Osterweis et al. (1984) emphasized that clinicians typically assume "that the absence of grieving phenomena following bereavement represents some form of personality pathology" (p. 18). Similarly, Horowitz (1990) has stated that those who show little overt grief or distress following a loss are "narcissistic personalities" who "may be too developmentally immature to have an adult type of relationship and so cannot exhibit an adult type of mourning at its loss" (p. 301; see also Raphael, 1983). It has also been suggested that some people fail to exhibit distress because

they were only superficially attached to their spouses (Fraley & Shaver, 1999; Rando, 1993).

### EVIDENCE FOR INTENSE DISTRESS

Among people who have faced the loss of a loved one, is it true that distress is commonly experienced? Will distress or depression emerge at a later date among those who fail to exhibit distress in the first several weeks or months following the loss? We identified several studies that provide information bearing on these questions. Most of these studies focused on the loss of a spouse (Boerner, Wortman, & Bonanno, 2005; Bonanno, Moskowitz et al., 2005; Bonanno et al., 2002; Bonanno & Field, 2001; Bonanno et al., 1995; Bournstein, Clayton, Halikas, Maurice, & Robins, 1973; Lund et al., 1986; Vachon, Rogers et al., 1982; Vachon, Sheldon et al., 1982; Zisook & Shuchter, 1986); with several of these examining response to loss following a time of caregiving for a chronically ill loved one (Aneshensel, Botticello, & Yamamoto-Mitani, 2004; Bonanno, Moscowitz et al., 2005; Chentstova-Dutton, et al., 2002; Li, 2005; Schulz et al., 2003; Zhang, Mitchell, Bambauer, Jones, & Prigerson, 2008). A few studies examined reactions to the death of a child (Bonanno, Moskowitz et al., 2005; Wortman & Silver, 1992; Wijngaards-de Meij et al., 2008). These studies assessed depression or other forms of distress in the early months following the death, and then again anywhere from 13 to 60 months after the loss. The construct of depression/distress was operationalized differently in the different studies. For example, some studies utilized the Symptom Checklist 90 (SCL-90) depression subscale and/or *Diagnostic and Statistical Manual of Mental Disorders* (DSM)-based Structured Clinical Interview for Disorders (SCID; e.g., Bonanno, Moscowitz et al., 2005); other studies used the Center for Epidemiologic Studies of Depression (CESD) scale (e.g., Bonanno et al., 2002). For each study, the investigators determined a cutoff score to classify respondents as high or low in distress or depression.

The longitudinal studies identified here provide evidence regarding the prevalence of different patterns of grief. "Normal" or "common" grief, which involves moving from high distress to low distress over time, was found among 41% of participants in a study on loss of a child from sudden infant death syndrome (SIDS; Wortman & Silver, 1987), and anywhere between 9% and 41% in studies on conjugal loss (35% in Bonanno et al., 1995; 29% in Bournstein et al., 1973; 9% in Lund, Caserta, & Dimond, 1986; 41% in Vachon, Rogers et al., 1982;

and 20% in Zisook & Shuchter, 1986). Furthermore, in these studies, evidence for "minimal" or "absent" grief, which involves scoring low in distress consistently over time, was found for 26% (Wortman & Silver, 1987), 41% (Bonanno et al., 1995), 57% (Bournstein et al., 1973), 30% (Vachon, Rogers et al., 1982), 78% (Lund et al., 1986), and 65% (Zisook & Shuchter, 1986) of respondents.

In a prospective study on conjugal loss among older adults that included data from 3 years pre-loss to 18 months post-loss (Bonanno et al., 2002; Bonanno, Wortman, & Nesse, 2004), nearly half of the participants (46%) experienced low levels of distress consistently over time and were labelled "resilient." Only 11% showed "normal" or "common" grief. Another trajectory in this study referred to as "depressed-improved" reflected elevated distress before the loss and improvement after the loss (10%). A similar pattern of reduced distress levels following the loss was detected in prospective studies that included both pre- and post-loss data on caregivers of dementia patients (Aneshensel et al., 2004; Schulz et al., 2003; Zhang et al., 2008), as well as on caregiver samples that included a variety of illnesses (Li, 2005). In two of these studies (Aneshensel et al., 2004; Zhang et al., 2008), only about 17% showed a pattern of distress reflecting "common" grief following the death. Moreover, Aneshensel and colleagues observed a pattern of stable but low distress (64%) and absent distress (11%) in a majority of their participants, and Zhang and colleagues found persistently absent depression in about half of their sample.

Taken together, in all studies, less than half of the sample showed "normal" grief, and in many, such a reaction was shown by only a small minority of respondents. In fact, in the prospective study on conjugal loss by Bonanno et al. (2002), the relatively small proportion of those who showed "normal" grief (11%) was almost equal to those who showed a depressed-improved pattern of being more distressed before the loss, followed by improvement after the loss (10%). Most important, however, the available evidence shows that "minimal" or "absent" grief is very common. The number of respondents failing to show elevated distress or depression at the initial or final time point was sizable, ranging from one-quarter of the sample to more than three-quarters of the sample. In fact, a comparison of nonbereaved and bereaved individuals (who lost either a child or a spouse; Bonanno, Moskowitz et al., 2005) showed that, in terms of distress levels, slightly more than half of the bereaved did not significantly differ from

the matched sample of nonbereaved individuals when assessed at 4 and 18 months post-loss.

It should be noted that category labels such "minimal" or "absent" grief do not mean that there was absolutely no distress at any moment after the loss, but rather that, despite brief spikes in distress around the time of the death (Bonanno, Moskowitz et al., 2005) or a short period of daily variability in levels of well-being (Bisconti, Bergeman, & Boker, 2004), people who showed these patterns had generally low distress levels and managed to function at or near their normal levels (Bonanno, 2005). The prevalence of the "minimal" or "absent" grief reaction alone calls into question the assumption that failure to show distress following a loss is pathological. In fact, it suggests that learning more about why many people do not exhibit significant distress following a loss should become an important research priority.

## STUDIES WITH ASSESSMENT OF MILD DEPRESSION

When we have described these findings in the past (e.g., Bonanno et al., 2002; Wortman & Silver, 1989, 2001), it was sometimes suggested that the data may underestimate those who show significant distress following a loss. This is because most of the studies we reviewed classify respondents as depressed only if their score exceeds a cutoff believed to reflect clinically significant levels of depression. Respondents who do not exhibit major depression may still be evidencing considerable distress or depression. The previous studies do not speak to this issue, since they do not include measures of mild depression.

Fortunately, such measures have been included in a number of studies. For example, Bruce, Kim, Leaf, and Jacobs (1990) assessed dysphoria as well as depression in a study of conjugally bereaved individuals (aged 45 and older). Dysphoria was defined as feeling "sad, blue, depressed, or when you lost all interest and pleasure in things you usually cared about or enjoyed" for 2 weeks or more. About 60% of the respondents had experienced dysphoria. However, a significant minority (almost 40%) did not go through even a 2-week period of sadness following their loss. Similarly, Zisook, Paulus, Shuchter, and Judd (1997) conducted a study of elderly widowers and widows in which their ratings on symptom inventories were used to classify them into *DSM-IV* categories of major depression, minor depression, subsyndromal depression (endorsing any two symptoms from the symptom list), and no depression (endorsing one or no items reflecting depression). Two months after the partner's death, 20% were classified as showing major depression, 20% were classified as exhibiting minor depression, and 11% were classified as evidencing subsyndromal depression. Forty-nine percent of the respondents were classified as evidencing no depression (for similar results, see Cleiren, 1993). These studies provide compelling evidence that, following the death of a spouse, a substantial percentage of people do not show significant distress.

## DELAYED GRIEF

Is it true that if the bereaved do not become depressed following a major loss, a "delayed grief reaction," or physical health problems, will emerge at some point in the future? The data from the longitudinal studies we identified fail to support this view. In two studies, there were no respondents showing a delayed grief reaction (Bonanno et al., 1995; Bonanno & Field, 2001; Zisook & Shuchter, 1986). In the remaining studies, the percentage of respondents showing delayed grief was .02%, 1%, 2%, 2.5%, and 5.1%, respectively (Boerner et al., 2005; Bournstein et al., 1973; Lund et al., 1986; Wortman & Silver, 1987; Vachon, Rogers et al., 1982). It should be noted that in two of these studies (Lund et al., 1986; Zisook & Shuchter, 1986), bereaved respondents were interviewed at frequent intervals during the course of the study. There were very few respondents who moved from low distress to high distress on any subsequent interview. These studies indicate that "delayed grief" does not occur in more than a small percentage of cases. Nor do physical symptoms appear to emerge among those who fail to experience distress soon after the loss. Both the Boerner et al. (2005) and Bonanno and Field (2001) studies are convincing on this point, because conjugally bereaved individuals were assessed over a 4- and 5-year period, respectively, using multiple outcome measures. Data failing to support the "delayed grief" hypothesis were also obtained by Middleton et al. (1996). Based on cluster analyses of several bereaved samples, she concluded that "no evidence was found for . . . delayed grief." Nonetheless, in the previously described survey conducted by Middleton et al. (1993), a substantial majority of researchers and clinicians (76.6%) indicated that delayed grief does occur.

## PREDICTORS OF "MINIMAL" DISTRESS

The hypothesis that some people fail to become distressed following a loss because they were not attached to the loved one, or because they were cold and unfeeling, has only recently been subject to empirical research. Bonanno et al. (2002) tested the prediction that those who reported low levels of depression from pre-loss through 18 months of bereavement (resilient group) would score higher on pre-loss measures of avoidant/dismissive attachment than those in other groups (depressed-improved, common grief, chronic grief, and chronic depression). They also examined whether those in the resilient group would evaluate their marriage less positively and more negatively, and whether they would be rated by interviewers as less comfortable and skillful socially, and as exhibiting less warmth compared with the other groups at the pre-loss time point. The resilient group did not appear to differ from the other groups on any of these variables. A follow-up study yielded similar results with respect to variables on processing the loss (Bonanno et al., 2004). For example, the resilient group scored relatively high on comfort from positive memories of the deceased, a finding that also argues against the view that they were not strongly attached to the deceased. Furthermore, in their study on the loss of spouse or child, Bonanno, Moskowitz, et al. (2005) found that the friends of bereaved participants who showed resilience following the death rated them more positively, and reported having more contact and closer relations with them. Taken together, these findings do not support—and even contradict—the hypothesis that the absence of intense distress following loss is a sign of lack of attachment to the deceased or the inability to maintain close relationships.

Thus, available evidence clearly indicates that the so-called "normal" grief pattern is not as common as was assumed in the past, and that a significant proportion of bereaved individuals experience relatively little distress following a loss, without showing delayed grief or other signs of maladjustment. It should be noted, however, that such a reaction is far more prevalent following some kinds of losses than others. For example, elderly people who lose a spouse are more likely to show consistently low distress than are younger individuals who lose a spouse or parents who lose a child. In fact, research on the loss of a child under sudden or violent circumstances suggests that it is normative to experience intense distress following such a loss. In her study of the violent death of a child, for example, Murphy (1996) found that 4 months after the loss, more than 80% of the mothers and 60% of the fathers rated themselves as highly distressed. Thus, there is clear evidence that both the nature of the death and the circumstances surrounding the loss play a critical role in people's response to loss. These and other factors associated with long-term difficulties in adaptation to loss will be discussed in the section on recovery.

## FUTURE DIRECTIONS

Given the prevalence of resilience or low distress following a loss, we need to learn more about the potential costs and benefits of this response. As described previously, there is evidence that, for the bereaved person, resilience, or showing consistently low distress following the loss, appears to be an adaptive response. However, it would be interesting to address whether any disadvantages are associated with resilience. For example, there could be negative social implications of a resilient pattern in response to bereavement. In some cases, the resilient person may elicit negative reactions from others because others expect the bereaved to show more distress. Others may interpret low levels of distress as an indication of aloofness or indifference. In other cases, showing resilience may reflect positively on the bereaved because it is easier for others to be with a less-distressed person. Another intriguing question is what happens in families or other social groups when one person shows a low distress pattern after a loss, whereas the other members in this social system experience intense distress. In such a case, would those who are more distressed be likely to benefit from the presence or availability of a resilient person? Or, would the lack of congruence in the experience of individual members be more likely to lead to misunderstandings and individual coping efforts that interfere with one another? These questions are likely to assume considerable importance in couples following the death of a child. For example, one spouse may feel uncomfortable expressing feelings of distress about the loss if it appears that the partner is not as distressed (e.g., Wortman, Battle, & Lemkau, 1997). Future work addressing these questions would make an important contribution because people rarely face a loss in a social vacuum.

## Positive Emotions Are Typically Absent

### DESCRIPTION

The most influential theories of grief and loss, such as Freud's (1917/1957) psychoanalytic model and Bowlby's (1980) attachment model, emphasize the importance of working through the emotional pain associated with the loss. Amid the despair and anguish that often accompany grief, positive emotions may seem unwarranted, even inappropriate (Fredrickson, Tugade, Waugh, & Larkin, 2003). When they are mentioned at all, positive emotions are typically viewed as indicative of denial and as an impediment to the grieving process (Deutsch, 1937; Sanders, 1993; see Keltner & Bonanno, 1997, for a review). With notable exceptions (e.g., Folkman, 1997b, 2008; Folkman & Moskowitz, 2000; Fredrickson, 2001; Lazarus, Kanner, & Folkman, 1980), theories focusing specifically on the grieving process, or more generally on coping with adversity, have failed to consider the role that may be played by positive emotions.

In the 1980s, Wortman and her associates became interested in whether positive emotions were experienced by people who had encountered major losses, and if so, whether they could perhaps sustain hope and facilitate adjustment. Therefore, they decided to measure positive as well as negative emotions in two studies, one focusing on permanent paralysis following a spinal cord injury, and one focusing on loss of a child as a result of SIDS; see Wortman and Silver (1987) for a more detailed discussion. In conducting the first study, they encountered extreme resistance from the hospital staff, who felt it was "ridiculous" to ask people who were permanently disabled about their positive emotions. In the second study, they experienced similar problems from their interviewers, who did not want to ask people who had lost a child how many times they had felt happy in the past week. Only through careful pilot work and much persuading were they able to convince the staff, and the interviewers, that the project was indeed feasible and worthwhile.

## EVIDENCE FOR POSITIVE EMOTIONS FOLLOWING LOSS

Both of these studies provided evidence that positive emotions are quite prevalent following major loss. At 3 weeks following the death of their infant to SIDS, parents reported experiencing positive emotions such as happiness as frequently as they experienced negative feelings. By the second interview, conducted 3 months after the infant's death, positive affect was more prevalent than negative affect, and this continued to be the case at the third interview, conducted at 18 months after the loss. Respondents were asked to describe the intensity as well as the frequency of their feelings. These measures were included so that the investigators could determine whether negative feelings, although no more prevalent than positive ones, were more intense. However, this did not turn out to be the case. At all three interviews, feelings of happiness were found to be just as intense as feelings of sadness. In fact, at the second and third interviews, respondents reported that their feelings of happiness were significantly more intense than their feelings of sadness.

Subsequent studies have corroborated that positive emotions are surprisingly prevalent during bereavement. For example, when caregivers of men who died of AIDS were asked to talk about their experiences, about 80% evidenced positive emotions during the conversation, whereas only 61% conveyed negative emotions (Folkman, 1997a, 2001; Folkman & Moskowitz, 2000; Stein, Folkman, Trabasso, & Christopher-Richards, 1997). Except for just before and just after the death, caregivers' reports regarding positive states of mind were as high as community samples (Folkman, 1997a). Bonanno, Moskowitz, et al., examined positive affect scores of caregivers from eight months preloss to 8 months postloss. They demonstrated that the presence of positive emotions even within a few weeks before and after the death. Comparable findings have been obtained from a study that went beyond self-report data. At 6 months post-loss, Bonanno and Keltner (1997) coded facial expressions of conjugally bereaved respondents while they were talking about their relationship with the deceased. Videotapes of the interviews were then coded for the presence of genuine or "Duchenne" laughs or smiles, which involve movements in the muscles around the eyes. Positive emotion was exhibited by the majority of participants. Moreover, the presence of positive affect was associated with reduced grief at 14 and 25 months post-loss. Those who exhibited Duchenne laughs or smiles also evoked more favorable responses in observers (Keltner & Bonanno, 1997). In addition to rating them more positively overall, observers rated those who engaged in laughs and smiles as healthier, better adjusted, less frustrating, and more amusing. These findings suggest that one way positive emotions may facilitate coping with loss is by eliciting positive responses from those in the social environment.

### REVISED STRESS AND COPING MODEL

Drawing on her research on caregivers of men who died of AIDS, Folkman (1997b) concluded that it is important to learn more about how positive psychological states are generated and maintained during a major loss, as well as how they help to sustain coping efforts. In her revision of Lazarus and Folkman's original model of the coping process (1984), Folkman (1997b, 2001, 2008) has proposed that, when people are distressed as a result of a loss event, they can generate positive emotions by infusing ordinary events with positive meaning. This observation came about in an interesting way. In her study of caregiving partners of men with AIDS, Folkman (1997a) had initially focused exclusively on stressful aspects of the caregiving situation. Respondents were questioned about these aspects every 2 months. Shortly after the study began, several participants "reported that we were missing an important part of their experience by asking only about stressful events; they said we needed to ask about positive events as well if we were to understand how they coped with the stress of caregiving" (p. 1215). Consequently, Folkman added a question in which respondents were asked to describe "something you did, or something that happened to you, that made you feel good and that was meaningful to you and helped you get through the day" (p. 1215). Such events were reported by 99.5% of the respondents. Events focused on many different aspects of daily life, such as enjoying a good meal, receiving appreciation for something done for one's partner, or going to the movies with friends. Folkman has hypothesized that events of this sort generate positive emotion by helping people feel connected and cared about, by providing a sense of achievement and self-esteem, and by providing a respite or distraction from the stress of caregiving. She has suggested that engaging in activities that generate positive emotions, and positive emotions themselves, are likely to help sustain coping efforts in dealing with a stressful situation. Recent empirical evidence is consistent with this prediction. Positive affect is not only quite prevalent at times of adversity but also appears to ameliorate bereavement-related distress (Bonanno, Moskowitz et al., 2005; Moskowitz et al., 2003). For example, in a study on the role of daily positive emotions during bereavement, Ong, Bergeman, and Bisconti (2004) found that the stress–depression correlation was significantly reduced on days in which more positive emotion was experienced.

### BROADEN-AND-BUILD THEORY OF POSITIVE EMOTIONS

Another theory that has important implications for understanding the role that positive emotions may play in coping with loss is Fredrickson's broaden-and-build theory of positive emotions (Fredrickson, 1998, 2001; Fredrickson & Losada, 2005; Fredrickson et al., 2003). Fredrickson has maintained that positive emotions can broaden people's attention, thinking, and behavioral repertoire, bringing about an increase in flexibility, creativity, and efficiency and thereby improving their ways of coping with stress. She maintains that, over time, this helps people to accumulate important resources, including physical resources (e.g., health), social resources (e.g., friendships), intellectual resources (e.g., expert knowledge), and psychological resources (e.g., optimism). In brief, her work suggests that efforts to cultivate positive emotions in the aftermath of a stressful life experience will pay off in the short run by improving the person's subjective experience, undoing physiological arousal, and enhancing coping, and in the long term by building enduring resources.

## FUTURE DIRECTIONS

In subsequent work, it will be important to learn more about how people cultivate and maintain positive emotions in the midst of coping with a major loss. Are there particular strategies that people use to generate and maintain such emotions during a crisis? Are those with certain personality characteristics or belief systems (e.g., those with particular spiritual beliefs) more likely than others to experience positive emotions in the context of adversity? We also need to know more about the impact of positive emotions on adaptation to a major life event such as bereavement. Specific hypotheses could be derived from the Frederickson model, addressing the mechanisms through which positive emotions are thought to improve coping with stress. For example, one could assess whether those who experience positive emotions following a loss indeed show higher flexibility, creativity, and efficiency in terms of their thinking and coping behavior, and if so, whether this buffers the negative impact of the loss on people's adjustment. As Folkman (1997b) has pointed out, it would also be useful to determine whether positive psychological states must reach a certain level of intensity or duration in order to sustain or facilitate coping with loss. Future work in this area is particularly important because strategies that help generate positive emotions in the face of loss are a concrete tool that can be taught as part of an intervention (cf. Fredrickson, 2001). It will also be important to learn more about difficulties the bereaved may encounter in experiencing or expressing positive emotions following a loss. For example, some people may feel guilty if they enjoy something because their loved one is "missing out" on enjoyable experiences. Experiencing or expressing positive emotions may also make people feel that they are being disloyal toward their loved one.

## *The Importance of Working Through the Loss*
### DESCRIPTION

Among researchers as well as practitioners in the field of grief and loss, it has been commonly assumed that to adjust successfully to the death of a loved one, a person must "work through" the thoughts, memories, and emotions associated with the loss. The term *grief work* was originally coined by Freud (1917/1957), who maintained that "working through" our grief is critically important—a process we neglect at our peril. Although there is some debate about what it means to "work through" a loss, most grief theorists assert that it involves an active, ongoing effort to come to terms with the death. Implicit in our understanding of grief work is that it is not possible to resolve a loss without it. As Rando (1984) has stated, "For the griever who has not attended to his grief, the pain is as acute and fresh ten years later as it was the day after" (p. 114). Attempts to deny the implications of the loss, or block feelings or thoughts about it, are generally regarded as maladaptive. As noted earlier, this view of the grieving process has constituted the dominant perspective on bereavement for the past half century (Bonanno, 2001). It is only within the past several years that investigators have begun to question these ideas (see, e.g., Bonanno & Kaltman, 1999; Stroebe, 1992–1993; Wortman & Silver, 1989, 2001).

However, an examination of the most influential books on grief therapy suggests that clinicians still regard "working through" as a cornerstone of good treatment (see, e.g., Rando, 1993; Worden, 2008). Consequently, a major treatment goal for clinicians typically involves facilitating the expression of feelings and thoughts surrounding the loss (see Bonanno, 2001, for a more detailed discussion). Clinicians have also emphasized the importance of expressing negative feelings that are directed toward the deceased, such as anger or hostility (see, e.g., Lazare, 1989; Raphael, 1983). In fact, practitioners have frequently argued against the use of sedative drugs in the early phases of mourning because they may interfere with the process of "working through" the loss (see Jacobs, 1993, for a more detailed discussion). As Jacobs (1993) has indicated, such attitudes are prevalent among practicing clinicians despite the fact that there is "little or no evidence for the idea" (p. 254).

### EVIDENCE ON "THE VALUE OF WORKING THROUGH"

Over the past decade, several studies relevant to the construct of "working through" have appeared in the literature. These studies have assessed such constructs as confronting thoughts and reminders of the loss versus avoiding reminders and using distraction (e.g., Bonanno et al., 1995; Bonanno & Field, 2001; M. Stroebe & Stroebe, 1991), thinking about one's relationship with the loved one (e.g., Nolen-Hoeksema et al., 1997), verbally expressing or disclosing feelings of grief or distress (e.g., Lepore, Silver, Wortman, & Wayment, 1996), exhibiting negative facial expressions (e.g., Bonanno & Keltner, 1997; Keltner & Bonanno, 1997), or expressing one's feelings through writing about the loss (Lepore & Smyth, 2002; Pennebaker, Zech, & Rime, 2001; Smyth & Greenberg, 2000). These studies have provided limited support for the notion that "working through" is important for adjustment to the death of a loved one. Some have found support for the grief work hypothesis on only a few dependent measures, some have not found any support for this hypothesis, and some have reported findings that directly contradict this hypothesis.

## CONFRONTING VERSUS AVOIDING LOSS

In one of the earliest studies on grief work, M. Stroebe and Stroebe (1991) assessed five kinds of behaviors associated with confronting the loss of one's spouse (e.g., disclosed one's feelings to others) or with avoidance (e.g., avoided reminders), at 4 to 7 months, 14 months, and 2 years post-loss. At the final time point, there were no differences between widows who had showed evidence for confronting their loss at either of the first two time points and those who did not. However, different findings emerged for widowers. The less frequently they used avoidance as a coping strategy at prior time points, the greater was their improvement in depression scores at the final time point. Overall, these results provide limited support for the grief work hypothesis, leading M. Stroebe and Stroebe (1991) to conclude that the statement "'Everyone needs to do grief work' is an oversimplification" (p. 481).

In a study of gay men who lost a partner to AIDS, Nolen-Hoeksema and colleagues (1997) examined the impact of thinking about one's relationship with the partner versus avoiding such thoughts. Those who had thought about their life without their partner, and how they had changed as a result of the loss, showed more positive morale shortly after the death than those who did not. However, this group showed more depression over the 12 months following the loss.

In another study comparing those who used avoidant versus more confrontative coping styles (Bonanno et al., 1995; Bonanno & Field, 2001),

respondents who had lost a spouse were asked to talk about their relationship to the deceased, and their feelings about the loss, at the 6-month point following their loss. Physiological data assessing cardiovascular reactivity were also collected. Respondents who evidenced emotional avoidance (i.e., little emotion relative to their physiological reactivity) showed low levels of interviewer-rated grief throughout the 2-year study. Among respondents who initially showed emotional avoidance, there was no evidence of delayed grief. Although respondents with an avoidant style did show higher levels of somatic complaints at 6 months post-loss, these symptoms did not persist beyond the 6-month assessment and were not related to medical visits. Even stronger evidence for the adaptive benefits of emotional avoidance, also termed *repressive coping*" comes from a recent study of bereaved individuals who lost a spouse or parent (Coifman, Bonanno, Ray, & Gross, 2007). Emotional avoidance predicted fewer psychological symptoms and somatic complaints, a less significant medical history, and ratings of better adjustment from friends, both concurrently and over time (up to 18 months post-loss). No health costs of emotional avoidance were detected at any point in this study.

Taken together, the results of these studies indicate that, under some circumstances, confrontative coping is beneficial whereas, under other circumstances, it has no effect or has a detrimental impact on adjustment. In these studies, many respondents did not make an active, ongoing effort to confront the loss but nonetheless evidenced good adjustment following bereavement. Apparently, focusing attention away from one's emotional distress can be an effective means of coping with the loss of a loved one.

## TALKING ABOUT NEGATIVE FEELINGS

A study by Bonanno and Keltner (1997) casts doubt on the value of expressing negative feelings. These investigators assessed the expression of negative emotion in two ways: through self-report and through facial expressions. An advantage of studying facial expressions is that they can be assessed independently of self-report and even without participant awareness. Those who expressed negative feelings or manifested negative facial expressions while talking about the decreased 6 months post-loss showed higher interviewer-rated grief at 14 months post-loss. This was particularly the case for facial expressions of anger, the emotion most consistently believed by grief work theorists to require expression (Belitsky & Jacobs, 1986).

As Bonanno (2001) has indicated, it was not clear from this study whether the expression of negative emotions actually influenced subsequent grief, or whether individuals in a more acute state of grief merely tended to express more negative emotions—in other words, the expression of negative affect may have simply been a by-product of grief. To address this concern, Bonanno (2001) reanalyzed the facial expression data controlling for the initial level of grief and distress, which enabled him to isolate the extent to which expressing negative emotion was related to subsequent grief. Even under these stringent conditions, facial expressions of negative emotion were still related to increased grief at 14 months post-loss. These studies by Bonanno and his associates suggest that minimizing the expression of negative emotion results in reduced grief over time, which is just the opposite of what the grief work hypothesis would predict.

## WRITING ABOUT NEGATIVE FEELINGS

Pennebaker et al. (2001) agreed with Bonanno that results of prior studies were difficult to interpret because current distress is the best predictor of future distress, and high initial distress may merely be a reflection on grief. To provide a more convincing test of the value of expressing one's distress, Pennebaker and his associates developed an intervention that involved expression of emotion by writing about the trauma or loss. Participants are asked to write essays expressing their deepest thoughts and feelings about the most traumatic event they can remember. Control participants are asked to write about innocuous topics, such as their plans for the day. Typically, participants write for 20–30 minutes on several consecutive days (see, e.g., Pennebaker & Beall, 1986). When given these instructions, people are indeed willing to write about experiences that are very traumatic and upsetting. According to Pennebaker et al. (2001), "Deaths, abuse incidents, and tragic failures are common themes" (p. 530).

It has been shown that writing has a positive impact on health outcomes such as health center visits and immunologic status. The literature on the impact of writing on mood and psychological well-being is somewhat mixed (see Pennebaker et al., 2001, for a review; see also Chapter 18, by Pennebaker, & Chung, 2011, this volume). However, a meta-analysis suggests that overall, mood and psychological well-being being improve following writing. The results also indicate that writing can affect health outcomes as well as behavioral changes, such as an improvement in grades, or the ability to get a new job after being laid off. Hence, the results illustrate that the impact of writing is not restricted to any one outcome. Smyth's (1998) study suggested that the respondents who completed the writing task showed significant improvements in several domains. Specifically, they scored higher on reported physical health, psychological well-being, physiology functioning, and general functioning. The effect sizes that emerged in this study were similar in magnitude to those of other psychological interventions.

Do these writing effects apply to individuals who have lost a loved one? Pennebaker et al. (2001) have estimated that, across the studies conducted in his lab, approximately 20% of participants write about the death of a close friend or family member. According to these investigators, people who write about death benefit as much as people who write about other topics. However, studies focusing on the value of emotional expression among the bereaved have produced inconclusive findings (see M. Stroebe, Stroebe, Schut, Zech, & van den Bout, 2002, for a review). For example, Segal, Bogaards, Becker, and Chatman (1999) conducted a study with elderly people who had lost a spouse an average of 16 months previously. Respondents were instructed to talk into a tape recorder about the loss and to express their deepest feelings. When compared with a delayed treatment control condition, those who expressed their feelings showed a slight but nonsignificant improvement in hopelessness. No significant effects emerged on other measures of distress, such as depression and intrusion/avoidance.

Two studies by Range and her associates (Kovac & Range, 2000; Range, Kovac, & Marion, 2000) also fail to support the value of written emotional expression among the bereaved. In the first study (Range et al., 2000), undergraduates who had experienced the loss of a friend or family member as a result of an accident or a homicide were asked to write about their deepest thoughts and feelings surrounding the death. A control group was asked to write about a trivial issue. The results revealed that both groups showed improvements in symptoms of depression, anxiety, and grief during the course of the study. There was no indication of greater improvement among respondents who were assigned to express their feelings. There were also no differences among the two groups in doctor visits. In the second study, people who had lost a loved one to suicide were invited to express their deepest feelings or to write about a trivial issue. The study included many dependent measures such as intrusion/avoidance, doctors' visits, and grief. On the majority of measures, there were no differences between the groups. Similar results were also obtained in an intervention study by Bower, Kemeny, Taylor, and Fahey (2003). Women who had lost a close relative to breast cancer were assigned to write about the death or about neutral topics. Writing did not appear to facilitate adaptation to the loss.

Stroebe et al. (2002) conducted two exceptionally well-designed studies to determine whether expression of emotions facilitates recovery among the bereaved. In the first study, the authors focused on disclosures of emotion made by the bereaved in everyday life. A large sample of people who had lost a spouse were asked to complete a questionnaire designed to assess disclosure of emotion to others at four points over a 2-year period. The results provided no evidence that disclosure facilitated adjustment to loss. In the second study, people who lost a spouse from 4 to 8 months previously were randomly assigned to one of three writing conditions or to a no-writing control condition. Participants in the first writing condition were instructed to focus on their emotions. Those in the second condition were told to focus on problems and difficulties they have to deal with as a result of the death. The final group was asked to focus on both their feelings and problems. The results of this study provided no evidence whatsoever for a general beneficial effect of emotional expression. None of the experimental groups was better off than control respondents on any measures.

To determine whether the emotional expression of grief may be beneficial under specific conditions, M. Stroebe et al. (2002) further examined whether writing effects were a function of the type of loss. When they compared bereaved participants who expected the loss with those who had encountered a sudden, unexpected loss, there was no indication that emotional expression through writing was more beneficial for the latter group. They also investigated whether the expression of emotions may work only among people who have not yet had much opportunity to disclose their feelings. However, they found no evidence to suggest that those who had rarely disclosed their feelings in the past benefited more from the writing intervention than those who had disclosed their feelings more frequently. In fact, these investigators found that low disclosers were less likely to suffer from intrusive thoughts, and had fewer doctor visits, than did high disclosers.

Similar findings were obtained by Seery, Silver, Holman, Ence, and Chu (2007) in a study of the impact of expressive thoughts following the September 11, 2001 catastrophe. Members of a large, representative sample were given the opportunity to express their feelings about the terrorist attacks of September 11, 2001 on that day and the following few days. Follow-up surveys were conducted to assess mental and physical health outcomes over the next 2 years. Contrary to expectation, participants who chose not to express any initial reactions to the attacks reported better outcomes over time than did those who expressed feelings about the attacks. Among respondents who chose to express their reactions at the time of the attacks, longer responses were associated with worse outcomes over time. These results suggest that rather than indicating pathology, reluctance to express negative feelings appears to reflect resilience in the face of trauma.

## GRIEF WORK, AVOIDANCE, AND RUMINATION

Bonanno, Papa, Lalande, Zhang, and Noll (2005) conducted a study on grief processing and deliberate grief avoidance among bereaved spouses and parents in two cultures: the United States and the People's Republic of China. These investigators tested different versions of the grief work hypothesis, using a comprehensive measure of grief processing that included thinking and talking about the deceased, having positive memories, expressing feelings, and searching for meaning. They also developed a measure of grief avoidance that included avoidance of thinking, talking, and expressing feelings about the deceased. This study addressed (a) the traditional hypothesis that grief processing was a necessary step toward positive adjustment, and that the absence of grief processing reflects avoidance or denial; (b) the conditional hypothesis that grief work may be beneficial for those with severe grief; and (c) another modified hypothesis that grief work was more akin to rumination, with the prediction that those who scored high on grief processing initially would continue to score high on this measure and show poorer adjustment at the 18-month follow-up than those who did not score high on initial grief processing.

Support was found for the third but not for the first two hypotheses. Grief processing and avoidance each predicted poorer adjustment for U.S. participants, even for those who had shown more severe grief initially. The authors interpreted this as contradictory to both the traditional and the conditional grief work hypothesis but as consistent with the grief work as rumination hypothesis. Grief processing and avoidance did not emerge as significant predictors of outcome among the Chinese participants, which may have reflected cultural differences in terms of mourning rituals and practices. Overall, the authors concluded that these findings cast doubt on the usefulness of grief processing and argued that it may be inadvisable to encourage the bereaved to focus on processing the loss.

When reviewing the different studies that have tested the grief work hypothesis, it is important to keep in mind how grief work was conceptualized in each study, and how this may have affected the findings. For example, it is possible that Bonanno, Papa, et al. (2005) failed to find positive effects of grief processing because their grief processing measure included the expression of feelings, which, as discussed previously, has been found to predict worse outcome in some studies, and searching for meaning, which may be regarded as reflective of ruminative thinking. There is evidence that rumination, if defined as engaging in thoughts and behaviors that maintain one's focus on negative emotions (Nolen-Hoeksema, 1991), heightens distress, interferes with problem solving, and may drive away potential supporters.

More recently, it has been argued that rumination represents a form of avoidance and that it should be distinguished from other efforts to confront the reality of the death, such as finding meaning in loss or making plans for one's life beyond the loss. The idea is that rumination tends to involves a deliberate pondering on a narrow aspect of the loss (e.g., the event leading up to it and what one could have done to prevent it), a focus that prevents the person from "facing up to the reality of the loss" (Stroebe et al., 2007; p. 470). This reconceptualization of rumination as avoidance is in line with findings by Boelen and colleagues that rumination (e.g., thinking about who is to blame for the death) and behavioral avoidance (avoiding places that remind of the deceased) items loaded on a single factor (Boehlen, van den Bout, & van den Hout, 2006). This finding and the related conceptual discussion of the nature of rumination underscore the importance of identifying the content and focus of thoughts and actions pertaining to the loss, rather than relying on simple contrasting of broad concepts such as confrontation and avoidance.

**FUTURE DIRECTIONS**

In future work, it will be important to include separate assessments of constructs pertaining to working through, such as thinking about the loss, talking about what has happened, crying, or searching for meaning. This would help to clarify how these constructs are related to one another and to identify the role played by each in the process of recovery. When comparing findings from different studies on this issue, and in particular when drawing conclusions about adaptiveness, it is extremely important to be clear about what kind of grief processing is talked about in each specific case. This also leads to the more general question regarding what kind of grief processing may be beneficial for whom, and under which circumstances. For example, one reason the literature on "working through" may be so inconsistent is because some studies may have included people who did not need to "work through" what happened, some who may have been reluctant to engage fully in the process, and some who were made worse by being required to confront the trauma. Those who may have difficulty expressing their emotions may benefit the most from interventions such as writing about their experience (Lumley, Tojeck, & Macklem, 2002; Norman, Lumley, Dooley, & Diamond, 2004). Furthermore, it is possible that "working through" may be more beneficial for certain kinds of events, such as those that are particularly traumatic and/or likely to shatter the survivors' views of the world. We also need to know more about the conditions under which emotional expression reduces the bereaved person's distress, helps him or her to gain insight or cognitively structure what has happened, and helps to elicit support and encouragement from others. Hopefully, subsequent research will assist us in specifying the conditions under which "working through" one's loss is more or less likely to be beneficial, and if it is indicated, how this grief processing needs to be done to truly facilitate recovery and adjustment.

### Breaking Down Attachments
#### DESCRIPTION

According to the traditional view on grief, espoused by Freud (1917/1957) and other psychoanalytic writers (e.g., Volkan, 1971), it is necessary to disengage from the deceased in order to get on with life. These writers believed that, for grief work to be completed, the bereaved person must withdraw energy from the deceased and thus free him- or herself from attachment to an unavailable person. This view remained influential for many years, with its advocates maintaining that if attachments are not broken down, the bereaved will be unable to invest his or her energy in new relationships or activities. It is generally believed that bereaved people accomplish this task by carefully reviewing thoughts and memories of the deceased, as well as both positive and negative aspects of the relationship (see, e.g., Rando, 1993; Raphael, 1983). Clinicians have traditionally maintained that the failure to break down bonds with the deceased is indicative of a need for treatment. Until recently, relinquishing the tie to the deceased has been a major goal of grief therapy (see, e.g., Humphrey & Zimpfer, 1996; Raphael & Nunn, 1988; Sanders, 1989).

During the past decade, this view has been called into question (see Stroebe & Schut, 2005, for a review). Indeed, an increasing number of researchers now believe that it is normal to maintain a continuing connection to the deceased, and that such a connection may actually promote good adjustment to the loss (Attig, 1996; Klass, Silverman, & Nickman, 1996; Neimeyer, 1998; Shmotkin, 1999). Others have maintained that it is time to move beyond the dichotomy of disengagement versus continuing connection (Boerner & Heckhausen; 2003; Russac, Steighner, & Canto, 2002). For example, Boerner and Heckhausen (2003) conceptualized adaptive bereavement as a process of transforming mental ties to the deceased that involves features of both disengagement and continuing connection. They further proposed that this process of transforming the relationship occurs by substituting mental representations of the deceased for the lost relationship. Some mental representations may simply reflect experiences that are retrieved from memory (e.g., remembering what the deceased said in a particular situation). Others may be newly constructed by adding new aspects to one's preexisting image (e.g., imagining what the deceased would say). Boerner and Heckhausen (2003) also noted that different ways of transforming the relationship may be more or less adaptive for a particular person. Stroebe and Schut (2005) extended this view by arguing that certain types of continuing bonds, as well as certain types of relinquishing bonds, can be helpful or harmful. Their notion of relinquishing ties, however, is one of "relocating" rather than "forgetting" the deceased, reflecting the idea of transforming the nature of the relationship to symbolic, internalized, imagined levels of relatedness (Boerner & Heckhausen, 2003; Shuchter & Zisook, 1993; Stroebe & Schut, 2005).

Historically, one of the first theorists to question the importance of breaking down attachments was Bowlby (1980). In his later writings, Bowlby maintained that continuing attachments to the deceased, such as sensing his or her presence or talking with him or her, can provide an important sense of continuity and facilitate adjustment to the loss. A similar view has been expressed by Hagman (1995, 2001), who argued that there had been too much emphasis on relinquishment of the bond with the deceased. In fact, Hagman indicated that, in some cases, it is more adaptive to restructure one's memories of the deceased so as to allow a continuing connection. In their influential book, *Continuing Bonds*, Klass et al. (1996) also emphasized the potential value of maintaining a connection with the deceased. These investigators noted that their training led them to expect grief resolution to be accompanied by breaking down attachments to the deceased. However, this is not what they found in their research or in their clinical work. Instead, their work indicated that most people experienced a continuing connection with the deceased and that these connections "provided solace, comfort, and support, and eased the transition from the past to the future" (p. xvii).

Just as it was previously maintained that breaking the bond between the bereaved and deceased should be an important goal of therapy, many clinicians now argue that such bonds should be facilitated as part of bereavement counseling. Silverman and Nickman (1996) concluded that the tie between the bereaved and the deceased loved one should be viewed as a strengthening resource, and that it should be explicitly encouraged in bereavement interventions. Along similar lines, Fleming and Robinson (1991) have argued that it is important for the bereaved to confront such questions as what he or she has learned from the deceased, and how he or she has changed as a result of the relationship with the deceased. Neimeyer (2000, 2001) has proposed a number of innovative methods for developing an ongoing connection with the deceased, such as writing a biographical sketch of the deceased or writing letters to the deceased along with imaginary answers, which are to be written by the bereaved from the deceased person's perspective. Other investigators have provided specific suggestions about how to learn more about the deceased and his or her possible influence on one's life. For example, Attig (2000) has indicated that it can be helpful to explore records such as letters or diaries, as well as sharing memories with others who knew the deceased. He has suggested that the bereaved can benefit considerably by talking with people who may have a different perspective on the deceased. For example, a wife might seek out opportunities to talk with her deceased husband's coworkers, or parents may make an effort to talk with the friends of their deceased adolescent son.

## EVIDENCE FOR PREVALENCE AND TYPES OF CONTINUING CONNECTIONS

Does empirical evidence support the view that continuing attachments to the deceased are common, and that they facilitate good adjustment? Since the 1970s, studies have appeared in the literature suggesting that many forms of attachment to the deceased are common (see, e.g., Glick, Weiss, & Parkes, 1974; Parkes & Weiss, 1983; Rees, 1971). The most frequently studied forms of attachment include sensing the presence of the deceased, seeing the deceased as protecting or watching over oneself, and talking to the deceased (see Klass & Walter, 2001, for a review). For example, Zisook and Shuchter (1993) found that 13 months after their spouse's death, 63% of the respondents indicated that they feel their spouse is with them at times, 47% indicated that he or she is watching out for them, and 34% reported that they talk with their spouse regularly. Similar results have been reported by Stroebe and Stroebe (1991), who found that 2 years following the death of a spouse, a third of the bereaved still sensed the presence of the deceased. Results suggesting a continuing connection between the deceased and the bereaved have also been reported by Bonanno, Mihalecz, and LeJeune (1999) in a study of the emotional themes that emerge during bereavement. These investigators have reported that, 6 months after the loss, more than 80% of the bereaved described emotional themes indicative of an enduring positive bond. Similar findings were obtained by Richards, Acree, and Folkman (1999) in their study of bereavement among caregivers of men who died of AIDS. These investigators reported that 3–4 years post-loss, 70% of the bereaved caregivers reported an ongoing inner relationship with their deceased partner. Continuing ties with the deceased took many forms: some deceased partners were thought to serve as guides, some were believed to be present at times, and some "talked with" the bereaved partner. A sense of closeness with the deceased persisted even though most of the men had made life changes (e.g., changing jobs or living situations). As Richards et al. (1999) have indicated, "The continued relationship to the deceased did not appear to be an aspect of clinging to the past but, rather, a part of a reorganized present where the deceased assumed a new position in the living partner's world scheme" (pp. 122–123).

Data from the Harvard Child Bereavement Study (Silverman & Worden, 1992) indicate that it is common for children to maintain a connection with deceased parents. Silverman and Nickman (1996) reported that 4 months after losing a parent, 74% of the children had located their parent in heaven, and most viewed the parent as watching out for them. Moreover, nearly 60% of the children reported that they talked with the deceased parent, and 43% indicated that they received an answer. A year following the loss, these attachment behaviors were still very prevalent, with nearly 40% of the children indicating that they talked with their deceased parent.

There has also been interest in connections in which the deceased loved one serves as a moral compass or guide (see, e.g., Klass & Walter, 2001; Marwit & Klass, 1996). Although this form of continuing bond has received less study than those mentioned earlier, Glick, Weiss, and Parkes (1974) found that at 1 year following the loss, 69% of those who lost a spouse expressed agreement with the statement that they try to behave as the deceased would want them to. Similarly, Stroebe and Stroebe (1991) found that at 2 years following the death of their spouse, half of the respondents indicated that they consulted the bereaved when they had to make a decision. Several similar kinds of attachment behavior have been described in the literature, including relying on the deceased as a role model, incorporating virtues of the deceased into one's character, working to further the deceased's interests or values, and reflecting on the deceased person's life and/or death to clarify current values or value conflicts (Marwit & Klass, 1996; Normand, Silverman, & Nickman, 1996).

In a related study, Field, Gal-Oz, and Bonanno (2003) assessed the frequency of a wide variety of attachment behaviors. They included such items as attempting to carry out the deceased's wishes, having inner conversations with the deceased, taking on the spouse's values or interests, using the spouse as a guide in making decisions, reminiscing with others about the spouse, experiencing the spouse as continuing to live through oneself, having fond memories of the spouse, and seeing the spouse as a loving presence in one's life. The results indicated that most of these types of connection were quite prevalent even at 5 years after the loss. On average, participants endorsed these items in the range of "moderately true." Items that received the highest scores included keeping things that belonged to one's spouse, enjoying reminiscing with others about one's spouse, seeing the spouse as a loving presence in one's life, expressing awareness of the positive influence of one's spouse on who one is today, and having fond memories of one's spouse. Items endorsed less frequently at 5 years post-loss included seeking out things that remind one of the spouse, awareness of taking on one's spouse's values or interests, and having conversations with one's spouse.

## CONTINUING CONNECTIONS AND ADAPTATION

Although many studies have examined the prevalence of continuing connections to the deceased among the bereaved, only a few have examined the relationship between such connections and adaptation to the loss. These studies have yielded inconclusive evidence. In studies assessing the frequency of sensing the presence of the deceased or talking with him or her, the majority of respondents experience these encounters as comforting (Klass & Walter, 2001). Silverman and Nickman (1996) have also noted that the ties that children developed with their deceased parents were apparently beneficial. Many children made spontaneous comments such as "It feels good to think about him." In fact, when the children were asked what they would advise another bereaved child to do, they gave answers such as "Just think of them as often as you can." However, as other investigators have noted (cf. Fraley & Shaver, 1999), a significant number of survivors report that ongoing connections are not always comforting. For example, nearly 60% of the children in the study by Silverman and Nickman (1996) indicated that they were "scared" by the idea that their parents could watch them from heaven. In fact, some children regarded their deceased parent as a ghost whose presence was frightening and unpredictable (Normand, Silverman, & Nickman, 1996). In a follow-up analysis of these data, Silverman, Baker, Cait, and Boerner (2003) found that many of the children who showed emotional and behavioral problems after the loss had a continuing bond with the deceased that was primarily negative. These "high-risk" children carried troubling legacies related to their deceased parent's health, personality, or role in the family. Health-related legacies, for example, reflected children's fear that they will die from the same condition or disease that killed their parent. Role-related legacies reflected children's sense that they needed to assume the role in the family that was once filled by the parent, creating a burden that was clearly too heavy for these children.

Datson and Marwit (1997) found that 60% of those who had lost a loved one within the previous 4 years reported sensing the presence of their deceased loved one at some point, and the vast majority (86%) regarded the experience as comforting. However, those who reported that they had sensed the presence of their loved one scored higher in neuroticism than those who did not. These findings suggest that, in some cases, sensing the presence of the deceased loved one may be more an indication of greater distress than a sign of good adjustment.

In a study by Field, Nichols, Holen, and Horowitz (1999), interviewers rated the extent to which bereaved individuals manifested four different kinds of attachment behaviors 6 months after the loss. Those who tended to maintain the deceased person's possessions as they were when he or she was alive, or who tended to make excessive use of the deceased's possessions for comfort, exhibited more severe grief symptoms over the course of the 25-month study. These respondents also showed less of a decrease in grief symptoms over time. Attachment strategies that involved sensing the deceased spouse's presence, or seeking comfort through memories of their loved one, were not related to the intensity of grief. These findings suggest that whether continuing bonds are adaptive or maladaptive may depend on the form that the connection takes.

To address this question, Field et al. (2003) conducted a follow-up study on this same sample, in which they assessed a wide variety of attachment behaviors at 5 years post-loss (see earlier discussion). Results showed that each of the continuing bond items, as well as a composite score based on all of the items that were assessed, was associated with more severe grief as assessed 6 months after the death. There was a strong positive correlation between continuing bonds assessed 5 years after the death and grief assessed at the same time point. The relationship between continuing bonds and other forms of well-being was much weaker, suggesting that the relationship between continuing bonds and adjustment is largely restricted to grief-related measures.

In another study, Field and Friedrichs (2004) examined the use of attachment behaviors as a way of coping with the death of a husband. Fifteen early-bereaved widows (4 months post-loss) and 15 later-bereaved widows (more than 2 years) completed continuing bond and mood measures four times each day for 14 consecutive days. Greater use of continuing bond coping was related to more positive mood among the later- but not the early-bereaved, and more negative mood in both groups. Furthermore, in time-lagged analyses, greater use of continuing bond coping was predictive of a shift toward more negative mood among early-bereaved but not among later-bereaved widows. These findings suggest that continuing bond coping may be less effective in mood regulation earlier than later on after the death. As the authors noted, however, neither this nor the prior two studies allowed for an investigation of the direction of causality between continuing bonds and grief symptoms. Hence, it is not clear whether continuing bonds are simply correlates of bereavement-related distress or whether the formation of such bonds in fact plays a causal role in impending adjustment to bereavement. In fact, it has been argued that the association between continuing bonds and grief intensity is at least partially due to conceptual overlap between the two constructs, and that this may have led to overestimating the strength of this association (Schut, Stroebe, Boelen, & Zijkerveld, 2006). This group of researchers conducted a prospective analysis of continuing bonds (7–12 months post-loss) and grief (9 months later; Boelen, Stroebe, Schut, and Zijkerveld, 2006). In order to deal with the conceptual overlap between continuing bonds and grief symptoms, they removed continuing bonds–like items from the grief scale. They found that maintaining bonds through comforting memories, but not cherishing possessions of the deceased, continued to predict later grief symptoms severity. Thus, when considered together, the available studies demonstrate that continuing bonds should not be regarded as exclusively adaptive.

In summary, our belief in the value of continuing attachments between the bereaved and the deceased has shifted markedly over the past few decades. Initially, it was believed that it was essential to break down ties to the deceased. At present, such ties are widely regarded as normal and generally beneficial. Because so few studies have examined the role such ties may play in adjustment to loss, there is little evidence to support this current view. In fact, the few studies that have explored the matter suggest that continuing bonds are sometimes adaptive and sometimes maladaptive.

## FUTURE DIRECTIONS

In future work, it will be important to learn more about whether certain kinds of continuing bonds may facilitate good adjustment while others do not. Some types of behaviors may in fact reflect the presence of continuing bonds, whereas others may signal the presence of other psychological processes. Maintaining the deceased person's possessions as they were, for example, may reflect failure to accept the loss rather than a continuing attachment to the deceased.

Results of the studies by Field et al. (1999, 2003) also suggest that whether continuing bonds are adaptive may depend on how much time has elapsed since the death. At this point, we do not know whether

those who make the best adjustments to a loss experience continuing bonds for several years into the future, or whether these bonds gradually fade over time as the bereaved become involved in other relationships and activities. By examining a large and representative class of continuing bonds from shortly after the loss through the next several years, it should be possible to address critical questions about the possible causal role continuing bonds may play in facilitating adjustment. Such questions could also be addressed through experimental studies in which respondents are randomly assigned to participate in exercises believed to promote continuing bonds, such as discussions about what the deceased loved one has meant to them.

Even if continuing bonds are generally found to facilitate adjustment, it is important to identify conditions under which this is not the case. Negative legacies from past relationships can be related to aspects of the deceased's life (e.g., burdensome responsibilities that were once filled by the deceased, such as caring for an elderly relative, that now fall on the bereaved), or to aspects of the relationship with the deceased (e.g., if the relationship was abusive or destructive in other ways). If the bereaved is left with such a negative legacy, what kind of a connection to the deceased, if any, should the bereaved attempt to develop? In some cases, perhaps reviewing the relationship, and the negative legacy that is attached to this relationship, can help the bereaved to attain important self-knowledge. However, it may be this self-knowledge (e.g., I deserved to be with someone who treated me better), rather than a positive tie with the deceased, that is helpful to the person under such conditions.

In the process of clarifying the relationship between various continuing bonds and adjustment, it would be valuable to have a greater understanding about how particular sorts of connections are experienced and perceived by the bereaved. For example, although it is common for the bereaved to talk with the deceased and to report that this is comforting, little is known about what transpires in such conversations or what psychological needs they may fulfill. It will also be important to determine whether circumstances exist that might impede or facilitate the development of continuing bonds that facilitate adjustment. For example, the opportunity to talk with others who knew and valued the deceased may help to facilitate the development of such bonds. It may be more difficult for the bereaved to develop such bonds following particular kinds of losses, such as a loss that cannot be acknowledged or shared

(Boerner & Heckhausen, 2003). Finally, future research should address not only the conditions under which continuing bonds are beneficial, but also try to identify conditions under which the relinquishment of such bonds may promote better adjustment to bereavement (see Field, Gao, & Paderna, 2005; Stroebe & Schut, 2005).

## Expectations About Recovery

### DESCRIPTION

Traditionally, it has been believed that once people have completed the process of "working through" the loss and "relinquishing their ties to the deceased," they will reach a state of recovery. Most prior work has conceptualized recovery in terms of a return to prebereavement or baseline levels of psychological distress. As Weiss (1993) has emphasized, however, it is important to examine a broader set of indicators when trying to determine whether a person has recovered from a loss. These include freedom from intrusive or disturbing thoughts and the ability to encounter reminders without intense pain; the ability to give energy to everyday life; the ability to experience pleasure when desirable, hoped-for or enriching events occur; hopefulness about the future and being able to make and carry out future plans; and the ability to function well in social roles such as spouse, parent, and member of the community.

In the past, bereavement has been viewed as a time-limited process, with people resuming "normal life" once they reach the end point (Malkinson, 2001). It was sometimes assumed that grief work would be completed in approximately 12 months (Malkinson, 2001; Wortman & Silver, 2001), although most discussions of recovery did not include a specific time frame. Those who failed to recover after an "appropriate" amount of time were often viewed as displaying "chronic" grief (see, e.g., Jacobs, 1993), a pattern of grieving that has been regarded as an indication of "pathological mourning" (Middleton et al., 1993). Over the past decade, however, this view of the recovery process has begun to change. Malkinson (2001) has noted that at this point, the 12-month time period is viewed as "mythological" and that there is wide recognition that the process can take far longer.

Moreover, recovery is no longer viewed as a process with a discrete end point. As widows and widowers sometimes express it, "You don't get over it, you get used to it" (Weiss, 1993, p. 277). Several investigators have pointed out that terms like *resolution* and *recovery* are becoming unpopular, and that they are not applicable to most losses because they imply a once-and-for-all closure that does not occur (see, e.g., Klass, Silverman, & Nickman, 1996; Rando, 1993; Stroebe, Hansson et al., 2001; Weiss, 1993). Similarly, there is a growing consensus that bereaved individuals may never return to their pre-loss state. Weiss (1993) has argued that a major loss will almost invariably produce changes in a person's character. Miller and Omarzu (1998) have suggested that returning to one's pre-loss state may not be an optimal goal. As Malkinson (2001) has expressed it, recovery can be "a lifelong process of struggling to find the balance between what was and what is" (p. 675).

### EVIDENCE FOR CHRONICITY

Empirical evidence suggests that while most bereaved individuals do not seem to experience intense distress for extended periods of time (see the earlier section on the expectation of intense distress), a significant minority of people develop long-term difficulties. This was found in the longitudinal studies mentioned previously that included several post-loss time points and provided evidence for different patterns of grief. "Chronic" grief, which involved scoring consistently high in distress at post-loss time points, was found among 30% of participants in the study on the loss of a child from SIDS (Wortman & Silver, 1987), and anywhere between 8% and 26% in studies on conjugal loss (24% in Bonanno et al., 1995; 13% in Bournstein et al., 1973; 8% in Lund et al., 1986; 26% in Vachon, Rogers et al., 1982; and 20% in Zisook & Shuchter, 1986). Recent caregiving studies have found similar percentages for the chronic grief trajectory among bereaved caregivers (ranging from 8% to 17%; e.g., Aneshensel et al., 2004; Zhang et al., 2008). It should be noted that the highest percentage of respondents showing a pattern of consistently high levels of distress following the loss came from the study on death of a child to SIDS (Wortman & Silver, 1987). Another important consideration is the striking difference among the studies on conjugal loss in the percentage of respondents evidencing chronic grief. This may be related to differences in the age of the respondents, and hence the untimeliness of the loss. For example, the study by Lund et al. (1986) focused on elderly bereaved, whereas the study by Vachon, Rogers, et al. (1982) focused on loss of a spouse at midlife.

In our prospective work on conjugal loss (Bonanno et al., 2002), the availability of pre-loss data made it possible to further distinguish a chronic grief pattern, in which respondents scored low before the loss and consistently high afterward (16%), from chronic depression (8%), which involved scoring high prior to the loss and at all post-loss time points. To further elucidate the nature of these patterns, Bonanno et al. (2002) identified their pre-loss predictors. Chronic grievers were likely to have had healthy spouses, to rate their marriage positively, and to show high levels of pre-loss dependency (e.g., agreeing that no one could take the spouse's place). The chronically depressed group was less positive about their marriage than were chronic grievers, but as dependent on their spouse. Further analyses examined the context and processing of the loss at 6 and 18 months post-loss (Bonanno et al., 2004). Results indicate that chronic grief stems from an enduring struggle with cognitive and emotional distress related to the loss, whereas chronic depression results more from enduring emotional difficulties that are exacerbated by the loss. For example, at 6 months post-loss, chronic grievers were more likely to report current yearning and emotional pangs, and they reported thinking and talking about the deceased more often than did chronically depressed individuals.

Most classic grief theorists (e.g., Jacobs, 1993) discuss the notion of chronic grief but fail to indicate how long it typically lasts and whether it abates at some point. To address this issue, we conducted a follow-up analysis investigating whether the chronic grievers and the chronically depressed would remain distressed up to 48 months post-loss (Boerner et al., 2005). Overall, the chronic grief group experienced an intense and prolonged period of distress. Measures of outcome and processing the loss measures, however, indicated a turn toward better adjustment by the 48-month time point, which suggests that this group does not remain chronically distressed as a result of the loss. In contrast, the chronically depressed group clearly demonstrated long-term problems, with little indication of improvement between 18 and 48 months. This group not only showed the poorest adjustment 4 years after the loss but also struggled the most with questions about meaning. These differential findings for the chronic grief and chronic depression group underscore the need to further refine the criteria that are used to identify those who are at risk for long-term problems.

## RISK FACTORS

Over the past decade, it has become increasingly clear that reactions to loss are highly variable, but that a significant minority shows enduring effects. Consequently, researchers have become interested in identifying factors that may promote or impede successful adjustment to the death of a loved one. Studying risk factors has the potential to advance

bereavement theory by helping to clarify the mechanisms through which loss influences subsequent mental and physical health. Perhaps even more important, knowledge about risk factors can aid in the identification of people who may benefit from bereavement interventions.

Several broad classes of risk factors have been studied in the literature (see Archer, 1999; Jordan & Neimeyer, 2003; and Stroebe & Schut, 2001; Stroebe, Schut, & Stroebe, 2007, for reviews). These include *demographic factors,* such as age, gender, and socioeconomic status; *background factors,* including whether the respondent has a history of mental health problems or substance abuse, or has experienced prior losses or traumas; *factors describing the type and nature of the relationship,* such as whether it was a child, spouse, or sibling who was lost and whether the relationship was emotionally close or conflictual; *personal and social resources,* including personality traits, attachment history, religiosity, and social support; and *the context in which the loss occurs,* which refers to the circumstances surrounding the death, whether the surviving loved one was involved in caregiving, the type and quality of the death, and the presence of concomitant stressors such as ill health of the surviving loved one. A comprehensive review of these risk factors is beyond the scope of this chapter. However, in this section, we wish to highlight selected areas of research on risk factors that we believe are of emerging interest and importance.

Most of the research on *gender differences* following the loss of a loved one has focused on the loss of a spouse. There is clear evidence that, in comparison to married controls, widowed men are more likely to become depressed and to experience greater mortality than are widowed women (see Stroebe et al., 2007, and Miller & Wortman, 2002, for reviews). Interestingly, such deaths are especially likely among younger bereaved men. Major causes of death among bereaved men include alcohol-related illness, accidents and violence, suicide, and chronic ischemic heart disease.

One possible explanation for these gender differences is that men may benefit more from marriage than do women, and may therefore be more adversely affected when the marriage ends. Consistent with this view, several studies have shown that women typically have many more close social relationships than men, who rely primarily on their wives for support. In addition, women usually perform more housework and child care than do men. Because men often rely on their wives in these domains, they may find it difficult to handle these matters on their own. However, research suggests that, although social ties and household responsibilities are related to gender differences following conjugal loss, they account for relatively little variance in the relationship between widowhood and mortality or depression (Miller & Wortman, 2002).

A second mechanism that may account for gender differences has been suggested by Umberson (1987, 1992), who has demonstrated that women typically take greater responsibility for their partner's health care, diet, nutrition, and exercise than do men. For example, married women are typically the ones who schedule doctor appointments and regular checkups for themselves and their spouses. They are also more likely to monitor whether their husbands are taking prescribed medications, and to offer reminders if necessary. Married women are also more likely to place constraints on negative health behavior, such as drinking and driving. Umberson concludes that the poor health of men following the death of their spouse is caused in part by the loss of this positive influence on their health behavior.

Studies of child loss have consistently found that mothers experience more distress than do fathers. Available research indicates that this is the case following perinatal death, death in infancy or childhood, and the death of older children (see Archer, 1999, for a review). Women also show higher distress than men following several different kinds of child loss. Dyregrov and her associates (2003) conducted a study of the predictors of grief among parents who lost a child through suicide, accidents, or SIDS. Across all three samples, mothers evidenced higher levels of posttraumatic reactions and complicated mourning than fathers. Mothers also experienced more intrusive thoughts, bodily symptoms, depression, anxiety, and grief than did fathers. Gender differences among parents who suffered different kinds of loss also emerged in a study conducted by Murphy and her associates (Murphy, Chung, & Johnson, 2002; Murphy, Das Gupta et al., 1999; Murphy, Johnson, Chung, & Beaton, 2003; Murphy, Johnson, & Wu, 2003). Parents who lost a child as a result of an accident, suicide, or homicide were interviewed at several points in time following the death. These investigators found significant gender differences on many indices of mental distress, including depression, anxiety, somatic complaints, and cognitive functioning. In each case, mothers scored higher than fathers. Women continued to show greater overall distress

than men as the study continued. In fact, gender was one of the best predictors of changes in distress over time. Mental distress of fathers showed a greater decline over time than the mental distress of mothers (Murphy, Chung, & Johnson, 2002).

Available research suggests that gender differences also exist in the coping strategies that are most helpful in dealing with the death of a spouse or child (see Archer, 1999, for a review). In a treatment study conducted by Schut et al., for example, widows showed a greater decline in distress following counseling that focused on day-to-day problems. In contrast, widowers showed a greater decline following counseling that facilitated emotional expression. According to Archer, such findings reflect a sociocultural pattern of gender differences involving the inhibition of emotional expression by boys and men. A similar pattern of findings emerged from studies on how parents cope with the death of a child. Mothers typically deal with such a loss by seeking support or by communicating with other family members. In contrast, fathers attempt to conceal their feelings, which they claim is to protect their wives. Interestingly, wives often tend to complain that their husbands are not willing to share their feelings (see Archer, 1999 for a more detailed discussion).

Murphy, Das Gupta et al. (1999) report findings consistent with this view. Their results showed an interesting shift in the symptom patterns for fathers and mothers starting in the second year of the study. At that point, mothers' symptoms declined. Fathers, who started out with lower distress than their wives, reported slight increases in five of the ten symptoms that were assessed. This suggests that, consistent with Archers' (1999) analysis, men may "hold in" their grief initially in an effort to be strong for their families (Martin & Doka, 2000). According to Archer (1999), such finding "can be seen as part of a widespread pattern of male inexpressiveness" (p. 245).

Virtually all of the studies that have examined how bereavement is affected by the *nature of the relationship* have focused on the loss of a spouse. Historically, clinical writings on loss have maintained that chronic grief results from conflict in the marital relationship or feelings of ambivalence toward the spouse (see, e.g., Bowlby, 1980; Freud, 1917/1957; Parkes & Weiss, 1983). However, well-controlled studies fail to provide support for this view (Bonanno et al., 2002; Carr et al., 2000). Clinicians have also maintained that excessive dependency on one's spouse is a risk factor for chronic grief (see, e.g., Lopata, 1979; Parkes & Weiss, 1983). Available evidence suggests that this is indeed the case. In the Bonanno et al. (2002) study described earlier, chronic grievers showed significantly higher levels of dependency on their spouse, as well as of general interpersonal dependency than did respondents in some of the other trajectory groups. It would be interesting to determine whether the nature of the relationship is an important risk factor in other kinds of relationships. For example, do parents have more difficulty resolving their grief following the death of an adolescent child if the relationship was conflictual?

Regarding personal and social resources, some of the most important work linking personality with bereavement outcome has been conducted by Nolen-Hoeksema and her colleagues (see, e.g., Nolen-Hoeksema & Larson, 1999; Nolen-Hoeksema, 2001). In a study on coping with conjugal loss, she identified two personality variables that played an important role: dispositional optimism and a ruminative coping style. Those who scored high on dispositional optimism (i.e., the tendency to be optimistic in most circumstances) showed a greater decline in symptoms of depression following the loss and were also more likely to find meaning or benefit in the loss than were pessimists. As mentioned earlier, a ruminative coping style involves a tendency to "engage in thoughts and behaviors that maintain one's focus on one's negative emotions and the possible causes and consequences of those emotions" (Nolen-Hoeksema, 2001, p. 546). Nolen-Hoeksema's findings indicate that those who engage in rumination following loss show little decrease in distress over time. Although bereaved ruminators believed that focusing on the loss would solve their problems, this was not the case: They were significantly less likely to become actively engaged in effective problem solving than were nonruminators.

Several studies have provided evidence that the loss of a child leads to more intense and prolonged distress than any other type of loss (Cleiren, 1993; Cleiren, Diekstra, Kerhof, & van der Wal, 1994; Nolen-Hoeksema & Larson, 1999). In an important study comparing the loss of a child, spouse, sibling, or parent, Cleiren et al. (1994) found that the kinship relationship influenced virtually all aspects of functioning after the loss, with mothers most strongly affected, followed by widowers and sisters. Sisters is a group that heretofore had not been identified as vulnerable.

In recent years, there has been increasing interest in the role that religious or spiritual beliefs may play in dealing with a loved one's death (see Stroebe, Hansson, Schut, Stroebe, & Van den Blink, 2008, for a more detailed discussion). Many investigators have suggested that religious beliefs may ease the sting of death and facilitate finding meaning in the loss, by providing a ready framework of beliefs for incorporating negative events (Pargament & Park, 1995). It has also been argued that specific tenets of one's faith, such as the belief that the deceased is in a better place, or that the survivor and deceased will be reunited in the afterlife, may mitigate the distress associated with the death of a loved one. Unfortunately, most of the studies that have examined variables of this sort are methodologically weak, and the results are conflictual. However, there are indications in the literature that religious beliefs facilitate finding meaning in the death of a child (McIntosh, Silver, & Wortman, 1993; Murphy, Johnson, & Lohan, 2003). Moreover, available evidence suggests that those with spiritual beliefs are more likely to use positive reappraisal and effective problem solving than are those who do not hold such beliefs (Richards et al., 1999; Richards & Folkman, 1997).

As noted earlier, there is also a great deal of interest in the relationship between a person's attachment style and his or her reaction to the loss of a loved one (see Shaver & Tancredy, 2001; Stroebe, Schut, & Stroebe, 2005a; Zhang et al., 2006, for a more detailed discussion). For example, Shaver and Tancredy (2001) have maintained that individuals with a secure attachment style find it easy to be close to others, and typically react to loss with normal but not overwhelming grief. Those with an insecure-dismissing orientation to relationships have difficulty trusting others or allowing themselves to depend on others, and are "compulsively independent" (Stroebe, Schut, & Stroebe, 2005a). These individuals would be expended to suppress and avoid attachment-related emotions, and to show relatively little distress following a major loss. Those with an anxious or preoccupied orientation to relationships have a strong desire to be close to others but are often preoccupied or worried that their partner will abandon them. Such individuals would be expected to react to the loss with intense distress and to remain upset and preoccupied with the loss. Although few studies have tested these hypotheses, some limited evidence suggests that attachment style may be important. For example, Wayment and Vierthaler (2002) found that persons with a secure attachment style showed lower levels of depressive symptoms following the loss of a loved one than did those with a preoccupied style, who expressed more distress and were more likely to engage in rumination.

At present, some of the most exciting work on risk factors has focused on various factors associated with *the context in which the death occurs*. One contextual factor that is generating increasing research interest concerns the *circumstances surrounding the loss*. Accumulating evidence clearly suggests that grief is more likely to be intense and prolonged following the sudden, traumatic loss of a spouse or child.

In an early study examining the effects of losing a spouse or child in a motor vehicle crash 4–7 years previously (Lehman, Wortman, & Williams, 1987), comparisons between bereaved and control respondents, matched on a case-by-case basis, revealed significant differences on depression and other psychiatric symptoms, role functioning, and quality of life. The bereaved experienced more strain in dealing with surviving children and family members, and felt more vulnerable to future negative events. Bereavement was associated with an increased mortality rate, a decline in financial status, and, in the case of bereaved parents, a higher divorce rate. A majority of respondents indicated that they were still experiencing painful thoughts and memories about their loved one.

Another study focusing on how parents are affected by the sudden, traumatic loss of a child (Murphy et al., 2002) found that 5 years post-loss, 61% of mothers and 62% of fathers met diagnostic criteria for mental distress. The findings demonstrated that 28% of the mothers met diagnostic criteria for PTSD, which was nearly three times higher than the rate for a normative sample. For fathers, 12.5% met the diagnostic criteria for PTSD. This was two times higher than the rate for men in the normative sample. In a follow-up study, Murphy, Johnson, Wu, et al. (2003) examined the influence of type of death (accident, suicide, homicide) and time since death on parent outcome. Those who lost a child through homicide were more likely to manifest symptoms of PTSD. However, a majority of parents reported that it took them 3 or 4 years to put the loss into perspective and continue with their lives, and this assessment was not affected by the child's cause of death.

Similar results were obtained in a study by Dyregrov et al. (2003), who focused on parents who lost a child as a result of suicide, SIDS, or an accident. The results showed that 1.5 years after the death of their child, a considerable proportion of parents showed symptoms of PTSD and complicated grief (CG) reactions. Rates of problems were highest for those who lost loved ones through accidents or suicide. As many as 78% of these parents were "above the risk zone of maladaptive symptoms of loss and long-term dysfunction" (p. 155). On the basis of these findings, the authors concluded that "to lose a child suddenly and in traumatic circumstances is a devastating experience for the survivors, most often resulting in a tremendous and long-lasting impact" (p. 156).

Available evidence also suggests that the sudden, traumatic death of a spouse is associated with intense and prolonged distress. In addition to the aforementioned study by Lehman et al., two more recent studies help to clarify the impact of such losses. Zisook, Chentsova-Dutton, and Shuchter (1998) followed a large number of respondents longitudinally for the first 2 years after losing a spouse. Those whose spouse died as a result of an accident, homicide, or suicide were more likely to develop PTSD symptoms than were those who experienced a sudden, unexpected death due to natural causes (e.g., heart attack). Those who scored high on PTSD symptoms also scored high on depression. Similarly, Kaltman and Bonanno (2003) compared respondents whose spouses died of natural causes with those who experienced the death of a spouse as a result of an accident, homicide, or suicide. The latter group manifested a significantly higher number of PTSD symptoms as long as 25 months after the loss. Moreover, those who lost a loved one through natural causes showed a decline in depressive symptoms, whereas those who lost a loved one as a result of an accident or suicide showed no drop in depressive symptoms over the 2-year course of the study. Among the natural death cohort, there were no significant differences in PTSD symptoms or the persistence of depression between bereaved individuals who had sudden, unexpected losses and those who had expected losses.

Taken together, these studies provide compelling evidence that the death of a spouse or child under traumatic or violent circumstances is linked to more intense and prolonged grief. It is important to note that such deaths are associated with PTSD symptoms, as well as with symptoms of depression. This means that, in addition to dealing with such symptoms as yearning for the deceased and profound sadness, survivors of sudden, traumatic losses must contend with such symptoms as intrusive thoughts and flashbacks, feelings of detachment or estrangement, irritability, and problems in concentration.

The studies reviewed here have focused primarily on the untimely death of a spouse or child. Do the circumstances under which the death occurs have an impact on survivors when a loved one dies following a life-threatening illness or when an elderly person dies? For people aged 65 and older, chronic illnesses such as cancer, heart disease, and diabetes account for more than 60% of all deaths. Over the past decade, a great deal of research has focused on the impact of caregiving (see Schulz, Boerner, & Hebert, 2008, for a review). Studies have shown that caregivers are more stressed and depressed and have lower levels of well-being than noncaregivers (Pinquart & Sorensen, 2003a, 2003b). Depressive symptoms increase as the number of hours one engages in caregiving increases (Schulz et al., 2001).

In recent years, investigators have begun to examine the impact of caregiving on adjustment to the loss following the loved one's death. This research demonstrates that the relationship between caregiving and adjustment to bereavement is complex. Although stressful caregiving is associated with poor psychological adjustment when the spouse is alive, many overly taxed caregivers seem to rebound to relatively high levels of functioning after the death (Schulz et al., 2003). However, a minority of strained caregivers demonstrated intense and prolonged grief, and investigators are attempting to uncover the determinants of this reaction. Thus far, research indicates that high levels of caregiving burden, feeling exhausted and overloaded, and lack of support (Gross, 2007; Hebert et al., 2006) put caregivers at risk for more intense and prolonged grief reactions.

Research with dementia caregivers found that among the caregivers with poor adjustment were not only those who were in difficult caregiving situations (e.g., caring for a more cognitively impaired patient), but also some who reported very positive features of the caregiving experience (Boerner et al., 2004; Schulz et al., 2006). This intriguing finding suggests that there may be some positive caregiving experiences that can also put a person at risk for difficulties following the loved one's death. This may be the result of two related factors: losing their loved one deprives these individuals of a meaningful and important role, and a positive view of caregiving may be a reflection of an extremely close relationship between caregiver and the person they cared for.

Another aspect of the caregiving situation that has emerged as a potential risk factor is preparedness for the death. Although the research on this issue is only in its infancy, it seems clear that, despite providing high-intensity care, often for years, many bereaved caregivers perceive themselves as unprepared for the death. Those who have such feelings tend to deal with more complications in their grieving process (Hebert et al., 2006). However, we need to gain a better understanding of what it means to be prepared for a loved one's death. Based on a series of focus groups with caregivers, Hebert and colleagues proposed that preparedness has emotional (e.g., being at peace with prospect of death), pragmatic (e.g., having funeral arrangements planned), and informational (e.g., medical aspects of end-of-life) components (Hebert et al., 2009). This study also showed that, for example, a person could feel prepared with respect to the informational and pragmatic components, but yet feel entirely unprepared emotionally. Overall, this work suggests that even the relatively certain prospect of death does not necessarily translate into being prepared for what lies ahead, and that this might be an important area for professionals to address in their encounters with caregivers, before and after the loss.

An important issue that is discussed primarily in the context of caregiving for terminally ill patients is how to help a dying person to experience a "good death." According to Carr (2003), a "good death" is characterized by physical comfort, support from one's loved ones, acceptance, and appropriate medical care. Carr is one of the first bereavement researchers to suggest that whether a loved one dies a "good death" may have implications for the grief experienced by surviving family members. In analyses based on the Changing Lives of Older Couples (CLOC) data, she found that those who reported that their spouses were in severe pain showed elevated levels of yearning, anxiety, and intrusive thoughts following the loss. Those who believed that their spouse's medical care was negligent reported elevated anger symptoms.

Several studies have shown that unique stresses are associated with caring for a loved one who is dying (see Carr et al., 2006, for a more detailed discussion). For example, Prigerson and her associates (2003) examined quality of life among hospice-based dying patients and their caregivers, who included spouses and children. The caregivers had cared for their relatives for 2 years, on average, prior to the hospice admission. More than three-quarters of the caregivers reported that they had witnessed the patient in severe pain or discomfort, and 62% said they had witnessed this daily. Nearly half reported that their loved one was unable to sleep or unable to eat or swallow on a daily basis. These findings are particularly striking when one considers that one of the core goals of hospice care is pain management.

Several studies have shown that family members report more positive evaluations of their spouse's quality of care at the end of life and better psychological adjustment following the death when their loved one spent his or her final weeks using in-home hospice services rather than receiving care in nursing homes, hospitals, or at home with home health nursing services (see, e.g., Teno, Clarridge, & Casey, 2004). In fact, a study by Christakis and Iwashyna (2003) indicates that hospice use can reduce the increased mortality risk associated with bereavement. These investigators conducted a matched cohort study with a sample of nearly 200,000 respondents in the United States. At 18 months after the loss, significantly fewer deaths occurred among wives whose husbands had received hospice care than among those whose husbands received other types of care (typically a combination of home care with occasional hospital stays). Mortality was also lower for husbands whose wives received hospice care, but the effect fell short of statistical significance. These studies suggest that in-home hospice care may be more conducive to a "good death" for the patient and, consequently, his or her surviving loved ones.

## COMPLICATED GRIEF AS A DISTINCT PSYCHIATRIC DISORDER

Despite the progress that has been made in identifying risk factors for chronic grief, there are no standard guidelines to determine how complications following bereavement should be diagnosed and when they should be treated. Among theorists as well as clinicians, there has been a long-standing awareness that bereavement can result in psychiatric problems. As Jacobs (1993) has indicated, most research has focused on the prevalence of clinically significant depression and anxiety disorders among the bereaved. More recently, as was described earlier, researchers have become interested in the prevalence of PTSD following the loss of a loved one, particularly among survivors of sudden, traumatic losses.

In an important new line of research, Prigerson and her associates (e.g., Prigerson, 2004; Jacobs, Mazure, & Prigerson, 2000; see Lichtenthal, Cruess, & Prigerson, 2004; Prigerson, Vanderwerker, & Maciejewski, 2008; Zhang, El-Jawahri, & Prigerson, 2006, for a review) have focused on the development of diagnostic criteria to identify those individuals who exhibit chronic grief and who would benefit from clinical intervention. Drawing from epidemiological, pharmacological, and clinical case studies, these investigators have identified a unique pattern of symptoms called *complicated grief*.[1] They have maintained that these symptoms are associated with enduring mental and physical health problems that are typically slow to resolve and that can persist for years if left untreated. To obtain a diagnosis of CG, individuals must experience intense yearning for the deceased daily or to a disabling degree. They must also experience five or more additional symptoms during the past month: feeling stunned, dazed or shocked by the death; trouble accepting the death; difficulty trusting others; excessive bitterness or anger related to the loss; feeling uneasy about moving forward; feeling that life is empty and holds no meaning without the deceased; and numbness (absence of emotion) since the loss. These symptoms must cause marked and persistent dysfunction in social, occupational, or other important roles, and the symptom disturbance must last at least 6 months. Research has shown that these symptoms form a unified cluster and that they are distinct from depression, anxiety, or PTSD. For example, feeling sad and blue is characteristic of depression but not of CG, and avoidance and hyperarousal are characteristic of PTSD but not of CG. Unlike these other disorders, vulnerability to CG is believed to be rooted in insecure attachment styles that are developed in childhood. Consistent with this notion, evidence has shown that childhood abuse and serious neglect are significantly associated with CG during widowhood (Silverman, Johnson, & Prigerson, 2001).

Evidence has shown that the prevalence of CG among individuals who have lost a loved one is between 10% and 20%. The symptoms of CG typically last for several years. They are predictive of morbidity (e.g., suicidal thoughts and behaviors, incidence of cardiac events, high blood pressure), adverse health behaviors (e.g., increased alcohol consumption and use of tobacco), and impairments in the quality of life (e.g., loss of energy). Interestingly, bereaved people with CG are significantly less likely to visit a mental health or physical health care professional than those without grief complications. People with severe mental anguish may have difficulty mobilizing themselves to go into treatment. They may also avoid treatment because they believe it would be unbearably painful to focus on the loss.

## FUTURE DIRECTIONS

We now know that a significant minority of individuals experience enduring difficulties following the loss of a loved one, and we have a reasonably good understanding of the risk factors for grief complications. However, important questions remain unanswered about exactly how people do recover from a loss. As Archer (1999) has observed, "It is commonly believed that it is not time itself that is the healer but some process which occurs during this time" (p. 108). At this point, however, there is considerable confusion about what this process involves. It is now clear that some people recover from a loss without "working through" the implications of what has happened. But how do people come to accept the loss, to encounter reminders without distress, and to become engaged in new interests or pursuits?

In evaluating the impact of a major loss, it is important to recognize that the survivor may also be coping with additional losses. The death of child, for example, may require surviving parents to face the loss of their hopes and dreams for the future, the loss of their belief in God as a benevolent protector, and the loss of their beliefs in their ability to control important outcomes. The death of a spouse is often accompanied by concurrent stressors, including loss of income or struggling with tasks formerly performed by the deceased. Documenting the frequency of such secondary losses (Rando, 1993) will help to clarify our understanding of the bereavement experience and provide valuable information for intervention.

Although most research on the enduring effects of loss has focused on mental and physical health problems, there is increasing recognition that losses can bring about positive psychological changes (Tedeschi & Calhoun, 1996, 2004). Several researchers have documented, for example, that following the loss of a spouse, the surviving spouse reports greater feelings of self-confidence, a greater awareness of one's strengths, and a greater inclination to try new experiences (see Wortman, 2004, for a review). It less clear whether sudden, traumatic losses of a spouse or child are typically accompanied by personal growth. There are some indications that survivors of trauma resent the implication that they should be able to find something good in what has happened, and that others' exhortations to this effect often heighten survivors' feelings of inadequacy and shame (see Wortman, 2004, for a more detailed discussion).

## Conclusion

In previous papers, we have described several common assumptions about coping with loss that appear to be held by professionals in the field as well as by laypersons. We conducted a careful evaluation of each assumption and concluded that most were not supported, and were often contradicted, by the available data. Indeed, this is why these assumptions were originally referred to as "myths of coping with loss."

It has been 20 years since the first articles on the myths of coping appeared in the literature (Wortman & Silver, 1987, 1989). As the scientific evidence pertaining to these myths has continued to accumulate, there have been some shifts in the prevailing views about how people cope with loss. The main purpose of this chapter has been to summarize the most important research bearing on the validity of each "myth of coping," and also to highlight how the myths themselves have changed over time.

Here, we first summarize how, in our judgment, these assumptions are currently viewed by researchers. We then examine the extent to which the myths of coping are still influential among practicing clinicians. We discuss the relationship between belief in these myths and grief counseling and therapy as it is currently practiced in the United States today. In particular, we highlight extensive research evidence suggesting that treatment for grief is in many cases not effective. We then consider the extent to which the myths of coping continue to influence other health care providers who come into contact with the bereaved, such as clergy and general practitioners. Next, we consider the extent to which these myths of coping are maintained by the bereaved themselves and their potential support providers. We also explore whether these beliefs impact the amount and quality of support the bereaved are likely to receive.

### Implications for Research

Over time, it appears that researchers' assumptions about the process of coping with loss have changed in important ways. For example, most researchers would probably agree that a large minority of respondents fail to experience even mild depression following an important loss, that delayed grief is rare, that positive emotions are common following a loss and are associated with a good recovery, that not everyone may need to actively confront their thoughts and feelings about the loss, that continuing attachment to the loved one is normal, and that recovery from a loss is highly variable and depends on many factors, including the nature of the relationship and the circumstances surrounding the death.

Awareness of this body of work is leading researchers to ask new and important questions about the process of coping with loss. As was noted earlier, for example, many of the early studies on grief focused solely on depression and other negative emotions and symptoms; questions about positive emotions experienced during grieving were typically not included. At this point, however, researchers not only are including measures of positive emotions but also are attempting to identify the role that such emotions may play in facilitating adjustment to a loss. In terms of outcome measures, it has become clear that we must examine the possibility that losses can bring about enduring positive changes, such as increased self-confidence and independence, altered life priorities, and enhanced compassion for others suffering similar losses (for a more detailed discussion of growth following loss, see Wortman, 2004).

Despite these advances, it is important for researchers to ask themselves whether they may hold assumptions or beliefs about the coping process that are limiting the scope of their scientific inquiry into loss. In a collaborative study called the Americans' Changing Lives, for example (see Nesse, Wortman, & House, 2006), personal interviews were conducted with a national sample of people who had lost a spouse anywhere from 3 months to 60 years previously. Several of the investigators wanted to eliminate questions about widowhood for all respondents whose loss occurred longer than 10 years ago, assuming that there would be no effects after that point. Ultimately, the decision was made to ask these questions of all respondents. This was fortunate because the results enhanced our knowledge about the ways such losses continue to influence the surviving spouse. For example, several decades after the loss, it was common for people to have thoughts and conversations about their spouse that made them feel sad or upset (see Carnelley, Wortman, Bolger, & Burke, 2006).

### Implications for Treatment

Earlier, we have attempted to argue that, in most cases, researchers no longer take the prevailing cultural assumptions about coping with loss at face value and instead appear to recognize the extraordinary variability in response to loss. It is less clear, however, whether the accumulation of research findings has filtered down to clinicians or other health care providers working with the bereaved, to potential support providers of the bereaved, or to the bereaved themselves.

#### CLINICIANS

A review of books and articles written for and by clinicians indicates that assumptions about the importance of going through a period of distress and of working through the loss are still widely held. For example, in what is perhaps the most widely used book on grief counseling written for clinicians and other mental health professionals, Worden (2008) suggests that if negative feelings are not expressed, psychological difficulties may emerge at a later point.

Since the 1990s there has been a proliferation of grief counseling and therapy. This is reflected in a wide variety of workshops, professional conferences, and publications on the topic, as well as in countless individual and group-based treatments offered in virtually all communities (Neimeyer, 2000). Most treatments for loss are based on the assumption that individuals must "work through" their feelings to accommodate the loss (see, e.g., Rando, 1993; Worden, 2008). As Neimeyer (2000) has indicated, most people assume that grief counseling is "a firmly established, demonstrably effective service, which, like psychotherapy in general, seems to have found a secure niche in the health care field" (p. 542). And indeed, most clinicians who treat the bereaved believe that what they do is helpful and necessary (Jordan & Neimeyer, 2003).

To date, however, available research has failed to provide evidence that grief treatments are efficacious. During the past decade, several reviews of grief and mourning treatment studies have appeared in the literature. Some authors have published narrative reviews (e.g., Jordan & Neimeyer, 2003; Larson & Hoyt, 2007; Schut & Stroebe, 2010; Schut, Stroebe, Van den Bout & Terheggen, 2001). Others have conducted meta-analytic reviews of grief and mourning treatment studies (e.g., Allumbough & Hoyt, 1999; Kato & Mann, 1999; Fortner & Neimeyer, 1999; (summarized in Neimeyer, 2000)). These reviews have focused on somewhat different sets of studies and have employed a variety of analytic approaches. With one exception (Larson & Hoyt, 2007), however, each of these reviews came to basically the same conclusion: that the scientific basis for the efficacy of grief counseling is weak.

Currier, Neimeyer, and Berman (2008) have recently published a meta-analysis of grief treatment studies that is far more comprehensive than the others and that uses state-of-the-art statistical procedures. Their analyses demonstrated that interventions had a small effect when respondents were assessed at post-treatment, but no discernible effect at follow-up, which was, on average, about 36 weeks later. Currier et al. (2008) pointed out that despite the absence of overall effects, there was considerable variation in the impact of the grief treatments that were studied. They conducted additional analyses in order to learn more about the conditions under which grief and mourning treatments may be effective. One finding to emerge from their analyses is that the benefits derived from treatment were strongly influenced by respondents' level of distress. If respondents were selected because they had experienced a loss, without regard to their level of distress, positive treatment effects were unlikely. In contrast, in those studies focusing on participants who were experiencing high distress surrounding the loss, the results showed a clear benefit at post-treatment and also at follow-up. According to Currier et al. (2008), in those studies in which the target of intervention was respondents who were manifesting significant distress as a result of the loss, effect sizes (a measure of clinical relevance) compare favorably with the positive outcomes shown for psychotherapy in general.

Jordan and Neimeyer (2003) have identified some additional factors that may influence the findings from grief treatment studies. They have suggested that some studies may have failed to find a robust positive effect for grief counseling because the studies were small and there may not have been enough statistical power to detect differences between groups. In other studies, findings may not have emerged because the treatment offered did not include enough sessions (most included 8–12 sessions). Alternatively, the intervention may not have been offered at the most appropriate time. Neimeyer (2000) found that interventions that were delivered shortly after the death had significantly smaller effect sizes than those delivered at a later time. Jordan and Neimeyer (2003) have suggested that there may be a "critical window of time" (p. 774) when it is best to offer interventions, perhaps 6–18 months after the loss, "before problematic patterns of adjustment have become entrenched" (p. 774). These investigators also emphasized that the types of counseling needed shortly after the loss may differ from what is needed a year or more after the loss, noting that investigators should try to customize the type of intervention to particular points in the bereavement trajectory.

Taken together, these findings suggest that, in many cases, people may not need therapy following a loved one's death, but that some subgroups are likely to benefit substantially from treatment. It would be useful to develop interventions that are designed specifically to address the problems of mourners in high-risk categories, such as those who have already developed CG. Shear and her associates (2005) have recently completed a randomized, clinical trial comparing an intervention designed for people with CG to a more standard treatment for depression (interpersonal therapy). The multifaceted CG intervention draws from research on the treatment of PTSD.

For example, clients are given exercises to help them confront avoided situations. In addition, they are asked to tell their story into a tape recorder and to play it back during the week. The average length of treatment was 19 weeks. Although both treatments produced improvement in CG symptoms, there was a higher response rate and a faster time to response in the CG treatment. This treatment would appear to hold considerable promise for people who are struggling with CG.

Perhaps the main implication of this work for practicing clinicians is that they should not assume that one type of intervention will work best for everyone. As Jordan and Neimeyer (2003) have emphasized, "It is a truism that grief is unique to each individual, yet this wisdom is rarely reflected in the design and delivery of services to the bereaved" (p. 782). They suggest that treating clinicians focus more attention on such issues as whether the client has experienced previous traumas or losses, as well as the client's personality structure, coping style, and available support resources.

This work suggests that it is essential for program administrators to focus their efforts on identifying high-risk mourners. This task could be facilitated by the development of screening tools that make it possible to identify people at risk for subsequent problems. As was described earlier, Prigerson and her associates (2008) have developed an Inventory of Complicated Grief (now called Prolonged Grief) that has predictive validity regarding those who are likely to develop CG.

One consistent finding that has emerged from the intervention studies reviewed here is that those who seek treatment are likely to show better results from grief therapy than those who are recruited into a treatment (see Stroebe, Schut, & Stroebe, 2005b, for a more detailed discussion). It is not clear whether this occurs because those who seek treatment are more likely to have serious problems and hence benefit more from the treatment, or whether other important factors underlie this effect. However, as was noted earlier, there is evidence to indicate that individuals with CG are less likely to seek treatment than are those whose grief is not associated with complications. This suggests that those most in need of help may be least likely to seek and obtain it. At this point, little is known about what percentage of high-risk mourners seek help. It would also be highly useful to understand the reasons why high-risk mourners often do not seek help. Clearly, it is important for administrators and policy makers to find ways of reaching out to high-risk mourners who do not avail themselves of treatment.

## OTHER CARE PROVIDERS

Although research on help-seeking is limited, available research suggests that only a small percentage of those who experience major mental health problems following bereavement seek professional help (see Jacobs, 1993, for a more detailed discussion). To the extent that they seek assistance at all, bereaved individuals are far more likely to approach physicians, nurses, or clergymen than they are to seek formal grief counseling or therapy. Hence, it is important to ask whether these care providers may hold assumptions about the grieving process that interfere with their ability to provide effective help and support to the bereaved.

Evidence suggests that physicians and nurses do not receive much training about grief, and an examination of commonly used textbooks suggests that such books often perpetuate the myths of coping. For example, books written for nurses and physicians frequently maintain that people go through stages of emotional response as they come to terms with the loss, and that failure to exhibit distress is indicative of a problem (see, e.g., Potter & Perry, 1997). Clearly, it is important for care providers to recognize that, particularly with certain kinds of loss, it is normative to exhibit little distress, and that this may be indicative of resilience.

How much do physicians and clergy know about the risk factors associated with complications of bereavement? Do they know, for example, that a large percentage of parents who experience the sudden, traumatic loss of a child experience high levels of symptoms for years after the loss? If they are not aware of these findings, they may convey to bereaved parents that they should be over the loss, thus contributing to the burden such parents are already shouldering. In our experience, it is common for physicians and those in the clergy to assume that prolonged grief is indicative of a weakness or coping failure on the part of the bereaved. It is also important for physicians and clergymen to have a good understanding of the symptomatology that accompanies particular types of loss. For example, they could be far more helpful to those who encounter sudden, traumatic losses if they understand that such losses are often accompanied by posttraumatic stress symptoms. Many studies have suggested that following the traumatic death of a loved one, survivors are frightened by such symptoms as memory loss, concentration problems, and intrusive thoughts or images of the deceased (Dyregrov et al., 2003), Physicians and clergymen are in a unique position to normalize disturbing symptoms among bereaved who are not receiving grief therapy or treatment. Bereaved individuals are likely to benefit from learning that their symptoms are understandable, given what they have been through, and that they do not convey mental illness or coping failure.

Knowledge of risk factors would not only help to ensure that bereaved people are treated more compassionately by their physicians and clergymen but would also increase the likelihood that those who would benefit from counseling are encouraged to seek help. At present, little is known about how common it is for these care providers to make referrals, or whether they are knowledgeable about how or where to refer bereaved people for grief counseling.

Considering the impact of bereavement on mortality, particularly among men who lose their spouses, it would also be prudent for clergy to encourage these men to see their physicians. These men would benefit from encouragement, from physicians as well as clergymen, to take other positive steps to maintain their health. Clergymen may also be in a good position to mobilize support for the bereaved, particularly for widowed men who may have relied primarily on their wives for support and companionship.

### The Bereaved and Their Support Providers

At present, what expectations or assumptions about the grieving process are prevalent among laypersons? When a person experiences a loss, does he or she expect to go through stages of grief, beginning with intense distress? If intense distress is not experienced, is this a source of concern? How knowledgeable are laypersons about the symptoms of grief, and how do they judge and evaluate their own reactions? Do they believe that it is necessary to "work through" the loss, and if so, what kinds of behaviors do they engage in to facilitate this? Do they assess their progress according to a timetable concerning when they think they should be recovered? Are laypersons aware that symptoms are more intense and prolonged following certain kinds of losses, or do they hold themselves up to unrealistically high standards and judge themselves harshly if they are not able to move on within a year or so? Given that most bereaved do not seek grief counseling or therapy, where do they turn for assistance, and to what extent are they able to obtain information and/or support that is beneficial? It is also important to ascertain whether certain assumptions or beliefs about coping with loss are held by members of the bereaved person's support network and, if so, whether these facilitate or impede the receipt of effective support.

Unfortunately, few studies have focused on these questions, and at present little is known about how the grief process is viewed by the bereaved or by those in their support network. However, there are some indications in the literature that many laypersons still believe in stages of emotional response. Elison and McGonigle (2003) describe a case in which one woman asked her therapist to do something to make her angry. When the therapist asked why she should do so, the client replied, "My neighbor told me that at this stage, I should be angry, and I'm not. I'm afraid I'm not doing this right" (p. xxiii).

It also appears that laypersons have strong expectations that the bereaved will go through a period of intense distress. Those who do not appear to be showing enough distress may elicit judgmental reactions from others. A person who fails to react with sufficient distress may also be thought to be "in denial," with friends conveying the sentiment that "it hasn't hit her yet." Elison and McGonigle (2003) have pointed out that in cases of deaths that occur under suspicious circumstances, failure to show distress may be shown as evidence as guilt. They maintained that the failure of John and Patty Ramsey to show distress following the murder of their daughter, JonBenet, "convicted them in the court of public opinion."

In their insightful book *Liberating Losses,* Elison and McGonigle (2003) describe several situations in which people feel relieved or liberated following the loss of a loved one. For example, they note that it is common to experience feelings of relief after a long period of caregiving. Such feelings are also prevalent when a person has been involved in a relationship with someone who has been a constant source of criticism, abuse, or oppression. In these cases, the death may be viewed as a "God given divorce" (see also Sanders, 1999). Elison and McGonigle (2003) note how outsiders' comments are often unhelpful. For example, a friend may say "It's okay to cry," or "You must miss him terribly," thus making the survivor feel even more guilty and conspicuous. Or, they may make comments like, "I can't believe you're getting rid of his things already," implying that the survivor's reactions are inappropriate.

Regarding expectations about recovery, some studies suggest that the bereaved judge themselves harshly if they continue to show intense distress beyond the first few months. A frequent complaint of the bereaved is that others expect them to be recovered from the loss far sooner than they are.

There is also evidence that others attempt to encourage a prompt recovery following the loss, and that the bereaved do not find this helpful (Ingram et al., 2001; Lehman, Ellard, & Wortman, 1986). For example, following the death of a spouse, friends might try to arouse the surviving spouse's interest in new activities or in the resumption of old hobbies or interests. It is also common for others to bring up the topic of remarriage. Discussions of this topic are often initiated within a few days or weeks of the spouse's death.

Other kinds of responses that are frequently made by potential support providers but that are not regarded as helpful by the bereaved include attempts to block discussions about the loss or displays of feelings (e.g., "Crying won't bring him back"); minimization of the problem (e.g., "You had so many good years together"); invoking a religious or philosophical perspective (e.g., "God needed him more than you did"); giving advice (e.g., "You should consider getting a dog; they're wonderful companions"); and identification with feelings (e.g., "I know how you feel—I lost my second cousin"). It is also common for those in the support network to ask inappropriate questions. They may ask about such matters as how the death occurred (e.g., "Was he wearing a seat belt?"); about financial matters (e.g., "How are you going to spend all of that insurance money?"); or about the loved one's possessions (e.g., "What are you going to do with his tools?"). Studies have shown that unsupportive social interactions account for a significant amount of the variance in depression among the bereaved, beyond the variance explained by the level of present grief (Ingram et al., 2001). Such comments are more likely to be made by relatives or close friends than they are among casual acquaintances of the survivor (see Wortman, Wolff, & Bonanno, 2004, for a more detailed discussion).

What types of responses from support providers do the bereaved regard as beneficial? Research indicates that they value the opportunity to talk with others about their feelings when they elect to do so (Lehman et al., 1986; Marwit & Carusa, 1998). In fact, there is evidence that if people want to talk about the loss and are blocked from doing so, they become more depressed over time (Lepore et al., 1996). The bereaved also find it helpful when others convey a supportive presence (e.g., "I am here for you") or express concern (e.g., "I care what happens to you"). Tangible assistance, such as help with errands or meals, is typically regarded as helpful. Finally, contact with a similar other is judged to be very helpful. Unlike those who have not experienced such a loss, they may have a more accurate understanding of what the bereaved has been through. Contact with similar others can also reassure the bereaved that their own feelings and behaviors are normal.

In our judgment, it would be beneficial for the bereaved themselves, and their potential support providers, to have greater awareness of the extraordinary variability in responses to loss. We believe that awareness of the conditions under which the bereaved may fail to experience or exhibit distress, or may experience grief that is more intense and prolonged than the norm, would also have a positive impact. Hopefully, greater understanding of the available research will result in treatment of the bereaved that is less judgmental and more compassionate.

## Notes

1. More recently, Prigerson and colleagues have referred to complicated grief as "prolonged grief disorder" (Prigerson, Vanderwerker, & Maciejewski, 2008). However, since the term *complicated grief* is still more commonly used in the literature, we choose to retain this terminology for the purpose of clarity.

## References

Allumbaugh, D.L., & Hoyt, W.T. (1999). Effectiveness of grief therapy: A meta-analysis. *Journal of Counseling Psychology, 46,* 370–380.

Aneshensel, C.S., Botticello, A.L., & Yamamoto-Mitani, N. (2004). When caregiving ends: The course of depressive symptoms after bereavement. *Journal of Health and Social Behavior, 45,* 422–440.

Archer, J. (1999). *The nature of grief: The evolution and psychology of reactions to loss.* New York: Routledge.

Archer, J. (2008). Theories of grief: Past, present, and future perspectives. In M. Stroebe, R. Hansson, H. Schut, & W. Stroebe (Eds.), *Handbook of bereavement research and practice: 21st century perspectives* (pp. 45–65). Washington, DC: American Psychological Association Press.

Attig, T. (1996). *How we grieve: Relearning the world.* New York: Oxford University Press.

Attig, T. (2000). Anticipatory mourning and the transition to loving in absence. In T.A. Rando (Ed.), *Clinical dimensions of anticipatory mourning: Theory and practice in working with dying, their loved ones, and their caregivers* (pp. 115–133). Champaign, IL: Research Press.

Balk, D. (1983). Adolescents' grief reactions and self-concept perceptions following sibling death: A study of 33 teenagers. *Journal of Youth and Adolescence, 12,* 137–161.

Baltes, M.M., & Skrotzki, E. (1995). Tod im alter: Eigene endlichkeit und partnerverlust [Death in old age: Finality and loss of spouse]. In R. Oerter, & L. Montada (Eds.), *Entwicklungspsychologie* (3rd ed., pp. 1137–1146). Munich, Germany: PVU.

Batten, M., & Oltjenbruns, K.A. (1999). Adolescent sibling bereavement as a catalyst for spiritual bereavement as a catalyst for spiritual development: A model for understanding. *Death Studies, 23,* 529–546.

Belitsky, R., & Jacobs, S. (1986). Bereavement, attachment theory, and mental disorders. *Psychiatric Annals, 16,* 276–280.

Bisconti, T.L., Bergeman, C.S., & Boker, S.M. (2004). *Social support as a predictor of variability: An examination of recent widows' adjustment trajectories.* Manuscript submitted for publication.

Boelen, P.A., Stroebe, M.S., Schut, H.A., & Zijerveld, A.M. (2006). Continuing bonds and grief: A prospective analysis. *Death Studies, 30*(8), 767–776.

Boelen, P.A., van den Bout, J., & van den Hout, M.A. (2006). Negative cognitions and avoidance in emotional problems after bereavement: A prospective study. *Behavioral Research and Therapy, 44*(11), 1657–1672.

Boerner, K., & Heckhausen, J. (2003). To have and have not: Adaptive bereavement by transforming mental ties to the deceased. *Death Studies, 27,* 199–226.

Boerner, K., Schulz, R., & Horowitz, A. (2004). Positive aspects of caregiving and adaptation to bereavement. *Psychology and Aging, 19,* 668–675.

Boerner, K., Wortman, C.B., & Bonanno, G. (2005). Resilient or at risk? A four-year study of older adults who initially showed high or low distress following conjugal loss. *Journal of Gerontology: Series B: Psychological Sciences and Social Sciences, 60B,* 67–73.

Bonanno, G.A. (2001). Grief and emotion: A social-functional perspective. In M.S. Stroebe, & R.O. Hansson (Eds.), *Handbook of bereavement research: Consequences, coping, and care* (pp. 493–515). Washington, DC: American Psychological Association.

Bonanno, G.A. (2005). Resilience in the face of potential trauma. *Current Directions in Psychological Science, 14,* 135–138.

Bonanno, G.A., & Field, N.P. (2001). Evaluating the delayed grief hypothesis across 5 years of bereavement. *American Behavioral Scientist, 44,* 798–816.

Bonanno, G.A., & Kaltman, S. (1999). Toward an integrative perspective on bereavement. *Psychological Bulletin, 125,* 760–786.

Bonanno, G.A., & Kaltman, S. (2001). The varieties of grief experience. *Clinical Psychology Review, 21,* 705–734.

Bonanno, G.A., & Keltner, D. (1997). Facial expressions of emotion and the course of conjugal bereavement. *Journal of Abnormal Psychology, 106,* 126–137.

Bonanno, G.A., Keltner, D., Holen, A., & Horowitz, M.J. (1995). When avoiding unpleasant emotion might not be such a bad thing: Verbal-autonomic response dissociation and midlife conjugal bereavement. *Journal of Personality and Social Psychology, 46,* 975–985.

Bonanno, G.A., Mihalecz, M.C., & LeJeune, J.T. (1999). The core emotion themes of conjugal loss. *Motivation and Emotion, 23,* 175–201.

Bonanno, G.A., Moskowitz, J.T., Papa, A., & Folkman, S. (2005). Resilience to loss in bereaved spouses, bereaved parents, and bereaved gay men. *Journal of Personality and Social Psychology, 88,* 827–843.

Bonanno, G.A., Papa, A., Lalande, K., Zhang, N., & Noll, J.G. (2005). Grief processing and deliberate grief avoidance: A prospective comparison of bereaved spouses and parents in the United States and the People's Republic of China. *Journal of Consulting and Clinical Psychology, 73,* 86–98.

Bonanno, G.A., Rennicke, C., & Dekel, S. (2005). Self-enhancement among high-exposure survivors of the September 11th terrorist attack: Resilience or social maladjustment? *Journal of Personality and Social Psychology, 88,* 984–998.

Bonanno, G.A., Wortman, C.B., Lehman, D., Tweed, R., Sonnega, J., Carr, D., et al. (2002). Resilience to loss, chronic grief, and their pre-bereavement predictors. *Journal of Personality and Social Psychology, 83*, 1150–1164.

Bonanno, G.A., Wortman, C.B., & Nesse, R.M. (2004). Prospective patterns of resilience and maladjustment during widowhood. *Psychology and Aging, 19*, 260–271.

Bournstein, P.E., Clayton, P.J., Halikas, J.A., Maurice, W.L., & Robins, E. (1973). The depression of widowhood after thirteen months. *British Journal of Psychiatry, 122*, 561–566.

Bower, J.E., Kemeny, M.E., Taylor, S.E., & Fahey, J.L. (2003). Finding positive meaning and its association with natural killer cell cytotoxicity among participants in a bereavement-related disclosure intervention. *Annals of Behavioral Medicine, 25*, 146–155.

Bowlby, J. (1969). Attachment. In *Attachment and loss* Vol. 1. New York: Basic Books.

Bowlby, J. (1973). Separation: Anxiety and anger. In *Attachment and loss* Vol. 2. New York: Basic Books.

Bowlby, J. (1980). Loss: Sadness and depression. In *Attachment and loss* Vol. 3. New York: Basic Books.

Bruce, M.L., Kim, K, Leaf, P.J., & Jacobs, S. (1990). Depressive episodes and dysphoria resulting from conjugal bereavement in a prospective community sample. *American Journal of Psychiatry, 147*, 608–611.

Carnelley, K.B., Wortman, C.B., Bolger, N., & Burke, C.T. (2006). The time course of adjustment to widowhood: Evidence from a national probability sample. *Journal of Personality and Social Psychology, 91*(3), 476–492

Carnelley, K.B., Wortman, C.B., & Kessler, R.C. (1999). The impact of widowhood on depression: Findings from a prospective survey. *Psychological Medicine, 29*, 1111–1123.

Carr, D. (2003). A "good death" for whom? Quality of spouse's death and psychological distress among older widowed persons. *Journal of Health and Social Behavior, 44*, 215–232.

Carr, D. (2004). Black/white differences in psychological adjustment to spousal loss among older adults. *Research on Aging, 26*, 591–622.

Carr, D., House, J.S., Kessler, R.C., Nesse, R.M., Sonnega, J., & Wortman, C. (2000). Marital quality and psychological adjustment to widowhood among older adults: A longitudinal analysis. *Journal of Gerontology: Series B: Psychological Sciences and Social Sciences, 55B*, S197–S207.

Carr, D., Wortman, C.B., & Wolff, K. (2006). How Americans die. In D. Carr, R. Nesse, & C.B. Wortman (Eds.), *Spousal bereavement in late life* (pp. 49–78). New York: Springer.

Carver, C.S., & Vargas, S. (2011). Stress, coping, and health. In H.S. Friedman (Ed.), *The Oxford handbook of health psychology*. New York: Oxford University Press.

Chentsova-Dutton, Y., Shuchter, S., Hutchin, S., Strause, L., Burns, K., Dunn, L., et al. (2002). Depression and grief reactions in hospice caregivers: From pre-death to 1 year afterwards. *Journal of Affective Disorders, 69*, 53–60.

Christakis, N., & Iwashyna, T. (2003). The health impact on health care on families: A matched cohort study of hospice use by decedents and mortality outcomes in surviving, widowed spouses. *Social Science and Medicine, 57*, 465–574.

Cleiren, M.P.H.D. (1993). *Bereavement and adaptation: A comparative study of the aftermath of death*. Philadelphia: Hemisphere.

Cleiren, M., Diekstra, R., Kerkhof, A., & van der Wal, J. (1994). Mode of death and kinship in bereavement: Focusing on "who" rather than "how." *Crisis, 15*(1), 22–36.

Coifman, K.G., Bonanno, G.A., Ray, R.D., & Gross, J.J. (2007). Does repressive coping promote resilience? Affective-autonomic response discrepancy during bereavement. *Journal of Personality and Social Psychology, 92*, 745–758.

Currier, J.M., Neimeyer, R.A. & Berman, J.S. (2008). The effectiveness of psychotherapeutic interventions for bereaved persons: A comprehensive quantitative review. *Psychological Bulletin, 134*, 648–661.

Datson, S.L., & Marwit, S.J. (1997). Personality constructs and perceived presence of deceased loved ones. *Death Studies, 21*, 131–146.

Deutsch, H. (1937). Absence of grief. *Psychoanalytic Quarterly, 6*, 12–22.

Dyregrov, K., Nordanger, D., & Dyregrov, A. (2003). Predictors of psychosocial distress after suicide, SIDS and accidents. *Death Studies, 27*, 143–165.

Elison, J., & McGonigle, C. (2003). *Liberating losses: When death brings relief*. Cambridge, MA: Perseus.

Field, N.P., & Friedrichs, M. (2004). Continuing bonds in coping with the death of a husband. *Death Studies, 28*, 597–620.

Field, N.P., Gal-Oz, E., & Bonanno, G.A. (2003). Continuing bonds and adjustment at 5 years after the death of a spouse. *Journal of Consulting and Clinical Psychology, 71*, 110–117.

Field, N., Gao, B. & Paderna, L. (2005). Continuing bonds in bereavement: An attachment theory based perspective. *Death Studies, 29*, 1–23.

Field, N.P., Nichols, C., Holen, A., & Horowitz, M.J. (1999). The relation of continuing attachment to adjustment in conjugal bereavement. *Journal of Consulting and Clinical Psychology, 67*, 212–218.

Fleming, S., & Robinson, P.J. (1991). The application of cognitive therapy to the bereaved. In T.M. Vallis, & J.L. Howes (Eds.), *The challenge of cognitive therapy: Applications to non-traditional populations* (pp. 135–158). New York: Plenum.

Folkman, S. (1997a). Introduction to the special section: Use of bereavement narratives to predict well-being in gay men whose partner died of AIDS—Four theoretical perspectives. *Journal of Personality and Social Psychology, 72*, 851–854.

Folkman, S. (1997b). Positive psychological states and coping with severe stress. *Social Science and Medicine, 45*, 1207–1221.

Folkman, S. (2001). Revised coping theory and the process of bereavement. In M.S. Stroebe, & R.O. Hansson (Eds.), *Handbook of bereavement research: Consequences, coping, and care* (pp. 563–584). Washington, DC: American Psychological Association.

Folkman S. (2008). The case for positive emotions in the stress process. *Anxiety Stress Coping, 21*(1), 3–14.

Folkman, S., Chesney, M., Collette, L., Boccellari, A., & Cooke, M. (1996). Postbereavement depressive mood and its pre-bereavement predictors in HIV+ and HIV–gay men. *Journal of Personality and Social Psychology, 70*, 336–348.

Folkman, S., & Moskowitz, J.T. (2000). Stress, positive emotion, and coping. *Current Directions in Psychological Science, 9*, 115–118.

Fortner, B.V., & Neimeyer, R.A. (1999). Death anxiety in older adults: A quantitative review. *Death Studies, 23*, 387–411.

Fraley, R.C., & Shaver, P.R. (1999). Loss and bereavement: Bowlby's theory and recent controversies concerning "grief work" and the nature of detachment. In J. Cassidy, & P.R. Shaver (Eds.), *Handbook of attachment theory and research: Theory, research, and clinical applications* (pp. 735–759). New York: Guilford.

Fredrickson, B.L. (1998). What good are positive emotions? *Review of General Psychology, 2*, 300–319.

Fredrickson, B.L. (2001). The role of positive emotions in positive psychology: The broaden-and-build theory of positive emotions. *American Psychologist, 56*, 218–226.

Fredrickson B.L., & Losada, M.F. (2005). Positive affect and the complex dynamics of human flourishing. *American Psychologist, 60(7)*, 678–686.

Fredrickson, B.L., Tugade, M.M., Waugh, C.E., & Larkin, G.R. (2003). What good are positive emotions? A prospective study of resilience and emotions following the terrorist attacks on the United States on September 11, 2001. *Journal of Personality and Social Psychology, 84*, 365–376.

Freud, S. (1957). Mourning and melancholia. In J. Strachey (Ed.), *The standard edition of the complete works of Sigmund Freud* Vol. 14 (pp. 152–170). London: Hogarth Press. (Original work published 1917).

Glick, I.O., Weiss, R.S., & Parkes, C.M. (1974). *The first year of bereavement.* New York: Wiley.

Gowell, E.C. (1992). *Good grief rituals: Tools for healing.* New York: Station Hill Press.

Gross, J. (2007, November 19). Study finds higher outlays for caregivers of older relatives. *New York Times*, p. A18.

Hagman, G. (1995). Mourning: A review and reconsideration. *International Journal of Psycho-Analysis, 76*, 909–925.

Hagman, G. (2001). Beyond decathexis: Toward a new psychoanalytic understanding and treatment of mourning. In R.A. Neimeyer (Ed.), *Meaning, reconstruction and the experience of loss* (pp. 13–31). Washington, DC: American Psychological Association.

Haley, W.E., Bergman, E.J., Roth, D.L., McVie, T., Gaugler, J.E., & Mittelman, M.S. (2008). Long-term effects of bereavement and caregiver intervention on dementia caregiver depressive symptoms. *The Gerontologist, 48(6)*, 732–740.

Hebert, R.S., Dang, Q., & Schulz, R. (2006). Preparedness for the death of a loved one and mental health in bereaved caregivers of patients with dementia: Findings from the REACH study. *Journal of Palliative Medicine, 9(3)*, 683–693.

Hebert, R.S., Schulz, R., Copeland, V.C., & Arnold, R.M. (2009). Preparing family caregivers for death and bereavement. Insights from caregivers of terminally ill patients. *Journal of Pain Symptom Management, 37(1)*, 3–12.

Hogan, N.S., & DeSantis, L. (1994). Things that help and hinder adolescent sibling bereavement. *Western Journal of Nursing Research, 16*, 132–153.

Horowitz, M.J. (1976). *Stress response syndromes.* Oxford, England: Jason Aronson.

Horowitz, M.J. (1985). Anxious states of mind induced by stress. In A.H. Tuma, & J.D. Maser (Eds.), *Anxiety and the anxiety disorders* (pp. 619–631). Hillsdale, NJ: Erlbaum.

Horowitz, M.J. (1990). A model of mourning: Change in schemas of self and other. *Journal of American Psychoanalytic Association, 38*, 297–324.

Humphrey, G.M., & Zimpfer, D.G. (1996). *Counseling for grief and bereavement.* Thousand Oaks, CA: Sage Publications.

Ingram, K.M., Jones, D.A., & Smith, N.G. (2001). Adjustment among people who have experienced AIDS-related multiple loss: The role of unsupportive social interactions, social support, and coping. *Omega: Journal of Death and Dying, 43*, 287–309.

Jacobs, S. (1993). *Pathological grief: Maladaptation to loss.* Washington, DC: American Psychiatric Press.

Jacobs, J.R., & Bovasso, G.B. (2009). Re-examining the long-term effects of experiencing parental death in childhood on adult psychopathology. *The Journal of Nervous and Mental Disease, 197(1)*, 24–27.

Jacobs, S., Mazure, C., & Prigerson, H. (2000). Diagnostic criteria for traumatic grief. *Death Studies, 24*, 185–199.

Jordan, J.R., & Neimeyer, R.A. (2003). Does grief counseling work? *Death Studies, 27*, 765–786.

Kaltman, S., & Bonanno, G.A. (2003). Trauma and bereavement: Examining the impact of sudden and violent death. *Journal of Anxiety Disorders, 17*, 131–147.

Kato, P.M., & Mann, T. (1999). A synthesis of psychological interventions for the bereaved. *Clinical Psychology Review, 19*, 275–296.

Keltner, D., & Bonanno, G.A. (1997). A study of laughter and dissociation: Distinct correlates of laughter and smiling during bereavement. *Journal of Personality and Social Psychology, 73*, 687–702.

Klass, D., Silverman, P.R., & Nickman, S.L. (1996). *Continuing bonds: New understandings of grief.* Philadelphia: Taylor and Francis.

Klass, D., & Walter, J. (2001). Processes of grieving: How bonds are continued. In M.S. Stroebe, & R.O. Hansson (Eds.), *Handbook of bereavement research: Consequences, coping, and care* (pp. 431–448). Washington, DC: American Psychological Association.

Kovac, S.H., & Range, L.M. (2000). Writing projects: Lessening undergraduates' unique suicidal bereavement. *Suicide and Life-Threatening Behavior, 30*, 50–60.

Kübler-Ross, E. (1969). *On death and dying.* New York: Springer.

Larson, D.G., & Hoyt, W.T. (2007). What has become of grief counseling? An evaluation of the empirical foundations of the new pessimism. *Professional Psychology: Research and Practice, 38*, 347–355.

Lazare, A. (1989). Bereavement and unresolved grief. In A. Lazare (Ed.), *Outpatient psychiatry: Diagnosis and treatment* (2nd ed., pp. 381–397). Baltimore: Williams and Wilkins.

Lazarus, R., & Folkman, S. (1984). *Stress, appraisal, and coping.* New York: Springer.

Lazarus, R.S., Kanner, A.D., & Folkman, S. (1980). Emotions: A cognitive-phenomenological analysis. In R. Plutchik, & H. Kellerman (Eds.), *Emotions: Theory, research, and experience* Vol. 1 (pp. 189–217). New York: Academic Press.

Lehman, D.R., Ellard, J.H., & Wortman, C.B. (1986). Social support for the bereaved: Recipients' and providers' perspectives on what is helpful. *Journal of Consulting and Clinical Psychology, 54*, 438–446.

Lehman, D.R., Wortman, C.B., & Williams, A.F. (1987). Long-term effects of losing a spouse or child in a motor vehicle crash. *Journal of Personality and Social Psychology, 52*, 218–231.

Lepore, S.J., Silver, R.C., Wortman, C.B., & Wayment, H.A. (1996). Social constraints, intrusive thoughts, and depressive symptoms among bereaved mothers. *Journal of Personality and Social Psychology, 70*, 271–282.

Lepore, S.J., & Smyth, J.M. (2002). *The writing cure: How expressive writing promotes health and emotional well-being.* Washington: American Psychological Association.

Li, L.W. (2005). From caregiving to bereavement: Trajectories of depressive symptoms among wife and daughter caregivers. *Journals of Gerontology, 60B*, 190–198.

Lichtenstein, P., Gatz, M., Pedersen, N.L., Berg, S., & McClearn, G.E. (1996). A co-twin control study of response to widowhood. *Journal of Gerontology. Series B, Psychological Sciences and Social Sciences, 51*, 279–289.

Lichtenthal, W.G., Cruess, D.G., & Prigerson, H.G. (2004). A case for establishing complicated grief as a distinct mental disorder in *DSM-V. Clinical Psychology Review, 24*, 637–662.

Lopata, H.Z. (1979). *Women as widows: Support systems.* New York: Elsevier.

Lumley, M.A., Tojeck, T.M., & Macklem, D.J. (2002). The effects of written and verbal disclosure among repressive and alexithymic people. In S.J. Lepore, & J.M. Smyth (Eds.), *The writing cure: How expressive writing promotes health and emotional well-being* (pp. 75–95). Washington, DC: American Psychological Association.

Lund, D.A., Dimond, M.F., Caserta, M.S., Johnson, R.J., Poulton, J.L., & Connelly, J.R. (1986). Identifying elderly with coping difficulties after two years of bereavement. *Omega, 16,* 213–224.

Lund, D.A., Caserta, M.S., & Dimond, M.F. (1986). Impact of bereavement on the self-conceptions of older surviving spouses. *Symbolic Interaction, 9,* 235–244.

Maciejewski, P.K., Zhang, B., Block, S.D., & Prigerson, H.G. (2007). An empirical examination of the stage theory of grief. *JAMA: Journal of the American Medical Association, 297,* 716–723.

Malkinson, R. (2001). Cognitive-behavioral therapy of grief: A review and application. *Research on Social Work Practice, 11,* 671–698.

Malkinson, R., Rubin, S.S., & Witztum, E. (2000). *Traumatic and nontraumatic loss and bereavement: Clinical theory and practice.* Madison, CT: Psychosocial Press.

Marris, P. (1958). *Widows and their families.* London: Routledge and Kegan Paul.

Martin, J.L., & Doka, K. (2000). *Men don't cry . . . women do: Transcending gender stereotypes of grief.* Philadelphia: Brunner/Mazel.

Marwit, S.J., & Carusa, S.S. (1998). Communicated support following loss: Examining the experiences of parental death and parental divorce in adolescence. *Death Studies, 22,* 237–255.

Marwit, S.J., & Klass, D. (1996). Grief and the role of the inner representation of the deceased. In D. Klass, & P.R. Silverman (Eds.), *Continuing bonds: New understandings of grief* (pp. 297–309). Philadelphia: Taylor and Francis.

McIntosh, D., Silver, R., & Wortman, C.B. (1993). Religion's role in adjustment to a negative life event: Coping with the loss of a child. *Journal of Personality and Social Psychology, 65,* 812–821.

Mendes de Leon, C.F., Kasl, S.V., & Jacobs, S. (1994). A prospective study of widowhood and changes in symptoms of depression in a community sample of the elderly. *Psychological Medicine, 24,* 613–624.

Middleton, W., Burnett, P., Raphael, B., & Martinek, N. (1996). The bereavement response: A cluster analysis. *British Journal of Psychiatry, 169,* 167–171.

Middleton, W., Moylan, A., Raphael, B., Burnett, P., & Martinek, N. (1993). An international perspective on bereavement related concepts. *Australian and New Zealand Journal of Psychiatry, 27,* 457–463.

Middleton, W., Raphael, B., Burnett, P., & Martinek, N. (1998). A longitudinal study comparing bereavement phenomena in recently bereaved spouses, adult children and parents. *Australian and New Zealand Journal of Psychiatry, 32,* 235–241.

Miller, E.D., & Omarzu, J. (1998). New directions in loss research. In J. Harvey (Ed.), *Perspectives on loss: A sourcebook* (pp. 3–20). Washington, DC: Taylor & Francis.

Miller, E., & Wortman, C.B. (2002). Gender differences in mortality and morbidity following a major stressor: The case of conjugal bereavement. In G. Weidner, S.M. Kopp, &

M. Kristenson (Eds.), *Heart disease: Environment, stress and gender* (pp. 251–266). Washington, DC: IOS Press.

Moskowitz, J.T., Folkman, S., & Acree, M. (2003). Do positive psychological states shed light on recovery from bereavement? Findings from a 3-year longitudinal study. *Death Studies, 27,* 471–500.

Moskowitz, J.T., Folkman, S., Collette, L., & Vittinghoff, E. (1996). Coping and mood during AIDS-related caregiving and bereavement. *Annals of Behavioral Medicine, 18,* 49–57.

Murphy, S.A. (1996). Parent bereavement stress and preventive intervention following the violent deaths of adolescent or young adult children. *Death Studies, 20,* 441–452.

Murphy, S.A., Chung, I., & Johnson, L.C. (2002). Patterns of mental distress following the violent death of a child and predictors of change over time. *Research in Nursing & Health, 25,* 425–437.

Murphy, S.A., Das Gupta, A., Cain, K.C., Johnson, L.C., Lohan, J., & Wu, L., et al. (1999). Changes in parents' mental distress after the violent death of an adolescent or young adult child: A longitudinal prospective analysis. *Death Studies, 23,* 129–159.

Murphy, S.A., Johnson, L.C., Chung, I., & Beaton, R.D. (2003). The prevalence of PTSD following the violent death of a child and predictors of change 5 years later. *Journal of Traumatic Stress, 16,* 17–25.

Murphy, S.A., Johnson, L.C., & Lohan, J. (2002). The aftermath of the violent death of a child: An integration of the assessment of parents' mental distress and PTSD during the first 5 years of bereavement. *Journal of Loss and Trauma, 7,* 203–222.

Murphy, S.A., Johnson, L.C., & Lohan, J. (2003). Finding meaning in a child's violent death: A five-year prospective analysis of parents' personal narratives and empirical data. *Death Studies, 27,* 381–404.

Murphy, S.A., Johnson, L.C., Wu, L., Fan, J.J., & Lohan, J. (2003). Bereaved parents' outcomes 4 to 60 months after their children's death by accident, suicide, or homicide: A comparative study demonstrating differences. *Death Studies, 27,* 39–61.

Neimeyer, R.A. (1997). Problems and prospects in constructivist psychotherapy. *Journal of Constructivist Psychology, 10,* 51–74.

Neimeyer, R.A. (1998). *Lessons of loss: A guide to coping.* Boston: McGraw-Hill.

Neimeyer, R.A. (1999). Narrative strategies in grief therapy. *Journal of Constructivist Psychology, 12,* 65–85.

Neimeyer, R.A. (2000). Searching for the meaning of meaning: Grief therapy and the process of reconstruction. *Death Studies, 24,* 541–558.

Neimeyer, R.A. (2001). *Meaning, reconstruction and the experience of loss.* Washington, DC: American Psychological Association.

Neimeyer, R.A. (2006). Widowhood, grief and the quest for meaning: A narrative perspective on resilience. In D. Carr, R.M. Nesse, & C.B. Wortman (Eds.), *Spousal bereavement in late life* (pp. 227–252). New York: Springer.

Nesse, R.M., Wortman, C.B., & House, J.S. (2006). Introduction: A history of the changing lives of older couples study. In D. Carr, R. Nesse, & C.B. Wortman (Eds.), *Spousal bereavement in late life* (pp. xxi–xxxi). New York: Springer.

Nolen-Hoeksema, S. (1991). Responses to depression and their effects on the duration of depressive episodes. *Journal of Abnormal Psychology, 100,* 569–582.

Nolen-Hoeksema, S. (2001). Ruminative coping and adjustment to bereavement. In M.S. Stroebe, & R.O. Hansson (Eds.), *Handbook of bereavement research: Consequences, coping, and care* (pp. 545–562). Washington, DC: American Psychological Association.

Nolen-Hoeksema, S., & Larson, J. (1999). *Coping with loss.* Mahwah, NJ: Erlbaum.

Nolen-Hoeksema, S., McBride, A., & Larson, J. (1997). Rumination and psychological distress among bereaved partners. *Journal of Personality and Social Psychology, 72,* 855–862.

Norman, S.A., Lumley, M.A., Dooley, J.A., & Diamond, M.P. (2004). For whom does it work? Moderators of the effects of written emotional disclosure in women with chronic pelvic pain. *Psychosomatic Medicine, 66,* 174–183.

Normand, C.L., Silverman, P.R., & Nickman, S.L. (1996). Bereaved children's changing relationships with the deceased. In D. Klass, & P.R. Silverman (Eds.), *Continuing bonds: New understandings of grief* (pp. 87–111). Philadelphia: Taylor and Francis.

Ong, A.D., Bergeman, C.S., & Bisconit, T.L. (2004). The role of daily positive emotions during conjugal bereavement. *Journals of Gerentology: Series B: Psychological Sciences and Social Psychology, 59B,* 168–176.

Osterweis, M., Solomon, F., & Green, F. (1984). *Bereavement: Reactions, consequences, and care.* Washington, DC: National Academy Press.

Pargament, K.I., & Park, C.L. (1995). Merely a defense? The variety of religious means and ends. *Journal of Social Issues, 51,* 13–32.

Parkes, C.M., & Weiss, R.S. (1983). *Recovery from bereavement.* New York: Basic Books.

Pennebaker, J.W., & Beall, S.K. (1986). Confronting a traumatic event: Toward an understanding of inhibition and disease. *Journal of Abnormal Psychology, 95,* 274–281.

Pennebaker, J.W., & Chung, C.K. (2011). Expressive writing: Connections to physical and mental health. In H.S. Friedman (Ed.), *The Oxford handbook of health psychology.* New York: Oxford University Press.

Pennebaker, J.W., Zech, E., & Rime, B. (2001). Disclosing and sharing emotion: Psychological, social, and health consequences. In M.S. Stroebe, & R.O. Hansson (Eds.), *Handbook of bereavement research: Consequences, coping, and care* (pp. 517–543). Washington, DC: American Psychological Association.

Pinquart, M., & Sorenson, S. (2003a). Differences between caregivers and noncaregivers in psychological health and physical health: A meta-analysis. *Psychology and Aging, 18,* 250–267.

Pinquart, M., & Sorenson, S. (2003b). Associations of stressors and uplifts of caregiving with caregiver burden and depressive mood: A meta-analysis. *Journals of Gerentology: Series B: Psychological Sciences and Social Sciences, 58B,* P112–P128.

Potter, P.A., & Perry, A.G. (1997). *Fundamentals of nursing: Concepts, process, and practice* (4th ed.). St. Louis, MO: Mosby.

Prigerson, H. (2004). Complicated grief: When the path of adjustment leads to a dead-end. *Bereavement Care, 23,* 38–40.

Prigerson, H.G., Cherlin, E., Chen, J.H., Kasl, S.V., Hurzeler, R., & Bradley, E.H. (2003). The stressful caregiving adult reactions to experiences of dying (SCARED) scale: A measure for assessing caregiver exposure to distress in terminal care. *American Journal of Geriatric Psychiatry, 11,* 309–319.

Prigerson, H.G., Vanderwerker, L.C., & Maciejewski, P.K. (2008). A case for inclusion of prolonged grief disorder in DSM-V. In M.S. Stroebe, R.O. Hansson, & H. Schut (Eds.), *Handbook of bereavement research and practice: Advances in theory and intervention* (pp. 165–186). Washington, DC: American Psychological Association.

Ramsay, R.W., & Happee, J.A. (1977). The stress of bereavement: Components and treatment. In C.D. Spielberger, & I.G. Sarason (Eds.), *Stress and anxiety: IV* (pp. 53–64). Oxford, UK: Hemisphere.

Rando, T.A. (1984). *Grief, dying, and death.* Champaign, IL: Research Press.

Rando, T.A. (1993). *Treatment of complicated mourning.* Champaign, IL: Research Press.

Range, L.M., Kovac, S.H., & Marion, M.S. (2000). Does writing about the bereavement lessen grief following sudden, unintentional death? *Death Studies, 24,* 115–134.

Raphael, B. (1983). *The anatomy of bereavement.* New York: Basic Books.

Raphael, B., & Nunn, K. (1988). Counseling the bereaved. *Journal of Social Issues, 44,* 191–206.

Rees, W.D. (1971). The hallucinations of widowhood. *British Medical Journal, 4,* 37–41.

Richards, T., Acree, M., & Folkman, S. (1999). Spiritual aspects of loss among partners of men with AIDS: Postbereavement follow-up. *Death Studies, 23,* 105–127.

Richards, T.A., & Folkman, S. (1997). Spiritual aspects of loss at the time of a partner's death from AIDS. *Death Studies, 21,* 527–552.

Russac, R.J., Steighner, N.S., & Canto, A. (2002). Grief work versus continuing bonds: A call for paradigm integration or replacement? *Death Studies, 26,* 463–478.

Sanders, C.M. (1989). *Grief: The mourning after.* New York: Wiley.

Sanders, C.M. (1993). Risk factors in bereavement outcome. In M. Stroebe, W. Stroebe, & R.O. Hansson (Eds.), *Handbook of bereavement: Theory, research and intervention* (pp. 255–267). New York: Cambridge University Press.

Sanders, C.M. (1999). *Grief: The mourning after* (2nd ed.). New York: Wiley.

Schulz, R., Beach, S.R., Lind, B., Martire, L.M., Zdaniuk, B., Hirsch, C., et al. (2001). Involvement in caregiving and adjustment to death of a spouse: Findings from the caregiver health effects study. *Journal of the American Medical Association, 285,* 3123–3129.

Schulz, R., Boerner, K., Shear, K., Zhang, S., & Gitlin, L.N. (2006). Predictors of complicated grief among dementia caregivers: A prospective study of bereavement. *The American Journal of Geriatric Psychiatry, 14*(8), 650–658.

Schulz, R., Boerner, K, & Hebert, R.S. (2008). Caregiving and bereavement. In M. Stroebe, R. Hansson, H. Schut, & W. Stroebe (Eds.), *Handbook of bereavement research and practice: 21st century perspectives* (pp. 265–285). Washington, DC: American Psychological Association Press.

Schulz, R., Mendelson, A.B., & Haley, W.E. (2003). End-of-life care and the effects of bereavement on family caregivers of persons with dementia. *New England Journal of Medicine, 349,* 1936–1942.

Schut, H., & Stroebe, M. (2010). Effects of support, counselling and therapy before and after the loss: Can we really help bereaved people? *Psychologica Belgica, 50,* 89–102.

Schut, H.A., Stroebe, M.S., Boelen, P.A., & Zijerveld, A.M. (2006). Continuing relationships with the deceased: Disentangling bonds and grief. *Death Studies, 30*(8), 757–766.

Schut, H., Stroebe, M.S., van den Bout, J., & Terheggen, M. (2001). The efficacy of bereavement interventions: Determining who benefits. In M.S. Stroebe, R.O. Hansson, W. Stroebe, & H. Schut (Eds.), *Handbook of bereavement research: Consequences, coping, and care* (pp. 705–737). Washington, DC: American Psychological Association.

Seery, M.D., Silver, R.C., Holman, E.A., Ence, W.A., & Chu, T.Q. (2007). Expressing thoughts and feelings following a collective trauma: Immediate responses to 9/11 predict negative outcomes in a national sample. *Journal of Consulting and Clinical Psychology, 29*, 1–11.

Segal, D.L., Bogaards, J.A., Becker, L.A., & Chatman, C. (1999). Effects of emotional expression on adjustment to spousal loss among older adults. *Journal of Mental Health and Aging, 5*, 297–310.

Shaver, P.R., & Tancredy, C.M. (2001). Emotion, attachment, and bereavement: A conceptual commentary. In M.S. Stroebe, R.O. Hansson, W. Stroebe, & H. Schut (Eds.), *Handbook of bereavement research: Consequences, coping, and care* (pp. 63–88). Washington, DC: American Psychological Association.

Shear, K., Frank, E., Houck, P.R., & Reynolds, C.F., III. (2005). Treatment of complicated grief: A randomized controlled trial. *Journal of the American Medical Association, 293*, 2601–2608.

Shear, K., Monk, T., Houck, P., Melhem, N., Frank, E., Reynolds, C., & Sillowash, R. (2007). An attachment-based model of complicated grief including the role of avoidance. *European Archives of Psychiatry and Clinical Neuroscience, 257*, 453–461.

Shmotkin, D. (1999). Affective bonds of adult children with living versus deceased parents. *Psychology and Aging, 14*, 473–482.

Shuchter, S.R. (1986). *Dimensions of grief: Adjusting to the death of a spouse.* San Francisco, CA: Jossey-Bass.

Shuchter, S.R., & Zisook, S. (1993). The course of normal grief. In M.S. Stroebe, & W. Stroebe (Eds.), *Handbook of bereavement: Theory, research, and intervention* (pp. 23–43). New York: Cambridge University Press.

Silverman, P.R., Baker, J., Cait, C., & Boerner, K. (2003). The effects of negative legacies on the adjustment of parentally bereaved children and adolescents. *Omega: Journal of Death and Dying, 46*, 335–352.

Silverman, P.R., Johnson, J., & Prigerson, H.G. (2001). Preliminary explorations of the effects of prior trauma and loss on risk for psychiatric disorders in recently widowed people. *Israel Journal of Psychiatry and Related Sciences, 38*, 202–215.

Silverman, P.R., & Nickman, S.L. (1996). Children's construction of their dead parents. In D. Klass, P.R. Silverman, & S.L. Nickman (Eds.). (1996). *Continuing bonds: New understandings of grief* (pp. 73–86). Philadelphia: Taylor and Francis.

Silverman, P.R., Nickman, S., & Worden, J.W. (1992). Detachment revisited: The child's reconstruction of a dead parent. *American Journal of Orthopsychiatry, 62*, 494–503.

Silverman, P.R., & Worden, J.W. (1992). Children's reactions in the early months after the death of a parent. *American Journal of Orthopsychiatry, 62*, 93–104.

Smyth, J.M. (1998). Written emotional expression: Effect sizes, outcome types, and moderating variables. *Journal of Consulting and Clinical Psychology, 66*, 174–184.

Smyth, J.M., & Greenberg, M.A. (2000). Scriptotherapy: The effects of writing about traumatic events. In P.R. Duberstein, & J.M. Masling (Eds.), *Psychodynamic perspectives on sickness and health* (pp. 121–160). Washington, DC: American Psychological Association.

Stein, N.L., Folkman, S., Trabasso, T., & Christopher-Richards, A. (1997). Appraisal and goal processes as predictors of well-being in bereaved care-givers. *Journal of Personality and Social Psychology, 72*, 863–871.

Stroebe, M.S. (1992–1993). Coping with bereavement: A review of the grief work hypothesis. *Omega: Journal of Death and Dying, 26*, 19–42.

Stroebe, M.S., Folkman, S., Hansson, R.O., & Schut, H. (2006). The prediction of bereavement outcome: development of an integrative risk factor framework. *Social Science and Medicine, 63*(9), 2440–2451.

Stroebe, M.S., Hansson, R.O., Schut, H., & Stroebe, W. (Eds.). (2008). *Handbook of bereavement research and practice: 21st century perspectives.* Washington, DC: American Psychological Association Press.

Stroebe, M.S., Hansson, R.O., Schut, H., Stroebe, W., & Van den Blink, E. (2008). *Handbook of bereavement research and practice: Advances in theory and intervention.* Washington, DC, US: American Psychological Association.

Stroebe, M.S., Hansson, R.O., & Stroebe, W. (1993). Contemporary themes and controversies in bereavement research. In M.S. Stroebe, W. Stroebe, & R.O. Hansson (Eds.), *Handbook of bereavement: Theory, research, and intervention* (pp. 457–476). Cambridge, England: Cambridge University Press.

Stroebe, M.S., Hansson, R.O., Stroebe, W., & Schut, H. (Eds.). (2001). *Handbook of bereavement research: Consequences, coping, and care.* Washington, DC: American Psychological Association.

Stroebe, M., & Schut, H. (1999). The dual process model of coping with bereavement: Rationale and description. *Death Studies, 23*, 197–224.

Stroebe, M.S., & Schut, H. (2001). Meaning making in the dual process model of coping with bereavement. In R.A. Neimeyer (Ed.), *Meaning reconstruction and the experience of loss* (pp. 55–73). Washington, DC: American Psychological Association.

Stroebe, M., & Schut, H. (2005). To continue or relinquish bonds: A review of consequences for the bereaved. *Death Studies, 29*, 477–494.

Stroebe, M., Schut, H., & Stroebe, W. (2005a). Attachment in coping with bereavement: A theoretical integration. *Review of General Psychology, 9*, 48–66.

Stroebe, W., Schut, H., & Stroebe, M.S. (2005b). Grief work, disclosure, and counseling: Do they help the bereaved? *Clinical Psychology Review, 25*, 395–414.

Stroebe, M., Schut, H., & Stroebe, W. (2007). Health outcomes of bereavement. *Lancet, 370*, 1960–1973.

Stroebe, M., & Stroebe, W. (1991). Does "grief work" work? *Journal of Consulting and Clinical Psychology, 59*, 479–482.

Stroebe, M.S., Stroebe, W., & Hansson, R.O. (Eds.). (1993). *Handbook of bereavement: Theory, research, and intervention.* New York: Cambridge University Press.

Stroebe, M., Stroebe, W., & Schut, H. (2001). Gender differences in adjustment to bereavement: An empirical and theoretical review. *Review of General Psychology, 5*, 62–83.

Stroebe, M., Stroebe, W., Schut, H., Zech, E., & van den Bout, J. (2002). Does disclosure of emotion facilitate recovery from bereavement? Evidence from two prospective studies. *Journal of Consulting and Clinical Psychology, 70*, 169–178.

Taylor, S.E. (2011). Social support: a review. In H.S. Friedman (Ed.), *The Oxford handbook of health psychology.* New York: Oxford University Press.

Tedeschi, R.G., & Calhoun, L.G. (1996). The posttraumatic growth inventory: Measuring the positive legacy of trauma. *Journal of Traumatic Stress, 9*, 455–472.

Tedeschi, R.G., & Calhoun, L.G. (2004). Target article: "Posttraumatic growth: Conceptual foundations and empirical evidence." *Psychological Inquiry, 15*, 1–18.

Teno, J.M., Clarridge, B.R., & Casey, V. (2004). Family perspectives on end-of-life care at the last place of care. *Journal of the American Medical Association, 29*, 88–93.

Umberson, D. (1987). Family status and health behaviors: Social control as a dimension of social integration. *Journal of Health and Social Behavior, 28*, 306–319.

Umberson, D. (1992). Gender, marital status and the social control of health behavior. *Social Science and Medicine, 34*, 907–917.

Umberson, D. (2003). *Death of a parent.* New York: Cambridge University Press.

Vachon, M.L.S., Rogers, J., Lyall, W.A., Lancee, W.J., Sheldon, A.R., & Freeman, S.J.J. (1982). Predictors and correlates of adaptation to conjugal bereavement. *American Journal of Psychiatry, 139*, 998–1002.

Vachon, M.L.S., Sheldon, A.R., Lancee, W.J., Lyall, W.A.L., Rogers, J., & Freeman, S.J.J. (1982). Correlates of enduring distress patterns following bereavement: Social network, life situation and personality. *Psychological Medicine, 12*, 783–788.

Volkan, V. (1971). A study of a patient's "re-grief work" through dreams, psychological tests and psychoanalysis. *Psychiatric Quarterly, 45*, 244–273.

Wayment, H.A., & Vierthaler, J. (2002). Attachment style and bereavement reactions. *Journal of Loss and Trauma, 7*, 129–149.

Weiss, R.S. (1993). Loss and recovery. In M.S. Stroebe, W. Stroebe, & R.O. Hansson (Eds.), *Handbook of bereavement: Theory, research, and intervention* (pp. 271–284). New York: Cambridge University Press.

Wijngaards-de Meij, L., Stroebe, M., Schut, H., Stroebe, W., van den Bout, J., van der Heijden, P.G., & Dijkstra, I. (2008). Parents grieving the loss of their child: Interdependence in coping. *British Journal of Clinical Psychology, 47*, 31–42.

Wolff, K., & Wortman, C.B. (2006). Psychological consequences of spousal loss among the elderly. In D. Carr, R. Nesse, & C.B. Wortman (Eds.). *Spousal bereavement in late life* (pp. 81–115). New York: Springer.

Worden, J.W. (2008). *Grief counseling and grief therapy: A handbook for the mental health practitioner* (4th ed.). New York: Springer.

Wortman, C.B. (2004). Post-traumatic growth: Progress and problems. *Psychological Inquiry, 15*, 81–90.

Wortman, C.B., Battle, E.S., & Lemkau, J.P. (1997). Coming to terms with sudden, traumatic death of a spouse or child. In R.C. Davis, & A.J. Lurigio (Eds.), *Victims of crime* (pp. 108–133). Thousand Oaks, CA: Sage.

Wortman, C.B., Boerner, K. (2007). Reactions to the death of a loved one: Myths of coping versus scientific evidence. In H.S. Friedman, & R.C. Silver (Eds.), *Foundations of health psychology* (pp. 285–324). Oxford University Press.

Wortman, C.B., & Silver, R.C. (1987). Coping with irrevocable loss. In G.R. VandenBos, & B.K. Bryant (Eds.), *Cataclysms, crises, and catastrophes: Psychology in action (Master Lecture Series)*, Vol. 6 (pp. 189–235). Washington, DC: American Psychological Association.

Wortman, C.B., & Silver, R.C. (1989). The myths of coping with loss. *Journal of Consulting and Clinical Psychology, 57*, 349–357.

Wortman, C.B., & Silver, R.C. (1992). Reconsidering assumptions about coping with loss: An overview of current research. In S.H. Filipp, L. Montada, & M. Lerner (Eds.), *Life crises and experiences of loss in adulthood* (pp. 341–365). Hillsdale, NJ: Erlbaum.

Wortman, C.B., & Silver, R.C. (2001). The myths of coping with loss revisited. In M.S. Stroebe, R.O. Hansson, W. Stroebe, & H. Schut (Eds.), *Handbook of bereavement research: Consequences, coping, and care* (pp. 405–430). Washington, DC: American Psychological Association.

Wortman, C.B., Wolff, K., & Bonanno, G. (2004). Loss of an intimate partner through death. In D. Mashek, & A. Aron (Eds.) *The handbook of closeness and intimacy* (pp. 305–320). Mahwah, NJ: Erlbaum.

Zhang, B., El-Jawahri, A., & Prigerson, H.G. (2006). Update on bereavement research: Evidenced-based guidelines for the diagnosis and treatment of complicated bereavement. *Journal of Palliative Medicine, 9*(5), 1188–1203.

Zhang, B., Mitchell, S.L., Bambauer, K.Z., Jones R, & Prigerson, H.G. (2008). Depressive symptom trajectories and associated risks among bereaved Alzheimer disease caregivers. *American Journal of Geriatric Psychiatry, 16*(2), 145–155.

Zisook, S., Chentsova-Dutton, Y., & Shuchter, S.R. (1998). PTSD following bereavement. *Annals of Clinical Psychiatry, 10*, 157–163.

Zisook, S., Paulus, M., Shuchter, S.R., & Judd, L.L. (1997). The many faces of depression following spousal bereavement. *Journal of Affective Disorders, 45*, 85–94.

Zisook, S., & Shuchter, S.R. (1986). The first four years of widowhood. *Psychiatric Annals, 16*, 288–294.

Zisook, S., & Shuchter, S.R. (1993). Major depression associated with widowhood. *American Journal of Geriatric Psychiatry, 1*, 316–326.

# Family Consultation for Couples Coping with Health Problems: A Social Cybernetic Approach

Michael J. Rohrbaugh *and* Varda Shoham

**Abstract**

We describe a *social-cybernetic* view of health behavior problems and a *family consultation* (FAMCON) intervention based on that view. Resurrecting foundational ideas from cybernetic family systems theory, this approach takes relationships rather than individuals as a primary unit of analysis, attaches more importance to problem maintenance than to etiology, downplays linear causality, and blurs the conceptual boundary between an individual patient and factors such as stress or support in his or her social environment. Intervention aims to interrupt two types of interpersonal problem maintenance—*ironic processes* and *symptom–system fit* (conceptualized, respectively, as positive and negative feedback cycles)—and to mobilize *communal coping* as a relational resource for change. Although this chapter draws primarily on a couple-focused intervention project with health-compromised smokers to illustrate both the clinical approach and supporting research, we have also applied both the FAMCON format and the social cybernetic view of problem maintenance to help couples and families cope with problems ranging from heart disease, cancer, and chronic pain to alcoholism, anxiety, and depression. If FAMCON proves effective with health problems that do not respond to other, more straightforward behavioral approaches, it could offer a useful alternative to psychoeducational and cognitive-behavioral interventions in the framework of stepped care.

**Keywords:** Family consultation, couples, coping, chronic illness, smoking, social-cybernetics

How are close relationships relevant to chronic health problems and addictions? Research in health psychology provides persuasive evidence that causal arrows go both ways: Positive support from family members (or its opposite, conflict and criticism) predicts the future course of diverse problems such as heart disease, cancer, renal disease, arthritis, diabetes, alcoholism, dementia, and pain (Fisher, 2006; Rohrbaugh, Shoham, & Coyne, 2006; Weihs, Enright, & Simmens, 2008); yet it is also clear that a patient's chronic illness can burden or disrupt family relations, even to the point of putting family caregivers at risk for health problems themselves (Schulz & Beach, 1999; Vitaliano, Zhang, & Scanlan, 2003). Each of these causal paths suggests an approach to intervention, such as attempting on one hand to improve the social support chronically ill patients receive from spouses and other family members (Martire & Schulz, 2007), or on the other hand, to reduce caregiver burden directly (Belle, Burgio, Burns, Coon, Czaja, Gallagher-Thompson, et al., 2006).

Our own work aligns mainly with the first path, addressing how close relationships simultaneously "get under the skin" (Taylor, Repetti, & Seeman, 1997) *and* provide a vital resource for clinical change. Yet, we depart from mainstream health psychology by downplaying both linear causality and the conceptual boundary between an individual patient and factors such as stress or support in his or her social environment. For more than 15 years, we have investigated the role close relationships play in maintaining and resolving various "individual" problems ranging from alcoholism to adolescent drug abuse, and from change-resistant smoking to coping with chronic heart disease. Reflecting our shared background as systemic family psychologists, we assume these problems rarely occur in a vacuum: Rather, they persist as an aspect of current close relationships in which causes and effects appear inextricably interwoven, with one person's behavior feeding back to set the stage for what another person does, and vice versa, in ongoing, circular sequences of interaction.

We call this approach "cybernetic" to highlight the circularity embodied in feedback systems, in which the effect or result of some problem behavior operates to modify, control, or regulate that very same behavior. Although internal feedback loops (e.g., physiological homeostasis) are well known in clinical biology, the transposition of this idea to systems of behavior outside the skin is less familiar—hence we add the modifier "social" to underscore the primacy of feedback control circuits operating *between* people rather than within them. This social-cybernetic view takes relationships rather than individuals as a primary unit of analysis and attaches more importance to problem maintenance than to etiology: What keeps a problem going is usually much more relevant to intervention than whatever may have initiated the problem in the first place. A corollary is that patterns of problem maintenance—and the interventions we design to interrupt them—are inherently idiographic, or case specific. This is because problem-maintaining interpersonal cycles can take drastically different, even opposite forms across cases involving topographically similar complaints (e.g., nagging vs. protecting a spouse who smokes, overeats, or shows distress).

This chapter describes a *social-cybernetic* view of health behavior problems and a *family consultation* (FAMCON) intervention format based on that view. The conceptual underpinnings of social-cybernetics are not new, but date back at least 50 years to Gregory Bateson, Don Jackson, and the beginnings of the family therapy movement (Hoffman, 1981; Nichols, 2008). Unfortunately, subsequent dilution by individualist and post-modern trends obstructed the focused empirical examination we think social-cybernetic ideas still deserve—and which we aim to resurrect here. Similarly, the consultation format we use to apply these ideas, consisting essentially of an assessment phase followed by strategic pattern interruption introduced in a carefully prepared "opinion" session, borrows elements from earlier work in family systems medicine (e.g., Wynne, McDaniel, & Weber, 1986) and strategic/systemic family therapy

(e.g., Fisch, Weakland, & Segal, 1982; Selvini-Palazzoli, Boscolo, Cecchin, & Prata, 1978). Although the present chapter focuses on couples and uses an intervention project with health-compromised smokers to exemplify central principles, procedures, and research methods, we routinely apply both the FAMCON format and the cybernetic view of problem maintenance to other problems and client configurations as well.

Finally, the approach we take here may interest some readers because it challenges several common assumptions in clinical health psychology. For example, in contrast to most psychoeducational and cognitive-behavioral approaches, we do *not* assume that effective interventions require understanding the development or etiology of an individual patient's problems or teaching the patient better coping or health management skills. Rather, we assume that identifying and interrupting current cycles of persistent problem maintaining social interaction between the patient and intimate others can be sufficient to initiate sustainable change in diverse problems of health and behavior, including behavior relevant to such topographically distinct risk factors as nicotine addiction, depression, and obesity. Indeed, the lines of inquiry implied here portend shifts of emphasis on multiple dimensions: from individual to relational problem units, from problem development (etiology) to problem maintenance (course), from instructive skill building interventions to strategic pattern interruption, and from group-based comparisons of average outcomes to bottom-up analyses of idiographic, yet rule-governed change.

## Two Social-Cybernetic Feedback Processes

A key distinction in the cybernetic framework is between *positive feedback*, referring to the enhancement or amplification of an effect by its own influence on the process that gives rise to it (e.g., an arms race, amplifier gain in electronics), and *negative feedback*, referring to the dampening or counteraction of an effect by its own influence on antecedent processes (e.g., the operation of a simple thermostat, inhibition of hormone secretion by high hormone levels in the blood). Analogously, two patterns of social-cybernetic problem maintenance reflecting positive and negative feedback loops are of particular interest in the realm of behavior: *Ironic processes* are deviation-amplifying positive feedback cycles that occur when well-intended, persistently applied "solutions" keep problem behavior going or make it worse. *Symptom–system fit*, on the other hand, refers to deviation-minimizing negative feedback cycles in which a problem or risk behavior appears to preserve some aspect of relational stability for the people involved.

Where human problems persist, ironic positive feedback processes are ubiquitous: They happen when trying harder to fall asleep keeps a person awake; when demands for intimacy provoke withdrawal; when urging one's spouse to eat, drink, or smoke less leads her to do it more; when encouraging a depressed partner to cheer up results in more despondency; and when attempting to resolve a disagreement through frank and open discussion serves only to intensify the conflict. Although social psychologist Dan Wegner (1994) first coined the term "ironic process" to describe ironic effects of attempted thought suppression on mental control, it captures well a much broader range of ironic phenomena introduced decades earlier by family therapists at Palo Alto's Mental Research Institute (Weakland, Fisch, Watzlawick, & Bodin, 1974; Watzlawick, Weakland, & Fisch, 1974; Fisch et al., 1982). Whether occurring within or between people, these processes persist because problem and attempted solution become intertwined in a vicious cycle, or positive feedback loop, in which more of the solution leads to more of the problem, leading to more of the same solution, and so on. Most important, formulations of ironic problem–solution loops provide a template for assessment and strategic intervention: They tell us where to look to understand what keeps a problem going (look for "more of the same" solution) and suggest what needs to happen for the problem to be resolved (someone must apply "less of the same" solution). Thus, to resolve a problem, it should not be necessary to understand or change its antecedent cause (assuming that can be determined), but simply to break the ironic pattern of problem maintenance by promoting less of the same solution. If this can be done—even in a small way—virtuous cycles can develop that lead to further positive change (cf. Rohrbaugh & Shoham, 2001, 2005; Shoham & Rohrbaugh, 1997).

Problem maintenance via *negative* feedback, which is emphasized in the writings of family therapists like Jackson (1957), Haley (1976), and Minuchin (1974), relates to the interpersonal functions a problem serves, not so much for the patient, but for the current close relationships in which he or she participates. Thus, problem behavior may persist because it provides a basis for the restoration or preservation of some vital relationship parameter (e.g., marital cohesion, conflict reduction, engagement of a disengaged family member) in a kind of interpersonal homeostasis. In the addictions arena, clinicians have observed that drinking and smoking can serve important communication functions in family relationships, particularly for regulating emotional closeness and distance (Doherty & Whitehead, 1986; Leipman, Silvia, & Nirenberg, 1989; Steinglass, Bennett, Wolin, & Reiss, 1987; Whitehead & Doherty, 1989). The pattern we call *symptom–system fit* occurs when a problem such as drinking or smoking appears to have adaptive consequences for a relationship, at least in the short run (Rohrbaugh, Shoham, & Racioppo, 2002; Rohrbaugh, Shoham, Trost, Muramoto, Cate, & Leischow, 2001; Shoham, Butler, Rohrbaugh, & Trost, 2007). For example, in couples where both partners smoke or drink, shared substance use might create a context for mutually supportive interactions or help partners stay positive, even when they disagree. Because one can only hypothesize about what interpersonal "function" a problem might serve based on observing the interaction sequences in which it occurs, identifying symptom–system fit typically involves more inference than identifying an ironic process. Formulations of symptom–system fit are nonetheless useful because they suggest approaches to pattern interruption that target this aspect of problem maintenance directly (e.g., helping a couple disagree or stay connected without smoking or drinking).

Finally, to anticipate a common confusion, the cybernetic usage of "negative feedback" has little to do with giving or receiving criticism, and "positive feedback" relates only tangentially to reinforcement or praise. On the other hand, positive close relationships do matter: In fact, a crucial flip side of social-cybernetic problem maintenance is the fact that positive, collaborative relationships not only confer health benefits but also provide a powerful resource for helping people change. For this reason, cultivation of *communal coping* has a central place in the FAMCON intervention format we will describe shortly.

## Why Look Beyond the Patient?

As the root word "psyche" suggests, psychology has long been concerned with events and processes occurring inside the skin—and more recently, the brain—of the individual. Yet, to understand health and health behavior, there are also good reasons to look outward, at least as far as the close relationships in which individuals participate. Prospective epidemiological studies controlling for initial health status show unequivocal health-protective effects of close relationships, linking both their quantity and quality

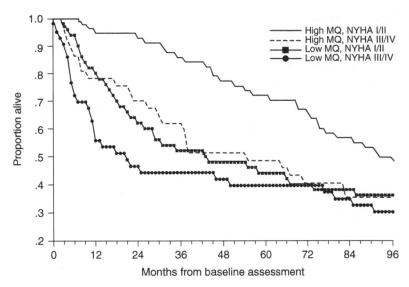

**Fig. 20.1** Patient survival for subgroups formed by crossing high/low marital quality (MQ) and high/low HF severity (NYHA class): High MQ, NYHA I/II (*n* = 58), High MQ, NYHA III/IV (*n* = 38), Low MQ, NYHA I/II (*n* = 50), Low MQ, NYHA III/IV (*n* = 43). Cox regression shows significant main effects for both marital quality and NYHA class (*p* <.001), and the two predictors do not interact. From Rohrbaugh, M. J., Shoham, V., & Coyne, J. C. (2006). Effects of marital quality on 8-year survival of patients with heart failure. *American Journal of Cardiology, 98,* 1069–1072. Reprinted with permission of the publisher, Elsevier.

to future morbidity and mortality (Berkman, 1985; House, Landis, & Umberson, 1988). Thus, people with high levels of social support are less likely to become sick, more likely to recover rapidly when illness does occur, and less likely to die from an established disease. Such findings span problems ranging from the common cold (Cohen, Doyle, Skoner, Rabin, & Gwaltney, 1997) to pain, diabetes, multiple sclerosis, pregnancy complications, heart and lung disease, various forms of cancer, and psychological distress (Brown, Sheffield, Leary, & Robinson, 2003; Collins, Dunkel-Schetter, Lobel, & Scrimshaw, 1993; Stone, Mezzacappa, Donatone, & Gonder, 1999).

Research in this area also highlights diverse pathways along which relationships may affect health: for example, by buffering the effects of stressful life experiences (Cohen & Hoberman, 1983); by influencing crucial health *behaviors* such as diet, exercise, alcohol or tobacco use, and adherence to medical regimen (DiMatteo, 2004); and by influencing physiological and neuroendocrine responses directly (Uchino, Cacioppo, & Kiecolt-Glaser, 1996). Interestingly, the emerging field of social neuroscience is finding evidence that, in very fundamental ways, "we are wired to connect" (Goleman, 2006): Our ongoing interactions with other people (especially those we care about most) appear to have far-reaching biological consequences, with brain-to-brain links triggering hormones that regulate, among other things, how partners' cardiovascular and immune systems function.

A compelling illustration of the power of close relationships comes from our own studies of couples coping with heart failure, a chronic condition that makes stringent and complex demands on patients and their families. In a study of 189 heart failure patients (139 men and 50 women) and their spouses, we found that interview and observational measures of marital quality predicted all-cause patient mortality over the next 8 years, independent of how well the patient's heart functioned at baseline (Rohrbaugh et al., 2006; see Figure 20.1). Marital quality was a substantially stronger predictor of survival than individual (patient-level) risk and protective factors such as psychological distress, hostility, neuroticism, self-efficacy, optimism, and breadth of perceived emotional support—and the overall statistical effect of marital quality was greater for female patients than males (cf. Coyne, Rohrbaugh, et al., 2001; Rohrbaugh, Shoham, et al., 2004).

A related justification for looking beyond the patient comes from evidence of so-called "partner" or "transitive" effects in couples, where an individual attribute of one partner (e.g., a personality characteristic or level of psychological distress) predicts some health outcome for the other partner, independent of what the same attribute in the actor can predict (Kenny, 1996; Ruiz, Mathews, Scheier, & Schulz, 2006). For example, a striking spouse-to-patient partner effect in the heart failure study was that a spouse's confidence in the patient's ability to manage day-to-day aspects of the illness predicted patient survival over and above what the patient's own cardiac self-efficacy (an actor effect) could predict (Rohrbaugh et al., 2004). And with another sample of heart failure patients and their spouses, we found a partner effect of the spouse's psychological distress, which predicted worsening of the patient's cardiac symptoms over the next 6 months (Rohrbaugh, Shoham, Cleary, Berman, & Ewy, 2009). Although the presence of such a statistical partner effect implies interpersonal influence, explicating the nature or mechanism of that influence often requires taking into account possibly relevant third variables. Thus, the partner effect of spouse confidence on survival appeared largely due to the spouse's confidence correlating with (and serving as a proxy for) the broader construct of dyadic marital quality; however, in Rohrbaugh et al. (2009), we could not explain the partner effect of spouse distress by taking into account either marital quality or the patient's adherence to medical regimen.

Another finding in the heart-failure studies—that the frequency of a couple's useful discussions about the patient's illness strongly predicted survival (Rohrbaugh et al., 2006)—highlights a component of marital quality we think has special relevance to intervention. This is a couple's propensity for *communal coping*, which involves defining a health problem as "ours" rather than "yours" or "mine" and taking cooperative action to solve it (Lyons, Mickelson, Sullivan, & Coyne, 1998). Consistent with this idea, a follow-up study with a different sample of heart patients found that communal coping, unobtrusively measured by a spouse's first-person plural pronoun use (*we* talk) during a conjoint coping interview, predicted a favorable heart failure symptom course over the next 6 months (Rohrbaugh, Mehl, Shoham, Reilly, & Ewy, 2008). Strikingly, we also found that increased *we* talk during the course of a couple-focused (FAMCON) intervention for smokers with heart or lung disease predicted stable cessation a year after the smoker had quit (Rohrbaugh, Shoham, Skoyen, Jensen, & Mehl, in press). Not coincidentally, a central thrust of FAMCON is to promote and mobilize communal coping to support social-cybernetic intervention.

Whereas other researchers have documented direct (physiological) pathways between marital conflict and neuroendocrine systems related to cardiovascular and immune function (Kiecolt-Glaser & Newton, 2001), our own work focuses more on indirect (behavioral) pathways through which marital interaction facilitates or undermines health *behavior*, such as a patient's adherence to dietary, exercise, medication, and stress management regimens that, in turn, influences the course of cardiovascular and other chronic illnesses. For example, we find diminished patient adherence associated with ironic demand–withdraw couple interaction, in which one partner (usually the spouse) criticizes, complains, and pressures for change, while the other resists, avoids, and withdraws (Shoham & Rohrbaugh, 2006). This positive feedback pattern is also common in couples where one partner smokes against the other's wishes; hence, the connection to our work with health-compromised smokers, for whom smoking is an indirect (behavioral) pathway to poor cardiac health.

## An Application to Change-resistant Smoking

To illustrate both the social-cybernetic model of problem maintenance and the FAMCON intervention format, we will draw on work with couples in which at least one partner has a health problem directly aggravated by continued tobacco use. Despite increasing societal prohibitions, cigarette smoking remains a pressing public health problem: A substantial minority of U.S. adults continues to smoke, and many do so despite having smoking-related illnesses (Brandon, 2001). Although effective cessation treatments exist, their overall success rates are modest, and they rarely reach the high-risk, health-compromised smokers who need them most (Compas, Haaga, Keefe, Leitenberg, & Williams, 1998; Fiore et al., 1996, 2000, 2008; Lichtenstein & Glasgow, 1992). In addition, average effect sizes in controlled clinical trials appear to have diminished over the past few decades (Irvin & Brandon, 2000), perhaps reflecting a residual core of treatment-resistant smokers (Hughes, 2003; Hughes, Goldstein, Hurt, & Shiffman, 1999).

We focus here on patients at the intersection of two overlapping risk groups: (a) those ambivalent about giving up tobacco use and (b) those with established smoking-related health problems who nonetheless continue to use tobacco. The overlap is not complete because many ambivalent smokers have no established health problem (at least not yet), and some smokers with health problems have no interest in quitting. Survey data indicate that surprisingly high proportions of patients continue to smoke despite having chronic illnesses like emphysema (37.9%), asthma (24.8%), heart disease (20.3%), hypertension (19.5%), and diabetes (18.5%), and despite receiving medical advice to quit (Agency for Healthcare Research and Quality, 2006). Even if these percentages have declined somewhat in the past few years, it is evident that health-compromised smokers have moved beyond the mere possibility of suffering from a tobacco-related disease; they face a heightened likelihood of further negative impact and a trajectory of deteriorating health that cessation can help to attenuate or reverse (Chuahirun et al., 2004; Dresler & Leon, 2007).

Curiously, evidenced-based cessation treatments recommended in successive versions of the Public Health Service (PHS) Clinical Practice Guideline (Fiore et al., 1996, 2000, 2008) focus almost exclusively on the individual smoker, even though substantial evidence indicates that social support provided by significant others, especially spouses, predicts whether smokers are able to quit and stay abstinent (Campbell & Patterson, 1995; Roski, Schmid, & Lando, 1996). More than a dozen studies link the success of a smoker's cessation efforts to spousal support and the absence of spousal criticism, yet clinical trials of so-called "social support" interventions based on teaching partners better support skills have had consistently disappointing results (Lichtenstein, Glasgow, & Abrams, 1986; Lichtenstein & Glasgow, 1992; Palmer, Baucom, & McBride, 2000; Park, Tudiver, Schultz, & Campbell, 2004). The latter findings apparently prompted the PHS panel to exclude relationship-focused interventions from the Guideline. Unlike the 1996 and 2008 Guideline documents, the 2000 document did recommend helping smokers enlist support for quitting from people outside the treatment context (Fiore et al., 2000, pp. 65–69); for example, by training them how to solicit support from friends, family, and coworkers, but this component is typically packaged with other kinds of behavioral skill training and does not focus on couple-specific relationship patterns that facilitate or hinder stable cessation.

We have argued elsewhere that the failure of social support training should not deter attempts to develop more effective couple and family-level interventions for change-resistant smoking (Rohrbaugh, Shoham, Trost, et al., 2001; Shoham, Rohrbaugh, Trost, & Muramoto, 2006). One reason is that the early interventions apparently also failed to increase the targeted mediating variable of social support (Lichtenstein et al., 1986). In addition, some of these interventions occurred in formats that mixed dual- and single-smoker couples in the same treatment group, whereas others made little distinction between committed partners and other relatives or acquaintances. The most crucial problem may be that teaching one-size-fits-all support skills and

problem solving strategies in group formats detracts attention from how particular support behaviors fit (or don't fit) idiosyncratic couple relationships: In some couples, for example, a spouse's persistent positive encouragement provokes resistance, and in others, a spouse's refusal to allow smoking in the house (counted as "negative" support in some studies) actually functions to help a smoker stay abstinent.

Converging lines of research suggest further that taking relationships as a unit for intervention may pay special dividends when the patient is female and/or has a partner who also smokes. For example, the *quality* of marital relations appears generally more crucial to the health of women than of men (Kiecolt-Glaser & Newton, 2001; Rohrbaugh et al., 2006): women who smoke tend to have more difficulty quitting and staying abstinent than men (Bjornson et al., 1995; Escobedo & Peddicard, 1996; Wetter et al., 1999), having a partner who smokes is a major risk factor for continued smoking and failure in future quit attempts (Ferguson, Bauld, Chesterman, & Judge, 2005; Murray, Johnston, Dolce, Lee, & O'Hara, 1995), and women who attempt to quit are more handicapped by a smoking partner than men are (Derby, Lasater, Vass, Gonzalez, & Carleton, 1994; Homish & Leonard, 2005).

Against this background, we developed and pilot tested a FAMCON intervention for couples in which one partner (the primary smoker) continued to smoke despite having or being at significant risk for heart or lung disease, and despite receiving repeated advice to quit. Based on social-cybernetic and family systems principles, the FAMCON approach is substantially different in concept and format from social support interventions tested in the past. As we detail below, the preliminary results were promising, as primary smokers achieved a 50% rate of stable abstinence over at least 6 months, which compares favorably to cessation benchmarks in the literature, especially those reported for smokers initially unmotivated to quit (Shoham, Rohrbaugh, Trost, & Muramoto, 2006). There were also indications that FAMCON may be particularly well suited to female smokers and tobacco users whose partner also smokes, two sub-groups at the highest risk for relapse.

### The Family Consultation Approach
Family systems theory provides a useful perspective on how close relationships can both maintain, and be maintained by, change-resistant smoking–and why including family members can enhance treatment outcome (Doherty & Whitehead, 1986). The FAMCON intervention we designed for health-compromised

smokers differs in several key respects from the social support interventions tested in the past (Rohrbaugh et al., 2001). Whereas the latter assume that cessation depends on whether individual smokers and their partners learn and implement various problem solving, coping, or support skills (Lichtenstein & Glasgow, 1992), FAMCON assumes that (a) smoking is inextricably interwoven with the family and social relationships in which it occurs, (b) these relationships can play a key (albeit inadvertent) role in maintaining change-resistant smoking, and (c) partners and important family members should be involved in treatment, not merely as adjunct therapists or providers of social support, but as full participants with a stake in the process of change (Doherty & Whitehead, 1986).

Consistent with these ideas, FAMCON focuses on the two types of interpersonal problem maintenance mentioned earlier—*ironic processes* and *symptom–system fit* (conceptualized, respectively, as positive and negative feedback cycles)—and aims to mobilize *communal coping* as a relational resource for change. An ironic process occurs when well-intentioned but persistent "solutions" to a problem feed back to keep the problem going or make it worse (Fisch et al., 1982; Rohrbaugh & Shoham, 2001, 2005; Shoham & Rohrbaugh, 1997). For example, a partner's nagging may lead to more smoking, which leads to more nagging, and so on. Symptom–system fit, on the other hand, occurs when a problem, such as smoking or drinking, appears to have adaptive consequences for a relationship, at least in the short run. Thus, smoking could help to regulate closeness and distance for a couple—or more commonly, when both partners smoke, it could provide a context for mutually supportive interactions (Doherty & Whitehead, 1986; Rohrbaugh et al., 2002; Rohrbaugh, Shoham, Butler, Hasler, & Berman, 2009; Shoham, Butler, Rohrbaugh, & Trost, 2007). Interventions aimed at interrupting ironic processes or helping partners realign their relationship in ways not organized around smoking can vary substantially from couple to couple, depending on the (case-specific) dynamics of problem maintenance. In all cases, however, FAMCON emphasizes the importance of partners working together (coping communally) to help one or both smokers achieve stable cessation. Finally, unlike most treatments for tobacco dependence, FAMCON avoids educational or prescriptive approaches to change, relying instead on strategic interventions that emphasize client choice. In this way, it is less an alternative treatment than a complementary format that can incorporate empirically supported components such as pharmacotherapy, behavioral skills training, and even smoking reduction, if clients so choose, as long as this occurs in ways that fit and protect the partners' relationship.

Procedurally, FAMCON provides up to 10 "consultation" sessions for single- or dual-smoker couples, ideally proceeding through a *preparation* phase (sessions 1–3), a *quit* phase (sessions 4–5), and a *consolidation* phase (session 6+). The treatment typically unfolds over 4 months, with sessions 1–3 conducted during the first month in a structured format and subsequent sessions allocated according to each couple's quit plan and progress. The preparation phase includes indirect interventions (e.g., solution-oriented questions and a daily diary procedure), as well as detailed assessment of smoking-related interaction patterns, past quit attempts (and how they failed), and couple strengths. In session 3, after reviewing assessment information with the treatment team, the consultant presents a carefully tailored "opinion," providing specific observations and feedback about how smoking fits the couple's relationship; why/how quitting will be difficult; reasons to be optimistic about success; and issues for the couple to consider in developing a quit plan. The opinion session also includes gently proffered suggestions intended to interrupt certain interaction patterns, and it typically concludes with an invitation for the couple to consider a quit date. Following principles outlined below, the remaining FAMCON sessions in the quit and consolidation phases focus on helping the couple develop, implement, and sustain a quit plan for one or both partners while preserving and building upon communal qualities of their relationship.

Couple-specific dynamics are relevant throughout FAMCON, both as factors in smoking maintenance and resources for successful cessation. Thus, to understand problem maintenance, the therapist-consultant pays close attention to ironic interpersonal cycles fueled by well-intentioned attempts to control or protect a smoker, as well as to the function(s) smoking appears to serve in the couple's relationship.

### Ironic Processes

As noted above, an ironic process occurs when persistent, well-intentioned attempts to solve a problem feed back to keep the problem going or make it worse. The following vignettes illustrate how such positive feedback loops might help to maintain change-resistant smoking:

- A husband (H) smokes in the presence of his nonsmoking wife (W), who comments how bad it smells and frequently waves her hand to fan away the smoke. H, who had two heart attacks, shows no inclination to be influenced by this and says, "The more she pushes me, the more I'll smoke!" Although W tries not to nag, she finds it difficult not to urge H to "give quitting a try." (She did this when he had bronchitis, and he promptly resumed smoking.) Previously, H recovered from alcoholism, but only after W stopped saying, "If you loved me enough, you'd quit": When she said instead, "I don't care what you do," he enrolled in a treatment program.

- H, who values greatly his 30-year "conflict-free" relationship with W, avoids expressing directly his wish for W to quit smoking. Although smoke aggravates H's asthma, he fears that showing disapproval would upset W and create stress in their relationship. W *confides* that she sometimes finds H's indirect (nonverbal) messages disturbing, although she too avoids expressing this directly, and when he does this she feels more like smoking (Rohrbaugh et al., 2001, p. 20).

A central aim in FAMCON is to identify and interrupt ironic positive feedback cycles such as these. As it turns out, most ironic patterns tend to involve either doing too much, as in the first example, or doing too little, as in the second. They may also bear on smoking either directly (e.g., nagging to quit) or indirectly (e.g., pushing exercise or a particular quit strategy). To interrupt an ironic process successfully, the therapist-consultant must (a) accurately identify particular solution efforts that maintain or exacerbate the problem (here, smoking), (b) specify what less of those same solution behaviors might look like, and (c) persuade at least one of the people involved to do less or the opposite of what they have been doing (Fisch et al., 1982; Rohrbaugh & Shoham, 2001). Thus, if the thrust of a spouse's solution effort is to push directly or indirectly for change (and this has the ironic effect of making change less likely), we will look for ways he or she might do "less of the same"—for example, by declaring helplessness, demonstrating acceptance, or simply observing. On the other hand, if the spouse's main solution is to *avoid* dealing with the smoking, we will encourage more direct courses of action, such as gently taking a stand. Compared to the alcohol-involved couples we studied earlier (Rohrbaugh et al., 2002; Shoham et al., 1998), our sample of health-compromised smokers tended to show more

ironic patterns centered on avoidance and protection than on direct influence. Consequently, interventions more often aimed to *increase* partner influence attempts than to decrease them.

### Symptom–System Fit

The negative feedback construct of symptom–system fit calls attention to the interpersonal functions a problem serves, particularly for the current close relationships in which the problem bearer participates (Haley, 1976; Hoffman, 1981; Minuchin, 1974). From this perspective, problem maintenance involves a kind of interpersonal homeostasis, modeled on a cybernetic negative feedback loop, in which the problem behavior provides a basis for the restoration or perpetuation of some vital relationship parameter (e.g., marital cohesion, conflict reduction). For couples in which both partners smoke or drink, shared substance use might create a context for mutually supportive interactions or help partners stay positive, even when they disagree. For example:

- H and W have an early morning ritual of smoking together in their garage on favorite lawn chairs. W says smoking together is the only thing H will let her initiate: "If we didn't smoke in the garage I doubt we'd talk much—and he wouldn't even miss me." When the couple does talk, W feels that H calms her down—and they mostly talk when they smoke. W had quit smoking some years previously but resumed "because I felt such a distance between us."

- H and W have mostly nonsmoking friends but say, "We enjoy our forbidden pleasure together. We like being outside the mainstream." W says, "If one of us quits and the other doesn't, I think our relationship would change—and probably not for the better" (Rohrbaugh et al., 2001, p. 22).

The clinical aim of addressing symptom–system fit is to help couples realign their relationship in ways not organized around tobacco use. For example, if partners anticipate relational difficulties likely to accompany cessation attempts, they can practice exposing themselves to such situations before attempting to quit, or work toward establishing substitute rituals and activities that do not involve smoking. In this way, they begin to make nonsmoking fit the system—a collaborative strategy we think may pay special dividends in managing symptoms of nicotine withdrawal.

## Communal Coping

The third central construct in FAMCON is communal coping, which concerns mobilizing resources for change in ways that complement social-cybernetic pattern interruption. Thus, regardless of whether one or both partners smoke, the consultant encourages them to view this as a communal problem ("ours," not "yours" or "mine") and work together toward solving it. We also promote communal coping by attending to and reinforcing partners' recollections of how they have successfully resolved difficulties together in the past, and perhaps most directly, by requesting partner agreement and framing suggestions in terms of benefiting "you as a couple."

## Procedural Considerations

Several features of FAMCON for change-resistant smoking deserve special comment: First, although substantially different in format, this couple-focused treatment is fundamentally compatible with, and in some ways parallel to, recommendations in the PHS Guideline. Like the Guideline, for example, FAMCON encourages uses of pharmacologic quit aids and incorporates empirically supported elements of "practical counseling" to help smokers prepare for and sustain cessation (e.g., identifying high-risk situations, practicing coping strategies, and sometimes smoking reduction). The difference is that FAMCON redefines and repackages these elements with the couple as a primary focus of intervention and a resource for helping the smoker(s) change. Thus, while mindful of ironic processes and symptom–system fit, the consultant encourages a communal approach to decisions about which cessation strategies make most sense for the patient *and* the couple, with both partners fully involved in this process. Also like the Guideline, FAMCON pays close, personalized attention to smokers' readiness to quit, with the consultant adopting a stance not unlike Motivational Interviewing; but the focus again is more relational than individual. By involving the spouse or partner, FAMCON is well positioned to recruit real-life motivational leverage beyond the patient—a strategy used effectively in other family-focused motivational interventions for addiction (Smith & Meyers, 2004).

Other features of FAMCON go well beyond the PHS Guideline. For example, the assessment phase includes several forms of indirect intervention, such as a *daily diary phone-in exercise* that calls attention to key smoking-related patterns of interaction and a series of *circular and solution-oriented questions* that highlight individual and couple strengths or imply pathways to future (communal) change (Rohrbaugh et al., 2001). The diary procedure requires that both partners independently call our clinic voice mail each morning for at least 14 consecutive days, leaving answers to a series of questions about the previous day. The questions concern specific problem and solution patterns relevant to the case, as well as mood and relationship quality (e.g., How many cigarettes did you smoke yesterday? How much did you try to discourage your partner from smoking? How close and connected did you feel?). Because answers to the questions are quantitative (most on 0–10 scales), it is possible to identify couple-specific trends over time, such as the extent to which what one person does (e.g., frequency of smoking) correlates from day to day with what the other partner does (e.g., intensity of influence attempts). In addition to using this data in research, we find that presenting selected daily diary results in the feedback/opinion session enhances the credibility of the consultant's observations and therapeutic recommendations. Couples also do a shortened version of the daily call-ins again later, for at least a week before and after their planned quit date, and this *quit diary* procedure provides a basis for regular contact during the critical transition to nonsmoking. (Participants agree in advance to receive a reminder call if they neglect to phone in).

In addition to conjoint planning and problem solving, the quit phase of FAMCON often includes one or more *enactment modules* aimed at addressing ironic processes or symptom–system fit. The principle here is to bring problem-maintaining interaction patterns into the consulting room in a way that highlights their contribution to smoking maintenance and provides an occasion for what family therapists call *enactment-based intervention*. Thus, if a spouse or partner persistently engages in some counterproductive support behavior such as nagging (or conversely, avoiding difficult conversations about the patient's health), the consultant may encourage the couple to enact a typical interaction sequence in the session to illustrate this, then invite the partner(s) to try a "less of the same" approach (again via enactment) to solving the problem at hand. Similarly, if smoking seems to "fit" the couple's relationship by helping the partners maintain cohesion or avoid conflict, the consultant may use an enactment-based exposure approach to help them prepare for the (often difficult) transition to tobacco-free family interaction.

In general, negative feedback cycles (reflecting symptom–system fit) appear more difficult to conceptualize, operationalize, and target for intervention than positive feedback cycles (reflecting ironic processes). This is because the former typically require more inference than the latter, particularly in regard to the presumed "function" of a symptom in regulating relationships. Also, negative feedback cycles sometimes involve triadic (rather than dyadic) interaction sequences and can therefore be more complex. The clinical implications of symptom–system fit sometimes translate to a kind of relationship-level exposure intervention, in which the consultant effectively arranges for clients to experience whatever a symptom such as smoking, drinking, or overeating helps them approach or avoid as a couple, but without engaging in the symptom (e.g., consuming a substance). For this reason, we sometimes characterize working with symptom–system fit as requiring a more "muscular" approach than, say, interrupting an ironic process by getting someone to do less of some specific "solution" behavior.

During the treatment development project, we made several adjustments to the original protocol (Rohrbaugh et al., 2001), and these appear in the current manual for FAMCON with change-resistant smokers (Shoham, Rohrbaugh, & Trost, 2006). For example, we elevated the importance of communal coping (collaborative problem solving) and added the in-session enactment modules outlined above. We should also note that the name "FAMCON" may be slightly misleading due to the predominant couple-level focus of this intervention, at least as we use it with health-compromised smokers. Although the FAMCON format does allow for involvement of family members other than the spouse (e.g., adult children concerned about a parent's health), we do not typically pursue this in the smoking research unless it is evident that other close relations play a key role in problem maintenance or could be a valuable resource for change. On the other hand, involving other family members is fairly common in our work with other problems, as well as with younger patients and older adults who smoke, when interaction sequences reflecting cross-generation coalitions and other forms of triangulation figure prominently in problem maintenance.

## Supporting Research
The next few sections exemplify our research with the FAMCON/social-cybernetic approach, mainly in relation to change-resistant smoking. This work both connects to and departs from the broader literatures on social influence and health-related behavior change. For example, there are clear connections to research on "social control," concerned with the regulatory role

relationships play in encouraging (or sometimes hindering) a healthy lifestyle (Lewis & Rook, 1999; Tucker, 2002), and also to recent literature on "dyadic coping" (Lewis et al., 2006; Manne, Sherman, Ross, Ostroff, Heyman, & Fox, 2004; Revenson, Kayser, & Bodenmann, 2005). When our work departs from these traditions, it is usually in the direction of taking dyadic rather than individual processes as a unit of analysis. Thus, a social control study aiming to explain how a partner's influence attempts affect an individual recipient might focus on disentangling the recipient's affective and behavioral responses to different influence strategies (Tucker, Orlando, Elliot, & Klein, 2006; Umberson, 1992). A social-cybernetic approach, on the other hand, would look for circular redundancies in the interconnected behaviors of *both* participants— what does the patient do in response to the influence attempt, how does the partner responds, what does the patient do then, and so on—and would use this formulation to fashion a dyadic description of the regulatory process. Similarly, although an interdependence theory analysis of dyadic or communal coping might emphasize internal processes like "transformation of motivation" (Lewis et al., 2006), the social-cybernetic lens attaches less importance to what partners think than to what they actually *do* as participants in observable, repeating sequences of behavior.

We begin with preliminary data on FAMCON treatment outcomes, then move to studies of the three putative mechanisms of change: communal coping, ironic processes, and symptom–system fit.

### Promising Cessation Outcomes
In a treatment development study (Shoham et al., 2006), we tested FAMCON with 20 couples in which one partner (the patient) continued to smoke despite having or being at significant risk for heart or lung disease. In eight couples, the other partner smoked as well. On average, couples participated in eight FAMCON sessions and had quit outcomes that compare favorably to benchmarks in the literature. For example, the 50% rate of stable abstinence achieved by primary smokers at 6 months is approximately twice that cited in Fiore et al.'s (2000) meta-analysis involving other, comparably intensive interventions. For the entire sample of 28 smokers, stable coverified cessation rates were 54% and 46% over 6 and 12 months, respectively (Table 20.1). Encouragingly, the FAMCON intervention appeared well-suited to female smokers and smokers whose partner also smoked—two subgroups at high risk for

**Table 20.1** FAMCON cessation outcomes by smoking status and follow-up interval

| Follow-up interval | Primary smokers (*n* = 20) | Secondary smokers(*n* = 8) | All smokers (*n* = 28) |
|---|---|---|---|
| | **30-day abstinence (point prevalence)** | | |
| 1 month | 55% | 75% | 61% |
| 6 months | 50 | 63 | 54 |
| 12 months | 40 | 63 | 46 |
| | **Percent abstinent days during follow-up interval** | | |
| 1 month | $M = 65$ ($SD = 43$) | $M = 75$ ($SD = 46$) | $M = 68$ ($SD = 43$) |
| 6 months | 53 (46) | 73 (46) | 58 (46) |
| 12 months | 48 (47) | 68 (47) | 54 (47) |

From Shoham, V., Rohrbaugh, M. J., Trost, S. E., & Muramoto, M. (2006). A family consultation intervention for health-compromised smokers. *Journal of Substance Abuse Treatment, 31*, 395–402. Reprinted with permission of the publisher, Elsevier.

relapse (Figure 20.1). Although *n*'s were small, virtually all cessation, health, and client satisfaction indices were in the direction of better outcomes for women than men, which could reflect the fact that FAMCON, more than most other cessation interventions, explicitly takes relationship dynamics into account. Similarly, the fact that dual-smoker couples were at least as successful as single-smoker couples is consistent with the possibility that FAMCON's emphasis on relational functions of smoking (symptom–system fit) helped to neutralize the risk factor of spousal smoking status.

This pilot outcome study has obvious limitations, notably its small sample size, lack of a control group, and self-report assessment of cessation outcomes. Although having a serious health problem (e.g., a myocardial infarction) may not, on its own, increase the likelihood of giving up smoking (Andrikopoulos et al., 2001), only a randomized clinical trial can unambiguously rule out the possibility that other, individually focused interventions would have worked just as well, or that a substantial proportion of our health-compromised smokers would have somehow managed to quit on their own.

Although it was not possible to document with quantitative rigor *how* FAMCON helped smokers quit and stay abstinent, our clinical observations were consistent with the family systems principles on which the intervention is based. For example, cessation tended to be most successful when partners worked together and accepted the communal-coping frame for doing so; in fact, each of the three couples in which primary smokers failed to abstain at all (even for 2 days) essentially never bought the communal coping idea and resisted suggestions to view smoking as "our" problem (rather than just the individual smoker's problem). Cessation seemed

most successful when couples found satisfactory ways to protect their relationship during the quit phase, and when the partners freely and conjointly chose and prepared for a quit date without explicit or implicit pressure from the therapist-consultant. It was also evident that rather different patterns of couple interaction served to maintain smoking in different ways for different couples, and that correspondingly different intervention strategies (e.g., encouraging a spouse to back off vs. take a stand) helped to facilitate constructive change.

### Ironic Processes

An ironic process occurs when persistent attempts to solve a problem keep the problem going or makes it worse (Shoham & Rohrbaugh, 1997). In the health arena, for example, research on "social control" suggests that repeated attempts by spouses and social network members to influence health-compromising behavior such as smoking, drinking, and noncompliance with medical regimen often appear to increase those behaviors (Helgeson, Novak, Lepore, & Eton, 2004; Lewis & Rook, 1999). Our own studies of couples coping with smoking and other health problems (e.g., heart disease, alcoholism) have used both self-report and observational methods to capture ironic aspects of interpersonal influence attempts (Rohrbaugh et al., 2009; Shoham & Rohrbaugh, 2006). One approach has involved adapting a self-report measure of smoking-specific partner "support" (Cohen & Lichtenstein's, 1990, *Partner Interaction Questionnaire* [PIQ]; Roski et al., 1996) for this purpose. As the quotes around "support" imply, partner behaviors intended to promote cessation do not always have supportive consequences in the sense of helping the smoker quit. In fact, a key implication of partner support research is that negative support (nagging, criticism, etc.) tends not only to be ineffective but could also serve to perpetuate the very behavior a partner wants to eliminate. To assess possible ironic interpersonal influence, we included a bipolar item capturing perceptions of whether the partner's net influence attempts made it easier or more difficult for a smoker to approach abstinence. In addition, by administering the modified PIQ to both partners in the couple (rather than just smokers, as other studies have done), it was possible to estimate interpartner agreement and take this into account when examining later quit outcomes (Pollak, Baucom, Palmer, Peterson, Ostbye, & Stanton, 2006).

Data from 34 couples with a health-compromised primary smoker (the 20 FAMCON couples plus 14 from another assessment-only study) indicate that almost half of the respondents rated the helpfulness of partner influence attempts in the negative range of our bipolar response scale (i.e., more toward "makes me want to smoke more" than toward "helps me smoke less"), which points to the likely relevance of ironic interpersonal processes. The modified PIQ results also indicate that women who continued to smoke despite having a health problem received less support for quitting from their spouse or partner than male smokers did, regardless of whether the support was positive or negative, whether the partner also smoked, or whether it was the smoker or partner who rated the partner's support behavior (Rohrbaugh, Shoham, & Dempsey, 2009). At the same time, the *quality* of partner support smokers received appeared to predict later quit success or failure more for women than for men, particularly if the support was negative or seen by the patient and partner as unhelpful. A similar gender-linked pattern of prediction emerged from observational ratings of partner-demand/patient-withdraw interaction during a baseline discussion of health-related disagreements (Shoham & Rohrbaugh, 2006). These findings are consistent with a broader literature linking gender, relationships, and health—specifically, with evidence that women are generally more oriented to relationships than men (Taylor, 2006), and that associations between marital quality and health tend to be stronger for women than for men (Kiecolt-Glaser & Newton, 2001; Rohrbaugh et al., 2006; Saxbe, Repetti, & Nishina, 2008).

Ironic positive feedback loops can also occur in connection with a rather different interpersonal coping strategy, common in chronic illness, where one partner tries to protect the other from distress by hiding negative emotions and avoiding potentially upsetting topics. Studies of such "protective buffering" in couples coping with heart disease and cancer suggest ironic associations with *increased* distress, not only for the person who protects but also for the "protected" spouse (Coyne & Smith, 1991; Hagedoorn, Kuijer, Buunk, DeJong, Wobbes, & Sanderman, 2000; Manne, Norton, Ostroff, Winkel, Fox, & Grana, 2007). We have seen this, too, in studies of partner protection with heart failure (Butler, Rohrbaugh, Shoham, Trost, & Ewy, 2004; Trost, 2004). In fact, a daily process analysis of covariation between protection and distress found asymmetrical partner effects, wherein protection by the spouse predicted the patient's daily distress more than patient protection predicted spouse distress (Butler et al., 2004).

Last, the ironic process idea helps illuminate how well intentioned *therapeutic* efforts might go wrong. This could occur, for example, when "working through" a couple complaint in supportive individual therapy makes it possible for the partners to avoid resolving the problem directly, or when pushing a spouse to change recapitulates a problem maintaining solution applied by the clients themselves. The latter pattern is illustrated by a study comparing two treatments for couples in which the husband abused alcohol (Shoham, Rohrbaugh, Stickle, & Jacob, 1998). The two treatments, cognitive-behavioral therapy (CBT) and family systems therapy (FST), differed substantially in the level of demand they placed on the drinker for abstinence and change. Although drinking was a primary target for change in both approaches, CBT took a firm stance about expected abstinence from alcohol, using adjunctive breathalyzer tests to ensure compliance, and FST employed less direct strategies to work with clients' resistance. Before treatment began, we obtained observational measures of how much each couple engaged in demand–withdraw interaction, focusing on the pattern of wife's demand and husband's withdraw during a discussion of the husband's drinking. The retention and abstinence results were striking: When couples high in this particular demand–withdraw pattern received CBT, they attended fewer sessions and tended to have poorer drinking outcomes, whereas for FST, levels of this pattern made little difference. Thus, for high-demand couples, CBT may have ironically provided "more of the same" ineffective solution: The alcoholic husbands appeared to resist a demanding therapist in the same way they resisted their demanding wives.

## Symptom–System Fit

Although rarely invoked in the smoking literature, family systems theory provides a useful perspective on why having a spouse or partner who smokes has negative prognostic implications for successful cessation (Doherty & Whitehead, 1986; Homish & Leonard, 2005). As noted above, the pattern we call symptom–system fit occurs when a problem such as smoking or drinking appears to have adaptive consequences for a relationship, at least in the short run (Rohrbaugh et al., 2001, 2002). Thus, in couples where both partners smoke, shared smoking might create a context for mutually supportive interactions by providing soothing joint experiences or helping partners stay positive, even when they disagree. In a laboratory demonstration of this phenomenon, 25 couples in which one or both partners smoked discussed a health-related disagreement before and during a period of actual smoking (Shoham et al., 2007). Immediately afterward, the partners used independent joysticks to recall their continuous emotional experience during the interaction while watching themselves on video. Participants in dual-smoker couples reported increased positive emotion contingent upon lighting up, while in single-smoker couples both partners (nonsmokers and smokers alike) reported the opposite. Strikingly, changes in individuals' emotional experience from baseline to smoking depended mainly on a couple-level variable (partner smoking status), with no apparent unique contribution from individual characteristics, such as a participant's gender, psychological distress, or even (in the case of single-smoker couples) whether he or she was smoking at the time of the assessment.

In interpreting the Shoham et al. (2007) results, we speculated that dyad-level emotion regulation might help to explain why smokers have more trouble quitting and remaining abstinent when a spouse or partner also smokes. Still, the results left open the question of whether symptom–system fit in dual-smoker couples amounted simply to a surge of positive emotion in each partner as an individual, or whether something inherent in what the partners experienced *together* as a couple played a role as well. To examine more directly the couple as a dynamic, interacting unit, we reanalyzed the same data to determine if the coordination or *synchrony* of partners' moment-to-moment emotional experience also changed coincident with active smoking. The results showed that a couple-level index of *affective synchrony*, operationalized as correlated moment-to-moment change in partners' reported emotional experience, tended to increase during smoking for dual-smoker couples and decrease for single-smoker couples (Rohrbaugh, Shoham, Hasler, et al., 2009). This finding was independent of the parallel mean-level changes in emotional valence reported in Shoham et al. (2007), suggesting that couple-level synchrony represents a different aspect of partners' immediate response to smoking than simply how positive or negative each feels as an individual. In fact, the dual-smoker couples in our sample tended to increase either their affective synchrony *or* their absolute level of positive emotion in response to laboratory smoking, but not both.

Taken together, these results suggest that emotional correlates and consequences of change-resistant smoking have an important social dimension, depending not only on biological or psychological characteristics of the individual smoker, but also on the specific relational context in which smoking occurs. An immediate practical implication of the symptom–system fit idea is that clinicians can usefully intervene by helping couples in smoking partnerships realign their relationship in ways not organized around substance use.

## We Talk and Communal Coping

Finally, some intriguing preliminary data on *communal coping*, a central FAMCON mechanism of action, come from automatic text analysis of participants' speech before and during the intervention. In theory, FAMCON aims to mobilize communal coping by encouraging partners to define the smoking problem as "ours" rather than "yours" or "mine" and take cooperative action to solve it (Lyons et al, 1998; Shoham, Rohrbaugh, Trost, & Muramoto, 2006). Building on evidence that first-person plural pronoun use (*we* talk) marks effective relational problem solving (Seider, Hirschberger, Nelson, & Levenson, 2009; Simmons, Gordon, & Chambless, 2005) and has prognostic significance in couples coping with heart failure (Rohrbaugh et al., 2008), we obtained conjoint speech samples from health-compromised smokers and their partners before and during the FAMCON intervention, then obtained pronoun counts from transcripts of each sample using Pennebaker et al.'s (2001) Linguistic Inquiry Word Count (LIWC) software. Of interest was whether pretreatment *we* talk, and especially *change* in *we* talk during the course of treatment, would predict later cessation outcomes. To check this, we examined outcome in relation to partners' *we* talk during FAMCON session 4 (immediately following the opinion/intervention) and the final session, using word counts from a pretreatment marital interaction task as a baseline covariate. Results for the 20 treated FAMCON couples described above show that increases in *we* talk by both partners during therapy (controlling for baseline *we* talk) predicted stable cessation 1 year later (Rohrbaugh et al., in press). This result provides preliminary documentation of communal coping as an empirically supported change mechanism and highlights the potential utility of automatic text analysis in intervention research.

## Other Clinical Applications

Although working in a couple format with health-compromised smokers and clear-cut behavioral outcomes is useful for research, we also apply the FAMCON social-cybernetic approach clinically to other client configurations and other clinical problems. In fact, when other complaints or behavioral risk factors (e.g., depressed mood, hypertension, obesity) appear intertwined with tobacco use in couples, we typically try to address those additional complaints as well.

Table 20.2 outlines a generic version of FAMCON we have used to help couples and families resolve problems related to conditions such as alcoholism, heart disease, dementia, depression, cancer, traumatic brain injury, bipolar disorder, metabolic syndrome, posttraumatic stress, and prescription drug abuse. The generic FAMCON approach is essentially similar to the smoking protocol in both concept and format. In other words, regardless of the specific behavioral or emotional complaint, we begin with a careful assessment of social-cybernetic problem maintenance, then initiate intervention in the form of an expert "opinion" aimed at interrupting problem patterns and mobilizing communal resources for change. The main variations from the smoking protocol involve (a) greater attention in the preparation phase to defining the relevant client system (whom to see in what format), (b) flexible expansion to triadic and structural formulations of problem maintenance (e.g., cross-generation coalition sequences involving other family members or helpers), and (c) more reliance on strategic reframing for interrupting social-cybernetic patterns. In addition, when the target complaint does not involve substance use, the invitation to consider a specific behavior change (offered at the end of the opinion session) is more likely to focus on interrupting some specific aspect of problem maintenance than on initiating change in the problem itself by setting a quit date.

**Table 20.2    A Generic Template for Family Consultation (FAMCON) Intervention**

I. Preparation (preconsultation phone contact)
- Decide whom to see in what format
- Frame clinical work as "consultation" rather than "therapy"

II. Assessment (2 sessions plus daily phone-ins)
- Define complaint(s) in behavioral terms
- Investigate solution patterns (ironic processes), structural alignments, and symptom–system fit
- Understand clients' preferred views
- Intervene indirectly (e.g., to promote communal coping) with circular and solution-focused questions
- Invite daily diary phone-ins for 14+ days (optional)
    - Track complaint and solution/relationship patterns
    - Identify patterns of covariation over time, especially patterns relevant to problem maintenance
- [Prepare opinion]

III. Feedback, opinion (1 session)
- Compliment couple/family strengths, noble intentions
- Frame change as difficult but offer reasons to be optimistic
- Present selected diary data to highlight relevant patterns (optional)
- Offer direct or indirect suggestions for "less of the same" solutions (interrupting ironic processes)
- Highlight relational consequences of change (accommodating symptom–system fit)
- Encourage communal problem solving and support (by "you as a couple")
- Invite couple-level consideration and/or commitment to a specific change (e.g., a quit date for smokers)

IV. Follow-up (2–7 sessions)
- Adjust suggestions and tactics according to clients' response to intervention
- Introduce enactment modules to interrupt ironic interaction patterns or challenge symptom–system fit (optional)
- Nurture and solidify incipient change

## Reflections and Directions

Having conveyed our enthusiasm for social-cybernetic analyses of health behavior problems and the FAMCON intervention format, we will now stand back a bit and reflect on both the strengths and limitations of this approach as we see them. In keeping with Dr. Friedman's charge to contributors to this volume, we will also attempt to capture some "deeper truths" about important things we have come to understand, including how our approach fits (and doesn't fit) with broader currents in the field and where we would like to go from here.

### Deeper Truths

Cutting to the chase, here are five "truths" we regard as useful in a psychosocial approach to change-resistant health problems, especially when simpler, more direct approaches have failed. (These are not the only truths, or even the most important truths we can construct—and of course they may not be "truths" at all if the meaning of events and behavior is mainly a matter of social construction).

- *Truth 1. How a problem persists, as an aspect of current social interaction, is more relevant to intervention than how the problem originated.* A paper by our mentors from the 1970s and 1980s captures nicely this basic assumption of the social-cybernetic approach:

Regardless of their origins and etiology—if, indeed, these can ever be reliably determined— the problems people bring [to clinicians] persist only if they are maintained by ongoing current behavior of the client and others with whom he interacts. Correspondingly, if such problem-maintaining behavior is appropriately changed or eliminated, the problem will be resolved or vanish, regardless of its nature, or origin, or duration. (Weakland et al., 1974, p. 144)

- *Truth 2. What one calls psychosocial intervention is not a trivial matter.* With health complaints, the term "consultation" is usually preferable to "treatment," "counseling," or (perhaps especially) "family therapy." In our experience, it is rarely a good idea to push people toward acknowledging and addressing relationship problems in the context of helping them cope with physical illness, even when such problems may be obvious to an observer. In fact, suggesting or implying that patients might benefit from couple or family "therapy" can easily turn ironic, as it is likely to arouse resistance when partners or family members avoid overt conflict with each other (a not uncommon correlate of chronic somatic complaints) or if one member of the client system favors a "therapy" solution while another does not. A better approach is to frame the clinical encounter as an in-depth "consultation" about how to handle the complaint, where several heads are better than one and a communal orientation by the people involved will increase the likelihood of success.

- *Truth 3. To understand a clinical problem and plan intervention, it is more useful to investigate what people* do *than what they* have. From our perspective, attempting to identify and explicate psychological "disorders" is usually more handicapping than helpful: As a rule, we prefer to focus not on what people have (in terms of some disorder), but on what they do. Asking what people do when they have problem such as depression, anxiety, or pain is a short step from following on with questions about what other people do in response. This leads to what happens next, and voila a circular sequence of interaction may emerge, suggesting a social-cybernetic formulation of how (and why) the problem persists. In this way, the locus of problem maintenance moves more easily from inside to outside the skin, where we think it often belongs.

- *Truth 4. The path to clinical change is often bumpy and can appear more discontinuous than continuous.* Change follows from interrupting what people habitually do with each other, and their doing something differently (less of the same) may require starts and stops and even minor crises before new patterns of interaction take hold to replace the old ones.

- *Truth 5. The more entrenched a problem and the interaction patterns supporting it, the more helpful are indirect, strategic approaches to intervention.* This includes tactics such as using metaphor, framing suggestions in terms consistent with people's own idiosyncratic language and preferred views, restraining people from precipitous change, prescribing the very experience clients aim to avoid, or providing feedback about change-resistant patterns by having clients listen from behind a mirror to the clinical team discussing their situation. Also useful can be direct, enactment-based strategies in which the clinician elicits, then attempts to restructure, problematic interaction patterns in the consulting room. Whatever the approach, interrupting entrenched relational patterns usually requires more than educating clients about their condition or teaching them better coping skills.

In the next (and final) few sections of this chapter, we will reflect on a number of challenges we face and outline some avenues we hope to explore in future work.

### Scientific Challenges

A central scientific challenge is to investigate the efficacy and effectiveness of FAMCON with specific clinical populations in randomized clinical trials. Starting with health-compromised, change-resistant smokers, one approach could compare FAMCON to a more accessible, individually focused smoking cessation intervention based on the current PHS Clinical Practice Guideline (Fiore et al., 2008). A limitation, however, is that the two treatments would also differ in dosage or intensity, a confound necessary from a public-health standpoint to test whether a best-shot approach such as FAMCON justifies the additional time and expense involved. Alternatively, one could aim to maximize internal validity by comparing FAMCON to an equally intensive control intervention that perhaps even allows spouse participation in some way.

A related line of inquiry is to investigate *for whom* the intervention works best, or is most indicated—a question bearing on the possibility of stepped care. In general, we hypothesize that FAMCON will have the largest effect sizes relative to standard individually focused treatments (a) when the problem or complaint has not changed in response to other intervention efforts, (b) when the principal complainant is female, and (c) when participating partners or family members are concordant for the problem or risk behavior targeted for intervention.

We would also like to explore systematic applications of FAMCON to other pressing health problems, particularly metabolic syndrome and treatment-resistant posttraumatic stress disorder (PTSD). With metabolic syndrome (characterized by abdominal obesity, elevated blood pressure, blood fat disorders, and insulin resistance), a key initial step is to assess and define a patient-specific set of problem maintaining *behaviors* related to eating, exercise, stress management, or other aspects of medical regimen that, by their commission or omission, help to perpetuate the physiological syndrome. The next step, of course, is to identify couple or family interaction

patterns in the form of ironic processes or symptom–system fit (e.g., concordant overeating) that help to maintain the targeted patient behaviors. This in turn sets the FAMCON stage for interrupting problem maintaining patterns while promoting communal coping by the people involved.

Almost by definition, PTSD is a condition that encourages linear-etiological accounts of the presenting symptoms and individually focused intervention. When PTSD symptoms persist, however, a social-cybernetic analysis focused on current, ongoing social interaction may suggest alternative avenues of intervention. For example, a spouse or family members may be responding to a combat veteran's distress in ways that inadvertently help to perpetuate it, or a veteran may disengage from the very people who could help most because "they can't understand what I've been through." Careful tracking of interaction sequences in the FAMCON format can open possibilities for productive pattern interruption and revitalized communal coping by the veteran and his or her important others.

The most difficult scientific challenge is to study *how* these interventions work. In pursuing this, we hope to make more and better use of idiographic methods, both to examine mechanisms of action in the FAMCON intervention format, and to examine basic aspects of social-cybernetic problem maintenance. Although nomothetic group designs (like RCTs) have dominated behavioral research for over a century, findings from such analyses of *inter*-individual variation generalize poorly to understanding and explaining *intra*-individual variation at the level of any given case (Molenaar, 2004). In other words, what applies for everyone on average says little about anyone in particular. Without demeaning the importance of aggregate mediation analyses, we see underappreciated benefits of idiographic strategies that illuminate rather than obscure the anatomy of case-level behavior change. Fortuitously, the FAMCON format, with several weeks of assessment preceding the initiation of intervention in a carefully prepared feedback session, provides a convenient interrupted time-series framework for examining idiographic (case-level) questions. The central idiographic questions are (a) whether fluctuations over time in relevant social process variables (e.g., influence and protection attempts, relational cohesion) correlate as predicted with fluctuations in target risk behaviors within any given case; (b) whether changes in problem maintaining social-cybernetic patterns are demonstrable following intervention in any given case; and

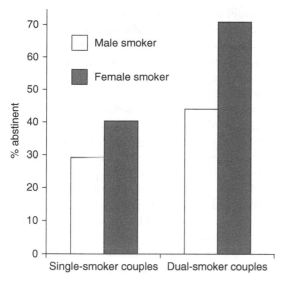

**Fig. 20.2** FAMCON 12-month point-prevalence cessation rates by gender and partner smoking status. From Shoham, V., Rohrbaugh, M. J., Trost, S. E., & Muramoto, M. (2006). A family consultation intervention for health-compromised smokers. *Journal of Substance Abuse Treatment, 31*, 395–402. Reprinted with permission of the publisher, Elsevier.

(c) whether dynamics of social-cybernetic problem maintenance, reflected in covariation over time between relationship and risk behavior variables, change from before to after intervention as predicted. To address these questions, we envision analyzing time-series data from individual FAMCON cases using both straightforward statistical techniques (Borckardt, Nash, Murphy, Moore, Shaw, & O'Neil, 2007) and more sophisticated ones (Hamaker, Dolan, & Molenaar, 2005).

A more basic challenge is how best to study social-cybernetic processes per se, apart from whether or not they change in response to intervention. To document an ironic process, for example, one needs to establish bidirectional functional links between the persistent application of some solution behavior and the persistence or exacerbation of the very problem that solution is intended to remedy. Moreover, given the idiographic nature of ironic problem maintenance (i.e., that drastically different solution patterns can maintain the same clinical problem), a truly relevant methodology must allow for heterogeneous problem–solution dynamics in different cases and situations, even with the same clinical problem. This implies a methodology capable of detecting and documenting *within-case* associations between problem and solution patterns (either within or between people) through repeated observations over time. Thus, if repeated applications of some solution behavior (e.g., exhorting one's child

or partner to change) covary over time with the frequency or intensity of some targeted problem behavior, we have—*for that case*—an empirical pattern consistent with ironic process. Further quantitative refinements, such as testing for lagged associations between solution and problem components, can strengthen the inference that more solution leads (ironically) to more of the problem, and vice versa. Another potentially promising methodology involves using state space grids to examine how dyadic systems change, often discontinuously, from one state to another (Hollenstein, 2007). In dynamic systems terms, any given system tends to stabilize in only a small subset of all possible states or patterns: *Attractors* are stable and recurrent states to which a system frequently returns (e.g., a particular problem–solution loop, or a period of reciprocated positivity), and *phase transitions* involve a period of increased behavioral variability and unpredictability as the system reconfigures toward a different attractor state.

Several current projects in our laboratory apply these ideas. For example, in studies of heart patients and change-resistant smokers we use daily diary reports to document ironic within-couple associations between one partner's smoking and perceptions of the other's influence attempts, and likewise between the two partners' protective buffering and distress. Another methodology uses micro-analytic, stimulated recall data (based on joystick ratings by couples watching themselves on video tape) to link moment-to-moment fluctuations in one partner's ongoing intention to protect versus engage with the other partner's experience of positive versus negative affect. A common aim of these methods is to examine dynamic within-couple associations between health-related complaint behaviors (here, smoking and negative affect) and a spouse's attempted solutions to those complaints.

### Clinical and Conceptual Challenges

As a clinical matter, it is fair to ask when and for whom the social-cybernetic FAMCON model might *not* apply. First, we see this approach as most suited to stable, persistent problems, in which clients or clinicians in some way feel stuck; it is probably least suited to crisis situations, health transitions (e.g., adapting to a cancer diagnosis), or prevention aims—although some forms of consultation or education based on other (e.g., social learning or biomedical) assumptions might well be useful in those contexts. Second, the FAMCON approach may not be ideal as a first-line treatment: If other, more straightforward, empirically supported approaches work, we should use them. Fourth, because communal coping is a central change mechanisms, FAMCON seems to work best when there are stable relationship on which to build: Having to treat couple problems first can be an overload.

Finally, one might ask: What are the most common and telling criticisms of this model, and how do we respond to them?

*Criticism 1. This is a superficial, oversimplified theory of problems and change: Interrupting problems isn't enough because people will just get stuck again in the same old ways.* The idea here is that the social-cybernetic model makes unrealistic assumptions about how people change and/or ignore aspects of the clinical situation that may be crucial to appropriate intervention. For example, some critics find implausible the rolling-snowball idea that a few well-targeted interventions producing small changes in clients' interactions can kick off a process that will lead to significant shifts in the problem pattern; others grant that brief interventions sometimes produce dramatic changes, but doubt that those changes last. Not surprisingly, clinicians from competing theoretical persuasions object to our ignoring personality and past relationship dynamics that, from other perspectives, may be fundamental to the problems at hand. For example, a psychodynamic clinician might be skeptical about how interrupting a demand–withdraw sequence of marital interaction could possibly address a problem rooted in one partner's insecure attachment or life-long fear of intimacy. Defenders of a social-cybernetic approach would reply that such "iceberg" assumptions about what lies beneath a couple's complaint serve only to complicate the clinician's task and make meaningful change more difficult to achieve.

*Criticism 2. The approach discounts individual determinants of behavior.* It is well known that stable individual differences in personality (e.g., Big 5, Type A and D) predict health behavior and well-being, as do individually based motivational constructs like cognitive dissonance and psychological reactance. How, then, can the FAMCON social-cybernetic approach basically ignore such factors? In the past, we have written about individual constructs such as "psychological reactance" in connection with some of the same problems and interpersonal phenomena described here (Rohrbaugh, Tennen, Press, & White, 1981; Shoham-Salomon, Avner, & Neeman, 1989). We also appreciate the obvious relevance of constructs like attachment security (Shaver & Mikulincer, 2007) and autonomy support (Williams et al., 2006) to health behavior change in close relationships.

The problem we have with embracing or integrating such ideas with a social-cybernetic analysis is that individual constructs are simply too seductive: They distract attention from circular, complimentary relational aspects of the situations in which a particular problem is embedded. If we are "wired to connect," as the Goleman quote cited earlier suggests, we may also be wired to think individually and linearly, at least insofar as prevailing individualistic cultural injunctions might shape the relevant neural circuitry. Identifying the social-cybernetic sequences crucial to FAMCON requires deliberately setting aside more familiar and convenient individualistic schemas— and this doesn't come easily. In actuality, relatively stable individual factors—especially participants' preferred views of the problem, themselves, and each other—*do* play an important role in FAMCON intervention. That role is secondary, however, as we are more likely to accept and *use* a particular view to frame suggestions for pattern interruption rather than treating the view itself (even if it appears problematic) as a target for change. (We are reminded here of a remark attributed to family therapy pioneer Carl Whittaker, who described his own conceptual evolution as nearing a point where "I don't 'see' individuals any more—I see only fragments of families.")

*Criticism 3. By focusing only on pattern interruption, this approach fails to teach people the skills and insights they will need to solve similar problems in the future.* For better or worse, it is true that our approach attaches little importance to traditional curative factors such as understanding, skill acquisition, and emotional catharsis. The focus is entirely on interrupting ironic processes in the present, with no assumption that insight or understanding is necessary for such interruption to happen. History may be relevant to clients' views, which are in turn relevant to how a therapist encourages less-of-the-same solution behavior; however, "interpretations" (or frames) offered in this context are pragmatic tools for effecting change, not attempts to illuminate any psychological "reality."

*Criticism 4. Because the therapist/consultant is not always explicit with clients about the rationale for strategic intervention, the social-cybernetic intervention approach is unnecessarily manipulative.* In our view, responsible behavioral intervention is inherently manipulative, and as Truth 5 above suggests, the strategic stance is most indicated when clinical problems or the relational patterns supporting them have been resistant to change. We prefer to create situations in which people construct their own explanations of why change happens and endures: This is in contrast to imposing our own explanations, as psychoeducational approaches typically do. We also assume that constructive change is more dependent upon getting people to *do* something differently than to think or feel differently. In other words, cognitive and emotional change is more likely to follow behavior change than vice versa.

*Criticism 5. Because systems of human behavior are open rather than closed, cybernetic concepts originally applied to closed systems are not truly applicable.* In a strict sense this is true, as Moyer (1994), McHale and Sullivan (2008), and others have pointed out. On the other hand, the conceptual abstractions of "open" systems theory do not translate easily to tangible operations and clinical interventions. As a conceptual road map guiding where and how to intervene, we much prefer the more pragmatic (if epistemologically flawed) social-cybernetic metaphors outlined here.

## Coda

Commentators from de Toqueville to Malcolm Gladwell have noted our culture's preoccupation with the individual, which reaches almost caricature proportions in the prevailing paradigms of psychology and psychiatry. The social-cybernetic ideas we present here challenge individualistic explanations of problematic behavior and behavior change by shifting attention from individuals to relationships and offering alternatives to medication, psychoeducation, skill building, and cognitive-behavioral intervention.

## Acknowledgments

We thank the many colleagues and students who contributed to the work described in this chapter.

This research was supported by awards R21-DA13121, R01-DA17539–01, U10-DA13720, and U10-DA15815 from the National Institute on Drug Abuse; award 0051286Z from the American Heart Association; award AA08970 from the National Institute on Alcoholism and Alcohol Abuse; and by supplemental grants from the University of Arizona Agricultural Experiment Station and the Sarver Heart Foundation.

## References

Agency for Healthcare Research and Quality. (2006, June 30). *AHRQ news and numbers, 204*. Retrieved from http://www.ahrq.gov/news/enews/enews204.htm#2.

Andrikopolous, G.K., Richter, D.J., Dilaveris, P.E., Pipilis, A., Zaharoulis, A., Giafolis, J.E., et al. (2001). In-hospital mortality of habitual cigarette smokers after acute myocardial infarction: The "smokers paradox" in a countrywide study. *European Heart Journal, 22*, 776–784.

Belle, S.H., Burgio, L., Burns, R., Coon, D, Czaja, S.J, Gallagher-Thompson, D., et al. (2006). Enhancing the quality of life of dementia caregivers from different ethnic or racial groups: A randomized, controlled trial. *Annals of Internal Medicine, 145*, 727–738.

Berkman, L. (1985). The relationship of social networks and social support to morbidity and mortality. In S. Cohen, & S.L. Syme (Eds.), *Social support and health* (pp. 241–262). Orlando, FL: Academic Press.

Bjornson, W., Rand, C., Connett, J.E., Lindgren, P., Nides, M., Pope, F., et al. (1995). Gender differences in smoking cessation after 3 years in the Lung Health Study. *American Journal of Public Health, 85*, 223–230.

Borckardt, J., Nash, M.R., Murphy, M.D., Moore, M., Shaw, D., & O'Neil P. (2007). Clinical practice as natural laboratory for psychotherapy research: A guide to case-based time-series analysis. *American Psychologist, 63*, 77–95.

Brandon, T.H. (2001). Behavioral tobacco cessation treatments: Yesterday's news or tomorrow's headlines? *Journal of Clinical Oncology, 19*, 64s–68s.

Brown, J.L., Sheffield, D., Leary, M.R., & Robinson, M.E. (2003). Social support and experimental pain. *Psychosomatic Medicine, 65*, 276–283.

Butler, E.A., Rohrbaugh, M.J., Shoham, V., Trost, S., & Ewy, G.A. (2004, April). *A diary study of protective buffering in couples facing heart disease*. Western Psychological Association, Phoenix, AZ.

Campbell, T.L., & Patterson, J.M. (1995). The effectiveness of family interventions in the treatment of physical illness. *Journal of Marital and Family Therapy, 21*, 545–583.

Chuahirun, T., Simoni, J., Hudson, C., Seipel, T., Khanna, A., Harrist, R.B., et al. (2004). Cigarette smoking exacerbates and its cessation ameliorates renal injury in type 2 diabetes. *American Journal of the Medical Sciences, 327*, 57–67.

Cohen, S., & Hoberman, H.M. (1983). Positive events and social supports as buffers of life change stress. *Journal of Applied Social Psychology, 13*, 99–125.

Cohen, S., & Lichtenstein, E. (1990). Partner behaviors that support quitting smoking. *Journal of Consulting and Clinical Psychology, 58*, 304–309.

Cohen, S., Doyle, W.J., Skoner, D.P., Rabin, B.S., & Gwaltney, J.M. (1997). Social ties and susceptibility to the common cold. *Journal of the American Medical Association, 277*, 1940–1944.

Collins, L., Dunkel-Schetter, C., Lobel, M., & Scrimshaw, S.C.M (1993). Social support in pregnancy: Psychosocial correlates of birth outcomes and postpartum depression. *Journal of Personality and Social Psychology, 6*, 1243–1258.

Compas, B.E., Haaga, D.A.F., Keefe, F.J., Leitenberg, H., & Williams, D.A. (1998). Sampling of empirically supported psychological treatments from health psychology: Smoking, chronic pain, cancer, and bulimia nervosa. *Journal of Consulting and Clinical Psychology, 66*, 89–112.

Coyne, J.C., & Smith, D.A. (1991). Couples coping with a myocardial infarction: A contextual perspective on wives' distress. *Journal of Personality and Social Psychology, 61*, 404–412.

Coyne, J.C., Rohrbaugh, M.J., Shoham, V., Sonnega, J.S., Nicklas, J.M., & Cranford, J.A. (2001). Prognostic importance of marital quality for survival of congestive heart failure. *American Journal of Cardiology, 88*, 526–529.

Derby, C.A., Lasater, T.M., Vass, K., Gonzalez, S., & Carleton, R.A. (1994). Characteristics of smokers who attempt to quit and of those who recently succeeded. *American Journal of Preventive Medicine, 10*, 327–334.

DiMatteo, M.R. (2004). Social support and patient adherence to medical treatment: A meta-analysis. *Health Psychology, 23*, 207–218.

Doherty, W.J., & Whitehead, D. (1986). The social dynamics of cigarette smoking: A family systems perspective. *Family Process, 25*, 453–549.

Dresler, C., & Leon, M. (2007). Tobacco control: Reversal of risk after quitting smoking. *IARC Handbooks on Cancer Prevention No. 11*. Lyon, FR: World Health Organization.

Escobedo, L.G., & Peddicord, J.P. (1996). Smoking prevalence in U.S. birth cohorts: The influence of gender and education. *American Journal of Public Health, 86*, 231–236.

Ferguson, J., Bauld, L., Chesterman, J., & Judge, K. (2005). The English smoking treatment services: One year outcomes. *Addiction, 100*, 59–69.

Fiore M.C., Jaen, C.R., Baker, T.B., Bailey, W.C., Benowitz, N.L., Curry, S.J., et al. (2008). *Treating tobacco use and dependence: 2008 update. Clinical practice guideline* No. 18. Rockville, MD: US Department of Health and Human Services, Public Health Service, Agency for Health Care Policy and Research.

Fiore, M.C., Bailey, W.C., Cohen, S.J., Dorfman, S.F., Goldstein, M.G., Gritz, E.R., et al. (1996). *Smoking cessation. Clinical practice guideline* No. 18. Rockville, MD: US Department of Health and Human Services, Public Health Service, Agency for Health Care Policy and Research (AHCPR Publication No. 96–0692).

Fiore, M.C., Bailey, W.C., Cohen, S.J., Dorfman, S.F., Goldstein, M.G., Gritz, E.R., et al. (2000). *Treating tobacco use and dependence. Clinical practice guideline*. Rockville, MD: US Public Health Service.

Fisch, R., Weakland, J.H., & Segal, L. (1982). *The tactics of change*. San Francisco: Jossey-Bass.

Fisher, L. (2006). Research on the family and chronic disease among adults. *Families, Systems & Health, 24*, 373–380.

Goleman, D. (2006). *Social intelligence: The new science of human relationships*. New York: Random House.

Hagedoorn M., Kuijer R.G., Buunk B.P., DeJong G.M., Wobbes T., & Sanderman, R. (2000). Marital satisfaction in patients with cancer: Does support from intimate partners benefit those who need it the most? *Health Psychology, 19*, 274–282.

Haley, J. (1976). *Problem solving therapy*. San Francisco, CA: Jossey-Bass.

Hamaker, E.L., Dolan, C.V., & Molenaar, P.C.M. (2005). Statistical modeling of the individual: Rationale and application of multivariate stationary time series analysis. *Multivariate Behavioral Research, 40*, 207–233.

Helgeson, V.S., Novak, S.A., Lepore, S.J., & Eton, D.T. (2004). Spouse social control efforts: Relation to health behavior and well-being among men with prostate cancer. *Journal of Social and Personal Relationships, 21*, 53–68.

Hoffman, L. (1981). *Foundations of family therapy*. New York: Basic Books.

Hollenstein, T. (2007). State space grids: Analyzing dynamics across development. *International Journal of Behavioral Development, 31*, 384–396.

Homish, G.G., & Leonard, K.E. (2005). Spousal influence on smoking behaviors in a US community sample of newly married couples. *Social Science and Medicine, 61*, 2557–2567.

House, J.S., Landis, K.R., & Umberson, D. (1988). Social relationships and health. *Science, 241*, 540–545.

Hughes, J.R. (2003). Motivating and helping smokers to stop smoking. *Journal of General Internal Medicine, 18*, 1053–1057.

Hughes, J.R., Goldstein, M.G., Hurt, R.D., & Shiffman, S. (1999). Recent advances in the pharmacotherapy of smoking. *Journal of the American Medical Association, 281*, 72–76.

Irvin, J.E. & Brandon, T.H. (2000). The increasing recalcitrance of smokers in clinical trials. *Nicotine & Tobacco Research, 2*, 79–84.

Jackson, D.D. (1957). The question of family homeostasis. *Psychiatric Quarterly Supplement, 31*, 79–90.

Kenny, D.A. (1996). Models of interdependence in dyadic research. *Journal of Social and Personal Relationships, 13*, 279–294.

Kiecolt-Glaser, J.K., & Newton, T.L. (2001). Marriage and health: His and hers. *Psychological Bulletin, 127*, 472–503.

Leipman, M., Silvia, L., & Nirenberg, T. (1989). The use of behavior loop mapping for substance abuse. *Family Relations, 38*, 282–287.

Lewis, M.A., & Rook, K.S. (1999). Social control in personal relationships: Impact on health behaviors and psychological distress. *Health Psychology, 18*, 63–71.

Lewis, M.A., McBride, C.M., Pollak, K.I., Puleo, E., Butterfield, R.M., & Emmons, K.M. (2006). Understanding health behavior change among couples: An interdependence and communal coping approach. *Social Science and Medicine, 62*, 1369–1380.

Lichtenstein, E., & Glasgow, R.E. (1992). Smoking cessation: What have we learned over the past decade? *Journal of Consulting and Clinical Psychology, 60*, 518–527.

Lichtenstein, E., Glasgow, R.E., & Abrams, D.B. (1986). Social support in smoking cessation: In search of effective interventions. *Behavior Therapy, 17*, 607–619.

Lyons, R.F., Mickelson, K.D., Sullivan, M.J., & Coyne, J.C. (1998). Coping as a communal process. *Journal of Personal and Social Relationships, 15*, 579–605.

Manne, S., Norton, T., Ostroff, J., Winkel, G., Fox, K., & Grana, G. (2007). Protective buffering and psychological distress among couples coping with breast cancer: The moderating role of relationship satisfaction. *Journal of Family Psychology, 21*, 380–388.

Manne, S., Sherman, M., Ross, S., Ostroff, J., Heyman, R.E., & Fox, K. (2004). Couples' support-related communication, psychological distress, and relationship satisfaction among women with early stage breast cancer. *Journal of Consulting and Clinical Psychology, 72*, 660–670.

Martire, L.M., & Schulz, R. (2007). Involving family in psychosocial interventions for chronic illness. *Current Directions in Psychological Science, 16*, 90–94.

McHale, J.P., & Sullivan, M.J. (2008). Family systems. In M. Hersen, & A. M Gross (Eds.), *Handbook of clinical psychology* Vol. 2: *Children and adolescents* (pp. 192–226). Hoboken, NJ: John Wiley & Sons.

Minuchin, S. (1974). *Families and family therapy*. Cambridge, MA: Harvard University Press.

Molenaar, P.C.M. (2004). A manifesto on psychology as idiographic science: Bringing the person back into scientific psychology, this time forever. *Measurement, 2*, 201–218.

Moyer, A. (1994). Cybernetic theory does not explain family and couple process: System theory and dialectical metatheory. *American Journal of Family Therapy, 22*, 2273–2281.

Murray, R.P., Johnston, J.J., Dolce, J.J., Lee, W.W., & O'Hara, P. (1995). Social support for smoking cessation and abstinence: The Lung Health Study. *Addictive Behaviors, 20*, 159–170.

Nichols, M.P. (2008). *Family therapy: Concepts and methods.* Boston, MA: Allyn & Bacon.

Palmer, C.A., Baucom, D.H., & McBride, C.M. (2000). Couple approaches to smoking cessation. In K.B. Schmaling, & T.G. Sher (Eds.), *The psychology of couples and illness: Theory, research, & practice* (pp. 311–336). Washington, DC: American Psychological Association.

Park, E., Tudiver, F., Schultz, J.K., & Campbell, T. (2004). Does enhancing partner support and interaction improve smoking cessation? A meta-analysis. *Annals of Family Medicine, 2,* 170–174.

Pennebaker, J.W., Francis, M.E., & Booth, R.J. (2001). Linguistic inquiry and word count (LIWC): LIWC 2001 [Computer program]. Mahwah, NJ: Erlbaum.

Pollak, K.I., Baucom, D.H., Palmer, C.A., Peterson, B.L., Ostbye, T., & Stanton, S. (2006). Couples' reports of support for smoking cessation predicting women's late pregnancy cessation. *American Journal of Health Promotion, 21,* 90–96.

Revenson, T.A., Kayser, K., & Bodenmann, G. (2005). *Couples coping with stress: Emerging perspectives on dyadic coping.* Washington, DC: American Psychological Association.

Rohrbaugh, M., Tennen, H., Press, S.E., & White, L. (1981). Compliance, defiance and therapeutic paradox: Guidelines for strategic use of paradoxical interventions. *American Journal of Orthopsychiatry, 51,* 454–467.

Rohrbaugh, M.J., Shoham, V., & Racioppo, M.W. (2002). Toward family-level attribute x treatment interaction research. In H. Liddle, D. Santisteban, et al. (Eds.), *Family Psychology: Science-Based Intervention* (pp. 215–237). Washington, DC: American Psychological Association.

Rohrbaugh, M.J., & Shoham, V. (2001). Brief therapy based on interrupting ironic processes: The Palo Alto model. *Clinical Psychology: Science and Practice, 8,* 66–81.

Rohrbaugh, M.J., & Shoham, V. (2005). Ironic processes in brief therapy and research. *Journal of Brief Therapy, 4,* 59–71.

Rohrbaugh, M.J., Cranford, J.A., Shoham, V., Nicklas, J.M., Sonnega, J., & Coyne, J.C. (2002). Couples coping with congestive heart failure: Role and gender differences in psychological distress. *Journal of Family Psychology, 16,* 3–13.

Rohrbaugh, M.J., Mehl, M.R., Shoham, V., Reilly, E.S., & Ewy, G. (2008). Prognostic significance of spouse "we-talk" in couples coping with heart failure. *Journal of Consulting and Clinical Psychology, 76,* 781–789.

Rohrbaugh, M.J., Shoham, V., & Coyne, J.C. (2006). Effects of marital quality on 8-year survival of patients with heart failure. *American Journal of Cardiology, 98,* 1069–1072.

Rohrbaugh, M.J., Shoham, V., & Dempsey, C.L. (2009). Gender differences in quit support by partners of health-compromised smokers. *Journal of Drug Issues, 39,* 1045–1061.

Rohrbaugh, M.J., Shoham, V., Butler, E.A., Hasler, B.P., & Berman J.S. (2009). Affective synchrony in dual- and single-smoker couples: Further evidence of "symptom-system fit"? *Family Process, 48,* 55–67.

Rohrbaugh, M.J., Shoham, V., Cleary, A., Berman, J.S., & Ewy, G.A. (2009). Health consequences of partner distress in couples coping with heart failure. *Heart and Lung: Journal of Acute and Critical Care, 38,* 298–305.

Rohrbaugh, M.J., Shoham, V., Coyne, J.C., Cranford, J.A., Nicklas, J.M., & Sonnega, J. (2004). Beyond the "self" in self-efficacy: Spouse confidence predicts survival following heart failure. *Journal of Family Psychology, 18,* 184–193.

Rohrbaugh, M.J., Shoham, V., Trost, S., Muramoto, M., Cate, R., & Leischow, S. (2001). Couple-dynamics of change resistant smoking: Toward a family-consultation model. *Family Process, 40,* 15–31.

Rohrbaugh, M.J., Shoham, V., Skoyen, J.A., Jensen, M., & Mehl, M.R. (in press). We-talk, communal coping, and cessation success in couples with a health-compromised smoker. *Family Process.*

Roski, J., Schmid, L.A., & Lando, H.A. (1996). Long-term associations of helpful and harmful spousal behaviors with smoking cessation. *Addictive Behaviors, 21,* 173–185.

Ruiz, J.M., Mathews, K.A., Scheier, M.F., & Schulz, R. (2006). Does who you marry matter for your health? Influence of patients' and spouses' personality on their partners' psychological well-being following coronary artery bypass surgery. *Journal of Personality and Social Psychology, 91,* 255–267.

Saxbe, D.E., Repetti, R.L., & Nishina, A. (2008). Marital satisfaction, recovery from work, and diurnal cortisol among men and women. *Health Psychology, 27,* 15–25.

Schulz, R., & Beach, S.R. (1999). Caregiving as a risk factor for mortality: The caregiver health effects study. *Journal of the American Medical Association, 282,* 2215–2219.

Seider, B.H., Hirschberger, G., Nelson, K.L., & Levenson, R.W. (2009). We can work it out: Age differences in relational pronouns, physiology, and behavior in marital conflict. *Psychology and Aging, 24,* 604–613.

Selvini-Palazzoli, M., Boscolo, L., Cecchin, G., & Prata, G. (1978). *Paradox and counterparadox.* New York: Jason Aronson.

Shaver, P.R., & Mikulincer, M. (2007). Adult attachment strategies and the regulation of emotion. In J.J. Gross (Ed.), *Handbook of emotion regulation* (pp. 446–465). New York: Guilford Press.

Shoham-Salomon, V., Avner, R., & Neeman, R. (1989). You're changed if you do and changed if you don't: Mechanisms underlying paradoxical interventions. *Journal of Consulting and Clinical Psychology, 57,* 590–598.

Shoham, V., & Rohrbaugh, M.J. (1997). Interrupting ironic processes. *Psychological Science, 8,* 151–153.

Shoham, V., & Rohrbaugh, M.J. (2006). *Demand-withdraw marital interaction and the maintenance of health-compromising behavior.* International Association for Relationship Research, Rethymnon, Crete, Greece.

Shoham, V., Butler, E.A., Rohrbaugh, M.J., & Trost, S.E. (2007). System-symptom fit in couples: Emotion regulation when one or both partners smoke. *Journal of Abnormal Psychology, 116,* 848–853.

Shoham, V., Rohrbaugh, M.J., & Trost, S.E. (2006). *Family consultation (FAMCON) for change-resistant smokers: A treatment manual.* Family Research Laboratory, Department of Psychology, University of Arizona.

Shoham, V., Rohrbaugh, M.J., Stickle, T.R., & Jacob, T. (1998). Demand-withdraw couple interaction moderates retention in cognitive-behavioral vs. family-systems treatments for alcoholism. *Journal of Family Psychology, 12,* 557–577.

Shoham, V., Rohrbaugh, M.J., Trost, S.E., & Muramoto, M. (2006). A family consultation intervention for health-compromised smokers. *Journal of Substance Abuse Treatment, 31,* 395–402.

Simmons, R.A., Gordon, P.C., & Chambless, D.L. (2005). Pronouns in marital interaction: What do "you" and "I" say about marital health? *Psychological Science, 16,* 932–936.

Smith, J.E., & Meyers, R.J. (2004). *Motivating substance abusers to enter treatment: Working with family members.* New York: Guilford Press.

Steinglass, P., Bennett, L., Wolin, S., & Reiss, D. (1987). *The alcoholic family.* New York: Basic Books.

Stone, A.A., Mezzacappa, E.S., Donatone, B.A., & Gonder, M. (1999). Psychological stress and social support are associated with prostate-specific antigen levels in men: Results from a community screening program. *Health Psychology, 18*, 482–486.

Taylor, S.E. (2006). Tend and befriend: Biobehavioral bases of affiliation under stress. *Current Directions in Psychological Science, 15*, 273–277.

Taylor, S.E., Repetti, R.L., & Seeman, T. (1997). Health psychology: What is an unhealthy environment and how does it get under the skin? *Annual Review of Psychology, 48*, 411–447.

Trost, S.E. (2004). *Protective buffering among couples coping with heart disease: Behavior, intentions, and psychological distress.* Unpublished doctoral dissertation, University of Arizona, Tucson, AZ.

Tucker, J.S. (2002). Health-related social control within older adults' relationships. *Journal of Gerentology: Psychological Sciences, 57B*, 387–395.

Tucker, J.S., Orlando, M., Elliot, M.N., & Klein, D.J. (2006). Affective and behavioral responses to health-related social control. *Health Psychology, 25*, 715–722.

Uchino B.N., Cacioppo J.T., & Kiecolt-Glaser, J.K. (1996). The relationship between social support and physiological processes: A review with emphasis on underlying mechanisms and implications for health. *Psychological Bulletin, 119*, 488–531.

Umberson, D. (1992). Gender, marital status, and the social control of health behavior. *Social Science and Medicine, 34*, 907–917.

Vitaliano P.P., Zhang J., & Scanlan J.M. (2003). Is caregiving hazardous to one's physical health? A meta-analysis. *PsychologicalBulletin, 129*, 946–972.

Watzlawick, P., Weakland, J.H., & Fisch, R. (1974). *Change: Principles of problem formation and problem resolution.* New York: Norton.

Weakland, J.H., Fisch, R., Watzlawick, P., & Bodin, A. (1974). Brief therapy: Focused problems resolution. *Family Process, 13*, 141–168.

Wegner, D.M. (1994). Ironic processes of mental control. *Psychological Review, 101*, 34–52.

Weihs, K.L., Enright, T.M., Simmens, S.J., et al. (2008). Close relationships and emotional processing predict mortality in women with breast cancer: Preliminary evidence. *Psychosomatic Medicine, 70*, 117–124.

Wetter, D.W., Fiore, M.C., Young, T.B., McClure, J.B., de Moor, C.A., & Baker, T.B. (1999). Gender differences in response to nicotine replacement therapy: Objective and subjective indexes of tobacco withdrawal. *Experimental and Clinical Psychopharmacology, 7*, 135–144.

Whitehead, D., & Doherty, W.J. (1989). Systems dynamics in cigarette smoking: An exploratory study. *Family Systems Medicine, 7*, 264–273.

Williams, G.C., McGregor, H.A., Sharp, D., Levesque, C., Kouides, R.W., Ryan, R.M., & Deci, E.L. (2006). Toward a self-determination intervention for motivating tobacco cessation: Supporting autonomy and competence in a clinical trial. *Health Psychology, 25*, 91–101.

Wynne, L.C., McDaniel, S.H. & Weber, T.T. (Eds.). (1986). *Systems consultation: A new perspective for family therapy.* New York: Guilford Press.

# Childhood Health and Chronic Illness

Barbara J. Tinsley *and* Mary H. Burleson

**Abstract**

Children's health has profound and sustained consequences for later life. Although child morbidity and mortality have been greatly reduced over the past few decades due to medical discoveries, immunization efforts, and improved technology, many children continue to face poor health due to poverty or related issues, behavioral risk factors, and chronic illness or disability. In this chapter, we provide a state-of-the-art summary of research on children's health and its developmental consequences.

**Keywords:** Children, health, chronic illness, disability, methodology

Physical health tends to decline with age, and is widely expected to be at its highest peak during childhood. However, concern about children's health continues to be the most pressing issue for contemporary families, both in the United States and around the world (Foster, Bass, Zamora, Tinsley, & Gonzalez, 2008). Childhood mortality has greatly decreased in the last century, and medical breakthroughs and technology have changed the shape of pediatric care. Immunization programs and antibiotic therapies have radically lowered both child mortality and morbidity in pediatric populations. New disease-specific therapies allow children with a wide variety of metabolic and congenital problems to survive into adolescence.

Nevertheless, although the health of most children has improved in recent years, lifestyle-related diseases (e.g., obesity) are becoming more prevalent. Today's pediatricians are increasingly called upon to provide behavioral information and counseling, in contrast to their historical focus on caring for children with severe infectious and communicable diseases. In addition, wide health inequalities persist between and across children in various sociodemographic groups in the United States. In spite of the changing nature of health care for children overall,

child morbidity remains disproportionately high in children from lower sociodemographic homes. Children from more deprived and disadvantaged backgrounds tend to have poorer health and higher rates of mortality from major diseases such as heart disease, diabetes, and cancer in adulthood. Especially for children, the origins of poor health can be multiple and complex, and addressing the root causes can be equally complex. Wider determinants—the influencing factors responsible for everyone's health—are more significant for children. Some differences in health are unavoidable, but many are reversible or preventable and the result of unfairness or inequality in circumstance, access to services, or lifestyles and behavior, which are themselves often determined by these wider societal issues.

Why is it imperative to understand the psychosocial dynamics of children's health? Most importantly, health problems during childhood cause much distress and suffering to children and their families. Childhood illness is costly to communities in terms of both well-being and dollars, and any knowledge that can contribute to ameliorating these conditions or the problems they cause is vitally important. In addition, early experience has profound life-long consequences for health, both positive and negative.

Many unhealthy lifestyles begin during childhood. Prenatal, infancy, childhood, and adolescent health issues are strong predictors of poor health outcomes later in life, and problems left too long without intervention may never be remedied effectively.

Theory and empirical evidence conclusively demonstrate strong relations between good health in childhood and positive concurrent or later outcomes in many developmental domains. These include school attendance and achievement, which are in turn associated with better employment and more opportunities to make a positive contribution to society (Challenger, 2009). Other developmental domains affected by children's physical health include social-emotional competence, motor control, and cognitive functioning. Early intervention and preventive services focused on the young are critical for breaking intergenerational cycles of health inequalities. In other words, improving children's health outcomes in the short term can have significant short- and long-term benefits for children, families, and society as a whole.

In this chapter, an overview and synthesis of research focused on the psychology of children's health will be presented. First, we will address some potential mechanisms by which childhood health conditions may influence or predict adult health. Second, we discuss some noteworthy characteristics of children's health psychology research. Third, children's understanding of health and health behaviors are examined, focusing on cognitive-developmental and individual differences perspectives. Fourth, the contribution of children's social and demographic environments to their health status is explored. Fifth, consequences of children's health status (especially childhood chronic disease and disability) are considered. Sixth, prevention and intervention strategies are addressed. We conclude with implications of this overview and synthesis for future research in these areas and for physical health policy.

## Mechanisms for Childhood Health Effects in Adulthood

As we increasingly recognize, many lines of evidence, including epidemiologic data and data from extensive clinical and experimental studies, indicate that early life health events play a powerful role in influencing later health. What are the possible mechanisms of these relations?

One possibility is that prenatal and early infant neurological or biochemical environments set the foundation for developmental consequences in later life (Bateson et al., 2004). Epidemiological studies indicate that smaller size at birth and during infancy is associated with increased rates of coronary heart disease, stroke, type 2 diabetes mellitus, adiposity, metabolic syndromes, and osteoporosis in adult life (Bateson et al., 2004; Cooper et al., 1997; Frankel, Sweetnam, Yarnell, & Smith, 1996; Hales & Barker, 1992; Kensara et al., 2005; Osmond, Barker, Winter, Fall, & Simmonds, 1993). Perinatal events appear to exert effects that are independent of environmental risk factors in adults (Barker, Forsen, Uutela, & Osmond, 2001; Frankel et al., 1996) or may be amplified by other risk factors (Bhargava et al., 2004). Slow growth in utero may be associated with increased allocation of nutrients to adipose tissue during development and may then result in accelerated weight gain during childhood (Barker, 1998; Hovi et al., 2007), which may contribute to a relatively greater risk of coronary heart disease, hypertension, and type 2 diabetes mellitus. There is a continuous positive relation between low birth weight and future risk—not just for extreme low weights but also for normal weights (Hofman et al., 2004). Prematurity itself, independent of size for gestational age, has been associated with insulin resistance and glucose intolerance in prepubertal children (Hovi et al., 2007) that may track into young adulthood and may be accompanied by elevated blood pressure (Gluckman, Hanson, Cooper, & Thornburg, 2008).

Another level of influence may occur through early environmental conditions. Stress, stability, safety, and nurturing influence children's psychological, behavioral, and social development, with strong implications for their later health (Rutter, 1981). Families with high levels of overt conflict and aggression or coldness and neglect can impair children's emotional expression and regulation, leading to problematic social functioning and risky health behaviors such as substance abuse (Repetti, Taylor, & Seeman, 2002). In addition, adaptation to chronic stress may accumulate physiological costs and lead to potentially irreversible alterations in nervous system structure and function. These stress-related changes in neuroendocrine regulatory systems in turn may contribute to development of diseases, and further exacerbate risky behavior with many serious long-term health consequences (Seeman, Singer, Rowe, Horwitz, & McEwen, 1997). All of these effects are exacerbated by hostile or impoverished social contexts (Taylor, Repetti, & Seeman, 1997). Children who grow up in lower socioeconomic homes with limited incomes and educations are often exposed to social and physical environments that negatively affect physical health and development (e.g., abuse, lead paint). Rearing children in these impoverished conditions can result in lack of knowledge and ability to improve their circumstances.

## Issues in Children's Health Psychology Research

Recent developmental psychology models of the etiology of children's physical health demonstrate that neither biological nor experiential factors alone yield adequate understanding of development, and only by combining these components can one better understand children's physical health in a developmental perspective. Sameroff's transactional model of development suggests that two major influences—a continuum of reproductive causality, which includes both genetic constitutional factors as well as birth-related trauma, and a continuum of caretaking causality, which includes the social, intellectual, and physical environment—are critical for the prediction of developmental outcomes (Sameroff, 2009). Other models, such as systems theory, similarly underscore the necessity of considering the complex interplay between biological and experiential factors in determining children's physical health status at any point in time (Mackner, Black, & Starr, 2003).

Adult health psychology is more cohesive than pediatric health psychology. In the adult health field, the divisions among research on prevention, health status, and chronic illness are more fluid than in children's health research. For example, research on adult hypertension often studies a combination of behavioral etiology, biologic consequences, and implications for prevention. However, in child health research, there is a dichotomy between research focused on disease prevention/well-child care/acute illness and investigations of children's chronic illness. Child health studies combining these two foci are few and far between.

Of course, some central concerns are common to both chronic and acute/wellness in childhood. First, much of children's health care is determined by others, rather than by the child (Wilkinson, 1988). This is especially true of younger children: Medical values and decisions are imposed on young children by adults. Parents' and other adults' relative control of children's health behavior increasingly reverts to children themselves in later childhood and adolescence. One aspect of this control relates to parents' communication on behalf of their children, a relatively neglected area of research in health communication. The pediatric context is substantially different from most other health care communication situations.

In most pediatric encounters, there exists a triad consisting of a parent or guardian, the physician, and the child patient. Depending on the age of the child, to varying degrees, the parent is the sole or primary information giver and co-decision maker with the pediatrician or the family practice specialist. In the case of very young children, there is little communication between the actual patient and the physician; the interaction primarily occurs between the physician and the parent or caregiver at least until the child is 6 to 12 years of age (Mendelsohn, Quinn, & McNabb, 1993).

## Prevention, Wellness, and Acute Illness
### Children's Understanding of Health and Health Behavior

One common focus of research on psychosocial aspects of children's health is the extent to which children understand the way that health "works," and how this knowledge changes as they mature. This work reflects the cognitive-structural tradition, as exemplified by Piaget (1970), and focuses on development-related normative changes in children's attitudes and ideas about health. The main topic addressed by this literature is children's understanding of health-related concepts (e.g., illness etiology, health knowledge, mechanisms of health).

Early work in this area described developmental patterns in children's understanding of illness and body systems (Gellert, 1962, 1978; Nagy, 1951; Nagy, 1953; Rashkis, 1965). These studies documented the increasing ability of children to accurately categorize complex health concepts. In the late 1970s, other investigations continued to employ Piagetian theory to analyze children's systematic understanding of health and illness (Bibace & Walsh, 1980; Campbell, 1975; Natapoff, 1978; Perrin & Gerrity, 1981; Simeonsson, Buckley, & Monson, 1979). These studies suggest that children in the preoperational stage of cognition have health and illness understandings that confuse cause and effect and lack differentiation. By the concrete operational period, according to these studies, children's conceptual understanding of health and illness increasingly parallels that of adults, although fairly simplistically. For example, children at this stage believe that germs cause all illness or that wellness is dependent on following specific rules (Bibace & Walsh, 1980; Perrin & Gerrity, 1981). By the formal operational period, youth are able to understand and use appropriately more sophisticated concepts such as infection and preventive health behavior (Simeonsson et al., 1979). The findings of these studies are limited, however, by the populations studied (i.e., mostly hospitalized and sick children), inconsistent measure development (i.e., little attention paid to determining psychometrics), lack of control groups, differing criteria for the specification of Piagetian stages, confusion between chronological age and developmental status, and a focus on illness, at the expense of examining children's understanding of wellness.

Piagetian theory has not been the exclusive framework through which children's ideas about health and illness vis-a-vis their cognitive status have been examined. Other models include script theory, the intuitive/naïve scientist approach, and Vygotskian theory. In *script theory*, children are thought to develop script-like, sequential representations of everyday, commonplace events such as eating breakfast (Baker-Ward, Ornstein, & Starnes, 2009; Nelson, 1986; Principe, Ornstein, Baker-Ward, & Gordon, 2000). Eiser demonstrated that children develop scripts for health events, such as going to the doctor, and are able to recall and relate specific circumstances that occur within these events (Eiser, 1989). The *intuitive/naïve scientist approach* is consistent with a developmental perspective on children's health learning but refutes the structured notion of the Piagetian-based studies to suggest that children's understanding is unconstrained by stage of cognitive development (Carey, 1985). With this perspective, children's concepts of health can be traced from preschoolers' simple and often inaccurate explanations of body functioning to preadolescents' "intuitive" biological understanding of the importance of body functioning for the maintenance of life (Hergenrather & Rabinowitz, 1991). A *Vygotskian approach* may also aid in illuminating the relations between children's cognitive development and health socialization. For young children, parents create supported learning situations, termed *scaffolding*, in which their children can extend their skills and knowledge to a higher level of competence (Rogoff, 1990). Scaffolding can be applied to the way that children learn any number of novel tasks, including but not limited to health and safety behaviors such as tooth brushing, food selection, and caring for minor injuries (Lees & Tinsley, 2000).

Although few data exist to validate the usefulness of these alternate theories for understanding children's concepts of health, these models suggest intriguing alternatives for conceptualizing developmental patterns in children's health understanding. It seems apparent that children's understanding of illness and other health concepts does evolve in a systematic and predictable sequence, perhaps consistent with Piaget's theory of cognitive development; nevertheless, individual differences also exist in how children understand health.

### Relations Between Children's Health Understanding and their Health Behavior

How do studies of child health beliefs and understanding inform our ability to predict child health behavior? Unfortunately, few studies have been able to link children's knowledge of and beliefs about health to their actual health behavior. These null findings correspond with the notion that, for young children especially, routine or preventive health care is a manifestation of parents' health directives and behaviors. In early childhood, children are taken for health care when they are perceived by adults to have an illness or other condition requiring professional attention. At these ages, children self-initiate medical care only under unusual circumstances, such as visiting a school nurse. This pattern is consistent with more general theories concerning parents' management of young children's lives and the distinction between parent-initiated and child-initiated health behaviors of the child (McDowell & Parke, 2009).

Investigations with older children have shown mixed results. For example, health knowledge and health beliefs predicted avoidance of risk behaviors in 6- to 17-year-old children (Rashkis, 1965; Rimal, 2003). However, other studies have found little relation between children's health knowledge, beliefs, and behaviors (Tinsley, Holtgrave, Erdley, & Reise, 2003). Given the limited predictive relation between knowledge and behavior in adults, the ambiguity of these findings should not be surprising. Additional work is needed to further investigate the association between children's health-related attitudes and a wide range of wellness and illness health behaviors.

### Individual Differences in Children's Health Attitudes, Understanding, and Behavior

In contrast to a Piagetian-stage approach, an individual differences perspective on children's acquisition of health attitudes and behavior shifts from a maturational focus on the unfolding of abilities in these domains to the personality, social, and cultural variables that mediate this acquisition. Research on how individual difference factors impact child health attitudes and behavior occurred mostly between 1975 and 1988. These studies focused on how children's motivation and perceived vulnerability influenced their health knowledge and beliefs (Gochman,

1987; Parcel & Meyer, 1978). Investigations of children's health-related locus of control indicate a relation between internal health locus of control and more sophisticated understanding of the clues used to identify health and illness (Neuhauser, Amsterdam, Hines, & Steward, 1978). Children's health vulnerability, defined as the perceived likelihood of experiencing health problems, increases between the ages of 8 and 13, and decreases thereafter (Gochman, 1987). Unfortunately, this group of studies has not demonstrated that these individual difference factors can predict child health behavior.

However, in contrast to an assumption that children's health-related attitudes and knowledge unfold in a fixed, invariant sequence dependent on their cognitive level, a focus on individual differences in these areas has different implications. Specifically, the individual differences perspective raises the issue of the nature and range of the modifiers of children's health attitudes and how they interact with cognitive development. One highly important modifier of children's health attitudes and behavior is the family.

## Family Modifiers of Children's Health Attitudes and Behavior

Family influences on child wellness and illness include sociodemographic factors, families' efforts to teach their children health attitudes and behavior, and the extent to which families provide environments conducive to the development of positive health behavior in their children.

### SOCIODEMOGRAPHIC FACTORS

Sociodemographic influences on children's health behavior and status have been traditionally a starting point for examination of family influences on children's health. Social class and ethnicity are used worldwide to document patterns of wellness and illness in childhood. Many explanations for how socioeconomic status (SES) affects children's health center on factors associated with poverty (e.g., inadequate diet). Epidemiological studies suggest that SES is related to child health outcomes in a monotonic fashion; each decreasing SES level is associated with an increasing prevalence of disease. In other words, not only do those children who live in poverty experience worse health than children who do not live in poverty, but individuals at each level of SES also experience better health than those just below them (Chen, Matthews, & Boyce, 2002). From a developmental perspective, the relations between children's SES and their health is complex; these relations may change with age or achieving

certain developmental milestones (Chen et al., 2002).

Research demonstrates that children from low social class families experience illnesses such as gastroenteritis, influenza, meningitis, and rheumatic fever more often than do children from higher social class homes, even when ethnicity is controlled (Hart, et al., 2003). However, the mechanisms accounting for these demographic effects are not fully known. Many explanations for how SES affects children's health center on factors associated with poverty (e.g., inadequate diet or less access to primary care services such as immunizations and dental care). In addition, low-SES families often live in environments characterized by high stress as well as few resources and little support (Hart et al., 2003).

Empirical studies suggest strong bidirectional patterns between unmet child health needs and child health status. Children who do not receive adequate health care are less well, and less well children often do not receive the health care that they need. For example, Stephens used multiple logistic regression modeling to examine parents' concerns about their children's health status and developmental risk. Additional outcome variables consisted of three measures of basic access to health care: telephone contact with a physician, well-child visit in the past year, and missed or delayed needed care. Controlling for other family factors, having more demographic risk factors was associated with poorer health status (i.e., percent reported "good/fair/poor" vs. "excellent/ very good") and being at higher risk for developmental delays. For example, the likelihood of having either poorer health or developmental delay increased in a dose–response pattern with each risk factor. A higher number of risk factors was also associated with poorer health care access, which may further degrade health. In light of the fact that children with higher profiles of risk are also more likely to lack access to care, the results of this study indicate that children who most need care have the greatest difficulty obtaining it (Dowd, 2007; Larson, Russ, Crall, & Halfon, 2008; Stevens, 2006). Unfortunately, about one-third of (or 3.1 million) young children in the United States have two or more demographic risk factors for poor health (Evans, Keenan, & Shipton, 2007).

One thought-provoking feature of the literature linking child health and sociodemographic status is the finding from several studies documenting the influence of maternal education, in comparison to other demographic variables such as maternal employment or family income, on child health status

(Inkelas, Halfon, Wood, & Schuster, 2007). This suggests that education may expose mothers to better-quality information about the contributors to health and change their health-related interaction with children. Thus, it is the distribution of parent and family health behaviors within social class, and not social class per se, that is important for utilization of child health services and child health status. Even more importantly, the identification of sociodemographic group differences in child health services utilization and child health status is a useful starting point, but additional attention to the processes underlying social class differences is required. A more productive approach to conceptualizing the links between social class and child health status would be to focus on the family processes associated with the development of children's behavior and health rather than examining descriptive variables such as social class.

## FAMILY SOCIALIZATION FACTORS

Two approaches have characterized research on the ways in which families socialize children's health behavior: studies in which the individual child's attitudes and behaviors are the outcomes of interest versus studies in which the family as a whole is the unit of analysis. Child-focused studies include the extent to which children's health behaviors resemble parents' health beliefs and behavior, the impact of child-rearing practices on child health behavior, and parents' impact on child health understanding and health behavior. In general, three principal categories of parenting variables—parenting practices (i.e., what parents do), parenting goals (i.e., why they do it), and parenting style (i.e., how they do it)—are shown to influence children's health socialization and, ultimately, their behaviors (Jackson & Dickinson, 2009). For example, in a study of girls and their parents, lower reports of positive parenting practices by daughters were correlated with parents' underestimation of children's risk behavior (O'Donnell et al., 2008). As another example, recent work demonstrates that children's sleep problems were adversely affected (increased more/decreased less over time) when, in third grade, mothers experienced more negative emotions and displayed a less sensitive style and the mother–child relationship was characterized by less closeness/more conflict (absence of the father and youth of the mother were also associated with sleep problems) (Bell & Belsky, 2008).

A somewhat different approach to untangling the sources of family influence on child health behaviors is to consider the family as a health socialization unit.

Studies focusing on the family as a unit use multivariate models to study the complexities and multiple sources of families' influences on children's health behavior as embedded in more general socialization influences. The few studies approaching the determinants of child health behavior in this manner highlight the bidirectional effects and multiple factors that moderate or mediate pathways to child health status. The findings from studies using multivariate approaches illustrate their value for representing the complexity and multiple sources of influence on children's health attitudes and behavior.

What is the significance of identifying family-level influences on child health? Our current models of health, as discussed previously, posit interactions of biological, social, and environmental factors. Families are the major component of young children's social and environmental contexts, and examination of these contextual contributions is a critical ingredient of any model of childhood health. Familial influence on children's health must also be examined from multiple perspectives. The role of individual family members is obviously very important. For example, studies indicate that mothers play a pivotal role in determining the health of their children (Carolan, 2007). This includes such behaviors as their decision making as to use of health services, escorting children to physicians, and in providing home nursing for ill children. However, it is still an empirical question whether the role of fathers, other family members, or families as a unit in determining child health attitudes, behavior, and status can account for additional portions of the variance in these child health outcomes (Baker & Silverstein, 2008; Fägerskiöld, 2006; Franckel & Lalou, 2009).

Sallis, Nader, and their colleagues have conducted a series of systematic studies over the past 25 years aimed at investigating family determinants of health behavior (Barr-Anderson et al., 2007; Sallis, Patterson, McKenzie, & Nader, 1988; Sallis, Rosenberg, & Kerr, 2009). One major objective of many of these studies has been to examine similarities and differences in health-related variables across family members. For example, there are statistically significant correlations among parent–child, sibling–sibling, and spouse–spouse blood pressures. Similar correlations are found with serum cholesterol, lipoproteins, and body fat (obesity). Although genetic influences may account for part of the variance in parent–child and sibling–sibling similarities, this is not the case for spouse–spouse similarities. Therefore, some of the correspondence in biomarkers of risk is likely due to the family context. Sallis and Nader

(Sallis, Patterson, McKenzie, & Nader, 1988) discuss three possible influences: smoking, diet, and exercise. There is a great deal of evidence that smoking habits, health-related dietary habits, and physical activity habits are very similar within families. However, many of the studies that provide this evidence are limited in their scope in terms of their attention to family structure, demographic factors, and the explication of the comparative strengths and interactions of various influences (Sallis et al., 1988). Moreover, similar inquiries concerning such issues as one-parent families and families varying in ethnicity and culture have rarely been undertaken. Many empirical questions remain unanswered and prevent us from achieving a thorough understanding of the role of the family in determining children's health attitudes and behavior.

## Other Socialization Influences on Children's Health Understanding and Behavior

Family socialization is a substantial influence on children's emerging health awareness and behavior. Nevertheless, other societal and social influences (peers, schools, and media) have important roles in accomplishing health socialization in childhood.

### PEER AND SCHOOL INFLUENCES ON CHILDREN'S HEALTH

As children develop, peers play an increasingly important role in determining their attitudes and behavior. Peers provide either complementary or competing sources of influence, along with families or other socializing forces. For the most part, studies documenting the extent to which peers impact children's health behavior are concerned with peer influences on risk behavior, such as drug use (Farruggia & Sorkin, 2009; Fonseca, Matos, Guerra, & Gomes, 2009; Wang, Simons-Morton, Farhart, & Luk, 2009). However, a few studies have investigated the extent to which peers have positive influence on children's health behavior, and find limited peer influence compared with that of other socialization agents. For example, in an investigation of positive aspects of adolescents' health (lack of emotional and somatic symptoms, positive subjective health, and self-reported happiness), as predicted by their relationships with parents and peers and their perceptions of school, positive perceptions of the school and relations with parents predicted positive health behavior, whereas peer and sibling relationships were not significant (Peltzer, 2007). The results from this study provide evidence of the greater influence of parents compared with that of peers in the health behavior context.

Schools have been demonstrated to significantly influence children's behavior, apart from the family. In addition to the physical health education they provide to students, they can be the site for interventions designed to improve students' health (Au, Suen, & Kwok, 2010; Moseley & Gradisar, 2009; Yager & O'Dea, 2009). However, these programs are often unsuccessful in their goals of achieving better health behaviors in children, possibly because the programs are often offered on a one-time basis, with little follow-up, and delivered by teachers with little preparation for teaching children about health.

### MEDIA INFLUENCES ON CHILDREN'S HEALTH

Television and other screen viewing among children are at an all time high. On average, children aged 2–5 spend 32 hours a week in front of a TV—watching television, DVDs, DVR, and videos, and using a game console. Children aged 6–11 spend about 28 hours a week in front of the TV. The vast majority of this viewing (97%) is of live TV (McDonough, 2009). The level of access is also high: 8% of 8- to 18-year-olds have a TV in their bedroom, 54% have a DVD/VCR player, 37% have cable/satellite TV, and 20% have premium channels (Roberts, Foehr, & Rideout, 2005). In 63% of households, the TV is "usually" on during meals (Roberts et al., 2005).

Television and other screen programming have the potential to both educate teens and foster discussion with parents about health, sex, responsible behavior, and safety; however, this is rarely the case. In the most recent research on the effects of media on the health and well-being of children and adolescents, studies have shown that media can provide information about safe health practices and can foster social connectedness (Strasburger, Jordan, & Donnerstein, 2010). However, other recent evidence raises concerns about media's effects on aggression, sexual behavior, substance use, disordered eating, and academic difficulties (Strasburger et al., 2010). Currently, we have few ways to increase the benefits and reduce the harm that media can have for the developing child and adolescents.

A great deal is known about the effects of screen viewing (e.g., television programming, cable TV, and computer use) on children's health, because there have been numerous studies on the subject. Screen viewing is a public health issue for children in several different ways. Children get lots of information about health from advertisements. Advertisements do not generally give true or balanced information about healthy lifestyles and food choices, and the majority of children who watch health-related commercials believe what the advertising tells them (Harris, Bargh, & Brownell, 2009). TV viewing starts earlier than other forms of media, often beginning before age 2. Spending time watching TV can take time away from children's healthy activities like active play outside with friends. Thus, watching lots of television and other screen viewing can contribute to childhood overweight and obesity. Television viewing is also associated with altered sleep patterns and sleep disorders among children and adolescents. A recent study found that infants and toddlers who watch television have more irregular sleep schedules (Johnson, Cohen, Kasen, First, & Brook, 2004; Thompson & Christakis, 2005). These sleep disturbances may persist; teens who watched 3 or more hours of TV per day had higher risk of sleep problems by early adulthood (Thompson, Flores, Ebel, & Christakis, 2008). Finally, screen viewing can promote risky behavior, such as trying dangerous stunts, substance use and abuse, and irresponsible sexual behavior (Kunkel, Eyal, Finnerty, Biely, & Donnerstein, 2005).

Injuries are the leading cause of death in childhood, and watching unsafe behavior on TV may increase children's risk-taking behavior. Children have been injured trying to repeat dangerous stunts they have seen on television shows. Many children watch TV sporting events. Researchers surveyed TV sports event ads to assess what children are viewing. Almost half of all commercial breaks during sporting events contained at least one advertisement that portrayed unsafe behavior or violence (Tamburro, Gordon, D'Apolito, & Howard, 2004).

The presence of alcohol on television and other screen programming runs the gamut from drinking to talking about drinking beer and liquor on prime-time shows to logos displayed at sporting events. Children and youth see, on average, about 2,000 beer and wine ads on TV each year (Strasburger, 2002). Many studies have shown that alcoholic drinks are the most common beverage portrayed on screen, and that they are seldom portrayed in a negative light (Robinson, Chen, & Killen, 1998). Exposure to alcohol use on television and in music videos (such as on MTV) is also a risk factor for increased drinking in adolescents (Snyder, Milici, Slater, Sun, & Strizhakova, 2006). Advertisements on television and other screens portray people as being happier, sexier, and more successful when they drink. Alcohol advertising, including TV ads, contributes to increased drinking among youth (Outley & Taddese, 2006). Television advertisements for alcohol that combines the sweet taste of soda pop in a liquor-branded malt beverage

(i.e., "alcopop,") may target youth, especially African American children (Mekemson & Glantz, 2002). The Center on Alcohol Marketing and Youth at Georgetown University found that, in 2003, the top 15 prime time programs most popular with adolescents all included alcohol advertisements (Robinson et al., 1998). Alcohol is increasingly advertised during screen programs that young people are more likely to watch than people of legal drinking age (CAMY, 2006; Snyder et al., 2006).

Even though tobacco ads are banned on TV, young people still see people smoking on programs and movies shown on television. The tobacco industry uses product placement in films. Smoking in movies increased throughout the 1990s and early 2000s (Mekemson & Glantz, 2002). Internal tobacco industry documents illustrate that the tobacco industry purposefully markets their product to youth. The industry uses subtle strategies, such as imposing logos at sporting events, product placement, and celebrities smoking, to get around the ban on TV advertising for their products (CAMY, 2006; Cummings, Morley, Horan, Steger, & Leavell, 2002). Children who engage in screen viewing start smoking at an earlier age (Gutschoven & Van den Bulck, 2005). The relationship between television viewing and age of starting smoking was stronger than that of peer smoking, parental smoking, and gender (Mekemson & Glantz, 2002).

Sexual content is a real presence on TV. Soap operas, music videos, prime time shows, and advertisements all contain a great deal of sexual content, but usually nothing about contraception or safer sex. The number of sex scenes on TV has nearly doubled since 1998, with 70% of the top 20 most-watched shows by adolescents including sexual content (Cummings et al., 2002). Fifteen percent of scenes with sexual intercourse depict characters who have just met having sex. Of the shows with sexual content, an average of five scenes per hour involves sex. Watching sex on TV increases the chances a teen will have sex, and may cause teens to start having sex at younger ages. Even viewing programming with characters talking about sex increases the likelihood of sexual initiation (Collins et al., 2004).

We now turn to issues that are more relevant for the smaller proportion of children who experience chronic disease or disabilities. Although there are more similarities than differences across well and chronically ill or disabled children, many chronically ill or disabled children experience unique challenges due to their health status. In the next section of this chapter, we highlight some of these considerations.

## Chronic Disease in Childhood

Advances in medicine and surgery have increased the number of children with chronic illnesses that are surviving into adolescence. By 2015, worldwide, 1.2 billion children aged 5–14 years will have some type of significant chronic disease (Huff, McClanahan, & Omar, 2008). Approximately 10%–15% of U.S. (between 10 and 20 million) children are estimated to have an ongoing physical health condition (Bramlett & Blumberg, 2008). Although most of these conditions are relatively mild and interfere little with a child's usual activities, at least 10% of children with physical illness have symptoms severe enough to have an impact on their daily lives (Bethell, Read, Blumberg, & Newacheck, 2008). More than one-quarter of all U.S. children have a chronic health condition, a significant increase over the rate seen in earlier decades, and a statistic that looms large for the nation's efforts to subdue rising health care costs (Bramlett & Blumberg, 2008).

Although specific medical conditions in children can be associated with unique stressors and issues, many common features also exist across conditions. The assumption made in this chapter is that the psychosocial needs of children with various medical conditions are more similar than they are different (Schaeffer, Weist, & McGrath, 2003). The major challenge for health care professionals who care for infants, children, and young adults and for those who will treat them as they age into adulthood has become the management of chronic disabilities and diseases (DeAngelis & Zylke, 2006).

### Coping with Childhood Chronic Illness

By definition, chronic diseases cannot be cured, but treatment may lessen some consequences of the disease, and often, overall deterioration can be prevented or slowed. Physical disabilities and chronic disease can substantially impede children's developmental trajectories. Children with chronic diseases and disabilities must develop academically, socially, and physically at the same time that they cope and adjust to frequent disabling treatment, parental worry, demands of self-care, and challenges to their self-image (Boekaerts & Roder, 1999). They must develop independence from parents despite the fact that they are more dependent on them than other children are on their parents, form stable identities, and cope with the physical and psychological effects of the disease or disability and medication side effects (Burns, Sadof, & Kamat, 2006).

There is consensus among child health clinicians and researchers that children's chronic diseases and disabilities affect many more people than the children themselves. Instead, chronically ill and disabled children impact their parents, siblings, peers, teachers, and communities. From the time before they were diagnosed, many of these children are in need of daily care (often complex care), and impact the family's instrumental, social interactional, physical, emotional, and financial resources available. Depending on their specific care requirements, specific diseases and disabilities generate differing demands on these resources (Bockaerts & Roder, 1999).

The results of some studies of children with chronic illness and disabilities suggest that coping with a chronic illness may lead to more effective coping with everyday stressors (Boekaerts & Roder, 1999). Evaluating the effectiveness of coping styles in children with chronic illness is important to improve interventions to help ill and disabled children cope with their conditions (Hampel, Rudolph, Stachow, Lass-Lentzsch, & Petermann, 2005). A review (Lavigne & Faier-Routman, 1992; Patterson & Blum, 1996) and meta-analysis by Lavigne and Faier-Rothman (Lavigne & Faier-Routman, 1992) compared the relations among illness characteristics and adjustment. With this perspective, the adjustment of chronically ill and disabled children can be organized around aspects such as functional status, type of disease/disability, duration and severity of the condition, prognosis, visibility of the condition, the extent of pain suffered by the child, and coping. Among these features, research centered on children's coping mechanisms is most promising (Brown, Daly, & Rickel, 2007). The results of studies aimed at investigating children's coping behavior as a mediating mechanism in the relations between disability or chronic illness and adjustment suggest that this perspective is a fertile approach (Hanna & Guthrie, 2001). However, as with most studies concerning disabled or chronically ill children, serious methodological concerns exist. In this case, a substantial number of these concerns are focused on assessment. There is little agreement about how to measure children's coping or adjustment. Added to this methodological brew is a wide range of possible coping mechanisms depending on specifics of the disease or disability. Within the stress and coping literature as applied to adjustment in disabled or chronically ill children, the stresses are perceived stresses (as perceived by the child), and the coping behaviors are specific to each disability and chronic disease (Steele, Cushing, Bender, & Richards, 2008). Thus, researchers recognize that it is very hard to develop a typology of perceived stresses experienced by disabled or chronically ill children, and equally difficult to typify their coping mechanisms, much less link them in any meaningful way (Boekaerts & Roder, 1999; Zehnder, Prchal, Vollrath, & Landolt, 2006).

Findings about the influence of coping on psychological adjustment in children with different medical conditions have been largely based on cross-sectional data and are inconsistent (Zehnder et al., 2006). One of the few prospective studies evaluated the effect of various coping strategies on children's posttraumatic stress symptoms and behavioral problems 1 month and 1 year after an accidental injury or the diagnosis of a chronic disease in 161 pediatric patients 6–15 years of age. Effects of coping strategies on psychosocial adjustment were found: Religious coping was associated with reduced posttraumatic stress symptoms, and active coping strategies predicted lower levels of internalizing and externalizing behavioral problems. However, support-seeking strategies, distraction, and avoidance had no impact on long-term psychosocial adjustment (Zehnder et al., 2006). This study suggests that, from the ill or disabled child's perspective, the ability to cope depends on family environment, functional status, and verbal intelligence, which is not all that different from the ability of well children to cope with non–health condition aspects of their lives (Cohen, 1999).

### Comparing Chronically Ill with Non–Chronically Ill Children

One frequent research question for those addressing the needs of disabled and chronically ill children has been the extent to which they differ in their psychological health and functioning from children who are not disabled or chronically ill. A meta-analytic review of more than 80 studies of children's adjustment to physical disorders found increased risk for overall adjustment problems and internalizing and externalizing symptoms. However, studies comparing ill children to well-child control groups were less likely to find significant differences than studies comparing ill children to behavioral norms derived from well children (Lavigne & Faier-Routman, 1992). Individual studies and other reviews considering results from multiple studies suggest fewer negative consequences than might be assumed (Lavigne & Faier-Routman, 1992).

In studies of this genre, three aspects of functioning are usually examined: academic, psychological, and social. Regarding academic performance, disabled and chronically ill children appear overall to be just as successful as their well and nondisabled peers

(Vitulano, 2003). Despite documented disparity in school days missed, significant discrepancies are not found in the academic development of these two groups of children.

The most common mental health outcomes used to make comparisons in the psychological realm are levels of depression, anxiety, and behavior problems. Many studies have compared these constructs in the two groups, and across these studies, results are equivocal. Finding differ depending on (a) which behavior problems or categories (internalizing vs. externalizing) are chosen; (b) whether disabled and chronic ill children are compared with children with no chronic disease, normative groups, or children with acute illnesses; and (c) whether parents or children themselves provided the ratings (Boekaerts & Roder, 1999). Another issue relevant to these studies is the extent to which levels of dysfunction in the chronically ill or disabled groups actually reach clinical significance (Boekaerts & Roder, 1999). Inconsistencies in the findings of these studies, perhaps related to the variability in study measures, samples, and design, suggest that there is a substantial need for more consistency in methods before strong conclusions can be drawn regarding how disabled and chronically ill children actually differ in their psychological functioning from other groups of children.

Knowledge regarding the self-concept of disabled/chronically ill versus abled and non–chronically ill children is similarly unclear. When compared on dimensions of self-concept including academic performance, physical appearance, anxiety, popularity, happiness, physical competence, and overall self-perception of competence, some studies have found no significant differences between the two groups (Hazzard & Angert, 1986; Nelms, 1989). Other studies indicate differences, with chronically ill and disabled students having either lower or higher scores in these self-concept domains than children who do not experience chronic health challenges or disabilities (Hazzard & Angert, 1986; Kiernan, Guerin, & MacLachlan, 2005). Further, many findings did not hold up when the sample matching was more carefully done and the two groups of children were compared to norms for these measures (Boekaerts & Roder, 1999).

The third domain of functioning empirically examined in past literature is social functioning. Consistent with the literature on academic and psychological functioning, when abled and non–chronically ill children are compared with their disabled or chronically ill peers, findings are mixed. Studies that focus on social functioning find that some chronically ill children are socially isolated, and others are not (Alderfer, Wiebe, & Hartmann, 2002; Spirito, DeLawyer, & Stark, 1991). For example, preschoolers with at least one medical condition experienced a greater frequency of peer rejection and bullying compared with healthy peers. Depressive symptoms mediated the relationship between illness and social behavior (Curtis & Luby, 2008). These disparate findings regarding the extent of social isolation suggest that disability and chronic illness in childhood should be studied more systematically and carefully, for a better understanding of their effects on children's social competence.

It has long been a tenet of special education that there are more similarities than differences between well and chronically ill or disabled children. These similarities are considered to be more useful foci for research than examining differences among children in order to understand the behavior of chronically ill and disabled children. With the latter approach, there is the substantial risk that, with the perspective of children's dysfunction as the center of attention, the results of such studies will distract researchers and those who work with chronically ill and disabled children by connecting maladjustment directly to being chronically ill or disabled. Instead, it has been recommended that researchers utilize a social capital or social resources perspective to create a picture of these children's adjustment (Eiser, 1990; Hobfoll, 1989). For example, such resources as perceived availability of social support, coping mechanisms, and attitudes toward the disease or disability may be more important than illness per se.

## Comparing Children with Different Chronic Illnesses

A second common research focus is how children with one type of disability or chronic illness differ in their adjustment from children with different kinds of disability or chronic illness (Boekaerts & Roder, 1999). Some studies report findings on academic functioning that indicate differences between children with different afflictions (Fowler, Johnson, & Atkinson, 1985). For example, chronic diseases such as sickle-cell disease, diabetes mellitus, and epilepsy are associated with poorer academic functioning (Parent, Wodrich, & Hasan, 2009).

Studies comparing psychosocial functioning outcomes between children with two different conditions provide equivocal findings, with some differences being found (McMahon, Grant, Compas, Thurm, & Ey, 2003). For example, children with asthma seem to have more internalizing behaviors and lower self-concepts than do children with diabetes (Kashani, Konig, Shepperd, Wilfley, & Morris, 1988; McQuaid, Kopel, & Nassau, 2001). A meta-analysis found interdisease differences, but only in a few studies. Children with neurological disorders such as epilepsy seemed to be most at risk for psychological maladjustment (Lavigne & Faier-Routman, 1992).

The comparison of children's social functioning across specific diseases and conditions reveals that the quality of peer relations is inversely associated with the level of physical disfigurement or physical activity inabilities. For example, children with cancer or epilepsy engender more negative responses from children without disabilities or conditions than do children with diabetes or cardiac conditions (Spirito et al., 1991).

Many researchers believe that there is more variability within diagnostic groups than between them (Morison, Bromfield, & Cameron, 2003; Stein & Jessop, 1989). Methodological problems and inconsistencies in these literatures compound the problem of relating different levels or types of adjustment to specific diseases, and there is a critical need for within-group designs to identify variables that affect the quality of adjustment. Inconsistent findings also may result from the use of informants with different roles in children's lives (e.g., clinicians, parents, teachers, peers), as this research finds relatively low interrater reliability across informants (Brown, Riley, & Wissow, 2007; Coie, Lochman, Terry, & Hyman, 1992). This may be accounted for by the differing "windows of opportunity" affordable to informants with respect to observing child behavior. Nevertheless, this multi-informant approach is useful in creating a behavioral portrait of the whole child and offers unique predictive contributions for each informant (Coie et al., 1992; Tinsley, Holtgrave, Erdley, & Reise, 1997).

## Sources of Stress and Sources of Support

A variety of social influences (e.g., families, schools, medical professionals) can be both stressors and sources of support for disabled or chronically ill children. Moreover, some of the effects of stressors on the entities in the social environment of these children can be characterized as bidirectional, as those who provide social support for children with chronic disease or disability can be stressed and have their own needs for support. In this next section, some aspects of the roles of families, medical professionals, teachers and schools, and peers in the lives of disabled or chronically ill children are briefly explored, and some of the stressors and supports for these social environmental agents are also detailed.

## FAMILIES

The family systems perspective best conceptualizes the bidirectional effects between families and the adaptation of their disabled or chronically ill children (Kazak, Simms, & Rourke, 2002). Brown (2002) argues that cultural systems, family systems, peers, schools, and health care providers influence the adjustment and adaptation of children with chronic illness and that in turn, these children have reciprocal influences on the systems. Prior research suggests that psychopathology in some aspect of the family system is commonly found in families of disabled or chronically ill children (Kazak, 1989; Kazak, Rourke, & Crump, 2003). Factors associated with psychopathology in families with disabled or chronically ill children include family structure and function, coping resources (including medical, psychosocial, and educational), and characteristics of the issues brought about by specific diseases or disabilities (Kazak et al., 2003).

In a review of studies examining child illness and disability demands on the family and family resources, Cohen developed a typology of four important results (Cohen, 1999): (a) the demands of childhood chronic illness impose severe strains on families, including stresses on family structure and function; (b) total family resources (including psychosocial, financial, and instrumental) influence the course and impact of the chronic illness or disability; (c) the most influential factors affecting family coping with a child's chronic illness or disability are related to the whole family, and include the meanings of illness and disability for the family (e.g., is the illness viewed as a challenge or a threat?); and (d) biopsychosocial illness or disability factors (e.g., the extent to which a treatment requires intense family involvement) can affect the relations among family factors, child illness or disability, and the child's outcomes (Cohen, 1999). Gustafsson and colleagues (Gustafsson, Bjorksten, & Kjellman, 1994), in a prospective study designed to determine the extent to which family factors predicted development of asthma, found instead that families coping with a child's asthma and the related stress are more likely to develop dysfunctional family dynamics. Moreover, the psychological demands of having an asthmatic child in a family were most exacerbated by two factors: the extent to which the illness manifested symptoms unpredictably and the perceived vulnerability of the child for complications.

Canam (1993) identified some of the common adaptive tasks facing parents of children with chronic conditions, including acceptance of the condition, managing the child on a daily basis, meeting the child's developmental needs, coping with stress, assisting family members with their emotions, and educating others about the child. Other studies implicate shifting caregiving roles and boundaries (e.g., the role changes experienced by siblings, such as more responsibility for organizing the everyday life of the family—activities that previously were the purview of parents), financial burdens (Looman, O'Connor-Von, Ferski, & Hildenbrand, 2009), and the necessity to interact with professionals and institutions outside the home when that might not fit with the family's style (Cohen, 1999; Wood, 1995). Psychosocial distress also appears to have the most negative effects on the family when the child's condition involves functional limitations, regardless of whether the condition affects single or multiple domains (Cohen, 1999).

As with other aspects of research on the effects of child chronic disease or disability, many inconsistencies and methodological artifacts limit the usefulness of the findings. Research design issues permeate this literature; most of the empirical work in this field is cross-sectional in nature and does not permit the examination of change over time in these relations.

## INDIVIDUAL FAMILY MEMBERS

As noted above, the type, severity, and duration of chronic illness in children significantly influence their ability to psychologically adjust (Lavigne & Faier-Routman, 1992; Patterson & Blum, 1996). However, family and parent variables have been identified in two meta-analyses (Bennett, 1994; Lavigne & Faier-Routman, 1992) as more influential than these illness variables. Child coping and adjustment are related to the family environment, most powerfully in terms of parental health locus of control and child health status (Cohen, 1999). The extent to which the parents of ill or disabled children perceive internal control of their children's health events appears to make a substantial difference in the quality of the family environment and the health status of the children.

Parents are stressed by the additional demands inherent in the presence of a chronically ill or disabled child in the family. This strain can contribute to or exacerbate marital problems. Research has demonstrated that marital discord is a powerful and long-lasting stressor for most children exposed to their parents' conflict (Cummings & Merrilees, 2010). However, for chronically ill and disabled children, the relations among the quality of parents' relationships, stress, and adjustment are more complex, intense, and bidirectional (Cohen, 1999; Vrijmoet et al., 2008). Marital distress not only impacts family functioning as a whole, but parenting behaviors specifically (Story & Bradbury, 2004), and include decreases in parenting sensitivity, responsiveness, positivity, and involvement (Cummings, Davies, & Campbell, 2002; Grych & Fincham, 2001; Owen & Cox, 1997; Webster-Stratton & Hammond, 1999). Chronically ill or disabled children may be directly stressed by marital conflict, but also indirectly affected by the consequences of marital discord: less availability of parental support due to the distraction of marital disagreements.

As individual parents, mothers and fathers also face challenges associated with caring for a disabled or chronically ill child. Historically, most of the relevant studies have focused on mothers; mothers have been culturally conceptualized as the main caregivers for well and chronically ill or disabled children (McDougal, 2002). Moreover, until recently, mothers have been the main informants in investigations of the effects on parents of raising chronically ill or disabled children (Cohen, 1999; Drotar, Agle, Eckl, & Thompson, 1996). In the past few years, fathers' reports of these effects are also included in such studies (Gavin & Wysocki, 2006). Various studies have documented the specific stressors that impact parents. One such study held focus groups of parents with chronically ill children to report the range of stressors that the parents perceived (Kratz, Uding, Trahms, Villareale, & Kieckhefer, 2009). Qualitative analyses identified commonly perceived challenges, including social isolation, strained relationships, and ongoing frustrations with health care and educational systems.

A small number of studies in this literature specifically focus on differences between mothers and fathers with respect to the differential roles they assume in caregiving and the nature of the consequential effects of parenting a chronically ill or disabled child (Higham, 2009). Across studies, mothers still appear to have more involvement in managing children's access to medical providers and have higher levels of interaction with these providers. Home caregiving is disproportionately borne by mothers (Navaie-Waliser, Spriggs, & Feldman, 2002). In turn, the effects of parenting chronically ill or disabled children are manifested in different ways for mothers and fathers. Mothers, as a group, appear to exhibit more distress than fathers (perhaps due to their assumption of the majority of the caregiving). However, fathers suffer in their own way,

demonstrating financial distress and emotional withdrawal from the child (Seiffge-Krenke, 2002). In an analysis of these patterns, Dashiff concluded that mothers and fathers are uniquely vulnerable to different aspects of such parenting, and find different gender-based ways to cope with the upset; fathers seem to use distraction and distancing to cope, whereas mothers are more likely to engage in activities to control the health issue and its medical regimens to cope (Dashiff, 1993).

Methodological issues are also part of this research literature—most studies have compared psychological functioning in parents of chronically ill or disabled children and those parenting well children, which is an inappropriate control group since the differences between the groups are inherent in any comparison of healthy and unhealthy individuals. Control groups within children's specific illness, age, severity, or visibility of the affliction are better matches. Results from these studies often find significant differences in psychological functioning between these two groups of parents; for example, several studies find mean differences in depression levels, with the parents of chronically ill or disabled children reporting more depression than parents of well children. However, although parents of disabled or chronically ill children appear more depressed, very rarely does their depression exceed clinical boundaries.

Research on the siblings of chronically ill children has shown increased levels of emotional stress and behavioral symptoms (Gardner, 1998). Past research has documented that over half of well siblings exhibit psychological and behavioral symptoms (Gardner, 1998). However, evidence from meta-analyses demonstrates that, although children are at slightly elevated risk of psychosocial distress, only a minority of these well siblings display symptoms reaching clinical levels (Barlow & Ellard, 2006). The mechanisms of these effects are complicated and best considered within a family systems perspective. Direct effects include the manner in which siblings of ill or disabled children are treated by their parents. Usually, this is manifested in differential parental treatment for the well child vis-à-vis the chronically ill or disabled child. Parents are often overprotective of a chronically ill or disabled child, leaving the well sibling with less attention and daily care (Cameron, Young, & Wiebe, 2007). Another possible dynamic of this type is that such parents will have less time overall to engage in activities with their well children. Other, more indirect effects can also be detected in many of these families, in which siblings of chronically ill or disabled children interact with parents and other caregivers who are depressed, anxious, or withdrawn. The social environments of siblings of ill or disabled children are characterized by less overall interaction with parents and other caregivers, as well as less positivity in these interactions (Cohen, 1999). Intervention studies designed to modify the negative experiences of siblings have been helpful to the siblings of chronically ill children, particularly during periods of hospitalization of the ill child. Reports indicate that siblings who receive interventions stressing cognitive-based age appropriate educational experiences concerning their hospitalized brother or sister (e.g., explanations of the treatment being given to the child) are less anxious than children who did not receive the educational treatment (Barlow & Ellard, 2006).

## OTHER SOCIAL INFLUENCES

Other social influences in the lives of chronically ill and disabled children are peers and teachers. The extent to which these individuals affect the psychosocial lives of such children often is mediated by the visible nature of the condition (Cohen, 1999; Duggan, Medway, & Bunke, 2004; Nabors, Lehmkuhl, & Warm, 2004). In general, children with chronic conditions do not have more problems in their peer relations than other youth, although children with medical conditions that are stigmatizing or that involve the central nervous system (CNS) may encounter peer difficulties. Social support from friends and classmates appears to facilitate these children's disease adaptation and may help with the lifestyle aspects of treatment regimens. Adolescent peer-crowd affiliations (e.g., "brains," "jocks") that are linked with health-promoting behaviors may prove beneficial to disease management and health. Results from studies examining the role of peers for children with chronic conditions highlights the need for helping children and adolescents disclose their medical condition to peers in positive ways and for including close friends in the treatment process and in school-reentry programs after extended medical care (La Greca, Bearman, & Moore, 2002).

La Greca and her colleagues (2002) suggest that further study is needed to tease out factors that contribute to interventions that promote peer acceptance. In a study examining the impact of scripts, the authors presented either positive or explanatory information, on children's attitudes about a line drawing of either a typical child or one in a wheelchair. Findings indicated that gender and age were significantly related to children's perceptions. Girls provided higher playmate preference ratings for both the typical child and the one sitting in a wheelchair than did boys, and older children (aged 6 years, 4 months to 9 years) reported higher ratings than did younger children. Physical status of the child in the line drawing did not impact children's opinions (Nabors & Larson, 2002). It may be that children in the developmental period of middle childhood do not hold negative attitudes toward peers who are wheelchair-bound. Because no stigma was attached to the child in either condition, type of information did not influence children's attitudes.

An examination of teachers' experiences of chronic illness in their pupils demonstrated relationships with the extent to which they feel responsible for addressing such problems, and to the amount of training they have to deal with these problems (Duggan et al., 2004). Nearly every teacher (98.7% of 480) reported knowing a student in the school with a chronic illness, and 43% felt moderately to very responsible for dealing with issues of chronic illness; 59% reported no academic training and 64% reported no on-the-job training for dealing with issues of students' chronic illness. The researchers concluded that teachers are ill-prepared to deal with issues of chronic illness in the schools (Clay, Cortina, Harper, Cocco, & Drotar, 2004). Teachers often are unaware when students in their classes have seizure disorders; a child with seizure disorders may never have a seizure at school. In contrast, limitations of children with cerebral palsy or orthopedic impairments are usually more visible and color peer and teacher perceptions of the abilities and restrictions of these children (Nabors et al., 2004). In addition, condition-related symptoms common to all children but exacerbated by a child's medical condition (e.g., inattentiveness due to pain) may be perceived by other students or teachers as misbehaving (Perrin, Ayoub, & Willett, 1993).

Culture also impacts ill and disabled children's adjustment and coping, often mediated by the family environment of the child. Culturally influenced health beliefs, perceptions of wellness and illness roles, decision-making conventions, and other rituals and behaviors are examples of the ways in which culture can be a determinant of adjustment and coping in ill or disabled children and their families (Turner, 1996). For example, if cultural understandings are used to define the sources or cause of an illness, there will be consequential influences on treatment plans.

## Intervention Strategies
### Illness Prevention

Intervention and prevention strategies focus on enhancing children's physical health and/or preventing illness. Contemporary viewpoints of health and wellness promotion address issues outside of the physical body, including social and psychological aspects of children's lives. By developing and implementing prevention and intervention programs, a variety of health and education entities endeavor to promote physical (and mental) health during childhood.

Childhood obesity is widely recognized to be a very serious and growing health problem, and many interventions have been developed in an effort to reverse the trend. These programs illustrate the variety of approaches that can be applied to prevention strategies against many child health problems. Among over 60 randomized controlled trials of obesity prevention programs, some focused on increasing physical activity, some on decreasing calorie intake, and some combined both approaches. Because most children spend most of their waking hours during the week at school, some strategies were designed to be school-based, in order to manage both children's physical exercise and their diet. Other approaches were community-based, taking a public health approach. Because family cultural beliefs and patterns influence children's health, other programs combined school- and family-based interventions, with instruction in school about the causes of obesity and homework assignments related to obesity and its causes that require parents and children to work together (Sallis et al., 1993).

Mercy and Saul (2009) reviewed the effectiveness of several prevention and intervention programs aimed at transforming children's rearing environments to improve child physical and mental health outcomes. Based on this review, they offered policy recommendations for facilitating such programs in the future. They argue that the United States must develop the infrastructure to scale up from studies documenting effective programs to transform these small-scale studies into national studies affecting many children and families. To accomplish this goal, three actions are necessary. The first is to develop a mechanism to make accessible to health professionals a database of effective prevention and intervention approaches that is easily understood. A second proposal involves creating the social capital to enable neighborhoods and communities to execute effective prevention and intervention programs. Third, local, state, and national agencies would be supported in instantiating the evidence-based prevention and intervention activities (Mercy & Saul, 2009).

Overall, it appears that the most fundamental ways of assisting children to grow up healthy are programs that work with families as a unit, rather than with only the children. Courses of action that seek to improve parents' abilities to establish and maintain nurturing and safe rearing conditions for their children or to provide other types of parental support to help parents manage the stress levels in children's lives have been somewhat successful in improving child rearing patterns (Repetti et al., 2002). However, less research is available to determine how best to support parents' efforts to change social environmental conditions (Taylor & Biglan, 1998).

Interestingly, the program that has been most successful in facilitating more effective parenting and environments was devised and evaluated with careful randomized controlled trials more than 20 years ago: the Nurse–Family Partnership (Olds, Henderson, Chamberline, & Tatelbaum, 1986). This program was developed by David Olds and involved nurse visitations to low-income first mothers during pregnancy and their child's infancy. The purpose of the nurse home visits was to facilitate mothers' efforts to provide safe prenatal environments for their babies through reducing such threats to development as substance use or lack of access to health care, teaching the young mothers-to-be positive child care methods, and support for initiatives to improve socioeconomic conditions (Olds et al., 1986). Findings from a series of studies aimed at revealing the child outcomes resulting from mothers' participation in this program were very encouraging: less abuse and unintentional injuries, and better cognitive and social emotional development were found in the Nurse–Family Partnership families compared with families in the control groups. A follow-up study 15 years after the initial investigation indicated that both the mothers and the children in the experimental group were less involved in crime and other antisocial behaviors (Olds et al., 1998).

### Interventions for Children with Chronic Illness or Disabilities
#### COMPLIANCE WITH MEDICAL REGIMENS
One major issue addressed by intervention strategies for children with chronic illness or disabilities is compliance with medical regimens, especially those that are painful, complicated, time-intensive and stigmatizing. Compliance with self-care in chronic disease has been studied across a range of disciplines including nursing, medicine, psychology, and sociology. It appears that psychosocial factors (e.g., the positive personal meaning of illness and treatment, attitude, therapeutic motivation, emotional well-being) exert

the greatest influence on adolescents' compliance, but family, peer, and health care provider support are essential to the promotion of compliance. However, the factors that influence compliance are somewhat idiosyncratic, and for this reason no study is able to offer a universally acceptable picture of compliance and its related factors. Understanding health-related behaviors and the interrelated factors that influence them is essential to health care providers for both the diagnosis of noncompliance and the support of compliance (LaGreca & Schuman, 1995).

To improve compliance, greater attention should be given to children themselves and especially to their lifestyles. Children should be looked upon as individuals with a chronic disease who are passing through a particularly critical period in their lives. Individualized, tailor-made care planning and personal goal setting should be emphasized. Also, compliance-promoting interventions in addition to education should be emphasized. A focus on behavior-centered and/or organizational interventions is needed (Kyngäs, Kroll, & Duffy, 2000).

There is also a need for improvement in the support offered to children. They need frequent support, encouragement, and positive feedback as they strive to manage simultaneously their chronic illness and normal developmental crises. Lack of support may increase the likelihood of noncompliance.

Although Kyngäs (Kyngäs, 1999) developed a theoretical model of compliance of youth with diabetes, in general, researchers of compliance among children have not sufficiently incorporated study findings into theory building, measurement development, and clinical practice (LaGreca & Schuman, 1995). Existing models of health behavior, such as the health belief model (Becker, 1974; Rosenstock, 1974) and the theory of reasoned action (Fishbein & Ajzen, 1975) have found wide applicability in health behavior research but have not received much attention in compliance research (Mullen, Hersey, & Iverson, 1987). Other frameworks such as the locus of control (Karoly, 1993) and medical models (Dracup & Meleis, 1982) have also been largely omitted from this literature.

Furthermore, there is a need for studies of personal meaning in chronic disease. Very little is known about the personal meaning or the perceived impact of a chronic disease on the lives of adolescents. Family support has been found to be an essential factor to improve compliance; however, it has been argued that the family does not influence compliance directly, but through mediating factors (Kyngäs, Hentinen, Koivukangas, & Ohinmaa, 1996; Miller-Johnson

et al., 1994). Future research is needed to clarify the role of the context of family and peer relationships on adolescent compliance. Also, the need for more research to improve the treatment of children and adolescents with a chronic disease is immediate, as the long-term costs and consequences of poor compliance affect the individual, family, and society.

## INTERVENTIONS TO PROMOTE ADJUSTMENT
The other major area of intervention research on chronic disease and disability in children addresses prevention and intervention strategies to enhance their psychosocial development. Two themes are predominant in this literature. One theme directly addresses methods to modify these children's stress and the psychosocial effects of the disease or disability, whereas the other perspective focuses on modifying parents' and other family members' stress or inability to cope related to their children's condition, in the effort to support children coping with their own stresses.

There have been remarkably few controlled evaluations of interventions to improve the adjustment of children with chronic physical disorders. Among the few that exist, Perrin and colleagues assessed the effects of a combined education and stress management program on children with asthma compared to a control condition (Perrin, MacLean, Gortmaker, & Asher, 1992). Children in the intervention group were reported by parents to exhibit improvements in adjustment and functional status compared with those in the control condition. As another example, Varni and colleagues (Varni, Katz, Colegrove, & Dolgin, 1993) evaluated social skills to manage the challenges associated with returning to school following the intensive phase of cancer treatment. Social-cognitive problem solving, assertiveness training, and ways of handling peer problems provided greater positive effects on child adjustment at a 9-month follow-up, compared with those found with a traditional supportive intervention.

Family-focused interventions are somewhat more common, but still sparse. A psychosocial intervention with families of children newly diagnosed with leukemia over a 6-year follow-up period was evaluated by Kupst and her colleagues (Kupst & Schulman, 1988; Kupst et al., 1982). Subjects were randomly assigned to one of three interventions: (1) total or (2) moderate coping skills intervention or (3) a no coping intervention control condition. Although coping skills intervention was effective in enhancing adjustment of mothers at the time of diagnosis, it was not related to subsequent adjustment of the child. Kupst and Schulman (1988) concluded that, after the critical times passed and life returned to normal in those families, there may have been less need for continuous intervention. Ireys and colleagues (Ireys, Sills, Kolodner, & Walsh, 1996) evaluated a 15-month social support intervention for mothers of children with juvenile rheumatoid arthritis. Mentors (mothers of young adults who had had juvenile rheumatoid arthritis since childhood) were joined to mothers of 2- to 11-year-old children with this disease. Both child and parent adjustment and perceived social support improved in this program compared with that of a control group.

Positive psychology has been another source of ideas for intervention with ill or disabled children. A longstanding area of intervention for adult patients with life-threatening diseases is based on the premise that positive emotions contribute to psychological and physical well-being via more effective coping (Tugade, Fredrickson, & Barrett, 2004). Recently, researchers are investigating this approach with chronically ill children. For example, benefit-finding (demonstrating awareness of the potential benefits of the illness; e.g., understanding the value of life) was measured among survivors of childhood cancer. Results indicated that benefit-finding in children with cancer is associated with optimism about the course of their disease. The authors speculate that positive outcomes may develop following childhood cancer, and may be facilitated by appropriate counseling (Michel, Taylor, Absolom, & Eiser, 2009).

Unfortunately, the many differences among studies of such intervention programs make it difficult to assess the extent to one approach is more effective than the others. These studies use a variety of outcome measures and frequently use different methods to measure the same variables. Many studies measure independent and dependent variables using non-objective methods or lack control groups. Very few investigations assess fidelity to the intervention method chosen, and many do not indicate how children or families are selected for treatment groups, suggesting the possibility of unreported selection bias (Yetter, 2009).

## Conclusion
Research on the factors and mechanisms impacting children's health status has now achieved considerable momentum. Several consistent findings have emerged. To begin, children's health understanding seems to proceed in a developmental fashion, with increasing complexity and sophisticated thinking as children age. Taking a more nuanced individual differences perspective has contributed to better understanding of the complex relations among psychosocial factors and health outcomes. Moreover, the theoretical and empirical work summarized in this chapter illustrates the continuities and discontinuities in the health information and messages children receive across family, peers, schools, the media, and other socialization agents. As a result, the burden of synthesizing these socialization messages falls on the child. Additionally, this review suggests that a direction-of-effects issue permeates the child health research area. Many variables that influence children's health attitudes and behavior are in turn affected by those attitudes and behaviors. Evidence cited in this review also indicates that these pathways of influence are not always direct, but instead in many cases are mediated by other variables, such as stress.

Another conclusion is that chronic illness in childhood is not necessarily as detrimental to children's academic, psychological, and social development as has been assumed. Many investigators expected to find deficits in chronically ill and disabled children, but their results suggest that factors other than illness itself may better explain poor outcomes. In many cases, children and their families are resilient, although coping is further facilitated by a wide range of support resources. The theories and studies surveyed in this chapter also suggest that variations in children's health status can provide opportunities for illuminating the ways in which children cope with stressful change and how support resources can best be utilized during health and other types of crises.

Ethnicity and social class are not consistently incorporated in many of the studies reviewed in this chapter, and therefore the findings may not generalize to populations other than those in each investigation's sample. Inconsistencies and inadequacies in designs and measures across studies exist within most subareas of this literature. Although these problems have limited the development of a coherent data base to address children's health problems, prevention and intervention strategies have become more comprehensive. Given new understandings of the malleability of neurological, psychological, and social characteristics as children develop, interventions can now be tailored to address targets with the highest potential to effect long-lasting change.

## Future Directions
A plethora of issues in childhood health remain to be effectively addressed. Although child health

researchers are already an interdisciplinary group, additional investment of researchers from disciplines that have not yet been involved in efforts to understand the variables and mechanisms that affect child health status is important. Very few areas of scientific inquiry are limited in their relevance for studying children's wellness and illness. The idea of plasticity, defined as the ability of an organism to develop in various ways, depending on the particular environment or setting, provides a relatively new conceptual basis for future research in the continuities and discontinuities associated with the development of health status in childhood. Methodological problems in the child health research literatures and the lack of theory-driven research remain limitations; attention and coordination concerning research designs and variables that can be used to replicate and expand findings from child health research are critical to moving the field forward with collaboration and interdisciplinarity.

Future studies in the area of factors and pathways to children's health should proceed both at the level of individual specifications of important variables, as well as in testing of overarching models. In light of the importance of children's health for a variety of developmental domains, bidirectional effects of health variables and other areas of development (e.g., social, academic) should be studied and applied to programs aimed at improving children's health in the context of the whole child. Such issues warrant more sustained and systematic inquiry. Until very recently, the science of psychosocial aspects of prevention in children's health has received little attention, and more examination of how prevention can be facilitated and improved in childhood is critical for future studies of how children can learn to be healthy. Furthermore, more attention should be paid to well children, and how their health beliefs, behavior, and social and physical environment contribute to wellness, as opposed to a focus on the etiology of disease and disability. It is more constructive to understand the commonalities across well children than to delve into the differences of ill children.

The potential for great achievement in the fields of child health research and application is upon us. Exponentially increasing mastery of technology, as well as maturation of the science of social policy, assures healthier children in the years to come.

## References

Alderfer, M.A., Wiebe, D.J., & Hartmann, D.P. (2002). Predictors of the peer acceptance of children with diabetes: Social behavior and disease severity. *Journal of Clinical Psychology in Medical Settings, 9*, 121–130.

Au, W.H., Suen, L.K.P., & Kwok, Y.L. (2010). Handwashing programme in kindergarten: A pilot study. *Health Education & Behavior, 110*, 5–16.

Baker-Ward, L., Ornstein, P.A., & Starnes, L.P. (2009). Children's understanding and remembering of stressful experiences. In R.F.J.A. Quas (Ed.), *Emotion and memory in development: Biological, cognitive, and social considerations* (pp. 28–59). New York, NY: Oxford University Press.

Baker, L.A., & Silverstein, M. (2008). Preventive health behaviors among grandmothers raising grandchildren. *The Journals of Gerontology: Series B: Psychological Sciences and Social Sciences, 63B*, S304–311.

Barker, D.J.P. (1998). In utero programming of chronic disease. *Clinical Sciences, 95*, 115–128.

Barker, D.J.P., Forsen, T., Uutela, A., & Osmond, C. (2001). Size at birth and resilience to effects of poor living conditions in adult life: Longitudinal study. *British Medical Journal, 323*, 1273–1276.

Barlow, J.H., & Ellard, D.R. (2006). The psychosocial well-being of children with chronic disease, their parents and siblings: An overview of the research evidence base. *Child: Care, Health and Development, 32*, 19–31.

Barr-Anderson, D.J., Young, D.R., Sallis, J.F., Neumark-Sztainer, D.R., Gittelsohn, J., Webber, L., et al. (2007). Structured physical activity and psychosocial correlates in middle-school girls. *Preventive Medicine: An International Journal Devoted to Practice and Theory, 44*, 404–409.

Bateson, P., Barker, D., Clutton-Brock, T., Deb, D., D'Udine, B., Foley, R.A., et al. (2004). Developmental plasticity and human health. *Nature, 430*, 419–421.

Becker, M.H. (1974). *The health belief model and personal health behaviour*. Thorofare, NJ: Slack.

Bell, B.G., & Belsky, J. (2008). Parents, parenting, and children's sleep problems: Exploring reciprocal effects. *British Journal of Developmental Psychology, 26*, 579–593.

Bennett, D. (1994). Depression among children with chronic medical problems: A meta-analysis. *Journal of Pediatric Psychology, 19*, 149–169.

Bethell, C.D., Read, D., Blumberg, S.J., & Newacheck, P.W. (2008). What is the prevalence of children with special health care needs? Toward an understanding of variations in findings and methods across three national surveys. *Journal of Maternal & Child Health, 12*, 1.

Bhargava, S.K., Sachdev, H.S., Fall, C.H.D., Osmond, C., Lakshmy, R., Barker, D.J.P., et al. (2004). Relation of serial changes in childhood body-mass index to impaired glucose tolerance in young adulthood. *New England Journal of Medicine, 350*, 865–875.

Bibace, R., & Walsh, M.W. (1980). Development of children's concepts of illness. *Pediatrics, 66*, 912–917.

Boekaerts, M., & Roder, I. (1999). Stress, coping, and adjustment in children with a chronic disease: A review of the literature. *Disability and Rehabilitation, 21*, 311–337.

Bramlett, M.D., & Blumberg, S.J. (2008). Prevalence of children with special health care needs in metropolitan and micropolitan statistical areas in the United States. *Journal of Maternal & Child Health, 12*, 488.

Brown, J.D., Riley, A.W., & Wissow, L.S. (2007). Identification of youth psychosocial problems during pediatric primary care visits. *Administration and Policy in Mental Health and Mental Health Services Research 34*, 269–281.

Brown, R.T. (2002). Society of pediatric psychology presidential address: Toward a social ecology of pediatric psychology. *Journal of Pediatric Psychology, 27*, 191–201.

Brown, R.T., Daly, B.P., & Rickel, A.U. (2007). *Chronic illness in children and adolescents.* Ashland, OH: Hogrefe & Huber Publishers.

Burns, J.J., Sadof, M., & Kamat, D. (2006). Managing the adolescent with a chronic illness. *Psychiatric Annals, 36*, 715–719.

Cameron, L.D., Young, M.J., & Wiebe, D.J. (2007). Maternal trait anxiety and diabetes control in adolescents with Type I diabetes. *Journal of Pediatric Psychology, 32*, 733–744.

Campbell, J.D. (1975). Illness is a point of view: The development of children's concepts of illness. *Child Development, 46*, 92–100.

CAMY, Center for Alcohol Marketing and Youth. (2006). *Alcohol advertising on television, 2001 to 2003: More of the same.* Retrieved from http://camy.org/research/tv1004/report.pdf.

Canam, C. (1993). Common adaptive tasks facing parents of children with chronic conditions. *Journal of Advanced Nursing, 18*, 46–53.

Carey, S. (1985). *Conceptual change in childhood.* London: Methuen.

Carolan, M. (2007). Health literacy and the information needs and dilemmas of first-time mothers over 35 years. *Journal of Clinical Nursing, 16*, 1162–1172.

Challenger, A. (2009). *Health: Why does it matter?* Paper presented at the Healthy Lives, Brighter Futures conference.

Chen, E., Matthews, K.A., & Boyce, W.T. (2002). Socioeconomic differences in children's health: How and why do these relationships change with age? *Psychological Bulletin, 128*, 295–329.

Clay, D.L., Cortina, S., Harper, D.C., Cocco, K.M., & Drotar, D. (2004). Schoolteachers' experiences with childhood chronic illness. *Children's Health Care, 33*, 227–239.

Cohen, M.S. (1999). Families coping with childhood chronic illness: A research review. *Family, Systems & Health, 17*, 149–164.

Coie, J.D., Lochman, J.E., Terry, R., & Hyman, C. (1992). Predicting early adolescent disorder from childhood aggression and peer rejection. *Journal of Consulting and Clinical Psychology, 60*, 783–792.

Collins, R.L., Elliott, M.N., Berry, S.H., Kanouse, D.E., Kunkel, D., Hunter, S.B., et al. (2004). Watching sex on television predicts adolescent initiation of sexual behavior. *Pediatrics, 114*, e280–289.

Cooper, C., Fall, C., Egger, P., Hobbs, R., Eastell, R., & Barker, D. (1997). Birth weight and risk of cardiovascular disease in a cohort of women followed up since 1976. *British Medical Journal, 315*, 396–400.

Cummings, E.M., Davies, P.T., & Campbell, S.B. (2002). Developmental psychopathology and family process: Theory, research, and clinical implications. *Journal of the American Academy of Child & Adolescent Psychiatry, 41*, 886.

Cummings, E.M., & Merrilees, C.E. (2010). Identifying the dynamic processes underlying links between marital conflict and child adjustment. In M.S. Schulz, M.K. Pruett, P.K. Kerig, & R.D. Parke (Eds.), *Strengthening couple relationships for optimal child development: Lessons from research and intervention* (pp. 27–40). Washington, DC: American Psychological Association.

Cummings, K.M., Morley, C.P., Horan, J.K., Steger, C., & Leavell, N.R. (2002). Marketing to America's youth: Evidence from corporate documents. *Tobacco Control, 11*, 15–17.

Curtis, C.E., & Luby, J.L. (2008). Depression and social functioning in preschool children with chronic medical conditions. *Journal of Pediatrics, 153*, 408–413.

Dashiff, C. (1993). Parents' perceptions of diabetes in adolescent daughters and its impact on the family. *Journal of Pediatric Psychology, 8*, 361–369.

DeAngelis, C.D., & Zylke, J.W. (2006). Theme issue on chronic diseases in infants, children, and young adults. *Journal of the American Medical Association, 296*, 1780.

Dowd, J.B. (2007). Early childhood origins of the income/health gradient: The role of maternal health behaviors. *Social Science & Medicine, 65*, 1202–1213.

Dracup, A., & Meleis, A.J. (1982). Compliance (An interactional approach). *Nursing Research, 31*, 31–36.

Drotar, D., Agle, D.P., Eckl, C.L., & Thompson, P.A. (1996). Impact of the repressive personality style on the measurement of psychological distress in children and adolescents with chronic illness: An example from hemophilia. *Journal of Pediatric Psychology. Special Issue: Assessment in pediatric psychology, 21*, 283–293.

Duggan, D.D., Medway, F.J., & Bunke, V.L. (2004). Training educators to address the needs and issues of students with chronic illnesses: Examining their knowledge, confidence levels, and perceptions. *Canadian Journal of School Psychology, 19*, 149–165.

Eiser, C. (1989). Children's concepts of illness: Towards an alternative to the "stage" approach. *Psychology and Health, 3*, 93–101.

Eiser, C. (1990). Psychological effects of chronic disease. *Journal of Child Psychology and Psychiatry and Allied Disciplines, 3*, 85–98.

Evans, S., Keenan, T.R., & Shipton, E.A. (2007). Psychosocial adjustment and physical health of children living with maternal chronic pain. *Journal of Paediatrics and Child Health, 43*(4), 262.

Fägerskiöld, A. (2006). Support of fathers of infants by the child health nurse. *Scandinavian Journal of Caring Sciences, 20*, 79–85.

Farruggia, S.P., & Sorkin, D.H. (2009). Health risks for older US adolescents in foster care: The significance of important others' health behaviours on youths' health and health behaviours. *Child: Care, Health and Development, 35*, 340–348.

Fishbein, M., & Ajzen, I. (1975). *Belief, attitude, intention and behaviour.* New York: Reading, Addison-Wesley.

Fonseca, H., Matos, M.G., Guerra, A., & Gomes, P.J. (2009). Are overweight and obese adolescents different from their peers? *International Journal of Pediatric Obesity, 4*, 166–174.

Foster, K.N., Bass, L., Zamora, A., Tinsley, B., & Gonzalez, B. (2008). *Mothers' reports of protective strategies for promotion of children's safety: A focus group approach.* Paper presented at the 88th annual convention of the Western Psychological Association, Irvine, CA.

Fowler, M., Johnson, M., & Atkinson, S. (1985). School achievement and absence in children with chronic health conditions. *Journal of Pediatrics, 106*, 683–687.

Franckel, A., & Lalou, R. (2009). Health-seeking behaviour for childhood malaria: Household dynamics in rural Senegal. *Journal of Biosocial Science, 41*, 1–19.

Frankel, S.E.P., Sweetnam, P., Yarnell, J., & Smith, G.D. (1996). Birthweight, body-mass index in middle age and incident coronary heart disease. *Lancet, 348*, 1478–1480.

Gardner, E. (1998). Siblings of chronically ill children: Towards an understanding of process. *Clinical Child Psychology and Psychiatry, 3*, 213–227.

Gavin, L., & Wysocki, T. (2006). Associations of paternal involvement in disease management with maternal and family outcomes in families with children with chronic illness. *Journal of Pediatric Psychology, 31,* 481–489.

Gellert, E. (1962). Children's conceptions of the content and functions of the human body. *Genetic Psychology Monographs, 61,* 293–405.

Gellert, E. (1978). What do I have inside me? How children view their bodies. In E. Gellert (Ed.), *Psychological Aspects of Pediatric Care* (pp. 19–35). New York: Grune & Stratton.

Gluckman, P.D., Hanson, M.D., Cooper, C.C., & Thornburg, K.L. (2008). Effect of in utero and early-life conditions on adult health and disease. *The New England Journal of Medicine, 359,* 61–73.

Gochman, D.S. (1987). *Youngsters' health cognitions: Cross-sectional and longitudinal analyses.* Louisville, KY: Health Behavior Systems.

Grych, J.H., & Fincham, F.D. (Eds.). (2001). *Interparental conflict and child development: Theory, research, and applications.* New York, NY: Cambridge University Press.

Gustafsson, P., Bjorksten, B., & Kjellman, N. (1994). Family dysfunction in asthma: A prospective study of illness development. *Journal of Pediatrics, 125,* 493–498.

Gutschoven, K., & Van den Bulck, J. (2005). Television viewing and age at smoking initiation: Does a relationship exist between higher levels of television viewing and earlier onset of smoking? *Nicotine & Tobacco Research, 7,* 381–385.

Hales, C.N., & Barker, D.J. (1992). Type 2 (non-insulin-dependent) diabetes mellitus: The thrifty phenotype hypothesis. *Diabetologia, 35,* 595–601.

Hampel, P., Rudolph, H., Stachow, R., Lass-Lentzsch, A., & Petermann, F. (2005). Coping among children and adolescents with chronic illness. *Anxiety, Stress & Coping: An International Journal, 18,* 145–155.

Hanna, K.M., & Guthrie, D. (2001). Parents' and adolescents' perceptions of helpful and nonhelpful support for adolescents' assumption of diabetes management responsibility. *Issues in Comprehensive Pediatric Nursing, 24,* 209–223.

Harris, J.L., Bargh, J.A., & Brownell, K.D. (2009). Priming effects of television food advertising on eating behavior. *Health Psychology, 28,* 404–413.

Hart, C.L., Taylor, M.D., Smith, G.D., Whalley, L.J., Starr, J.M., Hole, D.J., et al. (2003). Childhood IQ, social class, deprivation, and their relationships with mortality and morbidity risk in later life: Prospective observational study linking the Scottish mental survey 1932 and the Midspan studies. *Psychosomatic Medicine, 65,* 877–883.

Hazzard, A., & Angert, L. (1986). Knowledge, attitudes, and behavior in children with asthma. *Journal of Asthma, 23,* 61–67.

Hergenrather, J.R., & Rabinowitz, M. (1991). Age-related differences in the organization of children's knowledge of illness. *Developmental Psychology, 27,* 939–952.

Higham, S. (2009). An exploration of mothers and fathers views of their identities in chronic-kidney-disease management: Parents as students? *Journal of Clinical Nursing, 18,* 2773–2775.

Hobfoll, S.E. (1989). Conservation of resources: A new attempt at conceptualizing stress. *American Psychologist, 44,* 513–524.

Hofman, P.L., Regan, F., Jackson, W.E., Jefferies, C., Knight, D.B., Robinson, E.M., et al. (2004). Premature birth and later insulin resistance. *New England Journal of Medicine, 351,* 2888.

Hovi, P., Andersson, S., Eriksson, J.G., Jarvenpaa, A., Strang-Karlsson, S., Makitie, O., et al. (2007). Glucose regulation in young adults with very low birth weight. *New England Journal of Medicine, 356,* 2053–2063.

Huff, M.B., McClanahan, K.K., & Omar, H.A. (2008). The effects of chronic illness upon mental health status of children and adolescents. *International Journal on Disability and Human Development. Special Issue: Adolescents, chronic illness and disability, 7,* 273–278.

Inkelas, M., Halfon, N., Wood, D.L., & Schuster, M. (2007). Health reform for children and families. In R.M.R. Andersen, T.H. Rice, G.F. Kominski (Eds.), *Changing the U.S. health care system: Key issues in health services policy and management* (3rd ed., pp. 405–438). San Francisco, CA: Jossey-Bass.

Ireys, H.T., Sills, E.M., Kolodner, K.B., & Walsh, B.B. (1996). A social support intervention for parents of children with juvenile rheumatoid arthritis: Results of a randomized trial. *Journal of Pediatric Psychology, 21,* 633–641.

Jackson, C., & Dickinson, D.M. (2009). Developing parenting programs to prevent child health risk behaviors: A practice model. *Health Education Research, 24,* 1029–1042.

Johnson, J.G., Cohen, P., Kasen, S., First, M.B., & Brook, J.S. (2004). Association between television viewing and sleep problems during adolescence and early adulthood. *Archives of Pediatric & Adolescent Medicine, 158,* 562–568.

Karoly, P. (1993). Enlarging the scope of the compliance construct: Toward developmental and motivational relevance. In L. Epstein, N.A. Krasnegor, S. Bennett-Johnson, & S.J. Yaffe (Eds.), *Developmental aspects of health compliance behavior* (pp. 11–27). Hillsdale, NJ: Erlbaum.

Kashani, J.H., Konig, P., Shepperd, J.A., Wilfley, D., & Morris, D.A. (1988). Psychopathology and self-concept in asthmatic children. *Journal of Pediatric Psychology, 13,* 509–520.

Kazak, A.E. (1989). Families of chronically ill children: A systems and social-ecology model of adaptation and challenge. *Journal of Consulting and Clinical Psychology, 57,* 25–30.

Kazak, A.E., Rourke, M., & Crump, T.A. (2003). Families and other systems in pediatric psychology. In M.C. Roberts (Ed.), *Handbook of pediatric psychology* (3rd ed., pp. 159–175). New York, NY: Guilford Press.

Kazak, A.E., Simms, S., & Rourke, M.T. (2002). Family systems practice in pediatric psychology. *Journal of Pediatric Psychology, 27,* 133–143.

Kensara, O.A., Wootton, S.A., Phillips, D.I., Patel, M., Jackson, A., & Elia, M. (2005). Fetal programming of body composition: Relation between birth weight and body composition measured with dual-energy X-ray absorptiometry and anthropometric methods in older Englishmen. *American Journal of Clinical Nutrition, 82,* 980–987.

Kiernan, G., Guerin, S., & MacLachlan, M. (2005). Children's voices: Qualitative data from the "Barretstown studies." *International Journal of Nursing Studies, 42,* 733–741.

Kratz, L., Uding, N., Trahms, C.M., Villareale, N., & Kieckhefer, G.M. (2009). Managing childhood chronic illness: Parent perspectives and implications for parent-provider relationships. *Families, Systems, & Health, 27,* 303–313.

Kunkel, D., Eyal, K., Finnerty, K., Biely, E., & Donnerstein, E. (2005). *Sex on TV.* Menlo Park, CA: Kaiser Family Foundation.

Kupst, M.J., & Schulman, J.L. (1988). Long-term coping with pediatric leukemia: A six-year follow-up study. *Journal of Pediatric Psychology, 13,* 7–23.

Kupst, M.J., Schulman, J.L., Henig, G., Maurer, H., Morgan, E., & Fochtman, D. (1982). Family coping with childhood leukemia: One year after diagnosis. *Journal of Pediatric Psychology, 7,* 157–174.

Kyngäs, H. (1999). The theoretical model of compliance of young diabetics. *Journal of Clinical Nursing, 8*, 73–80.

Kyngäs, H., Hentinen, M., Koivukangas, P., & Ohinmaa, A. (1996). Young diabetics' compliance in the framework of the MIMIC model. *Journal of Advanced Nursing, 24*, 997–1005.

Kyngäs, H.A., Kroll, T., & Duffy, M.E. (2000). Compliance in adolescents with chronic diseases: A review. *Journal of Adolescent Health, 26*, 379–388.

La Greca, A.M., Bearman, K.J., & Moore, H. (2002). Peer relations of youth with pediatric conditions and health risks: Promoting social support and healthy lifestyles. *Journal of Developmental & Behavioral Pediatrics, 23*, 271–280.

LaGreca, A.M., & Schuman, W.B. (1995). Adherence to prescribed regimens. In M.C. Roberts (Ed.), *Handbook of pediatric psychology* (2nd ed., pp. 55–83). New York: Guilford Press.

Larson, K., Russ, S.A., Crall, J.J., & Halfon, N. (2008). Influence of multiple social risks on children's health. *Pediatrics, 121*, 337–344.

Lavigne, J.V., & Faier-Routman, J. (1992). Psychological adjustment to pediatric physical disorders: A meta-analytic review. *Journal of Pediatric Psychology, 17*, 133–157.

Lees, N.B., & Tinsley, B.J. (2000). Maternal socialization of children's preventive health behavior: The role of maternal affect and teaching strategies. *Merrill-Palmer Quarterly, 46*, 632–652.

Looman, W.S., O'Connor-Von, S.K., Ferski, G.J., & Hildenbrand, D.A. (2009). Financial and employment problems in families of children with special health care needs: Implications for research and practice. *Journal of Pediatric Health Care, 23*, 117–125.

Mackner, L.M., Black, M.M., & Starr, R.H., Jr. (2003). Cognitive development of children in poverty with failure to thrive: A prospective study through age 6. *Journal of Child Psychology and Psychiatry, 44*(5), 743.

McDonough, P. (2009, October 26). TV viewing among kids at an eight-year high. *Neilsenwire*. Retrieved from http://blog.nielsen.com/nielsenwire/media_entertainment/tv-viewing-among-kids-at-an-eight-year-high/.

McDougal, J. (2002). Promoting normalization in families with preschool children with type 1 diabetes. *Journal for Specialists in Pediatric Nursing, 7*, 113–120.

McDowell, D.J., & Parke, R.D. (2009). Parental correlates of children's peer relations: An empirical test of a tripartite model. *Developmental Psychology, 45*, 224–235.

McMahon, S.D., Grant, K.E., Compas, B.E., Thurm, A.E., & Ey, S. (2003). Stress and psychopathology in children and adolescents: Is there evidence of specificity? *Journal of Child Psychology & Psychiatry & Allied Disciplines, 44*, 107–133.

McQuaid, E.L., Kopel, S.J., & Nassau, J.H. (2001). Behavioral adjustment in children with asthma: A meta-analysis. *Journal of Developmental & Behavioral Pediatrics, 22*, 430–439.

Mekemson, C., & Glantz, S.A. (2002). How the tobacco industry built its relationship with Hollywood. *Tobacco Control, 11*, 181–191.

Mendelsohn, J., Quinn, M.T., & McNabb, W.L. (1993). Practicing pediatricians' views of the child's role in the pediatric interview. *Academic Medicine, 68*(1), 90.

Mercy, J.A., & Saul, J. (2009). Creating a healthier future through early interventions for children. *Journal of the American Medical Association, 301*, 2262–2264.

Michel, G., Taylor, N., Absolom, K., & Eiser, C. (2009). Benefit finding in survivors of childhood cancer and their parents: Further empirical support for the benefit finding scale for children. *Child: Care, Health and Development, 36*, 123–129.

Miller-Johnson, S., Emery, R.E., Marvin, R.S., Clarke, W., Lovinger, R., & Martin, M. (1994). Parent–child relationships and management of insulin-dependent diabetes mellitus. *Journal of Consulting and Clinical Psychology, 62*, 603–610.

Morison, J.E., Bromfield, L.M., & Cameron, H.J. (2003). A therapeutic model for supporting families of children with a chronic illness or disability. *Child and Adolescent Mental Health, 8*, 125–130.

Moseley, L., & Gradisar, M. (2009). Evaluation of a school-based intervention for adolescent sleep problems. *Sleep: Journal of Sleep and Sleep Disorders Research, 32*, 334–341.

Mullen, P.D., Hersey, J.C., & Iverson, D.C. (1987). Health behaviour models compared. *Social Science & Medicine, 11*, 973–983.

Nabors, L.A., & Larson, E.R. (2002). The effects of brief interventions on children's playmate preferences for a child sitting in a wheelchair. *Journal of Developmental and Physical Disabilities, 14*, 403–413.

Nabors, L.A., Lehmkuhl, H.D., & Warm, J.S. (2004). Children's acceptance ratings of a child with a facial scar: The impact of positive scripts. *Early Education and Development, 15*, 79–91.

Nagy, M.H. (1951). Children's ideas on the origins of illness. *Health Education Journal, 9*, 6–12.

Nagy, M.H. (1953). The representation of "germs" by children. *Journal of Genetic Psychology, 83*, 227–240.

Natapoff, J.N. (1978). Children's views of health: A developmental study. *American Journal of Public Health, 68*, 995–1000.

Navaie-Waliser, M., Spriggs, A., & Feldman, P. (2002). Informal caregiving: Differential experiences by gender. *Medical Care, 40*, 1249–1259.

Nelms, B.C. (1989). Emotional behaviors in chronically ill children. *Journal of Abnormal Child Psychology, 17*, 217–223.

Nelson, K. (1986). *Event knowledge: Structure and function in development*. Hillsdale, NJ: Erlbaum.

Neuhauser, C., Amsterdam, B., Hines, P., & Steward, M. (1978). Children's concepts of healing: Cognitive development and locus of control factors. *American Journal of Orthopsychiatry, 48*, 335–341.

O'Donnell, L., Stueve, A., Duran, R., Myint-U, A., Agronick, G., Doval, A.S., et al. (2008). Parenting practices, parents' underestimation of daughters' risks, and alcohol and sexual behaviors of urban girls. *Journal of Adolescent Health, 42*, 496–502.

Olds, D.L., Henderson, C.R.J., Chamberline, R., & Tatelbaum, R. (1986). Preventing child abuse and neglect: A randomized trial of nurse home visitation. *Pediatrics, 78*, 65–78.

Olds, D.L., Henderson, C.R.J., Cole, R., Eckenrode, J., Kitzman, H.D.L., et al. (1998). Long-term effects of nurse home visitation on children's criminal and antisocial behavior: 15-year follow-up of a randomized controlled trial. *Journal of the American Medical Association, 280*, 1238–1244.

Osmond, C., Barker, D.J.P., Winter, P.D., Fall, C.H.D., & Simmonds, S.J. (1993). Early growth and death from cardiovascular disease in women. *British Medical Journal, 307*, 1519–1524.

Outley, C.W., & Taddese, A. (2006). A content analysis of health and physical activity messages marketed to African American children during after-school television programming. *Archives of Pediatric & Adolescent Medicine, 160*, 432–435.

Owen, M.T., & Cox, M.J. (1997). Marital conflict and the development of infant–parent attachment relationships. *Journal of Family Psychology, 11*, 152–164.

Parcel, G.S., & Meyer, M.P. (1978). Development of an instrument to measure children's health locus of control. *Health Education Quarterly, 6*, 149–159.

Parent, K.B., Wodrich, D.L., & Hasan, K.S. (2009). Type 1 diabetes mellitus and school: A comparison of patients and healthy siblings. *Pediatric Diabetes, 10*, 554–562.

Patterson, J., & Blum, R.W. (1996). Risk and resilience among children and youth with disabilities. *Archives of Pediatrics & Adolescent Medicine, 150*, 692–698.

Peltzer, K. (2007). Predictors of positive health among a sample of South African adolescents. *Psychological Reports, 100*, 1186–1188.

Perrin, E.C., Ayoub, C., & Willett, J. (1993). In the eyes of the beholder: Family and maternal influences on perceptions of adjustment of children with a chronic illness. *Journal of Developmental & Behavioral Pediatrics, 14*, 94–105.

Perrin, E.C., & Gerrity, P.S. (1981). There's a demon in your belly: Children's understanding of illness. *Pediatrics, 67*, 841–849.

Perrin, J.M., MacLean, W.E.J., Gortmaker, S.L., & Asher, K.N. (1992). Improving the psychological status of children with asthma: A randomized controlled trial. *Developmental and Behavioral Pediatrics, 13*, 241–247.

Piaget, J. (1970). *Psychology and epistemology: Towards a theory of knowledge.* Harmondsworth, UK: Penguin.

Principe, G.F., Ornstein, P.A., Baker-Ward, L., & Gordon, B.N. (2000). The effects of intervening experiences on children's memory for a physical examination. *Applied Cognitive Psychology, 14*, 59–80.

Rashkis, S.R. (1965). Children's understanding of health. *Archives of General Psychiatry, 12*, 10–17.

Repetti, R.L., Taylor, S.E., & Seeman, T.E. (2002). Risky families: Family social environments and the mental and physical health of offspring. *Psychological Bulletin, 128*, 330–366.

Rimal, R. (2003). Intergenerational transmission of health: The role of intrapersonal, interpersonal, and communicative factors. *Health Education & Behavior, 30*, 10–28.

Roberts, D.F., Foehr, U.G., & Rideout, V. (2005). *Generation M: Media in the lives of 8–18 year-olds.* Menlo Park, CA: Kaiser Family Foundation.

Robinson, T.N., Chen, H.L., & Killen, J.D. (1998). Television and music video exposure and risk of adolescent alcohol use. *Pediatrics, 102*, E54.

Rogoff, B. (1990). *Apprenticeship in thinking: Cognitive development in social context.* New York: Oxford University Press.

Rosenstock, I.M. (1974). The health belief model and preventive health behaviour. *Health Education Monographs, 2*, 354–386.

Rutter, M. (1981). *Maternal deprivation reassessed* (2nd ed.). Hammondsworth, UK: Penguin.

Sallis, J.F., McKenzie, T.L., Alcaraz, J.E., Kolody, B., Hovell, M.F., & Nader, P.R. (1993). Project SPARK: Effects of physical education on adiposity in children. *Annals of the New York Academy of Sciences, 699*, 127–136.

Sallis, J.F., Patterson, T.L., McKenzie, T.L., & Nader, P.R. (1988). Family variables and physical activity in preschool children. *Journal of Developmental & Behavioral Pediatrics, 9*, 57–61.

Sallis, J.F., Rosenberg, D., & Kerr, J. (2009). Early physical activity, sedentary behavior, and dietary patterns. In L.J. Heinberg, & Thompson, J. Kevin (Eds.), *Obesity in youth: Causes, consequences, and cures* (pp. 37–57). Washington, DC: American Psychological Association.

Sameroff, A. (Ed.). (2009). *The transactional model of development: How children and contexts shape each other.* Washington, DC: American Psychological Association.

Schaeffer, C.M., Weist, M.D., & McGrath, J.W. (2003). Children with special health care needs in school: Responding to the challenge through comprehensive school-based health care. In M.D.E. Weist, S.W. Evans, N.A. Lever (Eds.), *Handbook of school mental health: Advancing practice and research. Issues in clinical child psychology* (pp. 223–235). New York: Kluwer Academic/Plenum Publishers.

Seeman, T.E., Singer, B.H., Rowe, J.W., Horwitz, R.I., & McEwen, B.S. (1997). Price of adaptation—allostatic load and its health consequences. *Archives of Internal Medicine, 157*(19), 2259–2268.

Seiffge-Krenke, I. (2002). "Come on, say something, Dad!": Communication and coping in fathers of diabetic adolescents. *Journal of Pediatric Psychology, 27*, 439–450.

Simeonsson, R.J., Buckley, L., & Monson, L. (1979). Conceptions of illness causality in hospitalized children. *Journal of Pediatric Psychology, 4*, 77–84.

Snyder, L.B., Milici, F.F., Slater, M., Sun, H., & Strizhakova, Y. (2006). Effects of alcohol advertising exposure on drinking among youth. *Archives of Pediatric & Adolescent Medicine, 160*, 18–24.

Spirito, A., DeLawyer, D.D., & Stark, L.J. (1991). Peer relations and social adjustment of chronically ill children and adolescents. *Clinical Psychology Review, 11*, 539–564.

Steele, R.G., Cushing, C.C., Bender, J.A., & Richards, M.M. (2008). Profiles and correlates of children's self-reported coping strategies using a cluster analytic approach. *Journal of Child and Family Studies, 17*, 140–153.

Stein, R.E., & Jessop, D.J. (1989). What diagnosis does not tell: The case for a noncategorical approach to chronic illness in childhood. *Social Science & Medicine, 29*, 769–778.

Stevens, G.D. (2006). Gradients in the health status and developmental risks of young children: The combined influences of multiple social risk factors. *Maternal & Child Health Journal, 10*, 187–199.

Story, L.B., & Bradbury, T.N. (2004). Understanding marriage and stress: Essential questions and challenges. *Clinical Psychology Review, 23*, 1139–1162.

Strasburger, V.C. (2002). Alcohol advertising and adolescents. *Pediatric Clinics of North America, 49*, 353–376.

Strasburger, V.C., Jordan, A.B., & Donnerstein, E. (2010). Health effects of media on children and adolescents. *Pediatrics, 125*, 756–767.

Tamburro, R.F., Gordon, P.L., D'Apolito, J.P., & Howard, S.C. (2004). Unsafe and violent behavior in commercials aired during televised major sporting events. *Pediatrics, 114*, e694–698.

Taylor, S.E., Repetti, R.L., & Seeman, T.E. (1997). Health psychology: What is an unhealthy environment and how does it get under the skin? *Annual Review of Psychology, 48*, 411–447.

Taylor, T.K., & Biglan, A. (1998). Behavioral family interventions for improving child-rearing: A review of the literature for clinicians and policy makers. *Clinical Child & Family Psychological Review, 1*, 41–60.

Thompson, D.A., & Christakis, D.A. (2005). The association between television viewing and irregular sleep schedules among children less than 3 years of age. *Pediatrics, 116*, 851–856.

Thompson, D.A., Flores, G., Ebel, B.E., & Christakis, D.A. (2008). Comida en venta: after-school advertising on

Spanish-language television in the United States. *Journal of Pediatrics, 152,* 576–581.

Tinsley, B.J., Holtgrave, D.R., Erdley, C.A., & Reise, S.P. (1997). A multimethod analysis of risk perceptions and health behaviors in children. *Educational and Psychological Measurement, 57,* 197–209.

Tinsley, B.J., Holtgrave, D.R., Erdley, C.A., & Reise, S.P. (2003). *How children learn to be healthy.* New York, NY: Cambridge University Press.

Tugade, M.M., Fredrickson, B.L., & Barrett, L.F. (2004). Psychological resilience and positive emotional granularity: Examining the benefits of positive emotions on coping and health. *Journal of Personality, 72,* 1161–1190.

Turner, D.C. (1996). The role of culture in chronic illness. *American Behavioral Scientist. Special Issue: Perspectives on chronic illness: Treating patients and delivering care, 39,* 717–728.

Varni, J.W., Katz, E.R., Colegrove, J.R., & Dolgin, M. (1993). The impact of social skills training on the adjustment of children with newly diagnosed cancer. *Journal of Pediatric Psychology, 18,* 751–767.

Vitulano, L.A. (2003). Psychosocial issues for children and adolescents with chronic illness: Self-esteem, school functioning and sports participation. *Child and Adolescent Psychiatric Clinics of North America, 12,* 585–592.

Vrijmoet, C.M.J., van Klink, J.M.M., Kolk, A.M., Koopman, H.M., Ball, L.M., & Egeler, R.M. (2008). Assessment of parental psychological stress in pediatric cancer: A review. *Journal of Pediatric Psychology, 33,* 694–706.

Wang, J., Simons-Morton, B.G., Farhart, T., & Luk, J.W. (2009). Socio-demographic variability in adolescent substance use: Mediation by parents and peers. *Prevention Science, 10,* 2009.

Webster-Stratton, C., & Hammond, M. (1999). Marital conflict management skills, parenting style, and early-onset conduct problems: Processes and pathways. *Journal of Child Psychology and Psychiatry, 40,* 917–927.

Wilkinson, S.R. (1988). *The child's world of illness: The development of health and illness behavior.* Cambridge UK: Cambridge University Press.

Wood, B.L. (1995). A developmental biopsychosocial approach to the treatment of chronic illness in children and adolescents. In D. -D. Lusterman, R.H. Mikesell, & S.H. McDaniel (Eds.), *Integrating family therapy: Handbook of family psychology and systems theory* (pp. 437–455). Washington, DC: American Psychological Association.

Yager, Z., & O'Dea, J. (2009). Body image, dieting and disordered eating and activity practices among teacher trainees: Implications for school-based health education and obesity prevention programs. *Health Education Research, 24,* 472–482.

Yetter, G. (2009). Exercise-based school obesity prevention programs: An overview. *Psychology in the Schools, 46,* 739–747.

Zehnder, D., Prchal, A., Vollrath, M., & Landolt, M.A. (2006). Prospective study of the effectiveness of coping in pediatric patients. *Child Psychiatry & Human Development, 36,* 351–368.

# Transplantation

Mary Amanda Dew *and* Andrea F. DiMartini

### Abstract

This chapter discusses the health psychology of organ transplantation and the relevance of this field to the broader study of psychological issues in chronic disease. It begins with an overview of the evolution and prevalence of transplantation, and describes the time-line of events that typically occur as patients and prospective living organ donors advance through the transplantation process. Evidence regarding ethnic, gender-related, and other disparities in access to and availability of organ transplantation is reviewed, and strategies undertaken to reduce these disparities are described. Then, from the perspective of the individual transplant recipient, his or her family caregiver, and the living donor, the chapter discusses stressors and psychological and behavioral outcomes associated with each phase of the transplantation (and organ donation) process. General quality of life, mental health, and medical adherence are considered. Intervention strategies to improve these outcomes are discussed. The chapter lists important questions to guide future research.

**Keywords:** Organ transplantation, organ donation, transplant recipient, living donor, family caregiver, disparities, mental health, medical adherence

Organ transplantation is the optimal treatment for many end-stage organ diseases. Most major medical centers in the United States operate programs to transplant kidneys, livers, hearts, lungs, pancreases, and/or intestines. Transplantation shares with many other medical interventions the goals of extending and improving the quality of individuals' lives. Nevertheless, the notion of receiving a new organ can seem exotic and mysterious, even to some clinicians and researchers. Moreover, the individuals who benefit from transplantation or who volunteer as living donors are often seen as unique groups who have little in common with—and therefore little to tell us about—either individuals who have other illnesses or who engage in other charitable acts.

The purpose of this chapter is not only to dispel these various misperceptions but to provide examples from our own and others' research demonstrating that the organ transplantation process provides a useful model for better understanding a number of

issues that arise as patients and their families face life-threatening chronic disease and its treatment. Issues of timely and equitable access to transplantation are similar to those arising in other areas of health care, particularly where demand exceeds available resources. The ongoing care required during the transplantation process—involving repeated medical evaluations, major surgery, and a complex medical regimen—is similar to the multifaceted care associated with many chronic diseases. Like other chronic diseases, the stressors that arise for patients during the transplantation process include both acute events and ongoing health and psychosocial strains. Furthermore, end-stage organ disease and transplantation exemplify situations of loss and revitalization that most of us experience in different forms during the life course. Transplant patients' families also confront a wide range of stressors—some experienced vicariously through observing their loved one's illness and medical care, but others linked directly to daily life with a person with chronic disease, including caregiving responsibilities, financial burdens, and altered family relationships. Finally, as in other chronic diseases, families' reactions to one member's illness can motivate them to take action: in the transplant context, they may volunteer to become living donors for the ill family member, a friend, or even a stranger. This is not unlike motives for medical altruism arising in other contexts. An individual's desire to help others often stems from first-hand experiences with a family member or close friend who has serious illness. Psychological benefits, as well as costs can be associated with this helping behavior.

The value of studying organ transplantation goes beyond its relevance to broader concerns involving equitable health care access, psychological adaptation to chronic disease, and medical altruism. It is an important area of study in its own right. The ongoing organ shortage makes efforts to increase the organ supply a priority. Receiving a new organ is no longer an unusual medical event and, given the organ shortage, serving as a living donor has become considerably more common. Transplantation can extend life by years or even decades, and thousands of transplants are performed annually. Thus, the population of individuals who have received this medical intervention or who have been directly affected by the organ transplant enterprise (e.g., family members, donors) continues to grow. Indeed, organ transplantation is just one form of an expanding pool of organ replacement strategies, which includes artificial alternatives to human organs, new domains of transplantation such as those involving the face and hand, and experimental work in areas such as organ regeneration. These strategies are likely to play increasingly prominent roles in health care due to the combination of rising life expectancies, the growing prevalence of end-stage organ disease, and an expanding range of other conditions for which transplantation provides effective treatment.

Given this set of factors, it is important for health psychologists to understand key issues confronting researchers and clinicians in this field. It is also imperative that patients, their families, and prospective living donors know what to expect during the transplantation process and thereafter. Education about the circumstances under which transplantation is considered a suitable treatment option will help these individuals to decide whether they want to embark on this process. Education regarding the likely stressors as well as the potential benefits of transplantation will help to equip all persons affected by it with tools and resources needed to achieve optimal health and quality-of-life (QOL) outcomes.

Moreover, it is only through knowledge about the nature of transplant-related stressors that we will be able to develop and test new intervention strategies to maximize posttransplant outcomes.

Because organ transplantation is less familiar to many health psychologists than are other areas of health care, in the following sections of the chapter we first provide a brief overview of the evolution and current prevalence of organ transplantation and describe the time-line of events that typically occur as patients or prospective living donors move through the transplantation process. We then discuss the social and health psychology research issues of key concern for ensuring access to and availability of organ transplantation across all segments of the population. Next, we turn to the transplantation process itself. We consider stressors as well as psychological and behavioral outcomes observed during this process in transplant patients and their families. We review evidence concerning similar issues in living donors. For patient and family outcomes, as well as living donor outcomes, we note research findings that not only inform the clinical care of populations affected by transplantation, but provide insight into more general behavioral and health issues faced by persons living with chronic disease or by those individuals seeking to help them. In the final section of the chapter, we delineate the most pressing clinical and research issues for future work in the health psychology of organ transplantation. Throughout the chapter, although we consider some issues relevant to transplantation in all age groups, our primary focus is on transplantation in adults.

## Evolution and Prevalence of Organ Transplantation

The modern era of transplantation is less than 30 years old. Surgical techniques for organ transplantation in humans were well-developed by the 1950s and 1960s, and the first successful kidney transplant was performed between identical twins in 1954. One reason for its success was that no immune barriers exist between identical twins. However, most individuals do not have an identical twin, and these patients typically receive organs from deceased donors. There were initially few effective strategies to prevent these organ recipients' bodies from rejecting the foreign tissue. Thus, early excitement regarding the promise of transplantation as an effective organ replacement strategy gave way to pessimism and to the closing of many fledging transplant programs by the late 1960s due to the intractably high graft loss rates and mortality rates in recipients of deceased donor organs (Starzl, 2005). The September 17, 1971 cover of *Life Magazine* stated

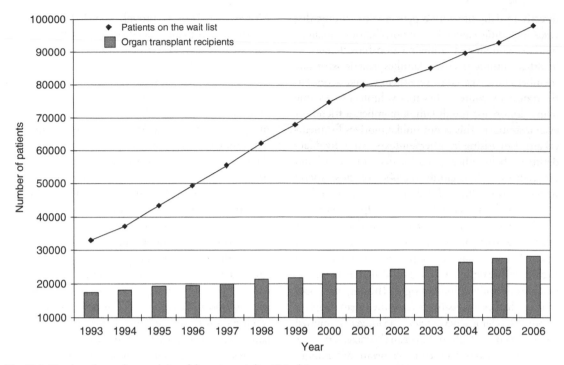

**Fig. 22.1** Number of transplants and size of the active wait list, United States.
*Source*: 2002 and 2007 Annual Reports, United States Organ Procurement and Transplantation Network and the Scientific Registry of Transplant Recipients (http://optn.transplant.hrsa.org). Includes kidney, liver, heart, lung, heart-lung, pancreas, and intestine transplants.

the dismal conclusion already reached by many in the field: ". . . an era of medical failure: The tragic record of heart transplants." The cover photograph showed six recipients, all smiling and apparently healthy, all several months posttransplant, and all dead within a few months of their group photograph.

The discovery and development of cyclosporine, a potent drug that provided more highly targeted immunoregulation without the toxicity associated with other agents, revitalized this clinical enterprise in the early 1980s. This drug, used in combination with other immunosuppressive agents, increased the survival time after transplantation from months to years. It thus paved the way for organ transplantation to quickly evolve from an experimental procedure into the standard of care of many end-stage diseases. The numbers of transplant candidates grew exponentially. In response to growing demand, the United States and other countries worldwide developed systems to efficiently and safely allocate organs, based on such factors as medical need and how long an organ could be preserved during transport to a patient's medical center.

Today, the greatest obstacle to receiving a transplant is the organ shortage. As shown in Figure 22.1, the number of individuals on the United States wait list greatly exceeds the number of transplants. Organ donation rates are rising, but the size of the wait list is growing even more rapidly. Although time spent on the wait list varies by factors such as the type of organ required and the patient's medical condition and blood type, 66% of transplant candidates in the United States wait for 1 year or longer (Organ Procurement and Transplantation Network [OPTN], 2009). Individuals awaiting a kidney can be maintained for extended periods of time by dialysis. Selected heart transplant candidates may be similarly "bridged" to transplant with mechanical circulatory support devices. Both such patient groups face significant mortality risks even with these interventions. No long-term alternative treatments exist for other organ candidates and thus, given the organ shortage, their prospects are even more dire.

Organs from living donors have helped to reduce the waiting times. Living kidney donation is most common, and living liver donation is possible for some patients (OPTN, 2008). Living donation of other organs is possible in some circumstances but remains rare. Living donors are most typically biologically and/or emotionally related to the recipient (e.g., a sibling or the spouse). Not only may patients who have a living donor avoid waiting on the list for a transplant but, by reducing the total wait list size, living donation increases the chance for patients without living donors to receive deceased donor transplants. Furthermore, living donor organs can result in better transplant recipient health and survival outcomes: the donated organ is usually superior to a deceased donor organ because living donors must meet stringent medical criteria, organ preservation time is minimal, and the donated organ has not been subject to the pathophysiological effects of poor perfusion and related factors. Living donation is not without risk to the donor. However, in the United States and many other countries, the risk–benefit ratio is favorable, especially for kidney donation (Tan, Marcos, & Shapiro, 2007). We discuss steps taken to ensure donor physical and psychological safety later in this chapter.

Figure 22.2 shows the total numbers of deceased donor transplants and living donor transplants that were performed for each type of organ in the United States in 2007. Overall, kidney transplantation (involved either deceased or living donors) is the most prevalent, and intestine and heart–lung transplants are the most rare. Similar distributions are reported in other Western countries. The predominance of kidney transplantation is due in large part to the fact that a individual requires only one kidney for adequate function. Thus, each deceased donor can help two patients in need, and each living donor can donate to one patient yet maintain their own kidney function. In addition, the medical costs of the patient's kidney transplantation surgery are federally financed through Medicare in the United States. Other types of transplants do not receive this coverage.

Survival is good to excellent for many types of organ transplantation. Kidney recipients, especially those with living donors, show the highest survival rates (OPTN, 2008). At 1 year posttransplant, 98% of recipients of living donor kidneys are alive, and 77% survive 10 years or more. Deceased donor kidney recipients, and pancreas, liver, and heart recipients show slightly lower survival rates, ranging from 87% to 95% at 1 year, and 54% to 61% at 10 years posttransplant. Survival rates for intestine recipients and lung recipients are good at 1 year (73% and 84%, respectively), but only a minority are alive at 10 years (42% and 27%, respectively). However, these rates, like those for other types of transplant recipients, have markedly improved in the past decade. Given mortality rates that range up to 26% per year in transplant candidates (OPTN, 2008), it is clear that transplantation provides a significant extension of life for many patients.

## Steps in the Process of Receiving or Donating an Organ

Organ transplantation is best considered not as a single event (i.e., the surgery), but as a series of events and time periods. These events and periods are each associated with a variety of unique issues concerning

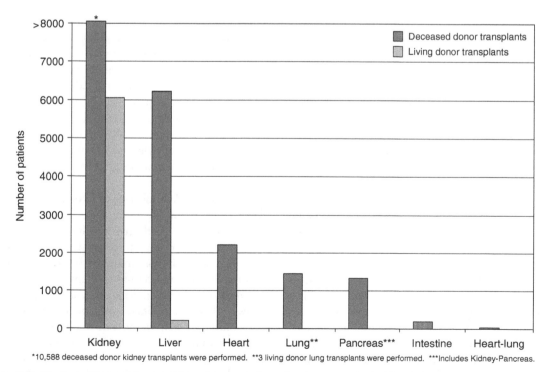

**Fig. 22.2** Numbers of deceased donor and living donor transplants of each organ type in the United States in 2007.
*Source*: Organ Procurement and Transplantation Network, United Network for Organ Sharing (http://optn.transplant.hrsa.org).

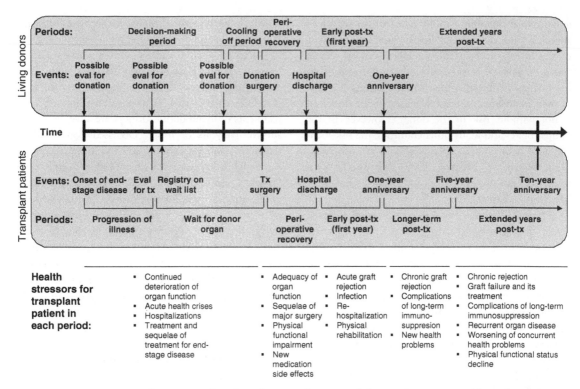

| Health stressors for transplant patient in each period: | Continued deterioration of organ function | Adequacy of organ function | Acute graft rejection | Chronic graft rejection | Chronic rejection |
|---|---|---|---|---|---|
| | • Acute health crises | • Sequelae of major surgery | • Infection | • Complications of long-term immuno-suppression | • Graft failure and its treatment |
| | • Hospitalizations | • Physical functional impairment | • Re-hospitalization | | • Complications of long-term immunosuppression |
| | • Treatment and sequelae of treatment for end-stage disease | • New medication side effects | • Physical rehabilitation | • New health problems | • Recurrent organ disease |
| | | | | | • Worsening of concurrent health problems |
| | | | | | • Physical functional status decline |

Fig. 22.3 Organ transplantation time-line: Critical events and time periods for transplant patients and living donors.

access to care, key health-related stressors, and patient health and behavioral outcomes (Dew et al., 2007b; Olbrisch, Benedict, Ashe, & Levenson, 2002). Figure 22.3 illustrates the typical time-line for both patients and living donors. For patients, the process usually begins when their end-stage disease can no longer be effectively managed with standard outpatient care (e.g., self-administered medications, lifestyle changes). The initiation of heightened care—often inpatient hospitalization and/or major interventions such as dialysis for kidney failure or mechanical circulatory support for heart failure—prompts referral for the formal evaluation by the transplant team. The evaluation is followed by the wait for an organ, the transplant surgery and perioperative recovery period, and the short- and longer-term years following the surgery.

The patient's medical evaluation and onset of the waiting period can precipitate the search for a living donor (when living donation is medically possible). Thus, living donors may enter the process near to the time a patient undergoes the formal medical evaluation for transplant, although in some cases they are not identified or do not come forward until the patient has been on the wait list for some time. Thereafter, donors experience a similar series of events and time periods involving the surgery, recovery, and life post-donation. Some elements of the

transplantation (and donation) process can vary considerably in their duration, depending on such factors as the rapidity with which the patient's medical condition declines, the length of the wait for a donor organ, and the medical complications that the patient or living donor develop perioperatively. However, the essential ordering of events and time periods is similar for all patients and living donors. Figure 22.3 also lists health-related stressors that patients typically experience during each time period. We will return to a consideration of these stressors, as well patient and donor psychological outcomes, after reviewing issues concerning access to organ transplantation for persons in need.

## Access to and Availability of Organ Transplantation

Particularly when an effective health or social intervention is in short supply, disparities are likely to arise in access to it. Identifying both the disparities and the factors contributing to them is critical for the development of strategies to ensure equitable access. Alternatively, increasing the intervention's availability may help to mitigate the impact of factors that serve as barriers or increase disparities in access. Organ transplantation has provided fertile ground for work on these issues. The findings have proven relevant for addressing similar concerns in other areas of health care (e.g., Smedley et al., 2003).

## Disparities in Access to Transplantation

We noted earlier that organ allocation systems in the United States and most other countries are based largely on factors such as the medical need of the transplant candidate. Nevertheless, there are well-documented sociodemographic disparities in access to transplantation. Ethnic minorities, women, individuals residing in rural areas, those with lower education or socioeconomic status (SES), and those with limited or no health insurance have reduced access: they are less likely to be referred for an evaluation for transplant, they are referred later in their illness course, and they are less likely to complete the evaluation, be entered onto the wait list, receive a deceased organ transplant, or identify and receive a transplant from a living donor (Alexander & Sehgal, 1998; Axelrod et al., 2008; Epstein et al., 2000; Lederer et al., 2008; Nguyen, Segev, & Thuluvath, 2007; Schaeffner, Mehta, & Winkelmayer, 2008; Segev, et al., 2009; Weng, Joffe, Feldman, & Mange, 2005; Young & Little, 2004). These disparities do not arise because these individuals are in any less need for transplantation. For example, ethnic minorities are disproportionately affected by many end-stages diseases that would be best treated by transplantation, including renal, liver, and heart disease (Myaskovsky et al., 2007). In addition, although characteristics such as ethnicity, SES, and insurance status are interrelated, the literature on access to transplantation indicates that each characteristic adds independently to the disparities. The fact that SES and insurance status disparities exist even for government-financed kidney transplantation is particularly noteworthy.

More than 20 years of research characterizes these disparities and the factors underlying them. Some factors are health care system structural barriers. For example, rural–urban differences in transplant rates appear to reflect the fact the medical centers with transplant programs are clustered primarily in large urban areas. Furthermore, urban centers themselves are not evenly distributed within a given country, and this contributes to broad regional differences in transplant rates (Axelrod et al., 2008; Kasiske et al., 2008). In addition, organ allocation policies have inadvertently contributed to disparities. For example, in many countries, allocation policies for deceased donor kidneys have favored close blood group and human leukocyte antigen (HLA) matching of donors and recipients. This matching fosters better transplant outcomes in general but places ethnic minorities at a disadvantage: because minorities in the United States and Europe are overrepresented in the end-stage renal disease population (relative to their proportions in the general population), and underrepresented in the pool of available donors, they wait longer on the list and are less likely to receive transplants (Rudge, Johnson, Fuggle, & Forsythe, 2007; Young & Kew, 2005).

Factors at the level of the health care provider and the patient also appear to underlie disparities in access to transplantation, but it has been challenging to disentangle the relative impact of elements such as provider uncertainty and bias versus patient preferences and treatment refusal. Moreover, a relatively narrow range of provider and patient factors have received empirical study. On the provider side, several studies have shown that providers are likely to view women and ethnic minorities as less appropriate kidney transplant candidates even when they have medical histories similar to other patients (Soucie, Neylan, & McClellan, 1992; Thamer et al., 2001). Health care providers have been found to mention liver transplantation as an option less often in medical encounters with African American than European American patients, even after other factors such as medical comorbidities have been taken into account (Julapalli, Kramer, & El-Serag, 2005).

A landmark study by Ayanian et al. (1999, 2004) is particularly informative. They surveyed a United States population-based sample of end-stage renal disease patients and their nephrologists. The nephrologists were less likely to believe that kidney transplantation improves survival in African Americans than that it improves survival in European Americans. (There are survival benefits in both groups.) Factors most often cited by the nephrologists for why African Americans are less likely to be evaluated for transplantation included patient preferences and limited availability of living donors. Physician–patient communication and trust, and physician bias were least often cited. Interestingly, if nephrologists did not believe that physician–patient communication was an important contributor to ethnic group differences in referral for transplant, their own African American patients were significantly more likely than their European American patients to report receiving little or no information about transplantation. In contrast, among physicians who felt that physician–patient communication and trust were important causes of disparities, there were no differences between black and white patients' reports of how much information they received.

Evidence delineating patient-related factors, such as preferences for care, beliefs, health concerns, and past health care or social experiences, comes primarily from work focused on ethnic group differences in end-stage kidney disease patients. Thus, Ayanian et al. (1999), in the study described above, found that African American dialysis patients were less likely to want a transplant or believe that it would lengthen survival or improve QOL. Ozminkowski et al. (1997) documented similar preferences and beliefs, and noted that African American dialysis patients were more averse to receiving a deceased organ transplant than were European Americans. African Americans more often cited religious objections to deceased donor transplantation, and they were more likely to have financial and health-related concerns about posttransplant life. Their religious beliefs and health-related and financial concerns were, in turn, related to their lower willingness to be placed on the transplant wait list. Klassen et al. (2002) found that African Americans (not unexpectedly) reported greater exposure to racial discrimination, and that this exposure itself was associated with a reduced likelihood of being listed for transplant and less patient interest in receiving a transplant. In a review of information recorded in patients' medical records, Sequist et al. (2004) noted that Native American and Hispanic American dialysis patients were more likely than European American patients to refuse to consider transplantation and, among those who refused, ethnic minority patients were more likely to cite financial and other psychosocial concerns (e.g., cultural or religious beliefs, or worries about the transplantation process). Given this study's methodology, the authors could not distinguish between patient perceptions versus health care providers' perceptions of patients' views. Nevertheless, the findings are important because little research has examined these ethnic minority groups' preferences regarding transplantation.

Finally, disparities related to patient ethnicity may reflect differences in knowledge about and willingness to consider living kidney donation, which itself provides a major alternative to a lengthy wait on the national list for a deceased donor organ. Although transplant candidates of all ethnic groups are hesitant to ask anyone to consider serving as a living donor (Kranenburg et al., 2009a; Lunsford et al., 2007; Reese et al., 2008), the hesitation, ambivalence, and/or unwillingness appear highest in ethnic minority groups (Gourlay, Stothers, & Liu, 2005; Rodrigue, Cornell, Kaplan, & Howard, 2008b). Such reactions have been found to be related to concerns that the donor could have health or financial problems caused by the donation, and worries about feeling guilty if the graft failed or feeling indebted to the donor (Pradel, Limcangco, Mullins, & Bartlett, 2003; Rodrigue et al., 2008b).

Fewer studies have examined patient preferences and beliefs in relation to gender disparities. Within a sample of patients found eligible for heart transplantation, women were less likely than men to agree to be listed for transplant (Aaronson, Schwartz, Goin, & Mancini, 1995). Among dialysis patients, Klassen et al. (2002) found women to express less interest in transplantation than men. Moreover, similar to findings for African Americans, women reporting lifetime gender-based discrimination were less likely to be placed on the wait list or desire a transplant. As the authors note, these findings are consistent with a larger literature on physical and mental health consequences of lifetime discrimination (Kessler, Michelson, & William, 1999; Kreiger, 2000).

The disparities on which most research in transplantation has focused—that is, ethnicity, gender, geographical differences—are widely acknowledged by transplant and other health care professionals to be inequities that must be overcome. But what about disparities linked to individuals' social or behavioral history? For example, should individuals who have alcoholic liver disease (ALD) have the same access to transplantation as patients who did not "cause" their condition? Given the organ shortage, persons with ALD were at one time viewed as less deserving for precisely this reason (Moss & Siegler, 1991). Concerns were also voiced that their posttransplant health outcomes might be poorer due to a return to alcohol use and concomitant nonadherence to the medical regimen. However, ALD patients have been found to have posttransplant survival rates equal to patients transplanted for other conditions, and the great majority remain abstinent and show good medical adherence after transplant (Dew et al., 2008b). There is now widespread acceptance in the transplant community that it is unethical to bar them from transplantation, once they receive medical and psychosocial intervention for their alcohol use and show evidence of commitment to abstinence (DiMartini, Weinrieb, & Fireman, 2002). Yet, health care providers outside of transplantation do not appear to share this view. Persons with ALD continue to be less likely to be referred for evaluation or informed that transplantation is a treatment option, even when their medical condition is otherwise similar to non-ALD patients (Julapalli et al., 2005; Tuttle-Newhall, Rutledge, Johnson, & Fair 1997). Surveys indicate that up to 40% of health care providers deem ALD patients to be unsuitable for transplantation (Kotlyar, Burke, Campbell, & Weinrieb, 2008).

There are other social groups for whom—even in the transplant community—there remains little consensus regarding access to transplantation. One such group is prisoners. Organ allocation policy and recommendations in the United States and internationally take a clear position that allocation should not be based on social characteristics or judgments of social worth (Participants in the International Summit, 2008; Organ Procurement and Transplantation Network/United Network for Organ Sharing [OPTN/UNOS] Ethics Committee, 2007; OPTN/UNOS Policies, 2009). However, public and health care professional opinion is divided over whether transplantation should be an option for prisoners, and whether offering it to them is "fair" to others in need of a transplant, given the organ shortage (e.g., McKneally & Sade, 2003). Even if one rejects the notion of choosing transplant candidates based on social worth, legitimate psychosocial concerns can exist about whether prisoners have (or, after prison, will have) the social supports and financial and health care resources to maintain adherence to the complex posttransplant medical regimen. Similar concerns, about both fairness and psychosocial issues, have been voiced about persons with mental disabilities (e.g., Leonard, Eastham, & Dark, 2000), despite the fact that, at least in the United States, blanket denial of health care to persons with a particular condition is prohibited under the Americans with Disabilities Act (Orentlicher, 1996). Unease has also arisen regarding patients with social histories typically found to be repugnant (e.g., histories of violent or sexual crimes; Paris et al., 2005). In all such situations, the question of who should be entitled to receive consideration for transplant (the issue of access) must be separated from psychosocial issues that legitimately must be weighed case-by-case in determining eligibility for transplantation. We return to the role of psychosocial factors in the transplant evaluation process later in the chapter. Independent of these factors, our point here is that membership in stigmatized social groups is not only likely to be associated with disparities in access to transplantation, but may be viewed by both laypersons and health care professionals as a reason to deny this intervention to some individuals in the face of organ scarcity.

## Strategies to Reduce Disparities in Access to Transplantation

The 2002 Institute of Medicine (IOM) report on racial and ethnic disparities in health care recommended that a variety of strategies be deployed to address these inequities (Smedley et al., 2003). These recommendations, many of which generalize to other types of disparities, were developed in part from findings on access to organ transplantation. At the most general level, the IOM advocated for increased awareness of health care disparities among all stakeholders, including patients, health care providers, and the general public. Aligned with this were more specific recommendations to address provider-related factors, including greater use of evidence-based guidelines to promote consistency of care and the development of interventions to enhance patient–provider communication. In terms of patient-related factors, recommendations focused on the need for strategies to better educate patients in how best to access care and participate in treatment decisions. Finally, in addition to calling for more research to identify factors underlying the disparities and to test promising interventions, the IOM called for data collection and monitoring to chart progress toward the elimination of disparities.

What progress have we made toward these goals within the field of organ transplantation? Research documenting the continued existence of disparities is burgeoning. Unfortunately, only a relatively small literature examines factors that account for the disparities. Because most studies employ cross-sectional and/or retrospective designs, they cannot establish whether provider- or patient-related correlates of disparities truly lead to disparities, or are instead outcomes of unequal access to transplantation. There is little evidence of any intervention development or testing to address these correlates of the disparities.

However, there is one area for which organ transplantation serves as a model: data collection, monitoring, and intervention on health care system-level factors in order to promote equity in access to transplantation among patients waiting for transplants. In the United States, for example, there is ongoing study of whether modifications in the deceased donor organ allocation system have reduced sociodemographic disparities. Specifically, the OPTN, administered under federal contract by UNOS, is charged with the fair and equitable allocation of organs (U.S. Department of Health and Human Services, 1999). Under this charge, OPTN/UNOS engages in ongoing research and policy developments to address and remove inequities in allocation, and progress is charted by examining extensive patient outcomes data collected by the OPTN and maintained in the Scientific Registry of Transplant Recipients (www.ustransplant.org).

One example of this work concerns the allocation system for deceased donor liver transplantation. In 2002, with the goal of reducing disparities, policy modifications were adopted so that liver allocation was based primarily on objective indicators of transplant candidate illness severity rather than on a combination of subjective indicators and a patient's accrued time on the wait list. Steps were also taken to minimize geographic variability in the supply of all types of deceased donor organs, because these variations had been found to be linked to disparities for ethnic minorities and economically disadvantaged groups. Analyses then examined the impact of these changes. Moylan et al. (2008) found that, before the revision, African Americans were less likely than European Americans to receive liver transplants, and they were more likely to die or become too sick for transplantation within 3 years of registering on the United States wait list. These differences no longer held after the allocation system was revised, although African Americans continued to be added to the wait list at more advanced stages of disease than European Americans.

Gender disparities were not reduced under the revised system: women remained less likely to receive transplants and more likely to die or become too sick for transplantation. Moylan et al. suggested women's smaller size (which could limit the pool of suitable donors) or other physiological variables not included in the previous or current allocation system might contribute to the gender difference. Geographical disparities were also not eliminated: patients living in regions with higher numbers of deceased donors continued to have greater access to liver transplantation (Moylan et al., 2008). Additional analyses under the revised allocation system have shown that at higher-volume liver transplant centers, patient waiting times are shorter, and patients who receive transplants have lower disease severity than at centers performing fewer transplants (Ahmad, Bryce, Cacciarelli, & Roberts, 2007). The implication of geographic, center volume, and other such differences is that patients without the financial or personal/familial resources needed to travel to certain regions or to larger centers continue to be at a disadvantage for transplant (Axelrod & Pomfret, 2008).

In short, although more work needed in order to remove important disparities in the United States organ allocation system, careful data collection and monitoring activities are essential for targeting areas of the system for research and policy development or revision. This does not obviate the need to study provider- and patient-related factors that also contribute to disparities. However, it suggests the value of large patient registries when examining health care system structural barriers that are associated with disparities in access to care; similar approaches are likely to be critical in other areas of health care as well.

### The Availability of Transplantation

Aside from promoting equity in access to a fixed supply of organs, another approach that may reduce disparities is to increase the supply. For example, ethnic minorities' chances of receiving transplants could be improved by increasing the availability of histocompatible kidneys in the deceased donor pool. In addition, with a larger organ supply, debates about fairness in access for stigmatized social groups—which become heated when the supply is inadequate and the consequences are life versus death—might be lessened and/or largely replaced by discussions of how to promote optimal outcomes in transplant recipients with varying psychosocial risk profiles.

Two avenues of work on the availability of organs for transplant have been undertaken. First, research has examined factors related to, and interventions to increase, the rate of deceased organ donation in the general population, as well as in population subgroups that are underrepresented in the donor pool relative to their representation among those in need of a transplant (e.g., African Americans, Asian Americans). Second, research has examined similar issues in living organ donation.

#### DECEASED ORGAN DONATION
*Factors Affecting Donation*
Rates of deceased organ donation are affected by factors ranging from government legislation and health care system structural characteristics to variables at the level of individual prospective donors and their families (Rhee, Kern, Cooper, & Freeman 2009). As shown in the upper half of Figure 22.4, deceased donation rates vary dramatically across countries. Laws regarding brain death, cultural norms, and the ways in which organ procurement is organized contribute to these differences. For example, despite legislation sanctioning brain death criteria in Asian countries, the notion of brain death is largely unacceptable to the general population and thus deceased organ donation remains rare (Bowman & Richard, 2003). Factors related to the organization of and consent required for organ procurement activities

also affect donation rates. Thus, in some (primarily European) countries, willingness to be an organ donor is presumed and only individuals registered as not wishing to donate are routinely excluded from organ procurement activities at their death. In other countries, including the United States, prior consent from the potential donor and/or family consent at the time of death must be obtained. In Spain, both presumed consent laws and a 1989 national reorganization of the organ procurement system have been credited with producing the highest donation rate in the world (34 donors per million population, see Figure 22.4). Under the "Spanish model" (Matesanz, 2003), organ procurement activities are the responsibility of highly trained hospital physicians and transplant coordinators, with extensive further coordination at regional and national levels. Other countries, including the United States, utilize a more decentralized approach and rely on organ procurement organizations (OPOs) that collaborate with but are independent of hospitals and transplant programs.

Even if organ procurement activities are modified to come closer to the Spanish model, legislation permitting presumed consent for donation remains unlikely in the United States and in many other countries (Orentlicher, 2009). Thus, most research has focused on better understanding and attempting to increase individuals' and their families' willingness to consent to organ donation. As in other

Western countries, the majority of Americans have positive attitudes about donation: A 2005 survey of a nationally representative sample of 2,341 adults found that 78% said they would be likely or very likely to have their organs donated, and 53% stated that they had given permission for organ donation on a driver's license or an organ donor card (Gallup Organization, 2005). These percentages were only 73% and 28%, respectively, in a 1993 Gallup survey. However, despite increasingly positive attitudes, a number of factors remain associated with willingness to become an organ donor, including most prominently ethnicity and level of education.

Ethnic minority groups have been consistently found to be less willing to agree to deceased organ donation (Kurz, Scharff, Terry, Alexander, & Waterman, 2007; Myaskovsky et al., 2007). In the 2005 Gallup survey, European Americans were most likely to express willingness to donate and to have signed up to be organ donors (82% and 61%, respectively), followed by Hispanic Americans (75% and 39%) and Asian Americans (also 75% and 39%). African Americans showed lower percentages (64%, 31%). Correlates of African Americans' lesser willingness to donate include past experiences of discrimination, and mistrust of the medical system (for example, beliefs that health care providers would not do everything possible to save the donor's life and that racial discrimination exists in organ

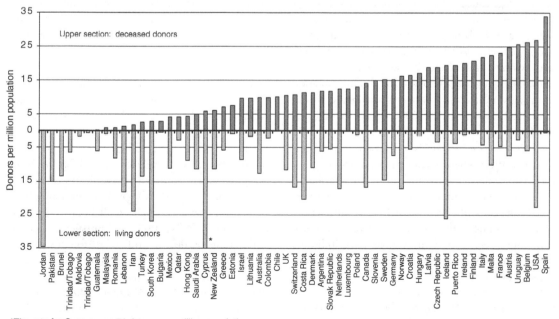

*The rate for Cyprus was 54 donors per million population.

**Fig. 22.4** Rates of deceased and living organ donation reported worldwide in 2006.
*Source*: IRODat (International Registry of Organ Donation and Transplant) database, Sanz et al., 2007.

allocation) (Boulware et al., 2002a; Morgan, Miller, & Arasarathnam, 2003; Siminoff & Saunders Sturm, 2000). The impact of religious beliefs on African Americans' willingness to donate is unclear, with some studies finding that religious objections led to a reduced willingness to donate but others finding that religious beliefs were cited to support donation (Kurz et al., 2007; Myaskovsky et al., 2007). Fewer studies have examined correlates of donation intentions in other ethnic minority groups. There is some evidence that Hispanic Americans voice mistrust of the medical system and that Asian Americans and Native Americans are likely to cite cultural, religious, or spiritual beliefs as reducing their willingness to donate (e.g., Fahrenwald & Stabnow, 2005; Frates, Rohrer, & Thomas, 2006; Lam & McCullough, 2000).

Although sociocultural factors have an undeniable influence on willingness to agree to deceased donation (e.g., Bowman & Richards, 2003; Myaskovsky et al., 2007), general level of education, as well as accuracy and extent of specific knowledge about organ donation and transplantation, may together account for a large component of the association of ethnicity with willingness to donate. Thus, the Gallup survey supports other research over the past 20 years (e.g., Haustein & Sellers, 2004) in showing that a greater level of education is strongly related to greater intentions to donate: 86% of college graduates stated that they would be likely or very likely to donate their organs, compared to 78% of those with some college education and 68% of those with a high school education or less (Gallup, 2005). Furthermore, with greater levels of education, ethnic group differences were attenuated. Additional work shows that both within and across ethnic groups, extent of knowledge about organ donation and transplantation is strongly related to willingness to donate (Frates et al., 2006; Kurz et al., 2007; Pham & Spigner, 2004).

Willingness to donate is only one of several factors that affect whether consent is ultimately given for organ donation at the time of death. Families of patients who meet brain death criteria are routinely asked for consent, even though it is not legally required under the United States Uniform Anatomical Gift Act if individuals have indicated their intentions on a driver's license or in a donor registry (Wendler & Dickert, 2001). Furthermore, individuals may never have registered their intentions to donate, and family members may be unaware of their loved ones' wishes. The 2005 Gallup survey found that 97% of Americans said they would donate a family member's organs if that person's

wishes to donate were known, but only 71% would agree to the donation if they did not know the person's wishes. Analyses of hospital records in the United States and the United Kingdom have found that fewer than half of families consent to donation and that lack of family consent is the primary reason that potential donors' organs are not retrieved (Department of Health, 2007; Sheehy et al., 2003).

A growing literature has examined factors associated with family consent to donation, and the most critical factors pertain to how, when, and by whom the communication of the request for donation is made. Requests made in private settings, made separately from notification of the patient's death, and made by carefully trained individuals are associated with higher consent rates (Simpkin, Robertson, Barber, & Young, 2009). Families who are provided with clearly communicated information about the process and need for organ donation, those who are satisfied with their loved one's care, and those who do not feel rushed into a decision are also more likely to consent (e.g., DeJong et al., 1998; Siminoff, Gordon, Hewlett, & Arnold, 2001). In addition to process factors, sociodemographic variables and family members' beliefs and attitudes about deceased organ donation each play a role. European American families are not only more likely to be asked to donate their loved one's organs (e.g., Guadagnoli et al., 1999), but they are more likely to consent to donation than are ethnic minority families (Kurz et al., 2007; Siminoff et al., 2001). Families whose members themselves are willing to donate are more likely to consent to donation of their loved one's organs (Siminoff et al., 2001).

*Strategies to Increase Deceased Donation*
Extensive activities—with some including research components—have been undertaken at many societal levels, including (a) legislation (e.g., "first-person consent" laws allowing OPOs to pursue donation in the absence of family consent; UNOS, 2009); (b) government-initiated reorganizations of organ procurement (e.g., the Organ Donation and Transplantation Breakthrough Collaboratives; Shafer et al., 2008; OPTN, 2008); (c) campaigns to increase willingness to donate, offered through the mass media or in schools, workplaces, or minority communities (e.g., Alvaro, Jones, Robles, & Siegel, 2006; Callender, Hall, & Branch, 2001; Harrison, Morgan, & Di Corcia, 2008; Piccoli et al., 2006; Quinn, Alexander, Hollingsworth, O'Connor, & Meltzer, 2006); and (d) interventions to increase family consent (e.g., Linyear & Tartaglia, 1999;

Riker & White, 1995). These activities are consistent with and were accelerated by the 2006 IOM recommendations on strategies to increase donation (Childress & Liverman, 2006). Moreover, in the fields of social and health psychology, studies testing interventions to increase donation have provided a valuable context for applying and refining theories about attitude–behavior relationships, and conceptual models of persuasion, message framing, and behavior change (Feeley, 2007; Jeffres, Carroll, Rubenking, & Amschlinger, 2008; Radecki & Jaccard, 1999; Siegel et al., 2008).

Have these activities been effective? The largest body of work has focused on interventions at the level of the individual prospective donor (as opposed to those at the levels of the family or health care system). These interventions have aimed to increase individuals' intentions and behaviors related to donating (e.g., signing a donor card) through receipt of educational material regarding the value and need for organ donation. Much of the published work is descriptive, reporting—for example—on the development of culturally sensitive materials for specific ethnic minority groups (e.g., Fahrenwald, Belitz, Keckler, & Sharma, 2007; Thomas, 2002; Wong, Cárdenas, Shiu-Thornton, Spigner, & Allen, 2009). The strength of these descriptive studies is that they illustrate community-based collaborative efforts to tackle a public health issue, and the resulting educational strategies provide potentially valuable resources for use and evaluation.

However, some research has incorporated more formal evaluation of intervention effectiveness. Notable examples include work by Alvaro et al. (2006), showing that Spanish-language television and radio advertisements promoting organ donation among Hispanic Americans successfully increased pro-donation beliefs and family discussion among people exposed to the advertisements (relative to individuals who were not exposed). Quinn et al. (2006), in a randomized controlled trial involving 12 corporations and 40 work sites, found that educational strategies focused on the need for organ donors led to increases in participants' and their family members' rates of signing donor cards. Finally, Callender et al. (2001, 2003) developed and evaluated the impact of the National Minority Organ Tissue Transplant Education Program (MOTTEP®), a grassroots effort to increase awareness of the need for donation in minority communities. They found that the percentages of program recipients who were willing to donate, had signed donor cards, and had discussed donation with family

members all increased after program exposure. A novel feature of the program is that it provides education not only about donation but about diseases and lifestyle issues in minority communities that can lead to a need for transplant. However, because program evaluations do not included control groups (a limitation shared by much of the research in this area), it is difficult to reach firm conclusions about program impact. Nevertheless, one of MOTTEP's® strengths is that it has demonstrated sustainability and the ability to be disseminated: program activities have been under way for over 10 years, and the program is now offered in more than 10 cities (Callender et al., 2003; www.NationalMOTTEP.org). Few other interventions to increase donation have shown similar accomplishments.

Last, a health care system-level intervention (with a family-focused component) is also noteworthy. In 2003, the United States Department of Health and Human Services launched a major initiative to increase donation rates: it collaborated with OPOs, donor centers, and transplant centers to apply a series of "best practices" to improve the family consenting process and all other organizational activities that are involved in obtaining potential donors' organs at their deaths (Shafer et al., 2006). For example, its strategies for how best to structure communications with families were based on past research on this issue. Unlike the Spanish approach described earlier, the United States Organ Donation Breakthrough Collaborative (ODBC) incorporated empirical assessments to chart program effectiveness. During the ODBC's first year, the number of donors obtained in hospitals/OPOs enrolled in the program increased 14%, compared with 8% in nonprogram hospitals/OPOs (Shafer et al., 2008). Additional analyses showed that the annual increases in organ donation at participating hospitals/OPOs after program inception outpaced established yearly trends at these sites. Moreover, the total number of organ donors in the United States increased 22.5% over 3 years of the program, compared to a 5.5% increase during the 3 years before the program began (Shafer et al., 2008).

## LIVING ORGAN DONATION
### Factors Affecting Donation
Similar to deceased donation, factors affecting rates of living donation range from governmental and policy differences across countries, to factors at the level of the individual prospective donor. The lower half of Figure 22.4 shows the range of living donor transplant rates worldwide. Cultural differences that

make deceased donor transplantation unacceptable in some countries ensure that, if transplants are performed in those countries, they are largely limited to organs from living donors. Countries also differ in whether financial incentives are provided for organ donation (Rhee et al., 2009). In some countries, including India and Iran, living donor organ sales are legal. In others, including Pakistan, the Philippines, and Egypt, such sales are illegal but remain the norm (Budiani-Saberi & Delmonico, 2008). (Because the activity is illegal, it is not captured in Figure 22.4.) Although most countries do not condone organ vending, the organ shortage has given rise to a global crisis in the exploitation of humans as organ donors and the trafficking of organs. This includes "transplant tourism," in which individuals desperate for transplants and judging it unlikely that they will receive one within their own national health care system go where donors are more plentiful (legally or illegally) (Delmonico & Dew, 2007; Merion et al., 2008). The direction of the tourism is from wealthy countries to impoverished ones. The "tourists" are also ultimately exploited in terms of deadly health risks linked to the acquired organs. As we discuss later in this chapter, there are major psychological costs to organ vendors (i.e., the individuals who sell their own organs), with little evidence of any benefit— financial or otherwise—from the sale. Furthermore, organ trafficking is not limited to living donation but includes organs confiscated from executed prisoners in countries such as China (Budiani-Saberi & Delmonico, 2008). The World Health Organization (WHO) is coordinating efforts to ensure that all countries, as they address the need to increase both deceased and living organ donation, adopt procedures to respect human rights, prevent coercion, and guarantee informed consent (Participants in the Global Summit, 2008). Nevertheless, the growth in organ trafficking and transplant tourism illustrates the grim consequences of demand versus supply imbalances in a life-giving area of health care.

Within countries and legal systems that already prohibit organ vending and work to ensure human rights protections, research has examined the extent to which individuals are willing to serve as living donors and factors associated with willingness to donate. The 2005 Gallup survey described earlier found that 62% of Americans stated that they would be very likely to serve as a living donor for a family member. This percentage is similar to that found in previous surveys conducted over the past 35 years (e.g., Fellner & Schwartz, 1971) and mirrors the 62% of spouses and 60% of adult children of dialysis patients who reported in one recent study that they had already discussed with their family member the possibility of donating a kidney to them (Boulware et al., 2005). Fewer Gallup survey respondents stated that they were very likely to donate to a close friend (31%) or a stranger (8%). Overall, these percentages resemble the distribution of actual living donors in the United States: in 2008, family members (e.g., siblings, adult children, spouses) made up 72% of all living donors, with the remaining 28% consisting of unrelated donors (e.g., friends, acquaintances, and anonymous donors) (OPTN, 2009).

Willingness to donate does not appear to be strongly linked to demographic characteristics such as gender, ethnicity, or education (Gallup, 2005). However, African Americans are less likely to be accepted as living donors because of higher rates of the same medical problems that lead African Americans to need transplants (Young & Kew, 2005). In addition, women in the United States and many other countries are more likely than men to become living donors (Biller-Andorno, 2002; Csete, 2008). It is not known whether this reflects medical factors (e.g., men may have medical conditions that more often rule them out as donors) and/or sociocultural factors (e.g., men may be at greater risk for lost wages since they are more likely to be employed; men may be less available due to military service or incarceration; women are more likely to have social roles as caregivers and nurturers, and this may be perceived to include donating an organ). Furthermore, the gender imbalance may reflect coercive elements, especially in cultural groups in which the family elder has absolute decision-making capacity and where gender-based social inequalities are the norm (Csete, 2008). No matter what the factors responsible for the gender imbalance, it emphasizes the importance of careful psychosocial evaluation of prospective donors to ensure that they have not come forward out of coercion and that their well-being will not be adversely affected by donation, as we discuss later.

Beliefs and attitudes are potent correlates of willingness to serve as a living donor. For example, a general population survey in the United States revealed that concerns about donation surgery, mistrust in hospitals, and believing that economic, gender-based, or racial discrimination exists in the provision of health care were each associated with reduced willingness to become a living donor (Boulware et al., 2002b). In contrast, factors such as sociodemographics, comorbid medical conditions, and religious or spiritual beliefs did not affect willingness to donate. Willingness to become a deceased donor and—in particular—attitudes affirming the importance of helping others through organ donation, are associated with greater willingness to become a living donor (e.g., Landolt et al., 2001; Simmons, Marine, & Simmons, 1987). This is consistent with a large literature on attitudes and motives linked to helping behaviors in medical and nonmedical contexts (Batson, 1998; Penner, Dovidio, Piliavin, & Shroeder, 2005; Piliavin & Callero, 1991). We consider the role of motives in greater depth later in this chapter when we discuss factors affecting living donors' health and psychological outcomes.

Survey research can be criticized on the grounds that willingness and intentions may not translate into behavior. Unfortunately, most studies that query individuals who have decided to donate (or have already donated) do not also include individuals who chose not to donate. Without considering both types of individuals, it is not possible to establish whether any given variable is a correlate of the decision to donate. Moreover, by surveying living donors after they have decided to donate (or actually donated), such studies are subject to biases associated with retrospective designs: Respondents' memories of factors that led to their decision may differ from what they would have reported if they had been queried earlier in the process.

Although retrospective in design, work by Simmons et al. (1987) is noteworthy because of its careful examination of a wide range of psychosocial characteristics in kidney transplant recipients' family members who did versus did not volunteer to serve as donors. They found that family member volunteers had higher status occupations and were younger than nonvolunteers. There were no gender differences. The nature of the family relationship mattered: parents and adult children were more likely than siblings and other relatives to volunteer. In addition, among siblings, those who volunteered were closer in age to the patient. Simmons et al. further examined differences between the subgroup of volunteers who actually went through with donation and the nonvolunteers. Nonvolunteers had a history of fewer social contacts with the patient, and seemed to have stronger social allegiances or commitments within their own immediate families: they were more likely to be married and have children, and were considerably more likely to have a spouse who opposed the donation. In addition, nonvolunteers had more worries and medical concerns about donating, and they had less favorable general attitudes about living donation. Stothers et al. (2005) reported similar differences between donors

and nondonors in degree of medical concerns and general attitudes.

Whether the correlates of volunteering to serve as a living donor would extend beyond family (related) donors to unrelated donors is unknown. However, work in unrelated, anonymous bone marrow donation suggests that they would generalize. Specifically, Switzer et al. (1999) surveyed individuals who had joined a national registry of persons willing to serve as bone marrow donors. They questioned potential donors shortly after they had been asked to undergo additional testing as potential matches for patients. Findings indicated that individuals who declined further testing (and dropped out of the registry) expressed more worries and medical concerns about donation, and they were more likely to report that family and friends had discouraged them from joining the registry. They were also less likely to have a history of medical volunteerism (e.g., blood donation)—a factor found to be important for predicting new episodes of helping behavior in many contexts and thought to reflect the development of an internal self-image consistent with helping others (Penner et al., 2005). There were no demographic differences between those who continued with testing versus those who dropped out.

Last, living organ donor volunteers are sometimes are found to be incompatible with their intended recipient, based on blood or HLA typing, and thus are unable to donate to them. Would these individuals be willing to serve as unrelated donors to other transplant candidates? This scenario arises in, for example, donor-exchange programs (Hanto, Reitsma, & Delmonico, 2008; Segev et al., 2005). In these programs, an incompatible donor donates to another transplant recipient, so that his or her intended recipient will receive a kidney from another living donor (paired donation) or from the deceased donor pool (list donation). Waterman et al. (2006) surveyed individuals who were incompatible with their intended recipients about their general willingness to participate in exchange programs. (No such programs were actually available to them.) They were also asked whether they would be willing to serve as nondirected donors, a choice that would not help their own family member to receive a transplant. Respondents were considerably more willing to participate in paired donation (64%) than list donation (38%) or nondirected donation (12%). Higher scores on a measure of empathy were associated with willingness to engage in each of these forms of donation. Individuals willing to participate in paired donation were likely to be first-degree relatives of their intended recipients (rather than more distant relative or friends), whereas individuals willing to become nondirected donors were more likely to be distant relatives or friends of their intended recipient.

*Strategies to Increase Living Donation*

The idea of explicitly attempting to increase living donation rates has historically been controversial. For many years, the WHO maintained that efforts should focus on increasing deceased donation rather than living donation because of the risks to living donors (WHO, 1991). In contrast to all other populations that undergo surgery, living donors undergo removal of critical organ mass for reasons completely unrelated to their own health. This raises the difficult ethical issue of whether allowing donation violates the *primum non nocere* (do no harm) precept in medicine (Childress & Liverman, 2006) and has resulted in the transplant community's mandate to ensure that donors do not experience negative long-term medical or psychosocial consequences, as we discuss later in this chapter. However, in a global environment in which living donor transplantation has dramatically expanded as a key strategy to address the organ shortage, the WHO and the transplant community recognize that the only responsible course of action is to facilitate and support activities to increase living donation—but only those activities that recognize and protect human rights and that do not feed into organ trafficking (Delmonico, 2005; Delmonico & Dew, 2007; Participants in the Global Summit, 2008).

The transplant community is developing novel strategies to increase the rates of living donation through exchange programs (described above) and their variants (e.g., Hanto et al., 2008). Societal strategies to facilitate living donation include legislative activity to provide limited financial compensation to living donors, since it is well known that donors can incur significant financial burden above what will be reimbursed by the transplant recipient's medical coverage (Clarke, Klarenbach, Vlaicu, Yang, & Garg, 2006). These burdens include, for example, lost wages, childcare costs, and nonreimbursable travel expenses associated with donation. In the United States, the Organ Donor Leave Act of 1999 was passed to provide additional paid leave for federal employees who are living donors, and several states have implemented legislation offering various forms of support to donors, including paid or unpaid leave for extended time periods and tax benefits. Boulware et al. (2008) evaluated changes in living donation rates from before to after the enactment of

federal and state legislation supporting donors. Results show that rates of living related donation (the most common type of donation) did not increase after legislative changes. However, rates of living unrelated donation increased, suggesting that the legislative activities had a selective effect on barriers to unrelated donation.

Any form of financial compensation or incentives has been subject to considerable debate, however, and those who reject such payments cite the potential for exploitation of individuals with limited economic resources and the possibility of minimizing the altruistic value of the donated organ (e.g., Childress & Liverman, 2006; Friedman & Friedman, 2006). Thus, additional intervention activities, undertaken mostly at the level of individual transplant candidates and their families, focus on educational efforts to inform these individuals about living donation rather than to convince any given individual to donate. Many of the reports in this area describe specific transplant programs' or other organizations' plans or current educational activities (e.g., Callender, Hall, & Miles, 2002; Hays & Gladding, 2007; Hays & Waterman, 2008; Kranenburg et al., 2009b). Although they provide no empirical evaluation of effectiveness, they are informative in describing the range of strategies that might be utilized, including the provision of written, video taped or internet-based materials; role-playing activities (focused, for example, on how to ask someone to consider serving as a living donor); and use of peer educators and mentors.

Among the smaller group of studies with evaluative components, two are noteworthy. Schweitzer et al. (1997) found an increase in the percentage of kidney transplant candidates who approached at least one potential donor after their transplant program instituted a structured multicomponent education program (with verbal, written, and video information) aimed at patients and their families. The increase was greatest in African American and older patients—subgroups that had previously been the least likely to identify living donors. Total rates of living donor transplants increased during the study period as well. This study's chief limitation—failure to include a control group—was remedied in a recent randomized controlled trial by Rodrigue et al. (2007, 2008). They evaluated the effectiveness of a home-based education program that involved discussion and interaction among the educator, transplant candidate, and family members. Their comparison condition was the standard, didactic education program utilized in the transplant clinic setting. The home-based program led to increased patient willingness to discuss living donation with other persons, a higher number of living donor inquiries to the transplant program, more donor evaluations, and more living donor transplants. The home-based program was tailored to be culturally sensitive, and additional analyses comparing program impact in African Americans and European Americans showed that it helped to close the gap between these groups in numbers of donors coming forward and in actual living donor transplants.

## Summary

A large literature documents factors from macro to micro level that affect rates of deceased and living donation. Strategies to increase donation will continue to be needed at each level to address sociocultural factors that limit donation and organizational and interpersonal barriers to donor identification. At the same time, the global health and transplant communities must stem commercial and trafficking activities that promote organ vending, violate human rights, and imperil donors' and recipients' health and well-being. In countries and cultures that oppose trafficking, considerable attention has been devoted to delineating correlates of individuals' willingness to volunteer to serve as deceased and/or living donors, and families' willingness to consent to the donation of their loved ones' organs. The potential donor's expressed intentions, attitudes, and beliefs, and knowledge about organ donation appear to be critical. Intervention efforts to date have largely been focused on providing education about these issues. Some short-term results have been encouraging. However, the ability of most interventions to be disseminated and sustained is unknown and represents a prime area for future work.

## Stressors and Outcomes in Organ Transplant Patients and Their Families

The transplantation process involves a series of events, time periods, and significant health-related stressors that affect patients and their families, as delineated in Figure 22.3. Access to and availability of organs affect whether and when patients will reach the point of transplant. Psychological and behavioral factors, usually assessed during the evaluation for transplantation, can also influence patient selection for transplantation. We discuss those factors below. We then consider psychological and behavioral responses to the transplantation process. Like many other medical interventions, the success of organ transplantation is ultimately judged not only by its ability to extend life but to maximize

QOL (Cupples et al., 2006; Krakauer, Bailey, & Lin, 2004). Patients' psychological well-being and their behavioral functioning—namely, their ability to adhere to each of the multiple components of their medical regimen—are integral components of QOL. Moreover, psychological and behavioral outcomes posttransplant are important because they predict longer-term transplant-related physical morbidity and mortality. We summarize evidence concerning these associations below, and we also consider the smaller literature on family psychological outcomes during the transplantation process. Finally, we summarize information on interventions' effectiveness at treating or preventing psychological and behavioral difficulties in transplant patients and their families.

## Psychological and Behavioral Factors in Patient Selection for Transplantation

When patients undergo a transplant program's formal evaluation to determine eligibility for organ transplantation, they complete both medical and psychosocial evaluations. Important elements receiving at least some degree of consideration include lifetime history of psychiatric disorders; history and current use of alcohol, nicotine, and other substances; past and current level of adherence to medical regimens; cognitive capacity and ability to understand what will be required for posttransplant care; social history and current status (including employment and financial circumstances, marital status, social supports, and coping strategies for managing health issues); and personal expectations and knowledge about transplantation (Dew et al., 2000b; DiMartini, Dew, & Crone, 2009; Olbrisch et al., 2002). Of these elements, psychiatric history, substance use, intellectual functioning, and medical adherence have the greatest bearing on program decisions about whether a patient is listed for transplant. However, surveys of United States transplant programs show that there is substantial variability in whether problems in these areas (e.g., current mood disorders, schizophrenia, suicidal ideation, drug abuse, mental retardation, and histories of medical nonadherence) are viewed as absolute or relative contraindications to transplantation, or do not serve as contraindications at all (Corley et al., 1998; Levenson & Olbrisch, 1993, 2002). Heart and lung programs have been found to be most likely to turn down patients due to such factors, kidney programs are the most lenient, and liver programs lie between these extremes. Kidney programs may be more lenient because graft loss does not result in patient death (dialysis remains an option), and transplantation is ultimately less expensive than dialysis. Depending on the reason, decisions against listing a patient for transplant may be temporary and may be reversed upon the patient's completion of psychological or behavioral interventions and/or demonstration that certain problems are being addressed. For example, United States and European liver programs routinely require that individuals with a substance use diagnosis (one of the most common indications for liver transplant) show evidence of abstinence for at least 6 months before they are listed for transplantation (Kotlyar et al., 2008). Similarly, organ transplant programs may require that patients with histories of medical adherence difficulties show that they are able to follow care requirements for some period of months before they are listed.

Programs are more likely to intervene to assist patients to address psychosocial concerns than to view those concerns as absolute contraindications to transplantation for several reasons. Of primary importance, psychological and behavioral difficulties identified during the evaluation or pretransplant waiting period are not consistently found to predict poor posttransplant medical outcomes (e.g., reduced survival time, increased rates of graft rejection, and other medical complications). This inconsistency in findings is evident in clinical case reports (e.g., Le Melle & Entelis, 2005; Lurie et al., 2000; Orr, Johnston, Ashwal, & Bailey, 2000; Shakil et al., 1997) as well as in larger-scale empirical evaluations of the impact of psychiatric disorders or substance abuse or dependence histories (e.g., Chacko, Harper, Gotto, & Young, 1996; Chang et al., 1997; Liu et al., 2003; Owen, Bonds, & Wellisch, 2006; Pageaux et al., 1999; Skotzko, Rudis, Kobashigawa, & Laks, 1999). Impaired intellectual functioning also does not appear to result in poorer posttransplant survival (Martens, Jones, & Reiss, 2006), although the number of cases studied to date is small. Relatively little evidence is available concerning pretransplant adherence to the medical regimen (beyond abstinence from substance use) as a predictor of posttransplant medical outcomes. A few reports have found that expert evaluators' qualitative global ratings of pretransplant "psychosocial risk"—incorporating their views about patients' adherence, psychological, and other psychosocial characteristics—can provide better-than-chance prediction of posttransplant morbidity and mortality (e.g., Chacko et al., 1996; Owen et al., 2006; Shapiro, Schulman, & Bagiella, 2003; Shapiro et al., 1995). However, it is difficult to determine the specific components of psychosocial risk responsible for these associations, or whether such

risk ratings were (or could be) made reliably. There is no risk index in widespread use in transplant programs in the United States or elsewhere.

The generally inconsistent predictive effects likely stem from multiple factors (Dew et al., 2000b; 2002; DiMartini et al., 2009). Foremost among these are the stressful circumstances that patients face during the psychosocial evaluation and the wait for an organ: they are very ill, and they are afraid that they will be denied a transplant or that a donor organ will not become available in time. In the evaluation itself, patients have legitimate reasons to be concerned about how the information they impart will be used, and evaluators may vary in their skills at putting patients at greater ease in order to obtain accurate information, as well as in their skills at detecting attempts at deception. Changes in patients' mental status due to end-stage illness (resulting in forgetfulness, confusion, or apathy) can further complicate the evaluation and reduce its reliability. Accurately predicting whether problems identified during the evaluation will resolve or be exacerbated by transplantation is difficult in these circumstances. During the waiting period, even if patients with, for example, histories of substance abuse successfully control their addiction when they are ill and afraid, this information may have little predictive value for their behavior posttransplant, when they feel better. Alternatively, patients' apparent lack of responsiveness to interventions for psychological or behavioral problems may not be representative of their ability to respond to similar interventions posttransplant when they feel physically better.

Overall, a flexible case-by-case approach to patient selection for transplantation is more likely to be appropriate than is the application of rigid psychosocial criteria, and this is an encouraging conclusion: it recognizes the possibility that even those patients with apparently major psychological and behavioral vulnerabilities can have successful transplant medical outcomes. In terms of predicting posttransplant medical outcomes, it may be more fruitful to focus on patients' early posttransplant psychological responses, as well as other factors in their posttransplant social environment (e.g., social supports) that may affect their recovery and subsequent health. These conclusions are likely relevant to health interventions well beyond organ transplantation. For example, similar issues and concerns about the predictive power and general utility of psychosocial selection criteria have arisen in newer fields of surgical intervention for life-threatening conditions (e.g., bariatric surgery; Wadden & Sarwer, 2006).

What has been learned in the context of transplant candidate selection is already informing work in the bariatric surgery patient population (e.g., Bauchowitz et al., 2005).

## Psychological and Behavioral Outcomes During the Transplantation Process

### PROGRESSION OF ILLNESS AND THE WAIT FOR A DONOR ORGAN

Both before and after the formal evaluation for transplantation, the most critical stressors facing patients and their families are the patient's deteriorating physical health and functional capacity. Although there is a large literature on the psychological sequelae of major physical illness (Dew, 1998; Evans et al., 2005), patients' reactions specifically to the prospect of organ transplantation in this context have largely focused on (a) their willingness to consider transplantation (discussed earlier in this chapter) and (b) psychiatric disorders and psychological distress experienced while they are on the wait list for a donor organ.

Both patients and their families describe the waiting period as the most psychologically stressful part of the transplant experience (Stukas et al., 1999). Because of the uncertainty as to whether and when a donor organ will become available, patients are faced with the mutually opposing prospects of preparing to live and preparing to die (Abbey & Farrow, 1998; Larson & Curtis, 2006). The risk for episodes of psychiatric disorders and clinically significant distress is consequently high. Mood and anxiety-related disorders are the most common diagnosable psychiatric disorders among transplant candidates, although there is considerable variability in prevalence rates reported across studies. As many as three-quarters of all transplant candidates may experience these disorders or clinically significant symptom levels during the waiting period (Barbour, Blumenthal, & Palmer, 2006; Dew et al., 2000b; Dobbels et al., 2001, 2007; Spaderna, Smits, Rahmel, & Weidner, 2007; Telles-Correia et al., 2008). Transplant candidates show higher rates of psychiatric disorders than the rates reported in other chronic disease populations or the general population (Dew, Martire, & Hall, 2003; Dobbels et al., 2001). The disorders are more prevalent in heart, lung, and liver candidates than among kidney candidates, perhaps reflecting the more limited end-stage organ disease treatment options for the former groups. Depression appears more prominent than anxiety disorders in heart, liver, and kidney candidates, whereas anxiety disorders appear more common in lung candidates. Lung disease, with its associated hypoxia and shortness of breath, may have a unique etiologic relationship to anxiety disorders such as panic disorder (Parekh et al., 2003).

Work examining putative predictors or immediate consequences of psychiatric disorder and distress during the waiting period is limited almost exclusively to cross-sectional studies. Demographic and background factors known to increase risk for depression and anxiety in the general population (e.g., lifetime psychiatric history) increase risk in transplant candidates as well (e.g., Rocca et al., 2003). Other correlates of poorer psychological well-being include physical symptom severity and physical functional impairments, greater use of avoidant coping strategies, and poorer social supports (e.g., Burker et al., 2005b; Myaskovsky et al., 2003; Parekh et al., 2003; Rocca et al., 2003; Singh, Gayowski, Wagener, & Marino, 1997; Telles-Correia, Barbosa, Mega, & Monteiro, 2009). In the absence of longitudinal studies, the predictive direction of most associations with cannot be determined.

Although there are few data, it seems likely that psychiatric disorders and elevated psychological distress levels could adversely affect transplant candidates' ability to adhere to their medical regimen. Alternatively, any impact of mental health problems might be trumped by transplant programs' requirements for and close monitoring of candidates' adherence. Indeed, the great majority of patients on the wait list (85% to over 95%) maintain abstinence from substance use (e.g., Evon et al., 2005; Gish et al., 2001; Iasi et al., 2003). One recent report examining heart, liver, and lung candidates found that over 91% had missed at most just a single medication dose in the 2 weeks before assessment (Dobbels et al., 2005). These authors found no statistically reliable association between psychological distress levels and medication adherence.

Finally, the waiting period for transplant can place considerable strain on transplant candidates' family members. Role changes within the family, changes in daily living activities and schedules, and financial burdens (arising from formal and informal care required by the patient), add to the stressors already associated with the patient's deteriorating medical condition (Dew et al., 2000a). Up to 50% of family caregivers (who are usually patients' spouses) exhibit mood and anxiety symptoms (Bolkhir, Loisell, Evon, & Hayashi, 2007; Claar et al., 2005; Rodrigue & Baz, 2007), and the majority of caregivers report increases in caregiving tasks and subjective feelings of caregiver burden (Morelon, Berthoux, Brun-Strang, Flor, & Volle, 2005; Rodrigue & Baz, 2007).

These findings are similar to those noted for caregivers to other chronic disease populations (Lim & Zebrack, 2004; Schulz & Sherwood, 2008), although there is some evidence that transplant candidates' caregivers show distress and burden levels even higher than those of other caregiver cohorts (Meltzer & Rodrigue, 2001). Family caregivers' psychological and overall well-being appears to be closely linked to that of the transplant candidate (Myaskovsky et al., 2005; Rodrigue, Widows, & Baz, 2006). Other correlates of greater caregiver distress and caregiving burden include the caregiver's use of avoidant or passive coping strategies (e.g., Burker et al., 2005a; Claar et al., 2005), the patient's use of such strategies (e.g., Myaskovsky et al., 2005), and longer duration of the patient's disease (e.g., Rodrigue & Baz, 2007). This literature remains too small to discern differences between caregivers by the type of transplant patients require, and similar to studies of transplant candidates, most investigations of their caregivers are cross-sectional.

## POSTSURGICAL RECOVERY AND THE YEARS AFTER TRANSPLANTATION

The common expression, "Is the glass half full or half empty?" captures the range of interpretations of the evidence on patients' psychological, behavioral, and general QOL outcomes after transplantation. There is little doubt but that QOL—incorporating the dimensions of physical functioning, mental health, and social well-being—is improved with transplantation. Even in the late 1990s, when survival time and medical outcomes were somewhat less favorable than they are now, we found in a systematic review of 218 studies conducted over the prior three decades that there were clear benefits to transplantation: Patients' QOL in all domains improved from pre- to posttransplant in the majority of studies (Dew et al., 1997). Nevertheless, gains were less consistently observed for mental health (and social functioning) than for either physical functional QOL or global QOL perceptions. In addition, in no specific domain of QOL was there consistent evidence that transplant recipients' well-being equaled that of healthy nonpatient comparison samples.

In fact, transplant recipients and their families are routinely counseled not to expect that recipients' level of well-being will rival that of individuals who have never had end-stage disease; they are instead trading one chronic disease for another (Dew et al., 2002). After transplantation, they must follow a complex medical regimen for the remainder of their lives. They face major morbidities associated with

the transplant (acute and chronic graft rejection), as well as complications secondary to immunosuppression (e.g., diabetes, hypertension, renal damage, and malignancies). At the same time, however, they have been given "extra" years of life that they would not otherwise have had, and they compellingly describe the value of those years (Craven & Farrow, 1993). Below we discuss the mental health and behavioral consequences of exposure to this unique set of circumstances.

### Psychiatric Disorders and Psychological Distress Post Transplantation

In the weeks following transplantation, once patients have begun to recover from the immediate effects of major surgery and any early medical complications, most patients and their families voice high levels of optimism and even elation about prospects for full rehabilitation and enhanced well-being (DeVito Dabbs et al., 2004; Dew et al., 2002). However, this "honeymoon" period is often ended by the realization that physical recovery is slower and more difficult than may have been anticipated. Up to two-thirds of transplant recipients go on to experience mood disorders (including major depression, dysthymia, and adjustment disorders) during the first several years after transplantation, and up to one-third experience anxiety disorders (including panic disorder, generalized anxiety disorder, posttraumatic stress disorder [PTSD], and adjustment disorders) (Dew & DiMartini, 2005; DiMartini, Dew, & Trzepacz, 2005). Similar to differences among transplant candidates, kidney recipients appear to be at lower risk than recipients of other organs. Regardless of whether individuals meet criteria for diagnosable disorder, elevated levels of psychological symptomatology are also common (Dew et al., 2001b; Dobbels, Verleden, Dupon, Vanhaecke, & De Geest, 2006; Olbrisch et al., 2002).

For many patients, risk for new episodes of disorder or clinically significant psychological distress abates with time posttransplant (Dew et al., 2005; DiMartini et al., 2005; Dobbels et al., 2006), and this pattern mirrors that observed after exposure to many types of major life events (Dohrenwend, 1998; Kessler, 1997). In addition, the factors that patients report to precipitate episodes of disorder or elevated distress "normalize" with time to become less transplant-specific and more highly linked to routine life events and stressors that nonpatient populations also experience (Dew et al., 2001b).

One disorder with an onset almost exclusively during the first year posttransplant is PTSD related to the transplant. For example, in a sample of heart transplant recipients, we found that 16% had experienced PTSD by 12 months posttransplant, whereas only an additional 1% had new onsets of PTSD during the subsequent 2 years (Dew et al., 2001b). Interestingly, factors capable of precipitating PTSD in transplant populations may include not only actual events surrounding the transplant experience (e.g., critical medical events during the waiting period, or the surgery itself) but patients' experiences of hallucinated events or delusions during perioperative delirium (DiMartini, Dew, Kormos, McCurry, & Fontes, 2007). Because delirium is common after major surgery, such findings suggest that the currently employed criteria for a diagnosis of PTSD may need to be expanded to include both objectively defined events and psychically induced experiences. The ability of such experiences to provoke PTSD is consistent with a larger literature documenting heightened psychological distress among patients who have previously experienced delirium during stays in intensive care units (Breitbart, Gibson, & Tremblay, 2002; Jones, Griffiths, Humphris, & Skirrow, 2001).

There is no evidence on the prevalence or nature of psychiatric disorders beyond the first several years posttransplant. However, although general QOL perceptions remain high even many years posttransplant (e.g., Grady et al., 2007), a small body of evidence suggests that psychological distress levels begin to rise once again as transplant recipients enter the late-term years of their lifespan, when physical morbidities become more prominent (Bunzel & Laederach-Hofmann, 1999; Dobbels et al., 2004; Martinelli et al., 2007; Vermeulen et al., 2003). Whether depressive or anxiety symptoms predominate during the late-term years remains unknown.

Numerous studies have sought to identify factors that increase individuals' risk for psychiatric disorders and elevated distress during the posttransplant years. Most of this work focuses on the first several years after surgery. We and others have employed a vulnerability model or diathesis–stress approach (Dohrenwend, 2000; Ormel & De Jong, 1999) to conceptualizing the range of factors likely to provoke or contribute to psychological dysfunction. In this conceptualization, transplant recipients who possess certain vulnerabilities (e.g., intrapersonal characteristics such as a poor sense of mastery, or interpersonal factors such as poor support from their primary family caregiver) are hypothesized to be particularly likely to have poor psychological outcomes, given exposure to ongoing, chronic transplant-related stressors (e.g., Dew et al., 1994). These poor outcomes include not only the sheer occurrence of mood and anxiety disorders and elevated distress, but whether the disorders and distress are sustained (vs. abating relatively quickly). Beyond well-established risk factors (e.g., lifetime history of disorder), the factors most consistently found associated with increased vulnerability in transplant recipients are poor relationships and supports from the family caregiver, other family members, and friends (e.g., Dew et al., 1994, 2001b, 2005; Stilley et al., 1999; Stukas et al., 1999); fewer social connections and involvements in social activities (e.g., Littlefield et al., 1996; Dobbels et al., 2004); use of avoidant or passive coping strategies (e.g., Dew et al., 1996a; Nickel, Wunsch, Egle, Lohse, & Otto, 2002; Stilley et al., 1999); a poor sense of personal control or mastery (e.g., Evangelista, Moser, Dracup, Doering, & Kobashigawa, 2004; Kugler et al., 1994); and low levels of characteristics such as optimism, hope, or positive expectations for the future (e.g., Evangelista, Doering, Dracup, Vassilakis, & Kobashigawa, 2003; Goetzmann et al., 2007; Leedham, Meyerowitz, Muirhead, & Frist, 1995). In our own work, we have found that the effects of such factors are additive: the presence of an increasing number of factors bears a dose–response relationship to likelihood that psychiatric disorders will develop (e.g., Dew et al., 2001b).

One important limitation in this literature is that the bulk of studies are cross-sectional and thus whether factors truly increase vulnerability cannot be established. Even in prospective studies (e.g., Dew et al., 2001b), it is not possible to conclude that identified predictors were in fact causal agents. Another limitation of most studies is that they fail to consider a full range of potential vulnerability factors, including sociodemographic and background factors, and intrapersonal, interpersonal, and environmental characteristics that have the potential to affect psychological outcomes. Thus, it is difficult to determine whether some factors exert stronger predictive effects than others or are more important for certain segments of a given patient sample than for others (e.g., for men vs. women). In addition, individual studies generally focus on only single-organ transplant populations and have not examined whether certain factors vary in their impact depending on type of transplant received. Since rates of depressive and anxiety disorders differ by type of organ transplantation, as noted earlier, it is possible that potential vulnerability factors could be differentially important as well. Finally, it is not clear whether factors that increase vulnerability to poor psychological outcomes early posttransplant have similar effects on later posttransplant outcomes.

The presence of posttransplant mood or anxiety disorders or elevated psychological symptoms increases the risk for transplant-related morbidities and mortality. Two studies in heart recipients have documented such effects, independent of other risk factors for poor outcomes. Havik et al. (2007) reported that recipients who had high depressive symptom levels at routine medical evaluations were almost three times more likely to die during the next 6 years of follow-up than were those with low depression levels. Dew et al. (1999) found that persistently elevated depression symptom levels during the first year after heart transplantation led to over a fourfold greater risk that patients would develop chronic graft rejection (a major morbidity associated with transplantation) in the next 2 years. Recipients who developed PTSD during the first year posttransplant were more than 15 times more likely to die during the next 2 years. Neither of these studies could examine the mechanism by which depression or anxiety affected physical health outcomes. It is likely that both behavioral factors (e.g., nonadherence to the medical regimen) and physiological changes serve as mediators of these effects, as suggested in a large body of literature examining linkages between mental and physical well-being (e.g., Evans et al., 2005; Fenton & Stover, 2006). In organ transplantation, however, the impact of patients' psychological status on risk for nonadherence has not yet received detailed consideration, as we discuss below.

Family members provide significant care and assistance to transplant recipients, and their posttransplant mental health outcomes are also important to consider. Organ transplantation presents an interesting context for testing hypotheses about family caregiver well-being in the face of their loved one's chronic disease. On the one hand, based on the evidence on mental health effects of family caregiving in other chronic disease populations (e.g., Schulz & Sherwood, 2008), we would hypothesize that transplant family caregivers would show high rates of psychiatric disorders and clinically significant distress, especially as the period of caregiving grows longer. On the other hand, life after transplantation differs from life with most other chronic conditions because—rather than the deteriorating course typical in chronic disease—transplantation leads to a reversal of previous disability, at least for some period of years. This suggests that transplant family caregivers might show lower rates of mental health problems than other caregiver populations, particularly in the early years posttransplant, before patients develop new morbidities. In fact, the rates of psychiatric disorders in family caregivers during the first several years posttransplant are as high as those observed in other caregiver populations. Moreover, family caregivers are at least as likely as transplant recipients themselves to develop mood and anxiety disorders and to show high distress levels during this time (Bohachick, Reedeer, Taylor, & Anton, 2001; Bunzel, Laederach-Hofmann, Wieselthaler, Roethy, & Wolner, 2007; Dew et al., 2004b; Stukas et al., 1999).

Among the most important risk factors for poor family caregiver mental health posttransplant is caregiver burden, including the numbers of household and nursing care tasks for which the caregiver is responsible, as well as the subjectively perceived burden in providing care (Cohen, Katz, & Baruch, 2007; Dew et al., 2004b; Ullrich, Jansch, Schmidt, Struber, & Niedermeyer, 2004). A poorer-quality relationship with the recipient is also a robust correlate and predictor of risk for poor caregiver mental health (Chowanec & Binik, 1989; Dew et al., 2004b). There is additional evidence that caregivers' physical health status is entwined with their mental health, with each affecting the other (Cohen et al., 2007; Dew et al., 1998). Other predictors of poor psychological status in caregivers posttransplant are similar to factors we identified as correlates among caregivers to transplant candidates. The posttransplant literature is stronger in terms of collecting longitudinal (rather than only cross-sectional) data in caregivers, but does not address any differences in outcomes among them according to type of transplant their family member received.

*Adherence to the Medical Regimen Posttransplantation*

Adherence to the regimen is the key behavioral issue confronting transplant recipients. All recipients must follow a life-long, multifaceted regimen that includes taking multiple immunosuppressive medications, attending regular follow-up medical evaluations, completing blood work and other tests, regularly monitoring vital signs and other health parameters, following exercise and dietary requirements, abstaining from tobacco and drug use, and limiting or abstaining from alcohol. As with other prescribed health care regimens in acute and chronic disease (Kravitz & Melnikow, 2004), patients' adherence to the posttransplant regimen is a major determinant of their health outcomes. Nonadherence to medications and to other components of this regimen has repeatedly been found to predict post-transplant morbidity and mortality (for reviews, see Butler, Roderick, Mullee, Mason, & Peveler, 2004; De Geest, Dobbels, Fluri, Paris, & Troosters, 2005; Denhaerynck et al., 2005; Dew et al., 2000b; Fine et al., 2009).

Given the psychosocial evaluation process for transplantation, as well as extensive patient education about health risks posttransplant (Dumas-Hicks, 2003), it might be assumed that adherence—that is, the degree to which patients' behavior coincides with posttransplant medical recommendations (Sabaté, 2003)—would be very high. Unfortunately, like patients with other chronic diseases, many transplant recipients have difficulty maintaining high levels of adherence. In a recent meta-analysis, we examined nonadherence outcomes in 147 studies of organ transplant recipients published since the advent of modern immunosuppression in the early 1980s (Dew et al., 2007a). The average nonadherence rates ranged from 1% to 4% of patients annually for substance use (tobacco, alcohol, illicit drugs), to 19% to 25% of patients annually for nonadherence to immunosuppressants, diet, exercise, and other health care monitoring requirements. The rate of nonadherence to immunosuppressants, at 23% of patients annually, is particularly disturbing given these medications' roles in preventing graft rejection. However, patients experience many unpleasant side effects from these medications, and failure to take them does not produce immediate morbidity. Graft rejection can develop insidiously, with no symptoms until it is severe. Hence, despite ongoing education, patients may not fully comprehend the risks they take in missing medications.

We found surprisingly few differences based on the type of organ transplant patients received. Of particular note, immunosuppressant nonadherence was highest in kidney recipients (34% of patients annually), with heart and liver recipients showing lower rates (15% and 7%, respectively). (There were too few studies of recipients of other types of transplants to include them in these comparisons.) The nonadherence rate may have been highest kidney recipients due either to less stringent psychosocial selection criteria, as discussed earlier, or because the consequences of graft loss are less severe.

Beyond average rates of nonadherence, other important issues pertain to the timing of nonadherence relative to the transplant: How early might nonadherence problems emerge, and how do they unfold over time? The evidence shows that nonadherence in some areas can begin as soon as patients are discharged from the hospital after the transplant. For example, Nevins et al. (2001) used electronic medication monitoring to chart the course of nonadherence to azathioprine, a medication that has typically been included in the "cocktail" of immunosuppressants that recipients take. They found that 19% of kidney recipients missed 4 days or more of medication even in the first month post-discharge. As in other chronic disease populations (e.g., Montgomery & Kasper, 1998; Rudd, 1995), nonadherence in most areas of the regimen worsens with time, particularly beyond 6–7 months posttransplant (e.g., Chisholm, et al., 2000; Dew et al., 1996b, 2008a, 2008b; Grady, Jalowiec, & White-Williams, 1998). Levels of nonadherence appear to stabilize after the first few years (De Geest et al., 2005; Dew et al., 2001a; Grady et al., 1998). Interestingly, nonadherence in any given area of the regimen does not necessarily indicate that individuals will have difficulty in other areas. The areas are not highly interrelated and there appears to be little evidence of an overall "profile" of typical nonadherence among transplant recipients (e.g., Berlakovich et al., 2000; Dew et al., 1996b; 2008a; Liu & Zaki, 2004).

Predictors of nonadherence in transplant recipients remain incompletely understood. Recently, the WHO conceptualization of five categories of risk factors likely to be important for adherence to chronic disease treatment regimens (Sabaté, 2003) has guided the inclusion of variables in studies in this literature. These categories include sociodemographic characteristics, health care system and treatment provider factors (e.g., insurance coverage, provider communication skills), disease-related characteristics (e.g., symptoms or complications; health perceptions), treatment-related factors (e.g., medication side effects), and patient-related psychosocial factors (e.g., coping strategies, social supports). There appears to be at least some support for the role of variables in all five categories, although the evidence is often inconsistent (De Geest et al., 2005; Denhaerynck et al., 2005; Dew et al., 2001a; Fine et al., 2009). In our meta-analysis, we were hampered in examining risk factors' impact because many studies failed to include putative risk factors or included only a small set of them (Dew et al., 2007a). Thus, we could not examine, for example, the impact of patient psychological distress on outcomes, despite evidence from other chronic disease research implicating depression, in particular, as an important risk factor (DiMatteo, Lepper, & Croghan, 2000). Our results did indicate, however, that demographic characteristics, social supports, and perceived health showed at best weak associations with any area of posttransplant adherence.

One strong risk factor emerged in our analyses: Pretransplant substance use was highly predictive of nonadherence to posttransplant substance use restrictions (Dew et al., 2007a). Indeed, in a separate meta-analysis focused on 54 studies of individuals receiving transplants for diseases resulting from substance use (as opposed to the studies of general transplant samples discussed thus far), we found that nonadherence to posttransplant substance use restrictions was higher than in the general transplant samples: 4% of patients annually for illicit drug and 6% annually for alcohol use, compared to 1% and 4%, respectively, for general samples (Dew et al., 2008b). We also found that a shorter duration of pretransplant abstinence predicted a higher likelihood of relapse, supporting the pretransplant abstinence requirements imposed by many transplant programs. Nevertheless, the relapse rates we observed were considerably lower than might be expected based on the clinical literature regarding relapse in substance abusing populations, perhaps due to heightened screening and monitoring of transplant candidates with substance abuse histories.

## STRATEGIES FOR IMPROVING TRANSPLANT PATIENT AND FAMILY PSYCHOLOGICAL AND BEHAVIORAL OUTCOMES

Despite evidence of mental health and adherence-related difficulties linked to organ transplantation, relatively few interventions have been mounted and tested. One might presume that interventions found effective in other community-based or patient populations would be useful in transplant populations as well (e.g., psychopharmacologic agents; educational or social support strategies; various types of psychotherapy). Antidepressants and anxiolytics are indeed frequently prescribed to transplant recipients and have been found in routine clinical practice to be safe and useful for them (DiMartini et al., 2005). Some attempts have been made to utilize traditional, multisession psychotherapeutic interventions (e.g., Abbey & Farrow, 1998; Baines, Joseph, & Jindal, 2004; Gross et al., 2004). However, most such interventions have been difficult to implement or formally evaluate due to important constraints in the transplant population (Dew et al., 2004a). First, as is typical with highly specialized care, transplant centers are dispersed geographically, and many patients travel long distances to them. After surgery, patients return to their center infrequently, and thus ongoing face-to-face interventions are often impractical. Second, in the absence of major complications, hospital stays after transplant surgery are relatively brief (e.g., about 5 days for kidney transplantation). There is little time for intervention during this period. Third, during the stressful period of waiting for an organ and during the perioperative recovery period, patients and families are unable to absorb much of what they are told to expect in the long term after discharge. When they return for follow-up medical appointments, insufficient time is available for intensive psychological or behavioral interventions. Finally, restrictions on third-party payments and hospital budgets mean that transplant teams have few resources available to develop and empirically evaluate intervention services.

Given these constraints, transplant programs have developed intervention alternatives that do not rely heavily on frequent face-to-face contact or the use of trained mental health professionals. These include bibliotherapy (e.g., Hodges, Craven, & Littlefield, 1995), peer mentoring and support (e.g., Faulk, 1999; Wright et al., 2001), telephone- or internet-based psychotherapeutic or educational strategies (e.g., Goedecke, Winsett, Martin, Hathaway, & Gaber, 2001; Napolitano et al., 2002; Schäfer-Keller et al., 2009), and the use of home-based self-monitoring tools (e.g., Chlan et al., 1998; Schneider, Winsett, Reed, & Hathaway, 2001). In addition, brief, intensive educational or support services have been developed for the short inpatient period after transplant surgery; these interventions are often accompanied by telephone follow-up sessions (e.g., Bass, Galley-Reilley, Twiss, & Whitaker, 1999; Klein, Otto, & Kramer, 2009; Lisson, Rodrigue, Reed, & Nelson, 2005; Traiger & Bui, 1997). A few efforts have focused on brief counseling and feedback strategies, mostly for medication-taking, during posttransplant follow-up clinic visits (e.g., Hardstaff, Green, & Talbot, 2003). Much of the work is descriptive and has not included an evaluative component. However, at least anecdotally, the strategies have been reported to be useful within individual transplant programs and thus may warrant formal evaluation (for reviews, see De Bleser, Matteson, Dobbels, Russell, & De Geest, 2009; Dew et al., 2007b; Dew & DiMartini, 2005).

Several efforts that have undergone more rigorous testing merit comment. With respect to psychological outcomes, Blumenthal and colleagues (2006; Napolitano et al., 2002) evaluated an 8- to 12-week telephone intervention utilizing supportive counseling with cognitive-behavioral techniques to improve lung transplant candidates' ability to cope with stressors arising during the waiting period. Patients had lower anxiety and depressive symptoms, better perceived global mental health, lower levels of somatic complaints, and better perceived social support at the conclusion of the intervention, compared with individuals randomized to receive usual medical management by the transplant team. Rodrigue et al. (2005, 2006) evaluated a similar telephone-based program in lung transplant candidates and obtained similar results. However, they also assessed family caregivers. Although these caregivers did not participate in the telephone sessions, they benefitted as well: they had lower depression levels and better QOL than did caregivers of patients in the comparison condition, and these benefits were maintained during the 3-month post-intervention follow-up period. Finally, we evaluated an internet-based intervention that included components to address stress management and psychological well-being using problem solving therapy principles in a workshop-based format (Dew et al., 2004a). Heart transplant recipients and their family caregivers who had access to the website were compared to a historical comparison group of patients (and caregivers) who received usual care from the transplant team. The intervention group patients showed improved depression and anxiety symptoms, and caregivers had improved anxiety symptoms, relative to the comparison groups, after 4 months of website exposure.

With respect to medical adherence posttransplant, Chisholm et al. (2001) tested an intervention involving pharmacist counseling to patients either at routine transplant clinic follow-up visits or by telephone. The intervention group showed better medication adherence during the 12-month study period than did patients receiving usual follow-up care. In our internet-based intervention study, we included a problem-solving therapy-based workshop focused on maximizing adherence to all components of the medical regimen in heart recipients (Dew et al., 2004a). Although we observed no adherence benefits in intervention versus comparison group patients, the subgroup of patients who specifically used the adherence workshop component of the intervention website showed significant improvements in keeping clinic appointments, completing blood work, and following dietary requirements relative to the comparison group. Finally, DeVito Dabbs et al. (2009) evaluated a hand-held personal digital assistant (PDA) with customized software to allow patients to monitor symptoms and well-being. Compared to patients receiving standard care (which included the use of paper-and-pencil diaries to monitor health), patients using the PDA showed higher levels of self-efficacy for managing their regimen, performed self-care behaviors at higher rates (including monitoring of symptoms, body temperature, and blood pressure, and spirometry to assess lung function), and showed higher overall levels of adherence to the posttransplant medical regimen than the comparison group during the 2 months of study follow-up.

### Summary

Transplantation improves patient QOL. Nevertheless, like other populations exposed to a range of acute and chronic stressors, transplant candidates, recipients, and their families are at increased risk for psychiatric disorders and elevated psychological symptom levels. Nonadherence to the multifaceted posttransplant medical regimen is common and worsens with time. With few exceptions (e.g., the strong association between pretransplant substance use and risk for such use posttransplant), it has been difficult to identify strong pretransplant predictors of poor psychological or behavioral outcomes posttransplant. However, a growing literature documents posttransplant factors that predict or are correlated with psychological difficulties in both patients and their family caregivers. Moreover, patients' posttransplant psychological distress and nonadherence to the medical regimen increase their risk for poor physical health outcomes. This field has been hampered by limited longitudinal or prospective research (relative to cross-sectional work), by difficulties in developing interventions due to logistical issues typical in populations receiving specialized care, and by infrequent empirical evaluation of interventions' effectiveness. Interventions tested to date show that improvements in psychological and behavioral outcomes are possible. Whether intervention benefits can be maintained over time will be an important issue for future studies.

### Stressors and Outcomes in Living Organ Donors

Throughout the history of human organ transplantation, living donation has served as a unique and important form of gift giving. It has features that distinguish it from other types of helping behaviors, including no expectation of reciprocity (the transplant recipient will never provide an organ in return) and the unparalleled ability of the gift of a living organ to prolong life (Dew et al., 2007d; Simmons et al., 1987). Donors face major stressors: they undergo significant discomfort, inconvenience, unreimbursable financial expenses, and physical risk in order to donate. The decision to donate may take place during a crisis situation in which the patient's health is rapidly deteriorating. Alternatively, a donor may come forward in order to enable an individual to receive a transplant before a health crisis occurs. This set of factors suggests that there are important psychological issues to consider before donation, and also indicates the need to carefully monitor donors' postdonation physical and psychological outcomes. Figure 22.3 delineates the acute events and time periods associated with living donation, and in this section we discuss issues pertinent to the psychosocial evaluation of prospective living donors, followed by a summary of the evidence on psychological and psychosocial outcomes associated with living donation.

## The Psychosocial Evaluation and Individuals' Motives for Donation

Like potential transplant candidates, prospective living donors undergo an extensive medical and psychosocial evaluation. The components of the psychosocial evaluation are also similar to those administered to transplant candidates, and there is an equally great—if not greater—emphasis on ensuring that donors do not have major mental health or substance use problems and have stable social and financial circumstances (Dew et al., 2007a, 2007b; Olbrisch, Benedict, Haller, & Levenson, 2001). In addition, heavy emphasis is placed on evaluating donors' understanding of the risks and benefits of donation (for both the recipient and the donor), as well as their motives for donation. Once donors have been determined to be medically and psychosocially suitable for donation, most transplant programs provide a "cooling off period" in order to ensure that donors have an opportunity to think about and reconsider any decision about donation before the surgery takes place. The psychosocial evaluation and the cooling off period are designed to protect donors' safety; they reflect transplant programs' strong imperative to ensure that donors have made an informed decision and that donors' well-being will be preserved (Abecassis et al., 2000; Ethics Committee, 2004; Pruett et al., 2006).

Earlier in the chapter, we discussed a number of factors that have been found to be associated with individuals' willingness to serve as living organ donors. Donors themselves emphasize the importance of helping others. Both clinical and research activity has focused on understanding why donors feel this way, whether this fully captures their reasons for coming forward, and whether theories of altruism apply specifically to living donation. For example, a noteworthy debate in the altruism research literature has concerned whether any gift-giving behavior is truly altruistic (i.e., driven by selfless compassion and care for others) or is driven largely by self-serving motives (Batson, 1998; Cialdini et al., 1987; Penner et al., 2005). It has been argued that almost all ostensible altruism hides egoistic and self-serving motives, even if the aim is only to increase one's happiness or relieve one's own negative emotional state (Cialdini et al., 1987). This debate mirrors a concern among transplant professionals that potential donors' motives must be completely examined during the required psychosocial evaluation, and that it may be an unfavorable sign if donors express self-serving motives.

In fact, most donors' motives reflect a complex interweaving of selfless desires (e.g., to relieve the suffering of another), self-serving desires (fear of losing a loved one to death), and other factors (e.g., social or familial pressures or norms). Furthermore, the combination of motivational forces appears to vary depending on whether a donor is related (biologically or emotionally) to the patient, or is unrelated. For example, studies over the past 30 years have found that living related donors most typically cite a desire to help the transplant candidate as a key motive, but may also express beliefs that the donation will make their own lives more worthwhile, feelings of moral or religious duty, a desire to make amends for past actions, and sometimes a desire to acquiesce to perceived pressure to donate from family, friends, and/or medical personnel (e.g., Franklin & Crombie, 2003; Lennerling, Forsberg, & Nyberg, 2003; Papachristou et al., 2004; Simmons et al., 1987). Unrelated donors also express a preponderance of motives related to altruistic or humanitarian goals, but usually in combination with feelings of moral and religious obligation or identity, and beliefs that their self-worth will be increased (e.g., Henderson et al., 2003; Jacobs, Roman, Garvey, Kahn, & Matas, 2004).

Do motives matter for postdonation outcomes? Given that most donors express multiple motives, the most important issue concerns the particular combination and expression of motives (and not whether altruism is the only motive present). Thus, research has shown that, even when donors state a desire to help others, if they are also equally or more strongly motivated to atone or make amends for past actions, they are likely to have poorer psychological outcomes postdonation (e.g., Schover, Streem, Boparai, Duriak, & Novick, 1997; Sharma & Enoch,

1987; Simmons et al., 1987). Furthermore, not only the nature of the motives but the strength with which they are held is linked to donor outcomes. In particular, ambivalence about donating—lingering feelings of uncertainty and hesitation about donating—reflects weaker motivation or desire to donate. Ambivalence is a strong and consistent predictor of poorer physical, psychological, and psychosocial outcomes after donation (e.g., DiMartini et al., 2008; Hayashi et al., 2007; Simmons et al., 1987; Smith et al., 1986; Switzer, Simmons, & Dew, 1996). Finally, coercion—either emotional or based on financial inducement—results in poorer donor psychological and psychosocial outcomes. Outcomes in organ vendors provide the most striking evidence in this regard: studies of individuals selling their kidneys indicate that not only do they ultimately experience financial hardship even greater than that which led them to sell their kidneys, but they experience both physical and mental health problems (Rizvi, Naqvi, Zafar, & Ahmed, 2009). Iranian kidney vendors, for example, have reported marked psychological distress, including hate and anger at the recipient, and resentment and anguish over a perceived lack of gratitude from the recipient (e.g., Zargooshi, 2001a, 2001b). Such findings strongly suggest that altruistic motives provide the bedrock needed to ensure that living organ donation yields a favorable balance of benefits to risks for donors. In short, "helping behavior" without a strong altruistic component can ultimately be quite damaging to the helper, and this may further inform theoretical perspectives in the field of altruism research.

## Psychological and Psychosocial Outcomes Postdonation

The imperative to ensure that the risks of living donation are minimal provides the impetus for most research on postdonation outcomes. Earlier in the chapter, we noted the greater emphasis being placed on living donor transplantation worldwide in recent years, and this has resulted in a proliferation of studies examining medical and psychosocial outcomes in living donors. Most of this work focuses on, at most, the first several years postdonation. At least during these initial years, many of the findings in (nonvendor) living donors are highly favorable. From a psychosocial standpoint, for example, no matter whether donors are queried shortly after donation or many years later, studies consistently show that (a) very few donors (0%–4%) regret having donated (e.g., Fehrman-Ekholm et al., 2000; Jacobs, Johnson, Anderson, Gillingham, & Matas, 1998), (b) the vast majority (95%–100%) affirm that they would still donate if they had it to do again (e.g., Peters et al., 2000; Verbesey et al., 2005), and (c) most (90%–95%) perceive their act of donation to have been a very gratifying experience that has benefited them personally (e.g., Corley, Keswick, Sergeant, & Scott, 2000; Simmons et al., 1987). These findings hold for kidney donors (who constitute the largest group of donors) and individuals who donate a segment of their livers. (Little is yet known about lung lobe donors.) Moreover, studies show that donors' average scores on generic QOL instruments are equal to or well exceed normative levels in all domains (for reviews, see Clemens et al., 2006; Dew et al., 2007d).

Nevertheless, sizable minorities of living donors experience psychological and other psychosocial difficulties postdonation. Three areas appear to be particularly affected. First, across existing studies, an average of about 10% of living donors have been found to meet criteria for mood or anxiety disorders, and about one-quarter show clinically significant psychological symptom levels (e.g., Erim et al., 2006; Heck, Schweitzer, & Seidel-Wiesel, 2004; Jordan et al., 2004; Walter et al., 2002). Time since donation (at least during the first several years) has not been found to be strongly related to the rates of psychological distress or to the other difficulties noted below.

Second, family relationships frequently show increased strain after donation. Although donors typically report that their relationship with the transplant recipient is unchanged or improved postdonation, about 10%–15% of donors report that relationships with other family members are worsened (e.g., Karliova et al., 2002; Reimer et al., 2006; Sterneck et al., 1995). Studies generally do not specify which types of relationships have been affected (e.g., spousal vs. other relationships). However, the spousal relationship may be at particular risk for strain after donation, given anecdotal reports of postdonation separations and divorces (e.g., Reimer et al., 2006; Schover et al., 1997). In general, these anecdotal accounts suggest that the donation precipitated the ending of already-fragile marriages.

Finally, sizable proportions of donors report that their physical functional QOL is worse than before donation: on average, across studies in this literature, approximately 25% of donors voice major concerns about their health, including concerns about new or future health problems, and worries about whether their remaining organ is or will continue to function adequately (Corley et al., 2000; Neuhaus et al. 2005;

Stothers, Gourlay, & Liu, 2005). Although donors are typically assessed well beyond the early months of recovery, worsened health since donation, persistent pain, enduring fatigue, and negative body image changes (related primarily to the surgical scar) are problems that are each noted in about 25% of donors (Giessing et al., 2004; Kim-Schluger et al. 2002; Stothers et al., 2005; Trotter et al., 2001; Walter et al., 2002).

Predictors and correlates of postdonation outcomes remained poorly defined and, perhaps for this reason, there has been no study of interventions to address negative postdonation outcomes. Aside from predonation motives, neither demographic characteristics, predonation psychological distress, nor postoperative donor medical complications consistently predict poor donor outcomes (Dew et al., 2007d). In addition, whether the transplant was successful or not (i.e., the recipient lost the graft or died) is not a consistent predictor. This is noteworthy because of longstanding fears in the transplant community that poor recipient outcomes would lead to lasting psychological damage to donors (Ingelfinger, 2005; Simmons et al., 1987). However, qualitative studies' exploration of this issue show that, although donors experience bereavement in the aftermath of recipient graft loss or death, they frequently comment that they were grateful that they could do as much as possible for the recipient (e.g., Sadler, Davison, Carroll, & Kountz, 1971; Switzer et al., 1998).

## Summary

Living donation can allow individuals to express compassion and altruism for others facing end-stage kidney disease and, under some circumstances, other end-stage organ diseases. Motives reflecting altruism commonly coexist with a variety of other reasons for donating. The nature and strength of motives for donating affects postdonation psychosocial outcomes in living donors. Although postdonation outcomes are overwhelmingly positive in living donors, evidence that significant minorities of donors experience psychological or somatic distress or strained interpersonal relationships supports ongoing efforts to monitor donor health and QOL outcomes in the long term following donation. Continued focus on the careful psychosocial evaluation of prospective donors will help to identify the donors who have the best chances for positive outcomes and allow for appropriate counseling when donation is unlikely to be in an individual's best interests (Dew et al., 2007c; Olbrisch et al., 2001).

## Conclusion
### Future Directions

The health psychology of organ transplantation encompasses a wide spectrum of clinical and research issues. Issues regarding access to and availability of transplantation are connected to broad social concerns pertaining to equity in health care and the unfortunate fact that disparities across ethnic, gender, social, and geographic lines continue to affect which patients receive life-saving treatment. Limited availability of organs heightens tensions surrounding how best to determine which individuals are in greatest need or are most likely to benefit from transplantation. Strategies to increase organ availability rely in large part on the good will and altruism of individuals who commit their organs to donation at the time of their deaths or who come forward as living donors. Clearly, skilled clinicians and researchers are needed to delineate the social and psychological factors that perpetuate disparities in access, that make individuals more or less likely to consider donation, and that render larger health care system changes (e.g., in organ allocation schemas) more versus less likely to promote equitable access and increase the availability of transplantation.

Attention is equally necessary at the level of the individual patient, his or her family, and the living donor as they negotiate the steps and the stressors involved in the transplantation (and donation) process. Organ transplantation significantly extends life, but QOL can only be maximized through the concerted efforts of all parties involved in this endeavor. Both clinical acumen and empirical data are needed to identify individuals at risk for psychological and behavioral difficulties before the transplantation surgery, as well as after it. Careful evaluation of prospective transplant candidates and living donors is important in this regard, as is the application of timely interventions to remedy outstanding psychosocial problems that could interfere with successful adaptation after the surgery. Monitoring not only of medical outcomes posttransplant (and postdonation) but psychological and behavioral well-being is critical for the care of transplant recipients and donors. Such monitoring is also essential to identify long-term health issues that demand focused research attention. These activities will ensure that transplant recipients and their families fully benefit from organ transplantation, and that the risks that living donors incur in providing the "gift of life" are minimal and do not lead to long-term psychological or other health problems.

**Table 22.1  Future directions for research in organ transplantation psychology**

| Domain of Study | Research Questions |
| --- | --- |
| Access to and availability of organ transplantation | • Beyond the continued documentation of disparities in access to organ transplantation, what is the full range of patient-, provider-, and health care system-level factors that contribute to the disparities?<br>• Aside from disparities related to ethnicity, can we better characterize the nature and determinants of disparities associated with gender and other social and geographic characteristics?<br>• Can we develop and empirically evaluate interventions directed toward patients and health care providers, in order to reduce disparities in access to transplantation?<br>• Can we increase the range of evidence-based interventions available to increase deceased and living organ donation? Can we mount quality improvement/quality assurance initiatives to examine ongoing program activities, and/or conduct and disseminate the results of research testing novel interventions in this area? |
| Stressors and outcomes in organ transplant patients and their families | • Which transplant recipients and family caregivers are at risk for poor psychological outcomes posttransplant? Can we prospectively identify not only patient and caregiver factors that increase risk, but provider- and health care system-level factors affect these outcomes?<br>• Can we prospectively identify a full range of patient-, provider-, and health care system-level factors that affect transplant recipients' levels of adherence to the posttransplant medical regimen?<br>• Among transplant recipients, what are the psychological and behavioral consequences of entering the late-term years posttransplant, when medical burden typically increases? How can we maximize psychological well-being and minimize suffering in the face of late-term posttransplant morbidities?<br>• Can we increase the range of evidence-based interventions available to address psychological and medical adherence-related difficulties posttransplant? Can we mount quality improvement/quality assurance initiatives to examine ongoing clinical practices, and/or conduct and disseminate the results of research testing novel interventions in this area? |
| Stressors and outcomes in living donors | • What are the long-term psychological and general QOL outcomes in living donors beyond the first several years postdonation?<br>• How can we better identify prospective donors at risk for poor outcomes and effectively intervene to prevent those problems? |

In our view, ten questions represent critical future directions for the field. These questions, spanning the major topic areas of this chapter, are listed in Table 22.1. They build on both the findings from and limitations in existing research. For example, they reflect the need throughout the field to move beyond cross-sectional studies that cannot establish the predictive direction of effects between variables. They reflect the fact that intervention work to date remains relatively rare, and that interventions developed and utilized in clinical practice may not yet have received formal empirical evaluation. With respect to outcomes in patients, families, and living donors, the research questions for the future reflect the importance of looking beyond the first several years posttransplant to chart the nature and predictors of outcomes during the extended years after the transplantation surgery. A full accounting of the costs and benefits of organ transplantation requires that we consider outcomes in the late-term years with as much care as we consider issues pertaining to access and short-term results in the organ transplantation enterprise. Equally important, progress made in addressing the research questions in Table 22.1 may ultimately benefit not only the field of organ transplantation but also our general understanding of issues affecting access to optimal health care, adaptation to chronic disease and its treatment, and the conditions under which individuals step forward to provide significant help to others in medical need.

## Acknowledgement

Preparation of this chapter was supported in part by Grant MH072718 from the National Institute of Mental Health and Grant NR011149 from the National Institute of Nursing Research, Bethesda, MD.

## References

Aaronson, K.D., Schwartz, J.S., Goin, J.E., & Mancini, D.M. (1995). Sex differences in patient acceptance of cardiac transplant candidacy. *Circulation, 91*, 2753–2761.

Abecassis, M., Adams, M., Adams, P., Arnold, R.M., Atkins, C.R., Barr, M.L., et al. Live Organ Donor Consensus Group. (2000). Consensus statement on the live organ donor. *Journal of the American Medical Association, 284*(22), 2919–2926.

Abbey, S., & Farrow, S. (1998). Group therapy and organ transplantation. *International Journal of Group Psychotherapy, 48*, 163–185.

Ahmad, J., Bryce, C.L., Cacciarelli, T., & Roberts, M.S. (2007). Differences in access to liver transplantation: Disease severity, waiting time, and transplantation center volume. *Annals of Internal Medicine, 146*(10), 707–713.

Alexander, G.C., & Sehgal, A.R. (1998). Barriers to cadaveric renal transplantation among blacks, women, and the poor. *Journal of the American Medical Association, 280*(13), 1148–1152.

Alvaro, E.M., Jones, S.P., Robles, A.S.M., & Siegel, J. (2006). Hispanic organ donation: Impact of a Spanish-language organ donation campaign. *Journal of the National Medical Association, 98*(1), 28–35.

Axelrod, D.A., Guidinger, M.K., Finlayson, S., Schaubel, D.E., Goodman, D.C., Chobanian, M., et al. (2008). Rates of solid-organ wait-listing, transplantation, and survival among residents of rural and urban areas. *Journal of the American Medical Association, 299*(2), 202–207.

Axelrod, D.A., & Pomfret, E.A. (2008). Race and sex disparities in liver transplantation. Progress toward achieving equal access? *Journal of the American Medical Association, 300*(20), 2425–2426.

Ayanian, J.Z., Cleary, P.D., Keogh, J.H., Noonan, S.J., David-Kasdan, J.A., & Epstein, A.M. (2004). Physicians' beliefs about racial differences in referral for renal transplantation. *American Journal of Kidney Diseases, 43*(2), 350–357.

Ayanian, J.Z., Cleary, P.D., Weissman, J.S., & Epstein, A.M. (1999). The effect of patients' preferences on racial differences in access to renal transplantation. *New England Journal of Medicine, 341*(22), 1661–1669.

Baines, L.S., Joseph, J.T., & Jindal, R.M. (2004). Prospective randomized study of individual and group psychotherapy versus controls in recipients of renal transplants. *Kidney International, 65*, 1937–1942.

Barbour, K.A., Blumenthal, J.A., & Palmer, S.M. (2006). Psychosocial issues in the assessment and management of patients undergoing lung transplantation. *Chest, 129*, 1367–1374.

Bass, M., Galley-Reilley, J., Twiss, D.E., & Whitaker, D. (1999). A diversified patient education program for transplant recipients. *American Nephrology Nurses Association, 26*(3), 287–292, 343.

Batson, C.D. (1998). Altruism and prosocial behavior. In: D.T. Gilbert, S.T. Fiske, & G. Lindzey (Eds.). *The handbook of social psychology* Vol. 2 (4th ed., pp. 282–316). New York: McGraw-Hill.

Bauchowitz, A.U., Gonder-Frederick, L.A., Olbrisch, M.-E., Azarbad, L., Ryee, M. -Y., Woodson, M., et al. (2005). Psychosocial evaluation of bariatric surgery candidates: A survey of present practices. *Psychosomatic Medicine, 67*, 825–832.

Berlakovich, G.A., Langer, F., Freundorfer, E., Windhager, T., Rockenschaub, S., Sporn, E., et al. (2000). General compliance after liver transplantation for alcoholic cirrhosis. *Transplantation International, 13*, 129–135.

Biller-Andorno, N. (2002). Gender imbalance in living organ donation. *Medicine, Health Care and Philosophy, 5*, 199–204.

Blumenthal, J.A., Babyak, M.A., Carney, R.M., Keefe, F.J., Davis, R.D., LaCaille, R.A., et al. (2006). *Journal of Consulting and Clinical Psychology, 74*(5), 535–544.

Bohachick, P., Reedeer, S., Taylor, M.V., & Anton, B.B. (2001). Psychosocial impact of heart transplantation on spouses. *Clinical Nursing Research, 10*(1), 6–25.

Bolkhir, A., Loiselle, M.M., Evon, D.M., & Hayashi, P.H. (2007). Depression in primary caregivers of patients listed for liver or kidney transplantation. *Progress in Transplantation, 17*(3), 193–198.

Boulware, L.E., Meoni, L.A., Fink, N.E., Parekh, R.S., Kao, W.H.L., Klag, M.J., et al. (2005). Preferences, knowledge, communication and patient-physician discussion of living kidney transplantation in African American families. *American Journal of Transplantation, 5*, 1503–1512.

Boulware, L.B., Ratner, L.E., Cooper, L.A., Sosa, J.A., LaVeist, T.A., & Powe, N.R. (2002a). Understanding disparities in donor behavior: Race and general differences in willingness to donate blood and cadaveric organs. *Medical Care, 40*, 85–95.

Boulware, L.E., Ratner, L.E., Sosa, J.A., Cooper, L.A., LaVeist, T.A., & Powe, N.R. (2002b). Determinants of willingness to donate living related and cadaveric organs: Identifying opportunities for intervention. *Transplantation, 73*(10), 1683–1691.

Boulware, L.E., Troll, M.U., Plantinga, L.C., & Powe, N.R. (2008). The association of state and national legislation with living kidney donation rates in the United States: A national study. *American Journal of Transplantation, 8*, 1451–1470.

Bowman, K.W., & Richard, S.A. (2003). Culture, brain death, and transplantation. *Progress in Transplantation, 13*(3), 211–217.

Breitbart, W., Gibson, C., & Tremblay, A. (2002). The delirium experience: Delirium recall and delirium-related distress in hospitalized patients with cancer, their spouse/caregivers, and their nurses. *Psychosomatics, 43*, 183–194.

Budiani-Saberi, D.A., & Delmonico, F.L. (2008). Organ trafficking and transplant tourism: A commentary on the global realities. *American Journal of Transplantation, 8*, 925–929.

Bunzel, B., & Laederach-Hofmann, K. (1999). Long-term effects of heart transplantation: The gap between physical performance and emotional well-being. *Scandinavian Journal of Rehabilitation Medicine, 31*, 214–222.

Bunzel, B., Laederach-Hofmann, K., Wieselthaler, G., Roethy, W., & Wolner E. (2007). Mechanical circulatory support as a bridge to heart transplantation: What remains? Long-term emotional sequelae in patients and spouses. *Journal of Heart & Lung Transplantation, 26*(4), 384–389.

Burker, E.J., Evon, D.M., Ascari, J.C., Loiselle, M.M., Finkel, J.B., & Mill, M.R. (2005a). Planning helps, behavioral disengagement does not: Coping and depression in the spouses of heart transplant candidates. *Clinical Transplantation, 19*, 653–658.

Burker, E.J., Evon, D.M., Marroquin Loiselle, M., Finkel, J.B., & Mill, M.R. (2005b). Coping predicts depression and disability in heart transplant candidates. *Journal of Psychosomatic Research, 59*(4), 215–222.

Butler, J.A., Roderick, P., Mullee, M., Mason, J.C., & Peveler, R.C. (2004). Frequency and impact of nonadherence to immunosuppressants after renal transplantation: A systematic review. *Transplantation, 77*(5), 769–776.

Callender, C.O., Hall, M.B., & Branch, D. (2001). An assessment of the effectiveness of the MOTTEP model for increasing donation rates and preventing the need for transplantation—Adult findings: Program years 1998 and 1999. *Seminars in Nephrology, 21*(4), 419–428.

Callender, C.O., Hall, M.B., & Miles, P.V. (2002). Increasing living donations: Expanding the National MOTTEP community grassroots model. *Transplantation Proceedings, 34*, 2563–2564.

Callender, C.O., Miles, P.V., & Hall, M.B. (2003). Experience with national minority organ tissue transplant education program in the United States. *Transplantation Proceedings, 35*, 1151–1152.

Chacko, R.C., Harper, R.G., Gotto, J., & Young, J. (1996). Psychiatric interview and psychometric predictors of cardiac transplant survival. *American Journal of Psychiatry, 153*, 1607–1612.

Chang, G., Antin, J.H., Orav, E.J., Randall, U., McGarigle, C., Behr, H.M. (1997). Substance abuse and bone marrow transplant. *American Journal of Drug and Alcohol Abuse, 23*, 301–308.

Childress, J.F., & Liverman, C.T. (Eds.) and the Committee on Increasing Rates of Organ Donation, Board on Health Sciences Policy, Institute of Medicine. (2006). *Organ donation. Opportunities for action*. Washington, DC: The National Academies Press.

Chisholm, M.A., Mulloy, L.L., Jagadeesan, M., & DiPiro, J.T. (2001). Impact of clinical pharmacy services on renal transplant patients' compliance with immunosuppressive medications. *Clinical Transplantation, 15*, 330–336.

Chisholm, M.A., Vollenweider, L.J., Mulloy, L.L., Jagadeesan, M., Wynn, J.J., Rogers, H.E., et al. (2000). Renal transplant patient compliance with free immunosuppressive medications. *Transplantation, 70*, 1240–1244.

Chlan, L., Snyder, M., Finkelstein, S., Hertz, M., Edin, C., Wielinski, C., & Dutta, A. (1998). Promoting adherence to an electronic home spirometry research program after lung transplantation. *Applied Nursing Research, 11*, 36–40.

Chowanec, G.D., & Binik, Y.M. (1989). End stage renal disease and the marital dyad: An empirical investigation. *Social Science & Medicine, 28*(9), 971–983.

Cialdini, R.B., Schaller, M., Houlihan, D., Arps, K., Fultz, J., & Beaman, A.L. (1987). Empathy-based helping: Is it selflessly selfishly motivated? *Journal of Personality and Social Psychology, 52*(4), 749–758.

Claar, R.L., Parekh, P.L., Palmer, S.M., Lacaille, R.A., Davis, R.D., Rowe, S.K., et al. (2005). Emotional distress and quality of life in caregivers of patients awaiting lung transplant. *Journal of Psychosomatic Research, 59*, 1–6.

Clarke, K.S., Klarenbach, S., Vlaicu, S., Yang, R.C., & Garg, A.X. (2006). The direct and indirect economic costs incurred by living kidney donors—A systematic review. *Nephrology Dialysis Transplantation, 21*, 1952–1960.

Clemens, K.K., Thiessen-Philbrook, H., Parikh, C.R., Yang, R.C., Karley, M.L., Boudville, N., et al. (2006). Psychosocial health of living kidney donors: A systematic review. *American Journal of Transplantation, 6*(12), 2965–2977.

Cohen, M., Katz, D., & Baruch, Y. (2007). Stress among the family caregivers of liver transplant recipients. *Progress in Transplantation, 17*(1), 48–53.

Corley, M.C., Keswick, R.K., Sergeant, C.C., & Scott, S. (2000). Attitude, self-image, and quality of life of living kidney donors. *Nephrology Nursing Journal, 27*(1), 43–52.

Corley, M.C., Westerberg, N., Elswick, R.K., Connell, D., Neil, J., Sneed, G., et al. (1998). Rationing organs using psychosocial and lifestyle criteria. *Research in Nursing and Health, 21*, 327–337.

Craven, J., & Farrow, S. (1993). *Surviving transplantation: A personal guide for organ transplant patients, their families, friends and caregivers*. Toronto: University of Toronto Press, 1993.

Csete, M. (2008). Gender issues in transplantation. *Anesthesia & Analgesia, 107*(1), 232–238.

Cupples, S.A., Dew, M.A., Grady, K.L., De Geest, S., Dobbels, F., Lanuza, D., et al. (2006). Report of the Psychosocial Outcomes Workgroup of the Nursing and Social Sciences Council of ISHLT. The present status of research on psychosocial outcomes in cardiothoracic transplantation: Review and recommendations for the field. *Journal of Heart & Lung Transplantation, 25*, 716–725.

De Bleser, L., Matteson, M., Dobbels, F., Russell, C., & De Geest, S. (2009). Interventions to improve medication-adherence after transplantation: A systematic review. *Transplant International, 22*(8), 780–797.

De Geest, S., Dobbels, F. Fluri, C., Paris, W., & Troosters, T. (2005). Adherence to the therapeutic regimen in heart, lung, and heart-lung transplant recipients. *Journal of Cardiovascular Nursing, 20*(5S), S88–S98.

DeJong, W., Franz, H.G., Wolf, S.M., Nathan, J., Payne, D., Reitsma, W., et al. (1998). Requesting organ donation: An interview study of donor and nondonors families. *American Journal of Critical Care, 7*, 13–23.

Delmonico, F.L. (2005). Commentary: The WHO resolution on human organ and tissue transplantation. *Transplantation, 79*(6), 639–640.

Delmonico, F.L., & Dew, M.A. (2007). Living donor kidney transplantation in a global environment. *Kidney International, 71*, 608–614.

Denhaerynck, K., Dobbels, F., Cleemput, I., Desmyttere, A., Schäfer-Keller, P., Schaub, S., et al. (2005). Prevalence, consequences and determinants of nonadherence in adult renal transplant patients: A literature review. *Transplantation International, 18*(10), 1121–1133.

Department of Health. (2007). *On the state of public health: Annual report of the Chief Medical Officer 2006*. Report No. 28175. London: Department of Health. Retrieved from http://www.dh.gov.uk/en/Publicationsandstatistics/Publications/AnnualReports/DH_076817.

DeVito Dabbs, A., Dew, M.A., Myers, B., Begey, A., Hawkins, R., Ren, D., et al. (2009). Evaluation of a hand-held, computer based intervention to promote early self-care behaviors after lung transplant. *Clinical Transplantation, 23*, 537–545.

DeVito Dabbs, A., Hoffman, L.A., Swigart, V., Happ, M.B., Dauber, J.H., McCurry, K.R., et al. (2004). Striving for normalcy: Symptoms and the threat of rejection after lung transplantation. *Social Science & Medicine, 59*, 1473–1484.

Dew, M.A. (1998). Psychiatric disorder in the context of physical illness. In B.P. Dohrenwend (Ed.), *Adversity, stress and psychopathology* (pp. 177–218). New York: Oxford University Press.

Dew, M.A., & DiMartini, A.F. (2005). Psychological disorders and distress after adult cardiothoracic transplantation. *Journal of Cardiovascular Nursing, 20*(5 Suppl.), S51–S66.

Dew, M.A., DiMartini, A.F., DeVito Dabbs, A., Myaskovsky, L., Steel, J., Unruh, M., et al. (2007a). Rates and risk factors for nonadherence to the medical regimen after adult solid organ transplantation. *Transplantation, 83*, 858–873.

Dew, M.A., DiMartini, A.F., DeVito Dabbs, A.J., Zomak, R., De Geest, S., Dobbels, F., et al. (2008a). Adherence to the medical regimen during the first two years after lung transplantation. *Transplantation, 85*(2), 193–202.

Dew, M.A., DiMartini, A.F., & Kormos, R.L. (2007b). Organ transplantation, Stress of. In: G. Fink (Ed.), *Encyclopedia of stress* Vol. 3 (2nd ed., 35–44). Oxford, UK: Academic Press (Elsevier).

Dew, M.A., DiMartini, A.F., Steel, J., DeVito Dabbs, A., Myaskovsky, L., Unruh, M., & Greenhouse, J. (2008b). Meta-analysis of risk for relapse to substance use after transplantation of the liver or other solid organs. *Liver Transplantation, 14*, 159–172.

Dew, M.A., Dunbar-Jacob, J., Switzer, G.E., DiMartini, A.F., Stilley, C., & Kormos, R.L. (2001a). Adherence to the medical regimen in transplantation. In: J.R. Rodrigue (Ed.), *Biopsychosocial perspectives on transplantation* (pp. 93–124). New York: Kluwer Academic/Plenum Publishers.

Dew, M.A., Goycoolea, J.M., Harris, R.C., Lee, A., Zomak, R., Dunbar-Jacob, J., et al. (2004a). An internet-based intervention to improve psychosocial outcomes in heart transplant recipients and family caregivers: Development and evaluation. *Journal of Heart & Lung Transplantation, 23*, 745–758.

Dew, M.A., Goycoolea, J.M., Stukas, A.A., Switzer, G.E., Simmons, R.G., Roth, L.H., et al. (1998). Temporal profiles of physical health in family members of heart transplant recipients: Predictors of health change during caregiving. *Health Psychology, 17*(2), 138–151.

Dew, M.A., Goycoolea, J.M., Switzer, G.E., & Allen, A.S. (2000a). Quality of life in organ transplantation: Effects on adult recipients and their families. In: P.T. Trzepacz, & A. DiMartini (Eds.), *The transplant patient: Biological, psychiatric and ethical issues in organ transplantation* (pp. 67–145). New York: Cambridge University Press.

Dew, M.A., Jacobs, C.L., Jowsey, S.G., et al. (2007c). Guidelines for the psychosocial evaluation of living unrelated kidney donors in the United States. *American Journal of Transplantation, 7*(5), 1047–1054.

Dew, M.A., Kormos, R.L., DiMartini, A.F., Switzer, G.E., Schulberg, H.C., Roth, L.H., et al. (2001b). Prevalence and risk of depression and anxiety-related disorders during the first three years after heart transplantation. *Psychosomatics, 42*(4), 300–313.

Dew, M.A., Kormos, R.L., Roth, L.H., Murali, S., DiMartini, A., & Griffith, B.P. (1999). Early post-transplant medical compliance and mental health predict physical morbidity and mortality one to three years after heart transplantation. *Journal of Heart & Lung Transplantation, 18*(6), 549–562.

Dew, M.A., Manzetti, J., Goycoolea, J.R., Lee, A., Zomak, R., Venzak, J.L., et al. (2002). Psychosocial aspects of transplantation. In: S.L. Smith, & L. Ohler (Eds.), *Organ Transplantation: Concepts, Issues, Practice and Outcomes*, Chapter 8. New York: Medscape Transplantation, WebMD, Inc. Retrieved from http://www.medscape.com/viewpublication/704_about1.

Dew, M.A., Martire, L.M., & Hall, M. (2003). Depression: Epidemiology and risk factors. In: M.E. Thase, & J. Potokar

(Eds.), *Advances in the management and treatment of depression* (pp. 1–39). London: Martin Dunitz/Taylor & Francis.

Dew, M.A., Myaskovsky, L., DiMartini, A.F., Switzer, G.E., Schulberg, H.C., & Kormos, R.L. (2004b). Onset, timing and risk for depression and anxiety in family caregivers to heart transplant recipients. *Psychological Medicine, 34*, 1065–1082.

Dew, M.A., Myaskovsky, L., Switzer, G.E., DiMartini, A.F., Schulberg, H.C., & Kormos, R.L. (2005). Profiles and predictors of the course of psychological distress across four years after heart transplantation. *Psychological Medicine, 35*, 1215–1227.

Dew, M.A., Roth, L.H., Schulberg, H.C., Simmons, R.G., Kormos, R.L., Trzepacz, P.T., & Griffith, B.P. (1996a). Prevalence and predictors of depression and anxiety-related disorders during the year after heart transplantation. *General Hospital Psychiatry, 18*(6), 48S–61S.

Dew, M.A., Roth, L.H., Thompson, M.E., Kormos, R.L., & Griffith, B.P. (1996b). Medical compliance and its predictors in the first year after heart transplantation. *Journal of Heart & Lung Transplantation, 15*, 631–645.

Dew, M.A., Simmons, R.G., Roth, L.H., Schulberg, H.C., Thompson, M.E., Armitage, J.M., & Griffith, B.P. (1994). Psychosocial predictors of vulnerability to distress in the year following heart transplantation. *Psychological Medicine, 24*, 929–945.

Dew, M.A., Switzer, G.E., DiMartini, A.F., Matukaitis, J., Fitzgerald, M.G., & Kormos, R.L. (2000b). Psychosocial assessments and outcomes in organ transplantation. *Progress in Transplantation, 10*, 239–261.

Dew, M.A., Switzer, G.E., DiMartini, A.F., Myaskovsky, L., & Crowley-Matoka, M. (2007d). Psychosocial aspects of living organ donation. In H.P. Tan, A. Marcos, & R. Shapiro (Eds.), *Living donor transplantation* (pp. 7–26). New York: Informa Healthcare.

Dew, M.A., Switzer, G.E., Goycoolea, J.M., Allen, A., DiMartini, A., Kormos, R.L., et al. (1997). Does transplantation produce quality of life benefits? A quantitative review of the literature. *Transplantation, 64*(9), 1261–1273.

DiMartini, A., Dew, M.A., Kormos, R., McCurry, K., & Fontes, P. (2007). Posttraumatic stress disorder caused by hallucinations and delusions experienced in delirium. *Psychosomatics, 48*(5), 436–439.

DiMartini, A., Porterfield, K., Fitzgerald, M.G., Dew, M.A., Switzer, G.E., Marcos, A., et al. (2008). Psychological profile of living liver donors and post-donation outcomes. In W. Weimar, M.A. Bos, & J.J. van Busschbach (Eds.), *Organ transplantation: Ethical, legal and psychosocial aspects. Towards a common European policy* (pp. 216–220). Lengerich, Germany: Pabst Science Publishers.

DiMartini, A.F., Dew, M.A., & Crone, C.C. (2009). Organ transplantation. In B.J. Sadock, V.A. Sadock, & P. Ruiz (Eds.), *Kaplan and Sadock's comprehensive textbook of psychiatry* Vol. 2 (9th ed., pp. 2441–2456). Philadelphia: Lippincott Williams & Wilkins.

DiMartini, A.F., Dew, M.A., & Trzepacz, P.T. (2005). Organ transplantation. In J.L. Levenson (Ed.), *The American Psychiatric Publishing textbook of psychosomatic medicine* (pp. 675–700). Washington, DC: The American Psychiatric Press, Inc.

DiMartini, A., Weinrieb, R., & Fireman, M. (2002). Liver transplantation in patients with alcohol and other substance use disorders. *Psychiatric Clinics of North America, 25*(1), 195–209.

DiMatteo, M.R., Lepper, H.S, & Croghan, T.W. (2000). Depression is a risk factor for noncompliance with medical treatment: Meta-analysis of the effects of anxiety and depression on patient adherence. *Archives of Internal Medicine, 160*(14), 2101–2107.

Dobbels, F., De Geest, S., Cleemput, I., Fischler, B., Kesteloot, K., Vanhaecke, J., et al. (2001). Psychosocial and behavioral selection criteria for solid organ transplantation. *Progress in Transplantation, 11*(2), 121–132.

Dobbels, F., De Geest, S., Martin, S., Cleemput, J., Droogne, W., & Vanhaecke, J. (2004). Prevalence and correlates of depression symptoms at 10 years after heart transplantation: Continuous attention required. *Transplant International, 17*(8), 424–431.

Dobbels, F., Vanhaecke, J., Desmyttere, A., Dupont, L., Nevins, F., & De Geest, S. (2005). Prevalence and correlates of self-reported pretransplant nonadherence with medication in heart, liver, and lung transplant candidates. *Transplantation, 79*, 1588–1595.

Dobbels, F., Vanhaecke, J., Nevens, F., Dupont, L., Verleden, G., Van Hees, D., et al. (2007). Liver versus cardiothoracic transplant candidates and their pretransplant psychosocial and behavioral risk profiles: Good neighbors or complete strangers? *Transplant International, 20*, 1020–1030.

Dobbels, F., Verleden, G., Dupont, L., Vanhaecke, J., & De Geest, S. (2006). To transplant or not? The importance of psychosocial and behavioural factors before lung transplantation. *Chronic Respiratory Disease, 3*, 39–47.

Dohrenwend, B.P. (Ed.) (1998). *Adversity, stress, and psychopathology.* New York: Oxford University Press.

Dohrenwend, B.P. (2000). The role of adversity and stress in psychopathology: Some evidence and its implications for theory and research. *Journal of Health and Social Behavior, 41*, 1–19.

Dumas-Hicks, D.H. (2003). Immunosuppression. In S.A. Cupples, & L. Ohler (Eds.), *Transplantation nursing secrets* (pp. 67–74). Philadelphia, PA: Hanley & Belfus, Inc.

Epstein, A.M., Ayanian, J.Z., Keogh, J.H., Noonan, S.J., Armistead, N., Cleary, P.D., et al. (2000). Racial disparities in access to renal transplantation. *New England Journal of Medicine, 343*(21), 1537–1544.

Erim, Y., Beckmann, M., Valentin-Gamazo, C., Malago, M., Frilling, A., Schlaak, J.F., et al. (2006). Quality of life and psychiatric complications after adult living donor liver transplantation. *Liver Transplantation, 12*, 1782–1790.

Ethics Committee of the Transplantation Society. (2004). The consensus statement of the Amsterdam Forum on the care of the live kidney donor. *Transplantation, 78*(4), 491–492.

Evangelista, L.S., Doering, L.V., Dracup, K., Vassilakis, M.E., & Kobashigawa, J. (2003). Hope, mood states and quality of life in female heart transplant recipients. *Journal of Heart & Lung Transplantation, 22*, 681–686.

Evangelista, L.S., Moser, D., Dracup, K., Doering, L., & Kobashigawa, J. (2004). Functional status and perceived control influence quality of life in female heart transplant recipients. *Journal of Heart & Lung Transplantation, 23*, 360–367.

Evans, D., Charney, D.S., Lewis, L., Golden, R.N., Gorman, J.M., Krishnan, K.R., et al. (2005). Mood disorders in the medically ill: Scientific review and recommendations. *Biological Psychiatry, 58*, 175–189.

Evon, D.M., Burker, E.J., Sedway, J.A., Cicale, R., Davis, K., & Egan, T. (2005). Tobacco and alcohol use in lung transplant candidates and recipients. *Clinical Transplantation, 19*, 207–214.

Fahrenwald, N.L., & Stabnow, W. (2005). Sociocultural perspective on organ and tissue donation among reservation-dwelling American Indian adults. *Ethnicity & Health, 10*(4), 341–354.

Fahrenwald, N.L., Belitz, C., Keckler, A., & Sharma, M. (2007). Sharing the gift of life: An intervention to increase organ and tissue donation for American Indians. *Progress in Transplantation, 17*(4), 281–287.

Faulk, J.S. (1999). Peer-to-peer transplant mentor program: The San Diego experience. *Transplantation Proceedings, 31*(4A) 75S.

Feeley, T.H. (2007). College students' knowledge, attitudes, and behaviors regarding organ donation: An integrated review of the literature. *Journal of Applied Social Psychology, 37*(2), 243–271.

Fellner, C.H., & Schwartz, S.H. (1971). Altruism in disrepute. Medical versus public attitudes toward the living organ donor. *New England Journal of Medicine, 284*(11), 582–585.

Fehrman-Ekholm, I., Brink, B., Ericsson, C., Elinder, C.G, Dunér, F., & Lundgren, G. (2000). Kidney donors don't regret: Follow-up of 370 donors in Stockholm since 1964. *Transplantation, 69*(10), 2067–2071.

Fenton, W.S., & Stover, E.S. (2006). Mood disorders: Cardiovascular and diabetes comorbidity. *Current Opinion in Psychiatry, 19*, 421–427.

Fine, R.N., Becker, Y., De Geest, S., Eisen, H., Ettenger, R., Evans, R., et al. (2009). Nonadherence consensus conference summary report. *American Journal of Transplantation, 9*(1), 35–41.

Franklin, P.M., & Crombie, A.K. (2003). Live related renal transplantation: Psychological, social, and cultural issues. *Transplantation, 76*(8), 1247–1252.

Frates, J., Rohrer, G.G., & Thomas D. (2006). Promoting organ donation to Hispanics: The role of the media and medicine. *Journal of Health Communication, 11*(7), 683–698.

Freidman, E. A, & Friedman, A.L. (2006). Payment for donor kidneys: Pros and cons. *Kidney International, 69*, 960–962.

Gallup Organization. (2005). *2005 national survey of organ and tissue donation attitudes and behaviors.* US Department of Health and Human Services. Retrieved from http://www.organdonor.gov/survey2005/index.shtm.

Giessing, M., Reuter, S., Schönberger, B., Deger, S., Tuerk, I., Hirte, I., et al. (2004). Quality of life of living kidney donors in Germany: A survey with the Validated Short Form-36 and Giessen Subjective Complaints List-24 questionnaires. *Transplantation, 78*(6), 846–872.

Gish, R.G., Lee A., Brooks, L., Leung, J., Lau, J.Y., & Moore, D.H. (2001). Long-term follow-up of patients diagnosed with alcohol dependence or alcohol abuse who were evaluated for liver transplantation. *Liver Transplantation, 7*(7), 581–587.

Goedecke, P.A., Winsett, R.P., Martin, J.C., Hathaway, D.K., & Gaber, A.O. (2001). Development of a web site for transplant patient education. *Progress in Transplantation, 11*(3), 208–213.

Goetzmann, L., Klaghofer, R., Wagner-Huber, R., Halter, J., Boehler, A., Muellhaupt, B., et al. (2007). Psychosocial vulnerability predicts psychosocial outcome after an organ transplant: Results of a prospective study with lung, liver, and bone-marrow patients. *Journal of Psychosomatic Research, 62*(1), 93–100.

Gourlay, W.A., Stothers, L., & Liu, L. (2005). Attitudes and predictive factors for live kidney donation in British Columbia: A comparison of recipients and wait-list patients. *Canadian Journal of Urology, 12*, 2511–2520.

Grady, K.L., Jalowiec, A., & White-Williams, C. (1998). Patient compliance at one year and two years after heart transplantation. *Journal of Heart & Lung Transplantation, 17,* 383–394.

Grady, K.L., Naftel, D.C., Kobashigawa, J., Chait, J., Young, J.B., Pelegrin, D., et al. (2007). Patterns and predictors of quality of life at 5 to 10 years after heart transplantation. *Journal of Heart & Lung Transplantation, 26*(5), 535–543.

Gross, C.R., Kreitzer, J.J., Russas, V., Treesak, C., Frazier, P.A., & Hertz, M.I. (2004). Mindfulness meditation to reduce symptoms after organ transplant: A pilot study. *Advances in Mind-Body Medicine, 20*(2), 20–29.

Guadagnoli, E., McNamara P., Evanisko, M.J., Beasley, C., Callender, C.O., & Poretsky, A. (1999). The influence of race on approaching families for organ donation and their decision to donate. *American Journal of Public Health, 89,* 244–247.

Hardstaff, R., Green, K., & Talbot, D. (2003). Measurement of compliance posttransplantation–The results of a 12-month study using electronic monitoring. *Transplantation Proceedings, 35,* 796–797.

Hanto, R.L., Reitsma, W., & Delmonico, F.L. (2008). The development of a successful multiregional kidney paired donation program. *Transplantation, 86*(12), 1744–1748.

Harrison, T.R., Morgan, S.E., & Di Corcia, M.J. (2008). Effects of information, education, and communication training about organ donation for gatekeepers: Clerks at the Department of Motor Vehicles and organ donor registries. *Progress in Transplantation, 18*(4), 301–309.

Haustein, S.V., & Sellers, M.T. (2004). Factors associated with (un)willingness to be an organ donor: Importance of public exposure and knowledge. *Clinical Transplantation, 18*(2), 193–200.

Havik, O.E., Sivertsen, B., Relbo, A., Hellesvik, M., Grov, I., Geiran, O., et al. (2007). Depressive symptoms and all-cause mortality after heart transplantation. *Transplantation, 84,* 97–103.

Hayashi, A., Noma, S., Uehara, M., Kuwabara, H., Tanaka, S., Furuno, Y., et al. (2007). Relevant factors to psychological status of donors before living-related liver transplantation. *Transplantation, 84*(10), 1255–1261.

Hays, R., & Gladding, H. (2007). Helping helpers: A living donor mentor program. *Nephrology News & Issues, 21*(5), 41–51.

Hays, R., & Waterman, A.D. (2008). Improving preemptive transplant education to increase living donation rates: Reaching patients earlier in their disease adjustment process. *Progress in Transplantation, 18,* 251–256.

Heck, G., Schweitzer, J., & Seidel-Wiesel, M. (2004). Psychological effects of living related kidney transplantation–Risks and chances. *Clinical Transplantation, 18,* 716–721.

Henderson, A.J.Z., Landolt, M.A., McDonald, M.F., Barrable, W.M., Soos, J.G., Gourlay, W., et al. (2003). The living anonymous kidney donor: Lunatic or saint? *American Journal of Transplantation, 3*(2), 203–213.

Hodges, B, Craven, J., & Littlefield, C. (1995). Bibliotherapy for psychosocial distress in lung transplant patients and their families. *Psychosomatics, 36*(4), 360–368.

Iasi, M.S., Vieira, A., Anez, C.I., Trindade, R., Codovani, N.T., Favero S.S., et al. (2003). Recurrence of alcohol ingestion in liver transplantation candidates. *Transplantation Proceedings, 35*(3), 1123–1124.

Ingelfinger, J.R. (2005). Risks and benefits to the living donor. *New England Journal of Medicine, 353*(5), 447–449.

Jacobs, C., Johnson, E., Anderson, K., Gillingham, K., & Matas, A. (1998). Kidney transplants from living donors: How donation affects family dynamics. *Advances in Renal Replacement Therapy, 5*(2), 89–97.

Jacobs, C.L., Roman, D., Garvey, C., Kahn, J., & Matas, A.J. (2004). Twenty-two nondirected kidney donors: An update on a single center's experience. *American Journal of Transplantation, 4*(7), 1110–1116.

Jeffres, L.W., Carroll, J.A., Rubenking, B.E., & Amschlinger, J. (2008). Communication as a predictor of willingness to donate one's organs: An addition to the theory of reasoned action. *Progress in Transplantation, 18*(4), 257–262.

Jones, C.M., Griffiths, R.D., Humphris, G., & Skirrow, P.M. (2001). Memory, delusions, and the development of acute posttraumatic stress disorder-related symptoms after intensive care. *Critical Care Medicine, 29,* 573–580.

Jordan, J., Sann, U., Janton, A., Gossmann, J., Kramer, W., Kachel, H.G., et al. (2004). Living kidney donors' long-term psychological status and health behavior after nephrectomy–A retrospective study. *Journal of Nephrology, 17*(5), 728–735.

Julapalli, V.R., Kramer, J.R., & El-Serag, H.B. (2005). Evaluation for liver transplantation: Adherence to AASLD referral guidelines in a large veterans affairs center. *Liver Transplantation, 11*(11), 1370–1378.

Karliova, M., Malago, M., Valentin-Gamazo, C., Reimer, J., Treichel, U., & Franke, G.H. (2002). Living-related liver transplantation from the view of the donor: A 1-year follow-up survey. *Transplantation, 73*(11), 1799–1804.

Kasiske, B.L., Snyder, J.J., Skeans, M.A., Tuomari, A.V., Maclean, J.R., & Israni, A.K. (2008). The geography of kidney transplantation in the United States. *American Journal of Transplantation, 8*(3), 647–657.

Kessler, R.C. (1997). The effects of stressful life events on depression. *Annual Review of Psychology, 48,* 191–214.

Kessler, R.C., Michelson, K.D., & William, D.R. (1999). The prevalence, distribution and mental health correlates of discrimination in the United States. *Journal of Social Behavior, 40,* 208–230.

Kim-Schluger, L., Florman, S.S., Schiano, T., Schiano, T., O'Rourke, M., Gagliardi, R., et al. (2002). Quality of life after lobectomy for adult liver transplantation. *Transplantation, 73*(10), 1593–1597.

Klassen, A.C., Hall, A.G., Saksvig, B, Curbow, B., & Klassen, D.K. (2002). Relationship between patients' perceptions of disadvantage and discrimination and listing for kidney transplantation. *American Journal of Public Health, 22*(5), 811–817.

Klein, A., Otto, G., & Kramer, I. (2009). Impact of a pharmaceutical care program on liver transplant patients' compliance with immunosuppressive medication: A prospective, randomized, controlled trial using electronic monitoring. *Transplantation, 87*(6), 839–847.

Kotlyar, D.S., Burke, A., Campbell, M.S., & Weinrieb, R.M. (2008). A critical review of candidacy for orthotopic liver transplantation in alcoholic liver disease. *American Journal of Gastroenterology, 103,* 734–743.

Krakauer, H., Bailey, R.C., & Lin, M.J.Y. (2004). Beyond survival: The burden of disease in decision making in organ transplantation. *American Journal of Transplantation, 4,* 1555–1561.

Kranenburg, L.W., Richards, M., Zuidema, W.C., Weimar, W., Hilhorst, M.T., Ijzermans, J.N.M., et al. (2009a). Avoiding the issue: Patients' (non)communication with potential living kidney donors. *Patient Education and Counseling, 74,* 39–44.

Kranenburg, L.W., Zuidema, W., Weimar, W., Hilhorst, M., Ijzermans, J., Passchier J., et al. (2009b). Strategies to advance living kidney donation: A single center's experience. *Progress in Transplantation, 19,* 71–75.

Kravitz, R.L., & Melnikow, J. (2004). Medical adherence research: Time for a change in direction? *Medical Care, 42*(3), 197–199.

Kreiger, N. (2000). Discrimination and health. In L.P. Berkman, & I. Kawachi (Eds.). *Social epidemiology* (pp. 36–75). NY: Oxford University Press Inc.

Kugler, J., Tenderich, G., Stahlhut, P., Posival, H., Körner, M.M., Körfer, R., et al. (1994). Emotional adjustment and perceived locus of control in heart transplant patients. *Journal of Psychosomatic Research, 38,* 403–408.

Kurz, R.S., Scharff, D.P., Terry, T., Alexander, S., & Waterman, A. (2007). Factors influencing organ donation decisions by African Americans. *Medical Care Research and Review, 64*(5), 475–517.

Lam, W.A., & McCullough, L.B. (2000). Influence of religious and spiritual values on the willingness of Chinese-Americans to donate organs for transplantation. *Clinical Transplantation, 14,* 449–456.

Landolt, M.A., Henderson, A.J.Z., Barrable, W.M., Greenwood, S.D., McDonald, M.F., Soos, J.G., et al. (2001). Living anonymous kidney donation: What does the public think? *Transplantation, 71*(11), 1690–1696.

Larson, A.M., & Curtis, J.R. (2006). Integrating palliative care for liver transplant candidates: "Too well for transplant, too sick for life." *Journal of the American Medical Association, 295*(18), 2168–2176.

Lederer, D.J., Benn, E.K., Barr, R.G., Wilt, J.S., Reilly, G., Sonett, J.R., et al. (2008). Racial differences in waiting list outcomes in chronic obstructive pulmonary disease. *American Journal of Respiratory and Critical Care Medicine, 177*(4), 450–454.

Leedham, B., Meyerowitz, B.E., Muirhead, J., & Frist, W.H. (1995). Positive expectations predict health after heart transplantation. *Health Psychology, 14,* 74–79.

Le Melle, S.M., & Entelis, C. (2005). Heart transplant in a young man with schizophrenia. *American Journal of Psychiatry, 162*(3), 453–457.

Lennerling, A., Forsberg, A., Nyberg, G. (2003). Becoming a living kidney donor. *Transplantation, 76,* 1243–1247.

Leonard, J., Eastham, R., & Dark, J. (2000). Heart and heart-lung transplantation in Down's syndrome. The lack of supportive evidence means each case must be carefully assessed. *British Medical Journal, 320*(7238), 816–817.

Levenson, J.L., & Olbrisch, M.E. (1993). Psychosocial evaluation of organ transplant candidates: A comparative survey of process, criteria, and outcomes in heart, liver, and kidney transplantation. *Psychosomatics, 34,* 314–323.

Levenson, J.L., & Olbrisch, M.E. (2002). Psychosocial evaluation of organ transplant candidates: Comparative survey of process criteria and outcomes 1989 and 2000. *Psychosomatics, 43,* 167–168.

Lim, J.W., & Zebrack, B. (2004). Caring for family members with chronic physical illness: A critical review of caregiver literature. *Health and Quality of Life Outcomes 2,* 50. Retrieved from http://www.hqlo.com/content/2/1/50.

Linyear, A.S., & Tartaglia, A. (1999). Family communication coordination: A program to increase organ donation. *Journal of Transplant Coordination, 9*(3), 165–174.

Lisson, G.L., Rodrigue, J.R., Reed, A.I., & Nelson, D.R. (2005). A brief psychological intervention to improve adherence following transplantation. *Annals of Transplantation, 10*(1), 52–57.

Littlefield, C., Abbey, S., Fiducia, D., Cardella, C., Greig, P., Levy, G., et al. (1996). Quality of life following transplantation of the heart, liver, and lungs. *General Hospital Psychiatry, 18,* 36S–47S.

Liu, L.U., Schiano, T.D., Lau, N., O'Rourke, M., Min, A.D., Sigal, S.H., et al. (2003). Survival and risk of recidivism in methadone-dependent patients undergoing liver transplantation. *American Journal of Transplantation, 3,* 1273–1277.

Liu, W.J., & Zaki, M. (2004). Medication compliance among renal transplant patients: A Hospital Kuala Lumpur experience. *Medical Journal of Malaysia, 59,* 649–659.

Lunsford, S.L., Simpson, K.S., Chavin, K.D., Mensching, K.J., Miles, L.G., Shilling, L.M., et al. (2007). Can family attributes explain the racial disparity in living kidney donation? *Transplantation Proceedings, 39*(5), 1376–1380.

Lurie, S., Shemesh, E., Sheiner, P.A., Emre, S., Tindle, H.L., Melchionna, L., et al. (2000). Nonadherence in pediatric liver transplant recipients—An assessment of risk factors and natural history. *Pediatric Transplantation, 4*(3), 200–206.

Martens, M.A., Jones, L., & Reiss, S. (2006). Organ transplantation, organ donation and mental retardation. *Pediatric Transplantation, 10,* 658–664.

Martinelli, V., Fusar-Poli, P., Emanuele, E., Kiersy, C., Campana, C., Barale, F., et al. (2007). Getting old with a new heart: Impact of age on depression and quality of life in long-term heart transplant recipients. *Journal of Heart & Lung Transplantation, 26*(5), 544–548.

Matesanz, R. (2003). Factors influencing the adaptation of the Spanish model of organ donation. *Transplantation International, 16,* 736–741.

McKneally, M.F., & Sade, R.M. (2003). The prisoner dilemma: Should convicted felons have the same access to heart transplantation as ordinary citizens? Opposing views. *The Journal of Thoracic and Cardiovascular Surgery, 125*(3), 451–453.

Meltzer, L.J., & Rodrigue, J.R. (2001). Psychological distress in caregivers of liver and lung transplant candidates. *Journal of Clinical Psychology in Medical Settings, 8*(3), 173–180.

Merion, R.M., Barnes, A.D., Lin, M., Ashby, V.B., McBride, V., Ortiz-Rios, E., et al. (2008). Transplants in foreign countries among patients removed from the US transplant waiting list. *American Journal of Transplantation, 8,* 988–996.

Montgomery, S.A., & Kasper, S. (1998). Side effects, dropouts from treatment and cost consequences. *International Clinical Psychopharmacology, 13*(S2), S1–S5.

Morgan, S.E., Miller, J.K., & Arasaratnam, L.A. (2003). Similarities and differences between African Americans' and European Americans' attitudes, knowledge, and willingness to communicate about organ donation. *Journal of Applied Social Psychology, 33,* 693–715.

Morelon, E., Berthoux, F., Brun-Strang, C., Flor, S., & Volle, R. (2005). Partners' concerns, needs and expectations in ESRD: Results of the CODIT Study. *Nephrology Dialysis Transplantation, 20*(8), 1670–1675.

Moss, A.H., & Siegler, J. (1991). Should alcoholics compete equally for liver transplantation? *Journal of the American Medical Association, 265,* 1295–1298.

Moylan, C.A., Brady, C.W., Johnson, J.L., Smith, A.D., Tuttle-Newhall, J.E., & Muir, A.J. (2008). Disparities in liver transplantation before and after introduction of the MELD score. *Journal of the American Medical Association, 300*(20), 2371–2378.

Myaskovsky, L., Dew, M.A., Switzer, G.E., Hall, M., Kormos, R.L., Goycoolea, J.M., et al. (2003). Avoidant coping with health problems is related to poorer quality of life among lung transplant candidates. *Progress in Transplantation, 13*(3), 183–192.

Myaskovsky, L., Dew, M.A., Switzer, G.E., McNulty, M.L., DiMartini, A.F., & McCurry, K.R. (2005). Quality of life and coping strategies among lung transplant candidates and their family caregivers. *Social Science & Medicine, 60*, 2321–2332.

Myaskovsky, L., Switzer, G.E., Crowley-Matoka, M., Unruh, M., DiMartini, A.F., & Dew, M.A. (2007). Psychosocial factors associated with ethnic differences in transplantation. *Current Opinion in Organ Transplantation, 12*, 182–187.

Napolitano, M.A., Babyak, M.A., Palmer, S., Tapson, V., Davis, R.D., Blumenthal, J.A., et al. (2002). Effects of a telephone-based psychosocial intervention for patients awaiting lung transplantation. *Chest, 122*(4), 1176–1184.

Neuhaus, T.J., Wartmann, M., Weber, M., Landolt, M.A., Laube, G.F., & Kemper, M.J. (2005). Psychosocial impact of living-related kidney transplantation on donors and partners. *Pediatric Nephrology, 20*, 205–209.

Nevins, T.E., Kruse, L., Skeans, M.A., & Thomas, W. (2001). The natural history of azathioprine compliance after renal transplantation. *Kidney International, 60*(4), 1565–1570.

Nguyen, G.C., Segev, D.L., & Thuluvath, P.J. (2007). Racial disparities in the management of hospitalized patients with cirrhosis and complications of portal hypertension: A national study. *Hepatology, 45*, 1282–1289.

Nickel, R., Wunsch A., Egle, U.T., Lohse, A.W., & Otto, G. (2002). The relevance of anxiety, depression, and coping in patients after liver transplantation. *Liver Transplantation, 8*(1), 63–71.

Olbrisch, M.E., Benedict, S.M., Ashe, K., & Levenson, J.L. (2002). Psychological assessment and care of organ transplant patients. *Journal of Consulting and Clinical Psychology, 76*(3), 771–783.

Olbrisch M.E., Benedict, S.J., Haller, D.L., & Levenson, J.L. (2001). Psychosocial assessment of living organ donors: Clinical and ethical considerations. *Progress in Transplantation, 11*(1), 40–49.

Orentlicher, D. (1996). Psychosocial assessment of organ transplant candidates and the Americans with Disabilities Act. *General Hospital Psychiatry, 18*(6 Suppl.), 5S–12S.

Orentlicher, D. (2009). Presumed consent to organ donation: Its rise and fall in the United States. *Rutgers Law Review, 61*(2), 295–331.

Organ Procurement and Transplantation Network/United Network for Organ Sharing Ethics Committee (2007). *Ethics Committee position statement regarding convicted criminals and transplant evaluation*. US Department of Health and Human Services, Washington, DC. Retrieved from http://optn.transplant.hrsa.gov/resources/bioethics.asp?index=3.

Organ Procurement and Transplantation Network/United Network for Organ Sharing (2009). *Policies*. US Department of Health and Human Services, Washington, DC. Retrieved from http://optn.transplant.hrsa.gov/policiesAndBylaws/policies.asp.

Organ Procurement and Transplantation Network and the Scientific Registry of Transplant Recipients (2009). *Data Tables*. Department of Health and Human Services, Health Resources and Services Administration, Healthcare Systems Bureau, Division of Transplantation, Rockville, MD; United Network for Organ Sharing, Richmond, VA; University Renal Research and Education Association, Ann Arbor, MI. Retrieved from http://www.optn.transplant.hrsa.gov.

Organ Procurement and Transplantation Network and the Scientific Registry of Transplant Recipients (2008). *2008 Annual Report, Transplant Data 1998–2007*. Department of Health and Human Services, Health Resources and Services Administration, Healthcare Systems Bureau, Division of Transplantation, Rockville, MD; United Network for Organ Sharing, Richmond, VA; University Renal Research and Education Association, Ann Arbor, MI. Retrieved from http:www.ustransplant.org/annual_report/current/default.htm, or http://optn.transplant.hrsa.gov/data/annualreport.asp.

Ormel, J., & De Jong, A. (1999). On vulnerability to common mental disorders: An evidence-based plea for a developmental perspective. In M. Tansella, & G. Thornicroft (Eds.), *Common mental disorders in primary care. Essays in honour of Sir David Goldberg* (pp. 34–52). London: Routledge.

Orr, R.D., Johnston, J.K., Ashwal, S., & Bailey, L.L. (2000). Should children with severe cognitive impairment receive solid organ transplants? *Journal of Clinical Ethics, 11*(3), 219–229.

Owen, J.E., Bonds, C.L., & Wellisch, D.K. (2006). Psychiatric evaluations of heart transplant candidates: Predicting post-transplant hospitalizations, rejection episodes, and survival. *Psychosomatics, 47*(3), 213–222.

Ozminkowski, R.J., White, A.J., Hassol, A., & Murphy, M. (1997). Minimizing race disparity regarding receipt of a cadaver kidney transplant. *American Journal of Kidney Diseases, 30*, 749–759.

Pageaux, G.P., Michel, J., Coste, V., Perney, P., Possoz, P., Perrigault, P.F., et al. (1999). Alcoholic cirrhosis is a good indication for liver transplantation, even for cases of recidivism. *Gut, 45*, 421–426.

Papachristou, C., Walter, M., Dietrick, K., Danzer, G., Klupp, J., Klapp, B.F., et al. (2004). Motivation for living-donor liver transplantation from the donor's perspective: An in-depth qualitative research study. *Transplantation, 78*, 1506–1514.

Parekh, P.I., Blumenthal, J.A., Babyak, M.A., Merrill, K., Carney, R.M., Davis, R.D., et al. (2003). Psychiatric disorder and quality of life in patients awaiting lung transplantation. *Chest, 124*, 1683–1688.

Paris, W., Miller, R., Hille, C., Nour, B., & Griggs, J. (2005). Pedophiles and stalkers as transplant candidates: One program's experience. *Progress in Transplantation, 15*(4), 323–328.

Participants in the International Summit on Transplant Tourism and Organ Trafficking. (2008). The Declaration of Istanbul on organ trafficking and transplant tourism. *Transplantation, 86*(8), 1013–1018.

Penner, L.A., Dovidio, J.F., Piliavin, J.A., & Shroeder, D.A. (2005). Prosocial behavior: Multilevel perspectives. *Annual Review of Psychology, 56*, 365–392.

Peters, T.G., Repper, S.M., Jones, K.W., Walker, G.W., Vincent, M., & Hunter, R.D. (2000). Living kidney donation: Recovery and return to activities of daily living. *Clinical Transplantation, 14*, 433–438.

Pham, H., & Spigner, C. (2004). Knowledge and opinions about organ donation and transplantation among Vietnamese Americans in Seattle, Washington: A pilot study. *Clinical Transplantation, 18*(6), 707–715.

Piccoli, G.B., Soragna, G., Putaggio, S., Mezza, E., Burdese, J., Vespertino, E., et al. (2006). Efficacy of an educational programme for secondary school students on opinions of renal transplantation and organ donation: A randomized controlled trial. *Nephrology Dialysis Transplantation, 21*, 499–509.

Piliavin, J.A., & Callero, P.L. (1991). *Giving blood: The development of an altruistic identity.* Baltimore, MD: Johns Hopkins University Press.

Pradel, F.G., Limcangco, J.R., Mullins, C.D., & Bartlett, S.J. (2003). Patients' attitudes about living donor transplantation and living donor nephrectomy. *American Journal of Kidney Diseases, 41,* 849–858.

Pruett, T.L., Tibell, A., Alabdulkareem, A., Bhandari, M., Cronin, D.C., Dew, M.A., et al. (2006).The ethics statement of the Vancouver Forum on the live lung, liver, pancreas, and intestine donor. *Transplantation, 81*(10), 1386–1387.

Quinn, M.T., Alexander, G.C., Hollingsworth, D., O'Connor, K.G., & Meltzer, D. for the Corporate Contributions for Life Consortium. (2006). Design and evaluation of a workplace intervention to promote organ donation. *Progress in Transplantation, 16,* 253–259.

Radecki, C.M., & Jaccard, J. (1999). Signing an organ donation letter: The prediction of behavior from behavioral intentions. *Journal of Applied Social Psychology, 29,* 1833–1853.

Reese, P.P., Shea, J.A., Berns, J.S., Simon, M.K., Joffe, M.M., Bloom, R.D., et al. (2008). Recruitment of live donors by candidates for kidney transplantation. *Clinical Journal of The American Society of Nephrology, 3*(4), 1152–1159.

Reimer, J., Rensing, A., Haasen, C., Philipp, T., Pietruck, F. & Franke, G.H. (2006). The impact of living-related kidney transplantation on the donor's life. *Transplantation, 81*(9), 1268–1273.

Rhee, J., Kern, B., Cooper, J., & Freeman, R.B. (2009). Organ Donation. *Seminars in Liver Disease, 29*(1), 19–39.

Riker, R.R., & White B.W. (1995). The effect of physician education on the rates of donation request and tissue donation. *Transplantation, 59*(6), 880–884.

Rizvi, A.H.S., Naqvi, A.S.A., Zafar, N.M., & Ahmed, E. (2009). Regulated compensation donation in Pakistan and Iran. *Current Opinion in Organ Transplantation, 14,* 124–128.

Rocca, P., Cocuzza, E., Rasetti, R., Rocca, G., Zanalda, E., & Bogetto, F. (2003). Predictors of psychiatric disorders in liver transplantation candidates: Logistic regression models. *Liver Transplantation, 9*(7), 721–726.

Rodrigue, J.R., & Baz, M.A. (2007). Waiting for lung transplantation: Quality of life, mood, caregiving strain and benefit, and social intimacy of spouses. *Clinical Transplantation, 21*(6), 722–727.

Rodrigue, M.R., Baz, M.A., Widows, M.R., & Ehlers, S.L. (2005). A randomized evaluation of quality-of-life therapy with patients awaiting lung transplantation. *American Journal of Transplantation, 5,* 2425–2432.

Rodrigue, J.R., Cornell, D.L., Kaplan, B., & Howard, R.J. (2008a). A randomized trial of a home-based educational approach to increase live donor kidney transplantation: Effects in blacks and whites. *American Journal of Kidney Diseases, 51*(4), 663–670.

Rodrigue, J.R., Cornell, D.L., Kaplan, B., & Howard, R.J. (2008b). Patients' willingness to talk to others about living kidney donation. *Progress in Transplantation, 18,* 25–31.

Rodrigue, J.R., Cornell, D.L., Lin, J.K., Kaplan, B., & Howard, R.J. (2007). Increasing live donor kidney transplantation: A randomized controlled trial of a home-based education intervention. *American Journal of Transplantation, 7,* 394–401.

Rodrigue, J.R., Widows, M.R., & Baz, M.A. (2006). Caregivers of lung transplant candidates: Do they benefit when the patient is receiving psychological services? *Progress in Transplantation, 16*(4), 336–342.

Rudd, P. (1995). Clinicians and patients with hypertension: Unsettled issues about compliance. *American Heart Journal, 130*(3), Part 1, 572–577.

Rudge, C., Johnson, R.J., Fuggle, S.V., & Forsythe, J.L.R. (2007). Renal transplantation in the United Kingdom for patients from ethnic minorities. *Transplantation, 83*(9), 1169–1173.

Sabaté, E., & World Health Organization. (2003). *Adherence to long-term therapies: Evidence for action.* Geneva: World Health Organization. Retrieved from http://whqlibdoc.who.int/publications/2003/9241545992.pdf or http://www.who.int/chp/knowledge/publications/adherence_report/en/print.html.

Sadler, H.H., Davison, L., Carroll, C., & Kountz S.L. (1971). The living, genetically unrelated, kidney donor. *Seminars in Psychiatry, 3,* 86–101.

Sanz, A., Boni, R.C., Ghirardini, A., Costa, A.N., & Manyalich, M. (2007). IRODaT 2006. International donation and transplantation activity. *Organs and Tissues and Cells, 2,* 77–80.

Schaeffner, E.S., Mehta, J., & Winkelmayer, W.C. (2008). Educational level as a determinant of access to and outcomes after kidney transplantation in the United States. *American Journal of Kidney Diseases, 51*(5), 811–818.

Schäfer-Keller, P., Dickenmann, M., Barry, D.L., Steiger, J., Bock, A., & De Geest, S. (2009). Computerized patient education in kidney transplantation: Testing the content validity and usability of the Organ Transplant Information System (OTIS). *Patient Education & Counseling, 74*(1), 110–117.

Schneider, S., Winsett, R.P., Reed, L., & Hathaway, D.K. (2001). Use of structured self-monitoring in transplant education. *Progress in Transplantation, 11*(2), 133–136.

Schover, L.R., Streem, S.B., Boparai, N., Duriak, K., & Novick, A.C. (1997). The psychosocial impact of donating a kidney: Long-term followup from a urology based center. *Journal of Urology, 157*(5), 1596–1600.

Schulz, R., & Sherwood, P.R. (2008). Physical and mental health effects of family caregiving. *American Journal of Nursing, 108*(S9), 23–27.

Schweitzer, E.J., Yoon, S., Hart, J., Anderson, L., Barnes, R., Evans, D., et al. (1997). Increased living donor volunteer rates with a formal recipient family education program. *American Journal of Kidney Diseases, 29*(5), 739–745.

Segev, D.L., Gentry, S.E., Warren, D.S., Reeb, B., & Montgomery, R.A. (2005). Kidney paired donation and optimizing the use of live donor organs. *Journal of the American Medical Association, 293,* 1883–1890.

Segev, D.L., Kucirka, L.M., Oberal, P.C., Parekh, R.S., Boulware, L.E., Powe, N.R., et al. (2009). Age and comorbidities are effect modifiers of gender disparities in renal transplantation. *Journal of the American Society of Nephrology, 20,* 621–628.

Sequist, T.D., Narva, A.S., Stiles, S.K., Karp, S.K., Cass, A., & Ayanian, J.A. (2004). Access to renal transplantation among American Indians and Hispanics. *American Journal of Kidney Diseases, 44*(2), 344–352.

Shafer, T.J., Wagner, D., Chessare, J., Schall, M.W., McBride, V., Zampiello, F.A., et al. (2008). US organ donation breakthrough collaborative increases organ donation. *Critical Care Nursing Quarterly, 31*(3), 190–210.

Shafer, T.J., Wagner, D., Chessare, J., Zampiello, F.A., McBride, V., & Perdue, J. (2006). Organ donation breakthrough collaborative: Increasing organ donation through system redesign. *Critical Care Nurse, 26,* 33–49.

Shakil, R.P., Pinna, A., Demetris, J., Lee, R.G., Fung, J.J., & Rakela, J. (1997). Survival and quality of life after liver transplantation for acute alcoholic hepatitis. *Liver Transplant Surgery, 3*(3), 240–244.

Shapiro, P.A., Schulman, J.K., & Bagiella, E. (2003). Prediction of posttransplant survival by psychiatric evaluation of heart transplant candidates: A preoperative study. *Psychosomatics, 44*(2), 164–165.

Shapiro, P.A., Williams, D.L., Foray, A.T., Gelman, I.S., Wuklich, N., & Sciacca, R. (1995). Psychosocial evaluation and prediction of compliance problems and morbidity after heart transplantation. *Transplantation, 60*, 1462–1466.

Sharma, V.K., & Enoch, M.D. (1987). Psychological sequelae of kidney donation. A 5–10 year follow up study. *Acta Psychiatrica Scandinavica, 75*, 264–267.

Sheehy, E., Conrad, S.L., Bingham, L.E., Luskin, R., Weber, P., Eakin, M., et al. (2003). Estimating the number of potential organ donors in the United States. *New England Journal of Medicine, 349*(7), 667–674.

Siegel, J.T., Alvaro, E.M., Crano, W.D., Lac, A., Ting, S., & Jones, S.P. (2008). A quasi-experimental investigation of message appeal variations on organ donor registration rates. *Health Psychology, 27*(2), 170–178.

Siminoff, L.A., Gordon, H., Hewlett, J., & Arnold, R.M. (2001). Factors influencing families' consent for donation of solid organs for transplantation. *Journal of the American Medical Association, 286*(1), 71–77.

Siminoff, L.A., & Saunders Sturm, C.M. (2000). African-American reluctance to donate; Beliefs and attitudes about organ donation and implications for policy. *Kennedy Institute Ethics Journal, 10*, 59–74.

Simmons, R.G., Marine, S.K., & Simmons, R.L. (1987). *Gift of life: The effect of organ transplantation on individual, family, and societal dynamics.* New Brunswick, NJ: Transaction Publishers, Inc.

Simpkin, A.L., Robertson, L.C., Barber, V.S., & Young, J.D. (2009). Modifiable factors influencing relatives' decision to offer organ donation: Systematic review. *British Medical Journal, 338*, 1–8.

Singh, N., Gayowski, T., Wagener, M.M., & Marino, I.R. (1997). Vulnerability to psychologic distress and depression in patients with end-stage liver disease due to hepatitis C virus. *Clinical Transplantation, 11*, 406–411.

Skotzko, C.E., Rudis, R., Kobashigawa, J.A., & Laks, H. (1999). Psychiatric disorders and outcome following cardiac transplantation. *Journal of Heart & Lung Transplantation, 18*, 952–956.

Smedley, B.D., Stith, A.Y., & Nelson, A.R. (Eds.), Committee on Understanding and Eliminating Racial and Ethnic Disparities in Health Care, Board on Health Sciences Policy, Institute of Medicine. (2003). *Unequal treatment: Confronting racial and ethnic disparities in health Care, 2002 report.* Washington, DC: National Academies Press.

Smith, M.D., Kappell, D.F., Province, M.A., Hong, B.A., Robson, A.M., Dutton, S., et al. (1986). Living-related kidney donors: A multicenter study of donor education, socioeconomic adjustment, and rehabilitation. *American Journal of Kidney Diseases, 8*(4), 223–233.

Soucie, J.M., Neylan, J.F., & McClellan, W. (1992). Race and sex differences in the identification of candidates for renal transplantation. *American Journal of Kidney Diseases, 19*, 414–419.

Spaderna, H., Smits, J.M.A., Rahmel, A.O., & Weidner, G. (2007). Psychosocial and behavioural factors in heart transplant candidates–an overview. *Transplant International, 20*, 909–920.

Starzl, T.E. (2005). The mystique of organ transplantation. *Journal of the American College of Surgeons, 201*(2), 160–170.

Sterneck, M.R., Fischer, L., Nischwitz, U., Burdelski, M., Kjer, S., Latta, S., et al. (1995). Selection of the living liver donor. *Transplantation, 60*(7), 667–671.

Stilley, C.S., Dew, M.A., Stukas, A.A., Switzer, G.E., Manzetti, J.D., Keenan, R.J., et al. (1999). Psychological symptom levels and their correlates in lung and heart-lung transplant recipients. *Psychosomatics, 40*, 503–509.

Stothers, L., Gourlay, W.A., & Liu, L. (2005). Attitudes and predictive factors for live kidney donation: A comparison of live kidney donors versus nondonors. *International Society of Nephrology, 67*, 1105–1111.

Stukas, A.A., Dew, M.A., Switzer, G.E., DiMartini, A., Kormos, R.L., & Griffith, B.P. (1999). Post-traumatic stress disorder in heart transplant recipients and their primary family caregivers. *Psychosomatics, 40*, 212–221.

Switzer, G.E., Dew, M.A., Magistro, C.A., Goycoolea, J.M., Twillman, R.K., Alter, C., et al. (1998). The effects of bereavement on adult sibling bone marrow donors' psychological well-being and reactions to donation. *Bone Marrow Transplantation, 21*, 181–188.

Switzer, G.E., Dew, M.A., Stukas, A.A., Goycoolea, J.M., Hegland, J., & Simmons, R.G. (1999). Factors associated with attrition from a national bone marrow registry. *Bone Marrow Transplantation, 24*, 313–319.

Switzer, G.E., Simmons, R.G., & Dew, M.A. (1996). Helping unrelated strangers: Physical and psychological reactions to the bone marrow donation process among anonymous donors. *Journal of Applied Social Psychology, 26*, 469–490.

Tan, H.P., Marcos, A., & Shapiro, R. (Eds.). (2007). *Living donor transplantation.* New York: Informa Healthcare.

Telles-Correia, D., Barbosa, A., Mega, I., Direitinho, M., Morbey, A., & Monteiro, E. (2008). Psychiatric differences between liver transplant candidates with familial amyloid polyneuropathy and those with alcoholic liver disease. *Progress in Transplantation, 18*, 134–139.

Telles-Correia, D., Barbosa, A., Mega, I., & Monteiro, E. (2009). Importance of depression and active coping in liver transplant candidates' quality of life. *Progress in Transplantation, 19*, 85–89.

Thamer, M., Hwang, W., Fink, N.E., Sadler, J.H., Bass, E.R., Levey, A.S., et al. (2001). US nephrologists' attitudes towards renal transplantation: Results from a national survey. *Transplantation, 71*(2), 281–288.

Thomas, C. (2002). Development of a culturally sensitive, locality-based program to increase kidney donation. *Advances in Renal Replacement Therapy, 9*(1), 54–56.

Traiger, G.L., & Bui, L.L. (1997). A self-medication administration program for transplant recipients. *Critical Care Nursing, 17*, 71–79.

Trotter, J.F., Talamantes, M., McClure, M., Wachs, M., Bak, T., Trouillot, T., et al. (2001). Right hepatic lobe donation for living donor liver transplantation: Impact on donor quality of life. *Liver Transplantation, 7*, 485–493.

Tuttle-Newhall, J.E., Rutledge, R., Johnson, M., & Fair, J. (1997). A statewide, population-based, time series analysis of access to liver transplantation. *Transplantation, 63*, 255–262.

Ullrich, G., Jansch, H., Schmidt, S., Struber, M., & Niedermeyer, J. (2004). The experience of the support person involved in a lung transplant programme: Results of a pilot study. *European Journal of Medical Research, 9*(12), 555–652.

558 | TRANSPLANTATION

United Network for Organ Sharing (2009). *Fact Sheet: Donor Designation (First Person Consent) Status by State, 2009.* Department of Health and Human Services, Washington, DC. Retrieved from http://www.unos.org/inTheNews/fact-sheets.asp?fs=6.

U.S. Department of Health and Human Services, Health Resources and Services Administration (1999). Organ Procurement and Transplantation Network Final Rule. *Federal Register, 64,* 56650–56661.

Verbesey, J.E., Simpson, M.A., Pomposelli, J.J., Richman, E., Bracken, A.M., Garrigan, K., et al. (2005). Living donor adult liver transplantation: A longitudinal study of the donor's quality of life. *American Journal of Transplantation, 5*(11), 2770–2777.

Vermeulen, K.M., Ouwens, J.P., van der Bij, W., de Boer, W.J., Koëter, G.H., & TenVergert, E.M. (2003). Long-term quality of life in patients surviving at least 55 months after lung transplantation. *General Hospital Psychiatry, 25*(2), 95–102.

Wadden, T.A., & Sarwer, D.B. (2006). Behavioral assessment of candidates for bariatric surgery: A patient-oriented approach. *Obesity, 14*(S2), 53S–62S.

Walter, M., Bronner, E., Pascher, A., Steinmüller, T., Neuhaus, P., & Klapp, B.F. (2002). Psychosocial outcome of living donors after living donor liver transplantation: A pilot study. *Clinical Transplantation, 16,* 339–344.

Waterman, A.D., Schenk, E.A., Barrett, A.C., Waterman, B.M., Rodrigue, J.R., Woodle, S.S., et al. (2006). Incompatible kidney donor candidates' willingness to participate in donor-exchange and non-directed donation. *American Journal of Transplantation, 6,* 1631–1638.

Wendler, D., & Dickert, J. (2001). The consent process for cadaveric organ procurement. *Journal of the American Medical Association, 285,* 329–333.

Weng, F.L., Joffe, M.M., Feldman, J.L., & Mange, K.C. (2005). Rates of completion of the medical evaluation for renal transplantation. *American Journal of Kidney Diseases, 46*(4), 734–745.

Wong, K.A., Cárdenas, V., Shiu-Thornton, S., Spigner, C., & Allen, M.D. (2009). How do communities want their information? Designing educational outreach on organ donation for Asian Americans. *Progress in Transplantation, 19,* 44–52.

World Health Organization (WHO). (1991). Guiding principles on human organ transplantation. World Health Organization. *Lancet, 337,* 1470–1471.

Wright, L., Pennington, J.J., Abbey, S., Young, E., Haines, J., & Ross, H. (2001). Evaluation of a mentorship program for heart transplant patients. *Journal of Heart & Lung Transplantation, 20,* 1030–1033.

Young, C.J., & Kew, C. (2005). Health disparities in transplantation: Focus on the complexity and challenge of renal transplantation in African Americans. *Medical Clinics of North America, 89,* 1003–1031.

Young, L.E., & Little, M.A. (2004). Women and heart transplantation: An issue of gender equity? *Health Care for Women International, 25,* 436–453.

Zargooshi, J. (2001a). Iranian kidney donors: Motivations and relations with recipients. *Journal of Urology, 165,* 386–392.

Zargooski, J. (2001b). Quality of life of Iranian kidney "donors." *Journal of Urology, 166,* 1790–1799.

Lydia Temoshok

**Abstract**

This chapter discusses key human immunodeficiency virus (HIV)/acquired immune deficiency syndrome (AIDS) issues, developments, research, and clinical/policy implications for the United States. The first section focuses on psychoneuroimmunology (PNI) and biobehavioral HIV research. It summarizes critical information and biomedical research on HIV, and then reviews in some detail examples of PNI and biobehavioral HIV/AIDS research, especially research on plausible PNI mechanisms in HIV progression that is conversant with the basic science discoveries starting in the mid-1990s. The second section considers the much more voluminous record of psychosocial and behavioral clinical research, including interventions. It argues that this research, which has addressed almost exclusively two main areas—HIV behavioral prevention and adherence to HIV medications—would be more successful in terms of impacting these areas if this research and these interventions were better informed by biomedical research. Thus, a critical consideration of the impact of this research, as well as future research directions, will necessarily include references to significant biomedical research in the areas of HIV prevention and treatment.

**Keywords:** HIV infection, AIDS, psychoneuroimmunology, biobehavioral HIV research, HIV prevention, biomedical research

For health psychology and other behavioral researchers, as well as for practitioners, to make credible and important contributions to understanding and impacting significant problems concerning any disease, it is critical to understand the basic biology of disease etiology, pathogenesis, and progression, as well as the biomedical and epidemiological context for disease prevention and treatment. Perhaps the most challenging disease in terms of keeping abreast of key developments in biomedical and clinical research is acquired immune deficiency syndrome (AIDS), which is caused by chronic infection with the human immunodeficiency virus (HIV-1). HIV/AIDS is the largest pandemic in contemporary history, killing more than 40 million people worldwide as of this writing, while over 30 million more are still living with the infection.

This chapter will not address comprehensively or in depth the myriad biomedical developments and progress in behavioral science in the field of HIV/AIDS over the past three decades, but will, instead, discuss topics and key issues in the field that are particularly relevant for the student, researcher, and/or practitioner in health psychology and behavioral medicine. Woven into the presentation of psychosocial and behavioral HIV/AIDS research will be the key strands of biomedical research that are considered the essential foundation for conducting informed and relevant HIV behavioral science research, as well as psychosocial/behavioral interventions.

Because of the immense global scope of the pandemic, this chapter will focus on key HIV/AIDS issues, developments, research, and clinical/policy implications for the United States. The first main section of this chapter will focus on the research area that has the closest biomedical linkages: psychoneuroimmunology (PNI) and biobehavioral HIV research. The most relevant of this research is grounded in a basic understanding of HIV pathogenesis and progression, and collaborative partnerships with biomedical HIV researchers. Thus, this first section of the chapter will summarize critical information and biomedical research on HIV, and then review in some detail examples of PNI and biobehavioral HIV/AIDS research, especially research on plausible PNI mechanisms in HIV progression that is conversant with the basic science discoveries starting in the mid-1990s.

The second main section of the chapter will take a wider perspective and overview, with less detail on individual studies and references, in considering the much more voluminous record of psychosocial and behavioral clinical research, including interventions. It will be argued that this research, which has addressed almost exclusively two main areas, HIV behavioral prevention and adherence to HIV medications, would be more successful in terms of impacting these areas if this research and these interventions (e.g., to prevent HIV sexual acquisition and transmission and to promote optimal adherence to life-saving HIV treatments) were better informed by biomedical research. Thus, a critical consideration of the impact of this research, as well as future research directions, will necessarily include references to significant biomedical research in the areas of HIV prevention and treatment.

## Biobehavioral HIV Research
### The Dawn of the AIDS Era

The first published recognition of the health problem that would later be called AIDS was in 1981, although the clear linkage of AIDS to its causative agent—infection by a virus that would, much later, be called HIV—would remain a mystery until 1984 (e.g., Sarngadharan et al., 1984; Safai et al., 1984). There were actually several 1981 publications: the June 1981 report by the Centers for Disease Control and Prevention (CDC) on a cluster of rare cases of *Pneumocystis carinii* pneumonia (PCP) in five homosexual men (Centers for Disease Control and Prevention [CDC], 1981), and three converging clinical reports in the December issue of the *New England Journal of Medicine* of *P. carinii* pneumonia and chronic ulcerative herpes simplex among homosexual men in Los Angeles (Gottlieb et al., 1981) and New York City (Masur et al., 1981; Siegel et al., 1981), which the authors had the prescience to recognize as evidence for a new acquired cellular immunodeficiency. In 1983–1984, two groups of scientists, Robert Gallo and his group at the National Institutes of Health in Bethesda, Maryland, and the Luc Montagnier/Chermann group in Paris, France,

reported growing from AIDS patients isolates of a new retrovirus (HIV, but then called HTLV-III [human T cell leukemia virus, distinguished from HTLV-1 and 2] and LAV [lymphadenopathy virus]) in the premier journal *Science* (Barre-Sinoussi, et al., 1983; Popovic et al., 1984). As of this writing, almost three decades of research have informed biomedical understanding of the main AIDS virus, HIV-1, and how it causes disease, the impact of HIV infection on immune function, the dynamics of the acute and chronic infection, how HIV is transmitted, and how it can be prevented and treated (for a health psychology-friendly overview, see Klimas, Koneru, & Fletcher, 2008). Although a closely related virus, HIV-2 has been described, it is associated with apparently less severe clinical outcomes and is much more restricted geographically; thus, in this chapter, we will discuss only HIV-1 and call it simply "HIV."

### HIV Pathogenesis and Progression

CD4 is the primary and first to be discovered cell surface molecule (receptor) on T lymphocytes and other immune cells, to which the virus binds and then enters and infects these cells. (In a later section, the role of the subsequently discovered HIV coreceptors CCR5 and CXCR4 will be discussed). HIV affects the immune system by infecting CD4$^+$ T lymphocytes, also called *T helper cells*. These immune cells play a central role in marshalling, sustaining, and then appropriately shutting down the immune response when its job is done, signaling other cells such as the cytotoxic T cell, B cells, phagocytes, and macrophages, as well as other cells involved with host immunity, such as monocytes and thymocytes (Fahey et al., 1990; Ho Tsong Fang, Colantonio, & Uittenbogaart, 2008; Nilsson et al., 2007). Thus, HIV causes not only a gradual loss of key immune cells in terms of numbers, but also a profound disorganization and dysregulation of the immune system's coordinated response to pathogens and internally arising abnormal cells and mutations, which could become cancerous.

The initial phase of acute HIV infection typically lasts several weeks, during which there is a great deal of HIV in the blood (viremia), and the person often experiences flu-like symptoms and/or a rash (Levy, 2006). HIV is a retrovirus, composed of single-stranded RNA, instead of the related double-stranded DNA found in humans and most organisms. When the virus enters a host's immune cells, its RNA integrates itself into the DNA and genetic machinery of the immune cells, hijacking the host's protein-making functions to make proteins for HIV. When most of the HIV has left the bloodstream and has been incorporated into immune cells, this ushers in the so-called *latent phase* of infection, which can last 10 years or even longer in a healthy person. During this time of chronic but latent infection, although the person generally feels and appears well, there is still replication of the virus, a gradual loss of CD4+ T cells, and deterioration of immune function.

There are three categories of disease progression in the CDC's Classification System for HIV-infected Adults and Adolescents. "Category A" includes the short phase of acute HIV infection, asymptomatic (yet infected) states, and persistent generalized lymphadenopathy (PGL; CDC, 1993). The normal number of CD4+ T cells is between 800 and 1,200 cells per cubic millimeter (mm³) of blood (Nilsson et al., 2007). Typically, when the CD4+ T cell count drops below 500 mm³, HIV-infected persons may experience "Category B" symptoms (which are not A or C symptoms), including cold sores (herpes simplex), condyloma (warts), fungal infections, thrush and vaginal candidiasis, minor infections, or other symptoms (e.g., fatigue, night sweats, and chronic diarrhea). When the number of measurable CD4+ T cells declines below 200 cells/mm³, as determined by blood tests, infected persons are at risk for serious opportunistic infections and cancers, considered "Category C" or AIDS indicator conditions, including *P. carinii* pneumonia, toxoplasmosis, cytomegalovirus infections of the eye or intestine, debilitating weight loss, lymphoma, and other cancers, including the normally rare cancer Kaposi's sarcoma. The CDC classification system also includes in the definition of ("full-blown") AIDS as having a CD4+ T cell count below 200 cells/mm³ (CDC, 1993).

*Viral load*, the amount of HIV RNA (viral genetic material) that can be measured in the blood, is another indicator of disease severity and the ability of the immune system and/or treatment to control (suppress) the virus. Typically, as the disease progresses from the latent phase into AIDS, there is a steep increase in HIV RNA in the bloodstream. The rate of progression of HIV infection can vary greatly from person to person. Some of the well-recognized factors affecting the rate of disease progression include coinfection (e.g., hepatitis), age, host genetic makeup, use of antiretroviral therapy (ART), and adherence to ART medication regimens (to be discussed in the second third of this chapter).

### Individual Variation in HIV Disease Progression

Despite the success of effective treatments in delaying progression to full-blown AIDS and mortality, there continues to be great individual variation in HIV disease progression. Some people stay healthy for many years, either with or without medication, while others experience rapid immune system decline and succumb within a year or two of the first opportunistic infection. Much of this variation cannot be explained by biological or medication factors. Since the earliest days of the AIDS epidemic, there has been a great deal of interest in understanding what factors might explain why a very small percentage of HIV-infected individuals progress much more slowly than do the majority. These rare individuals—termed more recently *natural viral suppressors* or *elite controllers*, and previously *long-term non-progressors*—are able to control/suppress HIV-1 for years, usually without symptoms, and without the use of ART. These individuals, who have been studied intensively in terms of their immune responses and relevant genetic markers, do not seem to have been infected with a weaker or less virulent form of HIV.

### Biological Characteristics of Elite Controllers

A subset of HIV-infected persons who are able to control viremia to below the limits of an assay's detection (<50 RNA copies/mL plasma, or the previous limits of detection of <400 RNA copies/mL) without ART has been termed elite controllers (ECs; Bailey et al., 2006; Blankson et al., 2007; Deeks & Walker, 2007; Pereya et al., 2008). ECs appear to be equivalent to natural viral suppressors (NVS), individuals who have the ability to naturally suppress HIV-1 to undetectable levels (Sajadi et al., 2007). Previously, before HIV RNA (viral load) testing was performed routinely, HIV-infected individuals who appeared healthy for years after diagnosis with HIV were called long-term nonprogressors (LTNPs) in the earlier literature. Studies on cohorts of LTNPs often had conflicting findings (Ashton et al., 1998; Cao et al., 1995; Pantaleo et al., 1995), probably attributable to the heterogeneous viral loads of individuals in these cohorts, as well as uncertainty about the exact date of HIV infection and seroconversion to *seropositive status* (when there are measurable antibodies to HIV in the blood).

Among ECs, certain HLA class I alleles are overrepresented, strongly suggesting that HIV-specific cytotoxic T lymphocyte (CTL) responses restricted by these alleles may be important for control of viremia (Pereya et al., 2008). There is no clear explanation, however, for why some individuals with this protective HLA allele can control viremia, yet others cannot. Moreover, a significant number of ECs do not have this allele, suggesting that other mechanisms are responsible for their ability to control viremia. Key factors suggested are immune activation, density and expression of CCR5 (the primary and early disease coreceptor by which HIV binds to and enters immune cells) (Berger, Murphy, & Farber, 1999), binding by natural ligands (chemokines) for the coreceptors, and effects on cell-mediated immunity (Dolan et al., 2007; Jacobson et al., 2009).

## Psychosocial Characteristics of Long-term Nonprogressors

Psychoneuroimmunology is the study of reciprocal interactions among psychological processes and the nervous and immune systems (related terms are neuroimmunomodulation [NIM] and psychoneuroendocrinimmunology [PNEI]). The theoretical possibility of PNI influences on the course of HIV/AIDS was suggested at the dawn of the epidemic (Coates, Temoshok, & Mandel, 1984; for decade-encompassing reviews, see Cole & Kemeny, 2001; Leserman & Temoshok, 2010; Solomon, Kemeny, & Temoshok, 1991). Although hypotheses concerning the contribution of psychosocial characteristics associated with long-term survival after AIDS diagnosis were posed relatively early in the epidemic (Solomon & Temoshok, 1987; Solomon et al., 1987), there are only a few studies addressing the psychosocial characteristics of a true cohort of LTNPs; that is, individuals demonstrating a qualitatively different course of HIV infection, rather than simply a slower course. One case-control study in which 41 LTNPs were matched with 41 rapid progressors (progression to AIDS within 6 years of seroconversion) found that LTNPs had higher incomes, were more likely to have finished secondary school, and were more likely to have higher-status occupations (Schechter et al., 1994). These data might suggest that LTNPs, compared with rapid progressors, may be subject to less chronic stress, which has been linked more recently to inflammation (Irwin, 2008) and exacerbation of immune activation and HIV replication (e.g., Temoshok et al., 2008b, discussed more in depth in a later section).

A longitudinal study comparing LTNPs ($n = 51$), intermediate progressors ($n = 82$), and rapid progressors ($n = 33$) initially reported no significant differences on a battery of measures including assessments of personality, coping, distress, and social support (Troop et al., 1997). However, a later report by the same team found that a pattern emerged over 30 months, in which "acceptance coping" was associated with lower risk of progression (Thornton et al., 2000). "A positive outlook" and positive health behaviors were identified as key factors to which patients attributed their nonprogressor status in two studies (respectively, $n = 62$ nonprogressors and 72 controls; $n = 25$ nonprogressors without controls; Barroso, 1999; Troop et al., 1997). Interestingly, patients did not tend to attribute their healthy status to ART.

There has been considerable research into the relations between various psychosocial factors and HIV disease progression (Bower et al., 1998; Ironson et al., 2005a, b; Leserman, 2008; Leserman et al., 2000; Vassend, Eskild, & Halvorsen, 1997). Most research on this topic has examined indices of HIV progression over a set follow-up period, using outcome variables such as CD4+ cell loss, time to an AIDS-defining diagnosis, or more rarely, mortality (vs. survival) or time to death. Probably the first study of actual survival outcomes, in 21 men with AIDS and not on any treatment, conducted by this chapter's author, found that a moderate increase in heart rate in response to a laboratory emotional stress task, followed by an approximate return to that individual's resting baseline, was the strongest and most significant predictor of longer survival over a 2-year follow-up period, controlling for baseline CD4+ cell count and AIDS-defining condition (O'Leary et al., 1989; Temoshok et al., 1987). These findings were interpreted in terms of the hypothesized role of physiological-immunological homeostasis and stress/HIV-induced dysregulation of that homeostasis in HIV progression (Temoshok, 1990, 2000). It was theorized that maladaptive coping responses or patterns such as Type C keeps the individual in a chronic state of unrecognized and unaddressed stress, and concomitant dysregulation of homeostatic responses, including inappropriate physiological responses to stressors (i.e., increased physiological reactivity and decreased recovery).

Multiple studies have suggested that positive coping strategies are associated with slower HIV disease progression, whereas negative coping strategies, such as denial, have deleterious effects (discussed more in depth in Temoshok et al., 2008a). Proactive problem solving was associated with slower disease progression in 104 men and women (Vassend et al., 1997), and 65 gay men with HIV (Vassend & Eskild, 1998). An optimistic outlook has been associated with lower mortality ($N = 31$ men; Blomkvist et al., 1994) and slower HIV disease progression ($N = 177$ men and women; Ironson & Hayward, 2008), although findings in this area have been mixed (Reed et al., 1994). A study of 40 gay men followed for 2–3 years found that coping by finding meaning in HIV-related stressors was associated with lower mortality (Bower et al., 1998).

The use of religious coping strategies, such as prayer and visualization, was associated with lower risk of mortality in a sample of 901 persons with HIV, but only among those not on ART (Fitzpatrick et al., 2007). This finding is probably explained by the fact that ART makes such a significant impact on disease progression that it accounts for nearly all the variance among those on ART regimens. Another study of religious coping ($n$ = 76) found that "spiritual transformation" was associated with lower HIV-related mortality (Ironson et al., 2005a). A study of long-term survivors with HIV ($N$ = 46) found that they were distinguished from an equivalent seropositive comparison group ($N$ = 89) by their emotional expressiveness and the depth of their processing of past traumas (O'Cleirigh et al., 2003). The key finding of this study was that emotional material must be deeply processed rather than simply expressed. Finally, a large longitudinal study of 773 HIV-positive women found that an array of coping-related variables designated as "psychological resources" (positive affect, positive expectancies regarding health outcomes, and the ability to find meaning in challenging circumstances) were associated with slower CD4$^+$ count decline and less mortality during the 5-year follow-up period (Ickovics et al., 2006).

In contrast, passive coping strategies (e.g., denial, behavioral and mental disengagement) have been found to predict negative outcomes in HIV. Faster progression to AIDS during 7.5 years of follow-up among 82 gay men was associated with persistently high denial scores (Leserman et al., 2000). Concealment of homosexual identity, a related concept and form of denial, has been associated with an accelerated course of HIV infection in 80 gay men followed for 9 years (Cole et al., 1996). An Italian study of 100 HIV-positive men and women (Solano et al., 1993), found that HIV progression was related to stronger maladaptive Type C coping, characterized by difficulty in recognizing internal cues of stress and distress and in expressing one's emotions and needs (Temoshok, 1985; Temoshok & Dreher, 1992). Also in Italy, a larger study of 200 participants found that stronger Type C coping significantly predicted HIV progression at 6- and 12-month follow-ups among the 100 originally asymptomatic patients with compromised immunity (baseline CD4$^+$ counts < 500 cells/mm$^3$) (Solano, Costa, Temoshok, et al., 2002).

Social support has also been associated with disease progression outcomes in persons with HIV, although findings are not consistent. A 9-year longitudinal study of 96 men found that those with larger social networks and greater social support were less likely to progress to AIDS (Leserman et al., 2002). Other studies with larger sample sizes ($N$s of 143 to 185), however, have failed to show a relationship between social support and disease progression (Ironson & Hayward, 2008; Miller et al., 1997; Thornton et al., 2000), possibly because of differences in how social networks and social support were measured across these studies.

### Stress, Depression, and Coping in HIV Disease Progression

This section will focus on longitudinal studies before and after the advent of highly active ART (HAART), which have evaluated whether stressful life events, depression, or coping affect CD4$^+$ T cells, HIV viral load, and disease progression. Previous literature reviews (Leserman, 2008; Temoshok et al., 2008a) have documented consistent and adverse effects of depression, stress, and dysfunctional coping on HIV disease progression; however, the most compelling evidence comes from studying cohorts over long time intervals because HIV tends to advance slowly. In addition, because psychosocial variables change over time, the most methodologically sound studies account for chronicity of depression or stress rather than focusing on a single baseline measure (Chida & Vedhara, 2009).

A recent meta analysis (Chida & Vedhara, 2009) of 17 years of data from 35 prospective cohorts (33,252 sample participants; 38% of studies with 3 or more years follow-up) found a robust and significant relationship between adverse psychosocial factors (e.g., depression, anxiety, stressful life events, and avoidant and denial coping) with HIV disease progression (e.g., decline in CD4$^+$ T cells or clinical status). These psychosocial–HIV disease relationships were maintained even when controlling for HAART, medication adherence, and socioeconomic status. What follows is a brief review of some of this evidence, both before and after the advent of HAART, focusing on longer prospective studies and those examining the chronic effects of psychosocial factors.

### Before Era of HAART: Depression, Stress, and Coping

The San Francisco Men's Health Study, a 9-year longitudinal study of about 400 asymptomatic HIV-infected gay men, found that those who were depressed at study entry progressed to AIDS on average 1.4 years sooner than those who were not depressed (Page-Shafer et al., 1996). Chronic depression was associated with a 67% increased risk of mortality after 7 years compared to no depression

(Mayne et al., 1996). These findings were not altered when adjusting for baseline demographic variables, CD4 T lymphocyte count, HIV-related medical symptoms, ART, and health habits.

The Coping in Health and Illness Project (CHIP) examined the change in depressive symptoms and stressful life events every 6 months for up to 9 years in 96 initially asymptomatic HIV-infected gay men (Leserman et al., 1999, 2000, 2002). Higher cumulative-average stressful event scores were predictive of faster progression to AIDS during 5.5- (Leserman et al., 1999), 7.5- (Leserman et al., 2000), and 9-year follow-up (Leserman et al., 2002), controlling for demographic variables, baseline CD4$^+$ cells and viral load, ART, and serum cortisol. At study end, 74% of those above the median in stress progressed to AIDS compared with 40% below the median. Cumulative average depressive symptoms was also associated with increased risk of AIDS at 5.5 years (Leserman et al., 1999), and the risk of a clinical (Category B) condition but not AIDS at 9 years (Leserman et al., 2002). Using denial as one's main coping mechanism was linked to faster progression to AIDS at 7.5 years. Although cumulative cortisol was associated with faster disease progression, cortisol did *not* mediate the relationship between stress and depression with disease change (Leserman et al., 2002).

The stress of bereavement has been associated with more rapid decline in CD4$^+$ T cells during a 3- to 4-year study (Kemeny & Dean, 1995), as well as with increased serum neopterin (an immune activation marker associated with increased risk of AIDS) (Kemeny et al., 1995). A large longitudinal study of 1,716 women with HIV followed over 7.5 years found that those who were chronically depressed were significantly more likely to die from HIV/AIDS (O'Cleirigh et al., 2003). A 6- to 8-year study of 996 Tanzania women without access to HAART showed that chronic depression was associated with a 61% increased risk of clinical progression and over twice the hazard of death (Antelman et al., 2007).

Although these studies reported significant findings relative to the role of psychosocial factors and biomarkers of HIV disease progression, a number of negative studies exist as well. The difference may be attributed to the fact that most of these studies tended to examine baseline psychosocial measures rather than chronicity of stress or depression.

### Studies in the HAART Era: Depression, Stress, and Coping

As more effective treatments for HIV became available, researchers interested in PNI relationships wondered if psychosocial factors would still have an impact on HIV disease markers or if potent antiretroviral medications would obscure these effects. Because strict adherence to HIV medication regimens is an important predictor of therapy success, controlling for adherence is important in these studies.

Ickovics and colleagues followed HIV-infected women ($N$ = 765) during a 7-year period when HAART began to be available (Ickovics et al., 2001). Women with chronic depressive symptoms were about two times more likely to die from AIDS and had greater declines in CD4$^+$ T lymphocytes than those never experiencing depression; these effects were especially pronounced among those with low baseline CD4$^+$ T cells. Control variables included baseline CD4$^+$, HIV viral load, HIV-related symptoms, and ART. In a recent reanalysis of these data, women with more adaptive psychological coping (e.g., positive affect, finding meaning, and positive HIV expectancy) had greater decreases in AIDS-related mortality (Ickovics et al., 2006).

The Women's Interagency HIV Study (WIHS), a 7.5-year investigation of 1,716 women from five U.S. cities, showed that those with chronic depressive symptoms were more likely to die from HIV (13%) than were those with few or no depressive symptoms (6%) (Cook et al., 2004). Findings held when controlling for demographic variables, illegal drug use, baseline CD4$^+$, viral load, HIV symptoms, and type of ART used. Depression was also associated with poorer virologic response, and greater risk of immunological failure, AIDS-defining illness, and all-cause death among a subset initiating HAART use (Anastos et al., 2005).

Depression was found in a sample of 96 men to be associated with a substantially increased risk of progressing from HIV infection to AIDS status over a 5-year follow-up (Fitzpatrick et al., 2007). A study of 490 HIV-infected men and women followed for up to 41 months found that each standard deviation increase in depressive symptoms was related to a 49% increased risk of AIDS mortality, controlling for demographic variables, CD4, viral load, and ART (Leserman et al., 2007). In addition, patients with more childhood and adult traumatic events had significantly more opportunistic infections and faster all-cause and AIDS-related mortality.

A 2-year study of 177 HIV-infected patients found that those with high cumulative depression and avoidant coping had twice the rate of decline in CD4$^+$ T cells and greater increases in viral load compared to low scorers, controlling for HAART and adherence (Ironson et al., 2005a). Furthermore, those with more adverse life events had greater increases in viral load, but not change in CD4+ T cells. Depression at the time of first HAART initiation has been linked with (a) over five times the risk of clinical HIV progression (Bouhnik et al., 2005); (b) greater risk of AIDS and virologic failure, controlling for medication adherence (Parienti et al., 2004; Villes et al., 2007); and (c) shorter survival (Lima et al., 2007).

## Biopsychosocial Interventions

It is not surprising that the numerous studies that have documented the important role of stress, coping, and depression in HIV disease progression have influenced subsequent studies examining how these relationships might be mitigated or reversed by biopsychosocial or biobehavioral interventions. In fact, there have been several meta-analyses of this literature. The most thorough meta-analysis evaluated 35 randomized controlled trials through 2006 that tested the efficacy of 46 separate stress management interventions in a total of 3,077 HIV-infected persons (Scott-Sheldon et al., 2008). Interventions, both small-group (36%) and individual sessions (64%), included the following: coping skills (59%), interpersonal skills (50%), relaxation practice (48%), HIV/AIDS education (37%), social support (37%), exercise education and practice (26%), and medication adherence (13%). Compared with controls (74% were assessment-only controls), the stress management interventions were shown to reliably reduce anxiety, depression, and fatigue and improve quality of life at the first posttreatment assessment. The interventions in the meta-analysis did not differ from controls on change in CD4+ T cells, HIV viral load, or hormonal outcomes (e.g., cortisol, dehydroepiandrosterone sulfate [DHEA-S]). Similarly, another meta-analysis of 15 randomized controlled trials of cognitive-behavioral interventions for those infected with HIV showed similar effect sizes for changes in depression and anxiety, with little evidence for intervention effects on CD4+ T cells (Crepaz et al., 2006).

However, a number of notable limitations in the literature concerning biopsychosocial interventions make it difficult to interpret these studies. First, the follow-up time periods evaluated have been, generally, 1 week to 3 months post intervention, which is too short to evaluate immunological and clinical changes in HIV, particularly impact on disease progression. Second, many studies fail to control for patients' medical status upon entering the study, to control for medical treatment, or for medication adherence, all critical factors that affect disease progression

and outcome. Third, the control groups tend to be inadequate, given that the majority were assessment only (e.g., waiting list, usual/standard care) controls. With more equivalent controls, the effect sizes of the interventions on mental health might be considerably smaller. A final limitation to be noted is that most study samples were not chosen based on the need for stress management treatment (e.g., clinically depressed or anxious mood); many actually exclude those with mental health or substance abuse diagnoses, severely limiting their generalizability to the majority of persons living with HIV/AIDS in the second decade of the 21st century.

A recent review of cognitive-behavioral stress management (CBSM) interventions in HIV has a slightly different interpretation of this literature (Carrico & Antoni, 2008). This review focused on 14 randomized controlled trials (e.g., CBSM, relaxation training) examining immune status and/or neuroendocrine outcomes, and concluded that, irrespective of treatment modality, studies that improve psychological adjustment tend to have beneficial effects on immune status and/or neuroendocrine regulation. For example, in a study of mildly HIV symptomatic gay men, those receiving CBSM showed decreases initially as well as over time in depressive symptoms, anxiety, poor coping, 24-hour cortisol, and norepinephrine (NE), and increases in the naïve CD4+ T cell subset (an indicator of immune system reconstitution) and T cytotoxic/suppressor (CD3+ CD8+) lymphocytes compared to a modified waiting list control (Antoni et al., 2000, 2005). Decreased anxiety was associated with decreases in NE (Antoni et al., 2000). Reductions in cortisol output and depressed mood during the intervention mediated the changes in naïve CD4 T cells during the 6- to 12-month follow-up (Antoni et al., 2005). Finally, greater reductions in NE during CBSM buffered declines after 1-year in cytotoxic/suppressor (CD8+) T cells (Antoni et al., 2000).

Another study comparing CBSM plus supportive/expressive therapy to a control of watching stress management videos showed no effect of the experimental intervention on CD4+ counts or HIV viral load at the end of treatment However, those who increased in self-efficacy during the intervention had significant increases in CD4+ T cells and decreases in viral load (Ironson et al., 2005b). Another study also showed no effects of cognitive-behavioral treatment on CD4+ T cell count, but found that persons with lower distress tended to have the largest increases in CD4+ cell count (Mülder et al., 1995).

In a study that examined the effects of CBSM plus medication adherence training versus an adherence only control in 130 HIV-infected gay men, the combination treatment group had reductions in depression and denial coping compared to the controls (Antoni et al., 2006). Among those with detectable viral load at baseline, the CBSM group had significantly greater decreases in HIV viral load through the 15-month follow-up, compared with those receiving only adherence training.

In a sample of HIV-positive and HIV-negative bereaved gay men, those who were randomly assigned to a bereavement support group showed significant decreases in dysphoria, plasma cortisol, and health care visits, and significant increases in CD4$^+$ count and total T lymphocytes at 6 months compared with standard care controls (Goodkin et al., 1998). Men with decreased cortisol had significantly increased CD4$^+$ T cells.

## Immunological Factors in the Pathogenesis and Progression of HIV/AIDS

### CHRONIC IMMUNE ACTIVATION

The central conundrum of HIV pathogenesis is that, although HIV infection is characterized by a progressive decline of CD4$^+$ cell count, which renders the individual susceptible to infection by opportunistic pathogens, researchers have concluded that the chief pathogenic culprit is the persistent and excessive ("promiscuous") immune response to HIV (Hazenberg et al., 2003). This chronic but ineffective immune activation has been shown to contribute significantly to HIV disease progression to AIDS (Lawn et al., 2001).

Immune activation per se has not been assessed in published studies to date that examined PNI relationships to HIV progression and/or possible mechanisms. It is recommended that future research use CD38 receptor expression on leukocytes, including CD4$^+$, CD8$^+$, B, and natural killer (NK) cells (Malavasi et al., 2008) as a marker of cell activation, primarily because its prognostic value has been shown to be more potent than that of CD4$^+$ cell counts, HIV coreceptor (CCR5 or CXCR4) usage, plasma viremia, and HLA-DR expression (another HIV activation marker) (Giorgi et al., 1999). The function of CD38 is to cleave substrates that are released by cells undergoing apoptosis (programmed cell death). Thus, it is conceivable that the increased expression of CD38 in HIV-infected patients reflects abnormally high levels of apoptosis (Gougeon et al., 1996). For AIDS, in particular, high levels of CD38 expression on CD8$^+$ T cells are associated with worse

prognosis (Kolber, 2008; Mekmullica et al., 2009). In HIV-infected patients undergoing therapy, lower levels of CD38 expression are associated with improved immune reconstitution (Al-Harthi et al., 2000; Tilling et al., 2002). Another reason for PNI HIV researchers to be interested in CD38 is a report that acute stress increases the expression of CD38 on T lymphocytes (Atanackovic et al., 2006), suggesting that a causal link may exist between psychological stress and CD38$^+$ expression, possibly induced by neuromediators.

### Natural Killer Cells

Natural killer cells are large, granular, unprimed lymphocytes that constitute a large component of innate immunity, providing a first line of immune defense (Herberman, 1986). Natural killer cells have direct cytolytic activity against certain tumor and virus-infected cells, including HIV-1-infected lymphocytes, and play a central role in determining the quality of the host's immune response to infection (Tyler et al., 1990). A recent review of the role of NK in HIV infection suggests that several mechanisms and processes involving NK cells are implicated in controlling HIV (Alter & Altfeld, 2009). Commonly in HIV disease progression, a "shift" occurs from a Th1 immune response (activated lymphocytes releasing cytokines that express anti-inflammatory properties) to a predominantly Th2-type response (involving cytokines that express proinflammatory properties). It is now recognized that the proliferation of NK cells soon after acute HIV infection is critical in early containment of viral replication and in inducing/regulating a strong antiviral-adaptive immune response. The induction of proinflammatory cytokines (e.g., interferon-$\gamma$) results in the potentiation of virus-specific CD8$^+$ T cells, which attempt to control viral replication during the chronic (so-called *latency*) phase of HIV infection.

In addition to these mechanisms, recent research has also revealed the complex role for killer immunoglobulin receptors (KIR), which are preferentially expressed on the cytotoxic NK cell subsets and bind to HLA class 1 molecules. The combined expression of specific KIRs in conjunction with their HLA class 1 ligands is protective in HIV disease, and have been identified in highly HIV-exposed but uninfected individuals (Alter & Altfeld, 2009).

HIV has evolved a number of mechanisms to evade or deflect these antiviral and protective NK cell responses. For example, HIV induces expansion of highly dysfunctional NK cell subsets that lack the majority of NK cell effector functions, including killing, cytokine secretion, and antibody-dependent cellular toxicity. Natural killer function, generally speaking, is compromised by HIV viremia, although these mechanisms are not well understood (Ward & Barker, 2008).

Although NK activity or cytotoxicity is the most commonly assessed immune factor in PNI HIV research, mainly because it is so sensitive to stress and psychosocial variation, there is little biomedical evidence that NK activity, per se, is a key factor or mediator of HIV progression later in HIV infection, which is when it has been assessed in most PNI studies involving NK. It is more likely that higher NK cytotoxic function during HIV infection *reflects* rather than causally contributes to the success of the host's overall immune response in controlling HIV. In the same sense, CD4+ cell count also reflects the host's overall immune system health and function relative to HIV's attack on the system. Thus, NK cytotoxicity may be more accurately viewed as a bio-marker of disease progression, rather than a causal mediator of it. An example of this interpretation of the role of NK cells in HIV are studies from the University of Miami, which found that relative preservation of NK cell counts and function was protective of health in HIV-infected persons *with very low CD4 cell counts* (Ironson et al., 2001). This group also found that NK cells mediated between emotional–cognitive processing of trauma and the maintenance of health in this same sample (O'Cleirigh et al., 2008).

In an early study of HIV-infected men, bereavement was associated with lower NK cell cytotoxicity and lymphocyte proliferation to phytohemagglutinin (PHA; Goodkin et al., 1996). Bereavement has also been associated with increased serum neopterin, an immune activation marker associated with increased risk of progression to AIDS (Kemeny et al., 1995). Other studies, however, found no association between stressful life events and NK cell cytotoxicity in African American women coinfected with HIV and human papillomavirus; pessimism was related to lower NK cell cytotoxicity and CD8+ T cell percentage (CD8+ T cells are, in addition to CD4+ T cells, a target of HIV infection; Byrnes et al., 1998). A 2-year follow-up of HIV-infected men found that the combination of stressful events and depressed mood was related to greater declines in NK cell counts (CD56+ and CD16+ subsets) and CD8+ T lymphocytes (Leserman et al., 1997). A cross-sectional study of 200 HIV-infected adults found the relationship between distress (anxiety, depression) and disease severity (higher HIV viral load and

lower CD4+ count) was mediated, statistically, by lower NK cell count and cytotoxicity and by increased cytotoxic CD8+ T cell activation (Greeson et al., 2008). This latter finding is particularly promising for future research, given the central role of immune activation in HIV immunopathogenesis.

## Cytokines, Chemokines, and the HIV Coreceptors

A complex network of interactions exist between cytokines and chemokines that influences HIV pathogenesis (Kinter et al., 2000). Research has focused on the balance between cytokines that either stimulate (inflammatory cytokines) or inhibit (β chemokines) in vivo HIV replication. The β chemokines macrophage inflammatory protein (MIP)-1α and MIP-1β bind to the CCR5 coreceptor, potently suppressing infection by CCR5 viral strains (Cocchi et al., 1995). Increased production of these β chemokines, the first recognized natural inhibitors of HIV, is associated with more favorable clinical status, disease-free HIV infection, and protection from infection (Garzino-Demo et al., 1999; Ullum et al., 1998). Congruently, suppression of CCR5 coreceptor expression is increasingly viewed as a critical mechanism for the natural and therapeutic control of HIV disease. It has also been shown that variations in the genes encoding CCR5 and MIP-1α influence HIV pathogenesis, viral burden, and HIV clinical course through their effects on cell-mediated immunity, in addition to their better-known effects on viral-entry mechanisms (Dolan et al., 2007).

Interleukin 6 (IL-6) is a proinflammatory cytokine secreted by T cells and by monocytes in the acute-phase response to inflammation, mediating fever. Increases in IL-6 production have been observed both in vitro and in vivo in sera from HIV-infected individuals (Lafeuillade et al., 1991), as well as in the cerebrospinal fluid of HIV-positive individuals with AIDS dementia (Perrella et al., 1992). Considered an HIV progression factor, IL-6 can induce HIV replication in monocytes in vitro (Poli et al., 1990), upregulate the CCR5 HIV coreceptor to facilitate entry of R5 viruses (the most commonly transmitted strain and the predominant strain found earlier in infection), increase HIV replication via (most likely) increased immune activation, and induce apoptosis—all of which are associated with accelerated HIV progression (Lawn et al., 2001).

Interleukin-10 has been characterized as a cytokine "shared between the immune and neuroendocrine systems," which potentially serves a negative feedback role to counter (regulate) proinflammatory cytokines in the central nervous system, as well as in the homeostatic functioning of the hypothalamic-pituitary-adrenal (HPA) axis (Blalock & Smith, 2007; Couper et al., 2008). In HIV infection, the role of IL-10 might seem less than straightforward, based on apparently contrasting claims on the levels of IL-10 in HIV-infected subjects or in primate models of HIV infection (Hofmann-Lehmann et al., 2002). It is has been shown, however, that IL-10 can inhibit HIV infection in vitro (Bento et al., 2009). Furthermore, a polymorphism in the IL-10 promoter that increases IL-10 production is associated with better HIV prognosis (Shin et al., 2000). Increased IL-10 production in vitro was found to be associated with improved disease outcome (Betts et al., 2006). In contrast, however, another research group reported that production of IL-10 is correlated inversely with CD4+ cell counts in HIV-infected patients (Salvaggio et al., 1996). Most of the studies that indicated a negative effect of IL-10 levels on HIV progression were performed using serum samples or cells activated with PHA, a polyclonal stimulator. Because production from cells activated with antigens is predictive of better outcome, measurement of IL-10 production from antigen-activated cells may constitute an improved marker of progression as compared to measurements from serum or PHA-activated cells (Garzino-Demo et al., 1999).

## PNI Studies of Cytokines, β-Chemokines, and Coping Factors

Few clinical (i.e., human) studies have examined PNI relationships with these cytokine and β-chemokine mediators of HIV progression. In the first study of this kind, Temoshok and her colleagues investigated the relationships of psychological factors, specifically Type C coping (lack of or very low emotion/stress/need recognition, expression, and communication) and the related construct of alexithymia (problems in cognitively processing and regulating emotion, resulting in difficulties describing and identifying feelings) and psychophysiological stress responses (exaggerated heart rate and blood pressure reactivity and underrecovery following experimental emotional stress tasks) to cytokine mediators of HIV progression (antigen-stimulated production of IL-6, and of the anti-HIV β-chemokines MIP-1α and MIP-1β) (Temoshok et al., 2008b). This study was performed in a baseline sample of 200 HIV-infected, predominantly African American outpatients attending an HIV primary care clinic in inner-city Baltimore. Stronger Type C coping was significantly associated

with higher in vitro antigen-stimulated production of the proinflammatory cytokine IL-6 at baseline, controlling for age and CD4+ count (Temoshok et al., 2008b). This significant positive relationship between IL-6 production and stronger Type C coping was found at 36-month follow-up, when the biomarker CD4+ cell count was also predicted (significant negative association) by higher baseline Type C coping (Temoshok et al., 2011). Because IL-6 is considered a HIV progression factor, these findings suggest that stress-related production of IL-6 (there is increased stress because of the inherent fragility of the Type C coping style) is a candidate mediator for the previously reported relationship between stronger Type C coping and subsequent disease progression (Solano et al., 1993, 2002).

The Type C coping style, deployed strongly and exclusively (relative to other coping styles) in response to chronic stressors, is theorized to contribute to a dysregulated stress response, including exaggerated physiological and immunological reactivity/activation, and decreased recovery to a stable state of homeostasis (Temoshok, 1990, 2000). Stronger Type C coping has been linked to disease progression in HIV and other immunologically mediated disorders (Temoshok et al., 2008a).

Coping styles that are conceptually related to Type C in terms of the emotional dysregulation involved, such as reduced emotional expressiveness and repressive coping, have also been associated with decreased immune function and faster disease progression in HIV-positive patients (Ashton et al., 2005; O'Clerigh et al., 2003; Wald, Dowling, & Temoshok, 2006). Alexithymia (literally "no words for feelings"; [Taylor, 2004]) is an important and well-researched construct that is closely related, theoretically, to Type C coping. Unlike strong Type C copers, who are not conscious of being distressed, alexithymic individuals may report undifferentiated and diffuse psychological distress, such as "being upset" (Garssen & Remie, 2004). Alexithymia was found to be related to illness behavior but not to CD4+ count among HIV-infected individuals (Lumley, Tomakowsky, & Torosian, 1997). In addition, alexithymia has been associated with increased cardiovascular reactivity (Waldstein et al., 2002), which, under some conditions, has also been linked to HIV progression (Cole et al., 2003).

In the same study of 200 largely African American HIV-infected individuals in Baltimore, alexithymia was correlated with significantly lower stimulated production of the HIV-inhibiting β chemokines MIP-1α and/or -β at baseline (Temoshok et al.,

2008b), at 24-month follow-up (Temoshok et al., 2009b), and at 36-month follow-up, when CD4$^+$ cell count was also predicted (Temoshok et al., 2011). Thus, the adjacent constructs of Type C and alexithymia, both of which describe aspects of emotional dysregulation, are associated with reciprocal immune factors related in the predicted directions to either HIV progression (IL-6) or protection (MIP-1$\alpha$/$\beta$). Although alexithymia and Type C coping are phenotypically similar, alexithymia may be more common in socioeconomically and educationally disadvantaged populations, such as the inner-city outpatient population of HIV-infected individuals in which this study was conducted, than would Type C coping, which was first characterized in an almost exclusively white middle-class sample in northern California (e.g., Temoshok, 1985) and found to be related to significantly shorter survival with AIDS among middle-class gay white males in San Francisco (Temoshok et al., 1987).

Independent of alexithymia, greater heart rate reactivity and poorer heart rate recovery in response to experimental emotional stress (role-playing) tasks were also significantly associated with lower production of MIP-1$\alpha$, adjusted for cardiovascular medications, methadone use, CD4$^+$ count, and age at baseline (Temoshok et al., 2008b). In multiple regression analyses, adjusted for these same factors, decreased production of MIP-1$\alpha$ and/or MIP-1$\beta$ at 24 months was significantly predicted by baseline assessments of higher diastolic and/or systolic blood pressure (DSP/SBP) and/or heart rate reactivity, as well as poorer SBP and/or DBP recovery following the emotional stress tasks (Temoshok et al., 2009a). Evidence for a pattern of psychophysiological, as well as emotional, dysregulation that may result in chronic suppression of anti-HIV $\beta$-chemokine production (in which these $\beta$ chemokines bind to the HIV coreceptor CCR5, thus preventing HIV entry into immune cells) was strengthened by consistent findings at 36-month follow-up (Temoshok et al., 2011). The finding that Type C coping, alexithymia, and heart rate reactivity/recovery are associated independently and differentially with specific aspects of HIV progression-relevant immune functioning may reflect distinct biobehavioral pathways that contribute to HIV progression.

### Neuroendocrine Dysregulation in the Pathogenesis and Progression of HIV/AIDS
#### Cortisol and Catecholamines
HIV infection is associated with and appears to induce a number of abnormalities in immunological and neuroendocrinological functions. An active

sector of PNEI research in HIV has been concerned with mapping out the effects of stressors on immune cells and the respective contributions of the HPA axis hormones adrenocorticotropic hormone (ACTH) and cortisol, as well as the sympathetic-adrenal-medullary (SAM) axis hormones, epinephrine and NE.

Some biomedical investigators have observed that elevated cortisol, the adrenal steroid secreted during stress and the most important human endogenous glucocorticoid, appears to play a central role in the pathogenesis of HIV infection and progression to AIDS (Corley, 1996). An important animal model of social stress found that simian immunodeficiency virus (SIV)-infected rhesus macaques that experienced unstable social conditions had, ultimately, shorter survival (Capitanio et al., 1998). The investigators found that unstable social stress was associated with *lower* basal cortisol concentrations, which they hypothesized resulted from enhanced negative feedback regulation of the HPA axis due to chronic stress (e.g.,Yehuda et al., 1995). A subsequent study by the Capitanio group, also in rhesus macaques, similarly found that sustained submission by macaques in unstable social groups (high stress) was associated with lower basal plasma cortisol concentrations (Capitanio et al., 2008). Another study found that cortisol did not mediate the effects of stress and depression on HIV disease progression; however, higher serum cortisol was associated with faster disease progression and mortality during 9-year follow-up (Leserman et al., 2002). Other studies that experimentally manipulated glucocorticoid levels have either not shown alterations in CD4$^+$ T lymphocytes or HIV viral load (Andrieu & Lu, 2004), or shown improvements in these disease markers (Ulmer et al., 2005).

It has been proposed that DHEA, a naturally occurring adrenal steroid whose declining levels have been shown to predict progression to AIDS, may act as a cortisol antagonist to maintain cortisol homeostasis (e.g., decreasing stress-related hypercortisolemia) and enhance immune functioning (Clerici et al., 1997). A randomized controlled study of a 10-week CBSM intervention in HIV-positive men showed that the intervention buffered decreases in DHEA-S (sulfate, as found in the bloodstream), increased the cortisol-to-DHEA-S ratio, and reduced mood disturbance and perceived stress (Cruess et al., 1999).

The inconsistent findings regarding the role of cortisol in mediating stress effects in HIV disease progression (Cole, 2008) may be understood in light of more recent evidence that has challenged the classical view that glucocorticoids are always anti-inflammatory (Sorrells & Sapolsky, 2007). These authors reviewed the evidence that, in some cases, glucocorticoids can increase proinflammatory cytokine production and cell migration, which could account for some of the apparently contradictory reports in the PNEI literature. In addition, diurnal variation in cortisol may also contribute to inconsistent findings regarding the role of the HPA-axis in HIV.

In vitro research in animals (rhesus macaques) has shown that catecholamines associated with the sympathetic nervous system, particularly NE, can accelerate and/or are associated with SIV replication (Sloan et al., 2007). There is limited evidence, however, for these effects in vivo in studies of human HIV progression, despite the reasonable hypothesis that the influence of stress on disease processes is mediated through their effects on physiological stress-response systems (Capitanio et al., 2008).

One of the few studies in humans that incorporated neuroendocrine measures found that higher perceived stress and NE levels predicted worse HIV viral load response to starting a new protease inhibitor (one of the main HAART medications) (Ironson et al., 2008). These investigators reported that NE mediated the relationship between perceived stress and change in viral load, whereas cortisol was unrelated to viral load. On the other hand, dysregulated physiological stress patterns (increased heart rate reactivity and poorer recovery) following a laboratory emotional stress task were not found to mediate the effect of higher alexithymia on lower production of anti-HIV β chemokines; rather, alexithymia and increased reactivity/poorer recovery were independent influences on these key HIV antiprogression factors (Temoshok et al., 2008b).

### Neurotransmitters

The decreased quality of life and depression commonly experienced by persons living with HIV/AIDS has been hypothesized to be biologically mediated, in addition to being the sequelae of the more readily apparent psychological factors of stigma, and of having a serious and often fatal chronic disease for which there is no cure (e.g., Solomon, Kemeny, & Temoshok, 1991). Immune-mediated catabolism of the essential amino acid tryptophan, which commonly occurs in the HIV progression–related shift from a Th2 immune response to a predominantly Th1-type response, impairs the synthesis of the neurotransmitter serotonin (Schroecksnadel et al., 2007). Decreased serotonin and its precursor tryptophan are

implicated in the pathogenesis of mood disturbances and depression (Widner et al., 2002). The conversion of tryptophan to kynurenine by the enzyme indoleamine-(2,3-) dioxygenase (IDO) is triggered by the cytokine interferon-γ, a key mediator of Th1-type immune response (Brown et al., 1991). There are interesting parallels and links between immune activation, as reflected in elevated plasma neopterin concentrations (a prognostic marker for HIV progression), the development of depression, and enhanced tryptophan degradation (Schroecksnadel et al., 2008), as well as the inhibition of both neopterin formation and tryptophan degradation by effective ART (Zangerle et al., 2002).

### Conclusions and Directions for Future Biobehavioral HIV Research.

Both before and after the advent of HAART, biobehavioral studies have suggested that stressful events, depression, and dysregulated coping may affect immunological and clinical decline in HIV infection. In many studies, these PNI relationships appear to be robust, even when adjusting for other markers and/or predictors of HIV disease progression. It is important to remember, however, that the *direction* of the relationship—with the attendant causal implications—between psychosocial factors such as stress, depression, and coping, and disease progression requires further clarification because advancing illness certainly affects these factors. Many of the studies cited examined psychosocial variables before changes in disease status—although after diagnosis; thus, longitudinal studies with longer follow-up times (e.g., at least 2 years) would be the most able to suggest psychosocial factors that may influence HIV disease progression.

As with most associations in PNI research, biological and behavioral relationships are bidirectional, interactive, synergistic, and involve positive and/or negative feedback loops. For example, less generally resilient styles of coping with stress will become further strained under the significant stressor of an HIV diagnosis, causing further breakdowns in the ability to cope with this and other life stressors, increased depression, and so forth. A tendency to react with depressed mood may escalate into clinical depression and/or hopelessness in confronting the multiple challenges of trying to live as normally as possible with what had been widely perceived until fairly recently as a lethal disease, but which is now considered a chronic disease, albeit one which must be treated indefinitely. Moreover, it is clear that cognitive-behavioral and other interventions can change health behaviors that have a subsequent impact on health and, potentially, on disease progression. The two primary pathways of influence linking psychosocial/behavioral factors to health outcomes—biobehavioral (PNI, PNEI) factors and health behaviors (e.g., smoking, exercise, adherence to prescribed regimens)—are probably mutually reinforcing and/or synergistic (e.g., Temoshok, 1995).

### Interventions

Few studies evaluate, in sufficiently powered studies, psychosocial interventions intended to influence disease progression in HIV-infected persons. More research is needed to address whether psychosocial/ biobehavioral interventions can impact stress, immune, and disease relationships in HIV. Such studies need to have longer time frames, because it is not clear the extent to which these interventions affect longer-term clinical outcomes ($\geq 2$ years), in addition to mood and cognitive/behavioral factors. It is important that this research be performed with persons in need of psychological intervention (e.g., clinical depression vs. simply depressed mood), and with persons who are at risk for disease progression (e.g., who have detectable or uncontrolled viral load, in spite of medical treatment). Despite some positive findings from the research cited above, other studies found no relationship between CBSM interventions and immunological or neuroendocrine changes (Scott-Sheldon et al., 2008). Many of these studies demonstrated no or minimal effects on depressed mood (Carrico & Antoni, 2008). Moreover, there is little evidence that changing depressed mood per se affects key biomedical HIV progression–related mediators. Thus, the verdict is still out whether CBSM or other interventions for HIV-positive persons can have demonstrable causal effects on HIV immune and neuroendocrine biomarkers that are associated with and/or mediate HIV progression, and what mechanisms might account for changes in immunological and clinical status.

CBSM is the intervention most often evaluated in PNI HIV studies (although mindfulness-based stress reduction is becoming popular, it has yet to demonstrate convincing results). "Traditional" PNI interventions tested over the years have not yielded impressive evidence for improved clinical status, health functioning, or survival among people living with HIV/AIDS. Although some biological markers of improved health have been observed, their overall potential for slowing HIV disease has been disappointing. There is an obvious need for future research to evaluate the effects on biomedical processes and

HIV outcomes of innovative interventions that have been developed rationally on the basis of PNI HIV research.

It is sobering to reflect that the ground-breaking research published in *Science* that first put PNI on the map, demonstrating behavioral conditioning of immune responses in mice (Ader & Cohen, 1982), has never been applied to developing conditioning interventions designed to enhance more appropriate and salutary cognitive, emotional, physiological, and cytokine/immune responses in HIV-positive persons. The possibility of conditioning-based interventions for HIV-positive persons was first suggested, with great but ultimately unfulfilled excitement, in a National Institutes of Mental Health (NIMH)-sponsored workshop on PNI and HIV convened early in the course of the HIV/AIDS epidemic (Temoshok, 1987). Behavioral conditioning in one or more biological systems could constitute the basis for "natural" PNI interventions that elicit endogenous health processes that contribute to slowing progression of HIV disease and improving health outcomes. In addition, immunogenic PNI behavioral conditioning interventions could reduce, theoretically, the need for higher doses of often-toxic HIV medications. This idea is a logical implication and extension of the first human study to suggest the benefits of behavior conditioning; psoriasis patients treated under a partial schedule of pharmacologic (corticosteroid) reinforcement could be maintained with low treatment doses (e.g., only one-quarter or one-half the usual amount of prescribed medication) that were "relatively ineffective" under standard treatment conditions (Ader, et al., 2010; Schedlowski & Pacheco-López, 2010).

### Need for Studies Incorporating Mechanisms

Nearly three decades of HIV PNI research have revealed a number of replicated linkages between psychosocial factors (e.g., stress, coping, depression) and biomarkers of HIV progression. A fundamental limitation of most of these studies is that few have hypothesized or discussed—much less examined within the same study—immunological or endocrinological mechanisms underlying these associations. There are several exceptions: For example, the consideration of mechanisms by which dispositional optimism could predict slower disease progression in HIV (Ironson et al., 2005a), and the early study of predictors of longer survival for men with AIDS (Temoshok et al., 1987), interpreted in terms of the hypothesized role of physiological-immunological homeostasis and stress/HIV-induced dysregulation of homeostasis in HIV progression (Temoshok, 1990, 2000).

For future research, it would be important for PNI researchers seeking to understand the protective or pathogenic influences of hypothesized psychosocial/behavioral factors on HIV progression to collaborate with biomedical researchers to elucidate the *mechanisms* linking these factors to progression-relevant immunologic processes, such as NK cell–mediated induction of Th1 and CD8$^+$ T cell responses soon after HIV infection (which leads to establishment of a lower viral set point) and the protective effect of KIR-mediated activation of NK cells. Critically needed is more research documenting the potential mediating role of neuroendocrine and immune markers (e.g., proinflammatory cytokines and chemokines) linking psychosocial factors and HIV disease course. It is expected that future research will reveal the extent to which serotonin and tryptophan are biomarkers or correlates of HIV progression, whether they play mechanistic roles in linking the well-documented associations between depression and HIV progression, and/or whether they play a more causal role in HIV immunopathogenesis (Boasso & Shearer, 2007).

Studies evaluating psychosocial interventions in HIV need to incorporate into their research design and elucidate (not just speculate, post hoc) the mechanisms by which any intervention-induced changes may have influenced immune and neuroendocrine functioning relevant to HIV progression. Further, there are no studies (as of this writing) that evaluate the ability of interventions to modulate specific immune factors for which there is strong biomedical evidence for mediating or influencing HIV progression. The term *psychogenicity* has been proposed to refer to the ability of a psychological or biobehavioral intervention to modify in a salutary direction individual differences on psychosocial factors that have been explicitly linked to disease progression (HIV, in the present context), mechanisms/mediators of progression, and/or relevant progression and antiprogression factors (Temoshok, 2004; Temoshok & Wald, 2002a).

The dearth of studies of mechanisms linking psychosocial factors and HIV progression may be attributed to several related factors. Chiefly, biomedical HIV research during the 1980s and the first half of the 1990s had yet to make key discoveries about the HIV coreceptors CCR5 and CXCR4, the central role of immune activation, and the importance of certain chemokines and cytokines as HIV progression or protective factors. These complex, basic science

studies were difficult for behavioral scientists to keep up with, much less contemplate integrating into their research. Further, the new biomedical HIV research on HIV pathogenesis exploded into scientific journals in the mid-1990s, along with the advent of HAART in 1996, which drastically changed the clinical picture for persons living with HIV/AIDS. The majority of behavioral HIV researchers chose at that point to take the more academically congruent path of studying behavioral factors influencing adherence to the new medications, and/or to continue along the well-paved route (although not yet a super highway) of studying behavioral prevention of HIV, research areas that will be considered next.

## HIV Behavioral Research
### Behavioral Prevention
#### A HISTORICAL SUMMARY OF HIV BEHAVIORAL PREVENTION EFFORTS 1985–1999
##### The Demedicalization of HIV/AIDS
A special issue of the *American Psychologist* published in November 1984, included the first articles written by psychologists (or by any other behavioral scientists) on the newly recognized health problem now called AIDS (which replaced the earlier and unfortunate term *gay-related immunodeficiency disease* or GRID). Although one article discussed a number of points of intersection between AIDS as a deadly disease and public health crisis and psychological research considered more broadly as *biopsychosocial*, including the possibility that psychosocial factors could contribute to disease progression through PNI mechanisms (Coates, Temoshok, & Mandel, 1984), the other articles in that issue focused on the behavioral, psychological, and mental health aspects of AIDS, particularly as they concerned gay men and sexual transmission (e.g., Batchelor, 1984; Morin, Charles, & Malyon, 1984).

It is not clear whether that publication influenced or merely heralded the separation of psychological research on HIV/AIDS from a foundation in biomedicine, as was the case, for example, in psycho-oncology research. What is clear, in hindsight, is that behavioral and psychosocial "prevention," particularly preventing sexual exposure to the virus, quickly became "demedicalized" and redirected away from the biomedical and public health issues concerned with addressing a growing epidemic and a devastating life-threatening disease for infected individuals toward prevention of HIV/AIDS discrimination and stigma among at-risk gay and bisexual men. This was perhaps inevitable, given that, unlike cancer or other diseases, HIV/AIDS in the 1980s afflicted almost exclusively gay and bisexual men in San Francisco, and predominantly elsewhere in the United States and Europe, although the New York City metropolitan area had a high concentration of AIDS cases in injecting drug users (IDUs) at that time (Des Jarlais & Friedman, 1990). Having two already stigmatized populations (i.e., gay men and IDUs) become recognized as being at increased risk for HIV/AIDS compounded this situation.

Although one of the most important biomedical milestones in the short history of the HIV pandemic was the development of the antibody blood test for HIV by Robert Gallo and colleagues (Safai et al., 1984), this test was not universally embraced as an important prevention tool by nonmedical scientists and practitioners. In fact, at that time, "activist" AIDS organizations such as ACT-UP viewed the test as the primary way to identify HIV-positive individuals and thus subject them to job, housing, and insurance discrimination. In the absence of any effective or even partially effective treatment for the devastating symptoms and diseases associated with AIDS, activists argued that HIV (antibody) testing was virtually moot, and likely to cause only psychological distress, social stigma, and ostracizing of individuals who tested HIV-positive.

A convergence of social and political pressures culminated in an unprecedented situation in 1985: Testing for HIV was conducted largely in anonymous (i.e., no name linkage) CDC-sponsored testing centers, where HIV-positive persons would *not* be reported to public health agencies for contact tracing and notification of partners as was/is the case for every other sexually transmitted infection (STI) in the United States, or where positive persons would *not* be considered as having been diagnosed with a serious disease and followed-up medically, as was/is the case for every other disease in the United States. Moreover, the *diagnosis* of HIV, now termed "positive test result," would be given, not by a physician or nurse who had medical credentials and training, but by a "HIV test counselor," who may have received, at best, a weekend course in what to tell people about the test's meaning and what they should do next, medically and psychologically (unfortunately, this is still the case as of this writing in 2011). HIV-positive persons were reassured, euphemistically, that having antibodies in their blood against the HIV virus meant that they had been exposed to HIV, not that they had dreaded "full-blown" AIDS.

## Misinformation About HIV/AIDS

During the mid-1980s, public health announcements (usually developed and promulgated by media/communications specialists, not behavioral scientists) emphasized that *anyone* could have HIV, from your grandmother to your 8-year-old neighbor boy. Prominent television spots proclaimed, "when you have sex with someone, you are having sex with every person that person ever slept with," and depicted a long line of increasingly sleazy partners. Viewers were exhorted to use a condom every single time they had sex, even with spouses, because even your spouse had a line of previous partners who certainly could not be trusted, even if you could trust your spouse with not cheating now. All this so-called public health "information" was very misleading and scientifically inaccurate. For example, if your current partner is HIV-positive, you are indeed at risk of acquiring HIV through genital or anal intercourse; however, if that person is not infected and you are not infected, it doesn't matter how many of your or your partner's past partners were HIV-positive (as long as they stayed in the past, and those relationships have not been renewed); you both managed to "dodge a bullet" and fortunately, neither one of you became infected. Subsequent biomedical research would show the surprisingly low statistical probabilities of transmission per each (sexual) act when one partner was infected.

By the end of the 1980s, it was evident even to people who were not epidemiologists that, although it was theoretically possible for your 85-year-old grandmother or your wife to be infected with HIV, this was highly unlikely (in the United States, at that time); it was *statistically* much more likely that the 24-year-old gay man down the street was infected. Such obvious inaccuracies (e.g., that anyone could be infected, so use condoms each and every time you have sex, no matter with whom), which were promulgated by well-meaning but unscientific "AIDS awareness campaigns" undermined the public's trust in the credibility of this information, which led, in turn, to mistrusting much of what the government and the CDC put out in terms of accurate information (see Temoshok, Grade, & Zich, 1989).

Many behavioral studies on HIV/AIDS in the mid to late 1980s were concerned with documenting knowledge, awareness, and beliefs (KAB research) of HIV/AIDS in various populations (e.g., DiClemente, Zorn, & Temoshok, 1986; Temoshok, Sweet, & Zich, 1987). Most preventive interventions during this period, as well as for the next two decades, were based on the commonsense notion that if people have more knowledge about how HIV can be transmitted and prevented, they will adopt these preventive behaviors, primarily using condoms. Unfortunately, there was little or no evidence for the effectiveness of AIDS awareness campaigns or interventions based only on education (Sherr, 1987). Incredibly, there was little or no evaluation of HIV/AIDS prevention education programs, especially those conducted outside academic settings; thus, no one knew that they didn't work.

It could be contended that the nadir in the public's trust in HIV/AIDS information coming from government and public health sources occurred in 2004, concerning the spermicide nonoxynol-9 (N-9), which had been promoted by AIDS educators for almost two decades as the best lubricant to enhance the preventive effectiveness of condoms (public health departments across the U.S. distributed boxes of N-9 lubricated condoms to HIV and STI clinics). A study sponsored by the United Nations Programme on AIDS (UNAIDS), which followed nearly 1,000 sex workers in Africa from 1996 to 2000, showed a 50% *higher* HIV infection rate among those who used N-9 gels compared to placebos, as well as a higher incidence of vaginal lesions, which were thought to have facilitated HIV transmission (van Damme, 2000). These findings were confirmed and extended in a National Cancer Institute study, which found that that regular use of N-9 increased the risk of infection with the sexually transmitted human papillomavirus (HPV) that can cause cervical cancer (Marais et al., 2006).

### The Neglected Focus on Secondary Prevention

It was deemed politically incorrect in the 1980s and for the following decades to refer to "high-risk persons" or even persons at high risk for acquiring HIV/AIDS, because these terms could subject these persons or groups to discrimination. Instead, it was argued, somewhat logically but very effectively, that it was less stigmatizing to refer to "risky behaviors" or behaviors that increased the chances of acquiring HIV. Although referring to "risky behaviors" seems rational at first glance, this had unintended consequences when these words were put into misleading prevention messages, which emphasized the importance of avoiding anal sex to prevent acquiring HIV. Although passive anal sex was linked statistically in a number of studies during the 1980s with a higher likelihood of acquiring HIV, this was not because this behavior was inherently "risky," but because if you were a man being the recipient of anal sex, your partner is a man and statistically more likely to be infected with HIV. Moreover, if one partner is HIV-positive, HIV is statistically more likely to be transmitted through the behavior of anal sex because it involves a volume of seminal fluid which, contains relatively high concentrations of the HIV virus, which could enter the bloodstream via lesions in the unlubricated and thus more tearable anus and rectum. If your partner is not HIV-infected, however, you could have "risky" anal sex all day long (theoretically) and not become infected with HIV (Temoshok, 1992).

The politically correct but scientifically inaccurate focus on sexual behaviors, not the persons more likely to be infected with HIV, not only engendered misleading public health messages, as discussed above, but obscured recognition of the importance of secondary HIV prevention; that is, the transmission of HIV by HIV-infected persons to uninfected partners. Although HIV-positive persons were encouraged to use condoms during sex, during the 1980s and 1990s, there was little emphasis on the fact that they could transmit this deadly virus to their sexual partner(s) if condoms were not used correctly, if they slipped or broke, occurrences which are much more likely during anal sex. HIV counselors were told by gay activists and HIV advocates that they should not question HIV-positive persons very much or at all about the number of their sexual partners, whether they used condoms during sexual intercourse, or whether they had problems using them correctly, as this would make people feel guilty about their sexuality. Counselors were further exhorted not to imply that infected individuals had a responsibility for taking actions to prevent the transmission of HIV to their sexual partners; the concept of responsibility was too close to the concept of guilt, and this would constitute "blaming the victim." At least one study, however, demonstrated that individuals with HIV/AIDS were quite aware of the distinction between blame and responsibility in terms of health behavior change, and quite willing to accept responsibility when this was clearly and non-judgmentally articulated (Moulton, Sweet & Temoshok, 1987).

In the misguided attempt to prevent discrimination against HIV-infected persons, many activists in the 1980s and 90s insisted, incorrectly, that it didn't matter whether your partner was infected or not— you should just use a condom each and every time you have sex, whether with a "one-night stand," a sex worker (prostitute), or with your spouse. Such statements flew in the face of common sense, and led many people to think, for example, "I've had dozens of condomless sexual encounters with prostitutes/ one-night stands/casual partners and didn't get infected, so I must be immune," or ". . . so I am probably already infected," concluding in the case of all these examples, ". . . so I might as well keep doing what I have been doing," or ". . . so condoms really don't matter, I don't like them, so why bother?"

Thus, by focusing only on primary prevention (i.e., the acquisition of HIV) and one prevention strategy (i.e., educating people that using condoms will help prevent HIV/AIDS), behavioral prevention efforts until the late 1990s were severely crippled, minus one of the two major arms of public health: secondary prevention. Although Des Jarlais and his colleagues were the first to sound the alarm about the enhanced HIV transmission rates among IDUs and their heterosexual partners, and to promote effective but highly politically controversial interventions such as needle exchange programs (Des Jarlais et al., 1984, DesJarlais & Friedman, 1990), the first mention of secondary HIV prevention to prevent the sexual transmission of HIV from an infected person to an uninfected partner was at a plenary session during the 1992 HIV/AIDS conference in Amsterdam, the Netherlands (Temoshok, 1992). The first time in the literature that secondary prevention was defined for HIV, following the model of other infectious diseases, was in 1998 (Temoshok & Frerichs, 1998).

Around this time, several published reports indicated that a surprisingly high percentage of HIV-positive persons did not disclose their status to some or all of their sexual partners, and admitted to inconsistent use of condoms during penetrative vaginal or anal sex with uninfected or status-unknown sexual partners (e.g., Kalichman, 2000). Disturbing levels of HIV transmission risk-relevant behaviors were reported even among HIV-infected members of the U.S. military, where there were severe sanctions for violating safe sex orders (Temoshok & Patterson, 1996).

### HIV Behavioral Prevention Efforts: 2000–2010

With the initial decline in new infections halting at an unacceptably high rate of approximately 40,000 per year since 1992 (CDC, 2000), the CDC announced a new prevention strategy in 2001 (Janssen et al., 2001). The Serostatus Approach to Fighting the Epidemic (SAFE) was aimed at reducing the risk of transmission, and was targeted specifically to seropositive individuals, but also to those who are currently unaware of their serostatus. The five essential components/objectives of SAFE are to: (a) increase the number of HIV-infected persons who know their serostatus, (b) increase the use of health care and preventive services, (c) increase high-quality care and treatment, (d) increase adherence to therapy by individuals with HIV, and (e) increase the number of individuals with HIV who adopt and sustain HIV-STD risk reduction behavior.

In 2003, the CDC issued new recommendations for health care providers to prioritize screening and brief interventions to reduce transmission risk–relevant behaviors among their HIV-positive patients (CDC, 2003a). These recommendations were part of a new federal HIV prevention strategy that emphasized wider HIV testing, early detection, and treatment of HIV infection (CDC, 2003b). The CDC had recognized, finally, the need to focus on and fund secondary prevention initiatives, dubbed "prevention for positives."

### HIV Prevention Integrated into Medical Care and Treatment

HIV screening and early detection are critical to getting HIV-infected persons into medical care and treatment, and to prevent further transmission to sexual or injecting drug-sharing partners, and perinatally, from mother to child. Based on the 2006 HIV testing recommendations from the CDC (Branson et al., 2006, Branson, 2007), all patients in health care settings, regardless of risk factors, should be notified and then screened for HIV unless they decline, in what is referred to as *opt-out screening*. In the U.S., it is now standard practice to ask every pregnant woman to be HIV tested early in her pregnancy, so that, if she is found to be HIV-positive, appropriate measures can be taken to greatly reduce the chances that her baby will be born HIV-infected, as well as to treat her condition (Panel on Antiretroviral Guidelines for Adults and Adolescents, 2008). These recommendations by the CDC have been extremely successful in reducing the risk of perinatal HIV transmission in the United States to less than 2% through the use of this combination of HIV testing, obstetrical interventions if the mother is HIV-positive (i.e., elective cesarean section at 38 weeks' gestation), and antiretroviral regimens during the last months of pregnancy (i.e., nevirapine or zidovudine; Coovadia, 2004).

Although the new emphasis in prevention strategies by the CDC to promote HIV secondary (transmission) prevention in health care settings (i.e., among patients infected with HIV) was met initially with considerable resistance from HIV activist and advocacy groups (discussed in Gerbert et al., 2006), they were welcomed by many HIV biomedical and behavioral experts as a long-overdue return to dealing with HIV/AIDS as the serious medical condition that it is, in an appropriate medical setting. Qualitative evaluations of 15 demonstration sites, which were funded under the Health Resources and Service Administration (HRSA) initiative on Prevention with Positives in Clinical Settings, revealed that interventions that were well matched both to the clinical environment and the patient populations were feasible and acceptable to health care providers and behavioral "prevention interventionists," as well as to clinic staff (Koester et al., 2007).

## Promoting Adherence to Antiretroviral Medications

With the introduction of effective ART in 1996, HIV infection was transformed from a life-threatening and ultimately fatal disease to a chronic condition. When HIV treatment consists of several medications, typically at least three drugs belonging to two classes of ART, this treatment is referred to as HAART. The wide use of HAART since 1996 has been responsible for dramatic reduction in viral burden and improved immune functioning, quality of life, and longevity in persons infected with HIV (Broder, 2009). Currently, 20 antiretroviral drugs have been approved for use in the treatment of HIV, and six classes of antiretroviral therapies are available that interrupt different stages in HIV's life cycle of replication: nucleoside/nucleotide reverse transcriptase inhibitors (NRTI), non-nucleoside reverse transcriptase inhibitors (NNRTI), protease inhibitors (PI), fusion inhibitors, CCR5 coreceptor antagonists, and integrase inhibitors (Panel on Antiretroviral Guidelines for Adults and Adolescents, 2008).

These drugs control viral replication as long as they are taken regularly, and near-exactly as prescribed. When viral replication is contained at a very low level (<50 RNA copies/mL blood), the virus (RNA) cannot be detected through currently available blood tests, at which point the patient is said to be "undetectable," which is a highly positive achievement for both the patient and the treating physician. As long as HIV is controlled at these very low levels, the immune system, particularly the key CD4 T lymphocytes can recover in terms of number and function (Lange et al., 2002). Even individuals presenting with late-stage infection may expect to have a normal lifespan, as long as they have continued access to ART, expert medical care, and cooperate and participate fully in their health care.

The promise and effectiveness of these HIV therapies rest, however, almost entirely on an individual's ability to adhere to often complicated and sometimes toxic regimens. Strict adherence (90–95+%) to antiretroviral medication regimens is necessary to maintain HIV viral suppression and prevent drug-resistant strains of the virus from arising and rendering first-line regimens ineffective (e.g., Bangsberg et al., 2000; Bangsberg, Kroetz, & Deeks, 2007). Unfortunately, adherence is often poor; therapeutic effects have been reported to be suboptimal in 30%–70% of HIV-infected patients (e.g., Low-Beer, et al., 2000). Although dozens of studies have been published to date in the health psychology and HIV/AIDS literature on approaches to promote and enhance adherence to prescribed regimens, few have demonstrated even modest increases in long-term adherence. The most effective interventions are those which address the objective of increasing adherence to therapy in combination with the objective of increasing the adoption and maintenance of HIV/STI risk reduction behaviors, as recommended in steps 4 and 5 of CDC's SAFE strategy (Janssen et al., 2001, discussed above). The best example of these combined preventive interventions has been developed and carried out by Kalichman and his colleagues (Kalichman, 2008).

## Gaps and Challenges in HIV Behavioral Prevention Research and Its Translation

### TRANSMISSION OF DRUG-RESISTANT HIV AND THE POTENTIAL FOR BIODISPARITY

The highly mutable nature of HIV has led to numerous virus mutations that cause drug resistance, which severely compromises and complicates effective HIV ART. Drug resistance constitutes a serious problem for the individual, leading to treatment failure, limited options for alternative treatments, and ultimately, disease progression. Genotypic assays can detect drug resistance mutations when present in viral genes. Phenotypic assays measure the ability of a virus to grow in different concentrations of antiretroviral drugs. Resistance to some drugs may confer cross-resistance to other classes of antiretrovirals, further complicating the selection of appropriate drug regimens (Klimas, Koneru, & Fletcher, 2008).

A growing body of evidence suggests that significant numbers of treatment-naïve patients—20% or more of patients in some studies—have evidence of drug resistance (which they could only have acquired from HIV-positive sexual and/or drug-sharing partners who have themselves developed resistance), and that much of this resistance is to the best-tolerated and easiest to use drugs (Poggensee et al., 2007; Weinstock et al., 2004). Although the risk of new infections with drug-resistant virus has received the most attention, HIV-positive sexual or IDU partners of drug-resistant individuals are also at risk for "super infection" with drug-resistant viral strains (e.g., Yerly et al., 2004). Transmission risk behaviors among HIV-positive individuals vary according to partner serostatus, with the highest rates of unprotected intercourse occurring with partners known to be seropositive (Elford, 2006; Wald & Temoshok, 2002). Although such "serosorting" does decrease the likelihood of new HIV infections, it places HIV-positive individuals and their HIV-positive sex partners at greater risk of super infection with drug-resistant strains (Temoshok & Wald, 2008).

A number of studies have shown that suboptimal adherence to HIV ART fosters the selection and emergence of mutated and resistant strains. Evidence from a variety of sources suggests that patients who are most likely to have drug-resistant HIV because of poor adherence to ART are also at increased risk of transmitting resistant HIV to others, particularly via sexual transmission (Diamond et al., 2005; Flaks et al., 2001; Remien et al., 2007; Wilson et al., 2002).

This converging evidence suggests the possibility that multi–drug resistant HIV strains will spread within segregated sexual networks. To the extent that these sexual networks are characterized by differences in socioeconomic status, geography (e.g., socially isolated neighborhoods), HIV risk-relevant behaviors (e.g., injecting drug use, men having sex with men [MSM]), and/or ethnicity/race, the result may be stratification of drug-resistant HIV into particular communities and subpopulations (Temoshok & Wald, 2002b, 2008). If this happens, the currently observed social disparities in HIV outcomes resulting from disadvantaged socioeconomic conditions and reduced access to health services and medications may become biologically entrenched, as drug-resistant strains of HIV that are more difficult to treat appear more commonly in disadvantaged communities. The term *biodisparity* has been coined to refer to this biological entrenchment of social and economic disparities (Temoshok & Wald, 2002b, 2008).

## Unabated High Rates of HIV Within Certain Ethnic and Transmission Risk Stratifications

The combination of HIV screening of pregnant women in health care settings and antiretroviral treatment to prevent mother-to-child transmission have demonstrated extremely high preventive efficacy, as discussed above. Although there was extremely rapid spread of HIV among IDUs in the first two decades of the U.S. epidemic, there are many examples of preventive risk reduction programs for IDUs that have been very effective both in preventing initial epidemics and in bringing existing epidemics under control (Des Jarlais & Semaan, 2008). Recent statistics by the CDC (analyzed through 2008) suggest that prevention efforts have not been successful, however, in reducing the number of new HIV infections or their prevalence within certain race/ethnic and transmission risk stratifications. Notably, CDC reported that, from 2005 to 2008, the estimated rate of diagnoses of HIV infection remained stable among whites, decreased among Hispanics/Latinos (although the number increased), and increased among blacks/African Americans. In 2008, blacks/African Americans accounted for 52% of all diagnoses of HIV infection.

Considering transmission risk stratification, the number of annual diagnoses of HIV infection among MSM increased from 2005 to 2008. In 2008, MSM (54%) and persons exposed through heterosexual contact (32%) accounted for 86% of all HIV diagnoses in the 37 U.S. states included in these analyses (CDC, HIV Surveillance Report, 2010). The top five cities in terms of the percentages of HIV infection among gay men were Baltimore (38%), New York (29%), Dallas (26%), Houston (26%), and Miami (25%). The high rate of infection among MSM in Baltimore may be related, in addition to the high percentage of black/African Americans, to the increase in the percentage who are unaware of their HIV status—73% in this report, up from 62% in 2005.

## Conclusion, Recommendations, and Directions for Future Behavioral Prevention Research

### NEED TO ADDRESS HIGH RATES OF HIV IN CERTAIN ETHNIC AND TRANSMISSION RISK STRATIFICATIONS

These extremely high–and increasing—rates of HIV, particularly among MSM reflect the failure of behavioral primary prevention efforts. The mainstay of most prevention programs (outside of state and federally funded initiatives and academically based research) is still education, despite the fact that research over the past nearly three decades has shown education alone to be ineffective in changing HIV and STI exposure and transmission risk–relevant behaviors, the behavior of actually getting HIV-tested, and adherence to ART for those who are HIV-positive. There is an urgent need for behavioral scientists to address the interrelated problems that are contributing to these high rates, including the limited uptake among MSM, particularly men of color, of HIV testing and of available evidence-based behavioral interventions. New research is needed to examine the interaction of biological, psychosocial, and behavioral determinants of risk to identify new intervention targets. It is critical for HIV behavioral scientists and clinicians to design and test innovative strategies and multifaceted, integrated intervention approaches to address multiple risk factors, including mental health problems and substance use (e.g., Temoshok & Wald, 2008).

## Need to Incorporate Biomedical Research on HIV Infectiousness

Epidemiologists have long been aware of an apparent contradiction in HIV transmission data: relatively high rates of heterosexual transmission, despite the fact that the estimated likelihood of HIV transmission in a single heterosexual encounter is extremely low: 1 in 700 to 1 in 3,000 for female-to-male vaginal transmission, and 1 in 200 to 1 in 2,000 for male-to-female vaginal transmission (Royce et al., 1997). This apparent contradiction is accounted for by periods of *amplified* infectiousness, in which the risk of transmission per sexual encounter is many times higher than normal (Cohen, 2006). Unfortunately, important biomedical findings on factors that increase HIV *infectiousness*—which amplifies HIV transmission—have been largely neglected by behavioral scientists conducting HIV research (Temoshok & Wald, 2008).

The first factor shown to amplify infectiousness is acute HIV infection, the period of days to a few weeks shortly after infection, during which there are very high levels of HIV in the bloodstream (viremia), and the risk of vaginal transmission of HIV may be as high as 4% per coital act, whereas the risk per act of anal intercourse is much higher than for vaginal transmission (Pilcher et al., 2004). It is, therefore, critical to develop strategies for identifying HIV infection early in the acute phase, and to enhance linkages and referral of HIV-positive persons in the acute phase of HIV infection to health care services in order to provide rapid medical treatment to reduce viral loads, behavioral assessments to identify HIV transmission risk to partners, and intensive prevention interventions to reduce enhanced transmission risk. A major problem is that patients with acute HIV infection are difficult to identify, as they either do not experience or pay attention to symptoms of

acute infection. Behavioral practitioners, in addition to primary care physicians, emergency room personnel, and other professionals who provide services to high-risk individuals need to have accurate information about the symptoms of acute HIV infection. Testing strategies designed to identify acute HIV infection also show promise, particularly when they are combined with screening for risk behaviors associated with HIV acquisition, partner notification, and thorough and persistent contact tracing efforts (Pilcher et al., 2004).

The second main factor shown to increase both HIV infectiousness and susceptibility to HIV is the presence of STIs, such as syphilis, gonorrhea, and genital herpes (herpes simplex virus-2, HSV-2) infection (Fleming & Wasserheit, 1999; Rottingen, Cameron, & Garnett, 2001). HSV-2 is perhaps the most significant STI involved in amplified HIV transmission risk, due to its wide prevalence and multiple biological interactions with HIV (Corey et al., 2004). Although ulcerative STIs such as HSV-2, syphilis, and chancroid are associated with the greatest increase in HIV transmission risk, non-ulcerative STIs also increase the likelihood of HIV transmission. In men with HIV, urethritis from *Chlamydia* or gonorrhea infection is associated with a higher seminal viral load (Cohen et al., 1997). Treatment for those STIs lowers seminal viral load (Eron et al., 1996).

These findings suggest that prompt diagnosis and treatment of STIs in both HIV-positive individuals and their HIV-negative (serodiscordant) partners are of critical importance in HIV prevention. Additionally, the acquisition of one or more STIs from a seroconcordant partner enhances HIV infectiousness in both partners, thus magnifying transmission risk for both. Thus, seroconcordant transmission risk behaviors by persons with HIV also represent a significant public health danger, which has not been addressed in most Prevention with Positives programs (Temoshok & Wald, 2008). It may be beneficial for HIV clinics to establish partner testing clinics in which full STI screening, treatment, and behavioral prevention services are made available to partners, regardless of HIV status (Sahasrabuddhe & Vermund, 2007).

## Microbicides and Other Biomedical Preventive Interventions

To the extent that condom usage has a number of practical limitations, including social, religious, and cultural taboos, combined with the persistent observation that men often resist the proposed use of a condom by their sex partners, developing an effective vaginal microbicide to enable women to protect themselves without requiring the cooperation of their partners is a public health priority (Quinn & Overbaugh, 2005). Results of a large ($N = 900$) trial that demonstrated that a topically applied vaginal gel containing the ART drug tenofovir was able to block HIV transmission were announced at the 2010 International AIDS Conference in Vienna (Cohen, 2010). and published shortly thereafter (Abdool Karim, Abdool Karim, Frolich et al., 2010). This is the first time any biological intervention against HIV transmission has shown such convincing efficacy. Overall, those who received the gel had a 39% lower chance of becoming infected with HIV than did those who received a placebo. Subset analyses revealed that the "high adherers" who used the gel as advised more than 80% of the time had a 54% reduction in risk of infection, which is in stark contrast to the subgroup who used the gel less than half the time, in whom risk reduction plummeted to 28%. Thus, there is a significant role for behavioral scientists to play, working in concert with biomedical colleagues, in developing innovative and effective interventions to enhance adherence and to reduce attitudinal, knowledge, and practical barriers to optimal use of this and future effective microbicides.

Another biomedical strategy that has been demonstrated to have a significant protective effect for men against HIV is male circumcision (Johnson & Quinn, 2009), although this is probably more of an issue for some countries in Africa than in the United States. Given the effectiveness of this relatively simple and inexpensive preventive intervention, there is a critical need for behavioral studies, conducted in collaboration with biomedical colleagues, regarding the barriers to and facilitators of uptake, and on developing and testing strategies to facilitate uptake of male circumcision (e.g., Eaton & Kalichman, 2009).

### Adherence Research That Addresses Biomedical Questions

Nearly all HIV adherence research has been concerned with either delineating factors associated with better or with worse adherence, or with interventions to promote adherence to prescribed ART medications. Biomedical/pharmaceutical questions with behavioral implications have rarely been pursued by behavioral researchers. It may be useful, therefore, to describe an example of adherence research that addresses such a question. *Pill burden* has been assumed, by HIV clinicians as well as by behavioral scientists, to be a contributing factor

to nonadherence. In response, the pharmaceutical industry has developed pills combining two or three medications (e.g., Combivir, Trizivir, Truvada, Epzicon, Atripla). A study that evaluated how this combination pill strategy contributed to ART adherence and clinical outcomes in a sample of 178 largely African American HIV-positive men and women found that patients who have trouble taking several pills are just as likely to have trouble taking one pill containing two or three medications (Temoshok & Smith, 2011). Moreover, results suggested that missing one pill with two or three medications will result more quickly in treatment failure (detectable viral load) and a lower CD4$^+$ cell count (which reflects overall health and functioning of the immune system). These findings call into question the commensense idea that pill burden is one of the primary causes of nonadherence and treatment failure, and they have important implications for medical and public health practices of prescribing ART and promoting adherence.

## Conclusion

The recurring theme in the biobehavioral and behavioral prevention research considered in this chapter is that it is critical for behavioral scientists conducting research or interventions in the HIV/AIDS arena to acquire a good working knowledge of the biomedical research in their area of inquiry, and to collaborate actively with biomedical HIV researchers and clinicians. It is not sufficient to stay merely abreast of current research in HIV pathogenesis, epidemiology, treatment, and prevention; for behavioral scientists to have a significant impact on important outcomes (slowing HIV progression, reducing HIV acquisition and transmission, increasing adherence to effective treatments), they must get ahead of the curve by being in a position to recognize future directions and opportunities for research that will have a positive, widespread, and significant impact on public health, as well as individual patients' health outcomes.

## References

Abdool Karim, Q, Abdul Karim, S.S., Frolich, J.A., Grober, A.C., Baxter, C., et al. (2010). Effectiveness and safety of tenofovir gel, an antiretroviral microbicide, for the prevention of HIV infection in women. *Science, 329*, (5996): 1168–74.

Ader R., & Cohen, N. (1982). Behaviorally conditioned immunosuppression and murine systemic lupus erythematosus. *Science, 215*, 1534–1536.

Ader, R., Mercurio, M.G., Walton, J., James, D., Davis, M., Ojha, V., et al. (2010). Conditioned pharmacotherapeutic effects: A preliminary study. *Psychosomatic Medicine, 72*(2), 192–197. (Published ahead of print as 10.1097/PSY.0b013e3181cbd38b).

Al-Harthi, L., Siegel, J., Spritzler, J., Pottage, J., Agnoli, M., & Landay, A. (2000). Maximum suppression of HIV replication leads to the restoration of HIV-specific responses in early HIV disease. *AIDS, 14*, 761–770.

Alter, G., & Altfeld, M. (2009). NK cells in HIV-1 infection: Evidence for their role in the control of HIV-1 infection. *Journal of Internal Medicine, 265*, 29–42.

Anastos, K., Schneider, M.F., Gange, S.J., Minkoff, H., Greenblatt, R.M., Feldman, J., et al. (2005). The association of race, sociodemographic, and behavioral characteristics with response to highly active antiretroviral therapy in women. *Journal of Acquired Immune Deficiency Syndrome, 39*, 537–544.

Andrieu, J.M., & Lu, W. (2004). Long-term clinical, immunologic and virologic impact of glucocorticoids on the chronic phase of HIV infection. *BMC Medicine, 2*, 17.

Antelman, G., Kaaya, S., Wei, R., Mbwambo, J., Msamanga, G.I., Fawzi, W.W., & Smith Fawzi, M.C. (2007). Depressive symptoms increase risk of HIV disease progression and mortality among women in Tanzania. *Journal of Acquired Immune Deficiency Syndrome, 44*, 470–477.

Antoni, M.H., Carrico, A.W., Duran, R.E., Spitzer, S., Penedo, F., Ironson, G., et al. (2006). Randomized clinical trial of cognitive behavioral stress management on human immunodeficiency virus viral load in gay men treated with highly active antiretroviral therapy. *Psychosomatic Medicine, 68*, 143–151.

Antoni, M.H., Cruess, D.G., Cruess, S., Lutgendorf, S., Kumar, M., Ironson, G., et al. (2000). Cognitive-behavioral stress management intervention effects on anxiety, 24-hr urinary norepinephrine output, and T-cytotoxic/suppressor cells over time among symptomatic HIV-infected gay men. *Journal of Consulting & Clinical Psychology, 68*, 31–45.

Antoni, M.H., Cruess, D.G., Klimas, N., Carrico, A.W., Maher, K., Cruess, S., et al. (2005). Increases in a marker of immune system reconstitution are predated by decreases in 24-h urinary cortisol output and depressed mood during a 10-week stress management intervention in symptomatic HIV-infected men. *Journal of Psychosomatic Research, 58*, 3–13.

Ashton, L.J., Carr, A., Cunningham, P.H., Roggensack, K.M., Law, M., Robertson, M., Cooper, D.A., & Kaldor, J.M. (1998). Predictors of progression in long-term nonprogressors. *AIDS Research and Human Retroviruses, 14*(2): 117–121.

Ashton, E., Vosvick, M., Chesney, M., Gore-Felton, C., Koopman, C., O'Shea, K., et al. (2005). Social support and maladaptive coping as predictors of the change in physical health symptoms among persons living with HIV/AIDS. *AIDS Patient Care and STDS, 19*, 587–598.

Atanackovic, D., Schnee, B., Schuch, G., Faltz, C., Schulze, J., Weber, C.S., et al. (2006). Acute psychological stress alerts the adaptive immune response: Stress-induced mobilization of effector T cells. *Journal of Neuroimmunology, 176*, 141–152.

Bailey, J.R., Williams, T.M., Siliciano, R.F., Blankson, J.N. (2006). Maintenance of viral suppression in HIV-1-infected HLA-B*57+ elite suppressors despite CTL escape mutations. *Journal of Experimental Medicine, 203*, 1357–1369.

Bangsberg, D.R., Hecht, F.M., Charlebois, E.D., Zolopa, A.R., Holodniy, M., Sheiner, L., et al. (2000). Adherence to protease inhibitors, HIV-1 viral load, and development of drug resistance in an indigent population. *AIDS, 14*, 357–366.

Bangsberg, D.R., Kroeta, D.L., & Deeks, S.G. (2007). Adherence-resistance relationships to combination HIV antiretroviral therapy. *Current HIV/AIDS Reports, 4*, 65–72.

Barroso, J. (1999). A review of fatigue in people with HIV infection. *Journal of Associated Nursing and AIDS Care, 10*(5), 42–49.

Batchelor, W.F. (1984). AIDS: A public health and psychological emergency. *American Psychologist, 39*(11), 1279–1284.

Barre-Sinoussi, F., Chermann, J.C., Rey, F., Nugeyre, M.T., Chamaret, S., Rozenbaum, W., & Montagnier, L. (1983). Isolation of a T-lymphotropic retrovirus from a patient at risk for acquired immune deficiency syndrome (AIDS). *Science, 220*, 868–871.

Bento, C.A., Hygino, J., Andrade, R.M., Saramago, C.S., Silva, R.G., Silva, A.A., et al. (2009). IL-10-secreting T cells from HIV-infected pregnant women downregulate HIV-1 replication: Effect enhanced by antiretroviral treatment. *AIDS, 23*, 9–18.

Berger, E.A., Murphy, P.M., & Farber, J.M. (1999). Chemokine receptors as HIV-1 coreceptors: Roles in viral entry, tropism and disease. *Annual Review of Immunology, 17*, 657–700.

Betts, M.R., Nason, M.C., West, S.M., De Rosa, S.C., Migueles, S.A., Abraham, J., et al. (2006). HIV nonprogressors preferentially maintain highly functional HIV-specific CD8+ T cells. *Blood, 107*, 4781–4789.

Blalock, J.E., & Smith, E.M. (2007). Conceptual development of the immune system as a sixth sense. *Brain, Behavior, and Immunity, 21*, 23–33.

Blankson, J.N., Bailey, J.R., Thayil, S., Yang, H.C., Lassen, K., Lai, J., Gandhi, S.K., et al. (2007). Isolation and characterization of replication-competent human immunodeficiency virus type 1 from a subset of elite suppressors. *Journal of Virology, 81*, 2508–2518.

Blomkvist, V., Theorell, T., Jonsson, H., Schulman, S., Berntorp, E., & Stiegendal, L.(1994). Psychosocial self-prognosis in relation to mortality and morbidity in hemophiliacs with HIV infection, *Psychotherapy and Psychosomatics, 62*, 185–192.

Boasso, A., & Shearer, G.M. (2007). How does indoleamine 2, 3-dioxygenase contribute to HIV-mediated immune dysregulation. *Current Drug Metabolism, 8*, 217–223.

Bouhnik, A.D., Preau, M., Vincent, E., Carrieri, M.P., Gallais, H., Lepeu, G., et al. (2005). Depression and clinical progression in HIV-infected drug users treated with highly active antiretroviral therapy. *Antiviral Therapy, 10*, 53–61.

Bower, J.E.,Kemeny, M.E.,Taylor, S.E., & Fahey, J.L. (1998). Cognitive processing, discovery of meaning, CD4 decline, and AIDS-related mortality among bereaved HIV-seropositive men; *Journal of Consulting and Clinical Psychology, 66*, 979–986.

Branson, B.M., Handsfield, H.H., Lampe, M.A., Janssen, R.S., Taylor, A.W., Lyss, S.B., Clark, J.E., & the Centers for Disease Control, Prevention (CDC). (2006). Revised recommendations for HIV testing of adults, adolescents, and pregnant women in health-care settings. *MMWR Recommendations and Reports 22, 55*(RR-14), 1–17.

Branson, B. (2007). Current HIV epidemiology and revised recommendations for HIV testing in health-care settings. *Journal of Medical Virology, 79*, S6–S10.

Broder, S. (2009). The development of antiretroviral therapy and its impact on the HIV-1/AIDS pandemic. *Antiviral Research, 85*, 1–18.

Brown, R.R., Ozaki, Y., Datta, S.P., Borden, E.C., Sondel, P.M., & Malone, D.G. (1991). Implications of interferon-induced tryptophan catabolism in cancer, auto-immune diseases and AIDS. *Advance in Experimental Medicine and Biology, 294*, 425–435.

Byrnes, D.M., Antoni, M.H., Goodkin, K., Efantis-Potter, J., Asthana, D., Simon, T., et al. (1998). Stressful events, pessimism, natural killer cell cytotoxicity, and cytotoxic/suppressor T cells in HIV+ black women at risk for cervical cancer. *Psychosomatic Medicine, 60*, 714–722.

Cao, Y., Shaw, G.M., Saag, M.S., Kokka, R. Todd, J., Urdea, M., & Ho, D.D. (1995). Comparison of branched DNA (bDNA) amplification technique with end-point dilution culture, p24 antigen assay and polymerase chain reaction (PCR) in the quantitation of HIV-1 in plasma. *AIDS Research and Human Retroviruses, 11*, 353–361.

Capitanio, J.P., Abel, K., Mendoza, S.P., Blozis, S.A., McChesney, M.B., Cole, S.W., & Mason, W.A. (2008). Personality and serotonin transporter genotype interact with social context to affect immunity and viral set-point in simian immunodeficiency virus disease. *Brain, Behavior, and Immunity, 22*, 676–689.

Capitanio, J.P., Mendoza, S.P., Lerche, N.W., & Mason, W.A. (1998). Social stress results in altered glucocorticoid regulation and shorter survival in simian acquired immune deficiency syndrome. *Proceedings of the National Academy of Sciences of the United States of America, 95*, 4714–4719.

Carrico, A.W., & Antoni, M.H. (2008). Effects of psychological interventions on neuroendocrine hormone regulation and immune status in HIV-positive persons: A review of randomized controlled trials. *Psychosomatic Medicine, 70*, 575–584.

Centers for Disease Control and Prevention. (1981). *Morbidity and Mortality Weekly Report, 30*(21), 1–3.

Centers for Disease Control and Prevention. (1993). *Revised Classification System for HIV Infection and Expanded Surveillance Case Definition for AIDS Among Adolescents and Adults.* Retrieved from http://www.cdc.gov/mmwr/preview/mmwrhtml/00018871.htm.

Centers for Disease Control and Prevention. (2000). *HIV/AIDS Surveillance Report, 12*(1),1–42.

Centers for Disease Control and Prevention. (2003a). Incorporating HIV prevention into the medical care of persons living with HIV. *Morbidity and Mortality Weekly Review (MMWR), 52*, 1–24.

Centers for Disease Control and Prevention. (2003b). Advancing HIV prevention: New strategies for a changing epidemic—United States, 2003. *Morbidity and Mortality Weekly Review (MMWR), 52*, 329–332.

Centers for Disease Control and Prevention. (2010). Diagnoses of HIV infection and AIDS in the United States and dependent areas, 2008. *HIV/AIDS Surveillance Report, 20*, 1–142.

Chida, Y., & Vedhara, K. (2009). Adverse psychosocial factors predict poorer prognosis in HIV disease: A meta-analytic review of prospective investigations. *Brain, Behavior, and Immunity, 23*, 434–445.

Clerici, M., Trabattoni, D., Piconi, S., Fusi, M.L., Ruzzante, S., Clerici, C., & Villa, M.L. (1997). A possible role for the cortisol/anticortisols imbalance in the progression of human immunodeficiency virus. *Psychoneuroendocrinology, 22*(Suppl. 1), S27–S31.

Coates, T.J., Temoshok, L., & Mandel, J. (1984). Psychosocial research is essential to understanding and treating AIDS. *American Psychologist, 39*, 1309–1314.

Cocchi, F., DeVico, A.L., Garzino-Demo, A., Arya, S.K., Gallo, R.C., & Lusso, P. (1995). Identification of RANTES, MIP-1 alpha, and MIP-1 beta as the major HIV-suppressive factors produced by CD8+ T cells. *Science, 270*, 1811–1815.

Cohen, J. (2010). At last, vaginal gel scores victory against HIV. *Science, 329*, 374–375.

Cohen, M.S. (2006). Amplified transmission of HIV-1: Missing link in the HIV pandemic. *Transactions of the American Clinical and Climatological Association, 117*, 213–225.

Cole, S.W. (2008). Psychosocial influences on HIV-1 disease progression: Neural, endocrine, and virologic mechanisms. *Psychosomatic Medicine, 70*, 562–568.

Cole, S.W., & Kemeny, M.E. (2001). Psychosocial influences on the progression of HIV infection. In R. Ader, D.L. Felten, & N. Cohen (Eds.), *Psychoneuroimmunology* (3rd ed., pp. 583–612). San Diego: Academic Press.

Cole, S.W., Kemeny, M.E., Fahey, J.L., Zack, J.A., & Naliboff, B.D. (2003). Psychological risk factors for HIV pathogenesis: Mediation by the autonomic nervous system. *Biological Psychiatry, 54*, 1444–1456.

Cole, S.W., Kemeny, M.E., Taylor, S.E., & Visscher, B.R. (1996). Elevated physical health risk among gay men who conceal their homosexual identity. *Health Psychology, 15*, 243–251.

Cook, J.A., Grey, D., Burke, J., Cohen, M.H., Gurtman, A.C., Richardson, J.L., et al. (2004). Depressive symptoms and AIDS-related mortality among a multisite cohort of HIV-positive women. *American Journal of Public Health, 94*, 1133–1140.

Coovadia, H. (2004). Antiretroviral agents—How best to protect infants from HIV and save their mothers from AIDS. *New England Journal of Medicine, 351*, 289–292.

Corey, L., Wald, A., Celum, C.L., & Quinn, T.C. (2004). The effects of herpes simplex virus-2 on HIV-1 acquisition and transmission: A review of two overlapping epidemics. *AIDS, 35*, 435–445.

Corley, P.A. (1996). Acquired immune deficiency syndrome: The glucocorticoid solution. *Medical Hypotheses, 47*, 49–54.

Couper, K.N., Blount, D.G., & Riley, E.M. (2008). IL-10: The master regulator of immunity to infection. *Journal of Immunology, 180*, 5771–5777.

Crepaz, N., Lyles, C., Wolitski, R., Passin, W.F., Rama, S.M., Herbst, J., et al. (2006). Do prevention interventions reduce HIV risk behaviours among people living with HIV? A meta-analytic review of controlled trials. *AIDS, 20*, 143–157.

Crepaz N., Passin, W.F., Herbst, J.H., Rama, S.M., Malow, R.M., Purcell, D.W., & Wolitski, R.J. (2008). Meta-analysis of cognitive-behavioral interventions on HIV-positive persons' mental health and immune functioning. *Health Psychology, 27*, 4–14.

Cruess, D.G., Antoni, M.H., Kumar, M., Ironson, G., McCabe, P., Fernandez, J.B., et al. (1999). Cognitive-behavioral stress management buffers decreases in dehydroepiandrosterone sulfate (DHEA-S) and increases in the cortisol/DHEA-S ratio and reduces mood disturbance and perceived stress among HIV-seropositive men. *Psychoneuroendocrinology, 24*, 537–549.

Deeks, S.G., & Walker, B.D. (2007). Human immunodeficiency virus controllers: Mechanisms of durable virus control in the absence of antiretroviral therapy. *Immunity, 27*, 406–416.

Des Jarlais, D.C., Chamberland, M.E., Yancovitz, S.R., Weinberg, P., & Friedman, S.R. (1984). Heterosexual partners: A large risk group for AIDS [letter]. *Lancet, 8415*, 1346–1347.

Des Jarlais, D.C., & Friedman, S.R. (1990). Target groups for preventing AIDS among intravenous drug users. In L. Temoshok, & A. Baum (Eds.), *Psychosocial perspectives on AIDS: Etiology, prevention, and treatment* (pp. 35–50). Hillsdale, NJ: Lawrence Erlbaum Associates, Publishers.

Des Jarlais, D.C., & Semaan, S. (2008). HIV prevention for injecting drug users: The first 25 years and counting. *Psychosomatic Medicine, 70*, 606–611.

Diamond, C., Richardson, J.L., Milam, J., Stoyanoff, S., McCutchan, J.A., Kemper, C., et al. (2005). Use of and adherence to antiretroviral therapy is associated with decreased sexual risk behavior in HIV clinic patients. *AIDS, 39*, 211–218.

DiClemente, R.J., Zorn, J., Temoshok, L. (1986). Knowledge, attitudes, and beliefs of high school students about AIDS. *American Journal of Public Health, 76*, 1143–1145.

Dolan, M.J., Kulkarni, H., Camargo, J.F., He, W., Smith, A., Anaya, J.M., et al. (2007). CCL3L1 and CCR5 influence cell-mediated immunity and affect HIV-AIDS pathogenesis via viral entry-independent mechanisms. *Nature Immunology, 8*, 1324–1336.

Eaton, L., & Kalichman, S.C. (2009). Behavioral aspects of male circumcision for the prevention of HIV infection. *Current HIV/AIDS Reports, 6*(4), 187–193.

Elford, J. (2006). Changing patterns of sexual behavior in the era of highly active antiretroviral therapy. *Current Opinion in Infectious Diseases, 19*, 26–32.

Eron, J.J., Jr., Gilliam, B., Fiscus, S., Dyer, J., & Cohen, M.S. (1996). HIV-1 shedding and chamydial urethritis. *Journal of the American Medical Association, 275* (1), 36.

Fahey, J.L., Taylor, J.M. G., Detels, R., Hofmann, B., Melmed, R., Nishanian, P., & Giorgi, J.V. (1990). The prognostic value of cellular and serologic markers in infection with human immunodeficiency virus type 1. *New England Journal of Medicine, 322*, 166–172.

Fitzpatrick, A.L., Standish, L.J., Berger, J., Kim, J.G., Calabrese, C., & Polissar, N. (2007). Survival in HIV-1-positive adults practicing psychological or spiritual activities for one year. *Alternative Theapies in Health and Medicine, 13*(5),18–20, 22–24.

Flaks, R.C., Burnman, W., Gourley, P., Rietmeijer, C., & Cohn, E.D. (2001). HIV transmission risk behavior and its relation to antiretroviral treatment adherence. *Sexually Transmitted Diseases, 77*, 184–186.

Fleming, D.T., & Wasserheit, J.N. (1999). From epidemiological synergy to public health policy and practice: The contribution of other sexually transmitted diseases to sexual transmission of HIV infection. *Sexually Transmitted Infections, 75*, 3–17.

Garssen, B., & Remie, M. (2004). Different concepts or different words? In I. Nyklíček, L. Temoshok, & A. Vingerhoets (Eds.), *Emotional expression and health* (pp. 117–136). New York: Brunner-Routledge, Hove.

Garzino-Demo, A., Moss, R.B., Margolick, J.B., Cleghorn, F., Sill, A., Blattner, W.A., et al. (1999). Spontaneous and antigen-induced production of HIV-inhibitory beta-chemokines are associated with AIDS-free status. *Proceedings of the National Academy of Sciences USA, 96*, 11986–11991.

Gerbert, B., Danley, D.W., Herzig, K., Clanon, K., Ciccarone, D., Gilbert, P., & Allerton, M. (2006). Reframing "Prevention with Positives": Incorporating counseling techniques that improve the health of HIV-positive patients. *AIDS Patient Care and STDs, 20*, 19–29.

Giorgi, J.V., Hultin, L.E., McKeating, J.A., Johnson, T.D., Owens, B., Jacobson L.P., et al. (1999). Shorter survival in advanced human immunodeficiency virus type 1 infection is more closely associated with T lymphocyte activation than with plasma virus burden or virus chemokine coreceptor usage. *Journal of Infectious Diseases, 179*, 859–870.

Goodkin, K., Feaster, D.J., Asthana, D., Blaney, N.T., Kumar, M., Baldewicz, T., et al. (1998). A bereavement support group intervention is longitudinally associated with salutary effects on the CD4 cell count and number of physician visits. *Clinical & Diagnostic Laboratory Immunology, 5*, 382–391.

Goodkin, K., Feaster, D.J., Tuttle, R., Blaney, N.T., Kumar, M., Baum, M.K., et al. (1996). Bereavement is associated with time-dependent decrements in cellular immune function in asymptomatic human immunodeficiency virus type 1-seropositive homosexual men. *Clinical & Diagnostic Laboratory Immunology, 3*, 109–118.

Gottlieb, M.S., Schroff, R., Schanker, H.M., Weisman, J.D., Fan, P.T., Wolf, R.A., & Saxon, A. (1981). *Pneumocystis carinii* pneumonia and mucosal *candidiasis* in previously healthy homosexual men: Evidence of a new acquired cellular immunodeficiency. *New England Journal of Medicine, 305*(24), 1425–1430.

Gougeon, M.L., Lecoeur, H., Dulioust, A., Enouf, M.G., Crouvoiser, M., Goujard, C., et al. (1996). Programmed cell death in peripheral lymphocytes from HIV-infected persons: increased susceptibility to apoptosis of CD4 and CD8 T cells correlates with lymphocyte activation and with disease progression. *Journal of Immunology, 156*, 3509–3520.

Greeson, J.M., Hurwitz, B.E., Llabre, M.M., Schneiderman, N., Penedo, F.J., & Klimas, N.G. (2008). Psychological distress, killer lymphocytes and disease severity in HIV/AIDS. *Brain, Behavior, and Immunity, 22*, 901–911.

Hazenberg, M.D., Otto, S.A., van Benthem, B.H., Roos, M.T., Coutinho, R.A., Lange, J.M., et al. (2003). Persistent immune activation in HIV-1 infection is associated with progression to AIDS. *AIDS, 17*, 1881–1888.

Herberman, R.B. (1986). Natural killer cells. *Annual Review of Medicine, 37*, 347–352.

Hofmann-Lehmann, R., Williams, A.L., Swenerton, R.K., Li, P.L., Rasmussen, R.A., Chenine, A.L., et al. (2002). Quantitation of simian cytokine and beta-chemokine mRNAs, using real-time reverse transcriptase-polymerase chain reaction: Variations in expression during chronic primate lentivirus infection. *AIDS Research and Human Retroviruses, 18*, 627–639.

Ho Tsong Fang, R., Colantonio, A.D., & Uittenbogaart, C.H. (2008). The role of the thymus in HIV infection: A 10 year perspective. *AIDS, 22*(2), 171–184.

Ickovics, J.R., Hamburger, M.E., Vlahov, D., Schoenbaum, E.E., Schuman, P., Boland, R.J. & Moore, J. (2001). Mortality, CD4 cell count decline, and depressive symptoms among HIV-seropositive women: Longitudinal analysis from the HIV epidemiology research study. *Journal of the American Medical Association, 285*, 1460–1465.

Ickovics, J.R., Milan, S., Boland, R., Schoenbaum, E., Schuman, P., & Vlahov, D. (2006). Psychological resources protect health: 5-year survival and immune function among HIV-infected women from four US cities. *AIDS, 20*, 1851–1860.

Ironson, G., Balbin, E., Solomon, G., Fahey, J., Klimas, N., Schneiderman, N., & Letcher, M.A. (2001). Relative preservation of natural killer cell cytotoxicity and number in healthy AIDS patients with low CD4 counts. *AIDS, 15*, 2065–2073.

Ironson, G., Balbin, E., Stieren, E., Detz, K., Fletcher, M.A., Schneiderman, N., & Kumar, M. (2008). Perceived stress and norepinephrine predict the effectiveness of response to protease inhibitors in HIV. *International Journal of Behavioral Medicine, 15*, 221–226.

Ironson, G., & Hayward, H.S. (2008). Do positive psychosocial factors predict disease progression in HIV-1? A review of the evidence. *Psychosomatic Medicine, 70*, 546–554.

Ironson, G., O'Cleirigh, C., Fletcher, M.A., Laurenceau, J.P., Balbin, E., Klimas, N., et al. (2005a). Psychosocial factors predict CD4 and viral load change in men and women with human immunodeficiency virus in the era of highly active anti-retroviral treatment. *Psychosomatic Medicine, 67*, 1013–1021.

Ironson, G., Weiss S., Lydston, D., Ishii, M., Jones, D., Asthana, D., Tobin, J., et al. (2005b). The impact of improved self-efficacy on HIV viral load and distress in culturally diverse women living with AIDS: the SMART/EST women's project. *AIDS Care, 17*, 222–236.

Irwin, M.R. (2008). Human psychoneuroimmunology: 20 years of discovery. *Brain, Behavior, and Immunity, 22*, 129–139.

Jacobson, M.A., Ditmer, D.P., Sinclair, E., Martin, J.N., Deeks, S.G., Hunt, P., Mocarski, E.S. & Shiboski, C. (2009). Human herpesvirus replication and abnormal CD8+ cell activation and low CD4+ T cell couns in antiretroviral-suppressed HIV patients. *PLoSOne, 4* (4), e5277.

Janssen, R.S., Holtgrave, D.R., Valdiserri, R.O., Shepherd, M., Gayle, H.D., & De Cock, K.M. (2001). The serostatus approach to fighting the HIV epidemic: Prevention strategies for infected individuals. *American Journal of Public Health, 91*, 1019–1024.

Kalichman, S.C. (2000). HIV transmission risk behaviors of men and women living with HIV/AIDS: Prevalence, predictors, and emerging clinical interventions. *Clinical Psychology: Science and Practice, 7*, 32–47.

Kalichman, S.C. (2008). Co-occurrence of treatment non-adherence and continued HIV transmission risk behaviors: Implications for positive prevention interventions. *Psychosomatic Medicine, 70*, 593–597.

Kemeny, M.E., & Dean, L. (1995). Effects of AIDS-related bereavement on HIV progression among New York City gay men. *AIDS Education and Prevention, 7*, 36–47.

Kemeny, M.E., Weiner, H., Duran, R., Taylor, S.E., Visscher, B., & Fahey, J.L. (1995). Immune system changes after the death of a partner in HIV-positive gay men. *Psychosomatic Medicine, 57*, 547–554.

Kinter, A., Arthos, J., Cicala, C., & Fauci, A.S. (2000). Chemokines, cytokines and HIV: A complex network of interactions that influence HIV pathogenesis. *Immunology Review, 177*, 88–98.

Klimas, N., Koneru, A.O., & Fletcher, M.A. (2008). Overview of HIV. *Psychosomatic Medicine, 70*(5), 523–530.

Koester, K.A., Maiorana, A., Vernon, K., Myers, J., Rose, C.D., & Morin, S. (2007). Implementation of HIV prevention interventions with people living with HIV/AIDS in clinical settings: Challenges and lessons learned. *AIDS and Behavior, 11*, S17–S29.

Kolber, M.A. (2008). CD38+CD8+ T-cells negatively correlate with CD4 central memory cells in virally suppressed HIV-1-infected individuals. *AIDS, 22*, 1937–1941.

Lafeuillade, A., Poizot-Martin, I., Quilichini, R., Gastaut, J.A., Kaplanski, S., Farnarier, C., et al. (1991). Increased interleu-kin-6 production is associated with disease progression in HIV infection. *AIDS, 5*, 1139–1140.

Lange, C.G., Lederman, M.M., Madero, J.S., Medvik, K., Asaad, R., Pacheko, C., et al. (2002). Impact of suppression of viral replication by highly active antiretroviral therapy on immune function and phenotype in chronic HIV-1 infection. *Journal of Acquired Immune Deficiency Syndrome, 30*, 33–40.

Lawn, S.D., Butera, S.T., & Folks, T.M. (2001). Contribution of immune activation to the pathogenesis and transmission of human immunodeficiency virus type 1 infection. *Clinical Microbiology Reviews, 14*, 753–77.

Leserman, J. (2008). Role of depression, stress, and trauma in HIV disease progression. *Psychosomatic Medicine, 70*, 539–545.

Leserman, J., Jackson, E.D., Petitto, J.M., Golden, R.N., Silva, S.G., Perkins, D.O., et al. (1999). Progression to AIDS: The effects of stress, depressive symptoms, and social support. *Psychosomatic Medicine, 61*, 397–406.

Leserman, J., Pence, B.W., Whetten, K., Mugavero, M.J., Thielman, N.M., Swartz, M.S., & Stangl, D. (2007). Relation of lifetime trauma and depressive symptoms to mortality in HIV. *American Journal of Psychiatry, 164*(11), 1707–1713.

Leserman, J., Petitto, J.M., Golden, R.N., Gaynes, B.N., Gu, H., Perkins, D.O., et al. (2000). The impact of stressful life events, depression, social support, coping and cortisol on progression to AIDS. *American Journal of Psychiatry, 157*, 1221–1228.

Leserman, J., Petitto, J.M., Gu, H., Gaynes, B.N., Barroso, J., Golden, R.N., et al. (2002). Progression to AIDS, a clinical AIDS condition, and mortality: Psychosocial and physiological predictors. *Psychological Medicine, 32*, 1059–1073.

Leserman, J., Petitto, J.M., Perkins, D.O., Folds, J.D., Golden, R.N., & Evans, D.L. (1997). Severe stress, depressive symptoms, and changes in lymphocyte subsets in human immunodeficiency virus-infected men. *Archives of General Psychiatry, 54*, 279–285.

Leserman, J., & Temoshok, L.R. (2010). HIV/AIDS: Immunological, neuroendocrinological, psychosocial, and biopsychosocial intervention factors in the pathogenesis and progression of HIV disease. In U. Ehlert & R. von Känel (Ed.), *Psychoendokrinologie und psychoimmunologie* (pp. 325–340). Berlin-Heidelberg: Springer-Verlag.

Levy, J.A. (2006). HIV pathogenesis: Knowledge gained after two decades of research. *Advances in Dental Research, 19*, 10–16.

Lima, V.D., Geller, J., Bangsberg, D.R., Patterson, T.L., Daniel, M., Kerr, T., et al. (2007). The effects of adherence on the association between depressive symptoms and mortality among HIV infected individuals first initiating HAART. *AIDS, 21*, 1175–1183.

Low-Beer, S., Yip, B., O'Shaughnessy, M., Hogg, R., & Montaner, J. (2000). Adherence to triple therapy and viral load response. *Journal of Acquired Immune Deficiency Syndrome, 23*, 360–361.

Lumley, M.A., Tomakowsky, J., & Torosian, T. (1997). The relationship of alexithymia to subjective and biomedical measures of disease. *Psychosomatics, 38*, 497–502.

Malavasi, F., Deaglio, S., Funaro, A., Ferrero, E., Horenstein, A.L., Ortolan, E., et al. (2008). Evolution and function of the ADP ribosyl cyclase/CD38 gene family in physiology and pathology. *Physiological Review, 88*, 841–886.

Marais, D., Carrara, H., Kay, P., Ramjee, G., & Williamson, A.L. (2006). The impact of the use of COL-1492, a nonoxynol-9 vaginal gel, on the presence of cervical human papillomavirus in female sex workers. *Virus Research, 121*(2), 220–222.

Masur, H., Michelis, M.A., Greene, J., Onorato, I., Vande Stouwe, R.A., Holzman, R.S., Wormer, et al. (1981). An outbreak of community-acquired *Pneumocystis carinii* pneumonia: Initial manifestation of cellular immune dysfunction. *New England Journal of Medicine, 305*(24), 1431–1438.

Mayne, T.J., Vittinghoff, E., Chesney, M.A., Barrett, D.C., & Coates, T.J. (1996). Depressive affect and survival among gay and bisexual men infected with HIV. *Archives of Internal Medicine, 156*, 2233–2238.

Mekmullica, J., Brouwers, P., Charurat, M., Paul, M., Shearer, W., Mendez, H., et al. (2009). Early immunological predictors of neurodevelopmental outcomes in HIV-infected children. *Clinical Infectious Diseases, 48*, 338–346.

Miller, G.E., Kemeny, M.E., Taylor, S.E., Cole, S.W., & Visscher, B.R. (1997). Social relationships and immune processes in HIV seropositive gay and bisexual men. *Annals of Behavioral Medicine, 19*(2), 139–151.

Moulton, J.M., Sweet, D.M., & Temoshok, L. (1987). Attributions of blame and responsibility in relation to distress and health behavior change in people with AIDS and AIDS-related complex. *Journal of Applied Social Psychology, 17*, 493–506.

Morin, S.F., Charles, K.A., & Malyon, A.K. (1984). The psychological impact of AIDS on gay men. *American Psychologist, 39*, 1288–1293.

Mülder, C.L., Antoni, M.H., Emmelkamp, P.M., Veugelers, P.J., Sandfort, T.G., van de Vijver, F.A., & de Vries, M.J. (1995). Psychosocial group intervention and the rate of decline of immunological parameters in asymptomatic HIV-infected homosexual men. *Psychotherapy & Psychosomatics, 63*, 185–192.

Nilsson, J., Kinloch-de-Loes, S., Granath, A., Sönnerborg, A., Goh, L.E., & Andersson, J. (2007). Early immune activation in gut-associated and peripheral lymphoid tissue during acute HIV infection. *AIDS, 21*(5), 565–574.

O'Cleirigh, C., Ironson, G., Antoni, M., Fletcher, M.A., McGuffey, L., Balbin, E., et al. (2003). Emotional expression and depth processing of trauma and their relation to long-term survival in patients with HIV/AIDS. *Journal of Psychosomatic Research, 54*, 225–235.

O'Cleirigh, C., Ironson, G., Fletcher, M.A., & Schneiderman, N. (2008). Written emotional disclosure and processing of trauma are associated with protected health status and immunity in people living with HIV/AIDS. *British Journal of Health Psychology, 13*(4), 81–84.

O'Leary, A., Temoshok, L., Jenkins, S.R., & Sweet, D.M. (1989). Autonomic reactivity and immune function in men with AIDS. *Psychophysiology, 26*, S47.

Page-Shafer K., Delorenze, G.N., Satariano, W., & Winkelstein, W., Jr. (1996). Comorbidity and survival in HIV-infected men in the San Francisco Men's Health Survey. *Annals of Epidemiology, 6*, 420–430.

Panel on Antiretroviral Guidelines for Adults and Adolescents. (2008, January 29). *Guidelines for the use of antiretroviral agents in HIV-1 infected adults and adolescents.* Department of Health and Human Services, Washington, DC.

Pantaleo, G., Menzo, S., Vaccarezza, M., Graziosi, C., Cohen, O.J., Demarest, J.F., et al. (1995). Studies in subjects with long-term nonprogressive human immunodeficiency virus infection. *New England Journal of Medicine, 332*, 209–216.

Parienti, J.J., Massari, V., Descamps, D., Vabret, A., Bouvet, E., Larouze, B., & Verdon, R. (2004). Predictors of virologic failure and resistance in HIV-infected patients treated with nevirapine- or efavirenz-based antiretroviral therapy. *Clinical Infectious Diseases, 38*, 1311–1316.

Pereya, F., Addo, M.M., Kaufmann, D.E., Liu, Y., Miura, T., Rathod, A., et al. (2008). Genetic and immunologic heterogeneity among persons who control HIV infection in the absence of therapy. *Journal of Infectious Diseases, 197*(4), 563–571.

Perrella, O., Carrieri, P.B., Guarnaccia, D., & Soscia, M. (1992). Cerebrospinal fluid cytokines in AIDS dementia complex. *Journal of Neurology, 239*, 387–388.

Pilcher, C.D., Eron, J.J., Glavin, S., Gay, C., & Cohen, M.S. (2004). Acute HIV revisited: New opportunities for treatment and prevention. *Journal of Clinical Investigation, 113*, 937–945.

Poggensee, G., Kücherer, C., Werning, J., Somogyi, S., Bieniek, B., Dupke, S., et al. (2007). Impact of transmission of drug-resistant HIV on the course of infection and the treatment success. Data from the German HIV-1 Seroconverter Study. *HIV Medications, 8*, 511–519.

Poli, G., Bressler, P., Kinter, A., Duh, E., Timmer, W.C., Rabson, A., et al. (1990). Interleukin 6 induces human immunodeficiency virus expression in infected monocytic cells alone and in synergy with tumor necrosis factor alpha by transcriptional and post-transcriptional mechanisms. *Journal of Experimental Medicine, 172*, 151–158.

Popovic, M., Sarngadharan, M.G., Read, E., & Gallo, R.C. (1984a). Antibodies reactive with human T-lymphotropic retrovirses (HTLV-III) in the serum of patients with AIDS. *Science, 224*, 506–508.

Popovic, M., Sarngadharan, M.G., Read, E., & Gallo, R.C. (1984b). Detection, isolation, and continuous production of cytopathic retroviruses (HTLV-III) from patients with AIDS and pre-AIDS. *Science, 224*, 497–500.

Quinn, T.C, & Overbaugh, J. (2005). HIV/AIDS in women: An expanding epidemic. *Science, 208*, 1582–1583.

Reed, G.M., Kemeny, M.E., Taylor, S.E., Wang, H.Y., & Visscher, B.R. (1994). Realistic acceptance as a predictor of decreased survival time in gay men with AIDS. *Health Psychology, 13*, 299–307.

Remien, R.H., Exner, T.M., Morin, S.F., Ehrhardt, A.A., Johnson, M.O., Correale, J., et al. (2007). Medication adherence and sexual risk behavior among HIV-infected adults: Implications for transmission of resistant virus. *AIDS and Behavior, 11*, 663–675.

Rottingen, J.A., Cameron, D.W., & Garnett, G.P. (2001). A systematic review of the epidemiologic interactions between classic sexually transmitted diseases and HIV: How much really is known? *Sexually Transmitted Diseases, 28*, 579–597.

Royce, R.A., Sena, A., Cates, W.J., & Cohen, M.S. (1997). Sexual transmission of HIV. *New England Journal of Medicine, 336*, 1072–1078.

Sahasrabuddhe, V.V., Vermund, S.H. (2007). The future of HIV prevention: Control of sexually transmitted infections and circumcision interventions. *Infectious Disease Clinics of North America, 21*, 241–257.

Safai, B., Sarngadharan, M.G., Groopman, J.E., Arnett, K., Popovic, M., Sliski, A., et al. (1984). Seroepidemiological studies of human T-lymphotropic retrovirus type III in acquired immunodeficiency syndrome. *Lancet, 1*(8392), 1438–1440.

Sajadi, M.M., Heredia, A., Le, N., & Constantine, N. (2007). HIV-1 natural viral suppressors: Control of viral replication in the absence of therapy. *AIDS, 21*, 517–519.

Salvaggio A., Balotta C., Galli M., & Clerici M. (1996). CD4 count in HIV infection is positively correlated to interferon-gamma and negatively correlated to interleukin-10 in vitro production. *AIDS, 10*, 449–451.

Schechter, M.T., Hogg, R.S., Aylward, B., Craib, K.J., Le, T.N., Montaner, J.S. (1994). Higher socioeconomic status is associated with slower progression of HIV infection independent of access to health care. *Journal of Clinical Epidemiology, 47*(1), 59–67.

Schedlowski, M., & Pacheco-López, G. (2010). The learned immune response: Pavlov and beyond. *Brain, Behavior, and Immunity, 24*, 176–185.

Schroecksnadel, K., Sarcletti, M., Winkler, C., Mumelter, B., Weiss, G., Fuchs, D., et al. (2008). Quality of life and immune activation in patients with HIV-infection. *Brain, Behavior, and Immunity, 22*, 881–889.

Schroecksnadel, K., Zangerle, R., Bellmann-Weiler, R., Garimorth, K., Weiss, G., & Fuchs, D. (2007). Indoleamine-2, 3-dioxygenase and other interferon-gamma-mediated pathways in patients with human immunodeficiency virus infection. *Current Drug Metabolism, 8*, 225–236.

Scott-Sheldon, L.A., Kalichman, S.C., Carey, M.P., & Fielder, R.L. (2008). Stress management interventions for HIV+ adults: A meta-analysis of randomized controlled trials, 1989 to 2006. *Health Psychology, 27*, 129–139.

Sherr, L. (1987). An evaluation of the UK Government Health Education Campaign. *Psychology and Health, 1*, 61–72.

Shin, H.D., Winkler, C., Stephens, J.C., Bream, J., Young, H., Goedert, J.J., et al. (2000). Genetic restriction of HIV-1 pathogenesis to AIDS by promoter alleles of IL10. *Proceedings of the National Academy of Sciences USA, 97*, 14467–14472.

Siegel, F.P., Lopez, C., Hammer, G.S., Brown, A.E., Kornfeld, S.J., Gold.J., et al. (1981). Severe acquired immunodeficiency in male homosexuals manifested by chronic perianal ulcerative herpes simplex lesions. *New England Journal of Medicine, 305*(24), 1439–1444.

Sloan, E.K., Collado-Hidalgo, A., & Cole, S.W. (2007). Psychobiology of HIV infection. In R. Ader (Ed.), *Psychoneuroimmunology* (4th ed., pp. 1053–1076). Burlington, MA: Elsevier Academic Press.

Solano, L., Costa, M., Salvati, S., Coda, R., Aiuti, F., Mezzaroma, I., & Bertini, M. (1993). Psychosocial factors, clinical evolution in HIV-infection: a longitudinal study. *Journal of Psychosomatic Research, 37*, 39–51.

Solano, L., Costa, M., Temoshok, L., Salvati, S., Coda, R., Aiuti, F., et al. (2002). An emotionally inexpressive (Type C) coping style influences HIV disease progression at six and twelve month follow-ups. *Psychology & Health, 7*, 641–655.

Solomon, G.F., Kemeny, M., & Temoshok, L. (1991). Psychoneuroimmunologic aspects of human immunodeficiency virus infection. In R. Ader, D.L. Felten, & N. Cohen (Eds.), *Psychoneuroimmunology II* (pp. 1081–1113). Orland, FL: Academic Press.

Solomon, G.F., & Temoshok, L. (1987). A psychoneuroimmunologic perspective on AIDS research: Questions, preliminary findings, and suggestions. *Journal of Applied Social Psychology, 17*, 286–308.

Solomon, G.F., Temoshok, L., O'Leary, A., & Zich, J. (1987). An intensive psychoimmunologic study of long-surviving persons with AIDS: Pilot work, background studies, hypotheses, and methods. *Annals of the New York Academy of Sciences, 496*, 647–655.

Sorrells, S.F., & Sapolsky, R.M. (2007). An inflammatory review of glucocorticoid actions in the CNS. *Brain, Behavior, and Immunity, 21*, 259–272.

Taylor, G.J. (2004). Alexithymia: 25 years of theory and research. In I. Nyklíček, L. Temoshok, A. Vingerhoets (Eds.), *Emotional expression and health*. Hove and New York: Brunner-Routledge.

Temoshok, L. (1985). Biopsychosocial studies on cutaneous malignant melanoma: Psychosocial factors associated with prognostic indicators, progression, psychophysiology, and tumor-host response. *Social Science & Medicine, 20*, 833–840.

Temoshok, L. (1987). *Report on the First National Conference on Psychoneuroimmunology and HIV/AIDS*. Bethesda, MD: The National Institutes of Mental Health.

Temoshok, L. (1990). On attempting to articulate the biopsychosocial model: Psychological-psychophysiologicahomeostasis. In H. Friedman (Ed.), *Personality and disease*, (pp. 203–225). New York, NY: Wiley.

Temoshok, L. (1992). *Preventing HIV transmission by HIV infected individuals: The forgotten focus*. Plenary address, VIII International Conference on AIDS/III STD world congress, Amsterdam, The Netherlands.

Temoshok, L. (1995). On biobehavioral models of cancer stress and disease course. *American Psychologist, 50*, 1104–1105.

Temoshok, L. (2000). Complex coping patterns and their role in adaptation and neuroimmunomodulation: Theory, methodology, and research. *Annals of the N,Y, Academy of Sciences, 917*, 446–455.

Temoshok, L.R. (2004). Rethinking theory and research in biopsychosocial oncology. *Psycho-oncology, 13*, 460–467.

Temoshok, L., & Dreher, H. (1992). *The type C connection: The behavioral links to cancer and your health*. New York: Random House.

Temoshok, L.R., & Frerichs, R.R. (1998). Secondary HIV prevention. *Focus: A Guide to AIDS Research and Counseling, 13*(7), 1–4.

Temoshok, L., Garzino-Demo, A., Smith, L., & Wiley, J.A. (2011). Dysregulated physiological and emotional responses to stress are associated with cytokine and chemokine HIV progression mediators and with CD4+ count at 36-month follow-up. *Journal of Acquired Immune Deficiency Syndromes, 56*, 88.

Temoshok, L., Grade, M., & Zich, J. (1989). Public health, the press, and AIDS: An analysis of newspaper articles in London and San Francisco. In I. Corliss, & M. Pittman-Lindeman (Eds.), *AIDS: Principles, practices, and politics* (pp. 525–542). New York: Harper & Row.

Temoshok, L.R., & Patterson, T.L. (1996). Risk of HIV transmission in infected US military personnel. [research letter]. *The Lancet, 347*, 697.

Temoshok, L., & Smith, L. (2011). Defining HIV medicine adherence as number of prescribed medications vs. doses taken is the best predictor of clinical outcomes. *Annals of Behavioral Medicine, 41*, s63.

Temoshok, L., Sweet, D.M., & Zich, J. (1987). A three-city comparison of the public's knowledge and attitudes about AIDS. *Psychology & Health, 1*, 43–60.

Temoshok, L.R., Synowski, S.J., Wald, R.L., & Garzino-Demo, A. (2009a). Baseline cardiovascular reactivity predicts significantly lower production of HIV entry-inhibiting beta-chemokines at 24-month follow-up. *Brain, Behavior, and Immunity, 23*, 504–505.

Temoshok, L.R., & Wald, R.L. (2002a). Change is complex: Rethinking research on psychosocical interventions and cancer. *Integrative Cancer Therapies, 1*, 135–145.

Temoshok, L.R., & Wald, R.L. (2002b). The potential for biodisparity in disadvantaged communities: An illustration from inner-city Baltimore. *Journal of Human Virology, 5*(91), 252.

Temoshok, L.R., & Wald, R.L. (2008). Integrating multidimensional HIV prevention programs into health care settings. *Psychosomatic Medicine, 70*, 612–619.

Temoshok, L.R., Wald, R.L., Synowski, S., & Garzino-Demo, A. (2008a). Coping as a multi-system construct associated with pathways mediating HIV-relevant immune function and disease progression. *Psychosomatic Medicine, 70*, 555–561.

Temoshok, L.R., Wald, R.L., Synowski, S.J., Garzino-Demo, A., & Wiley, J.A. (2009b). Baseline alexithymia predicts stimulated production of a key HIV anti-progression factor over 24 months of follow-up. *Annals of Behavioral Medicine, 37*, S19.

Temoshok, L.R., Waldstein, S.R., Wald, R.L., Garzino-Demo, A., Synowski, S.J., Sun, L., & Wiley, J.A. (2008b). Type C coping, alexithymia, and heart rate reactivity are associated independently and differentially with specific immune mechanisms linked to HIV progression. *Brain, Behavior, and Immunity, 22*, 781–792.

Temoshok, L., Zich, J., Solomon, G.F. & Stites, D.P. (1987, June). An intensive psychoimmunologic study of long-surviving persons with AIDS. Paper presented at the III International Conference on AIDS. Washington, D.C.

Thornton, S., Troop, M. Burgess, A.P., Button, J., Goodall, R., Flynn, R., Gazzard, B.G., Catalán, J., & Easterbrook, P.J. (2000). The relationship of psychological variables and disease progression among long-term HIV-infected men. *International Journal of STD & AIDS, 11*, 734–742.

Tilling, R., Kinloch, S., Goh, L.E., Cooper, D., Perrin, L., Lampe, F., et al. (2002). Parallel decline of CD8+/CD38++ T cells and viraemia in response to quadruple highly active antiretroviral therapy in primary HIV infection. *AIDS, 16*, 589–596.

Troop, M., Easterbrook, P., Thornton, S., Flynn, R., Gazzard, B., & Catalan, J. (1997). Reasons given by patients for "non-progression" in HIV infection. *AIDS Care, 9*, 133–142.

Tyler, D.S., Stanley, S.D., Nastala, C.A., Austin, A.A., Bartlett, J.A., Stine, K.C., et al. (1990). Alterations in antibody-dependent cellular cytotoxicity during the course of HIV-1 infection. Humoral and cellular defects. *Journal of Immunology, 144*, 3375–3384.

Ullum, H., Cozzi, L.A., Victor, J., Aladdin, H., Phillips, A.N., Gerstoft, J., et al. (1998). Production of beta-chemokines in human immunodeficiency virus (HIV) infection: Evidence that high levels of macrophage inflammatory protein-1beta are associated with a decreased risk of HIV disease progression. *Journal of Infectious Diseases, 177*, 331–336.

Ulmer, A., Muller, M., Bertisch-Mollenhoff, B., & Frietsch, B. (2005). Low dose prednisolone reduces CD4+ T cell loss in therapy-naive HIV-patients without antiretroviral therapy. *European Journal of Medical Research, 10*, 105–109.

van Damme, L. (2000, July 14). *Advances in topical microbicides.* Presented at the XIII International AIDS Conference, Durban, South Africa.

Vassend, O., Eskild, A., & Halvorsen, R. (1997). Negative affectivity, coping, immune status, and disease progression in HIV infected individuals. *Psychology & Health, 12*, 375–388.

Vassend, O., & Eskild, A. (1998). Psychological distress, coping, and disease progression in HIV-positive homosexual men. *Journal of Health Psychology, 3*, 243–257.

Villes, V., Spire, B., Lewden, C., Perronne, C., Besnier, J.M., Garre, M., et al. (2007). The effect of depressive symptoms at ART initiation on HIV clinical progression and mortality: Implications in clinical practice. *Antiviral Therapy, 12*, 1067–1074.

Wald, R.L., Dowling, G.C., & Temoshok, L.R. (2006). Coping styles predict immune system parameters and clinical outcomes in patients with HIV. *Retrovirology, 3*(Suppl. 1), P65.

Wald, R.L., &Temoshok, L.R. (2002). Transmission risk behaviors in HIV patients attending an inner-city HIV primary care clinic. *Journal of Human Virology, 5*, 91.

Waldstein, S.R., Kauhanen, J., Neumann, S.A., & Katzel, L.I. (2002). Alexithymia and cardiovascular risk in older adults: Psychosocial, psychophysiological, and biomedical correlates. *Psychology & Health, 17*, 597–610.

Ward, J., & Barker, E. (2008). Role of natural killer cells in HIV pathogenesis. *Current HIV/AIDS Reports, 5*, 44–50.

Weinstock, H.S., Zaidi, I., Heneine, W., Bennett, D., Garcia-Lerma, J.G., Douglas, J.M., Jr., et al. (2004). The epidemiology of antiretroviral drug resistance among drug-naïve HIV-1-infected persons in 10 US cities. *Journal of Infectious Diseases,189*, 2174–2180.

Widner, B., Laich, A., Sperner-Unterweger, B., Ledochowski, M., & Fuchs, D. (2002). Neopterin production, tryptophan degradation, and mental depression—What is the link? *Brain, Behavior, and Immunity, 16*, 590–595.

Wilson, T.E., Barrón, Y., Cohen, M., Richardson, J., Greenblatt, R., Sacks, H.S., & Young, M. (2002). Adherence to antiretroviral therapy and its association with sexual behavior in a national sample of women with human immunodeficiency virus. *AIDS, 34*, 529–534.

Yehuda, R., Boisoneau, D., Lowy, M.T., & Giller, E.L., Jr. (1995). Dose-response changes in plasma cortisol and lymphocyte glucocorticoid receptors following dexamethasone administration in combat veterans with and without posttraumatic stress disorder. *Archives of General Psychiatry, 52*, 583–593.

Yerly, S., Jost, S., Monnat, M., Telenti, A., Cavassini, M., Chave, J.P., et al. (2004). HIV-1 co/super-infection in intravenous drug users. *AIDS, 18*, 1413–1421.

Zangerle, R., Widner, B., Quirchmair, G., Neurauter, G., Sarcletti, M., & Fuchs, D. (2002). Effective antiretroviral therapy reduces degradation of tryptophan in patients with HIV-1 infection. *Clinical Immunology, 104*, 242–247.

# PART 4

# Health Behaviors and Change

Ralf Schwarzer

**Abstract**

An overview of theoretical constructs and mechanisms of health behavior change is provided, based on a self-regulation framework that makes a distinction between goal setting and goal pursuit. Risk perception, outcome expectancies, and task self-efficacy are seen as predisposing factors in the goal setting phase (motivational phase), whereas planning, action control, and maintenance/recovery self-efficacy are regarded as influential in the goal pursuit phase (volitional phase). The first phase leads to forming an intention, and the second phase leads to actual behavior change. Such a mediator model serves to explain social-cognitive processes in health behavior change. Adding a second layer on top of it, a moderator model is provided in which three stages are distinguished to segment the audience for tailored interventions. Identifying persons as preintenders, intenders, or actors offers an opportunity to match theory-based treatments to specific target groups. Research examples serve to illustrate the application of the model to health promotion.

**Keywords:** Self-regulation, risk perception, outcome expectancies, self-efficacy, preintenders, intenders, health promotion

Many health conditions are caused by risk behaviors, such as problem drinking, substance use, smoking, reckless driving, overeating, or unprotected sexual intercourse. The key question in health behavior research is how to predict and modify the adoption and maintenance of health behaviors. Fortunately, human beings have, in principle, control over their conduct. Health-compromising behaviors can be eliminated by self-regulatory efforts, and health-enhancing behaviors can be adopted instead, such as physical exercise, weight control, preventive nutrition, dental hygiene, condom use, or accident prevention. Health self-regulation refers to the motivational, volitional, and actional processes of abandoning such health-compromising behaviors in favor of adopting and maintaining health-enhancing behaviors (Leventhal, Weinman, Leventhal, & Phillips, 2008).

This chapter highlights some current issues in health behavior research. In the first section, various psychological constructs are described that have been found useful. These are intention, risk perception, outcome expectancies, perceived self-efficacy, and planning. In the second section, theoretical perspectives on the health behavior change process are discussed. From a metatheoretical viewpoint, stage models are contrasted to continuum models. Following is one example of a continuum model (theory of planned behavior) and one example of a stage model (transtheoretical model). Then a two-layer hybrid framework is introduced (health action process approach). In the third section, some unresolved issues in health behavior research are discussed. All sections are illustrated by research findings and suggestions for further research.

## Constructs and Principles
### Intention, Motivation, Volition
Changes in health behaviors can be influenced by opportunities and barriers, by explicit decisions,

or by random events. In this chapter, we are dealing solely with intentional changes that happen when people become motivated to alter their previous way of life and set goals for a different course of action. For example, they may consider to quit smoking, or they make an effort to do so. Thus, intention represents a key factor in health behavior change. This construct had been suggested by Fishbein and Ajzen (1975) to operate as a mediator to overcome the attitude–behavior gap. Since behaviors could not be well predicted by attitudes, intention appeared to be a useful mediator and a better proximal predictor of many behaviors. Since then, there is consensus that intention is an indispensable variable when it comes to explaining and predicting behaviors. In the process of motivation, intention has been regarded as a kind of "watershed" between an initial goal setting phase and a subsequent goal pursuit phase. Lewin, Dembo, Festinger, and Sears (1944) described a *motivation phase* of goal setting that is followed by a *volition phase* of goal pursuit. This distinction has been elaborated and called the *Rubicon model* by Heckhausen (1980, 1991), Heckhausen and Gollwitzer (1987), and Kuhl (1983). Motivation is a preintentional process, whereas volition refers to a postintentional process. When describing health behavior change, it is most helpful to follow this distinction. For example, to gauge the progress of an individual who is supposed to quit smoking and to design therapeutic interventions, the first question to ask should be whether this person is either preintentional or postintentional. To which degree is the person motivated (goal setting), or to which degree is the person making explicit efforts to quit (goal pursuing)? The terms *motivation* and *goal setting* pertain to the preintentional phase, whereas the terms *volition* and *goal pursuit* pertain to the postintentional phase. These distinctions will be discussed in more detail in the section on stage models.

Although the construct of intention is indispensable in explaining health behavior change, its predictive value is limited (Schwarzer, 1992; Sheeran, 2002). When trying to translate intentions into behavior, individuals are faced with various obstacles, such as distractions, forgetting, or conflicting bad habits. Godin and Kok (1996), who reviewed 19 studies, found a mean correlation of .46 between intention and health behavior, such as exercise, screening attendance, and addictions. Abraham and Sheeran (2000) reported behavioral intention measures to account for 20%–25% of the variance in health behavior measures. If not equipped with means to meet these obstacles, motivation alone does not suffice to change behavior (Baumeister, Heatherton & Tice, 1994). To overcome this limitation, further constructs are required that operate in concert with the intention. Volitional factors can help to bridge the intention–behavior gap (Sheeran, 2002) since people do not fully act upon their intentions (e.g., Abraham, Sheeran, & Johnston, 1998). *Implementation intentions* are one such volitional factor (Gollwitzer, 1999) that can be interpreted as postintentional mental simulation or planning strategies. A detailed discussion follows below in the section on planning.

A concept related to intention is behavioral willingness (Gibbons & Gerrard, 1997; Gibbons, Gerrard, & Lane, 2003). The authors believe that health-compromising behavior is often not intentional, but is rather a spontaneous reaction to social circumstances. Gibbons and Gerrard define behavioral willingness as an openness to risk opportunity (i.e., what an individual would be willing to do under certain circumstances).

### Risk Perception

At first glance, perceiving a health threat seems to be the most obvious prerequisite for the motivation to overcome a risk behavior (e.g., smoking). Consequently, a central task for health communication is not only to provide information about the existence and magnitude of a certain risk, but also to increase the subjective relevance of a health issue to focus the individuals' attention on information pertaining directly to their own risk. However, general perceptions of risk (e.g., "Smoking is dangerous") and personal perceptions of risk (e.g., "I am at risk because I am a smoker") often differ to a great extent. Individuals could be well informed about general aspects of certain risks and precautions (e.g., most smokers acknowledge that smoking can cause diseases), but, nevertheless, many might not feel personally at risk (Klein & Cerully, 2007).

Especially when it comes to a comparison with similar others, one's view of the risk is somewhat distorted (see Suls, 2011, Chapter 12, this volume). On average, individuals tend to see themselves as being less likely than others to experience health problems in the future. For example, when asked how they judge their risk of becoming infected with human immunodeficiency virus (HIV) compared to an average peer of the same sex and age (the *average risk*), participants typically give a below-average estimate (e.g., Hahn & Renner, 1998). This has been coined "unrealistic optimism" or "optimistic bias" (Weinstein, 1980, 1988). It reflects the difference between the perceived risk for oneself and that for others, belonging to the broader construct of defensive optimism (Taylor & Brown, 1994).

*Defensive optimism* represents an underestimation of risk that hinders the adoption of precautionary behaviors, whereas *functional optimism* promotes their adoption (Radcliffe & Klein, 2002; Schwarzer, 1994). People who are optimistic may be so in two ways: They underestimate risks, but are optimistic about their capability to overcome their bad habits. Since both kinds of optimism are confounded, risk perceptions are often poor predictors of behavior.

People with a high-risk status (e.g., high blood pressure, obesity, and high cholesterol) should perceive a higher pressure to act, and they are more inclined to form an intention to change their habits than are people who are not at risk (cf. Croyle, Sun, & Louie, 1993; Renner, 2004). The actual risk status should be related to perceived risk for future health problems and diseases. However, the relationship between current objective risk status and risk perception varies considerably, suggesting that they might contribute differently to intention forming.

Renner and Schwarzer (2005) found that objective risk predicted risk perception, but the latter did not translate into an intention to eat a healthy diet. Thus, risk communication might be a dead end, resulting in higher risk perception, but not leading to intention formation. The relation between objective risk status, risk perception, and risk behavior is still not well understood and represents a challenge for further research (Brewer, Weinstein, Cuite, & Herrington, 2004; Panzer & Renner, 2008). Both the objective and subjective risk may not be functional for health behavior change if not accompanied by other motivational and volitional factors.

An example for the ambiguous role of fear appeals in health promotion is the current debate on the introduction of graphic warning labels on cigarette packs. Although good research on fear appeals has been published for half a century (e.g., Leventhal, Singer, & Jones, 1965), public health agents seem to be unaware of the psychological mechanisms that are involved in risk communication. Some epidemiological studies provide evidence for the effectiveness of graphic warning labels. However, this kind of evidence is methodologically weak because studies are nonexperimental and do not allow for causal inferences. Typically, in such studies telephone interviews are conducted based on random-digit dialing, and a subsample of volunteers report about reading warning labels and what they believe is the impact on their intentions not to smoke, and eventually, on their attempts at quitting. It can be assumed that respondents constitute a positive selection of intenders or contemplators who are interested in the topic, and who consider quitting anyway. Such studies are typically not guided by health behavior theories but are rather data driven. It is indeed very hard to collect valid data on this issue because there might be no good way to design a randomized controlled trial. Experimental work on risk communication mainly takes place in the laboratory, where internal validity is high, but external (ecological) validity is low. One such experiment was recently conducted to investigate the impact of cigarette warning labels on cognitive dissonance in smokers. Smokers' and nonsmokers' risk perceptions with regard to smoking-related diseases were measured with response latencies before and after presentation of warning labels. Responses showed an impact of confrontation with smoking-related health risks rather than an impact of warning labels themselves.

The adoption of health behaviors should not be viewed simplistically as a response to a health threat. Risk information alone does not help people to change risky behaviors because it does not provide meaningful information about how to manage behavioral changes. Initial risk perception seems to be advantageous in helping people become motivated to change, but later, other factors are more influential in the self-regulation process. This state of affairs has encouraged health psychologists to design more complex models that combine risk perception with other determinants and processes of change.

### Outcome Expectancies

In addition to being aware of a health threat, people also need to know how to regulate their behavior. They need to understand the links between actions and subsequent outcomes. These outcome expectancies can be the most influential beliefs in the motivation to change. The term *outcome expectancies* is most common in social-cognitive theory (Bandura, 1997). The equivalent terms *pros and cons* are used in the transtheoretical model (Prochaska & Velicer, 1997), in which they represent the decisional balance in people who are contemplating whether to adopt a novel behavior or not. In the theory of reasoned action (Fishbein & Ajzen, 1975), the corresponding term is *behavioral beliefs* that act as precursors of attitudes.

The pros and cons represent positive and negative outcome expectancies. A smoker may find more good reasons to quit ("If I quit smoking, then my friend will like me much more") than reasons to continue smoking ("If I quit, I will become more tense and irritated"). This imbalance in favor of positive outcome expectancies will not lead directly to action, but it can help to generate the intention to quit. Outcome expectancies can also be understood as means–ends relationships, indicating that people know proper strategies to produce the desired effects. Many of those cognitions represent social outcome expectancies (normative beliefs) by pertaining to the social consequences of a particular behavior (Trafimow & Fishbein, 1995).

The perceived contingencies between actions and outcomes need not be explicitly worded; they can also be rather diffuse mental representations, loaded with emotions (Trafimow & Sheeran, 1998). Social cognition models are often misunderstood as being rational models that deal with "cold cognitions." In line with the "bounded rationality" view, emotions would only be an error term. In contrast, health behavior change, to a large degree, is an emotional process that turns into a cognitive one after people have been asked about their thoughts and feelings, thus making them aware of what is going on emotionally. Recent studies have, therefore, focused on emotional outcome expectancies (Dunton & Vaughan, 2008; Lawton, Conner, & McEachan, 2009; Trafimow et al., 2004). An example of an emotional outcome expectancy is anticipated regret ("If I do not use a condom tonight, then I will regret it tomorrow"). Behavior is followed by an expected emotion (Abraham & Sheeran, 2003; Conner, Sandberg, McMillan, & Higgins, 2006). Emotional content of outcome expectancies seems to be most influential in intention formation.

Another important aspect of outcome expectancies is the focus on either gains or losses. A gain-framed message refers to a positive outcome expectancy, such as "Protect yourself from the sun and you will help yourself stay healthy," whereas a loss-framed message can be a negative outcome expectancy, such as "Expose yourself to the sun and you will risk becoming sick" (item examples from Detweiler, Bedell, Salovey, Pronin, & Rothman, 1999). A similar distinction is the promotion versus prevention focus of outcome expectancies or health messages.

Outcome expectancies change over time. The distance between cognitions and actions plays a role for the decisional balance. When thinking of the consequences of lifestyle changes such as more physical activity and dietary improvements, the positive side is more valued. However, when it comes to micro-level intentions, when imminent health behaviors are at stake, the negative side comes into play. When people contemplate long-term outcomes (e.g., "I will stay slim and become healthier"), the pros might dominate the cons. When they anticipate immediate outcomes (e.g., "I will be exhausted; desserts are tempting"), the cons move into the foreground. This instability of the decisional balance changes the intention levels and reduces the subsequent likelihood of taking action. Thus, failure to act upon one's intentions can be due to intention instability, which, in turn, emerges as a result of the reevaluation of the pros and cons, as the situation for the intended action approaches. This is in line with *construal level theory* (Eyal, Liberman, Trope, & Walther, 2004). According to this theory, mental representations of an event depend on psychological distance, which may be more or less the temporal distance to the event. More distal events are construed at a high level, whereas more proximal events are construed at a low level. Low-level construals are contextualized, concrete, and often short-term outcomes, whereas high-level construals are more decontextualized, abstract, and often long-term outcomes. Pros about an event tend to represent higher-level construals, whereas cons represent lower-level construals (Eyal et al., 2004). As a consequence for the design of interventions, one would make short-term and emotional outcome expectancies more salient (e.g., "You will feel more energetic after exercise; you will enjoy the taste of fresh fruits; you will regret not having used a condom"). A favorable decisional balance can be achieved even by parsimonious interventions (Göhner, Seelig, & Fuchs, 2009).

### Perceived Self-efficacy

Perceived self-efficacy portrays individuals' beliefs in their capabilities to exercise control over challenging demands and over their own functioning (Bandura, 1997, 2000). It involves the regulation of thought processes, affective states, motivation, behavior, or changing environmental conditions. These beliefs are critical in approaching novel or difficult situations, or in adopting a strenuous self-regimen. People make an internal attribution in terms of personal competence when forecasting their behavior (e.g., "I am certain that I can quit smoking even if my friend continues to smoke"). Such optimistic self-beliefs influence the goals people set for themselves, what courses of action they choose to pursue, how much effort they invest in given endeavors, and how long they persevere in the face of barriers and setbacks. Self-efficacy influences the challenges that people take on, as well as how high they set their goals (e.g., "I intend to reduce my smoking," or "I intend to quit smoking altogether"). Some people harbor self-doubts and cannot motivate themselves. They see little point in even setting a goal if they believe they do not have what it takes to succeed. Thus, the intention to change a habit that affects health depends to some degree on a firm belief in one's capability to exercise control over that habit.

Perceived self-efficacy has been found to be important at all stages in the health behavior change process (Bandura, 1997), but it does not always constitute exactly the same construct. Its meaning depends on the particular situation of individuals who may be more or less advanced in the change process. The distinction between action self-efficacy, coping self-efficacy, and recovery self-efficacy has been brought up by Marlatt, Baer, and Quigley (1995) in the domain of addictive behaviors. The rationale for the distinction between several phase-specific self-efficacy beliefs is that, during the course of health behavior change, different tasks have to be mastered and different self-efficacy beliefs are required to master these tasks successfully. For example, a person might be confident in his or her capability to be physically active in general (i.e., high action self-efficacy), but might not be very confident to resume physical activity after a setback (low recovery self-efficacy).

*Action self-efficacy* (also called "preaction self-efficacy") refers to the first phase of the process, in which an individual does not yet act, but develops a motivation to do so. It is an optimistic belief during the preactional phase. Individuals high in action self-efficacy imagine success, anticipate potential outcomes of diverse strategies, and are more likely to initiate a new behavior. Those with less self-efficacy imagine failure, harbor self-doubts, and tend to procrastinate. Although preaction self-efficacy is instrumental in the motivation phase, the two following constructs are instrumental in the subsequent volition phase and can, therefore, also by summarized under the heading of volitional self-efficacy.

*Maintenance self-efficacy* represents optimistic beliefs about one's capability to cope with barriers that arise during the maintenance period. (The equivalent term "coping self-efficacy" has also been used in a different sense; therefore, we now prefer the term "maintenance self-efficacy.") A new health behavior might turn out to be much more difficult to adhere to than expected, but a self-efficacious person responds confidently with better strategies, more effort, and prolonged persistence to overcome such hurdles. Once an action has been taken, individuals with high maintenance self-efficacy invest more effort and persist longer than those who are less self-efficacious.

*Recovery self-efficacy* addresses the experience of failure and recovery from setbacks. If a lapse occurs, individuals can fall prey to the "abstinence violation effect," that is, they attribute their lapse to internal, stable, and global causes, dramatize the event, and interpret it as a full-blown relapse (Marlatt et al., 1995). Highly self-efficacious individuals, however, avoid this effect by attributing the lapse to an external high-risk situation and by finding ways to control the damage and to restore hope. Recovery self-efficacy pertains to one's conviction to get back on track after being derailed. The person trusts his or her competence to regain control after a setback or failure and to reduce harm (Marlatt, 2002).

A functional difference exists between these self-efficacy constructs, whereas their temporal sequence is less important. Different phase-specific self-efficacy beliefs may be harbored at the same point in time. The assumption is that they operate in a different manner. For example, recovery self-efficacy is most functional when it comes to resuming an interrupted chain of action, whereas action self-efficacy is most functional when facing a novel challenging demand (Luszczynska, Mazurkiewicz, Ziegelmann, & Schwarzer, 2007).

This distinction between phase-specific self-efficacy beliefs has proven useful in various domains of behavior change. Action self-efficacy tends to predict intentions, whereas maintenance self-efficacy tends to predict behaviors. Individuals who had recovered from a setback needed different self-beliefs than did those who had maintained theirs levels of activity (Scholz, Sniehotta, & Schwarzer, 2005). Several authors (Rodgers, Hall, Blanchard, McAuley, & Munroe, 2002; Rodgers & Sullivan, 2001; Rodgers, Murray, Courneya, Bell, & Harber, 2009) have found evidence for phase-specific self-efficacy beliefs in the domain of exercise behavior (i.e., task self-efficacy, coping self-efficacy, and scheduling self-efficacy). Phase-specific self-efficacy differed in the effects on various preventive health behaviors, such as breast self-examination (Luszczynska & Schwarzer, 2003), dietary behaviors (Schwarzer & Renner, 2000), and physical exercise (Scholz et al., 2005).

## Planning

Good intentions are more likely to be translated into action when people develop success scenarios and preparatory strategies of approaching a difficult task. Mental simulation helps to identify cues for action. The terms *planning* and *implementation intentions* have been used to address this phenomenon. Research on action plans for health behaviors has been suggested by Lewin (1947), for example, in the context of food choice. Lewin distinguished between an overall plan and a specific plan to take the first step toward a dietary goal. Leventhal, Singer, and Jones (1965) have argued that fear appeals can facilitate health behavior change only when combined with action plans; that is, specific instructions on when, where, and how to perform them.

Renewed attention to planning emerged when the concept of implementation intentions was introduced from the perspective of motivation psychology (Gollwitzer, 1999). An implementation intention represents a mental "if-then" association that links the when and where of a situation (if-condition) to a specific action (then-condition). Holding an if-then cognition in a critical situation is assumed to lead to a behavioral response without much conscious awareness. An if-then cognition facilitates increased information processing in terms of enhanced accessibility, detection, and discrimination of critical cues (Webb, Hendricks, & Brandon, 2007). To date, research has accumulated abundant evidence for the effectiveness of implementation intentions in the laboratory, as well as in the field where participants generate plans themselves (Wiedemann, Schüz, Sniehotta, Scholz, & Schwarzer, 2009). In many studies, action planning was found to mediate the relations between intentions and behaviors, such as physical activity (Conner & Norman, 2005; Norman & Conner, 2005). Meta-analyses have summarized their effects on health behaviors (for an overview, see Gollwitzer & Sheeran, 2006).

Another way of planning is the anticipation of barriers and the generation of alternative behaviors to overcome them. This has been called *coping planning* (Scholz, Sniehotta, Burkert, & Schwarzer, 2007; Sniehotta, Scholz, & Schwarzer, 2006; Sniehotta, Schwarzer, Scholz, & Schüz, 2005). People imagine scenarios that hinder them in performing their intended behavior, and they develop one or more plans to cope with such a challenging situation. For example: "If I plan to run on Sunday, but the weather does not permit it, I will go swimming instead," or "If there is something exciting on TV tonight that I do not want to miss, I will reschedule my workout to the afternoon." Coping planning might be a more effective self-regulatory strategy than action planning, partly because it implies action planning. After people contemplate the when, where, and how of action, they imagine possible barriers and generate coping strategies. Thus, coping planning comes on top of action planning (Scholz, Schüz, Ziegelmann, Lippke, &

Schwarzer, 2008). Planning is an alterable variable. It can be easily communicated to individuals with self-regulatory deficits. Quite a few randomized controlled trials have documented the evidence in favor of such planning interventions (e.g., Chapman, Armitage, & Norman, 2009; Luszczynska, 2006; Luszczynska, Tryburcy, & Schwarzer, 2007; Van Osch, Lechner, Reubsaet, Wigger, & de Vries, 2008). It has also been found that action planning and coping planning have a synergistic effect on physical activity (Araújo-Soares, McIntyre, & Sniehotta, 2009).

## Mechanisms and Models of Health Behavior Change
### Meta Theory: Stage Models and Continuum Models
Health behavior change encompasses a variety of social, emotional, and cognitive factors. Some of these determinants are assumed to operate in concert. Therefore, researchers have aimed at identifying the optimal set of factors that allow for the best prediction or explanation of health behavior change. Such models or theories are subject to debate in health psychology. For example, which model is the most parsimonious and makes the best prediction of regular condom use? From which model can we derive clinical strategies to modify refractory dietary risk behaviors? Which model suggests a good policy to promote smoking cessation at the workplace? The models of health behavior change preferred currently overlap in terms of some of the crucial factors, but major differences are found in terms of the underlying philosophy. This section provides a brief overview of some models.

Models of health behavior change postulate a pattern of factors that may improve motivation and that would eventually lead to sustained behavior change. A distinction is made between stage models and continuum models. In continuum models, individuals are placed along a range that reflects the likelihood of action. Influential predictor variables are identified and combined in one prediction equation. The goal of an intervention is to move the individual along this route toward action. Such models assume that a person's behavior is the outcome of an intention (e.g., "I intend to run four times a week for at least 30 minutes each time"). Intention forming is seen as being determined by beliefs and attitudes (Fishbein & Ajzen, 1975). Therefore, the focus is on identifying a parsimonious set of predictors that includes constructs such as perceived barriers, social norms, disease severity, personal vulnerability, attitudes, or perceived self-efficacy. These are then combined into a prediction equation for explaining behavioral intention and behavior change. The most prominent approach of this kind is the theory of planned behavior (see below). A general characteristic of continuum models is that they better account for intention variance than for behavior variance.

There are two debatable aspects of continuum models. First, a single prediction rule for describing behavior change implies that cognitive and behavioral changes occur in a linear fashion, and that a "one-size-fits-all" intervention approach is suitable for all individuals engaging in unhealthy behaviors. Consequently, it excludes qualitative changes during the course of time, such as changing mindsets, phase transitions, or recycling back and forth. According to continuum models, it is not important whether an intervention approach is targeted first toward changing perceived vulnerability, perceived consequences, or perceived self-efficacy. Hence, interventions are not required to move forward in any certain sequence, but they could be applied in any order, or even simultaneously.

Second, traditional continuum models typically did not account for the postintentional phase, in which goals are translated into action. The segment between intentions and behaviors is a black box, also called the *intention–behavior gap* (Sheeran, 2002). It is quite common that people do not behave in accordance with their intentions. For example, unforeseen barriers emerge, and people give in to temptations. In a postintentional phase, various factors can compromise or facilitate the translation of intentions into action. Some of these postintentional factors have been identified, such as maintenance self-efficacy and recovery self-efficacy (Luszczynska & Schwarzer, 2003; Scholz, Sniehotta, & Schwarzer, 2005), as well as action planning and coping planning (Lippke, Ziegelmann, & Schwarzer, 2004, 2005; Luszczynska, Sobczyk, & Abraham, 2007; Sniehotta, Scholz, & Schwarzer, 2005, 2006; Ziegelmann, Lippke, & Schwarzer, 2006). Theorizing about health behavior change should not be reduced to the motivation phase only, while omitting the subsequent action phase that is more decisive for behavior change. Advanced continuum models, therefore, need to include factors that help to bridge the intention–behavior gap (Sniehotta, 2009a). In doing so, it is implicitly assumed that there are at least two phases of behavior change: a motivational one that ends with an intention, and a volitional one that ends with successful performance. Thus, any extension of

traditional continuum models into this direction implicitly adopts the idea of distinct processes, stages, or phases in health behavior change.

To overcome the limitations of continuum models, stage theorists have made an attempt to consider process characteristics by proposing a number of qualitative stages. The transtheoretical model of behavior change (TTM; e.g., DiClemente & Prochaska, 1982; Prochaska & DiClemente, 1983; Prochaska, DiClemente, & Norcross, 1992; Velicer, Prochaska, & Redding, 2006) has become the most popular stage model. Stage models can only be seen as superior to continuum models if empirical evidence emerges that attests to the discontinuity between stages and to the successful tailoring of interventions to subgroups of individuals who have been identified at such stages. Moreover, the critical factors that move people from one stage to another need to be identified (Armitage & Arden, 2002).

Whereas the focus of continuum models lies in the prediction of intention and behaviors, the focus of stage models lies in stage-matched interventions. However, administering matched treatments may not necessarily be the most productive approach to encourage health behavior change—combination treatments might be even more successful. In terms of utility, Abraham (2008) argued that as long as targeting stage-defined audiences is problematic and causes additional costs, investment in stage-specific interventions is not justified. Combining interventions that are designed to promote a variety of cognitive changes might be less expensive, since this does not require prior screening for action preparedness within the audience. Above all, they might be even more successful. Nonetheless, it would be premature to conclude that stage-tailored interventions are not useful since they can only be as good as the underlying stage definitions. Refining stage definitions or different stage conceptions might generate stronger support for the stage framework.

A variety of stage models have been proposed, for example the *precaution adoption process approach* (PAPM; Weinstein, 1988). Another older stage model has only recently been applied to health behaviors is the *model of action phases* (MAP), also called the Rubicon model. Heckhausen (1980, 1991), Heckhausen and Gollwitzer (1987), and Kuhl (1983) have distinguished between a motivation phase of goal setting that is followed by a volition phase of goal pursuit. This approach has evolved from German motivation psychology since the early 20th century (e.g., Lewin et al., 1944), and it has inspired the *health action process approach* (HAPA; Schwarzer, 1992).

Overviews of leading health behavior theories are provided in some book chapters (health belief model, reviewed by Abraham & Sheeran, 2005; protection motivation theory, reviewed by Norman, Boer, & Seydel, 2005; social cognitive theory, reviewed by Luszczynska & Schwarzer, 2005; transtheoretical model, reviewed by Sutton, 2005; theory of planned behavior, reviewed by Conner & Sparks, 2005; Biddle, & Fuchs, 2009; Sniehotta, 2009b). In the following sections, three models will be described briefly.

## Theory of Planned Behavior

The theory of planned behavior (TPB; Ajzen, 1991) represents a revised version of the theory of reasoned action (TRA; Fishbein & Ajzen, 1975). It is a continuum model that includes distal and proximal antecedents of a given behavior. The core of the model consists of eight variables (see Figure 24.1).ntention reflects a person's readiness to perform a health behavior. The intention is based on attitude toward the behavior, subjective norm, and perceived behavioral control. Intention mediates between these three factors and the behavior. Attitude toward a behavior is an indicator of the positive or negative value that is associated with the performance of the behavior. It is determined by a set of behavioral beliefs. Subjective norm is the perceived social pressure to engage or not to engage in a behavior. It is determined by a set of normative beliefs. Perceived behavioral control pertains to one's perceptions of the ability to perform a health behavior. It is determined by a set of control beliefs. It is about the same as perceived self-efficacy (Bandura, 1997). Behavioral beliefs reflect the contingency between a behavior and expected outcomes. Thus, this is the same as outcome expectancies (Bandura, 1997). These beliefs are multiplied with the subjective values of the expected outcomes. This product is seen to determine

the attitude toward the behavior. Normative beliefs pertain to the perceived behavioral expectations of significant others such as a partner, coworker, teacher, or friend. These beliefs are multiplied with one's motivation to comply with these specific expectations. This product, then, is seen to determine the subjective norm. Control beliefs refer to factors that may facilitate or impede performance of a behavior. These beliefs are multiplied with the perceived power of each control factor. This product is seen to determine the perceived behavioral control.

The TPB has been applied to many health behaviors, and it has become the most frequently used continuum model. There are more than one thousand publications referring to this model. The model has been evaluated as being successful in predicting intentions, but less successful in predicting behaviors, which is obvious because there are no postintentional variables in the model. In a meta-analysis, Armitage and Conner (2001) reported an average of 39 percent of explained intention variance, as opposed to an average of 27 percent explained behavior variance. These percentages are high because many studies in this area are only cross-sectional correlation studies based upon self-reports. Due to such research designs, the coefficients are inflated, whereas in longitudinal studies, using objective behavioral outcomes, and in experimental studies, the predictive value of the theory is very limited (Sniehotta, 2009b). Thus, the TPB is mainly an intention theory. To transform it into a more powerful behavior change theory, it needs to be extended by postintentional predictors that are more proximal to the behavior in question. Several recent studies have added action planning as a mediator between intentions and behavior, which has made a substantial improvement (Sheeran, Milne, Webb, & Gollwitzer, 2005).

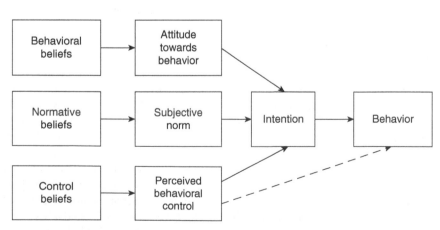

**Fig. 24.1** Theory of planned behavior (TPB).

### The Transtheoretical Model of Behavior Change

To overcome the limitations of continuum models, stage theories offer an alternative that address the existence or usefulness of action phases or stages. One such approach is based on clinical research on addictions, and now has become the dominant model of health behavior change: the transtheoretical model of behavior change (TTM), also called stages of change (SOC) model (DiClemente & Prochaska, 1982; Prochaska, & Velicer, 1997). Its main feature is the implication that different types of cognitions and behaviors may be important at different stages of the health behavior change process. The most common version of the TTM includes five discrete stages of health behavior change that are defined in terms of one's past behavior and future plans (precontemplation, contemplation, preparation, action, maintenance; see Figure 24.2). For example, at the precontemplation stage, a problem drinker does not think about quitting in the future. At the contemplation stage, he or she reflects about quitting sometime within the next 6 months, but does not make any specific plans for behavior change. At the preparation stage, the problem drinker resolves to quit within the next month and prepares for this step. The action stage includes individuals who have taken successful action for any period of time. If abstinence has lasted for more than 6 months, the person is categorized as being in the maintenance stage. The five stages are expected to be mutually exclusive and qualitatively different. Sometimes a termination stage is added, for example in the case of smokers who have been abstinent for at least 5 years.

People could make multiple attempts to progress from preaction to action stages. However, relapses could occur anytime, resulting in a spiral-like progression through the behavior-change process. In contrast to continuum models, stage models such as the transtheoretical model assume that factors producing movement toward action differ in respect to a person's stage. The identification of stages bears implications for interventions because matching a treatment to the current stage of a target group would lead to better outcomes.

In addition to the described basic stages of change, the TTM also includes ten processes of change, decisional balance (the perceived pros and cons of changing), perceived self-efficacy, and temptation. Processes of change are conceptualized as causes for the transitions between the stages, whereby it is assumed that different factors influence different stage transitions.

Decisional balance, as well as self-efficacy/temptation, are usually described as dependent variables. Thus, as people move through stages, they arrive at a more favorable decisional balance and at higher levels of self-efficacy. On the other hand, is seems more plausible to understand these factors as causes of stage movement. Decisional balance is one of the oldest constructs in psychology. Benjamin Franklin (1706–1790) had already suggested to list all the pros and cons on a sheet of paper when it comes to making a difficult decision (that's why it is also

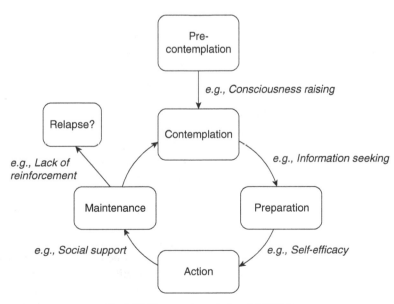

**Fig. 24.2** The transtheoretical model (TTM).

called the *Franklin method*). In decision making theories, balancing plays a key role (Janis & Mann, 1977). Thus, it can be assumed that balancing is mainly a preintentional process, in particular in the contemplation stage, and that it facilitates intention formation.

In TTM, the ten processes of change constitute clusters of treatment strategies that were derived from an examination of 24 psychotherapy models (Prochaska & DiClemente, 1983). These are consciousness raising (the extent to which people seek and assimilate new information), dramatic relief (identification and expression of emotions pertaining to the problem behavior), environmental reevaluation (gauging the effects of the risk behavior on the physical and social environment), self-reevaluation (appraising one's values in terms of a problem behavior), social liberation (perceptions of whether the social world is supportive of a person's choices), counter-conditioning (substituting the problem behavior with alternatives), helping relationships (provision and use of social support), reinforcement management (use of rewards in making changes), self-liberation (commitment to changing the problem behavior), and stimulus control (controlling the situation that evokes the problem behavior).

An abundance of studies have used the TTM, providing support for the usefulness of stages. Evidence has emerged suggesting that the notion of stages of behavior change is meaningful and has pragmatic value (Velicer, Redding, Sun, & Prochaska, 2007). A meta-analysis on tailoring interventions pointed to empirical evidence in favor of stage-matched treatments (Noar, Benac, & Harris, 2007). The TTM's practicability for interventions is very appealing.

The TTM has been criticized by some researchers (e.g., Adams & White, 2003; Bandura, 1997). Weinstein, Rothman, and Sutton (1998) and Sutton (2005) argued that the stages might not be genuinely qualitative, but are rather arbitrary distinctions within a continuous process. In particular, passage of time might not be the ideal criterion for defining stages (Lippke, Ziegelmann, Schwarzer, & Velicer, 2009). Kraft, Sutton, and McCreath Reynolds (1999) demonstrated within a sample of daily smokers that precontemplators, contemplators, and preparers were not at different qualitative stages, but rather at different places along an underlying continuum. Similarly, Courneya, Nigg, and Estabrooks (1998) reported that continuous measures of intention explained more variance in exercise behavior than did the stage algorithm proposed by the TTM. Armitage and

Arden (2008) found a correlation of .78 between intention and stages of change, indicating that the stages seem to reflect a linear process of readiness for change. However, such a high correlation sheds doubt on the usefulness of the stage construct because arbitrary cutoffs of a behavioral intention measure would then become an equivalent means to segment the audience into more homogeneous target groups for interventions (Armitage, 2009). The stages of change construct is supposed to be a "fast and frugal decision tree" blending intentions (precontemplation, contemplation, preparation) and behavior (action, maintenance). Therefore, it should be sufficiently distinct from any behavioral intention measure. In other words, a moderate intercorrelation between intentions and stages would reflect discriminant validity. Other researchers have found that processes of change did not predict smoking stage movements (Herzog & Blagg, 2007), and that stage-matched and stage-mismatched interventions with young adult smokers did not yield the hypothesized results (Quinlan & McCaul, 2000). Stages of change did not predict success in weight control in adult women (Jeffery, French, & Rothman, 1999). De Vet, de Nooijer, de Vries, and Brug (2008) provided matched versus mismatched treatments for precontemplators, contemplators, and actors, but they did not find that matching was superior.

Thus, evidence in favor of the TTM is mixed. The critique mainly addresses the conceptual notion of stages, their operationalization, the failure to move people from one stage to the next, or the failure to achieve stage-matched effects. A major problem that TTM shares with all other models is the validity of the key constructs. Stage allocation is based on a simple algorithm (a fast and frugal decision tree) asking people whether they act or not, and if not, whether they intend to do so or not, etc. Sensitivity and specificity need to be addressed to determine the number of false positives, for example. Passage of time might not be the ideal criterion to identify cutoff points in the process of change (Lippke, Ziegelmann, Schwarzer, & Velicer, 2009). Self-reports for stages or intentions are subject to intraindividual fluctuation and, therefore, may result in different decisions depending on the time of day, mood, or social influence. Thus, if a particular stage algorithm is not sufficiently valid in a particular health promotion setting, any stage-matched intervention will fail. Moreover, if validity is perfect, but the treatment contents or implementation methods are not well designed, the interventions will also fail. Also, tailoring per se may have a placebo effect that undermines the genuine effects of the matched treatments (Webb, Hendricks, & Brandon, 2007). Thus, an unsuccessful research project based on a stage of change model should not be counted as a disconfirmation of the theory.

Some authors have been critical about the assumption of stages and have discarded the TTM as a whole. This is unjustified because it not only consists of the five stages, but also of ten processes of change and decisional balance, and self-efficacy/temptation. The TTM had been proposed as an integration of theories (Prochaska & Velicer, 1997). It includes a number of promising components that are not yet well tested and deserve more experimental scrutiny.

Processes such as stimulus control, counter-conditioning, consciousness raising, and receipt of social support are included as components in many interventions without explicitly referring to TTM. Planning, for example, can involve content that reflects some of the ten processes. Armitage (2008) has studied implementation intentions that were inspired by TTM processes. Thus, many components of the TTM appear in studies without an explicit link to this model. It does not come as a surprise that specific components have been found successful, given the fact that they were originally taken from leading psychotherapy models. All 14 variables of the TTM as a whole are hard to test. Therefore, the TTM might be seen rather as a useful heuristic framework than as a closed, testable theory (Armitage, 2009; Lippke & Ziegelmann, 2008).

### The Health Action Process Approach: A Two-layer Framework

The traditional continuum models have been mainly criticized because of the intention–behavior gap.

A model that explicitly includes postintentional factors to overcome this gap is the HAPA (Schwarzer, 2008). The model suggests a distinction between (a) preintentional motivation processes that lead to a behavioral intention and (b) postintentional volition processes that lead to the actual health behavior. Within the two phases, different patterns of social-cognitive predictors may emerge (see Figure 24.3). In the initial motivation phase, a person develops an intention to act. In this phase, risk perception is seen as a distal antecedent (e.g., "I am at risk for cardiovascular disease"). Risk perception in itself is insufficient to enable a person to form an intention. Rather, it sets the stage for a contemplation process and further elaboration of thoughts about consequences and competencies. Similarly, positive outcome expectancies (e.g., "If I exercise five times per week, I will reduce my cardiovascular risk") are chiefly seen as being important in the motivation phase, when a person balances the pros and cons of certain behavioral outcomes. Further, one needs to believe in one's capability to perform a desired action (perceived self-efficacy, e.g., "I am capable of adhering to my exercise schedule in spite of the temptation to watch TV"). Perceived self-efficacy operates in concert with positive outcome expectancies, both of which contribute substantially to forming an intention. Both beliefs are needed for forming intentions to adopt difficult behaviors, such as regular physical exercise.

After a person develops an inclination toward a particular health behavior, the "good intention" has to be transformed into detailed instructions on how to perform the desired action. Once an action has been initiated, it has to be maintained. This is not

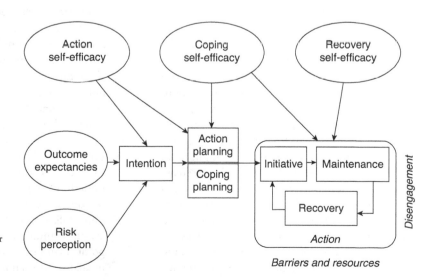

**Fig. 24.3** The continuum layer of the health action process approach (HAPA).

achieved through a single act of will, but involves self-regulatory skills and strategies. Thus, the postintentional phase should be further broken down into more proximal factors, such as planning and recovery self-efficacy. Other social cognition models do not address explicitly postintentional factors (Luszczynska & Schwarzer, 2005).

Including planning and self-efficacy as volitional mediators renders the model into an implicit stage model because it implies the existence of (at least) two phases: a motivational one and a volitional one. The purpose of such a model is twofold: It allows a better prediction of behavior, and it reflects the assumed causal mechanism of behavior change. Research based on this model, therefore, employs path-analytic methods (e.g., Lippke, Ziegelmann, & Schwarzer, 2005; Luszczynska & Schwarzer, 2003; Renner et al., 2008; Richert, Reuter, Wiedemann, Lippke, Ziegelmann, & Schwarzer, 2010; Schwarzer et al., 2007; Schwarzer et al., 2010).

However, when it comes to the design of interventions, one can consider turning the implicit stage model into an explicit one. This is done by identifying individuals who reside either at the motivational stage or the volitional stage. Then, each group becomes the target of a specific treatment that is tailored to this group. Moreover, it is theoretically meaningful, and has been found to be useful, to subdivide further the volitional group into those who perform and those who only intend to perform. In the postintentional preactional stage, individuals are labeled "intenders," whereas in the actional stage they are labeled "actors." Thus, a suitable subdivision within the health behavior change process yields three groups: preintenders, intenders, and actors. The term "stage" in this context was chosen to allude to the stage theories, but not in the strict definition that includes irreversibility and invariance. The terms "phase" or "mindset" may be equally suitable for this distinction. The basic idea is that individuals pass through different mindsets on their way to behavior change. Thus, interventions may be most efficient when tailored to these particular mindsets. For example, preintenders are supposed to benefit from confrontation with outcome expectancies and some level of risk communication. They need to learn that the new behavior (e.g., becoming physically active) has positive outcomes (e.g., well-being, weight loss, fun) as opposed to the negative outcomes that accompany the current (sedentary) behavior (such as developing an illness or being unattractive). Moreover, it has been found that preintenders benefit more from gain-framed than from loss-framed outcome expectancies (Detweiler et al., 1999).

In contrast, intenders should not benefit much from such health messages in the form of outcome expectancies because, after setting a goal, they have already moved beyond this mindset. Rather, they should benefit from planning to translate their intentions into action. Finally, actors do not need any treatment at all unless one wants to improve their relapse prevention skills. Then, they should be prepared for particular high-risk situations in which lapses are imminent.

The HAPA is designed as an open architecture based on a collection of various principles, rather than on specific testable assumptions. It was developed in 1988 (Schwarzer, 1992) as an attempt to integrate the model of action phases (Heckhausen, 1980) with social-cognitive theory (Bandura, 1986). It has five major principles that make it distinct from other models.

- Principle 1: *Motivation and volition.* The first principle suggests that one should divide the health behavior change process into two phases. A switch of mindsets occurs when people move from deliberation to action. First comes the motivation phase in which people develop their intentions. Afterward, they enter the volition phase.
- Principle 2: *Two volitional phases.* In the volition phase, there are two groups of individuals: those who have not yet translated their intentions into action, and those who have. There are inactive as well as active persons in this phase. In other words, in the volitional phase, one finds intenders as well as actors, who are characterized by different psychological states. Thus, in addition to health behavior change as a continuous process, one can also create three categories of people with different mindsets depending on their current point of residence within the course of health behavior change: Preintenders, intenders, and actors.
- Principle 3: *Postintentional planning.* Intenders who are in the volitional preactional stage are motivated to change, but do not act because they might lack the right skills to translate their intention into action. Planning is a key strategy at this point. Planning serves as an operative mediator between intentions and behavior.

- Principle 4: *Two kinds of mental simulation.* Planning can be divided into action planning and coping planning. Action planning pertains to the when, where, and how of intended action. Coping planning includes the anticipation of barriers and the design of alternative actions that help to attain one's goals in spite of the impediments.
- Principle 5: *Phase-specific self-efficacy.* Perceived self-efficacy is required throughout the entire process. However, the nature of self-efficacy differs from phase to phase, because there are different challenges as people progress from one phase to the next one. Goal setting, planning, initiative, action, and maintenance pose challenges that are not of the same nature. Therefore, one should distinguish between preactional self-efficacy, coping self-efficacy, and recovery self-efficacy. Sometimes the terms *task self-efficacy* instead of preaction self-efficacy, and *maintenance self-efficacy* instead of coping and recovery self-efficacy are preferred.

In sum, HAPA is a health-behavior change framework with an open architecture. The HAPA has two layers, a continuum layer and a phase (or stage) layer. Depending on the research question, one might choose the one or the other. The HAPA is designed as a sequence of two continuous self-regulatory processes, a goal setting phase (motivation) and a goal pursuit phase (volition). The second phase is subdivided into a preaction phase and an action phase. One can superimpose these three phases on the continuum model as a second layer and regard phase as a moderator. This two-layer architecture allows a switch between the continuum model and the stage model, depending on the given research question. The stage layer is useful when designing stage-matched interventions. For preintenders, one needs risk and resource communication, for example by addressing the pros and cons of the critical behavior. For intenders, planning treatments are helpful to support people who lack the necessary skills to translate their intentions into behavior. And for actors, one needs to stabilize their newly adopted health behaviors through relapse prevention strategies.

The HAPA allows both the researcher and the practitioner to make a number of choices. Although it was initially inspired by distinguishing between a motivational and a volitional stage, and later extended to the distinction between preintenders, intenders, and actors, one need not necessarily group individuals according to such stages. If the purpose is to predict behavior change, one would specify a mediator model that includes postintentional constructs (such as planning and volitional self-efficacy) as proximal predictors of performance (Scholz, Nagy, Göhner, Luszczynska, & Kliegel, 2009).

For the purpose of stage-tailored interventions, however, usually three stage groups are established. This does not exclude the possibility of generating more than three stages. For example, for some research questions, one might want to subdivide the preintenders into precontemplators and contemplators, according to the TTM (Velicer & Prochaska, 2008), or opt for a distinction between preintenders who are either (a) unaware of an issue, (b) aware but unengaged, or (c) deciding (Weinstein, Lyon, Sandman, & Cuite, 1998. Thus, the HAPA is not a puristic stage model, but a versatile theoretical framework that allows for a variety of approaches.

## General Issues in Health Behavior Change
### Goal Conflict, Goal Hierarchies, and Priority Management in Health Self-regulation

Studies are usually limited to one behavior and a corresponding behavioral goal (intention). This is a deliberate choice because the more complex the research question, the less likely it becomes to find the evidence. But we need to acknowledge the fact that people do have multiple goals that are often in conflict. For example, the intention to work out every day might serve the goal to become slim, which, in turn, may serve the broader goal to become attractive for a potential partner, and so on. Depending on the value placed on the superordinate goal, the subordinate goal might have a certain chance to be pursued while competing goals (enjoying dinner parties) are being downgraded. A variety of action-control components operate in the volition phase that help a person adhere to a chosen regimen. Relapse prevention and harm reduction strategies are needed to stabilize intentions and behaviors in times of conflict. Such strategies need to be part of interventions designed to preclude people from regressing from action to earlier stages.

Goal setting, intention formation, effort investment, planning, action control, and disengagement are self-regulatory constructs. Health self-regulation encompasses a broad range of cognitions and behaviors. Studies could benefit from work in other fields, for example from relapse prevention theory (Marlatt, 2002; Marlatt et al., 1995) and self-regulation theories (Baumeister & Vohs, 2004; Carver & Scheier, 1998;

Cervone, Shadel, Smith, & Fiori, 2006; Kuhl, 2001; Maes & Karoly, 2005).

Self-regulatory constructs other than self-efficacy might help to further explain postintentional processes of health behavior change. Theories of volition emphasize that self-regulation refers to an individual's ability to focus attention on the task at hand and to keep a favorable emotional balance. Self-competencies that refer to regulation of attentional and emotional components of goal-directed behavior might play a crucial role across all phases of health behavior change. In different stages of goal pursuit, people need to pay attention and stay with the task at hand. They need to concentrate even when an interfering task emerges. Moreover, controlling interfering emotions such as boredom, anger, distress, exhaustion, anxiety, or reluctance requires a number of cognitive skills. Self-regulation of attention and emotion might also be seen as a stable personal disposition, an individual difference characteristic that enables habitual control over recurrent actions, as well as in the process of behavior change (see Cervone et al., 2006; Kuhl, 2001).

From the perspective of modeling health behavior change, the question arises how many and which volitional factors should be included to bridge the intention–behavior gap. After the inclusion of planning and volitional self-efficacy, action control would be a third promising candidate. Future research needs to find out to which degree an accumulation of further volitional factors would account for substantial variance of health behaviors, or whether this would rather violate the postulate of parsimony. In some studies, we have added the construct of action control to the model (Schüz, Sniehotta, Mallach, Wiedemann, & Schwarzer, 2009; Sniehotta, Nagy, Scholz, & Schwarzer, 2006). Although planning is a prospective strategy—that is, behavioral plans are made before the situation is encountered—action control is a concurrent self-regulatory strategy, in which the ongoing behavior is continuously evaluated with regard to a behavioral standard. A study on dental flossing (Schüz et al., 2009) has investigated stage-specific effects of an action control treatment (a dental flossing calendar). The intervention led to higher action control levels at follow-up, thus indicating volitional effects. However, the action control intervention did not improve intention formation, and, thus, had no motivational effect, as hypothesized. Action control facilitated flossing behavior in volitional individuals only. In other words, a beneficial effect emerged only in the stage-matched

condition. This result suggests that only intenders and actors benefit from self-regulatory treatments. A very parsimonious intervention, such as the provision of dental calendars for self-monitoring, may bring forth notable effects if correctly addressed to individuals who are in a volitional phase.

A further question is whether we should judge the quality and usefulness of a model only in terms of explained behavioral variance. Gaining insight into mediating processes upgrades the importance of such mediators as secondary outcomes. The mediators are relevant criteria by themselves. Even if we cannot immediately change a certain refractory behavior, we might move a crucial step further by changing one of the proximal mediators into the right direction.

### The Debate About Continuum Versus Stage Models

When identifying individuals with different mindsets and separating them for particular analyses or treatments, we are dealing with a stage model. By this, we go beyond the quest for mediating factors. Stage is supposed to operate as a moderator with two or more levels (e.g., preintenders, intenders, actors). The assumption is that the mean values of social-cognitive variables and behavior differ between these subgroups. Moreover, the mediating mechanism may differ as well. Technically, the analysis reflects a moderated mediation (Lippke, Wiedemann, et al., 2009). How exactly individuals with different mindsets differ in terms of the causal mechanisms of health behavior change remains a research agenda for the future. Evidence in favor of moderated mediation would support the discontinuity hypothesis, which means that change does not reflect a continuum, but rather a process that involves two or more qualitative stages (mindsets). This notion of discontinuity has been demonstrated in a number of contributions (Armitage, Povey, & Arden, 2003; Lippke, Ziegelmann, et al., 2009). There are also studies that attempt to combine a continuum model (TPB) with the stages approach (Courneya, Nigg, & Estabrooks, 1998).

A better way of demonstrating the usefulness of a stage distinction is documented by experimental effects when manipulating one or more of the proposed mediators. Improving self-efficacy in women who were motivated to practice breast self-examination has resulted in higher levels of this behavior (Luszczynska, 2004). Improving action planning and coping planning in patients motivated to increase their physical activity has also been successful (Luszczynska, 2006; Sniehotta, Scholz, & Schwarzer, 2006; Ziegelmann, Lippke & Schwarzer, 2006). If a proposed mediator is effective at a particular stage, but not at the other, then we need to identify which individuals reside at which stage and tailor the treatment (e.g., planning, self-efficacy interventions) to one group.

The usefulness of stages also depends on the validity of their assessment. Stages are based upon discontinuity, thus the assessment tool must identify individuals who belong to a relatively homogeneous group that is clearly distinct from the previous and/or subsequent group. The stage algorithm, thus, must produce such homogeneous groups on the basis of relevant criteria. This, however, poses a major problem. In the TTM, the main criterion for grouping is the passage of time. For example, someone is judged to be a preparer when she or he intends to change within a month, or someone is promoted from actor to maintainer after adhering to the desired behavior for 6 months. Obviously, this is based upon average clinical experience. Therefore, we rather avoid time as a criterion and use psychological variables, in particular intention and behavior, to build a staging algorithm (Lippke, Ziegelmann, Schwarzer, & Velicer, 2009). Nevertheless, all criteria suffer from some arbitrariness.

Indistinct boundaries exist between stages, and these make misclassification likely. Even the best set of social-cognitive variables cannot attain perfect validity because personal characteristics are often instable. Intentions may change within a day, rendering the staging outcome unreliable. However, intention instability is not a problem germane to stage theories. It causes trouble in continuum theories as well. Predicting Time 2 performance by Time 1 intention may be biased due to changes in intention during the observation period. Instability of predictors is a general problem in all approaches that deal with change. Misclassification of individuals would, however, be a serious matter if these persons were treated with an adverse intervention. So far, there is not much evidence of harm created by stage mismatch (except for selective dropout from treatment). All treatments appear to be more or less beneficial or are, at worst, ineffective (Dijkstra, Conijn, & De Vries, 2006). A stage assessment procedure of poor validity may underestimate the usefulness of stages and lead to unsuccessful health-promotion efforts. But if stage-matched individuals, on average, gain more than mismatched or unmatched individuals, they do have an advantage.

The debate about stages of change as opposed to a continuum of change resembles a debate on the scientific truth about the objective world. The quest for the existence of stages assumes that the nature of health behavior change is either one or the other, and that the only task is to "discover" whether stages truly exist. However, stage is a construct, not nature. We invent the notion of stages to help us understand how people change and to provide better treatment to those who have difficulties in changing their behaviors. We construct stages to open another window that allows for a different view on the change process. Thus, the question is not whether stages truly exist, but whether stage is a useful construct.

Moreover, there is no difference between stages and "pseudostages." The latter term refers to a categorization of a "truly existing continuum" into stages. However, continuum is also a construct. A continuum is frequently subdivided into categories, although this is accompanied by the loss of some information because it is regarded as useful to illustrate unique characteristics of a variable's distribution or its relationship to others. Then, the question remains: When does the assumption of stages appear to be more useful than the continuum hypothesis?

If we find that certain groups of individuals undergoing a change process share common features and have similar mindsets that are distinct from those in a different group at a different point in the change process, then we might want to label them as residents of a particular stage, such as preintenders, intenders, or actors. This is useful because we obtain a fresh view on the features of individuals within a hypothetical change process. Whether this process is truly a series of qualitative steps or an underlying action-readiness continuum remains a matter of judgment. We do not discover the existence of one or the other; we rather choose a construct that provides a convenient template for subsequent research efforts. If, for example, scientists regard some individuals as "inclined abstainers," they have deliberately chosen a category and created a label that improves communication about the phenomenon in question. Due to its biological connotations, the choice of the stage label may have been unfortunate, but, meanwhile, it has proven useful and has led to a success history in health psychology. The focus is not on the illusion of scientific truth, but on practicability, and one important aspect of the latter is therapeutic effectiveness. If stage-tailored interventions turn out to be more effective than untailored ones, the construct of stage has proven useful.

## Understanding the Mechanisms of Health Behavior Change

To understand better the mechanisms of health behavior change, we need to identify mediator effects as well as moderator effects. The HAPA, for example, as a parsimonious mediator model does not explicitly include moderators, except of stage. Stage as a moderator indicates that a prediction model within one stage group operates in a different way than a prediction model within an adjacent stage group. This is similar to the assumption that one set of social-cognitive variables can move people from stage A to B, whereas a different set of variables can move people from stage B to C.

Although action planning has been found to mediate the intention–behavior relation (Gollwitzer & Sheeran, 2006), some studies have failed to find such mediation effects (Norman & Conner, 2005). This suggests that the relationships among intentions, planning, and behavior might also depend on other factors. For example, the degree to which planning mediates between intentions and behavior has been found to be higher in older than in younger individuals (Renner, Spivak, Kwon, & Schwarzer, 2007; Scholz, Sniehotta, Burkert, & Schwarzer, 2007). This represents a case of moderated mediation. Perceived self-efficacy is one potential moderator for the degree to which planning has an effect on subsequent behaviors. It is expected to moderate the planning-behavior relation because people harboring self-doubts might fail to act upon their plans. For persons with a high level of self-efficacy, planning might be more likely to facilitate goal achievement. Self-efficacious people feel more confident about translating their plans into actual behavior. In other words, whether planning interventions (independent variable) actually affect behavior (dependent variable) might depend on the individual's level of self-efficacy (moderator). In a study on physical activity, longitudinal data from an online survey were used to examine similar interrelationships (Lippke, Wiedemann, et al., 2009). Only those persons who had a sufficiently high level of exercise self-efficacy acted upon their plans. Conversely, participants who were harboring self-doubts failed to act upon their plans (see also Gutiérrez-Doña, Lippke, Renner, Kwon, & Schwarzer, 2009).

Mediator models work well in some groups, but not in others. By comparing men and women, younger and older individuals, and those from different cultures, we identify relevant moderators (Renner, Spivak, Kwon, & Schwarzer, 2007; Reuter, Ziegelmann, Wiedemann, Lippke, Schüz, & Aiken, 2009; Ziegelmann, Lippke, & Schwarzer, 2006). When a mediator model (be it a simple three-variable model, or a more complex one) has strong interrelations within one category of people, but weak associations within a different category of people, then this is a case of moderated mediation. The amount to which the mediator translates the effect of the independent variable on the dependent variable depends on the levels of a moderator variable. Such moderators can be sex, age, culture, and the like, but also can be psychological variables that are closely related to the constructs used in health behavior models (Hankonen, Absetz, Ghisletta, Renner, & Uutela, 2010). Temporal stability of intention, for example, may be a moderator (Conner, 2008). Moderated mediation is also possible with psychosocial variables, such as intention or planning. For example, the intention–behavior link is mediated by planning, and this mediator effect can be moderated by level of intention (Wiedemann, Schüz, Sniehotta, Scholz, & Schwarzer, 2009). Here, we have a special case in which the independent variable (intention) of a mediator model serves the function of a moderator in addition. In other words, only in highly motivated persons does the intention operate via planning on the improvement of adherence, whereas in poorly motivated persons no such mediator effect is visible.

The best way to demonstrate the mechanisms of health behavior change is the experimental manipulation of those variables that are supposed to produce behaviors or to move people from one stage to another (Michie, Rothman, & Sheeran, 2007; Reuter, Ziegelmann, Wiedemann, & Lippke, 2008; Weinstein, 1993). Various experimental studies have shown that self-efficacy interventions do make a difference, which attests to the fact that self-efficacy is indeed an operative construct that facilitates volitional processes, such as effort and persistence (Luszczynska, Tryburcy, & Schwarzer, 2007).

The finding that a model fits the data does not prove that the chosen model is the only one or the best one that fits. The question is whether this model appears to be empirically superior to alternative models. Finding the best model for a particular research context requires consideration of several questions: Which model accounts for most of the criterion variance? Which one provides the best insight into the causal mechanism of health behavior change? Is the model that makes the best prediction also the best one for the design of interventions? Which is the most parsimonious one?

To test the validity of a model in comparison with other theories of health behavior change, experimental studies are required (Weinstein, Lyon, Sandman, & Cuite, 1998). So far, most of the studies that aim at comparing determinants from different theories are mainly correlational ones. A minority of studies includes experimental manipulations and examines the maintenance of behavior change by means of follow-up assessment. Future research should include the manipulation of constructs from one theory in one sample, and manipulation of the constructs from a different theory (such as TPB) in another sample. For example, at the stage of intention development, one group could be treated by improving positive attitudes and subjective norms (TPB), whereas the other group could be treated by improving self-efficacy, outcome expectancies, and risk perception (HAPA). At the stage of goal pursuit, on the other hand, one group could be treated by improving perceived behavioral control (TPB), whereas the other could be treated by enhancing a combination of self-efficacy, action planning, and relapse prevention (HAPA). It is unlikely that one will ever find an acid test to compare all models with each other since they are partly incompatible—as are, for example, stage models versus continuum models. Researchers tend to prefer eclectic approaches, such as selecting attractive elements from one model and implanting them into another, which also can be seen as a means of theory evolution (Lippke & Ziegelmann, 2008; Sniehotta, 2009a, 2009b).

## Conclusion

Health behavior change is a major challenge to health psychology and public health research. The key question is how to predict and modify the adoption and maintenance of health behaviors such as physical exercise, weight control, preventive nutrition, dental hygiene, condom use, and accident prevention, as well as the modification of problem drinking, substance use, smoking, reckless driving, overeating, or unprotected sexual intercourse. Public health efforts aim at changing environments, for example, when imposing a ban on smoking in certain places. Such policy decisions must be based upon sound research that identifies causes and effects and also predicts the likelihood of compliance with such measures. On the other hand, most lifestyle changes are based on individual health self-regulation that includes the motivational, volitional, and actional processes of abandoning health-compromising behaviors in favor of health-enhancing behaviors. We have described various psychological constructs such as

intention, risk perception, outcome expectancies, perceived self-efficacy, and planning. None of them constitutes a "magic bullet." They need to operate in concert, and that is why theories and models are needed to better understand the mechanisms of diverse health behavior change processes. The distinction between continuum models and stage models is helpful to grasp the general philosophy of certain approaches. To illustrate very different viewpoints, we have provided one example of a continuum model (theory of planned behavior) and one example of a stage model (transtheoretical model). Then, a two-layer hybrid framework was introduced (health action process approach). All models are meaningful and justified to serve as starting points for research. Depending on context and research questions, one might see a particular model as being more reasonable than others. All currently discussed models have limitations and cannot account fully for the complexity of behavior change mechanisms. As an example for such a mechanism that is not included in any theory, we have chosen moderated mediation. This method refers to why change takes place, as well as in whom change takes place. There are populations for whom a particular mediator model might make the best predictions, whereas another mediator model might work superiorly in a different population. Whatever mechanism is studied in the adoption and maintenance of health behaviors, it is most important to make our implicit theories explicit, because insight does emerge from data without theory (Rothman, 2000; Weinstein et al., 1998).

## References

Abraham, C. (2008). Beyond stages of change: Multi-determinant continuum models of action readiness and menu-based interventions. *Applied Psychology: An International Review, 57*, 30–41.

Abraham, C., & Sheeran, P. (2000). Understanding and changing health behaviour: From health beliefs to self-regulation. In P. Norman, C. Abraham, & M. Conner (Eds.), *Understanding and changing health behaviour* (pp. 3–24). Amsterdam: Harwood.

Abraham, C., & Sheeran, P. (2003). Acting on intentions: The role of anticipated regret. *British Journal of Social Psychology, 42*, 495–511.

Abraham, C., & Sheeran, P. (2005). The health belief model. In M. Conner, & P. Norman (Eds.), *Predicting health behavior* (pp. 28–80). Maidenhead: Open University Press.

Abraham, C., Sheeran, P., & Johnston, M. (1998). From health beliefs to self-regulation: Theoretical advances in the psychology of action control. *Psychology & Health, 13*, 569–591.

Adams, J., & White, M. (2003). Are activity promotion interventions based on the transtheoretical model effective? A critical review. *British Journal of Sports Medicine, 37*, 106–114.

Ajzen, I. (1991). The theory of planned behavior. *Organizational Behavior and Human Decision Processes, 50*, 179–211.

Araújo-Soares, V., McIntyre, T., & Sniehotta, F.F. (2009). Predicting changes in physical activity amongst adolescents: The role of self-efficacy, intention, action planning and coping planning. *Health Education Research, 24*, 128–139.

Armitage, C.J. (2008). A volitional help sheet to encourage smoking cessation: A randomized exploratory trial. *Health Psychology, 27*, 557–566.

Armitage, C.J. (2009). Is there utility in the transtheoretical model? *British Journal of Health Psychology, 14*, 195–210.

Armitage, C.J., & Arden, M.A. (2002). Exploring discontinuity pattern in the transtheoretical model: An application of the theory of planned behavior. *British Journal of Health Psychology, 7*, 89–103.

Armitage, C.J., & Arden, M.A. (2008). How useful are the stages of change for targeting interventions? Randomized test of a brief intervention to reduce smoking. *Health Psychology, 27*, 789–798.

Armitage, C.J., & Conner, M. (2001). Efficacy of the theory of planned behaviour: A meta-analytic review. *British Journal of Social Psychology, 40*, 471–499.

Armitage, J.C., Povey, R., & Arden, M.A. (2003). Evidence for discontinuity patterns across the stages of change: A role for attitudinal ambivalence. *Psychology & Health, 18*, 373–386.

Bandura, A. (1986). *Social foundations of thought and action.* Englewood Cliffs, NJ: Prentice Hall.

Bandura, A. (1997). *Self-efficacy: The exercise of control.* New York: Freeman.

Bandura, A. (2000). Cultivate self-efficacy for personal and organizational effectiveness. In E.A. Locke (Ed), *The Blackwell handbook of principles of organizational behavior* (pp. 120–136). Oxford, England: Blackwell.

Baumeister, R.F., Heatherton, T.F., & Tice, D.M. (1994). *Losing control: How and why people fail at self-regulation.* San Diego, CA: Academic Press.

Baumeister, R.F., & Vohs, K.D. (Eds.). (2004). *Handbook of self-regulation: Research, theory, and applications.* New York: Guilford Press.

Biddle, S.J.H., & Fuchs, R. (2009). Exercise psychology: A view from Europe. *Psychology of Sport and Exercise, 10*, 410–419.

Brewer, N.T., Weinstein, N.D., Cuite, C.L., & Herrington, J.E. (2004). Risk perceptions and their relation to risk behavior. *Annals of Behavioral Medicine, 27*, 125–130.

Carver, C.S., & Scheier, M.F. (1998). *On the self-regulation of behavior.* New York: Cambridge University Press.

Cervone, D., Shadel, W.G., Smith, R.E., & Fiori, M. (2006). Self-regulation: Reminders and suggestions from personality science. *Applied Psychology: An International Review, 55*, 333–385.

Chapman, J., Armitage, C.J., & Norman, P. (2009). Comparing implementation intention interventions in relation to young adults' intake of fruit and vegetables. *Psychology & Health, 24*, 317–332.

Conner, M. (2008). Initiation and maintenance of health behaviors. *Applied Psychology: An International Review, 57*, 42–50.

Conner, M., & Norman, P. (Eds.). (2005). *Predicting health behavior: Research and practice with social cognition models* (2nd ed.). Buckingham, England: Open University Press.

Conner, M., Sandberg, T., McMillan, B., & Higgins, A. (2006). Role of anticipated regret in adolescent smoking initiation. *British Journal of Health Psychology, 11*, 85–101.

Conner, M., & Sparks, P. (2005). The theory of planned behaviour and health behaviours. In M. Conner, & P. Norman (Eds.), *Predicting health behaviour: Research and practice with social cognition models* (2nd ed., pp. 170–222). Maidenhead, UK: Open University Press.

Courneya, K.S., Nigg, C.R., & Estabrooks, P.A. (1998). Relationships among the theory of planned behavior, stages of change, and exercise behavior in older persons over a three year period. *Psychology and Health, 13*, 355–367.

Croyle, R.T., Sun, Y., & Louie, D. (1993). Psychological minimization of cholesterol test results: Moderators of appraisal in college students and community residents. *Health Psychology, 12*, 503–507.

Detweiler, J.B., Bedell, B.T., Salovey, P., Pronin, E., & Rothman, A.J. (1999). Message framing and sunscreen use: Gain-framed messages motivate beach-goers. *Health Psychology, 18*, 189–196.

de Vet, E., de Nooijer, J., de Vries, N.K., & Brug, J. (2008). Testing the transtheoretical model for fruit intake: Comparing web-based tailored stage-matched and stage-mismatched feedback. *Health Education Research, 23*, 218–227.

DiClemente, C.C., & Prochaska, J.O. (1982). Self-change and therapy change of smoking behavior: A comparison of processes of change in cessation and maintenance. *Addictive Behaviors, 7*, 133–142.

Dijkstra, A., Conijn, B., & De Vries, H. (2006).A match-mismatch test of a stage model of behaviour change in tobacco smoking. *Addiction, 101*, 1035–1043.

Dunton, G.F., & Vaughan, E. (2008). Anticipated affective consequences of physical activity adoption and maintenance. *Health Psychology, 27*, 703–710.

Eyal, T., Liberman, N., Trope, Y., & Walther, E. (2004). The pros and cons of temporally near and distant action. *Journal of Personality and Social Psychology, 86*(6), 781–795.

Fishbein, M., & Ajzen, I. (1975). *Belief, attitude, intention, and behavior: An introduction to theory and research.* Reading, MA: Addison-Wesley.

Gibbons, F.X., & Gerrard, M. (1997). Health images and their effects on health behavior. In B.P. Buunk, & F.X. Gibbons (Eds.), *Health, coping, and well-being: Perspectives from social comparison theory* (pp. 63–94). Mahwah, NJ: Erlbaum.

Gibbons F.X., Gerrard, M., & Lane, D.J. (2003). A social-reaction model of adolescent health risk. In J.J. Suls, & K.A. Wallston (Eds.), *Social psychological foundations of health and illness* (pp. 107–136). Oxford, England: Blackwell.

Godin, G., & Kok, G. (1996). The theory of planned behavior: A review of its applications to health-related behaviors. *American Journal of Health Promotion, 11*, 87–97.

Göhner, W., Seelig, H., & Fuchs, R. (2009). Intervention effects on cognitive antecedents of physical exercise: A 1-year follow-up study. *Applied Psychology: Health and Well-being, 1*, 233–256.

Gollwitzer, P.M. (1999). Implementation intentions: Strong effects of simple plans. *American Psychologist, 54*, 493–503.

Gollwitzer, P.M., & Sheeran, P. (2006). Implementation intentions and goal achievement: A meta-analysis of effects and processes. *Advances in Experimental Social Psychology, 38*, 69–119.

Gutiérrez-Doña, B., Lippke, S., Renner, B., Kwon, S., & Schwarzer, R. (2009). How self-efficacy and planning predict dietary behaviors in Costa Rican and South Korean women: A moderated mediation analysis. *Applied Psychology: Health & Well-Being, 1*, 91–104.

Hahn, A., & Renner, B. (1998). Perception of health risks: How smoker status affects defensive optimism. *Anxiety, Stress, and Coping, 11*, 93–112.

Hankonen, N., Absetz, P., Ghisletta, P., Renner, B., & Uutela, A. (2010). Gender differences in social cognitive determinants of exercise adoption. *Psychology & Health, 25*(1), 55–69. doi:10.1080/08870440902736972.

Heckhausen, H. (1980). *Motivation und handeln. Lehrbuch der motivationspsychologie* [Motivation and action. Textbook of motivation psychology]. Berlin: Springer-Verlag.

Heckhausen, H. (1991). *Motivation and action.* Berlin: Springer.

Heckhausen, H., & Gollwitzer, P.M. (1987). Thought contents and cognitive functioning in motivational vs. volitional states of mind. *Motivation and Emotion, 11*, 101–120.

Herzog, T.A., & Blagg, C.O. (2007). Are most precontemplators contemplating smoking cessation? Assessing the validity of the stages of change. *Health Psychology, 26*, 222–231.

Janis, I.L., & Mann, L. (1977). *Decision making: A psychological analysis of conflict, choice, and commitment.* London: Cassel & Collier Macmillan.

Jeffery, R.W., French, S.A., & Rothman, A.J. (1999). Stage of change as a predictor of success in weight control in adult women. *Health Psychology, 18*, 543–546.

Klein, W.M.P., & Cerully, J.L. (2007). Risk appraisal. In R.F. Baumeister, & K.D. Vohs (Eds.), *Encyclopedia of social psychology* Vol. 2 (pp. 756–758). Thousand Oaks, CA: Sage.

Kraft, P., Sutton, S.R., & McCreath Reynolds, H. (1999). The transtheoretical model of behaviour change: Are the stages qualitatively different? *Psychology & Health, 14*(3), 433–450.

Kuhl, J. (1983). *Motivation, konflikt und handlungskontrolle.* [Motivation, conflict, and action control]. Berlin: Springer.

Kuhl, J. (2001). *Motivation und persönlichkeit. Interaktionen psychischer systeme* [Motivation and personality: Interactions of mental systems]. Göttingen, Germany: Hogrefe.

Lawton, R., Conner, M., & McEachan, R. (2009). Desire or reason: Predicting health behaviors from affective and cognitive attitudes. *Health Psychology, 28*, 56–65.

Leventhal, H., Singer, R., & Jones, S. (1965). Effects of fear and specificity of recommendation upon attitudes and behavior. *Journal of Personality and Social Psychology, 2*, 20–29.

Leventhal, H., Weinman, J., Leventhal, E., & Phillips, L.A. (2008). Health psychology: The search for pathways between behavior and health. *Annual Review of Psychology, 59*, 477–505.

Lewin, K. (1947). Group decision and social change. In T.M. Newcomb, & E.L. Hartley (Eds.), *Readings in social psychology* (pp. 330–344). New York: Holt.

Lewin, K., Dembo, T., Festinger, L.A., & Sears, P.S. (1944). Level of aspiration. In J. McV. Hunt (Ed.), *Personality and the behavior disorders* Vol. 1 (pp. 333–378). New York: Ronald.

Lippke, S., Wiedemann, A.U., Ziegelmann, J.P., Reuter, T., & Schwarzer, R. (2009). Self-efficacy moderates the mediation of intentions into behavior via plans. *American Journal of Health Behavior, 33*, 521–529.

Lippke, S., & Ziegelmann, J.P. (2008). Theory-based health behavior change: Developing, testing and applying theories for evidence-based interventions. *Applied Psychology: International Review, 57*, 698–716.

Lippke, S., Ziegelmann, J.P., & Schwarzer, R. (2004). Initiation and maintenance of physical exercise: Stage-specific effects of a planning intervention. *Research in Sports Medicine, 12*, 221–240.

Lippke, S., Ziegelmann, J.P., & Schwarzer, R. (2005). Stage-specific adoption and maintenance of physical activity: Testing a three-stage model. *Psychology of Sport & Exercise, 6*, 585–603.

Lippke, S., Ziegelmann, J.P., Schwarzer, R., & Velicer, W.F. (2009). Validity of stage assessment in the adoption and maintenance of physical activity and fruit and vegetable consumption. *Health Psychology, 28*, 183–193.

Luszczynska, A. (2004). Change in breast self-examination behavior: Effects of intervention on enhancing self-efficacy. *International Journal of Behavioral Medicine, 11*, 95–103.

Luszczynska, A. (2006). An implementation intentions intervention, the use of planning strategy, and physical activity after myocardial infarction. *Social Science and Medicine, 62*, 900–908.

Luszczynska, A., Mazurkiewicz, M., Ziegelmann J.P., & Schwarzer, R. (2007). Recovery self-efficacy and intention as predictors of running or jogging behavior: A cross-lagged panel analysis over a two-year period. *Psychology of Sport and Exercise, 8*, 247–260.

Luszczynska, A., & Schwarzer, R. (2003). Planning and self-efficacy in the adoption and maintenance of breast self-examination: A longitudinal study on self-regulatory cognitions. *Psychology and Health, 18*, 93–108.

Luszczynska, A., & Schwarzer, R. (2005). Social cognitive theory. In M. Conner, & P. Norman (Eds.), *Predicting health behaviour* (2nd ed. rev., pp. 127–169). Buckingham, UK: Open University Press.

Luszczynska, A., Sobczyk, A., & Abraham, C. (2007). Planning to reduce weight: Implementation intentions intervention helps to reduce body weight among overweight or obese women by prompting action planning. *Health Psychology, 26*, 507–512.

Luszczynska, A., Tryburcy, M., & Schwarzer, R. (2007). Improving fruit and vegetable consumption: A self-efficacy intervention compared to a combined self-efficacy and planning intervention. *Health Education Research, 22*, 630–638.

Maes, S., & Karoly, P. (2005). Self-regulation assessment and intervention in physical health and illness: A review. *Applied Psychology: An International Review, 54*, 267–299.

Marlatt, G.A. (2002). *Harm reduction: Pragmatic strategies for managing high-risk behaviours.* New York: Guilford.

Marlatt, G.A., Baer, J.S., & Quigley, L.A. (1995). Self-efficacy and addictive behavior. In A. Bandura (Ed), *Self-efficacy in changing societies* (pp. 289–315). New York: Cambridge University Press.

Michie, S., Rothman, A.J., & Sheeran, P. (2007). Advancing the science of behaviour change. *Psychology and Health, 22*, 249–253.

Noar, S.M., Benac, C.N., & Harris, M.S. (2007). Does tailoring matter? Meta-analytic review of tailored print health behavior change interventions. *Psychological Bulletin, 133*, 673–693.

Norman, P., & Conner, M. (2005). The theory of planned behavior and exercise: Evidence for the mediating and moderating roles of planning on intention-behavior relationships. *Journal of Sport & Exercise Psychology, 27*, 488–504.

Norman, P., Boer, H., & Seydel, E.R. (2005). Protection motivation theory. In M. Conner, & P. Norman (Eds.), Predicting health behavior (pp. 81–126). Maidenhead, UK: Open University Press.

Panzer, M., & Renner, B. (2008). To be or not to be at risk: Spontaneous reactions to risk information. *Psychology & Health, 23*, 617–627.

Prochaska, J.O., & DiClemente, C.C. (1983). Stages and processes of self-change of smoking: Toward an integrative model of change. *Journal of Consulting and Clinical Psychology, 51,* 390–395.

Prochaska, J.O., DiClemente, C.C., & Norcross, J.C. (1992). In search of how people change: Applications to addictive behaviors. *American Psychologist, 47,* 1102–1114.

Prochaska, J.O., & Velicer, W.F. (1997). The transtheoretical model of health behavior change. *American Journal of Health Promotion, 12,* 38–48.

Quinlan, K.B., & McCaul, K.D. (2000). Matched and mismatched interventions with young adult smokers: Testing a stage theory. *Health Psychology, 19,* 165–171.

Radcliffe, N.M., & Klein, W.M.P. (2002). Dispositional, unrealistic, and comparative optimism: Differential relations with knowledge and processing of risk information and beliefs about personal risk. *Personality and Social Psychology Bulletin, 28,* 836–846.

Renner, B. (2004). Biased reasoning: Adaptive responses to health risk feedback. *Personality and Social Psychology Bulletin, 30,* 384–396.

Renner, B., Kwon, S., Yang, B.-H., Paik, K.-C., Kim, S.H., Roh, S., et al. (2008). Social-cognitive predictors of dietary behaviors in South Korean men and women. *International Journal of Behavioral Medicine, 15,* 4–13.

Renner, B., & Schwarzer, R. (2005). The motivation to eat a healthy diet: How intenders and nonintenders differ in terms of risk perception, outcome expectancies, self-efficacy, and nutrition behavior. *Polish Psychological Bulletin, 36*(1), 7–15.

Renner, B., Spivak, Y., Kwon, S., & Schwarzer, R. (2007). Does age make a difference? Predicting physical activity of South Koreans. *Psychology and Aging, 22,* 482–493.

Reuter, T., Ziegelmann, J.P., Wiedemann, A.U., & Lippke, S. (2008). Dietary planning as a mediator of the intention-behavior relation: An experimental-causal-chain design. *Applied Psychology: An International Review. Special Issue: Health and Well-Being, 57,* 194–207.

Reuter, T., Ziegelmann, J.P., Wiedemann, A.U., Lippke, S., Schüz, B., & Aiken, L.S. (2009). Planning bridges the intention-behavior gap: Age makes a difference and strategy use explains why. *Psychology & Health* (in press). http://dx.doi.org/10.1080/08870440902939857.

Richert, J., Reuter, T., Wiedemann, A.U., Lippke, S., Ziegelmann, J., & Schwarzer, R. (2010). Differential effects of planning and self-efficacy on fruit and vegetable consumption. *Appetite, 54,* 611–614. doi: 10.1016/j.appet.2010.03.006.

Rodgers, W.M., Hall, C.R., Blanchard, C.M., McAuley, E., & Munroe, K.J. (2002). Task and scheduling self-efficacy as predictors of exercise behaviour. *Psychology and Health, 27,* 405–416.

Rodgers, W.M., Murray, T.C., Courneya, K.S., Bell, G.J., & Harber, V.J. (2009). The specificity of self-efficacy over the course of a progressive exercise program. *Applied Psychology: Health and Well-Being, 1,* 211–232.

Rodgers, W., & Sullivan, M.J.L. (2001). Task, coping and scheduling self-efficacy in relation to frequency of physical activity. *Journal of Applied Social Psychology, 31,* 741–753.

Rothman, A.J. (2000). Toward a theory-based analysis of behavioral maintenance. *Health Psychology, 19,* 64–69.

Scholz, U., Nagy, G., Göhner, W., Luszczynska, A., & Kliegel, M. (2009). Changes in self-regulatory cognitions as predictors of changes in smoking and nutrition behaviour. *Psychology & Health, 24,* 545–561.

Scholz, U., Schüz, B., Ziegelmann, J.P., Lippke, S., & Schwarzer, R. (2008). Beyond behavioural intentions: Planning mediates between intentions and physical activity. *British Journal of Health Psychology, 13,* 479–494.

Scholz, U., Sniehotta, F.F., Burkert, S., & Schwarzer, R. (2007). Increasing physical exercise levels: Age-specific benefits of planning. *Journal of Aging and Health, 19,* 851–866.

Scholz, U., Sniehotta, F.F., & Schwarzer, R. (2005). Predicting physical exercise in cardiac rehabilitation: The role of phase-specific self-efficacy beliefs. *Journal of Sport & Exercise Psychology, 27,* 135–151.

Schüz, B., Sniehotta, F.F., Mallach, N., Wiedemann, A., & Schwarzer, R. (2009). Predicting transitions from preintentional, intentional and actional stages of change: Adherence to oral self-care recommendations. *Health Education Research, 24,* 64–75.

Schwarzer, R. (1992). Self-efficacy in the adoption and maintenance of health behaviors: Theoretical approaches and a new model. In R. Schwarzer (Ed.), *Self-efficacy: Thought control of action* (pp. 217–243). Washington, DC: Hemisphere.

Schwarzer, R. (1994). Optimism, vulnerability, and self-beliefs as health-related cognitions: A systematic overview. *Psychology and Health, 9,* 161–180.

Schwarzer, R. (2008). Modeling health behavior change: How to predict and modify the adoption and maintenance of health behaviors. *Applied Psychology: An International Review, 57,* 1–29.

Schwarzer, R., & Renner, B. (2000). Social-cognitive predictors of health behavior: Action self-efficacy and coping self-efficacy. *Health Psychology, 19,* 487–495.

Schwarzer, R., Richert, J., Kreausukon, P., Remme, L., Wiedemann, A.U., & Reuter, T. (2010). Translating intentions into nutrition behaviors via planning requires self-efficacy: Evidence from Thailand and Germany. *International Journal of Psychology, 54,* 260–268.

Schwarzer, R., Schüz, B., Ziegelmann, J.P., Lippke, S., Luszczynska, A., & Scholz, U. (2007). Adoption and maintenance of four health behaviors: Theory-guided longitudinal studies on dental flossing, seat belt use, dietary behavior, and physical activity. *Annals of Behavioral Medicine, 33,* 156–166.

Sheeran, P. (2002). Intention-behavior relations: A conceptual and empirical review. *European Review of Social Psychology, 12,* 1–36.

Sheeran, P., Milne, S., Webb, T.L., & Gollwitzer, P.M. (2005). Implementation intentions and health behaviours. In M. Conner, & P. Norman (Eds.), *Predicting health behaviour: Research and practice with social cognition models* (2nd ed., pp. 276–323). Maidenhead, England: Open University Press.

Sniehotta, F.F. (2009a). Towards a theory of intentional behaviour change: Plans, planning, and self-regulation. *British Journal of Health Psychology, 14,* 261–273.

Sniehotta, F.F. (2009b). An experimental test of the theory of planned behavior. *Applied Psychology: Health and Well-Being, 1,* 257–270.

Sniehotta, F.F., Nagy, G., Scholz, U., & Schwarzer, R. (2006). The role of action control in implementing intentions during the first weeks of behaviour change. *British Journal of Social Psychology, 45*(1), 87–106.

Sniehotta, F.F., Scholz, U., & Schwarzer, R. (2005). Bridging the intention-behaviour gap: Planning, self-efficacy, and action control in the adoption and maintenance of physical exercise. *Psychology & Health, 20,* 143–160.

Sniehotta, F.F., Scholz, U., & Schwarzer, R. (2006). Action plans and coping plans for physical exercise: A longitudinal intervention study in cardiac rehabilitation. *British Journal of Health Psychology, 11*, 23–37.

Sniehotta, F.F., Schwarzer, R., Scholz, U., & Schüz, B. (2005). Action planning and coping planning for long-term lifestyle change: Theory and assessment. *European Journal of Social Psychology, 35*, 565–576.

Suls, J. (2011). Social comparison processes: Implications for physical health. In H.S. Friedman (Ed.), *The Oxford handbook of health psychology*. New York: Oxford University Press.

Sutton, S. (2005). Stage models of health behaviour. In M. Conner, & P. Norman (Eds.), *Predicting health behaviour: Research and practice with social cognition models* (2nd ed., pp. 223–275). Maidenhead, UK: Open University Press.

Taylor, S.E., & Brown, J.D. (1994). Positive illusions and well-being revisited: Separating fact from fiction. *Psychological Bulletin, 116*, 21–27.

Trafimow, D., & Fishbein, M. (1995). Do people really distinguish between behavioral and normative beliefs? *British Journal of Social Psychology, 34*, 257–266.

Trafimow, D., & Sheeran, P. (1998). Some tests of the distinction between cognitive and affective beliefs. *Journal of Experimental Social Psychology, 34*, 378–397.

Trafimow, D., Sheeran, P., Lombardo, B., Finlay.K.A., Brown, J., & Armitage, C.J. (2004). Affective and cognitive control of persons and Behaviours. *British Journal of Social Psychology, 43*, 207–224.

Van Osch, L., Lechner, L., Reubsaet, A., Wigger, S., & de Vries, H. (2008). Relapse prevention in a national smoking cessation contest: Effects of coping planning. *British Journal of Health Psychology, 13*, 525–535.

Velicer, W.F., & Prochaska, J.O. (2008). Stage and non-stage theories of behavior and behavior change: A comment on Schwarzer. *Applied Psychology: An International Review, 57*(1), 75–83.

Velicer, W.F., Prochaska, J.O., & Redding, C.A. (2006). Tailored communications for smoking cessation: Past successes and future directions. *Drug and Alcohol Review, 25*, 47–55.

Velicer, W.F., Redding, C.A., Sun, X., & Prochaska, J.O. (2007). Demographic variables, smoking variables, and outcome across five studies. *Health Psychology, 26*, 278–287.

Webb, M.S., Hendricks, P.S., & Brandon, T.H. (2007). Expectancy priming of smoking cessation messages enhances the placebo effect of tailored interventions. *Health Psychology, 26*, 598–609.

Weinstein, N.D. (1980). Unrealistic optimism about future life events. *Journal of Personality and Social Psychology, 39*, 806–820.

Weinstein, N.D. (1988). The precaution adoption process. *Health Psychology, 7*, 355–386.

Weinstein, N.D. (1993). Testing four competing theories of health-protective behavior. *Health Psychology, 12*, 324–333.

Weinstein, N.D., Lyon, J.E., Sandman, P.M., & Cuite, C.L. (1998). Experimental evidence for stages of health behavior change: The precaution adoption process model applied to home radon testing. *Health Psychology, 17*, 445–453.

Weinstein, N.D., Rothman, A.J., & Sutton, S.R. (1998). Stage theories of health behavior: Conceptual and methodological issues. *Health Psychology, 17*, 290–299.

Wiedemann, A.U., Schüz, B., Sniehotta, F.F., Scholz, U., & Schwarzer, R. (2009). Disentangling the relation between intentions, planning, and behaviour: A moderated mediation analysis. *Psychology & Health, 24*, 67–79.

Ziegelmann, J.P., Lippke, S. & Schwarzer, R. (2006). Adoption and maintenance of physical activity: Planning interventions in young, middle-aged, and older adults. *Psychology & Health, 21*, 145–163.

# Advancing Health Behavior Theory: The Interplay Among Theories of Health Behavior, Empirical Modeling of Health Behavior, and Behavioral Interventions

Leona S. Aiken

**Abstract**

Intervention research aimed at modifying health behavior can go beyond merely assessing behavioral outcomes to characterizing the putative mechanisms by which interventions bring about behavior change. To characterize these mechanisms, a two-stage research program is required. The first stage involves the development and evaluation of a psychosocial model of the putative determinants of a particular health behavior. This may be a hybrid model that draws constructs from existing theories and models, and it may also integrate constructs from related areas of scholarship. The second stage involves translation of the psychosocial model into a multicomponent intervention to encourage behavior adoption. Here, each model construct is transformed into a component of the intervention and becomes a candidate mechanism by which the intervention may bring about behavior change. The intervention is evaluated in an experimental trial, followed by mediation analysis to examine putative linkages from the intervention to change on model constructs to change on behavior outcomes. This two-stage approach is illustrated with examples of health behaviors aimed at disease detection and prevention, at distal and proximal threats to health, and at private and public health-related behaviors. Examination of the putative mechanisms by which interventions bring about behavior change reverses the flow of information from health behavior model to intervention. Instead, the findings from health behavior interventions can lead to theoretical advances in our understanding of health protective behavior.

**Keywords:** Hybrid model, multiple component intervention, mediation analysis of intervention, preventive intervention, mechanisms of health behavior change, mediators

Health psychology has a rich array of models and theories from which to draw in characterizing the determinants of health risk and health protective behavior. Much effort has been expended on testing existing models. Further, classic models have been elaborated through the creation of hybrid models. Hybrid models integrate constructs from both existing models and related literatures, with the goal of forming more complete representations of how health-related behavior accrues and is sustained. Health psychology also undertakes to change health-related behavior in service of greater health.

Interventions are implemented, and their impact on behavior is assessed.

The goal of this chapter is to join together these three aspects of health psychology: theoretical models of health behavior, model testing and elaboration, and health behavior change intervention. The unidirectional flow from existing theoretical models first to the development of empirically supported models of the putative determinants of health behavior and then to the translation of empirically supported models into model driven interventions has great potential to yield stronger, more effective behavior change interventions. Yet, there is another great opportunity—to use what we learn from health behavior interventions to improve our models of health behavior. Interventions can be designed, implemented, and evaluated in such a way that the mechanisms by which the interventions bring about behavior change (or fail to bring about change or even undermine behavior change) can be uncovered. Then, the unidirectional flow from model to intervention can be reversed, and the outcomes of intervention trials can lead to theoretical advances in our understanding of health risk and protective behavior. The underlying theme of this chapter—that knowledge can flow from appropriately designed, implemented, and evaluated interventions to theory in health behavior—has been articulated before by myself and my collaborator of many years, Stephen G. West (West, Aiken, & Todd, 1993; West & Aiken, 1997). My aim here is to illuminate this theme with my program of research in women's health across the lifespan, carried out with our doctoral students who have gone on to their own careers in health psychology; their work is discussed herein.[1,2]

## Two-stage Approach to Advancing Health Behavior Theory

Underlying the use of intervention trials to enhance health behavior theory is a two-stage research agenda (West & Aiken, 1997). Stage One involves development, testing, and refinement of a multiple-construct psychosocial model of a particular health behavior. Stage Two involves faithful translation of this model into a multicomponent intervention to bring about behavior change, followed by the examination of both intervention outcomes on behavior and the putative mechanisms by which the intervention brought about behavior change. The first stage is familiar—we specify a model of constructs that we hypothesize to underlie a particular health behavior. We address distinct measurement of each construct. We then test the model through modeling of data that captures the constructs and modeled behaviors. In the best of circumstances, there is sensitivity to time—we gather pretest measures that reflect time before the assessment of model constructs, and we gather outcome data at some later point.

Stage Two is multifaceted, with many requirements. The psychosocial model is translated into the content of the intervention, with a one-to-one mapping of constructs of the model into components (i.e., specific content) of the intervention. Adequate measures are established for each construct in the model that is driving the intervention; these measures are typically drawn from the preceding psychosocial phase of the research. The intervention is implemented, and the outcome evaluated, ideally in a randomized controlled trial (but see West et al., 2008). Then, mediation analyses follow (MacKinnon, 2008) to uncover the mechanisms by which the intervention brought about (or failed to bring about) behavior change. It is this final phase of Stage Two that permits the intervention to provide information that can lead to the refinement of our model of the health behavior. We have adopted this two-stage approach in our own work on women's health across the lifespan, including mammography screening, condom use, sun protection, and calcium consumption.

## Two Levels of Theory and the Two-stage Approach

Figure 25.1 illustrates the theoretical structure underlying our two-stage approach. Several constructs from the health belief model (HBM; Rosenstock, 1974) are included for illustrative purposes. The right-hand side of the figure represents *psychosocial theory*, which specifies the relationships among a set of constructs and their relationship to a health behavior. Psychosocial models of health behavior are familiar territory in health psychology. In the simple model of Figure 25.1, all three constructs independently predict behavior. In addition, perceived susceptibility also influences perceived benefits; the model specifies that the perception of personal vulnerability to a health threat enhances the perceived benefits of a prescribed health behavior (Aiken, Gerend, & Jackson, 2001). The left-hand side of Figure 25.1 represents *program theory*, which specifies the linkage from individual components or segments of an intervention to model constructs. These two layers of theory underlie theory-based intervention. The two neatly distinguish the accuracy of the theory of the putative determinants of a health behavior (psychosocial theory) from the adequacy of an intervention to produce change on these putative determinants (program theory). I note that these two aspects of theory also have been termed *conceptual theory* and *action theory*, respectively, by other authors (Chen, 1990; Donaldson, 2001).

## The Two-stage Approach and Mediation Analysis

The two-stage approach directly maps onto the use of mediation analysis to examine the mechanisms through which interventions bring about behavior

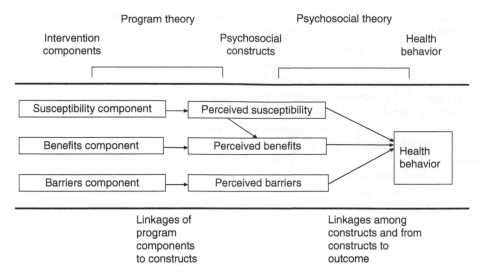

Program theory          Psychosocial theory

Intervention components       Psychosocial constructs       Health behavior

Linkages of program components to constructs       Linkages among constructs and from constructs to outcome

**Fig. 25.1** Underlying structure of the two-stage approach to intervention research. Adapted from West, S. G., & Aiken, L. S. (1997). Towards understanding individual effects in multiple component prevention programs: Design and analysis strategies. Chapter 6. In K. Bryant, M. Windle, & S. West (Eds.). *The science of prevention: Methodological advances from alcohol and substance abuse research* (Chapter 6, p. 195). Washington, D. C.: American Psychological Association, with permission of the publisher.

change. I introduce this idea now and return to it in greater depth later in the chapter. Figure 25.2 illustrates the specification of a model for mediation analysis of an intervention $X$, in which two constructs, $M_1$ and $M_2$, are targeted for behavior change. Change on two constructs is hypothesized to produce change in behavior $Y$. In this specification, the constructs from the psychosocial model developed in Stage One (psychosocial modeling) become the putative mediators of the impact of the intervention on behavior in Stage Two. In a mediational model of

the intervention, the paths $b_1$ and $b_2$ from putative mediators to behavior provide an examination of whether changes in levels on the mediators (here, increased perceived susceptibility and perceived benefits) are associated with change in behavior $Y$, thus informing psychosocial theory. The paths $a_1$ and $a_2$ from the intervention to the mediators assess whether the content specifically built into an intervention to produce change on a mediator actually produces the desired change, thus informing program theory. Finally, the path $c'$ represents the effect

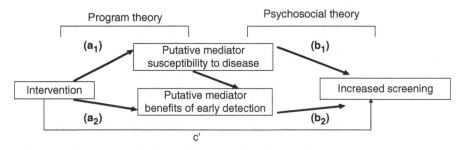

Figure 2a. Model of mechanisms of a two-construct intervention.

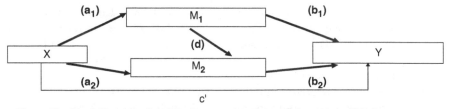

Figure 2b. Mediational model of the two construct intervention, where X is the intervention, $M_1$ and $M_2$ are the two mediators, and Y is the outcome behavior.

**Fig. 25.2** Mapping of mediation analysis of intervention outcomes on the psychosocial and program theory components of the two-stage approach to Intervention.

of the intervention on outcome Y that is not explained by the mediational model underlying the intervention..

## Adventures in Modeling and Manipulating Health Behavior

There are two broad alternative approaches to the study of health behavior. One fruitful approach is to focus on a particular behavior (e.g., risky sexual behavior, smoking), or on closely linked behaviors that relate to a single outcome (e.g., diet and exercise in relation to weight and obesity). Such problem-focused programs of research have been highly productive from the perspective of psychosocial theory and effective intervention. The work is cumulative and progresses over time. As new methodologies emerge, they can be integrated into the study of a single behavioral phenomenon. For example, computer-based interventions based on stages of change models have been fruitfully applied to smoking interventions (Velicer, Prochaska, & Redding, 2006). Neural imaging to understand possible brain mechanisms in sensation seeking and behavioral control that are associated with risky sexual behavior has been undertaken (Lee, Leung, Fox, Gao, & Chan, 2008). Through an iterative process, interventions can be honed for efficiency and effectiveness and for translation to wide application.

An alternative approach to a program of research in health behavior modeling and intervention is to let theoretical issues that are of interest in the study of health behavior drive the selection of behaviors to investigate. This has been the approach that I and my students have followed: We have chosen to study a variety of health behaviors that permit us to raise issues of theoretical interest about the design of both psychosocial models and model-based interventions. These issues include detection versus prevention, proximal (near-term) versus distal (far-term) threats, public versus private behaviors, potentially opposed behaviors that convey risk versus protection with regard to a single health threat, behaviors with strong emotional components, and behaviors that do versus do not involve significant others. We began with a study of mammography screening for detection of breast cancer (Aiken, West, Woodward, & Reno, 1994a; Aiken, West, Reno, Woodward, & Reynolds, 1994b). This study required a consideration of how to communicate risk information and the contingency between understanding risk and perceiving benefits of a health action. We moved to prevention, with our study of condom use by young women (Bryan, Aiken, & West, 1996, 1997).

Enhancing self-efficacy for condom use, particularly for addressing impediments to condom use from partners, became an important focus. An interest in publicly observable behavior led us to study sun protection against skin cancer among young women (Jackson & Aiken, 2000, 2006). This work surfaced new challenges. First, the threat of skin cancer is viewed by young women as a distal threat that may lie far in the future, something that they believe people contract when they are old. Second, tanning is subject to powerful normative influences—being tanned is stylish and therefore desirable. Third, sun protection against skin cancer versus sun exposure for the purpose of tanning are juxtaposed behaviors; however, they are certainly not mutually exclusive. A continued interest in intervening to change proximal behavior associated with distal risks coupled with public concern about the costs of osteoporosis among older women led us to efforts to increase calcium consumption among young women (Schmiege, Aiken, Sanders, & Gerend, 2007; Schmiege & Aiken, 2011). Here, the health threat of osteoporosis is truly distal, perhaps half a century away in the lives of young women.

Developing interests and opportunities continue to drive our research program. An opportunity to carry out the mediation analysis of an existing eight-session intervention with specific content staged over time has resulted in our consideration of strategies to characterize intervention mechanisms manifested over time (Ranby et al., 2009). Until recently, models of health behavior that have driven our interventions have been cognitive in nature, addressing norms, attitudes, efficacy, and other familiar constructs. New interest in the role of emotion in health behavior led to our incorporating emotion into both modeling of health behavior and intervention to modify health behavior. We began this work with consideration of a health-related decision that has a strong emotional component: elective breast augmentation in young women (Moser & Aiken, 2011). We are now incorporating emotional arousal into a health promotion intervention (Moser, 2011). The relative weakness of health behavior models in understanding the link between behavioral intention and sustained health behavior has led us to consider the role of ongoing social support and social influence from a significant other in sustaining health behavior, specifically the role of husbands in their wives' health behavior (Ranby, 2009). Each of these steps in our work, we believe, has given us new insights into the putative determinants of a range of health-related behaviors and experience with interventions to modify these behaviors. The work has also provided the opportunity to study the same behavior across populations—including condom use among young adult women versus their male peers (Bryan, Schindeldecker, & Aiken, 2001) versus adolescent incarcerated youth (Bryan, Aiken, & West, 2004), mammography screening among middle-class predominantly Caucasian women versus underserved Hispanic women (Aiken, Jackson, Castro, & Pero, 2000), and sun protection against skin cancer among young women (Jackson & Aiken, 2000, 2006) and among a community sample of older women (Reid, 2010).

Along with psychosocial modeling of health behaviors and implementation of interventions to modify these behaviors, we have undertaken the study of constructs themselves. Models of health behavior explicitly or implicitly assume that perception of vulnerability or susceptibility to some health threat is a motivational force to take health-protective action (Aiken, Gerend, & Jackson, 2001; Aiken, Gerend, Jackson, & Ranby, in press). This has led us to an intensive consideration of the determinants of perceived susceptibility (Aiken, Fenaughty, West, Johnson, & Luckett, 1995; Gerend, Aiken, & West, 2004; Gerend, Aiken, West, & Erchull, 2004; Gerend, Erchull, Aiken, & Maner, 2006), and how the measurement approach to perceived susceptibility impacts the identification of its apparent correlates (Ranby, Aiken, Gerend, & Erchull, 2010). Our interest in behavior that has both normative and attitudinal roots has led us to consider classes of normative influence and the interplay between norms and attitudes in health behavior (Reid, Cialdini, & Aiken, 2010).

## Stage 1: The Psychosocial Model
### From Classic Models to Expanded and Hybrid Models

I distinguish three broad classes of models (with fuzzy boundaries) in current health behavior literature. These include extant classic models of behavior, extended/appended forms of the classic models, and hybrid models.

EXTANT CLASSIC MODELS OF BEHAVIOR IN GENERAL AND HEALTH BEHAVIOR IN PARTICULAR

A substantial body of classic and more recent models of health behavior are applied precisely as these models are specified, completely and without any modification. These include continuous behavior models, among them the HBM (Rosenstock, 1974),

the theory of reasoned action (TRA; Fishbein & Ajzen, 1975), theory of planned behavior (TPB; Ajzen, 1991), protection motivation theory (Rogers, 1975), social-cognitive theory (Bandura, 1986), and the health action process approach (HAPA; Schwarzer, 2008). They also include stage models of behavior adoption, among them, the protection adoption process model (Weinstein, 1988) and the transtheoretical model of change (Prochaska, DiClemente, & Norcross, 1992). These theories or models, in fact, share core constructs, although these constructs go by different names and have unique nuances of definition across formulations. These constructs include knowledge/information, risk perceptions, attitudes, norms, self-efficacy, and intentions (Noar & Zimmerman, 2005). Of course, not all constructs appear in all the classic models of health behavior (e.g., perceptions of risk are explicit in the HBM but not the TRA).

EXTENDED/APPENDED FORMS OF THE CLASSIC MODELS

Second are models that employ the well-specified existing models described above and append them with additional constructs. In fact, the makers of the original theories or models have themselves added to their own original proposals. Themes of behavioral control or self-efficacy have been added to the original specifications of the TRA and the HBM (Ajzen, 1991). The TPB is the TRA with the addition of perceived behavioral control. In 1988, Rosenstock, Strecher, and Becker wrote that the HBM had been originally designed for one-shot behaviors (e.g., vaccination), and that for sustained health behaviors the concept of self-efficacy was a necessary addition to the model. Following the rich distinction between injunctive norms (i.e., what others say, I should do) versus descriptive norms (i.e., what others actually do) by Cialdini (Cialdini, Reno, & Kallgren, 1990), Fishbein (2000) expanded the TRA to include descriptive norms. Fishbein's original characterization of norms in the TRA had included only injunctive norms. Newer, expanded models that themselves have received substantial attention integrate older models as the core. For example, the HAPA (Schwarzer, 2008) draws on social-cognitive theory, emphasizing self-efficacy throughout health behavior adoption and maintenance. The contribution of the HAPA is the specification of important forces that operate to bridge the gap between intentions and behavior. Additions to existing models reflect the *Zeitgeist* in psychology. Now that the study of emotion is once again central in psychology, we see the integration of emotion and anticipated emotion into models of health behavior adoption. Current emphases in psychology on diversity and on the powerful force of culture lead us to expect the integration of constructs from research on culture and diversity into classic models of health behavior.

## HYBRID MODELS

Third are hybrid models. These are models that draw constructs from more than one existing theory or model and, in addition, may integrate constructs from related areas of scholarship. Hybrid models integrate multiple constructs, specifying not only the relationships of individual constructs to behavior but, in addition, potentially causal relationships among the constructs themselves. Hybrid models have emerged with the goal of bringing together what is known about a health behavior from multiple sources, to provide a more complete characterization of the behavior (Nigg & Jordan, 2005). Researchers who develop hybrid models and who use them to guide intervention design assume that certain factors are unique both to particular behaviors and to the populations for which interventions are designed, and that effective interventions will consider these unique factors.

### *Hybrid Models as Reflections of the Current State of Knowledge*

In our own work, we employ hybrid models, and begin the study of a particular behavior by constructing a model of the behavior. Here, we find the distinction between theory and model provided by Nigg and Jordan (2005) to be useful. They state, "A theory is a system of assumptions and rules to describe, predict, and explain the nature of specified phenomena. A model is a description of a system that accounts for what is known" (Nigg & Jordan, op. cit, p. 291). Our hybrid models for specific health behaviors have drawn on at least four streams of information: past literature on relationships of individual constructs in existing models to the target behavior in the target population, similar literature that addressees the target behavior in other populations, findings on related behaviors and related health issues, and intensive discussions about the behavior in the population of interest in the form of focus groups.

Certainly, the models we construct and on which we base our interventions draw upon core constructs that appear in one form or another in leading models of health behavior. These constructs include perceptions of risk for a health threat, attitudes toward the health protective behavior, normative influences, self-efficacy, and intentions. The selection of these constructs is based on literature that supports the relationship of each construct to the behavior or to intentions to perform the behavior. We include intentions as well as behavior, since so much literature in health psychology focuses on behavioral intentions (Webb & Sheeran, 2006), and we are interested in the intention–behavior link.

The literature from which we draw necessarily has involved populations other than those we are targeting. Our interest in interventions to change young women's behavior to protect against distal risks has required that we draw on literature that studies older women, for whom the risk is much more proximal. To study calcium consumption in young women, we were forced to draw mainly on studies of older women, since there was little research on younger women. Similarly, in our study of elective plastic surgery among young women, we turned to literature on plastic surgery on somewhat older women. Our interest in young women's health also has been motivated in part by a lack of focus on younger women. When we began our work on condom use among relatively sexually inexperienced young women, most of the existing literature addressed men—either heterosexual men or men who have sex with men.

We also turn to existing literature that addresses different but related questions. For example, in our consideration of risky sexual behavior in young women, we turned to a more complete related literature on unwanted pregnancy and the factors associated with failure to use birth control. This led us to consideration of work by Gerrard (1987) on women's acceptance of their own sexuality, a willingness of a young woman to acknowledge to herself that she is sexually active and to be proactive in protecting herself from risks associated with sexual intercourse.

Finally, we ask our populations. Focus groups have provided insights and have revealed overlooked factors. Focus groups with young women revealed to us barriers to use of sunscreen, and also young women's lack of awareness that photoaging begins when one is very young. Focus groups with young women identified for us barriers to their consuming calcium, namely, the strong concern that calcium-rich foods are fattening. Our most recent focus groups addressing why young women want breast implants revealed a complex of motivational dimensions, as well as a series of steps in which they engage over time as they consider and finally decide about breast implants. As we exported our whole mammography intervention from middle-class predominantly Caucasian women to underserved Hispanic women, focus groups again guided our hands in both expansion of our then existing psychosocial model of screening and later, in intervention design.

## The Central Issue of Measurement

Having specified a model, the next intensive step is measurement development. We use existing scales from the literature in whole or in part—as with our sources of model content, we draw from related populations and related behaviors. We modify existing scales to be appropriate to our own research problem and population. We also develop our own items that we hope will capture ideas in our models. Over the years, we have created and accumulated our own scales, which we generalize from one behavior to another, rewriting parts of items to apply in new settings. We aim to have sufficient items per scale so that, if our psychometric analysis reveals badly behaved items, we may trim out these items and still have sufficient items for construct measurement.

With only very rare exceptions, we employ multiple-item scales, rather than relying on individual items. There rare items in the health psychology literature are classic and stand alone; for example, the classic direct comparative risk item, "Compared to other people your own age (or like you), how at risk are your for developing disease?" (Weinstein, 1982). We carry out extensive psychometric work to establish, first, that the items of each scale represent a unitary construct (i.e., that a one-dimensional confirmatory factor model reproduces the data for each scale adequately with all items having substantial loadings). If an item proves problematic in terms of distribution and psychometric properties in the single-factor model, it is discarded. We then pass through a discriminant validity phase of modeling in which we establish that the constructs in the model are distinct. For this, we estimate a confirmatory factor model including all the constructs, permitting all the interconstruct correlations to be freely estimated. Where a pair of constructs exhibits high intercorrelation, we test whether the two constructs psychometrically can be argued to reflect one underlying dimension. In the multiconstruct confirmatory factor model, we force the correlation between the pair of constructs to equal 1.0, and test whether model fit deteriorates. If it does, then we have evidence for the distinctiveness of the constructs. When we have multiple related constructs (e.g., injunctive

norms, descriptive norms from peers, broad societal norms), we also estimate a measurement model for this subset of constructs and examine the distinctiveness of the subset of constructs. This measurement work pays off in testing the psychosocial model in Stage One, and later in Stage Two, when we move to intervention and explore, through mediation analysis, potential mechanisms by which the intervention may have brought about behavior change. Examples of our psychometric work as part of model development can be found in Aiken et al., 1994a; Bryan et al., 1997; Jackson & Aiken, 2000, Moser & Aiken, 2011; Schmiege et al., 2007).

## Model Testing, Re-specification, and Replication

Having addressed the measurement of each construct, we examine the adequacy of our hypothesized model in two stages. First, we estimate the model as we have specified it and examine overall model fit, plus the significance of all the individual relationships specified in the model. We search for aspects of the model that have failed to fit, and we make small modifications in the original model, if there is strong evidence in our data that supports the modifications. In rare instances, we may slightly modify a measure to improve it. Then we replicate the model in an independent sample. We re-examine the measurement models, and we estimate the revised model from the first sample. In recent times, we have used a stacked structural equation model to examine the extent to which the re-specified model from the first sample is reproduced in the second sample. We identify any discrepancies, particularly relationships that fail to replicate. This becomes important in the mediation analysis phase of the intervention. Schmiege et al. (2007) and Moser and Aiken (2011) provide examples of the replication strategy.

## Temporal Issues in Psychosocial Modeling of Behavior and Behavior Change
### ONGOING BEHAVIOR VERSUS BEHAVIOR CHANGE

An inherent discontinuity exists between a psychosocial model of a behavior and a model of an intervention. In most instances, psychosocial models of health behavior characterize ongoing behavior in the absence of formal intervention or other factors that would result in behavior change. In contrast, the intervention aims to produce change, and it is change that we want to explain when we undertake to characterize the mechanisms underlying behavior in response to intervention. The issue is thus whether the constructs that predict ongoing behavior also predict behavior change. Much has been said about this issue, even with the recommendation to develop models only of new behaviors, at the point of their initiation. Yet, what we often study in health psychology are ongoing behaviors.

## TEMPORAL ISSUES

The approach we have taken is to address temporal precedence in our modeling phase. Most obviously, we avoid "postdiction" In postdiction, one asks questions about recent behavior, measures current status on psychosocial constructs in the same questionnaire, and the uses the psychosocial constructs as "predictors" of the recent past behavior. Suppose one asks, "How often did you exercise in the past month?" In the same interview, one asks for current judgments of self-efficacy for exercise and norms for exercise. Then, one specifies a model in which the psychosocial constructs of self-efficacy and norms serve as predictors of exercise in the past month; this is postdiction. It goes without saying that postdiction must be avoided in modeling behavior.

## TWO PANELS OF DATA FOR PSYCHOSOCIAL MODELING

We now undertake two panels of data collection for the development of the psychosocial model. The top part of Figure 25.3 illustrates these two panels of data collection; Schmiege et. al. (2007) provides an example. The first panel of data collection actually addresses three time frames: (1) recent past behavior (e.g., dietary content in the past month measured with a food frequency questionnaire), (2) current status on psychosocial constructs (e.g., dietary norms), and (3) intention to diet in the near future. A second panel of data collected some time later (e.g., 6 months later) addresses two more time frames: (4) recent past behavior (again, diet in the past month), and (5) intention to diet in the near future. Two distinct options for modeling the data that reflect these time frames are illustrated in Figure 25.3. Model A of Figure 25.3 does not include behavior assessed at Time 1. It models *ongoing behavior* at Panel 2, without any accounting for behavior measured at Panel 1. Model B includes behavior at Panel 1, which predicts behavior measured at Panel 2. Following Ajzen (2002) and Hennessy et al. (2010), initially measured behavior also predicts model constructs, under the assumption that model constructs underlie the stability of behavior over time. In model B, the prediction of behavior at Panel 2 is actually prediction of the residual of behavior at Panel 2 not accounted for by behavior at Panel 1; that is, any random fluctuation and/or systematic change in behavior across panels. The interplay between intentions and behavior is also

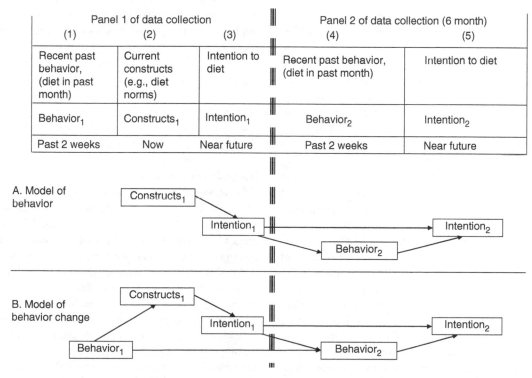

**Fig. 25.3** Temporal issues in the psychosocial modeling of health behavior.

explored in model B. These temporal issues in psychosocial modeling are complex. Weinstein (2007) has well characterized these complexities. He argues that Model A without initial behavior overestimates the relationship of psychosocial constructs to behavior, but that Model B, which includes initial behavior, underestimates these same relationships. These points are well taken. My view is that, often in psychology, we are able to achieve at most the direction of relationships, rather than magnitude of relationships. In the psychosocial modeling phase, the observation of associations often provides useful directions for intervention.

Once in a while, we are fortunate to have a natural event of large magnitude that converts our study of ongoing behavior or small behavioral fluctuations to a study of behavior change. An example is our work on predictors of use of hormone therapy with estrogen and progesterone (HRT) in a cohort of peri- and postmenopausal women (Gerend, Aiken, Erchull, & Lapin, 2006). Our first data collection occurred in 1995–1996, followed by repeated data collection in 1998–1999, 2001, 2002, and 2003. From 1995 through mid-2002, medical recommendations for use of hormone therapy were generally positive, and there was a sense among a large group of women that hormone therapy was the fountain of youth. Use versus nonuse of HRT was quite stable in our cohort between 1995 and 2002; the psychosocial variables we measured in 1995 continued to predict HRT use for 7 years. Then, on July 9, 2002, the Women's Health Initiative (WHI), the largest study of women's health ever funded in the United States, which had enrolled 40,000 women into a randomized trial of HRT, announced that it was terminating one arm of the HRT study (use of combined estrogen and progestin) because the health risks exceeded the benefits. At that time, 8 million women in the United States were taking combined HRT, including about half of the cohort we were studying, none of whom were participants in the WHI. Suddenly, we had the opportunity to study potential behavior change in the face of a natural intervention from the WHI. We found that the barriers or safety concerns expressed by users of HRT in 1995, concerns that had lain dormant in the golden "be forever young" years of HRT, predicted whether these women terminated use after the WHI announcement. Another less dramatic example of environmental forces was the intense international debate about whether mammography screening was useful for women in their 40s, which played out in the early 1990s; we were following a

cohort of women and studying their ongoing screening at the time, and we were able to examine the impact of the debate on women in their 40s who had been receiving regular screening (Aiken, & Jackson, 1996; Aiken, Jackson, & Lapin, 1998).

With two-panel models, we are attempting to establish *temporal precedence*; that is, in our observational psychosocial studies that inform intervention, we intend that the status on a psychosocial construct (say, self-reported self-efficacy for exercise) precedes in time the behavior it is purported to predict (here, exercise). Of course, even if we measure a construct at Panel 1 and then later assess the behavior at Panel 2, but the behavior was in place even before Panel 1 as "past behavior," then this "past behavior" may serve as the common cause of both the construct and later behavior. We are the first to admit our temporal precedence structure in data collection does not rule out spurious correlations; we try to address this issue by predicting future behavior from past behavior and asking for the unique contribution of construct measures to prediction of behavior over and above behavior stability. Eventually, we move to randomized trials, in which we manipulate constructs such as self-efficacy through intervention content and then examine subsequent behavior, in order to do a better job of ruling out spurious effects in our search for predictors of behavior change.

I have said that when we model behavior with past behavior partialed out, we are actually modeling behavior change, and this is so. However, we are measuring behavior changes that may be relatively small fluctuations in the absence of intervention. Again, we make an inductive leap from natural behavioral change to intervention driven behavior change when we apply our findings from psychosocial models of behavior to the design of interventions. We are willing to make this leap.

## Stage 2: Intervention
### Characteristics of Our Interventions
There are five over-arching characteristics of all our interventions. First, the psychosocial model from Stage One becomes the roadmap of the constructs to be targeted in the intervention, hence the term, *model-based intervention*. Second, given multiple construct psychosocial models, our interventions aim to change participants' levels on multiple constructs. Third, distinct content of the intervention is targeted to each construct. Fourth, the logical relationships among constructs in the psychosocial model are preserved in the intervention; we present the content of the intervention that relates to individual constructs

in an order that follows from the psychosocial model. Fifth, we aim to move beyond merely determining whether the intervention produced a change in behavior to an examination of the processes by which the intervention produced behavior change. Thus, we have thorough measurement of each construct that is included in the psychosocial model underlying the design of the intervention.

We break the intervention endeavor into a series of phases. Phase 1 involves intervention design. Phase 2 entails implementation of the intervention in a randomized trial. Phase 3 encompasses analyses of the impact of the intervention on intentions, behavioral outcomes, and also on the constructs targeted with the components of the intervention. Phase 4 involves mediation analysis to uncover the apparent processes by which the intervention produced intervention outcomes. It is Phase 4, the final phase of the intervention endeavor, that permits us to reverse the time-honored expectation that theory informs application; the results of the mediation analysis provide information that may lead to refinement of health behavior theory.

Following from the psychosocial model (and with some inductive leap to be sure), we create an intervention in which change on model constructs is expected to produce change in behavioral outcomes. This is hardly a novel expectation; it is implicit in every intervention that content of the intervention will engage processes within the recipients that lead to behavior change. What the two-stage approach accomplishes is to make this assumption explicit and to base program design on evidence of the relationships of constructs to behavior gleaned from systematic modeling of the behavior in psychosocial Stage One.

## Model Constructs and Intervention Components

Throughout the intervention endeavor, we distinguish *constructs* in the psychosocial model from *components* of the intervention. By an intervention component, we mean the content of the intervention specifically designed to produce change on one construct from the psychosocial model. The focus during the design phase of the intervention (Phase 1) is to create components that will produce change on the constructs in service of inducing behavior change (e.g., changing participants' perceptions of peer norms, diminishing negative attitudes to the behavior, increasing self-efficacy for the behavior, all to support behavior adoption and maintenance). The mediation analysis in Phase 4 establishes the linkages between change on the constructs and change in

behavior; here the constructs of the psychosocial model serve as the putative mediators through which the intervention brings about change.

Why is Phase 4, mediation analysis, absolutely necessary for intervention design to inform behavior theory? Phase 4 provides evidence of the linkage between change on constructs and change in behavior in the context of a randomized trial. A counterexample is useful here. Tailored intervention is a modern approach in intervention design; individual participants receive health risk–related information that is specific to themselves (Kreuter, Farrell, Olevitch, & Brennan, 2000). In interventions to increase cancer screening, information is provided about each individual's particular level of risk for some cancer, under the assumption that increased perceived risk will lead to increased screening. Tailored interventions have been shown to modify risk perception; the same interventions have been shown to enhance screening rates. However, in more than one instance, the changes in perceived risk have been unrelated to changes in screening; that is, the linkage illustrated in Figure 25.2 from intervention to putative mediator to outcome has not been realized. Absent this last step, to establish the relationship of change on a construct (here, perceived risk) to change on an outcome (here, screening), we cannot claim that change on the targeted construct was the mechanism by which behavior change was induced. See Aiken et al. (in press) for further discussion of this issue.

### Phase 1: Designing the Intervention

The psychosocial model becomes the heart of the design of the intervention. Again examine Figure 25.1. In the left-hand area representing program theory, we show three program components, each with an arrow to one construct. The arrow from each component to a construct indicates that the content of that component is designed specifically to change the level on that construct. Typically, we create an intervention component for each construct in the psychosocial model for which we found support in our psychosocial modeling. There are exceptions here. In our psychosocial model of young women's condom use (Bryan et al., 1997) a link from perceived benefits of condom use to affective attitudes toward condoms (e.g., condoms are disgusting) to intentions to condom use was estimated and replicated. In the intervention based on the psychosocial model (Bryan et al., 1996), we had content devoted to increasing the perception of benefits of condom use. We deliberately had no program component directly targeted to change affective attitudes (e.g., that condoms ruin the mood, that they are disgusting) because we wanted to test whether change in perceived benefits would be associated with change in affective attitudes. In fact, in the intervention, an increase in perceived benefits was associated with lessening of the negative attitude to condoms (Bryan et al., 1996).

The particular content of the program components is guided by multiple sources. We draw on what has worked in our previous interventions and in related interventions in published research. For example, there is a large and currently accumulating literature on methods for communicating risk to the lay public. We have also drawn on basic laboratory research in the social psychology of compliance (see Aiken et al., 1994b; Reynolds, West, & Aiken, 1990). We are the first to admit that some of our intervention content is trial and error, and that things don't always translate from the experimental laboratory to field interventions. An early mistake we made was to implement a form of our mammography intervention that included a number of exercises shown to increase compliance in laboratory settings—e.g., publicly contracting to carry out some behavior, imagining carrying out the behavior. When we implemented these same exercises in the field with mature women, the negative reaction of some participants was visible. Moreover, the quiet settings in the laboratory in which these exercises had been employed with success in no way resembled some of the field settings in which we presented the mammography program (among them a restaurant while women dined and enjoyed libations).

The psychosocial model is just this, a model; it is not a manifesto. By this I mean that we are not complete slaves to our psychosocial models. We have included intervention content that is not supported by the psychosocial model, particularly when we have strong theoretical interest in a particular construct that has failed in the psychosocial phase. Jackson and Aiken (2000), in our psychosocial modeling phase of sun protection against photoaging and skin cancer among young women, assessed what we termed *image norms*. These were the appearance norms with regard to being tanned or pale exhibited by aspirational peers in the media, that is, people who set beauty standards, including actresses and models. Previous literature on sunbathing had suggested the role of celebrities in shaping tanning, although we found no empirical studies of this relationship. Our measure of image norms was unrelated to intentions to sunbathe in the psychosocial phase. Nonetheless, we included an extensive component of the intervention directed to image norms, for theoretical interest. We found a

powerful effect of the intervention on image norms; change in image norms was strongly associated with change in perception of the advantages of tanning and also change in outcome behaviors of sun protection and sunbathing.

## DISTAL AND PROXIMAL THREATS DRIVE INTERVENTION DESIGN

The distinction between proximal and distal threats to behavior is important in intervention design. By proximal threats we mean health threats with near-term potential consequences (e.g., unintentional injury from a single episode of heavy drinking), whereas distal threats are those in which the consequences of a health risk behavior manifest themselves far into the future (e.g., liver damage from cumulative alcohol consumption). We have learned through our work with young women that, when we aim to change behavior to protect against a distal threat to health, incorporating proximal threats and proximal benefits into intervention is effective. In our efforts to increase both sun protection and calcium consumption among young women of college age, we have had to find ways to make distal health threats meaningful for our target population. We have learned that young women perceive that skin cancer happens to older women, like their mothers, if not their grandmothers, and that osteoporosis is something that happens to very old women like great-grandmothers. In our work with young women, we have taken two approaches to addressing distal threat. First, we have sought other threats to health and well-being that would lead to the same behavior. Sun protection provides an example. Our intervention aim in Jackson and Aiken (2006) was to increase sun protection against skin cancer; our intervention content focused heavily on a more proximal threat, photoaging. We vividly brought home the message that photoaging begins in one's 20s, and that the time was now to protect one's skin against the ravages of the sun. This is not to say we ignored the threat of skin cancer. We used a testimonial from a woman in her 30s who contracted melanoma in her early 20s sunbathing on the roof of a dormitory at the university where we carried out this research.

Second, we have sought proximal benefits of behaviors aimed at protecting against a distal threat. At the time we were working on calcium consumption, literature on weight loss and weight loss maintenance was reporting that calcium consumption was associated with more effective weight loss and weight loss maintenance. Our focus groups with young women had revealed that young women resisted consumption of calcium-rich foods because these foods were fattening. We incorporated the current literature on weight and calcium into our intervention to counter this barrier.

## CHOOSING AMONG FOCI TO AVOID REACTANCE

There is a lesson to be learned from Mark Twain's (1889) observation that there is "more than one way to skin a cat" and from Charles Kingsley's (1855) quip that there are "more ways of killing a cat than choking it with cream." Sometimes a focus on a behavior that is relatively neutral rather than one that is more positively or negatively emotionally tinged can be an effective intervention strategy. In our work on sun protection against skin cancer (Jackson & Aiken, 2006), we never said, "Don't sunbathe." The reason is simple—women reported to us that suntans made them look more attractive and healthier, and moreover made them feel more confident and even more competent. We did say, "Sun protect." Our intervention increased sun protection to be sure; but it also decreased sunbathing. In our work on calcium consumption (Schmiege & Aiken, 2011), we focused on encouraging women to take calcium supplements. We chose to do this for a number of reasons. Taking a calcium supplement once a day after a meal is much easier than changing one's diet to include calcium-rich food, particularly among college women for whom the norms against milk consumption are strong in social settings. Second, calcium supplements are not fattening, and some calcium-rich foods are. We directed the intervention to teaching women when to take calcium supplements and how to make it easy to do so.

## THE COMPLEXITY OF NORMATIVE MANIPULATIONS

Of all the constructs with which we have dealt, social norm manipulations pose among the greatest challenges. It is well to consider the important distinction between injunctive norms of what significant others say we should do and descriptive norms of what our peers actually do (Cialdini et al., 1990). In interventions, we often buck the existing descriptive norm. For example, in the sun protection intervention, with publicly observable tanned peers, we could not try to manipulate the descriptive norm by saying, "Your friends really aren't tanned." In the calcium consumption intervention, we knew from our prior work that, in fact, the strong majority of college women are deficient in calcium consumption. In the first draft of our intervention, we included a descriptive norm message that deplored this sorry state, "Three-quarters of young women at this university do not get enough calcium." The use of this message in the intervention would have created the descriptive norm that not getting enough calcium is usual, typical (and therefore acceptable).[3] For health behavior, this is a serious problem, because there is no observable consequence of getting insufficient calcium when one is 20 years of age—the consequences are 40 to 50 years down the road. We have learned to be acutely aware of our descriptive normative messages.

## DESIGN ISSUES: COMBINING MULTIPLE COMPONENTS INTO AN INTERVENTION

In laboratory experimental research, the design of choice is typically the complete factorial design. Moreover, we often counterbalance the order of presentation of materials across participants to avoid carryover effects. This is standard classic laboratory experimental fare. Imagine a health promotion intervention with four distinct components, each representing one of the four constructs of the HBM: susceptibility to health threat, severity of health threat, benefits of health action, and barriers to health action. Further imagine that we plan to implement an evaluation of this health communication in the classic experimental mode: a complete factorial design with four factors, each factor having two levels (component present, component absent) and a careful counterbalancing of orders of presentation of components. This yields $2 \times 2 \times 2 \times 2 = 16$ different versions of the intervention, of which one is a no-treatment control, the remainder are all possible combinations of one, two, three, or all four components of the HBM. Even incomplete counterbalancing would at least double the number of unique conditions of the experiment.

Is this how health intervention research, implemented in the field, with constraints on funding and on access to participant settings, takes place? It does not. Does it even make sense, given infinite money and infinite participants and infinite time, to approach intervention research in this way? It does not. The approach we take in intervention research is to implement the *strongest design possible*, in the hopes of producing behavior change. We include components in the intervention that target most or all of the constructs of our psychosocial model. Moreover, the order of presentation of intervention components is driven by a logical structure. For mammography screening, we presented data on susceptibility and severity of breast cancer first; then we moved to the great benefits of early detection of breast cancer for survival and the benefits of mammography for early detection. Finally, we addressed barriers to screening. It made little sense to begin the intervention with a discussion of barriers to getting mammograms, or to talk about the benefits of screening without first setting up the health threat (combining susceptibility and severity). Counterbalancing the order of components of an intervention can create forms of the intervention that do not unfold logically; in short, that simply do not make sense. Further, in the complete factorial design, some of the partial intervention conditions (i.e., those in which only one or two components are present) also may make no sense. In complete factorial tradition, one would have an intervention condition that addressed only barriers to mammography screening, and another condition that addressed only the severity of breast cancer and barriers to screening. Neither condition could be imagined to encourage screening.

The use of specialized incomplete factorial designs in intervention research can yield useful information about the incremental impact of individual constructs (Collins, Murphy, Nair, & Strecher, 2005; Nair et al., 2008; West & Aiken, 1997). A judiciously selected subset of conditions (for example, out of the 16 possible conditions of the $2 \times 2 \times 2 \times 2$ design) can yield information about main effects of each component and some important interactions between components. Interpretability of effects in incomplete factorial designs requires the strong assumption that some effects, particularly higher-order interactions, are zero in the population.

Other design alternatives are possible: For example, a constructive research strategy in which components are added to a base design (West & Aiken, 1997). One might implement a base intervention focused on benefits and barriers of a health behavior and also a second enhanced intervention in which information about susceptibility preceded the benefits and barriers components. This addition of a susceptibility component prior to the benefits and barriers components would address the important theoretical question of whether one must feel susceptible to a disease threat before fully appreciating and acting on the benefits of the prescribed health action and overcoming the barriers to that action.

In sum, the message here is that what we implement and evaluate in multicomponent interventions are those strong communications that include most or all components of our models. We may implement a judiciously chosen small set of variations on the complete communication that answer important theoretical questions. Order of inclusion of intervention components is driven by logic of arguments that build one from the other. As elaborated below, intensive measurement preceding and following the intervention is critical for unpacking the mechanisms of the intervention.

## Phase 2: Implementation of the Randomized Trial

### MEASUREMENT OF OUTCOMES

Phase 2 consists of implementation of the intervention in a randomized trial. Here, our extensive work on measurement of each construct in the psychosocial model, carried out in the psychosocial modeling phase of the intervention, is critical. For evaluation of the efficacy of the design to produce behavior change, we must have excellent measures of the outcome behavior(s) taken first in a pretest before the intervention. As in our psychosocial modeling, we measure intentions to behave immediately at the end of the intervention. Then, at a later follow-up, we assess outcome behavior and also reassess intentions. We often go beyond the target behavior (e.g., using sun screen for sun protection, taking calcium supplements) and inquire about related effects. We ask for other evidence that participants have acted on our messages (e.g., purchasing and carrying condoms, sun screen, calcium supplements, or talking to friends about the content of the program).

### MEASUREMENT OF PUTATIVE MEDIATORS

The need for measurement, however, goes far beyond intentions to behave and outcomes. In order that we be in a position to examine the processes by which the intervention brought about behavior change (or failed to do so) through mediation analysis, we require measures of each construct in the psychosocial model that underlies the intervention design. This includes all the constructs for which there are corresponding components in the intervention. It also includes constructs in the model we do not target directly in the intervention (e.g., affective attitudes to condom use in Bryan et al., 1996), but which we expect to change as a function of change on other constructs. This measurement is required both before and after the intervention. Absent both pretest and posttest measurement of all constructs that may serve as putative mediators of the intervention, mediation analysis of intervention mechanisms is not possible.

### IMPLEMENTATION EVALUATION

Part of Phase 2, implementation of the intervention, involves documentation of the integrity of the delivery of the intervention, each and every time the intervention is delivered. Our implementation evaluation instrument consists of a complete checklist of every point to be delivered in the intervention in the order in which it is to be presented. A research assistant observes the intervention and verifies that each point was made in the prescribed order, and documents any points that were missed or whether any content, not in the intervention script, was included. For exercises to be carried out during an intervention (e.g., role playing informing a potential sexual partner that one wants to use a condom), the assistant documents how the exercise proceeded, whether all participants joined in. The research assistant also documents events that occur during the intervention session that change the very nature of the intervention. For example, in one presentation of our mammography screening intervention, a participant who had recently had a mastectomy stopped the program and talked about the whole experience of having breast cancer; we were neither able to deliver the complete program nor to collect posttest data. These implementation evaluation records are useful in explaining why data of a group of participants may be exceptional in particular instances.

## Phase 3: Evaluation of Outcomes

This phase is straightforward, examining outcomes. Even though we have random assignment, we statistically adjust outcomes for pretest levels, thus examining adjusted gain scores. We address three classes of outcomes: two are the typical foci of outcome evaluation—change in intention at immediate posttest and change in behavior at follow-up. The third is less typical, assessing change on each of the constructs of the psychosocial model that now serve as putative mediators of the impact of the intervention, as was illustrated in Figure 25.2. Changes in level on these psychosocial constructs are proximal outcomes of the intervention.

## Phase 4: Mediation Analysis of Intervention Outcomes

The mediation model of the intervention in our two-stage approach arises directly from the psychosocial model developed, tested, and replicated in Stage One. Only those constructs that change as a function of the intervention are included in the mediation analysis of intervention effects. Thus, there may be a construct included in both the psychosocial model and in the intervention that did not respond to the intervention; such a construct cannot appear as a mediator in the mediation analysis of the intervention, which focuses on how the intervention produced behavior change.

## STATISTICAL MATTERS IN MEDIATION ANALYSIS

Much has been written about mediation analysis. MacKinnon's 2008 book, *Introduction to Statistical Mediation Analysis,* is a comprehensive reference work. Mediation analysis can be carried out in a series of regression analyses, as specified in Baron and Kenny (1986). With the growth of structural equation modeling and complex models of mediation, mediational models are now very often estimated in the context of structural equation models. The focus in mediation analysis of intervention is whether paths can be established from the intervention through putative mediators to the outcome. Path coefficients are estimated for each of the paths in the model. In Figure 25.2B, the mediated path from intervention through perceived benefits to outcome is represented by the path coefficient $a_2$ from intervention $X$ to benefits $M_2$ and the path $b_2$ from benefits to outcome. The magnitude of the *mediated effect* is the product of the path coefficients $(a_2 \times b_2)$. Beginning with Sobel (1982) a plethora of approaches has been proposed to testing significance of the mediated path. These approaches are summarized in MacKinnon, Lockwood, Hoffman, West, and Sheets (2002). The original Sobel approach has proven to be severely underpowered. New approaches yield much higher-power tests of mediation. Among the new approaches are including those based on the use of bootstrapping to estimate the standard error of a mediated effect, followed by tests of significance that employ the bootstrapped standard error as the error measure for the test statistic. Although this may sound obscure, bootstrapped standard errors and tests of mediated effects are easily obtained in standard structural equation modeling software (see MacKinnon, 2008, Chapter 12 for a discussion of bootstrap methods in mediation analysis).

## MAMMOGRAPHY INTERVENTION, AN OFF-THE-SHELF MODEL

The mammography intervention (Aiken et al., 1994b; Reynolds et al., 1990) illustrates use of a standing classic model of health behavior in intervention design. We followed the HBM directly in creating the intervention, with an intervention component directed to each of the four health beliefs in the model: perceived susceptibility to a threat, perceived severity of the threat, perceived benefits of a health protective action, and perceived barriers to the action. Of these four constructs, perceived susceptibility to breast cancer and perceived benefits of mammography screening were both increased by the intervention. However, there was no change in either perceived severity of breast cancer (which, not surprisingly, was very high before intervention) or perceived barriers to mammography screening. The mediation analysis of this early intervention effort in Aiken et al. (1994b) was thus quite simple, but it is illustrative of the approach to unpacking interventions. We first separately examined the individual mediated effect from the intervention through perceived susceptibility to intention and from intervention through perceived benefits to intention. Each of these effects was significant. Then, we turned to the model in Figure 25.2B. We estimated a mediational model with both these paths included (but without the path from susceptibility to benefits, path *d* in Figure 25.2B). In this model, only the mediated effect of perceived benefits was significant, and model fit was poor. Following theorizing by Ronis (1992), which characterized perceived susceptibility as an important precursor to perceived benefits, we then added the path *d* from susceptibility to benefits; this yielded a well-fitting model and yielded significant mediation from both susceptibility and benefits. This revised model that included path *d* suggested a much stronger role for susceptibility than the role in the model without the *d* path (see also Aiken et al., 2001; Aiken et al., in press). The *total mediated effect* of perceived susceptibility in the model in Figure 25.2B was the sum of two mediated paths: Path 1,

a simple mediated path, the path Intervention → Susceptibility → Intentions; and Path 2, a complex mediated path involving two mediators in sequence, the path Intervention → Susceptibility → Benefits → Intentions. Together, Path 1 plus Path 2 led to an estimate of the total mediated effect of susceptibility that was three times the size of that from Path 1 alone (see West & Aiken, 1997, pp. 185–191 for the full exploration of the role of perceived susceptibility in this model). The final model of the intervention is given in Figure 25.4, which also includes the link from intentions to behavior. It also includes perceived severity and perceived barriers; however, these are not mediators. Rather, they are *covariates* in the model, included because perceived severity was a positive correlate of perceived benefits, and perceived barriers was a strong negative correlate of behavior.

What could we take away from this mediational analysis? It appears that both perceived susceptibility and perceived benefits, both of which were modified by the intervention, contributed to change in intentions and to screening. The mediational analysis also suggested that perceived susceptibility might well have its effect in part through impact on perceived benefits. Of course, we could not say that susceptibility was causally related to perceived benefits. Such a claim would have required a second form of the intervention in which perceived susceptibility was not included in the model. Nor could we say that changes in perceived benefits and perceived susceptibility caused changes in outcomes. The effects of the intervention on the putative mediators are experimentally produced through a randomized trial; however, the

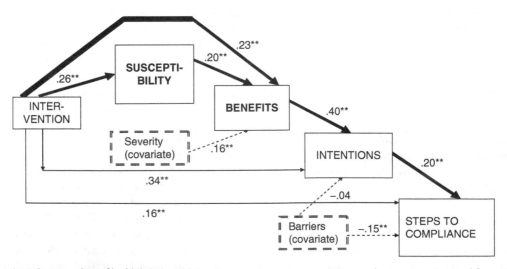

**Fig. 25.4** Mediation analysis of health-belief model–based intervention to increase mammography screening. Reprinted from Aiken, L. S., West, S. G., Reno, R. R., Woodward, C., & Reynolds. (1994b). Increasing screening mammography in asymptomatic women: Evaluation of a Second Generation, theory-based program. *Health Psychology, 13,* 526–538, with permission of the publisher.

effects of these mediators to outcomes are correlational in nature. That the second half of the mediation chain (i.e., from change in a mediator to change in outcome) is inherently correlational constrains our conclusions about mechanisms underlying an intervention to be those that are plausible rather than causal in nature.

## SUN PROTECTION INTERVENTION

Our work on sun protection began with the development of a psychosocial model that targeted two behaviors: sun protection and sunbathing. These are not diametrically opposed behaviors—people use sunscreen and then expose themselves to the sun. The psychosocial model (Jackson & Aiken, 2000) was far more complex than the "off-the-shelf" HBM for the mammography intervention. For sun protection and sunbathing, we developed a hybrid model with constructs drawn from the HBM, the TRA, and social-cognitive theory. To this we added the construct of image norms of the paleness versus tanness of aspirational peers (movie stars and models), described above. Our psychosocial modeling showed mediational linkages from susceptibility to skin cancer and photoaging, norms for sun protection, barriers and self-efficacy for sun protection, to intention to sun protect; susceptibility also related to intentions to sunbathe, as did norms for sunbathing and advantages of tanning. In the intervention that followed (Jackson & Aiken, 2006) we targeted seven distinct constructs, listed as putative mediators in Table 25.1. For susceptibility, severity, and benefits, we considered photoaging and skin cancer as two distinct threats. There were separate intervention components for susceptibility to and severity of photoaging, for susceptibility to and severity of skin cancer, and for benefits of sun protection for both photoaging and for skin cancer. As mentioned previously, even though image norms had not been predictive in psychosocial modeling, we included a strong image norm component in the intervention. In service of increasing self-efficacy

**Table 25.1  Analysis of Jackson and Aiken (2006). Effect size $d$, and correlation of residualized change on constructs with residualized intentions and behavior**

| Construct | Effect size $d$ for impact of intervention | Correlations among residualized change on intentions and behavior, and correlations of residualized change on putative mediators with residualized change in intentions and behavior | | | | |
| | | Intention Sun protect | Intention Sunbathe | Body Sun Protection | Face Sun Protection | Hours Sunbathing |
|---|---|---|---|---|---|---|
| Intentions and Outcome Behaviors | | | | | | |
| Intention, sun protect, posttest | $d = .92$ | — | | | | |
| Intention, sunbathe, posttest | −1.31 | −.46* | — | | | |
| Body sun protection, follow-up | .20 | .28* | −.36* | — | | |
| Face sun protection, follow-up | .44 | .20* | −.30* | .60* | — | |
| Hours sunbathing, follow-up | −.21 | −.09 | .15+ | −.18* | .06 | — |
| Correlations of Putative Mediators (Model constructs) with Intentions and Outcomes | | | | | | |
| Susceptibility, photoaging (cancer)[1] | .47 (.44) | .16* | −.28* | .18* | .18* | −.22* |
| Severity, photoaging (cancer)[1] | .39 (.20) | .12+ | −.21* | .14 | .03 | −.10 |
| Benefits, photoaging (cancer)[1] | .88 (.71) | .33* | −.26* | .16+ | .16+ | −.02 |
| Barriers to sun protection | .28 | −.20* | −.30* | −.07 | −.04 | .25* |
| Self-efficacy for sun protection | 1.08 | .46* | −.48* | .25* | .19* | −.19* |
| Advantages of tanning | −1.03 | −.25* | .43* | −.23* | −.17* | .26* |
| Image norms for paleness | 1.27 | .30* | −.38* | .21* | .23* | −.07 |

* $p \leq .05$ at least; + $p \leq .10$.
[1]Effect size for photoaging health belief with effect size for skin cancer health belief in parentheses.

for sun protection, the intervention suggested simple strategies for incorporating sun protection into daily life, for example, using after-bath moisturizers that contain sun protection.

Effect sizes of the impacts of the intervention are provided in Table 25.1. We found significant increases in the intentions to sun protect; actual protection of both face and body increased as well. We also found significant decreases in intention to sunbathe and in sunbathing itself. This was so even though we never admonished participants to refrain from sunbathing (in order to avoid reactance). We also found significant impact of the intervention in the desired direction for all putative mediators except severity of skin cancer. The effect sizes of the intervention on critical constructs were notably large (among them, $d = 1.27$ for image norms for paleness; $d = -1.03$ for advantages of sunbathing, $d = 1.08$ for self-efficacy for sun protection, $d = .92$ for intention to sun protect, and $d = -1.31$ for intention to sunbathe). Changes in behavior were small to moderate. As shown in Table 25.1, there were notable correlations of residualized change on putative mediators with residualized change in both intentions and behavior; the most consistently correlated putative mediators were susceptibility to photoaging, self-efficacy for sun protection, advantages of tanning, and image norms for paleness.

Our mediation analysis included the seven putative mediators; we chose to include only health beliefs with regard to photoaging, since photoaging

was the proximal threat and had yielded slightly larger effect sizes in the analysis of outcomes. Our final mediational model shown in Figure 25.5. The mediational model supported that the cognitive health beliefs (susceptibility, severity, benefits) and self-efficacy for sun protection mediated the relationship of the intervention to intention to sun protect. In contrast, the normative and attitudinal measures of image norms and advantages of tanning, respectively, were mediators of intention to sunbathe. The full mediational model was well fitting. In addition, we carried out a series of *focused tests* of specific mediational paths within the model; highlights are given here. First, a focused test supported what we had observed in the mammography intervention—that perceived susceptibility to photoaging served as a mediator of the effect of the intervention on perceived benefits of sun protection (i.e., the mediated path, Intervention → Perceived Susceptibility → Benefits). In turn, benefits mediated the relationship of the intervention on intention to sun protect (i.e., the mediated path, Intervention → Benefits → Intention to Sun Protect). Image norms mediated the impact of the intervention on advantages of tanning (i.e., the path Intervention → Image Norms → Advantages of Tanning). Perceived susceptibility to photoaging and advantages of tanning were juxtaposed mediators of the intervention effect on sunbathing.

What did we gain from the mediation analysis, above and beyond the demonstration that intentions

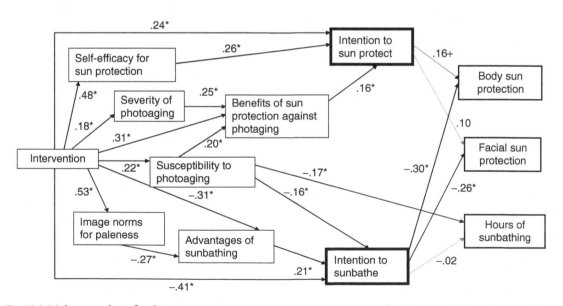

**Fig. 25.5** Mediation analysis of multicomponent intervention to increase sun protection and to decrease sunbathing. Reprinted from Jackson, K., & Aiken, L. S. (2006). Evaluation of a multi-component appearance-based sun-protective intervention for young women: Uncovering the mechanisms of program efficacy. *Health Psychology, 25,* 34–46, with permission of the publisher.

and behavior changed in the targeted direction? First, this mediation analysis lends support to the utility of hybrid models for particular health-related behaviors; that is, models that draw together constructs from multiple established models of health behavior in service of a more complete characterization of the putative determinants of a particular health behavior. Second, the mediation analysis suggested roles for cognitive beliefs from the HBM and self-efficacy from social-cognitive theory for changing intentions to sun protect. In contrast, norms and attitudes were strong mediators of the intervention on intentions to sunbathe. Third, the mediational role of image norms for paleness on decreasing intentions to sunbathe was the first demonstration of its kind. Fourth, the mediational sequence Image Norms → Advantages of Tanning → Intentions to Sunbathe suggests that manipulation of image norms might be an effective method of changing attitudes without causing the reactance that can accrue from directly targeting strongly held attitudes (e.g., the great attractiveness of a tan). We are the first to admit that we cannot claim any causal relationship here, just as we could not with susceptibility and benefits in the mammography intervention. Nonetheless, these findings have led us to consider image norms in relation to another appearance-related behavior among women that has potentially serious negative medical sequelae, specifically, breast augmentation (Kucera, 2008).

## MEDIATION ANALYSIS OF A MULTISESSION, MULTISITE INTERVENTION

The most complex mediation analysis of an intervention in which I been involved[4] is the analysis of a large-scale multisite intervention (Athletes Targeting Healthy Exercise and Nutrition Alternatives [ATHENA]; Elliot et. al., 2004, 2006). The mediation analysis examined the mechanisms underlying the ATHENA intervention, which aimed both to prevent unhealthy weight control strategies (e.g., diet pills, purging) and to prevent the use of sport-enhancing drugs (anabolic steroids, creatine) among high-school women athletes (Ranby et al., 2009). The intervention was delivered in an eight-session intervention carried out over a 5-month period (see Elliot et al., 2004, 2006 for description of the intervention).

The delivery of the intervention components over sessions was a special boon to mediation analysis because it set the *temporal precedence* of the content of the intervention components. The sequencing of intervention content is depicted in Figure 25.6;

the numerical value in the lower corner of each construct box indicates the session in which the intervention component targeted to that construct was presented. For example, Sessions 1 and 2 conveyed information on the effects of anabolic steroids; sessions 5 and 6 targeted outcome expectancies for use of steroids; and session 8 assessed intentions to use steroids, with behavior measured 9 months later. The full mediational model reflected the complexity and multidimensional nature of the intervention, with 11 mediators predicting two distinct proximal outcomes: intention to use steroids/creatine and intention to engage in unhealthy weight loss practices. Due to the great complexity of the intervention and the extensive set of mediators, we undertook a sequence of mediational analyses to clarify the apparent action of the program through these 11 mediators on two outcomes. All these mediational analyses necessarily took account of the clustered nature of the data; specifically, that the intervention was delivered to 29 sports teams within nine different schools.

We first estimated a series of simple single mediator models (Intervention → Mediator → Intention) and estimated the proportion of the total effect of the intervention that was carried through the single mediational path in each single-mediator analysis, referred to as the *proportion mediated*. Since mediators were correlated, the single-mediation models accounted for overlapping mediation of the intervention.[5] Only those individual mediators that actually evidenced significant mediation were retained for further mediation analysis. In these single-mediation analyses of the intervention, social norms, outcome expectancies, self-efficacy, and knowledge emerged as powerful mediators.

Our next step was to estimate the full mediational model, which contained seven mediational paths from intervention to intentions to use steroids and another seven mediational paths from intervention to intention to engage in unhealthy weight loss behavior. With one exception, all paths in the model, including those from intervention to each mediator, from mediator to mediator, and mediator to intention, were significant; moreover, the model fit adequately.

We then moved to a third stage of analysis in which we examined each of the mediational paths in the full model and estimated the unique proportion of the total mediation attributable to each path. We did this separately for each of the two intention measures. For illustrative purposes, four of the seven mediation paths from intervention to intention to

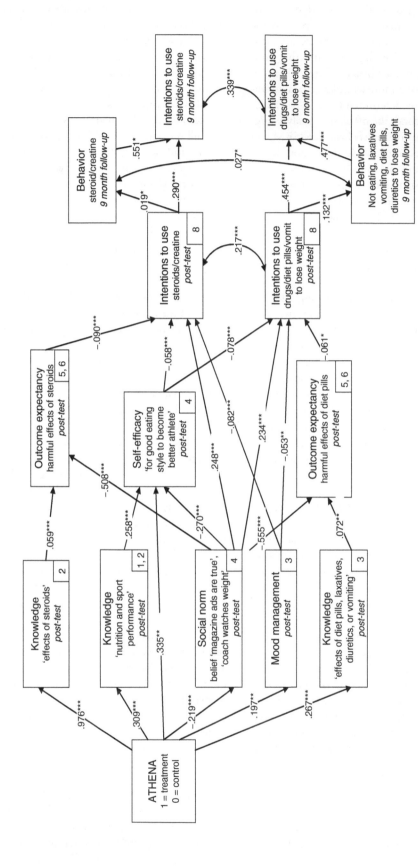

**Fig. 25.6** Multiple mediator model of the ATHENA intervention. Reprinted from of Ranby, K.W., Aiken, L. S., MacKinnon, D. P., Elliot, D. L., Moe, E. L., McGinnis, W., & Goldberg, L. (2009). A mediation analysis of the ATHENA intervention for female athletes: Prevention of athletic-enhancing substance use and unhealthy weight loss behaviors. *Journal of Pediatric Psychology, 34(10),* *1069–1083,* with permission of the publisher.

use steroids/creatine were as follows (session numbers in parentheses):

a. Intervention → social norm (4) → intentions to use steroids (8)

b. Intervention → social norm (4) → outcome expectancies for steroids/creatine (5,6) &→ intentions to use steroids/creatine (8)

c. Intervention → social norm (4) → self-efficacy for healthy eating (4) → intentions to use steroids/creatine (8);

d. Intervention → mood management (3) → intentions to use steroids/creatine (8)

Note that the first three paths share the mediator social norm in common, whereas path d shares no mediators with the other three paths. For each of the two dependent variables, the proportion mediated by each path was a partialed effect, the unique mediational effect of a single path, with all other paths held constant. Thus, proportions of the total intervention mediated by each of the seven paths from intervention to intention to use steroids summed to 1.00; that is, the proportion accounted for by each of the paths was unique. A parallel set of estimates of unique proportion mediated by individual paths was carried out for intention to engage in unhealthy weight loss behaviors. Social norms on its own (i.e., in the path Intervention → Social Norms → Intentions) accounted for the largest unique proportion of the total mediated effect for both intention to use steroids/creatine (proportion unique mediated = .45) and intention for unhealthy weight loss methods (proportion unique mediated = .40). Self-efficacy on its own (i.e., in the path Intervention → Self-Efficacy → Intentions) was the next most important mediator (proportion unique mediated =. 17 and .20, respectively).

Given the strategy of estimating the unique proportions mediated through different paths, it is possible to sum the proportion mediated for all paths in which a particular mediator appears to obtain an estimate of the total mediational effect associated with that mediator. Consider paths a, b, and c above for mediation paths from intervention to social norm and ultimately to intention to use steroids/creatine. These individual paths accounted for .45 + .04 + .03 = .52 proportion of the total mediated effect of the intervention on intention to use steroid/creatine, reinforcing the power of social norms in the intervention. The parallel values for intention for unhealthy weight loss behaviors were .40 + .06 + .04 = .50. The methodology for estimating unique proportions mediated is provided in Appendix 2 of Ranby et al. (2009).

In summary, the multistage mediational analysis of the ATHENA intervention first identified individual mediators of the intervention, then tested whether a system of mediation illustrated in Figure 25.6 was plausible from the perspective of model fit, and finally estimated the role of individual mediational chains and individual mediators in the full multiple-mediator model.

## Some Lessons from Psychosocial Modeling
### Utility of Developing Hybrid Psychosocial Models

Our work has involved the development and testing of hybrid psychosocial models of behavior. This strategy has been informative, in and of itself, in characterizing health behavior. Moreover, hybrid models have effectively guided intervention design. The hybrid model strategy has also permitted consideration of constructs that apply to unique classes of behaviors, for example, image norms that may underlie appearance-related behaviors, and emotions that underlie elective plastic surgery. There is a certain simplicity and elegance in working with an existing model that stands on a large body of research, as in the classic models of health behavior; also, one's own work contributes to the accumulated body of knowledge about the model. However, the hybrid modeling approach may provide a broader perspective on particular health behaviors, a perspective that is enriched by the breadth of health behavior models and related literatures from which to draw.

### Core Models and Population-specific Constructs

The study of a single behavior in multiple populations affords special opportunities to study the generalizability of models across demographic groups, as well as to identify specific factors relating to behavior in particular strata of individuals. As previously mentioned, one example in our work is condom use among young college women (Bryan et al., 1996, 1997), young college men (Bryan et al., 2001), and incarcerated youth (Bryan et al., 2004). Another is our work on mammography screening in predominantly middle-class Caucasian women reported here versus with underserved Hispanic women (Aiken et al., 2000). From this work, we have learned two things. First is that a single construct (e.g., control) may have different meanings for different populations, so that the application of a broad general model requires tailoring of constructs to specific populations. In the case of control and condom use, our characterization of control in our work with young college women and condom use (Bryan et al., 1996, 1997) addressed their sense of control of the sexual encounter, whether and when sex would occur. With young college men (Bryan et al., 2001), this control construct had no predictive utility. A different casting of control in terms of sexual self-control, being able to put on a condom, keep the partner interested, and continue toward intercourse was predictive for males. Self-efficacy for men was more along the lines of purchasing condoms and the mechanics of condom use, whereas for women, it was being able to negotiate condom use with their partner and to deal with partner dissatisfaction about condom use. A second observation from working on a common behavior across populations is that, in addition to core constructs like susceptibility, attitudes, norms, benefits, and barriers, there may be additional more population-specific constructs that can be added to existing models for greater explanatory power. For Hispanic women, acculturation to the dominant Anglo culture predicted mammography screening (Aiken et al., 2000), whereas this construct was not applicable in a Caucasian middle-class U.S. born population. Among incarcerated young males (Bryan et al., 2004), optimism about the future and self-esteem were predictive of condom use, two constructs not included in our modeling with middle-class college males.

## What Have We Learned from Mediation Analysis of Interventions?
### Lessons Learned About Health Behavior
I began the chapter with the argument that mediational analysis of the mechanisms by which interventions bring about changes in health behavior could inform our models of health behavior. From each of our mediational analyses of interventions we have learned something about health behavior. From both the mammography and the sun protection interventions, we have gleaned evidence that one important contribution of perceived susceptibility may be as a factor that strengthens the perception of perceived benefits of a health action. This has shaped our own theorizing about perceived susceptibility as an early factor in a chain of constructs that lead to health behavior (Aiken et al., 2001, in press). Second, from our early intervention work on condom use (Bryan et al., 1996) and our work on sun protection (Jackson & Aiken, 2006), we have learned about the precursors of attitudes and how changing those precursors appears to result in

change in attitudes. This suggests that, in modifying health behavior, we can avoid engendering reactance that would result from directly attempting to modify attitudes (e.g., "condoms are disgusting," or "I am more attractive with a tan") by intervening on constructs that appear to be upstream from attitudes. In the case of condom use, our hypothesized upstream construct was benefits of condom use; for sun protection, image norms for paleness. Third, the sun protection intervention also highlighted the importance of media norms, in addition to injunctive and descriptive norms. For appearance-related behaviors like tanning, health behavior models should include powerful media influences (Reid et al.,2010). Fourth, from our work on distal threats to health that are perceived to be far in the future (young women and skin cancer, osteoporosis), we have learned that by intervening with a proximal benefit of a protective behavior (e.g., sun protection against photoaging; the hypothesized weight control benefits of calcium), we were able to bring about salutary health behavior. This leads us to an enhanced understanding of what motivates health protective behavior, at least in young people; that is, immediate, personally relevant positive health and well-being outcomes rather than remote threats to health somewhere in the unforeseen future. The mediation analysis of the ATHENA intervention, targeted to high school-aged women, reinforced the important role of proximal threats through content that showed how unhealthy behaviors undermine current athletic performance. This same mediation analysis further supported the powerful role of normative influences, particularly from athletic coaches, but also more subtle influences, for example, the influence of mood control (affect) in prevention of unhealthy behavior in our observation of mood management as a significant mediator of the intervention effect on intention to use steroids.

### For the Future: The Search for Moderators
It is possible that the mechanisms by which interventions bring about behavior change differ across individuals. Put another way, there may be variables that modify or moderate the components of mediational paths underlying interventions. These *moderators*, as they are termed, may change the relationship from the intervention to a mediator (the $a_1$ and $a_2$ paths in Figure 25.2) or from the mediator to the outcome (the $b_1$ and $b_2$ paths in Figure 25.2). In our work on sexual behavior among young men and women, gender could be said to moderate the impact of perceived control of the sexual encounter

on condom use. Control over whether and when to have sex predicted condom use for young women but not for young men. Personality variables are likely candidates for moderators of intervention. For example, conscientiousness (Kern & Friedman, 2008), might modify the relationship between the mediator of acquired knowledge about appropriate health-protective behavior the one hand and actual sustained health-protective behavior on the other. The identification of such moderators will permit a more nuanced understanding of interventions, integrating the questions of how and for whom interventions work. Modern statistical frameworks make it possible to ask these questions. Fairchild and MacKinnon (2009) have recently provided a general framework for simultaneous examination of both mediation and moderation of intervention effects (see also Edwards & Lambert, 2007; Preacher, Rucker, & Hays, 2007). We have just begun to examine the role of moderators in explaining health behavior, for example, to understand how age moderates the relationship between planning for regular exercise and actual exercise maintenance (Reuter et al., 2010) and how the status of a male–female relationship as casual versus committed moderates the mediators of condom use (Reid & Aiken, in press). We anticipate that the identification of moderators of intervention mechanisms is fertile ground for health psychology.

## Conclusion

My choice of which health behaviors to study has been driven by what we considered the most interesting theoretical questions. Core conceptual issues have included screening to detect disease versus disease prevention; public versus private behaviors; behaviors in which the threats to health are proximal (near-term) versus distal (far-term); and pairs of behaviors that support a common health goal, or that work in opposition. Importantly, the creating of intervention components has been guided by comprehensive models. I and my students have particularly enjoyed developing strategies to encourage behavior change that avoid reactance—pressure to resist the intervention. To make all this feasible, an important part of our work has been on the measurement of central constructs in health psychology; specifically, our work on perceived susceptibility and on establishing adequate measures of psychosocial constructs through psychometric analysis. Finally, an exciting part of this work has been utilization of statistical developments in mediation analysis and the integration of mediation

analysis into the structural equation modeling framework. These developments have permitted us to examine models of increasing complexity with greater statistical power and ever greater refinement.

### The Value of Hybrid Models

The aggregation of our intervention work has led us to believe strongly in the value of hybrid models that draw together important putative determinants of behavior from multiple sources to create a rich resource to guide intervention research. To be sure, such hybrid models have informed our intervention design. Beyond this, they have surfaced important mediators of intervention effects. These mediators have, in turn, provided insights into the putative determinants of health-protective behavior. There are proponents of the use of extant models exactly as they are specified. They have argued against hybrid models, and particularly against separating out unique influences on behavior that may be construed to fall within a larger theoretical category (e.g., separating the sexual partner's norm for condom use from a more general injunctive norms from others). The argument is that programmatic research on an existing model as it is specified in its pure form contributes to the body of what is known about an individual theory or model, the breadth of its applicability, its strengths and limitations.

In contrast to this position, it is our experience that the development of hybrid psychosocial models that draw on both multiple models of health behavior and on potentially rich related literatures, and that incorporate unique factors relating to specific behaviors for specific populations, has proved informative in intervention design. In turn, the model-based multicomponent interventions that flow from such hybrid models can be implemented and evaluated in a manner that surfaces the apparent mechanisms by which the intervention brings about behavior change. This research process reverses the unidirectional flow from model to intervention. Careful examination of the putative mechanisms by which health behavior interventions bring about behavior change can lead to theoretical advances in our understanding of health risk and protective behavior.

### Notes

1. Our students over the years have contributed greatly to the research: Kim D. Reynolds, Claremont Graduate University; Angela D. Bryan, University of Colorado; Kristina M. Jackson, Brown University; Mary A. Gerend, Florida State

University; Mindy J. Erchull, University of Mary Washington; Sarah J. Schmiege, University of Colorado Denver; Krista W. Ranby, Duke University; Allecia E. Reid, Yale University and Stephanie E. Moser, current doctoral student.

2. I thank Howard Friedman for his wise counsel and exceptional editorial expertise, and Kristina Jackson for her critical review of this chapter.

3. We were fortunate that our colleague Robert Cialdini pointed out the error of our ways in this communication, and we did not convey this message in the intervention.

4. I was not involved in the design and implementation of the intervention, but only in the mediational analysis of intervention effects in collaboration with those who created and implemented the intervention.

5. The analysis of correlated mediators in single mediational models is parallel to having two correlated predictors X and Z and of a single outcome Y and estimating two one-predictor regression analyses, each with one of the two predictors, $\hat{Y} = b_1 X + b_0$ and $\hat{Y} = b_1 Z + b_0$. Since the two predictors X and Z are correlated, the two regression analyses would account for overlapping variation in the outcome. The sum of the proportion of variation predicted by X alone, plus the proportion of variation predicted by Y alone in their separate regression equations—that is, $R^2_{YX}$ plus $R^2_{YZ}$—would be greater than the proportion predicted by the two predictors in the same equation— that is, $R^2_{YXZ}$ from the regression equation $\hat{Y} = b_1 X + b_2 Z + b_0$.

# References

Aiken, L.S., Fenaughty, A.M., West, S.G., Johnson, J.J., & Luckett, T.L. (1995). Perceived determinants of risk for breast cancer and the relationships among objective risk, perceived risk, and screening behavior over time. *Women's Health: Research on Gender, Behavior, and Policy, 1,* 27–50.

Aiken, L.S., Gerend, M.A., & Jackson, K.M. (2001). Subjective risk and health protective behavior: Cancer screening and cancer prevention. In A. Baum, T. Revenson, & J. Singer (Eds.), *Handbook of health psychology* (pp. 727–746). Mahwah, NJ: Lawrence Erlbaum.

Aiken, L.S. Gerend, M.A., Jackson, K.M., & Ranby, K. (in press). Subjective risk and health protective behavior. In A. Baum, T. Revenson, & J. Singer (Eds.), *Handbook of health psychology* (2nd ed.). New York: Taylor & Francis.

Aiken, L.S., & Jackson, K.M. (1996). Mammography benefits for women under 50: A closer look at the controversy. *Women's Health: Research on Gender, Behavior, and Policy, 2*(4), 235–242.

Aiken, L.S., Jackson, K.M., Castro, F.G., & Pero, V.I. (2000). Mediators of the linkage from acculturation to mammography screening compliance among urban Hispanic women. *Women and Cancer, 2,* 4–16.

Aiken, L.S., Jackson, K.M., & Lapin, A. (1998). Mammography screening for women under 50: Women's response to medical controversy and changing practice guidelines. *Women's Health: Research on Gender, Behavior, and Policy, 4,* 169–197

Aiken, L.S., West, S.G., Woodward, C., & Reno, R.R. (1994a). Health beliefs and compliance with mammography screening recommendations. *Health Psychology, 13,* 122–129.

Aiken, L.S., West, S.G., Reno, R.R., Woodward, C., & Reynolds. (1994b). Increasing screening mammography in asymptomatic women: Evaluation of a Second Generation, theory-based program. *Health Psychology, 13,* 526–538.

Ajzen, I. (1991). The theory of planned behavior. *Organizational Behavior and Human Decision Processes, 50,* 179–211.

Ajzen, I. (2002). Residual effects of past on later behavior: Habituation and reasoned action perspectives. *Personality and Social Psychology Review, 6,* 107–122.

Bandura, A. (1986). *Social foundations of thought and action: A social cognitive theory.* Englewood Cliffs, NJ: Prentice-Hall.

Baron, R.M., & Kenny, D.A. (1986). The moderator-mediator variable distinction in social psychological research: Conceptual, strategic, and statistical considerations. *Journal of Personality and Social Psychology, 51,* 1173–1182.

Bryan, A.D., Aiken, L.S., & West, S.G. (1996). Increasing condom use: Evaluation of a theory-based intervention to prevent sexually transmitted disease in young women. *Health Psychology, 15,* 371–382.

Bryan, A.D., Aiken, L.S., & West, S.G. (1997). Young women's condom use: The influence of acceptance of sexuality, control over the sexual encounter, and perceived susceptibility to common STDs. *Health Psychology, 16,* 468–479.

Bryan, A.D., Aiken, L.S., & West, S.G. (2004). HVI/STD risk among incarcerated adolescents: Optimism about the future and self-esteem as predictors of condom use self-efficacy. *Journal of Applied Social Psychology, 34,* 912–936.

Bryan, A., Schindeldecker, M.S., & Aiken, L.S. (2001). Sexual self-control and male condom use outcome beliefs: Predicting heterosexual men's condom-use intentions and behavior. *Journal of Applied Social Psychology, 31,* 1911–1938.

Chen, H.-T. (1990). *Theory-driven evaluation.* Newbury Park, CA: Sage.

Cialdini, R.B., Reno, R.R., & Kallgren, C.A. (1990). A focus theory of normative conduct: Recycling the concept of norms to reduce littering in public places. *Journal of Personality and Social Psychology, 58,* 1015–1026.

Collins, L.M., Murphy, S.A., Nair, V., & Strecher, V. (2005). A strategy for optimizing and evaluating behavioral interventions. *Annals of Behavioral Medicine, 30,* 65–73.

Donaldson, S.I. (2001). Mediator and moderator analysis in program development. In S. Sussman (Ed.), *Handbook of program development for health behavior research and practice* (pp. 470–500). Newbury Park, CA: Sage.

Edwards, J.R., & Lambert, L.S. (2007). Methods for integrating moderation and mediation: A general analytical framework using moderated path analysis. *Psychological Methods, 12,* 1–22.

Elliot, D.L., Goldberg, L., Moe, E.L., DeFrancesco, C.A., Durham, M.B., & Hix- Small, H. (2004). Preventing substance use and disordered eating: Initial outcomes of the ATHENA (athletes targeting healthy exercise and nutrition alternatives) program. *Archives of Pediatric and Adolescent Medicine, 158,* 1043–1049.

Elliot, D.L., Moe, E.L., Goldberg, L., DeFrancesco, C.A., Durham, M.B., & Hix- Small, H. (2006). Definition and outcome of a curriculum to prevent disordered eating and body-shaping drug use. *Journal of School Health, 76,* 67–73.

Fairchild, A.J., & MacKinnon, D.P. (2009). A general model for testing mediation and moderation effects. *Prevention Science, 10,* 87–99.

Fishbein, M. (2000). The role of theory in HIV prevention. *AIDS Care, 12*(3), 273–278.

Fishbein, M., & Ajzen, I. (1975). *Belief, attitude, intention, and behavior: An introduction to theory and research.* Reading, MA: Addison Wesley.

Gerend, M.A., Aiken, L.S., Erchull, M.J., & Lapin, M.A. (2006). Women's use of hormone therapy before and after the women's health initiative: A psychosocial model of stability and change. *Preventive Medicine, 43,* 158–164.

Gerend, M., Aiken, L.S., West, S.G, & Erchull, M.J. (2004). Beyond medical risk: Investigating the psychological factors underlying women's perceptions of susceptibility to breast cancer, heart disease, and osteoporosis. *Health Psychology, 23,* 247–258.

Gerend, M.A., Aiken, L.S., & West, S.G. (2004). Personality factors in older women's perceived susceptibility to diseases of aging. *Journal of Personality, 72,* 243–270.

Gerend, M.A., Erchull M.J., Aiken, L.S., & Maner, J.K. (2006). Reasons and risk: Factors underlying women's perceptions of susceptibility to osteoporosis. *Maturitas, 55,* 227–237.

Gerrard, M. (1987). Sex, sex guilt, and contraceptive use revisited: Trends in the 1980s. *Journal of Personality and Social Psychology, 52,* 975–980.

Hennessy, M., Bleakley, A., Fishbein, M., Brown, L., DiClemente, R., Romer, D., et al. (2010). Differentiating between precursors and control variables when analyzing reasoned action theories. *AIDS and Behavior, 14,* 225–236.

Jackson, K.M., & Aiken, L.S. (2000). A psychosocial model of sun-protection and sunbathing in young women: The impact of health beliefs, attitudes, norms, and self-efficacy for sun-protection. *Health Psychology, 19,* 469–478.

Jackson, K., & Aiken, L.S. (2006). Evaluation of a multi-component appearance-based sun-protective intervention for young women: Uncovering the mechanisms of program efficacy. *Health Psychology, 25,* 34–46.

Kern, M.L., & Friedman, H.S. (2008). Do conscientious individuals live longer? A quantitative review. *Health Psychology, 27,* 505–512.

Kingsley, C. (1855). Westward Ho! Quote retrieved from http://www.worldwidewords.org/qa/qa-mor1.htm.

Kreuter, M.W., Farrell, D., Olevitch, L., & Brennan, L. (2000). *Tailoring health messages: Customizing communication with computer technology.* Mahwah, NJ: Lawrence Erlbaum.

Kucera, A.M. (2008). *Psychosocial factors influencing young women's decisions for elective cosmetic breast augmentation.* Unpublished honors thesis, Arizona State University, Tempe, Arizona.

Lee, T.M., Leung, A.W., Fox, P.T., Gao, J.H., & Chan, C.C. (2008). Age-related differences in neural activities during risk taking as revealed by functional MRI. *Social, Cognitive and Affective Neuroscience, 3*(1), 7–15.

MacKinnon, D.P. (2008). *Introduction to statistical mediation analysis.* New York: Lawrence Erlbaum Associates, Taylor & Francis Group.

MacKinnon, D.P., Lockwood, C.M., Hoffman, J.M., West, S.G., & Sheets, V. (2002). A comparison of methods to test mediation and other intervening variable effects. *Psychological Methods, 7,* 83–104.

Moser, S.E. (2011). *Development and evaluation of an intervention to increase sun protection in young women.* Unpublished doctoral dissertation, Arizona State University, Tempe, AZ.

Moser, S.E., & Aiken, L.S. (2011). Cognitive and emotional factors associated with elective breast augmentation among young women. *Psychology and Health, 26,* 41–60.

Nair, V., Strecher, V., Fagerlin, A., Ubel, P., Resnicow, K., Murphy, S., et al. (2008). Screening experiments and the use of fractional factorial designs in behavioral intervention research. *American Journal of Public Health, 98,* 1354–1359.

Nigg, C.R., & Jordan, P.J. (2005). Commentary: It's a difference of opinion that makes a horserace. *Health Education Research, 20,* 291–293.

Noar, S.M., & Zimmerman, R.S. (2005). Health behavior theory and cumulative knowledge regarding health behaviors: Are we moving in the right direction? *Health Education Research, 20,* 275–290.

Preacher, K.J., Rucker, D.D., & Hayes, A.F. (2007). Addressing moderated mediation hypotheses: Theory, methods, and prescriptions. *Multivariate Behavioral Research, 42,* 185–227.

Prochaska, J.O., DiClemente, C.C., & Norcross, J.C. (1992). In search of how people change: Applications to addictive behaviors. *American Psychologist, 47,* 1102–1114.

Ranby, K.W. (2009). *Spousal influences on adult women's exercise: An expansion of the health action process approach model.* Unpublished doctoral dissertation, Arizona State University, Tempe, Arizona.

Ranby, K.W., Aiken, L.S., Gerend, M.A., & Erchull, M.J. (2010). Perceived susceptibility measures are not interchangeable: Absolute, direct comparative and indirect comparative risk clarified. *Health Psychology, 29,* 20–28.

Ranby, K.W., Aiken, L.S., MacKinnon, D.P., Elliot, D.L., Moe, E.L., McGinnis, W., & Goldberg, L. (2009). A mediation analysis of the ATHENA intervention for female athletes: Prevention of athletic-enhancing substance use and unhealthy weight loss behaviors. *Journal of Pediatric Psychology, 34,* 1069–1083.

Reid, A.E. (2010). *Uncovering mechanisms through which injunctive norms influence health behavior: A randomized trial.* Unpublished doctoral dissertation, Arizona State University, Tempe, Arizona.

Reid, A.E., & Aiken, L.S. (in press). Integration of five health behaviour models: Common strengths and unique contributions to understanding condom use. *Psychology and Health.*

Reid, A.E., Cialdini, R.B., & Aiken, L.S. (2010). Social norms and health behavior. In A. Steptoe (Ed.), *Handbook of behavioral medicine: Methods and applications.* New York, NY: Springer. Chapter *19,* 263–275.

Reuter, T., Ziegelmann, J.P., Wiedemann, A.U., Lippke, S., Schüz, B., & Aiken, L.S. (2010). Planning bridges the intention-behavior gap: Age makes a difference and strategy use explains why. *Psychology and Health, 27,* 873–887.

Reynolds, K.D., West, S.G., & Aiken, L.S. (1990). Increasing the use of mammography screening: A pilot program. *Health Education Quarterly, 17,* 429–441.

Rogers, R.W. (1975). A protection motivation theory of fear appeals and attitude change. *Journal of Psychology, 91,* 93–114.

Ronis, D.L. (1992). Conditional health threats: Health beliefs, decisions, and behaviors among adults. *Health Psychology, 11,* 127–134.

Rosenstock, I.M. (1974). The health belief model and preventive health behavior. *Health Education Monographs, 2,* 354–386.

Rosenstock, I.M., Strecher, V.J., & Becker, M.J. (1988). Social learning theory and the health belief model. *Health Education Quarterly, 15,* 175–183.

Schmiege, S.J., Aiken, L.S., Sanders, J.L., & Gerend, M. (2007). Osteoporosis prevention among young women: Psychosocial models of calcium consumption and weight-bearing exercise. *Health Psychology, 26,* 277–287.

Schmiege, S.J., & Aiken, L.S. (2011). *A multi-component, theoretically-based intervention randomized controlled trial to increase calcium intake among young women.* Manuscript in preparation, Arizona State University.

Schwarzer, R. (2008). Modeling health behavior change: How to predict and modify the adoption and maintenance of health behaviors. *Applied Psychology: An International Review, 57,* 1–29.

Sobel, M.E. (1982). Asymptotic confidence intervals for indirect effects in structural equation models. *Sociological Methodology, 13,* 290–312.

Twain, M. (1889). A Connecticut Yankee in King Arthur's court. Quote retrieved from http://www.worldwidewords.org/qa/qa-mor1.htm.

Velicer, W.F., Prochaska, J.O., & Redding, C.A. (2006). Tailored communications for smoking cessation: Past successes and future directions. *Drug and Alcohol Review, 15,* 49–57.

Webb, T.L., & Sheeran, P. (2006). Does changing behavioral intentions engender bahaviour change? A meta-analysis of the experimental evidence. *Psychological Bulletin, 132*(2), 249–268.

Weinstein, N.D. (1982). Unrealistic optimism about susceptibility to health problems. *Journal of Behavioral Medicine, 5,* 441–461.

Weinstein, N.D. (1988). The precaution adoption process. *Health Psychology, 7,* 355–386.

Weinstein, N.D. (2007). Misleading tests of health behavior theories. *Annals of Behavioral Medicine, 33,* 1–10.

West, S.G., & Aiken, L.S. (1997). Towards understanding individual effects in multiple component prevention programs: Design and analysis strategies. In K. Bryant, M. Windle, & S. West (Eds.), *The science of prevention: Methodological advances from alcohol and substance abuse research* (pp. 167–209). Washington, DC: American Psychological Association.

West, S.G., Aiken, L.S., & Todd, M. (1993). Probing the effects of individual components in multiple component prevention programs. *American Journal of Community Psychology, 21,* 571–605.

West, S.G., Duan, N., Pequegnat, W., Gaist, P., Des Jarlais, D.C., Holtgrave, D., et al. (2008). Alternatives to the randomized controlled trial. *American Journal of Public Health, 98*(8), 1359–1366.

# The Perception of Health Risks

Britta Renner *and* Harald Schupp

## Abstract

This chapter first examines how risk experts and nonexperts construe health risks and indicates systematic differences between the lay and expert risk estimates. Second, it analyzes the difference between general risk perceptions and personal risk perceptions, with particular emphasis on typical biases in personal risk perceptions, such as the optimistic bias and differences in personal risk perceptions across the lifespan. Third, it examines how people respond to health risk information indicating that they are at risk by highlighting the question of whether the core motivational fabric of reactions toward personalized risk information is made up of self-defensive or adaptive strivings.

**Keywords:** Health risks, risk assessment, risk perception, risk information

On April 12, 2009, the Government of Mexico responded to a request by the World Health Organization (WHO) for verification of an outbreak of acute respiratory infections in the small rural community of La Gloria, Veracruz. During April 22–24, 2009, a new influenza A (H1N1) virus infection, commonly called "swine flu," was confirmed in several patients. On June 11, 2009, the pandemic H1N1 2009 was declared by the WHO. All countries were advised to be on high alert and to strengthen infection control measures in health facilities. In September 2009, over 254,206 laboratory-confirmed cases of pandemic H1N1 and at least 2,837 deaths were reported by the WHO (Pandemic H1N1 2009, update 64, 2009). As a consequence, fears were rising that, during the winter months in 2009, a second wave of pandemic spread would occur, and many countries were planning national vaccination campaigns. At the same time, many citizens were not convinced that the new influenza A (H1N1) virus posed a serious health threat to them (Reuter & Renner, 2011). A survey conducted by the German news magazine *Spiegel* (August 29, 2009) showed that only 38% of German citizens stated that they will "definitely" or "likely" take part

in the upcoming immunization program. This raised great concern in public health authorities that the planned immunization program might suffer the same fate as the National Influenza Immunization Program (NIIP), launched on October 1, 1976, as reaction to a swine flu outbreak in the United States. After only 3 months, the NIIP was effectively halted since public reactions were highly negative. By that time, only 22% of the U.S. population had been immunized. Luckily, the virus did not develop the feared deadly potential of the 1918–1920 flu pandemic. The examples of the new influenza A and the swine flu outbreak in 1976 reveal that a key to the impact that public health intervention programs can achieve depends greatly on how individuals perceive health risks. This holds true not only for preventive efforts in case of infectious diseases but also in case of noninfectious diseases caused by behavior-related risk factors such as tobacco and alcohol consumption, being overweight, high blood pressure, high cholesterol, and unprotected sexual intercourse, behaviors that are responsible for more than 60% of all deaths worldwide (World Health Organization [WHO], 2002). Given the global burden of health risks, the question is: How can we implement more effective risk avoidance and reduction in the future?

It seems inherently plausible that people need not only to be aware of an existing health risk ("Many people get infected with a new influenza type"), but they also need to feel personally at risk ("I might catch the new influenza myself") in order to take protective action. Thus, to optimize health promotion efforts, it appears especially important to understand (a) how people construe and evaluate health risks in general (general risk perception), (b) how they gauge their own personal risk (personal risk perception), and (c) how they react to information indicating that they are personally at risk. This chapter is organized along these three topics. First, we examine how risk experts and nonexperts construe health risks, and we indicate systematic differences between the lay and expert risk estimates. Second, we examine the difference between general risk perceptions ("Smoking may cause lung cancer") and personal risk perceptions ("I may get lung cancer because I smoke"), with particular emphasis on typical biases in personal risk perceptions such as optimistic bias and differences in personal risk perceptions across the lifespan. Third, we examine how people respond to health risk information indicating that they are at risk by highlighting the question of whether the core motivational fabric of reactions toward personalized risk information is made up of self-defensive or adaptive strivings.

## General Risk Perception: How Do Experts and Laypeople Construe Health Risks?

In general, risks to health cannot be sensed—we cannot touch, feel, see, or smell the magnitude of health risks. Nonetheless, people have been interested in identifying and measuring risks to health throughout history. During the past several decades, this interest has intensified, and the field of risk analysis has grown rapidly, focusing on the identification, quantification, and characterization of threats to human health—a set of activities broadly called *risk assessment*.

### What Is Risk?: Risk Assessment

Risk experts across various disciplines and domains (e.g., health, finance, engineering) commonly define risk as a combination of the likelihood of an occurrence of a hazardous event or exposure and the severity of injury or disease (e.g., lung cancer) caused by it. Accordingly, "risk" encompasses two core elements: (a) the chance or probability of adverse health outcomes, and (b) the severity of the expected adverse outcomes. Risk described as being proportional to both the *probability* and *severity* of the event (risk = probability × severity of the event occurring) implies that greater loss and greater event likelihood result in a greater overall risk (Fischhoff, Bostrom, & Quadrel, 2000; Slovic, 2000a; WHO, 2002).

Determining numerically the probability of adverse events for different hazards and risk factors, and to assess the scale and range of possible adverse consequences, is one of the main challenges for scientific risk assessment (Slovic, 1987, 2000a; WHO, 2002). Ideally, risks to health should be assessed in terms of a "common currency." Two such common measures of risk are the number of deaths per year (mortality) and the number of cases of disease per year (morbidity). A great advantage of having common currencies for measuring risks is that highly divergent hazards, such as automobiles, swine flu, nuclear power plants, or smoking, can be projected on one measurement scale, thus enabling a comparison between and a prioritizing of risks. For example, in 2006, heart diseases caused 631,636 of all deaths in the United States, whereas accidents were responsible for 121,599 of all deaths (Heron et al., 2009; Figure 26.1). Accordingly, heart diseases pose a five times greater risk in comparison to accidents (26% vs. 5%).

The number of deaths indicates the probability component of the risk term and the event "death" represents the severity component, which can be combined and reduced to a single dimension "expected losses" (e.g., expected deaths, cf. also Bostrom, 1997). The impact of hazards such as behavioral risk factors (e.g., smoking, physical inactivity) can alternatively be expressed in morbidity rates instead of mortality rates. The WHO (2002), for example, suggested a principal metric for measuring risk on the basis of the disability-adjusted life year (DALY), whereby 1 DALY represents the loss of 1 healthy life year.

On the basis of mortality or morbidity rates, two common types of risk measures can be calculated. The *absolute risk* describes the chances of adverse health outcomes for a specific group (e.g., smokers). For example, 152 out of 1,000 men aged 65 who have smoked at least 100 cigarettes in their lifetime will die in the next 10 years from lung cancer, which is equivalent to a probability of .152. The *relative risk* (RR) describes the ratio of the probability of the disease occurring in the exposed group (e.g., smokers) and a nonexposed group (nonsmokers). For example, seven out of 1,000 men aged 65 who have

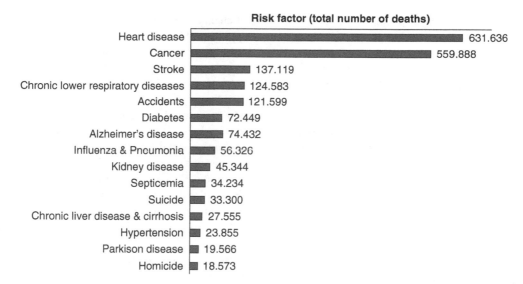

**Risk factor (total number of deaths)**

|  |  |
|---|---|
| Heart disease | 631.636 |
| Cancer | 559.888 |
| Stroke | 137.119 |
| Chronic lower respiratory diseases | 124.583 |
| Accidents | 121.599 |
| Diabetes | 72.449 |
| Alzheimer's disease | 74.432 |
| Influenza & Pneumonia | 56.326 |
| Kidney disease | 45.344 |
| Septicemia | 34.234 |
| Suicide | 33.300 |
| Chronic liver disease & cirrhosis | 27.555 |
| Hypertension | 23.855 |
| Parkison disease | 19.566 |
| Homicide | 18.573 |

**Fig. 26.1** The 15 leading causes of death for the total population in 2006 in the United States Compiled from Heron, M., Hoyert, D. L., Murphy, S. L., Xu, J., Kochanek, K. D., & Tejada-Vera, B. (2009). Deaths: Final data for 2006. *National Vital Statistics Reports, 57*(14), 1–134. *Note:* In 2006, the total number of deaths was 2.426.264.

never smoked will die in the next 10 years from lung cancer. Accordingly, the relative risk of lung cancer associated with smoking is RR = (152/1000)/(7/1000) = 21.71. Thus, smokers aged 65 years are about 22 times as likely as nonsmokers to die of lung cancer in the next 10 years. This represents a quite substantial relative risk since, for other diseases, such as pneumonia, the 10-year relative risk for smokers aged 65 years is also increased but "only" by a factor of RR = 1.8. (Numbers were adapted from 10-year probability of death estimations by Woloshin, Schwartz, and Welch, 2002a, based on the Multiple Cause of Death Data 1998, National Center of Health Statistics). Thus, the risk of lung cancer due to smoking as any other risk can be expressed in various "risk metrics," which are normatively equivalent but might cause quite different impressions within various stakeholders.

## CONTROVERSIES ABOUT UNIVERSALLY VALID RISK MEASURES: THE DEBATE ABOUT SURVIVAL AND MORTALITY RATES

Risk assessment is commonly considered as yielding an objective measure of risk that is based on empirical evidence and is following a scientifically logical sequence (see for further discussion Bostrom, 1997; Fischhoff et al., 2000; Slovic, 2000a; WHO, 2002). However, it is important to realize that an objective or universally valid risk measure does not exist. Taking mortality rates as example, the number of fatalities per year metric ascribes to the death of a 5-year-old child the same value as to the death of an

88-year-old adult. Conversely, focusing on the years of life lost yields a dramatically different picture, giving far less weight to fatalities of older adults. Thus, using mortality rates versus number of years of life lost as risk measure involves a subjective weighting of the value of life at different ages.

The immense impact of the chosen measure of risk becomes immediately apparent when contrasting 5-year survival and mortality rates for assessing health risk and treatment effectiveness. Five-year survival rates are very common in medical research for estimating the effect of health interventions, such as cancer treatments (cf. 5-year cancer survival rates in Europe; Gondos, Bray, Hakulinen, & Brenner, 2009). Imagine that you read the following statement in the *New York Times,* from the principal investigator of a large medical trial, after using a new screening method for detecting lung cancer:

> If cancer nodules are detected and removed in their initial phase, the 5-year survival from lung cancer can exceed 70%. In contrast, the overall rate of cure for lung cancer is 12%. We're saying we could change survival from 12% or 15% to 80% . . . there are 172,000 new cases a year. Think of 12% or 15% compared to 80%. (Cited from Woloshin, Schwartz, & Welch, 2002b)

Probably, most readers would be impressed and convinced that the new lung cancer screening method will help to significantly decrease the burden of annual fatalities due to lung cancer. If a new lung cancer screening leads to a 65% increase in the number of people who are alive 5 years later, many experts, as well as many laypeople, will consider this a tremendous step forward in terms of health risk reduction.

Unfortunately, an improved 5-year survival for cancer patients does not mean that cancer treatment has improved and that fewer patients die of cancer (Welch et al., 2007). Gilbert Welch, Lisa Schwartz, and Steven Woloshin (2000) analyzed the 20 most common solid tumors in the United States. From 1950 to 1995, for each of the 20 tumor types, an increase in 5-year survival was observed. The absolute increase in 5-year survival ranged from 3% (pancreatic cancer) to 50% (prostate cancer). However, changes in 5-year survival were completely uncorrelated with changes in mortality ($r$ = .00). Accordingly, higher survival does not mean longer life but may actually reflect changes in diagnosis. First, finding more people with early-stage cancer with unchanged time of death can significantly inflate 5-year survival rates by setting the time of diagnosis earlier, even if no life is prolonged or saved (Gigerenzer, Gaissmaier, Kurz-Milcke, Schwartz, & Woloshin, 2008). A hypothetical scenario serves to illustrate this so-called *lead-time bias*. Imagine a group of cancer patients who did not undergo screening. At the age of 67, the first symptoms occurred and cancer was diagnosed. Three years later, at age 70, all of them were deceased. Each patient survived only 3 years and thus the 5-year survival is 0%. With screening, they would have been diagnosed with cancer much earlier, say, at age 60 and received treatment earlier. However, they all still die at age 70. Focusing on the 5-year survival rate, the message would nonetheless be very positive: "We're saying we could change survival from 0% to 100%." Since all have now survived 10 years, their 5-year survival rate is 100%. Even though the survival rate has changed dramatically, the time of death remains unchanged: Whether diagnosed at age 67 or at age 60, all patients die at age 70 (Gigerenzer et al., 2008). Another bias that also can inflate the 5 year-survival diagnosis is the *overdiagnosis bias*. The overdiagnosis bias inflates 5-year survival by the detection of cancers that will never progress to cause symptoms in the patient's lifetime (nonprogressive cancer). In particular, for highly sensitive screenings, the likelihood that nonprogressive cancers are detected is increased (Woloshin et al., 2002b). However, if a new screening method leads to disproportionally more detections of nonprogressive cancer in comparison to detections of progressive cancer, the survival rate would change dramatically, whereas the number of people who die

will change only slightly (Gigerenzer et al., 2008). Supporting this notion, the change in 5-year cancer survival was positively correlated with the change in the tumor incidence rate with Pearson $r$ = .49 (Welch et al., 2000).

Adding to the complexity of risk assessment, the chain of events leading to an adverse health outcome includes both proximal and distal causes. Whereas proximal factors act directly to cause disease, distal causes are further back in the causal chain and act via a number of intermediary causes. Behavioral risk factors such as a poor diet have an adverse effect on blood pressure, lipid profiles, and insulin sensitivity, which in turn causes heart diseases. Ideally, the whole causal chain is modeled in the assessment of risks to health. Moreover, risks to health do not occur in isolation. Many risks to health (e.g., smoking and alcohol consumption) act jointly to cause disease or injury. For example, the Asia Pacific Cohort Studies Collaboration (2009) with 378,579 participants showed that smoking amplifies the positive association between body mass index (BMI) and coronary heart disease (CHD). For a 2 kg/m² increment in BMI, the increase in the CHD risk for smokers was four percentage points greater than for nonsmokers (13% vs. 9%). Similarly, data from the Framingham Study (Fox et al., 2008) showed that the lifetime (30-year) risk of cardiovascular disease (CVD) among normal-weight women with diabetes is 55%, whereas among obese women with diabetes the risk is 79%. If two risk factors have a synergistic relationship, rigorous lifestyle modification may contribute to greater reduction in disease burden than in case of an additive relationship.

As these examples depict, risk assessment is a highly complex process since risk can numerically be expressed in many different metrics that inevitably convey only parts of the bigger picture. Moreover, adverse health outcomes are often caused by multiple proximal and distal behavioral and nonbehavioral risk factors, further adding to the complexity of risk assessment. To develop an effective and efficient targeting of limited prevention resources, risk reduction commonly focuses on selected, major health risks.

## LOOKING BACK INTO HISTORY: THE HEALTH RISK TRANSITION

An indispensable basis for identifying major health risks is the prevalence and incidence rates of the leading causes of death and illness. Therefore, in many countries, public institutions such as the National Center for Health Statistics in the United States or the German Federal Statistical Office

(*Statistisches Bundesamt*) register the causes of death and new cases of diseases (e.g., heart disease, lung cancer) according to the International Statistical Classification of Diseases and Related Health Problems (ICD-10). The standardized registration allows estimating how common a disease is within a population over a certain period of time (prevalence rate) and the number of new disease cases during a certain period of time (incidence rate). These data show that, in many countries during the last century, a long-term shift in mortality and disease patterns has occurred whereby pandemics of infection were replaced by degenerative, chronic diseases. For example, the disease transition, or "cross-over" of communicable to noncommunicable diseases as leading cause of death, occurred around 1968 in South Korea, whereas in the United States, the disease transition took place around 1920 (see Figure 26.2).

The dramatic peak of infectious diseases in the 20th century was the so-called Spanish flu pandemic, which scoured the world from 1918 to 1920. During the Spanish flu pandemic, one-third of the world's population (or approximately 500 million persons) were infected, and total deaths were estimated at 50 million or more (Taubenberger & Morens, 2006). During 1918, in the United States, more than 460,000 out of 1,430,079 people died due to an influenza infection. In comparison, heart diseases claimed only 135,585 lives during 1918. After 3 years, in 1921, the impact of the Spanish flu had lessened, and influenza and pneumonia as the leading causes of death switched ranks with heart diseases (cf. Figure 26.2). Seventeen years later, in 1938, pneumonia and influenza (third) switched

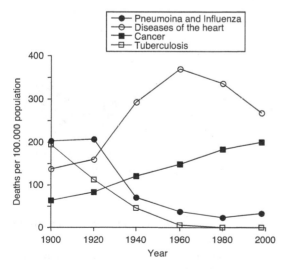

**Fig. 26.2** Disease transition in the United States (data adapted from the National Center for Health Statistics).

rank as second leading causes of death with a newly emerging threat to health: cancer (second). Since then, the two noncommunicable diseases, heart disease and cancer, are by far the leading causes of death in the United States and in most other industrialized countries. Changes in disease patterns are also reflected in public health interventions. When infectious diseases prevailed, the focus was on protection against influenza or tuberculosis through daily gargling or by avoiding "careless" spitting, coughing, or sneezing (see also Box 26.1 for an illustration of public health promotion campaigns) rather than focusing on a healthy diet and exercising.

### What Is Risk? Lay Perceptions of Risk

An important consequence of the disease transition was that individual people were increasingly seen as being mainly responsible for handling their own risks to health, since many risks were characterized as behavioral in origin and, therefore, largely under individual control (WHO, 2002). This in turn led to the lifestyles approach in health promotion (see Box 26.1 for examples). For instance, a great deal of attention was paid to combating CHD through health promotion aimed at increasing exercise and lowering dietary cholesterol, cigarette smoking, and alcohol consumption. Since the late 1970s, for instance, numerous public health campaigns have focused on CVD risk factors in order to inform the public about the involved health risk and preventive behaviors. Between 1979 and 1990, general knowledge about what a person can do to keep her- or himself from having a heart attack or a stroke improved significantly (Frank, Winkleby, Fortmann, & Farquhar, 1993; Gans, Assmann, Sallar, & Lasater, 1999). As another consequence, the image of and knowledge about smoking and its health risks has changed tremendously across the past decades. Until the late 1950s, smoking was positively portrayed in the media. Many brands were using the image of idealized, noble, wise doctors who recommended a specific tobacco brand as advertising strategy (see Box 26.2). At that time, in the United States, over 50% of adult males smoked, and smoking was accepted in offices, airplanes and elevators; even TV cartoon programs were sponsored by cigarette brands. This predominately positive image of smoking started to change when the Surgeon General's report in 1964 declared that smoking causes cancer. After extensive public health campaigns portraying the adverse health risks of smoking, the image of smoking has become predominantly negative, and the prevalence of smoking has dropped to 28% in 1991.

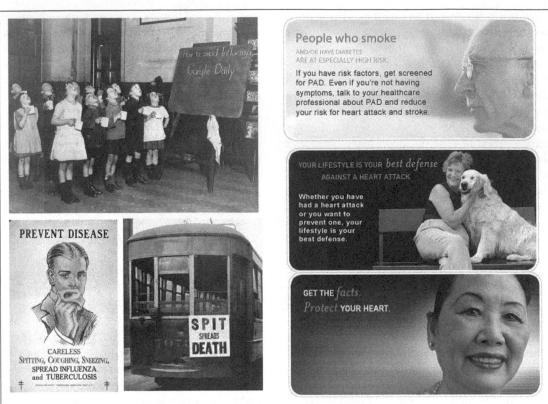

**Box 26.1** Public health promotion during the Spanish flu era 1918–1920 (left side, source: Wiki Commons) and current examples (right side, source: www.americanheart.org).

**Box 26.2** Smoking-related ads from 1939, 1946, and 2005. From the collection of Stanford University (http://tobacco.stanford.edu) and http://home2.nyc.gov/html/doh/html/pr2007/pr026–07.shtml).

Nowadays, most people, including smokers, are convinced that smoking causes severe life-threatening diseases such as lung cancer (Oncken, McKee, Krishnan-Sarin, O'Malley, & Mazure, 2005; Weinstein, 1998; Weinstein, Slovic, & Gibson, 2004). The very thought of medical doctors and celebrities advertising tobacco smoking is, for most people, impossible.

Thus, taking a long-term perspective shows that public health risk communication targeting major health risks such as smoking have made a noticeable difference in risk perceptions and population behavior. Beside these considerable changes in risk perceptions and behaviors across the last decades, numerous people do not exercise regularly, nor do they follow a healthy diet or refrain from smoking, although they appear to be more concerned about genetically modified food, toxic waste, or mobile phones. This leads to the question: Which factors determine lay understanding and perceptions of risk?

## THE NUMBERS OF RISK

A pioneering study on risk perceptions by Lichtenstein, Slovic, Fischhoff, Layman, and Combs (1978) showed that laypeople, compared with experts, tend to overestimate rare causes of death while underestimating common causes of death (see also Hertwig, Pachur, & Kurzenhäuser, 2005). Slovic, Fischhoff, and Lichtenstein (1985) concluded that experts and lay risk estimations differ because most experts equate risk with yearly fatalities, whereas laypeople do not. Since then, a vast number of studies have been devoted to the topic how laypeople estimate the numbers of risks; and the idea that experts view risks more veridically than laypeople is commonly accepted within risk researchers, managers, and policy makers (Bostrom, 1997; Kraus, Malmfors, & Slovic, 1992; Savadori et al., 2004; Slovic, 2000a). However, differences between laypeople and expert view on risks do not necessarily imply that expert judgments are more valid. Rowe and Wright (2001) analyzed empirical studies comparing expert and laypeople risk judgments and, contrary to the common notion, found little supporting empirical evidence in their meta-analysis for the idea that experts are more veridical in their risk assessments. In a subsequent rigorous study, Wright, Bolger, and Rowe (2002) examined risk judgments from experts (life underwriters) and laypeople (business students) for 31 hazards (lung cancer, smoking, asthma, etc.) and compared them to the factual risk (annual fatalities). The results showed that laypeople were as veridical in their ordering of risks as experts. The correlation between risk judgments and the factual risk was $r = .73$ for the laypeople and $r = .66$ for the experts. Thus, both laypeople and experts showed a relatively good performance in terms of ordering the absolute risk in the metric of annual fatalities (see also Raude, Fischler, Setbon, & Flahault, 2005). The studies by Rowe and colleagues showed that laypeople are as capable of rank-ordering risks in terms of their lethal potential as experts. However, rank-ordering or prioritizing risks in terms of the expected deaths, is only one (albeit a very important) way to measure risk.

When it comes to estimating more complex numbers of risk, the accuracy of lay perceptions commonly decreases, and systematic deviations between normative risk estimations and lay perceptions occur. A comprehensive study by Weinstein (2000) examined the relationship between severity and likelihood for over 200 different hazards. Normatively, risk can be represented as a probability by severity interaction. Thus, if the likelihood of an adverse health outcome is zero, the resulting perceived risk and motivation to act should also be zero, regardless of how serious the adverse health outcome may be. Consistent with the normative view, for every participant, an interaction between severity and likelihood was observed. Motivation to take precautions essentially vanished when either severity or likelihood was zero. However, the type of the relationship among severity, likelihood, and motivation to act varied with the severity and likelihood of the hazard. For high-serious and low-probability events, as well as for low-serious and low-probability events, an interaction could be observed that represents the assumed synergism between the two variables. In contrast, individuals showed insensitivity to variations in likelihood once likelihood had reached the threshold of a 50–50 chance. Weinstein (2000) suggested that people make finer distinctions at the low end of the likelihood scale than at the high end. Therefore, individuals confronted with a hazard with a 60% chance of occurring may display the same reaction as individuals who are confronted with a hazard with an 80% chance of occurring. This could explain why, for instance, many individuals view smoking and high cholesterol as cardiovascular risk factors of similar magnitude, although smoking is far more dangerous. Moreover, insensitivity to probability variations appears to be dependent on the seriousness of the expected adverse health outcome. Rottenstreich and Hsee (2001) showed that more serious outcomes (e.g., painful electric shock vs. losing $20) induced a more pronounced insensitivity to probability variations. Thus, the more serious the expected event is, the more people overweight small probabilities and react adversely to events, even though they are unlikely to happen (cf. Loewenstein, Weber, Hsee, & Welch, 2001).

Accordingly, people become insensitive to variations and deviate from the normative probability × severity algorithm when the likelihood or severity exceeds a certain threshold. This finding might at least partly explain why people are more worried about "risky" technologies such as genetic engineering or nuclear power than about health risk behaviors such as a lack of physical exercise or an unhealthy diet. Technologies are more likely to be associated with disasters and extremely serious and fatal outcomes (e.g., nuclear meltdown, contamination of water and food supply), whereas health risk behaviors are commonly associated with less severe outcomes (see also Slovic, 1987). The associated catastrophic outcomes with technologies might be outside "the window of risk" and therefore, people might be very unresponsive to probability arguments put forward by experts in favor of technologies. Conversely, outcomes of health risk behaviors might appear comparably "harmless" but quite likely. This could also represent an obstacle for risk communication since high probability perceptions could induce a relative insensitivity toward differences in likelihood of negative outcomes between different health risk factors and behaviors. This might induce a "seen one, seen 'em all" mindset, in which different risk behaviors are not appropriately differentiated. In view of that, effective risk communication should supply information about the relative risks of acquiring one disease versus another to help people anchor the likelihood of occurrence and severity in appropriate ways. Otherwise, individuals may ignore considerable differences between risks and consequently fail to take appropriate measures to protect themselves.

## HOW SMALL NUMBERS ADD UP:
### ESTIMATING CUMULATIVE RISKS

Many health risks have a relatively low probability of severe adverse health outcomes for any single exposure. This poses a great challenge to risk communication since people often have difficulties with the representation of small numbers or probabilities (cf. Lipkus, 2007; Peters et al., 2009; Schwartz, Woloshin, Black, & Welch, 1997; Visschers, Meertens, Passchier, & de Vries, 2009). For example, people on average greatly overestimate the absolute risk for contracting human immunodeficiency virus (HIV) through a single unprotected sexual intercourse by a factor of 10 (Cohen & Bruce, 1997; Pinkerton, Wagner-Raphael, Craun, & Abramson, 2000). However, these initial small probabilities add up over repeated exposures to create a substantial overall risk. Even if people are accurately aware that a certain behavior increases the risk of becoming ill, and that risk increases with greater exposure, they fail to apply appropriate rules when estimating the danger of increasing exposure to certain risks (cf. Visschers et al., 2009). For example, Sastre,

Mullet, and Sorum (1999) asked 155 French adults to estimate the risk of developing lung cancer for certain smoking habits (see also Eiser, Reicher, & Podpadec, 1995). They found that all participants, smokers as well as nonsmokers, believed that the risk of lung cancer increases as the number of consumed cigarettes increases. Nonetheless, the estimated strength of this dose–response effect was negatively accelerated. After surpassing a threshold of 15 cigarettes per day, an increase in consumption led only to a small rise in perceived risk. However, the actual relationship between smoked cigarettes per day and lung cancer risk is at least proportional. Replicating this finding, Weinstein, Marcus, and Moser (2005) compared actual and perceived lung cancer risk in a national survey with more than 1,200 smokers and found that smokers greatly underestimated the cumulative risk of smoking. In a similar vein, many adolescent smokers see no health risk from smoking regularly for the first few years (Slovic, 2000b). This underestimation of cumulative short-term risks, coupled with a tendency to underestimate the addictive properties of tobacco, indicates that many adolescent smokers have dramatic misconceptions about the cumulative risks from smoking cigarettes. The tendency to underestimate cumulative risk might be even more pronounced when the risk behavior is associated with positive aspects and outcomes. Knäuper, Kornik, Atkinson, Guberman, and Aydin (2005) showed that people particularly underestimate the cumulative risk of infection with sexually transmitted diseases by appealing prospective sexual partners. Misjudging the cumulative risk of increasing exposure to risks could jeopardize appropriate behaviors, and in the worst case, encourage extensive risk behaviors.

Unfortunately, not only the implications of repeated risk behavior can be misunderstood, but also the long-term effectiveness of precautions can be misconstrued. Birth control, for example, needs a continuing process of risk management. The risk of conception is relatively low on a single occasion of sexual intercourse, but accumulates over repeated occasions. Imagine a contraceptive method with a 1-year reliability of .98. Of 100 women who apply this method, two will be become pregnant during 1 year of use. This outcome appears reassuring. However, with each additional year, the number of unwanted pregnancies will further increase. After a 10-year period, 20% of the same group of women will be pregnant, although they might still perceive their risk as 2%. Shaklee and Fischhoff (1990) showed that most laypersons do not realize that contraceptive effectiveness declines over time (cf. also Doyle, 1997). Thus, a short-term perspective on effectiveness may promote unrealistically optimistic estimations about long-term outcomes since individuals are not aware how rapidly small risks add up. Since most effectiveness information about birth control methods is only presented for 1 year of use, individuals may have too much confidence in their precautions. Likewise, Linville, Fischer, and Fischhoff (1993) showed that the cumulative protective effectiveness of condom use is often overestimated. They asked male college students to rate the probability of an HIV transmission from male to female in one case and in 100 cases of protected sex. On average, the one-case probability of an HIV infection was overestimated, while the mean estimate for 100 cases was highly underestimated. Accordingly, public risk communication that does not emphasize how the risk of an HIV infection accumulates over repeated exposures, even for protected intercourse, could give recipients a dangerously wrong impression about their safety.

Hence, from a health education perspective, protective effectiveness information should be presented for short as well as long time periods to assist people in making informed choices. Communicating only the effectiveness for short time periods can create impressions of inflated preventive effectiveness, thereby "persuading" individuals to make behavior changes associated with negative outcomes in the long run. In a similar vein, to prevent misconceptions about cumulative risks, public health campaigns are needed that explicitly inform the public about how risk accumulates in the long run. Ideally, risk and effectiveness estimates should be presented for all the time periods that are relevant to people's decisions, in order to support informed decisions and to prevent exaggerated perceptions of threat and preventive effectiveness.

## HOW DIFFERENT RISKS ADD UP: ESTIMATING SYNERGISTIC EFFECTS

Estimating a health risk becomes even more complex when multiple risks are considered. Certain risk behaviors, such as smoking and alcohol consumption, result in a combined risk that is greater than the sum of the single risks. However, empirical evidence shows that people have problems in understanding such synergistic relations (cf. French, Sutton, Kinmonth, & Marteau, 2006). Hermand, Mullet, and Lavieville (1997) demonstrated that smokers and nonsmokers believed that engaging in only one risk behavior (heavy alcohol consumption or heavy smoking) results in the same risk as engaging in both at the same time. Hence, the two risks have been considered as disjunctive instead of synergistic (see also Hermand, Mullet, Sorum, & Tillard, 2000). In a similar vein, Hampson, Andrews, Lee, Lichtenstein, and Barckley (2000) reported that smoking was seen as dangerous as the combination of smoking and exposure to radon. Thus, combined-hazard risk perceptions seem to be a subadditive combination of the two single-hazard risks (French et al., 2006; Hampson et al., 1998, 2000). French et al. (2006) argue that the often-found subadditive effect may be caused by a methodological artifact resulting from using range-restricted rating scales. However, even using an unbounded rating scale yielded only a weak synergistic interaction. Interestingly, Bonnin-Scaon, Lafon, Chaisseigne, Mullet, and Sorum (2002) showed that laypeople can be trained to use the multiplicative rule that is consistent with the normative notion instead of the subadditive rule. They asked laypeople to judge the risk of esophageal cancer associated with different levels of smoking and alcohol consumption. Prior to the training session, participants used a subadditive rule to combine the risks from smoking and alcohol consumption. However, after the training session, as well as 1 month later, they used the multiplicative rule.

As these examples demonstrate, "getting the numbers of risk right" is a highly complex and challenging task. Considering the complexity of the task at hand, such as the accumulative impact of small risks over time, the synergistic effects of multiple risk factors, or the impact of diverse adverse health outcomes, it is not surprising that most laypeople and often also experts fail to make accurate estimations. Communication about harmful effects of hazards should include information about potential synergistic or additional effects, as otherwise people might seriously misconstrue their overall risk. Giving comprehensive and complete risk information for example, providing information about the relative risks of acquiring one disease versus another, or providing information about the cumulative increase of the risk over time supports people in anchoring the likelihood of occurrence and severity in more appropriate ways.

## PRESENTATION FORMATS AND THE UNDERSTANDING OF THE NUMBERS OF RISK

In addition to providing comprehensive risk information instead of bits and pieces of it, research has reliably demonstrated that the numeric and visual format used to represent the numbers of risks can significantly facilitate the understanding of risk (Edwards, Elwyn, Covey, Matthews, & Pill, 2001; Lipkus, 2007; Visschers et al., 2009). The magnitude of risk can be framed in many numeric formats, such as percentages (e.g., having a 5% chance of getting the disease), probabilities (e.g., 0.05), or natural frequencies (e.g., 5 out of 100) and in many different visual formats (e.g., bar charts or icons displaying the number of individuals affected). All these numeric formats represent equally valid representation of the numbers of risk, but certain formats seem to be in general easier to understand than others (in-depth discussions and recommendations of best practices for formats of conveying health risks can be found in Gigerenzer et al., 2008, Lipkus, 2007, and Visschers et al., 2009).

One of the most striking effects on the understanding of risk has been demonstrated empirically by comparing relative and absolute numeric risk formats (see also the section What Is Risk?). Relative risk formats describe risk in conditional probabilities, percentages, or ratios without defining the baseline or absolute risk level. Thus, a risk factor may be described as conferring "50% more risk" than another, even when the absolute increase is only from 2% to 3%. Without information about the baseline risk level, people tend to overestimate not only the impact of risk factors but also the impact of precautionary measures (Lipkus, 2007). For example, a company advertises a new toothpaste by emphasizing that new clinical studies have shown that the number of users suffering serious gum disease has been decreased by 50% relative to standard toothpaste users. Communicating the number of individuals who stand to benefit from the improved toothpaste relative to the standard toothpaste is a reasonable and commonly used risk metric. However, as "standalone" risk information, it creates a much more positive impression about the effectiveness of the protective measure than when absolute or "background" risk information that is, the base rate of users suffering from serious gum disease is additionally provided (Stone et al., 2003). Adding the absolute risk or base rate would read as follows: Out of 5,000 standard toothpaste users, 30 users suffer from serious gum disease; out of 5,000 improved toothpaste users, 15 users suffer from serious gum disease. Thus, we have an absolute risk reduction of 0.3% (from 0.6% to 0.3% users) and a relative risk reduction of 50% (from 30 to 15 users). Both formats are numerically valid risk metrics, but the latter format suggests a much greater impact than the former format and thus, creates a greater willingness to take preventive action (Gigerenzer et al., 2008; Lipkus, 2007; Stone et al., 2003).

Conveying risk in *natural frequencies* instead of in conditional probabilities, and in a Bayesian format, also appears to facilitate the understanding of risk within laypeople, as well as within experts (cf. also Gigerenzer et al., 2008). Imagine that a man gets the information that he tested positive in the Hemoccult test, which is an early indicator for colorectal cancer. Now, he is wondering how likely it is that he actually has colorectal cancer. His physician tells him that the probability of colorectal cancer is 0.3% (base rate) and if a person has colorectal cancer, the probability that the hemoccult test is positive is 50% (sensitivity). If a person does not have cancer, however, the probability that he still tests positive is 3% (false-negative rate). The Bayes' theorem would tell us that the probability that a person has colorectal cancer, if the test indicates a positive test result, is $(0.3 \times 50)/(0.3 \times 50 + 99.7 \times 3) = .048 \sim 5\%$. This risk format is not only difficult for laypeople to grasp, but also for experts. Hoffrage, Lindsey, Hertwig, and Gigerenzer (2000) provided 24 physicians with the above case information and asked them to estimate the probability that the described man actually has colorectal cancer. Since this is a task medical doctors face quite frequently, and one that is of great importance for their patients, they should easily be able to answer the question correctly. However, the result was devastating: only 1 out of 24 physicians gave the correct answer. Restating the task in natural frequencies reads as follows: Out of 10,000 people, 30 have colorectal cancer (= 0.3% base rate). Of these, 15 will have a positive Hemoccult test (50% sensitivity). Out of the remaining 9,970 people without colorectal cancer, 300 will still test positive (3% false-negative rate). When the task was presented in natural frequencies, 16 out of 24 physicians gave the correct answer: 15 out of 315 (i.e., 5%).

Various studies including laypeople and experts have demonstrated that understanding the numbers of risk and the willingness to act upon numbers is moderated by the communication format. Thus, the sometimes pessimistic view that the public is not capable of understanding the numbers of risk may at least partly be the result of using suboptimal formats of risk communication. Instead of expecting people to adapt to certain risk communication formats, risk communication formats should be adapted to the needs and competencies of the general public. Sound and reliable risk communication should therefore provide transparent information by providing preferably absolute and relative risk information, mortality rates and survival rates, or natural frequencies, in addition to conditional probabilities (Gigerenzer et al., 2008; Lipkus, 2007; Visschers et al., 2009).

## Personal Risk Perceptions

At first glance, perceiving a health threat seems to be the most obvious prerequisite for the motivation to change a risk behavior. Consequently, improving knowledge about the nature, magnitude, and significance of health risks is a central goal for public health campaigns aiming at disease prevention. Generally, it is implicitly assumed that, by increasing the awareness of a health threat, corresponding increases in personal risk perceptions and the motivation to change behavior are automatically stimulated. However, from a psychological perspective, the process is far more complex. Health behavior change theories such as the health belief model (HBM), the protection motivation theory (PMT), or the health action process approach (HAPA) share the assumption that people need not only to be aware of a certain health risk but they need to feel personally at risk in order to take protective action (Armitage & Conner, 2000; Brewer et al., 2007; Renner & Schwarzer, 2003; Weinstein, 1993, Weinstein, 2003). However, general perceptions of risk ("Many people get infected with a new influenza type") and personal perceptions of risk ("I might catch the new influenza myself") often differ to a great extent (French & Marteau, 2007; Renner & Schwarzer, 2003; Weinstein, 1998). Individuals can be well informed about health risks and precautions (e.g., most smokers acknowledge that smoking can cause diseases such as lung cancer), but, nevertheless, they might not feel personally at risk. Thus, for optimizing health promotion efforts, it appears especially important to understand how individuals construe their personal risk of a certain health threat (Renner & Schwarzer, 2003).

### Absolute Personal Risk Perceptions

One of the most common ways of assessing people's perceptions of their own health risks is to ask them to give a numerical risk estimate for their personal absolute risk. Comparing personal absolute risk perceptions with epidemiological or actuarial risk estimates shows that they often greatly deviate from each other. Similar to general risk perceptions, the likelihood for becoming oneself a victim of disease is often drastically overestimated (van der Pligt, 1998). This is even the case for widely known risks such as smoking or breast cancer. Based on the examination of British doctors over a period of 40 years, the overall mortality rates in smokers were about twice as great as in nonsmokers. Thus, about half of the deaths among smokers were caused by tobacco (Doll, Peto, Wheatley, Gray, & Sutherland, 1994). British smokers estimated their own personal risk of getting lung cancer to be 41% and their risk of getting a heart disease to be 47%. Thus, smokers substantially overestimated their lifetime risk for these diseases (Sutton, 1998). Similarly, a national sample of Norwegian smokers estimated their risk of dying from lung cancer given that they continue to smoke to be 39%, which is also too pessimistic (Rise, Strype, & Sutton, 2002). In a similar vein, Lipkus et al. (2000) asked adult women between the ages of 45 and 54 years to estimate their life-time breast cancer risk. In addition, they measured the actual breast cancer risk through the Gail score, which calculates breast cancer risk on the basis of seven risk factors (age, race, age of menarche, age at first live birth, number of first-degree relatives with breast cancer, number of previous breast biopsies, and a history of atypical hyperplasia). Compared to their actual life-time risk (8%), they greatly overestimated their lifetime breast cancer risk (34%). Similarly, Graves et al. (2008) recently showed in sample of women from Central and South America that 81% overestimated their life-time breast cancer risk in comparison to their actual risk based on the Gail score.

Most researchers agree that inaccurate numerical estimations are due to a lack of knowledge and difficulties with numerical operations (French & Marteau, 2007). In particular, most risks have only a small probability; for example, the likelihood of becoming infected with HIV through unprotected sexual intercourse with an infected partner is approximately .001, which is very difficult for people to understand and to translate into meaning (Pinkerton et al., 2000). Similar to general risk perceptions, it has been found that certain numerical formats facilitate more accurate estimations. For example, the overestimation error appears to be less pronounced when risk perception are assessed by using a natural frequency scale ("How many women like you out of 100 will get breast cancer in your lifetime?") than by using a percentage scale ("What is your personal risk of getting breast cancer in your lifetime? Please answer on a scale of 0% to 100%"). However, the overestimation bias for breast cancer risk was less pronounced but still substantial (Schapira, Davids, McAuliffe, & Nattinger, 2004).

## Comparative Personal Risk Perceptions: Unrealistic Optimism

Although people often overestimate their personal absolute risk, they nonetheless are often convinced that their risk is lower than that of other people. The same women who dramatically overestimated their personal absolute breast cancer risk in the study by Lipkus et al. (2000) were at the same time convinced that their comparative risk is below average (see also Woloshin, Schwartz, Black, & Welch, 1999 for similar results). Numerous studies have shown that when people are asked to rate their chances of experiencing certain illnesses, accidents, and other problems, most of them report that their risk is below average (for reviews see Helweg Larsen & Shepperd, 2001; Shepperd, Carroll, Grace, & Terry, 2002). For example, when asked how they judge their risk of becoming HIV-infected compared to an average peer of the same sex and age (the average risk), participants typically give a below-average estimate (e.g., Hahn & Renner, 1998). However, if people believe on average that their risk is below average, they are systematically underestimating their personal risk. This bias in comparative risk perception has been labeled as *unrealistic optimism* or *optimistic bias* (Perloff & Fetzer, 1986; Weinstein, 1980) and reflects the difference between the perceived risk for oneself (personal risk perception) and the perceived risk for others (general risk perception).

### MEASUREMENT AND CONSEQUENCES OF UNREALISTIC OPTIMISM

There are two widely used methods for establishing an optimistic bias. In the direct method, participants are asked directly to estimate their risk relative to their peers (Weinstein, 1980). For example, participants are asked to compare their risk with that of the average person of their age and sex ("Compared to an average person of my age and sex, my chances of getting lung cancer in the future are -3 [much below average]; 0 [average]; +3 [much above average]"). An optimistic bias has been established if the participants, on average, view their risk as below average. In the indirect method, participants are asked to make two separate judgments (Perloff & Fetzer, 1986). Specifically, they are asked to rate their own absolute risk ('How likely do you think you are to get lung cancer at some point in the future?') and the absolute risk for an average person ("How likely do you think an average person of your age and sex is to

get lung cancer at some point in the future?"). If the difference between these two absolute judgments is not zero, an optimistic bias has been established.

Both methods have been successfully used to demonstrate optimistic bias, although, in most studies, the direct method yielded stronger evidence of a systematic bias (e.g., Covey & Davies, 2004; Hahn & Renner, 1998; Hevey, French, Marteau, & Sutton, 2009; Sutton, 2002; Welkenhuysen, Evers-Kiebooms, Decruyenaere, & Van Den Berghe, 1996). However, the two measures are usually only modestly correlated, ranging from $r = .20$ to $r = .50$ (French & Hevey, 2008). Taking lung cancer again as an example shows that both methods indicated an optimistic bias in a U.K. sample (Covey & Davies, 2004) as well as in a German sample (Hahn & Renner, 1998). However, the two methods correlated only modestly in both samples, with $r = .44$ in the U.K. sample and $r = .48$ in the German sample. Thus, the two measures appear to capture different aspects of comparative risk. It appears obvious that this lack of parallelism between the two measures may be at least partly due to the two different modus operandi for determining the difference between the risk for the self and the average peer. People seem not simply to calculate a difference score as implied by the indirect method but rather use a different algorithm or heuristic for comparison (Hahn & Renner, 1998; Hevey et al., 2009; Rose, Endo, Windschitl, & Suls, 2008; also see Chambers & Windschitl, 2004, for a discussion of the processes that may underlie the difference between the two methods).

It is important to note that both methods—the direct and indirect method for detecting an optimistic bias-operate at the level of the group. However, they are silent with regard to the question of who gave unrealistically biased risk estimates. A man who says that his risk of heart disease is "below average" might give a somewhat optimistic risk rating, but if he is of normal weight, does not smoke or drink, and is physically active, his optimistic rating may actually be a realistic perception of his risk status (cf. Armor & Sackett, 2006; Weinstein, 2003). Thus, by using the direct or indirect measure, it is not possible to identify which person gave biased risk estimations. For assessing the optimistic bias at the individual level, objective risk measures are required. Only a small number of studies have used objective health risk appraisal instruments (HRA) for determining the actual individual risk status. Health risk appraisals are designed to estimate a person's mortality or morbidity risk for various diseases based on characteristics such as medical history, blood pressure, and smoking habits. Avis, Smith, and McKinlay (1989), for example, assessed the actual comparative heart attack risk and the comparative perception of heart attack risk from 732 men and women aged 25–65 years. A total of 42% of the respondents underestimated their comparative risk, whereas only 18% overestimated their comparative risk, and 40% were accurate.

Gramling et al. (2008) examined the long-term consequences of perceiving one's comparative CVD risk to be lower than established clinical tools would estimate. They conducted a 15-year mortality surveillance study of more than 2,800 adults who had no history of myocardial infarction. Men who rated their CVD risk to be lower than men of their same age had nearly a three times lower incidence of CVD-related mortality compared with all others. The striking finding was that this holds true, even when controlling for differences in known risk factors such as cholesterol ratio, blood pressure, smoking status, obesity, first-degree family history of early-onset CHD, and current use of medication. Thus, holding optimistic perceptions of risk led to advantages, at least for men (see also McKenney, Lapane, Assaf, & Carleton, 1995 for similar results). In a similar vein, data drawn from the Aging in Manitoba Study, examining a representative sample of Manitoba residents of 70 or more years of age, also showed that a positive social comparison of one's health lowered the odds of hospitalization and mortality measured 2 and 6 years later (Bailis, Chipperfield, & Perry, 2005). Moreover, each unit of increase in the positive social comparison scale corresponded to a reduction of 74% in the odds of hospitalization and of 82% in those of mortality. Bailis et al. (2005) noted that the observed effect size for positive social comparison was comparable to the influence of behavioral risk factors, such as obesity or exercise. Thus, perceiving oneself less at risk than others, might be grounded in reality, capturing substantial aspects of one's health that are not detected currently by established clinical tools.

**UNREALISTIC OPTIMISM ACROSS THE LIFESPAN**
The notion that risk perceptions are grounded in reality is further supported by the finding that people feel more at risk with increasing age. Renner, Knoll, and Schwarzer (2000) examined a German community sample between 18 and 89 years of age and found that people felt more at risk for cardiovascular diseases with increasing age. From a normative perspective, this indicates "relative accuracy" in risk perceptions for the self since major health risks (e.g., CVD, cancer) increase across the lifespan. Moreover, major biological systems, such as cardiovascular function, lung volume, or muscle strength, start to decline in young and middle adulthood—at the age of 35 to 40 at the latest (Rybash, Roodin, & Hoyer, 1995). It is important to note that these physical changes do not imply that people actually feel ill or that they suffer from a disease. Nonetheless, people may notice physical changes (e.g., decline in muscle strength) and, therefore, become more aware of their susceptibility to diseases in general, which might induce changes in subjective health conceptions and goals (Renner, Spivak, Kwon, & Schwarzer, 2007). Supporting this notion, biological changes are mirrored by psychological changes, which emerge in the 30s. Specifically, health becomes an increasingly important life goal (Hooker & Kaus, 1994; Nurmi, 1992; Staudinger, Freund, Linden, & Maas, 1999), and people start to invest increasingly more time and energy in pursuing health-related goals (Ebner, Freund, & Baltes, 2006). Interestingly, the motivational impact from feeling at risk on health behavior change appears also to increase with increasing age. Comparing younger adults (<35 years) and older adults from a German sample showed that risk perception motivated the intention for protective behavior within older adults but had no significant impact on younger adults' intentions and health behavior (Schwarzer & Renner, 2000). Specifically, the more older adults felt at risk, the more they intended to follow a healthy diet, and the healthier was their diet half a year later. Conversely, within young adults, risk perception had no substantial impact on intention or nutritional behavior. A highly similar pattern was found within a Korean sample examining the relationship between risk perception for CVD and physical activity within younger and older adults (Renner et al., 2007).

However, acknowledging that one's risk does increase with increasing age does not necessarily imply that people become less optimistic about their risk in comparison to their peers. In fact, the phenomena of *unrealistic optimism* has been observed not only in children (Albery & Messer, 2005), adolescents (Cohn, Macfarlane, Yanez, & Imai, 1995; Millstein & Halpern-Felsher, 2002; Quadrel, Fischhoff, & Davis, 1993), and students (Weinstein, 1982), but also in middle-aged and older adults (Renner et al., 2000; Weinstein, 1987). On the contrary, unrealistic optimism may even increase with increasing age. With increasing experiences of age-related declines and increasing feelings of threat through impending age-related loss, a greater activation of the use of downward comparisons may occur (Bauer, Wrosch, & Jobin, 2008; Cheng, Fung, & Chan, 2007; Heckhausen & Brim, 1997; Heckhausen & Krueger, 1993). Although people may acknowledge that their risk increases with increasing age, they may at the same time believe that their peers are even worse off, and this tendency may become more accentuated the older people become. Accordingly, considered from a lifespan perspective, people may demonstrate evidence for relative accuracy in absolute risk perceptions for the self while demonstrating evidence for an age-differential optimistic bias. Renner, Gutiérrez-Dona, Kwon, and Schwarzer (2011) examined absolute risk perception for self and the average peer in community samples from Germany and Costa Rica, two predominately individualistic countries, and South Korea, a predominately collectivistic country (Figure 26.3). Germans and Costa Ricans, as well as South Koreans, showed evidence for relative accuracy in their absolute risk perceptions for the self since, with increasing age, they perceived themselves more at risk. Nonetheless, older adults in all three samples showed a clear evidence for unrealistic optimism (see Figure 26.3). Thus, older participants from different cultural backgrounds acknowledged that they are at greater risk with increasing age, but were simultaneously still convinced that bad things are more likely to happen to others than to themselves. Thus, unrealistic optimism appears to be a robust phenomenon across the lifespan.

Furthermore, an increasingly pronounced unrealistic optimistic bias was observed across the age groups. Specifically, below 30 years of age, South Koreans attributed a similar degree of invulnerability to their peers, demonstrating an unbiased comparative risk perception (cf. also Heine, 2004; Heine & Buchtel, 2009). However, this unbiased view of one's peers' risk turned into an increasingly pessimistic view with increasing age, indicating an age-differential accelerated shift in risk perceptions for the peer versus the self (see also Inumiya, Choi, Yoon, Seo, & Han, 1999). An age-differential shift in risk perceptions for the self versus peers was also apparent in Costa Ricans, but not in Germans (for a more detailed discussion of cultural differences, please see Heine, 2004; Heine & Hamamura, 2007; Rose et al., 2008; Sedikides, Gaertner, & Vevea, 2005). Thus, with increasing age, Westerners as well as Easterners believed that they are more at risk, and they also increasingly believed that they are less bad off than their peers. These findings are in line with

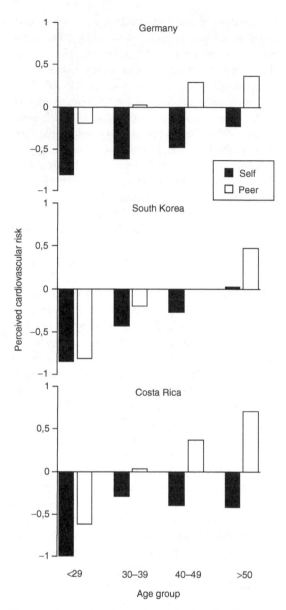

**Fig. 26.3** Perceived cardiovascular risk for the self and an average peer across age groups and countries. From Renner, B., Gutiérrez-Dona, B., Kwon, S., & Schwarzer, R. (2011, submitted). Risk perception across age groups and countries: Becoming more vulnerable but being still invincible.

lifespan research postulating increasingly compensatory social downward comparisons with increasing experiences of age-related declines.

## DETERMINANTS OF UNREALISTIC OPTIMISM
Why do people feel less at risk than others? Research has posited various explanations for the intriguing phenomena, involving both motivational and cognitive processes (Chambers & Windschitl, 2004; Helweg-Larsen & Shepperd, 2001; Klein & Weinstein, 1997; Shepperd et al., 2002).

Motivational accounts postulate that at the heart of the optimistic bias is a motivation to self-enhance or to protect and maintain a positive view of one's health (Armor & Taylor, 1998; for reviews see Helweg-Larsen & Shepperd, 2001; Klein & Weinstein, 1997; Shepperd et al., 2002). Accordingly, the fact that individuals harbor pessimistic biases for others may represent a mechanism by which people maintain a comparatively optimistic outlook for themselves, despite realizing that health-related risks do increase with age. This might satisfy a need for accuracy by acknowledging more objective risk at an absolute level, while also serving self-protective needs by maintaining a pessimistic view of others at the same time (Armor & Taylor, 1998; Taylor & Shepperd, 1998; Whitley & Hern, 1991). However, a purely motivational account does not sufficiently explain the phenomena. If people bias comparative risk perceptions predominantly because they want to maintain a positive view of the self, serious diseases should provoke an increased degree of optimistic bias since they are particular threatening for the self. Contrary to the idea that biased comparative risk perceptions are a defense against feelings of threat and anxiety, unrealistic optimism is generally no greater for serious, life-threatening hazards than for more mundane problems (Helweg-Larsen & Shepperd, 2001; Weinstein, 2003). For example, developing cancer is commonly not associated with unrealistic optimism, although it is highly threatening for people (Weinstein, 1980). Furthermore, Harris, Griffin, and Murray (2008) analyzed different studies with more than 1,400 participants in total and found no consistent support for the severity–denial hypothesis.

From a cognitive perspective, it has been argued that the bias might result from our tendency to focus more on our own health-related factors than on those of peers when comparing our risk to others (Chambers & Windschitl, 2004; Weinstein & Lachendro, 1982). Supporting this notion, empirical studies typically show that comparative risk judgments correlate to a higher degree with absolute risk judgments for the self than with absolute risk judgments for peers (Klar & Giladi, 1999; Kruger, Windschitl, Burrus, Fessel, & Chambers, 2008; Pahl, Eiser, & White, 2009; Ranby, Aiken, Gerend, & Erchull, 2010; Rose et al., 2008). Interestingly, the "egocentric" bias is not limited to the self since focusing on another individual produces similar biases in comparative judgment as does focusing on the self. People show the same sort of egocentric biases when the self is not relevant and they are focusing on others (Klar

& Giladi, 1999; Moore & Kim, 2003). Weinstein and Lachendro (1982; see also, Kruger et al., 2008) showed that that egocentrism and optimistic bias was reduced, but not eliminated, when people's knowledge about the comparison group increased. However, the egocentrism account has been criticized as providing a restatement rather than an explanation of the observed phenomena (Moore, 2007). Specifically, the egocentrism account proposes that people think differently about themselves as opposed to others, and therefore a bias in comparisons involving the self occurs. Clearly, people know more about themselves than they do about other individuals (Baumeister, 1998; Klar & Giladi, 1999; Kruger et al., 2008) and thus, the self holds a unique status in cognition.

Another possibility to gain insight into the underlying mechanism of the optimistic bias is to examine which type of hazard elicits a particularly strong unrealistic bias (Weinstein, 2003). Interestingly, some hazards appear to be associated with a strong and reliable bias (e.g., STDs, alcohol problems, suicide), whereas other hazards commonly elicit only a weak or no bias (e.g., cold, cancer). A first and agenda-setting study by Neil Weinstein (1980) observed that the more frequently a hazard is perceived, the less optimistic are comparative risk perceptions ($r = -.29$) (see also Rose et al., 2008). Personal experience also reduced the amount of bias ($r = -.42$). Conversely, Weinstein (1980) observed a strong facilitating effect on unrealistic optimism for the perceived controllability of the hazard ($r = .67$) and the salience of a clear stereotype of a victim for the hazard ($r = .76$). Almost 30 years later, based on more than 1,400 participants from seven different samples, Harris et al. (2008) also found clear evidence for the facilitating effect of controllability and stereotype salience (see also Moore & Rosenthal, 1991). Interestingly, controllability of the event and stereotype salience are highly correlated (Weinstein, 1980), indicating that, for controllable events, people find it easy to picture typical victims variously referred to as "high-risk victim prototype," "unhealthy prototype," "typical at-risk person," or as "high-risk stereotype" (Gibbons & Gerrard, 1997; Hahn & Renner, 1998; Lek & Bishop, 1995; Perloff & Fetzer, 1986; Thornton, Gibbons, & Gerrard, 2002; Weinstein, 1980). This may explain why lung cancer typically elicits a pronouncedly unrealistic optimism, whereas cancer in general does not. Lung cancer in comparison to cancer is perceived as a controllable and behavior-dependent disease, and people can easily picture a typical victim (Hahn & Renner, 1998).

Well-articulated, stereotypic beliefs about high-risk individuals are already developed by children and adolescents (e.g., smoker image or heavy drinker image; Andrews & Peterson, 2006; Chassin, Tetzloff, & Hershey, 1985; Leventhal & Cleary, 1980).

Choosing to compare with a high-risk stereotype is likely to leave the individual with a false sense of invulnerability. And this, in essence, might be the basis of the bias (cf. Gibbons & Gerrard, 1997; Helweg Larsen & Shepperd, 2001; Klein & Weinstein, 1997; Misovich, Fisher, & Fisher, 1997). Presumably, the less similar a person believes he or she is to the high-risk stereotype, the safer the person will perceive him- or herself (Perloff & Fetzer, 1986). However, only few studies have assessed the risk profile of risk stereotypes. Hahn and Renner (1998) asked smokers who smoked on average 16 cigarettes a day for 19 years to characterize the typical smoking behavior of a person who is at high risk for getting lung cancer. On average, the smokers estimated that a person at high risk for getting lung cancer smokes about 24 cigarettes a day for 14 years. These subjective estimates for the "high-risk stereotype" were compared with participants' own smoking behavior. Thus, for each smoker, the similarity between the self and the high-risk stereotype was assessed by calculating a difference score (own smoking behavior minus high-risk stereotype smoking behavior). As Figure 26.4 depicts, when the number of smoked cigarettes per day reported by the smokers equated the estimated number of cigarettes for the high-risk stereotype (= "0" on the x-axis), smokers believed that their own risk for lung cancer is only slightly above average in comparison to their peers (= "0" on the y-axis). Or, to put this effect more bluntly, even smokers who demonstrated a smoking behavior that they themselves judged as highly risky nonetheless viewed their own personal risk as only average in comparison to their peers (including smokers and nonsmokers!). Thus, these results support the notion that unrealistic optimistic risk perception might stem from a comparison with a high-risk stereotype.

The impact of risk stereotypes on comparative risk judgments has been conceptualized as a "pure" cognitive effect resulting from the representativeness heuristic (Kahneman & Tversky, 1972). Specifically, the representativeness heuristic assumes that people judge their comparative risk by assessing the fit of their own risk profile to the prototype of the disease category (= risk stereotype). In accordance with this notion, smokers believed that they were at average risk for getting lung cancer if their personal risk profile equated the risk profile of their risk

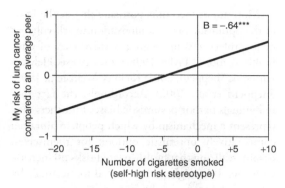

**Fig. 26.4** Comparative risk judgments as a function of the difference between one's own consumed number of cigarettes per day and the consumption ascribed to the high-risk stereotype (relative frequency). Reprinted from Hahn, A., & Renner, B. (1998). Perception of health risks: How smoker status affects defensive optimism. *Anxiety, Stress and Coping, 11*(2), 93–112, with permission of the publisher Taylor & Francis.

stereotype for lung cancer. Also, following this logic, Harris et al. (2008) argued that increasing the concreteness and closeness of the comparison target (e.g., "friend" vs. "average peer") is associated with less bias through a reduced activation of target stereotypes and thus decreased estimates of other-risk (cf. also Perloff & Fetzer, 1986).

Conversely, the comparison with a high-risk stereotype has also been conceptualized from a motivational perspective as an active, downward comparison process. Specifically, it is proposed that people distance themselves psychologically from risks by construing high-risk stereotypes as a function of their own behavior in order to sustain a distance between the image of risk and the self (Chambers & Windschitl, 2004; Gibbons & Gerrard, 1997; Klein & Weinstein, 1997; Tennen, McKee, & Affleck, 2000). In support of this notion, studies showed that people tend to associate more negative than positive personality attributes with a person who behaves in a risky way (e.g., Gerrard, Gibbons, Lane, & Stock, 2005; Gump, Kulik, & Henderson, 1998). Moreover, a survey with a random national sample of 3,820 French smokers and nonsmokers suggests that smokers adapted their beliefs about a high-risk behavior profile to their own risk behavior. The more cigarettes participants have smoked per day or the longer they have smoked, the more extreme were their beliefs about the behavior attributed to a person at risk (Peretti-Watel et al., 2007).

One intriguing conclusion from this research is that public health education campaigns may often facilitate, instead of reduce, unrealistic optimistic risk perceptions. The guiding principles proposed by campaigns for health risk reduction usually include vivid presentations of risk factors and show high-risk persons. This may foster risk stereotypes that are perceived as dissimilar and thus, may lead to an underestimation of personal risk because individuals think that many risk factors do not apply to them (Renner & Schwarzer, 2003; Weinstein & Klein, 1995). Consequently, risk communication that provides only information about general risk may make people aware of a risk ("Smoking causes coronary heart disease"), but at the same time may lead to the underestimation of the risk for the self ("It is unlikely that this will happen to me") by creating high-risk stereotypes.

One possibility to reduce unrealistic optimism is to provide additional information about the risk faced by an average peer. Weinstein and Lachendro (1982), for instance, asked participants to come up with a number of possible risk-reducing factors that typical peers might list. This experimental intervention resulted in lower unrealistic optimism since the participants were encouraged to explicitly consider moderating factors in other persons that they usually only relate to themselves. Such additional information may help people locate their risk status more accurately and become motivated to change risky behaviors. Still, with this type of message, recipients have to infer the magnitude of their personal risk, leaving considerable leeway for a positive view of one's risk. One possibility to reduce this ambiguity and interpretation leeway about one's risk status is to inform people about their actual health risk through providing personalized risk feedback.

## Reactions Toward Personalized Risk Feedback

Imagine your general practitioner routinely runs a cardiovascular check and tells you that your cholesterol level is too high and that your risk for CVD may be elevated. How would you possibly react? From a psychological perspective, personalized risk feedback represents self-relevant, negative, and threatening information for the self. Numerous studies have been conducted to study how people react toward negative, self-relevant feedback. Research in the area of persuasive communication, impression formation, judgment and decision-making, and risk communication have consistently shown that people accept negative feedback to a lesser degree than positive feedback (Baumeister, Bratslavsky, Finkenauer, & Vohs, 2001; Carroll, Sweeny, & Shepperd, 2006; Lench & Ditto, 2008; Rothman & Salovey, 2007; Sedikides & Green, 2000; Taylor & Brown, 1988; Wyer & Frey, 1983).

In the domain of health risk research, Jemmott, Ditto, and Croyle (1986) invented an experimental procedure to study reactions toward health risk feedback. An often replicated finding is that participants who were made to believe that they suffer from a hypothetical thiamine acetylase (TAA) deficiency perceived their test result as less accurate and rated a TAA deficiency as a less serious threat to their health than their experimental counterparts, who were made to believe that they did not have a TAA deficiency (for a review see Croyle, Sun, & Hart, 1997). Similar asymmetrical acceptance patterns were found in experimental studies of appraisals of cholesterol and blood pressure test results (Croyle, 1990; Croyle, Sun, & Louie, 1993), gum disease test results (McCaul, Thiesse-Duffy, & Wilson, 1992), a hypothetical bacterial condition (Cioffi, 1991), a hypothetical fibrocystic disease (Kunda, 1987), and diabetes (Orbell & Hagger, 2006). An asymmetrical acceptance pattern has also been observed by Croyle, Sun, and Louie (1993) within a community cholesterol screening (cf. also Croyle et al., 2006). These studies demonstrate that people accept negative health risk information to a lesser degree than they do positive information. Thus, the asymmetrical acceptance is a very robust phenomenon, evident across a wide range of diseases and samples. This leads to the question: Why is bad news less accepted than good news?

### What We Don't Like, We Don't Accept: A Motivated Reasoning Perspective

The lower acceptance of negative in comparison to positive health risk feedback is commonly seen as clear-cut evidence for "self-defensive denial" or "motivated reasoning" (e.g., Agostinelli, Sherman, Presson, & Chassin, 1992; Baumeister et al., 2001; Croyle et al., 1997; Dawson, Gilovich, & Regan, 2002; Kunda, 1990; Pyszczynski, & Greenberg, 1987; Sedikides & Green, 2000; Taylor & Brown, 1988). Specifically, Croyle et al. (1997) have argued that people who are informed that they have an elevated risk of disease derogate the validity of the risk factor test and minimize the seriousness of the health threat posed by the risk factor in order to maintain a favorable sense of their health. Thus, people appear to have basically two different lines of self-defense when they are confronted with threatening information, as depicted in the model of illness threat appraisal (Figure 26.5; Ditto, Jemmott, & Darley, 1988; Ditto & Lopez, 1992). The first line of defense is the derogation of the validity of the threatening information, also called "denial of fact." For example, a person might interpret an elevated

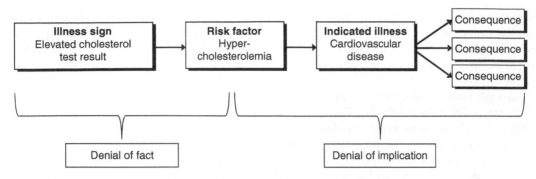

**Fig. 26.5** Model of illness threat appraisal. Adapted from Ditto, P. H., Jemmott, J. B., & Darley, J. M. (1988). Appraising the threat of illness: A mental representational approach. *Health Psychology, 7*(2), 183–201; and Ditto, P. H., & Lopez, D. F. (1992). Motivated skepticism: Use of differential decision criteria for preferred and nonpreferred conclusions. *Journal of Personality and Social Psychology, 63*(4), 568–584.

cholesterol test reading as just a transient elevated cholesterol level rather than as an indicator for hypercholesterolemia, which increases the risk for CVD. The second line of defense, also called "denial of implications," encompasses the derogation of the specific consequences of the elevated risk status. For example, hypercholesterolemia might be perceived only as weakly related to CVD and serious consequences. Accordingly, the disregarding of negative risk feedback information can enfold on different stages within the illness threat appraisal process and appears to be the result of "motivated reasoning" because self-defensive motives employ various processing strategies that question the given negative information. Most researchers are convinced that self-defensive reactions toward negative feedback represent the "norm" because they are inherent in the fabric of human nature. For example, Wiebe and Korbel (2003, p. 191) concluded that "defensive self-protection is a widespread, normative response to health threats" and likewise Eisenstadt and Leippe (1994, p. 623) emphasized that "self-enhancing responses to feedback are the norm" (see also Campbell & Sedikides, 1999).

At first glance, the motivated reasoning account poses a simple and straightforward explanation for the often-observed asymmetrical acceptance pattern: People don't like bad news and consequently, they try to derogate it with superficial rational strategies. However, on a second look, the motivated reasoning account has some critical limitations in terms of empirical evidence and theoretical conceptions (cf. Ditto & Lopez, 1992; Ditto, Scepansky, Munro, Apanovitch, & Lockhart, 1998; Panzer & Renner, 2009; Renner, 2004).

First, the empirical evidence does not provide a clear-cut case for self-defensive reactions toward

negative feedback. People receiving bad news (e.g., "Your blood pressure is too high") rate the test result as less reliable and valid than people receiving good news ("Your blood pressure is optimal"). This asymmetrical acceptance pattern is typically interpreted as a *rejection bias*: People reject negative feedback to a higher degree than they do positive feedback. However, the same pattern of findings can be taken as evidence for an acceptance bias: People are more willing to accept positive feedback than negative feedback. Importantly, framing the asymmetrical acceptance pattern as evidence for a rejection bias focuses on the negative feedback group and implies that their judgments are biased. Conversely, framing the findings as evidence for an acceptance bias focuses on the positive feedback group, implying that their judgments are biased. In fact, both interpretations are justifiable, and one could even argue that both groups are biased. Accordingly, although the classical asymmetrical acceptance pattern tells us that there is a difference between the positive and negative feedback group, this research is silent with regard to which group shows a bias.

Second, at the heart of the motivated reasoning account is the assumption that people derogate negative risk feedback without noticing it. If people are confronted with negative feedback, self-defensive motivations become activated that induce motivational biased information processing targeted at undermining the given threatening information (Balcetis, 2008; Kunda, 1990). However, the inherent assumption of self-deception is in conflict with numerous studies demonstrating that negative information draws greater attention, induces more elaborate cognitive processing, and causes a mobilization reaction (Baumeister et al., 2001; Pratto & John, 1991). For example, Liberman and Chaiken

(1992) reported that individuals receiving health-threatening information invested more effort in reading the message than did individuals receiving less health-threatening information. Similarly, Ditto and Lopez (1992) observed that participants whose (self-administered) test indicated a TAA-deficiency went to greater length to examine their test strip and showed more frequent retesting behavior (e.g., conducting a second test with a new test strip). To reconcile these findings with the motivated reasoning account, one must assume that people pay more attention to and spend more processing resources on negative risk feedback to inevitably reach the conclusion that the information is not valid (cf. also Ditto, Scepansky, Munro, Apanovitch, & Lockhart, 1998; Renner, 2004).

Third, if people predominately derogate negative information, maladaptive and counterproductive behaviors seem to be the logical consequence. If people are not convinced that the given negative risk feedback is valid and are reluctant to accept it, they should not be motivated to change their behavior. Thus, a motivated reasoning account inevitably results in an "adaptive paradox" (Ditto et al., 1998; Panzer & Renner, 2009; Renner, 2004; Renner, Schüz, & Sniehotta, 2008): The predominant response to threatening information should be a defensive or persistent behavior pattern, rather than adaptive behavior changes that are required to avoid future serious harm. However, studies assessing behavior-proximal variables, such as intentions and behavior change, commonly report adaptive response patterns instead of the expected unresponsiveness to information signaling a health threat: People who received bad news were more inclined to change behaviors than were people who received good news (e.g., Bowen, Fries, & Hopp, 1994; Kreuter & Strecher, 1996; Panzer & Renner, 2008; Panzer & Renner, 2009; Renner, 2004). For explaining these conflicting results, various "reloaded" versions of motivational reasoning have been put forward. For example, Ditto and Croyle (1995) argued from a dual-processing perspective that people may simultaneously engage in fear- and danger-control processes (cf. also Leventhal, Leventhal, & Contrada, 1998). Accordingly, derogating the threatening risk feedback serves primarily to control fear and negative affect, whereas the adoption of instrumental behavior serves to control the immediate danger. Other authors argue that people's reactions are not completely biased, but are constrained by their wish to construe plausible justifications for their judgments and behaviors (Baumeister et al., 2001; Kunda,

1990). However, these extended motivated reasoning accounts do not provide much insight into when and how people resist information about their risk. Furthermore, they seem to be immunized against empirical falsification: Resistance against threatening information is due to motivated reasoning, and acceptance is due to reality constraints. Hence, any pattern of finding can be explained post-hoc without providing a firm basis for predicting specific results.

### Is the Danger Real? A Quantity of Processing Perspective

Did you lately observe some gum inflammation or gum bleeding when brushing your teeth? Did you know that this might put you at a substantially higher risk for CHD, even if you don't have any other risk factors? A recently published meta-analysis is suggesting that periodontal disease, including gingivitis with gum inflammation and bleeding, is a risk factor for CHD that is independent of traditional CHD risk factors (Humphrey, Fu, Buckley, Freeman, & Helfand, 2008). You might think that the range and number of risk factors for major diseases such as CVD is steadily increasing, until it is now almost impossible to attend and react to all the provided information. Indeed, this represents a core challenge for human functioning. We have only a limited capacity of attentional and processing resources, and thus the question arises: What is the most effective way to invest these precious and sparse resources in order to avoid serious harm?

Given that we have only limited resources for too many competing stimuli, it appears to be most adaptive to preferably invest these resources in survival-relevant stimuli. In general, negative events are more likely to represent survival-relevant stimuli than are positive events since they are more strongly related to adverse health outcomes, they are typically of greater time urgency, and thus, they more often require an immediate response (Baumeister et al., 2001; Cacioppo, Gardner, & Berntson, 1999; Ditto & Lopez, 1992; Ditto, Munro, Apanovitch, Scepansky, & Lockhart, 2003; Ditto et al., 1998; Pratto & John, 1991; Renner, 2004; Schwarz, 1998; Taylor, 1991). As a consequence, negative as compared to positive information more often requires behavioral changes. Since behavioral changes are more cost-intensive for the organism than maintaining the status quo, it appears reasonable to scrutinize negative information more carefully than positive information in order to determine whether the danger is real or imaginary.

Based on this line of reasoning, Ditto and Lopez (1992; Ditto et al., 2003; Ditto et al., 1998) suggested in their quantity of processing (QOP) view that often-found asymmetrical acceptance is simply caused by the fact that negative information triggers more elaborate cognitive analyses than does positive information. If people think more deeply about negative information, they are more likely to consider plausible alternative explanations, producing greater uncertainty regarding the validity of the information. As a consequence, negative information is less likely to be accepted than is positive information. Accordingly, the QOP view conceptualizes common asymmetrical acceptance as an unintentional by-product of a highly adaptive strategy of directing elaborate cognitive processing toward potentially threatening stimuli, which is an attempt to determine whether a threat actually exists. If it does not, valuable resources will not be expended in mobilizing to cope with an imagery danger. Thus, in contrast to the motivational reasoning view, the QOP view considers people as unbiased and adaptive information processors.

Relying on a very common strategy in social-cognitive research to demonstrate elaborate cognitive processing, Ditto et al. (1998, Study 3) tested whether people who received negative health risk feedback were more sensitive to differential information quality than were people who received positive health risk feedback. If negative health risk information triggers more elaborate cognitive processing than does positive information, people receiving negative information should be sensitive to differences in information quality, whereas people receiving positive information, triggering only a heuristic processing mode, should be rather insensitive to information quality. Supporting this prediction of the QOP view, participants who received negative TAA feedback accepted feedback of low quality less readily than TAA feedback of high quality. Interestingly, negative information was accepted to a similar degree as positive information when participants had reason to believe that the information was of high quality. Conversely, positive feedback was highly accepted regardless of whether it was of high or low quality. The found pattern of result is in line with the QOP view that negative risk information triggers more elaborate processing than does positive risk information, and therefore negative information is less likely accepted than positive information. However, from a motivational reasoning perspective, one could still argue that people receiving highly valid negative TAA risk feedback finally accepted it because there was virtually no leeway for derogating the information (von Hippel, Lakin, & Shakarchi,

2005). Thus, the unambiguous acceptance of good news and the differential acceptance of bad news are still inconclusive of whether this indicates an adaptive or a self-defensive reaction pattern.

## Why Good News Does Not Always Induce Acceptance and Reassurance: A Cue-adaptive Reasoning Perspective

The main focus of public health risk screening programs, as well as of risk research, has been on people who are at risk and on the question of how bad news is "digested" by the recipients. The reception of good news (e.g., "Your cholesterol test result is optimal") has comparably been neglected. Commonly, it has been assumed that positive health risk feedback is met with great acceptance and reassurance (Wardle et al., 2003). Curiously, this seems not always to be the case. Weinstein, Atwood, Puleo, Fletcher, Colditz, and Emmons (2004), for example, examined primary care patients between 40 and 70 years who received computerized risk assessment feedback about their colon cancer risk. Most of the patients greatly overestimated their risk, as comparisons between prefeedback risk perceptions and actual risk scores revealed. Thus, for most patients, the risk feedback indicted a lower risk status than they had expected. According to the motivated reasoning and QOP views, receiving such good news should have resulted in pronounced acceptance of the feedback and in reduced postfeedback risk perceptions. Although most participants correctly recalled their actual risk status, as presented by the computer, many did not accept the risk feedback as being accurate, with a large majority still believing their actual risk to be higher. Similar resistance toward positive feedback or "lack of reassurance" has been observed in various empirical studies (Channer, James, Papouchado, & Russel Rees, 1987; Dillard, McCaul, Kelso, & Klein, 2006; Marteau, Roberts, LaRusse, & Green, 2005; McCaul, Canevello, Mathwig, & Klein, 2003; Michie et al., 2002; Scott, Prior, Wood, & Gray, 2005). The resistance toward positive feedback has also been observed in the context of severe diseases. For instance, a study with cancer patients undergoing chemotherapy revealed that unexpected positive health information (rapid tumor shrinking), as opposed to expected information (gradual tumor shrinking), elicited marked distress and negative affect (Nerenz, Leventhal, Love, & Ringler, 1984; see also Hilgart, Phelps, Bennett, Hood, Brain & Murray, 2010). This raises the question: How can the resistance toward good news be explained, and could this contribute to our understanding of reactions toward personalized risk feedback in general?

The cue-adaptive reasoning account (CARA) suggested that the often-observed asymmetrical acceptance of risk feedback might not only be consequent on the valence of the feedback information, but may also arise when risk feedback information is inconsistent with preexisting risk perceptions (Panzer & Renner, 2008, 2009; Renner, 2004). Social cognition research has shown that unexpected information, conflicting with held beliefs and attitudes, is generally perceived as less trustworthy and diagnostically accurate than is information that is concordant with preexisting expectancies (e.g., Edwards & Smith, 1996; Shrauger, 1975; Swann, Griffin, Predmore, & Gaines, 1987). Moreover, several lines of research suggest that unexpected information triggers more elaborate stimulus analysis than expected information (e.g., Edwards & Smith, 1996; Hilton, Klein, & von Hippel, 1991). For instance, research on argument evaluation showed that belief-incompatible arguments induce a longer reading time and more thought, and are judged as weaker than belief-compatible arguments (Edwards & Smith, 1996; Lord, Ross, & Lepper, 1979; Petty & Cacioppo, 1986). Accordingly, the CARA assumes that both negative as well as risk feedback that conflicts with preexisting risk perceptions serve as cues that draw attentional resources for elaborate stimulus processing (Renner, 2004). If people spend more cognitive resources on negative or unexpected risk information, plausible alternative explanations are more likely taken into account, producing greater uncertainty regarding the reliability and validity of the information, and, as a consequence, negative or unexpected risk information is less likely to be accepted than is expected positive risk information. One important implication of assuming that unexpected risk feedback triggers more rigorous cognitive processing is that not only unexpected bad news but also unexpected good news is received with greater reluctance.

The assumption that unexpected good news is subjected to more elaborate processing might appear on a first glance counterintuitive and certainly contrasts clearly with the motivated reasoning and QOP views. If people predominately strive to attain or maintain a positive view of the self, individuals who believe that they are at high risk but receive an "all-clear" feedback should readily accept the feedback as valid information. However, from the CARA perspective, individuals receiving unexpected positive risk feedback should scrutinize the information as rigorously as participants receiving negative risk feedback. Especially in the context of personally consequential feedback, this might represent a highly adaptive response. If people believe that their risk is elevated but then receive an all-clear "normal" test result, they might scrutinize the unexpected positive risk information quite carefully to determine the validity of the all-clear information. This is a very reasonable and resource-saving strategy since acting on false all-clear health risk feedback means that already-taken protective actions and changes in beliefs and behavior will erroneously be terminated. In this case, resources previously invested in preventive actions would be expended, while severe harm would not be prevented by protective action since the "protective shields" would be prematurely taken down. Following more general conceptions on the affect system and self-regulation (cf. Baumeister et al., 2001; Taylor, 1991), the CARA view considers the preferential allocation of processing resources to negative or unexpected information as an adaptive response. In a world where many stimuli and varying demands compete for processing resources, investment of processing resources to self- and survival-relevant stimuli fosters successful adaptations to environmental challenges and demands (c.f., Baumeister et al., 2001; Ditto et al., 1998). Accordingly, the lack of reassurance in the face of all-clear health risk feedback and the often-found asymmetrical acceptance of negative and positive risk feedback are conceptualized from the CARA view as an unintentional by-product of an adaptive allocation of cognitive processing resources.

Considering how people react toward unexpected good news might also provide an explanation for why experimental research using fictional risk feedback (for review see Croyle et al., 1997) typically found a resistance toward bad news, whereas studies on "real" risks also report a resistance toward good news (e.g., Weinstein et al., 2004). Previous experimental studies providing health feedback might have inadvertently confounded preexisting risk perceptions with risk feedback valence. Considering that individuals tend to harbor positive perceptions about their health risks (e.g., Weinstein, 1980, 2003; see also 3.2), differential acceptance of health feedback was presumably observed because people who received positive risk feedback received it expectantly, since it matched their preexisting positive risk perceptions. Conversely, negative risk feedback probably took them by surprise, since it contrasted with their positive risk perceptions. This might be particularly true since experimental studies were almost exclusively based on reactions of (healthy) graduate students, whereas field studies are typically based on middle-aged and older adults. According to the CARA account, expected positive risk feedback should be readily accepted, whereas unexpected negative risk feedback should be subjected to elaborate cognitive processing explaining the found asymmetrical acceptance. In field studies that include a wider age range, it is more likely that participants perceived their risk less optimistically, and thus a substantial number of people might had expected to receive bad news. If they received good news that contrasted with their preexisting negative risk perceptions, the CARA account would predict that they closely scrutinize the given positive risk feedback information, thus explaining the observed reluctance to accept good news (Hilgart et al., 2010, but see also Bennett et al., 2009).

The proposed assumptions of the CARA account were subjected to a more rigorous test within a community health screening, with 590 participants receiving feedback about their actual cholesterol level (Renner, 2004). If, as the CARA notion suggests, negative or unexpected risk information is processed in a more detail-oriented manner, individuals receiving unexpected negative, expected negative, or unexpected positive risk feedback should be more likely to accept high-quality risk feedback

than low-quality risk feedback. Conversely, expected positive risk feedback should initiate little cognitive analysis, and individuals should therefore demonstrate relative insensitivity to risk feedback quality. As in previous experimental studies, an asymmetrical acceptance was found: Participants who received an elevated cholesterol reading accepted the negative risk feedback to a lesser degree than did participants who received an optimal reading. Importantly, a more detailed analysis of the data showed that this typical observed main effect for feedback valence was qualified by risk perceptions (feedback expectancy) and feedback quality, as predicted by the CARA account (see Figure 26.6). Specifically, participants who received unexpected or expected negative risk feedback were clearly sensitive to the quality of the given feedback, since acceptance was significantly higher for risk feedback of high quality than of low quality. Importantly, participants receiving unexpected positive risk feedback also showed sensitivity to feedback quality: When the feedback was of low quality, it was rated as less accurate than when it was of high quality. The only group that was not sensitive to the quality of the feedback was the group that received expected positive risk feedback information. They accepted the given positive feedback to a high degree. A similar pattern was also found for behavioral-proximal measures: Participants

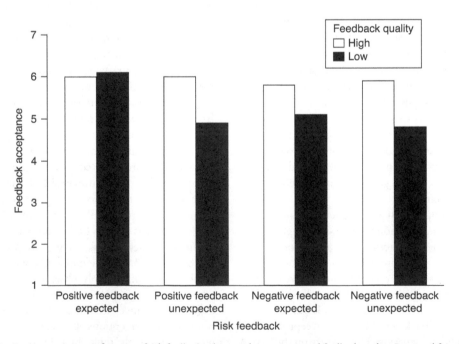

**Fig. 26.6** Feedback acceptance as a function of risk feedback valence, risk expectancy, and feedback quality. Reprinted from Renner, B. (2004). Biased reasoning: Adaptive responses to health risk feedback. *Personality and Social Psychology Bulletin, 30*, 384–396, with permission of the publisher, Sage Publications.

receiving unexpected or expected negative feedback felt a greater need to change their behavior and to take precautionary action when receiving feedback of high quality than of low quality. In a similar vein, when participants received unexpected positive feedback of low quality, the feedback lacked its reassuring effect, whereas when it was of high quality, participants felt reassured and had no need for further protective action. Thus, unexpected or expected negative feedback, as well as unexpected positive feedback, elicited sensitivity toward the quality of the given feedback information. Conversely, those who received expected positive feedback were insensitive toward feedback quality. Even when receiving feedback of low quality, they were convinced that they were safe and did not need to take precautionary action. Accordingly, participants demonstrated a highly adaptive response pattern in the face of personally consequential feedback.

## Conclusion

It is widely agreed that people's understanding of health risks is of central relevance for effective risk communication and health interventions. However, health risk perception and communication are broad and general constructs that cut across scientific disciplines. Accordingly, many questions have been raised and multiple perspectives invoked, resulting in a vast but rather fragmented literature. The present chapter suggests a conceptual framework for integrating various lines of risk research by organizing the literature according to three core questions: The first and most basic question is how people construe and evaluate health risks in general; the second question is, when people are aware that a certain health risk exists, how do they construe their own personal risk; and the third question is how people respond to risk communication that is tailored to their personal health risk status. Each of these three issues needs to be considered when devising effective risk communication, and some implications and suggestions for delivering risk information on the basis of the presented empirical evidence are indicated.

Being aware of health risks is certainly a precondition for accurate risk perception. Estimates of numerical risk and its consequences are delivered at all levels of risk communication, ranging from broad public media channels to face-to-face interactions. However, risk information is a multifaceted phenomenon and selecting what kind of risk information is provided represents a complex and difficult, rather than a simple and straightforward decision. For instance, numerical risk estimates can be based on single or cumulative exposure rates, on short-versus long-term time windows, and on specific populations, thus creating a thorny jungle of risk estimates for the audience. Risk communicators can portray rather different messages, focusing on the risk of one exposure in comparison to cumulative exposure or by varying the chosen length of the communicated time horizon. However, to support comprehension and informed choice, instead of persuading people into behavior change, people should be informed about the absolute and relative risk of acquiring one disease versus another, the impact of various risk factors over time, and the benefits derived from changing a targeted behavior. Overall, to prevent misapprehension in the audience, effective risk communication inevitably requires a focus on selected risk estimates, which should be oriented on the scope and needs of the audience rather than being in the service of special interest groups. Furthermore, the example of the 5-year mortality statistics for cancer highlights the ethical dimension of providing risk information and the need to develop common standards for the professional communication of health risks.

Even when a risk for a certain population or reference group is well understood, this does not mean that people believe that they are personally at risk. Public health interventions depicting testimonials of disease victims or portraying people at high risk may create high-risk stereotypes and, as consequence, induce a paradox effect: People may be well informed about the magnitude of risk, but at the same time they might be convinced that this misfortune will not happen to them because they feel highly dissimilar to the high-risk stereotype. Thus, general risk perceptions might be substantial, but personal risk perceptions might be low and optimistically biased. Interestingly, the discrepancy between general and personal risk perceptions seems to be a very general phenomenon observed across age groups and cultures. To cross the Rubicon between general and personal risk perceptions, recipients should be informed about their risk relative to similar others, or, even better, should receive personalized risk information. However, people are not a tabula rasa, in whom risk communication can determine the agenda. Personalized risk information is filtered through preexisting risk perceptions. If risk information conflicts with these perceptions and beliefs, it is scrutinized carefully before it is accepted. Interestingly, this holds not only for negative risk feedback, but appears also to apply to positive risk feedback. To avoid retesting and increased feelings of worry within the recipients, an "all-clear" nonelevated risk status should be as carefully explained and discussed as an elevated risk status.

Finally, it is important to note that, while becoming aware of one's own risk is a necessary prerequisite to motivating health behavior change, it is by no means sufficient. Successful health behavior change depends on additional self-regulatory resources, such as self-efficacy and planning (cf. Renner & Schwarzer, 2003; Renner et al., 2007, Renner, Hankonen, Ghisletta, & Absetz, 2011). Thus, perception of health risk is a crucial starting point for becoming motivated to change behaviors, but self-regulatory resources and competencies are needed to change complex behaviors successfully. Accordingly, effective risk communication should not only provide information about health risks but also include communication about resources to initiate health behavior changes. A risk and resource perspective shifts the focus toward the actual means and opportunities of behavior change, as well as the optimistic beliefs of being competent to handle challenging risk situations. Risk communication, which only portrays the risk without offering realistic and detailed information on how to cope with the threat, might induce anxiety, frustration, and even helplessness. Scaring people may be easily achieved, but effective risk communication can only lead to sustainable behavior change if people are encouraged to master their health goals.

## Acknowledgements

This research was supported by the German Research Foundation (RE 1583/3-1 granted to Britta Renner & Harald Schupp).

## References

Agostinelli, G., Sherman, S.J., Presson, C.C., & Chassin, L. (1992). Self-protection and self-enhancement biases in estimates of population prevalence. *Personality and Social Psychology Bulletin, 18*(5), 631–642.

Albery, I.P., & Messer, D. (2005). Comparative optimism about health and nonhealth events in 8- and 9-year-old children. *Health Psychology, 24*(3), 316–320.

Andrews, J.A., & Peterson, M. (2006). The development of social images of substance users in children: A Guttman unidimensional scaling approach. *Journal of Substance Use, 11*(5), 305–321.

Armitage, C.J., & Conner, M. (2000). Social cognition models and health behaviour: A structured review. *Psychology & Health, 15*(2), 173–189.

Armor, D., & Taylor, S.E. (1998). Situated optimism: Specific outcome expectancies and self-regulation. *Advances in Experimental Social Psychology, 30*, 309–379.

Armor, D.A., & Sackett, A.M. (2006). Accuracy, error, and bias in predictions for real versus hypothetical events. *Journal of Personality and Social Psychology, 91*(4), 583–600.

Avis, N.E., Smith, K.W., & McKinlay, J.B. (1989). Accuracy of perceptions of heart attack risk: What influences perceptions and can they be changed? *American Journal of Public Health, 79*(12), 1608–1612.

Bailis, D.S., Chipperfield, J.G., & Perry, R.P. (2005). Optimistic social comparisons of older adults low in primary control: A prospective analysis of hospitalization and mortality. *Health Psychology, 24*(4), 393–401.

Balcetis, E. (2008). Where the motivation resides and self-deception hides: How motivated cognition accomplishes self-deception. *Social and Personality Psychology Compass, 2*(1), 361–381.

Bauer, I., Wrosch, C., & Jobin, J. (2008). I'm better off than most other people: The role of social comparisons for coping with regret in young adulthood and old age. *Psychology and Aging, 23*(4), 800–811.

Baumeister, R.F., Bratslavsky, E., Finkenauer, C., & Vohs, K.D. (2001). Bad is stronger than good. *Review of General Psychology, 5*(4), 323–370.

Baumeister, R.F. (1998). The self. In D.T. Gilbert, S.T. Fiske, & G. Lindzey (Eds.), *The handbook of social psychology* Vols. 1 and 2 (4th ed., pp. 680–740). New York, NY: McGraw-Hill.

Bennett, P., Wilkinson, C., Turner, J., Edwards, R.T., France, B., Griffin, G., et al. (2009). Factors associated with intrusive cancer-related worries in women undergoing cancer genetic risk assessment. *Familial Cancer, 8*(2), 159–165.

Bonnin-Scaon, S., Lafon, P., Chasseigne, G., Mullet, E., & Sorum, P.C. (2002). Learning the relationship between smoking, drinking alcohol and the risk of esophageal cancer. *Health Education Research, 17*(4), 415–424.

Bostrom, A. (1997). Risk perceptions: "Experts" vs. "lay people." *Duke Environmental Law and Policy Forum, 8*(1), 101–113.

Bowen, D.J., Fries, E., & Hopp, H.P. (1994). Effects of dietary fat feedback on behavioral and psychological variables. *Journal of Behavioral Medicine, 17*(6), 589–604.

Brewer, N.T., Chapman, G.B., Gibbons, F.X., Gerrard, M., McCaul, K.D., & Weinstein, N.D. (2007). Meta-analysis of the relationship between risk perception and health behavior: The example of vaccination. *Health Psychology, 26*(2), 136–145.

Cacioppo, J.T., Gardner, W.L., & Berntson, G.G. (1999). The affect system has parallel and integrative processing components: Form follows function. *Journal of Personality and Social Psychology, 76*(5), 839–855.

Campbell, W.K., & Sedikides, C. (1999). Self-threat magnifies the self-serving bias: A meta-analytic integration. *Review of General Psychology, 3*(1), 23–43.

Carroll, P., Sweeny, K., & Shepperd, J.A. (2006). Forsaking optimism. *Review of General Psychology, 10*(1), 56–73.

Chambers, J.R., & Windschitl, P.D. (2004). Biases in social comparative judgments: The role of nonmotivated factors in above-average and comparative-optimism effects. *Psychological Bulletin, 130*(5), 813–838.

Channer, K.S., James, M.A., Papouchado, M., & Russel Rees, J. (1987). Failure of a negative exercise test to reassure patients with chest pain. *Quarterly Journal of Medicine, 63*(240), 315–322.

Chassin, L.A., Tetzloff, C., & Hershey, M. (1985). Self-image and social-image factors in adolescent alcohol use. *Journal of Studies on Alcohol, 46*(1), 39–47.

Cheng, S.-T., Fung, H., & Chan, A. (2007). Maintaining self-rated health through social comparison in old age. *The Journals of *Gerontology: Series B: Psychological Sciences and Social Sciences, 62*(5), 277–285.

Cioffi, D. (1991). Asymmetry of doubt in medical self-diagnosis: The ambiguity of "uncertain wellness." *Journal of Personality and Social Psychology, 61*(6), 969–980.

Cohen, D.J., & Bruce, K.E. (1997). Sex and mortality: Real risk and perceived vulnerability. *Journal of Sex Research, 34*(3), 279–291.

Cohn, L.D., Macfarlane, S., Yanez, C., & Imai, W.K. (1995). Risk-perception: Differences between adolescents and adults. *Health Psychology, 14*(3), 217–222.

Covey, J.A., & Davies, A.D.M. (2004). Are people unrealistically optimistic? It depends how you ask them. *British Journal of Health Psychology, 9*(1), 39–49.

Croyle, R.T. (1990). Biased appraisal of high blood pressure. *Preventive Medicine, 19*(1), 40–44.

Croyle, R.T., Loftus, E.F., Barger, S.D., Sun, Y.-C., Hart, M., & Gettig, J. (2006). How well do people recall risk factor test results? Accuracy and bias among cholesterol screening participants. *Health Psychology, 25*(3), 425–432.

Croyle, R.T., Sun, Y.-C., & Hart, M. (1997). Processing risk factor information: Defensive biases in health-related. In K.J. Petrie, & J.A. Weinman (Eds.), *Perceptions of health and illness: Current research and applications* (pp. 267–290). Amsterdam, Netherlands: Harwood Academic Publishers.

Croyle, R.T., Sun, Y. -C., & Louie, D.H. (1993). Psychological minimization of cholesterol test results: Moderators of appraisal in college students and community residents. *Health Psychology, 12*(6), 503–507.

Dawson, E., Gilovich, T., & Regan, D.T. (2002). Motivated reasoning and performance on the Wason Selection Task. *Personality and Social Psychology Bulletin, 28*(10), 1379–1387.

Dillard, A.J., McCaul, K.D., Kelso, P.D., & Klein, W.M.P. (2006). Resisting good news: Reactions to breast cancer risk communication. *Health Communication, 19*(2), 115–123.

Ditto, P.H., & Croyle, R.T. (1995). Understanding the impact of risk factor test results: Insights from a basic research program. In R.T. Croyle (Ed.), *Psychosocial effects of screening for disease prevention and detection* (pp. 144–181). New York, NY: Oxford University Press.

Ditto, P.H., Jemmott, J.B., & Darley, J.M. (1988). Appraising the threat of illness: A mental representational approach. *Health Psychology, 7*(2), 183–201.

Ditto, P.H., & Lopez, D.F. (1992). Motivated skepticism: Use of differential decision criteria for preferred and nonpreferred conclusions. *Journal of Personality and Social Psychology, 63*(4), 568–584.

Ditto, P.H., Munro, G.D., Apanovitch, A.M., Scepansky, J.A., & Lockhart, L.K. (2003). Spontaneous skepticism: The interplay of motivation and expectation in responses to favorable and unfavorable medical diagnoses. *Personality and Social Psychology Bulletin, 29*(9), 1120–1132.

Ditto, P.H., Scepansky, J.A., Munro, G.D., Apanovitch, A.M., & Lockhart, L.K. (1998). Motivated sensitivity to preference-inconsistent information. *Journal of Personality and Social Psychology, 75*(1), 53–69.

Doll, R., Peto, R., Wheatley, K., Gray, R., & Sutherland, I. (1994). Mortality in relation to smoking: 40 years' observations on male British doctors. *British Medical Journal, 309*(6959), 901–911.

Doyle, J.K. (1997). Judging cumulative risk. *Journal of Applied Social Psychology, 27*(6), 500–524.

Ebner, N.C., Freund, A.M., & Baltes, P.B. (2006). Developmental changes in personal goal orientation from young to late adulthood: From striving for gains to maintenance and prevention of losses. *Psychology and Aging, 21*(4), 664–678.

Edwards, A., Elwyn, G., Covey, J., Matthews, E., & Pill, R. (2001). Presenting risk information - A review of the effects of "framing" and other manipulations on patient outcomes. *Journal of Health Communication, 6*(1), 61–82.

Edwards, K., & Smith, E.E. (1996). A disconfirmation bias in the evaluation of arguments. *Journal of Personality and Social Psychology, 71*(1), 5–24.

Eisenstadt, D., & Leippe, M.R. (1994). The self-comparison process and self-discrepant feedback: Consequences of learning you are what you thought you were not. *Journal of Personality and Social Psychology, 67*(4), 611–626.

Eiser, J.R., Reicher, S.D., & Podpadec, T.J. (1995). Smokers' and non-smokers' estimates of their personal risk of cancer and of the incremental risk attributable to cigarette smoking. *Addiction Research, 3*(3), 221–229.

Fischhoff, B., Bostrom, A., & Quadrel, M.J. (2000). Risk perception and communication. In T. Connolly, H.R. Arkes, & K.R. Hammond (Eds.), *Judgment and decision making: An interdisciplinary reader* (2nd ed., pp. 479–499). New York, NY: Cambridge University Press.

Fox, C.S., Pencina, M.J., Wilson, P.W., Paynter, N.P., Vasan, R.S., & D'Agostino, R.B., Sr. (2008). Lifetime risk of cardiovascular disease among individuals with and without diabetes stratified by obesity status in the Framingham heart study. *Diabetes Care, 31*(8), 1582–1584.

Frank, E., Winklcby, M., Fortmann, S.P., & Farquhar, J.W. (1993). Cardiovascular disease risk-factors: Improvements in knowledge and behavior in the 1980s. *American Journal of Public Health, 83*(4), 590–593.

French, D.P., & Hevey, D. (2008). What do people think about when answering questionnaires to assess unrealistic optimism about skin cancer? A think aloud study. *Psychology, Health & Medicine, 13*(1), 63–74.

French, D.P., & Marteau, T. (2007). Communicating risk. In S. Ayers, A. Baum, C. McManus, S. Newman, K. Wallston, & J. Weinman (Eds.), *Cambridge handbook of psychology, health and medicine* (pp. 431–435). Cambridge, UK: Cambridge University Press.

French, D.P., Sutton, S., Kinmonth, A.L., & Marteau, T.M. (2006). Assessing perceptions of risks due to multiple hazards. *Journal of Risk Research, 9*(6), 657–682.

Gans, K.M., Assmann, S.F., Sallar, A., & Lasater, T.M. (1999). Knowledge of cardiovascular disease prevention: An analysis from two New England communities. *Preventive Medicine: An International Journal Devoted to Practice and Theory, 29*(4), 229–237.

Gerrard, M., Gibbons, F.X., Lane, D.J., & Stock, M.L. (2005). Smoking cessation: Social comparison level predicts success for adult smokers. *Health Psychology, 24*(6), 623–629.

Gibbons, F.X., & Gerrard, M. (1997). Health images and their effects on health behavior. In B.P. Buunk, & F.X. Gibbons (Eds.), *Health, coping, and well-being: Perspectives from social comparison theory* (pp. 63–94). Mahwah, NJ: Lawrence Erlbaum Associates Publishers.

Gigerenzer, G., Gaissmaier, W., Kurz-Milcke, E., Schwartz, L.M., & Woloshin, S. (2008). Helping doctors and patients make sense of health statistics. *Psychological Science in the Public Interest, 8*(2), 53–96.

Gondos, A., Bray, F., Hakulinen, T., & Brenner, H. (2009). Trends in cancer survival in 11 European populations from 1990 to 2009: A model-based analysis. *Annals of Oncology, 20*(3), 564–573.

Gramling, R., Klein, W., Roberts, M., Waring, M.E., Gramling, D., & Eaton, C.B. (2008). Self-rated cardiovascular risk and 15-year cardiovascular mortality. *Annals of Family Medicine, 6*(4), 302–306.

Graves, K.D., Huerta, E., Cullen, J., Kaufman, E., Sheppard, V., Luta, G., et al. (2008). Perceived risk of breast cancer among Latinas attending community clinics: Risk comprehension and relationship with mammography adherence. *Cancer Causes and Control, 19*(10), 1373–1382.

Gump, B.B., Kulik, J.A., & Henderson, G.R. (1998). Blaming the same-sex victim in HIV-prevention messages: Further examination of the self-protective similarity bias. *Basic and Applied Social Psychology, 20*(2), 123–132.

Hahn, A., & Renner, B. (1998). Perception of health risks: How smoker status affects defensive optimism. *Anxiety, Stress and Coping, 11*(2), 93–112.

Hampson, S.E., Andrews, J.A., Lee, M.E., Foster, L.S., Glasgow, R.E., & Lichtenstein, E. (1998). Lay understanding of synergistic risk: The case of radon and cigarette smoking. *Risk Analysis, 18*(3), 343–350.

Hampson, S.E., Andrews, J.A., Lee, M.E., Lichtenstein, E., & Barckley, M. (2000). Radon and cigarette smoking: Perceptions of this synergistic health risk. *Health Psychology, 19*(3), 247–252.

Harris, P.R., Griffin, D.W., & Murray, S. (2008). Testing the limits of optimistic bias: Event and person moderators in a multilevel framework. *Journal of Personality and Social Psychology, 95*(5), 1225–1237.

Heckhausen, J., & Brim, O.G. (1997). Perceived problems for self and others: Self-protection by social downgrading throughout adulthood. *Psychology and Aging, 12*(4), 610–619.

Heckhausen, J., & Krueger, J. (1993). Developmental expectations for the self and most other people: Age grading in three functions of social comparison. *Developmental Psychology, 29*(3), 539–548.

Heine, S.J. (2004). Positive self-views: Understanding universals and variability across cultures. *Journal of Cultural and Evolutionary Psychology, 2*(1–2), 109–122.

Heine, S.J., & Buchtel, E.E. (2009). Personality: The universal and the culturally specific. *Annual Review of Psychology, 60*, 369–394.

Heine, S.J., & Hamamura, T. (2007). In search of East Asian self-enhancement. *Personality and Social Psychology Review, 11*(1), 1–24.

Helweg-Larsen, M., & Shepperd, J.A. (2001). Do moderators of the optimistic bias affect personal or target risk estimates? A review of the literature. *Personality and Social Psychology Review, 5*, 74–95.

Hermand, D., Mullet, E., & Lavieville, S. (1997). Perception of the combined effects of smoking and alcohol on cancer risks in never smokers and heavy smokers. *Journal of Health Psychology, 2*(4), 481–491.

Hermand, D., Mullet, E., Sorum, P., & Tillard, B. (2000). Perception of the combined effects of smoking and alcohol on cancer risks in alcoholics. *European Review of Applied Psychology, 50*(3), 321–326.

Heron, M., Hoyert, D.L., Murphy, S.L., Xu, J., Kochanek, K.D., & Tejada-Vera, B. (2009). Deaths: Final data for 2006. *National Vital Statistics Reports, 57*(14), 1–134.

Hertwig, R., Pachur, T., & Kurzenhäuser, S. (2005). Judgments of risk frequencies: Tests of possible cognitive mechanisms. *Journal of Experimental Psychology: Learning, Memory, and Cognition, 31*(4), 621–642.

Hevey, D., French, D.P., Marteau, T.M., & Sutton, S. (2009). Assessing unrealistic optimism: Impact of different approaches to measuring susceptibility to diabetes. *Journal of Health Psychology, 14*(3), 372–377.

Hilgart, J., Phelps, C., Bennett, P., Hood, K., Brain, K., & Murray, A. (2010). "I have always believed I was at high risk . . ." The role of expectation in emotional responses to the receipt of an average, moderate or high cancer genetic risk assessment result: A thematic analysis of free-text questionnaire comments. *Familial Cancer 9*(3), 469–472.

Hilton, J.L., Klein, J.G., & von Hippel, W. (1991). Attention allocation and impression formation. *Personality and Social Psychology Bulletin, 17*(5), 548–559.

Hoffrage, U., Lindsey, S., Hertwig, R., & Gigerenzer, G. (2000). Communicating statistical information. *Science, 290*(5500), 2261–2262.

Hooker, K., & Kaus, C.R. (1994). Health-related possible selves in young and middle adulthood. *Psychology and Aging, 9*(1), 126–133.

Humphrey, L.L., Fu, R.W., Buckley, D.I., Freeman, M., & Helfand, M. (2008). Periodontal disease and coronary heart disease incidence: A systematic review and meta-analysis. *Journal of General Internal Medicine, 23*(12), 2079–2086.

Inumiya, Y., Choi, I. -H., Yoon, D. -H., Seo, D. -H., & Han, S.-Y. (1999). The relationship between unrealistic optimism and independent-interdependent construals of self in Korean culture. *Korean Journal of Social & Personality Psychology, 13*(1), 183–201.

Jemmott, J.B., 3rd, Ditto, P.H., & Croyle, R.T. (1986). Judging health status: Effects of perceived prevalence and personal relevance. *Journal of Personality and Social Psychology, 50*(5), 899–905.

Kahneman, D., & Tversky, A. (1972). Subjective probability: A judgment of representativeness. *Cognitive Psychology, 3*(3), 430–454.

Klar, Y., & Giladi, E.E. (1999). Are most people happier than their peers, or are they just happy? *Personality and Social Psychology Bulletin, 25*(5), 585–594.

Klein, W.M., & Weinstein, N.D. (1997). Social comparison and unrealistic optimism about personal risk. In B.P. Buunk, & F.X. Gibbons (Eds.), *Health, coping, and well-being: Perspectives from social comparison theory* (pp. 25–61). Mahwah, NJ: Lawrence Erlbaum Associates Publishers.

Knäuper, B., Kornik, R., Atkinson, K., Guberman, C., & Aydin, C. (2005). Motivation influences the underestimation of cumulative risk. *Personality and Social Psychology Bulletin, 31*(11), 1511–1523.

Kraus, N., Malmfors, T., & Slovic, P. (1992). Intuitive toxicology - expert and lay judgements of chemical risks. *Risk Analysis, 12*(2), 215–232.

Kreuter, M.W., & Strecher, V.J. (1996). Do tailored behavior change messages enhance the effectiveness of health risk appraisal? Results from a randomized trial. *Health Education Research, 11*(1), 97–105.

Kruger, J., Windschitl, P.D., Burrus, J., Fessel, F., & Chambers, J.R. (2008). The rational side of egocentrism in social comparisons. *Journal of Experimental Social Psychology, 44*(2), 220–232.

Kunda, Z. (1987). Motivated inference: Self-serving generation and evaluation of causal theories. *Journal of Personality and Social Psychology, 53*(4), 636–647.

Kunda, Z. (1990). The case for motivated reasoning. *Psychological Bulletin, 108*(3), 480–498.

Lek, Y.-Y., & Bishop, G.D. (1995). Perceived vulnerability to illness threats: The role of disease type, risk factor perception and attributions. *Psychology & Health, 10*(3), 205–219.

Lench, H.C., & Ditto, P.H. (2008). Automatic optimism: Biased use of base rate information for positive and negative events. *Journal of Experimental Social Psychology, 44*(3), 631–639.

Leventhal, H., & Cleary, P.D. (1980). The smoking problem: A review of the research and theory in behavioral risk modification. *Psychological Bulletin, 88*(2), 370–405.

Leventhal, H., Leventhal, E.A., & Contrada, R.J. (1998). Self-regulation, health, and behavior: A perceptual-cognitive approach. *Psychology & Health, 13*(4), 717–733.

Liberman, A., & Chaiken, S. (1992). Defensive processing of personally relevant health messages. *Personality and Social Psychology Bulletin, 18*(6), 669–679.

Lichtenstein, S., Slovic, P., Fischhoff, B., Layman, M., & Combs, B. (1978). Judged frequency of lethal events. *Journal of Experimental Psychology: Human Learning and Memory, 4*(6), 551–578.

Linville, P.W., Fischer, G.W., & Fischhoff, B. (1993). AIDS risk perceptions and decision biases. In J.B. Pryor, & G.D. Reeder (Eds.), *The social psychology of HIV infection* (pp. 5–38). Hillsdale, NJ: Lawrence Erlbaum Associates.

Lipkus, I.M. (2007). Numeric, verbal, and visual formats of conveying health risks: Suggested best practices and future recommendations. *Medical Decision Making, 27*(5), 696–713.

Lipkus, I.M., Kuchibhatla, M., McBride, C.M., Bosworth, H.B., Pollak, K.I., Siegler, I.C., et al. (2000). Relationships among breast cancer perceived absolute risk, comparative risk, and worries. *Cancer Epidemiology Biomarkers & Prevention, 9*(9), 973–975.

Loewenstein, G.F., Weber, E.U., Hsee, C.K., & Welch, N. (2001). Risk as feelings. *Psychological Bulletin, 127*(2), 267–286.

Lord, C.G., Ross, L., & Lepper, M.R. (1979). Biased assimilation and attitude polarization: The effects of prior theories on subsequently considered evidence. *Journal of Personality and Social Psychology, 37*(11), 2098–2109.

Marteau, T.M., Roberts, S., LaRusse, S., & Green, R.C. (2005). Predictive genetic testing for Alzheimer's disease: Impact upon risk perception. *Risk Analysis, 25*(2), 397–404.

McCaul, K.D., Canevello, A.B., Mathwig, J.L., & Klein, W.M.P. (2003). Risk communication and worry about breast cancer. *Psychology, Health & Medicine, 8*(4), 379.

McCaul, K.D., Thiesse-Duffy, E., & Wilson, P. (1992). Coping with medical diagnosis: The effects of at-risk versus disease labels over time. *Journal of Applied Social Psychology, 22*(17), 1340–1355.

McKenney, J.L., Lapane, K.L., Assaf, A.R., & Carleton, R.A. (1995). The association between perceived risk and actual cardiovascular-disease. *Epidemiology, 6*(6), 612–616.

Michie, S., Weinman, J., Miller, J., Collins, V., Halliday, J., & Marteau, T.M. (2002). Predictive genetic testing: High risk expectations in the face of low risk information. *Journal of Behavioral Medicine, 25*(1), 33–50.

Millstein, S.G., & Halpern-Felsher, B.L. (2002). Perceptions of risk and vulnerability. *Journal of Adolescent Health, 31*(Suppl.1), 10–27.

Misovich, S.J., Fisher, J.D., & Fisher, W.A. (1997). Social comparison processes and AIDS risk and AIDS preventive behavior. In B.P. Buunk, & F.X. Gibbons (Eds.), *Health, coping, and well-being: Perspectives from social comparison theory* (pp. 95–123). Mahwah, NJ: Lawrence Erlbaum Associates Publishers.

Moore, D. (2007). When good = better than average. *Judgment and Decision Making, 2*(5), 277–291.

Moore, D.A., & Kim, T.G. (2003). Myopic social prediction and the solo comparison effect. *Journal of Personality and Social Psychology, 85*(6), 1121–1135.

Moore, S., & Rosenthal, D.A. (1991). Adolescent invulnerability and perceptions of AIDS risk. *Journal of Adolescent Research, 6*(2), 164–180.

Nerenz, D.R., Leventhal, H., Love, R.R., & Ringler, K.E. (1984). Psychological aspects of cancer chemotherapy. *International Review of Applied Psychology, 33*(4), 521–529.

Nurmi, J.-E. (1992). Age differences in adult life goals, concerns, and their temporal extension: A life course approach to future-oriented motivation. *International Journal of Behavioral Development, 15*(4), 487–508.

Oncken, C., McKee, S., Krishnan-Sarin, S., O'Malley, S., & Mazure, C.M. (2005). Knowledge and perceived risk of smoking-related conditions: A survey of cigarette smokers. *Preventive Medicine, 40*(6), 779–784.

Orbell, S., & Hagger, M. (2006). Temporal framing and the decision to take part in type 2 diabetes screening: Effects of individual differences in consideration of future consequences on persuasion. *Health Psychology, 25*(4), 537–548.

Pahl, S., Eiser, J.R., & White, M.P. (2009). Boundaries of self-positivity: The effect of comparison focus in self-friend comparisons. *Journal of Social Psychology, 149*(4), 413–424.

Panzer, M., & Renner, B. (2008). To be or not to be at risk: Spontaneous reactions to risk information. *Psychology & Health, 23*(5), 617–627.

Panzer, M., & Renner, B. (2009). Spontaneous reactions to health risk feedback: A network perspective. *Journal of Behavioral Medicine, 32*(4), 317–327.

Peretti-Watel, P., Constance, J., Guilbert, P., Gautier, A., Beck, F., & Moatti, J.P. (2007). Smoking too few cigarettes to be at risk? Smokers' perceptions of risk and risk denial, a French survey. *Tobacco Control, 16*(5), 351–356.

Perloff, L.S., & Fetzer, B.K. (1986). Self-other judgments and perceived vulnerability to victimization. *Journal of Personality and Social Psychology, 50*(3), 502–510.

Peters, E., Dieckmann, N.F., Vastfjall, D., Mertz, C.K., Slovic, P., & Hibbard, J.H. (2009). Bringing meaning to numbers: The impact of evaluative categories on decisions. *Journal of Experimental Psychology: Applied, 15*(3), 213–227.

Petty, R.E., & Cacioppo, J.T. (1986). Communication and persuasion: Central and peripheral routes to attitude changes. New York, NY: Springer-Verlag.

Pinkerton, S.D., Wagner-Raphael, L.I., Craun, C.A., & Abramson, P.R. (2000). A quantitative study of the accuracy of college students' HIV risk estimates. *Journal of Applied Biobehavioral Research, 5*(1), 1–25.

Pratto, F., & John, O.P. (1991). Automatic vigilance: The attention-grabbing power of negative social information. *Journal of Personality and Social Psychology, 61*(3), 380–391.

Pyszczynski, T., & Greenberg, J. (1987). Toward an integration of cognitive and motivational perspectives on social inference: A biased hypothesis-testing model. In L. Berkowitz (Ed.), *Advances in experimental social psychology* Vol. 20 (pp. 297–340). San Diego, CA: Academic Press.

Quadrel, M.J., Fischhoff, B., & Davis, W. (1993). Adolescent (in)vulnerability. *American Psychologist, 48*(2), 102–116.

Ranby, K.W., Aiken, L.S., Gerend, M.A., & Erchull, M.J. (2010). Perceived susceptibility measures are not interchangeable: Absolute, direct comparative, and indirect comparative risk. *Health Psychology, 29*(1), 20–28.

Raude, J., Fischler, C., Setbon, M., & Flahault, A. (2005). Scientist and public responses to BSE-related risk: A comparative study. *Journal of Risk Research, 8*(7), 663–678.

Renner, B. (2004). Biased reasoning: Adaptive responses to health risk feedback. *Personality and Social Psychology Bulletin, 30,* 384–396.

Renner, B., Gutiérrez-Dona, B., Kwon, S., & Schwarzer, R. (2011). *Risk perception across age groups and countries: Becoming more vulnerable but being still invincible.* Manuscript submitted for publication.

Renner, B., Hankonen, N., Ghisletta, P., & Absetz, P. (2011). *Dynamic psychological and behavioral changes in the adoption and maintenance of exercise.* Manuscript submitted for publication.

Renner, B., Knoll, N., & Schwarzer, R. (2000). Age and body weight make a difference in optimistic health beliefs and nutrition behaviors. *International Journal of Behavioral Medicine, 7,* 143–159.

Renner, B., Schüz, B., & Sniehotta, F. (2008). Preventive health behaviour and adaptive accuracy of risk perceptions. *Risk Analysis, 28*(3), 741–748.

Renner, B., & Schwarzer, R. (2003). Social-cognitive factors in health behavior change. In J. Suls, & K.A. Wallston (Eds.), *Social psychological foundations of health and illness* (pp. 169–196). Malden, MA: Blackwell Publishing.

Renner, B., Spivak, Y., Kwon, S., & Schwarzer, R. (2007). Does age make a difference? Predicting physical activity of South Koreans. *Psychology and Aging, 22*(3), 482–493.

Reuter, T., & Renner, B. (2011). *Who takes precautionary action in the face of a new emerging H1N1 influenza?* Manuscript submitted for publication.

Rise, J., Strype, J., & Sutton, S. (2002). Comparative risk ratings and lung cancer among Norwegian smokers. *Addiction Research & Theory, 10*(3), 313–320.

Rose, J.P., Endo, Y., Windschitl, P.D., & Suls, J. (2008). Cultural differences in unrealistic optimism and pessimism: The role of egocentrism and direct versus indirect comparison measures. *Personality and Social Psychology Bulletin, 34*(9), 1236–1248.

Rothman, A.J., & Salovey, P. (2007). The reciprocal relation between principles and practice: Social psychology and health behavior. In A.W. Kruglanski, & E.T. Higgins (Eds.), *Social psychology: Handbook of basic principles* (2nd ed., pp. 826–849). New York, NY: Guilford Press.

Rottenstreich, Y., & Hsee, C.K. (2001). Money, kisses, and electric shocks: On the affective psychology of risk. *Psychological Science, 12*(3), 185–190.

Rowe, G., & Wright, G. (2001). Differences in expert and lay judgments of risk: Myth or reality? *Risk Analysis, 21*(2), 341–356.

Rybash, J.W., Roodin, P.A., & Hoyer, W.J. (1995). *Adult development and aging.* Madison, WI: Brown & Benchmark.

Sastre, M.T., Mullet, E., & Sorum, P.C. (1999). Relationship between cigarette dose and perceived risk of lung cancer. *Preventive Medicine, 28*(6), 566–571.

Savadori, L., Savio, S., Nicotra, E., Rumiati, R., Finucane, M., & Slovic, P. (2004). Expert and public perception of risk from biotechnology. *Risk Analysis, 24*(5), 1289–1299.

Schapira, M.M., Davids, S.L., McAuliffe, T.L., & Nattinger, A.B. (2004). Agreement between scales in the measurement of breast cancer risk perceptions. *Risk Analysis, 24*(3), 665–673.

Schwartz, L.M., Woloshin, S., Black, W.C., & Welch, H.G. (1997). The role of numeracy in understanding the benefit of screening mammography. *Annals of Internal Medicine, 127*(11), 966–972.

Schwarz, N. (1998). Warmer and more social: Recent developments in cognitive social psychology. *Annual Review of Sociology, 24,* 239–264.

Schwarzer, R., & Renner, B. (2000). Social-cognitive predictors of health behavior: Action self-efficacy and coping self-efficacy. *Health Psychology, 19,* 487–495.

Scott, S., Prior, L., Wood, F., & Gray, J. (2005). Repositioning the patient: The implications of being "at risk." *Social Science & Medicine, 60*(8), 1869–1879.

Sedikides, C., Gaertner, L., & Vevea, J.L. (2005). Pancultural self-enhancement reloaded: A meta-analytic reply to Heine (2005). *Journal of Personality and Social Psychology, 89*(4), 539–551.

Sedikides, C., & Green, J.D. (2000). On the self-protective nature of inconsistency-negativity management: Using the person memory paradigm to examine self-referent memory. *Journal of Personality and Social Psychology, 79*(6), 906–922.

Shaklee, H., & Fischhoff, B. (1990). The psychology of contraceptive surprises: Cumulative risk and contraceptive effectiveness. *Journal of Applied Social Psychology, 20*(5), 385–403.

Shepperd, J.A., Carroll, P., Grace, J., & Terry, M. (2002). Exploring the causes of comparative optimism. *Psychologica Belgica, 42*(1–2), 65–98.

Shrauger, J.S. (1975). Responses to evaluation as a function of initial self-perceptions. *Psychological Bulletin, 82*(4), 581–596.

Slovic, P. (1987). Perception of risk. *Science, 236*(4799), 280–285.

Slovic, P. (2000a). *The perception of risk.* London: Earthscan Publications.

Slovic, P. (2000b). What does it mean to know a cumulative risk? Adolescents' perceptions of short-term and long-term consequences of smoking. *Journal of Behavioral Decision Making, 13*(2), 259–266.

Slovic, P., Fischhoff, B. & Lichtenstein, S. (1985). Characterizing perceived risk. In R.W. Kates, C. Hohenemser, & J.X. Kasperson (Eds.), *Perilous progress: Managing the hazards of technology* (pp. 91–123). Boulder, CO: Westview.

Staudinger, U.M., Freund, A., Linden, M., & Maas, I. (1999). Self, personality, and life management: Psychological resilience and vulnerability. In P.B. Baltes, & K.U. Mayer (Eds.), *The Berlin aging study: Aging from 70 to 100* (pp. 302–326). New York, NY: Cambridge University Press.

Stone, E.R., Sieck, W.R., Bull, B.E., Yates, J.F., Parks, S.C., & Rush, C.J. (2003). Foreground:background salience: Explaining the effects of graphical displays on risk avoidance. *Organizational Behavior and Human Decision Processes, 90*(1), 19–36.

Sutton, S. (1998). How ordinary people in Great Britain perceive the health risks of smoking. *Journal of Epidemiology and Community Health, 52*(5), 338–339.

Sutton, S. (2002). Influencing optimism in smokers by giving information about the average smoker. *Risk, Decision & Policy, 7*(2), 165–174.

Swann, W.B., Griffin, J.J., Predmore, S.C., & Gaines, B. (1987). The cognitive-affective crossfire: When self-consistency confronts self-enhancement. *Journal of Personality and Social Psychology, 52*(5), 881–889.

Taubenberger, J.K., & Morens, D.M. (2006). 1918 influenza: The mother of all pandemics. *Emerging Infectious Diseases, 12*(1), 15–22.

Taylor, K.M., & Shepperd, J.A. (1998). Bracing for the worst: Severity, testing, and feedback timing as moderators of the optimistic bias. *Personality and Social Psychology Bulletin, 24*(9), 915–926.

Taylor, S.E. (1991). Asymmetrical effects of positive and negative events: The mobilization minimization hypothesis. *Psychological Bulletin, 110*(1), 67–85.

Taylor, S.E., & Brown, J.D. (1988). Illusion and well-being: A social psychological perspective on mental health. *Psychological Bulletin, 103*(2), 193–210.

Tennen, H., McKee, T.E., & Affleck, G. (2000). Social comparison processes in health and illness. In J. Suls, & L. Wheeler (Eds.), *Handbook of social comparison: Theory and research* (pp. 443–483). Dordrecht, Netherlands: Kluwer Academic Publishers.

The Asia Pacific Cohort Studies Collaboration. (2009). Impact of cigarette smoking on the relationship between body mass index and coronary heart disease: A pooled analysis of 3264 stroke and 2706 CHD events in 378579 individuals in the Asia Pacific region. *BMC Public Health, 9*, 294–304.

Thornton, B., Gibbons, F.X., & Gerrard, M. (2002). Risk perception and prototype perception: Independent processes predicting risk behavior. *Personality and Social Psychology Bulletin, 28*(7), 986–999.

van der Pligt, J. (1998). Perceived risk and vulnerability as predictors of precautionary behaviour. *British Journal of Health Psychology, 3*(Part 1), 1–14.

Visschers, V.H.M., Meertens, R.M., Passchier, W.W.F., & de Vries, N.N.K. (2009). Probability information in risk communication: A review of the research literature. *Risk Analysis, 29*(2), 267–287.

von Hippel, W., Lakin, J.L., & Shakarchi, R.J. (2005). Individual differences in motivated social cognition: The case of self-serving information processing. *Personality and Social Psychology Bulletin, 31*(10), 1347–1357.

Wardle, J., Williamson, S., Sutton, S., Biran, A., McCaffery, K., Cuzick, J., et al. (2003). Psychological impact of colorectal cancer screening. *Health Psychology, 22*(1), 54–59.

Weinstein, N.D. (1980). Unrealistic optimism about future life events. *Journal of Personality and Social Psychology, 39*(5), 806–820.

Weinstein, N.D. (1982). Unrealistic optimism about susceptibility to health problems. *Journal of Behavioral Medicine, 5*(4), 441–460.

Weinstein, N.D. (1987). Unrealistic optimism about susceptibility to health problems: Conclusions from a community-wide sample. *Journal of Behavioral Medicine, 10*(5), 481–500.

Weinstein, N.D. (1993). Testing four competing theories of health-protective behavior. *Health Psychology, 12*(4), 324–333.

Weinstein, N.D. (1998). Accuracy of smokers' risk perceptions. *Annals of Behavioral Medicine, 20*(2), 135–140.

Weinstein, N.D. (2000). Perceived probability, perceived severity, and health-protective behavior. *Health Psychology, 19*(1), 65–74.

Weinstein, N.D. (2003). Exploring the links between risk perceptions and preventive health behavior. In J. Suls, &

K.A. Wallston (Eds.), *Social psychological foundations of health and illness* (pp. 22–53). Malden, MA: Blackwell Publishing.

Weinstein, N.D., Atwood, K., Puleo, E., Fletcher, R., Colditz, G., & Emmons, K.M. (2004). Colon cancer: Risk perceptions and risk communication. *Journal of Health Communication, 9*(1), 53–65.

Weinstein, N.D., & Klein, W.M. (1995). Resistance of personal risk perceptions to debiasing interventions. *Health Psychology, 14*(2), 132–140.

Weinstein, N.D., & Lachendro, E. (1982). Egocentrism as a source of unrealistic optimism. *Personality and Social Psychology Bulletin, 8*(2), 195–200.

Weinstein, N.D., Marcus, S.E., & Moser, R.P. (2005). Smokers' unrealistic optimism about their risk. *Tobacco Control, 14*(1), 55–59.

Weinstein, N.D., Slovic, P., & Gibson, G. (2004). Accuracy and optimism in smokers' beliefs about quitting. *Nicotine & Tobacco Research, 6*, 375–380.

Welch, H.G., Schwartz, L.M., & Woloshin, S. (2000). Are increasing 5-year survival rates evidence of success against cancer? *The Journal of the American Medical Association, 283*(22), 2975–2978.

Welch, H.G., Woloshin, S., Schwartz, L.M., Gordis, L., Gøtzsche, P.C., Harris, R., et al. (2007). Overstating the evidence for lung cancer screening: The international early lung cancer action program (I-ELCAP) study. *Archives of Internal Medicine, 167*(21), 2289–2295.

Welkenhuysen, M., Evers-Kiebooms, G., Decruyenaere, M., & Van Den Berghe, H. (1996). Unrealistic optimism and genetic risk. *Psychology & Health, 11*(4), 479–492.

Whitley, B.E., & Hern, A.L. (1991). Perceptions of vulnerability to pregnancy and the use of effective contraception. *Personality and Social Psychology Bulletin, 17*(1), 104–110.

Wiebe, D.J., & Korbel, C. (2003). Defensive denial, affect, and the self-regulation of health threats. In L.D. Cameron, & H. Leventhal (Eds.), *The self-regulation of health and illness behaviour* (pp. 184–203). New York, NY: Routledge.

Woloshin, S., Schwartz, L.M., Black, W.C., & Welch, H.G. (1999). Women's perceptions of breast cancer risk: How you ask matters. *Medical Decision Making, 19*(3), 221–229.

Woloshin, S., Schwartz, L.M., & Welch, H.G. (2002a). Risk charts: Putting cancer in context. *Journal of the National Cancer Institute, 94*(11), 799–804.

Woloshin, S., Schwartz, L.M., & Welch, H.G. (2002b). Tobacco money: Up in smoke? *Lancet, 359*(9323), 2108–2111.

World Health Organization. (2002). *The World Health Report 2002: Reducing risk, promoting health life.* Retrieved from http://www.who.int/entity/whr/2002/en/whr02_en.pdf.

World Health Organization. (2009). *Pandemic (H1N1) 2009 - Update 64.* Retrieved from http://www.who.int/csr/don/2009_09_04.

Wright, G., Bolger, F., & Rowe, G. (2002). An empirical test of the relative validity of expert and lay judgments of risk. *Risk Analysis, 22*(6), 1107–1122.

Wyer, R.S., & Frey, D. (1983). The effects of feedback about self and others on the recall and judgments of feedback-relevant information. *Journal of Experimental Social Psychology, 19*(6), 540–559.

# Physical Activity and Health: Current Research Trends and Critical Issues

Dawn K. Wilson, Nicole Zarrett, *and* Heather Kitzman-Ulrich

**Abstract**

The field of health psychology may offer unique theoretical and practical approaches for promoting physically active lifestyle changes. This chapter addresses relevant theoretical mediating and moderating factors ranging from cognitive, emotional, and physical to social and environmental influences on improving physical activity (PA) across the lifespan. It highlights the critical need for theoretically driven research that focuses on understanding mediational factors that may explain behavior and behavior change processes. It also focuses on understanding the balance between conducting science-based research using randomized controlled trials (RCTs) versus the need for involving communities in more participatory research for improving community engagement. In addition, it highlights the need for incorporating a developmental perspective and outlines key issues relevant to understanding PA behavior across the lifespan.

**Keywords:** Physical activity research, health, exercise, health psychology, behavior change, disease prevention, randomized controlled trials

Physical inactivity has been shown to be linked to serious public health problems such as obesity, chronic disease, morbidity, and mortality. Being inactive doubles an individual's risk for developing coronary heart disease and has been estimated to result in 23% of all deaths in the United States (Hahn, Teutsch, Rothenberg, & Marks, 1990). National estimates indicate that only slightly over half the population is engaging in leisure time physical activity (PA) on a daily basis (U.S. Department of Health and Human Services [USDHHS], 2008). The important influence of PA on chronic disease reduction, including obesity, and increased longevity has been well-established (Centers for Disease Control and Prevention, 2000; Pate, Davis, Robinson et al., (2006). The CDC-American College of Sports Medicine (ACSM) concluded that moderate-intensity activity equivalent to a brisk walk results in enough benefit to prevent a number of poor health outcomes and death (Pate et al., 2006). A study by Dunn, Marcus, Kampert, et al. (1999) showed that similar fitness levels can be obtained by individuals performing lifestyle activities compared with structured exercise. Despite the beneficial relationship between engagement in PA and health, more than half of the U.S. population is not regularly active at recommended levels of 30 minutes a day, most days of the week (Haskell, I-Min, Pate, et al., 2007; Nelson, Rejeski, Blair et al., 2007). In youth, 37% of students do not participate in 20 minutes of vigorous PA on 3 of the previous 7 days, and African American, Hispanic, and female students are less likely than their white male counterparts to participate in vigorous PA at recommended levels (Pate, Davis, Robinson, et al., 2006). National studies also show that inactivity is more prevalent among African American (35%) than Caucasian (18%) adults (Jones et al., 1998). This has led to national efforts to develop more knowledge about the determinants and mediating factors of inactive behaviors (Baranowski, Anderson, & Carmack, 1998; Wilson, 2008).

National studies have shown that engaging in physically active lifestyles can significantly reduce the risks of chronic disease, morbidity, and mortality.

Regular PA reduces the risk for cardiovascular morbidity and all-cause mortality, and helps to maintain and enhance weight loss (USDHHS, 1996, 2008). Prospective studies indicate that regular PA reduces the risk of non–insulin dependent diabetes mellitus and improves insulin sensitivity (Manson, Nathan, Krolewski, et al., 1992; Manson, Rimm, Stampfer, et al., 1991). The National Heart, Lung, and Blood Institute (NHLBI) convened the Expert Panel on the Identification, Evaluation, and Treatment of Overweight and Obesity in Adults (NHLBI, 1998) and concluded that weight loss among those who are overweight and obese leads to a reduction in risk factors for diabetes and cardiovascular disease. Strong evidence indicates that weight loss reduces blood pressure, reduces serum triglycerides, increases high-density lipoprotein cholesterol, and produces some reduction in total serum cholesterol, low-density lipoprotein cholesterol, blood glucose, and HbA1c (NHLBI, 1998, Kaplan, Wilson, & Hartwell, et al., 1985). This report also concluded that PA is an important component of weight loss treatment, and is one of the best predictors of long-term weight maintenance. A review by Ross, Freeman, Janssen, et al. (2000) also indicated that, when energy deficit is held constant, PA can induce a comparable level of weight loss as caloric reduction. Further, even with modest weight loss, PA has a significant effect of improving the pattern of obesity by reducing abdominal fat (Ross et al., 2000).

The field of health psychology may offer unique theoretical and practical approaches for promoting physically active lifestyle changes. This chapter addresses relevant theoretical mediating and moderating factors ranging from cognitive, emotional and physical to social and environmental influences on improving PA across the lifespan. The mediating variable model proposes a framework for designing interventions and for understanding how interventions work to promote improvements in health behaviors, including the increasing engagement in PA (Baranowski, Anderson, & Carmack., 1998; Baranowski, Cullen, Nicklas, Thompson, & Barnowski, 2003; Wilson, St. George, & Zarrett, 2010). The assumption underlying this approach is that interventions result in behavior change due to changes in mediating variables. Moderating variables may also advance our understanding of intervention effects on improving health behaviors such as PA. More complex moderating factors may be required to advance our knowledge of behavior change processes (Resnicow & Vaughan, 2006).

The purpose of this chapter is to provide the state of the art of critical issues for understanding the impact of PA research on improving health, preventing chronic disease, and for moving the field forward in innovative and important ways. The chapter highlights the critical need for theoretically driven research that focuses on understanding mediational factors that may explain behavior and behavior change processes. We also focus on understanding the balance between conducting science-based research using randomized controlled trials (RCTs) versus the need for involving communities in more participatory research for improving community engagement (Israel, Schulz, Parker et al., 2001). In addition, we highlight the need for incorporating a developmental perspective and outline key issues relevant to understanding PA behavior across the lifespan.

## Importance of Conceptual Frameworks for Guiding Progress

Participation in PA can be best understood through a dynamic systems perspective of human development (see Baltes, 1997; Bronfenbrenner, 2005; Eccles, Wigfield, & Schiefele, 1998; Lerner, 2006; Magnusson & Stattin, 2006; Overton, 2006; Schwartz, 1982; for examples of the conceptualization and application of this theoretical framework). Although a number of different systems models exist, all share the core belief that behavior is influenced by the synergistic relation between individuals and multiple levels of individual and environmental subsystems over time (Bronfenbrenner, 2005; Bronfenbrenner & Morris, 2006; Sallis, Cervero, Ascher, et al., 2006). In particular, Bronfenbrenner's (2005) bioecological model provides a strong macro-paradigm for looking at development as resulting from a complex system of interactions between individuals and the various levels of their environment over time. Specifically, the bioecological model provides a framework for understanding development of health behaviors as shaped by environmental subsystems that include the integration of intrapersonal factors, microsystemic factors (families and institutions), mesosystemic factors (interactions between family and institutions), exosystemic factors (communities, policies), and macrosystemic effects (all systems, micro-, meso-, and exo-, as related to a culture or subculture).

Bronfenbrenner's earlier work stressed the interplay within and across levels of individuals' environments as the primary influence on development, and focused less on the biological contributions and the child's own role in the developmental process. However, more recent versions of the bioecological theory emphasize that all characteristics of the individual—biological, psychological, social, and emotional—must be considered to understand the developmental process (Bronfenbrenner & Morris, 2006). In this more recent model, the child is seen as an active, purposeful agent in the developmental process; characteristics of the whole child both affect and are affected by the interactions that occur within their various environments in a reciprocal fashion over time. A direct implication of this proposition is that understanding adolescent development requires that the network of relations between characteristics of the individual and the ecologies in which he or she develops must be studied in an integrated and temporal manner (Magnusson & Stattin, 2006). Moreover, this idea of a multilevel developmental system emphasizes the potential for change both in the individual and the contexts in which individuals develop in the process of promoting positive development. This underscores the general assumption guiding most modern developmental theories: Development occurs through a process of systemic interactions within and between the individual and the environment, over time (cf., Cairns, Elder, & Costello, 1996; Magnusson & Stattin, 1998; Mahoney & Bergman, 2002). Specifically, developmental period will dictate the type, duration, and intensity of PA. For example, whereas 30–60 minutes of daily activity are recommended for both children and adolescents, to engage preadolescent children in PA, it may be more effective for the activity to be broken down into 15-minute segments throughout the day, given their shorter attention spans and physical abilities (Strong, Malina, Blimkie, et al., 2005).

Applying the bioecological model to individuals' motivation to engage in PA stresses the importance of examining the connected nature between individuals and the social and material influences that characterize their various daily contexts. Put another way, PA choices involve reciprocal processes between the contextual constraints and opportunities for participation within the family, school, and community, and individuals' own motivations to participate (Bouffard, Wimer, & Caronongan et al., 2006; Elder & Conger, 2000; Mahoney, Larson, & Eccles, 2005). For example, in addition to youth PA-based interest and perceived ability, youth participation in a community-based sports program also depends on availability and access to these opportunities in the community (Hirsch, Roffman, Deutsch, et al., 2000; Quinn, 1999), as well as parent support and resources to promote youth interest and involvement (Fredricks

& Eccles, 2005; Zarrett, 2007). A combination of multiple safe, nurturing, and caring environments facilitates adolescents initial and continued engagement by enabling youth to explore a variety of options and roles, establish positive mentor relationships, and develop personal assets (e.g., self-esteem, social skills) (Dunbar, 2002; Roffman, Suaurez-Orozco, & Rhodes, 2003).

Although the bioecological model, and systems theories more generally, provides a broad perspective for explaining behavior, important supplemental theories help to identify the specific intrapersonal (e.g., cognitive, biological, psychosocial) and environmental factors that interact to influence health behaviors such as PA. Bandura's social cognitive theory (SCT) assumes that individual-cognitive factors, environmental events, and behavior are interacting and reciprocal determinants of each other (Bandura, 1991, 1997). In its simplest form, the theory views behavior (in this case, the choice to engage in PA) as resulting from a cyclical process in which an individual's PA self-efficacy (and other attributions) and feedback from the environment encourage or discourage initial and continued pursuit of the activity. In particular, the reciprocal interaction of cognitive factors, such as self-efficacy, and social factors such as instrumental and emotional support from parents and peers, have been important predictors of PA engagement and general health-related trajectories across the lifespan (Bandura, 1991,1997; Wilson, Evans, Williams, et al. 2005).

The Eccles' expectancy-value model (Eccles, 1983; Eccles, Wigfield, & Schiefele, 1998), and its extension, the Eccles' et al. socialization model (Eccles, 1993), also stresses the importance of the bidirectional process that occurs between individuals' competence beliefs and social supports (e.g. socializers' beliefs and behaviors), along with other key factors within the social context that affect achievement behaviors related to health behaviors (e.g., engagement in PA). This model identifies subjective task value (e.g., enjoyment, utility, etc.) as a key intrapersonal factor that influences choices. Specifically, the Eccles' expectancy-value model is founded on the premise that activity-related choices (e.g., engagement in PA etc.) are directly linked to whether the individual attaches importance to the activity (value), and whether he/she feels he/she is good at and expects future success in the activity (expectancy). Eccles and her colleagues have identified multiple factors that contribute to individuals' development of these expectancies and values that cut across multiple ecological levels. An individual's activity choices and his/her activity-specific beliefs, values, and behaviors are both influential on, and influenced by parent behaviors and beliefs, which are all influenced by the resources and supports in the family and child assets, as well as the neighborhood, schools, and the broader cultural milieu. All levels play a key role in determining how individuals select to participate in specific activities such as PA (Eccles, 1993).

In summary, engagement in PA is the product of the combined influence of intrapersonal factors such as motivation/cognitions (e.g., self-efficacy, value of PA, etc.) and genetics (e.g., body type, natural drive to be active), with environmental/contextual factors such as social support, access to resources, value, and role-modeling of PA. These factors remain important in understanding engagement in PA throughout the lifespan from childhood through adulthood.

## Importance of Qualitative Data for Guiding the Field

An increasing use of qualitative data has been the focus of recent studies. Specifically, qualitative data are thought to provide the opportunity to give researchers insights into understanding critical issues related to barriers for engaging in PA, as well as other health behaviors. In addition, qualitative data may provide innovative ideas about conceptual factors that may guide the development of unique and effective interventions that may sustain engagement in healthy behaviors such as PA over a lifetime.

A report by Masse, Dassa, Gauvin, Giles-Corti, and Motl (2002) has highlighted the importance of using qualitative methods to better understand theoretical constructs that may mediate behavior change. A number of focus group studies have been conducted (Griffin, Wilson, Wilcox, et al., 2008; Wilson, Williams, Evans, et al. 2005; Wright, Wilson, Griffin et al., 2010) that indicate several clear barriers to PA exist, especially in underserved populations (low income, minorities). Focus groups were conducted by Wilson, Griffin, Ainsworth, and colleagues (Griffin et al., 2008) with citizens in a rural southeastern community (a low-socioeconomic status [SES], high-crime region) that assessed the needs of a low-income African American community for developing an intervention to increase PA and walking on trails. Three general themes for increasing PA were identified: safety, access, and family and community involvement. Findings from these focus groups revealed that barriers to PA among participants primarily included lacking the motivation to engage in PA and not having role models or social support for PA. Additional barriers for PA among participants of lower income and education were not having access to facilities and opportunities for PA and concerns about safety (both crime- and traffic-related).

Previous investigators (Eyler, Baker, Cromer, et al., 1998; Nies, Vollman, & Cook, 1999) have also conducted focus groups with African American women in rural counties of the United States. These focus groups revealed that cultural beliefs were related to barriers of PA. For example, cultural and social norms related to body image were discussed, and feelings of not wanting to be too skinny or fit were common among African American women. Family obligations were also seen as important and as a barrier in some cases to being physically active. Environmental barriers included hot weather, lack of maintained sidewalks, lack of facilities, safety concerns (due to crime, traffic, and stray dogs), poor transportation, and monetary costs.

In summary, as an example, the results of the focus groups (primarily among low-SES, African Americans) indicate that key environmental barriers to PA include concerns about safety, stray dogs, lack of group participation, lack of available facilities and sidewalks. In addition, African Americans had psychosocial barriers that included lack of self-motivation, cultural body image issues, and lack of time due to family obligations. These data have implications for developing community interventions. This work has led to the funding of a trial known as Positive Action for Today's Health (PATH; Wilson, Trumpeter, St. George, et al. 2010). Specifically, PATH is testing the efficacy of a police-patrolled walking program plus social marketing program that combines an RCT approach with a community engagement participatory research approach (Wilson et al., 2010). The social marketing approach targets psychosocial factors related to attitudes and barriers for PA and addresses issues of motivation, self-efficacy (self-confidence), and social norms related to PA. In addition, the PATH project has marked a walking route and implemented a police-patrolled walking program that may help to reduce concerns about safety and access to PA opportunities. The PATH trial is an innovative example of how qualitative research led to the development of a community-based intervention that specifically tests the efficacy of an intervention that includes both police-patrolled walking and social marketing elements to increase PA in low-income African Americans (compared to a police-patrolled walking program only and a general health education program in two demographically matched communities).

Further research is needed that utilizes such an approach, which involves obtaining qualitative data about barriers and facilitators of PA across the lifespan and in subgroups that may be at increased risk for developing chronic disease and increased rates of mortality. The example of the PATH trial (Wilson et al., 2010) demonstrates that with ongoing community input, RCT trials can be developed that not only test scientific premises but have a high probability of success because community engagement is enhanced by integrating community input throughout the developmental, implementation, and evaluation processes.

## The Importance of RCT Evidence for Guiding the Field

The use of RCTs is important for the field of PA in that scientific integrity promotes evidence-based research that can advance the field in meaningful ways. Randomized controlled trials are considered the gold standard of research designs in that systematic error is minimized and results represent "true" findings (Kaptchuk, 2001). In its simplest form, an RCT aims to evaluate the effects of an intervention by randomizing participants to either an active intervention or a comparison condition. A cornerstone of RCTs is the random assignment of participants, such that the probability of each participant being assigned to a specific group is equal, and the assignment sequence is concealed and not predictable (Altman et al., 2001; Kazdin, 2003). Random assignment of participants reduces threats to internal validity and increases the extent to which group differences can be attributed to the intervention under study (Kazdin, 2003). Another component of well-conducted RCTs is blind assessment of measures, which assures that treatment and outcome measures are not influenced by bias (Kaptchuk, 2001). Findings from RCTs guide clinical practice and the development of future research hypotheses, and are also critical in establishing evidence-based practice guidelines (Kao, Tyson, Blakely, & Lally, 2008). Therefore, well-conducted RCTs are an essential component of the process for developing evidence-based results for dissemination of efficacious interventions to clinical practice and public health interventions. However, the tight scientific rigor can sometimes limit the engagement and willingness of community members to engage in the research process. We discuss these sensitive issues in greater depth below (see Importance of Community-based Trials for Guiding the Field).

Although RCTs are the gold standard of research designs, there are many challenges to conducting RCTs in community-based settings. Studies conducted at the community level, such as in schools, present challenges to traditional RCT methodology (Sanson-Fisher, Bonevski, Green, & D'Este, 2007). For example, utilizing schools as the unit of randomization requires an adequate number of available schools that are geographically distant in order to reduce possible contamination effects. Additionally, a cohort design is typically necessary to obtain a large enough sample of schools necessary for adequate statistical power. For example, in the Active by Choice Today (ACT) trial, a motivational and skill-building after-school program to improve PA levels in underserved (low-income, ethnic minority) sixth-graders, 24 schools were needed to obtain adequate statistical power (Wilson et al., 2008). However, few studies have the resources to conduct an intensive after-school program in 24 schools concurrently; therefore in the ACT study, a cohort design was employed in which six schools were matched on demographic variables and randomized each year over 4 years. Additional challenges in community-based populations include the variety and complex systems inherent within each community (Sanson-Fisher, Bonevski, Green, & D'Este, 2007). For example, in the ACT school-based after-school intervention (Wilson et al., 2008), the climate of the school environment, such as staff motivation and functionality of the school, directly impacted the fidelity of intervention delivery. Efforts were made by staff in the ACT trial to improve intervention fidelity in schools with less than optimal environments through standardized training protocols, internal process evaluations that provided critical feedback to ACT after-school intervention staff, external process evaluations, and booster sessions (Wilson, Griffin, Saunders et al., 2009). Overall, intervention fidelity ratings were high, although somewhat variable, in all 24 schools. The ACT after-school intervention provides one example of a community-based RCT and the challenges faced by researchers conducting these labor-intensive interventions in complex community settings.

Guidelines have been established to encourage sound methodology and accurate reporting of RCTs. To that end, a group of scientists developed the CONSORT statement that was originally published by Begg and colleagues (1996) and has recently been revised by Moher and colleagues (Moher, Schulz, & Altman, 2001). Several peer-reviewed medical and health-related journals require authors to follow the

CONSORT statement (Freemantle, Mason, Haines, & Eccles, 1997; Kaplan, Trudeau, & Davidson, 2004), and data suggest that the implementation of CONSORT has improved the quality of reporting from RCTs (Moher, Schulz, & Altman, 2001). The CONSORT statement includes a checklist and flow diagram to assist authors in accurate reporting of RCTs (Altman et al., 2001). Altman and colleagues (2001) published an explanation and elaboration of the revised CONSORT statement to assist authors in using the guidelines, and their work includes examples of appropriate reporting for each checklist item. Due to the importance of randomization procedures in an RCT, it is especially important to accurately describe how participants were randomized to treatment conditions. Studies have indicated that approximately 50%–70% of published reports do not describe an adequate method for generating random numbers used for randomization (Altman & Dore, 1990; Schulz, Chalmers, Grimes, & Altman, 1994). Additionally, the CONSORT statement describes the importance of specifying whether intent-to-treat analysis was employed, in which all participants enrolled at baseline are included in subsequent analyses. This is particularly relevant as studies that do not use an intent-to-treat analysis may report biased treatment effects (Hollis & Campbell, 1999). Overall, the CONSORT statement provides a tool for researchers to accurately describe their RCT, which in turn will improve the design and conduct of RCTs in the future (Freemantle, Mason, Haines, & Eccles, 1997). Accurate reporting is also vital for consumers of health research to develop policy and conduct syntheses of research findings.

The CONSORT statement has also been endorsed by behavioral medicine journals, such as the *Annals of Behavioral Medicine* and the journal *Health Psychology*. The Society of Behavioral Medicine established the Evidence Based Behavioral Medicine Committee, which published an explanation of how the CONSORT statement is relevant to behavioral medicine studies, such as those dealing with the prevention and treatment of chronic illness, and including PA promotion (Davidson et al., 2003). Behavioral medicine intervention studies provide unique issues related to the CONSORT statement that are highlighted in a statement from the Evidence Based Behavioral Medicine Committee (Davidson et al., 2003). This statement, published by Davidson and colleagues (2003) describes each section of the CONSORT checklist and outlines special issues for behavioral intervention research. One area highlighted by Davidson and colleagues (2003), which is not explicitly included in the CONSORT statement, is how participants were recruited to participate in a study. Authors should note whether participants volunteered to participate or were recruited through representative outreach methods. Another area highlighted in this statement is the need for adequate reporting of intervention details. The authors provide a useful table that highlights the minimal information that should be provided on intervention specifics, including content, provider, format, setting, recipient, intensity, duration, and fidelity. Additionally, behavioral medicine interventions need to describe and justify the selection of primary and secondary outcome measures, along with any mediational variables evaluated in the RCT. Blinding of research staff and participants can also be a challenge in behavioral interventions, as compared to drug studies in which active and placebo drugs look similar. It is difficult to keep intervention staff and study participants blind when implementing a behavioral intervention; however, efforts can be made to assure that individuals collecting outcome measures are blind to the study participant's group allocation. Davidson and colleagues (2003) also provide five additional items to the CONSORT statement that include information on training of treatment (intervention) providers, supervision of treatment (intervention) providers, patient and treatment provider preferences for treatment or group allocation, success of treatment (intervention) delivery or integrity of intervention delivery, and adherence to treatment protocols. The areas highlighted in this statement raise important considerations for researchers who are conducting RCTs.

Meta-analyses or research syntheses play a critical role in the consumption of health intervention research, guide the development of best-practice approaches and policy, and identify gaps in the current knowledge base related to PA promotion (Walker, Hernandez, & Kattan, 2008). Meta-analyses aim to summarize the results of several studies that address a similar problem or intervention approach, and may include smaller studies in addition to larger RCTs (Walker, Hernandez, & Kattan, 2008). Meta-analyses use specific reproducible statistical techniques to integrate findings from heterogeneous studies evaluating similar outcomes (Knight, Fabes, & Higgins, 1996). Walker and colleagues (Walker, Hernandez, & Kattan, 2008) describe four critical issues for a well-designed meta analysis. When meta-analyses are conducted appropriately, they can provide more generalizable findings, as compared to a single RCT that may be biased or dependent on a specific population (Halpern, Karlawish, & Berlin, 2002). However, care is needed to not draw causal inferences from meta-analyses, and consumers need to be aware of the pitfalls associated with meta-analyses (Bailar, 1997; Knight, Fabes, & Higgins, 1996). For example, due to differences in statistical techniques or inclusion criteria, two meta-analyses on the same topic may arrive at different conclusions. Additionally, large RCTs may conflict with the findings of meta-analyses (LeLorier, Gregoire, Benhaddad, Lapierre, & Derderian, 1997). One particularly helpful resource is the Cochrane Collaboration, which is an international nonprofit organization that specializes in the production and dissemination of systematic reviews related to health care interventions. These reviews are published in the Cochrane Database of Systematic Reviews as part of the Cochrane Library, which is typically available at most university libraries. To develop a detailed and well-informed opinion in the field of PA research, readers should utilize all resources available, including meta-analyses and well-designed RCTs.

The Cochrane Database has published several meta-analyses on PA promotion in youth and adults. Dobbins and colleagues (Dobbins, De Corby, Robeson, Husson, & Tirilis, 2009) conducted a review of school-based PA promotion studies in children and adolescents between the ages of 6 and 18 years. Selection criteria included whether the study was conducted in a school setting, attempted to improve PA levels, was relevant to public health practice and could be conducted by public health units, reported PA outcomes for children or adolescents, and used a prospective design with a control condition. During the screening process, the authors identified 395 distinct studies by searching scientific databases (Medline, BIOSIS, PyscInfo, etc.), contacting experts in the field, and reviewing reference lists of relevant articles and other meta-analyses and reviews. From those studies, 104 were considered relevant, and 26 studies were included in the meta-analysis. The authors provide detailed information on the data extraction process and how studies were deemed eligible. All of the studies included implemented a PA intervention in a school setting, with some studies also targeting community and home variables. Interventions targeted a wide range of variables, including teacher training, curriculum and materials for students and parents, enhanced physical education classes, the provision of PA equipment, integration of PA education into other courses, and increased youth leisure time PA. Primary outcomes included leisure time (non school-time) moderate to vigorous PA (MVPA), overall MVPA (leisure and school-time), and television viewing. Secondary outcomes included systolic (mm Hg) and diastolic blood pressure (mm Hg), blood cholesterol (mg/dL), body mass index (BMI; kg/m$^2$), maximal oxygen consumption (VO$_2$ max), and pulse rate (beats/minute). Results demonstrated that school-based PA interventions were effective at improving duration of MVPA, especially during school-time hours, and in reducing television viewing. However, results indicate that school-based PA programs are not as successful at improving leisure time PA rates. Surprisingly, only seven of the 26 studies reviewed included an outcome related to leisure time PA, and only two of these studies reported an improvement in leisure time MVPA. Furthermore, these two studies only reported short-term improvements in leisure time MVPA as long-term outcomes were not assessed. School-based PA interventions were also found to improve blood cholesterol and fitness levels, but did not have an impact on blood pressure, BMI, or pulse rate. This review provides good evidence that school-based PA programs are successful at improving duration of PA during school-time hours, and at improving some fitness and physiological variables. However, areas highlighted by the authors for future research include the development of interventions to significantly alter leisure time PA that integrate other variables thought to improve PA levels, such as behavioral skills and family involvement. Additionally, future research needs to assess long-term PA outcomes. This review provides a good example of how a well-conducted meta-analysis can provide an informative summary of PA interventions, highlight gaps in the field, and point to future research directions.

Another Cochrane review evaluated programs to promote recommended PA levels in individuals 16 years of age or older (Hillsdon, Foster, & Thorogood, 2005). Inclusion criteria included RCTs to improve PA levels in free-living sedentary adults, had at least 6-months of follow-up data from the start of intervention implementation, and used an intent-to-treat analysis or had no greater than a 20% loss of study participants. Traditional search methods were used to identify articles, such as searching electronic databases and references lists of relevant articles, and making personal contact with scientists in the field. The authors identified 287 studies, of which 35 studies met inclusion criteria and 29 studies were included in the meta-analysis. Hillsdon and colleagues (Hillsdon, Foster, & Thorogood, 2005) provide a detailed flowchart to illustrate the inclusion process in their review. Hillsdon and colleagues (2005) also provide a detailed description of participant characteristics for studies included in this review. Interventions used to promote PA varied greatly and included one-to-one or group counseling and advice; prescribed PA; home- or facility-based PA; ongoing support, including face-to-face, telephone, or written materials; and self-monitoring. Primary outcomes included measures of PA and cardiorespiratory fitness ($VO_2$ max). Results of the meta-analysis indicate a positive but moderate effect of PA interventions to improve self-reported PA and cardiorespiratory fitness in individuals over 12 months of follow-up. Of the 19 studies reporting PA as their primary outcome, only seven demonstrated significant effects. Only two of ten studies using a dichotomous PA outcome found positive significant improvements in PA. Eleven studies measured cardiorespiratory fitness as a primary outcome, of which five demonstrated significant improvements. Overall, the authors indicated that the quality of studies included in the review were less than ideal, with only six studies meeting all quality criteria. Several studies did not use an intent-to-treat analysis, failed to report randomization procedures, and utilized staff that were not blind to collect main outcome measures. Hillsdon and colleagues (2005) concluded that a mix of professional guidance, self-directed materials, and ongoing support show promise for improving PA outcomes. Future research needs to include more objective assessments of PA, include longer follow-up periods, and conduct better-quality research. Additionally, future studies need to evaluate PA interventions in a variety of SES and ethnic groups.

In summary, the review of the importance of RCTs, CONSORT guidelines, and meta-analyses are an important component for the advancement of understanding the impact of PA on the field of health in general. However, there are also a number of limitations that scientific rigor can produce in developing effective community-based interventions. As long as RCTs are based on qualitative input and continue to integrate the communities' values and beliefs throughout the developmental stage, then the more likely will they be successful in engaging the community in the process of change and sustaining those changes overtime. Sometimes, this approach reduces scientific rigor, such as not keeping measurement staff blind to data collection, since community members often are better able to maintain relations with participants over long-term follow-up periods. Further issues concerning the interface of RCT and community participatory approaches are discussed below. In general, it is a balancing act to implement scientifically rigorous studies and, at the same time, promote community engagement and input in successful research programs.

## The Importance of Community-based Trials for Guiding the Field

Community researchers have argued for more community-based participatory research approaches to better understand and sustain intervention effects over the long term (Israel, Schulz, Parker, & Becker, 2001). However, very few studies have focused on evaluating the efficacy of long-term interventions that specifically alter community-level supports for PA. There is an increasing need to develop longitudinal studies that allow for detailed documentation of the change process as interventions are implemented and sustained over time. As noted, issues of safety and access to PA opportunities remain an important issue from an underserved community perspective. Several cross-sectional studies have evaluated associations between safety, access for walking trails, and PA in underserved communities. The CDC analyzed data from the 1996 Behavioral Risk Surveillance System in Maryland, Montana, Ohio, Pennsylvania, and Virginia (MMWR, 1999). This report was the first to document the higher prevalence of physical inactivity among persons who perceive their neighborhoods as unsafe, and these findings remained after controlling for other factors. Wilson, Kirtland, Ainsworth, and Addy (2004) studied racial/ethnic disparities in safety and access for PA by stratifying neighborhoods as either low or high in SES based on U.S. Census data. Compared with the higher-SES group, fewer adults in the low-SES group met the PA recommendations for moderate and vigorous PA. The low-SES group reported higher perceptions of neighborhood crime, unattended dogs, unpleasantness of neighborhoods, untrustworthy neighbors, and less access to public recreation facilities as compared with the higher-SES group. Having and using trails also predicted PA and walking for individuals from low-SES areas, but not for individuals from high-SES areas. In another study by Reed, Ainsworth, Wilson et al. (2004), 56% of residents in a rural community reported being aware of walking trails in their neighborhood, although only 33% reported utilizing those trails. Brownson, Housemann, Brown, et al. (2000) also examined the association between PA and proximity to walking trails in rural counties in Missouri. Residents from 12 counties were randomly sampled and participated in a phone survey. Among persons with access to walking trails, 38.8% had used the trails. Of those who reported using the trails, 55.2% reported that they had increased their amount of walking since they began using the trail. Women and persons with a high school education or less were more than twice as likely to have increased the amount of walking since they began using the walking trails.

Several community-based interventions have demonstrated that walking programs that involve trails and the promotion of trails have been successful in increasing PA in adults. Brownson, Smith, Pratt, et al. (1996) examined the impact of community coalitions to foster PA in rural Missouri. Activities of these coalitions included developing walking clubs, aerobic classes, and fitness festivals with exercise demonstrations. Among well-organized coalitions, these activities significantly decreased sedentary behavior. In a study by Fisher and Li (2004), community residents in a metropolitan area of Portland, Oregon, were recruited and randomized to participate in either a neighborhood peer-led walking group or an information-only control group. Intervention participants participated in a peer-led neighborhood walk and received information materials and monthly newsletters. Neighborhoods in the control condition received health education information only. Compared to the control neighborhoods, results of the multilevel intervention showed increases in walking after 6 months of intervention. Based on these studies, it is not clear that simply building a walking trail will promote walking without active engagement of the community residents. Thus, in the PATH trial (Wilson et al., 2010), an ecological approach was implemented that targeted the built environment (identified a walking trail), safety (led by neighborhood safety captains and off-duty police officers), and psychosocial factors related to attitudes and barriers for PA, motivation, self-efficacy (self-confidence), and social norms related to PA. The PATH trial (Wilson et al., 2010) expands on this previous research by testing the efficacy of a patrolled walking program plus social marketing intervention in low-SES, high-crime neighborhoods. We hypothesized in the PATH trial that the patrolled walking trail plus social marketing intervention would result in greater increases in total minutes per day of moderate and vigorous PA, as compared to a patrolled walking trail-only intervention or no walking intervention (general health education). Importantly, we also hypothesized that social environmental measures associated with increasing

community connectedness would also mediate changes in walking and PA over time.

In summary, community-based participatory studies have become increasing more valued in the field of PA and health sciences overall in recent years. This is partly due to the fact that evidence for long-term outcomes has been limited to relying on RCTs alone. Future studies should focus on efforts to blend RCT approaches with community-participatory approaches in promoting PA changes in high-risk populations. Although compromises will be made along the way, the end result will potentially be more sustainable for communities that are allowed to engage in the process of changing their communities and neighborhood environments to increase support for PA.

## Issues Across the Lifespan

Addressing health issues, such as increasing PA, from a lifespan perspective provides an important foundation for intervention/prevention research that considers normative growth, individuals' capacity to engage in PA, and continuity in growth and behavior over time, as well as critical periods during which greater opportunities for change occur. Developmental theories have been in existence since the inception of the field of psychology; however, successful integration of developmental theories in understanding the formation and development of long-term health-related lifestyle preferences (e.g., engagement in PA over a lifetime) has not been forthcoming. Much progress in understanding the appropriate theoretical approaches to influencing health behaviors will depend upon fully understanding and integrating critical elements of developmental theory into systematic and scientifically designed studies. Previous investigators have proposed a future orientation be given to prevention and the promotion of positive lifestyle development from very early on in a child's lifetime (Maddux, Roberts, Sledden, & Wight, 1986). Investigators taking a developmental perspective have also argued that prevention and treatment approaches must be targeted to specific issues during each critical period of a child's developmental lifespan (Maddux et al., 1986). We first outline continuity in PA across the lifespan and differences consistently observed by demographic factors. We follow with a discussion of the organized systematic changes in the biological/physical, cognitive, and psychosocial development across the lifespan, identifying critical points for promoting positive exercise habits and preventing obesity. In addition to the mediational factors that are predictive of PA across the lifespan discussed above (e.g., self-efficacy, value, social support), we identify other mediational factors that explain behavior and behavior change processes at particular, critical periods of the lifespan.

### Trends in PA Across the Lifespan

Physical activity participation peaks very early in the lifespan, reaching its maximum between the ages of 10 and 13 for a majority of individuals (Weinberg & Gould, 2007). Thereafter, age-related declines in PA are observed through the remainder of adolescence, and these declines continue throughout adulthood (Gordon-Larsen et al., 2004; Livingstone, Robson, Wallis, & McKinley, 2003; Weinberg & Gould, 2007). Despite these declines, researchers have found some indication that the continuity of PA participation, with corresponding early participation in positive health behaviors (during middle childhood and adolescence), predicts sustained health behaviors through adulthood (Busseri et al., 2006; Malina, 2001; Taylor, Blair, Cummings et al., 1999). Specifically, participation in PA during the earlier years of development, as well as having PA skills and being physically fit, are all predictive of PA participation in later adolescence and adulthood (Pate, Dowda, O'Neill, & Ward, 2007; Malina, 2001; Taylor et al., 1999). Stability of sedentary behaviors over time has also been documented. For example, boys who spent the greatest amount of time watching television, and boys and girls who spent the most time playing video games during childhood were more likely to have highly frequent sedentary behaviors during adolescence (Janz et al., 2000, 2005).

There is great continuity in the effects of leading a healthy lifestyle, so that how one cares for his or her health during youth and the early adult years will play a major role in determining health profiles during middle and late adulthood (Friedman, Martin, Tucker, et al., 2008). Healthy older adults have both "good" or "forgiving" genes and have led life-long, healthy lifestyles. Their less fortunate counterparts have a less forgiving genetic profile and/or earlier lifestyles that set them on a pathway that was not protective in the face of the inevitable changes that occur after the age of 50 years (Friedman, et al., 2008).

Although studies have documented age-related PA declines for both boys and girls, these declines have consistently been found to be greater, and to occur earlier in development, for girls than boys (Nelson, Neumark-Sztainer, Hannan, et al., 2006;

Janz et al., 2000). Whereas declines in girls PA begins during mid to late childhood, boys tend to increase their vigorous PA through the transition into early adolescence, with PA declining during mid to late adolescence. During middle childhood, the higher rates of PA among boys than girls are due mainly to girls' greater decreases in PA during the evening hours. Morning and afternoon activities of boys and girls remain similar during these years. For girls, greater PA declines that emerge during the mid to late childhood years have been shown to continue into and throughout adulthood.

### Physical Developmental Influences on PA

Major developmental changes in physical growth are paralleled by changes in individuals' needs, values, and abilities related to PA. Two important growth spurts occur during the early period of the lifespan and are critical for both identifying potential risks for the onset of obesity and for changes in individuals' PA choices and abilities. Children grow rapidly within the first 2 years of their life, reaching an average of 50% of adult stature by age 2. Growth then continues at a slower, but steady rate until the onset of puberty, during which another growth spurt begins (ages 11–12 for girls and ages 13–14 years for boys) (Tanner & Davies, 1985; Abbassi, 1998). The growing ends of the bones fuse about 2–3 years after the adolescent growth spurt begins and normal growth ceases. Weight gain is directly related to growth patterns from infancy to late adolescence. Moreover, fat deposition varies in direct relation to growth patterns and changes in muscle mass. On average, an infant's birth weight triples within the first year of life, with the child gaining between .5 to 2 pounds per month (Insel, Turner, & Ross, 2007). Declines in body fat typically occur between 9 months and 6 years, when it reaches adiposity rebound (the point of maximum leanness), before its gradual increase through adolescence and adulthood (Whitaker, Pepe, Wright, et al., 1998). Children who experience early adiposity rebound (defined as <4.8 years of age) are at greater risk for higher BMI during adolescence and adulthood (Taylor, Grant, Goulding, & Whitaker et al., 1998; Williams, 2005). Researchers have identified the preschool years as a critical period during which screening for early adiposity rebound can be used as a tool for implementing measures of prevention prior to the child's actual onset of obesity (Taylor et al., 2005). From childhood to the onset of puberty, children gain an average of just 5 pounds a year.

The first 2 years following the onset of puberty has been identified as another critical period for risk of obesity onset and potential changes in PA abilities and choices. During the adolescent growth spurt, on average, girls gain 35 pounds and boys gain 45 pounds per year. However, if adolescents' gain even slightly more weight per year during this period, they become at risk for obesity (Insel et al., 2007). Muscle mass peaks at puberty, between the ages of 16 and 20 in females and 18 and 25 in males (Wilmore & Costill, 1994), with body fat averaging at 23% and 15% of total body weight at physical maturity for females and males, respectively (Spear, 2002).

Physiological maturation of children's nervous, cardiovascular, and respiratory systems during the first 18 years of life results in measurable improvements in physical fitness ability from childhood to young adulthood. Although limited during childhood, gradual increases in motor ability, strength (in terms of both increased muscle mass and neuromuscular control), heart size, blood volume, and lung capacity lead to improvements in both anaerobic and aerobic capacity that are comparable to adults by late adolescence. However, the more children and adolescents engage in PA, the greater their aerobic and anaerobic improvements (Wilmore & Costill, 1994). The body continues to evolve during adulthood, during which physical maturity and motor performance peak during the 20s before beginning to decline during the 30s. Shrinking of disks in the spinal vertebrae and in the bones results in the loss of about half an inch of height between the ages of 30 and 50 (Schulz & Salthouse, 1999). Declines in physical strength become noticeable between the ages of 40 and 45 years and continues to decline about 5% per decade from that point forward. As fat gradually replaces muscle fiber, there is a corresponding decrease in basal metabolism, slowing about 3% every 10 years starting in early adulthood. On average, women gain weight until their mid-50s and men until their mid-40s, at which point they begin to lose weight due to the considerable loss of muscle mass, water, bone, and lean tissue (Ogden, Fryar, Carroll, et al., 2004).

As body fat increases, there is an increasing risk for the onset of obesity as individuals transition from the early to middle adulthood years. However, individuals who remain physically active and engage in muscle-bearing exercise can maintain much of their muscle mass and stay fit (van Pelt, Dinneno, Seals, & Jones, 2001). In fact, exercise can offset declines in muscle mass to such a degree that, until

age 60, major declines observed in muscle size, weight, strength, and endurance are still due more to lack of use than aging. However, after age 60, muscle mass decline speeds up enough so that even individuals who are physically fit are unable to maintain the same level of strength. Fat and connective tissue replace muscle fiber, leading to both stiffer muscles and longer recovery times from injury. Despite the physical challenges as individuals transition into late adulthood, older adults who get regular aerobic exercise have been shown to be more fit than middle-aged adults who lead inactive lifestyles. There are incredible benefits to staying active during late adulthood, including decreasing the risk of heart disease, high blood pressure, strokes, colon cancer, and diabetes, and providing pain relief for arthritis (Rowe & Kahn, 1998), as well as benefits in social and cognitive functioning including reducing depression and the risk for dementia (Abbott, White, Ross, et al., 2004; Kramer & Willis, 2002) and Alzheimer disease (Verghese, Lipton, Katz, et al., 2003; Wilson & Bennett, 2003). For example, Abbott and colleagues (2004) found that taking a long walk daily significantly reduced the risk of developing dementia.

Across the lifespan, growth, muscle mass, and fat accumulation depend on healthy habits (diet, PA, etc.) and heredity. Overall, individuals who exercise report having more positive emotions, feel that their lives are more meaningful, and have longer life expectancies than their nonactive counterparts (d'Epinay & Bickel, 2003; Fukukawa, Nakashima, Tsuboi, et al., 2004; Kahana, Lawrence, Kahana, et al., 2002).

### Cognitive Developmental Influences on PA

The gradual development of self-regulation skills through the child and adolescent years results in the maturing child's different ways of thinking about his or her PA performance, related emotions, and goals. Until a child becomes a self-regulated learner, he or she will take a more passive role in managing play, relying heavily on external feedback to evaluate performance and attributing failures to factors outside his or her control. In contrast, an individual with self-regulation has the skills to self-monitor progress and focus on self-improvement, manage emotions, and seek help from others. They are active participants who initiate, maintain, and achieve self-directed goals.

There are three primary elements of self-regulated learning: self-directed behavior, self-oriented feedback, and the motivation to engage in these strategies

(Zimmerman, 2000). The individual's ability to engage in self-directed behavior, whereby he/she believes he/she plays an instrumental role in achieving his/her goals, involves the ability to initiate and successfully employ a number of strategies to improve his/her skills. Until 12 years of age, children have less mature cognitive abilities, including coding processes and rehearsal strategies, as well as attentional and decision-making skills (Gallagher, French, Thomas, & Thomas, 1996). In addition, novice participants will possess less sport-specific knowledge or cognitive representations than more experienced "experts" (French & McPherson, 2003). Therefore, self-directed behavior is limited in younger children, who are unable to process information or apply complex strategies as effectively as older children. Self-oriented feedback involves individuals' ability to assess the effectiveness of the strategies which they employed, and use this feedback in their decision to either employ or change their strategies in future attempts (future orientation). Feedback from internal standards of competence (self-efficacy) are built upon past experiences, observations of others (modeling), and the reinforcements/rewards they receive for their performance from others. As a child moves into preschool years, he/she develops short-term memory and concrete cognitive abilities, such as being able to understand simple notions of self-oriented beliefs. However, the most prominent cognitive growth of the preschool period is the increased understanding and sensitivity to environmental cues, such as simple positive and negative reinforcers of behavior, and the modeling of socializers' behaviors (Flavell, 1999). Therefore, the preschool and childhood years are viewed as a critical period for developing early healthy lifestyle habits through observational learning or modeling of behaviors (McCullagh & Weiss, 2002; Weir, Etelson, & Brand, 2006; Weiss, McCullagh, Smith, & Berlant, 1998). As children mature and cognitive processes become more advanced (e.g., attentional skills), they become increasingly more capable of learning from models (Gallagher et al., 1996), and thus parents, siblings, peers, and other key socializers continue to play a primary role in youth engagement in PA.

Last, motivation to engage in PA is liable to wane during adolescence, when the ability to think abstractly prompts adolescents to think about their world and themselves in new ways. In particular, the ability to assess their "ideal" selves in comparison to their "real" selves leads to increased self-awareness and, at times, to self-doubt (Harter, 1999; Harter, 2003). As discussed, an adolescent will be motivated to engage in PA and seek out increasingly more challenging physical activities in the future if they feel highly competent in the activity and express value (e.g., high interest) in the activity (Eccles et al., 1998). Self-efficacy, future orientation, social comparison orientation, and perceived behavior of others (e.g., peers) are all employed to make decisions about initial and continued engagement in PA, and to formulate their own health attitudes, beliefs, goals, and intentions (Luszczynska et al., 2004).

### Psychosocial Influences on PA

Even as early as infancy and the toddler years, children are able to recognize their parents' simple health beliefs and respond to simple behavioral and environmental cues (Flavell, 1999). However, the preschool years have been identified as a particularly critical period in development for building and establishing life-long healthy habits (Brent & Weitzman, 2004; Pate, Pfeiffer, Trost, et al., 2004). Corresponding with the cognitive shift that occurs during preschool outlined above, children at this age experience increased sensitivity to environmental cues and depend more highly on family members and other prominent socializers to act as social references that guide behavior (Bandura, 1999). Therefore, parents, siblings, and other socializers are especially important for providing opportunities and encouraging a child's PA, as well as for role modeling the importance of PA by incorporating PA into their own lives (Eccles, 1993). Parents are key facilitators of positive health behaviors through creating a positive context (both socially and behaviorally) that supports their child's engagement in PA practices. Corresponding to the cognitive development of preschool and early school-aged children discussed above, parents can act as role models by incorporating PA into their own lives. In fact, research suggests both a concurrent relation between parent and youth activity levels (e.g., Babkes & Weiss, 1999), as well as a longitudinal influence of parents' own activity involvement on their child's subsequent participation in activity through adolescence (Anderson, Funk, Elliot, & Smith, 2003; Fredricks & Eccles, 2002; 2005; Huebner & Mancini, 2003; Simpkins, Fredricks, Davis-Kean, & Eccles, 2006). For example, parental behaviors such as mothers' frequency of walking were associated with PA scores in youth (Spurrier, Magarey, Golley, et al., 2008). During this stage of their children's development, parents are also able to begin encouraging their children to pursue healthy behaviors by exposing them to these behaviors in various ways. Such support can include parents participating with their adolescent in the activity (coactivity), which gives parents the opportunity to actively coach and teach their children skills and to provide performance feedback including direct positive reinforcements for participating (Eccles et al., 1998; Fredricks & Eccles, 2005). Similarly, aspects of the physical home environment (e.g., number of items of outdoor play equipment) have been linked to higher engagement in PA of children (Spurrier et al., 2008; Fredricks & Eccles, 2005). Parental support and involvement, including provision of resources (e.g., transportation, equipment) and acting as interpreters of experience (e.g., parent perception of child ability, encouragement, coactivity) continue to predict youth engagement in PA throughout childhood and adolescence (Eccles, 1993; Fredricks & Eccles, 2005; Jacobs, Vernon, & Eccles, 2005; Sallis, Prochaska, & Taylor, 2000; Heitzler, Martin, Duke, & Huhman, 2006; Trost, Sallis, Pate, et al., 2003).

Prior to the age of 4, children should be encouraged to engage in free play. From the preschool years through the early childhood years however, children become increasingly physically, cognitively, and socially capable of engaging in organized team play. The increasing drive/need for social interaction with peers from the preschool years through the adolescent years results in the increasing role that peers play in influencing the frequency, duration, intensity, and type of PA in which youth engage (Springer, Kelder, & Hoelscher, 2006). In particular, the relation between activity participation and peers during adolescence, commonly referred to as a "leisure culture," has been well documented (Eccles, Barber, Stone, & Hunt, 2003; Eder & Kinney, 1995; Mahoney & Cairns, 1997). Much empirical research has shown that adolescents' friend groups (e.g., "crowd"), and the social identities they attach to this affiliation, are critical predictors of the types of activities in which adolescents participate (Eccles & Barber, 1999; Hartup & Stevens, 1997; Luthar, Shoum, & Brown, 2006). Moreover, youth report "spending time with friends" as a central motivating factor for why they first chose to participate in an activity, their enjoyment in the activity, as well as whether they persist or drop out of an activity (Borden, Perkins, Villarruel, & Stone, 2005; Huebner & Mancini, 2003; Loder & Hirsch, 2003; Persson et al., 2007). For example, Springer, Kelder, and Hoelscher (2006) examined the importance of understanding social determinants of health

behaviors at the middle school age, when interactions with peers become more important, and found that encouragement from friends was the only variable positively associated with vigorous PA in youth.

The development for increasing autonomy during the adolescent years introduces another emerging challenge for engaging youth in PA. Gaining greater responsibility for their own leisure activity choices, PA options must be "enticing enough" to continue to engage youth (and compete with other leisure activities, like video games). Some of the observed declines in PA during early adolescence (age 11) result from granting adolescents greater autonomy and aiding them in exercising their newly developed skills for niche-picking (Dennisen, Zarrett, & Eccles, 2007; Zarrett, 2007). For example, Aaron and colleagues (2002) found that much of the decline in PA observed across a 4-year period of adolescence was due to a decrease in the number of activities in which youth participated, rather than the amount of time youth spent in PA. Other reasons for observed declines that have been documented include increases in school-related requirements and routines, increases in leisure-time computer use (Nelson et al., 2006), playing video games, and watching television (Janz et al., 2000, 2005). Although PA self-efficacy, social support, and enjoyment are predictive of engaging in PA throughout the lifespan, these factors are particularly salient during this critical period when youth are given greater freedom to choose and when a variety of leisure time opportunities are most plentiful (DeBourdeaudjuij, Lefevre, Deforche, et al., 2005; Eccles et al., 2003; Jacobs, Lanza, Osgood, et al., 2002; Neumark-Sztainer, Story, Hannan, et al., 2003).

Moreover, access to neighborhood resources, such as parks, community centers, playing fields, and positive adult mentors who implement and oversee the activity is significantly associated with increases in youth participation (Duncan & Brooks-Gunn, 2000; Mahoney, Cairns, & Farmer, 2003; Pederson & Seidman, 2005; Quinn, 1999; Rural School & Community Trust, 2005). During early and middle adolescence, not only do almost all youth attend school, but many of these same youth receive additional support from community youth organizations. By late adolescence, when community and school supports may be at their most needed, these supports diverge or disappear altogether, with fewer community programs and recreational leagues targeted toward high school students, and fewer school-based opportunities to engage in PA as sports teams become more competitive/selective (Eccles & Gootman, 2002; Zarrett & Eccles, 2006). Despite these challenges during late adolescence, early participation (during middle childhood and adolescence), in which youth build their activity-specific skill set and increase internal motivation, predicts sustained participation in healthy PA (Busseri et al., 2006; Jordan & Nettles, 2000; Mahoney, et al., 2003) even when activities become competitive in high school (Quiroz, 2000; Simpkins, Ripke, Huston, & Eccles, 2005).

Although the most precipitous declines occur during adolescence, another less steep decline occurs during early adulthood (ages 18–29) and again during older adulthood (over age 50), marking two additional critical periods for increased initiatives to encourage initial and sustained participation in PA (Whaley, 2004). In comparison to childhood and adolescence, developmental change during adulthood is less predictable and is much more dependent upon social, as opposed to maturational, influences. Ruble and Goodnow (1998) have argued that the social timetable is more likely to matter than the biological timetable at this developmental stage. As a consequence, many of the declines in PA observed during early adulthood result from the increasing occupational and social (family) responsibilities that demand and consume waking hours. Research has consistently found a relation between number of years of education and adult health, even after controlling for obvious third variables. A primary reason for this relation is that more-educated people tend to have more fulfilling jobs that provide a sense of personal control, social support, and most importantly, opportunities to live a healthier lifestyle. For example, those who stayed in school longer were more likely to exercise and stay at the recommended weight (Mirowsky & Ross, 2003).

In contrast, declines in PA participation during later adulthood are due primarily to the accrual of physical limitations that individuals experience as they age. However, almost as prominent an influence on older adults' motivation to participate in PA is the degree in which they endorse/internalize existing societal stereotypes that older adults do not, and should not, exercise because of possible health risks. For example, when both children and older adults (60 years and older) were asked to assess the age-appropriateness of involvement in various strenuous (e.g., marathon running; racquetball) and less strenuous (e.g., archery) activities for 20- to 80-year-olds (in 20-year increments), both children and older adults viewed all PAs as less appropriate as

the age of the referent person increased, and that PAs were more appropriate for males than for females (with the exception of ballet) (Behlendorf, MacRae, & Vos Strache, 1999; Ostrow & Dzewaltowski, 1986).

Similar to other critical periods in the lifespan, older adults' perceptions of physical self-efficacy (or physical competence) is highly predictive of their engagement in PA (Estabrooks & Carron, 1998; Li, McAuley, Harmer, et al., 2001; McAuley, 1993). However, unlike in younger periods of the lifespan, during older adulthood, self-perceptions of low physical efficacy are supported by societal beliefs. The combination of declining health and the endorsement of these stereotypes sets in motion a vicious cycle in which a physical ailment or limitation supports the elderly person's perception that she/he possesses low efficacy to engage in the PA. In turn, the lack of PA contributes to additional medical conditions, physical limitations, and declining psychological well-being, which lead the elderly to develop increasingly low physical efficacy. This cycle supports a self-fulfilling prophecy, further endorsing the societal conception that older adults should not engage in PA. In sum, ageism (and sexism), among its many injuries to humanity, have also contributed to the major barriers to PA for many older adults.

Although changing social attitudes and advances in knowledge about the physical, social, and cognitive benefits of PA have helped to break down some of these barriers to PA involvement of older individuals in the United States, these stereotypes continue to be pervasive enough to impede the PA involvement of older individuals in our society. For example, Goggin and Morrow (2001) found that, although 89% of the older adults they surveyed acknowledged the important health benefits of participating in PA, 69% of them were not participating in sufficient levels of PA to reap these benefits.

## Conclusion

This chapter has provided an innovative perspective on integrating state-of-the-art of critical issues for conducting PA research and for improving health and preventing chronic disease. The chapter specifically outlined the critical need for theoretically driven research that focuses on understanding mediational factors that may explain behavior and behavior change processes related to PA across the lifespan. It was argued that future research should strive to balance the use of scientifically rigorous RCTs with community-based participatory approaches in an effort to develop effective and long-lasting improvements in PA and health. These efforts will more likely succeed in influencing policy and public health interventions because community input will more likely lead to dissemination of successful approaches/methods. Additionally, the use of meta-analyses to gather information on the state of PA research was presented, and challenges and limitations were highlighted. The need to incorporate a developmental perspective, and key issues relevant to understanding PA behavior across the lifespan was also highlighted and should provide important critical issues to consider for future research. In particular, biological, cognitive, social, and environmental issues were considered across the lifespan. Although many individuals are aware of the benefits of engaging in PA across the lifespan, there are myths and barriers to continuity of PA. These barriers must be further studied and understood through qualitative in-depth analyses, in order to better develop appropriate interventions with community input. These approaches will need to address multiple ecological issues and will be more likely to result in long-term success if community engagement is enhanced as part of the process.

## References

Aaron, D., Storti, K., Robertson, R., Kriska, A., & LaPorte, R. (2002). Longitudinal study of the number and choice of leisure time physical activities from mid to late adolescence: Implications for school curricula and community recreation programs. *Archives of Pediatrics & Adolescent Medicine, 156*(11), 1075–1080.

Abbassi, V. (1998). Growth and normal puberty. *Pediatrics, 102*(2), 507–511.

Abbott, R.D., White, L.R., Ross, G., Masaki, K.H., Curb, J., & Petrovitch, H. (2004). Walking and dementia in physically capable elderly men. *Journal of the American Medical Association, 292*(12), 1447–1453.

Altman, D.G., & Dore, C.J. (1990). Randomisation and baseline comparisons in clinical trials. *Lancet, 335*(8682), 149–153.

Altman, D.G., Schulz, K.F., Moher, D., Egger, M., Davidoff, F., Elbourne, D., et al. (2001). The revised CONSORT statement for reporting randomized trials: Explanation and elaboration. *Annals of Internal Medicine, 134*(8), 663–694.

Anderson, J.C., Funk, J.B., Elliot, R., & Smith, P.H. (2003). Parental support and pressure and children's extracurricular activities: Relationships with amount of involvement and affective experience of participation. *Journal of Applied Developmental Psychology, 4*(2), 241–257.

Babkes, M.L., & Weiss, M.R. (1999). Parent influence on cognitive and affective responses in children's competitive soccer participation. *Pediatric Exercise Science, 11*, 44–62.

Bailar, J.C. (1997). The Promise and Problems of Meta-Analysis. *New England Journal of Medicine, 337*(8), 559–561.

Baltes, P.B. (1997). On the incomplete architecture of human ontogeny: Selection, optimization, and compensation as foundations of developmental theory. *American Psychologist, 52*, 366–380.

Bandura, A. (1991). Self-regulation of motivation through anticipatory and self-reactive mechanisms. In R. Dienstbier (Ed.), *Nebraska symposium on motivation 1990: Perspectives on motivation* (pp. 69–164). Lincoln, NE: University of Nebraska Press.

Bandura, A. (1997). Self-efficacy: The exercise of control. New York: W.H. Freeman.

Bandura A. (1999). Social cognitive theory of personality. In L.A. Pervin, & O.P. John (Eds.), *Handbook of personality: Theory and research* (pp. 154–196). New York: Guilford.

Baranowski, T., Anderson, C., & Carmack, C. (1998). Mediating variable framework in physical activity interventions: How are we doing? How might we do better? *American Journal of Preventive Medicine, 15*, 266–297.

Baranowski, T., Cullen, K.W., Nicklas, T., Thompson, D., & Barnowski, J. (2003). Are current health behavioral change models helpful in guiding prevention of weight gain efforts? *Obesity Research, 11*, 23S–43S.

Behlendorf, B., MacRae, P.G., & Vos Strache, C. (1999). Children's perceptions of physical activity for adults: Competence and appropriateness. *Journal of Aging and Physical Activity, 7*, 354–373.

Begg, C., Cho, M., Eastwood, S., Horton, R., Moher, D., Olkin, I., et al. (1996). Improving the quality of reporting of randomized controlled trials. The CONSORT statement. *Journal of the American Medical Association, 276*(8), 637–639.

Bouffard, S., Wimer, C., Caronongan, P., Little, P., Dearing, E., & Simpkins, S.D. (2006). Demographic differences in patterns of youth out-of-school time activity participation. *Journal of Youth Development*. Retrieved from http://www.nae4ha.org/directory/jyd/intro.html.

Borden, L.M., Perkins, D.F., Villarruel, F.A., & Stone, M.R. (2005). To participate or not to participate: That is the question. In G.G. Noam (Ed.), H.B. Weiss, P.M.D. Little, & S.M. Bouffard (Issue Eds.), *New Directions for Youth Development* Vol. 105: *Participation in youth programs: Enrollment, attendance, and engagement* (pp. 33–50). San Francisco: Jossey-Bass.

Brent, R.L., & Weitzman, M. (2004). The pediatricians' role and responsibility in educating parents about environmental risks. *Pediatrics, 113*, 1167–1172.

Bronfenbrenner, U. (2005). *Making human beings human: Bioecological perspectives on human development*. Thousand Oaks, CA: Sage.

Bronfenbrenner, U., & Morris, P. (2006). The bioecological model of human development. In W. Daman, & R.M. Lerner (Eds.-in-Chief), R.M. Lerner (Vol. Ed.), *Handbook of child psychology: Vol. 1. Theoretical models of human development* (pp. 793–828). Hoboken, NJ: John Wiley & Sons.

Brownson, R.C., Housemann, R.A., Brown, D.R., Jackson-Thompson, J., King, A.C., Malone, B.R. et al. (2000). Promoting physical activity in rural communities: Walking trail access, use, and effects. *American Journal of Preventive Medicine, 18*(3), 235–241.

Brownson, R.C., Smith, C.A., Pratt, M., et al. (1996). Preventing cardiovascular disease through community-based risk reduction: The Bootheel heart health project. *American Journal of Public Health, 86*, 206–213.

Busseri, M.A., Rose-Krasnor, L., Willoughby, T., & Chalmers, H. (2006). A longitudinal examination of breadth and intensity of youth activity involvement and successful development. *Developmental Psychology, 42*, 1313–1326.

Cairns, R.B., Elder, G.H., Jr., & Costello, E.J. (Eds.). (1996). *Developmental science*. Cambridge: Cambridge University Press.

Centers for Disease Control and Prevention. (1999). Neighborhood safety and the prevalence of physical inactivity—selected states, 1996. *Morbidity and Mortality Weekly Report, 48*, 143–146.

Center for Disease Control and Prevention. (2000). *Physical activity and good nutrition: Essential elements for good health*. Atlanta, GA. Retrieved from http://www.cdc.gov/nccdphp/dnpa/dnpaaag:htm.

Davidson, K.W., Goldstein, M., Kaplan, R.M., Kaufmann, P.G., Knatterud, G.L., Orleans, C.T., et al. (2003). Evidence-based behavioral medicine: What is it and how do we achieve it? *Annals of Behavioral Medicine, 26*(3), 161–171.

De Bourdeaudhuij, I., Lefevre, J., Deforche, B., Wijndaele, K., Matton, L., & Philippaerts, R. (2005). Physical activity and psychosocial correlates in normal weight and overweight 11 to 19 Year Olds. *Obesity Research, 13*(6), 1097–1105.

Dennisen, J., Zarrett, N., & Eccles, J.S. (2007). I like to do it, I'm able and I know I am: Longitudinal couplings between domain-specific achievement, self-concept, and interest. *Child Development, 78*(2), 430–447.

d'Epinay, C.J., & Bickel, J.F. (2003). Do "young-old" exercisers feel better than sedentary persons? A cohort study in Switzerland. *Canadian Journal of Aging, 22*, 155–165.

Dobbins, M., De Corby, K., Robeson, P., Husson, H., & Tirilis, D. (2009). School-based physical activity programs for promoting physical activity and fitness in children and adolescents aged 6–18. *Cochrane Database Systematic Reviews 1*(1), CD007651.

Dunbar, C. (2002). *Alternative schooling for African American youth: Does anyone know we're here?* Princeton, NJ: Princeton University Press.

Duncan, G.J., & Brooks-Gunn J. (2000). Family poverty, welfare reform, and child development. *Child Development, 71*(1), 188–196.

Dunn, A., Marcus, B., Kampert, J., Garcia, M., Kohl, H., & Blair, S. (1999). Comparison of lifestyle and structured interventions to increase physical activity and cardiorespiratory fitness: a randomized trial. *Journal of the American Medical Association, 281*(4), 327–334.

Eccles, J.S. (1983). Expectancies, values, and academic behaviors. In J. Spence (Ed.), *Achievement and achievement motivation* (pp. 75–146). San Francisco: Freeman.

Eccles, J.S. (1993). School and family effects on the ontogeny of children's interests, self-perceptions, and activity choice. In J. Jacobs (Ed.), *Nebraska symposium on motivation, 1992: Developmental perspectives on motivation* (pp. 145–208). Lincoln: University of Nebraska Press.

Eccles, J.S., & Barber, B. (1999). Student council, volunteering, basketball, or marching band: What kind of extracurricular participation matters? *Journal of Adolescent Research, 14*, 10–43.

Eccles, J.S., Barber, B.L., Stone, M., & Hunt, J. (2003). Extracurricular activities and adolescent development. *Journal of Social Issues, 59*(4), 865–889.

Eccles, J.S. & Gootman, J.A. (Eds.) (2002). *Community programs to promote youth development*. Washington, DC: National Academy Press.

Eccles, J.S., Wigfield, A., & Schiefele, U. (1998). Motivation to succeed. In W. Damon (Series Ed.), & N. Eisenberg (Vol. Ed.), *Handbook of child psychology*: Vol. 3 *Social, emotional and personality development* (5th ed., pp. 1017–1094). New York: Wiley.

Eder, D., & Kinney, D.A. (1995). The effects of middle school extracurricular activities on adolescents' popularity and peer status. *Youth & Society, 26*, 298–324.

Elder, G.H., & Conger, R. (2000). *Children of the land*. Chicago: University of Chicago Press.

Estabrooks, P.A., & Carron, A.V. (1998). The role of the group with elderly exercisers. *Small Group Research, 30*, 438–452.

Eyler, A.A., Baker, E., Cromer, L., King, A.C., Brownson, R.C., & Donatelle, R.J. (1998). Physical activity and minority women: A qualitative study. *Health Education & Behavior, 25*(5), 640–652.

Fisher, K.J., & Li, F. (2004). A community-based walking trial to improve neighborhood quality of life in adults: A multilevel analysis. *Annals of Behavioral Medicine, 28*, 186–194.

Flavell, J.H. (1999). Cognitive development: Children's knowledge about mind. *Annual Review of Psychology, 50*, 21–45.

Fredricks, J.A., & Eccles, J.S. (2002). Children's competence and value beliefs from childhood through adolescence: Growth trajectories in two male-sex-typed domains. *Developmental Psychology, 38*(4), 519–533.

Fredricks, J.A., & Eccles, J.S. (2005). Family socialization, gender, and sport motivation and involvement. *Journal of Sport & Exercise Psychology, 27*, 3–31.

Freemantle, N., Mason, J.M., Haines, A., & Eccles, M.P. (1997). CONSORT: An important step toward evidence-based health care. Consolidated standards of reporting trials. *Annals of Internal Medicine, 126*(1), 81–83.

French, K.E., & McPherson, S.L. (2003). Development of expertise in sport. In M.R. Weiss (Ed.), *Developmental sport and exercise psychology: A lifespan perspective* (pp. 403–423). Morgantown, WV: Fitness Information Technology, Inc.

Friedman, H.S., Martin, L.R., Tucker, J.S., Criqui, M.H., Kern, M.L., & Reynolds, C.A. (2008). Stability of physical activity across the lifespan. *Journal of Health Psychology, 13*(8), 1092–1104.

Fukukawa, Y., Nakashima, C., Tsuboi, S., Kozakai, R., Doyo, W., Niino, N., et al. (2004). Age Differences in the Effect of Physical Activity on Depressive Symptoms. *Psychology and Aging, 19*(2), 346-351.

Gallagher, J.D., French, K.E., Thomas, K.T., & Thomas, J.R. (1996). Expertise in youth sport: Relations between knowledge and skill. In F.L. Smoll, & R.E. Smith (Eds.), *Children and youth in sport: A biopsychosocial perspective* (pp. 338–358). Madison, WI: Brown & Benchmark.

Goggin, N.L., & Morrow, J.R. (2001). Physical activity behaviors of older adults. *Journal of Aging and Physical Activity, 9*, 58–66.

Gordon-Larsen, P., Nelson, M.C., & Popkin, B.M. (2004). Longitudinal physical activity and sedentary behavior trends: Adolescence to adulthood. *American Journal of Preventative Medicine, 27*(4), 277–283.

Griffin, S.F., Wilson, D.K., Wilcox, S., Buck, J., Ainsworth, B.E. (2008). Physical activity influences in a disadvantaged African American community and the communities' solutions. *Health Education Practice, 9*, 180–190.

Hahn, R.A., Teutsch, S.M., Rothenberg, R.B., Marks, J.S. (1990). Excess deaths from nine chronic diseases in the United States, 1986. *Journal of the American Medical Association, 264*, 2654–2659.

Halpern, S.D., Karlawish, J.H., & Berlin, J.A. (2002). The continuing unethical conduct of underpowered clinical trials. *Journal of the American Medical Association, 288*(3), 358–362.

Harter, S. (1999). *The construction of the self: A developmental perspective*. New York: Guilford.

Harter, S. (2003). The development of self-representations during childhood and adolescence. In M.R. Leary, & J.P. Tangney (Eds.), *Handbook of self and identity* (pp. 610–642). New York: Guilford.

Hartup, W.W., & Stevens, N. (1997). Friendships and adaptation in the life course. *Psychological Bulletin, 121*, 355–370.

Haskell, W.L., I-Min, L., Pate, R.R., Powell, K.E., Blair, S.N., Franklin, B.A. et al. (2007). Physical Activity and Public Health: Updated Recommendation for Adults from the American College of Sports Medicine and the American Heart Association. *Medicine & Science in Sports & Exercise, 39*(8), 1423–1434.

Heitzler, C.D., Martin, S.L., Duke, J., & Huhman, M. (2006). Correlates of physical activity in a national sample of children ages 9–13 years. *Preventive Medicine, 42*, 254–260.

Hillsdon, M., Foster, C., & Thorogood, M. (2005). Interventions for promoting physical activity. *Cochrane Database Systematic Reviews* (1), CD003180.

Hirsch, B.J., Roffman, J.G., Deutsch, N.L., Flynn, C.A., Loder, T.L., & Pagano, M.E. (2000). Inner-city youth development organizations: Strengthening programs for adolescent girls. *Journal of Early Adolescence, 20*(2), 210–230.

Hollis, S., & Campbell, F. (1999). What is meant by intention to treat analysis? Survey of published randomised controlled trials. *British Medical Journal, 319*(7211), 670–674.

Huebner, A.J., & Mancini, J.A. (2003). Shaping structured out-of-school time use among youth: The effects of self, family, and friend systems. *Journal of Youth and Adolescence, 32*(6), 453–463.

Insel, P., Turner, R.E., & Ross, D. (2007). Nutrition (3rd Edition). In P. Insel, R.E. Turner, & D. Ross (Eds.), Sudbury, MA: Jones and Bartlett Publishers.

Israel, B.A., Schulz, A.J., Parker, E.A., & Becker, A.B. (2001). Community-based participatory research: Policy recommendations for promoting a partnership approach in health research. *Education for Health, 14*, 182–197.

Jacobs, J.E., Lanza, S., Osgood, D.W., Eccles, J.S., & Wigfield, A. (2002). Changes in children's self-competence and values: Gender and domain differences across grades one through twelve. *Child Development, 73*(2), 509–527.

Jacobs, J.E., Vernon, M.K., & Eccles, J.S. (2005). Activity choices in middle childhood: The roles of gender, self-beliefs, and parents' influence. In J.L. Mahoney, R.W. Larson, & J.S. Eccles (Eds.), *Organized activities as contexts of development: Extracurricular activities, after-school and community programs* (pp. 235–254). Mahwah, New Jersey: Lawrence Erlbaum Associates.

Janz, K.F., Burns, T.L., & Levy, S.M. (2005). Tracking of activity and sedentary behaviors in childhood: The Iowa bone development study. *American Journal of Preventative Medicine, 29*(3), 171–178.

Janz, K.F., Dawson, J.D., & Mahoney, L.T. (2000). Tracking physical fitness and physical activity from childhood to adolescence: The Muscatine study. *Medicine & Science in Sports & Exercise, 32*(7), 1250–1257.

Jones, D., Ainsworth, B., Croft, J., Macera, C., Lloyd, E., & Yusuf, H. (1998). Moderate leisure-time physical activity: who is meeting the public health recommendations? A national cross-sectional study. *Archives Of Family Medicine, 7*(3), 285–289.

Jordan, W.J., & Nettles, S.M. (2000). How students invest their time outside of school: Effects on school-related outcomes. *Social Psychology of Education, 3*, 217–243.

Kahana, E., Lawrence, R., Kahana, B., Kercher, K., Wisniewski, A., Stoller, E., et al. (2002). Long-term impact of preventive proactivity on quality of life of the old-old. *Psychosomatic Medicine, 64*(3), 382–394.

Kao, L.S., Tyson, J.E., Blakely, M.L., & Lally, K.P. (2008). Clinical research methodology I: introduction to randomized trials. *Journal of the American College of Surgeons, 206*(2), 361–369.

Kaplan, R.M., Trudeau, K.J., & Davidson, K.W. (2004). New policy on reports of randomized clinical trials. *Annals of Behavioral Medicine, 27*(2), 81.

Kaplan, R.M., Wilson, D.K., Hartwell, S.L., Merino, K.L., & Wallace, J.P. (1985). Prospective evaluation of HDL cholesterol changes after diet and physical conditioning programs for patients with type II diabetes mellitus. *Diabetes Care, 8*, 343–348.

Kaptchuk, T.J. (2001). The double-blind, randomized, placebo-controlled trial: Gold standard or golden calf? *Journal of Clinical Epidemiology, 54*(6), 541–549.

Kazdin, A.E. (2003). *Research design in clinical psychology* (4th ed.). Boston, MA: Allyn & Bacon.

Knight, G.P., Fabes, R.A., & Higgins, D.A. (1996). Concerns about drawing causal inferences from meta-analyses: An example in the study of gender differences in aggression. *Psychological Bulletin, 119*(3), 410–421.

Kramer, A.F., & Willis, S.L. (2002). Enhancing the cognitive vitality of older adults. *Current Directions in Psychological Science, 11*, 173–177.

LeLorier, J., Gregoire, G., Benhaddad, A., Lapierre, J., & Derderian, F. (1997). Discrepancies between meta-analyses and subsequent large randomized, controlled trials. *New England Journal of Medicine, 337*(8), 536–542.

Lerner, R.M. (2006). Developmental science, developmental systems, and contemporary theories of human development. In W. Damon & R.M. Lerner (Ed.), *Handbook of child psychology*, Vol. 1: *Theoretical models of human development* (6th ed., pp. 1–17. Hoboken, NJ: Wiley and Sons.

Li, F., McAuley, E., Harmer, P., Duncan, T.E., & Chaumeton, N.R. (2001). Tai Chi enhances self-efficacy and exercise behavior in older adults. *Journal of Aging and Physical Activity, 9*(2), 161–171.

Livingstone, M.B., Robson, P.J., Wallace, J.M., & McKinley, M.C. (2003). How active are we? Levels of routine physical activity in children and adults. *Proceedings of the Nutrition Society, 62*(3), 681–701.

Loder, T.L., & Hirsch, B.J. (2003). Inner-city youth development organizations: The salience of peer ties among early adolescent girls. *Applied Developmental Science, 7*(1), 2–12.

Luthar, S.S., Shoum, K.A., & Brown, P.J. (2006). Extracurricular involvement among affluent youth: A scapegoat for "ubiquitous achievement pressures"? *Developmental Psychology, 42*(3), 583–597.

Luszczynska, A., Gibbons, F.X., Piko, B.F., & Tekozel M. (2004). Self-regulatory cognitions, social comparison, and perceived peers' behaviors as predictors of nutrition and physical activity: A comparison among adolescents in Hungary, Poland, Turkey, and USA. *Psychology & Health, 19*, 577–593.

Maddux, J.E., Roberts, M.C., Sledden, E.A., & Wright L. (1986). Developmental issues in child health psychology. *American Psychologist, 41*, 25–34.

Magnusson, D., & Stattin, H. (1998). Person-context interaction theories. In W. Damon & R.M. Lerner (Eds.), *Handbook of* child psychology. *Volume 1: Theoretical models of human development* (pp. 685–759). New York: Wiley.

Magnusson, D., & Stattin, H. (2006). The person in the environment: Towards a general model for scientific inquiry. In R.M. Lerner (Ed.), *Handbook of child psychology Vol. 1: Theoretical models of human development* (6th ed., pp. 400–464). Hoboken, NJ: Wiley.

Mahoney, J.L., & Cairns, R.B. (1997). Do extracurricular activities protect against early school dropout? *Developmental Psychology, 33*(2), 241–253.

Mahoney, J.L., Cairns, B.D., & Farmer, T.W. (2003). Promoting interpersonal competence and educational success through extracurricular activity participation. *Journal of Educational Psychology, 95*, 409–418.

Mahoney, J.L., & Bergman, L.R. (2002). Conceptual and methodological issues in a developmental approach to positive adaptation. *Journal of Applied Developmental Psychology, 23*, 195–217.

Mahoney, J., Larson, R., & Eccles, J. (Eds.). (2005). *Organized activities as contexts of development: Extracurricular activities, after-school and community programs.* Hillsdale, NJ: Lawrence Erlbaum Associates.

Malina, R.M. (2001). Physical activity and fitness: Pathways from childhood to adulthood. *American Journal of Human Biology, 13*(2), 162–172.

Manson, J.E., Nathan, D.M., Krolewski, A.S., Stampfer, M.J., Willett, W.C., & Hennekens, C.H. (1992). A prospective study of exercise and incidence of diabetes among U.S. male physicians. *Journal of the American Medical Association, 268*, 63–67.

Manson, J.E., Rimm, E.B., Stampfer, M.J., Colditz, G.A., Willett, W.C., Krolewski, A.S., et al. (1991). Physical activity and incidence of non-insulin dependent mellitus in women. *Lancet, 338*, 774–778.

Masse, L.C., Dassa, C., Gauvin, L., Giles-Corti, B., & Motl, R. (2002). Emerging measurement and statistical methods in physical activity research. *American Journal of Preventive Medicine, 23*, 44–55.

McAuley, E. (1993). Self-efficacy and the maintenance of exercise participation in older adults. *Journal of Behavioral Medicine, 16*, 103–113.

McCullagh, P., & Weiss, M.R. (2002). Observational learning: The forgotten psychological method in sport psychology. In J.L. Van Raalte, & B.W. Brewer (Eds.), *Exploring sport and exercise psychology* (2nd ed., pp. 131–149). Washington, DC: American Psychological Association.

Mirowsky, J., & Ross, C.E. (2003). *Education, social status, and health.* New York: A. de Gruyter.

Moher, D., Schulz, K., & Altman, D. (2001). The CONSORT statement: revised recommendations for improving the quality of reports of parallel-group randomized trials. *Lancet, 357*(9263), 1191.

Nelson, M., Neumark-Stzainer, D., Hannan, P., Sirard, J., & Story, M. (2006). Longitudinal and secular trends in physical activity and sedentary behavior during adolescence. *Pediatrics, 118*(6), e1627–e1634.

Nelson, M.E., Rejeski, W., Blair, S.N., Duncan, P.W., Judge, J.O., King, A.C., et al. (2007). Physical activity and public health in older adults: Recommendation from the American College of Sports Medicine and the American Heart Association. *Medicine & Science in Sports & Exercise, 39*(8), 1435–1445.

Neumark-Sztainer, D., Story, M., Hannan, P., Tharp, T., & Rex, J. (2003). Factors associated with changes in physical activity: a

cohort study of inactive adolescent girls. *Archives Of Pediatrics & Adolescent Medicine, 157*(8), 803–810.

National Heart, Lung, and Blood Institute. (1998). Executive summary of the clinical guidelines on the identification, evaluation, treatment of overweight and obesity in adults. *Archives of Internal Medicine, 158*, 1855–1867.

Nies, M.A., Vollman, M., & Cook, T. (1999). African American women's experiences with physical activity in their daily lives. *Public Health Nursing, 16*, 23–31.

Ogden, C.L., Fryar, C.D., Carroll, M.D., et al. (2004). *Mean body weight, height, and body mass index, United States 1960–2002. Advance data from vital and health statistics,* No. 347. Hyattsville, MD: National Center for Health Statistics.

Ostrow, A.C., & Dzewaltowski, D.A. (1986). Older adults' perceptions of physical activity participation based on age-role and sex-role appropriateness. *Research Quarterly for Exercise and Sport, 57*, 167–169.

Overton, W.F. (2006). Developmental psychology: Philosophy, concepts, methodology. In R.M. Lerner (Ed.), *Handbook of child psychology,* Vol. 1: *Theoretical models of human development* (6th ed., pp. 18–88). Hoboken, NJ: Wiley.

Pate, R.R., Dowda, M., O'Neill, J.R., & Ward, D.S. (2007). Change in physical activity participation among adolescent girls from 8th to 12th grade. *Journal of Physical Activity and Health, 4*(1), 3–16.

Pate, R., Davis, M., Robinson, T., Stone, E., McKenzie, T., & Young, J. (2006). Promoting physical activity in children and youth: a leadership role for schools: a scientific statement from the American Heart Association Council on Nutrition, Physical Activity, and Metabolism (Physical Activity Committee) in collaboration with the Councils on Cardiovascular Disease in the Young and Cardiovascular Nursing. *Circulation, 114*(11), 1214–1224.

Pate, R.R., Pfeiffer, K.A., Trost, S.G., Ziegler, P., & Dowda, M. (2004). Physical Activity Among Children Attending Preschools. *Pediatrics, 114*(5), 1258–1263.

Pedersen, S., & Seidman, E. (2005). Contexts and correlates of out-of-school activity participation among low-income urban adolescents. In J.L. Mahoney, R.W. Larson, & J.S. Eccles (Eds.), *Organized activities as contexts of development: Extracurricular activities, after-school and community programs* (pp. 85–110). Mahwah, NJ: Lawrence Erlbaum Associates.

Persson, A., Kerr, M., & Stattin, H. (2007). Staying in or moving away from structured activities: Explanations involving parents and peers. *Developmental Psychology, 43*, 197–207.

Quinn, J. (1999). Where needs meet opportunity: Youth development programs for early teens. In R. Behrman (Ed.), *The future of children: When school is out* (pp. 96–116). Washington, DC: The David and Lucile Packard Foundation.

Quiroz, P. (2000). A comparison of the organizational and cultural contexts of extracurricular participation and sponsorship in two high schools. *Educational Studies, 31*, 249–275.

Reed, J.A., Ainsworth, B.E., Wilson, D.K., Kirtland, K., Mixon, G., & Cook, A. (2004). Environmental supports for physical activity: Awareness and use of walking trails. *Preventive Medicine, 39*, 903–908.

Resnicow, K., & Vaughan, R. (2006). A chaotic view of behavior change: A quantum leap for health promotion. *International Journal of Behavioral Nutrition and Physical Activity, 3*, 25.

Roffman, J.G., Suaurez-Orozco, C., & Rhodes, J. (2003). Facilitating positive development in immigrant youth: The role of mentors and community organizations. In F.A. Villarruel,

D.F. Perkins, L.M. Borden, & J.G. Keith (Eds.) *Community youth development: Programs, policies, and practices* (pp. 90–117). Thousand Oaks, CA: Sage.

Ross, R., Freeman, J.A., Janssen, I. (2000). Exercise alone is an effective strategy for reducing obesity and related comorbidities. *Exercise and Sports Sciences Reviews, 28,* 165–170.

Rowe, J.W., & Kahn, R.L. (1998). *Successful aging.* New York: Dell.

Ruble, D.N., & Goodnow, J.J. (1998). Social development in childhood and adulthood. In D.T. Gilbert, S.T. Fiske, & G. Lindzey (Eds.), *The handbook of social psychology* (4th ed., pp. 741–787). New York: Oxford University Press.

Rural School & Community Trust (2005). *Annual report.* Retrieved from http://www.ruraledu.org/site/c.beJMIZOCIrH/b.2820295/.

Sallis, J.F., Cervero, R.B., Ascher, W., Henderson, K.A., Kraft, M.K., & Kerr J. (2006). An ecological approach to creating active living communities. *Annual Review of Public Health, 27,* 297–322.

Sallis, J.F., Prochaska, J.J., & Taylor, W.C. (2000). A review of correlates of physical activity of children and adolescents. *Medicine and Science in Sports and Exercise, 32*(5), 963–975.

Sanson-Fisher, R.W., Bonevski, B., Green, L.W., & D'Este, C. (2007). Limitations of the randomized controlled trial in evaluating population-based health interventions. *American Journal of Preventive Medicine, 33*(2), 155–161.

Schwartz, G.E. (1982). Testing the biopsychosocial model: The ultimate challenge facing behavioral medicine? *Journal of Consulting and Clinical Psychology, 50,* 1040–1053.

Schulz, K.F., Chalmers, I., Grimes, D.A., & Altman, D.G. (1994). Assessing the quality of randomization from reports of controlled trials published in obstetrics and gynecology journals. *Journal of the American Medical Association, 272*(2), 125–128.

Schulz, R., & Salthouse, T. (1999). *Adult development and aging: Myths and emerging Realities* (3rd ed.). New York: Prentice Hall.

Simpkins, S.D., Fredricks, J., Davis-Kean, P., & Eccles, J.S. (2006). Healthy minds, healthy habits: The influence of activity involvement in middle childhood. In A.C. Huston, & M.N. Ripke (Eds.), *Developmental contexts in middle childhood* (pp. 283–302). New York: Cambridge University Press.

Simpkins, S.D., Ripke, M., Huston, A.C., & Eccles, J.S. (2005). Predicting participation and outcomes in out-of-school activities: Similarities and differences across social ecologies. In G.G. Noam (Ed.), H.B. Weiss, P.M.D. Little, & S.M. Bouffard (Issue Eds.), *New directions for youth development.* Vol. 105: *Participation in youth programs: Enrollment, attendance, and engagement* (pp. 51–70). San Francisco: Jossey-Bass.

Spear, B.A. (2002). Adolescent growth and development. *Journal of the American Dietetics Association, 102,* S23–S29.

Springer, A.E., Kelder, S.H., & Hoelscher, D.M. (2006). Social support, physical activity and sedentary behavior among 6th-grade girls: A cross-sectional study. *International Journal of Behavioral Nutrition and Physical Activity, 3,* 8.

Spurrier, N.J., Magarey, A.A., Golley, R., Curnow, F., & Sawyer, M.G. (2008). Relationships between the home environment and physical activity and dietary patterns of pre-school children: A cross-sectional study. *International Journal of Behavioral Nutrition and Physical Activity, 5,* 31–42.

Strong, W., Malina, R., Blimkie, C., Daniels, S., Dishman, R., Gutin, B., et al. (2005). Evidence based physical activity

for school-age youth. *The Journal Of Pediatrics, 146*(6), 732–737.

Tanner, J.M., & Davies, P.S. (1985). Clinical longitudinal standards for height and height velocity for North American children. *Journal of Pediatrics, 107*(3), 317–329.

Taylor, R.W., Grant, A.M., Goulding, A., & Williams, S.M. (2005). Early adiposity rebound: Review of papers linking this to subsequent obesity in children and adults. *Current Opinions in Clinical Nutrition and Metabolic Care, 8*(6), 607–661.

Taylor, W., Blair, S., Cummings, S., Wun, C., & Malina, R. (1999). Childhood and adolescent physical activity patterns and adult physical activity. *Medicine and Science in Sports and Exercise, 31*(1), 118–123.

Trost, S.G., Sallis, J.F., Pate, R.R., Freedson, P.S., Taylor, W.C., & Dowda, M. (2003). Evaluating a Model of Parental Influence on Youth Physical Activity. *American Journal of Preventive Medicine, 25*(4), 277–282.

U.S. Department of Health and Human Services. (1996). *Physical Activity and Health: A report of the surgeon general.* Atlanta, GA: National Center for Chronic Disease Prevention and Health Promotion, Centers for Disease Control and Prevention, U.S. Department of Health and Human Services.

U.S. Department of Health and Human Services (2008). 2008 Physical Activity Guidelines for Americans. Office of Disease Prevention and Health Promotion, Centers for Diseae Control and Prevention, U.S. Department of Health and Human Services.

van Pelt, R., Dinneno, F., Seals, D., & Jones, P. (2001). Age-related decline in RMR in physically active men: Relation to exercise volume and energy intake. *American Journal of Physiology. Endocrinology and Metabolism, 281*(3), E633–E639.

Verghese, J., Lipton, R., Katz, M., Hall, C., Derby, C., Kuslansky, G., et al. (2003). Leisure activities and the risk of dementia in the elderly. *The New England Journal Of Medicine, 348*(25), 2508–2516.

Walker, E., Hernandez, A.V., & Kattan, M.W. (2008). Meta-analysis: Its strengths and limitations. *Cleveland Clinic Journal of Medicine, 75*(6), 431–439.

Weinberg, R.S., & Gould, D. (2007). Children and sport psychology. In R.S. Weinberg, & D. Gould (Eds.), *Foundations of sport and exercise psychology* (pp. 514–532). Champaign, IL: Human Kinetics.

Weir, L.A., Etelson, D., & Brand, D.A. (2006). Parents' perceptions of neighborhood safety and children's physical activity. *Preventive Medicine, 43,* 212–217.

Weiss, M.R., McCullagh, P., Smith, A.L., & Berlant, A.R. (1998). Observational learning and the fearful child: Influence of peer models on swimming skill performance and psychological responses. *Research Quarterly for Exercise and Sport, 69,* 380–394.

Whaley, D.E. (2004). Seeing isn't always believing: Self-perceptions and physical activity behaviors in adults. In M.R. Weiss (Ed.), *Developmental sport and exercise psychology: A lifespan perspective* (pp. 289–311). Morgantown, WV, U.S.: Fitness Information Technology.

Whitaker, R., Pepe, M., Wright, J., Seidel, K., & Dietz, W. (1998). Early adiposity rebound and the risk of adult obesity. *Pediatrics, 101*(3), E5.

Wilmore, J.H., & Costill, D.L. (1994). Physiology of sport and exercise. In J.H. Wilmore, & D.L. Costill (Eds.), *Growth development and the young athlete* (pp. 400–421). Champaign, IL: Human Kinetics.

Wilson, R.S., & Bennett, D.A. (2003). Cognitive activity and risk of Alzheimer's disease. *Current Directions in Psychological Science, 12*, 87–91.

Wilson, D.K. (2008). Commentary for health psychology special issue: Theoretical advances in diet and physical activity interventions. *Health Psychology, 27*(Suppl. 1), S1.

Wilson, D.K., Evans, A.E., Williams, J., Mixon, G., Minette, C., Sirad, J., & Pate, R.A. (2005). Preliminary test of a student-centered program on increasing physical activity in underserved adolescents. *Annals of Behavioral Medicine. 30*, 119–124.

Wilson, D.K., Griffin, S., Saunders, R., Kitzman-Ulrich, H., Meyers, D.C., & Mansard, L. (2009). Using process evaluation for program improvement in dose, fidelity and reach: The ACT trial experience. *International Journal of Behavior Nutrition and Physical Activity*, 6, 79.

Wilson, D.K., Kirtland, K., Ainsworth, B., & Addy, C.L. (2004). Socioeconomic status and perceptions of access and safety for physical activity. *Annals of Behavioral Medicine, 28*, 20–28.

Wilson, D.K., Kitzman-Ulrich, H., Williams, J.E., Saunders, R., Griffin, S., Pate, R., et al. (2008). An overview of the "Active by Choice Today" (ACT) trial for increasing physical activity. *Contemporary Clinical Trials, 29*(1), 21–31.

Wilson, D.K., St. George, S.M., Zarrett, N. (2010). Developmental influences in understanding children and adolescent health behaviors. In J. Suls, K. Davidson, R. Kaplan (Eds.), *Handbook of health psychology.* New York: Guilford Press., p. 133–146.

Wilson, D.K., Trumpeter, M.S., St. George, S.M., et al. (2010). An overview of the "Positive Action for Today's Health" (PATH) trial for increasing walking in underserved communities. *Contemporary Clinical Trials. 31*, 624–633.

Wilson, D.K., Williams, J., Evans, A.E., Mixon, G., Minette, C., & Rheaume, C. (2005). A qualitative study of gender differences in preferences and motivational factors for physical activity in underserved adolescents. *Journal of Pediatric Psychology, 30*, 1–5.

Wright, M., Wilson, D.K., Griffin, S., Evans, A. (2010). The role of parental modeling and social support in promoting physical activity in underserved adolescents. *Health Education and Behavior. 25*, 224-232.

Zarrett, N.R. (2007). *The dynamic relation between out-of-school activities and adolescent development.* Doctoral dissertation, University of Michigan. *Dissertation Abstracts International, 67*(10), 6100B.

Zarrett, N., & Eccles, J.S. (2006). The passage to adulthood: Challenges of late adolescence. In S. Piha, & G. Hall (Vol. Eds.), *New directions for youth development. preparing youth for the crossing: From adolescence to early adulthood* (Issue 111, pp. 13–28). Wiley Periodicals Inc.

Zimmerman, B.J. (2000). Attaining self-regulation: A social cognitive perspective. In M. Boekaerts, P.R. Pintrich, & M. Zeidner (Eds.), *Handbook of self-regulation* (pp. 13–39). San Diego, CA: Academic Press.

# Alcohol Use and Alcohol Use Disorders

Kenneth J. Sher, Amelia E. Talley, Andrew K. Littlefield, *and* Julia A. Martinez

**Abstract**

Heavy alcohol use in the general population, especially among late adolescents and young adults, is highly prevalent and associated with a range of adverse health outcomes, such as unintentional injury and sexually transmitted infections, as well as fetal injury in pregnant women. Although heavy consumption tends to decrease as individuals age, the cumulative effect of alcohol exposure increases risk for some forms of cancer, gastrointestinal disease, dementing illnesses, and other serious conditions. Alcohol use can also interfere with treatments for medical illnesses via drug interactions and poor compliance with prescribed treatments. Against this backdrop of considerable health burden associated with alcohol use in the population are findings that, at least among certain subgroups of the population, there are health benefits of moderate consumption. Additionally, alcohol use disorders (AUDs; alcohol abuse and alcohol dependence), are among the most prevalent mental disorders in the United States and elsewhere. AUDs are frequently comorbid with other psychological disorders which in themselves have important implications for health. A number of approaches to the prevention and treatment of problematic alcohol use have been developed and are effective. Some of these can be employed during primary care visits or other contacts with health professionals (e.g., emergency room visits).

**Keywords:** Alcohol consumption, alcohol use disorders, assessment, comorbidity, epidemiology, medical illnesses, treatment

The majority of North Americans and adults in many cultures consume alcoholic beverages, and alcohol use disorders (AUDs) are among the most prevalent mental disorders in the United States. Although there appear to be some health benefits associated with moderate alcohol consumption in middle age, alcohol consumption is associated with numerous health-related problems across the lifespan, and AUDs carry with them significant consequences for the drinker, his or her friends and family, employers, the community, and the nation. Further, alcohol consumption and AUDs are frequently associated with other psychiatric and medical conditions; thus, their consequences can be far reaching and have implications for understanding a number of aspects of health-related behaviors and health outcomes.

## Definitions of Alcohol-related Concepts
### Alcohol Use Disorder

The *Diagnostic and Statistical Manual of Mental Disorders, Fourth Edition, Text Revision* (DSM-IV; American Psychiatric Association, 2000) defines two major classes of substance use disorders: substance dependence and substance abuse. The diagnostic criteria for AUDs follow those for substance use disorders, with *alcohol dependence* defined as "a maladaptive pattern of use, leading to clinically significant impairment or distress, as manifested by three (or more) of the following symptoms occurring at any time the same 12-month period: (1) tolerance, (2) withdrawal, (3) the substance is often taken in larger amounts or over a longer period than intended, (4) a persistent desire or unsuccessful efforts to cut down or control substance use, (5) a great deal of time is spent in activities necessary to obtain the substance, use the substance or recover from its effects, (6) important social, occupational, or recreational activities are given up or reduced because of substance use, and (7) the substance use is continued despite knowledge of having a persistent or recurrent physical or psychological problem that is likely to have been caused or exacerbated by the substance" (p. 197). The DSM-IV defines alcohol abuse as "a maladaptive pattern of substance use leading to clinically significant impairment or distress as manifested by one (or more) of the following occurring within a 12-month period: (1) recurrent substance use resulting in a failure to fulfill major role obligations at work, school, or home, (2) recurrent substance use in situations in which it is physically hazardous, (3) recurrent substance-related legal problems, and (4) continued substance use despite having persistent or recurrent social or interpersonal problems caused or exacerbated by the effects of the substance" (pg. 198). According to the DSM-IV's diagnostic hierarchy, individuals who meet criteria for alcohol dependence do not receive diagnoses for alcohol abuse, implying that dependence is the more severe of the two AUDs.

The abuse/dependence distinction made its debut in the third edition of the DSM (DSM-III, American Psychiatric Association, 1980), reflecting, in part, the distinction introduced by Edwards and Gross (1976) between alcohol dependence syndrome and alcohol-related disabilities, with the former construct reflecting the degree to which alcohol has come to dominate the drinker's life as evidenced by: narrowing in the drinking repertoire, salience of drink-seeking behavior, increased tolerance to alcohol, repeated withdrawal symptoms, relief or avoidance of withdrawal symptoms by further drinking, subjective awareness of compulsion to drink, and/or reinstatement after abstinence. In contrast, the alcohol-related disabilities construct reflected the degree to which the drinker experienced a range of problems, such as physical ailments (e.g., developing cirrhosis), occupational impairment, marital discord, and hazardous use (e.g., drinking and driving). Unlike Edwards and Gross's conceptualization of the dependence syndrome and alcohol-related disabilities as distinct but related dimensions, the categorical diagnostic approach embraced by the DSM to date viewed abuse and dependence as mutually exclusive categories, with a dependence diagnosis representing the more severe condition and precluding the ostensibly less severe abuse diagnosis. In the DSM-III, alcohol dependence was conceived as physiological,

indicated by tolerance or withdrawal and reflecting "neuroadaptation." This narrow concept of dependence was broadened in the revised criteria of DSM-III (DSM-III-R; American Psychiatric Association, 1987) and the DSM-IV to include behavioral signs of dependence, such as loss of control (i.e., drinking in larger amounts or longer than intended), inability to abstain, and other symptoms reflecting compulsive use. At present, the abuse–dependence distinction is coming under increasing scientific criticism (see Sher, Martinez, & Littlefield, 2011); these criticisms are based on both psychometric and construct validity concerns and, therefore, it seems likely that future revisions of the DSM and the International Diagnostic Code (ICD) will alter the coverage and boundaries of these two diagnostic categories.

### Alcohol Consumption
Current diagnostic criteria for AUDs do not include direct measures of alcohol consumption despite health concerns based on alcohol consumption patterns, regardless of whether someone meets AUD criteria or not. The U.S. government has recently provided safe drinking guidelines as part of its Dietary Guidelines for Americans, 2005 (U.S. Departments of Agriculture and of Health and Human Services, 2005). These guidelines discourage levels of consumption that exceed two drinks per day for men and one drink per day for women. Current estimates suggest that, among past-year drinkers 18 years of age and older, 46% of men and 32% of adult women in the United States exceed these safe drinking levels and are appropriate targets for interventions (Dawson, Grant, & Li, 2005).

In addition, there has been increasing concern in recent years over drinking patterns associated with high levels of consumption on drinking days (i.e., "binge" drinking). The National Institute of Alcohol Abuse and Alcoholism (NIAAA, 2004) defined binge drinking as "a pattern of drinking alcohol that brings blood alcohol concentration (BAC) to 0.08 gram percent or above. For the typical adult, this pattern corresponds to consuming five or more drinks (male), or four or more drinks (female), in about 2 hours," noting that such patterns represent significant risk for the drinker and society. From the standpoint of understanding the role of alcohol in health, it is important to distinguish among these various aspects of drinking behavior (frequency of consumption, amount typically consumed, binge drinking, cumulative alcohol exposure of the lifespan, abuse, and dependence), as well as the stage of life of the drinker because the health relevance of these various measures appears to differ in a number of critical ways. For example, with respect to alcoholic hepatitis and cardiomyopathy, cumulative consumption over the lifespan may be more critical than a few episodic heavy exposures (see Lucey, Mathurin, & Morgan, 2009; Nicolas et al., 2002; Stewart, Jones, & Day, 2001). In contrast, a few heavy drinking episodes during the first trimester may put a fetus at risk for fetal alcohol effects (see Abel, 1998; Gray & Henderson, 2006; Gray, Mukherjee, & Rutter, 2009). Additionally, although moderate alcohol consumption may have overall health benefits in middle-aged men, this is not the case in youth (Thakker, 1998). This age difference in the beneficial effects of alcohol is due to the significant morbidity and mortality associated with coronary artery disease and ischemic stroke that exists in middle age, a time in which alcohol has a salutary effect on these conditions (see Reynolds et al., 2003, for a meta-analysis). However, in youth, significant morbidity and mortality is associated with intentional and unintentional injury, and alcohol is a risk factor for these conditions. Thus, when considering the effects of alcohol on health, it is important to consider specific aspects of drinking patterns, stage of life, and specific health conditions.

## Epidemiology

Past-year rates of abstention from alcohol in the 2001–2002 National Epidemiologic Survey on Alcohol and Related Conditions (NESARC) indicate that 28.6% of individuals in the United States did not have more than a sip of alcohol in the prior year, whereas 65.4% reported at least some alcohol use (Falk, Yi, & Hiller-Sturmhofel, 2006). Lifetime abstention from alcohol use was estimated for 17.28% of the population (Falk et al., 2006). An earlier population-based study estimated that, from 1984 to 1985, approximately 15% of people in the United States were current alcohol abstainers, whereas 18% were lifetime abstainers (Rehm, Greenfield, & Rogers, 2001), suggesting considerable stability in the estimates of lifetime abstention over the past two decades. As of 2001, most current drinkers in the United States were classified as light drinkers (61.9%; i.e., three or fewer drinks per week), with smaller proportions being classified as moderate (21.3%; i.e., three to 14 drinks per week for men or three to seven drinks per week for women), and heavy drinkers (15.6%; more than two drinks per day for men or more than one drink per day for women) (Falk et al., 2006). The earlier National Alcohol Survey, by contrast, estimated that

most people in the United States from 1984 to 1985 drank zero-to-one (45%) or one-to-two (11%) drinks per day on average; the rest were estimated to drink two or more drinks per day (11%) on average (Rehm et al., 2001). By 2001, approximately 14% of adults in the United States were estimated to engage in binge drinking (defined as the consumption of five or more drinks on at least one occasion) in the previous 30 days (Naimi et al., 2003). It was estimated that each adult drinker engaged in approximately seven binge drinking episodes per year (Naimi et al., 2003). In 1985, approximately 30% of individuals had engaged in at least one binge drinking occasion in the prior year (Greenfield & Kerr, 2003).

Multiple population-based, epidemiological surveys indicate that the prevalence rates of AUDs are high, especially among those in late adolescence and early adulthood. Over the past 25 years, five large-scale, population-based epidemiological surveys using structured diagnostic interviews have provided estimates of AUDs in the United States. These include the Epidemiologic Catchment Area (ECA) Survey (Helzer, Burnam, & McEnvoy, 1991; Robins & Price 1991), the National Comorbidity Survey (NCS; Kessler, Crum, Warner, & Nelson, 1997; Kessler et al., 1994), the National Comorbidity Survey – Replication (NCS-R; Kessler, Berglund, Demler, Jin, & Walters, 2005; Kessler, Chiu, Demler, & Walters, 2005), the National Longitudinal Alcohol Epidemiologic Survey (NLAES; Grant, 1997; Grant, Harford, Dawson, Chou, et al., 1994; Grant & Pickering, 1996), and the National Epidemiologic Survey on Alcohol and Related Conditions (NESARC; Grant, Dawson, et al., 2004; Grant, Stinson, et al., 2004). Each of these major studies indicate very high lifetime and past-year prevalence rates of AUDs in the U.S. population (13.8% lifetime and 6.8% past-year DSM-III in ECA; 23.5% lifetime and 7.7% past-year DSM-IIIR in NCS; 18.2% lifetime and 7.41% past-year DSM-IV in NLAES; 30.3% lifetime and 8.46% past-year DSM-IV in NESARC; 18.6% lifetime and 4.4% past-year DSM-IV in NCS-R). In general, men are much more likely to be diagnosed with past-year alcohol abuse (6.9%) or dependence (5.4%) than are women (abuse: 2.6%; dependence: 2.3%; Grant, Dawson, et al., 2004). The prevalence of abuse is greater among Whites (5.1%) than among Blacks (3.3%), Asians (2.1%), and Hispanics (4.0%). The prevalence of dependence is higher in Whites (3.8%), Native Americans (6.4%), and Hispanics (4.0%) than Asians (2.4%).

## Drinking over the Life Course

The prevalence of both binge drinking and AUDs are highly age-graded. These changes in prevalence rates of AUDs over the life course argue for us to consider AUDs, in part, as developmental phenomena. The period intervening between adolescence and adulthood, known as "emerging adulthood" (Arnett, 2006) represents the time when individuals are at the highest risk for binge drinking and manifesting an AUD, with the highest prevalence of binge drinking and the peak hazard for onset for both alcohol abuse and alcohol dependence occurring around the age of 20 in the United States (Caetano & Tam, 1995; Grant, Dawson, et al., 2004; Grant, Moore, & Kaplan, 2003; Li, Hewitt, & Grant, 2004; Johnston, O'Malley, Bachman, & Schulenberg, 2007). This heightened risk is thought to reflect a time when individuals are relatively free of adult responsibilities but unrestrained by parental influence. However, as individuals progress into adulthood, perhaps undertaking a number of novel adult responsibilities (e.g., marriage and parenthood), rates of heavy consumption and AUDs typically decrease (i.e., "maturing out," Winick, 1962; see Arnett, 2006; Bachman, Wadsworth, O'Malley, Johnston, & Schulenberg, 1997; Donovan, Jessor, & Jessor, 1983; Littlefield & Sher, 2009).

Notably, there is significant cultural variation in these developmental patterns. In particular, Black men are likely to have later ages of onset of alcohol use disorder with increases during the third decade of life, whereas there is decreasing prevalence among White men of the same age (Grant, Dawson, et al., 2004; Herd & Grube 1996). These divergences in developmental paths may due to cultural variation in education, labor market participation, drinking motives, and marriage and parenting (Cooper et al., 2008; Dawson, 1998).

## Alcohol As a Drug
### Acute Effects

The neuropharmacology of alcohol (specifically ethanol, the form of alcohol contained in alcoholic beverages) affects virtually all major neurotransmitter systems, especially when alcohol is consumed at levels associated with intoxication. Alcohol operates both acutely and chronically with many central nervous system (CNS) neurotransmitter systems that play a key role in regulating cognition, affect, and behavior, as well as the subjective effects of alcohol, all of which may be factors in the development of alcohol addiction (Fromme & D'Amico, 1999; Vengeliene, Bilbao, Molander, & Spanagel, 2008).

For purposes of discussion, the subjective and hedonic effects of alcohol can be separated into three broad classes: (1) positive reinforcing effects (e.g., euphoric, arousing), (2) negative reinforcing effects (e.g., anxiolytic, antidepressant), and (3) punishing effects (e.g., depressant and acute discomfort such as flushing, nausea, and vomiting).

*Positively reinforcing effects of alcohol*, such as euphoria and increased arousal, are thought to be largely associated with enhanced monoaminergic (especially dopaminergic) effects and related opioid peptide activity (NIAAA, 1997). Opiate antagonists or blockers, in particular naltrexone and nalmefene, have been found to suppress the subjective stimulating effects of alcohol and craving in both social drinkers and non–treatment-seeking alcoholics (Drobes, Anton, Thomas, & Voronin, 2004).

*Negatively reinforcing acute subjective effects of alcohol*, including anxiolysis and possibly some antidepressant effects, are thought to be mediated by alcohol's effects on the $\gamma$-aminobutyric acid (GABA$_A$) receptor. It has been known for more than 50 years that alcohol has reliable effects on passive avoidance in rodents in a way quite similar to classic anxiolytic drugs, such as benzodiazepines (Harris, Mihic, & Valenzuela, 1998). Further, neuropharmacological studies have shown that alcohol works to enhance GABAergic activity through its action on the GABAA receptor. Drugs that have the opposite effect on this receptor (i.e., inverse agonists such as RO 15-4513) appear to reverse anxiolytic and related effects (Lister & Nutt, 1988), perhaps by competing for the same GABA$_A$ receptors as ethanol (Hanchar et al., 2006).

Some of the *punishing acute subjective effects of alcohol* (e.g., flushing) appear to be due to intermediary by-products of ethanol metabolism (specifically acetaldehyde, which is a toxic metabolite of alcohol; Eriksson, 1983; Eriksson, Mizoi, & Fukunaga, 1982). Further, it appears that many of the effects of acetaldehyde are manifested in the periphery. Other presumably punishing effects (e.g., sedation) are likely mediated by central GABAergic mechanisms within the hippocampus, septum, cerebral cortex, and cerebellum, and are more likely to be observed at high doses and on the descending limb of the blood alcohol curve (Fromme & D'Amico, 1999).

### ARE REINFORCING AND PUNISHING EFFECTS OF ALCOHOL DIRECT OR MEDIATED VIA COGNITIVE PROCESSES?

One of the most influential cognitive processing theories of psychological vulnerability is Josephs and Steele's (1990) "alcohol myopia" theory, which proposes that the effect of alcohol is contingent upon information processing of more or less salient features of the drinking context. This theory has received support across multiple domains and can provide a coherent explanation as to how alcohol can lead to either an animated, euphoric, and celebratory experience (i.e., *reinforcement*) or to a depressive "crying in one's beer" experience (i.e., *punishment*). In several studies, Steele and colleagues have shown that alcohol consumption, followed by distracting pleasant or neutral stimuli, can attenuate stress responses. However, when no distraction is present, low to moderate doses of alcohol do not reduce anxiety or produce anxiogenic effects (Josephs & Steele, 1990). However, at higher doses associated with intoxication, alcohol appears to have robust effects at reducing negative emotional states (e.g., Donohue, Curtin, Patrick, & Lang, 2007; Sher, Bartholow, Peuser, Erickson, & Wood, 2007). These findings suggest that at low and intermediate blood alcohol levels, many affective consequences of consumption are cognitively mediated and, thus, heavily context-dependent and moderated by individual differences related to appraisal processes. However, at higher doses, more direct effects of alcohol on brain centers responsible for mood and emotion are likely to be observed.

### Biphasic Effects of Alcohol

The reinforcing effects of alcohol typically are experienced on the ascending limb of the blood alcohol concentration (BAC) curve (measured from the time that drinking is initiated until individuals reach their peak BAC), and the punishing effects typically occur on the descending limb of the BAC curve (measured at the time subsequent to that when individuals have reached their peak BAC), rendering the net effect of alcohol as biphasic (Sher, Wood, Richardson, & Jackson, 2005). These biphasic effects are observable in the laboratory, and individuals also report expecting to experience such effects prior to drinking (Earleywine, 1994; Earleywine & Martin, 1993). Notably, heavier drinkers have been found more likely to experience stronger stimulant effects relative to sedative effects, whereas lighter drinkers have been found to experience the opposite (Earleywine, 1994). The biphasic effects of alcohol are subject to individual differences (Newlin & Thomson, 1990) as well as dosage (Holdstock & de Wit, 1998).

### Chronic Adaptation to Alcohol

Heavy, chronic drinkers often experience a range of persistent changes relevant to acute withdrawal symptoms and resultant emotional functioning. First, alcohol withdrawal symptoms are often associated with affective disturbance, particularly anxiety (Sellers, Sullivan, Somer, & Sykora, 1991; Sullivan, Sykora, Schneiderman, Naranjo, & Sellers, 1989). These associations can potentially create a vicious cycle whereby chronic alcohol use leads to affective disturbance, which in turn motivates further drinking. Second, some forms of anxiety and mood disorders appear to be "alcohol-induced" and, thus, differential diagnosis of substance-induced mood disorders is considered critical for nosology and treatment (American Psychiatric Association, 1994, 2000; Schuckit, 1994). Anxiety and mood disorders that remit spontaneously after a short period (less than a month) of abstinence and that only appear in the context of ongoing substance use should be considered substance-induced and not "independent." Third, even ostensibly independent anxiety and mood disorders often appear to temporally follow the occurrence of an AUD (especially true in the case of depression, Kessler et al., 1997). For example, in a multinational pool of five epidemiological studies (Merikangas et al., 1996), it was found that, among those with co-occurring alcohol dependence and depression, 20% reported that the onset of the disorders occurred together, 38% reported that depression came first, and 42% reported that alcohol dependence came first (the study did not compare order of onset for anxiety disorders and alcohol dependence).

A general perspective on changes associated with the chronic use of various drugs of abuse, including alcohol, is termed *allostasis* (i.e., adaptive homeostatic changes that occur in response to repeated drug challenges; e.g., Koob & LeMoal, 2001, 2008). According to this theory, an organism responds to drug challenges by producing counterdirectional (i.e., homeostatic) responses that increase over time. Thus, allostasis explains the phenomenon of acquired tolerance, the tendency for a given dose of a drug to elicit progressively less response over time, in a way similar to that proposed by Solomon and Corbit (1974) in their opponent-process theory and Siegel and colleagues (e.g., Siegel, Baptista, Kim, McDonald, & Weise-Kelly, 2000) in their Pavlovian account of tolerance development. However, the allostatic perspective goes further than these theories by specifically positing that repeated homeostatic challenges present an adaptive burden and result in a shift of a hedonic "set point" in the direction of the opponent process. Theoretically, such a process could explain intermediate- to long-term deviations in tonic emotional levels, resulting in a more depressed, irritable, and/or anxious alcohol dependent person. Such a perspective is also consistent with the general principle that acute and chronic effects of alcohol are opposite in direction with respect to both neuropharmacological effects and their behavioral correlates. These allostatic, chronic adaptations are believed to be mediated by the hypothalamic-pituitary-adrenal (HPA) axis via effects of corticotropin-releasing factor (CRF) (Koob & LeMoal, 2001, 2008); notably, current drug development efforts are targeting CRF antagonists to attempt to modulate these proposed allostatic influences.

## Genetic and Environmental Factors Associated with Alcohol Use and AUDs

The number of etiological factors contributing to alcohol use and AUDs are extensive, and both genetic and environmental factors, broadly construed, have been implicated as well as their interactions.

### Genetic Vulnerability

The existence of significant genetic influences on AUDs (among individuals who drink) has been firmly established in adoption studies (Cadoret, Yates, Troughton, Woodworth, & Stewart, 1995; Cloninger, Bohman, & Sigvardsson, 1981; Goodwin, Schulsinger, Hermansen, Guze, & Winokur, 1973; McGue, 1994) that show strong effects of biological parents independent of being reared with them. Moreover, classic twin studies (Heath, 1995; Heath et al., 1997; McGue, 1999) that compare concordance of alcohol-related phenotypes between monozygotic (identical) and dizygotic (fraternal) twins consistently show genes accounting for approximately half of the variance in AUD prevalence. Although the new era of molecular genetics has moved the focus from establishing the importance of genetic factors to identifying specific genes that are important in AUD etiology (Dick, Rose, & Kaprio, 2006), these twin and adoption studies remain useful in demonstrating both common genetic influences on AUDs and comorbid conditions, and the importance of gene × environment interaction in the absence of knowledge of specific genes involved.

For example, Slutske et al. (1998) showed that much of the comorbidity between childhood conduct disorder and AUDs can be attributed to shared additive genetic effects and, further, that temperamental traits (especially those related to poor self-control) appear to represent common genetically mediated

contributions to this disorder (Slutske et al., 2002). This suggests that, rather than looking for pure "alcohol genes," it might be fruitful to look for genes contributing to multivariate, spectrum phenotypes (Dick et al., 2008; Uhl et al., 2008), as well as for genes specific to alcohol dependence.

Similarly, genetically informative samples can be useful for identifying the presence of certain forms of gene × environment (GxE)interactions. In behavior-genetic rodent models of drinking, cross-fostering designs (in which the genetic background and rearing environment are experimentally crossed) can be extremely informative (Randall & Lester, 1975). However, the comparable design in humans, the adoption design, is problematic for several reasons. Human adoptions tend to select for strong genetic effects (due to deviant biological parents) and low variance in rearing conditions (i.e., adoption agencies tend not to place adoptees in problem homes). Moreover, in the classic twin design, GxE interactions are confounded with additive genetic effects (in the case of genes × shared environment) and with unique environmental effects (in the case of genes × unique environment). However, extended twin-family designs that control for genetic background in parents when examining differences in rearing conditions can elucidate where some GxE interactions might occur. Specifically, the absence of parental alcoholism (a protective environmental factor) can reduce the impact of high genetic risk for the development of AUDs in the offspring of (discordant) twins (Jacob et al., 2003; but see Slutske et al., 2008).

In recent years, increasing numbers of molecular genetic studies have sought to identify specific genes that confer risk. Much of this work focused on genes that play a role in alcohol metabolism, and subsequent subjective responses to alcohol. For example, variations in alcohol dehydrogenase (ADH) and aldehyde dehydrogenase (ALDH), two of the major enzymes involved in alcohol metabolism, have been linked to individual differences in subjective and physiological responses to alcohol (Chen, Loh, Hsu, Chen, Yu, & Cheng, 1996; Luczak, Elvine-Kreis, Shea, Carr, & Wall, 2002; Nakamura et al,, 1996). The most widely studied of these is allelic variation in a gene that encodes for ALDH. Individuals with one or two copies of the ALDH*2 allele have impaired acetaldehyde metabolism resulting in elevated acetaldehyde levels that lead to an alcohol-induced flushing response (Higuchi, Matsushita, Murayama, Takagi, & Hayashida, 1995). This mutation, which is present in a large minority of several Asian groups including Chinese, Japanese, and Koreans (but not Filipinos or Indians; Eng, Luczak, & Wall, 2007), is associated with a range of unpleasant effects, such as facial flushing, heart palpitations, and nausea, and is therefore thought to be protective against the development of alcohol dependence (Higuchi et al., 1995; Takeshita, Morimoto, Mao, Hashimoto, & Furuyama, 1994; Wall, Thomasson, Schuckit, & Ehlers, 1992). In a recent meta-analysis, Luczak, Glatt, and Wall (2006) found that presence of one (or two) copies of these alleles (that are linked with impaired acetaldehyde metabolism) were associated with a greatly reduced risk of alcohol dependence in Asian populations.

Although subjective response to alcohol as a function of variability in ADH genotypes has only just begun to be explored in alcohol challenge studies, there is evidence suggestive of etiologically relevant variability. Specifically, the presence of the ADH1B*2 allele leads to more rapid metabolism of alcohol to acetaldehyde (Crabb, 1995), which may generate an altered subjective response to drinking. This genotype occurs at a high base rate in Asians (especially Chinese, Japanese, and Koreans; Eng et al., 2007) and is associated with lower rates of AUDs in these populations (Luczak et al., 2006). The presence of at least one ADH1B*2 allele was also observed to be significantly more prevalent among young adult African Americans who do not have a family history of AUDs (Ehlers, Gilder, Harris, & Carr, 2001). Furthermore, in the same population, the presence of the ADH1B*2 allele was linked with higher levels of alcohol expectancies, which could be associated with greater subjective responses to alcohol as well.

Perhaps more relevant for understanding genetic influences in individuals of European descent, a number of genes associated with central brain neurotransmitter systems have been found to be associated with alcohol dependence. For example, GABA is a neurotransmitter involved in many of the anxiolytic and sedative effects of alcohol, and GABA receptors are involved in alcohol tolerance. Recent studies have established associations between $GABA_A$ receptor genes on chromosomes 4 (e.g., GABRA2, GABRB1) and 15 (e.g., GABRB3), and AUDs across human and animal studies (Dick & Beirut, 2006). Although genes associated with alcohol and acetaldehyde metabolism and the GABRA2 gene show replicable links to AUDs, there are a number of less consistent links with candidate genes associated with neurotransmitter function. Because of the possible role of some of these genes in comorbidity, it is worthwhile to mention them while noting the weaker empirical basis for some of these findings.

Serotonin is a neurotransmitter that is important in mood regulation, and it is associated with decreased alcohol consumption; however, the short 5-HTT allele is less efficient in transcription than the long allele and thus is thought to pose a risk for AUDs. There is also evidence for a relation between the short allele of the serotonin transporter (5-HTT) encoding gene and AUDs (Dick & Beirut, 2006; Dick & Feroud, 2003). Because interaction between this gene and childhood adversity has been shown in a primate model of drinking (Barr et al., 2004) and possibly in human depression (Caspi et al., 2003; but see Risch et al., 2009 and Karg et al., (in press)), it seems likely that this gene, in combination with early stressors, predisposes individuals to a range of pathology associated with affective disturbance.

Further, due to the importance of the dopamine system to the rewarding properties of alcohol and other drugs of abuse, there has been interest in whether genotypes related to the dopamine system (e.g., polymorphisms related to dopamine receptors $D_2$ and $D_4$ and to the dopamine transporter) have also been linked to AUDs. Despite a number of findings associated with allelic variation in $D_2$ and, to a lesser extent, $D_4$ receptor genes, data in this area are inconsistent (Dick & Beirut, 2006).

It should also be noted that there is increasing evidence that one of the genes associated with the acetylcholine muscarinic receptor (CHRM2) is associated with broad-spectrum pathology including AUDs, other drug use disorders, and related nonsubstance pathology (Dick et al., 2008; Luo, Kranzler, Zuo, Wang, Blumberg, & Gelernter, 2005).

At present, a number of large-scale genome-wide association studies are under way that will likely reveal additional genes that are reliably associated with the AUD (or closely related) phenotypes. However, as is true for all psychological disorders (Kendler, 2005, 2006), it seems unlikely that any single gene will reveal a strong bivariate association with AUDs, given the long and complex causal chain between gene action and the manifestation of alcohol-related pathology (Kendler, 2005, 2006; Sher, 1991) and the failure of genome-wide scans to identify strong single-gene effects of complex disorders (Goldstein, 2009).

### Environmental Factors Associated with AUDs and Related Constructs

The range of potential environmental influences on the development of alcohol dependence is vast and ranges from the chemical environment (e.g., ethanol and other drug exposures) to broad social factors (e.g., cultural influences) to life-stage specific factors (e.g., social roles that vary over the life course).

## PRENATAL ALCOHOL EXPOSURE

From a developmental perspective, the first alcohol-related environment for the developing human is the womb. Prenatal alcohol exposure can cause fetal alcohol syndrome (FAS), which is a clinical syndrome characterized by growth retardation, facial dysmorphology, and CNS deficits, including tremors and visual irregularities (Larkby & Day 1997; Manning & Eugene-Hoyme, 2007). Studies examining school-aged outcomes for children affected by FAS reveal a range of cognitive and behavioral problems that often persist and/or worsen as children mature, leading to high rates of antisocial behavior and the development of AUDs (Baer, Sampson, Barr, Connor, & Streissguth, 2003; Streissguth et al., 1994; Steinhausen, Willms & Spohr, 1993). These types of deficits and associated behavior problems are also common in children prenatally exposed to alcohol who are not diagnosed with full-syndrome FAS (Streissguth et al., 1990; Testa, Quigley, & Eiden, 2003) but have some subsyndromal spectrum disorder. Animal models suggest that fetal exposure to alcohol may lead to the development of specific drug sensitivities and preferences that may contribute to the development of AUDs (Abel, Bush, Dintcheff, 1981; Dominguez, Lopez, & Molin, 1998; Osborn, Yu, Gabriel, & Weinberg, 1998).

## ADOLESCENT ALCOHOL EXPOSURE

In addition to prenatal exposure to alcohol, increasing evidence indicates that youth exposure to alcohol may also be relevant to the development of AUDs. Accumulating research suggests that adolescents may be exquisitely sensitive to the neurotoxic effects of alcohol. Heavy exposure to alcohol in adolescence has been associated with structural and functional brain deficits, as well as deficits in cognitive functioning (Clark, Thatcher, & Tapert, 2008; De Bellis et al., 2000; Hargreaves, Quinn, Kashem, Matsumoto, & McGregor, 2009; Tapert, Brown, Baratta, Brown, 2004; Zeigler et al., 2005). The seemingly heightened sensitivity of the adolescent brain to alcohol-related insult is thought to be associated with neurodevelopmental vulnerability to disruption of the extensive remodeling of the brain that takes place in adolescence (e.g., synaptic pruning; Clark et al., 2008). The associated neurocognitive deficits, especially those associated with deficits in executive

functioning (Monti et al., 2005), could pose added risk for a range of externalizing behavior problems. Although a definite causal relation in humans has yet to be established, rodent models of adolescent ethanol exposure (Crews et al., 2000; Spear, 2000; Swartzwelder, Wilson, & Tayyeb, 1995) demonstrate that adolescence appears to be a time of heightened sensitivity to persistent neurologic damage.

One of the most reliable findings in the epidemiology of AUDs is that early onset of drinking is associated with increased likelihood of developing an AUD (Grant & Dawson, 1997; Hingson, Heeren, & Winter, 2006). What is not clear at this point is the extent that these findings represent a clear causal mechanism (perhaps because of increased sensitivity of the brain to alcohol or alcohol-related cues) or are an artifact of a common "third variable" associated with both early deviant behavior and the development of AUDs. Currently the data are ambiguous, with some evidence suggesting that the early alcohol consumption → AUD link is a spurious effect of correlated conduct problems (Prescott & Kendler, 1999), although it is unclear if a common third-variable causation is a sufficient explanation (McGue & Iacono, 2008; Odgers et al., 2008). Regardless of the mechanism of this association, early exposure, although associated with increased risk, does not appear to herald imminent alcohol dependence in younger adolescents. Indeed, Sartor, Lynskey, Heath, Jacob, and True (2007) and Hussong, Bauer, and Chassin (2008) found that, in early adulthood, earlier exposure is associated with longer duration from first drinking to dependence. This is likely due to limited opportunities for access and use in mid-adolescence, which constrains the dependence process (Sher, 2007).

## PARENTAL INFLUENCE

Parental influences on drinking and AUDs are usually viewed along three dimensions: modeling, parenting practices (i.e., nurturance and control), and abuse and neglect.

Alcoholic parents have been thought to inadvertently model their problematic drinking to their children, so that these children may emulate their parents' behavior as they get older (Ellis, Zucker, & Fitzgerald, 1997). Although there is poorer psychosocial adjustment in children of alcoholics (COAs) whose parents are actively drinking heavily versus those who are abstinent (Andreas & O'Farrell, 2007), the extent to which parents' modeling increases the risk of later AUDs in COAs is unclear (Chassin, Pitts, DeLucia, & Todd, 1999). For example, adoption and children-of-twins studies tend to show little evidence of modeling. That is, rates of alcoholism in the adoptive COAs do not appear to be elevated (Hopfer, Crowley, & Hewitt, 2003), and the offspring of twin pairs (that are discordant for AUDs) are not statistically different in their risk for AUDs after controlling for genetic and other environmental risk factors (Slutske et al., 2008).

Nonetheless, it might be less a matter of modeling and more a matter of general parenting practices that are of importance in considering the effects of parents on the development (or prevention) of AUDs. For example, parents who abuse alcohol are thought to demonstrate poor family management practices that are strongly linked with higher rates of internalizing and externalizing problems in children, such as lax and inconsistent discipline and inadequate supervision and monitoring. Also, poor parental monitoring puts children at risk for associating with substance-using peers. This peer association has been identified as a critical risk factor for early alcohol initiation and the development of alcohol problems (Hawkins, Catalano, & Miller, 1992). In addition to monitoring, a range of other familial factors have been found relevant to familial transmission of AUDs. These include communication, cohesiveness, social support, parent and sibling attitudes toward alcohol use, familial conflict, parental loss through divorce or separation, disruption of family rituals, and unfair and harsh disciplinary practices (Leonard & Eiden, 2007).

In addition to these more general facets of parenting and their relation to the development of AUDs, child maltreatment and neglect are two risk factors for AUDs worth noting separately, given their increased severity as risk factors for a number of mental health issues. Child maltreatment is a correlate of substance use in families and poor parenting practices overall; thus, it is difficult to identify how maltreatment contributes to the development of AUDs beyond simply being an environmental risk factor (Locke & Newcomb, 2004). However, child neglect has been found to contribute to the development of AUDs by increasing children's vulnerability to be pressured by peers to use alcohol at early ages (Clark, Thatcher, & Maisto, 2004; Dunn et al., 2002; Leonard & Eiden, 2007).

## PEER INFLUENCE
Peer influence is considered one of the strongest predictors of alcohol use, particularly in adolescence, with data suggesting near-perfect correlations between the alcohol use patterns of adolescent friends (Fowler et al., 2007). Peer influences on drinking may be stronger in adolescent girls than boys, although deviant peer associations have been found to exert influence on drinking behaviors in both boys and girls (Simons-Morton, Haynie, Crump, Eitel, & Saylor, 2001). This prompts the question of whether it is more often the case that peers socialize each other toward drinking behaviors, or whether it is more often that peers select into groups that are characterized by risky and heavy drinking behaviors (Sher, Grekin, & Williams, 2005). Data show that both selection and socialization effects are important aspects of peer influence on heavy drinking. Parental expectations moderate what types of peers children associate with and the amount to which the peers exert influence toward (or against) alcohol and substance use (Nash, McQueen, & Bray, 2005). As individuals move into adulthood, selection effects appear to become more important than socialization effects (Parra, Sher, Krull, & Jackson, 2007).

## INTIMATE PARTNER INFLUENCE
As result of assortative mating, heavier drinkers (including those who are alcohol dependent) often marry heavier drinkers, and spouses appear to influence each others' drinking and likelihood of having an AUD (Leonard & Eiden, 2007). Earlier reports suggest that husbands' drinking prior to marriage increases the likelihood of wives' drinking in the first year of marriage (Leonard & Eiden, 1999), although wives' heavy drinking has a longitudinal predictive effect of husbands' heavy drinking later in the course of marriage (Leonard & Mudar, 2004). More recent evidence (Leonard & Homish, 2008) suggests that, for both husbands and wives, spousal heavy drinking as well as post-marriage social networks (e.g., number of drinking buddies) are significant predictors of both partners' heavy drinking during the marriage. Decreased marital satisfaction and intimate partner violence are both causes and effects of heavy drinking in marriages, and heavy drinking has also typically been found to increase at the dissolution of a marriage (Leonard & Eiden, 2007). Further, higher levels of marital satisfaction appear to be protective against postmarital alcohol problems (Leonard & Homish, 2008). Thus, alcohol plays a role in the formation, maintenance, and dissolution of relationships, in which inequalities in drinking between partners tend to forecast increases in discord in the relationship and continued or increased drinking. At a broader level, however, family systems' perspectives of alcoholism recognize decreases in heavy drinking when spouses become parents (Leonard & Eiden, 2007).

## ADVERTISING AND MEDIA

Youths in the United States are heavily exposed to media promotions of alcohol. For example, it has been found that the average U.S. youth aged 10–14 years is exposed to, on average, 5.6 hours of alcohol use and 243.8 alcohol brand appearances, mostly from the youth-rated movies that children report watching (Dal Cin, Worth, Dalton, & Sargent, 2008). The majority of media depictions of drinking show positive, rather than negative, consequences (Grube & Waiters, 2005). Therefore, it is not surprising that modest associations have been found between exposure to television and magazine advertisements for beer and alcohol use in adolescents (Ellickson, Collins, Hambarsoomians, & McCaffrey, 2005). However, many studies are inconclusive or show very weak effects (Grube & Waiters, 2005). Therefore, the extent that advertising has a causal influence on consumption levels remains an area of controversy.

## CULTURE

The prevalence of AUDs varies dramatically across nations and often equally dramatically across subcultural groups within countries. For example, a recent global status report on alcohol estimated the lifetime prevalence of alcohol dependence to be 0.2% in Egypt, 3.8% in China, 7.7% in the U.S., 9.3% in Canada, 11.2% in Brazil, and 12.2% in Poland (World Health Organization [WHO], 2004a). Perhaps due to this variation, culture has long been viewed an important correlate of the development of AUDs, as certain societal cultures appear to be more permissive of alcohol than others or have drinking customs that might relate to the development of AUDS (Engs, 2001; MacAndrew & Edgerton, 1969).

Indeed, some have argued that one of the reasons that alcohol problems are so prevalent in the United States in comparison to certain Mediterranean countries (e.g., Italy) is that, in the United States, there is a 21-year-old minimum legal drinking age (MLDA). This restriction is thought to preempt the ability of youth to learn how to drink in a healthy way and thus creates a "forbidden fruit" phenomenon that leads to excess (Amethyst Initiative, 2008). However, recent research suggests rather comparable rates of drinking and alcohol problems in youths of different countries in Europe (which have lower MLDAs) and the United States (Grube, 2005), indicating that more research is necessary for understanding just how societal culture might play a role in the etiology of AUDs. In particular, with respect to effects of culture, the extent that alcohol is viewed as a drug versus a food stuff or that intoxication represents a socially sanctioned "time out" from normal roles and responsibilities (MacAndrew & Edgerton, 1969) may be much more important than the age at which it is legal to consume alcohol (Heath, 1995).

## Psychological Individual Differences in Risk for AUDs

The genetic data cited earlier clearly indicate that there are important individual differences in susceptibility to AUDs. Some of this variability appears to be related to how ethanol and its metabolites are processed by individuals (e.g., pharmacokinetics). However, the link between AUDs and genes associated with major motivational systems suggests that some of these genetic effects are mediated by what are traditionally thought of as motivational and personality processes. Psychological individual difference variables that have been implicated in AUD etiology are wide ranging and include neurocognitive processing, personality-related vulnerabilities, alcohol expectancies, and motives for use.

### Neurocognitive Deficits

Deficits in executive cognitive functioning (e.g., the regulation of goal-directed behavior, control of attention, planning, and cognitive flexibility) are associated with increased risk for AUDs (Giancola & Tarter, 1999). Such deficits are evident in children at elevated risk for alcoholism (Nigg et al., 2004). One particular endophenotypic measure of a neurocognitive deficit is reduced P300 amplitude, an electrophysiological index of inhibitory control. P300 amplitude has consistently been shown to be characteristic of individuals at high risk for AUDs (e.g., COAs) and is strongly associated with early-onset AUDs (Carlson, Iacono, & McGue, 2002; Carlson, McLarnon, & Iacono, 2007; Iacono, 1998), at least in boys and young men.

### Personality

Personality traits have long been considered an important feature of psychological theories of alcoholism. However, despite the apparent conceptual appeal of an "addictive personality," decades of empirical research have failed to identify a unique constellation of personality traits that characterize alcoholics. Rather, broad-based personality constructs appear to have etiologic relevance to alcohol abuse and dependence, particularly within the context of larger psychosocial models (Sher, Trull, Bartholow, & Vieth, 1999). Three broad-band personality dimensions have received particular attention: neuroticism/emotionality, impulsivity/disinhibition, and extraversion/sociability. For example, alcoholics exhibit significant elevations on measures of neuroticism/emotionality (Barnes, 1979, 1983; Sher et al., 1999), and many prospective studies have found neuroticism/emotionality to be predictive of subsequent alcohol involvement (Caspi et al., 1997; Chassin, Curran, Hussong, & Colder, 1996; Cloninger, Sigvardsson, Reich, & Bohman, 1988; Labouvie, Pandina, White, & Johnson, 1990; Sieber, 1981).

Impulsive/disinhibited traits appear to be some of the most etiologically significant personality dimensions for alcohol use and misuse, including such constructs as sensation seeking, aggressiveness, impulsivity, psychoticism, and novelty seeking (Sher & Trull, 1994). Prospective studies consistently indicate that traits such as aggression, conduct problems, impulsivity, unconventionality, and novelty seeking are strongly associated with the development of alcohol misuse, as well as other forms of substance misuse (Bates & Labouvie, 1995; Caspi et al., 1997; Cloninger et al., 1988; Hawkins et al., 1992; Pederson, 1991; Schuckit, 1998; Zucker, Fitzgerald, & Moses, 1995). Whiteside and Lynam (2001) utilized factor analyses to identify four distinct personality facets associated with impulsive-like behavior: sensation seeking, lack of planning, lack of persistence, and urgency (acting rashly when distressed). Further work has distinguished among positive and negative urgency (Cyders et al., 2007), resulting in five personality facets of impulsivity. These facets were shown to account for different aspects of risky behaviors, such that sensation seeking appeared to relate to the frequency of engaging in risky behaviors, including drinking-related behaviors, whereas urgency (particularly positive urgency, the tendency to act rashly while in a positive mood, see Cyders, Flory, Rainer, & Smith, 2009) appeared to relate to problem levels of involvement in those behaviors (e.g., Smith et al., 2007; see Cyders & Smith, 2008).

Although extraversion/sociability is considered a major personality dimension, reviews of the literature suggest that extraversion/sociability does not reliably distinguish alcoholic and nonalcoholic individuals (Barnes, 1983; Sher et al., 1999). However, some evidence from longitudinal studies suggests that extraversion/sociability predicts subsequent alcohol misuse (Jones, 1968; Kilbey, Downey, & Breslau, 1998; Sieber, 1981). Recent research (Park, Sher, Krull, & Wood, 2009) suggests that extraversion may be relevant to heavy consumption in late adolescence and early adulthood in that it is related to affiliation with certain types of highly sociable groups (e.g., Greek societies on college campuses) that often represent heavy drinking environments.

### Alcohol Outcome Expectancies

Another important aspect of psychological vulnerability is alcohol outcome expectancies. Alcohol outcome expectancies can be defined as beliefs that people have about the affective, cognitive, and behavioral effects of drinking alcohol (Goldman, Brown, & Christiansen, 1987). Goldman, Del Boca, and Darkes (1999) suggest that outcome expectancies can be categorized along three basic dimensions: positive versus negative expected outcomes (e.g., increased sociability versus increased aggressiveness), positive versus negative reinforcement (e.g., social facilitation versus tension reduction), and arousal versus sedation (e.g., stimulant versus depressant effects). Associations have been consistently found in cross-sectional studies between alcohol expectancies and both drinking behavior and drinking problems among children (Anderson et al., 2005; Dunn & Goldman, 2000), adolescents (Dunn & Goldman, 2000; Fromme & D'Amico, 2000), college students (Christiansen, Vik, & Jarchow, 2002; Palfai & Wood, 2001; Read, Wood, Lejuez, Palfai, & Slack, 2004), and adults (Lee, Greeley, & Oei, 1999; Pastor, & Evans, 2003). These studies suggest that drinking behavior is positively associated with positive outcome expectancies (assessed both individually and as a composite) but inconsistently associated with negative outcome expectancies (assessed both individually and as a composite). Moreover, the associations with positive expectancies are robust across a variety of drinking patterns and remain significant (although weaker) after controlling for demographics and previous drinking behavior (Carey, 1995; Jones, Corbin, & Fromme, 2001). Outcome expectancies tend to develop in childhood (Anderson et al., 2005; Christiansen, Goldman, & Inn, 1982; Dunn & Goldman, 2000; Jones, Corbin, & Fromme, 2001; Miller, Smith, & Goldman, 1990), strengthen during adolescence (Smith, Goldman, Greenbaum, & Christiansen, 1995), and weaken during early adulthood (presumably, following extended experience with drinking; Sher, Wood, Wood, & Raskin, 1996). Moreover, several prospective studies demonstrate that expectancies uniquely predict future drinking over extended time periods (Kilbey, Downey, & Breslau, 1998; Leonard & Mudar, 2000; Sher et al., 1996; Smith et al., 1995; Stacy, Newcomb, & Bentler, 1991). Although both cross-sectional and longitudinal studies suggest associations between expectancies and alcohol use, they do not necessarily implicate a causal relationship.

Somewhat surprisingly, the question of how individual differences in alcohol expectancies relate to individual differences in alcohol effects has not yet been systematically explored (Sher, Wood, Richardson, & Jackson, 2005). However, recent research focusing on individuals who possess different genotypes associated with ALDH (e.g., Hahn et al., 2006), dopamine, and GABA receptors (e. g., Young, Lawford, Feeney, Ritchie, & Noble, 2004) suggests that pharmacogenomic interactions between ethanol and specific genotypes can contribute to individual differences in alcohol expectancies.

In recent years, there has been increasing interest in implicit cognitive processes and how they relate to alcohol involvement (Wiers & Stacy, 2006). In contrast to explicit alcohol expectancies, which are assessed by self-report questionnaires and assume that these expectancies are conscious, implicit expectancies are assessed by any of a variety of behavioral tasks that are assumed to be automatic and largely unconscious. Both of these levels of cognition are thought to act in concert in "dual-process" models. Dual-process models predict that both more reflective explicit and more reflexive, automatic implicit cognitive processes influence behavior (e.g., Fazio & Towles-Schwen, 1999). Implicit alcohol-related cognitions (e.g., implicit alcohol expectancies) are thought to represent individual differences in memory associations between alcohol-related cues, outcomes, and behavior (Thush et al., 2008). Recent work has provided support for the utility of a range of implicit assessments (e.g., Implicit Association Test; Greenwald, Nosek, & Banaji, 2003) of implicit alcohol-related cognitions by showing that these measures predict drinking behavior over and above the prediction afforded by explicit measures of similar constructs (e.g., Thush & Wiers, 2007). Dual-process models of addiction also posit that controlled self-regulatory processes interact with both implicit and explicit expectancies (e.g., Thush et al., 2008) to predict alcohol use and alcohol-related outcomes. However, recent evidence has not supported that processes related to self-regulation interact with explicit alcohol expectancies to predict alcohol consumption or consequences (see Littlefield, Verges, McCarthy, & Sher, in press).

## MOTIVATIONS FOR USE

Individuals report a range of motives for consuming alcohol, and factor analyses of self-reported reasons for drinking reliably yield a multidimensional, four-factor structure (Cooper, 1994) which can be described as: (1) social motives (e.g., "to be sociable"), (2) enhancement motives (e.g., "to get high," "because it's fun"), (3) coping motives (e.g., "to forget your worries," "because it helps when you feel depressed or nervous"), and (4) conformity motives (e.g., "to fit in"). Notably, enhancement and coping motives (but not social or conformity motives) are strongly associated with drinking, heavy drinking, and drinking problems in both adolescents and adults (e.g., Cooper, 1994; Cooper, Frone, Russell, & Mudar, 1995; see Kuntsche, Knibbe, Gmel, & Engels, 2005). A growing body of literature indicates that the personality traits of extraversion and sensation-seeking tend to correlate with enhancement motives, and the personality trait of neuroticism tends to correlate with coping motives (Kuntsche, Knibbe, Gmel, & Engels, 2006). These findings point to specific motivational pathways arising from individual differences in temperamental/personality traits and, thus, link broad dispositional traits to alcohol etiology.

## Multiple Etiological Pathways

The literature on alcohol use motivations documents that AUDs are clearly multifactorial disorders and that there appear to be multiple pathways leading to the manifestation of an AUD (i.e., equifinality). The pathways are discussed below: *pharmacological vulnerability, general externalizing behavior,* and *affect regulation.* It is important to highlight the fact that these different pathways are not mutually exclusive and are likely additive or superadditive. In addition, they likely share common elements, and so some constructs, such as executive functioning, could relate to all three of the pathways considered. These pathways are considered in some detail in Sher, Martinez, and Littlefield (2011), and Littlefield and Sher (2010).

With respect to health psychology, the *affect regulation* pathway has received the most attention and deserves some discussion. Although the "self-medication" (e.g., Khantzian, 1985) view of the etiology of AUDs is widely held by both the lay public and many clinicians, the research literature indicates that alcohol can have variable effects on emotions and many, if not most, individuals do not drink to regulate negative moods. Some survey studies have found significant positive associations between stress and alcohol consumption and misuse (e.g., Cooper, Russell, Skinner, Frone, & Mudar, 1992; Scheier, Botvin, & Miller, 1999). Findings indicate that the association is stronger and more consistent with alcohol problems than alcohol consumption (McCreary & Sadava, 2000), suggesting the alcohol–stress relation is more relevant for pathological drinkers. Nevertheless, many studies find small or nonexistent relationships (Perreira & Sloan, 2001; Rohsenow, 1982; Welte & Mirand, 1995). Moreover, some research suggests that much of the alcohol–stress relation can be attributed to aversive events that directly result from drinking (e.g., losing a job due to alcohol use; Hart & Fazaa, 2004; O'Doherty, 1991).

Perhaps most critically, the research literature suggests that the alcohol–stress relation is highly conditional upon many factors, such as individuals' coping styles, beliefs about the utility of alcohol as a coping device, and the availability of alternative coping strategies, among other things (e.g., Sher & Grekin, 2007). As noted above, individuals higher in neuroticism/negative affectivity tend to report drinking to regulate negative moods, and endorsements of such reasons for drinking suggest a high likelihood for both heavy consumption and alcohol-related problems (Kuntsche et al., 2006). In addition, the literature on psychiatric comorbidity (discussed below) indicates that individuals with high levels of negative affect (as indicated by mood and anxiety disorder) are at high risk for the development of AUDs and, thus, directly implicates negative affect regulation as an important pathway into AUDs.

## Psychiatric and Medical Comorbidity

Individuals who have AUDs frequently have multiple psychiatric diagnoses, as well as various medical illnesses. In a companion volume, we consider psychiatric comorbidity more extensively (Sher, Martinez, & Littlefield, 2011). Here, we briefly consider psychiatric comorbidity but focus primarily on the health-damaging (and some health-promoting effects) of alcohol consumption.

### Psychiatric Comorbidity

Individuals with AUDs are more than twice as likely to exhibit another psychiatric disorder than are persons without an alcohol abuse/dependence diagnosis (Regier et al., 1990), but the nature of these beyond-chance associations is difficult to assess. For example, (a) AUD can be secondary to a primary psychiatric disorder, (b) a psychiatric disorder can be secondary to primary AUD, (c) both disorders could arise from a common diathesis or underlying vulnerability, (d) bidirectional influence can occur, and (e) overlapping diagnostic criteria can create artifactual associations (Clark, Watson, & Reynolds, 1995;

Schuckit, Irwin, & Brown, 1990; see Sher & Trull, 1996). Notably, comorbidity rates vary according to the population sampled, diagnostic approach employed, specific comorbid condition under consideration, extent of other drug use, and gender (Ross, Glaser, & Stiasny, 1988; NIAAA, 1993).

*Drug use disorders* are the conditions that are most comorbid with AUDs (Helzer, Burnam, & McEnvoy, 1991; Robins & Price, 1991; Kessler et al., 1997; Kessler et al., 1994; Grant, 1997; Grant et al., 1994; Grant & Pickering, 1996; Stinson et al., 2005). Additionally, tobacco use and tobacco dependence are strongly associated with alcohol use and AUDs (e.g., Jackson, Sher, & Schulenberg, 2005). Individuals with AUDs are more likely to smoke than are persons without AUDs (Jackson et al., 2005), social drinkers are more likely to smoke than nondrinkers (Istvan & Matarazzo, 1984), and individuals with diagnosable tobacco use disorder exhibit greater risk for AUDs (Breslau, 1995). Moreover, concurrent alcohol and tobacco use appear to interact synergistically to produce elevated health risks (Bien & Burge, 1990), including oral (Blot et al., 1988), laryngeal (Flanders & Rothman, 1982), and esophageal (Muñoz & Day, 1996) cancers.

AUDs commonly co-occur with *mood and anxiety disorders*. For example, of individuals with a current AUD who sought treatment during the same period, approximately 41% and 33% had at least one current independent mood or anxiety disorder, respectively (Grant, Stinson, et al., 2004), suggesting that mood and anxiety disorders should be addressed by substance abuse treatment providers. However, only a fraction of individuals with AUDs in the general population have a history of anxiety disorders (Schuckit & Hesselbrock, 2004), and only 19% and 17% of individuals with a past-year AUD were diagnosed with at least one mood and anxiety disorder, respectively, in the NESARC study (Grant, Stinson, et al., 2004). These findings suggest that mood and anxiety disorders are related to treatment seeking for those with AUDs.

#### PERSONALITY DISORDERS

In the DSM-IV-TR, personality disorders (PDs) are organized into three clusters, clusters A, B, and C, based on descriptive similarities. Cluster A (characterized as odd or eccentric) includes paranoid, schizoid, and schizotypal PDs. Cluster B (dramatic, emotional, erratic PDs) includes antisocial, borderline, histrionic, and narcissistic. Cluster C (fearful, anxious PDs) includes avoidant, dependent, and obsessive-compulsive PDs. Although several studies have examined the prevalence of PDs (notably antisocial PD) among individuals with AUDs (e.g., Verheul, van den Brink, & Hartgers, 1995; Sher & Trull, 2002; Trull, Sher, Minks-Brown, Durbin, & Burr, 2000), it is only recently that data have become available that systematically document the co-occurrence of different PDs with AUDs in the general population. Data from NESARC (Grant, Hasin, et al., 2004; Trull, Jahng, Tomko, Wood, & Sher, 2010) indicate that the co-occurrence of PDs with AUDs is pervasive in the U.S. population, and this is especially true for Cluster B (the dramatic, emotional, erratic cluster) PDs, such as antisocial, borderline, and histrionic PD.

## Medical Consequences

Alcohol affects virtually all major organ systems, and considerable medical morbidity and mortality is directly related to alcohol consumption (Rehm et al., 2003) from both injury (both intentional and unintentional; Rehm, Greenfield, & Rogers, 2001; Rehm et al., 2003) and diseases (including cardiovascular diseases, gastrointestinal [GI] diseases, cancer). In 2004, approximately 4% of all deaths worldwide were attributable to alcohol (Rehm et al., 2009), with most being the result of injury, cancer, cardiovascular disease, and liver cirrhosis. Excessive alcohol use (i.e., binge drinking or heavy use or both) has been identified as the third leading preventable cause of death in the United States (Mokdad, Marks, Stroup, & Gerberding, 2004). In 2001, among both men and women (Santibanez et al., 2004), the leading chronic condition resulting in death attributed to excessive alcohol use was alcoholic liver disease ($n = 12,201$), and the leading acute cause of death attributed to excessive alcohol use was injury from motor vehicle crashes ($n = 13,674$). In 2001 alone, 75,766 alcohol-attributed deaths occurred in the United States as a result of the harmful effects of excessive alcohol use (Santibanez et al., 2004). Of these alcohol-attributed deaths, approximately half were the result of chronic conditions ($n = 34,833$; 46%) and half were the result of acute causes ($n = 40,933$; 54%; Santibanez et al., 2004). A large majority of these alcohol-attributed deaths involved men ($n = 54,847$; 72%) and of these deaths among men, most included those aged 35 or older ($n = 41,202$; 75%). Years of potential life lost (YPLLs), indexing premature death, are calculated by multiplying age- and sex-specific alcohol-attributed death estimates by the respective estimate of life expectancy (Santibanez et al., 2004). In 2001, it was estimated that 2.3 million YPLLs were the result

of the effects of excessive alcohol use (Santibanez et al., 2004). Most of these YPLLs were attributable to acute causes of death (1,491,317; 65%) and, again, males (1,679,414; 74%) and specifically those over the age of 35 (973,214; 58%) were shown to have the highest YPLLs (Santibanez et al., 2004).

In addition to the deaths attributed to excessive alcohol use, alcohol misuse and abuse negatively impacts individuals' quality of life. In 1998, estimates of the economic burden in the United States due to alcohol use and abuse were $185 billion annually, with approximately half of the cost resulting from a loss of productivity attributed to alcohol-related illness (Harwood, 2000). Rehm et al. (2009) estimated that, in 2004, approximately 4.5% of the global burden of disease and injury was attributable to AUDs. The overall burden of disease is assessed using disability-adjusted life-years (DALYs), an index of total health burden, which is created by combining years of life lost due to premature death and years of life lived with disabilities into one indicator that assesses the total lost years of full health from specific causes. The World Health Organization, in 2004, ranked AUDs as one of the top 20 causes of DALYs globally, and as one of the top ten causes of DALYs in the United States (WHO, 2004b). Alcohol undoubtedly also contributes to other leading causes of DALYs, such as cardiovascular disease, cerebrovascular disease, cancer, and road traffic accidents (WHO, 2004b).

Given the health psychology focus of this volume, we first review the effects of acute alcohol poisoning, we then discuss the influence of alcohol on immune response, and finally, we review medical comorbidities that are important with respect to physical health, morbidity, and mortality.

## Alcohol Poisoning

Alcohol poisoning is the result of the acute toxic effects of consuming large quantities of alcohol in a relatively short period of time (Center for Disease Control [CDC], 2005). Because alcohol depresses the functioning of the central nervous system, which regulates involuntary actions (e.g., breathing), an overdose may be fatal. Excessive amounts of alcohol may also lead to death by asphyxiation (i.e., choking) during instances in which a person vomits while in an unconscious state. According to data from the Centers for Disease Control (Anderson et al., 2004), in 2001, 357 deaths in the United States were attributed to an overdose of ethanol. This reflected a 6% increase in the number of deaths estimated in 1999. Signs suggesting that alcohol poisoning has occurred include mental confusion, pallid color, an inability to rouse (unconsciousness), vomiting, hypoglycemic seizures, hypothermia, irregular or slowed breathing, and coma (Adinoff, Bone, & Linnoila, 1988). Currently, there exists no reliable and effective antagonist for the acute effects of ethanol. Treatment of alcohol poisoning entails supportive care, such as providing respiratory support and the administration of fluids and vitamins intravenously until alcohol is naturally metabolized and eliminated from the body (Adinoff, Bone, & Linnoila, 1988).

## Alcohol and Compromised Immunity

Evidence suggests that acute and chronic alcohol consumption has a suppressive effect on nearly all immune responses, including systems that detect and destroy cancerous cells (for reviews, see Cook 2008; Diaz et al., 2002; Messingham, Faunce, & Kovacs, 2002; Nelson & Kolls 2002). Generally, alcohol can affect both the immune system's response to pathogens during primary infection (i.e., inflammatory response) and the development of immunity to the infection. During primary infection, alcohol consumption can reduce the ability of the immune system to break down pathogens, alter levels of molecules that help coordinate immune response (i.e., cytokines), interfere with interactions between humoral and cellular-mediated immunity, inhibit the production of T cells, and change the production rate of oxygen radicals (Szabo, 1997, 1999). Moreover, both acute and chronic alcohol use can strain the cell-mediated immune response, resulting in (a) increased response in humoral immunity (which may be ineffective for infections that respond primarily to cell-mediated immune responses, such as tuberculosis [TB]), (b) alteration in the number and specific functionality of cells that mediate the immune response (i.e., T cells, B cells), and (c) possible impairment with regard to the destruction of viral and cancer cells (Szabo, 1997, 1999). All of these reactions contribute to abnormal immune responses and a weakened defense against pathogens, leading to more frequent and severe illness.

As a result of alcohol's effects on immune response, alcohol consumption may increase individuals' susceptibility to bacterial infections, increase their likelihood of contracting human immunodeficiency virus (HIV), and exacerbate trauma-induced immunosuppression. In chronic alcohol users, as compared to nonusers, an increased incidence of pneumonia is found, and these cases are more likely to result in death (Szabo, 1997). Alcohol use is also thought to contribute to a greater chance for initial HIV infection (perhaps by increasing individuals' propensity to engage in risking-taking behaviors) and acceleration of HIV progression. Finally, alcohol consumption may increase the likelihood of traumatic injury as well as comprise the subsequent immunosuppression response, contributing to higher rates of infection following injury (Brezel, Kassenbrock, & Stein, 1988; Smith & Kraus, 1988; Szabo, 1997). Although research in this area is ongoing, it is clear that the chronic and acute use of alcohol impairs the body's ability to appropriately and effectively respond to invading bacteria and viruses, regardless of gender (Kovacs & Messingham, 2002).

## Medical Comorbidities

More than 60 causes of death have been attributed to alcohol consumption (Rehm et al., 2003). Indeed, alcohol accounted for 6% of all attributable deaths in Canada for individuals under 70 in 2001 (Rehm, Patra, & Popova, 2006) and was the third leading cause of preventable death in the United States (Mokdad, Marks, Stroup, & Gerberding, 2004). As reviewed by Wood, Vinson, and Sher (2001), alcohol abuse and dependence have adverse effects on almost all physical illness. The relation between alcohol and injuries, cancer, liver disease, GI diseases, neurological disease, cardiovascular diseases, sexually transmitted infections, HIV disease, TB, diabetes, and chronic pain are outlined below.

### INJURIES

Alcohol misuse is frequently associated with injury; nonzero BACs are found in a substantial proportion of traffic fatalities and other traumatic deaths as well as nonfatal injuries (Hingson & Howland, 1993; Smith, Branas, & Miller, 1999). Further, deaths attributed to injuries account for approximately 45% of all alcohol-related deaths and for 80% of alcohol-related years of productive life lost (Shultz, Rice, & Parker, 1990; McGinnis & Foege, 1993). A number of studies have found that frequent binge drinking at baseline approximately doubles the risk of dying over an 8–9 year period compared to abstainers or non–binge drinkers (e.g., Anda, Williamson, & Remington, 1988; Klatsky & Armstrong, 1993), whereas data from a national study suggest that even infrequent binge drinking increases the risk of injury (Cherpitel, Tam, Midanik, Caetano, & Greenfield, 1995). Studies that examine alcohol levels at or shortly after the time of injury have found an exponential increase in the risk for injury in relation to BACs (e.g., Honkanen et al., 1983; Zador, 1991). In a recent meta-analysis exploring nonfatal injury in

16 countries, Borges et al. (2006) found that 21% of the sample reported drinking within 6 hours prior to injury, and societies with riskier consumption patterns had higher relative risk for injury. Additionally, a number of studies suggest that the amount of alcohol that increases the risk of injury may be relatively low (Roehrs, Beare, Zorick, & Roth, 1994; Yesavage Dolhert, & Taylor, 1994) and that hangovers also contribute to injury risk (Cherpitel, Meyers, & Perrine, 1998). However, it should be noted that dispositions associated with alcohol use, such as risk-taking, may be an important contributor to injury risk in general (Cherpitel et al.,1998), and thus, the relationship between alcohol and injury is likely a complex one.

Importantly, injuries related to alcohol involvement are not always unintended; injuries also result from the relation of alcohol with interpersonal violence and suicide (Abbey, 1991; Amaro, Fried, Cabral, & Zuckerman, 1990; Muscat & Huncharek, 1991; Ross, Bernstein, Trent, Henderson, & Paganini-Hill, 1990). With regard to suicide, for example, alcohol has been found to be involved in 10%–69% of completed suicides and 10%–73% of suicide attempts (within literature published between 1991 and 2001; Cherpitel, Borges, & Wilcox, 2004).

### CANCER
Total cancer mortality and alcohol consumption are linked beginning at consumption levels of three or more drinks per day (Blot, 1992); the risk for cancer is 50% greater for individuals who consume at least five drinks per day compared to nondrinkers (Boffetta & Garfinkel, 1990). The American Cancer Society (2006) asserts that men who consume two alcoholic drinks a day and women who ingest one alcoholic drink per day are at an increased risk for cancer. Although earlier work notes that causality has not been established (Rosenberg, Metzger, & Palmer, 1993; Schatzkin & Longnecker, 1994), a recent review on the relation between alcohol and cancer concludes that sufficient evidence now exists to support that there is a causal link between alcohol consumption and cancers of the oral cavity, pharynx, esophagus, liver, colon, rectum, and, in women, breast (Boffetta & Hashibe, 2006), and a casual association is suspected for other types of cancer. Nevertheless, for several types of cancer (e.g., bladder, stomach, ovarian) an association with alcohol is either unclear or absent (Adami et al., 1992; Boffetta & Hashibe, 2006; Gwinn et al., 1986; La Vecchia, Negri, Franceschi, & Gentile, 1992). Although the mechanisms by which alcoholic drinks exert their carcinogenic effect are not fully understood, evidence suggests that the risk of cancer for alcohol drinkers is at least partially modulated by genetic factors (Boffetta & Hashibe, 2006).

### LIVER DISEASE
The association between liver disease and alcohol is well established (Crabb, 1993). The spectrum of alcohol-related liver disease extends from transient and reversible conditions (e.g., acute fatty liver) to more severe (e.g., alcoholic hepatitis) and progressive and permanent (e.g., cirrhosis) conditions. Although acute fatty liver is common among people who consume large quantities of alcohol, only 15%–30% of heavy drinkers will develop cirrhosis (NIAAA, 1997). Risks for developing cirrhosis may vary by gender (Lieber, 1994a; Grant, Dufour, & Harford, 1988); the risk of cirrhosis for women begins to rise at lower levels of consumption compared to men (Bradley et al., 1998; Grant, Dufour, & Harford, 1988; Lieber, 1994a). These sex differences may be due to the fact that women exhibit a lower first-pass metabolism (Frezza et al., 1990) and that they attain higher blood alcohol levels for a given dose of ethanol (Lieber, 1994a).

Ethanol metabolism (i.e., the oxidation of ethanol to acetaldehyde and subsequently to acetate) increases the ratio of reduced nicotinamide adenine dinucleotide (NADH) to nicotinamide adenine dinucleotide (NAD), which is known to contribute to lipogenesis and the storage of fat in the liver (i.e., steatosis; Lucey et al., 2009). Steatosis is thought to increase the sensitivity of the liver to a number of other injurious mechanisms (Stewart et al., 2001). Evidence reviewed by Stewart et al. (see also Lucey et al., 2009; Song et al., 2006) suggests that oxidative stress and abnormal cytokine production (tumor necrosis factor [TNFα]), resulting from the metabolism of ethanol, are believed to be the mechanisms that contribute to necrosis and/or apoptosis, and, ultimately, to alcoholic liver disease. Malnutrition (Grant, Dufour, & Harford, 1988; Lieber, 1994b; Lucey et al., 2009; Stewart et al., 2001), interactions with viral hepatitis (Lieber, 1994b, 2000), sex (Stewart et al., 2001), and genetic predispositions (NIAAA, 1997; Stewart et al., 2001) are other important factors that may also determine the severity of alcoholic liver disease. Evidence from twin studies indicates that genetic factors may account for at least 50% of individual susceptibility, although studies have yet to reliably identify genetic markers for alcoholic liver disease (Stickel & Österreicher, 2006).

As of 1995, liver transplantation recipients who had been diagnosed with alcohol-liver disease (ALD; the most common cause of cirrhosis in Western countries) made up about 27% of patients (Pageaux et al., 2003). In the extant literature, it is estimated that between 11% and 49% of patients with ALD will relapse with regard to alcohol use following surgery (e.g., Bird et al., 1990; Lucey et al., 1997). For example, a recent report (Pageaux et al., 2003) found that 31% of ALD patients reinitiated alcohol use following a liver transplant. Moreover, approximately twice as many patients relapsed into heavy drinking (i.e., more than 14 units per week and/or periods of time with more than 4 units per day) than did into occasional drinking (i.e., less than 14 units per week). Although 8-year survival rates were comparable between postoperative heavy, occasional, and abstinent drinkers, the determined cause of death for relapsed heavy drinkers was related to alcohol in 15% of cases. Not surprisingly, in instances of liver rejection, the primary contributing factor, among relapsed drinkers, was poor adherence to immuno-suppression drugs. Despite some patients reinitiating alcohol use following liver transplantation, for many patients, the procedure itself provides effective alcohol relapse prevention (Vaillant, 1997).

## OTHER GASTROINTESTINAL DISEASES

The GI tract is the site at which alcohol is absorbed into the bloodstream. Chronic alcohol abuse may affect functioning of the oral cavity, esophagus, stomach, small intestine, and large intestine (Bode & Bode, 1997). That is, alcohol abusers may suffer from inflammation of the tongue, tooth decay, gum disease and tooth loss, and other related damage incurred in the oral cavity (Kranzler, Babor, Goldstein, & Gold,1990). Both acute and chronic alcohol use can also weaken the esophageal sphincter and increase the occurrence of heartburn, esophagitis, and other reflux-related conditions (e.g., Barrett's esophagus, Mallory-Weiss syndrome; Bode & Bode, 1992, 1997; Wienbeck & Berges, 1985). Among individuals who report chronic alcohol consumption (Gray, Donnelly, & Kingsnorth, 1993), there is an increased risk for the development of esophageal cancer (Bagnardi, Blangiardo, La Vecchia, & Corrao, 2001; Corrao, Bagnardi, Zambon, & La Vecchia, 2004). Additionally, acute and chronic alcohol consumption may result in deleterious effects on the stomach by altering the secretion of gastric acid, inducing gastric mucosal injury, and interfering with gastric motility (Bode & Bode, 1997). With regard to the lower GI system, alcohol use may interfere with the absorption of nutrients in the small intestine (for review see Bode & Bode, 1997), which may be a more significant problem in individuals with advanced liver disease and limited pancreatic function. Finally, alcohol enhances the propulsive motility of the large intestine (Mezey, 1985), but retards the impeding motility, contributing to diarrhea, especially among chronic alcohol abusers. In sum, alcohol interferes with the functioning of all parts of the GI tract, and, in general, damage to the GI tract has been linked to abdominal pain, intestinal bleeding, diarrhea, malnutrition, weight loss, and the presence of precancerous cells (Bode & Bode, 1997).

It is likely that alcohol acts in tandem with known carcinogens (e.g., cigarettes) to exacerbate the risk for certain GI-related conditions and cancers. Indeed, although alcohol consumption is commonly assumed to increase the risk of gastritis and other inflammatory conditions of the upper GI track mucosa, including peptic ulcers of the stomach or duodenum, empirical investigations suggest that much of the relation between alcohol and other GI conditions is confounded with cigarette smoking and that smoking modifies the risk due to alcohol (Chou, 1994). Nevertheless, taking into account cigarette use, heavy alcohol consumption has been independently found to contribute to a higher risk for certain types of GI-related cancers (Bode & Bode, 1997).

## NEUROLOGICAL DISEASE

Acute alcohol consumption has numerous effects on the brain (Peterson, Rothfleisch, Zelazo, & Pihl, 1990), including common acute effects such as "blackouts" (a period of time when recollection is impaired; Vinson, 1989). Although alcohol-induced blackouts have been thought to be an important early sign of alcoholism, research suggests that blackouts only modestly predict future AUDs (e.g., Anthenelli, Klein, Tsuang, Smith, & Schuckit, 1994) and that they are relatively common, especially among college students (Wechsler, Dowdall, Maenner, Gledhill-Hoyt, & Lee, 1998).

There is little evidence of any lingering impairment in neuropsychological tests following acute intoxication (Lemon, Chesher, Fox, Greeley, & Nabke, 1993; see Yesavage, Dolhert, & Taylor, 1994 for an exception), and most studies show little apparent effect among those who drink infrequently or moderately (Hebert et al., 1993; Parker, Parker, & Harford, 1991), especially when baseline neuropsychological performance is controlled (Arbuckle, Chaikelson, & Gold, 1994). However, neuropsychological impairment becomes increasingly likely with heavier drinking patterns (>21 standard drinks/week; Parsons & Nixon, 1998). Increasing evidence suggests that adolescents may be at especially high risk for alcohol-related neuropsychological impairments, perhaps because of the rapid rate of neurodevelopment occurring during this stage of life (Monti et al., 2005).

Despite these findings, severe alcohol dependence is associated with chronic brain diseases, such as Wernicke encephalopathy (characterized by neurological signs such as ataxia, nystagmus, and confusion) and Korsakoff psychosis (a combination of retrograde and anterograde amnesia; Victor, 1993, 1994). Wernicke and Korsakoff syndromes typically co-occur and are thought to be due to nutritional deficiency related to alcoholism rather than to the direct toxic effects of alcohol itself (Victor, 1993). Some symptoms of Wernicke-Korsakoff syndrome will resolve with improved nutrition and abstinence from alcohol, although the amnesia (classic Korsakoff syndrome) will resolve in only about 20% of patients (Victor, 1993). Further, predicting which patients with Wernicke-Korsakoff syndrome will improve is difficult (Berglund, 1991), yet prognosis tends to be poorer for sudden-onset cases and those in which patients do not abstain from alcohol consumption (Smith & Hillman, 1999). Finally, alcoholics who are seeking treatment tend to have more brain pathology, which can be used to diagnosis Wernicke-Korsakoff syndrome, than do alcoholics who are not seeking treatment (Fein & Landman, 2005). Sullivan and Pfefferbaum (2008) suggest that better nutrition habits or fewer predisposing factors among non–treatment-seeking alcoholics may account for this difference.

*Ischemic stroke*, in which blood flow to a part of the brain is stopped by a clot within an artery, and *hemorrhagic stroke*, in which bleeding in or around the brain occurs, are differentially related to alcohol. The association between alcohol and ischemic stroke risk appears to be J-shaped (Sacco et al., 1999; Reynolds et al., 2003), with the lowest risk among persons consuming less than one or between one and two drinks per day and the highest risk among those consuming more than five drinks per day (Reynolds et al., 2003). By contrast, the risk of hemorrhagic stroke increases monotonically with increasing alcohol consumption (Camargo, Jr. 1989; Klatsky, Armstrong, & Friedman, 1989; Reynolds et al., 2003), with the highest risk found for persons consuming more than five drinks per day (Reynolds et al., 2003). Additionally, the relative prevalence and mortality of ischemic stroke and hemorrhagic strokes varies depending on gender, ethnicity, and age of patients (Ayala et al., 2001; Ayala et al., 2002; Friday et al., 1989; Sarti, Rastenyte, Cepaitis, & Tuomilehto, 2000), suggesting distinct risk factors among subgroups.

The study of alcohol's effect on sleep dates back to the late 1930s (Roehrs & Roth, 2001). An extensive literature has been amassed since that time suggesting that alcohol has extensive effects on sleep as well as daytime sleepiness. Acute high alcohol doses disturb sleep in healthy subjects, but lower doses of alcohol appear to be beneficial for insomniacs. Nevertheless, tolerance to alcohol's sedative effects can develop rapidly, resulting in potentially excessive hypnotic use and, for insomniacs, potentially excessive daytime use (Roehrs & Roth, 2001). Further, recent prospective studies suggest that initial sleep problems are a risk factor for subsequent AUD onset and other alcohol-related consequences (Crum, Storr, Chan, & Ford, 2004; Wong, Brower, Fitzgerald, & Zucker, 2004). Additionally, findings have suggested that individuals with sleep disturbances and co-occurring anxiety disorders or dysphoria are at the highest risk to develop alcohol-related problems (Crum et al., 2004).

## CARDIOVASCULAR DISEASE

The consumption of one or two alcoholic drinks in the previous 24 hours may reduce the risk of a heart attack (McElduff & Dobson, 1997), and chronic low-level ethanol intake has been associated with cardiovascular health (Camargo et al., 1997; Okubo, Miyamoto, Suwazono, Kobayashi, & Nogawa, 2001; Corrao et al., 2004; Piano, 2005). Consistent with this, many studies have demonstrated an association between abstinence from alcohol and an increased risk of coronary artery disease, such as myocardial infarction (heart attack) and sudden cardiac death (see Maclure, 1993; but see Hart, Smith, Hole, & Hawthorne, 1999; Hanna, Chou, & Grant, 1997). Although the mechanism by which low-level alcohol consumption might lead to a decreased risk of coronary disease is uncertain, there is considerable evidence that the effect is mediated by alcohol's effects on (a) high-density lipoprotein (HDL) (Gaziano et al., 1993; NIAAA, 1997; Facchini et al., 1994; De Oliviera e Silva et al., 2000; Ellison et al., 2004); (b) increasing insulin sensitivity (Facchini et al., 1994, Flanagan et al., 2000), thus limiting the formation of advanced glycation end products (Vasdev, Gill, & Singal, 2006); and (c) plasma concentrations of endogenous tissue-type plasminogen activator (t-PA) that may promote lysis of intravascular clots (Booyse et al., 2007; Hendriks, Veenstra, Velthuis-te Wierik, Schaafsma, & Kluft, 1994; Ridker, Vaughan, Stampfer, Glynn, & Hennekens, 1994).

It is important to note that the findings of low to moderate alcohol use and reduced mortality risk from cardiovascular disease are not without controversy. Shaper, Wannamethee, and Walker (1988) hypothesized that most prospective studies assessing the relation between alcohol use and coronary heart disease contained systematic misclassification error. Specifically, Shaper et al. suggested people's alcohol consumption decreases, sometimes to the point of abstention, as they age and become ill or frail or increase use of medications. According to Shaper et al., if these people are included in the abstainer category, then it is not the absence of alcohol that elevates their risk for coronary heart disease but instead their compromised health. Although a number of studies have claimed to investigate and dispute this hypothesis (Klatsky, 1996; Maclure, 1993), a recent meta-analysis focused on studies that did not contaminate the abstainer category by including occasional or former drinkers (Fillmore, Kerr, Stockwell, Chikirtzhs, & Bostrom, 2006). The meta-analytic results indicated that abstainers and "light" or "moderate" drinkers were at equal risk for all-cause mortality, including coronary heart disease. Although the authors of this paper conclude that, based on laboratory science that demonstrates mechanisms for cardiac protection, alcohol can convey benefits to the heart; the authors also assert that actual outcomes in human populations for cardiac benefit may have been exaggerated (also see Andreasson, 2007; Holder, 2007; Klatsky, 2007; Mukamal, 2007; Rehm, 2007; Romelsjo, 2007; Shaper, 2007 for commentaries on Fillmore et al.).

Importantly, alcohol's effects on the heart are not universally salutary (e.g., Moushmoush & Abi-Mansour, 1991; Preedy, Atkinson, Richardson, & Peters, 1993; Zakhari, 1991). Among light to moderate drinkers, although alcohol consumption contributes to a lowered risk of hypertension among women (Klatsky, Friedman, Seigelaub & Gerard, 1977; Klatsky et al., 1986; Sesso, Cook, Buring, Manson, & Gaziano 2008; Witteman et al., 1990), it may contribute to a heightened risk among men (Sesso et al., 2008; but see Klatsky et al., 1977). Hypertension, defined as a blood pressure greater than or equal to 140/90 mm Hg, has been linked to both cardiovascular and cerebrovascular disease, as well as to renal failure (Neaton, Wentworth, Cutler, Stamler, & Kuller, 1993; Stamler, Stamler, & Neaton, 1993). In 2007, it was estimated that nearly one-fourth of adult Americans—at least 65 million individuals— had blood pressure levels that indicated hypertension (Rosendorff et al., 2007). Many studies have also provided evidence that hypertension is significantly associated with heavy alcohol consumption levels for both men and women (Ascherio et al., 1992; Camargo, & Rimm, 1996; Corrao et al., 2004; Klatsky, 1996; MacMahon, 1986; Reynolds et al., 2003; Witteman et al., 1990), even after controlling for other contributing confounds such as age, body weight, exercise, and smoking status. Moreover, hypertension is a prevalent comorbid medical condition among AUD patients (Klatsky, 1996; Luz & Coimbra, 2004; Parekh & Klag, 2001). Heavy alcohol consumption has also been shown to interfere with the pharmacological treatment of hypertension (Beevers, 1990). Indeed, among heavy drinkers, doctors commonly suggest the moderation or avoidance of alcohol consumption in addition to their normative recommendations for other nonpharmacologic interventions (e.g., exercise, sodium restriction; Pescatello et al., 2004; Sacks et al., 2001) to improve patients' prognosis.

Heavy and frequent drinking substantially increases the risk of damage to the myocardium (i.e., heart muscle), contributing to the development of cardiomyopathy and congestive heart failure (Richardson, Wodak, Atkinson, Saunders, & Jewitt, 1986), although the risk may be greater in men than in women (Wu, Sudhakar, Jaferi, Ahmed, & Regan, 1976). The severity of patients' alcohol-induced cardiomyopathy (Preedy, Atkinson, Richardson, & Peters, 1993) is usually related to their mean daily alcohol intake and duration of drinking. In the early stages of alcohol-induced cardiomyopathy, there is some evidence (e.g., Baudet, Rigaud, Rocha, Bardet, & Bourdarias, 1979; Nicolas et al., 2002) that the deleterious effects of ethanol on cardiac muscle may be reversed by abstaining from or reducing alcohol consumption.

In addition to precipitating myocardium damage, ethanol has been shown to contribute to certain cardiac arrhythmias (Greenspon & Schaal, 1983; Rosenqvist, 1998). Indeed, it has been estimated that alcohol is involved in 30%–60% of atrial fibrillation cases (the most common type of cardiac arrhythmia). Alcohol-related arrhythmias (i.e., "holiday heart syndrome") are usually preceded by binge drinking episodes and tend to terminate spontaneously (with cessation of alcohol consumption) or within 24–48 hours following the administration of β blockers (Rosenqvist, 1998). Although the aforementioned conditions are generally associated with heavy and frequent alcohol consumption patterns, smaller amounts of ethanol may also damage cardiac muscle over time (Kupari & Koskinen, 1993), for which the mechanisms of the injurious effects are unclear (Preedy, Atkinson, Richardson, & Peters, 1993).

## SEXUALLY TRANSMITTED INFECTIONS

A general association is reported between alcohol consumption and risky sex practices (Bolton, Vincke, Mak, & Dennehy, 1992; Bryant, 2006; Halpern-Felsher, Millstein, & Ellen, 1996; Leigh & Stall, 1993), such that greater levels of consumption relate to an increase in the likelihood of contracting a sexually transmitted infection (STI; e.g., HIV, human papillomavirus, syphilis). This increased likelihood for the contraction of STIs under the influence of alcohol is most likely due to the absence or ineffective use of prophylactics (Donovan & McEwan, 1995; Hingson, Strunin, Berlin, & Heeren, 1990). In one report, heavy drinkers (averaging five or more alcoholic drinks per day) were 2.8 times *less* likely to utilize condoms during sex, compared to alcohol-abstainers (Donovan & McEwan, 1995). Moreover, individuals with AUDs report a lifetime involvement in high-risk sexual behaviors, including multiple sex partners, unprotected sex, sex with high-risk partners, and sex in exchange for drugs or money (e.g., Avins et al., 1997; Boscarino et al., 1995; Gold, Karmiloff-Smith, Skinner, & Morton,, 1992; Kington & Bryant, 2002; Weinhardt, Carey, Carey, Maisto, & Gordan, 2001; Windle, 1997), placing them at greater risk for the acquisition of STIs.

Unlike studies assessing global associations between alcohol consumption and risky sexual behaviors, two types of event-level studies ask participants to report on the use of alcohol prior to specific sexual events. First, only about half of studies that assess drinking behaviors during two or three specific sexual encounters (e.g., first intercourse, most recent intercourse) reveal that alcohol use is related to subsequent condom use (e.g., Irwin, Morgenstern, Parsons, Wainberg, & Labouvie,, 2006; see Weinhardt & Carey, 2000 for a review). Second, studies assessing these associations across multiple sexual events (i.e., diary studies) have revealed tenuous evidence, at best, for the expected association between alcohol and risky sex (e.g., Harvey & Beckman, 1986; Leigh, 1993; Fortenberry, Orr, Katz, Brizendine, & Blythe, 1997; Leigh et al., 2008; Morrison et al., 2003; Weatherburn et al., 1993; Weinhardt et al., 2001).

Despite these equivocal findings, recent evidence suggests that moderators, such as age (Mustanski,

2008), gender (Barta et al., 2008; Scott-Sheldon et al., 2009; Weinhardt et al., 2001), partner's level of alcohol consumption (Barta et al., 2008), and partner type (i.e., casual vs. steady; Scott-Sheldon et al., 2009; but see Mustanski, 2008), may provide important information with regard to predicting under what conditions and for whom an association exists between risky sexual decisions and the consumption of alcohol on a given occasion (Cooper, 2002). Thus, studies suggest that certain individual and situational characteristics may increase the likelihood of engaging in risky sexual acts following drinking.

Alcohol use is thought to relate to an increase in risky sexual decision-making due to its direct influence on cognitions and its indirect influence of alcohol expectancies and shared-risk characteristics. That is, alcohol is known to reduce inhibitions and alter perceptions of risk (e.g., MacDonald, MacDonald, Zanna, & Fong, 2000; Fromme, D'Amico, & Katz, 1999; Cooper, 2002; Steele & Josephs, 1990). Additionally, alcohol expectancies are believed to play a role in the relation between alcohol use and sexual risk-taking. For example, people who believe that alcohol has positive effects on sexual arousal and performance are more likely to engage in risky sex practices following a drinking episode (e.g., Cooper, 2002; Dermen, Cooper, & Agocha, 1998; Dermen & Cooper, 2000). Indeed, some evidence suggests that individuals will consciously use alcohol as an excuse for engagement in inappropriate sexual encounters or to reduce awareness of risk behaviors (Dermen & Cooper, 1994; McKirnan, Vanable, Ostrow, & Hope, 2001). Alcohol may also indirectly contribute to risk by increasing the likelihood that individuals who are predisposed to high-risk lifestyles and possess certain personality characteristics (e.g., sensation seeking, impulsivity, agreeableness; Hoyle, Stephenson, Palmgreen, Lorch, & Donohew, 2002; Justus, Finn, & Steinmetz, 2000; Kalichman, Heckman, & Kelly, 1996; Velez-Blasini, 2008) are able to meet potential casual sex partners conveniently in bars or at parties.

## HUMAN IMMUNODEFICIENCY VIRUS

Individuals with AUDs are more likely to contract HIV compared to those without AUDs (Bryant, 2006). Specifically, heavy alcohol use has been found to increase the likelihood of contracting HIV as a result of more prevalent and riskier injection drug use (IDU) behaviors (Metzger, Navaline, & Woody, 1998; Stein et al., 2000; Windle, 1997). That alcohol consumption is closely tied to high-risk behaviors that are associated with HIV transmission (i.e., IDU, risky sexual behaviors) has led some to argue that alcohol treatment (in addition to drug use and sexual risk interventions) should be considered as a primary means of HIV prevention (Metzger et al., 1998; Purcell, Parsons, Halitis, Mizuno, & Woods, 2001). Consistent with the aforementioned literature that suggests a "global association" between alcohol consumption and STIs (e.g., HIV; Leigh & Stall, 1993; Seage et al., 2002), Hendershot, Stoner, George, and Norris (2007) found that sensation seeking predicted HIV risk directly as well as indirectly via sex-related alcohol expectancies and drinking in sexual contexts.

Individuals who are diagnosed with HIV are more likely to engage in problematic alcohol use (Meyerhoff, 2001; Petry, 1999). As reviewed by Samet et al. (2007), alcohol's impact on HIV disease progression has been examined in animal, in vitro, and human studies. In general, the combination of heavy alcohol use and HIV has been related to increased medical and psychiatric complications (Kington & Bryant, 2002), delays in seeking treatment (Samet et al., 1998), decreased medication compliance (Cook et al., 2001; Hendershot, Stoner, Pantalone, & Simoni, 2009; Wagner et al., 2001), and poor treatment outcomes (Lucas, Gebo, Caisson, & Moore, 2002; but see e.g., Dingle & Oei's [1997] findings that reveal no association between alcohol and HIV progression). Recent research suggests that, at least among people who do not receive antiretroviral therapy, heavy alcohol consumption is related to lower CD4+ cell counts and higher viral load counts (Samet, Horton, Traphagan, Lyon, & Freedberg, 2003, Samet et al., 2007).

Alcohol impairs immunologic function in HIV-infected persons through numerous mechanisms (Goforth, Lupash, Brown, Tan, & Fernandez, 2004). Animal models that examine the impact of alcohol on simian immunodeficiency virus (SIV) have found that alcohol-treated monkeys show a 64-fold increase in the SIV virus compared to sucrose-treated monkeys, suggesting alcohol either increased the infectivity of cells or increased the number of susceptible cells (e.g., Bagby et al., 2003). Additionally, alcohol may make some individuals diagnosed with HIV/AIDS more susceptible to the risk of infection as a result of medical comorbidities (i.e., AIDS-related complications), including TB, pneumonia, and hepatitis C (Kington & Bryant, 2002). In sum, research clearly shows that the consumption of alcohol may complicate the long-term prognosis of individuals diagnosed with HIV/AIDS.

Finally, among patients diagnosed with HIV/AIDS, adherence to antiretroviral therapy, which is thought to extend life by 15–20 years (Braithwaite et al., 2007; Karon, Fleming, Steketee, & De Cock, 2001), is also related to alcohol consumption. Indeed, alcohol consumption has been shown to be the most prevalent risk factor for decreased antiretroviral adherence in both cross-sectional (e.g., d'Arminio et al., 2005; Samet et al., 2004) and prospective (e.g., Braithwaite et al., 2005) studies.

### TUBERCULOSIS

Although only 5%–10% of people in the United States test positive for TB, it is estimated that one-third of the world's population is currently infected with TB (World Health Organization, 2009), and 10% will likely develop acute or reactivated symptoms (Flynn & Bloom, 1996). If left untreated, the illness is fatal in approximately half of those with active infections. Most individuals have immune systems that are able to effectively mobilize against TB, but those with comprised immune systems (e.g., alcoholics) may be less able. The immunosuppressive effects of alcohol dampen the initial response of the immune system to TB pathogens during both primary infection and cell-mediated immunity phases (Szabo, 1997). Alcoholics, especially those living in impoverished (e.g., homeless, indigent) and densely populated areas, are likely to be more susceptible to the contraction and accelerated advancement of TB (Szabo, 1997).

### DIABETES

In the United States, diabetes mellitus affects approximately 7.8% of adults over the age of 20, making it one of the most common chronic illnesses (Harris et al., 1998). Indeed, it is currently the sixth highest leading cause of death in the United States (Heron et al., 2009). A recent review of the extant literature (Howard, Amsten, & Gourevitch, 2004) suggests that the relationship between alcohol consumption and the risk for diabetes is U-shaped, with moderate drinkers (i.e., one drink/day in women; three drinks/day in men) having the lowest risk for the diagnosis of diabetes (e.g., de Vegt et al., 2002; Kao, Puddey, Boland, Watson, & Brancati, 2001; Wei, Gibbons, Mitchell, Kampert, & Blair 2000). Among those diagnosed with diabetes, approximately 50%–62% report consuming alcohol in the previous year (Ahmed et al., 2006; Lethbridge-Cejku, Schiller, & Bernadel, 2004). Because alcohol may influence the release of glucose into the bloodstream, which protects against low blood sugar, it can worsen the risk of hypoglycemia. That such large numbers of individuals are affected by this disease and so many of those diagnosed with diabetes consume alcohol, argues for a better understanding of the impact of alcohol consumption on the course of and complications with diabetes.

In samples of diabetic patients, mild to moderate consumption has been shown to improve cardiovascular functioning (Howard et al., 2004) and reduce the risk of cardiovascular heart disease (Solomon et al., 2000; Tanasescu, Hu, Willett, Stamfer & Rimm, 2001; the effect of alcohol on other diabetic complications [e.g., retinopathy, nephropathy, neuropathy] has yet to be fully understood). Despite these beneficial effects on cardiovascular functioning, a number of studies have revealed that, among individuals with diabetes, alcohol consumption is associated with poorer adherence to self-care recommendation guidelines (Ahmed, Karter, & Liu, 2006; Cox, Blount, Crowe, & Singh, 1996; Lerman et al., 2004). Moreover, these medical adherence behaviors are affected even among those persons who drink as little as one drink per day. Thus, it is necessary for researchers to further study the trade-off between the protective effects of alcohol on cardiovascular functioning in this population as well as the potential deleterious consequences to medical adherence and self-care.

## CHRONIC PAIN

Cross-national data suggests that chronic back or neck pain is comorbid with a number of mental disorders, including AUDs (Demyttenaere et al., 2007). In addition, alcohol consumption is thought to be an avoidant coping strategy for some chronic pain sufferers (Brennan, Schutte, & Moos, 2005; Melding, 1997). Although alcohol may have transient analgesic effects, overreliance on alcohol for pain relief may hinder more effective or permanent treatment strategies (e.g., physician visits) and may also result in problematic alcohol involvement (Brennan et al., 2005). Brennan et al. (2005) found that, among older adults, increased pain is associated with more use of alcohol to manage pain and that this relationship was stronger among individuals with drinking problems. Further, baseline drinking problems interacted with use of alcohol to manage pain to predict health problems and serious injury for men and increased drinking problems for women at a 3-year follow-up. Chronic pain also appears to relate to alcohol treatment outcomes and other drug behaviors. Chronic pain has been shown to hinder recovery from substance dependence, including

alcohol, in patients seeking help at detoxification programs (Larson et al., 2007). For patients taking opioids for chronic noncancer pain, family history of substance abuse and past problems with drugs or alcohol were predictors of aberrant drug behavior (Michna et al., 2003).

## Medication and Alcohol Use
### MEDICATION ADHERENCE
As noted above, substance abuse is a predictor of nonadherence to medicine therapy within both medical (Kresina et al., 2002) and psychiatric (Olfson et al., 2000) patient samples. For example, among those diagnosed with psychiatric pathologies, rates of nonadherence to medication regimens are higher among patients who have been diagnosed with a substance use disorder, compared to those with no such diagnosis (e.g., Magura, Laudet, Mahmood, Rosenblum, & Knight, 2002; Olfson et al., 2000). Weiss (2004) has argued that substance abuse is likely to contribute to medication nonadherence in general by increasing side effects, contributing to a disorganized lifestyle, impairing judgment about health behaviors, functioning as a mechanism for self-medication, and causing fear of combining medications.

Given the relation between alcohol consumption and noncompliance with regard to both general medical therapies and pharmacotherapy (Kranzler, Escobar, Lee, & Meza, 1996), research has begun to focus on improving adherence to the treatment of alcohol use disorders. Recent studies have attempted to match medication and behavioral treatments for alcohol-dependent individuals (COMBINE study; COMBINE Research Group, 2003) or have used a motivational model to change patients' consumption behaviors by focusing on how alcohol influences their daily lives (BRENDA; Volpicelli, Pettinati, McLellan, & O'Brien, 2001). These interventions are described below in the section on Treatment.

### DRUG–ALCOHOL INTERACTIONS
Although less serious events may go unreported, it has been estimated that alcohol–medication interactions may be involved in at least 25% of emergency room visits (Holder, 1992). A drug–alcohol interaction may occur via one of four primary pathways (Lieber, 1992). Acutely, alcohol may alter the rate at which a drug is metabolized by the body by competing for common enzymes. This may increase the time or enhance the effects of a drug at its site of action, increasing the likelihood of experiencing deleterious side effects from the drug. Next, chronic alcohol use

may activate drug-metabolizing enzymes, which may remain in the body for several weeks, and, as a result, dampen the beneficial effects of the medication. As such, heavy, chronic drinkers, compared to nondrinkers, may require higher or more frequent doses of certain medications to achieve maximum effectiveness. Additionally, chronic alcohol use may activate certain enzymes that increase the toxicity of some drugs (e.g., acetaminophen), causing damage to the liver or other organs. Finally, alcohol may exacerbate the inhibitory effects of certain drugs (e.g., sedatives, narcotics) at their sites of action in the brain. In subsequent sections, an examination of alcohol's interactions with other drugs is provided.

## INTERACTIONS WITH DRUGS OF ABUSE

The motivation for the use of two or more substances, defined as *polydrug use* (Grant & Harford, 1990; Martin, 2008), whether used concurrently (i.e., within a given time period [e.g., year]) or simultaneously (i.e., in combination at the same time), varies depending on the intentions of the user. Some users report the desire to achieve specific types of additive or interactive intoxication effects (Merchant & Macdonald, 1994; Uys & Niesink, 2005; Wibberley & Price, 2000), and thus are deliberate with their choice of drug combinations. Other users, by contrast, may "chase" one drug with another to alter or reduce the effects of another. For example, some individuals may use nicotine while consuming alcohol as a way to improve alertness and prolong their drinking occasion (Istvan & Matarazzo, 1984).

Although alcohol–nicotine is likely the most prevalent drug combination in the United States, with 21.7% of adults reporting concurrent use in the previous year (Falk, Yi, & Hiller-Sturmhofel, 2006; simultaneous use patterns are more difficult to estimate), individuals have also reported concurrent use of alcohol with a number of other drugs, such as marijuana (7%–28% adults report combined use; Collins, Ellickson, & Bell, 1998; Midanik, Tam, & Weisner, 2007; Norton & Colliver, 1988), sedatives (1.6%–2.3%; Collins et al., 1998; Grant & Harford, 1990), tranquilizers (3.3%; Grant & Harford, 1990), and cocaine (4.7%–5.3%; Collins et al., 1998; Grant & Harford, 1990). Although estimates are found to vary somewhat depending on the age (e.g., Midanik et al., 2007) and ethnicity (Epstein et al., 1999, 2002) of the user, there is evidence that alcohol is frequently combined with other psychoactive drugs to produce certain intoxication effects, and this has become increasingly common over the past 40 years (Martin, 2008).

Acute effects of combining alcohol with nonprescription drugs include significant intoxication and impairment (Martin, 2008), bodily harm (Gossop, 2001), and, in severe cases, death (Darke & Zador, 1996). Generally, the long-term consequences of polydrug use depend on whether they are used simultaneously or concurrently and may include greater physical health problems, psychological distress (Earleywine & Newcomb, 1997), and significant interpersonal problems (Midanik et al., 2007). As an example, the chronic effects of using alcohol and tobacco in combination may include physical health problems, such as cardiovascular disease and cancer (Mukamal, 2006; Pelucchi et al., 2006).

## PRESCRIPTION DRUG INTERACTIONS

Given the percentage of adults who are likely to consume alcohol at least occasionally (70%) and even daily (10%; Midanik & Room, 1992), and also considering that approximately half of American adults report taking at least one prescription medication (CDC, 2004), it is likely that these substances are being used in tandem at times. Moreover, it has been suggested that elderly adults may be most likely to experience the adverse effects of drug–alcohol interactions, as they consume up to 30% of prescribed medications (Gomberg, 1990) and are not without risk for being diagnosed with AUDs (Egbert, 1993). Indeed, a recent report (Pringle, Ahern, Heller, Gold, & Brown, 2005) revealed that 77% of all prescription drug users over the age of 65 were exposed to drugs that had known interactive effects with alcohol. Nineteen percent of those elderly patients who were taking prescription medications that were known to interact with alcohol reported the concomitant use of alcohol and drugs. An increased likelihood for the concomitant use of alcohol and drugs was shown for younger, male, and more educated elderly patients (Pringle et al., 2005).

With regard to the abuse of prescription medications (using drugs not prescribed to you by a physician or using drugs in a manner not intended by your physician), men and women who have been diagnosed with an AUD, compared to nondrinkers, are 18 times more likely to abuse prescription drugs (McCabe, Cranford, Morales, & Young, 2006). Moreover, young adults between 18 and 24 have been identified as those most likely to be polysubstance users, with 7% and 12% reporting concurrent and simultaneous use, respectively, of alcohol with the abuse of prescription medication within the past year (McCabe et al., 2006). Young adults are mostly likely to combine alcohol with opiates (e.g., Vicodin), followed, in prevalence, by stimulants (e.g., Ritalin), sedatives (e.g., Xanax), and sleeping medications (e.g., Ambien; McCabe et al., 2006).

Combining alcohol with certain prescription medications (which are sometimes used for non-prescribed purposes) may acutely result in alcohol poisoning, unconsciousness, respiratory distress, depression, and even death (Cone et al., 2003, 2004). Among young adults specifically, the combination of alcohol consumption with the abuse of prescribed drugs appears to increase the likelihood of unintentional injuries, fights, occupational problems, blackouts, vomiting, drunk driving, and unplanned sexual episodes (McCabe et al., 2006).

## Issues in Assessment
### Diagnostic Interviews
Several diagnostic interviews have been used to assess AUDs and other disorders in the United States, as they are defined by the DSM-IV of the American Psychiatric Association (1994). These include the Diagnostic Interview Schedule Version IV (DIS-IV: Robins, Cottler, Bucholz, & Compton, 1996), Composite International Diagnostic Interview (WHO CIDI: Version 3.0: Kessler & Üstün, 2004), Alcohol Use Disorder and Associated Disabilities Interview Schedule-IV (AUDADIS-IV: Grant and Dawson, 2000), Semi-Structured Assessment for the Genetics of Alcoholism (SSAGA), and Structured Clinical Interview for DSM-IV (SCID: First, Spitzer, Gibbon, & Williams, 2002).

Grant, Dawson, Stinson, Chou, Kay, and Pickering (2003) assessed the test–retest reliability of selected DSM-IV diagnoses as well as (among others) modules for alcohol consumption, alcohol abuse, and dependence appearing on the National Institute on Alcohol Abuse and Alcoholism's (NIAAA) website. Based on their findings, Grant et al. (2003) suggest that alcohol consumption exhibited "good to excellent" reliability (intraclass correlation [ICC] = 0.69–0.84), whereas alcohol abuse and dependence exhibited "good" reliability (past year diagnosis: $\kappa$ = .74). Despite the high reliability associated with these interviews, a number of practical drawbacks exist, such as the personnel and time required for data gathering. This has led clinicians and researchers to employ other assessments, including brief assessments that can be used efficiently in medical settings to screen for problematic drinking problems.

Although diagnostic interviews are useful in research and specialized treatment settings, they are often ill-suited for use in primary care and criminal justice settings where brevity and ease of administration are essential. To date, a large number of screening questionnaires have been developed for the purpose of identifying individuals with possible drinking problems in order to determine who might benefit from further evaluation and/or treatment.

One of the earliest such screening instruments is the Michigan Alcoholism Screening Test (MAST: Selzer, 1971). The MAST, consisting of 24 scored (differentially weighted) items, has been used in a variety of settings and has shown adequate psychometric properties (Ross, Gavin, & Skinner, 1990; Skinner, 1979; Teitelbaum & Mullen, 2000). Abbreviated forms of the MAST, including the 13-item Short MAST (Selzer, Vinokur, & van Rooijen, 1975) and 10-item Brief MAST (Pokorny, Miller, & Kaplan, 1972), have also been employed.

The Alcohol Use Disorders Identification Test (AUDIT: Babor et al., 1992) contains a 10-item questionnaire that measures quantity of alcohol consumption, alcohol dependence symptoms, and harmful consequences of drinking and comes in both self-administered questionnaire and interview versions (Babor et al., 2001). The AUDIT has been studied in a wide range of settings in a number of different countries and typically demonstrates high diagnostic sensitivity and specificity (Babor et al., 2001). There is also an eight-item complement that assesses physical effects of drinking and is normally used in medical settings (Bohn et al., 1995). This measure is fairly short and has good test–retest reliability and internal consistency (Maisto, Conigliaro, McNeil, Kraemer, & Kelley, 2000; Karno, Granholm, & Lin, 2000). Shorter versions have been developed but do not always perform as well as the full AUDIT (Gómez, Conde, Santana, & Jorrín, 2005).

Further, the CAGE, a four-item measure that is commonly used in various medical settings and usually orally administered by a health care provider, asks about "Cutting down," "Annoyance by criticism," "Guilty feelings," and "Eye-openers" (i.e., morning drinking, Ewing, 1984; Nyström, Peräsalo, & Salaspuro, 1993). Smart, Adiaf, and Kronke (1991) point out that the shortness of the questionnaire is one of its best attributes. The fact that the acronym makes it easy for practicing clinicians to remember undoubtedly contributes to its continued use by clinicians who can employ the items flexibly, often with additional questions about drinking patterns (O'Brien, 2008). Although the brevity of the scale can constrain its psychometric properties (Heck & Williams, 1995; Liskow, Campbell, Nickel, & Powell, 1995; Nyström et al., 1993), its ability to be integrated into regular practice represents a major virtue. A similar instrument, the TWEAK (Russell et al., 1994) was specifically designed to screen for the risk of drinking during pregnancy. This brief measure asks about "tolerance," "worry," "eye-openers," "amnesia," and "kut (cut)-down." Psychometric evaluation of the TWEAK reveals variable performance across different populations and, thus, further validation is needed to determine its value relative to other instruments (Chan et al., 1993; Bush et al., 2003).

### Assessment of Consumption

Drinking questionnaires account for the variation in drinking styles by focusing on both drinking frequency and quantity of consumption on a given drinking occasion. Because many individuals exhibit high intraindividual variability in drinking quantity, some researchers measure volume/variability in order to resolve drinking patterns further. More extensive assessments of drinking behavior, such as "graduated frequency" approaches (in which individuals are queried as to how often they drink varying numbers of drinks/occasions [1–2 drinks, 3–4 drinks, 5–6 drinks, etc.], Greenfield, 2000) are often employed to have sufficient data to measure intraindividual variability in drinking patterns. Another strategy is to measure typical quantity/frequency with supplementation using measures of heavy drinking to resolve drinking patterns that are likely to be associated with acute negative consequences, such as the 5/4 criteria (five drinks on an occasion for men and four drinks on an occasion for women) promoted by Wechsler and Austin (1998) as a measure of "binge drinking." Although this distinction appears somewhat crude, evidence suggests that this measure roughly corresponds to the NIAAA's (2004) recent definition of a "binge" episode as drinking that yields a blood alcohol concentration (BAC) of .08% or more.

An alcohol time-line follow-back interview (TLFB: Sobell & Sobell, 1992, 1995, 2000, 2003) is a drinking-assessment method that obtains detailed retrospective reports of alcohol use. By utilizing a calendar and memory aids to enhance recall (e.g., key dates that serve as anchors for reporting drinking), individuals provide retrospective estimates of their daily drinking over a specified time period that can vary up to 12 months from the interview date. The Alcohol TLFB has been shown to have good psychometric characteristics with a variety of drinker groups and can be flexibly scored to provide a range of measures relevant to drinking

and abstention patterns (Sobell, Brown, Leo, & Sobell, 1996). Although originally developed to be used in face-to-face assessments with a trained technician or clinician, both telephone and computer-based administrations have been shown to yield reliable results (Sobell et al., 1996).

### Daily Diary and Ecological Momentary Assessment Approaches

Most questionnaire-based assessments of alcohol use are cross-sectional and rely on retrospective reports of drinking. These data suffer from several shortcomings, including potential reporting bias and the inability to address questions about the temporal order of cause-and-effect relationships. Although some approaches, such as retrospective time-line follow-back assessments (Sobell & Sobell, 2003) and prospective panel studies resolve these issues to some degree, they fail to address shorter-term, dynamic associations between drinking and other variables of interest.

To address these issues, daily diary and ecological momentary assessment (EMA) methodologies have been developed. Participants in daily diary studies are instructed to record events or feelings that occurred during a specific day on structured palm-top computer recording forms (Carney, Tennen, Affleck, Del Boca, & Kranzler, 1998), via secure internet survey pages (e.g., Park, Armeli, & Tennen, 2004), or through interactive voice response systems over the telephone (Collins, Kashdan, & Gollnisch, 2003; Perrine, Mundt, Searles, & Lester, 1995). In EMA studies, however, drinkers are prompted several times per day to record drinking behaviors and other variables of interest in real time on palm-top computers. Thus, daily diary and EMA studies allow researchers to examine continually changing behaviors while utilizing naturalistic conditions and minimizing retrospective bias. In many clinical and research contexts, such assessments are burdensome; however, the value of obtaining real-time or near real-time data is increasingly recognized (Piasecki, Hufford, Solhan, & Trull, 2007).

### Biomarkers

Biomarkers of consumption derived from urine, blood, and expired air have traditionally been used to assess levels of alcohol use and treatment compliance (Allen, Litten, Strid, & Sillanauke, 2001; Lakshman & Tsutsumi, 2001; McClure, 2002), and biomarkers continue to be an active area of clinical research. Traditionally, blood markers, such as mean corpuscular volume (MCV) and carbohydrate deficient transferrin (CDT), and liver enzyme measures, such as γ-glutamyl transferase (GGT), aspartate aminotransferase (AST), and alanine aminotransferase (ALT), have been the primary markers used both in clinical research, and to varying extent, in clinical practice (see Conigrave, Davies, Haber, & Whitfield, 2003). Existing blood markers of chronic exposure are limited in that they are relatively insensitive to many drinking patterns and can be nonspecific (Conigrave et al., 2003), thus lacking both sensitivity and specificity. Additionally, they are not necessarily useful for assessing changes in patterns of drinking.

In recent years, there has been increasing interest in more direct assessments of alcohol consumption, such as blood alcohol level (BAL). Although BAL can be reliably estimated via simple devices that measure breath alcohol levels (e.g., Alcosensor IV, Intoximeters, Inc., St. Louis, MO), breath testing is only useful for assessing consumption when alcohol is still in the bloodstream. Given that the half-life of alcohol in the bloodstream is relatively brief, a legally intoxicated individual may show no blood alcohol several hours after reaching her or his peak BAL, thus limiting its use.

Although still in its infancy, wearable electrochemical devices that estimate BAC based on concentration of alcohol in sweat, referred to as transdermal ethanol sensors, provide objective real-time measures of consumption (Sakai, Mikulich-Gilbertson, Long & Crowley, 2006; Swift, 2000). These devices can store data over days and thus provide a quantitative, continuous measure of BAL levels over an extended time frame.

### Prevention

Alcohol prevention efforts can be categorized into universal, selective, and indicated prevention efforts. Universal prevention strategies seek to address an entire population (e.g., all adults in a community). Selective prevention strategies target subsets of the entire population that are thought to be at risk for problematic alcohol involvement (e.g., fraternity/sorority members). Indicated prevention efforts are designed to prevent the onset of a full-blown AUD in individuals who indicate early signs of dependence (e.g., mandated college students involved in problematic drinking).

### Universal Prevention Approaches

#### POLICY INTERVENTIONS

Most public policies on alcohol are conceived of and instituted with the express purpose of universally reducing alcohol use and related injuries and harms, either via penalties (sanctions) for risky behavior (e.g., drunk driving) or inducements (e.g., monetary appropriations) to support education and prevention efforts. Alcohol policies can be issued at federal, state, local, and institutional levels, and most commonly affect the pricing of alcohol (e.g., taxes, restrictions on happy-hour sales), how it is sold and its general availability (e.g., days of the week and hours that alcohol can be sold), where it is consumed (e.g., public places), enforcement (e.g., compliance checks, drunk driving laws), and underage access (Toomey & Wagenaar, 1999). Policies concerning the *price/taxation* of alcohol appear to be particularly effective. For example, a report of 112 studies on alcohol tax show a consistent moderately-strong association between higher taxes on alcohol and lower heavy drinking rates (Wagenaar, Salois, & Komro, 2009). Notably, taxation is a somewhat difficult policy for U.S. citizens to endorse as it is viewed by some as "punishing" moderate drinkers as well as heavy drinkers. Thus, such policies render the need for complicated tax formulas to achieve an optimal and agreeable tax rate for the general public (Pogue & Sgontz, 1989). Even if alcohol is not highly taxed, restrictions on happy hours and alcohol specials (which utilize low alcohol prices as a means of increasing alcohol sales) can be effective in reducing heavy drinking in some populations that are particularly receptive to such advertising (e.g., such as college students; Kuo, Wechsler, Greenberg, & Lee, 2003).

Restrictions on the availability of alcohol are also common deterrents of immoderate and problematic use, both in the general and underage population (Gruenwald, Ponicki, & Holder, 1993). For example, local policies that are placed on the *days/hours of operation* of premises that sell alcohol have been particularly effective in reducing alcohol-related traffic crashes (Ashe, Jernigan, Kline, & Galaz, 2003; McMillan & Lapham, 2006). Additionally, because adolescents and young adults have been found to be more likely to use alcohol if there is a higher local alcohol *outlet density* in the area in which they reside (Gruenwald, Johnson, & Treno, 2002; Treno, Ponicki, Remer, & Gruenwald, 2008; Weitzman, Folkman, Lemieux-Folkman, & Wechsler, 2003), local zoning limits on the density of alcohol outlets can help prevent alcohol use in these populations. Additionally, *server liability laws* (in which servers become liable for not responsibly "cutting off" drinkers) have also been shown to be slightly effective in reducing alcohol-related traffic crashes (Wagenaar & Holder, 1991). *Server training* is often suggested by researchers as an important potential prevention step; however, these policies are often created at the institutional level, and thus there is less evidence of its generalized effectiveness (Toomey & Wagenaar, 1999).

*Drunk driving laws* are also popular sanctions put in place to prevent both heavy drinking, and also drinking and driving. Blood alcohol concentration limit laws are common internationally and place a definable limit on one's BAC that is acceptable for driving (.08% in the U.S.). If the BAC is determined to be over this level, then the driver is punished, although the severity of such punishment differs widely by state (e.g., convictions, fines, and mandatory classes are common sanctions). Some states also institute zero-tolerance laws for underage drinkers, such that underage drivers are still liable for a BAC that is below .08% yet over .02%. These laws have been found to be effective in reducing alcohol-related crashes (Voas, Tippetts, & Fell, 2003). With regard to punishment for repeat offenders, vehicle sanctions in particular (e.g., impoundment) have been shown to slightly reduce recidivism rates (Voas & DeYoung, 2002).

Perhaps one of the best known underage alcohol policies is the National Minimum Drinking Age Act, instituted in 1984. The act withheld highway funding from states that did not impose a minimum legal drinking age (MLDA) of 21, in effect making age 21 the standard MLDA across the nation. The age of 21 also has historical value; it was the age that individuals could vote at the time that alcohol prohibition was repealed in 1933, and thus, most states deemed it as their MLDA (NIAAA, 2008a). When the voting age was lowered to 18, most states followed suit with their MLDA. Due to the high prevalence of alcohol-related traffic fatalities in youths and research showing that states with higher MLDAs suffered fewer fatalities, the Minimum Drinking Age Act was passed, resulting in vast reductions in alcohol-related traffic fatalities (American Medical Association, 2004; Mothers Against Drunk Driving, 2009; NIAAA, 2008a). However, there is recent interest in lowering the MLDA, given that underage drinking continues to be a problem in the United States (Amethyst Initiative, 2008; Johnston, O'Malley, Bachman, & Schulenberg, 2007). Notably, underage heavy drinkers tend to want a younger MLDA, whereas other underage youths do not report a preference (Martinez, Muñoz, & Sher, 2009). Insurance companies have suggested that if citizens want the MLDA to be lowered to 18, the driving age should simultaneously be *raised* to 18 (Rubin, 2008).

*School-based approaches* are usually aimed at educating elementary school youths and adolescents about the ill effects of alcohol and drugs, and how to resist peer pressure to use. School-based approaches can be affect-based (i.e., focused on self-esteem and self-efficacy), skills-based (i.e., focused on interpersonal interactions), knowledge-based (i.e., educating students about drugs and their effects), or a combination of the three (Tobler, 1986). Abstinence-only approaches that emphasize a "just say no" ideology toward alcohol consumption typically rely on education alone. Despite millions of dollars spent on programs that emphasize zero-tolerance approaches, such as Drug Abuse Resistance Education (D.A.R.E.), a consensus of empirical studies indicate that these approaches fail to reduce alcohol use and related consequences (Lynam et al., 1999; Moskowitz, 1989). Such programs, however, do successfully increase children's overall knowledge of drugs. Interventions that also incorporate skills training (e.g., Project ALERT) have been shown to reduce some hard drug use as well as improve self-efficacy and general decision making (Faggiano et al., 2008).

*Community-based approaches* are community efforts to prevent and reduce alcohol use and related problems. Much of what can be accomplished in a community-based approach is dependent on funding and the environmental risks and strengths of a particular community. Common elements in many community-based approaches are media campaigns, citizen monitoring, youth outreach programs, server-training programs, brief screening and/or counseling opportunities, and continuing education for professionals. Although evaluations of most of these locally based programs are unavailable, evaluations that do exist show modest effectiveness (Giesbrecht & Haydon, 2006).

### Selective Approaches

Selective approaches are common in college populations, which have characteristically high binge drinking rates. *Social norms marketing* (in which information is disseminated to correct misperceptions regarding peer drinking behavior) and *expectancy challenge* interventions (that focus on perceptions of alcohol's effects and provide accurate information) are two approaches that appear to have garnered empirical support (Cruz & Dunn, 2003; Perkins, Haines, & Rice, 2005), although results are somewhat mixed (Wechsler et al., 2003). Larimer and Cronce (2007) recently reviewed the literature on individual-focused prevention and treatment approaches for college drinking and found evidence for several similar efforts that appear to reduce drinking and/or related consequences, including normative reeducation programs, cognitive and behavioral skills-based interventions, motivational/ feedback-based interventions, and brief motivational interventions. Brief motivational interventions with personalized feedback were shown to be efficacious across a variety of modalities (e.g., delivered individually, in groups, or as stand-alone feedback with no in-person contact), highlighting the implemental flexibility of this approach.

In addition to these, *harm reduction approaches* (e.g., Marlatt & Gordon, 1985; Marlatt & Witkiewitz, 2002) promote strategies to avoid excessive levels of consumption and to minimize harmful consequences when intoxicated. Strategies that emphasize harm reduction approaches tailored to an individual's unique risk have been implemented for high school students, college students, and patients in medical settings (Neighbors, Larimer, Lostutter, & Woods, 2006). Interventions tailored for high school students that incorporate aspects of normative information and skill development for reducing risks associated with alcohol use (specifically drunk driving) are linked to reductions in risky drinking and other negative consequences from alcohol (Shope, Copeland, Marcoux, & Kamp, 1996). Similar programs that focus on drinking moderation skills and behavioral alternatives to high-risk alcohol-related behaviors have also been shown to result in reductions in risky drinking (D'Amico & Fromme, 2002).

### Treatment Approaches

Depending upon the nature and extent of excessive consumption, physical dependence, and alcohol-related problems, a variety of treatment approaches to address these problems may be relevant. Beyond the treatment of AUDs and other behavioral aspects of drinking is the treatment of medical conditions that may be largely attributable to alcohol consumption (e.g., liver transplantation for alcohol cirrhosis; Beresford & Everson, 2000). In this section, we highlight those treatments that are of most relevant to clinical psychologists.

### Treatment of Alcohol Withdrawal

Withdrawal from alcohol in individuals with moderate to severe alcohol dependence is associated with a common abstinence syndrome characterized by cardiovascular overactivity, sweating, sleep problems, tremor, and anxiety (see Kosten & O'Connor, 2003). Detoxification treatment is designed to control the potential psychological and medical complications that may temporarily arise after a period of sustained,

heavy use. Further, it is designed to do so in a way that is comfortable for the patient and to prepare the patient to make arrangements for future treatment of his or her dependence (Bayard, McIntyre, Hill, & Woodside, 2004; Kasser, Geller, Howell, & Wartenberg, 2004; Luty, 2006; Raistrick, 2000). A small minority of individuals who initially experience slight withdrawal reactions will progress to more severe reactions (e.g., alcohol withdrawal delirium, such as delirium tremens [Chick, 1989], hallucinosis, or seizure) that require skilled, hospital-based care.

Although the majority of individuals who are alcohol dependent can be withdrawn safely without medication (Whitfield et al.,1978), both human clinical and animal laboratory research suggests that there is a kindling-like process associated with withdrawal. That is, the likelihood of damage to certain brain regions (and corresponding behavioral deficits) increases with greater numbers of detoxifications (Becker, 1998), highlighting the potential value of medical treatments that dampen the withdrawal process or provide neuronal protection. Detoxification typically consists of monitoring withdrawal symptoms and responding with appropriate psychopharmacological interventions, such as benzodiazepines (Raistrick, 2000) and/or other drugs (e.g., antiepileptic drugs to treat seizures).

For many years, it was assumed that medical detoxification (using benzodiazepines or similarly acting drugs) in an inpatient facility was necessary to avoid having patients progress to major withdrawal. However, as discussed by Bischof, Richmond, and Case (2003), rising costs for inpatient treatment of alcohol abuse rose sharply during the 1980s, leading researchers to examine if outpatient services were as effective (Finney, Han, & Moos, 1996). As many of these less expensive alternatives were found to be at least as effective as traditional inpatient detoxification (e.g., Alterman, Hayashida, & O'Brien, 1988; Bischof et al., 1991; Feldman, Pattison, Sobell, Graham, & Sobell, 1975; Hayashida et al., 1989; Stinnett, 1982; see Bischof et al., 2003; Fleeman, 1997), other alternatives to hospital-based medical detoxification developed. These alternatives differed in both setting and in the use of medication. Some nonhospital medical detoxification programs moved treatment out of the more expensive hospital setting but continued to utilize medication routinely, whereas so-called *social setting detoxification* (Social Setting Detoxification, 1986) utilized a treatment process that provided a supportive, caring, and noninstitutional environment without the use of medication. Although several researchers concluded (based on empirical evidence) that social setting detoxification is an effective alternative to more costly hospital-based detoxification for most cases of withdrawal (e.g., O'Briant, Petersen, & Heacock, 1977), there may be concerns about the specific neurological sequelae of repeated unmedicated withdrawals.

### Brief Interventions

Brief interventions, which can be as short as 10–15 minutes (e.g., Fleming et al., 2000, 2002), are often used in primary care settings with drinkers who report having low levels of dependence and/or who are unwilling to pursue more intensive treatment regimens. These interventions often involve motivational approaches designed to encourage drinkers to consider changing their drinking behavior (Wilk, Jensen, & Havighurst, 1997). Typically, the role of the clinician is to help the drinker set drinking goals, agree on a plan to reduce or stop consumption, and provide advice and educational materials. Follow-up sessions are scheduled to monitor progress and renegotiate drinking goals and strategies. Brief interventions can be administered by a wide variety of providers in a range of treatment modalities and are relatively less expensive than extended treatment options (Heather, 1986). The NIAAA (2007) has developed a treatment manual, *Helping Patients Who Drink Too Much,* and supporting materials to encourage clinicians to screen and intervene with patients they see in their practices. The NIAAA has also recently added online training materials (2008b).

Meta-analyses of controlled trials indicate that brief interventions reduce alcohol consumption and drinking-related outcomes (compared to individuals that do not receive treatment) and appear to be as effective as extended treatment conditions (Moyer, Finney, Swearingen, & Vergun, 2002; Neighbors et al., 2006; Wilk et al., 1997). Further, these approaches appear to result in significant cost savings compared to the utilization of other health care services.

Recent studies also indicate that brief, motivational interventions delivered in an emergency room (ER) setting have been shown to reduce alcohol consumption, alcohol-related negative consequences, and recidivism, including among trauma patients (Bombardier & Rimmele, 1999; Gentilello, Ebel, Wickizer, Salkever, & Rivara, 2005; Monti et al., 1999). These brief ER interventions may be especially beneficial to patients who attribute their injury or diagnosis to alcohol consumption (Walton et al., 2008). Finally, there is evidence that individuals with higher levels of problematic alcohol use who are approached in ER settings are equally likely as those with lower levels to consent to enrollment in the intervention (Hungerford, Pollack, & Todd, 2000). As a result of these promising outcomes, brief motivational interventions are considered a "best-practice" recommendation in the United States (Neighbors et al., 2006).

### Cognitive-Behavioral Approaches

Although numerous cognitive-behavioral interventions to treat alcohol dependence have been developed and assessed (Miller, Zweben, DiClemente, & Rychtarik, 1995), a predominant model of cognitive - behavioral therapy (CBT) for AUDs is based on the work of Marlatt and Gordon (1985) regarding the relapse process. Marlatt's cognitive-behavioral model of relapse centers on high-risk situations and the individual's response in that situation (see Witkiewitz & Marlatt, 2004, 2008). Under this model, individuals that lack confidence to deal with the situation and/or lack an effective coping response are more likely to be tempted to drink. It is thought that the decision to use or not use is then mediated by the individual's outcome expectancies for the initial effects of using the substance (Jones, Corbin, & Fromme, 2001). This model provides the basis for relapse prevention interventions by identifying potential high-risk situations for relapse and challenging expectations for the perceived positive effects of a substance (Marlatt & Witkiewitz, 2002; Witkiewitz & Marlatt, 2004). A meta-analysis conducted by Irvin, Bowers, Dunn and Wang (1999) suggested that relapse prevention was a successful intervention for substance use and improving psychosocial adjustment, especially for individuals with alcohol problems.

A related component of CBT is social skills training (Monti & O'Leary, 1999). This approach assumes that increasing the repertoire of coping skills will reduce the stress of high-risk situations and provide alternatives to drinking. Techniques include assertiveness training and role-playing skills related to alcohol refusal. Several studies suggest social skills training is effective in reducing drinking (see Chambless & Ollendick, 2001).

Despite the apparent effectiveness of cognitive-behavioral approaches to treat AUDs, little is known about the cognitive-behavioral processes that underlie current definitions of coping (Morgenstern & Longabaugh, 2000; Witkiewitz & Marlatt, 2004, 2008). Although numerous studies have examined possible mediators (e.g., changes in coping skills) of cognitive-behavioral treatment for AUDs, there is little empirical support for the hypothesized mechanisms of action of CBT (Morgenstern & Longabaugh, 2000).

Based on the notion that alcohol-related cues (e.g., the sight and smell of an alcoholic beverage) can trigger a relapse for alcoholics, cue-exposure therapy repeatedly exposes patients to alcohol-related cues while preventing the usual response (drinking alcohol), with the desired outcome to reduce or eliminate urges to drink in response to cues (Monti & Rohsenow, 1999). Cue-exposure treatment draws from both classical learning models and social learning models of behavior. From the perspective of classical learning theory, environmental cues associated with past drinking elicit conditioned responses (e.g., Rohsenow et al., 1994) that are thought to play a role in relapse. As a corollary, repeated exposure to substance-associated cues while preventing conditioned responses should lead to an extinction of these reactions, decreasing the likelihood of craving and relapse and extending time to first relapse. Social learning theory suggests that the presence of cues increases risk of relapse because cues increase the relevance (salience) of positive effects of alcohol to the drinker, thus leading her or him to want to consume more alcohol (Monti & Rohsenow, 1999). Alcohol cues may also trigger cognitive and neurochemical reactions that undermine the drinker's ability to use coping skills and beliefs surrounding the use of skills (Monti & Rohsenow, 1999). Various approaches to implement cue exposure exist (Rohsenow et al., 1994), such as classical learning models that tend to focus on habituation and extinction of responses. Approaches based on social learning theory may also incorporate coping skills training. Cue-exposure is listed as a probably efficacious treatment for AUDs (Chambless & Ollendick, 2001), although some researchers have questioned the effectiveness of cue-exposure for treating substance use disorders (e.g., Conklin & Tiffany, 2002).

Although traditional cue-exposure techniques have focused on relatively passive exposures to alcohol cues (or various cues to drinking), it is possible that findings from recent research on implicit cognition in addiction can lead to techniques that enhance cue exposure (Wiers & Stacy, 2006). For example, Fadardi and Cox (2007) showed that the tendency for alcohol cues to grab a drinker's attention can be altered by training excessive drinkers to gain more control over their attentional bias via behavioral training. Critically, these changes in attentional bias appear to correlate with changes in drinking behavior. Based on recent research on implicit cognition, other behavioral techniques that try to alter automatic

reactions are also being evaluated. For example, Wiers et al. (2008) have exploited the finding that approach (pulling something towards oneself) and avoidance (pushing something away from oneself) movements are associated with more positive (pulling) and negative (pushing) emotions (e.g., Cacioppo et al., 1993). Specifically, preliminary data suggested that drinkers who were trained to "push" alcohol stimuli away showed reduced implicit positive attitudes toward alcohol as well as reduced craving.

It should also be noted that there is growing evidence from research on treatment of anxiety disorders that pharmacological manipulations can enhance exposure-based fear reduction (Norberg, Krystal, & Tolin, 2008). Specifically, D-cycloserine has been used to enhance extinction of alcohol seeking in rats (Vengeliene, Kiefer, & Spanagel, 2008), suggesting that such pharmacological enhancement of exposure-based treatments could be useful clinically in the future. These innovative approaches that exploit new findings on implicit cognition and the pharmacology of learning potentially open up a new era of research on exposure-based approaches.

### Generalized Self-regulation Training

Based on the perspective that (lack of) self-regulation (or self-control) contributes to AUDs, some researchers have recently suggested strengthening self-regulation as a treatment approach (e.g., Sher & Martinez, 2009). Recent research that suggests traits related to self-regulation, such as conscientiousness (Costa & McCrae, 1992), may be more mutable than previously thought (e.g., Roberts, Walton, & Viechtbauer, 2006). Experimental research has suggested that regular use of self-control will strengthen this attribute in a way akin to how muscles get stronger with regular use (Baumeister, Heatherton, & Tice, 1994; Muraven & Baumeister, 2000). This perspective provides novel approaches for training or rehabilitating self-control in persons suffering from substance use disorders. For example, self-control "exercises," such as dietary monitoring, regular physical exercise, money management planning, and working on improving study habits (Baumeister, Gailliot, DeWall, & Oaten, 2006), have led to improvements in other self-regulatory behaviors, such as smoking fewer cigarettes and drinking less alcohol. Thus, there is now increased interest in the treatment (and prevention) potential of self-control training for a range of behaviors affecting health and general role function.

### The Question of Patient–Treatment Matching
It has long been recognized that individuals with AUDs are extremely heterogeneous with respect to

etiology, symptomatology, and course of disorder. Because of this diversity, it has been speculated for many years that, rather than a "one-size-fits-all" approach to alcohol treatment, treatment outcomes might be optimized if patients could be matched to specific treatments based on their personal characteristics. In a large, multisite, randomized control trial, this general hypothesis was put to the test by examining the interaction between three psychosocial treatments (i.e., Twelve-Step Facilitation, Cognitive-Behavioral Coping Skills, or Motivational Enhancement Therapy) and several individual difference variables hypothesized to be related to responsiveness to specific treatment approaches (e.g., participant sex, coping skills; Project MATCH Research Group, 1993). Although numerous papers and chapters have been published based on Project Match, the outcomes of the primary study hypotheses not only failed to find differences among treatments as a main effect but also failed to find much evidence for the hypothesized interactions (Project MATCH Research Group, 1997). It is possible that future research will provide more convincing evidence of patient–treatment matching strategies with psychological and behavioral treatments. For example, as discussed in the section on naltrexone below, there appears to be evidence of patient–treatment matching for pharmacological treatments. It has also been suggested that the standard statistical approach to examining alcohol outcomes (e.g., relapse as a dichotomous outcome) may obscure important findings compared to more sophisticated approaches that conceptualize relapse as a nonlinear, dynamical process (Witkiewitz & Marlatt, 2007). Thus, although Project Match (and the theory underpinning it) has been popularly viewed as a failed approach, it is clearly premature to jettison patient–treatment matching as a viable strategy.

Indeed, other researchers (e.g., Conrod et al., 2000) have examined important individual differences, such as personality and drinking motives, in order to develop individually tailored treatments, predominantly targeted at substance use motivations associated with different personality dimensions. Preliminary empirical evidence suggests that treatment approaches that focus on individual differences in drinking motives related to sensation-seeking may result in slower increases in adolescent drinking and binge drinking following intervention (Conrod, Castellanos, & Mackie, 2008).

### Marital and Family Approaches
Alcohol use disorders often manifest themselves in the context of the family and have considerable consequences for spouses and other family members who often try to exert interpersonal influence over the drinker (Epstein & McCrady, 1998; Fals-Stewart et al., 2005). Consequently, it is not surprising that a number of interventions involve couples and the family unit.

At the couples' level, the most extensively studied approach is behavioral couples therapy (BCT). In addition to sharing many features of traditional cognitive-behavioral treatment for the drinker, BCT also targets cultivating partners' coping with drinking situations, reinforcing abstinence, and improving the dyadic relationship. A recent meta-analysis of BCT outcomes with regard to substance use disorders (in which eight of the 12 studies reviewed were for treatment of AUDs; Powers, Vedel, & Emmelkamp, 2008) demonstrated that this treatment approach was more effective than control treatments in improving relationship satisfaction as well as substance-related outcomes. Interestingly, the comparatively stronger salutary effect of BCT on substance-related outcomes was not evident immediately after treatment, when all treatments fared well but, rather, the couples' treatment effect strengthened relative to control treatments over time. This suggests that improved interpersonal relationships fostered better alcohol-related outcomes. Importantly, there was no relation between the number of sessions and outcomes, suggesting that BCT could be delivered as a relatively brief treatment.

A number of treatment approaches that target the entire family and larger social networks have also been developed (Copello, Velleman, & Templeton, 2005). Arguably the most systematically studied of these, the community reinforcement and family training approach (Smith & Meyers, 2004) is an extension of the community reinforcement approach (CRA, Sisson & Azrin, 1986). Under this approach, a friend or family member (e.g., spouse) either provides or removes agreed reinforcers (e.g., television access) to reward periods of sobriety or to punish drinking for the targeted individual. Further, the agreed-upon friend/family member may also encourage the alcohol dependent individual to enter treatment and supervise the use of disulfiram. Several studies suggest that CRA is an effective treatment for alcohol abuse and dependence (Carr, 2009; Chambless & Ollendick, 2001; Luty, 2006).

### Self-help Groups
Perhaps the most widely recognized treatment approach for AUDs is Alcoholics Anonymous (AA; AA World Services, 1978), a self-help movement

that has now been in existence for 75 years. AA describes itself as:

> [A] fellowship of men and women who share their experience, strength and hope with each other that they may solve their common problem and help others to recover from alcoholism. The only requirement for membership is a desire to stop drinking. There are no dues or fees for AA membership; we are self-supporting through our own contributions. AA is not allied with any sect, denomination, politics, organization, or institution; does not wish to engage in any controversy, neither endorses nor opposes any causes. Our primary purpose is to stay sober and help other alcoholics to achieve sobriety.

Based upon a disease model of alcoholism that posits that alcoholism is a relapsing illness that requires complete abstinence (Luty, 2006), new members are encouraged to recruit support from a sponsor (an AA member who has been sober for at least one year) and to attend 90 meetings in the first 90 days of treatment. Several studies suggest that AA is as effective as alternative treatments (Tonigan, Toscova, & Miller, 1996), although many studies are small, nonrandomized, or fail to account for the fact that many AA members are often concurrently involved in other forms of treatment.

Other self-help approaches have been developed that do not rely on abstinence goals. Specifically, *moderation management* (MM; Kishline, 1994) is based on the assumption that some individuals are problem drinkers yet not alcohol dependent and can learn to drink in nonproblematic ways. As noted by Humphreys (2003), both AA and MM share some assumptions. For example, both suggest that there is a difference between individuals who are alcohol dependent and less likely to be able to drink moderately and those individuals who may have problems with alcohol that are not due to an underlying dependence on alcohol. However, the two approaches differ to the extent that they believe the drinker is a good judge of how dependent he or she is and whether controlled drinking is a realistic outcome expectation. Specifically, AA and closely allied approaches embrace the notion that a hallmark symptom of alcoholism is denial (see Sher & Epler, 2004, for a discussion of this concept), and therefore, an individual is unable to realistically appraise his or her drinking. MM, on the other hand, views the individual as capable of rationally evaluating the appropriateness of controlled drinking goals. Comparisons of individuals who affiliate with AA and MM suggest that the two approaches draw from very different subpopulations of those with AUDs, with MM affiliates being more socially stable and less alcohol dependent than those who affiliate with AA (Humphreys & Klaw, 2001). Thus, although there has been considerable antagonism between advocates of the AA and MM approaches, it appears that the two approaches are, to a large extent, serving different populations with different clinical needs and goals.

### Pharmacotherapy

One of the most dramatic changes in treatment of AUDs to have occurred in the past 15 years is the introduction of the pharmaceuticals to curb craving and compulsive alcohol use. Although disulfiram (Antabuse) has been marketed for the treatment of alcohol dependence for more than 60 years, this medication (which causes an intense adverse reaction when the drinker consumes alcohol by blocking the enzyme that breaks down acetaldehyde, leading to a build-up of this toxic metabolite in the bloodstream) has not been shown to be effective as a major treatment modality by itself (although it may be useful as part of behavioral contracting).

In 1994, naltrexone (Revia) was the first new medication to receive U.S. Food and Drug Administration (FDA) approval for the treatment of alcohol dependence since disulfiram. Naltrexone, which blocks opiate receptors in the brain, appears to be a fairly effective medication in reducing heavy consumption and reducing risk of relapse (Srisurapanont & Jarusuraisin, 2005). Despite its apparent efficacy and low profile of side effects, many believe it is underutilized, perhaps because of physicians' reluctance to use medications to treat substance dependence. A long-acting, injectable form (Vivitrol) has recently been approved and appears to be effective as well (Garbutt et al., 2005). This long-acting form might prove to be useful in individuals who have difficulty in complying with oral pharmacotherapy. Additionally, recent findings (Kranzler et al., 2003) suggest that naltrexone can be taken on a targeted, as-needed basis (e.g., when a drinker wants to abstain or limit his drinking on a given occasion).

There appear to be important, genetically based individual differences in response to naltrexone (e.g., Oslin, Berttini, & O'Brien, 2006). Specifically, allelic variation in the $\mu$-opioid receptor moderates treatment response to naltrexone in alcohol dependent individuals. This finding may herald a new "pharmacogenomic" chapter in the history of patient–treatment matching attempts (e.g., Edenberg

& Kranzler, 2005). It is hoped by many that advances in both genomics and neurobiology will lead to other forms of "personalized medicine" (Zerhouni, 2006) in the treatment of alcohol dependence, in which the characterization of one's own genetic make-up will guide treatment efforts.

It should also be noted that two other drugs have empirical support for their use in the treatment of alcoholism, acamprosate (Campral) and topiramate (Topamax). Acamprosate is FDA approved for the treatment of alcohol dependence and is thought to work by restoring normal N-methyl-D-aspartate (NMDA) receptor tone in glutamate systems in the brain (Kiefer & Mann, 2005). However, in one recent, large, multicenter clinical trial in the United States, acamprosate was not found to be effective (Anton et al., 2006). Consequently, it has been speculated that this treatment only shows effectiveness in trials with patients with relatively severe dependence. Although topiramate has not received an indication for alcohol dependence from the FDA (it is approved for other conditions), this antiepileptic drug has been shown to be effective in a large, multisite, randomized control trial (Johnson et al., 2007), presumably by facilitating GABAergic neurotransmission and inhibiting glutaminergic pathways in the brain and thus reducing alcohol-mediated reward. A number of drugs with different targets and methods of action are under investigation currently, and it seems likely that the range of treatment options for alcohol dependence will increase over the coming years.

## Conclusion
### Future Directions
For the health psychologist, alcohol use and alcohol use disorders should be a topic of central concern. Exposure to alcohol affects individuals over the entire course of human development, including in utero exposures due to maternal consumption, during adolescence when most drinkers initiate drinking, and throughout adulthood into late life. Over this time, although the determinants and health-related risks and consequences change as a function life stage, alcohol consumption, overall, is a major source of health burden in the United States (Rehm et al., 2009). Unlike some licit (i.e., tobacco) and illicit drugs of abuse, there appear to be some significant positive health consequences, especially during mid-life. Further, only a minority of users abuse alcohol or are dependent upon it. Thus, our own and many other cultures' attitudes about alcohol are highly ambivalent; therefore, it seems likely that alcohol will continue to be an important part of our society, as well as continue to pose health risks for the population. It will be important to monitor how health risks associated with alcohol change as a function of the shifting health profile of the population. For example, with increasing prevalence of some disorders (e.g., type II diabetes; CDC, 2008; Kenny, Aubert, & Geiss, 1995) and decreasing prevalence of others (e.g., coronary artery disease; Fingerhut & Warner, 1997; Hu et al., 2000), will the general profile of health risks and benefits associated with alcohol change? Also, as we begin to understand genetic and epigenetic processes associated with various chronic diseases, will we be able to identify those individuals who are most vulnerable to specific forms of alcohol-related diseases and intervene preemptively or develop specific treatments that interfere with pathways of alcohol-induced illness and injury? Moreover, as new behavioral and pharmacological treatments for alcohol dependence are identified, will we be able to optimize treatment so that compulsive alcohol use and episodes of excessive consumption can be minimized? Finally, although screening and brief intervention for drinking problems have been demonstrated to be effective in primary care and ER settings, what factors are necessary to further disseminate these practices into usual care? Among medical practitioners and health psychologists, the answers to these questions carry significant weight and have far-reaching implications for better understanding a number of aspects of alcohol-affected health behaviors and outcomes.

## Acknowledgments
Preparation of this chapter was supported by NIH grants K05AA017242 and T32AA013526 to Kenneth J. Sher, F31 AA019596 to Andrew K. Littlefield, and F31AA018590 to Julia Martinez.

## References
Abbey, A. (1991). Acquaintance rape and alcohol consumption on college campuses: How are they linked? *Journal of American College Health, 39*, 165–169.

Abel, E.L. (1998). *Fetal Alcohol Abuse Syndrome.* New York: Plenum Press.

Abel, E.L., Bush, R., & Dintcheff, B.A. (1981). Exposure of rats to alcohol in utero alters drug sensitivity in adulthood. *Science, 212*, 1531–1533.

Adami, H., McLaughlin, J.K., Hsing, A.W., Wolk, A., Ekbom, A., Holmberg, L. et al. (1992). Alcoholism and cancer risk: A population-based cohort study. *Cancer Causes and Control, 3*, 419–425.

Adinoff, B., Bone, G.H.A., & Linnoila, M. (1988). Acute ethanol poisoning and the ethanol withdrawal syndrome. *Medical Toxicology, 3*, 172–196.

Ahmed, A.T., Karter, A.J., & Liu, J. (2006). Alcohol consumption is inversely associated with adherence to diabetes self-care behaviours. *Diabetic Medicine, 23*, 795–802.

Alcoholics Anonymous. (1978). *Twelve steps, twelve traditions.* New York: AA World Services.

Allen, J.P., Litten, R.Z., Strid, N., & Sillanauke, P. (2001). The role of biomarkers in alcoholism medication trials. *Alcoholism: Clinical and Experimental Research, 25*, 1119–1125.

Alterman, A.I., Hayashida, M., & O'Brien, C.P. (1988). Treatment response and safety of ambulatory medical detoxification. *Journal of Studies on Alcohol, 49*, 160–166.

Amaro, H., Fried, L.E., Cabral, H., & Zuckerman, B. (1990). Violence during pregnancy and substance use. *American Journal of Public Health, 80*, 575–579.

American Cancer Society. (2006). *Alcohol and cancer.* Retrieved from http://www.cancer.org/downloads/PRO/alcohol.pdf.

American Medical Association. (2004). *Minimum legal drinking age.* Retrieved from http://www.ama-assn.org/ama/pub/category/print/13246.html.

American Psychiatric Association. (1980). *Diagnostic and statistical manual of mental disorders* (3rd ed.). Washington, DC: Author.

American Psychiatric Association. (1987). *Diagnostic and statistical manual of mental disorders* (3rd ed., revised). Washington, DC: Author.

American Psychiatric Association. (1994). *Diagnostic and statistical manual of mental disorders* (4th ed.). Washington, DC: Author.

American Psychiatric Association. (2000). *Diagnostic and statistical manual of mental disorders* (4th ed., Text Revision). Washington, DC: Author.

Amethyst Initiative. (2008). *It's time to rethink the drinking age.* Retrieved from http://www.amethystinitiative.org/statement/.

Anda, R.F., Williamson, D.F., & Remington, P.L. (1988). Alcohol and fatal injuries among US adults. *Journal of the American Medical Association, 260*, 2529–2532.

Anderson, K.G., Smith, G.T., McCarthy, D.M., Fischer, S.F., Fister, S., Grodin, D., et al. (2005). Elementary school drinking: The role of temperament and learning. *Psychology of Addictive Behaviors, 19*, 21–27.

Anderson, R.N., Minino, A.M., Fingerhut, L.A., Warner, M., & Heinen, M.A. (2004). Deaths: Injuries, 2001. *National Vital Statistics Report, 52*, 1–87.

Andreas, J.B., & O'Farrell, T.J. (2007). Longitudinal associations between fathers' heavy drinking patterns and children's psychological adjustment. *Journal of Abnormal Child Psychology, 35*, 1–16.

Andreasson, S. (2007). The health benefits of moderate consumption called into question. *Addiction Research and Theory, 15*, 3–5.

Anthenelli, R.M., Klein, J.L., Tsuang, J.W., Smith, T.L., & Schuckit, M.A. (1994). The prognostic importance of blackouts in young men. *Journal of Studies on Alcohol, 55*, 290–295.

Anton, R.F., O'Malley, S.S., Ciraulo, D.A., Cisler, R.A., Couper, D., Donovan, D.M., et al. (2006). Combined pharmacotherapies and behavioral interventions for alcohol dependence. The COMBINE study: A randomized controlled trial. *Journal of the American Medical Association, 295*, 2003–2017.

Arbuckle, T.Y., Chaikelson, J.S., & Gold, D.P. (1994). Social drinking and cognitive functioning revisited: The role of intellectual endowment and psychological distress. *Journal of Studies on Alcohol, 55*, 352–361.

Arnett, J.J. (2006). Emerging adulthood: Understanding the new way of coming of age. In J.J. Arnett, & J.L. Tanner (Eds.), *Emerging adults in America: Coming of age in the 21st century* (pp. 3–19). Washington, DC: American Psychological Association.

Ascherio, A., Rimm, E.B., Giovannucci, E.L., Colditz, G.A., Rosner, B., Willett, W.C., et al. (1992). A prospective study of nutritional factors and hypertension among US men. *Circulation, 86*, 1475–1484.

Ashe, M., Jernigan, D., Kline, R., & Galaz, R. (2003). Land use planning and the control of tobacco, firearms, and fast food restaurants. *American Journal of Public Health, 93*, 1404–1408.

Avins, A.L., Lindan, C.P., Woods, W.J., Hudes, E.S., Boscarino, J.A., Kay, J., et al. (1997). Changes in HIV-related behaviors among heterosexual alcoholics following addiction treatment. *Drug and Alcohol Dependence, 44*, 47–55.

Ayala, C., Croft, J.B., Greenlund, K.J., Keenan, N.L., Donehoo, R.S., Malarcher, A.M., et al. (2002). Sex differences in US mortality rates for stroke and stroke subtypes by race/ethnicity and age, 1995–1998. *Stroke, 33*, 1197–1201.

Ayala, C., Greenlund, K.J., Croft, J.B., Keenan, N.L. Donehoo, R.S., Giles, W.H., et al. (2001). Racial/ethnic disparities in mortality by stroke subtype in the United States, 1995–1998. *American Journal of Epidemiology, 154*, 1057–1063.

Babor, T.F., de la Fuente, J.R., Saunders J., & Grant, M. (1992). *AUDIT: The alcohol use disorders identification test: Guidelines for use in primary health care.* Geneva: World Health Organization.

Babor, T.F., Higgins-Biddle, J.C., Saunders, J.B., & Monteiro, M.G. (2001). *AUDIT- The alcohol use disorders identification test: Guidelines for use in primary care.* Geneva: World Health Organization, Department of Mental Health and Substance Dependence.

Bachman, J.G., Wadsworth, K.N., O'Malley, P.M., Johnston, L.D., & Schulenberg, J.E. (1997). *Smoking, drinking, and drug use in young adulthood: The impacts of new freedoms and new responsibilities.* Mahwah, NJ: Lawrence Erlbaum Associates.

Baer, J.S., Sampson, P.D., Barr, H.M., Connor, P.D., & Streissguth, A.P. (2003). A 21-year longitudinal analysis of the effects of prenatal alcohol exposure on young adult drinking. *Archives of General Psychiatry, 60*, 377–385.

Bagby, G.J., Stoltz, D.A., Zhang, P., Kolls, J.K., Brown, J., Bohm, R.P., et al. (2003). The effect of chronic binge ethanol consumption on the primary stage of SIV infection in rhesus macaques. *Alcoholism Clinical and Experimental Research, 27*, 495–502.

Bagnardi, V., Blangiardo, M., La Vecchia, C., & Corrao, G. (2001). A meta-analysis of alcohol drinking and cancer risk. *British Journal of Cancer, 11*,1700–1705.

Barnes, G.E. (1979). The alcoholic personality: A reanalysis of the literature. *Journal of Studies on Alcohol, 40*, 571–633.

Barnes, G.E. (1983). Clinical and prealcoholic personality characteristics. In B. Kissin, and H. Begleiter (Eds.), *The biology of alcoholism* Vol. 6 (pp. 113–195). New York: Plenum.

Barr, C.S., Newman, T.K., Lindell, S., Shannon, C., Champoux, M., Lesch, K.P., et al. (2004). Interaction between serotonin transporter gene variation and rearing condition in alcohol preference and consumption in female primates. *Archives of General Psychiatry, 61*, 1146–1152.

Barta, W.D., Portnoy, D.B., Kiene, S.M., Tennen, H., Abu-Hasaballah, K.S., & Ferrer, R. (2008). A daily process investigation of alcohol-involved sexual risk behavior among economically disadvantaged problem drinkers living with HIV/AIDS. *AIDS & Behavior, 12*, 729–740.

Bates, M.E., & Labouvie, E.W. (1995). Personality environment constellations and alcohol use: A process-oriented study of intraindividual change during adolescence. *Psychology of Addictive Behaviors, 9*, 23–35.

Baudet, M., Rigaud, M., Rocha, P., Bardet, J., & Bourdarias, J.P. (1979). Reversibility of alcoholic cardiomyopathy with abstention from alcohol. *Cardiology, 64*, 317–324.

Baumeister, R.F., Gailliot, M., DeWall, C.N., & Oaten, M. (2006). Self-regulation and personality: How interventions increase regulatory success, and how depletion moderates the effects of traits on behavior. *Journal of Personality, 74*, 1173–1802.

Baumeister, R.F., Heatherton, T.F., & Tice, D.M. (1994). *Losing control: How and why people fail at self-regulation*. San Diego: Academic Press.

Bayard, M., McIntyre, J., Hill, K.R., & Woodside, J. (2004). Alcohol withdrawal syndrome. *American Family Physician, 69*, 1443–1450.

Becker, H.C. (1998). Kindling in alcohol withdrawal. *Alcohol, Health and Research World, 22*, 25–33.

Beevers, D.G. (1990). Alcohol, blood pressure and antihypertensive drugs. *Journal of Clinical Pharmacy and Therapeutics, 15*, 395–397.

Beresford, T.P., & Everson, G.T. (2000). Liver transplantation for alcoholic liver disease: Bias, beliefs, 6–month rule, and relapse—but where are the data? *Liver Transplantation, 6*, 777–778.

Berglund, M. (1991). Clinical and physiological implications and correlations. *Alcohol & Alcoholism, 1*, S399–S402.

Bien, T.H., & Burge, J. (1990). Smoking and drinking: A review of the literature. *International Journal of Addiction, 25*, 1429–1454.

Bird, G.L. A., Sheron, N., Goka, A.K. J., Alexander, G.J., & Williams, R.S. (1990). Increased plasma TNF in severe alcoholic hepatitis. *Annals of Internal Medicine, 112*, 917–920.

Bischof, G.H., Richmond, C., & Case, A. (2003). Detoxification at home: A brief solution-oriented family systems approach. *Contemporary Family Therapy, 25*, 17–39.

Bischof, G., Booker, J., Dyck, T., Graney, E., Hamblen, I., Hittinger, C., et al. (1991). Outpatient detoxification: An annotated bibliography. *Alcoholism Treatment Quarterly, 8*, 119–129.

Blot, W.J. (1992). Alcohol and cancer. *Cancer Research, 52*, S2119–S2123.

Blot, W.J., McLaughlin, J.K., Winn, D.M., Austin, D.F., Greenberg, R.S., Preston-Martin, S., et al. (1988). Smoking and drinking in relation to oral and pharyngeal cancer. *Cancer Research, 48*, 3282–3287.

Bode, C., & Bode, J.C. (1997). Alcohol's role in gastrointestinal tract disorders. *Alcohol Health & Research World, 21*, 76–83.

Bode, J.C., & Bode, C. (1992). Alcohol malnutrition and gastrointestinal tract. In R.R. Watson, & B. Watzl (Eds.), *Nutrition and Alcohol* (pp. 403–428). Boca Raton, FL: CRC Press.

Boffetta, P., & Garfinkel, L. (1990). Alcohol drinking and mortality among men enrolled in an American Cancer Society prospective study. *Epidemiology, 1*, 342–348.

Boffetta, P., & Hashibe, M. (2006). Alcohol and cancer. *Lancet Oncology, 7*, 149–156.

Bohn, M.J., Babor, T.F., & Kranzler, H.R. (1995). The alcohol use disorders identification test (AUDIT): Validation of a screening instrument for use in medical settings. *Journal of Studies on Alcohol, 56*(4), 423–432.

Bolton, R., Vincke, J., Mak, R., & Dennehy, E. (1992). Alcohol and risky sex: In search of an elusive connection. *Medical Anthropology, 14*, 323–363.

Bombardier, C.H., & Rimmele, C.T. (1999). Motivational interviewing to prevent alcohol abuse after traumatic brain injury: A case series. *Rehabilitation Psychology, 44*, 52–67.

Booyse, F., Pan, W., Grenett, H., Parks, D., Darley-Usmar, V., Bradley, K. et al. (2007). Mechanism by which alcohol and wine polyphenols affect coronary heart disease risk. *Annals of Epidemiology, 17*, S24–S31.

Borges, G., Cherpitel, C., Orozco, R., Bond, J., Ye, Y., Macdonald, S., et al. (2006). Multicentre study of acute alcohol use and non-fatal injuries: Data from the WHO collaborative study on alcohol injuries. *Bulletin of the World Health Organization, 84*, 453–460.

Boscarino, J.A., Avins, A.L., Woods, W.J., Lindan, C.P., Hudes, E.S., & Clark, W. (1995). Alcohol-related risk factors associated with HIV infection among patients entering alcoholism treatment: Implications for prevention. *Journal of Studies on Alcohol, 56*, 642–653.

Bradley, K.A., Badrinath, S., Bush, K., Boyd-Wickizer, J., & Anawalt, B. (1998). Medical risks for women who drink alcohol. *Journal of General Internal Medicine, 13*, 627–639.

Braithwaite, R.S., Conigliaro, J., Roberts, M.S., Shechter, S., Schaefer, A., Mcginnis, K. et al. (2007). Estimating the impact of alcohol consumption on survival for HIV+ individuals. *AIDS Care, 19*, 459–466.

Braithwaite, R.S., McGinnis, K.A., Conigliaro, J., Maisto, S.A., Crystal, S., Day, N., et al. (2005). A temporal and dose response association between alcohol consumption and medication adherence among veterans in care. *Alcoholism: Clinical & Experimental Research, 29*, 1190–1197.

Brennan, P.L., Schutte, K.K., & Moos, R.H. (2005). Pain and use of alcohol to manage pain: Prevalence and 3-year outcomes among older problem and non-problem drinkers. *Addiction, 100*, 777–786.

Breslau, N. (1995). Psychiatric comorbidity of smoking and nicotine dependence. *Behavior Genetics, 25*, 95–101.

Brezel, B.S., Kassenbrock, J.M., & Stein, J.M. (1988). Burns in substance abusers and in neurologically and mentally impaired patients. *Journal of Burn Care & Rehabilitation, 9*, 169–171.

Bryant, K.J. (2006). Expanding research on the role of alcohol consumption and related risks in the prevention and treatment of HIV_AIDS. *Substance Use & Misuse, 41*, 1465–1507.

Bush, K.R., Kivlahan, D.R., Davis, T.M., Dobie, D.J., Sporleder, J.L., Epler, A.J., et al. (2003). The TWEAK is weak for alcohol screening among female Veterans Affairs outpatients. *Alcoholism: Clinical and Experimental Research, 27*(12), 1971–1978.

Cacioppo, J.T., Priester, J.R., & Berntson, G.G. (1993). Rudimentary determinants of attitudes. II: Arm flexion and extension have differential effects on attitudes. *Journal of Personality and Social Psychology, 65*, 5–17.

Cadoret, R.J., Yates, M.D., Troughton, E., Woodworth, G., & Stewart, M.A. (1995). Adoption study demonstrating two genetic pathways to drug abuse. *Archives of General Psychiatry, 52*, 42–52.

Caetano, R., & Tam, T.W. (1995) Prevalence and correlates of DSM-IV and ICD-10 alcohol dependence: 1990

U.S. national alcohol survey. *Alcohol and Alcoholism, 30,* 177–186.

Camargo, C.A., & Rimm, E.B. (1996). Epidemiologic research on moderate alcohol consumption and blood pressure. In *Alcohol and the cardiovascular system* (pp. 25–62). (NIH publication No. 96–4133). Bethesda, MD: National Institute on Alcohol Abuse and Alcoholism.

Camargo, C.A., Hennekens, C.H., Gaziano, J.M., Glynn, R.J., Manson, J.E., et al. (1997). Prospective study of moderate alcohol consumption and mortality in US male physicians. *Archives of Internal Medicine, 157,* 79–85.

Camargo Jr., C.A. (1989). Moderate alcohol consumption and stroke: The epidemiologic evidence. *Stroke, 20,* 1611–1626.

Carey, K.B. (1995). Alcohol-related expectancies predict quantity and frequency of heavy drinking among college students. *Psychology of Addictive Behaviors, 9,* 236–241.

Carlson, S.R., Iacono, W.G., & McGue, M. (2002). P300 amplitude in adolescent twins discordant and concordant for alcohol use disorders. *Biological Psychology, 61,* 203–227.

Carlson, S. R., McLarnon, M. E., & Iacono, W. G. (2007). P300 amplitude, externalizing psychopathology, and earlier- versus later-onset substance use disorder. *Journal of Abnormal Psychology, 116,* 565–577.

Carney, M. A., Tennen, H., Affleck, G., del Boca, F. K., & Kranzler, H. R. (1998). Levels and patterns of alcohol consumption using timeline follow-back, daily diaries and real-time "electronic interviews." *Journal of Studies on Alcohol, 59,* 447–454.

Carr, A.A. (2009). The effectiveness of family therapy and systemic interventions for adult-focused problems. *Journal of Family Therapy, 31,* 46–74.

Caspi, A., Begg, D., Dickson, N., Harrington, H.-L., Langley, J., Moffitt, T.E., et al. (1997). Personality differences predict health-risk behaviors in adulthood: Evidence from a longitudinal study. *Journal of Personality and Social Psychology, 73,* 1052–1063.

Caspi, A., Sugden, K., Moffitt, T.E., Taylor, A., Craig, I.W., Harrington, H., et al. (2003). Influence of life stress on depression: Moderation by a polymorphism in the 5-HTT gene. *Science, 301,* 386–389.

Center for Disease Control. (2004). *Health, United States, 2004.* Hyattsville, MD: National Center for Health Statistics.

Center for Disease Control. (2005). *Quick stats: Information on alcohol use and health.* Retrieved from http://www.cdc.gov/alcohol/quickstats/general_info.htm.

Center for Disease Control. (2008). *Number of people with diabetes increases to 24 Million,* [Press release]. Retrieved from http://www.cdc.gov/media/pressrel/2008/r080624.htm.

Chambless, D.L., & Ollendick, T.H. (2001). Empirically supported psychological interventions: Controversies and evidence. *Annual Review of Psychology, 52,* 685–716.

Chan, A.K., Pristach, E.A., Welte, J.W., & Russell, M. (1993). Use of the TWEAK test in screening for alcoholism/heavy drinking in three populations. *Alcoholism: Clinical and Experimental Research, 17,* 1188–1192.

Chassin, L., Curran, P.J., Hussong, A.M., & Colder, C.R. (1996). The relation of parent alcoholism to adolescent substance use: A longitudinal follow-up study. *Journal of Abnormal Psychology, 105,* 70–80.

Chassin, L., Pitts, S.C., DeLucia, C., & Todd, M. (1999). A longitudinal study of children of alcoholics: Predicting young adult substance use disorders, anxiety, and depression. *Journal of Abnormal Psychology, 108,* 106–119.

Chen, W.J., Loh, E.W., Hsu, Y.P., Chen, C.C., Yu, J.M., & Cheng, A.T. (1996). Alcohol-metabolizing genes and alcoholism among Taiwanese Han men: Independent effect of ADH2, ADH3 and ALDH2. *British Journal of Psychiatry, 168,* 762–767.

Cherpitel, C.J., Borges, G.L., & Wilcox, H.C. (2004). Acute alcohol use and suicidal behavior: A review of the literature. *Alcoholism: Clinical and Experimental Research, 28,* S18–S28.

Cherpitel, C.J., Meyers, A.R., & Perrine, M.W. (1998). Alcohol consumption, sensation seeking and ski injury: A case-control study. *Journal of Studies on Alcohol, 59,* 216–221.

Cherpitel, C.J., Tam, T.W., Midanik, L.T., Caetano, R., & Greenfield T.K. (1995). Alcohol and non-fatal injury in the US general population: A risk function analysis. *Accident Analysis and Prevention, 27,* 651–661.

Chick, J. (1989). Delirium tremens. *British Medical Journal, 298,* 3–4.

Chou, S. (1994). An examination of the alcohol consumption and peptic ulcer association—results of a national survey. *Alcoholism, Clinical and Experimental Research, 18,* 149–153.

Christiansen, B.A., Goldman, M.S., & Inn, A. (1982). Development of alcohol-related expectancies in adolescents: Separating pharmacological from social-learning influences. *Journal of Consulting & Clinical Psychology, 50,* 336–344.

Christiansen, M., Vik, P.W., & Jarchow, A. (2002). College student heavy drinking in social contexts versus alone. *Psychology of Addictive Behaviors, 27,* 393–404.

Clark, D.B., Thatcher, D.L., & Maisto, S.A. (2004). Adolescent neglect and alcohol use disorders in two-parent families. *Child Maltreatment, 9,* 357–370.

Clark, D.B., Thatcher, D.L., & Tapert, S.F. (2008). Alcohol, psychological dysregulation, and adolescent brain development. *Alcoholism: Clinical and Experimental Research, 32,* 375–385.

Clark, L.A., Watson, D., & Reynolds, S. (1995). Diagnosis and classification of psychopathology: Challenges to the system and future directions. In J.T. Spence, J.M. Darley, & D.J. Foss (Eds.), *The annual review of psychology* Vol. 46 (pp. 121–153). Palo Alto, CA: Annual Reviews Inc.

Cloninger, C.R., Bohman, M., & Sigvardsson, S. (1981). Inheritance of alcohol abuse: Cross-fostering analysis of adopted men. *Archives of General Psychiatry, 38,* 861–868.

Cloninger, C.R., Sigvardsson, S., Reich, T., & Bohman, M. (1988). Childhood personality predicts alcohol abuse in young adults. *Alcoholism: Clinical and Experimental Research, 12,* 494–505.

Collins, R.L., Ellickson, P.L., & Bell, R.M. (1998). Simultaneous polydrug use among teens: Prevalence and predictors. *Journal of Substance Abuse, 10,* 233–253.

Collins, R.L., Kashdan, T.B., & Gollnisch, G. (2003). The feasibility of using cellular phones to collect ecological momentary assessment data: Application to alcohol consumption, *Experimental and Clinical Psychopharmacology, 11,* 73–78.

COMBINE Research Group. (2003). Testing combined pharmacotherapies and behavioral interventions in alcohol dependence: Rationale and methods. *Alcoholism: Clinical and Experimental Research, 27,* 1107–1122.

Cone, E.J., Fant, R.V., Rohay, J.M., Caplan, Y.H., Ballina, M., Reder, R.F., et al. (2004). Oxycodone involvement in drug abuse deaths: II. Evidence for toxic multiple drug-drug interaction. *Journal of Analytical Toxicology, 28,* 217–225.

Cone, E.J., Fant, R.V., Rohay, J.M., Caplan, Y.H., Ballina, M., Reder, R.F., et al. (2003). Oxycodone involvement in drug abuse deaths: A DAWN-based classification scheme applied to an oxycodone postmortem database containing over 1000 cases. *Journal of Analytical Toxicology, 27,* 57–67.

Conigrave, K.M., Davies, P., Haber, P., & Whitfield, J.B. (2003). Traditional markers of excessive alcohol use. *Addiction, 98*(Suppl. 2), 31–43.

Conklin, C.A., & Tiffany, S.T. (2002). Applying extinction research and theory to cue-exposure addiction treatments. *Addiction, 97,* 155–167.

Conrod, P.J., Castellanos, N., & Mackie, C. (2008). Personality-targeted interventions delay the growth of adolescent drinking and binge drinking. *Journal of Child Psychology and Psychiatry, 49,* 181–190.

Conrod, P.J., Stewart, S.H., Pihl, R.O., Côté, S., Fontaine, V., & Dongier, M. (2000). Efficacy of brief coping skills interventions that match different personality profiles of female substance abusers. *Psychology of Addictive Behaviors, 14,* 231–242.

Cook, R.L., Sereika, S.M., Hunt, S.C., Woodward, W.C., Erlen, J.A., & Conigliaro, J. (2001). Problem drinking and medication adherence among persons with HIV infection. *Journal of General Internal Medicine, 16,* 83–88.

Cook, R.T. (2008). Alcohol abuse, alcoholism, and damage to the immune system: A review. *Alcoholism: Clinical and Experimental Research, 22,* 1927–1942.

Cooper, M.L. (1994). Motivations for alcohol use among adolescents: Development and validation of a four-factor model. *Psychological Assessment, 6,* 117–128.

Cooper, M.L. (2002). Alcohol use and risky sexual behavior among college students and youth: Evaluating the evidence. *Journal of Studies on Alcohol, 14,* S101–S117.

Cooper, M.L., Frone, M.R., Russell, M., & Mudar, P. (1995). Drinking to regulate positive and negative emotions: A motivational model of alcohol use. *Journal of Personality and Social Psychology, 69,* 990–1005.

Cooper, M.L., Krull, J.L., Agocha, V.B., Flanagan, M.E., Orcutt, H.K., Grabe, S., et al. (2008). Motivational pathways to alcohol use and abuse among black and white adolescents. *Journal of Abnormal Psychology, 117,* 485–501.

Cooper, M., Russell, M., Skinner, J.B., Frone, M.R., & Mudar, P. (1992). Stress and alcohol use: Moderating effects of gender, coping, and alcohol expectancies. *Journal of Abnormal Psychology, 101,* 139–152.

Copello, A.G., Velleman, R.D. B., & Templeton, L.J. (2005). Family interventions in the treatment of alcohol and drug problems. *Drug and Alcohol Review, 24,* 369–385.

Corrao, G., Bagnardi, V., Zambon, A., & La Vecchia, C. (2004). A meta analysis of alcohol consumption and the risk of 15 diseases. *Preventative Medicine, 38,* 613–619.

Costa, P.T., & McCrae, R.R. (1992). Normal personality assessment in clinical practice: The NEO personality inventory. *Psychological Assessment, 4*(1), 5–13.

Cox, W.M., Blount, J.P., Crowe, P.A., & Singh, S.P. (1996). Diabetic patients' alcohol use and quality of life: Relationships with prescribed treatment compliance among older males. *Alcoholism: Clinical and Experimental Research, 20,* 327–331.

Crabb, D.W. (1993). Recent developments in alcoholism: The liver. In M. Galanter (Ed.), *Recent developments in alcoholism* Vol. 11: *Ten years of progress* (pp. 207–230). New York: Plenum Press.

Crabb, D.W. (1995). Ethanol oxidizing enzymes: Roles in alcohol metabolism and alcoholic liver disease. *Progress in Liver Diseases, 13,* 151–172.

Crews, F.T., Braun, C.J., Hoplight, B., Switzer, R.C., & Knapp, D.J. (2000). Binge ethanol consumption causes differential brain damage in young adolescent rats compared with adult rats: Alcohol effects on the fetus, brain, liver, and other organ systems. *Alcoholism: Clinical and Experimental Research, 24,* 1712–1723.

Crum, R.M., Storr, C.L., Chan, Y., & Ford, D.E. (2004). Sleep disturbance and risk for alcohol-related problems. *American Journal of Psychiatry, 161,* 1197–1203.

Cruz, I.Y., & Dunn, M.E. (2003). Lowering risk for early alcohol use by challenging alcohol expectancies in elementary school children. *Journal of Consulting & Clinical Psychology, 71,* 493–503.

Cyders, M.A., & Smith, G.T. (2008). Emotion-based dispositions to rash action: Positive and negative urgency. *Psychological Bulletin, 134,* 807–828.

Cyders, M.A., Flory, K., Rainer, S., & Smith, G.T. (2009). The role of personality dispositions to risky behavior in predicting first-year college drinking. *Addiction, 104,* 193–202.

Cyders, M.A., Smith, G.T., Spillane, N.S., Fischer, S., Annus, A.M., & Peterson, C. (2007). Integration of impulsivity and positive mood to predict risky behavior: development and validation of a measure of positive urgency. *Psychological Assessment, 19,* 107–118.

d'Arminio, M.A., Sabin, C.A., Phillips, A., Sterne, J., May, M., Justice, A., et al. (2005). The changing incidence of AIDS events in patients receiving highly active antiretroviral therapy. *Archives of Internal Medicine, 165,* 416–423.

D'Amico, E. & Fromme, K. (2002). Brief prevention for adolescent risk-taking behavior. *Addiction, 97,* 563–574.

Dal Cin, S., Worth, K.A., Dalton, M.A., & Sargent, J.D. (2008). Youth exposure to alcohol use and brand appearances in popular contemporary movies. *Addiction, 103,* 1925–1932.

Darke, S., & Zador, D. (1996). Fatal heroin "overdose": A review. *Addiction, 91,* 1765–1772.

Dawson, D.A., Grant, B.F., & Li, T.K. (2005). Quantifying the risks associated with exceeding recommended drinking limits. *Alcoholism: Clinical and Experimental Research, 29,* 902–908.

Dawson, D.A. (1998). Beyond black, white and Hispanic: Race, ethnic origin and drinking patterns in the United States. *Journal of Substance Abuse, 10,* 321–339.

De Bellis, M.D., Clark, D.B., Beers, S.R., Soloff, P.H., Boring, A.M., Hall, J., et al. (2000). Hippocampal volume in adolescent-onset alcohol use disorders. *American Journal of Psychiatry, 157,* 737–744.

De Oliveira e Silva, E.R., Foster, D., Harper, M.M., Seidman, C.E., Smith, J.D., Breslow, J.L. et al. (2000). Alcohol consumption raises HDL cholesterol levels by increasing the transport rate of apolipoproteins A-I and A-II. *Circulation, 102,* 2347–2352.

de Vegt, F., Dekker, J.M., Groeneveld, W.J., Nijpels, G., Stehouwer, C.D., Bouter, L.M., et al. (2002). Moderate alcohol consumption is associated with lower risk for incident diabetes and mortality: The Hoorn study. *Diabetes Research & Clinical Practice, 57,* 53–60.

Demyttenaere, K., Bruffaerts, R., Lee, S., Posada-Villa, J., Kovess, V., Angermeyer, M., et al. (2007). Mental disorders among persons with chronic back or neck pain: Results from the world mental health surveys. *Pain, 129,* 332–342.

Dermen, K.H., Cooper, M.L., & Agocha, V.B. (1998). Sex-related alcohol expectancies as moderators of the relationship between alcohol use and risky sex in adolescents. *Journal of Studies on Alcohol, 59,* 71–77.

Dermen, K.H., & Cooper, M.L. (1994). Sex-related alcohol expectancies among adolescents: II. Prediction of drinking in social and sexual situations. *Psychology of Addictive Behaviors, 8*, 161–168.

Dermen, K.H., & Cooper, M.L. (2000). Inhibition conflict and alcohol expectancy as moderators of alcohol's relationship to condom use. *Experimental and Clinical Psychopharmacology, 8*, 198–206.

Diaz, L.E., Montero, A., Gonzalez-Gross, M., Vallejo, A.I., Romeo, J., & Marcos, A. (2002). Influence of alcohol consumption on immunological status: A review. *European Journal of Clinical Nutrition, 56*, S50–S53.

Dick, D.M., & Beirut, L.J. (2006). The genetics of alcohol dependence. *Current Psychiatry Reports, 8*, 151–157.

Dick, D.M., & Feroud, T. (2003). Candidate genes for alcohol dependence: A review of genetic evidence from human studies. *Alcoholism: Clinical and Experimental Research, 27*, 868–879.

Dick, D.M., Aliev, F., Wang, J.C., Grucza, R.A., Schuckit, M., Kuperman, S., et al. (2008). Using dimensional models of externalizing psychopathology to aid in gene identification. *Archives of General Psychiatry, 65*, 310–318.

Dick, D.M., Rose, R.J., & Kaprio, J. (2006). The next challenge for psychiatric genetics: Characterizing the risk associated with identified genes. *Annals of Clinical Psychiatry, 18*, 223–231.

Dingle, G.A., & Oei, T.P. S. (1997). Is alcohol a cofactor of HIV and AIDS? Evidence from immunological and behavioral studies. *Psychological Bulletin, 122*, 56–71.

Dominguez, H.D., Lopez, M.F., & Molin, J.C. (1998). Neonatal responsiveness to alcohol odor and infant alcohol intake as a function of alcohol experience during late gestation. *Alcohol, 16*, 109–117.

Donohue, K.F., Curtin, J.J., Patrick, C.J., & Lang, A.R. (2007). Intoxication level and emotional response. *Emotion, 7*, 103–112.

Donovan, C., & McEwan, R. (1995). A review of the literature examining the relationship between alcohol use and HIV-related sexual risk-taking in young people. *Addiction, 90*, 319–328.

Donovan, J.E., Jessor, R., & Jessor, L. (1983). Problem drinking in adolescence and young adulthood: A follow-up study. *Journal of Studies on Alcohol, 44*, 109–137.

Drobes, D.J., Anton, R.F., Thomas, S.E., & Voronin, K. (2004). Effects of naltrexone and nalmefene on subjective response to alcohol among non-treatment-seeking alcoholics and social drinkers. *Alcoholism: Clinical and Experimental Research, 28*, 1362–1370.

Dunn, M.E., & Goldman, M.S. (2000). Validation of multidimensional scaling-based modeling of alcohol expectancies in memory: Age and drinking-related differences in expectancies of children assessed as first associates. *Alcoholism: Clinical and Experimental Research, 24*, 1639–1646.

Dunn, M.G., Tarter, R.E., Mezzich, A.C., Vanyukov, M., Kirisci, L., & Kirillova, G. (2002). Origins and consequences of child neglect in substance abuse families. *Clinical Psychology Review, 22*, 1063–1090.

Earleywine, M. (1994). Anticipated biphasic effects of alcohol vary with risk for alcoholism: A preliminary report. *Alcoholism: Clinical & Experimental Research, 18*, 711–714.

Earleywine, M., & Martin, C.S. (1993). Anticipated stimulant and sedative effects of alcohol vary with dosage and limb of the blood alcohol curve. *Alcoholism: Clinical & Experimental Research, 17*, 135–139.

Earleywine, M., & Newcomb, M. (1997). Concurrent versus simultaneous polydrug use: Prevalence, correlates, discriminant validity, and prospective effects on health outcomes. *Experimental and Clinical Psychopharmacology, 5*, 353–364.

Edenberg, H.J., & Kranzler, H.R. (2005). The contribution of genetics to addiction therapy approaches. *Pharmacology & Therapeutics, 108*, 86–93.

Egbert, A.M. (1993). The older alcoholic: Recognizing the subtle clinical clues. *Geriatrics, 48*, 63–69.

Ehlers, C.L., Gilder, D.A., Harris, L., & Carr, L. (2001). Association of the ADH2*3 allele with a negative family history of alcoholism in African American young adults. *Alcoholism: Clinical & Experimental Research, 25*, 1773–1777.

Ellickson, P.L., Collins, R.L., Hambarsoomians, K., & McCaffrey, D.F. (2005). Does alcohol advertising promote adolescent drinking? Results from a longitudinal assessment. *Addiction, 100*, 235–246.

Ellis, D.A., Zucker, R.A., & Fitzgerald, H.E. (1997). The role of family influences in development and risk. *Alcohol Health & Research World, 21*, 218–226.

Ellison, R.C., Zhang, Y., Qureshi, M.M., Knox, S., Arnett, D.K., & Province, M.A. (2004). Lifestyle determinants of high-density lipoprotein cholesterol: The national heart, lung, and blood institute family heart study. *American Heart Journal, 147*, 529–535.

Eng, M.Y., Luczak, S.E., & Wall, T.L. (2007). ALDH2, ADH1B, and ADH1C genotypes in Asians: A literature review. *Alcohol Research & Health, 30*, 22–30.

Engs, R.C. (2001). Past influences, current issues, future research directions. In E. Houghton, & A.M. Roche (Eds.), *Learning about drinking* (pp. 147–165). Philadelphia: Brunner-Routledge.

Edwards, G., & Gross, M.M. (1976). Alcohol dependence: Provisional description of a clinical syndrome. *British Medical Journal, 1*, 1058–1061.

Epstein, E.E., & McCrady, B.S. (1998). Behavioral couples treatment of alcohol and drug use disorders: Current status and innovations. *Clinical Psychology Review, 18*, 689–711.

Epstein, J.A., Botvin, G.J., & Diaz, T. (2002). Gateway polydrug use among Puerto Rican and Dominican adolescents residing in New York City: The moderating role of gender. *Journal of Child & Adolescent Substance Abuse, 12*, 33–46.

Epstein, J.A., Botvin, G.J., Griffin, K., & Diaz, T. (1999). Role of ethnicity and gender in polydrug use among a longitudinal sample of inner-city adolescents. *Journal of Alcohol and Drug Education, 45*, 1–12.

Eriksson, C.J. (1983). Human blood acetaldehyde concentration during ethanol oxidation (update 1982). *Pharmacology, Biochemistry & Behavior, 18*(Suppl. 1), 141–150.

Eriksson, C.J., Mizoi, Y., & Fukunaga, T. (1982). The determination of acetaldehyde in human blood by the perchloric acid precipitation method: The characterization and elimination of artifactual acetaldehyde formation. *Analytical Biochemistry, 125*, 259–263.

Ewing, J.A. (1984). Detecting alcoholism: The CAGE Questionnaire. *Journal of the American Medical Association, 252*, 1905–1907.

Facchini, F., Chen, I.Y., & Reaven, G.M. (1994). Light-to-moderate alcohol intake is associated with enhanced insulin sensitivity. *Diabetes Care, 17*, 115–119.

Fadardi, J.S., & Cox, W.M. (2007). Alcohol attention-control training program. *The Addictions Newsletter, 14*, 16–17.

Faggiano, F., Vigna-Taglianti, F.D., Versino, E., Zambon, A., Borraccino, A. & Lemma, P. (2008). School-based prevention for illicit drugs use: A systematic review. *Preventive Medicine, 46*, 385–396.

Falk, D.E., Yi, H., & Hiller-Sturmhofel, S. (2006). An epidemiologic analysis of co-occurring alcohol and tobacco use and disorders. *Alcohol Research & Health, 29*, 162–171.

Fals-Stewart, W., O'Farrell, T.J., Birchler, G.R., Cordova, J., & Kelley, M.L. (2005). Behavioral couples therapy for alcoholism and drug abuse: Where we've been, where we are, and we're we going. *Journal of Cognitive Psychotherapy, 19*, 229–246.

Fazio, R.H., & Towles-Schwen, T. (1999). The MODE model of attitude–behavior processes. In: S. Chaiken and Y. Trope (Eds.), *Dual-process theories in social psychology* (pp. 97–116). New York: Guilford.

Fein, G., & Landman, B. (2005). Treated and treatment-naive alcoholics come from different populations. *Alcohol, 35*, 19–26.

Feldman, D., Pattison, E., Sobell, L., Graham, T., & Sobell, M. (1975). Outpatient alcohol detoxification: Initial findings on 564 patients. *American Journal of Psychiatry, 132*, 407–412.

Fillmore, K.M., Kerr, W.C., Stockwell, T., Chikritzhs, T., & Bostrom, A. (2006). Moderate alcohol use and reduced mortality risk: Systematic error in prospective studies. *Addiction Research and Theory, 14*, 1–31.

Fingerhut, L.A., & Warner, M. (1997). *Injury chartbook. Health, United States, 1996–97.* Hyattsville, Maryland: National Center for Health Statistics.

Finney, J.W., Hahn, A., & Moos, R. (1996). The effectiveness of inpatient and outpatient treatment for alcohol abuse: The need to focus on mediators and moderators of setting effects. *Addiction, 91*, 1773–1796.

First, M.B., Spitzer, R.L., Gibbon, M., & Williams, J.B.W. (2002). *Structured clinical interview for DSM-IV Axis I disorders, research version, non-patient edition (SCID-I/NP).* New York: Biometrics Research, New York State Psychiatric Institute.

Flanagan, D.E., Moore, V.M., Godsland, I.F., Cockington, R.A., Robinson, J.S., & Phillips, D.I. (2000). Alcohol consumption and insulin resistance in young adults. *European Journal of Clinical Investigation, 30*, 297–301.

Flanders, W.D., & Rothman, K.J. (1982). Interaction of alcohol and tobacco in laryngeal cancer. *American Journal of Epidemiology, 115*, 371–379.

Fleeman, N.D. (1997) Alcohol home detoxification: a literature review. *Alcohol and Alcoholism, 32*, 649–656.

Fleming, M.F., Mundt, M.P., French, M.T., Manwell, L.B., Stauffacher, E.A., & Barry, K.L. (2000). Benefit-cost analysis of brief physician advice with problem drinkers in primary care settings. *Medical Care, 38*, 7–18.

Fleming, M.F., Mundt, M.P., French, M.T., Manwell, L.B., Stauffacher, E.A., & Barry, K.L. (2002). Brief physician advice for problem drinkers: long-term efficacy and benefit-cost analysis. *Alcoholism: Clinical and Experimental Research, 26*, 36–43.

Flynn, J.L., & Bloom, B.R. (1996). Role of T1 and T2 cytokines in the response to mycobacterium tuberculosis. *Annals of the New York Academy of Sciences, 795*, 137–146.

Fortenberry, J.D., Orr, D.P., Katz, B.P., Brizendine, E.J., & Blythe, M.J. (1997). Sex under the influence: A diary self-report study of substance use and sexual behavior among adolescent women. *Sexually Transmitted Diseases, 24*, 313–319.

Fowler, T., Shelton, K., Lifford, K., Rice, F., McBride, A., Nikolov, I., et al. (2007). Genetic and environmental influences on the relationship between peer alcohol use and own alcohol use in adolescents. *Addiction, 102*, 894–903.

Frezza, M., Di Padova, C., Pozzato, G., Terpin, M., Baraona, E., & Lieber, C.S. (1990). High blood alcohol levels in women: Role of decreased gastric alcohol dehydrogenase activity and first pass metabolism. *New England Journal of Medicine, 322*, 95–99.

Friday, G., Lai, S.M., Alter, M., Sobel, E., LaRue, L., Gil-Peralta, A., et al. (1989). Stroke in the Lehigh Valley: Racial/ethnic differences. *Neurology, 39*, 1165–1168.

Fromme, K., & D'Amico E.J. (1999). Neurobiological bases of alcohol's psychological effects. In.K. E. Leonard, & H.T. Blane (Eds.), *Psychological theories of drinking and alcoholism* (pp. 422–455). New York, NY: Guilford.

Fromme, K., D'Amico, E.J., & Katz, E.C. (1999). Intoxicated sexual risk taking: An expectancy or cognitive impairment explanation? *Journal of Studies on Alcohol, 60*, 54–63.

Fromme, K., & D'Amico, E.J. (2000). Measuring adolescent alcohol outcome expectancies. *Psychology of Addictive Behaviors, 14*, 206–212.

Garbutt, J.C., Kranzler, H.R., O'Malley, S.S., Gastfriend, D.R., Pettinatit, H.M., Silverman, B.I., et al. (2005). Vivitrex study group. Efficacy and tolerability of long-acting injectable naltrexone for alcohol dependence: a randomized controlled trial. *Journal of the American Medical Association, 293*, 1617–1625.

Gaziano, J.M., Buring, J.E., Breslow, J.L., Goldhaber, S.Z., Rosner, B., vanDenburgh, M., et al. (1993). Moderate alcohol intake, increased levels of high-density lipoprotein and its sub fractions, and decreased risk of myocardial infarction. *New England Journal of Medicine, 329*, 1829–1833.

Gentilello, L.M., Ebel, B.E., Wickizer, T.M., Salkever, D.S., & Rivara, F.P. (2005). Alcohol interventions for trauma patients treated in emergency departments and hospitals: a cost benefit analysis. *Annals of Surgery, 241*, 541–550.

Giancola, P.R., & Tarter, R.E. (1999). Executive cognitive functioning and risk for substance abuse. *Psychological Science, 10*, 203–205.

Giesbrecht, N., & Haydon, E. (2006). Community-based interventions and alcohol, tobacco, and other drugs: Foci, outcomes and implications. *Drug and Alcohol Review, 25*, 633–646.

Goforth, H.W., Lupash, D.P., Brown, M.E., Tan, J., & Fernandez, F. (2004). Role of alcohol and substances of abuse in the immunomodulation of human immunodeficiency virus disease: A Review. *Addictive Disorders & Their Treatment, 3*, 174–182.

Gold, R.S., Karmiloff-Smith, A., Skinner, M.J., & Morton, J. (1992). Situational factors and thought processes associated with unprotected intercourse in heterosexual students. *AIDS Care, 4*, 305–323.

Goldman, M.S., Brown, S.A., & Christiansen, B.A. (1987). Expectancy theory: Thinking about drinking. In H.T. Blane, & K.E. Leonard (Eds.), *Psychological theories of drinking and alcoholism* (pp. 181–226). New York: Guilford Press.

Goldman, M.S., Del Boca, F.K., & Darkes, J. (1999). Alcohol expectancy theory: The application of cognitive neuroscience. In H.T. Blane, & K.E. Leonard (Eds.), *Psychological theories of drinking and alcoholism* (pp. 203–246). New York: Guilford Press.

Goldstein, D.B. (2009). Common genetic variation and human traits. *New England Journal of Medicine, 360*, 1696–1698.

Gomberg, E.S.L. (1990). Drugs, alcohol and aging. In L.T. Kozlowski, H.M. Annis, & H.D. Cappell (Eds.), *Research advances in alcohol and drug problems* (pp. 182–194). New York: Plenum.

Gómez, A., Conde, A., Santana, J.M., & Jorrín, A. (2005). Diagnostic usefulness of brief versions of alcohol use disorders identification test (AUDIT) for detecting hazardous drinkers in primary care settings. *Journal of Studies on Alcohol, 66*(2), 305–308.

Goodwin, D.W., Schulsinger, F., Hermansen, L., Guze, S.B., & Winokur, G. (1973). Alcohol problems in adoptees raised apart from alcoholic biological parents. *Archives of General Psychiatry, 28*, 238–243.

Gossop, M. (2001). A web of dependence. *Addiction, 96*, 677–678.

Grant, B.F. (1997). Prevalence and correlates of alcohol use and DSM-IV alcohol dependence in the United States: Results of the national longitudinal epidemiologic survey. *Journal of Studies on Alcohol, 58*, 464–473.

Grant, B.F., & Dawson, D. (2000). *The alcohol use disorder and associated disabilities interview schedule-IV (AUDADIS-IV)*. Rockville, MD: National Institute on Alcohol Abuse and Alcoholism.

Grant, B.F., & Dawson, D.A. (1997). Age at onset of alcohol use and its association with DSM-IV alcohol abuse and dependence: Results from the national longitudinal alcohol epidemiologic survey. *Journal of Substance Abuse, 9*, 103–110.

Grant, B.F., Dawson, D.A., Stinson, F.S., Chou, P.S., Dufour, M.C., & Pickering, R. (2004). The 12-month prevalence and trends in DSM-IV alcohol abuse and dependence: United States, 1991–1992 and 2001–2001. *Drug and Alcohol Dependence, 74*, 223–234.

Grant, B.F., Dawson, D.A., Stinson, F.S., Chou, P.S., Kay, W., & Pickering, R. (2003). The alcohol use disorder and associated disabilities interview schedule-IV (AUDADIS-IV): Reliability of alcohol consumption, tobacco use, family history of depression and psychiatric diagnostic modules in a general population sample. *Drug and Alcohol Dependence, 71*, 7–16.

Grant, B.F., Dufour, M.C., & Harford, T.C. (1988). Epidemiology of alcoholic liver disease. *Seminars in Liver Disease, 8*, 12–25.

Grant, B.F., & Harford, T.C. (1990). Concurrent and simultaneous use of alcohol with cocaine: Results of national survey. *Drug and Alcohol Dependence, 25*, 97–104.

Grant, B.F., Harford, T.C., Dawson, D.A., Chou, P., Dufour, M., & Pickering, R. (1994). Prevalence of DSM-IV alcohol abuse and dependence: United States, 1992. *Alcohol Health & Research World, 18*, 243–248.

Grant, B.F., Hasin, D.S., Stinson, F.S., Dawson, D.A., Chou, S.P., Ruan, W.J., et al. (2004). Prevalence correlates and disability of personality disorders in the United States: Results from the National Epidemiological Survey on Alcohol and Related Conditions. *Journal of Clinical Psychiatry, 65*, 948–958.

Grant, B.F., Moore, T.C., & Kaplan, K. (2003). *Source and accuracy statement: Wave 1 national epidemiologic survey on alcohol and related conditions (NESARC)*. Bethesda, MD: National Institute on Alcohol Abuse and Alcoholism.

Grant, B.F., & Pickering, R.P. (1996). Comorbidity between DSM-IV alcohol and drug use disorders: Results from the national longitudinal alcohol epidemiologic survey. *Alcohol Health & Research World, 20*, 67–72.

Grant, B.F., Stinson, F.S., Dawson, D.A., Chou, P., Dufour, M.C., Compton, W., et al. (2004). Prevalence and co-occurrence of substance use disorders and independent mood and anxiety disorders: Results from the national epidemiologic survey on

alcohol and related conditions. *Archives of General Psychiatry, 61*, 807–816.

Gray, M.R., Donnelly, R.J., & Kingsnorth, A.N. (1993). The role of smoking and alcohol in metaplasia and cancer risk in Barrett's columnar lined oesophagus. *Gut, 34*, 727–731.

Gray, R., & Henderson, J. (2006). *Review of the fetal effects of prenatal alcohol exposure. Report to the department of health*. Oxford: National Perinatal Epidemiology Unit. Retrieved from http://www.npeu.ox.ac.uk/alcoholreport.

Gray, R., Mukherjee, R.A.S., & Rutter, M. (2009). Alcohol consumption during pregnancy and its effects on neurodevelopment: What is known and what remains uncertain. *Addiction, 104*, 1270–1273.

Greenfield, T.K., & Kerr, W.C. (2003). Tracking alcohol consumption over time. *Alcohol Research & Health, 27*, 30–38.

Greenfield, T.K. (2000). Ways of measuring drinking patterns and the difference they make: experience with graduated frequencies. *Journal of Substance Abuse, 12*, 33–49.

Greenspon, A.J., & Schaal, S.F. (1983). The "holiday heart": Electrophysiologic studies of alcohol effects in alcoholics. *Annals of Internal Medicine, 98*, 135–139.

Greenwald, A.G., Nosek, B.A., & Banaji, M.R. (2003). Understanding and using the implicit association test: I. An improved scoring algorithm. *Journal of Personality and Social Psychology, 85*, 197–216.

Grube, J. (2005). Youth drinking rates and problems: A comparison of European countries and the United States. Calverton, MD: Pacific Institute for Research and Evaluation and the Office of Juvenile Justice and Delinquency Prevention.

Grube, J.W., & Waiters, E. (2005). Alcohol in the media: Content and effects on drinking beliefs and behaviors among youth. *Adolescent Medicine Clinics, 16*, 327–343.

Gruenwald, P.J., Johnson, F.W., & Treno, A.J. (2002). Outlets, drinking and driving: A multilevel analysis of availability. *Journal of Studies and Alcohol, 63*, 460–468.

Gruenwald, P.J., Ponicki, W.R., & Holder, H.D. (1993). Relationship of outlet densities to alcohol consumption: A time series cross-sectional analysis. *Alcoholism: Clinical and Experimental Research, 17*, 38–47.

Gwinn, M.L., Webster, L.A., Lee, N.C., Layde, P.M., Rubin, G.I., & Cancer, Steroid, Hormone Study Group. (1986). Alcohol consumption and ovarian cancer risk. *American Journal of Epidemiology, 123*, 759–766.

Hahn, C.Y., Huang, S.Y., Ko, H.C., Hsieh, C.H., Lee, I.H., Yeh, T.L., et al. (2006). Acetaldehyde involvement in positive and negative alcohol expectancies in Han Chinese persons with alcoholism. *Archives of General Psychiatry, 63*, 817–823.

Halpern-Felsher, B., Millstein, S., & Ellen, J. (1996). Relationship of alcohol use and risky sexual behavior: A review and analysis of findings. *Journal of Adolescent Health, 19*, 331–336.

Hanchar, H.J., Chutsrinopkun, P., Meera, P., Supavilai, P., Sieghart, W., Wallner, M., et al. (2006). Ethanol potently and competitively inhibits binding of the alcohol antagonist Ro15-4513 to $\alpha_{4/6}$ $\beta_3\delta$ GABA$_A$ receptors. *Proceedings of the National Academy of Sciences, 103*, 8546–8551.

Hanna, E.Z., Chou, S.P., & Grant, B.F. (1997). The relationship between drinking and heart disease morbidity in the United States: Results from the national health interview survey. *Alcoholism: Clinical and Experimental Research, 21*, 111–118.

Hargreaves, G.A., Quinn, H., Kashem, M.A., Matsumoto, I., & McGregor, I.S. (2009). Proteomic analysis demonstrates adolescent vulnerability to lasting hippocampal changes following chronic alcohol consumption. *Alcoholism: Clinical and Experimental Research, 33*, 86–94.

Harris, M.I., Flegal, K.M., Cowie, C.C., Eberhardt, M.S., Goldstein, D.E., Little, R.R., et al. (1998). Prevalence of diabetes, impaired fasting glucose, and impaired glucose tolerance in U.S. adults: The third national health and nutrition examination survey, 1988-1994. *Diabetes Care, 21*, 518–524.

Harris, R.A., Mihic, S.J., & Valenzuela, C.F. (1998). Alcohol and benzodiazepines: Recent mechanistic studies. *Drug and Alcohol Dependence, 51*, 155–164.

Hart, C.L., Smith, G.D., Hole, D.J., & Hawthorne, V.M. (1999). Alcohol consumption and mortality from all causes, coronary heart disease, and stroke: Results from a prospective cohort study of Scottish men with 21 years of follow up. *British Medical Journal, 318*, 1725–1729.

Hart, K.E., & Fazaa, N. (2004). Life stress events and alcohol misuse: Distinguishing contributing stress events from consequential stress events. *Substance Use and Misuse, 39*, 1319–1339.

Harvey, S.M., & Beckman, L.J. (1986). Alcohol consumption, female sexual behavior and contraceptive use. *Journal of Studies on Alcohol, 47*, 327–332.

Harwood, H. (2000). *Updating estimates of the economic costs of alcohol abuse in the United States: Estimates, update methods, and data*. NIH Publication No. 98-4327. Rockville, MD: National Institutes of Health. Retrieved from http://pubs.niaaa.nih.gov/publications/economic-2000.

Hawkins, J.D., Catalano, R.F., & Miller, J.Y. (1992). Risk and protective factors for alcohol and other drug problems in adolescence and early adulthood: Implications for substance abuse prevention. *Psychological Bulletin, 112*, 64–105.

Hayashida, M., Alterman, A., McLellan, T., O'Brien, C., Purtill, J., Volpicelli, J., et al. (1989). Comparative effectiveness and costs of inpatient and outpatient detoxification of patients with mild-to-moderate alcohol withdrawal syndrome. *The New England Journal of Medicine, 320*, 358–365.

Heath, A.C. (1995). Genetic influences on alcoholism risk: A review of adoption and twin studies. *Alcohol Health & Research World, 19*, 166–171.

Heath, A.C., Bucholz, K., Madden, P., Dinwiddie, S., Slutske, W., Bierut, L., et al. (1997). Genetic and environmental contributions to alcohol dependence risk in a national twin sample: Consistency of findings in women and men. *Psychological Medicine, 27*, 1381–1396.

Heather, N. (1986). Minimal treatment intervention for problem drinkers. In G. Edwards (Ed.), *Current issues in clinical psychology* Vol. 4 (pp. 171–186). London: Plenum. heavy social drinking men. *Psychology of Addictive Behaviors, 7*, 311–315.

Hebert, L.E., Scherr, P.A., Beckett, L.A., Albert, M.S., Rosner, B., Talor, J.O., et al. (1993). Relation of smoking and low-to-moderate alcohol consumption to change in cognitive function: a longitudinal study in a defined community of older persons. *American Journal of Epidemiology, 137*, 881–891.

Heck, E.J., & Williams, M.D. (1995). Using the CAGE to screen for drinking-related problems in college students. *Journal of Studies on Alcohol, 56*(3), 282–286.

Helzer, J.E., Burnham, A., & McEvoy, L.T. (1991). Alcohol abuse and dependence. In L.N. Robins, & D.A. Regier (Eds.), *Psychiatric disorders in America: The epidemiologic catchment area study* (pp. 81–115). New York: The Free Press.

Hendershot, C.S., Stoner, S.A., George, W.H., & Norris, J. (2007). Alcohol use, expectancies and sexual sensation seeking as correlates of HIV risk behavior in heterosexual young adults. *Psychology of Addictive Behaviors, 21*, 365–372.

Hendershot, C.S., Stoner, S.A., Pantalone, D.W., & Simoni, J.M. (2009). Alcohol use and antiretroviral adherence: Review and meta-analysis. *Journal of Acquired Immune Deficiency Syndrome, 52*, 180–202.

Hendriks, H.F.J., Veenstra, J., Velthuis-te Wierik, E.J.M., Schaafsma, G., & Kluft, C. (1994). Effect of moderate dose of alcohol with evening meal on fibrinolytic factors. *British Medical Journal, 308*, 1003–1006.

Herd, D., & Grube, J. (1996). Black identity and drinking in the U.S.: A national study. *Addiction, 91*, 845–857.

Heron, M., Hoyert, D.L., Murphy, S.L., Xu, J., Kochanek, K.D., & Tejada-Vera, B. (2009). Deaths: Final data for 2006. *National Vital Statistics Report, 57*, 1–135.

Higuchi, S., Matsushita, S., Murayama, M., Takagi, S., & Hayashida, M. (1995). Alcohol and aldehyde dehydrogenase polymorphisms and the risk for alcoholism. *American Journal of Psychiatry, 152*, 1219–1221.

Hingson, R.W., Heeren, T., & Winter, M.R. (2006). Age of alcohol-dependence onset: Associations with severity of dependence and seeking treatment. *Pediatrics, 118*, 755–763.

Hingson, R.W., Strunin, L., Berlin, B.M., & Heeren, T. (1990). Beliefs about AIDS, use of alcohol and drugs, and unprotected sex among Massachusetts adolescents. *American Journal of Public Health, 80*, 295–299.

Hingson, R., & Howland, J. (1993). Alcohol and non-traffic unintended injuries. *Addiction, 88*, 877–883.

Holder, H.A. (2007). Warning shot across the bow? Comments on Fillmore, et al. *Addiction Research and Theory, 15*, 6–8.

Holder, H.D. (1992). What is a community and what are implications for prevention trials for reducing alcohol problems?. In H.D. Holder, & J.M. Howard (Eds.), *Community prevention trials for alcohol problems* (pp. 15–33). Westport, CT: Praeger.

Holdstock, L., & de Wit, H. (1998). Individual differences in the biphasic effects of ethanol. *Alcoholism: Clinical and Experimental Research, 22*, 1903–1911.

Honkanen, R., Ertama, L., Kuosmanen, P., Linnoila, M., Alha, A., & Visuri, T. (1983). The role of alcohol in accidental falls. *Journal of Studies on Alcohol, 44*, 231–245.

Hopfer, C.J., Crowley, T.J., & Hewitt, J.K. (2003). Review of twin and adoption studies of adolescent substance use. *Journal of the American Academy of Child & Adolescent Psychiatry, 42*, 710–719.

Howard, A.A., Arnsten, J.H., & Gourevitch, M.N. (2004). Effect of alcohol consumption on diabetes mellitus. *Annals of Internal Medicine, 140*, 211–219.

Hoyle, R.H., Stephenson, M.T., Palmgreen, P., Lorch, E.P., & Donohew, R.L. (2002). Reliability and validity of a brief measure of sensation seeking. *Personality and Individual Differences, 32*, 401–414.

Hu, F.B., Stampfer, M.J., Manson, J.E., Grodstein, F., Colditz, G.A., Speizer, F.E., et al. (2000). Trends in the incidence of coronary heart disease and changes in diet and lifestyle in women. *New England Journal of Medicine, 343*, 530–537.

Humphreys, K. (2003). *Circles of recovery: Self-help organizations for addictions*. Cambridge: Cambridge University Press.

Humphreys, K., & Klaw, E. (2001). Can targeting non-dependent problem drinkers and providing internet-based services expand access to assistance for alcohol problems? A study of the moderation management self-help/mutual aid organization. *Journal of Studies on Alcohol, 62*, 528–532.

Hungerford, D.W., Pollack, D.A., & Todd, K. (2000). Acceptability of emergency department-based screening and brief intervention for alcohol problems. *Academic Emergency Medicine, 7*, 1383–1392.

Hussong, A., Bauer, D., & Chassin, L. (2008). Telescoped trajectories from alcohol initiation to disorder in children of alcoholic parents. *Journal of Abnormal Psychology, 117*, 63–78.

Iacono, W.G. (1998). Identifying psychophysiological risk for psychopathology: Examples from substance use and schizophrenia research. *Psychophysiology, 35*, 621–637.

Irvin, J.E., Bowers, C.A., Dunn, M.E., & Wang, M.C. (1999). Efficacy of relapse prevention: A meta-analytic review. *Journal of Consulting and Clinical Psychology, 67*, 563–570.

Irwin, T.W., Morgenstern, J., Parsons, J.T., Wainberg, M., & Labouvie, E. (2006). Alcohol and Sexual HIV risk behavior among problem drinking men who have sex with men: An event level analysis of timeline follow-back data. *AIDS & Behavior, 10*, 299–307.

Istvan, J., & Matarazzo, J.D. (1984). Tobacco, alcohol, and caffeine use: A review of their interrelationships. *Psychological Bulletin, 95*, 301–326.

Jackson, K.M., Sher, K.J., & Schulenberg, J. (2005). Conjoint developmental trajectories of young adult alcohol and tobacco use. *Journal of Abnormal Psychology, 114*, 612–626.

Jacob, T., Waterman, B., Heath, A., True, W., Bucholz, K.K., Haber, R., et al. (2003). Genetic and environmental effects on offspring alcoholism: New insights using an offspring-of-twins design. *Archives of General Psychiatry, 60*, 1265–1272.

Johnson, B.A., Rosenthal, N., Capece, J.A., Wiegand, F., Mao, L., Beyers, K., et al. (2007). Topiramate for treating alcohol dependence: A randomized controlled trial. *Journal of the American Medical Association, 298*, 1641–1651.

Johnston, L.D., O'Malley, P.M., Bachman, J.G., & Schulenberg, J.E. (2007). *Monitoring the future national survey results on drug use, 1975–2005:* Vol. I, *Secondary school students* (NIH Publication No. 06-5883). Bethesda, MD: National Institute on Drug Abuse.

Jones, B.T., Corbin, W., & Fromme, K. (2001). A review of expectancy theory and alcohol consumption. *Addiction, 96*, 57–72.

Jones, M.C. (1968). Personality correlates and antecedents of drinking patterns in adult males. *Journal of Consulting and Clinical Psychology, 32*, 2–12.

Josephs, R.A., & Steele, C.M. (1990). The two faces of alcohol myopia: Attentional mediation of psychological stress. *Journal of Abnormal Psychology, 99*, 115–126.

Justus, A.N., Finn, P.R., & Steinmetz, J.E. (2000). The influence of traits of disinhibition on the association between alcohol use and risky sexual behavior. *Alcoholism: Clinical and Experimental Research, 24*, 1028–1035.

Kalichman, S.C., Heckman, T., & Kelly, J.A. (1996). Sensation seeking as an explanation for the association between substance use and HIV-related risky sexual behavior. *Archives of Sexual Behavior, 25*, 141–154.

Kao, W.H., Puddey, I.B., Boland, L.L., Watson, R.L., & Brancati, F.L. (2001). Alcohol consumption and the risk of type 2 diabetes mellitus: Atherosclerosis risk in communities study. *American Journal of Epidemiology, 154*, 748–757.

Karg, K., Burmeister, M., Shedden, K., & Sen, S. (in press). The serotonin transporter promoter variant (5-HTTLPR), stress, and depression Meta-analysis Revisited: Evidence of genetic moderation. *Archives of General Psychiatry.*

Karno, M., Granholm, E., & Lin, A. (2000). Factor structure of the alcohol use disorders identification test (AUDIT) in a mental health clinic sample. *Journal of Studies on Alcohol, 61*(5), 751–758.

Karon, J.M., Fleming, P.L., Steketee, R.W., & De Cock, K.M. (2001). HIV in the United States at the turn of the century: An epidemic in transition. *American Journal of Public Health, 91*, 1060–1068.

Kasser, C., Geller, A., Howell, E., & Wartenberg, A. (2004). *Detoxification: Principles and protocols.* Chevy Chase, MD: American Society of Addiction Medicine. Retrieved from http://www.asam.org/publ/detoxification.htm.

Kendler, K.S. (2005). Psychiatric genetics: A methodologic critique. *American Journal of Psychiatry, 162*, 3–11.

Kendler, K.S. (2006). Reflections on the relationship between psychiatric genetics and psychiatric nosology. *American Journal of Psychiatry, 163*, 1138–1146.

Kenny, S.J., Aubert, R.E., Geiss, L.S. (1995). Prevalence and incidence of non-insulin-dependent diabetes. In M.I. Harris, C.C. Cowie, G. Reiber, E. Boyko, M. Stern, & P. Bennett (Eds.), *Diabetes in America* (2nd ed., pp. 47–68). Washington, DC: US Government Printing Office.

Kessler, R.C., Berglund, P., Demler, O., Jin, R., & Walters, E.E. (2005). Lifetime prevalence and age-of-onset distributions of DSM-IV disorders in the national comorbidity survey replication. *Archives of General Psychiatry, 62*, 593–602.

Kessler, R.C., Chiu, W.T., Demler, O., & Walters, E.E. (2005). Prevalence, severity, and comorbidity in the national comorbidity survey replication. *Archives of General Psychiatry, 62*, 617–627.

Kessler, R.C., Crum, R.M., Warner, L.A., & Nelson, C.B. (1997). Lifetime co-occurrence of DSM-III-R alcohol abuse and dependence with other psychiatric disorders in the national comorbidity survey. *Archives of General Psychiatry, 54*, 313–321.

Kessler, R.C., McGonagle, K.A., Zhao, S., Nelson, C.B., Hughes, M., Eshleman, S., et al. (1994). Lifetime and 12-month prevalence of DSM-III-R psychiatric disorders in the United States: Results from the national comorbidity study. *Archives of General Psychiatry, 51*, 8–19.

Kessler, R.C., & Ustün, T.B. (2004). The world mental health (WMH) survey initiative version of the world health organization (WHO) composite international diagnostic interview (CIDI). *International Journal of Methods in Psychiatric Research, 13*, 93–121.

Khantzian, E.J. (1985). The self-medication hypothesis of addictive disorders: Focus on heroin and cocaine dependence. *American Journal of Psychiatry, 142*, 1259–1264.

Kiefer, F., & Mann, K. (2005). New achievements and pharmacotherapeutic approaches in the treatments of alcohol dependence. *European Journal of Pharmacology, 526*, 163–171.

Kilbey, M.M., Downey, K., & Breslau, N. (1998). Predicting the emergence and persistence of alcohol dependence in young adults: The role of expectancy and other risk factors. *Experimental & Clinical Psychopharmacology, 6*, 149–156.

Kington, R., & Bryant, K. (2002). Alcohol and HIV/AIDS - A commentary. *Alcohol Alert, 57*, 1–8.

Kishline, A. (1994). *Moderate drinking: The moderation management guide for people who want to reduce their drinking.* New York: Crown.

Klatsky, A.L. (1996). Alcohol, coronary disease, and hypertension. *Annual Review of Medicine, 47*, 149–160.

Klatsky, A.L. (2007). Errors in selection of "'error-free'" studies. *Addiction Research and Theory, 15*, 8–16.

Klatsky, A.L., & Armstrong, M.A. (1993). Alcohol use, other traits, and risk of unnatural death: A prospective study. *Alcoholism: Clinical and Experimental Research, 17*, 1156–1162.

Klatsky, A.L., Armstrong, M.A., & Friedman, G.D. (1989). Alcohol use and subsequent cerebrovascular disease hospitalizations. *Stroke, 20*, 741–746.

Klatsky, A.L., Friedman, G.D., & Armstrong, M.A. (1986). The relationships between alcoholic beverage use and other traits to blood pressure: a new Kaiser Permanente study. *Circulation, 73*, 628–636.

Klatsky, A.L., Friedman, G.D., Siegelaub, A.B., & Gerard, M.J. (1977). Alcohol consumption and blood pressure Kaiser-Permanente multiphasic health examination data. *New England Journal of Medicine, 296*, 1194–1200.

Koob, G.F., & Le Moal, M. (2001). Drug addiction, dysregulation of reward and allostasis. *Neuropsychopharmacology, 24*, 97–127.

Koob, G.F., & Le Moal, M. (2008). Addiction and the Brain Antireward System. *Annual Review of Psychology, 59*, 29–53.

Kosten, T.R., & O'Connor, P.G. (2003). Management of drug and alcohol withdrawal. *New England Journal of Medicine, 348*, 1786–1795.

Kovacs, E.J., & Messingham, K.A. (2002). Influence of alcohol and gender on immune response. *Alcohol Research & Health, 26*, 257–263.

Kranzler, H.R., Armeli, S., Tennen, H., Blomqvist, O., Oncken, C., Petty, N., et al. (2003). Targeted naltrexone for early problem drinkers. *Journal of Clinical Psychopharmacology, 23*, 294–304.

Kranzler, H.R., Babor, T.F., Goldstein, L., & Gold, J. (1990). Dental pathology and alcohol-related indicators in an outpatient clinic sample. *Community Dentistry & Oral Epidemiology, 18*, 204–207.

Kranzler, H.R., Escobar, R., Lee, D., & Meza, E. (1996). Elevated rates of early discontinuation from pharmacotherapy trials in alcoholics and drug abusers. *Alcoholism: Clinical and Experimental Research, 20*, 16–20.

Kresina, T.F., Flexner, C.W., Sinclair, J., Correia, M.A., Stapleton, J.T., Adeniyi-Jones, S., et al. (2002). Alcohol use and HIV pharmacotherapy. *AIDS Research and Human Retroviruses, 18*, 757–770.

Kuntsche, E.N., Knibbe, R., Gmel, G., & Engels, R. (2005). Why do young people drink? A review of drinking motives. *Clinical Psychology Review, 25*, 841–861.

Kuntsche, E., Knibbe, R., Gmel, G., & Engels, R. (2006). Who drinks and why? A review of socio-demographic, personality, and contextual issues behind the drinking motives in young people. *Psychology of Addictive Behaviors, 31*, 1844–1857.

Kuo, M., Wechsler, H., Greenberg, P., & Lee, H. (2003). The marketing of alcohol to college students: The role of low prices and special promotions. *American Journal of Preventive Medicine, 25*, 204–211.

Kupari, M., & Koskinen, P. (1993). Relation of left ventricular function to habitual alcohol consumption. *American Journal of Cardiology, 72*, 1418–1424.

La Vecchia, C., Negri, E., Franceschi, S., & Gentile, A. (1992). Family history and the risk of stomach and colorectal cancer. *Cancer, 70*, 50–55.

Labouvie, E.W., Pandina, R.J., White, H.R., & Johnson V. (1990). Risk factors of adolescent drug use: An affect-based interpretation. *Journal of Substance Abuse, 2*, 265–285.

Lakshman, M.R., & Tsutsumi, M. (2001). Alcohol biomarkers: Clinical significance and biochemical basis. *Alcohol, 25*, 171–172.

Larimer, M.E., & Cronce, J.M. (2007). Identification, prevention, and treatment revisited: Individual-focused college drinking prevention strategies 1999–2006. *Psychology of Addictive Behaviors, 32*, 2439–2468.

Larkby, C., & Day, N. (1997). The effects of prenatal alcohol exposure. *Alcohol, Health, and Research World, 2*, 192–198.

Larson, M.J., Paasche-Orlow, M., Cheng, D.M., Lloyd-Travaglini, C., Saitz, R., & Samet, J.H. (2007). Persistent pain is associated with substance use after detoxification: A prospective cohort analysis. *Addiction, 102*, 752–760.

Lee, N.K., Greely, J., & Oei, T.P. (1999). The relationship of positive and negative alcohol expectancies to patterns of consumption of alcohol in social drinkers. *Psychology of Addictive Behaviors, 24*, 359–369.

Leigh, B.C. (1993). Alcohol consumption and sexual activity as reported with a diary technique. *Journal of Abnormal Psychology, 102*, 490–493.

Leigh, B.C., & Stall, R. (1993). Substance use and risky sexual behavior for exposure to HIV: Issues in methodology, interpretation, and prevention. *American Psychologist, 48*, 1035–1045.

Leigh, B.C., Vanslyke, J.G., Hoppe, M.J., Rainey, D.T., Morrison, D.M., Gillmore, M.R. (2008). Drinking and condom use: Results from an event-based daily diary. *AIDS & Behavior, 12*, 104–112.

Lemon, J., Chesher, G., Fox, A., Greeley, J., & Nabke, C. (1993). Investigation of the "hangover" effects of an acute dose of alcohol on psychomotor performance. *Alcoholism: Clinical and Experimental Research, 17*, 665–668.

Leonard, K.E., & Eiden, R.D. (1999). Husbands and wives drinking: Unilateral or bilateral influences among newlyweds in a general population sample. *Journal of Studies on Alcohol Supplement, 13*, 130–138.

Leonard, K.E., & Eiden, R.D. (2007). Marital and family processes in the context of alcohol use and alcohol disorders. *Annual Review of Clinical Psychology, 3*, 285–310.

Leonard, K.E., & Homish, G.G. (2008). Predictors of heavy drinking and drinking problems over the first 4 years of marriage. *Psychology of Addictive Behaviors, 22*, 25–35.

Leonard, K.E., & Mudar, P. (2004). Husbands influence on wives' drinking: Testing a relationship motivation model in the early years of marriage. *Psychology of Addictive Behaviors, 18*, 340–349.

Leonard, K.E., & Mudar, P.J. (2000). Alcohol use in the year before marriage: Alcohol expectancies and peer drinking as proximal influences on husband and wife alcohol involvement. *Clinical & Experimental Research, 24*, 1666–1679.

Lerman, I., Lozano, L., Villa, A.R., Hernandez-Jimenez, S., Weinger, K., Caballero, A.E. et al. (2004). Psychosocial factors associated with poor diabetes self-care management in a specialized center in Mexico City. *Biomedicine & Pharmacotherapy, 58*, 566–570.

Lethbridge-Cejku, M., Schiller, J.S., & Bernadel, L. (2004). *Summary health statistics for US adults: National health interview survey, 2002.* Hyattsville, MD: National Center for Health Statistics.

Li, T.K., Hewitt, B., & Grant, B.F. (2004). Alcohol use disorders and mood disorders: A national institute on alcohol abuse and alcoholism perspective. *Biological Psychiatry, 56*, 718–720.

Lieber, C.S. (1994a). Alcohol and the liver: 1994 update. *Gastroenterology, 106*, 1085–1105.

Lieber, C.S. (1994b). Mechanisms of ethanol-drug-nutrition interactions. *Clinical Toxicology, 32*, 631–681.

Lieber, C.S. (1992). *Medical and nutritional complications of alcoholism: Mechanisms and management.* New York: Plenum Press.

Lieber, C.S. (2000). Alcoholic liver disease: New insights in pathogenesis lead to new treatments. *Journal of Hepatology, 32*, 113–128.

Liskow, B., Campbell, J., Nickel, E.J., & Powell, B.J. (1995). Validity of the CAGE questionnaire in screening for alcohol dependence in a walk-in (triage) clinic. *Journal of Studies on Alcohol, 56*(3), 277–281.

Lister, R.G., & Nutt, D.J. (1988). RO 15-4513 and its interaction with ethanol. *Advances in Alcohol and Substance Abuse, 7*, 119–123.

Littlefield, A.K., Vergés, A., McCarthy, D.M., & Sher, J.K. (in press). Interactions between self-reported alcohol outcome expectancies and cognitive functioning in the prediction of alcohol use and associated problems: A further examination. *Psychology of Addictive Behaviors.*

Littlefield, A.K., & Sher, K.J. (2009). Alcohol use disorders in young adulthood. In J.E. Grant, & M.N. Potenza (Eds.), *Young Adult Mental Health* (pp. 292–310). New York: Oxford University Press.

Locke, T.F., & Newcomb, M.D. (2004). Child maltreatment, parent alcohol- and drug-related problems, polydrug problems, and parenting practices: A test of gender differences and four theoretical perspectives. *Journal of Family Psychology, 18*, 120–134.

Lucas, G., Gebo, K., Chaisson, R., & Moore, R. (2002). Longitudinal assessment of the effects of drug and alcohol abuse on HIV-1 treatment outcomes in an urban clinic. *AIDS, 16*, 767–774.

Lucey, M.R., Carr, K., Beresford, T.P., Fisher, L.R., Shieck, V., Brown, K.A., et al. (1997). Alcohol use after liver transplantation in alcoholics: a clinical cohort follow-up study. *Hepatology, 25*, 1223–1227.

Lucey, M.R., Mathurin, P., & Morgan, T.R. (2009). Alcoholic hepatitis. *New England Journal of Medicine, 360*, 2758–2769.

Luczak, S.E., Elvine-Kreis, B., Shea, S.H., Carr, L.G., & Wall, T.L. (2002). Genetic risk for alcoholism relates to level of response to alcohol in Asian-American men and women. *Journal of Studies on Alcohol, 63*, 74–82.

Luczak, S.E., Glatt, S.J., & Wall, T.L. (2006) Meta-analyses of ALDH2 and ADH1B with alcohol dependence in Asians. *Psychological Bulletin, 132*, 607–612.

Luo, X., Kranzler, H.R., Zuo, L., Wang, S., Blumberg, H.P. & Gelernter, J. (2005). CHRM2 gene predisposes to alcohol dependence, drug dependence and affective disorders: results from an extended case-control structured association study. *Human Molecular Genetics, 14*, 2421–2434.

Luty, J. (2006). What works in alcohol use disorders. *Advances in Psychiatric Treatment, 12*, 13–22.

Luz, P.L. da, & Coimbra, S.R. (2004). Wine, alcohol and atherosclerosis: Clinical evidences and mechanisms. *Brazilian Journal of Medical and Biological Research, 37*, 1275–1295.

Lynam, D.R., Milich, R., Zimmerman, R., Novak, S.P., Logan, T.K., Martin, C., et al. (1999). Project DARE: no effects at 10-year follow-up. *Journal of Consulting and Clinical Psychology, 67*, 590–593.

MacAndrew, C., & Edgerton, R.B. (1969). *Drunken comportment: A social explanation.* Chicago: Aldine Publishing Company.

MacDonald, T.K., MacDonald, G., Zanna, M.P., & Fong, G. (2000). Alcohol, sexual arousal, and intentions to use condoms in young men: Applying alcohol myopia theory to risky sexual behavior. *Health Psychology, 19*, 290–298.

Maclure, M. (1993). Demonstration of deductive meta-analysis: Ethanol intake and risk of myocardial infarction. *Epidemiologic Reviews, 15*, 328–351.

MacMahon, S.W. (1986). Alcohol and hypertension: implications for prevention and treatment. *Annals of Internal Medicine, 105*, 124–26.

Magura, S., Laudet, A.B., Mahmood, D., Rosenblum, A., & Knight, E. (2002). Adherence to medication regimens and participation in dual focus self-help groups. *Psychiatric Services, 53*(3), 310–316.

Maisto, S.A., Conigliaro, J., McNeil, M., Kraemer, K., & Kelley, M.E. (2000). An empirical investigation of the factor structure of the AUDIT. *Psychological Assessment, 12*(3), 346–353.

Manning, M.A., & Eugene-Hoyme, H. (2007). Fetal alcohol spectrum disorders: A practical clinical approach to diagnosis. *Neuroscience and Biobehavioral Reviews, 31*, 230–238.

Marlatt, G.A., & Gordon, J.R. (1985). *Relapse prevention: Maintenance strategies in the treatment of addictive behaviors.* New York: Guilford Press.

Marlatt, G.A., & Witkiewitz, K. (2002). Harm reduction approaches to alcohol use: Health promotion, prevention, and treatment. *Psychology of Addictive Behaviors, 27*, 867–886.

Martin, C.S. (2008). Timing of alcohol and other drug use. *Alcohol Research & Health, 31*, 96–99.

Martinez, J.A., Muñoz, M.A., & Sher, K.J. (2009). A new minimum legal drinking age (MLDA)? Some findings to inform the debate. *Psychology of Addictive Behaviors, 34*, 407–410.

McCabe, S.E., Cranford, J.A., Morales, M., & Young, A. (2006). Simultaneous and concurrent polydrug use of alcohol and prescription drugs: Prevalence, correlates, and consequences. *Journal of Studies on Alcohol, 67*, 529–537.

McClure, J.B. (2002). Are biomarkers useful treatment aids for promoting health behavior change? An empirical review. *American Journal of Preventive Medicine, 22*, 200–207.

McCreary, D.R., & Sadava, S.W. (2000). Stress, alcohol use and alcohol-related problems: The influence of negative and positive affect in two cohorts of young adults. *Journal of Studies on Alcohol, 61*, 466–474.

McElduff, P., & Dobson, A.J. (1997). How much alcohol and how often? Population based case-control study of alcohol consumption and risk of a major coronary event. *British Medical Journal, 314*, 1159.

McGinnis, J.M., & Foege, W.H. (1993). Actual causes of death in the United States. *The Journal of the American Medical Association, 270*, 2207–2212.

McGue, M. (1994). Genes, environment, and the etiology of alcoholism. In R. Zucker, J. Howard & G. Boyd (Eds.), *The development of alcohol problems: Exploring the biopsychosocial matrix of risk. National Institute on Alcohol Abuse and Alcoholism Research Monograph* Vol. 26 (pp. 1–40) (NIH Publication No. 94-3495). Washington DC: National Institutes of Health.

McGue, M. (1999). Behavioral genetic models of alcoholism and drinking. In K.E. Leonard, & H.T. Blane (Eds.), *Psychological theories of drinking and alcoholism* (2nd ed., pp. 372–421). New York: Guilford.

McGue, M., & Iacono, W.G. (2008). The adolescent origins of substance use disorders. *International Journal of Methods in Psychiatric Research, 17*(Suppl. 1), S30–S38.

McKirnan, D.J., Vanable, P.A., Ostrow, D.B., & Hope, B. (2001). Expectancies of sexual "escape" and sexual risk among drug and alcohol-involved gay and bisexual men. *Journal of Substance Abuse, 13*, 137–154.

McMillan, G.P., & Lapham, S. (2006). Effectiveness of bans and laws in reducing traffic deaths: Legalized Sunday packaged alcohol sales and alcohol-related traffic crashes and crash fatalities in New Mexico. *American Journal of Public Health, 96*, 1944–1948.

Melding, P.S. (1997). Coping with pain in old age. In D.I. Mostofsky, & J. Lomranz (Eds.), *Handbook of pain and aging* (pp. 167–184). New York: Plenum Press.

Merchant, J., & Macdonald, R. (1994). Youth and rave culture: Ecstasy and health. *Youth Policy, 45*, 16–37.

Merikangas, K.R., Whitaker, A., Angst, J., Eaton, W., Canino, G., Rubio-Stipec, M., et al. (1996). Comorbidity and boundaries of affective disorders with anxiety disorders and substance misuse: Results of an international task force. *British Journal of Psychiatry, 168*(Suppl. 30), 58–67.

Messingham, K., Faunce, D., & Kovacs, E. (2002). Alcohol, injury, and cellular immunity. *Alcohol, 28*, 137–149.

Metzger, D.S., Navaline, H., & Woody, G.E. (1998). Drug abuse treatment as AIDS prevention. *Public Health Reports, 113*, S97–S106.

Meyerhoff, D.J. (2001) Effects of alcohol and HIV infection on the central nervous system. *Alcohol Research & Health, 25*, 288–298.

Mezey, E. (1985). Effect of ethanol on intestinal morphology, metabolism, and function. In H.K. Seitz, & B. Kommerell (Eds.), *Alcohol-related diseases in gastroenterology* (pp. 342–360). New York: Springer-Verlag.

Michna, E., Ross, E., Hynes, W., Nedeljkovic, S., Soumekh, S., Janfaza, D., et al. (2003). Predicting aberrant drug behavior in patients treated for chronic pain: Importance of abuse history. *Journal of Pain and Symptom Management, 28*, 250–258.

Midanik, L.T., & Room, R. (1992). The epidemiology of alcohol consumption. *Alcohol Health & Research World, 16*, 183–190.

Midanik, L.T., Tam, T.W., & Weisner, C. (2007). Concurrent and simultaneous drug and alcohol us: Results of the 2000 national alcohol survey. *Drug and Alcohol Dependence, 90*, 72–80.

Miller, P.M., Smith, G.T., & Goldman, M.S. (1990). Emergence of alcohol expectancies in childhood: A possible critical period. *Journal of Studies on Alcohol, 51*, 343–349.

Miller, W.R., Zweben, A., DiClemente, C.C., & Rychtarik, R.G. (1995). *Motivational enhancement therapy manual: A clinical research guide for therapists treating individuals with alcohol abuse and dependence*. Rockville, MD: U.S. Department of Health and Human Services.

Mokdad, A.H., Marks, J.S., Stroup, D.F., & Gerberding, J.L. (2004). Actual causes of death in the United States, 2000. *Journal of the American Medical Association, 291*, 1238–1245.

Monti, P.M., & O'Leary, T.A. (1999). Coping and social skills training for alcohol and cocaine dependence. *Psychiatric Clinics of North America, 22*, 447–470.

Monti, P.M., & Rohsenow, D.J. (1999) Coping-skills training and cue-exposure therapy in the treatment of alcoholism. *Alcohol Research and Health, 23*, 107–115.

Monti, P.M., Miranda, R., Nixon, K., Sher, K.J., Swartzwelder, H.S., Tapert, S.F., et al. (2005). Adolescence: Booze, brains and behavior. *Alcoholism: Clinical and Experimental Research, 29*, 207–220.

Monti, P.M., Colby, S.M., Barnett, N.P., Spirito, A., Rohsenow, D.J., Myers, M., et al. (1999). Brief intervention for harm reduction with alcohol-positive older adolescents in a hospital emergency department. *Journal of Consulting and Clinical Psychology, 67*, 989–994.

Monti, P.M., & Rohsenow, D.J. (1999). Coping-skills training and cue-exposure therapy in the treatment of alcoholism. *Alcohol Research & Health, 23*, 107–115.

Morgenstern, J., & Longabaugh, R. (2000). Cognitive-behavioral treatment for alcohol dependence: A review of evidence for its hypothesized mechanisms of action. *Addiction, 95*, 1475–1490.

Morrison, D.M., Gillmore, M.R., Hoppe, M.J., Gaylord, J., Leigh, B.C., & Rainey, D. (2003). Adolescent drinking and sex: Findings from a daily diary study. *Perspectives on Sexual and Reproductive Health, 35*, 162–168.

Moskowitz, J.M. (1989). The primary prevention of alcohol problems: A critical review of the research literature. *Journal of Studies on Alcohol, 50*, 54–88.

Mothers Against Drunk Driving. (2009). *The science behind the 21 law*. Retrieved from http://www.madd.org/Parents/Underage-Drinking.aspx.

Moushmoush, B., & Abi-Mansour, P. (1991). Alcohol and the heart: The long-term effects of alcohol on the cardiovascular systems. *Archives of Internal Medicine, 151*, 36–42.

Moyer, A., Finney, J.W., Swearingen, C.E., & Vergun, P. (2002). Brief interventions for alcohol problems: A meta-analytic review of controlled investigations in treatment-seeking and non-treatment seeking populations. *Addiction, 97*, 279–292.

Mukamal, K. (2007). Throwing the baby out with the bathwater: Some cautions for reviews of observational research on alcohol. *Addiction Research and Theory, 15*, 16–20.

Mukamal, K.J. (2006). The effects of smoking and drinking on cardiovascular disease and risk factors. *Alcohol Research & Health, 29*, 199–202.

Muñoz, N., & Day, N.E. (1996). Esophageal cancer. In D. Schoffenfield, & J.F. Fraumani Jr. (Eds.), *Cancer epidemiology and prevention* (pp. 681–706). New York: Oxford University Press.

Muraven, M., & Baumeister, R.F. (2000). Self-regulation and depletion of limited resources: Does self-control resemble a muscle? *Psychological Bulletin, 126*, 247–259.

Muscat, J.E., & Huncharek, M.S. (1991). Firearms and adult, domestic homicides: The role of alcohol and the victim. *The American Journal of Forensic Medicine and Pathology, 12*, 105–110.

Mustanski, B. (2008). Moderating effects of age on the alcohol and sexual risk taking association: An online daily diary study of men who have sex with men. *AIDS & Behavior, 12*, 118–126.

Naimi, T., Brewer, R., Mokdas, A., Denny, L., Serdula, M., & Marks, J. (2003). Binge drinking among U.S. adults. *Journal of the American Medical Association, 289*, 70–74.

Nakamura, K., Iwahashi, K., Matsuo, Y., Miyatake, R., Ichikawa, Y., & Suwaki, H. (1996). Characteristics of Japanese alcoholics with the atypical aldehyde dehydrogenase 2*2. I. A comparison of the genotypes of ALDH2, ADH2, ADH3, and cytochrome P-4502E1 between alcoholics and nonalcoholics. *Alcoholism: Clinical & Experimental Research, 20*, 52–55.

Nash, S.G., McQueen, A., & Bray, J.H. (2005). Pathways to adolescent alcohol use: Family environment, peer influence, and parental expectations. *Journal of Adolescent Health, 37*, 19–28.

National Institute on Alcohol Abuse and Alcoholism (NIAAA). (1993). *Eighth special report to the U.S. congress on alcohol and health* (NIH Publication No. 94-3699). Washington DC: Author.

National Institute on Alcohol Abuse and Alcoholism (NIAAA). (1997). *Ninth special report to the U.S. congress on alcohol and* health from the secretary of health and human services. Washington, DC: Author.

National Institute on Alcohol Abuse and Alcoholism (NIAAA). (2004). *NIAAA council approves definition of binge drinking, NIAAA Newsletter, No. 3*. Bethesda, MD: National Institute on Alcohol Abuse and Alcoholism.

National Institute on Alcohol Abuse and Alcoholism (NIAAA). (2007). *Helping patients who drink too much*. Rockville, MD: National Institute on Alcohol Abuse and Alcoholism.

National Institute on Alcohol Abuse and Alcoholism (NIAAA). (2008a). *Highlight on underage drinking*. Retrieved from http://alcoholpolicy.niaaa.nih.gov/index.asp?SEC-{DA5E054D-FB8E-4F06-BBBC-6EED9F37A758}&Type=B_BASIC_ftnref2.

National Institute on Alcohol Abuse and Alcoholism (NIAAA). (2008b). *NIAAA clinician's guide online training*. Retrieved from http://www.niaaa.nih.gov/Publications/EducationTraining-Materials/VideoCases.htm.

Neaton, J.D., Wentworth, D.N., Cutler, J., Stamler, J., & Kuller, L. (1993). Risk factors for death from different types of stroke. Multiple risk factor intervention trial research group. *Annals of Epidemiology, 3*, 493–499.

Neighbors, C., Larimer, M.E., Lostutter, T.W., & Woods, B.A. (2006). Harm reduction and individually focused alcohol prevention. *International Journal on Drug Policy, 17*, 304–309.

Nelson, S., & Kolls, J.K. (2002). Alcohol, host defence and society. *Nature Reviews: Immunology, 2*, 205–209.

Newlin, D.B., & Thomson, J.B. (1990). Alcohol challenge with sons of alcoholics: A critical review and analysis. *Psychological Bulletin, 108*, 383–402.

Nicolas, J.M., Fernandez-Sola, J., Estruch, R., Pare, J.C., Sacanella, E., Urbano-Marquez, A., et al. (2002). The effect of controlled drinking in alcoholic cardiomyopathy. *Annals of Internal Medicine, 136*, 192–200.

Nigg, J.T., Glass, J.M., Wong, M.M., Poon, E., Jester, J.M., Fitzgerald, H.E., et al. (2004). Neuropsychological executive functioning in children at elevated risk for alcoholism: Findings in early adolescence. *Journal of Abnormal Psychology, 113*, 302–314.

Norberg, M.M., Krystal, J.H., & Tolin, D.F. (2008). A meta-analysis of d-cycloserine and the facilitation of fear extinction and exposure therapy. *Biological Psychiatry, 63*, 1118–1126.

Norton, R., & Colliver, J. (1988). Prevalence and patterns of combined alcohol and marijuana use. *Journal of Studies on Alcohol, 49*, 378–380.

Nyström, M., Peräsalo, J., & Salaspuro, M. (1993). Screening for heavy drinking and alcohol-related problems in young university students: the CAGE, the Mm-MAST and the trauma score questionnaires. *Journal of Studies on Alcohol, 54*(5), 528–533.

O'Briant, R.G., Petersen, N.W., & Heacock, D. (1977). How safe is social setting detoxification? *Alcohol Health and Research World, 1*, 22–27.

O'Doherty, F. (1991). Is drug use a response to stress? *Drug and Alcohol Dependence, 29*, 97–106.

O'Brien, C.P. (2008). The CAGE questionnaire for detection of alcoholism: A remarkably useful but simple tool. *Journal of the American Medical Association, 300*(17), 2054–2056.

Odgers, C.L., Caspi, A., Nagin, D.S., Piquero, A.R., Slutske, W.S., Milne, B.J., et al. (2008). Is it important to prevent early exposure to drugs and alcohol among adolescents? *Psychological Science, 19*(10), 1037–1044.

Okubo, Y., Miyamoto, T., Suwazono, Y., Kobayashi, E., & Nogawa, K. (2001). Alcohol consumption and blood pressure in Japanese men. *Alcohol, 23*, 149–156.

Olfson, M., Mechanic, D., Hansell, S., Boyer, C.A., Walkup, J., & Weiden, P.J. (2000). Predicting medication noncompliance after hospital discharge among patients with schizophrenia. *Psychiatric Services, 51*, 216–222.

Osborn, J.A., Yu, C., Gabriel, K., & Weinberg, J. (1998). Fetal ethanol effects on benzodiazepine sensitivity measured by behavior on the elevated plus-maze. *Pharmacology Biochemistry and Behavior, 60*, 625–633.

Oslin, D.W., Berrettini, W.H., & O'Brien, C.P. (2006). Targeting treatments for alcohol dependence: The pharmacogenetics of naltrexone. *Addiction Biology, 11*, 397–403.

Pageaux, G.-P., Bismuth, M., Perney, P., Costes, V., Jaber, S., Possoz, P., et al. (2003). Alcohol relapse after liver transplantation for alcoholic liver disease: Does it matter? *Journal of Hepatology, 38*, 629–634.

Palfai, T., & Wood, M.D. (2001). Positive alcohol expectancies and drinking behavior: The influence of expectancy strength and memory accessibility. *Psychology of Addictive Behaviors, 15*, 60–67.

Parekh, R.S., & Klag, M.J. (2001). Alcohol: Role in the development of hypertension and end-stage renal disease. *Current Opinion in Nephrology and Hypertension, 10*, 385–390.

Park, A., Sher, K.J., Krull, J.L., & Wood, P.K. (2009). Dual mechanisms underlying accentuation of risky drinking via fraternity/sorority affiliation: The role of personality, peer norms, and alcohol availability. *Journal of Abnormal Psychology, 118*, 241–245.

Park, C.L., Armeli, S., & Tennen, H. (2004). Appraisal-coping goodness of fit: A daily internet study. *Personality and Social Psychology Bulletin, 30*, 558–569.

Parker, E.S., Parker, D.A., & Harford, T.C. (1991). Specifying the relationship between alcohol use and cognitive loss: The effects of frequency of consumption and psychological distress. *Journal of Studies on Alcohol, 52*, 366–373.

Parra, G., Sher, K.J., Krull, J., & Jackson, K.M. (2007). Frequency of heavy drinking and perceived peer alcohol involvement: Comparison of influence and selection mechanisms from a developmental perspective. *Psychology of Addictive Behaviors, 32*, 2211–2225.

Parsons O.A., & Nixon, S.J. (1998). Cognitive functioning in sober social drinkers: A review of the research since 1986. *Journal of Studies on Alcohol, 59*, 180–190.

Pastor, A.D., & Evans, S.M. (2003). Alcohol outcome expectancies and risk for alcohol use problems in women with and without a family history of alcoholism. *Drug and Alcohol Dependence, 70*, 201–214.

Pederson, W. (1991). Mental health, sensation seeking and drug use patterns: A longitudinal study. *British Journal of Addiction, 86*, 195–204.

Pelucchi, C., Gallus, S., Garavello, W., Bosetti, C., & La Vecchia, C. (2006). Cancer risk associated with alcohol and tobacco use: Focus on upper aero-digestive tract and liver. *Alcohol Research & Health, 29*, 193–198.

Perkins, H.W., Haines, M.P., & Rice, R. (2005). Misperceiving the college drinking norm and related problems: A nationwide study of exposure to prevention information, perceived norms and student alcohol misuse. *Journal of Studies on Alcohol, 66*, 470–478.

Perreira, K.M., & Sloan, F.A. (2001). Life events and alcohol consumption among mature adults: A longitudinal analysis. *Journal of Studies on Alcohol, 62*, 501–508.

Perrine, M.W., Mundt, J.C., Searles, J.S., & Lester, L.S. (1995). Validation of daily self-reported alcohol consumption using interactive voice response (IVR) technology. *Journal of Studies on Alcohol, 56*, 487–490.

Pescatello, L.S., Franklin, B.A., Fagard, R., Farquhar, W.B., Kelley, G.A., Ray, C.A., et al. (2004). Exercise and hypertension. *Medicine & Science in Sports & Exercise, 36*, 533–553.

Peterson, J.B., Rothfleisch, J., Zelazo, P.D., & Pihl, R.O. (1990). Acute alcohol intoxication and cognitive functioning. *Journal of Studies on Alcohol, 51*, 114–122.

Petry, N.M. (1999). Alcohol use in HIV patients: What we don't know may hurt us. *International Journal of STDS and AIDS, 10*, 561–570.

Piano, M.R. (2005). The cardiovascular effects of alcohol: The good and the bad. How low-risk drinking differs from high-risk drinking. *American Journal of Nursing, 105*, 87–91.

Piasecki, T.M., Hufford, M.R., Solhan, M., & Trull, T.J. (2007). Assessing clients in their natural environments with electronic diaries: Rationale, benefits, limitations, and barriers. *Psychological Assessment, 19*, 25–43.

Pogue, T.F., & Sgontz, L.G. (1989). Taxing to control social costs: The case of alcohol. *The American Economic Review, 79*, 235–243.

Pokorny, A.D., Miller, B.A., & Kaplan, H.B. (1972). The brief MAST: a shortened version of the Michigan alcoholism screening test. *American Journal of Psychiatry, 129*(3), 342–345.

Powers, M.B., Vedel, E., & Emmelkamp, P. (2008). Behavioral couples therapy (BCT) for alcohol and drug use disorders: A meta-analysis. *Clinical Psychology Review, 28*, 952–962.

Preedy, V.R., Atkinson, L.M., Richardson, P.J., & Peters, T.J. (1993). Mechanisms of ethanol-induced cardiac damage. *British Heart Journal, 69*, 197–200.

Prescott, C.A., & Kendler, K.S. (1999). Age at first drink and risk for alcoholism: A noncausal association. *Alcoholism: Clinical and Experimental Research, 23*, 101–107.

Pringle, K.E., Ahern, F.M., Heller, D.A., Gold, C.H., & Brown, T.V. (2005). Potential for alcohol and prescription drug interactions in older people. *Journal of the American Geriatrics Society, 53*, 1930–1936.

Project MATCH Research Group. (1993). Project MATCH: Rationale and methods for a multisite clinical trial matching alcoholism patients to treatment. *Alcoholism: Clinical and Experimental Research, 17*, 1130–1145.

Project MATCH Research Group. (1997). Matching alcoholism treatments to client heterogeneity: Project MATCH post-treatment drinking outcomes. *Journal of Studies on Alcohol, 58*, 7–29.

Purcell, D.W., Parsons, J.T., Halitis, P.N., Mizuno, Y., & Woods, W.J. (2001). Substance use and sexual transmission risk behavior of HIV-positive men who have sex with men. *Journal of Substance Abuse, 13*, 185–200.

Raistrick, D. (2000). Management of alcohol detoxification. *Advances in Psychiatric Treatment, 6*, 348–355.

Randall, C.L., & Lester, D. (1975). Social modification of alcohol consumption in inbred mice. *Science, 189*, 149–151.

Read, J. P, Wood, M.D., Lejuez, C.W., Palfai, T.P., & Slack, M. (2004). Gender, alcohol consumption and differing alcohol expectancy dimensions in college drinkers. *Experimental and Clinical Psychopharmacology, 12*, 298–308.

Regier, D.A., Farmer, M.E., Rae, D.S., Locke, B.Z., Keith, S.J., Judd, L.L., et al. (1990). Comorbidity of mental disorders with alcohol and other drug abuse. Results from the epidemiologic catchment area (ECA) Study. *Journal of American Medical Association, 264*, 2511–2518.

Rehm, J. (2007). On the limitations of observational studies. *Addiction Research and Theory, 15*, 20–22.

Rehm, J., Greenfield, T.K., & Rodgers, J.D. (2001). Average volume of alcohol consumption, patterns of drinking and all-cause mortality: Results from the US national alcohol survey. *American Journal of Epidemiology, 153*, 64–71.

Rehm, J., Patra, J., & Popova, S. (2006). Alcohol-attributable mortality and potential years of life lost in Canada 2001: Implications for prevention and policy. *Addiction, 101*, 373–384.

Rehm, J., Room, R., Graham, K., Monteiro, M., Gmel, G., & Sempos, C.T. (2003). The relationship of average volume of alcohol consumption and patterns of drinking to burden of disease: An overview. *Addiction, 98*, 1209–1228.

Rehm, J., Mathers, C., Popova., S., Thavorncharoensap, M., Teerawattananon, Y., & Patra, J. (2009). Global burden of disease and injury and economic cost attributable to alcohol use and alcohol-use disorders. *Lancet, 9682*, 2223–2233.

Reynolds, K., Lewis, B., Nolen, J.D., Kinney, G.L., Sathya, B., & He, J. (2003). Alcohol consumption and risk of stroke: a meta-analysis. *The Journal of the American Medical Association, 289*, 579–588.

Richardson, P.J., Wodak, A.D., Atkinson, L., Saunders, J.B., & Jewitt, D.E. (1986). Relation between alcohol intake, myocardial enzyme activity, and myocardial function in dilated cardiomyopathy. *British Heart Journal, 56*, 165–170.

Ridker, P.M., Vaughan, D.E., Stampfer, M.J., Glynn, R.J., & Hennekens, C.J. (1994). Association of moderate alcohol consumption and plasma concentration of endogenous tissue-type plasminogen activator. *The Journal of the American Medical Association, 272*, 929–933.

Risch N., Herrell R., Lehner T., Liang, L., Eaves, L., Hoh, J., et al. (2009). Interaction between the serotonin transporter gene (5-HTTLPR), stressful life events, and risk of depression: A meta-analysis. *Journal of the American Medical Association, 301*, 2462–2471.

Roberts, B.W., Walton, K.E., & Viechtbauer, W. (2006). Patterns of mean-level change in personality traits across the life course: A meta-analysis of longitudinal studies. *Psychological Bulletin, 132*, 1–25.

Robins, L.N., & Price, R.K. (1991). Adult disorders predicted by childhood conduct problems: Results from the NIMH epidemiologic catchment area project. *Psychiatry: Journal for the Study of Interpersonal Processes, 54*, 116–132.

Robins, L., Cottler, L., Bucholz, K., & Compton, W. (1996). *Diagnostic interview schedule, fourth version (DIS-IV)*. St. Louis, MO: Washington University.

Roehrs, T., & Roth, T. (2001). Sleep, sleepiness, sleep disorders and alcohol use and abuse. *Sleep Medicine Reviews, 5*, 287–297.

Roehrs, T., Beare, D., Zorick, F., & Roth, T. (1994). Sleepiness and ethanol effects on simulated driving. *Alcoholism: Clinical and Experimental Research, 18*, 154–158.

Rohsenow, D.J. (1982). Social anxiety, daily moods, and alcohol use over time among heavy social drinking men. *Addictive Behaviors, 7*(3), 311–315.

Rohsenow, D.J., Monti, P.M., Rubonis, A.V., Sirota, A.D., Niaura, R.S., Colby, S.M., et al. (1994). Cue reactivity as a predictor of drinking among male alcoholics. *Journal of Consulting and Clinical Psychology, 62,* 620–626.

Romelsjo, A. (2007). Moderate alcohol use and reduced mortality risk: Systematic error in prospective studies. *Addiction Research and Theory, 15,* 22–26.

Rosenberg, L., Metzger, L.S., & Palmer, J.R. (1993). Alcohol consumption and risk of breast cancer: a review of the epidemiologic evidence. *Epidemiological Review, 15,* 133–144.

Rosendorff, C., Black, H.R., Cannon, C.P., Gersh, B.J., Gore, J., Izzo, J.L., Jr., et al. (2007). Treatment of hypertension in the prevention and management of ischemic heart disease: A scientific statement from the American heart association council for high blood pressure research and the councils on clinical cardiology and epidemiology and prevention. *Circulation, 115,* 2761–2788.

Rosenqvist, M. (1998). Alcohol and cardiac arrhythmias. *Alcoholism: Clinical & Experimental Research, 22,* 318S–322S.

Ross, H.E., Gavin, D.R., & Skinner, H.A. (1990). Diagnostic validity of the MAST and the alcohol dependence scale in the assessment of DSM-III alcohol disorders. *Journal of Studies on Alcohol, 51*(6), 506–513.

Ross, H.E., Glaser, F.B., & Stiasny, S. (1988). Sex differences in the prevalence of psychiatric disorders in patients with alcohol and drug problems. *Addiction, 83,* 1179–1192.

Ross, R.K., Bernstein, L., Trent, L., Henderson, B.E., & Paganini-Hill, A. (1990) A prospective study of risk factors for traumatic death in the retirement community. *Preventative Medicine, 19,* 323–334.

Rubin, R. (2008). *Report makes a case for raising driving age. USA Today.* Retrieved from http://www.usatoday.com/news/2008-09—0-teen-drivers_N.htm.

Russell, M., Martier, S.S., Sokol, R.J., Mudar, P., Bottoms, S., Jacobson, S., & Jacobson, J. (1994). Screening for pregnancy risk-drinking. *Alcoholism: Clinical and Experimental Research, 18,* 1156–1161.

Sacco, R.L., Elkind, M., Boden-Albala, B., Lin, I., Kargman, D.E., Hauser, W.A., et al. (1999). The Protective Effect of Moderate Alcohol Consumption on Ischemic Stroke. *The Journal of the American Medical Association, 281,* 53–60.

Sacks, F.M., Svetkey, L.P., Vollmer, W.M., Appel, L.J., Bray, G.A., Harsha, D., et al. (2001). Effects on blood pressure of reduced dietary sodium and the dietary approaches to stop hypertension (DASH) diet. *The New England Journal of Medicine, 344,* 3–10.

Sakai, J.T., Mikulich-Gilbertson, S.K., Long, R.J., & Crowley, T.J. (2006) Validity of transdermal alcohol monitoring: Fixed and self-regulated dosing. *Alcoholism: Clinical and Experimental Research, 30,* 26–33.

Samet, J.H., Cheng, D.M., Libman, H., Nunes, D.P., Alperen, J.K., & Saitz, R. (2007). Alcohol consumption and HIV disease progression. *Journal of Acquired Immune Deficiency Syndrome, 46,* 194–199.

Samet, J.H., Freedberg, K.A., Stein, M.D., Lewis, R., Savetsky, J., Sullivan, L., et al. (1998). Trillion virion delay: Time from testing positive for HIV to presentation for primary care. *Archives of Internal Medicine, 158,* 734–740.

Samet, J.H., Horton, N.J., Traphagan, E.T., Lyon, S.M., & Freedberg, K.A. (2003). Alcohol consumption and HIV disease progression: Are they related? *Alcoholism: Clinical and Experimental Research, 27,* 862–867.

Samet, J.H., Horton, N.J., Meli, S., Freedberg, K.A., & Palepu, A. (2004). Alcohol consumption and antiretroviral adherence among HIV-infected persons with alcohol problems. *Alcoholism: Clinical and Experimental Research, 28,* 572–577.

Santibanez, T., Barker, L., Santoli, J., Bridges, C., Euler, G., & McCauley, M. (2004). Alcohol-attributable deaths and years of potential life lost—United States, 2001. *Morbidity and Mortality Weekly Report, 53,* 866–870.

Sarti, C., Rastenyte, D. Cepaitis, Z., & Tuomilehto, M.J. (2000). International trends in mortality from stroke, 1968 to 1994. *Stroke, 31,* 1588–1601.

Sartor, C.E., Lynskey, M.T., Heath, A.C., Jacob, T., & True, W. (2007). The role of childhood risk factors in initiation of alcohol use and progression to alcohol dependence. *Addiction, 102,* 216–225.

Schatzkin, A., & Longnecker, M.P. (1994). Alcohol and breast cancer: Where are we now and where do we go from here? *Cancer, 74,* 1101–1110.

Scheier, L.M., Botvin, G.J., & Miller, N.L. (1999). Life events, neighborhood stress, psychosocial functioning, and alcohol use among urban minority youth. *Journal of Child and Adolescent Substance Abuse, 9,* 19–50.

Schuckit, M.A. (1994). *Substance-related disorders. DSM-IV Sourcebook* Vol. 1. Washington, DC: American Psychiatric Association.

Schuckit, M.A. (1998). Biological, psychological and environmental predictors of the alcoholism risk: a longitudinal study. *Journal of Studies on Alcohol, 59,* 485–494.

Schuckit, M.A., & Hesselbrock, V. (2004). Alcohol dependence and anxiety disorders: What is the relationship? *American Journal of Psychiatry, 151,* 1723–1734.

Schuckit, M.A., Irwin, M., & Brown, S.A. (1990). The history of anxiety symptoms among 171 primary alcoholics. *Journal of Studies on Alcohol, 51,* 34–41.

Scott-Sheldon, L.A.J., Carey, M.P., Vanable, P.A., Senn, T.E., Coury-Doniger, P., & Urban, M.A. (2009). Alcohol consumption, drug use, and condom use among STD clinic patients. *Journal of Studies on Alcohol and Drugs, 70,* 762–770.

Seage, G.R., Holte, S., Gross, M., Koblin, B., Marmor, M., Mayer, K.H., et al. (2002). Case-crossover study of partner and situational factors for unprotected sex. *Journal of Acquired Immune Deficiency Syndrome, 31,* 432–439.

Sellers, E.M., Sullivan, J.T., Somer, G., & Sykora, K. (1991). Characterization of DSM-III-R criteria for uncomplicated alcohol withdrawal provides an empirical basis for DSM-IV. *Archives of General Psychiatry, 48,* 442–447.

Selzer, M.L. (1971). The Michigan alcoholism screening test: The quest for a new diagnostic instrument. *American Journal of Psychiatry, 127,* 1653–1658.

Selzer, M.L., Vinokur, A., & van Rooijen, L. (1975). A self-administered short Michigan alcoholism screening test (SMAST). *Journal of Studies on Alcohol, 36*(1), 117–126.

Sesso, H.D., Cook, N.R., Buring, J.E., Manson, J.E., & Gaziano, J.M. (2008). Alcohol consumption and the risk of hypertension in women and men. *Hypertension, 51,* 1080–1087.

Shaper, A.G. (2007). New baseline needed for alcohol and mortality studies. *Addiction Research and Theory, 15,* 26–29.

Shaper, A.G., Wannamethee, G., & Walker, M. (1988). Alcohol and mortality: explaining the U-shaped curve. *Lancet, 332,* 1268–1273.

Sher, K.J. (1991). *Children of alcoholics: A critical appraisal of theory and research.* Chicago: University of Chicago Press.

Sher, K.J. (2007). The road to alcohol dependence: Comment on Sartor et al. (2007). *Addiction, 102*, 185–187.

Sher, K.J., Bartholow, B.D., Peuser, K., Erickson, D.J., & Wood, M.D. (2007). Stress- -response dampening effects of alcohol: A systematic investigation of mediators, moderators, and outcomes. *Journal of Abnormal Psychology, 116*, 362–377.

Sher, K.J., & Epler, A.J. (2004). Alcoholic denial: Self-awareness and beyond. In B.D. Beitman, & J. Nair, J. (Eds.), *Self-awareness deficits in psychiatric patients: Neurobiology, assessment and treatment* (pp. 184–212). New York: W.W. Norton & Company.

Sher, K.J., & Grekin, E.R. (2007). Alcohol and affect regulation. In J. Gross (Ed.), *Handbook of emotion regulation* (pp. 560–580). New York: Guilford.

Sher, K.J., Grekin, E., & Williams, N. (2005). The development of alcohol problems. *Annual Review of Clinical Psychology, 1*, 493–523.

Sher, K.J., & Martinez, J.A. (2009). The future of treatment for substance use: A View from 2009. In L. Cohen, F.L. Collins, A.M. Young, D.E. McChargue, & T.R. Leffingwell (Eds.), *The Pharmacology and Treatment of Substance Abuse: An Evidence-Based Approach*, pp. 635–652. New York: Routledge.

Sher, K.J., Martinez, J.A., & Littlefield, A.K. (2011). Alcohol use and alcohol use disorders (clinical practice). In D. Barlow (Ed.), *Oxford handbook of clinical psychology*, p. 405–445. New York: Oxford.

Sher, K.J., & Trull, T.J. (1994). Personality and disinhibitory psychopathology: Alcoholism and antisocial personality disorder. *Journal of Abnormal Psychology, 103*, 92–102.

Sher, K.J., & Trull, T.J. (1996). Methodological issues in psychopathology research. *Annual Review of Psychology, 47*, 371–400.

Sher, K.J., & Trull, T.J. (2002). Substance use disorder and personality disorder. *Current Psychiatry Reports, 4*, 25–29.

Sher, K.J., Trull, T.J., Bartholow, B.D., & Vieth, A. (1999). Personality and alcoholism: Issues, methods, and etiological processes. In K. Leonard, & H.T. Blane (Eds.), *Psychological theories on drinking and alcoholism* (pp. 54–105). New York: Guilford Press.

Sher, K.J., Wood, M.D., Richardson, A.E., & Jackson, K.M. (2005). Subjective effects of alcohol I: Effects of the drink and drinking context. In M. Earleywine (Ed.), *Mind altering drugs: Scientific evidence for subjective experience* (pp. 86–134). New York: Oxford.

Sher, K.J., Wood, M.D., Wood, P.K., & Raskin, G. (1996). Alcohol outcome expectancies and alcohol use: A latent variable cross-lagged panel study. *Journal of Abnormal Psychology, 105*, 561–574.

Shope, J.T., Copeland, L.A., Marcoux, B.C., & Kamp, M.E. (1996). Effectiveness of a school-based substance abuse prevention program. *Journal of Drug Education, 26*, 323–337.

Shultz, J.M., Rice, D.P., & Parker, D.L. (1990). Alcohol-related mortality and years of potential life lost: United States, 1987. *Morbidity and Mortality Weekly Report, 39*, 173–178.

Sieber, M.F. (1981). Personality scores and licit and illicit substance abuse. *Personality and Individual Differences, 2*, 235–241.

Siegel, S., Baptista, M.A., Kim, J.A., McDonald, R.V., & Weise-Kelly, L. (2000). Pavlovian psychopharmacology: the associative basis of tolerance. *Experimental and Clinical Psychopharmacology, 8*, 276–293.

Simons-Morton, B., Haynie, D.L., Crump, A.D., Eitel, P., & Saylor, K.E. (2001). Peer and parent influences on smoking and drinking among early adolescents. *Health Education and Behavior, 28*, 95–107.

Sisson, R.W., & Azrin, N.H. (1986) Family-member involvement to initiate and promote treatment of problem drinkers. *Journal of Behavior Therapy and Experimental Psychiatry, 17*, 15–21.

Skinner, H.A. (1979). A multivariate evaluation of the MAST. *Journal of Studies on Alcohol, 40*(9), 831–844.

Slutske, W.S., D'Onofrio, B.M., Turkheimer, E., Emery, R.E., Harden, K.P., Heath, A.C., et al. (2008). Searching for an environmental effect of parental alcoholism on offspring alcohol use disorder: A genetically informed study of children of alcoholics. *Journal of Abnormal Psychology, 117*, 534–551.

Slutske, W.S., Heath, A.C., Dinwiddie, S.H., Madden, P.A., Bucholz, K.K., Dunne, M.P., et al. (1998). Common genetic risk factors for conduct disorder and alcohol dependence. *Journal of Abnormal Psychology, 107*, 363–374.

Slutske, W.S., Heath, A. C, Madden, P.A., Bucholz, K.K., Statham, D.J., & Martin, N.G. (2002). Personality and the genetic risk for alcohol dependence. *Journal of Abnormal Psychology, 111*, 124–133.

Smart, R.G., Adlaf, E.M., & Knoke, D. (1991). Use of the CAGE scale in a population survey of drinking. *Journal of Studies on Alcohol, 52*(6), 593–596.

Smith, G.S., & Kraus, J.F. (1988). Alcohol and residential, recreational, and occupational injuries: A review of the epidemiologic evidence. *Annual Review of Public Health, 9*, 99–121.

Smith, G.T., Fischer, S., Cyders, M.A., Annus, A.M., Spillane, N.S., & McCarthy, D.M. (2007). On the validity and utility of discriminating among impulsivity-like traits. *Assessment, 14*, 155–170.

Smith, G.T., Goldman, M.S., Greenbaum, P.E., & Christiansen, B.A. (1995). Expectancy for social facilitation from drinking: The divergent paths of high-expectancy and low expectancy adolescents. *Journal of Abnormal Psychology, 104*, 32–40.

Smith, G., Branas, C., & Miller, T. (1999). Fatal nontraffic injuries involving alcohol: A metaanalysis. *Annals of Emergency Medicine, 33*, 659–668.

Smith, I., & Hillman, A. (1999). Management of alcohol Korsakoff syndrome. *Advances in Psychiatric Treatment, 5*, 271–278.

Smith, J.E., & Meyers, R.J. (2004). *Motivating substance abusers to enter treatment: Working with family members*. New York: Guilford.

Sobell, L.C., Brown, J., Leo, G.I., & Sobell, M.B. (1996). The reliability of the alcohol timeline followback when administered by telephone and by computer. *Drug and Alcohol Dependence, 42*, 49–54.

Sobell, L.C., & Sobell, M.B. (1992). Timeline follow-back: a technique for assessing self-reported alcohol consumption. In R.Z. Litten, & J.P. Allen (Eds.), *Measuring alcohol consumption: Psychosocial and biochemical methods* (pp. 41–72). Totowa: Humana Press.

Sobell, L.C., & Sobell, M.B. (2000). Alcohol timeline followback (TLFB). In American Psychiatric Association (Ed.), *Handbook of psychiatric measures* (pp. 477–479). Washington, DC: American Psychiatric Association.

Sobell, L.C., & Sobell, M.B. (2003). Alcohol consumption measures. In P. Allen, & M. Columbus (Eds.), *Assessing alcohol problems: A guide for clinicians and researchers. National institute on alcohol abuse and alcoholism treatment handbook series* (2nd ed.) (pp. 78–99). Rockville, MD: National Institute on Alcohol Abuse and Alcoholism.

Sobell, M.B., & Sobell, L.C. (1995). Controlled drinking after 25 years: How important was the great debate? *Addiction, 90*, 1149–1153.

Social Setting Detoxification. (1986). *A tailored training program.* Available through Virginia Department of Mental Health and Mental Retardation Training Office, PO Box 1797, Richmond, VA 23214.

Solomon, R.L., & Corbit, J.D. (1974). An opponent-process theory of motivation: I. Temporal dynamics of affect. *Psychological Review, 81*, 119–145.

Solomon, C.G., Hu, F.B., Stampfer, M.J., Colditz, G.A., Speizer, F., Rimm, E.B. et al. (2000). Moderate alcohol consumption and risk of coronary heart disease among women with type 2 diabetes mellitus. *Circulation, 102*, 494–499.

Song, Z., Deaciuc, I., Song, M., Lee, D.Y., Liu, Y., Ji, X. et al. (2006). Silymarin protects against acute ethanol-induced hepatotoxicity in mice. *Alcoholism: Clinical and Experimental Research, 30*, 407–413.

Spear, L.P. (2000). The adolescent brain and age-related behavioral manifestations. *Neuroscience and Biobehavioral Reviews, 24*, 417–463.

Srisurapanont, M., & Jarusuraisin, N. (2005). Naltrexone for the treatment of alcoholism: A metaanalysis of randomized controlled trials. *International Journal of Neuropsychopharmacology, 8*, 267–280.

Stacy, A. W, Newcomb, M.D., & Bentler, P. M. (1991). Cognitive motivation and drug use: A 9-year longitudinal study. *Journal of Abnormal Psychology, 100*, 502–515.

Stamler, J., Stamler, R., Neaton, J.D. (1993). Blood pressure, systolic and diastolic, and cardiovascular risks. *Archives of Internal Medicine, 153*, 598–615.

Steele, C.M., & Josephs, R.A. (1990). Alcohol myopia: Its prized and dangerous effects. *American Psychologist, 45*, 921–933.

Stein, M.D., Hanna, L., Natarajan, R., Clarke, J., Marisi, M., Sobota, M., & Rich, J. (2000). Alcohol use patterns predict high-risk HIV behaviors among active injection drug users. *Journal of Substance Abuse Treatment, 18*, 359–363.

Steinhausen, H., Willms, J., & Spohr, H.L. (1993). Long-term psychopathological and cognitive outcome of children with fetal alcohol syndrome. *Journal of the American Academy of Child & Adolescent Psychiatry, 32*, 990–994.

Stewart, S., Jones, D., & Day, C.P. (2001). Alcoholic liver disease: New insights into mechanisms and preventative strategies. *Trends in Molecular Medicine, 7*, 408–413.

Stickel, F., & Österreicher, C.H. (2006). The role of genetic polymorphisms in alcoholic liver disease. *Alcohol and Alcoholism, 41*, 209–224.

Stinnett, J.L. (1982). Outpatient detoxification of the alcoholic. *The International Journal of the Addictions, 17*, 1031–1046.

Stinson, F.S., Grant, B.F., Dawson, D.A., Ruan, W.J., Huang, B., & Saha, T. (2005). Comorbidity between DSM-IV alcohol and specific drug use disorders in the United States: Results from the National Epidemiologic Survey on Alcohol and Related Conditions. *Drug and Alcohol Dependence, 80*, 105–116.

Streissguth, A.P., Barr, H.M., & Sampson, P.D. (1990). Moderate prenatal alcohol exposure: Effects on child IQ and learning problems at age 7 1/2 years. *Alcoholism: Clinical & Experimental Research, 14*, 662–669.

Streissguth, A.P., Sampson, P.D., Olson, H.C., Bookstein, F.L., Barr, H.M., Scott, M., et al. (1994). Maternal drinking during pregnancy: Attention and short-term memory in 14-year old offspring-a longitudinal prospective study. *Alcohol: Clinical and Experimental Research, 19*, 202–218.

Sullivan, E.V., & Pfefferbaum, A. (2008). Neuroimaging of the Wernicke-Korsakoff Syndrome. *Alcohol & Alcoholism, 44*(2), 155–165.

Sullivan, J.T., Sykora, K., Schneiderman, J., Naranjo, C.A., & Sellers, E.M. (1989). Assessment of alcohol withdrawal: The revised clinical institute withdrawal assessment for alcohol scale (CIWA-Ar). *British Journal of Addiction, 84*, 1353–1357.

Swartzwelder, H.S., Wilson, W.A., & Tayyeb, M.I. (1995). Age-dependent inhibition of long-term potentiation by ethanol in immature versus mature hippocampus. *Alcoholism: Clinical and Experimental Research, 19*, 1480–1485.

Swift, R. (2000). Transdermal alcohol measurement for estimation of blood alcohol concentration. *Alcoholism: Clinical and Experimental Research, 24*, 422–423.

Szabo, G. (1997). Alcohol's contribution to compromised immunity. *Alcohol Health & Research World, 21*, 31–38.

Szabo, G. (1999). Consequences of alcohol consumption on host defence. *Alcohol & Alcoholism, 34*, 830–841.

Takeshita, T., Morimoto, K., Mao, X., Hashimoto, T., & Furuyama, J. (1994). Characterization of the three genotypes of low Km aldehyde dehydrogenase in a Japanese population. *Human Genetics, 94*, 217–223.

Tanasescu, M., Hu, F.B., Willett, W.C., Stampfer, M.J., & Rimm, E.B. (2001). Alcohol consumption and risk of coronary heart disease among men with Type 2 diabetes mellitus. *Journal of the American College of Cardiology, 38*, 1836–1842.

Tapert, S.F., Brown, G.G., Baratta, M.V., & Brown, S.A. (2004) fMRI BOLD response to alcohol stimuli in alcohol dependent young women. *Addictive Behavior, 29*, 33–50.

Teitelbaum, L. & Mullen, B. (2000). The validity of the MAST in psychiatric settings: A meta-analytic integration. Michigan Alcoholism Screening Test. *Journal of Studies on Alcohol, 61*(2), 254–261.

Testa, M., Quigley, B.M., & Eiden, R.D. (2003). The effects of prenatal alcohol exposure on infant mental development: a meta-analytical review. *Alcohol & Alcoholism, 38*, 295–304.

Thakker, K.D. (1998). An overview of health risks and benefits of alcohol consumption. *Alcoholism: Clinical and Experimental Research, 22*, 285–298.

Thush, C., & Wiers, R.W. (2007). Explicit and implicit alcohol-related cognitions and the prediction of future drinking in adolescents. *Psychology of Addictive Behaviors, 32*, 1367–1383.

Thush, C., Wiers, R.W., Ames, S.L., Grenard, J.L., Sussman, S., & Stacy, A.W. (2008). Interactions between implicit and explicit cognition and working memory capacity in the prediction of alcohol use in at-risk adolescents. *Drug and Alcohol Dependence, 94*, 116–124.

Tobler, N.S. (1986). Meta-analysis of 143 adolescent drug prevention programs: Quantitative outcome results of program participants compared to a control or comparison group. *Journal of Drug Issues, 16*, 537–567.

Tonigan, J.S., Toscova, R., & Miller, W.R. (1996). Meta-analysis of the literature on Alcoholics Anonymous: Sample and study characteristics moderate findings. *Journal of Studies on Alcohol, 57*, 65–72.

Toomey, T.L., & Wagenaar, A.C. (1999). Policy options for prevention: The case of alcohol. *Journal of Public Health Policy, 20*, 192–213.

Treno, A.J., Ponicki, W.R., Remer, L.G., & Gruenwald, P.J. (2008). Alcohol outlets, youth drinking, and self-reported ease of access to alcohol: A constraints and opportunities approach. *Alcoholism: Clinical and Experimental Research, 32*, 1372–1379.

Trull, T.J., Jahng, S., Tomko, R.L., Wood, P.K., & Sher, K.J. (2010). Revised NESARC Personality Disorder Diagnoses: Gender, Prevalence, and Comorbidity with Substance Dependence Disorders. *Journal of Personality Disorders, 24,* 412–426.

Trull, T.J., Sher, K.J., Minks-Brown, C., Durbin, J., & Burr, R. (2000). Borderline personality disorder and substance use disorders: A review and integration. *Clinical Psychology Review, 20,* 235–253.

Uhl, G.R., Drgon, T., Johnson, C., Fatusin, O.O., Liu, Q.R., Contoreggi, C., et al. (2008). "Higher order" addiction molecular genetics: convergent data from genome-wide association in humans and mice. *Biochemical Pharmacology, 75,* 98–111.

U.S. Health and Human Services and U.S. Department of Agriculture (2005). *Dietary guidelines for Americans 2005* (6th ed.). Washington, DC: US Government Printing Office.

Uys, J.D.K., & Niesink, J.M. (2005). Pharmacological aspects of the combined use of 3,4-methylenedioxymethamphetamine (MDMA, ecstasy) and gamma-hydroxybutyric acid (GHB): A review of the literature. *Drug and Alcohol Review, 24,* 359–368.

Vaillant, G.E. (1997). The natural history of alcoholism and its relationship to liver transplantation. *Liver Transplantation Surgery, 3,* 304–310.

Vasdev, S., Gill, V., & Singal, P.K. (2006). Beneficial effect of low ethanol intake on the cardiovascular system: Possible biochemical mechanisms. *Vascular Health Risk Management, 2,* 263–276.

Velez-Blasini, C.J. (2008). Evidence against alcohol as a proximal cause of sexual risk taking among college students. *Journal of Sex Research, 45,* 118–128.

Vengeliene, V., Bilbao, A., Molander, A., & Spanagel, R. (2008). Neuropharmacology of alcohol addiction. *British Journal of Pharmacology, 154,* 299–315.

Vengeliene, V., Kiefer, F., & Spanagel, R. (2008). D-cycloserine facilitates extinction of conditioned alcohol-seeking behaviour in rats. *Alcohol & Alcoholism, 43,* 626–629.

Verheul, R., van den Brink, W., & Hartgers, C. (1995). Prevalence of personality disorders among alcoholics and drug addicts: an overview. *European Addiction Research, 1,* 166–177.

Victor, M. (1993). The Wernicke–Korsakoff syndrome. In R.D. Adams, & M. Victor (Eds.), *Principles of neurology* (5th ed., pp. 851–858). New York: McGraw-Hill.

Victor, M. (1994). Alcoholic dementia. *Canadian Journal of Neurological Sciences, 21,* 88–99.

Vinson, D.C. (1989). Acute transient memory loss. *American Family Physician, 39,* 249–254.

Voas, R.B., & DeYoung, D.J. (2002). Vehicle action: Effective policy for controlling drunk and other high-risk drivers? *Accident Analysis and Prevention, 34,* 263–270.

Voas, R.B., Tippetts, A.S., & Fell, J.C. (2003). Assessing the effectiveness of minimum legal drinking age and zero tolerance laws in the United States. *Accident Analysis and Prevention, 35,* 579–587.

Volpicelli, J.R., Pettinati, H.M., McLellan, A.T., & O'Brien, C.P. (2001). *Combining Medication and Psychosocial Treatments for the Addictions: The BRENDA approach.* New York: Guilford Press.

Wagenaar, A.C., & Holder, H.D. (1991). Effects of alcoholic beverage server liability on traffic crash injuries. *Alcoholism: Clinical and Experimental Research, 15,* 942–947.

Wagenaar, A.C., Salois, M.J., & Komro, K.A. (2009). Effects of beverage alcohol price and tax levels on drinking: A meta-analysis of 1,003 estimates from 112 studies. *Addiction, 104,* 179–190.

Wagner, J.H., Justice, A.C., Chesney, M., Sinclair, G., Weissman, S., & Rodriguez-Barradas, M. (2001). Patient- and provider-reported adherence: Toward a clinically useful approach to measuring antiretroviral adherence. *Journal of Clinical Epidemiology, 54,* S91–S98.

Wall, T.L., Thomasson, H.R., Schuckit, M.A., & Ehlers, C.L. (1992). Subjective feelings of alcohol intoxication in Asians with genetic variations of ALDH2 alleles. *Alcoholism: Clinical & Experimental Research, 16,* 991–995.

Walton, M.A., Goldstein, A.L., Chermack, S.T., McCammon, R.J., Cunningham, R.M., Barry, K.L., et al. (2008). Brief alcohol intervention in the emergency department; Moderators of effectiveness. *Journal of Studies on Alcohol and Drugs, 69,* 550–560.

Weatherburn, P., Davies, P.M., Hickson, F.C.I., Hunt, A.J., McManus, T.J., & Coxon, A.P.M. (1993). No connection between alcohol use and unsafe sex among gay and bisexual men. *AIDS, 7,* 115–119.

Wechsler, H., & Austin S.B. (1998). Binge drinking: The five/four measure. *Journal of Studies on Alcohol, 59,* 122–123.

Wechsler, H., Dowdall, G.W., Maenner, G., Gledhill-Hoyt, J., & Lee, H. (1998). Changes in binge drinking and related problems among American college students between 1993 and 1997. *Journal of American College Health, 47,* 57–68.

Wechsler, H., Nelson, T.F., Lee, J.E., Seibring, M., Lewis, C., & Keeling, R.P. (2003). Perception and reality: A national evaluation of social norms marketing interventions to reduce college students' heavy alcohol use. *Journal of Studies on Alcohol, 64,* 484–494.

Wei, M., Gibbons, L.W., Mitchell, T.L., Kampert, J.B., & Blair, S.N. (2000) Alcohol intake and incidence of type 2 diabetes in men. *Diabetes Care, 23,* 18–22.

Weinhardt, L.S., & Carey, M.P. (2000). Does alcohol lead to sexual risk behavior? Findings from event-level research. *Annual Review of Sex Research, 11,* 125–157.

Weinhardt, L.S., Carey, M.P., Carey, K.B., Maisto, S.A., & Gordan, C.M. (2001). The relation of alcohol use to HIV-risk sexual behavior among adults with a severe and persistent mental illness. *Journal of Consulting & Clinical Psychology, 69,* 77–84.

Weiss, R.D. (2004). Adherence to pharmacotherapy in patients with alcohol and opioid dependence. *Addiction, 99,* 1382–1392.

Weitzman, E.R., Folkman, A., Lemieux-Folkman, K., & Wechsler, H. (2003). The relationship of alcohol outlet density to heavy and frequent drinking and drinking-related problems among college students at eight universities. *Health & Place, 9,* 1–6.

Welte, J.W., & Mirand, A.L. (1995). Drinking, problem drinking and life stresses in the elderly general population. *Journal of Studies on Alcohol, 56,* 67–73.

Whiteside, S.P., & Lynam, D.R. (2001). The five factor model and impulsivity: Using a structural model of personality to understand impulsivity. *Personality and Individual Differences, 30,* 669–689.

Whitfield, C.L., Thompson, G., Lamb, A., Spencer, V., Pfeifer, M., & Browning-Ferrando, M. (1978). Detoxification of

1,024 alcoholic patients without psychoactive drugs. *Journal of the American Medical Association, 239*, 1409–1410.

Wibberley, C., & Price, J. (2000). Patterns of psycho-stimulant drug use amongst "social/operational users:" Implications for services. *Addiction Research, 8*, 95–111.

Wienbeck, M., & Berges, W. (1985). Esophageal and gastric lesions in the alcoholic. In H.K. Seitz, & B. Kommerell (Eds.), *Alcohol-related diseases in gastroenterology* (pp. 361–375). New York: Springer-Verlag.

Wiers, R.W., & Stacy, A.W. (Eds.). (2006). *Handbook of implicit cognition and addiction*. Thousand Oaks: Sage.

Wiers, R.W., Schoenmakers, T., Houben, K., Thush, C., Fadardi, J.S., & Cox, W.M. (2008). Can problematic alcohol use be trained away? New behavioural treatments aimed at changing and moderating implicit cognitive processes in alcohol abuse. In C.R. Martin (Ed.), *Identification and treatment of alcohol dependency* (pp. 187–207). Keswick, UK: M&K Publishing.

Wilk, A.I., Jensen, N.M., & Havighurst, T.C. (1997). Meta-analysis of randomized control trials addressing brief interventions in heavy alcohol drinkers. *Journal of General Internal Medicine, 12*, 274–283.

Windle, M. (1997). The trading of sex for money or drugs, sexually transmitted diseases (STDs), and HIV-related risk behaviors among multisubstance using alcoholic inpatients. *Drug and Alcohol Dependence, 49*, 33–38.

Winick, C. (1962). Maturing out of narcotic addiction. *Bulletin on Narcotics, 14*, 1–7.

Witkiewitz, K., & Marlatt, G.A. (2004). Relapse prevention for alcohol and drug problems: That was Zen, this is tao. *American Psychologist, 59*, 224–235.

Witkiewitz, K., & Marlatt, G.A. (2007). Modeling the complexity of post-treatment drinking: It's a rocky road to relapse. *Clinical Psychology Review, 27*, 724–738.

Witkiewitz, K., & Marlatt, G.A. (2008). Why and how do substance abuse treatments work? Investigating mediated change. *Addiction, 103*, 649–650.

Witteman, J.C., Willett, W.C., Stampfer, M.J., Colditz, G.A., Kok, F.J., Sacks, F.M., et al. (1990). Relation of moderate alcohol consumption and risk of systemic hypertension in women. *American Journal of Cardiology, 65*, 633–637.

Wong, M.M., Brower, K.J., Fitzgerald, H.E., & Zucker, R.A. (2004). Sleep problems in early childhood and early onset of alcohol and other drug use in adolescence. *Alcoholism: Clinical and Experimental Research, 28*, 578–587.

Wood, M.D., Vinson, D.C., & Sher, K.J. (2001). Alcohol use and misuse. In A. Baum, T. Revenson, & J. Singer (Eds.), *Handbook of health psychology* (pp. 281–318). Hillsdale, NJ: Erlbaum.

World Health Organization (2004a). *Global status report: Alcohol policy*. Geneva, Switzerland: World Health Organization.

World Health Organization (2004b). *The global burden of disease: 2004 update*. Geneva, Switzerland: World Health Organization. Retrieved from http://www.who.int/healthinfo/global_burden_disease/2004 report update/en/index.html.

World Health Organization. (2009). *Global tuberculosis control 2009*. Geneva, Switzerland: World Health Organization. Retrieved from http://www.who.int/tb/publications/global_report/2009/pdf/full_report.pdf.

Wu, C.F., Sudhakar, M., Jaferi, G., Ahmed, S.S., & Regan, T.J. (1976). Preclinical cardiomyopathy in chronic alcoholics: A sex difference. *American Heart Journal, 91*, 281.

Yesavage, J.A., Dolhert, N., & Taylor, J.L. (1994). Flight simulator performance of younger and older aircraft pilots: Effects of age and alcohol. *Journal of the American Geriatric Society, 42*, 577–582.

Young, R.M., Lawford, B.R., Feeney, G.F., Ritchie, T., & Noble, E.P. (2004). Alcohol-related expectancies are associated with the D2 dopamine receptor and GABAA receptor beta3 subunit genes. *Psychiatry Research, 127*, 171–183.

Zador, P.L. (1991). Alcohol-related relative risk of fatal driver injuries in relation to driver age and sex. *Journal of Studies on Alcohol, 52*, 302–310.

Zakhari, S. (1991). Vulnerability to cardiac disease. *Recent Developments in Alcoholism, 9*, 225–260.

Zeigler, D.W., Wang, C.C., Yoast, R.A., Dickinson, B.D., McCaffree, M.A., Robinowitz, C.B., et al. (2005). The neurocognitive effects of alcohol on adolescents and college students. *Preventive Medicine, 40*, 23–32.

Zerhouni, E.A. (2006). Clinical research at a crossroads: The NIH roadmap. *Journal of Investigative Medicine, 54*, 171–173.

Zucker, R.A., Fitzgerald, H.E., & Moses, H.D. (1995). Emergence of alcohol problems and the several alcoholisms: A developmental perspective on etiologic theory and life course trajectory. In D. Cicchetti, & D.J. Cohen (Eds.), *Developmental psychopathology*, Vol. 2: *Risk, disorder, and adaptation. Wiley series on personality processes* (pp. 677–711). New York, NY: John Wiley & Sons.

# Obesity

Emily L. Van Walleghen, Betsy A. Steeves, *and* Hollie A. Raynor

## Abstract

The prevalence of obesity has increased in recent years and is now considered a global epidemic. Due to the serious health and economic impacts of weight gain, an understanding of the consequences and causes of obesity is necessary in order to develop effective weight management strategies and implement weight loss programs. The objective of this chapter is to review the epidemiology, implications, etiology, and treatment of adult obesity. Obesity prevalence and trends, the health and economic implications of obesity, environmental and genetic determinants of obesity, benefits of weight loss treatment and treatment goals, obesity assessment, lifestyle, behavioral, and medical obesity treatment, and weight loss maintenance will be discussed.

**Keywords:** Obesity, weight loss, weight loss maintenance, obesity consequences, obesity etiology, obesity assessment, obesity treatment

Obesity is a consequence of positive energy balance, in which energy intake through consumption of food and beverages exceeds all three components of energy expenditure (resting energy expenditure, physical activity, and diet-induced thermogenesis). This imbalance in energy is believed to be multifaceted, and a consequence of genetic, hormonal, behavioral, and societal factors. As obesity increases the risk of developing several health comorbidities (Guh et al., 2009), and as the prevalence of obesity has increased dramatically over the past 30 years in all age groups and race/ethnicities (Wang & Beydoun, 2007), treatment of obesity has become a top priority of several health agencies in the United States (U.S. Department of Health and Human Services, 2000). The objective of this chapter is to review the epidemiology of obesity, consequences of obesity, etiology of obesity, and treatment of obesity. Due to differences between pediatric and adult obesity, particularly in terms of the assessment, prevalence, and treatment of obesity, this chapter will focus on adult obesity.

## Background
### Defining Obesity

Although obesity is technically characterized by excess body fat, methods for direct measurement of fat mass to determine obesity status are problematic in that they are generally time and cost prohibitive in a clinical setting and for population-based research. Instead, degree of adiposity is typically estimated using weight and height measurements to calculate body mass index (BMI), defined as weight in kilograms over height in meters squared ($kg/m^2$). The BMI standards are based upon the assumption that differences in weight between individuals at a given height are due to differences in body fat. Body fat status can then be classified according to BMI as underweight ($<18.5$ $kg/m^2$), normal weight ($18.5$–$24.9$ $kg/m^2$), overweight ($25.0$–$29.9$ $kg/m^2$), or obese ($\geq30.0$ $kg/m^2$). Level of obesity may be further categorized as class I ($30.0$–$34.9$ $kg/m^2$), class II ($\geq35$–$39.9$ $kg/m^2$), or class III ($\geq40$ $kg/m^2$). These cutoff points are independent of sex and age, and are utilized as standards to classify obesity in adults both within the United States and internationally. A BMI of ≥25 kg/m² is an indicator of excessive fat that may negatively affect health, with the risk of health consequences increasing progressively at higher levels of BMI (National Heart, Lung, and Blood Institute [NHLBI], 1998).

## Epidemiology of Obesity

It is currently estimated that between 1.3 and 1.6 billion adults worldwide, approximately one-third of the adult population, are overweight (BMI ≥25.0 kg/m²), whereas 400 million are obese (BMI ≥30.0 kg/m²) (Kelly, Yang, Chen, Reynolds, & He, 2008). The highest rates of obesity are typically found in economically developed regions, yet increases in obesity prevalence have occurred in recent years in economically undeveloped regions where obesity rates have historically been very low, reflecting a shift from obesity as a problem only in high-income countries to a global epidemic. In many regions throughout the world, the rates of obesity have more than tripled since 1980, with even greater increases in urban areas (Misra & Khurana, 2008).

In the United States, two-thirds of adults are overweight or obese and nearly one-third are obese (Wang & Beydoun, 2007), which is a prevalence similar to other Western countries (Kelly et al., 2008). Although the rates of overweight and obesity are not different between men and women among the general population, some minority groups are differentially affected, with a higher overweight and obesity prevalence in Hispanic and African American women compared to white women. The combined prevalence of overweight and obesity is also higher in older adults, with more than 70% of Americans over the age of 60 years overweight or obese. Compared to other regions of the United States, states in the southeast have disproportionately higher obesity rates, and larger increases in obesity prevalence over the past 15 years. Following world trends, the prevalence of obesity in all adults in the United States has increased sharply over the past 30 years, more than doubling since the late 1970s (Wang & Beydoun, 2007).

## Implications of Obesity

The increasing prevalence of obesity has resulted in a concurrent increase in the incidence of obesity-related morbidity and mortality. Obesity is associated with increased risk of cardiovascular disease (CVD), type 2 diabetes mellitus (DM), multiple cancers, and numerous other chronic physiologic and psychiatric conditions (Guh et al., 2009).

Overweight and obesity are the second leading cause of preventable death in the United States, only behind tobacco use, and obesity is associated with increased overall mortality risk (Flegal, Graubard, Williamson, & Gail, 2007; Mokdad, Marks, Stroup, & Grerberding, 2004). Excess adiposity also increases the risk of psychiatric disorders, social stigmatization, and decreases health-related quality of life. Importantly, as the prevalence of obesity has risen, so have health care expenditures associated with the diagnosis and treatment costs of comorbid conditions and work-related productivity losses attributable to morbidity and mortality associated with obesity (Finkelstein, Ruhm, & Kosa, 2005).

### MORBIDITIES

*Cardiovascular Disease and Type 2 Diabetes Mellitus*
Obesity has long been implicated in the pathogenesis of CVD, due to the negative effects of excess fat mass on blood flow and cardiac function. In recent years, however, it has been recognized that, in addition to serving as a fat storage depot, adipose tissue, in particular visceral adipose tissue, has important metabolic functions and is in itself an endocrine organ. Adipocytes are now known to release nonesterified fatty acids, hormones, proinflammatory cytokines, and other bioactive substances implicated in the promotion of insulin resistance and an inflammatory state leading to the development of CVD and type 2 DM (Bray, Clearfield, Fintel, & Nelinson, 2009).

*Cardiovascular Disease.* Cardiovascular disease is currently the leading cause of mortality in the United States, accounting for more than one in three deaths (Thom et al., 2006). Overweight and obesity have been shown to increase the risk of developing CVD (Wilson, D'Agostino, Sullivan, Parise, & Kannel, 2002), and to increase the risk of mortality from CVD (Flegal et al., 2007). Although analyses of National Health and Nutrition Examination Survey (NHANES) data indicate that the incidence of CVD risk factors, including hypertension and hypercholesterolemia, have decreased among overweight and obese individuals in the past 40 years, interpretation of these findings is complicated by concurrent improvements in the diagnosis and pharmacological treatment of these conditions (Gregg et al., 2005).

There is currently conflicting evidence regarding the existence of an "obesity paradox," a protective effect of a higher BMI, for some CV conditions including hypertension, coronary heart disease

(CHD), and heart failure (HF) in patients with existing CVD (Lavie, Milani, & Ventura, 2009). It is clear that further research is warranted; however, the vast majority of evidence supports national recommendations for the general population to maintain a normal body weight in order to minimize CVD risk (Eckel, Kahn, Robertson, & Rizza, 2006).

*Type 2 Diabetes Mellitus.* It is currently estimated that 8% of the United States population, or more than 24 million individuals, have DM (predominantly type 2 DM), which is responsible for annual direct and indirect costs of $174 billion (American Diabetes Association, 2008). The prevalence of DM is increasing, mirroring the increase in prevalence of overweight and obesity, with an additional one million diagnoses each year (American Diabetes Association, 2008). Analyses have found that obese individuals disproportionately account for the increase in diabetes prevalence cases in the past 25 years, and more than 80% of additional prevalence cases had a BMI ≥30 kg/m$^2$ (Gregg, Cheng, Narayan, Thompson, & Williamson, 2007). Although DM is an independent risk factor for CVD, the link between type 2 DM and CVD is also affected by obesity status. In Framingham Heart Study participants with type 2 DM, obesity was found to increase lifetime risk of CVD to nearly 80% in women and 90% in men (Fox et al., 2008).

*Cancer*
Overweight and obesity are related to the incidence of many types of cancer and to cancer mortality. Results of two meta-analyses based on prospective studies found positive associations between BMI and risk of endometrial, postmenopausal breast, renal, colorectal, and pancreatic cancer in women and colorectal and renal cancer in men (Guh et al., 2009; Renehan, Tyson, Egger, Heller, & Zwahlen, 2008). Analyses based on nationally representative samples have shown that risk mortality from all cancers in both sexes, as well as breast, uterine, cervical, and ovarian cancer in women and stomach and prostate cancer in men, increase linearly with increasing BMI, and findings based on NHANES data have shown that a BMI ≥30 kg/m$^2$ is associated with excess mortality from cancers considered obesity-related (Calle, Rodriguez, Walker-Thurmond, & Thun, 2003; Flegal et al., 2007). Although the mechanisms by which excess adiposity increase specific-site cancer risk are not yet fully understood, in general, obesity-related dysregulation of endogenous hormones

including insulin, insulin-like growth factor I, sex steroids, and adiponectin have been implicated in the pathogenesis (Renehan et al., 2008).

*Other Physiologic Morbidities*
Among the many additional medical conditions and diseases that have been linked to excess adiposity, there is clear evidence that obesity increases the risk of osteoarthritis (OA), chronic back pain, asthma, and gallbladder disease. Increased weight-bearing joint load and inflammation exacerbated by excess adiposity have been implicated in the pathogenesis of OA, and there is a strong association between obesity and knee OA (Messier, 2008). Analyses of NHANES data have found that the prevalence of both chronic knee pain and back pain among older Americans increases with increasing BMI (Andersen, Crespo, Bartlett, Bathon, & Fontaine, 2003). Other studies have shown that, in working-age adults, the risk of an acute back injury transitioning into chronic back pain is higher in obese compared to normal weight adults, as is the risk of disability retirement because of chronic back pain (Fransen et al., 2002; Hagen, Tambs, & Bjerkedal, 2002).

The prevalence of asthma in the United States has increased in parallel with the prevalence of overweight and obesity, and it has been proposed that the etiology of asthma is related to an inflammatory state that may be induced by obesity (Beuther, Weiss, & Sutherland, 2006). Similarly, obesity-induced inflammation and hyperinsulinemia have also been identified as a possible mechanism linking excess adiposity and gallbladder disease (Tsai, 2009). Although risk of hospitalized gallbladder disease has been found to increase at higher levels of BMI, other large prospective studies have identified abdominal obesity as an important predictor of gallstone development in both men and women (Tsai, Leitzmann, Willett, & Giovannucci, 2004; Tsai, Leitzmann, Willett, & Giovannucci, 2006).

MORTALITY
Recent estimates indicate that the annual number of deaths attributable to overweight and obesity in the United States is as high as 365,000 (Mokdad et al., 2004). Cause-specific excess deaths from overweight and obesity include CVD, diabetes, cancer, and kidney disease (Flegal et al., 2007). Obesity is associated with an increase in overall mortality risk (Adams et al., 2006; Flegal et al., 2007) and analyses restricted to healthy nonsmokers have found that the risk of death is greater in both

overweight and obese individuals, with increasing risk at higher levels of BMI, compared to those with a normal BMI (Adams et al., 2006). Moreover, it has been projected that overall life expectancy in the United States, which has steadily increased for more than 100 years, may decline within the first half of this century due to the increase in the prevalence of obesity and the effect of obesity on lifespan (Olshansky et al., 2005).

## PSYCHOLOGICAL IMPLICATIONS
### Psychiatric Disorders
The association between obesity and depression and other psychiatric disorders in adults is generally modest, however, the strength of the relationship varies according to degree of adiposity and sex. In nationally representative samples across all BMI categories, the prevalence of psychiatric disorders increases with increasing adiposity, and class III obese individuals have approximately twice the odds of a mood, anxiety, or personality disorder in comparison to normal weight individuals (Petry, Barry, Pietrzak, & Wagner, 2008). Further analyses have shown that although both overweight and obese women are at increased risk of any mood or anxiety disorder, only obese men are at elevated risk for the same conditions (Danielle, Robert, & Nancy, 2008). The prevalence of psychiatric disorders also increases in both sexes with any obesity-related comorbidity, including type 2 DM, CVD, and asthma, but is higher in women compared to men with the same comorbid conditions (Zhao et al., 2009). The mechanisms underlying increased depression and anxiety disorder risk in women and at higher levels of adiposity have not been fully defined, but the evidence based on U.S. data has been corroborated by pooled cross-national data analyses, indicating that this finding is independent of the obesity and psychiatric disorder prevalence of the population studied (Scott et al., 2007).

### Social Stigma
Weight bias is widespread in the United States, with research documenting weight prejudice and discrimination in employment, health care, and educational settings, as well as in interpersonal relationships and in the media, and it is estimated that the prevalence of weight stigmatizing experiences among Americans has increased by 66% in the last decade (Puhl & Heuer, 2009). There is a dose-dependent relationship between BMI and the prevalence of perceived weight bias in men and women, with higher rates of reported weight bias in women compared to

men overall in nationally representative samples (Hatzenbuehler, Keyes, & Hasin, 2009). Importantly, weight stigmatizing experiences have a detrimental impact on psychological health. Over half of overweight and obese individuals who perceive weight discrimination also meet the diagnostic criteria for at least one mood, anxiety, or substance abuse disorder, and are nearly 2.5 times more likely to have more than three psychiatric disorders than individuals who do not experience weight discrimination (Hatzenbuehler et al., 2009).

### Health-related Quality of Life
Health-related quality of life (HRQL) decreases with increasing BMI, and obesity is associated with an increased risk of experiencing poor health due to activity limitations, poor physical health, and poor mental health (Hassan, Joshi, Madhavan, & Amonkar, 2003). It has also been shown in examinations of Medical Expenditure Panel Survey (MEPS) data that the inverse relationship between HRQL and BMI exists regardless of chronic disease status, and that although the relationship is evident at any BMI $\geq 25$ kg/m$^2$, the reduction in HRQL in individuals with class II and class III obesity is comparable in magnitude to that associated with chronic diseases, including diabetes and asthma (Jia & Lubetkin, 2005). In class III obese individuals seeking weight loss treatment, impaired HRQL has also been shown to increase risk for symptoms of depression, suggesting that, in at-risk populations, impaired HRQL may further augment mood disorder risk (Fabricatore, Wadden, Sarwer, & Faith, 2005).

## ECONOMIC COSTS
The overall economic burden of obesity is attributable to both the direct medical costs of obesity-related disease diagnosis and treatment and the indirect costs of lost productivity in the labor force due to obesity-related morbidity and mortality. Recent estimates indicate the direct cost of obesity, including inpatient, outpatient, and prescription drug spending, is as high as $147 billion per year, or nearly 10% of all medical spending in the United States (Finkelstein, Trogdon, Cohen, & Dietz, 2009). Obesity increases per capita medical spending by over 40%, with an overall cost difference between an obese and normal weight individual of more than $1,400 per year based on MEPS data (Finkelstein et al., 2009). Although it has been suggested that lifetime medical costs for obese individuals may be lower due to reduced life expectancy, the majority of United States studies have found either no cost

reduction or an increase in lifetime medical costs with obesity, with increasing costs at higher levels of BMI (Finkelstein et al., 2008).

The indirect costs of obesity are more difficult to quantify due to the number of different potential contributors to excess spending including lost productivity from absenteeism, presenteeism (decreased productivity while at work), disability, and mortality, in addition to workers' compensation for workplace injury (Trogdon, Finkelstein, Hylands, Dellea, & Kamal-Bahl, 2008). Increased absenteeism and resulting costs based on MEPS data have been shown to increase with increasing BMI, and estimates of the overall costs of obesity-related absenteeism in the United States total $4.3 billion per year (Cawley, Rizzo, & Haas, 2007). Although fewer studies have investigated other sources of indirect costs, the currently available literature indicates that obesity is also associated with higher expenditures from presenteeism, disability, mortality, and workers' compensation (Trogdon et al., 2008).

## Etiology of Obesity

At the most basic level, obesity is due to an energy surplus that is stored as body fat. Interindividual variation in propensity to phenotypic obesity as a consequence of dysregulated energy intake and/or expenditure relative to requirements for maintenance of energy balance and body weight is multifaceted and involves a complex interaction between genetic susceptibility and environmental influence.

### *Regulation of Energy Homeostasis*

Body energy homeostasis is regulated by a intricate and overlapping neural network that receives and integrates peripheral signals of energy state and generates output resulting in adaptations to energy intake or expenditure to achieve energy balance and weight stability. Information regarding energy state from the periphery is conveyed primarily to neurons in the arcuate nucleus (ARC) of the hypothalamus, where this input is integrated and projected to second-order neurons signaling other areas of the brain to generate appropriate behavioral, autonomic, and endocrine adaptive responses necessary for energy homeostasis maintenance (Lenard & Berthoud, 2008).

Internal neural and hormonal signals of short- and long-term energy availability and stores arise from the chemosensory and gastrointestinal system, pancreas, liver, muscle, and adipose tissue, as well as from circulating metabolites, including glucose, free fatty acids, and amino acids, which can by sensed directly by the ARC of the hypothalamus (Lenard & Berthoud, 2008). Information regarding short-term situational energy needs affecting energy intake during individual meals mainly originates from hormones and peptides secreted from the gastrointestinal (GI) tract. Circulating levels of the majority of these hormones, such as cholecystokinin, glucagon-like peptide-1, and peptide YY, rise in response to a meal and are considered satiation signals influencing meal termination. In contrast, ghrelin is the only GI hormone known to stimulate food intake, with circulating levels falling upon meal initiation (Woods & D'Alessio, 2008).

Following absorption of meals, nutrients are either used immediately for fuel or stored for later use. Signals of energy stores are conveyed via the adiposity hormones insulin and leptin to regulate long-term energy balance and body fat maintenance. Basal circulating levels of insulin, secreted from pancreatic β cells, and leptin, secreted from adipocytes, are proportional to body fat, such that decreases in these hormones, reflecting a reduction in body fat stores, result in a compensatory increase in energy intake and reduction in energy expenditure to produce weight gain, whereas increases in circulating levels have an opposite effect. Although this mechanism is protective against excessive fat loss, the high circulating levels of insulin and leptin characteristic of obesity do not result in reductions in food intake or body weight, indicative of hypothalamic resistance to these hormones at higher levels of adiposity (Woods & D'Alessio, 2008).

In addition to the regulation of energy balance in response to metabolic requirements, food intake and activity expenditure can also be driven by mechanisms related to the reward system and the palatability or pleasure associated with specific food or activity stimuli originating in extra-hypothalamic areas of the brain. Because reward-based eating and behavior is dependent on environmental exposure to stimuli, it has been suggested that relatively weak homeostatic protection against weight gain is overridden by the reward system in the context of the modern environment (Zheng, Lenard, Shin, & Berthoud, 2009). Although interindividual differences in reward neurophysiology may predispose some individuals to increased food intake and obesity, it has also been demonstrated that signals influencing energy homeostasis including leptin, insulin, and peptide YY also affect areas of the brain regulating reward-driven behavior, emphasizing the importance of both internal metabolic signals and external environmental cues in body weight regulation (Batterham et al., 2007; Figlewicz & Benoit, 2009).

## Genetic and Epigenetic Determinants of Obesity

### GENETICS AND OBESITY

The genetic contribution to the development of obesity has been well documented, with heritability estimates for BMI ranging from 16% to 85% based on family, twin, and adoption studies (Yang, Kelly, & He, 2007). Although underlying genetic factors may confer protection against obesity to some individuals and increase susceptibility to weight gain in others, the genes responsible for these differences have largely not yet been identified. Although there are several known rare monogenic forms of human obesity resulting from gene mutations, in addition to other single-gene defects in homeostatic pathways (Yang et al., 2007), common human obesity is polygenic and cannot be explained by single gene mutations.

The first obesity susceptibility gene was the fat mass and obesity–associated gene (*FTO*), and subsequent studies have replicated the association between common *FTO* variants and BMI (Loos & Bouchard, 2008). Individuals inheriting a gene variant from each parent (approximately 16% of individuals of European decent) have a 1.67-fold higher risk of obesity and a 0.40–0.66 kg/m$^2$ increase in BMI compared to individuals without a risk variant, but the clinical relevance of *FTO* in predicting obesity is minimal, as variation in *FTO* accounts for only 1%–1.3% of BMI heritability (Loos & Bouchard, 2008).

### EPIGENETICS AND OBESITY

Although genetic variants contribute to explaining individual differences in obesity risk, epigenetic mechanisms affecting gene expression without altering the underlying DNA sequence may also be important determinants of body weight (Stoger, 2008). Defects in imprinted genes, normally expressed from only one parent as a result of epigenetic genomic modifications during gametogenesis, are known causes of some syndromic forms of obesity, such as Prader-Willi, but it has been suggested that dysregulation of genomic imprinting also affects body weight in nonsyndromic common forms of obesity (Stoger, 2008). In addition to genomic imprinting of gametes, however, nonimprinted genes can undergo epigenetic modifications throughout the lifespan, and those occurring in genes involved in regulating energy homeostasis and adipogenesis

during critical periods of early development, in response to specific environmental exposures, may influence future obesity risk (Campión, Milagro, & Martínez, 2009). Epidemiological studies have linked both maternal under- and overnutrition during embryogenesis to future obesity risk in offspring (Gillman et al., 2008; Roseboom, de Rooij, & Painter, 2006), and results of animal studies indicate that this association may be due to neonatal epigenetic changes induced by maternal diet (Campión et al., 2009). Human studies have found alterations in adipose tissue epigenetic profile in response to a hypocaloric weight loss diet in adults, as well as differences prior to treatment in those with greater body fat loss compared to those losing less body fat with diet, suggesting that epigenetic profiling may be useful in predicting individual treatment outcomes (Bouchard et al., 2009; Campión et al., 2009).

## Environmental Determinants of Obesity

Despite the importance of genetic variation in determination of obesity risk, evidence of epigenetic genomic modification in response to environmental exposures highlight the significance of the interaction between genes and environment in determining phenotype. The environment has the capacity to influence the development of obesity apart from gene expression, however, and it has been shown by differentiating between pure environmental effects and environmental effects on epigenetic factors in heritability estimates that both genetic components and common environmental factors, such as dietary intake and physical activity, predict BMI (Segal, Feng, McGuire, Allison, & Miller, 2008). Although these findings are indicative of the critical role the environment plays in determining obesity outcomes beyond inherent risk at the individual level, recent environmental changes at the population level—coinciding with dramatic increases in obesity prevalence since the early 1980s—have been implicated as a causative factor in the current obesity epidemic (J.O. Hill & Peters, 1998). Consideration of obesogenic environmental pressures on dietary and activity behaviors at both the individual and population level is therefore imperative for effective obesity prevention and treatment.

### FOOD ENVIRONMENTS, DIETARY INTAKE, AND OBESITY

Per capita food availability in the United States has risen dramatically over the past 30 years, and estimates of energy intake based on this increase indicate that adult daily energy intake is approximately 500 calories per day greater today than in the 1970s (Swinburn, Sacks, & Ravussin, 2009). In addition to the effect of overall food availability on increased intake, however, a number of other changes in the food environment may contribute to passive overconsumption and weight gain, such as increases in the variety of different foods available for consumption, with nearly 20,000 new food and beverage products introduced per year (Martinez, 2007). Portion sizes of fast foods, as well as of foods served at home and in restaurants, have also increased in the United States, as have consumption of energy-dense foods (foods containing more energy per gram) and sweetened beverages, such as sodas and punches (Nielsen & Popkin, 2003). The NHANES data indicate that higher energy intake is positively related to eating larger portion sizes and foods higher in energy density, and to drinking more sweetened beverages (Briefel & Johnson, 2004).

Experimental research has shown that an increase in dietary variety achieved by increasing the number of sensorially distinct foods within a meal results in overconsumption outside of conscious awareness, presumably by inhibiting sensory-specific satiety (H.A. Raynor & Epstein, 2001). Limiting dietary variety during obesity treatment has been shown to increase long-term sensory-specific satiety, and limiting the variety of high-fat foods has been associated with improvements in weight loss (H.A. Raynor, Jeffery, Tate, & Wing, 2004; H.A. Raynor, Niemeier, & Wing, 2006). Further, observational studies have shown that individuals successful at maintaining weight loss habitually consume a diet lower in variety within all food groups (H.A. Raynor, Wing, Jeffery, Phelan, & Hill, 2005), suggesting that decreasing the number of different types of foods available in the food environment may be an effective strategy for reversing current trends in obesity prevalence.

Basic eating research has also demonstrated that larger portion sizes of food increase energy intake, as a consequence of passive overconsumption outside of conscious awareness (Rolls, Morris, & Roe, 2002). Similarly, laboratory-based studies have found consumption of foods higher in energy density also contributes to passive overconsumption and increases energy intake compared to foods lower in energy density, as intake appears to be more influenced by the total weight of food consumed rather than by energy content (Rolls, 2009). Other experimental studies have shown that energy intake from sweetened beverages is not compensated for by a decrease in food intake, and increased consumption of both energy-dense foods and sweetened beverages has been associated with obesity in population-based studies (Malik, Schulze, & Hu, 2006; Rolls, 2009). Thus, changes in the food supply resulting in increased availability of larger portions of food, foods of higher energy density, and sweetened beverages may be important contributors to the obesity epidemic.

Beyond the types and amounts of foods available in the environment for consumption, individual dietary choices are influenced by food advertising, marketing, and pricing. The perceived value of large portions of energy-dense foods and sweetened beverages may override nutritional concerns regarding their consumption, and there is evidence that sales promotions have the capacity to alter food consumption patterns (French, 2003). Therefore, removing price incentives for these foods may limit their purchase and serve as an effective strategy for shifting food consumption patterns and decreasing energy intake (French, 2003).

## BUILT ENVIRONMENTS AND OBESITY

Broadly defined, built environments are those that are human-modified, encompassing urban design, land use, and transportation systems (Papas et al., 2007). The built environment is believed to influence both energy intake and expenditure. For intake, the built environment influences food availability and accessibility. For instance, frequency of fast food consumption, which is positively associated with energy intake (Briefel & Johnson, 2004), has risen over the past three decades, and currently one in four adults consumes fast food on any given day (Bowman & Vinyard, 2004). Importantly, this increase in consumption of fast food parallels the increase in the number of fast food outlets in the United States, which has grown from 30,000 to more than 230,000 since 1970 (Rosenheck, 2008). It has been shown that residents in areas with a higher density of fast food restaurants have a higher BMI and increased risk for obesity (Mehta & Chang, 2008). An association also exists between a reduction in access to supermarkets carrying fresh fruits and vegetables and other healthy food choices, which has occurred in urban areas since the conception of the obesity epidemic, and increased risk for obesity (Larson, Story, & Nelson, 2009).

In addition to its impact on energy intake, the built environment also influences energy expenditure, and aspects of the built environment that limit access to opportunities to engage in physical activity, such as reduced proximity to recreational facilities, higher residential density, and lower land-use mix and street connectivity, have all been associated with either increased BMI or obesity risk (Papas et al., 2007). Although less than half of American adults report meeting the minimum level of physical activity recommended to improve health status, meta-analysis of international environmental physical activity correlates has shown that neighborhood built environment variables, including low-cost recreational facilities, nearby shops, transit stops, bicycle facilities, and sidewalks on most streets, are related to meeting physical activity guidelines (Sallis et al., 2009). The same analysis showed that neighborhoods with the most attributes conducive to physical activity have 100% higher rates of meeting the recommended level of physical activity compared with those with the least attributes. Because economically disadvantaged neighborhoods with reduced opportunities for physical activity, as well as decreased access to healthy foods, are associated with higher obesity rates, improving the built environment may be an effective strategy for correcting obesity-related health disparities.

Besides the direct influence of the built environment on physical activity energy expenditure (PAEE), the built environment may also impact PAEE indirectly by affecting sedentary leisure-time behaviors such as television watching. Television viewing time has been found to be an independent risk factor for obesity in adults (Williams, Raynor, & Ciccolo, 2008), and it has been shown that those living in more walkable neighborhoods report both increased walking for transportation and decreased television viewing time (Sugiyama, Salmon, Dunstan, Bauman, & Owen, 2007). Other data indicate that the relationship between physical activity and BMI varies across levels of sedentary behavior, as BMI differences according to physical activity level have been demonstrated in individuals reporting low television viewing time, but not in those reporting high television viewing time (Dunton, Berrigan, Ballard-Barbash, Graubard, & Atienza, 2009). These results suggest that targeting aspects of the built environment affecting both physical activity and television viewing may be necessary to maximize the effectiveness of physical activity in weight management.

### Additional Potential Obesity Determinants

Although inherent energy regulatory systems conferring relatively weak protection against excess weight gain, combined with recent environmental changes supporting increased energy intake and reduced energy expenditure, may explain the origin of the obesity epidemic, the available data are not causal, leading some to suggest that additional factors that have undergone changes in the past 30 years (in addition to those related to the food environment and built environment) may also contribute (Keith et al., 2006). In terms of individual obesity risk, a growing body of evidence demonstrates a relationship between sleep duration and body weight, and although additional experimental research is needed, a meta-analysis of cross-sectional studies in adults found a pooled odds ratio of 1.55 for short sleep duration and obesity (Cappuccio et al., 2008). It has also been shown that other factors indirectly related to energy intake and expenditure, such as calcium intake and eating behavior characterized by high disinhibition and restraint, also predict obesity, indicating that future research examining the role of other potential contributors to the pathogenesis of obesity is warranted (Chaput et al., 2009).

## Treatment of Obesity
### Obesity Treatment Benefits

Although greater weight loss is associated with larger decreases in health risk, even modest weight loss in overweight and obese individuals is beneficial for risk factor reduction (NHLBI, 1998). Weight loss of only 5%–10% in individuals with CVD risk factors, including type 2 DM, hypertension, and dyslipidemia, has been associated with improvements in glycemic control, systolic and diastolic blood pressure, and plasma lipid profile (Van Gaal, Mertens, & Ballaux, 2005). For example, intensive weight loss programs resulting in a 10% reduction in body weight in obese individuals with type 2 DM has been shown to decrease fasting blood glucose by more than 25% (Anderson, Kendall, & Jenkins, 2003). In a meta-analysis of randomized controlled trials (RCTs) investigating the effects of weight reduction on blood pressure, it was found that for each kilogram of weight loss, both systolic and diastolic blood pressure decrease by approximately 1 mm Hg (Neter, Stam, Kok, Grobbee, & Geleijnse, 2003), while systematic review of the long-term effects of weight loss on lipid profile determined that a 10 kg weight loss in overweight and obese individuals can be expected to produce a 5% reduction in total cholesterol (Poobalan et al., 2004). Therefore, based on the benefits of modest weight loss in improving indicators of cardiometabolic disease, weight reduction is currently recommended by the American Diabetes Association, American Heart Association, and other expert groups as a component of lifestyle treatment for type 2 DM, hypertension, and dyslipidemia (NHLBI, 1998).

Evidence indicates that, in addition to treatment of CVD risk factors, weight loss may delay or prevent type 2 DM and hypertension in overweight and obese individuals without established disease. Results of the Diabetes Prevention Program (DPP), a United States multisite RCT, found that in individuals with impaired glucose tolerance, achieving 7% weight loss and maintaining 5% weight loss over 3 years reduced the incidence of diabetes by 58%, which was better than that achieved with medication (metformin) (Knowler et al., 2002). Results of the DPP are comparable to results of the Finnish Diabetes Prevention Study, in which a lifestyle intervention producing a mean weight loss of 4.2 kg reduced the risk of developing diabetes after 4 years by 58% (Tuomilehto et al., 2001). During follow-up after DPP, diabetes incidence over 10 years remained reduced by 34%, which is in agreement with follow-up results from the Finnish Diabetes Prevention Study. Results from both studies suggest that the benefits of weight loss in the prevention or delay of type 2 DM persist over the long term (Diabetes Prevention Program Research Group, 2009; Lindström et al., 2006).

The importance of weight loss in the prevention of hypertension has also been demonstrated. In another U.S. multicenter RCT, pre-hypertensive men and women who lost and maintained a weight loss of 4.5 kg decreased their systolic and diastolic blood pressure by 5 and 7 mm Hg, respectively, and had a lower relative risk of developing hypertension over 3 years (Stevens et al., 2001).

Additionally, studies have shown that weight loss may reduce the risk or symptoms of other obesity-related diseases, decrease risk of death, and improve health-related quality of life. For instance, weight loss is associated with a decreased risk of obesity-related cancer in postmenopausal women, and studies support weight loss for reducing postmenopausal breast cancer risk, with limited evidence for other cancer sites in men and women (Wolin & Colditz, 2008). It has also been suggested that weight loss could prevent a substantial number of knee and hip OA cases, and weight reduction has been shown to reduce pain and improve physical function in individuals with established knee OA (Messier, 2008). Finally, although not all studies have found benefits from weight reduction, the literature generally supports that weight loss has a positive impact on HRQL, with improvements in both physical and mental dimensions of health (Fontaine & Barofsky, 2001).

Although the relationship between mortality and voluntary weight loss is less clear than that between morbidity and voluntary weight loss, it has been proposed that the conflicting results are a consequence of inappropriate differentiation between intentional and unintentional weight loss (Coffey et al., 2005). Nonetheless, an association between intentional weight loss and reduction in mortality has been demonstrated in women and in individuals with type 2 DM, with intentional weight loss associated with a 25% decrease in total mortality (Poobalan et al., 2007; Williamson et al., 2000).

### Obesity Treatment Goals

Evidence-based obesity treatment guidelines set forth by the National Institutes of Health (NIH) recommend that weight loss treatment follow a two-step process, consisting of obesity assessment and management, with assessment used to inform individualized weight loss goals and treatment strategies based on risk status (NHLBI, 1998). General obesity treatment goals include weight loss, long-term weight loss maintenance, and prevention of further weight gain. An initial weight loss goal of 10% of body weight is advised, is achievable within a 6-month time frame, and can be maintained over the long-term. Achieving 10% weight loss over 6 months typically requires 0.5–1 lb of weight loss per week for overweight and class I obese individuals, and 1–2 lb per week for individuals with class II or III obesity. After 6 months of treatment, weight loss goals and rate of weight loss should be reassessed to determine strategies for continued weight loss or long-term weight loss maintenance (NHLBI, 1998). It is also important to determine each individual's own weight loss expectations and goals, which are typically higher than 10% and not achieved with weight loss treatment, as unrealistic weight loss expectations and goals may reduce treatment satisfaction, although effects on actual weight loss and weight loss maintenance are unclear (Gorin et al., 2007).

Approaches to weight loss may include dietary therapy, physical activity, behavior therapy, combined therapy, pharmacotherapy, or surgery. The appropriateness of these therapies is dependent upon initial BMI and the presence of comorbidities determined by obesity assessment (NHLBI, 1998). Combined therapy, consisting of dietary therapy, physical activity, and behavior therapy, has been

**Table 29.1 Weight loss therapy selection guidelines**

| Treatment | Body Mass Index (BMI) Category (kg/m²) | | | | |
|---|---|---|---|---|---|
| | 25.0–26.9 | 27.0–29.9 | 30.0–34.9 | 35.0–39.9 | ≥40.0 |
| Combined therapy | With comorbidities | With comorbidities | + | + | + |
| Pharmacotherapy | | With comorbidities | + | + | + |
| Surgery | | | | With comorbidities | + |

- Prevention of weight gain with lifestyle therapy is indicated in any patient with a BMI of ≥25.0 kg/m², even without comorbidities, whereas weight loss is not necessarily recommended for those with a BMI of 25.0–29.9 kg/m² or a high waist circumference, unless they have two or more comorbidities.
- Combined therapy, with a low-calorie diet (LCD), increased physical activity, and behavior therapy, provides the most successful intervention for weight loss and weight maintenance.
- Consider pharmacotherapy only if an individual has not lost 1 pound per week after 6 months of combined lifestyle therapy.

The + represents the use of indicated treatment regardless of comorbidities.
Adapted from National Heart, Lung, and Blood Institute (NHLBI) and the North American Association for the Study of Obesity (NAASO). (2000). *The practical guide: identification, evaluation, and treatment of overweight and obesity in adults*. Bethesda, MD: National Institutes of Health, Bethesda.

shown to be more effective for weight loss than any of these three treatments alone, and is recommended as a first line of treatment for weight reduction that can be continued indefinitely for weight maintenance. Pharmacotherapy should be used only in conjunction with combined therapy, and surgery is reserved for high-risk, clinically severely obese individuals when other treatment methods have failed (Table 29.1). Although treatment selection will be informed by individual obesity risk based on medical assessment, consideration of individual needs and preferences is also important (NHLBI, 1998).

## Obesity Assessment

Assessment begins with the identification and classification of degree of excess adiposity, allowing for the evaluation of relative associated health risk. Medical, diet and lifestyle, and behavioral assessments are also important to determine absolute risk and etiology of weight gain and to guide individualized treatment goals.

### OBESITY MEASUREMENT

Body mass index is the most widely accepted method for assessing body fat, and BMI tables are a simple reference requiring no calculation that can be used to determine BMI from height and weight measurements (Figure 29.1). In the general adult population, BMI is highly correlated with body fat and is an accurate indicator of excess adiposity, with correlation coefficients between BMI and percent body fat among NHANES subjects between 0.72 and 0.84 for women and 0.72 and 0.79 for men, depending on age group (Flegal et al., 2009). Because assessment of body fat according to BMI is based on the assumption that interindividual variation in weight at a given height is due to body fat rather than lean mass, under circumstances where lean body mass is disproportionate, BMI may incorrectly estimate adiposity. Although the correlation between BMI and body fat generally weakens with age, the majority of studies have found correlations in older adults remain strong, and the clinical utility BMI for measuring obesity in older individuals is not affected (McTigue, Hess, & Ziouras, 2006). Other studies have shown that the relationship between BMI and adiposity is affected by ethnicity, and is particularly evident in Asians, as individuals in this population typically have a lower proportion of lean body mass and thus a higher actual body fat percentage than indicated by BMI measurements. (Deurenberg, Deurenberg-Yap, & Guricci, 2002).

In addition to BMI, there are many additional less commonly used methods for measuring body fat. Although waist circumference measurements are typically used as a surrogate for abdominal adiposity to identify cardiometabolic risk, waist circumference is also correlated with total body fat percentage, and it has been shown that the strength of the relationship is similar to that of BMI and percent body fat (Flegal & Graubard, 2009). Measurements of skinfold thickness have been widely used for body fat assessment, but may not be valid for predicting body fat in obese individuals (Brodie, Moscrip, & Hutcheon, 1998). More accurate methods include air displacement plethysmography, dual-energy absorptiometry, and other imaging techniques. Although each of these methods has its own set of advantages and disadvantages, they are largely considered impractical for use in a clinical setting and

| BMI | 19 | 20 | 21 | 22 | 23 | 24 | 25 | 26 | 27 | 28 | 29 | 30 | 31 | 32 | 33 | 34 | 35 | 36 | 37 | 38 | 39 | 40 | 41 | 42 | 43 | 44 | 45 | 46 | 47 | 48 | 49 | 50 | 51 | 52 | 53 | 54 |
|---|---|---|---|---|---|---|---|---|---|---|---|---|---|---|---|---|---|---|---|---|---|---|---|---|---|---|---|---|---|---|---|---|---|---|---|---|
| Height (inches) | | | | | | | | | | | | | | | | | Body Weight (pounds) | | | | | | | | | | | | | | | | | | | |
| 58 | 91 | 96 | 100 | 105 | 110 | 115 | 119 | 124 | 129 | 134 | 138 | 143 | 148 | 153 | 158 | 162 | 167 | 172 | 177 | 181 | 186 | 191 | 196 | 201 | 205 | 210 | 215 | 220 | 224 | 229 | 234 | 239 | 244 | 248 | 253 | 258 |
| 59 | 94 | 99 | 104 | 109 | 114 | 119 | 124 | 128 | 133 | 138 | 143 | 148 | 153 | 158 | 163 | 168 | 173 | 178 | 183 | 188 | 193 | 198 | 203 | 208 | 212 | 217 | 222 | 227 | 232 | 237 | 242 | 247 | 252 | 257 | 262 | 267 |
| 60 | 97 | 102 | 107 | 112 | 118 | 123 | 128 | 133 | 138 | 143 | 148 | 153 | 158 | 163 | 168 | 174 | 179 | 184 | 189 | 194 | 199 | 204 | 209 | 215 | 220 | 225 | 230 | 235 | 240 | 245 | 250 | 255 | 261 | 266 | 271 | 276 |
| 61 | 100 | 106 | 111 | 116 | 122 | 127 | 132 | 137 | 143 | 148 | 153 | 158 | 164 | 169 | 174 | 180 | 185 | 190 | 195 | 201 | 206 | 211 | 217 | 222 | 227 | 232 | 238 | 243 | 248 | 254 | 259 | 264 | 269 | 275 | 280 | 285 |
| 62 | 104 | 109 | 115 | 120 | 126 | 131 | 136 | 142 | 147 | 153 | 158 | 164 | 169 | 175 | 180 | 186 | 191 | 196 | 202 | 207 | 213 | 218 | 224 | 229 | 235 | 240 | 246 | 251 | 256 | 262 | 267 | 273 | 278 | 284 | 289 | 295 |
| 63 | 107 | 113 | 118 | 124 | 130 | 135 | 141 | 146 | 152 | 158 | 163 | 169 | 175 | 180 | 186 | 191 | 197 | 203 | 208 | 214 | 220 | 225 | 231 | 237 | 242 | 248 | 254 | 259 | 265 | 270 | 278 | 282 | 287 | 293 | 299 | 304 |
| 64 | 110 | 116 | 122 | 128 | 134 | 140 | 145 | 151 | 157 | 163 | 169 | 174 | 180 | 186 | 192 | 197 | 204 | 209 | 215 | 221 | 227 | 232 | 238 | 244 | 250 | 256 | 262 | 267 | 273 | 279 | 285 | 291 | 296 | 302 | 308 | 314 |
| 65 | 114 | 120 | 126 | 132 | 138 | 144 | 150 | 156 | 162 | 168 | 174 | 180 | 186 | 192 | 198 | 204 | 210 | 216 | 222 | 228 | 234 | 240 | 246 | 252 | 258 | 264 | 270 | 276 | 282 | 288 | 294 | 300 | 306 | 312 | 318 | 324 |
| 66 | 118 | 124 | 130 | 136 | 142 | 148 | 155 | 161 | 167 | 173 | 179 | 186 | 192 | 198 | 204 | 210 | 216 | 223 | 229 | 235 | 241 | 247 | 253 | 260 | 266 | 272 | 278 | 284 | 291 | 297 | 303 | 309 | 315 | 322 | 328 | 334 |
| 67 | 121 | 127 | 134 | 140 | 146 | 153 | 159 | 166 | 172 | 178 | 185 | 191 | 198 | 204 | 211 | 217 | 223 | 230 | 236 | 242 | 249 | 255 | 261 | 268 | 274 | 280 | 287 | 293 | 299 | 306 | 312 | 319 | 325 | 331 | 338 | 344 |
| 68 | 125 | 131 | 138 | 144 | 151 | 158 | 164 | 171 | 177 | 184 | 190 | 197 | 203 | 210 | 216 | 223 | 230 | 236 | 243 | 249 | 256 | 262 | 269 | 276 | 282 | 289 | 295 | 302 | 308 | 315 | 322 | 328 | 335 | 341 | 348 | 354 |
| 69 | 128 | 135 | 142 | 149 | 155 | 162 | 169 | 176 | 182 | 189 | 196 | 203 | 209 | 216 | 223 | 230 | 236 | 243 | 250 | 257 | 263 | 270 | 277 | 284 | 291 | 297 | 304 | 311 | 318 | 324 | 331 | 338 | 345 | 351 | 358 | 365 |
| 70 | 132 | 139 | 146 | 153 | 160 | 167 | 174 | 181 | 188 | 195 | 202 | 209 | 216 | 222 | 229 | 236 | 243 | 250 | 257 | 264 | 271 | 278 | 285 | 292 | 299 | 306 | 313 | 320 | 327 | 334 | 341 | 348 | 355 | 362 | 369 | 376 |
| 71 | 136 | 143 | 150 | 157 | 165 | 172 | 179 | 186 | 193 | 200 | 208 | 215 | 222 | 229 | 236 | 243 | 250 | 257 | 265 | 272 | 279 | 286 | 293 | 301 | 308 | 315 | 322 | 329 | 338 | 343 | 351 | 358 | 365 | 372 | 379 | 386 |
| 72 | 140 | 147 | 154 | 162 | 169 | 177 | 184 | 191 | 199 | 206 | 213 | 221 | 228 | 235 | 242 | 250 | 258 | 265 | 272 | 279 | 287 | 294 | 302 | 309 | 316 | 324 | 331 | 338 | 346 | 353 | 361 | 368 | 375 | 383 | 390 | 397 |
| 73 | 144 | 151 | 159 | 166 | 174 | 182 | 189 | 197 | 204 | 212 | 219 | 227 | 235 | 242 | 250 | 257 | 265 | 272 | 280 | 288 | 295 | 302 | 310 | 318 | 325 | 333 | 340 | 348 | 355 | 363 | 371 | 378 | 386 | 393 | 401 | 408 |
| 74 | 148 | 155 | 163 | 171 | 179 | 186 | 194 | 202 | 210 | 218 | 225 | 233 | 241 | 249 | 256 | 264 | 272 | 280 | 287 | 295 | 303 | 311 | 319 | 326 | 334 | 342 | 350 | 358 | 365 | 373 | 381 | 389 | 396 | 404 | 412 | 420 |
| 75 | 152 | 160 | 168 | 176 | 184 | 192 | 200 | 208 | 216 | 224 | 232 | 240 | 248 | 256 | 264 | 272 | 279 | 287 | 295 | 303 | 311 | 319 | 327 | 335 | 343 | 351 | 359 | 367 | 375 | 383 | 391 | 399 | 407 | 415 | 423 | 431 |
| 76 | 156 | 164 | 172 | 180 | 189 | 197 | 205 | 213 | 221 | 230 | 238 | 246 | 254 | 263 | 271 | 279 | 287 | 295 | 304 | 312 | 320 | 328 | 336 | 344 | 353 | 361 | 369 | 377 | 385 | 394 | 402 | 410 | 418 | 426 | 435 | 443 |

**Figure 29.1.** Body mass index (BMI) table.

**Table 29.2  Classification of adults by body mass index (BMI)**

| Classification | BMI (kg/m²) | Risk of Comorbidities |
|---|---|---|
| Underweight | <18.5 | Low (but increased risk of other clinical problems) |
| Normal range | 18.5–24.9 | Average |
| Overweight | 25.0–29.9 | Increased |
| Obesity | | |
|   Class I | 30–34.9 | Moderate |
|   Class II | 35.0–39.9 | Severe |
|   Class III | ≥40.0 | Very severe |

Adapted from WHO. (1998). *Obesity: preventing and managing the global epidemic.* Geneva: World Health Organization.

are infrequently used. Bioelectrical impedance is a less costly alternative that is becoming more widely available, but the validity of this method across different populations has not been established, and it may underestimate body fat in obese individuals (Dehghan & Merchant, 2008).

## OBESITY CLASSIFICATION AND RELATIVE HEALTH RISK

The BMI cutoff values for classifying overweight and obesity in adults established by the NIH and WHO are based on the relationship between BMI and the risk of morbidity and mortality determined from observational and epidemiological studies (NHLBI, 1998). The cutoff values are arbitrary, given that the increase in risk with increase in BMI is continuous; however, it has been shown that BMI-defined obesity has a high specificity for identifying excess adiposity based on percent body fat (Romero-Corral et al., 2008), and the classifications are recommended for the estimation of relative risk compared to normal weight (Table 29.2) (NHLBI, 1998).

Due to the association between abdominal adiposity and cardiometabolic risk, NIH guidelines indicate that waist circumference should be measured as a surrogate of body fat distribution to evaluate relative risk in individuals with BMI measurements between 25.0 and 34.9 kg/m² (NHLBI, 1998). Increased relative risk according to waist circumference is defined by a measurement around the abdomen at the level of the iliac crest of greater than 102 cm (40 inches) in men and greater than 88 cm (35 inches) in women. It has been shown that elevated waist circumference is an independent predictor of CVD risk and that normal weight, overweight, and class I obese individuals with waist circumference measurements exceeding the established cutoffs have a higher risk of diabetes, hypertension, and dyslipidemia compared with those in the same BMI category with normal waist circumference measurements (Janssen, Katzmarzyk, & Ross, 2002). Because nearly all individuals with a BMI ≥35.0 kg/m² will be classified as high risk according to waist circumference, measurement of waist circumference in individuals with class II and class III obesity does not add to the predictive power of BMI in estimating health risk (NHLBI, 1998). Classification of overweight and obesity-associated relative disease risk based on both BMI and waist circumference is shown in Table 29.3.

## MEDICAL ASSESSMENT

Following establishment of relative risk from BMI and waist circumference measurements, medical assessment is necessary to evaluate absolute risk due to the presence of obesity-associated disease. Individuals with a high level of relative risk, based on anthropometric measurements, and high absolute risk, as a consequence comorbid conditions, may require more aggressive obesity treatment to prevent mortality compared with individuals with the same relative risk but lower absolute risk. Medical assessment can also help to determine factors that may contribute to the development of obesity, including medication use and underlying endocrine or genetic disorders.

**Table 29.3  Classification of adults by body mass index (BMI) and waist circumference**

| Classification | BMI (kg/m²) | Waist Circumference Normal | Waist Circumference High |
|---|---|---|---|
| Underweight | <18.5 | – | – |
| Normal range | 18.5–24.9 | – | – |
| Overweight | 25.0–29.9 | Increased | High |
| Obesity | | | |
|   Class I | 30–34.9 | High | Very high |
|   Class II | 35.0–39.9 | Very high | Very high |
|   Class III | ≥40.0 | Extremely high | Extremely high |

Adapted from NHLBI. (1998). Clinical guidelines on the identification, evaluation, and treatment of overweight and obesity in adults: The evidence report. *Obesity Research 6*, 51S–210S.

### Absolute Risk Assessment

National Institutes of Health guidelines state that absolute risk assessment is indicated for individuals with a BMI ≥25 kg/m². High absolute risk requiring intensive obesity treatment and disease management is evidenced by an elevated BMI combined with the presence or established history of CHD, other atherosclerotic disease, type 2 DM, or sleep apnea (NHLBI, 1998). Other CVD risk factors that increase absolute risk include cigarette smoking, hypertension, high low-density lipoprotein cholesterol, low high-density lipoprotein cholesterol, impaired fasting glucose, a family history of premature CHD, and age (male ≥45 years, female ≥55 years). Individuals with three or more of these CVD risk factors are also classified as having high absolute obesity-associated risk. Many additional comorbidities, such as OA, chronic back pain, asthma, gallbladder disease, and psychiatric disorders, may be detected during medical evaluation and require appropriate management, but do not generally impart increased absolute risk (NHLBI, 1998).

### Secondary Medical Causes of Obesity

Beyond risk assessment, medical evaluation is also useful to identify possible factors, including medication use and underlying disorders or diseases that, in addition to diet and lifestyle, may have contributed to weight gain and/or may impact the effectiveness of obesity treatment. Several specific drugs and categories of drugs commonly prescribed to treat chronic diseases and disorders have been associated with unintentional weight gain (Table 29.4).

**Table 29.4  Drugs reported to cause weight gain**

| Drug or Drug Category | Main Use |
| --- | --- |
| Insulin, sulfonylureas, thiazolidiones | Diabetes |
| β Blockers | Hypertension |
| Corticosteroids | Inflammatory disease |
| Cyproheptadine | Allergy, hay fever |
| Antipsychotics | Psychosis |
| Sodium valproate | Epilepsy |
| Tricyclic antidepressants | Depression |
| Lithium | Bipolar disorder |

Adapted and reprinted from Leslie, W. S., Hankey, C. R., Lean, M. E. J. (2007). Weight gain as an adverse effect of some commonly prescribed drugs: a systematic review. *Quarterly Journal of Medicine, 100,* 395–404, with permission of the publisher, Oxford Journals.

Endocrine diseases and disorders associated with obesity include hypothyroidism, Cushing syndrome, growth hormone deficiency, hypogonadism, polycystic ovarian syndrome, insulinomas, and conditions resulting in hypothalamic damage (Kokkoris & Pi-Sunyer, 2003). Identification of endocrine dysfunction in obesity assessment is important, as appropriate medical treatment for many of these conditions may reverse weight gain or improve weight loss outcomes. Rare genetic mutations may also result in endocrine or other types of abnormalities causing obesity, and include single-gene defects affecting hypothalamic control of energy intake, as well as syndromes such as Prader-Willi, which are typically characterized by obesity as a clinical feature in association with developmental delays and specific abnormal physical findings (Kokkoris & Pi-Sunyer, 2003). These conditions primarily present in early childhood, however, and are an improbable undiagnosed cause of obesity in developmentally normal adults.

### LIFESTYLE ASSESSMENT

Lifestyle assessment involves the evaluation of weight and dieting history, as well as current weight control practices, dietary intake and habits, and physical activity patterns, which can be used to inform the design of an effective individualized weight reduction treatment plan. As part of lifestyle assessment, resting energy expenditure and total energy expenditure can also be estimated from predictive equations to determine approximate daily energy requirements. These estimates may aid in establishing energy intake and physical activity goals to promote weight loss during treatment.

### Weight and Dieting History

Determining age of initial obesity onset may aid in identifying life events related to weight gain and other factors known to contribute to the etiology of obesity. Adult-onset weight gain is common, and it has been shown that, for normal weight adult men and women, the long-term risk over 10–30 years of becoming overweight or obese is approximately 50% (Vasan, Pencina, Cobain, Freiberg, & D'Agostino, 2005). Sustained weight gain may originate from marriage, postpartum weight retention, and smoking cessation, or may be triggered by other lifestyle factors related to obesity, including chronic stress and short sleep duration. Socioeconomic circumstances also influence the development of obesity, and exposure to socioeconomic disadvantage is associated with an increased risk of subsequent weight gain

(Giskes et al., 2008). There is also evidence that weight gain may be affected by social networks, with an individual's risk of obesity increasing by more than 50% if a friend becomes obese (Christakis & Fowler, 2007). Other individuals may report obesity onset in childhood, as childhood and adolescent weight status often persists into adulthood (Singh, Mulder, Twisk, Mechelen, & Chinapaw, 2008).

Dieting history may reveal previous unsuccessful efforts to reduce body weight or sustain weight loss. Frequent weight fluctuation, or weight cycling—as a consequence of intentional weight loss and subsequent unintentional weight regain—is a strong predictor of future weight gain in adult men and women. The relationship between weight cycling and future weight gain appears to depend on the magnitude of weight gain and loss with each cycle (Field, Manson, Taylor, Willett, & Colditz, 2004), however, and becomes much weaker when weight cycling is defined by weight loss and gain of only 5 or more pounds (Van Wye, Dubin, Blair, & Di Pietro, 2007). Past and current weight loss strategies, including over-the-counter medication and dietary supplement use, should also be ascertained as part of dieting history assessment, as the specific practices employed in efforts to control body weight may have important implications for treatment.

### Dietary Intake and Eating Habits/Patterns

Methods for dietary assessment used to quantify energy and nutrient intake include food records, 24-hour dietary recalls, and food frequency questionnaires (FFQs). Dietary records require the respondent to record all foods and beverages consumed, the portion size of each, as well as time and location of each meal or snack, typically for a period of 3–7 days. In the 24-hour recall, a trained interviewer prompts the respondent to describe all foods and beverages consumed over the previous 24 hours, including portion sizes and time and location of consumption. Food frequency questionnaires ask the respondent to report the number of times each food was consumed and the portion size over a given period of time from a list of foods. Several population-specific FFQs representative of typically eaten foods are available (Thompson & Byers, 1994).

Due to the subjective nature of dietary assessment measurement techniques and the reliance of these methods on a respondent's self-report, error in estimates of energy and nutrient intake is common. The prevalence of misreporting is dependent upon the population, and underreporting of energy intake

has been associated with a number of respondent characteristics such as gender, BMI, and social desirability and other demographic, psychosocial, and psychological characteristics (R.J. Hill & Davies, 2001). Obese adults may be especially prone to energy intake misreporting, and although the degree of energy intake underreporting has been shown to vary widely, studies have found reported intakes of nearly 60% less than actual daily energy intake (R.J. Hill & Davies, 2001). In general, energy intake estimates from dietary assessment should be interpreted with caution and should not be used in the determination of energy requirements necessary to produce weight loss.

Although each dietary intake assessment instruments can be imprecise, and all are equally accurate for measuring habitual energy intake (R.J. Hill & Davies, 2001), food records may be the most useful for individual dietary assessment because they allow for the quantification of energy and nutrient intake, as well as habitual dietary habits, whereas 24-hour recalls and FFQs do not allow for the determination of day-to-day eating patterns (Thompson & Byers, 1994). Several chronic dietary behaviors have been consistently associated with increased BMI or risk of obesity, and these can be identified from food records, including frequent restaurant and fast food consumption, large portion sizes, consumption of beverages with added sugar, low intake of fruits and vegetables, and skipping breakfast (Greenwood & Stanford, 2008).

### Physical Activity

Cardiorespiratory fitness (CRF), measured by maximal exercise test, is an important determinant of obesity-related mortality risk, with higher levels conferring a protective effect and lower levels exacerbating risk (LaMonte & Blair, 2006). Although CRF is influenced by demographic and genetic factors, the largest contributor is physical activity level (PAL). Therefore, PAL is frequently used as a surrogate measure when direct CRF testing is infeasible, and it has been shown to have a similar relationship to mortality as that of CRF (Warburton, Nicol, & Bredin, 2006). PAL can be measured using motion sensors including pedometers, which measure step count, and accelerometers, which measure acceleration in one or multiple planes of motion, as well as through the use of heart rate monitors and other direct methods. Although accelerometers are a frequently used, relatively low-cost method that can measure the intensity of duration and frequency of physical activity in daily life, PAL can also be measured indirectly by interview or diary. A number of validated questionnaires have been developed to measure PAL, such as the Paffenbarger Physical Activity Questionnaire, and these instruments offer the advantage of assessing both structured (planned) physical activity and unstructured activities of daily living (Paffenbarger Physical Activity Questionnaire, 1997).

In addition to structured exercise, it is also useful to assess nonexercise activities of daily living, as a sedentary job and more time spent in leisure time activities reduce energy expenditure and may therefore contribute to weight gain. Studies have also found that obese men and women sit between 2 and 2.5 hours more per day than their lean counterparts, accounting for a 300–350 calorie difference in activity energy expenditure each day (Levine et al., 2005). Therefore, a baseline activity level determined from assessment of both PAL and nonexercise activity will inform the design of initial and progressive physical activity goals for obesity treatment and aid in estimation of total daily energy expenditure and requirements for weight loss.

*Estimation of Energy Expenditure*

Resting energy expenditure (REE), the body's energy expenditure at complete rest in the postabsorptive state, is the largest component of total energy expenditure (TEE), generally accounting for more than 60% of TEE (Levine, 2005). The other primary component of TEE is PAEE, which includes energy expended in structured exercise and nonexercise activity. The REE can be assessed using indirect calorimetry, a method by which oxygen consumption and carbon dioxide production is measured and converted into an estimate of energy expenditure based on formulae. Noncalorimetric methods can also be used to measure REE, in which measurements of other variables related to energy expenditure, such as heart rate, are extrapolated to estimate energy expenditure (Levine, 2005). Although indirect calorimetry devices are becoming more available clinically, REE is more often calculated using predictive equations based on calorimetry measurements. An estimate of TEE can then be obtained by multiplying REE by an activity factor to account for PAEE based on an individual's habitual exercise and nonexercise activity level.

Several equations are available for predicting REE, with accuracy dependent upon the population studied. For example, the Mifflin-St. Jeor equation has been shown to predict REE in nonobese adults within 10% of REE measured by indirect calorimetry

with 82% accuracy and in obese adults with 70% accuracy, which was superior to estimates derived by other commonly used equations, including the Harris-Benedict and Owen (Frankenfield, Roth-Yousey, & Compher, 2005). Estimation of TEE in obese individuals from Institute of Medicine (IOM) Dietary Reference Intake (DRI) equations and activity factors may be preferable to other methods, as the prediction equations are based on doubly labeled water measurements, considered the gold standard for measurement of free living TEE, and obtained from sedentary individuals across a range of BMI categories. The accuracy of the IOM/DRI equations has also been corroborated by other investigations, showing a difference between TEE predictions based on DRI equations and actual TEE measured by doubly labeled water in middle-aged nonobese and obese men and women of approximately 6% and 7.5%, respectively (Tooze et al., 2007). The Mifflin-St. Jeor and IOM/DRI equations are shown in Table 29.5.

## BEHAVIORAL ASSESSMENT

A final area of assessment for treatment of obesity is motivational readiness for change in regards to eating and physical activity behaviors that produce weight loss. The concept of readiness to change is often framed within the transtheoretical model

**Table 29.5  Resting energy expenditure (REE) and total energy expenditure (TEE) predictive equations**

Mifflin-St. Jeor Equations [a]

For Females: REE (kcal/d) = $10 \times$ weight (kg) + $6.25 \times$ height (cm) − $5 \times$ age (y) − 161

For Males: REE (kcal/d) = $10 \times$ weight (kg) + $6.25 \times$ height (cm) − $5 \times$ age (y) + 5

---

Institute of Medicine Dietary Reference Intake Equations [b]

For Females: TEE (kcal/d) = $351.1 − 6.91 \times$ age (y) $\times$ PA $\times$ ($9.36 \times$ weight [kg] + $726 \times$ height [m])

For Males: TEE (kcal/d) = $661.8 − 9.53 \times$ age (y) $\times$ PA $\times$ ($15.91 \times$ weight [kg] + $726 \times$ height [m])

Activity factor (PA) = 1.0 (sedentary)

PA = 1.12 (low active)

PA = 1.27 (active)

PA = 1.45 (very active)

---

[a] Adapted from Mifflin, M. D., St Jeor, S. T., Hill, L. A., Scott, B. J., Daugherty, S. A., & Koh, Y. O. (1990). A new predictive equation for resting energy expenditure in healthy individuals. *American Journal of Clinical Nutrition, 51*, 241–247, with permission of the publisher, American Society for Nutrition.

[b] Adapted from Dietary Reference Intakes for Energy, Carbohydrate, Fiber, Fat, Fatty Acids, Cholesterol, Protein, and Amino Acids (Macronutrients). (2002). Washington, DC: National Academy Press.

(TTM), which consists of four dimensions of behavior change (DiClemente, 2003). In the TTM, the first dimension of behavior change is the five stages that individuals progresses through as behavior change occurs. These stages are precontemplation (not considering change in the near future), contemplation (considering change), preparation (developing a plan for change and increasing commitment to change), action (change is occurring), and maintenance (integrating new behaviors into lifestyle). A second dimension of TTM is the process of change, which enables an individual to move from one stage to another. These processes generally are geared to be more cognitive and experiential (i.e., increasing self-awareness), which are more generally associated with the precontemplation and contemplation stages, or behavioral (i.e., developing a plan, using reinforcement), which are geared more to the preparation, action, and maintenance stages. The third dimension of TTM focuses on markers of change, which include decisional balance (assessing the pros and cons of change), generally found in the contemplation phase, and self-efficacy, one's perceived ability to manage behavior change, occurring in the preparation, action, and maintenance stages. Finally, there is the context of change, which represents five broad areas of functioning (current life situation, beliefs and attitudes, interpersonal relationships, social systems, and enduring personal characteristics) that can make movement through the five stages easier or more difficult.

Using many of the dimensions of the TTM framework, several self-reported questionnaires have been developed to assess motivational readiness to change in relation to weight control (Cancer Prevention Research Center home of the Transtheoretical Model, 2004). These measures can be used to help identify the stage of change an individual might be at in regards to weight control. Once the stage of change is identified, an intervention can be developed that is more appropriate for an individual based upon the identified stage. It is hypothesized that, when the intervention is matched to the appropriate level of readiness to change, greater success will occur (DiClemente, 2003). For example, an individual who is in precontemplation and contemplation would require an intervention that focuses on increasing awareness of the need to change (i.e., increase understanding of the relationship between weight and other comorbidities that the individual might have) and/or increasing the benefits of change and decreasing the risks of change (DiClemente, 2003). Individuals in the preparation, action, and

maintenance stages would be more involved with behavioral strategies for change (i.e., setting achievable goals, and developing and implementing plans related to eating and physical activity behaviors).

## ADDITIONAL CONSIDERATIONS

For individuals eligible for weight loss therapy based on anthropometrics and health risk, and who are ready to begin a weight reduction program, it is important to determine any factors that may exclude an individual from obesity treatment prior to initiation. Exclusion criteria for weight reduction include pregnancy and lactation, serious uncontrolled psychiatric illness, other severe illness that may be exacerbated by calorie restriction, or history of anorexia nervosa (NHLBI, 1998). Although binge eating disorder has previously been considered a contraindication for obesity treatment due to the concern that dietary restriction might result in increased binge eating, it has been demonstrated that weight loss programs can reduce both bingeing and body weight, and it is proposed that standard behavioral weight loss programs may be a better treatment for binge eating disorder compared to cognitive-behavioral therapy programs specifically addressing binge eating (Stunkard & Costello Allison, 2003).

## Treatment Strategies
### LIFESTYLE INTERVENTION
Lifestyle interventions are composed of three components: dietary prescription, physical activity prescription, and cognitive-behavioral therapy. Cognitive-behavioral therapy teaches individuals skills for how to change eating and physical activity behaviors so that weight loss can occur.

### Diet
*Energy Intake.* For weight loss to occur, energy intake must be lower than energy expenditure, creating a negative energy balance. The size of the caloric deficit created will determine the amount of weight lost. One pound of adipose tissue stores approximately 3,500 kcal of available energy, therefore a 500 kcal deficit per day will create weight loss of about 1 pound per week, and a 1,000 kcal deficit per day will create a weight loss of about 2 pounds per week. A reduction in the number of kcal consumed per day is generally required to create an energy deficit of at least 500 kcal per day to produce subsequent weight loss, as it is incredibly challenging to engage in the amount of physical activity required to produce this size of energy deficit per day (approximately 1 hour and 40 minutes per day of

moderate-intense physical activity). A meta-analysis of RCTs of weight loss in which changes in physical activity, diet, or physical activity and diet were examined found that little weight loss occurred in trials in which only changes in physical activity occurred (Franz et al., 2007).

There are generally three energy prescriptions used in obesity treatment. The first prescription recommends the lowest energy intake, ≤800 kcal/day, and is called a very-low-calorie diet (VLCD). With VLCDs, medical supervision usually occurs, and food is generally provided in the form of meal replacements (nutritionally formulated foods, usually drinks or bars that are portioned controlled) or lean meat, fish, or fowl. Both the meal replacements and the focus on lean meats provide large amounts of protein to reduce the loss of lean muscle mass during weight loss. VLCDs have been shown to produce excellent initial weight losses (–20 kg at 12 weeks); this effect is due in part to the degree of energy restriction and in part to the increased structure of the diet (i.e., decreased dietary variety and the use of portion-controlled foods) (Wadden & Berkowitz, 2001). Given the large initial weight loss produced by VLCDs, it was hoped that combining this diet with behavior modification strategies would improve long-term weight loss. Although VLCDs do improve initial weight loss, they do not appear to produce better long-term weight loss than do low-calorie diets (LCDs) (Wadden, Crerand, & Brock, 2005). Difficulty with long-term weight loss with VLCDs generally appears when the transition from the VLCD to a diet composed of regular, conventional foods occurs.

The next energy prescription commonly used in obesity treatment is the LCD, which recommends 1,000–1,500 kcal/day, either in the form of conventional foods or a combination of meal replacements and conventional foods. Commonly, the LCD is also lower in fat, with around 20%–30% of energy from fat, and instructions are provided to follow the Dietary Guidelines for Americans (DGA) (Dietary Guidelines for Americans, 2005). Research shows that LCDs can create an average weight loss of about 8% of total body weight over a period of 6 months (NHLBI, 1998). The final method for providing an energy prescription for weight loss is to determine current TEE, based upon a method described previously, and then calculate a 500–1,000 kcal per day reduction from the TEE. This deficit should result in about 1–2 pounds of weight loss per week. As TEE is highly dependent on REE, which decreases with a reduction in body mass, as weight loss occurs, the energy prescription will need to be recalculated over time to achieve the same energy deficit.

As rate of weight loss with both LCDs and energy prescriptions based on TEE is slower than what occurs with a VLCD, medical supervision is not required but is recommended.

*Macronutrient Intake.* Although it is clear that for weight loss to occur, energy intake needs to be reduced, there is a great deal of debate as to what the ideal macronutrient composition (ratio of fat, carbohydrate, and protein) of the diet is for weight loss. Most research in obesity treatment has generally prescribed diets that are lower in fat (with <30% of calories coming from fat) and higher in carbohydrates (55%–60% of calories) (Strychar, 2006).

There are several reasons why a low-fat diet has been predominantly used in obesity treatment. Cross-sectionally, when the relationship between diet composition, energy intake, and weight status is examined, a stronger relationship between dietary fat and body weight, than between energy intake and body weight is found (Romieu et al., 1988). Longitudinal studies examining dietary predictors of weight change also find that changes in intake of high-fat foods and in energy from fat predict changes in weight in the general population (Klesges, Klesges, Haddock, & Eck, 1992) and in those trying to lose weight (Jeffery et al., 1984).

Experimental studies have also found that when dietary fat is reduced, significant weight loss occurs. For example, several recent meta-analyses of controlled trials comparing low-fat diets with normal-fat diets under ad libitum conditions have all found that reductions in dietary fat without restriction of energy intake causes decreases in energy intake and a consequential modest weight loss (Astrup, Grunwalk, Melanson, Saris, & Hill, 2000; Bray & Popkin, 1998). Furthermore, when the effect of a high-fat diet on energy intake is examined, passive overconsumption occurs, most likely due to the higher energy density of a high-fat diet (Rolls, 2009).

However, in the previous decade, research on the effect of a low-carbohydrate diet on weight loss has been examined. Many of the RCTs have used prescriptions that are similar to the Atkins diet (Atkins, 1998), which limits carbohydrate intake to 20 g/day for at least 2 weeks, and then increases carbohydrate intake to around 60–70 g/day (or, individuals are instructed to gradually increase carbohydrate intake until a desired weight is achieved). Low-carbohydrate diets do not include an energy prescription, allowing individuals to eat as much as desired, but only from allowed (e.g., low-carbohydrate) foods.

Several studies have compared low-carbohydrate diets to LCD low-fat diets (Brehm, Seeley, Daniels, & D'Alessio, 2003; G. Foster et al., 2003; Yancy, Olsen, Guyton, Bakst, & Westman, 2004). At 6 months, weight loss is greater in the low-carbohydrate diet as compared to the LCD low-fat diet (range: −9.7% to −12.9% body weight). However, few of these studies included a 12-month follow-up and those that did found no difference in weight loss between the two diets (G. Foster et al., 2003). Dietary measures found that carbohydrate intake decreased on the low-carbohydrate diet, and with the decrease in carbohydrate intake, there was a decrease in energy intake that was the same or slightly lower than reported with the LCD, low-fat diet. This change in caloric intake is believed to be responsible for the weight losses seen with the low-carbohydrate diet.

A recent RCT examined the effects of a reduced-calorie diet (750 kcal/day less than TEE) of differing macronutrient compositions on weight loss over a 2-year follow-up. Sacks and colleagues (Sacks et al., 2009) directly compared four diets, containing similar foods but of varying macronutrient contents (low-fat versus high-fat and average-protein versus high-protein, with additional analysis of the lowest and highest carbohydrate diets), in 811 participants. This study found that all diets, regardless of macronutrient content, resulted in clinically significant weight loss, with no differences in weight loss occurring between the four diets (Sacks et al., 2009).

*Dietary Structure.* The dietary challenge during obesity treatment is long-term adherence to reduced energy intake. One approach to improve long-term dietary adherence is to simplify the diet by adding more structure. For example, providing meal plans produces greater weight loss when compared to just providing an energy prescription (Wing et al., 1994). The use of meal replacements for at least two meals per day has improved weight loss outcomes as compared to diets composed of conventional foods (Heymsfield, van Mierlo, van der Knaap, Heo, & Frier, 2003). As basic eating research has found that greater variety in a meal (H.A. Raynor & Epstein, 2001), larger portion sizes (Rolls et al., 2002), and foods higher in energy density (Rolls, 2009) increase consumption, using dietary structure to

target these areas (i.e., reduce dietary variety [reduces choices], use portion-controlled foods [eliminates the need for measuring], and consume foods low in energy density) may help individuals more easily meet and adhere to a lower energy prescription over time.

*Physical Activity*

Physical activity is always a component of lifestyle interventions designed to produce weight loss. In 2007, The American College of Sports Medicine (ACSM) and the American Heart Association issued a revised version of Physical Activity and Public Health Guidelines, which are commonly regarded as the primary recommendations for physical activity in the United States for healthy adults aged 18–65 years (Physical Activity and Public Health: Updated Recommendation for Adults From the American College of Sports Medicine and the American Heart Association, Haskell et al., 2007). These guidelines state that, to promote and maintain health, all adults need a minimum of 30 minutes of moderate-intensity aerobic physical activity on 5 days per week or a minimum of 20 minutes of vigorous-intensity aerobic physical activity on 3 days per week. Moderate-intensity physical activity causes a noticeable increase in the heart rate and is similar to the intensity of a brisk walk. Vigorous-intensity physical activity is associated with a level of activity that causes rapid breathing and a substantial increase in heart rate, similar to the intensity of jogging. The guidelines also state that a combination of moderate- and vigorous-intensity physical activity and the accumulation of short bouts of physical activity (that are at least 10 minutes in duration and at the appropriate intensity levels) can be used to meet the recommendations. In addition to aerobic physical activity, the guidelines encourage healthy adults to perform strength training exercises on 2 nonconsecutive days per week, with a recommendation for doing 8–10 strength exercises with 8–12 repetitions of each exercise.

In 2009, the ACSM issued an additional position statement specifically addressing physical activity for weight loss and prevention of weight regain in adults (Donnelly et al., 2009). This position paper highlights the dose–response relationship that exists with physical activity, with greater weight losses being reported with greater amounts of physical activity. The ideal amount of physical activity for weight loss maintenance is undetermined as of yet; however, studies have shown that high levels of physical activity, 200–300 minutes per week, may aid in facilitating long-term maintenance of weight loss (Jakicic, Clarke, & Coleman, 2001).

As many overweight and obese individuals are sedentary, when physical activity is initiated, it is commonly recommended that this be lifestyle-based physical activity, which emphasizes brisk walking, as compared to structured physical activity (i.e., jogging) (Pal, Cheng, Egger, Binns, & Donovan, 2009). One method to increase brisk walking is to focus on steps accumulated per day using a pedometer. A meta-analysis of studies that provided adults with pedometers did find that using a pedometer increased the number of steps walked per day, with the current goal for adults being 10,000 steps per day (Bravata et al., 2007). As meeting these recommendations may seem very challenging, selection of type of physical activity performed should be based upon the individual's enjoyment of the activity and the ability to fit the activity into daily life (NHLBI, 1998). Additionally, supervision and cardiorespiratory testing may be indicated for high-risk individuals starting a physical activity program.

### Cognitive-Behavioral Therapy

Treatment for obesity has evolved over the past 30 years, and the success of the DPP (Knowler et al., 2002) has helped establish what is now known as "behavioral weight control" or "lifestyle intervention." This treatment is designed to modify eating, activity, and thinking habits that have contributed to a state of positive energy balance. Although this approach does recognize that weight is a consequence of more than just habits and behaviors, and that genetic, metabolic, and hormonal influences may predispose individuals to becoming obese, the behavioral approach assists individuals with developing a set of skills that allows weight loss to occur even in predisposed individuals (G.D. Foster, Makris, & Bailer, 2005; Wadden et al., 2005).

Lifestyle intervention is based in learning theory (i.e., behaviorism) and incorporates both classical and operant conditioning concepts in treatment. Lifestyle interventions also use cognitive strategies to help with changing behaviors, and thus are often cognitive-behavioral in overall structure (G.D. Foster et al., 2005). With lifestyle interventions, a functional analysis of behaviors related to energy balance is conducted to identify antecedents, behaviors, and consequences (ABCs) of eating and activity behaviors that are associated with overeating and physical inactivity (Wadden et al., 2005; Wing, 2004). This analysis identifies cues and events

(i.e., situations, emotions, thoughts, environmental stimuli) that may prompt problematic eating and inactivity behaviors, and the cognitive and emotional consequences of the behaviors that may reinforce the occurrence of the problematic behaviors (Wadden et al., 2005; Wing, 2004). The functional analysis identifies areas for intervention, with change in behaviors occurring as a consequence of the application of the skills supplied in lifestyle interventions (Wadden et al., 2005).

Behavioral interventions have three important characteristics (G.D. Foster et al., 2005; Wadden et al., 2005). The first of these characteristics is that behavioral interventions are goal directed. Goals in lifestyle interventions are very specific (i.e., a daily calorie goal, steps per day goal), providing the ability to ascertain degree of success during treatment. Behavioral treatments are also very process oriented. Thus, with the specified goals, individuals are encouraged to identify factors that help or hinder achievement of these goals, making plans to address these factors. If a goal is not achieved, or a plan is not set in motion, problem-solving skills are brought into play to identify barriers to success. With this approach, success is achieved by implementing skills as needed, rather than on relying on will power to make change (G.D. Foster et al., 2005). Finally, behavioral interventions focus on making small changes, rather than large changes. This concept is based upon the concept of successive approximation, in which incremental steps are made to achieve a goal that is much more distal (G.D. Foster et al., 2005). This allows individuals to achieve success fairly quickly, which can reinforce efforts in making continued behavior change.

Lifestyle interventions are composed of several components to change habits related to problematic eating and inactivity. These components can be taught in both individual and group sessions. Ideally, these components are taught over several months, allowing individuals to test the skills and receive feedback and support from interventionists as new behaviors are developed. Some of these components are based more in behaviorism, such as self-monitoring, goal-setting, stimulus control, behavioral substitution, and reinforcement, whereas other components—preplanning, problem solving, and cognitive restructuring—focus more on cognitive skills (G.D. Foster et al., 2005; Wadden et al., 2005; Wing, 2004).

*Self-monitoring.* Self-monitoring is a key component of behavioral interventions, as self-monitoring increases awareness of behaviors and also provides feedback on degree of success in achieving goals. A recent meta-regression of effective techniques in changing eating and activity behaviors found that self-monitoring combined with at least one other skill was significantly more effective than other interventions (Michie, Abraham, Whittington, McAteer, & Gupta, 2009) in changing behaviors. In lifestyle intervention, eating behavior (i.e., time and place of eating; amount, type of food, energy, and fat consumed) and physical activity (type of activity, minutes of moderate-intense physical activity, and steps) are recorded daily. Individuals are also instructed on how to read food labels to determine the energy and fat consumed from foods. As accurate self-monitoring of eating is very challenging, lifestyle intervention encourages daily self-monitoring of weight. This allows individuals to monitor their progress in weight loss and/or weight loss maintenance, and also enables the development of self-regulatory skills in regards to energy balance. Self-monitoring eating, physical activity, and weight allows an individual to understand the relationship between the behaviors and weight, so adjustments in eating and activity can be made appropriately. Although there have been concerns about negative psychological consequences from regular self-monitoring of weight, research in this area has not found this relationship (Wing et al., 2007).

*Goal-setting.* Goals in lifestyle interventions are observable, specific, and time-limited. For example, a dietary goal may be the following: "I will consume 1,200 to 1,400 kcal/day, as documented in my self-monitoring log, at least 5 days in the next week." Physical activity goals using observable measures of activity, such as a pedometer, are also helpful: "I will walk at least 10,000 steps per day at least 5 days in the next week." As mentioned earlier, smaller goals may be initially set to reach larger goals. Thus, often a baseline measure is taken (i.e., how many steps per day are taken at the start of the intervention), with a smaller goal made that is gradually increased over time until the larger goal is met (i.e., increase steps per day by 250 over a 7-day period, and when that is achieved, increase steps per day by another 250 over a 7-day period, etc.).

*Stimulus Control.* Stimulus control focuses on reducing cues in the environment that may prompt problematic eating behaviors or inactivity and increasing cues in the environment that encourage eating behaviors and activity that lead to weight loss. For example, individuals are encouraged to examine the home, work, and social environment for cues that lead to overeating and to remove these cues. This can include removing food from sight (getting rid of candy bowls and food on the counter in the kitchen), as well as removing problematic food from the environment (getting rid of ice cream and potato chips from the home and not buying them while grocery shopping). Cues can include things other than food, such as television watching. Many individuals develop a "habit," through classical conditioning, of eating while watching television, thus the television itself may prompt eating. Stimulus control also includes making sure healthy foods (i.e., fruits and vegetables) are available and ready to eat (i.e., washed and cut and stored in the refrigerator, so readily accessible to eat). The environment can also be changed to help individuals be active (i.e., making sure exercise clothes are out and in sight to prompt activity, exercise equipment is working and out in the open to encourage activity), and to be less sedentary (i.e., reduce the number of televisions in the house).

*Behavioral Substitution.* Although stimulus control is helpful for managing external cues that prompt behavior, overeating can also be cued by internal cues, such as emotions, through classical and operant conditioning. For example, if experiencing anxiety or anger are cues for overeating, an alternative behavior in response to this emotion can be substituted for eating. Ideally, this alternative behavior is not compatible with eating. Thus, doing things like writing, typing, housework, and exercise may be appropriate substitute behaviors.

*Reinforcement.* According to behaviorism, the consequences of a behavior will encourage the behavior to occur again, or to not occur again. For many individuals, weight loss, and its attendant improvement in health and quality of life, provides reinforcement for new eating and activity behaviors that are compatible with a lower weight. However, especially when the goal is weight loss maintenance, these naturally occurring reinforcers may not be so prominent and therefore may not be strong enough to encourage the continued occurrence of the new eating and activity behaviors. Thus, additional reinforcement may be needed. This reinforcement should be tied (contingent) to achieving set goals. For example, the goal may be achieving 250 minutes of moderate-intense physical activity in the week, with the reinforcer being a manicure.

Only when the goal is achieved should the manicure occur.

*Preplanning.* Preplanning involves making a specific plan to achieve a specified goal or to address a barrier. Often, preplanning involves having an individual actually write out the plan. Preplanning allows an individual to think through how to achieve the goal or address the barrier, which may involve the development and use of new behaviors in response to cues. For many people, eating out in restaurants is a cue for overeating. With preplanning, a new response for reacting to the cue of eating out in restaurants will have been thought through (i.e., a "healthier" restaurant is chosen, an option from the menu that meets dietary goals has been selected, the waiter will be asked to remove bread from the table, the dessert will be shared with an eating companion, etc.).

*Problem Solving.* Problem solving is composed of several steps, with the first step being to identify the problem in detail. Often, it is encouraged to identify the steps (behavioral chain) that led up to the problem. Several of these steps are targeted, and brainstorming occurs to identify all potential solutions to the identified steps. Then the pros and cons of each solution are defined, and a risk–benefit analysis of each solution occurs. The most feasible solution is chosen, and implementation of that solution is encouraged. After a brief period of implementation, an evaluation of the solution occurs. If the solution was not successful in reducing the problem, the process occurs again.

*Cognitive Restructuring.* In cognitive restructuring, individuals are taught to identify irrational thoughts that are becoming barriers to changing eating and activity behaviors. One of the most common irrational thoughts is "all-or-nothing" (black-and-white) thinking, in which an individual feels that if eating and activity behaviors are not engaged in perfectly, failure occurs (i.e., "I ate one more cookie than I had planned, thus I might as well give up my eating goals today and eat as much as I can"). In cognitive restructuring, individuals are taught to monitor their thoughts for dysfunctional patterns that are interfering with the ability to achieve their eating and activity goals, identify the distortion in the thoughts, and then modify those thoughts with rational thoughts.

## MEDICAL TREATMENT
### Pharmacotherapy

Pharmacotherapy for weight loss is only recommended for individuals with a BMI of ≥30 with no related disease risk factors, or for individuals with a BMI of ≥27 with obesity-related diseases or risk factors for disease. Additionally, it is recommended that drug treatment for obesity be combined with lifestyle intervention (NHLBI, 1998). Currently two medications are approved by the U.S. Food and Drug Administration (FDA) for long-term use in weight loss and weight loss maintenance: orlistat and sibutramine.

*Orlistat.* Orlistat (Xenical, Hoffman-LaRoche, Nutley, NJ), first approved by the FDA in 1998, acts as gastric and pancreatic lipase inhibitor and functions in the lumen of the gastrointestinal tract by inhibiting the lipase-initiated breakdown of approximately one-third of fat ingested in the diet, allowing it to pass through the GI tract unabsorbed (McNeely & Benfield, 1998).

A meta-analysis of 15 RCTs using orlistat (total sample size 9,833) showed that active treatment with orlistat produced 2.9 kg greater weight loss (95% confidence interval [CI] 2.5–3.2 kg) than placebo and increased the absolute percentage of participants reaching the 5% and 10% weight loss thresholds by 21% (18%–24%) and 12% (9%–14%), respectively (Rucker, Padwal, Li, Curioni, & Lau, 2007).

The recommended dosage for orlistat is three times daily with meals, and side effects most often reported with orlistat are gastrointestinal in nature, including fatty/oily stool, fecal urgency, oily spotting, and fecal incontinence (Padwal & Majumdar, 2007). Additionally, there is some concern of fat-soluble vitamin deficiency in orlistat users due to the drug's mechanism of action, and although incidence of deficiency is rare, coprescription of a fat-soluble vitamin supplement is recommended (Padwal & Majumdar, 2007).

*Sibutramine.* Sibutramine (Meridia, Abbott Laboratories, Abbott Park, IL), first approved for long-term treatment of obesity in 1997, was originally developed as an antidepressant (Padwal & Majumdar, 2007), but has found more popular use in weight loss. Sibutramine's proposed mechanism of action to aid in weight loss is two-fold: increasing satiety and, to a lesser extent, increasing thermogenesis. Sibutramine increases satiety by acting on the central nervous system by blocking serotonin and norepinephrine reuptake in monoamine pathways that modulate food intake (Bray, 2009); however, the mechanism by which sibutramine increases thermogenesis is less clear.

In a meta-analysis of eight studies using sibutramine, patients receiving sibutramine lost an additional 4.2 kg (3.6–4.7 kg) or 4.3% (3.7%–5.0%) beyond that of patients taking a placebo and increased the absolute percentage of patients reaching 5% and 10% weight loss by 32% (27%–37%, seven studies) and 18% (11%–25%, seven studies), respectively (Rucker et al., 2007).

Sibutramine is available for initiation of treatment in doses of 5, 10, and 15 mg units, and is increased or decreased depending on the patient's response to the drug; however, it is not recommended in doses over 15 mg (Bray, 2009). Reported side effects of sibutramine include insomnia, nausea, dry mouth, and constipation (Rucker et al., 2007). Additionally, when compared to placebo, sibutramine has been shown to increase systolic and diastolic blood pressure (Rucker et al., 2007) and increase pulse rate an average four to five beats per minute (Bray, 2009). Because of these potential side effects, sibutramine is not recommended for use in patients with a history of coronary artery disease, cardiac arrhythmias, congestive heart failure, or stroke (Bray, 2009).

*Other Weight Loss Medications.* Several short-term weight loss medications are approved by the FDA, including benzphetamine, diethylpropion, phendimetrazine, and phentermine. These drugs are approved for short-term use only, which is equivalent to 12 or less weeks in a 12-month period (Bray, 2009). All of these drugs are sympathomimetic amines, which are derived from amphetamine. Their mechanism of action is to stimulate neurons allowing for maintenance of high concentrations of dopamine and norepinephrine, thereby suppressing hunger signaling and decreasing appetite (Cannon & Kumar, 2009). Because of their mechanism of action, these drugs can increase heart rate and blood pressure and stimulate lipolysis, and therefore they are contraindicated in patients with CVD, moderate to severe hypertension, hyperthyroidism, glaucoma, pregnancy, and lactation. Of the short-term weight loss medications, phentermine is the most frequency prescribed, and it has been shown to produce modest weight losses over that of placebo. Phendimetrazine and benzphetamine are infrequently prescribed because they are classified as DEA schedule III drugs and have increased risk for developing physical tolerance (Cannon & Kumar, 2009).

*Weight Loss Surgery*

The use of bariatric surgery as a treatment mechanism for weight loss has gained popularity recently (Steinbrook, 2004). It is speculated that this is due in part to the fact that the current surgical procedures for weight loss are the only effective, long-term treatment available for severely obese patients (Steinbrook, 2004), with 80%–90% of bariatric surgery patients losing 50% of their excess body weight, whereas only 5%–10% of severely obese patients achieve and maintain significant weight loss through more traditional methods such as dieting, behavior modification, and use of pharmacotherapy (Varsha, 2006). Despite its effectiveness, bariatric surgery is still a major surgical procedure that potentially may involve short- and long-term complications. Therefore, it is only recommended for patients who have clinically severe obesity or morbid obesity, and have failed at other less-intense weight loss methods (NHLBI, 1998). The NIH guidelines recommend that, for weight loss surgery to be considered as a treatment option, the patient must have a BMI of >40 or >35 with comorbidities (NHLBI, 1998).

Three general categories of weight loss surgeries are currently available: malabsorptive surgeries (procedures that interfere with the digestions and absorption of nutrients, often by bypassing a portion of the intestines), restrictive surgeries (surgeries that limit the amount of food able to be held by the stomach), and malabsorptive/restrictive surgeries (surgeries that both limit the amount of food able to be held in the stomach and interfere with absorption of nutrients) (Buchwald, 2002). The most common types of surgeries now practiced in the United States are the restrictive and malabsorptive/restrictive surgeries.

*Restrictive Procedures.* The restrictive surgical weight loss procedures include the vertical-banded gastroplasty and the gastric band. These surgeries serve to decrease the holding capacity of the stomach by creating a small pouch in the proximal stomach, causing food consumed to be retained in the pouch, and thus allowing satiety to be induced with a smaller volume of food (Buchwald, 2002). In the vertical-banded gastroplasty, the stomach pouch is made by creating an opening through the stomach, which is held together by staple lines. An additional row of staples is placed vertically to create one wall of the pouch. A strip of polypropylene mesh is placed through the opening and around the other side of the stomach and sewn in place to create a ring. This ring serves as the other wall of the pouch, which allows food to pass through the pouch into the rest of the GI tract (Wadden & Stunkard, 2002).

In gastric banding, a small upper pouch is created by placing a silicone band around the proximal portion of the stomach, separating it from the larger distal stomach. The silicone band is sewn into place to prevent slipping, and the size of the opening of the band can be adjusted by increasing or decreasing the volume of saline in the silicone band through a port that is placed subcutaneously during surgery. This procedure is appealing to some because it is reversible and does not require stapling of the stomach (Wadden & Stunkard, 2002).

Complications for the purely restrictive bariatric surgery procedures are often related to the band, including band slippage, erosion, malfunction, or obstruction. Gastroesophageal reflux and vomiting are also reported (Varsha, 2006; Wadden & Stunkard, 2002). In vertical gastric banding, there is also the potential for complications associated with erosion of the staple line and stretching of the stomach pouch, with consequent weight regain when the postsurgical dietary instructions are not followed (Varsha, 2006).

*Malabsorptive/Restrictive Procedures.* The combination malabsorptive/restrictive procedure, the Roux-en-Y gastric bypass, is the most common form of bariatric surgery performed in the United States. In this procedure, a small gastric pouch is surgically created and a limb is made to connect the gastric pouch to the jejunum. This procedure can be modified by adjusting where the limb connects back into the small bowel, thereby changing the extent of the bypass, which at the minimum, includes a bypass of the distal stomach, duodenum, and the proximal jejunum (Buchwald, 2002).

Roux-en-Y gastric bypass is characterized by complications that are caused by changes in GI physiology, such as staple line disruption and ulcer formation with the creation of the gastric pouch (Varsha, 2006; Wadden & Stunkard, 2002); malabsorption, including iron and $B_{12}$ deficiency; and dumping syndrome, created by the bypass of the proximal small intestine (Buchwald, 2002).

*Health Outcomes of Bariatric Surgery.* Both health outcomes and operative mortality (defined as death within the first 30 days post-surgery) varies slightly with the types of surgery performed. In a meta-analysis of bariatric surgery procedures, the mortality for the restrictive procedures (gastric banding and gastroplasty) was 0.1% and 0.5% for gastric bypass procedures, respectively (Buchwald et al., 2004). Certain factors have been identified that may contribute to increases in mortality and medical complications post surgery, including advanced age of patient, increased obesity, and other medical conditions (Steinbrook, 2004). Additionally, surgeon experience is inversely related to mortality and operative complication rates, with centers/surgeons that perform more than 100 gastric bypass operations per year reporting two- to threefold lower rates of complications than those reporting fewer procedures (Schauer, 2005). Despite the risk of complications, the outcomes of bariatric surgery for most patients are very positive. A meta-analysis of 10,172 patients found that the overall weight loss for all surgeries combined was 61.2% (95% CI, 58.1–64.4%) at the assessed time point. This study also analyzed the weight loss outcomes for each type of procedure and found that percentage of excess weight loss (95% CI) was 47.5% (40.7%–54.2%) for gastric banding, 61.6% (56.7%–66.5%) for gastric bypass, and 68.2% (61.5%–74.8%) for gastroplasty (Buchwald et al., 2004).

### Long-term Weight Loss Maintenance

The goal of obesity treatment is to achieve long-term weight loss maintenance. One key step in investigating factors that may be important in achieving successful weight loss maintenance is to define successful weight loss maintenance. Wing and Hill, who cofounded the National Weight Control Registry (NWCR), have proposed that successful weight loss maintainers are "individuals who have intentionally lost at least 10% of their body weight and kept it off for at least 1 year" (Wing & Phelan, 2005). They highlight several important components of this definition. The first component is that the weight loss is intentional, as unintentional weight loss has been found to occur fairly frequently, and that unintentional weight loss may have different causes and consequences, particularly health-related, than weight loss achieved through intentional means. Wing and Hill have included the 10% criterion of weight loss because weight losses of this size have produced substantial reductions in risk factors for heart disease and diabetes. Finally, the 1-year time duration was is similar to criteria proposed by the IOM (Wing & Phelan, 2005).

As the research community now has a greater understanding of what produces weight loss, the focus of obesity treatment research has shifted to examine the criteria for successful long-term weight loss maintenance (Jeffery et al., 2000). Presently, few studies have used the definition developed by Wing and Hill to estimate the prevalence of successful weight loss maintenance. In general, those studies that have been conducted indicate that about 20% of overweight individuals become successful weight loss maintainers (Wing & Phelan, 2005). One study, the DPP, has followed overweight individuals randomized to a lifestyle intervention that had a weight loss goal of 7% for up to 4.6 years and found that of the approximately 1,000 participants randomized to this condition, the mean weight loss was 6% and 4% at 1- and 3-year follow-up, respectively (Knowler et al., 2002). However, at the end of the study, 37% of these participants had maintained a weight loss of 7% or more.

Most of the research that has been conducted to understand factors that are associated with successful long-term weight loss maintainers involves the NWCR. Wing and Hill established this registry in 1994, and the registry is a self-selected sample of more than 4,000 participants who are at least 18 years of age and have lost at least 30 lb and maintained that weight loss for at least 1 year (Wing & Phelan, 2005). Registry participants are followed yearly through completed questionnaires that assess how they maintain their weight loss.

Participants in the NWCR report having lost a mean of 72.6 lb, and have maintained the minimum weight loss of 30 lb for 5.7 years (Wing & Phelan, 2005). These participants have reduced their BMI from 36.7 kg/m$^2$ at their maximum weight to 25.1 kg/m$^2$. Registry participants are predominantly female (77%), college educated (82%), and white (95%). Most participants (89%) report achieving their weight loss through making changes in their diet and physical activity.

Specific strategies NWCR participants have used to maintain their weight loss have been examined. Studies investigating dietary components have found that registry members reported consuming a low-calorie (1,381 kcal/day), low-fat (24% energy from fat) diet (Wing & Phelan, 2005). Additionally, 78% report consuming breakfast daily (Wing & Phelan, 2005), and participants report a very consistent eating pattern marked by limited dietary variety (H. Raynor, Wing, Jeffery Phelan, & Hill, 2005). As a whole, the eating pattern of NWCR participants appears to be fairly inflexible and somewhat monotonous. Indeed, registry participants also

endorse engaging in a fairly high level of dietary restraint, a form of cognitive control over their eating (Wing & Phelan, 2005).

In regards to leisure-time activity, NWCR participants report engaging in high levels of physical activity, with women in the registry reporting expending 2,525 kcal/week and men reporting expending 3,293 kcal/week in physical activity (Wing & Phelan, 2005). This level of physical activity represents approximately 1 hour per day of moderate-intense physical activity. These participants also report watching little television, with 62% of participants at baseline reporting watching 10 hours or less of television per week (D.A. Raynor, Phelan, Hill, & Wing, 2006).

Finally, registry participants also report engaging in regular self-monitoring of their weight (Wing & Phelan, 2005). At entry into the registry, approximately one-third of participants weigh themselves at least once per day, and more frequent self-weighing is associated with lower BMI at entry into the NWCR.

Few RCTs have been conducted to examine factors that improve weight loss maintenance following weight loss in adults. One recent trial conducted by Wing and colleagues (Wing, Tate, Gorin, Raynor, & Fava, 2006) did find that face-to-face contact, in which daily self-weighing was encouraged, did significantly improve weight loss maintenance as compared to a newsletter control condition (5.5 lb regain in face-to-face condition vs. 10.8 lb regain in control condition). More research, particularly well-designed RCTs, are needed to better understand factors that can improve long-term weight loss maintenance in adults.

## Conclusion

Given the current prevalence of obesity and projections for the future spread of the obesity epidemic, as well as the serious health and economic consequences associated with obesity, public health initiatives and government legislation designed to change health-related behaviors are needed to prevent weight gain and promote weight loss. However, considering the multifaceted etiology of obesity at the individual level, obesity treatment requires a tailored approach informed by individual obesity assessment. Although modest weight loss is generally achievable with obesity treatment and associated with improvements in health and well-being, weight loss maintenance may be a greater challenge. Long-term weight loss success may require modification of the food environment and built environment in order to facilitate maintenance of behavior change.

## Future Directions

1. What types of public health initiatives should be implemented to reverse current obesity prevalence trends?

2. How can the detrimental health and economic consequences of obesity be reduced?

3. How can determination of individual etiological contributors to obesity be used to tailor treatment programs and predict treatment outcomes?

4. What strategies can be used to improve long-term weight loss maintenance?

## References

Adams, K.F., Schatzkin, A., Harris, T.B., Kipnis, V., Mouw, T., Ballard-Barbash, R., et al. (2006). Overweight, obesity, and mortality in a large prospective cohort of persons 50 to 71 years old. *New England Journal of Medicine, 355*(8), 763–778.

American Diabetes Association. (2008). Economic costs of diabetes in the U.S. in 2007. *Diabetes Care, 32*(10), 596–615.

Andersen, R.E., Crespo, C.J., Bartlett, S.J., Bathon, J.M., & Fontaine, K.R. (2003). Relationship between body weight gain and significant knee, hip, and back pain in older Americans. *Obesity Research, 11*(10), 1159–1162.

Anderson, J.W., Kendall, C.W.C., & Jenkins, D.J.A. (2003). Importance of weight management in type 2 diabetes: Review with meta-analysis of clinical studies. *Journal of the American College of Nutrition, 22*(5), 331–339.

Astrup, A., Grunwalk, G.K., Melanson, E.L., Saris, W.H.M., & Hill, J.O. (2000). The role of low-fat diets in body weight control: A meta-analysis of ad libitum dietary intervention studies. *International Journal of Obesity and Related Metabolic Disorders, 24*, 1545–1552.

Atkins, R.C. (1998). *Dr. Atkins' new diet revolution* (Rev. ed.). New York: Avon Books.

Batterham, R.L., Ffytche, D.H., Rosenthal, J.M., Zelaya, F.O., Barker, G.J., Withers, D.J., et al. (2007). PYY modulation of cortical and hypothalamic brain areas predicts feeding behaviour in humans. *Nature, 450*(7166), 106–109.

Beuther, D.A., Weiss, S.T., & Sutherland, E.R. (2006). Obesity and asthma. *American Journal of Respiratory Critical Care Medicine, 174*(2), 112–119.

Bouchard, L., Rabasa-Lhoret, R., Faraj, M., Lavoie, M.-E., Mill, J., Perusse, L., et al. (2009). Differential epigenomic and transcriptomic responses in subcutaneous adipose tissue between low and high responders to caloric restriction. *American Journal of Clinical Nutrition, 91*(2), 309–320.

Bowman, S.A., & Vinyard, B.T. (2004). Fast food consumption of US adults: Impact on energy and nutrient intakes and overweight status. *Journal of the American College of Nutrition, 23*, 163–168.

Bravata, D.M., Smith-Spangler, C., Sundaram, V., Gienger, A.L., Lin, N., Lewis, R., et al. (2007). Using pedometers to increase physical activity and improve health: A systematic review. *Journal of the American Medical Association, 298*, 2296–2304.

Bray, G.A. (2009). Medications for obesity: Mechanisms and applications. *Clinics in Chest Medicine, 30*(3), 525–538.

Bray, G.A., Clearfield, M.B., Fintel, D.J., & Nelinson, D.S. (2009). Overweight and obesity: The pathogenesis of cardio-metabolic risk. *Clinical Cornerstone, 9*(4), 30–42.

Bray, G.A., & Popkin, B.M. (1998). Dietary fat intake does affect obesity. *American Journal of Clinical Nutrition, 68*, 1157–1173.

Brehm, B.J., Seeley, R.J., Daniels, S.R., & D'Alessio, D.A. (2003). A randomized trial comparing a very low carbohydrate diet and a calorie-restricted low fat diet on body weight and cardiovascular risk factors in healthy women. *Journal of Clinical Endocrinology and Metabolism, 88*, 1617–1623.

Briefel, R.R., & Johnson, C.L. (2004). Secular trends in dietary intake in the United States. *Annual Review of Nutrition, 24*(1), 401–431.

Brodie, D., Moscrip, V., & Hutcheon, R. (1998). Body composition measurement: A review of hydrodensitometry, anthropometry, and impedance methods. *Nutrition, 14*(3), 296–310.

Buchwald, H. (2002). Overview of bariatric surgery. *Journal of the American College of Surgeons, 194*(3), 367–375.

Buchwald, H., Avidor, Y., Braunwald, E., Jensen, M.D., Pories, W., Fahrbach, K., et al. (2004). Bariatric surgery: A systematic review and meta-analysis. *Journal of the American Medical Association, 292*(14), 1724–1737.

Calle, E.E., Rodriguez, C., Walker-Thurmond, K., & Thun, M.J. (2003). Overweight, obesity, and mortality from cancer in a prospectively studied cohort of U.S. adults. *New England Journal of Medicine, 348*(17), 1625–1638.

Campión, J., Milagro, F.I., & Martínez, J.A. (2009). Individuality and epigenetics in obesity. *Obesity Reviews, 10*(4), 383–392.

Cancer Prevention Research Center (home of the Transtheoretical Model). (2004). Retrieved from http://www.uri.edu/research/cprc/about-us.htm.

Cannon, C.P., & Kumar, A. (2009). Treatment of overweight and obesity: Lifestyle, pharmacologic, and surgical options. *Clinical Cornerstone, 9*(4), 55–71.

Cappuccio, F.P., Taggart, F.M., Kandala, N.B., Currie, A., Peile, E., Stranges, S., et al. (2008). Meta-analysis of short sleep duration and obesity in children and adults. *Sleep, 31*(5), 619–626.

Cawley, J., Rizzo, J.A., & Haas, K. (2007). Occupation-specific absenteeism costs associated with obesity and morbid obesity. *Journal of Occupational and Environmental Medicine, 49*(12), 1317–1324.

Chaput, J.-P., Leblanc, C., Perusse, L., Despres, J.-P., Bouchard, C., & Tremblay, A. (2009). Risk factors for adult overweight and obesity in the Quebec family study: Have we been barking up the wrong tree. *Obesity, 17*(10), 1964–1970.

Christakis, N.A., & Fowler, J.H. (2007). The spread of obesity in a large social network over 32 years. *New England Journal of Medicine, 357*(4), 370–379.

Coffey, C.S., Gadbury, G.L., Fontaine, K.R., Wang, C., Weindruch, R., & Allison, D.B. (2005). The effects of intentional weight loss as a latent variable problem. *Statistics in Medicine, 24*(6), 941–954.

Danielle, B., Robert, H.P., & Nancy, M.P. (2008). Gender differences in associations between body mass index and DSM-IV mood and anxiety disorders: Results from the national epidemiologic survey on alcohol and related conditions. *Annals of Epidemiology, 18*(6), 458–466.

Dehghan, M., & Merchant, A. (2008). Is bioelectrical impedance accurate for use in large epidemiological studies? *Nutrition Journal, 7*(1), 26.

Deurenberg, P., Deurenberg-Yap, M., & Guricci, S. (2002). Asians are different from Caucasians and from each other in their body mass index/body fat percent relationship. *Obesity Reviews, 3*(3), 141–146.

Diabetes Prevention Program Research Group. (2009). 10-year follow-up of diabetes incidence and weight loss in the diabetes prevention program outcomes study. *Lancet, 374*(9702), 1677–1686.

DiClemente, C.C. (2003). *How addictions develop and addicted people recover.* New York, NY: Guilford Press.

US Department of Health and Human Services. (2005). *Dietary Guidelines for Americans.* Rockville, MD: Author. Retrieved from http://www.health.gov/DietaryGuidelines/default.htm.

Donnelly, J.E., Blair, S.N., Jakicic, J.M., Manore, M.M., Rankin, J.W., & Smith, B.K. (2009). Appropriate physical activity intervention strategies for weight loss and prevention of weight regain for adults. *Medicine & Science in Sports & Exercise, 41*(2), 459–471.

Dunton, G.F., Berrigan, D., Ballard-Barbash, R., Graubard, B., & Atienza, A.A. (2009). Joint associations of physical activity and sedentary behaviors with body mass index: results from a time use survey of US adults. *International Journal of Obesity, 33*(12), 1427–1436.

Eckel, R.H., Kahn, R., Robertson, R.M., & Rizza, R.A. (2006). Preventing cardiovascular disease and diabetes: A call to action from the American diabetes association and the American heart association. *Circulation, 113*(25), 2943–2946.

Fabricatore, A., Wadden, T., Sarwer, D., & Faith, M. (2005). Health-related quality of life and symptoms of depression in extremely obese persons seeking bariatric surgery. *Obesity Surgery, 15*(3), 304–309.

Field, A.E., Manson, J.E., Taylor, C.B., Willett, W.C., & Colditz, G.A. (2004). Association of weight change, weight control practices, and weight cycling among women in the nurses' health study II. *International Journal of Obesity and Related Metabolic Disorders, 28*(9), 1134–1142.

Figlewicz, D.P., & Benoit, S.C. (2009). Insulin, leptin, and food reward: Update 2008. *American Journal of Physiology Regulatory, Integrative and Comparative Physiology, 296*(1), R9–19.

Finkelstein, E.A., Ruhm, C.J., & Kosa, K.M. (2005). Economic causes and consequences of obesity. *Annual Review of Public Health, 26*(1), 239–257.

Finkelstein, E.A., Trogdon, J.G., Brown, D.S., Allaire, B.T., Dellea, P.S., & Kamal-Bahl, S.J. (2008). The lifetime medical cost burden of overweight and obesity: Implications for obesity prevention. *Obesity, 16*(8), 1843–1848.

Finkelstein, E.A., Trogdon, J.G., Cohen, J.W., & Dietz, W. (2009). Annual medical spending attributable to obesity: Payer-and service-specific estimates. *Health Affairs, 28*(5), w822–831.

Flegal, K.M., & Graubard, B.I. (2009). Estimates of excess deaths associated with body mass index and other anthropometric variables. *American Journal of Clinical Nutrition, 89*(4), 1213–1219.

Flegal, K.M., Graubard, B.I., Williamson, D.F., & Gail, M.H. (2007). Cause-specific excess deaths associated with underweight, overweight, and obesity. *Journal of the American Medical Association, 298*(17), 2028–2037.

Flegal, K.M., Shepherd, J.A., Looker, A.C., Graubard, B.I., Borrud, L.G., Ogden, C.L., et al. (2009). Comparisons of percentage body fat, body mass index, waist circumference, and waist-stature ratio in adults. *American Journal of Clinical Nutrition, 89*(2), 500–508.

Fontaine, K.R., & Barofsky, I. (2001). Obesity and health-related quality of life. *Obesity Reviews, 2*(3), 173–182.

Foster, G., Wyatt, H.R., Hill, J.O., McGuckin, B.G., Brill, C., Mohammed, B.S., et al. (2003). A randomized trial of a low-carbohydrate diet for obesity. *New England Journal of Medicine, 348*, 2082–2090.

Foster, G.D., Makris, A.P., & Bailer, B.A. (2005). Behavioral treatment of obesity. *American Journal of Clinical Nutrition, 82*, 230S–235S.

Fox, C.S., Pencina, M.J., Wilson, P.W., Paynter, N.P., Vasan, R.S., & D'Agostino, R.B. (2008). Lifetime risk of cardiovascular disease among individuals with and without diabetes stratified by obesity status in the Framingham heart study. *Diabetes Care, 31*(8), 1582–1584.

Frankenfield, D., Roth-Yousey, L., & Compher, C. (2005). Comparison of predictive equations for resting metabolic rate in healthy nonobese and obese adults: A systematic review. *Journal of the American Dietetic Association, 105*(5), 775–789.

Fransen, M.P., Woodward, M.P., Norton, R.P., Coggan, C.P., Dawe, M.B.A., & Sheridan, N.M.P.H. (2002). Risk factors associated with the transition from acute to chronic occupational back pain. *Spine, 27*(1), 92–98.

Franz, M.J., VanWormer, J.J., Crain, A.L., Boucher, J.L., Histon, T., Caplan, W., et al. (2007). Weight-loss outcomes: A systematic review and meta-analysis of weight-loss clinical trials with a minimum 1-year follow-up. *Journal of the American Dietetic Association, 107*(10), 1755–1767.

French, S.A. (2003). Pricing effects on food choices. *Journal of Nutrition, 133*(3), 841S–843.

Gillman, M.W., Rifas-Shiman, S.L., Kleinman, K., Oken, E., Rich-Edwards, J.W., & Taveras, E.M. (2008). Developmental origins of childhood overweight: Potential public health impact. *Obesity, 16*(7), 1651–1656.

Giskes, K., van Lenthe, F.J., Turrell, G., Kamphuis, C.B.M., Brug, J., & Mackenbach, J.P. (2008). Socioeconomic position at different stages of the life course and its influence on body weight and weight gain in adulthood: A longitudinal study with 13-year follow-up. *Obesity, 16*(6), 1377–1381.

Gorin, A.A., Marinilli Pinto, A., Tate, D.F., Raynor, H.A., Fava, J.L., & Wing, R.R. (2007). Failure to meet weight loss expectations does not impact maintenance in successful weight losers. *Obesity, 15*(12), 3086–3090.

Greenwood, J.L.J., & Stanford, J.B. (2008). Preventing or improving obesity by addressing specific eating patterns. *Journal of the American Board of Family Medicine, 21*(2), 135–140.

Gregg, E.W., Cheng, Y.J., Cadwell, B.L., Imperatore, G., Williams, D.E., Flegal, K.M., et al. (2005). Secular trends in cardiovascular disease risk factors according to body mass index in US adults. *Journal of the American Medical Association, 293*(15), 1868–1874.

Gregg, E.W., Cheng, Y.J., Narayan, K.M.V., Thompson, T.J., & Williamson, D.F. (2007). The relative contributions of different levels of overweight and obesity to the increased prevalence of diabetes in the United States: 1976–2004. *Preventive Medicine, 45*(5), 348–352.

Guh, D., Zhang, W., Bansback, N., Amarsi, Z., Birmingham, C.L., & Anis, A. (2009). The incidence of co-morbidities related to obesity and overweight: A systematic review and meta-analysis. *BMC Public Health, 9*(1), 88.

Hagen, K.B.P., Tambs, K.P., & Bjerkedal, T.M.D. (2002). A prospective cohort study of risk factors for disability retirement because of back pain in the general working population. *Spine, 27*(16), 1790–1796.

Haskell, W.L., Lee, I. –M., Pate, R.R., Powell, K.E., Blair, S.N., et al. (2007). Physical activity and public health: Updated recommendation for adults from the American college of sports medicine and the American heart association. *Circulation, 116*(9), 1081–1093.

Hassan, M.K., Joshi, A.V., Madhavan, S.S., & Amonkar, M.M. (2003). Obesity and health-related quality of life: A cross-sectional analysis of the US population. *International Journal of Obesity and Related Metabolic Disorders, 27*(10), 1227–1232.

Hatzenbuehler, M.L., Keyes, K.M., & Hasin, D.S. (2009). Associations between perceived weight discrimination and the prevalence of psychiatric disorders in the general population. *Obesity, 17*(11), 2033–2039.

Heymsfield, S.B., van Mierlo, C.A., van der Knaap, H.C., Heo, M., & Frier, H.I. (2003). Weight management using a meal replacement strategy: Meta and polling analysis from six studies. *International Journal of Obesity & Related Metabolic Disorders, 27*, 537–549.

Hill, J.O., & Peters, J.C. (1998). Environmental contributions to the obesity epidemic. *Science, 280*(5368), 1371–1374.

Hill, R.J., & Davies, P.S. (2001). The validity of self-reported energy intake as determined using the doubly labeled water technique. *British Journal of Nutrition, 85*, 415–430.

Jakicic, J.M., Clarke, K., & Coleman, E. (2001). Appropriate intervention strategies for weight loss and prevention of weight regain for adults. *Medicine and Science in Sports and Exercise, 33*(12), 2145–2156.

Janssen, I., Katzmarzyk, P.T., & Ross, R. (2002). Body mass index, waist circumference, and health risk: Evidence in support of current National Institutes of Health Guidelines. *Archives of Internal Medicine, 162*(18), 2074–2079.

Jeffery, R.W., Bjornson-Benson, W.M., Rosenthal, B.S., Lindquist, R.A., Kurth, C.L., & Johnson, S.L. (1984). Correlates of weight loss and its maintenance over two years of follow-up among middle aged men. *Preventive Medicine, 13*, 155–168.

Jeffery, R.W., Drewnowski, A., Epstein, L., Stunkard, A., Willson, G., Wing, R., et al. (2000). Long-term maintenance of weight loss: Current status. *Health Psychology, 19*(1 Suppl.), 37–41.

Jia, H., & Lubetkin, E.I. (2005). The impact of obesity on health-related quality-of-life in the general adult US population. *Journal of Public Health, 27*(2), 156–164.

Keith, S.W., Redden, D.T., Katzmarzyk, P.T., Boggiano, M.M., Hanlon, E.C., Benca, R.M., et al. (2006). Putative contributors to the secular increase in obesity: Exploring the roads less traveled. *International Journal of Obesity, 30*(11), 1585–1594.

Kelly, T., Yang, W., Chen, C.S., Reynolds, K., & He, J. (2008). Global burden of obesity in 2005 and projections to 2030. *International Journal of Obesity, 32*(9), 1431–1437.

Klesges, R.C., Klesges, L.M., Haddock, C.K., & Eck, L.H. (1992). A longitudinal analysis of the impact of dietary intake and physical activity on weight change in adults. *American Journal of Clinical Nutrition, 55*, 818–822.

Knowler, W.C., Barrett-Connor, E., Fowler, S.E., Hamman, R.F., Lachin, J.M., Walker, E.A., et al. (2002). Reduction in the incidence of type 2 diabetes with lifestyle intervention or metformin. *New England Journal of Medicine, 346*(6), 393–403.

Kokkoris, P., & Pi-Sunyer, F.X. (2003). Obesity and endocrine disease. *Endocrinology & Metabolism Clinics of North America, 32*(4), 895–914.

LaMonte, M.J., & Blair, S.N. (2006). Physical activity, cardiorespiratory fitness, and adiposity: Contributions to disease risk. *Current Opinion in Clinical Nutrition & Metabolic Care, 9*(5), 540–546.

Larson, N.I., Story, M.T., & Nelson, M.C. (2009). Neighborhood environments: Disparities in access to healthy foods in the U.S. *American Journal of Preventive Medicine, 36*(1), 74–81.

Lavie, C.J., Milani, R.V., & Ventura, H.O. (2009). Obesity and cardiovascular disease: Risk factor, paradox, and impact of weight loss. *Journal of the American College of Cardiology, 53*(21), 1925–1932.

Lenard, N.R., & Berthoud, H.-R. (2008). Central and peripheral regulation of food intake and physical activity: Pathways and genes. *Obesity, 16*(3s), S11–S22.

Levine, J.A. (2005). Measurement of energy expenditure. *Public Health Nutrition, 8*(7a), 1123–1132.

Levine, J.A., Lanningham-Foster, L.M., McCrady, S.K., Krizan, A.C., Olson, L.R., Kane, P.H., et al. (2005). Interindividual variation in posture allocation: Possible role in human obesity. *Science, 307*(5709), 584–586.

Lindström, J., Ilanne-Parikka, P., Peltonen, M., Aunola, S., Eriksson, J.G., Hemiö, K., et al. (2006). Sustained reduction in the incidence of type 2 diabetes by lifestyle intervention: Follow-up of the Finnish diabetes prevention study. *The Lancet, 368*(9548), 1673–1679.

Loos, R.J.F., & Bouchard, C. (2008). FTO: The first gene contributing to common forms of human obesity. *Obesity Reviews, 9*(3), 246–250.

Malik, V.S., Schulze, M.B., & Hu, F.B. (2006). Intake of sugar sweetened beverages and weight gain: A systematic review. *American Journal of Clinical Nutrition, 84*, 274–288.

Martinez, S.W. (2007). *The US food marketing system: Recent developments, 1997–2006.* Washington, DC: US Department of Agriculture.

McNeely, W., & Benfield, P. (1998). Orlistat. *Drugs, 56*(2), 241–249.

McTigue, K.M., Hess, R., & Ziouras, J. (2006). Obesity in older adults: A systematic review of the evidence for diagnosis and treatment. *Obesity, 14*(9), 1485–1497.

Mehta, N., & Chang, V. (2008). Weight status and restaurant availability a multilevel analysis. *American Journal of Preventative Medicine, 34*, 127–133.

Messier, S.P. (2008). Obesity and osteoarthritis: Disease genesis and nonpharmacologic weight management. *Rheumatic Disease Clinics of North America, 34*(3), 713–729.

Michie, S., Abraham, C., Whittington, C., McAteer, J., & Gupta, S. (2009). Effective techniques in healthy eating and physical activity interventions: A meta-regression. *Health Psychology, 28*, 690–701.

Misra, A., & Khurana, L. (2008). Obesity and the metabolic syndrome in developing countries. *Journal of Clinical Endocrinology and Metabolism, 93*, s9–s30.

Mokdad, A.H., Marks, J.S., Stroup, D.F., & Grerberding, J.L. (2004). Actual causes of death in the United States, 2000. *Journal of the American Medical Association, 291*, 1238–1245.

Neter, J.E., Stam, B.E., Kok, F.J., Grobbee, D.E., & Geleijnse, J.M. (2003). Influence of weight reduction on blood pressure: A meta-analysis of randomized controlled trials. *Hypertension, 42*(5), 878–884.

National Heart, Lung, and Blood Institute (NHLBI). (1998). Clinical guidelines on the identification, evaluation, and treatment of overweight and obesity in adults: The evidence report. *Obesity Research, 6*, 51S–210S.

Nielsen, S.J., & Popkin, B.M. (2003). Patterns and trends in food portion sizes, 1977-1998. *Journal of the American Medical Association, 289*, 450–453.

Olshansky, S.J., Passaro, D.J., Hershow, R.C., Layden, J., Carnes, B.A., Brody, J., et al. (2005). A potential decline in life expectancy in the United States in the 21st century. *New England Journal of Medicine, 352*(11), 1138–1145.

Padwal, R.S., & Majumdar, S.R. (2007). Drug treatments for obesity: Orlistat, sibutramine, and rimonabant. *The Lancet, 369*(9555), 71–77.

Paffenbarger, R.S., Wing, A.L., & Hyde, R.T. (1997). Paffenbarger Physical Activity Questionnaire. *Medicine & Science in Sports & Exercise, 29*(6), 83–88.

Pal, S., Cheng, C., Egger, G., Binns, C., & Donovan, R. (2009). Using pedometers to increase physical activity in overweight and obese women: A pilot study. *BMC Public Health, 9*, 309.

Papas, M.A., Alberg, A.J., Ewing, R., Helzlsouer, K.J., Gary, T.L., & Klassen, A.C. (2007). The built environment and obesity. *Epidemiologic Reviews, 29*(1), 129–143.

Petry, N.M., Barry, D., Pietrzak, R.H., & Wagner, J.A. (2008). Overweight and obesity are associated with psychiatric disorders: Results from the national epidemiologic survey on alcohol and related conditions. *Psychosomatic Medicine, 70*(3), 288–297.

Poobalan, A.S., Aucott, L., Smith, W.C.S., Avenell, A., Jung, R., Broom, J., et al. (2004). Effects of weight loss in overweight/obese individuals and long-term lipid outcomes; A systematic review. *Obesity Reviews, 5*(1), 43–50.

Poobalan, A.S., Aucott, L.S., Smith, W.C.S., Avenell, A., Jung, R., & Broom, J. (2007). Long-term weight loss effects on all cause mortality in overweight/obese populations. *Obesity Reviews, 8*(6), 503–513.

Puhl, R.M., & Heuer, C.A. (2009). The stigma of obesity: A review and update. *Obesity, 17*(5), 941–964.

Raynor, D.A., Phelan, S., Hill, J.O., & Wing, R.R. (2006). Television viewing and long-term weight maintenance: Results from the national weight control registry. *Obesity, 14*, 1816–1824.

Raynor, H.A., Jeffery, R.W., Phelan, S., Hill, J.O., Wing, R.R. (2005). Amount of food group variety consumed in the diet and long-term weight loss maintenance. *Obesity Research, 13*, 883–890.

Raynor, H.A., & Epstein, L.H. (2001). Dietary variety, energy regulation, and obesity. *Psychological Bulletin, 127*, 325–341.

Raynor, H.A., Jeffery, R.W., Tate, D.F., & Wing, R.R. (2004). Relationship between changes in food group variety, dietary intake, and weight during obesity treatment. *International Journal of Obesity, 28*, 813–820.

Raynor, H.A., Niemeier, H.N., & Wing, R.R. (2006). Effect of limiting snack food variety on long-term sensory-specific satiety and monotony during obesity treatment. *Eating Behaviors, 7*, 1–14.

Raynor, H.A., Wing, R.R., Jeffery, R.W., Phelan, S., & Hill, J.O. (2005). Amount of food group variety consumed in the diet and long-term weight loss maintenance. *Obesity Research, 13*, 883–890.

Renehan, A.G., Tyson, M., Egger, M., Heller, R.F., & Zwahlen, M. (2008). Body-mass index and incidence of cancer: A systematic review and meta-analysis of prospective observational studies. *The Lancet, 371*(9612), 569–578.

Rolls, B.J. (2009). The relationship between dietary energy density and energy intake. *Physiology & Behavior, 97*(5), 609–615.

Rolls, B.J., Morris, E.L., & Roe, L.S. (2002). Portion size of food affects energy intake in normal-weight and overweight men and women. *American Journal of Clinical Nutrition, 76*, 1207–1213.

Romero-Corral, A., Somers, V.K., Sierra-Johnson, J., Thomas, R.J., Collazo-Clavell, M.L., Korinek, J., et al. (2008). Accuracy of body mass index in diagnosing obesity in the adult general population. *International Journal of Obesity, 32*(6), 959–966.

Romieu, I., Willett, W.C., Stampfer, M.J., Colditz, G.A., Sampson, L., Rosner, B., et al. (1988). Energy intake and other determinants of relative weight. *American Journal of Clinical Nutrition, 47*, 406–412.

Roseboom, T., de Rooij, S., & Painter, R. (2006). The Dutch famine and its long-term consequences for adult health. *Early Human Development, 82*(8), 485–491.

Rosenheck, R. (2008). Fast food consumption and increased caloric intake: A systematic review of a trajectory towards weight gain and obesity risk. *Obesity Reviews, 9*(6), 535–547.

Rucker, D., Padwal, R., Li, S.K., Curioni, C., & Lau, D.C.W. (2007). Long term pharmacotherapy for obesity and overweight: updated meta-analysis. *British Medical Journal, 335*(7631), 1194–1199.

Sacks, F.M., Bray, G.A., Carey, V.J., Smith, S.R., Ryan, D.H., Anton, S.D., et al. (2009). Comparison of weight-loss diets with different compositions of fat, protein, and carbohydrates. *New England Journal of Medicine, 360*(9), 859–873.

Sallis, J.F., Bowles, H.R., Bauman, A., Ainsworth, B.E., Bull, F.C., Craig, C.L., et al. (2009). Neighborhood environments and physical activity among adults in 11 countries. *American Journal of Preventive Medicine, 36*(6), 484–490.

Schauer, P. (2005). Gastric bypass for severe obesity: Approaches and outcomes. *Surgery for Obesity and Related Diseases, 1*(3), 297–300.

Scott, K.M., Bruffaerts, R., Simon, G.E., Alonso, J., Angermeyer, M., de Girolamo, G., et al. (2007). Obesity and mental disorders in the general population: Results from the world mental health surveys. *International Journal of Obesity, 32*(1), 192–200.

Segal, N.L., Feng, R., McGuire, S.A., Allison, D.B., & Miller, S. (2008). Genetic and environmental contributions to body mass index: Comparative analysis of monozygotic twins, dizygotic twins and same-age unrelated siblings. *International Journal of Obesity, 33*(1), 37–41.

Singh, A.S., Mulder, C., Twisk, J.W.R., Mechelen, W.V., & Chinapaw, M.J.M. (2008). Tracking of childhood overweight into adulthood: a systematic review of the literature. *Obesity Reviews, 9*(5), 474–488.

Steinbrook, R. (2004). Surgery for severe obesity. *New England Journal of Medicine, 350*(11), 1075–1079.

Stevens, V.J., Obarzanek, E., Cook, N.R., Lee, I.-M., Appel, L.J., Smith West, D., et al. (2001). Long-term weight loss and changes in blood pressure: Results of the trials of hypertension prevention, phase II. *Annals of Internal Medicine, 134*(1), 1–11.

Stoger, R. (2008). Epigenetics and obesity. *Pharmacogenomics, 9*(12), 1851–1860.

Strychar, I. (2006). Diet in the management of weight loss. *Canadian Medical Association Journal, 174*(1), 56–63.

Stunkard, A.J., & Costello Allison, K. (2003). Two forms of disordered eating in obesity: Binge eating and night eating. *International Journal of Obesity Related Metabolism Disorders, 27*(1), 1–12.

Sugiyama, T., Salmon, J., Dunstan, D.W., Bauman, A.E., & Owen, N. (2007). Neighborhood walkability and TV viewing time among Australian adults. *American Journal of Preventive Medicine, 33*(6), 444–449.

Swinburn, B., Sacks, G., & Ravussin, E. (2009). Increased food energy supply is more than sufficient to explain the US epidemic of obesity. *American Journal of Clinical Nutrition, 90*(6), 1453–1456.

Thom, T., Haase, N., Rosamond, W., Howard, V.J., Rumsfeld, J., Manolio, T., et al. (2006). Heart disease and stroke statistics—2006 update: A report from the American heart association statistics committee and stroke statistics subcommittee. *Circulation, 113*(6), e85–e151.

Thompson, F.E., & Byers, T. (1994). Dietary assessment resource manual. *Journal of Nutrition, 124*(11S), 2245s–2317s.

Tooze, J.A., Schoeller, D.A., Subar, A.F., Kipnis, V., Schatzkin, A., & Troiano, R.P. (2007). Total daily energy expenditure among middle-aged men and women: The OPEN study. *American Journal of Clinical Nutrition, 86*(2), 382–387.

Trogdon, J.G., Finkelstein, E.A., Hylands, T., Dellea, P.S., & Kamal-Bahl, S.J. (2008). Indirect costs of obesity: A review of the current literature. *Obesity Reviews, 9*(5), 489–500.

Tsai, C.J. (2009). Steatocholecystitis and fatty gallbladder disease. *Digestive Diseases and Sciences, 54*(9), 1857–1863.

Tsai, C.J., Leitzmann, M.F., Willett, W.C., & Giovannucci, E.L. (2004). Prospective study of abdominal adiposity and gallstone disease in US men. *American Journal Clinical Nutrition, 80*(1), 38–44.

Tsai, C.J., Leitzmann, M.F., Willett, W.C., & Giovannucci, E.L. (2006). Central adiposity, regional fat distribution, and the risk of cholecystectomy in women. *Gut, 55*(5), 708–714.

Tuomilehto, J., Lindstrom, J., Eriksson, J., Valle, T., Hamalainen, H., Ilanne-Parikka, P., et al. (2001). Prevention of type 2 diabetes mellitus by changes in lifestyle among subjects with impaired glucose tolerance. *New England Journal of Medicine, 344*, 1343–1350.

U.S. Department of Health and Human Services (2000). *Healthy people 2010* (2nd ed.). Washington, DC: United States Government Printing Office.

Van Gaal, L.F., Mertens, I.L., & Ballaux, D. (2005). What is the relationship between risk factor reduction and degree of weight loss? *European Heart Journal Supplement, 7*, L21–L26.

Van Wye, G., Dubin, J.A., Blair, S.N., & Di Pietro, L. (2007). Weight cycling and 6-year weight change in healthy adults: The aerobics center longitudinal study. *Obesity, 15*(3), 731–739.

Varsha, V. (Ed.). (2006). *Health and treatment strategies in obesity* Vol. 27. Baltimore, MD: Karger.

Vasan, R.S., Pencina, M.J., Cobain, M., Freiberg, M.S., & D'Agostino, R.B. (2005). Estimated risks for developing obesity in the Framingham heart study. *Annals of Internal Medicine, 143*(7), 473–480.

Wadden, T.A., & Berkowitz, R. (2001). Very-low-calorie diets. In C.G. Fairburn, & K. Brownell (Eds.), *Eating disorders and obesity* (pp. 534–538). New York: Guilford.

Wadden, T.A., Crerand, C.E., & Brock, J. (2005). Behavioral treatment of obesity. *Psychiatric Clinics of North America, 28*, 151–170.

Wadden, T.A., & Stunkard, A. (Eds.). (2002). *Handbook of obesity treatment.* New York: The Guilford Press.

Wang, Y., & Beydoun, M.A. (2007). The obesity epidemic in the United States gender, age, socioeconomic, racial/ethnic, and geographic characteristics: A systematic review and meta-regression analysis. *Epidemiologic Reviews, 29*(1), 6–28.

Warburton, D.E.R., Nicol, C.W., & Bredin, S.S.D. (2006). Health benefits of physical activity: the evidence. *Canadian Medical Association Journal, 174*(6), 801–809.

Williams, D.M., Raynor, H.A., & Ciccolo, J.T. (2008). A review of TV viewing and its association with health outcomes in adults. *American Journal of Lifestyle Medicine, 2*, 250–259.

Williamson, D.F., Thompson, T.J., Thun, M., Flanders, D., Pamuk, E., & Byers, T. (2000). Intentional weight loss and mortality among overweight individuals with diabetes. *Diabetes Care, 23*(10), 1499–1504.

Wilson, P.W.F., D'Agostino, R.B., Sullivan, L., Parise, H., & Kannel, W.B. (2002). Overweight and obesity as determinants of cardiovascular risk: The Framingham experience. *Archives of Internal Medicine, 162*(16), 1867–1872.

Wing, R.R. (2004). Behavioral approaches to the treatment of obesity. In G.A. Bray, & C. Bouchard (Eds.), *Handbook of obesity: Clinical applications* (2nd ed., pp. 855–873). New York: Marcel Dekker, Inc.

Wing, R.R., Burton, L.R., Mullen, M., Jeffery, R.W., Thorson, C., & Raether, C. (1994). Provision of structured meal plans improves weight loss in overweight females. *Annals of Behavioral Medicine, 16*(Suppl.), S042.

Wing, R.R., & Phelan, S. (2005). Long-term weight loss maintenance. *American Journal of Clinical Nutrition, 82*, 222S–225S.

Wing, R.R., Tate, D.F., Gorin, A.A., Raynor, H.A., & Fava, J.L. (2006). A self-regulation program for maintenance of weight loss. *New England Journal of Medicine, 355*, 1563–1571.

Wing, R.R., Tate, D.F., Gorin, A.A., Raynor, H.A., Fava, J.L., & Machan, J. (2007). "STOP regain": Are there negative effects of daily weighing? *Journal of Consulting and Clinical Psychology, 75*(4), 652–656.

Wolin, K.Y., & Colditz, G.A. (2008). Can weight loss prevent cancer. *British Journal of Cancer, 99*(7), 995–999.

Woods, S.C., & D'Alessio, D.A. (2008). Central control of body weight and appetite. *Journal of Clinical Endocrinology and Metabolism, 93*(11, Suppl.1), s37–s50.

Yancy, W.S., Olsen, M.K., Guyton, J.R., Bakst, R.P., & Westman, E.C. (2004). A low-carbohydrate, ketogenic diet versus a low-fat diet to treat obesity and hyperlipidemia. *Annals of Internal Medicine, 140*, 769–777.

Yang, W., Kelly, T., & He, J. (2007). Genetic epidemiology of obesity. *Epidemiological Reviews, 29*(1), 49–61.

Zhao, G., Ford, E.S., Dhingra, S., Li, C., Strine, T.W., & Mokdad, A.H. (2009). Depression and anxiety among US adults: Associations with body mass index. *International Journal of Obesity, 33*(2), 257–266.

Zheng, H., Lenard, N.R., Shin, A.C., & Berthoud, H.R. (2009). Appetite control and energy balance regulation in the modern world: Reward-driven brain overrides repletion signals. *International Journal of Obesity, 33*(S2), S8–S13.

# CHAPTER
# 30

# Dispositional Optimism, Psychophysiology, and Health

Suzanne C. Segerstrom

**Abstract**

Dispositional optimism—the belief that the future generally holds positive but not negative events—appears to confer widespread benefit in terms of psychosocial well-being. An important question is whether this advantage extends to biological functions, such as immune activity, and to physical health. Although several studies have examined this question, the answer is still obscure. Amid studies demonstrating a physiological or health benefit to being more dispositionally optimistic are a substantial number of null findings. This chapter reviews these studies and considers why optimism is not more consistently associated with lower blood pressure, higher immune function, and lower morbidity and mortality.

**Keywords:** Dispositional optimism, psychosocial well-being, health

Dispositional optimism, the belief that the future generally holds positive but not negative events, appears to confer widespread benefit in terms of psychosocial well-being. An important question is whether this advantage extends to biological functions, such as immune activity, and to physical health. Although several studies have examined this question, the answer is still obscure. Amid studies demonstrating a physiological or health benefit to being more dispositionally optimistic are a substantial number of null findings. The goal of this chapter is not only to review these studies, but to illuminate why optimism is not more consistently associated with lower blood pressure, higher immune function, and lower morbidity and mortality.

## Psychosocial Qualities of Optimists

It may be beyond the scope of this volume, much less this chapter, to review the individual studies that link dispositional optimism to more positive and less negative affect, less psychopathology (e.g., depression), higher life satisfaction, more adaptive coping with and resistance to stress, more positive and long-lasting relationships, and so on.

Nonetheless, it is useful to briefly examine some foundational and meta-analytic results that illustrate the characteristics of dispositional optimism important to understanding optimism's effects on psychophysiology and other "hard" markers of health (e.g., survival). Although the relationship of optimism to these markers is complex, the straightforward findings that demonstrate how optimistic people approach stressful and demanding situations is particularly important in understanding how they differ physiologically from their more pessimistic counterparts.

Scheier and Carver (1985) developed the most commonly used measure of dispositional optimism, the Life Orientation Test (LOT), as a broad trait measure of optimistic outcome expectancies. In their theoretical model, optimistic expectancies determined an individual's self-regulatory approach: If expectancies were optimistic, persistence at a goal or toward a standard would follow; and if expectancies were pessimistic, disengagement would follow. In essence, the expectation of achieving a goal justified the effort involved in persisting toward achieving that goal. Without that expectation, no justification for expending effort existed, and disengagement was the reasonable response.

In the lab, optimistic expectancies for success at the task promoted persistence versus giving up in goal-directed behavior (Carver, Blaney, & Scheier, 1979; Scheier & Carver, 1982). Based on these findings, the dispositional form of optimism was proposed to promote better adaptation to challenges, stressors, and difficulties; the aggregation of these adaptations over time and situations should predict other multiply determined outcomes, such as health. Evidence accrued since the appearance of the LOT supports the original model with regard to expectancies and self-regulation. Dispositional optimism promotes persistence in the lab, much as specific expectancies do (Solberg Nes, Segerstrom, & Sephton, 2005). Meta-analysis indicates that dispositional optimism correlates with more active and approach forms of coping, whether directed at changing circumstances or emotions (Solberg Nes & Segerstrom, 2006).

In turn, this active, persistent mode of engaging one's circumstances or emotions can lead to better psychological and social health. In general, active and approach coping is more effective than disengagement in resolving all but very brief stressors (Suls & Fletcher, 1985), and coping at least partially mediates the relationship between optimism and psychological well-being (see Carver, Scheier, & Segerstrom, 2010, for a review). In one study, optimism promoted more active problem solving in couples, which partially mediated the relationship between optimism and the resolution of the conflict in question (Srivastava, McGonigal, Richards, Butler, & Gross, 2006). It is important to note that optimism is particularly likely to result in approach, persistence, and engagement with goals when the goal is high in importance (Geers, Wellman, & Lassiter, 2009), the benefits outweigh the costs (Segerstrom & Solberg Nes, 2006), and potentially more productive alternative goals are not available (Aspinwall & Richter, 1999). In sum, then, more optimistic people are more likely to adopt psychologically optimal self-regulatory strategies and enjoy more positive affect, less negative affect, and more life satisfaction as a result (Carver & Scheier, 1990). An early meta-analysis of the relationship of the LOT to negative affect found a medium to large, inverse relationship across diverse samples (see Table 30.1).

## Optimism and Health

The same meta-analysis found a small to medium, inverse relationship between dispositional optimism

Table 30.1 Meta-analytic results for the relationship between optimism and important outcomes

| Outcome | Effect size ($r$) | Source |
| --- | --- | --- |
| Negative affect | −.44 | Andersson, 1996 |
| Subjective health | .29 | Andersson, 1996 |
| Avoidance coping | −.21 | Solberg Nes & Segerstrom, 2006 |
| Subjective health | .21 | Rasmussen, Scheier, & Greenhouse, 2009 |
| Objective health | .11 | Rasmussen, Scheier, & Greenhouse, 2009 |

and symptom reporting, a subjective measure of health. A more recent meta-analysis found a similar effect size between optimism and symptom reporting[1] (see Table 30.1). In addition, optimism was associated with other health measures, including survival in the context of transplant, cancer, or aging. The effect size for all "hard" or objective markers of health, which included such outcomes as blood pressure, immune function, mortality, and survival, was small but significant and in the direction of optimism promoting better health (see Table 30.1).

Although small ($r = .11$), this effect size is consequential. It is larger than the effects of cognitive ability (IQ) and socioeconomic status on mortality risk (.02 and .06, respectively) and comparable to the effects of other personality traits, such as conscientiousness, on mortality risk (.09; Roberts, Kuncel, Shiner, Caspi, & Goldberg, 2007). Nonetheless, one might ask why the effects of optimism are substantially larger for psychological and subjective health outcomes than for objective markers of physiology and health. Two possibilities arise: the first has to do with mediation and the nature of causal chains, and the second has to do with moderation and the variability of the relationship between optimism and physical health.

First, if one examines the relationships of optimism to coping, affect, subjective health, and objective health (including physiology, morbidity, and mortality) shown in Table 30.1, one finds that optimism has the largest effect on how people *feel*, both in terms of their emotional well-being and in terms of their physical health. Although not proving specific pathways, these effect sizes are suggestive of potential causal chains. The suggestion arises from the logic of mediational pathways. In the mediational path that runs from A to B to C, then the relationship between A and B (AB) is necessarily larger than the relationship between A and C (AC), because AC is roughly the product of the values of AB and BC. If BC < 1, then AC < AB. Using this as a guideline, one is guarded about the possibility that optimism makes people feel physically healthier because they are objectively healthier, because the relationship between optimism and objective health is substantially smaller than the relationship between optimism and subjective health. One is less guarded about the possibility that optimism makes people *feel* physically healthier, which contributes to their objective health (Idler & Benjamini, 1997). Therefore, one possibility for the small effect of dispositional optimism on objective health is that objective health is at the tail end of a mediational chain.

Second, the adaptiveness of optimism for physiology and objective health may not be as clear-cut as for psychological adjustment and subjective health. I have not been able to locate any study that shows an inverse relationship between optimism and affect or psychological symptoms: that more optimism equals more depression, less happiness, and so on.[2] On the other hand, such findings are not uncommon for physiological markers. Even without considering moderated relationships—that is, examining only main effects of dispositional optimism on physiology—one finds that the mean effect size is embedded in a fairly large range. Figure 30.1 shows this range for studies of optimism and the immune system. Note that all effects have been coded such that positive numbers are in the "healthier" direction (for most people under most circumstances). Although the median effect size is small and positive (.06), the range is quite large (−.20 to .62).

Work reviewed in more detail below suggests why this might be true: The effect of dispositional optimism on physiology depends substantially if not entirely on the circumstances. Under one condition, optimism could be associated with better immune function and lower blood pressure; under another condition, the opposite could be true. Aggregating across all circumstances and conditions, there is a small net positive effect of being optimistic. This is indicated not only by the mean of the effect sizes across all main effects of optimism on physiology, but also the magnitude of the effects of optimism on morbidity (i.e., disease) and mortality (i.e., the fatal outcome of morbidity). These studies typically follow subjects for at least months and more typically years, effectively aggregating across the many situations, conditions, and circumstances encountered by the participants. Figure 30.1 superimposes the effect sizes for morbidity and mortality over those for immunity. One notes again the small median effect size (also .06), but in the context of a smaller range (.005 to .18).

The challenge for research on optimism and health, then, is to work backward from these small (but meaningful) effect sizes for morbidity and mortality to understand underlying physiology, the factors that contribute to variability in the effects of optimism on physiology, and the mechanisms that account for these factors. This challenge has been only partially answered at this point, but enough work has been done to sketch in the outlines. The remainder of this chapter will focus on work on two physiological parameters for which there is a substantial amount of work on the effects of optimism: blood pressure and immunity.

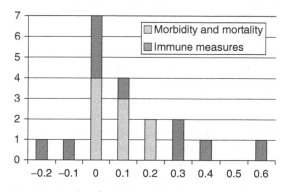

**Fig. 30.1** Number of studies (y axis) reporting various effect sizes (x axis) for the relationship of dispositional optimism to the immune system (dark bars) and to morbidity and mortality (light bars, superimposed). Most effect sizes were taken from Rasmussen et al. (2009). Three additional effect sizes from recent reports not included in Rasmussen et al. are also represented (O'Donovan et al., 2009; Segerstrom, 2006; Tindle et al., 2009).

## Optimism and Blood Pressure: Who and When
### The Nature and Significance of Blood Pressure in Brief
Blood pressure is the joint product of cardiac output and peripheral resistance. Cardiac output is determined by the volume of blood exiting the heart via contraction of the left ventricle; when that volume is relatively large, cardiac output is higher. Peripheral resistance is determined by the size of the blood vessels; when they are relatively constricted, resistance is higher. Because it is related to contraction of the ventricle, blood pressure is phasic. The highest pressure, systolic blood pressure (SBP), comes at the time at which the left ventricle contracts and sends a pressure wave into the circulatory system. Systolic BP is the top number in the usual expression of blood

pressure (e.g., the 120 in 120/80). When the ventricle relaxes, a lower pressure, diastolic blood pressure (DBP) results. Diastolic BP is the bottom number in the expression.

Cardiac output and peripheral resistance, and therefore blood pressure, are affected by the autonomic nervous system and especially the sympathetic branch. Sympathetic activation and parasympathetic withdrawal result in larger cardiac output, which tends to raise SBP. Effects on total peripheral resistance are more complicated. The parasympathetic branch has little effect on the vasculature, and the effects of sympathetic activation can depend on the location of the vasculature (e.g., skeletal vs. visceral tissue). The net effect of sympathetic activation, however, is generally an increase in total peripheral resistance and a resultant increase in both SBP and DBP. Overviews of the physiology and measurement of blood pressure can be found in Stern, Ray, and Quigley (2001) and Brownley, Hurwitz, and Schneiderman (2000).

Blood pressure, particularly SBP, is an important prognostic indicator for several kinds of morbidity, including heart attack and stroke, as well as mortality (Psaty et al., 2001). For example, each 10 mmHg decrease in SBP is associated with a one-third decrease in stroke risk (Lawes, Bennett, Feigin, & Rodgers, 2004). In addition, blood pressure stress reactivity—the degree to which blood pressure increases during stress—predicts the development of hypertension, atherosclerosis, and stroke (e.g., Everson et al., 2001).

### Optimism and Tonic Blood Pressure

Räikkönen and her colleagues have carried out two studies of dispositional optimism and ambulatory blood pressure. Ambulatory studies, in which blood pressure is measured intermittently over the course of hours to days, yield estimates that are more representative of an individual's typical blood pressure than are single assessments. The first study (Räikkönen, Matthews, Flory, Owens, & Gump, 1999) measured blood pressure during waking hours over 3 days in working adults. Dichotomizing dispositional optimism yielded significant differences between optimists and pessimists in both SBP and DBP, with pessimists having approximately 5 mm Hg higher SBP and DBP. The effects of optimism were particularly marked when negative mood at the time of the pressure reading was low. That is, when negative mood at the time of the pressure reading was high, both optimists and pessimists had relatively higher blood pressure; when negative mood was low, optimists had

relatively lower blood pressure, but pessimists' blood pressure remained high.

These results were partially replicated in a second study (Räikkönen & Matthews, 2008) that measured blood pressure during both waking and sleeping hours over 2 days and 1 night in adolescents aged 14–16. Again, optimism was associated with higher daytime and nighttime SBP and with higher daytime DBP, as well as the probability of exceeding the 95th percentile of blood pressure for age, weight, and height. Whereas optimistically phrased items (e.g., "In uncertain times, I usually expect the best") were somewhat more predictive of blood pressure in adults, pessimistically phrased items (e.g., "If something can go wrong for me, it will") were more predictive in adolescents, perhaps because they were more reliable in this sample. On the other hand, two pessimistically phrased items also predicted the development of clinical hypertension (blood pressure of 165/95 or higher) in a large sample of middle-aged men (Everson, Kaplan, Goldberg, & Salonen, 2000). Therefore, both optimistically and pessimistically phrased items have been predictive of blood pressure in these studies, and there is no systematic indication that it is better to be more optimistic versus less pessimistic.

Consistent with the generally positive effects of optimism on morbidity and mortality, then, optimism is associated with lower blood pressure on a daily and prospective basis. Furthermore, affect and depression did not mediate between optimism and blood pressure or hypertension. Rather, the interaction between optimism and negative mood (Räikkönen et al., 1999) indicated that optimists and pessimists were more alike when negative affect was high and more different when it was low. More pessimistic people may not benefit from lower blood pressure when their negative affect is lower than usual. The consequences of higher blood pressure among more pessimistic individuals may be the development and progression of atherosclerosis and, ultimately, cardiovascular mortality. Optimism is, in fact, associated with lesser progression of atherosclerosis and lower cardiovascular mortality in large-scale studies (Giltay, Kamphuis, Kalmijn, Zitman, & Knorhout, 2006; Matthews, Räikkönen, Sutton-Tyrrell, & Kuller, 2004; Tindle et al., 2009).

### Optimism and Blood Pressure Reactivity

The effects of optimism on blood pressure reactivity are more mixed. Two studies with undergraduates suggest that optimism predicts less blood pressure reactivity (Geers, Wellman, Helfer, Fowler, &

France, 2008; Williams, Riels, & Roper, 1990). Increases in DBP during mental arithmetic and a cold pressor task were significantly smaller for more optimistic students, and increases in SBP during the cold pressor task were marginally smaller for more optimistic students. Although neither study tested mediators, optimists also reported less pain during the cold pressor task and less anxiety during the mental arithmetic task. These differences in subjective experience may have accounted for the differences in blood pressure reactivity. Blood pressure reactivity could in turn mediate between optimism and outcomes such as tonic hypertension, atherosclerosis, and stroke.

Two other studies, however, suggest limits on or moderators of this effect. Both studies reported blood pressure reactivity as a function of the combined effects of optimism and chronic stressors that are more frequently experienced by racial minorities: violence exposure and discrimination. The first study (Clark, Benkert, & Flack, 2006) exposed inner-city black youth to a cognitive stressor (digits forward and backward). Violence exposure was inversely related to SBP and DBP reactivity; that is, youth who had been exposed to more violence in their homes and neighborhoods had smaller increases in blood pressure during the stressor. This finding supported a hypoarousal interpretation, in which desensitization to stressors occurs with higher violence exposure. Optimism moderated this relationship for SBP, such that the effect of violence exposure was stronger at higher levels of optimism; that is, more optimistic youth had more evidence for hypoarousal. This was not an effect of initial values, as baseline blood pressure was similar across levels of optimism and violence exposure. This study, therefore, is consistent with the previous studies in one sense—optimism was associated with less blood pressure reactivity—but also showed that the effects of optimism are context- and population-dependent. In fact, in this study, the highest reactivity was associated with low violence exposure and high optimism.

The second study likewise concluded that "the benefits of optimism (in particular) may be situationally dependent, particularly for Blacks" (Smart Richman, Bennett, Pek, Siegler, & Williams, 2007, p. 682). In this study, normotensive black and white adults underwent an anger recall task. There was a three-way interaction among race, optimism, and perceived discrimination over the past year that predicted DBP reactivity and recovery. The lowest reactivity and fastest recovery were among black participants who were optimistic and perceived less discrimination, whereas the highest reactivity and slowest recovery were among black participants who were optimistic and perceived more discrimination.

These two studies are consistent insofar as situational factors had the most marked effects on blood pressure reactivity among the most optimistic participants. However, the direction of the effect differed. For optimistic black youth, more violence exposure predicted less blood pressure reactivity, whereas for optimistic black adults, more perceived discrimination predicted more blood pressure reactivity. In both cases, optimism served to amplify the main effect of the stressor: hyporeactivity to violence exposure and hyperreactivity to discrimination. The difference in main effects may be attributable to the different physiological responses associated with trauma and chronic interpersonal stress (Segerstrom & Miller, 2004). But why does optimism amplify these effects? One possibility is that optimists' tendency to engage stressors makes them more sensitive to the physiological consequences of those stressors. Disengagement or distancing may decrease awareness of or sensitivity to stressors, although it should be noted that these coping styles may have their own negative consequences (Roth & Cohen, 1986).

The amplification of the blood pressure response under conditions of discrimination among optimistic black adults may parallel the effects of *John Henryism*. Like optimism, John Henryism is associated with more active and effortful coping. John Henryism is defined as "an individual's self-perception that he can meet the demands of his environment through hard work and determination" (James, Hartnett, & Kaslbeek, 1983, p. 263). This perception, in combination with challenging environmental circumstances such as low socioeconomic status (SES) or education, predicts higher blood pressure in black men (James et al., 1983). Although active coping is generally considered advantageous in terms of adjustment, the findings for both optimism and John Henryism suggest that there are limits to this advantage.

## Optimism and the Immune System: Who and When
### *The Nature and Significance of Immune Parameters in Brief*
The immune system comprises a complex network of tissues (e.g., lymph nodes), cells (e.g., T cells), and proteins (e.g., antibody) that together protects against invaders such as viruses and bacteria and may detect and attack some cancer cells. The immune

system can, however, also do harm to the host when it misidentifies benign substances or even self as threats, as in allergy and autoimmune disease, or when chronic activation promotes tissue damage. Therefore, although one can draw broad conclusions about what immune parameters are healthy when higher or lower, it is more correct to consider how that parameter relates to the population under study. For example, stronger cellular immune responses may indicate better ability to combat disease in a healthy, young adult or resistance to immunosenescence in an older adult, but excessive disease activity in autoimmunity.

The literature on optimism and immunity mainly concerns cellular immunity in healthy young adults, changes in helper T cells in human immunodeficiency virus (HIV)-infected adults, and pro- and anti-inflammatory cytokines, mainly in older adults. Therefore, this very brief review will give a general orientation to these immune parameters. For a more complete, accessible treatment of the immune system and its function in health and disease, see Clark (2008).

Cellular immunity is the immune system's response to intracellular pathogens such as viruses and some kinds of bacteria. As a rather gross oversimplification, it is mediated by antigen-sensing cells in the blood and tissues; helper T cells, which "turn on" the immune system; and cytotoxic T cells, natural killer cells, and macrophages, which destroy the offending pathogens. Although there are some in vitro assays that may reflect the robustness of components of this response, arguably the best indicators are in vivo tests that challenge the coordinated response of the system. The validity of these tests is bolstered by their ability to predict morbidity and mortality (Christou et al., 1995; Dolan et al., 1995; Wayne, Rhyne, Garry, & Goodwin, 1990). It is important to note that the ability of in vivo tests of cellular immunity to predict morbidity and mortality has been limited to vulnerable populations such as hospital patients or the elderly; on the other hand, many "normal" individuals will transition to being hospital patients or elderly, and so these tests have some relevance for them as well.

The HIV virus selectively infects the helper T cell, a cell that could be called the conductor of the immunological orchestra. As the virus kills these cells, the directorless immune system cannot effectively protect against pathogens, and death usually results from infectious disease (Sackoff, Hanna, Pfeiffer, & Tovian, 2006). The number of helper T cells is therefore both an indicator of disease progression and a prognostic factor for morbidity and mortality.

Cytokines are the proteins that immune cells (as well as some other tissues) produce to communicate with and direct the activity of other immune cells (as well as some other tissues). One important distinction between cytokines is whether they are proinflammatory or anti-inflammatory. Proinflammatory cytokines such as interleukin (IL)-6 increase risk for a number of diseases, including cardiovascular disease, myeloma, osteoporosis, and Alzheimer disease (Ershler & Keller, 2000; Papanicolaou, Wilder, Manolagas, & Chrousos, 1998). Anti-inflammatory cytokines such as IL-10 may be protective against these diseases.

### Optimism and Immunity in Healthy Adults

Initial reports of the relationship between optimism and in vitro immune parameters were not promising. Lee and colleagues (1995), in a study of Air Force Academy cadets, found very small correlations between the LOT and in vitro ability of immune cells to replicate and proliferate in response to stimulation. The largest correlation was in fact negative, $r = -.16$ between optimism and proliferation to phytohemagglutinin stimulation. Segerstrom and colleagues (1998), in a study of first-year law students, similarly reported null or small prospective correlations between the LOT and immune cell counts and function, with the largest correlation reflecting a positive relationship between optimism and number of cytotoxic T cells, $r = .25$.

Cohen and colleagues (1999) published the first study suggesting why these relationships were so (unexpectedly) small: The effect of dispositional optimism on the immune system is moderated by situational characteristics. In this study of healthy young adult women, dispositional optimism was associated with higher cytotoxic T-cell counts when stressors lasted less than 1 week, but lower counts when stressors lasted more than 1 week. A series of studies with first-year law students provided conceptual replications of the idea that optimism is associated with better cellular immunity when situations or stressors are straightforward to cope with, but worse immunity when they are complex. For law students who moved away from home, simplifying extracurricular demands on their time and energy, optimism was associated with higher T-cell counts and better in vivo cellular immunity. For law students who stayed home and confronted conflicts between law school and extracurricular demands, optimism was associated with lower T-cell counts and worse cellular immunity (Segerstrom, 2001, 2006).

This pattern also obtained in laboratory studies: When a noise stressor was controllable, optimism was associated with higher natural killer cell activity; but when it was uncontrollable, optimism was associated with lower activity (Sieber, Rodin, Larson, Ortega, Cummings, & Levy, 1992). A second study found that optimistic academic expectancies were associated with better in vivo cellular immunity after rest, but not after a demanding mental arithmetic task (Segerstrom, Castaneda, & Spencer, 2003).

Why would difficult tasks or circumstances reverse the effect of optimism on immune function? Some authors surmised that hallmark characteristics of optimists had harmful psychosocial and therefore immunological effects. A positive outlook might lead to disappointment when circumstance failed to have an easy resolution. For example, "situations which are highly stressful may provide to be demoralizing because the stressor continues, in conflict with the person's optimistic worldview" (Cohen et al., 1999, p. 170), and "those subjects who, by personal disposition, tend to expect positive and controllable outcomes are the most stressed when the actual outcome is contrary to their expectations" (Sieber et al., 1992, p. 154).

However, this interpretation faces several challenges. First, evidence is lacking that people who are more optimistic become demoralized or stressed in the face of outcomes that disconfirm their expectations. On the contrary, optimists maintained or even improved their adjustment relative to pessimists in the face of important events such as in vitro fertilization failure or a positive biopsy for breast cancer (Litt, Tennen, Affleck, & Klock, 1992; Stanton & Snider, 1993; see also Note 2). Second, if positive beliefs promote vulnerability to stressors, then negative beliefs should promote resilience to stressors. Evidence is also lacking in this domain. To the contrary, neuroticism, which reflects a predisposition to negative beliefs about oneself and one's world, increases depression in response to stressors (e.g., Bolger & Schilling, 1991). Third, in an explicit test of the model in first-year law students, negative affect and fatigue both failed to account for any of the relationship between optimism and cellular immunity (Segerstrom, 2006). Likewise, one study that found a negative relationship between optimism and immunity after a laboratory stressor also tested whether other personality characteristics could "stand in" for optimism. In this case, neuroticism did not produce the same effect, but conscientiousness did (Segerstrom et al., 2003). This finding suggests that it is the goal-directed aspect of optimism (i.e., its shared variance with conscientiousness) that produces the negative relationship between optimism and immunity, rather than distress.

I have proposed an alternative interpretation of the interaction between optimism and stressor difficulty or complexity that draws on the field of ecological immunology (Segerstrom, 2005, 2007). The premise of ecological immunology is that the resources required to mount an immune response may be appropriated to serve other functions for the organism. For example, mice that had the opportunity to acquire important assets such as social dominance, a mating opportunity, or a nest-box were more vulnerable to an experimentally administered parasite (Barnard & Behnke, 2001). In short, pursuit of social and physical goals in the outer world can compete for resources that are needed for immunological activity in the inner world. The tension between goal pursuit and the immune system is also evident in phenomena such as sickness behavior, the lethargy that reduces resource expenditure in goal pursuit when the immune response is prioritized (Dantzer et al., 2001). These are highly conserved responses that are evident across the phylogenetic spectrum from mollusks to insects to vertebrates (e.g., Adamo, 2006, 2008). As applied to optimism, then, high motivation and effort to pursue goals may associate with compromised immune function. This may be an adaptive response for a healthy organism insofar as minor decrements in immunity are unlikely to result in pathology, and goal achievement may have a net positive effect on health.

The physiological mechanisms by which these ecological effects obtain are not entirely clear. In insects, the limited resource may be a protein that provides fuel from stored fat (Adamo, Roberts, Easy, & Ross, 2008). In mammals, leptin may signal current energy availability and thereby moderate immunity (Demas, 2004). As ecological models gain more currency in humans, more research on the mechanisms of these effects should follow.

### Optimism and Immunity in HIV

The research literature describing how optimism affects immunity in people infected with HIV is similar in some ways to the literature describing how optimism affects immunity in healthy people. It is similar insofar as the measures typically reflect cellular immunity. These include immunity against latent herpes viruses, in which higher antibody titers reflect viral reactivation that is potentially the result of a lapse in cellular immunity, and cytotoxic cell (natural killer cell) function. The most common, and arguably most clinically relevant, measure is the number of CD4[+] helper T cells. As noted above, this measure is a marker of both immunocompetence and disease progression in HIV.

Finally, this literature is similar to that for healthy adults insofar as the results for the effects of optimism on immune markers in HIV are variable and often null. Table 30.2 summarizes the studies. In general, optimism appears to have the most potentially beneficial immunological correlates when markers other than number of CD4[+] helper T cells are examined. In both minority women and gay men, more optimism and less pessimism correlated with higher markers of cellular immunity, including cytotoxicity, number of cytotoxic (CD8[+]) cells, and—indirectly—immunity against latent viruses.

However, the results for number of CD4[+] helper T cells are less promising. Cross-sectional and prospective (over 18–24 months) analyses revealed few significant effects. One interesting exception was the nonlinear effect of optimistic items (net of pessimistic items) in predicting T-cell change (Milam, Richardson, Marks, Kemper, & McCutchan, 2004). The highest number of T cells at follow-up was a function of moderate optimism, followed by high optimism, and finally low optimism. The only study that reported a significant, longitudinal, linear effect of dispositional optimism on T cells also reported that there was a nonsignificant tendency for a quadratic effect ($p = .11$), but the nature of this effect was not described (Ironson et al., 2005).

The literature on optimism and immunity in HIV differs from that in healthy adults in that number of T cells has a different meaning in HIV. In this case, cell count is a cumulative indicator of disease process and progression. The mean number of CD4[+] T cells in these studies ranged from 297 to 508/mm[3] (see Table 30.2). This range typically indicates the disease stage at which T cells have declined to the point that symptoms—either nonspecific, such as night sweats, or acquired immune deficiency syndrome (AIDS)-defining, such as pneumonia—are emerging or present. It typically takes years for T cells to decline to this point. Therefore, cross-sectional relationships between optimism and CD4[+] T-cell counts are similar to the studies of morbidity and mortality reviewed earlier in this chapter: They reflect the effect of optimism on disease progression across many situations, conditions, and circumstances. If optimism has positive effects on cellular immunity in some cases and negative effects in others, one would expect generally null or small total effects, which is exactly what one finds in this literature.

### Optimism and Proinflammatory Cytokines

Perhaps the most promising results with regard to a protective effect of optimism on physiological parameters relevant to health comes from the few, mostly recent studies of optimism and proinflammatory cytokines. These studies use diverse methods. In a study of experimental pain induction in pain patients and controls, optimism was not related to IL-6 reactivity in controls, but pain patients with higher optimism had lower IL-6 reactivity (Costello et al., 2002). However, in another study of acute stress (Stroop and public speaking) in healthy, young, male adults, optimism was related to less IL-6 reactivity (Brydon, Walker, Wawrzyniak, Chart, & Steptoe, 2009). Another recent report found that optimism was inversely associated with tonic IL-6 in older women, accounting for an additional 37% percent of the variance above and beyond age and stress (O'Donovan et al., 2009).

There is some overlap between activation of cellular immunity and inflammation: For example, interferon-γ stimulates both arms of the immune system. Therefore, it is interesting to compare the effects of optimism on cellular immunity, which are mixed, to the effects on inflammation, which are negative. This contrasting pattern of results suggests that optimism may affect regulatory agents for inflammation rather than stimulatory agents. That is, optimism may promote more robust immune function as well as stronger regulatory responses. Supporting this hypothesis, higher optimism associated with more pronounced levels of IL-10, an anti-inflammatory cytokine, after older adults' cells were stimulated with influenza (Kohut, Cooper, Nickolaus, Russell, & Cunnick, 2002).

### Conclusion

Although the effects of dispositional optimism on psychosocial health seem fairly straightforward, the effects on physiology and therefore on physical health are clearly not. It seems that important characteristics of dispositional optimists, such as persistence at difficult goals, may benefit psychological well-being (Segerstrom & Solberg Nes, 2006) at the same time that they exact a physiological cost (Segerstrom, 2001, 2006). The benefit of optimism is enjoyed more by some people than others, as suggested by the blood pressure literature, and under

**Table 30.2  Studies of dispositional optimism and immunity in human immunodeficiency virus (HIV) infection**

| Study | Sample characteristics | Immune measure(s) | Relationship to optimism |
|---|---|---|---|
| Byrnes et al. (1998)[a] | 36 Black women coinfected with human papillomavirus (mean CD4$^+$ count = 508/mm$^3$) | NK cell cytotoxicity | $-.46$ ($\beta$) |
| | | CD8$^+$ T cell count | $-.34$ ($\beta$) |
| Cruess et al. (2000) | 40 gay men who experienced Hurricane Andrew (mean CD4$^+$ count = 312/mm$^3$) | Human herpesvirus IgG | $-.55$ ($pr$) |
| | | Epstein-Barr virus IgG | $-.32$ ($pr$) |
| | | Cytomegalovirus IgG | $-.28$ ($pr$) |
| Tomakowsky et al. (2001) | 78 primarily gay men (47 for follow-up) (mean CD4$^+$ count = 393/mm$^3$) | CD4$^+$ T-cell count | $-.05$ ($r$); $-.16$ ($\beta$) |
| | | CD4$^+$ T-cell change (2 yr) | $-.08$ ($\beta$) |
| Milam et al. (2004) | 363 men and 49 women (mean CD4$^+$ count = 435/mm$^3$) | CD4$^+$ T-cell count | Optimism: .07 ($r$) |
| | | | Pessimism: $-.04$ ($r$) |
| | | CD4$^+$ T-cell change (18 mo) | Linear optimism: $-.04$ ($\beta$) |
| | | | Linear pessimism: $-.05$ ($\beta$) |
| | | | Quadratic optimism: $-.46$ ($\beta$) |
| | | | Quadratic pessimism: $-.05$ ($\beta$) |
| Ironson et al. (2005) | 124 men and 53 women (mean CD4$^+$ count = 297/mm$^3$) | CD4$^+$ T-cell change (2 yr) | Linear: .19 ($\gamma$ from MLM; SE = .09) |
| | | | Quadratic: NS ($p = .11$) |

NK, natural killer; IgG, immunoglobulin G; MLM, multilevel model.
[a] Used the "premorbid pessimism" scale from the Millon Behavioral Health Inventory.

some circumstances but not others, as suggested by the psychoneuroimmunology literature.

There remains, however, a positive, if small, net effect of optimism on health outcomes such as cardiovascular morbidity and mortality, as well as markers of disease progression such as helper T-cell count in HIV. One possibility is that there are more people who benefit than people who don't. The blood pressure reactivity studies, for example, suggest that ethnic minorities may not benefit as much as those in the majority, who are less likely to experience prejudice. Likewise, across long periods of time, there may be more situations that are "easy" than "difficult."

This net effect may also result from pathways other than psychophysiology. Large-scale epidemiological studies indicate that more optimistic people engage in healthier behaviors. Higher dispositional optimism correlated with more physical activity, nonsmoking, and better diet (Giltay, Geleijnse, Zitman, Buijsse, & Kromhout, 2007; Tindle et al., 2009). Broadly speaking, therefore, the effects of optimism on health need to be considered across the multiple domains that define health, including all of those included in Table 30.1 (Rowe & Kahn, 1987). By this definition and

considering costs and benefits, higher dispositional optimism seems to be a good indicator that, in the long run, one will enjoy better health.

## Future Directions

- What personal and situational characteristics moderate the effects of dispositional optimism on physiology?
- What neurological or endocrine pathways account for optimism's effects on physiology?
- What is the influence of early or developmental factors that affect both optimism and health (e.g., early family environment)?
- Why and how do effects of optimism on cellular immune function and inflammation dissociate?
- Do optimistic and pessimistic items in optimism scales differentially predict physiological parameters?

## Notes

1. This effect size included studies using the Life Orientation Test (LOT) and its revision, as well as measures of optimistic attributional or explanatory style (the Attributional Style

Questionnaire). These measures are conceptually and empirically distinct (Ahrens & Haaga, 1993). However, less than 10% of the effect sizes came from studies employing attributional style, and so the effect size is attributable mainly to studies of dispositional optimism.

2. A figure in Chang and Sanna (2003, p. 107) would appear to indicate that higher dispositional optimism is associated with higher depression under circumstances of high life stress. However, it is important to note that this figure graphs the significant interaction effect (optimism by life stress) on depression ($R^2$ = .02) without incorporating the also significant and much more substantial main effect of optimism on depression ($R^2$ = .25). Therefore, although the slopes in this apparent cross-over interaction are represented correctly, the line representing pessimists' depression across levels of life stress should be located well above that for optimists. Even under circumstances of high life stress, optimists' predicted depression is actually approximately half that of pessimists in this study.

# References

Adamo, S.A. (2006). Comparative psychoneuroimmunology: Evidence from the insects. *Behavioral and Cognitive Neuroscience Reviews, 5*, 128–140.

Adamo, S.A. (2008). Norepinephrine and octopamine: Linking stress and immune function across phyla. *Invertebrate Survival Journal, 5*, 12–19.

Adamo, S.A., Roberts, J.L., Easy, R.H., & Ross, N.W. (2008). Competition between immune function and lipid transport for the protein apolipophorin III leads to stress-induced immunosuppression in crickets. *Journal of Experimental Biology, 211*, 531–538.

Ahrens, A.H., & Haaga, D.A.F. (1993). The specificity of attributional style and expectations to positive and negative affectivity, depression, and anxiety. *Cognitive Therapy and Research, 17*, 83–98.

Andersson, G. (1996). The benefits of optimism: A meta-analytic review of the Life Orientation Test. *Personality and Individual Differences, 21*, 719–725.

Aspinwall, L.G., & Richter, L. (1999). Optimism and self-mastery predict more rapid disengagement from unsolvable tasks in the presence of alternatives. *Motivation and Emotion, 23*, 221–245.

Barnard, C.J., & Behnke, J.M. (2001). From psychoneuroimmunology to ecological immunology: Life history strategies and immunity trade-offs. In R. Ader, D.L. Felton, & N. Cohen (Eds.), *Psychoneuroimmunology* Vol. 2 (3rd ed., pp. 35–47). San Diego: Academic Press.

Bolger, N., & Schilling, E.A. (1991). Personality and problems of everyday life: The role of neuroticism in exposure and reactivity to daily stressors. *Journal of Personality, 59*, 356–386.

Brownley, K.A., Hurwitz, B.E., & Schneiderman, N. (2000). Cardiovascular psychophysiology. In J.T. Cacioppo, L.G. Tassinary, & G.G. Berntson (Eds.), *Handbook of psychophysiology* (2nd ed., pp. 224–264). New York: Cambridge University Press.

Brydon, L., Walker, C., Wawrzyniak, A.J., Chart, H., & Steptoe, A. (2009). Dispositional optimism and stress-induced changes in immunity and negative mood. *Brain, Behavior, and Immunity, 23*, 810–816.

Byrnes, D.M., Antoni, M.H., Goodkin, K., Efantis-Potter, J., Asthana, D., Simon, T., et al. (1998). Stressful events, pessimism, natural killer cell cytotoxicity, and cytotoxic/suppressor T cells in HIV+ black women at risk for cervical cancer. *Psychosomatic Medicine, 60*, 714–722.

Carver, C.S., Blaney, P.H., & Scheier, M.F. (1979). Reassertion and giving up: The interactive role of self-directed attention and outcome expectancy. *Journal of Personality and Social Psychology, 37*, 1859–1870.

Carver, C.S., & Scheier, M.F. (1990). Origins and functions of positive and negative affect: A control-process view. *Psychological Review, 97*, 19–35.

Carver, C.S., Scheier, M.F., & Segerstrom, S.C. (2010). Optimism. *Clinical Psychology Review, 30*, 879–889.

Chang, E.C., & Sanna, L.J. (2003). Optimism, accumulated life stress, and psychological and physical adjustment: Is it always adaptive to expect the best? *Journal of Clinical and Social Psychology, 22*, 97–115.

Christou, N.V., Meakins, J.L., Gordon, J., Yee, J., Hassan-Zahraee, M., Nohr, C.W., et al. (1995). The delayed hypersensitivity response and host resistance in surgical patients: 20 years later. *Annals of Surgery, 222*, 534–548.

Clark, R., Benkert, R.A., & Flack, J.M. (2006). Violence exposure and optimism predict task-induced changes in blood pressure and pulse rate in a normotensive sample of inner-city black youth. *Psychosomatic Medicine, 68*, 73–79.

Clark, W.R. (2008). *In defense of self: How the immune system really works.* New York: Oxford.

Cohen, F., Kearney, K.A., Zegans, L.S., Kemeny, M.E., Neuhaus, J.M., & Stites, D.P. (1999). Differential immune system changes with acute and persistent stress for optimists vs pessimists. *Brain, Behavior, and Immunity, 13*, 155–174.

Costello, N.L., Bragdon, E.E., Light, K.C., Sigurdsson, A., Buntin, S., Grewen, K., & Maixner, W. (2002). Temporomandibular disorder and optimism: Relationships to ischemic pain sensitivity and interleukin-6. *Pain, 100*, 99–110.

Cruess, S., Antoni, M., Kilbourn, K., Ironson, G., Klimas, N., Fletcher, M.A., et al. (2000). Optimism, distress, and immunologic status in HIV-infected gay men following hurricane Andrew. *International Journal of Behavioral Medicine, 7*, 160–182.

Dantzer, R., Bluthé, R.M., Castanon, N., Chauvet, N., Capuron, L., Goodall, G., et al. (2001). Cytokine effects on behavior. In R. Ader, D.L. Felten, & N. Cohen (Eds.), *Psychoneuroimmunology* (3rd ed., pp. 703–727). San Diego: Academic Press.

Demas, G.E. (2004). The energetics of immunity: A neuroendocrine link between energy balance and immune function. *Hormones and Behavior, 45*, 173–180.

Dolan, M.J., Clerici, M., Blatt, S.P., Hendrix, C.W., Melcher, G.P., Boswell, R.N., et al. (1995). In vitro T cell function, delayed type hypersensitivity skin testing, and CD4+ T cell subset phenotyping independently predict survival time in patients infected with human immunodeficiency virus. *Journal of Infectious Diseases, 172*, 79–87.

Ershler, W.B., & Keller, E.T. (2000). Age-associated increased interleukin-6 gene expression, late-life diseases, and frailty. *Annual Review of Medicine, 51*, 245–270.

Everson, S.A., Kaplan, G.A., Goldberg, D.E., & Salonen, J.T. (2000). Hypertension incidence is predicted by high levels of hopelessness in Finnish men. *Hypertension, 35*, 561–567.

Everson, S.A., Lynch, J.W., Kaplan, G.A., Lakka, T.A., Sivenius, J., & Salonen, J.T. (2001). Stress-induced blood pressure reactivity and incident stroke in middle-aged men. *Stroke, 32*, 1263–1270.

Geers, A.L., Wellman, J.A., Helfer, S.G., Fowler, S.L., & France, C.R. (2008). Dispositional optimism and thoughts of well-being determine sensitivity to an experimental pain task. *Annals of Behavioral Medicine, 36*, 304–313.

Geers, A.L., Wellman, J.A., & Lassiter, G.D. (2009). Dispositional optimism and engagement: The moderating influence of goal prioritization. *Journal of Personality and Social Psychology, 96*, 913–932.

Giltay, E.J., Geleinjnse, J.M., Zitman, F.G., Buijsse, B., & Kromhout, K. (2007). Lifestyle and dietary correlates of dispositional optimism in men: The Zutphen elderly study. *Journal of Psychosomatic Research, 63*, 483–490.

Giltay, E.J., Kamphuis, M.H., Kalmijn, S., Zitman, F.G., & Kromhout, D. (2006). Dispositional optimism and the risk of cardiovascular death. *Archives of Internal Medicine, 166*, 431–436.

Idler, E.L., & Benyamini, Y. (1997). Self-rated health and mortality: A review of twenty-seven community studies. *Journal of Health and Social Behavior, 38*, 21–37.

Ironson, G., Balbin, E., Stuetzle, R., Fletcher, M.A., O'Cleirigh, C., Laurenceau, J.P., et al. (2005). Dispositional optimism and the mechanisms by which it predicts slower disease progression in HIV: Proactive behavior, avoidant coping, and depression. *International Journal of Behavioral Medicine, 12*, 86–97.

James, S.A., Hartnett, S.A., & Kalsbeek, W.D. (1983). John Henryism and blood pressure differences among black men. *Journal of Behavioral Medicine, 6*, 259–278.

Kohut, M.L., Cooper, M.M., Nickolaus, M.S., Russell, D.R., & Cunnick, J.E. (2002). Exercise and psychosocial factors modulate immunity to influenza vaccine in elderly individuals. *Journal of Gerontology: Medical Sciences, 57A*, M557–M562.

Lawes, C.M.M., Bennett, D.A., Feigin, V.L., & Rodgers, A. (2004). Blood pressure and stroke: An overview of published reviews. *Stroke, 35*, 1024–1033.

Lee, D.J., Meehan, R.T., Robinson, C., Smith, M.L., & Mabry, T.R. (1995). Psychosocial correlates of immune responsiveness and illness episodes in US air force academy cadets undergoing basic cadet training. *Journal of Psychosomatic Research, 39*, 445–457.

Litt, M.D., Tennen, H., Affleck, G., & Klock, S. (1992). Coping and cognitive factors in adaptation to *in vitro* fertilization failure. *Journal of Behavioral Medicine, 15*, 171–187.

Matthews, K.A., Räikkönen, K., Sutton-Tyrrell, K., & Kuller, L.H. (2004). Optimistic attitudes protect against progression of carotid atherosclerosis in healthy middle-aged women. *Psychosomatic Medicine, 66*, 640–644.

Milam, J.E., Richardson, J.L., Marks, G., Kemper, C.A., & McCutchan, A.J. (2004). The roles of dispositional optimism and pessimism in HIV disease progression. *Psychology and Health, 19*, 167–181.

O'Donovan, A., Lin, J., Dhabhar, F.S., Wokowitz, O., Tillie, J.M., Blackburn, E., & Epel, E. (2009). Pessimism correlates with leukocyte telomere shortness and elevated interleukin-6 in post-menopausal women. *Brain, Behavior, and Immunity, 23*, 446–449.

Papanicolaou, D.A., Wilder, R.L., Manolagas, S.C., & Chrousos, G.P. (1998). The pathophysiologic roles of interleukin-6 in human disease. *Annals of Internal Medicine, 128*, 127–137.

Psaty, B.M., Furberg, C.D., Kuller, L.H., Cushman, M., Savage, P.J., Levine, D., et al. (2001). Association between blood pressure level and the risk of myocardial infarction, stroke, and total mortality: The cardiovascular health study. *Archives of Internal Medicine, 161*, 1183–1192.

Räikkönen, K., & Matthews, K.A. (2008). Do dispositional pessimism and optimism predict ambulatory blood pressure during schooldays and nights in adolescents? *Journal of Personality, 76*, 605–629.

Räikkönen, K., Matthews, K.A., Flory, J.D., Owens, J.F., & Gump, B.B. (1999). Effects of optimism, pessimism, and trait anxiety on ambulatory blood pressure and mood during everyday life. *Journal of Personality and Social Psychology, 76*, 104–113.

Rasmussen, H.N., Scheier, M.F., & Greenhouse, J.B. (2009). Optimism and physical health: A meta-analytic review. *Annals of Behavioral Medicine, 37*, 239–256.

Roberts, B.W., Kuncel, N.R., Shiner, R., Caspi, A., & Goldberg, L.R. (2007). The power of personality: The comparative validity of personality traits, socioeconomic status, and cognitive ability for predicting important life outcomes. *Perspectives on Psychological Science, 2*, 313–345.

Roth, S., & Cohen, L.J. (1986). Approach, avoidance, and coping with stress. *American Psychologist, 41*, 813–819.

Rowe, J.W., & Kahn, R.L. (1987). Human aging: Usual and successful. *Science, 237*, 143–149.

Sackoff, J.E., Hanna, D.B., Pfeiffer, M.R., & Tovian, L.V. (2006). Causes of death among persons with AIDS in the era of highly active antiretroviral therapy: New York City. *Annals of Internal Medicine, 145*, 397–406.

Scheier, M.F., & Carver, C.S. (1982). Self-consciousness, outcome expectancy, and persistence. *Journal of Research in Personality, 16*, 409–418.

Scheier, M.F., & Carver, C.S. (1985). Optimism, coping, and health: Assessment and implications of generalized outcome expectancies. *Health Psychology, 4*, 219–247.

Segerstrom, S.C. (2001). Optimism, goal conflict, and stressor-related immune change. *Journal of Behavioral Medicine, 24*, 441–467.

Segerstrom, S.C. (2005). Optimism and immunity: Do positive thoughts always lead to positive effects? *Brain, Behavior, and Immunity, 19*, 195–200.

Segerstrom, S.C. (2006). How does optimism suppress immunity? Evaluation of three affective pathways. *Health Psychology, 25*, 653–657.

Segerstrom, S.C. (2007). Stress, energy, and immunity: An ecological view. *Current Directions in Psychological Science, 16*, 326–330.

Segerstrom, S.C., Castaneda, J.O., & Spencer, T.E. (2003). Optimism effects on cellular immunity: Testing the affective and persistence models. *Personality and Individual Differences, 35*, 1615–1624.

Segerstrom, S.C., & Miller, G.E. (2004). Psychological stress and the human immune system: A meta-analytic study of 30 years of inquiry. *Psychological Bulletin, 130*, 601–630.

Segerstrom, S.C., & Solberg Nes, L. (2006). When goals conflict but people prosper: The case of dispositional optimism. *Journal of Research in Personality, 40*, 675–693.

Segerstrom, S.C., Taylor, S.E., Kemeny, M.E., & Fahey, J.L. (1998). Optimism is associated with mood, coping, and immune change in response to stress. *Journal of Personality and Social Psychology, 74*, 1646–1655.

Sieber, W.J., Rodin, J., Larson, L., Ortega, S., Cummings, N., Levy, S., et al. (1992). Modulation of human natural killer cell activity by exposure to uncontrollable stress. *Brain, Behavior, and Immunity, 6*, 141–156.

Smart Richman, L., Bennett, G.G., Pek, J., Siegler, I., & Williams, R.B. (2007). Discrimination, dispositions, and cardiovascular responses to stress. *Health Psychology, 26*, 675–683.

Solberg Nes, L., & Segerstrom, S.C. (2006). Dispositional optimism and coping: A meta-analytic review. *Personality and Social Psychology Review, 10*, 235–251.

Solberg Nes, L., Segerstrom, S.C., & Sephton, S.E. (2005). Engagement and arousal: Optimism's effects during a brief stressor. *Personality and Social Psychology Bulletin, 31*, 111–120.

Srivastava, S., McGonigal, K.M., Richards, J.M., Butler, E.A., & Gross, J.J. (2006). Optimism in close relationships: How seeing things in a positive light makes them so. *Journal of Personality and Social Psychology, 91*, 143–153.

Stanton, A.L., & Snider, P.R. (1993). Coping with breast cancer diagnosis: A prospective study. *Health Psychology, 12*, 16–23.

Stern, R.M., Ray, W.J., & Quigley, K.S. (2001). *Psychophysiological recording*. New York: Oxford.

Suls, J., & Fletcher, B. (1985). The relative efficacy of avoidant and nonavoidant coping strategies: A meta-analysis. *Health Psychology, 4*, 249–288.

Tindle, H.A., Chang, Y.F., Kuller, L.H., Manson, J.E., Robinson, J.G., Roasl, M.C., et al. (2009). Optimism, cynical hostility, and incident coronary heart disease and mortality in the women's health initiative. *Circulation, 120*, 656–662.

Tomakowsky, J., Lumley, M.A., Markowitz, N., & Frank, C. (2001). Optimistic explanatory style and dispositional optimism in HIV-infected men. *Journal of Psychosomatic Research, 51*, 577–587.

Wayne, S.J., Rhyne, R.L., Garry, P.J., & Goodwin, J.S. (1990). Cell-mediated immunity as a predictor of morbidity and mortality in subjects over 60. *Journal of Gerontology: Medical Sciences, 45*, M45–M48.

Williams, R.D., Riels, A.G., & Roper, K.A. (1990). Optimism and distractibility in cardiovascular reactivity. *Psychological Record, 40*, 451–457.

PART 5

# Population and Sociocultural Issues

# Community Health

Marta Gil Lacruz

## Abstract

The social function of health psychology is the promotion of well-being and quality-of-life improvements, concepts that only become meaningful when they are analyzed in the real-life context of our communities. For social and community psychology, community health has always been a primary area for research and intervention, and the wide range of applications and theoretical frameworks that have been employed is a defining characteristic. This chapter discusses two such research models from the disciplines of mental health and community development: the ecological model and a model of empowerment and competence. Their origin and evolution encompass different geographical and epistemological circumstances and highlight the importance of cultural respect, risk prevention, and the optimization of community resources, with special emphasis placed on community participation.

**Keywords:** The social psychology of health, community psychology, personal well-being, social well-being, community health

## A definition of Health: The Classification of a Utopia

Throughout history, health has been an object of devotion and veneration. Rites, customs, and therapies related to health have evolved in parallel to the historical development of socioeconomic conditioning and our paradigm of thought. In Greece, the goddess of health was Hygeia, also goddess of harmony. Faith was based on reason: Men could improve their state of well-being if they followed "hygienist," preventative, and holistic precepts. From the 5th century BCE, the cult of Hygeia was superseded by Asclepias, god of medicine and healing. The pragmatism of Asclepias was reflected in a concern for well-being, order, preventative education, the idealization of medical skills, and a more personalized treatment of illness.

In the modern epoch, nature has been reinvented and humankind has appropriated aspirations of immortality. An obsession with the source of life and eternal youth has led to the establishment of an infinite variety of "natural" practices—from walking barefoot through a spring meadow in the morning dew to the daily workout at the gym; from the taking of vitamin supplements to visiting health spas and receiving cosmetic treatments: beauty, youth, and consumerism constitute a sophisticated trichotomy of contemporary health values.

A result of this process is that death and ageing are seen as abnormal, highly medicalized phenomena. Nevertheless, well-being and happiness do not simply involve the prolongation of health or the technical knowledge of remedies and healthy practices; more than anything else, well-being and happiness express the way in which the individual responds to the adaptive challenges of daily life in their context of reference (O'Connor, Friel, & Kellesher, 1997). Our capacity to imagine new challenges means that health cannot be defined as an absolute and permanent value (Baum, Revenson, & Singer, 2001); health is a concept that can, and must, be known by many different names and be seen in many different guises.

Community health psychology illustrates the evolution of this concept-value and the need to integrate those arguments that have generated debates and disagreements in the search for an understanding of social interaction (e.g., individual and social, theoretical and practical, health and sickness, sane and pathological). These psychosocial debates have fomented a new model of health that is closer to our social networks and further away from the operating theater. The next section of this chapter analyses origins and disciplinary repercussions, and this is followed by a discussion on collocation as a response to community health research and intervention.

## Health As a Psychosocial Question

Psychology and social psychology are disciplines that are closely related to health in that they deal with attitudes, values, social stratification, behaviors, and social conditions in the context of social reality. When psychologists speak of health, the focus is concentrated as much on the quality of life of the individual as on the attainment of social well-being (Harare, Waehler, & Rogers, 2005).

The cornerstone of the psychosocial approach is social interaction. Our personal relationships influence numerous variables that affect biological, cognitive, behavioral, and ecological processes (Baron & Byrne, 2005). From a complementary perspective, it should be noted that loneliness, or the lack of social interaction, is damaging to health. Since the 1960s, epidemiologic research has linked loneliness with somatic illnesses, physical ill-health, depression, alcoholism, obesity, sleep disorders, and a greater number of medical consultations. Feelings of loneliness are further associated with personality variables (susceptibility, anxiety, detachment, hostility, inhibition, and irritability) that affect the physical and mental condition of the individual (Yárnoz, 2008).

The study of these variables must include the different groups and social units with which we are involved: the individual, the family, the neighborhood, the workplace, friendships, the local community, etc. It is even the case that the risk of loneliness, in spite of its relatively high incidence (10%–30% of the population suffer intense loneliness at some time in their lives), is conditioned by social factors— single men, widows, and divorcees are higher-risk groups. To a certain extent, an emotional relationship seems to act as a protective shield (Yárnoz, 2008).

From this point of view, health is not the preserve of the medical profession but it must be approached from holistic and psychosocial perspectives. Health-related activities and behaviors are executed and learned in the context of social interaction. This leads to the question of how interaction functions within the complex abstraction that is health.

There is no simple answer. From a *micro-psychological* perspective, for example, in the patient–health professional dyad, patients are more likely to follow treatment instructions when they have a friendly relationship with their doctor, when they collaborate in their treatment plan, and when the treatment options are put forward in an attractive manner (Taylor, Helgeson, Reed, & Skokan, 1993; Thompson, Sobolew-Shubin, Galbraith, Schwankovsky, & Cruzen, 1993). Furthermore, the doctor's communication skills play a decisive role in patient satisfaction and correct observation of treatment guidelines (Goleman, 1991; Rall, Peskoff, & Byrne, 1994).

This underlines the importance of personal and demographic characteristics and intrapsychological processes, including attitudes, beliefs, attributions, and general cognitive representations. Conjectures of a physical ("It's something I ate"), psychological ("It's my nerves"), and religious ("It's punishment for my sinful behavior") nature are examples of different interpretive possibilities, and this process of interpretation has consequences for health: self-medication, seeking medical help, resigning oneself to the situation, etc. (DiMatteo, 1991). The many works that have analyzed the reciprocal interdependence of health, cognition, affect, and motivation include psychosomatic studies, pathogenic or health profiling, and research on personality characteristics (Friedman, 2000, 2008).

Nevertheless, the perspective does not fully respond to the debate on the impact of social interaction on health if the *macro-social* viewpoint is not taken into account. The social functioning of the individual is crucial for health (Totman, 1979, 1982). For example, in stressful circumstances, as in the case of hospitalization, patient recovery is more successful if individuals have the socioeconomic means to confront the situation, and they are integrated members of a social network (Luszczynska & Schwarzer, 2005; Salanova, Schaufeli, Llorens, Peiró, & Grau, 2000).

A social support network and the functions that it can perform on behalf of an individual therefore constitute essential reference points when studying the biopsychosocial adjustment of the individual to his or her surroundings or community. The manifestation of this support is varied and can be classified as expressive functions (e.g., unburdening oneself, empathy, motivation, etc.), informative functions (e.g., communicating solutions, providing examples and models, etc.), and instruments (e.g., financial loans, tools, services, products, etc.) (Gil-Lacruz, 2000). The flexibility of these support functions is of particular relevance to vulnerable groups facing difficult social conditions, for example, immigrants (Martínez, García, & Maya, 2001).

Gracia, Herrero, and Musitu (1995) argue that the relationship between the individual and his or her own perceptions should be recognized as an imperative conceptual tool in the analysis of the subject's immediate surroundings and a potent resource for the psychosocial professional. The study of social support and altruism is as much related to the recipient's perception of help as to the giver's feelings of well-being, a good example being blood or organ donations. Generous and cooperative individuals construct networks of solidarity that can stimulate the collaboration of others (a system known as *indirect reciprocity*). These individuals can also enjoy additional feelings of usefulness and meaning in their lives. This discussion leads to the critical juncture of the role of culture, context, and social agents in the treatment, rehabilitation, and promotion of health (Canals, 2004).

The discussion of the individual and his interpretation of the world that surrounds him does not exempt the analyst from contemplating other significant factors, such as the behavioral consequences of attributions, their social functionality, and their unequal distribution among social groups and social classes (Gil-Lacruz & Gil-Lacruz, 2010a). For example, adolescent risk behavior, such as excessive consumption of alcohol and/or use of drugs, is frequently associated with group behavior practices in which the importance of identification with peers and feelings of invincibility ("It'll never happen to me") are themselves risk factors.

The relationship between the study of well-being, psychological adjustment, and social interaction casts doubt on medical models or models that are solely based on the physical condition because psychosocial factors are determinants in the explanation of health and sickness.

The psychosocial model views the limitations of scientific medicalization as being based on the existential need to make sense of the body, physical, health, illness, and suffering. People demonstrate corporal symptoms, which represent a convergence of events, experiences, and interpretations that are of physical, psychological, social, and cultural origin. Problems based on beliefs such as the "evil eye" have no relevance from the point of view of strictly scientific medical practice, but they have a specific value,

with a corresponding clinical picture, for those who believe that they are the subject of envy or conspiracy (Gil-Lacruz, 2000, 2007a). Interpretations and experiences are shared and communicated throughout our social existence. Social interaction is both a cause and a consequence of our state of well-being.

Advances in research and techniques applied to our physical health have not been matched by progress in our knowledge and treatment of the impact of our beliefs and interpretations on our health (Labish, 1993). Well-being is reflected in our capacity for enjoyment, our participation in regular social activities, creative work, satisfying social relationships, and community competence (Winefield, 1992). The disciplines of health psychology and social psychology have a fascinating future, full of intriguing possibilities and research opportunities.

## Psychology and the Social Psychology of Health

The recognition of behavior and living conditions as determinants of health justifies the intervention of social psychology in the resolution of associated problems (Barriga, 2000).

The interactive and bidirectional nature of the organism and the environment means that psychology is the modulating factor in these exchanges (Rozanki & Kubzansky, 2005). The articulation of a psychosocial definition of health is important in terms of psychological research and intervention, and decisive in the design of the psychologist's educational and professional profile (Kenkel, DeLeon, Albino, & Porter, 2003; Kenkel, DeLeon, Matell, & Steep, 2005; Leventhal & Seime, 2004; Leventhal, Seime, Wedding, & Rozensky, 2005).

As the different psychological specialties are involved in these issues, an operative approximation to the study of health might consist in the determination of conceptual delimitation criteria. Figure 31.1 shows one attempt to map the disciplinary relationships from the viewpoint of two classic distinctions:

- *The type of health definition*: Clinical psychology and community psychology target the study of mental health, whereas cognitive medicine and health psychology is directed at physical health (Rodríguez Marín & Neipp, 2008).
- *The type of intervention*: Clinical psychology and cognitive medicine prioritize treatment and rehabilitation, whereas community psychology and health psychology prioritize prevention (Weiss, 1982).

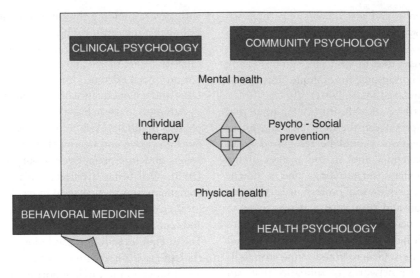

**Fig. 31.1** Disciplinary relationships of the psychology of health. From Godoy, J. F. (1999). Psicología de la salud: Delimitación conceptual. In M. A. Simón (Ed.), *Manual de psicología de la salud. Fundamentos, metodología y aplicaciones* (pp. 39–75). Madrid: Biblioteca Nueva.

The problem with this classification is that it tends to accentuate a series of dualisms that must be overcome in practice (e.g., physical–mental health, health promotion–treatment, health–illness, etc.). The specialization imposed by operational capability allows the maintenance of disciplinary distinctions, but it should never be forgotten that the most effective and desirable strategy is to be found in health promotion.

Health psychology is differentiated by its commitment to research on health needs and potential, and the knowledge of people and their contexts. To achieve these goals, the health psychologist often makes use of other branches of the discipline that include evolutionary, physiological, cognitive, industrial, and social psychology (Rodríguez Marín, 1991).

In the same way that health psychology is the scientific application of the psychology of health problems, the social psychology of health supposes the "healthy transformation" of social psychology. This delimitation does not resolve the difficulty of distinguishing between the psychological and psychosocial in the new standards and criteria on illness, healing, education, and prevention, although precedence is given to social interaction as the basis for explanation.

Social psychologists are therefore in a position to make a critical contribution to the question of health. Processes of health promotion, prevention, diagnosis, treatment, rehabilitation, improvements in the health system, and the development of health policies result from interactions between health system users and health professionals. Those involved in these processes work in a sociocultural context and acquire knowledge through interaction with their corresponding reference groups (Rodríguez Marín & Neipp, 2008).

The sociocultural context conditions our reactions to health and illness. Zborowski (1952) noted that, in American hospitals, Italians and Jews tended to exaggerate the expression of pain as this was not seen as personal weakness; the Irish, on the other hand, were much more stoical—the expression of pain did not accord with the value of strength, seen as a characteristic of their ethnic identity. Illness and disease have always been defined in terms of spatial and temporal coordinates. In ancient Israel, illness was often considered as atonement for guilt; for Christians, it implied a test that was to be overcome; and more recently, society views illness as a challenge to our innovative and technical abilities (Sapolsky, 1999).

As an axis of discourse, interaction integrates space, time, and their corresponding social factors (e.g., execution of roles in a given organizational context, group membership, etc.) and the individual's experience in terms of attitudes, emotional states, learning, and memory. Recent applications of these principles are involved in the concept of "resilience" and the protective process of psychosocial resources (Friborg, Hjemdal, Rosenvinge, & Martinussen, 2003). It has been estimated that optimism (as an ingredient of resilience) may be responsible for as much as an 18% increase in life-expectancy. The settings and situations in which an individual's resources are put to the test are clearly social (Gagne & Deci, 2005; Gallo, Ghaed, & Bracken, 2004).

The following section explains how the community development of social psychology paved the way for a paradigmatic shift in the concept of mental illness and affirmed the importance of a definition of health based on reference groups and environments. This was a somewhat polemical revision; the move away from welfare toward promotion, from the individual to the community, was met with stern resistance by many clinical professionals.

Community psychology arose as an alternative to clinical psychology; its orientation was to the comprehension and resolution of specific problems or pathologies that involved a significant socioenvironmental component (e.g., drug addiction, marginalization, social inequality, etc.). In addition to the work of criticism and denouncement, community psychology was interested in the teaching of social skills and personal competences as means for improving adjustment between people and their environments and quality of life in the community (Mann, 1978; Rappaport, 1977; Sarason, 1973, 1974).

The appearance of community psychology in the 1970s, initiated a review of the clinical medical models and their dependence on hospitalization for the resolution of problems that ignored the social dimension (Lowentalh & Blanco, 1985). Bernstein and Nietzel (1982) and Costa and López (1986) argue that this criticism provided the genesis for an alternative approach that involved the adoption of an ecological perspective (attention to the possible influences of socioenvironmental factors), social change (instead of individual), prevention (especially primary), crisis intervention, education for health, and the development of the psychological awareness of the community.

## The Origins of Community Psychology

The term *community psychology* seems to have first been employed in academic literature by Bennett in 1965 and Bennett, Anderson, Cooper, Hassol, Klein, and Rosemblum in 1966.

In spite of its diverse origins, American, European, and Latin American contributions concur in the definition of its central concepts: Buelga (2001) offers a geographical evolution of these definitions that begins with the European and American shift in mental health analysis and continues with the ideas of community development and intervention that emanated from Latin America.

### From Mental Illness to Community Mental Health: Europe and the United States

The scientific study of mental health, its causes and treatments, emerged in the climate of the French Revolution. The assertion of individual rights and the relevance of the social context were the foundations of the work of the alienist movement at the end of the 18th century. The movement's foremost representatives, Tuke (in England) and Pinel (in France), believed it was necessary to provide therapeutic environments in which patients could recover from illness (Rodado & Navarro, 1997). Paradoxically, these asylums were examples of carefully planned, rational, and ordered environments where work was seen as a privileged instrument for the generation of new habits, for overcoming emotions, and for instilling discipline and willpower.

Despite the alienist ideas of freedom and integration, the separation, isolation, and imprisonment of the disabled, delinquents, the sick, and the mentally ill would continue to be the de rigueur response of society to the affected individuals. There was criticism and the occasional, atypical experience (e.g., Kraepelin's objections to patient abuse and the colony at Gheel, 1917/1999) but the expansion of industrial capitalism and the domination of organic psychiatry blocked the advance of such progressive thinking.

The social problems caused by industrialization and urbanization would soon become apparent on both sides of the Atlantic. By the end of the 19th century, cities like Chicago and New York were theaters of social disintegration in which infants and young people were the protagonists. The child delinquent with no family, education, or social resources did not fit the profile of psychological imbalance and represented a severe challenge to the judicial, penal, and psychiatric systems of the day. Immigration and the attendant feelings of rootlessness were in the forefront of innumerable social conflicts. The response to these problems was diverse and varied, and the *mental hygiene* movement was one of the most distinguished.

The first step on the road to reform was social criticism. Visionaries such as Brees, Meyer, and James believed that social change was possible through education; for the hygienists, prevention was the key to mental health. Issues related to health promotion dominated social discourse and were soon institutionalized (e.g., mental hygiene committees were set up in Brazil, 1913; Canada, 1918; Britain, 1918; Czechoslovakia, 1921; and Spain, 1927).

The rapid expansion of the movement led to a variety of societal innovations and initiatives: social awareness campaigns, legislative reforms, outpatient clinics, and the development of child psychology (Buelga, Musitu, Vera, Avila, & Arango, 2009).

World War II provided further impetus for these progressive theories, despite the fact that, although the hygienists could be characterized by their ideological position, military psychology was very much ruled by pragmatic, operational principles. For example, Maxwell Jones was in charge of a hospital unit of 100 beds for soldiers who demonstrated reactions of anxiety, fatigue, or stress; he wrote of the absurdity of interviewing patient after patient when they all had the same symptoms. Why not have the same conversations with 100 patients at the same time? This was the birth of community therapy.

The sheer magnitude of the psychological and social disorders caused by the war (combat trauma, post-war social and family reinsertion, the devastation of the Nazi campaign, the climate of fear, and even the political phenomenon of post-war democratization) was reflected in the progressive psychiatry of intellects such as Bion, Bonnafé, Foulkes, Main, Jones, and Tosquelles, and instigated a movement that would see the traditional methodology of mental health replaced by the community model.

Self-help groups, crisis intervention units, the principles of self-management and mutual support, patient participation, and the promotion of relational resources are some of the strategies that aim to overcome the isolation and alienation of the patient. Cooperation and participation engender a sense of competence and give patients responsibility for the organization of their own time (Sánchez Vidal, 1991a).

This democratization of treatment runs parallel to the consolidation of the right to health. After World War II, most economically developed countries began work on embryonic social security systems that led to the establishment the welfare state.

Health is fundamental to welfare state politics; this became clear in the face of the evident inadequacy of the traditional systems (e.g., trade associations, charities, etc.) and the obvious need for an alternative (especially given the pressure of the workers' movements). The declaration of the Constitutional Charter of the World Health Organization (WHO, 1949) was a reflection of the prevailing social climate and the new definition of health. Three decades later, in 1978, the Declaration of Alma Ata explicitly recognized the responsibility of the state in this field. In 1986, Otawa Letter integrated the principles of health promotion (See Table 31.1).

From the first psychiatric theories, based on isolation, to models of prevention and integration, the definition of mental health has taken a Copernican turn that has been mirrored by treatment methods; from the days of the asylum to mental health centers, occupational workshops, and daycare, the community has become the protagonist. Pharmacological

**Table 31.1  The five key principles of health promotion according to the WHO (1986)**

- The implication of the population as a whole and in the context of its daily life, instead of being aimed at population groups at risk of specific illnesses

- The focusing of actions on the causes or determinants of health, to ensure that the environment, which is beyond the control of individuals, is favorable for health and well-being

- The combination of a variety of complementary theories and methodologies that include communication, education, legislation, physical measures, organizational changes, and community development

- The aspiration of the effective participation of the population, the fostering of self-help and encouragement for people to find their own ways of promoting health in their communities

- Although health promotion is basically a social activity, not a medical service, health professionals, especially those who work in primary care, can play a significant role in supporting and facilitating health promotion projects and actions.

advances (e.g., the discovery of narcoleptics that allow out-of-hospital treatment), new models of preventative psychiatry (e.g., Caplan), and the progressive policies of the 1960s all helped to kindle the fires of mental health reform (Erchul, 2009; Felner, Felner, & Morton, 2000).

The winds of change were to find legal expression in the British Mental Health Act of 1959, the French *Circulair* of 1960, and the American Community Health Act of 1963. The report of the Joint Commission on Mental Illness and Health, put before the U.S. Congress in 1960, not only exposed the terrible conditions of mentally ill patients, it also offered community strategies for change. Early intervention and crisis support were prioritized as part of primary and secondary prevention programs. At the same time, the report recommended the integration of the mental health services and other (not explicitly "medical") health professions (nursing, social work, psychology), in addition to training programs for paraprofessionals (Tenorio & Hernández, 2005). The Community Mental Health Act of 1963 was to implement these principles in the creation of Community Mental Health Centers.

The inclusion of psychologists and psychiatrists as part of interdisciplinary mental health teams prompted a revision of the psychologist's professional role and stimulated a profound debate that continues to the present (Hong & Leventhal, 2004;

Hong, Leventhal, & Seime, 2005). In 1965, a group of clinical psychologists met in Swampscott, near Boston, to discuss the issues; the result was the birth of community psychology. Plans were also drawn up for further meetings and a number of specialist publications (e.g., *Community Mental Health Journal*, 1965, *The American Journal of Community Psychology*, 1975).

This first meeting laid the foundations for a series of deliberations that are still relevant to contemporary social psychology: the importance of the application of theory and of theory being based on practical experience, the need to use scientific knowledge for the benefit of the community, and the social relevance of scientific knowledge and its diffusion. These debates brought about a radical change, from a model based on assistance to a model based on participation, development, the search for quality of life, and the fostering of community resources (Sánchez Vidal, 1991b).

The community perspective places special emphasis on environmental and sociocultural behavioral determinants (Hombrados, 1996) and the individual's interaction with the social or ecological system (Bullers, 2005). The role of the community psychologist cannot be circumscribed to the traditional mental health functions. The community psychologist requires interdisciplinary training in the social sciences (sociology, political science, anthropology), which can be applied to social intervention in groups, organizations, and community institutions.

The history of community psychology demonstrates that its evolution has been progressive and in accordance with its academic and institutional implementation; Newbrough (1992) details the following chronology:

- *From nascence, in 1965, to the Austin Conference of 1975*: This decade saw the delineation of the community psychologists' professional profile (education and training).
- *1975–1989*: The development of theoretical models for working in the community. The models highlighted prevention and advocated an ecological approach. The remit of the community psychologist was extended to include the social problems of the most socially disadvantaged groups and communities (Buelga, 2001).
- *1989 to the present*: This period can be referred to as a time of integration and diffusion; theoretical and methodological pluralism has become accepted.

## From Social Inequality to Latin American Community Development

Latin American community psychology features a series of idiosyncratic characteristics that are derived from its socioeconomic context. The history of resistance to the perpetuation of totalitarian regimes and the level of social inequality and injustice engendered a resolute and meaningful response from the social sciences. Social work, anthropology, popular education, and (later) psychology provided the bedrock upon which the new discipline of community psychology was constructed (Montero, 1999).

As previously mentioned, in the years after World War II, new political and social ideas were being debated and formulated in Europe and the United States. In the same way that the ideology of community health found expression in the WHO, the concept of fair development was expounded in international organizations like the United Nations (UN), the United Nations Educational Scientific and Cultural Organization (UNESCO), and the Organization of American States (OAE).

The social change planned by the new social services was squarely aimed at the mobilization of community resources. The next step was to replace the institutional objective of "organizing" with "developing" the active participation of the population (Campbell & Murray, 2004). Colombian sociologist Fals Borda was one of the founders of Participatory Action Research, which became a highly valued and widely employed instrument of social intervention (Buelga et al., 2009).

These models were to have profound influence on the process of Latin American agrarian reform that took place in the 1970s. The injustice and inequality in the distribution of wealth led Latin American social scientists to turn their attention to the problems of development and marginalization that were so commonplace in their countries (Wagner de Lima, 1999). In 1975, the University of Puerto Rico became the first institution to offer an academic specialty that focused on these issues (Sánchez, Wiesenfeld, & López, 1998). The position of Latin American social intellectualism was further consolidated by the hosting of a number of conferences, congresses, and meetings such as the 17th Inter American Congress of Psychology, in Lima, 1979, and the First and Second Regional Meetings of Community Psychology, in Sao Paolo, 1981 and Belo Horizonte, 1988.

In addition to this academic contribution, ground-breaking interdisciplinary pilot projects were undertaken in marginalized, indigenous, or rural communities by Fals Borda, Chaves, and Márquez, which questioned traditional social psychology methodology. As Lewin had already argued, a dynamic and changing reality makes it necessary to close the gap between research and action. The psychologist becomes involved in a community training and empowerment process that begins with the identification of needs and follows on with prioritization, the mobilization of social agents, and the organization of resources and activities, and concludes with the evaluation of the intervention program itself.

The adoption of this methodological model invoked a reconceptualization of the role of the social researcher and her professional profile (Buelga, 2007). The social psychologist directly intervenes in the research reality, and the accumulated scientific knowledge therefore responds to the community in which she is working. When the psychologist intervenes, this knowledge is imparted to the key stakeholders with the aim that *they* then become the true agents of change and development: One of the objectives of the social psychologist is the modification of reality through social action (Montero, 1994a).

New critical voices aligned themselves with the ideas of community development: Freire's "Education is the practice of freedom" was an attempt to unite the principles of Marxism, Christianity, and education (Ovejero, 1997). "Liberating education" can be understood as an interpersonal encounter for the common goals of knowledge and action (Grau, 2001). Dialogue and the problematization of daily life can generate a critical consciousness that can free people from feelings of defenselessness and fatalism (Montero, 1999).

A critical consciousness can be the stimulus for challenging and changing the established order. Once again, thought and action appear as two sides of the same coin (Anckermann et al., 2005). Authors such as Habermas (1999) agree that communication is a basic instrument; dialogue and communication among the critically conscious is the key to human liberty (Buelga et al., 2009).

Martín Baró (1985a,b), argues that, in the most marginalized and oppressed communities, psychology must be committed equally to education and the theology of liberation; such a commitment would free psychology from the social irrelevance with which it is often weighed down. "As De Corte [2001] points out, the work of Martín Baró is an exceptional example of a critical social psychology that does not renounce its moral obligation to attend to the human problems that define the surrounding social reality,

nor does it ignore its commitment to emancipation that gives meaning to similar intellectual endeavor" (Buelga, 2001, p. 208).

According to Montero (1996), the consolidation of this new approach was coincident with comparable tendencies in other countries: Lincoln and Guba (1985) in the United States; Parker (1989) in Britain; Seedat, MacKenzie, and Stevens (2004) in South Africa; and Ibáñez (1989) in Spain. These tendencies can be defined by the following characteristics:

- *The method follows the objective (not the reverse)*: This inevitably leads to the development of new procedures and instruments. Health is studied from the point of view that daily life and common sense are the producers of meaning and knowledge.
- *The individual is seen as an agent*: Reality is constructed collectively and dialectically, based on real-life experiences in which individuals and society mutually transform themselves by means of interaction. Conflict must be studied as a normal ingredient in the life of societies and processes of change.

In short, it can be said that community health psychology is binate in origin: the European and American school operates within a framework of community health and development that has its roots in the mental health reform movement, whereas the source of the Latin American sociocommunity model is the denunciation of social inequalities (Montero, 1994b). Both tendencies characterize the psychologist as a professional mediator for social change and view interaction as fundamental for their collective labor.

### Contemporary Issues
The product of community health psychology has come to be recognized as being of significant import and scientific impact. A range of scientific, epidemiological, and social factors have contributed to the formal acceptance of the community in the psychological study of health (Matarazzo, 1980, 1982; Miller, 1983; Rodríguez Marín, 1991), including:

- *Changes in causes of mortality and morbidity* and the importance of living conditions, environmental aspects, and social inequalities.
- *Improvements in epidemiological information media*: National statistics demonstrate that in the etiology of our mortality, cardiovascular disease, cancer, and accidents predominate, and these are closely linked to lifestyle.

- *A greater consciousness of how behavior affects health*. This is associated with scientific evidence on the relationship between the individual and his or her environment in pathology, treatment, and prevention.
- *The reorientation of natural medicine toward health* as an integral, holistic, and/or biopsychosocial phenomenon.
- *The raising of an ideal, a complete state of physical, mental, and social well-being*. Ironically, the existence of this ideal has meant that in a world of incredible medical advances, it is practically impossible to find the prototype of a person in perfect health: cholesterol imbalance, overweight, ageing, stress, and the proliferation of "syndromes" of every shape and form (pre/postvacation, pre/postoperation, pre/postnatal, pre/postschool, etc.) are a constant threat to the safety and integrity of the individual (Moral, 2008). We are much less tolerant of pain, although we happily "go under the knife" or submit our bodies to cosmetic torture in the pursuit of a homogenized image of aesthetic perfection.

The confluence of these factors was undoubtedly one of the reasons for the recognition, at the end of the 1970s, of the psychologist as a legitimate health professional. Psychology became part of the system at a time of crisis and reorganization of health services, and it played (and will continue to play) a role in their development. The emphasis on prevention and community action is especially relevant to primary health attention.

Simon (1999) has suggested that, conceptually, community psychology can be understood as being aimed at the comprehension, explanation, and solution of problems, transcending individual analysis and prioritizing actions for change and improvements in the environment (Bloom, 1984; Zax & Specter, 1978). For Rappaport (1977), community psychology is a discipline that accentuates the importance of an ecological perspective of interaction, meaning that improvements in adaptation between people and their environment can be effected with the creation of new health options and the development of personal resources, instead of achieving these goals through the elimination of individual and community weaknesses.

Godoy (1999, p. 50) gives us the following conclusion: "Although its practical consequences have yet to be evaluated, community psychology has made a substantial contribution toward health, especially in the importance of the psychosocial

variables at a conceptual and operative level and the emphasis on prevention and the fostering of individual competences as an alternative to a clinical model based on deficit."

## The Psychosocial Perspective of Community Health

From the psychosocial viewpoint, lifestyles are individual options that evolve in specific contexts. The family and reference groups determine our learning of health beliefs, acceptable health behaviors, and the health habits of nutrition, hygiene, and exercise (Echauri & Pérez, 2001). Huici (1985) asserts that social groups influence health through:

- Theories, definitions, or interpretations of illness. The family socializes the interpretation of symptoms, offers advice, and prescribes treatments. This can involve advocacy (or disapproval) of certain behaviors such as self-medication, seeking professional help, and compliance with treatment or therapy
- The expression of symptoms (e.g., the manifestation of pain)
- Behavior oriented toward health and healthy habits
- Relationships between the health professional and the patient
- The interaction between socioeconomic status, group structure, and the medical orientation of the professional.

### *A Study Object Beyond the Frontier*

Reference groups share a culture of health that "filters" our responses to well-being, illness, and associated behaviors. In fact, cultural diversity is one of the challenges faced on a daily basis in the maintenance and development of the health services. James and Prilleltensky (2002) ask if it is even possible for mental health practice to be integral and integrating. All health services (promotion, prevention, treatment, and rehabilitation) must make adjustments to react to social processes, such as financial and economic crises (Barriga, León, Martínez, & Rodríguez Marín, 1990).

Anthropology provides numerous examples of this symbiosis. The stereotypical American belief that life should be happy and controllable implies a conception of illness and death as failure, as battles that must be fought and won. On the other hand, in many Asian cultures, it is common to believe that life is full of suffering, and that this is not something that humans can control; illness and death are the result of bad luck, or of past actions, and must therefore be accepted (Baron & Byrne, 2005).

Different cultures offer different interpretations of health and illness. Calpe (2003) identifies three prototypes (magic, religious, and scientific) that are often interlinked. Returning to the East–West contrast, the same author (Calpe, 2003) notes that Chinese culture tends to accept scientific health interpretations when they are shrouded in mysticism and magic, whereas Western societies tend to accept "magical" acts (e.g., a miraculous recovery, the wonder of the birth of a child) if they are accompanied by a scientific explanation.

One of the primary sources of cultural influence is social stratification and social inequality (Gallo, Bogart, Vranceanu, & Mattews, 2005). Schnittker and McLeod (2005) refer to this field of study as "the social psychology of health disparities." The level of economic development of a society has a transparent influence on the health of the population as it conditions the standard of living (García, Sáez, & Escarbajal, 2000). A simple comparison of life expectancy in developed and developing countries is enough to illustrate the point: A baby girl born in Japan can expect to live for about 85 years; a baby girl born at the same time in Sierra Leone has a life expectancy of 37. The Japanese child will receive vaccinations, good nutrition, and good schooling. If she becomes a mother, she will benefit from high-quality maternity care; when she is older, she may develop chronic diseases, but excellent treatment and rehabilitation services will be available. This is clearly not the case for the child from Sierra Leone (WHO, 2007).

The disparity in access to economic resources finds expression in (Durán, 1983):

- Differences in knowledge and attitudes to health and health behavior
- Different risks of illness and risks of suffering specific illnesses
- Differences in health service access and efficiency of use
- Differences in treatment and recovery
- Differences in rehabilitation and social insertion
- Differences in the likelihood of death before reaching average life expectancy.

For the unprotected and disadvantaged, the health system is a particularly stressful institution (Friedman, 2002), but perhaps the most worrying aspect is that the system (whose theoretical objective is the promotion of health) perpetuates and exacerbates the differences listed above. Levels of assistance, satisfaction, and communication are not the same for those who have freedom of choice and those who have to face issues of health and illness with scant social, educational, and economic resources (Gil-Lacruz & Gil-Lacruz, 2010b).

Michael Moore's film *Sicko* opens with the case of an American citizen who has lost two fingers in an accident. His health insurance only covers the reattachment of one finger, so he must decide which of the fingers to save. This is the difference between a *national health service* and a health service that is controlled by the market. Free-market domination of health services tends to make treatment more expensive and increases social inequality. Nevertheless, both models must regulate access. In the national health systems of Europe, regulation is not established through price; it is established by waiting lists and service catalogues. In these systems, which are, a priori, more equitable, inequality is found in areas such as prevention: In Spain, for example, national insurance does not cover all dental, optical, and orthopedic services (Calero, 2009).

In addition to these health system inequalities, an individual's immediate environment also conditions and affects his or her health. Oliver (2003) points to the risk factors and social inequalities that can be observed in our great metropolises and their effect on mental health. In some of the transitional economies of Central and Eastern Europe, for example, the past decade has been a time of great social upheaval; the rural model has been replaced by uniformism, big cities, and crowded suburbs. As a consequence, deaths linked to alcohol abuse, accidents, violence, and suicide have all risen sharply (WHO, 2007).

Humans constantly modify their environments, and often in unnatural ways. These changes can obviously affect health, for example, with the appearance of new illnesses and diseases (Garrett, 1995); some of these are the result of mutations of infectious agents that become resistant to our medicines, whereas others are derived from lifestyle choices. diet, work, social activities, etc.

Environmental destruction is yet another cause of stress and illness in our communities. For example, an excessively humid, hot, and polluted atmosphere can provoke (among other things) a negative disposition, which, in turn, can result in adverse personal interactions, antisocial behavior, aggressive attitudes, and worse.

The most common strategies in the face of atmospheric pollution are measures to change the behavior of individuals (e.g., the banning of smoking in public places) and organizations (e.g., vehicle pollution emission regulations). However, what is really required is a much more profound political intervention, especially in terms of stricter control of contaminating industries and investment in public transport.

Community health environmental research can be divided into two phases:

- *The end of the 1950s to the mid-1980s*, when most research concentrated on the urban environment: the city, the workplace and institutions, and their interaction with human social behavior (Morales & Huici, 2003; Requena, 2000). One of the most significant findings of research in these decades was that immigrants, even when they maintain a degree of cultural homogeneity in their health habits (hygiene, diet, etc.), tend to assume the patterns of health and sickness of their new countries of residence (Anson, 2004; García, Sáez, & Escarbajal, 2000).
- *The mid-1980s to the present*: This period has witnessed a reorientation toward sustainability, as both the object and the objective. Research interest is also concerned with a sense of belonging to one's residential and environmental surroundings (Ng, Kam, & Pong, 2005). In recent decades, psychologists have turned their attention to the negative impact of humans on the environment, efforts to change behavior, and the promotion of healthy habits and attitudes.

A lesson that can be drawn from this discussion is the importance of integrating the individual and the collective in social interventions. All actions have an effect (however small) on the surrounding environment. From having children, driving a car, or using make-up, to recycling the rubbish and looking after a garden; all our actions have consequences for the environment, the community, and society as a whole.

The enormous task of convincing people to change their behavior and attitudes and to live and interact in mutually advantageous and healthy ways is a challenge that requires the knowledge, experience, and skills of the psychology professional (Katzev & Wang, 1994).

Measures designed by community professionals include family planning campaigns, recycling projects, and activities for the protection of natural habitats. Of equal importance, however, are campaigns aimed at fostering a new social consciousness of the citizen; social planning requires participation.

From a community perspective, context is not just an external reality: It has an influence on people's behavior, but it is also a construct that is the result of that behavior. Improvements in environmental conditions that prejudice health require new public policies that encourage community participation and convince individuals to adopt proactive roles in the improvement of their surroundings (Gil Rodríguez, León, & Jarana, 1995). An environment is not only defined by ecological, demographic, or economic characteristics; it is also defined by the culture of its protagonists, who shape the model of health and well-being (Aikins, 2004).

As with health, research and community action necessitates a holistic vision that is relevant and sensitive to social problems. It is a vision that must find a balance between theory and practice and demonstrate respect for cultural diversity (Morgan, 2000).

The limitations of impact and the generalized nature of community psychology interventions demand realistic, goal-oriented objectives (Páez, Marques, & Insúa, 1996). The experience of public health projects (e.g., preventative education, development of community resources, etc.) has highlighted the exigency of an exhaustive, tripartite evaluation of the identification of social needs, the implementation of the sociocommunity project, and a postimplementation assessment of the effectiveness of the project (Páez, 2003).

The significance of social values must never be ignored in this work; community psychology is a branch of scientific psychology but it should never forget its ideological perspective or its social conscience (Snow, Grady, & Gollete-Ewing, 2000). Assistentialism, victimization, and doctor-dependency do not generate social change; this objective can only be achieved by supra-individual, preventative, and interdisciplinary interventions (Fernández, Herrero, & Bravo, 2000).

### Aims and Objectives

Health promotion activity is inextricably linked to social and community resources and personal competences that offer individuals the possibility of assuming responsibility for their own health. "This means that it is desirable to involve the whole population, in their daily-life contexts and in the improvement of their health conditions; this should be facilitated by the available community resources (social education, social action, and organizations that form the backbone of the community) and the generation of any other resources that are deemed necessary for the adoption of measures that can modify the causes or determinants of health" (García, Sáez, & Escarbajal, 2000, p. 81).

The fostering of personal and community development through information, education for health, and life skills instruction must allow people to increase available options for the control of their own health and other social conditions that affect the community (García et al., 2000).

Community health objectives function in three distinct spheres:

- *Preventative*: The design of actions that impede potential problems or their aggravation
- *Promotional*: The optimization of psychosocial development, with the aim of improving social well-being
- *Therapeutic*: The resolution of social problems, such as marginalization and socioeconomic injustices.

The fundamental aim of community psychology and psychosocial intervention is the achievement of well-being; "the process by which the individual is able to maximize their current and potential abilities and achieve a state of complete self-actualization as a person and as a social entity" (Cuevas, 1996, p. 420).

It is therefore possible to identify objectives that are implicated in the tasks of intervention, research, and education:

- The promotion of health and the prevention of illness; the determination of psychosocial and lifestyle risk factors
- Diagnosis and assessment, treatment, and patient care, rehabilitation and patient adaptation to illness
- The evaluation, organization, and management of community health services.

The evaluation of projects undertaken in pursuit of these objectives has generally been positive, but it is clear that there is room for improvement. The achievements of preventative action programs, in spite of their diversity and utility, have often fallen short of expectation (Palomares, 1990). This has been due to the fact that these activities have not integrated the three essential requisites of such actions (Murray, Nelson, Poland, Maticka-Tyndale, & Ferris, 2004): a plan that respects the individual and community values of the object of the action; a program that is based on theoretical and methodological models of a scientific nature; and an emphasis on participation.

It should not, therefore, be the intention of the community psychologist to prepare differential pathological profiles between group elements and subsystems; nor should he or she aim to analyze the mental health problems that might affect specific social systems. The cornerstone of community psychology is the community, and intervention must analyze psychosocial processes within a framework that is delimited by particular time and space coordinates. Bunge (1972) explains that, as researchers, the job of community psychologists is to gain an understanding of problems and place them in a coherent and relevant body of knowledge in order to resolve them. The researcher must be a problematizer par excellence.

Recent developments in community psychology have shown that if it is to evolve in line with current health tendencies, it must be interventionist (Martín, Chacón, & Martínez, 1988). If, as Barriga (1987) has commented, the discipline is moving in the direction of greater social sensitivity and shared responsibility, the research and intervention work of the community psychologist must be based on the following values:

- The defense and promotion of sociocultural diversity
- The fight against inequality and discrimination
- The struggle to achieve an integrated health system
- The search for an individual and collective quality of life
- A conception of the individual as an active subject, capable of resolving his or her own problems in collaboration with peers.

In comparison with the traditional "individualist" model (also referred to as clinical, biological, passive, or medical), the community model postulates questions that are fundamental for social integration: How can the health system be improved? What is the perception of the work environment? How does the individual participate in social organizations and social processes? How do citizens feel about the proposed social solutions in their environment? (See Table 31.2).

The acceptance of interdisciplinarity assumes a conviction that the complex social reality is not the exclusive domain of one particular discipline; the questions posed by the psychologist are of equal importance and value as those issues raised by other social scientists (De Guevara, 1980) (see Table 31.3).

Nevertheless, this does not lessen the responsibility of the individual in society, as Barriga (1987) points out: the psychosocial model is not a sociological model; it values the individual experience of each member of each reference group and the extent to

**Table 31.2 Conceptions of health**

| Type of conception | Individualist | Community |
|---|---|---|
| The professional | Is the competent authority<br>Is the only one that can give an opinion<br>Is the only one that passes judgment<br>Uses technical jargon<br>Waits for users to seek help | Is an "advisor" to the community<br>Uses accessible language and pedagogic techniques<br>Draws up health measures and programs in conjunction with the community<br>Finds users |
| The user | Is a layperson<br>Does not offer opinions or suggestions<br>Obeys the professional<br>Seeks help (when ill) | Is knowledgeable<br>Is able to learn<br>Gives opinions and makes suggestions<br>Controls and develops self-management and self-awareness skills |

From García Martínez, Sáez, J., & Escarbajal, A. (2000). *Educación para la salud. Apuesta por la calidad de vida*. Madrid: Arán.

which that individual has interiorized (in their social representations and categories) the social medium in which they live.

## Theoretical Approaches

There is no consensus on a classification for community psychology models. A degree of clarity can be found if the visibility of models within the discipline is taken into consideration (although even this criterion is not free of criticism;- see Dyregrov, 2004). Rappaport and Seidman (2000) propose a dual systematization, based on the framework of origin:

- *The clinical-community approach*: Dominant in Europe and America, this includes the

**Table 31.3 Characteristics of community psychology**

| | |
|---|---|
| Causes of problems | The interaction relationship between people and social systems; the social support structure and social power |
| Degrees of analysis | Micro to macro; analysis of community organizations |
| Research methods | Qualitative methodology, research-action, case studies; "semi-experimental" approaches |
| Localization | Day-to-day social contexts; social relevance; emphasis on prevention |
| Provision of services | Proactive model; evaluation of need, especially in high-risk communities |
| Openness | A positive attitude toward both formal and informal shared psychological models; priority given to the creation of self-help and paraprofessional groups |

From Orford, J. (1993). *Community psychology: theory and practice*. England: John Wiley and Sons, with permission of the publisher.

community mental health model, Dohrenwend's psychosocial stress model (incorporating Lin and Ensel's model of well-being), and the community behavioral model. These models also integrate specific behavioral modification techniques, such as those of Banyard and LaPlant (2002).

- *The sociocommunity approach*: Developed in the Latin American context of social change; the ecological model is one of the most influential community instruments. In terms of the organizational and empowerment model, its relevance is in its capacity to generate research and community interventions (Shinn & Perkins, 2000).

By way of example, the following sections give an outline of two sociocommunity models that offer practical guidelines on health promotion in specific environments (Levine, Toro, & Perkins, 1993).

### THE ECOLOGICAL MODEL

According to Serrano-García and Alvárez (1992), the ecological model is the most representative community psychology model because it most clearly reflects the aspirations of social psychologists in their task of explaining the interdependent relationship between the individual and his environment (Durkheim, 1898/1971; Lewin, 1951; Simmel, 1902/1950; Thomas & Znaniecki, 1920; The Chicago school: Faris & Dunham, 1939; McKenzie, 1926). It also offers a perspective that underlines the effect that the physical medium (the setting) has on behavior.

Del Río, Guerrero, and Corazón (1979) put forward some basic questions for discussion: How does an environment influence the life-plan of an individual? How does the environment influence an individual's mental and sensorial development? What influence does an environment created by the mass media have on these life-plans and other personal projects?

Community factors are determinants, in that people must continually adapt to changes in the environment in which they live their lives. Attributes of change (e.g., interaction, cohesion, connection, community identity, etc.) are relevant when defining types of communities (from the most integrated to the most anomic) and understanding the reference group as a potentially therapeutic, adaptive system (Dench, 2002; Fondacaro & Weinberg, 2002). It is therefore widely assumed that every community is an ecological system (Von Bertalanfy, 1979), and the decay and deterioration of that system presupposes a serious risk to health and quality of life (Carlson, 1980).

However, individuals are not passive objects within their environments; influence is bidirectional and is reflected in different fields of ascendancy (Bronfenbrenner, 1979). The ecological environment can be seen as a conjunct of concentric structures (micro-, meso-, exo-, and macro-systems), each one integrated into the next (Trickett, 2009). This schematic has the advantage of an ordered formulation for the analysis of a social reality (of the environments in which the individual participates), and it also incorporates the individual's perception of those environments (from the micro-system or immediate environment to the macro-system that requires a greater degree of abstraction).

Once again, it can be noted that the multicausal nature of health and illness and the community perspective are recurrent themes. The providentialism of the origin of these processes and conditions is removed from these models at the point of analyzing their underlying causes (Kisnerman, 1987). Even the concept of health itself is affected by ecological aspects (San Martín & Pastor, 1984):

- A state of health is not absolute; it is inseparable from the ecological and social environment of the community. Health is an eminently processual concept and therefore variable.
- It is not possible to establish an indisputable standard that demarcates health and illness; there are only degrees and diverse expressions.
- There are at least three components to health: *subjective* (well-being); *objective* (functional capacity); and *psychoecological* (the mental, social, and biological adaptation of the individual).

Logically, these issues are expressed in the ecological model of health; a health system is developed with the validation of community knowledge and its transmission through organizational environments, for example, school students, university students, health professionals, etc. (Wandersman, 2003).

In Spain, health is a transversal axis in the school curriculum, which means that health issues are included in all subjects, irrespective of their scientific, technical, social, or humanistic/artistic content. Universities can also play a leading role in the promotion of health in the community through training, research, and dissemination of information. The WHO initiative for Health Promoting Universities (WHO/OPS 2003) highlights the ecological importance of universities' role in:

- Implementing transversal, multidisciplinary curricular designs on public health, health promotion, and healthy environments
- Studying the health needs of the university locality, running awareness campaigns on the importance of teaching, and developing life skills and competences
- Facilitating a harmonious and stimulating psychosocial environment, strengthening areas and opportunities for dialogue and decision making.

Public health institutions fundamentally respond to two ecological criteria:

- *Productive*: Service efficiency; health systems run exclusively in accordance with this criterion often suffer a lack of sensitivity in providing health service access. This is typically exemplified by the purchase of highly expensive, underused technological equipment at the cost of investment in other (arguably) more important areas such as prevention.
- *Distributive*: The attempt to establish health as a right for the population of a country (Embry, 2004). The distributive principle is institutionalized in Europe in the form of the National Health System: "[A] group of mechanisms through which human resources are organized in an administrative and medical-technological process in order to offer integral health services of sufficient quantity and adequate quality to cover the demand for those services by the entire population of a community and at a cost that is compatible with available funding" (WHO, 1972, p. 32).

Kelly (1986) believes that all community interventions must take into account four ecological principles: The interdependence of all elements in the system; the use of community resources that have been ignored in the first phase of the intervention; constant adaptation to the different settings; and a preventative attitude in the face of those changes that are produced in systems to avoid their corresponding dysfunctionalities.

These principles are clearly illustrated by the ecological analysis of nutrition: ecological factors like cultural habits, health and welfare system access, economic status, and commercial and social pressures determine health options. As global market forces control the food supply, healthy food is a political issue. The global food trade is big business.

Social and economic conditions affect dietary quality and contribute to health inequalities. The main dietary difference between social classes is the source of nutrients: In many countries, the economically disadvantaged substitute cheaper, processed food for fresh food. High fat intake is common and increases the possibility of cardiovascular diseases, cancer, degenerative sight conditions, obesity, and dental problems. Nutritional poverty lives alongside nutritional excess. People on low incomes, single-parent families, the elderly, and the unemployed are least able to eat well.

The Mediterranean culture (diet, climate, support networks, social interactions, pace of life, etc.) has a great influence on health in countries like Spain, Greece, Portugal, or Italy. The prevention of ecological decay and the preservation of the Mediterranean heritage require a global intervention: More research is needed on the consequences of the genetic engineering of fruit and vegetables; attention must be paid to public policy on nutrition, conservation, commercialization, and distribution; local values and products should be defended; and there should be alliances with social movements and nongovernmental organizations (e.g., the Slow Food Movement). There must also be healthy options in local settings; in the Mediterranean context, food and diet are not only related to a primary function, but also to living together, dialogue, and a celebration of our social life.

Environmental factors also determine the "quality" (support, solidarity, communication, etc.) or the "frailty" (competitiveness, isolation, hostility, etc.) of social relations. An ecological approach to social relationships allows us to learn about their decisive influence on the progress or degeneration of the quality of life, as much in terms of interaction with one's surroundings as in individual relationships. For Blocher and Biggs (1986), the ecological model is psychosocial in that it is interested in the interrelationships among the individual, the community,

and the environment—communication is ultimately an act of reflection and awareness (Gracia & Musitu, 2000).

### THE SOCIAL EMPOWERMENT AND COMPETENCE MODEL

This model accentuates the need for subjects to take control of their own lives and seek a solitary solution to their problems. The essential objective of psychosocial intervention is the empowerment of individuals and groups in the resolution of shared difficulties (Wolf, 1987).

In consonance with the ecological model, individual and group behavior is interpreted to the extent that the individual seeks maximum effectiveness in his interactions with his environments. One of the main differences between the two models is that the empowerment and competence model stresses the relevance of the independent variables of responsibility and the possibility of change for each of the elements involved.

The empowerment and competence model is commonly viewed as an alternative to Marxist-influenced models that criticize the ecological perspective for its excessive structuralism, the dominance of exterior relationships over the individual, and its social predetermination through accelerated technological and communication processes, etc. (Theodorson, 1974). For the empowerment model, autonomy and self-management are central to the acquisition of social competences in the interventions and actions that are implemented (Bruce & Thornton, 2004).

Laverack and Wallerstein (2001) believe that empowerment is a process that is initiated with personal development but continues with the development of self-help groups and community organizations and alliances that may lead to political and social actions. Goodman (1998) proposes an evaluation of this process in the community that is based on ten dimensions: community participation, leadership, solid social networks, the ability to articulate values, a sense of history, a sense of the community, critical reflection, the ability to mobilize resources, skills, and the ability to exercise power.

Irrespective of these debates, the model (along with those previously mentioned) can serve as a nexus between traditional health models and other alternatives that contemplate the significance of sociocultural factors, for example:

- *The medical-biological model (lack of illness or constant health–illness equilibrium)*: Fleck (1986) argues that this theoretical system is very much a modified version of age-old demonological conceptions in which the person is seen as being possessed; the body defends itself from attack, and health is therefore considered as an intrinsic condition of the organism (Esteban, 2001).

- *The sociocultural model (the antithesis of the aforementioned)*: This model establishes the relationship between the lack of illness and living conditions, which are determined by the physical environment and sociocultural practices (Ribes, 1990).

Ribes (1990, p. 21) further contends that the differences between the two positions can be reconciled: "The knowledge of the biological process of an illness and the social conditions of its epidemiology are not sufficient. What is needed is a model that is able to apply this knowledge in the form of effective measures in the day to day activities of real-life individuals, a dimension that transcends the molecular processes of the organism and the population statistics of the epidemiology."

The social empowerment and competence model offers an additional perspective on the concept of health from its organizational focus, which has a conception of the community as a conjunct of organizations that function in accordance with principles derived from organizational psychology and the study of social groups (Buelga, 2001). Organizational psychology provides community psychology with strategies for analysis that go beyond the individual. At the same time, community psychology enriches organizational psychology with its "lexicon of values," which prioritizes the well-being of the individual (Shinn & Perkins, 2000).

Organizational health can be defined as the capacity of the organization or community to survive, adapt, and grow, irrespective of the specific functions undertaken. According to Alonso (1994), research on organizational and community health refers to three criteria that condition the intervention:

- *Identity*: The specification of the mission and context of the organization, the shared understanding of its members, and the degree of consensus of these perceptions. It must be remembered that one of the most important contributions of community psychology is a sense of belonging (Townley & Kloos, 2009); Sarason (1974) said that this is a precept for any participative process or communal activity.
- *Adaptability*: The evaluation of the capacity of the organization to resolve problems and

react to the demands of its environment with its own resources; adaptation should respect organizational identity.
- *Integration*: The evaluation of how the organizational subsystems achieve their objectives and carry out their functions, both global and specific.

Community and organizational development (e.g., in the workplace) requires the participation of members in the acquisition of control competences that are tailored to their circumstances and environment (Klein, Ralls, Smith Major, & Douglas, 2000). This is a principle that has a long history in social psychology; Lewin devised group training techniques that have been effective in the improvement of interpersonal competence, reducing anxiety, and diminishing intergroup conflict (Rodríguez Molina, 2000).

The main task of community intervention is to convince the members that they possess the resources and strength to fulfill the role of an agent for change. Instead of helping to resolve problems, community intervention aims to equip people with the competences to resolve problems for themselves (Ander Egg, 1993). The community psychologist optimizes the use of resources, making every subject an agent of social intervention (Grande, Pons, Gil-Lacruz, & Marín, 1995).

Rodríguez (2009) suggests some specific psychosocial interventions for the empowerment of the members of a community:

- Actions that raise self-awareness and self confidence
- Actions developed within parameters of intergenerational and gender inclusion
- Actions that give communities access to information and communication technologies
- Actions that engender citizenship and productivity; these include instrumental knowledge and tools for the analysis of relevant economic and political dynamics
- Projects aimed at economic sustainability for vulnerable populations; community organizations, community networks, skills training, and socially productive programs
- Collective access to community spaces for taking political decisions and access to networks that transcend the closed circle of the community and the community's social capital.

This optimization is not just psychological; it is also a strengthening of the individual rights and personal opportunities of the citizens within their own environments—the neighborhood, workplace, or community organization (Musitu & Buelga, 2004). The different intervention levels (individual, organizational, community) are mutually interdependent if development strengthens the potential of others. Improving a community's quality of life implies analyzing the configuration of the social reality (Zimmerman, 2000). Empowerment through social structures (neighborhood associations, local organizations, etc.) leads to greater participation in society as a whole (Palmonari & Zani, 1980).

Resource development, political action, and the work of social scientists are three interdependent bases of the empowerment and competence model. Rappaport (1977, 1981) sees community psychology as inextricably linked to the adoption of values that guide intervention: diversity, cultural relativity, and an equitable distribution of resources. The scientific method guarantees that an understanding of the social reality gives coherence and validity to social interventions (Zimmerman, 2000).

In practice, however, this discourse can be compromised by mechanisms of local political control. Even within local organizations themselves, differences may exist in terms of objectives that reflect disagreements on the optimization of the social action, and this implies significant challenges that must be faced, especially in contexts of economic insecurity, corruption, a lack of solidarity, or the violation of human rights (Restrepo, 2000).

*Decentralization* and *participation* are frequently cited as the magic words of psychosocial intervention, but people do not always want to participate, and decentralization is often just a synonym for institutional dependency. Only those trapped in their ivory towers insist that participation, in and of itself, is a panacea of community empowerment. If participation is not based on a clear, concrete, and tangible objective, it can only lead to increased distrust and doubt (Rodríguez Villasante, 1994).

## Conclusion
### *The Psychological Dimension in the Promotion of Community Health: Old Battles and Future Directions*

The central tenet of this chapter is that social problems are multidimensional phenomena that must be tackled with due respect given to their structural, psychosocial, and environmental aspects (García Roca, 1992); as a consequence, well-being, quality of life, and health are the "result of a harmonious relationship between the individual and their natural and social environment" (p. 41).

Smith and Mackie (2007) say that good health may be the result of a good diet, regular exercise, or good genes, but this is clearly not the whole story; our emotional life, the stress we are under, our capacity to love and be loved, and our social relationships have as much influence on our bodies as on our minds (see studies on chronic pain and assimilation strategies by Pastor, López, Rodríguez Marín, Terol, & Sánchez, 1995; or studies on feelings of invulnerability and illusionary optimism by Sánchez, Rubio, Páez, & Blanco, 1998).

In the same way, the roots of ill-being can be uncovered in a negative relationship between the individual and her environment; lifestyles and social practices are fundamental to the quality of life, which is a determinant of health and well-being.

From this perspective, health is understood as a social and political question, and its phrasing and solution require the active participation of the community in its definition, in the management and control of the health system, and in interventions aimed at health promotion (WHO, 2005). The new concept of health demands a shift from a passive model to an active model of intervention and participation. We must work *on* the community *with* the community and *in* the community (Velásquez, 2003).

When health professionals promote exercise and take a stance against the use of drugs, when hospitals give patients greater control over their treatment, and when subsidies are given to groups that aid rehabilitation and recovery from illness and addiction, psychosocial processes are able to perform their role as promoters of health and generators of healthy minds and bodies (Miller & Shinn, 2005).

The goal is to engender a culture of health within the community itself. One of the essential components is education for health and the advocacy of healthy lifestyles (Gil Lacruz, 2007b).

Adopting measures that support the implementation of community orientation in the strategic enclaves of a society (e.g., schools and workplaces), involves the consideration of a series of underlying issues (Hombrados, 1996):

- *Socialization in the early years of life instills habits, attitudes, and values.* The school is one of the primary agents for this process (WHO, 1982). Education for health not only implies the acquisition of basic knowledge, but it reassesses the role of the teacher as an element of community change and psychosocial integration (Codd & Cohen, 2003; Snibbe & Markus, 2005).

- *Institutional and judicial powers need to understand the importance of health education.* Institutions must be made to recognize the economic benefits and the rationalization of resources that can result from prevention competencies that are learned at a young age, in sharp contrast to diagnosis and treatment in crisis situations later in life (Kratochwill & Shernoff, 2004; Kratochwill, Albers, & Shernoff, 2004).
- *Community and participative policies need to be implemented in the workplace,* in the study of treatment and accident risk prevention (Meliá, Arnedo, & Ricarte; 1996), ergonomic working practices (Llaneza, 2002), and adequate training (Ovejero, 2001).

- *A social capital approach offers an integral, promotional orientation* (Campbell, Cornish, & Mclean, 2004; Coleman, 2001; Lindstrom, 2005, 2006). The social capital model is associated with models of economic and social development (Moyano, 2001).
- *Health promotion empowerment is not simply linked to an informative model* (transmission of knowledge), or a motivational model (behavior modification), or even to the participation (in the sense of mere attendance) of the people involved in the programs or activities; health promotion empowerment is about change and people having control over their own lives. Unfortunately, in the contemporary health system, people are

**Table 31.4  Comparison of health tendencies**

| Comparison element | Curative tendency | Preventive tendency | Promotional tendency |
|---|---|---|---|
| User | Individual | Individual and population | Population groups |
| Initiative | Illness | Health and education services | Politicians, professionals, and the community |
| Choice | Wide-ranging | Restricted | Restricted |
| Access | Difficult | Easy | Easy |
| Attendance | Irregular | Regular | Constant |
| Continuity | Minimal | Minimal | High |
| Attitude of user | Obedience and submission | Individual and group action | Participative |
| Attitude of professionals | Aristocratic and technocratic | Technocratic | Democratic |
| Techniques | Diagnosis and treatment, advice | Research and control of illnesses; information and persuasion | Identification and solution of perceived problems; education and social change |
| Focus | Individual, unicausal hypothesis, search for certitude | Social–social groups, multicausal hypothesis, search for certitude | Community, familiar, group, and individual; multicausal hypothesis; tolerance of uncertainty |
| Characteristics | Business relationship; provision of services; reactive strategy | Public service; pro-active encouragement and prevention strategies | Public service; community resources |
| Finance | The user | The state; individual resources | The state; community resources |
| Evaluation | Patient attention | Avoidance of illnesses | Problems solved; improved quality of life |
| Value judgments | Quality | Cost effectiveness | Community development and improvement |
| Ideology | Liberal | Technocratic | Radical democratic |

From García Martínez, Sáez, J., & Escarbajal, A. (2000). *Educación para la salud. Apuesta por la calidad de vida.* Madrid: Arán.

generally seen as "clients" or "users" and not as citizens (Rodríguez, 2009).

The search for an intersection between the concepts of community health and community psychology reveals much common ground, based on (Costa & López, 1986):

- The relevance of physical, biological, and social ecosystems as the origin of social needs and the source of alternatives and solutions
- The belief that health education and prevention must be prioritized, at an individual level and in social organizations
- The necessity for the active, organized participation of the community in the evaluation of health problems and resolution strategies
- The ideal of a health service that uses epidemiological research to plan and manage successful health prevention and treatment programs for its entire population (see Table 31.4).

Despite scientific and governmental consensus on the importance of a community emphasis in the promotion of health, in practice, a range of problems threaten the viability of this ideal. Restrepo (2000) has written of the disappearance of multidisciplinary approaches, public health initiatives, and the fact that health service managers prioritize technocracy and the privatization of health services that endanger the health rights of the citizen.

In this context, psychology can often fall into the trap of placing too much responsibility on the individual for his or her risk behaviors: Is the smoker irrational and irresponsible, or a victim of one of the most powerful businesses organizations on the planet? Is a car accident the result of a careless driver, or of unnecessarily fast cars and overcrowded, badly maintained roads? Is the mother of an obese child negligent, or overworked and overwhelmed by the marketing strategies of the fast food industry? These questions place the psychologist squarely in the complex debate on rights, freedoms, and civic responsibilities, as well as forcing the health professional to consider their true objectives, target populations, and roles within the social services.

Community psychology and community health need to overcome the vision of health as an individual condition that is only appreciated in its absence. By definition and practice, quality of life and community development provide the foundations for both disciplines. Health psychology must be able to confront the challenges of the community with the necessary conceptual, professional, scientific, and technical training, and with the education and ideological reflection demanded by this new model of work, action, and intervention.

# References

Aikins, A.D.G. (2004). Strengthening quality and continuity of diabetes care in rural Ghana: A critical social psychological approach. *Journal of Health Psychology, 9,* 295–309.

Alonso, E. (1994). *Desarrollo organizacional: Un modelo de intervención en las organizaciones.* Madrid: Díaz Santos.

Anckermann, S., Dominguez, M., Soto, N., Kjaerulf, F., Berliner P., & Mikkelsen E.N. (2005). Psycho-social support to large numbers of traumatized people in post-conflict societies: An approach to community development in Guatemala. *Journal of Community and Applied Social Psychology, 15,* 136–152.

Ander Egg, E. (1993). *Técnicas de investigación social.* México: Humanitas.

Anson, J. (2004). The migrant mortality advantage: A 70 month follow-up of the Brussels population. *European Journal of Population, 20,* 191–218.

Banyard, V.L., & LaPlant, L.E. (2002). Exploring links between childhood maltreatment and empowerment. *Journal of Community Psychology, 30,* 687–707.

Barriga, S. (1987). La intervención, introducción teórica. En S. Barriga, J.M. León, & M. Martínez (Eds.), *Intervención psicosocial.* Barcelona: Hora.

Barriga, S. (2000). *Psicología general: Curso introductorio.* Barcelona: CEAC.

Barriga, S., León, J.M., Martínez, M., & Rodríguez Marín, J. (1990). Intervención en salud desde la psicología social. Simposio "contribuciones de la psicología social a los servicios de salud." En *Libro de simposios III congreso nacional de psicología social* (pp. 5–23.) Santiago de Compostela, SP.

Baron, R.A., & Byrne, D. (2005). *Psicología social.* Madrid: Prentice Hall.

Baum, A., Revenson, T.A., & Singer, J.E. (2001). *Handbook of health psychology.* Mahwah: Lawrence Erlbaum Associates.

Bennet, C.C. (1965). Community psychology: Impressions of the Boston conference of the education of psychologists for community mental health. *American Psychologists, 20,* 832–835.

Bennet, C.C., Anderson, L.S., Cooper, S., Hassol, L., Klein, D.C., & Rosemblum, G. (1966). *Community psychology: A report of the Boston conference on the education of psychologists for community mental health.* Boston: Boston University Press.

Bernstein, D.A. & Nietzel, M.T. (1982). *Introducción a la psicología clínica.* México: McGraw-Hill.

Blocher, S., & Biggs, L. (1986). *La psicología del counseling en medios comunitarios.* Barcelona: Herder.

Bloom, B.L. (1984). *Community mental health.* Monterrey: Brooks.

Bronfenbrenner, U. (1979). *The Ecology of Human Development: Experiments by Nature and Design.* Cambridge, MA: Harvard University Press.

Bruce, M.A., & Thornton M.C. (2004). It's my world? Exploring black and white perceptions of personal control. *Sociological Quarterly, 45,* 597–612.

Buelga, S. (2001). Psicología comunitaria. *Proyecto docente.* Valencia: Facultad de Psicología, Universidad de Valencia.

Buelga, S. (2007). El empowerment: La potenciación del bienestar desde la psicología comunitaria. En M. Gil-Lacruz

(Ed.), *Psicología social y bienestar: Una aproximación interdisciplinar* (pp.154–173). Zaragoza: Prensas Universitarias.

Buelga, S., Musitu, G., Vera, A., Ávila, M.E., & Arango, C. (2009). *Psicología social comunitaria*. México: Trillas.

Bullers, S. (2005). Environmental stressors, perceived control and health: The case of residents near large-scale hog farms in eastern North Carolina. *Human Ecology, 33*, 1–16.

Bunge, M. (1972). *La investigación científica*. Barcelona: Ariel.

Calero, J. (2009). Comparando dos modelos sanitarios. *El público, 665*, 5.

Calpe, I. (2003). *Qi Gong: Práctica corporal y pensamiento chino*. Barcelona: Kairos.

Campbell, C., & Murray, M. (2004). Community health psychology: Promoting analysis and action for social change. *Journal of Health Psychology, 9*, 187–195.

Campbell, C., Cornish, F., & Mclean, C. (2004). Social capital, participation and the perpetuation of health inequalities: Obstacles to African-Caribbean participation in partnerships to improve mental health. *Ethnicity and Health, 9*, 313–335.

Canals, J. (2004). La importancia de las dimensiones culturales en la asistencia y en la promoción de la salud. *Revista de Servicios Sociales y Política Social, 65*, 9–20.

Carlson, R.L. (1980). *Primavera silenciosa*. Barcelona: Grijalbo.

Codd, R.T., & Cohen B.N. (2003). Predicting college student intention to seek help for alcohol abuse. *Journal of Social and Clinical Psychology, 22*, 168–191.

Coleman, J.S. (2001). Capital social y creación de capital humano. *Zona Abierta, 94/95*, 47.

Costa, M., & López, E. (1986). *Salud Comunitaria*. Barcelona: Martínez Roca.

Cuevas, G. (1996). Intervención psicosocial. En L. Gómez Jacinto, & J.M. Canto (Eds.), *Psicología social* (pp. 415–423). Madrid: Biblioteca Eudema.

De Corte, L. (2001). *Memoria de un compromiso, la psicología social de Ignacio Martín-Baró*. Bilbao: Desclée de Brouwer.

De Guevara, L. (1980). Relación de la psicología con las ciencias sociales. En G. Musitu, E. Berjano, & J.R. Bueno (Eds.), *Psicología comunitaria*. Valencia: Nau Llibres.

Del Río, P., Guerrero, F., & Corazón, A. (1979). *La vida del barrio*. Sevilla: ProSevilla.

Dench, L.N. (2002). Exercise and movement as an adjunct to group therapy for women with chronical mental illness. *Women and Therapy, 25*, 39–55.

DiMatteo, M.R. (1991). *The psychology of health, illness and medical care: An individual perspective*. Pacific Grove: Brooks/ Cole Publishing.

Duran, M.A. (1983). *Desigualdad social y enfermedad*. Madrid: Tecnos.

Durkheim, E. (1971a, trad.). *El suicidio*. Buenos Aires: Schapire. (Original work published 1898).

Dyregrov, K. (2004). Strategies of professional assistance alter traumatic deaths: Empowerment or disempowerment? *Scandinavian Journal of Psychology, 45*, 181–189.

Echauri, M., & Pérez, M.J. (2001). *Estilos de vida. Promoción de a salud: Acciones colectivas y comunitarias*. Pamplona: Instituto de Salud Pública de Navarra.

Embry, D.D. (2004). Community-based prevention using simple, low-cost, evidence-based kernels and behavior vaccines. *Journal of Community Psychology, 32*, 575–591.

Erchul, W.P. (2009). Caplan´s contribution to the psychology consultation. *Journal of Educational and Psychological Consultation, 19*, 95–105

Esteban, M.L. (2001). *Re-producción del cuerpo femenino, discursos y prácticas acerca de la salud*. San Sebastian: Tercera Prensa.

Faris, R.E., & Dunham, H.W. (1939). *Manual disorders in urban areas*. Chicago: University of Chicago Press.

Felner, R.D., Felner, T.Y. & Morton, M. (2000). Prevention in mental health and social intervention. En S. Buelga (2001). (Ed.), *Psicología comunitaria. Proyecto docente*. Valencia: Facultad de Psicología, Universidad de Valencia.

Fernández, J., Herrero, J., & Bravo, A. (Eds.) (2000). *Intervención psicosocial y comunitaria: La promoción de la salud y la calidad de vida*. Madrid: Biblioteca Nueva.

Fleck, L. (1986). *La génesis y el desarrollo de un hecho científico*. Madrid: Alianza Universitaria.

Fondacaro, M.R., & Weinberg, D. (2002). Concepts of social justice in community psychology: Toward a social ecological epistemology. *American Journal of Community Psychology, 30*, 473–492.

Friborg, O., Hjemdal, O., Rosenvinge, J.H., & Martinussen, M. (2003). A new rating scale for adult resilience: What are the central protective resources behind healthy adjustment?. *International Journal of Methods in Psychiatric Research, 12*, 65–76.

Friedman, H.S. (2000). Long-term relations of personality and health: Dynamisms, mechanisms, tropisms. *Journal of Personality, 68*, 1089–1108.

Friedman, H.S. (2002). *Health Psychology*. Upper Saddle River: Pearson Education.

Friedman, H.S. (2008). The multiple linkages of personality and disease. *Brain, Behavior, and Immunity, 22*, 668–675.

Gagné, M., & Deci, E.L. (2005). Self-determination theory and work motivation. *Journal of Organizational Behavior, 26*, 331–362.

Gallo, L.C., Ghaed, S.G. & Bracken, W.S. (2004). Emotions and cognitions in coronary heart disease: Risk, resilience, and social context. *Cognitive Therapy and Research, 28*, 669–694.

Gallo, L.C., Bogart, L.M., Vranceanu, A.M., & Matthews, K.A. (2005). Socioeconomic status, resources, psychological experiences and emotional responses: A test of the reserve capacity model. *Journal of Personality and Social Psychology, 88*, 386–399.

García Martínez, Sáez, J., & Escarbajal, A. (2000). *Educación para la salud. Apuesta por la calidad de vida*. Madrid: Arán.

García Roca, J. (1992). *Público y privado en la acción social. Del Estado de Bienestar al Estado Social*. Madrid: Popular.

Garrett, L. (1995). *The coming plague: Newly emerging diseases in a world out of balance*. New York: Farrar, Straus and Giroux.

Gil-Lacruz, M. (2000). *Salud y fuentes de apoyo social: Análisis de una comunidad*. Madrid: Centro de Investigaciones Sociológicas.

Gil-Lacruz, M. (Ed.). (2007a). *Psicología social y bienestar*. Zaragoza: Prensas Universitarias.

Gil-Lacruz, M. (2007b). *Psicología social, un compromiso aplicado a la salud*. Zaragoza: Prensas Universitarias.

Gil-Lacruz, M., & Gil-Lacruz, A.I (2010a). Health attributions and health care behaviour interactions in a community sample. *Social Behavior and Personality, 30*, 845–858.

Gil-Lacruz, M., & Gil-Lacruz, A.I (2010b). Health Perception and Health Care Access: Sex Differences in Behaviors and Attitudes. *American Journal of Economics and Sociology, 69*, 783–801.

Gil Rodríguez, F., León J.M. & Jarana, L. (1995). *Habilidades sociales y salud*. Madrid: Pirámide.

Godoy, J.F. (1999). Psicología de la salud: Delimitación conceptual. En M.A. Simón (Ed.), *Manual de psicología de la salud*.

*Fundamentos, metodología y aplicaciones* (pp. 39–75). Madrid: Biblioteca Nueva.

Goleman, D. (1991, November 13). All too often, the doctor isn't listening, studies show. *New York Times*, pp. C1–C15.

Goodman, R.M. (1998). Identyfing and refining the dimensions of community capacity to provide a basis for measurement. *Health Education and Behaviour, 25*, 258–278.

Gracia, E., & Musitu, G. (2000). *Psicología social de la familia.* Barcelona: Paidós.

Gracia, E., Herrero, J., & Musitu, G. (1995). *Apoyo social.* Barcelona: PPU.

Grande, J.M., Pons, J., Gil-Lacruz, M., & Marín, M. (1995). El sentimiento de pertenencia a la comunidad y sus relaciones con la participación comunitaria. *Informació Psicológica, 57*, 24–28.

Grau, R. (2001). *Fundamentos de psicología social y de psicología social de la educación.* Castelló de la Plana: Publicacions de la Universitat Jaume I.

Habermas, J. (1999). Teoría de la acción comunicativa. Vol. II: *Crítica de la razón funcionalista.* Madrid: Taurus.

Harare, M.J., Waehler, C.A., & Rogers, J.R. (2005). An empirical investigation of a theoretically based measure of perceived wellness. *Journal of Counseling Psychology, 52*, 93–103.

Hombrados, M.I. (1996). *Introducción a la psicología comunitaria.* Málaga: Aljibe.

Hong, B.A., & Leventhal, G. (2004). Partnerships with psychiatry and other clinical disciplines: A key to psychology successes in U.S. medical schools. *Journal of Clinical Psychology in Medical Settings, 11*, 135–140.

Hong, B.A., Leventhal, G., & Seime, R.J. (2005). The association of American medical colleges and the association of medical school psychologists: Finding psychology's place in academic medicine. *Journal of Clinical Psychological in Medical Settings, 12*, 247–256.

Huici, C. (1985). Grupo social y comportamiento de salud y enfermedad. En J.F. Morales, A. Blanco, C. Huici, & J.M. Fernández (Eds.), *Psicología social aplicada.* Bilbao: Desclée de Brouwer.

Ibáñez, T. (1989). La psicología social como dispositivo desconstruccionista. En T. Ibáñez (coord.). *El conocimiento de la realidad social* (pp. 109–134). Barcelona: Sendai.

James, S., & Prilleltensky, I. (2002). Cultural diversity and mental health. Toward integrative practice. *Clinical Psychology Review, 22*, 1133–1154.

Katzev, R., & Wang, T. (1994). Can commitment change behavior?. A case study of environmental actions. *Journal of Social Behavior and Personality, 9*, 13–26.

Kelly, J.G. (1986). *A guide to conducting prevention research in the community.* Binghamton: Hawort.

Kenkel, M.B., Deleon, P.H., Matell, E.O. & Steep, A.E. (2005). Divided no more: Psychology's role in integrated health care. *Canadian Psychology, 46*, 189–202.

Kenkel, M.B., DeLeon, P.H., Albino J.E., & Porter, N. (2003). Challenges to professional psychology education in the 21st century–Response to Peterson, *American Psychologist, 58*, 801–805.

Kisnerman, N. (1987). *Salud pública y trabajo social.* Buenos Aires: Humanitas.

Klein, K.J., Ralls, S., Smith Major, V., & Douglas, C. (2000). Power and participation in workplace. En S. Buelga (Ed.). (2001). *Psicología comunitaria. Proyecto docente.* Valencia: Facultad de Psicología, Universidad de Valencia.

Kraepelin, E. (1999). *Cien años de psiquiatría.* Madrid: Siglo XXI. (Original work published 1917).

Kratochwill, T.R., & Shernoff, E.S. (2004). Evidence-based practice: Promoting evidence-based interventions in school psychology. *School Psychology Review, 33*, 34–48.

Kratochwill, T.R., Albers, C.A., & Shernoff, E.S. (2004). School-based interventions. *Child and Adolescent Psychiatric Clinics of North America, 13*, 885.

Labish, A. (1993). Características y condiciones de la actividad médica en la modernidad. En J. Portillo, y J. Rodríguez-Nebot (Eds.), *La medicalización de la sociedad* (pp. 231–251). Montevideo: Nordan-Comunidad.

Laverack, G., & Wallerstein, N. (2001). Measuring community empowerment: A fresh look at organizational domains. *Health Promotion Internacional, 16*, 2.

Leventhal, G., & Seime, R.J. (2004). Introduction to special issue: Psychology in academic health centers. *Journal of Clinical Psychology in Medical Settings, 11*, 75–76.

Leventhal, G., Seime, R.J., Wedding D., & Rozensky, R.H. (2005). The 2003 survey of academic medical center psychologists: Implications and outlook. *Journal of Clinical Psychology in Medical Setting, 12*, 209–220.

Levine, M., Toro, P.A., & Perkins, D.V. (1993). Social and community interventions. *Annual Review of Psychology, 44*, 525–558.

Lewin, K. (1951). *Field theory in social science.* New York: Harper and Row.

Lincoln, T., & Guba, E. (Eds.). (1985). *Naturalistic inquiry.* Beverly Hills: Sage.

Lindstrom, M. (2005). Ethnic differences in social participation and social capital in Malmo, Sweden: A population-based study. *Social Science and Medicine, 60*, 1527–1546.

Lindstrom, M. (2006). Psychosocial work conditions, social participation and social capital: A causal pathway investigated in a longitudinal study. *Social Science and Medicine, 62*, 280–291.

Llaneza, J. (2002). *Ergonomía y psicosociología aplicada: Manual para la formación del especialista.* Valladolid: Lex Nova.

Lowentahl, A., & Blanco, A. (1985). Intervenciones en problemas comunitarios. Psicología comunitaria. En M.A. Simón (Ed.). (1999). *Manual de psicología de la salud. Fundamentos, metodología y aplicaciones.* Madrid: Biblioteca Nueva.

Luszczynksa, A., & Schwarzer, R. (2005). Multidimensional health locus of control: Comments on the construct and its measurement. *Journal of Health Psychology, 10*, 633–642.

Mann, P.A. (1978). *Community psychology: Concepts and applications.* New York: The Free Press.

Martín-Baró, I. (1985a). *Acción e ideología. Psicología social desde Centroamérica.* El Salvador: Ucla Editores.

Martín-Baró, I. (1985b). El papel del psicólogo en el contexto centroamericano. *Boletín AVEPSO, 12*(3).

Martín, A., Chacon, F., & Martínez, J.M. (1988). *Psicología comunitaria.* Madrid: Visor.

Martínez, M.F., García, M., & Maya, I. (2001). Una tipología analítica de las redes de apoyo social en inmigrantes africanos en Andalucía. *Revista Española de Investigaciones Sociológicas, 95*, 99–125.

Matarazzo, J.D. (1980). Behavioral health and behavioral medicine. *American Psychologist, 35*, 807–817.

Matarazzo, J.D. (1982). Behavioral health's challenge to academic, scientific and professional psychology. *American Psychologist, 37*, 1–14.

McKenzie, R. (1926). The ecological approach to the study of the human community. En S. Buelga (Ed.) (2001). *Psicología comunitaria. Proyecto docente.* Valencia: Facultad de Psicología, Universidad de Valencia.

Meliá, J.L., Arnedo, M.T., & Ricarte, J.J. (1996). Efecto experimental del modelado de la conducta segura y del refuerzo de la conducta productiva sobre la seguridad y la productividad. *Psicológica, 17*, 229–248.

Miller, N.E. (1983). Behavioral medicine: Symbiosis between laboratory and clinic. *Annual Review of Psychology, 34*, 1–31.

Miller, R.L., & Shinn, M. (2005). Learning from communities: Overcoming difficulties in dissemination of prevention and promotion efforts. *American Journal of Community Psychology, 35*, 169–183.

Montero, M. (1994a). Un paradigma para la psicología social. Reflexiones desde el quehacer en América Latina. En J.L. Alvaro (Ed.). (1995). *Psicología social: Perspectivas teóricas y metodológicas.* Madrid: Siglo XXI.

Montero, M. (1994b). Indefinición y contradicciones de algunos conceptos básicos en la psicología social. En J.L. Alvaro (Ed.). (1995). *Psicología social: Perspectivas teóricas y metodológicas.* Madrid: Siglo XXI.

Montero, M. (1996). Paradigmas, corrientes y tendencias de la psicología social finisecular. En J.M. Sabucedo, O.D.´ Adamo, & V. García Beaudoux (Eds.). (1997). *Fundamentos de psicología social.* Madrid: Siglo XXI.

Montero, M. (1999). Perspectivas y retos de la psicología de la liberación. En S. Buelga(Ed.). (2001). *Psicología comunitaria. Proyecto docente.* Valencia: Facultad de Psicología, Universidad de Valencia.

Moral, M.V. (2008). Critica a la visión dominante de la salud–enfermedad desde la psicología social de la salud. Patologización preventiva de la vida cotidiana. *Boletín de Psicología, 94*, 85–104.

Morales, J.F., & Huici, C. (Eds.). (2003). *Psicología social.* Madrid: McGraw Hill.

Morgan, M. (2000). Applied community psychology: A ten year field trial. En S. Buelga (Ed.). (2001). *Psicología comunitaria. Proyecto docente.* Valencia: Facultad de Psicología, Universidad de Valencia.

Moyano, E. (2001). El concepto de capital social y su utilidad para el análisis de las dinámicas del desarrollo. *Revista de Fomento Social, 56*, 35–63.

Murray, M., Nelson, G., Poland, B., Maticka-Tyndale, E., & Ferris, L (2004). Assumptions and values in community health psychology. *Journal of Health Psychology, 9,* 315–326.

Musitu, G., & Buelga, S. (2004). Desarrollo comunitario y potenciación. En G. Musitu, J. Herrero, L. Cantera, & M. Montenegro (Eds.), *Introducción a la psicología comunitaria* (pp.167–195). Barcelona: UOC.

Newbrough, J.R. (1992). Community psychology for the 1990s. *Journal of Community Psychology, 20*, 7–15.

Ng, S.H., Kam, P.K. & Pong, R.W.M. (2005). People living in aging buildings: Their quality of life and sense of belonging. *Journal of Environmental Psychology, 25*, 347–360.

O'Connor, E.A., Friel, S., & Kellesher, C.C.F. (1997). Fashion consciousness as a social influence on lifestyle behaviour in young Irish adults. *Health Promotion International, 12*, 135–139.

Orford, J. (1993). *Community psychology: Theory and practice.* England: John Wiley and Sons.

Oliver, J.E. (2003). Mental life and the metropolis in suburban America. The psychological correlates of metropolitan place characteristics. *Urban Affairs Review, 39*, 228–253.

Ovejero, A. (1997). Paulo Freire y la psicosociopedagogía de la liberación. *Psicothema, 3*, 671–687.

Ovejero, A. (2001). *El trabajo del futuro y el futuro del trabajo: Algunas reflexiones desde la psicología social de la educación.* Madrid: Pirámide.

Páez, D., Marques, J., & Insúa, P. (1996). El estudio científico de los grupos: Representaciones prototípicas y de la variabilidad de los grupos. En S. Ayestarán (Ed.), *El grupo como construcción social.* Barcelona: Plural.

Páez, D. (coor.). (2003). *Psicología social, cultura y educación.* Madrid: Pearson-Prentice Hall.

Palmonari, A., & Zani, B. (1980). *Psicología sociale di comunita.* Bologna: Il Mulino.

Palomares Martínez, A. (1990). La promoción de la salud en la infancia. Factores en el diseño de programas. *Revista Española de Terapia de Comportamiento, 8*, 277–295.

Parker, I. (1989). *The crisis in modern social psychology and how to end it.* London: Routledge.

Pastor, M.A., López, S., Rodríguez Marín, J., Terol, M.C., & Sánchez, S. (1995). Evaluación multidimensional del dolor crónico en enfermos reumáticos. *Revista de Psicología de la Salud, 7*, 79–106.

Rall, M.L., Peskoff, F.S., & Byrne, J.J. (1994). The effects of information-giving behavior and gender on the perceptions of physicians: An experimental analysis. *Social Behavior and Personality, 22*, 1–16.

Rappaport, J. (1977). *Community psychology: Values, research and action.* New York. Holt, Rinehart and Winston.

Rappaport, J. (1981). In praise of paradox: A social policy of empowerment over prevention. *American Journal of Community Psychology, 9*, 1–25.

Rappaport, J., & Seidman, E. (Eds.). (2000). *Handbook of community psychology.* New York: Kluwer Academic Plenum.

Requena, F. (2000). Satisfacción, bienestar y calidad de vida en el trabajo. *Revista Española de Investigaciones Sociológicas, 92*, 11–44.

Restrepo, H.E. (2000). Incremento de la capacidad comunitaria y del empoderamiento de las comunidades para promover la salud. *Quinta Conferencia mundial de promoción de la salud.* Washington: Organización Panamericana de la Salud. Oficina Regional de la Organización Mundial de la Salud.

Ribes, E. (1990). *Psicología y salud: Un análisis conceptual.* Barcelona: Martínez Roca.

Rodado, J., & Navarro, F. (1997). La psiquiatría como campo científico: Modelos y tendencias. En S. Buelga (Ed.). (2001). *Psicología comunitaria. Proyecto docente.* Valencia: Facultad de Psicología, Universidad de Valencia.

Rodríguez Beltrán, M. (2009). Empoderamiento y promoción de la salud. *Red de Salud, 14*, 20–31.

Rodríguez Marín, J. (1991). Psicología de la salud: Situación en la España actual. *Revista de Psicología de la Salud, 3*, 55–91.

Rodríguez Marín, J., & Neipp, M.C. (2008). *Manual de psicología social de la salud.* Madrid: Síntesis.

Rodríguez Molina, I. (2000). *Psicología del trabajo. Proyecto docente.* Titularidad: Facultad de Psicología: Universidad de Valencia.

Rodríguez Villasante, T. (1994). *Las ciudades hablan: Identidades y movimientos sociales en seis metrópolis latinoamericanas.* Caracas: Nueva Sociedad.

Rozanski, A., & Kubzansky, L.D. (2005). Psychologic functioning and physical health: A paradigm of flexibility. *Psychosomatic Medicine, 67*, 47–53.

Salanova, M., Schaufeli, W., Llorens, S., Peiró, J.M., & Grau, R. (2000). Desde el burnout al engagement: ¿Una nueva perspectiva? *Revista de Psicología del Trabajo y de las Organizaciones, 16*, 117–134.

Sánchez Vidal, A. (1991a). *Psicología comunitaria. Bases conceptuales y métodos de intervención.* Barcelona: PPU.

Sánchez Vidal, A. (1991b). Evaluación social y comunitaria: Aspectos relacionales, valorativos y políticos. Santiago de Compostela: *Actas II Congreso Nacional de Psicología Social.*

Sánchez, F., Rubio, J., Páez, D., & Blanco, A. (1998). Optimismo ilusorio y percepción de riesgo. *Boletín de Psicología, 58*, 7–17.

Sánchez, E., Wiesenfeld, E., & López, R. (1998). Trayectoria y perspectivas de la Psicología Social Comunitaria en América Latina. En A. Martín González (ed.), *Psicología Comunitaria. Fundamentos y aplicaciones* (pp. 160–174). Madrid: Síntesis.

San Martín, H., & Pastor, V. (1984). *Salud comunitaria.* Madrid: Calero.

Sapolsky, R.M. (1999). The physiology and pathophysiology of unhappiness. In D. Kahneman, & E. Diener (Eds.). (1999). *Well-being: The foundations of hedonic psychology* (pp. 453–469), New York: Russell Sage Foundation.

Sarason, I.G. (1973). The evolution of community psychology. *American Journal of Community Psychology, 1*, 91–97.

Sarason, I.G. (1974). *The psychological sense of community: Prospects for community psychology.* San Francisco: Jossey Bass.

Schnittker, J., & McLeod, J.D. (2005). The social psychology of health disparities. *Annual Review of Sociology, 31*, 75–103.

Seedat, M., MacKenzie, S., & Stevens, G. (2004). Trends and redress in community psychology during 10 years of democracy (1994–2003): A journal-based perspective. *South African Journal of Psychology, 34*, 595–612.

Serrano García, I., & Álvarez, S. (1992). Análisis comparativo de marcos conceptuales de la psicología de la comunidad en Estados Unidos y América Latina. En S. Buelga (Ed.), *Psicología comunitaria. Proyecto docente.* Valencia: Facultad de Psicología, Universidad de Valencia.

Shinn, M., & Perkins, D.N. (2000). Contributions from organizational psychology. En S. Buelga (Ed.), *Psicología comunitaria. Proyecto docente.* Valencia: Facultad de Psicología, Universidad de Valencia.

Simmel, G. (1950). The metropolis and mental life. En S. Buelga (Ed.). (2001). *Psicología comunitaria. Proyecto docente.* Valencia: Facultad de Psicología, Universidad de Valencia. (Original work published 1902).

Simón, M.A. (Ed.). (1999). *Manual de psicología de la salud. Fundamentos, metodología y aplicaciones.* Madrid: Biblioteca Nueva.

Smith, E.R. & Mackie, D.M. (2007). *Social psychology.* New York: Psychology Press.

Snibbe, A.C., & Markus H.R. (2005). You can not always get what you want: Educational attainment, agency and choice. *Journal of Personality and Social Psychology, 88*, 703–720.

Snow, D., Grady, K., & Goyett-Ewing, M. (2000). A perspective on ethical issues in community psychology. En S. Buelga (Ed.). (2001). *Psicología comunitaria. Proyecto docente.* Valencia: Facultad de Psicología, Universidad de Valencia.

Taylor, S.E., Helgeson, V.S., Reed, G.M., & Skokan, L.A. (1993). Self generated feelings of control and adjustment to physical illness. *Journal of Social Issues, 47*, 91–109.

Tenorio, R., & Hernández, N. (2005). State of social work research within the scope of mental health. *Salud Mental, 28*, 18–32.

Theodorson, G.A. (1974). *Estudios de ecología humana.* Madrid: Labor.

Thomas, W.I., & Znaniecki, F. (1920). *The Polish peasant in Europe and America.* Boston: Badger.

Thompson, S.C., Sobolew-Shubin, A., Galbraith, M.E., Schwankovsky, L.V., & Cruzen, D. (1993). Maintaining perceptions of control: Finding perceived control in low control circumstances. *Journal of Personality and Social Psychology, 64*, 293–304.

Townley, G., & Kloos, B. (2009). Development of a measure of sense of community for individuals with serious mental illness residing in community settings. *Journal of Community Psychology, 37*, 362–380.

Totman, R. (1979). *Social causes of illness.* New York: Panteón.

Totman, R. (1982). Psychosomatic theories. En J.R. Eiser (Ed.), *Social psychology and behavioral medicine.* Chichester, UK: Wiley.

Trickett, E.J. (2009). Multilevel community-based culturally situated interventions and community impact: An ecological perspective. *American Journal of Community Psychology, 43*, 257–266.

Velasquez, N.R.P. (2003). Social psychology, health and community. *Revista Latinoamericana de Psicología, 35*, 214–216.

Von Bertanlafy, L. (1979). *Perspectivas en la teoría general de sistemas.* Madrid: Alianza.

Wagner de Lima, C. (1999). Estudio de la relación entre actividad comunitaria y conciencia personal. En S. Buelga (Ed.). (2001). *Psicología comunitaria. Proyecto docente.* Valencia: Facultad de Psicología, Universidad de Valencia.

Wandersman, A. (2003). Community science: Bridging the gap between science and practice with community-centered models. *American Journal of Community Psychology, 31*, 227–242.

Weiss, S.M. (1982). Health psychology: The time is now. *Health Psychology, 1*, 81–91.

Winefield, H.R. (1992). Doctor patient communication: An interpersonal helping process. *Interpersonal Review of Health Psychology, 1*, 167–187.

Wolf, T. (1987). Community psychology and empowerment: An activist insights. *American Journal of Communitarian Psychology, 15*, 151–166.

World Health Organization (1949). *Foundational letter.* Geneva: WHO.

World Health Organization (1972). *Health care system.* Geneva: WHO.

World Health Organization (1982). *United Nations inform.* Geneva: WHO.

World Health Organization (1986). *Ottawa letter.* Geneva: WHO.

World Health Organization/Organización Panamericana de la Salud (2003). *Construyendo universidades saludables.* Santiago de Chile: WHO.

World Health Organization (2005). *Bangkok letter (health promotion).* Geneva: WHO.

World Health Organization (2007). *The solid facts, social determinants of health*. Geneva: WHO.

Yárnoz, S. (2008). Spanish adaptation of the scale for evaluation of social and emotional loneliness in adults. *International Journal of Psychology and Psychology Therapy, 8*, 103–116.

Zax, M., & Specter, G.A. (1978). *Introducción a la psicología de la comunidad*. México: El Manual Moderno.

Zborowski, M. (1952). Cultural components in response to pain. In H.S. Friedman (Ed.). (2002). *Health psychology*. Upper Saddle River, NJ: Pearson Education.

Zimmerman, P. (2000). Empowerment theory: Psychological, organizational and community levels of analysis. En J. Rappaport, & E. Seidman (Eds.), *Handbook of community psychology* (pp. 43–64). New York: Kluwer Academic Plenum.

John M. Ruiz *and* Patrick Steffen

**Abstract**

Latinos, like other minorities, have a significant health risk factor profile marked by educational, economic, and disease challenges. Yet, despite these disparities, Latinos appear to live longer than non-Hispanic whites, an epidemiological phenomenon commonly referred to as the *Hispanic* or *Latino mortality paradox*. This surprising finding casts doubt on the generalizability of several tenets of psychosocial health and health disparities and spurs new questions regarding the cause of such resilience. This chapter begins by describing the characteristics of Latinos in the United States, before reviewing the evidence and complexity of the Latino mortality paradox. Emerging explanatory models for such effects are discussed and a conceptual model to guide future research is presented.

**Keywords**: Latino, Hispanic, mortality paradox, Latino health, health disparities

## Is There Something Unique About Hispanic Health?

One might wonder why a chapter is devoted specifically to Latino health. After all, Latinos share with other socially disadvantaged minorities a health risk factor profile marked by educational, economic, and disease challenges. Yet, despite these disparities, Latino's live longer than non-Hispanic whites, an epidemiological phenomenon commonly referred to as the *Hispanic* or *Latino mortality paradox*. This surprising finding casts doubt on the generalizability of several tenets of psychosocial health and health disparities and spurs new questions regarding the cause of such resilience. This chapter begins by describing the characteristics of Latinos in the United States, before reviewing the evidence and complexity of the Latino mortality paradox. We will discuss emerging explanatory models for such effects and present a conceptual model to guide future research. Importantly, this chapter is focused on Latino physical health as opposed to a broader discussion of well-being.

## A Note on Terminology

A number of umbrella terms including *Hispanic* and *Latino/a* are often used to collectively refer to people from Mexico, Central and South America, Spain, and Spanish-speaking or -influenced countries. The use of one term over another has been the subject of long debate (see Delgado & Stefancic, 1998; Hayes-Bautista & Chapa, 1987) that we will not enter into here. Most Latino people prefer to be recognized by their ancestral national origin such as Mexican, Mexican American, Cuban, Puerto Rican, and the like (De la Garza, DeSipio, Garcia, Garcia, & Falcon, 1992).

Beyond personal preference, umbrella terms have utility for summarizing data on a culturally similar group of people. There are also issues of precedent in data-gathering and ability to compare to such data. For example, the federal government standardized its collection of ethnicity data by adopting the term *Hispanic* in 1980 (Gibson & Jung, 2002) and revising terminology in 1997 to the phrase "*Hispanic or Latino*" (Greigo & Cassidy, 2001).

These terms are used in gathering all federal information on ethnicity, as well as in examining relationships with a wide range of outcomes including social, economic, educational, and health data. The scientific literature has followed suit by using these two umbrella terms across fields and disciplines. Although we recognize political, regional, and individual preferences regarding these terms, and we acknowledge conceptual distinctions between them, we will use the terms *Hispanic* and *Latino* interchangeably in this chapter.

## Latinos in the United States
### Growth and Diversity of the Latino Population in the United States

Latinos are the largest racial/ethnic minority group in the nation, accounting for over 15.4% of the total U.S. population (Pew Hispanic Center, 2010a). Between 2000 and 2008, the national census grew approximately 8.0% overall, with Latinos accounting for 51.3% of this increase compared to 19.6% growth among non-Hispanic whites and 13.6% growth among non-Hispanic blacks (Pew Hispanic Center, 2010a). These disparities in relative growth rates are altering the overall racial and ethnic distribution in the United States, such that, by 2050, non-Hispanic whites will no longer account for a majority of the population (see Figure 32.1). Over the same

time frame, the Latino population is projected to triple in size to roughly 29% of the population (Ortman & Guarneri, 2009).

Although nearly 48% of all Latinos live in California and Texas, migration is leading to significant populations in nearly every state. For example, between 2000 and 2008, the Latino population increased by 84% in Nebraska and by 111.9% in West Virginia (Pew Hispanic Center, 2010a). The most striking evidence of Latino migration may not be in cities and urban regions but in rural communities. The influx of Latinos to America's small towns is reversing population losses and reviving their economies (Coates & Gindlling, 2010). A recent analysis of U.S. population shifts found that, between 2000 and 2005, 221 counties (7% of all counties) experienced population increases only because Hispanic gains offset non-Hispanic declines (Johnson & Lichter, 2008).

Native births are by far the largest source of growth in the U.S. Latino population. Sixteen million or one in five children in the United States are Latino (Fry & Passel, 2009). Approximately 89% of these children were born in the United States and therefore, are U.S. citizens. It's estimated that by 2025, 30% of all children in the United States will be of Latino descent and that the generational make-up of this group will begin to shift toward a

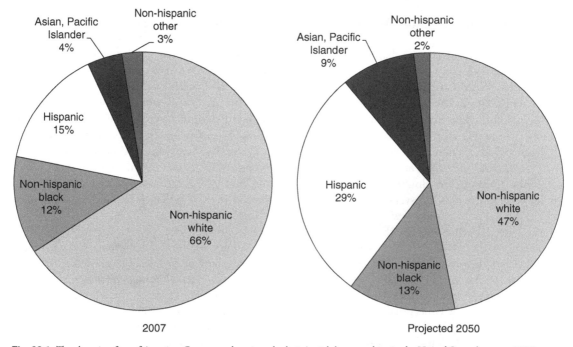

**Fig. 32.1** The changing face of America. Current and projected ethnic/racial demographics in the United States between 2007 to 2050. From Ortman, J. M., & Guarneri, C. E. (2009). *United States Population Projections: 2000 to 2050*. U.S. Census Bureau. http://www.census.gov/population/www/projections/analytical-document09.pdf; and Pew Hispanic Center (2010a). *Statistical Portrait of Hispanics in the United States, 2008*. http://pewhispanic.org/factsheets/factsheet.php?FactsheetID=58.

majority of third-generation and higher (Fry & Passel, 2009).

Immigration, legal and unauthorized, accounts for a substantial minority of growth. Of the 46.9 million Latinos currently residing in the United States, an estimated 38% are foreign-born (Pew Hispanic Center, 2010a, 2010b). Unauthorized immigrants account for 4% of the U.S. population, with a majority (59%) of undocumented immigrants coming from Mexico (Passel & Cohen, 2009). Migration between the U.S. and Mexico is bidirectional, and although there is a net flow into the United States, the rate of immigration varies considerably. For example, the net flow into the United States from Mexico decreased from approximately 547,000 in 2006 to 203,000 in 2008, a 63% reduction largely attributed to economic recession in the United States (Instituto Nacional de Estadistica Geografia e Informatica, 2007; Galindo & Ramos, 2009; Passel & Cohen, 2008).

Latinos in the United States are also strikingly heterogeneous, representing over 23 nationalities and speaking more than 12 languages and dialects (Pew Hispanic Center, 2008, 2010a). Approximately two-thirds of Latinos are of Mexican descent, followed by Puerto Ricans, Cubans, Salvadorans, and Dominicans (see Figure 32.2). Latino subgroups differ not only in terms of nationality and language but of culture as well (Parra-Cardona, Cordova, Holtrop, Villarruel, & Weiling, 2008). This diversity presents numerous health challenges, as equating

the preferences and behaviors of Latino subgroups can be akin to equating Iowans to New Yorkers (Weinick, Jacobs, Stone, Ortega, & Burstin, 2004). Although some Latino subgroups are regionally clustered (e.g., Cubans concentrated in Florida, Mexican and Mexican Americans concentrated in the Southwest), population growth and migration are contributing to a more national disbursement.

### Demographic Profile
The Latino population is unique from other major racial/ethnic groups on a number of demographic characteristics. For example, Latinos are by far the youngest group, with a median age of 27 years compared to a median age of 41 years for non-Hispanic whites, 32 years for non-Hispanic blacks, 36 years for non-Hispanic Asians, and a median age of 36 years for the total U.S. population (Pew Hispanic Center, 2010a). These age differences likely contribute to observed differences in marital rates and household statistics. Latinos are less likely to have ever been married compared to non-Hispanic whites (66.3% vs. 76.7%) but more likely to live in a family unit (i.e., household; 81% vs. 69%). Latino households tend to be larger than non-Hispanic white households and are more likely to be headed by a single parent (male or female). Perhaps as a function of cultural values, Latinos, specifically, U.S.-born Latinos are more likely to live with family members than are non-Hispanics of any race (Pew Hispanic Center, 2010a).

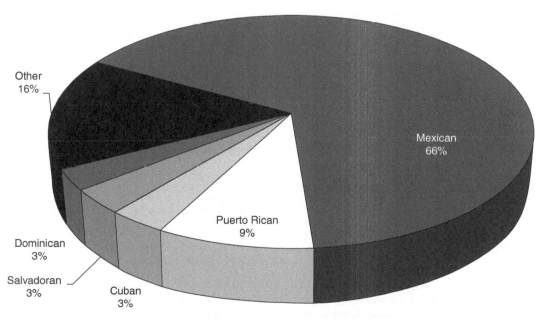

**Fig. 32.2** Distribution of the U.S. Latino population by country of origin. From Pew Hispanic Center (2010a). *Statistical Portrait of Hispanics in the United States, 2008.* http://pewhispanic.org/factsheets/factsheet.php?FactsheetID=58.

There are substantial differences between U.S. and foreign-born Latinos in the United States. For example, native-born Latinos are significantly younger (median age of 17 vs. 37 years) than foreign-born Latinos and are less likely to be married (40.9% vs. 57.9%, respectively: Pew Hispanic Center, 2010a, 2010b). Compared to U.S-born residents and legal immigrants, unauthorized immigrants are more likely to live with a spouse and children, and a majority of children of immigrants (73%) are born in the United States, thus making them second-generation Americans and U.S. citizens.

### What Makes Hispanics Hispanic?

Beyond demographics, Latinos are largely defined and differentiated from other groups by cultural values. Such values moderate everything from social behaviors to illness attributions and coping responses. Latino culture is *collectivistic*, reflecting an emphasis on the pursuit of group over individual goals. Specific values (see Table 32.1) such as *familismo, personalismo,* and *simpatio* motivate social interconnectedness and interpersonal harmony, which facilitates the collectivistic approach and may have important implications for health (Falicov, 1998; Zea, Quezada, & Belgrave, 1994). It's important to note that the Latino conceptualization of *family/familia* generally extends beyond the nuclear family to include relatives (parents, siblings, cousins, etc.) as well as close family friends. Strong family bonds create a protective, supportive network that is not necessarily insular but is self-sufficient. For example, childcare is often shared among parents, older siblings, aunts/uncles, cousins, and close family friends (Delgado, 2007). The importance of family harmony and valuing of children fosters the perception of this as a positively experienced opportunity, as opposed to a chore or duty.

In addition to social connectedness, Latinos place a great emphasis on social hierarchy and respect (*respeto*) for those of greater status (Calzada, Fernandez, & Cortes, 2010). Whereas men are seen as protectors and providers, women maintain a respected position as nurturers in the home. A marked difference between Latinos and mainstream American society is the valuing of elders. Elders maintain a high-status position in the Latino social hierarchy, which leads to significant inclusion in all manner of life. Prefixes such as *Don* (male) or *Donna* (female) to a first name (e.g., *Don* Howard) connote high respect and deference. In times of illness, *respeto* may be one social mechanism by which Latino elderly benefit from greater social support relative to non-Hispanics.

Although interpersonally centered cultural values may have health benefits, other values may be detrimental. Foremost is *fatalism/fatalismo* (Abraido-Lanza et al., 2007). Fatalism refers to the belief that fate, not the individual, exerts control over life events and outcomes. Some may find solace through

### Table 32.1 Select Latino cultural values

| | |
|---|---|
| *Familismo* | Importance for maintaining close family (broadly defined) connections |
| *Personalismo* | Valuing and building warm, affiliative interpersonal relationships |
| *Respeto* | Valuing social hierarchy and displaying deference to higher-status individuals, particularly elderly family members |
| *Simpatia* | Importance of displaying kindness and being polite and pleasant, particularly during times of interpersonal stress or conflict to maintain interpersonal harmony |
| *Fatalismo* | Belief that the course of fate cannot be changed and that events (e.g., cancer diagnosis) are beyond one's control |
| *Machismo* | Belief that it is a man's responsibility to protect and provide for his family |
| *Marianismo* | Belief that women should be nurturing, morally and spiritually strong, and emotional caretakers of the home |
| *Valuing children* | Importance of affection toward children and their inclusion in all manner of daily life; although children are expected to show respect for the social hierarchy, great tolerance is exercised, as inclusion is valued |
| *Valuing religion* | Religion is weaved into the fabric of daily life, offering direction and an explanation for events and experiences. Religion may also play a significant role in health care, with Latinos seeking care through prayer, church guidance, or from a *curandero* (spiritual healer) |

acceptance of a disease diagnosis as a result of fate. However, resigning health to fate may undermine motivation to adhere to medical regimens, change health behaviors, and set an expectation of death (Chavez, Hubbell, Mishra, & Valdez, 1997; Schwab, Meyer, & Merrell, 1994). The extent to which fatalism influences illness behaviors across health challenges is unclear, with some suggesting that it is potentially more problematic for diseases such as cancer (Natale-Pereira et al., 2008; Powe & Finnie, 2003).

### Socioeconomic Profile

Socioeconomic status (SES) is among the most robust psychosocial predictors of physical health (Ruiz, Steffen, & Prather, in press). Like other minority groups, Latinos experience significant economic disparities relative to non-Hispanic whites on a variety of indicators. One in five (19.5%) Latinos is classified as living below the poverty line, a rate similar to non-Hispanic blacks (21.9%) and significantly worse than non-Hispanic whites (8.2%; Pew Hispanic Center, 2010a). Latinos have the lowest median personal income among full-time, year-round workers ($28,820). Further examination reveals that foreign-born Latinos are actually the lowest-paid group among full-time workers, whereas native-born Latinos earnings are comparable to non-Hispanic blacks, yet still lag far behind non-Hispanic whites (Pew Hispanic Center, 2010b). This is in part due to differences in occupations. Latinos are overrepresented in unskilled labor (construction, food preparation, production, grounds keeping, and building maintenance) and underrepresented in management and technology (U.S. Bureau of Labor Statistics, 2009). In a slight deviation from personal income findings, Latinos, both native and foreign-born, have a higher median household income ($41,041) than non-Hispanic blacks ($35,644), reflecting larger households and more wage earners per household. However, Latino household income continues to trail that of non-Hispanic whites ($56,826) and the general population ($51,938).

Similar to non-Hispanic blacks, slightly less than half of all Latino households own their homes, compared to three-in-four non-Hispanic white households. During times of economic prosperity, home ownership rates climbed more rapidly among minorities as a whole compared to non-Hispanic whites (Kochhar, Gonzalez-Barrera, & Dockterman, 2009). However, during the economic downturn and the burst of the "housing bubble" between 2005 and 2009, black and Latino homeownership rates fell more dramatically compared to other groups and the national average. Housing disparities are further complicated by deficits in low-cost borrowing. Blacks and Latinos are far more likely than non-Hispanic whites to take higher-rate subprime mortgage loans (Kochhar et al., 2009). Unlike non-Hispanic whites, the use of these higher-interest rate loans is not inversely related to income. That is, higher-income earning Latinos are just as likely as low-income earning Latinos to take a higher-interest rate loan. This lending practice is troubling as it handicaps Latino income and may reflect knowledge deficits, stigma, and/or unfair lending practices.

Education is an important determinant of income earning potential and is often characterized as a "silver bullet" to reducing income disparities (Bils & Klenow, 2000; Jamison, Jamison, & Hanushek, 2007). Racial and ethnic groups differ significantly in terms of educational attainment. Latinos are at a significant educational disadvantage relative to all other racial and ethnic groups. At the low end of the education spectrum, nearly 40% of Latinos have less than a high school diploma, twice as high as any specific group, and substantially higher than the national average of 15.1% (Lopez, 2007). This high rate is largely driven by foreign-born Latinos of whom 34% have less than a 9th grade education. At the high end, Latinos have the lowest percentage of college graduates, at just 12.9% compared to the national average of 17.7% of non-Hispanic blacks, 30.7% of non-Hispanic whites, 50% of non-Hispanic Asians, and 27.7% of the population as a whole.

In contrast to educational attainment deficits, Latino attitudes toward education are markedly positive. Nine in ten Latinos, more than any other group, agree that a college education is important for success in life (Pew Hispanic Center, 2009). Additionally, more than three-quarters of young Latinos between 16 and 25 years report that their parents believe that going to college and attaining a degree is the most important goal following high school. Despite such positive attitudes, less than half (48%) of college-age Latinos believe a college degree is in their future (Kohut et al., 2007). Expectations are tied to country-of-origin, with foreign-born Latinos reporting lower expectations of attaining a college degree than native-born individuals. Nearly three-quarters of Latino youths who cut their education short report doing so out of pressure to provide financial support to their family (Pew Hispanic Center, 2009).

Among college-age Latinos, lack of active support from parents in attaining educational goals, differences in the cultural backgrounds between Latino students and their teachers/faculty, and limited English skills are also frequently cited reasons for the attainment gap.

## Summary

In summary, Latinos represent the largest racial/ethnic minority group and fastest growing segment of the U.S. population. The increase in the size of the Latino community is largely due to native births and is reflected in the strikingly young age of the population. Latino cultural values emphasize interpersonal connectedness and harmony generally and particularly within the family. This collectivistic emphasis is a marked distinction from the more individualistic values of the larger American society, although it varies as a function of acculturation among Latinos. Unfortunately, Latinos are at or near the bottom in most major socioeconomic indicators, a profile that robustly predicts worse physical health (Ruiz et al., in press). In the next section, we will examine whether this well-established relationship holds true for Latinos.

## Latino Health Status
### Perceived Health

Self-reported health is a reliable predictor of mortality (Idler & Benyamini, 1997; McGee, Liao, Cao, & Cooper, 1999). Given their socioeconomic challenges, it is reasonable to expect that Latinos would rate their health as lower in quality relative to non-Hispanic whites. In fact, data from several large cohort studies indicate the expected SES gradient on self-reported health whereby non-Hispanic whites rate their health as significantly better than most minorities, including Latinos (Perez-Stable, Napoles-Springer, & Miramontes, 1997; White, Philogene, Fine, & Sinha, 2009). For example, compared to non-Hispanic whites in the California Health Interview Survey, a self-report study with a representative sample of 50,000+ participants, Latinos were less likely to rate their health as "excellent" (22.7% vs. 11.9%) or "very good" (37.5% vs. 18.3%) and more likely to rate their health as "fair" (9.9% vs. 27.5%: Kandula, Lauderdale, & Baker, 2007). Although the magnitude of these effects were somewhat attenuated after controlling for a host of psychosocial covariates (age, sex, marital status, employment, SES), the pattern remained. Similar findings reported elsewhere (cf. Shetterly, Baxter, Mason, & Hamman, 1996) lead to the conclusion that Latinos are more likely to perceive their health as lower quality than non-Hispanic whites.

### Incidence of Major Diseases
#### COMMUNICABLE DISEASES

Communicable diseases refer to everything from H1N1 (i.e., swine flu) to hepatitis. The overall rates of infectious diseases are higher for Latinos compared to non-Hispanics. For example, Latinos accounted for 75.3% of the 4,499 diagnosed incidence of tuberculosis among U.S.-born persons in 2009 (Winston, Pratt, Armstrong, & Navin, 2010). Compared to non-Hispanic whites, Latinos were at twice the risk of hepatitis A (Heron et al., 2009), twice the risk for gonorrhea and syphilis (Centers for Disease Control and Prevention, 2009a), and three times the risk for chlamydia. With respect to the 2009 H1N1 pandemic, U.S. Latinos accounted for 30% of all cases, and they were 2.5 times more likely than non-Hispanic whites to be hospitalized (Centers for Disease Control and Prevention, 2010). Latino children were particularly hard hit, with children ages 5 years and under were nearly three times as likely to be hospitalized compared to non-Hispanic white children. Latinos under 18 accounted for 27% of all deaths attributed to H1N1 2009, exceeding their representation in the U.S. population (21%). The CDC (2010) reports that these disparities mirror general influenza patterns, which disproportionally affect Latinos and other minorities.

Human immunodeficiency virus and acquired immune deficiency syndrome (HIV/AIDS) remains a significant health challenge in the United States, despite improvements in testing and prevention. Despite constituting only 15% of the U.S. population, Latinos accounted for approximately 17% of all new HIV cases in 2006 and 17% of all persons living with HIV/AIDS in the United States (Centers for Disease Control and Prevention, 2009b). Latino men are nearly three times as likely, and Latino women are five times as likely to be diagnosed with AIDS compared to their non-Hispanic white counterparts. Following an AIDS diagnosis, Latino survival is comparable to non-Hispanic whites and significantly better than non-Hispanic blacks. Importantly, HIV/AIDS was among the top five causes of deaths for Latinos in the mid-1990s, but has since dropped out of the top ten (Heron, 2010).

#### HEART DISEASE AND HIGH BLOOD PRESSURE

Diseases of the heart have been the number one cause of death in the United States for over 100 years, with the exception of the 1918 influenza pandemic (American Heart Association, 2010; Heron, 2010). Overall, 11% of persons 18 years and over is diagnosed with heart disease (Pleis & Lucas, 2009). Despite their risk factor profile, including high rates of contributing diseases such as diabetes, Latinos are approximately 10% less likely to have heart disease compared to non-Hispanic whites (age-adjusted 5.7% Latino vs. 6.2% non-Hispanic white). Latinos have slightly higher rates of high blood pressure compared to non-Hispanic whites, an affect driven by women (19.2% vs. 15.9%, respectively).

### CANCER

Cancer is the second leading cause of death in the United States. Latinos experienced markedly lower incidence rates for overall cancer rates for men (430.3 per 100,000 vs. 556.6 national average) and women (326.8 vs. 414.8) for the top 15 cancers between 1997 and 2006 (Edwards et al., 2010). Latino incidence rates for several anatomical site-specific cancers are lower than for non-Hispanics, including lung, breast cancer in women, and prostate, melanoma, and urinary bladder cancer in men. However, Latino women are at 1.5 times greater risk for cervical cancer, and Latino men are at greater risk for cancers of the stomach, liver, and bile ducts than non-Hispanics, particularly non-Hispanic whites. Beyond incidence, Latinos surprisingly experience survival odds similar to non-Hispanic whites and better than most major minority groups (Clegg, Li, Hankey, Chu, & Edwards, 2002).

### DIABETES MELLITUS

The total prevalence of diabetes (types 1 and 2) in the United States is approximately 20.8 million people or 7.0% of the population (National Institute of Diabetes and Digestive and Kidney Diseases, 2008). Of this group, approximately 6.2 million (29.8%) people have undiagnosed diabetes. Latinos experience a disproportionate burden of the diabetes epidemic. Diabetes is significantly more prevalent in the Latino community, affecting 10.4% of Latinos compared to 6.6% of non-Hispanic whites. Rates vary among Latinos, with Cubans experiencing the lowest rates (8.2%) and Mexicans and Puerto Ricans experiencing some of the highest (11.9% and 12.6%, respectively). Data on ethnic differences in diabetes outcomes are mixed. For example, among persons with diabetes, Latinos are less likely to experience visual impairment than non-Hispanic whites, but 1.7 times more likely to initiate treatment for end-stage renal disease.

### Comparative Mortality Trends

Science loves a good challenge, and one of the most puzzling in psychosocial health research today concerns Latino mortality rates. Despite substantial socioeconomic disparities, Latinos appear to live as long, and in some cases, longer, than non-Hispanic whites (Abraido-Lanza, Dohrenwend, Ng-Mak, & Turner, 1999; Abraido-Lanza, et al., 2000; Markides, 1983; Markides, & Coreil, 1986; Sorlie, Backlund, Johnson, & Rogot, 1993). The first evidence for this surprising finding came from reviews of Hispanic health in the southwestern United States. Markides (1983; Markides, & Coreil, 1986) found that Hispanic health was similar to that of non-Hispanic whites despite a low SES more similar to blacks—an epidemiological paradox, given the strong association between lower SES and greater health risk (Ruiz et al., in press). The first empirical support for the phenomenon came from prospective national cohort studies matching census data to the National Death Index. Compared to non-Hispanic whites, U.S.-born Latinos were shown to have lower all-cause mortality (Sorlie et al., 1993). Since that time, this Hispanic mortality advantage is consistently evident in national mortality data, such as annual reports from the Center for Disease Control (CDC). For example, the most recent National Vital Statistics Report states that the 2006 age-adjusted death rate for the Hispanic population was 27.4% lower than that for non-Hispanic whites and 43.7% lower than for non-Hispanic blacks (see Figure 32.3; Heron et al., 2009). Despite small annual fluctuations in the specific numbers, the general trend has remained unchanged for over 15 years. Thus, the *Latino* or *Hispanic mortality paradox* refers to the epidemiological phenomenon whereby Hispanics live longer than non-Hispanic whites, despite the lower SES status of the former.

In addition to all-cause mortality, substantial evidence supports a Latino infant mortality advantage (Hessol & Fuentes-Afflick, 2005; Kitsantas, & Gaffney, 2010). For example, the 2006 National Vital Statistics data show that the Latino infant mortality rate was 5.41 per 1,000 live births compared to 5.58 for non-Hispanic whites and 13.35 for non-Hispanic blacks (see Figure 32.4; Matthews & MacDorman, 2010). Closer examination reveals that, although neonatal mortality is similar between Hispanics and non-Hispanic whites (3.74 vs. 3.64, respectively), Latino infants are more likely to survive following the neonatal period (28 days to 1 year), a trend observed elsewhere (Hessol & Fuentes-Afflick, 2005). When controlling for birth weight and gestational age, Latinos have slightly

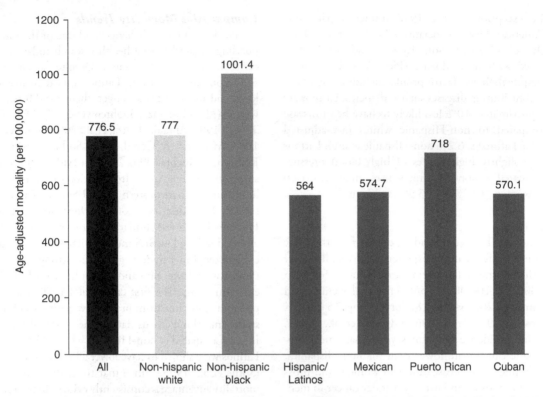

**Fig. 32.3** Age-adjusted mortality by race and ethnicity: 2006. From Heron, M., Hoyert, D. L., Murphy, S. L., Xu, J., Kochanek, K. D., & Tejada-Vera, B. (2009). Deaths: Final data for 2006. *National Vital Statistics Reports, 57*. Hyattsville, MD: National Center for Health Statistics.

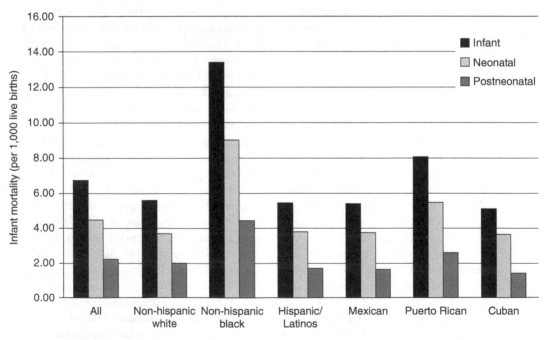

**Fig. 32.4** Infant mortality by race and ethnicity: 2006. Infant refers to birth to 1 year; Neonatal refers to birth to 28 days; Postneonatal refers to 28 days to 1 year. Adapted from Matthews, T. J., & MacDorman, M. F. (2010). Infant mortality statistics from the 2006 period linked birth/infant death data set. *National Vital Statistics Reports, 58*. Hyattsville, MD: National Center for Health Statistics.

lower mortality rates than non-Hispanic whites (Alexander et al., 2003; Alexander, Wingate, Bader, & Kogan, 2008). In contrast, non-Hispanic blacks experienced significant pre- and postneonatal infant mortality relative to all groups.

There is significant variation in mortality among Latinos. In general, persons of Mexican descent, as well as those from Central or South America, experience the lowest age-adjusted mortality and infant mortality. In contrast, Puerto Ricans experience the highest rates of both outcomes among Hispanic subgroups (Heron et al., 2009; Matthews & MacDorman, 2010). Reasons for this variation are unclear and should be the subject of future investigation. Regardless, Latinos as a group appear to experience better mortality outcomes than non-Hispanics.

### Leading Causes of Death
Table 32.2 shows the ten leading causes of death in the United States in 2006 (Heron, 2010). These circumstances account for 77.2% of all deaths in the United States; however, there are substantial racial/ethnic differences in their rankings and impact. These ten causes account for just 65.5% of Latino deaths, compared to 76% of all non-Hispanic white and 69.5% of non-Hispanic black deaths. Although disease of the heart and malignant neoplasms (cancer) are the leading cause of death for all three groups, they accounted for only 42% of Latino deaths, far less than the national average and

for any other racial/ethnic group. In contrast, Hispanics are more likely to die of accidents, assault, chronic liver disease, and diabetes mellitus, and Latino infants are more likely to die of perinatal (newborn) conditions (e.g., respiratory problems, infection) than the national average. Note that although Latino infants are more likely to die of perinatal conditions, they experience lower overall infant mortality (cf., Kitsantas, & Gaffney, 2010; Matthews & MacDorman, 2010).

### Doubts and Data Regarding the Validity of the Paradox
Naturally, paradoxical findings evoke healthy skepticism from the scientific community. An overarching concern with the national cohort data is the accuracy of census and death certificate reporting, which relies on representative counts and accurate classification of race and ethnicity (cf. Eschbach, Kuo, & Goodwin, 2006; Smith & Bradshaw, 2006). Annual reports from the National Center for Health Statistics add the caveat, "Mortality for Hispanics is somewhat understated because of net underreporting of Hispanic origin on the death certificate. Hispanic origin on the death certificate is underreported by an estimated 5%" (Heron et al., 2009, p. 5). However, Arias and colleagues (2010) recently demonstrated that ethnic misclassification is on U.S. death certificates is negligible and does not affect the observed Hispanic mortality trends. In addition, any such issues should not affect the infant

Table 32.2  2006 leading causes of death

| Rank | Total Population | | Latino Population | |
|------|------------------|--|-------------------|--|
| | Cause | % Total Deaths | Cause | % Total Deaths |
| 1 | Diseases of the heart | 26.0 | Diseases of the heart | 21.7 |
| 2 | Malignant neoplasms | 23.1 | Malignant neoplasms | 20 |
| 3 | Cerebrovascular diseases | 5.7 | Accidents | 9.1 |
| 4 | Chronic lower respiratory diseases | 5.1 | Cerebrovascular diseases | 5.3 |
| 5 | Accidents | 5.0 | Diabetes mellitus | 4.7 |
| 6 | Diabetes mellitus | 3.0 | Chronic liver disease | 2.7 |
| 7 | Alzheimer disease | 3.0 | Assault | 2.6 |
| 8 | Influenza, pneumonia | 2.3 | Chronic lower respiratory disease | 2.5 |
| 9 | Nephritis | 1.9 | Influenza, pneumonia | 2.2 |
| 10 | Septicemia | 1.4 | Perinatal conditions | 2.1 |

From Heron, M. (2010). Deaths: Leading causes for 2006. *National Vital Statistics Reports, 58.* Hyattsville, MD: National Center for Health Statistics.

mortality findings, which are largely based on matched birth and death certificate information (e.g., Matthews & MacDorman, 2010).

Two general hypotheses have been proposed to explain the paradox. The *Salmon bias hypothesis* posits that a sufficient number of Latino immigrants register in the United States (e.g., U.S. Census), but return to their home country before death, thus, appearing statistically immortal (no recorded death) in the United States. The *healthy migrant hypothesis* suggests that the Latino mortality advantage reflects a selection bias in that only the healthiest Latinos immigrate to the United States.

Abraido-Lanza and colleagues (1999) challenged the validity of these hypotheses by examining data from the 1995 National Longitudinal Mortality Study, which linked census data to the National Death Index for a maximum 9-year follow-up. Latino reverse migration was tested by examining mortality in two samples: Cuban immigrants who generally cannot return to their home country for fear of political retribution and, Puerto Ricans whose death in Puerto Rico would be recorded in U.S. records because it is a U.S. territory. In contrast to the Salmon bias hypothesis, both Puerto Ricans and Cubans lived longer than U.S.-born non-Hispanic whites. The healthy migrant hypothesis was tested by comparing longevity in Puerto Rican immigrants and nonimmigrants. Again, results were counter to the hypothesis. In particular, Latinos who lived out their life in their home country lived at least as long, and perhaps longer, than those who immigrated to the United States. Although these findings do not explain the mechanisms underlying the Latino mortality paradox, they refute the argument that the phenomenon is simply due to data limitations.

## Summary

Despite significant socioeconomic challenges, Latinos appear to live longer and experience lower infant mortality than do non-Hispanics. This conclusion is supported by consistency in national health statistics as well as evidence against potential reverse migration and healthy migrant effects. In the next section, we will discuss emerging explanatory models for such effects and introduce a conceptual model for guiding future research.

## Risk and Resilience Factors

Factors related to risk and resilience differ between Hispanics and non-Hispanic whites. One key difference is the effects of the social gradient on health.

As discussed previously, cultural factors such as collectivism and familialism appear to play key roles in the health of Hispanics and may account for their resilience in the face of stressors such as low SES. In this section, we begin by discussing ethnic differences in disease risk and resilience, and then discuss psychosocial and cultural factors that may contribute to risk and resilience differences. We end by discussing two models, the *reserve capacity model* and the *social capital model*, that provide overarching frameworks for understanding Hispanic health.

### Ethnic Differences in Disease Risk and Resilience

Hispanics and non-Hispanic whites differ in disease incidence and prevalence. Hispanics have lower rates of heart disease and stroke, but higher levels of cancer and HIV relative to whites (National Center for Health Statistics, 2008). Perhaps the most commonly known fact is that Hispanics are more likely to be diagnosed with diabetes relative to whites. Unfortunately, in addition to having higher rates of diabetes, Hispanics are also less likely to be aware of their diabetic status, thus decreasing opportunities for appropriate health interventions (Danaei et al., 2009). Two common themes appear to account for these ethnic differences in disease risk and resilience. First, heart disease and stroke are heavily influenced by lifestyle behaviors and stress. Second, cancer, HIV, and diabetes are heavily influenced by engagement in preventive medicine practices or medical treatment. Therefore, healthy lifestyle behaviors (and possibly psychosocial and cultural values that buffer against stress) may contribute to Hispanic resilience, and lack of engagement in preventive medicine and utilization of health care resources may contribute to Hispanic risk for disease.

Hispanics and non-Hispanic whites also differ in disease progression. For example, for whites, there is a strong relationship between SES and subclinical atherosclerosis, with increased SES being related to decreased subclinical atherosclerosis (Diez Roux et al., 2005; Lutsey et al., 2008). For Hispanics, however, the relationship between SES and disease progression changes with level of acculturation (Diez Roux et al., 2005), with increased acculturation to Western cultural being related to increased disease progression (Lutsey et al., 2008). In a study of subclinical atherosclerosis, less acculturated Hispanics showed a positive relationship between SES and disease (the classic Hispanic paradox), whereas more acculturated Hispanics showed a negative relationship between SES and disease (the typical social gradient; Gallo et al., 2009a). In other words, as Hispanics become acculturated to American culture, they begin to show health patterns similar to those of whites (Rumbaut, 1997). Interestingly, some researchers have proposed that acculturation to Western society be included as a risk factor for cardiovascular disease (CVD; Mooteri et al., 2004).

The relationship between established risk factors and disease outcomes appears to differ by ethnicity. The strongest predictors of CVD morbidity and mortality include high blood pressure, obesity, elevated triglycerides, and diabetes (Henderson et al., 2007). In spite of the fact that Mexican Americans have significantly lower rates of CVD morbidity and mortality, Mexican Americans score higher on risk factors for CVD such as higher blood pressure and higher levels of obesity and triglycerides compared to whites (Mitchell et al., 1990). And even though Hispanics are more likely to be diagnosed with diabetes, the relationship between diabetes and CVD appears to be weaker in Hispanics.

## Psychosocial and Cultural Factors Related to Health Risk

Psychological, social, and cultural factors have all been shown to play a role in physical health outcomes and therefore may play an important role in Hispanic–white differences in health (Rozanski, Blumenthal, & Kaplan, 1999). Mental health difficulties, particularly depression, have been related to increased CVD (Lesperance, Frasure-Smith, & Talajic, 1996). Lower SES is associated with higher incidence of depression and anxiety (Ansseau et al., 2008; Grant et al., 2005; Himmelfarb & Murrell, 1984; Warheit et al., 1975), anger (Mittleman et al., 1997; Ranchor, Bouma, & Sanderman, 1996), and hostility (Barefoot et al., 1991; Lynch, Kaplan, & Salonen, 1997; Scherwtiz, Perkins, Chesney, & Hughes, 1991). Some of these associations appear to be stronger among ethnic minorities (Barefoot et al., 1991; Scherwitz et al., 1991), and some studies suggest that the relationship begins in childhood (Gump, Matthews, & Raikkonen, 1999; Lynch et al., 1997).

Hispanic Americans are less likely to be diagnosed with depression compared to whites (Alegria et al., 2008; Andrade et al., 2003; Kessler et al., 1994) in spite of lower SES. This difference in depression rates may represent a pathway through which Hispanics are protected from CVD. In comparisons of depression rates between countries, Mexico has lower rates of major depression relative

to the United States (Andrade et al., 2003). As Hispanics acculturate to American culture, however, their rates of depression go up. Vega et al. (1998) found that there was a gradient of increased depression with increased time lived in the United States. Lifetime prevalence of major depressive episodes was 3.2% for Mexican immigrants who had lived less than 13 years in the United States, 7.9% for those living more than 13 years in the United States, and 14.4% for Mexican Americans born in the United States. As the prevalence of major depressive episodes increased, so did income and education, with U.S.-born Mexican Americans having significantly higher levels of SES as compared to immigrants. Given that Mexicans and Mexican immigrants are healthier than European Americans and U.S.-born Mexican Americans, and that acculturation to Western culture leads to an increase in both distress and SES, it is possible that cultural factors (such as socially oriented vs. individualistically oriented cultural values) explain the differences in health between immigrants and U.S.-born Americans.

Although Hispanics have lower rates of diagnosed depression, they have higher rates of self-reported levels of depressive symptoms (Bromberger et al., 2004) and levels of stress (Cuellar, Arnold, & Braccio, 2004; Cuellar & Roberts, 1997). It is interesting to note that, just as Hispanics are less likely to be diagnosed with CVD and yet have higher rates of CVD risk factors relative to whites, Hispanics are also less likely to be diagnosed with mental health problems such as major depression and yet self-report higher rates of depressive symptoms relative to whites. This is perhaps due to the fact that almost 50% of Hispanic Americans are foreign born and are likely still in the process of acculturation (National Research Council, 2006). As Hispanics become more acculturated, they begin to show levels of CVD and major depression similar to whites (Vega et al., 2004).

### DISCRIMINATION AND PREJUDICE

Racism remains a significant problem in the United States, despite improvements that have occurred over the last several decades (Clark et al., 1999). Although European Americans tend to view relationships with minority groups as being friendly and good-natured, minority groups report experiencing significant discrimination (Sigelman & Welch, 1993). In a large study examining the prevalence of perceived discrimination, it was found that approximately 90% of African Americans and 77%

of other minorities reported having been discriminated against because of race or ethnicity (Kessler, Mickelson, & Williams, 1999). This compares with 21% of European Americans who reported experience with racial discrimination.

Discrimination is a significant stressor for Hispanic immigrants to the United States, particularly as they attempt to adapt to a foreign culture. Finch, Kolody, and Vega (2000) found that, as Hispanic American immigrants become more acculturated to American society, they are more likely to report problems with racism and discrimination. As perceptions of discrimination increase, problems with mental health also increase. Perhaps this is not surprising given that racism can be a chronic stressor with far-reaching effects, impacting many different areas of a person's life. Hispanics may encounter racism when seeking employment, with respect to receiving equal pay, in obtaining educational opportunities, and in everyday interpersonal interactions (Williams, 1999). Discrimination can also negatively affect self-esteem and self-worth, leading to feelings of depression, and repeated exposure to racist messages can create doubt about one's personal worth and identity. In fact, depression has been the mental health problem most commonly associated with perceived racism (Williams, Neighbors, & Jackson, 2003).

## ENVIRONMENTAL STRESS AND RISK

Exposure to unhealthy environments appears to play an important role in the relationship between SES and health (Evans & Kantrowtiz, 2002; Taylor, Repetti, & Seeman, 1997). Lower-SES individuals are more likely to be exposed to hazardous waste, air and water pollution, high levels of noise in their neighborhoods and work environments, and live in crowded neighborhoods with higher levels of violence. Because people spend the majority of their time at home and at work, exposure to unhealthy environments is a chronic, constantly present condition. Unfortunately, there is evidence that even during recreation, lower-income individuals are more likely to be exposed to unhealthy conditions, such as swimming in contaminated waters (Cabelli & Dafour, 1983).

Exposure to crime and violence are particularly stressful (Evans & Kantrowitz, 2002). Crowded living conditions are related to increased stress and negative health outcomes (Baum, Garofalo, & Yali, 1999). Crowding is also associated with less satisfaction with living conditions and neighborhood quality (Nelson, 1978). Crowding appears to be particularly stressful for children, with crowding associated with higher behavioral problems and poor academic achievement, as well as with negative health outcomes (Evans, Lepore, Shejwal, & Palsane, 1998). Low-SES neighborhoods also have higher levels of crime and a greater likelihood of experiencing violence (Morenoff & Sampson, 1997).

Hispanics, however, appear to be protected from the stress of low-SES neighborhood when the neighborhood is predominately Hispanic. Hispanics in low-SES neighborhoods that are predominately Hispanic have better health than other groups living in low-SES neighborhoods (Cagney, Browning, & Wallace, 2007). One study found, however, that this was only true for Hispanics who spoke primarily Spanish at home (Johnson & Marchi, 2009). Hispanics who spoke English at home were not buffered from the stress of living in a low SES-neighborhood.

### Psychosocial and Cultural Resilience
An emerging hypothesis suggests that cultural values may moderate health outcomes and may at least partially account for Hispanic health outcomes (Steffen, 2006). Cultural values embodying psychosocial resilience factors such as social support may buffer against risk, leading to better health outcomes. For example, more collectivistic cultures, such as Hispanic culture, emphasizing community and interpersonal interconnectedness, are more likely to value social support, a well-established health moderator (House et al., 1988). Many non-Western cultures appear to be healthy in spite of low SES at least partly because of this emphasis on social support and community (Cockerham et al., 2001). In contrast, more individualistic cultures, such as the United States, may be health damaging through an emphasis on individual achievement and competition, which often requires adoption of social dominance and aggression, factors associated with disease risk (Siegman et al., 2000; Smith et al., 2008; Spence, 1985; Triandis, 1995; Waldron et al., 1982). Achievement and competition may also erode social support and fracture community ties, leading to adverse health outcomes. Moreover, for many Westerners, identity is strongly tied to SES (Spence, 1985), whereas non-Westerners are more likely to derive identify through group membership and social ties (Carpenter, 2000; Carpenter & Radhakrishnan, 2000; Dabul, Bernal, & Knight, 1995; Triandis, 1995). This cultural difference in how identity is defined may explain why the social

gradient works differently between Western and non-Western societies. That is, because SES is more important to an individual's identity in Western countries, lower SES may be stressful because it indicates less worth as a person.

Acculturation to Western society impacts cultural values and social orientation (Cuellar, Arnold, & Gonzalez, 1995; Marin & Gamba, 2003). In a study comparing high- and low-acculturated Mexican American immigrants with Anglo Americans, more-acculturated Mexican immigrants appeared more similar to Anglo Americans on a measure of cultural values than to less-acculturated Mexican immigrants (Domino & Acosta, 1987). Hispanics score significantly higher on measures of familialism as compared to European Americans, but as Hispanics acculturate to Western society, their scores on familialism tend to decrease (Sabogal et al., 1987).

Familialism, collectivism/allocentrism, and religiosity are specific cultural values held by Hispanics that may account for much of the positive health of Hispanics and the Hispanic paradox. Familialism and allocentrism are similar cultural concepts that emphasize a collectivist view in which the needs of the family or group are placed over the specific needs of the individual (Marin & Marin, 1991). Hispanics are more likely to be family-oriented, to have larger family networks, and to view their extended families the way whites view nuclear families. Higher family support is related to better psychological well-being and buffers against stress (Rodriguez et al., 2007). In regards to allocentrism, Hispanics living in neighborhoods with high concentrations of Hispanics tend to have better health (Browning & Cagney, 2002; Cagney, Browning, & Wallace, 2007).

Religiosity has been related to better health outcomes over a number of studies (McCullough et al., 2000). Although religiosity is positively related to social support and social networks and better health behaviors, controlling for these factors does not eliminate the relationship between religiosity and health (Hummer et al., 1999; Oman & Reed, 1998). Religiosity plays a central role in the lives of most Hispanics, more so than in whites. Not only are Hispanics more religious than whites, one study found that Hispanic immigrants are the most religious of any group in the United States (Hao & Johnson, 2000).

## Emerging Explanatory Models
### Reserve Capacity Model
The reserve capacity model emphasizes resources that an individual has that contribute to psychosocial risk

and resilience (Gallo et al., 2009b). Reserve capacity factors include tangible resources, interpersonal resources, intrapersonal resources, and culture-specific resources. The combination of these reserve capacity factors affects our ability to deal with negative events and affects our emotions and attitudes about these events in our lives. The interaction of reserve capacity factors with life events and emotions and attitudes leads to health risk factors and health outcomes. Reserve capacity factors develop over time in a sociocultural context. The SES of the individual and community interact with the cultural context of ethnicity, identity, acculturation, and cultural beliefs to create reserve capacity and thus lead to risk and resilience.

The reserve capacity model begins with the premise that individuals with low social status experience fewer positive events and more negative events, and therefore experience more stress relative to high-status individuals. Chronic exposure to negative events, such as racism, can lead individuals to perceive ambiguous events in a negative light because of previous negative experiences, leading to increased stress load over time. Low SES and minority status can interact synergistically to create high levels of stress that accumulate over time. Low-SES minorities probably have fewer opportunities to build and replenish resources, which then inhibits their ability to manage stressors or stressful situations effectively. In the language of the reserve capacity model, low-SES minorities have less reserve capacity to deal with stress.

In the case of Hispanics (particularly immigrants), however, Hispanics have significant psychosocial resources that help to balance or overcome the stress of low SES. As Hispanic immigrants acculturate to American society, they may lose significant psychosocial resources, such as strong social networks, to the degree that they adopt American cultural values. To the degree that Hispanics maintain traditional cultural values, such as familialism and allocentrism, they will likely have high levels of reserve capacity with which to deal with life stress.

### Social Capital Model
Whereas the reserve capacity model has been studied in health psychology and behavioral medicine, the social capital model has been focused on more in the areas of public health and epidemiology. Both models focus on the importance of social resources, although the social capital model focuses more on the levels of community and society. Social capital "refers to features of a social organization, such as

trust, norms, and networks that can improve the efficiency of society by facilitating coordinated actions" (Putnam, 1993, p. 167), and at the individual level consists of social trust, sense of belonging, volunteer activity, and community participation (Fujiwara & Kawachi, 2008; Islam, Merlo, Kawachi, Lindstrom, & Gerdtham, 2006; Kawachi, Kennedy, Lochner, & Prothrow-Stith, 1997).

High social capital predicts better self-reported mental and physical health (Fujiwara & Kawachi, 2008; Islam et al., 2006). Two factors that contribute to social capital are income inequality and relative deprivation. Income inequality focuses on income differences within a given country or community. A number of studies have found that increased differences in income predict negative health outcomes and increased mortality for those less fortunate (Kawachi et al., 1997; Wilkinson & Pickett, 2006). One interesting way to assess income inequality is to assess what is called the *Robin Hood index*, which is calculated by estimating the amount of income that must be redistributed from those above the mean to those below the mean to achieve income equality for everyone in a given community. The larger the index, the greater the income disparity. The Robin Hood index has been found to be strongly related to mortality in several studies, with correlations between .54 and .65 (Kawachi et al., 1997; Kennedy, Kawachi, & Prothrow-Smith, 1996). Perhaps not surprisingly, the Robin Hood index is also negatively correlated with measures of social capital, such as social trust and group membership.

Relative deprivation focuses on the emotions resulting from social comparisons involving inequality. Invidious social comparisons can lead to increased stress, maladaptive coping responses, and negative health behaviors as an attempt to deal with the negative emotions resulting from negative social comparisons (Subramanian & Kawachi, 2006; Wilkinson & Pickett, 2006). The Yitzhaki index of relative deprivation is frequently used to determine hierarchy and position relative to one's social reference groups. Studies have found that relative deprivation is related to worse self-reported mental and physical health (Kondo, Kawachi, Subramanian, Takeda, & Yamagata, 2008; Subramanyam, Kawachi, Berkman, & Subramanian, 2009).

The concepts of social capital, income inequality, and relative deprivation have been useful research tools for public health researchers interested in understanding how socioeconomic factors "get under the skin." These concepts also appear to provide a strong framework for understanding Hispanic health. Specifically, Hispanics may not have significant financial capital, but they are rich in social capital, which contributes to their positive health outcomes and resiliency.

## Future Directions

Despite a significant risk-factor profile, Latinos have surprisingly good health outcomes, including a mortality advantage relative to non-Hispanics. An important next step will be to examine the reasons for these effects. Although testing of potential resilience factors is exciting, one must know where the effect is before explaining it.

From a disease course perspective, a mortality advantage may reflect different levels of resiliency. First, a mortality advantage may reflect differences in disease vulnerability. That is, Latinos may live longer simply because they are healthier and less likely to get ill. Researchers could examine this possibility by examining potential differences in immune functioning, a clear moderator of illness risk (cf. Quan & Banks, 2007). Second, a mortality advantage may reflect differences in disease progression. It is possible that some major diseases progress more slowly among Latinos relative to non-Hispanics. Third, a mortality advantage may reflect differences in recovery following an acute medical crisis. By conceptualizing the mortality paradox in this way, researchers can identify and test resilience mechanisms that are more congruent with the specific phase of the disease course.

Future work should also address a number of challenges that will enable significant advances in the identification of Latino health challenges and guide effective interventions. Given their cultural heterogeneity and growing size, Hispanic subgroups need to be recruited into research and specifically identified in publication. There is also an increasing need for culturally sensitive measures and methods of diagnosis. Researchers must move beyond literal language translation of assessment instruments and develop culturally sensitive tools that capture differences in symptom manifestation. Finally, greater efforts need to be put into developing culturally tailored interventions to engage Latinos and fit treatment to their values and behavioral preferences. Prior efforts to tailor treatment have shown extraordinary promise that tailoring interventions is possible and beneficial. Future research should continue these efforts.

The Latino population is quite literally the future of America. It is imperative to understand and embrace their unique characteristics in order to meet their and America's future health care needs. Along the way, we have a rare opportunity to study what a group is doing right with regard to health, and perhaps, learn lessons that may lead to benefits for all.

## Further Reading

Abraido-Lanza, A.F., Dohrenwend, B.P., Ng-Mak, D.S., & Turner, J.B. (2000). Abraido-Lanza et al. respond. *American Journal of Public Health, 90*, 1798–1799.

Franzini, L., Ribble, J.C., & Keddie, A.M. (2001). Understanding the Hispanic paradox. *Ethnicity and Disease, 11*, 496–518.

Gallo, L.C., Penedo, F.J., Espinosa de los Monteros, K., & Arguelles, W. (2009). Resiliency in the face of disadvantage: Do Hispanic cultural characteristics protect health outcomes? *Journal of Personality, 77*, 1707–1746.

Shaw, R.J., Pickett, K.E., & Wilkinson, R.G. (2010). Ethnic density effects on birth outcomes and maternal smoking during pregnancy in the US linked birth and infant death data set. *American Journal of Public Health, 100*, 707–713.

Williams, D.R. (2005). Topic 3. Racial and ethnic inequalities in health: The health of U.S. racial and ethnic populations. *Journals of Gerontology, 60B*, 53–62.

## References

Abraido-Lanza, A.F., Dohrenwend, B.P., Ng-Mak, D.S., & Turner, J.B. (1999). The Latino mortality paradox: A test of the "Salmon bias" and healthy migrant hypotheses. *American Journal of Public Health, 89*, 1543–1548.

Abraido-Lanza, A.F., Viladrich, A., Florez, K.R., Cespedes, A., Aguirre, A.N., & De La Cruz, A. (2007). Fatalismo reconsidered: A cautionary note for health-related research and practice with Latino populations. *Ethnicity and Disease, 17*, 153–158.

Alegria, M., Canino, G., Shrout, P.E., Woo, M., Duan, N., Vila, D., et al. (2008). Prevalence of mental illness in immigrant and non-immigrant U.S. Latino groups. *American Journal of Psychiatry, 165*, 359–369.

Alexander, G.R., Kogan, M., Bader, D., Carlo, W., Allen, M., & Mor, J. (2003). US birth weight/gestational age-specific neonatal mortality: 1995–1997 rates for whites, Hispanics, and blacks. *Pediatrics, 111*, e61–e66.

Alexander, G.R., Wingate, M.S., Bader, D., & Kogan, M.D. (2008). The increasing racial disparity in infant mortality rates: Composition and contributors to recent US trends. *American Journal of Obstetrics and Gynecology, 198*, e1–9.

American Heart Association. (2010). Heart disease and stroke statistics 2010 update: A report from the American heart association. *Circulation, 121*, e46–e215.

Andrade, L., Caraveo-Anduaga, J.J., Berglund, P., Bijl, R.V., De Graff, R., et al. (2003). The epidemiology of major depressive episodes: Results from the international consortium of psychiatric epidemiology (ICPE) surveys. *International Journal of Methods in Psychiatric Research, 12*, 3–21.

Ansseau, M., Fischler, B., Dierick, M., Albert, A., Leyman, S., & Mignon, A. (2008). Socioeconomic correlates of generalized anxiety disorder and major depression in primary care: The GADIS II Study (generalized anxiety and depression impact survey II). *Depression and Anxiety, 25*, 506–513.

Arias, E., Eschbach, K., Schauman, W.S., Backlund, E.L., & Sorlie, P.D. (2010). The Hispanic mortality advantage and ethnic misclassification on US death certificates. *American Journal of Public Health, 100*, S171–S177.

Barefoot, J.C., Peterson, B.L., Dahlstrom, W.G., Siegler, I.C., Anderson, N.B., & Williams, R.B., Jr. (1991). Hostility patterns and health implications: Correlates of Cook-Medley hostility scale scores in a national survey. *Health Psychology, 10*, 18–24.

Baum, A., Garofalo, J.P., & Yali, A.M. (1999). Socioeconomic status and chronic stress: Does stress account for SES effects on health? In N.E. Adler, M. Marmot, B.S. McEwen, & J. Stewart (Eds.), *Socioeconomic status and health in industrial nations: Social, psychological, and biological pathways* (pp. 1–13). New York, NY: New York Academy of Sciences.

Bils, M., & Klenow, P.J. (2000). Does schooling cause growth? *American Economic Review, 90*, 1160–1183.

Bromberger, J.T., Harlow, S., Avis, N., Kravitz, H.M., & Cordal, A. (2004). Racial/ethnic differences in the prevalence of depressive symptoms among middle-aged women: The study of women's health across the nation (SWAN). *American Journal of Public Health, 94*, 1378–1385.

Browning, C.R., & Cagney, K.A. (2002). Neighborhood structural disadvantage, collective efficacy, and self-rated physical health in an urban setting. *Journal of Health and Social Behavior, 43*, 383–399.

Cabelli, V., & Dufour, A. (1983). *Health effects criteria for marine recreational waters.* Research Triangle Park, NC: U.S. Environmental Protection Agency.

Cagney, K.A., Browning, C.R., & Wallace, D.M. (2007). The Latino paradox in neighborhood context: The case of asthma and other respiratory conditions. *American Journal of Public Health, 97*, 919–925.

Carpenter, S. (2000). Effects of cultural tightness and collectivism on self-concept and causal attributions. *Cross-Cultural Research, 34*, 38–56.

Carpenter, S., & Radhakrishnan, P. (2000). Allocentrism and idiocentrism as predictors of in group perceptions: An individual difference extension of cultural patterns. *Journal of Research in Personality, 34*, 262–268.

Calzada, E.J., Fernandez, Y., & Cortes, D.E. (2010). Incorporating the cultural value of respeto into a framework of Latino parenting. *Cultural Diversity and Ethnic Minority Psychology, 16*, 77–86.

Centers for Disease Control and Prevention. (2009a). *Sexually transmitted diseases in the United States, 2008: National surveillance data for chlamydia, gonorrhea, and syphilis.* Atlanta, GA: U.S. Department of Health and Human Services, Centers for Disease Control and Prevention.

Centers for Disease Control and Prevention. (2009b). *HIV/AIDS surveillance report, 2007.* Atlanta, GA: U.S. Department of Health and Human Services, Centers for Disease Control and Prevention.

Centers for Disease Control and Prevention. (2010). *2009 H1N1 and seasonal flu and Hispanic communities: Questions and answers.* Retrieved from http://www.cdc.gov/h1n1flu/qa_hispanic.htm.

Chavez, L.R., Hubbell, F.A., Mishra, S.I., & Valdez, R.B. (1997). The influence of fatalism on self-reported use of Papanicolaou smears. *American Journal of Preventive Medicine, 13*, 418–424.

Clark, R., Anderson, N.B., Clark, V.R., & Williams, D.R. (1999). Racism as a stressor for African Americans: A biopsychosocial model. *American Psychologist, 54*, 805–816.

Cuellar, I., & Roberts, R.E. (1997). Relations of depression, acculturation, and socioeconomic status in a Latino sample. *Hispanic Journal of the Behavioral Sciences, 19*, 230–238.

Clegg, L.X., Li, F.P., Hankey, B.F., Chu, K., & Edwards, B.K. (2002). Cancer survival among US Whites and minorities: A SEER (surveillance, epidemiology, and end results) program population-based study. *Archives of Internal Medicine, 162*, 1985–1993.

Coates, D., & Gindlling, T. (2010). Are Hispanic immigrant families reviving the economies of America's small towns? *IZA Discussion Paper No. 4682*. Retrieved from http://papers.ssrn.com/sol3/papers.cfm?abstract_id=1545109.

Cockerham, W.C., & Yamori, Y. (2001). Okinawa: An exception to the social gradient of life expectancy in Japan. *Asia Pacific Journal of Clinical Nutrition, 10*, 154–158.

Cuellar, I., Arnold, B., & Braccio, S.M. (2004). Residency in the United States, subjective well-being, and depression in an older Mexican-origin sample. *Journal of Aging and Health, 16*, 447–466.

Cuellar, I., Arnold, B., & Gonzalez, G. (1995). Cognitive referents of acculturation: Assessment of cultural constructs in Mexican Americans. *Journal of Community Psychology, 23*, 339–356.

Dabul, A.J., Bernal, M.E., & Knight, G.P. (1995). Allocentric and idiocentric self-description and academic achievement among Mexican American and Anglo adolescents. *The Journal of Social Psychology, 135*, 621–630.

Danaei, G., Friedman, A.B., Oza, S., Murray, C.J.L., & Ezzati, M. (2009). Diabetes prevalence and diagnosis in US states: Analysis of health surveys. *Population Health Metrics, 7*, 16.

De la Garza, R.O., DeSipio, L., Garcia, F.C., Garcia, J., & Falcon, A. (1992). *Latino voices: Mexican, Puerto Rican & Cuban perspectives on American politics*. Boulder, CO: Westview Press.

Delgado, E.A. (2007). Latinos' use, desire, and type of non-parental child care arrangements. *Journal of Latinos and Education, 8*, 119–140.

Delgado, R., & Stefancic, J. (1998). *The Latino/a condition: A critical reader*. New York: New York University Press.

Diez Roux, A.V., Detrano, R., Jackson, S., Jacobs, D.R., Schreiner, P.J., Shea, S., & Szklo, M. (2005). Acculturation and socioeconomic position as predictors of coronary calcification in a multiethnic sample. *Circulation, 112*, 1557–1565.

Domino, G., & Acosta, A. (1987). The relation of acculturation and values in Mexican Americans. *Hispanic Journal of Behavioral Sciences, 9*, 131–150.

Edwards, B.K., Ward, E., Kohler, B.A., Eheman, C., Zauber, A.G., Anderson, R.N., et al. (2010). Annual report to the nation on the status of cancer, 1975–2006, featuring colorectal cancer trends and impact of interventions (risk factors, screening, and treatment) to reduce future rates. *Cancer, 116*, 544–573.

Eschbach, K., Kuo, Y.F., & Goodwin, J.S. (2006). Errors in ascertainment of Hispanic ethnicity on California death certificates: Implications for the explanation of the Hispanic mortality advantage. *American Journal of Public Health, 96*, 2209–2215.

Evans, G.W., & Kantrowitz, E. (2002). Socioeconomic status and health: The potential role of environmental risk exposure. *Annual Review of Public Health, 23*, 303–331.

Evans, G.W., Lepore, S.J., Shejwal, B.R., & Palsane, M.N. (1998). Chronic residential crowding and children's well being: an ecological perspective. *Child Development, 69*, 1514–1523.

Falicov, C. (1998). *Latino families in therapy: A guide to multicultural practice*. New York: Guilford Press.

Finch, B.K., Kolody, B., & Vega, W.A. (2000). Perceived discrimination and depression among Mexican-origin adults in California. *Journal of Health and Social Behavior, 41*, 295–313.

Fry, R., & Passel, J.S. (2009). *Latino children: A majority are U.S.-born offspring of immigrants*. Washington, DC: Pew Hispanic Center.

Fujiwara, T., & Kawachi, I. (2008). Social capital and health: A study of adult twins in the US. *American Journal of Preventive Medicine, 35*, 139–144.

Galindo, C., & Ramos, L.F. (2009). Un nuevo enfoque para estimar la migración internacional de Mexico [A new approach for estimating international migration from Mexico]. *La situación demográfica de Mexico 2008* (pp. 45–71). Mexico City: Consejo Nacional de Poblacion (CONAPO).

Gallo, L.C., Espinosa de los Monteros, K., Allison, M., Diez Roux, A., Polak, J.F., Watson, K.E., & Morales, L.S. (2009a). Do socioeconomic gradients in subclinical atherosclerosis vary according to acculturation level? Analyses of Mexican-Americans in the multi-ethnic study of atherosclerosis. *Psychosomatic Medicine, 71*, 756–762.

Gallo, L.C., Penedo, F.J., Espinosa de los Monteros, K., & Arguelles, W. (2009b). Resiliency in the face of disadvantage: Do Hispanic cultural characteristics protect health outcomes? *Journal of Personality, 77*, 1707–1746.

Gibson, C., & Jung, K. (2002). *Historical census statistics on population totals by race, 1790 to 1990, and by Hispanic origin, 1970 to 1990, for the United States, regions, divisions, and states*. Working paper series No. 56. Washington, DC: U.S. Census Bureau.

Grant, B.F., Hasin, D.S., Stinson, F.S., Dawson, D.A., June Ruan, W., Goldstein, R.B., et al. (2005). Prevalence, correlates, co-morbidity, and comparative disability of DSM-IV generalized anxiety disorder in the USA: Results from the national epidemiological survey on alcohol and related conditions. *Psychological Medicine, 35*, 1747–1759.

Greigo, E.M., & Cassidy, R.C. (2001). Overview of race and Hispanic origin: Census 2000 brief. Washington, DC: U.S. Census Bureau, March, 2001.

Gump, B.B., Matthews, K.A., & Raikkonen, K. (1999). Modeling relationships among socioeconomic status, hostility, cardiovascular reactivity, and left ventricular mass in African American and white children. *Health Psychology, 18*, 140–150.

Hao, L., & Johnson, R.W. (2000). Economic, cultural, and social origins of emotional well-being: Comparisons of immigrants and natives at midlife. *Research on Aging, 22*, 599–569.

Hayes-Bautista, D., & Chapa, J. (1987). Latino terminology: Conceptual bases for standardized terminology. *American Journal of Public Health, 77*, 61–68.

Henderson, S.O., Haiman, C.A., Wilkens, L.R., Kolonel, L.N., Wan, P., & Pike, M.C. (2007). Established risk factors account for most of the racial differences in cardiovascular disease mortality. *Plos One, 2*, e377.

Heron, M. (2010). Deaths: Leading causes for 2006. In *National vital statistics reports, 58*. Hyattsville, MD: National Center for Health Statistics.

Heron, M., Hoyert, D.L., Murphy, S.L., Xu, J., Kochanek, K.D., & Tejada-Vera, B. (2009). Deaths: Final data for 2006. In *National vital statistics reports, 57*. Hyattsville, MD: National Center for Health Statistics.

Hessol, N.A., & Fuentes-Afflick, E. (2005). Ethnic differences in neonatal and postneonatal mortality. *Pediatrics, 115*, e441–451.

Himmelfarb, S., & Murrell, S.A. (1984). The prevalence and correlates of anxiety symptoms in older adults. *Journal of Psychology, 116*, 159–167.

House, J.S., Landis, K.R., & Umberson, D. (1988). Social relationships and health. *Science, 241,* 540–545.

Hummer, R.A., Rogers, R.G., Nam, C.B., & Ellison, C.G. (1999). Religious involvement and U.S. adult mortality. *Demography, 36,* 273–285.

Idler, E.L., & Benyamini, Y. (1997). Self-rated health and mortality: A review of twenty-seven community studies. *Journal of Health and Social Behavior, 38,* 21–37.

Instituto Nacional de Estadistica, Geografia e Informatica. (INEGI: 2007). *Como se hace la ENOE. Metodos Y procedimientos,* Mexico. Retrieved from http://www.inegi.org.mx/prod_serv/contenidos/espanol/biblioteca/Default.asp?accion=1&upc=702825006541&s=est&c=10789.

Islam, M.K., Merlo, J., Kawachi, I., Lindstrom, M., & Gerdtham, U.G. (2006). Social capital and health: Does egalitarianism matter? A literature review. *International Journal for Equity in Health, 5,* 3–28.

Jamison, E.A., Jamison, D.T., & Hanushek, E.A. (2007). The effects of education on income growth and mortality decline. *Economics of Education Review, 26,* 771–788.

Johnson, K.M., & Lichter, D.T. (2008). Natural increase: A new source of population growth in emerging Hispanic destinations. *Population and Development Review, 34,* 327–346.

Johnson, M.A., & Marchi, K.S. (2009). Segmented assimilation theory and perinatal health disparities among women of Mexican descent. *Social Science & Medicine, 69,* 101–109.

Kandula, N.R., Lauderdale, D.S., & Baker, D.W. (2007). Differences in self-reported health among Asians, Latinos, and non-Hispanic whites: The role of language and nativity. *Annals of Epidemiology, 17,* 191–198.

Kawachi, I., Kennedy, B.P., Lochner, K., & Prothrow-Stith, D. (1997). Social capital, income inequality, and mortality. *American Journal of Public Health, 87,* 1491–1498.

Kennedy, B.P., Kawachi, I., & Prothrow-Stith, D. (1996). Income distribution and mortality: Cross-sectional ecological study of the Robin Hood index in the United States. *British Medical Journal, 312,* 1004–1007.

Kessler, R.C., McGongale, K.A., Zhao, S., Nelson, C.B., Hughes, M., Eshelman, S., et al. (1994). Lifetime and 12-month prevalence of DSM-III-R psychiatric disorders in the United States. *Archives of General Psychiatry, 51,* 8–19.

Kessler R.C, Mickelson K.D., & Williams D.R. (1999). The prevalence, distribution, and mental health correlates of perceived discrimination in the United States. *Journal of Health and Social Behavior, 40,* 208–230.

Kitsantas, P., & Gaffney, K.F. (2010). Racial/ethnic disparities in infant mortality. *Journal of Perinatal Medicine, 38,* 87–94.

Kochhar, R., Gonzalez-Barrera, A., & Dockterman, D. (2009). *Through boom and bust: Minorities, immigrants, and home-ownership.* Washington, DC: Pew Hispanic Center.

Kohut, A., Parker, K., Keeter, S., Doherty, C., Dimock, M., & the Pew Research Center for the People & Press. (2007). *How young people view their lives, futures and politics: A portrait of generation next.* Washington, DC: Pew Research Center.

Kondo, N., Kawachi, I., Subramanian, S.V., Takeda, Y., & Yamagata, Z. (2008). Do social comparisons explain the association between income inequality and health? Relative deprivation and perceived health among male and female Japanese individuals. *Social Science & Medicine, 67,* 982–987.

Lesperance, F., Frasure-Smith, N., & Talajic, M. (1996). Major depression before and after myocardial infarction: Its nature and consequences. *Psychosomatic Medicine, 58,* 99–110.

Lopez, M.H. (2007). Latinos and education: Explaining the attainment gap. Washington, DC: Pew Hispanic Center.

Lutsey, P.L., Diez Roux, A.V., Jacobs, D.R., Burke, G.L., Harman, J., Shea, S., & Folsom, A.R. (2008). Associations of acculturation and socioeconomic status with subclinical cardiovascular disease in the multi-ethnic study of atherosclerosis. *American Journal of Public Health, 98,* 1963–1970.

Lynch, J.W., Kaplan, G.A., & Salonen, J.T. (1997). Why do poor people behave poorly? Variation in adult health behaviors and psychosocial characteristics by stages of the socioeconomic life course. *Social Science & Medicine, 44,* 809–819.

Marin, G., & Gamba, R.J. (2003). Acculturation and changes in cultural values. In K.M. Chun, P.B. Organista, G. Marin (Eds.), *Acculturation: Advances in theory, measurement, and applied research* (pp. 83–93). Washington, DC: American Psychological Association.

Marin, G., & Marin, B.V. (1991). *Research with Hispanic populations.* Newbury Park, CA: Sage.

McCullough, M.E., Hoyt, W.T., Larson, D.B., Koenig, H. G, & Thoresen, C. (2000). Religious involvement and mortality: A meta-analytic review. *Health Psychology, 19,* 211–222.

Markides, K.S. (1983). Mortality among minority populations: A review of recent patterns and trends. *Public Health Reports, 98,* 252–260.

Markides, K.S., & Coreil, J. (1986). The health of Hispanics in the southwestern United States: An epidemiologic paradox. *Public Health Reports, 101,* 253–265.

Matthews, T.J., & MacDorman, M.F. (2010). Infant mortality statistics from the 2006 period linked birth/infant death data set. In *National vital statistics reports, 58.* Hyattsville, MD: National Center for Health Statistics.

McGee, D.L., Liao, Y., Cao, G., & Cooper, R.S. (1999). Self-reported health status and mortality in a multi8ethnic US cohort. *American Journal of Epidemiology, 149,* 41–46.

Mitchell, B.D., Stern, M.P., Haffner, S.M., Hazuda, H.P., & Patterson, J.K. (1990). Risk factors for cardiovascular mortality in Mexican Americans and non-Hispanic whites. San Antonio Heart Study. *American Journal of Epidemiology, 131,* 423–433.

Mittleman, M.A., Maclure, M., Nachnani, M., Sherwood, J.B., & Muller, J.E. (1997). Educational attainment, anger, and the risk of triggering myocardial infarction onset. The determinants of myocardial infarction onset study investigators. *Archives of Internal Medicine, 157,* 69–75.

Mooteri, S.N., Petersen, F., Dagubati, R., & Pai, R.G. (2004). Duration of residence in the United States as a new risk factor for coronary artery disease (the Konkani heart study). *American Journal of Cardiology, 93,* 359–361.

Morenoff, J.D., & Sampson, R.J. (1997). Violent crime and the spatial dynamics of neighborhood transition: Chicago, 1970–1990. *Social Forces, 76,* 31–64.

Natale-Pereira, A., Marks, J., Vega, M., Mouson, D., Hudson, S.V., & Salas-Lopez, D. (2008). Barriers and facilitators for colorectal cancer screening practices in the Latino community: Perspectives from community leaders. *Cancer Control, 15,* 157–165.

National Center for Health Statistics. (2008). *Health, United States, 2007, with chartbook on trends in the health of Americans* (report No. 76–641496). Hyattsville, MD: Centers for Disease Control, National Center for Health Statistics.

National Institute of Diabetes and Digestive and Kidney Diseases. (2008). *National diabetes statistics, 2007 fact sheet.* Bethesda, MD: US Department of Health and Human Services, National Institutes of Health.

National Resource Council. (2006). *Hispanics and the future of America*. Washington, DC: National Academies Press.

Nelson, F. (1978). Residential dissatisfaction in the crowded urban neighborhood. *International Review of Modern Sociology, 8*, 227–238.

Oman, D., & Reed, D. (1998). Religion and mortality among the community dwelling elderly. *American Journal of Public Health, 88*, 1469–1475.

Ortman, J.M., & Guarneri, C.E. (2009). *United States Population Projections: 2000 to 2050*. Washington, DC: U.S. Census Bureau. Retrieved from http://www.census.gov/population/www/projections/analytical-document09.pdf.

Parra-Cordona, J.R., Cordova, D. Jr., Holtrop, K., Villarruel, F.A., & Weiling, E. (2008). Shared ancestry, evolving stories: Similar and contrasting life experiences described by foreign born and U.S. born Latino parents. *Family Processes, 47*, 157–172.

Passel, J.S., & Cohen, D. (2009). *A portrait of unauthorized immigrants in the United States*. Washington, DC: Pew Hispanic Center.

Passel, J.S., & Cohen, D. (2008). *Trends in unauthorized immigration: Undocumented inflow not trails legal inflow*. Washington, DC: Pew Hispanic Center.

Perez-Stable, E.J., Napoles-Springer, A., & Miramontes, J.M. (1997). The effects of ethnicity and language on medical outcomes of patients with hypertension. *Medical Care, 35*, 1212–1219.

Pew Hispanic Center. (2008). *Latino settlement in the new century*. Retrieved from http://pewhispanic.org/files/reports/96.pdf.

Pew Hispanic Center. (2009). *Between Two Worlds: How Young Latinos Come of Age in America*. Retrieved from http://pewhispanic.org/files/reports/117.pdf

Pew Hispanic Center. (2010a). *Statistical portrait of Hispanics in the United States, 2008*. Retrieved from http://pewhispanic.org/factsheets/factsheet.php?FactsheetID=58.

Pew Hispanic Center. (2010b). *Statistical portrait of the foreign-born population in the United States, 2008*. Retrieved from http://pewhispanic.org/factsheets/factsheet.php?FactsheetID=59.

Pleis, J.R., & Lucas, J.W. (2009). Summary health statistics for U.S. adults: National health interview survey, 2007. *National Center for Health Statistics. Vital Health State, 10*(240).

Powe, B.D., & Finnie, R. (2003). Cancer fatalism: The state of the science. *Cancer Nursing, 26*, 454–467.

Putnam, R.D. (1993). *Making democracy work*. Princeton, NJ: Princeton University Press; 1993.

Quan, N., & Banks, W.A. (2007). Brain-immune communication pathways. *Brain, Behavior, and Immunity, 21*, 727–735.

Ranchor, A.V., Bouma, J., & Sanderman, R. (1996). Vulnerability and social class: Differential patterns of personality and social support over the social classes. *Personality and Individual Differences, 20*, 229–237.

Rodriguez, N., Mira, C.B., Paez, N.D., & Myers, H.F. (2007). Exploring the complexities of familism and acculturation: Central constructs for people of Mexican origin. *American Journal of Community Psychology, 39*, 61–77.

Rozanski, A., Blumenthal, J.A., & Kaplan, J. (1999). Impact of psychological factors on the pathogenesis of cardiovascular disease and its implication for therapy. *Circulation, 99*, 2192–2217.

Ruiz, J.M., Steffen, P., & Prather, C.C. (in press). Socioeconomic status and health. In A. Baum, T.A. Revenson, & J.E. Singer (Eds.), *Handbook of health psychology*. Mahwah, NJ: Lawrence Erlbaum Associates.

Rumbaut, R.G. (1997). Assimilation and its discontents: Between rhetoric and reality. *International Migration Review, 31*, 923–960.

Sabogal, F., Marin, G., & Otero-Sabogal, R. (1987). Hispanic familialism and acculturation: What changes and what doesn't? *Hispanic Journal of the Behavioral Sciences, 9*, 397–412.

Schwab, T., Meyer, J., & Merrell, R. (1994). Measuring attitudes and health beliefs among Mexican Americans with diabetes. *Diabetes Educator, 20*, 221–227.

Scherwtiz, L., Perkins, L., Chesney, M., & Hughes, G. (1991). Cook-Medley hostility scale and subsets: Relationship to demographic and psychosocial characteristics in young adults in the CARDIA study. *Psychosomatic Medicine, 53*, 36–49.

Shetterly, S.M., Baxter, J., Mason, L.D., & Hamman, R.F. (1996). Self-rated health among Hispanic vs. non-Hispanic white adults: The San Luis Valley health and aging study. *American Journal of Public Health, 86*, 1798–1801.

Siegman, A.W., Kubzansky, L.D., Kawachi, I., Boyle, S., Vokonas, P.S., & Sparrow, D. (2000). A prospective study of dominance and coronary heart disease in the normative aging study. *American Journal of Cardiology, 86*, 145–149.

Sigelman, L., & Welch, S. (1993). The contact hypothesis revisited: Black-white interaction and positive racial attitudes. *Social Forces, 71*, 781–795.

Smith, D.P., & Bradshaw, B.S. (2006). Rethinking the Hispanic paradox: Death rates and life expectancy for U.S. non-Hispanic white and Hispanic populations. *American Journal of Public Health, 96*, 1686–1692.

Smith, T.W., Uchino, B.N., Berg, C.A., Florsheim, P., Pearce, G., Hawkins, M., et al. (2008). Associations of self-reports versus spouse ratings of negative affectivity, dominance, and affiliation with coronary artery disease: Where should we look and who should we ask when studying personality and health? *Health Psychology, 27*, 676–684.

Sorlie, P.D., Backlund, E., Johnson, N.J., & Rogot, E. (1993). Mortality by Hispanic status in the United States. *Journal of the American Medical Association, 270*, 2464–2468.

Spence, J.T. (1985). Achievement American style: The rewards and costs of individualism. *American Psychologist, 40*, 1285–1295.

Steffen, P.R. (2006). The cultural gradient: Culture moderates the relationship between socioeconomic status (SES) and ambulatory blood pressure. *Journal of Behavioral Medicine, 29*, 501–510.

Subramanian, S.V., & Kawachi, I. (2006). Whose health is affected by income inequality? A multilevel interaction analysis of contemporaneous and lagged effects of state income on individual self-rated health in the United States. *Health Place, 12*, 141–156.

Subramanyam, M., Kawachi, I., Berkman, L., & Subramanian, S.V. (2009). Relative deprivation in income and self-rated health in the United States. *Social Science & Medicine, 69*, 327–334.

Taylor, S.E., Repetti, R., & Seeman, T.E. (1997). Health psychology: What is an unhealthy environment and how does it get under the skin? *Annual Review of Psychology, 48*, 411–447.

Triandis, H.C. (1995). *Individualism and collectivism*. Boulder, CO: Westview Press.

U.S. Bureau of Labor Statistics. (2009). *Labor force characteristics by race and ethnicity, 2008*. U.S. Department of Labor,

Report 1020. Retrieved from http://www.bls.gov/cps/cpsrace 2008.pdf.

Vega, W.A., Kolody, B., Aguilar-Gaxiola, S., Alderete, E., Catalano, R., & Caraveo-Anduaga, J. (1998). Lifetime prevalence of DSM-III-R psychiatric disorders among urban and rural Mexican Americans in California. *Archives of General Psychiatry, 55*, 771–778.

Vega, W.A., Sribney, W.M., Aguilar-Gaxiola, S., & Kolody, B. (2004). 12-month prevalence of DSM-III-R psychiatric disorders among Mexican Americans: Nativity, social assimilation, and age determinants. *Journal of Nervous and Mental Disease, 192*, 532–541.

Waldron, I., Nowotarski, M., Freimer, M., Henry, J.P., Post, N., & Witten, C. (1982). Cross-cultural variation in blood pressure: A quantitative analysis of the relationships of blood pressure to cultural characteristics, salt consumption, and body weight. *Social Science and Medicine, 16*, 419–430.

Warheit, G.J., Holzer, C.E., III, & Arey, S.A. (1975). Race and mental illness: An epidemiologic update. *Journal of Health and Social Behavior, 16*, 243–256.

Wei, M., Valdez, R.A., Mitchell, B.D., Haffner, S.M., Stern, M.P., & Hazuda, H.P. (1996). Migration status, socioeconomic status, and mortality rates in Mexican Americans and non-Hispanic whites: The San Antonio heart study. *Annals of Epidemiology, 6*, 307–313.

Weinick, R.M., Jacobs, E.A., Stone, L.C., Ortega, A.N., & Burstin, H. (2004). Hispanic health-care disparities: Challenging the myth of monolithic Hispanic population. *Medical Care, 42*, 313–319.

White, A.M., Philogene, G.S., Fine, L., & Sinha, S. (2009). Social support and self-reported health status of older adults in the United States. *American Journal of Public Health, 99*, 1872–1878.

Wilkinson, R.G. & Pickett, E. (2006). Income inequality and population health: A review and explanation of the evidence. *Social Science and Medicine, 62*, 1768–1784.

Williams, D.R., Neighbors, H.W., & Jackson, J.S. (2003). Racial/ethnic discrimination and health: Findings from community studies. *American Journal of Public Health, 93*, 200–208.

Williams, D.R. (1999). Race, socioeconomic status, and health: The added effects of racism and discrimination. *Annals of the New York Academy of Science, 896*, 173–188.

Winston, C., Pratt, R., Armstrong, L., & Navin, T. (2010). Decrease in reported tuberculosis cases–United States, 2009. *Morbidity and Mortality Weekly Report (MMWR), 59*, 289–294.

Zea, M.C., Quezada, T., & Belgrave, F.Z (1994). Latino cultural values: Their role in adjustment to disability. *Journal of Social Behavior and Personality, 9*, 185–200.

# Two Decades of Social Change in Central and Eastern Europe: Implications for Health

Irina L.G. Todorova

**Abstract**

This chapter explores the dynamics of changes in health indicators in Central and Eastern Europe over the last 20 years. It presents illustrations of the East–West health divide from different countries and compares groups of countries. It offers in-depth case studies from Bulgaria and Romania to represent further dimensions of the psychosocial and a sociocultural contextualization of health. The events in Eastern Europe illustrate the importance of bringing a contextual lens to health psychology phenomena. Behaviour change models need to take into account meanings of health and of health protective, preventive, or risk behaviours. Lifestyles cannot be conceptualized as purely individual choices, but are co-constructed within cultural values and contingent upon material conditions. Health care reform in Central and Eastern Europe needs to be undertaken in multiple directions simultaneously—structural and policy changes, health promotion, behavior change interventions, using participatory approaches coordinated with community groups—to ensure that health indicators will continue to improve.

**Keywords:** Health, social change, Eastern Europe, Central Europe, health psychology

Symbolically, this volume goes to print right after the 20th anniversary of the fall of the Berlin Wall in 1989 and the accompanying changes in all aspects of social, political, and economic life of the countries of Eastern Europe.[1] As existing systems of single-party rule and centrally controlled planned economies came to a halt or underwent radical revision in former communist countries, a period of transition to new political and economic systems and social structures commenced. It was believed that this transition would last a few years, and a free market economy would quickly work its magic to bring prosperity and economic growth. Now, 20 years later, the debate continues about whether the transition is over, and by what criteria this should be judged. The 20th anniversary of 1989, along with the 5-year anniversary of European Union (EU) accession for several countries of Central and Eastern Europe, motivated the publication of a broad comparative analysis of the tendencies and current state

of ten countries[2] in the region (Open Society Institute, 2009). This analysis concludes that EU accession has stimulated growth in economic areas, yet has not marked the end of the transitional period for these states, as much "unfinished business" is still evident. The area of health reform is among this unfinished business—since health care is considered a national competence area for EU members. Because it was not part of the accession agendas, it was not prioritized in the preaccession push for reforms. Reform and decentralization (Koulaksazov, Todorova, Tragakes, & Hristova, 2003) of the health care sector has been ongoing but slow, mainly because of the absence of long-term sustainable policies and financing, as ruling political parties do not sustain long-term plans, fragment frequently, and do not maintain consistent reforms through subsequent governments. Additionally, the outcomes of the implemented changes in health care system structures and policies have rarely been evaluated

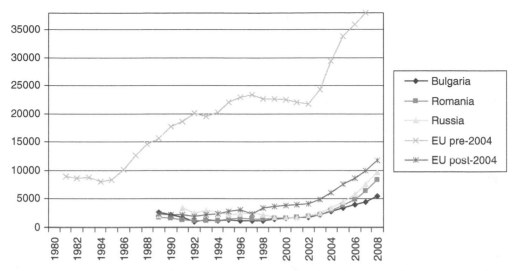

**Fig. 33.1** Gross National Product per capita for European Union (EU), pre-2004, EU post-2004, Bulgaria, Romania, and Russia (WHO Health for All Database, 2010).

(Rechel & McKee, 2009). Health care in Eastern Europe is characterized by underfunding when compared to public expenditures for health in other European countries (UNDP, 2007/2008), low wages for health providers, large regional and class disparities in access and affordability for some services, a conflict between private and public models, distrust and dissatisfaction with services, widespread informal payments (Balabanova & McKee, 2002c), divergence between existing documentation and actual practices, and general disorganization. Thus, the area of health care is considered one of the evident areas in which the transition is far from over for the new member states of the EU, and it requires further and long-term structural reforms (Open Society Institute, 2009).

Economic indicators of growth in these countries have shown "remarkable" progress (p. 26) during the last decade and particularly during the years since accession, and so have rates of employment (Open Society Institute, 2009; Figure 33.1). These trends are paralleled by similar improvement in the mortality and life expectancy statistics.[3] We can use such population-level morbidity- and mortality-related data to shed light on the question of where we are in the process of transition in countries of Eastern Europe. If we do so, we can see that, after dramatic drops in the early 1990s for most countries of the region, these indicators have now stabilized, returned to pre-1989 levels, or improved, indicating that at least the crisis has subsided. Taking into consideration the stabilization and gradual improvement in health and health system indicators

in the area at around the turn of the 21st century, some have concluded that the health crisis is over (Davis, 2000). This is true for some countries in Central and Eastern Europe, but for Russia and some new states, the indicators are still worse than they were before 1989 (Figures 33.2–33.5). And further, for all countries in the region, they are still less favorable than the same indicators in Western European states, thus sustaining the "East–West health divide." For the new member states, accession to the EU has been beneficial, but challenges of increasing inequalities within countries and health system reform are still quite relevant and have led some authors to express caution (McKee, Balabanova, & Steriu, 2007). The averaged national- and population-level data mask the growing inequalities within countries and regions, and thus relative health disparities. In Hungary, for example, the percentage of the population living below the national poverty line rose from 11% in 2000 to 16% in 2007 (Open Society Institute, 2009). These disparities require further explanation through quantitative analysis of differentials within and between countries, as well as through in-depth contextualized qualitative work.

During the last two decades, many publications have become available delineating the rapid changes observed in health indicators in countries of the former socialist block, including Central and Eastern Europe and the former Soviet Union. At the same time, considering the enormity of the health consequences and loss of life during this period of social change, it is surprising that much more

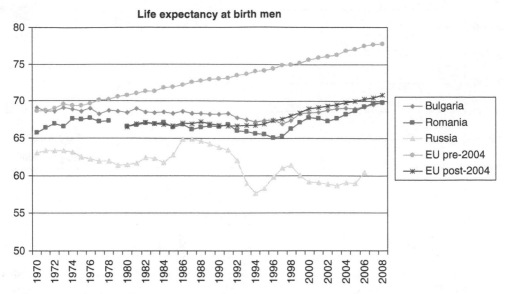

**Fig. 33.2** Life expectancy at birth for men in the European Union (EU) pre-2004, EU post-2004, Bulgaria, Romania, and Russia (WHO Health for All Database, 2010).

attention has not been devote to this topic, that only a few distinct research teams have been involved in its analysis, and that government responses and other attempts at intervention have been minimal (Kopp & Williams, 2006; Rechel & McKee, 2009). As Zatonski (2007) points out, a phenomenon of such dramatic worsening of health indicators in the late decades of the 20th century has been observed in only two areas of the globe—sub-Saharan Africa, in connection with the human immunodeficiency virus (HIV) epidemic, and in Eastern Europe (Zatonski, 2007).

This chapter gives us an opportunity to explore the dynamics of these changes during the last 20 years,

and from this vantage point, to summarize and make conclusions regarding the phenomena that have such powerful implications for the health of the population in the whole area. As change has been rapid and wide-reaching, it adds to our understanding of how contextual and social circumstances resonate with health, and of how health, health behaviours, and meanings of health and illness are enmeshed in their sociohistorical context. These interactions are complex, the influences on health are interconnected (Marks, 1996), and they differ depending on the preexisting conditions and historical circumstances in each country and region

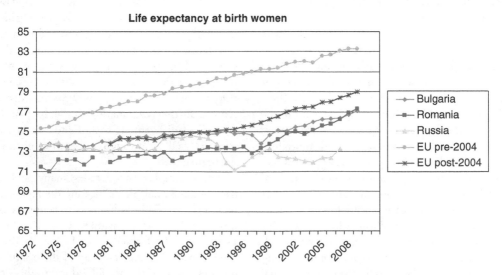

**Fig. 33.3** Life expectancy at birth for women in the European Union (EU) pre-2004, EU post-2004, Bulgaria, Romania, and Russia (WHO Health for All Database, 2010).

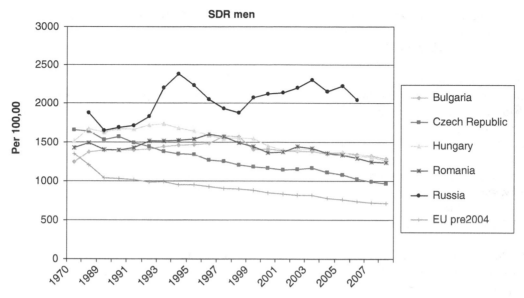

**Fig. 33.4** Standardized death rate per 100,000 in men, for selected countries (WHO Health for All Database, 2010).

(Bobak & Marmot, 2009; Leinsalu et al., 2009). As such, they offer a unique situation, happening right before our eyes, to observe both the relevance of health psychology to these phenomena and the implications of these phenomena for the field of health psychology.

The dramatic way in which health was impacted during social changes asks us to reflect on how the more individualistic health psychology constructs and models can be expanded to take into account these dimensions. An exclusively individualistic focus, conceptualizing lifestyle choices as individual decisions and cognitive determinants of health behaviours as intraindividual, can draw attention away from structural constraints and socioeconomic hierarchies (Murray & Campbell, 2003). So much of the health crisis was determined or influenced by sudden structural and systemic reforms, such as a radical dismantling of socialized medical systems, that we cannot ignore their resonance with the subjective experiences or health behaviours of individuals. We need to further draw these into the area of health psychology (Marks, 2008) and expand our understanding of the health impact of rapid

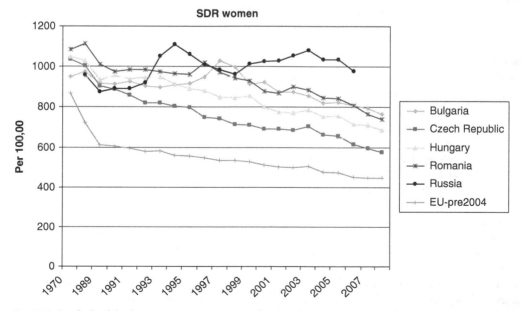

**Fig. 33.5** Standardized death rate per 100,000 in women, for selected countries (WHO Health for All Database, 2010).

social change. In analyzing the psychosocial dimensions of health changes, we are inevitably compelled to consider them as historically and locally situated, and thus reflect on the implications for health. Such a contextualized approach from health psychology is further pertinent at this time for Eastern Europe (Baban, 2006), as 20 years of transformations in health care policy and philosophy—as we shall see from our case studies—has shifted from a model of social and state responsibility for health, to neo-liberal discourses of individual responsibility, inadequacy, and blame (Todorova, Baban, Balabanova, Panayotova, & Bradley, 2006). Damaging structural conditions, cultural norms, and socioeconomic changes have been "medicalized" through stressing individual attitudes, coping abilities, and inability to adapt to change (Piko, 2002).

The social changes in Eastern Europe were, and are, contradictory, dynamic, and multilevel in their relevance to health, and particularly important in exacerbating inequalities and redefining power differentials. Thus, the phenomena in Eastern Europe also compel us to address social, economic, and health inequalities because they become impossible to ignore when observing the peaks and differentials in adverse health effects. The phenomena in Eastern Europe offer this opportunity for our profession to use the theoretical and methodological strengths of the discipline to solidly add this dimension to our research and practice endeavors.

Some of the implications for health were evident through dramatic changes in population-level demographic and epidemiological data, such as mortality, life expectancy, economic and poverty indicators, and thus offer an unprecedented look at health changes brought about by radical peace-time social change. These figures are useful in grounding us in the materiality of human lives (Murray & Campbell, 2003) during this period in Eastern Europe. Others are more subtle—they do not resonate as much in population-level indicators, but offer contextualized and historically situated opportunities for analyses of life, health, and illness in this region, and with it, a powerful understanding of people's experiences, strivings, successes, frustrations, and struggles. Qualitative health psychology has useful heuristic and methodological developments that allow us to elicit the experiences of people living through the health crisis, and to further elaborate on the contextualized nature of health problems, barriers, and behaviours. The shifting discourses of this period can serve to expand choices, or support discrimination and injustices (Murray &

Campbell, 2003). Further, studies of meanings of behaviours, health and illness, and the role of language in constructing health and the body, can be a path to expanding the theoretical basis of health psychology (Marks, 2008).

In the following pages, I will present illustrations of the East–West health divide from different countries and compare groups of countries, as well as offer several more in-depth case studies from Bulgaria and Romania to represent further dimensions of the psychosocial and a sociocultural contextualization of health.

## The East–West Health Divide

Several years ago, the widespread belief was that the transition would be over when the former communist countries on European territory joined the EU. When that happened, many believed, we would stop dividing countries into Eastern and Western Europe, sentiments expressed from an egalitarian mindset. However, this comparison between East and West, although problematic in its dichotomization and categorization, is still relevant and important to understand, so that we do not lose sight of sustained and newly emerging inequities.

The changes in Eastern Europe after World War II led to improvements in life expectancy, infant mortality, and general mortality, due to a large extent to the initial rapid gains of public health care systems. Thus, by the 1960s, there were few differences in health between Eastern and Western Europe; life expectancy was only 1–2 years apart (Zatonski, 2007). After the 1960s however, indicators in Eastern Europe became less favorable, especially as those health systems focused on infectious diseases and child mortality, while noncommunicable and chronic diseases increased. This trend, initially slow, created the East–West health divide, as life expectancy steadily increased in Western European countries from the 1960s through the first decade of the 21st century (Figures 33.2 and 33.3). The gap culminated in the aftermath of 1989, when mortality and morbidity spiked significantly in Eastern Europe, while continuing to decline in Western Europe. The sociopolitical changes in Eastern Europe were paralleled by multiple changes relevant to health and well-being, including what has been termed an "unprecedented" mortality crisis (Cockerham, 1997, 1999; Cornia & Paniccia, 2000) and a "health disaster" (Zatonski, 2007).

For many, the most evident illustration of the health gap between Eastern and Western Europe is the mortality gap (Zatonski, 2007). Consequently, we begin our discussion by examining the phenomenon of increased mortality, as it has been most striking and most troubling, and can also symbolize, in a visible way, many other changes in well-being in these countries.[4] Steep increases in mortality were evident immediately after 1989, for most countries in Eastern Europe. For some, such as Poland, the Czech Republic, and Slovenia, the trend reversed quickly, and within a few years, they recovered to previous levels (Zatonski, 2007). For others, however, recovery to pre-1989 levels became a reality only in the first decade of the 21st century, whereas for Russia, the situation is still concerning. The difference in life expectancy between the countries of Western Europe and those that joined the EU in 2004/2007 was 7 years in men and 5 years in women in 2006. For men, the difference in life expectancy between Russians and Western Europe was over 16 years in 1994 (at the peak of the crisis) and 17 years as late as 2006 (WHO Health for All Database, 2010). Even though life expectancy had slightly increased in Russia by 2008, since it had also increased in Western Europe, the gap was sustained.

The peaks in mortality were so striking that some doubted the validity of the statistics, although they were subsequently confirmed (Marmot & Bobak, 2000a). It has been estimated that these dynamics have led to millions of extra deaths during the first decade of the transition to a market economy for the region as a whole (Cornia & Paniccia, 2000). Although taking place in times of peace, the extent of loss of life is analogous to that of wartime, or to periods of famine and epidemics. It has since been concluded that the crisis was a unique phenomenon, with characteristics that are not analogous to past, similar phenomenon within Europe (Bacci, 2000) and that do not fit existing demographic models (Cornia, 2000). Additionally, analyses conclude that it cannot be considered a continuation of mortality trends existing from before 1989: although some decreases in life expectancy have been evident in Russia and countries of Eastern Europe since the mid 1960s (Zatonski, 2007), the surge in mortality observed during the first several years after 1989 is deemed quite unusual (Bacci, 2000; Shkolnikov & Cornia, 2000). Some of this health disaster's other characteristics are also unusual—it had a highest negative impact on young and middle-aged adults (rather than on children and the elderly, as might be expected), particularly working-age men.

Although a similar trend was initially observed for most countries of the region, with time, the directions of the mortality curves diverged. The study summarized in Cornia and Paniccia (2000) observed the initial rise in mortality in all 14 countries that were included in the survey. Some show a further upward trend in mortality or instabilities for several years, whereas for others the trend begins to drop soon afterward. For the Czech Republic, Slovakia, Poland, and former East Germany, for example, the surge is temporary (1990–1991), rather small, and life expectancy soon rebounded to pre-1989 levels (Cornia & Paniccia, 2000). For Bulgaria, Romania, and Hungary, on the other hand, a similar jump in mortality rates was observed initially, but the recovery occurred over a longer period. Mortality rates in Bulgaria and Romania peaked in 1995–1996, and only after 2000 can we say that they have recovered to pre-1989 levels (WHO Health for All Database, 2010; Figures 33.4 and 33.5).

Most worrying has been the mortality crisis in Russia and in some of the newly independent states at that time (Shkolnikov, McKee, & Leon, 2001), since life expectancy (particularly for men) fell for many years after the 1991 breakup of the Soviet Union. Mortality rates did not peak until 1994 (at 2,382 per 100,000, compared to 951 per 100,000 for the countries of the EU; WHO Health for All Database, 2010), and mortality trends created and sustained a very wide gender gap (Weidner & Cain, 2003). Life expectancy in 1998 fell to 57.62 for men in Russia, with a gender gap of 16.4 years (WHO Health for All Database, 2010). Much of this gender difference in mortality is attributed to cardiovascular incidents and external causes (Shkolnikov & Cornia, 2000). Additionally, increases in mortality were very much a function of age, dropping for children, remaining stable for the elderly, but increasing substantially for young and middle-aged adults (Shkolnikov et al., 2001). Mortality rates from homicides and suicides doubled from 1991 to 1994 (Shkolnikov et al., 2001). By the end of the century, homicides were 50 times higher than in Western Europe and five times higher than in the United States (Shkolnikov & Cornia, 2000). Similar patterns were observed also for Latvia, Estonia, and Lithuania, although they were of a smaller magnitude (Cornia & Paniccia, 2000).

The increase in mortality that followed immediately after 1989 has attracted the most attention because of its unexpectedness and widespread tragic outcomes. However, by 1998, the conclusions were that life expectancy in Russia had rapidly improved and was approaching the levels of the mid 1980s

(Shkolnikov et al., 2001), and analyses began to look for an explanation for this improvement. Unfortunately, before there was much time to focus on the improvement and the reasons for it, a new economic crisis in Russia, including skyrocketing inflation, devaluation of the ruble, and general destabilization, was paralleled by new jumps in mortality rates (WHO Health for All Database, 2010), accounting for millions of extra deaths during the total period of 1991–2001 than would have been predicted by rates at 1991 (Men, Brennan, Boffetta, & Zaridze, 2003). The characteristics of this wave of increased mortality are similar to that leading to the peak in 1994, and the reasons have been determined to be due to similar health conditions: cardiovascular disease and external causes, the largest absolute increase being for alcohol poisoning (Men et al., 2003).

Self-rated health (SRH), an outcome that adequately predicts mortality internationally (Bobak, Pikhart, Rose, Hertzman, & Marmot, 2000; Carlson, 1998; Idler & Benyamini, 1997), has been observed to be lower for people of Eastern Europe compared to Western Europe (Carlson, 1998, 2004). The prevalence of poor SRH was found to be different within Central and Eastern Europe, being lower in Poland and the Czech Republic, but higher in Russia, the Baltic states, and Hungary (Pikhart, 2002). Poor SRH has been shown to be high in Russia in a longitudinal population-based survey (Perlman & Bobak, 2008), and in the World Value Survey. Poor SRH was associated with higher mortality, but this association was not fully explained by alcohol consumption, smoking, life satisfaction, financial situation, and education (Perlman & Bobak, 2008).

Several studies have assessed the determinants of poor SRH for Eastern Europe (Balabanova & McKee, 2002b; Carlson, 1998; Perlman & Bobak, 2008; Pikhart, 2002). Economic insecurities (Balabanova & McKee, 2002b; Carlson, 2004), perceived control (Bobak et al., 2000; Perlman & Bobak, 2008), social capital (Carlson, 2004), and education (Balabanova & McKee, 2002b; Perlman & Bobak, 2008) were found to be associated with poorer SRH for Eastern European participants. Pikhart (2002) also found difference in SRH depending on years of education in seven national samples and five community samples of Eastern Europe. However, it has been suggested (Perlman & Bobak, 2008) that SRH in the context of the Russian health crisis might not have the same predictive determinants as mortality, since such a large portion of the deaths in Russia have been

sudden, possibly not accompanied by ill health beforehand. Also, although SRH was associated with mortality, it did not vary significantly during the years of the health crisis. The authors observe that the determinants are different—with education predicting both mortality and SRH, smoking predicting only mortality, income and life satisfaction predicting only SRH, and alcohol consumption determining the opposite, better SRH but higher mortality. They confirm that SRH has psychological dimensions, and is not simply an indicator of serious disease.

Using existing data from the World Value Survey, we observed gender, age, and marital status to be determinants of SRH in Bulgaria. During 1990–1997, there was a significant increase in unemployment rates in Bulgaria, and satisfaction with economic conditions also fell (for both men and women) (Todorova & Todorov, 2006). Although for younger men and women there was an improvement in SRH and life satisfaction, this positive change was not relevant for middle-aged and older people. So, we can say that during this period, well-being improves for younger people, and this is more visible for younger women compared with younger men. Self-rated health does not vary according to marital status in 1990, but by 1997 such difference is evident (interestingly, with people who are not married rating their health as better than those who are married). We controlled for age and observed that SRH improved for unmarried men, but remained similar for married men from 1990 to 1997. On the other hand, SRH improved for married women from 1990 to 1997, while remaining constant for unmarried women. The dynamics of SRH are different for different combinations of gender and marital status. Similarly, controlling for age, we found that life satisfaction was reduced for married men during that period yet it did not change for unmarried men. Life satisfaction dropped for married women from 1990 to 1997; however, that was a small change, compared to the more significant reduction in life satisfaction for unmarried women (Todorova & Todorov, 2006). We discuss some of the implications of these findings in the following sections.

Similar divides can be observed for children. The most recent wave of the Health Behaviour in School Aged Children survey showed highest levels of poor SRH among 11-, 13-, and 15-year-old students in Russia and the Ukraine, when comparing 41 participating countries (Currie et al., 2008). However, children in Bulgaria have rather higher levels of

SRH (Vassileva et al., 2008). Additionally, both boys and girls have higher scores of multiple health complaints in Eastern Europe compared to Western Europe (Currie et al., 2008). Multiple health complaints of children in Russia, Romania, Bulgaria, and the Ukraine are among the highest in the 41 countries. Girls in Eastern Europe additionally have lower levels of life satisfaction (Currie et al., 2008).

Studies addressing comparisons on measures of psychological distress are fewer, but also show an East–West divide. Depressive symptoms have been addressed, since depression highly contributes to disability and to somatic health (Steptoe, Tsuda, Tanaka, & Wardle, 2007), but with a reminder that the meaning of depression differs across cultures. Depressive symptoms were determined by socioeconomic status (SES),[5] and when taking a life-course perspective, were particularly influenced by current economic difficulties (Nicholson et al., 2008). Depressive symptoms and anger were observed to be higher in Russian women compared to women in the United States and compared to earlier studies in Russia (Shteyn, Schumm, Vodopianova, Hobfoll, & Lilly, 2003). This difference is evident also for young adults and children. The European Health and Behaviour Survey among university students showed significant differences in depressive symptoms between Eastern European[6] and Western European[7] students in 1989 (Steptoe & Wardle, 2001). Forty-three percent were above the cutoff points for moderate depression in Eastern Europe, compared to 23% in Western Europe. Ten years later, in 1999, we showed that the East–West difference in depressive symptoms persisted,[8] even though the students in this wave had been about 10 years old in 1989 (Wardle et al., 2004). This illustrates the continued tension and stress of life in Eastern Europe, despite the fact that, by then, the crisis had technically been over. Life satisfaction was also lower in students from Eastern Europe, although SRH did not show a difference (the proportion of poorer SRH was greater in Eastern Europe, but the average did not show a significant difference; Wardle, Steptoe, et al., 2004). Depressive symptoms were higher in countries that had higher gross national products (GNPs), since they exhibited greater ranges of income inequalities (Steptoe et al., 2007).

## Dimensions of the Health Crisis in Eastern Europe

Although the phenomenon of health decline has shown clear signs of improvement during the second decade since the transition, it continues to be of central interest both in terms of implications for the current health and well-being of the populations, and in terms of practical and theoretical lessons learned for the future. The analyses of the complexity of causes and explanations for the phenomenon continue. Understanding the health crisis must take into account this complexity of contributing factors, specific contexts, and meanings (Bobak et al., 2000; Marmot & Bobak, 2000b) and the way these different dimensions interact with each other. Many potential explanations of worsening of health status in Eastern Europe during the first years of the transition have been proposed: a continuation of trends of decreasing life expectancy from socialist times; a change in the way mortality statistics are reported, reflecting more openness; environmental factors; economic inequalities; impoverishment and malnutrition; health care reform and the inability of the health system to respond; changes in lifestyles and health behaviors (diet, physical activity, smoking, and alcohol consumption); and importantly, intense psychosocial stress of many dimensions. Some of these explanations for the mortality and morbidity crisis have been deemed inadequate to explain the sharp peaks (e.g., the continuation of preexisting trends) and also, none of them can adequately explain the specific features of the crisis on its own. Thus, I will address several dimensions that have been relevant to the experiences of people living in Eastern Europe during these two decades.

### Socioeconomic Inequalities in Health

Inequalities in health are evident between countries as well as within countries. Macro-level analyses have indicated that mortality and life expectancy are associated with the GDP of countries, as well as with the *Gini coefficient*[9] (Marmot & Bobak, 2000a). People living in conditions of lower income, with fewer years of education and lower social status, have greater morbidity, shorter lives, and spend larger parts of their lives in poorer health (Mackenbach, 2006). This report on health inequalities in Europe, commissioned by the European Commission, illustrates that the excess risk of dying could be up to 150% greater for those in lower-income groups compared with those in high-income groups.

The sociopolitical changes in Eastern Europe have been fast and in many ways radical. They have redefined the economic and political landscapes of societies, quickly shifting from planned socialist systems to privatization and market economies.

The GNP for many countries in the region decreased visibly during the first years of the transition (Figure 33.1), for example, by up to 60% in the Ukraine (Marmot & Bobak, 2000a). This freeing of the markets, as well as the removal of state support in many spheres invariably leads to greater inequality, especially affecting the unemployed, whose numbers increase (Heyns, 2005). Although income was low during socialist times, the distribution was more levelled, even when taking into account elite privileges. The new dynamics rapidly changed existing patterns of inequalities and created new ones, rapidly increasing the gap between groups.

Changes in economic conditions, for most groups, have not been of a magnitude that could directly lead to mortality from malnutrition, and the effects of poorer-quality diet and nutrients would also be slower to emerge and thus not able to explain the mortality crisis (Paniccia, 2000). In Russia, however, the percentage of people living in poverty rose visibly, up to 57% in 1992, and malnutrition had an important impact, especially for children (Shkolnikov & Cornia, 2000). Nevertheless, diseases and conditions directly associated with poverty have not increased at a magnitude that could explain the observed death rates. However, worsening of economic conditions has contributed significantly to poorer health through affecting access to health care, social capital, and psychosocial conditions, leading to stress, anxiety, insecurity, loss of status, and ultimately, to morbidity. Poor economic conditions and poverty are one pathway through which socioeconomic factors affect health, but relative inequalities and position in the social hierarchy are other, sometimes separate pathways (Marmot & Bobak, 2000a).

Relative differences in mortality between socioeconomic groups within countries are greater within Eastern European countries compared with Western European countries (Mackenbach, 2006). The Gini coefficient increased in countries of Eastern Europe, indicating greater disparities in income distribution, and its changes between 1989 and 1995 are associated with changes in life expectancy (Marmot & Bobak, 2000a). Further, the peaks in mortality observed during this period in Eastern Europe have affected predominantly middle-aged, working citizens (mostly men) in lower-paid jobs (Mackenbach, 2006; Marmot & Bobak, 2000a). Adult mortality in Eastern Europe is higher than would be expected by the GNPs of the countries (even in the period of falling GNP), so relative deprivation is considered to be key (Marmot & Bobak, 2000b). The exacerbated

relative deprivation (within countries), through the stress it evokes particularly for men, has been an important dimension of the role of socioeconomic context of health in Eastern Europe (Kopp, Skrabski, & Szedmák, 2000; Kopp & Williams, 2006). For some social groups in eastern countries, the relative deprivation people perceive when comparing their situations to those in western European countries is also an important factor, related to lower life satisfaction and lower optimism (Krastev, Dimitrova, & Garnizov, 2004), and potentially to poorer health.

Self-rated health also shows a gradient according to socioeconomic position (defined as income or education level), as illustrated in many studies of European countries (Mackenbach, 2006). Self-rated health was determined by current socioeconomic conditions in a sample of middle-aged Russian men and women (perceived social class and household income), but an important dimension was also the accumulation of hardships in childhood and over the years (Nicholson et al., 2008). In Bulgaria, income and self-assessed financial situation were both associated with SRH (Balabanova & McKee, 2002b). The subjective measure was used, since household income was considered an adequate reflection of financial status or hardship, considering the informal forms of payment and income that are widespread in the region. In the multivariate analysis, self-assessed financial situation (as well as education) was more consistently associated with SRH (Balabanova & McKee, 2002b). Pikhart (2002) also did not use income as the economic indicator, but rather developed an index of "material deprivation," measuring difficulties in buying basic items, and found an unexpectedly strong correlation with SRH in seven Eastern European countries.

Education is a particularly important socioeconomic indicator—in Eastern Europe, education level does not necessarily translate into economic advantage, but it does carry social prestige and thus has important psychosocial implications for health. Pikhart (2002) found that people with a primary-level education were twice as likely to report poor SRH compared with those having a university-level education. Leinsalu et al. (2009) observed that educational differences in mortality were not significant in the early 1990s between the four countries[10] they addressed. Yet, such differences emerged in the following decade. The changes were different among the countries: In Poland and Hungary, mortality rates decreased, except for the people with lowest education; in Estonia and Lithuania, however, mortality rates increased, except for the people in the highest educational group. External causes of death accounted for much of the educational difference in mortality (Leinsalu et al., 2009).

Self-rated health has shown associations with these individual level indicators of SES in Eastern Europe, but country level indicators of income and inequalities have also been tested: GDP, Gini coefficient, corruption index, and indicators of crime (Bobak, Murphy, Rose, & Marmot, 2007). In this analysis, SRH showed correlations with GDP, corruption index, and homicide rates, but not with society level indicators of inequalities in income distribution.

Socioeconomic gradients are observed in relation to morbidity and mortality from specific diseases, such as ischemic heart disease,[11] hypertension, and stroke, but not necessarily in the prevalence of cancer (Mackenbach, 2006). The probability for surviving for 5 years after being treated for cancer, however, is better for those in better socioeconomic positions in Europe. Symptoms of depression also show differences according to SES in Eastern Europe, including individual- and country-level indicators of inequality: Countries with higher Gini coefficients had higher levels of depressive symptoms (Steptoe et al., 2007).

## Case Study

Trends in mortality from cancers have generally not followed the steep increase characteristic for mortality from other diseases in Eastern Europe (Men et al., 2003). With few exceptions, cancer incidence and mortality is rarely discussed when analyzing the East–West health divide (Levi, Lucchini, Negri, Franceschi, & la Vecchia, 2000; Todorova, Baban, Alexandrova-Karamanova, & Bradley, 2009), which is one reason why we use it as an example. A less visible, but important dimension of the East–West health divide and of internal inequalities is that of cervical cancer incidence and mortality. Although one can argue that it does not contribute substantially to overall mortality statistics, the mortality gap from cervical cancer in Eastern Europe is striking when compared with that in Western European countries. The phenomenon of cervical cancer prevention serves as a perfect case study, encompassing many dimensions of the health issues in Eastern Europe.

The situation in Bulgaria and Romania specifically is particularly worrisome, since cervical cancer mortality has been rising during the past two decades, while it had been decreasing or stabilizing in the past (Figure 33.6). Western European countries, in contrast, show continuously decreasing rates of incidence and mortality (Levi et al., 2000). Most other Eastern European countries and Russia have also showed decreasing mortality rates, although remaining at a higher level than Western Europe. We use case examples from Bulgaria and Romania, for which this gap is most evident, to illustrate the dimensions of between-country and within-country inequalities in cervical cancer.

Although sustaining a regular screening program from the 1970s until the late 1980s that conducted routine Pap[12] smears in Bulgaria, during the restructuring of the health care system in the transitional period, this program was cancelled.[13] About 1.5 million women were screened annually in Bulgaria until 1989, after which this was abandoned and only 205,081 screening tests were reported in 1996 (Kostova & Zlatkov, 2006; Kostova, Zlatkov, & Danon, 1998). Thus, the example from Bulgaria illustrates vividly the effects of the rapid dismantling of the existing health care system on women's health and mortality.

On the other hand, in Romania, an organized national screening program did not exist either before or after 1989. A short-live program with limited success was introduced by the Romanian Ministry of Health in 1972, which approached women at their workplaces (Baban et al., 2005). However, this took place in a time of strict surveillance of pregnancies and aggressive bans on abortions and contraception (Baban, 1999), and the exams for Pap smears also allowed for the registration and monitoring of pregnancies. Romanian women avoided cervical exams as far as possible, and a general distrust of routine gynecological exams has persisted. Thus, the situation in Romania is an example of how the historical context of health care, and particularly women's reproductive health surveillance in parts of Eastern Europe, continues to resonate in the present and impacts attitudes and behaviors in ways that endangers women's health.

Thus, screening in both countries is currently conducted on an ad hoc opportunistic basis. Rather than taking Pap smears as part of a preventive program, when they are taken, it is usually as part of exams for other purposes, or when a diagnosis needs to be made. More recently, several attempts have been made by the Ministries of Health in both countries to develop contemporary strategies to reduce mortality from cervical cancer. So far, the process is stalled by lack of implementation of existing strategies and unclear legal framework, financial deficits, absence of linkages between elements of the system, and a de-emphasis on prevention as compared to curative medicine (even

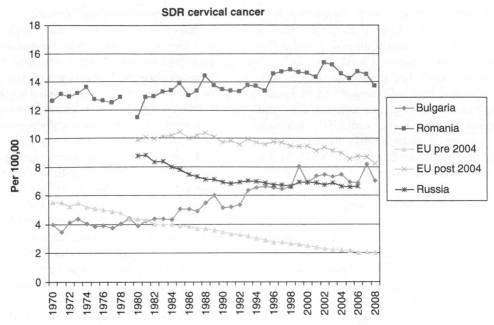

**SDR cervical cancer**

**Fig. 33.6** Cervical cancer mortality all ages, in the European Union (EU) pre-2004, EU post-2004, Bulgaria, Romania, and Russia (WHO Health for All Database, 2010).

though the laboratory capacities and expertise exist) (Avramova et al., 2005; Baban et al., 2005). Some tendencies toward a reduction in mortality from cervical cancer is being observed in the most current trends (WHO Health for All Database, 2010), which is probably due more to personal initiative; economic progress, which allows some women to pay for their tests; and greater media attention; and less to systemic and policy reforms.

### Between-country Gap

Screening for initial signs of cervical changes has reduced incidence and mortality from cancer, as illustrated by countries that have sustained such programs since the 1970s. For example, some of the lowest cervical cancer mortality rates per 100,000 women for 2006 (when the latest data were available for all cited countries) were 1.4 in Finland, 1.8 in France, and 2.0 in Sweden (WHO Health for All Database, 2010). In comparison, in Bulgaria, mortality from cervical cancer has been increasing between the late 1980 and 2006, from 3.9 per 100,000 in 1980, to 6.9 per 100,000 in 2006, which is more than three times the rate for Western European Union countries (Danon, Valerianova, & Ivanova, 2004; WHO Health for All Database, 2010). The highest levels of mortality were observed in 1999 (8.0 per 100,000), followed by a small drop (WHO Health for All Database, 2010). For Romania, the mortality rate was 14.72 per 100,000 women in 2006, which was the highest mortality rate

in Europe, and this has unfortunately been true for the past 20 years. This rate is seven times higher than the average of Western European Union countries (Figure 33.6). The highest rate was observed in 2002, at 15.37 per 100,000 (WHO Health for All Database, 2010). In summary, the gap in cervical cancer mortality rates is substantial, since the average in Eastern European countries[14] (8.75 per 100,000) is four times higher than that of Western European countries (2.03 per 100,000) in 2006. The mortality rates in Russia for 2006 were 6.62 per 100,000.

### Within-country Gaps

For Bulgaria and Romania disparities in access to screening are evident also within the countries. Women there face structural barriers that limit motivation, access, and uptake. In our international study, we investigated the prevalence of screening and its determinants, the existing barriers in both countries having to do with the organization of the health care system, and the doctor–patient relationship, as well as perceived stress and social support, which can contribute to inequalities in screening (Avramova et al., 2005; Baban et al., 2005). In nationally representative samples of women 20–65 years of age from Bulgaria and Romania, we found that relatively few women have ever had Pap smears—less than half in both countries: in Bulgaria (45.9%) and in Romania (21%) (Avramova et al., 2005; Baban et al., 2005).

Screening history differed according to sociodemographic conditions and depending on the extent of barriers faced in the health care system for both Bulgarian and Romanian women, thus offering an illustration of dimensions of inequalities (Todorova et al., 2009). Our study showed socioeconomic disparities in access to Pap smears, which further elucidate the low screening rates. The dimensions of inequalities were similar to those previously identified in the literature (Newmann & Garner, 2005), but in some cases the disparities between groups were very large. For both countries, women who had a lower probability of having had a Pap smear were those who had fewer socioeconomic resources (who lived in smaller towns, had fewer years of education, and lower financial resources), as well as those who were younger, unmarried, and were of ethnic minorities. Quite striking were the disparities between different ethnic groups. For example, 50.9% of women of Bulgarian ethnicity reported being screened, whereas 39.2% of Turkish and 8.8% of Roma women were screened. The situation was analogous in Romania, where only 5.2% of Roma women reporting being screened.

Socioeconomic conditions were also related to the extent to which the women reported facing health system barriers to screening (difficulties in access, transportation, price, communication with providers, etc.). The extent of facing systemic barriers was higher for minority women, for those from smaller towns (and thus with problematic access), and for women with fewer years of education and poorer perceived economic situation.

As an avoidable cause of death through screening, cervical cancer mortality is a vivid indicator of inequalities between and within countries, as well as of health system functioning. It also has gendered and psychosocial dimensions, which we will address below.

## Gendered Dimensions of Health Inequalities in Eastern Europe

The gendered dimensions and inequalities of the mortality and morbidity phenomena in Eastern Europe are quite striking and always intertwined with other dimensions. Thus, in this section, I will delineate some aspects of the complex ways in which social changes in Eastern Europe have influenced men's and women's lives differently, since the constructions of masculinity and femininity have also been changing (Kotzeva, 1999). Gender is a social, cultural, and psychological phenomenon, taking shape in social interaction. Gender constructions are historical and contextual, and thus have implications for health in the particular historical context of the transitional period. Importantly,

men's and women's health is closely interconnected. For example, in a study on the importance of life meaning for health in the transitional years, the authors observed that male mortality in specific regions of Hungary is more strongly correlated with averaged life meaning measures for the women in these regions, rather than for the men (Skrabski, Kopp, Rózsa, Réthelyi, & Rahe, 2005).

The social, political, and economic changes brought on evident consequences, particularly for men's health, as strikingly illustrated by the rise in mortality in working-aged men. This includes increases in men's suicides, cardiovascular incidences, alcohol poisoning, and other fatal events (Cockerham, 1999; Marmot & Bobak, 2000b; Möller-Leimkuhler, 2003; Shkolnikov et al., 2001; Weidner & Cain, 2003). The stress of unemployment has been one of the main sources of acute stress for the people of Eastern Europe, particularly considering that unemployment was almost an unknown phenomenon before 1989. Unemployment rates rose for all, but in some cases, the percent of unemployed men was higher than of women. Constructions of masculinity, having to do with the male breadwinner role, led to more negative and stigmatized meanings of men's unemployment compared to women's (Möller-Leimkuhler, 2003). These meanings could have had health implications, even though the direct economic consequences of being left without a job were particularly harsh for unemployed single mothers. Awareness of economic inequalities, particularly relative deprivation, the perceived position in social hierarchies, and social comparisons (Kopp, 2007), seems to have impacted men more than women. In Russia, Poland, and the Czech Republic, it was found that symptoms of depression were related to SES: levels of depressive symptoms were higher for women, but current disadvantage was more likely to impact psychological distress in men than in women (Nicholson et al., 2008). In Hungary, in 1988, lower income did not relate to psychological distress (depression) or to SRH for women, but it did so for men. By 1995, low income was related to poorer SRH for both men and women, but for men the relationship was mediated more strongly through depression (Kopp et al., 2000; Kopp & Williams, 2006).

An important concern has been that of a potential backlash for women and increasing gender inequalities at women's expense, as a result of the transition (Corrin, 1992; Einhorn, 1993; Funk, 1993; Gal & Kligman, 2000). Although in some aspects women were equal participants in the labor force before 1989, trends were already moving toward women losing this emancipation and a worsening of women's status and living conditions (reviewed by Molyneux, 1995).

Although mortality and life expectancy rates are important, it has been argued that they underestimate existing problems, since the extent of chronic illness becomes obscured (Andreev, McKee, & Shkolnikov, 2003). Much of the mortality in the transitional period, especially in Russia, has been due to sudden deaths, yet the chronic burden of disease is also important to address, and it is relevant particularly for women. Women's mortality has not increased at the same rate as men's (Figure 33.4 and 33.5); however, morbidity levels for women are higher than those for men (Szaflarski, 2001; Wroblewska, 2002). When taking into account expectancy of healthy life (i.e., years spent without chronic illness and disability), another dimension of the East–West health divide emerges. The probability of living in a healthy state shows a steeper decline for countries of Eastern Europe[15] compared with Western Europe,[16] and a very steep decline for Russia, which starts earlier than for the other countries (Andreev, McKee, et al., 2003). In summary, Russian men live fewer years in good health compared with men in Western Europe, but this is even truer for Russian women. This relative burden of poorer health is most striking for Russian women, but the same pattern in evident for other Eastern European countries, although at smaller magnitudes (Andreev, McKee, et al., 2003).

Women in Eastern Europe work in lower paid jobs, and even in similar jobs, there is an important income gap (Van der Lippe & Fodor, 1998). Women have a greater amount of tasks and workloads when they combine private and public spheres, and are more often parenting as single parents (as well as unemployed single parents). The increased cost and less availability of affordable childcare during the transition has also been relevant (Corrin, 1992; Lobodzinska, 1996). Domanksi (2002), working in six countries of Europe, shows that being in poverty is more probable for women than for men. Other studies have also shown greater gender economic inequalities and the "feminization of poverty" (Fodor, 2002), which becomes even more evident for older women.

From another perspective, since women work in lower-paid, usually service jobs, these jobs seem to have been less vulnerable to unemployment (Van der Lippe & Fodor, 1998). Education levels have been high among women, and it is hypothesized that this has been protective for them during the transition, since returns on education have been more substantial (Heyns, 2005). Perceptions of control, initiative, and choices also open up for women, particularly for young women (Kopp et al., 2000; Todorova & Kotzeva, 2003a). Our work on childlessness in Bulgaria has shown that becoming a mother remains central to a women's identity (Panayotova & Todorova, 2009; Todorova & Kotzeva, 2006); at the same time, more choices of roles and definitions of femininity have emerged, which is illustrated in the next Case Study.

## Case Study

The increase in mortality is visible mainly for men in Bulgaria, but for women it also increased, reaching a maximum (1,029 per 100,000) in 1997 (WHO Health for All Database, 2010). Life expectancy in Bulgaria was 68.29 years for men in 1989, reaching a low of 66.97 in 1997 and rebounding to 69.84 in 2008. Life expectancy for women was 74.89 in 1989, and although the drop was clear in 1997 (to 73.82), it was not as dramatic as it was for men, and has recovered to 77.11 in 2008 (WHO Health for All Database, 2010).

In a study we conducted using two waves of data from the World Values Survey (Inglehart et al., 2004), we followed shifts in values related to gender roles in Bulgaria from the early 1990s until the peak of the health crisis in 1997 (Todorova & Todorov, 2006). Gender values were assessed with questions about determining the greater right to a job in times of job scarcity, the necessity of children for a fulfilling life for women, the acceptability of a woman as a single mother, whether a working mother can be a nurturing mother, and whether both partners should contribute to the household income. We found that the importance of children as defining feminine identity was less strong from one wave to the next, and respondents endorsed to a greater extent the value that working women can also be nurturing mothers. These shifts are relative, since in other studies we still confirm strong pronatalistic cultural values and the motherhood mandate, with women being identified and self-identifying themselves predominantly as mothers (Kotzeva & Todorova, 2005; Todorova & Kotzeva, 2003b; Todorova & Kotzeva, 2006).

There were differences between men and women in the extent to which they held egalitarian gender values. Men more strongly endorsed the value that men have more of a right to a job in hard times, whereas women are more strongly in favor of the idea that both partners should contribute to the household income. Men were also less inclined to accept a woman's preference to have a child as a single mother, compared to women. In summary, from the early 1900s to the later 1990s, based on these data, women endorse egalitarian values to a greater extent than did men, an observation also made for Slovenia (Frieze et al., 2003).

Thus, we observed shifts in values regarding women's identities as mothers, but no observable shift in regard to the value of men taking on the responsibility for the economic security of the family, particularly in time of difficulties. The importance of the family also increased during this period, most probably having to do with the time of economic instability. More people feel that family is very important, increasing from 76.1% in 1990 to 87.9% in 1997, when economic hardships were most significant (Todorova & Todorov, 2006).

Our analyses were in contrast to conclusions in the literature, which find that married men in Eastern Europe are more protected in their health (Watson, 1995). The data from the WVS show that, for married men, there is a decrease in life satisfaction and SRH by the end of the 1990s. Married women and single men, on the other hand, were more protected during the critical period of the transition. Cultural constructions of masculinity and femininity most probably played an important role: married men are expected to be responsible for sustaining the family economically, especially in such critical times and thus are exposed to greater fear of failure; whereas married women are expected to sustain supportive social ties and nurturing relationships, which in turn protects their health.

After 1989, there was a sense of more choices in the construction of women's identity. Whether these choices are truly realistic for most women is a question, yet the available discourses do offer perceptions of possibilities and initiative. A more or less uniform model for women's identity was available in the 1980s and earlier (Kotzeva, 1999), whereas by the 1990s, options for different ways of combining work and family emerge for women— including not working, or working part-time. Ideas of female sexuality and body were also shifting. For example, women are getting married and having children later than previously (National Statistical Institute, 2004).

The economic crisis and unemployment have, however, threatened important signifiers of masculinity in the region (Van der Lippe & Fodor, 1998) having to do with being the provider. Roles associated with power and political influence were also threatened and lost for many. Activity in the political sphere opened up greater expectations, particularly for men, to be actively involved in the public sphere (Watson, 1995). As Courtenay points out, when the existing signifiers of masculinity are threatened or out of reach, men seek other ways of defining masculinity, such as risk taking, violence, and alcohol consumption (Courtenay, 2000). Constructions of masculinity are tied to acceptable ways of coping with acute personal, economic, and social stresses. The stress-reducing behaviors favored by existing cultural constructions of masculinity in the region tend to be more health-impairing ones (Courtenay, 2000; Watson, 1995).

Thus, the increased importance of traditional constructions of masculinity with limited alternatives and the increased social and personal perception of economic and political responsibility for men, as well as the preference for particular ways of coping with these stressors, can contribute to men's health risk during times of social change.

### Health Care System

The role of the destabilized health care system in increased morbidity and mortality is also important. Changes in the structure, organization, and responsiveness of the system have been widespread. To estimate the contribution of health system–level changes to the mortality gradient, one approach is to analyze the trends in preventable conditions and those treatable by medical care. According to some analyses, the characteristics of health conditions that were at the core of the mortality crisis are not those that would immediately increase from a poorly functioning health care system. If the health care system is seen to contribute most to preventing infectious diseases as "avoidable causes of death" (Cornia & Paniccia, 2000), then these aspects of health care have not contributed significantly to the steep rise in mortality, possibly with some exceptions for Russia (Shkolnikov & Cornia, 2000). However, deaths from ischemic heart disease, cerebrovascular disease, alcohol poisoning, and other primary contributors would be mitigated by a smoothly responsive health care system (Andreev, Nolte, Shkolnikov, Varavikova, & McKee, 2003). These authors conclude that if the health care system had been functioning in Russia as it was in the United Kingdom during this period, life expectancy for men would be increased by 1.7 years. It is possible that the implication of health care system restructuring has been different for the different countries in the area, increasing health-related expenditures in some, while decreasing them in others (UNDP, 2007/2008). Davis (2000) hypothesizes that, in the first group, in spite of a picture of worsening health and mortality indicators, the existing health systems might have prevented more serious deterioration, whereas for the second group (which includes Russia and Bulgaria), the rise in morbidity and mortality might be higher than would be explained by a rise in illness incidence (Davis, 2000). Additionally, there are more indirect aspects of the impact of health system transformations—limited access, attitudes that demotivate health-seeking behavior, etc.—and although not contributing significantly to the surge in mortality, they contribute to morbidity, stress, and disillusionment in many citizens (Kotzeva & Todorova, 2005; Panayotova & Todorova, 2006; Todorova et al., 2006).

## Case Study

Cervical cancer is an excellent example of an oncological disease easily preventable if a well-organized health system structure is functioning. Thus, the success in reducing cervical cancer incidence is a reflection of the workings of the health care system (Avramova et al., 2005; Baban et al., 2005).

Our findings indicate that health care system issues having to do with inadequate screening in Bulgaria are not related to the capacity of the system. There is sufficient capacity to conduct cervical cancer screening in Bulgaria, in terms of material resources (equipment, consumables, network of medical facilities, and cytological laboratories) and human skill and resources. Procedures for collecting and processing smears, and reporting of results are well established. As a matter of fact, there are concerns about underuse of the existing capacity of health facilities and laboratories, in view of the falling demand for screening in the 1990s (Avramova et al., 2005). Additionally, both in Romania and Bulgaria, the role of screening for controlling cervical cancer is widely acknowledged and supported. In Romania, even though there is less satisfaction with the capacity of the system to conduct screening in terms of material resources (equipment, consumables, and cytological laboratories) and qualified human resources (Baban et al., 2005), the main reasons for the low rates of coverage are still identified as having to do with organization and coordination among elements of the system. For one thing, communication within the health care system, and with other relevant institutions outside the system, was found to be problematic. There is limited engagement of policy makers with frontline practitioners who are confused by health care reforms, cervical cancer legislation, and the way that cervical cancer prevention is meant to be managed. There is lack of agreement about who should be taking the lead on communication efforts—health care staff, public health authorities, or civil society. Little information about cervical cancer prevention is available in the community, thought this has been changing in the last few years.

Other health care system barriers came from the fact that the existing legal and regulatory framework is interpreted in various ways by physicians and policy makers. Existing strategies and documentation have not been translated into explicit treatment guidelines on screening intervals, target groups, and screening coverage goals, and these are not linked to earmarked and allocated funding. Most providers rely on their basic medical training and personal opinions about who to screen and when. This situation has led to considerable variations in accessibility and quality of service provided. Without guidelines, this has led to a pattern of overtesting of young, low-risk women and limited screening in older higher-risk women. The result is that, even though the majority of women interviewed had visited the gynecologist in the past 5 years, only half of those had ever had a cervical smear (Avramova et al., 2005). Most women reported that their provider had never suggested a smear, pointing to the need to encourage gynecologists to remind clients about the importance of cervical screening when women visit them for other reasons.

In Bulgaria, the responsibility for cervical screening has changed several times over the past few years. Before the political reform of the early 1990s, gynecologists were responsible for screening, but this changed to general practitioners (GP), in an effort to demedicalize the health care system. However, because GP payment schedules were low, GPs felt untrained or unmotivated, clients were unhappy, and there was considerable discontent on the part of the gynecologists, this change was both unpopular and ineffective in raising screening coverage rates. Since 2003, screening has again become the responsibility of gynecologists, with referrals done by GPs. For their Pap smears to be covered by the National Health Insurance Fund (NHIF), women need a referral from a GP to a gynecologist. However, the NHIF has a system of rationed care (Rechel & McKee, 2009), which means that referrals are scarce, and providers prefer to save them for acute need rather than for prevention. This system can also foster potential inequalities through favoritism and connections. Both women and providers state that this practice significantly reduces the probability of conducting preventive smears (Avramova et al., 2005; Todorova et al., 2006):

There are a set number of free referrals for smear tests, and I have to play God, and decide who should get it and who shouldn't—it is not right for me to determine this according to my own views. (GP, small town)

As a result, even though theoretically covered by the NHIF, the price of the smear becomes an issue, since often the only way for a woman to obtain a smear is to circumvent the GP referral system and pay for the procedure herself. Thus, if they can afford it, women prefer to pay out of pocket in the private sector, rather than to fight for scarce monthly referral slips (Balabanova & McKee, 2002a, 2004). And many of those who cannot afford to bypass the referral system through the private sector do not participate in screening.

Women shared that they face barriers in getting a Pap smear, which included lack of insurance, absence of an ongoing relationship with primary care, having to devote too much time to travelling or waiting, the existing attitude within the system and culture of focusing on curative care, and an absence of initiative on the part of providers (Avramova et al., 2005; Baban et al., 2005). Other barriers that women reported were absence of sources of information and having to travel far for services. Some women reported traumatizing experiences, pain, and even harassment during exams. The most important barriers women reported were similar for Bulgarian and Romanian women (Avramova et al., 2005; Baban et al., 2005), even though the order of importance is slightly different.

Not having had a Pap smear was predicted strongly by the structural barriers women reported having come across in the health care system, and these barriers also mediated the effects of SES on screening history for both countries. Women who lived in more difficult socioeconomic situations also reported more significant barriers that were related to their screening history (Todorova et al., 2009).

On the whole, participants were quite disappointed with the health care reforms, in particular with the "GP as gatekeeper" model recently implemented in Bulgaria. Respondents also expressed discontent with certain shortages of supplies, but mostly with what the women perceive as commercialization of health care, corruption and informal payments, and depersonalization of care (Avramova et al., 2005).

Providers, on the other hand, shifted between nostalgia for the structured system of the past, critique of the current system, blaming individual women for their lack of awareness, or worrying about the consequences of health care reform for their health. Some providers saw women as suffering victims in the ongoing health care reforms, who have been left to care for themselves (Todorova et al., 2006). Others saw women as irresponsible, passive as a result of socialist health care mentality, needing control, surveillance, and sanctions in order to present for regular screening.

There was considerable support for an obligatory annual preventive gynecological check-up with sanctions such as fines and increases in monthly insurance premiums and user fees.

The conclusion is that, for asymptomatic women to navigate the rather chaotic system, they have to have adequate information about cervical cancer and prevention and about where to go, and they must be empowered to persist in requests for screening. This aspect of cervical cancer prevention will be further elaborated in the following section.

## Psychosocial and Behavioral Aspects

The dimensions discussed in the preceding Case Study are important for illuminating the complexity of health problems in Eastern Europe; however, the impact of psychosocial stress during the past two decades is deemed crucial to explaining the phenomena in Eastern Europe (Cornia & Paniccia, 2000; Marmot & Bobak, 2000b; Shkolnikov & Cornia, 2000) and is of central interest to health psychology. The experience of acute stress, unpredictability, and disillusionment can explain the specific characteristics of the mortality crisis in Eastern Europe, including the main causes of death and the temporal dynamics. The situation created by the rapid transformation of social, political, economic, and medical systems provided the exact conditions needed for acute stress: unexpected, disorienting changes resulting in new definitions of professional and interpersonal roles, new rules, and new values. These require new social, economic, psychological, coping, and other resources, which for many people are unavailable or unknown. This was true for the older and middle-aged working adults at that time, but even for younger ones who felt that the new rules were unclear, or that the transitional period was one of stagnation and loss of many of their productive years. Additionally, many felt it required a reevaluation of life's meaning and purpose, or even renunciation of one's previous life.

An empirical study did illustrate that meaning in life during the years of the transition was negatively associated with population-level mortality rates in 150 regions in Hungary, as well as with individual level assessments of well-being and SRH (Skrabski et al., 2005). These findings suggest that disorientation and reformulation of life's meaning during this period could have had important implications for well-being in the region.

Unemployment affected health both through immediate material deprivation and also through the stress of stigma, loss of identity, and purpose.

To avoid unemployment and to readapt in the rapidly changing labor market (including an expanding gray economy), people had to radically and immediately redefine their skills, approaches, and roles. For those who are employed, work that is stressful and requires high effort not balanced by adequate rewards is associated with poorer SRH (Salavecz et al., 2010). Even when employed, the stress of job insecurity was much higher during this period in Eastern European countries compared with previous years. Job insecurity was highest in the Czech Republic, Hungary, and Poland when comparing 16 countries in Europe, and was correlated with poor SRH and other health indicators (László et al., 2010).

Social ties and social participation were also affected through loss of jobs, migration, emigration, conflicts, and divorces, and social support decreased (Kopp et al., 2000). Social capital is related to SRH in Eastern Europe, although the connection is weaker than it is for economic hardships (Carlson, 2004).

Acute psychosocial stress can exacerbate those conditions that have most contributed to the morbidity and mortality crisis, such as sudden death from cardiovascular events, accidents, and alcohol poisoning (Cornia & Paniccia, 2000). The increased alcohol consumption including binge drinking is most likely provoked by higher psychosocial stress and is used as a stress reliever. Cardiovascular mortality, on the other hand, could be a direct result of acute stress, or is itself mediated by the effects of alcohol (Men et al., 2003).

As the events were rapid, unpredictable, and powerful, individuals' perception of having a sense of control, a role in decision making, and input in their social and professional lives was undermined. Perceived control over one's life has been shown to be low in Eastern Europe compared to Western Europe, and to be an important dimension of the East–West health divide (Bobak et al., 2000). Carlson (1998) analyzed SRH as it is related to economic conditions, social integration (participation in civic activities), and perceived control, using data from 25 European countries. In Eastern Europe, people felt they had less control over their lives than in Western Europe; they had lower economic satisfaction and poorer SRH, which on the other hand, was related to perceptions of control in all countries. In this analysis, people in Bulgaria had the lowest perceptions of life control, with Bulgarian women the very lowest—they evaluated their health as lowest, they had the least economic satisfaction, and the lowest level of perceived control and

decision making (Carlson, 1998). However, our analysis (Todorova & Todorov, 2006) showed differences according to age and gender within Bulgaria with time. For younger women, there was an increase in perceptions of control, whereas for men there was a tendency toward a decrease during 1990–1997 For older people, there was no increase in perceived control in 1997, and older women were more vulnerable than older men. There are no significant differences in perceived life control depending on marital status, and that is true for both 1990 and 1997 (Todorova & Todorov, 2006). Similarly, perceived control significantly decreased with time in Hungary, based on representative independent samples in 1988 and 1995, whereas depression visibly increased (Kopp et al., 2000). Perceived control was related to SRH also in the study based on data from the New Barometer surveys (Bobak et al., 2000). It was important as a mediator of the health consequences of economic vulnerability.

In summary, these phenomena of intensified stressful life events and chronic difficulties disrupted social relations, reduced perceived ability to cope, and lower perceived control, and could have impacted health through neuroendocrine and immune pathways (Marmot & Bobak, 2000b; Miller, Chen, & Cole, 2009; Uchino, 2006), as well as changing health behaviours.

Lifestyle explanations for the worsening health in Eastern Europe have been stressed by some (Cockerham, 1997; Feachem, 1994) and given less weight by others, who point to their inability to explain the crisis (Marmot & Bobak, 2000b). Lifestyle explanations have been assessed as inadequate to explain the mortality peaks, particularly because the implications of such changes would be observed over a longer time frame (with the exception of alcohol poisoning), compared to the immediate shifts observed in the first years of the transition (Shkolnikov & Cornia, 2000). Yet, they certainly contribute to health status and well-being, and their effects would be evident in the longer time frame of the transition. The acute and chronic stress experienced by people in the region could change health behaviours and thus impact health. From analyzing the context in Eastern Europe we can conclude that "lifestyle" cannot be assumed to be behaviours and values about health freely chosen by an individual (Cockerham, 1997). Social circumstances, large-scale reforms, and structural constraints change the meaning of lifestyle to make it much more contingent on circumstances, constraints, and social relations.

## Case Study

Psychosocial phenomena are of central importance in explaining the changes in health and aspects of the East–West health divide, particularly the high levels of acute stress that were characteristic of the early years of the transitional period. As described above, health system functioning and coordination is very relevant to the East–West divide in relation to cervical cancer incidence and mortality. Additionally, however, cervical cancer prevention has important psychosocial dimensions, which relate mainly to the role of stress, social support, beliefs, and attitudes in preventive health behaviors.

An important question we had was, considering that women who were more economically disadvantaged had a lower probability of having had a Pap smear test, what were the reasons for this inequality and how were they interconnected—was this related to the higher levels of stress they lived under, different attitudes and beliefs about the smear, or the significant barriers in the health care system they were facing, including affordability? We hypothesized that if people are living in stressful daily circumstances and have lower social support, for example, they would be less inclined to address preventive needs (Wardle, McCaffery, Nadel, & Atkin, 2004).

Romanian and Bulgarian women with overwhelming daily demands, with lower life satisfaction and control, with limited social support, or with social networks that have beliefs that forbid visits to gynecologists (all of which were exacerbated during the transitional period) have less possibility of engaging in screening. We did observe that women in both countries with higher experiences of perceived stress and low social support were less likely to have had Pap smears. Women with fewer resources had higher perceived stress and lower perceived social support, as well as a lower likelihood to have had a cervical smear (Avramova et al., 2005; Baban et al., 2005).

We also took into consideration cognitive dimensions of screening behaviors (Aiken, Gerend, & Jackson, 2001; Ajzen & Madden, 1986; Becker & Rosenstock, 1987; Bish, Sutton, & Golombok, 2000; Rosenstock, 1990), specifically the beliefs about the disease and the attitudes toward the screening test (Sutton & Rutherford, 2005). We used the constructs of perceived susceptibility to cervical cancer, perceived severity of cervical cancer, "costs"[17] of cervical smears versus benefits of smears,[17] attitudes toward screening, perceived behavioral control,[18] self-efficacy,[19] and subjective norms[20] (Bish et al.,

2000). Perceptions of susceptibility to and severity of the disease were not different depending on socioeconomic conditions for the Bulgarian women; however, women living in worse conditions perceived the benefits of the test as lower, and the "costs" as higher, and their attitudes were less positive. For Romanian women, poorer economic conditions were related to greater susceptibility to the disease, lower perceived benefits, and greater perceived "costs."

Returning to our main question regarding the reasons why women with more vulnerable socioeconomic situation were less likely to have been screened, we wanted to know if the effect of SES on screening history is mediated by perceived stress and social support, by cognitive factors, and/or by systemic barriers. We found that the structural barriers faced in the health care system were very important reasons for socioeconomic inequalities in screening history, even when their relevance was modelled in the context of beliefs and attitudes toward screening. The structural barriers the women faced in the health care system predicted not ever having had a cervical smear, and also mediated the effects of SES on screening, analyzed separately in both countries (Todorova & Bradley, 2006).

Women's perceptions of the "costs" of the test were also important and consistent reasons for lower screening history ("cost" included fear and stress from the test, discomfort, embarrassment, pain, and requiring too much time, whereas "price" was considered a systemic barrier). The perceived cost of the smear also was a major mediator of the effects of SES on screening history: Women with fewer resources saw the test as much more costly, and this was one of the reasons why they were less likely to have had a smear.

We also used intentions for future screening as an outcome variable for testing the different models to predict determinants of women's future behavior. The women in the study had rather high intentions for getting cervical smears, with 46.9% stating that they were confident or completely confident that they would have a Pap smear in the next 3 months (Avramova et al., 2005; Baban et al., 2005). When modelling future intentions for screening, however, the systemic barriers did not preserve their independent effects as mediators of the effects of SES on screening history as they did when modelling screening history (Todorova et al., 2009). Thus, we can conclude that when constructing their future intentions, women do not fully take into account the structural barriers they encounter, and they can preserve a more positive intent about what they will do in the future.

The quantitative data show that Bulgarian and Romanian women have a generally positive attitude toward preventive health practices (Avramova et al., 2005; Baban et al., 2005). Qualitative data confirm this, while also highlighting the complexity of the meanings of screening (Todorova, Baban, Kotzeva, & Bradley, 2008; Todorova & Bradley, 2008). It is important to understand the meanings of screening and preventive behaviors in the specific context of transition, health care reform, and cultural values related to health and prevention, as this can shed light on why intentions to present for screening are not always carried through (Mielewczyk & Willig, 2007).

Some women protest the regular presentation for screening, seeing it as medicalization of women's health and the intrusion of the medical gaze. In some cases, this was within a conceptualization of the body and femininity as private and mysterious, which carries traditional cultural meanings of female modesty and silence. However, the avoidance of encounters with the medical gaze is also a product of current negative experiences that women have in exposing the private body in a medical situation. Multiple encounters with barriers, authoritarian attitudes of providers, rising expenses and informal payments, insults and even harassment, lead women to avoid contact with the system, particularly in the absence of symptoms.

The avoidance of exposure to the medical gaze can also be seen as an outcome of experiences of control and surveillance from the medical and political system in the last few decades, particularly relevant for Romania during the pre-1989 era of control of reproductive health (Baban, 1999). The historical legacies of a paternalistic and intrusive health care system that monitors women's sexuality, sexual behaviors, and particularly, pregnancies and abortions, may also continue to reverberate and shape women's meanings of screening. Ultimately, as a result of the systemic problems, fear, embarrassment, and resistance to being intruded upon, many women state that they see a doctor only as a last resort, when they are "really" sick; some of them were proud that they had not needed or had decided not to see doctors, with the exception of the last weeks during their pregnancies: "When it is too much and I can't stand it, then [I go]" (Pavlina, Bulgaria).

Others, however, mainly younger women, have internalized visits to their gynecologist, including for screening, as "part of being a woman." They accept that gynecological exams are unpleasant but should be endured, or they can detach from the exam. They normalize screening and regular gynecological visits.

Bulgarian and Romanian women frequently referred to "national character" as an explanation for low rates of screening and prevalent avoidance of prevention. Statements such as "Bulgarians are generally negligent [about their health]" can be seen as a rationalization of not presenting for regular screening. The essentialistic explanation of national character, as something which is inevitable and difficult to change, offers comfort and acceptance of inactivity. On the other hand, this is also related to identity and belonging to a particular cultural context and local community. Behavior and attitudes toward prevention, which are perceived as being contradictory to those of the surrounding community, are difficult to implement and sustain. Thus, some avoid behavior that could be interpreted as an obsession with health, because of fear of being labelled as self-centered, a label particularly "inappropriate" for women.

For older women, an ambivalence about regular checkups was situated within a preference to be affiliated with the cultural norm of rejecting obsessions with health, and as enduring health problems as a strength and particularly of women's sacrifice. Even when they focus on prevention, it is for others:

> I myself take care of my health, mainly in order not to create troubles for those around me, not so much because I am afraid of illnesses. A person should be responsible and protect others from troubles, even forgetting about oneself, I see it that way. (Stefka, age 50, Bulgaria)

In the dilemma about localization of responsibility, the question of choice versus obligation certainly appears. According to some participants, women should have the right to choose or refuse preventive health care/ Pap smears. Others, more doubtful of the proactive stance, suggested that it might be useful for the system to control preventive medical exams, including Pap smears. Some suggested that "punitive actions" should be taken against women for ignoring preventive exams. (In many cases, this ambivalence was evident within a few sentences of the same narrative):

> There should definitely be compulsory exams. They have to think of something—like with immunizations, that are compulsory, and they immunize people born during a given year, it has to be compulsory, . . . so that the patient is obliged to go so that the doctor can see her, it has to be compulsory so that it can *make* women go, the doctor has to do it, something really compulsory. (Shirin, age 29)

Having experienced organized mass screening programs, older women both longed for the predictability of these programs and protested their invasiveness. Thus, ironically, even though they prefer a top-down system of screening and a model of more passive individuals, they exhibit more resistance to the normalization of screening and thus do not automatically adhere to the pressure to be screened. In this way, they can be more vocal about the barriers in the system and about their negative experiences. For middle-aged and older women, screening is tied to avoidance of intervention, as well as responsibility to others rather than self.

Younger women, however, saw themselves as being in a position to challenge the "national character" and perceived norms of female sacrifice, through their own behaviors and through motivating their mothers. Younger women situated their identities within a discourse of change and individual choice, and thus felt they could challenge existing norms and the prevailing passivity regarding prevention. They were more vocal about prevention being an individual initiative, and they saw a reliance on organized programs as less relevant. In this, they have become more accepting of the power of medicalization and susceptible to overscreening (often recommended as routine every 6 months). They normalize frequent and routine screening and gynecological visits, and Pap smears are associated with the way they construct femininity.

In summary, we identified multiple nuances and tensions in the meanings of screening, particularly in relationship to its normalization as a gendered behavior. Women's experiences exemplify an interweaving of psychosocial and cultural considerations that have implications for screening behavior. Women also negotiate the ambiguities of the historical legacies of social health care. The control of a paternalistic model of health care is protested, and at the same time they resort to it in their attempts to propose ideas for increasing uptake (through obligatory exams and sanctions). In these themes, the generational dimensions were quite evident. It must be stressed, however, that the generational dimensions of meanings of screening intersect, to a large extent, with the dimension of socioeconomic situation. The younger women in the samples tended to be also employed in well-paying jobs and tended to attend private gynecological consultations and thus screenings. As such, in some cases, they were being pulled into the commercialization of health care in the private sector, which resulted in overscreening. This can also desensitize to the significant structural and systemic barriers to preserving women's health.

## Conclusion

The events in Eastern Europe illustrate the importance of bringing a contextual lens to health psychology phenomena. Behavior change models need to take into account meanings of health protective, preventive, or risk behaviors. Lifestyles cannot be conceptualized as purely individual choices, but are co-constructed within cultural values and contingent upon material conditions. And concepts such as personal control become more useful if they are understood as resonating with the conditions within a society.

The gendered dimensions of health are particularly evident in Eastern Europe. Men's health has been seriously affected during the transition, and men's health status and behaviour has important implications for women's health and vice versa (Sabo, 1999; Skrabski et al., 2005). Health promotion interventions in Eastern Europe, informed by local meanings of gender, would also benefit from a relational gendered framework.

Our discussion has illustrated that health care reform in Eastern Europe needs to be undertaken in multiple directions simultaneously—structural and policy changes, health promotion, behaviour change interventions—to ensure that health indicators will continue to improve. Interventions can not be directed only toward knowledge or cognitive and psychological dimensions, since significant disparities and barriers stem from the organization and reform of the health care system, which require legislative and policy reconsiderations. At the same time, empowering individuals with stress-reducing and behaviour change approaches, grounded in local contexts, will also be beneficial in their efforts to mitigate the consequences of this stressful situation. These efforts to improve health can be most successful when conduced through participatory approaches and coordinated with community groups.

## Notes

1. Unless otherwise specified, by "Eastern Europe" I will mean the countries located in the area of Central and Eastern Europe, including Russia and the newly independent states from the former Soviet Union. Frequently in the literature, countries are grouped into those that were members of the European Union before 2004, those that became members in 2004, those that became members in 2007, and Russia and the newly independent states. The countries of former Yugoslavia will generally not be included, as the consequences of wars in the region have added additional morbidity and mortality. Since the reviewed literature uses data from different individual countries or groups of countries defined in different ways, they will be specified when necessary.

2. Bulgaria, Czech Republic, Estonia, Hungary, Latvia, Lithuania, Poland, Romania, Slovakia, Slovenia.
3. At the time of writing, the global economic crisis of 2008–2009 is affecting the countries of Eastern Europe and is predicted to potentially negate many of the gains in economic growth observed during the past decade and deepen inequalities. For example, in Bulgaria, the key indictors for economic growth fell for the first half of 2009. These changes are not a topic of analysis in this chapter, and all we can state is that hopefully, the achieved gains will serve as a support that will mitigate the potential negative impact on health.
4. Also, statistics about life expectancy and mortality are the few indicators that can be considered standardized and comparable from different countries of Europe.
5. In Russia, Poland, and the Czech Republic.
6. Former East Germany, Hungary, and Poland.
7. Austria, Belgium, Netherlands, Switzerland, and former West Germany.
8. The countries included for Eastern Europe were Bulgaria, Hungary, Poland, and Romania, and for Western Europe, Belgium, France, Germany, England, and the Netherlands.
9. An indicator of income distribution within countries.
10. Estonia, Lithuania, Poland, and Hungary.
11. Less so in Southern Europe compared with Northern Europe.
12. Papanicolaou smear of cervical cells, which can detect cervical abnormalities and precancerous cells.
13. These programs can be critiqued considering the fact that exams were conducted at work sites in quasi-mandatory ways, and the fact that women often were not informed what tests were being conducted; the screening did, however, generally keep mortality rates low.
14. The countries who joined the EU in 2004 and 2007 (Eastern), compared with those who were members before 2004 (Western).
15. Bulgaria, Czech Republic, Hungary, East Germany, Poland, and Romania.
16. Belgium, France, Ireland, Italy, Spain, West Germany, and United Kingdom.
17. "Costs" included experienced or anticipated fear of the test, distress and discomfort, embarrassment, painfulness, inconvenience, and extent to which they are time consuming. The price of the test is considered as part of the systemic barriers.
18. The extent to which the individual perceives that she has control over the behavior of screening.
19. Self-efficacy measures the extent to which the individuals feels confident in her ability to carry out the behavior.
20. Subjective norms measure whether the individual feels that those around her support the behavior.

# References

Aiken, L., Gerend, M., & Jackson, K. (2001). Subjective risk and health protective behavior: Cancer screening and cancer prevention. In A. Baum, T. Revenson, & J. Singer (Eds.), *Handbook of health psychology* (pp. 727–746). Mahwah, NJ: Erlbaum.

Ajzen, I., & Madden, T.J. (1986). Prediction of goal-directed behavior: Attitudes, intentions and perceived behavioral control. *Journal of Experimental Social Psychology, 22,* 453–474.

Andreev, E., McKee, M., & Shkolnikov, V. (2003). Health expectancy in the Russian federation: A new perspective on the health divide in Europe. *Bulletin of the World Health Organization, 81*(11), 778–789.

Andreev, E., Nolte, E., Shkolnikov, V., Varavikova, E., & McKee, M. (2003). The evolving pattern of avoidable mortality in Russia. *International Journal of Epidemiology, 32,* 437–446.

Avramova, L., Alexandrova, A., Balabanova, D., Bradley, J., Panayotova, Y., & Todorova, I. (2005). *Cervical cancer screening in Bulgaria: Psychosocial aspects and health systems dimensions.* Sofia, Bulgaria: Health Psychology Research Center & EngenderHealth.

Baban, A. (1999). Romania. In H. David (Ed.), *From abortion to contraception: A resource to public policies and reproductive behavior in central and eastern Europe from 1917 to the present* (pp. 191–221). Westport, CT: Greenwod Press.

Baban, A. (2006). The role of health psychology and behavioral medicine in narrowing the East-West health divide. *Cognitie, Creier, Comportament (Cognition, Brain, Behavior), X*(1), 1–7.

Baban, A., Balázsi, R., Bradley, J., Rusu, C., Szentágotai, A., & Tătaru, R. (2005). *Psychosocial and health system dimensions of cervical screening in Romania.* Cluj-Napoca, Romania: Romanian Association of Health Psychology, Department of Psychology, Babes-Bolyai University, EngenderHealth.

Bacci, M.L. (2000). Mortality crisis in a historical perspective: The European experience. In G.A. Cornia, & R. Paniccia (Eds.), *The mortality crisis in transitional economies* (pp. 38–58). Oxford: Oxford University Press.

Balabanova, D., & McKee, M. (2002a). Access to health care in a system of transition: The case of Bulgaria. *International Journal of Health Planning and Management, 17,* 377–395.

Balabanova, D., & McKee, M. (2002b). Self-reported health in Bulgaria: Levels and determinants. *Scandinavian Journal of Public Health, 30,* 306–312.

Balabanova, D., & McKee, M. (2002c). Understanding informal payments for health care: The example of Bulgaria. *Health Policy, 62*(3), 243–273.

Balabanova, D., & McKee, M. (2004). Reforming health financing in Bulgaria: The population perspective. *Social Science and Medicine, 58,* 753–765.

Becker, M.H., & Rosenstock, I.M. (1987). Comparing social learning theory and the health belief model. In W.B. Ward (Ed.), *Advances in health education and promotion* (Vol 2, pp. 245–249). Greenwich, CT: JAI Press.

Bish, A., Sutton, S., & Golombok, S. (2000). Predicting uptake of a routine cervical smear test: A comparison of the health belief model and the theory of planned behavior. *Psychology and Health, 15,* 35–50.

Bobak, M., & Marmot, M. (2009). Societal transition and health. *Lancet, 373,* 360–362.

Bobak, M., Murphy, M., Rose, R., & Marmot, M. (2007). Societal characteristics and health in the former communist countries of central and eastern Europe and the former Soviet Union: A multilevel analysis. *Journal of Epidemiology & Community Health, 61*(11), 990–996.

Bobak, M., Pikhart, H., Rose, R., Hertzman, C., & Marmot, M. (2000). Socioeconomic factors, material inequalities, and perceived control in self-rated health: Cross-sectional data from seven post-communist countries. *Social Science and Medicine, 51,* 1343–1350.

Carlson, P. (1998). Self-perceived health in east and west Europe: Another European health divide. *Social Science and Medicine, 46*(10), 1355–1366.

Carlson, P. (2004). The European health divide: A matter of financial or social capital? *Social Science & Medicine, 59*(9), 1985–1992.

Cockerham, W.C. (1997). The social determinants of the decline of life expectancy in Russia and eastern Europe: A lifestyle explanation. *Journal of Health and Social Behavior, 38*(2), 117–130.

Cockerham, W.C. (1999). *Health and social change in Russia and eastern Europe.* New York: Routledge.

Cornia, G.A. (2000). Short-term, long-term and hysteresis mortality models: A review. In G.A. Cornia, & R. Paniccia (Eds.), *The mortality crisis in transitional economies* (pp. 59–82). Oxford: Oxford University Press.

Cornia, G.A., & Paniccia, R. (2000). The transition mortality crisis: Evidence, interpretation and policy responses. In G.A. Cornia, & R. Paniccia (Eds.), *The mortality crisis in transitional economies* (pp. 3–37). Oxford: Oxford University Press.

Corrin, C. (1992). (Ed). *Superwomen and the double burden: Women's experiences of change in central and eastern Europe and the Former Soviet Union.* Toronto: Second Story Press.

Courtenay, W. (2000). Engendering health: A social constructionist examination of men's health beliefs and behaviors. *Psychology of Men and Masculinity, 1*(1), 4–15.

Currie, C., Gabhainn, S., Godeau, E., Roberts, C., Smith, R., Currie, D., et al. (2008). *Inequalities in young people's health: HBSC international report from the 2005/2006 survey* (Vol. 5). Copenhagen: WHO Regional Office for Europe.

Danon, S., Valerianova, Z., & Ivanova, T. (2004). *Cancer incidence in Bulgaria 2001.* Sofia: National Oncological Center, Bulgarian National Cancer Registry.

Davis, C. (2000). Transition, health production, and medical system effectiveness. In G.A. Cornia, & R. Paniccia (Eds.), *The mortality crisis in transitional economies* (pp. 174–203). Oxford: Oxford University Press.

Domanski, H. (2002). Is the east European underclass feminized? *Communist and Post-communist Studies, 35,* 383–394.

Einhorn, B. (1993). *Cinderella goes to the market: Citizenship, gender and women's movements in eastern Europe.* London: Verso.

Feachem, R. (1994). Health decline in eastern Europe. *Nature, 367,* 313–314.

Fodor, E. (2002). Gender and the experience of poverty in eastern Europe and Russia after 1989. *Communist and Post-communist Studies, 35,* 369–382.

Frieze, I.H., Ferligoj, A., Kogovšek, T., Rener, T., Horvat, J., & Šarlija, N. (2003). Gender-role attitudes in university students in the United States, Slovenia and Croatia. *Psychology of Women Quarterly, 27*(3), 256–261.

Funk, N. (1993). Introduction: Women and post-communism. In N. Funk, & M. Mueller (Eds.), *Gender politics and post-communism* (pp. 1–14). New York: Routledge.

Gal, S., & Kligman, G. (2000). *The politics of gender after socialism.* Princeton, NJ: Princeton University Press.

Heyns, B. (2005). Emerging inequalities in central and eastern Europe. *Annual Review of Sociology, 31,* 163–197.

Idler, I., & Benyamini, Y. (1997). Self-rated health and mortality: A review of twenty-seven community studies. *Journal of Health and Social Behavior, 38,* 21–37.

Inglehart, R., Basanez, M., Diez-Medrano, J., Halman, L., & Luijkx, R. (2004). *Human beliefs and values: A cross-cultural sourcebook.* Siglo: XXI Editores.

Kopp, M. (2007). Public health burden of chronic stress in a transforming society. *Psychological Topics, 16,* 297–310.

Kopp, M., Skrabski, A., & Szedmák, S. (2000). Psychosocial risk factors, inequality and self-rated morbidity in a changing society. *Social Science and Medicine, 51,* 1351–1361.

Kopp, M., & Williams, R. (2006). The impact of social, economic and political changes on health in central and eastern Europe: Is there a role for behavioral medicine scientists and practitioners for improving the health of our populations? *Cognitie, Creier, Comportament (Cognition, Brain, Behavior), X*(1), 15–29.

Kostova, P., & Zlatkov, V. (2006, May 6). *Prophylaxis and cervical screening in Bulgaria: Past, problems and future.* Paper presented at the EUROCHIP2 meeting, Sofia, Bulgaria.

Kostova, P., Zlatkov, V., & Danon, S. (1998). Cervical screening in Bulgaria. An analysis of the main indicators over the period 1970–1994. *Akusherstvo i Ginekologiya (Bulgarian), 37*(1), 27–29.

Kotzeva, T. (1999). Re-imaging Bulgarian women: The Marxist legacy and women's self identity. In C. Corrin (Ed.), *Gender and identity in central and eastern Europe* (pp. 83–98). London: Frank Cass.

Kotzeva, T., & Todorova, I. (2005). The social construction of infertility in Bulgarian society. *Sotsioogicheski problemi, 3–4,* 215–243.

Koulaksazov, S., Todorova, S., Tragakes, E., & Hristova, S. (2003). *Health care systems in transition: Bulgaria.* Copenhagen: European Observatory on Health Care Systems.

Krastev, I., Dimitrova, B., & Garnizov, V. (2004). *Optimistic theory about the pessimism of the transition.* Sofia: Initiative Global Bulgaria.

László, K.D., Pikhart, H., Kopp, M., Bobak, M., Pajak, A., Malyutina, S., et al. (2010). Job insecurity and health: A study of 16 European countries. *Social Science & Medicine, 70,* 867–874.

Leinsalu, M., Stirbu, I., Denny Vågerö, D., Kalediene, R., Kovács, K., et al. (2009). Educational inequalities in mortality in four eastern European countries: Divergence in trends during the post-communist transition from 1990 to 2000. *International Journal of Epidemiology, 38*(2), 512–525.

Levi, F., Lucchini, F., Negri, E., Franceschi, S., & la Vecchia, C. (2000). Cervical cancer mortality in young women in Europe: Patterns and trends. *European Journal of Cancer, 36*(17), 2266–2271.

Lobodzinska, B. (1996). Women's employment or return to "family values" in central-eastern Europe. *Journal of Comparative Family Studies, 27*(3), 519–544.

Mackenbach, J.P. (2006). *Health inequalities: Europe in profile.* Retrieved from http://ec.europa.eu/health/ph_determinants/socio_economics/documents/ev_060302_rd06_en.pdf.

Marks, D. (1996). Health psychology in context. *Journal of Health Psychology, 1,* 7–21.

Marks, D. (2008). The quest for meaningful theory in health psychology. *Journal of Health Psychology, 13*(8), 977–981.

Marmot, M., & Bobak, M. (2000a). International comparators and poverty and health in Europe. *British Medical Journal, 321*(7269), 1124–1128.

Marmot, M., & Bobak, M. (2000b). Psychosocial and biological mechanisms behind the recent mortality crisis in central and eastern Europe. In G. Cornia, & R. Paniccia (Eds.), *The mortality crisis in transitional economies* (pp. 127–148). New York: Oxford University Press.

McKee, M., Balabanova, D., & Steriu, A. (2007). A new year, a new era: Romania and Bulgaria join the European Union. *European Journal of Public Health, 17*(2), 119–120.

Men, T., Brennan, P., Boffetta, P., & Zaridze, D. (2003). Russian mortality trends for 1991–2001: Analysis by cause and region. *British Medical Journal, 327*(7421), 964–969.

Mielewczyk, F., & Willig, C. (2007). Old clothes and an older look: The case for a radical makeover in health behavior research. *Theory and Psychology, 17*(6), 811–837.

Miller, G., Chen, E., & Cole, S.W. (2009). Health Psychology: Developing biologically plausible models linking the social world and health. *Annual Review of Psychology, 60*, 501–524.

Molyneux, M. (1995). Gendered transitions: A review essay. *Gender and Development, 3*(3), 49–54.

Möller-Leimkuhler, A.M. (2003). The gender gap in suicide and premature death or: Why are men so vulnerable. *European Archives of Psychiatry and Clinical Neuroscience, 253*, 1–8.

Murray, M., & Campbell, C. (2003). Living in a material world: Reflecting on some assumptions of health psychology. *Journal of Health Psychology, 8*(2), 231–236.

National Statistical Institute. (2004). *Yearbook.* Sofia, Bulgaria: National Statistical Institute.

National Statistical Institute. (2009). *Key indicators for Bulgaria.* Retrieved from http://www.nsi.bg/KeyInd/KeyInd2009–07.pdf.

Newmann, S.J., & Garner, E.O. (2005). Social inequities along the cervical cancer continuum: A structured review. *Cancer Causes and Control, 16*, 63–70.

Nicholson, A., Pikhart, H., Pajak, A., Malyutina, S., Kubinova, R., Peasey, A., et al. (2008). Socio-economic status over the life-course and depressive symptoms in men and women in eastern Europe. *Journal of Affective Disorders, 105*(1), 125–136.

Open Society Institute. (2009). *Unfinished business of the fifth enlargement countries.* Retrieved from http://eupi.osi.bg/fce/001/0070/files/11_Comparative_report_online.pdf.

Panayotova, Y., & Todorova, I. (2006). *The politics of reproductive rights and reproductive technologies in Bulgaria.* Paper presented at the seminar on Ethical Issues in Reproductive Health, IUSSP.

Panayotova, Y., & Todorova, I. (2009). Cultural meanings of the infertility treatment procedures and new reproductive technologies: Women's voices from Bulgaria. In D. Birenbaum-Carmeli, & M.C. Inhorn (Eds.), *Assisting reproduction, testing genes: Global encounters with new biotechnologies* (pp. 61–85). New York: Berghahn Books.

Paniccia, R. (2000). Transition, impoverishment and mortality: How large an impact? In G.A. Cornia, & R. Paniccia (Eds.), *The mortality crisis in transitional economies* (pp. 105–126). Oxford: Oxford University Press.

Perlman, F., & Bobak, M. (2008). Determinants of self-rated health and mortality in Russia- are they the same? *International Journal for Equity in Health, 7*(19).

Pikhart, H. (2002). *Social and psychosocial determinants of self-rated health in central and eastern Europe.* Boston: Kluwer Academic.

Piko, B. (2002). Socio-cultural stress in modern societies and the myth of anxiety in eastern Europe. *Administration and Policy in Mental Health, 29*(3), 275–280.

Rechel, B., & McKee, M. (2009). Health reform in central and eastern Europe and the former Soviet Union. *Lancet, 374*(9696), 1186–1195.

Rosenstock, I.M. (1990). The health belief model: Explaining health behavior through expectancies. In K. Glanz, F.M. Lewis, & B.K. Rimer (Eds.), *Health behavior and health education: Theory, research and practice* (pp. 151–176). San Francisco: Jossey Bass.

Sabo, D. (1999). *Understanding men's health: A relational and gender sensitive approach* (Working Paper Series No. 99.14). Cambridge, MA: Harvard Center for Population and Development Studies.

Salavecz, G., Chandola, T., Pikhart, H., Dragano, N., Siegrist, J., Jöckel, K. -H., et al. (2010). Work stress and health in western European and post-communist countries: An east–west comparison study. *Journal of Epidemiology and Community Health, 64*, 57–62.

Shkolnikov, V., & Cornia, G.A. (2000). Population crisis and rising mortality in transitional Russia. In G.A. Cornia, & R. Paniccia (Eds.), *The mortality crisis in transitional economies* (pp. 253–279). Oxford: Oxford University Press.

Shkolnikov, V., McKee, M., & Leon, D.A. (2001). Changes in life expectancy in Russia in the mid-1990's. *The Lancet, 357* (9260), 917–921.

Shteyn, M., Schumm, J., Vodopianova, N., Hobfoll, S., & Lilly, R. (2003). The impact of the Russian transition on psychological resources and psychological distress. *Journal of Community Psychology, 31*(2), 113–127.

Skrabski, Á., Kopp, M., Rózsa, S., Réthelyi, J., & Rahe, R.H. (2005). Life meaning: An important correlate of health in the Hungarian population. *International Journal of Behavioral Medicine, 12*(2), 78–85.

Steptoe, A., Tsuda, A., Tanaka, Y., & Wardle, J. (2007). Depressive symptoms, socio-economic background, sense of control, and cultural factors in university students from 23 countries. *International Journal of Behavioral Medicine, 14*(2), 97–107.

Steptoe, A., & Wardle, J. (2001). Health behaviour, risk awareness and emotional well-being in students from eastern Europe and western Europe. *Social Science & Medicine, 53*(12), 1621–1630.

Sutton, S., & Rutherford, C. (2005). Sociodemographic and attitudinal correlates of cervical screening uptake in a national sample of women in Britain. *Social Science and Medicine, 61*(11), 2460–2465.

Szaflarski, M. (2001). Gender, self-reported health and health related lifestyles in Poland. *Health Care for Women International, 22*, 207–227.

Todorova, I., Baban, A., Alexandrova-Karamanova, A., & Bradley, J. (2009). Inequalities in cervical cancer screening in eastern Europe: Perspectives from Bulgaria and Romania. *International Journal of Public Health, 54*, 1–11.

Todorova, I., Baban, A., Balabanova, D., Panayotova, Y., & Bradley, J. (2006). Providers' constructions of the role of women in cervical cancer screening in Bulgaria and Romania. *Social Science and Medicine, 63*, 776–787.

Todorova, I., Baban, A., Kotzeva, T., & Bradley, J. (2008). *Meanings and experiences of cervical cancer screening in Bulgaria and Romania.* Paper presented at the 29th International Congress of Psychology, Berlin, Germany.

Todorova, I., & Bradley, J. (2006). *Inequalities in cervical cancer screening in eastern Europe.* Paper presented at the 26th Congress of IAAP, Athens, Greece.

Todorova, I., & Bradley, J. (2008). *Experiences of cervical cancer screening in Bulgaria.* Paper presented at the 116th annual convention of the American Psychological Association.

Todorova, I., & Kotzeva, T. (2003a). *A longitudinal view of women's self-perceived health in Bulgaria during the transitional period.* Paper presented at the "A Cross-Cultural Approach to Stress and Coping in Women: Research Perspectives." A roundtable presented at the 17th Conference of the European Health Psychology Society., Kos, Greece.

Todorova, I., & Kotzeva, T. (2003b). Social discourses, women's resistive voices: Facing involuntary childlessness in Bulgaria. *Women's Studies International Forum, 26*(2), 139–151.

Todorova, I., & Kotzeva, T. (2006). Contextual shifts in Bulgarian women's identity in the face of infertility. *Psychology & Health, 21*(1), 123–141.

Todorova, I., & Todorov, V. (2006). Gender and psychosocial aspects of health in Bulgaria. *Cognitie, Creier, Comportament (Cognition, Brain, Behavior)*, X(1), 31–51.

Uchino, B. (2006). Social support and health: A review of physiological pathways potentially underlying link to disease outcomes. *Journal of Behavioral Medicine*, 29(4), 377–387.

United Nations Development Programme. (2007/2008). *Human Development Report Statistics*. New York: Author. Retrieved from http://hdrstats.undp.org/en/indicators/50.html.

Van der Lippe, T., & Fodor, E. (1998). Changes in gender inequality in six eastern European countries. *Acta Sociologica*, 41, 131–149.

Vassileva, L., Alexandrova-Karamanova, A., Alexandrova, B., Bogdanova, E., Dimitrova, E., Kotzeva, T., et al. (2008). *Health behavior in school aged children: Results from the representative study in 11, 13, and 15 years old Bulgarian students* Sofia: Bulgarian Academy of Sciences & Health Psychology Research Center.

Wardle, J., McCaffery, K., Nadel, M., & Atkin, W. (2004). Socioeconomic differences in cancer screening participation: Comparing cognitive and psychosocial explanations. *Social Science and Medicine* 59(2), 249–261.

Wardle, J., Steptoe, A., Guliš, G., Sartory, G., Sęk, H., Todorova, I., et al. (2004). Depression, perceived control, and life satisfaction in university students from central-eastern and western Europe. *International Journal of Behavioral Medicine*, 11(1), 27–36.

Watson, P. (1995). Explaining rising mortality among men in eastern Europe. *Social Science and Medicine*, 41(7), 923–934.

Weidner, G., & Cain, V. (2003). The gender gap in heart disease: Lessons from eastern Europe. *American Journal of Public Health*, 93(5), 768–770.

World Health Organization. (2010). *European health for all database*. Geneva: Author. Retrieved from http://data.euro.who.int/hfadb/.

Wroblewska, W. (2002). Women's health status in Poland in the transition to a market economy. *Social Science and Medicine*, 54, 707–726.

Zatonski, W. (2007). The east-west health gap in Europe: What are the causes? *European Journal of Public Health*, 17(2), 121.

# Asian Meditation and Health

Yosuke Sakairi, Genji Sugamura, *and* Masao Suzuki

**Abstract**

This chapter explores the theory and methods of achieving well-being, focusing on meditation as a behavioral-physical-psychological training system. It includes a discussion of the training system of zen, yoga training, types of meditation methods, simple techniques for meditation, systems for practicing meditation, conditioning in meditation, mindfulness in meditation, and the effects of the meditation method.

**Keywords:** Well-being, meditation, zen, yoga training, mindfulness

So that medicine and psychology may contribute not only to pathological cures but also to disease prevention and health promotion, new approaches are needed in addition to the existing medical ones. One of these trends is the promotion of complementary and alternative medicine (CAM); and, as one of its main components, much attention is paid to meditation, which is an Asian traditional training of the mind and body (Haruki, Ishii, & Suzuki, 1996). One of the practical reasons for the need for CAM is medical cost restraint. Meditation necessarily enables many people to improve their health at a low cost.

In medical science, a specialist identifies negative points of health based on diagnosis and is personally involved in minimizing these negative points. Such an approach as this is effective when the number of the negative objects is small, as in the case of acute medical treatment for an individual, but it entails a too heavy financial burden if a large number of people are the focus, as in the case of disease prevention and health promotion. In addition, to promote continued health in many people with no diseases, it is necessary to intentionally assume negative points, such as the future possibility of contracting diseases. On the other hand, meditation is a good way of acquiring the skill of maximizing physical and mental functions (for example, mindfulness). Since this is an approach for multiplying affirmative points (new skills), it is possible for a lot of people with different personalities to form groups and conduct practical activities. Such a meditation system has been established through Asian traditions, which have been grappling with healthful improvements of mind and body for thousands of years. This system includes many treasures that can be helpful for modern people to solve health problems that they are facing today.

Essentially, however, meditation is not a heath care method but a training that one undertakes to acquire enlightenment and mindfulness. Rigorous traditional training, lasting for years, may cause not a few people to suffer health damage in the process. Therefore, simple methods are being taught or promulgated that prepare people for regular training, or that use methods for healing mental and physical disorders. A specialist who decides to utilize meditation for the health improvement of ordinary people must understand both the "big picture" as well as the essence of proper meditation, taking advantage of simple and easy methods suitable for beginners and stressing the importance of safety and effectiveness.

## Theory and Method of Well-being

In research on well-being, it is necessary to make a clear distinction between the theory and idea on what well-being means and the method and technology to promote it. The meaning of "well-being" differs depending on the time, culture, and individuals involved, and the whole of "well-being" is realized based on idea, culture, and religion. However, natural science, which essentially tries to obtain universal truths, has being seeking only after techniques as research objects, ignoring the sense of value, meaning, and so forth, that lie behind the method. The psychological research on meditation also has targeted only techniques such as postures and breathing methods, while putting aside the theories lying behind them (such as yoga and Buddhism), and has examined their psychological and physiological effectiveness with the use of scales that measure the alleviation of anxiety and depression.

On the other hand, if health psychology wishes to be an applied science dealing with health and well-being, it is necessary to indicate the direction in which the science is progressing and describe the standards used to clarify the extent to which health care has been promoted. Thus, it is necessary to grapple with the difficult and contradicting task of balancing science with value judgment. Although this issue remains unresolved, some progress has been made.

## Positive Concept of Well-being

People who wish to expand their conceptions beyond scientific limits conceive of psychological well-being as being based on the idea of a positive psychology that encompasses, among other things, concepts such as spirituality and quality of life (QOL). These concepts of well-being are helpful, but only if they are treated as limited hypotheses, always bearing in mind the importance of cultural and individual differences. Attempting to develop measuring scales to quantify well-being using a scientific approach would be foolhardy, because the preparation of those scales would invariably include the investigator's specific values, ideals, and religious beliefs.

Although it is appropriate for international organizations, such as World Health Organization (WHO), to discuss matters related to QOL and mental health in an effort to promote common understanding of these concepts, it would be inappropriate to create a common global scale for measuring them in one language (e.g., English), and then measure the mental health levels of people

with different cultural backgrounds using those scales simply translated into various languages. For example, in the WHO Subjective Well-being Inventory Japanese version (Ohno & Yoshimura, 2001), "sense of achievement" is used as one of the 11 scales for measuring degrees of mental health. Much care is required in the interpretation of the results, because although "sense of achievement" is regarded as an index based on respect for behavior *results*, "sense of fullness," based on respect for behavior *processes* can also be used as a scale for measuring health. In addition, there is a way of thinking in Asian cultures that regards it as "healthier" not to require achievements from the outset but to be content with and thankful for the present situations (*chisoku* 知足). The concept of well-being is specified based on individual conceptions of value, and its definition differs depending on culture and for each individual. It would be impossible to create global standards, so comparing and evaluating levels of mental health with one criterion must be avoided.

Regarding "health" problems, natural sciences can only deal with techniques (health methods and regimens) as research objects, so it is necessary to carefully define the meaning of health or well-being, depending on the purpose and situation.

In health regimens and medical science, importance is attached to mental and physical stability with reference to health, whereas in meditation a higher goal is set. The goal is to learn *han-nya* (般若; wisdom of understanding) by experience or to be unified with god-like beings. Trainers, who go have passed through literally life-and-death training toward that goal, may lose their health in the training process and even lose their life in asceticism. Since, in meditation, it is required to reach an absolutely peaceful state of mind, rather than to simply obtain temporary stability of mind and body, mental and physical health may be damaged its pursuit. Consequently, the far simpler methods presented in preparation for regular training and the techniques introduced for healing mental and physical disorder can be applied instead as health methods and regimens.

## Negative Concept of Well-being

People who seek scientific universality rather than individuality have avoided making value judgments based on what should be regarded as positive and have dealt with health problems merely from the standpoint of decreasing disease, pain, and death, which tend to be seen negatively by the majority of people. If only negative themes, such as depression and lifestyle-associated diseases, are discussed in textbooks of health psychology, it may represent the modest attitude of scientists attempting to stay within the boundaries of science. (Strictly speaking, the idea that it is good to decrease negatives and increase positives is simply one way of thinking. Asia embraces another, which attaches importance to the *balance* of positives and negatives, as indicated in the symbol for *Taiji* (太極). Development and growth have, to date, been unconditionally accepted as the highest good, but it is possible to predict that from now on, more attention will be paid to sustainability, with more importance attached to not only avoiding but also accepting negatives.)

In medical treatments, the definition of health based on disease is helpful in curing diseases, but many problems are involved when this definition is applied to matters related to disease prevention and health promotion. If a specific problem, such as a disease, comes to the fore, it seems necessary and effective to make a diagnosis, clarify its main cause, and take specific measures against the problem. However, in the case of prevention, the possible appearance of many problems, and many causes of such problems, may make such specification impossible. This may leave us with no choice but to determine, utilizing statistics and probability theories, certain behaviors (e.g., smoking and obesity) as risk factors. In essence, when developing preventive methods, it is necessary to tailor them to the individual, because each individual possibly has many different problems and many different causes of disease. However, because the number of people needing preventive measures is larger than the number of people in need of treatment, some specialists believe it is too costly and difficult to deal with individual cases for prevention, and they find it necessary to aim at improving statistic values through political or systematic interventions.

To remove risk factors, it is necessary to make continuous efforts to improve lifestyle, such as giving up smoking or increasing exercise, but the motivation for healthy people to do so is weak. If health is defined based on diseases, then there is no choice but to count as a motivation factor the future possibility of contracting cancer, diabetes, and so forth. In addition, people with a low risk excluded from the objects of intervention, relevant objects need to be selected and it would be difficult for the existing organizations such as companies to carry out such selection in groups.

As the term "lifestyle-associated diseases" goes, a lot of chronic diseases are largely influenced by the lifestyles followed by the patient for many years. Those regimens for health-maintaining lifestyles that introduce in great detail instructions on how and what to eat and drink, how and when to bathe and move the bowels seem most suited for preventing and improving lifestyle-associated diseases.

If Western medicine can be understood as pursuing a "means to decrease minuses" and as a "means to remove adverse parts," and Eastern medicine and health regimens understood as "means to maintain balance" (by refraining from both positive and negative excesses), then meditation can be understood as a "means to multiply pluses" in that it requires the learning of new techniques. Such a viewpoint is indispensable to improving mental and physical health.

- Western medicine approach: "Decrease minuses"; treat acute diseases
- Regimen and Eastern medicine: "Maintain balance"; prevent chronic diseases
- Meditation and Eastern practices: "Increase pluses"; promote mental and physical health

## Concept of Health As a Skill

Another viewpoint considers health as based on the skill with which the individual can control the mind and body, rather than on the condition of them. This encourages the acquisition of strengths and skills for dealing flexibly with changes and stresses in the environment. From this standpoint, promoting health means to improve strength and skill through therapy. Considering physical aspects, it can be expected that the stronger a person is physically, the stronger he is against diseases; that the more skillful he is in controlling his mind and body, the more stabilized his footsteps will be when walking and the less frequently he will hurt himself, and the higher his behavioral performance will be. Adding mental aspects to that and enhancing emotional, cognitive, and behavioral control skills, as well as physical control skills, will bring a variety of good results. Meditation is one effective way to bring about these good results.

Methods for controlling emotions, cognitions, and behaviors include various techniques in cognitive-behavioral psychotherapy, social skill therapy, and psychological skill therapy, used in sports psychology and so forth. Basically, meditation can be understood in the same "training" category as these methods. The difference is that scientific training uses different techniques depending on the nature of trainee's problem, whereas meditations use fixed methods (experience places) depending on the trainer. It is not that a meditation specialist understands his individual trainee's problem and shows him how to solve it, but rather that he will simply provide his trainee with a place in which to experience certain events and guide him through such experiences. Then, the trainee subjectively grapples with his problem, possibly together with others sharing the same experience place with him. For example, zen encompasses not only *zazen* (坐禅) as common self-training, but also *samu* (作務) as group work, and *sanzen* as private instruction by leaders, in which a system of compound group training is instituted.

The effectiveness of adopting such a system of group therapy for promoting mental and physical health has yet to be verified, but meditation is a system capable of being applied to many people at once, in which utilizing the effects of mass interactions and modeling, with the focus being on self-training, drastically reduces the cost of employing a specialist.

## Meditation As a Behavioral-Physical-Psychological Training System

By way of explaining a system of meditation, we will discuss zen and yoga here. For most people, the image of zen is *zazen* (sitting meditation), in which trainees sit quietly, and the image of yoga may be stretch exercises, in which practitioners adopt a variety of poses. However, these are only small parts of the systems of zen and yoga. *Zazen* is the main practice among the three therapies: *Kai, Jou,* and *E* (戒 定 慧), and yoga poses are only the third of eight parts of yoga: the āsana practice. In yoga, as well as in zen, training for self-regulations of behavior, physical functions (from involuntary to voluntary nervous systems), and mental functions are systematically conducted. To coordinate one's mind, it is necessary above all to coordinate one's body, so, in a very early stage of that process, it is necessary to keep in good order within the behaviors of daily life. *Kai* in zen and *yama* and *niyama* in yoga are the bases for these training systems, because they are not so much religious ideas as rules for behavior that lend themselves to enhancing physical functions.

## Training System of Zen

For some, the practice of zen training is undertaking through entering a communal life that is lived according to strict rules. In this way, the environment and lifestyle are coordinated. Not only *zazen* but also all behaviors of everyday life become training. Practices such as washing face, eating, cleaning,

and so forth are required to be made with mindfulness. If *zazen* is regarded as static meditation, eating and cleaning can be regarded as dynamic meditations. Dogen (1237/1991) considered life at large as practice, and specified that all meal manners had practice and a close relation, and were the practice itself.

Even while performing *zazen*, coordination moves from behavior to body (from muscles to breath) to mind (i.e., in increasing order of difficulty of self-regulation). For example, when practicing *zazen*, it is first necessary to learn the fixed way of entering the meditation hall, walking, bowing, and so forth. This is the coordination of behaviors. Then, the fixed poses are learned, such as sitting with legs crossed in the lotus position. At this time, only antigravity muscles tense to maintain position, and the others loose. This is the coordination of the muscle and bone system. Next, breathing is regulated, through deep exhalation and paying attention to slow breathing. This is the coordination of the visceral system through breathing. After completing these preparations, the self-monitoring of mental and physical movements commences. Doing nothing but observing various objects, which range from physical feelings and breathings to emotions and thoughts, while avoiding interpretation and maintaining mindfulness, is meditation.

As an example of the application of meditation, an upset heart causes the shoulders and the middle of the forehead to be tense and promotes anxiety. It is difficult to directly control the upset heart through willpower, so, to recover composure, it is necessary first to walk slowly, relax the shoulders, breathe deeply, and then observe one's own heart as if it were another's. In meditation, a trainee goes through the same motions every day, without changing his behaviors and physical conditions, and through this process mental conditioning is created; for the experienced practitioner, the recovery of composure has already been achieved while walking inside the meditation hall. This feature of meditation shares a common mechanism with "routine," which is a technique of sports psychology. A famous baseball player, Ichiro, walks the same way to enter batter's box and behaves the same way to take his position, so that he can bat under fixed and idealistic conditions of mind and body. In addition to baseball, players of various sports do their routines (the same behaviors) before set plays, such as free kick and free throw.

One suggestion that can be obtained from the meditation system is that, to keep mental and physical conditions in good order, it is necessary to take into comprehensive consideration behavioral, physical, and psychological aspects and intervene in them in an effective order. That is to say, it is important to deal with psychological matters only on the basis of the coordination of environments, lifestyles, behaviors, and physical conditions.

## Eight Parts of Yoga Training

Regarding yoga training, eight parts based on the *Yoga Sutra* or the yoga scriptures (Sahoda, 1980) are listed in Table 34.1. The first five parts are preparatory stages for coordinating social behaviors:1. Prohibition; 2. Precepts (personal behaviors); 3. Sitting (positions); 4. Breath (breathing) and 5. Withdrawal of the Senses (sensations). The sixth to eighth parts are the stages of psychological work in meditation: 6. dhāraṇā, in which attention is focused on specific objects, 7. dhyāna, in which nothing is done but observe objects without interpretation and with mindfulness maintained; and 8. samādhi, which is a condition in which there is no separation between the subject and object observed, and the observer is unified with the object.

In recent years, a variety of meditation methods and yoga have been used to promote mental and physical health, and the differences between them can be understood comprehensively by realizing that each method focuses importance on various combinations of the eight general parts of yoga.

For example, the type of meditation methods that focus attention on specific objects, such as mandalas and flames, attaches importance to the sixth part, dhāraṇā; whereas those meditation methods that require nothing but observation while maintaining mindfulness (like zen) focus on the seventh part, dhyāna. (In fact, the word *zen* is derived from *dhyāna*.)

Popularized meditation methods for beginners utilize some of the five parts of the preparation stages. Many popular yogas are based on the third part, āsana, whereas others focus on breathing techniques

**Table 34.1  Eight parts of yoga**

1. Restraints (yama)
2. Observances (niyama)
3. Postures (āsana)
4. Respiration (prāṇāyāma)
5. Control of the Senses (pratyāhāra)
6. Concentration (dhāraṇā)
7. Mindfulness (dhyāna)
8. Meditative absorption (samādhi)

from the fourth part. Some people who misunderstand the meaning of assuming unnatural positions in yoga regard it as merely physical training, gaining benefit from stretching. Originally, however, yoga was meant to be a meditation method that uses complicated physical positions to encourage the practitioner to self-monitor physical sensations and maintaining mindfulness. It is difficult for beginners to perform self-monitoring of internal thoughts and feelings; yoga's positions stimulate an awareness of physical sensations and breathing, encouraging the practitioner to breathe consciously and move slowly.

Meditation is often mistaken as a relaxation method. This idea may be traced to a treatise written by Wallace (1970), who studied physiological conditions during transcendental meditation (TM), a meditation practice widely known to Western researchers. TM's emphasis on hypometabolic conditions caused the misunderstanding that meditation is characterized by sitting still, resting mind and body, and not engaging in physical movements. However, the fact is that, even in TM, practitioners perform walking meditations, and in *zen* also, they perform slowly walking meditations called *Kinhin* (経行) in the intervals of *zazen*. The essence of meditation is not reducing metabolism, but self-monitoring. In this connection, methods like TM, in which trainees chant sounds called *mantras*, are performed as part of the second stage of yoga, niyama.

In essence, every meditation method includes factors of all the parts, and each is a practiced to deepen experiences by amassing expertise over time until reaching the eighth part, concentration. The question of which method is more effective depends on the purpose. So that average people may use meditation easily to promote their own health, simple meditation methods utilizing preparation stages are more appropriate than more advanced ones.

## Types of Meditation Methods

The meditation methods developed and practiced in Eastern cultures spread quickly among Western countries in the 1960s. During that period, Buddhist leaders left Tibet and went abroad, zen centers were established at various places in Europe and America, and Eastern- and inner-world–oriented trends were growing, mainly in North America. Transcendental meditation was promoted as a technique of simple meditation, and it spread quickly, mostly among youth worldwide. In addition to the advertising effect of its practice by the Beatles, TM owes its spread largely to a manualizing of the simple methods for its practice, instruction that is separated from any religious background, and the a verification of its psychological and physiological effectiveness through the use of natural science techniques (West, 1987; Wallace, 1991).

In the 1960s and 1970s, completely different techniques, ranging from *zazen* and Vipassana meditation to Hata Yoga and Taiji-Quan, were researched under the general term *meditation*. Consequently, later, to avoid confusion, an attempt was made to classify various meditation methods according to types. Goleman (1977) classified 15 types of meditation according to how the focus of attention was attained, and presented them under the following three categories: (1) *Concentration types*, in which attention is focused on fixed objects (mandala, mantra, etc.); (2) *mindfulness types*, in which mental and physical conditions continue to be observed as they are; and (3) *integration types*, which combine characteristics of either of the above types. Other researchers (Ornstein, 1972; Shapiro, 1982) also classified various techniques, utilizing basically similar frameworks. Practically speaking, however, it is impossible to strictly divide the techniques because the deeper the meditation experience goes, the greater the trend of paying attention to meditation rather than on concentration. Associating each type with the above-mentioned eight parts of yoga will make it easier to understand the classification of meditation types. The focused attention and mindfulness meditations correspond to the sixth part, concentration (dhāraṇā), and the seventh, meditation (dhyāna), respectively. Gradual instruction, inculcation, and meditation lead people to the eighth part, concentration. However, those advanced techniques are so difficult that they require practitioners to perform five-step preparations before practice. Because of the individual characteristics of those who wish to use meditation to maintain good health, it may be necessary to try several different approaches to meditation before finding an appropriate method.

In providing a comprehensive definition of meditation for the psychologist, Shapiro (1982, p. 268) said, "meditation refers to a family of techniques which have in common a conscious attempt to focus attention in a nonanalytical way and an attempt not to dwell on discursive, ruminating thought." Smith (1987, p. 140) said that common factors of meditation are "to focus your attention, maintain a stance of letting be, and be receptive to whatever may happen." Under either definition, the basic factor of meditation is regarded as learning "to maintain the

special way of paying attention: not react but just observe." Mindfulness meditation aims directly at this way of paying attention (mindfulness), whereas the focused-attention types of meditation, by restricting attention to a simple stimulation, halt thinking and reaction and change the active focus of attention to meditative attention.

It is generally difficult to practice mindfulness meditation, but the degree of difficulty varies depending on the object of attention. The easiest object of meditative attention is slow physical movements, such as those practiced in Taiji-Quan and Vipassana meditation; the second easiest is breathing and then physical sensation. The most difficult objects of meditative attention are psychological processes, such as emotion and thinking (Smith, 1987).

In *zazen*, the very difficult observation of mind is performed, but preparation to that level is made step-by-step, from body to mind, as indicated by an expression showing the essence of *zazen* "調身 (body coordination) → 調息 (breath coordination) → 調心 (mind coordination)," and comparatively easy methods are also provided, such as *Kinhin* (slow walking), which focuses attention on slow physical movements, and *Susokukan* (数息観; breath counting), which focuses attention on breathing. To use mindfulness meditation as a health method, practice should be restricted to relatively easy methods based on physical sensations such as body movements and breathing. A mindfulness meditation developed by Kabat-Zinn (1990) provides a method based on programming this type of technique, and it is practiced in medical settings to control pain and deal with stress. This program can become one of the models of mindfulness meditations used as a health method.

The focused-attention type meditations, in which unnecessary tension may be created by excessive efforts to focus attention, can cause negative results for health. Because of this, in cases where meditation is undertaken as a health-promotion method, the more relaxing types of meditation are more desirable. A model this type of meditation is *mantra meditation*, a type of meditation that uses simple words, such as *nianfo*, chanted without strain. In order to avoid strain, it is important to take attitudes of "commitment" or "trust" while chanting the words. Pure Land Buddhism is based on salvation by faith in Amitābha, and such an attitude prevents unnecessary strain.

Even regarding the positioning in Buddhism, *Shodomon* 聖道門 (Gateway of the Holy Path) of *Jiriki* 自力 (Self Power) is considered to be a

*Nangyoudou*難行道(difficult path), while *Joudomon* 浄土門 (Pure Land Buddhism) of *Tariki* 他力 (salvation by faith) to be *Igyoudou* 易行道 (easy path), which actually spreads among not monks but general people. In TM, innocence and naturalness are emphasized as attitudes taken while chanting mantra. In addition, Benson (1975), who researched meditation methods such as TM and Tummo yoga and advocated a concept and method of relaxation reaction, mentioned paying passive attention as a basic factor of meditation. *Autogenic therapy* (standard practices), which is not a meditation method per se, was developed by Shultz (1932) based on his research on self-hypnosis and yoga. It also employs techniques whose basis is to chant simple words while paying passive attention to physical sensations, so that it has much in common with meditation methods. Meditation methods that are based on single-word chants while maintaining a passive attitude seem to be the most promising as health-improvement techniques.

Other meditation methods utilize images that cause the mind and body to relax. For example, the 18th-century zen monk Hakuin (白隠) introduced the method of *Nanso* (軟酥) (Izusan,1983)as a therapeutic technique to help another, ill zen monk. To practice *Nanso*, imagines that you are sitting with an object on your head. This object is shaped like an egg made of gathered and rounded perfume pellets of beautiful color and fragrance. The egg is being melted gradually by the warmth of your body, and fragrant, warm liquid is flowing from your head to your legs, moistening the skin all over your body. The lower half of your body is warmed in the hot water into which the egg is melted. By repeating this imaginary physical sensation, you become refreshed, allowing uncomfortable sensations of the mind and body to flow away with the warm liquid.

*Nanso* is a therapeutic method of mediation, rather than true meditation, and it is used when the mind and body are already out of order, making it impossible to conduct meditation. Often misunderstood is meditation for having instant effects of stabilizing and relaxing heart.

Unfortunately, meditation (e.g., *zazen*) commenced immediately after losing health will prove completely useless, due to the mind being vexed with idle thoughts about the legs aching from unaccustomed positions, the sensation of pain in the back, and so forth. Meditation is a process, so it takes a time to achieve its effects.

In addition to the *Nanso* method, other techniques have been handed down as therapeutic methods for practitioners suffering from mental and physical disorder, and these techniques seem to be more effective than purely meditative practices.

## Simple Techniques of Meditation

Learning all the details of the meditation process is neither easy nor cheap. Instruction from experienced teachers is essential, and regular, continuing participation in the group practice of meditation is high desirable. The cost of pursuing detailed instruction in meditation may prove costly, both financially and in the possibility of harm from inexperienced teachers and less than trustworthy groups.

To use meditation methods for health enhancement, it is appropriate to begin at home, trying simple techniques by oneself. Once the basics have been learned, it is usual to join a group of people sharing the same concerns and receive specialist instruction in meditation practices. These meditation systems will be described in detail later, after a brief introduction to some simple, beginner-level techniques.

One of these simple techniques is a form of mindfulness meditation that utilizes slowed body movements. The technique is simply practiced by moving the body slowly and smoothly while paying careful attention to it. This is performed for only a few minutes every day, for example, by walking very slowly, like a super slow motion picture. Simply making daily movements slowly, as when washing the face or eating confectionary, makes it possible to experience richer feelings and to practice maintaining meditative attention. To move the body slowly and smoothly, one must continue to incessantly monitor each physical sensation, so that meditative attentions are maintained naturally, without needing the practitioner to do anything special in the way of paying attention. The practice of this technique may be expressed in a form of health lesson, such as, "Spare the time to move your body very slowly and smoothly once a day."

The mindfulness meditation technique developed and described by Kabat-Zinn (1990) is another of these types of techniques used in medicine and psychology. In addition, Vipassana meditation can also serve as a reference.

Another simple technique employs mantra meditation, which pays passive attention to chanting simple sounds and words. By chanting simple words and sounds to oneself, it is possible to relax both mentally and physically, allowing the body to be attentive to the natural experiences occurring within it, and paying attention to them in a passive and accepting attitude. When using TM, which is based on mantra meditation, it is recommended that the practice should be conducted twice per day for about 20 minutes at a time, although one report shows that even short meditations lasting 2–3 minutes are effective (Carrington, 1978). All that this technique requires is that the practitioner sit quietly and comfortably with eyes closed and silently and calmly chant a word. The practice may be expressed in the form of a health lesson such as, "Spend time in relaxation without doing anything once a day. During that time, sit comfortably with eyes closed and try to chant calmly to yourself the same word over and over again." Chanting silently is easier than "doing nothing" while meditating, because with the eyes closed and without something to focus on, various thoughts will appear in the mind and these may be difficult to ignore. It's much easier to try to calmly pay attention only to a single, repeated sound.

Another meditative technique used in medicine and psychology is the *relaxation reaction*, described by Benson (1975), which used TM as a model in its development and also features repetitive chanting.

In the case of TM, the instruction method is systematically programmed, but the details have yet to be made public. However, instruction manuals and tapes on clinical standard meditation methods, which faithfully imitate the instruction procedures of TM, have been published (Carrington, 1978). In addition, one of the most widely used and systematized of the chanting-type meditation techniques is *autogenic therapy* (Schultz, & Luthe, 1969). This is a medical technique without any religious overtones, so it is possible to give instruction at medical institutions or to have patients attend lecture meetings of the Japanese Society of Autogenic Therapy.

When selecting a word or sound to chant, in principle any word and sound will do, as long as it is one that the practitioner can calmly commit himself to. However, over time, the practitioner should carefully select words or sounds that are special to himself. In Benson's relaxation reaction (1975), the method suggested chanting the word "One" in time to breathing; later it was recommended that the practitioner use any favorite short word (Benson, 1984). In TM, the instructor chooses a mantra suited for the trainee and gives it to him as part of the ritual. Moreover, the trainee is required not to tell this mantra to others (Schulte, 1981). These procedures makes the mantra more special to him and enhances the continuity of his practice.

## System of Practicing Meditation

It's optimal if the simple methods of meditation introduced above can be performed as a daily habit, but this is difficult for many people to do by themselves. Once the basics are mastered, it's essential that the practitioner commit herself to learning the full range of meditative practices, under the instruction of a gifted teacher. This is no different than learning to change lifestyle habits to include taking moderate exercise, eating properly, and getting enough rest, all of which constitute effective life habits for health. Simply receiving information about appropriate exercises and dietary restrictions from sports trainers and dieticians, or hearing about the importance of sleep and rest from medical doctors and psychologists is not enough to guide a person to make these important changes, or if she does, to continue them. A teacher's order to "live life with calm heart" is meaningless without careful instruction; it is necessary to teach a person the skill of calming her heart and also to provide her with a system that allows her to continue to practice this effective health behavior.

Against the background of an aging society and ever-increasing medical costs, introducing a system by which the body and the mind can be self-regulated to promote better health seems quite useful. Compared to the costs of traditional Western medicine, the costs of implementing meditation as therapy are extremely low.

Just as therapeutic specialists such as physicians and counselors are needed in medicine and clinical psychology, so are special instructors and teachers needed in meditation. Unlike in the system of Western medicine, where a specialist treats each patient individually, and deals with his or her individual problems using various techniques, in the system of meditation, only one practice method is used, and the details of its application are minutely specified. This practice method is taught collectively and simultaneously to many people by the instructor. The students, after receiving instructions from the teacher, work on their own to perfect their practice and grapple with their individual problems. Therefore, the personnel costs spent to employ meditation specialists can be divided according to the size of the group, and these costs will disappear once students learn the techniques well enough to practice by themselves. In addition, the formation of a group of people practicing the same meditative technique encourages the building of supportive relationships, in which skilled students can be used as models, and participants can provide each other with feedback and encouragement.

Taken from an East–West perspective, systematic differences exist between the philosophies of health and healing. Western medicine is focused on treating disease; adverse health states are diagnosed and treated, usually on an individual level. Meditation, on the other hand, emphasizes learning mental and physical skills to preserve health. Once the mind and body are functioning correctly, exercises are done so that the individual can learn to coordinate the functioning of mind and body toward maintaining good health.

Because all persons learning a specific meditation technique learn to perform it in the same way, it becomes possible to deal with individual problems collectively. Because meditation is not used for acutely treating disease, but for promoting long-term health, it must be practiced daily, as a life habit, along with proper exercise and diet.

The collective practice system based on self-regulation training is a self-care system utilizing social support and modeling functions among the trainees, so it can be expected to not only reduce cost but also promote the continuity of practice.

## Mental and Physical Skills Obtained Through Meditation

The skills expected to be improved through continuous practice of meditation include those for self-monitoring to enhance awareness of one's own mental and physical conditions, and those for self-regulation to keep them in order. The concepts of *conditioning* and *mindfulness* enable the practitioner to coordinate mental and physical states.

The simple technique of mantra meditation is considered a conditioning technique, in that it promotes a specific mental or physical condition based upon the repeated chanting of particular sound (classical conditioning). The mindfulness-based meditations utilize an internal monitoring method to achieve results.

## Conditioning in Meditation

As described above for the practice of *zazen*, certain prescribed manners of walking into the meditation hall, sitting, and so forth must to be followed before entering into meditation. Meditation always follows certain fixed behaviors, positions, and breathings. A person in the meditative state experiences both a relaxed mind and intense concentration in a well-balanced percentage, a condition not limited to the mental aspect. His physical state, such as his muscular tenseness, breathing rhythm, and heartbeat rate, also become stabilized. In mantra meditation, an

identical sound is chanted while mind and body go into this stabilized condition through the daily practice of meditation. This conditioning practice, established through a repeated process, helps to coordinate the mental and physical condition to achieve a certain stabilized state. Thus, the effect of mantra meditation in coordinating mind and body can be explained using the concept of conditioning.

Most research work on cognitive modifications, such as a yoga trainee's special physiological reactions and a zen monk's enlightenment, has considered the special mental and physical conditions and experiences during meditation as mere curiosities. However, obtaining such effects requires intensive training for many years, and these effects differ from the mental and physical states acquired through simple meditation practices, performed by most people for health improvement. Referred to as *presence of mind* in zen, these states are not special, but normal conditions. They are neutral; neither especially good nor bad. However, it is the very nature of their neutrality that gives them value; when the practitioner can learn to return mental and physical levels to a neutral state at any time, he will have become adept in enhancing the stability or resilience of his body and mind. For example, in order to correct the disturbed state of mind and body, such as irritation and high blood pressure caused by unreasonable demands, it is considered very helpful to temporarily shift the mental and physical state to a neutral position, like shifting the gears in a car while driving.

If practicing mantra meditation enables a person to form a conditional reflex that will change mental and physical conditions in a fixed direction, it will help reduce the stress level by shifting attention away from unpleasant thoughts and emotional reactions.

## Mindfulness in Meditation

Meditation seeks to "to maintain a special manner of paying attention (mindfulness), where sheer observation without reactions is being performed." Mindfulness skills improve with the repeated practice of mindfulness-based meditation. But if mindfulness focuses attention on the reactions of the body, how then does it help reduce stress level, especially in the face of unpleasant thoughts or emotional reactions?

In the case of an uncomfortable condition of mind and body, such as pain and depression, it could be difficult to decide whether to monitor and become conscious of the condition, or remain unconscious of it. A person who is normally conscious of uncomfortable emotions, such as pain and unrest, may focus on these sensations more intensely or repeatedly go over negative thoughts, which may often intensify such emotions, rather than control them. In fact, it has been verified that a conscious attempt to control feelings and thoughts paradoxically intensifies intrusive thoughts (Wegner, 1994) and awakens the automatic nervous system (Gross, 1998).

However, mindfulness encourages the practitioner to do nothing but monitor these sensations, without making any attempts to control them. In this way, mindfulness gradually reduces uncomfortable emotions. In fact, it has been confirmed that practicing mindfulness meditation is effective for controlling chronic pain (Kabat-Zinn, Lipworth, & Burney, 1985) and preventing depression relapses (Teasdale et al., 2000).

The neural basis of brain is being clarified, and this may hold the key for the efficacy of mindfulness in controlling unwanted emotional responses. Ohira (2004), based on his overviews of recent researches, indicated that the ventral region of the prefrontal area, including the orbitofrontal area, is related to the coordinating function of emotional reactions caused by the amygdala. According to Ohira, it can be observed that when the ventral region is activated by an active attempt to control an emotion, sympathetic nerve activities are accelerated paradoxically. Moreover, while stressful stimulations are being calmly observed, as in mindfulness meditation, the dorsolateral region of the prefrontal area related to recursive consciousness is activated, and the activities of ventromedial region and amygdala are suppressed.

This result indicates that, when upset, it may be more effective to observe objectively one's self-condition and the surrounding situations rather than to make an unnatural effort to recover composure. Because it is not easy to conduct objective observations in stressful situations, learning meditation mindfulness skills is essential.

## Effects of Meditation Method

The mechanisms by which meditation alleviates anxiety have yet to be verified, but this author (Sakairi, 1999) is conducting research by observing changes in cognitive styles (an individual's outlook on things and his or her the way of thinking). The characteristics of changes that have to date been observed are enhanced flexibility, affirmativeness, and acceptability, which have much in common with the mental attitudes enhanced in other health regimes.

Regarding the work of enlivening one's spirit with a calm heart, the *Yojokun* (養生訓; Kaibara, 1713/1982) says:

> Have a calm mind and do not get upset; be slow and do not pressure anyone; relax and do not harden your mind; be taciturn and refrain from speaking or laughing loudly; be happy always and do not get angry without good reason; do not get sad easily and stop crying over spilt milk soon; do not blame yourself for your fault more than once; just accept Heaven's will and do not be sorry. These are the ways to cultivate your mind. (Vol. 2, 26)

The results of the research on observed changes in individual outlook and ways of thinking in 92 trainees in a meditation method (TM) during meditation are simply summarized in the following sections.

### Cognitive Changes
1. Affirmativeness: "My outlook on things and way of thinking became optimistic and affirmative."
2. Flexibility: "No longer as fussy about things and able to snap out of it more quickly."
3. Tolerance: "Now more tolerant toward others and able to forgive them more easily."
4. Acceptability: "Now I can accept things, situations, myself, etc."
5. Objectivity: "Now I can see things more objectively and with a broader mind."
6. Awareness: "Now I can think and feel about things more clearly and notice various things."

### Changes in Feelings and Emotions
1. Stability: "I've become less irritable and more composed."
2. Optimism: "I've become a happy person with a relaxed mind."
3. Simplicity: "Now I think of myself as a lucky person and more thankful."

Although it is not yet verified how actually effective the practice of meditation methods is for changing cognitive styles and emotions, the characteristics of the reported changes had much in common with the mental properties and situations targeted in other health-improvement regimens. The psychological changes brought about by meditation practice are summarized in order of the recommendations given in the *Yojokun* (quoted above) as follows:

1. Feelings become calmer and emotions more stabilized.
2. Acceptance of things, self, and others increases.

3. The way of thinking becomes more optimistic and affirmative, and feelings of gratitude are enhanced.

4. Enhanced flexibility helps mood change more quickly.

5. Enhanced objectivity makes it possible to make observations by putting a psychological distance between events and emotions.

Expecting only perfect results will make a person's view narrower and make him feel insecure and unhappy with those results, but being ready to accept whatever results are forthcoming—ranging from perfect success to utter failure—and committing himself to destiny will enable him not only to accept the result as it is but also to appreciate his luck when good results occur. Such an effect will extensively reset the framework of one's way of seeing and thinking about things using an utter failure criterion seems to be conspicuous in mindfulness meditations. Simply the attempt to deliberately walk slowly makes you feel how complicated and wonderful it is to move around normally, even as you do it unconsciously. When a disease makes a person unable to walk, he easily understands what he has lost; but if a person can actually feel the inconvenience while in good health, that person's dissatisfaction with his present situation would change to one of gratitude.

In addition, flexibility, which enables a person to make quick emotional shifts, can be remarkably improved by the passively performed Read Aloud (Svadiyaya) meditation. Formerly, this author advocated the "gear change model" to explain the mechanism of meditation effects (Sakairi, 1999), but the continued practice of meditation allows the individual to change both mental and physical states together. Irritability raises your blood pressures and nervousness makes your hands and feet cold. To freely change such mental and physical conditions—just as in the case of shifting the gears of a car—it is necessary to change your mental and physical levels temporarily into different states. Read Aloud meditation makes such change easier. In Read Aloud meditation, trainees are required only to repeatedly listen to the same sound everyday, while maintaining the same posture and in under the same certain relaxed psychological and physiological conditions. When the individual's emotions are running high, and she is in a disorderly state of mind, simply remembering will help to relax and ease the mind. Based on Pavlov's theory of conditioning, the sound can be utilized as a conditioning stimulus. In daily life, however, the mental and physical state of a person exercising this form of meditation may not readily respond to the sound; but once mental and physical levels return to normal, the subsequent changes would occur easily.

Although the volume of positive data is limited, if practicing meditation methods can enhance mental stability, objectivity, acceptability, flexibility, and so forth, it will be easier to maintain such mental attitudes as required by the *Yojokun*, and insecure and stressful situations will be alleviated naturally, too. To utilize meditation methods as a regimen and health technique, it is necessary to pursue further research.

## References

Benson, H. (1975). *The relaxation response.* New York: William Morrow and Company.

Benson, H. (1984). *Beyond the relaxation response.* New York: Times Books.

Carrington, P. (1978). *Clinically standardized meditation (CSM): Instructor's manual.* New Jersey: Pace Education Systems.

Dogen. (1991). *Tenzo kyokun or instructions for the Zen cook.* Tokyo: Koudansha. (Original work published 1237).

Goleman, D. (1977). *The varieties of the meditation experience.* New York: Irvington Publishers.

Gross, J.J. (1998). Antecedent- and response-focused emotion regulation: Divergent consequences for experience, expression, and physiology. *Journal of Personality and Social Psychology,* 74, 224–237.

Haruki, Y., Ishii, Y., & Suzuki, M. (Eds.). (1996). *Comparative and psychological study on meditation.* Delft, Netherlands: Eburon Publishers.

Izusan, K. (1983). *Hakuin-zenji Yasen-kanna.* Tokyo: Shunjusha Publishing.

Kabat-Zinn, J. (1990). *Full catastrophe living: Using the wisdom of your body and mind to face stress, pain, and illness.* New York: Dell Publishing.

Kabat-Zinn, J., Lipworth, L., & Burney, R. (1985). The clinical use of mindfulness meditation for the self-regulation of chronic pain. *Journal of Behavioral Medicine,* 8, 163–190.

Kaibara, E. (1982). *Yojokun.* Tokyo: Kodansha. (Original work published 1713).

Ohno, Y., & Yoshimura, K. (2001). *WHO the subjective well-being inventory: Japanese version.* Tokyo: Kaneko-shobo.

Ohira, H. (2004). Neural basis of emotion regulation: Control of prefrontal cortex over amygdalar activity. *Japanese Psychological Review,* 47, 93–118.

Ornstein, R.E. (1972). *The psychology of consciousness.* San Francisco: Freeman & Company.

Sahoda, T. (1980). *Yoga sutra.* Tokyo: Hirakawa Publishing.

Sakairi, Y. (1999). *Health psychological study on effects of meditation in reducing anxiety.* Tokyo: Kazama-shobo Publishing.

Schulte, T. (1981). *Transzendentale meditation und wohin sie furrt.* Stuttgart: Verlag Freies Geistesleben.

Schultz, J.H. (1932). *Das autogene training.* Stuttgart: Georg Thieme Verlag.

Schultz, J.H., & Luthe, W. (1969). *Autogenic therapy.* New York: Grune & Stratton.

Shapiro, D.H. (1982). Overview: Clinical and physiological comparison of meditation with other self-control strategies. *American journal of Psychiatry,* 139, 267–274.

Smith, J.C. (1987). Meditation as psychotherapy: A new look at the evidence. In M.A. West (Ed.), *The psychology of meditation* (pp. 136–149). Oxford: Clarendon Press, pp. 136–149.

Teasdale, J.D., Segal, Z.V., Williams, J.M.G., Ridgeway, V., Soulsby, J., & Lau, M. (2000). Prevention of relapse/recurrence in major depression by mindfulness-based cognitive therapy. *Journal of Consulting and Clinical Psychology, 68,* 615–623.

Wallace, R.K. (1970). Physiological effects of transcendental meditation. *Science, 167,* 1751–1754.

Wallace, R.K. (1991). *The neurophysiology of enlightenment.* Fairfield: Maharishi International University.

Wegner, D.M. (1994). Ironic processes of mental control. *Psychological Review, 101,* 34–52.

West, M.A. (1987). *The psychology of meditation.* Oxford: Clarendon Press.

# Health and Social Relationships in Nonhuman Primates: Toward a Comparative Health Psychology

John P. Capitanio

**Abstract**

Humans are not the only creatures that show rich and complex social relationships, nor are they the only creatures for whom health is a significant concern. A comparative approach to the study of social relationships and health is taken in the present chapter, with a focus on research conducted with nonhuman primates. Ecological, evolutionary, and mechanistic studies of monkeys, from both field and laboratory, are described. Characteristics of social relationships as studied by primatologists are discussed, and the roles of three such characteristics (complementarity [social dominance], "meshing" [social buffering], and stability) on endocrine, immune, and disease-related endpoints (including simian immunodeficiency virus [SIV] infection, atherosclerosis, and parasite abundance), are reviewed. Finally, several questions for future research are suggested.

**Keywords**: Primates, monkeys, dominance, social buffering, social relationships, immune system, endocrine system, atherosclerosis, simian immunodeficiency virus (SIV), parasites

It is obvious that humans are not the only creatures on the planet that show rich and complex social relationships, nor are they the only creatures for whom health is a significant concern. Humans are primates, sharing common ancestry with Old World monkeys (with divergence occurring approximately 23 million years ago [mya]) and apes (about 6 mya), and more distant ancestry with rodents (96 mya) (Nei & Glazko, 2002). Over the past couple of decades, data from several laboratories have examined how social relationships influence health in various nonhuman primate species. Some of these comparative studies, such as those conducted in the laboratory, are especially useful in that they permit study of disease-related mechanisms under well-controlled situations in a prospective fashion, something that is very hard to do with humans. And the phylogenetic proximity of humans to Old World monkeys suggests that similarities found between humans and these species may be due to homology (similarity owing to common descent) rather than analogy (similarity due to independent evolution of a

similar solution to a common problem; Campbell & Hodos, 1970). Homologous comparisons are extremely valuable, in that they increase the likelihood that underlying mechanisms are identical in the different species; with analogous comparisons, the similarities may be nothing more than superficial (although such comparisons are not without some value). Overall, then, studies with nonhuman primates form a link in the chain of translational research that ranges from *in vitro* work, to use of rodent models, to research involving human subjects.

A comparative approach can also provide a degree of experimental control that is impossible to achieve in human studies. In the laboratory, animals never miss appointments, always eat the proper foods, abstain from alcohol and drugs, and generally get better health care than most of the human population. This degree of control permits us to obtain good data using a surprisingly small number of animals, in fact a much smaller number than is usually possible with humans. Experimental control is also evident in the ability to "create" individuals with particular characteristics (e.g., through rearing in a nursery environment, rather than with a mother in a social setting) and to construct social settings that facilitate study of particular types and qualities of social relationships. The artificiality of the laboratory environment reminds us, however, that the animals are serving as *models*. Just as an engineer's model of a bridge tells her something (but not everything) about the qualities of the real structure, so too an animal model of a disease tells us something about the human disease.

A truly comparative approach, though, is broader than just modeling in animals a set of conditions that can tell us something about human diseases. A comparative orientation can also provide perspectives that may be hard to identify if our focus is only on humans—how disease fits into an ecological context, what adaptations animals have to avoid disease in the first place, and how disease shapes population structure and social relationships. Comparative study also confronts us with the single biggest difference between humans and all other animals: language. Nonhumans cannot tell us how they are feeling, whether they find their social relationships satisfying, or how their experiences as juveniles affect them as adults. Consequently, we are left with studying what animals actually *do*, and inferring from their behavior (and physiology) something about their psychological characteristics and states. Although one can argue the benefits and drawbacks of such an approach, it is an approach that is not unheard of in studies of human behavior: The field of human ethology, for example, involves study of human behavior using ethological techniques, with a focus on what people do, and not what they self-report doing, thinking, or feeling. An explicit focus on behavior often forces us to see phenomena somewhat differently.

Here, we describe data that have focused on the role of social relationships in health and immunity, but first we describe some "big picture" issues that reflect how a comparative approach can provide a different perspective on some familiar issues. For this discussion, I draw upon field studies of primate behavioral ecology. Recently, there has been a growing interest in the relationship between the life-history of primate species and disease (Huffman & Chapman, 2009; Nunn & Altizer, 2006). Unfortunately, this literature has developed largely independently of the field of health psychology, and of the large biomedical literature that employs animal models. It does, however, place some components of the study of social relationships and disease into broader ecological and evolutionary contexts, contexts that are relevant to health psychology, but that are often unacknowledged in the study of humans.

## A Comparative Approach to Health Psychology: Some "Big Picture" Issues
### Disease in Comparative Perspective

It is worth mentioning at the outset that the disease-related processes that have been examined in free-ranging populations of nonhuman primates are less closely related to the kinds of diseases that afflict humans from developed countries—cardiovascular disease, cancer, chronic respiratory disease—but, rather, are more like the diseases that afflict individuals from developing countries, and that killed people from developed countries as recently as a hundred years ago—in particular, acute infectious diseases that could lead, for example, to colitis and diarrhea, or to acute respiratory distress (Kaur & Singh, 2009; Taylor, 2009). These facts remind us that the diseases that we in developed countries live with daily are chronic, take a long time to develop, and are evident at least partially because of increased longevity resulting from better treatment of acute infectious diseases. These chronic diseases also have significant lifestyle components to them, associated with diet, exercise, and personal habits such as alcohol and tobacco use. Indeed, to model these diseases in animals, we usually must impose upon them extraordinary conditions, such as tobacco use or specially prepared atherogenic diets. Although some may question the validity of such models because they are not "natural," a comparative health psychologist might say "Exactly. And neither are the prevailing conditions for humans in developed countries today, relative to our evolutionary history." Humans—their social relationships and their immune systems—evolved in a context that included parasitism and acute infectious diseases as important agents of natural selection. Trans fats, high fructose corn syrup, an inactive lifestyle, menthol cigarettes, and other aspects of modern life that impair health were not relevant during millions of years of human evolution.

In a sense, then, we are presented with a problem of having immune systems that evolved to protect us primarily from one set of conditions—acute pathogens—and that are now being asked to protect us from very different conditions, brought on by substantial changes in lifestyle. And not only are our immune systems sometimes not up to the task, there is growing evidence that they may now be part of the problem. For example, inflammation, an important component of innate immunity that is usually protective, is now being implicated in a variety of chronic health conditions ranging from Alzheimer disease to heart disease to cancer, and this story is so well-supported that it has made its way into the popular press (Gorman, 2004; Stix, 2007). In addition, the greatly reduced exposure of humans in the developed world to relatively minor infectious agents that surround us may be skewing our immune responses toward hypersensitivity to substances that are actually fairly innocuous. This idea is usually described as the *hygiene hypothesis* and is often invoked to account for the explosion of cases of allergy and asthma in the developed world (Hopkin, 2009). Below, I will discuss how disease plays a role in shaping a species' characteristics, but it's worth noting that this process is still ongoing in our own species, and in the developed world, the shaping is largely driven by lifestyle choices that have accompanied economic development.

Finally, a comparative and ecological perspective on disease reminds us that, in terms of natural selection and evolution, the bottom line is fitness—transmission of one's genes into the next generation. Thinking in these terms is not common for most psychologists (health or otherwise); indeed, we tend to think that our cultural adaptations override natural selection—differences in reproduction between individuals in a population—if not worldwide, then at least in the developed world. To be sure, adaptations such as corrective eyewear, immunizations, and filtered water might result in relaxed selection on humans, but that doesn't mean selection is not occurring (Sabeti et al., 2006); rather, it suggests that we tend to think in too-narrow time-frames, and/or simply ignore such analyses for whatever reason. Genetically based individual characteristics—social, behavioral, physiological—that facilitated avoidance and/or successful management of a pathogen or disease process likely resulted in more successful reproduction (i.e., higher fitness) for some individuals over others. These characteristics would be evident in our species, and may continue to be selected. The influence of pathogens on fitness is not always direct in the sense of their being lethal, however; many pathogens can influence fitness owing to indirect, and especially additive, effects. For example, there is considerable comparative interest in pathogens, such as those that are sexually transmitted, that induce sterility, or at least reduce fecundity (Lockhart, Thrall, & Antonovics, 1996). Such pathogens may increase their own fitness at the expense of their host's fitness—a reminder that,

through natural selection, pathogens have their own evolutionary agenda, which might not coincide with that of the host. In addition, a pathogen could contribute to making the individual more susceptible to predation, either through making the animal more sluggish as its immune system fights the pathogen, or through more direct changes in behavior (Berdoy, Webster, & Macdonald, 2000; this example will be described below). Additive effects are seen when the effects of a pathogen may be exacerbated under conditions of food shortage, for example (e.g., Chapman et al., 2006). Such issues are not unknown in humans; the role of nutrition in health and disease is actively studied in people, and sick individuals are often warned against engaging in risky behavior, such as driving (other cars perhaps being the modern equivalent of "predators"), owing to reduced cognitive capabilities.

### Disease Is a Cost of Sociality

Humans are a very social species, as evidenced by complex social relationships of varying types between and within sexes that persist across the year. The same can also be said about most species of Old World monkeys and apes. That statement is not true about most animals, however, or even most mammals, nearly half of which are rodents (Wolff & Sherman, 2007). In fact, the social unit that is most common among terrestrial mammals consists only of a female with her immature offspring. Other social interactions for the typical mammal may be sporadic, revolving around territorial defense and mating, but during the active part of its day (which for many mammals is at night, as they are nocturnal), individuals forage alone (Eisenberg, 1981). Contrast this pattern with the predominant one among nonhuman primates, which involves permanent groups containing three or more adults (Kappeler & van Schaik, 2002). Rhesus macaques (*Macaca mulatta*) provide a good (and typical) example of the pattern seen in Old World monkeys. Groups are together year round, and range in size up to 100 or more animals, although a more common group size may be on the order of two or three dozen individuals. Adult females outnumber adult males on the order of three or four to one, and animals of all ages can be found in most groups. Females that are born into a group will nearly always live in that group for their entire lives. As such, females form the core of the social group and maintain strong social bonds, particularly with their female kin. Females are organized in matrilines, each of which comprises females that are related to each other and with whom they interact most often. Within a matriline, females show a dominance hierarchy, and in fact, matrilines themselves can be ranked, such that members of one entire matriline will outrank all members of a separate matriline. At sexual maturity, males typically leave the group, may spend time either solitary or with other males, and eventually work their way into a new social group. Males within a group are also arranged in a dominance hierarchy, and position in that hierarchy typically involves forming alliances with each other (Melnick & Pearl, 1987).

Given that the more typical mammalian pattern is much simpler than this, what factors could have led to the evolution of the rich social life displayed by rhesus monkeys and humans? Behavioral ecologists recognize several factors, an important one being protection from predators. An individual on his own has only one set of eyes and ears to keep watch for the carnivores and raptors that are hunting for lunch. But, in a group, there are many eyes and ears, and detection of a potential predator often results in a vocalization that serves to alert the other members of the group to the predator's presence (Cheney & Seyfarth, 2005). In addition to predator detection, the social group may also serve to actively drive the predator away by engaging in aggressive defense behavior. Not all species of mammals avail themselves of these benefits of social life, however, presumably because their feeding ecology won't support such groupings. Thus, in certain ecological conditions, there are definite survival advantages to living socially.

But social life also entails costs, and chief among them is the increased risk of infectious disease and parasite transmission (Alexander, 1974). If an individual is infected with a parasite of some type, the chances of infecting another individual may be higher if the animal lives in a social group. The relationship between sociality and disease risk is complex, however. For example, macaques spend a great deal of time grooming each other. Although this behavior serves a social function, namely to reflect and enhance social bonds, there is also an obvious hygienic function, in that *external* parasites can be removed from the body, especially in places that an animal itself cannot reach. Sociality, then, can result in decreased susceptibility to these types of pathogens (e.g., Sanchez-Villagra, Pope, & Salas, 1998). The process of grooming, however, often brings animals' heads in close proximity, which could increase the risk of transmission of an *internal* parasite, like a respiratory pathogen.

In fact, data indicate that degree of sociality is related to parasite load. In these analyses, population size and/or density is often used as a proxy measure for "sociality." In an analysis of 101 primate species and 231 different parasite taxa (including helminths, viruses, bacteria, fungi, and protozoa), Nunn et al. (2003) showed that host population density was a strong and significant predictor of parasite species richness (i.e., number of different parasite species present in animals), even after controlling for other influences. This relationship held not only for the combined parasite data, but also for the separate classes of parasites of viruses, helminths, and protozoan parasites, all internal pathogens. Of course, the role of population size and density and disease is well-known for humans as well. For example, an analysis of deaths from the plague in France in 1720–1722 showed that 100% of the towns that had more than 10,000 inhabitants were affected by the plague, but communities with lower populations were much less affected (Biraben, 1968). In general, then, although we may be very interested in understanding how the qualities of social relationships (e.g., social support) might be protective in the event of infection, a comparative perspective reminds us that the very phenomenon of our sociality puts us at increased risk of infection.

## Nonhuman Primates Have Strategies to Minimize the Health-related Costs of Social Living

Given that social life itself can be a risk factor for disease transmission, it is no surprise that animals have developed ways of minimizing these costs. In fact, arguments have been made that avoidance of pathogens has been an important selection factor in the evolution of primate sociality (Freeland, 1976, p. 12): "Selection for disease control and avoidance may be a potent force in determining parameters such as the level of integrity exhibited by a social group's individual composition, the size of social groups, and patterns of movement." Here, I briefly review such ideas. It is worth noting, however, that although many of these hypotheses were proposed more than 30 years ago by Freeland and others, they have only recently begun to be investigated; thus, the database is relatively small at this point, although it is a rapidly growing area of study.

### RESTRICTING ACTIVITIES TO THOSE ANIMALS WITHIN THE GROUP

Although parasite transmission within a group is a concern, groups that persist year round are likely to share a common pathogen load, and members of a given group are likely to become immune to most of those pathogens. Consequently, natural selection may favor individuals who minimize interactions with members of other groups, whose pathogen load may differ. In fact, this practice is widespread in primate species: Intergroup interactions often involve active avoidance (e.g., when groups see each other, they vocalize, which causes the groups to move farther apart) or outright hostility. When different groups do come together, usually little affiliative or sexual interaction occurs, and evidence suggests that, in those cases where affiliative intergroup interactions have been noted, the groups had recently fissioned or experienced migration of animals from one group to the other (Cheney, 1987), indicating that the groups probably shared a pathogen background, and so interaction may carry relatively lower risk.

## BEING SELECTIVE ABOUT WHO IS ADMITTED TO THE GROUP

Of course, groups cannot remain completely isolated from conspecifics; to do so would result in inbreeding and reduced fitness for group members. Consequently, there must be some migration between groups, and in most primate species this is accomplished by males, who emigrate from their natal groups around the age of sexual maturity. Being admitted to, and becoming established in, a group is not a simple or quick process, however; usually it takes place over many weeks, and during that time, the prospective immigrant is of low rank and subject to frequent chases and attacks by the high-ranked animals in the group. The likely effect of this process is stressful, and Freeland (1976) suggests that the stress imposed on the outsider may reveal the presence of latent infections, which can then result either in the diseased animal dying or the group members rejecting it. Although this explanation is speculative, owing largely to the rarity of observing the full process of immigration to a new group, there is evidence supporting aspects of the process. First, abundant evidence suggests that immigration and rising in rank in the new group typically takes a considerable period of time (Drickamer & Vessey, 1973; van Noordwijk & van Schaik, 1985). Second, we know that the period when males have left their natal group and attempt to immigrate to a new group is characterized by high mortality (Dittus, 1977). Third, stress does promote disease expression (e.g., see various contributions in this volume). Finally, there is some evidence that males that are solitary and not part of a group, may, in fact, suffer from disease (Nishida, 1966; but see Hamilton & Tilson, 1982).

## BEING SELECTIVE ABOUT WITH WHOM ONE MATES

Among mammals, females are typically the "choosier" sex, and males often compete with each other for access to receptive females (e.g., Bateson, 1983). This competition is stressful and can reveal (as described above) disease arising from latent infections, potentially enabling the female to assess male quality and choose the highest-quality male to sire her offspring (Freeland, 1976). There is evidence in the literature on nonhuman primates (Small, 1989), as well as on other taxa (Hamilton & Zuk, 1982), for the idea of female choosiness, and although the extent to which health is a major indicator of "quality" has been rarely examined in primates, there is evidence in other mammals that females prefer not to mate with infected males (Ehman & Scott, 2002). Cues (such as red facial coloration in the breeding season) are available, however, by which females can choose males (Waitt et al., 2003), and cues such as these have been considered indicators of health and quality (Folstad & Karter, 1992).

## BEHAVING SO AS TO MINIMIZE POSSIBLE INFECTION

I have already mentioned that social grooming is a behavior that serves a hygienic function of removing ectoparasites from body surfaces. Certainly, animals can groom themselves, and most animals do. But animals can rarely reach all parts of their bodies, and evidence suggests that these parts, including the head, neck, and back, are socially groomed significantly more than self-groomed (Barton, 1985). Of course, grooming is a complex behavior, and there is consensus that the social functions of grooming—involved in establishing and maintaining social bonds—are very important. Nevertheless, data do support a utilitarian function of removing ectoparasites (e.g., Sanchez-Villagra et al., 1998). Other behaviors can reduce infection as well. For example, there is some evidence that baboons alter their pattern of ranging so as to rotate among different sleeping sites because the ova and larvae of intestinal parasites excreted in feces are found in large numbers in the soil beneath the sleeping sites (Hausfater & Meade, 1982; see also Chapman, Rothman, & Hodder, 2009 for discussion of other strategies involving alteration of ranging patterns).

## MEDICATING WHEN NEEDED

It has been known for some time that the diets of wild primates contain substances that have minimal, if any, nutritional value, but that may be of therapeutic value in relieving distress from parasites. A variety of primate species consume soil, and often these soils have a clay basis and contain high concentrations of kaolin. Kaolin is an effective antidiarrheal for human and nonhuman primates, and is the main ingredient in Kaopectate (Pharmacia/Upjohn), a nonprescription pharmaceutical marketed as a treatment for gastrointestinal upset (Krishnamani & Mahaney, 2000). This has led to considerable interest in the study of self-medication in primates (reviewed by Huffman, 2007), and the data are compelling that animals use a variety of compounds therapeutically (although there is as yet no evidence to indicate that animals use these compounds prophylactically). One example of this work is leaf-swallowing by chimpanzees. Bristly leaves are chosen, folded between tongue and palate (not chewed), and swallowed on an empty stomach. They pass through the gut unchanged, but stimulate gut motility and scour the luminal surface, which facilitates the elimination of a nematode worm species, *Oesophagostomum*, that can cause abdominal pain and diarrhea (Huffman & Caton, 2001).

Many of the strategies described that minimize the health-related costs of sociality in nonhuman primates look strikingly similar to phenomena that occur in our own species. Some of these are obvious, such as use of medication and engaging in behaviors (e.g., hand-washing) to minimize possible infection. But what about some of the other strategies described? One interesting line of research in the past two decades has focused on fluctuating asymmetry (FA). Bilateral symmetry is the norm for developing organisms, and deviations from asymmetry (i.e., FA) can reflect instabilities during development due to genetic and/or environmental influence. These instabilities can be manifested as poor health and "bad genes" (Thornhill & Moller, 1997). In fact, evidence in humans exists that low FA (that is, greater bilateral symmetry) is associated with reduced morbidity and greater fecundity (Waynforth, 1998), and with more sexual partners (Thornhill & Gangestad, 1994). In short, humans, like nonhuman primates, may indeed be making reproductive decisions based upon health, as reflected in degree of body asymmetry; we simply may not know that (or why) we are doing it.

### Disease Affects Behavior and Social Life

Anyone who has been sick, regardless of the specific cause, knows that common side effects can include reduced energy, depression, anorexia, and reduced social interaction, a constellation of behavioral changes that are often referred to as "sickness behaviors," which arise from increased production of proinflammatory cytokines during infection (Johnson, 2002). There are more serious social consequences of disease, however. Some of the earliest data from nonhuman primates came from a field study of howler monkeys (*Alouatta palliata*) on Barro Colorado Island in the Panama Canal Zone in 1951 (Collias & Southwick, 1952). This was the same area that had been censused in 1932–1933, and a comparison of the datasets revealed a remarkable change in the structure of the population. Although the numbers of howler groups remained the same, the number of animals was less than half in 1951 compared to the earlier time point. More specifically, the composition of the individual groups changed, from a multimale–multifemale group composition, with an average of three adult males per group (26 of 28 groups had more than one adult male) in 1933, to one male–multifemale composition (23 of 29 groups) in 1951. It appears that this change in population density and group composition was the result of a recent epidemic of yellow fever. Of course, one need look no further than Africa to see the impact of disease on social structure in our own species (AVERT, 2009)— acquired immune deficiency syndrome (AIDS) has resulted in millions of orphaned children. Further, because the death of an adult results in households in South Africa being four times more likely to dissolve, the social disruption due to AIDS in the developing world will likely track closely the patterns of mortality (Hosegood, McGrath, Herbst, & Timaeus, 2004).

As mentioned earlier, it's often not appreciated that parasites are creatures that have their own agenda, and, like the hosts they invade, are subject to natural selection. Consequently, the parasite and the host are engaged in something like an arms race (which is played out over multiple generations), in which an advantage for one side results in a counterstrategy by the other. One implication of such a viewpoint is that parasites might alter the behavior of organisms to facilitate their own transmission. The classic example of this is found among rodents infected with *Toxoplasma gondii* (Berdoy et al., 2000). *T. gondii* is a protozoan parasite that can infect all mammals. In immunocompromised individuals, *Toxoplasma* can cause encephalitis and neurological disorders and problems with other organ systems, and in pregnant women, miscarriage or stillbirth. *T. gondii* has an "indirect" lifestyle, with cats as the final (or definitive) host, meaning the protozoan can only reproduce in cats, which then shed oocysts in their feces. Oocysts that are ingested by another mammal (the intermediate host) often result in cyst formation in various tissues, especially the brain, and subclinical infection. Cats, then, can become infected either by directly ingesting oocysts from the infected feces of another cat, or by consuming an intermediate host that is itself infected. Rats show a high prevalence of infection with *T. gondii*, and infected animals show increases in activity and decreases in fear-related behavior. Importantly, rats uninfected with *T. gondii* avoid areas with cat scent, as might be expected. Infected rats, however, actually seem to be attracted to these areas (Berdoy et al., 2000), a preference that is likely, in nature, to result in increased transmission of the parasite to cats, thereby serving the "needs" of the parasite at the expense of the intermediate host. Interestingly, a number of studies of humans have suggested that *T. gondii* infection is associated with differences in personality (e.g., lower novelty-seeking), lower reaction time, and psychoses such as schizophrenia (see review by Henriquez, Brett, Alexander, Pratt, & Roberts, 2009). Although it is difficult to know the direction of causality (e.g., Is lower novelty-seeking a result of infection, or are such individuals simply more likely to become infected?), it does appear that the genome of *T. gondii* contains genes for two enzymes that can affect dopamine and/or serotonin synthesis (Henriquez et al., 2009), thus contributing to the idea that this pathogen might be manipulating our own behavior.

Finally, disease can have an indirect and lasting effect on social processes and long-term health. One example of this was reported by Sapolsky and Share (2004) for a troop of olive baboons that had been under study since the 1970s. In the early 1980s, two troops of baboons took up residence near a garbage pit associated with a tourist lodge in Kenya. Some of the animals (termed refuse eaters) fed repeatedly from the dump, and these animals were among the most aggressive in the groups, typically adult males. Contaminated food at the dump resulted in an outbreak of tuberculosis in 1983, with the consequence that all of the refuse-eating adult males (46% of adult males) from one of the troops died. No other animals in that troop died. This event altered the sex ratio (fewer adult males in the group), but more importantly, the "culture" of the troop changed because the surviving adult males were considerably less aggressive than were those that died. Observations ceased on this group for a period of 7 years, after which detailed data were once again collected.

By this time, none of the resident adult males were the same ones that had survived the tuberculosis outbreak. However, the considerably more pacific culture in this troop persisted—rates of affiliation were high among adult males, rates of aggression directed at lower-ranking males were low, and physiological measures suggested less stress among subordinate males (see below). Baboons are like rhesus monkeys, in that groups of related females remain in the groups in which they are born, whereas males transfer at reproductive maturity. It appears that the more pacific behavior displayed by the replacement males was fostered by the behavior of the females, who more quickly interacted in an affiliative manner with immigrating males, "setting the tone" for the types of preferred interactions. Importantly for the subordinate males in this troop, the negative health consequences of social subordination that have been reported in wild baboon troops (see below) may have been avoided to a large degree.

A second example of the lasting effects of disease on social processes comes from a recent study of infant mortality patterns in two communities of chimpanzees in Cote d'Ivoire (Kuehl, Elzner, Moebius, Boesch, & Walsh, 2008). Respiratory pathogens (presumably contracted from humans) were found to be a significant source of mortality in infant chimpanzees in this population. Moreover, the numbers of infants and their mortality rate cycled regularly in these populations, but importantly, these cycles were out of phase with each other in the two communities, suggesting that the cycles were not driven by an environmental factor such as food availability. It appears that these cycles were organized around a peak of social play that occurs at 2–3 years of age among chimpanzees. Multiple deaths of infants due to a respiratory outbreak eventually synchronized the reproductive cycles of mothers, resulting in a peak of births. Social interactions among the infants in the birth cohorts increased until hitting the peak play age of 2–3 years, when infants play approximately twice as much, and with about twice as many partners, as animals of other ages. This increased contact then resulted in further outbreaks and mortality, and the cycle repeated. Together, these examples illustrate that disease can have an impact on specific subsets of animals, and this impact can have consequences for fundamental aspects of social life, such as group composition (howler monkeys), reproduction, and culture of the group, with positive (for the baboons) and negative (for the chimpanzees) health consequences for the most vulnerable in those societies.

## Social Relationships and Health in Nonhuman Primates

A growing literature examines the role of psychosocial factors in health-related outcomes among nonhuman primates. Some of this research has been conducted in field settings, where a strong focus has been on one specific component of social relationships—namely, social dominance—in which questions are of the form "Do low-ranked animals have greater parasite loads than high-ranked animals?" Considerably more research has been laboratory-based. Some of this has also focused on dominance; much of this research has employed the construct of "stress" to describe the independent variables of interest, and a large part of this body of work falls under the heading of psychoneuroimmunology. Before I describe some of the outcomes of this research, however, I would like to discuss briefly some of these points in more detail.

### Preliminary Issues: Relationships and Endpoints

#### HOW ARE SOCIAL RELATIONSHIPS STUDIED?

In animal behavior, discussion of what is meant by *social relationships* usually involves reference to the work of the eminent ethologist, Robert Hinde, who wrote a series of conceptual papers in the mid-1970s focused on the qualities of relationships. In Hinde's view (e.g., Hinde, 1976), relationships involve a series of interactions in time. These interactions can be described in terms of behavior (i.e., what A and B are doing with each other), but more important is *how* they are doing what they are doing: Are the two animals fighting in a savage or a perfunctory fashion? Is the interaction furtive or open? These aspects of interactions are examples of "qualities." Social relationships, then, can be characterized based upon the following qualities of the interactions (elements on this list are neither mutually exclusive nor exhaustive):

- *Content and complexity*: Consider the nature of the relationship between a pair of animals, the content of whose interactions comprises only agonistic behavior, versus another dyad whose content includes agonism but also affiliation. Relationships can be considered uniplex if the content involves only a single domain of behavior, or multiplex if it involves multiple domains.
- *Reciprocity versus complementarity*: Reciprocal interactions imply symmetry, by which is meant the display of similar behavior by the participants. Play interactions, for example, are usually quite symmetric, with animals chasing and being chased, play-biting and being bitten, etc. In contrast, some interactions are better described as complementary. The classic example here is of dominance–subordinance interactions, where one animal threatens a second, takes the second's food, and can keep the second away from a potential mate. The second, in turn, grooms the first more, avoids the first, and makes appeasement signals to avoid physical attack.
- *Meshing versus conflict*: Animals often behave toward each other as though the goals of one are aligned (i.e., mesh) with the goals of another. In a grooming interaction, for example, one animal may approach another animal and adopt a solicitation posture, after which the second animal begins grooming. This is in contrast to interactions that contain elements of conflict. To continue the grooming example, A may approach B and give a groom-present, at which point B relocates. A then approaches again and groom-presents, and B again relocates. This can continue until A gives up, B gives in, or something (or someone) intervenes to alter the situation. No aggression was displayed, but the interaction clearly suggests a conflict in goals between the two animals.
- *Temporal components*: Relationships involve a patterning of interactions over time, and so temporal aspects of the interactions become important. In fact, temporal components are critical for understanding changes in some relationships. For example, the rhesus monkey mother–infant relationship changes over time, as reflected in changes in the constituent interactions—infants are born very dependent on mother, and over the first few months develop increasing independence, until at weaning, conflictual interactions tend to peak in frequency. Another temporal aspect of interactions reflects stability. Are the interactions, and opportunities for interaction, stable over time? Lack of stability may result in only superficial relationships, or relationships in which particular forms of interaction (such as complementary interactions) predominate.

The focus of this discussion has been on describing dimensions of interactions that contribute to the establishment and maintenance of relationships between individuals. I will not discuss other relevant issues, such as extrapolating from dyadic relationships to descriptions of social networks, the contextual aspects of how some relationships can constrain others, whether some relationships are considered more important than others (e.g., for humans, these may be relationships that provide social support in times of crisis), or how relationships can be quantified using these qualities of interactions (but see Capitanio, 1985; Mason, Long, & Mendoza, 1993; Weinstein & Capitanio, 2008). Suffice it to say that this is a rich area of investigation and links comparative work with those components of social psychology and human ethology that are examining similar processes in humans.

With respect to comparative studies of social relationships and health, the preceding provides a framework to understand the studies that have been done. A substantial amount of work has focused on the complementarity component of relationships, with "dominance" serving as the organizing concept. Other studies have examined the health benefits of relationships with particular kinds of content; this direction includes research on the buffering effects on health that "friends" may exert (which suggests meshing). Finally, studies have examined the health consequences of stability or instability in social relationships. These three aspects of social relationships will be described below.

Unfortunately, no studies have examined the impact on health of multiple aspects of social relationships at one time. This is a deficiency in the literature, inasmuch as we don't know the relative contributions of these dimensions to health outcomes. This is made more problematic because the approaches taken have resorted to using a single term—stress—to describe the psychological state that presumably obtains when individuals are low in rank, do not have social buffers, or are in unstable social relationships. Are these three conditions equivalent psychologically or physiologically? Can one dimension substitute for another? And, what about individual difference factors: Might some animals be more affected than others by one or more of these qualities of social relationships? In short, the sophistication with which one can describe (and quantify) social relationships has, for the most part, not found its way into the comparative health psychology literature (although there are some exceptions, see below). Too often, in both the laboratory and the field literature, the complexity of social relationships is reduced to a single dimension, and that is most often

"dominance," with scant attention paid to other aspects of social relationships. This is unfortunate, inasmuch as the ability to manipulate some of these dimensions is much greater in nonhumans than in humans, which could result in a more sophisticated approach to understanding the role of relationships in health.

## WHAT ARE THE ENDPOINTS?

A variety of outcome measures have been utilized in the comparative literature. Studies of wild primates have typically relied on measures that are easily obtainable, inasmuch as blood sampling of animals is difficult. These field studies have usually employed measures such as number of parasites (or their eggs) found in fecal samples, or numbers of ectoparasites (e.g., ticks) quantified after darting of animals. Laboratory studies have often not relied on parasitology per se, but rather on other indicators of disease (such as viral load, serum cholesterol levels, or measures derived from histologic analysis) or immunity (ranging from cell counts to in vitro measures of cell function, to in vivo measures such as antibody responses, to other functional measures such as mRNA production for cytokines from stimulated blood cells). Others in this volume have described these measures, and I will not reiterate that discussion here. Rather, there are two issues to be raised about endpoints. First, as mentioned, something of a disconnect exists between field and laboratory studies in terms of the measures taken. Field studies generally focus on naturally occurring infections (although sometimes the infectious agent originates with humans), tissue access (e.g., blood) is limited, opportunities for histology are virtually nonexistent, and there is a strong desire to be minimally intrusive to the animals. What laboratory studies may lack in external validity (with respect to the natural situation for the animals), it makes up for in internal validity: Infectious agents can be introduced (or predisposing conditions can be imposed) at specific, known times, and tissue access, both pre- and post-necropsy, is typically excellent. This disconnect makes comparisons between field and laboratory research more difficult. The second issue is that it's important to keep the distinction between statistical and biological significance in mind. Many well-controlled psychoneuroimmunological studies have been conducted showing strong and significant effects of a manipulation on a particular immune measure (some of which studies will be described below). It is a leap to infer that a statistical effect is translated into a biological effect. It's possible, for example, that the protective effects of an immune response are not linear, but rather involve thresholds. So, a significant difference in antibody responses to a particular manipulation may have no actual health benefit, since levels for individuals in both the experimental and control groups may be well above some minimal threshold, above which additional antibody is likely to have little or no consequence for an actual infection.

## Complementarity in Relationships: Dominance

As described above, dominance is an important organizing feature of social life for Old World monkeys. At a minimum, dominance reflects an individual's priority of access to various resources—food, preferred resting sites, members of the opposite sex, etc. "Dominance" is truly a relationship-level concept; it emerges out of interactions between individuals, and an individual within a dominance hierarchy has a dominance rank. Rank, however, is contextual. If one takes the top-ranked animal from each of ten different monkey groups and puts them all together in a single cage, the animals will soon sort themselves into a dominance hierarchy, and the ranks will range from number 1 to number 10. Thus, in short order, an animal that had previously ranked 1 in its familiar group could now possess the 10th position in the hierarchy of the new group. It's important to understand that "dominance" describes an attribute of a relationship, and not an attribute of an individual. Certainly there are individual-level attributes that contribute to low or high rank in a hierarchy, but at this point it remains unclear what they are, although most primatologists would agree that it is some combination of, among other things, confidence and social skill. In addition, it is not the case that animals equivalent in rank in different groups necessarily possess the same characteristics (Sapolsky & Ray, 1989). A useful and still relevant discussion of the concept of dominance in primatology can be found in Bernstein (1981).

Because of the importance of dominance in the social life of primates, it is the relationship variable that has received the most attention in studies of disease and related physiology. Studies of dominance and health typically refer to the concept of stress and a naive hypothesis might go something like the following: Low-ranked animals experience greater stress; stress is associated with higher glucocorticoid levels and suppressed immune function; hence low-ranked animals have poorer health. Stress may well be the important intervening variable in understanding the relationship of dominance to health, but every phrase of the previous statement can be challenged by data,

some of which derive from the field literature exploring how dominance may related to parasite loads.

### "LOW-RANKED ANIMALS EXPERIENCE GREATER STRESS"

There is abundant evidence that this is not always so. Sapolsky (2005) has described a variety of situations in which high-ranked animals show greater indications of stress, and other situations in which low-ranked animals show greater indications of stress. For example, even among closely related species, such as macaques in the genus *Macaca*, variations occur in how dominance maps onto resource access. Some species, like rhesus macaques, are often described as "despotic." In such species, resource availability is skewed toward the high-ranked individuals, who attain their rank through aggression. In more "egalitarian" species like stumptail macaques (*M. arctoides*), resource distribution is far less skewed. Low rank tends to be associated with indicators of stress more in despotic than in egalitarian species. As a second example, even in despotic species, the relationship between rank and stress is variable. For example, under stable social conditions, low-ranked animals show greater signs of stress owing, presumably, to continued harassment, and lack of control and predictability in their lives. But, when the hierarchy becomes unstable, such as during challenges to the high-ranked animals from an immigrant, or during group formation in captivity, it is the high-ranked animals that show the greater evidence of stress. Finally, in a meta-analysis across the Primate Order, no consistent relationship was found between rank and physiological stress responses (Abbott et al., 2003). Rather, low rank was found to be associated with stress (as indexed by elevated levels of cortisol) only in species in which subordinate animals experience high rates of stressors, have little social support, and have few kin available.

### "STRESS IS ASSOCIATED WITH HIGHER GLUCOCORTICOID LEVELS"

Although it is often the case that stress (indexed through behavioral means) is associated with high cortisol, this is not always the case. In marmosets, small monkeys of the New World that typically live in family groups, subordinate females usually show reduced, and not elevated, basal levels of cortisol (Abbott et al., 2003). In this case, reduced cortisol is not associated with reduced levels of adrenocorticotropic hormone (ACTH), which is released from the pituitary and which stimulates cortisol release from the adrenal. Rather, reduced cortisol production is related to reduced responsiveness of the adrenal to the circulating ACTH. Although in this case, the hypocortisolism may not be related to subordination per se, but rather to the reproductive suppression imposed upon subordinate females by the dominant female, in other situations hypocortisolism is clearly associated with stress, particularly with chronic stress. In an experimental situation in which adult male rhesus monkeys were randomly assigned to stable or to unstable social conditions (see below), Capitanio et al. (1998) found that social instability resulted in reduced basal concentrations of cortisol. Pharmacologic probing of the hypothalamic-pituitary-adrenal (HPA) system by administration of the synthetic glucocorticoid dexamethasone suggested that the hypocortisolemia was associated with enhanced negative feedback in the HPA system. That is, in a normally functioning HPA system, release of cortisol "feeds back" to the hypothalamus and pituitary, ultimately causing a reduction in cortisol output. In this study, however, a standardized dose of dexamethasone decreased cortisol concentrations more in animals socialized in unstable conditions compared to animals in stable social groups. This is an important result because animals were randomly assigned to social condition—in situations in which chronic stress in humans has been associated with hypocortisolemia (e.g., posttraumatic stress disorder; Yehuda et al., 1995), the argument has been made that, since only a subset of chronically stressed individuals display the hypocortisolemia and enhanced negative feedback (Yehuda, 2006), perhaps the result reflects some preexisting HPA (or other) anomaly among those individuals. Such an argument is hard to justify when random assignment has occurred, which is, of course, impossible to implement with humans.

## "STRESS IS ASSOCIATED WITH SUPPRESSED IMMUNE FUNCTION"

As has been described elsewhere in this series, the immune system is a complex physiological system that has many different components, each with its own time-frame for operations, but which generally work together. However, it is a mistake to think of the immune system as a unitary system, with all components behaving in the same fashion. In fact, although there is substantial evidence that stress can suppress immunity, there is also evidence that stress can enhance immunity. Dhabhar (2009) describes situations in which stress can have immunoenhancing properties; for example, acute stress occurring at the time of immune activation can facilitate innate immune responses. This makes a certain amount of

sense from an evolutionary point of view. Given that our stress response systems probably evolved to help us deal with situations like escaping from a predator, it makes little sense that activation of those systems should put us at a disadvantage in the event of an injury arising from escape. Rather, it is the chronic activation of these systems that more consistently results in immunocompromise.

## "LOW-RANKED ANIMALS HAVE POORER HEALTH"

Just as low-ranked animals do not always experience the greatest stress, so too do they not always experience the worst health outcomes. Evidence describing the complex relationship between dominance and health come from field studies of dominance and parasitism, and from field and laboratory studies of dominance and atherosclerosis.

### Dominance and Parasite Loads

The results of the handful of field studies that have examined the relationship between dominance and parasite load have been somewhat mixed. Hausfater and Watson (1976), for example, found that high-ranked baboons had greater numbers of parasite ova per gram of feces than did lower-ranked baboons; rank was not related to parasite infection, however, for a different species of baboon (Müller-Graf, Collins, & Woolhouse, 1996). Similar to the Hausfater and Watson result, rank was associated with simian immunodeficiency virus (SIV) infection among female sooty mangabey monkeys (note that SIV is endemic and nonpathogenic in this species), with high-ranked females more likely to be infected than low-ranked females (Santiago et al., 2005). The relationship between rank and parasite load is even more complex, however: Hernandez, MacIntosh, and Huffman (2009) studied a troop of Japanese macaques and replicated Hausfater and Watson's 1976 result for females, but only for one of the two most prevalent parasite species— high-ranked females had more ova per gram of feces for *Oesophagostomum aculeatum* compared to low-ranked animals, but there was no relationship between rank and parasite load for a second parasite. Given the similar transmission biology of these two parasites, these results were puzzling.

### Dominance and Atherosclerosis

Clearer results on the role of dominance and health have been found in an ongoing, laboratory-based research program focused on atherosclerosis at Wake Forest University. The initial study (Kaplan,

Manuck, Clarkson, Lusso, & Taub, 1982) utilized adult male cynomolgus monkeys (*Macaca fascicularis*, a "despotic" species closely related to rhesus monkeys) that were fed a moderately atherogenic diet. Three groups of five animals each were formed, and the resulting social groups (referred to as stable social groups) remained together 24 hours per day. An additional three groups of five animals each were also formed into social groups, but these groups were reorganized periodically (every 4–12 weeks) by swapping members, so that animals were forced to reestablish dominance relationships. This was the unstable social condition. Both stable and unstable social conditions were maintained for 22 months, after which animals were necropsied and various measures were made of the coronary arteries. Animals were designated as high-ranked or as low-ranked based upon fight outcomes. Results of this study demonstrated convincingly that high-ranked animals displayed greater coronary artery atherosclerosis compared to low-ranked animals—but only among animals that were socialized in unstable social groups. There were no significant rank effects among animals in the stable groups.

Over the course of this research program, a variety of studies were conducted that incorporated the stable–unstable social manipulation for males. In some studies, all-female groups were formed as well, although these tended to be of the stable social configuration. Recently, a meta-analysis was published that examined the role of rank on measures of atherosclerosis, combining groups (especially control groups) from several studies (Kaplan, Chen, & Manuck, 2009). Altogether, data were presented on 200 females and 219 males. The results clearly showed that, for males in stable social groups, rank had no effect on development of atherosclerosis, although there was a nonsignificant trend for low-ranked males to show greater evidence of atherosclerosis. For females housed in similar, stable conditions, however, rank had a substantial effect, with subordinate animals showing the greatest development of atherosclerosis compared to dominant animals. Finally, high and low ranks were contrasted for males exposed to the social instability manipulation. Although the initial analysis showed a trend ($p = 0.08$) in the direction of dominant monkeys being at greatest risk, a subsequent analysis contrasted males in unstable groups in which an ovariectomized and estrogen-implanted female had been introduced, versus males in unstable groups in which no female was present. The results indicated that high-ranked males in unstable groups with a female had greater evidence of coronary artery atherosclerosis than did high-ranked males housed in unstable groups that did not include a female. The presence of a female, of course, induces competitive interactions among males, and would exacerbate the instability in a social hierarchy.

A few field studies conducted on intact and long-standing groups of monkeys support these results. Low-ranked animals (both males and females) in a stable group of captive vervet monkeys had significantly higher concentrations of serum total cholesterol (Bramblett, Coelho, & Mott, 1981), and among two stable troops of baboons in Kenya, subordinate males were found to have significantly lower concentrations of high-density lipoprotein (i.e., "good" cholesterol) compared to high-ranked animals (Sapolsky & Mott, 1987). Both of these results are consistent with the trend reported by Kaplan et al. (2009) that low-ranked adult males in stable groups showed greater evidence of atherosclerosis. Moreover, in a study of a free-ranging group of rhesus monkeys (Rawlins & Kessler, 1987), high-ranked animals were found to have significantly higher serum cholesterol levels; however, this was an unstable group, with several of the animals having recently experienced changes in rank, after the alpha male was deposed—again, consistent with the data reported by Kaplan et al. (2009).

Why might low rank be a risk factor for females, whereas for males high status in the context of social instability is more pathogenic than either low status during social instability or high status in stable conditions? Kaplan et al. (2009) suggest this has to do with natural differences between males and females in life-history. As described above for rhesus monkeys, male cynomolgus monkeys transfer between groups at reproductive maturity and, potentially, several times in adulthood. The social reorganization manipulation capitalizes on the fact that adult males encounter unfamiliar males at many points in their lives and must contest rank when they do. Some animals are more successful at this and become high-ranked. Once the hierarchy is established, however, and the group becomes stable, maintenance of the dominance hierarchy occurs through periodic (and usually ritualized) agonistic and competitive interactions. In fact, an important adaptive feature of dominance hierarchies is that they allow for relatively peaceful coexistence of unrelated animals—once everybody learns (and is reminded of) "the rules" about where the power is, all animals can get on with other aspects of social living. In unstable conditions, however, the rules keep changing, and one's high rank needs to be contested repeatedly. The life-history of females is quite different. Because females remain in their natal troops, their social lives revolve around relatives (within their matriline) and nonkin (across matrilines), and considerable time is involved in maintaining these rank relationships, particularly in despotic species. For example, in a comparison of aggressive behavior displayed, Bernstein et al. (1983) found that adult female rhesus monkeys displayed significantly more contact and noncontact aggression (e.g., biting and chasing, respectively) than did adult males. Altogether, then, the data are consistent with the picture that, in stable conditions, the at-risk animals are likely to be those (male or female) of low-rank as a result of continual reinforcement of the existing hierarchies, whereas in unstable conditions, the high-ranked animals experience the most stress, as they must work to both maintain their own positions and to maintain order in the group.

### A Note About Dominance in Monkeys and Socioeconomic Status in Humans

Like monkeys, humans also live in a hierarchical society, and parallels have been made between data showing that low rank in monkeys is a risk factor for disease, and data (reviewed by Adler et al., 1994) relating socioeconomic status (SES) in humans to health outcomes (e.g., Sapolsky, 2004). Although tempting, such comparisons must be done with extreme caution. First, as we've seen, it is not always the lowest-ranked monkeys that are at greatest risk for disease-related outcomes. Second, the human data suggest that it is not only the lowest-SES individuals at risk; that is, the model is not a threshold model, which is suggested by the nonhuman primate data, in which morbidity and mortality are increased only below some specific SES point. Rather, the human model is a graded one, in which the relationship between health and SES exists across the spectrum of SES (Adler et al., 1994). Finally, as Kaplan and Manuck (1999, pp. 157–158) indicate, the two phenomena, dominance hierarchy and SES, are conceptually distinct:

> In monkeys, status distinctions reflect behavioral asymmetries among individuals associated by common group membership. In contrast, SES in humans is generally defined in terms of demographic attributes that delineate strata of society and may thereby be taken to imply classes of individuals or groups effectively anonymous to each other. If human status is conceived in this latter sense, the relationship to monkeys with respect to patterns of disease is not clear, except insofar as class differences (between anonymous

strata) might evoke similar patterns of neuroendocrine response and similar disease sequelae. Here, the effects on health might share the same pathogenic mechanism as that seen in relation to primate social status, but not reflect the same behavioral construct—even though going by the same name (i.e., the "demoralization" of low SES, where such individuals are largely anonymous with respect to persons of higher "class" membership, versus low status derived from asymmetries of outcomes in competitive encounters among members of a primate social group).

Kaplan and Manuck (1999) then present a schema for understanding how their particular manipulations—stable and unstable social conditions—might be interpreted within a more "class"-oriented framework. I will not describe this aspect of their discussion, but rather raise the larger issue that phenomena that look similar may in fact be quite different in important respects. Consequently, comparisons must be made cautiously. The distinction parallels that drawn earlier in this essay between similarities that may be homologous (owing to common descent, in an evolutionary sense) versus analogous (functional similarity only); both can be useful, but generalizations must be more cautious in the latter situation compared to the former.

### Meshing in Relationships: Social Buffering

An important aspect of affiliative relationships is the degree to which the goals of the individuals are aligned. One way that this has been studied in nonhuman primates is in the context of social buffering, which refers to the process by which a familiar social partner can reduce the impact of stressful experiences. Challenging situations typically provide a focus for an individual that is directed at either overcoming the challenge or enduring it as well as possible. Companions that are in the same situation often share the same goals of overcoming and/or enduring, and if they are the "right" companions, can reduce for each other the behavioral and physiological arousal that is prompted by the situation. Certainly, this is a much-studied topic in human health psychology, but the ability to manipulate situations, to easily obtain physiological samples, and to study multiple species in order to understand what it is about the presence of a companion that reduces distress, makes a comparative approach a valuable one.

The effects of social buffering in nonhuman primates have been studied in a couple of different contexts, primarily in a mother–infant context, but also in a peer context for juveniles and adults.

The endpoints of such studies, however, have rarely been disease-related measures per se; rather, the focus has been on physiological measures pertaining to stress response systems and the immune system, with the implication (implied or stated) that repeated or chronic activation of these physiological responses is generally not good and can lead to (or exacerbate) a disease process. Thus, the effects that a companion has in reducing these responses should reduce the risk (or reduce the consequences) of disease. It is worth reiterating, however, that statistical significance does not necessarily imply biological significance, and the effects of buffering on disease might be studied most productively in a disease context.

The endpoint most commonly assessed in nonhuman primate studies of social buffering is plasma concentrations of cortisol (reviewed most recently by Hennessy, Kaiser, & Sachser, 2009). The procedure most often employed involves imposing a stressor on an individual (e.g., relocating it from its familiar environment to a novel room), manipulating the presence and identity (and sometimes number) of companions, and measuring whether cortisol concentrations differ from those seen in a control condition, either experienced by the same animal at a different time, or by different animals in a control group. Studies of this sort in nonhuman primates date back to the 1970s, and have been very informative in understanding the kinds of relationships that must exist for a buffering effect to be seen. These studies have also been useful in demonstrating how species differences in life-history relate to a buffering effect.

The classic example of how social buffering tracks the specifics of a species' life-history comes from a series of comparative studies involving squirrel monkeys (*Saimiri sciureus*) and titi monkeys (*Callicebus cupreus*), both of which are monkeys of the New World that can inhabit the same forests. Squirrel monkeys live in large groups with multiple adult males and females and offspring of various ages, not unlike rhesus monkeys. Interactions in squirrel monkey groups, however, tend to be sex-based (i.e., outside of the breeding season, males interact primarily with males, and females with females) to a much larger degree than is the case with rhesus macaques. Titi monkeys show a very different social organization. Here, a male and female form a pair bond and live together in small family groups with their offspring of various ages. Further, whereas squirrel monkeys (again, like rhesus) travel over a large home range, titi monkeys

confine themselves to small territories that are actively defended. Finally, squirrel monkeys show the typically mammalian pattern of parent–offspring relationships; namely, a close bond between mother and infant, with virtually no interaction between father and infant (or father and mother, for that matter). Titi monkeys, in contrast, are characterized by strong paternal care. Although they are obviously dependent on their mothers for nutrition early in life, titi infants spend approximately 70% of their time being carried by their fathers (Fragaszy, Schwarz, & Shimosaka, 1982).

The very different life-histories of these animals suggests different predictions about which animals might be the most effective buffers during stressful conditions: When infants are placed in stressful conditions, one might expect mothers would be the best buffers for squirrel monkeys, but that fathers would be for titi monkeys. This turns out to be the case (squirrel monkeys: Wiener, Johnson, & Levine, 1987; titi monkeys: Hoffman, Mendoza, Hennessy, & Mason, 1995), although it is worth noting that titi monkey mothers do provide some buffering of the cortisol response (Hoffman et al., 1995). Moreover, the presence of a heterosexual pair-bond among adult titi monkeys but not among adult squirrel monkeys suggests a differential effect of buffering in the adults of the two species. In fact, this is just what is found (Hennessy, Mendoza, Mason, & Moberg, 1995): When placed alone into novel surroundings, adult, pair-bonded titi monkeys show elevations in cortisol, but the presence of the partner buffers these elevations. This is not true for squirrel monkeys, even after males and females have been housed together as heterosexual pairs for months.

The preceding, however, should not be construed as suggesting that successful social buffering requires the presence of a tightly meshed relationship, such as exists when individuals show attachments to each other. Although attachment objects may buffer each other, buffering does not require an attachment relationship. The exact nature of the relationship that results in successful buffering is unknown, but there is some evidence that it requires something more than simple familiarity. In addition, it's important to recognize that social buffering of biobehavioral responses to stressful experiences may be somewhat selective to specific physiological systems.

## BUFFERING DOES NOT REQUIRE AN ATTACHMENT RELATIONSHIP

As described above, Wiener et al. (1987) demonstrated in squirrel monkeys that when infants are placed in a novel environment, their cortisol responses are lower when mother is present compared to when mother is absent and the infant is alone. However, when infants were allowed to remain in their familiar home environment, which included two other females and their infants, the increase in cortisol over baseline in response to separation was significantly attenuated compared to when the infant was separated and placed in the novel environment. Wiener et al. (1987) also examined responses to separation in infants that were not raised in a social group, but rather were raised in cages as dyads, one mother–infant pair per cage. In this situation, when mother was separated and the infant was allowed to remain in its familiar cage alone, the infant's cortisol concentrations were not different from those when the infant was separated into the novel environment. Thus, the buffering effect seen in the group-raised infants does not appear to be related to whether the infant was in the familiar physical environment, but rather appears to be related to the presence of familiar others in that physical environment, none of which were attachment objects.

A similar result has been found in comparisons of bonnet and pigtail macaques. Like rhesus, these are monkeys of the Old World, and although they demonstrate social organizations that are very similar to rhesus, pigtail monkeys are at the more "despotic" end of the dominance spectrum, whereas bonnets are at the more "egalitarian" end. When a pigtail infant's mother is removed from its social group for a few days, the infant displays a classic protest-despair response, as indicated by behavioral agitation on the day of separation accompanied by elevated heart rate (HR), typically followed on subsequent days by declines (below preseparation baseline) in HR, as well as behavioral evidence of depression (Reite, Short, Seiler, & Pauley, 1981). Infants that display substantial contact with peers during the separation, however, have attenuated HR responses, both for the initial increase in HR and in the subsequent decline (Caine & Reite, 1981). In a similar vein, bonnet macaques that experience the same maternal separation manipulation also show initial agitation and elevations in HR and BT followed by declines, but the elevations generally are lower compared to the pigtails, and the bonnets show less evidence of behavioral depression. This is likely due to the fact that each separated bonnet infant gets "adopted" by an adult female in the group, consistent with this species' reputation for tolerance (Reite, Kaemingk, & Boccia, 1989). In these two situations, then, physiological responses (HR in particular; unfortunately,

cortisol was not measured in these studies) were buffered by the presence of, and interaction with, social partners that were familiar, but to which the infant was not attached.

What is the nature of the relationship required to observe a buffering effect? The answer is unknown at this point, although anecdotal evidence suggests that there must be some relationship more complex than simple familiarity (if that can be considered a relationship). For example, one case report exists for a bonnet infant that was raised with its mother in a mixed-species group, including an adult male bonnet, four other adult bonnet females (two with infants), and three adult pigtail females (none with infants) (Reite & Snyder, 1982). Separation was accomplished by removing all of the bonnets from the group, leaving the infant bonnet with the three pigtail females in the familiar environment. This infant showed dramatic changes in HR, as well as in behavior (including depressed posture) and other physiological measures that were reminiscent of the responses that pigtail infants display. The pigtails were familiar, but the authors note: "Efforts on the part of the infant to contact the adult female pigtails were generally met with indifference, although one pigtail female did allow the infant to sleep next to her at night, and later in the separation period, to spend considerable time in physical contact with her during the day (p. 117)." These interactions, however, were insufficient to produce a buffering effect. Similarly, Reite et al. (1989) describe a case in which a separated pigtail infant was adopted by an infantless adult female pigtail within 7 minutes of the infant's mother being removed from the group. There was considerable interaction, yet the infant still showed physiological evidence of disturbance from the separation. Importantly, there was no evidence that this infant had ever spent any time in physical contact with this female prior to the separation. Thus, adoption by an animal that is merely familiar seems to be insufficient for buffering to be displayed.

## DIFFERENT PHYSIOLOGICAL SYSTEMS MAY ALSO BE BUFFERED, AND THEY MAY BE BUFFERED DIFFERENTLY

As mentioned, much of the work on social buffering has focused on the role of social partners in attenuating the cortisol response to a stressful situation. But the HPA axis is not the only physiological system activated in response to stress; for example, data described in the preceding section show that HR (which is often considered an indicator of autonomic nervous system activation) is affected as well.

Studies have also examined buffering of immune system responses. Boccia et al. (1997) demonstrated differences in immune responses between three bonnet macaque infants that had social support versus three that did not. Six infants were raised in a social group that included an adult male, six adult females (the mothers of the infants) and six juveniles (each an older sibling of one of the infants). Boccia et al. (1997) identified the preferred juvenile partner of each infant using a statistical procedure, then performed a separation, in which all animals were removed from the cage except for the six infants, and for three of those infants, their preferred juvenile partners. Behavioral data indicated that the presence of support reduced the depressive response to the separation. More importantly, a variety of effects were seen for functional immune measures, all of which were in the direction of supported infants showing better functional responses (e.g., greater proliferation of peripheral blood mononuclear cells [PBMCs] in response to stimulation with mitogens; and maintenance of natural killer cell function). In addition, although sample size was small, infants that received more affiliation from their juvenile friends showed the best immune function.

It's worth noting, however, that various physiological systems may not be buffered in the same way. Gust et al. (1994) studied seven adult female rhesus monkeys that were removed from their social group on two occasions. On one occasion, the animals were housed in a novel environment in individual cages, and on another occasion (order was counterbalanced), each female had a preferred partner present during the separation and relocation. Blood sampling was done prior to separation, then at 2, 24, and 96 hours later. Cortisol concentrations were elevated for all animals at the 2- and 24-hour time points and had returned to baseline levels by 96 hours. There was no buffering effect evident for cortisol. The PBMCs from those blood draws were phenotyped using flow cytometry, however, and a different picture emerged. At the 2-hour time point, substantial reductions (compared to preseparation values) were found for all animals for numbers of CD4+ T cells, CD8+ T cells, and CD20+ B cells. By the 24- and 96-hour time points, however, buffering effects were evident—the decline from preseparation values for CD4+ and CD8+ cell numbers was significantly attenuated for the females when they were with their companions. That is, the recovery to baseline values of T-cell numbers was faster when the animals were separated/relocated with their companions than when they experienced this situation

alone. Thus, buffering was seen for T-cell numbers in this study, but not for cortisol concentrations. Using a group formation rather than a social separation procedure, Gust et al. (1996) showed a similar result—the effects of social buffering on cortisol concentrations and on PBMC numbers were evident in different time frames.

The physiological response to a stressor is multifaceted, and consequently, the role that a social buffer plays may not be equivalent across all systems, as just described. Although many physiological systems can be activated, the principal stress–response systems are the HPA axis and the sympathetic-adrenal-medullary (SAM) system. Certainly, cortisol has broad effects on metabolism, but the neural (norepinephrine) and hormonal (epinephrine, mostly) effects of the SAM system can also have an impact (particularly on immune function; see below) that is more immediate than, and to some degree independent of, the HPA effect. Moreover, the role of the social buffer may be related differently to different physiological systems. It would be useful to know, for example, whether the types of behaviors displayed by the focal individual and its companion have effects on one stress response system over another.

### Stability in Social Relationships
When individuals interact with each other over a period of time, the relationship that develops is characterized by a certain degree of predictability. That is, the future interactions of the individuals are more likely to take the form (and have the qualities) of past interactions than they are to be completely novel. For example, as described earlier, one benefit of a society that includes dominance hierarchies is that, at least with respect to which individual gets access to which resource, competition does not have to accompany each interaction. This leads to greater predictability and reduced possibilities of injury. It has long been known that unpredictability is stressful; thus, the predictability inherent in stable social relationships is likely an important component of what makes social relationships so beneficial to health.

Study of the health consequences of stability in social relationships should imply a comparison between conditions that produce stable relationships with other conditions that would involve instability in social relationships. In field studies of primates, social instability occurs sporadically, such as when a new animal (for most species, a male) immigrates to a new group, or when rank within a group is contested, either among males or females (e.g., an overthrow of one matriline by members of another matriline). Such events are unpredictable, and it is hard to make clean comparisons with another group studied at the same time and under otherwise-similar ecological circumstances. Study of stable and unstable relationships is easily accomplished, however, in the laboratory, and in the experimental work on social relationships and health in nonhuman primates, social stability has been examined using two different paradigms. Of course, the results of these studies are usually described with respect to the concept of social stress; that is, the emphasis is on the deleterious effects of *unstable* conditions rather than on the beneficial effects of stable conditions.

The first approach to examining the role of stability in relationships is associated with the atherosclerosis research program, described above. This paradigm involves formation of stable social groups of five animals each (generally all males or all females) that live together 24 hours a day, and comparison with equal numbers of animals in an unstable condition that are housed similarly, but whose groups undergo reorganization every 4 weeks or more. Many of the results from this particular paradigm have centered on the role of rank, and in particular on the interaction of rank and social stability, as described earlier. Main effects of social stability, however, have been found for various health-related outcomes. For example, an early report from this laboratory noted that animals in the unstable condition had significantly more evidence of atherosclerosis than did animals in the unstable condition, regardless of rank (Kaplan et al., 1983). And other studies found that, compared to animals in the stable condition, animals in the unstable condition had a decreased cellular immune response when PBMCs were stimulated with the mitogen Concanavalin A (Cohen, Kaplan, Cunnick, Manuck, & Rabin, 1992); higher visceral adipose tissue mass, as indexed by computed tomography, despite no differences in body weight or body mass index (Jayo, Shively, Kaplan, & Manuck, 1993); and finally, increased antibody response to a booster immunization with tetanus toxoid (Cunnick et al., 1991). This last result is counter-intuitive, but only if one assumes that a higher antibody titer is necessarily an indicator of better function; in this case, the more parsimonious interpretation is that the social manipulations simply resulted in altered regulation of the immune response. Finally, social stability was not associated with a protective response to challenge with a respiratory pathogen, nor with basal concentrations of plasma cortisol and

catecholamines, compared to animals in unstable conditions. The reorganization of the unstable groups did lead to an increase in plasma norepinephrine (but not cortisol or epinephrine) that differed from concentrations among stable animals (which were not reorganized) taken at the same point in the study (Cohen et al., 1997). In short, this model of social stress and social stability has been productive and fairly consistent in revealing the protective effects of being housed in a social group that permits establishment of stable social relationships over long periods of time.

The second approach to studying stability in relationships has been taken in my own laboratory. One could argue that, in the procedure just described, considerable opportunity exists for stability in social relationships to develop even in members of the unstable social groups. Recall that these groups live together 24 hours per day, and are reorganized, at a minimum, at 4-week intervals. Consequently, once the initial dominance relationships are established (which often occurs within minutes: Mendoza & Barchas, 1983), the pattern of interactions likely becomes increasingly predictable. We were also interested in modeling social stability, but the unstable groups that served as our contrasting condition were more dynamically constructed. There were three principal differences between our procedure and that of Kaplan's. First, our animals' groups were formed for only 100 minutes per day, rather than the animals being continuously housed. Within a group, social dynamics can change dramatically as a result of a single incident, and we wanted to ensure that a human observer was present at all times that the animals were together, to record all such events. A second difference in procedure was that our stable groups comprised three adult males rather than five. Three is a minimal unit for complex social interactions to occur (e.g., two animals form an alliance against a third). We felt that the amount of added social complexity obtained by adding a third animal (instead of studying only dyads) was substantial, but that adding a fourth or fifth animal didn't produce commensurate increases in complexity. And, finally, our unstable social condition varied, on a daily basis, the number and identity of group members. That is, on any given day, two to four animals, drawn from a pool of nine or 12 monkeys (depending on the study), were formed into an unstable social group for 100 minutes. Thus, while animals in the unstable condition were often placed with animals that they had seen before (although all animals, in either the stable or unstable conditions, were initially unfamiliar with each other), the social context differed daily. For example, animals A, B, and C might be formed in a group on one day, and on the next, A could be placed with C, F, and G. The relationship between A and C would consequently have to be redefined for that session. In our unstable social conditions, then, the average group size was three (with a range of two to four), a number identical to the number of animals in each stable group, and the amount of social opportunity (100 min/day) was equal in both groups as well.

The difference in predictability between our stable and unstable social conditions was evident within a few days after the start of each study. All animals were transported from their individual living cages and were introduced into a large socialization cage one at a time. After a few days, the first animal admitted to a stable group would climb up onto a perch, and sit relaxed while the second animal, and then the third animal, were admitted using an entry chute. When each animal entered, they would typically signal to each other with friendly gestures such as lipsmacks, or, perhaps, ignore each other. In contrast, throughout the study (one of which lasted for more than 2 years), the first animal admitted to the cage in an unstable group would sit on a perch in a tense posture, with his gaze firmly directed to the entry chute. When the second animal became visible, the first animal's behavior changed quickly and included locomotion and/or social signalling. When the third animal (if there was one scheduled) was admitted, both animals already in the cage displayed this tension and visual fixation, and a similar response was seen if a fourth animal was scheduled. It was clear that animals in the unstable condition were very interested in identifying as soon as possible who the members were for each day. Once all animals were admitted, affiliative interactions among the stable animals usually occurred very quickly, involving social grooming, proximity, contact, and play. In contrast, tension in the unstable groups usually persisted for at least one animal (and often for all animals) throughout most of the 100-minute session.

Our use of the stable–unstable social groups procedure was aimed at testing hypotheses about whether and how stress contributes to AIDS disease progression. Some or all monkeys (depending on the study) were infected with SIV, which, in rhesus monkeys, causes a disease that is very similar to AIDS in humans (World Health Organization [WHO], 1988). The results of our first study were clear: Stable social relationships were protective (Capitanio,

Mendoza, Lerche, & Mason, 1998). Specifically, median survival (number of days from inoculation with SIV to euthanasia based on well-established veterinary criteria) for animals in the stable condition was 588.5 days, whereas median survival for animals in the unstable condition was significantly lower, 420.0 days. The harmful consequences of social instability was also evident in a variety of other measures made during these studies.

First, monkeys in unstable social conditions showed altered regulation of the HPA axis. Throughout the studies, we drew blood from the animals every 4 weeks during undisturbed conditions on days when the animals did not experience their social conditions. Samples were assayed for concentrations of cortisol, and results indicated that these basal cortisol values declined over the first 24 weeks of the study for animals in the unstable condition. Challenge tests (use of an acute, 2-hour stressor, with or without pretreatment of the animals with dexamethasone) revealed that the reduction in basal values was probably a result of enhanced negative feedback sensitivity in the HPA system (Capitanio et al., 1998), a result that is reminiscent of findings for posttraumatic stress disorder in humans (Yehuda, 2006).

Second, because glucocorticoids like cortisol can regulate immune function via known signal transduction pathways, we examined a measure of HPA-immune regulation, trafficking of lymphocytes in peripheral blood (Cole, Mendoza, & Capitanio, 2009). As expected, monkeys in stable social conditions displayed the expected negative relationship between cortisol concentrations and numbers of lymphocytes in peripheral blood: When basal concentrations of cortisol were high, lymphocyte numbers were low. In contrast, data from animals in unstable conditions were consistent with the idea that instability desensitizes immune cells to the effects of cortisol: For these animals, the correlation between cortisol concentrations and lymphocyte numbers was essentially zero. Thus, the altered HPA regulation resulting from experiencing unstable social conditions impacted at least one aspect of immunity.

Third, social instability was associated with increased density of sympathetic innervation in lymph nodes (Sloan et al., 2007). As with other target organs innervated by the sympathetic nervous system, nerves in lymph nodes secrete norepinephrine upon activation. *In vitro* studies have shown that norepinephrine stimulates HIV replication in infected cells through stimulation of β-adrenoreceptors (Cole, Korin, Fahey, & Zack, 1998), and in monkeys experiencing unstable social conditions, the density of sympathetic fibers in lymph nodes was significantly increased compared to density of animals in stable social conditions. This increased density was also associated with a reduced type I interferon response to infection (interferons are antiviral cytokines), and was noteworthy inasmuch as SIV replicates in lymph nodes preferentially in the vicinity of sympathetic nerve fibers (Sloan, Tarara, Capitanio, & Cole, 2006; Sloan et al., 2007).

Finally, social instability was associated with increased mRNA expression in PBMC of genes for inflammatory cytokines (Capitanio, unpublished). In one study, we had all animals in stable social conditions, then switched them to unstable conditions for a 5-week period, after which animals were switched back to their previous stable groups. We drew blood, isolated PBMC, and assessed mRNA expression for a variety of cytokines. In the initial stable condition, gene expression for inflammatory cytokines such as interleukin-6 and tumor necrosis factor-α was low, but during unstable conditions, significant elevations in gene expression were found. When stable conditions were reinstated 5 weeks later, levels of gene expression returned to those seen in the earlier stable condition. In terms of SIV and HIV disease, this is important because inflammatory cytokines can support viral replication (e.g., Landrø et al., 2009).

Although the effects of social instability were clear, it became evident that there were marked individual differences in many outcome measures, and we began exploring the contribution of individual difference factors such as personality and genotype. A complete discussion of the role of non-human primate personality in immunity and health is beyond the scope of the present chapter (but see Capitanio et al., 2008; Capitanio, 2011), but it is worth noting that, in a recent study, we found evidence that possessing a "risky" genotype or personality profile is harmful only if an animal is in unstable social conditions. Put another way, having stable social relationships buffers the effects of possessing risky traits. A good illustration of this involves the primate personality trait Sociability, which reflects a tendency to affiliate. This trait has been found in a variety of personality studies in nonhuman primates (e.g., Capitanio, 1999; Stevenson-Hinde & Zunz, 1978), and animals high in Sociability show greater frequencies of social approaches and less time spent in nonsocial activity (Capitanio, 1999), faster latencies to respond to social signals (Capitanio, 2002), and lower sympathetic innervation of lymph nodes

(Sloan et al., 2008). In a recent study (Capitanio et al., 2008), Sociability was unrelated to behavioral and physiological measures among SIV-infected monkeys in stable social conditions. In unstable conditions, however, we found a significant pattern of biobehavioral relationships involving Sociability: Animals that were low in Sociability showed lower basal cortisol concentrations (which we have demonstrated is a negative outcome in this model, see above), more submissive behavior (reflecting poor social skill), and higher expression of interferon-stimulated genes, which was related to higher SIV viral load (and which itself is strongly negatively correlated with survival). In short, being low-Sociable and in unstable social conditions put individuals at risk for higher viral loads and faster disease progression, but low-Sociable animals in stable conditions did not appear to be adversely affected.

# Conclusion
## Future Directions

One of the most influential papers in the field of behavioral biology was written by the ethologist Niko Tinbergen in 1963. In this paper, Tinbergen (1963) described four approaches to the study of behavior and other biological phenomena. Two of the approaches, causation and ontogeny, reflect questions about the influences of factors that operate within the time frame of the animal's life, and are usually described as "proximate" approaches. Causation refers to the physiological underpinning of the phenomenon of interest, and ontogeny refers to its development. The remaining two approaches ask questions about the function (or adaptive significance) and the evolution of the phenomenon. These "ultimate" questions reflect processes that have taken place in evolutionary time; what the "survival value" is (or was) of the phenomenon of interest, and how the phenomenon was shaped by natural selection to be in its present form. Obviously, one of these approaches is not superior, in any absolute sense, to the others; rather, they are different ways of understanding a phenomenon.

Comparative methods, involving study of similarities and differences between species, are important for all four of these approaches. In terms of proximate questions, which are those typically examined by psychologists, a comparative approach usually takes the form of modeling a phenomenon with animals. The studies referred to in the second half of this chapter are examples of animal models that have provided important insights into the mechanisms by which social relationships impact health. Not all animals models are created equal, however. As mentioned at the beginning of this chapter, some models reflect similarities owing to common ancestry (i.e., homology), and others do not (i.e., analogy). For example, in the study of infant–mother attachment, nonhuman primate models are valuable for understanding attachment in humans owing to the high likelihood that the common ancestor of rhesus monkeys and humans displayed such a relationship. Precocial birds, like geese, also display an attachment-like phenomenon; however, this is achieved in a process referred to as "imprinting." This is a good example of convergent evolution—natural selection favoring a similar solution to a common problem: keeping the young animal near its mother. But because the common ancestor of birds and humans is very unlikely to have displayed anything like this kind of filial relationship, this comparison represents analogy and not homology. Thus, knowledge of the physiological mechanisms subserving attachment in birds may not be as informative about the human situation, as is understanding such mechanisms in rhesus monkeys.

Why some models may be better than others, then, leads us back to ultimate approaches to behavior; in general, better models are likely to reflect common ancestry, with attachment in monkeys and humans having persisted in the evolutionary lines from the common ancestor because attachment continued to have adaptive significance for both species. So, ultimate approaches, although not necessarily recognized as such, are at the heart of the comparative method, even if that method is used to answer proximate questions. I've tried to show, in the first half of this chapter, that approaches that examine the adaptive significance of the role that social relationships play in health, and the role that disease can play in social life, can provide different insights into the study of this question in our own species: For example, the fact that our sociality is itself the reason why we study this question, and that other aspects of our behavior, such as mate choice and xenophobia, are likely to have evolved as (and may continue to be) adaptations that help to ensure the highest quality (i.e., healthiest) offspring and to limit exposure to disease, respectively.

This first pass at bringing together the primate parasite ecology and the health psychology/psychoneuroimmunology literatures has been aimed at stimulating thought in new directions, and this review raises some questions for the future:

1. We (human and comparative psychologists alike) need to develop a more sophisticated view of "social relationships" (e.g., Hinde, 1995). In particular, we need to better characterize the qualities of social relationships and examine their role in health outcomes. With respect to humans, this appears to be happening in the area of health consequences of variation in marital relationships (and particularly the presence of conflict and differences in attachment styles) (Gouin et al., 2009). What about the health-related consequences of other qualities of relationships, such as intimacy? And, what about the role of the qualities of other significant relationships, such as the parent–offspring relationship, for both human and nonhuman primates? What qualities of relationships result in social buffering? Although dominance is certainly important in the lives of monkeys and apes, it reflects only one aspect of the rich social lives of these animals.

2. There needs to be a better integration of laboratory and field approaches to understanding the impact of social relationships on health in nonhuman primate species. For the most part, laboratory and field primatologists interested in studying health-related issues have little scientific interaction. To be sure, the common thread of "disease" is approached from very different perspectives by these groups, as this chapter suggests, but that does not mean that the sharing of perspectives, methods, and ideas cannot enliven and enrich both groups of scientists. Integration is again an issue when one considers human health psychology; laboratory animal work is often acknowledged, but animal work in field settings is not recognized in human health psychology; nor is there much awareness of human health psychology among primate field workers. The field of human ethology may be the means by which these different groups find common ground.

3. Our conceptualization of risk must be broadened to include the notion of joint risk factors. Science's inherently reductionistic approach to questions often looks for main effects—this disease is exacerbated by personality, or by social stress, or by genotype, or by rank. It is becoming clear that the effects of many risk factors are contingent on the presence of other events or conditions. This is clear in the work described above on rank and disease
(i.e., high rank can be risky in unstable social conditions, but when social groups are stable, it is the low-ranked animals that may be at greater risk) and on personality and disease (being low-sociable in unstable conditions may be most risky).

4. Finally, we need to be more comprehensive about our endpoints. Individual scientists tend to have their favorite physiological system that often differs from that of their colleagues. These can include immune function, endocrine function, heart rate, gene expression, or more disease-specific processes. Going beyond one's familiar physiological system will likely require collaboration. As important, however, is how we think of our endpoints. Many of the endpoints we examine are components of regulated systems. What is contributing more directly to the disease: the component itself, or is it the system as a whole that is dysregulated? There is evidence, for example, that the effects of social relationships are regulatory; that is, they result in long-term alterations in the operating characteristics of systems, by altering set points, thresholds, rise times, and other dynamic features (e.g., Capitanio et al., 1998; Mendoza, Capitanio, & Mason, 2000). Moreover, since no physiological system exists in isolation, dysregulation in one system, like the HPA axis, may extend to other systems, such as the immune system. Thus, better measures may involve describing more dynamic components of physiological systems rather than just single measures that are components of the system.

# References

Abbott, D.H., Keverne, E.B., Bercovitch, F.B., Shively, C.A., Mendoza, S.P., et al. (2003). Are subordinates always stressed? A comparative analysis of rank differences in cortisol levels among primates. *Hormones and Behavior, 43*, 67–82.

Adler, N.E., Boyce, T., Chesney, M.A., Cohen, S., Folkman, S., et al. (1994). Socioeconomic status and health. The challenge of the gradient. *The American Psychologist, 49*(1), 15–24.

Alexander, R.D. (1974). Evolution of social behavior. *Annual Review of Ecology and Systematics, 5*, 325–383.

AVERT. (2009, August 19). Retrieved from http://www.avert.org/aidsimpact.htm.

Barton, R. (1985). Grooming site preferences in primates and their functional implications. *International Journal of Primatology, 6*, 519–532.

Bateson, P.P.G. (1983). *Mate Choice*. New York: Cambridge University Press.

Berdoy, M., Webster, J.P., & Macdonald, D.W. (2000). Fatal attraction in rats infected with Toxoplasma gondii. *Proceedings, Biological Sciences, 267*(1452), 1591–1594.

Bernstein, I.S. (1981). Dominance: The baby and the bathwater. *Behavioral and Brain Sciences, 4*, 419–457.

Bernstein, I., Williams, L., & Ramsay, M. (1983). The expression of aggression in old world monkeys. *International Journal of Primatology, 4*(2), 113–125.

Biraben, J.-N. (1968). Certain demographic characteristics of the plague epidemic in France, 1720–1722. *Daedalus, 97*, 536–545.

Boccia, M.L., Scanlan, J.M., Laudenslager, M.L., Berger, C.L., Hijazi, A.S., & Reite, M.L. (1997). Juvenile friends, behavior, and immune responses to separation in bonnet macaque infants. *Physiology and Behavior, 61(2)*, 191–198.

Bramblett, C.A., Coelho, A.J., & Mott, G.E. (1981). Behavior and serum cholesterol in a social group of Cercopithecus aethiops. *Primates, 22(1)*, 96–102.

Caine, N., & Reite, M. (1981). The effect of peer contact upon physiological response to maternal separation. *American Journal of Primatology, 1*, 271–276.

Campbell, C.B.G., & Hodos, W. (1970). The concept of homology and the evolution of the nervous system. *Behavior, Brain, and Evolution, 3*, 353–367.

Capitanio, J.P. (1985). Early experience and social processes in rhesus macaques (*Macaca mulatta*): II. Complex social interaction. *Journal of Comparative Psychology, 99*(2), 133–144.

Capitanio, J.P. (1999). Personality dimensions in adult male rhesus macaques: Prediction of behaviors across time and situation. *American Journal of Primatology, 47*, 299–320.

Capitanio, J.P. (2002). Sociability and responses to video playbacks in adult male rhesus monkeys (*Macaca mulatta*). *Primates, 43*, 169–178.

Capitanio, J.P. (2011). Nonhuman primate personality and immunity: Mechanisms of health and disease. In A. Weiss, J.E. King, & L. Murray (Eds.), *Personality, temperament, and behavioral syndromes in nonhuman primates*. New York: Springer.

Capitanio, J.P., Abel, K., Mendoza, S.P., Blozis, S.A., McChesney, M.B. et al. (2008). Personality and serotonin transporter genotype interact with social context to affect immunity and viral set-point in simian immunodeficiency virus disease. *Brain, Behavior, and Immunity, 22*, 676–689.

Capitanio, J.P., Mendoza, S.P., Lerche, N.W., & Mason, W.A. (1998). Social stress results in altered glucocorticoid regulation and shorter survival in simian acquired immune deficiency syndrome. *Proceedings of the National Academy of Sciences, 95*, 4714–4719.

Chapman, C.A., Rothman, J.M. & Hodder, S.A.M. (2009). Can parasite infections be a selective force influencing primate group size? A test with red colobus. In M.A. Huffman, & C.A. Chapman (Eds.), *Primate parasite ecology: The dynamics and study of host-parasite relationships* (pp. 423–440). Cambridge: University Press.

Chapman, C.A., Wasserman, M.D., Gillespie, T.R., Speirs, M.L., Lawes, M.J., Saj, T.L., et al. (2006). Do food availability, parasitism, and stress have synergistic effects on red colobus populations living in forest fragments? *American Journal of Physical Anthropology, 131*(4), 525–534.

Cheney, D.L. (1987). Interactions and relationships between groups. In B.B. Smuts, D.L. Cheney, R.M. Seyfarth, R.W. Wrangham, & T.T. Struhsaker (Eds.), *Primate societies* (pp. 267–281). Chicago: University Press.

Cheney, D.L., & Seyfarth, R.M. (2005). Constraints and preadaptations in the earliest stages of language evolution. *The Linguistic Review, 22*, 135–159.

Cohen, S., Kaplan, J.R., Cunnick, J.E., Manuck, S.B., & Rabin, B.S. (1992). Chronic social stress, Affiliation, and cellular immune response in nonhuman primates. *Psychological Science, 3*(5), 301–304.

Cohen, S., Line, S., Manuck, S.B., Rabin, B.S., Heise, E.R., & Kaplan, J.R. (1997). Chronic social stress, social status, and susceptibility to upper respiratory infections in nonhuman primates. *Psychosomatic Medicine, 59*, 213–221.

Cole, S.W., Korin, Y.D., Fahey, J.L., & Zack, J.A. (1998). Norepinephrine accelerates HIV replication via protein kinase A-dependent effects on cytokine production. *Journal of Immunology, 161*(2), 610–616.

Cole, S.W., Mendoza, S.P., & Capitanio, J.P. (2009). Social stress desensitizes lymphocytes to regulation by endogenous glucocorticoids: Insights from *in vivo* cell trafficking dynamics in rhesus macaques. *Psychosomatic Medicine, 71,* 591–597.

Collias, N., & Southwick, C. (1952). A field study of population density and social organization in howling monkeys. *Proceedings of the American Philosophical Society, 96*(2), 145–156.

Cunnick, J.E., Cohen, S., Rabin, B.S., Carpenter, B., Manuck, S., & Kaplan, J. (1991). Alterations in specific antibody production due to rank and social instability. *Brain, Behavior, and Immunity, 5,* 357–369.

Dhabhar, F. (2009). Enhancing versus suppressing effects of stress on immune function: Implications for immunoprotection and immunopathology. *Neuroimmunomodulation, 16,* 300–317.

Dittus, W.P.J. (1977). The social regulation of population density and age-sex distribution in the toque monkey. *Behaviour, 63,* 281–322.

Drickamer, L.C., & Vessey, S.H. (1973). Group changing in free-ranging male rhesus monkeys. *Primates, 14*(4), 359–368.

Ehman, K.D., & Scott, M.E. (2002). Female mice mate preferentially with non-parasitized males. *Parasitology, 125,* 461–466.

Eisenberg, J.F. (1981). *The mammalian radiations: An analysis of trends in evolution, adaptation, and behavior.* Chicago: University of Chicago Press.

Folstad, I., & Karter, A.J. (1992). Parasites, bright males, and the immunocompetence handicap. *American Naturalist, 139,* 603–622.

Fragaszy, D.M., Schwarz, S., & Shimosaka, D. (1982). Longitudinal observations of care and development of infant titi monkeys (*Callicebus moloch*). *American Journal of Primatology, 2,* 191–200.

Freeland, W.J. (1976). Pathogens and the evolution of primate sociality. *Biotropica, 8,* 12–24.

Gorman, C. (2004). The fires within. *Time, 163,* 38–46.

Gouin, J.P., Glaser, R., Loving, T.J., Malarkey, W.B., Stowell, J., Houts, C., & Kiecolt-Glaser, J.K. (2009). Attachment avoidance predicts inflammatory responses to marital conflict. *Brain, Behavior, and Immunity 23(7),* 898–904.

Gust, D.A., Gordon, T.P., Brodie, A.R., & McClure, H.M. (1994). Effect of a preferred companion in modulating stress in adult female rhesus monkey. *Physiology & Behavior, 55,* 681–684.

Gust, D.A., Gordon, T.P., Brodie, T.P., & McClure, H.M. (1996). Effect of companions in modulating stress associated with new group formation in juvenile rhesus macaques. *Physiology and Behavior, 59*(4/5), 941–945.

Hamilton, W.D., & Zuk, M. (1982). Heritable true fitness and bright birds: A role for parasites? *Science, 218*(4570), 384–387.

Hamilton, W.J., III, & Tilson, R.L. (1982). Solitary male baboons in a desert canyon. *American Journal of Primatology, 2,* 149–158.

Hausfater, G., & Meade, B.J. (1982). Alternation of sleeping groves by yellow baboons (*Papio cynocephalus*) as a strategy for parasite avoidance. *Primates, 23*(2), 287–297.

Hausfater, G., & Watson, D.F. (1976). Social and reproductive correlates of parasite ova emissions by baboons. *Nature, 262*(5570), 688–689.

Hennessy, M.B., Kaiser S., & Sachser, N. (2009). Social buffering of the stress response: Diversity, mechanisms, and functions. *Front Neuroendocrinology, 30*(4), 470–482.

Hennessy, M.B., Mendoza, S.P., Mason, W.A., & Moberg, G.P. (1995). Endocrine sensitivity to novelty in squirrel monkeys and titi monkeys: Species differences in characteristic modes of responding to the environment. *Physiology & Behavior, 57*(2), 331–338.

Henriquez, S.A., Brett, R., Alexander, J., Pratt, J., & Roberts, C.W. (2009). Neuropsychiatric disease and toxoplasma gondii infection. *Neuroimmunomodulation, 16*(2), 122–133.

Hernandez, A.D., MacIntosh, A.J., & Huffman, M.A. (2009). Primate parasite ecology: Patterns and predictions from an ongoing study of Japanese macaques. In M.A. Huffman, & C.A. Chapman (Eds.), *Primate parasite ecology: The dynamics and study of host-parasite relationships* (pp. 387–401). Cambridge: University Press.

Hinde, R.A. (1976). On describing relationships. *Journal of Child Psychology and Psychiatry, 17,* 1–19.

Hinde, R.A. (1995). A suggested structure for a science of relationships. *Personal Relationships, 2,* 1–15.

Hoffman, K.A., Mendoza, S.P., Hennessy, M.B., & Mason, W.A. (1995). Responses of infant titi monkeys, callicebus moloch, to removal of one or both parents: Evidence for paternal attachment. *Developmental Psychobiology, 28*(7), 399–407.

Hopkin, J. (2009). Genetic aspects of asthma, allergy and parasitic worm infections: evolutionary links. *Parasite Immunology, 31*(5), 267–273.

Hosegood, V., McGrath, N., Herbst, K., & Timaeus, I.M. (2004). The impact of adult mortality on household dissolution and migration in rural South Africa. *AIDS, 18*(11), 1585–1590.

Huffman, M.A. (2007). Primate self-medication. In C.J. Campbell, A. Fuentes, K.C. MacKinnon, M. Panger, & S.K. Bearder (Eds.), *Primates in perspective* (677–690). New York: Oxford Press.

Huffman, M.A., & Caton, J.M. (2001). Self-induced increase of gut motility and the control of parasitic infections in wild chimpanzees. *International Journal of Primatology, 22*(3), 329–346.

Huffman, M.A., & Chapman, C.A. (2009). *Primate parasite ecology: The dynamics and study of host-parasite relationships.* Cambridge: University Press.

Jayo, J.M., Shively, C.A., Kaplan, J.R., & Manuck, S.B. (1993). Effects of exercise and stress on body fat distribution in male cynomolgus monkeys. *International Journal of Obesity and related Metabolic Disorders, 17*(10), 597–604.

Johnson, R.W. (2002). The concept of sickness behavior: A brief chronological account of four key discoveries. *Veterinary Immunology and Immunopathology, 87,* 443–450.

Kaplan, J.R., Chen, H., Manuck, S.B. (2009). The relationship between social status and atherosclerosis in male and female monkeys as revealed by meta-analysis. *American Journal of Primatology, 71*(9), 732–741.

Kaplan, J.R., & Manuck, S.B. (1999). Status, stress, and atherosclerosis: The role of environment and individual behavior. *Annals of the New York Academy of Sciences, 896,* 145–161.

Kaplan, J.R., Manuck, S.B., Clarkson, T.B., Lusso, F.M., & Taub, D.M. (1982). Social status, environment, and atherosclerosis in cynomolgus monkeys. *Arteriosclerosis, 2,* 359–368.

Kaplan, J.R., Manuck, S.B., Clarkson, T.B., Lusso, F.M., Taub, D.M., & Miller, E.W. (1983). Social stress and atherosclerosis in normocholesterolemic monkeys. *Science, 220,* 733–735.

Kappeler, P.M., & van Schaik, C. (2002). Evolution of primate social systems. *International Journal of Primatology, 23,* 707–740.

Kaur, T., & Singh, J. (2009). Primate-parasitic zoonoses and anthropozoonoses: A literature review. In M.A. Huffman, & C.A. Chapman (Eds.), *Primate parasite ecology: The dynamics and study of host-parasite relationships* (pp. 199–230). Cambridge: University Press.

Krishnamani, R., & Mahaney, W.C. (2000). Geophagy among primates: Adaptive significance and ecological consequences. *Animal Behaviour, 59*, 899–915.

Kuehl, H.S., Elzner, C., Moebius, Y., Boesch, C., & Walsh, P.D. (2008). The price of play: Self-organized infant mortality cycles in chimpanzees. *PLoS One, 3*(6), e2440. doi:10.1371/journal.pone.0002440.

Landrø, L., Damås, J.K., Halvorsen, B., Fevang, B., Ueland, T., et al. (2009). CXCL16 in HIV infection - A link between inflammation and viral replication. *European Journal of Clinical Investigation, 39*(11), 1017–1024.

Lockhart, A.B., Thrall, P.H., & Antonovics, J. (1996). Sexually transmitted diseases in animals: Ecological and evolutionary implications. *Biological Reviews of the Cambridge Philosophical Society, 71*(3), 415–471.

Mason, W.A., Long, D.D., & Mendoza, S.P. (1993). Temperament and mother-infant conflict in macaques: A transactional analysis. In W.A. Mason, & S.P. Mendoza (Eds.), *Primate Social Conflict* (pp. 205–227). Albany, NY: State University of New York Press.

Melnick, D.J., & Pearl, M.C. (1987). Cercopithecines in multi-male groups: Genetic diversity and population structure. In B.B. Smuts, D.L. Cheney, R.M. Seyfarth, R.W. Wrangham, & T.T. Struhsaker (Eds.), *Primate societies* (pp. 121–134). Chicago: University Press.

Mendoza, S.P., & Barchas, P.R. (1983). Behavioral processes leading to linear status hierarchies following group formation in rhesus monkeys. *Journal of Human Evolution, 12*, 185–192.

Mendoza, S.P., Capitanio, J.P., & Mason, W.A. (2000). Chronic social stress: Studies in nonhuman primates. In G.P. Moberg, & J. Mench (Eds.), *The biology of animal stress* (pp. 227–247). New York, NY: CABI Publishing.

Müller-Graf, C.D., Collins, D.A., & Woolhouse, M.E. (1996). Intestinal parasite burden in five troops of olive baboons (*Papio cynocephalus anubis*) in Gombe Stream National Park, Tanzania. *Parasitology, 112*(Pt 5), 489–497.

Nei, M., & Glazko, G.V. (2002). Estimation of divergence times for a few mammalian and several primate species. *Journal of Heredity, 93*, 157–164.

Nishida, T. (1966). A sociological study of solitary male monkeys. *Primates, 7*, 141–204.

Nunn, C.L., & Altizer, S. (2006). *Infectious diseases in primates: Behavior, ecology and evolution*. Oxford University Press.

Nunn, C.L., Altizer, S., Jones, K.E., & Sechrest, W. (2003). Comparative tests of parasite species richness in primates. *The American Naturalist, 162*(5), 597–614.

Rawlins, R.G., & Kessler, M.J. (1987). Cholesterol and dominance rank in the Cayo Santiago macaques. *Puerto Rican Health Sciences Journal, 6*(2), 89–93.

Reite, M., Kaemingk, K., & Boccia, M.L. (1989). Maternal separation in bonnet monkey infants: Altered attachment and support. *Child Development, 60*, 473–480.

Reite, M., Short, R., Seiler, C., & Pauley, J.D. (1981). Attachment, loss, and depression. *Journal of Child Psychology and Psychiatry, and Allied Disciplines, 22*, 141–169.

Reite, M., & Snyder, D.S. (1982). Physiology of maternal separation in a bonnet macaque infant. *American Journal of Primatology, 2*, 115–120.

Sabeti, P.C., Schaffner, S.F., Fry, B., Lohmueller, J., Varilly, P., et al. (2006). Positive natural selection in the human lineage. *Science, 312*, 1614–1620.

Sanchez-Villagra, M.R., Pope, T.R., & Salas, V. (1998). Relation of intergroup variation in allogrooming to group social structure and ectoparasite loads in red howlers (*Alouatta seniculus*). *International Journal of Primatology, 19*, 473–491.

Santiago, M.L., Range, F., Keele, B.F., Li, Y., Bailes, E., et al. (2005). Simian immunodeficiency virus infection in free-ranging sooty mangabeys (*Cercocebus atys atys*) from the Taï Forest, Côte d'Ivoire: Implications for the origin of epidemic human immunodeficiency virus type 2. *Journal of Virology, 79*(19), 12515–12527.

Sapolsky, R.M. (2004). Social status and health in humans and other animals. *Annual Review of Anthropology, 33*, 393–418.

Sapolsky, R.M. (2005). The influence of social hierarchy on primate health. *Science, 308*, 648–652.

Sapolsky, R.M., & Mott, G.E. (1987). Social subordinance in wild baboons is associated with suppressed high density lipoprotein-cholesterol concentrations: The possible role of chronic social stress. *Endocrinology, 121*(5), 1605–1610.

Sapolsky, R.M., & Ray, J.C. (1989). Styles of dominance and their endocrine correlates among wild olive baboons (*Papio anubis*). *American Journal of Primatology, 18*, 1–13.

Sapolsky, R.M., & Share, L.J. (2004). A Pacific culture among wild baboons: Its emergence and transmission. *PLoS Biology, 2*(4), 534–541.

Sloan, E.K., Capitanio, J.P., Tarara, R.P., & Cole, S.W. (2008). Social temperament and lymph node innervation. *Brain, Behavior, and Immunity, 22*, 717–726.

Sloan, E.K., Capitanio, J.P., Tarara, R.P., Mendoza, S.P., Mason, W.A., & Cole, S.W. (2007). Social stress enhances sympathetic innervation of primate lymph nodes: Mechanisms and implications for viral pathogenesis. *Journal of Neuroscience, 27*, 8857–8865.

Sloan, E.K., Tarara, R.P., Capitanio, J.P., & Cole, S.W. (2006). Enhanced SIV replication adjacent to catecholaminergic varicosities in primate lymph nodes. *Journal of Virology, 80*, 4326–4335.

Small, M.F. (1989). Female choice in nonhuman primates. *Yearbook of Physical Anthropology, 32*, 103–127.

Stevenson-Hinde, J., & Zunz, M. (1978). Subjective assessment of individual rhesus monkeys. *Primates, 19*, 473–482.

Stix, G. (2007). A malignant flame. *Scientific American, 297*, 60–67.

Taylor, S.E. (2009). *Health psychology*. New York: McGraw-Hill.

Thornhill, R., & Gangestad, S.W. (1994). Human fluctuating asymmetry and sexual behavior. *Psychological Science, 5*, 297–302.

Thornhill, R., & Moller, A.P. (1997). Development stability, disease and medicine. *Biological Reviews, 72*, 497–548

Tinbergen, N. (1963). On aims and methods of ethology. *Zeitschrift fur Tierpsychologie, 20*, 410–433.

van Noordwijk, M.A., & van Schaik, C.P. (1985). Male migration and rank acquisition in wild long-tailed macaques (*Macaca fascicularis*). *Animal Behaviour, 33*, 849–861.

Waitt, C., Little, A.C., Wolfensohn, S., Honess, P., Brown, A.P., Buchannan-Smith, H.M., & Perrett, D.I. (2003). Evidence from rhesus macaques suggests that male coloration plays a role in female primate mate choice. *Proceedings of the Royal Society of London, B (Suppl), 270*, S144–S146.

Waynforth, D. (1998). Fluctuating asymmetry and human male life-history traits in rural Belize. *Proceedings, Biological Sciences, 265*(1405), 1497–1501.

Weinstein, T.A.R., & Capitanio, J.P. (2008). Individual differences in infant temperament predict social relationships of yearling rhesus monkeys (*Macaca mulatta*). *Animal Behaviour, 76*, 455–465.

World Health Organization (WHO). (1988). Animal models for HIV infection and AIDS: Memorandum/from a WHO meeting. *Bulletin of World Health Organization, 66*, 561–574.

Wiener, S.G., Johnson, D.F., & Levine, S. (1987). Influence of postnatal rearing conditions on the response of squirrel monkey infant relationships. *Physiology and Behavior, 39*, 21–26.

Wolff, J.O., & Sherman P.W. (Eds.). (2007). *Rodent societies: An ecological & evolutionary perspective.* Chicago: University of Chicago Press.

Yehuda, R. (2006). Advances in understanding neuroendocrine alterations in PTSD and their therapeutic implications. *Annals of the New York Academy of Sciences, 1071*, 137–166.

Yehuda, R., Kahana, B., Binder-Brynes, K., Southwick, S., Mason, J., & Giller, E. (1995). Low urinary cortisol excretion in Holocaust survivors with posttraumatic stress disorder. *American Journal of Psychiatry, 152*, 982–986.

# PART 6

# Conclusion

PART

Conclusion

# Conclusion: The Achievements and Promise of Health Psychology

Howard S. Friedman

**Abstract**

The preceding chapters in this handbook reveal that the influences that fostered the emergence of health psychology could become a threat to health psychology if psychologists abandon the unconventional ideas that led to the field's successful development. Health, recovery, and longevity are best approached with a science-based biopsychosocial model that often goes well beyond the traditional biomedical approach to disease. Hugely important are social relations, individual differences in reactions and behavior patterns across time, and interactions between biological predispositions and psychosocial environments. Improving population health and minimizing health disparities will likely require changes and improvements that go well beyond anything possible within the traditional biomedical health care system. Sophisticated research methods and sound measurements are a critical challenge of the complex biopsychosocial model but also a hallmark of excellent health psychology research.

**Keywords**: Health psychology, social support, social integration, health, biopsychosocial model

In 2001, the American Psychological Association added "promoting health" to its statements of vision and purpose. This striking change marked a formal shift from a traditional focus on mental health to a more direct and broader emphasis on health. As late as the 1970s, not even a formal *sub*-field existed called "health psychology," and few had viewed health promotion as an essential piece of psychology. Clearly, a deeper understanding of health has emerged, and health psychologists have been enormously successful in changing the position of psychology in health and health care.

Yet, as it assumes a significant role in studying and promoting health, the field faces many risks of a serious stumble. The productive factors that led to the early successes of health psychology are under continuing pressure. That is, the conditions that fostered the emergence of health psychology could become a threat to health psychology if psychologists abandon the unconventional ideas that led to its successful development.

Medical care and many health promotion efforts are still dominated by the biomedical model of health and disease, a model that is triumphant but seriously flawed. Also sometimes termed the "mechanical model" or the "traditional medical model," the biomedical model fundamentally views health as the absence of disease. It views injury as a breakdown to be repaired and it views illness as a problem to be treated and cured. The predominance of this model is based in part on its tremendous successes. Broken bones can be x-rayed and set, tumors can be excised, hips can be replaced, and clots can be busted. Bacterial infections can be cured with antibiotics, many viral infections can be slowed with anti-viral medications, high blood pressure can be lowered, and hormonal deficiencies can be supplemented. Many of the disease scourges of human history can now be diagnosed and successfully treated. Proper procedures have been standardized, and scientific research in medicine is focused and highly rigorous.

Despite its tremendous successes, the failings and limitations of the biomedical model of disease, however, have also been well-documented (Cuff & Vanselow, 2004; Kaplan, 2011, Chapter 5, this volume; Kohn, Corrigan, & Donaldson, 2000; Mechanic, 1983). These faults are both humanistic and scientific. The humanistic concerns range from dehumanization (and insufficient respect for human dignity) through assorted ethical challenges. The highly scientific concerns include incomplete models of healing, limited attention to prevention, neglect of social factors, insufficient consideration of development, preventable medical errors, and inadequate integration of public health measures.

In the United States alone, upwards of 100,000 patients a year die or are seriously injured by medical errors, often involving interpersonal matters like faulty lines of authority, or psychological matters like flawed decision-making. Beyond the errors, millions more people remain far from optimal health. Strikingly, it is the case that large numbers of individuals do not follow sensible prophylactic measures, and large numbers of patients do not fully cooperate with medical advice or treatments, for a variety of reasons that are not well addressed by the biomedical model.

The effects of emotions and personality and motivation on healing (and self-healing) are not easily incorporated into traditional treatments and are often dealt with unscientifically or simply ignored in medical settings. Alcohol and drug abuse, and levels of obesity, are at record levels. Treatable pain often goes untreated. And, millions of cases of illness and injury are preventable through known, inexpensive measures, which are not well implemented or followed. Many of the these problems involve psychological and social issues and are addressed in detail in this Oxford Handbook.

Health psychology stepped in to fill these gaps and correct these errors. In response to the limitations of the traditional biomedical approach, health psychology has developed a deep understanding of how various psychological and social variables combine with the biological ones to affect health—the so-called *biopsychosocial model* (Friedman & Adler, 2011, Chapter 1, this volume; Pickren & Degni, 2011, Chapter 2, this volume). This is much more than a fancy name for holistic health care, and in fact health psychology is very heavily scientific. Because health psychology developed not only out of knowledge of biology and psychophysiology but was also heavily influenced by social and clinical psychology, medical sociology, philosophy, public health, and cross-cultural epidemiology and anthropology, health psychology has the concepts and methods to address matters that go beyond the boundaries of biology but are still very relevant to medical care and to health (Matarazzo, 1994).

One of the key contributions is that psychology is not reductionist. Psychology focuses on human behavior rather than on organs, cells, or hormones. It needs to understand neuroscience, genetics, and cell biology to know the parameters of how human behaviors and reactions are affected by and affect organs, cells, and hormones, but psychology ultimately returns to the person. Analogously, psychology is not collectivist. It is informed by the influences of families, religions, and cultures, but ultimately returns to the person. This is a huge conceptual advantage for understanding and promoting health, for ultimately it is the individual who thrives or declines, lives or dies.

If, however, psychology (or health psychology) tries to imitate the more narrowly focused concepts and procedures of medicine and physiology, it may endanger the very reasons for its success. Not only is biomedical research more and more narrow and focused (often for very good scientific reason), but medical systems (and physicians) too are ever more specialized, marking increasing expertise and sophistication but necessarily losing insight into bigger pictures and processes. Further, medical systems are ever more guild-like and hierarchical, with the great benefits of increasing control and standardization but with potential losses of flexibility and of full interdisciplinary collaboration with the wide variety of professions knowledgeable about matters of health. Fortunately, topics and issues that are seen as peripheral or puzzling by the field of medicine remain interesting and researchable to psychologists.

The field of health psychology is bringing together diverse insights. By providing a dynamic and multilayered view into the nature of health, research in health psychology not only repeatedly reveals important limits of a traditional biomedical model that attempts to cure disease, but also reveals improved ways to proceed. From the perspective of health psychology, it is not the case that we are healthy until we become "sick." Further, it is not the case that mental problems or mental stresses are clearly distinguishable from physical problems or physical stresses. The human organism is launched with a particular genetic endowment into a specific yet complex and ever-changing environment, in which it reacts, copes, learns, strives, and ages, sometimes staying healthy and sometimes falling ill. But what does this mean in specific terms, and how are these matters represented in the *Oxford Handbook of Health Psychology*?

## Health Psychology and Health

Startling new insights emerge from the health psychology perspective. For example, it is not necessarily the case that providing more doctors (whether physician or psychologist) or more access is the best way to improve the health and well-being of the population (Kaplan, 2011, Chapter 5, this volume; Schwarzer, 2011, Chapter 24, this volume). Perhaps equally surprising and important, health psychology research documents that pain control is essentially a biopsychosocial process not a biomedical one, and a biopsychosocial approach provides much better interventions (Thorn, 2011, Chapter 16, this volume).

Health psychology suggests there may never be a simple "cure" for heart disease, or obesity, or pain, or aging. Notions of biopsychosocial homeostasis emphasize that the body and its environments are always changing—that health is dynamic. Homeostasis models have been confirmed as very fruitful, have been extended to multiple levels, and have been considered in an evolutionary context (Cacioppo & Berntson, 2011, Chapter 6, this volume). Many chapters in this handbook focus on dynamic processes and multiple causal links simultaneously in operation (Carver, 2011, Chapter 8, this volume; Friedman, 2011, Chapter 10, this volume; Kemeny, 2011, Chapter 7, this volume; Temoshok, 2011, Chapter 23, this volume). From the perspective of health psychology, obesity and alcohol abuse are not fundamentally diseases in the sense that the term is usually used (Sher et al., 2011, Chapter 28, this volume; Van Walleghen et al., 2011, Chapter 29, this volume). Similarly, viewing aging as a disease leads to various difficulties, but a new view of resilient or successful aging, a multifaceted and interdisciplinary notion, is becoming a major issue with the aging of many populations worldwide (Rook, Charles, & Heckhausen, 2011, Chapter 15, this volume).

There are vast clinical implications of health psychology approaches, as many common, traditional assumptions about treatment do not stand up to scientific review (Cacioppo & Berntson, 2011, Chapter 6, this volume; Rohrbaugh & Shoham, 2011, Chapter 20, this volume; Sakairi, Sugamura, & Suzuki, 2011, Chapter 34, this volume; Thorn, 2011, Chapter 16, this volume; Wortman & Boerner, 2011, Chapter 19, this volume). When the biomedical approach is replaced with a biopsychosocial approach, the full panoply of contributors to well-being are unleashed. More and more, the structural impediments to a more encompassing view of well-being are dissipating, and new views of health and optimal treatments are emerging.

Special considerations enter the picture when the patient is very young or old or stigmatized (Rook et al., 2011, Chapter 15, this volume; Ruiz, 2011, Chapter 32, this volume; Tinsley, 2011, Chapter 21, this volume). For example, ways of thinking about and coping with cancer are hugely complex biopsychosocial matters (Malcarne, 2011, Chapter 17, this volume). Analogously, organ transplantation, increasingly the optimal treatment for many diseases, is inherently complexly biopsychosocial (Dew & DiMartini, 2011, Chapter 22, this volume).

Although it is well-established that doctors and other health care providers function best when they communicate effectively with their patients, progress in improving communication should be based on a scientific understanding of practitioner–patient relations (Hall & Roter, 2011, Chapter 14, this volume; Rohrbaugh & Shoham, 2011, Chapter 20, this volume). Cooperation with treatment can never be fully addressed through simple protocols that parallel the protocols for disease management. That is, here too, the social science insights differ in a fundamental sense from a biomedical treatment model. Proper, effective communication, cooperation, and adherence are not at all what physicians call "the art of medicine." Rather they comprise the *science* of the art of medicine, a science that is contingent and probabilistic.

A popular model of health and disease involves stress, psychophysiological impairment (such as immune dysfunction), and resultant disease. There is no doubt that unusual challenges to the body (including psychological challenges) can disrupt internal homeostasis (Cacioppo & Berntson, 2011, Chapter 6, this volume; Carver, 2011, Chapter 8, this volume; Kemeny, 2011, Chapter 7, this volume; Segerstrom, 2011, Chapter 30, this volume; Temoshok, 2011, Chapter 23, this volume). But such links are not fully established as prime contributors to morbidity and mortality in humans. Because so many biological *and* psychological *and* social factors simultaneously contribute to health across time, there are few good studies showing specific effects of stressors, physiological mediators, and long-term significant disease or mortality risk. This is an area in which health psychology especially needs to be cautious in its claims, broad in its vision, and rigorous in its models and studies.

In fact, health behavior keeps emerging as a critical component of good health. That is, good nutrition, physical activity, sound sleep, cooperation with treatment, and avoidance of drug abuse and other risky activities are highly correlated with each other and with avoidance of chronic stress and psychophysiological health, and so it is nearly impossible to tease apart simple "stress" effects in humans (Aiken, 2011, Chapter 25, this volume; Sher et al., 2011, Chapter 28, this volume; Friedman, 2011, Chapter 10, this volume; Schwarzer, 2011, Chapter 24, this volume; Van Walleghen, Steeves, & Raynor, 2011, Chapter 29, this volume; Wilson, 2011, Chapter 27, this volume). Although some in the biomedical community disparage health psychology by asserting that there is little evidence for "pure" (nonbehavioral) effects of stress on illness, the reality is that it makes little sense to separate psychological and emotional states and motives from the various health behaviors that make up a person's day, week, or year. Lifespan and life-course perspectives on health emphasize the processes by which well-being is maintained in the face of ongoing challenges and age-related changes in functioning (Friedman, 2011, Chapter 10, this volume; Hampson & Friedman, 2008; Rook, Charles, & Heckhausen, 2011, Chapter 15, this volume). It is not enough to give people lists of health tips and recommendations; rather, it is important to set people on healthier long-term life paths (Friedman & Martin, 2011).

Health psychology continues to extend significantly its traditional role in assisting individuals to cope with disease, stress, and aging. How people think about, verbalize, and cope with challenges can have important direct and indirect effects on whether they enter the sick role and how they interface with the medical care system (Benyamini, 2011, Chapter 13, this volume; Carver, 2011, Chapter 8, this volume; Dew, 2011, Chapter 22, this volume; Malcarne, 2011, Chapter 17, this volume; Pennebaker & Chung, 2011, Chapter 18, this volume; Renner & Schupp, 2011, Chapter 26, this volume; Rohrbaugh & Shoham, 2011, Chapter 20, this volume; Rook, Charles, & Heckhausen, 2011, Chapter 15, this volume; Stanton & Revenson, 2011, Chapter 11, this volume; Tinsley, 2011, Chapter 21, this volume). Research on adaptation to chronic diseases has led to multifaceted conceptualizations of adjustment, as well as to attention to the reciprocal influences and intersections of emotions, cognition, behaviors, life roles, and culture. Similarly, studying personality as a predictor of health forces attention beyond a more narrow focus on psychoimmunology or unhealthy habits; it brings the view of how the pieces fit together in the whole person (Friedman & Adler, 2011, Chapter 1, this volume; Friedman, 2011, Chapter 10, this volume). By using a conceptual approach that goes well beyond treating "mental" health and leaving "physical" health to physicians, these health psychology efforts come much closer to the true nature of overall well-being. In fact, we may know that full success has been achieved when the term "wellness" has disappeared from use because the term "health" has become sufficiently and properly broadened.

The chapters in this *Oxford Handbook of Health Psychology* repeatedly reveal that a hugely important determinant of health, recovery, and longevity is social relations—variously termed social support or social integration. Social contact with others, a sense of belonging, and participation in social groups have been well documented to be significantly tied to many key aspects of health (including recovery from illness), and not always in a simple manner (Benyamini, 2011, Chapter 13, this volume; Capitanio, 2011, Chapter 35, this volume; Suls, 2011, Chapter 12, this volume; Taylor, 2011, Chapter 9, this volume; Todorova, 2011, Chapter 33, this volume). As noted, such matters are inherently outside the predominant biomedical approach to health, and in fact, in Western countries, family members are often pushed out of doctors' offices and hospitals, and may be referred to ancillary support groups. Most medical interventions are targeted at individuals, with insufficient attention to families and communities, despite known problems with this narrow approach. Of course, family members should not be crowding around the operating table, but the incompatibility in some such spheres of the technical biomedical demands and the psychosocial milieu in which the individual lives illustrates the many challenges that remain for a true biopsychosocial approach.

Perhaps nowhere is the importance and challenge of health psychology so apparent as in the issues of socioeconomic, ethnic, and cultural variations and disparities. These are areas that are inherently psychosocial. Minimizing (or eliminating) disparities will likely require changes and improvements that go well beyond anything possible within the traditional biomedical health care system. Communities, politics, ethnic identities and customs, social structures, and historical trajectories are key (Capitanio, 2011, Chapter 35, this volume; Gil-Lacruz, 2011, Chapter 31, this volume; Ruiz, 2011, Chapter 32, this volume; Sakairi, Sugamura, & Suzuki, 2011, Chapter 34, this volume; Taylor, 2011, Chapter 9, this volume; Todorova, 2011, Chapter 33, this volume).

Finally, and perhaps most importantly, sophisticated research methods and sound measurements are a critical challenge of the complex biopsychosocial model but also a hallmark of excellent health psychology research (see especially Aiken, 2011,

Chapter 25, this volume; Kaplan, 2011, Chapter 5, this volume; Smith, 2011, Chapter 3, this volume; Westmaas, Gil-Rivas, & Silver, 2011, Chapter 4, this volume). Biomedical-based research often tries to be atheoretical and data-driven, in an attempt to be more "objective" when dealing with matters of psychology and social relations, but social science by necessity often needs to employ rich concepts and complex models embedded with statistics and probabilities in an intricate nomological net (Cronbach & Meehl, 1955). Trying to oversimplify a construct like social support or stress or personality will, paradoxically, lead to research studies that are imprecise and misguided, as well as to treatment recommendations that are sterile or too simple.

Pushed by the U.S. Congress, the U.S. National Institutes of Health (NIH) opened the Office of Behavioral and Social Sciences Research (OBSSR) in 1995. The OBSSR aims to integrate a social and behavioral perspective across the research areas of the NIH, with an important goal being the initiation and promotion of studies to evaluate the contributions of behavioral, social, and lifestyle determinants in the development, course, treatment, and prevention of illness. Although much progress has been made, it remains to be seen whether a sociobehavioral perspective can be successfully overlaid on a biology-based and disease-focused health system; perhaps a more fundamental reorientation will be required.

## Conclusion

When the first issue of the journal *Health Psychology* was published (in 1982) under the editorship of George Stone, Stone himself wrote the first article. It was entitled "Health Psychology: A new journal for a new field" and outlined Stone's wide-ranging model of the "health system." Stone then raised a core issue, asking rhetorically, "With such an enormous range of approaches and topics, it is certainly appropriate to ask whether health psychology can exist as a cohesive and integrated field of specialization" (Stone, 1982, p. 3). The field of health psychology is still grappling with this matter. Sociobehavioral science research using health as an outcome now appears in a wide range of journals throughout psychology, the social sciences, and medicine, not only those dedicated to health psychology. And psychologists are now found throughout health care systems.

The secret to remaining cohesive and meaningful may lie in the forces that led to the successful and rapid emergence of health psychology in the first place. Health psychology will likely thrive as long as it continues to take advantage of its unusual abilities to integrate psychological, social, and biological concepts; to use sophisticated social science measures and statistical techniques; to view health as much more than the absence of disease; and to use the individual—the whole person rather than cells, organs, families or societies—as the unit of analysis. This, in turn, will likely require new and more sophisticated theories and models of health.

The first issue of *Health Psychology* also contained an address from the health psychology division's second president, Stephen M. Weiss, who was head of the recently formed behavioral medicine branch at the National Institute of Heart, Lung, and Blood (Weiss, 1982, p. 81; speech delivered in 1980). Weiss, hopeful but somewhat nervous about the future of the small field of health psychology, proclaimed, "If there ever was a time of opportunity for Health Psychology, that time is *now*." These words were a hope and a plea as much as a prediction, but the words were indeed prophetic, and the field of health psychology exploded during the following three decades—in research, in teaching, and in practice. As this *Oxford Handbook of Health Psychology* makes clear, health psychology is still growing and rapidly evolving, and it contributes significantly to other areas of psychology, health care, and the biosocial sciences. And, so long as health psychology maintains its core intellectual strengths, it will be continually enriched from these associated fields.

## References

Aiken, L.S. (2011). Advancing health behavior theory: The interplay among theories of health behavior, empirical modeling of health behavior, and behavioral interventions. In H.S. Friedman (Ed.), *The Oxford handbook of health psychology*. New York: Oxford University Press.

Benyamini, Y. (2011). Health and illness perceptions. In H.S. Friedman (Ed.), *The Oxford handbook of health psychology*. New York: Oxford University Press.

Cacioppo, J.T., & Berntson, G.G. (2011). The brain, homeostasis, and health: balancing demands of the internal and external milieu. In H.S. Friedman (Ed.), *The Oxford handbook of health psychology*. New York: Oxford University Press.

Capitanio, J.P. (2011). Health and social relationships in non-human primates: Toward a comparative health psychology. In H.S. Friedman (Ed.), *The Oxford handbook of health psychology*. New York: Oxford University Press.

Carver, C.S., & Vargas, S. (2011). Stress, coping, and health. In H.S. Friedman (Ed.), *The Oxford handbook of health psychology*. New York: Oxford University Press.

Cronbach, L.J., & Meehl, P.E. (1955). Construct validity in psychological tests. *Psychological Bulletin, 52,* 281–302.

Cuff, P.A., & Vanselow, N. (2004). *Improving medical education: Enhancing the behavioral and social science content of medical school education.* Washington, DC: National Academies Press.

Dew, M.A., & DiMartini, A.F. (2011). Transplantation. In H.S. Friedman (Ed.), *The Oxford handbook of health psychology*. New York: Oxford University Press.

Friedman, H.S. (2011). Personality, disease, and self-healing. In H.S. Friedman (Ed.), *The Oxford handbook of health psychology*. New York: Oxford University Press.

Friedman, H.S., & Adler, N.E. (2011). The intellectual roots of health psychology. In H.S. Friedman (Ed.), *The Oxford handbook of health psychology*. New York: Oxford University Press.

Friedman, H.S., & Martin, L.R. (2011). *The longevity project: Surprising discoveries for health and long life from the landmark eight-decade study*. New York: Hudson Street Press.

Gil-Lacruz, M. (2011). Community health. In H.S. Friedman (Ed.), *The Oxford handbook of health psychology*. New York: Oxford University Press.

Hall, J.A., & Roter, D.L. (2011). Physician–patient communication. In H.S. Friedman (Ed.), *The Oxford handbook of health psychology*. New York: Oxford University Press.

Hampson, S., & Friedman, H.S. (2008). Personality and health: A life span perspective. In O.P. John, R.W. Robins, & L. Pervin (Eds.), The handbook of personality (3rd ed., pp. 770–794). New York: Guilford.

Kaplan, R.M. (2011). Uncertainty, variability, and resource allocation in the health care decision process. In H.S. Friedman (Ed.), *The Oxford handbook of health psychology*. New York: Oxford University Press.

Kemeny, M.E. (2011). Psychoneuroimmunology. In H.S. Friedman (Ed.), *The Oxford handbook of health psychology*. New York: Oxford University Press.

Kohn, L.T., Corrigan, J.M., & Donaldson, M.S. (Eds). (2000). *To err is human: Building a safer health system*. Committee on quality of health care in America, Institute of Medicine. Washington, D.C.: National Academy Press.

Malcarne, V.L. (2011). Coping with cancer. In H.S. Friedman (Ed.), *The Oxford handbook of health psychology*. New York: Oxford University Press.

Matarazzo, J.D. (1994). Health and behavior: The coming together of science and practice in psychology and medicine after a century of benign neglect. *Journal of Clinical Psychology in Medical Settings, 1*(1), 7–39.

Mechanic, David (Ed.). (1983). *Handbook of health, health care, and the health professions*. New York: The Free Press.

Pennebaker, J.W., & Chung, C.K. (2011). Expressive writing: Connections to physical and mental health. In H.S. Friedman (Ed.), *The Oxford handbook of health psychology*. New York: Oxford University Press.

Pickren, W.E., & Degni, S. (2011). A history of the development of health psychology. In H.S. Friedman (Ed.), *The Oxford handbook of health psychology*. New York: Oxford University Press.

Renner, B., & Schupp, H. (2011). The perception of health risks. In H.S. Friedman (Ed.), *The Oxford handbook of health psychology*. New York: Oxford University Press.

Rohrbaugh, M.J., & Shoham, V. (2011). Family consultation for couples coping with health problems: A social-cybernetic approach. In H.S. Friedman (Ed.), *The Oxford handbook of health psychology*. New York: Oxford University Press.

Rook, K., Turk Charles, S., & Heckhausen, J. (2011). Aging and health. In H.S. Friedman (Ed.), *The Oxford handbook of health psychology*. New York: Oxford University Press.

Ruiz, J.M., & Steffen, P. (2011). Latino health. In H.S. Friedman (Ed.), *The Oxford handbook of health psychology*. New York: Oxford University Press.

Sakairi, Y., Sugamura, G., & Suzuki, M. (2011). Asian meditation and health. In H.S. Friedman (Ed.), *The Oxford handbook of health psychology*. New York: Oxford University Press.

Schwarzer, R. (2011). Health behavior change. In H.S. Friedman (Ed.), *The Oxford handbook of health psychology*. New York: Oxford University Press.

Segerstrom, S.C. (2011). Dispositional optimism, psychophysiology, and health. In H.S. Friedman (Ed.), *The Oxford handbook of health psychology*. New York: Oxford University Press.

Sher, K.J., Talley, A., Littlefield, A.K., & Martinez, J. (2011). Alcohol use and alcohol use disorders. In H.S. Friedman (Ed.), *The Oxford handbook of health psychology*. New York: Oxford University Press.

Smith, T.W. (2011). Measurement in health psychology research. In H.S. Friedman (Ed.), *The Oxford handbook of health psychology*. New York: Oxford University Press.

Stanton, A.L., & Revenson, T.A. (2011). Adjustment to chronic disease: progress and promise in research. In H.S. Friedman (Ed.), *The Oxford handbook of health psychology*. New York: Oxford University Press.

Stone, G.C. (1982). Health psychology, a new journal for a new field. *Health Psychology, 1*, 1–6.

Suls, J. (2011). Social comparison processes: Implications for physical health. In H.S. Friedman (Ed.), *The Oxford handbook of health psychology*. New York: Oxford University Press.

Taylor, S.E. (2011). Social support: A review. In H.S. Friedman (Ed.), *The Oxford handbook of health psychology*. New York: Oxford University Press.

Temoshok, L. (2011). HIV/AIDS. In H.S. Friedman (Ed.), *The Oxford handbook of health psychology*. New York: Oxford University Press.

Thorn, B.E. (2011). Chronic pain: Closing the gap between evidence and practice. In H.S. Friedman (Ed.), *The Oxford handbook of health psychology*. New York: Oxford University Press.

Tinsley, B.J., & Burleson, M.H. (2011). Childhood health and chronic illness. In H.S. Friedman (Ed.), *The Oxford handbook of health psychology*. New York: Oxford University Press.

Todorova, I.L.G. (2011). Two decades of social change in central and eastern Europe: Implications for health. In H.S. Friedman (Ed.), *The Oxford handbook of health psychology*. New York: Oxford University Press.

Van Walleghen, E.L., Steeves, B.A., & Raynor, H.A. (2011). Obesity. In H.S. Friedman (Ed.), *The Oxford handbook of health psychology*. New York: Oxford University Press.

Weiss, S.M. (1982). Health psychology: The time is now. *Health Psychology, 1*, 81–91.

Westmaas, J.L., Gil-Rivas, V., & Silver, R.C. (2011). Designing and conducting interventions to enhance physical and mental health outcomes. In H.S. Friedman (Ed.), *The Oxford handbook of health psychology*. New York: Oxford University Press.

Wilson, D.K., Zarrett, N., & Kitzman-Ulrich, H. (2011). Physical activity and health: Current research trends and critical issues. In H.S. Friedman (Ed.), *The Oxford handbook of health psychology*. New York: Oxford University Press.

Wortman, C.B., & Boerner, K. (2011). Beyond the myths of coping with loss: Prevailing assumptions versus scientific evidence. In H.S. Friedman (Ed.), *The Oxford handbook of health psychology*. New York: Oxford University Press.

# INDEX

Illness Perception Questionnaire (IPQ), 288–89, 300
  limitations, 289
Illness perceptions, 281–306. *See also* Personal risk perceptions
  absolute personal risk perceptions, 646–47
  aging and, 353
  assessment of, 287–89
  building blocks of, 284
  cardiovascular disease, 303
  causes, 285–86
  components of, 286–87
  consequences, 285
  contents of, 284–86
  controllability, 286
  curability, 286
  defining, 282–83
  family members, 298
  of fatigue, 295
  formation of, 290, 292–94
  future directions of study, 305–6
  health care providers, 298–99
  health outcome and, 294–96
  healthy individuals, 299–300
  hierarchical levels, 287–88
  identity, 284–85
  individual differences, 300
    age and, 301–2
    children and, 301–2
    culture, 304–5
    gender and, 302–4
    older adults and, 302
    personality and, 300–305
  of interest, 298
  interventions, 296–98
  neuroticism and, 300
  nonpatient, 299
  objective reality and, 306
  optimism and, 300
  representations, 291
  at risk individuals, 300
  schematic presentation of, 282*f*
  stability of, 290–91
    information and, 291
  structure of, 286–87
  subjective, 306
  timeline, 285
  treatment, 289–90, 296
Illness-wellness continuum, 355
Image norms, 622
IMIQ. *See* Implicit Model of Illness Questionnaire
IMMPACT. *See* Initiative on Methods, Measurement, and Pain Assessment in Clinical Trials
Immune cells, 142
  functions, 143*t*
Immune modulation, 130–31
Immune system, 142–43, 174
  affect and, 148–49
  cognitive representations, 151–52
  cortisol and, 177

  in depression, 149
  development, 153
  endocrine system and, 122
  interventions, 152–53
  learning and, 145–46
  neuroendocrine system and, 139, 140
  optimism and, 770–73
  physiological systems affecting, 143
  psychological factors and, 157
  stress and, 146–47, 870
Impairment, 355
Implicit Association Tests, 696
Implicit Model of Illness Questionnaire (IMIQ), 288
Impulsivity, 695
Inclined abstainers, 605
Indirect reciprocity, 783
Individual-cognitive factors, 667
Individual difference factors, 148
Individual inhibition, expressive writing and, 426–27
Individualistic cultures, 304
Individual-level interventions, 75
Inequality, 790
Infant mortality, by race/ethnicity, 812*f*
Infectious disease, 123–24
  nonhuman primate minimization of, 864
Inference, 52
Inflammation, 142
Informational support, 189
Informative relationships, 319
Inhibition
  individual, 426–27
  social, 426–27
Initiative on Methods, Measurement, and Pain Assessment in Clinical Trials (IMMPACT), 387
Injection drug users (IDUs), 574, 704
Injection therapy, 382*t*
Injury, 221
Insight, 431
Institute of Human Relations, 25
Institute of Medicine, 103, 529, 751
Instrumental activities of daily living (IADLs), 354
Instrumental methods, 52
Instrumental support, 190
Insulin, 749*t*
Integration, community health and, 796
Integration meditation, 853. *See also* Meditation
Intelligence, 232–33
  popular stereotypes, 232
Intender, 593, 602–5, 604
Intense distress, 443–47
  evidence for, 444–45
Intention-behavior gap, 597
Interactive circularity, 21
Interdisciplinary pain rehabilitation programs (IPRPs), 385, 386–87
Interdisciplinary sciences, 5

Interleukin-6 (IL-6), 149, 357, 773
Interleukin-10, 568–69
Internal parasites, 863
International Association for the Study of Pain (IASP), 376
International Classification of Diseases (ICD), 386
International Society of Critical Health Psychology, 35
Internet, 84, 404
Internet-based support groups, 206
Interpretation, 52
Interval scales, 53
Interventions, 73–89, 783
  adherence, 337–38
  age and, 353–54
  alcohol, 710–11, 713
  in childhood chronic disease, 512–15
  in chronic disease, 257–59
  community-level, 74–75, 87–88
  components, 621
  cooperation for, 85
  coping, 402
    desirability of, 405–6
    efficacy of, 402–3
  design, 83–85, 621–22
    distal and proximal threats driving, 622–23
    evaluation, 624–25
    multiple component, 623–24
    normative manipulations, 623–24
    putative mediators, 624
    randomized trial, 624–25
  enactment-based, 485
  ethical issues, 88
  FAMCON, 485
  future directions, 89
  health behavior change and, 79–80
  health behavior theories and, 620–21
  HIV, 566–67, 572
  illness perception, 296–98
  individual-level, 75
  mammography, 625–26
  mediation analysis of, 625
    statistical matters in, 625
  multisession, multisite, 629–30
  obesity, 752–57
  older adults, 353–54
  organizational-level, 74–75
  outcome evaluation, 86–87
  personality-based, 79
  population-level, 74
  population selection in, 82–83
  power analyses, 84–85
  primary, 74
  process evaluation, 85–86
  research finding dissemination, 88
  secondary, 74
  social support, 204–7
  sun protection, 627–29
  tertiary, 74
  waiting-room, 333
  web-based, 84

Intimate partners, alcohol and, 693–94
Intracranial pressure, 281
Intuitive/naive scientist approach, 502
Inui, T.S., 339
Invisible support, 194
IPQ. *See* Illness Perception
    Questionnaire
IPRPs. *See* Interdisciplinary pain
    rehabilitation programs
Ironic processes, 478
    family consultation and, 483–84
        supporting research, 487–88
IRT. *See* Item response theory
Ischemic stroke, 702
Italian Society of Psychosomatic
    Medicine, 34
Italy, 34
Item response theory (IRT), 60–61

**J**
Jackson, Andrew, 16
Jackson, Don, 478
Jackson, K., 622, 627*t*
Jackson, Kristina M., 633
Jacksonian populism, 16
Jacobs, S., 445
James, William, 4, 17
Janis, Irving, 10
Jemmott, J.B., 652
John Henryism, 770
Johns Hopkins University, 16, 217
Johnson, D.F., 873–74
Johnson, Lyndon, 31
Jones, S., 596
Jordan, J.R., 467
Jordan, P.J., 617
*Joudomon*, 854
*Journal of Consulting and Clinical
    Psychology*, 258
June bug incident, 275
Jung, Carl, 22

**K**
Kabat-Zinn, J., 411, 854
*Kai*, 851
Kaiser Permanente, 9
Kallgren, C.A., 616
Kampert, J., 665
Kaolin, 865
Kaopectate, 865
Kaplan, J.R., 872
Kay, W., 708
Kelly, J.G., 794
Keltner, D., 450
Kemper, Werner Walther, 19
Kennedy, John E., 31
Kenny, D.A., 625
Keshtgar, M.R., 410
Kidney donation, 524
Kiecolt-Glaser, Janice, 139
Killer immunoglobulin receptors (KIR),
    567
Kim, K., 445

King, Laura, 422
Kingsley, Charles, 623
*Kinhin*, 852
KIR. *See* Killer immunoglobulin receptors
Kirtland, K., 673
Klausner, Richard, 107
Knauper, B., 643
Knoll, N., 648
Kobasa, Suanne Ouellette, 219
Kohl, H., 665
Kornik, R., 643
Kraft, P., 600
Krantz, A.M., 428
Kübler-Ross, E., 440
Kupst, M.J., 515
Kyngäs, H., 514

**L**
Lachendro, E., 652
Lafon, P., 644
Lalande, K., 452
Language, emotions and, 428–29
Latin Americans, 255, 531, 543, 805–19
    college and, 809–10
    community development, 787–88
    comparative mortality trends, 811–13
    cultural values of, 808–9
        family in, 808
    defining, 805
    demographic profile of, 807–8
    diseases in, 810–11
        blood pressure, 810–11
        cancer, 811
        communicable, 810
        diabetes, 811
        heart disease, 810–11
    distribution of, 807*f*
    diversity of, 806–7
    education, 809
    explanatory models, 817–18
        reserve capacity model, 817
        social capital model, 817–18
    health of, 805
        perceived, 810
        self-reported, 810
    HIV in, 810
    mortality paradox, 805, 811, 813–14
    population growth, 806–7
    resilience, 814–18
        cultural of, 816–17
        psychosocial, 816–17
    risk factors, 814–18
        cultural, 815–16
        environmental, 816
        psychosocial, 815–16
    socioeconomic profile of, 809–10
Laverack, G., 795
Layman, M., 642
Lazarus, Richard, 11, 164–65, 247,
    395, 396
    on coping, 399
LCDs. *See* Low-calorie diets
Lead-time bias, 108, 640

Leaf, P.J., 445
League of Nations, 9
Leisure culture, 677
Lepore, Steve, 419, 420, 427
Leventhal, H., 166, 247, 283, 286, 297,
    596
Levi, Lennart, 20–21
Levine, S., 873–74
Lewin, K., 596, 788
Lewis, F.M., 405
Lewontin, Richard, 121, 123, 124, 132
Li, F., 673
Lichtenstein, S., 642
Life course correction, 432–33
Life expectancy, 8–9, 347. *See also* Age/
    Aging; Older adults
    EU and, 826*f*
        of women in, 826*f*
    future, 364
*Life Magazine*, 523–24
Life Orientation Test (LOT), 766
Lifestyle, 31–32
    diseases associated with, 850
Lindsey, S., 645
Linguistic Inquiry and Word Count
    (LIWC), 429, 431, 489
Linville, P.W., 644
Lithium, 749*t*
Lithuania, 832–33
Liver disease, alcohol use disorder and,
    700–701
Liver donation, 524
Liver transplantation, 701
Living organ donations, 524
    factors affecting, 533–37
    motives for, 546–47
    outcomes in, 545–46
    psychological outcomes after, 547–48
    psychosocial outcomes after, 547–48
    steps in, 525–26
    strategies for increasing, 536–37
    stressors in, 545–46
LIWC. *See* Linguistic Inquiry and Word
    Count
Lockwood, C.M., 625
Loma Prieta Earthquake, 424
Long-term costs, short-term
    gain *v.*, 129
Lopez, D.F., 655
Los Angeles, 99–101
Loss, 164. *See also* Bereavement;
    Coping; Grief
    avoiding, 450
    child, 460–61
    confronting, 450
    expected, 638
    positive emotions and, 447–49
    resilience and, 468
    spousal, 442–43, 458
    theories of, 439–42
    working through, 449–53
LOT. *See* Life Orientation
    Test

Neuroticism, 229–31, 276
    age and, 357
    illness perceptions and, 300
Neurotransmitters, 144
    HIV and, 571
Neutrophils, 142
    functions, 143*t*
New Barometer surveys, 840
Newman, S.P., 410
New Psychology, 16
New Thought, 16–17
*New Yorker* (magazine), 196
NHANES III. *See* National Health and
    Nutrition Education Survey
NHBPEP. *See* National High Blood
    Pressure Education Program
NHIF. *See* National Health Insurance
    Fund
NHLBI. *See* National Heart Lung and
    Blood Institute
NIAAA. *See* National Institute on Alcohol
    Abuse and Alcoholism
*Nianfo*, 853
NICE. *See* National Institute for Clinical
    Evidence in England
Nicholls, G., 422
Nichols, C., 456
Nickman, S.L., 456
Nicotinamide adenine dinucleotide
    (NAD), 700
Nicotine. *See* Smoking
NICUs. *See* Neonatal intensive care units
Nietzel, M.T., 785
Nigg, C.R., 600, 617
NIH. *See* National Institutes of Health
NIIP. *See* National Influenza
    Immunization Program
NIMH. *See* National Institutes of Mental
    Health
*Niyama*, 851
NKCA. *See* Natural killer cell activity
    assay
NK cells. *See* Natural killer cells
NLAES. *See* National Longitudinal
    Alcohol Epidemiologic Survey
NMDA. *See* N-methyl-D-aspartate
N-methyl-D-aspartate (NMDA), 717
NNRTI. *See* Non-nucleoside reverse
    transcriptase inhibitors
Nolen-Hoeksema, S., 460
Noll, J.G., 452
Nominal scales, 52–53
Nomological net, 50–51
Nonadherence, 337
Nonhuman primates, 860–80. *See also*
    *specific types*
    behavior, 865–66
    endpoints, 868–69
    future studies on, 878–80
    group activities, 863–64
    group admission in, 864
    heart rate activity, 874
    HPA system in, 874–75

infection minimization in, 864
mating selection in, 864
medication, 864–65
meshing in, 872–75
SAM system in, 875
social buffering in, 872–75
social life, 865–66
social relationships, 867–69
    complementarity in, 869–72
    stability in, 875–78
    study of, 867–69
strategies of, 863–65
stress in, 869–70
study of, 861
Non-nucleoside reverse transcriptase
    inhibitors (NNRTI), 577
Nonpatient illness perceptions, 299
Nonverbal behavior, patient satisfaction
    and, 334–36
Noradrenergic fibers, 144
Norepinephrine, 123, 130, 156, 566, 877
Norman, S.A., 453
Normative manipulations, 623–24
North Karelia, 33
NRC. *See* National Research Council
NRTI. *See* Nucleoside reverse transcriptase
    inhibitors
NTS. *See* Nucleus of tractus solitarius
Nucleoside reverse transcriptase inhibitors
    (NRTI), 577
Nucleus of tractus solitarius (NTS), 126
Nurse-Family Partnership, 513
Nutrition, 123
NWCR. *See* National Weight Control
    Registry

# O

O., Anna, 18
Obesity, 737–60
    absolute risk assessment, 749
    assessment, 745–46
    behavioral assessment, 751–52
    built environments and, 743–44
    cardiovascular disease and, 738–39
    CBT and, 755
    childhood, 513
    classification, 748
    defining, 737–38
    determinants, 744
    diabetes and, 738
    dietary intake and, 742–43, 750
    dietary structure, 754
    dieting history and, 749–50
    economic costs, 740–41
    endocrine system and, 738, 741,
        748–49, 749
    environmental determinants, 742–43
    epidemiology of, 738
    epigenetics and, 742
    etiology of, 741–42
        energy homeostasis, 741–42
    genetic determinants, 742
    HRQL and, 740

implications of, 738
lifestyle assessment and, 749–51
macronutrient intake in, 753–54
measurement, 745–46
medical assessment, 748–49
morbidities, 738–39
mortality and, 739–40
onset of, 675
osteoarthritis and, 739
physical activity, 750–51, 754–55
psychiatric disorders, 740
psychological implications, 740
relative health risk, 748
secondary medical causes of, 749
self-monitoring, 755–56
social stigma, 740
treatment of, 744–46
    additional considerations, 752
    bariatric surgery, 759
    behavioral substitution, 756
    benefits, 744–45
    cognitive restructuring, 757
    diet and, 752–53
    goals, 745–46
    goal setting, 756
    lifestyle intervention, 752–57
    malabsorptive procedures, 759
    medical, 757–59
    Orlistat, 757
    pharmacotherapy, 757
    preplanning, 757
    problem solving, 757
    reinforcement, 756–57
    restrictive procedures, 758–59
    Sibutramine, 757–58
    stimulus control, 756
    strategies, 752–57
    weight loss surgery, 758
    TTM of, 751–52
Objective health components, 794
Objective reality, 306
Obsessing, 424
OBSSR. *See* Office of Behavioral and
    Social Sciences Research
Obstacles, 163
Occupational health psychology, 35
ODBC. *See* Organ Donation
    Breakthrough Collaborative
OEDC. *See* Organization for Economic
    Development Cooperation
Office of Behavioral and Social Sciences
    Research (OBSSR), 891
Ohira, H., 857
Older adults. *See also* Age/Aging; Life
    expectancy
    future, 364–66
        antiaging medicine, 365–66
        health status, 364–65
        life expectancy, 364
    illness perceptions, 302
    physical functioning and, 348–55
        disease manifestation, 353
        medical intervention, 353–54

Posttraumatic stress disorder
(PTSD), 165–66, 461, 464
family consultation and, 492–93
rates of, 418
susceptibility to, 417–18
transplantation and, 540–41
Poverty, 836
Power analyses, 84–85
Prader-Willi, 742
Pratt, M., 673
Precaution adoption process approach, 597–98
Predispositions, 11
Prehypertension, 109
PreIntender, 602–5
Prejudice, Latin Americans and, 815–16
Prenatal conditions, 500
alcohol and, 692
Preparation phase, 483
Presence of mind, 856
Preventive behavior, 271
Preventive medicine, 102
Preventive tendency, 798*t*
Primary aging, 349–50
acute illness and, 350
everyday functioning, 349–50
homeostasis in, 349
physical decline, 349
reserve capacity, 349–50
Primary interventions, 74
Primates. *See* Nonhuman primates
Prisoners, 529
Proactive coping, 169–70
Problem-focused coping, 167–68
Problem solving therapy (PST),
for cancer, 408
Procedural terminology, 387–88
Process Analysis System, 323–24
study of, 326
Program theory, 613
Proinflammatory cytokines, 140, 146–47, 179, 357
Prolactin, 144
Prolotherapy injections, 382*t*
Promotional tendency, 798*t*
Proportion mediated, 629
Pros, 593
Prostate, Lung, Colorectal, and Ovarian
(PLCO) Screening, 106
Prostate cancer, 256
screening, 104–6
Prostatectomy, QALY after, 105*f*
Prostate-specific antigen (PSA), 103–4, 104, 112, 113*f*
Protection motivation theory (PMT), 646
Protective buffering, 253
Prototype approach, 284
Proximal threats, 622–23
PSA. *See* Prostate-specific antigen
Pseudo-tumor cerebri, 284
Psoriasis, 294
PST. *See* Problem solving therapy
Psyche, 479

Psychoanalysis, 18, 217
Psychoecological health components, 794
*Psychological Abstracts*, 32
Psychological Displacement in Diary
Writing (PDDP), 432
Psychologically mediated personality
factors, 224
Psychoneuroimmunology, 138–57
historical overview of, 139
Psychophysiological pathways of
influence, 172–73
Psychosocial adaptation, 47
Psychosocial disease pathways, 75–80
Psychosocial factors
in aging, 357–62
adaptation and, 360–61
concurrent health status, 358–60
personality, 357–58
rehabilitation, 361–64
social network influences, 362–64
community health, 789
in Eastern Europe, 839–43
in elite controllers, 563–64
in Latin Americans, 815–17
living organ donations, 547–48
in optimism, 766–67
physical activity and, 676–78
in rehabilitation programs, 361–64
in resilience, 816–17
risk, 55, 815–16
two-stage approach, 613
Psychosocial model, 21, 45, 613
core, 631–32
of health behavior theories, 616–17
hybrid, 631
issues in, 66–68
Psychosomatic medicine, 6–7
affirmation of, 18–19
new models of, 26–28
in United States, 21–26
*Psychosomatic Medicine* (journal), 26
Psychosomatic model, 21
Psychosomatics, 45
Psychoticism, 223
PsycINFO, 396
PTSD. *See* Posttraumatic stress disorder
Puberty, 675
Public campaigns, 273
Public campaigns, social norms and, 273, 274
Public health institutions, 794
Public health psychology, 35
Public health service (PHS), 482
Puleo, E., 655
Puska, Pekka, 33

## Q
QOL. *See* Quality of life
QOP. *See* Quantity of processing
Quality-Adjusted Life Years, 47, 68, 102–3
after prostatectomy, 105*f*
after RT, 105*f*

Quality of life (QOL), 657
physician-patient communication and, 338–39
transplantation and, 541
Quantity of processing (QOP), 655, 656
Question asking, 327
Quimby, Phineas P., 16–17
Quit diary, 485

## R
Race/ethnicity
chronic disease and, 255–56
infant mortality by, 812*f*
measurement, 46
mortality by, 812*f*
patient, 332–33
risk factors and, 814–15
Racioppo, M.W., 397
Radiation therapy (RT), 105*f*
Rahe, Richard, 29
Railway spine, 17–18
Ranby, Krista W., 634
Rando, T.A., 449
Randomized clinical trials (RCTs), 420, 666, 744
physical activity, 669–72
guidelines, 669–70
meta-analysis, 670–71
Range, L.M., 451
Rapaport, David, 24
Rappaport, J., 789, 793, 797
Ratio scales, 53
Rats, 865–66
RCTs. *See* Randomized clinical trials
Reach, 86
Reach, Effectiveness, Adoption,
Implementation, Maintenance
framework (RE-AIM), 83
Reactance, 623
RE-AIM. *See* Reach, Effectiveness,
Adoption, Implementation,
Maintenance framework
Real Aloud meditation, 858. *See also*
Meditation
Real wage, 123
Reasoned action, theory of, 598
Receiver operative curve (ROC), 61
Reciprocity, 867
Recovery, expectations, 458–65
background factors, 459
demographic factors, 459
relationship factors, 459
transplantation, 540
Recovery self-efficacy, 595
Recuperation, behavioral, 140
Recurrent pain, 376
REE. *See* Resting energy
expenditure
Reed, J.A., 673
Referents, 52
Referred pain, 379
Regulated variables, 124–25
Regulatory processes, 121–22

socioeconomic gradients and, 833
Self-worth, 249
Selye, Hans, 10, 27, 30, 128, 174
Sense of coherence, 229
Sensitivity, 61
Sequence, 339
Serostatus Approach to Fighting the
    Epidemic (SAFE), 576
Serotonin transporter gene, 199, 691
Serrano Garcia, I., 793
Server liability laws, 710
Server training, 710
Serviceman's Readjustment
    Act of 1944, 28
SES. See Socioeconomic status
Sex, measurement, 46
Sexual content, television and, 506
Sexually transmitted infection (STI), 574
    alcohol use disorder and, 704
Shaklee, H., 644
Shakow, David, 24, 28
Shalev, A.Y., 423
Shame, 154
Shaper, A.G., 702
Shapiro, D.H., 853
Share, L.J., 866
Shared decision making, 112–14
Sheeran, P., 592
Sheets, V., 625
Sherrington, Charles, 23
Short-term gain, long-term costs v., 129
Sibutramine, 757–58
Sickness behavior, 149, 178
Sicko (Moore), 790
Sifneos, Peter, 20
SIgA. See Secretory immunoglobulin A
Signal detection theory (SDT), 61–62
Significance, 249
Silver, R.C., 447, 452
Silverman, P.R., 456
Simian immunodeficiency virus
    (SIV), 154, 870, 877
Similar expert, 270
Simon, M.A., 789
Simpatia, 405
Singer, R., 596
SIV. See Simian immunodeficiency virus
Skin conductance level (SCL), 428
Slatcher, R.B., 425
SLE. See Systemic lupus erythematosus
Sleep, alcohol and, 702
Sleeping pills, 224
Sloan, D.M., 420
Slovic, P., 642
Slow Food Movement, 795
Small wins, 259
Smith, C.A., 673
Smith, E.R., 797
Smith, R.C., 333
Smoking, 639, 641
    advertisements, 642
    alcohol and, 707
    cessation, 80, 221, 273

change-resistant smoking and,
    481–82
    health behavior change and,
      81–82
    outcomes, 486–87
    high-risk stereotype, 651
    lung cancer and, 643
    perceived risks of, 646
    on television, 506
Smyth, Joshua, 419, 421, 425, 451
SNS. See Sympathetic nervous system
Sobel, M.E., 625
Sociability, 231–32
Social buffering, 872–75
    attachment relationships and, 873–74
Social capital model, 814
    Latin Americans and, 817–18
Social challenge, distress and, 177
Social change, 824–44
Social cognition, 271
Social cognitive theory (SCT), 76, 667
Social comparison processes, 269–77
    conceptual background, 269
    downward, 270, 275, 276
    upward, 270–72, 276–77
Social competence, 199
Social confrontation, 151
Social constraints, 253
Social control, 363
Social-cybernetic view, 478, 493
    beyond patient, 479–80
    feedback processes, 478–79
      ironic, 478
      negative, 478
      positive, 478
    health behavior, 480
Social dynamics, expressive writing and,
    432
Social ecological approach, 80–81
Social empowerment, 795–96
Social factors, expressive writing, 423
Social grooming, 864
Social hierarchy, 151
Social influences, health behavior change
    and, 79–80
Social inhibition, expressive writing and,
    426–27
Social instability, 871
Social isolation, 191, 193
Sociality, disease and, 862–63
Socialization, 797
    children's health and, 505–6
    family and, 504–5
Social life, disease and, 865–66
Social network influences, 362–64
Social norms, 271
    comparison feedback and, 274
    marketing, 711
    public campaigns and, 273, 274
    recalibrating, 274
Social psychology, 783–85
    mediated personality factors, 224
    research measurement in, 43

Social Readjustment Rating Scale, 29
Social relationships, study of, 867–68
Social self threats, HPA and, 155
Social setting detoxification, 712
Social stability, 875–78
Social stigma, obesity and, 740
Social support, 80, 151, 189–207
    benefits of, 190–91, 193–96, 203–4,
      252
    for bereavement, 468–70
    in chronic disease, 251
      in children, 510–12
      research, 253
    clinical trials, 482
    comparison processes in, 276
    costs of, 203–4
    culture and, 202–3
    defining, 189–90
    developmental approach to, 197–98
    effective, 195
    emotional, 190
    face-to-face, 206
    functional, 190
    gender and, 200–202
    groups, 205–6
      cancer, 406
    HIV and, 564
    informational, 189
    instrumental, 190
    Internet, 206
    interventions, 204–7
    invisible, 194
    literature on, 206
    mental health benefits, 190–91
    negative effects of, 252
    neuroendocrine system and, 192, 193
    origins of, 196–200
    pathways linking, to health, 191–93
    perceived, 202
    personality factors and, 227
    physical health benefits, 190–91
    providing, 203–4
    receivers of, 196–97
    research, 253
    resilience and, 254
    threats to, 195
    training, 482
Society of Behavioral Medicine, 670
Sociocultural ecological model, 796
Sociodemographic variations,
    aging, 355–57
Socioeconomic status (SES), 191, 219,
    233, 254
    childhood health and, 503–4
    chronic disease and, 254–55
    dominance and, 872
    Latin American, 809–10
    patient, 332–33
    self-rated health and, 833
    transplantations and, 527
Sodium valproate, 749t
Solomon, F., 444
Solomon, George, 139